LAKOTA DICTIONARY

LAKOTA DICTIONARY

Lakota–English / English–Lakota

New Comprehensive Edition

Compiled and edited by
Eugene Buechel and Paul Manhart

University of Nebraska Press
Lincoln and London

Library of Congress Cataloging-in-Publication Data
Buechel, Eugene.
Lakota dictionary: Lakota-English/English-Lakota / compiled and edited by Eugene Buechel and Paul Manhart.—New comprehensive ed.
p. cm.
Rev. ed. of: A dictionary of the Teton Dakota Sioux language. 1970.
Includes bibliographical references.
ISBN 0-8032-1305-0 (cloth: alk. paper)
ISBN 0-8032-6199-3 (pbk.: alk. paper)
1. Lakota dialect—Dictionaries—English. 2. English language—Dictionaries—Lakota.
I. Manhart, Paul. II. Buechel, Eugene. Dictionary of the Teton Dakota Sioux language.
III. Title.
PM1024.Z9 L333 2002
497'.5—dc21
2002018109

Contents

Preface

In 1967 four young Lakota men of the Pine Ridge Reservation started a community college. They hoped to educate Indian students in ways that support Lakota values. Specifically, the language of their tribe was to be studied and preserved. A brief chronology of the life and work of Father Eugene Buechel is in order because his love for the Lakotas and their language inspired the creation of this dictionary, which has gathered together the words and grammar of the people.

On 20 October 1874 Eugene Buechel was born in the town of Schleida in Thuringia, a southeastern province of Germany. He was educated in the Volkschule and Gymnasium in Fulda from 1881 to 1896. In 1896 and 1897, he studied at the seminary in Fulda and then entered the Society of Jesus, the Jesuit Order, in Blyenbach, Holland. In 1900, he came to the United States to master English.

Soon he was studying the Lakota Sioux language by teaching Lakota boys English at the St. Francis Mission school. Apparently during his first years there on the Rosebud Reservation, he traveled to the Episcopalian Mission on the Niobrara River for help with the Dakota dialect from clergy there who knew it well. Buechel began collecting Lakota words and writing down a few Lakota stories. In 1904 and 1905 he finished his theological studies in St. Louis, and in 1906 he was ordained a priest. He was back in St. Francis in 1907 and was assigned to the sister mission, Holy Rosary Mission, some 108 miles west of St. Francis, within sight of the Black Hills.

Day by day, with the help of Stephen Riggs's Dakota dictionary and Ella C. Deloria's works, Buechel's collection of words grew. He began to distinguish the three dialects of the Dakota peoples: the Dakota, Nakota, and Lakota, which was spoken by the more numerous groups living west of the Missouri River. Meanwhile, Buechel taught Peter Iron Shell, Ivan Stars Come Out, and several others to write Lakota, and they helped with collecting words, stories, and texts that had to do with the style of Indian life in those days. At Holy Rosary Mission he also started a collection of locally made artifacts and gathered forms of plant life as well as their Lakota names.

In about 1923 Buechel returned to St. Francis but continued gathering items for a future museum. So large was his word collection by then that he had a carpenter build a seven-drawer cabinet with each drawer divided to hold three rows of three-by-five-inch papers containing about twenty-eight thousand dictionary entries. Although he never saw a bound dictionary developed from his word collection, in 1924 he published a 350-page book, a Bible history that he and some others had translated from English into Lakota. In 1927 he published a Lakota prayer and hymn book, a pocket-sized book called *Sursum Corda* (which means "lift up your hearts"). In 1939 he published *A Complete Grammar of Lakota*. During those sixteen years at St. Francis and until his death he had continued collecting words and assisting in the pastoral work of the Mission.

Father Buechel died on 27 October 1954 at the mission. He was seven days into his eighty-first year. A special friend of the Lakotas passed away that day, as he had learned to speak and preach fluently in Lakota. He was also able to converse in the language with great delight, especially with some of his longtime friends, who would come to his residence daily, sit on benches in the yard, and chat together about recent news, asking "Taku toka hwo?"

The first edition of the Buechel Lakota dictionary was finally prepared by Father Paul Manhart and published in 1970 at St. Louis. Five thousand copies were printed, and in 1980, a second run of two thousand copies was ordered. Buechel's collection was in Lakota with English definitions. Lakota entry-words appeared with their pronunciation, part of speech, definition, examples of usage, and their sources. The first edition overcame constraints that had delayed its publication, not the least of which was rescuing Buechel's collection from permanent damage.

The seven-drawer cabinet and a footlocker filled with his books and correspondence had been moved to Holy Rosary Mission in 1955. The cabinet containing the word collection stood in the front office, where some children discovered it one day, opened the top drawer, and tore up about three hundred entry-words. Silas Left Hand Bull, secretary and interpreter for the mission superior, discovered the mischief the same day and collected all the pieces. Father John F. Bryde, principal of the school at Holy Rosary Mission and himself conversant in Lakota, asked Manhart if he would take the collection and bring it to publication, "so we would have a harder time losing it." Left Hand Bull and Manhart, in the summer of 1958, laid out the pieces of the torn-up word-entries on the large tables in the boys' dining room, sorted them out, found not one piece missing, and taped them all back together. After replacing them in the top drawer, Manhart moved the cabinet into his own room. In 1968 he took the collection to the Jesuit novitiate in St. Bonifacius, Minnesota, and within seventeen months, in February

1970, had a camera-ready manuscript prepared for printing in St. Louis. While the manuscript was being typed, Father George P. Casey, who also had become conversant in Lakota, composed a brief version of Buechel's *A Grammar of Lakota*, so that it could be included in the dictionary.

In June 1978, Manhart saw to publication in St. Louis another of Buechel's endeavors. *Lakota Tales and Texts* was prepared from a handwritten homemade book in Lakota left among Buechel's belongings. Father Buechel, Ivan Stars Come Out, and Peter Iron Shell had written it. In February 1973, during the occupation of Wounded Knee, this book was sitting on a shelf in Manhart's office. His library was rifled, but the *Lakota Tales and Texts* manuscript alone was untouched. It wasn't until 1993 that Father John Paul, then superior of Holy Rosary Mission, encouraged Manhart to take a year's sabbatical and then return to devote most of his time to translating and publishing Buechel's work. In 1998, Tipi Press in Chamberlain, South Dakota, published a two-volume set of *Lakota Tales and Text* in translation.

Thirty-some years after the publication of the first Buechel dictionary, some changes have been made. This second edition includes English translations of the many usage examples. Each Lakota entry-word is in bold face, shown with its syllabication. A separate entry within two back slashes indicates the entry-word's pronunciation. The part of speech follows in italics. The principal parts of most verbs are listed. Then in square brackets [ ] is indicated the root(s) of the entry-word. The colon indicates the definition—or definitions—which follow. Then in angle brackets < > are usage example(s). And at the end of the entry may come synonyms or sources. Much help is thereby provided for understanding a word and how it functions. Because many verbs are shown with their principal parts and changes in the stem, help is given between pairs of dots (·. . .·), where the ellipsis represents a pronoun inserted between the two dots.

This second edition also includes an English to Lakota section. In this part many words are sometimes grouped under a larger whole. For example, *chin* is grouped under *body* with many more anatomical terms. Similarly, a word may be grouped under a genus along with other specifics, such as *smartweed*, which is grouped under the genus *flower*. Another example is *paunch*, which can be found under *buffalo*. Grouping words this way helps with learning the context in which names or actions occur.

Many Lakota-speaking men and women have contributed to this large collection of Lakota words. They wanted explicitly to help build this dictionary for their children and so provide access to a precious heritage of the spirit. The study of language puts one in contact with the roots of a people. We must give a worthy account of how well we made use of every good gift brought to us through the tribes of this world. See in "Word Sources" the list of the many people who made this dictionary possible.

We also owe a debt of gratitude to the Louis W. Hill Family Foundation, to the William H. Donner Foundation, and to the University of Nebraska Press in Lincoln for their help in making possible the further study of the language treasure of the Dakota, Lakota, and Nakota peoples. The hope is that hereby the beauty, song, and wisdom written into Lakota might be further opened for all to experience something of this ancient heritage.

Send corrections, suggestions, and questions to Father Paul Manhart, S.J., *Lakota Dictionary* editor, 100 Mission Drive, Pine Ridge, SD 57770-2100. Lakota wicaša na tuwe c'eyaš yaecetupi kin iyuha *editor* ekta wahokiyaka po, Pine Ridge, SD 57770 k'el.

Fr. Paul Manhart, S.J.
Holy Rosary Mission

Introduction

Lakota Siouan Language

Three dialects of the Siouan language have long been spoken on the High Plains: Dakota, Lakota, and Nakota. In the early nineteenth century, people who spoke these dialects used the plains of the north-central United States for hunting. The largest spoken dialect, Lakota, was heard west of the Missouri River in North and South Dakota. The people were known as the Teton Sioux. North of the river in Montana, there was a mix of Dakota and Assiniboin. East of the river lived the Dakota and Nakota groups. The three dialects are quite close in vocabulary and grammar. Related to Lakota, the other two dialects interchange consonants and consonant clusters, and that gives the spoken language a unique sound readily understood by one who is Lakota. For instance, the Lakota for "very" is *lila,* whereas the Dakota is *dida* or *dina,* and the Nakota is *nina*. The grammar of the dialects is practically the same.

Phonetics helps to determine the Lakota alphabet in dealing with some particular sounds. Ella Deloria, for instance, distinguished two sounds, the mediate and the aspirate, for each of the consonants: *k, p, t, c,* and *g*. Later Buechel showed how, in dropping the character *d* from the Lakota alphabet, the *k, p,* and *t* can at the same time give an account for the merger of sounds with *g, b,* and *d*. Thus, when the *d* is dropped, *t* with a small dot over it, *ṫ*, can represent the sound merger of *t* and *d,* as in the word *anpetu,* "day"; the *t* unmarked is the common English *t* sound, and *t* with a hook over it, *ť*, is the aspirate (the *t* is gutturalized), as in the word *toka,* "enemy." And similarly with respect to *k* merged with *g,* and *p* merged with *b*. The *c* and *g* would each have only the mediate and aspirate sounds, as Deloria suggested.

k̇ as **g** in *give,* as in **k̇inhán**, *if* or *when* (or as **ch** in *machen,* German *to make*)
k as **k** in *kill,* as in **kínja**, *to whine*
ǩ as **k*** in *kill,* as in **ǩáta**, *hot*

ṗ as **b** in *bill,* as in **ṗa**, *to urge*
p as **p** in *pat,* as in **pa**, *bitter tasting*
p̌ as **p*** in *pill,* as in **p̌e** *top of the head* or *sharp*
ṫ as **d** in *day,* as in **ṫáku**, *something*

t as **t** in *take,* as in **tápa** *ball*
ṫ as **t*** in *tall,* as in **ṫanní,** *old* or *worn out*

ċ as **g** in *gentle,* as in **ċík'ala,** *small*
c or ć as **ch** in *chair,* as in **can** or **cinćá,** *child*

* The consonant is gutturalized.

Glottal and vowel stops occur with consonants, as in *k'in,* "to carry a load," and with very few vowels, as in *šk̄a',* "they say," or in *can'icipawege,* "a cross." Now, when *n* follows a vowel to indicate that the vowel is to be nasalized, the Greek ēta, *η,* is used in the pronunciation part only of the word-entry. See "Guide to Pronunciation."

Note 1: Most Lakota words are accented on the second syllable, so generally the accent is not written except in the pronunciation part, which is shown between backslashes \ \. When the accent is on the first or third syllable, it is inserted.

Note 2: A Lakota orthography has been developed over the course of more than two centuries. It now seems the neatness and clarity of the printed and written word reflect the expectation of Lakota speakers to lend dignity to the language. The quest has been to find a balance between the use of characters and diacritical marks so that when reading a text one is not burdened with a clutter of characters and marks. Linguists and learners strike a balance between sight and memory—sight of characters and recall of diacritical marks. Students yet discover that they cannot do without hearing the language spoken by a guide who has mastered pronunciation. Over time, the sound of a word heard and spoken well adds to memory, and what aids the eye is needed less. This effort at balancing characters has led to dropping some characters of the English alphabet: *d, f, q, r, v,* and *x,* reducing the number of Lakota characters to twenty. Diacritical marks are employed to help one express Lakota sounds, especially since dictionaries seem to require that sort of help be available. Of course once the memory is activated, most diacritics are superfluous and one can read more directly from the characters alone; that is, one can read without having characters also carry the load of diacritical marks, as was done early on in turning to the Greek ēta, *η,* to indicate the nasalizing of the vowel preceding it. But as the late Ella Deloria, herself a Dakota scholar, said about the *η,* it can be dropped, and the *n* and the *n* stop, *n',* used for that purpose, as in *cannunpa,* "pipe," and *tan'in,* "to appear."

Note 3: All vowels and consonants in Lakota are sounded, except the nasal indicators, *n*, and *n'*, even when vowels or consonants occur in a cluster. There are no diphthongs in Lakota. This leads to a limited set of rules for reading and writing the language.

Rules for Reading and Writing Lakota

Pertaining to the guttural *h*, *ȟ*:

ȟ need not be given a diacritical mark. It is assumed when

- *h* is the first consonant forming a cluster of consonants.
- *h* is the last character in a word.
- *h* is also a consonant stop, *h'*.

but it must be given one when *ȟ* is preceded by a space or vowel and followed by a vowel.

Pertaining to the nasal *n* and nasal stop, *n'*:

n is pronounced as in the word "name" and is commonly used in Lakota as it is in English, but it is also used as a nasal indicator when

- followed by a consonant or terminating a word.
- preceded by a nasal vowel and followed by a vowel, but then the nasal vowel must be stopped, thus *n'*.

Note 4: Vowels and nasal vowels—that is, *a*, *e*, *i*, *o*, *u*, and *an*, *in*, *on*, and *un*—are sounded much the same as they are in Latin. The short and the long vowel are marked thus: ă (the short a) and ā (the long a). The short vowel is briefly sounded; the long is dwelt upon. On the other hand, mediate consonants are sounded much like the English consonants that Lakota employs.

Note 5: In this dictionary the tilde (~) is often used in examples of word usage to represent the main entry-word to save space.

Guide to Pronunciation

Character		Sound as	In English	In Lakota
a		a	father	até
	a'	a–	fa'ther (the *a* is stopped short)	ška'
	an, an'	an	*blanc* (French)	ánpo *or* tan'ín
b		b	boy	buyá
c		ch	chair	séca
	ċ	j	joy	ċíscila
	c'	ch–	ch'air (*ch* alone is sounded)	ic'ú
e		e	they	cépa
	e'	e–	re'	ške'
g		g	big	ogná
	ġ, g'	ch, g–	*máchen* (German), g'o	káġa, šung'íte
h		h	hat	hánpa
	ḣ, ḣ', h'	h (gutturalized)	ḣog, ḣ', *or* h' stops	Ḣe Ska, nah'ón
i		i	machine	ilé
	in, in'	in	ink	k̇in *or* can'ícoga
j		s	fusion	cejí
k		k	kill	kínja
	k̇, k̇, k'	g, k̇, k'	give (k̇ gutturalized, k' stop)	k̇in, k̇áta, k'in
l		l	love	ilála
	l'	l–	sol'stice	lol'
m		m	man	máni
n		n	nose	na
	n, n', ŋ	(nasal indicator)	*blanc* (French)	can'ípame, caŋípame
o		o	oak	hoġán
on		oo (nasal)	soon	ónšila
p		p	pink	pa (*head*)
	ṗ, ṗ, p'	b, ṗ, p'	bill, (ṗ gutturalized, p' stop)	ṗahá, ṗejí, p'o
s		s	say	sinté
	s'	s–	s–ay	s'e
š		sh	show	ša
	š'	sh–	sh–ow	waš'aka
t		t	take	tápa
	ṫ, ṫ, t'	d, ṫ, t'	day (ṫ gutturalized, t' stop)	wašté, ṫanní, t'a
u		oo	boot	úta
un		oo (nasal)	soon	únpi
w		w	way	wakán
y		y	yonder	yanká
z		z	zero	wazíyata
	z'	z–	z–ink	maz'ípame

Note: Vowels when terminating a statement of fact may accept a stop: thus *han'*, *keyapí*, *ška'*, *ške'*, and so forth.

Using the Dictionary

Lakota–English

Entry-word and Parts of the Entry

- The entry word is in bold face. Syllables are separated by a dot (·). Subentries begin with a long dash (—) followed by a subentry word and its part of speech, definition, etc.
- The pronunciation is placed between two backslashes (\ \), and the syllables are separated by hyphens. Most diacritical marks can be found here.
- The abbreviation for the part of speech of the entry-word is in italic type.
- Most verbs display their principal parts, which are usually in the first, second, and third person, singular or plural.
- In square brackets ([ ]) root sources of the word and its composition are given.
- A bold colon (**:**) indicates the beginning of the definition.
- The definition or variation in meaning follow the colon.
- Examples of usage are set in angle brackets (<>), and the tilde (~) is used instead of printing the entry-word again.
- Finally, after a short dash (–) are synonyms and an abbreviation of the word source.
- The order for entries in the Lakota–English section follows the adapted English alphabet. The order for entries in the English–Lakota section follows the usual English order. Note: The hyphen (-), short dash (–), and long dash (—) all bring parts together.

LAKOTA–ENGLISH
a an (aŋ) b c c' e g g' h (ȟ) (ȟ') i in (iŋ) j k ḱ k' l l' m n (ŋ)
o on (oŋ) p ṗ p' s s' š š' t ṫ t' u un (uŋ) w y z z'

ENGLISH–LAKOTA
a b c d e f g h i j k l m n o p q r s t u v w x y z

Note: Parentheses around a character or a pair of characters, as in (ȟ), indicate that sometimes the *ȟ* does not have to be given the guttural diacritic mark because by rule the consonant cluster beginning with *h* always must be gutturalized; thus, *ihpéya*. Also the *h* glottal stop must always be gutturalized, as in *nah'ón*, just as also must be the *h* that ends a word, as in *hunh*. But when the guttural *h* occurs after a space or vowel and is followed by a vowel, the guttural mark must be given, as in *teȟíka*.

Parentheses around *η* indicate that the preceding vowel is nasalized. But this can be expressed when it is followed by a consonant or an *n* stop, *n'*. Thus, *canké* or *can'iyuwi*.

English–Lakota

Entry-word and Parts of the Entry

- The English entry word is in bold face.
- The part of speech noted before the colon is either that of the English entry-word or that of the first chosen Lakota word that follows the colon. This is meant to show a broadening of the field of meaning for the word.
- Subentries begin with a long or short dash (— or –) followed by the Lakota word and an English rendering in italics.
- A significant number of words related to one another are placed under a suggested entry-word, such as under the word "horse," where words for various kinds of horses and harness can be found. Therefore a given word may not occur by itself in its alphabetic place. Go to a word that has a close relationship, and under that entry find the specific word sought.
- Lakota has a way of contracting words, especially verbs and adjectives, to express plurality or repetition, being or condition, that the plural form of a word does not express. A variety of forms operate this way.

  - Reduplicated: Thus
    nakeca becomes *nagnakeca*
    nica becomes *nignica*
    lega becomes *leglega*
    leja becomes *lešleja*
    ceca becomes *cekceca*
    lila becomes *liglila*
    luta becomes *lugluta*
    zica becomes *zigzica*
  - Ability: as *pica(šni)* in *econpicašni*, "unable to do"
  - Diminutive: as *la*, in *šunkala*, "a puppy"
  - Causative: as *ya* or *yan* or *kiya*
  - Noun: as *pi* added to a verb
  - Reflexive: as *ici* or *ic'i*, as *gl* for *k* or *y*, *kp* for *p*
  - Reciprocal or prepositional insert: as *ki* or *kici*
  - Possessive: as *glo* or *gliyo* or *gla*

- Contracted: Thus *ata* becomes *al, eca* or *ca* becomes *el* or *l, ga* or *hca* become *ȟ, ja, š, ka* becomes *g, pa* becomes *b, tu* becomes *l, uta* becomes *ul, yan* becomes *ye, za* becomes *s.*
- Adverbial: Roots take suffixes, such as *han* to *ijehan, ka* to *kab, ke, ki(ci), kel, l, la, na, otan, pa, kiya, šniyan, s'e, ta, ata, tu, wapa, ya(n), yakel, yankel, tan, tanhan.* (Cf. Buechel's *A Grammar of Lakota,* #75 and #198, (1)–(3), on adverbial roots.)

A Lakota Grammar Brief

Based on *A Grammar of Lakota* by Eugene Buechel and edited by George Paul Casey

Contents

Parts of Speech in Lakota

Nouns

- *Gender:* Only real gender is used in Lakota, not grammatical gender. A few specific forms exist but are identified where *bloka* or *winyela* are added to the generic noun of the male or female.
- *Number:* There are singular, dual, and plural. Plural is indicated by the suffix *pi* for animate nouns, man and animal, and is not indicated for inanimate nouns, except by means of a quantitative adjective or adverb. For the dual see *A Grammer of Lakota,* E. Buechel, #31, #170.
- *Case:* There are no strict case forms.

Pronouns

With the exception of the relative pronoun and neuter *it,* all English pronouns have a Lakota equivalent. And though Lakota has separate personal pronoun forms, it is the inseparate forms, both objective and subjective, which are the most important. They must be used along with verbs, nouns, and adjectives, and these pronouns vary with each verb according to conjugation. See *A Grammer of Lakota,* #39.

Adjectives

- Descriptive adjectives usually follow their nouns and pronouns.
- Limiting adjectives usually precede nouns and pronouns.
- Plurality of adjectives often need not be expressed, but when expressed, the suffix *pi* is used, or in a complex process of differentiating a syllable of the adjective is reduplicated.
- There are separate and inseparate possessive adjectives; the inseparate are the more important and are incorporated with their objects. Different forms of these are used depending on the class of things to which the possessed object belongs.
- For comparison, Lakota does not use *-er,* as in "wiser," but rather *sam,* "more," as in "more wise," *sam ksapa.* The superlative suffix, *-est,* is not used but rather *iyotan,* "most," or some other like adverb, as in *iyotan ksapa.*

Adverbs

Adverbs usually precede the word they modify. Their use in Lakota is complicated by their large variety, euphonic variations, and lack of English equivalents, except by circumlocution.

Verbs
Generally the verb terminates the clause or sentence.

Conjunctions
A conjunction simply supplies the connection by way of addition of two things, and by way of adjectival or adverbial relationship of one idea to another.

Prepositions
A preposition joins nouns and verbs, adjectivally or adverbially. The preposition usually follows or incorporates its object.

Interjections
An interjection is a word related to a noun or verb, but somewhat independently, and it expresses attitude.

Particles
A particle is a word that communicates the attitude of the one acting.

Participles
A participle is a verb acting as an adjective.

Infinitives and Gerunds
Infinitives and gerunds are ways of using a verb as a noun.

SUBJECT AND PREDICATE

Rule	English	Lakota
Number Agreement: Animate Subject		
singular subject takes a singular predicate:	An owl is hooting.	Hinhan wan hoton.
	The baby is crying.	Hokšicala kin céya.
collective subject takes a plural predicate:	Your people are very numerous.	Nitaoyate kin lila ótapi.
indefinite pronoun may be plural in meaning:	None cried.	Tuweni céyapi šni.
or singular:	No one cried.	Tuweni céye šni.
compound subject takes a plural predicate:	The boy and girl cry.	Hokšicala kin na wicincala kin céyapi.
compound subject equally important and joined by *kici* or *ob* take a plural predicate:	Peter and Paul did not come.	Peter na Paul kici hípi šni.
unequal subjects, a singular predicate:	Peter and the baby did not come.	Peter hokšicala kin kici hi šni.
plural subject and predicate need one sign of plural:	The children are crying.	Wakanheja kin céyapi.
Number Agreement : Inanimate Subject		
plurality expressed by an adjective or adverb, not by the suffix *pi*:	Many trees grow there.	Can óta el icage.
Person Agreement:		
with two or more personal pronoun subjects, predicate plural in preferred order, 1st, 2nd, 3rd:	The boy and I will come.	Miš hokšila kin kici unyanpi kte.
with a plural pronoun in the partitive genitive, preceded by a numeral or pronoun, the verb must agree in person with the plural pronoun:	Three of us will go home.	Unkiyepi kin yámni unglapi kte.
Except when using *tukte wanji* "which or any one," the "of" phrase is omitted, or the inseparable personal pronoun is used:	Which one of you will go home?	Nitukte wanji yagni kta he?
Except the "of" phrase may always be omitted when the meaning is clear:	Three of us will go home.	Yámni unglapi kte.

THE LINKING VERB "TO BE"

Rule	English	Lakota
General Rule: When the predicate **identifies**	This man is the boss.	Wicaša kin le itancan kin he e.
the subject *e "to be"* (*epi*, the plural) is used	This is my child.	Le micinca kin e.
for all 3rd person subjects:	Who is this?	Le túwe hwo?
for 1st and 2nd person subjects, "e" is in the pronoun:	I am the boss.	Itancan kin he míye.
When the predicate **describes** the subject, no verb	This man is good.	Le wicaša kin wašte.
is used, the linking idea being expressed, either	This one is good.	Le wašte.
by the position of the noun and predicate for 3rd	This one will be boss.	Le itancan kte.
person subjects:	What is this?	Le táku he?
or by use of *kin heca*, " is such":	This man is boss.	Wicaša kin le itancan kin héca.
	This one is boss.	Le itancan kin héca.
and with 1st and 2nd person subjects, the pronoun	You are pitiful.	Ónnišike.
may be incorporated with the *kin heca*:	I am sad.	Cantemašice.
or incorporated with the *kin heca*:	I am a good boy.	Hokšila wašte kin hemaca.
Special Cases: When "it" is the subject of an impersonal verb, translate only the predicate:	It is cold.	Osni yelo.
grammatically *i.e.* Lakota uses a substantive:	It is good to cry.	Céyapi kin he wašte.
really meaning "the person" or "the thing":	It is a man. It is Peter. It is I.	Wicaša kin héca. Peter e. Míye yelo.
when "has" indicates a present state of being, a verb with *un*, "to be," is used:	He has come home.	Wána agli un.

Note: Most other English semi-copulative verbs have no Lakota equivalents; hence the thought must be rephrased.

THE SIMPLE SENTENCE

Direct Objects:		
a simple sentence:	God made the earth.	Wakantanka maka kin káge.
a double object is required after such verbs as to teach, to ask, *etc.*:	I will give you a horse.	Šúnkawakan cic'u kte.
	I will teach you Lakota.	Lakota iapi kin onspeciciyin kte.
or these verbs are used in their absolute form:	I taught him.	Waonspewakiye.
a double object is required when an object represents a part of a person:	I shake your hand.	Napeciyuze.
and when an animate object is had, *wica* is used:	I have children.	Wakanheja wicabluha.
a complement object is required for some verbs:	They made John chairman.	John itancan kágapi.
Indirect Objects:		
these are indicated by *ki* or *kici;* the more important of the two objects goes first	I will give the money to John.	Mázaska kin le John wak'u kte.
	:I will give John the money.	John Mázaska kin le wak'u kte.
Modifiers:		
adjective usually follows its noun:	John is a good man.	John wicaša wašte kin héca.
noun or pronoun used **descriptively,** they follow:	The land is mine.	Le makoce mitawa kin he e.
limiting, they precede:	The pine tree is very tall.	Wazi can kin líla hánska.
adverb usually precedes the word modified:	She is really sick.	Líla kúja.
phrase, as seen in the English infinitive, becomes a noun clausal substantive in most cases, *esp* if used as a noun:	It is good for us to be here.	Lel unkunpi kin he wašte.
adjectival, recast keeping adjectival meaning:	He is a man of great widom.	Wicaša wan líla ksápa kin héca.
adverbial, used prepositionally, it can be usually kept so:	Man does not live by bread alone.	Aguyapi kin ecéla on wicaša kin nípi šni.
infinitive of purpose is used with a verb of locomotion, but may be recast into an adverbial clausal substantive:	I came to see my child.	Micinca kin wanglaka wahi.

COMPLEX SENTENCES
Noun Clauses and Noun Clausal Substantives

Indirect Statements : are introduced by "that," *kin he* in this word order, noun clause – *kin he* – main clause:	I believe that he is a good man.	Wicaša wašte kin héca kin he wicawala.
Except in positive declarative sentences, *esp* after verbs like "to know", "to realize", "to see" *etc.*, the *kin he* becomes *ca*	I know that man is a sinner.	Wicaša kin he wahtani s'a ca slolwaye.
Indirect Quotations: the *kin* combines with *éya, ecín, epcá* to form *kéya, kécin, képca*:	He says he wants to eat.	Wóta cin kéye.
Direct Quotations: *éya, ekiya, ecin* all follow their quote:	"Hello!" he said.	"Hau!" éye.
unless they are used with *hécel* or *lécel*:	He spoke thus to him: "Who are you?"	Lécel ekiye, "Nituwe hwo?"
leyá, heyá, hecín precede the quote, but the corresponding *eya* or *ecin* may be repeated at the end:	They said: "What is this?" they said.	Heyápi, "Le táku hwo?" eyápi.
Indirect Statements: the *kin he* is often omitted in conversation, *esp* when the subordinate verb is in the future tense:	I believe you will give me the money.	Mázaska kin mayak'u kte wicawala.

Adjective Clauses

Note: Because Lakota lacks a relative pronoun, relative adjective clauses must be turned into adjectival clausal substantives, which are:

Restrictive: with the antecedent known to the speaker, use *kin he* for **singular** use:	The man whom you wish to see went home.	Wicaša wan wanlaka yacin kin he kigle.
for **plural** use: Note article change after antecedent.	The men whom you wish to see went home.	Wicaša k'eya wanwicalaka yacin kin hena kiglapi.
Restrictive: with the antecedent unknown to the speaker, use *héci, héci he, hécina*:	Whoever said that did not tell the truth.	Túwa heyá heci wicake šni.
Descriptive: make use of particles *ca, can, cána, cánahe,* or *canhe* :	He saw a man who was well dressed.	Wicaša wan tányan igluze ca wanyanke.
	He who has a good wife is really lucky.	Wicaša tawicu kin wašte canhe líla tányan wókini.
Identifying: *esp* as "it" introduces the antecedent, use *ca*:	It is John whom he meant.	John e ca ke.
	It is food which we came to buy.	Wóyute ca opeton unhipi.
	Who is it who hit you?	Túwe ca anipa he?
Additive or Explanatory: coordinate the clause with the rest of the sentence:	He gave me a book which I read.	Wówapi wan mak'u na blawa.

Adverbial and Substantive Clauses

Note: These clauses are introduced by relative adverbs; when **definite** use *kin,* when **indefinite** use *ca, can, cána.* Such clauses are of:

TIME : *tohanl ... hehanl:*	When the sun goes down, then you will come home.	Tohanl wi mahel iyaye kin, hehanl yaupi kte.
tohanyan ... hehanyan:	When he lived with his mother, then he was good.	Tohanyan hunku kin kici ti kin, hehanyan wašte.
	When he wants [then] he speaks to his friends.	Tohanl cin can [hehanl] takolaku kin wókiyake.
PLACE: *tuktel ... hel:*	Where they killed the man, there they buried him.	Wicaša kin he tuktel ktepi kin hel ȟápi.
	Where they killed an enemy, there they buried him.	Tuktel tóka wan ktepi cana hel ȟápi.
tohanyan ... hehanyan:	He went as far as he could.	Tohanyan okihi kin hehanyan iyaye.
MANNER: *tókel ... hécel, ecél, iyecel:*	You will do it as I did it.	Tókel ecamon kin he iyecel ecanonpi kte.
	Do it as he told you!	Tókel éya cana ecel econ po.

Note: Often in conversation one or other adverb may be omitted just as is done in English.

Some Adverbial Expressions

while	*k'el, el, icunhan:*	Talk to a boy when he is growing.	Hokšila wan icage k'el wókiyaka yo.
since	*etanhan, ehantanhan:*	It is three days since they came.	Hipi kin ehantanhan yámni can.
until	*itokab ... šni* in present time:	He did not die until he talked to me.	T'e šni itokab wómakiyaka.
before	*itokab* and future time:	I want to see you before I go.	Mni kte itokab wanciyanka wacin.
after	*óhakab, iyohakab:*	All eat after they wash their hands.	Nape glujajapi kin iyohakab iyuha wótapi kte.

Adverbial Clauses

or simply coordinate:	All wash their hands and afterward they will eat.	Iyuha nape glujajapi na iyohakab wótapi kte.
whither *tókiyab*:	Whither I am going you cannot come after me.	Tókiyab ble kin cin he mihatab yaupi oyakihipi šni.
whence *tókiyatanhan*:	Nobody will come whence I came.	Tókiyatanhan wahi kin tuweni u kte šni

Note: These adverbial clausal substantives are introduced by non-coordinating conjunctions, which in English are of themselves subordinating conjunctions; thus –

although *ešá, ešan, ešaš, šaš, yeša, yešan, yeš, weša, wešan, weš, keš, kayéš*:	Although they really shot at him, he got away unscathed.	Líla kutepi eša inihanšni hiyaye.
	Although it is only a lamb, you don't even give it to me.	Tóhanni tahcašunkala cincala kayeš mayak'u šni.
if, provided, unless *kin, kinhan, kinahán, ehantanš, ehantanhanš* :	If you have much, give to the poor.	Nitawoyuha kin óta ehantanš, wahpanica wicak'u w
if, doubting *hécihan, hécinahan, héci*:	If that is right tell it straight.	Hécetu hécihan owotanla oyaka yo.
because, since *ca, canke, héon, hecel, kin on, icin*:	I fired the man because he does not obey me.	Wicaša kin he namah'on šni ca, abluštan.
ca, canke are used postpositively:	I fired him; the man does not obey me, that is why [I fired him].	Abluštan; wicaša kin he namah'on šni ca.
icin is used prepositively:	I fired him for the man does not obey me.	Abluštan, icin wicaša kin he namah'on šni.
so that, in order that *ca*:	They stole the money in order to buy meat.	Talo opeton ca mázaska kin he manonpi.
or *hécel*:	They stole the money in order to buy meat.	Mázaska kin he manonpi, hécel talo opetonpi kte.
lest, in order that not *owekiš, owekinaš, owekinahanš* :	Don't kill that lest they will kill you.	Hécon šni ye, owekiš niktepi kte.
so, as a result *ca, hécel*:	He is very sick, so that he cannot walk.	Líla kuja ca máni okihi šni.
as … as *make a simple sentence of this*:	His clothes are as white as snow.	Tahayapi kin wa iyecel ska.
or *coordinate the sentence*:	You know as well as I.	Héna tányan slolwaye, na niš éya tányan slolyaye.
as if, as though *s'e, s'elececa*:	We go about as if lost sheep.	Táhcašùnkala s'e núniyan unkomanipi.
than, more than *sam, isam*:	I cannot find a man wiser than you.	Wicaša wan nisam ksapa ca iyewaya owakihi šni.

VERB TENSES AND MOODS

Note: the **dual form** is the same as the 1st person plural without the *pi* termination and is used when one person addresses another and includes him or her self in the action, being, or condition, thus: Father, let us go home. *Até, ungni kte.*

Indefinite Time: has two aspects –

Present: actually true now:	It is cold.	Osni yelo.
generally true now:	He never eats meat.	Talo yúte šni.
Past: took place in the past:	We saw him or her yesterday.	Ḣtálehan wanunyankapi.
was generally true:	The Lakotas usually ate much meat.	Lakota kin talo óta yútapi s'a.

Note: Adverbs help fix past and even present time.

Tense and Mood

Future: the indefinite with *kta, kte*

whenever used in English:	I will not go home.	Wagni kte šni.
when the *kta* is not repeated:	He will eat and go to bed.	Wótin na iyunkin kte.
when the verb is understood:	It will be warm today.	Lehanl mašte kte.
when used elliptically:	Will you come? I will not.	Yau kta he? Kte šni.
when used as a substitute for the imperative:	Give this to me.	Le mayak'u kte.
when with the infinitive of purpose:	I have much to tell you.	Táku óta eciciyapi kta bluha.
when with a clause of purpose, in this **order**: purpose clause – *kta on* – main verb:	They called for the boy that they might question him.	Hokšila kin he wiyungapi kta on kicopi.
with an imperative simply coordinate:	Turn him loose that he may go.	Kiyuška yo, iyayin kte.
with expressions as "is" or "was to," "going to," "sure to", *etc.* by *kta un*:	He who steals is sure to be in prison.	Túwa wamanon kin he kaškapi kta un.

Present Perfect: The indefinite

with some form of *yuštan* to complete, finish, together with a fixing adverb:	Now I have finished eating.	Wána wol miglustan.

Past Perfect:

use *k'un* or *un* with the verb:	I had told him long ago.	Ehanni owakiyake k'un.
indicate prior action by *nahahci … šni hanni*, not yet … when, or before:	The boy went to look for the horses before the sun had risen.	Nahahci wi hinape šni hanni hokšila kin šunkole iyaye.
or:	The sun had not yet risen when the boy went to look for the horses.	

Future Perfect: this tense is expressed by the **indefinite future**.

Progressive Tense:

indefinite with a verb suffix *han* or *he*:	They were walking home leisurely.	Asnikiya glahanpi.
infinitive with inflected *yanka* or *un*:	I was listening to it.	Nah'on manke.
	I am waiting for it.	Ape waun.

Emphatic Tense:

verb "do" with *kišto* or *kšto*:	Somebody is coming.	Ku kšto.
	I did do that.	Hécamon kšto.
imperative "do" or "be sure to," use *ecaš*:	Be sure to come [Do come]!	Ecaš u wo!

Subjunctive: a mood of –

wish, may, would that, use *toke … ni*:	I wish I were dead.	Toke mat'a ni.
toke eša … ni:	May God have mercy on me.	Toke eša Wakantanka onšimala ni.
… ni:	May God have mercy on me.	Wakantanka onšimala ni.
contrary to fact; subordinate clause … *k'eš* … main clause and *tka*:	If I had a stick I would kill the snake.	Can wan bluha k'eš, sintehla kin wakat'a tka.
subordinate clause and *tka*:	I would buy it [if I had the money].	Opeton tka [mázaska kin bluha k'eš].

uncertainty, use present or future tense, and the indicative, factual mood.

Imperative: the skeme of terminal particles to the sentence –

Addressee:	Conditions:	Addresser: Male	Female
singular	3rd person singular verb		
	if verb ends in *a, an, e, i, in* or negative:	yo.	ye.
	otherwise:	wo.	we.
plural	3rd person singular positive:	po.	pi.
	3rd person plural if negative:	yo.	ye.

Tense and Mood

Command: See terminal particles above –	Come!	U wo!
with [*ito*] use the future tense:	Let us pray.	[Ito] , waceunkiyapi kte.
verb in 2nd person with terminal *kilo* or *cin*:	Do not come near me.	[Ungna] , kiyela yau kilo!
Note: The latter is the strongest form; brackets [] mean optional use.		
Request:		
men and women use *yeto,* or *nito* only	Listen for a minute.	Anagoptanpi yeto.
women, to imply one's bidding be done at once for a good reason, or for just a minute		
Here *ito* is optional:	Now listen for a minute, friend.	Kóla, ito anagoptan yeto!
na or *yema* women say:	Listen to me!	Anamagoptan yema!
what is the matter you don't, eša – indicative – šni:	Give that money!	Eša mázaska omakiyanpi ye!
Entreaty: "Please."		
singular, 3rd person singular and *ye*:	Friend, help me!	Kóla, omakiyi ye.
plural, 3rd person plural and *ye*:	Friends, help me!	Kóla, omakiyanpi ye!
Consent: "very well *or* all right *etc.*"		
future indicative:	You may go.	Yin kte.
ho [*ca*] and the future:	You may go.	Ho, ca yin kte.
ho [*ca*] and the imperative:	You may go.	Ho, ca ya yo.

orders given to others, use *ho* and *wo* or *po* by men; *ho* and *we* or *pi* by women and terminal particle; orders including the speaker in the action men use *ho* and *ye, piye,* or *yo,* and women use *ho* and *na,* and *pi* and *na,* and the future indicative, thus

ADDRESSER		ADDRESSEE Singular	Plural
man	All right, go!	Hówo iyaya yo!	Hópo iyaya po!
woman	All right, go!	Hówe iyaya ye!	Ho, iyaye pi!
man	All right, let's go!	Hóye unyin kte!	Hópiye unyanpi kta!
woman	All right, let's go!	Hó na unyin kte!	Hópi na unyanpi kte!

MODAL AUXILIARY VERBS: The following verbs have equivalents in Lakota but only in a limited sense –

should *or* ought, it is fitting, use *iyececa*:	I should not do that.	Hécamon iyececa šni.
should, it is likely, use *iteka*:	He should be coming home now.	Wánna ku iteke.
would, customarily do *or* be, use *šna*:	John would be drunk.	John itomni kin héca šna. or
or:	John is usually drunk.	John itomni kin héca šna.
can *or* could, ability:	I can sing.	Walowan owakihi.
possibility:	This song cannot be sung.	Olowan kin he lowanpica šni.

INFINITIVE, PARTICIPLE, AND GERUND

Infinitive: may be a –

noun substantive becomes a clausal substantive:	Boys like to play.	Škátapi kin he hokšila kin iyokipipi.
adjectival modifier becomes an adjective:	He is a man to be trusted.	Wicaša wacinyepica kin héca.
or an appositive clausal substantive:	He is a man to be trusted.	Wicaša wan túwe ke éyaš wacinyan okihi kin héca.
adverbial complement, an infinitive:	He asked him to come.	U ši.
adverb of purpose, an infinitive with a verb of locomotion:	I shall go to fish.	Hokuwa mni kte.

Infinitive Clauses: These depend on the main verb, with word order –

subordinate clause … main clause,		
to wish, want, *i.e. cin:*	I want you to be good.	Niwašte kta wacin.
to believe, *etc., i.e. kécin*:	I believe this man is good.	Le wicaša kin he wašte kecanmi.
to declare one to, *i.e. kéya*:	He declared the people to have arrived.	Oyate wan ahi kta kéye.
to consider, think one (one's self) to be, *i.e. la, kága, yawa* and the reflexive forms:	I considered him good.	Íye wašte wala.
to see, hear, *wanyanka, etc.* with a noun object:	I saw a dog bite your boy.	Šúnka wan hokšila nitawa kin yahtaka wanblaka.
subordinate clause … *kin* or *ca* … main verb		
to know, *i.e. slolya*:	I know this man is good.	Wicaša kin le wašte ca slolwaye.
infinitive … main verb		
to command, ask, *etc., ši*:	You told me to come.	U mayaši.
NOTE: the infinitive with *cin*:	I want to wash myself.	Miglujaja wacin.
double objects for *wanyanka, nah'on,* and pronouns:	I saw you coming.	Yau wanciyanke.
substantival clauses with *apé*:	I was waiting for you to arrive.	Yahi acipe manke.

Participle and Gerund:

subjective participial complement:	He lay sleeping.	Ištinma hpáye.
use the infinitive:	Taking all his possessions he went away.	Tawoyuha oyas'in gluha iyaye.
	He took it without saying a thing.	Táku eyé šni icu.
or recast in the sense:	This looks bewildering to me.	Le awableze šni.
objective complement, a substantival clause:	I heard them singing.	Lowanpi nawah'on.
other participles and gerunds:	Having been blind, I now see.	Ištamagonge, k'éyaš wána watonwe.
use the appropriate clausal substantives:	I love going to school.	Wablawa kin he waštewalaka.

ADVERBS
Some Commonly Used

Lakota	English
ecána	soon
ehánni	long ago
lecála	a little while ago
lecáš	just a minute ago
nakéš	at last
tokáta	later on
ungnáhela	suddenly
wáncak	at once
watóhanl	sometime in the future
ijéhan	often
óhinni	always
téhan	for a long time
wancala	once
wána	now
hel, hétu, héci, héciya	there
kal, kákiya	yonder
kul, kúta	below
lel, létu, léci, léciya	here
mahétuya	within
tankál	outside
timá	inside
téhan	far
téhantu	far
tokánl	elsewhere
tokányan	elsewhere
tuktétu ke c'eyaš	in any place
tuktétu k'eyaš	in any place
wankál, wankáta	high up
hetán	from there
héciyatan	thence
kákiyatanhan	from yonder
kútanhan	from below
letán	from here
léciyatan	from here
mahétanhan	from within
tankátanhan	from without
tehántanhan	from afar
tokánltanhan	from somewhere
tókiyatanhan	from some place
wankátanhan	from on high
hecíyotan	thereabout
kakíyotan	somewhere yonder
lecíyotan	hereabout
tokíyotan	somewhere
akókiya	beyond

Lakota	English
héktakiya	backward
héciya, hétkiya	in that direction
kákiya, kátkiya	toward yonder place
kútakiya	downward
léciya, létkiya	toward this place
tóketkiya	toward some place
wankátkiya	upward
hógna	along that way
lógna	along this way
hehányan	that far
kahányan	that far
lehányan	this far
ecínšniyan	thoughtlessly
iwaštela	slowly
oh'ánkoya	quickly
šicáya	badly
tányan	well
witkótkoya	foolishly
ecél	so, thus
ecéhci	exactly so
hécel, hécelya	in that manner
iyécel	in that manner
iyécehci	in exactly the same manner
kákel	thus, so
lécel, lécelya	in this manner
hógna	in that way
lógna	in this way
tuktógna ke c'eyaš	in any manner whatever
áta, átaya	wholly, entirely
icéwinš	unusually
iyótan	most
kítanla	a little
kitányel	just a little
líla	very
hiyá	no
šni	not
to, hau, han, ohán	yes (men say)
han, toš	yes (women say)
tákuwe	why
tóhan	when
tókel	how
tuktél	where
tókiya	whither
tókiyatanhan	whence
séce, nacéca	perhaps
etc.	*etc.*

PERSONAL ADJECTIVES AND RELATIONSHIPS

Separate *poss adj*	Inseparate goods	Body Parts	Non-body Parts	Relationships
mitawa *my*	mita...	ma...	mi...	mi...
nitawa *your*	nita...	ni...	ni...	ni...
táwa *his/her*	ta...			...ku
unkitawapi *our*	unkita...pi	unk...pi	unk...pi	unki...pi
nitawapi *your*	nita...pi	ni...pi	ni...pi	ni...pi
táwapi *their*	ta...pi	...pi	...pi	...kupi

RELATIONSHIP	MAN'S	WOMAN'S	RELATIONSHIP	MAN'S	WOMAN'S
father	até	até	older brother	cíye	tibló
my father	atewaye kin	atewaye kin	my o. brother	ciyéwaye kin	mitíblo kin
your father	niyate kin	niyate kin	your o. brother	niciye kin	nitiblo kin
his/her father	atkuku kin	atkuku kin	his/her o. bro.	ciyeku kin	tibloku kin
I have for father	atewaya	atewaya	I have for o. bro.	ciyewaya	tiblowaya
mother	ína	← same	younger brother	misun	← same
my mother	ináwaye kin		my y. brother	misunkala kin	
your mother	nihun kin		your y. brother	nisunkala kin	
his/her mother	húnku kin		his/her y. bro.	sunkaku kin	
I have for mother	inawaya		to have for y. bro	sunkawaya	
grandfather	tunkašila	← same	older sister	tanké	cuwé
my grandfather	mitunkašila		my older sister	mitanke kin	cuwe kin
your grandfather	nitunkašila		your older sister	nitanke kin	nicuwe kin
his/her g. father	tunkašitku kin		his/her o. sister	tankeku kin	cuweku kin
I have for g. father	tunkašilawaya		I have for o. sis.	tankewaya	cuwewaya
grandmother	uncí	← same	younger sister	tankší	tanká
my grandmother	unciwaye kin		my y. sister	mitankši kin	mitánka kin
your grandmother	nikunši kin		your y. sister	nitankši kin	nitanka kin
his/her g. mother	kunšitku kin		his/her y. sister	tankšitku kin	tankáku kin
I have for g. mom.	unciwaya		I have for y. sis.	tankšiwaya	tankawaya
grandchild	takója	← same			
my grandchild	mitákoja kin				
your grandchild	nitakoja kin				
his/her grandchild	takojakpaku kin				
I have for g. child	takojawaya				

Note: other family relationships may be found in Buechel's *A Grammar of Lakota.*

PREPOSITIONS
Some Commonly Used

Lakota	English
ókšan	about
koákatan, ópta	across
opáya	along
égna, ópeya	among
ókšan, ohómni	around
ektá	at
aglágla	at the edge of
ohláteya	beneath
okó	between
akótanhan, koákatan	beyond
kaglá	by, near
on	by means of
etánhan	from
ektá, el, mahél, ógna, on	in
aglágla, kaglá	near
on	of
akánl, el	on
on	on account of
akótanhan, *or* koákatan	on the other side
ópta	over, across
óhan, ópta	through
ektá, el	to
ópeya	together with
étkiya	toward
ohláteya	under
el	unto
kicí, ob, on, ópeya	with
mahél	within

Lakota	English
aglágla	at the edge of
akánl	on
akótanhan	on the other side
égna	among
ékta	at, in
ektá	to
el	in, to, on
etánhan	from
étkiya	toward
iákanl	upon
ihákab	behind, after
íheciya	in that way from
ihéktab	behind
ihúkul	under
ihútab	downstream from
iȟéyata	in the hills from
ikíyela	near to
ilázatanhan	back of
imáhel	within
isákib	beside, near to
isánpa	beyond
itáhena	on this side of
itánkal	on the outside of
ítehan	far from
itókab	before
iwánkab	above
íyecana	soon, thereafter
iyóhakab	after
kaglá	by, near

Note: This list includes some prepositional adverbs.

Lakota	English
kicí	with [one]
koákatan	beyond
mahél	in, within
ob	with [many]
ógna	in
óhan	through
ohómni	around
ohláteya	under, beneath
okó	between
ókšan	around, about
on	of, with, by means of, in, on account of
opáya	along
ópeya	with, together with
ópta	through, across, over

Prepositional Suffixes

–ata, –ta	*insep suff*	at
–etu, –tu	*insep suff*	at
–na		at
–kiya		toward
–tanhan, tan		from
–wapa, –pa		beyond, *etc.*
–íyotan		in the vicinity of
–íyotanhan		about, in the neighborhood of

PREFIXES

"a" *insep:* the action is done on
"o" *insep:* place in or within which
"é" *insep:* place at which, accented
"i" *insep:* done or happens with on account of, for, with *ref* to

PREFIXES

"i" *pref to n*: after, following, next
"i" *pref to num card*: makes *num ord*
"i" *pref to adv of place or time and to some prep*: clarifies their relation to a preceding substantive

INTERJECTIONS AND INDEPENDENT ELEMENTS

a...a — Request to listen to or for
apá — Surprise
aš — Disapproval, but friendly
e — Joy to hear or see the pleasant
ecé — Surprise, and indignant
hahó...hahó — Gratitude and Joy for a gift
epelá — Joy at seeing much food
háun [man] — Pain or Sorrow
háye ... háye — Delight at a gift
hehé, hehehé — Regret at a misfortune
héi [man] — Attract one's attention
hěpela ... hépela — Joy, Surprise at seeing a friend
hiná ... hiná [woman] — Regret at another's mishap
hinún ... hinún [woman] — Regret at one's own luck
hókahe — Signal for action
hokahé — Welcome to visitors
hunhé ... hunhé — Regret
hunhunhé — Regret
ma [woman] — Being taken by Surprise
oȟ *or* ȟoȟ [man] — Disgust
tukí [woman] — Wonder
ši [woman] — Attract attention and many other meanings

tulá [man] — Surprise, but indignant
wan [man] — Surprise
ya [woman] — Fright, but pretended
yu [woman] — Disapproval, Prohibition
yun [woman] — Pain, Fatigue
itó ... — Come, Come on, Now then .... [to stir courage in one or one's self to do a thing. It precedes the sentence and takes the imperative or the future tense of the verb.]

ecéš [woman] — Surprise, Resentment at what another dares to say against the speaker
iyúwinškaš *or* icínyunškaš — Indignation at something said or done by another
mak'éye [woman] *or* wan k'éya [man] — The answer to a question or a joke one considers foolish.

túwa kakéša — This and the next three mean
túwa kakéšaš — Strong Indignation at a
túwehca škéka — statement considered
ohúnwela — foolish

wan ká wan — Surprise a sudden sight
wan lé wan [woman] — of something, thus: Look
ma ká wan — at this (that) !
ma lé wan [woman]

... séce — ... I think.
... nacéce — ... I suppose.
... kcáma — ... I thought. [I was sure!]
Akšáka — ... It is too bad ...
Lotkúnkešni ... — By the way ...
Únš'keyapika ... — By the way ... [returning to the topic]
nap'táhena — something undone because it slipped one's mind
ho *or* ho ca ... — Well *or* Well then ...
éya ... — Well then ... [to introduce one clause of a compound sentence when the other clause is coordinated with k'eyaš *or* tka]
ihó ... — Look, See, Behold ... [preceding a sentence to call attention to its topic.]
ínska *or* ínska in ... — Let me see ... [to indicate a pause to think, and can interrupt any sentence.]

syllables with changeable vowels

gla	hma	kša	pca	ska
ga	hpa	k̇a	psa	šma
han	hta	k'a	pta	špa
hca	kpa	ma	spa	tka
kca	ksa	man	ška	tkan
ṫa	tía	ya	yan	za

IN LAKOTA EACH CONSONANT AND VOWEL IS PRONOUNCED

But not in all words, as *ca pa wan*
In inflections of *bla ha la kta pa*

In suffixes:

1. *a* and *an* change to *e*:
   but sometimes the vowel may drop, *esp* where there is an elision and a change of consonants
   Changeable are: the endings of verbs, adverbs, adjectives, the sentence and coordinate clauses, but not before *ca*, and often not before *canke* and direct quotation, not at the end of indirect quotes, but before parenthetical expressions, but not before *ška*

   Changeable are: *a* or *an* that occur before words that begin with, the letters *e, hc, k, k', l, s, s', š,* and before articles, prepositions, some indefinite adjectives, and subordinate conjunctions and before particles that are adverbial, interrogative, imperative, declarative or subjunctive and before *ya, kiya, k̇, laka, ši, konza, napin, pica*

2. *a* or *an* change to *i* or *in* before *na, nainš, ye,* or the future tense

3. *i* of the plural ending *pi* changes to *e* in verbs before *lo*

THE FORMATION OF VERBS

1. waókiwicunkicicaksapi, We sever things in the middle for them.

absol	*prep*	*ki*	*pron*	*ki*	*kici*	*ka*	*pa*	*ya*	*yu*	*stem.*
wa –	o –	ki –	wicun –		kici –	ca –				ksapi

2. waókiwawicunkiciksapi, We cut things through the middle with a knife for them.

absol	*prep*	*ki*	*na, wa, wo*	*pron*	*ki*	*kici*	*stem.*
wa –	o –	ki –	wa –	wicun –		kici –	ksapi

3. wawéciyaotan'in, I make things manifest for one.

absol	*pron*	*ki, kici*	*ka, pa, ya, yu*	*prep*	*stem.*
wa –	we –	ci –	ya –	o –	tan'in

4. wanáowat'inza, I press things in tight with my foot.

absol	*na*	*prep*	*pron*	*ki, kici*	*stem.*
wa –	na –	o –	wa –		t'inza

5. wawówaoh'anko, I make lively by punching or shooting.

absol	*wa, wo*	*pron*	*ki, kici*	*prep*	*stem.*
wa –	wo –	wa –		o –	h'anko

6. Verbs with the following initial syllables follow rule No. 2 above:
   ca, ce, co, k̇o, k̇a, lo, ma, ṗa, šu, un as do their derivatives:
   ica, ice, waco, cok'in, wako, iko, waka, oma, wama, *etc.*

Note: The meaning of the additives to verbs :

... ka	act of striking with, or of some similar motion, even that of wind or water
... pa	act of pressing or weighing upon, pushing, sitting, lying upon
wa ...	the *absolute* form of the verb, *i.e.* incapable of taking an object
na ...	act of the feet, a spontaneous action
wa ...	action of a knife or saw
wo ...	an act done by shooting, poking, thrusting, or blowing with the mouth; Note: this is not the contraction of wa + o.
ya ...	action with the mouth, literally and figuratively
yu ...	action with the hands, action in general
k̇i ...	action performed in the middle
... ki	possessive form of the verb
... k ..., ... kici ...,	to or for someone
a ..., e ..., i ..., o ...	the inseparable preposition

VERBS OF LOCOMOTION

ya	to be on the way to some place
i	to have gone to some place
u	to be coming to this place
hi	to arrive at this place

to go to one's home	gla
to arrive at one's home	k̇i
to come to one's home here	ku
to arrive at one's home here	gli

suffix ... húnni indicates the arrival was not unexpected and the word is added to i, hi, ki, gli, thus: ihúnni, hihúnni, kihúnni, glihúnni

prefix	a ...	accompanied by something not one's own
	glo ...	accompanied by something one's own
	hiyo ...	to go for something not one's own
	gliyo ...	to go for something one's own

Double verbs: hiyúnka, to arrive at a place not one's own and spend the night [the fact being mentioned there]

Special double verbs:

hiyú	to start to come	iyáya	to start to go
hiyáya	to pass by	glicu	to start to come home
kigla	to start to go home	gligla	to pass by on one's way home

Illustration of the Use of the Eight Words of Locomotion

Suppose A takes a trip to B's house and returns, there being six steps of the journey:

A	1	2	3	B
	6	5	4	

C (a neighbor)

	1	2	3	4	5	6
A's point of view:	mni kte	ble	wahi	wagla	waku	wagli
B's point of view:	u kte	u	hi	gni kte	gla	ki
C's point of view:	yin kte	ya	i	gni kte	gla	ki

A says: (1) I shall go. (2) I go. (3) I arrived. (4) I go home. (5) I come home. (6) I arrived home.
B says: (1) He'll come. (2) He comes. (3) He arrived. (4) He'll go home. (5) He goes home. (6) He arrived.
C says: (1) He'll go. (2) He goes. (3) He arrived. (4) He'll go home. (5) He goes home. (6) He arrived back.

THE VERB "TO BE"–ITS USES

yanká: existence temporary or accidental, in a certain place when an event occurs, with an animate subject:	Many men were there when he died.	Wicaša óta yankapi kin hehanl t'e.
mere existance or presence in a certain place for an inanimate subject:	The money was there so I took it.	Mázaska kin he yanká, canké iwacu.
to form the progressive time:	I was listening to it.	Nah'on manké.
un: continued being in a place, an animate subject only:	That we are here is good. He is mute.	Lel unkúnpi kin he wašte. Ié šni un.
to form the progressive:	I am waiting for it.	Apé waún.
oúnyan: to remain as if it were one's home whereas it is not :	I stayed there six years.	Hel waníyetu šákpe owáunyan.
oúnyeya: to make one's home in a place	I lived there many years.	Hel waníyetu óta owáunyeya.
hiyéya: existance of inanimate things, singular in form but plural in meaning:	He cut all the trees there.	Can hiyéya kin kašléšleca.
yukán *or* **yuké:** to be "on hand": waníce: something is not on hand:	There is meat on hand. There is no meat.	Taló yuké. Taló waníce.
e *or* **épi:** the copulative "to be," for identification: for description ["is" is understood]:	 This man is boss. This man is good.	 Le wicaša kin itáncan kin he le e. Le wicaša kin wašte.

IRREGULAR VERBS

to be	**to eat something**	**to go**	*future*:	**to come forth**	
waún	wáta	bla	mni kte	wahíyu	wagní kte
yaún	yáta	la	ni kte	yahílu	yagní kte
un	yúta	ya	yin kte	hiyú	gni kte
unk'únpi	unyútapi	unyánpi	unyánpi kte	unhíyupi	unglápi kte
yaúnpi	yátapi	lápi	lápi kte	yahílupi	yaglápi kte
únpi	yútapi	yápi	yápi kte	hiyúpi	glápi kte

to go away		**to say something**	**to do**	**to lie down**
manká	iblábla	epá	ecámon	munká
nanká	ilála	ehá	ecánon	nunká
yanká	iyáya	éya	ecón	yunká
unyánkapi	unkíyayapi	éunkeyapi	ecúnkonpi	unyúnkapi
nankápi	ilálapi	ehápi	ecánonpi	nunkápi
yankápi	iyáyapi	eyápi	ecónpi	yunkápi

to carry away		**to think**	**to eat**	**to run**
ábla	iblámni kte	ecámi	wawáta	waímnanka
ála	iláni kte	ecáni	wayáta	yaínanka
áya	iyáyin kte	ecín	wóta	ínyanka
unkáyapi	unkíyayapi kte	unkécinpi	waúnyutapi	unkínyankapi
álapi	ilálapi kte	ecánipi	wayátapi	yaínyankapi
áyapi	iyáyapi kte	ecínpi	wótapi	ínyankapi

	to go home	**to use something**
ámni kte	waglá	mun
áni kte	yaglá	nun
áyin kte	gla	un
unkáyapi kte	unglápi	unkúnpi
álapi kte	yaglápi	núnpi
áyapi kte	glápi	únpi

SOME PARTICLES

Interrogative : these are *postp.* after the question
men: hwo, he, *or* so
women: huwé, he, *or* so

Declarative: ending the sentence as to fact
men: **yeló** (follows after e, i, in, an unchangeable a *or* an)
women: **we** (follows after o, on, u, un), ye (follows after i *or* in) **yelé** (follows an unchangeable a *or* an)

Note: No declarative particle is used by women after e or changeable a *or* an

CLASSES OF VERBS

English	Class 1 *pron prefix* to strike	Class 1 *pron insert* to receive	Class 2 *pron prefix* to praise	Class 2 *pron insert* to leave alone
I strike	wakáštaka	iwácu	blatán	ablúštan
I strike thee	cicáštaka	icícu	ciyátan	acíyuštan
I strike him	wakáštaka	iwácu	blatán	ablúštan
I strike you	cicáštakapi	icícupi	ciyátanpi	acíyuštanpi
I strike them	wicáwakaštaka	iwícawacu	wicáblatan	awícabluštan
thou strikest	yakáštaka	iyácu	latán	alúštan
thou strikest me	mayákaštaka	imáyacu	mayálatan	amáyaluštan
thou strikest him	yakáštaka	iyácu	latán	alúštan
thou strikest us	unyákaštakapi	unkíyacupi	unyálatanpi	unkáyaluštanpi
thou strikest them	wicáyakaštaka	iwícayacu	wicálatan	awícaluštan
he strikes*	kaštáka	icú	yatán	ayúštan
he strikes me	makáštaka	imácu	mayátan	amáyuštan
he strikes thee	nicáštaka	inícu	niyátan	aníyuštan
he strikes him	kaštáka	icú	yatán	ayúštan
he strikes us	unkáštakapi	unkícupi	unyátanpi	unkáyuštanpi
he strikes you	nicáštakapi	inícupi	niyátanpi	aníyuštanpi
he strikes them	wicákaštaka	iwícacu	wicáyatan	awícayuštan
we strike	unkáštakapi	unkicupi	unyátanpi	unkáyuštanpi
we strike thee	unníkaštakapi	unkínicupi	unníyatanpi	unkániyuštanpi
we strike him	unkáštakapi	unkícupi	unyátanpi	unkáyuštanpi
we strike you	unnícaštakapi	unkínicupi	unníyatanpi	unkániyuštanpi
we strike them	wicúnkáštakapi	iwícuncupi	wicúnyatanpi	awícunyuštanpi
you strike	yakáštakapi	iyácupi	latánpi	alúštanpi
you strike me	mayákaštakapi	imáyacupi	mayálatanpi	amáyaluštanpi
you strike him	yakaštakapi	iyácupi	latánpi	alúštanpi
you strike us	unyákaštakapi	unkíyacupi	unyálatanpi	unkáyaluštanpi
you strike them	wicáyakaštakapi	iwícayacupi	wicálatanpi	awícaluštanpi
they strike	kaštákapi	icúpi	yatánpi	ayúštanpi
they strike me	makáštakapi	imácupi	mayátanpi	amáyuštanpi
they strike thee	nicáštakapi	inícupi	niyátanpi	aníyuštanpi
they strike him	kaštákapi	icúpi	yatánpi	ayúštanpi
they strike us	unkáštakapi	unkícupi	unyátanpi	unkáyuštanpi
they strike you	nicáštakapi	inícupi	niyátanpi	aníyuštanpi
they strike them	wicákaštakapi	iwícacupi	wicáyatanpi	awícayuštanpi

*This form is also the form of the infinitive.

English	Class 1 *ki* long form *prefixed* to show to	Class 1 *ki* long form *inserted* to do to one	Class 1 *ki* short form *prefixed* to give back to
I ... to *or* for thee	cicípazo	ocícih'an	cicú
I ... him	wakípazo	owákih'an	wécu
I ... you	cicípazopi	ocícih'anpi	cicúpi
I ... them	wicáwakipazo	owícawakih'an	wicáwecu
thou ... me	mayákipazo	omáyakih'an	miyécu
thou ... him	yakípazo	oyákih'an	yécu
thou ... us	unyákipazopi	unkóyakih'anpi	unyécupi
thou ... them	wicáyakipzo	owícayakih'an	wicáyecu
he ... me	makípazo	omákih'an	mícu
he ... thee	nicípazo	onícih'an	nícu
he ... him*	kipázo	okíh'an	kicú
he ... us	unkípazopi	unkókih'anpi	unkícupi
he ... you	nicípazopi	onícih'anpi	nícupi
he ... them	wicákipazo	owícakih'an	wicákicu
we ... thee	unnícipazopi	unkónicih'anpi	unnícupi
we ... him	unkípazopi	unkókih'anpi	unkícupi
we ... you	unnícipazopi	unkónicih'anpi	unnícupi
we ... them	wicúnkipazopi	owícunkih'anpi	wicúnkicupi
you ... me	mayákipazopi	omáyakih'anpi	miyécupi
you ... him	yakípazopi	oyákih'anpi	yécupi
you ... us	unyákipazopi	unkóyakih'anpi	unyécupi
you ... them	wicáyakipazopi	owícayakih'anpi	wicáyecupi
they ... me	makípazopi	omakih'anpi	mícupi
they ... thee	nicípazopi	onícih'anpi	nícupi
they ... him	kipázopi	okíhíanpi	kicúpi
they ... us	unkípazopi	unkókih'anpi	unkícupi
they ... you	nicípazopi	onícih'anpi	nícupi
they ... them	wicákipazopi	owícakih'anpi	wicákicupi

Class 3 *verbs* *reflexive forms* to ... myself	
I am suffering	makákije
Thou art ...	nicákije
He is ...	kakíje
We are ...	unkákijapi
You are ...	nicákijapi
They are ...	kakíjapi
I am tired	wamátuka
Thou art ...	wanítuka
etc.	watúka
	waúntukapi
	wanitukapi
	watukapi
I deceive myself	mic'ignayan
Thou ... thyself	nic'ignayan
etc.	ic'ígnayan
	unkíc'ignayanpi
	nic'ígnayanpi
	ic'ígnayanpi
I said that to	hemíc'iye
myself. Thou ...	heníc'iye
He ...	heíc'iye
etc.	heúnkic'iyapi
	heníc'iyapi
	heíc'yapi
I appoint myself	migláhniga
You ...	nigláhniga
etc.	igláhniga
	unkíglahnigapi
	nigáhnigapi
	igláhnigapi
I rouse myself	mikpágica
etc.	nikpágica
	ikpágica
	unkíkpagicapi
	nikpágicapi
	ikpágicapi

Note: Class 1, *ki* short form —
a) we [wa + ki], ye, ni, mi, ci carry the accent, except mi in miye
b) *ki* is used always before *c* and c', usually before gl, gn, kc, ks, kš, and kt, sometimes before h, s, t.

Class 1 verbs: use *kici* only in the reciprocal plural form; *ic'i* is the reflexibe form pronoun, but a *ka* prefix becomes *igla,* and a *pa* prefix becomes *ikpa,* the latter inflect as a Class 3 verb. But the possessive form takes *ki* prefixed or inserted, and a *ka* prefix becomes *gla,* the *pa* prefix *kpa,* inflection follows Class 1.

English	Class 1 *ki* short form *inserted* to invite to	Class 1 *kici* *prefixed* to be for	Class 1 *kici* *inserted* to seek for	Class 1 *ki* and *kici* *inserted* to pray for
I ... thee	icíco	cícica	ocícile	wacécíciciya
I ... him	iwéco	wécica	owécile	wacéweciciya
I ... you	icícopi	cícicapi	ocícilepi	wacécíciciyapi
I ... them	iwícaweco	wicáwecica	owícawecile	wacéwicaweciciya
thou ... me	imíyeco	miyécica	omíyecile	wacemiyeciciya
thou ... him	iyéco	yécica	oyécile	wacéyeciciya
thou ... us	unkíyecopi	unyécicapi	unkóyecilepi	wacéunyeciciyapi
thou ... them	iwícayeco	wicáyecica	owícayecile	wacéwicayeciciya
he ... me	imíco	mícica	omícile	wacémiciciya
he ... thee	iníco	nícica	onícile	wacéniciciya
he ... him*	ikíco	kicíca	okícile	wacékiciciya
he ... us	unkíkicopi	unkícicapi	unkókicilepi	wacéunkiciciyapi
he ... you	inícopi	nícicapi	onícilepi	wacéniciciyapi
he ... them	iwícakico	wicákicica	owícakicile	wacéwicakiciciya
we ... thee	unkínicopi	unnícicapi	unkónicilepi	wacéunniciciyapi
we ... him	unkíkicopi	unkícicapi	unkókicilepi	wacéunkiciciyapi
we ... you	unkínicopi	unnícicapi	unkónicilepi	wacéunniciciyapi
we ... them	wícunkicopi	wicúnkicicapi	owícunkicilepi	wacéwicunkiciciyapi
you ... me	imíyecopi	miyécicapi	omíyecilepi	wacémiyeciciyapi
you ... him	iyécopi	yécicapi	oyécilepi	wacéyeciciyapi
you ... us	unkíyecopi	unyécicapi	unkóyecilepi	wacéunyeciciyapi
you ... them	iwícayecopi	wicáyecicapi	owícayecilepi	wacéwicayeciciyapi
they ... me	imícopi	mícicapi	omícilepi	wacémiciciyapi
they ... thee	inícopi	nícicapi	onícilepi	wacéniciciyapi
they ... him	ikícopi	kicícapi	okícilepi	wacékiciciyapi
they ... us	unkíkicopi	unkícicapi	unkókicilepi	wacéunkiciciyapi
they ... you	inícopi	nícicapi	onícilepi	wacéniciciyapi
they ... them	iwícakicopi	wicákicicapi	owícakicilepi	wacéwicakiciciyapi

Note: Class 2 verbs. The reciprocal plural form is used with *kici;* the reflexive form is had by changing the *y* of the prefix to *gl* and then inflect as a Class 3 verb. But the possessive form is similarly formed by changing the *y* of the prefix to *gl,* however the verb is then inflected as a Class 1 verb.

English	Class 2 *ki prefixed* to open to	Class 2 *ki inserted* to tell to	Class 2 *kici prefixed* to count for	Class 2 *kici inserted* to think for
I ... thee	cicíyugan	ocíciyaka	cíciyawa	icíciyukcan
I ... him	wakíyugan	owákiyaka	wécíyawa	iwéciyukcan
I ... you	cicíyuganpi	ocíciyakapi	cíciyawapi	icíciyukcanpi
I ... them	wicáwakiyugan	owícawakiyaka	wicáweciyawa	iwícaweciyukcan
thou ... me	mayákilugan	omáyakilaka	miyécilawa	imíyecilukcan
thou ... him	yakílugan	oyákilaka	yécilawa	iyécilukcan
thou ... us	unyákiluganpi	unkóyakilakapi	unyécilawapi	unkíyecilukcanpi
thou ... them	wicáyakilugan	owícayakilaka	wicáyecilawa	iwícayecilukcan
he ... me	makíyugan	omákiyaka	míciyawa	imíciyukcan
he ... thee	nicíyugan	oníciyaka	níciyawa	iníciyukcan
he ... him*	kiyúgan	okíyaka	kíciyawa	ikíciyukcan
he ... us	unkíyuganpi	unkókiyakapi	unkíciyawapi	unkíciciyukcanpi
he ... you	nicíyuganpi	oníciyakapi	níciyawapi	iníciyukcanpi
he ... them	wicákiyugan	owícakiyaka	wicákiciyawa	iwícakiciyukcan
we ... thee	unníciyuganpi	unkóniciyakapi	unníciyawapi	unkíniciyukcanpi
we ... him	unkíyuganpi	unkókiyakapi	unkíciyawapi	unkíciciyukcanpi
we ... you	unníciyuganpi	unkóniciyakapi	unníciyawapi	unkíniciyukcanpi
we ... them	wicúnkiyuganpi	owícunkiyakapi	wicúnkiciyawapi	iwícunkiciyukcanpi
you ... me	mayákiluganpi	omáyakilakapi	miyécilawapi	imíyecilukcanpi
you ... him	yakíluganpi	oyákilakapi	yécilawapi	iyécilukcanpi
you ... us	unyákiluganpi	unkóyakilakapi	unyécilawapi	unkíyecilukcanpi
you ... them	wicáyakiluganpi	owícayakilakapi	wicáyecilawapi	iwícayecilukcanpi
they ... me	makíyuganpi	omákiyakapi	míciyawapi	imíciyukcanpi
they ... thee	nicíyuganpi	oníciyakapi	níciyawapi	iníciyukcanpi
they ... him	kiyúganpi	okíyakapi	kíciyawapi	ikíciyukcanpi
they ... us	unkíyuganpi	unkókiyakapi	unkíciyawapi	unkíkiciyukcanpi
they ... you	nicíyuganpi	oníciyakakpi	níciyawapi	iníciyukcanpi
they ... them	wicákiyuganpi	owícakiyakapi	wicákiciyawapi	iwícakiciyukcanpi

Note: Class 2 verbs. The reciprocal plural form is used with *kici;* the reflexive form is had by changing the *y* of the prefix to *gl* and then inflect as a Class 3 verb. But the possessive form is similarly formed by changing the *y* of the prefix to *gl*, however the verb is then inflected as a Class 1 verb.

Word Sources

An	H. Antelope
AF	Francis Charles Apple
A	Frank Arrowside
B	Wm. Bergen
Ba	Alex Bordeaux
Bc	Charles Bordeaux
BD	Edward Bear Dog
Bd	Big Head
BE	Nicholas Black Elk
Be	Paul Black Elk
BF	Big Face
Bf	Felix Bordeaux
BH	Brave Hawk
Bh	Blue Horse
B.H.	*Bible History*, Buechel et al
BIW	Bear in the Woods
BL	Sam Broken Leg
Bl	Clarence W. Bull Ring
Bm	Wm. Bordeaux
BM	Benjamin Bull Man
BMj	John Bull Man
BN	Alexander Bull Nation
Bn	William Brown
Bo	Franz Boas
BR	J. E. Brown, *Sacred Pipe*
Br	John F. Bryde
BS	T. and J. Bone Shirt
Bs	J. Black Spotted Horse
BT	Big Turkey
Bt	Blue Thunder
Bu	Eugene Bush
Bw	Wm. Brown
CD	Wm. Cross Dog
CG	Crow Good Voice
CH	Charging Hawk
Ch	Henry Cottier
Cl	E. Clifford
CO	John Colombe
Co	Clown Horse
CR	Mrs. Crazy Horse
D	Ella Deloria, *Dakota Texts*
DE	Dog Ear Camp
De	M. Desersa
Du	John Dubray
EB	Wm. Eagle Bird
ED	Eagle Deer
Ed	Eagle Dog
EE	Jesse Eagle Elk
EEm	Maurice Eagle Elk
EF	R. Eagle Feather
EM	Eagle Man
ER	Eagle Road
ES	Owen Eagle Star
Es	Elk Sky
ET	Eagle Thunder
Et	Eagle Tail
F	Wm. Flood
FB	Fast Bull
FD	Frances Densmore, *Teton Sioux Music*
FE	Foolish Elk
FH	Fool Head
Fi	Fish
FN	Forget Nothing
FP	Fills Pipe
FR	Frank Four Horns
Fr	Joseph Frightened
FW	Fast Whirlwind
GA	A. Goes Among
GB	Mrs. Gray Buffalo
Gb	Joseph Good Bear
Gr	Charles Green
Gramm	E. Buechel, S.J., *Grammar of Lakota*
GS	Fred Good Shield
GT	Good Thunder
GV	Moses Good Voice
Gv	Jesse Good Voice
GW	Moses Good Will
H	James Howard
HC	Joseph Horn Cloud
HH	High Horse
Hh	Hunts Horse
HL	Horse Looking
HM	Leo Hawk Man
Hm	Holy Man
Ho	Hogán
HP	High Pipe
HT	Thomas Hoffman, S.J.
IB	Iron Bull
IS	Peter Iron Shell
Is	Allan Iron Shell
J	Wm. Janis
Ja	Joseph Jackson
JOH	Oscar Jealous of Him
K	Katola
Ka	Mrs. Kašna
KE	Frank Kills Enemy
KS	Charles Kills in Sight
KT	George Knock Off Two
L	Eugene Little
La	Tom Larvie
LB	Tom Little Bull
LC	Little Cloud
Lc	George Lone Cedar
LE	Frank Little Elk
LH	Little Hawk
Lh	Little Horse
LHB	Silas Left Hand Bull,
Lhb	P. Left Hand Bull
LM	Little Moccasin
LO	Lame Omaha
LP	Jacob LaPointe
LT	Robert Little Thunder
LTf	Frank Little Thunder
LWOW	E. Buechel, S.J., *Prayerbook...*
M	Wm. Metcalf
Me	George Menard
MF	Moccasin Face
MG	Makes Good
Mh	Makálhpaya
Mi	W. Mills
MN	Narcisse Moran
MO	Louis Mousseau
MS	E. Buechel, S.J., et al, *Lakota Tales and Text*
Mt	E. Buechel, unpublished *St. Matthew's Gospel*
MW	Make Noise in the Woods
NO	Noisy Owl
NP	Alfred Night Pipe
OE	James Old Eagle
OF	Owns Fire
OH	One Horn
OS	Michael One Star
P	E. Perrig, S.J., unpublished *Lakota Dictionary*
Pa	Martin Pacer
PB	Pretty Bird
Pb	(manuscript lost)
PD	Poor Dog
PLB	Peter Left Hand Bull
PO	Oliver Pine
R	S. R. Riggs, *Dakota Dictionary*
RA	Louis Runs Above

Ra	Wm. Randall
Rac	Charles Randall
RB	Louis Running Bear
Rb	Mrs. Red Bird
RC	Red Cloud
RE	Red Eyes
Re	Deacon Steven Red Elk
RF	Red Feather
Rf	Wm. Red Fish
RH	Charles Running Horse
Rh	Running Hawk
Rl	Ring Bull
RO	Charles Rooks
RT	Samuel Ring Thunder
RTj	John Red Tomahawk
RTt	Tom Red Tomahawk
RV	Mrs. Runs Close to Village
S	Tom, Norris, and Sam Shield
SB	Short Bull
Sb	Jake Standing Bull
Sbj	Mrs. J. Standing Bull
SC	Wm. Spotted Calf
SH	Stranger Horse
SE	Sore Eyes
SI	Ivan Stars Come Out
Si	B. Simpson
SLB	*same as* LHB
Sp	Mrs. Noah Stampede
ST	Spotted Tail
St	Pat Star
SW	A. Schweigman
Sw	Swift
Swb	(identity unknown) cf. glesyéla
ŠG	Šungleška
T	Antoine Trudell
TB	Two Bird
TH	Thunder Hawk
Ti	Titus
TT	Two Teeth
UW	Under Water
W	Alvina Walker
Wa	Mrs. Walking
WC	Clark Whissler, *Societies … in the Oglala Teton*
WE	George Walking Eagle
WF	White Feather
WH	Laban White Horse
Wh	Frank White
WHL	Louis and Daisy Whirlwind Horse
Wi	Emily White Hat
WI	J. Williamson *Dakota Dictionary*
WJR	J. R. Walker, *Oglala Sundance*
WL	Jesse White Lance
Wo	Wounded
WR	White Rabbit
Ww	Whitewash
WW	Whirlwind Soldier
Wwc	Charles White Wolf
WWS	same as WW
YH	Yellow Hair
Yh	Ed Yellow Hawk
YW	Yellow Wolf
#	Eugene Buechel, S.J. refers to his *Botanical Lists*

Abbreviations

a	active
abbrev	abbreviation
abs	absolute
adj	adjective, adjectival
adjp	adjective proper
adv	adverb, adverbial
altern	alternate, alternative
anto	antonym
archaic	archaic
art	article
aux	auxiliary
causa	causative
cf	confer
cl	clause
coll	collective
colloq	colloquial
com	command
comb	combination
comp	compounded
compos	composition
compar	comparative
conj	conjunction
contr	contrary
contrac	contraction
coord	coordinate
correl	correlative
dat	dative
defect	defective
def	definite
dem	demontrative
deriv	derivative, derived
dim	diminutive
diph	diphthong
dual	dual
e.g.	for instance
emph	emphasis, emphasized
encl	enclitic
entre	entreaty
esp	especially
etc.	et cetera, and so forth
euph	euphonic
exclam	exclamation
expl	explanative
express	expression
fig	figurative
fr	from
fut	future
idiom	idiomatic
i.e.	id est, that is
imper	imperative
imperf	imperfect, as to time
impers	impersonal
in compos	in composition
indefin	indefinite
indic	indicative, of fact
infin	infinitive
insep	inseparable
insert	insertion
interj	interjection
interrog	interrogative
invit	invitative
irreg	irregular
Lat	Latin
lit	literally
n	noun, substantive, topic *etc.*
neg	negative
neut	neutral
no	number
nomin	nominative
np	noun proper
num	number
num ord	ordinal number
num card	cardinal number
obj	object, objective
obsol	obsolete
opt	optative
p	past, time
part	participle
partic	particle
pf	perfect, said of time
ppf	past perfect time
pass	passive
pers	person
phr	phrase
pl	plural
poss	possessive
postp	post-positive
pred	predicate
pref	prefix
prep	preposition
pres	present
pron	pronoun
recip	reciprocal
red	reduplicate
ref	reference to
refl	reflexive
rel	relative to, relation to
sic	as meant, as intended
singl	singular
sl	slang
subj	subject, subjective
subjunc	subjunctive
subst	substantive
suff	suffix
superl	superlative
syll	syllable
syn	synonym
term	terminal
var	variant
v	verb
va	verb active, with an *obj*
vi	verb intransitive, no *obj*
vn	verb neutral
vt	verb transitive, with *obj*
vs	versus
vulg	a vulgar sense
~	the entry word is repeated

LAKOTA DICTIONARY

A

LAKOTA-ENGLISH DICTIONARY

[1]a \ă\ *exclam*, drawing others' attention on hearing the sound of a voice or of a noise < *A! Anagoptan po!* Hey! Listen here! > — *n* : the armpit or brisket, the space between the forlegs of quadruped animals < *A ohlate yumahel icu* She took it and hid it under her arm *i.e.* beneath her blanket > – D.59

[2]a \ă\ *insep prep pref*
1 : affixed to *v* and *adj* usually means "on" or "upon" < *amáni* to walk on > – Cf below
2 : affixed to some *v* it gives a causative meaning < *u* come, and *aú* bring; *ya* go, and *áya* take >
3 : affixed to *v* of motion it worms a *coll pl* < *aú* they come; *áya* they go; *ahí* they have arrived
4 : affixed to *n* it sometimes makes them *adv* < *wanica* none, and *awánil* or *awánilya* in a destroying manner >
5 : affixed to some *v* it makes them a *n* < *waptá* to cut off from, *awápte* a cutting on, thus *can'awapte* a cutting board >

a·be·be·ya \á-be-be-ya\ *adv red* [fr *ábeya* separately] : scattered as a flock, separaely; singly, and spreading out or scattering as a herd of buffalo when chased – *See* KAIYABEBEYA — **abe·kiya** *adv* : scattered, separately — **abe·ya** \á-be-ya\ *adv* : separately and scattering < ~ *iyayapi* or *akiyagle* Scattering they went away > – D.72

a·bla·gye·la \a-blá-gye-la\ *adv* : quietly, peacefully < *Tohanni ~ unpi šni* Never are they at peace (as is said when a married couple do not get along well with each other) > – BL

ablake·la \a-blá-ǩe-la\ *n* : a calm < ~ *ca wicaho htani ca tokiya eyaš nah'onpi kte* When there is a calm, where however is there a feeble voice that will be heard? > — **ablak hingla** \a-blák hiŋ-glà\ *v* : to turn calm suddenly – B.H.117.11 — *adj* : calm, still, without a wind < ~ *hingle* It was suddenly calm > – Bl D.21

a·bla·ska·bton·yan \á-bla-sǩa-btòŋ-yaŋ\ *adv* : aside of another; level, flat < ~ *unhpayapelo* We lay alongside of one another > — **ablaska·ya** \a-blá-sǩa-ya\ *adv* : level, without ridges

a·bla·ya \a-blá-ya\ *adj* : level on

a·ble·ca·han \a-blé-ca-haŋ\ *part* : scattered and fallen off, as from a pile of rocks *etc* – *Syn* OBLECAHAN

a·blel·ya o·yu·spa \á-blel-ya o-yù-spa\ *adv* : holding many things, as flowers or hair in the hand so the upper ends hang down on all sides evenly < ~ *han* He stood holding *e.g.* a bunch of plants set in a standing position > — Note: when things held are kept straight, they say: *ptayela han* it stands together – Cf oblélya

ables \a-blés\ *vn contrac* [fr *ableza* perceive] : to be clear < ~ *iyaya* or *áya* to become clear; ~ *amáyan* I became clear or visible. *Oyate kin tanyan ~ nayajinpi kte* You people should stand well visible > — **able·sya** *va* ables·wa·ya : to make clear or visible — *adv* : clearly, visibly

a·ble·za \a-blé-za\ *va* a·wá·ble·za : to look into, notice or perceive — *vn* a·má·bleza : **1** : to see clearly **2** : to pay attention **3** : to be sober

a·bli·he·ca \a-blí-he-ca\ *vn* a·ma·bliheca [fr *bliheca* to be active] : to be industrious in some regard — **ablihel·ic'iya** \a-blí-hel-i-c'i-ya\ *v refl* ablihel·mi·c'iya : to make one's self active or industrious — **ablihel·ya** *va* : to cause to be industrious about something — *adv* : industriously, stirringly

a·blo \a-bló\ *n* : the shoulder, the scapula < *Hehan ~ anunkatanhan wicahpi num owawa* I painted two stars on both the sides > — **ablo·hu** *n* : the shoulder bone or blade, the scapula — **ablo·iyokiju** *also* **ablo·iyokitahena** \a-bló-i-yo-ǩi-ju\ *n* : the part between the shoulders

a·blo·ke·tu \a-bló-ke-tu\ *v imperf* : to come summer, to have lived until summer < *Wana unk'abloketupelo* We are now making it through to summer > – Bl

a·blu·ke·ha·ha·ka \a-blú-ǩe-ha-ha-ka\ *v* : to pass over a thing very quickly, hence half-and-half, *i.e.* badly as in viewing arrows – Bl

a·ca·ga \a-cá-ǧa\ *vn* a·má·caga [fr *caga* to freeze] : to freeze in, on, or upon; to become ice on

a·ca·gle·gle \a-cá-gle-gle\ *adj* : scattered with things being far apart, with a motion this way and that — Note: *wakágege* I make stitches far apart – Bl — **acaglegle·yakel** *adv* [fr perhaps *canglegle* a thin stand of trees] : scattered haphazardly as when written with a letter placed here and there because of *e.g.* the shaking of the wagon < ~ *wakagelo* I executed it haphazardly > — *Syn* OKÁGLIGLE – Bl LHB

a·ca·hsna·sna \a-cá-ȟsna-sna\ *vn* [fr *acage* to freeze on + *snasna* repeated sound] : to rattle, as icicles formed on something

a·ca·hsu \a-cá-ȟsu\ *v* [fr *acaga* to freeze on + *su* the seed of something] : to form ice in droplets on something as on trees or grass *etc* < *Onštinmapihin acahmasu* Small ice drops formed on my eyelids, *Peji* ~ Ice formed in droplets on the grass > — **acahsu·su** *v red* : to form many drops of ice on < *Onštinmapihin ~ imayayelo* Droplets of ice aplenty formed on my eyelids > – Bl

a·ca·hšla·ya \a-cá-ȟšla-ya\ *adj* [fr *acaga* to freeze on + *šlayá* to make bare] : all icy or covered with ice, as are trees when rain is frozen on them

a·ca·je i·gla·ta \a-cá-je ì-gla-ta\ *v refl* [fr *caje* name + *iglatan* to praise one's self] : to give a name to one's self, to mention one's own name – B Bl LHB KE

a·ca·mni \a-cá-mni\ *vn* [fr *camni* a sprout] : to sprout on

a·can·can \a-cáŋ-caŋ\ *vn* a·má·cancan [fr *cancan* to shake or tremble] : to be shaking for some reason

a·can'·i·gla·ška yan·ka \a-cáŋ-i-gla-ška yaŋ-kà\ *v refl* [fr *acankaška* to bind wood on] : to be fortified – B.H.62.9

a·can·ka·ška \a-cáŋ-ka-škà\ *va* acán·wa·kaška [fr *can* + wood + *kaška* bind or tie] : to bind wood on, to fence in or inclose on — **acankaška·ya** *va* acankaška·wa·ya [fr *can* wood + *kaškaya* to cause to be inclosed] : to make a fence, to enclose *e.g.* a fort, to bind wood together on

a·can·kšin *or* **acakšin** \a-cáŋ-kšiŋ\ *va* acan·wa·kšin : to step over, pass or jump over – Note: *Wóacankšin* The Pasch – R Bl — **acankšin·ya** *va* acankšin·wa·ya : to cause to pass over — **acankšin·yan** *adv* : passing over

a·can·ku·ki·ya \a-cáŋ-ku-ki-ya\ *v* : to go by a certain place on one's way somewhere < *Hinhanni kin acankuwaya kte lo* I shall be passing by tomorrow > — **acanku·ya** \a-cáŋ-ku-ya\ *va* acanku·wa·ya [fr *a* on + *cankú* road,

\a\ father \e\ they \i\ machine \o\ smoke \u\ lunar \an, aŋ\ blanc Fr. \in, iŋ\ ink \on, oŋ, un, uŋ\ soon, confier Fr. \c\ chair \ǧ\ machen Ger. \j\ fusion \clusters: bl, gn, kp, hšl, etc...\ b[e]lo ... said with a slight vowel
See more in the Introduction, Guide to Pronunciation

way] : to make a road on, to pass through on — *adv* : lying on *e.g.* a road passing through – B.H.112.16, 200.4 WE

a·can·ni·yan \a-cáŋ-ni-yaŋ\ *va* acan·ma·niyan [fr *a* on account + *canniyan* to be angry at] : to be angry for or over

a·can·nun·pa \a-cáŋ-nuŋ-p̣a\ *va* acánnun·mun·pa [fr *cannunpa* to smoke tobacco] : to smoke on or after, as after eating a meal

a·can·te·ši·ca \a-cáŋ-ṫe-ši-ca\ *va* [fr *cante* heart + *šica* bad] : to be sad on account of — **acantešil·ya** *and* acantešil·yakel *adv* : sadly or sorrowfully for

a·can·ze \a-cáŋ-ze\ *va* a·ma·canze : to be angry at — **acanze·ka** \a-cáŋ-ze-ḳa\ *vn* : to be or get mad or angry at < *amacanzeka* he is angry with me, *awacanzeka* I am angry with him, *akicicanzekapi* they are angry with each other, *awicacanzekapi* or *acanwicazekapi* they are angry with them >

a·ca·pa \a-cá-pa\ *va* aca·wa·pa [fr *capá* pierce, stab] : to stab on, stick in; to take stitches in or on

a·ce·bya \a-cé-bya\ *va* ace·bwa·ya [fr *a* for + *cepa* fat] : to make fat for a certain purpose — **acebya·kel** *adv* : in a state of fattening for < ~ *gle* He set out for home well fattened >

a·ce·ji·ya \a-cé-ji-ya\ *va* [fr *a* purposely + *ceji* tongue + *ya* to cause] : to stick out the tongue to mock < *Acejimayalapelo* You stuck out your tongue at me > – Bl

a·ce·pa \a-cé-p̣a\ *va* [fr *cépa* fat] : to be or get fat for, *fig* to be in good order for

a·ce·sli \a-cé-sli\ *va* ace·wa·sli [fr *a* on + *ce* penis + *sli* trickle] : to excrete on something — *n* : something to urinate on, a diaper

a·ce·ti \a-cé-ti\ *va* ace·wa·ti [fr *a* on + *ceti* build a fire] : to make a fire on or at

a·ce·ya \a-cé-ya\ *va* a·wá·ceya unka·ceya·pi [fr *a* for + *ceya* weep] : to bemoan, bewail, cry out or for, to mourn or weep for — **aceya·pi** *part* : crying for, cried for

a·ci·ca·hlo \a-cí-ca-ȟlo\ *va* : to growl about, to complain of – Note: *ašicahlo* seems more correct – R Bl

a·co·ka·ta \a-có-ḳa-ṫa\ *adv* : going too far, exceeding ordinary prudence < ~ *imankeca* I'm such that I go too far as a man would say who wants more than what he gets > – Bc KE

a·co·pa \a-có-pa\ *va* aco·wa·pa [fr *copa* to wade in water : to wade into water for something < *Witka acope unyanpi kte* Let us go for eggs, *i.e.* those found in the bulrushes > – Bc

a·co·sya \a-có-sya\ *adv* : warmly

a·co·za \a-có-za\ *vn* [fr *cóza* warm] : to be warm on; to be comfortable

a·cu \a-cú\ *vn imperf* [fr *cu* dew] : to dew on, bedew — *prep* + *n* : with dew on

a·cun·ka·ška \a-cúŋ-ka-šḳa\ *va* acun·wa·kaška acunkaškapi : to fortify, surround with a fence or wall or palisade *etc* — **acunkaške** *or* **aconkaške** *n* : a fort, fortress, stronghold

a·cu·wi·ta \a-cú-wi-ṫa\ *va* a·má·cuwita [fr *cuwita* cold, feeling cold] : to be cold upon

a·cu·ya \a-cú-ya\ *va* acu·wa·ya : to cause dew upon; to lay out something overnight to have it bedewed – Bl – *Syn* KATATABYA

a·e·ce·la \á-e-ce-la\ *adv* : just that, ex-cluding or not including other things; < *Ihupa* ~ *iwacu* I took only the stem, ~ *yanka* to be destitute of everything, even of necessities > — **aecela·kel** *adv* : being without, not having with one – Bc B.H.115.17

a·e·ce·li·ye·i·c'i·ya \a-é-ce-li-ye-i-c'i-ya\ *v refl* : to shut up one's self, as in a room – B.H.192.15

a·e·ce·tu \a-é-ce-tu\ *vn* : to fit to do something < *Išta aemacetu šni yelo* My eyes are not right, *i.e.* I cannot see well as when they water, *Owakita aemacetu šni yelo* I cannot observe things well > – Bl LHB

a·e·gna·ka \a-é-gna-ka\ *va* : to add to – Bl

a·e·tu·la·ke·ci \a-é-ṫu-la-ḳe-ci\ *adv* : in a little while < ~ *wahi kte* I'll arrive in a short time > — **aetulake el** \á-e-ṫu-la-ḳe el\ *adv phr* : after a little while, rather at that time, very soon < *Na* ~ *winyan k'un hena iš eya ahihunni* Very soon these women themselves had also arrived > – B.H.137.14, 183.2, 259.5, 304.5

a·e·yo·ka·s'in \a-é-yo-ka-s'iŋ\ *v* aeyo·wa·kas'in aeyo·unkas'in·pi : to peep in at < *Yunkan paha k'on el ehunni na aeyokas'inpi el lila pte otapi* They had then arrived at a hill, and when they peeped, many indeed were the buffalo > – B.H.112.11

a·gan i·hpa·ya \á-ġaŋ i-ȟpa-ya\ *vn* : to fall or jump into water with a splash < *Áginhpaya yo* Go, jump in! >

a·gi \a-ġí\ *vn* [fr *gi* brown] **1** : to be covered with rust, to have a rusty or brown stain **2** : to be mildewed

a·gla \a-glá\ *va* a·wa·gla unka·gla·pi : to be carrying or taking home < *Pte pa wanjini ena ihpeya šni oyas'in* ~ *po* Everyone carry along back neither buffalo head nor what is disposed of > — *v coll pl* [fr *gla* to go home] : they go home < *Tona glinapapi kin hecena* ~ *ca miš eya wakiyagla na tiyata wagli* When those who were coming back got home, I too got home and went indoors > – Bl

a·gla·ge·ge \a-glá-ġe-ġe\ *va poss* [fr *a* on + *kagege* to sew] : to sew one's own on

a·gla·gla \a-glá-gla\ *adv* : along side of, in front of < ~ *inyanka* He ran in front of him, ~ *inajinpi* They stood before him, *Ecel* ~ *pazo au na nawajin el ahihunni* As it was they came presenting it before him, and when I stood up they came >

a·gla·han \a-glá-haŋ\ *vn* : to slip or slide out *e.g.* a tent pole when a number are dragged along, hence to be dropping as water continuously from a roof < *Mni* ~ Water is dripping > — *part perhaps* [fr *agla* to take home] : carrying home — *v coll pl* : they keep on going home, one after another, as after a meeting – IS

a·gla·hpa \a-glá-ȟp̣a\ *v poss* a·wa·glahpa [fr *a* on + *kahpa* to make fall] : to throw *e.g.* a garment over one's own, to cover one's own — **·gla·hpe·ki·ton** \a-glá-ȟp̣e-ḳi-toŋ\ *v poss* aglahpe·wa·ki·ton [fr *akahpeton* to throw on or cover] : to clothe or cover one's own — **aglahpe·ton** \a-glá-ȟp̣e-toŋ\ *v* aglahpe·wa·ton : to clothe one's own — **aglahpe·ya** *v poss* [fr *akahpeya* covering] : covering one's own — *v poss* aglahpe·wa·ya : to cover one's own

a·gla·ksa \a-glá-ksa\ *va poss* a·wa·glaksa [fr *a* on + *kaksa* to split] : to cut off one's own upon

a·gla·kšiš \a-glá-kšiš\ *vn* : to fall on top of one another; to be crossed, as in crossing one's legs; to fall or lie down upon, as does a dog – Cf aglaskica – YH

a·gla·kšun·yan yun·ka \a-glá-kšuŋ-yaŋ yuŋ-kà\ *v* : to lie on one's belly, prone or prostrate – Bl

a·gla·la \a-glá-la\ *va* [fr *a* on + *kalá* scatter] : to scatter one's own

a·gla·mna \a-glá-mna\ *va poss* a·wa·glamna [fr *a* for + *akamna* acquire in addition to] : to gather one's own, accumulate for a purpose

a·gla·pan \a-glá-paŋ\ *va poss* a·wa·glapan [fr *a* on + *kapan* to beat] : to beat out or thresh one's own upon

a·gla·pe·pe·ya \a-glá-p̣e-p̣e-ya\ *v* aglapepe·wa·ya : to make skip over – *See* cah'aglapepeya, mniaglapepeya – Bl

a·gla·po·ta \a-glá-ṗo-ṫa\ *va poss* [fr *a* on + *kapota* to fray] : to beat in pieces one's own upon — *vn perhaps* : to float upon

a·gla·psin·ta \a-glá-psiŋ-ṫa\ *va poss* [fr *akapsinta* to beat] : to strike or whip one's own, to correct

a·gla·pson \a-glá-psoŋ\ *va poss* [fr *a* on + *glapson* spill] : to spill one's own upon

a·gla·pšun \a-glá-pšuŋ\ *va poss* a·wa·glapšun [fr *a* on + *kapšun* to break by striking] : to put one's own out of joint — **aglapšun·yan** *adv* : bottom upwards, upside down; prone < ~ *ehpeya* or ~ *iyeya* to turn bottom-side up >

a·gla·pta \a-glá-ṗta\ *va* a·ma·glapta **1** : to cease to fall on or to rain **2** a·wa·glapta [fr *glapta* to lade out one's own] : to dip or lade out, as from one's own kettle – Cf oglapta

a·gla·ptus \a-glá-ptus\ *adv contrac* : prone < ~ *ihpaya* to fall flat on the ground > – *Syn* **AGLAPŠUNYAN**

a·gla·ski·ca \a-glá-ski-ca\ *va poss* a·wa·glaskica [fr *a* on + *kaskica* to press] : to press down on one's own; to lie on one's own – D.216

a·gla·skin \a-glá-skiŋ\ *part* : on the face < ~ *ihpeya* to throw down on the face, ~ *ihpaya* to fall down on one's own face > – Bl

a·gla·ški·ca \a-glá-ški-ca\ *v poss* a·wa·glaškica [fr *ayaškica* to press or chew] : to spit out on something of one's own – Note: the word *akaškica* seems not used

a·gla·šla \a-glá-šla\ *va poss* [fr *a* in addition to + *kašla* to shave] : to cut one's own in addition to – Bl

a·gla·šna \a-glá-šna\ *va poss* a·wa·glašna [fr *ayašna* to let fall from the mouth] : to make a mistake in speaking

a·gla·špa \a-glá-šṗa\ *va poss* [fr *a* on + *kašpa* strike off a piece] : to break a piece off one's own upon

a·gla·štan \a-glá-štaŋ\ *v poss* [fr *akaštan* or *ayaštan* to spill] **1** : to throw or spill *e.g.* water on one's own **2** : to cease speaking or eating

^{1}**a·gla·ta** \a-glá-ta\ *va* : to chorus to, to answer or respond to in music

^{2}**a·gla·ta** \a-glá-ta\ *v poss* a·wa·glata [fr *akata* to hoe around] : to hoe one's own, *e.g.* one's corn

a·gla·tkan \a-glá-tkaŋ\ *v poss* a·wa·blatkan [fr *a* on + *yatkan* to drink] : to drink one's own with or upon

a·gla·t'in·za \a-glá-t'iŋ-za\ *v* a·wa·glat'inza : to establish something for certain < *Ayaglat'inza he?* Did you confirm it? > – Bl

a·gle *or* **egle** \a-glé\ *va* *1st pers singl:* é·wa·gle or á·wa·gle *1st pers pl:* únka·gle·pi : to place or make stand on something, as a pitcher on a tray – Note: *3rd pers pl of* agla *means* they go home < *He aglá mánipelo* They stroll going there home > – B.H.171.10

a·gle·han \a-glé-haŋ\ *n* : a frame or groundworks, a foundation – D.222

a·gle·hi·ye·ya \a-glé-hi-ye-ya\ *part* : placed one after another

a·gle·ki·ya \a-glé-ki-ya\ *va* agle·wa·kiya : to cause to take home

a·gle·pa \a-glé-ṗa\ *va* a·wa·glepa [fr *glépa* to vomit] : to vomit upon

a·gle·ška \a-glé-ška\ *n* : an alligator — **agleška·la** *n* : a lizard

a·gle·ye·la \a-glé-ye-la\ *n* : an edge < ~ *ihunni* He reached the edge > – Bl LHB

a·gle·yus \a-glé-yus\ *v contrac* [fr *agleyuza* to hold against] : to hold against < ~ *kuté* to shoot, holding the gun against the object or very near it >

a·gle·yu·za \a-glé-yu-za\ *va* agle·blu·za : to hold against or near to; to come near to

a·gli \a-glí\ *va* a·wa·gli unka·gli·pi : to arrive at home; to bring home — *v coll pl* [fr *gli* to arrive back] : they *all* came back <*Maġá agli kte lo* The geese will be arriving back, as the Lakotas say on about February 7th or 8th>

a·gli·ce·ti \a-glí-ce-ti\ *v* : to come home and start a fire

a·gli·han \a-glí-haŋ\ *v* : to fall on < *Peta wan awicaglihin na* A fire descended upon them > — **agli·he** \a-glí-he\ *v* : to descend upon, to strike or hit by falling on < *Mahpiya wan akahpeya* ~ A cloud came down covering him >

a·gli·he·ya \a-glí-he-ya\ *va* : to shine on < *Wi kin Jonas natá kin* ~ The sun shone on Jonas' head > – B.H.61.10, 195.16, 240.14

a·gli·hun·ni \a-glí-huŋ-ni\ *va* a·wa·glihunni : to take something straight back home — *v coll pl* : they all arrived, coming straight back < *Na wanna unma kin* ~ And he took the other right back, *Awicaglihunnipi* They did bring them straight home, *Ecana* ~ *kte lo* They will soon arrive back > – Bl

a·gli·hpa·ya \a-glí-ȟpa-ya\ *vn* a·wa·glihpaya : to fall on, hitting the ground, to fall from above – *Syn* AHINHPAYA

a·gli·hpe·ya \a-glí-ȟpe-ya\ *va* aglihpe·wa·ya : to leave something on one's way home, *e.g.* a horse that is played out

a·gli·i·ya·pe \a-glí-i-ya-pe\ *v* agliiya·wa·pe [fr *agli* to come back + *iyape* to wait for] : to wait for their coming home

a·gli·na·jin \a-glí-na-jiŋ\ *v coll pl* : they came home and stood there, as a herd of horses do coming from the pasture

a·gli·na·pa \a-glí-na-ṗa\ *v* : to bring out one's own < *Na wanna wanjigjila tima iyayapi na* ~ *na taku yuja* ~ . *Yunkan pte optaye kin etan aglinapapi* And they went inside one by one and brought out what was a mix of things. Then from there they brought out a herd of cattle > – B.H. 223.6

a·gli·psi·ca \a-glí-psi-ca\ *v coll pl* : they come home and alight or dismount

a·gli·ti \a-glí-ti\ *v coll pl* : they come home and stay *i.e.* camp < *Tokša, ptayetu kin lel agliyatipi kte* Soon you should come home and stay here when together >

a·gli·to·ki·ci·kšu \a-glí-ṫo-ki-ci-kšu\ *v* : to bring along for somebody coming home < *Kola aglitomicikšu wo* Bring a friend along home for me > – Bl

a·gli·wan·yan·ka \a-glí-waŋ-yàŋ-ka\ *v coll pl* : they came back home to see their own

a·gli·wo·ta \a-glí-wo-ta\ *vn* agli·wa·wota : to stop for one's meal on the way home < *Na wanna anpo el ake akiya na wícokánhiyaya agliwotapi* And at daybreak, he again considered matters and during the afternoon they stopped for a meal on the way home >

a·gli·ya·cu *also* **agliyaku** \a-glí-ya-cu\ *va* a·wa·gliyacu : to be on one's way home bringing something, as one might bring a run-away boy — *v coll pl* : they are on their way home – D.251 B.H.48.1

a·gli·ya·gla \a-glí-ya-gla\ *va* : to pass by with some

\a\ father \e\ they \i\ machine \o\ smoke \u\ lunar \an, aŋ\ blanc Fr. \in, iŋ\ ink \on, oŋ, un, uŋ\ soon, confier Fr. \c\ chair \ġ\ machen Ger. \j\ fusion \clusters: bl, gn, kp, hšl, etc...\ $b^{e}lo$ ... said with a slight vowel
See more in the Introduction, Guide to Pronunciation

thing to any place, as a policeman who passes by with a prisoner — *v coll pl* : they all pass by < *Tan'inyan na glakinyan* ~ They all pass by in sight and crossing ahead on their way home, *Wanna unkisakib* ~` *eša inila* ~ Though they all passed by alongside us they passed in silence, *Wanna oyas'in lel witayela ku po, eya. Hecel el witayela* ~ *ca waš'ake owapa* "Now everyone come back here together," he said, and thus as they passed by in a group I joined the force > — **agliyagla·han** *v coll pl* : they continue to pass by, going home, as a column of soldiers does – Bl

a·gli·ya·han \a-glí-ya-haŋ\ *v coll pl* : they came up a hill and stopped in sight on their way home – Note: *gliyáhan* is used in speaking of one person only

a·gli·ya·ku *also* **agliyacu** \a-glí-ya-ku\ *va* a·wa·gliyaku [fr *agli* to arrive back + *aku* to come back bringing something] : to be coming home with something — *v coll pl* : they are coming home together < *Lel inkpata wakpala unhe iyohloke kin isam* ~, *i.e.* the enemies, *ca hecena ungliyacupi*, *i.e.* spies, Here at the head of that creek beyond its mouth they, enemies, were coming back together, and finally our scouts too came on back >

a·gli·ya·on·pa \a-glí-ya-oŋ-ṗa\ *v* agli·wa·onpa : to come and place on < *Inyan blaskaska ca el agliwicaonpapi* On a quite flat rock they came and placed them > – Cf aónpa

a·gli·yo·hi \a-glí-yo-hi\ *v coll pl* [fr *gliyohi* to arrive for one's own] : they reached home on returning – Bl

a·gli·yo·hpa·ya \a-glí-yo-ȟpa-ya\ *v coll pl* : they came down from a hill < *Na wanna zuya k'un* ~ *na wicoti el ukiya* So now they came down from the hill after they had been at war and were returning to camp > – MS.566 Bl

a·gli·yo·tka \a-glí-yo-tk̇a\ *v coll pl* : they stopped somewhere on their way home – Note: *gliyótaka* is used of speaking of only one

a·gli·yu·go \a-glí-yu-ġo\ *vn* agli·blu·go : to arrive at home tired out – RF

a·gli·yu·hpa \a-glí-yu-ȟpa\ *va* : to come home and lay down one's baggage, *i.e.* unload – Note: *awagliyuhpa* I come home and lie down, and *aglibluhpa* I unload – IS

a·glí·yu·kan \a-glí-yu-k̇aŋ\ *v coll pl* : they come home and remain < *Le wakpala cik'ala kin opaya ukiya tka agliyukin kte šni s'elececa* yelo They returned along this little creek, but it was only as if they would not be coming home to stay >

a·gli·yun·ka \a-glí-yuŋ-k̇a\ *v* : to come home and sleep — *v coll pl* : they all camped on the way home – Note: *gliyúnka* is used to refer to one only < *Na hetan ukiya na wakpala wan na šakowin agliyunkin. Wakinyan iglag ukiye k'on agliyunkelo* And from there they made their return, they had seven overnights, and finally arrived home. they came home travelling in thunder and lightning > – Bl

a·glo·gla \a-gló-gla\ *v* a·wa·glogla : to carry home – Bl

a·glu·blu \a-glú-blu\ *v poss* a·wa·glublu [fr *yablu* to make fine by chewing] : to plow one's own upon

a·glu·ga·ta \a-glú-ġa-ṫa\ *v poss* a·wa·glugata [fr *yugata* to extend hand and arm upwards] : to open out *e.g.* one's hand on anything

a·glu·ha \a-glú-ha\ *v poss* a·wa·gluha [fr *ayuha* to hold on] : to have or take one's own on account of, to provide for some occasion, keep one's own for a certain occasion or purpose

a·glu·he·te \a-glú-he-ṫe\ *v poss* [fr *ayuhete* to concentrate on] : to wait upon one's own sole object of one's thoughts

a·glu·ho·mni \a-glú-ho-mni\ *v coll pl* : they all turn around to see – Note: *iglúhomni* is used in referring to one only – Bl

a·glu·ȟi·ca \a-glú-ȟi-ca\ *v poss* a·wa·gluȟica [fr *a* on + *yuȟica* to waken] : to waken one's own upon

a·glu·ka·ka \a-glú-k̇a-k̇a\ *v* : to repair one's own *e.g.* feathers; to renew or refurbish – Bl KE – *Syn* APIICI'YA

a·glu·kan \a-glú-kaŋ\ *va* a·wa·glukan : to leave unmolested

a·glu·ka·wa \a-glú-k̇a-wa\ *v poss* [fr *yukawa* to open] : to open up one's own *e.g.* wound

a·glu·kcan \a-glú-kcaŋ\ *v poss* a·wa·glukcan [fr *yukcan* to comprehend] : to understand one's own upon or in relation to

a·glu·man \a-glú-maŋ\ *v poss* a·wa·gluman [fr *yuman* to grind, sharpen] : to grind one's own upon

a·glu·so·ta \a-glú-so-ṫa\ *v poss* a·wa·glusota [fr *yusota* to make an end of] : to use one's own up on

a·glu·sto \a-glú-sṫo\ *v poss* a·wa·glusto [fr *yusto* to make smooth] : to smooth one's own down on, as one's hair

a·glu·su·ta \a-glú-su-ṫa\ *v poss* a·wa·glusuta [fr *yusuta* to strengthen] : to make hard one's own upon

a·glu·ški·ca \a-glú-ški-ca\ *v poss* [fr *yuškica* to squeeze] : to press out one's own upon

a·glu·šlu·šlu·ta \a-glú-šlu-šlu-ta\ *v* : to let slip < *Kan iwapsake wan imicik'ege šni ca awaglušlušlutin kte lo* A cutting knife for tendons since it was dull for my use, I shall let it keep slipping. > – Cf yušluta *and* oglikiya

a·glu·šna \a-glú-šna\ *v poss* [fr *yušna* to let slip or miss] : to make a mistake over

a·glu·štan \a-glú-štaŋ\ *v poss* a·wa·gluštan [fr *ayuštan* to let alone] : to leave off something pertaining to one's self

a·glu·šte \a-glú-šte\ *vn* : to be lame in < *Si amaglušte* I sprained by foot > — **aglušte·šte** *v red* : to be numb or lame < *Amaglušte šte* I feel numb > – Bl

a·glu·ta \a-glú-ṫa\ *v poss* [fr *yúta* to eat on, or fr *ayuta* to look at] : to eat one's own with something upon something, *or* to look at one's own < *Awicagluta yelo* He gazed at them > – B.H.53.2,197.11

a·glu·ti·tan \a-glú-ṫi-ṫaŋ\ *v poss* [fr *yutitan* to pull] : to stretch one's own upon; to pull down

a·glu·we·ga \a-glú-we-ġa\ *v poss* [fr *yuwega* to break but not entirely] : to bend or break upon

a·glu·wi \a-glú-wi\ *v poss* a·wa·gluwi [fr *yuwi* to bind up] : to wrap one's own around, as one's leggings on one's legs

a·glu·za \a-glú-za\ *v poss* [fr *yúza* to take hold of] : to hold one's own to

a·gna \a-gná\ *adv* and perhaps *prep* : *at once* < *Yunkan lila kpeyela iyeya na* ~ *wounka na psunpsunkiya agliyunka* Then came a very loud report, all at once it fell, and they came home lying face-down, ~ *mni k'un wankal hiyu* All at once the water had risen > — **agna·gna** *adv red* : at once repeatedly – D.217-218, 269

a·gna·han \a-gná-haŋ\ *vn* [fr *gnahan* to fall of itself] : to fall on, as fruit in anything

a·gna·ka \a-gná-k̇a\ *va* a·wa·gnaka unka·gnaka·pi : to place on anything, to apply externally *e.g.* medicine, poultice, *etc*

a·gna·la \a-gná-la\ *adv* : only with, with so many only

a·gna·wo·ta·pi \á-gna-wo-ta-pi\ *n* : a table, or anything to eat on, as a box *etc*

agni \a-gní\ *v 3rd pers singl of agla* to take home : he took it home – Note: it is so changed when the word *na* follows

a·gu \a-ġú\ *vn* [fr *ġu* to burn] : to burn on anything, to burn on account of or by reason of anything < *We agu s'e* It is as if blood burns, *i.e.* 'all is bloody' > — **agu·gu·ya** *va red* [fr *aguya* to set fire on] : to cause to burn on — **agu·ya** *va* agú·wa·ya : to make something burn on

a·gu·ya·pi \a-ġú-ya-ṗi\ *n* : wheat bread

~ *blu* flour | ~ *owašlece* a slice of bread
~ *inaze* a flour sifter | or ~ *waksápi wanji*
~ *gmigmela* biscuits | ~ *sáka* hard bread, crackers
~ *ha* chaff | ~ *skúya* pastry, sweet crackers, or ~ *skuyéla*
~ *hu* straw *i.e.* of wheat | ~ *skuyéla gmigméla yuhlokab* doughnuts
~ *icapa* a flail | ~ *su* a grain of wheat, seed wheat
~ *ikácoco* a bread raiser | ~ *špan ha* bread crust
~ *išpánye* a baking pan
~ *okaġe* a bakery
~ *ošpanyan* a baker over

~ *tacáġu* a loaf of bread (which is light and spongy like to lungs)
~ *zípela* or ~ *zibzípela* pancakes

a·gu·ya·pi su o·ka·la \a-ġú-ya-ṗi su o-kà-la\ *v* : to sow wheat

a·ha·ha·ye·la \a-há-ha-ye-la\ *adv* : not firmly, in a movable way – Cf haháyela

a·ha·he \a-ha-ĕ'\ *interj* : *exclam* of Thanks to one for a gift, something like: "Three cheers for ... ", thus : "N. ahahé!" which is then repeated – BT

a·ha·kab \a-há-k̇ab\ *adv* : after, afterward

a·han \a-háŋ\ *vn* a·wa·han [fr *han* to stand] : to stand or rest on — *v imper* or *interj* : "Look out!", "Be careful!" as is said when something is losing its balance and will drop, as a lamp on the edge of a table < ~ *hinhpayin kta!* Look out! It might fall! > — Ahan *np* : a man in days of old who went out on some nice day in March, and he was not prepared for cold weather. So he froze to death when a blizzard suddenly came upon him. So when a blizzard comes in the month of March, people say: "Ahán taanpetu welo." Once George Rogers used the word as a warning for somebody to stop annoying one of the family, and he pronounces the word: Hehán – R WE Cf anbhánk̇eya D.197

a·han·han \a-háŋ-haŋ\ *v red* [fr *ahan* to stand on] : to stand upon < Pajola *waz'ahanhan* A hill beset with many pines > – Bl

a·han·he·pi·i·c'i·ya \a-háŋ-he-pi-i-c'i-ya\ *v refl* : to wait until night overtakes one – B.H.77.4

a·han·ke·ya \a-háŋ-ke-ya\ *adv* : immediately then, following, immediately behind < *hócoka kin* ~ immediately outside the camp center > — **ahanke·yela** \a-háŋ-ke-ye-la\ *adv* : just before, previously – D.246

a·han·ki·kta·pi \a-háŋ-k̇i-kta-pi\ *n* : a wake, a watching at the body of a deceased person – Bl

a·han·na·jin ku·wa \a-háŋ-na-jin kù-wa\ *v* : to bother one constantly – Bl

a·han·zi \a-háŋ-zi\ *vn imperf* a·ma·hanzi : to be shady, over-shadowed — **ahanzi·ya** *va* ahanzi·wa·ya : to over-shadow or cause shade upon, to make dark upon, to screen from the sun < *Wanagi ahanzimayanpelo* Spirits cast their shadow over me, *i.e.* I am happy > – BT

a·he·ce·ca \a-hé-ce-ca\ *vn* a·ma·hececa unka·hececa·pi : to be rather better, to recover a little — **ahececa·ke** *adj* a·ma·hececake : rather better — **a·he·cel** \a-hé-cel\ *adv contrac of ahececa* : in getting better — **ahecel·ya** \a-hé-cel-ya\ *adv* : pretty well, middling – Bl

a·he·ce·tu·ka \a-hé-ce-tu-k̇a\ *adj perhaps* : small while something else is large – Bl

a·he·he·ye·la \a-hé-he-ye-la\ *adv* : not firmly < ~ *yanka* He sat unsteadily >

a·he·ki·ya \a-hé-k̇i-ya\ *vn* [fr *ahan* to stand on + *kiya* to cause] : to cause to stand on, perhaps to step on < ~ *po* "Step on that!" *i.e.* to crush a bug > – Bl

a·he·yun \a-hé-yuŋ\ *va* ahe·mun ahe·nun [fr *heyun* to wrap or pack] : to tie up a bundle on

a·hi \a-hí\ *va* a·wá·hi : to arrive at a place, bringing something — *v coll pl* : they have come < *Wanbli wan hiyomahi na wicoti ekta amaki k'on na ake amahi k'on* An eagle came for me, it took me to camp, and it arrived again bringing me >

a·hi·gla·hta·ka \a-hí-gla-ḣta-ka\ *va* : to grind one's teeth or with one's teeth

a·hi·gle \a-hí-gle\ *va* ahi·wa·gle : to bring and place, to set < *Wanna woyute kin aupi na lel* ~ *po. Hoipate kin opuze kin ekta ahi yuslohan* ~ Now bring the meal and set it here. They brought dragging the net to shore > – Note: *ahigle kte* to place a bet – B.H.274.17, 302.8

a·hi·gna·ka \a-hí-gna-ka\ *va* : to come or bring and put down < *Hecel wana cokab ahignakapi. Na inyan tob* ~ So they came and put it down in their midst. And he came and set down four stones > – D.98

a·hi·hun·ni \a-hí-huŋ-ni\ *v coll pl* : they arrive < *Na wanna glihunnipi icunhan iš eya wamakaškan caje oyas'in* ~ *na wanna ataya okawing au. Ecel aglagla pazo au na nawajin el* ~. *Wanna akicita* ~ *kte lo* And while they had all but arrived home, every sort of creeping creature themselves arrived, and they came together circling about. Thus they came presenting themselves before them; I stood when they arrived. Now the warriors will come in >

a·hi·i·cu \a-hí-i-cu\ *v* : to have come and taken < *Tancan kin ahiicupi* They have come and taken the body > – B.H.99.4, 269.17

a·hi·ju *also* **ahítokšu** \a-hí-ju\ *va* ahi·wa·ju [fr *ahi* to arrive bringing + *ju* to lay up] : to bring and pile up

a·hi·ki·ci·gla \a-hí-ki-ci-gle\ *vn* ahi·we·cigle ahi·un·kicigle·pi : to bet for one

a·hi·kte \a-hí-kte\ *vn* : to kill in battle – Bl

a·hi·k'u \a-hí-k'u\ *v* : to bring and give < *Hunku kin hanpa eya* ~ His mother brought and gave him some moccasins > – MS.563

a·hi·mni·ci·ya \a-hí-mni-ci-ya\ *v* [fr *ahi* arrive bringing something + *mniciya* come together] : to assemble, to keep coming in one after another

a·hi·na·pa \a-hí-na-pa\ *vn* : to come out on, as do many sores — *v coll pl* : they come in sight, to come out on – Note: *ahinape* is used referring to one only — *va* : to have one come out < *Pilate ake Jesus tankal ahinapin* Pilate again had Jesus come out > – B.H.264.19

a·hin·han \a-híŋ-haŋ\ *vn* a·ma·hinhan [fr *hinhan* precipitate] : to rain upon, to fall as rain does on things < *Ahinhe* It is raining, *i.e.* it rains >

a·hin·he·ki·ya *or* **ahínheya** \a-híŋ-he-k̇i-ya\ *va* ahinhe·wa·kiya ahinhe·wa·ya : to cause to fall on, as does rain

a·hin·hpa·ya \a-híŋ-ḣpa-ya\ *vn* a·ma·hinhpaya unka·hinhpaya·pi : to fall on anything < *Yunkan keya kin wicaša wan nata kin akan* ~ When he said that, the man fell over on his head > — **ahinhpaya·ic'iya** *va* : to make fall on one's own self — **ahinhpaye·ya** *va* a·ma·

\a\ father \e\ they \i\ machine \o\ smoke \u\ lunar \an, aŋ\ blanc Fr. \in, iŋ\ ink \on, oŋ, un, uŋ\ soon, confier Fr. \c\ chair \ġ\ machen Ger. \j\ fusion \clusters: bl, gn, kp, hšl, etc...\ b[e]lo ... said with a slight vowel
See more in the Introduction, Guide to Pronunciation

hinhpayeya : to cause to fall on – Bl LHM

a·hi·o·yu·spa \a-hí-o-yu-spa\ *va* : to have come and captured – B.H.256.24

a·hi·pa·ni \a-hí-pa-ni\ *v* ahi·wa·pani [fr *ahi* arrive + *paní* to elbow one] : to shove with the elbow, to push or crowd against

a·hi·te·bya \a-hí-te-bya\ *v* : to come and devour – B.H. 200.4

a·hi·ti \a-hí-ti\ *v* ahi·wa·ti ahi·un·ti·pi : to come and pitch one's tent — *v coll pl* : they come and pitch their tents

a·hi·to·kšu \a-hí-to-kšu\ *va* : to pile up – Cf ahíju

a·hi·ton·wan \a-hí-toŋ-waŋ\ *va* ahi·wa·tonwan : to look towards one, to look to or upon, to regard < *Kul ~ yanka. Kuta ahiwatonwan. Kul ahitonwin ye* He sat looking down at him. I looked down at him. Please have a lowly regard for him > — **ahitonwe·kiya** \a-hí-toŋ-we-ki-ya\ *va* ahitonwe·wa·kiya : to cause to look towards — **ahitonwe·ya** *va* ahitonwe·wa·ya : to cause to look to

a·hi·un·pa \a-hí-uŋ-pa\ *v* ahi·wa·unpa : to bring and place — *va* : to have come and lain down – B.H.99.5,120.7, 187.8

a·hi·wi·co·ti \a-hí-wi-co-ti\ *n* : an on-coming crowd < *Israel oyate ~ kin wanyankapi* The approaching crowd of Israelite people saw him > – B.H.69.2, 131.17

a·hi·wi·ta·ya \a-hí-wi-ta-ya\ *v 3rd pers pl* : they have come together – B.H.64.21

a·hi·wi·yo·pe·ya \a-hí-wi-yo-pe-ya\ *va* : to have arrived somewhere and sold something – B.H.31.2

a·hi·wo·ta \a-hí-wo-ta\ *va* : to arrive and press against –B.H.71.12

a·hi·ya·gle \a-hí-ya-gle\ *va* and *vn* : to bring home and place on — *v coll pl* : they come and go on toward home — **ahiyagle·ya** *part* : coming and going – Bl

a·hi·ya·han \a-hí-ya-haŋ\ *vn* : to come and alight on, as a flock of birds on a field — *v coll pl* : they came up, *i.e.* on the other side of a hill and stood in sight – Note: *hiyáhan* is used in referring to one only < *Wanna akicita kin ~ na wancak natan ahiyu* The soldiers came up on the other side, and at once they came on the attack > – Bl

a·hi·yan·ka \a-hí-yan-ka\ *vn* : to come, *i.e.* many, and stay around < *K'ós'e ahiyankelo* Apparently they came to stay > – Bl

¹a·hi·ya·ya \a-hí-ya-ya\ *va* a·wa·hiyaya a·yá·hilale un-ka·hiyaya·pi : to take and carry around, to hand round *e.g.* the pipe < *Tancan kin el nape ~ šni yo* Do not lay a hand on him > – B.H.42.21, 90.1 — *v coll pl* : they passed by

²a·hi·ya·ya \a-hí-ya-ya\ *va* : to sing a tune < *Olowan num ~* He sang two songs, *Olowan wan ayahilale kinhan* At the time you sang a song, *T'ebleze šni wawiyahpahpaya ayahilale* You sang it franticly making a fake attack >

a·hi·yo·hpa·ya \a-hí-yo-ȟpa-ya\ *v coll pl* : they came down a hill < *Hehanl ungna paha wan etan wicaša ota ~ na au na ahi* Many men had then perhaps come down from the hills, they came and arrived. *Yunkan lila wicotapi na ahiwicoti* Then they were very much a crowd and were approaching >

a·hi·yo·ka·kin \a-hí-yo-ka-kiŋ\ *v* ahiyo·wa·kakin : to come and peep in

a·hi·yo·ka·s'in \a-hí-yo-ka-s'iŋ\ *v* ahiyo·wa·kas'in ahi-yo·un·kas'in·pi : to look in at a window or door, to peep in – Note: *iblokas'in* is used in *ref* to one only < *Heciyatanhan ~ yanke* He sat looking on from there > – D.39 — **ahiyokas'ins'in** *v red* : to appear and disappear; to peep and peep again

a·hi·yu \a-hí-yu\ *va* ahi·bu : to be coming and bringing < *Na he, i.e. cricket, lila i etan we ~* And blood was really coming from its (the cricket's) mouth > – B.H.67.-38, 76.33 — *v coll pl* : they are on their way home, as reported by somebody < *Natan ~ na kinil awicaupi. Lena tohanl okicize wanji el unpi na kuwa awicahiyupi eša napapi kte šni yelo* They came on the attack and brought almost all of them with them. When these were in a fight, and though they tried to bring them along home, they will not flee > – Bl D.103

a·hi·yu·kan \a-hí-yu-kaŋ\ *v* ahi·blu·kan : to come and make room, to come and shake off

a·hi·yun·ka \a-hí-yuŋ-ka\ *vn* [fr *ahi* arrive + *yunka* lie down] : to come and sleep, *i.e.* collectively — *va perhaps* : to bring and lie down

a·hi·yu·slo·han \a-hí-yu-slo-haŋ\ *vn* : to come dragging along — *adv perhaps* : moving out < *Hoipate kin opuze kin ekta ~ ahigle* The came dragging the net and putting it on shore > –B.H.301.27 LHB

a·hi·yu·štan \a-hí-y-štaŋ\ *v* ahi·blu·štan [fr *ahi* to arrive + *yuštan* to finish] : to come and finish, to come to the end, as the last word in a talk < *Ho, lecala ahiunyuštanpi* Well, lately we finished, *i.e.* we are now at the end of our fast, for we have plenty of meat > – Bl

a·hi·yu·we·ga \a-hí-yu-we-ġa\ *v coll pl* : they cross; they came and broke it

a·ho·co·ka \a-hó-co-ka\ *adv* [fr *hocoka* center-camp] : in the midst — **ahocoka·ya** *adv* : around, surrounding < *~ unyanpi* We went around it > — *va* ahocoka·wa·ya : to surround

a·ho·ki·pa \a-hó-ki-pa\ *v poss* aho·wa·kipa [fr *ahopa* to keep or observe] : to value as one's own, to respect one's own, as one's husband; to take care of

a·ho·kši·win·kte \a-hó-kši-wiŋ-kte\ *v* ahokši·wa·winkte : to get angry at *e.g.* a child; to act like a child towards one

a·ho·pa \a-hó-pa\ *va* aho·wa·pa aho·un·pa·pi : to take care of; to keep or observe a regulation or commandment < *Tanyan ~ yo. Ahokicipapi* Take good care of him. They cared for each other >

a·ho·pe·ki·ya *or* **ahopeya** \a-hó-pe-ki-ya\ *va* ahope·wa·-kiya : to cause to respect; to keep or observe — *part* : respecting, honoring, observing — *adv* : obediently

a·ho·tan \a-hó-taŋ\ *va* aho·wa·tan : to make a noise around one — **ahotan·ka** \a-hó-taŋ-ka\ *n* : one who makes noise around

a·ho·ton \a-hó-toŋ\ *va* [fr *a* for + *hoton* to cry out] : to cry out for, as a bird for food — **ahoton·ton** *v red* : to cry out for repeatedly, to bawl for anything

a·ho·ya·so·tka·ya \a-hó-so-tka-ya\ *vn* : to make expressions of anger < *Okiwaš'ag nišicelo ahoyasotkamaya yelo* I am speechless to express my anger with you > – YH Bl

a·ho·ye·ki·ci·ya·pi \a-hó-ye-ki-ci-ya-pi\ *n* : a scolding of each other; a quarreling with others; mutual recriminations — **ahoye·ya** \a-hó-ye-ya\ *vn* ahoye·wa·ya a-hoye·un·yan·pi : to quarrel < *Ahoyekiciyapi* They quarreled with each other >

a·hu·tkan·yan \a-hú-tkaŋ-yaŋ\ *adv* : branching, having many prongs or roots

a·ȟa·bya \a-ȟá-bya\ *v* aȟa·bwa·ya [fr *ȟabya* frighten away] : to scare *e.g. game*

a·ȟan·ȟan \a-ȟáŋ-ȟaŋ\ *interj exclam* : of some disgust, as in finding one's hands affected by touching poison ivy < *~ yelo* Rats! >

a·hco \a-ȟcó\ *n* : the upper part of the arm – Cf istó

a·ȟe·yun·ka \a-ȟé-yuŋ-ka\ *vn* [fr *a* on + *ȟeyúnka* frost] :

to be frost on anything < *Can'áȟeyunke* There is a frost on the trees, as at times durng the winter >

a·ȟi·ca·han *or* **agicahan** \a-ȟí-ca-haŋ\ *v* [fr *a* on + *ȟicahan* to misstep] : to stumble and fall on < *Aȟicahe konze* He pretended to stumble and fall on >

a·hlo \a-ȟló\ *vn* [fr *a* for + *hlo* to growl] : to growl over or about a thing, as does a dog over a bone

a·hmun \a-ȟmúŋ\ *va* : to drown one in noise, to be noisy about one < *Lila amayahmun. Inila yanki ye, amayahmunke lo* You smother me with your noise. Be quiet. You are drowning me in your noise, *i.e.* when a person is not wishing to get angry > - Bl

a·hni·yan \a-ȟní-yaŋ\ *va* : to be angry, to take hold of angrily — **ahniyan·yan** *v red* a·wa·hniyanyan a·ma·hniyanhan : to be angry at, to take hold of one in anger < *Amayahniyanyan hwo?* Are you angry with me? > - Note: the word does not indicate the fondling or handling *e.g.* a baby lovingly - Bl

a·hta·ni \a-ȟtá-ni\ *v* [fr *a* for + *htani* to work on] **1** : to labor for one, to work at anything **2** : to sin or break a law

a·hta·ta *also* **ahtateca** \a-ȟtá-ṫa\ *adj* : languid, feeble, weak — **ahtatešniyan** \a-ȟtá-te-šni-yaŋ\ *adv* : without stopping or rest, continually in respect to something - Bl

a·hwa·i·c'i·ya \a-ȟwá-i-c'i-ya\ *v refl* : to make one's self sleepy < *Ahwaic'iye s'e manke lo* I was making as if I were sleepy > — **ahwaic'iye·la** *adv* : quietly < ~ *yanka po* Be quiet! *or* Sit quietly! > - Bl

a·hwa·ya *or* **ahwayela** \a-ȟwá-ya\ *adv* : mildly, patiently, gently, easily - Cf iwaštela

a·h'a \a-ȟ'á\ *vn* : to make noise, as does rain or hail striking a window < *Ah'ayelo* It is pitter-pattering > - Cf h'ayéla

a·h'an·h'an \a-ȟ'áŋ-ȟ'aŋ\ *va* a·wá·h'anh'an : to do a thing carelessly not having one's mind on it — **ah'an·h'an·ka** \a-ȟ'áŋ-ȟ'aŋ-ka\ *adj* : careless, negligent

a·h'a·ye·ton \a-ȟ'á-ye-toŋ\ *v* : to glue or paste *e.g.* colored plumes on the tips of feathers fitted on a warbonnet; to decorate a horse for parade - LHB

a·h'e·ca \a-ȟ'é-ca\ *n* : things of minor importance, in opposition to important matters < ~ *kin oblakin kte šni* I'll not relate things of little importance > - BD

a·h'e·h'e·ya \a-ȟ'é-ȟ'e-ya\ *adv* : raggedly < ~ *yanke lo* She is in rags > - S

a·h'in·h'in·ci·ya \a-ȟ'íŋ-ȟ'iŋ-ci-ya\ *va* : to make one's way carefully < *Ah'inh'inciyelahci mawani yelo* I did indeed walk with care! *e.g.* among cactus or sharp rocks > - Bl

a·h'inl·h'inl·ci·ye·la·kel \a-ȟ'íŋl-ȟ'iŋl-ci-ye-la-kel\ *adv* : slowly and painfully < ~ *mani* He walked, perhaps even groaning, as a person suffering from rheumatism > - Bl

a·h'o·ka·ka \a-ȟ'ó-ka-ka\ *adj* : skillful, adept < *Itowapi kaga ah'okake lo* He is skillful in taking pictures > - Bl

a·i \a-í\ *va* a·wá·i unká·i·pi : to carry or take to a place — *v coll pl* [fr *i* to have gone] : they reached a place < *Wanna hocokata ai. Na wanna ake zuya ai na el opa* They had got to center-camp. And when they again got on the warpath, he joined up >

a·i·a \a-í-a\ *va* ai·wa·ya ai·ya·ya ai·wicun·yan·pi **1** : to speak evil of, to slander < *Oyate kin ake ainiyanpi kte lo. Tuwa tokeca aie hwo?* The people will again talk about you. Was it some one else he spoke of? > - B.H.316.16 — **aia·pi** \a-í-a-pi\ *n* : a consultation; a slander

a·i·cab \a-í-cab\ *v contrac* [fr *aicapa* to open the mouth against one] : to offend in speech - Cf aícapa

a·i·ca·ga \a-í-ca-ġa\ *v* [fr *a* in + *icaga* to grow] : to grow on or in, to yield, produce, accrue < *Taku maka ~ , hena mitawa yelo* What grows on earth is mine > — **aicage** \a-í-ca-ġe\ *n* : interest, as of money - B.H.268.22

a·i·cah \a-í-caȟ\ *v contrac* [fr *aicaga* to grow on] : to produce — **aica·hya** \a-í-ca-ȟya\ *va* aica·hwa·ya : to cause to grow on, to make produce

a·i·ca·mna \a-í-ca-mna\ *vn* [fr *a* on + *icamna* to storm] : to storm upon, to blow furiously on

[1]**a·i·ca·pa** \a-í-ca-pa *or* a-í-ca-pa\ *va* [fr *a* on + *i* mouth + *kapa* to beat] : to open the mouth against anyone

[2]**a·i·ca·pa** \a-í-ca-pa\ *va* aica·wa·pa [fr *a* on + *i* by means of + *capá* to stab] : to stab one thing through or on another

a·i·ca·ptan·ptan \a-í-ca-ptaŋ-ptaŋ\ *vn* a·mi·captanptan : to roll over and over on anything

a·i·ca·zo \a-í-ca-zo\ *va* ai·wa·kazo [fr *i* for + *kazo* mark a line] : to have drawn for a time upon, to take credit on account of

a·i·ci·ki·ni·ca \a-í-ci-ki-ni-ca\ *v* : to dispute among themselves < *Yunkan Juda wicaša kin aicikinicapi na heyapi* It was said the Jews disputed among themselves > - B.H.227.21

a·i·ci·ma·ni \a-í-ci-ma-ni\ *vn* aicima·wa·ni [fr *ici* together + *mani* to travel] : to journey upon, to make a journey with for some purpose <*Ota Makoce Šica ekta aicimanipi* Many journey to the Bad Lands >

a·i·ci·ta·ki·gna \a-í-ci-ta-ki-gna\ *adv* : on the other, *i.e.* folded on, doubled - Cf aítagnaka Bl

a·i·ci·yo·pte·pte·ya \a-í-ci-yo-pte-pte-ya\ *adv* : crosswise as four things at the four quarters about a point of reference < ~ *yankapi* They stood crosswise > - Bl

a·i·co·ga \a-í-co-ġa\ *vn* [fr *icoga* to drift on] : to gather on or drift on anything

a·i·co·za \a-í-co-za\ *vn* ai·ma·coza [fr *a* on + *icoza* to be warm] : to be warm on or with

a·i·c'i·ble·za \a-í-c'i-ble-za\ *v* : to understand, realize concerning one's self; to notice on one's behalf, on one's self < *Akisni ~. Mani kin aic'ibleze šni na ihanble s'elececa* She realized she had got well. She did not realize she walked since it was as though she were dreaming > - B B.H.250.34, 322.3 D.215.12

a·i·c'i·ca·ga \a-í-c'i-ca-ġa\ *va* a·mi·c'icaga unka·ic'icaga·pi : to make on one's self *e.g.* the Sign of the Cross < *Can'ic'ipawega ~ po* All make the Sign of the Cross >

a·i·c'i·ki·ta \a-í-c'i-ki-ta\ *v refl* a·mi·c'icita [fr *akita* to hunt for] : to seek one's self, to regard one's own interests

a·i·c'i·ki·ya \a-í-c'i-ki-ya\ *v refl* a·mi·c'ikiya [fr *akiya* to consider] : to be diligent, make effort, bestir one's self — *adj* : diligent < ~ *waun* I am industrious >

a·i·c'i·kta·šni \a-í-c'i-kta-šni\ *v* **1** : to neglect one's self **2** [fr *aktašni* to despise] : to despise, not to heed, to reject or slight - Cf aktá

a·i·e \a-í-e\ *v* [fr *aia* to speak about one] : to slander - Cf aía

a·i·e·ki·ya \a-í-e-ki-ya\ *va* **1** : to cause to talk about, *i.e.* in either a good or bad sense **2** : to consult with

a·i·gla·gcan·ku·ya \a-í-gla-gcaŋ-kù-ya\ *v* : to break camp for the road - Bl KE

\a\ father \e\ they \i\ machine \o\ smoke \u\ lunar \an, aŋ\ blanc Fr. \in, iŋ\ ink \on, oŋ, un, uŋ\ soon, confier Fr. \c\ chair \ġ\ machen Ger. \j\ fusion \clusters: bl, gn, kp, hšl, etc...\ b°lo ... said with a slight vowel **See more in the Introduction, Guide to Pronunciation**

a·i·gla·gya \a-í-gla-gya\ *v refl* [fr *iglaka* to move camp] : to make move camp – Bl LHB

a·i·gla·hpa \a-í-gla-ȟpa\ *v refl* a·mi·glahpa [fr *a* on + *kahpa* to make fall] : to cover one's own — **aiglahpe·ya** \a-í-gla-ȟpe-ya\ *va* aiglahpe·wa·ya : to cast about one < *Taku aiglahpeyapi* They threw on some (clothes *i.e.*) >

a·i·gla·ka \a-í-gla-ka\ *v* : to break camp – B LHB

a·i·gla·la \a-í-gla-la\ *v refl* [fr *aglala* to scatter] : to cast or throw upon one's self < ~ *waštemna* perfume powder >

a·i·gla·ptan·yan \a-í-gla-ptaŋ-yaŋ\ *v* : to get something unexpectedly, what one has been wishing for – Bl

a·i·gla·p'o \a-í-gla-p'o\ *v refl* [fr *a* on + *kap'o* raise dust] : to get dusty, as by moving about < *Makahlu nisipi kin el aniglap'opi kin hena glatata po* Shake off the dust you picked up on your feet > – B.H.222.17

a·i·gla·štan \a-í-gla-štaŋ\ *v refl* a·mi·glaštan [fr *a* on + *kaštan* to spill] : to pour out or spill on one's self

a·i·gla·tan \a-í-gla-ṫaŋ\ *v refl* a·mi·glatan [fr *yatan* to praise] : to praise one's self for some quality or capacity

a·i·glu·ha \a-í-glu-ha\ *v refl* [fr *yuha* to have] **1** : to have or retain for one's own use, to provide for one's self **2** : to be a citizen

a·i·glu·ho·mni \a-í-glu-ho-mni\ *v refl* : to turn on, to throw one's self at, as in battle – B.H.101.23

a·i·glu·hle·ca \a-í-glu-ȟle-ca\ *v refl* : to tear one's own — **aigluhle·hleca** *v red* : to tear one's own to pieces — **aigluhle·hlel** *part contrac* : ripping one's own – B.H. 34.37

a·i·glu·hpa \a-í-glu-ȟpa\ *v refl* a·mi·gluhpa [fr *yuhpa* to pull or make fall] : to cause to fall on one's self, to bring on one's self < *Amigluhpa* He made it fall on myself, *Wóteȟi amigluhpe* He brought trouble for me >

a·i·glu·ksa \a-í-glu-ksa\ *v refl* [fr *yuksa* to break off] : to break off, as a limb of a tree on one's self

a·i·glu·po·ta \a-í-glu-ṗo-ṫa\ *v refl* [fr *glupota* rend one's own] : to tear or rend *e.g.* one's own garment on one's self

a·i·glu·ptan·yan \a-í-glu-ptan-yan\ *v refl* [fr *a* on + *igluptanyan* to turn around] : to turn over on or roll over on < *Canke el mahel (cega) iyunka na* ~ So when it lay down in a bucket it turned over on it >

a·i·glu·so·ta \a-í-glu-so-ta\ *v refl* : to use up one's own; to go all away, to migrate, as do ducks and geese

a·i·glu·ši·ca \a-í-glu-ši-ca\ *v refl* a·mi·glušica [fr *yušica* to cause trouble] : to get one's self into difficulty with

a·i·glu·ške·han \a-í-glu-ške-haŋ\ *v refl* [fr *yuškehan* to make wild] : to get busy on one's own self, to bestir one's own self, as a horse is supposed to do when a certain place must be reached – Bl

a·i·glu·šla \a-í-glu-šla\ *v refl* [fr *yušla* make bald] : to cut *e.g.* grass and cover one's self with it < *Peji amiglušla* Mown grass covered me >

a·i·glu·tan \a-í-glu-ṫaŋ\ *v refl* **1** : to pull the trigger of a gun on one's self **2** : to besmear one's self with one's own emission, to pollute one's self

a·i·glu·za \a-í-glu-za\ *v refl* a·mi·gluza [fr *gluza* to take one's own] : to dress or prepare one's self for an occasion

a·i·han \a-í-haŋ\ *v coll pl* : they go and stand on anything

a·i·han·bla \a-í-haŋ-bla\ *vn* ai·wa·hanbla [fr *ihanble* to dream] : to dream about < *Tatanka pizi wan ota latka ca on (tatanka wan) aiyahanble lo* For the fact that you drank much of a buffalo bull's gall (a buffalo bull's), you had dreams. >

a·i·ȟa·t'a \a-í-ȟa-t'a\ *v* : to laugh or giggle at < *Aiȟaunt'api* They laughed at him >

a·i·hpa·ya \a-í-ȟpa-ya\ *vn* [fr *ihpaya* to fall] : to fall on, as do leaves on anything

a·i·hpe·ya \a-í-ȟpe-ya\ *va* aihpe·wa·ya **1** : to throw or place on **2** : to leave or entrust with one < *Hokšila kin miye aihpemaya yo* Entrust me with the boy > – B.H.42.16 **3** : to communicate, endow, bequeath, dispose by will < *Aihpemaya* I inherited it > — **aihpeya·pi** *n* : a legacy or inheritance

a·i·i·c'i·la \a-í-i-c'i-la\ *v refl* : to act as though one had brought in – B.H.310.7

a·i·ka·pa \a-í-ka-ṗa\ *va* ai·wa·kapa [fr *i* mouth + *kapa* to beat] : to open the mouth on, to scold

a·i·kca·pta \a-í-kca-ṗta\ *v* : to talk much to, to reprove or scold

a·i·ki·a \a-í-ki-a\ *v poss* ai·wa·kia [fr *aia* to talk about one] : to talk about something that concerns one's self, to consider or talk against

a·i·ko·yag \a-í-ko-yag\ *v contrac* [fr *aikoyaka* to stick to] : to be sticking to — **aikoya·gya** *va* aikoya·gwa·ya : to cause to stick to or to link to or on

a·i·ko·ya·ka \a-í-ko-ya-ka\ *vn* : to stick to or one, to cleave to, to be fastened to

a·i·kpa·bla·ya *also* **aikpajuju** \a-í-kpa-bla-ya\ *v refl* a·mi·kpablaya : to make a fool of one's self by talking or acting foolishly < *Taku epe cin ecehci ecanon šni kin, anikpablaye lo, tak tokamon tan'in šni yelo* What I misplaced has not come to light, you made a fool of yourself when you did not do exactly what I said, *Ka tinskoya anikpablaye* How far will you go making a fool of yourself! *lit* you have spread yourself flat, *i.e.* you are making a complete fool of yourself > – Note: while *pablaya* is *archaic*, it lends the *fig* to make one's self be a laughing stock, to be helpless with one's back on the ground – BT D.72, 75 note 1

a·i·kpa·gan \a-í-kṗa-ġaŋ\ *v refl* a·ma·kpagan [fr *pagan* able to spare : to part with one's self for any purpose — **aikpagan·yan** *part* : parting with one's self for

a·i·kpa·ju·ju \a-í-kṗa-ju-ju\ *v refl* : to make a fool of one's self – Bl *Syn* AIKPABLAYA

a·i·kpa·tan \a-í-kṗa-ṫaŋ\ *v refl* a·mi·kpatan [fr *patan* to take care of] : to reserve for one's self *e.g.* for any duty or purpose — **aikpatan·yan** *part* : reserving one's self for

a·i·kpo·gan \a-í-kpo-ġaŋ\ *v refl* [fr *a* on + *pogan* to blow] : to blow on one's self, as with the mouth using water, medicine, *etc* < *Na tohanl okicize econonpi ca (pejuta kin le)* ~ *po* And when you are to engage in battle, blow (this medicine on yourselves >

a·i·kšin·ki·ya \a-í-kšiŋ-ki-ya\ *va* aikšin·wa·kiya : to make faces at

a·i·le \a-í-le\ *vn* [fr *ile* to burn] : to burn or blaze on

aile·šaša *adv* : in the red flame < ~ *yuza* to hold in the red flame > — **ailešaša·ya** *va* ailešaša·wa·ya : to put in and hold in the red flame to scorch

a·i·le·ya \a-í-le-ya\ *va* aile·wa·ya : to cause to burn on or around, to set fire to < *Na wanna cega wan lila tanka ca ogna wizila k'on itiyopa el aileyapi* They had set fire to that old tipi in a very large barrel near the door > — *part* : setting fire to

a·i·mni·ci·ya \a-í-mni-ci-ya\ *v coll pl* : they gather together for some purpose

a·i·na·pa \a-í-na-pa\ *va* aina·wa·pa [fr *a* on + *inapa* to emerge] : to come in sight of or upon

a·i·na·ta·gya \a-í-na-ta-gya\ *adv* : beyond a hill < ~ *na-*

jin It stood, perhaps tied, beyond the hill > – Bc
a·i·ni·han \a-í-ni-haŋ\ *vn* ai·ma·nihan : to be afraid on account of — **ainihan·yan** *adv* : excitedly, fearfully
a·i·ni·la \a-í-ni-la\ *adv* : stilly or silently for, as in making the approach to game < ~ *osni* cold without wind >
a·in·ki·ca·ton \a-íŋ-ki-ca-toŋ\ *va* ain·we·caton : to put on around one an overcoat, shawl, or anything warm, as around a child — **ainki·ton** \a-íŋ-ki-toŋ\ *v* ain·we·ton : to wear an overcoat or shawl over one's clothes – Bl
a·in·yan·ka \a-íŋ-yaŋ-ka\ *v* a·wa·imanka a·ya·inanka unka·inyanka·pi [fr *inyanka* to run] : to run on *e.g.* a floor, to run for, run to get – Cf for more under ínyanka
a·i·pi·ya·ka \a-í-pi-ya-ka\ *va* : to tie around one's self, to gird one's self < *Minihuhe ska wan aipiyake* He tied about himself a white cloth > – Note: the word is sometimes written *mnihúha* though not *deriv* from *mni* water
a·i·po·gan \a-í-po-ġaŋ\ *va* ai·wa·pogan [fr *ipogan* to exhale] : to blow upon
a·i·sin·yan \a-í-sin-yaŋ\ *adv* : out of sight, behind something else < ~ *iyaya*. ~ *iyotakapi* He got out of sight. They sat down out of sight > – D.39.71 Cf akotanhan
a·i·šta·cel·ya \a-í-šta-cel-ya\ *va* : to catch a side glance or glimpse of anything < *Aištacelwaye s'elececa* It seemed I caught a glimpse of a signal > – Bl
a·i·šta·e·cel·ya \a-í-šta-e-cel-ya\ *va* : to see, understand < *Miyeš aištaecelwaye šni* I do not understand > – Bl
a·i·šta·gnag \a-í-šta-gnag\ *v contrac* [fr *aištagnaka* gaze at] : to gaze at < ~ *kuwa* He caught sight of something and kept peering at it > — **aištagnag·ya** *adv* : looking at intently < ~ *kuwa* He watched it closely > — **aištagnagya·kel** *adv* : intently looking at – Bl
a·i·šta·gna·ka \a-í-šta-gna-ka\ *va* aišta·wa·gnaka [fr *a* on + *išta* eyes + *gnaka* to place, set] : to place the eyes upon, to look at intently — **aištagnake·šni** \a-í-šta-gna-ke-šni\ *v* : to neglect, not look after *e.g.* one's child –Bl
a·i·štin·ma \a-í-štiŋ-ma\ *vn* a·mi·štinma [fr *a* on + *ištinma* to sleep] : to sleep on
a·i·ta·gla·hwe *or* **áitaglahwe·kiya** *or* **áitaglahwe·ya** \á-i-ta-gla-hwe\ *adv* : with the wind < ~ *bla* I go downwind, ~ *unyanpi* We go with the wind, ~ *unglapi* We have the wind to our backs > – Bl
a·i·ta·gna·gya \a-í-ta-gna-gya\ *adv* : placing something on top of another < ~ *k'in* He carried something on top of another > – Bl
a·i·ta·gna·ka \a-í-ta-gna-ka\ *va* aita·wa·gnaka : to place one on top of another, as is done in carrying – R Bl
a·i·tan·can \a-í-taŋ-caŋ\ *n* : the ruler over < *Taku ainitancan heci hena nici* What, whatever was it for you to be king over these people? > – B.H.94.21
a·i·te·yu·šin·ki·ya \a-í-te-yu-šiŋ-ki-ya\ *va* aiteyušin·wa·kiya : to knit the brows or cut faces at
a·i·tkob \a-í-tkob\ *adv* : around < ~ *u* to come around as around a horse to walk to it from the front so as to catch it > — **aitko·kib** \a-í-tko-kib\ *adv* : towards < ~ *inyanka* to run towards it > – Bl
a·i·tku \a-í-tku\ *adv* : spoon-like, as in describing the lower lip of a baby crying
a·i·to-he-ki·ci·ya·pi \a-í-to-he-ki-ci-ya-pi\ *v pl* : they answer each other sharply – Bl
a·i·to·he·ya \a-í-to-he-ya\ *v* aitohe·wa·ya [fr *ite* face + *oheya* a place to say] : to turn one's face on, to look at; to answer accusations or hard words, to give one back < ~ *yo* Answer back!, *Tohanl tuwa aitohewaya can šna tokel wacin ecel wakuwa yelo* When I must confront one, I treat him just as I choose. *Tuwa aitohewaya can wahmunge lo* I bewitch, believe anyone I look at > – Bc Cf D.101, 103
a·i·to·kab \a-í-to-kab\ *adv* : before, *i.e.* in time
a·i·ton·šni \a-í-toŋ-šni\ *v* ai·wa·tonšni : to tell lies on one
a·i·wan·ca·ya·pi \a-í-waŋ-ca-ya-pi\ *v 3rd pers pl* : they all talk bad about each other – Bl
a·i·ya·cin·yan \a-í-ya-ciŋ-yaŋ\ *adv* : prudently, circumspectly < ~ *econ* He did it with circumspection > – Bl *Syn* KAIWANYANGYA, OWAHECELYA
a·i·ya·gle \a-í-ya-gle\ *vn* : to lead to, reach to, as does a road; to lead to as a result of conduct — **aiyagle·ya** *va* aiyagle·wa·ya : to lead to **a** : to bring upon one's self **b** : to deserve or merit — *adv* : leading to, even to; until
a·i·ya·hpa·ya \a-í-ya-hpa-ya\ *va* aiyahpa·wa·ya : to fall upon
a·i·ya·hpe·ya \a-í-ya-hpe-ya\ *va* aiyahpe·wa·ya **1** : to throw on or over, as a rope in catching a horse **2** : to communicate to one *i.e.* a disease, to infect
a·i·ya·kab *or* **aiyakapa** \a-í-ya-kab\ *v contrac, archaic* [fr *aiyakapa* to surpass] : to exceed, surpass
a·i·ya·ka·pte·ya \a-í-ya-ka-pte-ya\ *adv* : uphill, ascending < *Yunkan tuwa ocanku wan ogna ya ca ecel ihektab bla na ~ ya ca ecel bla na paha wan el iyahan ca miš eya el iyawahan. Paha wan tanka ~ bla na iyawahan* Then since some one went in the direction of the road, I went that way after him; when he went uphill, I went that way; and since he went up onto the hill, I too went onto it. I went ascending a tall mountain and went and stood on it > – R Cf iyákapteya
a·i·ya·ka·ška \a-í-ya-ka-ška\ *va* aiya·wa·kaška : to tie one thing on another < *Inyan on wokpanpi wanji tahu aiyakaškapi* They bound a stone to the nap of a grinder handle >
a·i·ya·pe \a-í-ya-pe\ *va* aiya·wa·pe [fr *a* on + *iyape* to ambush] : to lie in wait for
a·i·ya·pe·mni \a-í-ya-pe-mni\ *va* aiya·wa·pemni [fr *iyapemni* wrap up in] : to wrap around, wrap up with
a·i·ya·sa·ka \a-í-ya-sa-ka\ *vn* aiya·ma·saka : to stiffen or become hard, as raw hide
a·i·ye·cel·ya \a-í-ye-cel-ya\ *adv* : in much the same manner, in a way a little less to one than another < *Iyohila tokel oškinciyapi kte kin ~ owicak'u* He lent them each a bit less as they might be kept busy >
a·i·yo·hans·ya \a-í-yo-haŋs-ya\ *adv* : in the shade < ~ *hpaye* He lay in the shade > — *va* : to overshadow < *Mahpiya wan aiyohanswicaye. Nagi kin aiyohanswicaye* A cloud overshadowed them. The spirit cast a shadow over them >
a·i·yo·hpe·ya \a-í-yo-hpe-ya\ *adv* : downhill — *n* : a declivity < *Na paha k'on he ~ wicoti etkiya bla. Na ungnahela ~ tuwa kici ble ehanl weksuye. ~ mani. ~ iyaye* I had gone down the hill toward camp. And all at once on the way down, I recalled then I went with some one. He walked downhill. He went on down the hill > – Note: the word is also applied *fig*, to a man older than 50 years – IS D.9, 67
a·i·yo·jan·jan \a-í-yo-jaŋ-jaŋ\ *vi* : to shine on — **aiyojanjan·ic'i·ya** *v refl* : to have lighted one, be illuminated by — **aiyojanjan·ya** *va* : to throw light on, illumine, as by a lighted match – Bl

---

\a\ father \e\ they \i\ machine \o\ smoke \u\ lunar \an, aŋ\ blanc Fr. \in, iŋ\ ink \on, oŋ, un, uŋ\ soon, confier Fr. \c\ chair \ġ\ machen Ger. \j\ fusion \clusters: bl, gn, kp, hšl, etc...\ b^e^lo ... said with a slight vowel
See more in the Introduction, Guide to Pronunciation

a·i·yo·ki·pi \a-í-yo-ki-pi\ *adj* : pleasant, agreeable — **aiyokipi·ya** *adv* : agreeably

a·i·yo·kpa·za \a-í-yo-kpa-za\ *vn* : to be darkened; *fig* to be confused < *Anpahan wi kin aiyokpazin kte* In daylight the sun will be darkened >

a·i·yo·pte·ca \a-í-yo-pte-ca\ *adv* : less than — **aiyoptel** \a-í-yo-ptel\ *or* **aiyopte·tu** \a-í-yo-pte-tu\ *and* **aiyoptetu·ya** *adv* : less; towards, in the direction of

a·i·yo·pte·ya \a-í-yo-pte-ya\ *v* : to match with what one contributes < *Takunl aiyoptemayaye cin hignaciyin kte* Because you are a match for me I'll marry you, as a girl would say to her lover, that he should buy her, *i.e.* give her something so that he does not throw her away > — *adv* : in a straight line or direction < ~ *iyayapi* They went on straightway, directly one place to another, *Kaiciopteya kipazo* He pointed directly square across for him, *i.e.* right opposite on a line with >

a·i·yo·tan \a-í-yo-taŋ\ *adv* : more than, greater than, beyond < *aiyotanhci* quite a bit more than or beyond > — **aiyotan·i·c'i·la** \a-í-yo-taŋ-i-c'i-la\ *v refl* : to push one's self ahead of others - Bl

a·i·yu·ȟe·ya \a-í-yu-ȟe-ya\ *adv* : extremely, wonderfully < ~ *wašte* extremely good, ~ *luzahan* superbly fast > - Bl

a·i·yu·hta·ta \a-í-yu-ȟta-ta\ *v* : to let loose on, give rope to *e.g.* a horse seemingly strangled - B

a·i·yu·kcan \a-í-yu-kcaŋ\ *va* : to think of something or to think over something; to think much of one

a·i·zi·ta \a-í-zi-ta\ *vn* [fr *a* for + *izita* to be smoking] : to smoke or burn *e.g.* incense for some purpose

a·ja·ya \á-ja-ya\ *adv* : plainly, clearly < ~ *owicakiyake* He spoke plainly to them >

a·ji·ji \a-jí-ji\ *v* a·wa·jiji : to whisper about a person or thing - Note: *ojíji* is used by men

a·jo \a-jó\ *v* : to whistle for - Cf ajójo

a·jo·jo \a-jó-jo\ *v* : a·wa·jojo : to whistle about, to call by whistling, as for a dog — **ajojo·kiya** \a-jó-jo-ǩi-ya\ *va* ajojo·wa·kiya : to cause to whistle for

a·jun·tka \a-júŋ-tka\ *n* : the kidneys

a·ju·ton \a-jú-toŋ\ *v* aju·wa·ton : to add a little lie to one's narrative - Bl

a·kab \a-ǩáb\ *prep* : over, beyond, upon < ~ *iyeya* to throw beyond, ~ *iyaya* to overflow; or *fig* to be pressed for work that is not done yet, *Wanna cega* ~ *iyaya* The bucket overflowed, ~ *iyayešni makuwapi ca ecamon šni* Since they expected me not to go beyond that, I did not do so, or No end was there to bother with, so I could not do it, *i.e.* what you wanted done > - Bc

a·ka·bhan \a-ǩá-bhaŋ\ *adj* or *adv* : standing on the outside, as one does on the outside of a nest of tubs or kettles

a·ka·bla \a-ǩá-bla\ *va* a·wa·kabla [fr *kabla* to slice] : to cut into thin slices or strips, to slice in addition to

a·ka·bla·bla·ga \á-ka-bla-bla-ġa\ *v red* [fr *akablaga* to spread] : to open out < *Hehanl ungna wanbli ca yanka na* ~ At the time it was perhaps an eagle that was perched and unfurled its wings >

a·ka·bla·ga \á-ka-bla-ġa\ *vn* : to spread out over, as one's wings, to open *e.g.* the armpits or underparts of the wings for - D.81 — **akablah** \á-ǩa-blaȟ\ *vn contrac of* akablaga < ~ *iyeya* to spread over quickly, as a bird its wings >

a·ka·bla·ja \á-ǩa-bla-ja\ *va* á·wa·kablaja : to straddle, to spread the legs apart, to go astride

a·ka·blas \á-ǩa-blas\ *vn contrac of* akablaza : to tear open < ~ *iyeya* to tear or rip open suddenly >

a·ka·blaš \á-ǩa-blaš\ *va contrac of* akablaja : to go astride < ~ *inajin* to stand astride of >

a·ka·bla·ya \á-ǩa-bla-ya\ *vn* : to spread out over, as with one's wings < *El ewatonwan ehanl wanbli wan akokiya* ~ *na itannunk wicahpi* When I looked at it, then there was an eagle with unfurled wings in the beyond, and on either side a star >

a·ka·bla·za \a-ǩá-bla-za\ *vn* : to tear open on, as a bag on a horse

a·ka·ble·ca \a-ǩá-ble-ca\ *va* a·wa·kableca [fr *kableca* to break] : to break *e.g.* an instrument by striking it on something, to break one thing lying on another by striking — **akablel** \a-ǩá-blel\ *vn contrac of* akableca : to break into pieces on < ~ *iyeya ihpeya* He threw it down of a sudden breaking it to pieces >

a·ka·blu \a-ǩá-blu\ *va* a·wa·kablu [fr *a* on + *kablu* to pulverize] : to break up fine upon < *Amayakablu welo* You raised dust settling on me, hence the meaning: to strike dust and make it settle on someone > - Bl Cf *akápsica* — *vn* : to go up in dust < *Wipa kin paogmus egle yo, tušu ipatan ton wo, maka etan kaspayin na wiluzignag ton wo, hecel* ~ *kta šni yelo* Set shut the windflaps, have lodge pole braces, dampen some of the ground, and have it (the tent) insulated so that dust be not disturbed > - Bl

a·ka·e·con s'e \a-ǩá-e-coŋ s'e\ *adv* : over-much, excessively < ~ *econ* He over-did it > - FH *Syn* AOKAGA

a·ka·ga \a-ǩá-ġa\ *va* [fr *a* on + *kaga* to make] **1** : to make on anything, to add **2** : to tell a lie about or to speak evil of **3** : to exaggerate < *He wicoh'an kin el akage šni po* Do not add to this custom >

a·ka·gal \á-ka-ġal\ *adv* : stretching out to < ~ *hapya* He lay with arms reaching outstretched, as a little child towards its mother > - R Bl — **akagal·kiya** \á-ǩa-ġal-ǩi-ya\ *adj* : spread out or outstretched, as the hand or arm - BD Cf kagálkiya — **akagal·tkiya** \á-ǩa-ġal-tki-ya\ *adv* : stretched out, as the arms < ~ *un* He is sprawled >

a·ka·ga·pi \a-ǩá-ġa-pi\ *n* : something made in addition, and exaggeration, a falsehood

a·ka·ge·ge \a-ǩá-ġe-ġe\ *va* a·wa·kagege [fr *kagege* to sew] : to sew on or to, to patch on something else

a·ka·ȟa·pa \a-ǩá-ȟa-pa\ *v* a·wa·kaȟapa [fr *a* on + *kaȟapa* drive by whipping] : to drive or whip on

a·ka·ȟa·ya \a-ǩá-ȟa-ya\ *va* : to spread news, all the while exaggerating it - Bl

a·ka·hla \a-ǩá-ȟla\ *va* a·wa·kaȟla : to rattle, make sound by striking at or on account of < *Na hlahla kin awicakahlapi na cancega kin kabupi na šiyotanka kin yajopi na awicaš'api* The bell rang for them, the drum was beat, the grouse honked, and they shouted at them >

a·ka·hpa \a-ǩá-hpa\ *va* a·wa·kahpa : to cover, throw on or over; to cover up, conceal < *Amakahpa yo. Yunkan el šina kpanyanpi wan el* ~ *egnaka na lowan.* ~ *ihpeya* Throw a cover on me. Then she sang while putting on a tanned blanket to cover. She left him under covers >

aka·hpe \a-ǩá-ȟpe\ *n* **1** : a bed cover, spread or quilt **2** : a covering, a veil or shroud < *canpagmiya* ~ a wagon-cover, *ite* ~ a veil, *hiyete* ~ a cloak or mantle >

a·ka·hpe·ki·ci·ci·ya \a-ǩá-ȟpe-ǩi-ci-ci-ya\ *v* akahpe·we·ciciya : to cover up for one or pass by a matter, to forgive — **akahpekici·ton** \a-ǩá-ȟpe-ǩi-ci-toŋ\ *va* akahpe·we·citon : to cover for one — **akahpeki·ton** \a-ǩá-ȟpe-ǩi-toŋ\ *v poss* akahpe·we·ton : to cover one's own

a·ka·hpe·ton \a-ǩá-ȟpe-toŋ\ *va* a·wa·kahpeton : to cover up, throw on *e.g.* a covering; to cover up, conceal *e.g.* one's real opinion, *i.e.* when used with *ia* < ~ *iwaye* I hid my thoughts > — *part* : covered, concealed — **akahpeton·ton** *v red* : to cover up < ~ *ia* He spoke not being open >

a·ka·hpe·ya \a-ká-ȟpe-ya\ *adv* : covering < *Mahpiya wan šapa ca ~ he* A cloud that was dark stood covering over, ~ *agliha* It came down covering him > - B.H.56. 16, 61.10 D.224

a·ka·hpi·hpe·ya \a-ká-ȟpi-ȟpe-ya\ *va* : to throw over, cover over, as a blanket over a trunk *etc* - Bl

a·ka·htan \a-ká-ȟtaŋ\ *vn* 1 : to soak into and come through on the other side, as grease through a skin 2 : to boil over, flow over < *Watage ota yelo waslipa po; unnihan ~ yelo* There is much foam, lick it off; shortly it overflows > — **akahtan·yan** *va* akahtan·wa·ya 1 : to cause to cook in 2 : to cut and make rough on– B. H.108.16 BT

a·ka·hwo·gya \a-ká-ȟwo-gya\ *va* : to let fly over one < *Pešnija akahwogmayaye lo* You let the sparks, *i.e.* in smoking, fly over me > - Bl

a·ka·ji·pa \a-ká-ji-pa\ *va* a·wa·kajipa : to shave with a knife or drawing knife upon

a·ka·kan \a-ká-kaŋ\ *va* a·wa·kakaŋ unka·kakan·pi [fr *a* on + *kakan* strike off] 1 : to beat, to strike off on anything *e.g.* cherries off a bush onto a shawl spread out below 2 : to hew on anything - R Cf okákan

a·ka·kpan \a-ká-kpaŋ\ *va* a·wa·kakpan [fr *a* on + *kakpan* to pound] : to pound fine on anything, to pound in addition to what is already done

a·ka·kpi \a-ká-kpi\ *va* a·wa·kakpi : to crack on, as a nut on anything

a·ka·ksa \a-ká-ksa\ *va* a·wa·kaksa [fr *a* on + *kaksa* to cut off] : to cut off on something, cut off from, cut off in addition to

a·ka·kša \a-ká-kša\ *va* a·wa·kakša : to coil up on, as a rope

aka·kšan \a-ká-kšaŋ\ *va* a·wa·kakšan a·ma·-kakšan : to go around to prevent or to see one — *adv as well as* **akakšan·yan** *adv* : around, not in a straight course, as in going in a round-about way to catch a horse < *Na wanna ~ natan unyanpi* We went a circuitous route to make an attack > - Bl

a·ka·kši·ja \a-ká-kši-ja\ *va* a·wa·kakšija : to bend into or round, as a piece of iron — **aka·kšiš** \a-ká-kšiš\ *v contrac of* akakšija : to bend < ~ *iyeya* to quickly bend >

a·ka·tan \a-ká-ktaŋ\ *va* a·wa·kaktan : to bend onto, to bend around

a·ka·ku·ka \a-ká-ku-ka\ *va* a·wa·kakuka : to pound to pieces on

a·ka·la \a-ká-la\ *va* a·wa·kala : to pour out on, as grain, not liquids < ~ *hiyuya* to take one *fig* by surprise > - Note: the *fig* sense is also conveyed in *apable hiyuya* - Bl — **akala·la** *v red* : to pour out on anything < ~ *iyeya* suddenly to pour out on >

a·kal·ya \a-kál-ya\ *va* akal·wa·ya [fr *a* on + *kalya* to heat] : to cause to heat upon - Bl

a·ka·mna \a-ká-mna\ *va* a·wa·kamna [fr *a* on + *kamna* to rip] 1 : to acquire in addition to 2 : to tear open on, as at a seam

a·ka·mni i·ya·ya \á-ka-mni i-yá-ya\ *vn* : to separate with a splash, *e.g.* snow with stepping on it when water is underneath

¹a·kan \a-kaŋ\ *prep* : on, upon < *Maka ~. Maka kin le nitawapi kte lo ca ~ ota inicagapi kte lo* On earth. This land will be ours and thereon many of you shall grow up > - Note: the word is used with and without the final *n,* as in *aká* or *akán* Cf akánl

²a·kan \a-káŋ\ *vn* a·ma·kan : to become old on, or with

a·kan·han·pa \a-káŋ-haŋ-pa\ *n* : overshoes

a·kan i·ye·i·c'i·ya \a-káŋ i-yè-i-c'i-ya\ *v refl* : to jump on *e.g.* a horse, to mount

a·kanl *and* **akan** \a-káŋl\ *prep* : on, upon < *maka ~* on earth , *Yunkan inyan tanka wan glipha keye. Canke ~ inajin* Then he stated that a great stone fell. So he stood upon it, ~ *ogle* an overcoat, ~ *zizipila* a dister >

a·kanl wa·un·yan·pi \a-káŋl wa-ùŋ-yaŋ-pi\ *n* : an altar - Note other names for an altar: ~ waunyeyapi, ~ waunyeyin kte, *and* ~ wawágluwakanpi, this last indicating *on* something one's own is consecrated - B.H.11.10, 58.5, 108.1 Pb.33

a·kan·mna \a-káŋ-mna\ *vn* : to smell like something burning - Note: the word is doubtfully from *káta* + *omna*. Here the *k* is soft, k - R Me

a·kan·tu \a-káŋ-tu\ *adv* : above < *paha ~* above the hill > — *n* : the top one — *adj* : living, in authority, common < *Wicaša ~* living men, men in authority, common man > - B.H.294.6 — **akantu·ic'iya** \a-káŋ-tu-i-c'i-ya\ *v* : to make much of one's self - Bl *Syn* IGLUTAN'IN — **akantu·ya** *and* **akantuya·kel** *adv* : above, high up; on the outside, without < *wicaša ~* man above > - B.H. 70.4 — **akantu·yela** *adv* : outside, on the surface, almost on the top, above or high up - Bl

a·kan wa·pa·bla·pi \a-káŋ wa-pà-bla-pi\ *n* : an ironing board

a·kan wa·un·yan·pi \a-káŋ wa-ùŋ-yaŋ-pi\ *n* : an altar - B.H.110.6

a·kan·yan·ka \a-káŋ-yaŋ-ka\ *v* akan·man·ka akan'·un·yanka·pi : to ride a horse < *Nupin hinkceka sapa akanwicayankapi* They rode both dark bay horses > — **akanyanka·pi** *n* : a seat, a place to sit

a·kan·yun·ka \a-káŋ-yuŋ-ka\ *v* akan·mun·ka : to lie on something

¹a·ka·pa *or* **akapan** \a-ká-pa\ *v* a·wa·kapa : to beat or thresh off on, to pound

²a·ka·pa \á-ka-pa\ *adv* : larger somewhat, implying a comparison

a·ka·pa·tan·han \a-ká-pa-taŋ-haŋ\ *adv* 1 : on the outside, exteriorly 2 : from another side or place 3 : from above

a·ka·pe·ca \á-ka-pe-ca\ *adv* : having something to spare — **akape·ya** \a-ká-pe-ya\ *adv* : having to spare as a coat, more than, greater or higher < *Tipi kin le ~ wiyopeyapi* This house sold for more > - Bl

a·ka·pol·pol \a-ká-pol-pol\ *v red contrac of* akapolpota : to beat — **akapolpo·ta** \a-ká-pol-po-ta\ *v red* [fr *akapota* to beat] : to beat to pieces in many places on

a·ka·po·ta \a-ká-po-ta\ *va* a·wa·kapota [fr *a* on + *kapota* to tear or shred] : to beat to pieces on anything

a·ka·psi·ca \a-ká-psi-ca\ *va* : to make jump *etc* on striking, as by splashing water on one < *Amayakapsice lo. Hanta yo, anicapsicin kte* You made me jump. Get away! I'll make you jump > - Bl Cf akáblu

a·ka·pta \a-ká-pta\ *va* a·wa·kapta [fr *a* on + *kapta* bail out] : to cut off on, as a part of a stick

a·ka·pte·ce·la \a-ká-pte-ce-la\ *va* a·wa·kaptecela : to

\a\ father \e\ they \i\ machine \o\ smoke \u\ lunar \an, aŋ\ blanc Fr. \in, iŋ\ ink \on, oŋ, un, uŋ\ soon, confier Fr. \c\ chair \ġ\ machen Ger. \j\ fusion \clusters: bl, gn, kp, hšl, etc...\ b^e^lo ... said with a slight vowel **See more in the Introduction, Guide to Pronunciation**

make shorter, to cut off a piece from *e.g.* a stick

a·ka·san·pa \a-k̇á-saŋ-pa\ *or* **akasanpa·ta** \a-k̇á-saŋ-pa-ṫa\ *or* **akasanpata·han** *adv* : opposite, across, on the other side, as of a river – Note: the word is a bit *archaic* — **akasanpa·tanhan** \a-k̇á-saŋ-pa-ṫaŋ-haŋ\ *adv* : on the other side, from beyond, from the other side < *Mni* ~ , or *hutasanpata* from the other side of the water > – Note: this word is of the Santee dialect. Tetons say *koakatanhan*

a·ka·ska \a-k̇á-sk̇a\ *vn* a·wa·kaska : to be greedy – *archaic* — *adj* : greedy, voracious

a·ka·ski·ca \a-k̇á-sk̇i-ca\ *vn* : to be pressing down, to press down

a·ka·sni \a-k̇á-sni\ *va* a·wa·kasni [fr *kasni* to cool] : to extinguish on, as fire

a·ka·stag \a-k̇á-sṫag\ *v contrac of* akastaka : to daub < ~ *ehpeya* They threw daubing, chinking *e.g.* a house > — **akastag·ya** *adv* : sticking on or in — **akastagya·kel** \a-k̇á-sṫa-gya-k̇el\ *adv* : clinging to sticking on

a·ka·sta·ka \a-k̇á-sṫa-k̇a\ *va* a·wa·kastaka unka·kasta-ka·pi : to throw or daub on *e.g.* plaster, to bespatter < *Ištinma* ~ He dropped off to sleep, a saying not often used. *tiakastaka* to daub a house > – IS

a·ka·sto \a-k̇á-sṫo\ *va* a·wa·kasto unka·kasto·pi : to smooth down on, as the hair on the head

a·ka·s'o \a-k̇ā'-s'o\ *v* a·wa·kas'o [perhaps fr *a* on + *kasol* deplete] : to chop off a piece from on

a·ka·ška \a-k̇á-šk̇a\ *va* a·wa·kaška [fr *kaška* bind] : to bind upon

a·ka·šla \a-k̇á-šla\ *va* a·wa·kašla [fr *a* on + *kašla* to cut down] : to cut or mow down upon, as grass upon a hay field

a·ka·špa \a-k̇á-šṗa\ *va* a·wa·ka [fr *a* on + *kašpa* to separate] : to cut or break off on < *Na can eya šeca ca aletka kin hena akašpapi. Maka kin tan'inšniyan owanjila yanka ške lo* (many buffalo) *ca ikanyela euntipi na ~ icu wanaunsapi kte lo* These branches were some of the dry wood they cut. They say since the (many buffalo) were at rest making the ground invisible, we set up camp nearby so we might take to the chase and pare them down > — *vn* a·ma·kašpa : to be provoked or beyond endurance — **akašpe·ya** *vn* a·ma·kašpeya : to remain longer than one can well endure — *va* akašpe·wa·ya : to provoke

a·ka·špu \a-k̇á-šṗu\ *va* a·wa·kašpu [fr *a* on + *kašpu* to knock off] : to cut off a piece by striking, to cut off on

a·ka·štaka \a-k̇á-šṫa-k̇a\ *va* a·wa·kaštaka [fr *a* on + *kaštaka* to beat] : to beat one on another

a·ka·štan \a-k̇á-šṫaŋ\ *va* a·wa·kaštan unka·kaštan·pi [fr *a* on + *kaštan* to pour liquid] : to pour out on, to spill on, as water to baptize

[1]**a·ka·ta** \a-k̇á-ṫa\ *vn* a·wa·kata [fr *a* on + *kata* hot] : to be hot on

[2]**a·ka·ta** \a-k̇á-ta\ *va* a·wa·kata : to draw a bow, bend as a bow < *Na itazipa k'on ecel icu na wahinkpe ecel ~ na wanna ena wankatakiya iyeya* And he did thus take the bow, so drew an arrow on it, and sent it right aloft >

[3]**a·ka·ta** \a-k̇á-ta\ *va* a·wa·kata unka·kata·pi : to hoe, to dig about with a hoe, to hill up, as corn, to cover with dirt, to cultivate < *Wagmeza* ~ He hoed corn, *Peji* ~ (*i.e.* a hole) *ca otan'in šni* He who was hoeing grass was out of sight, *i.e.* he was *in* a hole >

a·ka·ta·han *or* **akantanhan** \a-k̇á-ṫa-haŋ\ *adv* : above, overhead, on top, on the surface – R

a·ka·tan·han \á-ka-ṫaŋ-haŋ\ *adv* : on the outside < *hin* ~ hair (of the robe) outside > – Note: the accent on *1st syll* The reason may be the *hin* hair

a·ka·te·ya \a-k̇á-te-ya\ *va* akate·wa·ya : to cause to hoe

a·ka·tin \á-ka-ṫiŋ\ *va* a·wa·katin : to straighten on, as the arms, to measure with the arms outstretched on — **akatin·pi** *n* : the measure from fingertip to fingertip, an ell, *i.e.* the length or distance of the fingers when the arms are stretched out — **akatin·tin** \á-ka-ṫiŋ-ṫiŋ\ *v red* : to make a measure of < ~ *mani* to walk moving the arms sideways, as in giving signs, *Pejuta wan aikpogan na* ~ He blew on himself a medicine from side to side > — **akatin·yan** *va* : to straighten slowly one way something that is crooked

a·ka·t'iŋs \a-k̇á-t'ins\ *v contrac of* akat'inza : to pound

a·ka·tin·za \a-k̇á-t'iŋ-za\ *v* [fr *a* on + *ka* striking + *t'inza* to pound] : to press anything down tight, as a weight over — **akat'in·sya** *va* akat'ins·wa·ya : to press down on anything by means of weights

a·ka·ung \a-k̇á-uŋg\ *v contrac of* akaunka : to fell

a·ka·un·ka \a-k̇á-uŋ-k̇a\ *va* a·wa·kaunka [fr *a* on + *kaunka* to fell] : to cut down *e.g.* a tree on anything, to make fall by cutting

a·ka·un·yan \a-k̇á-uŋ-yaŋ\ *adv* : lying across, as a body on a horse

a·ka·we·ga \a-k̇á-we-ġa\ *va* a·wa·kawega [fr *a* on + *kawega* break in striking] : to break or fracture by striking on anything — **akaweh** \a-k̇á-weȟ\ *v contrac of* akawega : to fracture < ~ *ehpeya* Broken they abandoned it >

a·ka·win·ga \a-k̇á-wiŋ-ġa\ *vn* : to go round and round, as an eagle makes its gyrations — **akawinh** \a-k̇á-wiŋȟ\ *v contrac* : to go round and round –R Bl

a·ka·win·ja \a-k̇á-wiŋ-ja\ *va* a·wa·kawinja : to bend down on, as grass on anything — **akawinš** *v contrac* : to bend < ~ *iyeya* to suddenly bend down, ~ *hinhpaya* to fall suddenly , as a tree falling against a bank and not on the ground > – Bl

a·ka·za·mni \a-k̇á-za-mni\ *va* a·wa·kazamni [fr *a* on + *kazamni* to open out] : to open upon one, to throw open as one's blanket < ~ *ehpeya* to set it open, ~ *han* to stand ajar > — **akazamni·yan** \a-k̇á-za-mni-yaŋ\ *part* : opened on

a·kce·ya \a-kcé-ya\ *va* a·wa·kceya : to cook or roast *e.g.* ribs partly and then to dry

a·ke \a-k̇é\ *adv* : again, a second time, repeated, as in numbering, thus:
akéwanji or *akéwanjila* eleven
akénunpa or *akénonpa* or contrac *akénom* twelve
akéyamni thirteen
akétopa or contrac *akétob* fourteen
akézaptan fifteen
akéšakpe sixteen
akéšakowin seventeen
akéšaglogan eighteen
akénapciyunka nineteen

a·ke e·ce·ca \a-ké e-ce-ca\ *vn* : to recur

a·ke·i·ye·na·ke·ca \a-ké-i-yè-na-ke-ca\ *adv* : as much again

a·keš \a-k̇éš\ *adv emph of* aké : really again

a·ke·šna·šna \a-k̇é-šna-šna\ *adv* : again and again – B. H.88.9

a·ke·ya \a-k̇é–ya\ *va* ake·wa·ya : to place on, to make a roof on, to place on the roof, make one roof on another

a·ki \a-k̇í\ *va* a·wa·ki unka·ki·pi : to arrive at home carrying something — *v coll pl* : they reach home < *Hokšila kin he mni el ~ kiye* The boy got home by water >

a·ki·a \a-k̇í-a\ *va* : to try one – Cf akíya *ref* to spelling

a·ki·ble·za \a-ǩí-ble-za\ *v* : to think about < *Oh'an ekta akibleze* He thought about the treatment he had given him (*i.e.* David) > – B.H.90.14, 108.22, 240.16

a·ki·ca·ga \a-ǩí-ca-ġa\ *va* a·we·caga : to make on, to add to; to be unreasonable, to go too far — **akica·geca** \aǩí-ca-ġe-ca\ *va* a·we·cageca : to overreach, to cheat, to want more than is right, to be unreasonable — **aki·cah** \a-ǩí-caȟ\ *v contrac of* akicaga : to be demanding — **akica·hya** \a-ǩí-ca-ȟya\ *adv* : unreasonably

a·ki·ca·ška \a-ǩí-ca-šǩa\ *va* aki·wa·kaška [fr *a* on + *kaška* to bind] : to bind to or on, bind together < *Canke akicaškapi s'e inyanke* He seemed to run (cross-legged, knock-kneed) > — **akicaška·ška** *v red* aki·wa·kaškaška : to baste on, sew on as in basting, temporarily tacking

a·ki·ce·pa \a-ǩí-ce-ṗa\ *vn* a·ma·kicepa : to become fleshy for or again

a·ki·ce·ti \a-ǩí-ce-ti\ *vn* : to arrive at home and start a fire, *i.e.* when one's home is somewhere else

a·ki·ce·ya \a-ǩí-ce-ya\ *v poss* a·wa·kiceya unka·kiceya·pi [fr *ki* for + *aceya* bewail] : to cry for or weep over one's own, to mourn for one as a dead relative

a·ki·ci·ca·ta \a-ǩí-ci-ca-ta\ *v* a·we·cecata a·mi·cicata [fr *akata* to hoe] : to hoe for one, to hoe for

a·ki·ci·ci·ta \a-ǩí-ci-ci-ṫa\ *v* a·wé·cicita [fr *akita* to search for] : to hunt a thing for another — **akicikcita** *v poss* a·we·cikcita : to hunt one's own – R Bl

a·ki·ci·ki·pa·pi \a-ǩí-ci-ǩi-pà-pi\ *v pl* [fr *akipa* to come upon one] : they met each other

a·ki·ci·kši·ja \a-ǩí-ci-kši-ja\ *v* : to retain anything not one's own for one, as a mother retains things in the name of her child – B

a·ki·ci·kta \a-ǩí-ci-kta\ *v* a·wé·cikta [fr *akta* give heed to] : to receive or accept from another; to have respect for another — **akicikta·šni** *v* a·we·ciktašni [fr *aktašni* to despise] : to refuse or reject when offered by one

a·ki·ci·kton·ja \a-ǩí-ci-ktoŋ-ja\ *va* : to forgive one

a·ki·ci·ni·ca \a-ǩí-ci-ni-ca\ *va* a·we·cinica [fr *anica* to lay claim to] : to withhold from, retain for < *Woahtani awicakinicapi kta* Their sins will be retained >

[1]**a·ki·ci·pa** \a-ǩí-ci-pa\ *v* a·we·cipa unka·kicipa·pi [fr *apa* to smite one] : to strike for one

[2]**a·ki·ci·pa** \a-ǩí-ci-ṗa\ *n* : a flat tableland that lies higher than a creek < *Wakpala iwankab ~ k'el etipi kte lo* They pitched camp at a flat above a creek > – Bl

a·ki·ci·pa·pi \a-ǩí-ci-pa-ṗi\ *v pl* [fr *akipa* to meet] : they met each other

a·ki·ci·pe \a-ǩí-ci-ṗe\ *v* a·we·cipe unka·kicipe·pi : to wait for one, to hope for

[1]**a·ki·ci·ta** \a-ǩí-ci-ṫa\ *v* a·we·cita [fr *akita* to search for] : to hunt for another

[2]**a·ki·ci·ta** \a-ǩí-ci-ta\ *n* a·ma·kicita : a head warrior, one next to the chief, a warrior soldier, a policeman, thus in order and rank with other military terms:

~ *awanyang najin* a sentinel, sentry, guard
~ *ehanna ayuštanpi iyunwin* pension
~ *hayapi* military dress, uniforms, regimentals
~ *ikceka* a soldier of Private rank
~ *itancan* an officer, lieutenant, captain, commander, colonel
~ *itancan ȟantkahu zi (ska) yuha* corporal, sergeant
~ *itancan okihe* an Adjutant
~ *itancan tanka* a General
~ *itancan taokiye* or *tawahoši* an orderly
~ *iyecinka opa* a volunteer
~ *kicipasipi* a maneuver
~ *omanipi* a parade
~ *optaye* a company, a corps
~ *optaye itancan* a captain or commanding officer
~ *optaye itancan taokiye* a Lieutenant
~ *optaye tanka* a division or brigade
~ *optaye tanka itancan* a Brigadier
~ *ošpaye tanka* an army
~ *ošpaye tanka opa* a regular
~ *ota* troops
~ *owe* a troop, detachment, regiment
akicitapi hca rank and file
~ *tamaza wakan* or *ikce okšupi* a muzzle loader – Bl
~ *teca* a recruit
~ *tipi* barracks, soldiers' quarters, a fort or garrison
~ *tipi acunkaškapi* a fortified camp, a fortress
~ *tonweya omanipi* a patrol
šunk'akanyankapi ~ cavalry
~ *kicipasi* to drill
akicitakte *v* akicita·wa·kte [fr ~ + *kte* to kill] : to punish officially for the violation of law
~ *najin* *vn* akicita na·wa·jin : to stand guard, as a warrior soldier
~ *natantan kaonspe* *v* : to drill

a·ki·ci·ton·wan \a-ǩí-ci-ṫoŋ-waŋ\ *v* a·we·citonwan a·mi·citonwan [fr *atonwan* look to or at] : to look at for one, to have the oversight for one

a·ki·ci·yu·kyu·ta \a-ǩí-ci-kyu-ṫa\ *v red of* akiciyuta : to look at one another – B.H.253.11 — **akici·yul** *adv* [fr *akiciyuta* look at each other] : face to face, looking at each other

a·ki·ci·yu·pta·pi o·wo·gla·ke \á-ki-ci-yu-ṫa-pi o-wò-gla-ke\ *n* : a dialogue

a·ki·ci·yu·ta \a-ǩí-ci-yu-ṫa\ *adv* : face to face

a·ki·ci·zu·ya \á-ki-ci-zu-ya\ *v* [fr *a* on + *kici* each other + *zuya* to war] : to make war on one another – B.H.245.9

a·ki·cons \a-ǩí-coŋs\ *v* [fr *akiconza* say and not do] : to keep one in suspense, to avoid granting a thing with excuses < ~ *iapi* They expressed excuses, ~ *iwaye* I spoke giving excuses, ~ *aya* He began giving excuses >

a·ki·con·za \a-ǩí-coŋ-za\ *v* : to make resolutions without carrying them out — **akiconza·ha** *perhaps adv* : speaking indecisively

a·ki·c'un·c'un \a-ǩí-c'uŋ-c'uŋ\ *v* a·we·c'unc'un : to do a thing repeatedly, to glory in — **akic'unc'un·ka** \a-ǩí-c'un-c'un-ka\ *v* a·we·c'unc'unka : to do a thing repeatedly, to overdo, be importunate, to act or play recklessly or defiantly, *i.e.* contrary to orders – Note: the word is not *akicic'unc'unka*, but *akic'un*...

a·ki·c'u·ya \a-ǩí-c'u-ya\ *adv* : much, plentifully < ~ *mak'u wo* Give me much >

a·ki·gla·gki·ci·ton \a-ǩí-gla-gki-ci-toŋ\ *v* akigla·gwe·citon : to patch for one — **akiglagki·ton** *v poss* akigla·gwe·ton [fr *akiglagton* to patch] : to patch one's own — **akigla·gton** \a-ǩí-gla-gtoŋ\ *v* akigla·gwa·ton : to put on a patch, to patch, to sew on a hole — *part* : patched, having a patch on — **akigla·gya** *va* akigla·gwa·ya : to patch, to put on or use for a patch – R Bl

a·ki·gla·ke \a-ǩí-gla-ǩe\ *n* : a sole of a shoe or moccasin (one sewed on) < *hanpákiglake* a moccasin sole > –

\a\ father \e\ they \i\ machine \o\ smoke \u\ lunar \an, aŋ\ blanc Fr. \in, iŋ\ ink \on, oŋ, un, uŋ\ soon, confier Fr. \c\ chair \ġ\ machen Ger. \j\ fusion \clusters: bl, gn, kp, ȟšl, etc...\ b[e]lo ... said with a slight vowel
See more in the Introduction, Guide to Pronunciation

Note: the word is used only in connection with *hanpa*

a·ki·gla·ski·ca \a-k̇í-gla-sk̇i-ca\ *v* : to press down one's own by sitting on it, as in sitting on one's overcoat, to sit on one's own, as in resting on one's heels - Cf akiglaskin — *adj* : face downwards, prone — *v* : to lie on one's own — **akiglaski** *or* **akiglaskin** *v contrac of* akiglaskica : to press down < *Si kin sanni ~ yanka* He sat (resting) on one foot (placed below one) while the other is only bent, *Si kin nupin ~ yanka* He rests on both feet while the knees are bent, *Siyete sanni ~ yanka* He sat (rested) on the heel of one foot while the other leg (knee) is bent > — **akigla·skil** *v contrac of* akiglaskica : to press down < *~ ehpeic'iya* He threw his self on his face > — **akiglaski·lya** \a-k̇í-gla-sk̇i-lya\ *adv* : lying on the face, prone - R RF

a·ki·gla·ške \a-k̇í-gla-ške\ *v* : to tie or bind one's self together with another < *Niyeš sipa kayeš ~ yaun welo* You are hobbling your very own feet, as a man would say in refusing to marry a woman > - Bl KE

a·ki·gle \a-k̇í-gle\ *adv* : again, more than once, once again; times, and is used with numerals < *nunpa ~* twice > - Note: *lit* the word means "set one on top of another" Added to any number, it means "so many times in succession" — *v poss of* agle : to place or make stand some thing on one's own, as once some took pith, put it in the hand or on the lower arm and lit it. To stand this was a display of bravery. Such marks have been observed, and the display is called to *pelákigle, pelá·wa·kigle* — **akigle·gle** *adv red of* akigle : many times - D.97

a·ki·gle·gle·pa \a-k̇í-gle-gle-ṗa\ *vn* aki·wa·gleglepa : to vomit on one's own reaching home

a·ki·gle·ya \a-k̇í-gle-ya\ *adv* [fr *akigle* again + *ya* cause] : repeatedly

[1]**a·ki·gna** \a-k̇í-gna\ *v* : to sit, as a hen on eggs, to have care for as for offspring, as said of birds < *~ iyayelo* She has given extra care > - Bl

[2]**a·ki·gna** \a-k̇í-gna\ *adv* : through and through < *Šungila kin ~ o ške. ~ cawapin kte lo. ~ caic'ipe* It is said he shot the fox through and through. Let me stab it thoroughly. (But in a perfect job) he stabbed himself, *i.e. fig* he ate himself full > - Cf glakínyan

a·ki·gnag \a-k̇í-gnag\ *v poss of* akignaka : to place on — **akigna·gya** *adv* : placed on

a·ki·gna·ka \a-k̇í-gna-k̇a\ *v poss* a·we·gnaka a·ye·gnaka [fr *agnaka* to apply *e.g.* a medicine on] : to place one's own on

a·ki·he·ca \a-k̇í-he-ca\ *adv* : close together - Bl

a·ki·he·ce·ca \a-k̇í-he-ce-ca\ *vn* : to become so on reaching home, *i.e.* to get sick or well on one's arrival home < *Akihemaceca* I felt good arriving home >

a·ki·he·na·ke·ca \á-k̇i-he-na-ke-ca\ *adv* : equally many or much - *Syn* AKILECELYA

a·ki·ȟo·ka \a-k̇í-ȟo-ka\ *n* : one who is skillful — **akiȟoka** \a-k̇í-ȟo-k̇a\ *adj* : skillful, skilled in

a·ki·h'an \a-k̇í-h'aŋ\ *vn* a·ma·kih'an unka·kih'an·pi : to be without food, be hungry, to starve < *Le wahinkpe kin, tohanl amicih'anpi ca oyate kin witaya šna lapi na yeyayapi ktelo* When they are hungry for me, the people will be continually petitioning for this Arrow and will launch it > — **akih'an·pi** *n* : a famine, a starving — **akih'an·t'a** *v* akih'an·ma·t'a : to starve to death, die of hunger — **akih'ant'e·ya** *va* akih'ant'e·wa·ya : to cause to die of hunger — **akih'an·yan** *va* : to cause to starve < *akih'an'ic'iya* one's self to fast > — *adv* : in a way fasting

a·ki·i·c'i·ya \a-k̇í-i-c'i-ya\ *v refl* aci·mi·c'iya : to prefer one's self - WW

a·ki·jal \á-k̇i-jal\ *adj contrac of* akijata : forked — **akijal·ya** *vn* : to fork, as a stream — *adv* : in a manner forked < *~ woeye* a forked *i.e.* insincere or deceptive saying > - Bl

a·ki·ja·ta \á-k̇i-ja-ta\ *adj* : forked, as a stream

a·ki·ka·ška *or* **akicaška** \a-k̇í-k̇a-ška\ *v* : to tie two things together - B.H.11.15

a·ki·ki·gla·ška \a-k̇í-k̇i-gla-ška\ *v* aki·we·glaška : to tie together, as one's torn moccasins, to tie up or hobble one's horse - Bl

a·ki·ki·šni·ya \a-k̇í-k̇i-šni-ya\ *adv* : all, entirely < *Taku ~ oyas'in ociciyake lo* I told you absolutely everything > - Bl

a·ki·kši·ja \a-k̇í-kši-ja\ *v poss* a·we·kšija [fr *akšija* to dispossess] : to bend down *e.g.* the hand on, to retain anything

a·ki·kta \a-k̇í-k̇ta\ *v poss* a·wa·kikta [fr *akta* to respect] : to give heed to

a·ki·kton·ja \a-k̇í-k̇toŋ-ja\ *va* a·we·ktonja unka·kiktonja·pi a·ci·ktonja a·mi·ktonja : to forget, not remember — **akiktonš** *va contrac of* akiktonja : to forget — **akikton·šya** *va* : to make forget — *adv* : in a manner forgetful

a·kil \a-k̇íl\ *v contrac of* akita : to seek for < *~ iyaya* He has gone hunting, *Cuwintku kin tokel kte kta hecihan he ~ ece-un ške* They say she was constantly (being only) on the look-out for a good way how she might kill the daughter > - D.167

a·ki·le·ce·ca \á-k̇i-le-ce-ca\ *adj* : equal to, of equal size < *Tipi kin oyasin ~* All the houses were the same size > — **akile·cel** *adv* : like to, equal to — **akilece·lya** *adv* : equally < *~ kicic'u po* Give to each an equal amount, as is said when a sum of money is distributed with each receiving as much as the other, *Ikce wicaša kinhan wašicun kin nupin ~ oniwanjilapi kta okihišni yelo, tohanyan inicagapi hehanyan wicaša itancan unpi kin tolute ece koyakapi* Both common Indian and non-Indian are unable equally to feel at home; when you grow up, it is then only those who are head men who dress in purple > - Bl *Syn* IYECECA, AKIHENAKECA

a·ki·le·han \á-k̇i-le-haŋ\ *adv* : just as far — **akilehan·hankeca** *adj red of* akilehankeca : equal — **akilehan·yan** *adv red of* akilehanyan : equally far — **akilehan·keca** \á-k̇i-le-haŋ-ke-ca\ *adj* : of equal height, length, *etc* < *Kici akilemahankeca* I am as tall as he, *Iyuha ~* All of equal length, as a man would say in buying posts > - Cf for size, *akinskokeca* — **akilehan·wankatuya** *adj* : of the same height or length < *Iyuha ~* all of the same length > — **akilehan·yan** *adv* *adv* : equally far, alike far - Bl

a·ki·le·na·gna·ke·ca \á-k̇i-le-na-gna-ke-ca\ *adj red of* akilenakeca : alike — **akilena·keca** \á-k̇i-le-na-ke-ca\ *adj* : alike many, of equal number < *Akileunnakecapi* We are of equal number > - Cf iyénakeca

a·ki·le·na·na \á-k̇i-le-na-na\ *adj* : alike few

a·ki·me·ya \a-k̇í-me-ya\ *adv* : around

a·ki·mna·mna·i·c'i·ya \a-k̇í-mna-mna-i-c'i-ya\ *vn* : to collect everyone his own little supply < *~ unpahipi na unkic'upelo* We every one of us collected his own little supply, *e.g.* of sugar, coffee, *etc*, putting it together for use, *Hena ~ bluha* These I have in a collection > - Bl Cf akímnayan

a·ki·mna·yan \a-k̇í-mna-yaŋ\ *va* akimna·wa·ya : to collect one thing to another, consolidate < *Anpetu kin le el tipi kin le ekta miwoyuha lila ota akimnawaya yelo* Today I gathered together to this house my many possessions >

a·ki·mni·mni·ci·ya \a-ǩí-mni-mni-ci-ya\ *n* : each one's little bit that he brought < ~ *okiciyapi* They each helped one another with the little they brought > – Bl

a·ki·na·jin \a-ǩí-na-jiŋ\ *v* a·wa·kinajin : to return and stand < *Na wanna leci wakpala wan opaya ata ~ el ake lecel eya ... Hecel el witayela agliyagla ca miš ake owapa na najinpi k'on okšan ~* In this place along a creek, when he returned to stay and meet, he again said: ... So when he came by in his company and I had again followed and taken a stand, he returned in a roundabout way to stay > – B.H.59.7

a·ki·na·pa \a-ǩí-na-ṗa\ *v* : to take out and go home < *Lena ~ po* Take these out and go home > – B.H.179.11

[1]**a·ki·na·tan** \a-ǩí-na-ṫaŋ\ *v poss* akina·wa·tan [fr *anatan* to rush to one] : to rush for one's own

[2]**a·ki·na·tan** \a-ǩí-na-ṫaŋ\ *v* [fr perhaps *aki* arrive at + *natan* touch with the foot] : to reach or arrive at the goal

[1]**a·ki·ni·ca** \a-ǩí-ni-ca\ *va* [fr *anica* withhold] : to hold for one

[2]**a·ki·ni·ca** \a-ǩí-ni-ca\ *va* a·wa·kinica unka·kinica·pi : to dispute about something, claiming it as one's own < *wiakinicapi* they contend, as male animals do in fighting one another > – Bl

a·ki·ni·han·han \a-ǩí-ni-haŋ-haŋ\ *adv* : not knowing in fact really what happened < ~ *ia* to speak confusedly > – Note: *yat'insyakel ia* to speak plainly – Bl KE

[1]**a·ki·nil** \a-ǩí-nil\ *va contrac of* akinica : to hold for one < ~ *kignaka* to hold keeping something for one, *i.e.* to reserve something, placing it somewhere with the idea of getting it afterwards, to cache >

[2]**a·ki·nil** \a-ǩí-nil\ *va contrac of* akinica : to reserve for

a·ki·ni·lki·ya \a-ǩí-ni-lǩi-ya\ *v* akini·lwa·kiya : to cause to debate — **akini·lya** \a-ǩí-ni-lya\ *va* akini·lwa·ya : to cause to dispute or debate about, to quarrel about — *adv* : disputatiously, in a quarreling way

a·kin·glo·ta·ka \a-ǩíŋ-glo-ṫa-ka\ *v poss* [fr *akan* on + *iglotaka* sit one's self] : to saddle one's own, as one's ass < *Hinša gleška k'un he akinglotaki na ya* He had saddled the spotted sorrel horse and was gone > – B.H.79.17, 68.6 MS.563

a·kin·sko·ke·ca \á-ǩiŋ-sko-ǩe-ca\ *adj* : of the same size, of equal size, as two horses, two legs, *etc* < Nupin ~ opewaton wacin I want to purchse both of the same size (two or more things are compared), *Kici akinmaskokeca* I am the same size as he > — **akinsko·ya** \á-ǩiŋ-sǩo-ya\ *adv* : of equal size

a·kin·yan \a-ǩíŋ-yaŋ\ *va* [fr *a* on + *kinyan* to fly] : to fly over or on < *Lena suta k'eš akinye sekse unkiyayapi kte* If this (road) were hard *i.e.* smooth, we would seem to go flying over it >

a·kin·ye·i·c'i·ya \a-ǩíŋ-ye-i-c'i-ya\ *v* [fr *akan* on + *iyeic'iya*] : to push or thrust one's self upon or in upon < *Scili kin lila makuwapi. Tawa kin akinyemic'iye lo* The Pawnees gave me a real chase. His horse gave me a hot pursuit >

a·ki·on \a-ǩí-oŋ\ *va* a·wa·kion [fr *a* on + *aon* to place] : to place on, as wood on one's own fire, to place on for < *Yunkan oyate kin can ota eyaš tušu ece akionpi* The people then placed much wood on, but it was only tent poles >

a·ki·on·pa \a-ǩí-oŋ-ṗa\ *v* aki·wa·onpa : to return and place down

[1]**a·ki·pa** \a-ǩí-ṗa\ *v poss* [fr *ki* sign of *poss* + *apá* to strike] : to strike one's own

[2]**a·ki·pa** \a-ǩí-pa\ *v* a·wa·kipa unka·kipa·pi : to meet, as anyone travelling comes against or upon, to happen to or befall one < *Woteḣi akipapi* Trouble befell them, *Sinkpe ḣel amakipa hce lo* A muskrat indeed met me ashore, *Wana ca na tahena iktomi wan ~* Now it is at such time he encounters Iktomi >

a·ki·pab \a-ǩí-ṗab\ *adv* : divided, partaken of equally < ~ *egnaka* divided, separate, ~ *iyeya* to divide >

a·ki·pa·ja \a-ǩí-ṗa-ja\ *va* : to fold on, double over

a·ki·pa·pta·pi \á-ǩi-ṗa-pta-pi\ *v pl* : they break up and go in different directions < *Wana šun kipaptapi kte lo* Feathers will now break up and go in different directions > – Bl

a·ki·paš \a-ǩí-ṗaš\ *v contrac of* akipaja : to double over < ~ *iyeya* to suddenly double over >

a·ki·pa·ya \a-ǩí-ṗa-ya\ *va* : to cause to befall one

a·ki·pe \a-ǩí-ṗe\ *va* a·wa·kipe unka·kipe·pi : to wait for or for one, to expect or hope for

a·ki·pson·wa·he·ya \á-ǩi-psoŋ-wa-he-ya\ *adv* [fr *a* causative + *ki* one's own + *(pa)pson* spill + *wahe* betimes + *ya* sign of *adv*] : spreading out into a line < ~ *kušeya iyayapi* spreading out, they go on, *i.e.* to intercept the buffalo *etc;* the connotation is that of a whole crowd moving down to one place in a body > – Bl LC

a·ki·pša·pša \a-ǩí-pša-pša\ *adv* : close together, standing thick, as grain or grass, jammed together, as men or animals; full, as a lake of fish; or as is said of many children in a family — **akipšapša·ya** *adv red* : thickly, close together — **akipša·ya** *adv* : close together – R Bl

a·ki·ptan \a-ǩí-pṫaŋ\ *vn* unka·kiptan·pi : many to do together — *adv* : together, joining forces < ~ *unyanpi* We are going together, ~ *econpi* They did it together >

a·ki·sni \a-ǩí-sni\ *v poss* a·ma·kisni a·ni·kisni unka·kisni·pi [fr *asni* to get well] : to get well, recover from sickness or from anger – Note: this word is also said of the weather — **akisni·ya** *va* akisni·wa·ya : to cause one to get well, to cure — **akisni·yan** *adv* : getting well – Cf asníya — **akisniye·pica·šni** *adj* : incurable – B.H.184.23, 114.22

a·ki·šo·gya \a-ǩí-šo-gya\ *adv* : thick, close together – LC

a·ki·šo·ka \a-ǩí-šo-ǩa\ *adj* [fr *a* on + *šoka* dense] : thick on, as leaves thickly on and covering the ground < *Peji kin akišoke (kahihiyela) yunke* Thick grass lay carpeting the ground > – Bl

a·ki·š'a \a-ǩí-š'a\ *vn* : to shout, to cheer < *Akiš'api kin kowakipelo* I feared their shouting, *Wanna akiš'api na utapi.* They shouted and fired. *Hecel unkiš wanna awicunš'api na unkutapi* So we shouted at them and fired our guns > – D.44, 103

a·ki·š'ag \a-ǩí-š'ag\ *adj contrac of* akiš'aka : dense — **akiš'a·gya** *adv* : growing thickly, as wheat

a·ki·š'a·ka \a-ǩí-š'a-ǩa\ *adj* : thick, as grain or weeds growing in the field

a·ki·š'a·š'a \a-ǩí-š'a-š'a\ *v red of* akiš'a : to applaud < *Wanna pehan kin glinapin na ~* The crane came in sight on its way home, and they cheered for him >

a·ki·ta \a-ǩí-ṫa\ *va* a·wa·kita unka·kita·pi a·ci·cita : to seek or hunt for, as something lost, to make efforts to get

a·ki·ta·ku·ni·šni \a-ǩí-ṫa-ǩu-ni-šni\ *vn* a·ma·kitakunišni [fr *atakunišni* to begin to be extinct] : to become nothing, as in losing everything

---

\a\ father \e\ they \i\ machine \o\ smoke \u\ lunar \an, aŋ\ blanc Fr. \in, iŋ\ ink \on, oŋ, un, uŋ\ soon, confier Fr. \c\ chair \ǧ\ machen Ger. \j\ fusion \clusters: bl, gn, kp, hšl, etc...\ b^e^lo ... said with a slight vowel
See more in the Introduction, Guide to Pronunciation

a·ki·tan'·in·šni·šni \a-k̇í-taŋ-iŋ-šni-šni\ *adj* or *adv* : appearning now and then again < ~ *hingla* to become suddenly invisible every now and then, as do horses at a distance walking in hilly country > – Bl

a·ki·ta·pi \a-k̇í-ṫa-pi\ *n* : an effort, a research undertaken

a·ki·ti \a-k̇í-ti\ *vn* aki·wa·ti : to stop somewhere for the night on one's way, to spend an overnight < *Na glapi na akitipi na hihanna el wanna ake glapi* They were on their way home, spent an overnight, and in the morning were again on their way there > – Cf ahíti

a·ki·to \a-k̇í-to\ *v poss* a·we·to a·ye·to unka·kito·pi [fr *ato* to become blue] : to tatoo or make blue marks on the body – Note: an old belief has it that whoever tatoos himself will be well off in the other world. The old woman who stands on the road in the spirit world will let him pass on to God. Whoever does not do it will be killed by the woman

a·ki·ton·wan \a-k̇í-toŋ-waŋ\ *va* a·wá·kitonwan : to look for something lost – Cf *akicitonwan* to look for someone or something lost

a·ki·to·pi \a-k̇í-to-ṗi\ *n* marks made by tatooing — *part* : marked, tatooed

a·ki·t'a \ak̇í-t'a\ *vn* aki·ma·t'a : to die after getting home, as a warrior carried home wounded

a·ki·t'e·ya \a-k̇í-t'e-ya\ *adv* : crowded together, as books on a shelf – *Syn* AKIŠOKA

a·ki·wan·ya·ka \a-k̇í-waŋ-ya-ka\ *v* akiwan·bla·ka : to go and see one's own, as in the time of issue wagons at Pine Ridge, South Dakota – Note: *éwanyaka* they went to see something, *e.g.* a show

a·ki·ya \a-k̇í-ya\ *vn* a·wa·kiya : to practice, to give the mind to, to consider < *Na wanna heon wicaša itancanpi oyate el unpi k'un akiyapi na oyate kin nicitokab yaotan'inpi. Tokel econpi wašteka hecinhan he akiyapi* And for that reason, the leading men of the tribe considered it, tha the people well afford the honor before you. They conferred about how they might do the best thing for him > — *va* : to try one < *akimayapi* I am up for trial > – Note: *akia* is an *altern* spelling

a·ki·ya·gla \a-k̇í-ya-gla\ *va* a·wa·kiyagla [fr *aki* arrive at home + *awagla* to trim off] : to carry or take home — *v* : to go home — *v coll pl* : they all went or go home straightway < ~ *ške* They say they all left for home. *Na unma pte kin* ~. *Yunkan Šahiyela kin Wahin Wakpa etkiya iglaka* ~. *K'oyela* ~ He took along the other cow. Then the Cheyennes broke camp and went for Flint River.. Entirely all of them went directly home. (See the clouds *i.e* a storm passed by) > – Bl D.92, 72

a·ki·ya·ta·ka \a-k̇í-ya-ta-k̇a\ *v* : to be locked, as a horse's legs *etc*, or perhaps to be cramped < *Canke akih'an t'in kta ca cehupa kin ~ ca š'inš'inya wota ške* (the wolf). *Cankpe akiyatake s'e mani* And so when it was about to starve to death and its jaw locked, they say (the wolf) ate craning its neck. It walked seeming to have its knees cramped (cross-legged or knock-kneed) > — **akiyata·keca** *adv* : touching < *hiyete* ~ shoulders shrugged up, *hu* ~ knock-kneed, *cankpe* ~ *inyanka* to run with knees touching one another, cross-legged or knock-kneed > – Bl

a·ki·ye·han \á-k̇i-ye-haŋ\ *adv* : being flush or even — *vn* : to be flush or even – WE

a·ki·ye·la \a-k̇í-ye-la\ *adv* : near – *Syn* IKIYÉLA

a·ki·yo·ta·ka \a-k̇í-yo-ta-ka\ *v* : to mount a horse < *Iye kakeš glakca šni, najate kin pahin onz'akiyotake s'e* He soever does not groom himself, when he does not part his hair, is as if he were mounting (a horse) at the rump > – Bl

a·ki·yu·can·pi \a-k̇í-yu-caŋ-pi\ *v pl* : they shake anything when several things hit together

a·ki·yu·go \a-k̇í-yu-ġo\ *vn* aki·blu·go : to arrive somewhere tired out – Note: this is a newer word – RF

a·ki·yu·ha \a-k̇í-yu-ha\ *va* [fr *a* on + *ki* go taking home + *yuha* have or carry] : to have on, to hold on or lift up < ~ *aglapi* They take him home *e.g.* carrying him on their shoulders > –B.H.71.10, 197.7 — **akiyuha·pi** *v pl* : they bear or carry when several do it together < *Wicaša 60 seca (can wakan)* ~ Some 60 men went and carried the (sacred tree) back >

a·ki·yu·hpa \a-k̇í-yu-ḣṗa\ *v* aki·blu·hpa [fr *aki* carry home + *yuhpa* to hold] : to carry home and throw down

a·ki·yun·ka \a-k̇í-yuŋ-ka\ *v coll pl* : they stop for the night somewhere on their way, to spend an overnight < *Wanna wakpa cik'ala kin opaya akicita kin* ~ The soldiers bivouacked along the small creek >

a·ki·yu·ski·ca \a-k̇í-yu-sk̇i-ca\ *v* aki·blu·skica : to tie fastening together, to attach one to another

a·ki·yu·ti·tan·pi \a-k̇í-yu-ṫi-ṫaŋ-pi\ *v pl* : they pull different ways

a·ki·yu·we·ga \a-k̇í-yu-we-ġa\ *n* : a crossing, a ford < *Pankeska Wakpala kin lila mni hiyaya. Canke tokani akiyuwege šni* Shell Creek was in great flood. And so no way was there a crossing >

a·ki·yu·za \a-k̇í-yu-za\ *v pl* [fr *a* sign of *pl* number + *kiyuza* take hold of one] : they hold or take hold of one all around, to seize < *Akimayuzapi na oihpemaya po* Seize me and ... throw me in! > — **akiyuza·pi** *v pl* : they (two or more involved) hold or seize anything < *Yunkan winyan nunp el hipi ... eyaš ~ na eyayapi* Then two women arrived there ... but they seized and took him with them > – B.H.117.8 and 10

a·ko \a-k̇ó\ *exclam* : Welcome! – Note: this is an old word – *Syn* CANNAKO, WAŠTANMI — *adv* : beyond, on the other side of < *Winuhcala šica, ako gla yo. Ako econ wo* You bad old lady, go back to the other side! Do it over there > – Bl

a·ko·e·con \a-k̇ó-e-coŋ\ *v imper only perhaps* : Get away! < *Ya! Toskala* ~ Go! Get away from here, woodpecker! >

a·ko·i·to·he·ya \a-k̇ó-i-ṫo-he-ya\ *adv* : towards, with the face the other way, *i.e.* turned with the face away from < ~ *naṗe lo* He fled facing the other way beyond > – R Bl

a·ko·jal *or* **akajal** \a-k̇ó-jal\ *adv contrac of* akojata : straddling < ~ *najin* to stand over a thing, *e.g.* a log having it between the legs or as in riding horseback > – Note: *akojata* however is not used — **akoja·lya** *adv* : astride – D.37

a·ko·kab \á-k̇o-kab\ *adv* : across, straight across by a near way < ~ *ya* He made a shortcut > — **akoka·bya** *or* **akoka·byela** *v* : to go across, go by a near way — *adv* : by a near way, across – WE Bl

a·ko·ki·ya \a-k̇ó-k̇i-ya\ *adv* : beyond from one, away from one, the other way < *Ḣe Ska ~ . He e ca ~ glahan ške* The Rocky Mountains are the other way. Since that is so he started for home the other way > – D.220

a·ko·tan·han \a-k̇ó-ṫaŋ-haŋ\ *adv* : beyond, referring to place, time, and things: from beyond < *hinhanna* ~ the day after tomorrow, *htalehan* ~ the day before yesterday > – R

a·ko·wa·pa \a-k̇ó-wa-pa\ *adv* : further on, beyond a certain object mentioned < ~ *najin ye* Stand further from (the speaker) > — **akowapa·tanhan** \a-k̇ó-wa-pa-ṫaŋ-haŋ\ *adv* : from beyond – D.218.1

a·ko·za \a-k̇ó-za\ *va* a·wa·koza : to make a motion at, to attempt to strike < *Na wanna hunka eya yankapi k'on hena awicakozapi* And they tried to strike some of the relatives who had been seated >

a·kpa·ble·ca \a-kpá-ble-ca\ *va* [fr *a* on + *kableca* break by striking] : to break in pieces one's own on something - R Bl

a·kpa·gan \a-kpá-ġaŋ\ *va poss* a·wa·kpagan [fr *a* for + *kpagan* which is the *poss* of *pagan* to part with one's own] : to give away one's own for some purpose — **a-kpagan·yan** *adv* : giving away for

a·kpa·ha \a-kpá-ha\ *vn* : to be without help < *Aícikpaha manke* Nobody lends me a helping hand > - BT

a·kpa·hi \a-kpá-hi\ *va* [fr *a* on + *kpahi* the *poss of pahi* to pick up one's own] : to gather up one's own on something - R Bl

a·kpan·yan \a-kpáŋ-yaŋ\ *va* akpan·wa·ya : to tan over again, as when it is not done well, to tan hurriedly and carelessly - Bl

a·kpa·spa \a-kpá-spa\ *v* a·wa·kpaspa : to suffer patiently, endure until it has passed off < *Awakpaspin kte lo* I shall endure it, as a tired man would say who makes for the place of his destination in spite of being tired > - Bl — **akpaspe·ca** \a-kpá-spe-ca\ *n* : one who suffers patiently until his anger goes off without saying a word — **akpaspe·ya** *adv* **1** : patiently **2** : out of sight < ~ *iyeya* to rub hard pressing >

a·kpa·sya \a-kpá-sya\ *va* akpa·swa·ya : to cause darkness on, to darken — *adv* : benightedly, in ignorance

a·kpa·tan \a-kpá-taŋ\ *v poss* a·wa·kpatan [fr *a* for + *kpatan* and *patan* to save] : to reserve one's own purposely — **akpatan·yan** *adv* : reserving for a purpose

a·kpa·za \a-kpá-za\ *vn* a·ma·kpaza [fr *a* on + *kpaza* dark] : to come night on one, to become ignorant, benighted

a·kpa·zo \a-kpá-zo\ *v poss* a·wa·kpazo [fr *pazo* to point at] : to point at one's own

a·kša *or* **akša·ka** \a-kšá-ka\ *adv* **1** : more, in addition to < ~ *onmaspe šni*. ~ *econ owakihi šni* I did not know more how. I was unable to do more. *Freely*: It is a pity, *i.e.* too bad, to be unable to do more, *i.e.* again, for one reason or another > **2** : bent over from age < *Akšaka miyecu šni ye* Please, you do not have to return it to decrepit me, ~ *hel kušeya winyan wan wicaša šni ca un* It is where one is decrepit that there a woman is a burden, not a man > - Note: it seems this use refers in some way to *kšáka* - D.109

a·kšan·kšan \a-kšáŋ-kšaŋ\ *adv* : to and fro, across and back

a·kši·ja \a-kší-ja\ *va* a·wa·kšija : to take or retain something claimed by another — **akšiš** \a-kšíš\ *va contrac of* akšija : to retain < ~ *yuha* to have and to hold > - B.H.45.20

a·kšu \a-kšú\ *va* a·wa·kšu : to pile up on, to load on < *Paha Ska kin hel akanl emaonpapi na iȟ'e amakšu po. Na wanna inyan lila ota akanl akšupi* There on White Mountain lay me to rest and pile rocks on me. And on him they piled up a great many rocks > — *n* : a load — **a-kšu·ki·ya** \a-kšú-ki-ya\ *va* : to cause to pile up on - Note: R spells the word *ajúkiya*

¹a·kta \á-kta\ *adv* : again, over again - *Syn* AKÉ — *prep* : of, about, concerning

²a·kta \a-ktá\ *va* a·wa·kta : to have respect for, to regard, to keep in mind, to give heed to; to receive or accept one - Note: from this are formed: *akikta, akicikta, ihakta, wakta, etc.* to respect a person, one another, a guard, a sign ...

a·kta·kta \a-ktá-kta\ *adv red of* akta : again and again, repeatedly; gradually, little by little — **aktakta·ya** *adv* : repeatedly

a·kta·šni \a-ktá-šni\ *v* a·wa·ktašni [fr *aktá* to esteem] : to reject, despise — *adv* : not well < ~ *econ* to do a thing badly > — **aktašni·yan** *adv* : unwillingly, against one's will — Note: *"Ektašniyan" ipaweh etonwe šni ye* "Not according to him" did he look across

a·kton \a-któŋ\ *adv* : more than < *Wikcemna* ~ *bluha* I have more than ten >

a·kton·ja *or* **aktunja** \a-któŋ-ja\ *adj* a·ma·ktonja : forgetful — *v* : to forget — **akton·ktonja** \a-któŋ-ktoŋ-ja\ *adj* or *v red of* aktonja : to be absent-minded — **a-ktonktonš** *adj or v red contrac of* aktonktonja : frequently forgetful, or to forget often — **aktonkton·šya** *adv red of* aktonšya : forgetfully — **aktonš** *adj* or *v contrac of* aktonja : forgetful, or to forget — **akton·šya** *va* : to make forget < *Taku wan epin kte c'on aktonšmaya yelo* What I had been about to say made me forget > — **akton·yan** *adv* : forgetfully - Bl WE

a·ku \a-kú\ *va* a·wa·ku : to come bringing home, to bring — *v coll pl* : they are coming home < *Na iktomi wan hel un ca he ayakupi kte lo* And since there there was present an iktomi, you will come bringing it home > - R

a·ku·ka \a-kú-ka\ *vn* a·ma·kuka : to become old or rotten on one, as worn clothing

a·ku·ta ku·wa \a-kú-ta kù-wa\ *v* : to be after a thing again and again, as when inquiring repeatedly if a thing has been done - R Bc WE

a·k'a \a-k'á\ *v* a·ma·k'a : to dig on, make a mark as in playing a game, to win over another, in jumping and throwing farther than the other < *Ak'e lo* He deserves a mark, *i.e.* in the ground, in that sense digging >

a·k'in \a-k'íŋ\ *n* : something to pack on < ~ *ipatapi* a hide mounted with bead ornamentation and used as a saddle, ~ *ska* a clean horse blanket, ~ *kšupi* a beaded saddle blanket, *tatanka okise šunkak'in* a saddle blanket of half a buffalo hide >

a·k'o \a-k'ó\ *v* : to stick on - Cf ók'o

a·k'o·ka \a-k'ó-ka\ *v* : to talk to one incessantly < *Amayak'oke lo* You talked to me interminably > - Bl

a·la·ta \á-la-ta\ *adv abbrev of* álataya : all over < *owinja kin* ~, *canku kin* ~, *anpetu* ~ all over the bed, all over the road, all through the day, *Anpetu* ~ *ceyake. Anpetu kin* ~ *heconhe* He cried well for a whole day. That is what he was doing all day. *Pa kin* ~ *slolwicakiciye* He knew one another all over his head > — **alata·ya** *adv* : Cf álata - B.H.79.1,203.5 D.85

a·le·han·yank *or* **alehanyang** \á-le-haŋ-yaŋk\ *adv* : away from himself < ~ *niwicaye* Others he saved, implying "Himself he cannot save", ~ *egnaka* He set it far removed > - Cf ílehanyang B.H.266.7 Bl

a·le·ja \a-lé-ja\ *va* a·wa·leja : to urinage on something as dogs do — *n* : a diaper

a·le·le·ya \a-lé-le-ya\ *va* alele·wa·ya : to hold a green stick in the fire so it gets parched, to char - Bl

a·le·sab \a-lé-sab\ *adj* : frost-bitten, burnt or colored on the outside < ~ *iniyaya hwo?* Did you *e.g.* your hands get black and blue with the cold? > — **alesab·ya** *va* : to roast but little, so to eat it though still raw - Bl

a·le·tka \a-lé-tka\ *n* : a branch or limb of a tree < *can'á-*

\a\ father \e\ they \i\ machine \o\ smoke \u\ lunar \an, aŋ\ blanc Fr. \in, iŋ\ ink \on, oŋ, un, uŋ\ soon, confier Fr. \c\ chair \ġ\ machen Ger. \j\ fusion \clusters: bl, gn, kp, hšl, etc...\ bᵉlo ... said with a slight vowel
See more in the Introduction, Guide to Pronunciation

letka a tree limb > – D.34

a·li \a-lí\ *va* a·wa·li **1** : to climb up, ascend *e.g.* a hill < *Na wanna ówecinhan paha kin unkalipi. Canke can kin ali* And one after the next we climbed the hill. And so he climbed the tree > **2** : to step on < *Si amáli* He stepped on my foot. *Si acíli* I stepped on your foot >

a·li·a·gla \a-lí-a-gla\ *va* alia·wa·gla : to climb a hill and disappear on the other side, to cross a hill — **ali·kiya** \a-lí-ǩi-ya\ *va* : ali·wa·kiya : to make climb — **ali·li** *v red* : to do climbing < *Can kin ~ inyanka na glicu. Mni kin ~ inyanke* He ran to climb the tree and got back down. He ran stepping on the water > – D.57 MS.569

a·li·li·ya \a-lí-li-ya\ *adv red* [fr *aliya* climbing] : in a way climbing < *Na oyaya ~ muku sun on yuglakšinkšan owapi* And its limbs were painted zigzag with white earth in an ascending manner >

a·li·ya \a-lí-ya\ *adv* : climbing — *vn* ali·wa·ya : to go climbing — *n* : a hike, trek < ~ *kin ogna owa hececake lo ca ogna unyanpi kte lo* Let us go on the hike in such direction as he sketched, ~ *okit'eya* preventing climbing or hiking, as is said of a road leading upward on a narrow ridge > – LB RT — **a·li·ya·kel** *adv* : in a climbing manner

a·lo \a-ló\ *vn* : to be scorched, burnt, cooked < *Iȟanhan la keša* ~ He asks, *i.e.* for meat, in vain, but it is not yet cooked thoroughly, *Špan yeša* ~ *šni*, or *anapin šni* Though it cooked, it was not cooked, *or* it did not taste good > – *See* anapin Bl

a·lo·ki·kso·han \a-ló-ki-kso-haŋ\ *v poss of* aloksohan : to carry one's own under the arm

a·lo·kso·han \a-ló-kso-haŋ\ *va* alo·wa·ksohan : to carry putting under the arm *e.g.* a book, to carry tucked under the arm as one might a garment, to carry in the arms *e.g.* a child — *n* : the armpit – Note: *alokso* is not known D.49

a·los \a-lós\ *vn contrac of* aloza : to be scorched — **alo·sa·bya** \a-ló-sa-bya\ *va* : to let something get black while *e.g.* roasting it — **alos·hingle** *vn* : to geel a scorched sensation suddenly; to be frightened suddenly or suddenly angry < *Alos'hinglemayakiye lo* You have of a sudden frightened me > – *Syn* YUŠ'INYAYA, KAGAL HINGLA — **aloslo·syeca** *vn* aloslo·swa·yeca : to experience a burning sensation; to become angry – R Bl D.47 BT

a·lo·slo·za \a-ló-slo-za\ *vn red of* aloza : to be scorched but not cooked, as something held in a flame — **alo·sya** \a-ló-sya\ *va* alo·swa·ya : to scorch, as meat in a flame; – *fig* to have one's feeling touched by any circumstances, to be made angry

a·lo·wan \a-ló-waŋ\ *va* a·wa·lowan unka·lowan·pi : to sing in praise of anyone, to sing for, as for the death of an enemy

a·lo·wi·ta·ya \a-ló-wi-ṫa-ya\ *adv* : not well dried, as meat – Bl KE

a·lo·za \a-ló-za\ *vn* : to be scorched but not cooked

a·lu·slus *or* **aloslos** \a-lú-slus\ *v contrac of* alusluza or alosloza : to be scorched; to have the feeling all over one's body, teeth, *etc* caused by a grating sound < ~ *hingla* He suddenly shivered, ~ *mahingla* I suddenly shivered >

a·ma \a-má\ *interj exclam* : Bosh! Nonsense! , of surprise and incredulity at something said and one taps the arm of the speaker – *Syn* APA Bl

a·ma·ga·ju \a-má-ġa-ju\ *v* a·ma·magaju unka·magaju·pi [fr *a* on + *magaju* to be inclement weather] : to rain on — **amagaju·kiya** \a-má-ġa-ju-ǩi-ya\ *va* amagaju·wa·kiya : to cause to rain on — **amagaju·ya** *va* amagaju·wa·ya : to cause to rain on

a·ma·hpi·ya \a-má-ȟpi-ya\ *v imperf* : to cloud over — *adv* : cloudy, clouded over

a·ma·hpo·san·ta·gle·ya \a-má-ȟpo-saŋ-ṫa-glè-ya\ *adv* : silhouetted < ~ *najin i.e.* to stand on top of a hill, visible and in spite of the darkness one is set off against the sky > – Bc ED M

a·ma·ki·ni \a-má-ǩi-ni\ *v* : to walk on one's own < *Ṫo-ǩétu kec'eyaš oteȟi kta ca can wan yanke c'on hel amaunkinipi kte lo* As it is, there we ought to travel back on our own where there is a timber, since it will become a hard time, *i.e.* since fierce weather is on its way here > – Bl

a·ma·ni \a-má-ni\ *v* ama·wa·ni [fr *a* on + *mani* to travel] : to walk on

a·ma·šte \a-má-šte\ *vn* a·ma·mašte [fr *a* on + *mašte* warm] : to be warm on < *amašteic'iya yanka* to sit to sun and warm one's self >

a·ma·šte·na·pta·pta \a-má-šte-na-pta-pta\ *n* : the glimmering of vapor in the sun heat, the burning appearance of the prairie on a hot day, or on a heated stove

a·ma·šte·t'a \a-má-šte-t'a\ *vn* amašte·ma·t'a : to have a sun-stroke

a·ma·šte·ya \a-má-šte-ya\ *adv* : exposed to the heat, in the sun — **amašteya·kel** \a-má-šte-ya-ǩel\ *adv* : hotly

a·mi·c'i·ci·ya \a-mí-c'i-ci-ya\ *v refl* 1st *pers singl* [fr perhaps *aic'iciya* which is fr *aya* to lead along, but more probably fr *akiya* to consider] : I muse, am considering I am distracted – Note: a person says this when he remains sitting and thinks while somebody calls him – Bl

a·mna·i·c'i·ya \a-mná-i-c'i-ya\ *v refl* amna·mi·c'iya [fr *mnayan* gather] : to gather for himself, to be selfish — **amnan·yan** \a-mnán-yaŋ\ *va* amna·wa·ya [fr *a* on + *mnanyan* collect] : to collect, gather together to, add to

a·mni \a-mní\ *v* a·wa·mni unka·mni·pi [fr *a* on + *mni* set out to dry] : to spread out to dry on anything

a·mni·ci·ya·pi \a-mní-ci-ya-pi\ *v pl* amni·un·kiciya·pi [fr *a* for + *mniciyapi* they assemble] : they assemble to on account of

a·mni·mni \a-mní-mni\ *va* a·wa·mnimni unka·mnimni·pi a·ci·mnimni : to sprinkle on anything, to sprinkle with water *etc* — **amnimni·ya** *va* : to sprinkle on < *We kin tiyopa tankatahan amnimniyapi kte* They should sprinkle the blood on the outside of the door > – B.H.52.11

a·mni·tan \a-mní-ṫaŋ\ *vn* [fr *a* on + *mnitan* to overflow] : to flow on or over — **amnitan·ya** *va* amnitan·wa·ya : to cause to flow over, to water *i.e.* irrigate *e.g.* a field — **amnitan·yan** *adv* : in an overflowing manner

a·mon·mon·la \a-móŋ-moŋ-la\ *n* : a doll, a childish word

a·na·bla·ga \a-ná-bla-ġa\ *vn* [fr *a* on + *nablaga* to burst] : to open or spread out on, to unfurl on

a·na·blas \a-ná-blas\ *va contrac of* anablaza : to make burst by kicking < ~ *iyeya* to suddenly make burst >

a·na·bla·za \a-ná-bla-za\ *va* ana·wa·blaza : to tear open with the foot, to burst open on

a·na·ble·ca \a-ná-ble-ca\ *vn* : to spread out on, as grain when poured on anything — **anablel** *va contrac of* anableca < ~ *ehpeya* to scatter by pouring down >

a·na·blu \a-ná-blu\ *va* ana·wa·blu : to kick dust or dirt on something

a·na·bu \a-ná-bu\ *va* ana·wa·bu : to make a noise on with the feet, to stamp — **anabu·bu** *v red of* anabu : to do stamping

a·na·gi·bya \a-ná-ġi-bya\ *va* : to clamp, hold fast, to pin, as does the spring of a trap in catching *e.g.* a mouse

< *Ito, nape kin anagibyapi; canke ikikcu šni* Well, his hand was caught; so he failed to take it back > — **anagi·pa** *v* : to be held fast, clamped, pinned as by the spring of a trap *etc* < *Nape kin ena ~ ške. Ikto nape kin glutitan keš sutaya ~ ke.* They say right here his hand was pinned. Though Ikto pulled at his hand, he was securely pinned indeed > - D.27.22

a·na·gle·gle·ya·kel \a-ná-gle-gle-ya-kel\ *adv red of* anagleyakel : slowly, step-by-step, limping, the motion being that of one suffering from rheumatism < ~ *mawani* He walked torturously > — **anagle·yakel** *adv* : limping < ~ *mani* He walked with a limp, as often old people do, not setting their feet down firmly > - Bl

a·na·glo·ka \a-ná-glo-k̇a\ *va* : to knock and injure on, to sprain < *Iškahu anawagloka* I sprained my ankle >

a·na·glu·šte \a-ná-glu-šte\ *vn* : to be lame in the leg, to be limp; to break down, as one's leg does when they buckle < ~ *iyaya* He went lame > — **anaglušte·šte** *v red* - R Bl

a·na·go·ptan \a-ná-ġo-p̣taŋ\ *va* ana·wa·goptan ana·un·-goptan·pi : to listen to, hearken to; to obey — **anagoptan·ya** *va* anagoptan·wa·ya : to cause to listen to

a·na·gwag \a-ná-gwag\ *va contrac of* anagwaka : to complain < ~ *najin* He stood complaining, criticizing > - Bl

a·na·gwa·ka \a-ná-gwa-ka\ *va* [fr *nagwaka* to kick out] : to murmur against - B.H.55.2

a·na·ha \a-ná-ha\ *va* ana·wa·ha : to kick a ball, as used in a game, *esp* in a game where the ball is large and hangs on a string < ~ *iyeyapelo* It was given a swift kick > - Bl

a·na·ha·ha \a-ná-ha-ha\ *adv* : slowly, carefully - Note: ~ *mani* refers to one, whereas *nahaha mani* refers to more than one — *vn* ana·wa·haha : to walk or run noiselessly after one - F BD

a·na·hu·šte·šte·ya·kel \a-ná-hu-šte-šte-ya-kel\ *adv* : limpingly < ~ *mani* to walk limply, as a horse may do > - *Syn* ANÁPOKSANYANKEL Bl

a·na·ȟa \a-ná-ȟa\ *adj* : rough, roughened up

a·na·hla·ta \a-ná-ȟla-ṫa\ *v* ana·wa·hlata : to hold on carefully, as a man to a horse, to crawl up carefully on anything - R

a·na·hlo·hlo *or perhaps* **anagloglo** \a-ná-ȟlo-ȟlo\ *vn* : to bubble up, as in boiling

a·na·hlo·ka \a-ná-ȟlo-k̇a\ *va* ana·wa·hloka [fr *a* on + *nahloka* to wear a hole with the foot] : to wear a hole in, as in a moccasin on something

a·na·hma \a-ná-ȟma\ *va* ana·wa·hma : to hide, conceal — **anahman·pi** *n* : a concealing, concealment, cover-up — **anahme·ya** *adv* : secretly, slyly, covertly — **anahmeya·han** *adv* : secretly - B.H.302.7

a·na·hpa \a-ná-ȟp̣a\ *va* ana·wa·hpa [fr *a* on + *nahpa* to kick to fell] : to kick down on anything

a·na·hta·ka \a-ná-ȟṫa-k̇a\ *va* ana·wa·htaka [fr *a* on + *nahtaka* to kick anything] : to kick one on anything else

a·na·i·c'i·pson *or* **anaic'ipsun** \a-ná-i-c'i-psoŋ\ *v refl* ana·mi·c'ipson [fr *anapson* to spill by kicking] : to spill on one's self by kicking, as by kicking over a bucket of water

a·na·ji·pa \a-ná-ji-p̣a\ *v* ana·wa·jipa : to pinch with the feet

a·na·ki·ci·go·ptan \a-ná-k̇i-ci-ġo-p̣taŋ\ *v* ana·we·cigoptan [fr *anagoptan* to listen to one] : to hearken to for one, listen for one, to give ear or heed to for one — *v pl* ana·un·kicigoptan·pi : they listen to each other, one another — **anakicigoptan·yan** *adv* : listening to each other

a·na·ki·ci·kšin \a-ná-k̇i·ci·kšiŋ\ *v* : to come to one's aid - Cf anákikšin B.H.140.13

a·na·ki·ci·pta·pi \a-ná-k̇i-ci-p̣ta-pi\ *v pl recip* ana·un·kicipta·pi [fr *anapta* to hinder] : they stop or hinder each other

a·na·ki·ci·son \a-ná-k̇i-ci-soŋ\ *v* : to cross the legs or feet; to have intercourse, as husband and wife - Bl LHB

a·na·ki·ci·tan e·con·pi \a-ná-k̇i-ci-taŋ e-coŋ-pi\ *n* : the game boys play imitating the *zuya yapi*, the going to war - Bl

a·na·ki·go·ptan \a-ná-k̇i-ġo-p̣taŋ\ *v poss* ana·wa·kigoptan [fr *anagoptan* to obey] : to listen to, obey, as one's father

a·na·ki·hma \a-ná-k̇i-ȟma\ *va* and *poss* ana·wa·kihma : to hide, conceal; to refuse to tell, to deny, affirm that it is not so — **anakihman·pi** *n* : a concealing or denial — *part* : concealed

a·na·ki·hme·ya \a-ná-k̇i-ȟme-ya\ *va* anakihme·wa·ya : to cause to conceal — *adv* : covertly, secretly — **anakihmeya·han** *adv* : stealthily; privately

a·na·ki·kšin \a-ná-k̇i-kšiŋ\ *va* ana·we·kšin ana·ci·cikšin : to stand over and defend one, to interpose one's self for one in danger, to expose one's self for another or work for one to let him rest - D.223 B.H.155.25

a·na·ki·pa \a-ná-k̇i-pa\ *v* : to flee from - Bl SLB

a·na·ki·pta \a-ná-k̇i-pta\ *v* [fr *anapta* hinder] : to bring to a stop for one - Bl

a·na·kpa \a-ná-kp̣a\ *v* : to fly away from, as sparks from a wood fire < *Pelánamakpelo* Sparks landed on and burnt me > - Bl

a·na·ksa \a-ná-ksa\ *v* ana·wa·ksa [fr *a* on + *naksa* to step and break] : to break off a thing on something else with the foot

a·na·kši·ja \a-ná-kši-ja\ *v* ana·wa·kšija [fr *a* on + *nakšija* bend over by foot] : to bend down on with the foot, as grass on the prairie — **anakšiš** *v contrac* : to bend by foot < ~` *iyeya* to bend over quickly by foot >

a·na·ktan \a-ná-k̇taŋ\ *v* [fr *a* on + *naktan* bend by foot] : to bend on or over with the foot

a·na·k'e·za \a-ná-k'e-za\ *v* : to make smooth with the foot by treading on - Cf onák'eza, which may be the better word R

a·na·mna \a-ná-mna\ *va* ana·wa·mna [fr *a* on + *namna* to rip] : to rip on anything with the foot < *Hanpa inyan* ~ He ripped his moccasin on a stone >

a·na·mni \a-ná-mni\ *vn* : to give way under the foot, as does snow where there is water under it < ~ *iyeya* suddenly to give way underfoot >

a·nan·sa \a-náŋ-sa\ *va* anan·wa·sa [fr *a* on + *nansa* or *nasa* to go on a hunt] : to hunt or go after, as for buffalo

a·na·pa \a-ná-pa\ *va* ana·wa·pa [fr *a* for + *napa* run for] : to run to for refuge

a·na·pca \a-ná-pca\ *v* ana·wa·pca [fr *a* on + *napca* to swallow] : to swallow on or after something else

a·na·pin \a-ná-p̣iŋ\ *vn* : to be tasty < *Špan yeša ~ šni iyecel yaglicu (omayani) welo* Though cooked it did not taste good, so in a case like that you started for home (you walked) > - Note: this is said when somebody passes by in a hurry: *Špan yeša ~ šni naceca, inayahni* Though cooked it probably did not taste good. You

\a\ father \e\ they \i\ machine \o\ smoke \u\ lunar \an, aŋ\ blanc Fr. \in, iŋ\ ink \on, oŋ, un, uŋ\ soon, confier Fr. \c\ chair \ġ\ machen Ger. \j\ fusion \clusters: bl, gn, kp, hšl, etc...\ b^{e}lo ... said with a slight vowel
See more in the Introduction, Guide to Pronunciation

hurried on by. Bl mentioned both these phrases. The meaning is not quite clear. B gives the meaning: refuse to meat turned in a frying pan while frying

a·na·po·ksan·yan·kel \a-ná-po-ksaŋ-yaŋ-kel\ *adv* : in a limping manner < ~ *mani* He walks in a way limping, as does a horse with its head going up and down > - Cf anahušteštеyakel Bl

a·na·po·pa \a-ná-po-pa\ *vn* ana·ma·popa [fr *a* on + *napopa* to pop] : to burst on anything

a·na·po·ta \a-ná-po-ta\ *va* ana·wa·pota [fr *a* on + *napota* wear out with the feet] : to wear out on, as moccasin on anything

a·na·psa·ka \a-ná-psa-ka\ *va* ana·wa·psaka [fr *a* on + *napsaka* to bread by foot] : to break *e.g.* a string by foot on anything

a·na·pson *or* **anapsun** \a-ná-psoŋ\ *va* ana·wa·pson a-na·ma·pson ana·un·pson·pi : to kick over and spill on — *vn* : to boil over on anything

a·na·pša \a-ná-pša\ *va* : to break into a laugh after it had been suppressed — anapša·pša *vn red* : to bubble or boil up, as bubbles on foul water when disturbed - R BD

a·na·pšun \a-ná-pšuŋ\ *va* ana·wa·pšun [fr *a* on + *napšun* dislocate] : to dislocate, put out of joint on anything

a·na·pta \a-ná-pta\ *va* ana·wa·pta ana·un·pta·pi : to stop, hinder, to forbid — *vn* : to cease or stop < ~ *kuwa* He cornered it, ~ *aya* He surrounded them, as one drives them on > — **anapta·pi** \a-ná-pta-pi\ *part* : stopped, ceased < *on* ~ that which produces a stoppage hence the name for paregoric >

a·na·ptel \a-ná-ptel\ *adv* : less, less than — **anaptel·ya** *adv* : in a less manner — **anaptelya·kel** *adv* : less, in a lessened manner

a·na·pte·ton \a-ná-pte-toŋ\ *va* anapte·wa·ton : to prohibit, to lay a hindrance or embargo — *n* : a prohibition, obstruction, hindrance

a·na·ptu·ja \a-ná-ptu-ja\ *va* ana·wa·ptuja [fr *a* on + *naptuja* to split of itself] : to crack or split with the foot on anything

a·na·p'in \a-ná-p'iŋ\ *adj* or *adv* : frost-bitten and stiff < ~ *imayayelo* My hands are stiff from the cold > - Bl

a·na·p'o \a-ná-p'o\ *vn* ana·ma·p'o : to come all over one, as ashes or stream, to be fog on one

a·na·sa \a-ná-sa\ *vn* [fr *a* on + *nasá* to bristle] : to rise up on, as a hog's bristles on its back, to bristle up

a·na·sla·ta \a-ná-sla-ta\ *va* ana·wa·slata [fr *a* on + *naslata* creep up on] : to creep up to carefully, as a hunter to game — **anaslata·pi** \a-ná-sla-ta-pi\ *n* : a creeping up to game

a·na·šlo·ka \a-ná-šlo-ka\ *v* ana·wa·šloka : to kick off, as one's moccasins

a·na·ta \a-ná-ta\ *v* ana·wa·ta : to bury with the foot, to scrape dirt in with the foot

a·na·ta·kin·ye·ce \a-ná-ta-kiŋ-ye-ce\ *adv* : slantedly; concealing, so as to avoid something, surreptitiously < *tókinškinš* ~ carelessly avoiding > - Bl KE

a·na·tan \a-ná-taŋ\ *va* ana·wa·tan [fr *a* on + *natan* touch with the foot] : to flee to one, to rush on any person or thing — **anatan·pi** \a-ná-taŋ-pi\ *n* : an attack or assault, the offensive in war

a·na·ta·pši·ja \a-ná-ta-pši-ja\ *vn* : to bubble or come up as bubbles on water

a·na·ti·pa \a-ná-to-pa\ *vn* : to crisp, shrivel, be burned

a·na·ti·tan \a-ná-ti-taŋ\ *v* ana·wa·titan [fr *a* on + *natitan* to draw forward] : to push on with the foot, to pull back on account of

a·na·to·kel·ya·kel \a-ná-to-kel-ya-kel\ *adv* : using the feet in an unusual manner < ~ *mani* He walks strangely, as one who has sores, *Mani maptahanhan heon* ~ *mawani* Since my walking was quite peculiar, I walked in an unusual way >

a·na·tu·ka \a-ná-tu-ka\ *va* ana·wa·tuka [fr *a* on + *natuka* to stamp] : to wear off with the foot, as the hair from a buffalo hide moccasin

a·na·t'a \a-ná-t'a\ *va* ana·wa·t'a [fr *a* on + *nat'a* to kill by foot] : to kill with the foot on something

a·na·t'ins \a-ná-t'iŋs\ *va contrac of* anat'inza — **anat'in·sya** *adv* : firmly trodden

a·na·t'in·za \a-ná-t'iŋ-za\ *va* [fr *a* on + *nat'inza* to tramp] : to tramp down hard and tight, *fig* for dancing < *Anaunt'inzapi kte* We shall be dancing > - R

a·na·ung \a-ná-ung\ *va contrac of* anaunka : to gallop, to kick down — **anaun·gkiya** \a-ná-uŋ-gki-ya\ *va* : to cause to gallop on — **anaun·gya** *va* : to make gallop < ~ *owakihi yelo* I could not make *e.g.* the horse or cow gallop > - Note: the use of these forms of *anaung* is doubtful

a·na·un·ka \a-ná-un-ka\ *va* ana·wa·unka [fr *a* on + *naunka* to gallop] : to kick down on anything — *vn* : to gallop, as does a horse on anything - Bl

a·na·wab \a-ná-wab\ *adv* : over against or beyond

a·na·we·ga \a-ná-we-ga\ *v* aná·wa·wega [fr *a* on + *nawega* to break by foot] : to break on anything with the foot, but not to break off, rather to crack — **anaweh** \a-ná-weȟ\ *v contrac of* anawega : to break by foot < ~ *i-yeya* to crack suddenly with the foot >

a·na·win·ja \a-ná-wiŋ-ja\ *va* ana·wa·winja [fr *a* on + *nawinja* trample] : to bend down with the foot

a·na·win·lwin·ta \a-ná-wiŋ-lwiŋ-ta\ *v red* [fr *a* on + *nawinta* to scrape clear by foot] : to scrape the foot on

a·na·winš \a-ná-wiŋš\ *v contrac of* anawinja : to bend by foot < ~ *iyeya* of a sudden to bend down on by foot >

a·na·win·ta \a-ná-wiŋ-ta\ *v* ana·wa·winta [fr *a* on + *nawinta* to scrape] : to scrape the foot on

a·na·win·yan \a-ná-wiŋ-yaŋ\ *adv* : stealing up secretly by taking a round-about way; *fig* concealing by circumlocution - R Bl

a·na·zi·ca \a-ná-zi-ca\ *v* : to stretch with the foot something too short, *i.e.* holding it in the hands and bracing the foot against it, *e.g.* a belt - Bl

a·ni \a-ní\ *vn* a·wa·ni [fr *a* on *or* for + *ni* to live] : to live on or for

a·ni·ca \a-ní-ca\ *va* a·wa·nica : to withhold, keep back from, to retain something claimed by another, to lay claim to; to forbid or oppose - Note: from this word are formed *akinica* and *akicinica* to detain one - D.217

a·nil \a-níl\ *v contrac of* aníca : retain

a·ni·ni \a-ní-ni\ *n* : that which collects on, as soot, thick scum, *etc* < ~ *s'e hiyeya* It seemed to become smut or grime, as is said of soot that hangs loosely >

a·ni·ya \a-ní-ya\ *va* a·wa·niya unka·niyan·pi [fr *a* on + *niya* to breathe] : to breathe on

a·non·go·ptan \a-nóŋ-go-ptaŋ\ *va* : to obey, give ear to

a·nonh·ke·ci·ya \a-nóŋȟ-ke-cì-ya\ *va* : to lend an ear to, to listen to < ~ *manka* I sat listening >

a·non·wan \a-nóŋ-waŋ\ *va* a·wa·nonwan [fr *a* on or for + *nonwan* to swim] : to swim on, or for

a·nung \a-núng\ *adv contrac of* anunka : on both sides < ~ *opé* sharp on both sides, *i.e.* two-edged > - Note: anúnka is *obsol*

a·nun·gki·son \a-nún-gki-soŋ\ *n archaic* : a husband < ~ *wan kici waun kin he* he who is my "other half" I live with > – Note: this is an *archaic* word in the mouth of a man's wife WR

a·nun·gpa un \a-nún-gpa uŋ\ *v* : to agree to – Cf *anún-g'ite un* to oppose Bl

a·nun·gwa·ki·ca·ška \a-núŋ-gwa-ḱi-ca-šḱa\ *n* : saddle bags, *lit i.e.* something bound on both sides

a·nun·g'i·te un \a-núŋ-g'i-ṫe uŋ\ *v* : to oppose each other – Cf *contr*: *anungpa un* to agree – Bl

a·nun·ka·san \a-núŋ-ka-saŋ\ *n* : the bald or white-head eagle

a·nun·ka·tan \a-núŋ-ḱa-ṫaŋ\ *adv* : on or from both sides < *nap'anunkatan* with both hands, *nape sannila* with one hand, *Nap'anunkatan taku ojula icu na el* (on the blanket) *ognaka. Yunkan cahli na okala. Na ake nape sannila tau icu na ake el okala. Yunkan mazakan wahinša. Itokehan towicaya na pahte el kutakiya icazo na tapon kin ~ ecel na iku el oyas'in hecel owicawa* What was full he took with both hands and placed it on (the blanket). It was gunpowder and he scattered it. And again, with one hand he took something and again scattered it on it. They were gun caps. At first, he made them blue, and on the forehead he drew a mark downward and likewise on both cheeks, and so he drew a mark on everyone's chin > — **anunkatan·han** *adv* : on or from both sides, backward and forward < *Na hehan ablo ~ wicahpi num owawa* And then I drew on both sides of the shoulders two stars. > – B.H.156.14

A·nunk I·te \A-núŋk I-ṫè\ *np* : Double Face, a fabulous creature – D.245

a·nun·ki·yan \a-núŋ-ḱi-yaŋ\ *n* **1** : a cross-breed of any living thing **2** : an eagle – Note: *Situpi kin ataya skaska* Its tail feathers are entirely white (while its tail tips only are black) – Bl

a·nun·kpe·sto·la \a-núŋ-kpe-sto-la\ *n* : a pick axe

a·nun·wa·bya \a-núŋ-wa-bya\ *adv* : off to one side

an·bce·ya \aŋ-bcé-ya\ *v* : to cry in the daytime – Bl

An·bhan·ke·ya Wi *or* **A·han** \Aŋ-bháŋ-ke-ya Wi *or* A-hàŋ\ *np* : the old name for half of the months of March and April, about six weeks. The season when the weather changes frequently, half pleasant and half stormy, *"Anpetu-Hankeya* Day-At-Last" < *~ ca wa kin tke s'e hinhé lo* When it is the season of Day-At-Last, heavy snow seems to fall > – Note: it has been said that this is the name for the month of February

an·bši·ce·ca \aŋ-bší-ce-ca\ *n* : an unpleasant, rainy day < *~ yelo* It is a dreary day > – Bl

an·bwa·šte \aŋ-bwá-šte\ *n* : a pleasant day < *~ ca hlahla kin tehan hótan'in kte lo* When a pleasant day, the bells should sound their voices long > – Bl

anp *or* **anb** \áŋṗ\ *n contrac of* ánpa : daylight < *anp'icamna* a stormy day > – Bl

an·pa \áŋ-ṗa\ *n* : daylight, daytime < *Wanna ~, wanna ~ aya* Now it is daylight, it is becoming light > — **anpa·han** *adv* : in daylight < *~ el ipi kte. Hinhanna kin ~ ungni kte lo. ~ wi kin aiyokpazin kte* They should go in daylight. Tomorrow morning you and I shall go home. The sun will be darkened >

an·pa·ka·ble·za \áŋ-ṗa-ḱa-ble-za\ *n* : daybreaking, daybreak

an·pa·o·ho·ton·la \áŋ-ṗa-o-ho-ṫoŋ-la\ *n* : domestic fowls so named from their crowing in the morning – Note: the Holy Scriptures apply the word rather to the hour of the day only

an·pa·wi \áŋ-ṗa-wi\ *n* : the sun

an·pe·co·kan·ya \aŋ-ṗé-co-kàŋ-ya\ *n* : midday, noon – R Bl

an·pe·han \aŋ-ṗé-haŋ\ *adv* or *part* : today, *i.e.* today as past < *~ cogin ša wan owakahloke* Today I had struck a hole clean through a red core > – D.113

an·pe·ta·ca·gu \aŋ-ṗé-ta-ca-ġu *or* aŋ-ṗé-ta-cà-ġu\ *n* : a large grasshopper – Bl

an·pe·tu \aŋ-ṗé-ṫu\ *n* [fr *anpa* daylight + *étu* at] : day

an·pe·tu·han·ke·ye·la \aŋ-ṗé-ṫu-haŋ-ḱe-ye-la\ *adv* : before noon — **anpetu·la** \aŋ-ṗé-ṫu-la\ *n dim of* anpetu : a lovely day

an·pe·tu·ta·he·na \aŋ-ṗé-ṫu-ta-he-na\ *adv* : before the day is done

An·pe·tu·wa·kan \Aŋ-ṗé-ṫu-wa-kàŋ\ *np* : Sunday, *i.e.* a sacred day

an·pe·tu·wi \aŋ-ṗé-ṫu-wi\ *n* : the sun

[1]**an·po** \áŋ-ṗo\ *n* [fr *anpa* daylight + *o* in place] : dawn of morning < *ánpo kableze kin lehanl* as soon as it was daylight, or now that it was daylight > — *vn* : to dawn, as the morning comes < *Nahahci ~ šni hanni* It was before not quite dawn yet > B.H.186.1,134.13

[2]**an·po** \aŋ-ṗó\ *n* : a morning star

an·po·skanl *or* **anposkan·tu, anposkantu·ya, anposkantuya·kel** \aŋ-ṗó-šḱaŋl\ *adv* [fr *anpa* daylight + *oskantu* settling in] : by day, in the daytime – B.H.127.19

an·po wi·ca·hpi \áŋ-ṗo wi-cà-ȟpi *or* aŋ-ṗó wi-cà-ȟpi\ *n* : the morning star, perhaps the planet Jupiter, or perhaps *Ihúku Kigle* or *Itkób U* the star Arcturus < *~ Sunkáku* Brother Morning Star > – Note: word serves also as an *express*: "now the dawn of a new day" – Re

an·pta·ni·ya \aŋ-ptá-ni-ya\ *n* : breath of day, the very first glimmerings of morn; vapors raised by the sun

a·o·ci·kpa·kpa·ni \a-ó-ci-kṗa-kṗa-ni\ *adj red* : unequal in length — **aocikpani** \a-ó-ci-kṗa-ni\ *adj* : not equal in length — **aocikpani·ni** *adj red* : some longer and some shorter — **aocikpani·ya** *adv* : being not equal in length

a·o·cin \a-ó-ciŋ\ *v* [fr *a* causative + *ocin* to ask for] : to desire some of a thing

a·o·ci·ptel *or* **aociptel·ya** \a-ó-ci-ṗtel\ *adv* : not equal to, lacking — **aocipte·tu** *adv* : unequal, different

a·o·gi \a-ó-ġi\ *adj* : blurred, as the eye < *Wi kuwab ya ca na išta kin lemaceca yelo; ~ amaye lo* Whenever the sun went down, his eyes were like mine; mine became bleary, *Anpetu ~ yelo* It was a dreary day. *Wi kin ~ s'elececa. Išta aomagin* The sun seemed to be eclipsed, My eyes were blurred > — **aogin·ton** \a-ó-ġiŋ-toŋ\ *v* : to make indistinct; to hide — **aogin·yan** \a-ó-ġiŋ-yaŋ\ *adv* : in a blurred manner < *~ wáwakite lo* I cannot distinguish very well > — **aoginyan·kel** *adv* : in a blurry manner < *~ mun kte lo* I shall use it in an indistinguishable way > – B.H.238.22 Bl

a·o·gla·ka \a-ó-gla-ḱa\ *va* ao·wa·glaka [fr *a* in addition to + *oglaka* to tell] : to tell in regard to or in addition to; to be appealing to – B.H.256.20

a·o·gla·kin \a-ó-gla-ḱin\ *va* ao·wa·glakin : to peep around at one's own

a·o·gla·kšan \a-ó-gla-kšaŋ\ *v poss* [fr *kakšan* to bend around] : to come or go around, to turn or bend self in and around – KE

a·o·gla·tan \a-ó-gla-ṫaŋ\ *v poss* [fr *aokatan* to nail one on another] : to lock up, to nail up one's own, as one's

---

\a\ father \e\ they \i\ machine \o\ smoke \u\ lunar \an, aŋ\ blanc Fr. \in, iŋ\ ink \on, oŋ, un, uŋ\ soon, confier Fr. \c\ chair \ġ\ machen Ger. \j\ fusion \clusters: bl, gn, kp, hšl, etc...\ b[e]lo ... said with a slight vowel **See more in the Introduction, Guide to Pronunciation**

house when leaving - B

a·o·glu·ta \a-ó-glu-ta\ *vn* ao·ma·gluta : to close or fill up, as a hole or wound, to heal over — **aoglute·ya** \a-ó-glu-te-ya\ *va* aoglute·wa·ya : to close up, cause to heal over; to press around, surround or overwhelm, to close up on, as a war party might do — *part* : surrounding — *adv* : throngingly < *Le oyanke etanhan wašicun aogluteniyanpi tka cik'ayela šicaya yelo. Yunkan tima iyaya; canke oyate kin aogluteyapi* Whereas matters go badly in a tight situation, on account of this location, white men had you surrounded. So he entered the house and people closed in on him > - D.215, 220, 261, 5

a·o·gmi·gma \a-ó-gmi-gma\ *vn* : to roll on — **aogmigme·ya** *va* aogmigme·wa·ya : to cause to roll on anything — **aogmi·yanyan** *or perhaps* **aogmigme·yanyan** *adv* : round on anything

a·o·gna·ka \a-ó-gna-k̇a\ *va* ao·wa·gnaka [fr *ognaka* to place] : to set or place *e.g.* a cover upon

a·o·han·kton·yan \a-ó-haŋ-ktoŋ-yaŋ\ *adv* and *v* : to be around, to encircle, to sit around *e.g.* a warm stove in cold weather - BD

a·o·han·zi \a-ó-haŋ-zi\ *vn* [fr *a* on + *ohanzi* to shade] : to shade, overshadow, to be shade on — *adv* : in the shade, shade upon — **aohanzi·ya** *va* aohanzi·wa·ya : to cause shade upon, to overshadow — *adv* : shadowy or in the shade

a·o·hi·yu \a-ó-hi-yu\ *vn* [fr *a* upon + *ohiyu* to leak] : to come out upon, to leak upon

a·o·ho·mni \a-ó-ho-mni\ *adv* : around, surrounding < ~ *oglicu* to travel down around, as on a curved road, ~ *hiyu* to step around *e.g.* the bushes > - D.270 RT — *vn* ao·wa·homni : to go around, *i.e.* to avoid something, to avoid < *Na tehanyan ca na aohomnipi ca na he nakun slolyapi* And whenever far away they avoided it, whenever there they also knew about it > - Note: the word also carries another meaning of *wacín* perhaps to scheme D.117, 189 — **aohomni·pi** *n* : the circuit — **aohomni·ya** *v* aohomni·bla : to go around

a·o·h'an·han·han *or* **aoh'anhanhan·kel** \a-ó-ḣ'aŋ-haŋ-haŋ\ *adv* : very skillfully

a·o·jan·jan \a-ó-jaŋ-jaŋ\ *vn* ao·ma·janjan [fr *a* on + *ojanjan* to light] : to be light on anything — **aojanjan·ya** *va* aojanjan·wa·ya : to cause to be light upon, to light < *Tipi kin aojanjanyapi* The house was lit up > — **aojanjan·yan** *adv* : in an illuminating manner < ~ *wacipi* an evening dance near a big fire by those who intended to go on the warpath > - B.H.54.6 D.273 Bl

a·o·ka·ga \a-ó-k̇a-ġa\ *va* ao·wa·kaga : to add to, as in building, to make something in addition to, to do more than what one ought to do, to exaggerate < *Lena (olowan etc) aokagapi šni yo. Eceš ehaš aoyakage lo* Don't make more of these (the songs etc) than you should. No! You certainly exaggerate things > — *vn* ao·ma·kaga : to drift downstream — **aokage·ca** *va* ao·wa·kageca : to add to, to do or say more than is fitting; to be unreasonable — *n* : one who is unreasonable in his demands; an importunate person - Bl

a·o·ka·hi \a-ó-k̇a-hi\ *vn* : to hang over, as the hair over the face — **aokahi·ya** *adv* : through hanging hair or tresses < ~ *wakita* She looks out through the hair hanging over her face > - *Syn* KAOZAN S'E Bl

a·o·kah \a-ó-k̇aḣ\ *v contrac of* aokaga : to add to < ~ *oyaka* He said too much, or He embellished his talk >

a·o·ka·hni·ga \a-ó-k̇a-ḣni-ġa\ *va* ao·wa·kahniga [fr *a* concerning + *okahniga* understand] : to understand about, *i.e.* in consequence of

a·o·ka·hwog \a-ó-k̇a-ḣwog\ *vn contrac of* aokahwoka : to be drifting or floating on < ~ *iyaya* to go drifting on >

a·o·ka·hwo·ka \a-ó-k̇a-ḣwo-k̇a\ *vn* : to drift on, to float downstream

a·o·ka·hya \a-ó-k̇a-ḣya\ *adv* : extravagantly, as in talking — **aokahya·kel** \a-ó-k̇a-ḣya-k̇el\ *adv* : exaggeratedly

a·o·ka·ki \a-ó-k̇ak̇i\ *va* a·wa·okaki *or* awaokakin : to peep into, as through a keyhole or window, looking closely at something — **aokakinyan** *adv* : peeping into

a·o·ka·kšan·yan \a-ó-k̇a-kšaŋ-yaŋ\ *adv* : around about, by a round-about way

a·o·ka·mna \a-ó-k̇a-mna\ *v* ao·wa·kamna : to avoid, go around, to sneak around stealthily, as in hunting game; to slight one by avoiding noticing, and so honoring him when a person might do so - *Syn* OKAMNA, AYUKŠANYAN

a·o·ka·pol \a-ó-k̇a-ṗol\ *vn contrac of* aokapota : to be afloat, floating in a stream < ~ *iyaya* It went floating > — **a·o·ka·pol·ya** *va* aokapol·wa·ya : to cause to float

a·o·ka·po·ta \a-ó-k̇a-ṗo-ṫa\ *vn* : to float on, as a buoy, to rise to the top, *i.e.* anything in water

a·o·ka·sto \a-ó-k̇a-sṫo\ *va* ao·wa·kasto [fr *a* on + *okasto* leaving a trail in the grass] : to smooth down on

[1]**a·o·ka·ta** \a-ó-k̇a-ṫa\ *vn* ao·ma·kata : to be warm on

[2]**a·o·ka·ta** \a-ó-k̇a-ta\ *va* ao·wa·kata : to cover with earth

a·o·ka·tan \a-ó-k̇a-ṫaŋ\ *va* ao·wa·katan ao·un·katan·pi [fr *a* on + *okatan* to nail down] : to nail one thing on another - B.H.265.14

a·o·ka·ti·ca \a-ó-k̇a-ṫi-ca\ *va* ao·wa·katica : to draw or scrape snow on anything

a·o·ka·t'ins \a-ó-k̇a-t'iŋs\ *va contrac of* aokat'inza : to pound tight — **aokat'in·sya** *adv* : pressed in or on tight

a·o·ka·t'in·za \a-ó-k̇a-t'iŋ-za\ *va* ao·wa·kat'inza [fr *a* in + *okat'inza* press or pound] : to press or pound in tight, as in packing flour, to hammer on tight, as a hoop

a·o·ka·win·ga \a-ó-k̇a-wiŋ-ġa\ *va* ao·wa·kawinga : to encircle < *Na he oyate unkihakab ai k'on hena anatanpi na aokawingapi. Na ecel tona kujapi hena eqicaunkapi ca na aowicakawingapi. Na wanna lila wicakutepi na icunhan aowicakawingapi na ohanketa egnagna iyayapi* And there the people who had arrived after us attacked in an encircling operation. And so those who were indisposed, whenever they were given time to rest, were encircled. Now they were badly shot up, and meanwhile they were surrounded, and in the end they went right through their midst > - B.H.72.7 D.269

a·o·ki·ca·ga \a-ó-k̇i-ca-ġa\ *va* : to deal falsely < *Aomiyecagapelo* You deal dishonestly with me, *i.e.* although I treat you well — **aokicaga·pi** *n* : a falsehood >

a·o·ki·ca·ge·ca *and perhaps* **aákicageca** \a-ó-k̇i-ca-ġe-ca\ *n* : an importunate person - *Syn* AOKAGECA

a·o·ki·ci·pa·gi \a-ó-k̇i-ci-ṗa-ġi\ *v* ao·we·cipagi [fr *opagi* to cram a pipe] : to fill a pipe for one in addition to

a·o·ki·gna·ka \a-ó-k̇i-gna-k̇a\ *va* ao·we·gnaka [fr *a* in addition to + *okignaka* put in] : to put some in in addition to, to help one *e.g.* to food a second time

a·o·ki·hpa \a-ó-k̇i-ḣṗa\ *va* ao·wa·kihpa [fr *a* on + *okihpa* to rest] : to rest or lie by for

a·o·ki·me \a-ó-k̇i-me\ *va* ao·wa·kime : to encircle, go around; to clasp as with the arms, to embrace — **aoki·me·ya** *va* : to cause to encircle or go around — *adv* : encircling

a·o·ki·ya \a-ó-ki-ya\ *v* ao·wa·kiya ao·un·kiya·pi [fr *a* on + *okiya* to help one] : to get together and plan on , to make up something

a·o·ki·ye \a-ó-ki-ye\ *n* : a buggy or wagon top or cover - *See awokeya*

a·o·kpa·gi \a-ó-kpa-ġi\ *v poss* [fr *aopagi* to pack a pipe again] : to fill one's own pipe again

a·o·kpa·ni \a-ó-kpa-ni\ *vn* : to be wanting, not sufficient < *Heon owayawa kin tokata wakanyeja kin aokpanipi kta i-blukcan. Takuku aomakpani yelo* The reason is that when I go to school I first figure a child should be wanting. Little things are not sufficient for me, *i.e.* I am short on various things (which is an old saying) > — **aokpani·-yan** *adv* : insufficiently, less than - HH

a·o·kpas \a-ó-kpas\ *vn contrac of* aokpaza : to be dark on — **aokpas·ya** *va* aokpas·wa·ya : to darken or make dark upon — *adv* : obscurely, darkened

a·o·kpa·za \a-ó-kpa-za\ *vn* ao·ma·kpaza : to be dark on any place of thing

a·o·kpa·zan \a-ó-kpa-zan\ *va* ao·wa·kpazan : to push into, as an arrow into a quiver, or a feather into one's hair — **aokpazan·kiton** \a-ó-kpa-zaŋ-ki-toŋ\ *vn* : to have a sheath or case upon, to be sheathed or pushed in

a·o·k'o \a-ó-k'o\ *vn* [fr *a* causative + *ok'o* a noise] : to be a fuss made about — **aok'o·ya** *va* aok'o·wa·ya : to buzz about, to make a noise or fuss about

a·o·le \a-ó-le\ *v* ao·wa·le [fr *a* in addition + *ole* seek] : to seek for something in addition to

ao·mna \a-ó-mna\ *va* ao·wa·mna [fr *a* upon + *omna* to smell] : to smell upon, to smell in consequence of

a·o·na·ki·ta·ka \a-ó-na-ki-ta-ka\ *v poss* aona·wa·kitaka [fr *aonataka* fasten on] : to fasten *e.g.* a door on one

a·o·na·pa \a-ó-na-pa\ *va* aona·wa·pa [fr *a* at + *onapa* to take refuge in] : to flee to, take refuge at or in or on

a-o-na-slo-ka \a-ó-na-slo-ka\ *va* aona·wa·sloka : to run away from, to leave or desert *e.g.* a friend in danger

a·o·na·tag \a-ó-na-tag\ *va contrac of* aonataka : to lock up < ~ *iyeya* suddenly to lock up, *Aonaic'itag yankapi* They sat having locked up themselves, as did the Apostles out of fear >

a·o·na·ta·ka \a-ó-na-ta-ka\ *va* aona·wa·taka : to fasten on one, to lock up < *Tiyopa* ~ He fastened the door on him, or He shut him in, *mazaska* ~ a safe >

a·o·na·t'ins \a-ó-na-t'iŋs\ *va contrac of* aonat'inza : to pack tight < ~ *iyeya* suddenly to compress >

a·o·na·t'in·za \a-ó-na-t'iŋ-za\ *va* aona·wa·t'inza : to press down tight in *e.g.* a box or barrel

a·on *or* **aonpa** \a-óŋ *or* a-óŋ-pa\ *va* a·wa·on unká·-on·pi **1** : to lay or place on *e.g.* wood on a fire, to stoke a fire **2** : to smoke in addition to, on, or after - Note: this is a conversational meaning of the word; hence *acanmunpa* or *aomunpa* I smoke - BD

a·on·ši·ya \a-óŋ-ši-ya\ *adv* : more poorly, in a worse condition — **aonšiya·kel** \a-óŋ-ši-ya-kel\ *adv* : still worse, worse and worse

a·o·pa \a-ó-pa\ *v* aó·wa·pa [fr *a* with + *opa* follow] : to follow with

a·o·pa·gi \a-ó-pa-ġi\ *v* ao·wa·pagi [fr *a* in addition + *opagi* to pack] : to fill a pipe again or after eating

a·o·pa·ti·ca \a-ó-pa-ti-ca\ *v* : to stick or push in or under or on, as a quilt under the tick - Cf opática

a·o·pa·zan \a-ó-pa-zaŋ\ *n* **1** : eagle feathers **2** : anything a person man or woman used to stick in the hair of the head - Cf opázan, mitáaópazan, aókpazan

a·o·pe·mni \a-ó-pe-mni\ *va* ao·wa·pemni [fr *a* in + *ope-mni* wrap around] : to roll up in

a·o·pe·ya \a-ó-pe-ya\ *va* : to add to, to cause to follow with — *adv* : with, together with, included - D.37

a·o·po·gan \a-ó-po-ġan\ *va* ao·wa·pogan [fr *a* on + *opogan* blow out] : to blow on

a·o·pte·ca \a-ó-pte-ca\ *adj* : less, little — **aoptel** *adv contrac of* aopteca : less than — **aoptel·ya** \a-ó-pte-lya\ *va* aoptel·wa·ya : to diminish — *adv* : less — **aoptelya·kel** \a-ó-pte-lya-kel\ *adv* : less, less than — **aoptelye·la** *adv* : less, diminished

a·o·pte·tu \a-ó-pte-tu\ *adv* : less in size — **aoptetu·ya** *adv* : less, in a less manner

a·o·šla \a-ó-šla\ *n* : a bare spot, as a place where grass has been worn away by people or animals walking

a·o·šma \a-ó-šma\ *v* : to heap up in, on < *Amákiošma yo* Heap it on for me, *i.e.* food on a plate >

a·o·š'a·gya \a-ó-š'a-gya\ *adv* : tired out with difficulty < ~ *wahi* I arrived unwearied > - B.H.234.6 RH

a·o·ta·la·s'e \a-ó-ta-la-s'e\ *adv* : more < ~ *mak'u ye* Please give me more >

a·o·tan·hci \a-ó-taŋ-hci\ *adv* : chiefly, in the first place, before anything else, as caring for a very important matter < ~ *taku awacinpi iyececa* It is in the first place fitting they believe in something > - Cf iyótan B KE

a·o·tan'·in \a-ó-taŋ-iŋ\ *adv* and perhaps *vn* : approaching dusk, to be growing dim < ~ *lake cel unkihunnipi ktelo* We shall arrive when it is getting dark. *Tanyan wakita yo, aotan'in šni wanji yankelo* Do a good job watching; when it is not getting dark, a person is at home, as it is said when somebody is hiding somewhere > - Bl KE

a·o·te·han \a-ó-te-haŋ\ *vn* : to be far — **aotehan·tu** \a-ó-te-haŋ-tu\ *vn* : to be a long time, to be too late < *Aómatehantu* I was being a long time >

a·o·to·gna·ka *or* **aot'ognaka** \a-ó-to-gna-ka\ *vn* : to dare, to be foolhards, to risk one's life, to take one's chances at

a·o·t'ins \a-ó-t'iŋs\ *vn contrac of* aot'inza : to be tight on or in — **aot'ins·ya** *va* : to crowd or press about; to beset or besiege < *Aot'insmayan* He crowds me > — *adv* : crowding, besetting

a·o·t'in·za \a-ó-t'iŋ-za\ *vn* [fr *a* on or in + *ot'inza* to be tight in] : to be tight on one, as a garment, to be tight in, as one thing inside another < *Aomat'inza* It is tight on me >

a·o·t'o·gna·ka *or* **aotognaka** \a-ó-t'o-gna-ka\ *vn* aot'o·-wa·gnaka : to be foolhardy, to risk one's life, to dare

a·o·un·yan \a-ó-uŋ-yaŋ\ *v* [fr *a* on + *ounyan* stay in a place] : to be or abide on - Note: *Akan ounyan* He stayed on

a·o·we·han·han \a-ó-we-haŋ-haŋ\ *v red* aowe·wa·hanhan aowe·un·hanhan·pi [fr *aowehan*, but this word seems not used] : to jest, to make sport — **aowehanhan·yan** *adv* : jestingly, in sport

a·o·win·ški·ya \a-ó-wiŋ-ški-ya\ *va* : to make a bed on for, as in putting down a blanket for a child to play on

a·o·ya·ȟe \a-ó-ya-ȟe\ *vn* : to dry up on, soak in or evaporate on < *Casmu ca mini oyasin* ~ *iyaye* It was in sand all the water went and soaked in. ~ *ayanpa* It evaporated overnight, *i.e.* all the water disappeared overnight > - Bl

a·o·ya·ka \a-ó-ya-ka\ *v* ao·bla·ka : to add something

\a\ father \e\ they \i\ machine \o\ smoke \u\ lunar \an, aŋ\ blanc Fr. \in, iŋ\ ink \on, oŋ, un, uŋ\ soon, confier Fr. \c\ chair \ġ\ machen Ger. \j\ fusion \clusters: bl, gn, kp, hšl, etc...\ b^e^lo ... said with a slight vowel
See more in the Introduction, Guide to Pronunciation

when relating < *Ate tokel woniciyakapi kin aoyakapi ca heon lila canteunšicape* As Father told it to you, we became quite disconsolate because they embellished it > – B.H.283.11

a·o·yu·tku·ga \a-ó-yu-tku-ġa\ *va* : to shut out

a·o·ze·ze \a-ó-ze-ze\ *vn* : to dangle — **aozeze·ya** *adv* : danglingly, drooping

a·o·zi·ca \a-ó-zi-ca\ *va* ao·wa·zica : to reach out after

a·o·zi·gzi·ca \a-ó-zi-gzi-ca\ *va* ao·wa·zigzica : to stretch up after anything — **aozigzil** *va contrac of* aozigzica : to reach up for < ~ *najin* He stood stretching forth, ~ *wicapahi s'e toki ai* Wheresoever they arrived from he seemed to range far picking them, as is said when people from here and there go to some meeting *etc*, they being picked out here and there as it were on tiptoe > – Bl

a·o·zi·ya \a-ó-zi-ya\ *va* aozi·wa·ya : to cause to rest

[1]**a·pa** \a-ṗá\ *interj of surprise and incredulity* : "Bosh!" *or* "Nonsense!" < ~ *ayuštan* Stop? or Quit? ~ *owotanla* Pretend to be honest? *i.e.* recommending something bad as good > – Bl GV FP *Syn* AMÁ

[2]**a·pa** \a-ṗá\ *va* a·wa·pa a·ma·pa unka·pa·pi : to smite or strike a thing in any way < *Yunkan tokeya ie kin mila wan cuwi el apa na etan we hiyu* Then before he said a word, a knife struck him in the back and from it came blood >

a·pa·bla·ska \a-ṗá-bla-sk̇a\ *va* a·wa·pablaska [fr *a* on + *pablaska* flatten] : to make flat on anything

a·pa·bla·ya \a-ṗá-bla-ya\ *va* a·wa·pablaya [fr *a* on + *pablaya* to level] : to make level on anything; *fig* to fatigue one, play one out, to overcome as a man by talking or a horse by riding < *Acipablaya kte lo* I'll wear you down, implying: Well, I'll do it for you, or It's alright with me. *Ho wana ništinma ca acipablayelo. Wowapi kah waši k'on hankeya awapablayelo* Well now, since you were asleep, I wore you out. I played him out at last by my having ordered him to create a book > – Bl

a·pa·bla·za \a-ṗá-bla-za\ *va* [fr *a* on + *pablaza* burst] : to burst open on, to tear open on

a·pa·ble·ca \a-ṗá-ble-ca\ *va* a·wa·pableca [fr *a* on + *pableca* crush] : to break or crush on anything — *n* **a** : a hill in front of and joining a higher hill and so forming a ridge < *Paha wankatuya k'el tahena ~ wan yanke un hel* ... High up the hill on this side, there there is a ridge... > **b** : ground raised, a little hill < ~ *el najin* He stood at or on a small hill > – Note: the word may perhaps function as an *adj* : raised, elevated – Bc

a·pa·ble hi·yu·ya \a-ṗá-ble hi-yù-ya\ *v* : to surprise one, to take one by surprise – *Syn* AKÁLA HIYÙYA Bl

a·pa·blu \a-ṗá-blu\ *va* a·wa·pablu : to crush to powder on anything — *vn* a·ma·pablu : to belch, to bubble up as air from the water < *Keya mni mahe iyaya, unkan ~* A turtle went away into the water, and then it belched > — **apablu·blu** *vn red* : to bubble up with many bubbles

a·pa·can·can \a-ṗá-caŋ-caŋ\ *va* a·wa·pacancan [fr *a* on + *pacancan* push and cause trembling] : to push and make tremble on anything, to make one tremble by pushing

a·pa·co·za \a-ṗá-co-za\ *va* a·wa·pacoza [fr *a* on + *pacoza* to warm by rubbing] : to rub and make warm on anything

a·pa·ga \a-ṗá-ġa\ *vn* : to beset with prickles < *Amápagelo* I was covered with stickers, *Nape ~* His hands were beset with prickles > — **apaga·ya** *va* apaga·wa·ya : to cause to be assailed with prickles, as by throwing devil's grass or cactus *etc* on one – Bl

a·pa·gan \a-ṗá-ġaŋ\ *va* a·wa·pagan [fr *a* on + *pagan* able to spare or give] : to share or give away for a purpose

a·pa·gli·hpa·ya \a-ṗá-gli-ḣpa-ya\ *vn* apa·wa·glihpaya : to fall on one wounded < *Na ungna nitakuye wanji nikiyela ~ eša el eyatonwe kilo* I do not know but that a relative of yours fell on one near you, though you did not take a look at him >

a·pa·glu·šte \a-ṗá-glu-šte\ *vn* [fr *hušte* lame] : to be lame — **apaglušte·šte** *vn red* : to be crippled – Bl

a·pa·gmi·gma \a-ṗá-gmi-gma\ *va* a·wa·pagmigma [fr *a* on + *pagmigma* roll round] : to roll over on

a·pa·gmi·yan·yan \a-ṗá-gmi-yaŋ-yaŋ\ *va* a·wa·pagmiyanyan [fr *a* on + *pagmiyanyan* roll by hand] : to make round *e.g.* a ball on anything

a·pa·gmon *or* **apagmun** \a-ṗá-gmoŋ\ *va* a·wa·pagmon [fr *a* on + *pagmon* twist by hand] : to twist or roll on anything

a·pa·gna \a-ṗá-gna\ *va* a·wa·pagna : to shell *e.g.* corn

a·pa·go \a-ṗá-ġo\ *va* a·wa·pago [fr *a* on + *pago* carve or mark] : to carve or engrave on anything

a·pa·gu·ka \a-ṗá-ġu-k̇a\ *va* a·wa·paguka [fr *a* on + *paguka* sprain] : to sprain by rubbing on anything

a·pa·ha \a-ṗá-ha\ *va* a·wa·paha [fr *a* on + *paha* raise] : to raise on or over, as the hand to strike one < *Tohanl unci nazuspe kin he taku ~ can šna tokel niwacinpicašni yelo* Whenever my grandmother raised that axe over anything, then just so often it is no use your trying to live. *Can amapaha yešan icukiyelo* She lifted a stick at me, *i.e.* to hit me, but she took it down again, *i.e.* she restrained herself > – D.103 B.H.66.9 Bl

a·pa·ha he \a-ṗá-ha hè\ *phr* : on a low hill; *fig* on the one side of the rump < *Owanjila yanka yo; onze san ~ s'e škinnic'iyelo* Sit still. You move about as though on one side of your rump were light colored, so they say to a man in a meeting who moves about unnecessarily much, thus making himself busy over something > – BT KE

a·pa·ha·la·ka *or* **apahalake** \a-ṗá-ha-la-k̇a\ *n* : a low hill — *adv* : hill-like < *Na miš lel ~ wan el hunh najinpi ca el wakinawajin* And here at a small hill, when some were standing, I came back and stood > – R

a·pa·ha·ya \a-ṗá-ha-ya\ *adv* : convexlly

a·pa·hi \a-ṗá-hi\ *va* a·wa·pahi [fr *a* on + *pahi* collect] : to pick up or gather on anything

a·pa·hin·ta \a-ṗá-hiŋ-ṫa\ *va* a·wa·pahinta [fr *a* on + *pahinta* wipe off] : to brush on anything

a·pa·ho·mni \a-ṗá-ho-mni\ *va* a·wa·pahomni [fr *a* on + *pahomni* push about] : to push on or shove around on anything

a·pa·hun·hun·za \a-ṗá-huŋ-huŋ-za\ *va* a·wa·pahunhunza [fr *a* on + *pahunhunza* shake by hand] : to shake on anything

a·pa·ha·ka·ya·ya·pi \a-ṗá-ḣa-k̇a-yà-ya-pi\ *n* : something made rough or wrinkled or deformed by an injury – #

a·pa·ha·tka \a-ṗá-ḣa-tk̇a\ *adj* : against the grain, rough — **apahatka·ya** *adv* : roughly and against the grain

a·pa·hla·gan \a-ṗá-ḣla-ġaŋ\ *va* a·wa·pahlagan [fr *a* on + *pahlagan* to enlarge or lengthen] : to make large on anything

a·pa·hlal·ton \a-ṗá-ḣlal-toŋ\ *va* apahlal·wa·ton [fr *apahlata* embroider + *ton* to emanate] : to bind or embroider with ribbon

a·pa·hla·ta \a-ṗá-ḣla-ṫa\ *va* : to embroider — **apahlate** *n* : ribbon, ferret, a tape or binding < *šina ~* shawl ribbon > – R

a·pa·hle·ca \a-ṗá-ȟle-ca\ *va* a·wa·pahleca [fr *a* on + *pahleca* tear to pieces] : to tear or rend on anything, to rend by shoving with the hand *e.g.* the coat on one's back

a·pa·hlo·ka \a-ṗá-ȟlo-ka\ *va* a·wa·pahloka [fr *a* on + *pahloka* pierce] : to pierce or make a hole in on anything

a·pa·hpa \a-ṗá-ȟpa\ *va* a·wa·pahpa unká·pahpa·pi [fr *a* on + *pahpa* throw off] : to throw down on

a·pa·hpu \a-ṗá-ȟṗu\ *va* a·wa·pahpu [fr *a* on + *pahpu* pick or chip off] : to pick off on

a·pa·hta \a-ṗá-ȟṫa\ *va* apa·wa·hta apa·un·hta·pi [fr *a* on + *pahta* bind] : to bind or tie on anything < ~ *yuha* to tie a knot on *e.g.* one's handkerchief so as to remember something, ~ *yuha wagli yelo* I arrived home with it tied on >

a·pa·ja·ja \a-ṗá-ja-ja\ *va* a·wa·pajaja [fr *a* on + *pajaja* to wash] : to wash by rubbing or mopping on anything

a·pa·je·je \a-ṗá-je-je\ *adv* : at the edge or brim, as of a high bank, at the edge of a bench < ~ *najin (nainš iyotaka) yelo* He stood (or sat) at the (bank's) edge. *Koškalaka k'un maya ~ šunkaška yuha yekapinhca hpayahan ške* They say the lad with his dog on a leash was lying down indisposed at the edge of a river bend > — **apajeje·ya** *adv* : loosely, not securely, likely to fall, as a lamp placed on the edge of a table - BT D.225

a·pa·ji·pa \a-ṗá-ji-pa\ *va* a·wa·pajipa : to pinch by pressure on, as in sitting on

a·pa·jo·la \a-ṗá-jo-la\ *n* : just a little raise on the ground - B.H.189.14

a·pa·ju·ju \a-ṗá-ju-ju\ *va* a·wa·pajuju [fr *a* on + *pajuju* erase] : to wash by rubbing on anythng

a·pa·kin·ta \a-ṗá-k̇iŋ-ṫa\ *va* a·wa·pakinta [fr *a* on + *pakinta* to clean] : to wipe or rub off on anything

a·pa·kin·yan \a-ṗá-k̇iŋ-yaŋ\ *adv* : leaning over, as an old man does in walking, or as a tree to one side < ~ *mani* to walk with a lean > - *Syn* ATAKINYAN Bl

a·pa·ki·za \a-ṗá-k̇i-za\ *va* [fr *a* on + *pakiza* make creak] : to make a noise *e.g.* by filing or rubbing on

a·pa·ko \a-ṗá-ko\ *vn* [fr *pako* to be bent] : to bend over, to become crooked

a·pa·kpan \a-ṗá-kṗaŋ\ *va* a·wa·pakptan [fr *a* on + *pakpan* pulverize] : to crush or make fine on

a·pa·kpi \a-ṗá-kṗi\ *va* [fr *a* on + *pakpi* to mash] : to crack or mash on anything

a·pa·ksa \a-ṗá-ksa\ *va* a·wa·paksa [fr *a* on + *paksa* break by hand] : to break off on

a·pa·kson·lya \a-ṗá-ksoŋ-lya\ *va* : to have the last word in a quarrel, to win by talking - *Syn* KIPÁ Bl — **apakson·tkiciyapi** \a-ṗá-ksoŋ-tki-ci-ya-pi\ *n* : quarreling - *Syn* AHÓYEKICIYAPI

a·pa·kši·ja \a-ṗá-kši-ja\ *va* a·wa·pakšija [fr *a* on + *pakšija* to bend] : to bend, double up on anything

a·pa·ku·ka \a-ṗá-k̇uk̇a\ *va* a·wa·pakuka [fr *a* on + *pakuka* wear out] : to rub to pieces on anything

a·pa·k'e·ga \a-ṗá-k'e-ġa\ *va* a·wa·pak'ega [fr *a* on + *pak'ega* to scrape] : to rub smooth by hand, as with a tool on something - Note: Cl used *apabaga* with the same meaning

a·pa·k'e·za \a-ṗá-k'e-za\ *va* a·wa·pak'eza [fr *a* on + *pak'eza* smoothen] : to make smooth by scraping on

a·pa·k'o·za \a-ṗá-k'o-za\ *va* a·wa·pak'oza [fr *a* on + *pak'oza* to smoothen] : to rub and make smooth on

a·pa·la·pa \a-ṗá-la-ṗa\ *v* a·wa·palapa : to make or plane smooth

a·pa·ma·gle \á-pa-ma-gle\ *adv* : down-hill, descending — **apamagle·ya** *adv* : in a descending or down-hill manner < *Paha wan el šunkakanya wan ~ u* At the hill, here came descending a man on horse >

a·pa·man *or* **apame** \a-ṗá-maŋ\ *va* a·wa·paman [fr *a* on + *paman* to file or rub] : to file, rub, or polish on — **apame** *n* : a file, a rasp

a·pa·mni \a-ṗá-mni\ *va* a·wa·pamni [fr *a* on + *pamni* to distribute] : to divide out on

a·pa·pa \a-ṗá-pa\ *v red of* apá : to tap one or on something, as done with the hand — *n perhaps* : a tapping - KE

a·pa·po·pa \a-ṗá-po-ṗa\ *va* a·wa·papopa [fr *a* on + *papopa* squeeze and burst] : to make pop or burst on anything

a·pa·psa·ka \a-ṗá-psa-k̇a\ *va* a·wa·papsaka [fr *a* on + *papsaka* break in two] : to break in two *e.g.* a cord on anything

a·pa·pson \a-ṗá-psoŋ\ *va* a·wa·papson [fr *a* on + *papson* spill] : to spill on anything, as water < *We apapsonpi s'e* They were all bloody, *i.e.* as if their blood were spilled >

a·pa·pšun \a-ṗá-pšuŋ\ *va* a·wa·papšun [fr *a* on + *papšun* dislocated] : to put out of joint *e.g.* the arm, on any thing

a·pa·ptan \a-ṗá-ptaŋ\ *va* a·wa·paptan [fr *a* on + *paptan* turn over] : to roll over on anything — **apaptan·ptan** *v red* : to roll over and over on anything

a·pa·ptu·ja \a-ṗá-ptu-ja\ *va* a·wa·paptuja [fr *a* on + *paptuja* crack by hand] : to make crack or split on anything

a·pa·pu·za \a-ṗa-ṗu-za\ *va* a·wa·papuza [fr *a* on + *papuza* to dry by hand] : to wipe dry on anything

a·pa·si \a-ṗá-si\ *va* a·wa·pasi [fr *a* on + *pasi* inquire] : to follow after, to follow on, so as to deliver

a·pa·si·sa \a-ṗá-si-sa\ *va* a·wa·pasisa [fr *a* on + *pasisa* to stick in] : to stitch on, to patch; to stick in or through *e.g.* with a pin

a·pa·ski·ta \a-ṗá-ski-ṫa\ *v* : to press on hard - Bl KE

a·pa·sle·ca \a-ṗá-sle-ca\ *va* a·wa·pasleca [fr *a* on + *pasleca* to slit] : to slit by rubbing on anything

a·pa·slo·han \a-ṗá-slo-haŋ\ *va* a·wa·paslohan [fr *a* on + *paslohan* push along] : to shove or push along on anything

a·pa·snon \a-ṗá-snoŋ\ *va* a·wa·pasnon [fr *a* on + *pasnon* to roast on a spit] : to roast on or over anything

a·pa·sto \a-ṗá-sto\ *va* a·wa·pasto [fr *a* on + *pasto* to smoothen] : to make smooth, to brush down on anything

a·pa·su·ta \a-ṗá-su-ṫa\ *va* a·wa·pasuta [fr *a* on + *pasuta* make stiff] : to make hard or stiff by kneading on anything

a·pa·ši·ca \a-ṗá-ši-ca\ *va* a·wa·pašica [fr *a* on + *pašica* to soil by hand] : to soil or injure by rubbing on anything

a·pa·ši·pa \a-ṗá-ši-ṗa\ *va* a·wa·pašipa [fr *a* on + *pašipa* give another shape] : to break off close on anything; to put out of joint, to disjoint

a·pa·šli \a-ṗá-šli\ *va* : to squeeze out on — *vn* : to ooze out — **apašli·ya** *adv* : in an oozing manner

a·pa·šlo·ka \a-ṗá-šlo-k̇a\ *va* a·wa·pašloka [fr *a* on + *pašloka* push off] : to pull or shove off on, as one's coat

---

\a\ father \e\ they \i\ machine \o\ smoke \u\ lunar \an, aŋ\ blanc Fr. \in, iŋ\ ink \on, oŋ, un, uŋ\ soon, confier Fr. \c\ chair \ġ\ machen Ger. \j\ fusion \clusters: bl, gn, kp, hšl, etc...\ b[e]lo ... said with a slight vowel **See more in the Introduction, Guide to Pronunciation**

a·pa·šlu·ta \a-ṗá-šlu-ṫa\ *va* : to smear on – B.H.221.10

a·pa·špa \a-ṗá-šṗa\ *va* a·wa·pašpa [fr *a* on + *pašpa* to break off] : to break off a piece on anything

a·pa·špu \a-ṗá-šṗu\ *va* [fr *a* on + *pašpu* break or cut in pieces] : to pull off on anything, to pick or rub off, as one sticking on another

a·pa·šu·ja \a-ṗá-šu-ja\ *va* a·wa·pašuja [fr *a* on + *pašuja* crush by hand] : to mash or crush on anything

a·pa·šwog \a-ṗá-šwog\ *v contrac of* apašwoka : to come over on < ~ *iyeya* to inundate >

a·pa·šwo·ka \a-ṗá-šwo-k̇a\ *vn* [fr *a* on + *pašwoka* overflow] : to come up on or over, as water, to overflow

[1]**a·pa·ta** \a-ṗá-ṫa\ *va* a·wa·pata a·ma·pata·pi [fr *a* on + *pata* cut up] : to cut up on, as meat on a block; to operate on

[2]**a·pa·ta** \a-ṗá-ta\ *va* : to cut out and sew on, as in patching torn pants, to patch something

a·pa·tan \a-ṗá-taŋ\ *va* a·wa·patan [fr *a* on + *patan* care for or save] 1 : to reserve, to take care of for a purpose 2 : to push against – *Syn* APÁTITAN

a·pa·te·pa \a-ṗá-ṫe-ṗa\ *va* : to wear off short, as a pencil on paper

a·pa·ti·ca \a-ṗá-ṫi-ca\ *va* a·wa·patica [fr *a* on + *patica* push] : to scrape off from, as snow from the ground

a·pa·ti·tan \a-ṗá-ṫi-ṫaŋ\ *va* a·wa·patitan [fr *a* on + *patitan* push] : to push or brace against

a·pa·ton·ye·la \á-ṗa-toŋ-ye-la\ *adv* : singling out one thing from others, as one horse from a herd < ~ *wakuwa* I tried singling it out > – Cf áecela Bc

a·pa·tu·ja \a-ṗá-ṫu-ja\ *va* a·wa·patuja [fr *a* on + *patuja* bend over] : to stoop down on or over < ~ *po* Stoop down and you can do it, or Don't give up > – Note: the word seems to convey the same meaning as *akpaspa, fig* to stoop down with the view of being more able to carry something < *Toketu k'eyaš awakpaspin kte lo,* or *awapatujin kte lo* I will do it even if it be hard > – WE Bl

a·pa·tuš \a-ṗá-ṫuš\ *v contrac of* apatuja : to stoop over < ~ *yanka* He is in a stooping position > — **apatu·šya** *adv* : crouched

a·pa·tu·za *or* **apatuš** \a-ṗá-tu-za\ *v* : to stand stooping down on < *apatuza* or *apatuš inajin* to stand crouching over on > – Bl

a·pa·t'a \a-ṗá-t'a\ *va* a·wa·pat'a [fr *a* on + *pat'a* kill by pressing] : to kill by applying pressure on anything

a·pa·t'a·t'a \a-ṗá-t'a-t'a\ *vn red* : to become numb, as by freezing on

a·pa·t'in·za \a-ṗá-t'iŋ-za\ *va* a·wa·pat'inza [fr *a* on + *pat'inza* press tight] : to make stiff on, to press tight on, as in making a thumb mark < ~ *mazaska* to be stingy with money, tight with money >

a·pa·t'o \a-ṗá-t'o\ *vn* a·ma·pat'o : to oppose, obstruct, prevent progress —**apat'o·ya** *va* apat'o·wa·ya : to hinder, obstruct, stop — *adv* : in a way obstructing

a·pa·un·ka \a-ṗá-uŋ-k̇a\ *va* a·wa·paunka [fr *a* on + *paunka* push to make fall] : to push down on anything

a·pa·wa·ga \a-ṗá-wa-ġa\ *va* a·wa·pawaga : to pulverize with the hands by rubbing and to scatter over — **apawa·hwaga** *v red of* apawaga : to crumble by hand

a·pa·we·ga \a-ṗá-we-ġa\ *va* a·wa·pawega [fr *a* on + *pawega* to break by hand] : to break partly *e.g.* a stick on anything —**apaweh** \a-ṗá-weȟ\ *v contrac of* apawega < ~ *iyeya* to make break or crack of a sudden >

a·pa·win·ga \a-ṗá-wiŋ-ġa\ *vn* : to go around in circles on or over —**apawinh** \a-ṗá-wiŋȟ\ *v contrac of* apawinga : to be circling < ~ *iyaya* to go in circles >

a·pa·win·ja \a-ṗá-wiŋ-ja\ *va* a·wa·pawinja [fr *a* on + *pawinja* bend down] : to bend or press down *e.g.* grass on anything —**apawinš** *v contrac* : to bend down < ~ *iyeya* bend down suddenly >

a·pa·win·ta \a-ṗá-wiŋ-ṫa\ *va* a·wa·pawinta [fr *a* on + *pawinta* to rub] : to rub on < *Unkcela heca waksin na on* ~ It was cactus he cut and rubbed it on him >

a·pa·ye \á-ṗa-ye\ *n* : seasoning, *e.g.* anything like meat or grease boiled with corn – Cf wápaye —**apaye·ya** *va* ápaye·wa·ya : to use something for seasoning

a·pa·za \a-ṗá-za\ *v* : to stick up in a row, as bushes to sleep under < *Hi kin taku* ~ *šni* The teeth do not stand as something in a row, *i.e.* He has no teeth anymore, or He is now old > – Bl

a·pa·zo \a-ṗá-zo\ *va* a·wa·pazo [fr *a* on + *pazo* point to] : to show or point to on anything, to point at < *Nape amapazo* He pointed his finger at me, *ecannon šni ehantanš nap'acipazo kte lo* If you did not do it, I'll point you out >

a·pa·zun·ta \a-ṗá-zuŋ-ṫa\ *va* a·wa·pazunta [fr *a* on + *pazunta* to sew or lace] : to stitch or sew up in sewing on anything

[1]**a·pe** \a-ṗé\ **a** : a leaf of a tree, leaves **b** : a blade of common grass < *hoape* a fish's fin, *ȟupahu* a wing *e.g.* of a grass-hopper > – Cf apéša *etc*

[2]**a·pe** \a-pé\ *va* a·wa·pe unká·pe·pi : to wait for, hope for < *U* ~ He waited for one to come, *Ye* ~ He waited for one to go, or He desires one to go along, *Lel paha wan yanka ca el ye awicape ca kici el iyahanpi* Here since he awaited them to go to the hill where he was, they went up onto it together >

a·pe·han \a-ṗé-haŋ\ *va* a·wa·pehan [fr *a* on + *pehan* fold up] : to fold on anything

a·pe·ki·ya \a-pé-k̇i-ya\ *va* apé·wa·kiya : to cause to wait for

a·pe·la ta·pi·šle·ca·la i·ye·ce·ca \a-ṗé-la ta-ṗi-šle-ca-la i·yè-ce-ca\ *n* : prairie spurge, euphorbia petaloides eaplon; the name refers to the shape of the leaves – Bl

a·pe·ša \a-ṗé-ša\ *n* : a grass-hopper whose inner wings are red – Bl

a·pe ta·ca·gu \a-ṗé ta-cà-ġu\ *n* : a grass-hopper whose inner wings are black – Bl

a·pe·ya \a-pé-ya\ *adv* : waiting or hoping for

a·pe·yo·han \a-ṗé-yo-haŋ\ *n* : the mane of a horse

a·pe zi \a-ṗé zi\ *n* : a grass-hopper whose inner wings are yellow – Bl

a·pi·i·c'i·ya *or* **apic'iya** \a-ṗí-i-c'i-ya\ *v refl of* apiya : to revive, mend, as in selecting new officers in a society or organization

a·pi·ja \á-ṗi-ja\ *vn* a·ma·pija : to be wrinkled on anything

a·pi·ki·ya \a-ṗí-k̇i-ya\ *v* : to get ready one's own; to fix or make well < *Pelijanjanye kin* ~ He made ready, fixed, the lamp >

a·piš \á-ṗiš\ *v contrac of* apija : to be wrinkled —**apišpija** \á-ṗi-šṗi-ja\ *v red* : to be wrinkled on —**api·šya** *adv* : in a wrinkled manner

a·pi·ya \a-ṗí-ya\ *va* a·wa·piya 1 : to mend 2 : to apply medicine 3 : to revive, as in poking a fire, or in forming a society – Note: the probable meaning when applied to society is to elect new officers < *Paha Sapa kin le Wakantanka tohan maka kin piye šni hehanyan wagluha kte* When God has not revived the land, it is then that He will keep these Black Hills > Note also the meaning of the *refl* form of *apeya,* and *apéic'iya.* Cf apíc'iya ST

a·po \a-ṗó\ *vn* a·ma·po [fr *a* on + *po* to swell] : to swell on

a·po·gan \a-ṗó-ġaŋ\ *va* a·wa·pogan a·wica·pogan [fr *a* on + *pogan* to blow] : to blow on, as water, medicine, *etc* < *El pejuta* ~ He blew medicine on him >

a·po·hpo·gan \a-ṗó-ḣpo-ġan\ *v red of* apogan : to blow on medicine *etc* repeatedly or in different places - D.257

a·po·mna·mna \a-ṗó-mna-mna\ *va* apo·wa·mnamna [fr *a* causative + *pomnamna* shake the head] : to shake or wag the head about

a·pon·pon·ye·la \a-ṗóŋ-ṗoŋ-ye-la\ *adv* : like soft and rotten wood < *Woyuha kinhan he tohan cin kinhan he maka ~ yuha ni kte laka* When he wants this property, why should you not live having land gone bad like rotten wood > Note: the word is used in a *fig* sense, as is said to a fellow who will not lend out things - Bl

a·po·pa \a-pó-ṗa\ *vn* : to burst on, break upon — **apo·pa·han** *adv* or *part* : bursting open

a·po·ptan·ptan \a-pó-ptaŋ-ptaŋ\ *va* apo·wa·ptanptan [fr *a* causative + *poptanptan* shake the head] : to shake the head about, to dissent from - Cf apómnamna

a·po·šin \a-pó-šiŋ\ *v* apo·wa·šin : to make faces at < *Apomayašin so, toke?* Did you really make faces at me > — **apošin·šin** *va* apo·wa·šinšin : to make faces at, to wrinkle the nose - Bl D.37.41 note 5

a·po·tan \a-ṗó-ṫaŋ\ *adj* or *part* : torn up on, used up on, as a coat on somebody < *Le amapotahe lo* Now it's worn out on me > - Bl

a·psi·ca \a-psí-ca\ *va* a·wa·psica : to jump over anything < *Wakpala* ~ He jumped the creek > — **apsil** \a-psíl\ *v contrac of* apsíca

a·pša \a-pšá\ *va* a·wa·pša [fr *a* on + *pša* sneeze] : to sneeze on anything

a·pša·pša \a-pšá-pša\ *adj* : thick, close together, as grass *etc* — **apšapša·ya** *causa adj* : thickly set, in a close state - Bl

a·ptan \á-ptaŋ\ *vn* a·ma·ptan : to roll over, as one shot < *Enaš ~ keye* He stated it rolled over exactly here > — **aptan·ptan** \á-ptaŋ-ptaŋ\ *vn red* a·má·ptanptan : to roll about on — **aptan·yan** \a-ptáŋ-yaŋ\ *vn* a·má·-ptanyan : to roll over on, to fall over < *Han, mat'a eyin na ~ ke* Yes, he said "I was dead," when he meant to fall over >

a·ptan·ye·tu \a-ptáŋ-ye-tu\ *v* : the fall season comes on, to have reached the fall < *Wana unk'aptanyetupelo* We have now survived into the fall > - D.13 Bl

a·ptu·ja·han \a-ptú-ja-haŋ\ *part* : cracked or split on

a·pus \á-ṗus\ *v contrac of* apúza : to dry on

a·pu·ske·bya \a-ṗú-ske-bya\ *adv* : in a filtering manner

a·pu·ske·pa \a-ṗú-sk̇e-ṗa\ *vn* [fr *a* on + *puskepa* pour out] : to filter out on - Note: these two words are in doubtful use

a·pu·ski·ca \a-ṗú-ski-ca\ *va* a·wa·puskica : to press down tight upon — **apuskil** *v contrac of* apuskica

a·pu·spa \a-ṗú-sṗa\ *va* a·wa·puspa [fr *a* on + *puspa* to seal] : to stick or make stick on; to scab — **apuspa·pi** \a-ṗú-sṗa-ṗi\ *n* : mucilage; solder — **apuspe·ya** *adv* : in a sticking manner

a·pu·spu·za \a-ṗú-sṗu-za\ *v red of* apúza : to dry on

a·pu·stag \a-ṗú-stag\ *v* : to crouch < ~ *aya* to sneak or crouch up to, as to game > - Note: *aslohan* to crawl up on one's belly — **apusta·gya** *adv* : crouching - Bl

a·pu·sya \a-ṗú-sya\ *va* apu·swa·ya [fr *a* on + *pusya* to dry] : to cause to dry on — *adv* : in the manner of drying on

a·pu·tag \a-ṗú-tag\ *v contrac of* aputaka : to touch — **a-puta·gya** *va* : to cause to touch — *adv* : in the manner of touching

a·pu·ta·ka \a-ṗú-ta-ka\ *va* a·wa·putaka [fr *a* on + *putaka* to touch] : to touch, to lay on as the hands *etc* < *Na peslete el awicaputaka. Nape awicaputakapi* And he touched them on the top of the head. He laid his hands on them > - B.H.285.11

a·pu·t'ins \a-ṗú-t'iŋs\ *v contrac of* aput'inza : to press down — **aput'ins·t'ins** *v contrac red* — **aput'inst'insya** *adv* : firmly pressed upon — **aput'inst'inza** *v red* — **aput'insya** *adv* : firmly, as by hand

a·pu·t'in·za \a-ṗú-t'iŋ-za\ *va* a·wa·put'inza : to press down upon, as is done in making a thumb mark

a·pu·za \a-ṗú-za\ *vn* a·ma·puza [fr *a* on + *puza* dry] : to dry on, become dry on one, as clothes

a·p'e·ye·la \á-p'e-ye-la\ *adj* : very shallow, as is said of water such that one can walk through it without getting wet feet < *Mni kinhan ~ yunkelo* He lay where there was scarcely any water > - Bl

a·p'o \a-p'ó\ *vn* [fr *a* on + *p'o* to be fog] : to be fog on things

a·sa·ka \a-sá-k̇a\ *vn* a·ma·saka [fr *a* on + *saka* dried out] : to become dry or hard upon - B.H.112.4

a·san \a-sáŋ\ *vn* [fr *a* causative + *san* off-white] : to become whitish or grayish

a·san·pi \a-sáŋ-ṗi\ *n* [fr *aze* breast + *hanpi* juice] : milk of any kind
~ *gwugwu* thick milk
~ *ináze* or *inázeya* a milk serparator
~ *iyatke* what is used as a nipple - Cf napóštan EM
~ *niní* thick milk, cream
~ *pejuta* the ferrets food, *i.e.* the milkweed - Cf itópa sapa tapejuta, and šungleška
~ *skumnázi* or *asunpskumnazi* sour cream or sour milk
~ *súta* hard milk, *i.e.* cheese
~ *s'amná* bad smelling cheese
~ *wasná* cheese, perhaps also grated cheese
~ *wasná icáge* a churn
~ *wigli* or ~ *wasna* butter or cream

a·sa·pa \a-sá-ṗa\ *vn* [fr *a* on + *sapa* black] : to become black on

a·sa·sya *or* **asasyela** \a-sá-sya\ *adv* [fr *asaza* gentle] : slowly, gently, stilly

a·sa·za \a-sá-za\ *adj* : gentle - Note: the word is used mostly with the negative < ~ *šni* inconstant, unchaste >

a·scu \a-scú\ *v* a·wa·scu a·ma·scu : to look at others, apparently to marry them < He says: *Amayascu hwo?* Do you have your eye on me? She says: *Ya, he aciscu kacaš* Oh oh! Why is it you have your eyes on me, and then what? > - *Syn* AS'IN, perhaps Bl

a·sin·hte \a-síŋ-ḣte\ *adj* [fr *as'in* covet] : very desirable < *Mniša* ~ There is a passion for wine >

a·ska \a-ská\ *vn* [fr *a* on + *ska* white] : to become white on

[1]**a·skan** \a-skáŋ\ *vn* [fr *a* on + *skan* to melt] : to melt on, to thaw on, to disappear from, as snow < *Hehe, wana oyate unkotapi k'on ~ s'e unkayapelo* Too bad! We who had been once a numerous tribe became as though we had melted away > - Bl

[2]**a·skan** \á-skaŋ\ *n* [fr *aze* breast + *kan* vein] : the cords and veins of the breast

a·ske·pa \a-ské-ṗa\ *vn* [fr *a* on + *skepa* leak out] : to

\a\ father \e\ they \i\ machine \o\ smoke \u\ lunar \an, aŋ\ blanc Fr. \in, iŋ\ ink \on, oŋ, un, uŋ\ soon, confier Fr. \c\ chair \ġ\ machen Ger. \j\ fusion \clusters: bl, gn, kp, hšl, etc...\ b[e]lo ... said with a slight vowel **See more in the Introduction, Guide to Pronunciation**

leak out on

a·sla \a-slá\ *vn* [fr *a* on + *sla* oil] : to be greasy on anything — **asla·ya** *va* asla·wa·ya [fr *a* on + *slaya* anoint] : to make greasy, to grease — *adv* : in a greasy way

a·sli·pa \a-slí-p̣a\ *va* [fr *a* on + *slipa* lick] : to lick off, or lick from, as does a dog

a·slo·han \a-sló-haŋ\ *vn* a·wa·slohan [fr *a* on + *slohan* crawl] : to crawl along on anything — **aslohan·kel** *adv* slowly - Ed

a·slo·lya \a-sló-lya\ *va* aslo·lwa·ya [fr *a* on + *slolya* to know] : to know about, know all about, to be wise about

a·sna·sna \a-sná-sna\ *v* [fr *a* on + *snasna* to sound] : to ring or rattle

a·sni \a-sní\ *vn* a·ma·sni a·ni·sni unká·sni·pi : to recover, to get well from sickness; to recover from anger

a·sni·ki·ya \a-sní-ḳi-ya\ *vn* or *va* : to take a long rest or vacation - Note: *akisniya* to heal or cause to get well. Also, *ozikiya* to take a brief rest — **asnikiye·kiya** \a-sní-ḳi-ye-ḳi-ya\ *va* asnikiye·wa·kiya : to cause to get well — **asnikiye·ya** *va* : to make well - B.H.188.20, 188.17

a·sni·pi·ca \a-sní-p̣ica\ *adj* : curable

a·sni·sni·ki·ya \a-sní-sni-ḳi-ya\ *vi red of* asnikiya : to take a rest often < ~ *unyanpi kte lo.* ~ *hoyeyi na akešna ceyahe* Let us go resting often. He in often taking a rest cried out and wept again and again, or He lay shouting for help again and again > - D.28

a·sni·ya \a-sní-ya\ *v* asni·wa·ya : to cure *e.g.* a wound, to make something get well - Note: *akisniya* refers to persons, while *asniya* seems to refer to the thing to be cured — **asniya·kel** \a-sní-ya-ḳel\ *adv* : in the way of recovering

a·sni·ye·pi·ca·šni \a-sní-ye-p̣i-ca-šni\ *adj* : incurable

a·son \a-sóŋ\ *va* a·wa·son [fr *a* on + *son* to braid] : to plait or braid on anything

a·so·so \a-só-so\ *va* a·wa·soso [fr *a* on + *soso* cut into strings] : to cut up into strings on any place

a·span \a-sp̣áŋ\ *vn* [fr *a* on + *span* to thaw] : to become soft or melt on, as snow on anything

a·spa·ya \a-sp̣á-ya\ *vn* a·ma·spaya [fr *a* on + *spaya* to be wet] **1** : to become wet on **2** : to suck in water, as in drowning

a·spa·ye·i·c'i·ya \a-sp̣á-ye-i-c'i-ya\ *v refl of* aspaya : to inhale heavily < ~ *s'e unkupi* We are coming home slowly as though tired and pushing > - Bl

a·spe·ya \á-sp̣e-ya\ *va* áspe·wa·ya : to cause to sink down, as an anchor in water; to bury up, to weigh

a·stan \á-sṭaŋ\ *vn* : to be purple on, become purple

a·sto·ya \á-sṭo-ya\ *va* [fr *a* on + *stoya* to smoothen] : to smooth down upon

a·sun·kta \a-súŋ-ḳta\ *n* : the kidney < ~ *wayazan* I have kidney trouble >

a·sunp sku·mna·zi \a-súŋp sḳu-mna-zi\ *n* : sour milk or sour cream - Cf asánpi

a·su·ta \a-sú-ṭa\ *vn* a·ma·suta [fr *a* on + *suta* hard] : to become hard or strong upon

a·su·ton \a-sú-toŋ\ *vn* [fr *a* on + *suton* ripen] : to become ripe on or upon, as seeds

a·s'in \a-s'íŋ\ *vn* a·wa·s'in : to covet, secretly long for; to loiter about a place, to dally looking at something or somebody eating, wishing to get something too < *Amayas'in he?* Are you after getting me? (as is said to tease one) > — **as'in·s'in** *v red of* as'in : to keep dallying — **as'in·yan** \a-s'íŋ-yaŋ\ *adv* : desiringly < ~ *ayuta* He gazed on it, or ate it, with a passion > - B.H.149.16 Bl

a·ša \a-šá\ *vn* : to become reddish

a·šab \a-šáb\ *v contrac of* ašapa : to become blackish

a·ša·bya \a-šá-bya\ *va* aša·bwa·ya : to defile, to make dirty, to tarnish, to profane — *adv* : dirtily, in a defiled manner

a·ša·ka·gle \a-šá-ḳa-gle\ *adv* : holding loosely < ~ *yuha* to hold or brace something so it might not drop > — **ašakagle·ya** *adv* : loosely, tentatively < ~ *okuwa* He hardly tried, as is said when a man does something very difficult, hence with great pains, as when one fixes a piece of machinery or a car > — **ašakagleye·la** *adv* : in a way touching here and there < ~ *peji to yajunpelo* Here and there they cropped the first green blades of grass, ~ *okihi* or ~ *econ* He can, or He does with difficulty > - Note: a similar idea of contract with another is expressed thus: *Išpa ha yuzapi s'e* It was as though they grabbed him bythe skin of his elbow - LH J WE Cf išpá

a·ša·pa \a-šá-p̣a\ *vn* a·má·šapa [fr *a* on + *šapa* black] : to become black or dirty on anything

a·še·ca \a-šé-ca\ *vn* [fr *a* on + *šeca* dry] : to become dry or seasoned on anything

a·ši·ca \a-ší-ca\ *vn* [fr *a* on + *šica* bad] : to become bad or unpleasant on or for — **ašica·howaya** \a-ší-ca-ho-wa-ya\ *va* a·wa·šicahowaya : to cry out on account of — **ašica·ya** \a-ší-ca-ya\ *and* **ašicaya·kel** \a-ší-ca-ya-ḳel\ *adv* : badly, unpleasantly

a·ši·htin \a-ší-ȟṭiŋ\ *vn* : to be poorly on account of; to be defective

a·šil·wo·ya·ka \a-šíl-wo-ya-ka\ *v* : to speak evil of - B.H.164.6 LHB

a·šil·ya \a-ší-lya\ *and* **ašilya·kel** \a-ší-lya-ḳel\ *adv* : badly, sadly, unpleasantly

a·šin·hte \a-šíŋ-ȟte\ *adj* : no good, of poor quality, less good, worthless < *Woyuha* ~ The possessions are of poor quality, *Mniša* ~ It is wine of poor quality > — **ašinhte·yakel** \a-šíŋ-ȟte-ya-ḳel\ *adv* : in a less good condition - B.H.84.13,178.19 B

a·ška·ha·ye·la \a-šká-ha-ye-la\ *adv* : for a little while - *Syn* AŠKATUYELA, OPTELYELA Bl

a·škan·s'e \á-šḳaŋ-s'e\ *adv* : later than expected, rather late - Note: the word is opposed to *tanniš* sooner than expected < ~ *hi* He arrived rather late >

a·škan·škan \a-šḳáŋ-škan\ *vn* [fr *a* on + *škanškaŋ* move about] : to move about on anything — **aškanškan·yan** *adv* : moving about on

a·škan·šni·s'e \a-šḳáŋ-šni-s'e\ *adv* : sooner than ever expected so it seemed, seemingly in no time at all - D.27

a·škan·ye·la \á-šḳaŋ-ye-la\ *adv* : soon, quickly < ~ *unkihunnipi* or *unciupelo* We got across *or* were coming expeditiously, ~ *wahiyelo* I came in a hurry to leave soon again, (the contrary being said is: *Kat'éyetankahci wahiyelo* I came along leisurely, *i.e.* to stay for good) > - Note: Buechel questioned the word's meaning given by some to be: for a little while, not considering and in a hurry - BT

a·ška·ta \a-šḳá-ṭa\ *vn* a·wa·škata [fr *a* on + *šḳáta* to play] : to play on any place

a·ška·tu·la \a-šká-tu-la\ *adv* : lately, not long since - *Syn* LECALA — **aškatu·ya** *adv* : not long ago — **aškatuye·la** \a-šká-tu-ye-la *or* á-ška-tu-ye-la\ *adv* : lately, but a short time ago; near (in space) < ~ *hwo?* Is it near? *Taku* ~ *hošimakaglipi* They arrived home shortly ago with some message for me > - *Syn* KANYÉLA Ba Bl LH

a·ške \a-šḳé\ *n* : a tuft or bunch of hair that some Dakotas wear on the side of their head < *Lakota* ~ *gluwi-*

pi Lakotas bind up their own tuft of hair on the head >

a·ške·han \a-šké-haŋ\ *vn* a·ma·škehan [fr *a* causative + *škehan* carefree] : to do a thing carelessly < *Amáyaškehe lo* You don't seem to care for me, *i.e.* what I have to say > - Bl

a·škin·yan·ka·pi·la \a-škíŋ-yaŋ-k̇a-pi-la\ *adv* : in a short time, from a short distance < *Ho wana letan okanyela ca ~ onašlog unkihunnipi ktelo* Well now, since it is but a short distance from here, let us run off and reach it shortly, ~ *waglicu welo* I came back in a hurry from the little distance > - Bl

a·ški·yan·kel \a-škí-yaŋ-kel\ *adv* : a short distance - B

a·ški·yu·wi \a-škí-yu-wi\ *n* : a strip of leather, hide, or cloth wrapped around a bunch of hair, such as old men used to wear on both sides of the head < *aške yuwipi* the bunch of hair so tied up > - R BD

a·ško·bya \a-škó-bya\ *adv* : crookedly, in an arched manner

a·ško·pa \a-škó-ṗa\ *vn* [fr *a* on + *škopa* crooked] : to be crooked on or arched over

a·šla \a-šlá\ *vn* [fr *a* on + *šla* bare] : to be bare on anything - Note: the word is doubtfully used — **ašla·lyeta** \á-šla-lye-ta\ *adv* : bare, openly — **ašlašla·yela** \á-šla-šla-ye-la\ *adv perhaps* : entirely open, very plainly, clearly < ~ *wanblake lo* I saw it very clearly > — **ašla·ya** \a-šlá-ya\ *adv* : openly, plainly — **ašlaye·la** \á-šla-ye-la\ *adv* : openly, plainly < ~ *ociciyakin kte* I shall tell you plainly, ~ *slolyayin kte* you will know it clearly, ~ *kajuju* he paid cash. *Wi ~ hiyaye lo* It is clearly past noon. *Ecašni s'e canku kin ~ yunke lo* To be sure, it scarcely seemed there lay the road (implying there is no snow on the ground) > - Bc KE B.H.229.3

a·šlo \a-šló\ *vn* [fr *a* on + *šlo* melt] : to fuse or melt, as do metals, grease, *etc* - *Slang* to be drunk, intoxicated — **ašlo·ya** *va* ašlo·wa·ya : to cause to melt on, to solder, to weld

a·šlu·lya \a-šlú-lya\ *va* [fr *a* on + *šlulya* make slip] : to make slip on — **ašlušlu·ta** \a-šlú-šlu-ṫa\ *vn* [fr *a* on + *šlušluta* slippery] : to be slippery on

a·šma \a-šmá\ *vn* [fr *a* on + *šma* deep] : to be deep, as water, on any place < *Ašmélaka* It is somewhat deeper > — **ašme·ya** \a-šmé-ya\ *adv* : deeply, in a deep manner - D.223

a·šni·ja \a-šní-ja\ *vn* [fr *a* on + *šnija* withered] : to be wilted or withered on or for

a·šni·ya·ki·ya *or* **ašniyan** \a-šní-ya-ki-ya\ *v* : to tickle

a·šni·yan·yan \a-šní-yaŋ-yaŋ\ *vn* : to crawl or creep on, as a bug on one — *adv* : creeping along, in a crawling manner

a·šo·ka \a-šó-k̇a\ *vn* [fr *a* on + *šoka* thick] : to be thick, as a board, on anything

a·šo·ta \a-šó-ṫa\ *vn* [fr *a* on + *šota* smoky] : to be smoky on or at

a·špa·han \a-šṗá-haŋ\ *part* : worn off, as a nap of cloth, threadbare, worn out - Bl

a·špan \a-šṗáŋ\ *vn* [fr *a* on + *špan* cooked] : to be cooked, to be burnt on or by anything

a·štu·lya \a-šṫú-lya\ *va* aštu·lwa·ya : to cause to thaw on

a·štu·ta \a-šṫú-ṫa\ *vn* [fr *a* on + *štuta* thawed] : to thaw or warm on anything

a·šun·kt'e·ya \a-šúŋ-kt'e-ya\ *va* : to kill one for misdemeanor < *Tuwa nahmala wanasa ca na lila akicita ktepi, asunkt'eyapi nainš econpi šni ca na ti ayupotapi* Whenever a person went covertly hunting buffalo, warriors actually killed him; whensoever he was killed for misdemeanor or had not done so, his house was torn to pieces >

a·šun·ši·ya·kel \a-šúŋ-ši-ya-k̇el\ *adv* : but little at all < *Kitanyehci ~ wanblake lo* I saw with difficulty but little at all (as when wearing a poor set of eyeglasses, *etc*) > — **ašunšiye** \a-šúŋ-ši-ye\ *n* : a little bit only < ~ *lake wanblake lo* I recognized rather little at all > — **ašunšiyece** *n* : only a little < *Kitanyela ~ laka wanyanka* With difficulty does he see even only a little > - Bl

a·šu·ta \a-šú-ta\ *va* ašu·wa·ta : to miss, to fail of

a·šwu \a-šwú\ *vn* [fr *a* on + *šwu* to drop] : to drop *e.g.* water on anything — **ašwu·ya** *va* ašwu·wa·ya : to cause *e.g.* water to drop on

a·š'a \a-š'á\ *va* a·wa·š'a : to shout at < *akíš'a* to shout or cheer for one, *Awakiš'a* I cheered for him. *Wanna pehan kin hinapin na akiš'aš'a. Na kici tiwegna wahiya kin ayaš'api kta. Oyate kin Ikto aš'api* Now as the crane came in sight there was shouting at him. You should shout together when he arrives among the homes. The people shouted at Ikto > - D.112

a·š'ag \a-š'ág\ *vn contrac of* aš'aka : to be coated — **aš'a·gya** *adv* : in a coated manner < ~ *yanka* It was coated >

a·š'a·ka \a-š'á-k̇a\ *vn* : to be coated or furred, as the tongue in sickness; to be dirty, as a gun in need of being cleaned out — **aš'ake·ce** *v* a·wa·š'akece : to accumulate dirt, grease, *e.g.*

a·ta \á-ta\ *prep suff* : to, at, on - Note: *suff* to *n* ending in *a, ata* becomes *ta* alone. In other cases, *y* is introduced for euphony, thus: *tiyata* at home — *adv contrac of* átaya : entirely

a·ta·bya *or* **atabaya** \a-tá-bya\ *vn* : to go one after another, to follow in single file — *adv* : in a single filed order or manner

a·ta·bye·la \á-ṫa-bye-la\ *adj* : thin, as a slice of bread

a·ta·hna·ki·pca \a-tá-ȟna-k̇i-pca\ *v* atáhna·wa·kipca : to swallow one's saliva, as in desiring something - Note: the word is used when a person desires very much to eat an appetizing thing and begins already to swallow because of a watering mouth - Cf taǧé, napcá Bl

[1]**a·ta·ja** \a-ṫá-ja\ *vn* a·má·taja [fr *a* on + *taja* waves] : to be rough or in waves on one < *Amátajelo* It is rough on me >

[2]**a·ta·ja** \á-ta-ja\ *vn* : to be filled to the brim < *Ámatajelo* I'm full up, as one says who has gone the limit of eating > - Bl

a·ta·kin·yan \a-tá-k̇iŋ-yaŋ\ *adv* : leaning on, not perpendicular, slanting < *Wi ~ yanka* The sun is declining, as a tree leaning to one side > - *See* apákinyan Bl

a·ta·kpe \a-tá-kṗe\ *va* ata·wa·kpe [fr *a* on + *takpe* attack] : to make an attack on

a·ta·ku·ni·šni \a-ṫá-k̇u-ni-šni\ *vn* a·ma·takunišni : to come to naught, become enfeebled, to be ruined or become extinct, to wither away < ~ *amaha* I am reduced to a cypher > — **atakunišni·pica** \a-ṫá-k̇u-ni-šni-ṗi-ca\ *adj* : perishable — **atakunišni·yan** *va* atakunišni·wa·ya : to bring to naught, to annul - D.259, 262 LHB

a·tan \a-ṫáŋ\ *va* : to care for, to have respect for < *Atanpišni* They pay no attention to her > - B.H.241.2

a·tan'in \á-taŋ-iŋ\ *vn* a·ma·tan'in : to appear on, to be manifest < *Na wanna ~ ayapi. Atan'inšni aya na ~ iyaya*

Hecel ~ šni iyaya And they now began to appear. They did not show and went to put in an appearance. Thus did he go not showing up > — **atan'in'·in** \á-ṫaŋ-iŋ-iŋ\ *v red of* atan'in : to appear repeatedly — **atan'in·šniyan** \á-ṫaŋ-iŋ-šni-yaŋ\ *adv* : in a lost manner < *Ámatan'in-šniyan* I kept getting myself lost. *Yunkan iwankam taku ~ han ca wanblaka. ~ kinyan iyaya* Then up above I saw something that was kind of lost. It went away flying astray >

a·tan'·in·ya \á-ṫaŋ-iŋ-ya\ *va* áṫan'in·wa·ya : to make appear, to manifest < *Le lehanl atan'inwayin kte šni. Itunkasan Mato wakan atan'inyin kta. Na koškalaka nunp wakan atan'inyapi* This I shall not now reveal. It should make Weasel Bear appear special. And two young men made it clear he was special > — **atan'in·yan** \á-ṫaŋ-iŋ-yaŋ\ *adv* : appearing, manifestly, visibly < *Si kin ecela ~ najinpi* They stood, their feet alone appearing >

a·tan·ka \a-táŋ-k̇a\ *vn* [fr *a* on + *tanka* big] : to be large on, to be large; to be in addition to — **atanka·la** *v dim* : to be a bit less than large — **atanka·ya** *adv* : widely, extensively

a·tan'·onm \a-táŋ-oŋm\ *v contrac of* atan'onpa : to lean over < *~ iyaya* It was leaning, *i.e.* it had got past perpendicular > — **atan'on·mya** *adv* : in a leaning manner

a·tan'·on·pa \a-táŋ-oŋ-ṗa\ *vn* : to lean, as the sun does in the afternoon; to lean over, as a rider on a horse

a·tan s'e \a-ṫáŋ s'e\ *adv* : silently, stilly < *~ yunka* He lay still > — **atans'e·la** *adv* : motionless; restfully < *~ yanka* He sat without moving, or He took a long rest > - Bl

a·tan·s'in \a-ṫáŋ-s'iŋ\ *adv* : at a standstill < *~ un* It is at rest, *~ gluha* to keep one's own at par with, though one does not need or use it, *Wi kin ~ han. Wicahpi ~ han* The sun stood still. The star stood at rest > — **atans'in·s'in** *adv red* : idle < *~ yankapi* They sat idle > - Note: *atans'e* is the more correct form *Syn* OWANJILA YANKA B.H.25.24, 73.8, 105.43, 169.19, 52.4

a·tan·ton·šni \a-táŋ-toŋ-šni\ *v* : to have nothing of one's own, to be not able to save — **atanton·yan** *va* : to make one save so that he accumulates property - Cf tantónya WE

a·ta·pa \a-tá-pa\ *vn* a·wa·tapa [fr *a* on + *tapa* pursue] : to follow after on anything

a·ta·sa·ka \a-ṫá-sa-k̇a\ *vn* a·maßtasaka [fr *a* on + *tasaka* stiff] : to become stiff or hard on, as clothes

a·ta·šo·ša \a-tá-šo-ša\ *va* ata·wa·šoša ata·ci·šoša : to spit on anything

a·ta·šo·ša·pi·na na·bla·ga \a-tá-šo-ša-pi-na na-blà-ġa\ *n* : the large-flowered yellow flax, linum rigidum of the flax family. Same as *canhlogan nablaga,* and the word refers to the capsule - # 179 Bl

a·ta·šta·ja \a-ṫá-šta-ja\ *vn red of* ataja : to be rough or in waves of water on one

a·ta·ta·pe·šni \a-tá-ta-pe-šni\ *adv* : working something so as to keep it soft < *~ kuwa* He gave one no rest, *i.e.* being in pursuit of one, or He bothered one unceasingly > - Bl KE

a·ta·te·yan·pa \a-tá-ṫe-yaŋ-pa\ *va* [fr *a* on + *tateyanpa* a gale] : to blow upon anyting, as does the wind; here perhaps a gentle breeze - R Bl

a·ta·to·he·ya \á-ta-ṫo-he-ya\ *adv* : on the windward side

[1]**a·ta·ya** \á-ṫa-ya\ *adv* : all, everything, universally. wholly, altogether; alone, separately < *atayaš* entirely >

[2]**a·taya** \á-ṫa-ya\ *va* áta·wa·ya : to meet *e.g.* a person < *Iktomi kákena ya na Iya wan ~* Iktomi was going that there away and he met an Iya >

[3]**a·ta·ya** \a-ṫá-ya\ *vn* atá·wa·ya : to go directly, straight towards something

ataya·kel \á-ṫa-ya-k̇el\ *adv* : all of it < *Oyate kin ~ ahimniciye* The people gathered altogether > — **ataya·kinil** \á-ta-ya-k̇i-nil\ *adv* : pretty near all < *Na oyate kin ~ au na ecel can el aglagla inajinpi* Pretty near all the people came, and as it was they stood out in front of a woods > — **atayaš** \á-ta-yaš\ *adv emph of* átaya : entirely - B.H.295.11, 305.19

a·ta·ye·la \á-ṫa-ye-la\ *adv* : directly, personally, without a medium < *Yunkan šunka najinpi ~ unkihunnipi. ~ agliyagla. toka wan koyakipapi ca ~ wakte yelo. Niyatayela el ya ke* Then horses having stopped we went on across. They all passed directly by. And since you all feared an enemy I personally killed him. He meant he went there (to the camp) without you assisting > - D.269 B.H.238.3

a·ta·ye·ya \á-ṫa-ye-ya\ *v* átaye·wa·ya : to meet < *Na ob atayekiciyapi* Thus they met together > - B.H.121.4, 156.1, 155.23

a·te \a-ṫé\ *n* : a father, my father < *niyate* your father > — **ate·ku** \a-ṫé-ku\ *n* : his father - Note: *atkuku* is in use more commonly Cf ináku — **ate·ya** *va* ate·wa·ya : to have for a father - Note: the word sustains the relation of a child to a man. Among Dakotas one's father's brothers are also called *até*

a·te·bte·pa·he·ya·kel \a-ṫé-bte-ṗa-he-ya-k̇el\ *adv* : worn out like, tattered, threadbare, worn short < *Šina wan ~ in k'on* He had been wearing a threadbare blanket > - Cf tépa Bl

a·te·bya \a-ṫé-bya\ *va* até·bwa·ya [fr *a* on + *tebya* devour] : to cut up or devour on

a·te·ca \a-ṫé-ca\ *vn* [fr *a* on + *teca* new] : to become new on < *~ lake cin* the younger people, the youth > - B.H.283.6

a·te·pa·han \a-ṫé-ṗa-haŋ\ *part* : worn off short on

a·ti \a-ṫí\ *vn* [fr *a* on + *ti* to set up a house] : to build a house, to put up a tent at or on, to pitch a tent, to encamp at for a purpose

a·ti·gna·gya \a-ṫí-gna-gya\ *adv* : nearby - Note: implied is to be having a man staying nearby Bl

a·ti·o·le \a-ṫí-o-le\ *va* atio·wa·le : to live by relying on others' generosity - *Slang:* to sponge off others

a·tku·ku \a-tk̇ú-k̇u\ *n* : his or her father

a·to \a-tó\ *vn* a·ma·to [fr *a* on + *to* blue or green] **1** : to become blue or green on **2** : to tattoo - *Syn* AKITO

a·to·kan \a-tó-kaŋ\ *adv* : in or to another place

a·to·ke·ca \a-tó-k̇e-ca\ *vn* : to become different

a·to·kšu \a-ṫó-kšu\ *va* ató·wa·kšu [fr *a* on + *tokšu* carry] : to draw anything on, to pile up at or on, as a horse's pack

a·ton·wan \a-tóŋ-waŋ\ *va* a·wa·tonwan unka·tonwan·pi [fr *a* on + *tonwan* look] : to look to or at < *Ate, nata catkayatan winawizi wan imakoyakin kte lo, ca le ~ wo. Tuwehci napata yuzin kta ~* Father, on the left side of my head a cockle burr may have stuck on me, so take a look at it. Someone took a look so he might get it by hand > — **atonwan·yan** *va* atonwan·un·yan·pi **1** : to cause to look at **2** : to make a village at or on a place, perhaps such that it is situated on a vantage point for a view of the countryside by those who will live there, or perhaps on a promontory that leads people to catch sight of it

a·t'a·hya \a-t'á-ḣya\ *va* : to make dry and roughen, as a flour once wet and becomes rough through drying; hence to make not slippery - Cf šlušlutešni Bl

a·t'a·t'a·ka \a-t'á-t'a-ka\ *vn* [fr *a* causative + *t'at'aka* palsied] : to become palsied or numb < *Ungnahahci amaya-*

t'at'ake s'elececa It seems as though you may possibly be making me tremble (thus implying one is to handle one lovingly) > – Bl

a·t'e·ca \a-t'é-ca\ *adj* : lukewarm, as water

a·t'ins \a-t'íŋs\ *adj contrac of* at'inza : being tight on one — **at'in·sya** \a-t'íŋ-sya\ *adv* : tightly, in a squeezed way — **at'insya·kel** \á-t'iŋ-sya-kel\ *adv* : in a forced manner < ~ *wahi* I came impressed into coming but *e.g.* according to my promise, on definite terms > – SLB

a·t'in·za \a-t'íŋ-za\ *vn* a·ma·t'inza [fr *a* on + *t'inza* press] : to press on, to be tight on

a·t'o·za \a-t'ó-za\ *vn* [fr *a* on + *t'oja* blunt] : to become blunt or dull on

a·t'un·gya \a-t'úŋ-gya\ *va* at'un·gwa·ya : to suspect one or to have an inkling of < *Tan'akotanhan takunl at'ungyaye heci omakiyaka yo* Tell me whether you suspect some monstrosity > – BT

[1]**a·u** \a-ú\ *va* : to carry or bring anything towards < *Nape au yo* Shake hands. *fig* > — *v coll pl* : they come < *Lakota ehanna tokel icagapi kin wicahcala ehanna owecinhan oyak aupi* As once the Lakota were flourishing, it was then old men, one after the other, brought something to talk about how they were brought up. *Hecel ogna oyate au.* Hence people came to the place. *Lena nitunkašila yuha oyate kah aupelo.* These in company with your grandfather came to form a people. *Koškalaka wan wonicupi psa ca hetan yin kta keye lo, eya au.* They came saying: He stated that a young man would go forth from a reed basket. *Hecel wicowoyake aupi na ecel lehanl slolwaya,* So they brought things to talk about and so it was that I now know. *Yunkan anpetu wan el wicaša wan eyapaha au na lecel eya:* Then one day a man came bringing something to announce and said this: *Yunkan oyate kin wicakico au.* He brought the people an invitation. *Wowapi kin pazo au.* He brought a poster to display. *Le wicoh'an kin oyate econ aupi.* This custom people carry on. >

[2]**a·u** \a-ú\ *vn* [fr perhaps *a* on + *u* come] : to come out on, to ooze out or run, as does sap < *Mni au* It leaked water. >

a·un \a-úŋ\ *va* a·wa·un [fr *a* on + *un* to use] : to put *e.g.* wood on a fire — *vn* a·wa·un [fr *a* on + *un* to be] : to be on

a·un·yan \a-úŋ-yaŋ\ *vn* : to be on or over < ~ *iyaya* He passed on over *e.g.* a hill, a fence, *etc.* ~ *kute* to shoot on the wing, or as the bird flies over >

a·un·ye·ya \a-úŋ-ye-ya\ *va* aunye·wa·ya : to put on < *hinyete* ~ to put on the shoulder *e.g.* a patch or sack, *etc,* or to wear about the shoulders > – *Syn* AWINYEYA — *vn* : to approach from the windward side, *i.e.* to come with the wind – B.H.65.15, 265.3

a·un·ye·ya·pi \a-úŋ-ye-ya-pi\ *n* : sand-berries, ground-berries which, if approached from the windward side are said to become bitter, but if from the opposite direction, sweet — **aunyeyapi hu** *n* : the western sand-cherry, prunus bessayi bailey, the rose family; also the ground-cherry – Cf tahpíyogin *Syn* ICIWAGNUNI R # 14 BT

a·wa \a-wá\ *vn* a·ma·wa [fr *a* on + *wa* snow] : to snow upon anything – Cf awáhinhe

a·wa·bla \a-wá-bla\ *va* a·wa·wabla [fr *a* on + *wagla* to slice] : to cut in strips on

a·wa·bla·ya \a-wá-bla-ya\ *va* [fr *a* on + *wablaya* shave flat] : to smooth over, as by cutting with a knife, to shave off lumps on

a·wa·bla·za \a-wá-bla-za\ *va* a·wa·wablaza : to cut or rip open

a·wa·ble·ca \a-wá-bleca\ *va* a·wa·wableca : to break by cutting on anything, as on something brittle, to cut in pieces on — **awablel** *v contrac of* awableca : to cut < ~ *iyeya* to slash on >

a·wa·ci \a-wá-ci\ *va* awa·wa·ci [fr *a* on + *waci* to dance] : to dance on anything or in honor of < *Topa can awacicipi kte* I shall dance four days in your honor >

a·wa·cin \a-wá-ciŋ\ *va* awa·can·mi awa·can·ni awa·un·cin·pi *or* unka·wacin·pi [fr *a* on + *wacin* think] **1** : to think on or of, to meditate upon **2** : to believe in, to trust

a·wa·cin·kel \a-wá-ciŋ-kel\ *adv* : thinking upon — **awacin·pi** *n* : a thinking upon, a faith or trusting in

a·wa·cin·ya \a-wá-ciŋ-ya\ *va* awacin·wa·ya : to influence someone

a·wa·cin·ya·kel \a-wá-ciŋ-ya-kel\ *adv* : in the manner of thinking on

a·wa·cin·yan \a-wá-ciŋ-yaŋ\ *v* awacin·wa·ye : to influence another's thinking — *adv* : thinking upon

a·wa·gla \a-wá-gla\ *va* a·wa·wagla : to shave off with a knife, as the fat from the guts — **awagla·gla** *v red of* awagla : to shave off

a·wa·hin·he \a-wá-hiŋ-he\ *vn* [fr *awa* to snow on + *hinhe* to precipitate] : to snow upon — **awahinhe·ya** \a-wá-hiŋ-he-ya\ *v* awahinhe·wa·ya : to cause to snow upon — *adv* : to be snowing upon – Note: *adv* may also be *awahinhe·yan*

a·wa·hpa·ni \a-wá-ȟpa-ni\ *vn* : to be poor on account of — **awahpani·ca** \a-wá-ȟpa-ni-ca\ *vn* a·ma·wahpanica [fr *a* by means of + *wahpanica* destitute] : to become poor on account or by means of — **awahpani·ya** *va* awahpani·wa·ya : to make poor by means of — **awahpani·yan** *adv* : poorly off

a·wa·hta·ni \a-wá-ȟta-ni\ *va* awa·wa·htani : to transgress a usage or law, to sin, to fail to carry out a vow < *Awamic'ihtani* I transgressed or abused myself >

a·wa·hwa·ye·la \a-wá-ȟwa-ye-la\ *adv* : mildly, gently

a·wa·i·c'i·cin \a-wá-i-c'i-ciŋ\ *v refl* awa·mi·c'icin [fr *awacin* to think of] : to think much of one's own self, as do some people who are sickly < ~ *s'e mankahe lo* I was making as though I thought much of myself or I were important > – Bl

a·wa·i·c'i·hta·ni \a-wá-i-c'i-ȟta-ni\ *v refl of* awahtani : to transgress – Note: *awahtani* is to be guilty of sin, and *awaic'ihtani* is to transgress a law thereby becoming guilty, and thus hurting one's self < *Woahtani akipa* He meets a punishment > – Cf waic'ihtani R

a·wa·jal \a-wá-jal\ *v contrac of* awajata : to be astride < ~ *oštan* to sit or be placed on astride >

a·wa·ja·ta \a-wá-ja-ta\ *va* awa·wa·jata [fr *a* on + *wajata* to make forked] : to make a split on

a·wa·ka \a-wá-ka\ *va* awa·wa·ka [fr *a* on + *waka* to strip] : to cut or split *e.g.* the feather from a quill

a·wa·kan *or* **awakan·ka** \a-wá-kaŋ *or* a-wá-kaŋ-ka\ *vn* [fr *a* on account + *wakan* mysterious] : to be sacred or incomprehensible on some account — *n* : a supernanatural being — **awakan·yan** *adv* : mysteriously, supernatually

a·wa·ka·se·ya \a-wá-ka-se-ya\ *part*: obstructing, hindering, withstanding *e.g.* the snow < ~ *unglapi kte lo* We

---

\a\ father \e\ they \i\ machine \o\ smoke \u\ lunar \an, aŋ\ blanc Fr. \in, iŋ\ ink \on, oŋ, un, uŋ\ soon, confier Fr. \c\ chair \ġ\ machen Ger. \j\ fusion \clusters: bl, gn, kp, hšl, etc...\ b[e]lo ... said with a slight vowel
See more in the Introduction, Guide to Pronunciation

shall have the snow storm against us on our way home > – Bl

a·wa·ke·ya \a-wá-ke-ya\ *va* awake·wa·ya : to make a booth, to spread over *e.g.* with tree branches, to make an awning over, to make a shade — **awakeya·pi** *n* : a booth or shade

a·wa·ke·za \a-wá-ke-za\ *va* awa·wa·keza [fr *a* causative + *wakeza* to cut smoothly] : to cut off smoothly, as a feather for an arrow

a·wa·ki·cin \a-wá-ki-ciŋ\ *va poss of* awacin [fr *awacin* to think] : to give one's attention to

a·wa·kpan \a-wá-kpaŋ\ *va* awa·wa·kpan [fr *a* on + *wakpan* to cut fine, to shred] : to cut or make fine on, as in cutting tobacco

a·wa·ksa \a-wá-ksa\ *va* awa·wa·ksa [fr *a* on + *waksa* to cut off] : to cut off, as a stick, on anything, with a knife — **awaksa·ksa** *v red of* awaksa : to cut off repeatedly

a·wa·kši·ja \a-wá-kši-ja\ *va* awa·wa·kšija [fr *a upon* + *wakšija* to shut up] : to shut upon, as a pocket-knife — **awakšiš** *v contrac of* awakšija : to shut up < ~ *iyeya* It doubled or shut up, as a knife on anything >

a·wa·k'e·za \a-wá-k'e-za\ *va* awa·wa·k'eza : to cut off smooth, to split *e.g.* the feather end of a quill, or to cut off on *e.g.* the ribs of an animal

a·wa·ma·non \a-wá-ma-noŋ\ *v* [fr *manon* to steal] : to steal < *Awamawicanonpi* He stole from them > – B.H.-80.20

a·wa·mna \a-wá-mna\ *va* awa·wa·mna [fr *a* on + *wamna* to rip] : to rip on, as with a knife

a·wa·na·pi·škan·yan \a-wá-na-pi-škaŋ-yaŋ\ *va* : to play with, as babies do with dolls *etc* < *Awanamayapiškanyelo* You played with me (as if I were a play-thing) > – Bl

a·wa·ni·ca \a-wá-ni-ca\ *vn* awa·ma·nica [fr *a* on an account + *wanica* to lack] : to be or become nothing for some reason

a·wa·ni·c'i·gla·ka *or* **awaniglaka** \a-wá-ni-c'i-gla-ka\ *va* : to care for one's health – B.H.194.18 SLB

a·wa·nil \a-wá-nil\ *v contrac of* awanica : in a destroying manner < ~ *iyeya* devastatingly done> – Note: the word is used as an *adv*

a·wa·ni·ye·tu \a-wá-ni-ye-tu\ *v imperf* a·ma·waniyetu [fr *a* on + *waniyetu* winter] : to come winter on one < *Šunkawakan kin tawocola awaniyetupi ca ota t'api* Many of the horses died in dire need when winter came on. *Wana unk'awaniyetupelo* Winter came upon us > – BT Bl

a·wan·glag \a-wáŋ-glag\ *v contrac of* awanglaka : to care for

a·wan·gla·ka \a-wáŋ-gla-ka\ *v poss* awan·wa·glaka [fr *awanyanka* to see to] : to oversee, to take care of one's own

a·wan'·i·c'i·gla·ka \a-wáŋ-i-c'i-gla-ka\ *v* : to beware, to be on one's guard, to look to one's self

a·wan·kal \a-wáŋ-kal\ *adv* : above, overhead

a·wan·ki·ci·yan·ka \a-wáŋ-ki-ci-yaŋ-ka\ *v* awan·we·ciyanka [fr *awanyanka* to oversee] : to watch or oversee for one

a·wan·yang \a-wáŋ-yaŋg\ *v contrac of* awanyanka < ~ *waun* I am keeping watch, ~ *kuwa* He followed him with his eyes, *i.e.* watched closely, or kept watch on him > — **awanyan·gkiya** \a-wáŋ-yaŋ-gki-ya\ *va* awanyan·gwa·kiya : to cause to attend to or oversee – WE

a·wan·yan·ka \a-wáŋ-yaŋ-ka\ *va* awan·bla·ka [fr *a* on + *wanyanka* to see] : to look upon, to see to, to have the oversight of

a·wa·pol \a-wá-pol\ *v contrac of* awapota : to cut up

a·wa·po·ta \a-wá-po-ta\ *va* awa·wa·pota [fr *a* on + *wapota* destroy with a knife] : to cut in pieces on, destroy on anything by cutting with a knife

a·wa·psa·ka \a-wá-psa-ka\ *va* awa·wa·psaka [fr *a* on + *wapsaka* cut off] : to cut off on, as a cord or string, with a knife

a·wa·pšun \a-wá-pšuŋ\ *va* awa·wa·pšun [fr *a* on + *wapšun* to cut asunder] : to unjoint with a knife on anything

a·wa·pta \a-wá-pta\ *va* awa·wa·pta [fr *a* on + *wapta* to trim] : to cut off, as a piece, to cut on, as clothes on a board — **awapte** \a-wá-pte\ *n* : a cutting off from < *can* ~ a cutting board >

a·wa·ski·ca \a-wá-ski-ca\ *va* awa·wa·skica [fr *a* on + *waskica* to press out] : to press out on, as with a knife by cutting

a·wa·ski·ta \a-wá-ski-ta\ *va* awa·wa·skita [fr *a* on + *waskita* press on] : to press upon, as with a knife

a·wa·sku \a-wá-sku\ *va* awa·wa·sku [fr *a* on + *wasku* to pare] : to pare on, as an apple

a·wa·sle·ca \a-wá-sle-ca\ *va* awa·wa·sleca [fr *a* on + *wasleca* to rip or saw] : to split on

a·wa·smin \a-wá-smiŋ\ *va* awa·wa·smin [fr *a* on + *wasmin* shave off] : to cut or shave off close, as meat from bones

a·wa·so \a-wá-so\ *va See* awášo

a·wa·su·i·c'i·ya \a-wá-su-i-c'i-ya\ *v* awasu·mi·c'iya : to make one's self do something, to make a vow, take a pledge *e.g.* to be good or refrain from certain things < *Tuwa tehilapi ca na t'a ca nagi yuhapi na lila yuwakanpi na awasuic'iyapi* Whoever is cherished, when he dies, his soul is kept, consecrated, and pledges are made >

a·wa·ša·ka \a-wá-ša-ka\ *adj* : cheap, easily purchased — **awašaka·la** *adj* : cheap, as are some goods

a·wa·ši·pa \a-wá-ši-pa\ *va* awa·wa·šipa [fr *a* on + *wašipa* to prune] : to cut off or prune upon anything

a·wa·ški·ca \a-wá-ški-ca\ *va* awa·wa·škica [fr *a* on + *waškica* press out] : to press out upon, as by cutting with a knife

a·wa·šku \a-wá-šku\ *va* awa·wa·šku [fr *a* on + *wašku* to cut off] : to cut off upon, as corn from a cob

a·wa·šla \a-wá-šla\ *va* awa·wa·šla [fr *a* on + *wašla* make bare] : to make bare on, to shave off with a knife on, to cut *e.g.* grass in addition to what is already done

a·wa·šlo·ka \a-wá-šlo-ka\ *va* awa·wa·šloka [fr *a* on + *wašloka* to cut a hole] : to cut a hole in or on anything

a·wa·šma \a-wá-šma\ *adj* : deep, as is said of piles or hills of snow, leaves, *etc* – Bl

a·wa·šo *or* **awaso** \a-wá-šo\ *va* awa·wa·šo [fr *a* on + *waso* to cut a strip] : to cut off a string from, to cut a string on anything — **awašo·šo** *or* **awaso·so** *v red of* awaso : to cut strings from, or cut into strings on

a·wa·špa \a-wá-špa\ *va* awa·wa·špa [fr *a* on + *wašpa* to scalp] : to cut off on, as a piece of a stick

a·wa·špan·yan \a-wá-špaŋ-yaŋ\ *va* : to make a feast on account of a person or event < *He awašpanyanpi kte* He will be feasted > – GA

a·wa·špu \a-wá-špu\ *va* awa·wa·špu [fr *a* on + *wašpu* cut off] : to cut up on, to cut in pieces — **awašpu·špu** *v red* : to cut up on repeatedly

a·wa·šte \a-wá-šte\ *vn* a·ma·wašte [fr *a* on or for + *wašte* good] : to be good on or for, to become better than — **awašte·ka** \a-wá-šte-ka\ *vn* : to be good for, to be fit — **awašte·ya** *adv* : well, better than — **awašteya·kel** \a-wá-šte-ya-kel\ *adv* : better, in a better manner < ~ *amayan* I am becoming better >

a·wa·tan'·in·šni \a-wá-taŋ-iŋ-šni\ *adj* : dark, obscure, as in the dusk of evening < ~ *áye lo* It is getting dark > - BT
a·wa·t'e·ca \a-wá-t'e-ca\ *adv* : gently - Cf wawát'eca
a·wa·wa·pte \a-wá-wa-ṗte\ *n* : a cutting board
a·wa·ya·pi·ka \a-wá-ya-ṗi-ḱa\ *vn* awa·bla·pika [fr *a* concerning + *wayapika* fluent] : to be eloquent about anything, to be more eloquent than someone
a·wa·yu·pi·ka \a-wá-yu-ṗi-ḱa\ *vn* awa·blu·pika [fr *a* in *ref* to + *wayupika* skilled] : to be skillful about, to be more skillful than — **awayupi·ya** \a-wá-yu-ṗi-ya\ *adv* : skillfully, well
a·we \a-wé\ *vn* [fr *a* on + *we* bleed] **1** : to bleed on **2** : to become lean, as do cattle in the spring of the year
a·we·tu \a-we-ṫu\ *vn* a·ma·wetu [fr *a* on + *wetu* spring] : to become spring on one < *Tokécala awematu welo* Little by little the springtime came upon me. *Wana unkawetupe lo* We have reached springtime > - BT Bl
a·wi·ca·ka \a-wí-ca-ka\ *vn* awica·wa·ka : to be true on, to tell the truth — **awicake·han** \á-wi-ca-ḱe-haŋ\ *adv* : truly, of a truth — **awicake·ya** \á-wi-ca-ke-ya\ *adv* : truly < *Wanna (nazonspe) iwacu na wanna ~ awapa* I took the axe and gave it a real blow > - Note: this word is used perhaps in *ref* to one person — **awicakeya·han** \á-wi-ca-ḱe-ya-haŋ\ *adv* : of a truth — **awicakeya·kel** \á-wi-ca-ḱe-ya-kel\ *adv* : in earnest - B.H.80.23
a·wi·ca·š'a \a-wí-ca-š'a\ *n* [fr *a* on some account + *aš'a* to shout at] : shouting
a·wi·ca·ya·spu·ya \a-wí-ca-ya-sṗu-ya\ *n* : the itch, itching
[1]**a·win·ye·ya** \a-wíŋ-ye-ya\ *va* [fr *a* on + *in* to wear] : to put on, to wear - *Syn* AUNYEYA B.H.265.3
[2]**a·win·ye·ya** \a-wíŋ-ye-ya\ *adv* [fr *a* for + *winyeya* prepared] : ready for anything < *Hinyetawinyeya yo* Carry it on your shoulder, as one does a gun > - Cf wínyeya
a·win·ye·ya·pi hu \a-wíŋ-ye-ya-pi hù\ *n* : the groundcherry - Cf aúnyeyapi
a·wi·ya·kpa \a-wí-ya-kṗa\ *vn* [fr *a* on + *wiyakpa* shine] : to glisten on anything
a·wi·ya·ya \a-wí-ya-ya\ *v imperf* : not to return before the night, to stay away over-night - Note: the word corresponds perhaps to *ayanpa* BT
a·wi·yu·kcan \a-wí-yu-kcaŋ\ *v* awi·blu·kcan : to form an opinion on < *Šicaya awimayalukcanpi* You all have got a poor opinion of me > - B.H.161.3
a·wo·bla·za \a-wó-bla-za\ *va* awo·wa·blaza : to tear open by shooting on anything
a·wo·ble·ca \a-wó-ble-ca\ *va* awo·wa·bleca : to break in pieces by shooting or punching it — **awoblel** \a-wó-blel\ *v contrac of* awobleca : to break < ~ *iyeya* shatter >
a·wo·blu \a-wó-blu\ *vn* awo·ma·blu : to fill up quickly as a good well does; to blow up on, as by the wind; to bubble up on, as water; to gather about one, as might a multitude — **awoblu·blu** *v red of* awoblu : to be inflating - R
a·wo·can·gle \a-wó-caŋ-gle\ *v* : to whirl and tumble, to ricochet, as might an arrow < ~ *iyeya* to glance suddenly and tumble > - Note: the word is used of an arrow if it strikes its goal then whirls around summersault-like - Bl
a·wo·gla·ka \a-wó-gla-ḱa\ *va* : to appeal to one < *Awociglake* I appealed to you, *Awomayaglake šni* You told me nothing more > - Note: this is an alternate form of *aóglaka* which Cf
a·wo·hle·ca \a-wó-ȟle-ca\ *va* awo·wa·hleca [fr *a* on + *wohleca* to tear through] : to split by shooting or punching on anything
a·wo·hlo·ka \a-wó-ȟlo-ḱa\ *va* awo·wa·hloka [fr *a* on + *wohloka* make a hole] : to punch a hole in one thing on something else
a·wo·hpa \a-wó-ȟṗa\ *va* awo·wa·hpa [fr *a* on + *wohpa* to fell] : to make fall on by shooting
a·wo·ju·ju \a-wó-ju-ju\ *va* awo·wa·juju [fr *a* on + *wojuju* to crush] : to break all up on, to destroy upon
a·wo·ke·ya \a-wó-ḱe-ya\ *n* : a sort of roof < *Tiyobleca kin wazi ~ tipelo* They set up the tent with pine trees around it for a shelter > - LB
a·wo·ke·ya sa·pa \a-wó-ḱe-ya sà-ṗa\ *n* : a buggy
a·wo·kpan \a-wó-kṗaŋ\ *va* awo·wa·kpan [fr *a* on + *wokpan* to grind] : to pound fine on
a·wo·ksa \a-wó-ksa\ *va* awo·wa·ksa : to break off by shooting on, or by punching on
a·wo·ku·ka \a-wó-ḱu-ḱa\ *va* awo·wa·kuka [fr *a* on + *wokuka* to punch] : to shoot or punch to pieces on
a·wo·k'e·ga \a-wó-k'e-ġa\ *va* awo·wa·k'ega [fr *a* on + *wok'ega misfire*] : to misfire on, as in trying to shoot, to snap a gun on — **awok'eh** \a-wó-k'eȟ\ *v contrac of* awok'ega : to misfire on < ~ *iyeya* suddenly to misfire > - Cf awósna *Syn* AWOTO, AWOSKAPA
a·wo·pan \a-wó-paŋ\ *va* awo·wa·pan [fr *a* on + *wopan* pulverize] : to pound fine on, as corn
a·wo·po·ta \a-wó-ṗo-ṫa\ *va* awo·wa·pota [fr *a* on + *wopota* to riddle] : to shoot to pieces on anything
a·wo·psa·ka \a-wó-psa-ḱa\ *va* awo·wa·psaka [fr *a* on + *wopsaka* to break] : to break off, as a cord by shooting on
a·wo·pta \a-wó-pṫa\ *va* awo·wa·pta [fr *a* on + *wopta* to strike as with the end of a stick] : to punch off a piece, striking on anything, as with the end of a stick
a·wo·ptu·ja \a-wó-pṫu-ja\ *va* awo·wa·ptuja [fr *a* on or against + *woptuja* to crack] : to split or crack, as an arrow by shooting against anything, or as a stick in punching — **awoptuš** *v contrac of* awoptuja : to crack
a·wo·ska·pa \a-wó-sḱa-ṗa\ *va* awo·wa·skapa : to misfire on (the hammer not striking the cap rightly) - Cf awosna *Syn* AWOTO, AWOK'EGA
a·wo·sle·ca \a-wó-sle-ca\ *va* awo·wa·sleca [fr *a* on + *wosleca* to split] : to split by shooting upon
a·wo·sna \a-wó-sna\ *va* awo·wa·sna [fr *a* on + *wosna* to ring by shooting at] : to misfire on, as of a gun
a·wo·so·kso·lya \a-wó-so-kso-lya\ *adv red of* awosota : in a way being spent or used up or gone < ~ *unglihunnipelo* We reached home straightway covered with snow (as though everything disappeared, all but the snow) > - Bl
a·wo·so·ta \a-wó-so-ṫa\ *va* awo·wa·sota [fr *a* on + *wosota* use up shooting] : to use all up by shooting upon
a·wo·šla \a-wó-šla\ *va* awo·wa·šla [fr *a* on + *wošla* make bare shooting] : to make bare on by punching
a·wo·šle·ca \a-wó-šle-ca\ *va* awo·wa·šleca [fr *a* on + *wošleca* to split off] : to split off on, as a piece by shooting or punching
a·wo·šlo·ka \a-wó-šlo-ḱa\ *va* awo·wa·šloka [fr *a* on + *wošloka* to blow to clear out] : to shoot off on, to empty the contents of a gun on anything by shooting at
a·wo·šlu·šlul \a-wó-šlu-šlul\ *v contrac of* awošlušluta : to glance off of < ~ *iyayapi* They went glancing off of,

---

\a\ f<u>a</u>ther \e\ th<u>ey</u> \i\ mach<u>i</u>ne \o\ sm<u>o</u>ke \u\ l<u>u</u>nar \an, aŋ\ bl<u>anc</u> Fr. \in, iŋ\ <u>in</u>k \on, oŋ, un, uŋ\ s<u>oo</u>n, c<u>on</u>fier Fr. \c\ <u>ch</u>air \ġ\ ma<u>ch</u>en Ger. \j\ fu<u>s</u>ion \clusters: bl, gn, kp, hšl, etc...\ <u>b</u>[e]lo ... said with a slight vowel
See more in the Introduction, Guide to Pronunciation

as is said when soft snow sticks to a person and gets between the clothes > – M

a·wo·špa \a-wó-šṗa\ *va* awo·wa·špa [fr *a* on + *wošpa* to knock off] : to shoot a piece off on

a·wo·špu \a-wó-šṗu\ *va* awo·wa·špu [fr *a* on + *wošpu* to punch to pieces] : to knock off upon, as anything stuck on, by punching or stooting

a·wo·šta·ka \a-wó-šta-k̇a\ *vn* : to rebound, as an arrow on something hard and not going in – Bl

a·wo·ta·ku·ni·šni \a-wó-ṫa-k̇u-ni-šni\ *va* awo·wa·takunišni [fr *a* on + *wotakunišni* destroy, reduce to pieces] : to destroy by shooting or punching on anything

a·wo·to \a-wó-ṫo\ *va* awo·wa·to : to misfire on, the gun hammer not striking the cap rightly – *Syn* AWOSKAPA, AWOK'EGA Bl

a·wo·t'a \a-wó-t'a\ *va* awo·wa·t'a [fr *a* on + *wot'a* to be surfeited] : to kill on by punching

a·wo·wa·ši e·con \a-wó-wa-ši e-còŋ\ *v* awowaši ecannon : to work on something – B.H.115.7, 183.7, 209.7

a·wo·we·ga \a-wó-we-ġa\ *va* awo·wa·wega [fr *a* on + *wowega* break on falling] : to break on, as by shooting or punching

a·ya \á-ya\ *va* ábla ala amni kte ani kte **1** : to take or carry anything along **2** : to lead or rule < *Itancan kage k'on he itancan na oyate awicaya* He whom he had make chief is chief, and he led his people. *Le taku ca ala hwo?* What is it that you today rule? > **3** *v coll pl* [fr *ya* to go] : they go together < *Na wanna Oglala kin hunh waziyata aya na ake ḣelazatan aya* And some Oglalas were going north, and again they went together back behind the hills > **4** *vn* **a** : to be, to be in or on, to become < *Mašte áya* It is getting warm. *Wanna wicahcala na hunkešni aya* He now became an old and sickly man. *Tohanl oiyokpaz aya ca na wicaša lila waš'aka* Whenever it gets dark a man is very strong. *Wana anpa aya* It is now become daylight. *Lila wa šma aya* The snow has got very deep. *Wanna atan'in ayapi* Now they were getting to appear. *Wanna hunkešni amaye* Now I have got to be sickly > **b** : to be in or have the habit of < *Wotapi amáya* I am in the habit of eating. *Wotapi ayá* He has the habit of eating. *Lila šicaya amáya* I have a really bad habit. >

a·ya·bla·ska \a-yá-bla-sk̇a\ *va* a·bla·blaska [fr *a* on + *yablaska* to flatten] : to make flat with the mouth on anything

a·ya·bla·ya \a-yá-bla-ya\ *va* a·bla·blaya [fr *a* on + *yablaya* to level with the teeth] : to make level on with the teeth

a·ya·bla·za \a-yá-bla-za\ *va* a·bla·blaza [fr *a* on + *yablaza* to tear open] : to tear open on with the teeth

a·ya·ble·ca \a-yá-ble-ca\ *va* a·bla·bleca [fr *a* on + *yableca* crush by biting] : to crush on anything with the teeth

a·ya·blu \a-yá-blu\ *va* a·bla·blu [fr *a* on + *yablu* chew] : to chew fine on

a·ya·bu \a-yá-bu\ *va* a·bla·bu [fr *a* on + *yabu* make a sort of sound] : to growl about

a·ya·ce·ya \a-yá-ce-ya\ *va* a·bla·ceya [fr *a* on account of + *yaceya* to make cry] : to make cry by talking to

a·ya·gna·yan \a-yá-gna-yaŋ\ *va* a·bla·gnayan [fr *a* causative + *yagnayan* to deceive speaking] : deceive with the mouth, to tell a falsehood about

a·ya·go·pa \a-yá-ġo-ṗa\ *va* a·bla·gopa [fr *a* on + *yagopa to intake*] : to suck up on

a·ya·gwa \a-yá-gwa\ *va* a·bla·gwa : to chew, as it were on something soft, with the front teeth — **ayagwa·gwa** *v red of* ayagwa : to chew continually – Bl

a·ya·hin·ta \a-yá-hiŋ-ṫa\ *va* a·bla·hinta [fr *a* on + *yahinta* to brush off] : to brush off with the mouth

a·ya·ḣe·pa \a-yá-ḣe-ṗa\ *va* a·bla·ḣepa [fr *a* on + *yaḣepa* to drink up] : to drink up on

a·ya·hla·ya \a-yá-ḣla-ya\ *va* a·bla·hlaya [fr *a* on + *yahlaya* bite off] : to bite or peel off with the teeth on anything

a·ya·hle·ca \a-yá-ḣle-ca\ *va* a·bla·hleca [fr *a* on + *yahleca* to tear by teeth] : to tear with the teeth on

a·ya·hlo·ka \a-yá-ḣlo-k̇a\ *va* a·bla·hloka [fr *a* on + *yahloka* to gnaw] : to bit a hole in on anything

a·ya·hpa \a-yá-ḣṗa\ *va* a·bla·hpa [fr *a* on + *yahpa* to throw down by mouth] : to throw down with the mouth on anything

a·ya·hpu \a-yá-ḣṗu\ *v* a·bla·hpu [fr *a* on + *yahpu* bite off] : to bite off on, one thing on another

a·ya·hta·ka \a-yá-ḣṫa-k̇a\ *va* [fr *a* on + *yahtaka* to bite and hold] : to bit one thing on another

a·ya·h'u \a-yá-ḣ'u\ *va* a·bla·h'u [fr *a* on + *yah'u* to peel by biting] : to peel off

a·ya·i·c'i·ya \a-yá-i-c'i-ya\ *vn* : to have a habit of doing something < *Cannunpa* ~ He was in the habit of smoking >

a·ya·ji·pa \a-yá-ji-ṗa\ *va* a·bla·jipa : to pinch upon with the teeth

a·ya·kca \a-yá-kca\ *va* a·bla·kca [fr *a* on + *yakca* disentangle] : to untie with the teeth on anything

a·ya·ko·ka \a-yá-ko-k̇a\ *va* a·bla·koka [fr *a* on + *yakoka* rattle the teeth] : to clatter or gnash the teeth on or for anything

a·ya·kpa \a-yá-kṗa\ *va* a·bla·kpa [fr *a* on + *yakpa* bite out] : to bite out on

a·ya·kpan \a-yá-kṗaŋ\ *va* a·bla·kpan [fr *a* on + *yakpan* to chew] : to chew fine on

a·ya·kpi \a-yá-kṗi\ *va* : to crack with the teeth on anything

a·ya·ksa \a-yá-ksa\ *va* a·bla·ksa [fr *a* on + *yaksa* to bite off] : to bite off on

a·ya·kšan \a-yá-kšaŋ\ *va* a·bla·kšan [fr *a* on + *yakšan* to bend by mouth] : to bend with the mouth on

a·ya·kšija \a-yá-kši-ja\ *va* a·bla·kšija [fr *a* on + *yakšija* to double up] : to double up with the teeth on anything — **ayakšiš** *v contrac of* ayakšija : to double up

a·ya·ktan \a-yá-kṫaŋ\ *va* a·bla·ktan [fr *a* on + *yaktan* bend by mouth] : to bend with the mouth on

a·ya·ku·ka \ayá-k̇u-ka\ *va* a·bla·kuka [fr *a* on + *yakuka* to destroy with the teeth] : to bite or tear to pieces with the teeth on anything

a·ya·k'e·ga \a-yá-k'e-ġa\ *va* [fr *a* on + *yak'ega* gnaw] : to gnaw on anything

a·ya·k'e·za \a-yá-k'e-za\ *va* [fr *a* on + *yak'eza* to smoothen] : to make smooth with the teeth on anything

a·ya·k'o·ga \a-yá-k'o-ġa\ *va* [fr *a* on + *yak'oga* to bite off] : to bit or gnaw off on

a·ya·k'o·za \a-yá-k'o-za\ *va* [fr *a* on + *yak'oza* to eat smooth] : to bite off smooth, as do horses eating grass

a·ya·mna \a-yá-mna\ *va* [fr *a* on + *yamna* persuade] : to gain on or for, by speaking

a·yan·bi·c'i·ya \a-yáŋ-bi-c'i-ya\ *v refl of* ayanpa : to keep awake all night (with a purpose in mind) < *Palani kin tipi k'el ayanbmic'iye na wi wankab u kin hehan šunkawakan ota wicawaki yelo* I kept awake all night where the Pawnees lived, and when the sun rose, I then robbed them of many horses > – BT

a·yan·ka \a-yáŋ-k̇a\ *vn* [fr *a* on or for + *yanka* to be] : to be on or for, to be in such a condition

a·yan·pa \a-yáŋ-pa\ *vn* a·ma·yanpa unká·yanpa·pi : to come light on, come morning, *i.e.* to spend a sleepless night, being found sleepless by the dawn < *Awanyanka ayanpa* He spent a sleepless night watching, as for a sick [person. *Ištinme šni amayanpa. Ena hpaya* I spent all night not sleeping. Right here he lay down. *Yunkan ake išnala ~ ške. Hanhepi wocekiye wecaga el amayanpa* Then they say he again spent the night alone. I spent the whole night praying for him > – Cf awíyaya

a·ya·o·gwu \a-yá-o-gwu\ *v* a·bla·ogwu : to do something indistinctly — **ayaogwu·gwu** *v red of* ayaogwu : to do *e.g.* speaking but confusedly, without clarity

a·ya·o·ni·han \a-yá-o-ni-haŋ\ *vn* [fr *a* on or for + *yaonihan* to honor] : to praise on or for

a·ya·o·tan'·in \a-yá-o-taŋ-iŋ\ *va* a·bla·otan'in [fr *a* for + *yaotan'in* proclaim] : to make manifest on or for

a·ya·pe·han \a-yá-pe-haŋ\ *va* a·bla·pehan [fr *a* on + *yapehan* to fold using the teeth] : to fold up with the mouth on anything

a·ya·pe·mni \a-yá-pe-mni\ *va* [fr *a* on + *yapemni* to twist with the mouth] : to twist with the mouth on anything

a·ya·po·ta \a-yá-ṗo-ṫa\ *va* a·bla·pota [fr *a* on + *yapota* to bite in pieces] : to bite in pieces on anything

a·ya·psa·ka \a-yá-psa-ka\ *va* a·bla·psaka [fr *a* on + *yapsaka* to tear] : to bit off *e.g.* a string on something < ~ *icu* He stopped talking and avoided quarrelling, *fig* >

a·ya·pson \a-yá-psoŋ\ *va* a·bla·pson [fr *a* on + *yapson* to spill with the mouth] : to spill with the mouth on anything

a·ya·pšun \a-yá-pšuŋ\ *va* a·bla·pšun [fr *a* on + *yapšun* to pull out] : to pull out by the roots with the mouth on anything — **ayapšun·pšunyan** *adv red of* yapšun : in a manner uprooting < *Itušeš mapaganka hi ~ mayuta yanke* Indeed, he in sparing me teeth was eating me, roots and all (as an old man would say when much food is given to him) > – BS

a·ya·ptan·yan \a-yá-ṗtaŋ-yaŋ\ *va* [fr *a* on + *yaptanyan* to turn over with the mouth] : to turn over on anything with the mouth

a·ya·ptu·ja \a-yá-ṗtu-ja\ *va* [fr *a* on + *yaptuja* to crack with the mouth] : to crack or split with the mouth on anything

a·ya·skab \a-yá-sḱab\ *v contrac of* ayaskapa : to stick on — **ayaska·bton** \a-yá-sḱa-btoŋ\ *va* : to make stick on, as a postage stamp on a letter, to seal, to patch *e.g.* clothes — **ayaskabton·pi** *n* : the lining, as in a coat — **ayaska·bya** *va* : to stick on, to seal

a·ya·ska·pa \a-yá-sḱa-ṗa\ *vn* : to stick to or on, to adhere to

a·ya·sku \a-yá-sḱu\ *va* [fr *a* on + *yasku* to peel off] : to pull off on with the teeth

a·ya·sle·ca \a-yá-sle-ca\ *va* [fr *a* on + *yasleca* to split in biting] : to split with the teeth on anything

a·ya·smin \a-yá-smiŋ\ *va* [fr *a* on + *yasmin* bite off] : to pick off with the teeth or make bare with the teeth on

a·ya·sna \a-yá-sna\ *va* [fr *a* on + *yasna* to ring using the mouth] : to make ring, as a little bell, with the mouth on or over anything

a·ya·so·ta \a-yá-so-ṫa\ *va* a·bla·sota [fr *a* on + *yasota* to eat all up] : to eat up all

a·ya·spa·ya \a-yá-sṗa-ya\ *va* [fr *a* on + *yaspaya* to wet by the mouth] : to wet with the mouth on anything

a·ya·stan·ka \a-yá-sṫaŋ-ḱa\ *va* [fr *a* on + *yastanka* to wet by mouth] : to moisten on anything with the mouth

a·ya·sto \a-yá-sṫo\ *va* [fr *a* on + *yasto* to lick smooth] : to lick smooth on

a·ya·su \a-yá-su\ *va* a·bla·su [fr *a* on + *yasu* to decree] : to condemn on, for, or on account of

a·ya·su·ta \a-yá-su-ṫa\ *va* a·bla·suta [fr *a* causative + *yasuta* establish] : to make firm or establish with the mouth by speaking

a·ya·swa \a-yá-swa\ *va* [fr *a* on + *yaswa* pick to pieces] : to pick to pieces with the teeth on anything – R Bl

a·ya·ša·pa \a-yá-ša-ṗa\ *va* [fr *a* causative + *yašapa* soil with the mouth] : to blacken or defile with the mouth

a·ya·ška·he·ye·la \a-yá-ška-he-ye-la\ *v* : to speak of as near – Note: the word **ayaškatuyela** \a-yá-ška-ṫu-ye-la\ has the same meaning, but both words are of doubtful use

a·ya·ški·ca \a-yá-ški-ca\ *va* a·bla·škica [fr *a* on + *yaškica* to press with the mouth] : to press with the mouth upon, as in chewing tobacco

a·ya·ško·pa \a-yá-ško-ṗa\ *va* [fr *a* on + *yaškopa* to bite out] : to make crooked or twisted by biting on

a·ya·šlu·ta \a-yá-šlu-ṫa\ *va* [fr *a* on + *yašluta* to let slip] : to have the teeth slip on anything

a·ya·šna \a-yá-šna\ *va* a·bla·šna [fr *a* on + *yašna* to miss catching with the mouth] : to miss with the mouth, to let fall on from the mouth

a·ya·špa \a-yá-šṗa\ *va* a·bla·špa [fr *a* on + *yašpa* to bite off] : to bite a piece off on anything

a·ya·špu \a-yá-šṗu\ *va* [fr *a* on + *yašpu* to bite off what is stuck] : to bite off one, as one thing that adheres to another

a·ya·štan \a-yá-šṫaŋ\ *va* a·bla·štan [fr *a* causative + *yaštan* to finish speaking] : to cease from speaking or eating < *Na lecel eya, lowanpi ayaštanpi hehanl.... Oyate kin wanna wicaceya ~. Wanna miš wol ablaštan. Wota ~.* And this is what he said: When they finished singing then... ... The people now finished their crying. I am now finished eating. He finished eating >

a·ya·šu·ja \a-yá-šu-ja\ *va* [fr *a* on + *yašuja* crush] : to bite or mash up on with the teeth

a·ya·ta·ku·ni·šni \a-yá-ṫa-ku-ni-šni\ *va* [fr *a* on + *yatakunišni* destroy by mouth] : to destroy with the mouth on anything

a·ya·tan \a-yá-ṫaŋ\ *va* a·bla·tan [fr *a* for + *yatan* to give praise] : to praise for

a·ya·tan'·in \a-yá-taŋ-iŋ\ *va* a·bla·tan'in [fr *a* for + *yatan'in* to reveal by speaking] : to make manifest upon or for by speaking

a·ya·ti·tan \a-yá-ṫi-ṫaŋ\ *va* [fr *a* on + *yatitan* pull with the teeth] : to pull with the teeth on anything

a·ya·tkan \a-yá-tḱaŋ\ *va* a·bla·tkan [fr *a* on + *yatkan* to drink] : to drink *e.g.* water on or after eating — **ayatkan·yan** *adv* : drinking on or after – B.H.109.12,15

a·ya·to·gya \a-yá-to-gya\ *v* ayato·gwa·ye *or* a·bla·togye [fr *yatokeca* to distinguish] : to conceal, to change in the telling

a·ya·un·ka \a-yá-uŋ-ḱa\ *va* [fr *a* on + *yaunka* to pull down] : to throw down with the mouth on anything

a·ya·wa·ja \a-yá-wa-ja\ *v* a·bla·waja : to bite off on

a·ya·wa·šte \a-yá-wa-šte\ *va* a·bla·wašte [fr *a* on + *yawašte* to bless] : to bless upon

a·ya·we·ga \a-yá-we-ġa\ *va* [fr *a* on + *yawega* to crack

\a\ father \e\ they \i\ machine \o\ smoke \u\ lunar \an, aŋ\ blanc Fr. \in, iŋ\ ink \on, oŋ, un, uŋ\ soon, confier Fr. \c\ chair \ġ\ machen Ger. \j\ fusion \clusters: bl, gn, kp, hšl, etc...\ b[e]lo ... said with a slight vowel **See more in the Introduction, Guide to Pronunciation**

or break by mouth] : to fracture by biting on — **aya·we·hwe·ga** *v red* : to rebuke one < *Okiwaš'ag nišice lo, aho-yasotkamayaye lo, cehupa aciyawehwegin kta yunš, aciyawe-ga ye.* You refuse advice, I am speechless to express my anger over you; if I should rebuke you chatterbox, might I then be pleased to correct you. > – Bl

a·ya·za·mni \a-yá-za-mni\ *va* [fr *yazamni* to lay bare] : to open or uncover with the mouth by speaking

a·ya·zan \a-yá-zaŋ\ *vn* a·ma·yazan [fr *a* on + *yazan* to feel pain] : to be sick on

a·ya·zo·ka \a-yá-zo-ka\ *va* [fr *a* on + *yazoka* to sample] : to suck out on

a·ya·zun·ta \a-yá-zuŋ-ta\ *va* [fr *a* on + *yazunta* to praise falsely] : to connect or weave together, as in manipulating by talk

a·ye·ki·ya \á-ye-ki-ya\ *va* : to make one take along – Bl

a·ye·ya \á-ye-ya\ *va* áye·wa·ya : to make one take along

a·yo·ka \á-yo-ka\ *vn* : to take a look < *Tuwa ~ kin, iyopemiyanpi kte* Let those who taka a look pay me a price > – Bl

a·yo·ka·s'in \á-yo-ka-s'iŋ\ *va* ayo·wa·kas'in : to look into, to peep into – Note: *áokas'in* may exist also — **ayokas'in·yan** *adv* : peeping in upon

a·yo·ko·ka \á-yo-ko-ka\ *vn* : to look many times < *Tuwa ~ yakašigla iyececa yelo* One who just keeps looking is worthy of heavy criticism > – Bl

a·yu·bla·ska \a-yú-bla-ska\ *va* [fr *a* on + *yublaska* to flatten] : to make flat on

a·yu·bla·ya \a-yú-bla-ya\ *va* [fr *a* on + *yublaya* to lay open] : to spread out on, to unroll on

a·yu·bla·za \a-yú-bla-za\ *va* [fr *a* on + *yublaza* to burst open] : to burst open on; to make an incision on

a·yu·ble·ca \a-yú-ble-ca\ *va* a·blu·bleca [fr *a* on + *yubleca* to break or crush] : to break or crush on

a·yu·blu \a-yú-blu\ *va* a·blu·blu [fr *a* on *yublu* pulverize] : to pulverize, to plow, to make mellow on

a·yu·bu \a-yú-bu\ *va* [fr *a* on + *yubu* to drum] : to make a drumming sound on anything

a·yu·can \a-yú-caŋ\ *va* a·blu·can [fr *a* on + *yucan* to sift by shaking] : to sift or shake on or over — **ayucan·can** *va of* yucan : to cause to shake or tremble

a·yu·ce·ka \a-yú-ce-ka\ *va* [fr *a* on + *yuceka* to make stagger] : to make stagger on any place

a·yu·ce·ya \a-yú-ce-ya\ *va* [fr *a* on + *yuceya* to cause one to cry] : to make cry on

a·yu·co *or* **ayucoya** \a-yú-co\ *adv* : well, excellently < ~ kaga Well did he make it. ~ *econ* He did well. > — **a-yucoya·kel** *adv* : well, finished < ~ *econ* He did finishing touches >

a·yu·co·za \a-yú-co-za\ *va* [fr *a* on + *yucoza* to make comfortably warm] : to make warm on any place

a·yu·e·ce·tu \a-yú-e-ce-tu\ *va* [fr *a* on + *yuecetu* to fulfill or correct] : to fulfill or accomplish on

a·yu·e·ci·ya \a-yú-e-ci-ya\ *va* a·blu·eciya [fr *a* on + *yueciya* to turn inside out] : to turn the wrong side out on any thing

a·yu·ga \a-yú-ġa\ *va* a·blu·ga [fr *a* on + *yuga* to husk] : to husk on, as corn

a·yu·gal \a-yú-ġal\ *v contrac of* ayugata : to lift up one's arms < ~ *inajin* He stood up with his arms up-lifted. *Šina wan yuha hinapa na yublaya egnake na ake hanbloglaka na el ~ inajin na ungnahela šina el epazo* He came out with a blanket and laid it out flat, and again he related his vision, also when he stood up with up-lifted arms, and all at once he pointed at him in the blanket > — **ayugal-gata** *v red of* ayugata : to hold out *e.g.* the hand on anything, with the palm downward < *Yunkan le wanbli ca ~ pe el ca piya wanblakin kta* And here it was an eagle that spread out its claws over my head so I might see anew >

a·yu·gan \a-yú-ġaŋ\ *va* [fr *a* on + *yugan* to open] : to open *e.g.* the door on anything

a·yu·ga·pa \a-yú-ġa-pa\ *va* [fr *a* on + *yugapa* to strip off] : to strip or pull off on, as the skin of an animal

a·yu·ga·ta \a-yú-ġa-ta\ *va* a·blu·gata [fr *a* on + *yugata* to raise hand and arm upward] : to open out *e.g.* the hand or hands on anything, to lift one's hands over as in blessing, to lift the hands towards heaven < *Wicaša wan ataya ska igluza ca miwankab hinajin na amayugata* A man dressed entirely in white came and stood over me and imposed hands on me >

a·yu·gi·i·c'i·ya \a-yú-ġi-i-c'i-ya\ *v refl* [fr *ayugin* to slumber] : to make one's self slumber, to take a nap – Bl

a·yu·gin \a-yú-ġiŋ\ *vn* a·blu·gin : to slumber or nap

a·yu·gla \a-yú-gla\ *va* [fr *a* on + *yugla* to untwist] : to uncoil or untwist

a·yu·gmi·gma \a-yú-gmi-gma\ *va* [fr *a* on + *yugmigma* to make round] : to make round on

a·yu·gmu·za \a-yú-gmu-za\ *vn* a·blu·gmuza : to shut the eyes on, as when something gets in them, to shut upon, as the hand upon anything < *Nunge kin ayugmuze* He closed his ears > – D.268

a·yu·gna \a-yú-gna\ *va* [fr *a* on + *yugna* to shake off] : to shell *e.g.* corn, to shake off on *e.g.* fruit

a·yu·gna·yan \a-yú-gna-yaŋ\ *va* [fr *a* on + *yugnayan* to miss grasping] : to miss trying to catch hold of

a·yu·go \a-yú-ġo\ *va* [fr *a* on + *yugo* to mark on] : to make marks on

a·yu·gu·ka \a-yú-ġu-ka\ *va* [fr *a* on + *yuguka* to draw out, to sprain] : to draw out, as a sword from the scabbard, to sprain on

a·yu·gwe·za \a-yú-gwe-za\ *va* [fr *a* on + *yugweza* to roughen] : to make rough on – R Bl

a·yu·ha \a-yú-ha\ *va* a·blu·ha [fr *a* on + *yuha* to have or hold] : to have or possess on, to hold or lift on, to have for

a·yu·hel \a-yú-hel\ *adv* [fr *ayuhete* preoccupied with] : waiting for, constantly < ~ *manke* I am waiting (for them). ~ *makuwapi* They are constantly after me. *Hitunkala wan wote c'un el ~ kuwa* (The boy) kept edging around to where the mouse was gnawing. *Lila wojapi kin le ~ kuwa* He was very curious about this *wójapi*, often staying around > – D.96, 121

a·yu·he·te \a-yú-he-te\ *va* a·blu·hete a·lu·hete : to think of and be intent upon one thing < *Mazašala wanji waglušna inaniptecapelo, cicupi amayaluhetepi eš kolakiciyapi wašte kin hecela aluhetepi* You were prevented dropping a single penny, I restore it to you if you think of me, as you are intent only on a fine friendship >

a·yu·hin·han \a-yú-hiŋ-haŋ\ *v* a·blu·hinhan [fr *yuhinhan* to provoke] : to rake or harrow over

a·yu·hin·ta \a-yú-hiŋ-ta\ *va* [fr *a* on + *yuhinta* to sweep] : to sweep or rake off on

a·yu·ho·ho \a-yú-ho-ho\ *va* [fr *a* on + *yuhoho* to shake] : to shake on, as anything loose

a·yu·ho·mni \a-yú-ho-mni\ *va* a·blu·homni [fr *a* on + *yuhomni* to turn, rotate] : to turn around on, as in bringing a gun round and pointing it at one

a·yu·hun·hun·za \a-yú-huŋ-huŋ-za\ *va* [fr *a* on + *yuhunhunza* to shake *e.g.* a tree] : to shake on or over, as a tree over *e.g.* a blanket

a·yu·ȟa \a-yú-ȟa\ *vn* : to become attached to, stuck to
a·yu·ȟab \a-yú-ȟab\ *adv* : crawling, creeping on or towards < ~ *iyaya* He went on crawling >
a·yu·ȟe·pa \a-yú-ȟe-ṗa\ *vn* [fr *a* on + *yuȟepa* to ladle out] : to absorb on
a·yu·ȟe·ya·ta \a-yú-ȟe-ya-ṫa\ *va* [fr *a* on + *yuȟeyata* to reject] : to push back on or on one side
a·yu·ȟi·ca \a-yú-ȟi-ca\ *va* a·blu·ȟica [fr *a* on + *yugica* to awaken one] : to awaken one upon
a·yu·hla \a-yú-ȟla\ *va* [fr *a* on or over + *yuhla* to ring] : to ring or rattle over
a·yu·hla·gan \a-yú-ȟla-ġaŋ\ *va* [fr *a* on + *yuhlagan* separate from or leave] : to make large upon, to slacken *e.g.* a noose; to leave or forsake — **ayuhlagan·šni** *v* : not to leave or forsake, to be with constantly - R
a·yu·hla·ta \a-yú-ȟla-ṫa\ *va* [fr *a* on + *yuhlata* to scratch] : to scratch or claw on
a·yu·hle·ca \a-yú-ȟle-ca\ *va* a·blu·hleca [fr *a* on + *yuhleca* to rend] : to tear or rend on one, as a garment
a·yu·hlo·ka \a-yú-ȟlo-ḳa\ *va* a·blu·hloka [fr *a* on + *yuhloka* to make a hole] : to make a hole on or open on
a·yu·hmin \a-yú-ȟmiŋ\ *va* [fr *a* on + *yuhmin* to sling] : to sling or throw on one side, as a stone, on anything; to do crookedly, as in writing — **ayuhmin·yan** *adv* : done crookedly
a·yu·hmun \a-yú-ȟmuŋ\ *va* [fr *a* on + *yuhmun* to whizz] : to make buzz on; *fig* to talk incessantly to one while he is still - Bl
a·yu·hpa \a-yú-ȟṗa\ *va* a·blu·hpa [fr *a* on + *yuhpa* to topple] : to throw down on; to shut *e.g.* a window
a·yu·hpu \a-yú-ȟṗu\ *va* [fr *a* on + *yuhpu* to pick off a part] : to make crumble on
a·yu·hta·ta \a-yú-ȟta-ṫa\ *va* a·blu·htata a·wica·blu·htata : to lossen the lines on horses, so as to let them run - Note: the word may also be *ayuohtata*
a·yu·ȟu·ga \a-yú-ȟu-ġa\ *va* [fr *a* on + *yuȟuga* to crack by hand] : to break a hole in upon anything
a·yu·ȟun·ta \a-yú-ȟuŋ-ta\ *va* [fr *a* on + *yuȟunta* to soften by hand] : to make soft on by rubbing
a·yu·h'ol·h'o·ta \a-yú-ȟ'ol-ȟ'o-ta\ *v* : to ride, a vulgar word meaning to get on another's back as steer calves do - Bl
a·yu·h'u \a-yú-ȟ'u\ *va* [fr *a* on + *yuh'u* to peel] : to peel off on, as bark
a·yu·ja·ja \a-yú-ja-ja\ *va* [fr *a* on + *yujaja* to wash] : to wash on
a·yu·ji·pa \a-yú-ji-ṗa\ *va* a·blu·jipa [fr *a* on + *yujipa* to pinch] : to pinch upon with the hand
a·yu·ju·ju \a-yú-ju-ju\ *va* [fr *yujuju* to tear to pieces] : to destroy or take to pieces
a·yu·jun \a-yú-juŋ\ *va* [fr *a* on + *yujun* to pull out] : to pull out by the roots on anything
a·yu·kan \a-yú-kaŋ\ *va* : to go around, to give place to — **ayukan·yan** *adv* : going around - Cf kiyúkan
a·yu·ka·tin \a-yú-ḳa-ṫiŋ\ *va* [fr *a* on + *yukatin* straighten by hand] : to straighten out on with the hand
a·yu·ka·wa \a-yú-ḳa-wa\ *va* [fr *a* on + *yukawa* to open] : to cause to open on, as a wound
a·yu·kca \a-yú-kca\ *v* [fr *a* on + *yukca* to untie] : to untie on, to disentangle on
a·yu·kcan \a-yú-kcaŋ\ *v* : to comprehend - Cf yukcán
a·yu·kin·ca \a-yú-ḳiŋ-ca\ *va* a·blu·kinca : to scrape off on, as in cleaning a fish
a·yu·ki·pab \a-yú-ḳi-ṗab\ *adv* : separately, divided
a·yu·ki·pa·tu·ja \a-yú-ḳi-ṗa-ṫu-ja\ *va* : to cause to stoop or bow down on — **ayukipatu·šya** *va* ayukipatu·šwaya : to make bow down
a·yu·kpan \a-yú-kṗaŋ\ *va* a·blu·kpan [fr *a* on + *yukpan* to grind] : to grind or make fine on
a·yu·ksa \a-yú-ksa\ *va* a·blu·ksa [fr *a* on + *yuksa* break by hand] : to break off on, as limbs or sticks by hand
a·yu·kša \a-yú-kša\ *va* [fr *a* on + *yukša* to fold] : to fold, or bend, or double up on
a·yu·kšan·yan \a-yú-kšaŋ-yaŋ\ *adv* or *v* : to go around out of the way - Bl M,561
a·yu·kši·ja \a-yú-kši-ja\ *va* a·blu·kšija [fr *a* on + *yukšija* to double us] : to bend or double up on; to pull as a trigger of a gun on one
a·yu·ktan \a-yú-kṫaŋ\ *va* [fr *a* on + *yukta* to bend by hand] : to bend around on
a·yu·ku·ka \a-yú-ḳu-ḳa\ *va* [fr *a* on + *yukuka* to make rot] : to make rotten on
a·yu·kyu·ta \a-yú-kyu-ta\ *v red of* ayuta : to look at < *Akiciyukyutapi* They look at one another >
a·yu·k'e·ga \a-yú-k'e-ġa\ *va* a·blu·k'ega [fr *a* on + *yuk'ega* to scratch what itches] : to scratch or scrape the hands on anything - Cf yak'éga
a·yu·k'e·za \a-yú-k'e-za\ *va* [fr *a* on + *yuk'eza* to shear] : to make hard and smooth on, to shave off close, as a mule's mane
a·yu·k'o·ga \a-yú-k'o-ġa\ *va* [fr *a* on + *yuk'oga* roughen] : to scratch up, to make rough
a·yu·k'o·za \a-yú-k'o-za\ *va* [fr *a* on + *yuk'oza* to make smooth] : to make hard and smooth on
a·yul \a-yúl\ *v contrac of* ayuta : to look at < ~ *kuwa* or *yanka* to continue to look at, to stare at >
a·yu·man \a-yú-maŋ\ *va* [fr *a* on + *yuman* to sharpen] : to grind or file off on, to sharpen by grinding
a·yu·mni·ga \a-yú-mni-ġa\ *vn* [fr *a* on + *yumniga* shrink] : to shrink on, to settle on, as does snow < *Lehanl wa ayumnigayelo* or perhaps *ayumniyelo* Snow is now settled and hard, as on a road after traffic > — **ayumnih** \a-yú-mniȟ\ *v contrac of* ayumniga : to settle on < *Wa ~ iyaye* Snow is settling > - Bl
a·yu·mni·mni \a-yú-mni-mni\ *va* : to sprinkle on - B.H.58.6
a·yu·mni·mni·ja \a-yú-mni-mni-ja\ *vn* : to ruffle — *n* : a ruffle
a·yu·na-jin \a-yú-na-jiŋ\ *va* [fr *a* on + *yunajin* raise up] : to cause to stand on
a·yung \a-yúŋg\ *v contrac of* ayunka : to lie on
a·yun·gya \a-yúŋ-gya\ *v* ayun·gwa·ya : to cause to lie on or for — *vn* : to go and spend the night at - P
a·yun·ka \a-yúŋ-ḳa\ *vn* [fr *a* on + *yunka* lie down] : to be or lie on, to lie in wait, to spend the night out for, as for the purpose of killing deer
a·yu·o·hta·lya \a-yú-o-ȟta-lya\ *adv* : in a loose manner
a·yu·o·hta·ta \a-yú-o-ȟta-ṫa\ *v* : to loosen *e.g.* a noose
a·yu·pe·han \a-yú-ṗe-haŋ\ *va* [fr *a* on + *yupehan* to fold] : to fold up on
a·yu·pe·mni \a-yú-ṗe-mni\ *va* [fr *a* on + *yupemni* to twist] : to twist or turn to one side on
a·yu·po·ta \a-yú-po-ṫa\ *va* a·blu·pota [fr *a* on + *yupota* tear to pieces] : to wear out on; to tear to pieces or destroy on < *Ti ayupotapi* They tore the house to pieces >
a·yu·psa·ka \a-yú-psa-ḳa\ *va* [fr *a* on + *yupsaka* pull in

two] : to break or pull in two on anything, as a string
a·yu·pson \a-yú-psoŋ\ *va* [fr *a* on + *yupson* to spill] : to pour out or spill on, as water
a·yu·pšun \a-yú-šuŋ\ *va* [fr *a* on + *yupšun* to pull and break] : to pull out by the roots or to extract, as teeth, on anything
[1]a·yu·pta \a-yú-pta\ *va* a·blu·pta [fr *a* on + *yupta* to cut out] : to cut off on or pare, as a garment
[2]a·yu·pta \a-yū'-pta\ *va* a·blū·pta unka·yūpta·pi a·ci·yūpta a·maya·lūpta : to answer, to speak in return or opposition; to give or grant a thing when asked
a·yu·ptan·ptan \a-yú-ptaŋ-ptaŋ\ *va red* [fr *a* on + *yuptan* to roll] : to turn or roll back and forth — **ayuptan·yan** *va* a·blu·ptanyan : to turn or roll over on
a·yu·ptu·ja \a-yú-ptu-ja\ *v* : to drop *e.g.* an arrow in front of one's self by a slip of the hand while trying to shoot – Bl
a·yu·ske·pa \a-yú-ske-pa\ *va* [fr *a* on + *yuskepa* escape] : to make evaporate on or from
a·yu·ski·ca \a-yú-ski-ca\ *va* [fr *a* on + *yukica* to tighten] : to press down tight on
a·yu·ski·ta \a-yú-ski-ta\ *va* [fr *a* on + *yuskita* to bind] : to bind or bandage on — **ayuski·skita** *v red of* ayuskita : to tie or bandage on – D.220
a·yu·sku \a-yú-sku\ *va* [fr *a* on + *yusku* to peel off] : to peel or pare off on
a·yu·sle·ca \a-yú-sle-ca\ *va* [fr *a* on + *yusleca* to split] : to split on
a·yu·slo·han \a-yú-slo-haŋ\ *va* a·blu·slohan [fr *a* on + *yuslohan* to drag or draw] : to drag or draw along on; *fig* to tempt on by holding out alluring things < *Cah'áyuslohan watokšupi (1826)* In 1826 transportation was done by dragging on ice >
a·yu·slo·he·la·ka \a-yú-slo-he-la-ka\ *v* : to pull off something on, as bark on a tree, or a skin over an animal – Bl
a·yu·slu·ta \a-yú-slu-ta\ *va* [fr *a* on + *yusluta* to extract] : to pull out on
a·yu·sma·ka \a-yú-sma-ka\ *va* [fr *a* on + *yusmaka* to hollow out] : to indent on
a·yu·smin \a-yú-smiŋ\ *va* a·blu·smin [fr *a* on + *yusmin* to pick off] : to make bare
a·yu·sna \a-yú-sna\ *v* [fr *a* on + *yusna* to tinkle] : to ring on or over, as a bell
a·yu·so·ta \a-yú-so-ta\ *va* [fr *a* on + *yusota* spend] : to use up on, to expend on, to spend money on
a·yu·sto \a-yú-sto\ *va* [fr *a* on + *yusto* to smoothen] : to smooth down on, to make smooth, as hair on the head
a·yu·su·ta \a-yú-su-ta\ *va* [fr *a* on + *yusuta* to firm up] : to make firm on
a·yu·swa \a-yú-swa\ *v* : to dig under and make come down on, as sand, to undercut
a·yu·swu \a-yú-swu\ *va* [fr *a* on + *yuswu* to rattle] : to make a rattling noise on or over
a·yu·ša·pa \a-yú-ša-pa\ *va* [fr *a* on + *yušapa* to blacken] : to blacken or defile on anything
a·yu·ši·ca \a-yú-ši-ca\ *va* a·blu·šica [fr *a* on + *yušica* to spoil or ruin] : to spoil or make bad on
a·yu·ški·ca \a-yú-ški-ca\ *va* [fr *a* on + *yuškica* to wring] : to press out on
a·yu·ško·pa \a-yú-ško-pa\ *va* [fr *a* on + *yuškopa* to bend] : to make twist or warp on anything
a·yu·šla \a-yú-šla\ *va* a·blu·šla [fr *a* on + *yušla* to shear] : to shave off on, to cut *e.g.* grass, so as to cover one with < *Amiglušla* I cut on or for myself >
a·yu·šlo·ka \a-yú-šlo-ka\ *va* [fr *a* on + *yušloka* to pull off or out] : to pull out on
a·yu·šlu·šlu·ta \a-yú-šlu-šlu-ta\ *v red of* ayušluta : to make smooth on, or perhaps to sharpen < ~ *yo* Sharpen it > – GA
a·yu·šlu·ta \a-yú-šlu-ta\ *va* [fr *a* on + *yušluta* to slip out] : to draw or slip out on anything
a·yu·šna \a-yú-šna\ *va* [fr *a* on + *yušna* to drop] : to drop or let fall on
a·yu·špa \a-yú-špa\ *va* [fr *a* on + *yušpa* to break of divide] : to break off a piece on
a·yu·špi \a-yú-špi\ *va* [fr *a* on + *yušpi* to pick or gather] : to pick, as fruit on a place
a·yu·špu \a-yú-špu\ *va* [fr *a* on + *yušpu* to pull off] : to pick or pull off on < ~ *amayan welo* He sponges off me, as they would say if one asked them for a little of the same thing again and again > – Bl
a·yu·štan \a-yú-štaŋ\ *va* a·blu·štan : to stop or cease from, to let go, to let alone < *Amayuštan yo* Let me alone > — **ayuštan·kiya** \a-yú-štaŋ-ki-ya\ *va* : to put a check on, to make an end of, to put a stop to
a·yu·šu·ja \a-yú-šu-ja\ *va* : to sliver up on by twisting — **ayušu·šuja** *va red of* ayušuja : to keep meandering
a·yu·š'e \a-yú-š'e\ *va* a·blu·š'e : to make drop on, as medicine — *vn* : to fall in drops on — **ayuš'e·š'e** *v red of* ayuš'e : to drip continually — **ayuš'e·ya** *adv* : in a dripping manner – R B.H.199.2
[1]a·yu·ta \a-yú-ta\ *v* [fr *yúta* to eat] : to eat, eat upon or in addition to
[2]a·yu·ta \a-yú-ta\ *va* a·blu·ta **1** : to look at, look steadily at < *Itancan kin ~ wicaun wo. tunkašila, amayuta yo* The Lord is looking steadily at them. Good Father, look down upon me > **2** : to cultivate, cover with dirt – Note: this word is *archaic*, and not in use. Cf *akáta* which has this meaning
a·yu·ta·ku·ni·šni \a-yú-ta-ku-ni-šni\ *va* [fr *a* on + *yutakunišni* destroy] : to destroy or bring to naught on < *Sam ~ amayaupelo* You all make me more "broke" > – Bl
a·yu·tan \a-yú-taŋ\ *v* a·blu·tan [fr *a* on + *yutan* to touch] : to touch, to put the hand upon
a·yu·tan'·in \a-yú-taŋ-iŋ\ *va* [fr *a* on + *yutan'in* to manifest] : to make manifest upon
a·yu·teb \a-yú-teb\ *v contrac of* ayutepa : to wear off on < ~ *amayan welo* He is beginning to wear me out, as they would say if one asked for a portion of the same thing, *e.g.* food again and again > – Cf ayúšpu Bl
a·yu·te·ca \a-yú-te-ca\ *va* [fr *a* on + *yuteca* to renew] : to renew on
a·yu·te·pa \a-yú-te-pa\ *va* [fr *a* on + *yutepa* to wear off] : to wear off on
a·yu·ti·ca \a-yú-ti-ca\ *va* [fr *a* on + *yutica* to scrape with the hand] : to scrape or paw on
a·yu·ti·pa \a-yú-ti-pa\ *va* [fr *a* on + *yutipa* to cramp up] : to make cramp or draw up on
a·yu·titan \a-yú-ti-taŋ\ *va* a·blu·titan [fr *a* on + *yutitan* to pull or stretch] : to pull on
a·yu·to·gya·kel \a-yú-to-gya-kel\ *adv* : unchanging on, neither less nor more – B.H.68
a·yu·to·kan \a-yú-to-kaŋ\ *va* : to shove away, to put aside a little
a·yu·t'ins \a-yú-t'iŋs\ *v contrac of* ayut'inza : to squeeze < ~ *hingla* He pulled them suddenly tight together > – B.H.78.4
a·yu·t'in·za \a-yú-t'iŋ-za\ *va* : to squeeze
a·yu·un·ka \a-yú-uŋ-ka\ *va* a·blu·unka : to make fall on
a·yu·wa·kan \a-yú-wa-kaŋ\ *va* a·blu·wakan [fr *a* for + *yuwakan* to make holy] : to consecrate, make sacred for

a·yu·wan·kal \a-yú-waŋ-k̇al\ *va* [fr *a* on + *yuwankal* to exalt] : to exalt, make high for

a·yu·wa·šte \a-yú-wa-šte\ *va* [fr *a* on + *yuwašte* to bless] : to make good on or for

a·yu·wa·za \a-yú-wa-za\ *va* a·blu·waza : to scratch off with the fingernail on something – Bl

a·yu·we·ġa \a-yú-we-ġa\ *va* [fr *a* on + *yuwega* to break] : to break down on or fracture

a·yu·wi \a-yú-wi\ *va* [fr *a* on + *yuwi* to wrap] : to wrap on < *Hanpiška sutaya ~ yo, únnihan kih'an hi yelo* Wrap your upper boot firmly, a short time ago a storm arrived > – BT

a·yu·wi·ca·ka \a-yú-wi-ca-ka\ *va* [fr *a* for + *yuwicaka* to convince] : to assure one, to asseverate, affirm positively and earnestly

a·yu·wi·gnu·ni \a-yú-wi-gnu-ni\ *va* [fr *a* on + *yuwignuni* to destroy] : to cause to perish, to destroy on < ~ *mayakuwa* You distract, bewilder, disturb, mix me up in my work >

a·yu·win·ja \a-yú-wiŋ-ja\ *va* [fr *a* on + *yuwinja* to bend down] : to bend down on

a·yu·win·ta \a-yú-wiŋ-ṫa\ *va* [fr *a* on + *yuwinta* to overlay by hand] : to overlay, as wood with gold < *Mazaskazi ayuwintapi* They overlaid it with gold > – B.H.60.23

a·yu·za·mni \a-yú-za-mni\ *va* [fr *a* on + *yuzamni* to uncover] : to open, set open on, as a door; to unroll on

a·yu·ze \a-yú-ze\ *va* [fr *a* on + *yuze* to dip] : to dip or skim out on

a·yu·zi·ca \a-yú-zi-ca\ *va* [fr *a* on + *yuzica* to stretch] : to draw or stretch on

a·zan·gzan·ka \a-záŋ-gzaŋ-ka\ *v* : to whine, as do some babies – Bl

[1]**a·ze** \á-ze\ *vn* : to get aground, to stick fast, as a boat – Note: R gives the word as *azi*

[2]**a·ze** \a-zé\ *n* : the female breast, the cow's udder, *etc*

a·ze·in·kpa \a-zé-iŋ-kṗa\ *n* : the nipple of the breast

a·ze·ki·ya \á-ze-k̇i-ya\ *va* aze·wa·kiya : to run aground or cause to stick – Note: R gives the word as *azikiya*

a·ze·pin·kpa \a-zé-pin-kṗa\ *n* [fr *aze* + *pa* + *inkpa*, breast + top + nipple] : the nipple of the breast, the teat or dug of a cow, *etc*

a·ze·wi·ca·hin·šma \a-zé-wi-ca-hiŋ-šma\ *n* : a certain black caterpillar found in woods – Bl

a·ze·ya \á-ze-ya\ *va* aze·wa·ya [fr *áze* aground + *ya* to go] : to cause to go aground, to run aground, as a boat < *Paohaha yo, ~ un welo* Push the whole thing in, it's going aground > – Note: R gives the word as *aziya* — **aze·ze** \á-ze-ze\ *v red of* aze : to go aground often < ~ *unyanpi* We often go aground > – Note: the word is used also of dead fish, *etc* Bl

a·zi·i·c'i·ya *or* **oziic'iya** \a-zí-i-c'i-ya\ *v refl* : to rest self

a·zi·li·c'i·ya \a-zí-li-c'i-ya\ *v refl* : to apply smoke to one's self, to smoke one's self – D.197

a·zi·lki·ya \a-zí-lk̇i-ya\ *va* azi·lwa·kiya : to burn incense or to make a good smell by burning *e.g.* cedar leaves in certain religious rites or when one is sick

a·zi·lton \a-zí-ltoŋ\ *va* azi·lwa·ton : to make a pleasant smell by burning leaves, to incense < *Na wanna hehanl tatiye topa kin iyuha wazilyapi na azilmatonpi kta* They now at that time will incense all four directions and I shall be incensed >

a·zi·lya \a-zí-lya\ *va* azi·lwa·ya : to incense or smoke something, as meat < *Na cinca k'on ~* And he has had his child incensed >

a·zin \a-zíŋ\ *va* a·wa·zin : to suck or suckle, as does a child or the young of animals — **azin·kiya** \a-zíŋ-k̇i-ya\ *va* azin·wa·kiya : to give suck, suckle, to nurse as a mother her child

a·zi·ta \a-zí-ṫa\ *va* : to smoke upon, to burn *e.g.* incense

a·zi·ya \a-zí-ya\ *va* [fr *a* on + *ziya* make yellow] : to make yellow on anything

a·zu·ya \a-zú-ya\ *va* azu·wa·ya [fr *a* on or against + *zuya* to war upon] : to make war on someone, to go to war against a people – Note: also perhaps *azúyeya*

B

bla \blá\ *v 1st pers singl of* ya : I go — *pref to v* : A *v* commencing with *ya* changes *ya* to *bla* to form the 1st *pers singl*, and to *la* for the 2nd *pers singl* – Cf kabla
bla·bla·ta \bla-blá-ṫa\ *n* : an upland plain – Bl
bla·ȟa *or* **bláġa** \blá-ȟa\ *adj* : broad at one end and tapering
bla·ska *or* **bláske** \bla-sk̇á\ *adj* : flat, as a board — **blaska·ska** \bla-sk̇á-sk̇a\ *adj red* — **blaska·ya** \bla-sk̇a-ya\ *adv* : on the flat side, flat-wise, flatly
bla·ya \blá-ya\ *adj* : level, plain < ~ *hingla* He feels good *fig*, *Wašpanka ognake k'on tanyan iyojuwakiye lo ca ~ mahingle lo* I filled the grub-box well, brimful, so I feel good > – Bl
bla·ye \blá-ye\ *n* : a plain — **blaye·la** \blá-ye-la\ *adj* : plain, level-wise — **blaye·ya** \blá-ye-ya\ *adv* : evenly
bla·ye zi·tka·ta·can hu sto·la \blá-ye zi-tkà-ta-caŋ hu stòla \ *n* : hairy prairie clover; Petalostemum villosum; the pulse family; *casmu hu ȟolȟota* or *waptaya hu ȟolȟota* hairy prairie clover or snakeroot – Note: the roots make a good purge, but the leaves and blossoms are eaten for an inside swelling of the throat – BT Bc #136
bla·za \bla-zá\ *adv* : in strips — **blaza·han** \bla-zá-haŋ\ *part* : ripped open of itself, torn open
ble \blé\ *n* : a lake
ble·ble·ca \ble-blé-ca\ *adj red of* bleca : declining in health — **blebleca·han** \ble-blé-ca-haŋ\ *part red* : broken
ble·ble·sya \ble-blé-sya\ *v red of* blesya : to amuse one < *Bleblesic'iya* He amuses, regales himself >
ble·ca \ble-cá\ *adv* ma·bleca : getting poorer and poorer, as from sickness — **bleca·han** \ble-cá-haŋ\ *part* : broken of itself
ble·ga \blé-ġa\ *n* : the American white pelican, a large whitish water-bird with black spots – Bl FR
ble·i·yo·ka \ble-í-yo-ka\ *n* : little pools alongside a creek filled with weeds –Bl – *Syn* MINIYUŠPALA
ble·i·yo·ško·kpa \ble-í-yo-ško-kpa\ *n* : a buffalo wallow or hole where the water gathers after a rain – Bl
ble·ki·yu·te \ble-kí-yu-ṫe\ *n* [fr *ble* lake + *kiyute* channel] : a channel in a lake, a strait or isthmus
ble·la \blé-la\ *n* : a little lake, a pond
ble·o·ka·hmi \ble-ó-ka-ȟmi\ *n* : a bog or beech
ble·o·ško·kpa \ble-ó-ško-kṗa\ *n* : a lake basin
bles \blés\ *adj contrac of* bleza : clear — **ble·sya** \ble-syá\ *va* ble·swa·ya : to make clear, to cause to recover from stupidity — *adv* : clearly — **blesya·kel** \ble-syá-kel\ *adv* : clearly
ble·ya·ta \ble-yá-ṫa\ *adv* : at the lake
[1]**ble·za** *or more probably* **blóza** \blé-za\ *n* : the loon, the Great Northern Diver – BS
[2]**ble·za** \blé-za\ *adj* ma·bleza : clear, clear-sighted < *Išta ~* He is sober, *Wicableza s'e yalowan k'on aluštan* You stopped your singing as though they were sober *or* You stopped your cheering and singing > – Bl — **ble·ze·la** \blé-ze-la\ *adj* : clear, as water — **bleze·sni** \blé-ze-sni\ *adj* : desperate. reckless < ~ *s'e škan* He acted excitedly – Bl
ble·zi·c'i·ya \blé-zi-c'i-ya\ *v* 1 : to recruit 2 : to restore one's health
bli·he·ca \bli-hé-ca\ *vn* ma·blíheca ni·blíheca un·blíheca·pi : to be lively or active, industrious < *Le on lila niblihecapi kta ca eya, i.e. onwanpi* To this purpose he said that you ought to get about your business i.e. swimming > — *adj* : active, brisk, etc — **blihe·i·c'i·ya** \bli-hé-i-c'i-ya\ *v refl* : to take exercise or exert one's self, to practice — **bli·hel'·heca** \bli-hél'-he-ca\ *v red of* bliheca — **bli·he·ya** \bli-hé-ya\ *va* blihe·wa·ya : to make active or industrious — **blihe·i·c'i·ya** *or* **bli·hí·c'iya** \bli-hé-i-c'i-ya\ *v* blihe·mi·c'iya : to make one's self active, to get busy < *Kola, ~ yo* Friend, get busy > — *adv* : actively, industriously
blo \bló\ *n* 1 : a ridge or range of hills < *Yunkan ~ inamni pte hotonpi* So beyond a hill was the sound of buffalo > Note: this word was heard referring to the Black Hills 2 : an esuculent root eaten by Dakotas, in appearance and taste like the sweet potato, hence potatoes, the opirs tuberosa
blo·a·ka·tan \blo·á-ka-ṫaŋ\ *v* : to cultivate potatoes, i.e. by making hills around the plants
blo·a·li·ya \blo-á-li-ya\ *adv* : along the ridge
blo·blo·ska \blo-bló-sk̇a\ *n* : the trachea tube
blo·gyan·ka \blo-gyáŋ-ka\ *vn* blo·gman·ka blo·gun·yanka·pi : to remain at home when others go hunt
blo·hu \bló-hu\ *n* : potato tops, which are edible
blo·i·pa·tan \blo-í-ṗa-taŋ\ *n* : a potato masher
blo·ka \blo-k̇á\ *n* : the male of animals
blo·ka·sak \blo-k̇á-sak̇\ *n* : a belch
blo·ka·ska \blo-k̇á-sk̇a\ *vi* and *vt* blo·wa·kaska : to hiccup, hiccough < *Blowakaska lo talo watin kte lo* If I should eat fresh meat, I get the hiccups, as a man would say who got the hiccups >
blo·ke·co·kan·yan \blo-k̇é-co-k̇aŋ-yaŋ\ *n* : mid-summer — **bloke·han** *n* : last summer — **bloke·tu** \blo-ke-ṫu\ *n* : this summer, next summer, summer
blo·ki·t'a \bló-ki-t'a\ *v* : to be very tired or weary, as by walking, carrying a load < *Blomakit'e* I go weary, ~ *makal hpaya* He fell on the ground from weariness — **blokit'e·ya** *va* blokit'e·wa·ya : to make tired or weary, to tire out or fatigue – Bl R
blo·pa·hi a·gu·ya·pi \blo-pá-hi a-ġù-ya-ṗi\ *n* : potato-picking bread
blo·ta·hun·ka \blo-ṫá-huŋ-k̇a\ *n* : a chief, the leader of a warparty < *Tuwa wazuya itancan ca he ~. Miyeš le ~ wakte kte* One who leads a warparty is chief. This is the leader I shall kill >
blo·wan·ji·la *or* **blowanjia** \blo-wáŋ-ji-la\ *n* : a divide, a single upland plain between streams; the top of a ridge
blo·za \bló-za\ *n* : the pelican; a large gray-black water bird with a long bill – Note: Dakotas used to make medicine bags of the lower jaw with its sack – Bl
blu \blú\ *adj* : powdered, pulverized, made fine < *aguyapi ~* flour, *maka ~* dust — **blu·blu** \blu-blú\ *adj red of* blu : mellow and dry, as apples or turnips — *v 1st pers singl of* yublu : to mellow: to plough — **blu·yela** \blu-yé-la\ *adv* : in a powdered, pulverized condition < ~ *kaga* She made it into powdered form >
bu \bú\ *vn* : to make a noise, as of a drum that is beaten < *Ptegleška kin ho bupi. Pte ota yelo eyapi, na wanna buwicahingla ca miš kakel inawape, ehanl ekta ewatonwan. Oyate k'on he lila bu anatanpi* The cows were lowing. They say buffalo are many, and when they suddenly bellowed I went out that way; then I took a look at them. The people made quite a noisy attack > — **bubu** \bu-bú\ *v red* : to drum — *adj* : noisy < ~ *s'e* It is as if he were blustery, in a flurry, as is said of one who has a large head, etc., everything large; hence a chunky fellow, *Bubuke s'e* He is like a braggart > — **bubu·ya** \bu-bú-ya\ *adv red of* buya : noisily, with a noise < ~

mani He walked with a flurry > — **bu·ya** *or* **buyela** \bu-yá\ *adv* : noisely, in the manner of one lowing < ~ *mani* He walked noisely, ~ *apa* It hit with a thud > - D.217 — **buya·kel** \bu-yá-ǩel\ *adv* : in a noisy manner — **bu·ye·hci** \bu-yé-ȟci\ *adv* [fr *buya* noisily + *hci* indicating unpleasantness] : with a loud noise — **bu·yel** \bu-yél\ *adv* : noisily < ~ *inyanka* He ran up a storm > — **buye·la** \bu-yé-la\ *adv* : Cf buyá

C

ca

ca \ca\ *n* : a step, the distance one steps < ~ *nihanska* Your pace is long >
— *particle* : inferring a wish, as "Won't you?" It is put at the end of the statement < *Wagni kte, tokša yanka ca* I'll go home; would it not be soon? > - Note: under other circumstances if we omit *ca*, the statement becomes a command, thus < *Takoja, uwa ye, ungni kte, leciya untipi ca, eya* She said: Grandchild, come, let us go home, here is where we live >
— *def art* : It is employed to indicate a descriptive relative clause < *Yunkan wikoškalaka wan lila winyan wašte ca wanyanke. Yunkan winawizi wan catkayatanhan ikoyaka ca wanyanke. Yunkan itazipa wan lila hanska ca yuha najin na wahinkpe wan lila ȟanska ca nakun iyagna. Lila kahmi wan wašte ca el etipi. Tuwa okihi kinhan he šunkawakan ca wicak'u kte. Yunkan taku k'eya cikcik'ala ca el okala. Wamakaškan hutopa ca cic'upelo* A woman who was a very fine woman saw a young woman. She saw her a jealous person who stayed to her left. She stood holding a very long bow as well as a very long arrow along with it. They set up camp in a river bend that was convenient. One who could do so would give them a horse. Some things quite small she sowed in the ground. I give you a four-footed animal >
— *conj* : therefore - It is put at the beginning of a sentence < *Otan'in hecel slolwaya ca tanyan oblaka. Anpa ca wicocanlwakan yelo; na hanhepi ca otuyacin utapelo. Ate u maši ca wanna lena ociciyakapi kta ca wahi ca tanyan nah'on po. Hehé, le annpetu kin lowacin ca ina weksuye lo* So in this way I knew it to be clear, therefore I spoke well. In daylight therefore, they were cowards and at night then they fired off guns uselessly. Father told me to come, so I have come and shall tell you these things, therefore listen carefully. Alas, today I am hungry, therfore I recall my mother >
— *adv conj* : because, that is why; when - It is put at the end of a sentence < *Niš eya ecamon ca* Since I did you too did it (i.e. You are more than busy), *nišnala ca* when you are alone, *Siiyotiyewakiye tuweni makagege šni ca* I had trouble with my feet because no one mended my shoes, *Ho, ca eyaš wakokipe wicunkicapi kte lo. Itancan mitawa eyayapi na tuktel eunpapi tan'in šni ca hece* Well now, on the other hand, I was afraid we would put a demand on them. My Lord has been taken away and that is why it is not clear where they put him. > - B.H.271.7, 282.7

ca·e·gle \ca-é-gle\ *vn* cae·wa·gle [fr *ca* a step + *egle* to set] : to step, take a step — **caegle·pi** *n* : a step, steps < ~ *wanji* one step measure, a yard >

ca·ga \cá-ġa\ *n* : ice — *vn* : to freeze, become ice < ~ *s'e* icy > — **caga·ta** \cá-ġa-ta\ *adv* : at or on the ice

ca·ga·ta·ki·ya \cá-ġa-ta-ki-ya\ *adv* : out on the ice, i.e. iceward

ca·gla·wa \cá-gla-wa\ *v* : to count steps of one's own < ~ *maunnipi* We proceed slowly > - Bl

ca·gle *or* **caegle** \ca-glé\ *vn* : to step < ~ *ake zaptan* fifteen paces > — **cagle·pi** \ca-glé-pi\ *n* : a step, a pace < *câglegle iyutapi s'e mâni* to make big steps as though taking a measure of something > - D.99

ca·go·ti \cá-ġo-ti\ *n* : an ice-house

ca·gu \ca-ġú\ *n* **1** : the lungs **2** : lights

ca·gu·gu·ka·ca \ca-ġú-ġu-ka-ca\ *n* : a fool - Note: this can be said also: *witko oh'an s'a* as though acting crazy - Bc

ca·gu·ka \ca-ġú-ka\ *n* : a fool

ca·hal \ċa-hál\ *idiom interj* : "I don't quite know" - Note: the word is used by men and women - *Syn* TÓKCEL

ca han·ska·ska ma·ni \ca háŋ-ska-ska mà-ni\ *v express* : to take long steps in walking - Bl

ca·he·ce *or* **ca he·ce** \ca-hé-ce\ *conj* : the reason for, because

cah \cáȟ\ *n contrac of* caga : ice < ~ *kul* under the ice, ~ *iyaya* The ice is gone, ~ *hiyaya* ice floating

ca·ȟa·gle·ye·la \ca-ȟá-gle-ye-la\ *adv* : standing on ice seen from afar

ca·hka·hlo·ka \ca-ȟǩá-ȟlo-ǩa\ *v* : to make a hole in the ice by striking it, as for watering horses

ca·hka·t'a \ca-ȟǩá-t'a\ *v* ca·hma·kat'a : to be stunned or killed by a fall on ice, or by a block of ice falling on one

ca·hka·zo \ca-ȟǩá-zo\ *v* ca·hwa·kazo : to slide in one's moccasins on ice - Bl

ca·hli \ca-ȟlí\ *n* : charcoal, coal; gunpowder —
~ *iyúhpe* a large coal shovel
~ *óp'iye* a powder magazine
~ *oyúha* a powder flask, a powder horn
~ *šniyánpi* coal that yields little heat - RH
~ *típi* a powder house
~ *tokšú* a coal bucket

ca·hna·ju·ju \ca-ȟná-ju-ju\ *v* : to break up, as does ice in a river during the spring thaw

ca·ȟo·ta \ca-ȟó-ta\ *n* : ashes

ca·hsu \ca-ȟsú\ *n* [fr *cah* ice + *su* little droplets of ice : smooth or bare ice

ca·hswu·la \ca-ȟswú-la\ *n* : thin ice, ice not yet frozen solidly - Bl Ch

ca·ȟu·wa·ya·zan *also* **hohpá·wayazan** \ca-ȟú-wa-ya-zaŋ\ *n* : tuberculosis of the lungs - Note: this disease did not exist among tribes in the early days

ca·h'a·gla·pe·pe·ya \ca-ȟ'á-gla-ṗe-ṗe-ya\ *v* cah'aglapepe·wa·ya : to make a flat stone skip or bound over the ice, as boys might do - Bl

ca·h'a·li \ca-ȟ'á-li\ *v* cah'a·wa·li : to walk on ice

ca·h'i·ca·zo \ca-ȟ'í-ča-zo\ *n* : ice skates < ~ *kic'un nainš wec'un* He or I skate or slide on the ice >

ca·h'ku·wa \ca-ȟ'kú-wa\ *v* : to draw blocks of ice by means of a stick – Bl

Ca·h'o·ti·la \cá-ȟ'o-ti-la\ *n* : the name for Eskimo

ca·h'o·wan·ca·ya \ca-ȟ'ó-waŋ-ca-ya\ *adv* : ice all over < *Maka owancaya* ~ All over the Earth ice is everywhere, *Makoce ataya* ~ *Ice is entirely over the country* > – Bl

ca·h'o·wa·ta \ca-ȟ'ó-wa-ta\ *adv* : transparent, as newly formed ice

ca·h'pan·pan·la \ca-ȟ'paŋ-paŋ-la\ *v* : the ice to be soft < ~ *unkiyutapi kte* We should try how soft the ice is > – Bl

ca·h'su·ta \ca-ȟ'sú-ta\ *v* : the ice to be thick – Bl

ca·i·a \ca-i-a\ *v* ca·wa·ia [fr *ceya* to cry + *ia* to talk] : to talk crying – Note: the word is perhaps not used alone < ~ *iyaye* He talked crying, and not while walking, or He went to crying, ~ *iblable* I went away babbling >

ca·i·c'i·pa \ca-í-c'i-pa\ *v refl of* capa : to thrust into one's self; *fig* to eat one's self full < *Hehehe, camic'ipehce lo* What do you know, I've eaten myself full > – Bl

ca·i·gla·t'e \ca-í-gla-t'e\ *v* ca·mi·glat'e ca·ún·glat'a·pi : to sob, as one does before crying – Note: this word is used for the old word: *cowáiglazan* to shiver – WL

ca·je \ca-jé\ *n* : a name < *micáje* my name >

ca·je·glal \ca-jé-glal\ *v contrac of* cajeglata : to call one's self < ~ *hipi* They came identitfying themselves > – B.H.245.5 — **cajegla·ta** \ca-jé-gla-ṫa\ *v poss of* cajeyata : to call one's own by name < *cajéwaglata* I called my own by name >

ca·je·i·gla·ta \ca-jé-i-gla-ṫa\ *v refl* cajé·mi·glata : to speak one's own name

ca·je·ka·ga \ca-jé-ka-ġa\ *v* cajé·wa·kaga : to name or make a name for < *Na itazipa na wahinkpe hena ecel* ~ So he made a name for the bow and arrow

ca·je·ki·ya·ta \ca-jé-k̇i-ya-ṫa\ *v* cajé·wa·kiyata : to mention or speak of anything to one – B.H.168.24

ca·je·yal \ca-jé-yal\ *v* *contrac of* cajeyata : calling by name < ~ *wicakicopi* They invited them calling them by name >

ca·je·ya·ta \ca-jé-ya-ṫa\ *va* caje·bla·ta : to name, call by name; to speak the name of a person or thing; to mention by name

ca·ju·no·ka·po·ja \ca-jú-no-k̇a-ṗo-ja\ *n* : pneumonia

ca·ka \ca-k̇á\ *n* mi·cáka : the palate, roof of the mouth; gills

ca·ka·la \ca-k̇á-la\ *n* : a liar < *Nicákala* You're a liar >

ca·ka·po \ca-k̇á-po\ *n* : piarrhoea of the teeth

ca·ka·zi·gsi·tki·ya \cá-k̇a-zi-gsi-tki-ya\ *vn* : to make large strides < ~ *inyanka* He ran dragging his legs (as a tired horse) > – Bl SLB

ca·ki·ci·pa \ca-k̇í-ci-pa\ *v* ca·wé·cipa [fr *capa* to pierce] : to pierce for another e.g. a boil

ca·ki·pa \ca-k̇í-pa\ *v poss* ce·wa·kipa [fr *capa* to pierce] : to pierce one's own, as a boil by opening it with a pin

ca·ki·pa·tan \ca-k̇í-pa-taŋ\ *n* : a riding bridle bit

ca·ki·yu·hla·te \ca-k̇í-yu-ȟla-ṫe\ *n* [fr *caka* palate + *yuhlata* to scratch or claw] : a fish hook

ca·ksi \ca-ksí\ *n* : a wolf – *arch* yak'é – HM

ca·k'i·gla·ska \ca-k'i-gla-sk̇a\ *v* cak'í·wa·glaska : to eat up quickly the little one has, to get just a taste of it < ~ *iyeya* He suddenly devoured it > – Cf icáska — *n* salts

ca·lo·ki·mna \ca-ló-k̇i-mna\ *adv* [fr *cana* when + *okimna* gives an odor] : between the knees – Note: this is a vulgar word – R Bl — *Syn* CALOTAHENA

ca·mni *or* **canmni** \ca-mní\ *n* : a sprout, germ, or bud — **camni uya** \ca-mní uyà\ *v* : to sprout

[1]**ca·na** \cá-na\ *adv* : when, at such a time as – Note: the word always starts the sentence which may begin with *tuwa, tohan, tuktel*, etc, or with any word. The *na* of *cana* may be left out, or *hehanl* added < *Na hanhepi, cana hehanl inajin yapi* And whenever it was night, they went to rise and stand > – Gramm.148.1b

[2]**ca·na** \ca-ná\ *n* : the groin, inside the thigh; the gland in the groin

[1]**can** \caŋ\ *n* : a tree, trees; wood < ~ *stánka* wet wood

[2]**can** *or* **canna, cana** \caŋ, cáŋ-na, cá-na\ *adv conj* : when, or whenever (indefinite) – Note: the word follows *tohanl*, etc, and the dependent part of the sentence. When the word refers to indefinite time "whenever", it has the coordinate meaning "then". Cf above under *cána* – B.H.60.9, 23; 61a.7; 256.10

[3]**can** \caŋ\ *n* : a night or day – Note: the numeral *adj* always precedes the word < *Letan topa can ungni kte* Four days from now we shall go home >

can'·a·gna·ka·pi \caŋ-á-gna-ka-ṗi\ *n* : a bier < ~ *kin eupapi* They placed the bier – D.13

can'·a·kan·smi·yan \caŋ-á-k̇aŋ-smi-yaŋ\ *v* : to prune trees

can'·a·kan·yan·ka·pi \caŋ-á-k̇aŋ-yaŋ-k̇a-ṗi\ *n* : chair, bench, pew; anything to sit on

can'·a·ki·t'a \caŋ-á-k̇i-t'a\ *adv* : with much brush, many trees

can'·a·li·pi \caŋ-á-li-ṗi\ *n* : stairs; a ladder

can'·a·pa·kan *or* **can'apakinyan** \caŋ-á-ṗa-k̇an\ *n* : a crooked branch, one that grows or hangs downwards, such as children use for swinging

can·bla·ska \caŋ-blá-ska\ *n* : a board, or boards < ~ *zibzipela* shingles >

can·can \caŋ-cáŋ\ *vn* ma·cancan : to shake, tremble < *Lila macancan* I am badly shaking > — **cancan·kiya** \caŋ-cáŋ-k̇i-ya\ *va* cancan·wa·kiya : to make tremble or shake — **cancan·pi** \caŋ-caŋ-ṗi\ *n* : the ague, trembling — **cancan·s'e** \caŋ-cáŋ-s'e\ *adv* : hastily, quickly < ~ *škan* to act hastily, ~ *iyaya* to go away hurriedly > — **cancan·ya** \caŋ-cáŋ-ya\ *va* cancan·wa·ya : to make tremble or shake, as by telling bad news — **cancan·yan** *adv* : tremblingly, with the jitters

can·ce·ga \cáŋ-ce-ġa\ *n* : a drum < ~ *ha* a drumhead or hide, ~ *icábu* a drumstick

can·cin·ška \caŋ-cíŋ-ška\ *n* : a wooden spoon

can·gla·kin·yan \caŋ-glá-k̇iŋ-yaŋ\ *n* : a neckyoke

can·gle·gle \caŋ-glé-gle\ *n* : the scattering of trees < *Wakpala* ~ *un hel* There in a creek are trees here and there > – R — **canglegle·ka** \caŋ-glé-gle-k̇a\ *n* : trees that stand here and there

can·gle·pi \caŋ-glé-pi\ *n* : cord-wood; firewood < ~ *iyutapi wanji* a cord of wood >

can·gle·ška \caŋ-glé-šk̇a\ *n* : a hoop, a wheel — *adj* : round, wheel-like < *tahuka* ~ *a round sieve*, ~ *kute* to shoot through a hoop while it is rolling, a game >

can·gu·gu \caŋ-ġú-ġu\ *n* : a firebrand

can·gu·gu·ya gle·ška \cáŋ-ġu-ġù-ya gle-šk̇á\ *n* : the twohee or chewink – Note: its call: *kijó kijó kijó* and a smack with the lips – FR

can·gu·gu·ya ša \cáŋ-ġu-ġù-ya ša\ *n* : the wood thrush < ~ *s'e iwašicunlah* It's as if he were talkative as a wood thrush (as is said of a very talkative person), ~ *s'e ia can oegle wanil lila ie lo* Whenever he speaks he speaks as if a wood thrush, really without saying a sentence i.e. anything, as one might say when a person talked unduly long > – Bl

can·ha \caŋ-há\ *n* : bark, i.e. of a tree

can·han·ka·yan·ka·pi \caŋ-háŋ-ka-yaŋ-ka-pi\ *n* : a chair
can·han·pa \cáŋ-haŋ-p̣a\ *n* : shoes < ~ *iškahu hanska* boots >
can·han·pi \caŋ-háŋ-p̣i\ *n* : sugar, i.e. tree sap < ~ *blu* powdered sugar >
can·han·po·ka·ge \caŋ-háŋ-po-ka-ġe\ *n* : a shoemaker shop
can·ha·pa·šlo·tan·han \caŋ-há-p̣a-šlo-taŋ-haŋ\ *v* : to take off the inner bark of trees, e.g. maple, with a spoon to eat the sap and done in the spring when sap is rising - Bl
can·ha·san \caŋ-há-saŋ\ *n* **1** : the sugar of maple **2** : the white birch
can·ha·ša \caŋ-há-ša\ *n* : cinnamon bark
can·ha·šlo·tan·he *or* **canhašlotanhan** \caŋ-há-šlo-taŋ-he\ *vn* : to peel off, as bark does from some trees < *Canhašlotantanhešni k'el canšaša kaksa unyin kte lo* Let us go cut red willows whose bark hasn't been peeling > - Bl SLB
can·ha·yu·šlo·tan·han \caŋ-há-yu-šlò-taŋ-haŋ\ *v* : to take the inner bark of cottonwood trees, which was used for horse feed, and good as oats, they say - Bl
can·he·ya·la \caŋ-hé-ya-la\ *n* : the wren < ~ *išnala itancan* the wren, the "lone chief", a title given because of its loud voice
can·hu·ta \caŋ-hú-ṭa\ *n* : a stump of a tree < ~ *iyukse* a stump-puller
can·hu·te \cáŋ-hu-te\ *n* : the name of one of the four marks put on the hoop of the *painyankapi* (a hoop game)
can·hu·tkan \caŋ-hú-tkaŋ\ *n* : the root of a tree < ~ *sapa* a nigger head > - Note: the roots of a weed which are very tough, making roads over-rough and plowing an especially hard job
can·hu·ya·pi \cáŋ-hu-ya-pi\ *n* : crutches: stilts
can·ȟa·ȟa·ke \caŋ-ȟá-ȟa-ḳe\ *n* : a vertebra; a buffalo's hump — **canȟaȟake·ton** \caŋ-ȟá-ȟa-ke-ṫoŋ\ *vn* : to be humped, having a hump
can·ȟa·ka \caŋ-ȟá-ḳa\ *n* [fr *can* tree + *ȟaka* thick with branches] : brush; a bush
can·hcan·ga \caŋ-ȟcáŋ-ġa\ *vn red of* yacanga : to crunch or make a noise in chewing anything hard, as corn < *Blacánġa* I crunched it in my mouth > — *adj* : gristly, i.e. cartilaginous
can·ȟin·yan \caŋ-ȟíŋ-yan\ *va* canȟin·wa·ya : to be attached to one wishing always to be with him as fast friends, a loving couple < *He canȟinmaye šni* He is closely attached to me > -BD
can·hlo·gan \caŋ-ȟló-ġaŋ\ *n* : hollow stalks, weeds - Note: *waptaye* is a weed
~ **apé pepe** an herb resembling forget-me-nots; any white flowered species of oreocarya and related plants. Oreocarya perennis. Borage family - Bl #290
~ **ha šlušluta** white-flowered beard-tongue. Peatstemon albidus. Figwort family - Bl #167
~ **hu can swula** *or* **maka canšin hu** prairie pink - Note: *~ hu can swula un he tuktektel yuke this* prairie pink is in some places
~ **huhlá** *or* **húhla** evening primrose, night willow, herb oenothera biennis. Evening primrose family; its seeds are aromatic - BT #134
~ **hu pteptécela** low erigeron, daisy. Erigeron pumilus. The composite family - Bl #169
~ **hu sansán** prairie evening primrose, white-stemmed evening primrose. Oenothera pallida. Evening primrose family - Bl #190
~ **hutkán hanská** lance-leaved psoralea, tumble-weed. Psoralea lanceolata. Pulse family - Bl #211
~ **hutkan sabsapa** *also* **šunktawote** a species of buckwheat family. Erigeron flavum; it is found in the Bad Lands of South Dakota - Bl #109
~ **hu wanjila** *or* **hitunkala nakpala** the mouse-ear-everlasting. Antennaria apricate grane. Composite family. *Also* the hairy rock cress. Arabis hirsuta. Mustard family. *Also* the wing-angled loose strife. Lythrum alatum. The loose-strife family - Bl #177, 158
~ **hlahla** sharp-leaved beard tongue. Peatstemon acuminatus. Figwort family - RT #157
~ **inkpa gmigmela** lamb's quarters, pig weed. Chenopodium paganum. The goosefoot family - Note: the name belongs rather to the amaranth family - BT #37
~ **ištawiyaowicahpaya** froelichia. Froelichia floridanus. The amaranth family - Bl #103
~ **kcankcanla** the western Venus' looking glass. specularia leptocarpa. Blue bell family - Bl #248
~ **mah'áwanglakela** prairie lily, showy mentzelia. Mentzelia decapetala; the blossom opens at night - Bl #212
~ **maka ayublaya** *also* **tal'agnake** the stiff or hard-leaved golden-rod - BT #25
~ **makatola** *also* **perjuta wahinheya ipiye** purple fritillaria. Fritillaria atropurpurea. Lily family; it is pulverized and made into a salve and rubbed on scrophulous swellings - Bl #12
~ **nablaga** *or* **atášošapicana nablaga** the large-flowered yellow flax *or* the low lupine. Lupinus pusillus. Pulse family - Bl #179, 213
~ **ókiheton** the hairy umbrellawort. Oxybaphus hirsutus. *Also* sweet hallionia, the four-o'clock family - Cf huokiha hanskaska - K #202
~ **onzipakinte** ragweed - Cf canhlogan waštemna - Bl #21
~ **ówicak'o** winged pigweed. Cycloloma atriplici folium, the goosefoot family - Bl #42
~ **pa** the western wall-flower, yellow flox. Erysimum asperrimum, the mustard family. *Also* hu ȟolȟota, so named for its bitter taste after chewing leaves or root. *Also* wahcázi šícamna, for its disagreeable odor when the flowers wither away - Bl HH LB #150
~ **panpanla** spiderwort, widow's *or* Jobś tears. Tradescantia reflexa, the spiderwort family. *Also* hanp'inatapi, the blue flowers were used to paint moccasins and provided a blue, jelly-like paint -Bl #197
~ **panšpanjela** the great ragweed, horseweed, bitterweed. Ambrosia trifida - Cf yamnumnuga iyececa
~ **pepela** dense-flowered aster, white wreath aster. Aster hebecladus, the composite family - Bl #135
~ **sotka** prairie ragwort. Senecio platteasis, composite family - Bl #299
~ **suta** slender delea, Riddell's senecio. Senecio Riddellii, composite family - Cf heȟaka tapejuta - Bl DS #90, 219
~ **škiškita** cut-leaved nightshore. Solanum triflorum, nightshore family, the berries are used for a stomachache - BT #44
~ **wabluška hu** tumble mustard. Sisymbrium altissimum, its leaves are fringed, leg-like - Bl #65
~ **wahcazi panšpanjela** tufted loose-strife. Nauburgia thyrsiflora, the primose family - #173
~ **wakalyapi** golden coreopsis, the garden tickseed. Core-

\a\ father \e\ they \i\ machine \o\ smoke \u\ lunar \an, aŋ\ blanc Fr. \in, iŋ\ ink \on oŋ & un uŋ\ soon & confier Fr. \c\ chair \ġ\ machen Ger. \j\ fusion *clusters* bl, gn, kp, hšl, etc... \ b^e^lo ... said with a slight vowel
See more in the Introduction, Guide to Pronunciation

opsis tinctoria, the composite family, it is used for drinking tea that is very good – BS Bl #170
~ **wapoštan** *also* **payá pejuta** Geyer's spurge. Euphosbia geyeri, the spurge family, it is so called for it was used as a protection for the head – Bl BT #24
~ **wapoštan kagapi** Pursh's plantain. Plantago purshii, the Plantain family – Cf canhlogan wapoštan – K #200
~ **waštemna** ragweed, Roman wormwood, hogweed, wild pansy. Ambrosia alatior, the composite family. *Also* poipiye, as a tea from the leaves it is applied to swellings. Also *canhlogan onzipakinte, unma inkpa gmigmela,* i.e. a toilet weed, one round end. *Also* Canadian worm-wood. Artemisis canadensis, composite family, it has a pleasant odor. A tea is made from the root and is good for one who cannot urinate or whose bowels do not move, or for a woman who is finding it difficult to give birth to her child. The roots when pulverized make a perfume, and it is said when as such it is put on a sleep-ing man's face he will not wake up at night, and thus people can steal his horses – BT Bl #21 LE #47
~ **waštemna iyececa** Canada fleabane. Erigeron canadensis, the composite family – Bl #174
~ **wicagnaške** buttercup. Ranunculus cardiophyllus, the crowfoot family, so-called because the basal leaves look somewhat like thos of the gooseberry bush – HH #260
can·hlo·gu \caŋ-ȟló-ġu\ *n* : weeds, pigweeds, or any large weed
can·hlo·hsna·sna·la \caŋ-ȟló-ȟsna-sna-la\ *n* : alum root – Cf wahpe t'aga – BT #267
can·hloh su·ta \caŋ-ȟlóȟ sù-ta\ *n* : the woody sort of weeds – KE
can·hloh šlu·šlu·ta \caŋ-ȟlóȟ šlu-šlù-ta\ *n* : tall slick weeds – KE
can·ȟo·tka \caŋ-ȟó-tka\ *n* : a small straight shrub < ~ *hu* a stick of such a shrub, used for making arrows > — *adj* : frosty, covered with frost – Note: the bush referred to grows on the Platte River – Bl
can·hpan \caŋ-ȟpáŋ\ *n* : the American loot, mud hen, pied billed grebe. < *Zintkala kin ble k'el unpi, pasu skaskapi* The bird lives on lakes, their beaks are quite white > – Note: when a woman has been slandering and then goes away, they say of her: *Eyin na ~ ca miniali inyanke s'e ke gle* She says it and loot-like she scurries over the water on her way home — **canhpan ṗezí** *n* : king of loots — **canhpan ṗizí** *n* : gall of the loot – Bl B
can·hpi \cáŋ-ȟṗi\ *n* : a war club, a tomahawk
can·ȟu·na·ptan \caŋ-ȟú-na-ptan\ *n* : a group or bunch of bushes, as plum or buffalo berry bushes; or the side of a hill covered with trees – R
can i·ca·hpe hu \caŋ i-cá-ȟpe hu\ *n* : the tall nettle with stinging hairs. The roots are used for a tea taken for pains in the stomach. Urtica gracilis – BT #148
can'·i·ca·ji·pe \caŋ-í-ca-ji-pe\ *n* : a drawing knife or a plane
can'·i·ca·kan \caŋ-í-ca-kaŋ\ *n* [fr *can* wood + *kakan* hew] : an adze or any instrument used in hewing, adzing wood
can'·i·ca·šle·ce \caŋ-í-ca-šle-ce\ *n* [fr *can* wood + *kašleca* split by striking] : something to split wood with, a wedge
can'·i·ci·pa·we·ge *or* **can'icipawega** \caŋ-í-ci-pa-we-ġe\ *n* : a cross < ~ *aic'icaga po* Make the sign of the cross on yourselves > – Note: *cansuspeca,* the Dakota word B.H.-263.1 Phill.3.18
can'·i·co·ga \caŋ-í-co-ġa\ *n* : drift-wood
can'·i·c'i·k'oŋ·pa \caŋ-í-c'i-k'oŋ-ṗa\ *n* : two boards connected and serving for a cradle on which little babies were carried – Bl
can'·i·na·sle·lye \caŋ-í-na-sle-lye\ *n* : a saw-mill
can'·in·kpa \cáŋ-iŋ-kpa\ *n* : the ends of branches, buds
can'·in·kpa·ta \cáŋ-iŋ-kpa-ṫa\ *adv* : at the top of the tree – Bl
can'·i·pa·ji·pa \caŋ-í-ṗa-ji-ṗa\ *n* : a plane
can'·i·pa·ki·ze \caŋ-í-ṗa-ki-ze\ *n* [fr *can* wood + *pakiza* make creak by rubbing] : a violin; a piano
can'·i·pa·me \caŋ-í-ṗa-me\ *n* [fr *can* wood + *paman* to file] : a wood-rasp
can'·i·pa·ptan·ye \caŋ í-ṗa-ptaŋ-ye\ *n* : a lever
can'·i·sku·ye *or* **canwiskuye** \caŋ-í-sku-ye\ *n* : the honeysuckle sweet wood, a sweet-smelling shrub – Note: the connotation of it as a grocery is doubtful – R
can'·i·ta·zi·pa \caŋ-í-ta-zi-ṗa\ *n* : the aspen, perhaps
can'·i·to·kšu \caŋ-í-ṫo-kšu\ *n* : a mechanism replacing the wagon box, as a rack of a sort, for hauling wood
can'·i·wa·kse \caŋ-í-wa-kse\ *n* : a saw, a hand cross-cut saw
can'·i·ya·wi ci·k'a·la \caŋ-í-ya-wi cì-k'a-la\ *n* : the carrion flower or Jacob's ladder, otherwise known as *zuzeca tawote ptapta ikoyaka* what a snake eats sticks together – Bl #140
can'·i·yu·ho·mni ci·sci·la *or* **can'íyumni** \caŋ-í-yu-ho-mni cì-sci-la\ *n* : a gimlet, i.e. a tool to bore holes
can'·i·yu·hlo·ke \caŋ-í-yu-ȟlo-ke\ *n* : an auger, a gimlet or drill
can'·i·yu·ȟu·ge \caŋ-í-yu-ȟu-ġe\ *v* : to tie a rope to the top of a dry tree, and thus pull it down – Bl
can'·i·yu·ji·pe \caŋ-í-yu-ji-ṗe\ *n* : a drawing knife
can'·i·yu·ki·ze *or* **canyúkizaṗi** \caŋ-í-yu-ki-ze\ *n* : an organ or piano
can'·i·yu·me \caŋ-í-yu-me\ *n* : a rasp
can'·i·yu·mni \caŋ-í-yu-mni\ *n* : an auger for the boring of holes
can'·i·yu·slo·han \caŋ-í-yu-slo-haŋ\ *n* : a sled < *can'iyuslohe* a wood sled
can'·i·yu·ta·pi \caŋ-í-yu-ṫa-ṗi\ *n* : a cord of wood
can'·i·yu·wi *or* **can'iyuwiwi** \caŋ-í-yu-wi\ *n* : curly wood, a vine < ~ *cik'ala* the carrion flower > – Cf zuzeca tawote ptapta ikoyaka — **can'iyuwi iyececa** *n* : the virginia creeper, the woodbine, the false grape, the American ivy or the five-leaved ivy. Quinque folia psedera, the vine family, the roots are bad, *hutkan kin peta s'elececa* the root is like fire – Bl #198 — **can'iyuwi ówicak'o** *or* **ówicak'o hu** *n* : the western virginia bower, *skaska nahca* it is quite white indeed. Clema-tis ligusticifolia, the crowfoot family – Note: at times in the past when people had a headache, they made a tea of the roots. Horses eat the leaves – WE Bc Bw BT
can·ja·ta \caŋ-já-ṫa\ *n* : a forked stick
can·ka \caŋ-ká\ *n* **1** : the back or spine **2** : a fire-steel
can·ka·ga \caŋ-ká-ġa\ *n* : a log, any large piece of wood lying out < ~ *wan akan iyotaka* He sat on a log >
can·ka·gi·ca \caŋ-ká-ġi-ca\ *n* : touchwood, spunk or punk, i.e. soft, half-rotten wood – HM Bl
can·ka·gi·ȟa·ȟa \caŋ-ká-ġi-ȟa-ȟa\ *n* : shavings < ~ *wakagin kte* I shall whittle the stick so as to have shaving curls intermittently – Bl KE
can·ka·ho·hu \caŋ-ká-ho-hu\ *n* : the spine
can·ka·ho·ton \caŋ-ká-ho-toŋ\ *v* : to make wood ring; to play the harp, and such like < ~ *wayapika* He is skilled with the harp or guitar, etc, *cankahotonla* a zither > – B.H. 85.20
can·ka·hu \caŋ-ká-hu\ *n* [fr *canka* the back + *hu* bone] :

the backbone, spine, the vertebrae
can·ka·h'on·pa \caŋ-ká-ȟ'oŋ-ṗa\ *va* canka·hwa·onpa [fr *cankaga* log + *onpa* to place] : to lay or place logs to walk on, to bridge — **cankah'onpapi** \caŋ-ká-ȟ'oŋ-ṗa-ṗi\ *n* : a log laid across, a bridge < ~ *wan yunke lo* He laid a bridge across it >
can·ka·hpa·hpa \caŋ-ká-ȟpa-ȟpa\ *n* : shingles
can·ka·h'u \caŋ-ká-ȟ'u\ *v* : to peel the bark off a tree - Bl
can·ka·i·ci·o·pte·ya \cáŋ-ka-i-ci-yò-pte-ya\ *adv* : with the wood crossed
can·ka·i·le \caŋ-ká-i-le\ *v* : to make wood blaze by rubbing — **cankaile·pi** *n* : a match
can·ka·ki·za \caŋ-ká-ki-za\ *vn* : to swing and creak, as trees do in the wind
can·kal·ya·pi \caŋ-kál-ya-ṗi\ *n* : a tea made of a certain bark
can·kan·ka·pi \cáŋ-kaŋ-kà-pi\ *n* : a chair
can ka·p'o·je·la \cáŋ ka-p'ó-je-la\ *n* : a tree whose "wood is light"
can·ka·sku·sku \cáŋ-ka-sku-sku\ *v* cán·wa·kaskusku : to hew a log
can·ka·slu·te \caŋ-ká-slu-ṫe\ *n* : the spinal marrow
can·ka·ška \caŋ-ká-ška\ *v* can·wá·kaška [fr *can* wood + *kaška* to bind] : to bind wood together, to inclose with wood, to fence in < ~ *yanka* He sat bound — **canka-ška·pi** *n* : a fence, a fortification
can·ka·ško·kpa·pi \caŋ-ká-ško-kpa-ṗi\ *n* [fr *can* wood + *kaškopa* to strike crooked] : wood hewed out, a trough - B.H.46.9
can·ka·ta·pta·pa \caŋ-ká-ṫa-pta-ṗa\ *v* can·wa·kataptapa : to hew logs; to cut with a knife so the chips fly off - Bl
can·ka·zon·ta·pi *or* **cankazuntapi** \caŋ-ká-zoŋ-ta-pi\ *n* [fr *can* wood + *kazonta* or *kazunta* to weave] : thin sticks or reeds woven together so they can be rolled up and used for bed curtains; but it is more probable they were used for bed matting - Bl
can·ke *or* **cankeš** \caŋ-ké\ *adv* or *adv conj* : and so, and then, hence, therefore - Note: it BEGINS a sentence; but if it ENDS a sentence it acts as does *ca* : that is why - B.H.83.2; 136.10
can·ke·la·ka \caŋ-ké-la-ka\ *adv conj* : therefore
can·ki·ca·ton \caŋ-kí-ca-toŋ\ *v* : to play the harp for one - B.H.85.22
can·kin·ci·pa·gmi·yan \caŋ-kíŋ-ci-ṗa-gmi-yaŋ\ *n* : a wagon without its box
can·ko·gna·ke \caŋ-kó-gna-ke\ *n* : a case for a fire-steel - CF canka *and* ognake
can·ko·han \caŋ-kó-haŋ\ *n* : the parts along the backbone — **cankohan·šin** *n* : the fat along the back and sides
can·ko·o·pa \caŋ-kó-o-pa\ *n* : the back as of man, i.e. in the very middle
can·ko·ye *or* **cankuye** \caŋ-kó-ye\ *n* : a row, as of corn etc. - R
can·ko·ye·ton *or* **cankuyeton** \caŋ-kó-ye-toŋ\ *v* : to be in rows or furrows — **cankoyeton·ton** *v red* : to make rows or furrows, as does a plough — **cankoyetonton·-yan** *adv* : in rows or furrows - R
can·ko·za \caŋ-kó-za\ *v* can·wá·koza : to swing a stick to hit < *Pajoke s'e cankoze* He whips with rather the left hand > - Bl
can·kpe \caŋ-kṗé\ *n* : the knees or the tibia bone < ~ *hu* the knee bone — **cankpe·ška** *adv* [fr *cankpe* knees + *ška* they say *or perhaps* and yet] : on the knees < ~ *makagle najin* He knelt down - Note: *maka* earth, *agle* to set on, hence to kneel. Variants are: *caškémakagle, caškékamagle, caškékpamakagle* - Cf D.99 note 5
can·ksa \caŋ-ksá\ *n* : a policeman's club — **canksayuha** *n* : a policeman < ~ *kin le icu wo. Hehan wicahpi hinhpaya ~ wan icu* Take this club. Then when he took the club his star fell >
can·ksi·ksi·ze·ca \caŋ-ksí-ksi-ze-ca\ *adj* : saucy, morose
can·ku \caŋ-kú\ *n* : a road, way, path < ~ *iyutapi* a mile, ~ *icage* a road scraper >
can·ku·ji·pa \caŋ-kú-ji-ṗa\ *n* : the name of the stick or sticks (two) that are placed under the bedding on both sides (lengthwise) so as to prevent the bedding from spreading out too far on the ground or floor
can·ku·na·ptan \caŋ-kú-na-ptaŋ\ *n* : a slanting road, as one along a hill where one side is lower than the other - Bl B
can·ku·te \caŋ-kú-te\ *vn* : to shoot at a target
can·ku·ya \caŋ-kú-ya\ *v* canku·wa·ya : to make for a road, to have for a road - D.77
can·k'in·ya \caŋ-k'iŋ-ya\ *v* : to go to get firewood - D.66
can·la·ki·sni *also* **canlásni** \caŋ-lá-ki-sni\ *vn* canla·ma·-sni : to recover from anger or sorrow, to become composed - B.H.88.26 — **canlasnikiya** \caŋ-lá-sni-ki-ya\ *vn* : to recover from sorrow etc. < ~ *omanipi* They took a trip, recovering from their sorrow > - Bl
can·la·sni·yan \caŋ-lá-sni-yaŋ\ *va* canlasni·wa·ya : to cause to recover from sorrow - B
can·la·wa·kpan *also* **canlí awákpan** *or* **canlíawakpan** \caŋ-lá-wa-kṗaŋ\ *n* [fr *canli* tobacco + *awakpan* cut fine] : a board on which to cut and mix tobacco
can·le \caŋ-lé\ *va* can·wá·le : to gather firewood - D.12
can·li \caŋ-lí\ *n* : tobacco < ~ *ai, ahi, or yuška* to make peace - Note: in making peace, tobacco was brought and wrapped up in a blanket. When it was accepted and opened (yušká), the proposition was accepted - Bl
can·li a·wa·kpan \caŋ-lí a-wá-kṗaŋ\ *n* - Cf canlawakpan
can·li·ca·spe·ki·ton \caŋ-lí-ca-ṡpe-ki-ṫoŋ\ *v* : to satisfy one's self, as by eating - Bl — **canlicaspeki·ya** *v* canli-caspe·wa·kiya : to satisfy one - Cf canlicaspeya
can·li·ca·spe·ya \caŋl-í-ca-ṡpe-ya\ *va* canlicaspe·wa·ya : to satisfy the desires of the heart, whether good or bad
can·li·e·han·tan ka·ga·pi he·ca \caŋ-lí-ehaŋ-ṫaŋ kà-ġa-ṗi hé-ca\ *n* : a ready-made cigarette
can·li·i·ca·hi·ye \caŋ-lí-i-ca-hi-ye\ *n* : a root grown in the Rocky Mountains, which when mixed with tobacco makes it aromatic, and no snakes will stay where they scent it. When medicated with tobacco and inhaled, it is good for bronchitis; and when boiled and rubbed on a sore face, it relieves
can·li i·yo·pe-mni \caŋ-lí i-yò-ṗe-mni\ *n* : a cigarette
can·li·mna \caŋl-í-mna\ *v* : to be pleased with, satisfied with, to judge one satisfactory or up to standard < *Taku ecamon kin oyasin canlimayamna šni yelo* You judge me not up to standard in everything I do (as a man would say to his dissatisfied wife, *Canlicimna šni* I am not satisfied with you > - Bl LHB
can·li o·pe·mni·pi he·ca \caŋ-lí o-ṗè-mni-pi hé-ca\ *n* : a cigarette made when needed
can·li ya·ta·pi \caŋ-lí ya-tà-pi\ *n* : chewing tobacco
can·li·yu·gmun \caŋ-lí-yu-gmuŋ\ *v* : to twist tobacco, to

\a\ father \e\ they \i\ machine \o\ smoke \u\ lunar \an, aŋ\ blanc Fr. \in, iŋ\ ink \on oŋ & un uŋ\ soon & confier Fr. \c\ chair \ġ\ machen Ger. \j\ fusion \clusters bl, gn, kp, hšl, etc... \ b^e^lo ... said with a slight vowel
See more in the Introduction, Guide to Pronunciation

make cigars — **canlíyugmùn·pi** \ *n* : cigars < ~ *úŋpapi* a cigar >

can·li·yu·kpan·pi \caŋ-lí-yu-kp̄àŋ-p̄i\ *n* : a fine smoking tobacco

canl·ni·yan \caŋl-ní-yan\ *vn* canl·ma·niyan : to be angry, i.e. at women

can·lo·gu \caŋ-ló-ġu\ *n* : cigar ashes, tobacco remanents; dregs - Cf ogu - WL

can·lo·gu·ha \caŋ-ló-ġu-ha\ *n* [fr *canli* tobacco + *yuha* to hold] : a tobacco pouch

can·lo·pe \caŋ-ló-p̄e\ *adj* perhaps canló·ma·pe : glad, grateful for a favor done - B — **canlope·ya** *adv* : gladly < *Taku iyuškinyan econpi he ~ kapi* They gladly took it that they did it cheerfully > — *va* : to oblige one, to be good to one, to cheer one up - HC

can·lo·wan·ki·ya \cáŋ-lo-waŋ-k̄i-ya\ *v* [fr *can* wood + *lowankiya* make music or song] : to play on an instrument, as on a violin — **canlowakiya·pi** *n* : a musical box, an organ

canl·wa·hte·šni \caŋl-wá-ȟte-šni\ *adj* : looking forbidding or morose; displeased, as with somebody's visit - WE

canl·wan·ka \caŋl-wáŋ-ka\ *vn* canlwan·ma·ka canlwan·un·ka·pi : to be a coward — **canlwanka·ic'iya** *v refl* : to be afraid of everything, to fear for one's self, as in believing one's self sick - WE — **canlwanka·la** *adv* : cowardly — **canlwan·kan** *adj* or *n* [fr *cante* heart + *wan* behold + *kan* worn out] : a coward; weak-hearted < *Tuwa ~ ca lena el etonwan ca našlute lo* One who is weak-hearted, when he beholds this, goes down sliding > — **canlwanka·pi** *n* : cowardice

canl·wa·šte \caŋl-wá-šte\ *vn* : to be happy, contented — **canlwašte·ya** *va* canlwašte·wa·ya : to cheer one up, to make one feel good - *Syn* CANTOPEYA — *adj* : of good heart < ~ *un* to be encouraging > - B.H.88.24

can·lyu·ha \caŋl-yú-ha\ *vn* can·blu·ha : to be good-natured — **canlyuha·haka** *n* : one who is good-natured, kind-hearted habitually — **canlyuhaha·pi** *n* : good-heartedness — **canlyuha·ka** *n* : one who performed an act of kindness — **canlyuha·ya** *va* : to make one kindhearted or good-hearted < *Canlyúha·mayayapelo* You people made me kindhearted > - WE

can·mi·hce \caŋ-mí-ȟce\ *v 1st pers singl* [fr *awacanmi* I trust or believe + *hce* intensive sign] : I want it very badly - obsol BS

can·mi·lo·ka·tan·pi \caŋ-mí-lo-ka-taŋ-pi\ *n* : a weapon consisting of a wooden handle with two or three knife blades fixed in it towards one end along the center and used for striking by the Lakotas in war

can·na·han \cáŋ-na-haŋ\ *adv conj* : when, at such a time as < *Wetu ~ maga agli* In the spring of the year, the geese return >

can·na·hme·la k'el \caŋ-ná-ȟme-la k'el\ *n* perhaps : a place north of the *Wašun Wakpa* Hollow River where a bunch of trees is so located that one does not notice them until he is close by - Bl

can·na·ko *or* **akó** \caŋ-ná-k̄o\ *interj* : Welcome! - *Syn* WASTANMI which is *arch*

can·na·kpa \caŋ-ná-kp̄a\ *n* : a mushroom growing on trees

can·na·ksa \caŋ-ná-ksa\ *n* : a war club

can·na·kse·yu·ha \caŋ-ná-kse-yu-ha\ *n* : a policeman, one who carries a club

can·na·po·pa wi \caŋ-ná-po-p̄a\ *n* : the month of February, the moon when trees crack by reason of the cold - RH

can·na·slel·ya \caŋ-ná-slel-ya\ *va* cannaslel·wa·ya : to saw logs

can·ni·yan \caŋ-ní-yaŋ\ *vn* can·ma·niyan can'·un·niyanpi : to be angry at women, a word used of men only

can·ni·ye·ki·ci·ya·pi \caŋ-ní-ye-k̄i-ci-yà-pi\ *v* : they are angry with one another, husband and wife — **canniye·kiya** *va* canniye·wa·kiya : to make a man angry with his wife

can·ni·ye·ya \caŋ-ní-ye-ya\ *va* canniye·wa·ya: to be angry at or offended by a woman, as is said by men only

can·no·pa \caŋ-nó-pa\ *n* [fr *canna* when + *opa* perhaps i.e. a draw or ravine] : the crotch between the legs - Note: the word seems to be doubtful in meaning and origin. LHB suggests the word to be: *cannúnpa*

can·num·ki·ya \caŋ-núm-k̄i-ya\ *va* : to cause to smoke

can·nun·ga hu pte·pta·ce·la \caŋ-núŋ-ġa hu pte-pté-ce-la\ *n* : goldenrod. Solidago, the composite family - Bl

can·nun·ge \caŋ-núŋ-ġe\ *n* : a bunch, a lump on a tree, i.e. a certain type of mushroom - Cf nunge

[1]**can·nun·pa** \caŋ-núŋ-pa\ *n* : a pipe
~ *pahin iyapehanpi* a pipe with porcupine quill-work wrapped about the stem, such as is used in the *hunkalowanpi* ceremony
~ *iglaye* a wire pipe-stem cleaner - Cf glaya - BD
~ *p̄ahú* the bowl of a pipe
~ *sinte* the pipe stem
~ *wosláta* the original Indian pipe, consisting of a straight hollow deer bone - GA

[2]**can·nun·pa** \cáŋ-nun-pa\ *vn* cannun·mún·pa cannunnún·pa cannún·k'un·pa·pi [fr *canli* tobacco + *unpa* to smoke] : to smoke tobacco

can·nunp a·šlo·ye wa·kši·ca \caŋ-núnp a-šlò-ye wa-kšíca\ *n* : a tin plate, i.e. *maza wakšica* - Cf ašloya - *arch*

can·nunp ȟa·ka \caŋ-núnp ȟa-ka\ *n* : a rough pipe - Note: it is not a real pipe and is thought to be the *hunkata cannunpa* used in the *hunka lowanpi* ceremony - Bl

can'·o·gna·ka \caŋ-ó-gna-k̄a\ *n* : a wooden box < *canwognaka* a coffin >

can'·o·han·zi *or* **óhanziglepi** \caŋ-ó-haŋ-zi\ *n* : a bowery or the shade of trees, perhaps < *Ake ~ el iyotaka* He sat again in the shade of the trees >

can'·o·hlo·ge·ca *also* **can'óȟloka** \caŋ-ó-ȟlo-ġe·ca\ *n* : a hollow tree

can'·o·i·a·li *or* **oíali** \caŋ-ó-i-a-li\ *n* : a ladder

can'·o·ka·ji·pe \caŋ-ó-k̄a-ji-p̄e\ *n* : shavings

can'·o·ka·špu *also* **can'ókp̄an** *or* **can'ókpanla**\caŋ-ó-k̄a-špu\ *n* : chips - B.H.116.6

can'·o·na·kpan \caŋ-ó-na-kp̄aŋ\ *n* : sawdust

can'·o·ni·gla·t'a \cáŋ-o-ni-gla-t'a\ *n* : a breathless or awesome forest - *obsolete* - Note: *Taku keša wašakala kapi* They considered anything to be easy

can'·o·pa·ji·pe \caŋ-ó-p̄a-ji-p̄e\ *n* : shavings

can'·o·pa·mna \caŋ-ó-p̄a-mna\ *n* : sprouts growing up around a stump

can'·o·pa·tin·yan·pi s'e \cáŋ-o-p̄a-ṫiŋ-yaŋ-pi s'e\ *express* : tired of walking < ~ *wamatuka welo* I am exhausted as it were gotten stiff (walking) in the woods >

can'·o·pi·ye \caŋ-ó-p̄i-ye\ *n* : a storage trunk

can'·o·ptu·ȟa \caŋ-ó-ptu-ȟa\ *n* [perhaps fr *ópte* leavings] : small wood i.e. chips, kindling wood - Cf *yuptá*, that has the meaning: to cut out or off

can'·o·t'o·za \caŋ-ó-t'o-za\ *n* [fr *can* wood + *t'oza* smoothened] : a rounded stick

can'·o·wan·ca·ya \cáŋ-o-waŋ-ca-ya\ *n* : wood all over, i.e. a forest

can'·o·wo·ju \cáŋ-o-wo-ju\ *n* : an orchard < ~ *wašte* The Paradise >
can·pa \caŋ-pá\ *n* : choke-cherries
can·pa·gmi·ya i·pa·tan \caŋ-ṗá-gmi-ya i-pà-taŋ\ *n* : a spoke
can·pá·gmi·ya tàn·ka *n* : a lumber wagon
can·pa·gmi·yan·pi \caŋ-ṗá-gmi-yaŋ-pi\ *n* : a wagon; a chariot – in Dakota: *canpagmigma*
~ *cankáhu* the underboard, as of a wagon, connecting front and hind wheels
~ *cík'ala* a buggy without a top
~ *huǧáǧeca* a wagon without the box, just the gear and wheels – Cf huȟáka *or* húh'a
~ *hugmíyan* a wagon wheel
~ *hugmíyan hu nùnpa* a two-wheeled cart, a dray
~ *ihúpa* a wagon pole
~ *ipáhunhunze* a wagon spring
~ *oáye* a train
~ *škokpá* a wagon box
can·pa·gmi·yu·ti·tan \caŋ-ṗá-gmi-yu-ṫi-ṫaŋ\ *n* : a single or double tree; a whipple tree
can·pa·hu \caŋ-pá-hu\ *n* : a choke-cherry bush — **canpahu càn** *n* : the choke-cherry tree. Prunus Virginiana, the rose family; the limbs were used for the making of arrows – Bl #160
can·pa·ji·pa \cáŋ-ṗa-ji-pa\ *v* : to shave or plane wood
can·pa·ji·pe \caŋ-pá-ji-ṗe\ *n* : a carpenter
can·pa·ka·kan \caŋ-pá-ḱa-kaŋ\ *n* : the pigeon cherry
can·pa·ka·ski \caŋ-pá-ḱa-ški\ *n* : cherries that are mashed and dried, a favorite dish among the Dakotas
can·pa·ki·za \caŋ-pá-ki-za\ *vn* : to play on the violin
can·pa·ki·za·pi \caŋ-pá-ki-za-pi\ *n* : a piano
can·pa·ksa \caŋ-pá-ksa\ *n* [fr *can* tree + *paksa* break, *or* perhaps *canpa* choke-cherry + *ksa* separated] : a stump
can·pa·sa·pa \caŋ-pá-sà-pa wi\ *n* : the moon when the choke-cherries are black, i.e. July
can·pa·sla·ta \caŋ-ṗá-sla-ṫa\ *v* : to set posts — **canpaslata iyòk'e** *n* : a posthole digger
can·pa·sla·te \caŋ-ṗá-sla-ṫe\ *n* : a post or stake
can·pa·su on ki·ci·o·pi \caŋ-pá-su oŋ ki-cì-o-pi\ *n* : a mischievous pastime: children would eat a handfull of cherries and then sling one kernel after the other by means of a springy little stick, and so striking the bare skin of others. They held the kernel to that part of the stick that is drawn backward – Bl
can·pa·ta \caŋ-pá-ṫa\ *n* : a round bunch of bushes or trees – *archaic* – Cf *páta, canwita,* and *cunšoke* dense woods
can·pa·za na·jin \caŋ-ṗá-za nàjiŋ\ *n* : a tree – *obsolete* – Bl
can pe·jú·ta ci·k'a·la \caŋ pe-jú-ta cìk'ala\ *n* : mint, the strong form is taken from the root of the bush for making medicine for headaches; the weak form is taken from the leaves to make tea beverage, a common drink – KE
can·pe·pe \caŋ-ṗé-ṗe\ *n* : brambles – B.H.263.10
can·pe·ti·pi·ye \caŋ-ṗé-ti-ṗi-ye\ *n* : a stick a woman might use as a poker to move coals back into the fire < *winuhcala tacanpetipiye* an old lady's fire poker > – Note: *tacanpilipiye* seems to be an alternate pronunciation
can·pi·ško \cáŋ-ṗi-šḱo\ *n* : the American red start, a little bird living in the woods – Bl
can·psis un \caŋ-psís uŋ\ *v* : to be sad because neglected < *Ungnahahciš* ~ *onayajinke* You took refuge possibly for being sad from neglect > – Bl
can·pšun·ka \caŋ-pšúŋ-ka\ *n* : a block; large trees
can·pta·ya·han \caŋ-ptá-ya-haŋ\ *n* : the bush
can·sa·ka·la \caŋ-sá-ka-la\ *n* : a twig, switch, rod < *Oyasin* ~ *wicak'u* He gave them all a switch >
can·sa·pa \caŋ-sá-pa\ *n* : the walnut tree
can·sa·ta \caŋ-sá-te\ *n* : a horizontal stick on which they hang up meat to dry – ***Syn*** SATGLAKINYAN
can·ska \caŋ-ská\ *n* : a mulberry tree
can·ski·ske·ya \caŋ-skí-ske-ya\ *v* : to grow up in thinkets and undergrowth < *Canskiskemayayelo* or *Canteokic'unmayayelo* or *Canteokihišnimayayelo* I am all confused > – WE SLB
can·smna \caŋ-smná\ *adj* : unpleasant to the taste, as the flesh of wolves, otters, etc – R Bl
can·su \caŋ-sú\ *n* : the hickory nut; hickory wood — **cansu·hu** *n* : the hickory tree or the walnut of New England
can·su·spe·ca \caŋ-sú-spe-ca\ *n* : a wooden cross
can·swo·ju \caŋ-swó-ju\ *n* [fr *canswu* trees close-packed + *oju* plant] : a growth of trees in a bot-tom – Bl
can·šab·ša·pa \caŋ-šáb-ša-pa\ *n* : a group of trees standing against a *mayá* bank – Bl
can·ša·ša \caŋ-šá-ša\ *n* : dogwood, red osier dogwood . Cornus stolonifera, the dogwood family. It grows along running streams, as the Little White River, near Ḣe Peji Grass Mountainthe bark the Dakotas mix with bobacco for smoking – #162 — **canšášahcaka** *n* : a species of dogwood, the bark of which is considered the best for smoking
canšáša ipúsye *or* **cašaša ípusye** *n* : the constellation the Big Dipper, or perhaps Triangulum, so named for its likness to a willow stripped of its bark – WF – ***Syn*** WICA-KIYUHAPI
Can·ša·ša Wa·kpa \Caŋ-šá-ša Wa-kpà\ *np* : the James River in eastern South Dakota
can·ši·hu·ta \caŋ-ší-hu-ṫa\ *adj* : difficult to understand, complicated < *Ito iapi* ~ *wanji epin kte lo* Let me too say one thing hard-to-interpret, speaking briefly, *Šiyo s'e pa* ~ *laka ca yankin na* Stay around when your head like a grouse finds it rather difficult to understand (said of a person with a little nose) – Bl KE
can·šil \caŋ-šíl\ *adj contrac of* cantešica : grieved < *Maštincala kin* ~ *kigla* The rabbit went on home, grieving > — **canšil·ya** *va* canšil·wa·ya : to make sad — *adv* : sadly, sorrowfully — **canšilya·kel** *adv* : sorrowfully
can·šin \caŋ-šíŋ\ *n* [fr *caŋ* tree + *šin* sap] : the gum or resin that oozes from trees; pitch plaster, the pitch pine tree from which the gum oozes
can·šin·ka·hpu \caŋ-šíŋ-ḱa-ȟṗu\ *n* **1** : pine gum cut from oosings on the side of trees, trees; a resin deposit chipped from pine trees for chewing **2** : the downy woodpecker, a small species of bird – KE Swb
can·šin·ši·la \caŋ-šíŋ-ši-la\ *n* : a species of camomile perhaps, a plant from which gum oozes when it is broken off
can·ši·yo \cáŋ-ši-yo\ *n* : the bob white or prairie sharptailed grouse – FR
can·ška \caŋ-šká\ *n* : the large white-breasted hawk, a snake eater –Note: there are three kinds of such hawks: ~ *gi*, ~ *sapela*, and *wanblila*, a hawk or kite, something like an eagle or everglade kite. The *canška* is the rough-

---

\a\ father \e\ they \i\ machine \o\ smoke \u\ lunar \an, aŋ\ blanc Fr. \in, iŋ\ ink \on oŋ & un uŋ\ soon & confier Fr. \c\ chair \ǧ\ machen Ger. \j\ fusion *clusters* bl, gn, kp, hšl, etc... \ b[e]lo ... said with a slight vowel
See more in the Introduction, Guide to Pronunciation

legged hawk, the biggest species known in South Dakota. ~ *hoyázela* is the American osprey hawk, a fish hawk or marsh hawk, a fish eater. ~ *sápila*, perhaps the same as ~ *sapela*. ~ *šápela* the dark chicken hawk. ~ *únpi gi* the red-tailed hawk; *unpi* is as *upi*, as in *niupi*. ~ *unpígila* the yellow-tailed hawk - FR

can·ško·kpa \caŋ-škó-kpa\ *n* : a wagon box

can·špu·špu·la \caŋ-špú-špu-la\ *n* fr *can* wood + *yušpu* to strip off] : chips

can·šu·ška \cáŋ-šú-ška\ *n* : the boxelder tree. Negundo interior (Brittany), acer negundo (Latin), the maple family - Note: *tašuška* ants crawl up and look for the sweet sap - #123

can·ta·gle \caŋ-tá-gle\ *va* canta·wa·gle [fr *cante* heart + *agle* to set] : to set the heart upon, to wish for, desire, esp to set the heart on or for evil, to determine evil against one — **cantagle·pi** *n* : a determining of evil against — **cantagle·ya** *va* cantagle·wa·ya : to cause to set the heart against

can·ta·hca \cáŋ-ta-ḣca\ *n* : the Virginia white-tail deer - *Syn* SINTE HANSKA

can·ta·kse·ya \caŋ-tá-kse-ya\ *v* : to cause a big tree to fall by setting fire to it at the root - Bl

can·te \caŋ-té\ *n* : the heart < *micante* my heart >

can·te·e·la·i \caŋ-té-e-la-i\ *v* canteela·wa·i : to take to heart, to be displeased

can·te·el·yu·za \caŋ-té-el-yù-za\ *v* canteel·blu·za : to have or hold in the heart, to esteem

can·te·ha·ha·la \caŋ-té-ha-hà-la\ *adj* cante·ma·hahala : quick-tempered — **cantehaha·ye·la** *adj* : irascible

can·te·hun·ke·šni·yan \caŋ-té-hùŋ-ke-šni-yaŋ\ *adv* : discouraged - B.H.6.4

can·te·hu·ta *or* **cantehute** \caŋ-té-hù-ṫa\ *n* : the aorta of the heart - Bl

can·te·hni·yan·yan \caŋ-té-ḣnì-yaŋ-yaŋ\ *vn* cante·ma·hniyanyan : to be disturbed or distressed, as when one's foot hurts

can·te·i·ha·la yan·ka \caŋ-té-i-hà-la yaŋ-ká\ *v express* : to be irascible

can·te·i·ya·pa \caŋ-té-i-ya-pa\ *vn* : to be flurried or excited, to have the heart beat unnaturally — **canteiyapa·ṗi** *n* : heart-beating, excitement — **canteiyapa·ya** *adv* : excitedly

can·te·ka·ptan·yan \caŋ-té-k̇a-ptaŋ-yaŋ\ *adj* cante·ma·kaptanyan : to be changeable in one's views - Bl

can·te·ka·zan \caŋ-té-ka-zaŋ\ *vn* cante·ma·kazan : to be distressed, as when one is thirsty while eating, or when one has swallowed too much smoke or something heady

can·te·ki·ci·ci·ya·pi \caŋ-té-ki-ci-cì-ya-pi\ *n* : the loving each other

can·te·ki·c'un·yan \caŋ-ṫé-ki-c'uŋ-yaŋ\ *adv* : willingly, at one's own risk - Cf canteokic'unya - KE B.H.87.3

can·te·ki·ya \caŋ-ṫé-k̇i-ya\ *va* cante·wa·kiya : to love, to have an interest in or affection for, which prompts one to benevolent acts — **cantekiya·pi** *n* : love, benevolence; the one loved, the beloved

can·te·ki·yu·za \caŋ-ṫé-ki-yu-za\ *va* cante·wa·kiyuza : to hold in the heart for good or ill; to have an opinion of, whether good or bad < *Cincapi kinhe wanji ke s'e cantekiyuze* He loved it as if it were one of his own children > - B.H.93.12

can·te·mni·skan·o·ju·la \caŋ-té-mni-skaŋ-o-ju-la\ *adj* : very sad on account of suffering - Bl

can·te·o·gin *or* **cantogin** \caŋ-té-o-ġiŋ\ *n* : the pericardium, the membranus bag protecting the heart

can·te·o·ki·c'u·ni·ca \caŋ-té-o-ki-c'u-ni-ca\ *vn* canteo·we·c'unica : to be offended or angry at — **canteokic'u·nil** *v contrac of* canteokic'unica — **canteokic'unil·ya** \caŋ-té-o-ki-c'ù-nil-ya\ *va* canteokic'unil·wa·-ya : to offend, to make angry by opposition

can·te·o·ki·c'un·ya \caŋ-té-o-ki-c'ùŋ-ya\ *v* : canteokic'un·ma·yayelo : to do with heart, i.e. in a stirring manner - Note: *canteokihišnimayayelo* which stresses inability to sustain, and *canskiskemayayelo* which stresses being caught in confusion - WE

can·te·o·ki·hi·šni·ya \caŋ-té-o-ki-hi-šni-ya\ *v* : to have heart failure - Cf canteokic'unya - WE SLB

can·te·on·ši·ka \caŋ-té-oŋ ši ka\ *adj* canteon·ma·šika : low-spirited

can·te·o·yus·ya \caŋṫé-o-yus-ya\ *adv* : with the whole heart

can·te·o·yu·ze \caŋ-té-o-yu-ze\ *n* : an inclination or intention < *Nicanteoyuze kin ognayan makagi ye* Make me according to your intent > - Pb.32

can·te·ptan·yan \caŋ-ṫé-ptaŋ-yaŋ\ *vn* : to be angry; to be in a passion — *adj* : angry — **canteptan·yeya** *va* canteptanye·wa·ya : to make angry, to provoke

can·te·su·ta \caŋ-ṫé-su-ṫa\ *vn* cante·ma·suta : to be firm of heart, to be brave < ~ *kic'un* He wore his bravery > — *adj* : brave

can·te·ši·ca \caŋ-ṫé-ši-ca\ *vn* cante·ma·šica : to be sad, sorrowful < ~ *kiyuza* He was grieved by his enmity, ~ *makiyuza* He was grieve by my enmity > — **cantešica·ya** *adv* : sadly, sorrowfully - Bl

can·te·šil·i·c'i·ya \caŋ-ṫé-šil-i-c'i-ya\ *v refl of* cantešilya : to repent - Pb.40

can·te·šil·ya \caŋ-ṫé-šil-ya\ *va* cantešil·wa·ya : to make sad, sadden — *adv* : sorrowfully — **cantešilya·kel** *adv* : sadly

can·te·t'ins kic'un \caŋ-té-t'iŋs ki-c'ùŋ\ *v* : to take courage — **cantet'ins·t'in·za** *adj of* cantet'inza — **cantet'ins·ya** *va* cantet'in·swa·ya : to strengthen the heart, to encourage — *adv* : courageously - Bl

can·te·t'in·za \caŋ-ṫé-t'in-za\ *vn* cante·ma·t'inza : to be firm of heart, courageous < ~ *wacipi* Strong Heart dance, ~ *wápaha* the Strong Heart Lance, and seems to be a proper name

can·te·wa·hin·yan ši·ca \caŋ-té-wa-hiŋ-yaŋ ši-ca\ *adj* : irascible - Bl

can·te·wa·kan·he·ja \caŋ-ṫé-wa-kaŋ-he-ja\ *vn* : to be child-like, weak-hearted

can·te·wa·ni·ca \caŋ-ṫé-wā-ni-ca\ *vn* cante·ma·wānica : to be heartless, unprincipled, mean, wicked

can·te·wa·šte \cāŋ-ṫé-wa-šṫe\ *vn* cante·ma·wašte : to be glad, joyful < *Cantewašte po eya* He said: Rejoice! > — **cantewašte·ya** *adv* : joyfully, cheerfully — *va* cantewašte·wa·ya : to make glad, to gladden - Pb.45

can·te·ya·ši·ca \caŋ-ṫé-ya-ši-ca\ *va* cante·bla·šica : to make sad by talking, to dishearten

can·te·ya·šni·šni·ja \caŋ-té-ya-šni-šni-ja\ *vn* cante·ma·ya·šnišnija : to have a tickling in the throat; to have a spell of coughing - S

can·te·ya·t'ins \caŋ-ṫé-ya-t'iŋs\ *v contrac of* canteyat'inza

can·te·ya·t'in·za \caŋ-ṫé-ya-t'iŋ-za\ *va* cante·bla·t'inza : to cheer up by words, to comfort, strengthen

can·te·ya·wa·šte \caŋ-ṫé-ya-wa-šte\ *va* cante·bla·wašte : to make happy by words

can·te·ya·zan \caŋ-ṫé-ya-zaŋ\ *vn* : to be heart-sick, to have heart trouble; to be very hungry; a heart disease

can·te·yu·kan \caŋ-ṫé-yu-kaŋ\ *va* cante·ma·yukan : to have a heart, to be benevolent

can·te·yu·ke·ya \caŋ-ṫé-yu-ke-ya\ *adj* : reasonable

can·te·yu·šlog \caŋ-ṫé-yu-šlog\ *v* : to have a change of mind towards a more necessary good < ~ *iwekcu* I took it back changing my mind for the better > - BT

can·te·yu·za \caŋ-ṫé-yu-za\ *vn* cante·blu·za : to think, to form an opinion < *Tokel ~ he?* What is his opinion? >

can·ti·ca·spe·ya \caŋ-ṫí-ca-ṡpe-ya\ *vn* canticaspe·wa·ya : to satisfy the desires of the heart, whether good or bad; to gratify one's desires

can·ti·han·gya *or* **canteihangya** \caŋ-ṫí-haŋ-gya\ *va* cantihan·gwa·ya : to cause a heart-ache — **cantihan·g'i·c'iya** *v refl of* cantihangya : to give up, not being able to accomplish it - Bl

can·ti·han·ke \caŋ-ṫí-haŋ-ke\ *adj* canti·mi·hanke : worrying, sad, as when many children are sick in the family - Bl

can·ti·he·ya \caŋ-ṫí-he-ya\ *va* cantihe·wa·ya : to set the heart upon, to desire very much, to covet, yearn for, long for < *Wicaša kin iyuha (Wikoškalaka kin) cantiheyapi na yuzapi kta cinpi* Every man, every young woman, wants to win a spouse > - B.H.92.5 — *adj* : eager — **cantihe·ye** *n* : self-control; want or desire - D.46

can·ti·pan \caŋ-ṫí-ṗaŋ\ *n* : a coot or mud hen < *Zintkala kin ble k'el unpi pasu skaska* The bird living on a lake that has a white bill >

can·ti·ya·gle \caŋ-ṫí-ya-gle\ *vn* cantiya·ma·gle : to be angry or meditate evil — **cantiyagle·pi** *n* : malice, anger — **cantiyagle·ya** *va* cantiyagle·wa·ya : to be angry at or with, to make angry — *adv* : angrily

can·ti·ya·pa *or* **canteiyapa** \caŋ-ṫí-ya-pa\ *vn* : to be excited — **cantiyapa·pi** *or* **canteiyapapi** *n* : excitement, i.e. with a rapid heart-beat — **cantiyapa·ya** *or* **canteiyapa·ya** *adv* : excitedly

can·ti·ya·p'i·c'i·ya \caŋ-ṫí-ya-p'i-c'ì-ya\ *v* : to feel scared at one who has done something unintentionally - Bl

can·ti·yo·ki·pi·ya \caŋ-ṫí-yo-ki-pi-ya\ *adj* : hearty — *adv* : heartily

can·ti·yo·ki·ši·ca \caŋ-ṫí-yo-ki-ši-ca\ *va* cantiyo·wa·kišica : to be dissatisfied or outraged at something else < *Hankiya cantiyomayakišice* You became dissatisfied with me a little at a time > - BD

can·ti·yo·zi·ki·ya \caŋ-ṫí-yo-zi-k̇ì-ya\ *vn* : to get over one's anger, sorrow, etc. - Bl

can·tka·gi·ya \caŋ-ṫká-ġi-ya\ *va* : to let one wait and thus take his time < *Cantkagimayaye* You took up my time > - *Syn* OKANŠNIYA stresses causing one to have no time, < *okanšnimayaye* you caused me to have no time >, OUNC'ONNILYA stresses causing one to be delayed, < *oúnc'onnilmayaye* you delayed me >, and OHANNAJIN KUWA stresses trying to get one going < *ohannajin mayakuwa* you chased me to try to stand > - Bl WE

can·tki·ya \can-ṫkí-ya\ *va* canl·wa·kiya canl·ma·kiya : to love one, make him one's heart

can·tku \caŋ-ṫkú\ *n* : the chest < *Wakinyela s'e ~ kin ni-ško nankin na ~ nainš Wahacanka Sapa* Your chest is so large, like a morning dove's, and a chest otherwise like Black Shield's, (i.e. John Big Crow's grandfather, perhaps, invited many people to attend the wailing for his son who had been killed, and he heard the saying: *"Inše ~ ecela wicaša ota cin yelo; niconalapi eyaš bliheic'iya po* Only a chest do many men want; but you few keep active) >

can·tku·i·pa·si·se \caŋ-ṫkú-i-ṗa-si-se\ *n* : a breast pin, a badge

can·tku sa·pe·la \caŋ-ṫkú sà-pe-la\ *n* : the junco or chikadee, a little bird with a black breast, a tail *wanblupi s'e-lececa* with tail feathers like those of the eagle, the back black i.e. *ȟota* gray, and head like that of the *ištanica tanka* snowbird or horned lark - Bl

can·to·gin \caŋṫó-ġiŋ\ *n* : *See* canteogin

can·to·gna·gya \caŋ-ṫó-gna-gya\ *va* cantogna·wa·gya : to cause to place in the heart — *adv* : in a loving manner

can·to·gna·ka \caŋ-ṫó-gna-k̇a\ *va* canto·wa·gnaka [fr *cante* heart + *ognaka* to place in] : to place in the affections, to love — **cantognaka·pi** *n* : love

can·to·ju·ha \caŋ-ṫó-ju-ha\ *n* : a tobacco bag

can·to·ki·gna·ka \caŋ-ṫó-k̇i-gna-ka\ *v poss of* cantognaka canto·wa·kignaka : to place in one's heart

can·to·kpa·ni \caŋ-ṫó-kpa-ni\ *va* canto·wa·kpani [fr *cante* heart + *okpani* lacking in] : to long for < *Wahanpi kin cantokpani yelo. Lehanyan wahi kin locanteowakpani yelo* He was longing for the soup. When I had for so long arrived, I longed for food > — **cantokpani·pi** *n* : a longing for — **canto-kpani·yan** *va* cantokpani·wa·ya : to cause to long for — *adv* : longing for - Bl

can·to·pe·ya *or* **canlopeya** \caŋ-ṫó-ṗe-ya\ *va* cantope·wa·ya : to cheer up

can'·un·kce·mna *or* **can'unkcemna can** *or* **can'unkcemna hu** \caŋ-úŋ-kce-mna\ *n* : ill-scented sumac, skunk-bush. Rhus coriaria variety, trilobata, the gray cashew family. The leaves are mingled with tobacco and smoked - Bl #61

can·wa·ci·ki·ya·pi \cáŋ-wa-ci-k̇i-ya-pi\ *n* : a toy top

can·wa·hpa tan·ka \cáŋ-wa-ȟpa táŋ-ka\ *n* : the bronzed grackle. His says: *Mat'in ni* May I die, or *Cuhli* Sores impact, i.e. *tuwa koška ehantanš* if one if affected with a veneral disease

can·wa·kan \caŋ-wá-kaŋ\ *n* : a flag pole

can·wa·ksa \caŋ-wá-ksa\ *v* can·wa·waksa : to saw wood

can·wa·kši·ca \caŋ-wá-kši-ca\ *n* : a wooden dish or plate

can·wa·k'in \cáŋ-wa-k'iŋ\ *n* : a saddle < ~ *hu* the saddle bow, ~ *pasú* the saddle horn

can·wa·pe \caŋ-wá-ṗe\ *n* [fr *can* tree + *ape* leaf]: leaves or small branches < ~ *gi wi* September, i.e. the moon in which leaves turn brown. ~ *kasná wi* October, i.e. the moon in which the wind shakes off the leaves. ~ *wakan* mysterious leaves, ~ *wóȟešma* thick leaves or foliage, undergrowth - Cf can'iyuwi iyececa AF

can·wa·pto wi \caŋ-wá-pto wi\ *n* : May, the moon in which the leaves are green

can·wa·sle·ca \caŋ-wá-sle-ca\ *va* : to saw lengthwise — **canwasleca·pi** *n* : wood sawed lengthwise, a plank or boards, sawing or the making of boards — **canwa-sle·sle·ca** *va* : to saw boards, to saw lengthwise of the wood

can·wa·ta \caŋ-wá-ṫa\ *n* : a log canoe; a skiff

can·wi·ca·ji·pe \caŋ-wí-ca-ji-pe\ *n* : a drawing knife

can·wi·ci·pa·ga \caŋ-wí-ci-pa-ġa\ *n* : a cross

can·wi·lu·te \caŋ-wí-lu-ṫe\ *n* : logwood, containing red dye stuff

can·win·ja \cáŋ-wiŋ-ja\ *n* : a floor

can·wi·pa·snon \caŋ-wí-ṗa-snoŋ\ *n* : a spit or stick to take hold of and roast meat on

can·wi·ta \caŋ-wí-ṫa\ *n* : a little grove or island of trees

---

\a\ father \e\ they \i\ machine \o\ smoke \u\ lunar \an, aŋ\ blanc Fr. \in, iŋ\ ink \on oŋ & un uŋ\ soon & confier Fr. \c\ chair \ġ\ machen Ger. \j\ fusion *\clusters* bl, gn, kp, hšl, etc... \ b[e]lo ... said with a slight vowel
See more in the Introduction, Guide to Pronunciation

Syn CANPATA

can·wi·yo·wa \caŋ-wí-yo-wa\ *n* [fr *can* wood + *wiyowa* writing marker] : a pencil < *mázawiyowa* a pen >

can·wi·yu·te \caŋ-wí-yu-ṫe\ *n* : a wood measure, a cord stick

can·wi·yu·wi \caŋ-wí-yu-wi\ *n* : curled wood, a vine

can·wi·yu·ze \caŋ-wí-yu-ze\ *n* : a sharp stick to take meat out etc. from a kettle

can·wo·gna·ka \caŋ-wó-gna-ḳa\ *n* : a coffin – Note: a box is called *can'ognaka*

can·wo·ju·pi \caŋ-wó-ju-pi\ *n* : a park or a tree nursery; an orchard

can·wo·slo·han *or* **canwoslohe** \caŋ-wó-slo-haŋ\ *n* : a sled

can·wo·win·ge \caŋ-wó-wiŋ-ġe\ *n* : matted flooring < ~ *kaga* the banner (*wápaha)* used in the *Iḣoka Okolakiciye* Badger Society, a stick with an otter skin wrapped around it. ~ *mak'upi* I was given the Badger's banner, as is said when a person gets a certain job or office, as of collecting money for a certain purpose – Cf owinge – Bl

can·ya·h'u \caŋ-yá-ḣ'u\ *n* : the cottonwood tree, so called because in the olden times Indian horses would feed on its bark

can·yang \caŋ-yáŋg\ *vn contrac of* canyanka : to be sick of heart < ~ *yanka* He sat sick of heart, ~ *waecamon* I did it, groaning, i.e. worked in spite of sickness > – WE

can·yan·ka \caŋ-yáŋ-ḳa\ *vn* can·bla·ka can'unyankapi : to be heart-sick, to groan < *Na hehanl wicaša wan lila ~ ca el ahipi. Wicaša wan toki ~ ške'* And since the man was very heart-struck, they came to him. They say a man groaned somewhere > –D.224 B.H.230.1

can·yu·ki·za·pi \caŋ-yú-ḳi-za-ṗi\ *n* : an organ

can·yu·ktan \caŋ-yú-ktaŋ\ *n* : bent wood < *Canpagmiyanpi* ~ a wagon bow

can·yu·wa·ci·ki·za·pi \caŋ-yú-wa-ci-ḳi-zà-pi\ *n* : a toy top

can·yu·wa·ci·pi \caŋ-yú-wa-ci-pi\ *n* : a top, one that can be spun with two fingers

can·yu·wi·pi ka·ga·pi \caŋ-yú-wi-pi kà-ġa-pi\ *n* : two pieces of wood tied together which served as a boat for bows, guns, etc. while they were swimming across a river > – Bl

can·ze \caŋ-zé\ *vn* ma·canze *perhaps, or* can·ma·ze : to become incensed or angry < *Hehan wicahpi hinhpaya lila* ~ At the time Falling Star became very angry > – Pb.25 — **can·ze·ka** \caŋ-zé-ḳa\ *adj* can·má·zeka : angry — **canze·ya** \caŋ-zé-ya\ *va* canze·wa·ya : to make angry — *adv* : angrily

can·zi \caŋ-zi\ *n* : yellow wood, sumac, upland sumac, the cashew family. Rhus glabra – Note: Indians did smoke the leaves turned red – #16

ca·o·ki·t'a *also* **caokit'at'a** \ca-ó-ḳi-ṫ'a\ *vn* : to sob – Note: the original word was probably *ceyaokit'at'a* — **caokit'at'a·ya** *adv red of* caokit'aya : in a sobbing manner – B.H.229.23

ca on \ca òŋ\ *adv conj* : for that very reason – Cf ca *and* on – B.H.83.2

[1]**ca·pa** \cá-ṗa\ *n* : the beaver < ~ *s'e nakpa cikcik'a* His ears as little as those of a beaver, as is said of a big man with small ears > – Bl

[2]**ca·pa** \ca·pá\ *va* ca·wá·pa : to stab or pierce, to thrust into, as with a knife

ca·pa·pa \ca-pá-pa\ *v red* ca·wa·papa [fr *capá* to stab into : to thrust into, as a knife into flesh, in different places < *Na iyahpaya na ~ kte na pahá icu* So he seized him, killed stabbing him, and took the hill >

ca·pce·ya·kton \ca-pcé-ya-ktoŋ\ *n* : a beaver dam < ~ *ota yelo* Beaver dams are many > – Bl

ca·pce·ya·za·la \ca-pcé-ya-za-la *n* [fr *capa* beaver + *yaze* to pick out] : the wild black currant. Ribes Americanum of the middle United States. Saxifraga family. The plant grows along creeks with berries like gooseberries and sticky juice – RT #164

ca·pun·ka \ca-ṗúŋ-ḳa\ *n* : the mosquito < ~ *s'e* mosquito-like, ~ *s'e škatapi* They play like mosquitos >

ca·pun·kwo·ke·ya \ca-ṗúŋ-kwo-ḳe-ya\ *n* : a mosquito net

ca·pun·k'i·cu·wa \ca-ṗúŋ-k'i-cu wa\ *n* : a mosquito bar

ca·p'i·gmun·ke \ca-ṗ'i·gmuŋ-ḳe\ *n* : a beaver trap

ca·p'ti·gna·ka \ca-ṗt'í-gna-ka\ *n* : a beaver dam, a hole where a beavers gather their provisions – Bl

ca·p'ni·ge \ca-ṗ'ní-ġe\ *n* : a beaver stomach – Bl

ca·p'o·k'e \ca-ṗ'o-k'e\ *v* : to dig out beavers, i.e. after the dam waters have been let off

ca·p'o·na·ski·ski·ta \ca-ṗ'ó-na-skì-ski-ta\ *n* : a pastime for little children – Bl

ca·p'sin·te \ca-ṗ'síŋ-te\ *n* : a beaver tail – Bl

ca·p'sto \ca-ṗ'stó\ *n* : a fat, big beaver

ca·p'wi·ca·hca \ca-ṗ'wí-ca-ḣca\ *n* : an old beaver

ca·ska \ca-ska\ *suff* : together – Appended to numerals and making them *adv* < *Nunpincaska glipi* They both returned home together, *Ata iyuhacaska glipi* They all returned together >

[1]**ca·ske** \ca-ské\ *adj* ca·má·ske *or* ma·cáske : taking things not intended for one but for another < ~ *wicaša* a grasping man, *Wicaša kin ~ s'a* The man is as though he were grasping > – WE

ca·ske \ca-ské\ *v* ca·wa·ske : to take by mistake, as in supposing a thing was intended for some one when it was meant for another — **caske·ya** \ca-ské-ya\ *v* caske·wa·ya : to cause one to take by mistake, as in handing somebody something, while another, thinking it was meant for him, reaches out for it < *Caskemayaye lo* You overlook me while distributing things > – Bl

ca·smu \ca-smú\ *n* : sand

ca·smu i·ka·co·co \ca-smú i-kà-co-co\ *n* : a trowel

ca·smu hu·hol·ho·ta \ca-smú huḣol-ḣò-ta\ *n* : hairy prairie clover – *See* blaye zitkatacan hustola

ca·smu·ska \ca-smú-ska\ *n* : white sand

ca·smu·smu \ca-smú-smu\ *adj red of* casmu : sandy, much sand

caš \caš\ *adv* : then; but < *Hecegle ~ iye keye ca wana naunh'onpi* He said he heard us, so then he just as well (stop here). So therefore ... – B.H.75.1 (same as *tka*), 101.1, 105.25, 110.20, 174.17, 175.4 (*ca* is emph.), 208.4, 211.24, 264.22

caš·ki·ton \caš-kí-toŋ\ *v poss of* cašton caš·wa·kiton [fr *caje* name + *ki* for one's own + *ton* to have] : to give a name to one's own – D.106

caš·ton \caš-tóŋ\ *v* caš·wa·tonpi : to make a name for one's self — **cašton·pi** *part* : named

ca·š'a·ya \ca-š'á-ya\ *v* caš'a·wa·ya : to praise one's bravery – Note: perhaps also used is *cas'aya* – Bl

caš'·tan'in·yan \caš'táŋ-iŋ-yaŋ\ *adv* : having a great name < ~ *škan* His great reputation spread > – B.H.87.2

ca·ta \cá-ṫa\ *n* : cinders, i.e. hard ashes – Bl

ca·ta·na·šlo·gya \cá-ṫa-na-šlo-gya\ *v* catanašlog·wa·ya : to hill up corn with ashes – Bl

ca·tka \ca-tḳá\ *n* : the left hand < *micatka* my left hand > — *adj* ca·ma·tka : left-handed — **catka·yatan** *adv* : at the left side < *Ate, nata ~ winawizi wan imakoyakin kte lo* Father, at the left side of my head a cockleburr will stick to me > — **catkayatan·han** *adv* : at the left hand of < ~ *woglaka, wokilaka* He spoke crookedly, being one asking for food (to tell lies), *Unma hinzi kin le ~ iyayin kte lo. Yunkan nape ~ wase k'un he bluha* This other yellow hair horse on the left will leave. And then I held red coloring in my left hand >

ca·tku \ca-tǩú\ *n* : the back part of a tent or house, the part opposite the door, the place of honor < ~ *apahloka* an ornament fastened on the *catku*, i.e. the rear wall of the tent — **ca·tkul** \ca-tǩúl\ *adv* : at the back of a house or tent — **catku·ta** \ca-tkú-ṫa\ *adv* : at the back of the tent, opposite the entrance which is the place of honor < ~ *yanka* He sits in the honor place > — **catkutanhan** \ca-tkú-ṫaŋ-haŋ\ *adv* : at the back part of a tent

ca·u·kpe·pa·jo \ca-ú-kṗe-ṗa-jo\ *n* : the patella bone

[1]**ce** *or* **i·ce** *or* **ci** **cē**\ *interrog particle* : "Is it not so?" *or* "Is it not so?" *or* "Is it not right?" – It is used at the end of a sentence to which one expects an immediate affirmative answer. The voice is raised in pronouncing it. < *Wóeye kin le yuhapi ce?* They have (use) this word, do they not? *Lila woyute oteȟike ce?* Food is scarce, is it not? – Note: *ice* seems to be like to *au ce* Did they not come? *Icé* He arrived did he not? — *express* : "Say", being seemingly the equivalent in attracting somebody's attention < *Ho, takoja winyan kin he unyak'upi kta ce, eya ške'* Say now, grandchild, you will give us this woman, will you not? -- so they say he said, *Hitunkala he takula ca yatela so? Hanke wak'ula ye, miš eya watela kte. Ice, ice, etc.* Mr. Mouse, you eat what is but a bit, is it not so? Give him the little half, I too will eat a bit, won't you, won't you? *Katowotanla ku ye. Lehan wanciglak iblotaka ce* Please come back struck upright. I now sat down to see yours, did I not?, as is said when the men return from looking for buffalo > – D.97

[2]**ce** \ce\ *n* macé nicé : the penis

ce·a·kton \ce-á-ktoŋ\ *v* cea·wa·kton : to make a bridge — **ceakton·pi** *n* : a bridge

ce·bce·pa \ce-bcé-ṗa\ *adj red of* cepa : quite fat

ce·bki·ya \ce-bǩí-ya\ *va poss of* cebya ce·bwa·kiya : to fatten one's own

ce·blo·hu \ce-bló-hu\ *n* : the collar bone, the clavicle bone

ce·bya \ce-byá\ *va* ce·bwa·ya : to make fat, fatten — *adv* : fatly, liberally — **cebya·pi** \ce-byá-ṗi\ *part* : fattened, fatted — **ce·bye·la** \ce-byé-la\ *adj* : fat < *Wicaša* ~ The man is fat >

ce·ca \ce-cá\ *n* : the thigh

ce·ca·ho·hu \ce-cá-ho-hu\ *n* : the femur bone

ce·ca·o·wa·gle *or* **cecówagle** \ce-cá-o-wa-gle\ *n* : the femur bone, the hip-joint — **cecao·a·kle** \ce-cá-o-a-kle\ *n* : the pelvis

ce e·yaš \ce é-yaš\ *particle* : It universalizes *pron* – Cf ke c'éyaš *and* ke éyaš

ce·ga \cé-ġa\ *n* : a kettle, pot, pail, bucket — **cega·ska** \cé-ġa-ska\ *n* : a white tin kettle

ce·gnag \ce-gnág\ *v contrac of* cegnaka : to hold one's private parts as with a loincloth

ce·gna·ke \ce-gná-ǩe\ *n* : a breechcloth, a piece of cloth worn about the loins by Dakota men, loin cloth — **cegnake·kiton** \ce-gná-ǩe-ǩi-toŋ\ *v* cegnake·we·ton : to put on and wear a breechcloth — **cegna·kiton** \ce-gná-ǩi-toŋ\ *v* cegna·we·ton : to put on or wear a loincloth

ce·gu·gu \ce-ġú-ġu\ *adj* : burned black — **cegugu·ya** *va* ceguguwa·ya : to fry meat; to burn something black < *wašin* ~ to fry out fat > – BD

ce·gya \cé-gya\ *adv* [fr *céka* to stagger] : stumblingly

ce·g'i·yo·ka·ške \ce-g'í-yo-ka-ške\ *n* – Note: there are another two possible spellings: *ceh'iyokaške* and *ceȟiyokaške* this latter cf below

ce·hin·ka \ce-híŋ-ka\ *n* : an old man, *obsol* – *Syn* WICAHCALA – Bl

ce·hin·ka ta·pte \ce-híŋ-ka ta-ptè\ *n* : a large buffalo cow – Bl

ce·hu·pa \ce-hú-pa\ *n* : the under-jaw, the lower jaw

ce·hu·pa·gla·gla \ce-hú-pa-gla-gla\ *vn* cehupa·wa·glagla : to chatter, as do the teeth on account of the cold — *n* : the brown thrasher or the catbird, i.e. a bird whose name *deriv* from its chattering in the evening, so that people say that the weather will be cold. ~ *našlel kinica* The catbird tries to split things, or ~ *namašlel kinica* The catbird tries to split me, as is said when the jaws being tired refuse to move

ce·hu·pa o·a·gle \ce-hú-pa o-à-gle\ *n* : the place where the jaw connects – Cf paglá – Bl

ceh \céȟ\ *n contrac of* céga : kettle < ~ *sapa* a black kettle, ~ *ska* a white kettle >

ceh·ci·sci·la \ceȟ-cí-sci-la\ *n* : a small kettle or bucket

ceh·ka·hlo·ka \ceȟ-ka-ȟlo-ka\ *n* : a bucket or kettle with with a hole on either side in which a wire is fastened perhaps – Bl

ceh·hu·ha·tan \ceȟ-hú-ha-taŋ\ *n* : a kettle having legs

ceȟ·i·kan \ceȟ-í-kaŋ\ *n* : a kettle-bail, a kettle handle

ceȟ·i·yo·ka·ške \ceȟ-í-yo-ka-ške\ *n* : the stick or thing on which the kettle is hung – Bl – *Syn* SÁTA

ceh·na·ga *or* **cehnagi** *or* **cehnagila** \ceȟ-ná-ġa\ *n* : soot or whatever is black; dead coals < ~ *s'e ahiyaye* He passed by all dressed in black (as if covered with soot) > – Note: the alternate spellings: ceh'naga, ceh'nagi are less probable –Bl KE

ceh·ni·ge·ton \ceȟ-ní-ġe-toŋ\ *n* : a kettle that bulges in the middle – Bl

ce·hpi \ce-ȟṗí\ *n* mi·céhpi : flesh

ceh·pšun·ka \ceȟ-pšúŋ-ka\ *n* : a pail, small at the top and large at the bottom

ceh·p'o \ceȟ-p'ó\ *n* : the steam from a kettle

ceh·ska \ceȟ-ská\ *n* : a tin can

ceh·tan·kin·kin·yan \ceȟ-táŋ-kiŋ-kiŋ-yaŋ\ *n* : a large kettle – B.H.55.3

ceh·wo·ho·ta \ceȟ-wó-ho-ta\ *n* : a low wide, chubby kettle

ceh·wo·yu·te \ceȟ-wó-yu-te\ *n* : clay cakes etc. as little girls make < ~ *škatapi* They play at (making) cakes

ce·h'i·ha \ce-ȟ'í-ha\ *n* : a lid, cover for a kettle or bucket

ce·h'i·hu·pa \ce-ȟ'í-hu-pa\ *n* : a frying pan, or a long-handle kettle

ce·h'i·hu·pa·ton \ce-ȟ'í-hu-pa-toŋ\ *n* : a kettle or bucket with a bail, an over-arching handle

ce·h'o·ki·ye·ton \ce-ȟ'ó-ǩi-ye-toŋ\ *n* : a kettle such as a tea kettle

ce·ja·ka \ce-já-ka\ *adj* ce·ma·jaka ma·cejaka : pigeon-toed, as when one walks such that there is much space between the legs – Bl

ce·ji \ce-jí\ *n* mi·céji : the tongue — **ceji·hu·te** \ce-jí-hu-te\ *n* : the back part of the tongue — **ceji·in·kpa** *n* : the point of the tonue

ce·ji·ja·lya \ce-jí-ja-lya\ *adv* : deceitfully

\a\ father \e\ they \i\ machine \o\ smoke \u\ lunar \an, aŋ\ blanc Fr. \in, iŋ\ ink \on oŋ & un uŋ\ soon & confier Fr. \c\ chair \ġ\ machen Ger. \j\ fusion *clusters* bl, gn, kp, hšl, etc... \ b[e]lo ... said with a slight vowel **See more in the Introduction, Guide to Pronunciation**

ce·ji·ni·yan \ce-jí-ni-yaŋ\ *n* : a coated tongue as from a fever - *vn* ceji·ma·niyan : to have a sore tongue, as do babies
ce·jin \ce-jíŋ\ *n* : the penis erect
ce·ka \cé-ka\ *vn* ma·céka : to stagger — **ce·kceg** \cé-kceg\ *v contrac of* cekceka : to staagger — **cekce·gya** \ce-kcé-gya\ *adv* : staggeringly, reeling < ~ *mani* He is reeling on his feet > - **cekce·ka** \ce-kcé-ka\ *vn* : to stagger or reel
ce·ki·ca·ti \ce-kí-ca-ti\ *v* ce·we·cati [fr *ceti* start a fire] : to make a fire for me perhaps — **ceki·ci·ti** \ce-kí-ci-ti\ *v* ce·wé·citi : to make a fire for one - KE
ce·ki·ci·ya \cé-ki-ci-ya\ *v* cé·we·ciya *I for another* cé·ye·ciya *you for another* cé·un·kiciya·pi *we for others* cé·miye·ciya *you for me* [fr *cekiya* pray for] : to pray or supplicate for another - Note: God seems to be the object of this word - Cf cekiya, wacekiya
ce·ki·pa \ce-kí-pa\ *v* : to prepare meat for one < *Nape yuptanptan cewec'ipehce lo, peta kin oile ecetu šni ca* I prepared meat for myself nicely turning it by hand, since the fire did not break into flame > — **ce·ki·pa·pi** \ce-kí-pa-pi\ *n* : meat prepared for one, as *pápa* dried meat < *Icimani* ~ *wanji ceonpa yo* Roast a piece of *pápa* for a lonely traveller > - Bl
ce·ki·ti·pi \ce-kí-ti-pi\ *n* : a feast said to be partaken of by virgins and men who have known women
ce·ki·ya \cé-ki-ya\ *v* ce·wá·kiya ce·cí·ciya [fr *ceya* to cry] : to pray to < *Ceunniciyapi* We beseech you > — **cekiya·ya** \ce-kí-ya-ya\ *v red* or *adv of* cekiya : to implore one — *adv* : pleadingly < ~ *wokiyake* He spoke imploring him - B.H.227.6
ce·kpa \ce-kpá\ *n* macékpa : the navel, a twin < *Hau* ~ . *Hau kola* Hello, relative. Greetings, friend > — **cekpa·pi** *n* : twins — **cekpa agna·ke** \ce-kpá a-gnà-ke\ *n* : the afterbirth — **cekpa·ta** \ce-kpá-ta\ *adv* : by way of a twin < ~ *on slolya* He knew before birth > - IS
ce·kpi·yu·ski·te \ce-kpí-yu-ski-te\ *n* : a child's swaddling band
cel \cel\ *particle* : presumably it must be ... - It is placed at the end of a sentence - B.H.26.17, 64.13, 99.16 — *adv* [fr *ecel* or so] : about, approximately, nearly < *wikcemna cel* about ten, *Na tahasopi k'on hena on wihuta opahloke el cel ikanyan na can pteptecela on ecel okatan* And with these leather thongs in holes on the tent's lower edge, he presumably used as handle, and thus he nailed it fast with a very small piece of wood >
ce·li \ce-lí\ *n* : a seed-like grass with long joints — **celi·hu** \ce-lí-hu\ *n* : the seed stalk
ce·onp \ce-óŋp\ *va contrac of* ceonpa : to roast
ce·on·pa \ce-óŋ-pa\ *va* ce·wá·onpa : to roast, as meat
ce·pa \cé-pa\ *adj* ma·cépa ni·cepa un·cepa·pi : fleshy, fat
ce·pan \ce-páŋ\ *n* : sister-in-law - Note: this is a new word in regard to spelling and pronouncing perhaps
ce·pe·la tan·ka \cé-pe-la tàŋ-ka\ *n* : the black-billed cuckoo. It was described in 1940 as bigger than a wood thrush, lives in the woods, is brown shouldered, has a long tail, a whitish breast and belly, a black bill. It nests close to the ground and usually lays four greenish eggs. It returns in May and leaves in September, sings in the morning, at noon and in the evening, and not at night. Its song is a short note at first, then many. It is called *icó ka sápa* which cf . Reed's Bird Book describes the black-billed cuckoo which would be like the *cepela tanka*. But the yellow-billed cuckoo is also called cepela tanka, yet that variety is not called *icoka sapa* - FR
ce·sli \ce-slí\ *n* : dung — *vn* ce·wa·sli : to spread dung
ce·ši·kši·ce \ce-ší-kši-ce\ *n* : the fat covering the paunch - Bl
ce·ška \ce-šká\ *n* : the part of the breast near the collar bone
ce·ška·san·san kšu·pi \ce-šká-saŋ-saŋ kšú-pi\ *n* : a woman's beaded dress
ce·ški·kan \ce-škí-kaŋ\ *n* [fr *ceška* part near the collar bone above the breast + *ikan a* string] : a button
ce·ški·kan i·ye·ce·ca \ce-škí-kaŋ i-yè-ce-ca\ *n* : Geyer's yellow monkey flower, mimulus geyeri Torr. The leaves float on water - Bl #183
ce·ški·pa·zi·ze \ce-škí-pa-zi-ze\ *n* : a breast pin
ce·ški·yu·tan *or* **ceškaiyutan** \ce-škí-yu-taŋ\ *n* 1 : the suspenders 2 : the martingale, i.e. a harness strap connecting the head-gear with the belly-band
ce·ško·hlo·ke \ce-škó-hlo-ke\ *n* : the hollow place in the throat by the collar bone
ce·šlo·šlo \ce-šló-šlo\ *vn* : to have diarrhoea
ce·šlo·šlo pe·ju·ta \ce-šló-šlo pe-jù-ta\ *n* : the low milkweed - Bl #89 - *Syn* PEJI SWULA CIK'ALA
ce·tan \ca-táŋ\ *n* : a hawk
~ *glegléga* the sharp-skinned or red-shoulderedhawk
~ *šála* the sparrow hawk
~ *tánka* the big hawk - Note: three kinds of hawk were known: *cetan tanka, cetan šala* the chickenhawk, and *cetan watapela* the shrike. < *Cetan tanka s'e tuweni takuwaye šni* I have no relative like a big hawk >
~ *watápela* the loggerhead shrike. < ~ *s'e cik'ala tka pasu tanka* He is little like a loggerhead shrike, but his nose is large >
~ *watapela zi* the evening grossbeak, so called because the bird goes much after other birds, but it is not a shrike. The bird lives on seeds and berries - Bl BS
ce·te \ce-té\ *n* : the bottom of a vessel
ce·te·i·ya·ska·bye·la *or* **ceteyela** \ce-té-i-ska-bye-la\ *adv* : sticking to the bottom of a vessel, as a remnant of soap
ce·te·kan·ye·la *or* **ceteyela** \ce-té-kaŋ-ye-la\ *adv* : little in, as water in a pail
ce·te·sa·pa \ce-té-sa-pa\ *n* : suet, hard kidney fat
ce·te·ta \ce-té-ta\ *adv* : at the bottom of a vessel or a river < *minicéteta* at the river bottom >
ce·te·ta·la *or* **ceteyela** \ce-té-ta-la\ *adv* : having a little in, as in a ve-ssel - Cf cete - Bl
ce·ti \ce-tí\ *va* ce·wá·ti : to build a fire, make a fire
ce·tu \ce-tú\ *adv* : then: so much, just so
ce·tun·te \ce·túŋ-te\ *n* : the thigh bone
ce·tun·to·štan \ce-túŋ-to-štaŋ\ *n* : the neck or head of the femur, the articulation of the femur
ce·t'un·gla \ce-t'úŋ-gla\ *va* cet'un·wa·gla cet'un'un-gla-pi cet'uncigla : to doubt, to disbelieve — **ce·t'un·gla·ya** \ce-t'úŋ-gla-ya\ *va* cet'ungla·wa·ya : to cause to doubt
ce·ya \cé-ya\ *va* wa·céya : to weep, cry < ~ *iglala* to cry very hard, hysterically > - B.H.46.2
ce·ya·ka \ce-yá-ka\ *n* : mint, the generic name of mints; wild mint. Mentha canadensis, the mint family - Note: in Santee Sioux the word *ceyaka* means a dam, which explains the name *ceyaktonpi* bridge in Lakota. - Bl #216
ce·ya·kton *or* **ceákton** \ce-yá-ktoŋ\ *v* : to make a bridge - Note: *ceyáktonpi* is *ceáktonpi*. - Cf ceyaka, Note
ce·ya·na·ka \cé-ya-na-ka\ *vn* céya·ma·naka : to twitch under the eyes or about the mouth
ce·ya·o·ki·t'a \cé-ya-o-kì-t'a\ *v* : to sob, as children do -

Cf caókit'a – F

ce·ya·ya \ce-yá-ya\ *v red of* ceya : to sob < ~ *iyayapi* They went away sobbing > – Cf céya _– B.H.44.5

ce·yo·he \ce-yó-he\ *n* : the abdomen – Bl

ci \ci\ *1st and 2nd pers pron* wa-ni *contrac insert* : I-thee — *euph change of ki* after an *e* or an *i* becomes *ci* : for

ci·ca \ci-cá\ *adj* : rough; frizzled, tightly curled up hair

ci·ci·ye \ćí-ći-ye\ *n* : a bogeyman, a fabulous being mothers use to scare children with when putting them to sleep < *Takoja, ištinma ye; ~ wan u kte na eniyayin kte* Grandchild, go to sleep; a bogeyman will come and will take you away > – PD – *Syn* MMLA, H'EYA

ci·kci·k'a·la \ći-kćí-k'a-la\ *adj red of* cik'ala : very small, in *ref* to a singular *n* ; in *ref* to a plural *n* : cikcík'apila

ci·kci·k'a·ya \ći-kći-k'a-ya\ *adv* or *adj perhaps* : slender, spindle-like < *Šlošlola s'e hu ~ huoȟihe tankinkinyan kaca* Like an upland plover, his legs are very slim, his joints big clear out of proportion >

ci·kci·sci·la \ći-kćí-sci-la\ *adj red of* ciscila : quite small, in *ref* to a *singl n* ; in *ref* to a *pl n*, cikcíscipila < *Lena ~ yeš t'api šni yelo* Though these were little they did not die > – Pl

ci·k'a·la \ćí-k'a-la\ *adj* : little, very small, *ref* to a *singl n; ref* to *pl n* : cík'apila – Pl

ci·k'a·la·kel \ćí-k'a-la-kel\ *adv* : a little < ~ *icaske iyeunyin kte* Let us smoke the pipe a little, or eat a little, or etc. > – Bl

ci·k'a·la ška·ta·pi \ćí-k'a-la šká-ta-pi\ *n* : a toy for girls

ci·k'a·ya \ćí-k'a-ya\ *adj* and perhaps *adv* : small < *Ite ~* The head is small > – Bl

ci·k'a·ye·la \ćí-k'a-ye-la\ *adv* : pent up in a small place; small-wise

ci·lo *or* **kilo** \ci-ló\ *part* : meaning *šni yo*, or simply *šni* and is used after a 2nd *pers* or *imper* – Cf kilo

cin \ciŋ\ *va* wa·cin : to desire, to want — *def art* : the – It is used in place of *kin* when the *v* or *adj* preceding has changed a terminal *a* or *an* to *e* — *dem* : that < *Cin niyeš ehe kin* That is what you say, *Ake cin talo kin iyuha ayakšijin kte* [I suppose] you will again be claiming all the meat > – D.115

cin·ca \ciŋ-cá\ *n* mi·cinca ni·cinca : a child, the young of animals

cin·ca i·ya·ni·ca \ciŋ-cá ì-ya-ni-ca\ *n* : inability to give birth to the child > – Bl

cin·ca·ka·ga \ciŋ-cá-ka-ġa\ *v* cinca·wa·kaga : to beget a child

cin·ca·ki·ci·ton \ciŋ-cá-ki-ci-ṫoŋ\ *v* cinca·we·citon : to bear a child to or for one

Cin·ca·ki·ze \Cíŋ-ca-ki-ze\ *np* : the Apaches – R Bl

cin·ca·la \ciŋ-cá-la\ *n* : an offspring – It is more in use for the young of animals

cin·ca·ton \ciŋ-cá-ṫoŋ\ *va* cinca·wa·ton : to have or give birth to a child

cin·ca·ya \ciŋ-cá-ya\ *v* cinca·wa·ya : to have for a child, to adopt as a child

cin·co·ga *also* **can'icoga** \cíŋ-co-ġa\ *n* [fr *can* wood + *icoga* to lodge on] : bunches, as of dry grass, wood, etc left along a creek after a flood, hence driftwood – R

cin·co·pa·mna \ciŋ-có-ṗa-mna\ *n* : a bunch of children together with their parents – Cf can'opamna

cin·han *or* **kinhan** \ciŋ-háŋ\ *conj* : if, when

cin·hin·tku \ciŋ-híŋ-tku\ *n* : his or her stepchild – Bl

cin·htin \cíŋ-ȟtiŋ\ *adj* : crooked, *archaic* – Note: the meaning of this word has shifted to *škópa* crooked

cin·ka \cíŋ-ka\ *adv suff to pers pron* : voluntarily < *miyecinka* I freely, *niyecinka* you voluntarily > – *See* wacinka or wacín, both meaning to think, or I desire – R

cin·ki·ya \ciŋ-ḱí-ya\ *va* cin·wá·kiya : to cause to desire, to persuade or advise

cin·kpa \cíŋ-kṗa\ *n* [fr *can* wood + *inkpa* end point] : buds, a twig, the top of a tree, the end of a stick

cinkš \ciŋkš\ *n* : My child! as is said by fathers to their children

cin·kši \ciŋ-kší\ *n* : a son, a man's brother's son; or a woman's sister's son < *Micinca hokšila, wicincala. Nicinca hokšila, etc. Micinkši t'e šni itokab el u wo* My son's boy and girl. Your son's boy, etc. Come here before my son dies >

cin·kši·tku \ciŋ-kší-tku\ *n* : his or her son

cin·kši·ya \ciŋ-kší-ya\ *va* cinkši·wa·ya : to have for a son; to be a father to one

cin·kta·kta *or perhaps* **ceyinktakta** \cíŋ-kta-kta\ *v* wa·cinktakta : to cry sobbingly

cin·pi·ca \ciŋ-pí-ca\ *adj* : desirable

cin·ška \cin-šká\ *n* : a spoon < ~ *cik'ala* a teaspoon, ~ *tukiha* a shell-shaped spoon, or a very small spoon made of buffalo horn

cin·ška·sin·te yu·kan \ciŋ-šká siŋ-ṫè yu-kaŋ\ *n* : the Big Dipper constellation – Cf Wicakiyuhapi

cin·ška·ya·pi \ciŋ-šká-ya-pi\ *n* : a mountain sheep

cin·šni·yan·kel \ciŋ-šní-yaŋ-kel\ *adv* : detestingly < *Wowahtani ~ nitawoope kin ecel ecin kte* So let him consider your law in a way detesting sin > – Pb.44

cin·tok *or* **cintoka** \ciŋ-ṫók\ *adv* : certainly — *interj* : to be sure (*express* of assent)

cin·wa·kse \cíŋ-wa-kse\ *n* : a saw

cin·ya \ciŋ-yá\ *va* cin·wa·ya : to cause to desire, to persuade

cin·yan·kel \cíŋ-yaŋ-kel\ *adv* : desiringly < ~ *yanka* He sat harboring desire, *Tohanl mini kin škanškan can el iyayapi kte ~ yankapi* When the water was stirred then they would with desire go to get in it > – B.H.188.2, 192.13

ci·sci·la \ći-sći-la\ *adj* : small — **cisci·yela** *adj* : small, little; narrow, pent up, as a passage-way < ~ *wacinyayanpi.* ~ *tokeca* You put little trust. It was small difference — *adv* : a little, for a little while – R

ci·ya·nun \ci-yá-nuŋ\ *n* : a small *tahuka cangleška* hoop used in a game – *archaic*

ci·ye \ci-yé\ *n* : a man's older brother, my older brother < *niciye* your older brother > – Note: male cousins from the father's side older than one's self are also called *ciyé* — **ci·ye·ku** \ci-yé-ḱu\ *n* : his elder brother — **ciye·ya** *va* ciye·wa·ya : to have for an older brother

ci·yo·tan·ka \cí-yo-taŋ-ka\ *n* : a flute –*Syn* COTANKA, SIYOTANKA – R RT Bc Bl B.H.56.18

co \ċo\ *n* : the kernel or core, the meat of grain, the seed < ~ *áya* to become ripe > — *vn* : to ripen

co co \ċo ċo\ *exclam* : Oh, heavenly days! (of joy on seeing a friend unexpectedly) – BS

coco \ċo-ċó\ *adj* : soft, as mud, opposed to *t'inza* stiff and *suta* hard < ~ *hingla kaluza* It suddenly was soft to flow >

co·co·la \co-có-la\ *adj* : soft — **coco·ya** *adv* : made or left soft < ~ *špan* not well cooked >

co·gco·na·la \co-gcó-na-la\ *adj red of* conala : very few,

\a\ father \e\ they \i\ machine \o\ smoke \u\ lunar \an, aŋ\ blanc Fr. \in, iŋ\ ink \on oŋ & un uŋ\ soon & confier Fr. \c\ chair \ġ\ machen Ger. \j\ fusion *clusters* bl, gn, kp, hšl, etc... \ b°lo ... said with a slight vowel **See more in the Introduction, Guide to Pronunciation** very little

co·ge·ca \ċó-ġe-ca\ *adj* ma·cógeca : slovenly, with one's clothes not well put on

co·gin \ċo-ġíŋ\ *n* : pith, as of wood; the core of anything, as of an apple < *Wicagnaška hu hena ~ tanka* The gooseberry bush's pith is large > – D.12

co·hwan·ji·ca \co-ḣwáŋ-ji-ca\ *n* : the smaller willow < ~ *šaša* the low thin willow, ~ *tanka* the large willow

co·i·c'i·con *or* **icóic'ion** \co-í-c'i-coŋ\ *v* [fr *cokon* purpose evil] : to determine evil against one's self, to be resolute – R

[1]**co·ka** \co-k̇á\ *adj* : empty, without anything < *Šunkawakan ~ wagli mazaska etc. Yunkan lila wicaakih'an na le oyate omani ipi eša ~ agli. Waye wai tka ~ wagli yelo* Without a horse he brought home money etc. Then they were badly starving, and though now the people went travelling, they started for home without anything. I went to hunt for food, but I returned home empty-handed, i.e. a hunter for many but returned without any >

[2]**co·ka** \co-k̇á\ *n* : a low bottom, a place where there are lakes or marshes

co·kab \ċó-k̇ab\ *adv* : in the midst, central < *Mni ~ ihpeyapi* He was thrown in the water's midst > – Note: (to be fighting) *cokáb únmin* in the middle (while the hostile parties stand) on both sides – D.79 Bl

co·ka·ka \co-ká-ka\ *adj red of* coká : utterly empty

co·ka·ka·la \co-ká-ka-la\ *adv red of* cokala : quite naked

co·kal \co-k̇ál\ *adv contrac of* cokata : in the midst < *He itancan kaga na he ~ inajin. Itancan ~ ti. Yunkan ungnahela taji nump ~ hiyayapi* He made him king and he stood in the midst. The king dwelt in their midst. And of a sudden two red buffalo calves came by in the middle >

co·ka·la \co-ká-la\ *adj* : naked, bare < *Tanmácokala* I am without clothes, *Simácokala* I am without shoes, *Sicokala* He is without shoes > — *adj* : empty – Cf R and P in *ref* to *kokala* a small keg, which may suggest a shift in the meaning of the word

co·kan \co-k̇áŋ\ *n* : the middle < *Na lena okicize kin ~ lecel oh'anye ci wanyankapi heon lila cajeyatapi. Peta kin ~ inajin. Blaye ~ kinapapi. Wicaša wan ikanyela yanka; canke hu kin ~ kaksa ihpeya* His name was much mentioned since they saw him when he carried on this way in the midst of these battles. He made a stand in the midst of the fire. They came out in the midst of the valley. A man was nearby; so he threw him down and struck the middle of his legs >

co·kan·gna·gya \co-k̇áŋ-gna-gya\ *adv* : placed in the middle half < ~ *ya* She went halfway to the middle, *Miš ~ tima wai* I proceeded halfway indoors > – B.H.54.14

co·kan·hi·yu·c'i·ya *or* **cokanhiyuic'iya** \co-k̇áŋ-hi-yu-c'i-ya\ *v refl* : to thrust one's self into, to come uninvited

co·kanl \co-k̇áŋl\ *n* or *adv* : the middle, or in the midst < ~ *išnala omani na enana inajin.* ~ *wawagli kte lo* He walked alone in their midst, and so he stood up. Into your midst I shall bring game, e.g.: *Isto tasicoska nupin taajuntka ognake kin nupin tanitahu kin tata-hpa kin* Buffalo both leg and thigh meat, both kidney sacks, the backbone, the breast > – Bl

co·kan·yan \co-k̇áŋ-yaŋ\ *n* or *adv* : the middle; in the middle < *Yunkan hucan ~ hehanyan ataya we oha. Yunkan blaye kin ~ taku wan šayela u. Itancan kin ~ najin* Then blood adhered to arrow shaft all the way to its middle. And in the middle of the valley there came something afar off. The chief stood in their midst >

co·kan·yan·gna·ka \co-k̇áŋ-yaŋ-gna-ka\ *va* : to place across the middle, to place in the middle

co·ka·pa \co-k̇á-pa\ *adv* : in the midst, in the center

co·ka·ta \co-k̇á-ṫa\ *n* or *adv* : the middle; in the middle, in the midst < *Wicaša wan wakan ~ inajin* A priest stood up in their midst > — **cokata·kiya** \co-ká-ta-k̇i-ya\ *adv* : towards the middle — **cokata·wapa** \coká-ta-wa-pa\ *adv* : out in the middle, as of a stream

co·kco·na·la \co-kcó-na-la\ *adv red of* conala : a few

co·ke·hanl \có-k̇e-haŋl\ *adv* [fr *co* at the proper time + *kin* the + *ehanl* at that time] : at the proper time – Bl – *Syn* ĖTUKEHANL

co·kon \co-k̇óŋ\ *va* co·wa·kon : to purpose evil against one, to desire to take the life of one

co·ku \co-k̇ú\ *n* : the inside of the cuticle, the underside of the skin; the thickness or strip of the skin; the under part of the chin

co·ku·ki·ton \co-kú-k̇i-toŋ\ *v* coku·we·ton : to take on new flesh – B.H.44.14

co·k'in \co-k'íŋ\ *va* co·wa·k'in : to roast on spits over coals — **cok'in·pi** *part* : roasting

co·la \có-la\ *adj* : destitute, without, not having < *šina cola* without a blanket >

co·mni·gla·zan·zan \co-mní-gla-zaŋ-zaŋ\ *v red of* comniglazan comni·wa·glazanzan : to sob, esp as they do before crying out loud – *archaic* and note that *comniglazi* is not used

co·na·la \ċó-na-la\ *n* or *adj* : a few

co·na·la·ka \ċó-na-la-k̇a\ *n* or *adj* : not a few, i.e *conala šni*, hence *ota* many – Cf *k̇a* the equivalent of *šni*

co·ni·ca \ċo-ní-ca\ *n* : flesh, meat of any kind; the meat or kernel of grain

con·te·hi \ċóŋ-te-ḣi\ *n* : thick woods

con·wi·yu·go·ge \coŋ-wí-yu-go-ġe\ *n* : brush breaker

co·pa \co-pá\ *va* co·wá·pa : to wade, go into the water < *Mini cowapa* I waded in water >

co·pe·ki·ya \co-ṗé-k̇i-ya\ *va* : to make wade in water

cos \cos\ *adj contrac of* coza : uncomfortably warm — **co·sco·za** \co-scó-za\ *adj red* : oppressive in warmth — **cos·i·c'i·ya** \cos-í-c'i-ya\ *v refl* [fr *cosya* make dry] : to warm one's self — **cos·ya** \co-syá\ *va* cos·wa·ya : to cause to warm, as cooked victuals to dry and smoke, as meat < *Tašupe cosyapi wanji ciscila hci ceonpa na hoksila kin k'u* She roasted a quite small piece of cooked intestine and gave it to the boy > — *adv* : warmly < ~ *igluze omani yo* Travel warmly dressed > – Bl — **cosya·kel** \cos-yá-k̇el\ *adv* : in a warm state — **cos'·i·glu·za** \co-s'í-glu-za\ *v refl* or *poss* : to dress up warmly one's own self or posibly one's own

co·tan·ka \ċó-taŋ-ka\ *n* : a flute – Cf ciyotanka

co·za \ċó-za\ *adj* ma·cóza : warm, comfortable – The word is used both in regard to persons and things, as clothing, houses, etc

[1]**cu** \cu\ *interj* : Oh! – Said following the sound of a gun-shot – Bl

[2]**cu** \cu\ *n* : dew < ~ *šma* heavy dew > – R

cu·ci·c'in \cu-cí-c'iŋ\ *va* wá·cucic'in : to keep something with one's self, as a medicine in a bottle – Note: RF knew only *cutic'in* (which cf) and claimed that *cucic'in* to be a Yankton word, i.e. of the Nakota dialect

cu·glu·kan \cu-glú-k̇aŋ\ *v poss* [fr *cu* dew + *yukan* to shake off] : to shake off a dew, as would a tree in the wind shake off snow or ice etc – Note: we might also say *Inše canglukan* perhaps to shake it off a tree. The word is used when in spring ice forms on the branches of trees and drops; or when a cold spell comes in after warm weather in a change of weather – R

cu·han·zi \cu-háŋ-zi\ *v imperf singl* [fr *cu* dew + *óhanzi* shade, *fig* to thaw] : It is a day wrapped in a heavy wet fog < ~ *yelo,* as was said in earlier times when the grass was full of dew and the sky cloudy, thus indicating it would be a warm day > – RF *obsolete*

cu·hci \cu-ȟcí\ *adv* : by one's self – It is used with *pers pron* : miye, niye, etc, and sometimes with *num,* but it is never used alone < Niye ~ *econ wo* Do it yourself >

cu·hli \cuȟlí\ *express contrac* : *Mat'i ni, i.e. tuwa koška e-hantanš* May I die, i.e. if one is affected with venereal disease, such as AIDS – Note: *"Mat'i ni"* is the *canwahpa tanka olowan* the bronze grackle's song – GA

cu·i·yo·he \cu-í-yo-he\ *n* : moccasins, those made of old hides that have served as tents < *Wizihanpa wanji ~ micagege yo* Sew for me a pair of moccasins of old tent hides, i.e. a hide that does not turn hard from moisture, *Wimicahca ~ wanji micah yuha yo* My father-in-law, keep my grown-up pair of old tent hide moccasins > – Bl

cu·ma·hpi·ya \cu-má-ȟpi-ya\ *v* : to be cloudy

cu·mni \cú-mni\ *n* : dew-drops — **cumni·š'e** \cu-mní-š'e\ *n* : dew standing in droops, dew-drops – Cf oš'e — **cumniš'e·š'e** \cu-mní-š'e-š'e\ *n* : dew-drops all over anything

cu·ni·yan·t'a \cú-ni-yaŋ-t'a\ *n* : a faint – Cf sniyant'a

cun·ȟa·ka *or* **canȟáka** \cúŋ-ȟa-ǩa\ *n* : a brush or bush so dense that one cannot pass through – R

cun·hlo·ge·ca \cúŋ-ȟlo-ġe-ca\ *n* : dry wood that is rotten within

cun'·i·yu·ta·pi \cuŋ-í-yu-ta-pi\ *n* : a yard measure

cun'·i·yu·wi \cuŋ-í-yu-wi\ *n* : tree vines < ~ *ówicak'o* or *ówicak'ola hu* the the vines of the virgin's bower > – Cf· owicak'ola hu – WE #125

cun·ka·ške \cúŋ-ǩa-šǩe\ *n* : a fence or enclosure; a fort

cun·ka·ške i·yo·ka·tan \cúŋ-ǩa-šǩe i-yò-ǩa-ṫaŋ\ *n* : stapels

cun·ka·ške i·yu·t'in·ze \cúŋ-ǩa-šǩe i-yù-t'iŋ-ze\ *n* : wire stretcher

cunkš \cúŋkš\ *n* : my daughter, in addressing her – Both men and women use the word for girls — **cun·kši** \cuŋ-kší\ *n* mi·cúŋkši : a daughter, a man's brother's daughter, a niece, a woman' sister's daughter

cun·kši·la \cuŋ-kší-la\ *adj* : toy < ~ *wahinkpe* toy bows and arrows

cun·kši·tku \cuŋ-kší-tku\ *n* : his or her daughter – Note : most often used is *cunwitku*

cun·kši·ya \cuŋ-kší-ya\ *va* cunkši·wa·ya : to have for a daughter

cun·k'in \cúŋ-k'iŋ\ *n* : a back load of wood, i.e. as much as a woman can carry on her back

cun·k'in·ta \cúŋ-k'iŋ-ṫa\ *n* : any place where they go for wood

cun·pe·ška *or* **conpeška** *also* **peška** \cúŋ-pe-ška\ *n* : glue – Note: the Lakotas generally obtained glue from boiling buffalo heads, and the residue was used in fastening on the points of their arrows – R

cun·šo·ke \cúŋ-šo-ke\ *n* : dense woods < " ~ *kin hel waun kte wacin yelo,"* "I would want to have my home there in the dense woods, as said the magpie – D.260

cun·tan·ka \cúŋ-taŋ-ka\ *n* [fr *can* tree + *tanka* big] : high wood; groves of timber – Cf cúnšoke

cun·wan·ca \ċúŋ-waŋ-ca\ *n* : a forest

cun·win·zi·ye o·yu·ze \cuŋ-wíŋ-zi-ye o-yù-ze\ *n* : a certain place where the Lakotas picked from pine trees a certain yellow resin or so, which they boiledand used for dyeing yellow – Bl

cun·wi·sku·ye *or* **canwiskuye** \cuŋ-wí-sǩu-ye\ *n* : the honeysuckle perhaps, a species of plant – Cf míniskuya – R

cun·wi·sku·ye hu \cuŋ-wí-sǩu-ye hu\ *n* : the honeysuckle bush – Cf R

cun·wi·tku \cuŋ-wí-tku\ *n* : his or her daughter

cun·wi·ya·pe·ji·ji *or* **cunwiyape·zizi** \cuŋ-wí-ya-pe-ji-ĵi\ *n* : the yellow grape, vine, or fruit – KE

cun·wi·ya·pe·he *or* **cunwiyapehe·la** *or* **cúnyapehe** *or* **cunyápehe** \ċuŋ-wí-ya-ṗe-he\ *n* : grapes < ~ *iyuštaka* to press grapes, ~ *iyuwi* grape vines, the wild purple grape; vitus vulpina, ~ *ojupi* a vineyard > – A #124

cun·wi·ya·pe·he *or* **cúnyapehe puza** \cuŋ·wí-ya-ṗe-he pùza\ *n* : raisins – KE SLB

cun·wi·ya·wa \cun-wí-ya-wa\ *n* : a counting stick, one as used in games such as in ~ *kansu-kutepi* or ~ *kansu-hanpapeconpi*

cun·wo·ȟe·šma \cúŋ-wo-ȟe-šma\ *n* : dense woods, a forest

cu·pe \cu-ṗé\ *n* : marrow

cu·sni \cu-sní\ *adj* : cool, as are dewy mornings and evenings

cu·ti·c'in \cu-ṫí-c'iŋ\ *v* : to carry at the side, as a powder-horn strapped over the shoulder and coming down under the arm < *ptehecutic'in* a powder-horn, made from a cow's horn > – Note: this may be a doubtful translation. The word comes from *ikute* or *icute* and *k'in.* RF did not know the word *cucic'in.* – *See* cucic'in, above – Cf wacutic'in — **cuti·ki·c'in** \cu-ṫí-ki-c'iŋ\ *v poss* : to carry at the side for one

cu·wa·cu·lu·za \ċu-wá-cu-lu-za\ *n* : a scarecrow, a spirit pest – Note: the word is said to have been a Pawnee *express* originally – FD.81

cu·we \cu-wé\ *n* : a woman's older sister — **cuwe·ku** \cu-wé-ku\ *n* : her older sister — **cuwe·ya** \cu-wé-ya\ *va* : to have for an older sister

cu·wi \cu-wí\ *n* : the back, as the Oglala Lakotas say < ~ *mayazan* My back hurts or aches, ~ *nunga* a hunch-back, ~ *okiniya* to gasp, breathe as one dying, ~ *ozilkiya wakinyanka* He went soaring giving his back a long rest, ~ *kiton* to part with one's back, ~ *weton* I part with my back > – Note: all these are funny *express* for taking a smoke

cu·wi·gna·gya \cu-wí-gna-gya\ *va* cuwigna·gwa·ya : to use for a gown

cu·wi·gna·ka \cu-wí-gna-ka\ *n* : a non-Indian woman's dress < ~ *wiyakpakpa* a silk dress >

cu·wi o·gle \cu-wí o-glè\ *n* : Bedding < ~ *gliyomni kte* to go for my bedding > – Bl

cu·wi·o·ki·ni \cu-wí-o-ki-ni\ *vn* cuwio·wa·kini : to sigh Cf comniglazanyan — **cuwiokini·ya** *vn* cuwio·ma·kiniya : to gasp, as one dying; to groan, to breathe deeply < *Cuwipuskica mat'e kinica yelo* Being crushed in spirit, he was anxious that I die > – D.1 and 229 Bl B.H.119.29, 137.25

cu·wi·pa·ha \cu-wí-ṗa-ha\ *n* : the prominent part of the side below the arms

cu·wi·pu·ski·ca \cu-wí-ṗu-sǩi-ca\ *vn* cuwi·ma·puskica : to be oppressed with sorrow, not anger

cu·wi·pu·ski·ca·t'e·ki·ni·ca \cu-wí-ṗu-sǩi-ca-t'e-ǩì-ni-ca\ *v* cuwipuskica·ma·t'ekinica : to be dying with pent-up

---

\a\ father \e\ they \i\ machine \o\ smoke \u\ lunar \an, aŋ\ blanc Fr. \in, iŋ\ ink \on oŋ & un uŋ\ soon & confier Fr. \c\ chair \ġ\ machen Ger. \j\ fusion *clusters* bl, gn, kp, hšl, etc... \ b[e]lo ... said with a slight vowel **See more in the Introduction, Guide to Pronunciation**

sorrow, neither to rage nor to be in rage

cu·wi·ta \cu-wí-ṫa\ *adj* ma·cuwita un·cuwita·pi : cold, feeling cold

cu·wi·ta·gla \cu-wí-ṫa-gla\ *v* cuwita·wa·gla : to be trembling with cold – Bl

cu·wi·yu·ksa \cu-wí-yu-ksa\ *adj* : cut off at the waist < *ogle* ~ (not ~ *ogle)* a vest

cu·wi·yu·ski·te \cu-wí-yu-ski-ṫe\ *n* : a vest, or corset perhaps

cu·ya \cu-yá\ *va* cu·wa·ya : to cause dew

c'a \c'a\ *v* [fr *k'a* dig] : to dig – Cf kic'a

c'el \c'el\ *contrac altern phr for* k'el, i.e. kin el : in the ...

c'e·yaš \c'é-yaš\ *conj altern form for* k'eyaš : even if, although

c'on \c'oŋ\ *altern dem pron* or *def art* : that – *K'on* is changed to *c'on* after an *a* turned into an *e* < *Yunkan wanna emakiye c'on weksuye. Hecel miš tokel emakiye k'on ecel owakiyaka. Hehanl koškalaka eya waonspewicakiye c'on hena tacan kin icupi na tima eonpapi. Canke kolaye c'on ihunni na nupin wicao* Then I now remembered what he had said to me. So as it was I spoke to him about what he had said to me. At that time some young men whom he had taught took and placed the body inside. And then a close friend of his had got there and shot them both >

c'on·han \c'oŋ-háŋ\ *adv altern for* k'onhan : when (in ref to past time)

E

[1]e \e\ *pref* : It is commonly affixed to *v* .
 1 : signifying "to" or "at" and it is equivalent to *ektá* thus: *eihpeya* to throw away at a place. It makes a location "from" of the *v* and denotes that the action is done at a place, thus: *ewaksa* to saw off at. – Note: there are two other location *pref*, *"a"* and *"o"*
 2 : It makes a *coll pl* form of some *v* , thus: *inajin* he stands up, *enajin* they stand up

[2]e \e\ *v irreg* : to be < *he e* that is, *epi* they are or there are or there is > – Note: the word is used to *ref to* a person or thing mentioned before < *Pte san e ca okile hwo?* Is it a white buffalo he looks for?, *Na wanna ti iglukšan e enajin na lila wicotapi* And now they stood up, that is around a house, and they were very many, *Lakota num wicakahnigapi, unma Wahukeza Wašte e na unma Tašunke Luzahan e,* Two Lakotas were chosen, one that is Good Lance, the other being Fast Horse, *Yunkan he ate e ca koškalaka lila owanyank wašte.* Then there is a most handsome young man who is a Father, *Yunkan tipi kin e šni.* And then there was no house. *Wanna koškalaka kin e na tankšitku kin e na kunšitkula wan henakeca iglaka yapi keye.* Now he stated there were only so many, a young man, that is, his younger sister and his grandmother who went on a trip. *Tuwa e makagapi so?* Who is it they take me to be? > – B.H.67.7, 11.1, 167.5

[3]e \e\ *adv* : on the other hand, instead < *He e pila po* Rather you all be thankful > – B.H.51.19, 75.23, 123.4

e·ca \e-cá\ *adv* 1 : purposely < *Hogan tanka wan el eca yeya* In a great fish he continued on, for a purpose > 2 : anyhow, it's too bad, i.e. in *ref* to something done in the past; really, truly < ~ *wica wan akih'an t'in lo* Indeed, a man died starving, ~ *okihi šni yelo* Truly he was not able > — **eca ... laka** *conj* : it is ... there is < *Wicaša, eca tuwa wiwanciciyankapi nainš wacicikpamnipi kta makahnige laka?* Man, am I the one there is to select myself to judge or deal out things for you? > – Cf eháš SLB B.H.117.12, 195.3, 266.4, 224.2, 260.25

e·ca·ca \e-ċá-ċa\ *adv perhaps* 1 : for diversion, in fun <~ *lowan* to sing for a diversion > 2 : at all, by all means, so entirely, really, undoubtedly < ~ *tokah'an* She was really lost, ~ *ištinma* He was deep in slumber, *or* There is no doubting he was asleep, ~ ... *hiyu* He came here ... by all means > – Note: before a *v* it means to do thoroughly what the *v* indicates Cf D.26, 268

e·ca·e·con·ka \e-cá-e-còŋ-ka\ *vn* ecae·camon·ka 1 : to follow e.g. a business *or* occupation; to do as one likes, persistently against advice, to be self-willed 2 : to pretend

e·ca·han·ke·ya *or* **ecahankeyela** \e-cá-haŋ-ke-ya\ *adv* : immediately, right after; completely, continuously – Bl

e·ca·he·con·ka \e-cá-he-còŋ-ka\ *v* ecahe·camon·ka : to feign, pretend; not to do, or to do in spite of

e·ca·h'e *or* **ecaȟe** *or* **ecah'eke** \e-cá-ȟ'e\ *adv express of impatience* : indeed, truly, and is used only by women – R

e·ca·i·ci·je·na·ya \e-cá-i-ci-je-na-ya\ *v* ecaicijena·wa·ya : to mix together – Bl KE

e·ca·i·ci·šni·yan \e-cá-i-cii-šni-yaŋ\ *adv* : wrongly, entirely wrong – R Bl

e·ca·i·c'i·on *or* **ecakic'on** *also* **icoic'ion** \e-cá-i-c'i-oŋ\ *v refl* eca·mi·c'i-on : to do or determine e.g. evil to one's self – Cf ecakion R KE

e·ca·ka·leš *or* **ecakeleš** \e-cá-ka-leš\ *adv* : at any rate, nevertheless < ~ *cic'u kte šni* Nonetheless I shall not give it to you, as might be said when I want more for it, e.g. a horse, than what you offer > – Note: *ecakce* may be a related word in meaning but having no verification – SB

e·ca·kca·na \e-cá-kca-na\ *adv* : soon, *ref* to more than one event – Bl

e·ca·kel \e-cá-kel\ *adv* : purposely, but at the beginning < *Wo mak'u cin šni* ~ ; ~ *wo mak'u cin šni.* ~ *yahi* But from the start he did not want to give me food; but purposely he did not want to give me food. But then you arrived >

e·ca·ki·ci·on \e-cá-ki-ci-oŋ\ *va* [fr *econ* to do] : to do for one, perhaps < *Tokeške can šeca ecakicionpi kta hwo?* What in the world would they do with rotten wood? > – B.H.-74.2, 250.8, 265.18

e·ca·ki·con \e-cá-ki-coŋ\ *v* eca·we·con eca·ye·con eca·un·kicon·pi ecaci·con eca·miye·con [fr *econ* to do] : to do to one < *Na šunk luzahan num wicawacin yelo, eya.*

Na waun ecel ecakionpi. Na taku cinpi kin ecawicayecon kta keye k'on. Oyate tokel ecawicunkiconpi kta hwo? He said he wanted two first-rate horses. As it was being well off it was done for him. And when they wanted something he had said you would do it for them. How would we do it for the people? >

e·ca·ki·on \e-cá-ki-oŋ\ *v* eca·wa·kion eca·ma·kion [fr *econ* to do] : to do against < *Taku ecacicion welaka* What did I ever do against you? *i.e.* would you please let me know. > – B.H.68.18,112.6, 236.7, 237.11

e·ca·mna \e-cá-mna\ *adj* : having smell or taste, fragrant, savory – B.H.190.5

e·ca·na *or* **ecanna** \e-cá-na\ *adv* : soon < ~ *aglihunni kte lo* He will get back soon >

e·can·kin \e-cáŋ-kiŋ\ *va* ecan·wa·kin ecan·maya·kin : to think so of, form an opinion of one < *Heceš ipilapika ecankinpi. Tuweni lena wayakapi ecawicakin kte* This way they formed an opinion of those refusing. No one here should think this of captives > – D.202, 252

e·canl \e-caŋl\ *adv* : just then, at that instant when suddenly ... – Note: the word is often preceded by a verb in the *fut* tense: ... *kte.* But perhaps *tka ecanl* ... calls for *hcehanl* – Pb.68 B.H.69.4, 299.9 D.5

e·can·le·ha \e-cáŋ-le-ha\ *adv* : but instead – B.H.99

e·can·leš \e-cáŋ-leš\ *adv* : instead, in place of that; all the more, i.e. in a subordinate clause < *Na wanna kéya ónši íyahan* (i.e. on the blanket) *tka* ~ *inyan kin ko opemnipi* And now the miserable turtle climbed up on (the blanket), but all the more so was the rock as well wrapped in it > – B.H.212.7, 245, 255, 290, 311.41

e·ca·o·wan·ca·ya \e-cá-o-waŋ-ca-ya\ *adv* : all over – Bl

e·ca·o·yan·ke·ya \e-cá-o-yaŋ-ke-ya\ *adv* : by groups – Bl – *Syn* OŠPAŠPAYE

e·ca·o·ya·sin \e-cá-o-ya-siŋ\ *adv* : all *emph* – Bl – *Syn* OŠPAŠPAYE, ECAOYANKEYA

e·caš \e-cáš\ *express* : indeed, certainly, to be sure, to dispel any doubt < *Ecaš wau kte (i.e. you can depend on that). Na* ~ *topa can kin ake h'oká unhena el u wicaši* To be sure, I shall come. And certainly he told those singers to come there again after the four days > – B.H.41.22, 79.5

e·ca·šni \e-cá-šni\ *neg express* [fr *ecaš* indeed] : certainly not < ~ *s'e canku kin ášlayela yunke lo* The road lay as if not indeed clear (i.e. as though no snow had fallen on the road > – Bl

e·ca·un \e-cá-uŋ\ *v* : to be all alone by myself < *Miš lena tokel ecawicaun kin slolwaye šni. Cham tawicoicage kin iyuha kinil apica makoce el ecaunpi* I for one did not know why these were alone by themselves, Almost all Cham's off-spring were all alone in good country > – Bl B.H.-10.7

e·ca·ya·u·ke·ca \e-cá-ya-u-ke-ca\ *vn* eca·ma·yaukeca : to remain in one place — *n* : something permanent, a fixture

e·ca ... ye·la·ka \e-cá ... yè-la-ka\ *conj* : is it possible; it is ... therefore – Cf under *eca* < *Amayalupte šni, eca wica niglawa šni yelaka* You do not respond to me, is it possible a man does not rely on you? > – B.H.90.7, 113.19, 172.5, 177.18; 180.9, 184.8, 191.25, 210.17, 229.26, 239.12, 256.20, 264.12 SLB

e·ca·yu·h'i \e-cá-yu-h'i\ *n* : something all covered with buboes (inflammatory swellings), as does a toad — *adj* : rough, uneven on the surface

[1]**e·ce** *or* **ecela** \e-cé\ *adv* : only < *Yunkan huh'aka ece hpaye. Wi num ece tokanl waun. Ištogmus ece wayacipi kta. Wa ece skanyanpi na yatkanpi* Then he lay there only skin -and-bones. After only another two months he was well-off. You all will be dancing only with eyes shut. Snow alone did they melt and drink. >

[2]**e·ce** \ĕ-cĕ'\ *interj a friendly disappointment at a refusal* : Oh no!

e·ce·ca \e-cé-ca\ *vn* e·ma·ceca unke·ceca·pi : to be so, be affected with, as with a cold or disease; to be like < *Taku haye cin owasin taha* ~ . *Yunkan wicaša wan ataya huhu* ~ *ca na ha yelo hpaya* All that he had for clothes were like deer skin. Then since the man's limbs were altogether affected, he lay a dead-man > — *adv* : thus, so

e·ce·ca·ke \e-cé-ca-ke\ *adv* : just so, even so, that alone

e·ce·ce·ca \e-cé-ce-ca\ *adv red of* ececa : thus, so – Note: the word may function also as a *vn* – Bl

e·ce co·la yu·ha \é-ce co-la yu-hà\ *v* : to keep a horse free e.g. for work, to spare it < *Ece cola bluha kta* I might spare it, i.e. a horse > – Bl

e·ce·e \e-cé-e\ *adv* or *adj* : every < *Omaka wanji* ~ *econpi* It was done every year > – KE

e·ce·gla·la \e-cé-gla-la\ *adv* : only that – Bl

e·ce·hci \e-cé-hci\ *adv* : just so, exactly i.e. as one expected

e·ce·kce *or* **ecelkce** \e-cé-kce\ *adv* : in the proper place or way, in place < *Wanna ecelkce kiglapi* Each went his own way home, *Wowapi ecekce égnaka yo* Put books in their proper place > – B.H.35.10-13, 284.23

e·ce·kcel \e-cé-kcel\ *adv red of* ecel : in this manner or way; so and so, thus and thus – B.H.25.15 — **ecekcel·ya** *adv* : thus and thus

e·cel \e-cél\ *adv* : thus, so i.e. as it must be, as it was < *Tiyopa ecel icu* So he shut the door, *Tiyopa ecel iyeya* As it was he found the door >

[1]**e·ce·la** \ĕ'-ce-la\ *adj* : right, correct — *adv* : once, only < *Omaka wanjila* ~ *econpi* It was done in only one year >

[2]**e·ce·la** \e-cé-la\ *adv* : only, alone

e·ce·la·hcin \e-cé-la-hciŋ\ *adv* : just so much, that alone

e·ce·la·kel \é-ce-la-kel\ *adv perhaps* : itself alone, without help

e·cel·kce \e-cél-kce\ *adv* : in place – Cf ecekce

e·cel·ya \e-cél-ya\ *v* [fr *ecel* as it must be + *iyeya* of a sudden] : to make it quickly as it must be < *Tiyopa* ~ *yo* Shut the door >

e·ceš \e-céš\ *interj of unwillingness, used by women only* : of course < ~ *tuwá le* Of course, who is this? >

e·ce·ti \é-ce-ti\ *v* éce·wa·ti éce·un·ti·pi : to build a fire to or at

e·ce·tki·ya \e-cé-tki-ya\ *adv* : in some direction or other – Bl KE

e·ce·tu \e-cé-tu\ *vn* : to be accomplished or fulfilled < *Eyá letán nunpa can* ~ *kin unyanpi kte lo. Tokata lena* ~ *kte lo* Well, when it is two days from now, we shall go. In time yet to come it will be accomplished > — *adv* : so, thus, just right, about so many or so much < *Yamni* ~ It is about three > – B.H.112.1, 117.225 — **ecetu·kiya** \e-cé-tu-ki-ya\ *va* ecetu·wa·kiya : to make so, to accomplish or fulfill — **ecetu·šni** *adj* : null, void — **ecetu·šni·ya** *va* : to make a breach, i.e. of peace, a contract, etc; to rescind — **ecetu·ya** *va* ecetu·wa·ya : to fulfill, accomplish, to bring about — *adv* : about < *St. Francis Mission etan* west *etkiya* three miles ~ *ti* He lives about

---

\a\ father \e\ they \i\ machine \o\ smoke \u\ lunar \an, aŋ\ blanc Fr. \in, iŋ\ ink \on oŋ & un uŋ\ soon & confier Fr. \c\ chair \ġ\ machen Ger. \j\ fusion \clusters bl, gn, kp, hšl, etc... \ b^{e}lo ... said with a slight vowel **See more in the Introduction, Guide to Pronunciation**

three miles west from St. Francis Mission >

e·ce·wa·kta \e-cé-wa-kta\ *v* ecé·wa·wakta : to attend to, to pursue such a course; to be accustomed to — **ecewakta·ya** \e-cé-wa-kta-ya\ *adv* : attending to

e·ce·ya·nu·ni·ya \e-cé-ya-nu-ni-ya\ *va* : to lead astray

e·ci·a·i·yo·pte·ya \é-ci-a-i-yo-pte-ya\ *adv* : directly by, in the direction of – Bl

e·ci·ca·ska·ya \é-ci-ca-skà-ya\ *adv* : coming from all over < *Oyate kin witaya ~ okimniciye kta keyàpelo* They say the people coming from all over would return to meet together > – Bl

e·cin \e-cíŋ\ *vn* ecán·mi ecán·ni unki·cin·pi : to think, to suppose < *Na le tuwe hwo? Ecannipi nacece lo* And who is this? Perhaps you are supposing > – B.H.47.6 — *va* e·wa·canmi : to think of some one or of something – Note: the thought is expressed before the word *ecin*

e·cin·i·c'i·ci·ya \e-cíŋ-i-c'i-ci-ya\ *va* : to bring one's self to do something

e·cin·ka \e-cíŋ-ka\ *v* ecan·mi·ka [fr *ecin* think] : to think, to hesitate or waver in one's opinions

e·cin·šni \e-cíŋ-šni\ *adj* : thoughtless, foolish, vain — *adv* : thoughtlessly, foolishly, wrong < ~ *ecamon* I did it rechlessly >

e·cin·yan \e-cíŋ-yaŋ\ *adv* : hardly, barely < *Kitan ~ pawoslal iheya yanke* Hardly giving thought to it, straining to rise upright, he was expiring, as is said of a sick person when he is about ready to die > – LB KE

e·ci·pa \é-ci-pa\ *vn* [fr *akipa* to meet] : to meet together, as two ends of anything or as two armies in battle — **écipa·pi** *n* : an encounter, a meeting – D 215 — **ecipe·ya** \é-ci-pe-ya\ *va* écipe·wa·ya : to cause to meet together, as two ends of anything

e·ci·ptan \é-ci-ptaŋ\ *adv* [fr *akiptan* join forces] : together < ~ *ecunkonpi kte lo* We'll work at it together >

e·ci·škan·yan·kel \é-ci-škaŋ-yàŋ-kel\ *adv* : together – Bl

e·ci·ta·pa \é-ci-ta-pa\ *adj* : agreeing with each other, all of the same length; fitted to

e·ci·ya \e-cí-ya\ *va* e·wa·kiya un·ke·kiya·pi e·ni·ciya e·maya·kiya [fr *éya* say] : to say to one < *unkekiciyapi* we say to each other, *Niš tokel eniciya hwo?* Why did he say it to you? *Wowicake šni ca ayuštan yo, emakiya.* Since it is not the truth let him alone, he said to me > – Note: *c* changes back to *k* after the *a* of the pronoun. It seems the word is introduced from the Dakota of the Santee and therefore should be *ekiya*

e·ci·ya·pa·tan·han \e-cí-ya-pa-taŋ-haŋ\ *adv* : towards < *htayetu ~* towards evening > – B.H.17.11 SLB

e·ci·ya·pi *or* **ekiyapi** \e-cí-ya-pi\ *v 3rd pers pl* or *part of* eciya : called, named

e·ci·ya·tan \e-cí-ya-taŋ\ *adv* : from, thence, hence < *Na yamni can ehanl anpa ~ tokecela ayanpa. Yunkan taku wan skayela mahpiya ~ u* At the time in three days a little before daylight day came. There then came from the sky something quite white >

e·ci·ya·tan·han \e-cí-ya-taŋ-haŋ\ *adv* : from, of; on account of; concerning; hence < *tiyopa ~* from the door >

e·ci·ya·wa·pa s'e \e-cí-ya-wa-pa s'e\ *adv* : further on – *Syn* AKOWAPA

e·ci·yu·pta \é-ci-yu-pta\ *v* [fr *ayupta* to answer] : to answer one another

e·co·kon \e-có-koŋ\ *va* eco·wa·kon [fr *cokon* plot evil] : to determine evil against one for any cause

e·con \e-cóŋ\ *va* eca·mon *or* ecamun, eca·non *or* ecanun, e·cunkon·pi *or* ecunkunpi : to do, to work < *omniciye ~* to hold a meeting > – Note: WWH suggests the more proper spelling and pronunciation of *ecunkonpi* to be *ecunk'onpi*

e·con·ka·pin \e-cóŋ-ka-piŋ\ *v* econ·wa·kapin [fr *kapin* to be indisposed] : to be tired of doing, to want not to do

e·con·ki·ya \e-cóŋ-ki-ya\ *va* : to cause to do anything

e·con·pi·ca \e-cóŋ-pi-ca\ *v* : It can be done, is possible < ~ *šni* It cannot be done – Note: when joined to *v*, *pica* denotes possibility

e·con·pi·ca·ka \e-cóŋ-pi-ca-ka\ *v* It is possible, or perhaps: It is impossible – R Mi

e·co·pi·ca·šni·šni·yan \e-cóŋ-pi-ca-šnì-šni-yaŋ\ *adv red of* econpicašniyan : impossibly — **econpicašni·yan** *adv* : impractically

e·con·ši \e-cóŋ-ši\ *va* : to advise, to exact — **econšipi** *n* : orders

e·con·wa·cin·šni \e-cóŋ-wa-cìŋ-šni\ *v* : to be unwilling to do

e·cu·hci *or* **ecuhciš** \é-cu-hci\ *adv* : at least < *Ota aun wo: ite ~ naot'insya unyankapi kte lo. Lel hanhepi wanji ~ amayanpa na hehanl mni kte* Wear a whole lot: let us at least have crimped our face. I shall spend a night here, then I'll go > – D.228 Bl

e·cu·hci·kel \é-cu-hci-kel\ *adv* : nonetheless – Note: the word is equivalent to *écela eša* though only

e·e \e-é\ *v* hee lee etc which includes the substantive *v* : it is, that is < *Hecel wanna koškalaka num wicakahnigapi: unma Mato Topa ee, na unma Cetan Akicita ee. Na wana osnišni tka ee lila icamna na lila wašme* So two young men were chosen: one was Four Bears, and the other was Soldier Hawk. And it was not exactly cold, though there was real blowing snow and quite deep >

e·e ... e·e ... e·e \e-é ... e-é ... e-é\ *coord conj* : rather ... instead – B.H.184.22

e·eš \é-eš\ *adv* : indeed, that it is

e·e·ki·ya \é-e-ki-ya\ *va* : to substitute for, to put for another; to regard as being something — *adv* : instead of < *Ate, waku šni kinhan miye ~ wicaša kin le wanji u kta* Father, if I have not come home, this man instead of me should come >

e·ge·ju \é-ge-ju\ *v 3rd per pl* : they assembled – B.H.132.8

e·gla·ku \é-gla-ku\ *v poss* é·wa·glaku é·un·glaku·pi [fr *eyaku* take away : to take up again, to take back again, to take up one's own – Bl

e·gle \é-gle\ *va* é·wa·gle é·un·gle·pi : to place, set, or make stand in a place

e·gle·ga \é-gle-ga\ *v* é·wa·glega : to overtake

e·glu·kšan \é-glu-kšaŋ\ *v* : to return or turn around < *Isam ewaglukšan yelo* I went around at a greater distance (looking for something) > – Bl

e·glu·za \é-glu-za\ *v poss* é·wa·gluza [fr *eyuza* seize] : to overtake and take one's own

e·gna \é-gna\ *prep* : with, in amongst, in the midst of; through < *wicegna* amongst them, *oyate ~* with the people, *Ehanl pte otapi k'on ataya makop'o na ~ tan'inšniyan iyayapi* Those many buffaloes had then gone on clear through a cloud of dust and out of sight >

e·gnag \é-gnag\ *v contrac of* egnaka : to lay away < ~ *aya* to take and lay away

e·gna·gna \é-gna-gna\ *prep red of* egna : with, in, amongst, in the midst of, through < *Na ohankeya ~ iyayapi. Hena oyate ~ icahwicaye* And these after some time she raised in the tribe – B.H.104.23

e·gna·ka \é-gna-ka\ *va* é·wa·gnaka é·un·gnaka·pi *or* un·ké-gnaka·pi : to lay down or place, to lay away < *Éyagnake c'el isakib ~ yo* Put it away along side in the place where you had placed it – Bl

e·gna·la·hci \é-gna-la-hci\ *adv* : amongst

e·ha \é-ha\ *adv* : instead, on the contrary - B.H.68.9, 69.4 175.4 D.131 note 3, 204, 23

e·ha·ha·tun \e-há-ha-tuŋ\ *n* : chapped lips

e·ha·ka·leš *or* **eháeš** \e-há-k̇a-leš\ *express* : just for that, in that case < *Nonge nakpayemayelo* ~ . ~ *ecamon kte* My ears are hard of hearing in that case. Just for that I shall do it (a sort of *fig* used for *wicalašni k̇eš* though unbelievable) - R D.130, note 4 Bl SB

e·ha·ke \e-há-k̇e\ *n* : the last one — *adv* : yet, yet to come, a last time < ~ *wanjila* one more, *Heon* ~ *napeciyuzapi* So I shake your hand a last time

e·ha·ke·ke \e-há-k̇e-k̇e\ *adv* : for the very last time < ~ *niun welo* alive for the very last time, as a woman says to a dog when it is to be killed > -Bl LHB

e·ha·ke·la \e-há-k̇e-la\ *n* e·ma·hakela : the last one < *Miš emahakela kta keya. Šunkakanyanka ošpaye wanji* ~ *manipelo* He stated that I would be the last. A group on horseback were the last to travel > — *adv* : yet, yet a little while

e·ha·ke·la·ke·cin·han \e-há-k̇e-la-k̇e-ciŋ-haŋ\ *adv* : soon

[1]**e·han** \é-haŋ\ *vn coll pl of* ihan : they stand in or at < *Hihanna oyate kin taku kapi na kawita* ~ *ca miš el owapa* Next morning the people in question and those who stood in together I joined >

[2]**e·han** \e-háŋ\ *adv* : then, at that time or place; to, thus far < ~ *na he* ~ *winyunga* At that time, and thus far he raised questions > - Note: the word *ref* to past time

e·han·ke·c'un *or* **ehank'un** \e-háŋ-k̇e-c'uŋ\ *adv* : really, indeed < ~ , *Wakantanka Cinca kin he le e yelo. Wana* ~ *micunkši heceya cin šni* Really, this is the Son of God. Indeed, my daughter certainly did not want it, *canke* ~ and really, *Lakota* ~ *winyan kin slolyapi* It was plain she was a Lakota woman > - Cf *ehan'un* which seems related to the word. - GV B.H.268.12 D.157, 270.2

e·han·k'e·han \e-háŋ-k'e-haŋ\ *adv* : long ago, formerly < ~ *Homakšila wanna wimacahcala* Formerly I was a boy, now I am an old man - R B.H.190.22 *Syn* EHANNI, HANBLEBLEKEL KILELEKEL

e·han·k'un \e-háŋ-k'uŋ\ *adv* : indeed - Note: the word is used when one is informed or convinced of something which he has doubted or disbelieved, or has been ignorant of < *Takoja,* ~ *ecakel wasna kin mawayakinon ca wana slolwaye* Grandchild, I knew that you indeed purposely stole the wasna > - D.

e·hanl \e-háŋl\ *adv* : then, at that time, in *ref* to past time alone < ~ *wikoškalaka k'un t'a* Then the young woman had died >

e·han·na *or* **ehanni** \e-háŋ-na\ *adv* : long ago

e·han·ni·tan·han \e-háŋ-ni-t̀aŋ-haŋ\ *adv* : from a long time ago

e·han·tan \e-háŋ-t̀aŋ\ *adv* : already, ever since, from the outset < *He* ~ *yasupi kin heca yelo* It is he who is already judged, ~ *yuhapi* They had it already, before something else happened > - Note : *ehantan* plus a *v* means the first thing was already being done - B.H.-180.20, 191.8, 233.9 D.141, 154, 258, 261, 56

e·han·tan·han \e-háŋ-t̀aŋ-haŋ\ *adv* : from, from that time or place < *Hipi kin* ~ *yamni can* It is three days since they came from that place > - B.H.270.6

e·han·tan·hanš *or* **ehantanš** \e-háŋ-t̀aŋ-haŋš\ *conj* : if < *Tuwa tiwahe wašte kin he nakun cinca tewicaḣila* ~ *le wicoh'an kin econ kte lo* If one cherishes children and a good home, this custom should be kept > - Note: the probable meaning of the word: *Ehantanš, taogligle e yelo* If this be the case, it is his angel - B.H.98.23, 293.20

e·han·tu \e-háŋ-t̀u\ *adv* : at that time < *Hehan koškalaka cik'ala na nahahci tawicuton šni* ~ . *Ecel wagmeza k'on egnakapi le wetu* ~ Then the young man was immature and yet had not married at that time. So at that time that springtime the corn was laid in store > — **ehantu·hci** *adv* : just at that time — **ehantu·ke** *adv* : just then, then; indeed — **ehantu·lahci** *adv* : just then only - Bl

e·han'·un \e-háŋ-uŋ\ *adv* : so, just so, that is so, truly < *Ya,* ~ *le Israel cincapi kin wanjilą yelo. Misun,* ~ *toka šni* Yes, that is so, that this is the only one of the children of Israel. Little brother, that is so he is no stranger > - Note: the word implies one had doubted something before, and that it corresponds perhaps to the word *ehank'un* which *cf* - B.H.46.3, 104, 102.9 LHB

e·han·yan \e-háŋ-yaŋ\ *adv* : so far, as far as, up to a certain mark, as in filling a bottle < *Hu* ~ *lila atan'in šni* The legs up so far were not visible > - Cf hehanyan

e·haš \e-háš\ *adv* : surely, certainly, truly, indeed; unusually, undoubtedly < *Ho heci* ~ *kinšitku kici tila k'un wicaša itancan tunkanyan. Ito* ~ *tanyan wowak'u kte šni yešan, eya. Na kalehlege s'e šaic'iye* O.K., undoubtedly a leading man there who had taken sides with his grandmother is her father-in-law. "Come now, surely on the other hand I shall do well not giving her food," he said. And ideed, he blushed red as though he had struck a blaze > - Note: the word implies that it was too much, more than one can accept - Cf D.17 note 1

e·hun·ni \é-huŋ-ni\ *v coll pl of* ihunni : to reach, get across < *Na wanna Susunipi kin ikiyela* ~ And they reached the Shoshones nearby >

e·hu·we·hwe·gan·han \é-hu-we-ḣwè-ġaŋ-haŋ\ *v* : to be inert or slothful < *Toki le tuwa inahniyela wawaši ca iyaye c'on tok̇é ehuwehwegahe laka, toki iyaye tanin šni ye* Somewhere here some one whom I had been in a hurry to employ had gone, listen why don't you, they are all broken up; he's gone somewhere out of sight, as is said when a man was sent somewhere and stayed away longer than he ought to have > -Bl KE

e·ḣa \é-ḣa\ *va* é·wa·ḣa [fr *ḣa* bury] : to take and bury at a place, to bury there - B.H.103.1, 283.12

e·i·c'i·la \é-i-c'i-la\ *v refl* : to take one's self for a certain thing, esteem one's self as < *Wakantanka* ~ He takes himself to be God > - B.H.3.11

e·i·c'i·ya \é-i-c'i-ya\ *va* : to say to one's self or within one's self - Note: the word is put at the end of quotation - B.H.22.18

e·i·c'i·ca·ga \é-i-c'i-ca-ġa\ *v* : to claim to be < *Wakantanka Cinca eic'icagelo* He claims to be the Son of God > - B.H.264.9

e·i·gla·ku \é-i-gla-k̇u\ *v* : to help one's self to something when nobody gives it to us; to carry one's own back, as wood when nobody helps - Bl

e·i·glu·ja·ja \é-i-glu-ja-ja\ *v refl* : to wash one's self right there - B.H.221.11

e·i·hpe·i·c'i·ya·ya \é-i-ḣpe-i-c'i-ya-ya\ *va* : to betake one's self back, to throw out one'self and go; to be thrown out < *Ónamniyeta eihpeic'imayayapelo* You betook yourself leaving me stand until I caught up and then you again and again went back > - Bl

e·i·hpe·ki·ya \é-i-ḣpe-ki-ya\ *va* eihpe·wa·kiya : to take to and leave at, to throw away at

---

\a\ father \e\ they \i\ machine \o\ smoke \u\ lunar \an, aŋ\ blanc Fr. \in, iŋ\ ink \on oŋ & un uŋ\ soon & confier Fr. \c\ chair \ġ\ machen Ger. \j\ fusion \clusters bl, gn, kp, hšl, etc... \ b[e]lo ... said with a slight vowel **See more in the Introduction, Guide to Pronunciation**

e·i·hpe·ya \é-i-ḣpe-ya\ *va* : to take and leave at; to throw away at < *Mapehin he tehanl paha wan ekta eihpeyapi kta* They should take and leave my hair far off to a hill >

e·i·ya·pa·t'o \e-í-ya·ṗa-t'o\ *vn* : to strike against one < *eiyamapat'o* He struck against me >

e·ka·ga \é-ka-ġa\ *va* : to make a thing at a place < *"Wahpela Mato" kagin kta ca tipi wan ekagapi kte lo* A house will be built since Bear Leaf will make it

e·ka·hta·ka \é-ka-ḣta-k̇a\ *va* : to barely touch there < *Si kin mini kin ekahtakapi* Their feet barely touched the water – B.H.71.11, 116.14

e·ka·win·ga \é-ka-wiŋ-ġa\ *v* é·wa·kawinga : to turn around < *Isam éwakawingelo* I went around at a farther distance, as when looking for something, *Atan'inšniyan kinyan iyaya na ekawingin na ake glihunni. Kinyan iyaye na* ~ It went away flying out of sight, he turned around, and he made his way home > – MS.573

e·ke e·yaš \é-ke é-yaš\ – *See* kec'eyaš

e·ke·ki·ya \é-ke-ki-ya *v* [fr *keya* say that] : to say of one < *Hokšila kin he ayaupi šni ehantanš, wancakeš ayaupi kte šni yelo, eunkekiyapelo* "If you do not bring that boy at once, you will not bring him at all," we said of him – B.H.35.5 LHB

e·ke s'e \ē'-ke s'e\ *express for* : to seem yet to become better < ~ *wanji au wo* Bring one on that seems even better, *Hinhanna* ~ *hingni kta Tomorrow seems will be a* fine (day), *Unkihunnipi kin* ~ *hingni kte lo It seems* there will be joy when we arrive > – IS

e·ke šni \ē'-k̇e šni\ *express for* : to be delivered from, to get out and free without effort, i.e. without hindrance to the better – Cf under *eke s'e,* examples may incorporate *šni,* thus: *eke šni s'e* – Bl BT KE LHB

e·ki·ce·tu \e-kí-ce-tu\ *vn poss* e·má·kicetu [fr *ecetu* be fulfilled] : to recover, to become as before — **ekicetu·ya** \e-kí-ce-ṫu-ya\ *va* ekicetu·wa·ya : to cause to recover, to make right again, to restore, to raise up from the dead

e·ki·ci·ce·tu \e-kí-ci-ce-tu\ *vn* e·mi·cicetu e·ni·cicetu e·ún·kicicetu·pi : to become as before to or for one

e·ki·ci·gla·ku \é-k̇i-ci-gla-ku\ *v* : to help one another loading up, as wood on the back – Bl

e·ki·ci·gle \é-k̇i-ci-gle\ *v* é·we·cigle é·un·kicigle·pi [fr *egle* to place or put] : to place for one

e·ki·ci·glu·za \é-k̇i-ci-glu-za\ *v* é·we·cigluza [fr *egluza* to take one's own] : to overtake and take one's own from another, to retaliate

e·ki·ci·gna·ka \é-k̇i-ci-gna-ka\ *v* é-·we·cignaka é·mi·cignaka [fr *egnaka* lay away] : to lay away for one, to put away and keep for one

e·ki·ci·on·pa *also perhaps* **ékionpa** \é-k̇i-ci-oŋ-ṗa\ *v* é·we·cionpa : to place or set, as a trap for anything; to lay away or place something for another

e·ki·ci·pa \é-k̇i-ci-pa\ *v* [fr *akipa* wait for] : to meet and attack, as two hostile bands – Bl

e·ki·ci·pa·zo \é-k̇i-ci-ṗa-zo\ *v* é·we·cipazo [fr *pazo* to point : to point to for one

e·ki·ci·ya \e-kí-ci-ya\ *v used only in the dual and pl* : *unkékiciya* we two say to each other, *ekíciyapi* they said to each other or to one another

e·ki·ci·ya·ku \é-k̇i-ci-ya-k̇u\ *v* : to help one load wood on his or her back – Bl

e·ki·co \é-k̇i-co\ *va* [fr *kico* invite] : to call through – B.H.46.7

e·ki·gle \é-k̇i-gle\ *v poss* é·we·gle é·un·kigle·pi [fr *egle lay* away] : to place or lay away one's own < *Cunšoke ekta šunk ekiglepi* They lay away their horses in a forest >

e·ki·gle·ga \é-k̇i-gle-ġa\ *v* é·we·glega é·un·kiglega·pi é·wicun·kiglega·pi : to overtake one – B.H.54.2, 115.12, MS .563

e·ki·gna·ka \é-k̇i-gna-ka\ *v poss* é·we·gnaka é·un·kignaka·pi [fr *egnaka* lay away] : to lay away one's own < *Yunkan wak'in k'on ena pahpa* ~ *na akanl iyotaka* I then unloaded right here what I had toted, he laid it away and sat on it >

e·ki·hun·ni \é-k̇i-huŋ-ni\ *v* : to make it home, to come to the end, to finish the course < *Hena éwakihunni iyececa kin, hehanl ake wowaši ecunkon kte lo* When it is proper for me to make it home there, then you and I will again do work > Bl WHL

e·ki·on·pa \é-k̇i-oŋ-ṗa\ *v* : to place or set for anything – Cf ékicionpa

e·ki·pa·zo \é-k̇i-ṗa-zo\ *v* é·wa·kipazo [fr *epazo* to point at] : to show to one, point to or for one

e·ki·tan \é-k̇i-ṫaŋ\ *adv* : anyhow < *Yun! tókinahanš taku otaka ca* ~ *wamašipi kte hcin. Scepanši,* ~ *wawanyank unyin kte* Oh dear me! Maybe I shall be employed anyhow since there are many things (to do). Cousin, she will drop from sight to see (as they were warned not to do) >

e·ki·ya \e-k̇í-ya\ *v* : to say to, to have said to

e·ki·za \é-k̇i-za\ *va of* kiza : to fight them there – B.H. 73.10, 91.12

e·kšu \é-kšu\ *va* é·wa·kšu : to pile up, to lay up in a pile — **ékšu·pi** *part* : piled up

e·kta \e-k̇tá\ *prep* : to, at < *Wicoti* ~ *i na oyaka. Paha wan* ~ *i* He went to camp and spoke. He to a hill — **ekta·kiya** \e-ktá-k̇i-ya\ *adv* : to, towards — **ekta·kte** \e-k̇tá-k̇ta\ *prep red of* ekta : to

e·kta i·hce \é-k̇tá i-ḣce\ *express when another is taken in by a manipulation* : to bring one to go one's way < *Ekta maihce* He gives me just what I want, *Ekta mayáihce* You are giving me just what I want > – BT

e·kta·na \e-k̇tá-na\ *adv* : there behind, after < *Tuweni pa* (here, buffalo) *kin* ~ *ihpeyapi kte šni yelo. Ptepa wan* ~ *ihpeyayapi keye to eye lo, eya. Yunkan (šiyo kin) can kin* ~ *otka keyapi. Wicaša k'eya wanase ipi na* ~ *waceunpahapi* No one is to leave behind buffalo parts. Yes, he said he stated that you left behind a buffalo head. Then they say (the grouse) was hanging from a tree. Some men went on a buffalo hunt and afterwards they were doing roasting > B.H. 171.9 D.273

e·kta·šni·šni·yan \e-ktá-šni-šni-yaŋ\ *adv red* [fr *ektašniyan* not according to] : hardly according to < *Taku* ~ *waeconpi on lila šicapi* ... Scarcely according to what they were busy doing were they on that account very wicked ... > – B.H.80.18

e·kta·šni·yan \e-k̇tá-šni-yaŋ\ *adv* : not according to < ~ *ewatonwan inaniptecapelo* Not according to what I observed were you prevented >

e·kta·wa·pa \e-k̇tá-wa-ṗa\ *adv* : closeby something and facing it < *Tašunke Luzahan* ~ *inajin na leya. Wicoh'an ... hena tokata* ~ *ewagnake lo* Fast Horse stood closeby and this he said: "These customs I set aside for the future." > — **ektawapa·ya** *or* **éktawapàya** \e·k̇tá-wa-pà-ya\ *va* : to make closeby – Cf D.135

e·kte \e-kté\ *va* [fr *e* locative + *kte* kill] : to kill < *Hecena toka wan hpaye k'on he* ~ Finally he killed an enemy who had fallen >

e·kton·ja \é-k̇toŋ-ja\ *va* é·wa·ktonja é·ci·ktonja : to forget something

e·kton·je·s'a \é-k̇toŋ-je-s'a\ *adj* : light-headed, forgetful

e·ku·wa \é-k̇u-wa\ *va* : to follow right then and there, at once – B.H.54.1, 110.18, 115.12

e·k'e·yaš \e-k'é-yaš\ *universalizing particle* – Cf kec'éyaš

el \el\ *prep following a n* : in, at, to — *adv conj following a v* : when, i.e. it has the meaning of the Latin *cum temporale* time when < *Bluštan el owasin hecetu keyapi* They stated that all was O.K. when I finished it, *Wauncipi el ake emaceca* I was affected again when we danced, *Pte kin kiyela au el wanna wanji kute* When the buffaloes came near he shot one, *Kiyela u el hokšila k'on wanyankapi* When he came near the boy had been seen, *Le waniyetu omake ake napciyunka el hecel ecamon* I did this this winter when I was nineteen years old >

el·na·jin \el-ná-jiŋ\ *vn* elna·un·jin·pi : to stand at a place — **elnajin·ya** \el-ná-jiŋ-ya\ *va* elnajin·wa·ya : to cause to stand at; to bring to a stand, as one following a deer when he overtakes it

e·mni·ci·ya \é-mni-ci-ya\ *v coll pl* : tthey came together < *Ecana lila tipi wan tanka ca el* ~ They soon came together in what was a very large house, i.e. there to meet – B.H.206.6, 257.5, 293.15

e·na \é-na\ *adv* : right here < ~ *inajin* Stand right here, *Ho ca ~ un na ni wacin yo* Well now, stay right here and try to live, ~ *nankapi kin, niye ko henanipila kte lo* When you are right here, there will be you and only so many, *Wan, tanyeyela tawicu kicila otuwota ~ el unpi* Look, they are right here at an old camp site living right well with only his wife > — *conj* : and < *ogle wan ~ wicapaha* a shirt and scalp >

e·na·gna·la \e-ná-gna-la\ *adv* : now and then, sometimes

e·na·hci \é-na-ȟci\ *adv* [fr *ena* here + *hci* giving *emphto*] : quite close or near < *Tiyopa ~ iyotakapi* They sat very close to the door > – *Syn* KIYELA

e·na·jin \é-na-jiŋ\ *vn* éna·wa·jin : to stand at a place — *vn coll pl of* inajin : they stand – Cf *e*

e·na·ki·ya \e-ná-ki-ya\ *va* ená·wa·kiya : to finish; to quit, cease from < *Na wanna le okicize kin enakiyapi* And now this fight was finished >

e·na·na \e-ná-na\ *adv* : here and there; sometimes < *Cokanl išnala omani na ~ inajin na yanka na cannunpa wan okipagipi. Yunkan ~ leyapi: Lila zitkala otapelo, eyapi* He alone walked in the middle, here and there he stood, sat, and a pipe was packed for him. Then here and there he said this: "Very many are the birds," it is said > – *Syn* ENAGNALA perhaps — **enana·kiya** \e-ná-na-ki-ya\ *adv* : here and there < ~ *iyayapi.* ~ *mini olepi* They went away here and there. Here and there they found water > – B.H.54.4, 171.15 — **enana·tanhan** \e-ná-na-taŋ-haŋ\ *adv* : from here and there < *Na wanna okšantanhan ~ heyoka k'on au* And from round about and here and there clowns had come >

e·na·pa \é-na-pa\ *v coll pl of* inapa : they come in sight

e·o·ki·ya·ka \é-o-ki-ya-ka\ *va* : to go there and tell – B.H.293.18

e·on·pa \é-oŋ-pa\ *va* é·wa·onpa é·unk'on·pi : to place, to lay carefully < *Le hihanna kin mat'in kta ca tuktel paha wanji el tanyan emaonpa po* Since I am about to die this morning, lay me nicely to rest in a place where it is on a hill. >

e·o·ya·ka \é-o-ya-ka\ *va of* oyaka : to tell there, as would a messenger – B.H.46.6

e·pa·hpa \é-pa-ȟpa\ *va* é·wa·pahpa : to take to and lay down at

e·pa·ni \é-pa-ni\ *va* é·wa·pani : to crowd or shove, to push with the elbows one's way through a crowd

e·pa·tan \é-pa-taŋ\ *v* é·wa·patan : to touch with the hand

e·pa·zo \é-pa-zo\ *va* é·wa·pazo : to point at, point to < *Na tuweni waepazo kin on ~ šni, napahunka kin he on econpi. Na itazipa k'on tatiye topa ku oyasin ~* And no one points at one with the finger, it is done with the thumb. All at once he pointed at a blanket. And he pointed the bow at all four directions >

e·pca \e-pcá\ *v 1st pers singl, the only pers used* : I think < *Epcéhce* I gave it much thought > — **epca·pca** \e-pcá-pca\ *v 1st pers singl red of* epca : I thought so all the time but did not say so < *Epcápcahce* I spent much time thinking > – Bl

e·pce·ca \e-pcé-ċa\ *v 1st pers sing only* : I think so – R — **epce·ce** \e-pcé-ce\ *v red 1st pers singl perhaps of* epce : to come to mind < ~ *el epin kte* I shall say what comes to my mind, ~ *ecamon kte* I shall do what comes to my mind, i.e. *Tokša slolwayin kte* Soon I shall know it, what comes to mind > – Bc Mh

eš \eš\ *particle supposing something else cannot be done* : is it?, if < *Eš lecel ecamon kin wašte kta* It will be good if I do it this way, *Misun, lecel yaunke cin eš takuhci koyakipe sece lo* My brother, when you throw it down, does it not seem as though you are afraid of something indeed? *Eš tok, misun, tokaš* How about it, brother? *Nakun nimayayin na ecel eš micinkši wanwaglake* You inspire me also, and in this way is it not, nephew, that I am seeing myself? *Hecel eš cinka nake inila yanka ške'* So was it, they say, that he was at last silent about desiring it ? *Lila tehan glipi šni, canke ecel eš ewicaktonjapi* For very long they did not return, so at last is it that they are forgotten? > – D.9, 3, 26 B.H.126.18

e·ša \e-šá\ *adv perhaps* 1 : at the beginning of a sentence and followed by *šni* ; a wish is conveyed: I wonder if < *Eša mayak'u šni 150 dollars cic'u kte* I wonder if you will give the (horse) to me for 150 dollars, *Ito, eša wanbli gleška mahingni na kinyan ble šni* Well, I wonder if I shall suddenly become a spotted eagle and go flying? *Eša unkcekiȟa mahingle šni* I wonder if I might become a magpie > – D.144, 226 B.H.122.14, 181.23, 288.11 2 : *at the end of the sentence it means*: although < *Wašiglapi tuwa cinca t'in nainš tawicu eša* Though one's child or wife died they mourned for him/her, *Unkisakib agliyagla eša inila agliyagla* Although they passed alongside us, they passed in silence > 3 : after a *n* or *v* it means: also, some, any perhaps < *Can wiyopewagni kte nainš peji eša, inš šunkawakan eša* I'll go sell wood or some hay, or even a horse too. *Na hehantan wanna waniyetu ota itahena eša, lehanyan nahahci yuhapi* And already it has been many years since and yet they have only so much time, *Nanih'onpi šni eša ceya howaya po* Some did not hear you, cry out weeping! *Lila kutepi eša inihan šni hiyaya* There was much shooting and he went on passed unfrightened, *Hecel unglipi na lila el ewacanmi wawate eša inš imunka ko* So we arrived home and once in I was concerned with eating something or lying down as well > — *particle* : after *pron* it makes them universal < *taku eša* anything, *Tohan mat'e eša hehanl tokeca wanji (wahinkpe) yuha kta* Whensoever I die then he should carry one other (arrow), *Tuweni wicaša eša el yin kte šni* No man whatever will go there > – B.H.185.6, 227.9, 274.4, 275.20

\a\ father \e\ they \i\ machine \o\ smoke \u\ lunar \an, aŋ\ blanc Fr. \in, iŋ\ ink \on oŋ & un uŋ\ soon & confier Fr. \c\ chair \ġ\ machen Ger. \j\ fusion \clusters bl, gn, kp, hšl, etc... \ bᵉlo ... said with a slight vowel **See more in the Introduction, Guide to Pronunciation**

e·šan *also* **eša** \e-šán\ *adv* : also < *Lila* ~ Also as well > – B.H.274.24

e·šaš \e-šáš\ *conj emph of* eša : also < *Wowahtani on kakišunyayapi kte iyececa* ~ , *onšiyulapi ye* Because of sin it is also right that we should suffer; be merciful to us > — *interj* : indeed!

e·šeš \é-šeš\ *particle indicating finality and a mark of contrast in judgment or fact* : on the other hand, nevertheless, whereas < *Taku wanji econ šapi eyaš wicala šni ca* ~ *ecamon kte šni, eyin kte* He will say he has done something dirty, but nevertheless since he does not trust, I will do it, i.e. I do not have to, ~ *mni kte šni* I decidedly will not go, i.e. he lashes out when first he wanted to go along, whereas he did not for any indifferent reason. When one looks for another with whom he wanted to go some place, and when getting there he is told that his boy already went away, then he says: ~ *toka šni* Oh, it is alright. A priest tells John to persuade Joe to give up drinking; John tries hard but has no success; John tells the priest about Joe: ~ *okihipica šni* Oh well, he is unable, Clark thinks of going to Rosebud; then his brother Robert comes to his place in a car and says nothing about where he is going; Clark thinks Robert might go to Rosebud and hence says: *Robert, Rosebud ekta mni kta wacin tka* Robert, but I want to go to Rosebud. Then Robert says: ~ *heciya le ble lo, ca unyin kte* Whereas I am now going that way, let you and I go. If Robert did not intend to go then he could not use *éšeš* ; here it may mean: I have to, I have to anyhow, so you can come along. I told him to have his wife join the *Yatke Šni* Non-Drinkers; so he goes home and tells her, but she says she could not do so. Then Amos comes back to me to tell me so, saying: ~ *wicala šni* O my! He doesn't have confidence. Amos tells me that he and his wife will go to Winner tomorrow. I say that I too want to go then and that they should take me along. He promises. Then in the morning he comes to me saying: ~ *unyanpi kte šni* But now, let's not go. They changed their minds. *Wowapi cic'u tka,* ~ *ecamon šni. Ho ca* ~ *ena awape kte* I would give him a book whereas I did not. Alright, on the other hand I'll wait right here > – B.H.89.7, 118.3, 287.14

e·ta·kpa \é-ta-kpa\ *va* é·wa·takpe *or* éta·wa·kpe [fr *takpé* come up and attack] : to attack a certain person mentioned < *Na wanji najinyanpi ca etakpin na iyahpaya* And one attacked and seized him since they were standing >

e·tan \e-tán\ *prep* or *adv* [fr *etanhan* from] : from, on account of, concerning < *Na etan tima hiyu* And he came from out the house, *I* ~ He went out > — *pron* : some, somewhat < *Canblaska etan unkicupi. Can etan makau po* We took some lumber. Carry some wood >

e·tan·han \e-tan-han\ *prep* : from, on account of, concerning < *Maka gi oyuze el wicoti na* ~ *zuyayapi unketanhanpi. Oglala, S.D., ematanhan unketanhanpi* The camp was at a rich source of brown earth, and from it they made sorties. I am from Oglala, S.D., a conern of ours, X *etanhan na Y hetanhan* from X to Y > – B.H.50.2, 273.1

e·tan·han·han \e-tán-han-han\ *prep red* : from different places, kinds, etc. < *Na ake woyute* ~ *icu na tatiye topa ecel epazo* And again he received something to eat from different places, and so it was he pointed in every direction > – B.H.50.2

e·tan·hanš to·ka \e-tán-hanš tò-ka\ *express* : What difference does it make? < *Etanhanš he toka šni* That makes no difference > – Bl

e·tan·na han·pa \e-tán-na hàn-pa\ *n* : moccasins with no sole sewed on – Note: the Oglalas may say: *etannajin hanpa* – Bl

e·tanš \e-tánš\ *emph for* etan – B.H. 19.13, 259.22

e·tan·što·ka·ka \e-tán-što-ka-ka\ *adv express* : what difference does it make?

e·tan·tan \e-tán-tan\ *prep same as* etanhan

e·ta·pa \é-ta-pa\ *v* éta·wa·pa [fr *tapá* follow after] : to follow after

e·te·i·yo·ki·se·ya·zan \é-te-ì-yo-ki-sè-ya-zan\ *n* : neurology – Note: this is a new word

e·ti \é-ti\ *va* é·wa·ti é·un·ti·pi : to encamp at, to pitch a tent at < *Hehanl ake wakpala wan lila tanka ca el ihunnipi et etipi* They then again reached a very large creek and pitched their tent >

e·ti·ka·ga \é-ti-ka-ga\ *v* to camp at a certain place – B.H.5.5

e·ti·kel \é-ti-kel\ *adv* : travelling and camping at night, but slowly < ~ *unyanhanpi kte lo* Travelling and camping they will for awhile disappear from sight, i.e. as they make their way across the country to the Catholic Congress > – KS

e·ti·yo·yan·ka \é-ti-yò-yan-ka\ *v* : to live in a tent < *Toke ti šni yešan etiyoyankahe so?* Though he has no residence doesn't he for awhile live in a tent?, as a woman would say seeing a man live in a very small tent > – Bl

e·tki·ya \é-tki-ya\ *adv* : towards, to; with < *Wakantanka* ~ *taku okihipica šni wanice lo. Ca* ~ *iblabla* Nothing is impossible with God. So I am on my way with him > – B.H.161.7

e·to·ki·ci·kšu \é-to-ki-ci-kšu\ *v* éto·we·cikšu : to haul for another – Bl

e·ton·wan \é-ton-wan\ *va* é·wa·tonwan é·un·tonwan·pi é·ma·tonwan : to look to or towards < *El* ~ He looked towards him, or at him >

e·tu \é-tu\ *adv* : to, at, in there < *cuwi* ~ in the back, *Makoce wan tokeya el wai k'un he etu šni* The country to which I first had gone was not appropriate > – B.H.-196.19

e·tu·ke·hanl \é-tu-ke-hanl\ *adv* [fr *etu* to + *kin* the + *ehanl* then] : at the proper time < ~ *wowapi wagnuni* I lost a book just when I should have it > – *Syn* CÓKEHANL – Bl

e·tu·la·hci \é-tu-la-hci\ *adv* : just to, at, in

e·tu·la·ke \é-tu-la-ke\ *adv* : after a while, in a little while < ~ *kin* awhile > – *Syn* TOKŠA

e·un \é-un\ *v* é·wa·un : to go and dwell or be, to dwell at

e·wa·ce·ki·ya \é-wa-ce-ki-ya\ *v* : to pray there – B.H. 255.18

e·wa·cin *also* **éwacin·ka** \é-wa-cin\ *va* éwa·canmi éwa·un·cin·pi, éwa·canmi·ka éwa·canni·ka éwa·un·cin·ka·pi : to think of or concerning, to turn one's affections to < *Hecel unglipi na lila el ewacanmi wawate eša inš imunka ko* So we got back and once there I was thinking of doing some eating or else also going to bed, *Eya wacipi kin el owapa eša el ewacanmike šni* Well though I joined in the dance I did not give much thought to it >

e·wan·yan·ka \é-wan-yan-ka\ *v* : to look there – B.H. 271.1

e·we·hi·yu \é-we-hi-yu\ *v* : to hemorrhage (a new word)

e·wi·co·ti \é-wi-co-ti\ *v coll pl* : they camp together < *Inyan to oyuze el* ~ They camped at a blue stone quarry > – B.H.71.8

e·wi·ta·ya \é-wi-ta-ya\ *v* : to assemble there — *3 pers pl* : they assembled – B.H.107.6

e·wo·ya·ka \é-wo-ya-ka\ *v* [fr *woyaka* to tell] : to tell there

e·ya \é-ya\ *v* epá ehé un·kéya·pi : to say anything — *adv commencing a sentence* : Well, colloq < *Eya, tanyan unkunpelo* Well, we are fine >
conj : also, too < *miš eya* I also >
pron : some < *Na wakapapi eya mak'u* She gave me some pemmican > - Cf k'eya B.H.83.3
conj : although, anyhow - Note: the combination *Eya ... k'eyaš,* thus: *Eya lila wamatuka k'eyaš el mni kta* Though I am very worn out, still I should go there (*eya* must here be used), < *Lila wamatuka, k'eyaš eya el mni kte. Eya wacipi kin el owapa eša el ewaconmike šni* I am very worn out, but anyhow I shall go there. Although I joined in the dance I gave little thought to it > - Note: the form *eya ... eša is perhaps used also* < *Eya ayupta* Anyhow answer him, or You will answer him thus > - B.H.174.17 LHB

e·ya·ca·šton \é-ya-ca-štoŋ\ *v* : to give a name to - Cf cašton

e·ya ce·ki·ya \é-ya cè-ki-ya\ *v* : to have said praying - B.H.78.3, 80.9

e·ya ce·ya \é-ya cè-ya\ *v* : answering he wept - B.H.96.7

e·ya·han \é-ya-haŋ\ *v coll pl of* iyahan *in ref to the pres* : they go up a hill and stand on - Cf iyáhan — **eya·he** *v coll pl in ref to what is past* : they went up a hill and stood

e·ya hin·gla \e-yá hiŋ-glà\ *v* : to commence or burst out saying

e·ya ho·ye·ki·ya \é-ya hò-ye-ki-ya\ *v* : saying he yelled out to him - B.H.122.25 LHB

e·ya ho·ye·ye \é-ya hò-ye-ye\ *v* : to say with a loud voice - B.H.90.9

e·ya i·ce·ki·ye \é-ya i-cè-ki-ye\ *v* : saying he besought him - B.H.63.15 LHB

e·ya i·wa·ho·ya \é-ya i-wà-ho-ya\ *v* : saying he asked of me - B.H.94.11 LHB

e·ya i·wa·kta·ya \é-ya i-wà-kta-ya\ *v* : saying he was expecting - B.H.207.6 LHB

e·ya·ke \e-yá-ke\ *adv express* : you don't say < *Lila icamna lah* ~ It was a mighty storm – you don't say! > - Note: the *express* is used by women on hearing an unexpected bit of news or something that everybody knows and then ironically the word is used

e·ya ki·co \é-ya ki-cò\ *v* : saying he called him - B.H. 81.6 LHB

e·ya·ki·pan \e-yá-ki-paŋ\ *v* : saying he yelled at him - B.H.81.9 LHB

e·ya·kpa·ha \é-ya-kpa-ha\ *v poss* : to herald out one's own - B.H.192.6

e·ya·ku \é-ya-ku\ *va* é·bla·ku élaku é·un·yaku·pi : to take up, to take away < *Can ota* ~ He took away many trees > - Bl

e·ya·la s'e \e-yá-la s'e\ *adv* : seemingly all, apparently nothing but < *Unpšija (mud)* ~ *wagli yelo* I got home apparently covered, bespattered, with mud, *Wipatapi* ~ He is entirely covered with quill-work, i.e. he was so laden with such (porcupine quills) work that he seemed to be solid embroidery > - Note: this form extends also to other things such that we might speak of a camp thus: *wakablapi* ~ He is such a good provider, i.e. that it is as though you cannot see his home for all the racks of jerked beef drying around it - Bl D.51, note 2

eya lecel e-yá lé-cel\ *express of doubt* : do it if you can but you cannot - Note: this is a by-word used among friends as an answer to a big boast and expressing doubt. When the speaker adds it himself, he shows that he does not wish to be taken seriously

e·ya lo·wan \é-ya lo-wàŋ\ *v* : saying he sang - B.H.-88.4 LHB

e·ya o·ki·wa \é-ya o-kì-wa\ *v* : to write saying - B.H. 111.21 LHB

e·ya·pa·ha \é-ya-pa-ha\ *v* éya·wa·paha éya·un·paha·pi : to herald, proclaim aloud; to stand out and make a speech — *n* : a crier, herald, announcer - Note: the word may more properly be *iéyapaha,* which see, and may be derived from *ié* + *apaha* — **e·ya·pa·ha·ha** *v red of* ieyapaha : to announce over again - B.H.117.23

e·ya·pi e·ce·hce, e·ya u e·ce·hce \e-yá-pi e-cè-ȟce, e-yá u e-cè-ȟce\ *express of depreciation* : nothing but talk; nothing to it - GV

e·yaš \é-yaš\ *adv* : but then, as said familiarly < *Hecel hoopta ble* ~ *wicimani kin ataya kowakipapi.* So I went across the camp circle, but as I made my way I was entirely taken by fright. *Otiwota wicaša un wanji lel hi,* ~ *lila šicamna ca tima ye šni gle šipelo* One being an old-camp man arrived here, but because he was bad-smelling they told him to go home, not to go inside *Na* ~ *hehanyan wana oyate kin iye etkiya kicicupi kta on igluhomnipi* And however, then the people turned around toward him so he might be taken back > -B.H.94.10

e·ya šna \é-ya šna\ *adv* : every now and then, every time - B.H.70, 115,133, 137, 139, 159, 166, 191, 209, 307,192

e·ya·štan \é-ya-štaŋ\ *v coll pl of* yaštan : they finish speaking or eating or singing perhaps < *Ake lowanpi na eyaštanpi ehanl wicaša k'on he cokab inajin na lecel eya. Olowan kin le* ~ *el wanna ceyapi* When again they sang and finished speaking, then this man rose in the center and spoke in this way. When he finished the song they wept >

e·ya·što·ka \é-ya-što-ka\ *express* : I don't care, it makes no difference

e·yaš tu·ka \é-yaš tu-kà\ *adv* : as you should recall < ~ *unkicante kin unkoile s'elececa* Recall, our hearts were as though afire within us > - B.H.273.14

e·ya·wa *also* **e ya·wa** \é-ya-wa\ *v* : to take for, consider <*Jesus Messiah kin eyawapi* Jesus was taken for the Anointed One > - B.H.269.3

e·ya·we·la s'e \e-yá-we-la s'e\ *adj* : all bloody < ~ *ku* He came home all bloodied >

[1]**e·ya·ya** \é-ya-ya\ *va* éblable élala éun·yaya·pi : to take or to have taken with one < *Takoja, ištinma ye, ciciye wan u kta na éniyayin kte* Grandchild, go to sleep, a bogyman will come and will take you away, as a woman would say when putting children to sleep > - PD

[2]**e·ya·ya** \é-ya-ya\ *v coll pl of* iyaya : they have gone - Note: the same as *iyáyapi* - B.H.134.16

[3]**e·ya·ya** \e-yá-ya\ *v red* epápa unke·yaya·pi [fr éya say] : to say often, to repeat < *Tonhanyan oyakihipi ȟupahu koza po eyáyin* He kept saying: Flap your wings as long as you are able > - D.13

e·ya·ya·la·ka \e-yá-ya-la-ka\ *v red* epápa·laka : to lie

e·ye·ce·leš \e-yé-ce-leš\ *a by-word* : he said that a long time ago - WE LHB

e·ye le \e-yé le\ *express* : he said so, as is said when doubting a statement made by *men; by women: Eyá ke ... keyapi* He means to say ... it is said

---

\a\ father \e\ they \i\ machine \o\ smoke \u\ lunar \an, aŋ\ blanc Fr. \in, iŋ\ ink \on oŋ & un uŋ\ soon & confier Fr. \c\ chair \ġ\ machen Ger. \j\ fusion *clusters* bl, gn, kp, hšl, etc... \ bᵉlo ... said with a slight vowel
See more in the Introduction, Guide to Pronunciation

e·ye·pi·ca·šni \e-yé-pi-ca-šni\ *adj* : absurd

e·ye·šan \é-ye-šaŋ\ *express* : that is he < *He Ikpi Hunhunla iyekiyapi šni keye* He stated they failed to recognize Belly Shake, that is he, > – Note: the expression is a *deriv* of *iye + eša,* or *ee* + eša, perhaps

e·ye·ya \e-yé-ya\ *va* : to make say, to say something < *Ituśeka taku wanji eyemayayin kte hcin tka aciyuptin kte šni* I shall indeed keep saying something to you over and over again, but I will not give you an answer > – Bl

e·yo·ka·kin \é-yo-ka-kiŋ\ *va* éyo·wa·kakin : to look round into, as in a door partly open; to look out of

e·yo·ka·s'in \é-yo-ka-s'in\ *va* éyo·wa·kas'in éyo·un·kas'in·pi : to peep in, as through a keyhole; to look in by stealth < *Ohloka wan lila ciscila etun eyokas'inpi* They looked at him through a very tiny hole, *Cunwitku ti kin el* ~ He took a look in at his daugher's house, or She peeped into her daughter's tipi > – D.19

e·yo·ta·ka \é-yo-ta-ka\ *v coll pl of* iyotaka : they sat down < *Wol eyotake* They sat to eat > –B.H.124.3

e·yu·ġi·ca \é-yu-ġi-ca\ *vn* : to wake up right there, to go to and wake up – B.H.117.3, 134.15, 203.9

e·yu·hpa \é-yu-ḣṗa\ *va* é·blu·hpa : to take and lay down at, to take off one's pack and rest it, < *Íṗaḣe éyuhpapi (sic ipaġe)* They rested their packs before going on, e.g. to the place assigned for dinner > – Bl

e·yun·ka \é-yuŋ-ka\ *va* émunka énunka : to go and sleep at < *Iyayapi na wicoti kinikiyela* ~ They went and went to sleep out near the camp > – B.H.55.11 — *v coll pl of* iyunka : they went to bed

e·yu·tan \é-yu-taŋ\ *va* : to go near and touch < *Ungna emayalutan kilo* Beware lest you go touching me > – B.H.134.16, 137.9

e·yu·we·ge \é-yu-we-ġe\ *v coll pl of* iyuwega : they passed through or across – Note: *iyuwegapi has* the same meaning

e·yu·za \é-yu-za\ *va* é·blu·za : to go and take at, seize and hold at or on the way, to hold to or at

G

ga·ga·ya \ġa-ġá-ya\ *adv* : on the surface < ~ *špan* to fry a piece of meat on its flat side or surface, as a slice of bacon

ga·ge·ca \ġa-ġé-ca\ *n* : dross – Cf ginginca, below

gal·ga·ta \ġal-ġá-ta\ *adv* : forked, pronged; open, as a piece of cloth

gan \ġaŋ\ *adj* : mussed, dishevelled, as is said of hair standing up or sideways – Cf gan'íc'iya and wicágangan < *Pehin nigan* Your hair is mussed >

gan·gan \ġaŋ-ġáŋ\ *adj* : open, as is thin cloth

gan·gan'i·c'i·ya \ġaŋ-ġáŋ-i-c'i-ya\ *v refl red of* ġaŋ : to make hair stand on end – Cf gan'ic'iya

gan·gan·la \ġaŋ-ġáŋ-la\ *adj* : full of holes, as threadbare cloth appears to be etc *maganganla* i.e. I feel the cold because of this clothing, *Wana maganganla ca ťhanhan icaluza keš kagan mahiyu welo* Since for fun I was threadbare, the cold though came and passed right on through me > – Bl

gan·gan·šni \ġaŋ-ġáŋ-šni\ *adv* : crowded together, as men, animals, many wagons, etc < ~ *ahiyelo* They arrived there in a throng > — **ganganšni·yan** *adv* : jammed together, there being no room between – Cf R – WE B.H.51.19, 118.6

gan·gan·ye·la \ġaŋ-ġáŋ-ye-la\ *adv* : clearing, as thick clouds do when getting thinner < *Wana mahpiya* ~ *u welo* The sky is clearing up > — *adj* : very thin and sharp, as the blade or bit of an axe

gan·ge·ca \ġaŋ-ġé-ca\ *n* : dandruff – R

gan'·i·c'i·ya \ġaŋ-í-c'i-ya\ *v refl of* ġan : to make one's hair stand upright – Note: *pehin pawosla iyeya* is the equivalent in meaning

gan·ka \ġáŋ-ka\ *adj* : bushy, as of hair < *nata* ~ bushy pate, *Pehin maganka* I have a bushy head of hair >

gan s'e \ġáŋ s'e\ *adv* : with the hair standing on end, i.e. not combed and waving in the wind < ~ *manipi* They walk with their hair flying, *Le tuktel yugmin ikikicupi laka;* ~ *he ye* Here where he cleared it off, why is it not taken back? his hair stands on end – Bl —

gan·ye·la \ġaŋ-yé-la\ *adv* : with the hair standing up not combed

ge·bni·yan \ġé-bni-yaŋ\ *v* [fr *gepa* to gasp + *niyan* to breathe or inhale] : to breathe in a choking manner, as when the throat is swollen – *Syn* GEMNIYAN

ge·ge·i·c'i·ye·la \ġe-ġé-i-c'i-ye-la\ *adv* : walking upon and down in a room or so, in excitement < ~ *un* to be pacing back and forth – Cf ġeġeya – R Bl

ge·ge·ya *or perhaps* **gegéya** \ġé-ġe-ya\ *adv* : swinging, dangling < *Tipi wan el si nupin pahtapi na pa* ~ *otkeyapi. Peta pa kin kutakiya* ~ *okatanpi* In a house his both feet were bound, and his head hung swingling. Peter was nailed (to a cross) with his head hanging downward > – B.H.305.28 — *vi* : to swing e.g. one's arms, as a drunken person – Note: the refl form *gegeic'iya* – Cf R

ge·mni·yan \ġé-mni-yaŋ\ *v* : to gasp for breath – *Syn* GEBNIYAN

ge·pa \ġé-ṗa\ *vn* wa·gepa : to gasp for breath, and making a noise with the throat

gi \ġi\ *adj* : brown, dark gray, rusty-looking < *maka gi* brown earth >

gi·ca·han \ġi-cá-haŋ\ *vn in pres time* magicahaŋ : to slip, misstep, stumble and fall — **gicahe** *vn in p time* magicahe : to have slipped and fallen — **gicahe·ya** *va* gicahe·wa·ya : to cause to slip and fall

gi·gi \ġi-ġí\ *adj red of* ġi : brown, rusty — *n* : rust < *Wana peji* ~ *aye lo* The grass turned brown > – Bl — **gi·gi·ya** \ġi-ġí-ya\ *adv red of* ġiya : Brown < *Mahpiya* ~ *kahwoka. Tohanl mahpiya* ~ *kahwohwok ahiyaye cin hehantu kta ške'. Wana peji kin* ~ *aya* The dark cloud drifted away. When the dark cloud was floated by, they say it would at that time. The grass turned brown. >

gin·ca \ġíŋ-ca\ *vn* wa·ginca : to snivel, to grunt, to sob

gin·ce·la \ġíŋ-ce-la\ *adj* : aching; convalescing < ~ *ni k'un* He had lived with aches and pains, as is said when a man is recovering from illness. > – LB

gin·gin·ca \ġiŋ-ġíŋ-ca\ *n* : ear wax or dandruff; dross; quicksilver of looking-glasses; certain webs < *Nonge ~ omajula yelo* My ears are full of wax > - *Syn* GANGÉ-CA - Bl Cf R

ginl·gin·ca \ġiŋl-ġíŋ-ca\ *v red of* ġínca : to make a noise like one choking

ginl·gin·ca·la \ġíŋl-ġiŋ-ca-la\ *n* : the Wilson snipe, so-called on account of the noise it makes - Bl

gi·tka \ġi-tk̇á\ *adj* : grayish — **gitka·tka** \ġi-tk̇á-tk̇a\ *adj red of* ġitka : reddish, brownish, or yellowish

gi·ya \ġi-yá\ *adv* or *adj* : appearing brown < *Mato cincála-hakáktala wan giyehci yanke lake* The youngest little bear cub can you believe is apparently quite brown, i.e. in its very brown coat, *~ špan* She fried it well-done > - D.116 — *va* : to make brown, to roast, as corn or coffee

[1]**gla** \gla\ *syll used to make the poss form of v commencing with* ka *and* ya . Thus, k̲a̲ksa, g̲l̲a̲ksa, while the *pron* are prefixed

[2]**gla** \gla\ *v* wa·gla : to go home < *Tiyatakiya wagla* I was on the way back toward my home > — *va* wa·glá : to detest something repulsive - Cf wóglaya - B

gla·bla·ya \gla-blá-ya\ *v poss of* kablaya, which Cf

gla·bla·za \gla-blá-za\ *v poss of* kablaza, *and* yablaza

gla·ble·ca \gla-blé-ca\ *v poss of* kableca, *and* yableca : to break in pieces one's own by striking e.g. something brittle, to bite in pieces or to pieces one's own < *Waglableca* I bit it to pieces > — **glablel** \gla-blél\ *contrac of* glableca : to break in pieces one's own < *~ iyeya* to break suddenly to pieces one's own >

gla·blu \gla-blú\ *v poss contrac of* kablu *or* yablu : to pulverize or masticate

gla·ce·ya \gla-cé-ya\ *v poss of* kaceya *or* yaceya : to make one cry by striking *or* speaking, *or* biting

glacoza \gla-có-za\ *v poss of* kacoza : to warm by striking

gla·ga·pa \gla-ġá-ṗa\ *v* : to tear or bruise a piece off

gla·ge·ge \gla-ġé-ġe\ *v poss* wa·glagege [fr *kagege* to sew] : to sew one's own

gla·gi·ca \gla-ġí-ca\ *v poss of* yaġica : to awaken one's own by talking

gla·gle·gle·ga \gla-glé-gle-ġa\ *vn poss* : one's self to be spotted < *Iktomi huhá glagleglelo* Spider's limbs are spotted, as they say when a fellow tells lies > - WE

gla·gna·yan \gla-gná-yaŋ\ *v poss of* yagnayan : to say falsifying

gla·go \gla-ġó\ *v poss of* kago : to put marks on one's own

gla·han \gla-háŋ\ *vn* : to ravel, to untwist, as a twisted string

gla·he \gla-hé\ *adv* : unrolled of itself

gla·he·ya \gla-hé-ya\ *adv* : continuously straight forward, without interruption < *~ ia* to speak continuously > — **glaheya·pi s'e** *adv* : doing or saying without halting or interruption < *~ omani hihunni* He arrived walking without stopping, i.e. doing what one wanted without stopping for anything else, thus without difficulties >

gla·hin·ta \gla-híŋ-ṫa\ *v poss of* kahinta : to sweep or brush one's own - B.H.174.9

gla·ho·ho \gla-hó-ho\ *v poss of* kahoho *or* yahoho : to loosen by striking or by shaking with the mouth one's own

gla·ho·mni \gla-hó-mni\ *v poss of* kahomni *or* yahomni : to turn one's own by striking *or* change one's own views through persuasion

gla·ho·ton \gla-hó-toŋ\ *v poss of* kahoton : to make one's own howl or to bite one's own and cry out

gla·hun·hun·za \gla-húŋ-huŋ-za\ *v poss of* kahunhunza *or* yahunhunza : to shake one's own by striking or shake one's own resolution by talking

gla·ȟa \gla-ȟá\ *v poss of* kaȟa : to curl or knot one's own - Bl

gla·ȟa·pa \gla-ȟá-ṗa\ *v poss of* kaȟapa *or* yaȟapa : to drive by striking one's own e.g. cattle or a team of horses, or to scare up one's own by talking

gla·ȟeb \gla-ȟéb\ *v poss contrac of* glaȟepa : to swallow one's own

gla·ȟe·pa \gla-ȟé-ṗa\ *v poss* wa·glaȟepa [fr *yaȟepa* drink up or empty] : to drink up one's own

gla·ȟi·ca \gla-ġí-ca\ *v poss of* yaġica, which cf

gla·ȟla·ȟla·ya \gla-ȟlá-ȟla-ya\ *v red of* glaȟlaya, cf

gla·ȟla·ya \gla-ȟlá-ya\ *v poss* wa·glaȟlaya [fr *yaȟlaya* to skin by biting] **1** : to bite obliquely, to bite off e.g. the skin of anything **2** : to tell a lie - Bl

gla·ȟle·ca \gla-ȟlé-ca\ *v poss* [fr *kaȟleca* break open by striking, or *yaȟleca* tear open by mouth] : to break open one's own by smiting, or teach open by biting — **gla·ȟlel** *v poss contrac of* glaȟleca : to break open one's own < *~ iyeya* suddenly to break or smash open one's own >

gla·ȟlo·ka \gla-ȟló-ka\ *v poss of* kaȟloka *and* yaȟloka : to break or bite a hole in one's own < *Waglaȟloke šni ca panpanla wanji mak'u wo* Give me a soft one since I did not bite a hole in it, i.e. I can't chew it, so ... > - Bl

gla·ȟni·ga \gla-ȟní-ġa\ *v poss* wa·glaȟniga [fr *kaȟniga* to choose] : to choose one's own

gla·ȟpa \gla-ȟṗá\ *v poss of* kaȟpa : to knock down one's own

gla·ȟpu \gla-ȟṗú\ *v poss of* wa·glaȟpu [fr *yaȟpu* bite off] : to pull or tear off with the teeth something of one's own that adheres to something else — **glaȟpu·ȟpu** \gla-ȟṗú-ȟṗu\ *v poss red of* glaȟpu

gla·ȟtag \gla-ȟtág\ *v contrac of* glaȟtaka : to bite one's own < *~ iyeya* suddenly to bite one's own >

gla·ȟta·ka \gla-ȟtá-k̇a\ *v poss* wa·glaȟtaka [fr *yaȟtaka* to bite] : to bite one's own

gla·ȟu·ga \gla-ȟú-ġa\ *v poss of* kaȟúġa *and* yaȟuga : to crush one's own by striking or by chewing - Cf glaȟuȟuga — **glaȟuh** \gla-ȟúȟ\ *v poss contrac of glaȟuga* — **glaȟuȟuga** \gla-ȟú-ȟu-ġa\ *v poss of* kaȟuȟuġa *and* yaȟuȟuġa : to smash or greak in one's own, as the skull of one's child, or as one's own kettle by pounding; to break up one's own with the teeth, as bones which belong to one's self

gla·h'u \glaȟ'ú\ *v* : to peel with the mouth, e.g. a turnip with the teeth - Bl

gla·i·le·ga \gla-í-le-ġa\ *v* : to enkindle again a fire, as in smoking a pipe - Bl WHL

gla·ja \gla-já\ *adj* or *vn* maglaja : to be sick or diseased and in a state of confinement - Note: but *wayazanka* ref to an attack of sickness — **glaja·ja** *v poss of* kajaja : to wash away one's own

gla·ja·ta \gla-já-ta\ *v poss of* yajalata : to bite and make forked one's own - Bl

gla·jib \gla-jíb\ *v contrac of* kajipa : to shave or plane < *~ iyeya* to slice off quickly, *~ yuta* to eat very slowly, to nibble away at or off >

\a\ f̲a̲ther \e\ th̲e̲y̲ \i\ mach̲i̲ne \o\ sm̲o̲ke \u\ l̲u̲nar \an, aŋ\ bl̲a̲nc Fr. \in, iŋ\ i̲n̲k \on, oŋ, un, uŋ\ s̲o̲o̲n, c̲o̲n̲fier Fr. \c\ c̲h̲air \ġ\ mac̲h̲en Ger. \j\ fus̲ion \clusters: bl, gn, kp, hšl, etc...\ b̲ᵉlo ... said with a slight vowel
See more in the Introduction, Guide to Pronunciation

gla·ji·pa \gla-jí-ṗa\ *va poss* wa·glajipa [fr *kajipa* shave off or plane] : to shave one's own e.g. stick, to bite off or nibble one's own food – Note: *yajipa* means to bite as does a mosquito, or to sting as does a bee

gla·jo \gla-jó\ *v poss* wa·glajo [fr *yajo* blow on an instrument] : to blow on one's own musical instrument

gla·ju·ju \gla-jú-ju\ *va poss* wa·glájuju [fr *kajuju* knock off or pay off] : to blot out or erase one's own; to pay one's debts

gla·jun·ke \gla-júŋ-k̇e\ *vn* or *adj* gla·šmun·ke [fr *glaja* afflicted + *un* have] : to be a confirmed invalid

gla·kan \gla-káŋ\ *v poss of* kakan : to hew one's own

gla·ka·wa \gla-k̇á-wa\ *v poss of* yakawa : to open or push back with the mouth one's own

gla·kca \gla-kcá\ *v poss* wa·glakca [fr *kakca* to comb] : to comb one's own

gla·ke \gla-k̇é\ *adj* : standing apart, alone, separated, as large trees without underbrush do; large-toothed, as a coarse comb – Cf canglegle *and* canglegleka, *archaic*

gla·ke·ke·ye·la \gla-k̇é-k̇e-ye-la\ *adv red of* glakeyela : not close together, but separated as men coming in a crowd and not close-packed, sparcely situated < ~ *yankapi, au, aye* They sparcely sat, came straggling, went dawdling along > – Bl

gla·ke·ya \gla-k̇é-ya\ *adv* : separately, at a distance from each other

gla·ke·ye·la \gla-k̇é-ye-la\ *adv* : here and there, as shocks of grain in a field – Bl BT

gla·kin·ca \gla-k̇íŋ-ca\ *v poss of* kakinca : to scrape off hair e.g. on a hide

gla·kin·kin·yan \gla-k̇íŋ-k̇iŋ-yaŋ\ *adv red* [fr *glakinyan* to traverse] : in a zigzag line < *Itancan k'on he ~ el u na kaȟol hiyuc'iya. Na ena ~ najin ca lila kutepi* This chief had come there in an uncertain course, and he caused himself to come gray. And right there they shot often since he stood in a crooked line > – B.H.12.3

gla·kin·yan \gla-k̇íŋ-yaŋ\ *adv* : transversely – Note: not crosswise which is called *kaicioptaya;* but as one man standing and another passes by, not crosswise as in a fourway intersection, but transversely, as at a T-junction. Thus a man ~ inajin, i.e. stood transversely to the people when he has them at his right or left side, hence at right angles

gla·ki·ski·za \gla-k̇í-sk̇i-za\ *v poss red of* yakiza : to grate one's own teeth – Cf higlakiskiza

gla·kpan \gla-kpáŋ\ *v poss of* kakpa : to beat or wink one's own < *Išta waglakpan* I wink my eyes >

gla·kpi \gla-kṗí\ *v poss of* kakpi *and* yakpi : to crack by striking, or to crack with the teeth

gla·ksa \gla-ksá\ *v poss* wa·kaksa [fr *kaksa* to cut + *yaksa* bite off] : to cut or bite off one's own – B.H.191.12 — **glaksa·ksa** *v red* wa·glaksaksa [fr *glaksa* to cut one's own] : to cut or bite one's own in many pieces

gla·kši·ja \gla-kší-ja\ *v poss of* yakšija : to double up one's own with the teeth

gla·ku·ka \gla-k̇ú-ka\ *v poss of* yakuka : to bite one's own to pieces

gla·k'e·za \gla-k'é-za\ *v poss of* yak'eza : to make a grating sound with one's teeth in smoothening

gla·k'o·ga \gla-k'ó-ġa\ *v poss of* yak'oga : to bite or gnaw off one's own

gla·la \gla-lá\ *v poss* wa·glála [fr *kala* to sow] : to scatter one's own

gla·mna \gla-mná\ *v poss* wa·glámna [fr *kamna* get or earn + *yamna* acquire by talking] : to acquire or collect e.g. property, or to acquire by talking

gla·o·ksa \gla-ó-ksa\ *v poss of* kaóksa : to cave in of one's own

gla·o·ni·han \gla-ó-ni-haŋ\ *v poss* wa·glaonihan [fr *yaonihan* to praise one] : to praise or honor one's own

gla·o·ta \gla-ó-ṫa\ *v poss of* yaóta : to count one's own many

gla·o·tan'·in \gla-ó-taŋ-iŋ\ *v poss* wa·glaotan'in [fr *yaotan'in* to declare] : to manifest or to declare one's own < *Hecel kéya ozuye tawa kin ohitika keya* ~ The turtle declared, so he says, his own war is courageous >

gla·pa \gla-pá\ *v poss* wa·glapa [fr *yapá* take in the mouth] : to take hold of one's own with the mouth

gla·pan \gla-ṗáŋ\ *v poss* wa·glapan [fr *kapan* to beat] : to beat or thresh out one's own, as one's own corn

gla·pa·pa \gla-ṗá-pa\ *v poss red of* glapa : to bite on one's own < *Šake ~ nawajin* I stood chewing on my fingernails >

gla·pe·han \gla-ṗé-haŋ\ *v poss* wa·glápehan [fr *yapehan* to fold with the teeth] : to fold up one's own with the mouth

gla·pe·mni \gla-ṗé-mni\ *v poss* : to turn or spin one's self around – Bl KE

gla·pol \gla-ṗól\ *v contrac of* glapota : to fray one's own < ~ *iyeya* to rip suddenly >

gla·po·pa \gla-pó-pa\ *v poss of* yapopa : to pop one's own, as in blowing on a leaf

gla·po·ta \gla-ṗó-ṫa\ *v poss* wa·glapota [fr *kapota* tear by the wind + *yapota* tear with the mouth] : to beat one's own to pieces; to bite to pieces, destroy one's own by biting

gla·psag \gla-pság\ *v poss of* glapsaka : to cut off one's own < ~ *iyeya* to suddenly cut off one's own >

gla·psa·ka \gla-psá-ka\ *v poss* [fr *kapsaka* cut off by striking + *yapsaka* bite off] : to cut off one's own by striking, e.g. a branch of one's tree; or to bite off one's own, e.g. one's string

gla·psan·psan \gla-psáŋ-psaŋ\ *v poss of* kapsánpsan : to move to and fro one's own, to swing one's own or sway back and forth < *Nape* ~ She moved her hand back and forth > – Cf sintónpsanpsan

gla·psin·psin·ta \gla-psíŋ-psiŋ-ṫa\ *v poss* wa·glapsinpsinta [fr *kapsinpsinta* to scourge] : to whip one's own child

gla·psin·ta \gla-psíŋ-ṫa\ *v poss of* kapsinta : to correct or whip one's own

gla·psun *or* **glapson** \gla-psúŋ\ *v poss* wa·glapsun [fr *kapsun* knock spilling or *yapsun* spill by mouth] : to spill one's own by striking, or to spill with the mouth

gla·pšun \gla-pšúŋ\ *v poss* wa·glapšun [fr *kapšun* to knock out or *yapšun* to bite out] : to knock out one's own by the roots, as a tooth, or to knock out of joint, as one's leg; to bite out or knock out one's own, as a horse does in shedding its teeth

gla·pta \gla-ptá\ *v poss of* kapta : to lade out one's own – Note: *yapta* may be the basic word for this – Bl

gla·ptan·yan \gla-ptáŋ-yaŋ\ *v poss of* kaptanyan : to turn over and over

gla·pte·ce·la \gla-pté-ce-la\ *v poss of* kaptecela *and* yaptecela : to break or to bite off short

gla·ptu·ja \gla-ṗtú-ja\ *v poss of* kaptuja : to crack one's own

gla·ptuš \gla-ṗtúš\ *v contrac of* glaptuja : to crack < ~ *iyeya* to crack of a sudden >

gla·ptu·za \gla-ptú-za\ *v poss of* kaptuza : perhaps to split or crack – Note: this may be an *altern* spelling of *glaptuja* – Bl

gla·pu·za \gla-ṗú-za\ *v poss of* yapuza : to dry with the mouth one's own - Bl

gla·skab \gla-sk̇áb\ *v contrac of* glaskapa : to clap

gla·ska·pa \gla-sk̇á-ṗa\ *v poss* wa·glaskapa [fr *kaskapa* to slap or clap] : to clap, to make strikes together < *Nape* ~ to clap one's hands >

gla·ske·pa \gla-sk̇é-ṗa\ *v poss of* kaskepa : to empty one's own slowly, as by drinking

gla·ski·ca \gla-sk̇í-ca\ *v poss* wa·gláskica [fr *kaskica* to press down *or* yaskica to suck or lick] : to press down or settle one's own; to press one's own with the mouth

gla·sku \gla-sk̇ú\ *v poss* wa·glasku [fr *yasku* peel off with the teeth] : to bite or peel off one's own

gla·sle·ca \gla-slé-ca\ *v poss of* kasleca : to split one's own i.e. wood with an axe

gla·slo·han \gla-sló-haŋ\ *v poss* [fr *kaslohan* make slide by striking *or yaslohan* drag with the mouth] : to slide, or to drag one's own

gla·sni \gla-sní\ *v poss* [fr *kasni* extinguish or *yasni cool by blowing]* : to extinguish one's own by beating, or to cool by blowing on one's own < *Peta unglasnipelo* We put the fire out beating the breeze, as they would say if the fire went out while they were talking - WH

gla·sol \gla-sól\ *v contrac of* glasota : to use or eat up < ~ *iyeya* to consume one's own suddenly >

gla·so·ta \gla-só-ṫa\ *v poss* wa·glasota [fr *kasota* use up or *yasota* eat up] : to cut all off, as one's timber; to use up words or language, i.e. to finish speaking, to eat up one's own

gla·sto \gla-sṫó\ *v poss of* kasto : to stroke and make smooth, as one does to her or his own hair

gla·su \gla-sú\ *v poss* wa·glasu [fr *yasú* to judge] **1** : to judge or condemn one's own **2** : to perfect, to finish perhaps - R

gla·su·ta \gla-sú-ṫa\ *v poss of* yasuta : to confirm one's own words

gla·s'i·c'i·ya \gla-s'í-c'i-ya\ *vn* : to be very lazy - Bl

glaš \glaš\ *v contra of* glajá : to be sick, in a sick condition

gla·ša·pa \gla-šá-ṗa\ *v poss of* yašapa : to soil one's own with the mouth

gla·ši·ca \gla-ší-ca\ *v poss of* yašica : to speak evil of one's own

gla·ška \gla-šk̇á\ *v refl* wa·glaška [fr *kaška* bind one] : to bind one's own < *Šunkunglaškapi ekta unkipi* We arrived at home with our horses in tether >

gla·ške·pa \gla-šké-pa\ *v poss of* yaškepa : to suck one's own dry, as does a calf its mother - Bl KE

gla·ški·ca \gla-šk̇í-ca\ *v poss* wa·glaškica [fr *yaškica* to chew on] : to press one's own with the mouth, as in chewing tobacco

gla·ški·pa \gla-škí-ṗa\ *v poss of* yaškipa : to bit one's own and fill up

gla·ško·pa \gla-škó-ṗa\ *v poss of* kaškopa *and* yaškopa : to make one's own crooked by striking or by the mouth

gla·šla \gla-šlá\ *v poss* wa·glašla [fr *kašla* to mow or shave, and *yašla* to graze] : to mow or to shave one's beard; to graze

gla·šlo·ka \gla-šló-k̇a\ *v poss of* kašloka : to knock out of one's own - B.H.191.9

gla·šlu·ta \gla-šlú-ṫa\ *v poss of* kašluta : to make one's own glance off

gla·šna \gla-šná\ *v poss* wa·glašna [fr *kašna* to miss, or *yašna* to blunder] : to miss in attempting to strike one's own; to blunder in speaking, talk incorrectly, to miss in taking food into the mouth —**glašna·šna** *v red of* glašna : to keep blundering —**glašnašna·yan** *adv* : blunderingly, as in talking incorrectly

gla·špa \gla-šṗá\ *v poss* wa·glašpa [fr *kašpa* knock off, or *yašpa* to bite off] : to knock or bite off a piece from one's own

gla·špu \gla-šṗú\ *v poss of* kašpu *and* yašpu : to knock or bite off

gla·šta·ka \gla-šṫá-k̇a\ *v poss* wa·glaštaka [fr *kaštaka* to beat of flog] : to strike or smite one's own

gla·štan \gla-šṫáŋ\ *v poss* wa·glaštan [fr *kaštan* pour out or *yaštan* spill with the mouth] : to pour out one's own, or to spill with the mouth e.g. coffee; *also* to finish eating or speaking

gla·šun·ka \gla-šúŋ-ka\ *v* perhaps and *n* : one who is often sick -MF

gla·šya \gla-šyá\ *adv perhaps* : afflicted < ~ *unpi ota akisniwicaye* Many who were afflicted he healed, *or* He healed any sort of sickness, ~ *makuja* I suffer from a persistent sickness >

gla·ta \gla-ṫá\ *v poss* wa·glata [fr *yata* to eat] : to taste one's own; to chew over again, i.e. ruminate as does a cow its cud

gla·tan \gla-ṫáŋ\ *v poss* wa·glatan [fr *yatan* to praise] : to praise one's own

gla·tan·ka \gla-ṫáŋ-k̇a\ *v poss of* yatanka : to speak of one's own as great or large

gla·tan·yan \gla-ṫáŋ-yaŋ\ *adv* or *v poss perhaps of* yatanyan : praising of one's own; to praise one's own - Bl

[1]**gla·ta·ta** \gla-ṫá-ṫa\ *v poss* wa·glatata [fr *katata* shake off] to knock and shake off e.g. one's own blanket; to take in the mouth and shake, as a dog does to something - Cf yata B.H.206.14

[2]**gla·ta·ta** \gla-ṫá-ṫa\ *v red* wa·glatata [fr *glaṫa* to taste or chew one's own] : to taste of chew over and over again < *Pejuta kin ikikca na* ~ He took back and kept chewing the medicine >

gla·teb \gla-ṫéb\ *v contrac of* glatepa : to wear off one's own, as the edge of one's teeth < ~ *iyeya* or *aya* to wear down quickly, or began to wear down >

gla·te·han \gla-ṫé-haŋ\ *v poss of* yatehan : to speak of one's own long or as far in the past or future

gla·te·pa \gla-ṫé-ṗa\ *v poss* wa·glatepa [fr *yatepa* cut or wear off] : to wear off one's teeth short < *Higlatepa* He wore his teeth short >

gla·ti·tan \gla-ṫí-ṫaŋ\ *v poss of* yatitan : to pull on one's own with the teeth

gla·tkan \gla-tk̇áŋ\ *v poss* wa·glatkan [fr *yatkan* to drink] : to drink one's own

gla·to·i·e \gla-ṫó-i-e *or* gla-ṫó-i-e\ *v* : to curse < *Takuwe šunka owanke kin le itancan wicašayatapi mitawa kin ~ hwo?* Why does this dog-like fellow curse my lord king? > - Cf šigla, ṫóie

gla·to·kan \gla-ṫó-k̇aŋ\ *v poss* wa·glatokan [fr *yatokan* speak as put elsewhere] : to put one's own in another place with the mouth, to speak of one's own as in another place

gla·to·ke·ca \gla-ṫó-k̇e-ca\ *v poss* wa·glatokeca [fr *yatokeca* alter with the mouth] : to speak of one's own as different

gla·to·na·na \gla-ṫo-na-na\ *v poss of* yatonana : to count

\a\ father \e\ they \i\ machine \o\ smoke \u\ lunar \an, aŋ\ blanc Fr. \in, iŋ\ ink \on, oŋ, un, uŋ\ soon, confier Fr. \c\ chair \ġ\ machen Ger. \j\ fusion \clusters: bl, gn, kp, hšl, etc...\ b^e^lo ... said with a slight vowel
See more in the Introduction, Guide to Pronunciation

one's own few – Cf glaota

gla·to·to \gla-ṫó-ṫo\ *v poss* wa·glatoto [fr *katoto* knock or rap] : to knock at one's own door

gla·t'a \gla-t'á\ *v poss* wa·glat'a [fr *kat'a* kill striking or *yat'a* kill biting] : to kill one's own by striking, or to bite one's own to death

gla·t'ins \gla-t'íŋs\ *v contrac of glat'inza* : to tighten one's own by driving, pounding, or by using the teeth

gla·t'in·za \gla-t'íŋ-za\ *v poss* wa·glat'inza [fr *kat'inza* tighten by striking, or *yat'inza* tighten using the teeth] : to make one's own tight by driving; to press one's own with the teeth

gla·un·ka \gla-úŋ-k̇a\ *v poss of* kaunka : to fell one's own – B.H.225.11

gla·wa \gla-wá\ *v poss* wa·glawa [fr *yawa* read or value] : to read one's own, to count or value one's own

gla·wa·ci \gla-wá-ci\ *v poss of* kawaci : to make spin, as a top by striking – Bl

gla·wa·kan \gla-wá-kaŋ\ *v poss* wa·glawakan [fr *yawakan* consider supernatural] : to call one's own sacred

gla·wan·kal \gla-wáŋ-k̇al\ *v poss of* yawankal : to raise one's own voice

gla·wa·šte \gla-wá-šṫe\ *v poss of* yawašte : to bless one's own

gla·wa·š'a·ka \gla-wá-š'a-ka\ *v poss of* yawaš'aka : to encourage one's own

gla·we·ga \gla-wé-ġa\ *v poss* wa·gláwega [fr *kawega* to fracture striking, or *yawega* to break with the teeth] : to break or fracture by striking, as one's own axe handle; to break partly off with the teeth

gla·weh \gla-wéḣ\ *v contrac of* glawega : to fracture — **glawe·hwega** *v red of* glawega : to keep breaking

gla·wi·ca·ka \gla-wí-ca-k̇a\ *v poss of* yawicaka : to affirm the truth about one's own

gla·wi·ya·kpa \gla-wí-ya-kpa\ *v poss of* yawiyakpa : to interpret or make shine one's own

gla·ya \gla-yá\ *va* gla·wa·ya : to push something through a small hole made e.g. by a wire down a pipe stem < *cannunpa iglaye* a wire pipe stem cleaner > – BD

gla·yung \gla-yúŋg\ *v contrac of* glayunka : to fell

gla·yun·ka \gla-yúŋ-k̇a\ *v poss* wa·glayunka [fr *kayunka* to fell by striking] : to cut down or fell one's own trees < ~` *iyeya* suddenly to fell >

gla·za·mni \gla-zá-mni\ *v poss* wa·glazamni [fr *kazamni* uncover] : to open or uncover one's own

gla·za·pa \gla-zá-ṗa\ *v poss* wa·glazapa [perhaps fr *kazapa* which may be *archaic*] : to cut off the fat with the skin, as in skinning animals

gla·ze \gla-zé\ *v poss* wa·glaze [fr *kaze* to dip out] : to lade out one's own, as one's food

gla·zo·ka \gla-zó-k̇a\ *v poss* wa·glázoka [fr *yazoka* to sip] : to suck one's own, as a child its own finger

gla·zun·ta *or* **glazonta** \gla-zúŋ-ṫa\ *v poss* wa·glazunta [fr *yazunta* unjustly to praise] : to connect one's words, to speak correctly; to praise or speak well of one's own

¹gle \gle\ *v of* gla : to go home

²gle \gle\ *va* : to put or have by one, to place, make stand, as is usually applied to things that stand on end, e.g. barrels, etc < *Mini wagle* I have water (put by me), *Yunkan winuhcala wan wiyohpeya gle keye* (to go), *wohan gle* (to set). *Ho, unci, iblabla kin le* micicat'in na ohan migle yo. Then he stated that an old lady went and threw into the kettle, setting out a feast. Yes, grandmother, while I am now on my way, put it to me and kill it for me > – Note: this word may be considered as the *vt* form of *han*

gleb \gleb\ *v contrac of* glepa : to vomit < ~ *kiyuya* to heave in vomitting > — **gleb·kiya** \gle-bk̇í-ya\ *va* gle·bwá·kiya: to cause to vomit

gle·ga \glé-ġa\ *adj* : spotted, or as calico with figured patterns

gle·gle \gle-glé\ *adj* : scattered here and there < *canglegle* a scattering of trees >

gle·gle·ga \gle-glé-ġa\ *adj red of* glega : spotted, speckled; brownish – R — **glegle·hya** *adv* : made spotted – Bl

gle·gle·ka \gle-glé-k̇a\ *adj* : scattered, separated one here and one there < *canglegleka* dispersed trees

gle·gle·za \gle-glé-za\ *adj* : striped, streaked

gle·gle·ze·la \gle-glé-ze-la\ *adj dim of* glezela : striped, streaked

gle·h'o·han \gle-ḣ'o-haŋ\ *v* : to wear a stripe on < *I kin gleh'owahan wacin yelo* When he went he expected to be wearng a stripe > – BT

gle·ki·ya \gle-k̇í-ya\ *va* gle·wa·kiya : to cause to go home, i.e. to send home

gle·pa \glé-ṗa\ *va* wa·glepa : to vomit, puke < *iglepa* to vomit up what one has eaten, *i·wá·glepa* I threw up >

gle·sye·la \gle-syé-la\ *adv* : wrinkled, folded; without order or geometric line or color as in the case of modern art < *Nige kinhan ṫanásula ognake s'e ~ nanke* You were warming your belly as though it were a storage room for animal brains, as is said when one is warming himself, his stomach > – Bl KE Swb

gle·ši \gle-ší\ *va* gle·wa·ši : to send home, to order to go home

gle·ška \gle-šk̇á\ *adj* : speckled, spotted

gle·ška·ška \gle-šk̇á-ška\ *adj red of* gleška : spotted, figured as calico

gle·ton \gle-tóŋ *or* gle-ṫoŋ\ *va* gle·wa·ton gle·mi·citon : to correct a mistake, to make right, mend, repair – *Syn* APIYA – WE

gle·za \glé-za\ *adj* **1** : striped, **2** : in ridges or rows, **3** : *fig* acting foolishly < *He gleze yelo* He makes a fool of himself > – WE

gle·ze·la \glé-ze-la\ *adj* : striped < *igmu ~* a stiped cat >

gle·ze·ze·ka \gle-zé-ze-ka\ *adj* or *n* : making a fool of one's self, a fool – *Syn* OILELEKA – WE

gli \gli\ *v poss of* hi : to arrive at home < *wagli* I got home

gli·a·pe \gli-á-pe\ *va* glia·wa·pe : to await one's coming home

gli·cu \gli-cú\ *v* **1** wa·gliyacu : to start to come home < *Yunkan ate inapa na ake ṫima ~* Then Father went out and again came in again, i.e. he left the tent and came in again > **2** : to get down or away from e.g. a wagon

gli·cu·ya \gli-cú-ya\ *va* glicu·wa·ya : to cause to start home, to cause to camp < *Leciya topa can hehanyan šna yujajape na hehanl oyate egna šna glicuwicayape* Here is where for four days they had washed, and then they again and again amongs the people started for home >

gli·gla \gli-glá\ *vn* : to pass by something or somebody, *glakinyan* i.e. alongside the road, going home < *Wanna wi glígle lo,* The sun passed by, as people said about January 15th in *ref* to the sun moving back to the east. *Wana ḣeyáta gligla po* Go now on back upland or Now walk along back > – D.92

gli·gle·ki·ya \gli-glé-ki-ya\ *adv* : doing one thing at a time, each in turn i.e. one thing at a time < *Cannunpa kin ~ iyatanpi* They in turn lit the pipe, *Na he icunhan cannunpa wan opagipi na catku el gnakapi ca he iyatanpi na ~ iyatanpi* And meantime a pipe was packed, and since it had been set aside to the left it was lit, and in turn they lit it, as in taking religiously the sweatbath > – MS.351 KE

gli·gle·ya·kel \gli-glé-ya-kel\ *adv* : hither and yon, here and there < ~ *omani* He travels here and there ~ *waun welo* I stayed hither and yon, as is said in watering trees here and there > – Bn Bw

gli·gni \gli-gní\ *v* : to come or go along towards one's house < *Nitakuye tona tewicayaȟilapi heci hena owewicakiceya po, eya okawinh* ~ "Those surely who are your relatives you cherish, them you ought to pray (cry) for", he said in the making of the rounds, as in doing the sundance

gli·han \gli-háŋ\ *vn* : to fall or come down and be standing, as an arrow < *Inyan wan* ~ *hpaya. Wahinkpe kin tanwankatuya ya na wanna makata* ~. ~ *glihpaya* A stone fell back down. The arrow went upward very high and came back down to the ground. It returned falling and stuck standing >

gli·he·ya \gli-hé-ya\ *adj* or *adv* : steep < *mayá* ~ *a steep bank, Maya* ~ *he lo* The bank rises steeply > – B.H. 68.11, 228.7

gli·hunni \gli-húŋ-ni\ *v poss* wa·glihunni [fr *hihunni* arrive at a place] : to reach home coming straightway

gli·hpa\gli-ȟpá\ *v* wa·glihpa : to fall down, i.e. once < *Yunkan inyan tanka wan* ~ *keya* Then he stated that a great stone fell > — **glihpa·ya** *vn* wa·glihpaya [fr *hinhpaya* to fall down] : to fall or lie down on coming home; to fall again: to fall and lie down, as a person or thing does < *Apá* ~ He fell wounded, *ta* ~ a fallen deer i.e. wounded > – B.H.283.5 D.199, 247

gli·hpe·ya \gli-ȟpé-ya\ *va* gliphe·wa·ya : to throw someone down, as in wrestling < *Yunkan iš wicaša wan ena winyan num hecel glihpewicayà* Then a man himself right there threw down two women >

gli·na·jin \gli-ná-jiŋ\ *v poss* wa·glinajin *or* wa·gli·na·-wa·jin [fr *hinajin* come and stand] : to return and stand < *Ecel wagliyacu na tankal waglinawajin. Nawajin k'on el waglinawajin* Thus I got down off and came and stood outside. I returned to where I had stood >

gli·na·pa \gli-ná-pa\ *v poss* wa·glinapa *or* wa·gli-na·wa·pa [fr *hinapa* come out of] : to come in sight coming home, to come out of

gli·nun·wan \gli-núŋ-waŋ\ *v* : to arrive at home swimming – Bl

gli owayawa \gli o-wá-ya-wa\ *n* : a day school

gli·psi·ca \gli-psí-ca\ *v poss* wa·glipsica [fr *hipsica* jump down or dismount] : to alight at home, to jump down again — **glipsil** *v poss contrac of* glipsica : to alight

gli·šni o·wa·ya·wa \glí-šni o-wá-ya-wa\ *n* : a boarding school

gli·tan'·in·ka \gli-táŋ-iŋ-ka\ *v* : to arrive suddenly at home, i.e. where the speaker is < *Toké tohinni tokiyatanhan yaglitan'inka so?* Where did you really come from to never suddenly arrive back home? > – Bl

gli·u \gli-ú\ *v* : to come to one's own home

gli·ya·cu *or perhaps* **glicu** \gli-yá-cu\ *v* wa·gliyacu ya-gliyacu agliyacu in *ref* to many : to be on one's way < *Gla po, hecel wanna miš wagliyacu na wagli* Be on your way home. So I am on my way and got home. *Ecel wagliyacu* (from a tent) *na tankal waglinawajin. Hecel miglahomni na wagli-yacu* As it was, I was on my way home with it (from a tent), and arriving I stood around outside. So I turned around and set out for home >

gli·ya·gla \glí-ya-gla\ *v* [as it were fr *yagli* + *yagla*] : to go from and return – Note: perhaps "*yagla* to go over there" is built on "*ya* to go" rather than rooted in the prefix meaning use of the mouth

gli·ya·gli \gli-yá-gli\ *v* wa·glíyagli: to go around or about a place, to have gone and come back, *esp* by another route < *Na wanna wagliyagli na wowiyuškinka* And I went and returned, and there was rejoicing – Note: the word may be a *deriv* of *gnayan* deceive, where *gna* seems to be changed to *gli* and the nasal sign dropped for euphony. J. Bear Shield suggested there is no such word. Moreover that *i* in *wagliyagli* is perhaps a contrac of *na*: *wagla-na-yagli*

gli·ya·han \gli-yá-haŋ\ *vn* wa·gliyahan agliyahan in *ref* to many : to appear on top of a hill in sight of one's way home < *Ecel paha wan el wahiyohpaye k'on he ake aiyakapteya waku na el wagliyahan* So at a hill from which I had come down, I again came back up on it, and there I appeared in sight of my home >

gli·ya·hpa·ya \gli-yá-ȟpa-ya\ *v poss* wa·gliyahpaya [fr *iyahpaya* to seize] : to come home and fall down upon one

gli·ya·ku \gli-yá-k̇u\ *v poss only 1st and 2nd pers are used, and 3rd pers is* glicu: wa·gliyaku ya·gliyaku un·gliyaku·pi : to return or start to come home < "*He Okiksahe*" *kin hogna yagliyakupi kte lo* You should return by way of the "Gorge" > – D.246

gli·yan·ka \gli-yáŋ-ka\ *v* [fr *gli* return + *oyanka* reside] : to go and be at home < *Šunka wawíyeke* (or *šunhpala wowiyuškin*) *s'e gliyankin kte lo* As one dining upon a dog (a puppy delight) he'll return home > – Bl

gli·yo \gli-yó\ *v poss of* hiyo : to come for something — **gliyo·hi** \gli-yó-hi\ *v poss* gliyo·wa·hi wica·gliyo-·wa·hi [fr *hiyohi* come for] : to arrive somewhere for one's own, as parents for the school children – Cf gliyoi

gli·yo·hpa·ya \gli-yó-ȟpa-ya\ *v* wa·gliyohpaya a·gliyo-hpaya (when many are involved) : to have come down from < *Na wanna wicaša zaptanpi k'on hena gliyohpayapi* (from a hill) And the five men came on down (from a hill). *Na oyate najinpi etkiya kupi na ikiyela glinajinpi* And they came back toward people standing and they returned and stood nearby >

gli·yo·i \gli-yó-i\ *v* gliyo·wa·i wica·gliyo·wa·i : to go somewhere for one's own, as parents for their school children

gli·yo·kpe·ca \gli-yó-kpe-ca\ *v poss* : to have come back home from somewhere < *Tokiyatanhan yagliyokpeca hwo?* Where is the place from which you have returned home? > – Cf kiyokpeca

gli·yo·ta·ka \gli-yó-ta-k̇a\ *v poss* wa·gliyotaka [fr *hiyotaka* to go and sit] : to sit down on one's way home < *Unkipi na wazi iyohanzi wan el ungliyotakapi. Wanna glinapapi na oyasin tankal gliyotakapi* We went home and sat in the shade of a pine tree. They came out (of the house) and all sat out of doors >

gli·yo·u \gli-yó-u\ *v poss of* hiyou : to come to take one's own home < *Hokšila gliyowau kte lo* I will come and take my boy home > – *See* gliyoya, to go to take

gli·yo·ya \gli-yó-ya\ *v poss* : to go and get one's own < *Hokšila mitawa kin hena wicagliyomni kta* I will go and get these boys of mine > – ST B.H.245.23 D.219

\a\ father \e\ they \i\ machine \o\ smoke \u\ lunar \an, aŋ\ blanc Fr. \in, iŋ\ ink \on, oŋ, un, uŋ\ soon, confier Fr. \c\ chair \ġ\ machen Ger. \j\ fusion \clusters: bl, gn, kp, hšl, etc...\ b^e^lo ... said with a slight vowel **See more in the Introduction, Guide to Pronunciation**

gli·yun·ka \gli-yúŋ-k̇a\ *v poss* wa·gli·munka un·gliyun-ka·pi [fr *hiyunka* to spend an overnight] : to come and sleep, to camp on the way home < *Psunpsunkiya* (or *psonpsonkiya*) ~ He lay face-down >

gli·yu·we·ga \gli-yú-we-ġa\ *v poss* wa·gliyuwega [fr *hi-yuwega* to ford] : to cross a stream by fording in coming home – B.H.204.1

¹glo \glo\ *pref to some v makes the poss form*

²glo \glo\ *v* : to grunt, make a noise as hogs and buffalo calves do < *Lila pte hotonpi na glopi* Buffalo grunt and sound off much >

glo·a·ya \glo-á-ya\ *v poss* wa·glóaya : to carry one's own toward a place < *Tipi kin he wanna ungloayapi* We transport this our own house > – B.H.47

glo·e·ya·ya \glo-é-ya-ya\ *v poss* wa·gloeyaya un·gloe-yaya : to take or have taken one's own with one going some place, as in taking one's child – B.H.270..12

glo·gla \glo-glá\ *v poss* wa·glogla : to carry one's own home < *Waglogni kte. Nupin waglogni k̇te* I shall go home. Both of us will go home > – D.120

glo·gle·ska *or* **gloglóska** \glo-glé-ska\ *n* : the gullet, esophagus

glo·gli \glo-glí\ *v poss* wa·glogli : to arrive at home with one's own

glo·gli·ya·cu \glo-glí-ya-cu\ *va* : to get something back, as after having loaned it out – B.H.61.6 MS.489 LHB

glo·glo \glo-gló *or* gló-glo\ *v red of* glo : to grunt, as do hogs, buffalo calves, or grouse < ~ *u* It came grunting > – D.84

glo·glo·lo·wan \glo-gló-lo-waŋ\ *v* : to sing with a hoarse voice – Bl

glo·glo·ska \glo-gló-ska\ *n* : the windpipe, i.e. throat

glo·hi \glo-hí\ *v poss* wa·glohi : to bring one's own to a place

glo·hi·na·pa \glo-hí-na-ṗa\ *v poss* : to lead one's own out – B.H.223.7

glo·i \glo-í\ *v poss* wa·gloi : to take or have taken one's own to a place – Pb.37

glo·in *or* **glowin** \gló-iŋ\ *v poss of* iŋ : to wear about the shoulders

glo·ki \glo-k̇í\ *v poss* wa·gloki : to arrive at home with one's own, as children, in speaking of others

glo·ki·ya·gla \glo-k̇i-ya-gla\ *v poss* wa·glokiyagla : to have taken away one's own and to be on the way home

glo·ku \glo-kú\ *v poss* : to be on the way home , bringing (home) one's own, as children < *Wanna* ~ He is on his way home bringing (his children) , as is said when you see him coming with his children >

glo·ni·ca \glo-ní-ca\ *v poss* wa·glonica [fr *anica* to withhold] : to refuse to give up what one claims, to forbid the use of one's own < *tiglónica* to forbid one's house, *tiyopa* ~ to hold the door, as an old saying goes > – Bl

glo·nil \glo-níl\ *v poss contrac of* glonica : to withhold — **glonil·kiya** *or* **glonilya** \glo-níl-ki-ya\ *va* glonil·-wa·kiya : to cause to hold as one's own

glo·u \glo-ú\ *v poss* wa·glou : to come bringing one's own, as children to school, to bring something over, as a horse one wants to sell – *Syn* AU

glo·win \gló-wiŋ\ *v poss* wa·glowin : to put around one his own, as a blanket < *Na wanna wicaša wan šina hin iakatan* ~ And a man put around himself his fur blanket on top > – Cf *in* to wear

glo·ya \glo-yá\ *v poss* : to go carrying one's own

glu \glu\ *pref poss* : to or for one's own – Note: *v* commencing with *yu* form the *poss* by converting *y* to *gl* . These *poss* forms have the *pron* prefixed

glu·a·ki·pab \glu-á-k̇i-ṗab\ *v poss of* yuakipab : to divide or separate one's own < ~ *ewagnaka* I make a division of my own >

glu·a·o·pte·tu \glu-á-o-pṫe-ṫu\ *v poss* wa·glúaoptetu [fr *yuaoptetu* to lessen] : to make one's own less

glu·bla·ya \glu-blá-ya\ *v poss* wa·glublaya [fr *yublaya* to open or spread out] : to spread out one's own, as one's blanket – D.268

glu·bla·za \glu-blá-za\ *va poss of* yublaza : to burst open one's own

glu·ble·ca \glu-blé-ca\ *v poss* wa·glúbleca [fr *yubleca* break or crush to pieces by hand] : to open out, take in pieces one's own — **glu·blel** \glu-blél\ *v contrac of* glubleca : to open outward and take in

glu·blu \glu-blú\ *v poss* wa·glúblu [fr *yublu* pulverize] : to plow or make mellow one's own field

glu·can \glu-cáŋ\ *v poss* wa·glucan [fr *yucan* to sift] : to shake or sift one's own — **glucan·can** *v poss red of* yucancan : to sift repeatedly

glu·can·ta·t'a yan·ka \glu-cáŋ-ṫa-t'a yaŋ-k̇à\ *v* : to have to wait long for a thing and so become impatient – Bc

glu·ce·ga \glu-cé-ġa\ *v* un·glúcega·pi : to dive with the head foremost – *Syn* GLUKŠEPI

glu·ce·ka \glu-cé-ka\ *v poss of* yuceka : to try to pull out one's own < *Na kunšitku tawala* (horse) *glucekahan keye* And his grandmother he stated tried to pull out her prize (horse), i.e. it got mired >

glu·ce·ya \glu-cé-ya\ *v poss of* yuceya : to make one's own cry

glu·co \glu-ċo\ *v poss* wa·gluco [fr *yuco* finish] : to perfect, finish one's own; to arrange one's own

glu·co·co \glu-ċó-ċo\ *v red* wa·glúcoco [fr *gluco* and *yucoco* soften by adding water] : to make soft one's own

glu·co·ka·ka \glu-có-ka-ka\ *v poss* wa·glucokaka [fr *yucokaka* make empty] : to empty one's own barrel

glu·co·za \glu-có-za\ *v poss of* yucoza : to make one's own comfortably warm

glu·e·ce·tu \glu-é-ce-ṫu\ *v poss* wa·gluecetu [fr *yuecetu* fulfill] : to make one's own right, to take back what one has said

glu·e·ci·ya \glu-é-ci-ya\ *v poss* wa·glueciya [fr *yueciya* reverse sides] : to turn one's own the other side out, as one's own bag

glu·ga \glu-ġá\ *v poss* wa·gluga [fr *yuga* to husk] : to pull off, as the husk of one's own corn

glu·gan \glu-ġáŋ\ *v poss* wa·glugan [fr *yugan* to open out] : to open out one's own, as one's blanket or one' door

glu·gal \glu-ġál\ *v contrac of* glugata : to extend one's hands *etc* < *Nape* ~ *najin* He stood with his hands extended in an attitude of supplication

glu·ga·ta \glu-ġá-ṫa\ *v poss* wa·glugata [fr *yugata* extend hands and arms upwards] : to spread out one's own, as one's hands in prayer

glu·ge \glu-ġé\ *v poss* wa·gluge [fr *yuge* take out by hand] : to pick or gather up scraps from one's floor — **gluge·ge** *v red* wa·glugege : to gather up one's own by handfuls – R Bl

glu·gla \glu-glá\ *v poss of* yugla : to untwist, uncoil, unroll; to loosen one's own, as one's own hair < *Pehin* ~ She straightened her hair – D.107

glu·glu·ka \glu-glú-k̇a\ *adj* : saucy, disrespectful to superiors

glu·gmi \glu-gmí\ *v poss of* yugmi : to clear off

glu·gmi·gma \glu-gmí-gma\ *v poss of* yugmigma : to

make round e.g. like a ball by hand
glu·gmun \glu-gmúŋ\ *v poss* wa·glugmun [fr *yugmun* to twist] : to twist one's own — **glugmun·gmun** *v red* : to twist < *Pehin* ~ She curled her hair > - Bl
glu·gna \glu-gná\ *v poss of* yugná : to make one's own fall off
glu·gnu·ni \glu-gnú-ni\ *v poss of* yugnuni : to make one's own wander
glu·go \glu-ġó\ *v poss of* yugo : to make marks or creases in one's own
glu·gu·ka \glu-ġú-ka\ *v poss of* yuguka : to draw one's knife from one's pocket < *Mila wan gluguke na winyeya najin* He drew a knife from his pocket and stood prepared> - D.246
glu·gwa \glu-gwá\ *v poss of* yugwa : to soften one's own by hand - Bl
glu·gwe·ze \glu-gwé-ze\ *adv* : swiftly, moving fast with the hands and with the face twitching, eyes, mouth *etc* as well < ~ *katka mani* He walked briskly fast, ~ *inyankelo* He ran straining > - Bl KE - *Syn* GLUŠNIYANYAHCE, GLUGWEZEHCE
glu·ha \glu-há\ *v poss* wa·glúha [fr *yuha* have] : to have or possess one's own — **glu·ha·ha** \glu-há-ha\ *v red of* gluha : to embrace one's own < ~ *ceyapi* They wept embracing her *or* They wailed over her > - D.270 B.H.39.17, 89.10
glu·ha·ki·ya \glu-há-k̇i-ya\ *va* : to put one in possession of his own, to make one keep his own < *Gluhawakiya. Mitoni kin le gluhamakiyi ye* I put him in possession of mine. Have me keep this my life > - Pb.41
glu·hin·ta \glu-híŋ-ṫa\ *v poss of* yuhinta : to rake one's own away
glu·ho·ho \glu-hó-ho\ *v poss* wa·glúhoho [fr *yuhoho* to shake] : to shake one's own, as one's teeth
glu·ho·mni \glu-hó-mni\ *v poss* wa·gluhomni : to turn one's own around < *Nakpa kin sanni wagluhomni kte lo* Let me turn the other ear >
glu·hun·huns \glu-húŋ-huŋs\ *v red contrac of* gluhunhunza : to shake something one's own
glu·hun·hun·za \glu-húŋ-huŋ-za\ *v poss* wa·gluhunhunza [fr *yuhunhunza* shake by hand] : to shake one's own, as one's tree
glu·ȟeb \glu-ȟéb\ *v contrac of* gluȟepa : to soak up
glu·ȟe·pa \glu-ȟé-ṗa\ *v poss* wa·gluȟepa [fr *yuȟepa* to lade out] : to soak up and wipe out, to dry up, as water from one's own canoe
glu·ȟe·ya·pa \glu-ȟé-ya-pa\ *v poss* wa·gluȟeyapa [fr *yuȟeyapa* take away] : to remove or take away one's own
glu·ȟe·ya·pa·ya \glu-ȟé-ya-pa-ya\ *v refl perhaps* : to get away from < *Wicaša šica wicagluȟeyapaya po* Stay away from evil men > - B.H.64.22,117.23, 212.6, 224.5
glu·ȟi·ca *or* **glugica** \glu-ȟí-ca\ *v poss* wa·gluȟica [fr *yuȟica* or *yuġica* to awake] : to wake up one's own
glu·hla \glu-ȟlá\ *v poss* wa·glúhla [fr *yuhla* to rattle] : to ring one's own bell
glu·hla·gan \glu-ȟlá-ġaŋ\ *v poss* wa·gluhlagan [fr *yuhlagan* to separate from] : to loosen a little e.g. one's belt; to leave, as a wife her husband < ~ *šni* to be constant, not to leave one's own >
glu·hla·ya \glu-ȟlá-ya\ *v poss* wa·glúhlaya [fr *yuhlaya* peel off] : to peel off the skin of one's own, as off one's potatoes
glu·hle·ca \glu-ȟlé-ca\ *v poss* wa·glúhleca [fr *yuhleca* tear to pieces] : to tear one's own, as one's coat — **glu·hle·hle·ca** \glu-ȟlé-ȟle-ca\ *v red* : to tear often
glu·hlel \glu-ȟlél\ *v poss contrac of* gluhleca : to tear
glu·hlog \glu-ȟlóg\ *v contrac of* gluhloka : to bore
glu·hlo·hlo·ka \glu-ȟló-ȟlo-ka\ *to red of* gluhloka
glu·hlo·ka \glu-ȟló-ka\ *v poss* wa·glúhloka [fr *yuhloka* to bore a hole] : to make a hole in one's own by boring
glu·hpa \glu-ȟpa\ *v poss* wa·gluhpa [fr *yuhpa* to take down] : to take down one's own, as a thing hung up < *Na winyan kin he taku wan k'in k'on he* ~ And the woman who had carried in the thing took it down > — **gluhpa·hpa** \glu-ȟṗá-ȟṗa\ *v red of* gluhpa
glu·hpan·hpan \glu-ȟṗáŋ-ȟṗaŋ\ *v poss red* wa·gluhpanhpan : to make soft one's own, as one's moccasins by putting them in water
glu·hpu \glu-ȟṗú\ *v poss* wa·gluhpu [fr *yuhpu* pick off] : to pull off one's own, as bark with one's hands — **glu·hpu·hpu** \glu-ȟṗú-ȟṗu\ *v red of* gluhpu
glu·h'e·h'e \glu-ȟ'é-ȟ'e\ *v poss of* gluh'eh'e : to do one's job only partly
glu·h'u \glu-ȟ'ú\ *v poss* wa·glúh'u [fr *yuh'u* to peel] : to pull off one's own, as bark with one's hands
glu·i·yu·pse \glu-í-yu-pse\ *v poss* : to take hold of one's own < *Nakpa* ~ *po* Listen attentively, or Give ear > - Cf iiglukse
glu·ja \glu-já\ *v poss* wa·gluje [fr *yuja* to stir or take] : to stir one's own; to take one's own, *e.g.* mush, *etc* - Cf gluzé
glu·ja·gja·ka \glu-já-gja-k̇a\ *v red of* glujaka : to keep pulling open one's own
glu·ja·ja \glu-já-ja\ *v poss* wa·glújaja [fr *yujaja* to wash something] : to wash one's own
glu·ja·ka \glu-já-k̇a\ *v poss* wa·glujaka [fr *yujaka* by hand to strain to open] : to pull open one's own, as one's eyes
glu·jib \glu-jíb\ *v contrac of* glujipa : to pinch one's own
glu·jin·ca \glu-jíŋ-ca\ *v poss* wa·glujinca [fr *yujinca* to pull or blow] : to pull or blow one's own nose < *Canke pahli glujincin kta* And so let him blow his nose clear >
glu·ji·pa \glu-jí-ṗa\ *v poss* wa·glujipa [fr *yujipa* pinch] : to pinch one's own
glu·ju·ju \glu-jú-ju\ *v poss* wa·glujuju [fr *yujuju* to destroy of void] : to pull down or destroy one's own
glu·jun \glu-júŋ\ *v poss* wa·glujun [fr *yujun* uproot] : to pull up one's own out by the roots, as one's tree < *Hin wan* ~ *na k'u* He pulled out a bit of fur and gave it to him > - MS.572
glu·kan \glu-káŋ\ *v poss* wa·glukan [fr *yukan* shake off] : to shake off one's own fruit
glu·ka·pa \glu-ká-ṗa\ *v poss of* yukapa : to catch in the hand of one's own
glu·ka·tin \glu-k̇á-ṫiŋ\ *v poss of* yukatin : to straighten out with one's own hands
glu·ka·wa \glu-k̇á-wa\ *v poss* wa·glukawa [fr *yukawa* to open with a grimace] : to open one's own, as one's mouth when one makes an effort with the hands, to cause a grimace in making an effort < *I waglukawa* I strained to go > - Cf *icapa* to gape
glu·kca \glu-kcá\ *v poss* wa·glukca [fr *yukca* untangle] : to untie one's own, to undo or unbraid, as a woman her hair
glu·kcan \glu-kcáŋ\ *v poss* wa·glukcan > to form an opinion of what concerns one's self, for an opinion of

---

\a\ father \e\ they \i\ machine \o\ smoke \u\ lunar \an, aŋ\ blanc Fr. \in, iŋ\ ink \on, oŋ, un, uŋ\ soon, confier Fr. \c\ chair \ġ\ machen Ger. \j\ fusion \clusters: bl, gn, kp, hšl, etc...\ b[e]lo ... said with a slight vowel
See more in the Introduction, Guide to Pronunciation

one's self
glu·ki·nun·kan \glu-k̇í-nuŋ-kaŋ\ *v poss of* yukinunkan : to divide one's own; *fig* to distract self
glu·kin·ca \glu-k̇íŋ-ca\ *v poss* wa·glukinca [fr *yukinca* to scrape off] : to scrape off *e.g.* dirt from one's own clothes by hand
glu·kin·yan \glu-k̇íŋ-yaŋ\ *v* : to put on more speed, to accelerate - Bl KE
glu·ki·pa·ja \glu-k̇í-ṗa-ja\ *v poss of* yukipaja : to double over - Bl
glu·ko·ka \glu-kó-k̇a\ *v poss of* yukoka : to ring one's own
glu·kpan \glu-k̇ṗaŋ\ *v poss* wa·glukpan [fr *yukpan* pulverize] : to grind one's own *e.g.* corn, *etc*
glu·ksa \glu-ksá\ *v poss* wa·gluksa [fr *yuksa* break off] : to break off one's own, as a stick with the hands — **gluksa·ksa** \glu-ksá-ksa\ *v poss red of* yuksaksa : to break off by hand frequently
glu·kša \glu-kšá\ *v poss of* yukša : to double up *e.g.* one's blanket
glu·kše \glu-kšé\ *v* : to turn or do a somersault, diving with head foremost < *Glukšepi* They dived head-first, *or* a dive head-first, *unglukšepi* or *ungluce-ga-pi* we dove *or* our diving > - Bl KE *Syn* GLU-CEGA
glu·kši·ja \glu-kší-ja\ *v poss of* yukšija : to to double up one's own
glu·ktan \glu-kṫaŋ\ *v poss* wa·gluktan [fr *yuktan* to bend] : to bend one's own
glu·ku·ka \glu-k̇ú-ka\ *v poss* wa·glukuka [fr *yukuka* to destroy] : to wear out or make old one's own
glu·k'e·ga \glu-k'é-ġa\ *v poss* wa·gluk'ega [fr *yuk'ega* to scratch or scrape] : to scrape or scratch one's own
glu·k'e·sk'e·za \glu-k'é-sk'-za\ *v red* wa·gluk'esk'eza [fr *gluk'eza* shave or rub smooth] : to shave off one's own close, as the hair of one's head, one's dog
glu·k'e·za \glu-k'é-za\ *v poss* wa·gluk'eza : to shave or rub smooth one's own, as one's arrows
glu·k'o·ga \glu-k'ó-ġa\ *v poss of* yuk'oga : to roughen
glu·k'o-za \glu-k'ó-za\ *v poss of* yuk'oza : to smooth and harden one's own
glul \glul\ *v contrac of* gluta : to eat one's own < ~ *waun* I am eating my food >
glu·man \glu-máŋ\ *v poss* wa·gluman un·gluman·pi : to grind and make sharp one's own, as one's axe or knife. -D.195
glu·mna \glu-mná\ *v poss* wa·glumna [fr *yumna* to rip] : to rip one's own
glu·na·jin \glu-ná-jiŋ\ *v poss* wa·glunajin [fr *yunajin* to make stand up] : to make one's own stand up
glu·na s'a \glu-ná s'a\ *v* : to veer in one's course, as does a ball struck not quite squarely, to slice or fowl curve - Bl KE
glu·o·ble·ca \glu-ó-ble-ca\ *v poss* wa·gluobleca [fr *yuo-bleca* to break scattering abroad] : to scatter out one's own
glu·o·blel \glu-ó-blel\ *v contrac of* gluobleca
glu·o·hla·gan \glu-ó-ȟla-ġaŋ\ *v poss of* yuohlagan : to loosen one's own a little, as one's girdle — **gluohlah** \glu-ó-ȟlaȟ\ *v contrac of* gluohlagan : to loosen a little or untie a knot
glu·o·ki·wan·ji·la \glu-ó-k̇i-waŋ-ji-la\ *v poss of* yuoki-wanjila : to place all one's own together, make one of them — **glu·o·ki·yu·ta** \glu-ó-k̇i-yu-ṫa\ *v poss of* yuo-kiyuta : to close up one's own *e.g.* wound *etc* < *Na oo kin* ~ And he closed up his own wound > - Cf R - *Syn* OKIZI
glu·o·ni·han \glu-ó-ni-haŋ\ *v poss* wa·gluonihan [fr *yuonihan* to honor] : to honor one's own
glu·o·ta \glu-ó-ṫa\ *v poss* wa·gluota [fr *yuota* multiply] : to multiply one's own
glu·o·tan'·in \glu-ó-taŋ-iŋ\ *v poss* wa·gluotan'in [fr *yu-otan'in* make appear] : to manifest one's own, *e.g.* a law
glu·o·tkon·za \glu-ó-ṫk̇oŋ-za\ *v poss* wa·gluotkonza [fr *yuotkonza* make of equal length, to finish] : to make e-qual one's own; to do like < *Wana yagluotkonza hwo?* Did you get your work done? > - Bl
glu·o·wan·ca·ya \glu-ó-waŋ-ca-ya\ *v poss* wa·gluowan-caya [fr *yuowancaya* make spread everywhere] : to cause to spread all over, to make one's own go all over
glu·pe \glu-ṗé\ *v poss of* yupe : to sharpen one's own
glu·pe·han \glu-ṗé-haŋ\ *v poss of* yupehan : to fold up one's own
glu·pe·mni \glu-ṗé-mni\ *v poss of* yupemni : to make one's own twist or warp
glu·pol \glu-ṗól\ *v contrac of* glupota : to tear to pieces one's own — **glu·pol·pota** \glu-ṗól-ṗo-ṫa\ *v red of* glu-pota
glu·po·pa \glu-pó-ṗa\ *v poss of* yupopa : to snap or burst one's own
glu·po·ta \glu-ṗó-ṫa\ *v poss* wa·glupota [fr *yupota* to tear] : to wear out one's own
glu·psag \glu-pság\ *v contrac of* glupsaka
glu·psa·ka \glu-psá-ka\ *v poss* wa·glupsaka [fr *yupsaka* break in two] : to break one's own with the hands, as a string or cord — **glupsa·psa·ka** *v red of* glupsaka
glu·psi·ca \glu-psí-ca\ *v poss* wa·glupsica [fr *yupsica* to make one jump] : to make one's own jump, as one's horse; to pull up with a hook and line one's own fish
glu·psil \glu-psíl\ *v contrac of* glupsica : to make jump — **glupsi·psica** \glu-psí-psi-ca\ *v red of* glupsica : to keep one's own jumping
glu·psun·psun *also* **glupsonpson** \glu-psúŋ-psuŋ\ *v poss of* yupsunpsun : to move back and forth one's own, as a cow her tail, to wag
glu·pšun \glu-pšúŋ\ *v poss* wa·glupšun [fr *yupšun* pull out] : to pull or extract one's own, as one's teeth
glu·pta \glu-pṫá\ *v poss of* yupta : to cut out one's own, as one's clothes
glu·ptan \glu-pṫáŋ\ - Cf gluptanyan
glu·ptan·yan \glu-pṫáŋ-yaŋ\ *v poss* wa·gluptanyan [fr *yuptanyan* pull to turn over] : to turn over one's own
glu·pte·ce·la \glu-pṫé-ce-la\ *v poss* wa·gluptecela [fr *yuptecela* shorten] : to shorten one's own
glu·ptu·ja \glu-pṫú-ja\ *v poss* wa·gluptuja [fr *yuptuja* to crack] : to crack or split anything of one's own by boring *etc* — **gluptu·ptuja** \glu-ptú-ptu-ja\ *v red of* glu-ptuja — **gluptuš** \glu-ptúš\ *v contrac of* gluptuja
glu·ptu·za \glu-ptú-za\ *v refl* : to bend self over, with buttocks upward - Bl KE
glus \glus\ *v contrac of* gluzá : to have or hold one's own < ~ *najin* to stand holding one's own >
glu·ska \glu-sk̇á\ *v poss of* yuska : to whiten, cleanse — **gluska·hcin** \glu-sk̇á-ȟciŋ\ *v* wa·gluskahcin : to smoke, in *ref* to clouds of smoke < *Wagluskahcin kte lo* I shall smoke mine, *Unglúskahcinpi kta lo* Let us smoke our own > - Bl
glu·ske·pa \glu-sk̇é-ṗa\ *v poss* wa·gluskepa [fr *yuskepa* make escape] : to absorb one's own; to cause one's own to leak out or e-vaporate
glu·ski·ca \glu-skí-ca\ *v poss of* yuskica : to press or to make tight

glu·skil \glu-skíl\ *v contrac of* gluskita : to tie up one's own
glu·ski·ski·ta \glu-skí-ski-ṫa\ *v red* wa·gluskiskita [fr *gluskita* wrap or tie] : to wrap or tie up one's own, as a Dakota woman does her baby
glu·ski·ta \glu-skí-ṫa\ *v poss* wa·gluskita [fr *yuskita* to wrap or tie] : to wrap or tie up one's own
glu·sku \glu-skú\ *v poss* wa·glusku [fr *yusku* to peel] : to cut close one's own, as the hair of one's child; to pare off, as the skin of one's own apple of potato — **glusku-sku** \glu-skú-sku\ *v red of* glusku : to keep paring
glu·sle·ca \glu-slé-ca\ *v poss of* yusleca : to be tearing
glu·slo·han \glu-sló-haŋ\ *v poss of* yuslohan : to drag or draw one's own
glu·slu·ta \glu-slú-ṫa\ *v poss* wa·glusluta [fr *yusluta* pull out from under] : to pull out, to draw out from under one's own < *Wowakan* ~ He drew out something strange >
glu·sna \glu-sná\ *v poss of* yusná : to ring one's own
glu·sni \glu-sní\ *v poss of* yusní : to put out or turn off
glu·sol \glu-sól\ *v contrac of* glusota : to use up one's own < ~` *iyeya* to quickly us up one's own > — **glusol·sota** \glu-sól-so-ṫa\ *v red of* glusota : to continue using up one's own
glu·so·ta \glu-só-ṫa\ *v poss* wa·glusota [fr *yusota* to use up all] : to use up all one's own
glu·sto \glu-sṫó\ *v poss of* yustó : to smooth down *e.g.* one's hair < pa ~ to smooth down one's own hair > — **glusto·sto** \glu-sṫó-sṫo\ *v red of* glustó : to be grooming one's own hair
glu·su·ksu·ta \glu-sú-ksu-ṫa\ *v red of* glusuta : to be making firm or establishing one's own
glu·su·ta \glu-sú-ṫa\ *v poss* wa·glusuta [fr *yusuta* make firm or established] : to make firm or to establish one's own
glu·šab \glu-šáb\ *v contrac of* glušapa : blacken, make dirty, or disfigure — **gluša·bšapa** \glu-ša-bša-ṗa\ *v red of* glušapa : to defile or soil, spoil one's own
glu·ši·ca \glu-ší-ca\ *v poss* wa·glušica [fr *yušica* cause to soil] : to make bad or to injure one's own
glu·ši·htin \glu-ší-ȟtiŋ\ *v poss* wa·glušihtin [fr *yušihtin* enfeeble] : to weaken or enfeeble one's own, as one's horse; to wear out, spoil, make bad , or injure one's own
glu·ši·kši·ca \glu-ší-kši-ca\ *v red of* glušica : to be continually defiling, spoiling
glu·ška \glu-šká\ *v poss* wa·gluška [fr *yuška* untie, loosen] : to untie or to let go one's own
glu·škan·škan \glu-škáŋ-škaŋ\ *v poss* wa·gluškanškan [fr *yuškanškan* make move about] : to make one's own move about
glu·ške·pa \glu-šké-ṗa\ *v poss of* yuškepa : to wring out one's own - Bl
glu·ški \glu-škí\ *v poss* wa·gluški [fr *yuški* to plait] : to pucker, gather, plait one's own
glu·ški·ca \glu-škí-ca\ *v poss of* yuškica : to press one's own with one's hands; to milk *e.g.* one's own cow
glu·škil \glu-škíl\ *v contrac of* gluškica : to press by hand — **gluški·škica** *v red of* gluškica
glu·ško·pa \glu-škó-ṗa\ *v poss of* yuškopa : to hollow out one's own
glu·šla \glu-šlá\ *v poss of* yušla : to shear one's own
glu·šlog \glu-šlóg\ *v contrac of* glušloka : pull off or out one's own < ~ *iyeya* quickly pull off *e.g.* one's clothes >
glu·šlo·ka \glu-šló-ka\ *v poss* wa·glušloka [fr *yušloka* pull off or out] : to pull off, as one's clothes; to pull out *e.g.* a cork — **glušlo·šloka** *v red of* glušloka
glu·šlu·ta \glu-šlú-ṫa\ *v poss of* yušluta : to let slip one's own out of hand
glu·šna \glu-šná\ *v poss* wa·glušna [fr *yušna* to err] : to miss in one's own regard — **glušna·šna** *v red of* glušna : to miss repeatedly in regard to one's own
glu·šni·yan·yan \glu-šní-yaŋ-yaŋ\ *v* : to get away in a hurry, swiftly < *Waglušniyanyanhce* I made a quick getaway indeed *i.e. kátka mani* walking away briskly > - Bl - *Syn* GLUGWEGEHCE
glu·špa \glu-špá\ *v poss of* yušpá : to break off or divide one's own
glu·špi \glu-špí\ *v poss of* yušpi : to pluck *e.g.* berries
glu·špu \glu-špú\ *v poss of* yušpu : to pull off something tight of one's own — **glušpu·ya** *v poss* wa·glušpuya [fr *yušpuya* to scratch] : to scratch one's own flesh — **glušpu·špuya** *v red of* glušpuya
glu·štan \glu-štáŋ\ *v poss* wa·gluštan [fr *yuštan* to complete] : to finish one's own, to come to a conclusion < *Wanna habloglaka na* ~ Now he finished telling his vision > — **gluštan·štan** *v red of* gluštan
glu·šte \glu-šté\ *adj* : numb, as one's foot when it is "asleep" < *Si nainš nape waglušte* My foot or my hands are numb >
glu·š'a·ka \glu-š'á-ka\ *v poss* wa·gluš'aka [fr *yuš'aka* to be heavily laden] : to be burdened with one's own
glu·ta \glú-ṫa\ *v poss* waglúta [fr *yúta* to eat] : to eat one's own as food
[1]**glu·tan** \glu-ṫáŋ\ *v poss* wa·glutan [fr *yutan* to honor] : to praise one's own
[2]**glu·tan** \glu-táŋ\ *v poss* wa·glutan [fr *yután* to touch] : to touch one's own
glu·tan'·in \glu-táŋ-iŋ\ *v poss* wa·glutan'in [fr *yutan'in* make appear or visible] : to make manifest one's own
glu·tan·ka \glu-táŋ-ka\ *v poss* wa·glutanka [fr *yutanka* make great or large] : to make large, enlarge one's own
glu·ta·ta \glu-tá-ta\ *v poss of* yutata : to shake one's own, as one's clothes
glu·te·ca \glu-ṫé-ca\ *v poss* wa·gluteca [fr *yuteca* make new] : to make new, renew one's own
glu·te·han \glu-ṫé-haŋ\ *v poss* wa·glutehan [fr *yutehan* prolong] : to make a long time; to put off, to defer
glu·te·pa \glu-ṫé-ṗa\ *v poss* wa·glutepa [fr *yutepa* wear off] : to make blunt, to wear off one's own
glu·ti·ca \glu-ṫí-ca\ *v poss* wa·glutica [fr *yutica* scrape away] : to scrape off *e.g.* snow from one's own place
glu·tin·to \glu-ṫiŋ-ṫo\ *v* wa·glutinto : to take all that has been staked in a game - Bl - *Syn* IGLUK'O
glu·ti·tan \glu-ṫí-ṫaŋ\ *v poss* wa·glutitan [fr *yutitan* pull] : to pull or stretch at one's own
glu·to·kan \glu-tó-kaŋ\ *v poss* wa·glutokan [fr *yutokan* reject] : to remove one's own to another place
glu·to·ke·ca \glu-ṫó-ke-ca\ *v poss* wa·glutokeca [fr *yutokeca* to alter] : to make one's own different
glu·t'a \glu-t'á\ *v poss* *wa*·glut'a [fr *yut'a* choke to death] : to kill one's own by hanging, choking, *etc*
glu·t'in·za \glu-t'íŋ-za\ *v poss of* yut'inza : to tighten one's own
glu·wa·ci \glu-wá-ci\ *v poss of* yuwáci : to make spin, as a top with thehand - Bl
glu·wa·hpa·ni·ca \glu-wá-ȟpa-ni-ca\ *v poss of* yuwa-

\a\ father \e\ they \i\ machine \o\ smoke \u\ lunar \an, aŋ\ blanc Fr. \in, iŋ\ ink \on, oŋ, un, uŋ\ soon, confier Fr. \c\ chair \ǧ\ machen Ger. \j\ fusion \clusters: bl, gn, kp, hšl, etc...\ b^e^lo ... said with a slight vowel
See more in the Introduction, Guide to Pronunciation

hpanica : to make poor one's own

glu·wa·hwa·la \glu-wá-ȟwa-la\ *v poss of* yuwahwala : to make gentle one's own

glu·wa·kan \glu-wá-kaŋ\ *v poss* wa·gluwakan [fr *yuwakan* make holy] : to make one's own sacred

glu·wan·ka \glu-wáŋ-ka\ *v poss* : to lift one's own < *Išta* ~ He raised his eyes > — **gluwankal** \glu-wáŋ-kal\ *v poss* wa·gluwankal [fr *yuwankal* raise up or lift] : to lift or raise up one's own - Cf yuwankal - B.H. 183.2, 230.7

glu·wa·šte \glu-wá-šte\ *v poss* wa·gluwašte [fr *yuwašte* make good : to make good one's own

glu·wa·š'a·ka \glu-wá-š'a-ka\ *v poss* wa·glúwaš'aka [fr *yuwaš'aka* make strong] : to make strong one's own

glu·wa·za \glu-wá-za\ *v poss of* yuwaza : to vex one's own

glu·we \glu-wé\ *v poss of* yuwe : to bleed one's own

glu·we·ga \glu-wé-ġa\ *v poss* wa·glúwega [fr *yuwega* to break] : to break or fracture one's own

glu·weh \glu-wéȟ\ *v contrac of* gluwega : to break — **glu·we·hwe·ga** \glu-wé-ȟwe-ġa\ *v red of* gluwega : to repeatedly fracture one's own

glu·wi \glu-wí\ *v poss* wa·gluwi [fr *yuwi* bind up] : to wrap up one's own, as with a string or thong < *Lakota ašké gluwipi* Lakotas bind up a hair tuft >

glu·wi·ca·ka \glu-wí-ca-ka\ *v poss* wa·gluwicaka [fr *yuwicaka* prove true] : to make true or prove one's own

glu·win·ga \glu-wíŋ-ġa\ *v poss of* yuwinga : to turn back - Bl

glu·win·ja \glu-wíŋ-ja\ *v poss* wa·gluwinja [fr *yuwinja* bend down] : to bend down *e.g.* one's own grass *etc* — **gluwinš** \glu-wíŋš\ *v contrac of* gluwinja — **glu·win·šwin·ja** \glu-wíŋ-šwiŋ-ja\ *v red of* gluwinja

glu·win·ta \glu-wíŋ-ta\ *v poss* wa·gluwinta [fr *yuwinta* to salute] : to stretch out the hand to implore, worship; to stroke one's own *e.g.* face

glu·win·ye·ya \glu-wíŋ-ye-ya\ *v poss of* yuwinyeya *and* winyeya : to make ready one's own

glu·wi·tan \glu-wí-taŋ\ *v poss* wa·gluwitan [fr *yuwitan* glorify] : to make proud, to glorify one's own

glu·wi·ta·ya \glu-wí-ta-ya\ *v poss of* yuwitaya : to gather or assemble with one's own - Cf witaya

glu·wi·ya·kpa \glu-wí-ya-kpa\ *v poss of* yuwiyakpa *and* wiyakpa : to make shine one's own; *fig* to interpret

glu·wo·sla·ta \glu-wó-sla-ta\ *v poss* wa·gluwoslata [fr *yuwoslata* set upright] : to place upright something of one's own

glu·za \glú-za\ *v poss* wa·glúza [fr *yúza* take a hold on] : to take or hold one's own

glu·za·mni \glu-zá-mni\ *v poss of* yuzamni : to uncover or disclose one's own

glu·ze \glu-zé\ *v poss* wa·gluze [fr *yuze* dip out] : to dip or lade out *e.g.* victuals from one's own kettle

glu·zo·ka \glu-zó-ka\ *v poss of* yuzoka : perhaps one who dips out food, as in a serving line - Note: the word may well be *gluzeka* the *v* becoming a *n* by the *suff "ka"*; the order of the word also suggests a misreading of *ó*

gmi·gma \gmi-gmá\ *vn* : to go around, like a wheel

gmi·gme·la \gmi-gmé-la\ *adj* : round, as is a wheel < *aguyapi* ~ biscuits, to be distinguished from: *aguyapi skuyela* ~ *yuhlokab* sweet bread with a round hole, *i.e.* doughnuts > — **gmigme·ya** *adv* : round and round, going round < *Taku wan* ~ *skayéla yanka* It was something light-colored that was going round and round, *i.e.* something white and spherical > - D.193

gmi·gmi·yan \gmi-gmí-yaŋ\ *adj* : round, perhaps like a ball — **gmigmiyan·yan** *adj red of* gmigmiyan

gmi·ka \gmí-ka\ *adj* magmika : light and small, as is said of men and animals < ~ *canke luzahan* It is light and little, and so, swift >

gmi s'e \gmi s'e\ *adv* [fr *yugmi* to clear off] : in the manner of clearing off, raking off *e.g.* grass from a field < ~ *únyan 'emayaye* As though they had been cleared off (the game I was after) got away from me > - *Syn* HÍN-TE S'E

gmi·yan \gmi-yáŋ\ *adj* : round, as a wheel — **gmiyan-yan** *adj red of* gmiyan — **gmiyanyan·la** *n* : any little round things

gmun \gmuŋ\ *adj* : twisted - Cf kagmun, yugmun

gmun·ka \gmúŋ-ka\ *va* wa·gmúnka : to set a trap, to trap anything, to catch in a trap < *Magmunkapi kin ehanni omáyuspapi tka* But when they set a trap for me, it was then they took hold on me, as they say when they go to the same house repeatedly > - B.H.258.8

gmunk wa·cin \gmúŋk wa-cìŋ\ *va* : to think of trapping one - B.H.241.23

gmun·smna \gmúŋ-smna\ *adj* : smelling like fish — **gmun·za** \gmúŋ-za\ *adj* : slimy, fish-like and smelling strong, i.e. like spoiled meat

gmus \gmús\ *adj contrac of* gmuza : shut — **gmus·ya** \gmús-ya\ *adv* : shut up

gmu·ya·pi s'e \gmu-yá-pi s'e\ *adv* : with many things together, bunched up, crowded together, as do children, horses, *etc* < *Waglula kin* ~ *etanhan ahinape* The worms emerged from it crowded together > - Bl B.H.155.14

gmu·za \gmú-za\ *adj* : shut, as the mouth or hand, *etc* - Cf ogmúza

gna·gna·lo·wan \gna-gná-lo-waŋ\ *v* : to sing a grunting song

gna·han \gná-haŋ\ *part* : fallen off of itself, as fruit

gna·ka \gná-ka\ *va* wa·gnaka : to lay or place, to lay away or lay up, as the dead; to inter < *Hanpšikšica wanjihci yagnaka hwo?* Haven't you laid away an old pair of shoes? *or* Haven't you an old pair of shoes for me? > - Bl

gnan·gnan s'e \gnaŋ-gnáŋ s'e\ *adv* : in an intermittent manner, as in laughing: "Ha-ha-ha" and making a wavering tune with the voice as in singing < ~ *olowan* a tremolo song > - SLB

gna·ška \gna-šká\ *n* : the common frog < ~ *hotonpi* frogs acroaking > — **gnaškacanli** *or* **gnaškacanlila** \gna-šká-caŋ-li\ *n* : a small kind of frog with a loud voice, a tree frog - Bl — **gnaškawakan** \gna-ška-wa-kàŋ\ *n* : the bull frog perhaps, a frog with a bray like that of a donkey, *šúnšunla iyececa* like that of a mule - Bl

gna·škin·yan \gna-škíŋ-yaŋ\ *vn* : to be wild, crazy, frantic < *šungnaškinyan* a mad dog > — **gnaškin-yan·yan** \gna-škíŋ-yaŋ-yaŋ\ *vn red* ma·gnaškinyan-yan : to be oppressed, overcome, frantic < *Hunh tokecapi na gnaškinyanyanpi na t'a ihpayapi* Some were sick, some frantic, and some lay dead >

gna·wa·han \gna-wá-haŋ\ *part same as* gnáhan : fallen

gna·yan \gná-yaŋ\ *va* wa·gnayan : to deceive, to cheat < *Gnáye akú wo,* Win him over, *i.e.* by good treatment, even if you don't feel like it > -Bl

gni \gni\ *v 3rd pers singl and used in the fut tense* [fr *gla* to go home] : to go to one's own home < *Wagni kte* I will go home > - Note: the *fut* of *gla* is properly *gni kte* - Cf mni

gnu·gnu·ška \gnu-gnú-ška\ *n* : the grasshopper < ~ *sapa* the black grasshopper or out-door cricket >

gnu·ni \gnú-ni\ *vn* wa·gnúni : to wander, be lost; to lose – Note: the word is perhaps the *contrac* of *kinuni*
go·bgo·bni·ya \go-bgó-bni-ya\ *vn* : to breathe hard
go·bi·štin·ma \ġo-bí-štiŋ-ma\ *v* go·bmi·štinma : to snore in sleep – WE — **go·bya** \ġó-bya\ *adv* : in a snoring manner
go·go s'e \ġo-ġó s'e\ *adv* : leaving a mark with one's foot < ~ *mani* to walk dragging one's feet over the ground and leaving marks, *Pahin s'e yuzica ~ mani* He walked leaving a mark from dragging his feet as though he were a porcupine stretching, as is said of old people who cannot lift their feet in walking > – Bl
gon·ga \ġóŋ-ġa\ *adj* : the eyes gently closed < ~ *manka*. ~ *un* My eyes are carefully closed. His eyes are discreetly closed, *i.e.* to be proud, not noticing others as though one were blind >
[1]**go·pa** *or* **ȟopa** \ġó-p̣a\ *adj* : attractive, beautiful, handsome < *wigópa* a pretty woman > – Cf gópeca
[2]**go·pa** \ġó-pa\ *vn* wa·gopa : to snore – D.272.33
go·pe·ca *or* **ȟopeca** \ġó-p̣e-ca\ *adj* : beautiful, well-formed
gu \ġu\ *vn* ma·gú ni·gú un·gú·pi : to burn, singe, or scorch; to be burnt
gu·ge·ca \ġu-ġé-ca\ also **guyeca** \ġu-yé-ca\ *n* : the soft, spongy part of bones in which there is oil – Note: compare *kagege* and *kayege*
gu·gna·gya *or* **ȟugnahya** \ġu-gná-gya\ *va* : to burn down, destroy by fire – P
gu·gu \ġu-ġú\ *v red of* ġu : to be burnt in
gugu·han \ġu-ġú-haŋ\ *adj* : senseless, witless, with no respect given < *He natá ~* He is foolish, crazy > – ED KE – *Syn* WITKO, GLUGLUKA
gu·gu ka·šla \ġu-ġú ka-šlà\ *adj* or *adv* : made bare by the hair being hacked to pieces with a knife, as is done sometimes as a sign of deep mourning < *Lila wašigla na ~ na ceyahan* He was in deep grief, had hacked off his hair, and was crying > KE
gu·gu·la \ġu-ġú-la\ *adj* : curled or ruffled as hair or fur – *Syn* YUMNIMNIJA
gu·gu·ya \ġu-ġú-ya\ *v red* gugu·wa·ya [fr *guyá* burn] : to cause to be burnt in different places, to burn in various places; to have more than one burn on a brand < *Pséhtin wan guguyi na canksa wan kage* He seared a piece of ash wood and made of it a policeman's club > –D.115
gu·he·he·ya \ġu-hé-he-ya\ *v red of* guhéya : to take away from circulation < *Wakpala oinkpa kin ~ yunkelo* The head of the creek lay along a way diverting him, *i.e.* there being a starting-point of many draws near together > – Bl KE
gu·he·ya \ġu-hé-ya\ *v* : to take from the course of travel somewhat, to produce a fanning out from an orientation point or line < *Canku kin kitanla ~ yunkelo* The road lay along a way diverting him a bit, *i.e.* many automobile trails on the prairie along a certain course giving the appearance of windrows > – Bl WHL
gu·h'cin·ca·ye·la \ġu-h'ciŋ-ca-ye-la\ *adv* : perching in such-wise as to avoid things and persons < ~ *unyanpi* We came, *i.e.* coming from very far, for a resting place > – Bl KE *Syn* NAHEBYELA
gu·i·c'i·ya \ġu-í-c'i-ya\ *v refl of* guyá : to burn one's self, as on a hot stove – *Syn* ŠPAN'ÍC'IYA
gu·mna \ġu-mná\ *adj* [fr *ġu* burnt + *omna* smelling] : smelling burnt < *Oná gumna* It smells like a prairie fire >
gun·ga *or* **gonga** \ġúŋ-ġa\ *adj* : proud, with eyes closed not minding others, haughty < ~ *yankahe* He was sitting haughtily > — **gunga·ga** *adj red of* gúnga : proud — **gungaga·ya** *adv* : proudly – D.73
gu·ši·ca \ġu-ší-ca\ *adj* : burnt and hence worthless
gu·ya \ġu-yá\ *va* gu·wa·ya : to burn, cause to burn
gu·ye·ca \ġu-yé-ca\ *n* : the soft and spongy part of bones which hold oil – Note: compare *kagege* and *kayege* – Cf gugeca
gwa·han \gwá-haŋ\ *part* : bad, over-ripe, as fruit; turning soft and bad, as meat – Bl
gwe·gwes \gwé-gwes\ *adj contrac of* gwegweza : striped, in *ref* to the ribs < *Tucuhu ~ hingla yaun welo* You are all but ribs, *i.e.* skin and bones, or wirey, as is said of very lean men or animals that still move about > – Cf R, under ȟwa — **gwegweza** \gwe-gwé-za\ *adj red of* gwéza : thin — **gwegwezela** \gwe-gwé-ze-la\ *adj red dim* : skinny, lean
gwe·za \gwé-za\ *adj* : lean, thin; ragged — **gwe·zela** \gwé-ze-la\ *adj dim of* gwéza : finely thin – Bl
gwu \gwu\ *adj* : curdled < *asanpi ~* curdled milk > — **gwu·gwu** \gwu-gwú\ *adj red* : remaining curdled
gwu·la \gwú-la\ *adj* : little, small, minute; fine, apt < *Maka akanl taku ~, taku kpanla hena oyasin owakiyake* On earth there are fine little things; I told him all the fine points > – Bl KE

H

ha \ha\ *n* : the skin or hide of animal or human person; the bark of trees or shrubs

ha·a·h'e·h'e \ha-á-ȟ'e-ȟ'e\ *adj* haá·ma·h'eh'e : having on ragged clothes — **haah'eh'e·ya** *adv* : in torn clothes - *Syn* HAÁKANHANHEYELA

ha·a·i·glu·hle·hle·ca \ha-á-i-glu-ȟle-ȟle-ca\ *v refl* : to tear up one's clothing - B.H.38.4

ha·a·kab \ha-á-k̇ab\ *adv* : on the outside, on the surface as said in *ref* to the skin — **haaka·byela** *adv* : on the surface, shallow, close under the skin, as *ópi* in opposition to *šogyéla ópi* a serious wound - Note: a *fig* use, ~ *eya* to be shallow in speaking, *i.e.* they do not mean what they say

ha·a·kan·han·he·ye·la \ha-á-k̇aŋ-haŋ-he-ye-la\ *adv* : in torn clothes - *Syn* HAAH'EH'EYA Bl

ha·a·kan·he·he·ye·la un \ha-á-k̇aŋ-he-he-ye-la uŋ\ *v red* : to have on torn clothes

ha·a·ka·pa \ha-á-k̇a-ṗa\ *adv* : on the outside — **haakapata** *adv* : externally — **haakapa·tanhan** *adv* : on the outer surface

ha·a·ka·ta·ta \ha-á-k̇a-ṫa-ṫa\ *v* haa·wa·katata haa·ci·catata : to give one the last one has, as in turning the box upside down and shaking it over someone's hands - Bl

ha·a·ku·ka \ha-á-k̇u-ka\ *v* : to have worn out clothes on < *Hehé, haámakuke lo* On my! I have on clothes worn out > - GA

ha·ci *or* **hacila** \ha-ċí\ *n* ha·má·ci : a very young man, a grown-up boy < *Ataya hamaci yelo* By all means I am but a grown boy. *Hacila kin kopi kayeš ópapi* The lads, mere children, were anxious as well to join in > - B.H.117.21

ha·cib \ha-ċíb\ *imper interj* : Sh-h-h - Note: this is an order to keep still or silent, *esp* used in games and *nahmapi kapi* meaning to be secretive - Cf iyóhōb BT

ha·ci·la \ha-ċí-la\ *n* : children - B.H.117.21

ha·co·co·la \ha-cō'-co-la\ *adj red* ha·má·cocola : naked, as said of men — **hacola** \ha-có-la\ *adj* : naked, without clothes - Note: the *pl* form, *hacó·pi·la* *Pl*

ha·e·ce \há-e-ċe *or* ha e-ċé\ *adj* or *adv* : empty < ~ *hinajin* He came and stood blank > - B.H.106.6

ha·ha·ke \ha-há-k̇e\ *adj* : feeling spurred on, urged to move *e.g.* out to another place, away < *Ons'mahahake s'elececa* It seemed I felt it urgent (to move on), as said when anxious to go somewhere now > - Bl KE

ha·ha·la *or* **hahayela** \ha-há-la\ *adv* ma·háhala : loose, easily moved as a lamp resting on the edge of a table < *Le anpetu kin mahahala yelo. Taku iyuha ecin wakinica yelo.* ~ *s'e inyanka* Today I am on edge. I was anxious to reflect on everything. He ran moving as though lively *e.g.* as a good horse >

ha·han \ha-haŋ\ *interj to cease from being an annoyance* : Quit being bothersome - Cf Ahán

ha·ha·yela \ha-há-ye-la\ *adj* : loose, not tight < ~ *okoyake* It is not tight in between, as is said of fence wire that is held tight by staples; or of a box standing on a table and liable to drop > - Cf hahála

ha·ho ha·ho \ha-hó ha-hó\ *express of joy on receiving something* < ~ *pilamaya* Oh great! I am glad! >

ha·hun·ta \ha-ȟúŋ-ṫa\ *n* : thread, twine, cord < ~ *iyapehanpi* spool-thread >

ha·i·glu·hle·hlel \ha-í-glu-ȟle-ȟlel\ *adv red contrac of* haiglu-hlehleca : scratching one's own < ~ *ceye* to cry tearing at one's own > - Cf iyúhlehlel B.H.90.25

ha·i·le·ya·pi s'e \ha-í-le-ya-pi s'e\ *adv* : like one whose clothes are burnt near fire; bringing close to the fire; being not afraid of fire < ~ *yanke lo* He sat close to the fire > - LB

ha·i·pa·ja·ja \ha-í-ṗa-ja-ja\ *n* : soap

ha·i·ye \ha-i-yē'\ *interj of joy at hearing good news* : Bless God!, as might be said when buffalo are near. *"Pilapi" he kapi* It's meaning is "rejoicing" - Note: *ai* in this word is pronounced as a diphthong, *i.e.* as a single vowel - RB HH

ha·i·yo·ti·ye·ki·ya \ha-í-yo-ṫi-ye-k̇i-ya\ *v* haiyotiye·wa·kiya : to suffer in consequence of poor clothing

ha·kab \ha-k̇áb\ *adv* : afterwards, in the meantime < ~ *le na iglaka enajin* Meantime here they stood stopping to pitch camp > - D.261

ha·ka·kša \hȧ-ka-kša\ *adj* : empty and folded after use < *Wojuha k'on ~ waglagli yelo* I had brought that full sack empty. *Pagé ~ ihpeyayelo* You left its belly empty, *i.e.* you gave your horse nothing to eat all day > - Bl

ha·ka·kta \ha-k̇á-k̇ta\ *adj* ha·ma·kakta ma·hakakta unhakakta·pi : last, the last, the youngest child, boy or girl < *Unma wica he tokapa na unma winyan ca he ~ hokšihamakakta yelo* One a man was first or oldest and another myself a woman was the very youngest child > - BT

ha·ka·ta \ha-k̇á-ṫa\ *n* : a man's or a woman's older or younger sister; a woman's brothers < *mahakta* my sister *Mihakata šunkawakan owicawakile yelo* I went searching for my younger sister and her horse > — **hakata·ku** \ha-k̇á-ṫa-ku\ *n* : her relatives - D.227 and 229 note 5 Bl

ha·ka·ta·ta \há-k̇a-ṫa-ṫa\ *v* : to give everything away < *Wana háwakatata yelo* Now I slough off my skin > - Bl

ha·ka·ta·ya \ha-k̇á-ṫa-ya\ *va* hakata·wa·ya : to have for an older or younger sister - Note: both men and women use the word - Bl

ha·ke *or* **hakela** *or* **hakakta** \ha-k̇é\ *n* : the youngest child, boy or girl

ha·ki·kta \ha-k̇í-kṫa\ *vn* ha·we·kta ha·ye·kta ha·un·kikta·pi : to look behind, look back, turn around to look — **hakikta·kta** *vn red of* hakikta : to look back often < ~ *inyankahanpi* They were looking back time and again > - D.56, 66, and 67

ha·ki·ton \hak̇í-toŋ\ *v* ha·wé·ton : to have clothes on, to be dressed - D.36

ha·ki·ya \ha-k̇í-ya\ *va* ha·wa·kiya : to clothe one, give one clothes

ha·la \há-la\ *n* : a flea, fleas < ~ *šaša* a red flea > - *Syn* PSICALA

ha·la·bla·ska \há-la-bla-ska\ *n* : a bedbug - Bl

hal·ha·te *or perhaps* **halhata** \hal-há-te\ *n* : a magpie, so called because of its squawking call or talk - WE

ha·mna \há-mna\ *adj* : smelling of skin, not smelling well as meat does at times

ha·na·hpu \há-na-ȟpu\ *v* : to shed — **hanahpu·hpu** *v red* : to appear ready to peel or drop off, as the rough bark of a tree or the skin *e.g.* of a snake

ha·na·sku \há-na-sku\ *vn* : to crack and peel — **hanasku·sku** *vn* : to crack and peel off, as the skin of potatoes do by boiling — **hanasku·ya** *va* hanasku·wa·ya : to cause to crack and peel off

[1]**han** *or final* **he** \haŋ\ *suff* : affixed to *v* or its *part* form. It indicates action is done repeatedly or for awhile < *Winyan wan céyahan, keye. Winyan wan heyata céyahe kin le, inayaye lo. Na wanna oyate kin kiblecahanpi* She stated that a woman was crying. This woman weeping in the hills was your mother. And the people were now dispersing > - Note: it seems to be a rule that a

v ending in *han* changes to *he* when it concerns past time. Thus *ahicahan* he stumbles and falls on one; *ahicahe* he stumbled and fell on one

²**han** *or* **hin** *or* **he** \haŋ\ *suff* affixed to *v* : they say, it is reported – Note: these three *suff* serve to give a word the meaning of *ške* < *Wanna micicau, hokšicala owáunpin ktelo, eyahe. Hecena iyaya ške; yahin na paha wan el asnikiya yanka ške. Eke blaye wan opta ya ške. Yahan, yunkan* It is said that she brought for me a baby for me to lay and bind it on a cradle board. Finally so they say, and she was sitting resting a long time on a hill, they say. The rumor is that she was going a goodly way across a prairie > – Note: the word *yahan* then may also be the *part* form

³**han** \haŋ\ *adv* of affirmation : Yes!

⁴**han** \haŋ\ *n contrac of* hanyetu : night < *han'icamna* a stormy night >

⁵**han** \haŋ\ *vn* : to stand upright, as of things, to remain, as said of grass, arrows that strike the ground and stand; also of cattle *etc* that remain or stay in a certain locality < *Hel hanpi ške. Tatanka optaye nunpa he lo* There they say is soup. There remain two herds of buffalo > – BT

⁶**han** \haŋ\ *adv* : before, Latin *ante* < *mat'ešni han* before I die > – B.H.39.7 *Syn* HANNI, ITOKAB

han·ble \haŋ-blé\ *vn* han·wa·ble : to fast and dream or attain vision; a religious prayer ceremonial – Note: one is said to be *ihanble* having visions

han·ble·ble *or* **hanbleble·kel** \haŋ-blé-ble\ \haŋ-blé-ble-k̇el \ *adv* perhaps : long ago < ~ *tak'eye* to say something long ago > – *Syn* EHANKEHAN, KILELEKEL

han·ble·ce·ya \haŋ-blé-ce-ya\ *vn* hanble·wa·ceya : to cry in the prayer of vision-seeking

han·blo·gla·gi·a \haŋ-bló-gla-ġi-ya\ *v* hanbloglagi·wa·ya : to tell dreams and visions — **hanblogla·gyakel** \haŋ-bló-gla-gya-k̇el\ *adv* : prophetically < ~ *leya oyake* He spoke saying this prophetically > – B.H.69.8

han·blo·gla·ka \haŋ-bló-gla-ka\ *va* hanblo·wa·glaka [fr *hanble* to fast + *oglaka* tell of one's own] : to tell of one's own intercourse with the spirits, to relate visions, to speak unintelligently; to pray < *Can kapestopi top yuha najin na* ~ He stood holding four wooden arrows, while he told visions >

han·co·kan \haŋ-có-kaŋ\ *n* : midnight < *Wana* ~ *nacece* It is now probably midnight > — **hancokan·yan** \haŋ-có-kaŋ-yaŋ\ *n* perhaps : midnight < *Na* ~ *enakiyapi. Ake lowanpi na* ~ *e ehanl hehanyela econpi* And they quit at midnight. Again they sang, and when it was midnight it was done only so far > – B.H.52.2

Han·ge·o·ku·te \Haŋ-ġé-o-ku-te\ *np* : the Santee clan of the Sisseton Indian Reservation in the extreme northeast corner of South Dakota

han·gla·wa·kel \haŋ-glá-wa-kel\ *adv* : counting the days and nights < ~ *un* to be counting the days and nights, *i.e.* to be biding his time day and night >

han·gna·gya \haŋ-gná-gya\ *adv* : being aware of things in a semi-conscious way, half-asleep < ~ *hpaya* to lie down ready to get up early > – *Syn* WINYEYA WHL

han·he·pi \haŋ-hé-ṗi\ *n* : night < ~ *cokanyan* midnight ~ *petijanjan* a lantern, *Petijanjan yuha omanipi* They travelled carrying a lamp, ~ *wašicun* The Power of the Night, its spirit of mystery, ~ *hmungapelo* the enchanted night, as is said when someone becomes sick very suddenly – Note: *wiwila hmungapelo* a bewitched spring >

han·he·pi wi \haŋ-hé-ṗi wi\ *n* : the moon

han'·i·gla·ka \haŋ-í-gla-ka\ *v* : to travel by night – Bl

han'·i·štin·ma \háŋ-i-štiŋ-ma\ *v* : to lie asleep at night < *Han'ištinme šni škan* He was restless lying awake at night > – WHL

han'·i·yan·pa *or* **hanwiyanpa** \haŋ-í-yaŋ-ṗa\ *n* : a moonlit night – LB

han'·i·ye·cin·ke šni \haŋ-í-ye-cin-ke šni\ *adv* : unexpectedly during the night < ~ *wahiyelo* I came very late, *i.e.* unexpectedly, in the night > – Bl WHL

han·ka \haŋ-ká\ *n* ni·hanka : a man's sister-in-law, *i.e.* his wife's sister or his brother's wife; my sister-in-law, perhaps < *nihanka* your sister-in-law > — **hanka·ku** *n* : his sister-in-law

han·ka·ši \haŋ-ká-ši\ *n* ni·hankaši : a man's female cousin, *i.e.* his mother's brother's daughter, but not his father's brother's daughter; my female cousin < *nihankaši* your female cousin > — **hankaši·tku** *n* : his female cousin — **hankaši·ya** *v* : to have for a female cousin, *i.e.* for a man to have

han·ka·ton \haŋ-k̇á-toŋ\ *va* hanka·wa·ton : to have for a sister-in-law — **hanka·ya** *va* hanka·wa·ya : to have for a sister-in-law, as a man his wife's sister and his brother's wife

han·ke \haŋ-k̇é\ *n* : half, a part of — **hanke·ke** \haŋ-k̇é-k̇e\ *n red of* hanke : half and half < ~ *wicak'u* He gave them each a half >

han·ke·ya \haŋ-k̇é-ya\ *adv* : at last, *i.e.* conveying the idea of having made good progress, having reached the middle, pretty much, little by little < *Tapškate ca* ~ *wayupika* He became fairly skilled at playing ball, *i.e.* learned how to play, *Hanhepi* ~ *etkiya napapi* They fled towards the middle of the night, *i.e.* through the night, ~ *wicota ohimniciye. Pte wan kacekcegyi na* ~ *t'a glihpaye.* ~ *kiblecahanpi* A goodly number [of people] were gathering for a meeting. A cow was staggering and at last it collapsed dead. Little by little they dispersed > — *n* : a near relative, a blood relation – Note: the word is not used in the *pl* , as it refers to only one < *Hemahankeya* He is a relative to me (One may not say: *hanke·wa·ya*) *Henihankeya* He is your relative > — *va* hanke·wa·ya : to halve, to have reached the middle — **hankeyaš** *adv emph* : being definitely average – B.H.54.5, 64.12, 82.1, 91.13, 170.6, 207.7, 29.5 D.52 EM

han·ki·gna·ka \haŋ-k̇í-gna-ka\ *v* : to delay, defer to the next morning, leave alone for the night < *Takuku cipasi kta* (last night) *tka onikan šni ca hancicignaka ca lehanl nitakuni šni* I might have inquired with you about trifles (last night), but since there is room for you and I deferred you to the morning, you have thusfar failed > – BT

han·ki·kta \haŋ-k̇í-k̇ta\ *vn* han·we·kta han'·un·kikta·pi : to rise very early in the morning, to wake while it is yet night

han·ko·ki·pa \haŋ-kó-ki-ṗa\ *va perhaps* hanko·wa·kipa : to fear the night, be afraid at night — *adv* : cowardly, fearing the night < *hankokipe·šni* not a fraid at night >

han·kpan \haŋ-kpáŋ\ *n* : a shoe string — **hankpan'o·hloka** *n* : the shoe string holes in or of a shoe

hanl i·ya·ya·pi s'e \haŋl i-yá-ya-pi s'e\ *adv* : in the manner of those having been told to begone, leaving resent-

---

\a\ father \e\ they \i\ machine \o\ smoke \u\ lunar \an, aŋ\ blanc Fr. \in, iŋ\ ink \on, oŋ, un, uŋ\ soon, confier Fr. \c\ chair \ġ\ machen Ger. \j\ fusion \clusters: bl, gn, kp, hšl, etc...\ b^e^lo ... said with a slight vowel
See more in the Introduction, Guide to Pronunciation

ner of those having been told to begone, leaving resentfully, indignantly, in a way of having been offended

han·lo·wan·pi \haŋ-ló-waŋ-pi\ *n* : a night song – *Syn* WIÓWEŠTE LOWANPI, WIOYEŠTE LOWANPI

han·ma·ni \haŋ-má-ni\ *v* hanma·wa·ni : to walk in the night, to be in the dark about anything; *fig* not to understand — **hanmani·pi·ke s'e** *adv* : unusually occurring < ~ *waun kin* I knowing absolutely nothing about it > – GA

han·mši·ce·la·hca·ke \haŋ-mší-ce-la-ȟca-ke\ *n* [fr *hanpa* moccasins + *šica* bad + *lahcaka* very] : a very poor pair of moccasins

han·mwi·tka \haŋ-mwí-tka\ *n* [fr *hanpa* moccasins + *witko* crazy] : fool moccasins, *i.e.* those showing no pattern in the beadwork – WE

han·napa \haŋ-ná-ṗa\ *v* : to escape at night – EE

han·na·tan·tan u \haŋ-ná-taŋ-tan u\ *v* : to come in the night feeling one's way with the feet — **hannatantan·kel** *adv* : feeling one's way with the feet through the night – Bl

han·ni \haŋ-ní\ *adv* : before, in *ref* to time and place < *El yapi šni* ~ They did not go there before > – B.H.61.6, 17.6, 177.23, 186.1, 204.6, 220.1, 226.17, 254.13 D.52

han·o·i·yo·ki·pi \haŋ-ó-i-yo-ki-pi\ *n perhaps* : a pleasant night < ~ *yelo* It was agreeable > – Bl

han·o·lu·ta \haŋ-ó-lu-ṫa\ *n* : a warm night

han·o·mani \haŋ-ó-man-ni\ *v* : to walk at night < ~ *omaspe šni* I did not get wet walking at night >

han·o·pta \haŋ-ó-pta\ *adv* : through the night < ~ *iglaka* He traveled through the night > – B.H.83.13

han·o·tkan \haŋ-ó-tk̇aŋ\ *n* : a dark, sultry night and perhaps stormy – *Syn* HANÓLULUTA Bl

han·pa \háŋ-ṗa\ *n* : moccasins

han·pa·i·ta·ke \háŋ-ṗa-i-ṫa-k̇e\ *n* *See* hánpitake

han·pa·ki·gla·ke *or* **hanp'akiglake** \haŋ-pá-k̇i-gla-k̇e\ *n* **1** : the sole of a shoe or moccasin **2** : a badge-like decoration worn on the chest in the Sundance – *Syn* WAKIGLAKA

han·pa kšu·pi \háŋ-ṗa kšù-pi\ *n* : beaded moccasins

han·pa·ku·te·pi \háŋ-ṗa ku-té-pi\ *n* : a pastime for young men – Bl

han·pa·pe·con·pi \háŋ-ṗa-pe-còŋ-ṗi\ *n* [fr *hanpa* shoe + *ape* await + *econ* to do] : a game in which a ball is hid in one of four moccasins or mittens and sought for by the opposite side; a hand game in which is sung: "Hanpa hiyu wo, wanna waktepi kte" – R MS

han·pi \haŋ-ṗí\ *n* : broth, soup, gravy, juice, sap < *canšuška* ~ the sap of boxelders *canpa* ~ *yatkanpi* a drink of chokecherry juice *Winuhca, papala wan cik'ala yégnake c'on* ~ *kaga yo, hanp'unglatkanpi kte lo* Mother-in-law, make some soup for which you have laid away a little bit of hot spice, we shall have a broth drink > – *Syn* WAHANPI Bl

han·pi·kce·ka \haŋ-ṗí-kce-k̇a\ *n* : common moccasins

han·pi·na·to·pi \haŋ-ṗí-na-to-pi\ *n* : the same as *canhlogan hlahla* the sharp-leaved beard-tongue, the wort family. Its blossoms are used to make blue paint for moccasins – Bl # 157, 197

han·pi o·ka·ške·ya \haŋ-ṗí o-k̇á-ške-ya\ *v* : to bind or lace a moccasin – Bl KE

han·pi·sa·bye \háŋ-ṗi-sa-bye\ *n* : shoe blacking, polish

han·pi·ška \han-ṗí-ška\ *n* [fr *hanpa* shoe + *iška* ankle] : the upper part of a moccasin that covers the ankle, the upper part of a shoe or boot < ~ *sutaya ayuwi yo, unnihan kih'an hi yelo* Wrap firmly the upper moccasin, shortly stormy weather arrives > – BT

han·pi·ška·ton \haŋ-ṗí-ška-toŋ\ *v* hanpiška·wa·ton : to sew an upper part to a moccasin, *i.e.* to make it like a rubber shoe for women – Bl

han·pi·ta·ke \han-ṗí-ṫa-k̇e\ *n* : the face or upper part of a moccasin, the tongue of a shoe or what serves as such

han·po·han \haŋ-ṗó-haŋ\ *v* hanpo·wa·han : to put on or wear moccasins

han·po·he·ki·ci·ci·ya \haŋ-ṗó-he-k̇i-ci-ci-ya\ *va* hanpohe·we·ciciya : to put moccasins on one

han·po·he·ki·ya \haŋ-ṗó-he-k̇i-ya\ *va* hanpohe·wa·kiya : to cause to put on moccasins

han·po·hya \háŋ-po-ȟya\ *adv* : losing one's way < ~ *wanunwehce lo* I was indeed swimming losing my way, as a man would say of himself who ran away moving arms and feet in excitement, *i.e.* as if to swim *nonwan* > – GA KE

han·po·ki·han \haŋ-ṗó-ki-haŋ\ *v poss* hanpo·wa·kihan [fr *hanpohan* put on a pair of moccasins] : to put on or wear one's own moccasins, to wear one's shoes < Han*natantan kte s'e hanpokihe lo* He put on his own shoes as though he might be feeling his way with his feet, as is said when a person's shoes are too wide >

han·po·na·šlo·ke *or* **hanp'onašloke** \han-ṗó-na-šlo-ke\ *n* : slippers – P

han·po·špu ho·kši·ca·la \haŋ-ṗó-šṗu ho-kšì-ca-la\ *n* : a doll

han·psi·cu \haŋ-psí-cu\ *n* : a piece of tanned hide cut to a size for a moccasin

han·pši·ši·ca \haŋ-pší-ši-ca\ *n* : an old and worn-out moccasin < ~ *ca owakihi yelo* A pair of worn-out moccasins I attained > – BT KE

han·ptan·ni \haŋ-ptáŋ-ni\ *n* : an old shoe or moccasin < ~ *wanjihci mak'u wo* Grant me but one old shoe > – Bl

han·p'a·ki·gla·ke \haŋ-p'á-k̇i-gla-k̇e\ *n* – *See* hanpakiglake

han·p'ce·ya·ka \haŋ-p'cé-ya-ka\ *n* : moccasins with porcupine quill work – Bl

han·p'hin·šma \haŋ-p'híŋ-šma\ *n* : moccasins made of buffalo fur with the hair inside

han·p'i·pa·ta \haŋ-p'í-ṗa-ta\ *n* : moccasins covered with porupine quill work

han·p'o·na·šlo·ke \haŋ-p'ó-na-šlo-ke\ *n* : slippers

han·p'ti·tin·yan·ka *or* **hanp'titilyanka** \haŋ-p'ṫí-yaŋ-ka\ *n* : slippers or moccasins for use in the house < ~ *wanji micaga yo* Make me a good pair of shoes for use in the house > – Bl KE

han·ska \háŋ-sk̇a\ *adj* : long, tall, of time and distance < *Waniyetu, canke hanhepi kin lila hanske* As to winter, the nights are very long > — **hanska·ska** *adj red of* hanska : quite long < *Pehin* ~ His is a quite long head of hair >

han·ske·ya \háŋ-ske-ya\ *adv* : far, extending, long < *Nupin wácinhin ikan* ~ *itowe el iyaglaškapi* Both headdress cords were tied on his forelock. ~ *eya* to dwell on a topic, or to speak long about something, *Unma na unma kin* ~ The one and the other were long>

han·šni \háŋ-šni\ *adv neg particle* : No! *i.e.* not Yes – *Syn* HÍYA

han·ta \háŋ-ṫa\ *v imper only* : Get away! Be gone! <~ *yo* You be gone! >

han·ta·he·na \háŋ-ta-he-na\ *adv* : before night < *Iyúpaga po, tokša* ~ *walašlapi kte lo* Lay hold on it, soon before night they'll be grazing. ~ *talo yutapi kte lo* Before night they'll be eating fresh meat > – B.H.55.7 BT

han·tan·hanš \háŋ-ṫaŋ-haŋš\ *adv* : if, in case that...

han·te·han \han-ṫé-haŋ\ *adv* : late in the night < *Wanna kitanla* ~ *ehanl wanna tonweya k'on henayos kupi. Nahahci* *taku ota oblakin kta tka wana ~ yelo* Now a little late into the night then these two scouts came home. Yet something much I should tell, but it is now late in the night > – Bl

han·te pe·pe i·ye·ce·ca \haŋ-té pe-pè i-ye-ce-ca\ *n* : the Illinois Mimosa, curly-podded legume. Acuan illinoiensis

han·tkan \haŋ-tkáŋ\ *n* : the fruit of a water plant called *wihúta hu* cattail, typha catifolia. When it is thoroughly ripe it is wooly. This material was once used by mothers to make a sort of quilt placed over sheeting and used for babies because it does not allow water to penetrate – # 231

han·tu·k'e \háŋ-tu-k'e\ *adv* : indeed, for once

han·t'e·ya \háŋ-t'e-ya\ *adv* : wearily, as the moving of a sick person

han·wa·ci·pi \haŋ-wá-ci-pi\ *n* : the Night Dance, name of a Dakota dance

han·wa·he·han·tu \haŋ-wá-he-haŋ-tu\ *n perhaps* : a fixed time of the night at which something usually takes place *etc* < *Wana ~* It is now its time of night > – Bl

[1]**han·wa·kan** \haŋ-wá-kaŋ\ *adj perhaps* : mysterious, as a strange thing going on in the night <*Hanhepi ~ s'elececa* It was as though the night was a bit eerie > – Bl

[2]**han·wa·kan** \háŋ-wa-kaŋ\ *n* : the aurora – P

han·wa·to·hanl·šna \haŋ-wá-to-haŋl-šna\ *adv* : anytime in the night, again and again in the night < *Na wanna ungnahanšna ~ wacipi na ecel anpa* And every now and then anytime in the night they danced even to sun-up >

han·wa·to·han·tu \haŋ-wá-to-haŋ-tu\ *adv* : sometime during the night < *~ k'eyaš wau kte lo* Sometime during the night though I shall come > – Bl

han·wi·yan·pa \haŋ-wí-yaŋ-pa\ *n* : moonlight < *Hanhepi wan el ~ oihokipi* One night there was pleasant moonlight >

han·ya·gu \haŋ-yá-ġu\ *n* : a robe dried out-of-doors in winter by freezing — **han·ya·gug** \haŋ-yá-ġug\ *v* : to spend the whole night in the cold < *Nape kin ~ imayayelo* My hands are gone stiff from the cold > – Bl KE

han·yan·ke·ci \haŋ-yáŋ-ke-ci\ *n of* hanyanke kinhan, or hanyankecihan, or hanyankecinhan : tomorrow –Note: *Hanhepi na hinhanna he kapi* Night and morning are together embraced by this word — **hanyanke·kecin** *or* **hanyake(ke)ci** \haŋ-yáŋ-ke-ke-ciŋ\ \haŋ-yá-ke-(ke)ci\ *n red of* hanyankeci : tomorrow, an over-night – B.H. 194.5

han·ye \haŋ-yé\ *adv contrac of* hanyétu : night

han·ye·co·kan \haŋ-yé-co-kaŋ\ *n* : midnight

han·ye·tu \haŋ-yé-tu\ *n* : night — **hanyetu·la** *n dim* : a brief night — **hanyetu·wi** *or* **hanye·wi** *n* : the moon < *~ yahilale ki* when you went past the moon, as addressed in prayer > – RF

han·yun·ka \haŋ-yúŋ-ka\ *vn* han·mun·ke : to remain overnight, as something killed and left until morning; or perhaps in *ref* to one staying overnight

ha·o·k'u \ha-ó'-k'u\ *v* hao·wa·k'u : to give, loan one's clothes to, or perhaps any clothes

ha·o·ya·sa·ka \ha-ó-ya-sa-ka\ *adj* : skin dried to the bone, very lean

ha·o·yu·h'u \há-o-yu-h'u\ *n* : a year's growth in a tree, *i.e.* with respect to its width of a ring < *~ ota yelo* There are many years' growth in the tree > – Bl

ha·pa·hla·ya \há-pa-hla-ya\ *v* : to throw off the skin, as do snakes

ha·pa·šlo·ka \ha-pá-šlo-ka\ *v* ha·wa·pašloka : to pull off skin, to chafe

ha·san·ni \ha-sáŋ-ni\ n : one of a pair, a mate, team < *~ manice* I lack a mate. *~ nahahci bluha šni* I do not have a mate yet > – KE

ha·stan \ha-stáŋ\ *adj* ha·má·stan : dark complexioned

haš \haš\ *interj of impatience, pride, discontentment* : Oh hell! – P

ha·ton \ha-tóŋ\ *vn* ha·ma·ton : to have chapped skin, as on the hands

hau \hau\ *interj of greeting or approbation* : Hello! Yes! Fine! Good! – Note: the vowels *a* and *u* are pronounced as a single vowel, a diphthong, sounding like the *o* in the English word: how Cf also Gramm 121

ha·un \há-uŋ\ *interj of severe pain* : Oh-h-h-h! – Note: the word is used by men Gramm 127

ha·ya \ha-yá\ *va* ha·wa·ya : to have for clothing < *Taku haye cin owasin taha ececa. Hena tahca šunkala tahaya koyagya el nihipelo* Everything he has for clothing is like deer skin. They have come clothed in sheep's clothing > – B.H.195.2

ha·ya·ke \ha-yá-ke\ *n* : clothes — **haya·pi** \ha-yá-pi\ *n* : clothes, wearing apparel of any kind

ha·ya·pi·yo·tke \ha-yá-pi-yo-tke\ *n* : a suit hanger

ha·yu·hpu \há-yu-hpu\ *vn* ha·wá·yu-hpu : to be scabbed – Note: the *refl*, ha·wá·gluhpu — **háyuhpu·hpu** *v red* : to be scabbing

ha·yu·za \há-yu-za\ *va* ha·blu·za : to skin, take off the skin of anything

ha·za \há-za\ *n* : the whortleberry, huckleberry

[1]**he** \he\

suff to v, indicative of repeated action etc. – Cf han

pron dem : that, *hená* those

adv : there, also *héna* or *hel.* It corresponds to *le* and *léna* or *lel*

< *Na wanna iglakapi na ake wakpala wan el etipi na he ake wicoh'an wan econ. Hena hinajin na taku ehin kta heci eya yo. Tuweni he šni*, or *Tuweni okapte šni* And they moved camp and again at a creek they pitched camp while there again they performed a ceremony. There he came and stood; say whatever you should say. No one is not there, or No one is left out, *i.e.* all are there > – Bl

interrog particle < *Wicáyala he?* Do you believe? >

[2]**he** \hē\ *interj calling for attention* : Look here!

[3]**he** \he\ *n* 1 : a horn, the horns of an animal 2 : a louse < *He can alikiyehce lo* He made the louse crawl the tree > – Cf heyópuza

he·a·ške·ton s'e \he-á-ške-toŋ s'e\ *adv* : with the hair braids standing out sideways – Bl

[1]**he·ca** \he-cá\ *n* : the buzzard, the turkey vulture < *Wana ~ wan gli yelo; wana osni wanice,* A buzzard is now returning; now there is no cold, *i.e.* its arrival meant the end of cold weather. *~ wan ku welo,* A buzzard has come back, as they say when a scout returns seemingly with good news > – Cf škipípila Bl

[2]**he·ca** \hé-ca\ *pron* and *adj* he·má·ca he·ún·ca·pi : such, such like; belonging to such a clan or such a description < *Tahca šunkala yuha kin heca* He is like the shepherd >

he·ca·c'unš \hé-ca-c'uŋš\ *adv* : nevertheless – B.H.244.3

he·ca·e·ša \hé-ca-e-ša\ *adv* : although it is such, not withstanding

he·ca·ki·ci·on \hé·ca·ki·ci·on\ *v* : to do that for one < *He-*

\a\ father \e\ they \i\ machine \o\ smoke \u\ lunar \an, aŋ\ blanc Fr. \in, iŋ\ ink \on, oŋ, un, uŋ\ soon, conifer Fr. \c\ chair \ġ\ machen Ger. \j\ fusion \clusters: bl, gn, kp, hšl, etc...\ b°lo ... said with a slight vowel **See more in the Introduction, Guide to Pronunciation**

cayecion iyececa He deserves you do that for him > – B.H.196.10, 250.7

he·ca·ki·con \hé-ca-k̇i-coŋ\ *va* heca·we·con [fr *hecon* to do that] : to do thus to one

he·ca·ki·on \hé-ca-k̇i-oŋ\ *v* [fr *hecon* to do that] : to do that, *i.e.* the same thing, to them – B.H.92.14

he·can·kin \he-cáŋ-k̇iŋ\ *va* hecán·wa·kin hecáŋ·ci·cin : to think so of one, to form such an opinion of one

he·ca·ška *or* **héecaška** \he-ca-šká\ *adv* : still, nevertheless

ha·ca yun·ka·pi \he-ćá yuŋ-kà-pi\ *n* : a place where buzzards, *hećá*, are nesting and shed many feathers – Bl

he·ce *or* **hecel** \hé-ce\ *adv* : thus, so, in this way, hence, therefore < *Tuweni waunšipi šni ca ~* In this way no one has hired us > – B.H.47.4, 67.9, 199.14, 235.6, 283.4, 290.5, 271.7

he·ce·ca \hé-ce-ca\ *adj* he·ma·ceca : like, such as, like that — *adv* : so, always so <*Tohanni lena ~ kta heci. Na ištogmus wowaci kin wacipi kin hena pte šake icicašla naunkapi kin ~ . Tohinni taku ~ wanyankapi šni* Never would these be such as that. For, these dances, the Shut Eye Dances, are such that cows' hoofs when they gallop knock bare together. Never has a thing like that been seen > – B.H.245.2

he·ce·ca can·keš \hé-ce-ca caŋ-kèš\ *adv* : therefore, since that is the case, since that is the way it is – B.H.26.2

he·ce·ca eša *or* **hececa eyáš** \hé-ce-ca e-šà\ *adv* : notwithstanding – B.H.51.11

he·ce·ca·ka \hé-ce-ca-k̇a\ *n* : such a one, as a mean fellow

he·ce·ca kin \hé-ce-ca kiŋ\ *adv* : if so – B.H.69.9, 111.7, 117.8, 190.6

he·ce·ca k'e·yaš \hé-ce-ca k'è-yaš\ *adv* : nevertheless – B.H.52.1

he·ce·gla *or* **hecegla·la** \hé-ce-gla\ *adv* : thus, so; only, only so far, only so little; that is all < *Heon ~ eye, eya* For that reason he said only so much, he said. *~ ška ecannon šni* And yet you did not do so little, *i.e.* it was only so little trouble and you could not do it. *Tanyan ecamonpica šni kin ~ kta* If I am unable to do so I shall do only so little. *Yunkan ~ wacin weksuye* Then I remembered to try only so far. >

he·ce·han \hé-ce-haŋ\ *adv* : really < *~ wowicake nainš wowicake šni heci* Is it really the truth or not the truth? or Is it really so or not? >

he·ce·hci \hé-ce-ȟci\ *adv* : just so, only so, altogether

he·ce·kce \hé-ce-kce\ *adv red of* hece : in this manner, so thus < *Ca on ~ iyahanbla* And so thus for this reason you had a vision. *~ iapi nawah'on. ~ omawani. ~ econpi* So thus I heard voices (words said), I made a journey, and so thus it was done, *i.e.* to one inquiring if he came for something special. *Talo nainš ~ yutapi* Otherwise in this manner they ate fresh meat > – B.H.45.13, 49.17, 55.6, 80.19, 136.19 Pb.28

he·ce·kce·ca·ka \hé-ce-kce-ca-k̇a\ *adj* : always such, bearing this character

he·ce·kce·ka \hé-ce-kce-ka\ *adj* : of such a sort < *Taku ~* Something on that line or order > – B.H.34.4

he·ce·kce·kel \hé-ce-kce-kel\ *adv red of* hecekcel *or* hecekce *perhaps* : thus < *Mazaskazi na canšin na pejuta waštemna ~ kahipi* Gold, tree gum, and sweet-smelling medicines were thus brought > – B.H.169.22

he·ce·kcel \hé-ce-kcel\ *adv red of* hecel : in this manner, so, thus, just as

he·ce·kce·tu \hé-ce-kce-ṫu\ *adv red of* hecetu : so, in this manner — **hecekcetu·ya** *adv* : after this manner

he·cel \hé-cel\ *adv* : thus, so, in this way; hence, therefore < *Taku ~ on Susanna aiapi slolyapi šni* Therefore they were unaware for what Susanna was slandered > – B.H. 138.5

he·ce·la \he-cé-la\ *adv* : that alone, only that – D.269

he·ce·la·ki·ya \he-cĕ'-la-k̇i-ya\ *adv* : only that way, that way only, that alone

he·ce·la·ya \he-cé-la-ya\ *va* hecela·wa·ya : to regard that alone

he·ce·lki·ya \hé-ce-lki-ya\ *adv* : that way – P

he·ce·lya \hé-ce-lya\ *adv* : so, thus, in that manner

he·ce·na \hé-ce-na\ *adv* : thus, conveying the idea that something keeps on happening, consequently, finally < *Hecel anpetu topa apepi eša, ~ t'a.* So though they waited four days, he finally died. *Ho ~ tiyatakiya inyanke na tawicu kin owicakiyake* Come now, she ran toward her house and his wife spoke to them. *Ekta nahahci lila wicotapi ca ~ waglicu* Consequently I started off for home since there was yet a very crowd. *Hecel wanna tipi iyohila kpamnipi, tka ecel ataya iyowicahi* In this way they distributed to each home, but as it was, it was entirely sufficient for them, *i.e.* coffee and sugar, *na ~ yusotapi šni* and consequently they were not used up. *Ho, misun, wanna wagni kte eya na ~ gla ca wanyank manka* Come now, my little brother, now I'll be going home, he said, and when I went I was there to see him. *~ econ* to keep at doing (work) *~ ya* to go right along > – P

he·ce·ni·ca·la \he-cé-ni-ca-la\ *n* : a yearling colt – R Bl

he·ceš \hé-ceš\ *adv emph of* héce : thus

he·ce·tki·ya \hé-ce-tk̇i-ya\ *adv* : in that direction < *~ iglaka gle na otiwota kin el akiti* He went in that direction, breaking camp and stopped overnight at an old encampment >

he·ce·tu \hé-ce-ṫu\ *adv* : as, so, thus; that is the way; right, well < *hecetuhca* just so, *Lena hecetuhca slolwaya* Just so, I knew about these >

he·cetuke \hé-ce-ṫu-k̇e\ *adv* : as is common, as is usual

he·ce·tu·la \hé-ce-ṫu-la\ *va* : to approve – B.H.175.5

he·ce·tu·la·ka \he-cé-ṫu-la-ka\ *vn* : to have an opinion, to think – *Syn* WICALA, SECELAKA

he·ce·tu·la·ka·pi \hé-ce-ṫu-la-ka-pi\ *n* : approval

he·ce·tu·wan·ji·ca \hé-ce-ṫu-waŋ-ji-ca\ *adj* : always the same < *~ el un* being always in the same place, *Ho, le ~ letan yuha ya po* All right, go now holding it from this time on always the same, which is in *ref* to a religious rite. *~ yankapi* They sat always the same >

he·ce·tu·ya \hé-ce-ṫu-ya\ *va* hécetu·wa·ya : to make so, cause to be so or right — *adv* : so, thus, in showing one how

he·ce·ya \hé-ce-ya\ *adv* : really, certainly < *Ho, wakokipa šni, ~ wani ye* Yes. Be not afraid, I am really alive > – B.H.101.1, 108.11, 118.3, 293.19 and 22 D.229, 269, 104

he·ci \hé-ci\ *adv* **1** : in or at that place, there, or away from the speaker **2** : whether, if, any *express* implying perhaps that I would like to know, *etc* < *Itokab tohanhci le iyecel owah'an ~ ?* Did I work here as at any time before? *Ca tuktogna oniglakin kta heci?* And whether he would tell you where of his own? *Ca tokeške waonspeic'iciya heci?* And how in the world did he ever teach himself? *Tokeške iyohipi kta heci?* How in the world would they ever reach here? > – Note: *heci* is paired thus: *tokel* how ... *heci*, *taku* what ... *heci*, *tohan* when ... *heci* – B.H.68.23, 174.19, 184.4, 208.9, 78.2, 252.16, 112.6, 245.2 Gramm 136.5

he·ci·na \hé-ci-na\ *adv* [fr *heci* + *na* and] : thus, so it is < *Makatanhan wicaša wan wicoh'an wan awahiyaya tka hena on onšimala yo, tuwa wankatanhan initancan* ~ I, a man from earth, sang a ceremonial song, a custom, but because of this pity me, if it is so you, one from above, are leader > — **hecina·han** *adv* : if, if it is so

he·cin \he-cíŋ\ *v* he·canmi he·canni he·unke·cin·pi [fr *he* that + *cin* to wish] : to think this, or that, with the thought expressed following – B.H.47.5, 199.3

he·cin·ška-ya-pi \hé-ciŋ-ška-ya-pi\ *n* : the mountain sheep, so called because its horns are used for spoons *cinšká*

[1]**he·ci·ya** \hé-ci-ya\ *adv* : at that place, there

[2]**he·ci·ya** \he-cí-ya\ *v* he·wa·kiya [fr *heya* to say that] : to say that to one < *hemakiya* he said that to me, *heciciya* I say that to you, *hekiciyapi* they say to each other > – Note: it is said that the word may have been introduced from the Santee dialect through the Bible, whereas it should be *hekiya*

he·ci·ya·pa·tan·han \hé-ci-ya-pa-ṫaŋ-haŋ\ *adv* : towards that time or place, on the side next to

he·ci·ya·tan \hé-ci-ya-ṫaŋ\ *adv* : from that place, thence — **heciyatan·han** *adv* : from that place, therefore

he·ci·yo·tan *or* **heciyotan·han** \he-cí-yo-taŋ\ *adv* : in that direction

he·con \hé-coŋ\ *v* hé·camon hé·cuŋ·kon·pi : to do that – Note: this word takes up the action of the preceding sentence and continues it < *Nazonspe cannunpa wan on huha kin kawehweh apa ške lo. Hecon na wicoti ekta i na oyaka* It is said with an axe-pipe he struck breaking his leg. That he did and he went to camp and told of it >

he·e \hé-e\ *v* : that is it, it is he – Note: this along with *lée* includes the *subst* and *dem pron*

he e·ca \he e-cá\ *adv* or *dem pron* : that person there < *Tuwa wiwicayunge ci he zuya itancan kin he wowaši tawa kin* ~ *hecon.* He who questioned them, that person there did the war chief's own work. *He eca u welo, eya* He said: that is he coming. *Yunkan unma cinca k'on he eca leya:* ... And then that other son had said this: ... > – KE

he e·ca eyaš \he e-cá é-yaš\ *adv* : nevertheless – B.H. 155.18

he·e·ca·ška \hé-e-ca-ška\ *adv* : still, nevertheless – Note: this may be *deriv* from *hee-ca-ška* they say that is it

he·e·han \hé-e-haŋ\ *adv* : at that time, in *ref* to the past

he·e·ki·ya \hé-e-k̇i-ya\ *adv* : in the place of — *va* hée-wakiya : to call or count that to be the person or thing, to substitute, to put one in place of another

he·ha·ha \he-há-ha\ *v red of 2nd pers singl of* héya : you are saying that

he·ha·ha·la·ka \h-há-ha-la-ke\ *v 2nd pers singl of* heyaya-laka : you lie, deceive

he·han \hé-haŋ\ *or perhaps* \he-háŋ\ *adv* : at that time, then

he·han·han·ke·ca \he-háŋ-haŋ-k̇e-ca\ *adv red of* hehan-keca : so long, each so long

he·han·han·yan \he-háŋ-haŋ-yaŋ\ *adv red of* hehanyan : at that time – Cf hehányan B.H.153.9, 208.10

he·han·hca \he-háŋ-ȟca\ *adv* : then and not until then

he·han·ke·ca \he-háŋ-k̇e-ca\ *adv* : so long

he·hanl \he-háŋl\ *adv* : at or to that place; then — **he-hanleš** *adv emph of* hehanl : to that very place – B.H. 49.7, 26.24

he·han·ni *and* **ehanni** \hé-haŋ-ni\ *adv* : then < *Cincala* ~ when it was young, at the time of its youth. *Kiyela yapi kin ~ itkob hinape* When they went near, he then came out again (to meet them), *or* He came to meet them as they approached > – D.152 B.H.93.10, 122.14

he·han·pi \he-háŋ-pi\ *n* : night, last night — *adv* : last night — **hehanpi wi** *n* : the moon – P

he·han·tan *and* **hehantanhan** \he-háŋ-ṫan\ *adv* : from that time therefore < *Oyate oyasin le lecetu na ~ waniyetu opawinge šni makoce le wanblaka* This is right for all people now, and now from that time therefore for hardly a hundred years I have seen the land. *Na ~ wanna waniyetu ota itahena eša, lehanyan nahahci (wahinkpe kin) yuhapi. He tonpi ~ hušte. ~ slolya waun.* And since then therefore, though it has been short of many years, it has been so long a time (the sacred arrow) has still been kept. Since then acquiring this it has been cripple. Since then therefore I am acquainted with it. > – D.100 B.H.86.22, 145.7, 156.3, 199.21, 280.2, 272.14

he·han·tu \he-háŋ-ṫu\ *adv* : at that time, then < *Wana wicoh'an tokaheya econ kte ci ~ . Wanna wi hinapa ~ keya. Wanna wicokan sanpa, ~ wanna wicokam tip wan el kagapi. Hokšiyuha kte kin ~ .* It is at this time now that he will do the first ceremony. He said the sun was at that time rising. Then it was after noon; then at noon a house was made there. It was at that time then when she would give birth > – MS.526 B.H.165.14, 246.3

he·han·tu·la \he-háŋ-ṫu-la\ *adv* : then — **hehantulahci** *adv* : just then – R Bl

he·han·yan *or* **hehanyan·kel** \he-háŋ-yaŋ\ *adv* : so far, in *ref* to places; so long, in *ref* to time; from that time, at that time, then < *Letanhan tohinni iyopewaye šni ye, tohanyan unni ~ . Yunkan hucan cokanyan ~ ataya we apa. Ḣe wankatuya wanca ~ ihunni. Eyaš ~ anpa canke.* Never from this time did I correct him, as long as you and I live, so long as we live. Then as far as the middle of the arrow shaft, so far did it entirely strike blood. Once on the mountain then he got across. But by that time that is why it was daylight > — **hehanyan·yan** *adv red of* hehanyan : so much further, longer – B.H.47.2, 73.24, 84.20, 189.1, 226.8, 200.21, 202.22, 233.8, 253.16, 255.22, 256.28, 32.6, 79.7

he·han·ye·la \he-háŋ-ye-la\ *adv* : so far, only so far < *Henihanyelapi* You all were only so far. *~ woglake* He talked only so long, or so far. *~ oihanke* The end is only so far out there. *Ho le wicowoyake kin ~ oyakapelo* Yes, this narrative was told only so far. *Lecel eya. ~ ecannonpi kte lo* Say it this way. You should do it only so far. *Ake lowanpi na hancokanyan e ehanl ~ econpi* They sang a song again and by the time it was midnight it was then done only so far. >

he·he \he-hé\ *interj* : alas < ~ *mat'a nunseca* Alas, it seems as though I should die > — **hehe·he** \he-he-hé\ *interj* : alas < ~ *wašicun ota el mahipelo, tka ota ónton-niyanpi šni* It is too bad, many white men came to me, but the many did not injure you >

he·he·la \he-hé-la\ *v dim of* heha : you said so – Note: this word is used in speaking to a child — *interj and a by-word* : You say so!

he·hu·te \he-hú-ṫe\ *n* : something, as a string, ribbon, or band, to hold the *aške* together, *i.e.* a tuft or bunch of hair that Lakota men once used to wear on the side of their head

he·hu·te·la \he-hú-ṫe-la\ *n* : an old buffalo whose horns

\a\ father \e\ they \i\ machine \o\ smoke \u\ lunar \an, aŋ\ blanc Fr. \in, iŋ\ ink \on, oŋ, un, uŋ\ soon, confier Fr. \c\ chair \ġ\ machen Ger. \j\ fusion \clusters: bl, gn, kp, hšl, etc...\ b[e]lo ... said with a slight vowel **See more in the Introduction, Guide to Pronunciation**

are worn off and damaged badly – Bl

he·ȟa·ka \he-ȟá-k̇a\ *n* [fr *he* horns + *ȟaka* branching] : the male elk, so called from its branching horns < ~ *iktomi* an elk with flat, broad horns, the prongs being short, a moose perhaps >

he·ȟa·ka he \he-ȟá-ka he\ *n* : the tall gaura, the small-flowered gaura. Gaura parviflora. – Cf wókahtan blaskaska Bl # 40, 119

he·ȟa·ka ta·pe·ju·ta \he-ȟá-k̇a tá-pe-jù-ta\ *n* : the slender dalea, dalea enlandra, the pulse family, the horsemint, wild bergawort. Menthaefolia graham, mint family. The Lakota distinguishes between the latter and *wahpe waštemna;* one grows in the open and the other in thickets. Also monarda mentaefolia graham. – Note: it is used for bad cuts with much blood issuing; the leaves are chewed and put under a bandage. This will stop the flow of blood. A tea of leaves strained and kept in a soft cloth placed over sore eyes overnight benefits them. The tea is also effective against whooping cough or other coughing, according to Crazy Hawk. The tea from the leaves is also good for people who faint. BT FD.178, 270-271

he·ȟa·ka·ta·wo·te \he-ȟá-ka-ta-wo-ṫe\ *n* : elk food – Note: this may be the same perhaps as *heȟakatapejuta*

He·ȟa·ka Wa·kpa \He-ȟá-ka Wa-kṗà\ *np* : the Yellowstone River, *i.e.* the Elk River, of the state of Montana and headed in and near the Yellowstone National Park

he·ȟak i·kto·mi \he-ȟák i-ktò-mi\ *n* : a moose

he·ȟa·kta·pe·ju·ta \he-ȟá-kta-ṗe-ju-ṫa\ *n* : elk medicine, a kind of mint – *See* heȟáka tápejùta

he·hlo·ge·ca \he-ȟló-ġe-ca\ *adj* : hollow-horned — **he-hlogeca iyececa** \hé-ȟlo-ġe-ca i-yè-ce-ca\ *n* : a buffalo cow with long horns, which is an exception – Bl

he·i·ca·kan \he-í-ċa-kaŋ\ *n* : a fine comb, a louse comb

he·i·c'i·ya \he-í-c'i-ya\ *v* : to say that to one's self, as at the beginning of a quotation

he·i·kan \he-í-k̇aŋ\ *n* : a string tying the end of the hair < *mazaša* ~ . ~ *iyaglaška.* a copper tiepin. A tie band bound her hair ends. >

he·i ... u yeto \hé-i ... ù ye-ṫo\ *v exclam* : to call to one, *i.e.* to men, to stop one, as "Hey! ... Hold it!

he·jan·jan \he-jáŋ-jaŋ\ *n* : an unhatched louse, a nit, a body louse, so called because it is translucent

he·ka·za \he-k̇á-za\ *n* : a yearling deer, *i.e.* with horns having one prong – Cf táhejata

he·ki·ci·na·ke·ca \he-k̇í-ci-na-k̇e-ca\ *vn* he·mi·cinakeca : to be all used up to or for one, to have no more

he·ki·ya \he-k̇í-ya\ *v* : to say this to

he·kta \hé-kṫa\ *n* that behind, what is passed or last, as applied to time and space < ~ *wetu* last spring > — *adv* : behind, back < ~ *u* He came behind. ~ *gla* He goes back home. ~ *wagluha wacin šni* I do not want it back > — **hektab** *adv* : behind, after < *mi·héktab* after me > — **hekta·kiya** \hé-kṫa-ki-ya\ *adv* : backward, whence one came < *Hecel ake ~ ble k'on he ogna waku* So again I came home in the direction in which I had gone in returning > — **hekta·kta·kiya** *adv red of* héktakiya : keeping going back from whence one came — **hekta·patan** \hé-kṫa-pa-taŋ\ *adv* : by or at the rear < *Si ~ wikan k'on iyakaška; canke iyutitan* A leather thong bound his foot to the back side, and so he pulled on it > — **hektapatan·han** *adv* : from behind, in the rear < ~ *iyotaka* to sit up behind, as behind a rider or driver > — **hekta·tanhan** \hé-kṫa-ṫaŋ-haŋ\ *adv* : behind — **hekta·wapa** *adv* : behind, after, backward — **hekta-wapa·tanhan** \hé-kṫa-wa-pa-ṫaŋ-haŋ\ *adv* : from behind — **hektawapa·ya** *adv* : behind, after, backward – B.H. 203.4 KE

hel \hel\ *adv* : in that place, there

[1]**hena** *or* **hel** \hé-na\ *adv* : in that place, there < ~ *ounyeya yo* There make your home >

[2]**he·na** \hé-na\ *pron pl of* he : those

he·na e·pi \hé-na è-pi\ *phr, pl of* hee [fr *hee* that is it, or it is he] : it is they < *Tona koškalaka tanšna unpi kin ~ kta keya* He says it will be those young men who are not married. *Wanyanka po! Lena nitakuyepi ehanna icagapi k'on ~ ca ekta lapi kta lo* See, you all! Since it is they a number of your relatives who had been brought up here long ago, they should proceed there>

he·na·gna·ke·ca \he-ná-gna-k̇e-ca\ *adv red of* henakeca : so many of each

he·na·ke \he-ná-k̇e\ *pron dem* : those there < ~ *mak'upelo* Those there gave it to me. ~ *agla yo* Take that there home > – KE

he·na·ke·ca \he-ná-k̇e-ca\ *adv* : so many, enough, sufficient; finished, all gone < *Waniyetu 67 henamakeca* I am 67 years old. *Tawicu kin e na cinca hokšila num ~ ob Egypt etkiya iyayapi* His wife and a two-year old boy child left together with him for Egypt > B.H.48.26

he·na·ke·hci \he-ná-k̇e-ȟci\ *adv* : all these, so great a quantity

he·na·kel \hé-na-k̇el\ *adj* : only so many, only so much – P Bl

he·na·ki·ya \he-ná-k̇i-ya\ *adv* : in so many ways

he·na·la \he-ná-la\ *adv* : only so many, or so much; none, all gone < *Henamala* Mine are all gone, or I have none. *Henákicila* All was gone for him, i.e. used up > – D.27

he·na·la·ki·ya \he-ná-la-k̇i-ya\ *adv* : only in so many ways or places

he·na·la·pi·la \he-ná-la-pi-la\ *adv pl of* henála : they have none

he·na·na \he-ná-na\ *pron red of* hená : these, those < ~ *oyakapi* These were speaking > – B.H.62.20

he·nan·gna·ke·ca \he-náŋ-gna-k̇e-ca\ *adv red of* henakeca : so many each — **henangnang** *adv contrac of* henangnakeca : each one so many

he·na·pi·la *or* **henalapi** \he-ná-pi-la\ *adv pl of* henala : they only so many < *Ena nankapi kin niye ko ~ kte lo. Ho, henalapi icunhan lecel wicaša wan eya* When you were right there, you too will be only so many. Yes, a man said in this way that in the meantime they are only so many >

he·na·yos *or* **heniyos** *or* **henayo·za** *or* **heniyoza** *or perhaps* **hiniyos** \he-ná-yos\ *pron* : these two

he·na·yu·za \hé-na-yu-za\ *pron* : those two — **he·na·-yu·za·ki·ya** *or* **heniyozakiya** \he-ná-yu-za-k̇i-ya\ *adv* : those two, these or those two times – Bl

he·on \hé-oŋ\ *adv* : for that, on that account, therefore

he·on·e·tan·han \hé-oŋ-e-ṫaŋ-haŋ\ *adv* : therefore

he·pa \he-ṗá\ *v* he·wa·pa he·ya·pa : to fight < *Kici heyapa inicipi šni yelo* You are unworthy fighting one another > – B.H.86.21

he·pca \he-pcá\ *v 1st pers singl* : I think that, I thought that – Note: this is the only form used. Cf epca, kepca — **hepca·pca** *v red of* hepcá : I think that – Bl

he·pce·ke·šni *or* **hepce·šni un** *v* : although I thought I would not < ~ *ecamon kte,* Though I had not intended to do it, I'll do it > – WE

he·pe·la \he-ṗe-lá\ *or* \hé-ṗe-la\ *interj of surprise when hearing or seeing something foolish said or done by others* : something like: "Sad to say!" < ~, *šicaya ehelo.* ~ , *eca-*

non yelo Alas, you have done badly. Alas, you did it. > Cf šku *Syn* HUNHUNHÉ, HÉPELA

he·pin *and* **hepa** \hé-p̣iŋ\ *v 1 pers singl of* héya : I say that

he·pi·ya \he-p̣í-ya\ *n* : the side or flank of a hill < *Ataya ~ el onakijinpi* They took refuge altogether on the side of a hill. *Na wanna paha wan ~ ca el inyan blaskaska ca el agliwicaonpapi. On cuwi-hepiya ewahunpe* And now on a hill side they came and placed them on a quite flat rock. With it (knives) they slashed an opening in the (bull's) back flank > - D.33, 218

he·pi·ye·la \he-p̣í-ye-la\ *adj* or *n* : on the grade of a hill < *hepyelahci canku* a road on very much of a grade of a hill > - Bl

he·po·la \he-p̣ó-la\ *n* : a buffalo bull horn - Bl

he·sla·tka·la \he-slá-tk̇a-la\ *n* : a young male elk

heš \heš\ *interj* : Why!, Well!, It may be < *eya heš tancan zanniyan tanyan waun welo* Well! Well! Healthwise I am doing well. *Heš hécon ehantanš tanyan kte šni* Well! If he did that it will not be well. *Heš nila yeš wahteyalašni k'on* Why! Though he demanded you, he is the one you had abominated > - D.204 B.H.48.7, 131.5, 184.12, 188.21, 193.18, 229.11

he·š'e·la·ke un \he-š'é-la-ke uŋ\ *express* : That was you again (guessing)

he·tan \he-ṫáŋ\ *adv contrac of* hetanhan : from that place, from that time, therefore, on that account < *Mato tipila ki ~ ilalapi kte lo. Itowe k'el mapehin kin ~ conala ate mayuha kta* You all shall go from the Bear's Lodge. In the forelock from a few hairs of my head Father will keep me >

he·tan·han \he-ṫáŋ-haŋ\ *adv* : from that place or time, therefore, on that account < *Iyaye k'on ~ anpetu ake nunpa* It was twelve days since he went >

he·tan·hanš \he-ṫáŋ-haŋš\ *adv emph of* hetanhan : definitly from that place or time, therefore, on that very account < *~ ṫóka* or *~ ṫók̇ak̇a* What difference is it? >

he·tka·la \he-tk̇á-la\ *n* : the ground squirrel, a kind of squirrel living in the woods or rocky places, *i.e. iġúġa el*, as in the Black Hills of South Dakota - Note: *tašnaheca iyececa gigi* the ground squirrel's color is like rusty *Syn* TAŠNÁHECA Bl

he·tki·ya \hé-ṫk̇i-ya\ *adv* : towards that place < *Wanna tipi k'on ~ ukiye* Now they are coming towards that house >

he·ton \he-tóŋ\ *adj* : horned — **heton cik'ala** \he-tóŋ cí-k'a-la\ *n* : an antilope - P

he·ton·ton \he-tóŋ-toŋ\ *adj red* : fearless, brave, faces up to difficulties < *Wan, ~ mic'ila* Brave, he demanded it of me for himself. *Wahacanka tanka wak'in s'elececa* It seemed I carried a great shield, as said by a person who suddenly got what he always wanted and so feels greatly encouraged > — **hetonton·ke** \he-tóŋ-toŋ-k̇e\ *n* : one who is fearless - Bl Bm KE

he·tu \hé-ṫu\ *adv* : at that place, there — **hetu·la** *adv* : there, then — **hetula·hci** \hé-ṫu-la-ȟci\ *adv* : just at that place or time - D.217

[1]**he·ya** \hé-ya\ *n* : a louse, lice, a head louse

[2]**he·ya** \he-yá\ *v* hep̣á hehá he·ún·k̇eya·pi [fr *he* that + *eya* to say] : to say that or this < *Heyéšni ciši k'a, eya. ~ ayupta* He said what he did not say was: I required you to dig. That is what he answered. *~ hoyeya* to say with a loud voice, *~ iyunga* That is the way he asked. *~ owa* to write the following, *~ pan* to let out a cry, *Heyapi šniš eyapika* They say that is not what they said, *i.e.* being indignant at a lie told. *~ wacekiya* to say the following prayer > - B.H.81.7, 199.10, 59.5, 76.5, 99.19, 108.2, 207.4, 236.7, 111.17, 236.4, 80.6

he·ya·pi·ke·šni \he-yá-pi-ke-šni\ *v pl* : they think one not able — *n* : one thought not able < *~ k'on hecon* One thought not able had done this > - Bl KE

he·ya·ya \he-yá-ya\ *v red* hepápa hehắha unkéyayapi [fr *heyá* to say that] : to say much, to keep saying - B.H.293.20

he·ya·ya·la·ka \he-yá-ya-la-k̇a\ *v red* hepápalaka hehắhalaka he·un·yaya·pi·laka heyayalaka·pi *or* heyaya·pi·laka [fr *heyá* to say that] : to tell lies - Cf eyáya WE

he·ye·ce·šni \he-yé-ci-šni\ *adj* : not thinking so, not informed about < *~ un welo* He is not informed > - Bl

he·ye·ki·ya \he-yé-k̇i-ya\ *va* heyé·wa·kiya : to cause to say that

he·yo·ka \he-yŏ'-ka\ *n* : a clown - Note: according to R this is the name of a Dakota personality called by some to be an anti-natural fellow. He is represented as a little old man with a cocked hat on his head, a bow and arrow in his hands and a quiver on his back. In winter he goes naked and in summer he wraps his buffalo robe around himself. *Osni, yunkan tiyoceyati šni naké mašte, yunkan ceyati šni ehan on le heyonika yelo* When it was cold and you started no fire in your home furnace, just now it was warm; and when you started no fire, then for this reason now you are indeed an anti-natural clown, *heyóka*, as is said to one when he once had a fire while they called it warm *weather*

he·yo·ka o·ti \he-yó-ka o-ṫì\ *n* : the house or place where a heyóka does his *wakán* work

he·yo·ka ta·pe·ju·ta \he-yó-ka ta-pe-jù-ta\ *n* : red false mallow, prairie mallow, malvastrum coccineum. A gray moss root. - Note: magicians once chewed the roots and rubbed their hands with it and so could dip them into the hottest water without being scalded. Sam Terry denied that it has the qualities just described. The roots chewed and laid on sores have a healing effect Cf FD. 167-8 NO Bl # 168

he·yo·ki·ci·le \he-yó-ki-ci-le\ *v* [fr *héya* lice + *ole* seek after] : to rid one of lice - D.109

he·yo·pa·špu \he-yó-p̣a-šp̣u\ *n* : a pin - Note: though the word is pronounced *heyopašpu, hiyopašpu* is more proper

he·yo·pu·za \he-yó-p̣u-za\ *adj* : lousy, full of lice or nits — *v* heyó·ma·puza : to be lousy - D.109

he·yo·ta·ke i·pa·špu \he-yó-ta-k̇e i-p̣a-šp̣u\ *n* : a toothpick - Note: *hiyotake* is the word but is said *heyotake*

he·yu·ȟa *or* **heyuġa** \he-yú-ȟa\ *n* : the name of all animals with branching horns

he·yu·ktan \he-yú-ktaŋ\ *adj* : bent-horned — *n* : an animal with bent horns < *Wicaša kin nakun iteha kiton na ~ wanjigji ca na makikceka iic'iyun* The man too had a mask, and while each one was bent-horned he rubbed himself with earthen soil >

he·yun \he-yúŋ\ *va* he·mun he·nun he·un·yun·pi : to tie up, wrap up a pack, pack up < *Taku henun kin suksutaya pahta yo, napecešni unkomani kte lo* What you wrapped up pack very very firmly, for we shall be traveling right along >

he·yun·pi \he-yúŋ-p̣i\ *n* : a wrapping, what is wrapped

\a\ father \e\ they \i\ machine \o\ smoke \u\ lunar \an, aŋ\ blanc Fr. \in, iŋ\ ink \on, oŋ, un, uŋ\ soon, confier Fr. \c\ chair \ġ\ machen Ger. \j\ fusion \clusters: bl, gn, kp, hšl, etc...\ b[e]lo ... said with a slight vowel **See more in the Introduction, Guide to Pronunciation**

around, as paper *etc*

[1]**hi** \hi\ *n* : a tooth, teeth; the bit or edge of an axe; the point of anything < *wicahi* human teeth, *mahi* my teeth >

[2]**hi** \hi\ *vn* wa·hi un·hi·pi : to arrive at < *El mahi* He came to me >

hi·a·ki·gle \hi-á-ǩi-gle\ *v* : to set the teeth firmly, as a dying person does < *Wanna t'in kte ca ~ . ~ woglake s'elececa* When he was about to die he set his teeth. He seemed to speak through his teeth > – EM

hi·a·pe \hi-á-ṗe\ *v* hia·wa·pe : to await one's coming

hi·a·yan·pa \hi-á-yaŋ-ṗa\ *v* [fr *hi* come + *ayanpa* come light on] : to come morning on, as in morning arriving

hi·bu \hi-bú\ *vn* wa·hibu : to come or arrive – *archaic*

hi·gla·ki·skis \hí-gla-ǩi-skis\ *v contrac of* higlakiskiza : to grate the teeth < ~ *waun* I grate my teeth >

hi·gla·ki·ski·za \hí-gla-ǩi-ski-za\ *v* he·wa·glakiskiza : to grate the teeth — **higlakiza** \hí-gla-ǩi-za\ *v* higla·wa·kiza : to grit or grind the teeth, as a cow or a man in his sleep, to crunch

hi·gla·ko·kog \hí-gla-ǩo-ǩog\ *v contrac of* higlakokoka : to gnash the teeth < ~ *waun* I gnashed by teeth >

hi·gla·ko·ko·ka \hí-gla-ǩoǩo-ǩa\ *v* hi·wa·glakokoka : to gnash the teeth, also perhaps to shatter the teeth

hi·gna \hi-gná\ *n* mi·higna nihigna : a husband < *hignaka* one who is a husband> — **higna·ku** *n* : her husband < ~ *wóǩic'u* She fed her husband (with meat above the knees of buffalos) > – HH Bl — **higna·ton** *vn* higna·wa·ton : to have a husband, to be married — **higna·ya** *v* higna·wa·ya : to have for a husband

hi·he·ya \hi-hé-ya\ *vn* [fr *hi* come + *iheya* go pass into or through] : to come and enter, as does a bullet or arrow — *v coll pl* : they assemble in one place

hi·han·na \hí-haŋ-na\ *n* : this morning – *See* hinhanna

hi·hi \hi-hí\ *adj* : soft, as fur or down < *hihi s'e* nappy, furry >

hi·hi·la \hi-hí-la\ *adj* : mellow, as ground or mud or sand < *Canku kin lila ~,* the road was very soft, *i.e.* the wheels going in deep, hence soft >

hi·hun·ni \hi-húŋ-ni\ *v* wa·hihunni : to arrive at any place < *Akicita najinpi k'on el ~ na wanji paiyotak ihpeya* He arrive at the place where the soldiers had stood, and he threw or made one sit down >

hi·h'a \hí-ȟ'a\ *v* : to gnash or show the teeth < *Máyašleca cinca hakakta s'e maku ~ kaca* It seemed the youngest coyote pup did not suck on its mothers teat, as is said of very lean people > – Bl — **hih'a·h'a** \hí-ȟ'a-ȟ'a\ *v red* : to gnash the teeth < ~ *inyanka* He ran with his teeth showing > — **hi·h'a·ki·ya** \hí-ȟ'a-ǩi-ya\ *vn* híh'a·wa·kiya : to show one's teeth, to grin — **hi·h'a·ye·la** \hí-ȟ'a-ye-la\ *adj* : thin, poor, emaciated < ~ *awayelo* Though poor and emaciated I led it. *Makú ~ yaun welo* Your breast is shrunken > – Bl — *adv* : showing one's teeth, as a person does that has been sick in bed for a long time and is now emaciated. *~ hpaya. Yunkan wicaša wan ataya huhu ececa ca na ~ hpaya ca wanyankapi ške lo* He lay open-mouthed. And then when the man, *húhu*, was altogether affected, then they say they saw him lying down with his teeth showing

hi·i·pa·ja·ja \hi-í-ṗa-ja-ja\ *n* : a tooth brush

hi·i·pa·špu \hi-í-pa-špu\ *v* hii·wa·pašpu : to pick the teeth

hi·i·šta \hi-í-šta\ *n* : the eyetooth – GV

hi·i·ya·t'in·ze \hi-í-ya-t'iŋ-ze\ *n* : cloves

hi·ma·za \hí-ma-za\ *n* : a gold tooth

hi·mni·ci·ya \hi-mní-ci-ya\ *v coll pl* : they come, assemble, to keep coming

hi·na *or* **hina·hina** \hi-nā'\ *or* \hi-ná-hi-ná\ *interj of surprise, used by women* : Well, well, well!

[1]**hi·na·jin** *or* **hinaja** *or* **hiwajatapi** \hi-ná-jiŋ\ *n* : the jaws of an arrow which hold the point

[2]**hi·na·jin** \hi-ná-jiŋ\ *vn* wa·hinajin *and perhaps* wa·hina·-wa·jin hina·un·jin·pi : to come and stand, to appear before <*Lehanl wicaša wan u na ~* Now the man came and he came and appeared > – Pb.27

hi·na·pa \hi-ná-pa\ *vn* wa·hínapa *or* wa·hina·wa·pa : to come in sight of, to come up, as something planted, or as the sun rising — **hinape·ya** \hi-ná-ṗe-ya\ *va* hinape·wa·ya : to cause to come in sight

hi·nu *or* **hinú·hinú** \hi-nū'\ *interj of gladness and surprise, as one meets a friend, used by women* : Oh-h-h-h! *or* That is funny. How funny! < ~ *, onapuza ca hanpi cola wówahele* Oh, with it all gone dry, I've cooked it to being no-soup > – D.115 BT

hi·num uya *or* **hinúm·bye** \hí-num ù-ya\ *n* : a two-year old colt

[1]**hin** \hiŋ\ *interj of disappointment over failure after a strained effort, used by men and women* : Oh well! — *interj of excuse when I did not mean it and accidentally offended another* : Whoops! – Note: the word is always said with a great expulsion of breath D.100 note 1

[2]**hin** \hiŋ\ *n* : hair, fur, down < ~ *naosakiya* it bristled up its hair >

hin'·a·kan·han·han *or* **hinkánhanhan** \hiŋ-á-ǩaŋ-haŋ-haŋ\ *adv* or *adj* : shedding one's hair, as do horses in spring

hin'·a·pa·ke \hiŋ-á-ṗa-ǩe\ *v* : to have winter hair < *Šunkawakan kin nahahci ~* The horse yet has its winter hair > – Bl

hin·gla *and* **hingni** \hiŋ-glá\ *vn aux* ma·hingla : indicating a sudden action or movement, to become, commence *etc* suddenly < *Otuyacin peta šaša hinglapi, utapi* For naught did fire suddenly flash turning red, they fired off their guns. *Yunkan taku eye, eyaš hi ece skaska hingle kin ecela wanyanke* He then said something, but he only arrived when it suddenly turned white, he saw it alone. *Yunkan (wahinkpe) iyoyanp ~ na tanwankatuya ya na wanna makata glihan* And then the arrow suddenly glowed, and when it went up very high it came back down and stuck in the ground. *Pte ota yelo, eyapi; ehanl ekta ewatonwan.* There are many buffalo, they said; they then went there to see. *Atan'in* šni ~ . Mat'a ~ , toka kte he? They simply disappeared. Supposing I were about to die, what would you do? *Iciyuta yunkan škan nihingle na kagal hihingla* I would try to get you jump in surprise and to get you to suddenly throw up your hands > – Note the following uses of *hingla* :

ablak ~ to die down, as does the wind
atan'inšni ~ to disappear
buwica ~ to charge one
ikópa ~ to be wary, leary of one
iyokišica or *iyokišil* ~ to fall into saddness
iyoyanp ~ to brighten, to light
kagal ~ to jump, to jerk, *kagal nihingla* to jump in surprise
kuja ~ to get sick
mat'a ~ I am just about dead
peta šaša hinglapi flashes, sparks
skaska ~ to whiten, turn white
škan nihingla you jumped in surprise
tonwan ~ to open one's eyes
wakokipa ~ to become afraid

hin·gnu \hiŋ-gnú\ *va* hin·wa·gnu : to singe off, as the down off a duck *etc* — **hingnu·pi** \hiŋ-gnú-ṗi\ *part* : singed off < ~ *s'e mahingle lo* I am shocked > – BT

[1]**hin·han** \hiŋ-háŋ\ *n* : an owl

~ *cik'ala* a small species of owl
~ *ġi* the short-eared owl – Cf the National Geographic Magazine, Feb. 1936, p. 217, Owls in North America
~ *hetonla* the horned owl
~ *kap'ipila* the long-eared owl; it is a little owl
~ *maǩótila* the burrowing owl, a little owl living in burrows with prairie dogs. < ~ *makotila cincala nataha s'e* the burrowing owl chicks seem to be a scalp, as is said when hair stands on end, unkempt. ~ *makotila ca kinyé s'e h'anhiyehci upelo* The burrowing owl also seems to fly with difficulty, as is said when people arrive very slowly > – Bl
~ *san* the gray owl
~ *sapa* the black owl
~ *ska* the white or snowy owl; it has black spots on the belly. Its deep trumpet voice is heard late in the late fall and even later on. It breeds in the winter on the prairie, coming down from the north – Bl
~ *ša* the great horned owl
~ *tánka* the large great horned owl – Noto: there are five kinds of owls whose song goes: who-who-who Spies were used to imitate this sound to indicate the enemy is near

[2]**hin·han** \hiŋ-háŋ\ *vn* : to fall, as rain or snow, hence to rain, or to snow, perhaps to precipitate < *Na wanna waniyetu anpetu wan el wa* ~ And now on a certain day of the winter it snowed. >

hin·han·ho·ton \hiŋ-háŋ-ho-toŋ\ *vn* : to hoot as an owl < *Na wanna yapi el ošpaye etan wanji* ~ *ca na inajinpi* And whenever in going along one from a group of animals gave a hoot, they came to a halt >

hin·han·ka·ga \hiŋ-háŋ-ǩa-ġa\ *n* : an owl — *v* : to hoot or shout as an owl, as young men do after dark; to act like an owl

hin·han ka·p'i·la \hiŋ-háŋ ka-p'ì-la\ *n* : the long-eared owl – Cf hinhán

hin·han·ke \hiŋ-háŋ-ke\ *n* or *adv* : a terminus, this end, a close, a stop; to come to an end, the end this way; < *Lehanyan* ~ ; *kahanyan* ~ Only so far is the end; this thus far is the end > – Bl KE

hin·han ma·ko·ti·la \hiŋ-háŋ ma-ǩò-ti-la\ *n* : the burrowing owl – Cf hiŋháŋ

hin·han·na *or* **hinhan·ni** \híŋ-haŋ-na\ *n* : this morning < *Ho wanna* ~ *el oyate kin witaya aya na oimniciye* Yes, on this morning the people gathered together and went for a meeting. ~ *kin winyan oyasin wayacipi kte lo* This morning (or possibly: Tomorrow) all you women will be dancing > – Cf hínhanna kin Note: *hihanna* is also used

hin·han·na·hci \híŋ-haŋ-na-ȟci\ *adv* : early in the morning – KE

hin·han·na kin *or* **hinhanna kin·han** \híŋ-haŋ-na k̇iŋ\ *or* \hín-haŋ-na k̇iŋ-hàŋ\ *n or perhaps adv* : tomorrow <~ *le ogna u kta* He should be coming in this way tomorrow. *Tohan hinhanna kinhan yaglapi kta he? Canke* ~ *eya* When will you all be going home tomorrow? And so he said: tomorrow. > – Note: *k̇in* here is pronounced simply *gi*

Hin·han·šun·wa·pa \Hiŋ-háŋ-šuŋ-wa-ṗa\ *np* : the Sicánġu or Brule nation, who wear a little owl feather on the head

hin·han·ta·han·pe \hiŋ-háŋ-ta-hàŋ-ṗe\ *n* **1** : an appendix to a buffalo heart **2** : the broad-leaved arrowhead – Note: the word is so called because of the shape of the leaves, arrowhead and rilled; sagittaria latifolia, of the water plantain family *Syn* PŠITOLA HU. BT Bl # 126

hin·he \hiŋ-hé\ *vn* : to rain — **hinhe·kiya** \hin-hé-ki-ya\ *va* : to cause to fall, as rain or snow — **hinhe·ya** *va* hinhe·wa·ya : to cause to rain *etc* – Cf hinhán

hin·hpa·ya \hiŋ-ṗá-ya\ *vn* ma·hinhpaya un·hiŋhpayapi : to fall, fall down

hin·hpe·ya \hiŋ-ȟpé-ya\ *va* hinhpe·wa·ya : to throw down or away what one has in the hand — *vn* : to be thrown down, to be lying down < *Wa oȟolya* ~ The snow remains lying in patches (giving the appearance of gray to the land), as is said when snow lies in spots here and there > – Bc

hin·hpi·hpi·la \híŋ-ȟpi-ȟpi-la\ *n* : a buffalo or horse in spring when they have shed their winter hair – Bl

hin·hte \hiŋ-ȟté\ *n* : thick fur, hair, or nap — **hinhte·ya** *adj* : furry, rough, the fir side out

hin'·i·kce·ka *or* **hin íkceka** *or* **hin·kce·ka** \hiŋ-í-kce-ka\ \hin í-kce-ca\ \híŋ-kce-ka\ *n* : a dark bay horse

hin·ji·ji·la \híŋ-ji-ji-la\ *adj* : downy, as young birds are — *n* : thin hair, as that on one's hands and arms

hin·ka·ci·ce·ye·la \híŋ-ka-ci-ce-ye-la\ *adv* : with the hair uncomed, matted < ~ *najin* He stood with hair unkempt > – Bl

hin·kpi·la \hiŋ-kṗí-la\ *n* : short hair or fur, as that on robes taken in summer; robes with short hair < *peji* ~ a certain short grass, that growing in mat-like patches of light green > – Bl D.21

hinl·ȟin·ca·la \híŋl-ȟin-ca-la\ *n* : the coot, a gray water bird, so called on account of the noise it makes – Bl

hin·na·sa·ki·ya \híŋ-na-sa-ki-ya\ *vn perhaps* : to have the hair standing up, as does an angry dog ready to attack – Bl

hin'·o·šku·šku \hiŋ-ó-šku-šku\ *v perhaps* : to shed old hair, as horses do in spring < *Šunkawakan hin'oškuškupelo* Horses shed their old hair > – Bl

hin·pa·hin \híŋ-pa-hiŋ\ *n* : a mouse-colored horse < *Miš* ~ *(i.e. horses) kin hena wicabluha kte lo* I shall hold these horses of mine >

hin·pa·hla \hiŋ-ṗá-ȟla\ *n* : a bunch of old thrown buffalo hair, which was held sacred and used as a *wótawe* charm *etc* < *Na tatanka* ~ *wan ku na pegnagkiya* And he brought home a buffalo bull hair charm, and had it worn in his hair >

hin·ska \hiŋ-ská\ *adj* : shed off, as is said of animals that have a new coat of hair, *lit* hair white – Note: *Mato Hinskála* Fresh Bear Coat was the name of Ribman of the village of Wounded Knee, South Dakota

hin·ske \hiŋ-ské\ *n* : the long upper or canine teeth of animals

hin·ske·ka·gya \hiŋ-ské-ka-gya\ *v* : to be ready to argue or say something in rebuttal <~ *iyemayelo* He put on pressure refuting me, *i.e.* he says the same as I did without having heard me > – Bl KE

hin·sko \híŋ-sǩo\ *adv* : so big, so large — **hinsko·keca** \híŋ-sǩo-ǩe-ca\ *adv* : so large, so great — **hinsko·la** *adv* : so small — **hinsko·skokeca** \híŋ-sǩo-sǩo-ke-ca\

\a\ father \e\ they \i\ machine \o\ smoke \u\ lunar \an, aŋ\ blanc Fr. \in, iŋ\ ink \on, oŋ, un, uŋ\ soon, confier Fr. \c\ chair \ġ\ machen Ger. \j\ fusion \clusters: bl, gn, kp, hšl, etc...\ b^e^lo ... said with a slight vowel
See more in the Introduction, Guide to Pronunciation

adv red : so large — **hinskoskoya** *adv red* : thus far — **hinsko·tanka** *adv* : so great — **hinsko·ya** *adv* : so far around, thus far — **hinskoye·la** *adv* : that big

hin·stan \hiŋ-stáŋ\ *n* : a chestnut colored horse

hin·ša \hiŋ-šá\ *n* : a sorrel horse — **hinša·ša** *n red of* hinša

hin·ta \híŋ-ṫa\ *n* : the bass, linden or lime wood < ~ *can* basswood or lilia > *Syn* PÁṪA GW

hin·te s'e \híŋ-te s'e\ *vt* [fr *yuhinta* to rake] : as if to rake *i.e.* a field or garden *etc* < ~ *našlog éyaya* As though they had been raked away, they (the game) bolted and got away > - Cf gmi s'e Bl

hin·tka *or* **hintka·la** \hiŋ-tká\ \híŋ-tka-la\ *n* : the nit or unhatched louse

hin·tkan \hiŋ-tkáŋ\ *n* : the common cattail or typha — **hintkan hu** *n* : the cattail stalk

hin·to \hiŋ-tő'\ *n* : a gray horse

hin·to·ke·ca \híŋ-to-ke-ca\ *n* : the color of something — *adj* : colored - P

hin·ya·ȟin \hiŋ-yá-ȟiŋ\ *interj of surprise in Dakota* : Well well! - Cf hiná, the Lakota word

hin·ya·ji·ce \hiŋ-yá-ji-ce\ *n* : fur, down, swan's down

hin·ya·kon \hiŋ-yá-koŋ\ *n* : stockings - Note: *hunyakon* is this word's adversative

hin·yan·ka \híŋ-yaŋ-ka\ *v used in imper usually* [fr *han* night + *yanka* sit] : to wait, hold on < ~ *yo* or *Ito ~ yo* or *Ito hinyanki yelo* Hold on! Well, wait! Well, he did wait. > - Note: the word is used in the *imper* if terminal *a* is used, but not when terminal *i* is used - B.H.43.17

hin·yan·ka·ga \híŋ-yaŋ-ḱa-ġa\ *n* : an owl - Note: when the wild pigeons wail, the children say "~ *hoton welo* The owl is hooting, *i.e.* There is a ghost!"

hin·yan·kah wa·ci·ya·pi \hiŋ-yáŋ-kaȟ wa-cì-ya-pi\ *n* : a pastime for boys - Note: the words perhaps mean: Believing the Owl Bl

hin·yan·se·la \hiŋ-yáŋ-se-la\ *adv* : badly, wickedly - R

hin·yan·sgla \hiŋ-yáŋ-sgla\ *v* hinyan·swa·gla : to be afraid on seeing something terrible - R Bl D.47 note 2

hin·yan·sya \hiŋ-yáŋ-sya\ *va* hinyan·swa·ya : to provoke — *adv* : sternly, crossly

hin·yan·za \hiŋ-yáŋ-za\ *vn* ma·hínyanza : to be stern, cross < *tawacin* ~ to be of surly disposition > — **hinyanze·ca** *adj* : stern, cross, sulky < *wicaša* ~ a sulky man > — **hinyanze·ke** \hiŋ-yáŋ-ze-ḱe *or* híŋ-yaŋ-ze-ḱe\ *adj* : stern or morose — **hinyan·ziyela** *adv* [fr *hinyanza*] : badly, wickedly

hin·ye·ta·on·pa \hiŋ-yé-ṫa-oŋ-ṗa\ *va* hinyeta·wa·onpa : to lay on the shoulder

hin·ye·te \hiŋ-yé-ṫe\ *n* : the shoulder, the whole shoulder

hin·ye·te·a·win·yan \hiŋ-yé-ṫe-a-wiŋ-yaŋ\ *v* hinyetea-win·wa·ya : to lay on the shoulder - Bl

hin·ye·te·wa·k'in \hiŋ-yé-ṫe-wa-k'iŋ\ *n* : a shoulder insignia of a military general's rank - WHL

hin·zi \híŋ-zi\ *adj* : buckskin or cream colored — *n* : a buckskin horse — **hinzi·ša** *n* : an orange colored horse

hi·o·na·h'a·ye·la \hí-o-na-ȟ'a-ye-la\ *adv* : showing the teeth, as a dying person, or as a skull, the lips removed < ~ *hpaya* to lie showing one's teeth, *i.e.* open mouthed>

hi·pa·šku \hí-pa-šku\ *v* : to pick the teeth - P

hi·psi·ca \hi-psí-ca\ *v* wa·hipsica : to jump down, as from a horse

hi·pson·pson·la \hí-psoŋ-psoŋ-la\ *adj perhaps* hi·ma·-psonpsonla : teeth on edge

hi·sto·la \hi-sṫó-la\ *n* : an arrow, or an arrowhead without barbs - Note: *kešlón* to have barb

hi·ta·kan·yu·wi \hi-tá-kaŋ-yu-wi\ *v* [fr *hi* a point + *takan deer* sinew + *yuwi* to bind] : to bind an arrowhead on the shaft

hi·ti·gla \hi-ṫí-gla\ *va* hiti·wa·gla : to loathe, dislike *e.g.* food — **hitigla·ya** *va* hitigla·wa·ya : to cause to loathe or dislike

hi·to·bu·ye \hí-ṫo-bu-ye\ *n* : a four-year old calf

hi·tun·ka·la \hi-túŋ-ka-la\ *n* : a mouse, mice

hi·tun·ka·la na·kpa·la \hi-túŋ-ka-la na-kṗà-la\ *n* : mouse ear, pussytoes, ladies'tobacco, white plantain; also the dwarf everlasting, the plantain-leaved everlasting, antennaria aprica grave, the composite family, so called because of the shape of the leaves. It serves as a medicine - Bl # 158

hi·tun·ka·la sa·pa \hi-túŋ-ka-la sà-pa\ *n* : the field mouse, or the mole - Note: *pangi gnakapi* they lay away artichokes

hi·tun·ka·la ta·wo·yu·te \hi-túŋ-ka-la ta-wò-yu-te\ *n* : the mouse's food - Cf tokala tapejuta hu bloka # 249 Bl

hi·tun·ka·la tun·kce \hi-túŋ-ka-la túŋ-kce\ *n* : the fall anemone, long-fruited anemone, the summer anemone, thimble weed; anemone cylindrica, the crowfoot family; so called for its leaves - B # 79

hi·tun·ka·san \hi-túŋ-ḱa-saŋ\ *n* : the large weasel; it is white in the winter, yellow in the summer - Note: the gopher is *wahinheya* Bl

Hi·tun·ka·san Wi·ca·ša \Hi-túŋ-ḱa-saŋ Wi-cà-ša\ *np* : a tribe of western Indians (unidentified) - Bl

hi·tun·ktan·ka \hi-ṫúŋ-ktaŋ·ka\ *n* : a rat < ~ *s'e nakpa tanktanka kaca* rat-like it seems to have very large ears, as is said of little men with long ears > - Bl

hi·tun·k'na·ȟa·bya·pi \hi-túŋ-k'na-ȟà-bya-pi\ *n* : a pastime for boys - Cf naȟáb Bl

hi·u·ya \hi-ú-ya\ *v* hiu·wa·ya : to grow teeth, as a baby does

hi·wa·ja·ta·pi \hi-wá-ja-ṫa-pi\ *n* : the jaws of an arrow that hold the head - *Syn* HINÁJIN Bl

hi·ya \hi-yá\ *adv* : no, of negation

hi·ya·gle \hi-yá-gle\ *vn* ma·híyagle un·hiyagle·pi : to reach to, as a road; to come upon one, as a temptation; it happens to one < *Šunkawakan k'innapapi mahiyagle* He came upon me running away with a horse > — **hiyagle·ya** *va* hiyagle·wa·ya : to cause to reach to; to bring upon one — *adv* : reaching to, leading to - B.H.7.22, 35.4, 42.1, 303.10

hi·ya·han \hi-yá-haŋ\ *vn* wa·hiyahan *or* wa·hiya·wa·-han ya·hiya·ya·han·pi un·hiya·un·han·-pi : to appear on top of a hill, so becoming visible - Note: *hiyahan* is used in *ref* to one; in *ref* to many: *ahiyahan*

hi·ya·hpe·ya \hi-yá-ȟpe-ya\ *v perhaps* : to throw over to one - Bl

hi·ya·ka·pta \hi-yá-ḱa-pṫa\ *vn* wahiya·wa·kapta : to come over *e.g.* a stream or hill

hi·ya·ki·gla \hi-yá-ḱi-gle\ *v* - Cf hiákigle

hi·ya·ki·gle·gle \hi-yá-ḱi-gle-gle\ *v* : to chatter, as from cold or chill

hi·yan·ka *or* **hinyanka** \hí-yaŋ-ka\ *v used in imper only* [fr *hi* arrive + *yanka* to be] : to stay where one has arrived, to wait a minute - Note: *Tate wan oyupemnipi s'e hiyanke lo* A whirlwind seemed to twist and now and then halt for a minute - Cf *tiyanka yo* Hold on a second! Bl D.56 note 2

hi·ya·nun \hi-yá-nuŋ\ *adj* ma·hiyanun : puny, small

and not able to grow – Cf koyánun

hi·ya·ta·gle \hí-ya-ta-gle\ *v* [fr *iyatagle* to surpass] : to have gone beyond, exceeded < *Ekta tonwéya ya po ungna ~ unyanpi kte lo* Go take a look in, perhaps we shall go further >

hi·ya·ya \hi-yá-ya\ *vn* wa·hiblabla ya·hilala : to go by, go past < *Wanna kiyela ~ po. Oyasin hocokata ~ po* Go by closely. Everyone go past the center. *Hanyewi, yahilale ki* O moon, do not pass by, as addressed in prayer. *Pankeska Wakpala kin lila mini ~ . Amáya wacin šni yahilale lo* The Platte River really carries water past. You pass by not thinking to take me along. > – Bl

hi·ya·ye *or* **ihíyaye** \hi-yá-ye\ *n* : semen – R

hi·ya·zan \hí-ya-zaŋ\ *vn* hí·ma·yazan : to have a tooth-ache — **hiyazan·pi** *n* : a tooth-ache

hi·ye·ya \hi-yé-ya\ *vn* : to become, to cause to be < *Najin ~* He had all stand. *hiyeye cin* Those who are, *i.e.* all, *Waptaye najin hiyeye kin* All weeds stood. *taku hiyeye cin* all things, *oyate hiyeye cin* all people, *unhiyeyapi* we are, *Paha hiyeye kin na wakpala yunke kin hena yuptokakin oškin'ic'iye* All hills and creeks they lie in he put himself to work looking around, *i.e.* hunting buffalo. *Wilwitaya eglepi* standing in shocks, *i.e.* the grain *ca wana enanala na zazecayela hiyeye lo* and all were here and there scattered about. *Hel enana úta lila ota hiyeye* In this place here and there occurred very many acorns > – Cf iyéya Gramm.319-320 D.77 Bl

hi·yo \hi-yó\ *v* : to come for something – Note: the word is used with verbs such as *i* , hi, iyaya, etc < *Woyute hiyomni kte* I shall go for something to eat. *Wanbli wan hiyomahi na wicoti ekta amaki* An eagle came for me and it arrived carrying me to camp. *Šunkawakan eya wicahiyomni kte* I shall come for some horses >

hi·yo·a·u \hi-yó-a-u\ *v* 3rd *pers pl* [fr *hiyo* come for + *au* they come] : They are coming for me – B.H.18.3

hi·yo·hi \hi-yó-hi\ *v* hiyó·wa·hi : to come, arrive for — **hiyohi·kiya** \hi-yó-hi-k̇i-ya\ *va* hiyóhi·wa·kiya : to cause to come for — **hiyohi·ya** *va* hiyohi·wa·ya : to cause to come for — **hiyo**

hi·yo·hpa·ya \hi-yó-ḣṗa-ya\ *vn* wa·hiyohpaya : to have come down from a hill, to be down, as said of a road < *gliyohpaya* to have come down from, as is said when one is coming down. *Ecel paha wan el wahiyohpaye k'on he ake aiyakapteya waku* So I was coming home going again uphill at a hill where I had come down >

hi·yo·hpe·ya \hi-yó-ḣpe-ya\ *va* : to come and let down – B.H.187.7

hi·yo·pa·ta·ke \hi-yó-ṗa-ta-k̇e\ *n* : a pin; a toothpick

hi·yo·ta·ka \hí-yo-ta-k̇a\ *vn* wa·hiyotaka [fr *hi* arrive + *iyotaka* sit] : to sit down, or stop on one's way someplace < *Manderson hel wahiyotaka. Hokšila, hel ~ yo* I stopped at Manderson on my way. Young lad, stop there on your way. >

hi·yo·t'in·za \hi-yó-t'iŋ-za\ *v* : to come and crowd together < *Iyuha hiyot'inze lo* Everyone came and crowded together > Bl

hi·yo·u \hi-yó-u\ *v* : to come for

hi·yo·ya \hi-yó-ya\ *va* : to bring or fetch – P

hi·yo·ya·ta·ke \hi-yó-ya-ta-k̇e\ *n* [fr *hi* teeth + *oyatake* to stick] : anything sticking between the teeth, as meat *etc* < *Hiyomayatake* A piece of *e.g.* meat got stuck between my teeth. *Hiyomayatake cin wakpašpu kte lo* A piece that got stuck in my teeth I shall loosen it, *i.e.* will pick it out > – Bl

hi·yu \hi-yú\ *vn* wa·hi·bu ya·hi·lu : to come from out of, as a child in parturition during birth, to come, come toward < *Tima ~ po* Come inside. *Tima ~ na tima iyotaka* Come inside and sit indoors. *Tankal ~* He came outside. *Canke wanbli k'on he wantanyeyela ti kin iwankab ~* And so the eagle came above the skilled archer's house. *Hacocola wahibu ca ake hamacocola kte lo. Tokeške tima yahilu hwo?* Since I came out naked, naked out again I shall go. How in the world did you get indoors, *i.e.* in the first place? > – B.H.43.12, 241.15

hi·yu·ki·ci·ci·ya \hi-yú-k̇i-ci-ci-ya\ *va* hiyu·we·ciciya : to hand to one his own

hi·yu·ki·ya \hi-yú-k̇i-ya\ *va* hiyu·wa·kiya : to cause to come to somebody; to send or hand to, as a letter

hi·yun·ka \hi-yúŋ-ka\ *vn* wa·hi·mun·ka : to arrive somewhere and stop for the night – B

hi·yu·ska·blu \hí-yu-ska-blu\ *n* : dentifrice, dental powder

hi·yu·we·ga \hi-yú-we-ġa\ *vn* hi·blu·wega : to cross a river or any water < *Canke wata nunp owecinhan hiyuwegapi keye* And so he stated that two boats made the crossing one after the other >

hi·yu·ya \hi-yú-ya\ *va* hiyu·wa·ya : to cause to come to, to send or hand to; to vomit

[1]ho \ho\ *pref to adv making them ref to a* circle of camps – Cf a number of such adverbs that follow

[2]ho \ho\ *adv* or *interj of affirmation* : Yes, all right < *Ho, ca* O.K. and > — *vn imper only perhaps* wa·ho un·hó-·pi : Come on, Come now, *etc* < *Ho wo* Come now, *Ho po* You all come now, *etc*, *Aiyopteya yapi na ake hopi ca na iš eya ecel hopi, na naunk nakicih'onpi. Šunkmanitu hopi. He wicaša akantu ho šni* They went in a straight line direction and again, come now, when he says so, come on, and they heard each other galloping. Come now, wolf. Come, this is not a common man > – Bl B.H.63.16, 294.6 — *n* : the voice either human or animal

ho·a·gla·gla \ho-á-gla-gla\ *adv* : along the tents of a camp circle, inside or outside < *hócokatonyan ~* along the circle of tents, *i.e.* inside, *holázatanhan ~ iyayapi* They went along the circle of tents, *i.e.* outside >

ho·a·i·ci·yo·pte·ya \ho-á-i-ci-yo-pte-ya\ *adv* : through the middle of the tent

ho·a·kab hi·yu·ya \ho-á-k̇ab hi-yú-ya\ *va* : to make one change in what he has said < *Ablezin na eyá yo; miyeš le taku hecetu ca ociciyake lo; tka inihanšni hoakab hiyumayayin kte hcin yelo* Notice and anyhow; I told you that this matter is alright; but fearlessly you will, yes, bring me around to change what I said >

ho·a·ki·ci·pa \ho-á-k̇i-ci-ṗa\ *v* hoa·we·cipa hoa·ci·cipa : to talk for one, put in a good word for one, recommend one – WE B.H.88.25, 237.9

ho·a·ki·ci·pa·pi \hó-a-k̇i-ci-pa-pi\ *n* : a salutation – P

ho·a·nunk \ho-á-nuŋk\ *adv* : on two sides of the camp inside the circle, as when two men walk around from opposite directions < *hoánunk hiyáyapi* going past, and so are opposite and on both sides, *i.e.* diagonally opposite within the circle. *Letanhan ~ ataya najinyeyapi na ecel tipi he el anunk ihunniyan po* From this place they stood in a row all the way on two sides of center camp, and thus when a tent stands make it reach to the two sides of the camp circle

ho·a·pa šin \hó-a-pa šiŋ\ *n* : hard fat on the *taníga* the

\a\ father \e\ they \i\ machine \o\ smoke \u\ lunar \an, aŋ\ blanc Fr. \in, iŋ\ ink \on, oŋ, un, uŋ\ soon, confier Fr. \c\ chair \ǧ\ machen Ger. \j\ fusion \clusters: bl, gn, kp, hšl, etc...\ b[e]lo ... said with a slight vowel
See more in the Introduction, Guide to Pronunciation

paunch – Bl

ho·a·pe \ho-á-ṗe\ *n* [fr *hogan* fish + *ape* fin] : fish fins

ho·a·pe·ša *or* **hoapeša·ša** \ho-á-ṗe-ša\ *n* : the red-fin, a species of fish; the short-headed red horse

ho·bla·ska \ho-blá-ska\ *n* : the gizzard shad, perhaps

ho·bu \hó-bu\ *n* ho·ma·bu : a rough, unpleasant voice — **hobu·kiya** \hó-bu-k̇i-ya\ *vn* hobu·wa·kiya : to speak with a gruff and unpleasant voice

ho·ca·ka \ho-cá-k̇a\ *n* [fr *hogan* fish + *caka* gills] : fish gills

ho·ca·tka·ya·tan·han \ho-cá-tka-ya-ṫaŋ-haŋ\ *adv* : at the left end of the open camp circle < ~ *tipi* they dwell at the left end of the open circle >

ho·ce·špu \ho-cé-šṗu\ *n* : fish scales – Note: the word *cešpú* in Dakota means a wart or scab

ho·ce·te \ho-cé-ṫe\ *n* : the direct road to a drove of buffalo, in opposition to a round about way taken by some hunters as all set upon them for the hunt < *Ho-nunpiyan unyanpi kte lo; akigle unyanpi kte lo* We shall go circling around; let us go once again > – Bl

ho·co·ka \hó-co-k̇a\ *n* : a courtyard, and area surrounded by tents or houses < *Na lila ~ otankaya na ištogmus wauncipi* The center area was very spacious, and they danced with eyes shut > – D.246

ho·co·kab *or* **hocokam** \hó-co-kab\ *adv* : in the middle of the camp circle of tents < *Tipi wašte wan ~ han ca el akiyuha akignakapi* A fine tent which stood in the center was carried and placed there >

ho·co·ka·ta \hó-co-ka-ta\ *n* : the center place, a vacant spot within a circle of tents — *adv* : in the center of a camp circle < ~ *hiyaya po* Go on past center camp >

ho·co·ka·ta·ki·ye \hó-co-ka-ta-ki-ye\ *adv* : towards the middle of the camp < ~ *bla* I went towards the center >

ho·co·ka·ta·han \hó-co-k̇a-ṫaŋ-haŋ\ *adv* : from the center or the midst of the camp < *Wicaša yamni ~ kupi ca el bla* When three men came back from center camp I went there >

ho·co·ka·ton·yan \hó-co-ka-ṫoŋ-yaŋ\ *adv* : In a circle < ~ *tipi* They dwell in a round village ~ *hoaglagla omani* He walked along the front of the tents, within the circle> — **hocokaton·tonyan** \hó-co-ka-ṫoŋ-ṫoŋ-yaŋ\ *adv red* : in their respective tribal circles < *Wicoti wanyanke* ~ He had a view of the encampment in their respective groups > – D.2

ho·co·špu *and perhaps* **hocošpi** \ho-có-šṗu\ *n* : a wart, a scab; scales of a fish

ho·ga·han \hó-ġa-haŋ\ *n* hó·ma·gahan : a rough, loud voice

ho·gan \ho-ġáŋ\ *n* : fish, the generic name for < ~ *mazognaka* a can of fish, as of sardines > — **hogan·mna** *adj* [fr *hogan* fish + *omna* an odor] : smelling of fish, fishy — **hogan·sanla** *or* **hogan·scila** *n* : little fish, minnows

ho·gan·tanka \ho-ġáŋ-tan-ka\ *n* : a big fish, a whale

ho·ga·ta \hó-ġa-ta\ *n* ho·ma·gata : a rough voice – *Syn* HÓGAHAN — **ho·gi·ta** \hó-ġi-ta\ *adj* hó·ma·gita : hoarse, as one's voice when the person has taken cold — **ho·gla·gita** \hó-gla-ġi-ta\ *v poss* hó·wa·glagita : to make one's self hoarse by speaking

ho·gle·gle·ga \ho-glé-gle-ġa\ *n* : the grass pike, or the rainbow fish – Bl SLB

ho·glu·wan·kal \hó-glu-waŋ-kal\ *adv* : with a high voice < ~ *lowan* She sang with a high pitch voice > – B.H.54.2

ho·gna \hó-gna\ *adv* : in that way or direction, in that manner < *Niye tokel yacin ~ kte* It will be that way just as you wish, or How is it you want it should be that way >

Ho·he \Hó-he\ *np* : An Assiniboin Indian

ho·he·ta·ma·hpi·ya \hó-he-ta-mà-ȟpi-ya\ *n* : the northern lights < ~ *ake tan'in* The northern lights again appeared > – Cf mahpiya tan'in Bl

ho·he·ta·pte \hó-he-ta-pte\ *n* : a buffalo cow apparently very thin and lean but found with much fat when killed, a very lean cow – B.

ho·hi \ho-hí\ *v imper only* : Take it. (It is used only when a man hands the burning pipe to someone else) – Cf na

ho·ho·la \ho-hó-la\ *adj* : loose, able to be shaken or moved < *Hi mahohola* My teeth are loose. >

ho·ho·pi·ca·šni \ho-hó-ṗi-ca-šni\ *adj* : immovable — **hohopicašni·yan** *adv* : immovably

ho·ho·šni \ho-hó-šni\ *adj obsol* : silent < ~ *yanka* He was silent >

ho·ho·te *or* **hohote·la** \hó-ho-ṫe\ *n* : a swing, a hammock, a seesaw; a swing as a grape vine hanging from a tree < ~ *kic'unpi, si on nahtakapi* They got on a swing, and with their feet they pushed> < ~ *akíciyapi* a sham fight between two groups of boys in which they use only their legs, ~ *kic'ún* to swing, to swing round ~ *we-c'un* I got on a swing ~ *kašká* to make a swing ~ *kaške unyin kte. Can'apakinyan wanice ke'eyaš can sakib unkaškin kte* Let's you and I go make a swing. Though there is lacking a tree with a leaning branch, let the two of us make a swing of trees side by side >

ho·hu *also* **huhu** \ho-hú\ *n* : a bone <~ *s'e tasáke* hard as a bone, as is said of something hard > – D.33

ho·hub \ho-húb\ *exclam of disappointment* : Oh rats! as might be said if a light was suddenly extinguished – WE

ho·hu·can·hpi \ho-hú-caŋ-ȟpi\ *n* : a club with a sharp horn attached to one end to kill animals with

ho·hu·i·ca·šle·ce \ho-hú-i-ca-šle-ce\ *n* : a primitive axe with which people split bones to get the marrow – Bl

ho·hu·i·ca·te \ho-hú-i-ca-ṫe\ *n* : a primitive hammer used to crack bones to get the marrow – Bl

ho·hu·ka·zun·ta \ho-hú-ka-zun-ta\ *n* : a sled made of buffalo bones < ~ *on óslohan kic'unpi* They put on buffalo bone skids to slide with >

ho·hu·mi·la \ho-hú-mi-la\ *n* : a bone knife – D.33

ho·hu·san s'e \ho-hú-saŋ s'e\ *adv and perhaps adj* : like whitish or yellowish bones < *Mahpiya kin ~ u welo* A yellowish cloud came > – Bl

ho·hu·šun·ka·kan *or* **hohušunka·wa·kan** \ho-hú-šuŋ-ka-kaŋ\ *n* : the astroyo-lus bone, part of the foot near the hoof – Bl SLB

ho·hu·wa·smin·pi \ho-hú-wa-smiŋ-pi\ *n* : a soup made of the back bones, a hash – Bl

ho·hu·ya·zan·pi \ho-hú-ya-zaŋ-pi\ *n* : rheumatism

ho·hu·yu·hmun·pi \ho-hú-yu-ȟmuŋ-pi\ *n* : a boy's toy

hoh \hóȟ\ *interj of displeasure at hearing what one does not like* : Aw -w -w -w - < ~, *niyeš ecanon šni* Aw- w- , you did it, *i.e. You* did it yourself > – Note: this is a word men use denoting objection or rejection of an idea that has been suggested

ho·ȟa-·pa \hó-ȟa-ṗa\ *n* ho·ma·ȟapa : a rough voice – Cf ȟapá

ho·ȟe·ceš \hó-ȟe-ceš\ *interj of disbeief* : Oh? - - - -

ho·hna·gi·ca·la \ho-ȟná-ġi-ca-la\ *n* : a certain sound, perhaps like a trill, made by women with the tongue and used in a cerrtain dance

ho·hni·yan·yan \hó-ȟni-yaŋ-yaŋ\ *vn* hó·wa·hniyanyan : to talk in a crying voice and in an excited manner, as is

done from bashfulness
ho·hpa \ho-ȟpá\ *vn* ho·wa·hpa : to cough < ~ *iglát'a* to cough convulsively ~ *miglat'a* I coughed spasmodically >
ho·hpa·h'an hanska \ho-ȟpá-ȟ'aŋ hàŋ-ska\ *n* : whooping cough
ho·hpa·ku·ja·pi \ho-ȟpá-ku-ja-pi\ *n* : consumption
ho·hpa·pi \ho-ȟpá-pi\ *n* : a cough, the having of a cold; consumption
ho·hpi \ho-ȟpí\ *n* : a nest — **hohpi·ya** *va* hohpi·wa·ya : to have a nest, to make a nest of
ho·hwa \ho-ȟwá\ *n* : the calamus. The leaves are eaten as well as the stalks by the Dakota. It is a kind of water grass; the roots are called *šunkcé*. The word designates more the leaves
Ho·hwo·ju Wi·ca·ša \Ho-ȟwó-ju Wi-cà-ša\ *np* : a clan of the Lakota Sioux commonly called the Húnkpapa or Húnkpapaya and living on the Standing Rock reservation in south central North Dakota
ho·hya·ze·la *or* **hoyázela** \ho-ȟyá-ze-la\ *n* [fr *hogan* fish + *yazela* taken by the mouth] : the kingfisher
ho·i·cu·wa \ho-í-cu-wa\ *n* [fr *hogan* fish + *kuwa* pursue] : a fish hook or a fishing apparatus
ho·i·gla·gi·ta *or* **hoglagita** \hó-i-gla-ǧi-ta\ *v poss* [fr *hoiyagita* to get hoarse] : to make one's self hoarse by speaking
ho·i·han·ke \ho-í-haŋ-ke\ *n* : either end of the camp circle, *i.e.* at the entrance to the camp circle
ho·i·kce·ya·kel \ho-í-kce-ya-k̇el\ *adv* : having not been educated or instructed; on the spur of the moment < ~ *oyaka* He talked with no expertise. ~ *lowan* He sang on the spur of the moment. > – Bl
ho·in·kpa·la \hó-iŋ-kṗa-la\ *adv perhaps* : being barely audible because very distant < *Hlahla kin* ~ *hotan'in* The bell was scarcely audible > – LB
ho·i·pa·te \ho-í-ṗa-ṫe\ *n* [fr *ṗatá* to cut and weave together] : a fishing net – Cf *ṗatá* to cut out and sew together BD
ho·i·šle·ya·tan·han \ho-í-šle-ya-ṫaŋ-haŋ\ *adv* : at the right end of an open camp circle < ~ *tipi* They live at the right end of the camp circle >
ho·i·šta \ho-í-šta\ *n* : a match
ho·i·to·ka·ga·tan·han \ho-í-ṫo-k̇a-ǧa-ṫaŋ-haŋ\ *adv perhaps* : at the south side of the camp < *Na wanna* ~ *kigla* And he now arrived at the south side of the camp >
ho·i·wo·tka \ho-í-wo-tka\ *n* : a carp, or the hog sucker < ~ *s'e i cik'a kaca* As if he were a carp, his mouth is not big, hence *fig* the word is applied to a person with a small mouth and who talks little. ~ *s'e tancan wašte* Like a carp, his body is well shaped, as they say or a well shaped horse > – Bl
ho·i·ye \ho-i-yé\ *interj* : Come along – *See* huyá
ho·i·yo·hpa·ya \ho-i-yó-ȟpa-ya\ *vn* hoiyó·ma·hpaya : to become hoarse, *i.e.* by the wind blowing on one and thus affecting the voice
ho·i·yo·ki·se \ho-í-yo-k̇i-se\ *n* : half of a company or camp
ho·i·yu·psi·ce \hó-i-yu-psi-ce\ *n* : a fish hook
ho·ja·han \hó-ja-haŋ\ *adv* : roughly, hoarsely < ~ *ia* to speak in a raucous way >
ho·ji·la \ho-ji-lā'\ *interj of admiration* : How beautiful! Simply splendid!
[1]**ho·ka** \ho-k̇á\ *n* : the eel
[2]**ho·ka** \ho-k̇á\ *n* : the thick-billed guillemot, Brunnich's murre
ho·ka ca han·ye kin·ye s'e \ho-k̇á ca haŋ-yé kiŋ-yè s'e\ *adj* : bewildered, hesitating, irresolute < ~ *unkunpi* We are confused > – L
ho·ka·ga·pi \ho-ká-ǧa-pi\ *n* : a flute, perhaps
ho·ka·ği·ca \ho-k̇á-ǧi-ca\ *n* : the snipe, a small kind of heron of the genus scolopax; the green-blue heron; the *dim* of course is *hok̇áǧicala* – R FR
ho·ka·gi·ta \hó-ka-ǧi-ta\ *v* hó·wa·kagita : to make the voice hoarse by speaking or singing
ho·ka·he \hŏ-k̇a-hé\ *interj of welcome* : Welcome! – Note: when a vistor has been bid to come in after rapping, by the invitation *Hau!* , on entering, the host says: ~ , *hel iyotaka* Welcome! Have a seat here. But if he fails to say this, the visitor is displeased
ho·kah·gle·pi *or* **ókahglepi** \ho-kaȟ-gle-pi\ *n* : something, as a fish tackle, tied to a stake; a thing moored, tied and left floating; *fig* those come first to a big meeting and put up their tents – Bl KE
ho·ka·ȟi·ca \ho-ká-ȟi-ca\ *n* : the stork
Ho·ka·ma·ni·pi·la \Ho-ká-ma-ni-ṗi-la\ *n* : a place on the Niobrara River in northern Nebraska where there used to be a large colony of nested cranes – Bl
ho·ka·psan·psan ia \hó-k̇a-psaŋ-psaŋ ià\ *v* : to whine
ho·ka·pta \ho-ká-pta\ *v* : to fill up < *Howákaptehce lo* I filled myself up, as with food > – Bl
ho·ka·to \ho-ká-to\ *n* : the blue heron
ho·ke·luta \ho-k̇é-lu-ta\ *n* : the full moon in the morning
ho·ke·mi·la *or* **hokemi** *or* **hokewin** \ho-k̇é-mi-la\ *n* : the "man in the moon", thought of as a woman by the old Lakota, with a lot of clothes on < ~ *ca najin yelo.* ~ *wanna wóze yelo (makalhpaya)* It is the "lady in the moon" standing. The "lady in the moon's" doing dipping (she lies upon the ground), *i.e.* at full moon she is stirring the kettle; similarly *wíaceic'iti* a ring around the moon, *i.e.* she makes a fire *(ceti)* > — **hoke·win s'e** \ho-k̇é-wiŋ s'e\ *adv* : like the woman, *i.e.* looking bulky, having on a lot of clothes, *makalhpaya* she lies on the ground – BT
ho·ki i·yo·kpa·za \hó-k̇i ì-yo-kpa-za\ *vn* : to get nowhere in using one's voice < *hók̇i wašte* to have a good loud voice, ~ *iyecehci waun welo* I am just like one unable to grasp anything. ~ *cokan waun* I am in the midst bewildered > – Cf hokómi Bl BT KE
ho·ki·tan·yan·kel \ho-k̇í-ṫaŋ-yaŋ-k̇el\ *adv* : noisily < ~ *natanpi* Noisily they made an attack > – B.H.134.14
ho·ki·ton \ho-k̇í-toŋ\ *v* ho·wé·ton : to holler, to sing out; to have a voice, the use of one's voice < *Šagya* ~ He has a voice to speak powerfully > – HM KE
Ho·ki·yo·hlo·ka Wa·kpa·la \Ho-k̇í-yo-ȟlo-ka Wa-kpá-la\ *np* : Pass Creek, in the eastern part of the Pine Ridge reservation
Ho·ko·mi *or* **Okomi** *or* **Yokomi** \Ho-kó-mi\ *np* : the name of a town in the state of Oklahoma in the 18 century perhaps, when beads, trinkets, and flannel were first sold to Indians in western United States – KE
ho·kši \ho-kší\ *n* : a child < ~ *wablenica ca onšiwicayalapi kte lo* You should take pity on a child who is an orphan >
ho·kši·ca·la \ho-kší-ca-la\ *n* : a baby < ~ *kagapi* a doll, ~ *toyunke* a cradle >

\a\ father \e\ they \i\ machine \o\ smoke \u\ lunar \an, aŋ\ blanc Fr. \in, iŋ\ ink \on, oŋ, un, uŋ\ soon, confier Fr. \c\ chair \ǧ\ machen Ger. \j\ fusion \clusters: bl, gn, kp, hšl, etc...\ b[e]lo ... said with a slight vowel
See more in the Introduction, Guide to Pronunciation

ho·kši·can·tki·ya·pi \ho-kší-caŋ-tki-ya-pi\ *n* : the beloved son, one universally esteemed

ho·kši·ce·kpa \ho-kší-ce-kpa\ *n* : the Pasch flower; a certain species of round mushrooms without stems, supposedly looking like a baby's navel in the healing process because of the color and form reminding one of the baby's umbilical cord and navel; a gosling, a wildblue flower appearing first in the spring; the twin flower, pulsatilla. The buttercup or crowfoot family. The state flower of South Dakota, and otherwise called *~ wanáhca* the (baby's) navel flower < *Wana ptehincala wicatonpi kte lo; wana ~ hinapelo* When calves are to be born, the navel flower sprouts, as is said in the springtime > - IS Bl BT # 149

ho·kši·ci·win·kte \ho-kší-ci-wiŋ-kte\ *adj* : childish, not man-like < *Miye hokšicimawinkte šni* I am not infantile. *Hokšiciwinktepi šni po* Don't be childish, *i.e.* Act like men, *He ~ s'a* He's always acting like a baby. > - WE

ho·kši ha·ka·kta *or* **hokši hakela** \ho-kší ha-ḱà-kta\ *n* : the youngest child

ho·kši·hi·yu·ki·ya \ho-kší-hi-yu-ḱi-ya\ *va* : to cause an abortion - Note: the word is not *hokšihiyuyekiya* — **hokšihiyu·ya** *v* : to have an abortion

ho·kši·i·kpi·gna·ka \ho-kší-i-kṗi-gna-ḱa\ *vn* hokšiikpi-·wa·gnaka : to be with child, to be pregnant

ho·kši·ka \ho-kší-ḱa\ *adj* ho·ma·kšika : yet a boy, a girl under-age

ho·kši·ka·ga \ho-kší-ḱa-ġa\ *va* hokši·wa·kaga : to beget a child, to impregnate

ho·kši·ke·šni \ho-kší-ke-šni\ *adj* : of age, not a boy, a girl

ho·kši·ki·ksu·ya \ho-kší-ki-ksu-ya\ *v* hokši·ye·ksuya : to be in labor, as before childbirth — **hokši·ksuya** *vn* hokši·we·ksuya hokši·ye·ksuya : to travail, be in childbirth, be in travail, to be in labor - B.H.160.12, 161.5, 164.10,15, 245.24

ho·kši·k'in \ho-kší-k'iŋ\ *va* hokši·wa·k'in : to carry or pack a child on the back

ho·kši·la \ho-kší-la\ *n* ho·ma·kšila hokši·pi·la ho·un·-kši·pi·la : a boy — **hokšila·la** *n dim* : a little boy

ho·kši·la wi·ca·hca \ho-kší-la wi-cà-ȟca\ *n* : a lazy young fellow, as if he were an old man

ho·kši·li·c'i·ya \ho-kší-li-c'i-ya\ *v* : to act in a childish manner - WE

ho·kši·ni·ge·šla \ho-kší-ni-ġe-šla\ *n* : an inexperienced young man or woman who tries to teach older people < *~ wan taku emakiyelo* The immature fellow said something to me > — **hokšinigešla·la** *n* : the last child in a family - *Syn* HAKÁKTA, HAKÉLA Bl

ho·kšin·win·kta \ho-kšíŋ-wiŋ-kta\ *v* hokšin·ma·winkta : to be angry and act like a child, to be pettish

ho·kšin·wi·tko·la \ho-kšíŋ-wi-tko-la\ *v* : to be childish, silly

ho·kší·o·un·pa·pi *or* **hokšiunpapi** \ho-kší-o-un-ṗa-pi\ *n* : an infant boy or girl - B.H.166.20,10, 169.15,19, 170.4

ho·kši·pa·slo·he \ho-kší-pa-slo-he\ *n* : a go-cart

ho·kši·šni·yan can·nun·pa \ho-kší-šni-yaŋ caŋ-nùŋ-pa\ *v* : to let the smoke pass through the nose while smoking - BT

ho·kši·to·ka·pa wo·i·yo·wa·ja \ho-kší-to-ka-pa wò-i-yo-wa-ja\ *n* : the first birthright - *Syn* WOTOKAPA WOIYOWAJA

ho·kši·un·ke \ho-kší-uŋ-ke\ *adj* : older, old enough < *~ eša hecon* Though old enough he did it. *~ šni ška hecon iyececa šni* They say he is not old enough that it be like him to do that > - KE

ho·kši·un·pa·pi \ho-kší-uŋ-pa-pi\ *n* - Cf hokšiounpapi

ho·kši·win·la \ho-kší-wiŋ-la\ *n* : a virgin according to the flesh, one who has not had a husband - Bl

ho·kši·yu·ha \ho-kší-yu-ha\ *v* hokši·blu·ha : to give birth to a child < *Piško s'e ~ wošikšiceke. ~ kte* Like the night hawk to give birth is quite troublesome. To give birth will be to conceive >

ho·kun·pe šni \ho-ḱúŋ-ṗe šni\ *adv* [fr *ho* voice + *ku* come back + *unpe* lay down] : *lit* not laying down the voice, hence babbling on < *~ wahoya* to talk to, or instruct, without interruption, *~ eya* to speak of something again and again. > - *Syn* YAPSAKE ŠNI LC

ho·cu·ta \ho-kú-ta\ *adv* : down stairs

ho·ku·wa \ho-ḱú-wa\ *v* ho·wa·kuwa : to fish, take or catch fish in any way

ho·la·za·ta \ho-lá-za-ta\ *adv* : outside a circle, beyond the camp circle — **holaza·tanhan** *adv* : outside the camp circle, at the rear of each tent < *~ hoaglagla hiyayapi* They passed along outside the camp > - D.251

ho·mna \hó-mna\ *adj* : with the odor of fish, fishy, smelling like fish

ho·mna·yan \hó-mna-yaŋ\ *v* homna·wa·ya : to gather or collect fish for a feast

ho·na·gi·la *or* **hona·witkala** \ho-ná-ġi-la\ \ho-ná-wi-tḱa-la\ *n* : tadpoles

ho·nun·pin·ya \ho-núŋ-ṗiŋ-ya\ *v* : to surround in a half circle, as after having made an approach to a herd < *Hinhanna kin honunpinwaya na wihpewayin kte* Tomorrow I shall surround (the herd) and give it away. > **ho·nun·pin·yan ya** \ho-núŋ-ṗiŋ-yaŋ ya\ *v* : to go around, surround going in a circle. - Note: on surrounding a buffalo herd they say: *Honunpinyan unyanpi kte lo; akigle unyanpi kte lo* Let us get clear around; let us go a second time. - Cf hocéte Bl

hon·hon *and* **honhon·zahela** \hoŋ-hóŋ\ *vn* \hon-hóŋ-za-he-la\ *adv* - *See* hunhún *and* hunhunzahela

ho·o·ka·winh \ho-ó-ka-wiŋȟ\ *adv* : around the camp inside, as a man walking around making announcements from one end of the circle to the other < *~ ieyapahapi. ~ hiyaya* It was announced around the camp circle. He passed around inside the camp circle. > - D.211, 225

ho·o·ki·hi·pi·ca·šni \hó-o-ki-hi-ṗi-ca-šni\ *v* : to be unable to get a chance to speak - Bl

ho·o·kšan \ho-ó-kšaŋ\ *adv perhaps* : around the circle outside

ho·o·pta \ho-ó-pta\ *adv* : across the camp circle; through the camp, *i.e.* the circle of tents < *~ iyaya. Hecel ~ ble* He went through the camp. So I crossed the camp circle. >

ho·o·ya·za s'e \ho-ó-ya-za s'e\ *adj* : crowded together like canned fish - NP

ho·pa·šku \ho-ṗá-šku\ *n* : fish-scales

ho·pa·tan \ho-ṗá-taŋ\ *v* ho·wa·patan : to spear fish

ho·pa·tan·ka·la \ho-ṗá-taŋ-ḱa-la\ *n* : a kind of fish like the perch - R Bl

ho·pa·wa·ta \ho-ṗá-wa-ta\ *n* : a fish - Bl

ho·pe·pe \ho-ṗé-ṗe\ *n* : a fish, the stone roller - Bl

ho·pe·ška s'e \ho-ṗé-ška s'e\ *adj* : with a comparison implied, as said of a knife with a long blade but short handle, or said of a fat man - *Syn* GMIGMELA S'E Bl

ho·pi·ški·ya \hó-pi-ški-ya\ *va* : to make the voice squeak, to speak with a squeaking voice

ho·pi·za \hó-ṗi-za\ *n* ho·ma·piza : a small squeaking voice

ho·po *or* **hówo** *or* **hóye** \hó-po\ *v imper* : All right! Very well! - B.H.62.7, 148.26
ho·sam \ho-sám\ *adv* : on the other side of, beyond the camp <~ *étonwan. Kákika ~ tiowa wan he kin heciya ye* He took a look beyond the camp. Over there on the other side he went there where stands a painted tipi > - *Syn* HOSÁNPATAHAN
ho·sa·mna \ho-sá-mna\ *adj* : smelling of fish, fishy - Cf hómna
ho·san \ho-sáŋ\ *n* : carp - Bl SLB
ho·san·ni·ca·ya \ho-sáŋ-ni-ca-ya\ *adv* : on one side < ~ *inajin* to stand up on one side > - B.H.64.15
ho·san·pa·ta·han \ho-sáŋ-pa-ta-haŋ\ *adv* : beyond the camp, on the other side of - *Syn* HOSÁM
hosan·pa·ta ya \ho-sáŋ-pa-ta ya\ *v* : to go visiting, *i.e.* away from the circle of tents < ~ *mni kte lo* I shall be going visiting > - B.H.86.2
ho·se·wi·mna \ho-sé-wi-mna\ *adj* : smelling like fish
ho·ši \ho-ší\ *v* : to tell news, to take word - Note: the word is used along with other *v*
ho·ši a·i \ho-ší a-ì\ *v* : to go there with a message - B.H.56.9
ho·ši·gla \ho-ší-gla\ *v* hoši·wa·gla : to go home carrying word - P
ho·ši·gli \ho-ší-gli\ *v* hoši·wa·gli : to arrive at home with news - P
ho·ši·gli·cu \ho-ší-gli-cu\ *v* hoši·wa·glicu : to be on the way home with news
ho·ši·gli·hun·ni \ho-ší-gli-huŋ-ni\ *v* hoši·wa·glihunni : to reach home with a message - B.H.43.6
ho·ši·hi \ho-ší-hi\ *v* hoši·wa·hi : to arrive somewhere with word - R
ho·ši·i \ho-ší-i\ *v* hoši·wa·i : to have gone to, or to have been at, to carry word - R
ho·ši·i·ya·ya \ho-ší-i-yà-ya\ *v* : to have gone to carry word
ho·ši·ka·gla \ho-ší-ka-gla\ *v* hoši·wa·kagla : to carry home word to one
ho·ši·ka·gli \ho-ší-ka-gli\ *v* hoši·wa·kagli : to arrive at home with word to one < *Taku áškatuyela hošimakaglipi. Mišnala wakpapta s'a hošicicagli* Lately they arrived home with word for me. I arrived home alone with word for you an escapee, or I an escapee arrived home alone with word for you. > - Bl B.H.42.27
ho·ši·ka·hi \ho-ší-ka-hi\ *v* hoši·wa·kahi : to arrive somewhere with word to one < *Taku wan wašte wanlakin kte lo, ca hošicicahi yelo* You shall see something good, so I have arrived with word for you. > - *See* B.H.43.3
ho·ši·ka·i \ho-ší-ka-i\ *v* hoši·wa·kai : to go in somewhere bringing word to one - B B.H.262.20
ho·ši·ka·ki \ho-ší-ka-ki\ *v* hoši·wa·kaki : to have taken word home to one
ho·ši·ka·ku \ho-ší-ka-ku\ *v* : to bring a message home to one < *Hošimakaku po* You all bring the message home to me > - B.H.169.15
ho·ši·ka·u \ho-ší-ka-u\ *v* : to come to ... with a message - B.H.272.8
ho·ši·ka·ya \ho-ší-ka-ya\ *v* hoši·wa·kaya : to take word to one
ho·ši·ki \ho-ší-ki\ *v* hoši·wa·ki : to have reached home with a message - R
ho·ši·ku *or* **hoší·u** \ho-ší-ku\ *v* hoši·wa·ku : to be coming home with a message - R
ho·ši·ši·pa \hó-ši-ši-pa\ *express used in song* - Note: children playing once used this as a word in song. They would then pinch others' hands, *i.e.* taking the skin between thumb and index finger and pulling upward, saying Šála. This was not supposed to hurt - FD.493
ho·ši·u \ho-ší-u\ *v* hoši·wa·u : to be coming with a message
ho·ši·ya \ho-ší-ya\ *v* hoši·bla : to go to take a message - R
ho·šna·šna ki·c'un \hó-šna-šna ki-c'ùŋ\ *v* : to hop on one leg, as children do for a pastime < ~ *kakicipa ecunkonpi kta* They will do a race, hopping on one leg > - Bl
ho·špe·ye·la \hó-špe-ye-la\ *adv* : loudly < ~ *pan* to call with a loud voice > - Bl
ho·šti \ho-ští\ *interj expressing strong disappointment and regret* : Oh, alas!
ho·š'a·gya \ho-š'a-gya\ *adv* : with a loud voice - B.H. 3.10
ho·tan'·in \hó-taŋ-iŋ\ *vn* ho·má·tan'in : to have one's voice heard < *Wanna maya k'el ikiyela inajinpi hotan'inpi* They had their voice·heard (echo) standing near the river bend. > - B.H.105.11
ho·tan·ka \hó-taŋ-ka\ *n* : a loud or great voice < *Canke ~ lecel eya ...* And so this is what a loud voice said ... > — **hotanka·kiya** \hó-taŋ-ka-ki-ya\ *adv* : with a great or loud voice — **hotanka·ya** *adv* : with a loud voice < *Lecel ~ eya: ...* In this way a loud voice said: ... >
Ho·tan·ke \Hó-taŋ-ke\ *np* : the Winnebago Indian
ho·tan·kin·kin·yan \hó-taŋ-kiŋ-kiŋ-yaŋ\ *adv* : with a voice of very great authority < ~ *heya pan* He called out saying this with a very great voice > - B.H.209.6
ho·ton \ho-tóŋ\ *v* ho·wá·ton : to cry out, put forth the voice as some animals do, as buffalo; to crow, to thunder < *Wakinyan ~ . Na wanna okšan ~ okawinjapi* The Thunderbird sounded. And now (the buffalo) matted it down honking round about > - Note: the word seems not applied to birds
ho·ton·kel *also* **hotonk'el** \ho-tóŋ-kel\ *adv* : groaning < *Iš ena patuš hotonk'el škan. Išnala tima iyayin na el ~ škanhin na ungna glinapa* He too moved about bent over moaning. He went alone indoors and there he started moving and got on his way home perhaps >
ho·ton·ki·ya \ho-tóŋ-ki-ya\ *va* hoton·wa·kiya : to cause to bawl or cry out
ho·ton·ton \ho-tóŋ-toŋ\ *v red* wa·hótonton [fr *hoton* to sound the voice] : to keep crying out < *Lila ~ kinyan* It (a magpie) flew away squawking >
ho·t'e·ca \ho-t'é-ca\ *n* : dead fish, such as are found in the spring
ho·un·ma \ho-úŋ-ma\ *n* : one of the sides of a surround on the buffalo hunt
ho·u·ya \hó-u-ya\ *va* hóu·wa·ya : to send the voice to, to cry out to one, to accost, shout < *Na wanna anpo ehanl Tašunke Luzahan lecel ~ . Ate, ahitonwan yo, hóuciciye ca nayah'on kta kihe k'un* And it was then daylight when Fast Horse shouted out this: Father, look, since I had kept busy crying out to you, you should hear. > D.244, 263
ho·wa·kan \hó-wa-kaŋ\ *vn* hó·ma·wakan : to wail < *Pa izitapi; canke ~ na óhanketa t'a* Its head was held in the smoke, and so it wailed and in the end it died >
ho·wa·pa·šin \hó-wa-pa-šiŋ\ *n* : the fat around the paunch - *Syn* TANIGA WAŠIN HH Bl

---

ho·wa·sa·pa \ho-wá-sa-pa\ *n* [fr *hogan* fish + *owasin* all + *sapa* black] : the catfish, or the black bass - Note: *hc-hasapa* [+ *ha* hide, rather than + *wa* of owásin] is perhaps the more correct Cf huhá, wójuha SLB

ho·wa·šte·ya \hó-wa-šte·ya\ *v* : to produce fine sound with the voice — *adv* : speaking with a grand voice < ~ *wacinksapa yo* Be clear-minded in using a fine sounding voice > - Bl

ho·wa·ya \ho-wá-ya\ *vn* ho·wá·waya *or* wahowabla yahowala : to cry out, to groan < *ceya* ~ to clamor noisily, to be noisy. *Na nanih'onpi šni eša, ceya ~ po* And though you didn't hear me, all of you clamor noisily > - R D.196 B.H.27.22, 262.26

ho·we \hó-we\ *adv* or *interj implying consent to* : All Right! - Note: the word is used by women, but Teton women may perhaps use *hóna* instead of *hówe* - Cf hówe D.9 note 4

ho·wi·wa·ci·pi \ho-wí-wa-ci-pi\ *n* : the Ghost Dance, perhaps, of the year 1891; a child's dance in which they say "Howí" - Cf Howíwicaša

Ho·wi·wi·ca·ša \Ho-wí-wi-ca-ša\ *np* : the Indians of the town at White Clay, Nebraska, on the edge of the Pine Ridge reservation, Oglalas, so called because they indulged in the Ghost Dance of 1891, in which they sang the word Howí, a word chosen because in the Ghost Dance the participants danced in a circle with hands joined just as in children's play (dance). They join hands and sing: Howí - LO

ho·wi·wo·tka \ho-wí-wo-tka\ *n* : a rack for drying fish

ho·wo \hó-wo\ *v imper* : All right! - Note: it carries the idea of consent or permission and is used by men. When addressing many they say: Hópo; women say: Hówe - Cf hóye B.H.48.2, 148.10

ho·wo·kšan *or* **hookšan** \ho-wó-kšaŋ\ *adv* : around the camp of tents, outside the camp; walking around outside, as is done by a spy

ho·ya \ho-yá\ *v* ho·wa·ya ho·ci·ya : to use the voice of another; to have another sing in one's stead

ho·ya·ze·la ci·k'a·la \ho-yá-ze-la cì-k'a-la\ *n* : the belted kingfisher - Note: the bird seems very *ohitika* courageous, and its cone is often used as *wotawe* a charm. The *heyoka kagapi* clown maker used it as a charm, tying it on a spear. The kingfisher's fighting qualities, thus considered *wayupika* expert, were often so associated with the use of *wotawe* a charm - Bl

ho·ya·ze·la tan·ka \ho-yá-ze-la tàŋ-ka\ *n* : the large kingfisher - Cf *hoyazela cik'ala* the belted kingfisher - KE

ho·ye \hó-ye\ *v imper* : All right! Very well! - Note: it means willingness in obeying an order or wish. It is used by men; in addressing many, we say: *Hópo*, or *Hói* - D.9 note 4 B.H.275.4

ho·ye·ki·ya \hó-ye-ki-ya\ *v* hoye·wa·kiya [fr *ho* voice + *yekiya* to bet] : to cry to, call to, pray to, address - B.H. 66.6, 90.6

ho·ye·ya \hó-ye-ya\ *va* hóye·wa·ya : to cause the voice to go to, to call, cry out < *Wankalkiya yugal najin na ~ . Ena nankapi kin niye ko henanipila kte lo, eya ~* He stood with arms outstretched upward and sent forth his voice. He cried out saying: You all sitting right here and you as well will be gone >

ho·ye·ye·ki·ya \hó-ye-ye-ki-ya\ *v red of* hoyekiya : to cry aloud to - B.H.107.20

[1]hu \hu\ *exclam* : Húhu huhu huhu - Note: the first *hu* is high pitched, the second is lower; this they call *wágla-š'api*. The sound is like that of a coyote and is made by by boys when they bring beef home

[2]hu \hu\ *n* mihu nihu wicahu **1** : the leg of man or animal; *fig* the wheel of a wagon or other vehicle < *Hu mayukan* It is my leg, or The leg is mine > **2** : the stock or stem of anything, as of a plant

hu·a·ki·š'a·ka \hu-á-ki-š'a-ka\ *adj* : strong in one's legs, not easily tired - Bl

hu·blo \hu-bló\ *n* : the shin bone, the lower part of the leg

hu·blo·yun·ke \hu-bló-yuŋ·ke\ *n* : the front muscle of the lower part of a man's leg - Cf hucó-gin GV

hu·can \hu-cáŋ\ *n* : the stem, the stock of a gun, the shaft of an arrow < *Wanna wahinkpe makata glihan. Yunkan ~ cokanyan hehanyan ataya we oha. Na ~ kin lila pašlušlutapi* Now the arrow coming back stuck in the ground. In the shaft's center, that far entirely blood adhered. And the shaft just kept popping up > - B.H.62.13

hu·cin·ška \hú-ciŋ-ška\ *n* : green milkweed. Acerates vividi flora, so called because of the shape of its leaves. - Note: pulverized roots when swallowed help children with diarrhoea. Tea of the whole plant is good for mothers who have no milk - L PLB # 258

hu·co·gin \hu-có-ġiŋ\ *n* : the calf of the leg, *i.e.* the muscle < ~ *namatipa* My calf cramped > - Cf hubló-yunke Bl

hu·gla·go \hu-glá-ġo\ *v poss* : to make cuts on one's own arms and legs, as in mourning - Bl

hu·gmi·ya a·yu·t'in·ze·la \hu-gmí-ya a-yù-t'iŋ-ze-la\ *n* : an iron ring, the rim of a wheel

hu·gmi·yan \hu-gmí-yaŋ\ *n* : a wagon wheel

hu·gmi·ya pe·pe·la \hu-gmí-ya pe-pè-la\ *n* : a circular saw

hu·ha \hu-há\ *n* : the limbs of the body, as the legs and arms; legs of a kettle < *šina ~* the hide of the feet left on a robe, *Šina ~ iyowakpatan kta* I'll patch the shawl that includes the four feet, *i.e.* patch all around the shawl > - WE

hu·ha·ton \hu-há-toŋ\ *vn* huha·wa·ton : to have legs or limbs

hu·ha·to·pa \hu-há-ṫo-ṗa\ *n* : a quadruped, particularly the wolf; a particular kind of quadruped - Note: *wahútopa* is the generic name R

hu·ha·ya \hu-há-ya\ *va* huha·wa·ya : to have for muscles, to use for legs

hu·ho·hu \hú-ho-hu\ *n* : the leg bones

hu·ȟa·ka \hu-ȟá-ka\ *adj* : lean, poor, nothing but bones; *fig* said of an empty hay rack < ~ *ece u welo* Skin-and-bones came only. > - Bl

hu·hla \hú-ȟla\ *n* : evening primrose, night willow - WE # 134

hu·hni·ye·ya \hú-ȟni-ye-ya\ *va* : to hurry one up, to make one lively, excited < *Huhniyeciye šni tka ociciyaka* I am not hurrying you, but I do tell you (what I want) > - Cf hníyeye s'e, wahúhniye s'e BT

hu·h'a \hú-ȟ'a\ *adj* : lean, boney - *Syn* TAMÁHECA — **huh'a s'e** *adv* : a kind of lean look appearing, lean-like, boney - Bl

hu·i·ci·gnu·ni·yan \hú-i-ci-gnu-ni-yaŋ\ *adv* : with bones mixed together < ~ *yunkapi* They lie with their bones mixed together, as is said of two friends who went on the warpath and being killed lie together dead > - Bl KE

hu·i·na·k'e·hye \hu-í-na-k'e-ȟye\ *n* : a wagon brake < ~ *ecel icu* to put on the wagon brake, ~ *ecel iyeya* to slam on the brake > - Cf inák'ehya

hu·i·na·ta·hye *or perhaps* **huina·t'age** \hu-í-na-ṫa-ȟye\ *n*

: a wagon brake — **huinat'a·hton** *v* : to put the (wagon) brake on - Bl

hu·i·pa·hte \hu-í-pa-ḣte\ *n* : hobbles

hu·i·ya·ka·ske \hu-í-ya-k̇a-ske\ *n* : a piece of buffalo hide tied around the ankles, as is done in the Sundance

hu·i·ya·ta \hu-í-ya-ṫa\ *adj* : bony, as very lean men or animals < *Ḣoká blóka s'e maku ~ heca* Like a badger he has a bony chest, as is said of persons with lean chests > - Bl

hu·i·yun \hu-í-yuŋ\ *adv* [fr *hu* leg + *íyun* to use] : on foot < *~ bla* I go on foot > - Note: the word *íyun* is here the Dakota for *un* meaning to use; hence a sign of the mixing of the Siouan dialects — **huiyun·kel** \hu-í-yuŋ-k̇el\ *adv* : on foot, *i.e.* walking

hu·i·yu·t'in·ze \hu-í-yu-t'iŋ-ze\ *n* : leggings

hu·ka \hu-k̇á\ *n* : the skin

hu·ka·gmi·ya \hu-k̇á-gmi-ya\ *n* : a wagon wheel

hu·ka·go·pi \hu-k̇á-ġo-pi\ *n* : the making of cuts into one's arms and legs, as some Indians once did when some relative died - Bl

hu·ka·i·ci·ca·win·yan yan·ka \hu-k̇á-i-ci-ca-wiŋ-yaŋ\ *v* : to cross one's legs while sitting - Bl — **hukaici·c'uya** *adv* : with legs crossed

hu·ka·we·ga·pi \hú-k̇a-we-ġa-pi\ *n* : a fracture of the limbs - Bl

hu·ki·tan·la \hú-ki-ṫaŋ·la\ *adv* : overloaded < *~ ku welo* He returned overloaded > Bl

hu·kpan·kos in·yan·ka \hu-kpáŋ-k̇os ìŋ-yaŋ-ka\ *v* : to run throwing the legs lively - *Syn* HNIYÁNYAN, ŠNIYÁNYAN

hu·kul \hu-k̇úl\ *adv* : under, beneath — **huku·ta** \hu-kú-ta\ *adv* : below, under, at the lowest place < *~ lila icamna* In the lowest places it really stormed >

hu·ku·ta·ki·ya \hu-k̇ú-ṫa-ki-ya\ *adv* : deep downward

hu·ku·tan·han \hu-k̇ú-ṫaŋ-haŋ\ *adv* : from below < *Okinyanke ocanku ḣe ~ el ewicoti* They set up camp together at the race track below the mountain >

hu·ku·ya \hu-k̇ú-ya\ *adv* : below, at the lowest places

hu·la·za·ta \hu-lá-za-ta\ *n* : the hind wheels

hu·na·po·bya \hu-ná-ṗo-bya\ *n* hunapo·bwa·ya : to have a blow-out in *e.g.* a tire

hu·na·pta \hu-ná-pta\ *v* huna·wa·pta : to have injured one's self and so to become lame - R Bl

hu·na·šte \hu-ná-šte\ *v* huna·wa·šte : to sprain one's leg - R Bl

hu·na·ti·pa \hu-ná-ṫi-ṗa\ *vn* : to have a cramp in the leg

hu·ni·šni \hu-ní-šni\ *adv* : motionless, still, quiet < *~ lecel mankahe lo* I sat here still. > - Bl

hu·nun·pa \hu-núŋ-pa\ *n* [fr *hu* leg + *nunpa* two] : a biped; Man, in the sacred language

hun \huŋ\ *n* nihun hunku : mother - Note: while *ina* my mother, *nihun* your mother, *hunku* his mother, *hun* is not used alone

hun·ca·je *and perhaps* **huncaje s'e** \húŋ-ca-je\ *n* : a garter, for stocking

hun·he \huŋ-hé\ *interj of astonishment or regret* : Oh no! - Gramm.127

hun·hun \huŋ-húŋ\ *vn* : to shake, tremble, as a tree in the wind - WE

hun·hun·he \huŋ-huŋ-hé\ *interj of regret* : Alas!

hun·huns \huŋ-húns\ *adj contrac of* hunhunza : shake — **hunhun·sya** \huŋ-húŋ·sya\ *va* hunhun·swa·ya: to cause to shake, to shake — *adv* : in a shaking manner

hun·hun·za \huŋ-húŋ-za\ *adj* ma·hunhunza — **hunhunza·han** *part* : shaken, shaking — **hunhunza·hela hela** *adv* : trembling, shaking, as on hearing bad news and is used also *fig* — **hunhunza·yela** *adj* : nervous < *Mahunhunzayela s'elececa* I am like one as if trembling, as is said when one is anxious to get away on a trip > - WE Bl

hunh \huŋḣ\ *pron* or *adj* : some, a part of — **hun·hunh** \húŋḣ huŋḣ\ *pron red* : some — **hun·hlala** \húŋ-ḣla-la\ *adv* : only a part

[1]**hun·ka** \huŋ-ká\ *n* : an ancestor - *Syn* TAKÚYE

[2]**hun·ka** \húŋ-ka\ *adj* : healthy in appearance < *Húnkehca kaca* He appears a bit sickly > - Cf húnkešni Bl

hun·ka·kan \huŋ-k̇á-k̇aŋ\ *v* hun·wa·kakan hun'·un·ka-kan·pi : to tell stories, yarns — **hunkakan·pi** *n* : stories, fables

hun·ka·ke \huŋ-k̇á-k̇e\ *n* mi·húnkake : an ancestor, one's father, mother, brothers and sisters, hence immediate relatives — **hunkake·ya** *va* hunkake·wa·ya : to have for an ancestor or relative - Bl Pb.35

hun·ka·lo·wan·pi \huŋ-k̇á-lo-waŋ-pi\ *n* : a rite or ceremony of the Dakotas, the Making of Relatives - BR.101

hun·ka·ta·can \huŋ-ká-ta-caŋ\ *n* : the pipe rack, consisting of two upright sticks, each having a crotch at the top and another lying over them; over against this rack the pipe rested

hun·ka·ta·can·nun·pa \hun-ká-ta-caŋ-nuŋ-pa\ *n* : a wand used in the *hunkalowanpi* and not a real pipe — **hun·ka·ta·can·nunp ti·o·wa·pi** \huŋ-k̇á-ta-caŋ-nuŋp tì-o-wa-pi\ *n* : a tipi with four pictures on the *hunkatacannunpa* wand painted on the surface outside - Note: the wand is otherwise called *canunp'ḣaka*

hun·ka·ta·wa·gmu·ha \huŋ-ká-ta-wa-gmu-ha\ *n* : a certain kind of rattle used in the *hunkalowanpi,* the Making Relatives ceremony

hun·ka·ya \huŋ-ká-ya\ *va* hunka·wa·ya : to consider and honor as a *hunká* a relative — **hunkaya·pi** *n* : one who is called *hunká* related

hun·ke·šni \húŋ-ke-šni\ *adj* : slow, not fast in walking or working; sickly < *Mahunkešni* I am sluggish > — *vn* wa·hunkešni : to be slow, sickly and lean, unable to do anything — **hunkešni·ya** *va* húnkešni·wa·ya : to render powerless

hun·kpa \húŋ-kpa\ *n* : the entrance to a camp when made in a circle or hollow square, with the entrance being made toward the west always < *~ kahya tipi* houses arranged as a *hunkpa,* with a space opening to the west >

Hun·kpa·pa *or* **Hunkpapa·ya** \Húŋ-kṗa-pa\ *np* : a clan or division of the Teton Lakota

Hun·kpa·ti *or* **Hunkpati·la** \Húŋ-kpa-ṫi\ *np* : the Lower Yanktonais, a clan of the Yanktonais Nakota

hun·ku \húŋ-ku\ *n* : his or her mother — **hunku·ya** \húŋ-k̇u-ya\ *va* húnku·wa·ya : to call mother, to have for a mother

hun·pe \húŋ-pe\ *n* : the stick used in digging wild turnips

hun·pe o·ki·ja·ta \húŋ-pe o-k̇i-ja-ṫa\ *n* : a stick with a crotch in one end and used for bracing tent-poles inside; two of them are used to support a horizontal bar on which meat is hung to dry and are called *saiglákinyan*

hun·ska \huŋ-ská\ *n* : leggings — **hunska·ya** *va* hunska·wa·ya : to have for leggings, to make leggings of

\a\ father \e\ they \i\ machine \o\ smoke \u\ lunar \an, aŋ\ blanc Fr. \in, iŋ\ ink \on, oŋ, un, uŋ\ soon, confier Fr. \c\ chair \ġ\ machen Ger. \j\ fusion \clusters: bl, gn, kp, hšl, etc...\ b[e]lo ... said with a slight vowel **See more in the Introduction, Guide to Pronunciation**

hun·ski·ca·ȟe \hun·skí-ca-ȟe\ *n* : garters – R Bl

hun·še \huŋ-šé\ *adv* : surely, there is no doubt about it I feel now, undoubtedly, most evidently – D.227,23,-56,120 B.H.26.22, 181.18, 101.1

hun·tka \húŋ-tka\ *n* : the cormorant, a large waterfowl, the double-crested cormorant – Note: *kangi iyececa* it is like a crow; *hena lila wakanpi* they are very remarkable; *mni mahel witka yuhapi* They lay their eggs in the water. Moreover, if an arrow hits them, they dive and return without it and so repeat their calls as if nothing ever happened. ~ *s'e icewin nunblala wicayuha* Cormorant-like she magnificently gives birth to only two, as is said of people who have only two children – Bl

hun·ya·kon \huŋ-yá-ǩoŋ\ *n* : stockings < ~ *iyáskabya, iyaskab·wa·ye, iyoskab·un·yan·pi, i.e.* to darn his, I darn my, we darn our stockings >

hu·o·ka·hmi \hu-ó-ka-ȟmi\ *n* : the hollow behind the knee

hu-o-ki·he \hu-ó-ǩi-he\ *n* : a joint < *Pehan s'e ~ miskosko* Like the crane, my joints are lumpy, as said when a man's joints are thick while his limbs are rather thin. ~ *nito* Your joints (knees) are green, *i.e.* are still limber, hence, You are still young > – Bl

hu·o·ki·he han·ska·ska \hu-ó-ǩi-he haŋ-skà-ska\ *n* : the narrow-leaved umbrella wort. Allinia linearis. The four-o'clock family – Note: a tea made with the roots is used when there is difficulty in urinating Bl # 215

hu·pa \hu-ṗá\ *n* : one of the poles used for a horse travois, tent-poles tied together to pack on; a travois < ~ *wanjila* a pony drag, ~ *wanjikšila* a one person drag > – Cf *šun'ónk'unpa* the dog travois D.229 note 4 R Bl BS

hu·pa·glu·za \hu-ṗá-glu-za\ *v* : to raise one's pipe while praying, as done by the Dakotas saying: ~ yo Smoke! – Note: *hupá* seems to be the root of *ihúpa* a stem or handle, in this case the pipe's stem, and *gluza* to hold one's own RF Bl

hu·pa·he·yun·pi \hu-ṗá-he-yuŋ-ṗi\ *n* : a travois, tent-poles tied together to pack on – *Syn* TUŠÚHEYUNPI

hu·pa·ki·yu·za \hu-ṗá-ǩi-yu-za\ *v* hupa·wa·kiyuza : to lift a pipe towards heaven while praying, as the Dakotas do – RF

hu·pa·wa·he·yun \hu-ṗá-wa-he-yuŋ\ *v* : to pack on a travois

hu·pa·wa·he·yun k'in·pi *or* **hupaheun k'inpi** \hu-ṗá-wa-he-yuŋ k'ìŋ-pi\ *n* : the original vehicle used by various tribes when there were no wagons; a travois, a French word for transport, having on it frequently an *initiyuktan*, a booth on a travois to transport a baby, mounted upon a *šunktacangleška*, a special travois for carrying children – Cf wahéyun HH

hu·pa·wan·ji·la \hu-ṗá-waŋ-ji-la\ *n* : a pony drag – Cf hupáwaheyun, wahéyun

hu·pa·za \hú-ṗa-za\ *adv* [fr *hu* legs + *ṗazá* to stick up bushes] : with the knees bent up and feet drawn to the body <~ *makagle hpaya* to lie flat on the back on the ground with the feet drawn towards the body, knees bent and sticking up, ~ *makagle yanka* to sit squatting on the ground, – Note: the idea behind " ~ *makagle inajin*" seems to be that the bent knees turned up ward look like sticks set up, standing, not expecting anyone in a deadly rest. > Perhaps the syllable *pa* is short for *pahá* hill. *Pazá* is a *va* to stick up bushes, as the Dakotas once did to sleep under when on a journey. But *pazá* also is a *n* meaning a holy name for wood; thus *canpáza najin* and ~ *makagle inajin,* both meaning to pray – Bl RF

hu·pa·za·gle \hú-ṗa-za-gle\ *v* húpaza·wa·gle : to sit with the legs bent up — **hupazagle·ya** *adv* : on the back with the knees sticking up < ~ *yunka* to lie in such a way >

hupe·pe \hu-ṗé-ṗe\ *n* : the hairy stickweed, lappsula redowskii occidentalis; also the sensitive briar, shrankia unicinata, the wild pulse family – Bl # 60, 270

hu·pe·sto·la *and* **hupesto·stola** *or* **pestostola** \hu-ṗé-sto-la\ \ṗe-stó-sto-la\ *n* : the yucca plant, the bayonet grass, bear grass, Spanish bayonet, soap weed, yucca glauca, of the lily family. – Note: the roots are used for a tea, and when mixed with the roots of the *unkcela blaska*, the flat cactus, mothers are helped when they cannot bring forth a child. But there is danger that this root also makes the *hokšiyuhapi šni pejuta*, a medicine for aborting a child, since it seems to cut off the foetus, as has been observed by some and not by others. Pulverized, the roots of the *hupestostola* can be mixed with tepid water and given to people who have a belly-ache. The root is also used for the making of soap. It also assumes a *lila wakan*, a very mysterious, use, *e.g.* in the catching of a wild horse. A person would burn the root and let its fumes reach the animal and then they would catch and halter it easily. A tea made of the roots is used also as a vermin killer by soaking the hair with it; and it also makes the hair grow. The stomach remedy was effective on October 28, 1917 – BD BT WE Bl # 141

hu·pe·yo·han \hu-ṗé-yo-haŋ\ *n* : an outer seam – Cf hupéyozan

hu·pe·yo·zan *or* **hupeyo·han** \hu-ṗé-yo-zaŋ\ *n* : the outer seam *e.g.* on a legging < *hunska* ~ an outer seam on a legging>

hu·pu can·sa·ka·la \hu-pú caŋ-sà-ka-la\ *n* : the bank swallow, a small but very swift bird living in holes on banks of streams – Bl

hu·pu wan·bli·la \hu-pú waŋ-blí-la\ *n* : the swallow-tailed kite

hu·san·gmi \hu-sáŋ-gmi\ *adj* : very lean — **husangmi-yela** *adj* : very thin < ~ *amaye lo* I am getting thin, poor > – *Syn* WAHPÁNICA Bl

hu·san·ni \hu-sáŋ-ni\ *n* : one of a pair, an odd one, as one leg – Cf sanní

hu·sli \hu-slí\ *n* : the lower part of the leg just above the ankle; the ankle < *Tahusliyeyapi s'e unkupelo* We came back as if we were horses gallopping with the clatter of hooves> – EB

hu·stag \hú-ṡtag\ *v contrac of* hustáka : to be faint — **husta·gya** *va* husta·gwa·ya : to enfeeble

hu·sta·ka \hú-ṡta-ǩa\ *vn* hú·ma·staka : to be faint, weak, weary, feeble in the legs

hu·šte \hu-šté\ *adj* hu·má·šte : lame — **hušte·kel** \hu-šté-ǩel\ *adv* : lamely < ~ *mani* to walk with a limp > — **hušte·šteyakel** *adv* : limping < ~ *mani* to walk with a stagger > — **hušte·ya** *va* hušte·wa·ya : to make lame — *adv* : limpingly — **hušteya·kel** \hu-šté-ya-ǩel *adv* : lamely

hu·tab \hú-ṫab\ *adv contrac of* hutapa : downstream, below – Note: *hútapa* seems not to be used, but only compounds of *hútab* — **huta·bkiya** \hú-ṫa-bki-ya\ *adv* : downstream, towards — **huta·bya** *and* **huta-bya·kel** \hú-ṫa-bya-ǩel \ *adv* : down-stream as opposed to *inkpátakiya* towards the stream head – R Bl

hu·ta·na·cu·te *or* **hutínacute** \hú-ta-na-cu-ṫe\ *n* : a rib of an ox or cow cut short, polished smooth, like a puck, and ornamented, then thrown (in a game) on the ice or

snow — *vn* : to play with the ~ , the puck, on ice - Bl
hu·ta·na·ku·te \hu-ṫá-na-ḱu-ṫe\ *vn* : to play with the *hútanacute*, the puck - R
hu·ta·san·pa·ta \hu-ṫá-saŋ-pa-ṫa\ *adv* : on the other side of a creek or lake - Cf hutátahenatanhan *Syn* MINI KIN KOÁKATAN *or* AKÁSANPATAHAN FB
hu·ta·ta \hu-ṫá-ṫa\ *adv* : at the water by the shore
hu·ta·ta·he·na·tan·han \hu-ṫá-ta-he-na-ṫaŋ-haŋ\ *adv* : on this side of a creek or lake - Cf hutásanpata *Syn* MINI KIN ITAHENA *or* ÓHUTATAHENATANHAN
hu·ta·wab \hú-ṫa-wab\ *adv* : further down *e.g.* a creek — **hutawa·bki·ya** \hú-ṫa-wa-bki-ya\ *adv* : in the downstream direction - KE
hu·ta·wa·pa \hú-ṫa-wa-pa\ *adv* : at the water by the shore
hu·te \hú-ṫe\ *n* : the root of a tree or plant, < *canhute* a stump with sprouts, the bottom of a tree, *Na wanna el ~ kin eungnakapi (canwakan)* And now we placed the root end of (the holy tree) in its place. > — *adj* : worn dull, as an axe
hu·te·i·yu·hpa \hu-ṫé-i-yu-ȟpa\ *adv* or *pron* : all, everything < *Eceš, ~ cic'u yacin yelo* You certainly do not want me to give you everything. > - Bl B.H.157.11
hu·te·la \hú-ṫe-la\ *n* : a pistol
hu·ti·pa·ksa \hu-ṫí-pa-ksa\ *va* : to break off - B.H.62.14
hu·ti·pa·k'o·ga *or* **hutipa·k'oh** \hu-ṫí-ṗa-k'o-ġa\ \hu-ṫí-ṗa-k'oȟ\ *v* and *v contrac* : to scoop up taking everything along, leaving nothing — **hutipak'o·yela** *adv* : all, everything, nothing excluded < *Hena ~ omáyakilakin kte* You should tell me absolutely all of this > - B.H.39.3 KE HC BS
hu·ti·pa·špu \hu-ṫí-ṗa-špu\ *v* : to drive away or back *e.g.* an enemy in battle; to push away, against, to cut and topple over < ~ *iyeya* to push and topple suddenly > - Bl KE
hu·ti·ya·gle·ya \hu-ṫí-ya-gle-ya\ *adv* : from top to bottom < ~ *kah'u; ~ šeca* He skinned it from top to bottom; it was rotten. > - Bl
hu·tkan \hu-tkáŋ\ *n* : a root, *fig* a blood relationship < *can ~* a tree's root >
hu·to·ka·pa·tan \hu-ṫó-ḱa-pa-ṫaŋ\ *n* : the forelegs, as of animals. - Note: in a *fig* sense the word means the front wheels of a vehicle; *hugmiyanyan* is the more proper word
hu·to·pa \hu-ṫó-ṗa\ *adj* : with or having four legs <*Wamakaškan ~ ca cic'upelo* I give you creatures that are four-legged > — *n* : a four-legged - Cf húnunpa
hu·wa·ki·š'a·ka \hu-wá-ki-š'a-ka\ *adj* : enduring, not easily tired, having stamina — **huwakiš'a·ke** \hu-wá-ki-š'a-ke\ *vn* : to be good on one's legs, to have strong legs < *Šunȟala s'e ~* He is agile on his feet like a young dog. >
hu·wa·ksa \hu-wá-ksa\ *v* : to amputate, perform an amputation
hu·wa·k'i·pe \hu-wá-k'i-ṗe\ *n* : the smaller bones in the lower leg and forearm: *cankpe ~* those in the lower leg from the *cankpe* knee to the ankle, *i.e.* the fibula, *išpa ~* those in the forearm from the *išpa* elbow to the wrist
hu·wi·ca·yu·ti·pa \hu-wí-ca-yu-ṫi-pa\ *n* : a little piece of meat that is found between the muscles below the knees of a buffalo - HH
hu·wo·ga \hú-wo-ġa\ *adj* : having the knees bent while holding the legs in the air from a sitting position < ~ *yanka* to sit with legs raised > - Bl
[1]**hu·ya** *or* **hu·ye** *or* **ho·i·ye** \hu-yá\ \hu-yé\ \ho-i-yé\ *interj of invitation* [fr *hiyú* come + *ye* please] : Come along < ~ , *hoapeša wan mini ceteta ape kahihiya nunke, le uciciye* Come now you, redfin, lie waiting paddling at the bottom of the water, I urge you now to come, so a person would say when throwing out a line to catch fish: *Huyá, He, misun, huya. Misun, Hey* Hey, say, my little brother, come here my little brother >
[2]**hu·ya** \hu-yá\ *v* : to have for a staff or leg < *canhuyapi* crutches > — **huyakel** \hu-yá-kel\ *adv* : using as a leg, as a person using a horse to ride instead of walking < *Le ~ omani yo* Travel using this as a leg > — **huya·ta** \hu-yá-ṫa\ *adv* : as the leg
hu·yu·kša \hú-yu-kša\ *adv* : drawing towards one's body with one's feet, as one does with his feet when in pain < ~ *yanka* or *manke* He *or* I sat cringing > - RF FR
hu·yu·ti·pa \hu-yú-ṫi-ṗa\ *v* : to have cramps in the calf of the leg < *Hehé, humáyutipe lo* Oh! my leg! My calf is cramped > - Bl
hu·za·ze·ca \hu-zá-ze-ca\ *n* : the spokes of a wheel - Bl
hwe *or* **hu·we** \hwe\, \hu-wé\ *adv of interrog, used by women as* hwo *is used by men to indicate a question*
hwo \hwo\ *adv of interrog, used by men*
Ȟ \the guttural *h*\ *abbrev of* ȟce : very < *ḱéyeȟ* for *kéyehce* he said that > - Note: *hca, hce, hci* as they relate to touching on the superlative: *hca* and *hce*, positive; *hci*, negative Cf hca, hce, hci
ȟa \ȟa\ *va* : to bury *e.g.* a dead person's body
ȟab \ȟáb\ *adj contrac of* ȟaṗá : stormy, inclement; raucous, harsh < ~ *hingla* to become stormy, ~ *iyaya* to get started *e.g.* something sacred >
ȟab·ȟa·bya \ȟab-ȟá-bya\ *adv red of* ȟabyá *of* ȟápa : with a rustling noise < ~ *iyaya* to go on with a rustling, *i.e.* to walk over *e.g.* dry leaves. *Mini k'on ~ púzelo* That pond is entirely dry > - Note: the word denotes the effect (the noise, or dryness) and the cause (the walking on dry leaves, or being entirely dry)
ȟab·ȟa·pa \ȟab-ȟá-pa\ *v red of* ȟápa : to make rustle
ȟab·ȟa·pe·la \ȟab-ȟá-ṗe-la\ *n* : a silk cloth of any kind, so called probably suggested by the rustling noise in handling cloth
ȟa·bya \ȟa-byá\ *va* ȟa·bwá·ya : to frighten or scare away anything, *e.g.* wild animals
Ȟa·ȟa·ton·wan \Ȟa-ȟá-ṫoŋ-waŋ\ *np* : the Chippewa or Ojibwa tribe, a name given by the Dakotas, as those who make their villages at the falls. It is believed the name came from Sault Ste. Marie, and not from the falls of the Mississippi
ȟa·ȟa·ya *or* **h'a·h'a·ya** \ȟa-ȟá-ya\ *v* : to patter on, as sleet on a tent < *Tipi kin iwankab taku hmun s'elececa na tipi kin ~ taku akalala hiyu na lila hececa* Up above the house there was something like a murmur, and there pattered on the house something coming out spilling, *i.e.* taking them by surprise, and it was really like that > - KE
[1]**ȟa·ka** \ȟá-ḱa\ *adj* : branching, having many prongs, as some deer horns < *heȟáḱa* elk >
[2]**ȟa·ka** \ȟa-ḱá\ *n* 1 : a shooting instrument in a game — *adj* 2 : ruffled, not smooth, made rough, as a feather
ȟa·ka·ku·te \ȟa-ḱá-ḱu-ṫe\ *v* : to play or shoot the *ȟaḱá*
ȟa·ka·ya \ȟa-ḱá-ya\ *adv* : branched < ~ *škan* to do var-

\a\ father \e\ they \i\ machine \o\ smoke \u\ lunar \an, aŋ\ blanc Fr. \in, iŋ\ ink \on, oŋ, un, uŋ\ soon, confier Fr. \c\ chair \ġ\ machen Ger. \j\ fusion \clusters: bl, gn, kp, hšl, etc...\ b[e]lo ... said with a slight vowel
See more in the Introduction, Guide to Pronunciation

ious things at the same time > - BE
ȟan \ȟaŋ\ *n* : a scab < ~ *hinhpaya* The scab has fallen off >
ȟan'·a·gna·ke·la s'e \ȟaŋ-á-gna-ke-la s'e\ *adv* : carefully and softly, as when touching a soft sore spot; gently < ~ *kúwa* to handle *e.g.* people carefully > - Bl
ȟan'·a·pa·ha \ȟaŋ-á-ṗa-ha\ *vn* ȟan'á·ma·paha : to have a thick scab on a wound - Bl
ȟan·ȟan \ȟaŋ-ȟáŋ\ *adj red* : scabby — **ȟanȟan·pi** *n* : sores — **ȟanȟan·yan** *va* : to cause to be scabby — *adv* : like a scab < ~ *hpaya* It lay scab-like > - R B.H.43.22, 227.6
ȟan'·i·t'a \ȟaŋ-í-t'a\ *v* ȟan'i·ma·t'a : to be covered with a rash, eruptions - Bl
ȟan'·i·ya·gna·ka s'e \ȟaŋ-í-ya-gna-ka s'e\ *adv* : cautiously < ~ *okuwa* to handle one very carefully > - WE WHL
ȟan·te \ȟaŋ-ṫé\ *n* : the cedar tree, the western cedar juniperus scopulorum. - Note: HC found that when its leaves are powdered and boiled make a fluid that, while absolutely harmless to man, will drive away potato bugs wherever it is poured. He saved his potato crop by using this broth on September 28, 1919
~ *can- hlogan* the common yarrow, milfoil, achillia millefolium of the composite family,
~ *iyececa* the low milkweed,
~ *pepe iyececa* the Illinois mimose, the curly-podded legume, acuan illinoensis, the pulse family,
ȟanteša or *ȟantešala* the red cedar >
- Cf pejí swula cik'ala # 192, 89, 244 Bl
ȟan·tkan·hu \ȟaŋ-tkáŋ-hu\ *n* : the upper arm bone
ȟan·tkan·hu·la \ȟaŋ-tkáŋ-hu-la\ *n* : one who means to be a leader everywhere — **ȟantkan·hunzi** *n* : a military rank arm stripe — **ȟantkan·oyuze** *or* **ȟan·tkunza** \ȟaŋ-tkúŋ-za *n* : an ornament arm band, an armlet, bands for holding up the shirt-sleeves - Bl WHL
¹ȟa·pa \ȟá-pa\ *vn* : to make a rustling noise, as in leaves or bushes, to rustle
²ȟa·pa \ȟa-ṗá\ *adj* : rough, as the wind or the voice < *hoȟáṗa* a throaty voice >
¹hca *or* **hcahca** \ȟca-ȟcá\ *adv* or *adv suff* or *adv red each post-positive* : very < *Le miye hca ca tokša oyate el unki kte, eya keya. Lena hecetu hca slolwaya. Wicaša wan šicahca* He stated saying: Since this is my very self we shall soon get to the tribe. I know these people are O.K. There is a man who is very bad. *Le miye ~ slolwaya na el owapa* I myself knew about this and joined in. >
²hca \ȟca\ *vn* : to blossom, bloom <~ *aya* to bloom, to begin blooming > — *n* : a flower blossom - *See* wahcá
hca·ka *or* **hca·ka·sa** \ȟcá-ka\ \ȟca-ká-sa\ *adv suff* : very < *tólahcaka* very blue, *waštehcaka* very good, *Wazihcaka* the beautiful Black Hills spruce, *Maštuštelahcake lo* I am very tired out. *Tokša he na ecamon kte kin le taku hcakasa eyin* This is very much what he said I should do soon. > - MS.95
hca·ya \ȟcá-ya\ *vn* : to blossom — *adv* : blossoming
hce \ȟce\ *adv* or *adv suff post-positive* : very < *Yunkan namah'onpi kin icantemawašte hce. Na macaje hce Cik'ala Wicakte emakiyapi* When they listened to me I was for that reason very glad. And I was given my name Little Killer >
hce·hanl \ȟce-háŋl\ *adv* : just then < ~ *šunkmanitu wan ... toki hiyaye* Just then a wolf came and went somewhere. > — **hcehanl ... na** *adv correl* : no sooner ... when < *Hcehanl winyan wanna ihunni na hecenaš tokápa kin pakáksa* No sooner now did the woman arrive when finally he struck off her head. > - Note: *Hepe hce, ehanl hi* No sooner did I say than he arrived - D.22
¹hci \ȟci\ *adv suff post-positive* : very < *hínhannahci* early in the morning, *ecanahci* very soon, *išnalahci* much alone, *ciscilahci* quite small >
²hci \ȟci\ *n* : a gap, as in the edge of an axe, a gash or cut scar — **hcihci** \ȟci-ȟcí\ *adj red* : gapped, notched, nicked, cut < *upi* ~ the fringed border of a garment, *Pute Hci, kuwi ye* Rabbit Lips, come here please, *Pute hcihcila* His lips are much cut up > — **hcihci·ya** *adv* : in a way torn < *Tatanka s'e nakpa ~ yankin na* Take it, like a buffalo bull's ears his are ragged, as they say of a man whose ear lobes are pretty well torn, gapped. *Wahinheya s'e loȟé* Like a gopher's are his jowls. > - Bl D.71, 113
hcin \ȟciŋ\ *suff of* hca : very < *Ktepi kte* ~ He will indeed be killed > - Note: the word is used with the *fut* tense
hci·wa·han \ȟci-wá-haŋ\ *part* : broken out in gaps, gapped
hco *or* **hco·ka** \ȟco\ \ȟcó-ka\ *adj* : slovenly, slatternly - Cf nahcohco — **hco·ya** *or* **hcoya·kel** \ȟcó-ya\, \ȟcó-ya-kel\ *adv* : slovenly, in a slovenly manner
ȟe \ȟe\ *n* : a high hill or ridge of hills, a mountain
ȟe·a·i \ȟe-á-i\ *va* : to have brought somewhere for burial
ȟe·blo *or* **ȟeblo·ka** \ȟé-blo\, \ȟé-blo-ka\ *n* : a hill top, a ridge
ȟe·he·pi·ya \ȟe-hé-ṗi-ya\ *adv* : part way up the hill
ȟe·hu·kul \ȟe-hú-kul\ *n* : the bottom or foot of a hill
ȟe·in·kpa \ȟe-íŋ-kṗa\ *n* : the brink or brow of a hill, the end of a hill
ȟe·i·pa \ȟe-í-pa\ *n* : the brow of a hill, *esp* the head or commencement of the cotes des prairies
ȟe·kpan·kpan·la \ȟe-kpáŋ-kpaŋ-la\ *n* : hilly land, *i.e.* all low hills - *Syn* PAHÁ KUTKÚCIYELA Bl
ȟe·ku \ȟe-kú\ *n* : the foot of a hill back from a river < ~ *unyanpi* We go at the foot of the hill. >
ȟel \ȟel\ *adv* [fr *ȟe* hill + *el* at] : ashore, when the water retreats <*Sinkpe ȟel amákiṗa hce* Muskrats met me ashore > - BT
ȟe·ma·ko·skanl *or* **ȟemakoskan·tu** \ȟe-má-ko-skaŋl\ \ȟe-má-ko-skaŋ-ṫu\ *adv* : in a desert place, an uninhabited place, a wilderness < ~ *etan oyate wan iglaka aya. ~ kin he itahena na Cahli Wakpa oinkpa kin ogna unkiyayapi. ~ yapi* In a wilderness the tribe began to break camp. We went on on this side of the wilderness and in the direction of the head of Coal Creek. > B.H.49.22
ȟe·ma·ko·ši·kši·ca \ȟe-má-ko-ši-kši-ca\ *n* : badlands - Bl
ȟe·ma·ni \ȟe-má-ni\ *v* : to walk on dry land
ȟe·ma·ya·can \ȟé-ma-ya-caŋ\ *n* : a wooded hill
ȟe·na·gi \ȟe-ná-ġi\ *n* : the shadow of a hill - Note: *Pahá ohanzizi yukelo* The shadow of a hill actually exists - Bl
ȟe·na·ke *or* **ȟenaptan** \ȟe-ná-ke\ *n* : a declivity, a slope - P
ȟe·o·hla·te \ȟe-ó-ȟla-ṫe\ *n* : the foot or bottom of a big hill
ȟe·o·pu·ze \ȟe-ó-ṗu-ze\ *n* - *See* ȟopúza R
ȟe·o·ški \ȟe-ó-ški\ *n* : rough lands — *adj* : hilly, rugged, uneven, as country cut with many canyons — **ȟeoški·ški** *adj red* : hilly - P R Bl B.H.89.1
ȟe·o·ta·he·na \ȟe-ó-ta-he-na\ *adv* : where one lives, in a desert place - R
Ȟe·ška \Ȟe-šká\ *np* : the Big Horn Mountains; the Rocky Mountains - D.225

ȟe·ta \ȟé-ta\ *adv* : on, to, or in the mountains
ȟe·ta·ki·ya \ȟé-ṫa-ǩi-ya\ *adv* : towards the hills - B.H. 154.6
ȟe·tko·za \ȟe-tkó-za\ *v* : to give things away often, as though one were rich, when in reality one is poor
ȟe·un·na·ptan \ȟe-úŋ-na-ṗtaŋ\ *n* : a hillside
Ḣe·wa·kto·kta \Ḣe-wá-kto-kṫa\ *np* : Arickaree Indian persons
ȟe·yab \ȟe-yáb\ *adv contrac of* ȟeyápa : away, elsewhere < ~ *iya yo* Go, or Get away, ~ *econ* He did his thing elsewhere, ~ *ihpeic'iya* to shy, as a horse, *Na inyan kin nakun iyuha* ~ *yanka* And the rock, as well as everything else were elsewhere > - D.204, 221
ȟe·ya·pa \ȟe-yá-pa\ *adv* : away from, as standing away from a hot stove *etc* < ~ *inajin.* ~ *yanka yo* Stand away. Sit elsewhere. > — *vn* ȟeya·wa·pa : to go away a little distance — **ȟeyapa·ya** *adv* : away a little distance
ȟe·ya·ta \ȟe-yá-ṫa\ *adv* : on or to the ridge, bluff, plateau *etc* , as in contrast with lower places, *esp* of the river bottoms *etc* - Cf ȟéta
ȟe·ya·tan·han \ȟe-yá-ṫaŋ-haŋ\ *adv* : on top of a hill < *Na wanna unkiyayapi na miš* ~ *waun* We now went on while I was on top of a hill. >
ȟe·yun·ka \ȟe-yúŋ-ka\ *n* : frost, hoarfrost - Cf aȟéyunka
hla \ȟla\ *vn* : to rattle < *sintehla* a rattle snake >
hla·gan \ȟla-ġáŋ\ *adj* : loose
hla·han \ȟla-háŋ\ *adv* : loosely, torn dangling
hla·hla \ȟla-ȟlá\ *n* **1** : a rattle **2** : a herald, crier < ~ *wanji igni po* Go look for a crier! > — *vn* wa·hláhla : to rattle
hla·hla hun·ca·je \ȟlá-ȟla hùŋ-ca-je\ *n* : garters with bells attached to them
hla·hla i·yo·gna·ka \ȟlá-ȟla i-yò-gna-ka\ *n* : the marsh wren, a little bird with a loud voice < ~ *s'e* It is like a marsh wren > - W
hla·hla tan·ka \ȟlá-ȟla ṫàŋ-ka\ *n* : bells
hla·hla·ya \ȟla-ȟlá-ya\ *adv* : rattling, loosely
hla·hla·yel \ȟla-ȟlá-yel\ *adv* : not securely — **hlahla·yela** *adv* : loosely, insecurely
hla·hya \ȟla-ȟyá\ *adv* : to a distance, removing — **hlahyeca** *vn* : to remove or go off to a distance — **hlahye·šni** *adv* : without leaving out or forgetting even one single thing, every single thing included - Bl
hla·in·šni \ȟla-íŋ-šni\ *adj* : capable, skillful < *Mahlainšni* I am skillful. *Wicaša* ~ *heca* Man is capable. > - BD
hla·ye·la \ȟla-yé-la\ *adv* : ringing, tinkling, as little bells do while a person is walking - *Syn* SNA S'E
hle·te \ȟle-té\ *n* ma·hlete : a very careless, irresponsible fellow who cares for nothing nor for anybody, and thus ruins everything - Wo
hli \ȟli\ *vn* ma·hlí : to break out in sores, to be sore, raw — *n* : a running sore, a raw place
hli·hli \ȟli-ȟlí\ *adj red* **1** : broken out in sores **2** : miring in mud — **hlihli·la** *adj* : miry, muddy < *Maka* ~ *on iic'iyun* He smeared himself with muddy earth. >
hlo \ȟlo\ *vn* wa·hlo : to growl, as a dog
hlo·ge·ca \ȟlo-ġé-ca\ *adj* : poor, thin, as a sick man; hollow, as a tree < ~ *un* He is sickly. ~ *amáye lo* I became thin > - R Bl
hlo·han \ȟlo-háŋ\ *adj* : slovenly, not well put on, as clothes — **hlohan·han** *adj red* : untidy, slovenly dressed or put on < *Taku ecanon kin, šunkpala wanji* ~ *kin he iyeniceca yelo* What you did, a slovenly dressed puppy, is like you, as is said when a man takes it too easy while working > — **hlohe·ca** \ȟlo-ḣé-ca\ *adj* : slovenly — **hlohe·ya** *adv* : in a slovenly manner - Bl
hlo·hlo \ȟlo-ȟló\ *v red of* hlo : to growl
hlo·hlo·ka \ȟlo-ȟló-ǩa\ *adj* : full of holes — **hlohlo·ka·han** *part* : perforated with holes — **hlohloka i·ca·ge** \ȟlo-ȟló-ǩa i-cà-ġe\ *n* : a crocket hoop
hlo·ka \ȟló-ǩa\ *adj* : hollow — *n* : a hollow — *part* : hollowed — **hloke·ce** \ȟló-ke-ce\ *n* : a hollow object
hlo·ki·ya \ȟlo-ǩí-ya\ *va* hlo·wá·kiya : to make growl — **hlo·ya** \ȟlo-yá\ *va* : to make growl — *adv* : growling
hlu·te \ȟlú-ṫe\ *adj* : long-necked, as is said of man and beast — **hlute s'e** *adv perhaps* : of a sort long-necked
hmin \ȟmiŋ\ *adj* : crooked, misshapen < *sihá* ~ a crooked foot > — **hmin·hmin** \ȟmiŋ-ȟmíŋ\ *adj red* : misshapen < *Canhpan s'e si* ~ *kaćá* She is like that, misshapen like the mud hen's feet, *i.e.* feet turned outward > — **hminhmin·yan** *adv red* : crookedly — **hmin·yan** *adv* : in a crooked manner, as in walking, *i.e.* sideways, fowl, sliced < ~ *škan* moving sideways, *Tapa* ~ *u* A ball came swerving > - Bl
hmun \ȟmuŋ\ *vn* : to buzz, hum, as the stones of a mill, the flapping of a bird's wings, a bullet ricocheting whistles < ~ *hingla* to break into a buzzing noise >
hmun·ga \ȟmúŋ-ġa\ *va* wa·hmunga : to cause sickness, to cause kindly enchantment, to bewitch < *kicihmungapi* to bewitch each other, *Tuwa aitohewaya can wahmunge lo* I fix my gaze on one as I bewitch him. > - B.H.70.6 D.103
hmun·hmun \ȟmuŋ-ȟmúŋ\ *v red of* hmun : to buzz
hmun·s'e *or* **hmun·s'e·kse** *or* **hmun·sececa** \ȟmúŋ-s'e\ *adv* : in a buzzing way, as people speaking or praying together, altogether in a chorus < ~ *cekiyapi, lowanpi* praying in unison, singing in chorus, *Na yamni t'api k'on hena titakuye kin hmuns'ekse wicaceye* Their close relatives wept wailing together over the three who had died. > — *n* : noise
hmun·ya \ȟmuŋ-yá\ *va* hmun·wa·ya : to cause to hum, make buzz — **hmun·yan** *or* **hmun·yĕla** *or* **hmun·yela** \ȟmuŋ-yáŋ\ \ȟmuŋ-yĕ'-la\ \ȟmuŋ-yé-la\ *adv* : whizzing or buzzing < *Mini kin* ~ *he lo* The waters stood crashing down. *Mini kin* ~ *hiyáye* The waters went rippling by > - Bl
hna \ȟna\ *vn* wa·hná : to snort, grunt, as does a person in anger
hna·han \ȟna-háŋ\ *adj* : slovenly, not tidy, hanging as a horse's lip — **hnahe·ya** *adv* : loosely, slovenly - R Bl
hna·hna \ȟná-ȟna\ *v red* wa·hnáhna [fr *hna* to grunt] : to grunt, to give forth the sound of a bear < *Lila* ~ *un* It is snorting very much, *i.e. groaning (haun* a painful groan), as one who is dying. > - D.219
hni·yan \ȟní-yaŋ\ *vn* : to be troubled, to have a stomachache — **hniyan·yan** \ȟni-yáŋ-yaŋ\ *adj red* ma·hníyanyan : afraid, quaking for fear < *Pute* ~ His lips quivered, as from cold *etc* . *Lehanl minagi kin mahniyanyan* My spirit is now shaken. > — **hni·yeye s'e** \ȟníyeye s'e\ *adv* : in haste, affrightedly - B.H.244.2
ȟo·ka \ȟo-ká\ *n* : the badger
ȟol·ȟo·ta \ȟol-ȟó-ṫa\ *adv red of* ȟota : gray
ȟol·wan·ca \ȟol-wáŋ-ca\ *adj* : all in gray < ~ *yelo* All

\a\ father \e\ they \i\ machine \o\ smoke \u\ lunar \an, aŋ\ blanc Fr. \in, iŋ\ ink \on, oŋ, un, uŋ\ soon, confier Fr. \c\ chair \ġ\ machen Ger. \j\ fusion \clusters: bl, gn, kp, hšl, etc...\ b[e]lo ... said with a slight vowel
See more in the Introduction, Guide to Pronunciation

are in gray, *i.e.* said when all are dressed in gray suits. Thus also: *Ȟolyápi s'e ahi* All came dressed in gray. > – Bl

ȟo·lya \ȟo-lyá\ *adv* : grayish, in a gray or mixed manner, as is said of putting paint on the face. < *Mato s'e sicúha ȟolyahci* Bear-like the soles of his shoes are hashed, as said when a man has torn soles. *Ȟolyápi s'e ahi* All came dressed in gray. > – R Bl

ȟo·lye·la \ȟo-lyé–la\ *adj perhaps* : grayish < *Yunkan winyan k'on u kin iwankab ~ han, mahpiya ekta iyagleyahan wanyankapi* Then the woman who had come stood above in a mist; they saw her going to heaven. >

ȟo·pu·ze \ȟo-p̌ú-ze\ *n* [fr *ȟe* hills of a countryside + *opuze* dry shore] : a dry land or wilderness, a desert or badlands so-called – R

ȟo·ta \ȟō'-ta\ *adj* : gray, brown; *fig* used or worn

hpa·han \ȟpa-háŋ\ *part* : thrown down, fallen down of itself

hpa·ka \ȟpá-ka\ *adj* : very slow – BS

hpan \ȟpaŋ\ *adj* : becoming softened, as corn in water — **hpan·kiyan** \ȟpaŋ-ǩí-yaŋ\ *v poss of* hpanyan : to soften one's own < *Ito, cante hpanwakiyin kte lo* Yes, I'll have a softened heart, as a hungry man says. *Máyašleca ca tahuka hpankiye s'e* A coyote hide is like a buffalo hide that has been softened, as is said when one hides some food in some place so as to eat it alone. > — **hpan·yan** \ȟpaŋ-yáŋ\ *va* hpan·wá·yan : to soak , steep in water – Bl

hpa·wa·han \ȟpa-wá-haŋ\ *part* : thrown off, down – R Bl

hpa·ya \ȟpá-ya\ *vn* wa·hpáya : to lie down, recline < *Kul* ~ He lies down. *T'a* ~ He lies dead, or He is dead. *Canku kin kal* ~ The road lies over there. > — **hpaye·la** *adv* : lying down — **hpaye·ya** \ȟpá-ye-ya\ *va* : to cause to lie down, to kill as in battle

hpe·ca·ka \ȟpé-ca-ka\ *adj* ma·hpécaka : faint, exhausted

hpe·la \ȟpé-la\ *adj* : weak < ~ *hingla* to be discouraged, diverted from, to turn suddenly being reminded of something sad, ~ *hingléǩiya* to make one sad suddenly > – Note: the word is not used alone Bl

hpe·yun·ka \ȟpe-yúŋ-ǩa\ *vn* : to stay with the young, to hover over, as a hen does over her brood, to brood over, as is said of a young man when his first child is born – Bl

hpi \ȟpi\ *v* : to hang down — *adj* : hanging down < *iha* ~ with a hanging lower lip, *Wapoštan mícihpi* Mine own hat was hanging down > — **hpi·hpi s'e** \ȟpi-ȟpí s'e\ *adv* : flapping from walking or running fast < ~ *inyanka* to run, hair aflying > — **hpi·ka** \ȟpí-ǩa\ *adj* : shaggy, bushy, as hair – KE

hpo \ȟpo\ *n* : scum, *esp* that which floats on the water of lakes or seas

hpu·hpu \ȟp̌u-ȟp̌ú\ *adj perhaps red of* ȟpu *obsol* : crumbled off — **hpuhpu·ya** *adv red of* hpuyá : crumbling away < *Oyute kin yuogmuza ye, keya s'e oyute kin* ~ Close up the sides, turtle-like your sides are crumbling away, said when a woman's dress is torn near the hip-bone. > — **hpu·wahan** \ȟp̌u-wá-haŋ\ *part* : crumbled off, come apart, as things formerly stuck together — **hpu·ya** \ȟp̌u-yá\ *adv* : crumbling off – Bl

hta·cu·šni \ȟta-cú-šni\ *n* : the cool of the evening

hta·he·pi·ye·la \ȟta-hé-p̌i-ye-la\ *adv* : before night, before retiring at night perhaps – Bl

hta-i-yo-kpa-za \ȟta-í-yo-kpa-za\ *vn* : to grow dark – B.H.54.1

hta·ki·ya·ka *or* **htakiya·kel** \ȟta-ǩí-ya-ǩa\ *adv* : towards evening

hta·le·han \ȟtá-le-haŋ\ *n* : yesterday < ~ *aǩotanhan* the day before yesterday >

hta·ma·ki·yo·kpa·za \ȟta-má-ǩi-yo-kpa-za\ *v* : to grow dusk – *Syn* AWATAN'INŠNI AYELO Bl

hta·ni \ȟta-ní\ *adj* : being poor < ~ *okile* to look for slowly and carefully. *Ablakela ca wicaho ~ ca tokiya eyaš nah'onpi kte* There was a calm, where the faint voice? but then they should hear it > – Note: *ȟtanišni* may more probably be the word, Cf Bl

hta·ni·šni \ȟta-ní-šni\ *adj* : motionless, without moving much < ~ *inyanka* to run with little movement, ~ *najin* to stand motionless > – Cf htaní *Syn* ŠKANŠKANŠNI WE

hta·o·jan·jan \ȟta-ó-jaŋ-jaŋ\ *n* : a dimming

hta·o·sni \ȟta-ó-sni\ *adj* : cold in the evening < ~ *ayelo* It grew cold as night drew on. > – Bl

hta·o·tan'·in·šni \ȟta-ó-taŋ-iŋ-šni\ *n* : dusk <*Wana ~ aye* It now became dusk. > – B.H.208.21

hta·o·ma·ni \ȟta-ó-ma-ni\ *v* : to walk about at night < *Maka wan iye t'in kta yeš ~ yelo* A skunk though it was about to die traveled about at night > – Ed BN

hta·ta \ȟtá-ťa\ *adj* ma·htáta : languid, weak — **htate·ca** \ȟtá-ťe-ca\ *adj* ma·htateca : weak, feeble

hta·ye \ȟtá-ye\ *adv* : in the evening, last evening < *Anpetu wan el ~ ehanl* It was then in the evening one day. >

hta·ye·ta·mna \ȟtá-ye-ťa-mna\ *adv perhaps* : at dusk < *Kangi s'e ~ iyunka* Like a crow he retires for the night at dusk, *i.e.* he goes to bed early. > Bl

hta·ye·tu \ȟtá-ye-ťu\ *n* : the evening

ȟu·ga·han \ȟu-ǧá-haŋ\ *part* : broken in, dented

ȟu·ge·ca \ȟu-ǧé-ca\ *n* : the soft part of bones – Cf ǧuǧeca

ȟu·gna·ga *or perahps* **ǧugnaǧa** \ȟu-gná-ǧa\ *vn* : to burn up, be consumed

ȟu·gna·ȟya *or perhaps* **ǧugnaȟya** \ȟu-gná-ȟya\ *va* ȟu·gna·ȟwa·ya : to cause to burn up, to consume

ȟu·gna·ya *also perhaps* **ǧugnaya** \ȟu-gná-ya\ *va* : to burn down, destroy by fire – P

ȟu·ha \ȟu-há\ *n* : the scraping or shavings of hides taken off in making them thin enough for robes and eaten by the Dakotas – Cf taȟuha

ȟu·hcin·ca·ye·la \ȟu-ȟcíŋ-ca-ye-la\ *adv* : very high, very far away, too high or too far away so as to be seen well; to be shot *etc*, as a bird on top of a house or game passing by < ~ *hiyaye lo* It came and went going far far away. Thus, *Oicušilya yanke* It is a place far away hard to get to. > – Bl

ȟu·ȟu·ga·he s'e \ȟu-ȟú-ǧe-he s'e\ *adv* : with a thundering noise < *Can kin ~ yunkahe. Wakinyan hoton s'e* The tree lay down with a crash. It was like the sound of thunder. > – MG

ȟu·h'cin·ca·ye·la \ȟu-ȟ'cíŋ-ca-ye-la\ *adv* : at a great distance, very high up < ~ *iyaye* to go a great distance, ~ *hiyaye* to go on a great distance further, *Lehanl ~ unkomanipi* Thus far we have traveled a great distance. > – Cf ȟuȟcinca-yela Bl

ȟu·in \ȟu-íŋ\ *vn* : to putrify

ȟun·win \ȟuŋ-wíŋ\ *vn* : to stink, become putrid as does meat – Cf ȟwin

ȟun·win·mna \ȟuŋ-wíŋ-mna\ *adj* : stinking, smelling purtrid <*Mato* ~ A bear smells foul. >

ȟun·win·ya \ȟuŋ-wíŋ-ya\ *va* ȟunwin·wa·ya : to cause to smell badly, make smell putrid

ȟu·pa·ho·ko·za \ȟu-ṗá-ho-ko-za\ *vn* [fr *ȟupahu* a wing + *o euph* + koza to beat or flap] : to flap or move the wings, to flutter

ȟu·pa·hu \ȟu-ṗá-hu\ *n* : the wing of a fowl

ȟu·pa·ki·gla·ke \ȟu-pá-ki-gla-k̇e\ *n* : a bat — **ȟupaki-glake·la** \ȟu-pá-ki-gla-k̇e-la\ *n* : the bird or part of a bird used as a *wotawe* charm

ȟu·pin·yun \ȟu-ṗíŋ-yuŋ\ *adv* : by the arms, without instruments, by main strength — **ȟupinyun·kel** \ȟu-ṗiŋ-yuŋ-k̇el\ *adv* : by main strength, not minding the things that are in the way, as bad weather *etc* < ~ *waun welo* I live by main strength. >

ȟu·pu can·sa·ka·la \ȟu-ṗú caŋ-sà-ka-la\ *n* : the cliff swallow, a little very swift bird living in holes on banks. The bank swallow, it lives not in round holes but in long narrow niches – Note: *ȟupu* may be a *contrac* of *ȟupa-hu* Bl

ȟu·pu wan·bli·la \ȟu-ṗú waŋ-blì-la\ *n* : the snow bunting. It stays summer and winter, has white feathers, but black wing feathers – Note: *ištanica tanka* the snow bird is only *hínskokeca* so large – Bl

ȟu·wa·pa·hpe \ȟu-wá-ṗa-ȟṗe\ *n* : the meat left sticking to a hide

ȟu·ya \ȟu-yá\ *n* : an aged eagle; a common eagle

hwa \ȟwa\ *adj* ma·hwá un·hwá·pi : sleepy, drowsy — **hwa·ka** \ȟwá-k̇a\ *adj* ma·hwáka : sleepy; mild, gentle — **hwa·ya** \ȟwá-ya\ *va* ȟwa·wá·ya : to make sleepy — *adv* : mildly, gently — **hwaye·la** \ȟwá-ye-la\ *adv* : slowly, softly, gently

hwin \ȟwiŋ\ *vn* : to stink, become putrid, as a dead body – *See* ȟunwín

hwin·mna \ȟwíŋ-mna\ *adj* : smelling putrid

h'a \ȟ'a\ *vn* : to smell bad, as meat, bones, cheese, *etc* when it has set for a few days < *Wanna* ~ *yelo* It now smells bad, they say of bones used for medicinal purposes when they are prepared just right, *i.e.* stinking > – Note: the word seems akin to "grayish" Cf oh'a-mna, oh'aya

h'a·h'a·ya \ȟ'a-ȟ'á-ya\ *v* : to patter on – *See* ȟaȟaya

h'a·kpa \ȟ'a-kṗá\ *adj* : not straight or level, a little curved or ruffled

h'a·mna \ȟ'a-mná\ *adj* : smelling like stale meat, tainted – *Syn* OS'ÁMNA

h'an \ȟ'aŋ\ *vn* wa·h'an : to do, to work, act < *Tókeške yah'an hwo? Na lila h'anpi kin slolya* Whatever have you been doing? And he knew how they really acted. >

h'an·han·ska \ȟ'áŋ-han-ska\ *vn* : to be long-winded, to be not soon tired

h'an·han·ska ho·hpa·pi \ȟ'áŋ-haŋ-ska ho-ȟṗà-pi\ *n* : whooping cough

h'an·hi \ȟ'aŋ-hí\ *vn* wa·h'ánhi ma·h'anhi : to be slow at work, to advance slowly or leisurely — **h'anhi·ka** \ȟ'aŋ-hí-k̇a\ *n* h'an·wá·hika : one who is slow at work, one who is incapable — **h'anhi·kiya** \ȟ'aŋ-hí-ki-ya\ *adv* : slowly, carefully, as in finishing a piece of work — **h'anhi·la** \ȟ'aŋ-hí-la\ *adj* ma·h'ánhila : very slow – Cf la

h'an·hi·ya \ȟ'aŋ-hí-ya\ *adv* : slowly, with difficulty < *Yunkan hinhan wan kuciyela* ~ *kinyan iyaya* And then an owl went flying slowly nearby. >

h'an·h'an·ka \ȟ'áŋ-ȟ'aŋ-ka\ *n* : one who creates disorder or mischief wherever he goes, as certain children do, so that the people know at once the mischief maker, an imp or villain – BH

h'an·li·ta \ȟ'aŋ-lí-ṫa\ *vn* : to be active, to make progress in work < ~ *waun* I am making progress. >

h'an·pi·ca \ȟ'aŋ-ṗí-ca\ *v* : It, or that, can be done < *Tokel?* ~ *šni* Why can it not be done? >

h'an·yan *or* **h'anye·ca** \ȟ'aŋ-yáŋ\ \ȟ'aŋ-yé-ca\ *vn* ȟ'an·wá·ya ȟ'an·wá·yeca : to fail, decline, sink away, as in sickness, to be near, approaching death, to be very tired

h'a·ye·la \ȟ'a-yé-la\ *adv* : making a noise like hail, rain, or sand falling on a roof or wall < ~ *akála* to throw or shoot all over a wall, *Tipi* ~ *he lo* 'Tis lashing the house. > – Cf ȟaȟáya

h'e·h'e \ȟ'e-ȟ'é\ *adj* : dangling, ragged < *hah'eh'e* ragged clothes, *haȟh'eh'e* to have on ragged clothes >

h'e·h'e·ya \ȟ'e-ȟ'é-ya\ *adv* : running or slobbering, as does a dog's mouth after a long run < *Šiyó šunka s'e imništan* ~ *yankelah* A grouse, like a dog, sat with much drivel drooling. > – *Syn* KALALA S'E Bl WHL

h'e·h'e·ye·la \ȟ'e-ȟ'é-ye-la\ *adv* : ragged, torn, dangling, as clothes < ~ *yanka* to be ragged > – Bl

h'e·ya \ȟ'e-yá\ *n archaic* : a fabulous being women use when putting restless children to sleep < *Owanjila hpaya;* ~ *wan u we* Lie quiet; an *h'eyá* is coming. > – Cf cíciye, mmla

h'o \ȟ'o\ *vn* : to stand, as hair < *Ítowe ah'o t'a* He died his forelock standing on end. >

h'o·ka \ȟ'o-k̇á\ *v* : to sing with the drum < *Wanna wa-h'óka* I now sing with a drum. > — *n* : a singer

h'un·hi·ki·ya \ȟ'úŋ-hi-k̇i-ya\ *va* : to finish, to perfect — *adv* : in a finished way, perfectly < ~ *ecamon* I did it by way of finishing it. > — **h'unhi·ya** \ȟ'úŋ-hi-ya\ *va* : to finish, to perfect — **h'unhiye·la** *adv* : exhausted, played out < ~ *waglihunni* Played out I came straight home. > – BT

h'un·hi·ye·šni \ȟ'úŋ-hi-ye-šni\ *v* h'úŋhi·wa·yešni : not to have as much – Note: we can also say similarly: *iyenakeca bluha šni* I do not have as much. Originally *h'un* may have been *h'an*

h'un·kpa·ni \ȟ'úŋ-kṗa-ni\ *vn* h'úŋ·wa·kpani : to play out, be unable to reach or do, to be unable to accomplish, to be in an unfinished state < ~ *waun* I'm not able to finish it. *H'unwakpani šni* I did not played out. > — **h'unkpani·kiya** \ȟ'úŋ-kṗa-ni-k̇i-ya\ *va* h'unkpani·wa·kiya : to leave in an unfinished state, to fail to accomplish — **h'unkpani·yan** \ȟ'úŋ-kṗa-ni-yaŋ\ *va* h'únkpani·wa·ya : to cause to fail to accomplish, to fail in finishing

h'un·t'a \ȟ'úŋ-t'a\ *vn* h'úŋ·ma·t'a : to give out at work, be laid up by work, be exhausted — **h'unt'e·ya** *va* [fr perhaps *h'an* to work + *on* because of + *t'eya* to cause death] : to cause to give out or exhaust one's strength, to oppress one with work < *Kaiwanyank ocicuwa kte lo, owékinaš h'unt'eciyin kte lo* I shall work at watching you, it may be I'll wear you out, *i.e.* lest I kill you by overworking you. > – Bl

h'un·wi·štan šni \ȟ'uŋ-wí-štaŋ šni\ *adj* : never quitting, incessant, persistent, all the time < *Tuwa* ~ *canku kin tanyan kag au welo* Somebody persistent has fixed a road well in every bad place as they came along. > Bl

h'un·yan \ȟ'úŋ-yaŋ\ *va* ma·h'únyan : to tire one – Note: the word is perhaps *obsol*

h'un·ye·la \ȟ'úŋ-ye-la\ *adv* : hardly, barely, scarcely < *Kogingin nankahelo;* ~ *wahiyelo* You were beckoning; I had hardly arrived. > – BT WHL

I

[1]**i** \i\ *pref* prefixed to :
v and *adj* : to, for, of, on, about, by means of, on account of, in consequence of
va : sometimes forms of them *n* of instrument, thus:
kajipa to shave, becomes *icajipa* a drawknife
num card : forms of them *num ord* , thus:
nunpa two, becomes *inunpa* second
adv : gives them the force of *prep* , thus:
tehan far, becomes *itehan* far from
n : signify time, meaning the next or succeeding one:
wetu spring, becomes *iwetu* the next spring
bloketu summer, becomes *ibloketu* next summer
ptanyetu autumn, becomes *iptanyetu* next fall
waniyetu winter, becomes *iwaniyetu* next winter
< *Paha Sapa iwoglakapi* They spoke in reference to the Black Hills, not "on" the Black Hills. *Oyate kin tokel tanyan unpi kte cin he iwanyanke* He looked to how the tribe might do well. > – Note: the meaning "on" is used less often than one would expect

[2]**i** \i\ *vn* wa·i unk·i·pi : to have gone to, to have been at < *Mitakuyepi, wašicuta wai na Tunkašila oti etanhan wašicun šakowin el mahipi* Ladies and gentlemen, I went over to the white man's town, and seven white men came to me from the President's mansion. > – R

[3]**i** \i\ *n* : the mouth < *mií, nií, wicái* my mouth, your mouth, the human mouth >

i·a *or* **iyá** \i-á\ *vn* i·wá·ya i·yá·ya un·kía·pi : to speak < *Tan'inyan ia okihi šni* He is not able to speak clearly. > — **ia·han** \i-á-haŋ\ *part* : speaking – B.H.278.9

i·a·kanl \i-á-k̇aŋl\ *prep* [fr *i* on + *akan* upon] : upon, on top of — **iakan·kanl** \i-á-kaŋ-kaŋl\ *prep red* : on top of more than one thing — **iaka·tanhan** \i-á-k̇a-ṫan-haŋ\ *adv* [fr *akan* upon] : on top of, upon; outside < *Šina hin ~ glowin* He put around himself a blanket with the fur outside. > – B.H.57.18, 60.21

i·a·ke \i-á-k̇e\ *adv* : again, so many more – Note: the word is not used alone — **iake·henakeca** \i-á-k̇e-he-na-k̇e-ca\ *adj* : so many more than ten — **iake·kana-keca** \i-á-k̇e-k̇a-na-k̇e-ca\ *adj* : that number more than ten

i·a·kel \i-á-k̇el\ *adv* : talking < *Wicegna ~ yapi* They went talking amongst themselves. >

i·a·kel·e·na·ke·ca \i-á-k̇e-le-na-k̇e-ca\ *adj* : so many more than ten

i·a·ke·le·na·la \i-á-k̇e-le-na-la\ *adj* : only so many more than ten

i·a·ke·na·pci·yun·ka \i-á-k̇e-na-pci-yuŋ-ka\ *num adj* : the nineteenth

i·a·ke·nun·pa \i-á-k̇e-nuŋ-ṗa\ *num adj* : the twelfth

i·a·ke·ša·glo·gan \i-á-k̇e-ša-glo-ġaŋ\ *num adj* : the eighteenth

i·a·ke·ša-ko-win \i-á-k̇e-ša-ko-wiŋ\ *num adj* : the seventeenth

i·a·ke·ša-kpe \i-á-k̇e-ša-kṗe\ *num adj* : the sixteenth

i·a·ke·to·pa \i-á-k̇e-ṫo-pa\ *num adj* : the fourteenth

i·a·ke·wan·ji·la \i-á-k̇e-waŋ-ji-la\ *num adj* : the eleventh

i·a·ke·ya·mni \i-á-k̇e-ya-mni\ *num adj* : the thirteenth

i·a·ke·za·ptan \i-á-k̇e-za-pṫaŋ\ *num adj* : the fifteenth

i·a·ki·cun·ni *also* **iyakicunni** \í-a-k̇i-cuŋ-ni\ *v* : to desist from, to grow tired and leave off – Cf iyakicunni

i·a·ki·c'u·ya \i-á-k̇i-c'u-ya\ *adj* : much – Cf iyakic'uya

i·a·ki·he·han·ke·ca \í-a-k̇i-he-haŋ-k̇e-ca\ *adv* : alike in length

i·a·ki·he·han·yan \í-a-k̇i-he-haŋ-yaŋ\ *adv* : alike in distance

i·a·ki·he·na·ke·ca \í-a-k̇i-he-na-k̇e-ca\ *adv* : of equal number with

i·a·ki·le·ce·ca \í-a-k̇i-le-ce-ca\ *adv* : alike, equal to, of one kind – Cf iyakilececa

i·a·ki·le·cel \í-a-k̇i-le-cel\ *adv* : like to equal to

i·a·ki·le·han·han·ke·ca \í-a-k̇i-le-haŋ-haŋ-ke-ca\ *adv red* [fr *iakilehankeca* equal in length to] : equal in size to

i·a·ki·le·han·han·yan \í-a-k̇i-le-haŋ-haŋ-yaŋ\ *adv red of* i-akilehanyan : alike in distance

i·a·ki·le·han·ke·ca \í-a-k̇i-le-haŋ-k̇e-ca\ *adv* : equal to in length < *Kici iakilemahankeca* I am as tall as he. >

i·a·ki·le·han·yan \í-a-k̇i-le-haŋ-yaŋ\ *adv* : alike in distance, as far as

i·a·ki·le·na·ke·ca \í-a-k̇i-le-na-k̇e-ca\ *adv* : as many as

i·a·ki·pa·pa \í-a-k̇i-pa-pa\ *v* ía·wa·kipapa [fr *i* mouth + *apa* to strike] : to strike on the mouth often, as you men do in shouting

i·a·ksa·pe \i-á-ksa-pe\ *adj* : wise in talking – B.H.85.25

i·a·na·pta \i-á-na-pta\ *va* : to detain, prevent beforehand from proceeding – Cf iyanapta

i·an·pe·tu \í-aŋ-ṗe-ṫu\ *n* : the same or next day < ~ *hankeyela* during that day, ~` *yamni* within the next three days > – B.H.177.1, 179.16

i·a·o·un·c'u·ni·ca \i-á-o-uŋ-c'u-ni-ca\ *v* iaoun·ma·c'unica : to stutter, stammer – Bl

i·a·pi \i-á-ṗi\ *n* : a talk, one's speech or language < ~ *kicága* to report one as saying things that he did not, ~ *micagapelo; epe šni yelo* They made a speech for me; I did not give it. ~ *otahena* an issue being re-examined > – WE

i·a·sni \i-á-sni\ *v* : to grow cold in or with *ref* to

i·a·š'a \í-a-š'a\ *v* ía·wa·š'a ía·un·š'a·pi : to halloo, make a loud inarticulate noise

i·a·ta·ye·la \í-a-ṫa-ye-la\ *pron adv* : that alone; personally, individually – Cf íyatayela

i·a·un·ca \i-á-uŋ-ca\ *va* : to imitate somebody's way of speaking – Note: únca is not used by the Oglalas

i·a·wan·yank \í-a-waŋ-yaŋk\ *v contrac of* iawanyanka : to keep one's eyes on < ~ *kuwa* to pursue something keeping it in sight > – B.H.77.6

i·a·wan·yan·ka \í-a-waŋ-yaŋ-ka\ *va* : to guard – B.H.133.23

i·a·wa·ya·pi·ka \i-á-wa-yà-ṗi-ka\ *v* : to speak nicely < *Winyan ca witkowin akisni s'e ~* A woman that's a loose woman speaks nicely as though she were recovering from a sickness, as is said when such a person speaks nicely to others. > – Bl

i·a·wi·ca·ka \i-á-wi-ca-ka\ *vn* iawica·wa·ka : to speak the truth

i·a·wi·ca·ke·han \i-á-wi-ca-k̇e-haŋ\ *adv* : truly, in truth

i·a·wo·gla·ka \i-á-wo-gla-ka\ *v* : to speak a language – B.H.278.4

i·ble·za \i-blé-za\ *vn* i·ma·bleza : to be enlightened about, to understand, as a person does gradually while waking up – Bl

i·bli·hel·ya \i-blí-hel-ya\ *va* iblihel·wa·ya : to stir up, excite – B.H.128.15

i·cab \i-cáb\ *v contrac of* icapa : to stick in < ~ *icu* to stick in and take out > — **ica·beya** \i-cá-be-ya\ *part* : pricked, injured in feelings — **ica·bheya** *adv* : right through, as pain going through the chest – Note: the word is becoming *obsol* R

i·ca·bla·ska \i-cá-bla-sk̇a\ *vn* [fr *i* on + *kablaska* strike flat] : to be flattened, as a bullet that is shot into wood

i·ca·bu \i-cá-bu\ *n* [fr *i* converts *v* to *n* + *kabu* to beat] :

a drum stick

[1]**i·ca·can** *or* **wícacan** \i-ċá-ċaŋ\ *n* : a sieve

[2]**i·ca·can** \í-ċa-ċaŋ\ *vn* í·wa·kacan : to trot, as does a horse < *íwakacan* I make it trot. >

i·ca·ga \i-cá-ġa\ *vn* i·má·caga [fr *kaga* to make] : to spring up, to grow as grass, a child, *etc* ; to become as a man < *inyan* ~ to turn into stone > – D.222

[1]**i·ca·ge** \i-ċá-ġe\ *n* [fr *i* for + *kaga* to make] : something to make a thing with, an instrument, a tool

[2]**i·ca·ge** \i-ċá-ġe\ *n* [fr *kage* to skim off] : to skim off < ~ *icu* to take up in a bucket *e.g.* water, to take off or skim, ~ *iwacu* I took it up skimming. >

i·ca·ge·ju·ya \i-ċá-ġe-ju-ya\ *v* icageju·wica·wa·ya : to come up and go along with a company — *adv* : together with, in company

i·ca·ge·ya \i-ċá-ġe-ya\ *adv* : together < *Oyate* ~ *tipi* People were camped together. >

i·ca·gi \i-ċá-ġi\ *vn* i·ma·kagi [fr *i* because of + *kagi* to be hindered] : to be hindered by an obstacle < *Taku* ~ *heci oyakin kta* If something is an obstacle let him say so. *Takuni imakagi šni omawani* I traveled with nothing hindering me. > — **icagi·šniyan** *adv* : without obstacles < *Takuni* ~ *omawani* I traveled without any hindrance. > — **icagi·ya** *or* **icageya** \í-ca-ġi-ya\ *va* : to bother, annoy one < *Ícage·maya·ye* You annoy me. *Ícageciye* I bother you. > – Bl

i·ca·gla *or* **icagla·la** *or* **icagla·ya** \i-ċá-gla\ *prep* [fr *i* to + *kagla* nearby] : by the side of, near to < ~ *ómakihan po* Follow me closely. *Paha wan otonwahe kin* ~ *han* A hill stands near the town.> – Bl B.H.184.25

i·ca·go \i-ċá-ġo\ *n* [fr *i* for + *kago* to draw a line] : a mark or line drawn — *va* i·wá·kago unki·cago·pi : to make a mark, draw a line, to sketch < *Le iyakago kin he itimahetanhan opimic'iye lo. Can wan on ... maka kin yumimeya* ~ *... yo* I took the initiative to act short of this line you drew. With a stick sketch a circular line on the ground. > D.34-35

i·ca·go·go \i-cá-ġo-ġo\ *v* [fr perhaps *kago* draw a line on the ground] : to make marks, with perhaps < *Pahin ca mani s'e onze* ~ *la s'e* So a porcupine walks so it seems as though its rump were going along to make marks, as is said of a woman who drags her too-long robe or dress over the ground, comparing her to a porcupine that drags its tail over the ground. > — **i·ca·go·pi** \i-ċá-ġo-pi\ *n* : a line — **icago·ya** *va* icago·wa·ya : to cause to mark — *adv* : marking, in the way of marking – Bl

i·ca·hi \i-ċá-hi\ *va* i·wa·kahi unki·cahi·pi [fr *i* on + *kahi* to stir] : to mix or stir up together — *vn* : to mix, to mingle < *Pte kin ataya iwicunkahipelo* We bunched the cattle all up together. > — **icahi·hi** \i-ċá-hi-hi\ *v red of* icahi : to mingle, mix together — **icahihi·ya** *adv* : mixed up with, together with — **icahi·kiton** \i-ċá-hi-ḱi-toŋ\ *v poss* : to mix together one's own < *Canlíwakpan hiyumiciya yo; canli icáhiweton kte lo* Hand me a tobacco cutting-board; I'll mix my tobacco. > – GA

i·ca·hin·te \i-ċá-hiŋ-ṫe\ *n* [fr *i* for + *kahinta* to sweep] : a broom

i·ca·hi·ton \i-ċá-hi-toŋ\ *va* icahi·wa·ton icahi·un·ton·pi : to mix together *e.g.* tobacco

i·ca·hi·ya \i-ċá-hi-ya\ *va* icahi·wa·ya : to mix together, adulterate < *taspícahiye* lemon extract >

i·ca·ho·mni \i-ċá-ho-mni\ *n* [fr *i* convert *v* to *n* + *kahomni make turn*] : something that is turned or turns, a wheel

i·cah \i-cáḣ\ *v contrac of* icaga : to grow, sprout < ~ *áya* It keeps growing. *Wana olute kin* ~ *ayapelo* Their thighs began growing, *i.e.* bones now growing fleshy, as during the spring. > – Bl

i·ca·ḣa·bḣa·pe·la \i-cá-ḣa-bḣa-pe-la\ *vn* : to rustle, as the grass in a gentle wind

i·ca·ḣa·pe \i-ċá-ḣa-ṗe\ *n* [fr *i* converts *v* to *n* + *kaḣapa* to drive] : something to drive with, a whip

i·ca·hci \i-ċá-ḣci\ *vn* [fr *kahci* break a gap] : to come off by wearing out *e.g.* a chain — **icahci·ya** *va* icahci·wa·ya : to make come off by wearing out

i·cah·ki·ya \i-cáḣ-ki-ya\ *va* ica·hwa·kiya : to cause to grow, to rear, raise *e.g.* a child or a domestic animal

i·cah·ko·ke·la \i-cáḣ-ḱo-ḱe-la\ *adj* : of quick growth – *See* oícah

i·ca·hli \i-cá-ḣli\ *v* i·wa·kahli : to step into mud < *Iyákahli kilo* Don't step in mud. > – Bl

i·ca·hmun \i-cá-ḣmuŋ\ *va* i·wa·kahmun : to make a buzz with < *inyan* ~ to buzz a stone, *i.e.* a sling > – B.H.87.7

i·ca·hnih \i-cá-ḣniḣ\ *v contrac* [fr *i* for + *kahniga* select] : to select, pick out < ~ *icu* to take a choice >

i·ca·ḣolḣo·ta \i-ċá-ḣo-lḣo-ṫa\ *n red of* icaḣota : drops of rain, flakes of snow, so called because they fall like ashes – Cf icáḣota

i·ca·ḣo-ta \i-ċá-ḣo-ṫa\ *n* [fr perhaps *caḣota* ashes] : drops of rain, flakes of snow, as they fall like ashes

i·ca·hpe hu \i-cá-ḣpe hu\ *n* : the narrow-leaved purple cone flower, niggerhead; brauneria angustifolia, the composite family – Note: it grows on the prairie < *makáblaye* ~ prairie cone flower >, otherwise it is called *ónglakcapi* snake-root which grows in the creeks, whereas the *icahpe hu* grows more on hills. As a medicine, it is chewed for toothache or for bellyache, or when one is thirsty or over-perspiring, as well as for swellings, for which last they chew the root and apply it to the swell – HM PLB

i·ca·htag \i-ċá-ḣtag\ *vn contrac of* icahtaka : to contact

i·ca·hta·gya \i-ċá-ḣta-gya\ *adv* icahta·gwa·ya : touching, as a cup-board does a wall, or as a man leaning against the wall *etc* ; relating to, concerning < ~ *han* to stand against, ~ *inajin* to stand leaning against > — *va* : to cause to touch — **icahtagya·kel** \i-ċá-ḣta-gya-ḱel\ *adv* : relating to

i·ca·hta-ka \i-ċá-ḣta-ḱa\ *vn* i·ma·kahtaka : to come in contact passing somebody, or as objects touch each other in a game, this being decided by the position; to touch *e.g.* poison ivy < *painyankapi* a game in which one tries to throw through a rolling hoop >

i·ca·hya \i-cá-ḣya\ *va* ica·hwa·ya : to cause to grow, to raise, rear, train up a child — *adv* : conformed to, made like

i·ca·i·je·na \i-ċá-i-je-na\ *v* i·wa·kaijena : to mix up – Bl

i·ca·ja \i-cá-ja\ *va* i·wa·caja : to think there is much or many, to do a thing much, as to give away much; to take more than proper; to do something in excess

i·ca·ja·ja \i-ċá-ja-ja\ *va* i·wá·kajaja : to wash by shaking *e.g.* a bottle < *Nasonspe on icajajapelo* The axe was washed by shaking it. > – Bl

i·ca·ja·pi \i-cá-ja-pi\ *n* : very much

\a\ father \e\ they \i\ machine \o\ smoke \u\ lunar \an, aŋ\ blanc Fr. \in, iŋ\ ink \on, oŋ, un, uŋ\ soon, confier Fr. \c\ chair \ġ\ machen Ger. \j\ fusion \clusters: bl, gn, kp, hšl, etc...\ b^{e}lo ... said with a slight vowel
See more in the Introduction, Guide to Pronunciation

i·ca·je \i-cá-je\ *adv* [fr *i* in + *caje* name] : in the name of — **icaje·ka** \i-cá-je-k̇a\ *vn* : to be named for or on account of — **icaje·yal** \i-cá-je-yal\ *adv contrac of* icajeyata : in the name of — **icajeya·ta** \i-cá-je-ya-ṫa\ *adv* : in the name of, in speaking the name of — **icajeyatapi** *n* : a candidate

i·ca·ju·ju \í-ca-ju-ju\ *n* : the fare, the pay - P Bl

i·ca·kan \i-čá-k̇aŋ\ *n* [fr *i* converts *v* to *n* + *kakan* to hew] : an adze — *va* i·wa·kakan unki·cakan·pi : to strike and cut a piece out of

i·ca·ki·ja \i-čá-k̇i-ja\ *vn* i·ma·kakija i·ni·cakija unki·cakija·pi : to be in want of, lacking, suffering for < *Na tuktel taku wanice naiš taku icakijapi ca niwicaya omani keyapi. Mini icakijapi* And where there was nothing, or they were lacking something, they say he is on his way to reviving them. They were lacking water. > - R B.H.66.19

i·ca·ki·je \i-čá-k̇i-je\ *n* [fr *i* converts to *n* + *kakija* to suffer] : affliction — **icakije·šniyan** *adv* : plentifully, not in want of

i·ca·kiš \i-čá-k̇iš\ *v contrac of* icakija : to suffer for < ~ *un* to be suffering for > — **icaki·šya** *va* icaki·šwa·ya : to cause to suffer for, to afflict — *adv* : in a suffering manner, scantily, inadequately

i·ca·kon·ta \i-čá-k̇oŋ-ta\ *va* [fr *kakonta* to wear or cut] : to cut a groove in, as one branch resting on another will do when swayed by the wind - Cf kakónta

i·ca·kpan \i-čá-kpaŋ\ *n* : a grinder, grater, pestle, mill — *adv* : completely crushed into small pieces < ~ *kablebleca* to break into pieces completely > - Bl WHL

i·ca·kša \i-cá-kša\ *v* [fr *kakša* to roll up] : to gather in a roll, as a blanket about the neck < *paícakša iyeya* to gather or roll together about the neck, *Paicakša imáyaye* I gathered it about my neck. >

i·ca·k'o·ge \i-cá-k'o-ġe\ *n* : a scraper

i·ca·k'os \i-cá-k'os\ *vn contrac of* icak'oza : to be made bare < ~ *iyaya* to have got bare >

i·ca·k'o·za \i-cá-k'o-za\ *vn* : to be made bare by *e.g.* the wind

i·ca·lu \í-ča-lu\ *n* [fr *i* converts *v* to *n* + *kalu* blow away] : a fan, a wing to fan one's self with

i·ca·lu·za \i-cá-lu-za\ *v* [fr *kaluza* flow rapidly] : to flow over, flow with < *Iwaštegla tate ~ ca maka woblu welo. Wicayajipa tacanhanpi ~* A wind that passes over slowly plows the ground. Bees' honey then is overflowing, *i.e.* the land is flowing with milk and honey. > - B.H.47.14

i·ca·ma \i-čá-ma\ *adj* : rough, as cloth or the beard; pricking, as do iron filings — *vn* : to hurt or prick, as anything in the eye or elsewhere < *Taku išta imákama* Something is hurting my eye. > — **icama·ma** *v red* : to prick — **icame·ca** \i-čá-me-ča\ *vn* : to be pricked, to have one's feelings injured by some little thing — **icameya** *adv* : pricked, injured in feelings < ~ *waun* My feelings are hurt. > - Cf icápa

i·ca·mna \i-čá-mna\ *vn* [fr *kamna* to rip] : to blow, bluster, storm, drive as wind or snow; to be torn by anything and lose the contents, as a bag of corn carried along <*Lila ~* There's a real storm. >

i·ca·na·h'o \í-ča-na-ḣ'o\ *v* : to glance causing matter to spray, to be carried away with the wind — **icana·s'a** *v* : to ricochet or glance off - WHL

i·can \i-čáŋ\ *adv* : whilst, in the meantime, just then

i·can·can \i-čáŋ-caŋ\ *vn* i·má·cancan [fr *i* on account of + *cancan* to shake] : to tremble for, shake on account of

i·canl *or* **ecanl** \i-čáŋl\ *adv* : but, just then < *Yamni t'api k'on hena titakuye kin hmunsekse wicaceya eša miš ~ lila wibluškin niwagli kin heon. Htayetu el wakpala wan el glihunni na ~ oiyokpaza* There was some sobbing and wailing when those three close relatives had died, but I was very glad because he brought you game. In the evening he arrived home at the creek and just then it was dark. > - MS.561

i·can·li·yu·ha \i-čáŋ-li-yu-ha\ *vn* : to be set and ready with all things needed, *i.e.* in a good mood, hence ready to do < *Taku icanliniyuha yelaka, winiš'oš'oke lo* Since you are ready with what is needed, you are ready for work > - Bl WHL

i·can·lka·spe·ya \i-čáŋ-lka-ṡpe-ya\ *v* icanlkaspe·wa·ya : to cheer up one's self, make one's self feel better by giving away *etc* after the death of a dear one - *Syn* CANTÍYOZIKIYA Bl

i·can·lši·ca \i-čáŋ-lši-ca\ *vn* : to be disaffected, displeased, hold hard feelings < *Takuni icanlšice un šni wo* Never keep holding hard feelings. > - Lc KE

i·can·lwa·šte \i-čáŋ-lwa-šte\ *vn* icanl·ma·wašte : to be glad for — **icanlwašte·ya** *adv* : gladly for

i·can·li·yu·ha·kel \i-čáŋ-li-yu-ha-kel\ *adv* : cheerfully < ~ *waun welo* I am doing cheefully. > - *Syn* CANTEWAŠTEYA St

i·can·ši·ca \i-čáŋ-ši-ca\ *vn* ican·ma·šica : to be sad for, as when someone died - B.H.302.24

i·can·ši·ca·pi \i-čáŋ-ši-ca-pi\ *n* : tribulation

i·can·šil \i-čáŋ-šil\ *vn contrac of* icanšica : to be sad for — **i·canši·lya** *va* icanši·lwa·ya : to make sad, grieve, to disappoint one by means of something — *adv* : sadly, distressingly

i·can·ta·gle \i-čáŋ-ṫa-gle\ *va* icata·wa·gle : to determine evil against one for some cause

i·can·te \i-čáŋ-ṫe\ *adv* : in or at the heart

i·can·te·ki·c'un \i-čáŋ-ṫe-k̇i-c'uŋ\ *vn* icante·we·c'un : to encourage one's self by reason of - *Syn* IŠPAKIC'UN — **icantekic'un·yan** *adv* : encouragingly

i·can·te·ni·ca \i-čáŋ-ṫe-ni-ca\ *vn* icante·ma·nica : to have no heart for, to be controlled by habit so that will-power is gone

i·can·te·ši·ca \i-čáŋ-ṫe-ši-ca\ *vn* icante·ma·šica : to be sad on account of < *Ehanl wikoškalaka k'un t'a; canke koškalaka k'un lila ~* That young woman at the time had died; and so on this account the young man was very sad. > — **icantešica·ya** *adv* : sadly on account of — **i·canteši·lya** \í-caŋ-ṫe-ši-lya\ *or* \i-čáŋ-ṫe-ši-lya\ *va* i·canteši·lwa·ya : to render happy by, make feel bad - R

i·can·te·t'ins \i-čáŋ-ṫe-t'iŋs\ *vn contrac of* icantet'inza : to be encouraged < ~ *kic'un wo* Put on encouragement. > - B.H.46.4, 122.7 — **icantet'in·sya** *va* icantet'in·swa·ya : to encourage one by reason of — *adv* : encouragingly

i·can·te·t'in·za \i-čáŋ-ṫe-t'iŋ-za\ *vn* icante·ma·t'inza : to be encouraged, sustained, or supported by

i·can·te·wa·šte \i-čáŋ-ṫe-wa-šte\ *vn* icante·ma·wašte : to be glad on account of < *Yunkan namah'onpi kin icantemawaštehce* And so when they heard me I was quite glad. > — **icantewašte·ya** *adv* : gladly on account of

i·can·to·gna·ka \i-čáŋ-ṫo-gna-ka\ *va* icanto·wa·gnaka : to place in the heart with *ref* to something, to purpose to give to one

i·can·to·kpa·ni \i-čáŋ-ṫo-kṗa-ni\ *v* icanto·wa·kpani : to long for in *ref* to

i·can·yan \í-caŋ-yaŋ\ *adv* : leaning against *e.g.* a chair half reclined and leaning against the wall, or as a man so leaning < *Tiícanyan yanke* He was leaning against the house. > – B.H.173.18

[1]i·ca·pa \i-ćá-ṗa\ *v* i·wa·kapa *or perhaps* i·wa·capa : to open the mouth, to open < ~ *glukawa* to open the mouth without effort >

[2]i·ca·pa \i-cá-pa\ *v* ica·wa·pa [fr *i* in + *capa* to stick in] : to stick into, to take a stitch, to stab with, to stick in *e.g.* a thorn or a stick < *Can icamapa. Na unma pestola k'on he el icapin na on yumni. Wašin ~ wacin yelo* A stick stuck me. And another stuck in the Diamond card and with it turned it around. He tried sticking into the fat. > – GA

i·ca·pan \i-ćá-paŋ\ *n* i·wa·kapan [fr *kapan* beat off] : a thresher, a threshing machine or combine, something to pound with — *va* : to pound to pieces – Bl

i·ca·pcab \i-cá-pcab\ *va* : to pierce through < *Peji to mini ~ he lo* Blue grass was piercing through water, *i.e.* drops of water on grass as it comes out of the ground. > Bl KE

i·ca·pe \i-cá-pe\ *n* [fr *i* converts *v* to *n* + *capa* pierce] : something that sticks in, a spear, a splinter, a stitch

i·ca·pe·pe·ya \i-cá-pe-pe-ya\ *or* \í-ca-pe-pe-ya\ *adv red of* icape : pierced or stuck in various places < *Maswiyokatan ~ yuwankal iyeyapi* Pierced with nails he was lifted up. > – B.H.265.23

i·ca·pe·ya \í-ca-ṗe-ya\ *adv* : more than that < ~ *wacin yelo* He considered more than that. >

i·ca·po·ga \i-cá-ṗo-ġaŋ\ *n* : a sudden blowing storm < ~ *hiyelo* There came a driving storm, ~ *wa hi* There started a snow storm, a blizzard. > Bl KE

i·ca·psa·ke \i-ćá-psa-ke\ *n* [fr *i* converts *v* to *n* + *kapsaka* to cut string or wire *etc*] : something used in cutting off strings < *pahin ~ a* porcupine quill cutter, a small knife >

i·ca·psin·te \i-ćá-psiŋ-ṫe\ *n* [fr *i* converts *v* to *n* + *kapsinta* to flog] : something to whip with, a whip < ~ *winšwinšahela* a flexible whip, a buggy whip >

i·ca·pšin·pšin·ca·la i·kpi ska \i-cá-pšiŋ-pšiŋ-ca-la i-kpì ska\ *n* : the tree swallow – Note: *upíjata* is the generic name for a swallow and practically synonymous

i·ca·pšin·pšin·ca·la i·kpi ša \i-cá-pšiŋ-pšiŋ-ca-la i-kpì ša\ *n* : the barn swallow

i·ca·pšun \i-ćá-pšuŋ\ *n* [fr *i* converts *v* to *n* + *kapšun* to strike and break out] : anything to pry out with or pull up by the roots

i·ca·pta \i-ćá-pṫa\ *vn* [fr *i* on account + *kapta* break out] : to break out, as the hold on meat in carrying it

i·ca·pta icu \í-ća-pta i-cù\ *v* : to dip, to ladle out – Bl

i·ca·ptan·ptan ki·c'un \i-ćá-pṫaŋ-pṫaŋ ki-c'uŋ\ *vn* [fr *kaptanptan* to make roll over] : to roll over much, to roll about < *(Šungleška kin) kul iyunki na ~* The spotted horse lay down and rolled about. > – D.257, 99

i·ca·p'o·šya \i-ćá-p'o-šya\ *v* : to make lighter, less heavy < *Wapahlaya na ~ s'e iblabla* I go as if peeling off and getting lighter. > – Bl

i·ca·p'tan·ktan·ka \i-ća-p'taŋ-ktaŋ-ka\ *adv* : with wide-open mouth < *Le tohan ceya ca ~ ceye* This one when he cries cries with a wide-open mouth. > – Bl

i·ca·san \i-ćá-saŋ\ *va* i·wá·kasan [fr *i* for + *kasan* to whiten] : to whiten, make fade by touching or striking

i·ca·ska \i-ćá-ska\ *v* : to eat a little lunch < ~ *iyeya* to eat a little lunch quickly, *Icask'iyewayin kte* I shall eat a bit of lunch. *Cik'alakel ~ iyeunyin kte,* Let you and I in small way in a hurry eat a bit of lunch *etc* ~ *iyewayin kte lo* Let me hurry and eat a little lunch. > – *Syn* CAK'I-GLAŠKA

i·ca·ski·ca \i-cá-ski-ca\ *vn* i·ma·kaskica : to be pressed down

i·ca·ski·ce \i-ćá-sḱi-ce\ *n* [fr *i* converts *v* to n + *kaskica* press down] : a press

i·ca·sle·ce \i-cá-sle-ce\ *n* [fr *i* for + *kasleca* to split] : something to split with, a wedge

i·ca·slo·he \i-cá-slo-he\ *n* : a marble, marbles; a stick made to slide along on snow or ice; the game of billiards < ~ *econpi* to play billiards >

i·ca·stan·ka \í-ća-staŋ-ka\ *v* : to moisten the mouth, as is done when people have little water < ~ *unyanpi kte* Let us go stanch our thirst. > – Bl

i·ca·še \i-ćá-še\ *n* [fr *i* converts *v* to *n* + *kaše* to strike against] : something rubbing against or fitted against, a hindrance — **icaše·ya** *va* icaše·wa·ya : to make a hindrance of, to hinder by means of

i·ca·ške \i-ćá'-šḱe\ *n* [fr *i* converts *v* to *n* + *kaška* to tie] : something to tie or bind around with, a girdle, a sash; a prize — *v* : to play for, run a race for, *etc* — **icaške-ya** *va* : to tie one with – B.H.229.25

i·ca·ški·ce \i-ćá-ški-ce\ *n* [fr *i* converts *v* to *n* + *kaškica* to pound] : something to pound with, a beetle, a heavy wooden hammer or pestle

i·ca·ški·ta \i-ćá-šḱi-ṫa\ *va* : to cut a little gash in, to cut notches – R Bl

i·ca·šla \i-cá-šla\ *n* [fr *i* converts *v* to *n* + *kašla* to mow] : something with which to mow < *peji ~* a mower or scythe, *putin ~* a razor >

i·ca·šle·ca \i-ćá-šle-ca\ *n* [fr *i* converts *v* to *n* + *kašleca* to split] : something with which to split, a wedge

i·ca·šlo·ka \i-cá-šlo-ka\ *adj perhaps* i·má·kašloka : knocked out; *colloq* to be all in, played out

i·ca·šlo·ke \i-ćá-šlo-ḱe\ *n* [fr *i* converts *v* to *n* + *kašloka* knock out] : a poker, cleaner < *cannunpa ~* a pipe tamper, a thin stick to press down the tobacco in a burning pipe, or to clean it >

i·ca·šo·ša \i-cá-šo-ša\ *v* i·wa·kašoša : to mix by shaking together

i·ca·špe \i-ćá-šṗe\ *n* [fr *i* converts *v* to *n* + *kašpa* strike off a piece] : an instrument for cutting out pieces < *mazicašpe* a cold chisel >

i·ca·špu \i-ćá-šṗu\ *vn* : to break off, as by over-heavy weight — *n* [fr *i* converts *v* to *n* + *kašpu* to knock off] : something to knock off with – R

i·ca·štan \í-ca-štaŋ\ *adv perhaps* : close up to one, as in running close up to one < ~ *manka* I am close up to him, ~ *mahiyanka* He ran (came) close up to me, *Hehanl wicaša wan ungnahela ~ mahiyankin na lecel omakiyaka* Then a man all at once came up close to me, and he told me this > – Cf icaštinyanka

i·ca·štin·yan·ka \í-ca-štiŋ-yan-ka\ *v* icaštin·man·ka : to catch up with another running after him < *Icaštinyanke na oyuspa na tuweceeyaš iyugnayan ca na he icaštan inyankin* He caught up with him, took hold of him, and when anybody was deceiving he would run right up close. >

i·ca·š'a·ka \i-cá-š'a-ka\ *vn* [fr *kaš'aka* strike with little force] : not to penetrate, as an axe that is dull

i·ca·ta \i-cá-ta\ *v* : to crowd together < ~ *iheya* to rush through crowded together >

i·ca·tan·tan \i-ćá-taŋ-taŋ\ *v* i·wá·katantan : to spread

---

or rub on *e.g.* glue all over < ~ *ehunni yo* Finish spreading it on.> — *adv* : daubing along, as in painting or smudging - Bl WHL

i·ca·tka·ya·tan *or* **icatkayatan·han** \i-cá-tk̇a-ya-ṫaŋ\ *adv* mi·catkayatan mi·catkayatanhan : to the left hand of - B.H.249.6

i·ca·tku·tan·han \i-cá-tku-taŋ-haŋ\ *adv* : to or at the back part of the tent from one

i·ca·t'a \í-ca-t'a\ *adv* : very < *šunkawakan ~ tanka* a very big (hence sluggish) horse >

i·ca·t'e \i-ċá-t'e\ *n* : anything to club to death with - Bl

i·ca·zo \i-ċá-zo\ *va* i·wa·cazo unki·cazo·pi : to draw a mark or line, to take credit, to owe, to be in debt — *n* : a mark, a line drawn — **icazo·kiya** \i-ċá-zo-k̇i-ya\ *va* icazo·wa·kiya : to cause to mark, to take things on credit, give credit to — **icazo·pi** \i-ċá-zo-pi\ *n* : credit(s) — **icazo·zo** *v red of* icázo : to incur credit

i·ce \i-cé\ *interrog particle* : Is it not so? - Cf cē

i·ce·bya \i-c'e-bya\ *va* ice·bwa·ya : to fatten by means of

i·ce·ki·ya \i-cé-k̇i-ya\ *va* ice·wa·kiya ice·ci·ciya [fr *ceki-ya* pray to] : to pray to one for something < *Le miye (Wakantanka Cinca) ca tokša taku icemayakiyapi ca na nawah'on kte lo* Since I am the (Son of God), soon whenever you pray to me, I shall listen. >

i·ce·pa \i-cé-ṗa\ *adj* i·má·cepa [fr *cepa* fat] : fat on or by, fat by reason on

i·ce·te \i-cē'-ṫe\ *n* : the rim or lip of a kettle

i·ce·ti \i-cé-ṫi\ *v* ice·wa·ti [fr *ceti* to start a fire] : to make a fire to or at < ~ *na mayujuju ye* Please undo what binds me and make a fire. > - D.228

i·ce·win \i-cé-wiŋ\ *adv* : grandly, magnificently < *Wicaša wan Kangi Tanka ~ Pasu Tanka keye* A man, Big Crow, Big Nose, grandly stated that, as is said of a man with a big nose. *Huntka s'e ~ nunpala wicayuha* Magnificently like a cormorant (itself like a crow) it has only two chicks, as is said of people with only two chil-dren. > — **i·ce·win la·ke·s'e** \i-cé-wiŋ la-ke-s'e\ *adv perhaps* : rather grandly < ~ *ištakte nuns'e amayuta yankelah* He was looking upon me strikingly, with piercing eyes. > — **icewinš** *adv* : very much, implying wonder < ~ *mayak'u* You gave me surprisingly very much. ~ *ṫak'ṫo-k̇onka* He is one that misplaces things. ~ *conamak'u we* Give me much more than a few. ~ *wokokipeka nacece* My! How awfully fearful he must be. > - D.153 Bl

i·ci \i-cí\ *pref* affixed to:
num card makes them *num ord* < *iciyamni* the third >
v makes them signify "together" < *koyaka* to put on, *ícikoyaka* to fasten together, *wanyanka* to see, *íciwanyanka* to compare >
prep and *adv* makes them convey the idea of space or time intervening between objects < *ícikiyela* near to each other, *ícitehan* far apart >

i·ci·ca·gmun \í-ci-ca-gmuŋ\ *va* íci·wa·kagmun [fr *kagmun* to spin or twist] : to tangle up

i·ci·ca·hi \í-ci-ca-hi\ *vn* : to mingle together, to mix — **icicahi·ya** *va* ícicahi·wa·ya : to mix together, mingle, stir up < *Wicaša na winyan ko ~ mimeya enanjin* Men and women mixed together stood in a circle. > — *adv* : mingled — **ícicahiya·kel** *adv* : altogether — **ícicahiya-pi** *part* : mixed together

i·ci·ca·ȟa·bha·pa *or* **icicaȟabhape·la** \í-ci-ca-ȟa-bȟa-ṗa\ *vn* : to rustle, as the grass in a gentle wind

i·ci·ca·ska·ya \í-ci-ca-ska-ya\ *va* : to mix < *Tašoše k'un he maka ~* He mixed dirt with his saliva. > - B.H.221.9

i·ci·ca·sni \í-ci-ca-sni\ *v* : to make cool, as hot coffee by pouring it to and fro from one cup to another - Bl

i·ci·ca·ška \í-ci-ċa-ška\ *v* : to bind together — **icicaške-ya** *adv* : tied together, united < ~ *eyapi* They said it all together. >

i·ci·ca·šla \í-ci-ca-šla\ *adv* : making each other bare by striking < *Pte na tahca ko naunkapi na šake ~ naunkapi* Buffalo and also deer galloped and they galloped clicking their hooves together. >

i·ci·ca·šla·šla·ye·la \í-ci-ca-šla-šla-ye-la\ *adv* : with a smash or clatter < *Makacega kin ~ kableblecapi* The pot broke with a clatter. > - B.H.76.4

i·ci·ca·šna·šna \í-ci-ca-šna-šna\ *v* : to clash, one thing striking another and making a ringing sound as do cymbals — *n* : cymbals

i·ci·ca·šo·ša \í-ci-ca-šo-ša\ *v* : to mix to cool off a liquid by pouring it to and fro from one cup to another -P Bl

i·ci·ca·win \í-ci-ca-wiŋ\ *adv* : back again by the same way < ~ *gla* to be on the way home by the same route, *anunk ~* back and forth, coming and going > — **icica-win·win** *adv red* : repeatedly back by the same way — **icicawin·yan** *adv* : back by the same way < ~ *inyanka* to meet running in opposite directions > - Bl

i·ci·c'u·ya \í-ci-c'u-ya\ *adv* : passing by each other when coming from opposite directions < ~ *iyayapi. Lenayos (lenaos) kakika paha wan lila tehanl yanke kin heci anunk ~ iyayapi kte lo* They went coming from opposite directions to pass one another. These two should be going back and forth passing in opposite dirctions over there where there is a very far-away hill. >

i·ci·gla·pšun·pšun·yan \í-ci-gla-pšuŋ-pšuŋ-yaŋ\ *adv* : piled on top of each other - Bl

i·ci·gle·gle·ga \í-ci-gle-gle-ġa\ *adj* : scattering, few - R — **iciglegleh** \í-ci-gle-gleȟ\ *adj contrac of* icigleglega : scattering <*Wanji ska (i.e.* porcupine quills), *wanji sapa, wanji zi, inš toto iyoyaza owecinhan iyeyapi ca he ~ oyazapi ecin api* She planned a pattern strung of (porcupine quills), stringing them one after the next: a white one, a black, a yellow, a blue. > - Note: the word is used when the same colors occur again and again in the same order

i·ci·gle·ška \í-ci-gle-ška\ *adj* : speckled, as corn of different colors — **icigleška·ška** *adj red* : speckled in various colors

i·ci·gni \i-cí-gni\ *va* i·wá·kigni i·un·kigni·pi : to beat or maltreat, as a man his wife < *Na tanyan ecanonpi šni kin hecegla la kta na niye inicignipi kte lo* You shall be beaten, and you should take only so much when you have not done well. >

i·ci·gnu·ni \í-ci-gnu-ni\ *v* : to be mixed up, so as not to be distinguished — **icignuni·ya** *va* icignuni·wa·ya : to cause not to be distinguished — **icignuniyan** *adv* : mingled, mixed up during that time - B.H.56.17, 201.6

i·ci·ha·kta·ya \í-ci-ha-kta-ya\ *adv* [fr *ihakta* to guard] : following each other

i·ci·he·han·han·yan \í-ci-he-haŋ-haŋ-yaŋ\ *adv red of* ici-hehanyan : so far apart

i·ci·he·han·yan \í-ci-he-haŋ-yaŋ\ *adv* : thus far apart

i·ci·hlo·gya \í-ci-ȟlo-gya\ *v* : to follow suit - KE

i·ci·hlo·ka \í-ci-ȟlo-ka\ *n* : a matching suit or number as in playing cards; a matching of bone rings, *obsol* < ~ *yuha* to have what matches, as is said of the game of dominos, cards, *etc* > - Bl KE

i·ci·hmin·yan \i-cí-ȟmiŋ-yaŋ\ *adv* : crookely, incorrectly, confusedly < ~ *nah'on* to hear incorrectly, ~ *wakaga* I made it wrong, differing from the other that is right. >

i·ci·i·yo·pe·ki·ci·ya·pi \í-ci-i-yo-ṗe-ki-ci-ya-pi\ *n* : a market

i·ci·i·yo·pe·ya \í-ci-i-yo-p̣e-ya\ *va* iciiyope·wa·ya [fr *iyopeya* to sell] : to barter, exchange one thing for another – **iciiyopeya·pi** *n* : barter, an exchange

i·ci·i·yo·pta \í-ci-i-yo-pta\ *adv* : in a range, in the same direction — **iciiyopte·ya** *adv* : in that direction, across or through

i·ci·je·han *or* **icije·na** \í-ci-je-haŋ\ *adv* : mingled, mixed up – R Bl

i·ci·kan·kan·ye·la \í-ci-kaŋ-kaŋ-ye-la\ *adv red of* icikanyela : near one another

i·ci·kan·ye·la \í-ci-kaŋ-ye-la\ *adv* : near together

i·ci·ki·ki·ye·la \í-ci-ki-ki-ye-la\ *adv red of* icikiyela : near to each other

i·ci·ki·ye·la \í-ci-ǩi-ye-la\ *adv* : close or near to each other

i·ci·ko·yag \í-ci-ǩo-yag\ *v contrac of* icikoyaka : to fasten

i·ci·ko·ya·gya \í-ci-ǩo-ya-gya\ *va* icikoya·gwa·ya : to fasten one to another — *adv* : linked, joined < *Isto ~ manipi* They walked with arms linked. >

i·ci·ko·ya·ka \í-ci-ǩo-ya-ǩa\ *vn* : to be fastened on to another — *adj* : united

i·ci·kpu·kpe·ya \í-ci-kpu-kpe-ya\ *adv* : scattered, mixed up – Cf kpukpéya

i·ci·kte \i-cí-kte\ *v* : to kill one's self, commit suicide – Cf ic'ikte BD

i·ci·lo·wan \í-ci-lo-waŋ\ *v* : to wail alone (to one's self), as at the death of a relative — **icilowan·pi** *n* : a death song

i·ci·ma \i-cí-ma\ *adv* : ever, again < *han'icima, hehan* the night before >

i·ci·ma·ni \í-ci-ma-ni\ *vn* ici·wa·mani icima·un·ni·pi : to travel, to go on a journey without one's family, to visit or go on an extended trip to another tribe or band — *n* : a traveler – D.116 note 2

i·ci·ma·ni ce·ki·pa·pi \í-ci-ma-ni ce-ǩì-p̣a-pi\ : soft meat under the shoulders of buffalo – HH Bl

i·ci·ma·ni·pi \í-ci-ma-ni-pi\ *n* : traveling, visiting

i·ci·ma·ni ti·pi \í-ci-ma-ni tì-pi\ *n* : an hotel – Bl

i·ci·mna *or* **ic'imna** \í-ci-mna\ *v* : to have confidence in one's self < *~ šni* to have no confidence in one' self, to be diffident > – B.H.74.21

i·ci·na·kšin·pi *or* **écinakšinpi** \í-ci-na-kšiŋ-pi\ *v coll pl* [fr *anakikšin* to stand in for another] : They stand up for each other, shield each other, help each other – Note: the word is used with the *pl* ending on itself or a *v* following though that is unusual R KE

i·ci·na·pci·yun·ka \i-cí-na-pci-yuŋ-ǩa\ *num ord adj* : ninth – Note: this form is not much used, Cf ínapciyunka

i·ci·nun·pa \i-cí-nuŋ-pa\ *num ord adj* : the second; — *adv* : a second time, again < *icinunpani šni* not a second time, *Icinunpani ihangwacawayin kte šni* He will not destroy them again. > – B.H.9.2, 181.20

i·cin \i-cíŋ\ *conj* : namely, for you know ... < *Mni kin hel ihpeyapi ehantanš ni iyayin kte cin he (kéya kin) slolkiya; ~ kéya kin mini mahel unpi* The turtle knows himself: if he is thrown there into the lake he will go away alive; for you know turtles live in water. > — *v* : to desire one thing for another, to desire more of in addition, as in asking more money for an object, thus for another < *Okise iwakicin kte* I desire a half for him. *~ eyaš* but namely ... > – B.H.157.20

i·cin·ca \i-cíŋ-ca\ *n* : a child, *i.e.* in *ref* to < *Toke nicincapi kin icincapi kin na wicoicage iciyamni na itopa hehanyan wanwicayaglakapi ni* I suppose of course you may see for some time your children, children of the third and fourth generation. > – B.H.125.13

i·cin'·in \i-cíŋ-iŋ\ *v* i·wa·kin'in [fr *kin'in* to assail] : to throw at, to strike with

i·cin·kcin \í-ciŋ-kciŋ\ *adv* : angrily, roughly, as one in speaking

i·cin·ya \i-cíŋ-ya\ *va* icin·wa·ya : to cause to desire, entice

i·cin·yun·škaš \i-cíŋ-yuŋ-škaš\ *interj of reproof* : "For heaven's sake!" < *~ Wakantanka ohoyalapi šni kin* For goodness' sake! You surely do not honor God! > – *Syn* ÍYUWINŠKAŠ B.H.55.20

i·ci·onb \i-cí-oŋb\ *adv* : off to one side, off from, out at one side of < *Tipi kin ~ bla* I went off to one side of the house. *~ ya* to swerve > — **icion·bya** *adv* : out of the way, off to the side < *~ hpaya* to lie down out of the way, as a strip of wood nailed under and serving to brace > – P

i·ci·pa \í-ci-pa\ *vn* : to meet, to clash < *Hecel iyawicapapi na ob icipapi na ob econpi* So they struck them, clashed, and engaged. > – KE

i·ci·pa·ha·ha \í-ci-p̣a-ha-ha\ *adv* : piled up, men and things < *~ egnakapi* It was put away piled. > — **icipahaha·ya** *adv* : on top of one another – B.H.71.12, 302.8

i·ci·pa·ja \í-ci-p̣a-ja\ *adv perhaps* : dove-tailed together at the ends, inserted, laminated, fitted

i·ci·pa·si·sa \í-ci-p̣a-si-sa\ *va* [fr *pasisa* to pin] : to stick to one another, to sew together, sew across < *Iciwapasisa wicao ške* It's said he shot sticking them all, *i.e.* he pierced them all with one shot. > — **icipasise·ya** *adv* : pinned into one another, put close to one another < *~ yapi wanyanke* He saw them going put close to one another. > – D.113 B.H.22.6

i·ci·paš \í-ci-p̣aš\ *adv contrac of* icipaja : back by the same way that one had left on < *~ glicu* to start coming back arriving the same way they left on. > — **icipa·špaš** \í-ci-p̣a-šp̣aš\ *adv* : backwards and forward, doubled on – D.227

i·ci·pa·tkuh \í-ci-p̣a-tǩuȟ\ *adv contrac of* p̣atǩuǥa : to be close together, to be adjacent <~ *yankapi* They sat close together. > – *Syn* OKOWANILYA, ICIPAT'INS Bl KE

i·ci·pa·t'ins \í-ci-p̣a-t'iŋs\ *v* : to push tightly together – Cf icipatkuh Bl KE

i·ci·pa·wa·hwah \í-ci-p̣a-ȟwaȟ\ *adv perhaps* : crossing in all directions *etc*, as wood piled disorderly, or as hair tangled up < *Can šeca ota yelo, ~ hpayelo* Much is the dry wood, lying piled haphazardly. > – Bl

i·ci·pa·we·ga \í-ci-p̣a-we-ǥa\ *vn* [fr *pawega* break by hand] : to cross, or to lie across — **icipaweh** *v contrac of* icipawega : to lie crosswise < *~ okatan* to nail on crosswise, to crucify > — **icipawe·hwega** *v red* : to cross — **icipawe·hya** \í-ci-p̣a-we-ȟya\ *adv* : crosswise, across

i·ci·pi·ye·la \í-ci-p̣i-ye-la\ *adv* : sufficiently for one's self < *~ owinja gluha wahi yelo* I came bringing just enough bedding for myself. *~ yanka* to have barely enough room to sit on, *okáglayakel yanka* (the opposite) to have plenty room to sit on > – Bl

i·ci·sam *or* **icisanb** \í-ci-sam\ *adv* : interruptingly < *~ wómayakilake* You spoke interrupting me all the while. >

\a\ father \e\ they \i\ machine \o\ smoke \u\ lunar \an, aŋ\ blanc Fr. \in, iŋ\ ink \on, oŋ, un, uŋ\ soon, confier Fr. \c\ chair \ǧ\ machen Ger. \j\ fusion \clusters: bl, gn, kp, hšl, etc...\ b^e^lo ... said with a slight vowel
See more in the Introduction, Guide to Pronunciation

i·ci·san·ni·ca \i-cí-saŋ-ni-ca\ *v* : to go to one side, to be off center, out of balance < *Wi ~ ye k'on ceti yelo, tate kte lo* The sun having gone over half its course started a fire, the wind will start up. > — **icisannicab** *v* : to have made over one-half of one's way < *Wanaš ~ yapelo* They now are gone half-way there. > – Bl BT KE

i·ci·sku·ya \í-ci-sku-ya\ *adj* [fr *skuya* sweet] : alike, sour or sweet < *kici ~* alike sweet with >

i·ci·ša·glo·gan \i-cí-ša-glo-ġaŋ\ *num ord* : the eighth

i·ci·ša·ko·win \i-cí-ša-ḱo-wiŋ\ *num ord* : the seventh

i·ci·ša·kpe \i-cí-ša-kṗe\ *num ord* : the sixth

i·ci·šle·ca \í-ci-šle-ca\ *adv* or *v* : to be or stand so close together that one shot will kill more than one < ~ *un nainš najin* to be or stand close together > — **icišleca·ya** *adv* : mixedly close together < ~ *wicoti* to camp close together, *i.e.* with tents being close together and mixed up apparently but a few in line. Game may at times stand this way, where more than one can be shot with one bullet. ~ *yankapi* to be mixed together, or ~ *kaot'ins yankapi* to be packed close together as people in a room. > – Note: they say to many, though *obsol* : *iciyaiyopteya*, or ~ *au* or *aya* they came or began to be compact *Syn* ICIT'EYELA

i·ci·šni·yan *or* **wicišniyan** \í-ci-šni-yaŋ\ *adv* : away off, not near anything – R Bl

i·ci·ta·ki·gnag \í-ci-ta-ki-gnag\ *adv* : on top of each other while carried by somebody — **icitakigna·gna** *adv red* : on top of one another < ~ *au welo* They are coming one bunch after another. > – *Syn* ICIKANKANYELA Bl

i·ci·tan'·in·šni \í-ci-taŋ-iŋ-šni\ *vn* [fr *tan'in* appear] : not to be manifest, *i.e.* that which is the one between two or more

i·ci·te·han *also* **icitehan·han** \í-ci-ṫe-haŋ\ *adv* : far apart — **icitehan·yan** *adv* : far apart from each other < *Hecel nupin lila ~ iyayapi* So both went on very far apart. >

i·ci·tko·kib \í-ci-tḱo-ḱib\ *adv* : meeting face to face, *i.e.* opposite each other

i·ci·tko·ki·pa·pi \í-ci-tḱo-ḱi-ṗa-ṗi\ *v pl of* itkokipa : They met face to face

i·ci·to·han *also* **icitohanhan** *and* **icitohanhanyan** \í-ci-ṫo-haŋ\ *adv interrog* : how long from? — **icitohan·yan** *adv* : how far apart?

i·ci·to·ke·ca \í-ci-to-ke-ca\ *adj* : different from each other

i·ci·to·na \í-ci-ṫo-na\ *adj interrog indef* : how many? *i.e.* in comparison to someone else's < *Šunkawakan ~ yuha so* How many horses has he compared to others? > – KE

i·ci·to·pa \i-cí-ṫo-ṗa\ *num card* : the fourth

i·ci·t'e·ya \í-ci-t'e-ya\ *adv* : very close together, crowding each other badly — **icit'eye·la** *adv* : crowded together – Cf icišlecaya

i·ci·wan·yan·ka \í-ci-waŋ-yaŋ-ḱa\ *va* iciwanblaka iciwan'·un·yanka·pi [fr *wanyanka* to see] : to look at things together, to compare — **iciwanyanka·pi** *n* : a comparison

i·ci·wa·šte \i-cí-wa-šte\ *vn* : to be good with or for < *Taku ~* With what is it good? >

i·ci·wi·kce·mna \i-cí-wí-kce-mna\ *num ord* : the tenth

i·ci·wo·to·pi \í-ci-wo-ṫo-pi\ *v 3rd per pl of* woto : they knock with the end of something < *Ṗe íciwotopi* They run with their heads together, as do rams. > – Bl

i·ci·ya \i-cí-ya\ *va* i·wa·kiya unki·kiya·pi i·ma·kiya : to take sides with, assist in a dispute or controversy

i·ci·ya·cin \í-ci-ya-ciŋ\ *v* íciblacin [fr *iyacin* compare] : to liken several things to each other; to think equal — **iciyacin·yan** *adv* : likening to one another

i·ci·ya·gla·ski·ski·ya \í-ci-ya-gla-ski-ski-ya\ *adv red* : in layers of flat or straight things, one upon another and horizontally; piled on top of each other – Cf óciyuštanštan, ócibcib – Bl

i·ci·ya·gla·ski·ya \í-ci-ya-gla-sḱi-ya\ *adv* : one above another, pressing on each other, as is said of flat or straight things; one on top of another – Cf agláskica, óciyuštanštan B.H.239.2, 244.4

i·ci·ya·gla·ška \í-ci-ya-gla-šḱa\ *v poss* iciya·wa·glaška : to unite together, or tie one to another of one's own < *Nape iciyaglaške oyuspa* He clasped grasping his hand. >

i·ci·ya·gle \í-ci-ya-gle\ *vn* : to reach one to another — *v red* : to be reaching to another repeatedly — **iciyagle·gleya** *adv* : reaching to another — **iciyagle·ya** *adv* : reaching one to another — *va* iciyagle·wa·ya : to cause one to reach to another, cause to meet

i·ci·ya·hlah \í-ci-ya-ħlaħ\ *v* : to cross or lock together < *nape ~ iyeya* to fold the hands for prayer, crossing the fingers > – Cf iciyaskabya Bl KE

i·ci·ya·hlal \í-ci-ya-ħlal\ *adv* [fr *yahlata* speak as if dying] : speaking as one gasping for breath and dying < *Nape ~ okiciyuspewicakiya au na lecel eya* He brought him and had them clasp one another's hands as he gasped for breath, and this is what he said: *Nape ~ ogluspa* Hold my hands as I breathe my last > – SI

i·ci·ya·hpa·ya \í-ci-ya-ħṗa-ya\ *va* : to catch from one another, to communicate to others *e.g.* an infectious disease

i·ci·ya·i·gla·ška·pi \í-ci-ya-i-gla-šḱa-pi\ *v pl* : to unite one to another, to tie each other together as man and wife

i·ci·ya·i·yo·pte·ya \í-ci-ya-i-yo-pte-ya\ *adv* : randomly close together – Cf ícišlecaya

i·ci·ya·ka·ška \í-ci-ya-ka-šḱa\ *va* íciya·wa·kaška : to tie or unite things mutually

i·ci·ya·ki·gle \í-ci-ya-ḱi-gle\ *adv* : one by one, one after another — **íciyakigle·gle** *adv red* : in succession

i·ci·ya·mni \i-cí-ya-mni\ *num ord* : the third, the third time < *Na ake ~ ai na ake iyena wicaopi na agli* And again a third time they went and again as many were shot and they returned home. >

i·ci·ya·pa \í-ci-ya-pa\ *vn* iciya·ma·pa : to bump into somebody < *Tate ~ yelo* He bucked a wind. *Toke unšipi šni ca iciyawicawapa ni* May I bump into those who do not give orders, as a woman would say out of jealously in regard to two big men that she married. > — **iciyapa·pi** *n* : a collision – Cf iyóto, iyápa Bl

i·ci·ya·pu·spa \í-ci-ya-pu-spa\ *va* iciya·wa·ppuspa [fr *iyapuspa* to glue] : to stick two or more things together

i·ci·ya·skab \í-ci-ya-sḱab\ *v contrac of* iciyaskapa : to stick to each other — **iciyaska·bya** *va* íciyaska·bwa·ya : to cause to adhere or stick to each other — *adv* : adhering to each other < *nape ~ ogluspa* to place the hands together with palms together, as in going to Holy Communion. > – Bl

i·ci·ya·ska·pa \í-ci-ya-sḱa-ṗa\ *vn* [fr *iyaskapa* to stick on] : to adhere or stick one to another

i·ci·ya·sya·za \í-ci-ya-sya-za\ *adv red of* iciyaza : in rows, in a range

i·ci·ya·wa \í-ci-ya-wa\ *va* íci·bla·wa [fr *yawa* to read] : to count up together

i·ci·ya·za \í-ci-ya-za\ *adv red of* iyaza : in rows, in a range, from one to another, as in passing a thing around < *Lena wicoicage ~ aupi* These bring one generation to another. > — **iciyaza·za** *adv red* : one after the other, from one to the other – P

i·ci·ye·han·yan \í-ci-ye-haŋ-yaŋ\ *adv* : equally long - Bl

i·ci·yo·ki·he \í-ci-yo-ki-he\ *adj* : adjoining < ~ *un* to join, be adjoining > — **iciyokehe·ya** *va* íciyokihe·wa·ya : to connect things, as two ropes, so as to make it longer — *adv* : over again and again, repeatedly, one after another

i·ci·yo·ta·tkons \í-ci-yo-ta-tkoŋs\ *adv* [fr *iyotatkonza* even with] : opposite to each other, equal to , even with

i·ci·yu·gmun \í-ci-yu-gmuŋ\ *va* íci·blu·gmun : to twist together *e.g.* two threads < *Wapepe iciyugmunpi tešlagkiyapi* They made him wear a crown woven of thistle. > — **iciyugmun·yan** *adv* : twisted < *Canpepe ~ yuktanpi* Brambles were bent and twisted together. > - Pb.38 B.H.263.10

i·ci·yu·mna·he s'e \í-ci-yu-mna-he s'e\ *adv* : in various directions < ~ *wicomani yelo* Their traveling is in diverse directions, *i.e.* many people traveling in all directions. > - Bl

i·ci·yun·ga \í-ci-yuŋ-ġa\ *va* ici·mun·ga ici·nun·ga unki·ciyunga·pi : to cross-question, to examine by cross-questioning — **iciyunga·pi** *n* : an examination

i·ci·yu·o·ta \í-ci-yu-o-ṫa\ *va* íci·blu·ota [fr *yuota* to multiply] : to multiply together

i·ci·yu·wi \í-ci-yu-wi\ *v* : to get entangled, entangle one's self - P

i·ci·za·ptan \i-cí-za-pṫaŋ\ *num ord* : the fifth

i·co·ga \í-co-ġa\ *vn* : to lodge on, drift and lodge on, as a log of wood - B.H.8.4

i·co·kab \i-có-kab\ *adv* micókab unki·cokab wicicokab [fr *icokapa* before] : before < *Tipi kin ~ énajin. Na el can wan glakinyan otka na ~ wazilyapi* They stood in front of the house. And there he suspended a piece of wood transversly, and it was made to smolder amidst them. > — **icoka·bya** \i-có-ka-bya\ *adv* : before, between < *Wanji unyankapi kin ~ iyotakin na taku hoyeya ...* One person sat down between us who were sitting and he cried out something ... >

i·co·kan·yan \i-có-kaŋ-yaŋ\ *adv* : in the middle, between - B.H.54.5

i·co·ka·pa *or* **icokab** \i-có-ka-pa\ *adv* [fr *cokapa* in the midst] : before, amidst — **icokapa·tanhan** \i-có-ka-pa-ṫaŋ-haŋ\ *adv* : before, in the midst, inside of

i·co·ka sa·pa \i-có-ka sà-pa\ *n* : the black-billed cuckoo, a bird whose mouth is black inside, whose tail is long, it lives in the woods and leaves in the fall, it is big as the *canwahpa tanka* - Cf hin'ikcekapila, and cépela tanka - Bl

i·co·ka·ta \i-có-ka-ta\ *adv* : in the middle of < *Ahimniciya kin ~* They are assembling in center camp. > - B.H. 83.24

i·co·lya \i-čó'-lya\ *v* : to make a base of operations < *Tuktel icolyaya hwo?* Where do you stay, or make your home? > - Bl

i·co·ma *or* **icomi** \i-có-ma\ *va* : to draw up around the shoulders *e.g.* one's blanket, to wear a blanket held tightly around the body, the arms holding the edges in front of the body < *Šina iwácoma. Koškalaka kin tilazata pamahel ~ najin* I drew a blanket up around myself. He in pushing the young man in behind the house stood drawing one up around him. > - D.47

i·co·pa \i-có-pa\ *v* icó·wa·pa [fr *copa* to wade] : to wade in, as in one's moccasins

i·cos \i-cós\ *v contrac of* icoza : to be warm by — **icosya** \i-có-sya\ *va* ico·swa·ya : to make warm with

i·co·za \i-có-za\ *vn* i·ma·coza [fr *coza* warm and comfortable] : to be warm by means of *e.g.* clothing

i·co·mi *or* **icomin** *or* **icoma** \i-có-mi\ *va* : to draw up around the shoulders *e.g.* a blanket < *Winyan wan šina pamahel icomin na olowan wan yawankal éyaye* A woman drew up pushing in around her a blanket and she took with her a song as she raised her voice. > - R D.261

i·cu \i-cú\ *va* i·wa·cu : to take, take up anything, to accept, receive

i·cu·cu \i-čú-ču\ *v* : to have or take more or plenty of something <*Iyacucu lakelo* Should you not take plenty, *blihic'iya yo* get busy with it, as is said encouragingly to one who is on the point of winning a race. Also said is: *Yakalu lakelo,iyótanla icu wo. Miye iwácucu kaca; eya šna wau welo* Try fanning yourself, and receive the high regard. As for me, I am taking no more; well I do come every now and then. > - Bl

i·cu·hca \i-cú-ȟca\ *adv* : the very one, the only one < *Wanjila ~ au yo* Bring it though it be only one. > - Note: the word is not the same as *icuhcin*

i·cu·ki·ya \i-cú-ki-ya\ *va* icu·wa·kiya : to cause to receive, to hold one's self back in self-control

i·cun·han \i-cúŋ-haŋ\ *adv* : whilst, during the time, in the meantime < *Wanna anpetu num mani kin ~ wicaša wan el hi. Yunkan ~ taku owicakiyake ci he kiksuya. Na hecel nupin kawingapi na kiglapi le ~ , oyate kin okihpayapi kte keyapi. Na ena lila tehan manka ~ , tanke ena ate kici tokena yankapi* Meanwhile a man came there after traveling for two days. Then during the time he recalled what he told them. And so both turned and went back and then got home while the people stated they would take some rest. And right here in the meantime I stayed a very long time, their older sister along with their father remained while the others moved on. > - Note: the word is used also without a noun, as in the use of "meanwhile"

i·cun·han·la·hci \i-cúŋ-haŋ-la-ȟci\ *adv* : just at that time

i·cun·kši·la \i-cúŋ-kši-la\ *n* : a little bow, such as small boys us

i·cun'·onb *or* **icíonb** \i-cúŋ-oŋb\ *adv contrac of* icun'onpa : out at one side of < *Tipi kin ~ bla* I went off to one side of the house. >

i·cun'·on·pa \i-cúŋ-oŋ-pa\ *adv* : off to one side, off from, out of the way < *micun'onpa* off from me >

i·cun'·on·pa·tan·han \i-cúŋ-oŋ-pa-ṫaŋ-haŋ\ *adv* : out of the way, off to one side

i·cun·sya \i-cúŋ-sya\ *v* icun·swa·ya : to be dilatory, not to do much, to have no mind to work, to work only for the pay — **icunsya·kel** \i-cúŋ-sya-kel\ *adv* : not heartily, pretending — **icunsye·ca** *n* : one who is not faithful, or one who does not do his duty well - Note: the word may be a *diriv* of *econ* or of *konza* - R Bl

i·cunš \i-cúŋš\ *v contrac of* kunza : to pretend - Note: icunza is *obsol*

i·cu·pi·ca \i-cú-pi-ca\ *adj* : available - P

i·cu·te \i-cú-te\ *n* [fr *kute* to shoot] : something to shoot with, as the arrows one uses in a game < ~ *wahinkpe* the name for the sticks used in the game called *painyankapi* the hoop game > - R

i·cu·tu \i-cú-tu\ *n* : a round stone to grind corn *etc* on

i·cu·wa \i-cú-wa\ *n* [fr *kuwa* to hunt] : something with which to hunt or catch anything < *hoícuwa* a fish-

---

hook >

i·c'i \i-c'í\ *pron refl signifying* **a** : the action of the *v* returns upon the actor, and sometimes **b** : the action is done for one's self < *ic'icaga* to make one's self >

i·c'i·ble·ble·ca \i-c'í-ble-ble-ca\ *v refl red* : to shake one's self, as a horse does < *Kul iyunkin na hnahna na icaptanptan kic'un na inajin na ~ na eciyatanhan maka gi wobluya* It lies down, grunts, rolls about, stands up, and shakes itself and for all that brown dirt blows away. >

i·c'i·ca·ga \i-c'í-ca-ġa\ *v refl* mi·c'icaga [fr *kaga* to make] : to make one's self, to make for one's self

i·c'i·can \i-c'í-caŋ\ *v refl* mi·c'ican : to cry over one's own self – Cf **kicán** BD

i·c'i·can·yan \i-c'í-caŋ-yaŋ\ *adv* : standing or planted firmly, as a post, a hay-stack, a person < *Wopte wan lécegla ~ hiyeye cin eya ške'* It's said he said a stack of all the trimmings was standing close. >

i·c'i·ca·ška \i-cí-ca-ška\ *v refl* mi·c'icaška [fr *kaška* to bind] : to bind or tie one's self, to deliver up one's self to authorities

i·c'i·cons \i-c'í-coŋs\ *v contrac of* ic'iconza : to determine < ~ *opa* to follow on one's own decision, to make a profession of religion > — **ic'icon·skiya** *va* : to cause one to determine for himself

i·c'i·con·za \i-c'í-coŋ-za\ *v refl* mi·c'iconza [fr *konza* pretend] : to determine for one's self, make up one's mind, to vow <*Ekta yin kta ~ . Eya anpetu kin lehanl mic'iconza ca wana wahi yelo* He decided he would go. Moreover, since I now determined the day I came, *i.e.* I came as I had promised. > – Bl

i·c'i·c'u·ya \i-c'í-c'u-ya\ *adv* [fr *k'u* to give] : giving one's self up, being devoted < ~ *econ* He acts devotedly. >

i·c'i·gla·lu \i-c'í-gla-lu\ *v refl of* kalu : to fan one's self

i·c'i·gle \i-c'í-gle\ *v refl* mi·c'igle [fr *gle* to place] : to lay up for one's self < *Taku ic'iglepi* They set aside something for themselves, as furniture perhaps. > — **ic'igleka** \i-c'í-gle-ka\ *n* : one who has much, one who is always accumulating, a thriving person

i·c'i·gna·ka \i-c'í-gna-ka\ *v refl* mi·c'ignaka [fr *gnaka* lay up or away] : to place or locate one's self, to lay up for one's self < *Taku ic'ignakapi* They set aside something for themselves, as furnishings perhaps. >

i·c'i·gna·yan \i-c'í-gna-yaŋ\ *v refl* mi·c'ignayan [fr *gnayan* deceive] : to deceive one's self

i·c'i·h'an \i-c'í-h'aŋ\ *v refl* : to extricate one's self, to help one's self – B.H.76.14

i·c'i·ksa·pa \i-c'í-ksa-ṗa\ *v* : to save for one's self, to have gained experience, to be wise < *Lenáke mic'iksapelo* This precious bit is saved for me, or This little nest I keep for tomorrow. *Hecel oyate woyute ic'iksapapi* So the people saved for him something to eat. > – Bl

i·c'i·ksu·ya \i-c'í-ksu-ya\ *v refl* mi·c'iksuya [fr *kiksuya* to recall] : to remember one's self, to come to one's self

i·c'i·kte \i-c'í-kte\ *v refl* [fr *kte* to kill] : to kill for one's self – Note: to commit suicide however is *icíkte* BD

i·c'i·la \i-c'í-la\ *v refl* [fr *la* to esteem] : to say of or to consider one's self < *wašte ~* to consider one's self good >

i·c'i·mna *or* **icimna** \i-c'í-mna\ *v* : to have confidence in one's self

i·c'i·mni·kel \i-c'í-mni-kel\ *adv* : sprawled < ~ *munkelo* I lie sprawled or stretched out. >

i·c'in \i-c'íŋ\ *n* : a harness — **ic'in'·ikan** *n* : harness lines — **ic'in·pasu** *n* : the hame — **ic'in·yuhlate** *n* : a snap

i·e *or* **ia** *or* **iye** *or* **iya** \i-é\ *v* : to speak

i·e·ca·na *or* **iyecana** \í-e-ca-na\ *adv* : soon after

i·e·gla·šna \i-é-gla-šna\ *v poss* [fr *ieyašna* to talk without discretion] : to blunder in speaking, to stammer, to speak falsely of one's own, as in telling one's dreams or visions — **ie-glašna s'a** *n* : a blunderer — **ieglašna·šna** *vn* : to stammer, stutter

i·e·ka·pin \i-é-ka-ṗiŋ\ *vn* [fr *kapin to* be indisposed] : to be tired of speaking, to be unwilling to speak

i·e·ki·ya \i-é-ki-ya\ *va* ié·wa·kiya : to cause to speak, to make a speaker of, to have for an interpreter

i·e·ksa·pa \i-é-ksa-ṗa\ *vn* ié·ma·ksapa : to be wise in one's speech, to be eloquent

i·e·la·ya \i-é-la-ya\ *v* : to put everything in the mouth, as babies often do < ~ *abla* I was in the habit of putting everything in my mouth. > – Bl

i·el·gle \í-el-gle\ *v* íel·wa·gle : to reproach, blame

i·e·ska \i-é-ska\ *n* iyé·ma·ska iyé·ni·ska : one who speaks well, an interpreter — *vn* ie·ma·ska : to be fluent, to speak a language intelligibly — **ieska·kiya** \i-é-ska-ki-ya\ *va* ieska·wa·kiya : to have for interpreter or cause to interpret from one language to another

i·e·slo·ta \i-é-slo-ta\ *adj* : spoken candidly, telling the truth, speaking aware of the situation – Bl

i·e·šni \i-é-šni\ *v* : to be unable to speak, to be dumb

i·e·wi·ca·ka \i-é-wi-ca-ka\ *vn* iewica·wa·ka : to tell the truth — **iewicake·ya** *adv* : truly – P

i·e·ya·pa·ha \i-é-ya-ṗa-ha\ *v* iéya·wa·paha : to proclaim, publish — *n* : a public crier, a herald – Note: the incorrect form is *éyapaha*

i·e·ya·šna \i-é-ya-šna\ *v* ié·bla·šna : to talk just as one pleases, to talk falsely — **ieyašna·šna** *v red* : to ventilate

i·gla \i-glá\ *pref* – It makes the *refl* form of verbs beginning with *ka* and *ya* < *iglablaska* to flatten one's own by striking; *i·wa·glablaska* I flattened my own by striking. > – Bl

i·gla·cin \i-glá-ciŋ\ *v poss* i·wa·glacin i·mi·glacin : to liken one's own or one's self to

i·glag \i-glág\ *v contra of* iglaka : to travel about < ~ *unyanpi* We are going touring. >

i·gla·gle·gle·ga \i-glá-gle-gle-ġa\ *v refl* : to stripe one's self with colors, to make a fool of one's self – KE

i·gla·gna·škin·yan \i-glá-gna-škiŋ-yaŋ\ *v* [fr *iyagnaškinyan* say foolish things] : to storm

i·gla·go·go \i-glá-ġo-ġo\ *v refl* [fr *kagogo* to gash marks] : to cut one's self in many places – B.H.108.10

i·gla·gya·ke *or* **iglagyakel** \i-glá-gya-ke\ *adv* [fr *iglaka* to move camp] : loaded down with some of one's own luggage < ~ *hi* to have come with all one's belongings, as on a trip >

i·gla·ho·gi·ta \i-glá-ho-ġi-ta\ *vn* [fr *yahogita* to become hoarse] : to become hoarse from speaking

i·gla·ho·mni \i-glá-ho-mni\ *v refl* mi·glahomni [fr *yahomni* to persuade] : to turn one's self around, to change one's own opinion < *Na wanna tiyatakiya ~ na tipi etkiya glapi. Na wanna ~ na tima kigla* And now he turned round headed homeward, and they were on their way back toward their house. Now he turned around to go inside on his arrival. >

i·gla·hni·ga \i-glá-hni-ġa\ *v* : to choose for one's self, to choose one's self as the object – B.H.220.10 KE

i·gla·ja·ta \i-glá-ja-ta\ *v refl* mi·glajata [fr *yajata* seduce one] : to contradict one's self

i·gla·ji·ca \i-glá-ji-ca\ *v refl* [fr *yajica* speak as rich] : to speak of one's self as rich – Cf ijica — **iglajica·ka** \i-glá-ji-ca-ka\ *n* : one who counts himself rich

i·gla·ka \i-glá-k̇a\ *vn* i·wa·glaka unki·glaka·pi : to move, to travel about with a family, pitching one's tent at short stages, to go camping

i·gla·ka·ta \i-glá-ka-ta\ *v refl* : to make one's self warm by moving the arms rhythmically - Bl

i·gla·ksa \i-glá-ksa\ *v refl* mi·glaksa [fr *kaksa* to split or *yaksa* to bite off] : to cut or bite off one's own

i·gla·lu *also* **ic'iglalu** \i-glá-lu\ *v refl* mi·glalu [fr *kalu* to fan] : to fan one's self

i·gla·mna \i-glá-mna\ *v refl* mi·glamna unki·glamna·pi [fr *kamna* to get or obtain, or *yamna* to win over] : to turn one's self around, to gain for one's self, to get back one's own <*Miš ena miglamna* I got back right here myself. >

i·gla·ta·ta \i-glá-ta-ta\ *v refl of* katata : to shake dust off one's self

i·gla·o·co·za \i-glá-o-co-za\ *v refl of* ocoza : to make one's self warm by moving the arms rhythmically - Bl

i·gla·o·ni·han \i-glá-o-ni-haŋ\ *v refl* mi·gláonihan [fr *yaonihan* to honor] : to praise one's self

i·gla·on·spe \i-glá-oŋ-spe\ *v refl* [fr *kaonspe* to train] : to train one's self, train by one's self <*Hena on šunkawakan iglaonspepi na hena on oyate icagapi kta* For that reason horses were trained and for the same reason people would develope. > - WHL

i·gla·on·ši·ka \i-glá-oŋ-ši-ka\ *v refl of* yaonšika : to speak of one's self as miserable - B.H.74.16

i·gla·o·tan'·in \i-glá-o-taŋ-iŋ\ *v refl* mi·glaotan'in [fr *yaotan'in* to make manifest] : to manifest one's self, to proclaim one's self

i·gla·pe·mni \i-glá-ṗe-mni\ *v refl* [fr *kapemni* make go awry] : to turn swinging self around <*Hinhan Cik'ala ~ škan* Little Owl spun around in haste. > - KE

i·gla·sto \i-glá-sto\ *va* i·wa·glasto : to smooth one's self or one's hair; *fig* to be left out, incomplete < *Imáglasto tka* I almost got left out, *i.e.* it almost did not reach me. > - Bl KE WHL

i·gla·su \i-glá-su\ *v refl* [fr *yasu* to decree or judge] : to judge one's self, to see one's own wrong-doing and promise to do better - IS

i·gla·ši·ca \i-glá-ši-ca\ *v refl* : to speak evil, to blame one's self

i·gla·ška \i-glá-šk̇a\ *v refl* mi·glaška [fr *kaška* to bind] : to bind one's self, to deliver one's self up to be punished

i·gla·šna \i-glá-šna\ *v refl* [fr *yašna* to miss with the mouth, *fig* to blunder in speaking] : to miss biting one's self, as a dog does in trying to bite its own tail — **iglašna·šna** *v red* : to keep missing with the mouth

i·gla·špa \i-glá-šṗa\ *v refl* mi·glašpa [fr *yašpa* bite off, *kašpa* cut loose] : to bite one's self loose; to break loose — **iglašpa·špa** *v red* : to bite or break one's self free

i·gla·štan \i-glá-štaŋ\ *v refl* mi·glaštan : to finish speaking or eating one's own food < *Le yaglapi na tanyan wol miglaštanpi hehanl* I then finished eating well my own food as I bit this off. >

i·gla·šya·kel \i-glá-šya-kel\ *adv* : sickly - WHL

i·gla·ta·ma·he·ca \i-glá-ta-ma-he-ca\ *v refl* : to become leaning by speaking *esp* by talking or slandering < *Šunka tamaheca s'e iwašicunpi c'on ~* Like a scrawny dog he had begun to lean on being talkative. > - Bl

[1]**i·gla·tan** \i-glá-ṫaŋ\ *v refl* mi·glatan [fr *yatan* to praise] : to praise one's self, to brag, boast

[2]**i·gla·tan** \i-glá-taŋ\ *v poss* i·wa·glatan [fr *iyatan* to light, as a pipe] : to light one's own *e.g.* a pipe < *Ilege mak'u wo; iwaglatan kte* I want to light mine; let me have your (burning) cigaret. >

i·gla·ta·ta \i-glá-ta-ta\ *v refl* [fr *katata* shake off] : to shake *e.g.* dust off one's self

i·gla·to·kan \i-glá-to-kaŋ\ *v refl* mi·glatokan [fr *yatokan* speak as if in another place] : to clear one's self, to prove an alibi

i·gla·t'a \i-glá-t'a\ *v* mi·glat'a : to have convulsions < *hohṗáiglat'a* to cough convulsively > — *v refl* [perhaps fr *kat'a* strike dead] : to strike dead one's own < *Can on ~ omani* He walked his own struck fatally with a club, *i.e.* walking slowly without paying attention to anything. > - Bl WHL

i·gla·t'e \i-glá-t'e\ *v refl* mi·glat'e [perhaps fr *yat'a* bite to death] : to give in, to grant - WE

i·gla·wa \i-glá-wa\ *v refl* mi·glawa i·ya·glawa [fr *yawa* to count] : to count one's self, to esteem one's self < *wašte ~* to consider one's self good, *wakan ~* to count one's self holy > - *Syn* WAŠTEIC'ILA B.H.111.5

i·gla·ye·ki·ya \i-glá-ye-k̇i-ya\ *v* : to push into, as a straw to clear out a pipe stem

i·gla·ye·ya \i-glá-ye-ya\ *n* : a pipe stem cleaner

i·gla·zo \i-glá-zo\ *v poss* i·wa·glazo [fr *icazo* to mark] : to mark one's self, to make marks on one's own *e.g.* blanket

i·gla·zun·ta \i-glá-uŋ-ṫa\ *v refl* mi·glazunta : to praise one's self

i·gle \í-gle\ *v* í·wa·gle : to use abusive language, to murmur < *Moses el iglepi. Wicaša el iglepi* They used abusive language on Moses. They murmured against a man. > - B.H.54.6, 235.13

i·gleb \i-gléb\ *v contrac of* iglépa : to vomit — **iglebkiya** \i-glé-bk̇i-ya\ *va* igle·bwa·kiya : to cause one to vomit up what he has eaten - D.33

i·gle·gle·hya \i-glé-gle-ḣya\ *adv* : with a whole assortment of things < *~ škan* : to be busy with many things (at the same time) > — **igleglehya·kel** *adv* : without a clear distinction between things, in an assortment of various things < *~ taku econ* fickly to perform, *~ pahi* to pick up worthless things > - Bl WHL

i·gle·gle·pa \i-glé-gle-ṗa\ *v red* i·wa·gleglepa [fr *iglepa* to vomit] : to vomit or throw up what one has eaten

i·gle·pa \i-glé-ṗa\ *vn* i·wá·glepa : to vomit, throw up on account of

i·gli \i-glí\ *n* : the soft fat of animals, grease, oil

i·glo·a·ya \i-gló-a-ya\ *v* : to pay attention to one's self — *v refl* [fr *aya* to lead] : to advance one's self, to get along well - B.H.130.10

i·glo·e·ya·ya \i-gló-e-ya-ya\ *v* : to go on one's own, to make one's own way -WHL

i·glo·hi \i-gló-hi\ *v refl* mi·glohi [fr *hi* to have arrived] : to bring one's self to a place, as a deer that might come to be shot

i·glo·i \i-gló-i\ *v refl* mi·gloi [fr *i* to have gone to] : to take one's self to, to take one's own to

i·glo·ku \i-gló-k̇u\ *v refl* mi·gloku [fr *ku* to come toward home] : to bring one's self towards home

i·glo·ni·ca \i-gló-ni-ca\ *v refl* i·wa·glonica : to forbid one's self, to balk, to refuse to go, as men too may do

i·glo·u \i-gló-u\ *v refl* [fr *u* to come] : to bring one's self towards a place, *fig* to induce one, as by studying

---

\a\ father \e\ they \i\ machine \o\ smoke \u\ lunar \an, aŋ\ blanc Fr. \in, iŋ\ ink \on, oŋ, un, uŋ\ soon, confier Fr. \c\ chair \ġ\ machen Ger. \j\ fusion \clusters: bl, gn, kp, hšl, etc...\ b^{e}lo ... said with a slight vowel
See more in the Introduction, Guide to Pronunciation

etc to bring one's self into the Church, or into doing something – Bl

i·glo·ya \i-glǒ-ya\ *v refl* mi·gloya [fr *ya* to be going] : to take one's self to a place, to take to one's self

i·glu \i-glú\ *pref* to *v* in *yu* making them the *v refl*, to make one's self ...

i·glu·ble·za \i-glú-ble-za\ *v refl* [fr *ibleza* to understand] : to make one's self see or think clearly

i·glu·can·ze \i-glú-caŋ-ze\ *v refl* [fr *yucanze* to make angry] : to hurt one's self and so get angry, to fail to accomplish something and so get angry – Bl

i·glu·ce·ya \i-glú-ce-ya\ *v refl* [fr *yuceya* to make cry] : to do something and so have tears come to one's eyes – Bl

i·glu·co·sco·za \i-glú-co-sco-za\ *v refl* : to warm one's self at a stove – *Syn* OKÁLIC'IYA

i·glu·e·ce·tu \i-glú-e-ce-tu\ *v refl* mi·gluecetu [fr *yuecetu* to correct] : to make one's self right, to reform, repent

i·glu·e·ki·ce·tu \i-glú-e-ki-ce-tu\ *v refl* mi·gluekicetu : to make one's self right, as before; to raise one's self from the dead, as did Christ

i·glu·gu·ka \i-glú-ġu-ka\ *v refl* : perhaps to make a fool of one's self, exposing one's self – WE

i·glu·ha \i-glú-ha\ *v refl* mi·gluha [fr *yuha* to have] : to possess one's self, be free; to restrain one's self, act well; to be able to carry one's own goods *etc* — **igluha·ya** *va* : to cause one to be free < *iyecinka igluhaya* to set free on one's own > – Pb.20

i·glu·hi \i-glú-hi\ *v refl* [perhaps fr *yuhi* to drive off] : to busy or arouse one's self < *Unkigluhipi kte lo* Let us get busy, arouse ourselves. > — **igluhi·ka** \i-glú-hi-ka\ *v refl* [fr *yuhika* shake off] : to quit a job to do something that wants attention immediately – Bl

i·glu·hin·han \i-glú-hiŋ-haŋ\ *v refl* mi·gluhinhan [fr *yuhinhan* to tease] : to lose one's patience, one's temper on account of being teased and when one wants peace <*Igluhinhe wakapin* I'm tired of him losing his temper at being teased, *i.e.* too angry to be teased. > — **igluhinhe·ya** *va* igluhinhe·wa·ya : to get one excited and make one lose his patience – Bl

i·glu·ho·mni \i-glú-ho-mni\ *v refl* mi·gluhomni [fr *yuhomni* to turn around] : to turn one's self around, to twirl — **igluhomni·ya** *va* : to cause one to turn himself around, *fig* to be converted

i·glu·hu·ku·ci·ye·la \i-glú-hu-ku-ci-ye-la\ *v refl* : to lower one's self – B.H.168.3

i·glu·hu·kul \i-glú-hu-kul\ *v contrac of* igluhukuya : to humble self < ~ *iyeic'iya* to put one's self down >

i·glu·hu·ku·lya \i-glú-hu-ku-lya\ *v refl* [fr *yuhukuya* to put self down] : to put one's self down — **igluhuku·ya** *v refl* mi·gluhukuya : to lower one's self, to be humble

i·glu·hci \i-glú-ȟci\ *v poss of* iyuhci : to tear or break out one's own button hole or eye of a needle <*Hehé iwagluhci* Alas! I broke out my button holes. >

i·glu·ȟi·ca \i-glú-ȟi-ca\ *v refl* mi·gluȟica [fr *yuȟica* or *yuġica* to awaken] : to waken one's self up — **iglu·ȟil** \i-glú-ȟil\ *v contrac* : to waken <~ *un wo* Keep your eyes open, or Watch out, or *Keep awake.* > – BT

i·glu·hla·hla·ta \i-glú-ȟla-ȟla-ta\ *v red* : to scratch one's self much or many times – D.40

i·glu·hla·ta \i-glú-ȟla-ta\ *v refl* mi·gluhlata [fr *yuhlata* to scratch] : to scratch one's self, to pinch one's self

i·glu·hlo·ka \i-glú-ȟlo-ka\ *v refl* mi·gluhloka [fr *yuhloka* make a hole] : to open or unbosom one's self, to open for one's self

i·glu·hni·ga \i-glú-ȟni-ġa\ *v refl* mi·gluhniga [fr *yuhniga* to dress one] : to dress up

i·glu·ȟo·pa \i-glú-ȟo-pa\ *v refl* : to make one's self look pretty – B.H.112.9

i·glu·hta·ni·ka·pin \i-glú-ȟta-ni-ka-pìŋ\ *v refl* igluhtani·wa·kapin [fr *htani* weak + *kapin* to be tired] : to be unable to move one's self, as when sick in bed, or when one is very lazy – *Syn* IGLUŠKAŠKANKAPIN WE Bl

i·glu·i·pa·we·htu \i-glú-i-pa-we-ȟtu\ *v refl* : to leave the straight road – B.H.119.20

i·glu·ja·ja \i-glú-ja-ja\ *v refl* mi·glujaja [fr *yujaja* to wash] : to wash one's self

i·glu·ju·ju \i-glú-ju-ju\ *v refl* mi·glujuju [fr *yujuju* destroy] : to pull to pieces one's own, as one's own bundle

i·glu·ka·wa \i-glú-ka-wa\ *v poss* i·wa·glukawa [fr *i* mouth + *glukawa* to open one's own] : to open one's mouth

i·glu·kcan \i-glú-kcaŋ\ *v refl* mi·glukcan [fr *yukcan* to understand] : to have an opinion of one's self, to understand one's self, to examine one's self, to make up one's opinion

i·glu·ksa \i-glú-ksa\ *v refl* mi·gluksa [fr *yuksa* break off] : to break one's own < *Yunkan pa* ~ And then he broke his head. >

i·glu·kšan \í-glu-kšaŋ\ *adv* : around, round about anything < *Na wanna ti* ~ *e enajin* They now stood, that is, around their house. > — **iglukšan·tanhan** *adv* : around from all sides — **iglukšan·yan** *adv* : round about

i·glu·ku·ya \i-glú-ku-ya\ *v refl* : to humble one's self – *Syn* IGLUHUKUYA

i·glu·k'e·ga \i-glú-k'e-ġa\ *v refl* [fr *yuk'ega* to scratch when itching] : to scratch one's self, to itch self – Bl

i·glu·k'o \i-glú-k'o\ *v* : to take it all, as to take all in a game that has been staked – *Syn* GLUTINTO Bl

i·glu·na·jin \i-glú-na-jin\ *v refl* [fr *yunajin* raise to stand] : to rise by one's self – Pb.15

i·glu·nun·pa \i-glú-nuŋ-pa\ *v refl* mi·glununpa [fr *yununpa* divide in two] : to make two of one's self, to have two pursuits on hand at the same time

i·glu·o·co·sco·za \i-glú-o-co-sco-za\ *v refl* [fr *yuocoscoza* make one warm *e.g.* by clothing] : to make one's self warm by putting on much clothing – Bl

i·glu·o·ki·ni·han \i-glú-o-ki-ni-haŋ\ *v poss* : to make one's own honorable

i·glu·o·ni·han \i-glú-o-ni-haŋ\ *v refl* mi·gluonihan [fr *yuonihan* to honor] : to honor one's self

i·glu·on·ši·ka \i-glú-oŋ-ši-ka\ *v refl* [fr *yuonšika* reduce to littleness] : to humble one's self – B.H.215.7, 232.14

i·glu·o·ta \i-glú-o-ta\ *v refl* mi·gluota [fr *yuota* multipy] : to multiply one's self, to do many things at the same time, to multiply – Pb.44 B.H.45.3

i·glu·o·tan'·in \i-glú-o-taŋ-iŋ\ *v refl* mi-glúotan'in [fr *yuotan'in* make manifest] : to manifest one's self

i·glu·o·tkon·za \i-glú-o-tkoŋ-za\ *v refl* [fr *yuotkonza* make of equal length] : to have become equal to others, to have become ready with everything like others, as in having things ready for a trip while others are waiting – Bl

i·glu·o·wo·tan·la \i-glú-o-wo-taŋ-la\ *v refl* mi·gluowotanla [fr *yuowotanla* make straight or right] : to straighten one's self up, to stand straight, to make one's self upright or righteous

i·glu·psi·ca \i-glú-psi-ca\ *v refl* mi·glupsica [fr *yupsica* make jump] : to prance or jump about, as does a frisky horse

i·glu·ptan \i-glú-ptaŋ\ *v refl* : to roll over — **igluptan·ptan** \i-glú-ptaŋ-ptaŋ\ *v refl* : to roll over again and again < *Icapšinpšincala wan ~ iyaye* A swallow rolled over and over. > — **igluptan·yan** *v refl* [fr *yuptanyan* turn over by hand] : to turn around; *fig* to change one's mind – P MS.570 B D.35

i·glus \i-glús\ *v refl contrac of* igluza : to dress up

i·glu·so·ta \i-glú-so-ṫa\ *v refl* mi·glusota [fr *yusota* use up, make and end of] : to use one's self up, to use up one's own, perhaps *fig* to finish speaking

i·glu·su·ta \i-glú-su-ṫa\ *v refl* mi·glusuta [fr *yusuta* to make firm] : to make one's self firm, to establish one's self

i·glu·su·ya·kel \i-glú-su-ya-kel\ *adv* : in the state of being ready < ~ *yanka* to be on the spot and ready, ~ *mankelo* I am on ready-alert. > – Cf yusú egle

i·glu·ša·pa \i-glú-ša-ṗa\ *v refl* mi·glušapa [fr *yušapa* defile or blacken] : to blacken, to defile one's self

i·glu·ši·ca \iglú-ši-ca\ *v refl* mi·glušica [fr *yušica* make bad, to spoil] : to make one's self bad, get one's self into difficulty

i·glu·ši·htin \i-glú-ši-ḣtiŋ\ *v refl* mi·glušihtin [fr *yušihtin* enfeeble or debase] : to enfeeble or injure one's self in any way

i·glu·ška \i-glú-ška\ *v refl* mi·gluška : to untie, to loose one's self – D.220

i·glu·škan·škan·ka·pi(ŋ) \i-glú-škaŋ-škaŋ-k̇a-ṗi(ŋ)\ *v refl* igluškanškan·wa·kapi [fr *yuškanškan* cause to move + *kapin* be adverse to] : to be unable to move one's self, as a sick person in bed – *Syn* igluhtanikapi WE

i·glu·šlo·ka \i-glú-šlo-k̇a\ *v refl* mi·glušloka [fr *yušloka* pull off or out] : to pull or put off one's own, to divest one's self of *e.g.* one's garments

i·glu·špa \i-glú-šṗa\ *v refl* [fr *yušpa* break off] : to tear off one's self, as pieces of skin, scab, *etc*, to tear one's self loose – B.H.25.5

i·glu·štan \i-glú-štaŋ\ *v refl* mi·gluštan [fr *yuštan* to finish] : to finish or complete the things pertaining to one's self < *Wakantanka el wocekiye eyin kta na he ~ kinhan hehanl ... Lol'ih'an nigluštan kinhan can k'in unyin kte* Let him say a prayer to God, and having finished it, then ... When you are finished preparing food then we shall go to carry wood. > – Bl

i·glu·š'a·ka \i-glú-š'a-ka\ *v refl* iglu·ma·š'aka [fr *yuš'aka* to be heavily laden] : to be pregnant, to be overburdened with one's self

i·glu·š'in·š'in \i-glú-š'iŋ-š'iŋ\ *v refl* [fr *yuš'inš'in* to tickle] : to tickle one's self repeatedly – D.40

i·glu·ta \i-glú-ta\ *v poss* i·mi·gluta [fr *iyuta* to measure] : to measure one's self, to measure or try one's own

i·glu·ta·ku·ni·šni \i-glú-ṫa-ku-ni-šni\ *v refl* mi·glutakunišni [fr *yutakunišni* to destroy] : to destory one's self

i·glu·tan \i-glú-taŋ\ *v refl* mi·glutan unki·glutan·pi : to paint one's self, to put on fine clothes or dress < *Hecel wanna oyate k'on iglutanpi* So now the people had dressed fine. > – B.H.108.1

i·glu·tan'·in \i-glú-taŋ-iŋ\ *v refl* mi·glutan'in [fr *yutan'in* to reveal] : to manifest one's self < *togyé* ~ to simulate >

i·glu·tan·ka \i-glú-taŋ-k̇a\ *v refl* mi·glutanka [fr *yutanka* enlargen] : to make one's self great

i·glu·tan·tan \i-glú-taŋ-taŋ\ *v refl* [fr *yutan* to touch] : to touch as with one's dirty hands, to touch often

i·glu·ta·ta \i-glú-ta-ta\ *v poss red* [fr *iyuta* to try, weigh, measure] : to measure, one's self, to try *e.g.* a coat *etc*, to try, attempt repeatedly < *Kinyan ~ yanka* It tried flying time and again. >

i·glu·te·ca \i-glú-ṫe-ca\ *v refl* mi·gluteca [fr *yuteca* renew] : to make one's self new

i·glu·te·mni \i-glú-ṫe-mni\ *v* mi·glutemni : to perspire

i·glu·ti·tan \i-glú-ṫi-ṫaŋ\ *v refl* [fr *yutitan* to pull] : to struggle to tear one's self away – D.163, 206

i·glu·to·kan \i-glú-to-kaŋ\ *v refl* mi·glutokan : to remove one's self to another place – Bl

i·glu·to·ke·ca \i-glú-to-k̇e-ca\ *v refl* mi·glutokeca [fr *yutokeca* to alter] : to make one's self different, to disguise one's self

i·glu·t'a \i-glú-t'a\ *v refl* [fr *yut'a* to choke to death] : to kill one's self < ~ *wikan on* to kill by hanging >

i·glu·wa·hpa·ni·ca *or* **igluwahpanica·la** \i-glú-wa-ḣṗa-ni-ca\ *n* : one who throws away everything he has, a squanderer, spend-thrift

i·glu·wan·ka·tu·ya \i-glú-waŋ-k̇a-ṫu-ya\ *v refl* mi·gluwankatuya : to raise one's self, to be proud

i·glu·wa·šte \i-glú-wa-šṫe\ *v refl* [fr *yuwašte* to bless or make good] : to make one's self good, to make reparation for a wrong done

i·glu·wa·š'a·ka \i-glú-wa-š'a-ka\ *v refl* mi·gluwaš'aka [fr *yuwaš'aka* to strengthen] : to strengthen one's self

i·glu·wa·za \i-glú-wa-za\ *v refl* [fr *yuwaza* to twist and turn] : to rub one's self, as on account of a little itching – Bl

i·glu·wi \i-glú-wi\ *v refl* mi·gluwi [fr *yuwi* to bind] : to wrap or tie on one's own, as one's leggings

i·glu·win·ye·ya \i-glú-wiŋ-ye-ya\ *v refl* mi·gluwinyeya [fr *yuwinyeya* to make ready] : to make one's self ready or to get ready – *Syn* KENUN'IC'IYA

i·glu·wi·ta·ya \i-glú-wi-ṫa-ya\ *v refl* [fr *yuwitaya* collect or assemble] : to concentrate – P

[1]**i·glu·za** \i-glū́'-za\ *v refl* mi·gluza: to dress up, put on a dress, to paint one's self < *Wicaša wan ataya ska ~ . Takuwe migluze k'on iyecel ecannon hwo?* A man painted himself entirely white. Why was it you did such as I had done in arraying myself? > – Note: the word is used instead of *aigluza*

[2]**i·glu·za** \i-glú-za\ *v refl* [fr *yuza* take hold of] : to refuse to give up one's own, to defend one's self – IS WE

i·glu·ze·ze \í-glu-ze-ze\ *v refl* i·mi·gluzeze : to hold up one's self by, to cling to < *Inyan kin le he Wakantanka tawa lakaš tohinni wakanšica yujujupi okihi šni ca ikce wicaša he ~ icagapi* Of course since God is this rock of his and never able to be destroyed by satan, the common man grows up clinging to it. > — **igluzeze·ya** *adv* : clinging to – MS.658

i·glu·zi·ca \i-glú-zi-ca\ *v refl* mi·gluzica [fr *yuzica* to stretch] : to stretch one's self, to stand up on tiptoe < *Ungna tatanka wan inajin na ~* I guess a buffalo bull stood and stretched>

i·gmu \i-gmú\ *n* : a cat – Note: the word is an *abbrev* of *igmušunkala*, its original name – Bl
igmugleška the spotted wild cat, the genet
igmugleza or *igmuglezela* the bobcat, the tiger
igmuhota the gray wild cat, the lynx
igmušunka the domestic cat
igmutanka a lion; *fig* an Indian inspector

---

a\ father \e\ they \i\ machine \o\ smoke \u\ lunar \an, aŋ\ blanc Fr. \in, iŋ\ ink \on, oŋ, un, uŋ\ soon, confier Fr. \c\ chair \ġ\ machen Ger. \j\ fusion \clusters: bl, gn, kp, hšl, etc...\ b^{e}lo ... said with a slight vowel
See more in the Introduction, Guide to Pronunciation

igmuwatogla a mountain lion, a wild cat – Bl

i·gmun·ke \i-gmúŋ-ḳe\ *n* : a snare, trap, a poison to trap with

i·gna·gna·yan \i-gná-gna-yaŋ\ *v red* i·wa·gnagnayan [fr *ignayan* to deceive with or for] : to sport with; to deceive by

i·gna·gna·ye s'e \í-gna-gna-ye s'e\ *adv* : appearing enticing, bringing one along < ~ *aupelo* They came drawn along coming one after the other. > – Bl

i·gna·škin·yan \i-gná-škiŋ-yaŋ\ *vn* i·ma·gnaškinyan : to be possessed with, to be demonized; to be crazy for or by reason of

i·gna·yan \i-gná-yaŋ\ *va* i·wá·gnayan unkí·gnayan·pi : to deceive with or for – R

i·gni \i-gní\ *va* i·wa·gni unki·gni·pi : to hunt, seek for, to follow after *e.g.* game; to call names < *Can ~ yo* Go after some wood. *Šunkmanitu imagni* He called me a wolf. *Na oyate kin koškalaka top iwicagnipi* And the people searched for four young men. >

i·gni·gla \i-gní-gla\ *va* i·wa·gnigla : to go home for

i·gni·ya \i-gní-ya\ *va* : to go for, take a journey for, to procure

i·gnu \i-gnú\ *va* i·wa·gnu : to blame or charge with < *eya ignupi* to utter slander > – B.H.113.11

i·gu·ga \i-ġú-ġa\ *n* : rock, perhaps a rocky place < *Hetkala ~ el ti* The ground squirrel lives in a rocky place. > – Cf the bird, *~otila* D.262

i·gu·ga·o·ti·la \i-ġú-ġa-o-ṫi-la\ *n* : a wren perhaps, one living in the clefts of rock, thus *iguga oti* to live in the clefts < *Igugala ecel un, na ḣolḣotala na canheya hinskokeca* *i.e.* a cleft dweller lives that way, is brown-gray, and a wren just so big, very small and with white stripes; perhaps a common sparrow. > – Bl

i·ha \i-há\ *n* : the lower lip; *fig* the lid or cover of anything — **iha·hpi** \i-há-ḣpi\ *n* : hanging lips — **iha·i·slaye** \i-há-i-sla-ye\ *n* [fr *iha* lips + *islaye* grease for] : grease for the lips, a lip ointment

i·ha·kab \i-há-ḳab\ *adv* mi·hakab unki·hakab : after, *i.e.* in place, behind < *Cihakab waun* I am after you. *~ yapi* They go after. *Mihakab u po* Come come behind me. > — **ihaka·bya** *va* : to follow — **ihaka·pa** \i-há-ḳa-ṗa\ *adv* : after, behind — **ihakapa·tanhan** \i-há-ḳa-pa-ṫaŋ-haŋ\ *adv* : from behind

i·ha·ki·ci·kta \i-há-ki-ci-kta\ *va* ihá·we·cikta [fr *ihakta* have regard for] : to accept of, take of one

i·ha·ki·kta \i-há-ki-kta\ *v poss* ihá·we·kta or perhaps ihá·wa·kikta : to have regard for one's own

i·ha·kta \i-há-kta\ *va* ihá·wa·kta : to see to, be intent upon, to watch over, guard; to have regard for, love; to obey, follow; to wait for one < *Ihamakta yo* Wait for me! as might be said when one walks faster than the other. > — **ihakta·kta** *v red* : to follow often

i·ha·kta·pi·la \i-há-ḳta-ṗi-la\ *n* : a pet

i·ha·kta·ya \i-há-kta·ya\ *va* ihakta·wa·ya : to cause to have regard for — *adv* : having regard for

i·ha·mna·pi s'e \i-há-mna-pi s'e\ *adv* : much appealing to one's appetite < *Wašpanka ~ ahimayakigle kin le ibluškin* I am delighted with this your bringing me most tasty cooked food. > – BT Bl WHL

i·han \i-háŋ\ *vn* i·wá·han i·ún·han·pi : to stand in or at, to remain < *Na ehake hakela ecela ~ keya. Yunkan itancan k'on hena witayela ihanpi na lecel eyapi. Wana nišnala inihan* And in the end he stated the youngest alone remained. And then those who had been chiefs remained together. Now you are the only one left. >

i·han·bla \i-háŋ-bla\ *v* i·wá·hanbla unkí·hanbla·pi : to dream, to have visions < *Taku iyahanbla hwo* What did you dream? *Tatanka wan iwahanble lo. Yuwipi wašicun ca iwicawahanbla* I had a vision of a buffalo bull. I dreamt of the yuwipi power stones. >

i·han·ce·ti \i-háŋ-ce-ti\ *n* : shavings laid ready in the evening to start a fire with in the morning, *i.e. can lecel kajipapi un hanhepi ehan uncetipi. ~ on ipoganpi* When it is evening wood shavings are made, then we start a fire. Shavings are blown upon (to set ablaze). – Bl B

i·hang \i-háŋg\ *v contrac of* ihanke : to come to an end — **ihan·gkiya** \i-háŋ-gki-ya\ *va poss* ihan·gwa·kiya : to destroy one's own or for one — **ihan·gya** *v* ihan·gwa·ya [fr *ihanke* an end] : to destroy, to bring to an end – Cf ihánkeya

i·han i·yu·pta \í-haŋ i-yù-pta\ *adv* : through most of the night, through the night < ~ *wau welo* I was acoming through the night. > – Bl

i·han·ke \i-háŋ-ḳe\ *n* : the end, termination, the border or boundary < *He ~ ca el Šahiyela okitipi. Ḣe Ska akokiya ~ kin el lecel womayakiyaka. Ti ~ el unglapi* There the Cheyennes are camped at the border. Beyond the Rocky Mountains at the border I have spoken to you this way. We are on our way home to a house near completion. > — *vn* i·ma·hanke : to end, come to an end — **ihanke·ta** \i-háŋ-ke-ṫa\ *adv* : at the end, at the last — **ihanke·ya** *adv* : at the end, at the end, at the last or lowest part < *Pte kin tukte ~ cepe kin iyuha awicunglipelo ca nakeš tantan wayatin kte lo* Since we brought home all whichever buffalo were at the end fat, right now you should eat very well. >

I·han·kton·wan \I-háŋ-ktoŋ-waŋ\ *np* [fr *ihanke* border + *tonwan* to look or be present at] : the Yanktons, name of one of the divisions of the Dakota people

i·ha·ton \í-ha-toŋ\ *v* íha·ma·ton : to have chapped lips < *Ihamaton ca i slawakiyin ktelo* When I have chapped lips I should anoint my mouth (lips). > – Bl

i·he \i-hé\ *v* i·wa·he : to use sarcasm or cutting words at one < *wayátiktil ~* to nag, to find fault with others when there is no reason for it > – Cf tiktíca LB WHL

i·he·ce·gla \í-he-ce-gla\ *adv* : at once, immediately — **ihecegla·la** \i-hé-ce-gla-la\ *adv* : right at that moment < *Yunkan ~ tonwe* And then at that very moment he saw > – B.H.108.23, 117.10

i·he·ci·ya \í-he-ci-ya\ *adv* : in that way from — **iheciya·tan** \í-he-ci-ya-ṫaŋ\ *adv* : in that direction from — **iheciyatan·han** \í-he-ci-ya-ṫaŋ-haŋ\ *adv* : on that side of — **iheci·yotan** \i-he-cí-yo-ṫaŋ\ *adv* : in that direction from – R

i·he·han·han·yan \í-he-haŋ-haŋ-yaŋ\ *adv* : so so far from

i·he·han·yan \í-he-haŋ-yaŋ\ *adv* : so far from

i·he·ki·ya \i-hé-ki-ya\ *v poss* ihé·wa·kiya : to have remaining < *Hehe kola, Iktomila s'e léceglala ihewakiye lo* Too bad, friend, like dear little Spider I have remaining only this much. – Note: the word implies one has but little left. > Cf D.56

i·he·ktab \i-hé-ḳtab\ *prep* mi·hektab : behind, after one

i·he·kta·bya \i-hé-ḳta-bya *or* í-he-ḳta-bya\ *adv* : behind

i·he·kta·pa \i-hé-ḳta-pa\ *adv* : behind < *mihektapa* behind me > — **ihektapa·ta** \i-hé-kta-pa-ṫa\ *adv* : at the back, behind — **ihektapa·tanhan** \i-hé-ḳta-pa-ṫaŋ-haŋ\ *adv* : from behind

i·he·ya \i-hé-ya\ *v* **a** : to go or pass through < *iyopta ~* to discharge from the bowels, *Mini ecela ~* Only water discharged. *Cunkaške kin ~ wanjila ihekiyapi* They have only one fence row left. > **b** : to shoot or hit < *Wakangli makata iheyapi* Lightning struck the ground. *Wan-*

wicayank ~ he Did he see them get hit at once? *Kaotan ~* He pounded it in tight. > d : to assemble, *i.e. witaya ~, katá ~, wanyag ~,* and are *coll pl* – D.28, 58, 92, 271

i·hin·han·na \i-híŋ-haŋ-na\ *n* : the day following, the next morning < *Anpetu Wakan ~* Monday *Na wana ~ el wiyohpatanhan wicaša wan hihunni* And now on the next day a man from the west arrived. >

i·hi·ṫi \í-hi-ṫi\ *adj* : insisting on one's own opinion < *Taku owakiyaka nah'on šni piyeleš ~ yelo* He did not hear what I said to him heedlessly insisting on what was his own idea. > – Bl

i·ho \i-hó\ *v imper only* : Behold, Listen, See then, Be it so < *~ le icinunpa wicoh'an econ eša lila šogya econ yawapi. ~ micinkši, lena aokagapi šni yo. Leci ku wo eya.* Look now, though he kept the custom again, he very seriously considered keeping it. Listen son, do not do more of this than you ought. He said come here. *Hecel ekta mni na el wai; yunkan "~ taku tokel slolyaye kin olakin kte lo," eya* So I went to and into the water; and then he said: "Be it so, you should tell what and how you know." *~ misun, wanna yagni kta* Look my brother, you should be off for home. > – Note: *iho ... wo* and *iho ... po* are doubtfully *deriv* of the word. *Iho* seems to infer arousing one to do something, the speaker including himself.

i·ho·e·ceš \i-hó-e-ceš\ *adv* : just as well, might as well < *~ hecel ecunkonpi kte* So we might as well should do it. > – Cf itóeceš, itóceš

i·ho·hu·ca·ṫe \i-hó-hu-ca-ṫe\ *n* : a big stone hammer with which to break up bones in order to retrieve the marrow – Cf *ihonicata* the small hammer Bl

i·ho·ni·ca·ta \i-hó-ni-ca-ta\ *n* : a stone hammer with which to pound meat and cherries – Note: the word *ihúnicata* is incorrect Cf *ohúnnicata* D.16

i·ho·ye·ya \i-hó-ye-ya\ *va* : to utter with *ref* to, to pronounce < *Ungna ... woyašica ihoyeyaya kilo* Beware ... you are not to utter evil deeds. > – B.H.67.16

i·hu *or* **hu** \i-hú\ *v* : to penetrate < *onze ihu* to commit sodomy > – Note: the word is an obscene by-word relating to copulation

i·hu·blo·ya \í-hu-blo-ya\ *v* íhublo·wa·ya : to strike on the lower part of the legs as punishment, to flog < *Ihublociyin kta. Hecanon šni kinhan, ihublociyin kte lo* I should flog you. I shall flog you unless you did not do that. > – IS

I·hu·k̇u Ki·gle \I-hú-k̇u Ki-glè\ *n* : Arcturus, a first magnitude star, alpha Bootes, in that northern constellation, and otherwise known as *Itkob U,* or *Ánpo Wicáhpi Sunkáku* – WE

i·hu·ku·ku·ya \i-hú-k̇u-k̇u-ya\ *adv red of* ihukuya : beneath, under anything

i·hu·kul \i-hú-k̇ul\ *adv contrac of* ihukuya : under, beneath < *oyunke ~* under the bed, *~ iyeya* to put underneath >

i·hu·ku·ya \i-hú-k̇u-ya\ *adv* mi·hukuya : under, beneath anything, down below

i·hun·ni \i-húŋ-ni\ *vn* i·wá·hunni : to reach, get across, to finish, to come to the end of < *Anpetu 60 niopeyapi waun kte lo. Na he ~ kin ate ekta wagni kte lo. Hel unkihunnipi* I'll be together with you for sixty days. And I'll be going home to my father when I finish there. We got to the place in the end. >

[1]**i·hun·ni·ki·ya** \i-húŋ-ni-k̇i-ya\ *va* : to cause to reach

[2]**i·hun·ni·ki·ya** \i-húŋ-ni-k̇i-ya\ *va* ihunni·wa·kiya : to go through with, finish, complete, as the reading of a book < *Waawanyanke k'un he ihunnikiye* He had finished standing watch. > – B.H.160.9

i·hun·ni·yan \i-húŋ-ni-yaŋ\ *adv* : clear through, entirely < *Wicokanhiyaye ci ~ taku talo ke eyaš yatapi kte šni* We shall not eat any meat through to the next afternoon. > — *va* ihunni·wa·yan : to cause to reach < *Letanhan hoanunk ataya najinyeyapi na ecel tipi he el anunk ~ po. Wanna tipi kin tice kin hehanyan ~ wa šma kin* They all stood in a row on both sides of center camp from this time on; and so make both sides reach at that tent. the The snow was surely deep reaching as far as the tipi smoke-vent. >

i·hu·pa \i-hú-ṗa\ *n* : the bail or handle of anything; a stem, shaft, thill *etc* ; a wagon tongue, an axe handle < *~ iyuhomni* a crank > — **ihupa·kiciton** \i-hú-ṗa-k̇i-ci-toŋ\ *va* ihupa·we·citon : to put in a handle *etc* for one — **ihupakiton** \i-hú-ṗa-k̇i-toŋ\ *v poss* ihupa·we·ton : to bail or handle one's own — **ihupa·ton** \i-hú-ṗa-toŋ\ *v* ihupa·wa·ton : to have a handle or bail to anything – P

i·hu·tab \i-hú-ṫab\ *adv* : down-stream of, below

i·hu·ta·wab \i-hú-ṫa-wab\ *prep* or *adv* : downstream beyond, below (local), at the end of, as of the month < *Wašin Wakpa iyohloke el kitanla ~ he ewicoti* There a little downstream they set up camp at the mouth of the South Fork of the Platte River. >

i·ȟa \i-ȟá\ *v* i·wa·ȟa i·ma·ȟa [fr *i* mouth + *ȟa* to bury] : to laugh, to laugh at, make fun of — **iȟa·ȟa** \i-ȟá-ȟa\ *v red* i·wa·ȟaȟa [fr *iȟa* to laugh at] : to ridicule, laugh at < *~ ia* to commit rape (a doubtful meaning), *~ kuwa* to treat one like a boy, to imitate him > — **iȟaȟa·ke** \i-ȟá-ȟa-k̇e\ *n* : one who is always jesting, a fool — **iȟaȟa·ya** \i-ȟá-ȟa-ya\ *va* iȟaȟa·wa·ya : to cause to jest or laugh at — *adv* : laughingly, jestingly – Pb.24 Bl BD

i·ȟa·hpi·ya *or* **ihahpiya** \i-ȟá-ȟpi-ya\ *adv* : with hanging lips – Bl

i·ȟa·ke \i-ȟá-k̇e\ *v* i·wa·ȟake : to laugh, jest

i·ȟa·ki·ya \i-ȟá-k̇i-ya\ *va* iȟa·wa·kiya : to cause to laugh

i·ȟan·han \í-ȟaŋ-haŋ\ *adv* : jestingly, in fun, not in earnest for awhile < *~ el waun kte* I shall wear it in jest. *~ šunkawakan bluha kte* Let me hold a horse in fun. *~ kin inyankapi* (without a prize) They ran for fun, *i.e.* temporarily. > — **iȟanhan caje** \í-ȟaŋ-haŋ ca-jè\ *n* : a nickname – D.260

i·ȟa·t'a \i-ȟá-t'a\ *vn* i·wá·ȟa-t'a : to laugh hard — **iȟa·t'a·t'a** \i-ȟá-t'a-t'a\ *vn* iȟa·ma·t'at'a : to lugh immoderately — **iȟa·ya** \i-ȟá-ya\ *va* iȟa·wa·ya : to cause to laugh, to be the occasion of laughter

i·hca \í-ȟca\ *vn* [fr *i* to have gone + *hca* verily] : to be sure to have gone to, to be sure to be there < *Ihcin kte. Waihcin kta.* He will be sure to come. I should be there for sure. >

i·hci·wa·han \i-ȟcí-wa-haŋ\ *part* : broken out in gaps, gapped; torn, as a buttonhole

i·ȟe·yab \i-ȟé-yab\ *adv* : away from < *Wicaša kin le ayuštan na ~ iyaya yo* Let this man alone and stay away from him. > – B.H.203.8

i·ȟe·ya·ta \i·ȟé-ya-ṫa\ *adj* or *prep* mi·ȟeyata [fr *ȟeyata* in the uplands] : back from, behind < *tipi kin ~* back of the house > — **iȟeya·tanhan** *or* **iȟeyata·tanhan** \i-ȟé-ya-ṫaŋ-haŋ\ \i-ȟé-ya-ṫa-ṫaŋ-haŋ\ *adv* : from behind

---

a\ f<u>a</u>ther \e\ th<u>e</u>y \i\ mach<u>i</u>ne \o\ sm<u>o</u>ke \u\ l<u>u</u>nar \an, aŋ\ bl<u>anc</u> Fr. \in, iŋ\ <u>in</u>k \on, oŋ, un, uŋ\ s<u>oo</u>n, <u>con</u>fier Fr. \c\ <u>ch</u>air \ġ\ ma<u>ch</u>en Ger. \j\ fu<u>s</u>ion \clusters: bl, gn, kp, hšl, etc...\ <u>b</u>[e]<u>l</u>o ... said with a slight vowel
See more in the Introduction, Guide to Pronunciation

i·ȟe·ya·ti·ye·ya \i-ȟé-ya-ti-ye-ya\ *va* [fr *iȟeyata* behind + *iyeya* to shove at] : to thrust – P

[1]**i·ȟli** \í-ȟli\ *n* or *adj* í·ma·ȟli : a sore mouth

[2]**i·ȟli** \i-ȟlí\ *vn* i·máȟli : to have a sore breaking out in consequence of

i·ȟna·han \í-ȟna-haŋ\ *vn* i·ma·ȟnahan : to have the under lip hanging down

i·ȟni·yan·yan \i-ȟní-yaŋ-yaŋ\ *vn* i·ma·ȟniyanyan : to be troubledwith, excited about

I·ȟo-ka \Í-ȟo-ka\ *np* : the name of a class or band of Tetons; perhaps also the name of a dance < ~ *okolakiciye* the Badger Society, a military organization >

i·ȟpa·ya \i-ȟpá-ya\ *vn* i·wa·ȟpaya i·ya·ȟpaya unki·ȟpa-ya : to fall, fall down; to become sick < *T's iȟpayapi* They fell down dead, *or* They became fatally sick. >

i·ȟpe·ki·ci·ci·ya·pi \i-ȟpé-ki-ci-ci-ya-pi\ *n* : a divorce, a throwing each other away

i·ȟpe·ki·ci·ya \i-ȟpé-ki-ci-ya\ *v* : to throw away for or to — **iȟpeki·ya** \i-ȟpe-ki-ya\ *va poss* iȟpe·wa·kiya : to throw away, to forsake, leave one's own – Note: the form *eȟpeya* does not exist

i·ȟpe·ya \i-ȟpé-ya\ *va* iȟpe·wa·ya : to throw down, to throw away; to leave, forsake < *Kaksa ~ okicaslel* He parted it, throwing it down and splitting it. >

i·ȟta·he·pi \i-ȟtá-he-pi\ *n* : before night, before the day is out

i·ȟta·le·han \í-ȟta-le-haŋ\ *adv* or *prep* : further from the day before yesterday — **iȟtalehan·han** *adv* : often in days past

i·ȟta·ye·tu \í-ȟta-ye-tu\ *n* : the next evening, the evening following the time mentioned

i·ȟu·ȟa·o·ti·la *or* igugaotila \i-ȟú-ȟa-o-tì-la\ *n* : a sparrow

i·ȟun·win \i-ȟúŋ-wiŋ\ *vn* : to smell of, to stink — *n* : a bad smell, a stink

i·ȟwa·ȟwa s'e \í-ȟwa-ȟwa s'e\ *adv* : slowly, gradually in a drowsy manner < ~ *igluwinyeya* gradually to ready one's self > – L Bl

i·h'an \i-ȟ'aŋ\ *vn* i·wa·h'an [fr *h'an* to act or do] : to do, work, do in *ref* to , to be busy with something < *canpa* ~ to work on berries, *i.e.* picking, pounding, *etc* cherries. > – Bl

i·h'e \i-ȟ'é\ *n* : a rock or gravel < ~ *tipi* a concrete building, *Paha Ska kin hel emaonpapi na ~ amakšu po* Lay me to rest there at White Mountain and heap rocks over me. >

i·h'e·h'e can·hlo·gan \i-ȟ'é-ȟ'e caŋ-ȟlò-ġaŋ\ *n* : the silky or low townsendia, or perhaps more correctly the townsendia ex scapa, townsendia grandiflora, the composite family – Bl # 285

i·h'e ma·ka ce·ya·ka \i-ȟ'é ma-ka ce-yà-ka\ *n* : the long-flowered penny royal. Hedeoma longiflora, the mint family. – Note: it is used in *wahanpi* soup, the leaves being stirred into it – Bl # 269

i·h'e swu·la \i-ȟ'é swū-la\ *n* : little stones, as found on ant hills or at the bottom of a river, gravel, fine rocks

i·i·c'i·cel \í-i-c'i·cel\ *adv contrac* [fr perhaps *iic'icita* to guard self] : watching one's self lest doing wrong – Bl

i·i·c'i·gni \i-í-c'i-gni\ *v refl* imic'igni [fr *igni* to hunt for one] : to hunt *e.g.* game for one's self

i·i·c'i·ȟa-ȟa \i-í-c'i-ȟa-ȟa\ *v refl* i·mi·c'iȟaȟa [fr *iȟa* to laugh] : to make one's self a laughing-stock, as is said of one who commits adultery

i·i·c'i·kcu \i-í-c'i-kcu\ *v refl* i·mi·c'ikcu [fr *icu* to take] : to help one's self, take what one is to have

i·i·c'i·yun \i-í-c'i-yuŋ\ *v refl* [fr *iyún* to apply by rubbing] : to rub on one's self *e.g.* medicine – D.257

i·i·glu·ge \i-í-glu-ġe\ *v* i·mi·gluge i·ni·gluge : to act absurdly, to blunder – *Syn* AIKPABLAYA

i·i·glu·kse \i-í-glu-kse\ *v refl* : to break or cut off one's own for a purpose < *"A" eyapi "na nakpa ~ po"* "Ah!" they said, "and cut off your ears." perhaps the saying: "Lend me your ears." or simply: "Attention!" > – Cf gluíyupse MF

i·i·kcu \i-í-kcu\ *v* [fr *icu* to take] : to take or obtain what one expects < *Ptan he taku kin húnkešni ca yuptanyan ~ canna ake luzahan hecel on tunkašila ptan eyacajewicašton* Whenever otter gets by pulling over what he expects to be sickly, then because he is so much faster grandfather gives otters the name. > BT

i·i·ki·ya \í-i-ki-ya\ *v* : to ask back what one has given

i·i·kpa·kin·te \i-í-kpa-kiŋ-te\ *n* : a napkin, anything to wipe one's mouth with – Bl

i·i·kpu·stan \i-í-kpu-staŋ\ *v poss of* ipustan : to push up against one's own

i·i·kpu·ta·ka \í-i-kpu-ta-ka\ *v poss* ii·wa·kputaka [fr *iiputaka* to kiss] : to kiss one's own, as one's relatives

i·in·kpa·ta \í-iŋ-kpa-ta\ *adv* : at the point of anything

i·i·pu·ta·ka \í-i-pu-ta-ka\ *v* íi·wa·putaka : to kiss < *Hehanl hiyu na iiputake na leya* ... She then came up and kissed him and said this ... >

i·i·šla·ya·tan·han \í-i-šla-ya-taŋ-haŋ\ \i-í-šla-ya-taŋ-haŋ\ *adv* : to the right side of – B.H.159.11, 249.5, 260.6

i·i·tkob \í-i-tkob\ *adv* : in reply — **iitko·patanhan** \í-i-tko-pa-taŋ-haŋ\ *adv* : returning the compliment, as in saying to another what is fitting to be said to him alone

i·i·yu·wi \í-i-yu-wi\ *n* : something to tie around the mouth < *šung ~* a halter >

i·jan·jan \i-jáŋ-jaŋ\ *vn* : to give light, as a candle — *n* : a light — **ijanjan·ya** *va* ijanjan·wa·ya : to light *e.g.* a candle, to cause to give light — **ijanjan·yan** *adv* : giving light for

i·ja·ta \í-ja-ta\ *adj* : forked mouth, double tongued

[1]**i·je·han** \í-je-haŋ\ *adv* : among, into the midst < ~ *iyaya* He went among them. >

[2]**i·je·han** \i-jé-haŋ\ *adv* : often, frequently, repeatedly, right along < *Šunkawakan ~ bluha kte lo* Oh, that I might have a horse right along (a prayer)... > — **ijehan·yan** *adv* : often — **ijehanyan·kel** *adv* : frequently

i·je·na \i-jé-na\ *adv* : mixed up, *e.g.* different kinds together

i·ji·ca \i-jí-ca\ *vn* : to be rich in goods – Note: thus in distinction from *wašeca* and *iwášeca* to be rich in provisions

i·ji·lya \i-jí-lya\ *va* ijil·wa·ya : to cause to be rich — *adv* : richly

i·ji·mna \i-jí-mna\ *vn* : to smell like something burning as fat or bones or cloth

i·jog \í-jog\ *v contrac of* íjoka : to purse, pucker the lips

i·jo·ka \í-jo-ka\ *vn* : to have the lips pushed out — **ijo-kiya** \í-jo-ki-ya\ *v* ijo·wa·kiya : to push out the mouth at, to twist the mouth, to whistle – Cf jo

i·ka·blu·ya \i-ká-blu-ya\ *adv* : crushing fine — *v* : to crush < ~ *iyukpan* to grind fine as dust > – B.H. 240.14

[1]**i·ka·can** \i-ká-caŋ\ *va* i·wa·kacan : to shake as in sifting

[2]**i·ka·can** \í-ka-caŋ\ *vn* : to trot, as a horse does — *va* í-·wa·kacan : to adjust something carried on the back, as a baby by jerking it upward — **ikacan·can** \í-ka-caŋ-caŋ\ *vn* [fr *i* towards + *kacancan* to trot] : to trot towards, as a horse does, perhaps — *n* : the trot of a horse < ~ *wanna el u na tipi tiyopa aiyopteya wahpe wan paslatapi ca han* A horse trot came there, and it came to a

halt straight toward the house door since a leaf was pinned to it. > – WHL

i·ka·gi \i-k̇á-ġi\ *vn* : to be hindered – *See* icági

i·ka·han *and* **ikahan·yan** \í-k̇a-haŋ\ *adv* : so far from

i·ka·ke·in \i-k̇á-k̇e-iŋ\ *v* : to lean on something bending, as trees or tree limbs might, to knock against and cause a slight tilt – Cf íkaki, keínyanhan

i·ka·ki *or* **ikaki·ya** \í-k̇a-k̇i\ *adv* : on that side of — **ikakiya·tanhan** *adv* : in that way from, on that side — **ikaki·yotan** *adv* : in that direction from

i·ka·mna \i-k̇á-mna\ *v* i·wá·kamna : to rip by striking < *Ogle* ~ He ripped his pants. >

i·kan *also* **wíkan** \i-káŋ\ *n* : a cord, string, rope, the bail of any-thing

i·kan·co·la \i-káŋ-co-la\ *n* : a bow-like spear used by members of the *Tokala Okolakiciye*, otherwise known as the *Tokala Tawahukeza*, which is perhaps the *Tokala Tawokonze*

i·kan·co·la ma·s'a·pa·pi \i-káŋ-co-la ma-s'a-ṗa-pi\ *n* : a radio, a wireless < ~ *wan yuha s'elececa* It's as though she holds a radio, as one would say to a woman who gossips much about other people. > – *Syn* MAZACOLA WINAH'ON, TATUYE ON WINAH'ON

i·kan·ki·ci·ton \i-káŋ-k̇i-ci-toŋ\ *va* ikan·we·citon : to put or tie a string or strap on for one to carry by — **ikankiton** *v poss of* ikan·we·ton [fr *ikanton* to tie on a handle] : to tie a string on one's own pack to carry it by

i·kan·ton \i-káŋ-toŋ\ *va* ikan·wa·ton : to put a string or strap on a bag *etc* to carry it by < *Na hanpošpu hokšicala wan anok ikantonpi ca yuhapi* And they carried a doll tied supported on both sides. > — **ikanton·ton** *v red* : to tie numbers of holds to carry by – D.211

i·kan·yan \i-k̇áŋ-yaŋ\ *va* ikan·wa·yan : to have for a string or handle

i·kan·ye \i-káŋ-ye\ *adv* : towards the center, as towards the fire

i·kan·ye·la \i-k̇áŋ-ye-la\ *adv* : near to – Note: the more proper form seems to be *ikiyéla* near to one thing

i·kan·ye·tan \i-k̇áŋ-ye-taŋ\ *adv* : in front of < *mikanyetan* in front of me > — *n* : the front — **ikanyetan·han** *adv* : on the river or lake side of an object, in front of < *mikanyetanhan* on my side of the lake or river >

i·ka·pa \í-k̇a-ṗa\ *va* í·wa·kapa í·ma·kapa [fr *i* mouth + *kapá* thresh or beat] : to open the mouth on, talk loud to — **ikapa·ka** \í-k̇a-ṗa-k̇a\ *n* : one who scolds, perhaps, a talkative person — **ikapa·s'a** *n* : one who scolds, a scold

i·ka·pe·ya \i-ká-ṗe-ya\ *adv* : beyond, more than

i·ka·pta \i-k̇á-pṫa\ *adv* : through < ~ *hinhpaya* to fall through >

i·ka·skab \í-k̇a-sk̇ab\ *v contrac of* íkaskapa : to slap — **ikaska·bya** *adv* : smiting on the mouth

i·ka·ska·pa \í-k̇a-sk̇a-ṗa\ *va* í·wa·kaskapa : to slap on the mouth

i·ka·sli \i-k̇á-sli\ *v* i·má·kasli : to have one's self, a finger or so, bruised by something, as by a door

i·ka·to \í-k̇a-to\ *vn* : to gallop, as does a horse

i·ka·wa·wa \í-k̇a-wa-wa\ *vn red* : to move the lips, open the mouth often – Cf íšpašpa Bl

i·kcan \i-kcáŋ\ *v* i·ma·kcan : to want to do a thing but with you first trying it – Bl

i·kca·pta \i-kcá-pṫa\ *v poss* mi·kcá-pta unkí·kcapta·pi [fr *icapta* to break out] : to be angry and talk badly

i·kce \i-kcé\ *adj* : common, wild, in a state of nature < ~ *wicaša* an Indian person > — *adv* : for nothing, freely, in the common way < ~ *mac'u* He gave it to me for nothing, *i.e.* gave it for nothing, ~ *heya* He said that in the common way. > — **ikce·ka** \i-kcé-k̇a\ *adj* : common — **ikce·kce** *adv red of* ikce : commonly, wildly — **ikcekce·ka** \i-kcé-kce-k̇a\ *adj red of* ikcéka : common — **ikcekce·ya** *adv red of* ikceya : ordinarily, in a common manner, naturally

i·kce o·kšu·pi \i-kcé o-kšù-pi\ *n* : a muzzle-loader or shotgun – *Syn* AKICITA TAMAZAWAKAN Bl

i·kce wi·ca·ša \i-kcé wi-cà-ša\ *n* : common men, Indians and not white men, wild men

i·kce·wo·a·i·e o·we o·pa \i-kcé-wo-a-i-e o-wè o-pa\ *np* : a democrat — **ikcewoaie·pi** *n* : a democracy – P

i·kce·ya \i-kcé-ya\ *adv* : in a common manner, commonly, naturally, ordinarily, freely, wildly < *Lehanl* ~ *wanwicalakapi kte lo* They will see them ordinarily at this time, *i.e.* they see spirits without being sacred or special, ~ *u wanice* He does not come without a special reason. > — **ikceya·kel** \i-kcé-ya-k̇el\ *adv* : ordinarily – WE

i·kci·a \i-kcí-a\ *v* [fr *ikce* freely + *ia* to speak] : to speak frankly, truthfully < ~ *niwánicelo* You are a liar. > – BT

i·ci·ble·za \i-k̇í-ble-za\ *v* [fr *i* consequently + *kibleza* to sober up] : to recover from drunkenness on account of – Cf kibléza

i·ki·ca·ga \i-kí-ca-ġa\ *vn* i·ma·kicaga [fr *icaga* to grow, develop] : to become, to grow to be

i·ki·ca·zo \i-k̇í-ca-zo\ *va* i·we·cazo i·mi·cazo [fr *icazo* to draw a line] : to take credit of one

i·ki·ci·ca·ga \i-k̇í-ci-ca-ġa\ *vn* i·mi·cicaga [fr *icaga* to grow] : to grow for one

i·ki·ci·cu \i-k̇í-ci-cu\ *v* i·we·cicu i·mi·cicu [fr *icu* take or receive] : to take or get for one

i·ki·ci·gni \i-k̇í-ci-gni\ *v* i·we·cigni [fr *igni* to hunt something] : to hunt *e.g.* deer *etc* for one

i·ki·ci·han \i-k̇í-ci-haŋ\ *v* i·mi·cihan [fr *han* to stand] : to remain for one

i·ki·ci·ḣa·ḣa·pi \i-k̇í-ci-ḣa-ḣa-pi\ *v recip* : they laugh at each other

i·ki·ci·ksa·pa \i-k̇í-ci-ksa-ṗa\ *v* i·we·ciksapa [fr *iksapa* to be preoccupied with] : to be wise for one, instruct one in the right way

i·ki·ci·lo·wan \i-k̇í-ci-lo-waŋ\ *v* i·we·cilowan [fr *ilowan* to sing in praise of one] : to sing to one, to praise one for another

i·ki·cin \í-k̇i-ciŋ\ *va* í·we·cin *or* í·wa·kiciŋ : to desire something for what one has given or will give

i·ki·ci·yu·kcan \i-k̇í-ci-yu-kcaŋ\ *v* i·we·ciyukcan i·mi·ciyukcan iciciyukcan [fr *iyukcan* to understand] : to judge of or from another opinion about anything for another

i·ki·ci·yun \i-k̇í-ci-yuŋ\ *v* i·we·ciun *or* i·we·ciyun [fr *yun* to anoint] : to rub on for – B.H.199.2

i·ki·ci·yu·škin \i-k̇í-ci-yu-škiŋ\ *v* : to congratulate – P

i·ki·ci·yu·štan \i-k̇í-ci-yu-šṫaŋ\ *v* i·we·ciyuštan [fr *iyuštan* to finish] : to take care of *e.g.* a sick person

i·ki·co \i-k̇í-co\ *va* i·we·co i·mi·ci : to invite to, as to eat corn or meat

i·ki·gni \i-k̇í-gni\ *v poss* : to hunt one's own

i·ki·ḣa \i-k̇í-ḣa\ *v poss* i·wa·kiḣa [fr *iḣa* to laugh at] : to laugh at one's own — **ikiḣa·ḣa** *v red of* ikiḣa : to

---

a\ father \e\ they \i\ machine \o\ smoke \u\ lunar \an, aŋ\ blanc Fr. \in, iŋ\ ink \on, oŋ, un, uŋ\ soon, confier Fr. \c\ chair \ġ\ machen Ger. \j\ fusion \clusters: bl, gn, kp, hšl, etc...\ b[e]lo ... said with a slight vowel **See more in the Introduction, Guide to Pronunciation**

make fun of one's own

i·ki·h'an \i-ǩí-ȟ'aŋ\ *v* i·wa·kih'an : to cook, cook meat for < *Talo* ~ He cooked meat for him. *Toká cik'ala imáki-h'an yo* First cook me a bit of meat, said when a sick person wants something and one gives it to him. > – Bl WHL

i·ki·ji·ca \i-kí-ji-ca\ *vn* : to be rich in goods < *Tunkaši-la mazaska išnala ~ kte* The President will be rich only in money. > – BT

i·ki·kcu \i-ǩí-kcu\ *v poss* i·we·kcu [fr *icu* to take] : to take back what one has given, to take one's own < *Hece wicaša kin mazawakan ~ na ekta ~* Therefore the man took his own gun and took it back to him. >

i·ki·ki·ye·la \i-ǩí-ǩi-ye-la\ *adv red of* ikiyéla : near to many things, as houses – Note: *ikiyéla* near to one thing

i·ki·ksab \i-ǩí-ksab\ *v contrac of* ikiksapa : to make one wise — **ikiksa·bya** *va* ikiksa·bwa·ya : to cause one to be wise in *ref* to one's own — *adv* : wisely, cautiously

i·ki·ksa·pa \i-ǩí-ksa-p̣a\ *vn* i·wa·kiksapa : to be wise for one's own, to consult

i·ki·k'o \i-ǩí-k'o\ *v* : to be excited by tumult < *Waná hinhanna canke taku hmun s'e ikik'opi* It was now morning and the camp got into an uproar *Taku ikik'opi* There was an uproar about something. > — **ikik'o·k'o** *v red of* ikik'o : to create a disturbance, in *ref* to many – B.H.239.4, 263.3, 250.7 D.269, 78

i·ki·ni·ca \i-ǩí-ni-ca\ *va* : to grab, try to get something, as a bunch of dogs a cat, or boys candy < *Na el Pehin Hanska,* i.e. General G. Custer, *natan hi na ecel iwicakinicapi. Na wanna heyoka unmapi k'on cega k'on ikinicapi* And there Long Hair, General Custer, came on the attack, and as it was they tried to get them. Now they had grabbed they a bucket, the other a clown. > — **iki·nil** \i-ǩí-nil\ *v contrac of* ikinica : to try to get, where persons are crowded together grabbing for or trying to get; to kill, each trying to kill < ~ *awicaupi* They came trying to get and kill them. >

i·kin·ta \i-ǩíŋ-ṫa\ *vn* i·ma·kinta : to be defective, not as usual – *Syn* IPINTA Bl

i·kin·te·šni \i-ǩíŋ-ṫe-šni\ *adj* : dull, as an axe *etc* that cannot be used < *Kan íwapsake wan imicikintešni* The knife with which I cut sinew is dull. > – BD Bl

i·kin·ye·la \i-ǩíŋ-ye-la\ *adv* : near to, in *ref* to time and place < *Tipi wan ena han ca ~ šunkawakan kin hu pawicahtin na tipi k'on tima i* He had gone into the house after he hobbled his horse near the house standing right there. >

i·ki·pa·ci·ca \i-kí-p̣a-ci-ca\ *v* : to wear away *e.g.* something's hair < *Wan, owekiš hin imayakipacicin kte lo* Oh oh, you will perhaps wear away my hair. > – Cf kipácica

i·ki·pa·jin \i-ǩí-p̣a-jiŋ\ *va* i·wa·kipajin [fr *kipajin* to oppose] : to quarrel with one for or on account of anything — **ikipajin·yan** *adv* : opposing < *tawacin ~* denying one's self > – B.H.214.12, 70.8

i·ki·pan \i-ǩí-p̣aŋ\ *va* i·wa·kipan [fr *kipan* to call to] : to call to one for something

i·ki·pa·ti·tan \i-ǩí-p̣a-ti-taŋ\ *va* i·wa·kipatitan i·ma·ki-patitan : to push one sideways as in running a race and trying to beat one – WE

i·ki·pe·mni \i-ǩí-p̣e-mni\ *v* i·ma·kipemni : to wrestle with and take from – Bl

i·ki·pi \i-ǩí-p̣i\ *v* [fr *kipi* to be sufficient for] : to need for one's self < ~ *šni* to be unworthy, *Imakipi šni* I am not worthy. ~ *šni iwanglake* He deemed himself unworthy. *Mazaska ota ~* He needed much money. *Unkikipipi kte* We shall be in need. > – B.H.55.15, 111.5, 175.3, 226.16, 295.15 Pb.31

i·ki·ya \i-ǩí-ya\ *v* : to assist, to side with, take sides with < *Jesus el imayakiyin kta iceciciye* I pray to you Jesus that you should come to my assistance. > – Note: See *iciya*, it may be the same word B.H.46.12, 197.1 Pb.10

i·ki·ye·la \i-ǩi-yé-la\ *adv* : near – Cf ikikiyela

i·ki·yun \i-ǩí-yuŋ\ *v poss* i·wa·kiyun *or* iwakiun unki·-kiyun·pi : to rub on one's self < *Nape maka ~* He rubbed dirt on his hands. > — **ikiyun·yun** *v red* : to rub on one's self, in *ref* to many < *Na wana pejuta išta nonge ko ikiyunyunpi* And now they rubbed medicine on their eyes and ears. >

i·ki·yu·ta \i-ǩí-yu-ṫa\ *va* : to measure out to, perhaps < *Makoce kin yušpašpaya iwicakiyuta* He measured out to them the land in parcels. > – B.H.73.13

i·ki·yu·wi \i-ǩí-yu-wi\ *va* : to bridle, to put a rope in the mouth of one's horse, *obsol*

i·ko·a·ka·tan·han \i-ǩó-a-ǩa-ṫaŋ-haŋ\ *adv* : across the river from B.H.203.3

i·ko·gla·mna·ya *also* **ikoglamnayan iyaya** \i-ǩó-gla-mna-ya\ *va* ikoglamna·wa·ya : to get ahead of somebody and put one's self in the way, to get before, as a horse by making short cuts or a round-about way Bl

i·ko·kab \i-ǩō'-ǩab\ *adv* : before, out in front, in both time and place < *Tka he ~ Tašunke Luzahan tokeya wan eyapi* They would say in front of him in first place was Fast Horse. >

i·ko·kto·pa·win·ge \i-kó-kto-p̣a-wiŋ-ġe\ *num ord adj* : the one thousandth

i·ko·pa \i-kó-pa\ *va* iko·wa·pa : to be afraid of, to fear *e.g.* some event – B.H.136.16 Pb.45

i·ko·pe·gla \i-kó-p̣e-gla\ *vn* ikope·wa·gla : to be in the state of fear on account of — **ikope·kiya** \i-kó-pe-ǩi-ya\ *va* ikope·wa·kiya : to cause to be fearful

i·ko·yag \i-ǩó-yag\ *v contrac of* ikoyaka : to adhere to — **ikoya·gya** *va* ikoya·gwa·ya : to fastern to, as a horse to a cart, to join one thing to another, to clothe or put on — *adv* : fastened to < ~ *han* to stand fastened to > — **ikoyagya·kel** *adv* : fastened to – B.H.76.7

i·ko·ya·ka \i-ǩó-ya-ǩa\ *vn* iko·ma·yaka iko·un·yaka·pi : to adhere to, stick to, to be fastened to < *Na talo tukte-ni ikoyake šni* Nowhere did the meat stick. *Ate, nata catkayatan winawizi wan imakoyakin kte lo* Father, a burr will stick to the left side of my head. *Na heon cehpi ekta waconica tanka inikoyaka* And for that reason a large piece of venison stuck to your flesh. >

i·ko·ze \i-ǩó-ze\ *v* i·wa·koze : to shake, move with the hand < *Na le can eya wiyaka iyakaškapi kin hena icu na "lena hunka ~ yelo"* And he took the feathers and the rod to which they were tied, and he said "their movement was well and hearty". >

i·kpa·gan \i-kp̣á-ġaŋ\ *v refl* mi·kpagan [fr *pagan* give away] : to spare one's self, yield up one's self

i·kpa·ge \i-kp̣á-ġe\ *n* : the notch in the end of an arrow by which the string is pulled backwards < ~ *ecela tan'-inyan wao welo* I shot, only the notch being visible, *i.e.* an arrow went so deep only the notch was visible.> – Bl

i·kpa·gi·ca \i-kp̣á-ġi-ca\ *v refl of* pagíca : to wake up < *Ikpagica po* You all, wake up! > – Bl

i·kpa·hi \i-kpá-hi\ *v refl poss of* pahí : to pick up for one's self < *Nunpa can kipiya ikpahipi* They picked up enough for two days. > – B.H.55.17

i·kpa·hin \i-kp̣á-hiŋ\ *vn* : to pillow head in one's hand

i·kpa·hun·hun·za \i-kp̣á-huŋ-huŋ-za\ *v refl poss of* pa-húnhunza : to shake by hand for one's self

i·kpa·hlo·ka \i-kp̣á-ȟlo-ǩa\ *v refl* mi·kpahloka [fr *pa-*

hloka to pierce] : to pierce through, to make a hole for one's self, as the muskrat does < *Hecena k̇eya šina kin etanhan ikpahloke na mini mahel wiyuškinškin* Finally the turtle made a hole out of the blanket and went frolicking in the water. >

i·kpa·hpa \i-kṗá-ȟṗa\ *v refl* mi·kpahpa [fr *pahpa* take or throw down] : to throw one's self off, as from a horse

i·kpa·kin·ta \i-kpá-k̇iŋ-ṫa\ *v refl* mi·kpakinta [fr *pakinta* to wipe] : to wipe, rub one's own < *Na peji ȟota on ikpakintapi* And they wiped themselves with sage. > - Cf kpakínta

i·kpa·ki·ški·ja \i-kpá-ki-ški-ja\ *v refl of* pakiškija : to make sore by rubbing perhaps < *Išta kin ~ na lila ic'icuwa* It made his eyes sore and really he caught himself unprepared. > - B.H.119.15

i·kpa·kpi \i-kṗá-kṗi\ *vn* : to pick a hole, break a hole, as a chick in its shell, to hatch out one's own - Note: the word is used in *ref* to chickens R

i·kpa·k'e·ga \i-kpá-k'e-ġa\ *v* mi·kpak'ega : to rub one's self against something to stop from itching - *Syn* IKPÁWAZA *and* IGLUWAZA, said of animals — **ikpak'ehk'ega** *v red of* ikpak'ega : to itch one's self - Bl

i·kpa·ptan \i-kṗá-ptaŋ\ *v refl* mi·kpaptan : to turn one's self over, to roll over — **ikpaptan·ptan** *v red* : to turn one's self over, roll over, as when not sleeping well, to toss — **ikpaptan·yela** \í-kpa-ṗtaŋ-ye-la\ *adv* : in the manner of rolling over < ~ *hci wahihunni yelo* I arrived really "on the roll". > - D.216 Bl BT

i·kpa·šlo·ka \i-kpá-šlo-ka\ *v refl of* pašloka : to slip out of, as out of a too big suit, to take off a garment - B.H.87.5

i·kpa·ta·ka \i-kṗá-ta-ka\ *v poss* : to lean on or brace one's own

i·kpa·tan \i-kṗá-ṫaŋ\ *v refl* mi·kpatan [fr *patan* to esteem] : to be careful of one's self — **ikpatan·yan** \i-kṗá-ṫaŋ-yaŋ\ *adv* : taking care of one's self carefully

i·kpa·ti·tan \i-kṗá-ti-ṫaŋ\ *v refl of* patitan : to push along, as a boat with a pole, to steer a boat

i·kpa·wa·za \i-kpá-wa-za\ *v refl* : to rub one's self against something, as cattle do on a tree < *(Sapa gleška kin) mni yatki na hehanl can wan el inajin na ikpawazahe* (The spotted black [cow]) drank water and then standing at a tree was rubbing itself. > - D.257

i·kpa·zo \i-kṗá-zo\ *v poss* mi·kpazo : to show one's self

i·kpi \i-kṗí\ *n* : the belly, abdomen — **ikpi·gnag** *v contrac of* ikpignaka : to place around the belly < ~ *iyeya* to wrap about the belly > — **ikpi-gna·gya** *adv* : placed in around the belly

i·kpi·gna·ka \i-kṗí-gna-ka\ *va* ikpi·wa·gnaka : to place in or put around the body, as a blanket when tied around one < *Inawaye kin ikpimagnake wi 7 k'el maton welo* My mother gave birth to me in the 7th month of her being pregnant with me. > - BT

i·kpi·pa·tan·han \i-kṗí-pa-ṫaŋ-haŋ\ *adv* : in around the belly

i·kpi·ska·ya·yun·ka \i-kṗí-sk̇a-yuŋ-ka\ *v* : to lie with the belly turned up, as does a dog

i·kpi·yo·na·pa \i-kṗí-yo-na-pa\ *v* : to take shelter in, to flee toward < *Ikpiyonacipelo, wawatin kte lo* I took shelter with you, I shall then eat, as a man would say coming in and wanting to eat. > - Bl

i·kpu·kpa *or* **ikpukpe·ya** \i-kṗú-kṗa\ *adv* : mixed up, as people of different nations dwelling together, or as different kinds of corn growing together in the same field

i·ksab \í-ksab\ *v contrac of* iksapa : to be wise about

[1]iksa·bya \í-ksa-bya\ *va* íksa·bwa·ya [fr *íksapa* to be wise in] : to make anything to do anything

[2]i·ksa·bya \i-ksá-bya\ *va* iksá·bwa·ya [fr *ksapa* wise] : to make wise for or concerning — *adv* : wisely

[1]i·ksa·pa \i-ksá-ṗa\ *vn* i·wa·ksapa : to be wise about anything

[2]i·ksa·pa \í-ksa-ṗa\ *vn* í·ma·ksapa : to be much engaged about something, to be unfortunate, not to obtain, to be burdened with *e.g.* other people's troubles - B.H. 129.22

i·kšin·ki·ya \í-kšiŋ-ki-ya\ *or perhaps* \í-kšiŋ-k̇i-ya\ *va* íkšin·wa·kiya íkšin·ma·kiya : to make faces at, to grimace at

i·kta·he·la \i-kṫá-he-la\ *adv* : moderately, carefully, gently - Bl

i·kte \i-kṫé\ *v* i·wa·kte [fr *kte* to kill] : to kill with anything — **ikte·ka** \i-kṫé-k̇a\ *n* : something to kill with, as a gun < ~ *manica* I have nothing to kill with. >

i·kto·mi \i-kṫó-mi\ *n* : a spider; a fabulous creature like the fox in English folklore < ~ *s'e cinca ota lahcak* He is like a spider having a great many children. > — **iktomi tawokaške** *or* **iktomi taokaške** *n* : a spiker web - Note: *wókaške* is a place of imprisonment. Children may have been heard to say incorrectly: *Iktomi tahókaške* Cf unktomi Bl

i·ku *or* **iku·hu** \i-kú\ \i-k̇ú-hu\ *n* : the chin

i·ku·ja \i-k̇ú-ja\ *vn* i·ma·kuja : to be sick or indisposed on account of

i·ku·ka \i-k̇ú-ka\ *vn* : to be decayed by reason of, worn out by; to be boiled to pieces together with — **ikuke·ya** \i-k̇ú-k̇e-ya\ *adv* : rotten or boiled to pieces with < ~ *špan* It is cooked all to pieces. >

i·ku·san *or* **ikusan·la** \í-k̇u-saŋ\ *n* : a mink, a small kind of mink with a light-colored jaw, mustela vison lacustris

i·ku·še \i-k̇ú-še\ *va* : to impede, to block < *Woecon kin le ~ najin* He stood there impeding this work. >

i·ku·ši·c'i·ya \i-k̇ú-ši-c'i-ya\ *v refl* : to prevent one's self — **ikuše·ton** *va* : to block the way with something < *Inyan tanka wan ikušetonpi na kiglapi* They have gone home since they blocked the way with a large stone. > — **ikuše·ya** *adv* : in the way of - B.H.269.12, 114.3, 230.2

i·ku·ta \i-k̇ú-ta\ *adv* or *prep* : below, downstream < *Nunpegnakapi ~ ewicoti* They encamped placing two camps downstream. >

i·ku·te *or the better form* **icute** \i-k̇ú-ṫe\ *n* : ammunition, something to shoot with, a gun — *va* : to direct something against another < *Wicoh'an šica imayakutepi* You aimed a bad work against me. > - B.H.88.13, 41.13

i·ku·te·ka \í-k̇u-te-ka\ *v* : to throw hints - B.H.99

i·ku·tku·te·ka \í-k̇u-tk̇u-ṫe-k̇a\ *vn* í·wa·kutkuteka : to make trial, to endeavor beforehand to know how one can succeed *e.g.* in asking for anything, try to evaluate

i·k'e·ge·šni \i-k'é-ġe-šni\ *adj* : dull, as a knife that cannot be used to scrape with < *Kan íwapsake wan imicik'ege šni*, or *imicikintešni* The sinew scraper is not of use to me for it being dull. > - *Syn* IKINTEŠNI Bl

---

\a\ father \e\ they \i\ machine \o\ smoke \u\ lunar \an, aŋ\ blanc Fr. \in, iŋ\ ink \on, oŋ, un, uŋ\ soon, confier Fr. \c\ chair \ġ\ machen Ger. \j\ fusion \clusters: bl, gn, kp, hšl, etc...\ b[e]lo ... said with a slight vowel
See more in the Introduction, Guide to Pronunciation

i·k'o \i-k'ó\ *v* : to get worried < *Ik'opi kta* They will get concerned. > – Bl

i·lag \i-lág\ *va contrac of* ilaka : to govern — **ila·gya** *va* ila·gwa·ya : to cause to serve, have for a servant, to make use of — **ila·ka** \i-lá-k̇a\ *va* i·wa·laka : to have for a servant, to control, govern, rule over – B.H.251.13

i·la·za·ta \i-lá-za-ṫa\ *adv* or *n* : back from, behind something < *milazata* by my side, *Wicaša wan nilazata najin he k'on he tuwe he? Ce ~ najin* Say, the man who had been standing beside you, who is he? He stood back from him. > — **ilazatan** \i-lá-za-ṫaŋ\ *adv* : from the side of — **ilazatan·han** *adv* : in the rear of, behind, from the side of < *Paha zizipela el ~ hel wicoti na etan zuya aya* At a narrow hill where behind it there was an encampment, some started a battle. >

i·le \i-lé\ *vn* : to burn, to blaze — *n* : a blaze

i·le·ci·ya *or* **ileciya·tan** \í-le-ci-ya\ \í-le-ci-ya-ṫaŋ\ *adv* : on this side of — **ileciyatan·han** *adv* : from this side of, in this way from — **ileci·yotan** *adv* : in this direction from

[1]**i·le·ga** \i-lé-ġa\ *vn* : to shine, glitter, as do stars < *Wicahpi wan lila ilege cin he waštewalaka* I love the star who shines brightly. > – MS.1

[2]**i·le·ga** \í-le-ġa\ *vn* i·ma·lega : to speak evil about somebody, to spoil one's reputation – *Syn* YATAKUNIŠNI Note: *wayatakunišni* is of a *va*

i·le·ge \i-lé-ġe\ *n* : a burning thing, a light < *~ mak'u wo; iwaglatan kte* Let me have your burning (cigaret); I would like to light mine. >

i·le·han \í-le-haŋ\ *adv* : so far off — **ilehan·han** *adv red of* ilehan : keeping so far off — **ilehan·yan** *adv* : so far off < *Ilehanyang egnaka* He set it just so far off. *Ilehanyang ic'icuwa yo* Get hold of yourself a bit. >

i·leh \i-léȟ\ *vn contrac of* iléġa : to shine

i·le·hle·ga \i-lé-ȟle-ġa\ *v red of* iléga : to shine, sparkle, twinkle, as do the stars < *Hehan wicahpi iyuha lila ~ waštešte* At that time all the stars shone most gloriously. > — **ile·hya** \i-lé-ȟya\ *adv* : in a shining manner — *va* : to cause to shine — **ilehya cannunpapi** *or* **ilehya únpapi** *n* : a cigar – MS.1 Bl

i·le·ni·lya·kel \i-lé-ni-lya-kel\ *adv* [fr *ile* a blaze + *nica* lacking, without] : with little enthusiasm left < ~ *wanasapi* They went to the hunt dispondently, there being only a few buffalo remaining. > – Bl

i·le·ya \i-lé-ya\ *va* ile·wa·ya : to burn, cause to burn, to set fire to

i·li·ta \i-lí-ṫa\ *v* : to be worried; to take an active part as in a game < ~ *škatapi opa* He joined taking an active part in playing. *Ilitapi kte lo* They will take an active part in it. > — **ilita·ka** \i-lí-ṫa-k̇a\ *vn* ili·ma·taka : to be animated for, brave for or on account of – Cf ik'ó Bl WHL

i·lo·cin \i-ló-ciŋ\ *v* : to be hungry on account of – B.H. 111.11

i·lo·wan \i-ló-waŋ\ *va* i·wa·lowan [fr *lowan* to sing] : to sing to or for, to sing the praises of, to praise one

i·ma·cu·ka \i-má-cu-ka\ *colloq express* i·ni·cuka : That gets me, *i.e.* implying one has a liking for a person or thing – *Syn* MAKTÉKA

i·ma·ga·ga \i-má-ġa-ġa\ *vn* i·ma·magaga [fr *magaga* amused] : to be amused with, cheered by — **imagaga·ic'iya** *v* : to recreate one's self

i·ma·ga·ju·ya \i-má-ġa-ju-ya\ *va* : to cause to rain by means of something – B.H.157.7

i·ma·hel \í-ma-hel\ *adv* : within — **imahe·lwapa** \i-má-he-lwa-pa\ *adv* : towards the inside, inwards — **imahe·ta** \i-má-he-ṫa\ *adv* : within < ~ *mayázan* It pains me inside. > — **imahe·tanhan** \i-má-he-ṫaŋ-haŋ\ *adv* : from within — **imahe·tu** \i-má-he-ṫu\ *adv* : within — **imahetu·ya** *adv* : inwards, within — **imahetuya·kel** \i-má-he-ṫu-ya-k̇el\ *adv* : in the inside of, within

i·ma·h'a·ka·te \i-má-ȟ'a-k̇a-ṫe\ *n* : a cultivator – WL

[1]**i·ma·ni** \i-má-ni\ *va* ima·wa·ni ima·un·ni·pi : to walk to or for a thing

[2]**i·ma·ni** \í-ma-ni\ *v* íma·wa·ni : to go home < *Miš eya imawani kte lo* I too shall go home. *Imaunnila kte lo* We will go the little way home. > – Bl WH

i·ma·s'o·yu·spe \i-má-s'o-yu-spe\ *n* : pincers, tongs

i·ma·zi·ya·pa \i-má-zi-ya-pa\ *n* : a hammer

i·mna \í-mna\ *vn* í·ma·mna í·un·mna·pi : to be satisfied, to have sufficient of < *Tawaonspe kin woitonpeyapi na imnapi* His knowledge of how came as a surprise to them and so they were satisfied. > — **imna·han** *adv* : satisfied, to satisfaction, sufficiently

[1]**i·mna·han·han** \í-mna-haŋ-haŋ\ *adv* : sufficiently, much, awfully < ~ *iȟaȟa* to ridicule terribly > – Cf wó imna B.H. 171.19

[2]**i·mna·han·han** \i-mná-haŋ-haŋ\ *n* : part of the guts of animals, perhaps the fourth or smallest manyple of animals

i·mna·han·yan \í-mna-haŋ-yaŋ\ *adv* : sufficiently — **imnahanyan·kel** \í-mna-haŋ-yaŋ-kel\ *adv* : very much, a great deal, sufficiently < ~ *econ* to do a great deal > — **imna·ic'iya** *v refl* [fr *imnayan* fill or satisfy] : to fill self with food, to satisfy one's self with – D.28

[1]**i·mna·yan** \i-mná-yaŋ\ *va* imna·wa·ya [fr *mnayan* to collect] : to gather together by means of

[2]**i·mna·yan** \í-mna-yaŋ\ *va* imna·wa·ya : to fill, satisfy — *adv* : filled, satisfied < ~ *wotapi* They ate being satisfied. > –B.H.208.15

i·mni·ca·hu \i-mní-ca-hu\ *n* : a bean – Note: it is the same as *omnicahu*, strophostyles pauciflora – Bl # 292

i·mni·ci·ya \i-mní-ci-ya\ *vn* imni·mi·ciya : to make an assembly for some purpose

i·mni·co·ya·pa \i-mní-co-ya-pa\ *v* : to use for wading < *Hanp'ceyaka wan imnicoyapelo* Quill-worked moccasins were used in wading. > – Bl WHL

i·mni·ja \i-mní-ja\ *adj* : chuck-full of water < *Ehaš ~ s'e cepelo* Certainly he is fat as if bloated with water, as is said of an unusually fat man or animal. > – Bl

i·mni·štan \i-mní-štaŋ\ *n* : water running from the mouth < ~ *au* to drivel, slaver, ~ *mau* The water is running from my mouth. *Šiyó šunka s'e ~ h'eh'eya yankelah* A grouse was sitting with its tongue dangling like a dog drivelling. > – Bl

i·mni·tan \i-mní-ṫaŋ\ *vn* : to spread out, inundate — *n* : a flood < ~ *kin u* The flood comes. > — **imnitan·yan** *va* imnitan·wa·ya : to flood – B.H.71.18, 195.16, 7.12

i·na \i-ná\ *n* : mother, my mother

i·na·bla·bla·za \i-ná-bla-bla-za\ *v red* [fr *inablaza* to kick open on account of] : to burst open because of something – B.H.112.17

i·na·bla·ska \i-ná-bla-ska\ *vn* ina·wa·blaska : to trample under foot < *Anpetu topa kinhan canku kin ~ ihpeyapi kte lo* The [sand] was thrown down for the road to be trampled for four days, *i.e.* the sand will be trampled hard and flat. > – Bl

i·na·bya \i-ná-bya\ *adv* : taking refuge in, sheltered by < *Tipi ~ waun* I am taking shelter in a house. > – Cf ináp̣a

i·na·gi·ha·ha \i-ná-ġi-ha-ha\ *vn* : to feel scared hearing something - RF

i·na·gna·ka \í-na-gna-ka\ *v* í·ma·nagnaka [fr *i* mouth + *nagnaka* to twitch] : to have the lips twitch < *Ímanagnakelo* My lips do twitch. > - Bl

i·na·ha·ha·ya \i-ná-ha-ha-ya\ *adv* : loosely, as wood corded badly

i·na·hci \i-ná-ḣci\ *va* ina·wa·hci : to pierce and have the hold break out of anything, to have the hold break out, as of a stirrup

i·na·hco \i-ná-ḣco\ *vn* : to be loosened - Cf nahcó

i·na·hlo·ka \i-ná-ḣlo-k̇a\ *va* ina·wa·hloka : to wear a hole with the foot by means of something, as in one's moccasins or stockings < *Hanpa inyan inawahloka* I wore a hole in my moccasins with a stone. >

[1]**i·na·hma** \i-ná-ḣma\ *va* or *vn* ina·wa·hma : to hide, keep secret, conceal - Cf D.56

[2]**i·na·hma** \í-na-ḣma\ *va* : to seduce, to commit fornication or adultery with one < *Ínawahme. ~ s'e (secretly) mila wan oglikiyi na yuha tima iyaye* I committed adultery. As though to seduce one I went indoors with a knife to sharpen. > - Cf wiinahma — **inahman·pi** \í-na-ḣmaŋ-pi\ *n* : seduction

i·na·hma·ya·kel \i-ná-ḣma-ya-kel\ *adv* : secretly, unknown to others - B.H.105.14

i·na·hme·ki·ci·ci·ya·pi \i-ná-ḣme-k̇i-ci-ci-ya-pi\ *n* : the game of hide-and-seek < *Ináhmekiciciya econpi* They played hide-and-seek. > - Note: inahmekiciyapi is a misspelling of the word

i·na·hme·ki·ya \i-ná-ḣme-k̇i-ya\ *va* inahme·wa·kiya : to hide from one — **inahme·ya** *adv* : secretly, covertly, silly — **inahmeya·han** *adv* : in secret, secretly

i·na·hni \i-ná-ḣni\ *vn* ina·wa·hni : to be in haste, in a hurry — *adv* : quickly, in haste < ~ *econpi* It was done quickly. > — **inahni·kel** *adv* : in a hurry - B.H.253.16 — **inahni·kiya** \i-ná-ḣni-k̇i-ya\ *va* inahni·wa·kiya : to cause to make haste, to hasten one — **inahni·pi** \i-ná-hni-ṗi\ *n* : a hastening, haste, hurry — **inahni·ya** *va* inahni·wa·ya : to hasten one, make hurry — **inahni·yan** *or* **inahniye·la** *adv* : in haste, hastily

i·na·hpe \i-ná-ḣṗe\ *n* [fr *nahpa* make fall] : that which is stepped on and sets off a trap, the pan of a trap — **inahpe·la** *n dim of* inahpe : a small trip on a trap

i·na·ḣu·ga \i-ná-ḣu-ġa\ *v* ina·wa·ḣuga : to mash by stepping on - Cf naḣúga *Syn* INÁKUKA — **inaḣu·ḣuga** *va* ina·wa·ḣuḣuga : to mash up or crush by trampling on

i·na·h'u·h'u \i-ná-ḣ'u-ḣ'u\ *v* : to scatter with the feet what has been piled up < ~ *ahiyu élale* You took it, came home, and scattered it. > - Bl

i·na·ja·bja·bye·la \i-ná-ja-bja-bye-la\ *adv* : going to ruin from the wear and tear of feet <*Wanišipeš šicala tanunka šni k'on, nakeš sipa kin ~ yaglilotake* Since you had been unwilling to do a little damage, at last on the way home you sat down the toes of your shoes ruined. > - Bl

i·na·ja·bja·pa \i-ná-ja-bja-pa\ *v red of* inajapa : to ruin or wear out the toe of one's shoe, to ruin completely by the wear of feet - Bl

i·na·ja·bya \i-ná-ja-bya\ *adv* : in a way ruinous to footwear - Bl WHL

i·na·ja·lye·ya \í-na-ja-lye-ya\ *v* : to keep the mouth open - Bl

i·na·ja·pa \i-ná-ja-pa\ *v* : to wear out the tip of one's shoes - Bl

i·na·jin \i-ná-jiŋ\ *vn* ina·wa·jin : to rise up to one's feet, to step to < *Miwankab hinajin na amayugata. Yunkan isakib inawajin* He came and stood over me and he raised his hands as in prayer. I then stood beside him. > — **inajin·kiya** \i-ná-jiŋ-k̇i-ya\ *va* : to cause to stand up, to raise up

i·na·ki·hma \í-na-ki-ḣma\ *v poss* ina·wa·kihma [fr *inahma* to entice] : to entice away one's own

i·na·ki·kšin \i-ná-k̇i-kšiŋ\ *v* ina·wa·kikšin : to take shelter in or behind, to make a shelter of, as of a tree

i·na·kin·lya \i-ná-k̇iŋ-lya\ *va* : to rub off, as mud from the feet with a mat or rug; *fig* to borrow from < *Cowinja akahpe he si ~ yo* Scrape your shoes off on the floor cover there. *Wólota kin inakinlmaya upelo* They came conning me into borrowing, *i.e.* they wanted to borrow from me but I would not do it. > - Bl WHL

i·na·kin·ta \i-ná-k̇iŋ-ṫa\ *v* ina·wa·kinta : to brush off on some account, *fig* to be able in no way to finish a job < *Hankeya inakintelo* Little by little he brushed it off. > - Bl

i·na·ki·pa \i-ná-k̇i-ṗa\ *v poss* ina·wa·kipa [fr *inapa* to take refuge in] : to take refuge in one's own, to trust in what sustains some relation to myself

i·na·ki·wi·zi \i-ná-k̇i-wi-zi\ *v poss* ina·wa·kiwizi [fr *inawizi* to be jealous] : to be envious of one's own relations, to be jealous of one's own

i·na·ku \i-ná-ku\ *n* : his or her mother - Cf atéku *Syn* HÚNKU Bl

i·na·ku·ka \i-ná-k̇u-k̇a\ *v* ina·wa·kuka [fr *nakuka* wear out by feet] : to crush or destroy with the foot

i·na·k'e·hya \i-ná-k'e-ḣya\ *v* : to make a scraping noise as a wagon brake < *huínak'ehye* a wagon brake >

i·na·k'e·sya \i-ná-k'e-sya\ *adv* : nearby, alongside

i·na·mni \i-ná-mni\ *adv* : beyond, over, as over the hill from < *Yunkan blo ~ pte hotonpi* And then buffaloes over the ridge were grunting. >

i·nan·gnang \í-naŋ-gnaŋg\ *v contrac of* inangnang : to move the lips

i·nan·gnan·ka \í-naŋ-gnaŋ-ka\ *v* í·ma·nangnanka : to move the lips, as in reading to one's self — **inangnanke s'e** \i-náŋ-gnaŋ·ke s'e\ *adv* : as if moving one's lips - WHL

i·na·pa \i-ná-pa\ *va* ina·wa·pa ina·un·pa·pi : to come out or up out, to come get things; to live through *e.g.* a winter; to take shelter or refuge in *e.g.* from a storm or any evil; to trust in - R

i·na·pan \i-ná-paŋ\ *v* : to be packed and made hard < *Anpetu yamni kinhan canku kin ataya ~ ihpeyapi kte lo* The entire road will be left packed hard after three days, *i.e.* the snow on the road. > - Bl WHL

i·na·pca·pca i·ye·ya \í-na-pca-pca i-yè-ya\ *v* : to suppress one's anger, to swallow one's anger, not answering < *Tuwa taku wanji eniciye c'eyaš ~ yo. ~ omawani yelo* Even if one says something to you, calm your anger. I may take a walk. > - Bl

i·na·pci·yun·yun·ka *or* **inapciyungyunka** \i-ná-pci-yuŋ-yuŋ-k̇a\ *num ord adj red of* napciyunka : every ninth one

i·na·pci·yun·ka *or* **inapcinyunka** \í-na-pci-yuŋ-k̇a\ *num ord adj* : the ninth

i·na·pe·ya \í-na-ṗe-ya\ *or* \i-ná-ṗe-ya\ *va* inápe·wa·ya : to cause to come in sight or come out of, to cause to appear on the other side; to shoot through; to cause to

\a\ father \e\ they \i\ machine \o\ smoke \u\ lunar \an, aŋ\ blanc Fr. \in, iŋ\ ink \on, oŋ, un, uŋ\ soon, confier Fr. \c\ chair \ġ\ machen Ger. \j\ fusion \clusters: bl, gn, kp, hšl, etc...\ b[e]lo ... said with a slight vowel
See more in the Introduction, Guide to Pronunciation

live through, as through a winter; to cause to trust in — *adv* : appearing, coming in sight, trusting in - R

i·na·pi·škan \i-ná-p̣i-škaŋ\ *va* iná·wa·piškan : to waste things foolishly, to squander — **inapiškan·yan** *v* iná·wa·piškanyan : to do little things to pass away time, to kill time — **inapiškanyan·pi** *n* : toys, playthings

i·na·po·ta \i-ná-p̣o-ṭa\ *va* ina·wa·pota [fr *napota* wear out with the feet] : to wear out *e.g.* one's moccasins by some means

i·na·psa·ka \i-ná-psa-ḳa\ *va* ina·wa·psaka [fr *napsaka* to break by foot] : to break off *e.g.* a string with the foot by some means or other

i·na·pša \i-ná-pša\ *vn* ina·wa·pša : to make a noise, as one walking with water slopping around in his moccasins — **inapša·pša** *v red* ina·wa·pšapša [fr *inapša slop about*] : to keep making a sloshing noise

i·na·pta \i-ná-p̣ta\ *va* ina·wa·pta : to wear out *e.g.* a shoe

i·na·pte·ca \i-ná-p̣te-ca\ *vn* : to be prevented by < *inaptecašni* not to be prevented by anything, *Inamaptecašni* I am not being prevented. *Mazašala wanji waglušna inaniptecapelo, cicupi amáyaluhetepi eš kolakiciyapi wašte kin heuncapi kta* You are prevented dropping a penny; is it that I should give it to you? but if you are after me ours should be a fine friendship. >

i·na·p'i·bi·ye·ya \í-na-p'i-bi-ye-ya\ *va* ínap'ibiye·ma·ye ínap'ibiye·un·ya·pi : to drop the lower lip, as when on the point of crying, *i.e.* to contract the muscles below the mouth, as is specially noticed in children — **inap'i·p'i·yeya** *va* : to make one start crying, *i.e.* to drop (wear about the neck) the lower lip before crying, as is noticed in babies < *Ínap'ip'iyemayelo* He made me start crying. >

i·na·sa·ka \í-na-sa-ḳa\ *v* ína·ma·saka : to spring and strike, as does a branch along a path when walking < *Išta can inamasaka* A splinter struck my eye, *i.e.* when a splinter flew in one's eye. > - Bl WHL

i·na·sli \i-ná-sli\ *va* iná·wa·sli : to crush with the foot

i·na·šlo·ka \i-ná-šlo-ḳa\ *v* iná·wa·šloka **1** : to pass on beyond, to wear through, wear out something *e.g.* shoes **2** : to get one's self away, to escape, as from danger **3** : to slip off, as a cover from somethng

i·na·ta·ke \i-ná-ta-ke\ *n* [fr *i* by means of + *nataka* to close up] : a fastener, *e.g.* a bolt, lock, bar, a fence, a fort, *etc*

i·na·tan \í-na-ṭaŋ\ *va* : to press upon with the foot to gain support < *siínatan* a stirrup >

i·na·ti·bya \i-nä'-ṭi-bya\ *v* : to roast hurriedly, as meat on coals, to make curl up - R

i·na·t'a·ge \i-ná-t'a-ġe\ *n* : a brake of a wagon - HUINAK'EHYE

i·na·t'a·hya \i-ná-t'a-ḣya\ *va* : to use the brake on a wagon - Cf inák'ehya — *adv* : in a sliding careful way < ~ *ya* to go walking carefully on slippery ground so as not to fall, walking in a sliding way >

i·na·wi·zi \i-ná-wi-zi\ *v* ina·wa·wizi : to be jealous, to be envious of — **inawizi·pi** *n* : jealousy, envy — **inawizi·ya** *va* inawizi·wa·ya : to cause to be jealous — *adj* : enviable - P

i·na·ya \i-ná-ya\ *va* ina·wa·ya : to call mother, to have for a mother

i·ni \i-ní\ *vn* i·wa·ni i·ya·ni unki·ni·pi : to take a vapor bath, to steam one's self, to take a sweat - Note: to make this bath *wakan*, one would wash and steam himself four times by pouring water over hot stones and accompanying this with singing *etc*. This was once done ceremonially after killing an enemy or a royal eagle - R

i·ni·han \i-ní-haŋ\ *vn* i·ma·nihan unki·nihan·pi : to be scared, frightened; to be amazed, astonished — **inihan·pi** *n* : amazement - *See* wówinihan, wóinihan

i·ni·han·šni \i-ní-haŋ-šni\ *adv* : fearlessly, persistently < *Lila kutepi eša* ~ *hiyaya* Though they did a very much shooting he fearlessly went on ahead. > — **inihanšni·yan** *adv* : persistently - B.H.213.6

i·ni·han·ya \i-ní-haŋ-ya\ *va* inihan·wa·ya : to frighten, scare, amaze, astonish one < *Optelyela inihanmayanpelo* I was frightened a little while. > — **inihan·yan** *adv* : in amazement - Bl

i·ni·hin·ci·ya \i-ní-hiŋ-ci-ya\ *v* : to be alarmed on seeing *etc* something because of something else < *Heya nah'onpi k'un hecena* ~ *hinglapi* They were in the end suddenly alarmed on hearing him say that. > — **ini·hinciye·šniyan** *adv* : fearlessly - B.H.67.5, 172.4, 128.1 302.18 Bl

i·ni·ka·ga \i-ní-ḳa-ġa\ *vn* [fr *ini* to take a vapor bath + *kaga* to make] : to take a vapor bath, *lit* to make *ini*, or *initi*, or *iniopa* < *inikagapi wókeya* a sweatlodge >

i·ni·la \i-ní-la\ *adj* : still, silent < ~ *manka* I sat quiet. ~ *agliyagla* He was silent passing by. *Inila un* He is being silent, *fig* He is a gentle snake. > — **inila·ya** *va* ini·la·wa·ya : to cause to be silent, make still

i·ni·o·pa \i-ní-o-pa\ *vn* : to take a vapor bath with others

i·ni·pi \i-ní-p̣i\ *n* : a steaming, sweating

i·ni·ti \i-ní-ti\ *n* : a sweat-house — *vn* ini·wa·ti : to take a vapor bath; to make a little house and sweat in it

i·ni·ti·yu·ktan \i-ní-ṭi-yu-ḳtaŋ\ *n* : the little booth fastened on two poles and drawn by horses or dogs, in which babies are transported — *v* initi·blu·ktan : to bend willows over for a booth - Bl

i·ni·wo·ke·ya \i-ní-wo-ḳe-ya\ *n* : a sweat house

i·ni·ya \i-ní-ya\ *va* i·wa·niya [fr *niyá* to breathe] : to breathe from

i·ni·yan pe·ju·ta *or* **iniyanpi** \í-ni-yaŋ pe-jù-ta\ *n* : the annual erigeron, erigeron annuum; the buckwheat family - Note: it is so called because it is used for children with sore mouths, *i* . A tea is made from the whole plant. It is also used as a tea for those who cannot urinate well - BT Bl

i·num \i-núm\ *num ord contrac of* inunpa : second — **inu·mnun** \i-nú-mnum\ *num ord contrac of* inumnunpa : every other one — **inumnun·pa** *num ord adv* : every second one

¹i·nun·pa \i-núŋ-pa\ *num ord adj* : the second

²i·nun·pa \í-nuŋ-pa\ *n* [fr *i* mouth + *nunpa* two] : two mouths < *mazakan* ~ a two-barrelled gun >

i·nun·wan \i-núŋ-waŋ\ *v* : to swim - Bl

¹in \iŋ\ *adv neg obsol,* hiyá *altern* form : no — *va* wa·in ya·in unk'in·pi : to wear around the shoulders *e.g.* a blanket < *Šina hin akatahan in* He wears a blanket with hair outside. > - BD

²in *or* **in ska** \iŋ\ *or* \íŋ-ṡka\ *interj of hesitancy when not finding the right word* : Let me see, Ahhhh..., Let me see, Ahhhh..., You know, Uhhhh...

in·ki·ya \iŋ-ḳí-ya\ *va* in·wa·kiya : to cause to wear *e.g.* a shawl

in·kpa \íŋ-kp̣a\ *n* : the end of anything, the small end, the head or source, as of a stream < *Yunkan can* ~ *kin iwankam gla na ecel atan'inšni iyaya* The top end of the tree towered above and as it was went out of sight. — **inkpa·ta** \íŋ-kp̣a-ṭa\ *adv* : at the end, head, or source; upstream, above — **inkpata·han** *adv* : from end or head of, as of a stream — **inkpata·kiya** \íŋ-kp̣a-ṭa-kiya\ *adv* : upstream, towards the head of a stream, as opposed to *hútabya* downstream — **inkpata·las'e** *adv* : near the head or top of something < *Onjinjintka Wakpala he el okijata el ~ ewicoti* They camped at the fork in the Rosebud Creek. >

in·ska *or* **inska in** \íŋ-ska\ *interj of hesitancy* : Let me see, Wait a minute - B.H.47.2

in·sko·ke·ca \íŋ-sko-ke-ca\ *adv* : so large < *Na tacan kin šunkawakan tacan ~* And the carcass is as large as the body of a horse. >

in·sko·ki·ni·ca \íŋ-sko-ki-ni-ca\ *vn* : to be doubtful which is the largest - Note: *hinskokinica*, which is *deriv* from *hinsko* how large, and *akinica* is disputed

inš *or* **naínš** \iŋš\ *conj* : or < *Hecel unglipi na lila el ewacanmi wawate eša ~ imunka ko. ~ wanyanka yo* So though I was concerned about my eating or spending the night as well, we got home. Or see into it. > - Note: *ko* usually ends a sentence.

in·še \íŋ-še\ *adv perhaps* : only, just; of course, evidently, implying excuse or explanation < *~ eca ca ecamon* I did it only for fun. *~ le šungmanitu tawote ca waun welo* I use only this wolf's food. *Wanikan šni tka ~ hetatanka pizi wan ota latkan ca on aiyahanble lo.* You dream about being holy but it is because you only drink much gall of a buffalo horn. *Kola, nišnala gla po, ena wan kte, eya ške'* They say he said: Friends, go home alone, right here an arrow killed him. *Yunkan oyasin "Hiya, lena ~ waniyetu el icagapi ca osni kin okihipelo" eyapi.* And then everyone said: "No. Only these can take it because they grow in the winter. *~ he toka šni ška hepelo* I said they say he just is not an enemy. *Le ~ oyate wowicawak'a kta ca lecamon* I did this only so I might do digging up people, *i.e.* it is just an excuse. *Mini kin hel ihpeyapi ehantanš niyayin kte cin he (keya kin) slolkiya; icin kéya kin mini mahel unpi , tka ~ wicagnayan* If it is thrown in the water, the turtle knows it will live; because the turtle lives in water, but it deceived them. *Eya takuni ota epin kte šni tka ~ takuku iciyungin kte lo* Besides, I shall not say much of anything, but of course I'll cross-examine you about all sorts of things. > - B.H.88.13, 306 D.71, 77, 20 note 1 Gram. 201

in·še·še·kel \íŋ-še-še-kel\ *adv* : losing one's own train of thought or a point to be made in a talk < *~ he wóyak mašipi k'un* I lost the point I had been asked to tell. > - *Syn* ÚNŠ'KEYAPIKA *or* UNŠKEYAPIKA, LOTKUNKEŠNI

in·še·še·la·keš \íŋ-še-še-la-keš\ *n* : an instance — *adv* : for instance - P

in·še·ya·pi·ka \íŋ-še-ya-pi-ka\ *adv* : being distracted, forgetful - *Syn* UNŠKEYAPIKA MN

inš he·cel *or* **inš he·ce** \íŋš hé-cel\ *express* : It is all the same to me. That is all right. I do not care. So the saying goes

inš to·ka *or* **inš tok** *express at the end of a questioning attitude* : Or else? < *Ho eca ína-iyokihe kin he ~* All right, anyhow, this is his second-mother (or step-mother, *etc*), or else? > - D.9 B.H.198.2

in·š'un·ma·ke·ci *or* **unš'unmakeci** \íŋ-š'uŋ-ma-ke-ci\ *interj of excuse* : Oh yes! Just because!

in·yan \íŋ-yaŋ\ *n* : a stone, stones < *~ cega* a stone jar, *~ icahmun* a sling > - Note: *imnija* is the word in Dakota, whereas in Lakota *imníja* means bloated

in·yang \íŋ-yaŋg\ *v contrac of* inyanka : to run < *~ ble kta* I shall go on a run. *~ škan* the sport of track >

in·yan·ha \íŋ-yaŋ-ha\ *n* : a sea-shell

in·yan·he \íŋ-yaŋ-he\ *n* : a rocky hill

in·yan·ka \íŋ-yaŋ-ka\ *vn* waímnanka yaínanka unkin·yanka·pi : to run - Note: the word is said to be the same as *i-yanka wa-i-mnanka ya-i-nanka*

in·yan ka·pe·mni \íŋ-yaŋ ka-pe-mni\ *n* : a stone war-club

in·yan maka \íŋ-yaŋ maka\ *n* : cement

in·yan on·ye·ya·pi \íŋ-yaŋ oŋ-ye-ya-pi\ *n* : a sling with which to throw little stones

in·ya sa·pa \íŋ-yaŋ sa-pa\ *n* : a slate

in·yan ša o·k'e *or* **inyan šok'e** \íŋ-yaŋ ša o-k'e\ *n* : a place at Black Pipe in South Dakota where is found red earth to paint with - Bl

In·yan Wo·slol Han \Íŋ-yaŋ Wo-slól Haŋ\ *np* : the Standing Rock Agency - D.222-223

i·o·a·pe \i-ó-a-pe\ *n* : an hour < *~ yamni hehanl* three hourse after this > - B.H.283.6

i·o·blu·la \í-o-blu-la\ *n* : a sheltered place where the wind does not blow

i·o·gla·mni·yan \i-ó-gla-mni-yaŋ\ *adv* : following around the curves, as of a stream

i·o·gmus \í-o-gmus\ *v contrac of* íogmuza : to be with mouth shut < *~ manka* I keep my mouth shut. *~ yatapi* You were eating with your mouth closed. *~ yuza* to gag, *~ gluza* to clamp one's palm over one's mouth > — **iogmu·sya** *va* : to cause to shut the mouth - D.268, 2, 6

i·o·gmu·za \í-o-gmu-za\ *n* : a closed mouth — *vn* ío·wa·gmuza : to have the mouth shut, to lay the hand on the mouth

i·o·gnag \i-ó-gnag\ *v contrac of* iógnaka : to put in the mouth — **iogna·gkiya** \i-ó-gna-gki-ya\ *va* iogna·gwa·kiya : to put in the mouth of another, to give to eat, to cause to eat — **iogna·gya** *va* iogna·gwa·ya : to cause to put into the mouth, to give food to - B.H.144.3

i·o·gna·ka \i-ó-gna-ka\ *va* ió·wa·gnaka [fr *i* mouth + *ognaka* to place in] : to put into the mouth *e.g.* food

i·o·hi·ti·ka \í-o-hi-ti-ka\ *adj* : being brave in words, pugnacious

i·o·ju·gju·ya \í-o-ju-gju-ya\ *v red* : to fill all the way < *Wata kin nupin iojugjuyapi* Both the boats were brim-full (with water), > - Cf íojuya B.H.186.12

i·o·ju·la \í-o-ju-la\ *adj* [fr *ojula* full] : full to the brim — **iojula·ya** *v* : to make full, to fill < *Anpetu tahena pustag mahingni iojulawayelo* Before evening of the day I was full up suddenly crouched down, i.e. I'll do much work today. > — **iojuya** \í-o-ju-ya\ *va* io·wa·juya : to fill to the brim - B.H.71.18 Bl

i·o·ka·pa·za *or* **íokàza** \i-ó-ka-pa-za\ *vn* io·wa·kapaza : to be pungent in the mouth, as pepper - BD

i·o·ka·tan \i-ő'-ka-taŋ\ *or* \í-o-ka-tan\ *va* io·wa·katan : to nail one thing on another, to nail and hold an axe or other heavy weight on the other side to buttress - BD

i·o·ka·winh \i-ő'-ka-winh\ *adv* : following around the circle

i·o·ko·gna \i-ó-ko-gna\ *adv* : in the midst, between - B.H.7.11

i·o·kpa·kpas \i-ó-kpa-kpas\ *adv* : moving the lips < *~ yanka* He sat moving his lips. >

i·o·ma·ka \í-o-ma-ka\ *n* : the year next to, the next year - B.H.78.5, 112.1

\a\ father \e\ they \i\ machine \o\ smoke \u\ lunar \an, aŋ\ blanc Fr. \in, iŋ\ ink \on, oŋ, un, uŋ\ soon, confier Fr. \c\ chair \ġ\ machen Ger. \j\ fusion \clusters: bl, gn, kp, hšl, etc...\ b^e^lo ... said with a slight vowel **See more in the Introduction, Guide to Pronunciation**

i·on·ši·la \i-óŋ-ši-la\ *v* ionši·wa·la [fr *onšila* to pity] : to have mercy or compassion on one in *ref* to something, to grant, bestow — **ionšila·ya** *adv* : having compassion on one in *ref* to something

i·on·wi·yu·ta \í-oŋ-wi-yù-ta\ *v* ionwibluta : to make a motion with the mouth, to gesture to one with the mouth

i·o·pa·win·ge \i-ó-ṗa-wiŋ-ġe\ *num ord adj* or *n* : the one hundredth

i·o·štan *or* **ioštanpi** \i-ŏ'-štaŋ\ *or* \i-ó-štan-ṗi\ *n* [fr *oštan* put in or on] : a cork, stopper for a vial *etc*

i·o·wa \i-ó-wa\ *n* [fr *owá* write] : something to write or paint with, a pen or pencil or *etc*

i·o·wo·i·c'i·šlo·ka \í-o-wo-i-c'i-šlo-ka\ *v* : to dig out in a hurry *e.g.* some turnips < *Iowomic'išlokin kta ca hecamon we* I did this so I might go in a hurry to digging (turnips). > – Bl

i·o·ya·škan \í-o-ya-škaŋ\ *va* io·bla·škan : to get one to talk < *Ioblaškan na on lila woglake* I got him to talk, so he talked very much. > – PO

i·o·yu·spe \i-ó-yu-spe\ *n* : a handle – B.H.60.11

¹i·pa \i-ṗá\ *n* : a sort of sausage – Cf talípa

²i·pa \i-ṗá\ *n* : the top of anything, the high end hill of a ridge; a cape, a promentory *etc* are said to be *ȟe ipa* < ~ *k'el akanl iyotaka yo; hecon na tanyan wáȟita yo* Sit down on the the ridge at the high end; do this and keep watch. > – Bl

i·pa·ce·ka \í-ṗa-ce-ka\ *va* i·wa·paceka : to push and make stumble – Bl

i·pa·ci·ca \i-ṗá-ci-ca\ *vt* [fr *pacica* to mix up] : to ruffle *e.g.* one's hair with the hands < *Pehin kin ipacicapi s'e* It seems his hair was all messed, as is said when a man's hair is disheveled and pressed down. > – Bl

i·pa·ga *or* **ipaȟe** \í-ṗa-ġa\ *adv* or *n* : before dinnertime, or the place of dinner < *Hinhanna kin wancag ~ maunnipi kte lo* Tomorrow we shall travel at once before the time for dinner. ~ *éyuhpapi* They took down their packs to rest before reaching the assigned place for dinner. > – Bl

i·pa·gan \i-ṗá-ġaŋ\ *v* [fr *pagan* to open by pushing] : to push aside, as a tent door, for the purpose of looking out

i·pa·glo·ka \i-ṗá-glo-ka\ *v* : to be dislocated, as a joint, by anything

i·pa·gmung \i-ṗá-gmuŋg\ *v contrac of* ipagmunka : to be able to dip up *e.g.* water with a vessel < *Cega kin mni kin ekta ~ ojula icu wacin* I tried to dip up to a full bucket of water, *i.e.* tried to dip out a pailfull of water. > D.223

i·pa·gmun·ka \i-ṗá-gmuŋ-ka\ *vn* : to be capable of being dipped up with a bucket

i·pa·go \i-ṗá-ġo\ *n* [fr *i* for + *pago* to carve] : something to carve or engrave with, a carving implement

i·pa·go·ya \i-ṗá-ġo-ya\ *adv* : passing by, exceeding in speed, as when one horse outruns another

i·pa·ha \i-ṗá-ha\ *v* : to raise up, as a curtain, to hoist up < *Wipa kin ~ egle* They set raising up the vent flaps. ~ *iyeya* to raise up quickly > – D 196-7

i·pa·hin \i-ṗá-hiŋ\ *n* : a pillow — *vn* i·wa·pahin : to lean the head against, to have for a pillow — **ipahin·ki·ton** \i-ṗá-hiŋ-ki-toŋ\ *v* : to rest, to make a resting place out of — **ipahin·ya** *vn* : to have for, use for a pillow

i·pa·ho·ton·pi \i-ṗá-ho-toŋ-pi\ *n* : a pop-gun, as once the Lakota used to make them

i·pa·hla·hla·ya \i-ṗá-ȟla-ȟla-ya\ *adv red* : row-on-row

i·pa·hla·la *or* **ipahla·lya** \i-ṗá-ȟla-la\ *adv* : in a row, facing one way, lined up like soldiers in rank formation < ~ *najinpi* They stood lined up in ranks. ~ *au* They came on lined up. *Catku el ~ ewicagnaka* They arranged them in a line in the honor place. *Ošpašpaye ecel ~ au* They came as it was by groups in rows. ~ *k'in canglakinyan* a neckyoke for a four-horse evener > – D.77

i·pa·hlo·ka \i- ṗá-ȟlo-ka\ *va* : to make a hole in, to punch through

i·pa·hna \i-ṗá-ȟna\ *adv* : through, through and through, as a needle is sent through cloth in sewing < ~ *o* to shoot through something, so the point is visible on the other side, *Canke apaha najin na ~ o* And so he stood taking aim and sent his arrow piercing it. ~ *iheya* He struck through it. > – Note: R gives the Dakota: *ipahdan* Sb D.193 and 117 KE

i·pa·hna·he·ya \i-ṗá-ȟna-he-ya\ *adv* : right through < ~ *yazan* to be pain right through, ~ *o* to pierce > – Cf D.112 *Syn* IPÁZEYA

i·pa·ho \i-ṗá-ȟo\ *v* i·wa·paȟo : to brush up, as hair from the forehead, to brush into a curl

¹i·pa·hte \i-ṗá-ȟte\ *n* [fr *i* for + *pahta* to tie up] : something with which to tie up, a string

²i·pa·hte \í-pa-ȟte\ *n* [fr *i* mouth + *pahta* to tie up] : a bridle

¹i·pa·jin \i-ṗá-jiŋ\ *vn* i·ma·pajin : to be prevented by something from proceeding, to come to a stand, not to be able to go on

²i·pa·jin \í-ṗa-jiŋ\ *v* í·wa·pajin : to resist difficulties, to overcome difficulties, to go on bravely, not to fear dying — **ipajin·yan** \i-ṗá-jiŋ-yaŋ\ *adv* : prevented by, in opposition, opposing

i·pa·ji·pa \i-ṗá-ji-ṗa\ *va* i·wa·pajipa [fr *pajipa* to prick] : to stick in, to prick with — **ipajipe** *n* : something that pricks, a pricker

i·pa·jun·ta \i-ṗá-juŋ-ṫa\ *va* i·wa·pajunta : to give when it is not wanted, to force upon one

i·pa·ka \i-ṗá-ka\ *vn* i·wa·paka : to draw back, as meat from ribs when cooked, or as husks of corn when ripe < ~ *yuha* to hold together like a bunch or handful of feathers, grass, *etc* > – Bl

i·pa·kin·ja \i-ṗá-kiŋ-ja\ *v* i·wa·pakinja : to rub, as one's eyes with the hands

i·pa·kin·ta \i-ṗá-kiŋ-ṫa\ *va* i·wa·pakinta : to wipe off — **ipakinte** *n* [fr *i* for + *pakinta* to wipe off] : something with which to wipe, a towel

i·pa·ko·te \i-ṗá-ko-ṫe\ *n* : a probe

i·pa·kšan \i-ṗa-kšaŋ\ *n* : a bend in a river *etc* – D.249

i·pa·la *or* **ipa** \i-ṗá-la\ *n* : something corresponding to sausage < *Nata kin ~ s'e wau welo* (or *waun welo*) I came, my head like a sausage (*or* My head is like a link of sausage), as is said when a man has lost his hair above the forehead. > – Cf *talípa* fr *talo* meat + *ipa* like sausage Bl

i·pa·man \i-ṗá-maŋ\ *va* i·wa·pame [fr *paman* to file] : to rub, rub on, as in filing a piece of wood or metal

i·pa·me \i-ṗá-me\ *n* : something to rub with or to file with < *can* ~ a wood file, *wan* ~ a stone with which to rub arrows >

i·pan·ho·ye·ya \i-ṗáŋ-ho-ye-ya\ *adv* [perhaps fr *pan* to shout + *hoyeya* to utter a sound with the voice] : screamingly, yelling above the natural voice

i·pa·psa·ke \i-ṗá-psa-ke\ *n* : a small knife for cutting porcupine quills

i·pa·ptan \i-ṗá-ptaŋ\ *v* : to turn over < ~ *ehpeic'iya* to turn one's self over > – Bl

i·pa·pu·za \i-ṗá-ṗu-za\ *n* : something with which to wipe dry, a towel

i·pa·san \i-ṗá-saŋ\ *va* i·wa·pasan : to put on white paint with the end of a stick, to make white dots, to rub on and whiten with

i·pas·han \i-ṗás-haŋ\ *or* \i-ṗá-s'haŋ\ *n* : anything that comes through and holds, a trip or trigger, *i.e.* a small iron that comes over and holds a set trap, a needle

i·pa·si·sa \i-ṗá-si-sa\ *va* i·wa·pasisa : to stick in, as a needle or pin, to fasten, as with a wiping-screw — **ipasise** *n* [fr *i* for + *pasisa* to pin together] : a pin

i·pa·sli \i-ṗá-sli\ *va* i·wa·pasli : to crush by pressing against something < *Si kin maya* ~ The bank collapsed under the pressure of his foot. > - B.H.68.12

i·pa·sli·ya \í-ṗa-sli-ya\ *va* i·wa·pasliya : to press one against the wall — *adv* : pressing against something < *Tiipasliya yuza yo* Hold him up against the wall of the house. > - Bl

i·pa·smin·yan \i-ṗá-smiŋ-yaŋ\ *n* : the ramrod for a gun < *mazawakan* ~ a gun ramrod> - BD

i·pa·so·tka \i-ṗá-so-ṫka\ *adj* : conspicuous, extending up, as a tall tree or steeple, one thing larger or taller than others, as the protruding ends of the logs in a log cabin — **ipasotka·ya** *adv* : conspicuously < *tipi* ~ a tall house, a tower > - Bl

i·pa·spa \i-ṗá-sṗa\ *va* i·wa·paspa : to drive in, as tent pins or a stake

i·pa·spa·ya \i-ṗá-spa-ya\ *vn* : to become wet, as by sitting on moist ground - Bl

i·pa·swa·ya·zan \i-ṗá-swa-ya-zaŋ\ *n* : pleurisy

i·pa·ški·ca \i-ṗá-ški-ca\ *v* i·wa·paškica [fr *paškica* press out by hand] : to rub, *e.g.* clothes on a washboard

i·pa·šlog \i-ṗá-šlog\ *contrac of* ipašloka : to shed one's clothing < ~ *iyeya* to take off *e.g.* a shirt >

i·pa·šlo·ka \i-ṗá-šlo-ḱa\ *va* : to draw off over the head *e.g.* a T-shirt - Note: in a transfered sense: to live or to make it through a winter or a sickness

i·pa·šp̣e·yunk \i-ṗá-šp̣e-yuŋk\ *v* : to be close and jolting, knocking against one another < ~ *inyanka* to run close together and jolt one another, as in a narrow path > - Bl

i·pa·ta \i-ṗá-ta\ *v* i·wa·pata : to embroider, to work quills of the porcupine < *Hanpa wan lila yupiyela iye he* ~ He worked very beautifully quills on a pair of moccasins. *Hanpa k'el glakinkinyan ipatapi* Quills were worked in a zigzag pattern on the moccasins. > - D.226-7

i·pa·tag \i-ṗá-tag\ *va contrac of* ipataka : to have for a support — **ipata·gton** *va* ipata·gwa·ton [fr *ipatage* a brace + *ton* give rise to] : to brace out or stretch, as in drying hides and skins < *Cana kin can ipatagtonpi s'e inyanke* When he ran at such a time, it was as if sticks gave him support, *i.e.* he ran with feet far apart. > — **ipata·gya** *va* ipata·gwa·ya : to cause to brace out or up, to sustain, reinforce - Bl

i·pa·ta·ka \i-ṗá-ta-ḱa\ *va* i·wa·pataka : to stretch out by means of cross-sticks; to have for a staff or support, be dependent upon — **ipatake** *n* [fr *i* for + *patake* come to a stop] : a prop or brace, a stick to stretch a skin on < *sinkpe ha* ~ a brace on which to stretch a muskrat skin >

[1]**i·pa·tan** \i-ṗá-ṫaŋ\ *n* : a prop or brace < *Tušu* ~ *ton wo; wakinyan ukiye eyaš lila tate kte lo* Gain tent pole braces; the Thunderbird is coming, but then there will be much wind. > - Bl

[2]**i·pa·tan** \i-ṗá-taŋ\ *va* i·wa·patan : to mash up one thing on another

i·pa·tan·gle \i-ṗá-ṫaŋ-gle\ *va* : to brace

i·pa·ta·pi \i-ṗá-ta-ṗi\ *n* : embroidery, ornamental work

i·pa·tku·ga \i-ṗá-tku-ġa\ *adv* : abreast, in a row, in a phalanx — **ipatku·hya** \i-ṗá-ṫku-ḣya\ *adv* : in a row, abreast - R Bl

i·pa·t'in·za \i-ṗá-t'iŋ-za\ *va* i·wa·pat'inza : to make firm by means of — *n* [fr *i* by means of + *pat'inza* to firm up] : anything that makes firm, sustenance, nourishment

i·pa·wa·ga \i-ṗá-wa-ġa\ *v* i·wa·pawaga : to rub, scrub or scour *e.g.* a floor < *Pehin kin ipawagapi s'e hpayelo* He lay as though his hair was scrubbed, *i.e.* his hair uncombed or matted. > - Bl

i·pa·we·ga \i-ṗá-we-ġa\ *vn* : to bend across, to intersect, to come into or cross, as one road does another - Note: the word is perhaps *obsol*

i·pa·weh \i-ṗá-weḣ\ *vn contrac of* ipawega : to cross < ~ *econ* to do something incorrectly > — **ipawe·hwehya** *adv red of* ipawehya : aside, out of the way, incorrectly — **ipawe·hya** *va* ipawe·hwaya : to cause to intersect — *adv* : crossing, aside out of the way; incorrectly

i·pa·win·ta \i-ṗá-wiŋ-ta\ *va* i·wa·pawinta : to rub on with

i·pa·ze·ya *or* **ipaseya** \i-ṗá-ze-ya\ *adv* : right through, as a pain runs right through the chest < ~ *mayazan* The pain runs clear through me. > - Cf ipásisa Note: the word is perhaps *obsol* RF Rh

i·pa·zi·ca \i-ṗá-zi-ca\ *adv* : bulged out, as a tent when one leans against it

i·pa·zi·lya \i-ṗá-zi-lya\ *adv* or *adj* : convex, as opposed to *škokpá* concave < ~ *han* to stand humped up, *tipi* ~ a house high up, a tower > - Bl Bt

i·pe·sle·tan·han \i-ṗé-sle-ṫaŋ-haŋ\ *adv* : from the head side or end < *Tancan kin hpaya tka k'un hel* ~ *iyotakin na* ... He sat however away from the head end of the place where the body had lain ... — **ipeslete** *adv* : at the head end < ~ *tka k'un hel* but at the head end of the place where ... > - B.H.271.4, 109.10

i·pi *or* **wípi** \í-pi\ *adj* or *vn* í·ma·pi : full, satisfied, as from eating < *Mazaska* ~ *nit'e. Íwicapi.* You died having plenty money. They were satisfied. > - BT B.H.55.8

i·pi·ga \i-ṗí-ġa\ *vn* [fr *píga* to boil] : to boil *e.g.* water, to foam — *n* : the foam of boiling water

i·pi·glag \i-ṗí-glag\ *v poss contrac of* ipiglaka : to gird one's self — **ipigla·gki·ton** \i-ṗí-gla-gki-toŋ\ *va* ipigla·gwe·ton : to put on one's girdle, to gird one's self — **ipigla·gton** *va* ipigla·gwa·ton : to put on a girdle, to be girded

i·pi·gla·ka \i-ṗí-gla-ḱa\ *v poss* [fr *ipiyaka* to gird self] : to put on one's own girdle — **ipiglake** *n* : a girdle

i·pih \i-ṗíḣ\ *v contrac of* ipiga : to boil

i·pi·i·c'i·ya \í-ṗi-i-c'i-ya\ *v refl of* ipiya : to fill one's self with < *Mini ipiic'iyapi* They filled themselves with water > - B.H.55.25

i·pi·la \i-ṗí-la\ *va* ipi·wa·la : to deny to, refuse to give, to withhold from, as too good for one < *Pel'ipimayala ca nacicipin kte lo* Since you have withheld fire from me, I shall flee from you. > - Bl D.202 note 3, 53 note 2

i·pi·la·ye \i-ṗí-la-ye\ *n* : something that gladdens

i·pin·ta \i-ṗíŋ-ṫa\ *vn* i·ma·pinta : to be defective in some part, to be too short or too little, to be not as usual - R Bl

---

\a\ f<u>a</u>ther \e\ th<u>e</u>y \i\ mach<u>i</u>ne \o\ sm<u>o</u>ke \u\ l<u>u</u>nar \an, aŋ\ bl<u>an</u>c Fr. \in, iŋ\ <u>in</u>k \on, oŋ, un, uŋ\ s<u>oo</u>n, <u>con</u>fier Fr. \c\ <u>ch</u>air \ġ\ ma<u>ch</u>en Ger. \j\ fu<u>s</u>ion \clusters: bl, gn, kp, hšl, etc...\ <u>b</u>ᵉlo ... said with a slight vowel
See more in the Introduction, Guide to Pronunciation

i·pi·ya \í-ṗi-ya\ *va* ípi·wa·ya : to make full, to fill

i·pi·yag \i-ṗí-yag\ *va contrac of* ipiyaka : to gird self — **ipiya·gkiciton** \i-ṗí-ya-gḳi-ci-toŋ\ *va* ipiya·gwe·ci-ton : to gird one, to put on a girdle for one — **ipiya-gki·ton** *va poss* ipiya·gwe·ton : to put on one's girdle, to be girded — **ipiya·gton** *vn* ipiya·gwa·ton : to gird, put on a girdle, to be girded, perhaps

i·pi·ya·ka \i-ṗí-ya-ḳa\ ipi·bla·ka *va* : to gird one's self, to put on a girdle

i·pi·ya·ka·sa·pa \i-ṗí-ya-ḳa-sa-pa\ *n* : a strap buckle
ipiyakasapa iyuhloke : a harness punch
ipiyakasapa onzoge hin-šma : cowboy riding pants

i·pi·ya·ke \i-ṗí-ya-ḳe\ *n* : a girdle, sash belt < ~ *kšupi* a beaded belt >

i·pi·ye \i-ṗí-ye\ *n* : something to repair with

i·po \i-ṗó\ *n* : a swelling

i·po·gan \i-ṗó-ġaŋ\ *vn* i·wa·pogan : to breathe out, exhale < ~ *yo* Blow on it, *i.e.* to make a fire blaze by blowing at it. > — **ipoh** \i-ṗóḣ\ *vn contrac of* ipogan : to blow on, blow in, blow away < ~ *iyeya* to cause blowing on > — **ipo·hya** *va* ipo·hwa·ya : to cause to breathe out, exhale — *adv* : blowing perhaps - Bl

i·psi·ca \i-psí-ca\ *vn* i·wa·psica unki·psica·pi : to jump down from, to jump, to jump over < *Cokan inajin na ungnahela jinlhingni na tokanl* ~ He stood up in the center, all at once he was about to whistle, and he jumped somewhere else. > — **ipsil** *vn contrac of* ipsíca : to jump — **ipsi·psica** *vn red* : to hop, as a grasshopper < ~ *iyaye* to go on hopping > — **ipsipsil** *v red* : to be jumping < ~ *iyaye* to have gone jumping > - B.H.280.10

i·pšin·ca·la \i-pšíŋ-ca-la\ *adj* : in the likeness of a small swallow < *Ite ~ kaca* That fellow's face is like that of a little swallow, as they say of a man with a small and wrinkled face. >

i·pu·hni·yan \i-pú-ḣni-yaŋ\ *adj* : anxious, eager, in a hurry to do something, as may horses, *i.e. yapi cinpi* they want to get going

i·pu·ske·pa \i-ṗú-ske-ṗa\ *n* : a strainer - P Bl

i·pu·ski·ca \í-ṗu-sḳi-ca\ *vn* í·ma·puskica : to be close to, to touch or press on < ~ *wicaša ota hipi* He was close to many men who were arrived. > — **ipuskice·la** *adv* : pressed together < ~ *iyotakapi* They sat close together. > — **ipuskil** *vn contrac* : to be close together — **ipuski-lya** *va* ipuski·lwa·ya : to cause to press on — *adv* : pressed together — **ipuskiskil** \í-ṗu-sḳi-sḳil\ *adv* : close packed < ~ *iyeya* to shove close together >

i·pu·sli \í-ṗu-sli\ *vn* í·ma·pusli : to be close to, to press upon, to touch anything — **ipusli·ya** *va* ipusli·wa·ya : to cause to press on — *adv* : touching < *makipusliya* on the ground, touching the ground >

i·pu·spa \i-ṗú-sṗa\ *va* i·wa·puspa : to stick, paste, glue on — **ipuspe** \i-ṗú-sṗe\ *n* : anything that sticks to, as a seal, a wafer < ~ *s'e yankelo* He sat as though stuck to something, or *fig* He holds his peace. >

i·pu·stag \i-ṗú-sṫag\ *v contrac of* ipustaka : to be flat < *makipustag ihpeic'iya* to throw one's self flat on the ground>

i·pu·sta·ka \i-ṗú-sṫa-ka\ *vn* i·ma·pustaka : to be flat, to be wanting, defective

i·pu·stan \i-ṗú-sṫaŋ\ *adv* : pushing up against < ~ *yuza* to clap up against, as might a coal of fire > - Bl

i·pu·sye *or* **wípusye** \i-ṗú-sye\ *n* : something to dry on or with, a dryer

i·pu·š'in \i-pú-š'iŋ\ *n* : the outside of a bend or curve as in a river - Bl

i·pu·ta·ka \i-ṗú-tag\ *va contrac* i·wa·putaka [*fr iputaka* to kiss] : to touch, kiss

i·pu·za \í-ṗu-za\ *vn* i·ma·puza : to have the mouth dry, to be thirsty — **ipuza·pi** *n* : thirst — **ipuza·t'a** *vn* ípuza·ma·t'a : to die or be dying of thirst, to be very thirsty, to suffer from thirst

i·p'o \i-p'ŏ\ *n* [*fr p'o* to be foggy] : steam, a mist

i·p'o·za \i-p'ó-za\ *vn* : to be cranky — **ip'oze·ca** *vn* i·ma·p'ozeca : to be out of humor about anything, to be cross, irritable

i·sa·bye \i-sá-bye\ *n* : blacking

i·sa·kib \i-sá-ḳib\ *adv* : on the side of, along side of < *Canku ~ iyotaka* He said on the side of the road. *Mísakib* at my side, *Unkísakib akiyagle* They passed by on the side of us. > — **isaki·bya** *adv* : on the side of, beside - B.H.36.19

i·sam \i-sám\ *adv* [*fr isanpa* beyond, more] : beyond that place or time < *Hecel ~ iblabla* So I went on beyond. *Yunkan ~* (beyond the woods) *lila wicoti na lila iyokipi* Then beyond (beyond the woods) there was a large village and they were much pleased. > — **isam·tu** *or* **isanbtu** *or* **isanpa·tu** *adv* : more than < *Wicatancan kin he wokoyake kin ~ šni hwo?* Is the body not more than the clothing? > — **isamya** \i-sá-mya\ *or* \i-sa-myá\ *adv* : further on, on the other side of, beyond < ~ *hehanl. Misamya waš'agya unpi* It was then further on. They have become stronger than I. > — **isamyeš** *adv* : more than before, all the more - B.H.193.23, 261.11, 263.2 Bt

I·san·a·ti \I-sáŋ-a-ṫi\ *np* [*fr isan* knife + *ati* they dwell at] : the Santee division of the Dakota peoples, so called because they used to stay long at the place where they got the material for their stone knives, hence *isan* knife in the Dakota dialect, whereas it is in Lakota *mila* - WE

i·sanb \í-saŋb\ *adv* [*fr isanpa* more] : more than — **isan·btu** *or* **isamtu** \í-saŋ-btu\ *adv* : more, increasingly — **isan·bya** \í-saŋ-bya\ *adv* : more, increasingly < *Misanbya waš'agya unpi. Taku kin oyas'in ~ cantececiye* They became stronger than I. I loved you more than all things. > - Cf samyé B.H.67.19, 252.18, 193.23, 78

i·san·pa \í-saŋ-pa\ *adv* : beyond that place or time, more than < *Tanyan ecannonpi kin ake ~ ecannonpi kte lo. Inisanpapi. Isanpapi.* When you do well, you will again do more. You who are far away. Those who are in the beyond. > — **isanpa·tanhan** \í-saŋ-pa-ṫaŋ-haŋ\ *adv* from beyond that, beyond < *Yunkan ~ makoce wan lila canwape to na makoce kin toyéla yunká* Then from beyond that there is a land very much in green leaves, and the land lies there quite green. > — **i·san·pa·ya** \í-saŋ-ṗa-ya\ *adv* : more than < *Niyepi kin hena wicinisanpayapi šni hwo?* You, are you not of more value than they? > - B.H. 193.26, 194.6

i·san·yan \i-sáŋ-yaŋ\ *va* isan·wa·ya : to communicate the whiting *e.g.* from one's robe to another by rubbing against it

I·san·ya·ti \I-sáŋ-ya-ṫi\ *np* : the Santee Dakota - Cf I-san'ati

i·sa·pa \i-sá-ṗa\ *vn* i·ma·sapa : to be blackened by anything

i·si \i-sí\ *adv* : at or on the foot < ~ *wagluha kte. Na el ite makipastoya glihpeic'iyi na wopila eye* He will keep himself at his feet. And there he threw himself face down at his feet and gave thanks. > - Pb.23

i·si·tu·te·ce *or* **išitutece** \i-sí-ṫu-ṫe-ce\ *adj or adv* : lacking the necessities < ~ *šni u* He came well prepared, *i.e.* having made all preparations. > —Cf išitutece šni LC

i·si·ya·tan·han \i-sí-ya-ṫaŋ-haŋ\ *adv* : near the feet of < *Tancan kin hpaya tka k'un hel iyotake ca* Where he sat down there the body would have been lying. > - B.H. 271.4

i·sku·ya \í-sk̇u-ya\ *adj* í·ma·skuya : the mouth watering for — **iskuya·gla** *vn* ískuya·wa·gla : to have one's mouth water for different kinds of food — **iskuye·ya** *va* ískuye·wa·ya *or* skuye·wa·ya : to make one's mouth water for, to salt or perhaps to sweeten

i·sla·ye \i-slá-ye\ *n* : ointment, salve < ~ *ojuha* an oil bag >

i·slo·lya \i-sló-lya\ *va* islo·lwa·ya : to know by means of - D.246

i·span·span·he·ca *or* **uspanspanheca** \i-sṗáŋ-sṗaŋ-he-ca\ *n* : American hop hornbeam, ironwood *can maza* or *iťúhu* black walnut, leverwood; of the ostrya virginica, the birch family perhaps - Note: its flowers look like hops, the leaves like those of the elm tree. It was used for bows, and its blossoms for painting the face, hence the saying: *Ša wóilag ota yelo* Red are the many put to use - R BT Bl HM # 19

i·sti·ko·ya·gya \i-sṫí-ko-ya-gya\ *va perhaps* : to hold with the arms - B.H.77.24

i·sti·ho·hi·ya \i-sṫí-ho-hi-ya\ *v* : to reach with the arm — *adv* : within arm's reach

i·sto \i-sṫó\ *n* : the arm of a person, *i.e.* the lower part of the arm perhaps — **isto·glukatin** \i-sṫó-glu-k̇a-ṫiŋ\ *v poss* isto·wa·glukatin : to stretch out one's arms — **istoglu·kšan** *v poss* : to bend one's arm — **isto·iyohiya** *v* istoiyohi·wa·ya : to reach with the arm — *adv* : within arm's reach — **isto·katinkiya** \i-sṫó-k̇a-ṫiŋ-k̇i-ya\ *va* istokatin·wa·kiya : to cause to stretch out the arm — **isto·pakšan** \i-sṫó-ṗa-kšaŋ\ *n* : the bend of the arm — **istopa·kšija** *v* isto·wa·pakšija : to bend the arm — **isto·staka** \i-sṫó-sta-k̇a\ *adj* : tired in one's arms - B.H.56.2

i·sto·šni·ški·ye *v* - Note: the word may more properly be *ištokšinkiye*

i·sto·ye·ya \i-sṫó-ye-ya\ *v* : to stretch out one's hand or arm - *Syn* NAPEYEYA Bl

i·sto·yu·kan \i-sṫó-yu-kan\ *v* istó·ma·yukan : to have arms

i·sto·yu·kši·ja \i-sṫó-yu-kši-ja\ *v* isto·blu·kšija : to bend up the arm

i·swu \i-swú\ *n* : small stones — **iswu·la** *n dim* : gravel

iš \iš\ *pron* iš, íye : he, she, it, < *iš iye* he himself >

i·ša·glo·gan \i-šá-glo-ġaŋ\ *num ord adj* : the eighth — **i·šaglo·gloglogan** \i-šá-glo-glo-ġaŋ\ *num ord red adj* : every eighth one

i·ša·ko·win \i-šá-ko-wiŋ\ *num ord adj* : the seventh — **išakowin·win** *num ord red adj* : every seventh one

i·ša·kpe \i-šá-kṗe\ *num ord adj* : the sixth — *n* : a six-shooter, a pistol — **išakpe·kpe** *num ord adj* : every sixth one

i·ša·mna \i-šá-mna\ *adj* : dark red < ~ *s'e* to seem to be reddish, *Na hocokam oyate kin ~ s'e oimniciye* And the people gathered in the center seemed to be red, *i.e.* the whole crowd seemed to be red. >

i·ši \i-ší\ *v* i·wa·ši : to pay wages — *n perhaps* : wages

i·ši·ca \i-ší-ca\ *vn* i·ma·šica : to be hurt, harmed, injured - Cf iwícawašte Bl D.59

i·ši·ca·wa·cin \i-ší-ca-wa-ciŋ\ *vn* : to be greedy, covetous, desiring more

i·ši·co·la \i-ší-co-la\ *adv* [fr *wiši* remuneration + *cola* not having] : without remuneration

i·ši·gla \i-ší-gla\ *v* iši·lwa·gla *perhaps* : to be angry about

i·ši·htin \i-ší-ḣtiŋ\ *vn* i·ma·šihtin : to be feeble from, be injured by, to be enfeebled

i·ši·kcin *or* **išínhcin** *or* **išíkcin** \i'-ši-kciŋ\ *adv* [fr perhaps *i* on account of + *šica* bad + *cin* desire] : angrily, crossly < ~ *kuwa* to treat somebody mean > - C P GV

i·ši·ki·cin \i-ší-k̇i-ciŋ\ *v* iši·we·cin : to want pay

i·ši·ki·gla \i-ší-k̇i-gla\ *vn* i·ma·šikigla : to be angry on account of, to be sad about, affected by or for — **išiki·gla·ya** *va* išikigla·wa·ya : to make angry by, to make angry and torment, to afflict for

i·šil a·ya \i-šíl á-ya\ *v* : to be or become bad on account of - B.H.155.15

i·šin·htin \i-šíŋ-ḣtiŋ\ *vn* - Cf išihtin Bl

i·šin·ki·htin \i-šíŋ-k̇i-ḣtiŋ\ *v* išin·we·htin : to be injured or harmed by one's own

i·šinl \í-šiŋl\ *adv* : quickly < ~ *kah wacanmi tka owakihi šni* I tried to make it speedily but I could not. >

i·ši·tu·te·ca \i-ší-ṫu-ṫe-ce\ *adv* : being unprepared for < ~ *šni* being equipped with everything before starting on a journey *etc* > - *Syn* WAPIKIYECE LC

i·ška·hu \i-šk̇á-hu\ *n* : the ankle bones < *canhanpa ~ hanska* boots >

i·ška·hu·ton *va* iškahu·wa·ton : to put tops on moccasins

i·ška·kan \i-šk̇á-kaŋ\ *n* : the large tendon extending from the heel up the leg, the large tendon in the back of the neck, perhaps

i·škan \i-šk̇áŋ\ *v* : to move for a purpose < *petiškan* to come near the fire, draw up to the fire, to warm one's self >

i·škan·ka·pin \i-šk̇áŋ-k̇a-ṗiŋ\ *v* i·má·škankapin : to be lazy by reason of

i·škan·škan a·ki·ta \í-šk̇aŋ-šk̇aŋ a-k̇ì-ṫa\ *express* : to look at with a hungry mouth, as children do when others eat < ~ *amáyakita ye, tuktehan akih'an t'emayayin kte* You look at me with a hungry look; sometime you will make me die of hunger, as a woman would say to her grandchildren. >

i·škan·yan \í-šk̇aŋ-yaŋ\ *va* iškan·wa·ya : to get one to talk by teasing *etc* - Bl

i·ška·ta \i-šk̇á-ta\ *va* i·wa·škata : to play to or for anything

i·ški·ške·ye·ce \i-šk̇í-ške-ye-ce\ *n* : an interference by one in another's talk, speech, or game - Bl WHL

i·ško·gin \i-šk̇ō'-ġiŋ\ *n* : the long hair on a horse's ankle, a bare spot on part of the forelegs above the knees, its odor being ugly - Note: the word seems to be a *deriv* of *iška* ankle + *ogin* to clothe or sheath, whereas more proximately the *deriv* being *ogingin* to nod, which raises a question about *ogingin* itself.

i·šla·ya·pa·tan·han \i-šlá-ya-pa-ṫaŋ-haŋ\ *adv* : from the right side - BD

i·šla·ya·tan *or* **išlayatan·han** \i-šlá-ya-ṫaŋ\ *adv* : at or to the right hand of < *Na unma hinša kin le ~ iyayin kte lo* And this other red horse will go on to the right. >

i·šlo·ye \í-šlo-ye\ *n* : something with which to hold or melt metal, a pair of tongs or a ladle < *mazasu ~* a pot

---

\a\ father \e\ they \i\ machine \o\ smoke \u\ lunar \an, aŋ\ blanc Fr. \in, iŋ\ ink \on, oŋ, un, uŋ\ soon, confier Fr. \c\ chair \ġ\ machen Ger. \j\ fusion \clusters: bl, gn, kp, hšl, etc...\ b^{e}lo ... said with a slight vowel
See more in the Introduction, Guide to Pronunciation

or crucible in which to melt a metal > – Bl

i·šna·la \i-šná-la\ *pron* mi·šnala ni·šnala unki·šna·pi·la : alone, he or she alone < *Hokšila ~ yuhapi kin hemaca* I am the only boy they had. > — **išna·šnala** \i-šná-šna-la\ *pron red* : each one by himself – B.H.123.8 D.157

i·šna·ti \i-šná-ṫi\ *vn* : to have the menses; *lit* to dwell alone or in a separate house — *n* : menstruation, the menses < *~ wanjini kiyela* (or *nikiyela) u kte šni* She (You) will not be coming near any onset of her (your) menses. > — **išnati·pi** \i-šná-ṫi-ṗi\ *n* : dwelling alone, the menses

i·šna·wo·gla·ka \i-šná-wo-gla-ka\ *v* mi·šnawo·wa·glaka : to talk to one's self

i·šni·ka·leš \i-šní-k̇a-leš\ *adv* : within a little, nearly, pretty near

i·šo·kšo·ka·pi·la \í-šo-kšo-k̇a-ṗi-la\ *n* : thick lips

i·šo-ta \i-šó-ṫa\ *n* : smoke, cloud, atmosphere, environment < *Maká kin ohinni ~ wan el kakišyapi* A skunk is always is made to endure being in its own atmosphere. >

i·špa \i-špá\ *n* : the elbow < *~ tainšpa akipa* His elbow's elbow met with disaster. *~ ha yuzapi s'e owakihi yelo (ohiwayelo)* I was able as it was to grasp his elbow's hide (I won over him), *i.e. fig* I carried a thing through though they may even have caught a hold of the skin of one's elbow, which is held up for protection. > – Bl GA

i·špa·hu \i-špá-hu\ *n* : the bones of the lower part of the arm, the radius and ulna

i·špa ki·c'un \i-špá k̇i-c'uŋ\ *v* : to use one's elbows, perhaps < *Išpa kic'unpi canna (cana) okihipelo* They used their elbows when they were able. > — **išpakic'un** \i-špá-ki-c'uŋ\ *vn* : to take courage, to busy one's self – *Syn* BLIHEIC'IYA — **išpa kic'un·yan** *adv* : using the elbows < *~ maka hawayelo* Using my elbows I had earth for my clothing. > – GA CH Bl

i·špan·špan·he·ca \i-špáŋ-špan-he-ca\ *n* – Cf *ispanspanheca* for an alternative spelling – HP

i·špa·špa \í-špa-špa\ *vn* : to move the lips as some persons do when reading to themselves < *~ manka* I sat moving my lips. > – *Syn* ÍKAWAWA R Bl

i·špa·zi·hin \i-špá-zi-hiŋ\ *n* : a buffalo's elbow – Bl

i·špu·ki·ton \i-špú-k̇i-toŋ\ *v* išpu·wa·kiton : to eat little because there is little on hand – Bl

i·šta \i-štá\ *n* mi·išta unkí·šta·pi : the eye, eyes < *Le maišta on wanblaka* I saw this with my own eyes. >

i·šta·a·ka·hpe \i-štá-a-ka-ȟpe\ *n* : the eye-blinds for horses

i·šta·bles \i-štá-bles\ *vn contrac of* ištableza : to be sharp-sighted — **ištable·sya** *va* ištable·swa·ya : to make clear-sighted

i·šta·ble·za \i-šta-ble-za\ *vn* išta·ma·bleza : to be clear-sighted

i·šta·gla·kpa \i-šta-gla-kṗa\ *v poss* išta·wa·glakpa [fr *ištakakpa* to put out one's eyes] : to put out one's own eyes

i·šta·gon·ga \i-štá-ġoŋ-ġa\ *vn* išta·ma·gonga : to be blind, not able to see well — **ištagonga·pi** *n* : blindness — **ištagonga·ya** *adv* : in a blind state < *~ tonpi* He was born blind. > — *va* ištagonga·wa·ya : to make blind, to blind

i·šta·gon·ge \i-šta-ġoŋ-ġe\ *n* : a blind person

i·šta·ha \i-štá-ha\ *n* : the eyelid

i·šta·hca \i-štá-ȟca\ *vn* : to have obscure vision, to be snow-blind < *Šiyo ištahcapi* The grouse are snow-blind, as they say when it is very foggy in the spring or winter. *Tuwa yatonwanpi kinhan, ištanihcapi kte lo* If you look at a person, you will have poor vision. > – D.21

i·šta·ȟe \i-štá-ȟe\ *n* : the ridge above the eyebrows – Note: *ištaȟepi* is doubtfully used for eyebrows — **ištaȟe·hin** *n* : the eyebrow — **ištaȟe hin·šmašma** *express* : He has very thick eyebrows, as is said when playing cards and one does not deposite money because he has none

i·šta·ȟe·pi·hin \i-štá-ȟe-ṗi-hiŋ\ *n* : the eye-lashes – R Bl

i·šta·ȟe yu·šla \i-štá-ȟe yu-šlà\ *n* : a tool, pincers, to pull out hairs, as those of the eyebrows, beard *etc*

i·šta·hmin \i-štá-ȟmiŋ\ *adj* : cross-eyed

i·šta·i·yo·hi·ya \i-štá-i-yo-hi-ya\ *adv* : as far as the eye can see

i·šta·i·yo·šni·ja \i-štá-i-yo-šni-ja\ *vn* : to have the eyes blinded or dazzled by the light — *va* : to dazzle, perhaps — **ištaiyošni·šya** *va* : to dazzle the eyes, as bright light does

i·šta·i·yo·ta·pa \i-štá-i-yo-ta-pa\ *v* : to look in the direction someone else is looking < *ištaiyota·wa·pa* I look in the direction someone else is looking, *ištaiyota·ma·pa* He is looking in the direction I am looking > – Note: the word is used for the *infin* of *otápa* imitate

i·šta jo·to·kte \i-štá jo-tò-kte\ *v* : to smoke or blind the eyes < *Ištajoto·ma·kte yelo* It blinded my eyes. >

i·šta·ka·kpa \i-štá-ka-kṗa\ *va* išta·wa·kakpa : to strike and put out an eye

i·šta·ka·kpan \i-štá-k̇a-kṗaŋ\ *v* išta·wa·kakpan : to wink the eye – Note: the *red* form *ištakakpankpan* is doubtfully used — **ištakakpan·pi s'e** *adv* : winking the eyes quickly, as is done in excitement *etc* < *Ehanni ~ škinmic'iye; yunkan lehanl owakihi šni yelo* I had flashed my eyes; and then I wasn't able. > Bl

i·šta·kpa \i-štá-kṗa\ *vn* išta·ma·kpa : to be blind, having the eye put out — **ištakpe·ya** *va* ištakpe·wa·ya : to make blind

i·šta·kšin \i-štá-kšiŋ\ *v* išta·ma·kšin : to be squint-eyed, or cross-eyed — **ištakšin·ka** \i-štá-kšiŋ-k̇a\ *n* : a squint-eyed person — **i·šta·kšin·kšin** *vn red* : to be squint-eyed

i·šta kte nun s'e \i-štá kte nuŋ s'e\ *adv express* : as with piercing eyes staring at one < *~ ayuta* to glare intently at one > – Bl

i·šta·maza \i-štá-ma-za\ *n* : eye-glasses

i·šta·mni·ga·ga \i-štá-mni-ġa-ġa\ *adv* : in tears, with tearful eyes running – Note: a variant spelling may be *ištamniȟaȟa*

i·šta·mni·han·pi \i-štá-mni-han-pi\ *n* : tears – Note: the more correct form is *ištamniyanpi*

i·šta·mni·o·jula \i-štá-mni-o-ju-la\ *adv* : with watering eyes, perhaps

i·šta·mni·o·šlo \i-štá-mni-o-šlo\ *adv* : with water standing in the eyes

i·šta·mni·yan \i-štá-mni-yaŋ\ *adv* : running at the eyes, being bleary-eyed < *~ kowakipe* I feared being with bleary eyes. > – Note: the form *ištamaniyan* is doubtful Pb.47 Bl

i·šta·na·gle·ski·ya \i-štá-na-glè-ski-ya\ *v* : to look sternly at one with eyes widely open – *Syn* IŠTANATOGKIYA

i·šta·na·gnan·ka \i-štá-na-gnaŋ-k̇a\ *vn red* išta·ma·nagnanka [fr *ištanaka* to twitch] : to have the eye twitch repeatedly

i·šta·na·ka \i-štá-na-k̇a\ *vn* išta·ma·naka : to have the eye twitch just once

i·šta·na·to·gki·ya \i-štá-na-tò-gk̇i-ya\ *v* : to look sternly at one, changing the eyes as it were — **ištanato·gyeya**

adv : to with an unnatural eye expression, as in fear or uncertainty < *Wicašayatapi kin ~ nacancan* The Chief trembled with dread. > – B.H.140.6 WHL

i·šta·ni·ca tan·ka \i-štá-ni-ca tàŋ-ka\ *n* : the horned lark or the snow-bird – Note: it is one of the first to be with us in the spring, and it stays here all winter, being seen along the roads; its call: Opteptecela, opteptecela. Its other name is *maštékola* which Cf

i·šta·ni·yan \i-štá-ni-yaŋ\ *v* išta·ma·niyan : to have sore eyes < *ištawicaniyanpi wi* month of those with sore eyes, *i.e.* the month of March > – Note: *íniyan* to have a sore inside the mouth — **ištaniyan·pi** *n* : soreness of the eyes, a disease some tribes are allergic to in the springtime – Bl

i·šta·o·hca \i-štá-o-hcà\ *adv express* : hanging over, as is said of the snow that forms ice in the eyes

i·šta·o·to·ya \i-štá o-tò-ya\ *va* išta oto·wa·ya : to give one a blue eye

i·šta·san·ki·ya \i-štá-saŋ-ki-ya\ *v* : to make a side glance, a snap of the eye expressing disgust < *~ kici unpi* They are tossing glances between them, *i.e.* out of jealousy. > – Bl WHL

i·šta·su \i-štá-su\ *n* : the eye-ball – Bl

i·šta·to·la·s'e a·yu·ta \i-štá-tò-la-s'e a-yú-ta\ *v* : to look at angrily < *He takuwe ištatolas'e amayaluta hwo* Look here! Why is it you look at me with eyes of anger? >

i·šta·wa·i·yo·jan·jan \i-štá-wa-i-yo-jaŋ-jaŋ\ *n* : snow-glare in the eyes <*Ištawaiyo·ma·janjan yelo* There is snow-glare in my eyes. >

i·šta·wa·ka·ške \i-štá-wa-kà-ške\ *n* : a disease of the eyes where the right corner of the right eye and the left corner of the left eye becomes red – KT

i·šta·wi·ca·ni·yan \i-štá-wi-ca-ni-yaŋ\ *n* : an epidemic of sore eyes < *~ wi* March, the moon of sore eyes > — **ištawica·yazan** \i-štá-wi-ca-ya-zaŋ\ *n* : sore eyes < *~ wi* March, the prevailing sore eyes month >

i·šta wi·yo·hpa·yin kte wan \i-štá wi-yò-hpa-yiŋ kte waŋ\ *express* : Why not let it get into the eyes!, as a spy made signs that buffalo are near while he was standing on a hill – Bl

i·šta·ye·ya \i-štá-ye-ya\ *v* ištaye·wa·ya : to look into the distance < *Yunkan tohanyan ištayeyapi hehanyan pte kin au* And then when they took a sighting as far as the eye can see, it was then the buffalos came. > – Bl

i·šte·ca \i-šté-ca\ *vn* i·ma·šteca : to be ashamed, to be bashful — **ištel** \i-štel\ *v contrac* : to be diffident

i·šte·li·c'i·ye·ya \i-šté-li-c'i-ye-ya\ *va* ištelic'iye·wa·ya : to baffle, make bewildered – Bl

i·šte·lki·ya \i-šté-lki-ya\ *vn* ište·lwa·kiya : to make one ashamed, to disappoint one

i·šte·lya \i-šté-lya\ *va* ište·lwa·ya ište·lma·yaya : to make ashamed, to dishonor

i·šti·han·ke \i-ští-haŋ-ke\ *n* : the outer corner of the eyes – Bl

i·štin·ma \i-štíŋ-ma\ *vn* mi·štinma : to sleep, be asleep

i·šti·ya·gna \i-ští-ya-gna\ *adv* : closely observing < *~ kuwa* to keep an eye out observing closely > – B.H.303.3

i·šti·yo·jan·jan·ya *or* **ištáiyojanjanya** \i-ští-yo-jaŋ-jaŋ-ya\ *va* : to dazzle one < *Ištiyojanjanmayayelo* (or *ištaiyowalmayayelo*) You excite my admiration, as a man would say if somebody came all dressed up. > – Bl

i·šti·yo·šni·ja *or* **ištaiošnija** \i-ští-yo-šni-ja\ *vn* ištio·ma·šnija : to have the eyes blinded or dazzled by the light — **ištiyošni·šya** *va* : to dazzle one – B.H.155.26

i·šti·yo·ta·pa \i-ští-yo-ta-pa\ *vn* : to look towards when somebody points < *Ištiyotawicapin* He looked at them in the direction he pointed. > – B.H.244.3

i·šti·yo·wa·lya \i-ští-yo-wa-lya\ *va* : to dazzle one < *Ištiyowalmayayelo* or *Ištiyojanjanmayayelo* You excite my admiration, *or fig* You knock my eyes out. > – Bl

i·što·gin \i-štó-ġiŋ\ *n* : the eyelids, perhaps, or the eye brows – Note: the proper word may be *ištahehin* the eye brow — **ištogin·kiya** *adv* : with eyes partly closed

i·što·gmus \i-štó-gmus\ *vn* [fr *ištogmuza* to shut the eyes] : to close the eyes < *~ waci* to dance with eyes closed > — **ištogmu·sya** *va* ištogmu·swa·ya : to cause to shut the eyes — *adv* : having the eyes shut

i·što·gmu·za \i-štó-gmu·za\ *vn* išto·wa·gmuza : to shut the eyes — *adj* : blind-folded, with the eyes shut

i·što·gna \i-štó-gna\ *adv* : in the eyes < *Na hlihlila on ~ šna apápi keye* And he says he kept being struck in the eyes with the mud. >

i·što·gna·ke \i-štó-gna-ke\ *n* : the socket or orbit off the eye – Bl

i·što·hli \i-štó-hli\ *adj* : bleary-eyed, having sore eyes

i·što·yu·ha \i-štó-yu-ha\ *n* : any cover for the eyes

i·što·ki·ci·ca·šta·ka·pi \i-štó-ki-ci-ca-šta-ka-pi\ *n* : a mischievous pastime in which children would chew the fruit of rose bushes, gather all the kernels in the hand and fling them into other people's faces – Bl

i·što·kšin \i-štó-kšiŋ\ *vn* išto·wa·kšin : to close one eye and look with the other — **ištokšin·kiya** *va* ištokšin·wa·kiya *va* : to look at with one eye closed – R Bl

i·šun·ma·ke·ci \í-šuŋ-ma-ke-ci\ *interj* or *adv* : incidentally < *~ he toki iyaya he* Incidentally, what became of him? > – Cf unš'unmakeci WHL

i·šu·ta \i-šú-ta\ *vn* išu·wa·ta : to fail accomplishing, to be unable to do a thing, to miss in shooting at — **išute·ya** \i-šú-te-ya\ *va* išute·wa·ya : to cause to fail doing

i·š'a·ke hun·ke·šni \i-š'a-ke huŋ-ke-šni\ *adj* : feeble, as is said of slow, sick, old men – Bl

i·š'o·š'o \i-š'ó-š'o\ *adj* i·ma·š'oš'o : scampering, not easily restrained, hasty, quick – Cf wiš'oš'o — **iš'oš'o·ka** \i-š'ó-š'o-ka\ *n* : one who obeys cheerfully, who is quick < *~ na walitake* He is quick and brave > – Cf wiš'oš'oka — **iš'oš'o·ya** *adv* : quickly, hastily, cheerfully, eagerly < *~ škanpi. Ikto iš'oš'oyehci aya ke* Iktoes (the tricksters, *Iktomi* Spider) are active. Ikto began pretty much eagerly. > – D.103

i·tab \í-tab\ *adv* : soon after, quickly – D.272, 56, 74

i·ta·gla·hwe \i-tá-gla-hwe\ *adv* : with the wind, the wind to the back < *Yunkan itaglahwetanhan šunkawakan ota au* And then many horses came with their backs to the wind. > — *n perhaps* : the leeward < *Paha ~ (ekta) unyanpi* We go to the leeward of the hill. > — **itagla·hwe·kiya** \i-tá-gla-hwe-ki-ya\ *adv* : with the wind — **itagla-hwe·tanhan** \i-tá-gla-hwe-taŋ-haŋ\ *adv* : from the direction whence blows the wind < *He ti kin ~ yau kte* You should bring that house downwind. *Na tohanl ~ iyayapi ca waštemna* And when they went on downwind there was a fragrant odor, *i.e.* the women did. > – Note: this word may occur as a *contrac* of *ištaglahwe*

i·ta·gna \i-tá-gna\ *adv* : with close observation < *~ kuwa* to watch closely > – Ww

i·ta·gna·gya \i-tá-gna-gya\ *adv* : placed one on top of

\a\ father \e\ they \i\ machine \o\ smoke \u\ lunar \an, aŋ\ blanc Fr. \in, iŋ\ ink \on, oŋ, un, uŋ\ soon, confier Fr. \c\ chair \ġ\ machen Ger. \j\ fusion \clusters: bl, gn, kp, hšl, etc...\ b[e]lo ... said with a slight vowel
See more in the Introduction, Guide to Pronunciation

another - R Bl

i·ta·gna·ka \i-tá-gna-ka\ *va* ita·wa·gnaka : to place one on top of another

i·ta·hena \i-tá-he-na\ *adv* : on this side of, in time or place — **itahena·tanhan** \i-tá-he-na-taŋ-haŋ\ or \í-ta-he-na-taŋ-haŋ\ *adv* : on this side of

i·ta·ka·ha \i-tá-ka-ha\ *n* : the instep or the top of the foot < *siitakaha* the foot instep >

i·ta·ka·hpe \i-tá-ka-ȟpe\ *n contrac of* iteakahpe : a cover for the face, a veil

i·ta·ke \i-tá-ke\ *n* : the upper part of a moccasin or shoe, as opposed to the sole - Bl

i·ta·ki·gnag \i-tá-ki-gnag\ *adv* : with something on top of something else

i·ta·mye \i-tá-mye\ *v* : to die < *Toki itamwaye kin* A marvelous moment when I die > - Note the principal parts: women say *iwátamye iyátamye itámye* ; men say *itamwaye itamyaye itamye*

[1]i·tan \i-táŋ\ *adv* [fr *tan* a side of *e.g.* beef] : on the side < ~ *anunk* on both sides, *mitantanhan* at my side, *mitankiyela* near me >

[2]i·tan \i-táŋ\ *n* : a packing strap < *Ceji ~ kin yuškapi* The tie of his tongue was loosed. > - Mark 7.35 HH

[3]i·tan \í-taŋ\ *vn* : to be proud

i·tan'·a·nunk *and* **itan'anunkatanhan** \i-táŋ-a-nuŋk\ \i-táŋ-a-nuŋ-ka-taŋ-haŋ\ *adv* : on both sides

i·tan·can \i-táŋ-caŋ\ *n* i·ma·tancan : a ruler, lord, master — **itancan·ka** \i-táŋ-caŋ-ka\ *n* : the chief one, lord or master

[1]i·tan·can·ki·ya \i-táŋ-caŋ-ki-ya\ *adv* : in a lordly manner, with authority

[2]i·tan·can·ki·ya *or* **itancan·ya** \i-táŋ-caŋ-ki-ya\ *va* itán-can·wa·kiya : to have for or acknowledge as master, to make lord or chief

i·tan·can·yan \i-táŋ-caŋ-yaŋ\ *adv* : with authority, chief-like < ~ *econ* to preside, *Yunkan Šunkmanitu Ohitika eciyapi wan ~ econ kta keyapi (wacipi). "Ito taku wan ~ oblakin kte cin he le e"* And then one called Brave Coyote, they say, would be in charge (of the dance). "Now then, this is the thing I shall say as director. > — **itancanyan·kel** *adv* : in the manner of a chief which one is not - BT

i·tan·glu·za·za \i-táŋ-glu-za-za\ *vn* itan·ma·gluzaza : to have a feeling of fright, to have a fearful scare — **itangluzaza·ya** *va* : to frighten one < *Itangluzazamayaye* You make me *fig* shine, glow. > - Cf tangluzaza Bl WHL

i·tan'·i·c'i·ya \i-táŋ-i-c'i-ya\ *v refl* : to improve one's self, *e.g.* one's health by eating, or one's property by working - WE

i·tan'·i·glu·kšan \i-táŋ-i-glu-kšaŋ\ *adv* : round about one

i·tan'·i·šla·ya·tan·han \i-táŋ-i-šla-ya-taŋ-haŋ\ *adv* : at the right side of somebody - B.H.286.3

i·tan·kal \i-táŋ-kal\ *adv* : without, outside of < *Tiyopa eciyatanhan ~ hinajinpi* They appeared outside towards the door. > — **itanka·ta** \i-táŋ-ka-ta\ *adv* : outside of < *otonwahe kin ~* outside of the town > — **itankatan·han** *adv* : from without - B.H.229.18 Pb.47

i·tan·ki·ye·la \i-táŋ-ki-ye-la\ *adv* mi·tankiyela : near to one

i·tan·nunk \i-taŋ-nuŋk\ *adv* [fr *itan'anunk* on both sides] : on both sides < *Tiyopa kin etanhan itokagatakiya ~ enajin* They stood on both sides facing south from the door. > - Cf itan

i·tan·nun·kwa·k'in·ki·ya·pi \i-tá-nuŋ-kwa-k'iŋ-ki-ya-pi\ *n* : a load carried by a horse on both sides without using tent-poles - Cf tušuheyunpi

i·tan'·o·kšan *or* **itaokšan** \i-táŋ-o-kšaŋ\ *adv* : around about, on all sides < ~ *eic'itonwan* He looked about himself. >

i·tan·pi \í-taŋ-pi\ *n* : pride, vainglory

i·tan·sak t'a \i-táŋ-sak t'a\ *v* [fr *tan* very + *saka* stiff + *t'a* to die] : frightened to death, terrified - B.H.280.13 WHL

i·tan·tan \í-taŋ-taŋ\ *v red* i·ma·tantan unki·tantan·pi [fr *itan* to be vain] : to be vain, proud of, to glory in — **i-tantan·pi** *n* : pride, glorying, arrogance

[1]i·tan·yan \í-taŋ-yaŋ\ *vn* itan·wa·ya : to be proud by reason of

[2]i·tan·yan \i-táŋ-yaŋ\ *adv* : well, on some account < *Ištinme kin, ~ kte lo* When asleep he will do well. > — *vn* : to be well off, by reason of *e.g.* working *etc* - B.H.229.1 WE

i·tan·ye·šni \í-taŋ-ye-šni\ *vn* í·ma·tanyešni : to receive no benefits from, to be of no use

i·ta·o·kšan *or* **itan'okšan** *or* **itawokšan** \i-tá-o-kšaŋ\ *adv* : round about on all sides, all around something, as a fence around property < *Tipi kin ~ canwape topakiya eglepi. Hecel wicitawokšan unyanpi na okiwanjila unkutapi* Round about the house branches were set out in four ways. So we went around them and continually fired off our guns. *Na hetanhan Paha Sapa ~ tiwahepi kin omaniyan unpi* And from there around the Black Hill the families were travelling. > - Cf R D.215

i·ta·šo-ša \i-tá-šo-ša\ *v* : to spit out

i·ta·to·wab *or* **itatowal** *or* **itatowapa** *or* **itatowapa-tanhan** \i-tá-to-wab\ \i-tá-to-wa-pa-taŋ-haŋ\ *adv* : to the windward side of, on this side of

i·ta·to·wa·ta \i-tá-to-wa-ta\ *adv* : in the direction whence the wind blows, against the wind, upwind, to the windward of - Cf tatowata

i·ta·wa·cin \i-tá-wa-ciŋ\ *n* : possession of mind or property < *Hunhunhe mazaska ~ šice lo* Sad to say, money renders an unstable mind, *i.e.* his mind on liberal use of money is to be stingy with it. > - BT WHL

i·ta·wan·ka·gle *or* **itawankagleya** \í-ta-waŋ-ka-gle\ *adv* : uphill, ascending, up a very steep hill

i·ta·zi·pa \i-tá-zi-pa\ *n* mi·tazipa : a bow to shoot with < ~ *ikan* a bow string, ~ *péconpi* or *pecónpi* a game, a boys' pastime > - Bl

i·te \i-té\ *n* mi·ite : the face

i·te·a·ka·hpe \i-té-a-ka-ȟpe\ *n* : a face cover, a veil

i·te·a·nung *or* **iteanunka·tanhan** \i-té-a-nuŋg\ *adv* : on both sides of the face

i·te a·šni·yan·pi \i-té a-šnì-yaŋ-pi\ *n* : squirrel-tail grass, fox-tail; hordeum jubatum, the grass family - Bl # 186

i·te a·wi·ca·šni·yan \i-té a-wì-ca-šni-yaŋ\ *n* : witch grass panicum capillare, the grass family - BT # 43

i·te·cin·hin \i-té-ciŋ-hiŋ\ *n* : the hair over the forehead, the forelock

i·te e·ye·šni *or* **ite yešni** \i-té e-yè-šni\ *adj* or *adv* : not paying attention to others, *i.e.* out of pride or anger < ~ *yanka* to sit giving no attention, pouting > - GA

i·te·ha \i-té-ha\ *n* 1 : a mask, as a medicine man once used < *Yunkan giic'iya ca ~ wan un he sinte-lulyapi kaga* And then when he painted himself brown, he made a red-tail deer mask to wear > 2 : a halter

i·te·han \í-te-haŋ\ *adv* [fr *téhan* far, long] : far from — **itehan·han** *and* **itehanhan·yan** *adv red* : far — **ite-han·lake** *adv* : after a while < ~ *ci; ~ ki. T'in na ~ wicaša wakan el kihi. Gla yo, ~ wau kte. Na ~ k'el eciyatan* *kupi* After a while he got back; after a bit he arrived back back. He died and after a while a priest then provided for him. "Go home, after a while I shall come." And after a while then they came back from there. >

i·te·han·tan·han *and* **itehan·yan** \í-ṫe-haŋ-ṫaŋ-haŋ\ *adv* : far away from

i·te·ho·hu \i-ṫé-ho-hu\ *n* : the cheek bones

i·te·i·ya·ska·bya \i-ṫé-i-ya-ska-bya\ *v* : to put a stamp on — **iteiyaskabye** *or* **wiciteiyaskabye** *n* : a postage stamp

i·te·ka \i-ṫé-k̇a\ *adv* or *v impers* : it is time for, due, timely, likely indeed; *lit* on the face of it, evidently, it appears < *Wanna hi ~* Now he ought to come. *Wana capa ota itekalo* There ought to be many beavers here. > – D.251 B.H.36.15

i·te·la·za·tan·han \i-ṫé-la-za-ṫaŋ-haŋ\ *adv* : behind the back

i·te·na·šin·šin·ki·ya \i-ṫé-na-šiŋ-šiŋ-ki-ya\ *v* : to cut faces – P

i·te·o·wa \i-ṫé-o-wa\ *v* : to draw, sketch — **iteowa·pi** *n* : a photograph, snapshot

i·te·o·yu·ze \i-ṫé-o-yu-ze\ *n* : a look, the case of the countenance, appearance, complexion < *~ wašte* a winsome, pleasant face >

i·te·pa·kin·te \i-ṫé-ṗa-k̇iŋ-ṫe\ *n* : a towel – *See* apákinta

i·te·ša hin·gle \i-ṫé-ša hiŋ-glè\ *v* : to blush – Bl

i·te·šin·ki·ya \i-ṫé-šiŋ-ki-ya\ *v* itešin·wa·kiya : to frown, to grin

i·te·šin·šin \i-ṫé-šiŋ-šiŋ\ *n* ite·ma·šinšin : a wrinkled face

i·te·šni·o·pa \i-ṫé-šni-o-ṗa\ *v* : to freeze the face – IS LHB

i·te·šni·šni·yan \i-ṫé-šni-šni-yaŋ\ *adv red of* itešniyan : truthfully — **itešniyan** *adv* : indeed, in fact, in reality – B.H.87.3, 259.9

i·te·tan·han \i-ṫé-ṫaŋ-haŋ\ *v* or *adv* : to be queer, as is said when a man who is considered good does something wrong; strangely, peculiarly, perhaps – B. Sb

i·te·tan·han \í-ṫe-ṫaŋ-haŋ\ *adv* : in front, face on toward a person or animal < *~ ya* to go or place one's self in front, as in approaching a horse lest one be kicked by being at its side > – Bl

i·te wa·to·gla \i-ṫé wa-tò-gla\ *n* : a horse that is very sensitive on the head, and hence dodges the bridle on being caught – Bl

i·te·we·s'e hin·gle *or* **iteša hingle** \i-ṫé-we-s'e hiŋ-glè\ *v* : to blush – Bl

i·te·ya *and* **iteyakel** \i-ṫé-ya\ *adv* : almost, apparently, likely, it stands to reason – D.67, 99 B.H.31.7, 121.4

i·te ye·šni \i-ṫé yè-šni\ *adj* or *adv* – *See* ite eyešni

i·te·yu·ko·ki·ya \i-ṫé-yu-ko-k̇i-ya\ *or* \i-ṫé-yu-ko-k̇i-ya\ : to frown, scowl, look severe

i·te·yu·kši·lki·ya \i-ṫé-yu-kši-lki-ya\ *vn* : to cut faces – P — **iteyukšin·kiya** \i-ṫé-yu-šiŋ-k̇i-ya\ *or* \i-ṫé-yu-kšiŋ-k̇i-ya\ *va* iteyušin·wa·kiya : to make faces at, to draw up the face at one, to frown at

i·te·yu·šin·šin \i-ṫé-yu-šiŋ-šiŋ\ *adj* : with face wrinkled

i·te·yu·šin·šin·ki·ya \i-ṫé-yu-šiŋ-šiŋ-ki-ya\ *v* : to cut faces – P

i·te·zi \i-ṫé-zi\ *n* : the stomach < *Taku ~ mayazan* Something pains by stomach, as is said when one is not satisfied with something. > – Bl

i·ti·ca·ga \i-ṫí-ca-ġa\ *v* iti·wa·kaga : to set up a tent for a certain purpose < *Hocokam tipi wanji iticicagepi kin, el wau na oyate k̇in wowicawakiyakin kte lo. Tipi wan tanka iticagapi k'un el agla na el ak̇i. Tipi wanji cokab iticagapi* When I set up a tent for you in camp center I came there, and I shall speak to the people. They went and arrived back at the big tent that had been erected. A tent was set up in the middle. > – MS.566 D.230

i·ti·ci·ca·ške \i-ṫí-ci-ca-ške\ *n* : the three first main tent poles, which are usually tied together

i·ti·gni·la \i-ṫí-gni-la\ *n* : the pocket gopher; a little animal that piles up provisions for the winter – FH Bl

i·ti·pa·kin·te \i-ṫí-pa-k̇iŋ-ṫe\ *n* : a towel

i·ti·sa·bye \i-ṫí-sa-bye\ *n* [fr *ite* face + *sabya* to blacken] : black for the face — *v* : to blacken the face with – Bl WHL

i·ti·yo·hi·la \i-ṫí-yo-hi-la\ *adj* : each one – Bl B.H.64.7

i·ti·yo·pa \í-ṫi-yo-ṗa\ *adv* : near the door < *Na wanna tipi kin ~ el can wan paslatapi. Kici ku na tipi k'on ~ el kinajinpi* And now a stake was driven in the ground near the door to the tipi. He is coming back with him, and they had arrived at the tipi close to the doorway. >

i·tka \i-ṫk̇á\ *n* : a blossom, the capsule, an egg, the seed of anything, the testicles — **itka·ska** \i-ṫk̇á-ska\ *n* : the white of an egg — **itka·zica** *n* : the yolk of an egg

i·tkob \i-ṫkō'b\ *adv* : again, back again, in return, in reply < *~ ahi* They returned. *~ wicaye* He went forward to meet them. > – D.230

I·tkob U \I-ṫk̇ób U\ *np* : Arcturus, a star of the first magnitude, alpha in the constellation of Bootes, one of the brightest stars rising in the northwest during the spring. It is so called because it comes to meet the returning birds from the southeast and south. And because below it they return and pass by, it is called *Ihuku Kigle* Below Return. When Itkob U stands in the mid heavens they say it is summer. – BT

i·tko·kib \í-ṫko-k̇ib\ *adv contrac* mi·tkokib [fr *itkokipa* to meet] : meeting, in the presence of, before

i·tko·ki·pa \í-ṫko-k̇i-pa\ *va* itko·wa·kipa : to meet, come together from opposite directions < *Itkokib u. ~ na kaška yuzi na agla. Cinca itkokib u. Tuweni Waziya itkokipin kta okihi šni* He came into his presence. He met him, took, laid hands on him and bound him. He came before the son. No one was able so that he might meet the spirits of the North. > – MS.566

i·tkon \i-ṫkóŋ\ *vn* : to burn, to blaze, as fire

i·tkons \í-ṫkoŋs\ *adv contrac of* itkoŋza : even with < *eye kin ~* when he said (this) at the same time (a cock crowed). > – B.H.259.4

i·tkon·ski·ya \í-ṫkoŋ-ski-ya\ *va* : to accomplish a task, to even up – Note: ítkonsya

[1]i·tkon·sya \i-ṫkóŋ-sya\ *or* \í-ṫkoŋ-sya\ *adv* : even with

[2]i·tkon·sya \í-ṫkoŋ-sya\ *va* : to make even; *fig* to have accomplished one's task < *Toh'an kin he itkoskiye* He has accomplished that task, or piece of work. > – B.H.73.16

i·tkon·ya·han \i-ṫkóŋ-ya-haŋ\ *part* : burning, alive, as coals — **itkon·yan** *va* itkóŋ·wa·ya : to make burn or blaze

i·tkon·za \í-ṫkoŋ-za\ *adv* : even with — **itkonze·la** *adv* : even with, coming up to the mark, not more and not less, as the fluid in a quart measure is even with the mark denoting the "qt" measure

[1]i·to \i-ṫó\ *vn* : to become blue by means of

\a\ father \e\ they \i\ machine \o\ smoke \u\ lunar \an, aŋ\ blanc Fr. \in, iŋ\ ink \on, oŋ, un, uŋ\ soon, confier Fr. \c\ chair \ġ\ machen Ger. \j\ fusion \clusters: bl, gn, kp, hšl, etc...\ b^{e}lo ... said with a slight vowel **See more in the Introduction, Guide to Pronunciation**

[2]i·to \i-ṫó\ *adv* or *interj* : Well, Come now < ~ *le hanhepi kin ake ewicunkizapi na tašunkepi kin oyasin wicunkipi ktelo. ~ wagni kte , eya ške; yunkan unma k'on he iš eya: Ito, wagni kte, eya ške. ~ ceye, wicoti ekta unyin kta* Well, tonight a second time we shall fight them, and we shall capture all their horses. They say he said: "I shall go on home;" and then the other fellow had said: "Come on, I'll go home," they say he said. Well, he cried: "Let us go on to camp together." >

i·to·btob \i-ṫó-btob\ *adj contrac of* itobtopa : every fourth one

i·to·bto·pa \i-ṫó-bṫo-ṗa\ *num ord adj of* itopa : every fourth one

i·to·ceš *or* **itoeceš** \i-ṫó-ceš\ *interj* of disappointment at not being welcome *etc*, thereupon giving way [fr *ito* Well! + *eceš* it's no use] : What good does it do! < ~ *ǩaǩi mni kte* Oh well! I'll go over that way. > – Cf ihóeceš

i·to·ci·ca·cu *or* **itooicacu** \i-ṫó-ci-ca-cu\ *n* : a camera

i·to·el \i-ṫó-el\ *conj* : but purposely before, but first

i·to·e·yaš \i-ṫo-é-yaš\ *conj* : but purposely before – Cf ṫóèyaš, ṫóèl

i·to·gla·za \í-ṫo-gla-za\ *n* : a head ornament, *i.e.* one tied on top of the head and connected at the other end with the hair braid – Ww

i·to·gna \i-ṫó-gna\ *adv* : in the face < ~ *ayap'api kte* You should slap him in the face, *or* Let him have a blow in the face. > — **itogna·gna** *adv red* : repeatedly in the face — **itogna·gya** *adj* : looking like a lord, with the appearance of a lord – B.H.256.9, 263.9

i·to·gna·ke \i-ṫó-gna-ke\ *n* mi·tognake : the face, countenance, visage, appearance, presence

I·to·gna O·pi \I-ṫó-gna Ò-pi\ *np* : Wounded Face, father of *Miwakan Yuha* Sword – RF

i·to·han \í-ṫo-haŋ\ *interrog adv* : how far from? how long from? < *Mahel najin yo; tanyan wanyanka yo; ~ iyewayin kte; tanyan awanyanka yo* Stand inside; look well; how far should I push ahead? Look well on things. > — **itohan·han** *adv red* : how long how long? — **itohan·yan** *adv* : a little ways off < *Na ~ ahinajin. ~ najin* And they came and stood a little ways off. He took his stand a bit away. > – Bl B.H.46.4, 259.8

i·to·he·he·ya \i-ṫó-he-he-ya\ *v red of* itoheya : in different directions < ~ *iyayapi* They went off in different directions. > – B.H.241.2

i·to·he·ki·ya \i-ṫó-he-ǩi-ya\ *v* : to go on home < *Itohewakiyin kta* I shall go on home. > – *Syn* ~ WAGNI KTE L Bl

i·to·he·ya \i-ṫó-he-ya\ *va* : to go on to any place < *Na Jordan Wakpala itaokšan makoce kin ataya ~ . Takuni etkiya itohewayin ktelo. Hektakiya ~* And he went into all the country around the Jordan River. I shall go on with nothing. He is goes on back home. > – L LWOW.180

i·to hin·yan·ka yo \i-ṫō' híŋ-yan-ka yo\ *imper express* : Wait a little! – B.H.93.21

i·to·hi·yan·ki ye·to \i-ṫó-hi-yaŋ-ka ye-ṫò\ *imper express* : Hold on! – B.H.20.26

i·to·ho·mni \í-ṫo-ho-mni\ *vn perhaps* : to turn round, end round < ~ *wec'un* I wore it [my hat] backwards, turned around. >

i·to·i·c'i·ko·wa *or* **itoic'ikuwa** \i-ṫó-i-c'i-ko-wa\ *v* : to have one's picture taken

i·to·ju·ha t'a ca \i-ṫó-ju-ha t'a ca\ *express, a saying used when a man is plain spoken* : He tells it as it is, *i.e.* he speaks frankly < *Itojuha nit'a canke iyeyaglašna sece* Your picture frame, or photo, is dead, and so it is as though you made a blunder, *i.e.* were missing something. > – Bl

i·to·ka \í-ṫo-ǩa\ *v* : to be without concern for, to be alright < *Yunkan onšilapi šni hekiyapi. Etanš he iuntokapi eša yelaka?* So they said they did not pity him. "Indeed, what concern is that also to us?" > – B.H.259.22,277.5 WHL

i·to·kab *or* **itokabtu** *or* **itokabtuya** \i-ṫó-ǩab\ \i-ṫó-ǩa-bṫu\ *adv* mi·-tokab : before, in *ref* to time and place < *Na ~ hinajin* And he came beforehand and stood. > – Note: whereas the word "before" in English and "ánte" in Latin operate sometimes as *prep*, the *itokab* in Lakota always follows *šni* and its *vb*, thus: *t'e šni itokab* before his death; and *kigle šni itokab* before he went. This is contrary to our English expectations: < *Le wicaša kin hinhanna wicokanhiyaye šni ecel kigni kte. Ti wegna ye šni ~ iglutokeca, owanyang šica ic'icaga.* So, this man will not set out for his home before tomorrow afternoon. Before he went among the tipis he disguised himself, making himself a sad sight. > — **itoka·bya** *adv* mi·tokabya ni·tokabya : before, up to that time – B.H. 32.1, 98.21, 75.1

i·to·ka·ga \i-ṫó-ǩa-ġa\ *n* : the South — *adv* : southward
itóǩaġaṫa *n* : the South — *adv* : at the south
itóǩaġaṫaǩiya *adv* : toward the south < *Tiyopa kin etanhan ~ itan'nunk enajin* They stood toward the south on both sides away from the door. >
itóǩaġaṫanhan *adv* : to the south of, on the south side of, from the south
itó-ǩaȟ *adv contrac of* itokaga : southward < ~ *bla* I am going south. ~ *iyaya* to have gone south (an euphemistic *phr for* : to have died. A soul was supposed to travel to spirit-land via the Milky Way, from north to south. One's fate was determined where the Milky Way divides into two branches in the south. >
itóǩaȟǩiya *adv* : toward the south, southwards
itóǩaȟwapa *adv* : towards the south – Sb

i·to·ka·mna *or* **itokabya** \i-ṫó-ǩa-mna\ *adv* : before that, up to that time – B.H.96.8, 97.2, 138.5, 303.7

i·to·kanl \í-ṫo-ǩaŋl\ *or* \i-ṫó-ǩaŋl\ *adv* : in another place away from, as opposed to *sakib* < ~ *iyaya* to go somewhere else away from > – B.H.293.25

i·to·ka·pa \i-ṫó-ǩa-pa\ *va* : to be before one in birth, to be older than < *Mitokapa* He is older than I. > — **itokapa·tanhan** *adv* : before, from before, from the presence of < *Mitokapatanhan* He is from before me. >

i·to·ka·šni \í-ṫo-ǩa-šni\ *v impers* í·ma·tokašni í·un·toka·pi·šni : it makes no difference, it does not concern or influence < *Na ena glakinkinyan najin ca lila kutepi eša ~ . Tahcašunkala kin el iwicatokešni* And right here where he stood in a crooked line, though they did much shooting, it made no difference. It made no difference to the sheep. > — **itokašni·yan** *adv* : in vain, without reason — **itoka-wacinšni** *v* : to be unconcerned in something, to be thoughtless – Cf itokašni B.H.220.7, 223.23, 28.3

i·to·ke·ca \i-ṫó-ǩe-ca\ *or* \í-ṫo-ǩe-ca\ *vn* i·ma·tokeca : to be altered, changed, to be affected by in any way — **itokeca·šni** *or* **itokeca šni** *v impers* i·ma·tokecašni : it makes one no difference, or no difference to — *vn* : to be unchanged, without a difference, to be not one's business – B.H. 303.19

i·to·ke·han \i-ṫó-ke-haŋ\ *adv* : at the first, formerly

i·to·ki \í-ṫo-ǩi\ *adv interrog* : where from? which way from? – Cf ṫoǩí

i·to·ki·ci·le \i-ṫó-ǩi-ci-le\ *vn* [fr *ite* face + *ole* look for + *kici* to each other] : to aim at one's face, seeking to strike – Bl

i·to·ki·ya *or* **itokiya·pa** *or* **itokiyapa·tanhan** \í-ṫo-ǩi-ya\

\í-to-k̇i-ya-pa-ṫaŋ-haŋ\ *adv interrog* : which way from? — **itokiya·tanhan** *adv interrog* : in what direction from?

i·to·ki·yo·pe·ya \í-ṫo-k̇i-yo-pe-ya\ *vn* : to trade, exchange - B.H.19.13

i·to·kšan \i-ṫó-kšaŋ\ *adv* [fr *ite* face + *okšan* around] : around the face, as in painting a circle < ~ *tokiyapi* A blue stripe was painted around his face. >

i·to·ktog \í-to-ktog\ *adv* : alternately — **itokto·gye** *adv* : in different ways — **itokto·kanl** \í-to-kto-k̇aŋl\ *adv* : alternately — **itokto·keca** \í-to-kto-k̇e-ca\ *adv* : alternately < ~ *econpi* They did it alternately. > - P Bl B.H.77.13

i·to·k'e·han \i-tó-k'e-haŋ\ *adv* : formerly, of old

i·to·k'e·yaš \i-tó-k'è-yaš\ *adv conj* : let me see, wait a little - Cf tóèyaš R

i·to·la kin he·han *or* **itola k'on hehan** \i-ṫõ'-la kiŋ hè-haŋ\ *adv* : long ago - Note: the word is *obsol* Cf itókab *Syn* LILA EHANNI

i·to·leš \i-ṫó-leš\ *interj calling into question in assuming another circumstance* : Really now! Supposing ... < ~ *wai šni kin toka kta he?* Well now, what if I did not go (what would happen?) ? ~ *heya ške c'un* Really! Suppose they had said he said that. > - Cf itóla Bl WHL

i·to·mni \i-ṫó-mni\ *adj* i·ma·tomni : drunk, dizzy from drinking - Cf itomnimni — **itomni·ic'iya** *vn* : to carouse, revel, get drunk — **itomni·mni** *adj* i·ma·tomnimni : dizzy, *i.e.* from sickness — **itomni·pi** *n* : drunkenness, a turning around of the head — **itomnis'a** *n* : a drunkard — **itomni·ya** *va* itomni·wa·ya : to make dizzy or drunk

i·to·na \í-to-na\ *adv* : of how many? Which number? — **itona·ka** \í-to-na-k̇a\ *adv* : of how many? — **itona-ke·ca** *adv* : of what number?

i·ton \i-tóŋ\ *vn* : to tell the truth - Note: the word is not used alone, *e.g.* as is *itonšni* to lie

i·ton'i·c'i·pa \i-tóŋ-i-c'i-pa\ *v perhaps* : to be astonished at one's self; to praise one's self to — **iton·kipa** \i-tóŋ-k̇i-pa\ *v poss of* itónpa : to wonder at one's self or one's own, to praise one's self — **itonkipe·ya** \i-tóŋ-ki-ṗe-ya\ *adv* : astonished at one's self, praising one's self

i·ton·pa \i-tóŋ-pa\ *va* itóŋ·wa·pa : to be astonished, to wonder, to praise one < *Le hecetu na oyate kin wanyankapi na lila itonpapi. Le takuwe itonyapapi hwo?* This is the way it was, the people saw it, and they praised him very much. Now why are you astonished? > — **itonpe·ya** *or* **itonpeya·han** \i-tóŋ-ṗe-ya\ *adv perhaps* : astonishingly, surprisingly, wonderfully, praiseworthily - B.H. 280.14

i·ton·pi·šni \i-tóŋ-pi-šni\ *n* : untruth, lies

i·ton·šni \i-tóŋ-šni\ *vn* i·wa·tonšni : to tell an untruth < *Akšakahci he ~ k'on* He had told more of that lie. > — **itonšni·šni** *v red of* itonšni : to keep lying — **itonšni·yan** *adv* : falsely

i·ton·wan \i-tóŋ-waŋ\ *vn* i·wa·tonwan [fr *tonwan* to look at] : to look or see with, as with one's eyes

i·to·o·i·ca·cu *or* **itocicacu** \i-ṫó-o-i-ca-cu\ *n* : a camera

i·to·o·pte·ya \i-ṫó-o-ṗte-ya\ *adv* : through, passing on, straight through - Cf iyopta R

i·to·pa \i-ṫó-ṗa\ *num ord adj* i·ma·topa : the fourth

i·to·pta sa·pa \i-ṫó-pṫa sà-pa\ *n* [fr *ite* face + *opta* across + *sapa* black] : the black-footed ferret, so called for a black stripe across its face - Note: its home is with prairie dogs and is very difficult to kill. Hence it is said to be *wakan;* and whoever kills one will soon die himself - BD

i·to·pta sa·pa ta·pe·ju·ta \i-ṫó-pṫa sa-pa ta-pe-jù-ta\ *n* : snow on the mountain, showy milkweed or spurge, white marginal spurge. A milkweed with blossoms half white and half green; euphorbia marginata, the spurge family. It grows in gumbo and near prairie dog homes - Note: it is also called *asanpi pejuta* . A tea from it is used by mothers without milk. Also, crushed leaves in warm water makes a liniment for swellings BT Bl # 214

i·to·to \i-ṫó-to\ *vn red of* itó : to be made blue by

i·to·wa·pi \i-ṫó-wa-ṗi\ *n* [fr *ite* face + *owapi* a sketch or painting] : a picture — **itowapo·gnake** *n* : a little frame in which photos are held — **itowapo·juha** *n* : a picture frame

i·to·we *or* **itoe** \í-to-we\ *n* : the forelock < ~ *k'el mapehin kin hetan cónala ate mayuha kta. Nupin wacinhin ikan hanskeya ~ el iyaglaškapi* My father will keep a few hairs from my forelock. Both a long string and the hairs were tied together on the forelock. > - Bl

i·to·ye *or* **itoye·hin** *or* **ito·e** \í-to-ye\ *n* : the forelock; the face, appearance — **itoye·kiton** *or* **itoekiton** \í-ṫo-ye-k̇i-toŋ\ *v poss* itoye·we·ton : to wear braids of hair or ornaments in front — **itoye·ton** *or* **itoeton** *vn* itoye·wa·ton : to have braids or ornaments dangling about one's face — **itoye·woblu** *or* **itoewoblu** *vn* : to have hair stand up, as from the wind blowing; *Psáloka heconpi* the Crow Indians do that — **itoye·yuh'o** *vn* itoye·ma·yuh'o : to have hair stand up on the head - R Bl

i·to·yu·ha \i-ṫó-yu-ha\ *vn* : to have on the face some expression < ~ *t'ékiya* to make or have a deadened expression on the face > - Bl WHL

i·tu \i-ṫú\ *adv* : wildly, without being planted or tamed < ~ *icaga* It has grown up of itself and for nothing. > - R Bl

[1]**i·tu·hu** \i-tú-hu\ *n* : the forehead; the frontal bone

[2]**i·tu·hu** \i-ṫú-hu\ *n* : the black oak < ~ *can* the black oak tree, wood > *Syn* ISPANSPANHECA Bl # 19

i·tu·hci *or* **otuhci** \i-ṫú-ḣci\ *adv* : for nothing, gratuitously, without cause

i·tu·ka·leš \i-ṫú-k̇a-leš\ *adv* : truly, indeed

i·tu·ma·ko·skan \i-ṫú-ma-k̇o-sk̇aŋ\ *adv* : in vain, to no purpose

i·tun·gtan·ka \i-ṫúŋ-gtaŋ-k̇a\ *n* : a rat

i·tun·kab \i-ṫúŋ-k̇ab\ *adv* : on the back, reclining backwards, as opposed to *aglapšunyan* upside down, prone < *Na tatanka ha wan owinjapi ca el ~ iyunka na hecina t'a. ~ naicabyeya ištinme* And he lay on his back on a buffalo robe mat, and he finally died. He was sleeping on his back with mouth wide open. > — **itunka·btu** \i-ṫúŋ-k̇a-bṫu\ *adv* : on the back — **itunka·byela** *adv* : on the back < ~ *glihpaya* He threw himself on his back on his return. ~ *hpaya* He lay on his back. > - WL Bl D.104, 272

i·tun·ka·la \i-ṫúŋ-k̇a-la\ *n* : a mouse

i·tun·ka·san *or* **itunkasan·la** \i-ṫúŋ-k̇a-saŋ\ *n* : the weasel

i·tun·psi·ca·la *or* **itunpsi·psicala** \i-ṫúŋ-psi-ca-la\ *n* : the field mouse

i·tu·pša·pša s'e *also* **pšapša s'e** \i-ṫú-pša-pša s'e\ *adv* : disorderly < ~ *un* to be disorderly in one's looks, *i.e.*

\a\ father \e\ they \i\ machine \o\ smoke \u\ lunar \an, aŋ\ blanc Fr. \in, iŋ\ ink \on, oŋ, un, uŋ\ soon, confier Fr. \c\ chair \ġ\ machen Ger. \j\ fusion \clusters: bl, gn, kp, hšl, etc...\ b^e^lo ... said with a slight vowel **See more in the Introduction, Guide to Pronunciation**

with ragged clothes, dishevelled hair *etc* > - Bl
i·tu·še·ka \i-ṫú-še-ka\ *adv* : by all means, nevertheless; by repetition, perseverance in doing it over and over again < ~ *owakihi kte lo.* ~ *taku wanji eyemayahin kte hcin, tka aciyuptin kte šni yelo.* I shall be able through perseverance. He will have made me say something repeating it over and over, but I shall not answer him. > Note: the word is incorrectly spelled *itušaka* - Bl
i·tu·šeš \i-ṫú-šeš\ *adv* : indeed < ~ *išica mawacinka pcelyela mayuta tanke* Indeed he tried to hurt me, for awhile it was my older sister that looked my way. >
i·tu·tu \i-ṫú-ṫu\ *adv red of* itu : in a wild state — **ítutu·ya** *adv red of* ituya : gratuitously — **itu un** *v* : to be in a wild state
itu·ya \i-ṫú-ya\ *adv* : for nothing, without a cause, gratuitously — **ituya·kel** \i-ṫú-ya-ḱel\ *adv* : without cause, gratuitously - R Bl
i·t'a \i-t'a\ *v* : to die for some reason - Bl LHB
i·t'e·ca \i-t'é-ca\ *adj* : slightly warm, lukewarm, tepid, as is said of fluids only — **it'e·lya** \i-t'é-lya\ *va* : to make slightly warm or tepid, *e.g.* water
i·t'e·ni·han \i-t'é-ni-haŋ\ *adj* : bothered, disturbed for some reason or other so that action is impeded < ~ *šni* not to be bothered *Taku* ~ *econšnimayapelo* What is bothersome you do giving me no time to do my work. ~ *wotešni* being bothered so one eats little > - Bl
i·t'e·wa·cin \i-t'é-wa-ciŋ\ *v* : to intend to die on account of < *Tokeš'unlaka wayatkanpi kin* ~ It being as it was, he intended to die from the drinking. > - Bl
i·t'ins \i-t'íŋs\ *v contrac of* it'inza : to be firm — **it'insya** *va* it'in·swa·ya : to make firm by means of
i·t'in·za \i-t'íŋ-za\ *vn* : to be firm by reason of
i·t'in·ze \i-t'íŋ-ze\ *n* : a fastener, a tightener, as an elastic garter
i·t'un·gki·ya \i-t'úŋ-gḱi-ya\ *v* : to suspect concerning one's self
i·t'un·gya \i-t'úŋ·gya\ *v* : to suspect — **it'un·keca** \i-t'úŋ-ḱe-ca\ *vn* i·ma·t'unkeca : to be suspected of, to be unwilling to do - BD
i·wa·cin \í-wa-ciŋ\ *v* íwa·canmi : to think of going to
i·wa·cin·gnu·ni·yan \i-wá-ciŋ-gnu-ni-yaŋ\ *adv* : causing bewilderment, wonder, as at the first sight of a giant machine's complication < *Kinyekiyapi wan tima tokel kagapi kin wanyankin na* ~ *ayuta* He looked upon with wonder and saw how the inside of an airplane was made. > - Bl WHL
i·wa·cin·ja·ta \i-wá-ciŋ-ja-ta\ *vn* iwacin·ma·jata : to be undecided about anything
i·wa·cin·ko \i-wá-ciŋ-ko\ *vn* iwacin·ma·ko : to be impatient about, be out of humor on account of
i·wa·cin·to·kan·kan·gna·gna·ya \i-wá-ciŋ-to-kaŋ-kaŋ-gna-gna-ya\ *adv* : with the mind not concentrating on any particular subject or idea, ruminating casually perhaps with a grunting sound < *Ca hecel kohan* ~ *omawani yelo* And so meanwhile I took a walk ruminating over matters. > - Bl
i·wa·cin·ton \i-wá-ciŋ-toŋ\ *v* iwacin·wa·ton : to be intelligent by reason of
i·wa·cin·yan \i-wá-ciŋ-yaŋ\ *va* iwacin·wa·ya iwacin·ci·ya : to trust in for, or in *ref* to < *Le anpetu kin el taku wan iwacinciyelo* Today I trust you in one thing. (So what he wants follows). > — *adv* : trustingly
i·wa·cin·ye·hci \i-wá-ciŋ-ye-ȟci\ *v* : to depend on another's ability, to hold great trust, to stand in great need of help - Pb.41 WHL
i·wa·gla·mna \i-wá-gla-mna\ *n* : an extra or fresh horse < *Na ecel* ~ *yuha najinpi kin el aglihunni* And as it was they came straight back to where they stood with the fresh horses. > - Note: in former days the Dakotas would have another horse along in case the one they were riding played out, or a horse were needed for an escape or the carrying of meat home
i·wa·ho·ki·ci·ya·pi \i-wá-ho-ḱi-ci-ya-pi\ *v* [fr *iwahoya* to let one know] : they promise to each other < *Olowan kin he unkahiyayapi kta kéya i.e. iwahounkiciyapi k'un* We agreed *i.e.* had promised to sing that song. > - D.224
i·wa·ho·kon·ki·ya \i-wá-ho-ḱoŋ-ḱi-ya\ *va* iwahokon·wa·kiya : to instruct in regard to, to counsel or advise concerning — **iwahokonkiya·pi** *n* : instruction, counsel
i·wa·ho·ya \i-wá-ho-ya\ *va* iwaho·wa·ya : to send word to concerning anything; to promise, grant, permit; to warn, let one know < *Yúsyus iwahociyin kte. Hecel wanna oyuspa. Yunkan iyokipi. Hecel wanna iwahoyin na "Hinhanna kin anpahan unyin kte lo" eya. Niyate taku tona iwahomaye* I shall be sure to instruct you. So then he took hold on him. And then he was pleased with him. So he let him know and he said: "Tomorrow morning in daylight let's you and I go." Your father let me know a number of things. > - D.11, 13, 236 B.H..112.7
i·wa·hu·ke·za \i-wá-hu-ke-za\ *n* : a bayonet < *Akicita num* ~ *yuhapi.* ~ *yamni yuha.* Two soldiers are holding a bayonet. He is holding three bayonets. > - B.H.95.26
i·wa·hte·la·šni \í-wa-ȟte-la-šni\ *va* iwahte·wa·la·šni : to dislike on some account, to dislike something in one, to disesteem, think lightly of for some reason, to be disgusted with one on account of - D.33, 268
i·wa·hwa·ye·la \i-wá-ȟwa-ye-la\ *adv* : gently, quietly, peacefully < *Hankeya* ~ *glapelo* Little by little they went quietly homewards, *i.e.* the storm clouds passed by without much noise. > - Bl
i·wa·h'an'·i·c'i·la \i-wá-ȟ'aŋ-i-c'i-la\ *v refl* iwáh'an·mi·c'ila : to be proud
i·wa·i·c'i·ni·yan \i-wá-i-c'i-ni-yaŋ\ *v refl of* iwakiniya : to be dissatisfied with one's self
i·wa·kan \í-wa-kaŋ\ *adj* : talkative, tattling, gabbling — *n* : a babbler
[1]**i·wa·kan·yan** \í-wa-kaŋ-yaŋ\ *adv* : in a babbling manner
[2]**i·wa·kan·yan** \i-wá-kaŋ-yaŋ\ *adv* : supernaturally
i·wa·kan·ye·ja \i-wá-kaŋ-ye-ja\ *adj* : poor and easily satisfied, being in distress < *Taku keša imawakanyeja yelo* I am satisfied with any amount, be it ever so little. > - Note: the Tetons rarely use the *adj* Bl
i·wa·ki·ci \i-wá-ḱi-ci\ *vn* iwa·wa·kici : to dance for one, as in praise of one *e.g.* in the Scalp Dance - R
i·wa·ki·ci·hci \i-wá-ḱi-ci-ȟci\ *v* iwá·mi·cihci [fr *i* for + *wahci* to cut out] : to tear off and take for one; to make fringes < Iwakicihcipi kte. *Na wana* ~ *mila on* They will make fringes. And he made fringes with a knife. > - Note: *pahcí* to cut or break out notches by cutting R
I·wa·ki·ci Wa·ci·pi \I-wá-ḱi-ci Wa-cì-pi\ *np* : the Scalp Dance
i·wa·ki·con·za \i-wá-ḱi-coŋ-za\ *va* iwa·we·conza [fr *konza* pretend] : to influence one, to command one in regard to — **iwakicon·ze** *n* : a commandment, decree
i·wa·ki·ni·ya \i-wá-ḱi-ni-ya\ *va* iwa·wa·kiniya : to get out of humor with, to neglect or contemn
i·wa·kta \i-wá-kṫa\ *vn* iwa·wa·kta : to be on one's guard, to be on the look-out, to guard — *n* : a mark, a sign; a pledge - B.H.160.10, 174.9
i·wa·kta·ya \i-wá-kta-ya\ *va* iwakta·wa·ya : to have a

look-out for, to put on one's guard, to forewarn, admonish —*adv* : guardedly - B.H.55.14, 157.22

i·wa·kte·gla \i-wá-kte-gla\ *vn* iwakte·wa·gla : to go home in triumph having taken scalps

i·wa·kte·gli \i-wá-kṫe-gli\ *vn* iwakte·wa·gli : to come home in triumph bringing scalps

i·wa·kte·ki·ya·gla \i-wá-kte-k̇i-ya-gla\ *va* : to cause one to go home in triumph, having taken scalps as trophies < *Waniyetu amakešakowin el Scili kin iwaktemakiyaglapelo* In my seventeenth year the Pawnees went home in triumph. > - BT

i·wa·ku·wa \i-wá-k̇u-wa\ *va* : to provoke one, make one angry

i·wa·li·ta·ke \i-wá-li-ta-k̇e\ *adj* : active < *Iwalitakelo* He is active. > - *Syn* IYUŠKINYAN ŠKAN

i·wa·na·gi·ye·ya \i-wá-na-ġi-ye-ya\ *va* : to trouble one in regard to, to disturb one with

i·wa·ni·ti \i-wá-ni-ṫi\ *vn* iwani·wa·ti : to go and spend the winter at for some purpose

i·wa·ni·ye·tu \í-wa-ni-ye-ṫu\ *n* : the succeeding winter, the next winter

i·wan·glag \i-wáŋ-glag\ *v contrac of* iwanglaka : to be concerned for one's own

i·wan·gla·ka \i-wáŋ-gla-ka\ *v poss* iwan·wa·glaka [fr *i-wanyanka* to look at] : to look to, have regard for one's own < *Ikipišni iwanglake* He deemed himself unworthy > — **iwan'ic'iglaka** *v refl* : to look at one's self, to guard one's self < *Iwanmic'iglaka* I watch after myself. > - B.H.175.3

i·wan'·i·glag \i-wáŋ-i-glag\ *v contrac of* iwán'iglaka : to watch over one's self

i·wan'·i·gla·ka \i-wáŋ-i-gla-k̇a\ *v* iwan·mi·glaka : to look at one's self as in a glass; to watch over, guard one's self, to set a guard

i·wan·ji·ca \i-wáŋ-ji-ca\ *v* : to control, check *e.g.* one's anger < *Wacin ~ šni* He fails to control his desires (thus he get angry easily). > - Bl WHL

i·wan·kab \i-wáŋ-k̇ab\ *adv* : above something < *mi-wankab* above me *Na tipi kin ~ ikiyela hinajin* It (a cloud) came and stood nearby above the house. *Na wa kin ~ iyeya* And the snow was suddenly on top of it. >

i·wan·ka·bi·c'i·ya \i-wáŋ-k̇a-bi-c'i-ya\ *v refl* : to exalt one's self - B.H.161.2

i·wan·ka·btu *or* **iwankabtu·ya** *or* **iwankabtuya·kel** *or* **iwankal** \i-wáŋ-ka-bṫu-ya-kel\ \i-wáŋ-kal\ *adv* : above, up

i·wan·ka·pa *or* **iwanka·pata** \i-wáŋ-k̇a-pa\ \i-wáŋ-k̇a-pa-ṫa\ *adv* : above, up above one — **iwanka·tahan** \i-wáŋ-k̇a-ṫaŋ-haŋ\ *adv* : from above one < *Hunh wakpala kin opaya ya po; na hunh ~ ya po* Some of you go along in the creek; others go along above it. >

i·wan·ki·ci·yan·ka \i-wáŋ-k̇i-ci-yaŋ-k̇a\ *v* iwan·we·ci-yanka iwan'·un·kiciyankapi : to look to, watch over for one < *iwankiciyankapi* they look to, to watch over one another >

i·wan·yang \i-wáŋ-yaŋg\ *v contrac of* iwanyanka : to look to or at — **iwanyan·gya** *adv perhaps* : watching out, being careful < ~ *conala etan cantewašteya wicak'u wo* In taking care give gladly from the little you have. > — **iwanyangye·hci** *adv* : examining very carefully, keeping one's eyes open < ~ *omani* He walks with his eyes open. > — **iwanyank** *v contrac of* iwanyanka : to look to or at - B.H.120.15, 153.18 Bl

i·wan·yan·ka \i-wáŋ-yaŋ-k̇a\ *va* iwan·bla·ka : to look to or at, to survey, examine, spy on, watch at; to judge < *Hetanhan hinhanna ca na tuktogna oti iwašte kin he ogna kahnigapi nainš iwanyankapi na tokiyatanhan oge wašte kin he ogna na oyate tonakecapi kin hena tanyan iyukcanpi* When it was morning, from that time on, they understood well how many people there were, where comes their good ways, and they took a look at and chose the better place to live. > — **iwanyanka·pi** *n* : spies, surveyors — **iwanyanke** *n* : something by which to see, an eye-piece, the sight of a gun, a telescope, or field glass - Note: *maziwanke* an opera glass or a telescope - B.H.89.12, 45.5, 194.13

i·wa·pe \i-wá-ṗe\ *v* iwa·wa·pe : to make sharp by — **iwape·šni** *v* : to make dull on

i·wa·pe·tog \i-wá-ṗe-tog\ *n contrac of* iwapetokeca : what is used as a mark, a sign — **iwapeto·gton** *va* iwapeto·gwa·ton : to mark or brand with

i·wa·pe·to·ke·ca \i-wá-ṗe-to-ke-ca\ *n* : a mark, a sign

i·wa·psa·ka \í-wa-psa-ka\ *v* : to cut off with, as with a knife or some other thing < *Kan iwapsake wan imicikinte-šni* The tendon cutter was too dull for me. >

i·wa·sa·za \i-wá-sa-za\ *vn* iwa·ma·saza : to take hard, to get sick over

i·wa·še·ca \i-wá-še-ca\ *vn* iwa·ma·šeca : to be rich provisions *esp*

i·wa·ši \i-wá-ši\ *va* : to employ for a certain purpose - B.H.7.18, 85.20, 227.7

i·wa·ši·cun \í-wa-ši-cuŋ\ *vn* i·ma·wašicun : to be talkative, to talk badly

i·wa·šte \i-wá-šte\ *vn* i·ma·wašte [fr *wašte* good] : to be better by means of, to be benifited by < *Hetanhan hinhanna ca na tuktogna oti ~ kin he ogna kahnigapi* When it was morning, from that time on, they took a look at and chose the better place to live. >

i·wa·šte·gla \i-wá-šte-gla\ *adv* : carefully — **iwaštegla-la** *adv red* : slowly - Cf iwaštela

i·wa·šte·ka \i-wá-šṫe-ka\ *vn* : to be none the better for

i·wa·šte·la \i-wá-šte-la\ *adv* : slowly, moderately, carefully < *Hehanl ~ ie ši* Then he bade him speak slowly. >

i·wa·šte·ya \i-wá-šṫe-ya\ *adv* : better — **iwašteya·kel** \i-wá-šṫe-ya-k̇el\ *adv.* : a little better

i·wa·š'ag \i-wá-š'ag\ *vn contrac of* iwaš'aka — **iwaš'a·gya** *va* iwaš'a·gwa·ya : to strengthen by means of

i·wa·š'a·ka \i-wá-š'a-ka\ *vn* iwa·ma·š'aka : to be strong by reason of or for < *cehpi ~* to be strong as to the flesh > — *n* : strength, the source of strength < *~ šni* to be weak, be unable to recover *Cehpi imáwaš'ake šni* My source of strength is not in flesh. >

i·wa·to·hanl *or* **iwatohan·tu** \í-wa-ṫo-haŋl\ *adv perhaps* : sometime, one day in *ref* to something < *~ ungna wicacokam wašicun wan hinajin na atayaš wanjini unkayuta-pi šni* Possibly sometime a white man came standing in their midst, and not so much as one of us did look at him. > -B.H.8.3, 32.1, 74.18, 259.8, 31.6, 90.17

i·wa·to·ki·ya \i-wá-ṫo-ki-ya\ *vn* : to be much concerned by < *Waeyapi kin on lila iwatokiyapi ške'* He stated that they were really much concerned by their speaking. > — **iwatokiya·šni** *vn* iwa·ma·tokiyašni : to be none of one's business — **iwatokiya·tanhan** \í-wa-ṫo-k̇i-ya-ṫaŋ-haŋ\ *adv* : out of concern - D.225 BT

i·wa·to·pe·ki·ya \i-wá-ṫo-ṗe-ki-ya\ *n* : an oar, paddle, anything with which to row a boat

---

\a\ father \e\ they \i\ machine \o\ smoke \u\ lunar \an, aŋ\ blanc Fr. \in, iŋ\ ink \on, oŋ, un, uŋ\ soon, con-ťier Fr. \c\ chair \ġ\ machen Ger. \j\ fusion \clusters: bl, gn, kp, hšl, etc...\ b^{e}lo ... said with a slight vowel
See more in the Introduction, Guide to Pronunciation

i·wa·tu·ka \i-wá-ṫu-ka\ *vn* : to be tired of or on account of anything
i·wa·tu·kte \í-wa-ṫu-kte\ *adv* : from hence < *Mato Ša tipi kin he ~ el ti yelo* Red Bear lives over there in that house. > - BT WHL
i·wa·wi·ku·wa \i-wá-wi-ku-wa\ *va* iwawi·wa·kuwa to do something to make one angry, to provoke one
i·wa·ya·zan \i-wá-ya-zaŋ\ *vn* iwa·ma·yazan : to be sick in consequence of
i·wa·yu·pi·ka \i-wá-yu-ṗi-ka\ *vn* iwá·blu·pika : to be skillful, handy on account of or in doing — **iwayupi·ya** *adv* : handily, nicely, well < *~ španyan* She cooked it nicely. > - B.H.20.19, 77.11
i·wa·zi·ya·pa *and* **iwaziyapa·tanhan** \i-wá-zi-ya-pa\ \i-wá-zi-ya-pa-ṫaŋ-haŋ\ *adv* : to the north of — **iwaziya·ta** *adv* : at the north of — **iwaziya·tanhan** \i-wá-zi-ya-ṫaŋ-haŋ\ *adv* : northward of
i·we \i-wé\ *vn* i·ma·we : to bleed by reason of
i·we·ce·ya \i-wé-ce-ya\ *va* iwece·wa·ya : to have regard for, to do as one commands
i·we·hi·yu \í-we-hi-yu\ *v* íwe·ma·hiyu : to bleed from the mouth — **iwehiyu·pi** *n* : a bleeding from the mouth, a sickness among some Sioux — **iwehiyu·ya** *v* íwehiyu·wa·ya : to raise blood, spit blood - Bl
i·we·šle·ka \i-wé-šle-ka\ *vn* iwe·wa·šleka : to do something worthy of honor, to wear or have as evidence of bravery - Note: the custom was in an earlier time to wear a split feather as a sign of having been wounded by the enemy - R Bl
i·we·tu \i-wé-ṫu\ *n* : the next or following spring
i·we·yo·ša-ya \i-wé-yo-ša-ya\ *adv perhaps* [fr *i* mouth + *we* blood + *ošaya* to be red in] : with a bloody mouth < *Na tahca na pte ko ~ kacegceg omanipi* And a deer and a buffalo too traveled struck and staggering along. > - Note: *kacegceg* is better spelled *kacekcek*
i·wi·ca·ble·za \i-wí-ca-ble-za\ *n* : enlightenment
i·wi·ca·ca·ga \i-wí-ca-ca-ġa\ *n* : a generation < *~ šakowin hehanyan ocic'u ktelo* I shall then give you seven generations. > - Bl MS.514
i·wi·ca·gna·yan \i-wí-ca-gna-yaŋ\ *n* [fr *gnayan* to deceive] : deception
i·wi·ca·hu·pi \i-wí-ca-hu-pi\ *n* [fr *hu* the stock of a plant] : sodomy - Note: the word is now vulgar
i·wi·ca·kca·šla \i-wí-ca-kca-šla\ *n* : a clipper
i·wi·ca·mna \í-wi-ca-mna\ *adj* [fr *imna* be satisfied] : satisfying, furnishing much nourishment
i·wi·ca·po \i-wí-ca-ṗo\ *n* [fr *po* to swell] : a swelling, an inflation on account of
i·wi·ca·pu·za \í-wi-ca-pu-za\ *n* [fr *puza* dry] : thirst
i·wi·ca·šte·ca \i-wí-ca-šte-ca\ *n* [fr *išteca* to be ashamed] : shame, bashfulness
i·wi·ca·wa·šte \i-wí-ca-wa-šte\ *adj* : nourishing, nutritious, as food; being good for them, as certain things might be - P Bl
i·wi·ca·yu·tan \i-wí-ca-yu-ṫaŋ\ *adj* : lovely, tempting - P Bl
i·wi·kce·mna \i-wí-kce-mna\ *num ord adj* : the tenth — **iwikcemna·mna** *adj red* : every tenth one — *n* : tithes
i·win·kte \i-wíŋ-kte\ *vn* i·ma·winkte i·unki·winkte·pi : to glory in, to be proud of — **iwinkte·kte** *v red* : to be vain or boastful — **iwinkte·pi** *n* : a glorying in — **i-winkte·ya** *va* iwinkte·wa·ya : to cause to glory in — *adv* : glorying, proudly
i·wi·štan \i-wí-štaŋ\ *va* i·wa·wištan : to treat well, as a sick person
i·wi·tko \i-wí-tko\ *vn* i·ma·witko [fr *witko* foolish] : to be drunk on < *taku ~* something that intoxicates, liquor > — **iwitko·tkoka** *vn* : to become foolish by means of — **iwitko·ya** *va* iwitko·wa·ya : to make drunk with
i·wi·yo·hi·yan·pa·ta \í-wi-yo-hi-yaŋ-pa-ṫa\ *adv* : at the east of — **iwiyohiyanpa·tanhan** *adv* : to the east of
i·wi·zi·lye \i-wí-zi-lye\ *n* : frankincense; weed *etc* - P
i·wo·bla·ska·ye·la \i-wó-bla-sǩa-ye-la\ *adv* : made flat, flatened by force of < *Yunkan maza su num ~ mahel un* And two flatened bullets are within. >
i·wo·blu \i-wó-blu\ *vn* : to be blowy, snowy, to bluster; to drift, blow up *e.g.* snow or dust — *n* : a blizzard < *~ tanka* a great blizzard > — **iwoblu·blu** *v red* : to blow persistently - D.249
i·wo·ca·je·ya·lya \i-wó-ca-je-ya-lya\ *v* : to sing one's praises on account of — *adv* : in praise of one < *~ woglaka* to talk in praise of one's own affairs > - Bl
i·wo·c'u \i-wó-c'u\ *n* [fr *woc'ú* to churn] : a churn
i·wo·ga·ga \í-wo-ġa-ġa\ *n* : a rifle < *Le koškalaka kin wahinkpe na ~ wan hecel yuha hpaya ška. ~ s'e haiyotiyekiya* They say this young man lay in this way holding his arrows and a rifle. It is as if a rifle made him suffer for lack of proper clothing, as though many bullets went through them > - Bl
i·wo·gla·ka \i-wó-gla-ka\ *v poss* iwo·wa·glaka [fr *woyaka* to tell] : to speak in *ref* to one's own
i·wo·hin·yan·sya·kel \i-wó-hiŋ-yaŋ-sya-kel\ *adv* : in a threatening or irate manner < *~ wakinyan ukiye* An awful thunderstorm is coming. > - Bl
i·wo·hta·ka \i-wó-ȟta-ka\ *vn* iwo·ma·htaka : to hit or strike against, bump — *va* iwó·wa·htaka : to strike something - *Syn* IWÓTO
i·wo·hta·ke \i-wó-ȟta-ke\ *n* : a billiard stick or cue, the hammer of a gun
i·wo·i·c'i·to \i-wó-i-c'i-ṫo\ *v* [fr *iwoto* to hit] : to run one's self against - Note: *ipustan* and its *refl* form *ikpustan* - Bl
i·wo·ju \i-wó-ju\ *n* : a seed drill < *wagmeza ~* a corn drill, *~ su* seed for a drill > - B.H.200.3
i·wo·ko·ki·pe·ke \í-wo-ko-ki-ṗe-ke\ *n* : one with a sharp tongue - Bl
i·wo·kpan \í-wo-kpaŋ\ *va* : to crash to pieces - Bl WHL
i·wo·na s'a \í-wo-na s'a\ *n* : what goes on a straight or even course but not in the desirable direction, as a ball going beyond its target < *~ iyeyapi s'e unkiyayapelo* We went on as though it were driven in an unwanted direction, as a speeding automobile over high and low places. *~ iyaye s'e hiyu* He came here as if he were going on a straight course. *iwonas'iyaya* to pass over a target and high into the air, as an arrow might do > - Note: íwowanka Bl WHL
i·wo·pan \i-wó-paŋ\ *v* [fr *wopan* to pound fine] : to shoot to pieces — *n* : a pestle
i·wo·psil \í-wo-psil\ *v* : to flip off, to ricochet < *~ wao* I struck it with a ricochet shot. > - *Syn* IWOWANKA
i·wo·sla \i-wó-sla\ *adj* or *adv* : in an upright manner < *nakpa ~ ikikcu* to prick up one's ears; or it could be said: *nakpa yuwankal ikikcu* > - Bl
i·wo·sli \i-wó-sli\ *n* : a squirt, a syringe, a squirt gun which is made by Dakota boys out of the common elder or boxwood
i·wo·slo·han \i-wó-slo-haŋ\ *v* : to blow along lengthwise < *~ iyeya* to blow or burst > — **iwoslohan·han** *v red* : to fly over the ground, as snow in a blizzard < *waiwoslohanhan* snow drifting > - Bl

i·wo·šo \í-wo-šō\ *n* : pouting lips — **iwošo·ka** \í-wo-šō-ka\ *adj* : pouting with the mouth pushed up — **iwošo·kiya** \í-wo-šō-ki-ya\ *vn* íwošo·wa·kiya : to push out the lips, to pout - R Bl

i·wo·š'a·ka \i-wó-š'a-ka\ *v* iwo·wa·š'aka [fr *woš'aka* shoot lightly] : to hit with little force, to indent < *wacin* ~ to be discouraged, *Hecel wacin iwomaš'akin kte šni* So I shall not be discouraged. > - Pb.42

i·wo·tan'·in·šni·yan \i-wó-taŋ-iŋ-šni-yaŋ\ *adv* : visible only very close by < ~ *han na kaska iyaya* It was being hardly visible, and it cleared off. >

i·wo·to *or* **iyoto** \i-wō'-to\ *vn* iwo·ma·to : to hit or strike against, butt against < *iwoic'ito* to hit one's self >

i·wo·wan·ka o \í-wo-waŋ-ka o\ *v* íwowanka wa·o : to hit something after first striking another thing, as an arrow the ground first < *Iwowanka iyeyapi s'e unkiyayapelo* We went on as though suddenly first glancing off something else, as in going fast in an automobile through a draw to a higher point. > - Bl

i·wo·ya·ka \i-wó-ya-ka\ *va* iwó·bla·ka : to relate, tell of, to speak to in *ref* to

[1]**i·ya** *or* **ia** \i-yá\ \i-á\ *vn* i·wá·ya i·yá·ya unki·ya·pi : to speak - Note: iáa *vn red* where the "y" is dropped Cf D.105 note 1

[2]**I·ya** \Í-ya\ *np* : a fabulous creature famous for the fact that it eats

i·yab \i-yáb\ *v contrac of* iyapa : to strike against something < *Tiyopa* ~ *iblabla* I went and struck against the door. >

i·ya·bla·gye·la \i-yá-bla-gye-la\ *adv* : calmly < *Anpetu wan okatakin wanica ca* ~ *helo* The day without a stir stood calmly. > - Bl

i·ya·ble·za \í-ya-ble-za\ *va* : to watch with *ref* to something < *Miniyatkanpi kin iyawicableza yo* When they are taking a drink of water take a good look at them. > - B.H.75.14

[1]**i·ya·bya** \i-yá-bya\ *adv* **1** : singly, separately scattered, as in hunting < ~ *unyanpi* We go separately. > **2** : butting or striking against

[2]**i·ya·bya** \í-ya-bya\ *adv* : scattering around, dispersedly < ~ *najinpi* Scattering about they came to a stop. ~ *unkolepi* Scattering ourselves around we hunted. >

i·ya·ci·ca \i-yá-ci-ca\ *adj* : rough, ruffled up, as is said of hair or feathers

i·ya·cin \i-yá-ciŋ\ *va* i·blá·cin : to liken to, compare with — **iyacin·kel** \i-yá-ciŋ-kel\ *adv* : by way of comparison — **iyacinpi** *n* : a likeness, resemblance — **iyacin·yan** *adv* : like to, in like manner, equal to; parabolically, metaphorically — **iyacinyan·kel** \i-yá-cin-yaŋ-kel\ *adv* : somewhat like

i·ya·ge·gnag *or* **iyage** \i-yá-ġe-gnag\ \i-yá-ġe\ *n* : a cluster-like group, as of grapes — **iyage·ya** \i-yá-ġe-ya\ *adv* : in clusters, bunches - R P Bl

i·ya·gi \i-yá-ġi\ *v* : to be rusty perhaps - Bl

[1]**i·ya·gla·pšin-yan** \i-yá-gla-pšiŋ-yaŋ\ *va* : to turn over upon anything

[2]**i·ya·gla·pšin-yan** \í-ya-gla-pšiŋ-yaŋ\ *adv* : bottom upwards

i·ya·gla·ski \i-yá-gla-ski\ *vn contrac of* iyaglaskica : to press on < ~ *ma·yanka* It is pressing on me. >

i·ya·gla·ski·ca \i-yá-gla-ski-ca\ *vn* iya·ma·glaskica [fr *aglaskica* press on] : to lie on, press on, to cover

i·ya·gla·ski·lya \i-yá-gla-ski-lya\ *va* iyaglaski·lwa·ya : to cause to press upon

i·ya·gla·ška \i-yá-gla-ška\ *v poss* iya·wa·glaška [fr *iyakaška* to tie to] : to tie one's own to < *Nupin wácinhin ikan hanskeya itowe el iyaglaškapi.* Both tied to the forelock a long string head-piece. *yuónjincayela* ~ to tie up short, *i.e.* to tuck up one's robe or dress. > - Bl

i·ya·gla·šna *or* **ieglašna** \i-yá-gla-šna\ *vn* iya·wa·glašna : to make a mistake, to blunder in speaking

i·ya·gle \i-yá-gle\ *vn* : to go or come to, to reach to, extend or lead to, as does a road; to meet, come upon one - Cf iyagleya

i·ya·gle·gle·ga \i-yá-gle-gle-ġa\ *v* iya·ma·gleglega : to tell lies - Bl

i·ya·gle·i·c'i·ya \i-yá-gle-i-c'i-ya\ *vn* : to get one's self into trouble or difficulties that one cannot overcome, as does a thief, to be in for trouble, to meet obstructions on one's way - *Syn* IYOKAIC'IYA

i·ya·gle·ton \i-yá-gle-toŋ\ *va* : to have on or over < ~ *econ* She does it on something else, as to knit on. > — **iyagleton·yan** *adv* : over, having something under < ~ *kaksa* to cut one stick, *e.g.*, off on another >

i·ya·gle·ya \i-yá-gle-ya\ *va* iyagle·wa·ya iyagle·ma·ya : to cause to reach to , to lead or bring one to, as a man into trouble < *Pte otapi el ai na maya wan el iyaglewicayapi. Yunkan winyan k'on u kin iwankab holyela han, mahpiya ekta ~ han wanyankapi* They brought them to a bend when they came upon many buffalo. Then they saw the woman up above standing in a mist and leading him to heaven. > — *adv* : leading somewhere, as does a road, reaching to, even to; on top of something, as a house on its foundation < *Canku kin le Manderson (otonwahe) ~ ihunni. Htayetu ~ heconhanpi. ~ han. Petijanjan ~ egle yo, i.e.* put it on; or, *Ptejanjan agle egle yo. Le woeye kin lehan ~* This is the road leading the way to Manderson (a town). In the evening they were doing the trip. Even into night. Set up on top a lamp, or Set up a lamp stand. Now it has led to this saying > - Note: this is an old word in use until the present day, *le anpetu kin ~* until this day B.H.113.7, 274.13, 108.3

i·ya·glu·ha \i-yá-glu-ha\ *v poss* iya·wa·gluha iya·blu·ha [fr *iyayuha* to follow after] : to follow after one's own, as a colt its mother

i·ya·glu·pta \i-yá-glu-pta\ *v refl* iya·ma·glupta iyaniglupta : to slip away, break loose, escape, as an animal one has tried to kill - Bl

i·ya·glu·za \i-yá-glu-za\ *v* : to have or hold for one's own protection, ecouragement or support; to take back one's words < *Hecélahci wana iyawagluzelo* With that alone I am well cared for (*i.e.* having given everything away). > Bl KE

i·ya·gna \i-yá-gna\ *prep* : after, behind, following; with, together with < *Yunkan itazipa wan lila hanska ca yuha najin na wahinkpe wan lila hanska ca nakun ~ . Wanna yamni can miyagna unpi* (Mark 8.1) . *Mahpiyašapa iyagna u kin* And then he stood holding a very long arrow together with a very long bow. Now they are following me for three days. In fact a black cloud came afterwards. > — **iyagna·gna** *prep red* : keeping together with — **iyagna·kel** \i-yá-gna-kel\ *adv* : in the manner of following - *Syn* IYAYUSTOG St B.H.258.7

i·ya·gna·škin·yan \i-yá-gna-škiŋ-yaŋ\ *v* iya·ma·gnaškinyan : to say foolish things in anger - Bl

i·ya·gton \i-yá-gtoŋ\ *v* iya·gwa·ton [fr *iyake* a feather

\a\ father \e\ they \i\ machine \o\ smoke \u\ lunar \an, aŋ\ blanc Fr. \in, iŋ\ ink \on, oŋ, un, uŋ\ soon, confier Fr. \c\ chair \ġ\ machen Ger. \j\ fusion \clusters: bl, gn, kp, hšl, etc...\ b'lo ... said with a slight vowel **See more in the Introduction, Guide to Pronunciation**

end of quill or arrow] : to put a feather on an arrow

i·ya·gu·ya \i-yá-ġu-ya\ *v* : to burn, as a little mush in a kettle after the water is evaporated – Note: *iyáġu* also is perhaps used

i·ya·gya \i-yá-gya\ *va* : to make fit the feather end, *i.e.* of arrows < *Wanbli hupahu wiyaka ca iyagyapi* It was eagle wing feathers made to fit the feather end of the arrows. > – Cf iyáke

i·ya·gya·ta·ye·la \í-ya-gya-ṫa-ye-la\ *adv red of* iyatayela : individually, personally, self alone – B.H.60.4

¹i·ya·han \i-yá-haŋ\ *va* iya·wa·han unki·yahan·pi : to go up a hill and stand, *i.e.* in *ref* to one person; to many persons, *éyahan* is used < *Paha kin kal iyawahe* I ascended the hill there. > — *part* : speaking

²i·ya·han \í-ya-haŋ\ *va* íya·wa·han : to put the foot on, step on anything < *Na wannaš šina wan inyan eya ko el ahipi na wanna kéya onši* ~ And right now they brought there a blanket as well as a stone, and he stepped on the poor turtle. >

i·ya·ȟa·gye·la \í-ya-ȟa-gye-la\ *adv* : too little left, too short < ~ *tókanl iyawakaške šni* I did not tie the other end of the string, *i.e.* the two ends of the string were too short to tie them together. *Tuwa iyaȟagyelahci omiglaptelo* One left for me too little of my own, *i.e.* one left me very little. > – Bl

i·ya·hpa·hpa·ya \i-yá-ȟpa-ȟpa-ya\ *vn* : to scramble < *iyakicihpayapi* they scramble > – P Bl

i·ya·hpa·ya \i-yá-ȟpa-ya\ *vn* iya·wa·hpaya iya·un·hpa-ya·pi : to fall upon, grab, seize < *Na kici iyakicihpayapi. Hunku kin ceya iyayin na (hokšila tawa) iyakihpaya kéye* They together seized him. He stated he seized his own (his own boy) and his mother went away crying. – R

i·ya·hpe·ki·ci·ci·ya \i-yá-ȟpe-ḱi-ci-ci-ya\ *va* : to put or throw on for one, *e.g.* a load on a horse

¹i·ya·hpe·ki·ya \i-yá-ȟpe-ḱi-ya\ *va* : to put on or throw over *e.g.* the back of a horse, as in loading it < *Hō-o-o wanna* ~ *yo* OK, load him up now! as an old man called out before moving on. >

²i·ya·hpe·ki·ya \i-yá-ȟpe-ḱi-ya\ *va* a : to give or hand to one *e.g.* the pipe b : to touch the ground with and then hold up the pipe to heaven, as is done before smoking the pipe

i·ya·hpe·ya \i-yá-ȟpe-ya\ *va* iyahpe·wa·ya : to throw over or on, to throw out, as a rope on a horse's head or as a fishline < *Wakantanka* ~ to make God favorable by *e.g.* prayer, which is a saying used in former times. *Cannunpa* ~ *po* Have a smoke! > – RF Bl

i·ya·i·c'i·kpe·han \i-yá-i-c'i-kpe-haŋ\ *v refl of* iyapehan : to wrap one's self around, as does a snake < *Zuzeca wan hiyu na Paul nape el* ~ A serpent came up and wrapped itself around Paul's hand. > – B.H.304.2

i·ya·i·c'i·pa \i-yá-i-c'i-pa\ *v* : to knock against, as one's head against a wall < *Wanun* ~ *yelo* He accidentally bumped up against it. > – P Bl

i·ya·i·gla·ška \i-yá-i-gla-ška\ *v refl* iyá·mi·glaška [fr *iyakaška* to tie to] : to tie one's self, to give one's self up to be bound

i·ya·ka \í-ya-ḱa\ *n* : a glutton, one who eats too much

i·ya·kab \í-ya-ḱab\ *adv* [fr *i* go + *akab* beyond] : in addition, more than what is due, than what one needs, to spare < *Taku oyasin* ~ *yuha* He has everything to spare. ~ *econ* to overdo, ~ *iyeya* to surpass > – P B.H.149.22

i·ya·ka·btu *or* **iyakab** \í-ya-ka-btu\ *adv* : surpassingly – R Bl

i·ya·ka·hpe \í-ya-ka-ȟpe\ *n* [fr *akahpa* to cover] : a cover or lid for the mouth of anything — **iyakahpe·ya** *adv* : serving as a cover < ~ *han* to stand as a cover > – B.H.60.20, 23.6

i·ya·kan·win·la·ke s'e \i-yá-kaŋ-wiŋ-la-ke s'e\ *adv* : speaking so as to leave the possible suggestion of a doubt about what is said < ~ *tak'eye* He says so but I doubt it. > – Bl

i·ya·ka·pa \í-ya-ka-pa\ *vn* íya·ma·kapa : to be larger than, to surpass

¹i·ya·ka·pa·tan·han \i-yá-ḱa-pa-ṫaŋ-haŋ\ *adv* : afterwards, behind

²i·ya·ka·pa·tan·han \í-ya-ḱa-pa-ṫaŋ-haŋ\ *adv* : over or on top

i·ya·ka·pe·i·c'i·ya \í-ya-ka-ṗe-i-c'i-ya\ *v refl* : to go beyond one's self, to be intemperate — **iyakape·peya** \í-ya-ka-ṗe-ṗe-ya\ *adv red of* iyakapeya : passing beyond – B.H.178.9

i·ya·ka·pe·ya \í-ya-ḱa-ṗe-ya\ *va* iyakape·wa·ya : to pass, go beyond, to overcome, to persuade or succeed in persuading — *adv* : more than surpassing

i·ya·ka·pta \i-yá-ḱa-pta\ *va* iya·wa·kapta iya·un·kapta·pi *or* unki·yakapta·pi : to climb, as a hill, to reach the top, to pass over or beyond — **iyakapte·ya** *v* iyakapte·wa·ya : to cause to pass up or over — *adv* : beyond, going over, going up-hill

i·ya·ka·san·ni \i-yá-ḱa-saŋ-ni\ *n* : one side or half of something — **iyakasanni·la** *n* : one side only

i·ya·ka·ška \i-yá-ḱa-ška\ *va* iya·wa·kaška [fr *kaška* to tie] : to tie one thing to or on another < *Na le can eya wiyaka iyakaškapi kin hena icu* And he took this stick and wing feather that were tied together. >

i·ya·ka·tin \i-yá-ka-ṫiŋ\ *v* iyá·wa·katin [fr *akatin* straighten out] : to measure by means of *e.g.* a yardstick

i·ya·ka·win \í-ya-ḱa-wiŋ\ *vn* [fr *akawin* exaggerate or to lie, a Dakota word] : to exceed, go beyond bounds, to overflow, as a river does its banks – R

i·ya·ke \i-yá-ḱe\ *n* : a feather end of a quill, the feather on an arrow

i·ya·ki·ca·ška \i-yá-ḱi-ca-ška\ *v* : to be tied or roped together < ~ *ówahehce* I tried hard to tie it up, as a man says to another who is very lazy and does not want to be disturbed, and so wants to help him along. ~ *ócicihehce* I am trying hard to get you engaged (*i.e.* in work and for me to follow you closely). ~ *ómakihan yo* Follow close behind me, *lit* study me to get yourself involved. > – Bl KE

i·ya·ki·ci·hpa·ya \i-yá-ḱi-ci-ȟpa-ya\ *v* : to bounce on each other

i·ya·ki·ci·yu·ha *or* **iyakicihuȟa** \i-yá-ḱi-ci-yu-ha\ *vn* iya·we·ciyuha [fr *iyayuȟa* have an attachment] : to be attached to, as one horse to another, to follow those one loves – Note: *iyábluȟa* I am attached to it

i·ya·ki·cun·ni \í-ya-ḱi-cuŋ-ni\ *vn* íya·we·cunni : to become tired and leave off, to give up < *Na wana iyawicakicunnipi na awicayuštanpi* And they now let them go and gave up on them. > – D.59 MS.565

i·ya·ki·cun·ni·ya \í-ya-ḱi-cuŋ-ni-ya\ *va* í-yakicunni·wa·ya : to cause to leave off or cease from — **iyakicunni-yan** *adv* : leaving off

i·ya·ki·c'u \i-yá-ḱi-c'u\ *vn* : to be much, to increase — *adv* : much more than one needs

i·ya·ki·c'un·c'un·ka \i-yá-ḱi-c'uŋ-c'uŋ-ka\ *n* : one who does more than is usual; one who keeps on begging

i·ya·ki·c'u·ya \i-yá-ḱi-c'u-ya\ *adv* : much, a good deal, plentifully, in abundance < ~ *bluha* I have a great deal > — *va* iyákic'u·wa·ya : to have more than one needs

- Cf akic'uya

i·ya·ki·gle \i-yá-k̇i-gle\ *adv* : times < *zaptan ~* five times > — *vn* : to surpass, overlap, reach beyond the time, as old corn lasting until the new comes — *adv* : like to, as < *Wetu ~ mašte* It is as warm as spring. > - Cf akígle B.H.37.7 Pb.36

i·ya·ki·gle·ga \í-ya-k̇i-gle-ġa\ *v* : to go on and overtake - R Bl

i·ya·ki·gle·gle *adv red* : over and over again, repeatedly

i·ya·ki·gleh \í-ya-ki-gleȟ\ *v contrac of* íyakiglega : to overtake

i·ya·ki·gle·ya \i-yá-k̇i-gle-ya\ *va* iyakigle·wa·ya : to cause to reach round to, to make surpass — *adv* : surpassing < *nunpa ~* twice, *šakowin ~* times seven > - B.H.112.8, 217.2

i·ya·ki·gna \i-yá-k̇i-gna\ *adv* : in layers, one on another

i·ya·ki·hpa·ya \i-yá-k̇i-ȟpa-ya\ *v poss of* iyahpaya : to grab, seize one's own, as one's gun - D.248, 266

i·ya·ki·ju \i-yá-k̇i-ju\ *adv perhaps* [fr *ju* to set or place] : together united, put, placed, laid up together, as seed or plants in a garden < *hocokab tipi ~ iyahpeya* to throw a cover over the tipi put together in the camp circle, *i.e.* to join two to four tents into one big one for meeting purposes. *Na el akicita wóhanpi na oceti šakowin el iwoglakapi. Hinhanna kin hocokab tipi ~ iyahpeyapi kta ške lo* And there was held a warriors' feast and there the seven camp fires held conferences. In the morning they say a tent would be opened out and put together in center camp. > — **i-yakiju·ya** *adv* : together < *~ okala. ~ omaka 102 ni un na t'e* He planted together. He lived for 102 years and died. > - B.H.128.11

i·ya·ki·le·ce·ca \í-ya-k̇i-le-ce-ca\ *adv* : like, alike — **iyakilecel** \í-ya-k̇i-le-cel\ *adv* : alike - Note: *iyákilecel* is a doubtful form B B.H.191.20-21, 235.10

i·ya·ki·le·han·ke·ca \í-ya-k̇i-le-haŋ-ke-ca\ *adv* : of the same length with — **iyakilehan·yan** *adv* : of equal distance — **iyakile·nakeca** *adv* : of equal number — **iyakilena·la** *adv* : as few as

i·ya·ki·li \i-yá-ki-li\ *va* : to climb up on one's own, perhaps - B.H.8.5

i·ya·ki·ni·sko·ke·ca \í-ya-k̇i-ni-sk̇o-k̇e-ca\ *adv* : of the same size

i·ya·ki·pa·pa \í-ya-ki-pa-pa\ *v* : to strike on the mouth - Cf íakipapa

i·ya·ki·pe \i-yá-k̇i-ṗe\ *va* iya·wa·kipe : to wait for, hope for; to befall, happen to < *~ mankelo,* or *ape mankelo. i-háwakta na ena mankelo. Iyamakipe yo* I waited for him, I watched and right there was I. Wait for me. > — **iyakipe·ya** *adv* : waiting for - Bl D.202, 219

i·ya·ki·š'a \í-ya-k̇i-š'a\ *v* : to shout at one's own — **iyakiš'a·š'a** *v red* : to keep shouting at one's own - Cf íyaš'a

¹i·ya·ki·ta \i-yá-k̇i-ṫa\ *va* : to urge on *e.g.* slow horses, to chase away *e.g.* dogs < *Iyawicakita yo* Urge them on, *i.e.* the horses, to hurry them up if you want to get home. > - RTj

²i·ya·ki·ta \í-ya-k̇i-ṫa\ *va* iya·wa·kita [fr *akita* look for] : to have an eye to, keep watch on, lest one commit some depredation, to hunt for charges against one

i·ya·ki·tan'·in \i-yá-k̇i-taŋ-iŋ\ *v* : to arrive when it is yet light and things are visible and clear < *~ lake unki kinhan wašte yelo* If you and I go for home to arrive at dusk, would it be good? *i.e.* better to go in daylight. *Anpetu ~ šni yelo* It is not a day to arrive at dusk, *i.e.* it is foggy. > - Bl KE

i·ya·ko \í-ya-ko\ *adv* [fr *akó* beyond] : beyond anything — **iyako·tanhan** \í-ya-ko-taŋ-haŋ\ *adv* : beyond, from beyond

i·ya·ksa·pa \i-yá-ksa-ṗa\ *va* : to make wise by talking

i·ya·kta·šni \i-yá-k̇ta-šni\ *va* iya·wa·ktašni íya·un·kici-kta·pi šni [fr *aktašni* despise] : to disregard - Note: the word *iyákta* is not used - Bl

i·ya·k'in·ton \i-yá-k'iŋ-toŋ\ *v* : to sew, glue, lay something on, as a piece of leather - Bl

i·ya·k'o·za \i-yá-k'o-za\ *n* : a horse that has big knuckles, *i.e.* are swollen and *iyanunga* they become hard < *Kul Wicaša ~ wan yuhapi* The Lower Brule have a horse with swollen knuckles. > - *Syn* WOHÉ Bl

i·ya·li \i-yá-li\ *va* iya·wa·li [fr *ali* to climb up] : to climb up on

i·ya·mni \i-yá-mni\ *num ord adj* : the third — **iyamnila** *num ord adj* : only the third one

¹i·ya·mni·mni \i-yá-mni-mni\ *num ord adj red* : every third one

²i·ya·mni·mni *or* **iamnimni** \i-yá-mni-mni\ *v* iya·wa·mnimni [fr *amnimni* to sprinkle on] : to sprinkle, as water on anything

i·ya·na·ji·ca \i-yá-na-ji-ca\ *v* iyána·wa·jica : to run with what one has taken, as a run-away horse with a wagon, or a man with a horse < *Tašunke kin zaptan iyanawajice lo* I ran off with his five horses. > - BT

i·ya·na·pta \i-yá-na-ṗta\ *va* iyana·wa·pta [fr *anapta* to stop or hinder] : to detain, to go before and prevent from proceeding < *~ kuté* to obstruct, step in the way, and shoot > - Bl

i·ya·ni·ca \i-yá-ni-ca\ *vn* iya·ma·nica iya·un·nica·pi : to be prevented, detained or hindered by; to remain fast, be unable to go on < *Magaju kin he iyamanica* I was prevented by the rain to go on. > - D.22

i·ya·nun·ga \i-yá-nuŋ-ġa\ *vn* iya·ma·nunga : to become hard, callous or unfeeling, as a scarred place - Note: this is said of the knuckles of a horse when they are swollen *Syn* IYAK'OZA

i·ya·nunh \i-yá-nunȟ\ *vn contrac of* iyanunga : to get hard < *~ iyeya* quickly to become callous > — **iyanunȟya** *va* iyanun·ȟwa·ya : to cause to become callous

i·ya·o·pe·mni \i-yá-o-ṗe-mni\ *va* iyao·wa·pemni : to cover, enclose, shroud - P Bl

¹i·ya·pa \i-yá-pa\ *va* iya·wa·pa iya·ma·pa iya·un·pa·pi iyaic'ipa : to beat or strike against, to beat, as the heart; to strike or knock against, as the the foot < *Lila cante ~ wanyank yankahan. Lila cante iyamapa. Tokša iyacicipe kte* He was seeing his heart beating fast. My heart really beat. Soon I shall thrash you. >

²i·ya·pa \í-ya-pa\ *n* : a snow storm < *~ wan hi yelo* A storm came. > - GA B.H.69.12

i·ya·pa·ha·ye·la \í-ya-ṗa-ha-ye-la\ *adv* : brimful, much of anything, as is said of dry things as grain that heaps on top - *Syn* ÍYAPAŠNIŠYELA Cf íyujibyela Bl

i·ya·pa·kel \i-yá-pa-kel\ *adv* : unexpectedly, all of a sudden < *~` wanblake lo* I saw it all of a sudden. > - Bl

i·ya·pa·pa \i-yá-pa-pa\ *v red of* iyapa : to beat < *Icapšinpšincala ic'icage na mni ~ kinyan ya* A swallow raised itself and went flying beating the water. > - MS.573

i·ya·pa·šni·šye·la \í-ya-ṗa-šni-šye-la\ *adj* : brimful - *Syn* ÍYAPAHAYELA P Bl

---

\a\ father \e\ they \i\ machine \o\ smoke \u\ lunar \an, aŋ\ blanc Fr. \in, iŋ\ ink \on, oŋ, un, uŋ\ soon, confier Fr. \c\ chair \ġ\ machen Ger. \j\ fusion \clusters: bl, gn, kp, hšl, etc...\ b^e^lo ... said with a slight vowel
See more in the Introduction, Guide to Pronunciation

i·ya·pa·štag \í-ya-p̣a-štag\ *vn contrac of* iyapaštaka : to surprised — **iyapašta·gya** *va* iyapašta·gwa·ya : to creep up and fall upon before one is away, to take by surprise - R Bl

i·ya·pa·šta·ka \í-ya-p̣a-šta-ka\ *vn* íya·ma·p̣aštaka : to be taken by surprise - R Bl

i·ya·pa·tan \í-ya-p̣taŋ\ *adv* : pushing or shoving onto, right up against one < ~ *glus kat'iyewayelo* I shot holding it from close up, nearby. > - Bl

i·ya·pa·t'o *or* **iyapat'o·la** \í-ya-p̣a-t'o\ *vn* íya·ma·pat'o : to butt against, be struck by; to press on, be cramped by *e.g.* a short moccasin < *Hanpa iyamapat'ola. Si iyamapat'o ca si mapani ye* My shoes are a bit tight on me. Please jog me with the foot, the foot that is cramped, as is said when the shoes are too short. > - Bl

i·ya·pa·t'o·ya \í-ya-p̣a-t'o-ya\ *va* iyapat'o·wa·ya : to run against, to hinder, prevent — **iyapat'oya·kel** *or* **iyapat'oye·la** \í-ya-p̣a-t'o-ya-ḳel\ *adv* : in the manner of pressing against, pressed together, cramped together, close together, as in sitting close together or as books stand close together on a shelf < ~ *unyankapi* We sat cramped together. >

i·ya·pa·ya \i-yá-pa-ya\ *va* iyapa·wa·ya : to run against, be thrown against, as in an automobile - Bl

iyapaya·kel \i-yá-pa-ya-ḳel\ *adv* : encountering, as stormy weather < ~ *wan'unkiciyankapi ca takuni tanyan unkoglakapi šni yelo* When we ran onto seeing one another, we did not talk affairs and accomplish anything. > - Bl

[1]**i·ya·pe** \í-ya-p̣e\ *adv* : near, close < *míyape* near me, *níyape* near you, *Tanká miyape yanka* My younger sister was close to me. >

[2]**i·ya·pe** \í-ya-p̣e\ *va* íya·wa·pe [fr *ape* wait for] : to wait for, lie in wait for, lie in ambush < *Tokša iyácicipe kte* Sometime I'll wait for you. >

i·ya·pe·han \i-yá-p̣e-haŋ\ *va* iya·wa·pehan [fr *pehan* fold up] : to fold up with, to wind on, as the thread on a spool, to wrap around < *hahunta iyapehanpi* spoolthread, *cannunpa pahin iyapehanpi* a pipe stem wrapped around with porupine quill-work, *Tašupa can iyawapehan na cewaonpin kte lo* I wrapped the intestines around a board and will roast them. > — **iyapehan·yan** *adv* : folding up - Bl

i·ya·pe·kel \i-yá-p̣e-ḳel\ *adv* : waiting for an opportunity, keeping a careful watch < ~ *kuwa* to watch so to catch, wait for a chance to catch > - B.H.230.11 KE

i·ya·pe·la \í-ya-p̣e-la\ *adv* : near, close at hand

i·ya·pe·mni \i-yá-p̣e-mni\ *va* iya·wa·pemni [fr *aopemni* wrap up in] : to wrap around, wind up in — **iyapemni·yan** *adv* : wrapped up in

i·ya·pe·ya \i-yá-p̣e-ya\ *va* iyape·wa·ya [fr *iyape* wait for] : to cause to lie in wait for — *adv* : lying in wait for

i·ya·pu·spa \i-yá-p̣u-sp̣a\ *va* iya·wa·puspa : to glue, stick on with glue or paste — *vn* iya·ma·puspa : to stick to, as wet clothes; to be glued, as sore eyes

i·ya·pu·spe·ya \i-yá-p̣u-sp̣e-ya\ *va* iyapuspe·wa·ya : to cause to glue on — *adv* : in a glued or sticking manner

i·ya·p'o·p'o·ya \i-yá-p'o-p'o-ya\ *adv* : misty < ~ *hiyaya ca osni yelo. Mahpiya gigiya kahwog hiyaye lo* It was cold when it turned misty. A dark cloud floated on by. > - Bl

i·ya·p'o·sp'os \i-yá-p'o-sp'os\ *n* : turbulent cloud formations < ~ *ahiyaye lo* Chaotic cloud formations went about, as is said when the sky is very cloudy and then clears. > - Bl KE

i·ya·p'o·ye·la \í-ya-p'o-ye-la\ *adv* : with a thick mist - B..H.56.16

i·ya·sag \i-yá-sag\ *vn contrac of* iyasaka : to be dried

i·ya·sa·ka \i-yá-sa-ḳa\ *vn* iya·ma·saka : to be dried hard on, as skin or garments on one

i·ya·skab \i-yá-sḳab\ *v* [fr *iyaskapa* stick to] : to adhere to — **iyaska·bya** *va perhaps* : to make stick to, as a postage stamp — *adv* : sticking to — **iyaskabye** *n* : glue - WE

i·ya·ska·pa \i-yá-sḳa-p̣a\ *vn* iya·ma·skapa : to stick to or on, adhere to < *Inyan kin ena* ~ It stuck right here to the rock. > - B.H.135.4 D.73

i·ya·ski \i-yá-sḳi\ *va contrac of* iyaskica : to press on

i·ya·ski·ca \i-yá-sḳi-ca\ *va* i·bla·skica : to press or suck one thing on another, as corn on the cob — **iyaski·lya** *adv* : pressing, sucking on

i·ya·ski·ska \i-yá-sḳi-sḳa\ *vn* iya·ma·skiska : to be smoothed down, as the hair on an animal by swimming in the water

i·ya·sni \i-yá-sni\ *vn* iya·ma·sni [fr *asni* recover] : to become still, as a noise deasing, to recover from, as from anger or sickness, to die down, as a fire with only coals left - D.197

i·ya·sni·ya \i-yá-sni-ya\ *va* iyasni·wa·ya : to give to one unexpectedly, to make quiet, pacify

i·ya·su \i-yá-su\ *va* i·bla·su [fr *yasu* to decree] : to judge of, judge on account of, to condemn for

i·ya·s'e \í-ya-s'e\ *n* [fr *iya* a fabulous character noted for eating everything] : a glutton

i·ya·ška \i-yá-ška\ *or* \í-ya-ška\ *adj* : loose-tongued < *Yunkan hokšila kin he* ~ *hokšila ic'icaga ke* And then what do you know: a boy grows up on his own, and that boy is loose-tongued, *i.e.* cares not what and how he talks. >

i·ya·šla·lya\í-ya-šla-lya\ *va* íyašla·lwa·ya : to prove one to be a liar, to catch one in a suspected action - D.279

i·ya·šla·ta \í-ya-šla-ta\ *vn* iya·ma·šlata : to be found guilty of a lie < *El ayakage cinhan tokata Tunkašila ekta wai kin iyanišlatin kta ca tanyan econ wo* If at the start you have exaggerated matters, do well so that you are not found guilty of a lie when I go to the President, as was said to a government representative. >

i·ya·šla·ya \í-ya-šla-ya\ *adv* : plainly, clearly

i·ya·šo·ta \i-yá-šo-ṭa\ *v* : to make smoke, steam, as with one's breath < ~ *s'e omawani* I walked long as though I were making steam, *i.e.* making my breath a fog in the cold weather. > - Bl KE

i·ya·š'a \í-ya-š'a\ *v* iya·wa·š'a [fr *aš'a* to shout] : to shout at or against — **iyaš'a·yapi** *n* : a war-whoop - P Bl

i·ya·š'a-pi \í-ya-š'à-pi\ *n* : an acclamation - Bl

[1]**i·ya·ta** \i-yá-ta\ *va* i·bla·ta : to say what one intends < *Iyatahe c'on wan k'u welo* He gave one what he said he had intended, *i.e.* to a person absent - Cf R Bl

[2]**i·ya·ta** \i-yá-ta\ *v* : to chew something with something else < *Tap̣í ca wašinlo iyatapi s'e* It was as though they were chewing liver and the juiciest fat, as is said when through disputing much confusion is created. > - Bl

i·ya·tab \i-yá-tab\ *adv* : after, soon, soon again < *Miyatab u wo* Follow me. ~ *ya* He goes soon. > — **iyata·byela** \í-ya-ta-bye-la\ *adv* : soon after - B.H. 177.14, 205.1, 234.3 D.73

[1]**i·ya·ta·gle** \í-ya-ta-gle\ *adj* iya·ma·tagle : going beyond, surpassing, going beyond ordinary bounds, being excessive — *adv* : full, running over < *Le anpetu kin iyamatagle ca heon oškinc'iye mašice lo, ca ito le hanhepi kin ake ewicunkiyapi kte lo. Ungna taku iyanitable kin ikan lupsake cin otehi wan slolyayin kta* Today was too much for me, since mine was a worthless job; and come now,

this night we shall again speak to them. Perhaps what is in excess for you you will know of the difficulty when you break the cord. >

[2]**i·ya·ta·gle** \í-ya-ṫa-gle\ *v* or *adj* iya·ma·tagle iya·ni·tagle : to be speechless from surprise

i·ya·ta·gle·i·c'i·ya \í-ya-ta-gle-i-c'i-ya\ *vn* : to surfeit, to be immoderate < ~ *šni* to be moderate, temperate > – P

i·ya·ta·gle·ya \í-ya-ta-gle-ya\ *va* iyatagle·wa·ya : to go beyond, surpass, to do more than is right or exact, to do too much, to cause to go beyond, to be intemperate — *adv* : too much

[1]**i·ya·tan** \i-yá-ṫaŋ\ *va* i·bla·tan : to light *e.g.* a pipe < *Na cannunpa unhe wanna iyatanpi na unpwicakiyapi. Ilatan hwo? Hau, iwaglatan. Na gliglekiya iyatanpi* And that pipe was now lighted and they had them smoke it. Did you light it? Yes, I lit my own. And it was lighted one at a time. >

[2]**i·ya·tan** \i-yá-taŋ\ *va* i·bla·tan : to touch with the mouth

i·ya·tan'·in·lake \i-yá-ṫaŋ-iŋ-la-k̇e\ *n* : the while it is yet daylight < ~ *c'el ecamon ktelo* I shall do it in the daylight > – Bl

i·ya·ta·sag \i-yá-ṫa-sag\ *vn of* iyatasaka : to become stiff — **iyatasa·gya** *adv* : stiffly

i·ya·ta·sa·ka \i-yá-ṫa-sa-k̇a\ *vn* iya·ma·tasaka [fr *tasaka hardened*] : to become hard or stiff on one, as skin that has been wet and dried stiff or frozen on

i·ya·ta·ye·la *or* íatayela \í-ya-ṫa-ye-la\ *adv pron* : personally, indivi-dually, it alone < ~ *šunkawakan kipi* It alone cost one horse. >

i·ya·un·pa \i-yá-uŋ-ṗa\ *va* iya·wa·unpa [fr *aonpa* place on] 1 : to lay or place on 2 : to accuse of, blame with < *Lena taku iyaniunpapi kin takuni alupta šni he?* Did you respond with nothing when these accused you of something? > — **iyaunpa·pi** \i-yá-uŋ-ṗa-ṗi\ *n* : an accusation — **iyaunpe·picašni** \i-yá-uŋ-ṗe-ṗi-ca-šni\ *adj* : blameless < *Le weyapi kin iyaunpemapicašni yelo* He could not accuse me of this shedding of blood. > — **iyaunpepicašni·yan** *adv* : blamelessly — **iyaunpe·ya** *adv* : in a blaming or accusing way

i·ya·wa \i-yá-wa\ *va* i·bla·wa [fr *yawa* to count] : to count by or according to, count together, to figure with, to settle – B.H.33.2, 217.4

i·ya·wan·yan·gki·ci·ya *or* **iawanyangkiciya** \i-yá-waŋ-yaŋ-gki-ci-ya\ *v* : to accompany and watch over along the way < *Wakantanka taogligle wašte wan iawanyangkiciyin kte he wicawala yelo* I believe that God's good angel accompanies and guards a person. > – B.H.122.19

i·ya·ya \i-yá-ya\ *vn* : to have gone; to exceed, be more than enough, to go over, to be a surplus < *Wicokan sam* ~ It us afternoon. *Na tona* (*i.e.* sugar and coffee) *iyaye k'on hena kala iyeya, tka ayuta naunjinpi kin hecena takuni šni* Some sugar and coffee that was more than enough suddenly scattered, but in the end when we stood up to look there was nothing. *Unkiyayapi* We then left. >

i·ya·ya·han *part of* iyaya *of* iya *or* ia : talking, chatting – Pb.24

i·ya·ye·ki·ya \i-yá-ye-k̇i-ya\ *v* iyáye·wa·kiya : to pretend to go away, to act as though one was going away – Bl

i·ya·ye·ya \i-yá-ye-ya\ *va* iyaye·wa·ya : to cause to go or have gone; to send; to turn away, to rout < *Na šunkawakan kin unyan iyayewicunyapi kte. Wiyatke kin le miyopteya iyayeyi ye* And we'll send the horses out of sight. This cup may it pass me by. > – Pb.41

i·ya·yuh \i-yá-yuȟ\ *v contrac* [fr *iyayuȟa* to be a follower] : to go closely behind another < ~ *un* It goes close behind. ~ *iyaya* He went on behind it. ~ *ocimani yacin* You wish that I walk behind you. *Mitaoyate kin nahahci waziyata pte* ~ *unpi ca tohanl agli kinhan iwanweglakin kta* Since my people, yet in the north, are going closely behind the buffalo, I shall then keep an eye out for them whensoever they arrive home. > – OH

i·ya·yu·ȟe \i-yá-yu-ȟe\ *v* iya·blu·ȟe iya·ci·yuȟe : to have an attachment for, be a follower of, the Latin *cara* to be dear or familiar with < *Iyaciyuȟa yacin* You wish that I be your close friend. *Iyamaluȟepi šni* You have no attachment to me. > – B.H.101.15, 107.10

i·ya·yu·hki·ya *or* iyayuhya \i-yá-yu-ȟk̇i-ya\ *adv* : following < *Wicahpi kin he* ~ *yapi* They went following the star. > – B.H. 169.18, 112.3 KE

i·ya·yu·kšan \i-yá-yu-kšaŋ\ *prep* : around < *otonwahe* ~ around town > – B.H.72.12

i·ya·yus \i-yá-yus\ *v contrac of* iyayuza : to hold to < ~ *yuza* to hold anything close to another >

i·ya·yu·sco·la \i-yá-yu-sco-la\ *adj* : unarmed – BD

i·ya·yu·stak *or* iyayustag \i-yá-yu-ṡtak\ *v of* iyayustaka : to hold together, with, together with < *Wowapi nunpa* ~ *yuha* He holds two books together (in his hand). >

i·ya·yu·sta·ka \i-yá-yu-ṡta-k̇a\ *v* : to hold one thing securely to another < *iyayustag heyun* to tie up one thing on another, *Iyayustag hemun* I bound it to another. > – KE

i·ya·yu·wi \i-yá-yu-wi\ *v* iya·ma·yuwi iya·ni·yuwi : to grow warped, become curled or twisted < *Leceya nape kin can iyamayuwi kte lo* My hands really became warped wood, *i.e.* became stiff. *Nape can iyaniyuwi hca hwo?* Did your hands really become twisted wood? > – Bl

i·ya·yu·za \i-yá-yu-za\ *va* iya·blu·za [fr *yuza* to grasp] : to hold to or at — *n* : a holder, as a cloth with which to hold a hot iron

i·ya·za \i-yá-za\ *adv* : one after another, as when going from one home to another < *Tipi* ~ *omani. Tiíyaza. Wópate kin* ~ *wol omani hi. Hecel Wicahpi Hinhpaya oyate* ~ *omani na taku econpica šni econ keyapi* He traveled from house to house. From house to house. He came on foot to eat the meat scraps one after the next. So they say Falling Star travels from tribe to tribe, and what he is incapable to do he does. > – Note: *oyáza* to string *e.g.* beads.

i·ya·zan \i-yá-zaŋ\ *vn* i·ma·yazan [fr *yazan* feel pain] : to be sick on account of or by means of, to be affected by sympathy with or for

i·ya·zi \i-yá-zi\ *v* : to be convalescent < *Tohan watuka iyanizi keci hehanl* ... When exhausted you are resting pretty much nonetheless, then ..., *i.e.* When you have recovered ... , > – Bl

i·ya·zil \i-yá-zil\ *vn contrac of* iyazita : to make smoke — **iyazi·lya** *va* iyazi·lwa·ya : to burn *e.g.*sweet leaves, to burn incense

i·ya·zi·ta \i-yá-zi-ta\ *vn* : to burn *e.g.* cedar leaves, to smoke and make a pleasant odor.

i·ye \í-ye\ *pron* : he, she, it, *iyepi* they

i·ye·ca·na \í-ye-ca-na\ *adv* : soon after, near to, soon < ~ *yahi* You came soon after. ~ *wau kta* I shall come soon. >

\a\ father \e\ they \i\ machine \o\ smoke \u\ lunar \an, aŋ\ blanc Fr. \in, iŋ\ ink \on, oŋ, un, uŋ\ soon, confier Fr. \c\ chair \ġ\ machen Ger. \j\ fusion \clusters: bl, gn, kp, hšl, etc...\ b[e]lo ... said with a slight vowel
See more in the Introduction, Guide to Pronunciation

i·ye·ce·ca \i-yé-ce-ca\ *vn* iye·ma·ceca : to be like to; to be fitting, proper < *Hécamon kta ~* It is right that I should do that. > — *adv* : like, like as, like that, such as, the same as

i·ye·ce·ca·šni·yan \i-yé-ce-ca-šni-yaŋ\ *adv* : unlike, such as not < *Itazipa ... na yuwegapi ~ suta ca econpi* A bow that is strong and one broken unlike it did it. >

i·ye·ce·hci \i-yé-ce-ȟci\ *adv* : just like < *Hokṡiyokpaza ~ waun welo* I am just like one unable to make my voice clear (hence I cannot grasp anything I say). *He (zitkala) ~ hehanl šinasapa wicablumihan yelo* Just like that (bird), I was then making the rounds with catholic priests. > – BT

i·ye·ce·kce·ca \i-yé-ce-kce-ca\ *adv red of* iyececa : like, such as < *Hunhunhé, le unci si ~ yelo* Oh how hers are like grandmother's feet. > — **iyecekce·lya** *adv red of* iyecelya : a bit like, less, much – D.55 B.H.63.11

i·ye·cel \i-yé-cel\ *prep* or *adv* : like, in like manner < ~ *econ* to conform to, to be consistent, to imitate, *Le t'inkte ~ oh'an yelo* As he conducted himself so he shall die. > – B.H.1.20, 258.12

i·ye·ce·lya \i-yé-ce-lya\ *adv* : like; a little less, not much < ~ *šica ayapi* They began to be a little less bad. > – B.H. 9.3

i·ye·ce·tu \i-yé-ce-ṫu\ *vn* : to be so, become so, to be as expected; to come to pass or take place — *adv* : so, thus, right — **iyecetu·ya** *adv* : so — **iyecetuya·kel** \i-yé-ce-ṫu-ya-ǩel\ *adv* : in this manner

i·ye·cin·ka \i-yé-ciŋ-ǩa\ *adv* mi·yecinka : of one's self, of one's own accord, without advice < ~ *iglúha* to be a citizen > — **iyecinka·la** *adv* mi·yecinkala unki·yecinkalapi : of one's own accord < ~ *hena iyagnipi kta* You of your own accord should go out to hunt. >

i·ye·cin·kin·yan·ka \i-yé-ciŋ-ǩiŋ-yaŋ-ka\ *n* : an automobile

i·ye·eš \í-ye-eš\ *pron emph* : he, she, it

i·ye·ha \i-yé-ha\ *adv* eha : instead, rather he or she < *Yunkan hankaku kin ~ nagiyeya ške'* And then they say instead his sister-in-law bothered him. > – Note: the word indicates something like: It is you who does it, as is said when one is accused of doing what the speaker is doing – LP

i·ye·han \i-yé-haŋ\ *adv* : at the appointed time < *Wanna iyemicihan* Now my time is on, *i.e.* for my being on duty. >

i·ye·han·han·ke·ca \i-yé-haŋ-haŋ-ke-ca\ *adv red of* iyehankeca : being of the same length — **iyehanhan·tu** \i-yé-haŋ-haŋ-ṫu\ *adv red of* iyehantu : at the times referred to, at referred to places perhaps — **iyehanhan·yan** *adv red of* iyehanyan : being even — **iyehan·keca** *or* **iyehanyan** *adv* : being of the same length, as two things compared

i·ye·hanl \i-yé-haŋl\ *adv* : at the time, just then – Note: the word refers to past as well as future time *Syn* WAHEHANL B.H.22.2, 53.3, 61.17

i·ye·han·tu \i-yé-haŋ-ṫu\ *adv* : at the time, now, it being the time now < *Na wanna anpetu wan el kipi kte ci ~ wicokanyan to eyaš asnikiyapi. ~ Kinhan ake wau kta. Na wotapi kte k'un he wana ~ . Na wanna ~ k'on hehan ukiya* And now on the day they shall arrive home, it will be noon, but first they take a good rest. At the time I shall come again. And now at the time it will be time for dinner. And when it is time they will then reach home *i.e.* at the appointed time, when it was time. > — **iyehantu·la** \i-yé-haŋ-ṫu-la\ *adv* : just at the time — **iyehantula·hci** *adv* : exactly at the time — **iyehantu·šni** \i-yé-haŋ-tu-šni\ *adv* : not time yet

i·ye·han·wa·pa \i-yé-haŋ-wa-pa\ *adv* : towards the time – R Bl B.H.148.14

i·ye·han·yan *or* **iyehankeca** \i-yé-haŋ-yaŋ\ *adv* or perhaps *adj* : being even, of the same size, length, and height *etc* < ~ *šni* not being even, *i.e.* it does not come up to the mark, one being smaller than the other. ~ *cin* He wants the same, as is said when one is in buying a hat and wants the same size he had before. *Tuweni ~ un šni* No one wears the same size. *Tuweni ~ šni han.skin* No one is of the same height. *Tuweni iyenihanyan kte šni* No one will be of the same size as you. *Takuni niyehanyan tanka šni* Nothing is of a size big as yours. > – Note: the word is used in comparing or measuring two things and seems always to call for an *adj* , at least in the mind

i·ye·i·c'i·ya \i-yé-i-c'i-ya\ *v refl of* iyeya : to find one's self, to put or thrust one's self < *ogna ~* to push, crowd one's self in >

i·ye·ja·ka·keš \i-yé-ja-ǩa-ǩeš\ *adv* : unable, failing by a little, as in what one is accustomed

i·ye·ka·eš *or* **iyékaleš** \i-yé-ǩa-eš\ *pron* : even he or she

i·ye·ka·pin \i-yé-ǩa-ṗiŋ\ *vn* : to be tired of speaking – Cf iékapin

i·ye·ki·ci·han·tu \i-yé-ǩi-ci-haŋ-ṫu\ *vn* iyé·mi·cihantu i·ye·unki·cihantu : to be suitable for one, be fitting or belonging to one; to be the time or opportunity for one – B.H.172.3

i·ye·ki·ya \i-yé-ǩi-ya\ *va poss of* iyeya : to find one's own, to recognize; to put or push one's own in < *Ate, iyemayakiyin kta. Wímakan nitawa ojuha el ~ yo* Father, you should recognize me. Put my straps in your bag. >

i·ye·kta·šni \i-yé-kṫa-šni\ *adv* : incorrectly, not according to rule

i·ye·na \i-yé-na\ *pron* : as many, as many as, so many < *Tipi tonakeca kin yawapi na lena* (coffee and sugar) *~ wicak'upi kte lo. Na ake iciyamni ai na ake ~ wicaopi na agli. Oyate peji ~ . Na ~ ca mini yatkanpi šni nainš wotapi šni ... wanna enakiyapi* They counted how many houses there were, and as many as there were of these, coffee and sugar, were given them. And they brought a thirteenth and again as many were wounded and went home. A nation as many as the blades of grass. And so many there were who had not drunk water or eaten ... were now finished. > – B.H.111.5

i·ye·na·ka \i-yé-na-ǩa\ *adv* : so many as — **iyena·keca** *adj* or *pron* iye·ma·nakeca iye·un·nakeca·pi : as many, as much < *Ake econpi na ake ~* (buffalos) *naceca wicaopi* A second time they did (went on the hunt), and again as many buffalos were probably shot. > — **iyenan·gnakeca** *adv red of* iyenakeca : as many, much

i·ye·na·yan \i-yé-na-yaŋ\ *vn* iyena·wa·ya : to give up, to be tired of < ~ *unpi* They are giving up. > – P BD Bl B.H.118.12

i·ye·pi·šni \i-yé-pi-šni\ *v* [fr *iyepi* they + *šni* not] : They did not seem to be the same people anymore < ~ *s'e kunšitku kici kas'ala yankapi keye* He said they were putting on airs with his grandmother as though they were no longer the same people. >

i·ye·ska *or* **ieska** \i-yé-ska\ *v* : to speak a language

i·yeš *or* **iyeeš** \i-yéš\ \í-ye-eš\ *pron emph* : he, she, it < *Itancan kin itokab wawahtani kte šni ca ~ wašte ye* He the Lord is good so I might not sin before him. > – B.H. 138.1 and 2

i·ye·ška·la·ka \í-ye-ška-la-ka\ *pron* : he himself, even he – Cf D.71 R *Syn* IYEK'E (Yankton), IYEŠTUKALAKA

i·ye·šni·ca \i-yé-šni-ca\ *interj* : You don't say so!, It cannot be!

i·ye·štu·ka \i-yé-štu-ka\ *pron* : he who ought < ~ *laka* he who did what another ought to have done, *Unkíyeštuka he wanbli yeš kte yešan* We though who ought to have, but he killed the eagle, *i.e.* it was fooled in spite of his smartness. ~ *oyuspe* He caught it, *i.e.* while everyone else had missed it. *Yunkan ~ wakan; canke ...* And then he must have been gifted with special powers; hence ... *i.e.* he had supernatural powers. > - Bl D.158 and 119 B.H.88.3 KE

i·ye·ya \i-yé-ya\ *v aux emph* iye·wa·ya iye·un·yan·pi : indicates quickness or suddenness of action - Note: the word is appended to *v* commencing with *ka na pa wa wo ya yu* , and to some *adv* and generally lends an express action done quickly — *va* iye·wa·ya : to find; to put, place, thrust into, shove at < *Na wa kin iwankal* (on the house) *iyeya* And the snow suddenly piled up (on the house). *Taku wan iyewayelo ca iwacu welo* Something I found I took. > — **iyeya·ya** \i-yé-ya-ya\ *va red emph of* iyeya : to keep putting in; to be finding - P

i·yo \i-yó\ *prep in comp* : to, in, into - Note: the *euph* "y" place between *i* and *o*

i·yo·bla·ye \i-yó-bla-ye\ *n* [fr *oblaye* a level place] : a plain extending from, as from a hill

i·yo·blu·la *or* **ioblula** \i-yó-blu-la\ *adv* : sheltered — *n* : a sheltered place

i·yo·co·ka·ya \i-yó-co-ka-ya\ *adv* [fr *i* in + *ocokanya* in the midst] : in the midst of; all put into the mouth, all swallowed up in

i·yo·co·sya·kel \i-yó-co-sya-kel\ *adv* : with added cover on, as on the feet < ~ *owahelo* I wore it for added cover. > - *Syn* IYOWINHAHAYAKEL Bl

i·yo·co·za \i-yó-co-za\ *vn* : to be warm in, as in a coat < *He imacoza* I am warm in that. >

i·yo·gla·gla \i-yó-gla-gla\ *adv* : rattling < ~ *s'e iyaya* He went by as if rattling. > - Note: the word indicates a noise as of a bullet put into the muzzle of a gun and going down with a certain rattling sound

i·yo·gla·mna \i-yó-gla-mna\ *adv* : circuitously, round all the crooks and turns — **iyoglamna·yan** *or* **iyoglamniyan** *adv* : circuitously, particularly *i.e.* in utter detail < ~ *woglaka* to speak going round and round the topic >

i·yo·gli \i-yó-gli\ *n* : a razor strap, a steel hone perhaps — **iyogli·ya** *va* iyogli·wa·ya : to rub back and forth, as in whetting or strapping a razor

i·yo·glu·št'e·ya \i-yó-št'e-ya\ *v* iyoglušt'e·wa·ya : to pile up words of criticism to the point of discouraging one < *Iyoglušt'emayayelo* You nag me, as a man who wants to live in peace would say to another who is always after him, meaning: You make me sick with your talking. > - Bl KE

i·yo·glu·ze \i-yó-glu-ze\ *n* : wearing apparel - Bl

i·yo·gmus *or* **iogmus** \í-yo-gmus\ *vn contrac* : to be with shut mouth - Cf íogmusya, íogmuza

i·yo·gnag *or* **iognag** \i-yó-gnag\ *va contrac of* iyognaka : to place in the mouth < ~ *iyeya* to suddenly put something in the mouth > - Cf iognagkiya, iognagya

i·yo·gna·ka *or* **iognaka** \i-yó-gna-ka\ *va* iyo·wa·gnaka : to put into the mouth *e.g.* food

i·yo·ha·kab \í-yo-ha-kab\ *adv* : after in time, subsequent to — **iyohaka·bton** \í-yo-ha-ka-btoŋ\ *v* : to close or seal, as a full box or letter after it is finished - Bl

i·yo·ha·ka·btu \í-yo-ha-ka-btu\ *adv* : afterwards — **iyohakabtu·ya** *adv* : afterwards — **iyohakabtuya·kel** \í-yo-ha-ka-btu-ya-kel\ *adv* : a little after

i·yo·han \i-yó-haŋ\ *va* iyo·wa·he [fr *ohán* to boil] : to boil one thing with another

i·yo·han·zi \i-yó-haŋ-zi\ *n* [fr *ohanzi* shade] : a shady place, a bower < *Wazi ~ wan el ungliyotakapi* We got home and sat in a pine bower. >

i·yo·he \í-yo-he\ *n* : something wrapped around the feet, socks or stockings

[1]**i·yo·hi** \i-yó-hi\ *adj* : each, every one

[2]**i·yo·hi** \i-yó-hi\ *va* iyo·wa·hi iyo·ma·hi iyo·un·hi·pi : to reach, get to, to arrive at a place; to be sufficient for, to reach to one, as in a division of articles; to be large enough for, as a garment < *Hecel tipi opawinge sam iyaye yawapi, na hena waksica ogna pamnipi na ecel ataya iyowicahi.* So they counted more than a hundred tents, and to these dishes were distributed, and thus there was enough for all. *Hecel tipi iyohila kpamnipi* (*i.e.* coffee and sugar), *tka ecel ataya iyowicahi na hecena yasotapi šni* So (coffee and sugar) were distributed to each tent, yet as it was it got around to all, and in the end not everything was eaten. >

i·yo·hi·ki·ya \i-yó-hi-ki-ya\ *va* iyohi·wa·kiya : to cause to reach or arrive at; to give to each one, make go around, as in dividing articles

i·yo·hi·la \i-yó-hi-la\ *adj* : each one

i·yo·hi·šni \i-yó-hi-šni\ *v* : not to reach to — **iyohišniyan** *va* : to cause not to reach to

i·yo·hi·ya \i-yó-hi-ya\ *va* iyohi·wa·ya : to cause to reach a place, to extend the hand to, make reach to all

i·yo·hob \i-yó-hōb\ *interj obsol warning to keep silent* - Note: when playing hide-and-seek all hide themselves; one would say "Iyohob!" and thus start the one seeking *Syn* HACIB BT Bl

i·yo·ȟa \i-yŏ'-ȟa\ *n* : the lower part of the face, the side of the face, the upper jaw of animals, the gills of fish < *Bléga s'e ~ ziyela. ~ cannunpa* It was like a pelican, the lower part of the side of the face being yellowish. the common short-stemmed pipe > - Bl

i·yo·ȟa·hin \i-yó-ȟa-hiŋ\ *n* : whiskers

i·yo·ȟa-ȟa \i-yó-ȟa-ȟa\ *n* : falls < *mini iyoȟaȟa* waterfalls >

i·yo·hla·te \i-yó-ȟla-te\ *adv* : underneath < ~ *inajin* to stand up underneath > — **iyohlate·ya** *adv* [fr *ohlateya* under] : underneath - B.H.109.5, 95.22

i·yo·hlo·gya \i-yó-ȟlo-gya\ *adv* : by, through, by means of < *Niye ~ wicoicage oyasin wicayawaštepi ktelo* Through you every generation will be blessed. *ieska wan ~ wokiyake* to speak through an interpreter. *Wicaša šica ~ yuakagal oyakatanpi* Through wicked men you crucified him. > - B.H.10.10, 35.5, 136.3, 279.22

i·yo·hlo·ke \i-yó-ȟlo-ke\ *n* : the mouth of a river or of two rivers that form a confluence < *Wakpala kin le ~ el iyawicunpepi kta* At the confluence of this creek we shall lie in wait for them. > - *Syn* OKIJATA

i·yo·hpa·ya \i-yó-ȟpa-ya\ *vn* iyo·wa·hpaya : to go down from a hill, away from the speaker

i·yo·hpe·ki·ya *or* **iyohpeya** \i-yó-ȟpe-ki-ya\ *va* : to throw in

i·yo·hpe·ya \i-yó-ȟpe-ya\ *va* iyohpe·wa·ya : to throw or cast into; to cook, throwing meat into the kettle

---

\a\ f<u>a</u>ther \e\ th<u>e</u>y \i\ mach<u>i</u>ne \o\ sm<u>o</u>ke \u\ l<u>u</u>nar \an, aŋ\ bl<u>anc</u> Fr. \in, iŋ\ <u>in</u>k \on, oŋ, un, uŋ\ <u>soon</u>, <u>con</u>fier Fr. \c\ <u>ch</u>air \ġ\ ma<u>ch</u>en Ger. \j\ fu<u>s</u>ion \clusters: bl, gn, kp, hšl, etc...\ <u>b</u>^{e}<u>l</u>o ... said with a slight vowel
See more in the Introduction, Guide to Pronunciation

i·yo·i·c'i·kte·ka \í-yo-i-c'i-kte-k̄a\ *v refl of* iyokteka : to reprove one's self, to repent – *Syn* IYOPEICIYA

i·yo·ja \i-yó-ja\ *v* : to amplify sound, *esp* harsh sound < *Tasiha tanka wan iyojahe s'e ye unyanpelo* They went playing a big game of *Tasiha* as though it were sound amplified, as might be said while following retreating enemies. *Canpagmiyanpi iyojahe s'e* A wagon seemed to be making an extra loud clatter, as when the rattling of a wagon is heard from a distance. > – Cf jahan Bl

i·yo·jan·jan \i-yó-jaŋ-jaŋ\ *n* [fr *ojanjan* a light] : light — *vn* : to shine, shine into, to give light to < *Iyonijanjanpi el mani po* Walk when light is given to you. > — **iyojanjan·yan** *vn* : to shine, to shine into, to give light — *adv* : shining, giving light — **iyojanjan·ye** *n* : light < *Maka kin ~ kin he miye yelo* I am the light of the world. > – B.H.244.15, 221.8

i·yo·ju·ki·ya \í-yo-ju-k̄i-ya\ *v poss of* iyojuya : to make one's own brimful < *Wašpanka ognake k'on tanyan iyojuwakiyelo* I had made my pan of cooked food nicely brimful. > — **iyoju·ya** *va* : to make brimful – Bl

i·yo·ka·ga *or* **iyokaga·tanhan** \í-yo-k̄a-ġa\ \í-yo-k̄a-ġa-taŋ-haŋ\ *adv* [fr *okaga* to make a copy] : south of — **iyokah** *and* **iyoka·hkiya** \í-yo-k̄aȟ\ and \í-yo-k̄a-ȟk̄i-ya\ *adv contrac of* iyokaga : south of — **iyoka·hwapa** *adj* : in a southerly direction

i·yo·ka·hmin \i-yó-ka-ȟmiŋ\ *n* : a point of land

i·yo·ka·i·c'i·ya \i-yó-ka-i-c'i-ya\ *v* : to get one's self into trouble – *Syn* IYÁLEICIYA

i·yo·ka·ki·šya \í-yo-k̄a-k̄i-šya\ *v* iyokaki·šwa·ya : to give a sharp answer after one has kept silent for a while – Bl

i·yo·kal \i-yō'-k̄al\ *adv contrac of* iyokata : to be warm on some account < ~ *španyan* to toast or roast by holding to the fire, ~ *aya* to hold near fire to make warm > – Bl

i·yo·ka·la \i-yó-k̄a-la\ *vn* iyo·wa·kala [fr *okala* pour out] : to empty or pour into, as grain — *n* : something into which anything is poured, and so to measure with, a measure

i·yo·ka·li·c'i·ya \i-yó-k̄a-li-c'i-ya\ *v* : to get one's self into trouble by too much talking, and thus to be caught as a liar, to become an unwilling creditor, as when one gives away something good but receiveds a thing less valuable < *Iyokalmic'iye lo* I got myself into trouble. >

i·yo·ka·lu·za \i-yó-k̄a-lu-za\ *n* : air in motion, a breeze — *adj* : airy, cool

i·yo·ka·lya \i-yō'-k̄a-lya\ *va* iyoka·lwaya : to warm, make hot in, to heat with *e.g.* a stove a room; *fig* to make hot, excited — *adv perhaps* : by the heat

i·yo·ka·ni·yan \i-yó-k̄a-ni-yaŋ\ *vn* iyo·ma·kaniyaŋ : to be jarred or shaken by a striking

i·yo·kan \i-yó-k̄aŋ\ *adj* : open, roomy < *Tipi ~ el can wicayakaku kte lo* You should start bringing them wood in at the open shed. > – Bl

i·yo·ka·pa \i-yó-k̄a-pa\ *v* iyo·wa·kapa [fr *kapá* excel] : to surpass

i·yo·ka·pas \i-yó-k̄a-pas\ *vn contrac of* iyokapaza : to be pungent — **iyokapa·sya** *va* iyokapa·swa·ya : to exert an evil influence upon, as on a sick person by one's presence, to make one worse — **iyokapasye·ca** *or* **iyokapasya** *va* : to have a negative influence on one

i·yo·ka·pa·tan·han \í-yo-k̄a-pa-taŋ-haŋ\ *adv* mí·yokapatanhan : behind, after; younger than

i·yo·ka·pa·za \i-yó-k̄a-pa-za\ *vn* iyo·ma·kapaza : to be pungent, make smart, as does pepper or mustard seed in the mouth

i·yo·ka·pte \i-yó-ka-p̄te\ *n* [fr *kapta* to lade or bail out] : something with which to dip, a dipper, ladle – Cf okapta

i·yo·ka·ski·ca \i-yó-k̄a-ski-ca\ *v* : to clog, congest < *Pahli iyomakaskicelo* My nose is stuffed. > – Bl WHL

i·yo·ka·še·ye·la \í-yo-k̄a-še-ye-la\ *adv* : closely, close to, as in holding a horse's halter close to the mouth < ~ *kaška yuze,* ~ *okatan* to hold it close bound, to drive a nail in up to the head >

i·yo·ka·ške \i-yó-k̄a-šk̄e\ *n* [fr *kaška* to tie] : something that connects or is used to bind with

i·yo·ka·štan pe·sto·la \í-yo-k̄a-štaŋ pe-stò-la\ *n* : a funnel – Bl

i·yo·ka·ta \i-yó-ka-ṫa\ *vn* [fr *okáta* to be warm inside] : to be warm in, warm by reason of, to be hot inside, as from liquor

i·yo·ka·tan \i-yó-k̄a-ṫaŋ\ *va* iyo·wa·katan [fr *okátan* to nail] : to drive in, as a nail on something

i·yo·ka·tku·ge \i-yó-k̄a-ṫku-ġe\ *n* [fr *katkuga* strike off] : a nail, a screw, a nut of a screw

i·yo·ka·win·ga \i-yó-k̄a-wiŋ-ġa\ *v* : to turn round and round — **iyokawinh** *or* **iokawinh** \i-yó-k̄a-wiŋȟ\ *v* : to turn, rotate

i·yo·ki \i-yó-k̄i\ *va* : to permit, encourage, allow – Note : the word is not used except with *šni* or in a negative way

i·yo·ki·ca·sle·ca \i-yó-k̄i-ca-sle-ca\ *va* iyoki·wa·kasleca [fr *kasleca* to split, as wood] : to split in two in the middle

i·yo·ki·ca·ška \i-yó-k̄i-ca-šk̄a\ *va* iyoki·wa·kaška [fr *kaška* to tie] : to tie together, as two strings — **iyokicaške·ya** *adv* : tied together, connected or following each other, as the seasons of the year without any intervening time

i·yo·ki·ca·špa \i-yó-k̄i-ca-šp̄a\ *va* iyoki·wa·kašpa [fr *kašpa* to cut loose] : to divide in the middle

i·yo·ki·gnag \i-yó-k̄i-gnag\ *va contrac* [fr *okignaka* to put in one's own] : to place one's own in < ~ *hingla* at the same instant, as said of guns fired off simultaneously >

i·yo·ki·gna·ka \i-yó-k̄i-gna-k̄a\ *va* iyo·wa·kignaka [fr *akignaka* to put in one's own] : to put or place in together, to put in one's own mouth

[1]**i·yo·ki·he** \i-yó-k̄i-he\ *n* : a joint

[2]**i·yo·ki·he** \í-yo-k̄i-he\ *vn* iyo·wa·kihe : to be next to, be second — *adj* : second, next to – Cf D.3 note 2

[1]**i·yo·ki·he·ya** \í-yo-k̄i-he·ya\ *adv* : lengthened out, added to, next to, following, succeeding

[2]**i·yo·ki·he·ya** \i-yó-k̄i-he-ya\ *v* iyokihe·wa·ya : to continue something commenced by others, perhaps

i·yo·ki·hi \i-yó-k̄i-hi\ *va* iyo·wa·kihi [fr *okihi* to be able] : to be able for; to come upon, to come up with

i·yo·ki·hi·ya \i-yó-k̄i-hi-ya\ *va* iyokihi·wa·ya : to make able for — *adv* : ably

i·yo·ki·ni·han \i-yó-k̄i-ni-haŋ\ *adj* [fr *okinihan* to single out for praise] : honored for — **iyokinihan·yan** *adv* : honorably

i·yo·ki·pi \i-yō'-k̄i-p̄i\ *va* iyo·wa·kipi : to please, be pleasing to others — *vn* iyo·ma·kipi iyo·un·kipi·pi : to be pleased with, to like < *iyonimakipi* I am pleased with you, *or* you are pleasing to me > – Pb.35

i·yo·ki·pi·šni·ya \i-yó-k̄i-p̄i-šni-ya\ *va* : to cause one to feel displeased — **iyokipišniyan·kel** *adv* : unpleasantly < ~ *najinpi* They felt awkward standing. > – B.H.277.17

i·yo·ki·pi·ya \i-yó-k̄i-p̄i-ya\ *va* iyokipi·wa·ya : to cause to be pleased, to please — *adv* : delightfully, pleasantly

i·yo·ki·se \i-yó-k̄i-se\ *n* [fr *okíse* a part of] : the half of anything cut in two < *Maka ~ tatanka ota nawah'on. Tawoyuha kin wicak'u* I heard many buffalo, a half of the land. He gave them their own property. > — **iyokise·ya** *adv* : half < *Maka ~ tatanka ota nawah'on. Ito, taku unkaglipi kin he ~ unk'upi kte* I heard many buffalo as half the land. Well now, what we brought back half will be given to us. > - BT Bl B.H.125.5, 127.4

i·yo·ki·ši·ca \i-yó-ǩi-ši-ca\ *vn* iyo·ma·kišica iyo·ni·cišica iyo·un·kišica·pi : to be sad, sorry, grieved — **iyokišica-pi** *n* : sadness, sorrow — **iyokišica·ya** *va* : to make sad, to sadden — *adv* : sadly

i·yo·ki·šil \i-yó-ǩi-šil\ *vn contrac of* iyokišica : to be sad — **iyokiši·lya** *va* iyokiši·lwa·ya : to sadden, grieve, displease, disappoint — *adv* : in a manner producing sadness, sadly < *~ najin* to be wrapped in grief > - D.14

i·yo·ki·šni \i-yó-ǩi-šni\ *va* iyó·wa·ki·šni iyo·un·ki·pi·šni iyo·ma·kišni : to forbid, prevent, hinder; to advise vigorously against something - Cf iyóki NOTE R D.116

i·yo·ki·tan'·in \i-yó-ǩi-taŋ-iŋ\ *n* [fr *otan'in* to be visible] : manifestation — **iyokitan'in·yan** *adv* : manifestly

i·yo·ki·win \í-yo-ǩi-wiŋ\ *v* íyo·wa·kiwin íyo·ma·kiwin : to motion, point somewhere with one's mouth — **iyo-kiwin·win** *v refl* iyo·wa·kiwinwin : to point at one's own - Bl

i·yo·ki·yu·sle·ca \í-yo-ǩi-yu-sle-ca\ *vn* [fr *yusleca* to split] : to split in two, be divided in customs — **iyokiyuslel** *vn contrac of* iyokiyusleca

i·yo·ko \i-yō'-ǩo\ *n* : space, as between heaven and earth < *Maka kin na mahpiya ~ el waun* I dwell in space between heaven and earth. *Hel ~ ogna iyotaka yo* Sit down there in that space. > - D.58

i·yo·ko·gna *or* **iokogna** \i-yō'-ǩo-gna\ *adv* [fr *iyoko* a space + *ogna* in] : between places, between one place and another

i·yo·ko·pe·ya \í-yo-ǩo-ṗe-ya\ *adv* : opposite to, beyond in sight

i·yo·kpa·ni \i-yó-kpa-ni\ *vn* iyo·ma·kpani : to lack, be wanting; to be less than, not enough; to fail, not to reach in time, not to accomplish

i·yo·kpa·ni·ya \i-yó-kṗa-ni-ya\ *va* iyokpani·wa·ya : to cause to lack *etc* — **iyokpani·yan** *and* **iokpaniyan** *adv* : lacking, failing of < *Wiciyokpaniyan yaun šni* You are not failing them. > - B.H.169.10

i·yo·kpa·ta \i-yō'-kṗa-ta\ *va* iyo·wa·kpata : to sew on, to put a patch on one's own < *Šiná huhá iyowakpatin kta* I shall put a patch on my shawl that includes the legs. >

i·yo·kte·ka \í-yō-kte-ǩa\ *va* iyo·wa·kteka : to scold, reprove, speak sharply to — **iyokte·kteka** *v red* íyo·wa·ktekteka : to scold often

i·yo·mna·ya \i-yó-mna-ya\ *va* iyomna·wa·ya : to put much in the mouth, as corn, cherries, *etc* - Bl

i·yo·na·ni·yan \i-yó-na-ni-yaŋ\ *vn* iyona·wa·niyan : to be jarred or shaken by foot

i·yo·na·pa \i-yó-na-pa\ *v* : to take shelter in < *Egypt makoce kin ~ yo* Take refuge in the land of Egypt. > - B.H.170.3

i·yo·na·ta·ke \i-yó-na-ta-ǩe\ *n* : a bar, anything with which to bar or to close up

i·yo·na·tan \í-yo-na-taŋ\ *v* : to urge one, urge upon one, as with the foot < *~ mayakuwayelo* You urge me to push on to act, *i.e.* give me time and I'll do it. > - Bl

i·yo·ni·yan \i-yó-ni-yaŋ\ *adv* : in the distance, faintly audible, slightly felt < *Hlahla kin ~ hotan'in* The crier's voice was scarcely audible, *i.e.* dimly audible because very distant. > - LB WHL

i·yo·pa·ski·ca \i-yó-ṗa-ski-ca\ *va* : to press in, ram in, as in loading a gun

i·yo·pa·štag \í-yo-ṗa-štag\ *va contrac of* iyopaštaka : to actuate < *~ waun* I am exciting. > — **iyopašta·gya** *adv* : encouragingly

i·yo·pa·šta·ka \í-yo-ṗa-šta-ǩa\ *va* íyo·wa·paštaka : to excite, incite, encourage, actuate, urge - D.221

i·yo·pa·ta \i-yó-ṗa-ta\ *va* iyó·wa·pata : to patch, sew a piece on < *Hakéla pehin šikšicela k'eyaš huhá k'el ecuhcin iyowapatin kte* Though my youngest child's hair is a bit thin, I shall at least put a patch on his hide with legs, *i.e.* to cover his head. > - D.87

i·yo·pa·tan \í-yo-ṗa-ṫaŋ\ *va* íyo·wa·patan : to push one abruptly, to make one go on, *i.e.* without constant pressure

[1]**i·yo·pa·zan** \í-yo-ṗa-zaŋ\ *va* iyo·wa·pazan [fr *i* mouth + *opazan* push into or under] : to put into the mouth

[2] **i·yo·pa·zan** \i-yó-ṗa-zaŋ\ *n* : something to bind or hold in, as a ferrule (a bushing); the brass ring that holds in the ramrod of a gun, or the ramrod itself; the bore of a gun - R Bl

i·yo·pe·i·c'i·ya \i-yō'-ṗe-i-c'i-ya\ *v refl* iyópe·mi·c'iya [fr *iyopeya* to correct] : to blame one's self, reprove one's self, to repent — **iyopeic'iya·pi** *n* : a blaming one's self, repentance, contrition

i·yo·pe·ki·ya \i-yó-ṗe-ǩi-ya\ *va* iyope·wa·kiya : to reprove, chide, scold, punish

i·yo·pe·mni \i-yó-pe-mni\ *n* : a cigaret

[1]**i·yo·pe·ya** \i-yō'-ṗe-ya\ *va* iyope·wa·ya : to reprove, correct, punish

[2]**i·yo·pe·ya** \i-yó-ṗe-ya\ *va* iyope·wa·ya : to make one tree lodge on another - Note: the word in Dakota is *iyepeya* - Cf R Bl

[3]**i·yo·pe·ya** \i-yó-ṗe-ya\ *v* : to exchange, sell < *Mazaska iyopeyaye kin hena yagluha oyakihi tka* You would be able to have for yourself those things for which you exchange money. > — *n* : the price paid, exchange - B.H.283.1

i·yo·psi·ca \i-yó-psi-ca\ *vn* iyo·wa·psica : to hop, jump down < *Wanmayanka po, miš iyowapsicin ktelo* Watch me. I'll jump down. *Mni kin ekta iyopsicapi* They hopped to the water. >

i·yo·psi·lka·ki·ci·pa e·con·pi \i-yó-psi-lka-ǩi-ci-pa e-còŋ-pi\ *n* : a pastime game for boys

i·yo·pša s'e \i-yó-pša s'e\ *adv* : with a muffled sound, as of a gun-shot — **iyopša·ya** *vn* : to be just slightly audible in the distance — *adv* : with a slightly audible sound - Bl WHL

i·yo·pša·pša \i-yó-pša-pša\ *vn* : to boil up in bubbles

i·yo·pša·ya \i-yó-pša-ya\ *adv perhaps* : with a hardly audible report as of a gun-shot - Bl

i·yo·pta \i-yó-pṫa\ *v* : to pass through or between < *Tokša iyounptin ktelo* Soon we shall pass through, *i.e.* will leave now. *~ iyaya* to pass through, pass on, *~ iyeya* to purge > — **i-yoptaiyeyapi** \i-yó-pta-i-yè-ya-pi\ *n* : a purge, cathartic

i·yo·pte \i-yó-pte\ *prep* : through, by way of < *miyopte šni ehantanš* except through me > - B.H.254.22

[1]**i·yo·pte·ya** \i-yó-pṫe-ya\ *adv* : through, straight through, passing on < *~ ya. Miyopteya iyayeyi ye* He went on through. Have it pass me on by. *Hecel emakiya kin hehanl wanna ~ iblabla. Hehanl ake ~ icimani ya* So when he said

\a\ father \e\ they \i\ machine \o\ smoke \u\ lunar \an, aŋ\ blanc Fr. \in, iŋ\ ink \on, oŋ, un, uŋ\ soon, confier Fr. \c\ chair \ǧ\ machen Ger. \j\ fusion \clusters: bl, gn, kp, hšl, etc...\ b°lo ... said with a slight vowel **See more in the Introduction, Guide to Pronunciation**

it to me I now then went on through. Then again he went passing through on a trip. *Wiyatke kin le miyopteya iyayeyi ye* Would you have this cup pass me by. > – B.H. 255.9, 54.9 Pb.41

²i·yo·pte·ya \i-yó-pte-ya\ *vn* iyopte·wa·ya : to have acquired some skill, made some progress

i·yo·pti·ye·ya \i-yó-pti-ye-ya\ *va contrac* [fr *iyopta* pass through + *iyeya* cause to go] : to cause to pass through

i·yo·pu·hli \i-yó-ṗu-ȟli\ *n* : a cork wadding for a gun — **iyopuhli·ya** *va* : to use for gun wadding

i·yo·pu·ski·ce \i-yó-ṗu-ski-ce\ *n* : a ramrod

i·yo·sni·yan \i-yó-sni-yaŋ\ *adj* : chilly, cool < *Tate wan ~ uye lo; wasu hinhin kte laka* The wind became chilly; sleet might well precipitate. > — **iyosni·yaya** *va* iyó sniya·wica·ya : to cool < *Tate wan iyosniyawicaye* A wind cooled them down. > – B.H.139.23 Bl WHL

i·yo·ša·la s'e \i-yó-ša-la s'e\ *adv* : all in red < ~ *ahiyaye* They passed by all dressed more or less in red. > – Bl

i·yo·šni·ja \i-yó-šni-ja\ *vn* iyo·ma·šnija : to be blinded by the sun or snow < *Išta kin wi iyošnije* The sun blinded her eyes, *or perhaps* The sunlight reflected in her eyes blinded the mother so she could not see well. > – D.222

i·yo·štan *or* **iyoštan·pi** \i-yó-štaŋ\ *n* [fr *óštan* put in *or* on] : something pushed into the mouth of anything, a vial cork, a stopper

i·yo·tag \í-yo-ṫag\ *v contrac of* iyotaka : to sit < ~ *hiyeya* to become seated > — **iyota·gkiya** \í-yo-ṫa-gk̇i-ya\ *va* íyota·gwa·kiya : to cause to sit down

i·yo·ta·he·na \i-yó-ta-he-na\ *adv obsol* : meantime forgotten < *Iapi ~ epin kte* I shall speak of what was forgotten but said before, *i.e.* something that, as you remember, we had talked about. ~ *owanjigjila yanka yo* Take your forgotten rest, *i.e.* Stay at home, as said to a fellow who always bums around. > – *Syn* NAPTAHENA Cf lotkunkešni WE RF

i·yo·ta·he·pi \i-yó-ta-he-pi\ *adv* : between one place and another — **iyotahepi·ya** \i-yó-ta-he-ṗi-ya\ *adv* : on the way, this side of the place of destination – B.H.39.14

i·yo·ta·ka \í-yo-ṫa-k̇a\ *vn* : to sit, be sitting, to sit down, rest, to camp perhaps < *Wayawa iblotaka. Na wanna wizipan paha kin ohlate wakpala el iyotakapi* I sat down to read. And they rested their bedrolls at a creek below the hill. > — **iyotakė·han** *part* : sitting

i·yo·tan \i-yŏ'-ṫaŋ\ *adv* : very, most < ~ *wašte* very good > — *adj used in comparing one thing with another* i·ma·yotan : great, greater, greatest, chief — **iyotan·hci** *adv* : most of all, chiefly

i·yo·tan'·in \i-yó-ṫaŋ-iŋ\ *v* : to shine on account of < *Mahpiya kin lila ~* The cloud shone very brightly. > – B.H.166.4

i·yo·tan·la \i-yó-ṫan-la\ *va* : to regard something above all else, such as money, property, ownership, show < *Woyuha kin iyotanyala* You regard property above all else, hence to show one's pride. > — *adv perhaps but obsol* : well, meaning *tanyan* < ~ *oyah'an yelo* You have done well. ~ *omayakih'an yelo* You have done me well. *Sagye kin le e ca yacin heci, icu na ~ icu wo* Take and take well, would it be this cane you want. > – Note: the *adv* tanyan is generally replacing the *adv* iyotanla Pb.26 RF BT WHL

i·yo·tan·la·ka \i-yó-ṫaŋ-la-k̇a\ *va* iyotan·wa·laka : to esteem most, value most highly

i·yo·tan·yan \i-yó-ṫaŋ-yaŋ\ *adv* : greatly

i·yo·ta·tkons \i-yó-ta-ṫkoŋs\ *adv contrac of* iyotatkonza : over against, opposite to — **iyotatkon·sya** *adv* : even with, opposite to

i·yo·ta·tkon·za \i-yó-ta-ṫkoŋ-za\ *adv of* otatkonza : over against, even with, opposite to

i·yo·ti·tan·la \í-yo-ṫi-ṫaŋ-la\ *adj* : tightly fitted < *Ogle í-yomatitanla yelo* The coat is tight-fitting on me, *i.e.* too tight, too small for me. > – Bl WHL

i·yo·ti·ye·ki·ya \i-yó-ṫi-ye-k̇i-ya\ *vn* : to have troubles, to suffer, find it hard < ~ *yaunpi* or *iyotiyeyakiya* You all are finding it hard. *Miye ekta ~ mayahipi* You came to me having troubles. *haiyotiyekiya* to suffer from poor clothing, *haiyotiyewakiye* I had trouble with clothing, *si-iyotiyekiya* to suffer from one's feet > — **iyotiye·ic'iciya** *v refl* : to bring troubles on one's self – Note: there is some doubt about the spelling of the *v refl* – WE

i·yo·to \i-yŏ'-to\ *vn* : to bump against < *Tiyopa iyówato* I bumped against the door. > *Syn* ÍCIYAPA

i·yo·t'o·gnag \i-yó-t'o-gnag\ *vn contrac of* iyot'ognaka : to risk life

i·yo·t'o·gna·ka \i-yó-t'o-gna-ka\ *vn* : to hazard life, risk one's life, go into danger

i·yo·t'ins·t'ins \í-yo-t'iŋs-t'iŋs\ *v contrac red* : to take mouthful after mouthful < *Wana peji to kin ~ yašlapi iyececa* It was as though they cropped off the blue grass mouthful by mouthful, *i.e.* they shined themselves with grass. > – Bl WHL

i·yo·wa \i-yó-wa\ *n* : writing materials

i·yo·wa·ja \i-yó-wa-ja\ *or* \í-yo-wa-ja\ *adv perhaps* iyo·ma·waja iyo·un·waja·pi [fr *owaja* be concerned in] : near to, equal to, relating to, concerned in, having a right to — **iyowaja·ka** \í-yo-wa-ja-k̇a\ *adv neg meaning* iyowajašni : unrelated to, unconcerned in — **iyowaja·šni** *or* **iyowajašni·šniyan** \i-yó-wa-ja-šni\ *adv* : not near to, not equal to, having nothing to do with

i·yo·wa·lya \i-yó-wa-lya\ *v* : to have something as an excuse – Cf wal'iyowalya D.124 WHL

i·yo·wang \i-yó-waŋg\ *n contrac of* iyowanke : an example — **iyowan·gya** \í-yo-waŋ-gya\ *va perhaps* : to have one to be imitated, to set an example for, be imitated < *iyowan·gwa·ya* I am his example, *i.e.* he does as I do, *iyowan·gma·ya* He is my example, *i.e.* I do as he does. > – Cf owángya Bl

i·yo·wan·ke \i-yó-waŋ-k̇e\ *n* : an example set for

i·yo·waš \i-yó-waš\ *vn contrac of* iyowaja : to be near to < ~ *waun šni* I am not near to, ~ *yuha* to have a concern in > – B.H.19.13

i·yo·wa·ta \i-yŏ'-wa-ṫa\ *v* or *adj perhaps* : to reflect, as is said of a sunrise on a cold winter morning when a long ray of bright light goes straight up meaning cold weather < *Wi kin ~*, or simply *iyowata* The sun turns back, *or* It reflects. *Miyoglas'in on iyowatwayin kte* I shall reflect (the light) with a mirror, as is said when signals are given with a looking glass. *Tipi wan ~* A house glows, as said when in the distance a house is visible on account of a fire throwing its light on it. > — **iyowa·tya** *va* : to make visible by throwing light on – Cf iyowata

i·yo·wi·ca·jan·jan s'e \i-yó-wi-ca-jan-jaŋ s'e\ *adv* : gleaming as it were < ~ *koyaka* to dress very attractively > – *Syn* KALEHLEGAPI S'E Bl

i·yo·win·ha·ha·ya·kel \i-yó-wiŋ-ha-ha-ya-kel\ *adv* : with added cover on, as on the feet <~ *owahelo* I put it on with more cover. >

i·yo·win·ȟa·la \i-yó-wiŋ-ȟa-la\ *adv* : in jest, jestingly

i·yo·win·ȟa·la \í-yo-wiŋ-ȟa-la\ *va* iyowinȟa·ci·la : to fulfil somebody's wishes – Bl

i·yo·win·ȟa·ye·la \i-yó-wiŋ-ȟa-ye-la\ *adv* : in jest, jectingly – Bl

i·yo·win'·i·c'i·ya \i-yó-wiŋ-i-c'i-ya\ *v refl of* iyowinyan :

to declare one's willingness – D.221

i·yo·win·ki·ya \i-yó-wiŋ-ǩi-ya\ *va* iyowin·wa·kiya iyowin'·un·kiya·pi : to permit, allow < *iyówinmakiya yo* Allow me. >

i·yo·win·yan \i-yó-wiŋ-yaŋ\ *va* iyowin·wa·ya : to bear, endure, to be sufficient for, permit, consent, accept < *Ate hecel iyowinye šni. Canke unmapi unhena iyowinyanpi* Father therefore did not consent to it. And then they both accepted it. *Hecel winyan kin ~* So the woman gave her consent. > — **iyowinye·šni** *adv* : without leave, contrary to orders, insufficient, inoperative as medicine

i·yo·wi·wi·la s'e \i-yó-wi-wi-la s'e \ *adv* : as though springing water, like a spring welling forth; *fig* in appearance fatty, quite fleshy – Bl WHL

i·yo·wo·tan'·in \i-yó-wo-taŋ-iŋ\ *n* : a place from which one can see to a great distance, as a hill, a visibility vantage point — *adj perhaps* : visible < *Wana maka ~ šni hingla* Of a sudden the ground was out of sight. > — *v irreg perhaps* : there is visibility on account of < *P'o wan ~ šni* A heavy fog filled the land. > — **iyowotan'in·šniyan** *adv* : invisibly < *Hecena mahpiya eciyatan ošota s'e hiyu na ~ najin.* In the end, he came as from a cloud of smoke and stood unseen. > — **iyowotan'inšniye·la** *adv* : beyond sight, invisibly < *Šota ~ kuwapi ška opi šni gli yelo* He arrived home unscathed, they say they followed the smoke without being seen. > – MS.563 D.208

i·yo·ya \i-yó-ya\ *vn* iyo·wa·ya : to gape, yawn – Note: BD used iyówawa. Cf icápa

i·yo·yag \i-yó-yag\ *vn contrac of* iyoyaka : to be displeased

i·yo·ya·gwa·gwa \i-yó-ya-gwa-gwa\ *v* : to chew in a way, *i.e.* with the front teeth, what cannot be chewed as something soft, in order to taste it – Bl

i·yo·ya·gya \i-yó-ya-gya\ *va* iyoya·gwa·ya : to displease, hurt one's feelings, to offend or make one sick – Bl

i·yo·ya·ka \i-yó-ya-ka\ *vn* iyo·ma·yaka : to be offended, displeased, to be made sick

i·yo·ya·ke·ca \i-yó-ya-ke-ca\ *vn* iyo·ma·yakeca : to be sorrowful, distressed

i·yo·ya·lal \i-yó-ya-lal\ *adv of* iyoya : in a sleeping manner < *~ ecunkonpi* We worked at it lackadaisically. >

i·yo·yam \i-yó-yam\ *vn contrac of* iyoyanpa : to shine — **iyoyam·ya** *va* iyoyam·wa·ya [fr *iyoyanbya* shine on, or illuminated] : to shine on, illuminate, enlighten — *adv* : illuminated, in an illuminated manner

i·yo·yan·bya \i-yó-yaŋ-bya\ *va* [fr *iyoyanpaya* cast light on] : to enlighten one – Cf iyoyamya Pb.29

i·yo·yan·bye·la \i-yó-yaŋ-bye-la\ *adv* : being in the light < *Ile s'e ~ hinajin* He came and stood as if he were afire in its light. > – B.H.113.4

i·yo·yan·pa \i-yó-yaŋ-p̌a\ *vn* : to shine, give light — *n* : light < *Yunkan (taku wan) iyoyap hingla na tanwankatuya ya na wanna makata glihan* Then something suddenly shone with light, went very high upward, and came down to came down to stick in the ground. *Taku wan ite kin ataya iyoyam mahingle na toyela iyaya* Suddenly something happened, my face entirely glowed and turned blue. *Wanna ake iyoyam mahingle. Hehanl ungnahela ite kin iyoyam mahingla na ecel wanna lila mat'in kta seca.* Again I suddenly glowed. Then all at once my face glowed and thus it seemed I was on the very point of dying. *Yunkan ataya iyoyam hingla na atan'in šni* Then again it shone and was not visible. *Wankatanhan toyela ~ ca* It shone blue from above, *i.e.* the water was blue. >

iyoyanpa·ya *va* iyowanpa·wa·ya : to enlighten, shine on

i·yo·ya·s'in \i-yó-ya-s'iŋ\ *adv* : with, on < *pa he* a head with the horns on, *šunkwinyela cincala ~* a mare along with her colt > – Note: one could not say *pa wapoštan ~* a head with a hat on — **iyoyas'in·yan** *adv* : with, on – Note: the word may perhaps not be used by the Tetons who use rather *iyoyas'in. Iyówas'inyan* is D's spelling B.H.238.4 D.28 and 98

i·yo·ya·ya \i-yó-ya-ya\ *va* : to make yawn

i·yo·ya·za \i-yó-ya-za\ *v* : to string, as beads, or to put a string through a needle

i·yo·zi \i-yó-zi\ *n* [fr *ózi* to rest] : rest, repose — **iyozi·kiya** \i-yó-zi-ǩi-ya\ *va* iyozi·wa·kiya : to cause to rest — **iyozi·ya** *adv* : at rest — **iyozi·ziya** *adv red* : leisurely

i·yu·blah \i-yú-blaȟ\ *v* : to open out < *tipi ~ iyeya* to open the whole front part of the tent, *i.e.* to raise the walls of a tent, *Yunkan wanna tipi kin ~ iyeyapi. Wanna tipi ~ iyeyapi wan eglepi* They now set out a tent whose walls were raised. >

i·yu·can \i-yú-caŋ\ *va* i·blu·can 1 : to riddle, sift — *vn* 2 : to be short of things < *Canli imayucan* I am short on tobacco. *Lol'iyucankelo* He has little to eat. *Woyute iyucanpi šni* They are not short on food. > – Bl B.H.106.8

i·yu·can·te·ši·ca \i-yú-caŋ-ťe-ši-ca\ *va* : to make feel bad on account of, in consequence of

i·yu·can·yan·kel \i-yú-caŋ-yaŋ-kel\ *adv* : a little, very little of, as food < *~ yuha* to have a little, *~ yanke* to be very little of, *Peji ~ najinpi kte šni nacecelo* It may be when there is little grass they will not stand, meaning the horses. > – Bl

i·yu·e·ce·tu \i-yú-e-ce-tu\ *va* i·blu·ecetu : to perfect, make right by means of

i·yu·ge·ya \i-yú-ǧe-ya\ *adj* : all, the whole

i·yu·gmi·gma \i-yú-gmn-gma\ *n* [fr *yugmigma* make into a ball] : something that turns a thing, a turner, as a water-wheel

i·yu·gna·yan \i-yú-gna-yaŋ\ *vn* i·ma·yugnayan [fr *yugnayan* to miss in trying] : to be deceived, as in the prospect of receiving something < *Iyugnayenic'iyelo* You were yourself deceived. *Woyute eciyatanhan ~ ayapi* They began to be deceived concerning food. > – MS.488 B.H.55.10

i·yu·gu·ka \i-yú-ǧu-ka\ *v* i·blu·guka : to injure by a hard pull, to strain, to sprain *e.g.* a tendon < *Cekpa ibluguka ca hece* So when I pulled a tendon, as a man says when a friend always wants him back. > – Bl WLH

i·yu·ha \i-yú-ha\ *adj* : all < *~ kaska* all in all, being clear > — **iyuha·ha** *adj red* : really all – P B.H.50.3

i·yu·ha·ha·ya \i-yú-ha-ha-ya\ *adv red of* iyuhaya : slovenly

i·yu·ha·ya \i-yú-ha-ya\ *adv* : lossely, slovenly

i·yu·hin·he \i-yú-hiŋ-he\ *n* : a harrow

i·yu·hin·ta \i-yú-hiŋ-ta\ *va* i·blu·hinta : to rake away the intestines — **iyuhinte** *n* : anything with which to rake < *makiyuhinte* a rake used on the ground >

i·yu·ho·mni \i-yú-ho-mni\ *n* [fr *yuhomni* turn around] : something with which to turn, as a door knob

i·yu·ho·ta \i-yú-ho-ťa\ *n* : intestines, all the inside organs of an animal < *~ kin ataya wankatakiya mau* My entire innerds came up, *i.e.* the feeling to vomit. >

\a\ father \e\ they \i\ machine \o\ smoke \u\ lunar \an, aŋ\ blanc Fr. \in, iŋ\ ink \on, oŋ, un, uŋ\ soon, confier Fr. \c\ chair \ǧ\ machen Ger. \j\ fusion \clusters: bl, gn, kp, hšl, etc...\ b[e]lo ... said with a slight vowel
See more in the Introduction, Guide to Pronunciation

i·yu·hci \i-yú-ḣci\ *va* i·blu·hci unki·yuhci·pi : to break out, make it break, as the eye of a needle, to tear a button hole < *nakpa* ~ to tear one's ear > – Bl

i·yu·ḣe·pe \i-yú-ḣe-ṗe\ *n* [fr *yuḣepa* to empty out] : an absorber, a sponge –P Bl

i·yu·hla·hla·ya \i·yu·ḣla-ḣla-ya\ *adv* : peeling or pulling off and uncovering sores or wounds, by removal of scabs and bandages < *Wokoyake kin coku kin ekta iyaskapa keš kiyušlokapi* The clothing was pulled off though it stuck to the underskin, hence to open sores. > – WHL

i·yu·hla·ta \i-yú-ḣla-ta\ *va* i·blu·hlata [fr *yuhlata* to scratch] : to catch hold of with, as with a hook, to scratch with, to claw — **iyuhlate** *n* [fr *i* instumental + *yuhlata* to scratch] : something with which to catch or scratch with, a claw

i·yu·hle·hlel \i-yú-ḣle-ḣlel\ *adv* : being scratched < ~ *icu* tearing up while taking it, *Onjinjintka oju wan el iyayapi na* ~ *iyayapi* They entered a rose garden and scratched they went. >

i·yu·hlo·ke \i-yú-ḣlo-ke\ *n* [fr *yuhloka* to make a hole] : something with which to open or make a hole < *tiyopa* ~ a door opener, a key >

i·yu·hmin \í-yu-ḣmiŋ\ *vn* i·blu·hmin : to be distorted, as a word difficult to say well < *Wanagi* ~ His soul is contorted, as people say when a person's face, half of it, and as happens among the Dakotas, is distorted. *Wanagi imayuhmin* My spirit is bent up. >

i·yu·hmun \i-yú-ḣmuŋ\ *n* [fr *yuhmun* to make whizz] : a sling, a slingshot

i·yu·hpa \i-yú-ḣṗa\ *v* : to be all, completed and indicating: That's it, or That's all. — *adj* : all, the whole – Cf iyuha < *Tóke léceya cante* ~ *niwanica hwo?* Am I to suppose you are without a whole heart in saying this? > — **iyuhpa·la** *and* **iyuhpa** *adj* : all, the whole – B.H.95.23 Bl

i·yu·hpe \i-yú-ḣṗe\ *n* [fr *yuhpa* pull loose] : something to pull down with

i·yu·h'e·ya·ya·pi \i-yú-ḣ'e-ya-ya-pi\ *n* : a certain part of the meat on the shoulder blades of a buffalo – *Syn* TISTO CONICA HH Bl

i·yu·i·je·na \i-yú-i-je-na\ *v* i·blu·ijena : to mix – Cf iyukpukpa Bl

i·yu·ja·ja \i-yú-ja-ja\ *va* [fr *yujaja* to wash] : to wash with, to be washed with, to wring out — *n* : something with which to wash, as a wash-tub, wash-board, *etc*

i·yu·ji·bye·la \í-yu-ji-bye-la\ *adv* : brimful, as of fluids – *Syn* ÍYAPAHAYELA Bl

i·yu·ji·pa \i-yú-ji-ṗa\ *n* [fr *i* mouth + *yujipa* to pinch] : the upper end of the forehead where the hair begins < ~ *el o* He wounded him on the forehead. > — **iyujipe** *n* **a** : the front lock of a man's hair **b** : something with which to pinch or lay hold with, as *maziyujipe* tongs < ~ *pakihte cin etulahci kute* He shot just at the clip that bound his forelock. > – Note: little girls often had their hair fixed together in this sort of fastener or clip — *v perhaps* : to pinch with an instrument or pull out hairs – MS.77 D.88

i·yu·ka·ki·ja \i-yú-k̇a-ki-ja\ *va* : to cause to suffer by — **iyukaki·šya** *adv perhaps* : causing pain < ~ *ecakiconpi* They did it to him causing pain. > – B.H.266.4, 167.11

i·yu·kcan \i-yú-kcaŋ\ *va* i·blu·kcan unki·yukcan·pi i·ci·yukcan i·mayalu·kcan [fr *yukan* understand] : to understand, have an opinion or understanding of, to think or guess; to judge — **iyukcan·ke** \i-yú-kcaŋ-k̇e\ *n* : one who forms an opinion — **iyukcan·kel** *adv* : guessing < ~ *aya* to go on guessing > — **iyukcan·yan** *va* iyukcan·wa·ya : to cause to understand — *adv* : thinking, having an understanding of

i·yu·kin \i-yú-k̇iŋ\ *va* i·blu·kin : to wrench, pry — **iyukin·kin** *v red* i·blu·kinkin : to pull to and fro as a fence post in order to loosen it — **iyukin·yan** *adv* : prying — **iyukinyan icu** *v* : to apply a lever on a fulcrum to lift or move – Note: the word implies prying with a lever *Syn* IYUPSEYA ICU Bl

i·yu·ki·pab \i-yú-k̇i-ṗab\ *adv* : divided, *archaic*

i·yu·kol·tke·ye·la \i-yú-kol-tke-ye-la\ *adv* : hanging without touching down < ~ *otke lo* It hangs without touching the ground, as a piece of wood or a bag on a fence > – Bl

i·yu·kpan \i-yú-k̇ṗaŋ\ *va* [fr *yukpan* pulverize] : to rub up fine, as with the fingers; perhaps to pulverize by means of < *ikabluya* ~ to pulverize rubbing fine as dust > — *n* : something with which to make fine, a mill – B.H.240.14

i·yu·kpu·kpa \i-yú-k̇ṗu-k̇ṗa\ *va* i·blu·kpukpa [fr *yukpukpa* to crumble and scatter] : to break up fine and mingle together, as also in mixing tobacco and *canšaša* a bark chipped from the red willow tree – *Syn* IYUIJENA Bl

i·yu·ksa \i-yú-ksa\ *va* i·blu·ksa [fr *yuksa* to break] : to break off with, cut off with — **iyukse** *n* : something with which to break or cut off, a pair of snips

i·yu·kšan \i-yú-kšaŋ\ *vn* : to go off, curve off, as a road

i·yu·k'e·ge \i-yú-k'e-ġe\ *n* [fr *yuk'ega* to scratch an itch] : something with which to scratch, as a piece of wood – R Bl

i·yu·k'e·ze \i-yú-k'e-ze\ *n* [fr *yuk'eza* clip off] : a scraper

i·yu·k'o \i-yú-k'o\ *v* i·blu·k'o : to enlarge a hole by reaming < *Hi* ~ *welo* He reamed out a tooth (cavity). > – Bl WHL

i·yul \i-yúl\ *v contrac of* iyuta : to eat with, as one thing with another — **iyul·kiton** \i-yúl-k̇i-toŋ\ *n* : something with which to eat, *i.e.* a sauce — **iyul·ton** *n* : something to eat with other things, sauce, contiment

i·yu·man *or* **iyume** \i-yú-maŋ\ *n* [fr *yuman* to sharpen] : something with which to rub or grind, a file, stone, *etc*, hence *maziyume* a metal file

i·yu·mni \i-yú-mni\ *n* [fr *yumni* to turn around] : something that turns around < *tate* ~ a whirlwind, *can* ~ an auger

i·yun \í-yuŋ\ *va* í·wa·yun únki·yun·pi : to rub on, to apply, as ointment or soap *etc* < *Na maka hlihlila on iic'iyun. Le wicaša tuwa ayin kta cin he pejuta iwayun kta. Sla wakan imáyunpi* And he rubbed himself with muddy earth. This will be the man on whom I shall rub a medicine. I was anointed with Holy Oil. > – Pb.45

i·yung \i-yúng\ *v contrac of* iyunka : to lie out as for deer

i·yun·ga \i-yúŋ-ġa\ *va* i·mun·ga i·nun·ga : to inquire of one, as one a question < *Unkiyanungapi* You asked us > — **iyunga·pi** *n* : an inquiry

i·yunh \i-yúŋḣ\ *v contrac of* iyunga : to question one

i·yun·ka \i-yúŋ-k̇a\ *vn* i·mun·ka i·nun·ka unki·yunka·pi : to lie down, go to bed < *Wakpala wan el iyunkin kta iyukcan* He decided he would be overnight at a creek. >

i·yun·ka·la \i-yúŋ-ka-la\ *adv* : personally < *Iye* ~ *he* He He stood in person. *Atkuku kin iye* ~ *tankal hinajin* His father came personally and stood outside. > – B.H.14.10, 53.1, 88.10, 102.5, 300.16 D.203

i·yun·kel \í-yuŋ-k̇el\ *adv* : travelling < *hu* ~ travelling on or by foot > – KE WHL

i·yun·pi or **wiyunpi** \i-yúŋ-pi\ \wí-yuŋ-pi\ *n* : unction, anoinment – B

i·yun·ton \i-yúŋ-toŋ\ *va* iyun·wa·ton : to put grease or brains on a skin, a hide, in order to dress it

i·yun·win \i-yúŋ-wiŋ\ *n* : remuneration, something with which to pay < ~ *yukan* to be pay > — **iyunwin·ton** *v* iyunwin·wa·ton : to have the means to pay, have something to give for — **iyunwin·yan** *va* iyun-win·wa·ya : to have or use as pay

i·yu·pa·ga \i-yú-pa-ġa\ *va* : to gather up in the hand *e.g.* the mouth of a bag for tying, to seize, lay hold of, to arrest *e.g.* a desparate fellow. – Note: this meaning seems *obsol* whereas *iyupah icu* is used < *Iyupah icu po* Get along! as said in goading horses to hurry. ~ *po, tokša hantahena wašlašlapi kte lo* Get along! Soon before night, they (the horses) will have it cropped. > – BT

i·yu·pah \i-yú'-paȟ\ *va contrac* iyupaga : to gather up together in the hand, in a bunch with none missing < ~ *naunk au* They (with some missing perhaps) came gathered together on the gallop. ~ *yuza* to clasp tight in a bunch, *i.e.* as by the mouth of a bag, ~ *okala* to gather up by hand and sow > — **iyupa·hya** \i-yú-pa-ȟya\ *adv* : grouping, into bunches < ~ *okala* to sow in bunches > – R Bl B.H. 39.2

i·yu·pan \i-yú-paŋ\ *va* i·blu·pan : to break or rub up, as in the hand

i·yu·pi·za \i-yú-pi-za\ *adj* : wrinkled

i·yu·pse·pse·ya \i-yú-pse-pse-ya\ *adv red of* iyupseya : in many crooks

i·yu·pse·ya \i-yú-pse-ya\ *adv* : crookedly, zigzag < ~ *icu* to lift something with a stick by inserting a fulcrum under it to operate as a lever > – *Syn* IYUKINYAN — **iyupseya·kel** *adv* : crookedly perhaps, in a mess < ~ *taku tokanon* You misplaced something in the confusion > – Note: *iyupsiya* seems commonly to be avoided in favor of the form, *iyupseya* Bl

i·yu·pša·ya \i-yú-pša-ya\ *adv* : mixed up, all together, as good and bad

i·yu·pta \i-yú-pta\ *v* : to take up with a spade, to dig and take up, as in spading < ~ *icu, iwacu* He, I took it up in spading >

I·yu·pta·la \Í-yu-pta-la\ *np* : a society like the Omaha Dance Society

i·yu·pu·za \i-yú-pu-za\ *va* i·blu·puza [fr *yupuza* wipe dry] : to make dry with — **iyupuze** *n* : something with which to make dry, a towel

i·yu·sa·ke \i-yú-sa-ke\ *n* : a gad, a whip

i·yu·ska·pa \i-yú-ska-pa\ *va* : to crack a whip and strike something or somebody

i·yu·ski·te \i-yú-ski-te\ *n* : a bandage – Note: yuskita

i·yu·slo·han \i-yú-slo-haŋ\ *v* : to drag something < ~ *eyaya* to have taken dragging it along, *i.e.* dragging or taking along with all that is lying on it, as a blanket *etc* > — **iyuslohe** *n* [fr *yuslohan* to tow] : something to drag along — **iyuslohe·ton** *v* iyuslohe·wa·ton : to drag something along — **iyusloheton·yan** *and* **iyuslohe·ya** *adv* : in a way of dragging – Bl

i·yu·sna i·ye·ya \i-yú-sna i-yè-ya\ *v* : to pull out, as pins from a tent < *Na wanna tipi k'on he wiceška ~ iyeyapi, na wanna h'oká etanhan hinapapi* And quickly the tipi pins were pulled out, and on that account the singers came out. >

i·yu·sol \i-yú-sol\ *va contrac of* iyusota : to use up < ~ *eyaya* All passed by. >

i·yu·so·ta \i-yú-so-ta\ *va* i·blu·sota [fr *yusota* expend] : to use all up with, to use up for

i·yu·so·tka \i-yú-so-tka\ *v* : to clear up < ~ *iyaya* The clouds cleared away. > – Note: the word is used only in *ref* to clouds of a thunderstorm or clouds of smoke disappearing – LP

i·yu·sto \i-yú-sto\ *v* i·blu·sto : to smooth down, as the hair < *Pešlete el awicaputakiya na etanhan anunk kutakiya si ekta iyagleya ~ ewicayaya* She kissed them on the top of the head, and therefore she took them to groom their hair reaching on both sides down to the feet. >

i·yu·s'e·ya \i-yú-s'e-ya\ *adv* : barely, hardly < ~ *miglu-štan* Scarcely was I finished. ~ *otan'in* It is hardly visible. > – Note: compare the *adv iyuzeya*

i·yu·s'o \i-yú-s'o\ *vn* [fr *yus'o* to swim as does a duck] : to come up for air, as is said when a man rides through water and gets wet in spite of lifting his legs – Bl

i·yu·s'o·ya \i-yú-s'o-ya\ *adv* : in an exhausted condition, reluctantly, with difficulty < ~ *iyowinkiye* to reluctantly allow, ~ *ihunni* to reach the end with difficulty > — **iyus'oya·hci** *adv* : with difficulty — **iyus'oyakel** *adv* : just a little, hardly < *Kitanyel ~ iyewayelo* Hardly a little could I find, or That is all I could find. ~ *kini* It is hard to live again. > – B.H.109.4, 38.12 LB

i·yu·ši·ca \i-yú-ši-ca\ *v* [fr *yušica* make one bad] : to injure by means of, make bad with < *iglušica* to get one's self into difficulty > — **iyušice** *n* : something that makes bad or injures

i·yu·šin·ktin·yan \i-yú-šiŋ-ktiŋ-yaŋ\ *adv* : leaning one way or another < ~ *najin* to stand leaning one way > – Bl

i·yu·ška \i-yú-ška\ *n* [fr *yuška* untie] : something by means of which to untie *e.g.* a bundle

i·yu·ški \i-yú-ški\ *va contrac of* iyuškica : to press

i·yu·ški·ca \i-yú-ški-ca\ *va* i·blu·škica : to press on and cut accidentally as with a knife, to wring out, as out of water — **iyuškice** *n* : a press

i·yu·škin \i-yú-škiŋ\ *vn* i·blu·škin : to rejoice, be glad, to rejoice in — **iyuškin·kiya** \i-yú-škiŋ-ki-ya\ *va* iyu-škin·wa·kiya : to cause to rejoice — **iyuškin·škin** *v red* : to be continually glad — **iyuškinškin·yan** *adv red of* iyuškinyan : rejoicing

i·yu·škin·yan \i-yú-škiŋ-yaŋ\ *va* iyuškin·wa·ya : to make glad, to gladden, rejoice — *adv* : gladly, rejoicingly

i·yu·šla \i-yú-šla\ *n* [fr *yušla* to shear] : shears, scissors < *mitaiyušla* my scissors > – D.59

i·yu·šlok \i-yú-šlok\ *v contrac of* iyušloka : to pull off or out with, to slip off, to divest one's self of *e.g.* a sweater. < *Šiná kin ecela ~ kipi* They took away pulling off only the blanket. >

i·yu·šlo·ka \i-yú-šlo-ka\ *n* [fr *yušloka* pull off, out] : something with which to pull off or out, as a cork screw, an extractor — **iyušloke** *n* : a key

i·yu·šlu·šlu·ta \i-yú-šlu-šlu-ta\ *n red* [fr *yušlušluta*] : something with which to make smooth, a polisher

i·yu·šna \i-yú-šna\ *n* [fr *yušna* let slip] : one that has lost its mate, an odd one

i·yu·šṕa \i-yú-špa\ *va* i·blu·špa [fr *yušpa* break off, divide] : to pick off from, as from a scab

i·yu·špe·šni \í-yu-špe-šni\ *adj* : silent, not opening one's mouth < ~ *mankelo* I remained silent. > – Cf išpašpa

---

\a\ father \e\ they \i\ machine \o\ smoke \u\ lunar \an, aŋ\ blanc Fr. \in, iŋ\ ink \on, oŋ, un, uŋ\ soon, confier Fr. \c\ chair \ġ\ machen Ger. \j\ fusion \clusters: bl, gn, kp, hšl, etc...\ b°lo ... said with a slight vowel
See more in the Introduction, Guide to Pronunciation

i·yu·špe·ye·ya \i-yú-špe-ye-ya\ *adv* : with one having neglected to do something < ~ *econ* to do somebody's work that he neglected, *i.e.* doing work besides one's own > - WE WHL KE

i·yu·špu \i-yú-špu\ *va* i·blu·špu [fr *yušpu* pull off] : to pick off from, as corn from the strings

i·yu·šta·ka \i-yu·šta-ka\ *v* : to soften, make soft, press < *Cunwiyapehe iyuštakapi s'e* I was as though the grapes were pressed, and suggesting the color purple. >

i·yu·štan \i-yú-štaŋ\ *va* i·blu·štan [fr *yuštan* to finish] : to finish inside, to finish for

i·yu·š'in·ya·ya \i-yú-š'iŋ-ya-ya\ *and* \i-yu-š'íŋ-ya-ya *v* : to be surprised at or with regard to - B.H.163.1, 181.9, 252.1 MS.157

i·yu·š'in·ye·ya \i-yú-š'iŋ-ye-ya\ *vn* i·ma·yuš'inyeya : to be frightened - B.H.289.5

[1]**i·yu·ta** \i-yú-ta\ *v* i·wá·ta i·yá·ta *possible forms of 1st and 2nd person* [fr *yuta* to eat] : to eat with, as one thing with another

[2]**i·yu·ta** \i-yú-ta\ *va* i·blu·ta i·ci·yuta : to measure, weigh, to try or attempt < *Yunkan ibluta nihingla na kagal hingla* And then I suddenly tried you, and he threw up his hands, *i.e.* being disappointed in what he got *etc.* > - BT

[3]**i·yu·ta** \i-yú-ta\ *va* [fr *utá* to try] : to taste

[1]**i·yu·tan** \i-yú-taŋ\ *v* i·ma·yutan : to tempt; to be tempted or tried < *Tušu iyutanton wo; wakinyan ukiye eyaš lila tate kte lo* Have the tent poles tested having been roped down; thunder is coming but it will be very windy. > - Cf *ipátan* to brace — *n* : the trigger of a gun Bl

[2]**i·yu·tan** \i-yū'-taŋ\ *va* i·blu·tan : to put in grease and mix up, to mix up *e.g.* grease and cherries to make pemmican; to mingle

i·yu·tan·tan \i-yū'-taŋ-taŋ\ *va* i·blu·tantan [fr *yután* to touch, feel] : to touch, to feel in several places

i·yu·tan·yan \i-yú-taŋ-yan\ *adv* : stretched out, as was Christ's body on the cross < ~ *otke* to be hung up stretched out, *i.e.* crucified > - Cf iyútitanyan — *va* iyutan·wa·ya : to tempt, to try or prove — *adv* : tempting, trying

i·yu·ta·pi \i-yú-ta-pi\ *n* : a measure
makiyutapi or *makaiyutapi* a surveyor's chain
tekuiyutapi a pound
wójuiyutapi or *wójiyutapi* an acre

i·yu·te·ki·ya \i-yú-te-ki-ya\ *va* iyute·wa·kiya 1 : to cause to measure 2 : to adjust, arrange 3 : to appoint

i·yu·te·pa \i-yú-te-pa\ *vn* [fr *yutepa* wear off] : to be worn out by anything

i·yu·te·pi·ca·šni \i-yú-te-pi-ca-šni\ *adj* : unmeasuable, immense, fathemless - P

i·yu·te·ya \i-yú-te-ya\ *va* iyute·wa·ya — *adv* : by measure

i·yu·ti·tan \i-yú-ti-taŋ\ *n* : a tug or double-tree — *va* i·blu·titan [fr *yutitan* to pull] : to pull by — *vn* : to be stretched or pulled by — **iyutitan·yan** *adv* : stretched by

i·yu·tku·ge \i-yú-tku-ge\ *n* : something with which to fasten or lock, a key

i·yu·ton \i-yú-toŋ\ *va* i·blu·ton : to grease, as a hide when it is to be tanned - Bl

i·yu·tu·tka·ya·kel \i-yú-tu-tka-ya-kel\ *adv* : partly and imperfectly < ~ *econ* to do partly > - LP

i·yu·wan·ka \i-yú-waŋ-ka\ *adv* : up < *Wicaša num wicakico na wihuta yujunpi na ~ eglepi* He called two men who raised the tipi's lower border and placed it up. >

i·yu·wa·šte \i-yú-wa-šte\ *v* i·blu·wašte [fr *yuwašte* to bless] : to make good, benefit by means of — *n* : something that benefits, a benefit

i·yu·we·ga \i-yú-we-ga\ *va* i·blu·wega : to pass through, to cross or ford *e.g.* a stream

i·yu·weh \i-yú-weh\ *va contrac of* iyuwega : to pass through < ~ *iyaye* to ford a stream > — **iyuwe·hya** *adv* : crossing, fording

i·yu·wi \i-yú-wi\ *vn* : to curl, twist, as a vine or curled wood — *n* : anything twisted or tied, a vine — **iyuwi-cola** *adj* : not bandaged or dressed, as a sore — *n* : anything not twisted or tied

i·yu·win \i-yú-wiŋ\ *n* : remuneration, pay - Note: the more proper word is spelled *iyunwin which Cf*

i·yu·win·ška·la·ke s'e \i-yú-wiŋ-ška-la-ke s'e\ *adv* or *interj of anger or disgust at what is said or done by another* : How frightful it is said! - Bl WHL

i·yu·win·škaš *or* **iyuwinška** \i-yú-wiŋ-škaš\ *exclam interj said with a reproving tone* : For heaven's sake! < ~ *taku wan okihi wacinpi he kapi* For heaven's sake! They meant they tried something they were able, *i.e.* for a long time. > - *Syn* ICINYUNŠKAŠ

i·yu·wi·ya \i-yú-wi-ya\ *adv* : tangled, in a snarl, as hair or thread

i·yu·za \i-yú-za\ *va* i·blu·za [fr *yuza* to seize] : to hold on or to, to put the hand on and hold < *nape* ~ to lay hands on, *i.e.* to be in one's power > — **iyuze** *n* : something with which to hold, a holder, handle; something with which to take out, a ladle - B.H.42.20

i·yu·zi·gzil \i-yú-zi-gzil\ *v contrac red* [fr *yuzica* to stretch] : to stretch < *Oyaya kin yuakagal ~ okatanpi* The limbs were nailed outstretched. > - Cf yuzigzica B.H. 265.22

i·yu·zi·ya \i-yú-zi-ya\ *adv* : partly in sight, as is said of anything seen over a hill — **iyuzi·ziya** *adv red* : in sight

i·za·ptan \i-zá-ptaŋ\ *adj* : the fifth — **izaptan·ptan** *adj red* : every fifth one

i·ze·ze·ya \i-zé-ze-ya\ *adv* : dangling < *Taku ~ ikoyake* It stuck to what was dangling. >

i·zi·gzi·ta \i-zí-gzi-ta\ *vn red* izigzi·lwa·ya izi·lwa·ya [fr *izita* to smoke] : to smoke, as from something burning < *Ehanl ~ na ungna yuile* It smoked at the time and I do not know but that he set it afire. > - Note: the *contrac* form seems to be used in the conjugation of the word Cf izita

i·zil \i-zíl\ *vn contrac of* izita : to smoke — **izil·ton** *va* izi·lwa·ton: to make a smoke, to smoke anything

i·zil·ya \i-zí-lya\ *va* izi·lwa·ya : to cause to smoke *e.g.* a deer skin, to incense < *Na wanna wizilya eya icu na ~ . Taku waštemna waštehce kin izilyapi* And he took and offered incense and incensed it. What was a delightful odor was made to smoke. > - B.H.61.2

i·zi·ta \i-zí-ta\ *vn* : to smoke, as a prairie fire or a firebrand, or fat held over a fire — *va perhaps* : to smoke something, holding it in smoke < *Pa gegeya otkeyapi na ohlate cetipi na pa izitapi. Wakeya wan lila tanka ca etanhan šota izitahe* They hung up dangling the head, and beneath it a fire was set, and the head was smoked. It was giving off smoke from the very large tent. > - D.47

i·zo \i-zó\ *n* : an upland plain that is a peninsula - R Bl

i·zu·ya·pi \i-zú-ya-pi\ *n* : the Palledium of an expedition, sometimes a pipe, other times an animal's skin, carried by Dakotas when going off to war

i·zu·za \i-zú-za\ *n* : a large, rough whetstone for the grinding of axes *etc* - Note: the *míogle* is used to sharpen knives, which Cf

J

ja \ja\ *a language root e.g. yujá* to mix or make mush
jag \jag\ *adj contrac of* játa : forked
ja·gja·lya *or* **jagjalya·kel** \ja-gjá-lya\ *adv red of* jalyá *and* játa : forkedly, doubly < ~ *wanyanka* to have double vision, *i.e.* to see one thing multiplied by a defect of the eyes, as at time in old age, ~ *wakita* to look seeing things doubly from bad eyes >
ja·gja·ta \ja-gjá-ṫa\ *adj red of* játa : forked, rough
ja·han \ja-háŋ\ *adj* : rough, harsh, making loud noice, as an animal might do < *ho* ~ a gruff voice > — **jahan-han** *adj* : rough, unpleasant, grating < *Hojáhanhan* Its voice was grating. >
ja·he·s'e \ja-hé-s'e\ *adv* : noisily, unpleasantly < ~ *apa* to strike making a loud noise, ~ *ia* to speak hoarsely >
ja·he·ya \ja-hé-ya\ *adv* : roughly, harshly, not melodiously, as said of the voice < ~ *ia* to speak with a mellow voice > - Bl
ja·ja \ja-ja\ *a language root red* - Cf yujája
ja·ja·han \ja-já-haŋ\ *vn* : to be in need of washing < *Unkcela heca waksin na on apawinta ca he tohinni jajahe šni* It was cactus he cut, and so (the painted hide) he had rubbed on was never in need of washing. > - MS.482
ja·ja·ya \já-ja-ya\ *adv* : clearly, plainly < *jájayehci* very plainly > — **jajaye·la** *adv* : clearly, distinctly < ~ *wanyanka* to see accurately >
ja·ka \já-ka\ *adj* : rolling or straining, as the eyes
jal \jal\ *adj contrac of* játa : forked — **ja·lya** \ja-lyá\ *adv* : forkedly < ~ *wiyukcan* to be of two minds, to be undecided >
jan·jan \jaŋ-jáŋ\ *n* : a vial, a bottle, a glass of any kind; window glass < ~ *okášleca* or ~ *okábleca* pieces of broken glasses or bottles , ~ *wakšica* a drinking glass > — **janjan·la** *adj perhaps* : clear, transparent, as glass beads < *pšitó* ~ transparent beads > — **janjan·yela** *adv* : clearly, distinctly < ~ *wanyanka* to see distinctly >
ja·ta \jă'-ṫa\ *adj* : forked, as a stick or stream or road
je·na *or* **šena** \jé-na\ *adj* : having used up - Cf šena
ji \ji\ *adj* : thin and bristly, as the hair on the hands and arms, and as on a young duck < *išpá ji* a thin bristly elbow, *héji* thin or frail horns >
ji·a·le·pa *or* **tajiagnunpa** \ji-á-le-pa\ \ta-jí-a-gnun-pa\ *n* : the meadow lark - BE Wo
ji·ca \jí-ca\ *adj* ma·jíca : rich < *Jicinicagelo* You've grown rich, as they say to a man who watches everywhere that nothing be wasted or spoiled. > — **jica·ka** \ji-cá-ka\ *adj* ma·jicaka : rich
ji·ji \ji-jí\ *v* wa·jiji : to whisper — **jiji·lowan** *v* jiji-·wa·lowan : to sing in a low whispering, drawling manner
ji·ji·ya \ji-jí-ya\ *adv red of* jíya : standing up, as the hair on one's hands

ji·ji·ya·han \ji-jí-ya-haŋ\ *adv* : whispering
ji·la \jí-la\ *adj* : thin and bristly, as hair
ji·lya \ji-lyá\ *va* ji·lwa·ya : to make rich — **ji·lyeca** \ji-lyé-ca\ *va* ji·lwa·yeca : to make rich
jin \jiŋ\ *vn* ma·jin : to stand erect, stiffen up, as is said of a man's penis
jin·ca \jíŋ-ca\ *vn* wa·jinca : to blow out from the nose, to blow the nose, snuff up; to hiss perhaps < ~ *yo* Blow (your nose)! >
jinl·hin·gla \jíŋl-hiŋ-gla\ *v* jinl·ma·hingla [fr *jinca* to blow out + *hingla* done suddenly] : to whistle, pushing air out suddenly < *Cokan inajin na ungnahela jinlhingni na tokanl ipsica* It stood in the center, and all at once it blew and jumped somewhere else. > - SI
ji·pa \jí-ṗa\ *v* : to smoothen, clear off — **jipa·han** *and* **jipa·heca** \ji-ṗá-haŋ\ *part* : becoming smooth or hollowed out of itself
ji·ya \jí-ya\ *adv* : thin and standing up, as hair; thinly scattered and sparkling in the sunbeams
ji·ya·han \ji-yá-haŋ\ *adv perhaps* : whispering, soft, with a subdued voice < ~ *lowan.* ~ *cekiya* to sing softly, to pray for one in a low voice > — **jiyahan·lowan** *v* : to sing in a low, whispering, drawling manner, as while practising - *Syn* ḢWAYELA LOWAN
ji·ye·la \ji-yé-la\ *adv* : thinly, sparcely, as the hair on the hands
jo \jō\ *v* wa·jo : to whistle, as a man does — **jo·hoton** \jo-hō'-toŋ\ *v* : to whistle, as birds — **johoton·la** *n* : the bobwhite, whose call is like whistling to somebody (*jo*) - *Syn* PAKÓŠKALA
jo·jo \jō'-jo\ *v red* wa·jójo [fr *jo* to whistle] : to whistle for a while, to whistle for — **jojo·lowan** \jo-jó-lo-waŋ\ *v* jojó·wa·lowan : to whistle a tune
jo·jo·ya·gton \jo-jó-ya-gtoŋ\ *v* : to make a loop, noose, or a lasso — *adv* : in a noose < ~ *icu* to make it into a noose > — **jojoya·ke** *n* : a noose or slip-knot - R Bl
jo·lo·wan \jo-ló-waŋ\ *v* wa·jolowan : to whistle a tune — **jolowan·wan** *v* : to whistle a tune < ~ *nanke lo* You were sitting whistling a tune. >
jo·to·kte \jo-tó-kte\ *v* [fr *šóta* smoke + *okte* a killing] : to suffer from smoke, be affected by smoke < *Išta jotomakte yelo, wipapiya po* My eyes suffer from smoke (blinding them), open up the smoke flaps! >
ju \ju\ *v* wa·ju : to root; to put, place, lay up - Cf ojú — **ju·ju** \jú-ju\ *v* : to pay off, break up - Cf kajuju
ju·ju·wa·han \ju-jú-wa-haŋ\ *part* : broken, fallen to pieces, as a house; to become loose
jun \juŋ\ *v* : to pull out - Cf yujun
ju·ton \ju-tóŋ\ *v* ju·wa·ton : to fill one's self with food - Bl

K

k \k\ *pref* – it makes the *poss* form of *v* commencing with "p", *e.g.* *pagan* to part with becomes *kpagan* which means to part with one's own

[1]**ka** \k̇a\ *interrog partic, placed at the end of the question* — *art* : the < *Tokel cin ka lecel un wicaši* He bade them conduct themselves as he thus wished. *Inš toka tokeca wanji unkapepi kte ka* A-a-a, shall we lay in wait for another enemy? *Tokantanhan oniciyakapi ka?* Does he speak to you with some one else's authority? *Ito, tuwa icu ka* Let's see, who gets it? *Ito, Elias u na eglaku ka yanke* Well now, is Elias to come and take back his own? *Canke hecel omani ka ...* While he traveled thus, ... *Tohanl iyokipi ka can kakišwicayahe* When he was pleased then he was causing them suffering. *Cunkš, tohan yacin ka lel un wo* Daughter, stay here as long as you like. *Wacin ka yunkanš ehannihci cacipapakta tka ye lo* And so I adesired quite a long time ago to have surpassed you. *Toki yacin ka ya ye* Please go somewhere you want. > – B.H.133.14, 198.3, 242.2, 266.4, 268.4, 318, 87 D.60, 71, 98

[2]**ka** \k̇a\ *pref* – it makes a class of *v* whose action is performed by striking, as with the hand or with an axe, club or other instrument, or by the action of the wind or water, but note: *pron* of the *v* are prefixed

[3]**ka** \ka\ *suff* – attached to *v* and *n*, in most cases it does not seem materially to alter the meaning, yet it seems that "ka" *emph* a word that a thing is done well, or is a very good thing or done by all. It makes a *v* into a *n*. < *Na wanna wagliyagli na wowiyuškinka na toeyaš tohanl wicaakih'an kin ake wonic'upi kta keyapelo, eya* And I went and returned, there was real joy, but first he said: when they were starving, they stated that he would again give you food. > — **ka** \ka\ *adv neg suff* : not – Note: attached to words is the equivalent of *šni* not. It may be used ironically, as *wašte* good, *wašteka* not good; *ota* many: *otaka, otašni conala* few: conalaka, conalašni < *Ota tase heca ka* Sad to say it is not that much. > These are all indicative of the *neg.* *Otan'inka* may be used in the sense of *otan'inšni* not appearing, not manifest. < *Taku otan'inka*, or *Taku wan otan'inšni* There is no news. Or *Taku onspeka* There is no learning. *Taku isanp kokipepicaka* What further fear should I have than that? > — *adv pos suff* : almost < *T'aka* or perhaps *Tka* He almost died. *Hinhpayaka* He almost fell down. > — **ka** *and* **laka** \ka\ *adv* : rather, pretty much < *Wicaša tanktanka ka unpi* Men were rather very big. *Juda oyate kin waptanyanpi ka* The Jewish people were rather lucky. *Le kagišnišni oh'anke lah* He rather did this more so just as he pleased. > – R B.H.179.18, 222.4, 111.16, 143 D.103 Bl

[4]**ka** \k̇a\ *va* or *vt* wa·ka ci·ca : to mean, signify, take for, consider; to ask for, demand < *He wake* That is what I mean. *oyate taku kapi* the people in question *Ic'ice ki (kin)* He means himself. *Šunka mayaki yelaka* Evidently am I a dog that you come to me? >

[5]**ka** \k̇a\ *adv* : there, yonder < *Tohanl iyokipi ka can kakišwicaye* When he was pleased there he caused them to suffer. > –B.H.76.14

[6]**ka** \k̇a\ *dem pron* : that yonder, there – Note: the *pl* form is *kaná*. The word is used when the thing spoken of is not quite close, when we use *le*; the tree yonder *kacáŋ*, the house there < *Katipi wan tanka he kin he untipi ca el ungni kte lo. Ito, ka cik'ala imakih'an yo* Let us start to go to that large house where we live. Now then, he meant "Cook me a little bit." > – Gramm.23

ka·a·be·ya \k̇a-á-be-ya\ *adv* : scattered, as horses < ~ *iyaya* to go on scattering >

ka·a·blel iyeya \k̇a-á-blel i-yè-ya\ *v* : to scatter by striking < *kaablel yeyá* to scatter, as one's hair by loosening one's braids *Yunkan witanšna un k'on nupin kaablel yeyapi* And then that virgin's both braids were loosed. >

ka·a·gla·pšin *or* **kaaglapšin·yan** \k̇a-á-bla-pšiŋ\ *adv* : bottom side up, turned over < ~ *ihpeya* to throw upside down >

ka·a·i·yo·hpe·ya \k̇a-á-i-yo-ḣpe-ya\ *adv* : down-hill, down a steep descent

ka·a·ko·ki·ya \k̇a-á-ko-ki-ya\ *adv* : in another direction, another way < *Wanbli wan ~ kinyan iyaya* And eagle went on flying in another direction. > – MS.574

ka·a·o·ptel \k̇a-á-o-ṗtel\ *v contrac of* kaaopteca (this form is unknown) : to be less than < ~ *econ* to do less than > — **kaaopte·tu** \k̇a-á-o-apṫe-tu\ *v* : to lessen < ~ *econ* to do less, or make it less > — **kaaoptetu·ya** *adv* : in the way of diminishing — **kaaoptetuya·kel** \k̇a-á-o-pṫe-tu-ya-k̇el\ *adv* : diminishingly – BD WHL

ka·a·pa·ma·gle *or* **kaapamagle·ya** \k̇a-á-pa-ma-gle\ *adv* : sloping down- hill, gently sloping

ka·a·ta·kin·yan \k̇a-á-ta-kiŋ-yaŋ\ *adv* : leaning

ka·a·ta·ku·ni·šni \k̇a-á-ta-k̇u-ni-šni\ *va* : to destroy by striking

ka·a·ya \k̇a-á-ya\ *va* wa·káaya unka·aya·pi : to be taking to one

ka·a·ya·skab \k̇a-á-ya-sk̇ab\ *adv* : clinging to or touching < ~ *inajin* to lean on, cling to, standing touching one > – Bl

ka·bla \k̇a-blá\ *va* wa·kábla : to cut meat thin for drying, as Lakota women do, to slice up — **kabla·blapi** \k̇a-blá-bla-ṗi\ *n* : the preparing meat for drying by slicing thin, hence, slices – Cf wakablapi P

ka·bla·ga \k̇a-blá-ġa\ *v* : to spread out, as a bird does its wings — **kablah** \k̇a-blaḣ\ *v contrac* : to unfurl < ~ *iyeya* to quickly unfurl >

ka·bla·ja \k̇a-blá-ja\ *va* wa·kablaja : to spread open, as the legs, to straddle < *Kablaje s'e iyunka* He lay down as though straddling, *i.e.* indicating perhaps tiredness. > – Bl

ka·bla·pi \k̇a-blá-pi\ *n* : something cut up in slices or thin pieces, as meat for drying

ka·blas \k̇a-blás\ *va contrac of* kablaza : to rip open

ka·bla·ska \k̇a-blá-ska\ *va* wa·kablaska : to flatten by beating, to make flat by striking, as a leaden bullet, or as done with an axe; to hew

ka·bla·ski·ya \k̇a-blá-ski-ya\ *va* kabla·swa·kiya : to cause to rip of burst open

ka·blaš \k̇a-bláš\ *va contrac of* kablaja : to spread apart < ~ *inajin* to straddle or stand astride anything > — **kabla·šya** *va* kabla·šwa·ya : to cause to straddle

ka·bla·ya \k̇a-blá-ya\ *va* wa·kablaya : to make level by beating *e.g.* a holy place — *vn* : to open, as the eyes of a young dog for its first sight – LB

ka·bla·za \k̇a-blá-za\ *va* wa·káblaza : to make rip open or burst by striking or throwing down, as a ball by striking

ka·ble·ble·ca \k̇a-blé-ble-ca\ *va red* wa·kablebleca : to break to pieces — **kable·blel** \k̇a-blé-blel\ *va red contrac* : to break into pieces

ka·ble·ble·si·c'i·ya \k̇a-blé-ble-si-c'i-ya\ *v refl* : to rest one's mind by walking around after hard work < *Kableblesmic'iyin kte* I took a break walking about. > – *Syn* KAZILIC'IYA MG

ka·ble·ca \k̇a-blé-ca\ *va* wa·kableca : to break something brittle by striking *e.g.* glass — **kablel** \k̇a-blél\ *v contrac of* kableca : to throw down and break to pieces < ~ *iyeya* to break by striking, ~ *ihpeya* to throw down and break into pieces, *peji kinhan* ~ to tromp down the grass *Najinpi ktelo* They (the horses) must stand, as is said of them when hay in plentiful to eat. ~ *hingni kte* He will be crushed. > — **kablel·kiya** \k̇a-blél-k̇i-ya\ *va* kablel·wa·kiya : to cause to break - Bl B.H.240.13

[1]**ka·blel·ya** \k̇a-blé-lya\ *va* : to cause to break to pieces

[2]**ka·ble·lya** \k̇á-ble-lya\ *adv* : scattered, loosened < *Pehin* ~ *škatapi* They play with their hair loosened. >

ka·bles \k̇a-blés\ *vn contrac of* kableza : to clear off — **kables·glepi s'e** *adv* : distinctly, clearly < ~ *un* It clearly is. *anpetu* ~ *a* clear day, *i.e.* without any mist *Tohunhunniyan k'eyaš* ~ *unpi šni* But clearly they did not live forever. > — **kable·sya** *va* : to cause to be clear, to clear off, as the wind does fog - Bl

ka·ble·za \k̇a-blé-za\ *vn* : to become clear, clear off, as fog clears away < *Anpó* ~ . *Ecel anpa na kableze el koškalaka k'on inapin na leya ...* A morning star became clear. So when there was daylight and it broke, that young man came out and this he said... > — **kableze-šni** *vn* : to be still foggy or dark, *i.e.* before the day dawns — *va* wa·kablezešni : to strike and make frantic

ka·blo·blo \k̇a-bló-blo\ *v red* : to hit hard many times, hence perhaps to cause swellings by striking - Bl D. 196 B.H.68.16

ka·blu \k̇a-blú\ *va* wa·káblu : to pound fine, to pulverize, to strike *e.g.* ground *etc* < *Na makoce kin ataya kahminpi na kablupi* The entire countryside was struck and misshapened. > — **kablu·blu** *v red* : to strike over and over again — **kablu·kiya** \k̇a-blú-k̇i-ya\ *va* kablu·wa·kiya : to cause to make fine — **kablu·pi** *n* : something fine, as powdered sugar — **kablu·ya** *va* : to cause to make fine

ka·bu \k̇a-bú\ *va* : to beat, as on a drum < *Cancega kin kabupi* They beat the drum. > — **kabu·bu** *v red* wa·kabubu : to beat often — **kabubu·ya** *adv red of* kabuya : knocking — **kabu·ya** *adv* : striking, knocking

ka·ca \k̇a-cá\ *neg suff* : not < *Okihi kaca* He cannot do it. > — *vn* : to be like, fitting, proper, worthy - Note: the word is often used as a *v* , thus the meaning *hececa, i.e. he + iyececa* - B.H.62.13

ka·can \k̇a-cáŋ\ *va* wa·kacan : to shake, clear by shaking; to sift — *vn* : to shiver < *Óblula wanice ca unkacanpi kte lo* We'll be shivering since it (the house) is without weather-proof. *Wakacanhelo* I was shivering, as would be said while one moved his body and drew his clothing tighter for feeling cold. > — **kacan·can** *vn red* : to trot, as does a horse — *va red* wa·kácancan : to clean by shaking, as in sifting, to shake — **kacancan·yan** *and* **kacancanye·la** *adv* : shaking, shivering with cold - Bl

ka·can·gle·gle·ya \k̇a-káŋ-gle-gle-ya\ *v* : to roll a wheel, to turn cart-wheels < *Húnpe kacanglegleyapi s'e inyankelo* His turnip stick (*i.e.* his leg) went running as though it were turning cart-wheels. > - Bl

ka·can·gle i·ye·ya \k̇a-cáŋ-gle- i-yè-ya\ *v* : to throw something round, as a hoop, and thus make it go on, as in a game

ka·can·he \ka-cáŋ-he\ *v* wa·kacanhe : to shake with the cold

ka·canl \k̇a-cáŋl\ *v* : to move the heart to sadness or to gladness < *Cante* ~ *šice* His heart moved toward sadness. *Cante* ~ *wašte* His heart moved with gladness, *fig* to sift as flour. >

ka·can·lab i·ye·ya *or* **kacanlwašte iyeya** \k̇a-cáŋ-lab i-yè-ya\ *v* : to cheer one up - Bl

ka·caš \k̇a-cáš\ *interrog of doubt or hesitation* : What then? *or* What of it? < *Tase, le ciciyuha* ~ *, hanke cicu ka* Of course not! What then, am I to keep this for you, when I received from you but a part? > - Note: the less detailed *interrog* interest in: *Waštekaca* It is not good R Gramm. 361(3)

Ka·ce·gu Un \K̇a-cé-ġu Uŋ\ *np* [fr *kacegu* short-coated] : a Congregationalist, a christian group - Sw

ka·ce·gya \k̇a-cé-gya\ *adv* : staggering, in a staggering manner < ~ *mani* to walk staggering >

ka·cek \k̇a-cék\ *va red of* kaceka : to stagger something < ~ *iyeya* to make stagger by striking > — **kaceka** \k̇a-cé-k̇a\ *va* wa·káceka : to strike and make stagger — **kace·kcegya** *adv red of* kacegya : staggering — **kace-kcek** \k̇a-cē'-kcēk\ *va red contrac of* kaceka : to be staggering <~ *najin* to stand unsteadily, ~ *ya* to go staggering > — **kacekce·ka** *vt* and *vi* ma·kácekceka [fr *kaceka* to light a stunning blow] : to stagger < *Tate waš'akelo on makacekcekelo. Mahunkešni ca makacekceke* I staggered because of the strong wind. I staggered since I was very feeble. > - D.119, 114

ka·cel \k̇a-cél\ *partic postp* indicating uncertainty *tan'in-šni* < *Tokel ... ekta mni kte* ~ Howsoever ... I shall go to a place, *tuwa* ~ someone or other > - B.H.147.7, 222.7

ka·ce·sli·sli \k̇a-cé-sli-sli\ *v* : to go along with a bounce and a sway < ~ *s'e mani* to walk as though with a bounce and a sway, *i.e.* weak-kneed > - Bl

ka·ce·ya \k̇a-cé-ya\ *va* wa·káceya [fr *ceya* to cry] : to make cry by striking

ka·ci·ca \k̇a-cí-ca\ *va archaic* wa·kácica : to soften and smoothen *e.g.* a hide or a plowed field, giving it a finishing touch by rubbing with a tool, or a harrow - RF Bl WHL

ka·ci·k'a·la \k̇a-cí-k'a-la\ *va* wa·kacik'ala [fr *cik'ala* little] : to make small by chopping off — **kacik'a·yela** *va* [fr *cik'ayela* small, pent up] : to make small by striking — **kaci·scila** *va* : to make small by cutting

ka·co·co \k̇a-có-co\ *va* wa·kácoco : to mix up, as eggs, to beat up

ka·co·za \k̇a-có-za\ *va* : to make warm by striking - R

ka·e \k̇á-e\ *pron express* : that is he

ka·e·ce·tu \k̇a-é-ce-tu\ *va* wa·kaecetu : to make right or accomplish by striking

ka·e·han \k̇a-é-haŋ\ *adv* : before that event takes place - Note: the word is somewhat like *kohan* meanwhile < ~ *migluwinyeya kte* I shall get ready beforehand. *Winyan kin t'in kte kin heon* ~ *canwognaka ikignipi kte* They will hunt for a coffin before because the lady will die. > - M

ka·e·kta·wa·pa·ya \k̇a-é-kta-wa-pa-ya\ *adv perhaps* : far < ~ *laka ca kohan miye wapami kte hcelo* Since it must be far, meanwhile I shall move away slowly indeed. >

ka·eš \k̇a-éš\ *pron express emph* : that one < *Wanjila* ~ *el unpi šni* Not one of them was in. *Hee* ~ *hi šni* That is the one that did not come, *i.e.* the one expected did not come or appear. >

ka·e·tu·la·ke el \k̇a-é-tu-la-ke el\ *adv phr* : in a little while < ~ *peji owayašla kin wanil aye* In a short while the pasture full of grass died out. > - *Syn* TOKŠA B.H.11.2

\a\ father \e\ they \i\ machine \o\ smoke \u\ lunar \an, aŋ\ blanc Fr. \in, iŋ\ ink \on, oŋ, un, uŋ\ soon, confier Fr. \c\ chair \ġ\ machen Ger. \j\ fusion \clusters: bl, gn, kp, hšl, etc...\ b[e]lo ... said with a slight vowel
See more in the Introduction, Guide to Pronunciation

ka·e·ya·ya \ka-é-ya-ya\ *vt* wa·káeblabla [fr *eyaya* take along] : to have taken something belonging to another, to have carried away < *Unkcekiha wan wososo ~ c'on iyatap ye* The strip of meat a magpie had carried away was chewed away at. > – D.73

ka·ga \ká-ġa\ *va* wa·kága : to make, form, execute, to cause to be, to be the cause or author of — **kage yuza** \ka-ġé yu-zà\ *v express* : to take hold of me, perhaps – Bl

ka·gab \ka-ġáb\ *v contrac of* kagapa : to make spread out, to lay open by cutting < *~ iyeya* to lay open > — **kaga·bya** *adv* : gaping open, as a wound

ka·ga·lga·ta \ka-ġa-lġa-ta\ *adv red of* kagata : to extend *e.g.* the hands

ka·gal hin·gle \ka-ġál hiŋ-glè\ *vn* kagal ma·hingle : to be disappointed suddenly in one's expectations, to throw up one's hands, *i.e.* with the idea of falling over on one's hands, perhaps < *Kagal hinglemayakiyelo* You are a total disappointment to me. > – Cf alos hingle BT B.H.38.4

ka·ga·lki·ya \ka-ġá-lki-ya\ *adv* : spread out, stretched out, as the hand or arm

ka·gan \ka-ġáŋ\ *vn* : to open, make an opening in, to come through, as the wind does through one's clothing, to open by itself or by the wind < *Tate kin ~ mahiyu. Wana maganganla ca ihanhan icaluza keš, ~ mahiyuwelo* The wind came through to me. Though it blew for a time when full of holes, it came through to me. > – R Bl PD

ka·gan·gan·yan \ka-ġaŋ-ġaŋ-yaŋ\ *adv red of* kaganyan : open — **kagan·yan** *adv* : open, spread out

ka·ga·pa \ka-ġá-pa\ *va* wa·kagapa : to cut, spread open by cutting, to lay open

ka·ga·ta \ka-ġá-ta\ *adv* : spread out, as the hands or fingers

ka·ga·tki·ya \ka-ġá-tki-ya\ *adv* – Note: this a variant spelling of *kagalkiya*

ka·ge \ka-ġé\ *va* wa·káge : to skim off *e.g.* cream from milk < *asanpi ~* to skim off milk >

ka·ge·ge \ka-ġé-ġe\ *va* wa·kagege **1** : to sew **2** *v red indicating repetition of the v attached* [perhaps fr *kage* to skim] < *~ icu* to take out repeatedly, *i.e.* by handfuls; to take out a handful is rendered *kage icu* > – Note: the word is not used alone

ka·gi \ka-gí\ *v* wa·kagi ma·kagi **a** : to stop one's progress, to be in one's way, as a river; not to be able to proceed **b** : to hold in esteem, to respect

ka·gi·ca *and* **kahica** \ka-ġí-ca\ *va* wa·kagica : to wake up by striking – D.26

ka·gin·lgin·ca \ka-ġíŋ-lġiŋ-ca\ *va* : to strike and make spit fumes, as it were – *Syn* KAJINKJINCA Bl

ka·gi·šni \ka-ġí-šni\ *adv* : without obstruction < *~ iyaye* to pass on without hindrance > — **kagišni·šni** *or* **kagišnišni·yan** *adv red* : not hindered, not influenced by any number of people present, doing as one pleases, without fear or regard for anything < *~ oh'an* to act without regard for anyone. *Unhcegila s'e ~ wala yelo* I regarded it without fear as if it were a mastodon. *~ woglaka* to talk without regard for others > – *Syn* WITONPEŠNI B.H.282.3

ka·gi·ya \ka-ġí-ya\ *va* kagi·wa·ya kagi·un·yan·pi : to hinder, obstruct, to make go slow, to bother < *Kagimayaya. Nihunkešni ni ca kagimayayin kta ca ni kte šni yelo, eya* You bother me. He said he means it is you who are sickly, so that you will be a hindrance to me, as said in *ref* to going to war. > —*adv* : hindering

[1]**ka·gla** \ka-glá\ *adv* : by the side of, nearby < *kaglalaka hwo?* Is it near? >

[2]**ka·gla** \ka-glá\ *va* wa·kagla [fr *agla* take home] : to take home to one < *He ~ yo* Take that home to him. > — *vn* : to unfold, to stretch out to full length, uncoil, as a snake or rope < *Wikan ~ . Šupe kin ~ hinhpaye* A leather thong uncoiled. The intestines fell and unravelled > – D.247

ka·gla·gla \ka-glá-ga\ *adv red* [fr *kagla* by the side of] : alongside of

ka·gla·kin·yan \ka-glá-kiŋ-yaŋ\ *adv* : sticking, perhaps sideways, from the side < *Tate ~ unglapi ktelo* We will have the wind from the side. > – Cf glakínyan

ka·gla·la \ka-glá-la\ *adv red of* kagla : nearby < *~ hiyaya yo* Come and go alongside. >

ka·gla·ya \ka-glá-ya\ *adv* : by the side of

ka·gle·ga *and* **kagle·glega** \ka-glé-ġa\ *va* wa·kaglega [fr *glega* spotted] **1** : to mark across, or to make figures, or stripes across by cutting **2** : to make rough

ka·gle·gle·za \ka-glé-gle-za\ *v red of* kagleza : to cut a mark across or around

ka·gle·pa \ka-glé-pa\ *va* : to make one vomit by striking on the back, as one in whose throat something got stuck — *vn* ma·kaglepa : to vomit on account of dizziness caused by rapid circular motions

ka·gle·za \ka-glé-za\ *va* wa·kagleza [fr *gleza* striped] : to mark across or around by cutting, to make in stripes or figures — **kagleze·la** *va* : to stripe, make striped – R

ka·gli \ka-glí\ *va* wa·kagli [fr *k(i)* to + *agli* bring home] : to bring home to one < *Wanna wašin wan yapa ~ ške'* Now they say he brought home a piece of fat held in his mouth. >

ka·glog \ka-glóg\ *va contrac of* kagloka : to put out of joint < *~ iyeya* suddenly to knock out of joint >

ka·glo·glo \ka-gló-glo\ *v red* [fr *ka* striking + *glo* to grunt] : to hit hard in anger, to make howl

kaglo-glo·ka *va red of* kagloka : to shake *e.g.* in the way an old wagon-box or wagon jars one riding in it – Bl

ka·glo·ka \ka-gló-ka\ *va* wa·kagloka : to put out of joint by striking — *vn perhaps* : to make a misstep, thus feeling pain but without a dislocation, *i.e. kapšun* < *Tahuka ~* He stumbled over a buffalo hide. >

ka·gmi\ka-gmí\ *va* wa·kágmi **a** : to cut all down, to clear away, as timber, grass *etc* **b** : to hoe – R

ka·gmi·gma \ka-gmí-gma\ *va* wa·kagmigma : to make round by striking or rolling — *vn perhaps* : to roll along < *Tapa kin le wankayewaya kin hehan kuta ~ iyaye ci, kuwapi kte lo* They will chase after this ball once I throw it high up then goes rolling down. >

ka·gmi·pi s'e \ka-gmí-pi s'e\ *adv* : as though cut all down, slash-cut < *~ yankapi* They have nothing whatsoever left, entirely poor. > – Note: the *syn express: Keye cola yankapi* He stated they were destitute – Bl

ka·gmi·yan·yan \ka-gmí-yaŋ-yaŋ\ *va* wa·kagmiyanyan : to make roll by striking, as a ball *esp* in playing games

ka·gmun \ka-gmúŋ\ *v* wa·kagmun : to spin or twist with the extended hand

ka·gna \ka-gná\ *va* wa·kagna : to shake off by striking *e.g.* corn, striking off the kernels, or fruit, from a tree

ka·gna·yan \ka-gná-yaŋ\ *va* wa·kagnayan [fr *gnayan* to cheat] : to miss partly while striking, as in splitting wood and striking off a little piece

ka·go \ka-ġó\ *va* wa·kago **1** : to draw a line, *i.e.* on land, as a reservation line, to mark, make marks, cuts, or gashes **2** : to vaccinate

ka·go·go \k̇a-ġó-ġo\ *va red* : to make marks, to gash

ka·go·pa \k̇a-ġó-ṗa\ *va* wa·kagopa [fr *ka* striking + *gopa* to snore] : to strike one asleep, to wake partly up and make snore

ka·gug \k̇a-ġúg\ *va contrac of* kaguka : to lengthen a little by striking

ka·gu·ka \k̇a-ġú-ka\ *va* wa·kaguka : to sprain or strain *e.g.* a tendon, to lengthen a little by striking – R

ka·gwa \ka·gwá\ *v* : to bruise one, to strike and skin < ~ *iyeya* to bruise suddenly, ~ *iyemayayelo* You bruised me of a sudden. > – Bl

ka·gwe·za \ka-gwé-za\ *va* wa·kagweza : to make rough by striking – Bl

ka·gwu \k̇a-gwú\ *v* wa·kagwu : to make curdle, thick, by striking or moving

ka·gye·la \ka-gyé-la\ *adv* : rattling, like an old wagon *etc*

ka·han \k̇a-háη\ *adv* : to this, thus far < ~ *niš toka hwo?* Is there anything the matter with you to date? > – Note: the word is used when one is pointing at the same time, as in saying: "He emptied the bottle so far." *See* ehan, lehan, kehan, iyehan — **kahan·han** *or* **kahanhan·keca** *or* **ka-hanhan·yan** *adv red* : thus far — **kahan·keca** \k̇a-háη-k̇e-ca\ *adv perhaps* : to this, thus far, so long — **kahanl** *adv* : to or at this, thus far — **kahan·tu** \k̇a-háη-ṫu\ *adv* : to that, so far, so long < ~ *kinhan* it be-ing so long > — **kahantu·k'e** *or* **kahantuk'el** *adv* : now then < ~ *katkaηhanyan wiyukcan po* Now then, think well. > — **kahantu·ya** *adv* : so far — **kahan·yan** *adv* : thus far <~ *inajin yo* Stand up thus far. > — **kahanyan-ka** *adv* : some distance off, as in counting relationship — **kahan·yela** *adv* : only so far, only so long – P Bl

ka·ha·ye·ya \k̇a-há-ye-ya\ *v* : to go away, leave < *Hihanna kin kaháyewayin kte* I shall leave tomorrow. > – Note: R gives *kaha iyeya* < *Wana kaha iyeya po* Leave now! which is said when they prepared to go and are now ready, being said by the leader or one of the group > – Bc Bl Rb

ka·he·kta·ki·ya \k̇a-hé-kta-k̇i-ya\ *adv* : backwards < ~ *kacekcekapi* They staggered backwards. > – B.H.256.11

ka·he·pi·ya \k̇a-hé-pi-ya\ *adv and perhaps n* : on the side of < *Canku kin he ~ hpaya* That road goes along the hill, *i.e.* on it. *Yunkan ~ wan el taku wan hpaya* Then something lay along on the hill-side. > – MS.160

ka·hi \ka-hí\ *va* wa·kahi [fr *ahi* to bring] **1** : to bring to one, to arrive bringing something to one < *Le cik'ala cicicahi ye. Pte kin ataya iwicunkahpelo* I brought you this little one. We fell everyone of the buffalo, *i.e.* we bunched them up. > **2** : to stir, to rummage

ka·hi·hi·ya \k̇a-hí-hi-ya\ *adv* : moving, wafting one's way along, as a fish's fins in water, or as feathers in the wind < *Huyé* or *Hoiyé, hoapeša wan mini ceteta ape ~ nunke, le uciciye* Come now, you red-fin fish, who lie waiting and wafting your way at the bottom of the water, I would have you come now, so a person would say when throwing out a line to catch fish. > – Bl

ka·hi·hi·ye·la \k̇a-hí-hi-ye-la\ *adj* : thickly covered < *Peji kin ~ yunke* The grass lay thick, *i.e.* much grass. > – Bl

ka·hin·hpe·ya \k̇a-híη-ȟpe-ya\ *va* : to run over something, to make fall over or down, to overthrow < *Na wasabglepi kin he ~ glicupi. Hecena ~ iyaya na kte* And they got off and knocked down the land markers that were set up. In the end he went running over them and put an end to them. > – MS.521

ka·hinl \k̇a-híηl\ *va contrac of* kahinta : to brush or sweep off or out < ~ *iyeya* to sweep out, ~ *ehpeya* They swept and threw things away >

ka·hin·ta \k̇a-híη-ṫa\ *va* wa·kahinta : to sweep or brush up, as a floor < *owan* ~ to sweep the floor >

ka·hin·tu ska \k̇a-híη-ṫu ska\ *adv* : sweeping clean < ~ *iyaya* to go by sweeping clean, as when the wind clears a place, sweeping it clean > – Bl

ka·hi·ya·ya \ka-hí-ya-ya\ *v* : to go through a tune, to sing a song or tune < *olowan* ~ to sing a song or hymn, *Hogluwankal olowan - . U na wanjila eša, i.e. olowan wan* (at least one) *unkicahiyayapi* He raised his voice to sing a song. He came and though it was but one, *i.e.* at least one song, we sang along. > – D.20 B.H.54.2

ka·ho·ho *or* **kahoho·la** \k̇a-hó-ho\ *va* wa·kahoho : to loosen something by striking, as a fence post, to strike and knock loose, as a torch or stick set in the ground < *Wihuta iyuha ~ po* Knock loose all lower tent borders, as is announced before breaking camp. >

ka·ho·mni \k̇a-hó-mni\ *va* wa·káhomni : to make something turn around by striking, as a top, to turn around, as a wheel by striking, to spin, as a top — **kahomni·mni** *va red* : to spin *e.g.* a top – B.H.87.17

ka·ho·ton \k̇a-hó-toη\ *va* wa·kahoton : to make animals cry, however not dogs, by striking *e.g.* pigs; to make howl by striking — **kahoton·ton** *va red* : to make an animal sqweal – Bl

ka·ho·wa \k̇a-hó-wa\ *v* : to make dogs howl by striking them

ka·hu·kul \k̇a-hú-k̇ul\ *adv* : down < ~ *iyeya* to put down by striking > — **kahuku·lwapa** *adv* : striking down

ka·hun\k̇a-húη\ *va* wa·káhun : to make a mark by striking with an axe

ka·hun·huns \k̇a-húη-huηs\ *va contrac of* kahunhunza : to shake by striking, thus ~ *iyeya* — **kahunhun·sya** *adv* : shaking < ~ *han* It stands shaking, >

ka·hun·hun·za \k̇a-húη-huη-za\ *va* wa·kahunhunza : to shake, make shake by striking, as a tree, or as the wind does trees — *vn* ma·káhunhunza : to be shaken, as on a wagon, rocking chair, *etc*

ka·hun·kun·za \k̇a-húη-kuη-za\ *va* : to pretend to strike with an axe

ka·hu·te \k̇a-hú-ṫe\ *va* wa·kahute : to wear to a stump by striking as with an axe — **kahute·la** *part perhaps* : worn to a stump

kah \k̇aȟ\ *v contrac of* káġa : to make < ~ *áya* to continue making >

ka·ȟa \k̇a-ȟá\ *va* wa·kaȟa : to curl, to knot, to roughen or notch by striking — *n* : a curl, a knot

ka·ȟab \k̇a-ȟáb\ *va contrac of* kaȟapa : to ride herd, to drive along *e.g.* horses or cattle < ~ *aya* They went together *e.g.* on a cattle drive. > — **kaȟa·bȟapa** \k̇a-ȟá-bȟa-ṗa\ *v red* : to beat against and make a rustling noise, as the wind blowing against grass

ka·ȟa·ȟa \k̇a-ȟá-ȟa\ *vn red of* kaȟa : to curl up, as a flame, to sparkle or send up sparks

ka·ȟa·pa \k̇a-ȟá-ṗa\ *va* wa·kaȟapa : to drive along, as a team or bunch of cattle, to drive, whip

ka·hci \k̇a-ȟcí\ *va* wa·kahci : to gap, to break a gap in something, as in the edge of an axe — **kahci·hci** *v red*

\a\ father \e\ they \i\ machine \o\ smoke \u\ lunar \an, aη\ blanc Fr. \in, iη\ ink \on, oη, un, uη\ soon, confier Fr. \c\ chair \ġ\ machen Ger. \j\ fusion \clusters: bl, gn, kp, hšl, etc...\ b^e^lo ... said with a slight vowel **See more in the Introduction, Guide to Pronunciation** wa·kahcihci : to break out gaps from the edge of an axe — **kahci·ya** *va* kahci·wa·ya : to cause to break a gap in an axe

ka·ȟeb \k̇a-ȟéb\ *va contrac of* kaȟepa : to bail or empty out < ~ *ihpeya* to empty by lading out > – Note: the word is used only of liquids

ka·ȟe·pa \k̇a-ȟé-ṗa\ *va* wa·kaȟepa : to bail or throw out, as water with the hand or a cup *etc* until it is all gone

ka·ȟe·ya·ta \k̇a-ȟé-ya-ṫa\ *adv* [fr *ȟeyata* on or to a ridge] : back on one side < ~ *iyeya* to shove or throw back or to one side >

ka·hka·ga \k̇a-ȟk̇á-ǧa\ *v* : to cough, belch, pretending to cough up something that got into the person by magic < *Yunkan heceglala unma k'on ~ . Na ake unma k'on he ~ na iš ake unma k'on econ.* And the one had belched only so much. And again another had belched, and again another had done it. > – Note: the sound of *kaȟ*

ka·hki·ya \k̇a-ȟk̇í-ya\ *va* ka·hwa·kiya : to cause to make < *Na canli wapahta kin hena kahkiyapi* And they had made those tobacco ties made. >

ka·hla \k̇a-ȟlá\ *va* wa·kahla : to make sound by striking, to ring *e.g.* a bell

ka·hla·gan \k̇a-ȟlá-ǧaŋ\ *vn* : to lengthen out, become long, to extend < ~ *yeya* to cause to extend to, *e.g.* to give away what has been given one > — **kahlah** \k̇a-ȟláȟ\ *vn contrac* : to extend < ~ *áya* It lengthens out. >

ka·hla·hla \k̇a-ȟlá-ȟla\ *v red* wa·kahlahla [fr *kahla* to ring] : to rattle perhaps

ka·hla·hla·gan \k̇a-ȟlá-ȟla-ǧaŋ\ *v red of* kahlagan : to become long — **kahlahlah** \k̇a-ȟlá-ȟlaȟ\ *v contrac of* kahlahlagan : to be lengthening — **kahlahla·hya** \k̇a-ȟlá-ȟla-ȟya\ *adv* : lengthening out < ~ *aya* to become long or lengthen out, as the days of the year >

ka·hla·ta \k̇a-ȟlá-ṫa\ *va* : to catch something with a sharp hook, as with a fish hook, or a hawk preying on an animal

ka·hla·te \k̇a-ȟlá-ṫe\ *adv* : below something < ~ *owák'a* I dug into it below. > — **kahlate·ya** *adv* : below, undermining perhaps < ~ *wak'a* I dug ground below. >

ka·hla·ya \k̇a-ȟlá-ya\ *va* kahla·wa·ya : to cause one to ring or sound — *vn* : to fall off, as a sticking plaster, to come off, as paint or paste or scales – D.248

ka·hla·ye·la \k̇á-ȟla-ye-la\ *adv* : causing to ring or sound something; *fig* one's full utterance being given < ~ *iyuha onspeciciyelo* I have taught you everything I know. > – Bl

ka·hle·ca \k̇a-ȟlé-ca\ *va* wa·kahleca : to tear open by striking, to split open, to fracture — **kahle·hleca** *va red* wa·kahlehleca : to break in *e.g.* the skull, to fracture — **kahlel** \k̇a-ȟlél\ *v contrac of* kahleca : to break in < ~ *iyeya* to fracture suddenly > — **kahle·lya** *va* kahle·lwa·ya : to cause to fracture

ka·hli \k̇a-ȟlí\ *vn* wa·kahli : to mire, stick in the mud — **kahli·hli** *v red* : to mire in mud — **kahli·ya** *va* kahli·wa·ya : to cause to mire – D.77

ka·hlo·ge·ca \k̇a-ȟló-ǧe-ca\ *adj* : poor, empty, hungry < *Hunhe, ~ yeyele* It's too bad, he does indeed go hungry continually, as a woman would say when a man asks for food continually. *Owipi woteȟi. ~ yewáyehcelo* He has trouble getting full. I'm continually getting hungry for sure, as one who eats endlessly. *Wan, lila wawata ška ~ yewayelo* Wow! They say I really eat, I'm continually getting hungry, *i.e.* I'm still hungry in spite of having eaten much. > – Bl

ka·hlo·go·štan·pi \k̇a-ȟló-ǧo-štaŋ-pi\ *n* : a vest, a garment made without sleeves

ka·hlo·gya \k̇a-ȟló-gya\ *va* kahlo·gwa·ya : to cause to make a hole in, to break into, as a burglar into a house < *Pahte kin kahlogmayehcelo* It has made a hole in my forehead, *i.e.* so cold has it been. > — *adv perhaps* : breaking a way in < *Pahte kin ~ wicatasakelo* Their foreheads were frozen the cold breaking its way in. > P Bl

ka·hlo·hlo·ka \k̇a-ȟló-ȟlo-k̇a\ *v red of* kahloka : to break a hole in – B.H.274.19

ka·hlok \k̇a-ȟlók\ *va contrac of* kahloka : to knock a hole in < ~ *iyeya* suddenly to knock a hole in, ~ *ya* to go on, *fig* without minding anything, *Unkigluštanpi na ~ unkigni ktelo* We shall start for home once we are finished *e.g.* with our work. *Kahlohlok iyaye ole* He looked for it in all directions. >

ka·hlo·ka \k̇a-ȟló-k̇a\ *va* : to break a hole in anything, to make a hole by striking, as with an axe or club into ice

ka·hlu·hla·ta \k̇a-ȟlú-ȟla-ta\ *adv* : hanging in abundance, drooping < ~ *hiyu* *e.g.* leaves coming out in abundance and drooping, ~ *hiyuic'iya* to burgeon and hang down, or *fig* to stand up and talk too often. ~ *ihpeic'iyapi* They threw themselves down at his feet. > – Note: *kah* and *yuhlata*, *kah* and *luhlata* WE

ka·hlu·hlul \k̇a-ȟlú-ȟlul\ *adv contrac* : hanging in abundance, drooping, hanging down – WHL

ka·hmi \k̇a-ȟmí\ *n* : an inside corner, a bend in a river, a bay, a point of land, *etc* – R

ka·hmin \k̇a-ȟmíŋ\ *va* wa·kahmin : to bend by striking

ka·hmun \k̇a-ȟmúŋ\ *va* wa·kahmun : to make buzz, to whirl and cause to make noise — *vn* : to buzz < *Can lila ~ tate ca* Trees rustle a great deal when there is wind. > — **kahmun·hmun** *v red* : to buzz steadily — **kahmunhmun·yan** *adv* : buzzing — **kahmun·yan** *adv* : whirring, buzzing

ka·hni·ga \k̇a-ȟní-ǧa\ *va* wa·kahniga : to choose, select, to appoint < *Koškalaka nump wicakahniga po* You select two young men. > — **kahnih** \k̇a-ȟníȟ\ *va contrac* : to choose < ~ *icu* to take one's choice > — **kahni·hkiya** \k̇a-ȟní-ȟk̇i-ya\ *va* kahni·hwa·kiya : to cause to choose — **kahnihni·ga** \k̇a-ȟní-ȟni-ǧa\ *v red of* kahniga : to choose often — **kahnihnih** *v red contrac* : to choose — **kahni·hpica** \k̇a-ȟní-ȟpi-ca\ *adj* : eligible — **kahni·hya** *adv* : choosing

ka·ȟo·ta *or* **kaȟol** \k̇a-ȟó-ṫa\ *vn* or *vn contrac* wa·kaȟota : to make gray by striking < ~ *iyeya* to make gray >

ka·hpa \k̇a-ȟṗá\ *va* wa·kahpa : to knock down anything hanging up, to make something fall < ~ *iyeya yo* Quickly bring things down, as is said before breaking camp. >

ka·hpa·hpa \k̇a-ȟṗá-ȟṗa\ *v red* wa·kahpahpa : to strike and make pieces fly off, as from wood or ice

ka·hpe·ki·ya \k̇a-ȟṗé-k̇i-ya\ *va* kahpe·wa·kiya : to cause to knock down

ka·hpu \k̇a-ȟṗú\ *va* wa·kahpu : to knock off something sticking, as pine gum, to scale off — **kahpu·hpu** *v red* : to scale off — **kahpu·ya** *adv* : scaling, falling off

ka·hši \k̇a-ȟší\ *va* : to get a thing done, to order something

ka·hta·ke·ke \k̇a-ȟtá-k̇e-k̇e\ *va* wa·kahtakeke : to bother, to irk one, *i.e.* one's words displease another though nothing bad is said – Bl WHL

ka·htan \k̇a-ȟtáŋ\ *vn* : to soak up, to soak in, as does grease in wood – R Bl

ka·htan·ka \k̇a-ȟtáŋ-ka\ *v* : to be attached to, have an

affection for, as one animal has for another – R Bl
ka·htan·yan \k̇a-ȟtáŋ-yaŋ\ *va* : to cause to spread, as one does grease – R Bl
ka·hta·ta \k̇a-ȟta-ṫa\ *v* wa·kahtata : to enfeeble, make unwell by striking
ka·htu·te·šni \k̇a-ȟtú-ṫe-šni\ *adv* : not well made
ka·ȟu·ga \k̇a-ȟú-ġa\ *va* : to break up or break in *e.g.* the skull by striking, to crack something by striking — *vn* : to be deformed by being dropped or knocked about < *Cega* ~ The bucket is out of shape. > — **kaȟuh** \k̇a-ȟúȟ\ *va contrac* : to crack something by striking < ~ *iyewaya* I cracked it with a sudden blow. *Yunkan wicaša wan icu na keya* ~ *apin kte kecin* Then a man took it and figured that he would strike cracking the turtle. > — **kaȟu·hkiya** \k̇a-ȟú-ȟk̇i-ya\ *va* kaȟu·hwa·kiya : to cause to break or knock in — **kaȟu·ȟuga** *v red* : to smash *e.g.* eggs, a head, or anything brittle — **kaȟu·ȟya** *adv* : breaking or staving in
ka·ȟun-ta *or* **kaȟunte** \ka-ȟúŋ-ta\ *v* : to wear out gradually and soften, as a church bell rope – A
ka·hwa \k̇a-ȟwá\ *va* [fr *hwa* to be sleepy] : to make sleepy by striking or shaking, as in a wagon < *Canpagmiyan makahwa* The bumpy wagon rocked me to sleep. >
ka·hwog \k̇a-ȟwóg\ *v contrac of* kahwoka : to be carried away < ~ *iyaya* It has drifted off, carried along by wind or tide, *i.e.* blown off. ~ *iyeya* to blow away > — **kahwo·gya** *va* kahwo·gwa·ya : to cause to drift, to wave as a flag — **kahwo·hwog** *vn red of* kahwohwoka : to drift, float, wave < *Tohanl mahpiya gigiya* ~ *ahiyaye cin hehantu kta ške* They say it will be then when brown clouds are carried *i.e.* drift in the wind. >
ka·hwo·hwo·ka \k̇a-ȟwó-ȟwo-k̇a\ *v red of* kahwoka : to be carried by the wind – D.92
ka·hwo·ka \k̇a-ȟwó-ka\ *vn* : to be carried away by wind, to float like the clouds or wave as a flag < *Tate ca wowapi kahwokelo. Ókah u* It was the wind that carried the letter away. He comes floating down river. > – BT
ka·hya \k̇a-ȟyá\ *n* [fr *kaga* to make] : a make, a kind, a sort — *adv* : make like, like, in the form of < *Iktomi tawogmunke* ~ made like a spider's web, *wakiyela* ~ in the form of a dove, *Lakol* ~ *wicoh'an* a sort of Lakota work, *wah'eca* ~ *hinhelo* Like sleet rain fell. > — **kahya·kel** *adv* : in appearance < *tuwa tokeca* ~ one different in appearance, *i.e.* looking like someone else, disguised, with the form of another, with meaning unknown > – B.H.272.3
ka·hya·pa·ya·la·ke s'e \ka-ȟyá-pa-ya-la-ke s'e\ *adv* : towards the front side < *Wana lowan kta ca* ~ *omniciye* There was a meeting out towards the front so he might do singing. > – MS.159
ka·hyu·hla·ta \k̇a-ȟyú-ȟla-ta\ *v* [fr *kaga* to make + *yuhlata* to claw or scratch] : to make a scratch, as does a cat or other clawed animal or bird
ka·h'a·kpa \k̇a-ȟ'á-k̇pa\ *va* wa·kah'akpa : to hollow out, as in whittling or notching, to make a hollow place by cutting with an axe – Bl
ka·h'an·hi·ya \k̇a-ȟ'áŋ-hi-ya\ *adv* [fr *h'anhiya* in a labored way] : a little slower, slowly, as in walking, reading, speaking, *etc*
ka·h'e \k̇a-ȟ'é\ *vt* : to exhaust every detail, to elaborate, develop < *Ptepa kah'epi s'e oyaka* He told something with all its details. > – Bw WHL
ka·h'ol \k̇a-ȟ'ól\ *v aux* [fr *kah'ota* but is *obsol*] ~ iyeya : to throw away *e.g.* a ball < ~ *hiyuc'iye* (of *uya* to have thrown down) He got off a horse, or down from a wagon, ~ *yeic'iya* to give one's self up, surrender to > – Bl
ka·h'u \k̇a-ȟ'ú\ *va* : to peel off by striking, to skin, as a potato thrown on a hard surface — **kah'u·h'u** *v red* wakah'uh'u : to make rough by breaking the bark or skin in many places
ka·i \k̇a-í\ *va* wa·kai unka·i·pi [fr *ai* take to] : to go in, bringing something to one, to take to one
ka·i·can·yan *or* **icanyan** \k̇a-í-caŋ-yaŋ\ *adv* : leaning against < ~ *egle* to lean against, ~ *najin* to lean standing against something >
ka·i·ci·c'u·ya \k̇a-í-ci-c'u-ya\ *adv* : crossing each other, crookedly < *hukaicic'uya yanka* to cross one's legs while sitting > – RF
ka·i·ci·o·pte·ya *or* **kaic'iopteya** \k̇a-í-ci-o-pte-ya\ *adv* : crosswise, as two roads intersecting < ~ *iyaya* to go by crosswise, ~ *ikázo* to make or mark with a cross > – Cf glakínyan D.4
ka·i·ci·san·ni·ca \k̇a-í-ci-saŋ-ni-ca\ *adv* : striking sideways, towards the side < ~ *ahiyayelo, ecel egnaka yo* The wind *etc* have blown it half off, *i.e.* the tablecloth, so put it back on. >
ka·i·ci·ya·pe·han \k̇a-í-ci-ya-ṗe-haŋ\ *adv* [fr *apehan* to fold on anything] : tangled up < *si* ~ *yanka* to sit with one foot lying on the other, *hu* ~ *yanka* to sit, on the ground, with legs crossed, *i.e.* in an Indian fashion, before one, *hu* ~ *najin* to stand with feet lying on one another > — **kaiciyapehe·ya** *adv* : having them crossed < *hu* ~ *hpaya* to lie with legs crossed > – Bl
ka·i·co·ga \k̇a-í-co-ġa\ *vn* : to come off, slide away as wood in water, to gather in bunches as old hay, twigs, *etc* — **kai·coh** \k̇a-í-coȟ\ *v contrac* : to gather in bunches
ka·i·ge·ju·ya \k̇a-í-ġe-ju-ya\ *adv* : crowding in
ka·i·glu·win·yan \k̇a-í-glu-wiŋ-yaŋ\ *v* : to make a woman of, to become effeminate < ~ *hiyayelo* He became effeminate. > – Bl
ka·i·ha·kte·ya \ka-í-ha-kte-ya\ *adv* : not as much, not fully < ~ *s'e magaju* It rains but a few drops. > – Bl WHL
ka·i·ȟe-ju \k̇a-í-ȟe-ju\ *vn* : to be sore from riding as on horseback – *Syn* KATUTA Bl
ka·i·ȟe·ju·ju·ya \k̇a-í-ȟe-ju-ju-ya\ *adv red of* kaiȟejuya : being sore from riding < ~ *unpelo* We are sore from riding. > – Note: the word is almost the same as *kaiȟeya;* the difference is uncertain — **kaiȟeju·ya** *va* : to make one sore riding
ka·i·ȟe·ya \k̇a-í-ȟe-ya\ *adv* : drawing up behind, grouping < ~ *aya, ahinajin* to begin to gather, to come together into groups or bunches, as is said of people, or things as driftwood into clusters or piles > – Bl
ka·i·je·na \k̇a-í-je-na\ *va* : to confuse, mix up as the wind does < *Tate* ~ Wind stirs confusion. > – Bl
ka·i·le \k̇a-í-le\ *v* [fr *ile* to blaze] : to make blaze by fanning, or as the wind does — **kaile·hlega** *va* : to strike *e.g.* a fire and cause to send sparks — **kaile·le** *v red* : to keep blazing – Bl
ka·i·na·hni \ka-í-na-ȟni\ *v* : to hurry up in working, to be busier < ~ *yo* Be busier! > — **kainahni·la** *v* wa·kainahnila : to hurry up, run, in the manner of old people — **kainahni·yan** *adv* or *v perhaps* : hurriedly

\a\ father \e\ they \i\ machine \o\ smoke \u\ lunar \an, aŋ\ blanc Fr. \in, iŋ\ ink \on, oŋ, un, uŋ\ soon, confier Fr. \c\ chair \ġ\ machen Ger. \j\ fusion \clusters: bl, gn, kp, hšl, etc...\ b^{e}lo ... said with a slight vowel
See more in the Introduction, Guide to Pronunciation

ka·in·yang i·ye·ya \k̇a-íŋ-yang i-yè-ya\ *v* : to throw and make run, as a rabbit, *etc* < ~ *iyaya* to throw and make run on by > – Bl

ka·in·yan·ke·la·ka \k̇a-íŋ-yaŋ-ke-la-ka\ *v* wa·káinyankelaka : to run like old people do, taking short steps and advancing fast – Bl

ka·i·pa·tku·hya \k̇a-í-ṗa-tku-ḣya\ *adv* : in a line fronting

ka·i·pa·zi·lya \k̇a-í-ṗa-zi-lya\ *adv* : high < ~ *lake s'e han* He stands higher than the others. > – Bl

ka·i·psi·lya·la·ke s'e \k̇a-í-psi-lya-la-ke s'e\ *adv* : keeping pace ahead of others < ~ *inyanka* to be running a little ahead of others > – Note: this is said also of the middle finger on the hand – Bl WHL

ka·i·pu·sta·gya \k̇a-í-ṗu-sṫa-gya\ *adv* : crowding, pressing against

ka·i·šlo·šlog \k̇a-í-šlo-šlog\ *v* : to jolt < ~ *iyaya* to go jolting along > – *Syn* KAIŠUTATA

ka·i·šta·mi·ni·han·pi hi·yu·ya *or* **kaištamini·oju iyeya** \k̇a-í-šṫa-mi-ni-han-pi hi-yù-ya\ *v perhaps* : to bring tears into one's eyes, as the wind does – Bl

ka·i·šu·ta \k̇a-í-šu-ta\ *v* : to stumble, *i.e.* once, to make a misstep < ~ *iyaya* to go and stumble, or to go jolting as is said when speaking of a wagon when it jolts going transversely over ruts *etc*, ~ *iblabla* I am jolting along, as on hard snow. > — **kaišuta·ta** *v* : to stumble and labor until one gets on one's feet again < ~ *iyaya* to go stumbling > – Note: it is used with other *v*

ka·i·teb \k̇a-í-ṫeb\ *adv* : diagonally, not straight — **kaite·bya** *adv* : crosswise, slanting diagonally, slanting < ~ *kaksa* to split crosswise >

ka·i·te·ce·ca·šni \ka-í-ṫe-ce-ca-šni\ *v* [fr *ite* face + *ececa* to be affected] : to change one's facial expression as by a slap, a blow, or by a reproving remark < ~ *iyemayayelo* Suddenly you made me change in expression, which is said in fun and means: You make me angry. > – Bl WHL

ka·i·te·han·la·ke \ka-í-te-haŋ-la-ke\ *adv* : a little farther off in *ref* to place, a little later in *ref* to time < *Na ake ~ ehanl ake u* And when he came a second time a little farther off, he then came again. >

ka·i·te·pa \k̇a-í-ṫe-ṗa\ *va* wa·kaitepa : to cut diagonally

ka·i·te·ye·šni i·ye·ya \k̇a-í-ṫe-ye-šni i-yè-ya\ *v perhaps* : to make one suddenly serious by a hurting remark – Bl

ka·i·tkob \k̇a-í-tk̇ob\ *adv* : back again < ~ *glihpaya* to fall back again, to rebound >

ka·i·tko·bya \k̇a-í-tk̇o-bya\ *adv* : opposite but a little to one side, no looking quite straight at one

ka·i·tko·kib \k̇a-í-tko-k̇ib\ *adv* : with the face towards one, meeting — **kaitkoki·bya** *adv* : facing one — **kaitkoki·patanhan** \k̇a-í-tk̇o-k̇i-pa-ṫaŋ-haŋ\ *adv* : opposite to, fronting one

ka·i·to·kab *or* **kaitokabya** \k̇a-í-to-k̇ab\ *adv* : before, in advance of, as of a travelling party < ~ *gli* to come home before the rest, ~ *ya* to go before, *i.e.* to prepare or break the way >

ka·i·to·kanl \k̇a-í-to-kaŋl\ *adv* : out to one side < ~ *iyeya* to shove aside >

ka·i·to·kpas \k̇a-í-ṫo-kṗas\ *va contrac* wa·kaitokpaza [fr *kaitokpaza* to spread darkness over] : to bring darkness over for a little while by smiting, to stun by striking

ka·i·to·mni \k̇a-í-to-mni\ *vn* ma·káitomni : to be dizzy having been struck on the head or been turning swiftly around on or in, as on a merry-go-round

ka·i·tun·kab *and* **kaitunkabya** \k̇a-í-ṫun-k̇ab\ *adv* : reclining one's body, as when riding horseback < ~ *glihpaye* He fell backwards, *i.e.* losing his balance, while reclining in the saddle. > – Note: *itunkab* flat on the back, lying looking upward Bl

ka·i·wan·yan·gya \ka-í-waŋ-yaŋ-gya\ *adv* : prudently, circumspectly, carefully, as in carrying a load without dropping things < ~ *econ* to do it carefully, ~ *magaju* to rains but only a few drops > – *Syn* OWAHECELYA, KAIYACINYAN, AIYACINYAN Bl

ka·i·wan·yank \ka-í-waŋ-yaŋk\ *v* [fr *kaiwanyanka* to watch one] : to watch one < ~ *ocicuwa kte lo, owekinaš h'unt'eciyin ktelo* I shall keep a good watch for you, lest I should overburden you. > – Note: the word *kaiwanyanka* seems not to be used or even to exist

ka·i·yab \k̇a-í-yab\ *adv* : without warning < *Šunkmanitu ~ Ihan, i.e.* He Meets a Wolf Without Warning, he coming from the opposite direction. This happens to be EM's Indian name. *Oyate wan tanka wicoti ca ~ ihan* Without warning he came upon a great camp of human beings. > – Bl D.207-208

ka·i·ya·be·be·ya \k̇a-í-ya-be-be-ya\ *or* \k̇a-í-ya-ṗe-ṗe-ya\ *adv red* : in all directions — **kaiyabe·yekiya** \k̇a-í-be-ye-ki-ya\ *or* \k̇a-í-ṗe-ye-ki-ya\ *adv* : scattered < ~ *iyayekiyapi* They are running in all directions, as horses that are being chased. > – B.H.304.4

ka·i·ya·cin·yan \k̇a-í-ya-ciŋ-yaŋ\ *adv* : carefully < ~ *econ* He does it carefully, as in carrying a load without dropping anything. > – *Syn* KAIWANYANGYA Bl

ka·i·ya·ka·pe·ya \k̇a-í-ya-ka-ṗe-ya\ *adv* : exceeding, a little more than — **kaiyakapeya·la s'e** *adv* : a little ahead < ~ *inyanka* to be a little ahead of others in running >

ka·i·ya·ka·pte·ya \k̇a-í-ya-k̇a-pṫe-ya\ *adv* : uphill

ka·i·ya·ki·c'u·la s'e \k̇a-í-ya-k̇i-c'u-la s'e\ *adv* : by a little more than the usual amount < ~ *mak'u šni, icewinš conala mak'u we* He did not give me more than usual, he did give me a few in a grand way, *i.e.* I expected much but received little. ~ *yahipi kin icanlmawašte* When you brought it I was glad for it. > – Bl WHL

ka·i·ya·ki·c'u·ya \k̇a-í-ya-k̇i-c'u-ya\ *adv* : a little more

ka·i·ya·pe·ha \k̇a-í-ya-ṗe-haŋ\ *v* : to get entrangled, swung around – B.H.95.23

ka·i·yo·ca·tka \k̇a-í-yo-ca-tka\ *n* : a left-handed performance – WHL

ka·i·yo·hpe·ya \k̇a-í-yo-ḣpe-ya\ *adv* : down hill, downward – Bl WHL

ka·i·yo·kpan·ni·yan \ka-í-yo-kpaŋ-ni-yaŋ\ *adv* : unevenly – Note: a similar use: *Ócihišnišniyan econpi he kapi* They meant it was done unevenly, unequally spaced – Bl

ka·i·yo·tag \k̇a-í-yo-ṫag\ *v contrac of* kaiyotaka : to be seated < ~ *glihpaya* to fall down in attempting to be seated > — **kaiyotag·tag** *v contrac red* : to be seated < ~ *glihpaya* to bump up and down as when seated in a wagon on a bad road > – Bl

ka·i·yo·ta·ka \k̇a-í-yo-ṫa-k̇a\ *v* : to be seated < ~ *glihpaya* to fall down when being seated >

ka·i·yo·was \k̇a-í-yo-was\ *va* [fr *kaiyowaza* to cause an echo] : to cause on echo by striking < ~ *iyeya* to strike an echo suddenly >

ka·i·yo·wa·za \k̇a-í-yo-wa-za\ *va* wa·kaiyowaza : to make echo with the hand, make resound

ka·i·yo·ya·gya \k̇a-í-yo-ya-gya\ *v* : to shake slightly, to quiver as do the chin or cheeks when one rides over rough roads < *Kawankaka iyaya ca iyoḣa kin ~ iyeye.* Since he went on being jostled about, his jowels suddenly quivered. > – Note: similarly: *Tapon naškan s'e inyanke*

He ran as though his cheeks were being jostled - Bl WHL

ka·i·yu·sya·tan·han \k̇a-í-yu-sya-taŋ-haŋ\ *adv* : - *See* kaiyuzeya *and* kaiyuzeyatanhan

ka·i·yu·ze·ya *and* **kaiyuzeya·kel** \k̇a-í-yu-ze-ya\ *adv* : a little way off, not a long way off < ~ *icu* to take by reaching, to reach for, ~ *hinajin* to come and stand not far off, ~ *enajin* they stood a bit away > — **kaiyuzeya·tanhan** *adv* : from a distance < ~ *o* to hit though one is very far away, ~ *yešan, apelo* Though not far off he hit it. > - Note: the word is perhaps a *syn* for *kaiyusyatanhan*

ka·ja \k̇a-já\ *va* wa·kaja : to split a little, to make gape, to hit and split < ~ *wao* I hit and split it. > - *Syn* KAŠLEL Bl

ka·ja·bja·pa \k̇a-já-bja-ṗa\ *v red of* kajapa : to put a nick in, make dull < *Makájabjapelo* I am very tired from riding. >

ka·ja·han \k̇a-já-haŋ\ *va* wa·kajahan [fr *jahan* harsh, rough] : to make open out by striking, to press open — **kajahan·han** *v* : to open gradually by applying pressure

ka·ja·ja \k̇a-já-ja\ *va* wa·kajaja : to wash away, as a bridge by a flood, to wash away by pulling back and forth < ~ *iyaya* to go on washing away >

ka·ja·ka \k̇a-já-k̇a\ *va* wa·kajaka : to squeeze open, as a wound, to strain or knock open

ka·jal \k̇a-jál\ *va contrac of* kajata : to make forked < ~ *iyeya* to part suddenly > — **kaja·lya** \k̇a-já-lya\ *adv* : with objects spread or stretched apart < *Tiškakan* ~ *yanka* The neck muscle was stretched apart, as is said when with a lean person the two muscles on the neck are protruding and there is a hollow between the two. > - Bl WHL

ka·jan·jan *or* **kajanjan·ka** \k̇a-jáŋ-jaŋ\ \k̇a-jáŋ-jaŋ-k̇a\ *vn* [fr *janjan* glass] : to become light, as clouds after rain clear, to dawn — **kajanjan·yan** *adv* : dawning < ~ *u* It is dawning, *i.e.* coming dawn. > - B.H.186.2

ka·ja·pa \k̇a-já-ṗa\ *va* : to strike and make dull, as an axe or knife by hitting it on something hard, so that the thin part of it turns around, to nick - Bl

ka·ja·ta \k̇a-já-ṫa\ *va* wa·kájata : to make forked by cutting with an axe

ka·jib \k̇a-jíb\ *va contrac of* kajipa : to shave off quickly or by a stroke < ~ *iyeya* to suddenly shave off > — **ka·ji·bji·pa** \k̇a-jí-bji-ṗa\ *va red* : to shave off

ka·ji·ni·ca šni \ka-jí-ni-ca šni\ *v* : to be ostensibly in want < *takuni* ~ *keš* although not clearly in want of anything > - Note: a doubtful meaning is applied to a person who took the whole of something instead of only a part of it TH

ka·jin·kjin·ca \k̇a-jíŋ-kjiŋ-ca\ *va* : to strike and make spit fumes as it were - *Syn* KAGINLGINCA

ka·ji·pa \k̇a-jí-ṗa\ *va* wa·kajipa : to shave with a knife or drawing-knife, to plane

ka·jo \k̇a-jó\ *vn* wa·kájo **a** : to purge, have diarrhoea **b** : to whistle as does the wind < ~ *iyeya* to pass or evacuate suddenly, *Tate* ~ . *Nónge tate makajo ca tanyan nawah'on šni* Wind whistled. My ears didn't hear well since I passed wind. > - Bl

ka·jo·jo·ye·ya \ka-jó-jo-ye-ya\ *v red* [fr *kajo* to whistle + *yeya* to cause] : to throw as a piece of wood with a whizzing sound - Note: the word *ref* also to diarrhoea Bl

ka·ju \ka-jú\ *va* : to uproot, as a strong wind does to trees, to break off < *Tinpsinla wana hukaju* The wild turnip stems now break off, as is said in August when the stems of the wild turnip are dry and break off. > — **kaju·ju** \k̇a-jú-ju\ *va* **1** : to knock off, to blot out, efface **2** : to pay off, as one's debts -A Sb

ka·jun \k̇a-júŋ\ *va* : to knock out somebody's tooth by hitting with a ball or by striking, to pull up, as birds do corn, to come out or moult, as the quills of geese R WHL

ka·jun·he s'e \k̇a-júŋ-he s'e\ *adv* : knocked fast into mud < ~ *inajin* to get something knocked standing mired in mud > Bl WHL

[1]**ka·ka** \ká-k̇a\ *adj* : stiff, rattling as a stiff hide when beaten, sounding dull as a bell sometimes does < *Iyeš* ~ *wowaši econ* He does work that rattles You, as one would say to another to incite him to work pointing at another (*iyeš*) who does work hard. > - BE

[2]**ka·ka** \k̇a-k̇á\ *n* : a baby's word for grandfather

ka·kab \k̇a-k̇áb\ *v contrac of* kakapa : to knock something away from a place < ~ *iyeya* to bat or knock something away from, ~ *ihpeya* to strike and throw one down, *si* ~ *iyeya* to trip one by holding the foot in his way while he is moving > - *Syn* KAHAYEYA, KAHINHPEYA LT WHL

ka·kag \k̇á-kag\ *va contrac of perhaps* kakáka : to sound or rattle like an old kettle when shaken with stones in it < ~ *hingla* suddenly to make rattle > — **kaka·gya** \k̇a-ká-gya\ *adv* : rattling, as a old kettle when shaken, rattling, as an empty wagon — **kakagya·kel** \k̇a-ká-gya-k̇el\ *adv* : rattling

ka·ka·ka \k̇a-ká-k̇a\ *va* wa·kákaka : to make a dull noise by beating, pounding, an old kettle or a stiff hide

[1]**ka·kan** \k̇a-káŋ\ *va* wa·kákan **a** : to hew, as a log, to adze **b** : to knock off, as fruit from a tree

[2]**ka·kan** \k̇a-k̇áŋ\ *v* wa·kákan : to make marks, notches into something hard — **kakan·kan** \k̇a-k̇áŋ-k̇aŋ\ *v* : to cut notches in or knobs on

ka·ka·pa \k̇a-ká-ṗa\ *va* wa·kakapa : to strike a ball that is thrown and send it back - Cf pakápa

ka·ka·tin \k̇a-ká-ṫiŋ\ *va* wa·kakatin : to straighten out by striking, as round or coiled wire, or a horse shoe

ka·ka·wa \k̇a-ká-wa\ *va* wa·kákawa : to make open by striking, *i.e.* to strike something off and thus open it partly, *e.g.* a tin can

ka·kca \k̇a-kcá\ *va* wa·kákca : to comb, as hair, to disentangle

[1]**ka·ke·ca** \ká-k̇e-ca\ *adv* : in this manner, thus

[2]**ka·ke·ca** \ká-k̇e-ca\ *adj* : stiff, making a noise when felt or handled, as parchment - Cf kák̇a

ka·kel \ká-k̇el\ *adv* **a** : so, thus < ~ *econ wo* Do it in this manner. ~ *ecamon we* That way I do, *i.e.* that's the trick I work. ~ *na* ~ thus and so > **b** : in some direction somewhere < *Na* ~ *kawinh iyayapi* And they went on turning in some direction. > — **kake·lya** \ká-k̇é-lya\ *adv* : thus, so

ka·ke·na \ká-k̇e-na\ *adv* : somewhere, in some direction < *Iktomi* ~ *ya na Iya wan ataya* Iktomi (Spider) was going somewhere and he met up with an Iya (Monster Eater). >

ka·ke·ston \k̇a-ké-stoŋ\ *va* kake·swa·ton : to make barbed, as an arrow — **kakeston·yan** *adv* : with barbs

\a\ father \e\ they \i\ machine \o\ smoke \u\ lunar \an, aŋ\ blanc Fr. \in, iŋ\ ink \on, oŋ, un, uŋ\ soon, confier Fr. \c\ chair \ġ\ machen Ger. \j\ fusion \clusters: bl, gn, kp, hšl, etc...\ b^e^lo ... said with a slight vowel
See more in the Introduction, Guide to Pronunciation

-R Bl

ka·keš \k̇a-k̇éš\ *adv indef* : any, at random < *Tukte unma* ~ What one, no matter which? *tuktektetu* ~ anywhere, *Iye ~ glakca šni najute kin pahin onz'ákiyotake s'e* He so ever does not comb the back of the head mounts [a horse's] rump as if it were a porcupine> — **kake·škeš** \k̇a-k̇é·šk̇eš\ *adv red* : any < *taku* ~ anything > - Bl B.H. 108.10, 60.3 SW

ka·ke·tu *and* **kaketu·ya** \k̇a-k̇é-ṫu\ *adv* : in this way, so, thus

[1]**ka·ki** \k̇á-k̇i\ *adv* : there, yonder < ~ *mni kte* I shall go yonder. ~ *ka* yonder ~ *ka cancega wan hotan'in kin hel niyate ti yelo* Yonder where a drum is singing is your father's house. > - Cf *leci* and *heci* in *ref* to place D.208

[2]**ka·ki** \k̇a-k̇í\ *va* wa·káki [fr *aki* to arrive home carrying something] : to have taken home, or somewhere else to one < *unkakipi* we arrive home carrying, *Miye talo kin he wakaki* I got home carrying that fresh meat. > - D.244

ka·ki·ci·pa·pi \ka-k̇í-ci-pa-pi\ *n* [fr *kapa* to excel] : a race, contest < *kignun* ~ a swimming game, as an underwater race >

ka·ki·ci·pe·han \k̇a-k̇í-ci-ṗe-haŋ\ *v* : to wave, form waves as in water < *mini* ~ water waves > - B.H.71.12 WHL

ka·ki·ja \k̇a-k̇í-ja\ *vn* ma·kakija ni·cakija : to suffer, be afflicted —*adj* : suffering, afflicted

ka·ki·ka *and* **kaki ka** *or* **kakiya** \k̇á-k̇i-k̇a\ \k̇á-k̇i ka\ \k̇á-k̇i-ya\ *adv* : over there, yonder < *Hehanl lenayos ~ paha wan lila tehan yanke kin heci anunk icic'uya iyayapi kte lo. Nitanke niyate ob ~ tipi wan he kin he tipelo* At the time the two will go yonder there where there is a very long hill to pass one another on both sides. Your older sister along with your father live in that house over there. >

ka·ki·nunk \k̇a-k̇í-nuŋk\ *adv* : each one his own way < ~ *iyayapi* they went on each his own way. > - B.H.89.10

ka·ki·nun·kan \ka-k̇í-nuŋ-kaŋ\ *adv* : apart < ~ *iyeya* to force apart, to separate, *Tate hiyu na can k'un hena ~ iyeye* Wind came and these trees were forced apart. > — **kakinunkan·kiya** \k̇a-k̇í-nuŋ-k̇aŋ-k̇i-ya\ *adv* : forced to separate, go apart < *Mini kin ~ iyaye* The water went and parted> - B.H.112.4, 113.9 D.22

ka·kin·ca \k̇a-k̇íŋ-ca\ *va* wa·kakinca : to scrape *e.g.* hair from a hide — **kakinl** \k̇a-k̇íŋl\ *va contrac of* kakinca : to scrape < ~ *iyeya* to scrape off > — **kakin·lkinca** *v red of* kakinca : to scrape from - Bl

ka·ki·pa \ka-k̇í-pa\ *v* ka·wa·kipa [fr *kapa* to excel] : to surpass, excel one, to get through successfully < *Oiyohpaye kin šica ca kawakiipe cinhan iyowakita kte lo* If I get successfully through the bad crossing, he will keep watch on it. > - Bl

ka·ki·paš *and* **kakipaš·paš** \k̇a-k̇í-ṗaš\ *adv* and *adv red* : wrinkled, loose-fitting

ka·kis \k̇a-k̇ís\ *v* [fr *kiza*]: to make creak by rubbing < ~ *iyeya* suddenly to creak > — **kaki·skiza** \k̇a-k̇í-sk̇i-za\ *v red* : to keep squeaking

ka·kiš \k̇a-k̇íš\ *vn contrac of* kakija : to suffer — **kaki·šic'iya** *v refl* : to make one's self suffer — **kaki·šya** *va* kaki·šwa·ya : to inflict or make suffering, to punish — *adv* : afflicted, suffering — **kakišya·kel** \k̇a-k̇í-šya-k̇el\ *adv* : in pain < ~ *waun* I am in pain. >

ka·ki·ya \k̇á-k̇i-ya\ *adv* : yonder, there — **kakiya·tanhan** \k̇á-k̇i-ya-ṫaŋ-haŋ\ *adv* : from yonder place, in this wise, in this way, by this means

ka·ki·yo·tan \k̇a-k̇í-yo·taŋ\ *adv* : in that direction — **kakiyotan·lahci** *adv* : just that way, just in that direction

ka·ki·za *or* **kakinza** \k̇a-k̇í-za\ *v* : to make creak by rubbing, as two trees do that rub against each other, or as door hinges that are not well oiled < *Tiyopa* ~ The door does creak. *Can numb icicameya han canke tate hiyu can icicakinzahan ške* They say two trees stood remaining close to one another, and so the wind came up making the trees creak, *i.e.* the two trees rubbed together making a loud squeaking noise. *Can numb tate can iyena icicakinzahan* There were two among so many trees the wind was making creak. > - D.21.26

ka·kmin \k̇a-kmíŋ\ *va* wa·kakmin : to clear off *e.g.* weeds from a field < *Na makoce kin oyate kin ataya kakminpi na kablupi* And the people beat and cleared off the field entirely. >

ka·kog \k̇a-kóg\ *va contrac of* kakoka : to make a dull sound by striking < ~ *hingla* to suddenly strike a muffled sound > — **kako·gya** *or* **kakogna·kel** \k̇a-kó-gya-k̇el\ *adv* : rattling

ka·ko·ka *or* **kako·koka** \k̇a-kó-k̇a\ *va* wa·kakoka : to produce a dull sound by striking - Note: but a sound not by drumming which is *kabú* to drum

ka·kon·ta \k̇a-kóŋ-ṫa\ *va* wa·kakonta : to cut in ridges, to wear thin a rope, a strap, *etc* by striking — **kakon·tkonta** *va red* wa·kakontkonta : to hollow out in grooves or ridges

ka·kpa \k̇a-kṗá\ *va* wa·kakpa : to strike and make a hole in, to cut a vein < *Tezi* ~ He punctured the stomach. *Išta kin nupin kakpapi* Both his eyes were put out. ~ *iyeya* to shoot through, as an arrow or bullet > - BT D.220

ka·kpan \k̇a-kṗáŋ\ *va* wa·kakpan **1** : to beat fine, to mash up **2** : to wink, as the eye - Cf ištákakpan

ka·kpi \k̇a-kṗí\ *va* wa·kákpi : to crack or break, as a nut — **kakpi·yeya** *va* : to pierce through < *Pte* ~ He pierced through the buffalo. > - Bl

ka·ksa \k̇a-ksá\ *va* wa·kaksa : to separate by striking, as with an axe, to split, to cut off, as with an axe or by striking < *Pa* ~ He struck off its head. > — **kaksa·ksa** *va red* wa·kaksaksa : to cut off often, to cut up, as wood for fire < *Wana mahpiya ~ ca kask'iyayin kte lo* Since the clouds are now breaking up the weather will clear. *cankaksaksapi* to cut off one piece after another, as pieces from a stick, to whittle > - WE Bl

ka·ksi·hpe·ya \ka-ksí-ḣpe-ya\ *va* [fr *kaksa* cut off + *ihpeya* throw down] : to strike and sever - B.H.133.26

ka·kša \k̇a-kšá\ *va* wa·kakša : to coil, roll up, as a *wikan* a rope, to wind up, as yarn, to fold up — *adv* : coiled up < *Pagé hákakša omawani yelo* My belly is rolling up as I walk around, *i.e.* indicating to be hungry. *tuwa* ~ one rolled up, as a man says to another when doubting his truthfulness > — **kakša·kša** *or* **kakša·la** *adv red* : coiled up, in coils, rolled round - Bl LB

ka·kšan \k̇a-kšáŋ\ *va* wa·kakšan : to bend, bend up — **kakšan·kšan** *or* **kakšankšin** *adv red* : crookedly, in a zigzag manner < ~ *inyanka* to run staggering > - Bl

ka·kši·ja \k̇a-kší-ja\ *va* wa·kakšija : to bend up, double up by striking *e.g.* a leg opposite the knee, thus getting him on his knees, to shut up, as a pocket knife

ka·kši·kša \k̇a-kší-kša\ *vn* : to be tired < *Leceya makakšikšelo* I am really tired out. > - Note: the word is doubtful - Bl KE

ka·kši·kši·ja \k̇a-kší-kši-ja\ *v red of* kakšija : to fold up in parts, to collapse *e.g.* the knees in giving way - Note:

the meaning "to be tired from riding" is doubtful - Bl KE WHL

ka·kšiš \ǩa-kšíš\ *va contrac of* kakšija : to double up < ~ *iyeya* to suddenly collapse > — **kakši·šya** \ǩa-kší-šya\ *va* kakši·šwa·ya : to cause to shut up

ka·ktan \ǩa-ktáŋ\ *va* wa·kaktan : to bend by striking, to make something curved, as a horseshoe — **kaktan·ktan** \ǩa-ktáŋ-ktaŋ\ *v red* : to beat into a curved shape — **kaktan·yan** *adv* : bending

ka·ku \ǩa-ǩú\ *va of* aku : to start to bring home < *Wanji makaku yo. Tipi iyokan el can wicayakaku kte lo* Bring me back one. You should bring them wood into the empty shed. > - Bl

ka·ku·ka \ǩa-ǩú-ka\ *va* wa·kákuka : to wear out by friction, striking, *etc* - R

ka·kun·ta *and* **kakun·tkunta** \ǩa-ǩúŋ-ta\ *va* - *See* kakónta

ka·kye·la \ǩa-ǩyé-la\ *adv* : with a noise, perhaps of something dropping <*Taku ~ wakšica el ohinhpaya* Something fell into the dish with a clatter. >

ka·k'e·ga \ǩa-k'é-ǧa\ *va* wa·kak'ega : to make a grating noise

ka·k'es \ǩa-k'és\ *vn contrac of* kak'eza : to blow off and leave bare and hard, as when the wind blows the snow from the ground < ~ *iyeya* to drift heavily >

ka·k'e·za \ǩa-k'é-za\ *vn* : to leave hard and bare, as wind does the ground - Cf kak'óza

ka·g'o·ga \ǩa-k'ō'-ǧa\ *va* wa·kak'oga : to scrape off with a knife or stick, as dirt from shoes, clothes, or paint from the wall, *etc* — **kak'oh** *va contrac of* kag'oga : to scrape off < *Tinpsila ~ yutapi* They ate the turnips they scraped, or Scraping the turnips they eat them. >

ka·k'os \ǩa-k'ós\ *va contrac of* kak'oza : to make the ground hard < ~ *iyeya* to leave bare and hard >

ka·k'o·za \ǩa-k'ó-za\ *va* wa·kak'oza : to make the ground bare and thus harden it, to make hard, to leave hard and bare, as the wind does the ground, or by sweeping *etc*

[1]**kal** \ǩal\ *adv contrac perhaps of* kákiya : there, yonder < *Paha kin kal iyawahe* I went yonder and stood on the hill. ~ *ewicoti* They camp together over there. > - BT

[2]**kal** \ǩal\ *adj contrac of* káta : hot < *Kal aya* It is getting hot. >

ka·la \ǩa-lá\ *va* wa·kala : to scatter, as grain, to sow - Note: the word was once not applied to liquids

ka·lab \ǩa-láb\ *va perhaps of* kalápa : to rub smooth — **kalab iyekiya** \ǩa-láb i-yè-ki-ya\ *va* : to salute one < ~ *iyeunkiciyapi kta* We should salute one another. > - WE

ka·la·la \ǩa-lá-la\ *v red* wa·kalala [fr *kala* scatter] : to scatter, sow, throw, broadcast, doing so repeatedly < *Sipa kin ~ s'e yanka* The toe end was as if shredded, *i.e.* the toe end of moccasins was all torn. *Taku inayahni ca ~ s'e yainanke* You ran when you were in a hurry with what was like sowing, *i.e.* putting on clothes carelessly. > - Bl

ka·la·pa \ǩa-lá-p̂a\ *va* : to rub smooth and level - Note: *kalab iyekiya* is the form more often used - Bl

ka·le·ble·pa \ǩa-lé-ble-p̂a\ *v red* wa·kaleblepa [fr *kalepa* to notch] : to notch by cutting - R Bl

ka·le·ca·la \ǩa-lé-ca-la\ *adv* : soon, pretty soon — **kalecala·kes'e** *adv* : recently - Ww WHL

ka·le·ga \ǩa-lé-ǧa\ *va* : to fan or make shine by striking < *Hupáhu on peta kalegahin na ena t'a ške* It is said he was fanning the fire with a bird's wing and right here he died. > - MS.71

ka·le·han·yank \ǩa-lé-haŋ-yaŋk\ *v* : to separate parts, divide away < ~ *iyeya* to divide away rapidly > - B.H. 249.4

ka·le·hle·ga \ǩa-lé-ȟle-ǧa\ *v red of* kalega : to keep fanning *e.g.* a fire, to make shine as by polishing — **kalehlega·pi s'e** *adv perhaps* : sparkling < ~ *hingla* suddenly sparkling as it were, as a piece of metal that is being polished, ~ *koyaka* to dress very attractively > - *Syn* IYOWICAJANJAN S'E

ka·le·hya \ǩa-lé-ȟya\ *va* : to make shine by striking, as a fire

ka·le·kte·han \ǩa-lé-kte-haŋ\ *adv* : stumbling, tottering — **kalektehan·han** *adv red* : teetering — **kalektehan-han·yan** *adv* : stumblingly — **kalektehan·yan** *va* kalektehan·wa·yan : to cause to stumble along — *adv* : stumbling

ka·le·pa \ǩa-lé-p̂a\ *va* wa·kalepa : to cut a notch in

ka·lka·lya \ka-lká-lya\ *adv* : bitingly, in anger, bitterly < ~ *eya* to say it bitingly > - SH

ka·lki·ya \ká-lǩi-ya\ *v poss* : to heat one's own - Bl

ka·lob \ǩa-lób\ *va contrac of* kalópa : to mire, as in mud < ~ *iyaya* to go on mired > — **kalo·bkiya** \ǩa-ló-bǩi-ya\ *va contrac* kalo·bwa·kiya : to cause to mire — **kalo-blob** \ǩa-ló-blob\ *v contrac red* : miring, wading, as a horse in mud < ~ *iyaya* to keep miring > — **kaloblo·pa** \ǩa-ló-blo-p̂a\ *v red of* kalópa : to wade in, be stuck or mired — **kalo·bya** *va* kalo·bwa·ya : to cause to mire

ka·lo·cin \ǩa-lō'-ciŋ\ *vn* ma·kálocin : to be hungry from being shaken up, as from having ridden on a wagon or on horseback

ka·lo·pa \ǩa-ló-p̂a\ *va* : to strike something soft that does not give way, but at most shows a hole < *Pi ~* He struck into his liver. > — *vn* wa·kalopa : to mire, stick in the mud - *Syn* KAHLI

ka·lo·pe s'e \ǩa-ló-p̂e s'e\ *v* : to give a love tap < ~ *apa* to strike but without hurting one >

ka·lu \ǩa-lú\ *va* wa·kálu **a** : to blow or brush away a little with the hand **b** : to fan

ka·lu·la·ka *or* **kalu laka** \ǩa-lú-la-ǩa\ \ǩa-lú là-ǩa\ *n perhaps* : the fastest runner, men or horses < *Yakalu lakelo, iyotanla icu wo* Take it well, you are the fastest runner, *i.e.* you alone win, all others were far behind. > - Bl

ka·lu·lu \ǩa-lú-lu\ *v red* wa·kálulu [fr *kalú* to fan] : to be fanning < *Miglalu* I fan myself. *Lowan na icabu wan on el (šina kpanyanpi wan) ~ iyeya* He sang and with a drumb stick he brushed away on (a dressed robe). >

ka·lus \ǩa-lús\ *vn contrac of* kalúza : to flow rapidly — **kalu·sya** *va* kalu·swa·ya : to cause to flow — *adv* : flowing swiftly — **kalusya·lake s'e** \ǩa-lú-sya-la-ǩe s'e\ *adv* : fast, but as it were and not in reality < ~ *ungni ktelo* We shall go home fast. > - Note: the word is used by old people and children Bl

ka·lu·za \ǩa-lú-za\ *vn* **a** : to flow rapidly, as water **b** : to be filled with < *Ton ~. We ~* She gave birth rapidly. Blood flowed quickly. > - B.H.43.22, 49.18

ka·lya \ǩa-lyá\ *va* wa·kalya [supposedly fr *kataya* to heat] : to heat, as rocks < *Na inyan k'on hena ~* And these rocks he had heated. > — **ka·li·c'i·ya** \ǩa-lí-c'i-ya\ *v* : to warm one's self

ka·ma·kal i·ye·ya \ǩá-ma-kal i-yè-ya\ *va* : to strike down - Bl

---

\a\ father \e\ they \i\ machine \o\ smoke \u\ lunar \an, aŋ\ blanc Fr. \in, iŋ\ ink \on, oŋ, un, uŋ\ soon, confier Fr. \c\ chair \ǧ\ machen Ger. \j\ fusion \clusters: bl, gn, kp, hšl, etc...\ b[e]lo ... said with a slight vowel
See more in the Introduction, Guide to Pronunciation

ka·ma·ka·ta·ki·ya *or* **kamaka·tka** \ǩa-má-ǩa-ta-ǩi-ya\ *adv* : downward toward the earth or ground < ~ *uwate k'un. Tate wan ~ ihpemayelo* I had fired it [a gun] into the ground. A wind threw me to the ground. > – Bl

ka·ma·sya \ǩa-má-sya\ *adv* : as hard as iron < *Canku kin ~ yanka ca šlušlutelo* The road that was hard as iron was slippery. > – Bl

ka·ma·to \ǩa-má-to\ *va* wa·kámato : to provoke one and encounter resistance on his part, to anger or incite one < *Cicámato* I challenge you. > – Bl

ka·me·ya·kel \ǩa-mé-ya-kel\ *adv* : squatting down, meaning to remain somewhere < *Ka ~ manke* I sat yonder squatting. > – EB

ka·mi·ma \ǩa-mí-ma\ *va* wa·kámima : to make something flat and round by striking with an axe, as a wheel might be formed

ka·mna \ǩa-mná\ *va* wa·kamna : to get, obtain, earn — *vn perhaps* : to rip, as a seam, to come open, also to rip by striking, as a ball is ripped when struck often, to rip *e.g.* a coat

ka·mna·ki·ya *or* **kamnayan** \ǩa-mná-ǩi-ya\ *va* kamna·wa·kiya kamna·wa·ya : to cause to get or obtain

ka·mni·mni \ka-mní-mni\ *v red of* namni : to hang loosely, dangle, to swing, as a blanket in the wind — **kamnimni·la** *n* : earrings, such as always dangle and are made of a triangular shape < *Wapaha ~ el kšupi* They beaded on warbonnet earrings. > – Cf *owin* to wear *e.g.* earrings MS.153

ka·na \ka-ná\ *pron dem pl of* ka : those yonder – Gramm.23 D.38

ka·na·ke *and* **kanake·ca** *and* **kanake·hci** \ǩa-ná-ǩe\ *adv* : so many, so much, all these — **kana·kiya** \ǩa-ná-ki-ya\ *adv* : all these, so many, in so many ways

ka·ni *and* **ka·ni·ca** \ǩa-ní\ \ǩa-ní-ca\ *va* [fr *ka* striking + *nica* destitute] : to cut off, as meat from bones – *Syn* AKAŠPU Bl

[1]**kan** \ǩaŋ\ *adj* ma·kan un·kan·pi : aged, worn out with age < *Wanna ~* He is now enfeebled, *i.e.* in opposition to former youthful strength. >

[2]**kan** \kaŋ\ *abbrev of* kanta : a plum, plums < *Kan gigi yušpišpi s'e* They seem to pick russet colored plums. > – Note: the word is used in simile. There are red plums among the black ones that seem to be bad, but in reality are ripe and good. The meaning is something like: another kind. Or it indicates doing a thing poorly, *e.g.* writing, since one does not know how to write well – Bl

[3]**kan** \ǩaŋ\ *n* : a vein, artery, a sinew, tendon, nerve, a cord, string < ~ *masuksuta* My nerves are durable. *tahca ~ , pte ~* deer tendons, buffalo tendons, ~ wamaš'akelo My nerves are strong. >

kan'·a·ka·la·ya \kaŋ-á-ǩa-la-ya\ *adv* or *adj* : very lean < ~ *yanka* to be very lean, *i.e.* the veins being very visible and thick, *Pehan s'e napsu kin ~* The toes of a crane are skinny. > – Bl

kan·gi \kaŋ-ǧí\ *n* : a crow — **kangi cehupa ska** *n* : a white, vocal crow – Cf kangí tȧnka

kan·gi·ha mi·gna·ka \ǩaŋ-ǧí-ha mi-gnà-ka\ *n* : a feather disk, resembling the *unhcela kagapi* a bustle used in dancing and having a center like to that of the mescal bean in the upper flower-like part, along with crow feathers, *kangiha.* Hence, a feather ornament fastened on the back and dangling down; it is worn in the Omaha Dance – Bl

kan·gi o·yun·ke \kaŋ-ǧí o-yùŋ-ke\ *n* : a certain place where many crows are known to be nesting – Bl

kan·gi·ta·me \kaŋ-ǧí-ta-me\ *n* : black shale, a certain black soil, a black smooth stone found along the White River in southern South Dakota – MS.356

kan·gi tan·ka \kaŋ-ǧí tàŋ-ǩa\ *n* : the large crow, the raven – Note: there are three kinds of crow: *kangi tanka, uncišicala,* and *kangi cehupa ska.* The last cries out in the morning: "Wakalya, wakalya" and also: "Kah, kah, ..." They were taught to speak – Bl

Kan·gi Wi·ca·ša \Kaŋ-ǧí Wi-cà-ša\ *np* : a Crow Indian

kan·han \kaŋ-háŋ\ *adv* : dangling and falling off or out, tattered, old, falling, as ripe fruit *etc* < *hin ~* shedding hair, fur, as horses lose their hair in spring > — **kanhan·han** *adj* : tattered, ragged, dangling < *Iktomi ehakehcin ~ s'e iyaya ške* The say Iktomi (Spider) went on as if it were the very last time. > – Cf *haakanhanhan,* in *ref* to the clothes of old people; *hin'akanhanhan,* when speaking of horses as they shed their hair

kan·he \kaŋ-hé\ *vn* : to shell out, as ripe corn

kan·he·ca \kaŋ-hé-ca\ *adj* ma·kánheca : ragged, tattered, as one's clothes — **kanhe·heyela** *adv* : ragged < *Wicota kawél ~ , uwelo*A crowd came together poorly dressed, *i.e.* when many come in a hurry having on old clothes. > – Bl

kan·hi \ǩáŋ-hi\ *vn* kán·wa·hi : to live to be old, reach old age

kan·htal \ǩáŋ-ȟtal\ *adv* : with muscles relaxed, with a loss of tension < ~ *imacu* I feel lazy. > – Bl WHL

kan'·i·ca·kpe \kaŋ-í-ca-kṗe\ *n* [fr *kan* worn + *kakpa* to pierce] : a lancet

kan'·i·hun·ni \ǩáŋ-i-huŋ-ni\ *vn* kán'i·wa·hunni : to arrive at a ripe old age – *Syn* KANHI

kan'·i·na·ška·škan \kaŋ-í-na-ška-škaŋ\ *n* : a medical battery

kan'·i·t'a \ǩaŋ-í-t'a\ *vn* kan'i·ma·t'a : to die of old age

kan'·i·wa·psa·ke \ǩaŋ-í-wa-psa-ǩe\ *n* : something, as a knife, with which to cut off a sinew or string *etc* < ~ *wan imikinte šni,* or *imicik'eye* My knife is dull, *i.e.* is not sharp. > – Bl

kan'·i·ye·ya·pi s'e \ǩaŋ-í-ye-ya-pi s'e\ *adv* : as though without difficulties, being provided for all along the way < ~ *ya* or *u* to go or come cheerfully without meeting difficulties, ~ *oyaka* to tell well, in detail from start to finish > – Bl BE

kan·ka·kpa \kaŋ-ǩa-kṗa\ *va* kan·wa·kakpa : to cut a vein, to bleed one – *See* kankícakpa

kan·ke·ca *or* **kanke** \kaŋ-ǩé-ca\ \ǩaŋ-ǩé\ *n* : the pileated woodpecker or woodcock, or the red-headed woodpecker, a water bird with a thin long bill – Note: Bl said the bird, *hena wakan,* is as tall as a crane with a bill about one decimeter long, but along the Missouri River about three inches and yellow. The head was used as an ornament on the *hunkatacanunpa.* See a photograph in D.72. In Santee the *ǩanǩé* is said not to be a water bird and lives in the woods, a woodpecker the size of a wild pigeon with a black body, a red stripe on the head and a black heavy and sharp bill about one and a half inches long – Bl T D.71

kan·ki·ca·kpa \kaŋ-kí-ca-kṗa\ *va* kan·we·cakpa kan·ci·cakpa kan·mi·cakpa : to strike a vein for one, to bleed one

kan·na \kaŋ-ná\ *n* : blisters, that may appear on waist or ankles of men and horses < ~ *witka hiyu welo* Blisters waxed the size of an egg. > – Bl

kan·na·ce·ga \kaŋ-ná-ce-ġa\ *n* : the shape suggestive of a kettle < ~ *itazipa* a kettle shaped bow >

kan·na·ti·pa \káŋ-na-ṫi-ṗa\ \kaŋ-ná-ṫi-ṗa\ *vn* : to draw up, to cramp, as the nerves or muscles

kan·su \kaŋ-sú\ *n* 1 : plum stones, pits or seeds 2 : playing-cards 3 : any ticket — **kansu·kute** \kaŋ-sú-ǩu-te\ *va* kansu·wa·kute : to shoot plum stones, or to play cards — **kansukute·pi** \kaŋ-sú-ǩu-ṫe-ṗi\ *n* : playing cards

kan·su zin·tka·la \kaŋ-sú ziŋ-tkà-la\ *n* : the American redstart perhaps - Note: it is said *Škeluta iyececa* it is like the oriole or auduban, yet some call the redstart *guguya šku,* and also *canpiško*

kan·šni·šni·lak \ǩáŋ-šni-šni-lak\ *v* : to be surprised at, not expecting one < ~ *ataya* to meet one unexpectedly, one whom one had wanted to see > - IS

kan·ta \ǩáŋ-ṫa\ *n* : a plum, plums — **kanta·hu can** *n* : the plum tree, or plum bushes, prunus Americana — **kanta sapa** *n* : prunes — **kantaša wi** *n* : the month of August, when plums get red — **kantuhu** \kaŋ-ṫú-hu\ *n* : the plum bush - # 112

kan·winl \ǩaŋ-wíŋl i-yè-ya\ *v* : to sweep or brush by, move just touching in passing - KE

kan·ye \kaŋ-yé\ *adv* : inwards, towards the center, as of a house

kan·ye·ja \kaŋ-yē'-ja\ *n* : a child - Bl

kan·ye·la \kaŋ-yé-la\ *adv* : near < *Wanna pte otapi ca ~ yapi* They went near where there were many buffalo. >

kan·ye·ta \kaŋ-yé-ṫa\ *adv* or *n* : before, in front of — **kanye·tanhan** *adv* : on the inside of — **kanye·wapa** *adv* : within, towards the center

ka·o·bla·ga·he·ya \ǩa-ó-bla-ġa-he-ya\ *adv perhaps* : scattered out from a central place, as said of a line of men, as soldier, moving farther apart, lengthening the line, and thus being less likely to be hit < *Icitehanyan yapi he kapi* They intended they go far apart from each other. > - *Syn* NAOBLEL AYE S'E Bl

ka·o·ble·lya \ǩa-ó-ble-lya\ *adv* : scattered away from each other and leaving a free center < ~ *waci* to dance with a free center area > - Bl

ka·o·blo·ton \ǩa-ó-blo-toŋ\ *va* : to make edged, cornered by striking, to form a corner - Bl

ka·o·ci·kpa·ni \ǩa-ó-ci-kṗa-ni\ *va* wa·káocikpani : to make unequal sizes by striking — **kaocikpani·yan** *adv* : unequally

ka·o·cin·ši·ca \ǩa-ó-ciŋ-ši-ca\ *va* : to strike and make mean - Bl

ka·o·ci·pte·ca \ǩa-ó-ci-pte·ca\ *adv* : not equal — **kaocipteI** *adv contrac* : unequal, one large and one small, diminishing or increasing in size — **kaocipte·lya** *adv* : unequally — **kaocipte·tu** *adv* : unequal in size *etc* - R Bl

ka·o·gmi·gma \ǩa-ó-gmi-gma\ *v* : to make roll into something by striking, to make roll over and over by striking - R

ka·o·gna i·ye·i·c'i·ya \ka-ó-gna i-yè-i-c'i-ya\ *v refl* : to copulate, have intercourse - *Syn* KAOKAJAYA IYEIC'IYA - Bl

ka·o·he·ye \ka-ó-he-ye\ *adj* : slanted, as in toenailing wall studs in place - WHL

ka·o·hla·gan \ǩa-ó-ȟla-ġaŋ\ *vn* [fr *kahlagan* become long] : to get loosened, as bolts on a wagon, or as belts on any machine — **kaohla·gyela** *adv* : loosely, loose like a coat that is too big for one < ~ *nun* You wear too big a coat. > - A

ka·o·hla·hya·la·ka \ǩa-ó-ȟla-ȟya-la-ka\ *v imper perhaps* : be not near to and not very far from *e.g.* a place < *Nahahci* ~ Yet do not be very far from here. *Kitanla ~ ca yuinahni po* It is pretty far yet, so you better hurry up. >

ka·o·hla·ka·la \ka-ó-ȟla-ka-la\ *adj* : loose , as a wire on a car, which was once tight, or as one on a tree in which it once was imbed but now is loose

ka·o·hmin \ǩa-ó-ȟmiŋ\ *va* wa·kaohmin : to cause to move obliquely, as a man on horseback does with a running cow, going against her, to throw obliquely — **kaohmin·yan** *adv* : obliquely, moving sideways like a horse that is struck on one side < ~ *iyaya* to throw obliquely > - R Bl

ka·o·hpa \ǩa-ó-ȟṗa\ *va* wa·káohpa : to break through, to smash, to knock in *e.g.* somebody's skull — **kaohpe·kiya** \ǩa-ó-ȟpe-ǩi-ya\ *va* kaohpe·wa·kiya : to cause to knock a hole in — **kaohpe·ya** *va* : to cause to strike through — *adv* : in the manner of striking through - D.103

ka·o·hya \ǩa-ó-ȟya\ *adv* : leaning, sloping, twisting < ~ *egnaka* to place something leaning or sloping >

ka·o·h'an·ko \ǩa-ó-ȟ'aŋ-ko\ *va* wa·kaoh'anko [fr *oh'anko* to be quick at doing] : to strike and make go or work fast — **kaoh'anko·ya** *adv* : with greated hurry < ~ *škan yo* Be quick about what you are doing. > - B.H. 148.10 Bl

ka·o·i·yo·ki·pi \ka-ó-i-yo-ki-pi\ *v* : to be in good spirits - B.H.92.4

ka·o·ka·ja·ya i·ye·i·c'i·ya \ǩa-ó-ǩa-ja-ya i-yè-i-c'i-ya\ *v refl* : to have sexual intercourse, copulate - *Syn* KAOGNA IYEIC'IYA

ka·o·ka·ja·ya·ta e·kta i·ye·i·c'i·ya \ǩa-ó-ǩa-ja-ya-ta e-ktà i-yè-i-c'i-ya\ *v* : to get into the fork of a river so that one must retreat - Bl

ka·o·ki·c'u·ya \ǩa-ó-ǩi-c'u-ya\ *adv* : deluge-like, as is said of water spreading all over < ~ *iyaya* It went flooding everywhere. > - B.H.54.15

ka·o·ko·kab \ǩa-ó-ko-ǩab\ *adv* : around, across, before < ~ *ya* to go around, to hedge up the way, as in chasing buffalo >

ka·o·ksa \ǩa-ó-ksa\ *vn* : to fall off or over, to crumble down, as a bank, to fall in, cave in - *Syn* PTUH'A B.H.43.9, 72.15 Bl — *va* wa·kaoksa : to cut a hole into or through, as in ice — **kaokse·ya** *va* kaokse·wa·ya : to cause to break in, fall in, as an earthen bank

ka·o·ktan \ǩa-ó-ktaŋ\ *va* wa·kaoktan : to bend and pound in — **kaoktan·yan** *va* kaoktan·wa·ya : to cause to bend in — *adv* : bending into

ka·o·lu·i·c'i·ya \ka-ó-lu-i-c'i-ya\ *v refl* : to cool off by fanning one's self < ~ *yanka* to sit fanning one's self > - Note: the spelling *kaolusic'iya* is doubtful

ka·o·mni·mni \ǩa-ó-mni-mni\ *n perhaps* : a whirling around < ~ *iyecel canteluze lo* You formed an opinion like a whirlwind; ~ *iyecel wilukcan yelo* you understand like twister, as is said of one who makes all sorts of statements, *i.e.* he lies. > - BT

ka·o·na \ǩa-ō'-na\ *va* wa·káona : to drive or hammer on as an iron ring on a stick by striking

ka·on·spe \ǩa-óŋ-ṡpe\ *v* wa·kaonspe [fr *onspe* to teach] : to train, teach, as a horse, to break — **kaonspe·šni** *adj* : untrained, untaught

ka·on·ze wo·slal \ǩa-óŋ-ze wo-slàl\ *adv* : heels up < ~ *iyeya, ihpeya* to land erect, to threw down on end >

ka·o·p'o \ǩa-ó-p'o\ *v* : to raise dust, as in sweeping

ka·o·p'o·šya \ǩa-ó-p'o-šya\ *v* : to cause a stove to

\a\ father \e\ they \i\ machine \o\ smoke \u\ lunar \an, aŋ\ blanc Fr. \in, iŋ\ ink \on, oŋ, un, uŋ\ soon, confier Fr. \c\ chair \ġ\ machen Ger. \j\ fusion \clusters: bl, gn, kp, hšl, etc...\ b[e]lo ... said with a slight vowel
See more in the Introduction, Guide to Pronunciation

smoke by opening a room door *etc* - Bl
ka·o·sma·ka \k̇a-ó-sma-k̇a\ *va* [fr *osmaka* a gulch] : to make an indentation by striking, to make a hole through like into the ground
ka·o·sni \k̇a-ó-sni\ *adj* : made cool or cold — **kaosnii-c'iya** *v refl* : to cool down, refresh one's self in the open air, to cool off by fanning one's self - *Syn* KAOLUIC'I-YA — **kaosni·sni** *v red* : to be cooling off
ka·o·spa \k̇a-ó-sṗa\ *va* wa·kaospa : to strike and bruise in
ka·o·spe·ya \k̇a-ó-sṗe-ya\ *v* : to weigh down — **kao-speye·ton** *va* : to weigh anything
ka·o·swa \k̇a-ó-swa\ *v* : to slide down an incline, as of dirt or sand on a river bank, or of hay on a stack < ~ *hinhpaya* to fall sliding down a slope > WHL
ka·o·šlok i·ya·ya \k̇a-ó-šlok i-yà-ya\ *v* : to make a misstep and almost fall but then go on < *Yunkan ~ imayaya s'e hingla* Then suddenly it was as if I made a misstep and went right on. >
ka·o·šlo·šlog \k̇a-ó-šlo-šlog\ *v* : to stumble - *Syn* KAI-ŠUTA IYAYA
ka·o·špa \ka-ŏ'-špa\ *v* : to fall < ~ *hinhpaya* to fall off, as from a bank into a river > - Note: this word may well be incorrect since it seems confused with the word *kaóswa*
ka·o·ta la·ke s'e \k̇a-ó-ṫa là-k̇e s'e\ *adv* : a few more - B.H.67.18, 120.14
ka·o·tan \k̇a-ó-ṫaŋ\ *va* wa·kaotan : to pound tight into, as a board that stands out between others back among which it is knocked - Cf kaóna Bl D.58
ka·o·tan'·in \k̇a-ó-taŋ-in\ *va* wa·kaotan'in [fr *otan'in* to be visible] : to make manifest or apparent
ka·o·te·he·han \k̇a-ó-ṫe-he-haŋ\ *adv* : afar, distant, not yet time < *Nahahci ~ lakelo* It is yet pretty far. > - *Syn* KAOHLAHYALAKA Bl WHL
ka·o·tku·ga \k̇a-ó-tk̇u-ġa\ *vn* : to close and be locked of itself, as a door with a night-latch — **kao·tkuh** \k̇a-ó-tk̇uh̄\ *vn contrac* : to go and get on the other side, as a doorway, to go through and be on the other side of a door when slammed behind - Note: R gives *katkuh.* Bl BD
ka·o·t'ins \k̇a-ó-t'iŋs\ *va contrac of* kaot'inza : to pound tight < ~ *iyeya.* ~ *yankapi* He pounded it tight. They sat tightly packed, or They are crowded together, as in a room packed full. > - Bl
ka·o·t'in·za \k̇a-ó-t'iŋ-za\ *va* wa·kaot'inza [fr *ot'inza* tight in] : to drive or pound tight into a hole, as a fence-post or a screw into a hole that was there, to pound in tight something that is loose, as a loose nail in a wall
ka·o·wan·ya \k̇a-ó-waŋ-ya\ *vn* : to grow, be added to, increase < *Sanb kaowanye s'e* It is as though the story grew, *i.e.* while it is told to others. > - Bl WHL
ka·o·winh i·ya·ya \k̇a-ó-wiŋh̄ i-yà-ya\ *v* : to go, walk, in a circle < *Hinhanna el wanna wanase aya, na paha wan eya* (perhaps) *he ehanl ~ iyaya, na pte otayelo, eyapi* They said In the morning they went on a buffalo hunt, and since (perhaps) there was a hill they then travelled in a circle, for there were many buffalo. >
ka·o·wo·tan \k̇a-ó-wo-taŋ\ *va* wa·kaowotan : to do straightening out of beads or notches, as in wire by striking - Bl
ka·o·wo·tan'·in \k̇a-ó-wo-taŋ-iŋ\ *vn* : to clear away, as a storm or anything that obstructs vision, to clear off, become so that things can be seen at a distance
ka·o·wo·tan·la \k̇a-ó-wo-taŋ-la\ *va* [fr *owotanla* straight] wa·kaowotanla : to straighten, make straight by striking in any way
ka·o·ya·ȟe \k̇a-ó-ya-ȟe\ *v* wa·kaoyaȟe : to empty a vessel - Bl
ka·o·yu·tan·yan \k̇a-ó-yu-ṫaŋ-yaŋ\ *n perhaps* : a cut made into a tree with an axe and leaves it then later - B
ka·o·zan s'e \k̇a-ó-zaŋ s'e\ *adv* : as if hanging over the face, *i.e.* one's hair < ~ *wakita* to look through hair hanging over the face > - Cf aokahiya Bl
ka·o·ze·ze \k̇a-ó-ze-ze\ *vn* : to swing, dangle, as by the wind - *Syn* PAOZEZE — **kaozeze·ya** *adv* : swinging, dangling < ~ *yanka* to be dangling, or swinging >
[1]**ka·pa** *or* **kapan** \k̇a-pá\ *va* wa·kapa **1** to beat or thresh off, as corn, to pound up *e.g.* meat
[2]**ka·pa** \ka-pá\ *va* ka·wa·pa ka·un·pa·pi **a** : to pass by in running, to beat in a race, to excel, surpass in anything **b** : to go beyond, to transgress - D.107
ka·pan \k̇a-páŋ\ *va* wa·kapan : to beat or thresh off *e.g.* corn, to beat meat, make *pápa* — **kapan·pan** *va* wa·kapanpan : to beat soft, make mellow — **kapan·-yan** *v* : to beat, pummel, soften up < ~ *yanka, iyotaka yo* Make soft a spot for yourself and sit, *i.e.* by beating smoothe the hides *etc.* > - Bl
[1]**ka·pe** \k̇a-ṗé\ *va* : to chisel < *Inyan kapepi* They chiseled stone. > - B.H.100.7
[2]**ka·pe** \k̇a-ṗé\ *va* wa·kape [fr *pe* sharp or pointed] : to sharpen by pounding *e.g.* a scythe
[3]**ka·pe** *or* **kapa** \ka-ṗé\ \ka-pá\ *va* : to excel < *Ki inyankapi na Joe kape.* They came back running and Joe won, came in first. >
ka·pe·mni \k̇a-ṗé-mni\ *va* wa·kápemni [fr *pemni* crooked] : to make crooked or awry by striking < *Tahca topapi eyaš ~ k'in* But then he carried making it a crooked load of four deer. > — **kapemni·mni** *v red* : to make go awry — **kapemnimni·yan** *adv* : dangling < ~ *otkeic'iyapi* They had themselves hung dangling, *i.e.* in making giant strides. > — **kapemni·yan** *adv* : crookedly, dangling, swinging, as scissors tied by a string < *Ungna ~ mic'ignake ci* Surely perhaps I laid it up for myself readily available. > - MS.75 B.H.203.6 Bl
ka·pe·pe \k̇a-ṗéṗe\ *or* \k̇a-ṗé-ṗe\ *va red* [fr *k̇apé* to sharpen, and *kapé* to excel] : to be sharpening, and to be exceling
ka·pe·sto \k̇a-ṗé-sṫo\ *va* wa·kapesto [fr *pesto* sharp-pointed] : to make sharp-pointed with an axe < *Na can kapestopi top yuha najin* He stood holding four wooden sharp-pointed arrows. > — **kapesto·pi** *n* : an arrow all made of wood, the head end made sharp and thin to kill birds or other little animals
ka·pe·ya \ka-ṗé-ya\ *va* kape·wa·ya [fr *kapá* to excel] : to go or pass beyond, to do more, to cause to surpass — *adv* : beyond, further, greater than, surpassing
ka·pin \k̇a-ṗíŋ\ *vn* wa·ká-pin : to be indisposed or unwilling to do a thing, to be tired < *mani ~* to be too tired to walk, *econ ~* to be unwilling to do it, *ie ~* to be ill-disposed to say, *ape ~* to be tired of waiting > - D.81
ka·pin·ja \k̇a-ṗíŋ-ja\ *va* wa·kapinja : to shorten a horse's tail
ka·pis \k̇a-ṗís\ *va contrac of* kapiza : to make squeal
ka·pi·ye·han \k̇a-ṗí-ye-haŋ\ *adv* : sometime ago, a certain length of time, as implied in:. A long time ago I saw you and have seen you again; you were well and still are - Gb
ka·pi·za \k̇a-ṗí-za\ *va* wa·kápiza : to make squeak or squeal
ka·po \k̇a-ṗó\ *vn* ma·kápo : to swell, as one's flesh

ka·pob \k̇a-póḃ\ *va* [fr *kapopa* to make a popping noise] : to burst with a noise < ~ *iyaya* to go pop, ~ *iyeya* suddenly to pop, *or* to cause to burst >

ka·po·gan \k̇a-ṗó-ġaŋ\ *vn* : to puff out and become tied, to swell like a sail for the wind – *va* : to puff up a bladder — **kapoh** \k̇a-ṗóḣ\ *v contrac of* kapogan : to puff out, swell < ~ *iyeya* to make swell > — **kapo·hya** *va* kapo·hwa·ya : to make swell out, as anything filled with air — *adv* : rising, swelling out < *Mini ~ hiyotake* He came and sat down with a water swell, a blister. >

ka·po·lpo·ta \k̇a-ṗó-lṗo-ṫa\ *va red of* kapota : to tear or to reduce to shreds

ka·pon·ya \k̇a-ṗóŋ-ya\ *v* kapon·wa·ya : to remove the last rough places from a hide with the *wahintka* a hide scraper – Bl

ka·po·pa \k̇a-ṗó-ṗa\ *va* wa·kapopa : to make a popping noise by striking, *i.e.* smashing and making burst

kapopa·pi hu \k̇a-ṗó-ṗa-ṗi hu\ *n* : the closed or blind gentian and the bottle gentian. Gentiana Andrews-ii, the gentian family, also called *wahca wašte* beauty flower – Bc Bl

ka·po·ta \k̇a-ṗó-ṫa\ *va* or *vn* wa·kapota : to tear by striking, as clothes hung out and torn by the wind

ka·po·ya \k̇a-pó-ya\ *va* kapo·wa·ya : to brush *e.g.* one's coat

ka·psag \k̇a-pság\ *va* [fr *kapsaka* to cut or break something like a string] : to break violently < ~ *iyeya* or *ihpeya* to break *or* throw, ~ *hinhpaya* to fall breaking > — **kapsa·gya** *va* kapsa·gwa·ya : to cause to break — *adv* : broken, as a string

ka·psa·ka \k̇a-psá-k̇a\ : to cut something as a string or wire *etc*, limbed in two, to break *e.g.* a string by striking, — *vn* : to be cut in two < *Wikan kin kapsakahe* He was cutting the lasso limbed in two. > – D.66

ka·psan·psan \k̇a-psáŋ-psaŋ\ *vn* : to dangle, swing back and forth, to sway to and fro, as a limb in water — *vt perhaps* : to make something swing back and forth < *sicapsanpsan* to do pacing back and forth > – *See* sicápsan

ka·psa·psa·ka \k̇a-psá-psa-k̇a\ *v* [fr *kapsaka* to break or cut] : to be cutting in two *e.g.* a piece of string or wire

ka·psi·ca \k̇a-psí-ca\ *va* wa·kapsica : to make jump by striking, as in playing shinney < *tabkápsicapi* the game of shinney > — **ka·psil** \k̇a-psíl\ *va contrac* : to cause to jump – Note: the *contrac* is the same spelling as the *contrac* of *kapsinta* perhaps R

ka·psin·psin·ta \k̇a-psíŋ-psiŋ-ṫa\ *va* wa·kapsinpsinta : to whip, to correct by whipping, scourging – *Syn* YUPSINPSINTA

ka·psin·ta \k̇a-psíŋ-ṫa\ *va* wa·kapsinta : to whip, flog, to correct, as a child by whipping — **kapsinta·pi s'e** *adv* : whipping as it were < *Léceya, kola ~ škinmic'iye lo* Certainly, I am moved to seemingly whipping a friend. > – BT

ka·psi·psi·ca \k̇a-psí-psi-ca\ *va red* wa·kapsica [fr *kapsica* to make jump] : to make jump much by striking — **kapsi·psil** *v contrac* : to throw out and make skip about, as in fishing < ~ *iyeya* to make skip > – D.217

ka·pson \k̇a-psóŋ\ *va* wa·kapson : to spill something by striking — **kapson·pson** *va red* : to be spilling

ka·pšun \k̇a-pšúŋ\ *va* wa·kapšun : to break something by striking, as a ball hitting a tooth, to knock out *i.e.* a tooth, to dislocate *e.g.* a joint, by striking

ka·pšun·ka \k̇a-pšúŋ-k̇a\ *va* wa·kapšunka : to make round or knob-like

ka·pšun·pšun \k̇a-pšúŋ-pšuŋ\ *v red* [fr *kapšun* break by striking] : to strike and break out — **kapšun·yan** *va* kapšun·wa·ya : to cause to knock out of place

ka·pta \k̇a-ptá\ *va* wa·kapta : to lade or bail out, as water from a boat < ~ *iyaye* to break bursting under a heavy weight, as a sack whose contents are too heavy >

ka·ptan·ptan \k̇a-ptáŋ-ptaŋ\ *va* wa·kaptanptan : to turn over and over — **kaptan·yan** \k̇a-ṗtáŋ-yaŋ\ *va* wa·kaptanyan : to cause to fall over, to turn over, upset, as a canoe — *adv* : turning over — **kaptanye·ya** *va* kaptanye·wa·ya : to cause to fall over, to overturn

ka·pta·pta \k̇a-ṗtá-ṗta\ *vn* : to fall to pieces, as something rotten

ka·ptu·ga \k̇a-ptú-ġa\ *va* wa·kaptuga : to break off a piece by striking – BD

ka·ptu·h'a \k̇a-ptú-ḣ'a\ *va* : to scrape off, whittle off, as for kindling — **kaptuh'a·h'a** *va red* : to scrape off little things, as fibers from a hide – Bl

ka·ptu·ja \k̇a-ṗtú-ja\ *va* wa·kaptuja : to cause *e.g.* a board to crack and overlap by striking it on one end, to split or crack by striking, but not to split open — **kaptuptuja** *v red* : to make split or crack — **kaptu·ptuš** *va red contrac* : to be cracking < ~ *iyeya* to make crack > — **kaptuš** *v contrac* : to crack — **kaptuš·kiya** \k̇a-ṗtú-šk̇i-ya\ *va* kaptu·šwa·kiya : to cause to make crack

ka·ptu·za \k̇a-ptú-za\ *v* : to give a blow so as to make bend forward and over, as a blow to the pit of the stomach – Bl WHL

ka·pu·za \k̇a-ṗú-za\ *va* wa·kapuza : to make something dry by shaking it in the wind — *vn* : to become dry by being shaken by the wind, as one's laundry – Note: BT used the word also for voting "dry", *i.e.* to prohibit the sale of liquor in the state of South Dakota

ka·p'i \k̇a-p'í\ *v* : to float or wave, as in the wind < *Tate ca wowapi kap'iyelo* There was a wind that floated a letter away. > — **kap'i·p'i** *vn red perhaps* : to wink, blink, as when something gets into the eye or dazzles one < *Išta wiyohpemayin kte seca ca ~ wawakita yelo* I watched for what it seemed he threw into my eyes. >

ka·p'o \k̇a-p'ó\ *va* wa·kap'o : to raise dust, as in sweeping

ka·p'o·ja *or* **kap'oje·la** \k̇a-p'ó-ja\ *adj* : light, not heavy – Note: Kap'ojela was the name of the father of *Tašunke Witko* Crazy Horse – RF

ka·p'o·ši·c'i·ya \k̇a-p'ó-ši-c'i-ya\ *v* : to balance one's self — **kap'oš ki·c'un** *v* : to wear or walk lightly and carefully, as when passing on or over ice, in order not to break through — **kap'o·šp'o·ja** *adj red of* kap'oja : quite light, not heavy < *kap'ošp'oje s'e mani*, or *henala s'e mani* to walk as if one were plenty light, or to walk as though he were only so light. > — **kap'ošp'oje·la** *adv red of* kap'ojela : lightly, noiselessly < ~ *s'e mani* to walk as though lightly, without any noise> — **kap'ošye·la** *adv* : with care, lightly < *Taku oyasin ~ yacin* You lightly desire all things. > – Bl

ka·sa \k̇a-sá\ *va* wa·kasa : to bury in the snow, cover over with snow

ka·sa·bsa·bye·la \k̇a-sá-bsa-bye-la\ *adv red of* kasabyela : heavily < ~ *hinhpaye* She dropped to the ground repeatedly from weakness. > – D.270

\a\ father \e\ they \i\ machine \o\ smoke \u\ lunar \an, aŋ\ blanc Fr. \in, iŋ\ ink \on, oŋ, un, uŋ\ soon, confier Fr. \c\ chair \ġ\ machen Ger. \j\ fusion \clusters: bl, gn, kp, hšl, etc...\ b^{e}lo ... said with a slight vowel **See more in the Introduction, Guide to Pronunciation**

ka·sa·bye·la \k̇a-sá-bye-la\ *adv* : heavily < ~ *hinhpaya* to fall heavily, as from weakness > — Cf kasábsabyela

ka·sag \k̇a-sag\ *va contrac* [fr *kasaka* to whip] : to whip < ~ *iyeya* to keep whipping >

ka·sa·ka \k̇a-sá-k̇a\ *va* wa·kasaka : to switch, whip — **kasa·ksaka** *va red* wa·kasaksaka : to whip, to hit one

ka·san \k̇a-sáŋ\ *vn* wa·kasan : to turn white, as paint does from rain — *va* : to whiten by scraping — **ka-san·san** *v* wa·kasansan : to scrape and whiten

ka·se·pa \k̇a-sé-ṗa\ *vn* : to wash off, as the rain does paint - R B

ka·ska \k̇a-sk̇á\ *va* wa·kaska : to bleach by striking or dragging — *vn* : to become clear, to clear off, as clouds or smoke *etc* < *Mahpiya kin ~ iyaya* The cloud went and cleared off. *Na wicaša wan najin k'on el owotan'inšni na ~ iyaya na hecena oyate kin wanyank najinpi na ecel atan'in* And where the man had stood there was a haze, and it went and became clear, and finally the people stood seeing, and thus he was apparent. *Numbkaska* Two together became clear. > - Cf ícicaskaya WE

ka·skab \k̇a-sk̇áb\ *va contrac of* kaskapa : to strike off with the hand < ~ *iyeya* to swat >

ka·ska·pa \k̇a-sk̇á-ṗa\ *va* wa·kaskapa : to strike, as with the hand, to slap, to strike one's hands together - Note: the word is **not** *kaškapa*

ka·ska·ya \k̇a-sk̇á-ya\ *v* kaska·wa·ya : to make clear up < *Ošota ca kaskawaye* Since it was smoky I made it clear up. >

ka·skeb \k̇a-sk̇éb\ *va contrac* [fr *kaskepa* to empty by drinking] : to empty < ~ *iyeya* to bail out > — **kaske-bkiya** \k̇a-sk̇é-bk̇i-ya\ *va* kaske·bwa·kiya : to cause to bail out *e.g.* water from a canoe — **kaske·bya** *va* : to bail or empty out

ka·ske·pa \k̇a-sk̇é-ṗa\ *va* wa·kaskepa [fr *skepa* to leak or evaporate] : to empty something, as a bucket, gradually by drinking from it, to bail out, empty *e.g.* a pond *etc*

ka·ski·ca \k̇a-sk̇í-ca\ *vn* : to settle down, as does a stack of hay — *va* : to press, press down on by striking - Note: the latter meaning being the more correct - R

ka·ski·glag \k̇a-sk̇í-glag\ *adv* : without order or system, unpatterned < ~ *wicoti* to encamp together without order > - Bl

ka·skil \k̇a-sk̇íl\ *v contrac of* kaskica : to press down < ~ *yuza* to clasp in the arms > — **kaski·lya** *va* kaski·-lwa·ya : to cause to settle down or to press down

ka·ski·ska \k̇a-sk̇í-sk̇a\ *v* : to make rough or wavy by pounding — **kaskiska·ska** *v red* : to pound into various shapes or forms — **kaskiskaska·kel** *adv* : pounding in various patterns < ~ *kagege* to work out a pattern, map-like, as in beadwork *etc*, ~ *wakagege k'on wana kitanyankel wagluštan* I was now finished with the greatest difficulty with what I had worked out as a pattern. > - Bl WHL

ka·ski·ta \k̇a-sk̇í-ṫa\ *v* : to press, to clasp

ka·sku \k̇a-sk̇ú\ *va* wa·kasku : to peel off *e.g.* bark with an axe - BD

ka·sku·hya \k̇a-sk̇ú-ȟya\ *adv* : curring off squarely

ka·sk'i·ya·ya \k̇a-sk̇'í-ya-ya\ *vn* [fr *kaska* to clear + *iyaya* to have gone] : to clear up, as the weather - P Bl

ka·sla·la \k̇a-slá-la\ *adv* : slowly and carefully, not having expression < ~ *mani ya*, ~ *woglaka* to go walking carefully, to talk with care > - Cf sláta *Syn* KATÉ-YAKEL Bl

ka·sle·ca \k̇a-slé-ca\ *va* wa·kasleca : to split, *e.g.* wood, with an axe — **ka·slel** \k̇a-slél\ *va contrac* : to split < ~ *iyeya* to split quickly > — **kasle·lya** *va* kasle·lwa·ya : to cause to split — **kasle·slel** *va red contrac of* kasle-sleca : to cause splitting

ka·sli \k̇a-slí\ *va* wa·kasli : to strike and force something out, as water from a bladder or rubber ball, or grease from the same < ~ *kuté* to shoot at something many times > — **kasli·ya** *va* kasli·wa·ya : to cause one to press out - BD

ka·slo·han \k̇a-sló-haŋ\ *va* or *vn* : to make something or somebody slide by striking < ~ *iyeya* to make slide suddenly, ~ *yeya* or ~ *yemaya* to slide, as a wagon does on a slanting and slippery road *or* It made me slide, *Kaslohelo* He was sliding. ~ *glihpaye* Sliding he fell. > — **kaslohan·han** *v red* : to keep sliding, staggering < ~ *ihpaya* to fall again and again, like a staggering drunken man perhaps > - BT D.84

ka·sma·ka \k̇a-smá-k̇a\ *va* wa·kasmaka **a** : to indent or make concave by striking **b** : to make a track, as does a wagon

ka·smin \k̇a-smíŋ\ *va* wa·kasmin : to strike off something by means of an axe — **kasmin·yan** *v* : to make bare, as in striking off — **kasminyan·yan** *v red* : to be trimming bare

ka·sna \k̇a-sná\ *va* wa·kasna : to make ring or sound by striking *e.g.* a piece of iron or a kettle — **kasna·sna** *v red* wa·kasnasna **a** : to make ring **b** : to trim or cut off *e.g.* the limbs from a tree and so leave it bare

ka·sni \k̇a-sní\ *va* wa·kasni [fr *sni* cold] : to put out, extinguish by beating a fire, to cool *e.g.* food by shaking it or pouring it from one vessel into another — **kasni·-sni** *va red* : to stanch a flame - Bl

ka·sol \k̇a-sól\ *va contrac of* kasóta : to use up by striking — *vn* : to get or clear out of the way what is waste < ~ *iyeya* to use up quickly, ~ *eihpeya* to dispose throwing away, ~ *iyayelo* It went clearing out of the way, *i.e.* clouds were clearing away. - Cf kaska, *kaska iyayelo* the weather went and cleared up>

ka·so·ta \k̇a-só-ṫa\ *va* wa·kasota : to use up by striking as by felling trees and thus getting farm land, or by killing off cattle, or by having men fall in battle to use up — *vn* : to clear off, as the sky < *Kasol iyayelo* The weather cleared. >

ka·spa·ya \k̇a-sṗá-ya\ *va* wa·kaspaya [fr *spaya* to be wet] : to wet, moisten, as in sprinkling the floor before sweeping

ka·spe·ya \k̇a-sṗé-ya\ *va* kaspe·wa·ya : to weigh, *esp* something heavy — **kaspeye·la** *adv* : rather heavy < ~ *ku welo* He returned carrying too heavy a burden and sweating. > - Bl

ka·stag \k̇a-sṫág\ *va contrac of* kastaka : to throw on < ~ *ihpeya* to throw and make stick *e.g.* mud >

ka·sta·ka \k̇a-sṫá-k̇a\ *va* wa·kastaka : to throw on, as mud, to dump something, not liquid, *e.g.* mud or grain from a basin

ka·stan·ka \k̇a-sṫáŋ-k̇a\ *va* wa·kastanka : to moisten by pounding

ka·sto \k̇a-sṫó\ *va* wa·kasto : to smooth down, to stroke as hair with the hand < *Hena ~ wicunyuhapi*, perhaps: we value them highly. > — **kasto·sto** *va red* wa·kasto-sto : to make smooth, to stroke — **kasto·ya** *adv* : smoothly

ka·su·ksu·ta \k̇a-sú-ksu-ta\ *v red of* kasuta : to toughen

ka·su·ta \k̇a-sú-ṫa\ *v* wa·kasuta : to pound and make hard or tough, as in pounding a hide, to make *e.g.* tough boys by striking

ka·swa \k̇a-swá\ *va* wa·kaswa : to make lint, to curry

kaswa·ka \k̇a-swá-ka\ *va* : to make ragged, to shred – Cf kazá *Syn* KAZAZECA Bl D.36 WHL
ka·swa·swa \k̇a-swá-swa\ *v red of* kaswá : to curry
ka·swu \k̇a-swú\ *va* wa·kaswu : to cut into small strips, cut into dangles, make fringes — **kaswu·kiya** \k̇a-swú-k̇i-ya\ *va* kaswu·wa·kiya : to cause to cut into strips — **kaswu·pi** *n* : dangles, fringes — **kaswupi s'e** *adv* : fringed as it were, as is said of old torn clothes > — **kaswu·swu** *v red* wa·kaswuswu : to cut into strips and let hang
ka·s'a \k̇a-s'á\ *va* wa·kas'a : to strike and make hiss, as a snake < ~ *hanpi* They (the snakes) poised to strike. > — *vn* : to sail or glide in the air, as some birds do — **kas'a·kiya** \k̇a-s'á-k̇i-ya\ *v* : to extend one's hands over < *nape* ~ to hold one's hands spread out like wings *(kas'a)*, as over a stove to warm them, *Nape kas'awakiyelo* I had my hands to spread out. > — **kas'a·la** *adv* : proudly, putting on airs < *Wicaša* ~ *inajin* A man stood up putting on airs. *Wicaša* ~ *yanka* The man sat proudly > — **kas'ala·kel** *adv* : unconcerned < ~ *yanka* to be unconcerned about anything around one > – Note: *okas'a* to soar BD R Bl
ka·s'in·s'in \k̇a-s'íŋ-s'iŋ\ *v* : to dangle, drivel, as phlegm from the mouth of a sick person who is not strong enough to spit it all out < *Imništan* ~ He drivelled water from his mouth. > – Cf *s'ins'inya* to crane one's neck or throat — **kas'ins'in·yan** *adv red of* kas'inyan : drivelling < ~ *ikoyake* It stuck as he drivelled. > — **kas'in·yan** *adv* : dangling, like phlegm from the mouth of a cow *etc* –BD Bl
kaš *or perhaps* **ka** \kaš\ *encl emph* < ~ *iyunga yo* Well ask! > — *pron indef* : anyone, *cumque* in Latin, and perhaps the same as *k'eyaš* < *Tuweni ~ heca wanice. Tuweni ~ hecon kin he šni* Nobody whatever is wanting. Nobody whatever could do it, *or* Nobody could ever, I don't care who, do it, *i.e.* I am the very one. >
ka·še \k̇a-šé\ *vn* ma·kaše : to strike against, stumble < *Sipa* ~ It struck against his toes. > – Cf ptehu kaše
ka·še·ca \k̇a-šé-ca\ *va* wa·kášeca : to make dead or dry by striking, to deaden by cutting around, as around a tree — **kaše·lki·ya** \k̇a-šé-lk̇i-ya\ *va* kaše·lwa·kiya : to cause to deaden
ka·še·ya \k̇a-šé-ya\ *va* kaše·wa·ya : to obstruct, fend off — *adv* : hitting against
ka·šib \k̇a-šíb\ *va contrac of* kašipa : to knock or cut off < ~ *iyeya* to knock off suddenly >
ka·ši·bye·la \k̇a-ší-bye-la\ *adv* : bent < ~ *mani* to walk bent under a burden >
ka·ši·ca \k̇a-ší-ca\ *va* wa·kašica [fr *šica* bad, spoiled] : to spoil by striking, as in spoiling a table with an axe — **kašica·howaya** *va* wa·kašicahowaya : to cause to cry out by striking *e.g.* a dog — **kaši·kšil** *adv* : ruined, spoiled, infected < ~ *wakanpi sece* It seemed as though spirits infected him. > – D.196 BT
ka·ši·pa \k̇a-ší-ṗa\ *va perhaps* wa·kašipa : to knock or cut off close, as branches from a tree, legs from a chair or pot or rivets from a knife — *vn* : to be bent under the weight of something, as a hay rack
ka·ška \k̇a-šká\ *va* wa·kaška : to tie, bind, to imprison < ~ *yuha* to lead *i.e.* a horse, ~ *gle* to picket, ~ *gluza* to tie one's own, ~ *yus kte ayapi* They led him out to kill him. ~ *yus ayin kte* He will lead him away to bind him. *Zaptan-kaška wicincala k'un ole yapi* Prisoners-Five had gone to look for the girl. > — **kaška·han** *part* : tied, bound – D.227, 258, 157 MS.352 B.H.148.8, 130.6
ka·škan·škan \k̇a-škáŋ-škaŋ\ *vn* ma·kaškanškan : to be shaking, being shaken up, as when sitting on a heavy wagon, *i.e.* bumping or hitting – *Syn* NAŠKANŠKAN, KAHUNHUNZA
ka·ška-pa \k̇a-šká-ṗa\ *v* wa·kaškapa : to make a noise, as by striking water – *Syn* PAŠKAPA
ka·ška·pi·ya \k̇a-šká-ṗi-ya\ *va* kaškapi·wa·ya : to cause one to be bound, to have one arrested
ka·ška·ška \k̇a-šká-ška\ *va red of* kaška : to tie up one – B.H.217.15, 284.19
ka·škeb \k̇a-škéb\ *va* [fr *kašk̇epa* to press out] : to strike or press out by striking, as water from anything
ka·ške·han \k̇a-šké-haŋ\ *va* wa·kaškehan [fr *šk̇ehan* high spirited] : to make skip about by striking
ka·ške·pa \k̇a-šké-ṗa\ *va* wa·kaškepa : to strike and press out, as water
ka·ške·ya \k̇a-šké-ya\ *va* : to have one arrested < *Kaškewicaye* He had them arrested. > – B.H.286.4
ka·ški \k̇a-šk̇í\ *va* wa·kaški : to pound, grind *e.g.* cherries < *canpák̇aškipi* mashed cherries, a cherry grinder perhaps >
ka·ški·ca \k̇a-šk̇í-ca\ *va* wa·kaškica : to press by striking, to pound or to batter out *e.g.* clothes — **kaškil** \k̇a-šk̇íl\ *va contrac* : to press out < ~ *iyeya* to press >
ka·ški·ška \k̇a-šk̇í-ška\ *va* wa·kaškiška : to make rough by striking, as with an axe or stick
ka·ški·ški·ta \k̇a-šk̇í-šk̇i-ṫa\ *va* : to mark in equal lengths for cutting – Bl
ka·škob \k̇a-škób\ *va* : to make twisted
ka·ško·kpa \k̇a-škó-k̇pa\ *va* wa·kaškokpa : to hollow out, to make concave, cut out as a trough — **kaškokpa·kpa** \k̇a-škó-k̇pa-k̇pa\ *va red* : to rout out
ka·ško·pa \k̇a-škó-ṗa\ *va* wa·kaškopa : to make crooked or twisted by striking, but *not* to curve – Cf kaktán
ka·šku \k̇a-šků\ *va* : to scrape off, as scales from a fish, corn from a cob – Bl
ka·šla \k̇a-šlá\ *va* wa·kašla : to cut off, make bare, to shave, to mow — **kašla·šla** *v red* : to shave off — **kašla·ya** *va* kašla·wa·ya : to cause to make bare
ka·šle·ca \k̇a-šlé-ca\ *va* wa·kašleca ma·kašleca : to split, as wood by striking with an axe — **kašlel** \k̇a-šlél\ *va contrac* : to split < ~ *wao* I hit and split it. > – *Syn* KAJA — **kašle·šleca** *va red* wa·kašlešleca : to split up fine, *e.g.* wood < *Na tipi kin icokab can kašlešlecapi ota pahayela eglepi* And in the center of the tipi they set in a pile much split wood. >
ka·šlog \k̇a-šlóg\ *va contrac of* kašloka : to knock out
ka·šlo·ka \k̇a-šló-k̇a\ *va* : to knock off or out, as the helve from an axe or a nail from its hole, to fall out, as an arrow that has been shot into an animal, to clean out *e.g.* a pipe – B.H.116.3
ka·šlul \k̇a-šlúl\ *v contrac of* kašluta : to cause to glance off < ~ *iyeya* to make glance off, ~ *iyaya* to glance off, as an axe >
ka·šlu·šlu·ta \k̇a-šlú-šlu-ṫa\ *va red* wa·kašlušluta [fr *kašluta* to glance] : to polish, to smooth by striking, to planish
ka·šlu·ta \k̇a-šlú-ṫa\ *va* wa·kašluta : to strike and make glance off
ka·šme·ya·la·ke s'e \ka-šmé-ya-la-ke s'e\ *adv* : many sitting, perhaps together < ~ *nankapi* They are sitting

---

\a\ father \e\ they \i\ machine \o\ smoke \u\ lunar \an, aŋ\ blanc Fr. \in, iŋ\ ink \on, oŋ, un, uŋ\ soon, confier Fr. \c\ chair \ǧ\ machen Ger. \j\ fusion \clusters: bl, gn, kp, hšl, etc...\ b^e^lo ... said with a slight vowel
See more in the Introduction, Guide to Pronunciation

close-packed. > - Bl

ka·šna \k̇a-šná\ *va* wa·kašna : to miss in attempting to strike, as *e.g.* a ball — **kašna·šna** *v red* : to be missing

ka·šni·ja \k̇a-šní-ja\ *va* wa·kašnija [fr *šnija* withered] : to make wither by striking *e.g.* weeds

ka·šni·yan·yan \ka-šní-yaŋ-yaŋ\ *vn* : to break up, ripple or toss about < *mni* ~ water rippled, *i.e.* shallow water passing over rocks > — **kašniyanyan·la** *adv* : rippling along < *Mini kin* ~ *yunkelo* The water lay along tossing about, *i.e.* it rippled. > - Bl

ka·šo·ša \k̇a-šó-ša\ *va* wa·kašoša : to stir up and make turbid, as water with a stick or rock *etc*

ka·špa \k̇a-šṗá\ *va* wa·kašpa : to separate, to cut loose from, to strike off a piece, perhaps

ka·špa·pi \k̇a-šṗá-ṗi\ *n* : a dime, coin — **kašpapi·la** *n dim* : a dime pittance

ka·špe·pi·ca·šni \k̇a-šṗé-ṗi-ca-šni\ *adj* : not capable of being separated — **kašpepi·lpicašni** \k̇a-šṗé-ṗi-lṗi-ca-šni\ *adj* : solid, hard to chip, faithful to one's word < *Le tuwa* ~ , *oiekiton k'on*, This one who keeps his word had expressed only words, as is said when a man disappears suddenly having said he would stay. > - Bl WHL

ka·špe·ya \k̇a-šṗé-ya\ *va* kašpe·wa·ya : to cause to separate or break off

ka·špi \k̇a-šṗí\ *va* wa·kašpi : to knock off *e.g.* mulberries by striking the bush or tree under which a sheet has been spread, thus picking, *špi*

ka·špu \k̇a-šṗú\ *va* wa·kašpu : to knock off something by striking — **kašpu·špu** *va red* wa·kašpušpu : to chip away at - Note: the word implies knocking or striking off one piece after another from a log until it is used up, thus *cankášpušpupi* wood chips - Bl

ka·štag \k̇a-štág\ *va contrac of* kaštaka : to beat < ~ *yeya* to make strike, throw *e.g.* a *hutanacute* a cow's rib to play with >

ka·šta·ka \k̇a-šṫá-k̇a\ *va* wa·kaštaka : to strike, beat, whip

ka·štan \k̇a-šṫáŋ\ *va* wa·kaštan : to pour out - Note: the word is used in *ref* to liquids only Cf *papsún* to spill

ka·šta·štag \k̇a-štá-štag\ *va red contrac of* kaštaka : to strike < ~ *ogliya* to hone in the manner of striking, > - Bl

ka·štu·šta \k̇a-štú-šta\ *vn* ma·kaštušta : to be tired from riding - Bl

ka·šu·ja \k̇a-šú-ja\ *va* wa·kašuja : to bruise, batter, to mash, crush by striking < *pa* ~ to bruise the head, *i.e.* to make the nose bleed > — **kašuš** \k̇a-šúš\ *va contrac* : to bruise or mash down < ~ *iyeya* to bruise suddenly > — **kašu·šuja** *va red* : to batter — **kašušuš** *va red contrac* : to break or mash down < ~ *iyeya* to mash > — **kašušu·šya** *adv* : battered, bruised — **kašu·šya** *va* kašu·šwa·ya : to cause to batter — *adv* : bruisedly, batteredly

ka·šwu \k̇a-šwú\ *n* : urine < ~ *mahiyu welo* I urinated > - Bl

ka·š'ag \k̇a-š'ág\ *va contrac of* kaš'aka : to strike lightly — **kaš'a·gya** *va* kaš'a·gwa·ya : to cause to strike feebly

ka·š'a·ka \k̇a-š'á-k̇a\ *va* wa·kaš'aka : to strike with too little force to penetrate

ka·š'a·kiya \k̇a-š'á-k̇i-ya\ *v* : to strike lightly together

ka·š'in \k̇a-š'iŋ\ *vn* ma·kaš'in ni·kaš'in : to bend backwards, to be bent toward the inside, concavely, like the back of a sway-back horse, or a pug nose < *Mila* ~ . ~ *aya* The knife bends back. It has become bent back. > — **kaš'in·yan** *adv* : bent backwards

[1]ka·ta \k̇a-tá\ *va* wa·káta : to assemble together < ~ *iheya* to pass through and assemble, ~ *ihe unpi* They are using cutting words in assembling. *Hohu wakatin kte* I shall assemble the bones. > - Bl

[2]ka·ta \k̇á-ṫa\ *adj* ma·káta : warm, hot, as applied to persons and things

ka·ta·ga \ka-tá-ġa\ *v* [fr *tage* to foam] : to make froth or foam, as running water does — **katah̄** \ka-táh̄\ *v contrac* : to make to foam *e.g.* by beating eggs

ka·ta·ja \k̇a-tá-ja\ *v* [fr *taja* waves] : to make waves, as the wind does

ka·ta·kin \k̇a-tá-k̇iŋ\ *va* wa·katakin [fr *takin* to lean] : to strike and cause to lean sideways — **katakin·kin** *v red* : to be shaky and staggering < *Katakinkinhci wagli yelo* I got home and was quite shaky, *i.e.* staggering to right and left, as if having been hit. ~ *la s'e mawani yelo* I walked as though figuring he was staggering. > — **katakin·yan** \k̇a-tá-k̇iŋ-yaŋ\ *adv* : leaning < ~ *han* to stand leaning > - Bl WHL

ka·ta·ko·ha *or* **katakuyuha** *or* **katakoyuha** \k̇a-tá-k̇o-ha\ *va* wa·katakoha : to hold in one's arms *e.g.* a baby - D.247, note 1 B.H.129.16, 227.9

ka·ta·ku·ni·šni \k̇a-ṫá-ku-ni-šni\ *va* wa·tákunišni : to beat to pieces, to destroy, as by striking with an axe

ka·tan \k̇a-táŋ\ *va* wa·katan : to pound on *e.g.* beef before it is dried, to make beef steak or a piece of hide - Cf wák̇aṗe

ka·tan·bla·blas \k̇a-táŋ-bla-blas\ *adv perhaps* : on both sides of the back < ~ *glihpeic'iya* to throw or flop one's self on both sides of the back, as does an itching horse > - Cf ikpaptanptan Note: the word may not be used in *ref* to man Bl

ka·tan'·in \k̇a-taŋ-iŋ\ *va* wa·katan'in [fr *tan'in* to appear] : to make apparent, to clear off *e.g.* anything covered up

ka·tan·ka \k̇a-táŋ-k̇a\ *va* wa·kátanka [fr *tanka* large] : to beat out large, to enlarge by striking — **katanka·ya** *va* wa·katankaya : to make something larger that has been finished before

ka·tan'onb \k̇a-táŋ-oŋp\ *v contrac of* katan'onpa : to lean at an angle of about 45 degrees — **katan'on·bya** *adv* : leaning

ka·tan'·on·pa \k̇a-táŋ-oŋ-ṗa\ *v* [fr *katan* to place reclining] : to lean

ka·tan·tan \k̇a-táŋ-taŋ\ *va red of* katan : to pound on

ka·ta·pa \k̇a-tá-ṗa\ *va* : to shake and make dry, as the wind does clothes, to dry by shaking

ka·ta·pši·ja \k̇a-tá-ṗši-ja\ *va* wa·katapšija : to cause to rise, as buffles in water, by throwing something in — **kata·pšiš** *va contrac* : to create buffles in water < ~ *iyeya* to make bubbles by throwing something into water >

ka·ta·pta·pa \k̇a-ṫá-pta-ṗa\ *va* : to hew *e.g.* rocks < *can* ~ to hew off thin pieces of wood from a dry log, as for kindling, *cankataptapapi* kindling chips of wood, *inyan* ~ to chip stone > - Bl B.H.100.7

[1]ka·ta·ta \k̇a-ṫá-ṫa\ *va* wa·katata : to shake off *e.g.* dust from a blanket, perhaps to brush off with the hand or with a brush - R

[2]ka·ta·ta \ka-tá-ta\ *va* wa·katata : to make blunt by striking *e.g.* a tent pin at the upper end, the head where it is to be struck

ka·ta·ta·bya \k̇a-tá-ta-bya\ *va red* [fr *katatapa* shake to dry] : to make dry by shaking

ka·ta·ta·pa \k̇a-ṫá-ṫa-ṗa\ *va red* [fr *katapa* to dry by shaking] : to dry, as by flapping in the wind

ka·teb \k̇a-ṫéb\ *vn contrac* [fr *katepa* to wear out] : to wear out on its own < ~ *iyeya* to quickly wear, ~ *aya* to wear out from use >
ka·te·han \k̇a-ṫé-haŋ\ *adv* [fr *tehan* far] : far, at a distance — **katehan·yan** *adv* : at some distance, a little distance off
ka·te·pa \k̇a-ṫé-ṗa\ *vn* : to wear out by itself through striking against something — *va* wa·katepa : to cut to a stump, to cut tapering
[1]**ka·ti·ca** \k̇a-ṫí'-ca\ *va* wa·katica : to stir, or perhaps to mix up
[2]**ka·ti·ca** \k̇a-ṫí-ca\ *vn* : to be obstructed, as the nostrils
ka·ti·kti·ca \k̇a-ṫí-kṫi-ca\ *v red* [fr *katica* to stir] : to thicken by stirring
ka·tin \k̇a-ṫíŋ\ *adj* ma·katin : straight, straightened out, as the arm — **katin·kiya** \k̇a-ṫíŋ-ki-ya\ *va* : to stretch out, make straight < *Isto* ~ He had him straighten out his arm. >
ka·tin·tin·yeya *or* **katintim·yeya** \k̇a-ṫíŋ-ṫiŋ-ye-ya\ *adv* : continuously < *Šunkan s'e* ~ *omani* He just kept walking as though he were an old horse, *i.e.* walking apparently aimlessly here and there as old horses do although there be plenty of grass, as is said when one fails to catch a rabbit *etc* for food. *Lecala taku wan oye iyaya, tka* ~ *oye iyayelo* Lately there went something's track, but . >
ka·tin·yan \k̇a-ṫíŋ-yaŋ\ *adv* : straight, directly, non-stop or continuously, immediately or off-hand < *Wi k'on* ~ *yankelo, mašte kte lo.* ~ *econ šni* The sun had straightway set, so it will be hot weather. It did dally, *i.e.* did not do so immediately. > — **katinye·ya** *adv* : directly, continuously, without stop, straightened out < ~ *el hi.* ~ *owotanla ku wo. Ištinma owakihi šni* He came there directly. Come straight. I cannot sleep. > — *va* : to straighten out – P R Bl Mh BD Br
[1]**ka·tka** \k̇a-ṫká\ *vn* ma·kátka : to choke or be choked, as in eating, to stick in the throat
[2]**ka·tka** \ká-tka\ *adv* : briskly < ~ *mani* to walk briskly > *Syn* GLUGWEZEHCE, GLUŠNIYANYAHCE Bl
ka·tka·han·yan \k̇a-ṫkáŋ-haŋ-yaŋ\ *adv* : slowly, soundly < *Kahantuk'e* ~ *wiyukcan po* Now then, think well, soundly. > – *Syn* KAT'INSYA
ka·tkan·he·ya \k̇a-ṫkáŋ-he-ya\ *adv* : slowly, soundly < ~ *wikcan* to think slowly and soundly, a good trait > – Note: *tka-heya* suggests a *ref* to taking one's time as in thinking, and in opposition to *yuptanpila s'e wiyukcan* to think disorderly. Hence, ~ *škan* to move slowly. – Bl
ka·tke *and* **katka** \k̇a-ṫké\ *vn* : to choke — **katke·ya** *va* katke·wa·ya : to cause to choke
[1]**ka·tki·ya** \ká-tki-ya\ *adv* : that way, over yonder (and pointing) somewhere < *Hokšila* ~ *iyaya.* The boy went that way. *letkiya* this way > – Note: *kal, kakiya, kiya*
[2]**ka·tki·ya** *and* kalkiya \ká-tki-ya\ *v poss* : to heat one's own < *cuwi* ~ *yunka* to lie warming one's back > – Bl
ka·tku \k̇a-tkú\ *adj* : rather short of something, having very little, *e.g.* of sugar, coffee *etc* R Bl
ka·tku·ga \k̇a-ṫkú-ġa\ *va* wa·katkuga : to strike off square pieces – BD
ka·tkuns \k̇a-ṫkúŋs\ *va contrac of* katkunza : to cut off square — **katkun·tkunta** \k̇a-ṫkúŋ-ṫkuŋ-ṫa\ *v* – *See under kakuntkunta* — **katkunza** *va* wa·katkunza : to to cut off square < *Can* ~ *s'e mahpiya wan tan'in yelo* A cloud appeared like a board cut of square, *i.e.* when long clouds rise evenly, in a front, on the horizon. > – Bl
ka·tku·tku·ga \k̇a-ṫkú-ṫku-ġa\ *v red of* katkuga : to strike off square
ka·tku·ya·kel \k̇a-ṫkú-ya-kel\ *adv* : rather little, few of something, rather short – Bl
ka·to \k̇a-ṫó\ *va* wa·káto : to strike and not make an indentation, to rap, knock, make a sound —**kato·han** *v* : to stand and tap, as does a woodpecker on a tree
ka·to·na·ung \k̇a-ṫó-na-uŋg\ *vn of* katonaunka : to gallop < ~ *iyaya* to go on galloping, ~ *hiyaya* to pass by galloping, *Na ungna tahenakiya hiyu na lecegla* ~ *hiyaya ca akiš'api.* ~ *omawani ye* And perhaps he came out this way and when he came close by galloping they cheered him. I roamed about galloping. > — **katonaun·gkiya** *va* katonaun·gwa·kiya : to make gallop slowly
ka·to·na·un·ka \k̇a-ṫó-na-uŋ-k̇a\ *vn* : to gallop slowly, as a horse might
ka·to·to \k̇a-ṫó-ṫo\ *va red* wa·katoto [fr *kato* to rap] : to knock or beat on *e.g.* a door
ka·to·wo·tan·la \k̇a-ṫó-wo-taŋ-la\ *adv* : struck and set upright < ~ *kuye* beneath and set upright, *Lehan wanciglak iblotaka ce,* Did I not sit to look at yours thus far? as is said when the men return who looked for buffalo. > – BT
ka·to·ye·ya·pi s'e \k̇a-ṫó-ye-ya-pi s'e\ *adv* : alone < ~ *omawani* I went alone. *Wicahcala kin takošku kici* ~ *yankapi, ihunnipi* The old man and his son-in-law were alone, they got across, as is said when one or two are left alone by others. > – Bl
ka·tu·ka \k̇a-ṫú-k̇a\ *va* wa·katuka : to knock off *e.g.* fur, to destroy by smiting
ka·tunp \ka-ṫúŋp\ *adj* : thick and sticky < *Wašma iyecel unpšiš* ~ *omawani* I walked in thick and sticky mud as it were in deep snow, *i.e.* walking through gumbo. > – *Syn* TUNTUNPA WHL
ka·tu·ta \k̇a-tú-ta\ *vn* ma·katuta : to be sore from riding *etc* – *Syn* KAIḢEJU Bl
ka·tu·tka \k̇a-ṫú-tka\ *va* wa·katutka : to break in small pieces or to pound up fine – R Bl
ka·t'a \k̇a-t'á\ *va* wa·kat'a : to kill or stun by striking < ~ *iyeya* to kill by shooting, ~ *ehpeya* to knock over dead *Tuwa šigla ca kat'api* Those who became angry were killed. *Šni makat'elo* No he did not kill me. > — *vn* : to die by hitting an object – B.H.302.24
ka·t'a·ga \k̇a-t'á-ġa\ *va* : to shake and make dry, as the wind does a wet cloth < *Wana maka kin* ~ The ground is becoming dry now, as in the spring. *Mašte tate, hecel maka kin kat'agin ktelo* There is a wind that is hot, so it will dry out the land. > – Bl
ka·t'a·pt'a·pa *or* **kat'apt'ap** \ka-t'a-pt'a-pa\ *v* : to signify by a certain gesture of the head that expresses contempt, dislike, hatred *etc* . It consists in opening one's closed fist and moving it toward the object disliked and thus making the fingers outstretched, or in snapping one's finger in the sign of contempt – D.37, 88 RTj
ka·t'a·t'a \ka-t'á-t'a\ *v red of* kat'á : to keep killing < *Kat'at'api s'e u welo* He came as though he were exhausted, as is said of a man who comes *e.g.* on horseback very slowly and seemingly tired-out. > – A RTj
ka·t'e·la \ka-t'é-la\ *n* : a long drumstick used by women as a drumstick, a woman drummer's drumstick < ~ *tacancega icabu* their long drummer's drumstick > – Bl
ka·t'e·ya·kel \k̇a-t'e-ya-kel\ *adv* : slowly, leisurely < ~ *hi* to come slowly, ~ *ya* to go without being in a hurry,

\a\ father \e\ they \i\ machine \o\ smoke \u\ lunar \an, aŋ\ blanc Fr. \in, iŋ\ ink \on, oŋ, un, uŋ\ soon, confier Fr. \c\ chair \ġ\ machen Ger. \j\ fusion \clusters: bl, gn, kp, hšl, etc...\ b[e]lo ... said with a slight vowel
See more in the Introduction, Guide to Pronunciation

slowly > – *Sn* KASLASLAYA Bl

ka·t'e·ye·tan·ka \k̇a-t'é-ye-taŋ-ka\ *adv* : sitting still for a long time in a lazy manner, conveying the idea of being at leisure, not watching out, not being intent on anything, to sit in the Lakota fashion for men, with legs crossed almost under the buttox < ~ *yanka* to sit flat on the ground, with the legs outstretched and the knees bent partly out, ~ *nasunyan yanka* to sit flat on the ground with legs outstretched and both touching each other, ~ *mani* to walk about leisurely, ~ *najin* to stand unaware of anything, *i.e. watoglašni najin* stand composed. ~ *u,* to come leisurely, *i.e. iwaštegla u* to come slowly, *Kat'eyetankahci wahi* I came (to stay awhile), came very slowly. ~ *wowaši econ* to do one's work slowly, *i.e. ḣanhiyehci wowaši econ i.e.* to do work as in pain, where *ḣanhiyehci* is *archaic* > – Bl

ka·t'i·i·c'i·ya \k̇a-t'í-i-c'i-ya\ *v refl* : to shoot one's self – Bl

ka·t'in·hya \ka-t'íŋ-ḣya\ *adv* : grunting < ~ *glihpaya* to grunt while suddenly falling down >

ka·t'ins \k̇a-t'íŋs\ *va contrac of* kat'inza : to make firm — **kat'in·sya** *va* : to cause to be solid or at rest — *adv* : slowly, well, soundly < ~ *wiyukcan* to have a solid understanding > – *Syn* KATKANHANYAN — **kat'insya·kel** *adv* : pounded tight < ~ *manke* I am sitting here for good. > – EB

ka·t'in·za \k̇a-t'íŋ-za\ *va* wa·kat'inza [fr *t'inza* firm, brave] : to pound tight, make tight or firm

ka·t'i·ye·ya \k̇a-t'í-ye-ya\ *va* kat'iye·wa·ya : to kill by shooting

ka·t'o·za \k̇a-t'ó-za\ *va* wa·kat'oza : to dull or make blunt by striking

ka·t'un·ke·ca \k̇a-t'úŋ-k̇e-ca\ *va* wa·kat'unkeca : to suspect one — **kat'un·tunkeca** *v red* : to be suspecting one – R Bl

ka·u \k̇a-ú\ *va* wa·kau [fr *au* to bring or come to] : to be bringing something to < *Can etan makau po* Bring me some wood. *Cannunpa wan cicicaupi ca yanipi kte lo* You will live since I brought you a pipe. *Wigli waštemna k'on hena micaupi nito* Bring those perfumes to me, *i.e.* her perfume. > – B.H.137.16

ka·ung \k̇a-úng\ *va contrac of* kaunka : to cut down < ~ *ihpeya* to cut down and throw away > — **kaun·gkiya** *adv* – *See* kaúnkiya

ka·un·hye \k̇a-úŋ-ḣye\ *adj perhaps* – *See* kawínhye

ka·un·ka \k̇a-úŋ-ka\ *va* wa·kaunka : to cut down, fell *e.g.* trees, to strike down *e.g.* persons, to blow down, as the wind does trees — **kaunka·ka** \k̇a-úŋ-k̇a-ka\ *vn* : to be jolted or bounced up and down, as in a wagon < ~ *yemaya* It gave be a real jolting. > — **kaun·kiya** *or* **kaun·gkiya** \k̇a-úŋ-ki-ya\ \k̇a-uŋ-gki-ya\ *adv* : leaning over, as a half felled tree < *Can kin he ~ han* That tree is standing leaning over, half felled. >

ka·u·ta \k̇a-ú-ta\ *va* : to make a gun go off, by striking it — *vn* : to go off, accidentally by itself < *Kaúte* It discharged. >

ka·wa \k̇a-wá\ *v* : to open, as a flower – Bl

ka·wa·ci \k̇a-wá-ci\ *va* wa·kawaci [fr *ka* striking + *waci* to dance] : to cause to dance, by striking, to spin by whipping, as a boy does his top

ka·wa·cin·ksab \k̇a-wá-ciŋ-ksab\ *v contrac* : to bring about, restore consciousness < ~ *iyeya* to restore conscious awareness > WHL

ka·wa·han \k̇a-wá-haŋ\ *part* : opened

ka·wa·ja \k̇a-wá-ja\ *va* wa·kawaja : to work at a difficult thing, keep a thing though hardly able to do it

ka·wan·kab \k̇a-waŋ-k̇ab\ *adv* : upward < *wi ~ u kin lehanl* when at this time the sun came up > – B.H.118.4

ka·wan·ka·ka \k̇a-wáŋ-ka-ka\ *vn* : to be jolted or bounced up and down as in a wagon < ~ *imayaye* I was bounced. ~ *iyaya ca iyoḣa kin kaiyoyagya iyeye* Whe he went bouncing his lower jaw was made to quiver. > – *Syn* KAUNKAKA BD Bl

ka·wan·kal \k̇a-wáŋ-k̇al\ *adv* : upwards < ~ *iyeya* to knock upwards, *Na yaštan el ḣolyela he ake ~ iyaya* And when she finished speaking there again she went on upwards in a mist. *Na šna ~ kiglahanpi* And often they had been returning to the beyond. — **kawanka·lwapa** \k̇a-wáŋ-ka-·lwa-ṗa\ *adv* : a little up

ka·wa·swas \ka-wá-swas\ *va contrac and red* [fr *kawaza* to toss up] : to throw up *e.g.* dirt with a stick < *Caḣota kin ~ iyeye* He (the wolf) brushed the ashes off. > – D.22

ka·waš \k̇a-wáš\ *va contrac of* kawája : to work persistently at a hard job < ~ *yanka* He is keeping at it. >

ka·wa·šte \k̇a-wá-šṫe\ *va* : to make well, by striking or cutting with an axe, or by whittling, sewing, *etc* – Bl

ka·wa·š'a·ka \k̇a-wá-š'a-k̇a\ *vn* ma·kawaš'aka [fr *waš'aka* strong] : to be made strong by packing or carrying loads

ka·wa·tu·ka \k̇a-wá-ṫu-ka\ *vn* : to be tired from long riding on a wagon or on horseback, by reason of shaking (*ka*) < *Šunkakanyankapi makáwatuka* I am worn out riding horseback. *Canpagmiyanpi makawatuka* I am tired from riding a wagon. >

ka·wa·za \k̇a-wá-za\ *va* : to throw up *e.g.* ground or dirt with a stick – R Bl

ka·we·ga \k̇a-wé-ġa\ *va* : to break, crack by striking, but not to break entirely off — **kaweh** \k̇a-wéḣ\ *va contrac* : to crack < ~ *iyeya* to splinter > — **kawe·hwega** \k̇a-wé-ḣwe-ġa\ *va red* : to break often — **kawe·hweh** *va red contrac* : to fracture or break in several places < ~ *iyeya* to splinter, ~ *apa* to give a blow to splinter > — **kawe·hya** *va* kawe·hwa·ya : to cause to break — *adv* : breaking

ka·wel \k̇a-wél\ *adv* : together < *Wicota ~ kanheheyela u welo* A crowd came together attired in old clothes. *Tula, le tuwe kin witka welaka cu ~ hanp'ceyaka wan ohan hiyayele* Shame on you, indeed who is this egg, choo! he passed by together wearing a pair of moccasins with porcupine quill work > – Bl

ka·we·we \k̇a-wé-we\ *va* wa·kawewe : to strike and make bleed – Bl

ka·wi·gnu·ni \k̇a-wí-gnu-ni\ *va* wa·kawignuni : to destroy by striking, to break to pieces – R Bl

ka·wi·lwi·ta \k̇a-wí-lwi-ṫa\ *va* : to bunch, gather in groups < *Peji kin ~ ewagle kte* I am going to bunch the hay. > – WHL

ka·win·ga \k̇a-wíŋ-ġa\ *vn* wa·kawinga : to turn in one's course, turn around, go back < ~ *iyaya* He went and turned around. *Kola, ~ yo, heci yai kin, niktepi kta. Hecel nupin kawingapi na kiglapi* Friend, turn back, if you go they will kill you. So, they both went back and returned home. > — **kawinh** \k̇a-wíŋḣ\ *vn contrac* : to turn about < ~ *iyaya* to turn short, ~ *uši* : to call one back, or to tell one to come back >

ka·win·hye \k̇a-úŋ-ḣye\ *adj* : a hundred < *Nape nupin kaska ~* Both hands cleared a hundred. >

ka·win·ja \k̇a-wíŋ-ja\ *va* wa·kawinja : to beat down, mat down by striking *e.g.* grass *etc* — **kawinš** \k̇a-wíŋš\ *va contrac* : to beat down < ~ *iyeya* to trample, ~ *ihpeya* to beat and throw down > — **kawin·šwinja** *va red* : to down continually — **kawinšwinš** *va red contrac* : to mat down — **kawinšwin·šya** *adv* : matted down

ka·win·šya \k̇a-wíŋ-šya\ *va* kawin·šwa·ya : to cause to mat — *adv* : beaten down, fallen down

ka·wi·ta \k̇a-wí-ṫa\ *adv* : together < ~ *u po* Come together. ~ *awicakuwa* He went together after them. *Petaga kin ~ egle* He set up together the burning coal game. > — **kawita·ya** *adv* : together < ~ *agli el caje oglaka* When he brought him home he told his name. ~ *awicayapi* They were led together, *i.e.* rounded them into a small area. > - MS.568 D.211

ka·ye·ge *and* **kagege** \ka-yé-ġe\ *va* : to sew, stitch - Note: *kayege* is used in *ref* to present, *kagege* to the past where someone else is doing it; it is heard repeatedly among the Sicángu Sioux

ka·yeš \k̇a-yéš\ *adv emph* - It stresses a pronoun or other word < *miye* ~ I myself, *niye* ~ you yourself, *Iš iye ~ eye kin* He his very self surely said it. *Kawinga yo, miye ~ tehanyan ca owakihi šni* Turn back, I myself am not able since it is so far away. *Miye ~ wašicun kin ehanni maktepelo* I myself long ago was killed by the white man. *Heci Wakinyan Oyate kin el ~ maktepi šni yelo, eya* There he said: "In the Thunder Nation itself I was not killed. *Niyeš sipa ~ akiglaške šni yaun welo* You indeed are not hobbling your very own toes to his. > — *pron* : that one, even such < *Ungna tuwa tasicogin ~ ihpeyayapi kilo* Do not, I warn you, dispose of one's lower leg (it is supplied with many tendons). > - MS.155 Bl New B.H.54, 111, 126, 187, 196, 206, 208, 210, 245, 303

ka·ye·ya \k̇a-yê-ya\ *va* kaye·wa·ya : to wave *e.g.* a blanket < *Šiná wan kayeyelo* He waves a blanket, *i.e.* as a sign indicating the number of buffalo one sees. > - Bl

ka·yo·la wa·ci·pi \k̇a-yō'-la wa-cl-pi\ *n* : a dance, perhaps adapted by the Lakota and called *Isanyati wacipi* a Santee Indian dance - Bl

ka·yo·yo s'e \k̇a-yó-yo s'e\ *adv* : with fleshy parts shaking < ~ *mani* to walk like very fleshy, blabby men or animals. > - R Bl

ka·yunš \k̇a-yúŋš\ *adv conj* : if that is the case - Note: the word is used by one who tells something to another who already knows but had not divuiged the fact < *Hecetu ~ oyaka tka* If it had happened so, yet he did not tell. > - B.H.115.4 WHL

ka·za \k̇a-zá\ *va* wa·kaza : to pick to pieces, *e.g.* the *takan* sinew, tearing off one string after another and twisting it for use in sewing — *n* : a job < ~ *ota* There are many jobs. > - MO

ka·za·mni \k̇a-zá-mni\ *va* wa·kazamni : to uncover or open out, as anything covered, to push away by hand *e.g.* bed clothes < *Pámahe yaun kin ite ~* She uncovered her face if you wore it over your head. > — *vn* : to open, *e.g.* a door from a draft — **kazamni·mni** *vn* : to open and close continually, as a door does in the wind < *Tiyopa yuokiyuta yo, ~ iyayelo, tanyan iyakaška yo* Close the door, it has gone open, latch it well. > — **kazamni-mni·yela** *adv* : forcing open and flapping < ~ *tipi k'on* that tent flapping about, as is said of a tent not tied up in the wind > - WHL

ka·zan *or* **kazi** \k̇a-záŋ\ *va* wa·kazan : to hurt, to make feel pain by striking; to render motionless < *hinyete kazanpi* bruised shoulders > — *vn* : to fill up, have the sense of fullness < *Yunkan pi kazanpi ca na oniyan šice k'on iyemaceca amahi* Then when their liver seemed full then it brought on me that bad breath like mine. *Locin wawatin na cante makazan yelo* My heart had a sense of fullness and I was hungry eating. *Cante ~* to have heart burn, or *cante makazan* I have heart burn. > - R Bl B.H.265.3

ka·zan·pe·ya \k̇a-záŋ-ṗe-ya\ *va* : to smoothen a stick and make it sharp at one end - Bl

ka·zan·yan \k̇a-záŋ-yaŋ\ *adv* : parting, separating *e.g.* grass in passing through it - Note: the word seems to be derived from *kazá*

ka·za·za \k̇a-zá-za\ *va* wa·kazaza : to cut into fine strips and let hang, to slash - D.36

ka·za·za·pi \k̇a-zá-za-pi\ *n* : the ermine, so-called because the skin is cut up into strips to wear on the head

ka·za·ze·ca \k̇a-zá-ze-ca\ *v* : to shred, make ragged - *Syn* KASWAKA Bl

ka·ze \k̇a-zé\ *va* wa·kaze : to lade or dip out with a spoon or ladle < *Mícaze ye* Please lade out for me, *i.e.* serve me some. *Wakšica tanka wan ojula ~* She ladled out for me a big dish full, *i.e.* served me. > - D.54

ka·ze·la \k̇á-ze-la\ *adj* : shallow, not very deep, as water when a man can walk through without swimming - Bl

ka·ze·wi·e s'e \ka-zé-wi-e s'e\ *adv* : limping < ~ *u* to come limping like a horse, ~ *iyaya* to go on limping > - SC

ka·zi·li·c'i·ya \k̇a-zí-li-c'i-ya\ *v refl of* kazilya : to stretch one's self out, to lie down and rest leisurely, as after hard work or meals < *Kazilmic'iyin kte* I shall take a stretch. > - *Syn* KABLEBLESIC'IYA MG

ka·zi·lya \k̇a-zí-lya\ *v* : to stretch out, straighten

ka·zon·ta *or* **kazunta** \k̇a-zóŋ-ṫa\ *va* : to weave *e.g.* cloth, to twist in, as in making baskets or snow-shoes or bed folders (mats) - Cf *cankazontapi*

ka·zu·ksu·gye·la \ka-zú-ksu-gye-la\ *adv* : wet through, sopping wet, *i.e.* from rain or perspiration < ~ *omawani yelo* I traveled soaked in perspiration. > - Bl

kca \kca\ *adj* : loose, disentangled, straight — **kca·han** \kca-háŋ\ *part* : coming loose, untying of itself — **kca·kca** \kca-kcá\ *adj red* : often loosening < *Napsuhu ~ kacá* His finger seems to be loose, as is said when a person has long fingers. >

kca·ma \kcá-ma\ *v defect* : I thought - B.H.230.5, 232.2, 278.9

kcaǹ \kcaŋ\ *root word, never used alone* : *ref* to understanding - Cf yukcán

kcan·ka \kcáŋ-ka\ *n* : one who fails to do what he said he would - R Bl

kcan·kcan·la \kcaŋ-kcáŋ-la\ *adj* : tall and very movable as men or trees may be, unsteady, as may be said of a man's *tawacin* mind - Bl

kcan·pte·pte \kcaŋ-pté-pte\ *adv* : seemingly occupied with one's thoughts < ~ *hca mankelo* I was thinking deeply, in silence. ~ *hca amayaluta* You look at me as if you wanted to say something. > — **kcanptepte·kel** *and* **canpteptekel** : burdened with the knowledge of something < ~ *ku welo* He returns with a message. >

kca·wa·han \kca-wá-haŋ\ *part* : having come untied

kce·ki·ya \kcé-k̇i-ya\ *v* : to hold or hang over < *Nape ~ yaun welo* You are holding your hand over it, *i.e.* holding the spread-out hands over the stove to warm them, *i.e.* *nape kaš'akiya yaun welo* You knock your hands lightly. >

kce·ya \kce-yá\ *va* : to cook by hanging over the fire - Note: *wakceyapi* the roasting piece, the ribs of an animal

---

\a\ father \e\ they \i\ machine \o\ smoke \u\ lunar \an, aŋ\ blanc Fr. \in, iŋ\ ink \on, oŋ, un, uŋ\ soon, confier Fr. \c\ chair \ġ\ machen Ger. \j\ fusion \clusters: bl, gn, kp, hšl, etc...\ b°lo ... said with a slight vowel **See more in the Introduction, Guide to Pronunciation**

kco \kco\ *va abbrev of* kico : to call, invite

[1]**ke** \k̇e\ *encl abbrev of* ka itself and *abbrev of* laka : pretty much, nontheless < *he ianpetu tonakeca ke el* there in nonetheless a few days, *hecel unhe keci* so while he was there, *Taku mazaska zi keci on lila wiyakpayela he* What is it about gold that it glistens very much? *heconhanpi keci* while they were doing that, *Misun, lecelya un ke cin eš takuhci koyakipe sece lo* My little brother, it being pretty much so, is it you seem to be afraid of something. > – Note: *ke ci(n)* or *kéci,* an *abbrev* perhaps of *lake cin (kin* or *ci),* an *idiom* denoting: pretty much, nonetheless – D.3 note 3 B.H.113.18, 101.3, 89.5, 67.6, 226.5

[2]**ke** *or* **keya** \k̇e\ *n* : a turtle < *Kenatantan kte s'e hanpokihe lo* He put on his own moccasins as if continually the turtle was about to attack him, as is said when shoes are too wide. > – Note: the word is used commonly in connection with other words, *ke...*

ke·ca *and* **kecala** \k̇e-cá\ *n* : a long-haired dog

ke·can·h'a \k̇e-cáŋ-ḣ'a\ *n* : a turtle smelling of wood – Bl

ke·can·kin \k̇é-caŋ-k̇iŋ\ *va* kécan·wa·kin : to think of as such, to regard as

ke·ci \ke-cí\ *encl abbrev* : pretty much, nonetheless – Cf k̇e

ke·cin \k̇é-ciŋ\ *v* kécanmi kécanni ké·unke·cin·pi *or* kún·kecin·pi : to think that < *Wakan ~ šni yo* Do not think you are *wakan* endowed with power. *Kéwicakinpi* They think that of themselves, *or* They are thought to be that. > – B B.H.129.23, 137.6, 272.13

ke·ci·ya \k̇é-ci-ya\ *va* ké·wa·kiya ké·un·kiya·pi : to say to one that it is so and so – Note: the word is introduced from Santee through the Bible, hence the word should be *kékiya*

ke·con \k̇é-coŋ\ *v* kécamon kecanon kecunkonpi : to do that < *Tanyan ~ ic'ila ca* He thinks he has done that well, *or* When he considers himself he did that well. >

ke c'eyaš ke eyaš k'eyaš ce eyaš e k'eyaš e ke eyaš \ke c'é-yaš ke é-yaš k'é-yaš ce é-yaš e k'é-yaš e ke éyaš\ *encl* – It follows *pron* and makes them universal < *tuwé ~* anybody, *taku wato ke c'eyaš* whatever weeds > – B.H. 202.22

ke e·ša \ke e-šá\ *encl* – It follows *pron* to make them universal – Cf kešá

ke·e·yaš *or* **ke eyaš** \ke-é-yaš\ *adv* : although, all the same < *Ha-kela pehin šikšice ~ šina huhá iyowakpatin kta* I shall sew a patch on the shawl with the legs, although the child's hair is filthy. > — *encl* – It renders a *pron* universal – *See* ke c'éyaš

ke·gle·ze·la \k̇e-glé-ze-la\ *n* : a spotted or striped turtle living on land, the sand turtle perhaps – *See* patkáša

[1]**ke·ha** \k̇é-ha\ *v* 2nd *pers singl of* kéya : you say that

[2]**ke·ha** \k̇é-ha\ *n* [fr *keya* turtle + *ha* hide] : a tortoise shell

ke·hu·ku \k̇e-hú-k̇u\ *n* : an arrowhead diamond shaped – *See* keston, wismahin ikceka Bl

ke·h'an·la \k̇e-ḣ'áŋ-la\ *n* : a species of small turtle – GA

ke·in·yan·han \k̇e-íŋ-yaŋ-haŋ\ *part* : roof-like, sloping

ke·ki·ya \k̇e-kí-ya\ *v* ke·wa·kiya : to say that – B.H. 70.11, 111.20, 153.26, 196.8, 208.21, 217.7, 293.19

kel \kel\ *adv suff* : in a way, as it were, in a manner of speaking < *htalehankel* yesterday as it were > – Cf wínhahayakel Note: *itancanyan* to do something like a chief which one *is* , *itancanyankel* like a chief which one is *not*, as it were D.222.278

ke·nun'i·c'i·ya \k̇e-núŋ-i-c'i-ya\ *v* kenun·mi·c'iya : to get ready < *Kenun'ic'iya yo* Ready yourself. > – *Syn* I-GLUWINYEYA

ke·nun·nun·ja \k̇e-núŋ-nuŋ-ja\ *n* : the soft-shell turtle

ke·nun·yan \k̇e-núŋ-yaŋ\ *v* kenun·wa·ya : to know partly, to suspect – *Syn* AT'UNGYA

[1]**ke·pa** \k̇é-ṗa\ *v* 1st *pers singl of* kéya : I say that

[2]**ke·pa** \k̇é-pa\ *n* [fr *keya* turtle + *pa* head] : a tortoise's head

ke·pca \k̇é-pca\ *v* 1st *pers singl* : I thought that

ke·ston \k̇e-sṫóŋ\ *vn* [fr *keze* a barb + *ton* have] : to be barbed, have a barb, as a fish hook or arrow — *n* : a barbed arrow-head — **keston·šni** *n* : an arrow-head not barbed

ke·s'a·mna \k̇e-s'á-mna\ *n* : a species of turtle, the stink turtle – Ra Bl

ke s'e *or* **lake s'e** \ke s'é\ *encl suff* : rather, apparently pretty much more < *Inyankapi ~ wowaši econ. Le kagišnišni oh'an ke lah* They ran ahead to do work. He was not hindered working rather much more. *Ikanyela ~ hinajin. Taka lila iyoyake s'e yankahan ke* He came and stood much nearer. He was sitting roasting as though very displeased > – Bl B.H.58.7, 181.9, 236.23 D.8 note 6

keš \k̇eš\ *conj* : but, although < *Toka kin nicasotapi kte ~ iyuhaha wicawakte yelo* The enemy will wipe you out, but I shall kill them utterly. *Winyan wanji yuha ~ ihpeya hanke* The woman has one but she threw away half. > – Note: *Keš* although is always used in *ref* to *past* time. < *Tohanl wanasapi kta ~ kangi ska wan pte kin owicakiyaka ca lila napapi* Although when there was about to be a buffalo hunt they really fled since a white crow spoke to the buffalo > – MS.92

ke·ša \k̇e-šá\ *partic, perhaps adv* – It follows *pron* to make them universal < *tuwe ~* whoever, *taku ~* anything, *anpetu tukte ~* whichever day, *Miye ~ el ciyin kta iyececa šni.* It is not right that I whoever I am should go to you. *na nakun ~ unkiyepi na niye iyokoogna* and also so ever between us and you > – B.H.196.12, 228.6

ke·ško·kpa \k̇e-šk̇ō'-kpa\ *n* : a species of turtle – Bl

ke·wa·pa \ke-wá-ṗa\ *n* : the water lily, a water plant with round large leaves that lie flat in the water – Bl

ke·wo·yu·spa s'e \k̇e-wó-yu-spa s'e\ *adv* : as if a turtle being dragged from the mud, *fig* doing the impossible < *~ leniceca yelo* Such as you are doing the impossible, as is said of one who is strong and does things although they are hard to do, for it seems hard to drag a turtle out of the mud. > – BT

[1]**ke·ya** \k̇é-ya\ *v* képa kéha un·keya·pi : to say or state that < *Letan waniyetu topa kin oyate wan ahi kta keyelo* He stated that four winters (years) from now a people will have arrived. *~ cajeyata* He said he mentioned him by name. *~ iwahoya* He said he let him know. *~ okiyaka* He said he told him. > – Note: *kéya, kecankin* are from *éya* and of one class of *v* (to say, to think of) , *ecin, ecankin* are of a second (to think of). Those of the second class indicate that the subject of the preceding *v* is identical with the person who says or thinks, which those of the first class do not – B.H.64.2, 81.4, 205.5, 62.23, 94.1, 188.23, 256.14

[2]**ke·ya** \k̇é-ya\ *va* ke·wa·ya : to make a roof of < *Na hel canha keyapi* And a roof was built there of bark. >

[3]**ke·ya** \k̇é-ya\ *n* 1 : a roof < *Oyute kin yuogmuuza ye, ~ s'e oyute kin hpuhpuya* Close up the side (of your dress). The side like a roof is collapsing. > 2 : the large tortoise, turtle < *Keya s'e upihcihci* Like a great turtle's is the fringed lower border (of her dress). >

ke·ya·p' \k̇é-ya-p'\ *v* : they say that – Note: the word is used in non-eyewitness narration – D.1

ke·ye co·la *and* **keye cocola** \k̇é-ye cò-la\ \k̇é-ye co-có-la\ *adv* : entirely destitute, having nothing < ~ *yankapi* or *iyayapi* They were without anything *or* went on having nothing, entirely desititute. > - Bl *Syn* KAGMI S'E

ke·ze \k̇e-zé\ *n* : the barb of a fishhook, the sharp point of anything < ~ *šice* an arrow whose head hooks are also hooked and thus cannot be pulled out or brought backward > - St

ke' \ke'\ *va contrac of* ške' : it is said, they say - D.1

[1]**ki** \k̇i\ *pref* : an action is performed through the middle - Note: it is affixed to some *v*, thus *kiwaksa* to cut in two in the middle; it does not, however, draw the accent

[2]**ki** \k̇i\ *va* wa·ki : to take from one by force, to rob < *Tašunkepi kin oyasin wicunkipi kte lo. Na taku luhapi kin hena oyasin ko nicipi cinpi kte* Let us rob all their horses. And as well, all you who have something should wish to be without. > — *vn* wa·ki un·ki·pi : to arrive at one's home or where one lives - Note: the word is used when the person speaking is away from the home spoken of R

[3]**ki** \k̇i\ *prep in compos* : to, of - Note: **a** it is *pref* to or incorporated into *v* and always takes the accent of the *v*, thus *kícaga* to write a letter to. < *Wicakiyuajaja* He explained to them. > **b** when *pref* to *v* of motion commencing with a vowel, the "i" is dropped, thus *kaú* to bring to **c** in some instances it has the meaning of *kici* for — *pron poss in compos* : one's own < *okile* to seek one's own> - Note: this *ki* does not draw the accent — *abbrev of kin* the *or* kiló beware of, do not, which Cf < *Ungna wacinniwaš'akala ki* Perhaps you should not be easy to get, as for help. > - B.H. 73.7, 14, 68.18 MS.350

ki·a·gu·ya·pi \k̇i-á-ġu-ya-pi\ *v* : to turn into bread - B.H.175.15

ki·a·pe \k̇i-á-p̂e\ *vn* kia·wa·pe : to wait until one reaches home

ki·ble·ca \k̇i-blé-ca\ *vn of* bleca : to break up *e.g.* a gathering of people < *Na wanna oyate kin kiblecahanpi* And the people were dispersing. > - Note: *kiblecahan* seems to be the word always used

ki·ble·za \k̇i-blé-za\ *adj* : convalescent — *vn* wakibleza : to recover, as from a drunken fit, to get sober

[1]**ki·ca** \k̇í-ca\ *v poss* wa·kíca *or* wéca yéca un·kíca·pi [fr *ka* to mean, demand] : to mean one's own or demand one's own < *Nahahci weca šni* I still do not mean my own. I demand one thing that is mine, but they did not give it to me the way I am. > - Bl B.H.36.3, 179.19

[2]**ki·ca** \k̇i-cá\ *prep in compos* : for < *opeton* to buy, *opekicaton* to buy for >

ki·ca·ble·ca \k̇í-ca-ble-ca\ *v* we·cableca [fr *kableca* to break what is brittle] : to break for one by striking *e.g.* brittle ware

[1]**ki·ca·ga** \k̇i-ċá-ġa\ *vn of* cága : to become ice again

[2]**ki·ca·ga** \k̇í-ca-ġa\ *va* wé·caga mí·caga cí·caga [fr *káġa* to make] : to make to or for one < *wowapi* ~ to write a letter to, *woope* ~ to make a law for, *Tunkašitku kin wahinkpe ~ na wakute onspekiya* His grandfather taught him to make and shoot arrows. >

ki·ca·gla \k̇í-ċa-gla\ *vn* mi·cagla [fr *kagla* unfold] : to fall out or unroll for one

ki·ca·go \k̇í-ca-ġo\ *va of* kagó **1** : to make a mark for one **2** : to vaccinate

ki·ca·hi \k̇í-ca-hi\ *v* wé·cahi [fr *kahi* arrive with something] : to rummage for one

ki·ca·hpa \k̇i-cá-ȟpa\ *va* : to knock off for one, to remit to one *e.g.* his debts - B.H.217.11

ki·ca·kca \k̇i-cá-kca\ *v* we·cákca [fr *kakca* to comb] : to comb or curry one's own

ki·ca·kin·ca \k̇í-ca-k̇iŋ-ca\ *va* we·cakinca [fr *kakinca* to scrape from] : to scrape *e.g.* fish, for one

ki·ca·kpa \k̇í-ca-kp̂a\ *va of* kakpá : to strike into for one < *kan* ~ to cut a vein for one, to bleed one >

[1]**ki·ca·ksa** \k̇i-cá-ksa\ *va* ki·wá·kaksa **1** : to cut in two in the middle with an axe or by striking **2** : to break *e.g.* a law, to disobey

[2]**ki·ca·ksa** \k̇í-ca-ksa\ *va* wé·caksa [fr *kaksa* to split] : to cut in two for one, as a stick with an axe

ki·ca·ku·ka \k̇í-ca-k̇u-ka\ *va* wé·cakuka [fr *kakuka* wear out] : to pound to pieces or destroy for one *e.g. clothing*

ki·ca·la \k̇í-ċa-la\ *va* wé·cala [fr *kala* to sow] : to spill *e.g.* grain for another

[1]**ki·ca·mna** \k̇í-ca-mna\ *va* wé·camna [fr *kamna* to gain] : to earn for one

[2]**ki·camna** \k̇í-ca-mna\ *v* : to be in the midst, be beset, surrounded with *e.g.* an epidemic < *Wamniomni ~ yelo* He was in the midst of a whirlwind. *Wicaša ota ~* He was amidst many men. *Weco kuja okicamna el unkanpelo* When we were worn with age, I called him amidst an epidemic. > — **kicamna·yan** \k̇i-cá-mna-yaŋ\ *adv* : in an overwhelming way < ~ *ahiyaye* to pass by in large numbers. > - Bl WHL

ki·can \k̇i-cáŋ\ *v* wé·can un·kican·pi : to call on the dead, when wailing for them, as in crying: *Micinkši, micinkši*! My son, my son!

ki·can·i·c'i·ya *or* **kicinciya** \k̇i-cáŋ-i-c'i-ya\ *v refl* kican·mi·c'iya : to get ready, make one's self ready *e.g.* for a walk — **kican·kiya** \k̇i-cáŋ-k̇i-ya\ *v poss* : to arrange, get ready one's own, to pack up < *Owinja kin ~* He arranged the bedroll. > - B.H.290.8

ki·can·yan \k̇i-ċáŋ-yaŋ\ *va* kican·wa·ya : to work, till, cultivate *e.g.* the ground, to tend, care for < *talo ~* to dress out beef *etc*, *i.e.* cut into pieces > - D.199, 271

ki·ca·psag \k̇í-ca-psag\ *va of* kicapsaka : to cut in two < ~ *iyeya* to cut in two for one >

[1]**ki·ca·psaka** \k̇i-cá-psa-ka\ *va* ki·wa·kapsaka : to cut in two *e.g.* a string at the middle

[2]**ki·ca·psa·ka** \k̇í-ca-psa-ka\ *va* wé·capsaka [fr *kapsaka* to cut in half] : to cut in two *e.g.* a string for one

ki·ca·psun *or* **kicapson** \k̇í-ca-psuŋ\ *va* wé·capsun [fr *kpasun* to strike and break] : to knock over and spill out *e.g.* water for one

ki·ca·pšun \k̇í-ca-pšuŋ\ *v* wé·capšun [fr *kapšun* knock out] : to knock off *e.g.* a horse for one

ki·ca·sle·ca \k̇í-ca-sle-ca\ *v* wé·casleca [fr *kasleca* to split] : to split in two for one something soft or light

ki·ca·sto \k̇í-ca-sto\ *va* wé·casto : to smooth the hair for one - Bl

ki·ca·šla \k̇í-ca-šla\ *v of* kašla : to make bare for one, to cut low, to shave - B.H.76.6

ki·ca·šle·ca \k̇í-ca-šle-ca\ *v* wé·cašleca [fr *kašleca* to split] : to split in two for one something hard, to cut with effort

[1]**ki·ca·špa** \k̇i-cá-šp̂a\ *va* ki·wá·kašpa : to cut into the middle *e.g.* of an apple

[2]**ki·ca·špa** \k̇í-ca-šp̂a\ *v* wé·cašpa [fr *kašpa* separate or cut off] : to divide for one

---

\a\ father \e\ they \i\ machine \o\ smoke \u\ lunar \an, aŋ\ blanc Fr. \in, iŋ\ ink \on, oŋ, un, uŋ\ soon, confier Fr. \c\ chair \ġ\ machen Ger. \j\ fusion \clusters: bl, gn, kp, hšl, etc...\ b[e]lo ... said with a slight vowel
See more in the Introduction, Guide to Pronunciation

ki·ca·we·ga \k̇í-ca-we-ġa\ *v* wé·cawega [fr *kawega* to fracture] : to break partly or fracture one

ki·ca·wi·gnu·ni \k̇í-ca-wi-gnu-ni\ *v* wé·cawignuni [fr *kawignuni* strike to pieces] : to destroy for one *e.g.* a toy – R Bl

[1]**ki·ci** \k̇i-cí\ *prep* : with, together with < *Hehan Wicahpi Hinhpaya takolaku kin ~ iš eya yapi* At that time, he also went with his friend Falling Star. >

[2]**ki·ci** \k̇í-ci\ *prep in compos* : for < *Kíci maun* He is with me. > – Note: the syllable "*ki* " always keeps the accent of the *v* it is connected with

[3]**ki·ci** \k̇i-cí\ *prep or pron perhaps in compos* : to each other *i.e.* it makes the *recip* form of *v* < *Ecakiciconpi* They do to each other. *Waštekicilapi* They love each other. >

ki·ci·a·ta·ki·ci·ya \k̇i-cí-a-ṫa-k̇i-ci-ya\ *v* kiciata·we·ciya : to meet face to face, to meet squarely

ki·ci·ca \k̇i-cí-ca\ *vn* or *vt* : to be with, together with, following with, on the same side with, to have for a companion < *Wécica* I am with him. *He makicica* perhaps, He is with me. *He unkicicapi* He is with us. *Unkicicapi un* He is with us. *Na wica wan wécica k'on he icu, nazonspe, na iš eya ake kahunkonza* And a man I had for a companion took it, an axe, and he himself again made as if to strike with the axe. *Kicíca ota* There are many of his time, *i.e.* of the same age with. *Toke Itancan taogligle wakan kin yecicapi ni* Listen! May the Lord's angel be with you all. *Micica yaun* You are with me. > – B.H. 125.6, 164.16, 197.5, 227.11

ki·ci·ca·ble·ca \k̇í-ci-ca-ble-ca\ *v* wé·cicableca [fr *kableca* break to pieces] : to break up for one *e.g.* dishes by striking

ki·ci·ca·can \k̇í-ci-ca-caŋ\ *v* wé·cicacaŋ [fr *kacan* to shake] : to sift for one

ki·ci·ca·ga \k̇í-ci-ca-ġa\ *v* wé·cicaga un·kicicaga·pi [fr *kaga* to make] : to make anything for another – Note: *kícaga* to write a letter to one, *kícicaga* to write a letter for another *i.e.* other than the one to whom it is written

ki·ci·ca·ge·ge \k̇í-ci-ca-ġe-ġe\ *v* wé·cicagege [fr *kagege* to sew] : to sew anything for one

ki·ci·ca·gla \k̇í-ci-ca-gla\ *v* wé·cicagla [fr *agla* bring on the way home] : to take to one's home for him

ki·ci·ca·gli \k̇í-ci-ca-gli\ *v* wé·cicagli [fr *agli* bring arriving home] : to bring to one's home for him

ki·ci·ca·hi \k̇í-ci-ca-hi\ *v* wé·cicahi [fr *ahi* bring to a place] : to bring to a place for one

kici·ca·hin·ta \k̇í-ci-ca-hiŋ-ṫa\ *v* wé·cicahinta : to sweep for one

ki·ci·ca·hni·ga \k̇í-ci-ca-ḣni-ġa\ *v* wé·cicahniga [fr *kahniga* to choose] : to choose, select for one

ki·ci·ca·ḣu·ga \k̇í-ci-ca-ḣu-ġa\ *v* wé·cicaḣuga [fr *kaḣuga* to fracture] : to fracture for one, break in *e.g.* the skull or a barrelhead for one — **kicicaḣu·ḣuga** \k̇í-ci-ca-ḣu-ḣu-ġa\ *v red* : to keep fracturing for one

ki·ci·ca·i \k̇í-ci-ca-i\ *v* wé·cicai [fr *ai* to take to a place] : to take to a place for one

ki·ci·ca·i·c'i·ya \k̇i-cí-ca-i-c'i-ya\ *v refl* : to take sides with – B.H.3.12, 89.4

ki·ci·ca·ju·ju \k̇í-ci-ca-ju-ju\ *v* wé·cicajuju un·kicicajuju·pi [fr *kajuju* to pay, knock off] : to pay for anything for another, to erase for one, to forgive one

ki·ci·ca·kan \k̇í-ci-ca-kaŋ\ *v* wé·cicakan [fr *kakan* to hew] : to hew for one

ki·ci·ca·kca \k̇í-ci-ca-kca\ *v* wé·cicakca [fr *kakca* to comb] : to comb *e.g.* hair for one

ki·ci·ca·ki \k̇í-ci-ca-k̇i\ *v* wé·cicaki [fr *aki* to have taken to one's home] : to have taken to one's home for one

ki·ci·ca·kin·ca \k̇í-ci-ca-k̇iŋ-ca\ *v* wé·cicakinca [fr *kakinca* scrape] : to scrape for one

ki·ci·ca·ki·ya \k̇i-cí-ca-k̇i-ya\ *va* : to join one's own – Pb.43

ki·ci·ca·ksa \k̇í-ci-ca-ksa\ *v* wé·cicaksa [fr *kaksa* cut off] : to cut off *e.g.* a stick for one — **kicicaksa·ksa** *v red* : to cut up *e.g.* firewood for another

ki·ci·ca·ku \k̇í-ci-ca-k̇u\ *v* wé·cicaku [fr *aku* bring home] : to be bringing something home for one

ki·ci·ca·ku·ka \k̇í-ci-ca-k̇u-ka\ *v* wé·cicakuka [fr *kakuka* wear out] : to pound to pieces for one

ki·ci·ca·la \k̇í-ci-ca-la\ *v* wé·cicala [fr *kala* scatter] : to pour out or spill for one

ki·ci·ca·sle·ca \k̇í-ci-ca-sle-ca\ *v* wé·cicasleca [fr *kasleca* to split] : to split *e.g.* something light for one — **kicicasle·sleca** *v red* : to keep on splitting

ki·ci·ca·sni \k̇í-ci-ca-sni\ *va* wé·cicasni : to put out, extinguish *e.g.* a prairie fire for another – Bl

ki·ci·ca·ška \k̇í-ci-ca-šk̇a\ *v* wé·cicaška [fr *kaška* to bind] : to tie or bind for one

ki·ci·ca·šla \k̇í-ci-ca-šla\ *v* wé·cicašla [fr *kašla* to shave, mow] : to cut or make bare for one, as in mowing

ki·ci·ca·šle·ca \k̇í-ci-ca-šle-ca\ *v* wé·cicašleca : to split *e.g.* a log or something heavy for one — **kicicašleca·šleca** *v red* : to be splitting *e.g.* a large heavy log

ki·ci·ca·špa \k̇í-ci-ca-špa\ *v* wé·cicašpa [fr *kašpa* strike off a piece] : to deliver from, to relieve or free from one, to separate for one

ki·ci·ca·šta·ka \k̇í-ci-ca-šta-k̇a\ *v* wé·cicaštaka [fr *kaštaka* beat, whip] : to smite for one

ki·ci·ca·štan \k̇í-ci-ca-šṫaŋ\ *v* wé·cicaštan [fr *kaštan* pour out] : to pour out or spill for one, as in *ref* to liquids

ki·ci·ca·u \k̇í-ci-ca-u\ *v* wé·cicau mí·cicau : to bring for one

ki·ci·ca·we·ga \k̇í-ci-ca-we-ġa\ *v* wé·cicawega [fr *kawega*] : to break or partly break for one

ki·ci·ca·wo·ta \k̇i-cí-ca-wo-ṫa\ *n* : one of the same age < *Kicicamawota* I am of the same age as he, of one age with him. > – Cf kicíca

[1]**ki·ci·ca·ya** \k̇í-ci-ca-ya\ *v* wé·cicabla *or* perhaps wecicaya [fr *aya* take, carry to] : to take or carry to a place for one – *See* kaáya fr *áya*. The word may rather be *kícicaaya*

[2]**ki·ci·ca·ya** \k̇i-cí-ca-ya\ *or* \k̇í-ci-ca-ya\ *v* : to be with another < *Nícicaya maktepi kte* I shall be killed along with you. *Miyécicaya yaun kte* You will be with me. *Nicicaya unyankapi* We are with you. ~ *unpi* We are with him. > – B.H.254.11, 267.16, 292.6, 306.12

ki·ci·ca·zun·ta \k̇í-ci-ca-zun-ta\ *v* wé·cicazunta [fr *kazunta* or *kazonta* to weave] : to weave for one

ki·ci·ce·ya \k̇í-ci-ce-ya\ *va* : to bewail one – P

ki·ci·cin \k̇í-ci-ciŋ\ *v* wé·cicin mí·cicin [fr *cin* to desire, ask for] : to desire or ask for for one

ki·ci·co·pi \k̇i-cí-co-p̀i\ *v recip* un·kicico·pi [fr *kico* call or invite] : to call each other < *Na wanna hanhepi el ~ na el aya ca miš ake el owapa* And in the evening there was a call to one another, and since they were going there I joined in a second time. > — **kicico wotapi** \k̇i-cí-co wò-ṫa-pi\ *n* : a public feast, a feast in which a general invitation is given

ki·ci·cu·te \k̇í-ci-cu-ṫe\ *v* wé·cicute [fr *kute* to shoot] : to shoot anything for another

ki·ci·cu·te·pi \k̇i-cí-cu-ṫe-pi\ *v recip* un·kicicutepi : to shoot each other, as in the *wakan wacipi* a death dance

ki·ci·c'in \k̇í-ci-c'iŋ\ *v* wé·cic'in [fr *k'in* carry a load] :

to carry or pack for one
ki·ci·gle \k̇í-ci-gle\ *v* wé·cigle [fr *gle* to place something] : to place or set for one
ki·ci·glo·hi \k̇í-ci-glo-hi\ *v* wé·ciglohi [fr *glohi* to bring one's own to a place] : to bring one's own to him, to return his own - R Bl
ki·ci·glo·i \k̇í-ci-glo-i\ *v* wé·cigloi [fr *gloi* to have taken one's own] : to have taken one's own to him - R Bl
ki·ci·glo·ni·ca \k̇i-cí-glo-ni-ca\ *v* : to refuse to give up for one, as a mother prevents a child giving away its own - Bl
ki·ci·glo·ya \k̇í-ci-glo-ya\ *v* wé·cigloya [fr *gloya* to go taking one's own to a place] : to take one's own to him - Cf *hdoyá* in the R dictionary Bl shows rather the Lakota *gloyá in compos* only
ki·ci·gna·ka \k̇í-ci-gna-ka\ *v* wé·cignaka [fr *gnaka* lay up] : to lay away or lay up for one
ki·ci·han \k̇í-ci-haŋ\ *v* mi·cihan [fr *han* be or remain] : to be or remain for one
ki·ci·hi·yo·hi \k̇í-ci-hi-yo-hi\ *v* : to go and fetch for one
ki·ci·ȟa \k̇í-ci-ȟa\ *v* wé·ciȟa [fr *ȟa* to bury] : to bury for one
ki·ci·ȟa·pi \k̇i-cí-ȟa-pi\ *v 3 pers pl* : they laugh or smile at each other - Bl
ki·ci·hmun·ga·pi \k̇i-cí-ȟmuŋ-ġa-pi\ *v recip* un·kicihmungapi [fr *hmúnga* to bewitch] : to bewitch each other
ki·ci·h'an·yan \k̇í-ci-ȟ'aŋ-yaŋ\ *v* mí·cih'anyan [fr *h'anyan* fail, decline] : to fail or become worse for one, as one's sick child
ki·ci·i·c'i·ya \k̇i-cí-i-c'i-ya\ *v contrac of* kican'ic'iya : to make one's self ready - *See* kicínciya
ki·ci·kpa·mni \k̇i-cí-kṗa-mni\ *or* \k̇í-ci-kṗa-mni\ *v* [fr *pamni* distribute] : to divide among themselves < *Šunk kicikpamnipi na mazawakan ko tona na mazasu ko* Horses they distributed among themselves, a number of guns, and bullets as well. > — **kicikpamni·pi** *v recip* : to divide among themselves < *Unkicikpamnipi* We divided it among ourselves. >
ki·ci·ksu·ya \k̇í-ci-ksu-ya\ *or* \k̇i-cí-ksu-ya\ *v* wé·ciksuya [fr *kiksuya* remember] : to recollect for one
ki·ci·kšan \k̇i-cí-kšaŋ\ *or* \k̇í-ci-kšaŋ\ *v* : to wrestle with, to make love with, to have love-play < *Unkícikšan(pi)* You and I (we) had love-play together. >
ki·ci·kte·pi \k̇i-cí-kṫe-pi\ *v recip* : to kill each other < *Unkiciktepi* We killed each other. > — *n* : murder
ki·ci·ku·ja \k̇í-ci-k̇u-ya\ *v of* kúja : to be sick for one, as one's child
ki·ci·la \k̇i-cí-la\ *adv* : with, only with < ~ *ti* He lives only with her. >
ki·cin \k̇i-cíŋ\ *v of* cin : to desire one's own, to desire for or of one < *Taku mayakicin na hecanon hwo?* What did you do for me and did you do that? >
ki·cin·ci·ya \k̇i-cíŋ-ci-ya\ *v refl* : to get ready, make ready one's self, as for a walk - Cf iglúwinyeya *Syn perhaps* KICAN'IC'IYA
ki·cin'·in \k̇i-cíŋ-iŋ\ *v poss* wé·cin'in un·kicin'in·pi [fr *kin'in* assail] : to throw *e.g.* stones at one's own
ki·ci·pa \k̇í-ci-ṗa\ *va* wé·cipa cí·cipa **1** : to assist one *e.g.* with something to carry on a game in gambling **2** : to reserve, espouse *e.g.* a girl with the intention of marrying her, to keep for one
ki·ci·pa·ble·ca \k̇í-ci-ṗa-ble-ca\ *v* wé·cipableca [fr *pableca* to crush] : to break for one
ki·ci·pa·e·sya un·pi \k̇i-cí-ṗa-e-sya un-pi\ *v* : they are against each other as husband and wife - Bl
ki·ci·pa·gan \k̇í-ci-ṗa-ġaŋ\ *v* wé·cipagan [fr *pagan* to spare] : to part with for one — **kicipagan·pi** \k̇i-cí-ṗa-ġaŋ-pi\ *v recip* : to part with each other, as a man his wife < *Unkicipaganpi We parted with each other.* >
ki·ci·pa·gmun \k̇í-ci-ṗa-gmuŋ\ *v* wé·cipagmun [fr *pagmun* to roll up] : to twist or roll up *e.g.* a string for one
ki·ci·pa·go \k̇í-ci-ṗa-ġo\ *v* wé·cipago [fr *pago* carve or mark] : to carve for one
ki·ci·pa·hi \k̇í-ci-ṗa-hi\ *v* wé·cipahi mi·cipahi [fr *pahi* to gather, pick up] : to pick or gather up for one
ki·ci·pa·ja·ja \k̇í-ci-ṗa-ja-ja\ *v* wé·cipajaja [fr *pajaja* to wash or mop] : to wash out *e.g.* a gun for one
ki·ci·pa·jin·pi \k̇i-cí-ṗa-jiŋ-pi\ *v recip of* kipajin : they oppose each other < *Unkicipajinpi* We opposed each other. >
ki·ci·pa·ju·ju \k̇í-ci-ṗa-ju-ju\ *v* wé·cipajuju [fr *pajuju* erase] : to erase for one
ki·ci·pa·kca \k̇í-ci-ṗa-kca\ *v* wé·cipakca [fr *pakca* to comb] : to comb out straight for one
ki·ci·pa·kin·ta \k̇í-ci--ṗa-k̇iŋ-ṫa\ *v* wé·cipakinta [fr *pakinta* to wipe] : to wipe for one
ki·ci·pa·me \k̇í-ci-ṗa-me\ *v* wé·cipame [fr *paman* to file] : to file for one
ki·ci·pan \k̇í-ci-ṗaŋ\ *v* wé·cipan [fr *pan* to call or yell] : to call to one for another
ki·ci·pa·pson \k̇í-ci-ṗa-psoŋ\ *v* wé·ci·papson [fr *papson* to pour or spill] : to spill or pour out *e.g.* water for one
ki·ci·pa·si \k̇i-cí-ṗa-si\ *vn* : to drill, exercise as soldiers do - P
ki·ci·pa·snun \k̇í-ci-ṗa-snuŋ\ *v* wé·cipasnun [fr *pasnun* to roast on a spit] : to roast *e.g.* meat for one
ki·ci·pa·su·ta \k̇í-ci-ṗa-su-ṫa\ *v* wé·cipasuta [fr *pasuta* to stiffen] : to knead or make stiff *e.g.* bread for one
ki·ci·pa·ta \k̇í-ci-pa-ṫa\ *v* wé·cipata [fr *páta* to cut up] : to cut up or carve for one
ki·ci·pa·tan \k̇í-ci-ṗa-ṫaŋ\ *v* wé·cipatan [fr *patán* take care of] : to take care of for one
ki·ci·pa·zo \k̇í-ci-ṗa-zo\ *v* wé·cipazo [fr *pazo* to show to] : to point to for one
ki·ci·pe·han \k̇í-ci-ṗe-haŋ\ *v* wé·cipehan [fr *pehan* to fold up] : to fold up for one
ki·ci·pe·mni \k̇í-ci-ṗe-mni\ *vn* mi·cipemni [fr *pemni* warped] : to become crooked or twisted for one
ki·cis \k̇i-cís\ *v contrac of* kiciza : to fight or argue < ~ *wacinpi* They want to fight. >
ki·ci·son \k̇í-ci-soŋ\ *v* wé·cison [fr *son* to braid] : to braid for one
ki·ci·su·ta \k̇í-ci-su-ṫa\ *vn* mí·cisuta [fr *suta* hard, firm] : to become hard or firm for one
ki·ci·ši·ca \k̇í-ci-ši-ca\ *vn* mí·cišica [fr *šica* bad] : to become bad to or for one
ki·ci·ška·ta \k̇i-cí-ška-ta\ *n* : a playmate
ki·ci·šna·la \k̇i-cí-šna-la\ *pron* : alone with any one or any thing
ki·ci·te·han·yan·la·ke s'e \k̇í-ci-te-haŋ-yaŋ-la-ke s'e\ *adv* : a little apart, not far from each other < *Yunkan tipi nunp ~ han* Moreover two houses stood not far from each other. >
ki·ci·ton \k̇í-ci-toŋ\ *v* wé·citon mí·citon [fr *ton* to give birth to] : to bear or have a child to or for one

---

\a\ father \e\ they \i\ machine \o\ smoke \u\ lunar \an, aŋ\ blanc Fr. \in, iŋ\ ink \on, oŋ, un, uŋ\ soon, confier Fr. \c\ chair \ġ\ machen Ger. \j\ fusion \clusters: bl, gn, kp, hšl, etc...\ b^e^lo ... said with a slight vowel
See more in the Introduction, Guide to Pronunciation

ki·ci·t'a \ǩí-ci-t'a\ *v* : to die for - B.H.153.16

ki·ci·wa·šte \ǩí-ci-wa-šte\ *vn* mí·ciwašte [fr *wašte* good] : to be good or become good for one

ki·ci·ya \ǩí-ci-ya\ *v* wé·ciya mí·ciya : to go in place of another < *Miciya* He goes in place of me. *Niciya* He goes in place of you. >

ki·ci·ya·ȟe·pa \ǩí-ci-ya-ȟe-ṗa\ *v* wé·ciyaȟepa [fr *yaȟepa* to drink up] : to drink up for one

ki·ci·ya·hle·ca \ǩí-ci-ya-ȟle-ca\ *v* wé·ciyahleca [fr *yahleca* tear with the mouth] : to tear in pieces with the mouth for one — **kiciyahle·hleca** *v red* : continually tearing to pieces by mouth

ki·ci·ya·hta·ka \ǩí-ci-ya-ȟta-ka\ *v* wé·ciyahtaka [fr *yahtaka* to bite] : to bite for one

ki·ci·ya·mna \ǩí-ci-ya-mna\ *v* wé·ciyamna [fr *yamna* to win-over with talk] : to acquire for one by talking

ki·ci·yan·ka \ǩí-ci-yaŋ-ka\ *vn* mi·ciyanka [fr *yanka* to be] : to be or exist for one

ki·ci·ya·o·ni·han \ǩí-ci-ya-o-ni-haŋ\ *v* wé·ciyaonihan [fr *yaonihan* to praise, honor] : to praise for one

ki·ci·ya·o·tan'·in \ǩí-ci-ya-o-taŋ-iŋ\ *v* wé·ciyaotan'in [fr *yaotan'in* proclaim] : to make manifest, proclaim for one

ki·ci·ya·pa \ǩí-ci-ya-pa\ *v* wé·ciyapa [fr *yapa* take in the mouth] : to suck for one, as in conjuring, the affected part of a sick person

ki·ci·ya·po·ta \ǩí-ci-ya-ṗo-ṫa\ *v* wé·ciyapota [fr *yapota* to tear in pieces with the mouth] : to tear up with the mouth for one

ki·ci·ya·psa·ka \ǩí-ci-ya-psa-ǩa\ *v* wé·ciyapsaka [fr *yapsaka* tear in two by mouth] : to bite off *e.g.* a string for one

ki·ci·ya·su \ǩí-ci-ya-su\ *v* wé·ciyasu [fr *yasu* to judge, decree] : to judge or condemn for one — **kiciyasu·pi** \ǩi-cí-ya-su-ṗi\ *v recip* un·kiciyasu·pi : to judge or condemn each other

ki·ci·ya·špa \ǩí-ci-ya-šṗa\ *v* wé·ciyašṗa [fr *yašpa* bite off a piece] : to bite off a piece for one

ki·ci·ya·tan \ǩí-ci-ya-ṫaŋ\ *v* wé·ciyatan [fr *yatan* to praise] : to praise for one

ki·ci·ya·tan'·in \ǩí-ci-ya-taŋ-iŋ\ *v* wé·ciyatan'in [fr *yatan'in* declare] : to make manifest or declare for one

ki·ci·ya·wa \ǩí-ci-ya-wa\ *v* wé·ciyawa [fr *yawa* to read or count] : to count for one, to account to one

ki·ci·yu·bla·ya \ǩí-ci-yu-bla-ya\ *v* wé·ciyublaya [fr *yublaya* to open, unfold] : to spread out for one

ki·ci·yu·blu \ǩí-ci-yu-blu\ *v* wé·ciyublu [fr *yublu* pulverize] : to plow or break up for one

ki·ci·yu·can \ǩí-ci-yu-caŋ\ *v* wé·ciyucan [fr *yucan* to sift] : to shake for one

ki·ci·yu·ga \ǩí-ci-yu-ġa\ *v* wé·ciyuga [fr *yuga* to husk] : to husk *e.g.* corn for one - Note: the word is <u>not</u> "*yugan*" as is seen in R

ki·ci·yu·ga·ta \ǩí-ci-yu-ġa-ṫa\ *v* wé·ciyugata [fr *yugata* to stretch hands and arms out and up] : to open out *e.g.* the hand for one

ki·ci·yu·gmun \ǩí-ci-yu-gmuŋ\ *v* wé·ciyugmun [fr *yugmun* to twist] : to twist for one

ki·ci·yu·ha \ǩí-ci-yu-ha\ *v* wé·ciyuha un·kiciyuha·pi [fr *yuha* to have] : to have or keep for one

ki·ci·yu·han·ska \ǩí-ci-yu-haŋ-ska\ *va* : to lengthen out for one < *Taanpetu kin yeciluhanskin kte* You will give him length of days. > — Pb.40

ki·ci·yu·ho·mni \ǩí-ci-yu-ho-mni\ *v* wé·ciyuhomni [fr *yuhomni* to turn] : to turn around for one

ki·ci·yu·hun·hun·za \ǩí-ci-yu-huŋ-huŋ-za\ *v red* wé·ciyuhuŋhunza [fr *yuhunhunza* to shake, move by hand] : to shake, as a tree, for one

ki·ci·yu·hle·ca \ǩí-ci-yu-ȟle-ca\ *v* wé·ciyuhleca [fr *yuhleca* tear to pieces by hand] : to tear for one

ki·ci·yu·hlo·ka \ǩí-ci-yu-ȟlo-ǩa\ *v* wé·ciyuhloka [fr *yuhloka* make a hole by hand] : to open or make a hole for one

ki·ci·yu·ja \ǩí-ci-yu-ja\ *v* wé·ciyuja [fr *yuja* to mash or make mush] : to make mush for one

ki·ci·yu·ja·ja \ǩí-ci-yu-ja-ja\ *v* wé·ciyujaja [fr *yujaja* to wash] : to wash for one

ki·ci·yu·ju·ju \ǩí-ci-yu-ju-ju\ *v* wé·ciyujuju [fr *yujuju* tear down, to destroy] : to tear down or tear to pieces for one

ki·ci·yu·jun \ǩí-ci-yu-juŋ\ *v* wé·ciyujun [fr *yujun* to pull up as with the roots] : to pull out by the roots for one

ki·ci·yu·kpan \ǩí-ci-yu-kṗaŋ\ *v* wé·ciyukpan [fr *yukpan* to grind fine] : to grind *e.g.* grain for one

ki·ci·yu·ksa \ǩí-ci-yu-ksa\ *v* wé·ciyuksa [fr *yuksa* to break off by hand] : to break off for one

ki·ci·yu·kšan \ǩí-ci-yu-kšaŋ\ *v* wé·ciyukšan [fr *yukšan* to bend] : to bend for one

ki·ci·yu·man \ǩí-ci-yu-maŋ\ *v* wé·ciyuman [fr *yuman* sharpen] : to sharpen, grind *e.g.* an axe for one

ki·ci·yu·o·ta \ǩí-ci-yu-o-ta\ *v* wé·ciyuota [fr *yuota* to multipy] : to multiply for one - Pb.44

ki·ci·yu·o·wo·tan·la \ǩí-ci--yu-o-wo-taŋ-la\ *v* wé·ciyuowotanla [fr *yuowotanla* make right, straight] : to make straight, to straighten for one

ki·ci·yu·po·ta \ǩí-ci-yu-ṗo-ṫa\ *v* wé·ciyupota [fr *yupota* to wear out or pull to pieces] : to wear out or destroy for one

ki·ci·yu·psa·ka \ǩí-ci-yu-psa-ka\ *v* wé·ciyupsaka [fr *yupsaka* to break, pull in two] : to break *e.g.* a cord or string for another

ki·ci·yu·pšun \ǩí-ci-yu-pšuŋ\ *v* wé·ciyupšun [fr *yupšun* pull out] : to pull out or extract *e.g.* a tooth for one

ki·ci·yu·sa·pa \ǩí-ci-yu-sa-pa\ *v* wé·ciyusapa [fr *yusapa* to blacken] : to blacken for one

ki·ci·yu·ski·ski·ta \ǩí-ci-yu-sǩi-sǩi-ṫa\ *v red of* kiciyuskita : to bind up repeatedly for one

ki·ci·yu·ski·ta \ǩí-ci-yu-sǩi-ṫa\ *v* wé·ciyuskita [fr *yuskita* to tie tightly] : to bind up or wrap up for one

ki·ci·yu·so·ta \ǩí-ci-yu-so-ṫa\ *v* wé·ciyusota [fr *yusota* use up, spend] : to use up for one

ki·ci·yu·sto \ǩí-ci-yu-sṫo\ *v* wé·ciyusto [fr *yusto* make smooth] : to make smooth for one

ki·ci·yu·su·ta \ǩí-ci-yu-su-ṫa\ *v* wé·ciyusuta [fr *yusuta* make firm] : to make firm for one, to insure

ki·ci·yu·ša·pa \ǩí-ci-yu-šaṗa\ *v* wé·ciyušapa [fr *yušapa* to soil, defile, blacken] : to defile for one

ki·ci·yu·ši·ca \ǩí-ci-yu-ši-ca\ *v* wé·ciyušica [fr *yušica* to make bad, spoil] : to make bad or spoil for one

ki·ci·yu·šin·htin \ǩí-ci-yu-šiŋ-ȟtiŋ\ *v* wé·ciyušinhtin [perhaps fr *yušin* to wrinkle + *htata* weak, feeble] : to enfeeble or injure for one

ki·ci·yu·ška \ǩí-ci-yu-šǩa\ *v* wé·ciyuška [fr *yuška* loosen, untie] : to loosen for one

ki·ci·yu·šlo·ka \ǩí-ci-yu-šlo-ka\ *v* we·ciyušloka [fr *yušloka* pull off or out] : to pull off *e.g.* the clothes for one

ki·ci·yu·šna \ǩí-ci-yu-šna\ *v* wé·ciyušna [fr *yušna* let slip or drop] : to make a mistake for one

ki·ci·yu·špi \ǩí-ci-yu-špi\ *v* wé·ciyušpi [fr *yušpi* to pick or gather] : to gather or pick off *e.g.* berries for one

ki·ci·yu·štan \ǩí-ci-yu-štaŋ\ *v* wé·ciyuštan [fr *yuštan* to to finish, settle] : to finish or perfect for one

[1]**ki·ci·yu·ta** \ǩi-cí-yu-ṫa\ *v* kicí·wa·ta : to eat with one

[2]**ki·ci·yu·ta** \ǩí-ci-yu-ṫa\ *v* wé·ciyuta [fr *yuta* to eat] : to eat anything for one

ki·ci·yu·ta·ku·ni·šni \ǩí-ci-yu-ṫà-ku-ni-šni\ *v* wé·ciyutakunišni [fr *yutakunišni* destroy] : to destroy for another

ki·ci·yu·tan \ǩí-ci-yu-tan\ *v* wé·ciyutan [fr *yutan* touch] : to touch for one

ki·ci·yu·tan'·in \ǩí-ci-yu-taŋ-iŋ\ *v* wé·ciyutan'in [fr *yutan'in* make manifest] : to manifest for one

ki·ci·yu·tan·ka \ǩí-ci-yu-taŋ-ǩa\ *v* wé·ciyutanka [fr *yutanka* enlarge] : to enlarge for another

ki·ci·yu·te·ca \ǩí-ci-yu-ṫe-ca\ *v* wé·ciyuteca [fr *yuteca* to renew] : to make new for one

ki·ci·yu·te·han \ǩí-ci-yu-ṫe-haŋ\ *v* wé·ciyutehan [fr *yutehan* to delay, prolong] : to make a delay for one, prolong, put off ffor one < *T'in kte kin he yecilutehan* You made a delay for him who is about to die. > – Pb.41

ki·ci·yu·to·kan \ǩí-ci-yu-to-kaŋ\ *v* wé·ciyutokan [fr *yutokan* remove, reject] : to put in another place or remove for one

ki·ci·yu·to·ke·ca \ǩí-ci-yu-to-ǩe-ca\ *v* wé·ciyutokeca [fr *yutokeca* to alter, revoke] : to make different for one

ki·ci·yu·wa·šte \ǩí-ci-yu-wa-šte\ *v* wé·ciyuwašte [fr *yuwašte* bless] : to make good for one

ki·ci·yu·wa·š'a·ka \ǩí-ci-yu-wa-š'a-ǩa\ *v* wé·ciyuwaš'aka [fr *yuwaš'aka* strengthen] : to make strong for one

ki·ci·yu·we·ga \ǩí-ci-yu-we-ġa\ *v* wé·ciyuwega [fr *yuwega* to fracture] : to partly break for one, as a stick

ki·ci·yu·za \ǩí-ci-yu-za\ *v* wé·ciyuza [fr *yuza* grasp] : to hold for one

ki·ci·yu·za·mni \ǩí-ci-yu-za-mni\ *v* wé·ciyuzamni [fr *yuzamni* to uncover] : to open out or uncover for one

ki·ci·yu·za·pi \ǩi-cí-yu-za-pi\ *v recip* : to take each other as man and wife < *Wakan Kiciyuzapi* marriage, or the Sacrament of Matrimony >

ki·ci·za \ǩi-cí-za\ *v of* kiza : to fight < *kici* ~ to fight, quarrel with one, *Kici weciza* I quarreled with him. *Hanhepi ataya kici kicizelo* He quarreled with him the whole night through. > — **kiciza·pi** \ǩi-cí-za-pi\ *n* : a fight

ki·co \ǩi-có\ *va* wé·co mí·co : to call, invite *e.g.* to a feast

ki·con·za \ǩi-cóŋ-za\ *v* – *See* kicunza

ki·co·šni·yan \ǩi-có-šni-yaŋ\ *adv* : with being not invited, uninvited < *micošniyan* with me being uninvited > – B.H.147.7

ki·co·za \ǩi-có-za\ *va* : to wave at someone < *Nape wicakicozapi* They waved their hands at them. > – B.H. 186.1

ki·cu \ǩi-cú\ *v* wé·cu yé·cu un·kícu·pi mí·cu ní·cu cí·cu [fr *k'u* to give to] : to restore to one, give to one what belongs to him – Note: by analogy the word should be *kic'u*, but it is not. < *Na wanna tawicu cinca ko wicakicu ca ob oyate el gli* And his wife along with the child whom she was restoring to them arrived home in the tribe. >

ki·cun·ni \ǩi-cúŋ-ni\ *v* we·cúnni : to leave off, to abstain from what one was about to do, to give over, be discouraged, to excuse, not press any further — **kicunni·yan** \ǩi-cúŋ-ni-yaŋ\ *adv* : carelessly, not heartily — **kicunniyan·kel** *adv* : circumspectly, looking about carefully < ~ *omani* to go on carefully watching the road > – *Syn* IWÁNYANGYEHCI Bl

ki·cun·ske·han \ǩi-cúŋ-sǩe-haŋ\ *adv* : half full, as a vessel

ki·cun·za \ǩi-cúŋ-za\ *v* we·cúnza : to determine in regard to

ki·cu·wa \ǩi-cú-wa\ *n* : a friend < *Hau* ~ Hello friend! – *Syn* KOLA — *v poss* we·cúwa [fr *kuwa* pursue] : to follow up, pursue, as in trying to give medicine to one's child

ki·c'a \ǩi-c'á\ *v poss* we·c'a [fr *k'a* to dig] : to dig one's own, to dig for one

ki·c'in \ǩi-c'íŋ\ *v poss* we·c'ín un·kíc'in·pi : to carry or pack one's own, *e.g.* one's child or one's things – Note: *kic'in* is used in *ref* to carrying one one's back; whereas *k'in* is used in *ref* to carrying on one's shoulder, perhaps – BS

ki·c'un \ǩi-c'úŋ\ *va* wē'·c'un yē'·c'un un·kíc'un·pi : to put on or wear *e.g.* clothes, hat *etc* < *Na wase kic'unpi kin hena kpakintapi na glapi kte lo* And those who were painted red will wipe themselves off and be on their way home. – Note: when used with certain *v* the word shows that the action is done to themselves, thus: *itohomni* ~ to turn one's self around, *oslohan* ~ one's self to slip, *hošnašna* ~ to hop on one leg, *hohotela* ~ to swing one's self, *icaptanptan* ~ to roll about — **kic'un·kiciciya** \ǩi-c'úŋ-ǩi-ci-ci-ya\ *va* ki'un·we·ciciya : to put on for one, help one to put on *e.g.* clothes — **kic'unki·ya** \ǩi-c'úŋ-ǩi-ya\ *va* kic'un·wa·kiya : to cause to put on — **kic'un·skehanyan** *adv* : having little in, as perhaps in a vessel – *Syn* CETEYELA — **kic'un·ya** *va* kic'un·wa·ya : to cause to put on — **kic'un·yan** *adv* : in a clothed manner, perhaps < *tancan* ~ a body dressed > – B.H.69.11

ki·gla *also perhaps* **kigle** \ǩi-glá\ *vn* wa·kiyagla ya·kiyagla un·kiyagla·pi : to have gone home – Note: in all *pers* except the 3rd , "ya" is inserted, as if from the word *kiyagla* Cf kiglé

ki·gle \ǩi-glé\ *vn* : to have gone home — *v* we·gle [fr *gle* to place, set] : to place for, make ready for one, to place or lay up one's own — **kigle·kiya** \ǩi-glé-ǩi-ya\ *v* kigle·wa·kiya : to start home at once – Cf ukíya

ki·gle·ga \ǩi-glē'-ġa\ *va* we·glega : to overtake one < *Na wanji* ~ *ca na oyuspa* And when he overtook him he took hold on him. *Icizaptan can el wicakiglega* He overtook them on the fifth day. > – MS.353 D.56

ki·gle s'a \ǩi-glé s'a\ *n* : a truant, one who shirks his duty

ki·gle·ya \ǩi-glé-ya\ *va* kigle·wa·ya : to send off home

ki·gli \ǩi-glí\ *v* : to go straight home, to arrive home directly < *tokeya* ~ to arrive home first > – MW

ki·glu·špa \ǩi-glú-špa\ *v poss* ki·wa·glušpa : to break in two one's own

ki·gma \ǩi-gmá\ *vn* we·gmá *or* wa·kígma : to look like, resemble — **kigma·ic'iya** *v* : to imitate

ki·gna \ǩi-gná\ *va* we·gná ye·gná : to fondle *e.g.* a child, to caress, soothe < *He* ~ *yo* Caress him! >

ki·gnag \ǩi-gnág\ *va of* kignaka : to keep for one < ~ *wahi* I came to lay away something for one. >

ki·gna·gna \ǩi-gná-gna\ *v red of* ki-gna : to keep fondling one

ki·gna·gya \ǩi-gná-gya\ *va* kigna·gwa·ya : to cause to lay up one's own

---

\a\ f<u>a</u>ther \e\ th<u>e</u>y \i\ mach<u>i</u>ne \o\ sm<u>o</u>ke \u\ l<u>u</u>nar \an, aŋ\ bl<u>an</u>c Fr. \in, iŋ\ <u>in</u>k \on, oŋ, un, uŋ\ s<u>oo</u>n, <u>con</u>fier Fr. \c\ <u>ch</u>air \ġ\ ma<u>ch</u>en Ger. \j\ fu<u>s</u>ion \clusters: bl, gn, kp, hšl, etc...\ <u>b</u>ᵉ<u>l</u>o ... said with a slight vowel

See more in the Introduction, Guide to Pronunciation

ki·gna·ka \k̇i-gná-k̇a\ *va* we·gnáka ye·gnáka [fr *gnaka* to lay, place] **a** : to lay up for, keep for one, to lay up one's own **b** : to put off, to adjourn

ki·gna·škin·yan \k̇i-gná-škiŋ-yaŋ\ *v* : to turn crazy - B.H.204.10

ki·gna·yan \k̇i-gná-yaŋ\ *va* wa·kignayan perhaps : to fondle, caress

ki·gni kte \k̇i-gní-kte\ *vn irreg* : he will go home, *wagni kte* I shall go home, *yagni kte* you will bo home, *gla* he goes home - Cf Gramm.78 *See* kiglá

ki·gnug \k̇i-gnúg\ *vn contrac of* kignuka : to dive < ~ *iyaya* to go, dive underwater > — **kignu·gkiya** \k̇i-gnú-gk̇i-ya\ *va* kignu·gwa·kiya : to cause to dive

ki·gnu·ka \k̇i-gnú-k̇a\ *v* we·gnúka : to dive < *Mni kin el kignunk iblamni na cawapapa* I thrust him in and I go diving. *Kignunk ekta iyaye* He went in diving. >

ki·gnun \k̇i-gnúŋ\ *v* [fr perhaps *kignuka* to dive] : to dive < ~ *kakicipapi* an underwater distance swimming race, *i.e.* one would swim and then another, trying to swim the farthest > - Note: the word's *deriv* may be suggested further in the "*gnun*" : "g" *euph,* and "nun" *abbrev* of *nunwan* to swim, and "ka" *suff* which does not alter meaning Bl

ki·han \k̇i-háŋ\ *v* : to arrive and stand < *Tukte kawita unkihanpi kte lo* Which of us will assemble together? > - Note: *kawita unkihanpi kte* may be said also: *unkiwitayapi kte* - Bl

ki·he \k̇i-hé\ *v* : to make effort < ~ *laka yo* Stick to it, *or* Keep busy. > - IS WHL Re

ki·hi \k̇i-hí\ *vn* : to be fledged, as young birds, to be large enough, to provide for one's self - *Syn* UNCIHI

ki·hi·ya \k̇i-hí-ya\ *va* kihi·wa·ya : to raise *e.g.* a child, to train up to manhood - *Syn* UNCIHIYA

ki·ho·wa·ya \k̇i-hó-wa-ya\ *v* [fr *howaya* cry out] : to talk loud to - B.H.115.6

ki·hun·ni \k̇i-húŋ-ni\ *vn* wa·kihunni un·kihunni·pi : to get through, reach home or the goal *etc*

ki·hlo \k̇i-ȟló\ *v poss* ma·kihlo [fr *hlo* to growl] : to growl over one's own *e.g.* bone, as is said of dogs

ki·hpa·ya \k̇i-ȟpá-ya\ *v* : to bed down, to fall down - MW WHL

ki·h'an \k̇i-ȟ'áŋ\ *or* \k̇i-ȟ'áŋ\ *n* : stormy weather, a storm < *Hanpiška sutaya ayuwi yo, unnihan ~ hi yelo* Wrap firmly the upper moccasin, shortly weather comes. ~ *wan hi yelo* A storm came. *Tokel ~ kte k'un he ikopa keye* He said he had feared somewhere there would be a storm. > — **kih'an·ka** \k̇i-ȟ'áŋ-k̇a\ *v* : to have rather stormy weather < *Can wákih'ankelo* I am having a rather unpleasant day. > — **kih'an·yan** *v* ma·kih'anyan [fr *h'anyan* fail, decline] : to be likely to die to or for one, *e.g.* one's child - R Bl BT B.H.136.16

ki·i·gla·ksa \k̇i-í-gla-ksa\ *v refl* ki·mi·glaksa ki·ni·glaksa [fr *kicáksa* to cut in two, or to disobey] : to injure one's self

ki·i·glu·špa \k̇i-í-glu-špa\ *v refl* : to wrestle, free one's self < *Canke nahmakel kiiglušpin kta wacinyuze* And so, it was his intention secretly to divorce her. > - B.H.164.7

ki·in·yan·ka \k̇i-íŋ-yaŋ-k̇a\ *vn* [fr *ínyaŋka* to run] : to run with one for something, to race < ~ *wan kuwelo* He follows the races. *Kiinyankapi* They run races. *Kiinyank ape* He expects to run in races. > — **kiinyanka·pi** *n* : a running, a race - BT D.2, 107

ki·in·ye·ya \k̇i-íŋ-ye-ya\ *va* kiinye·wa·ya : to shoot or make fly an arrow — **kiinyeya·pi** *n* : a bow shot

ki·ja·ni·ca·šni \k̇i-já-ni-ca-šni\ *v* : to be unable to be grasped or held, to be elusive < ~ *yuha yo* Get hold of it even if it is impossible. > - Ba

ki·jo \k̇i-jó\ *va* wa·kijo [fr *jo* to whistle] : to whistle for, to call by whistling < *Le kijopica šni* This fellow is unable to whistle, as is said of a man with whom one has to be careful, for, not being able to stand a joke *etc*, he hits back. > — **kijo·jo** *v red* wa·kijojo : to whistle for, to call one's own *e.g.* one's dog by whistling - Bl

ki·kcan·pta \k̇i-kcáŋ-pta\ *va* **a** : to console, comfort one **b** : to take sides with, desire to help one < *Wicákikcanpte* a comforter, the Holy Spirit, *Cikcanptapi kte* I shall console you. > - Pb.40, 45

ki·ki·gla \k̇i-k̇í-gla\ *vn* ma·kikigla : to go home and leave one *e.g.* one's dog or horse

ki·ki·ka \k̇i-k̇í-k̇a\ *adj or n* : all covered with scrophulous sores - Bl

ki·ki·ya·kel \k̇i-k̇í-ya-k̇el\ *adv* : disorderly, in a way outside what is usual or customary < ~ *un* living in an unexpected way, as is said when a married couple, or other people, do not get along well with each other, *i.e.* *Tokinš cantewaštepi šni* They are carelessly unhappy. > - *Syn* OIGLUKIKI Bl WHL

ki·kpa·mni \k̇i-kṗá-mni\ *va* [fr *kpamni* to divide] : to divide or distribute one's own to

ki·ksa·pa \k̇i-ksá-pa\ *vn* wa·kiksapa [fr *ksapa* wise, prudent] : to become wise, to consult

ki·ksu·ya \k̇i-ksú-ya\ *va* we·ksúya mi·ksuya ci·ksuya **a** : to remember **b** : to be conscious of — **kiksuye·kiya** \k̇i-ksú-ye-k̇i-ya\ *va* kiksuye·wa·kiya : to cause to remember — **kiksuye·šni** *vn* : to be conscious in no way, to be unconscious, to be numb < *Nape weksuyešni* My hand is numb. > — **kiksuye·ya** *va* kiksuye·wa·ya : to cause to remember

ki·kšan \k̇i-kšáŋ\ *va* wa·kikšan **a** : to wrestle, perhaps **b** : to violate, commit rape on **c** : to take without leave — **kikšan·pi** *n* : rape

ki·kta \k̇i-ktá\ *vn* we·ktá : to awake from sleep, to be awaken < ~ *hiyaya* He came awake. ~ *iyotaka ke* He sat up pretty much awake, *or* He sat bold upright, having been lying on his back. > — **kikta·han** *part* : awake, keeping awake < ~ *un* He is keeping awake. > — **kikta iyotaka** *v* : to sit up, *i.e.* from a lying position — **kikta·ya** *adv* : awake < ~ *waun* I am awake. > - B.H. 109.10 D.105

ki·kte \k̇i-kté\ *va* we·kté [fr *kte* to kill] : to kill one's own, to kill for one

ki·ku·ja \k̇i-k̇ú-ja\ *v poss* ma·kikuja [fr *kuja* to be sick] : to be sick for one, to have one sick, *e.g.* a child

ki·ku·te \k̇i-k̇ú-ṫe\ *v* wa·kikute [fr *kuté* to shoot] : to shoot anything for another, such as ducks

ki·la \k̇i-lá\ *v* wa·kila [fr *la* to ask, beg of] : to ask or beg of one — *v poss* [fr *la* form an opinion of] : to think, esteem < *waštekila* to love one's own > - Note: the word is not used alone

ki·le·le *or* **kilele·kel** \k̇i-lē'-le\ \k̇i-lé-le-k̇el\ *adv* : long ago < ~ *tak eyé* just as it happens > - *Syn* EHANNI, EHANKEHAN, HANBLEBLEKEL R

ki·li \k̇i-lí\ *exclam in surprise of one's display of skill* : Wonderful!, Magnificent!, Ah-a-a-a-a < *Ata* ~ It's altogether brilliant! > - Bu

ki·lo \k̇i-ló\ *partic* : "...šni yo", "Beware of..." *or* "Do not..." < *Eyatonwe* ~ Pay no attention to it. *El le* ~ Do not go there. *Nita akicita kin ungna wicayagnaya* ~ I do not know but you should not cheat your soldiers. *Aktonš mayaye cilo* Do not let me forget it. > - Note: the word seems to follow the 2nd *pers* or *imper*. Women in speaking drop the "lo". B.H.176.4, 57.22, 47.7, 89.14

ki·lo·wan \ǩi-ló-waŋ\ *v* wa·kilowan [fr *lowan* to sing] : to sing to, as to a child - B.H.128.4

ki·lya·kel \ǩi-lyá-kel\ *adv* : steadfastly, with firm determination < ~ *econ* to do something slowly but surely > - Bl WHL

ki·ma·ka \ǩi-má-ǩa\ *v* : to turn into soil, as anything rotting in the ground

ki·mi·mi·la \ǩi-mí-mi-la\ *n* : a butterfly, and of sorts:
~ *gleglega* the speckled butterfly
~ *sapa* the black butterfly
~ *ska* the white butterfly, or the little moth that flies about at night and go for every light they notice, hence the saying: *Kimimila ska s'e takuni kokipapi šni* They are fearless as the little white moth.
~ *ša* the red butterfly
~ *to* the blue, purple, or green butterfly
~ *zi* the yellow butterfly - Bl

ki·mi·mi·la ta·wa·na·hca \ǩi-mí-mi-la ta-wa-nà-ȟca\ *n* : the large-flowered beard tongue, the figwort family, penstemon grandiflorus; also the bindweed, hedge bindweed, the morning glory, the morning glory family, convolvulus sepinus - Bl L BT # 2, 203

ki·mna·han \ǩi-mná-haŋ\ *vn* ma·kimnahan : to fall off, to rip off for one

ki·mni \ǩi-mní\ *v* we·mni ye·mni [fr *mni* hang out to dry] : to spread out one's own to dry in the sun

ki·na·han \ǩi-na-háŋ\ *conj* : if, when - Cf kinhán

ki·na·jin \ǩi-ná-jiŋ\ *v* wa·kina·wa·jin : to reach home and stand, to stand again in one's place, to recover one's position < *Na miš lel apahalaka wan el hunh najinpi ca el wakinawajin. Na blaye cokan* ~ I recovered my position when some stopped, when I stopped here on a hillock. And he stood again in the center of the flat. >

ki·na·ksa \ǩi-ná-ksa\ *also* \ǩi-ná-ksa\ *v poss* [fr *naksa* to break off] : to hurt one's foot by stepping on *e.g.* glass — *va* kiná·wa·ksa kina·un·ksa·pi : to break in two with the foot, to break in the middle

ki·na·pa \ǩi-ná-p̌a\ *v* wa·kinapa : to come or go forth out of, to have passed through in going home - B.H. 217.11, 185.10

ki·na·psa·ka \ǩi-ná-psa-ka\ *v* kina·wa·psaka [fr *napsaka* break in two by foot] : to break *e.g.* a string in two in the middle with the foot

ki·naš \ǩi-náš\ *interj* or perhaps *abbrev of* kinnahanš : then, well then < ~ *hunh mak'u we* Well then, give me some, *i.e.* expecting to get it. ~ *takuwe ecanon hwo?* Then why did you do it? ~ *he mayak'u šni* Well then, you did not give that to me, *i.e.* then give it. *Kinaš ina tokapa kin kici le šni* Then my mother was not only with her oldest. > - Note: the word is sometimes *contrac* to *kinš* and always begins a sentence which offers a suggestion "Well in that case ..." - C.9, note 1

ki·na·špa \ǩi-ná-šp̌a\ *v* kina·wa·špa [fr *našpa* break off by foot] : to break off about half with the foot

ki·ni \ǩi-ní\ *vn* wa·kini un·kini·pi [fr *ni* to live] : to live again, return to life from the dead, to revive, recover from fainting < *Kini Anpetu* Easter Day >

Ki·ni An·pe·tu \Ǩi-ní Aŋ-p̌è-ṫu\ *np* : Easter, Resurrection Day

ki·ni·ca \ǩi-ní-ca\ *vn* wa·kinica : to strive, try to, to be anxious to < *Econ wakinica* I tried to do it. *Na lila ake ekta ye wakinica* And I am really anxious again to go there, *i.e.* to the spirit land. >

ki·ni·han \ǩi-ní-haŋ\ *va* wa·kinihan : to honor, respect, reverence, to have confidence in — **kinihan·pi** *part* : honored, respected — **kinihan·šniyan** *adv* : dishonorably — **kinihan·yan** *adv* : honorably, respectfully

ki·ni·ki·ya \ǩi-ní-ǩi-ya\ *va* kini·wa·kiya : to cause to live again

ki·nil *or* **kinnil** \ǩi-níl\ *adv* : almost all but with a few missing < *Iyaye* ~ *manka* All but myself were going, *i.e.* trying to go. *Oyasin* ~ *inajinpi* All except a few stood up. *Hanke tan'in* ~ *oye iyaye lo* The trail went all but half distinguishable. *Temnit'e* ~ *kupi* The came home all but dying of sweat, *i.e.* almost overcome by perspiration. > - BT D.40

ki·ni·ya \ǩi-ní-ya\ *va* : to raise to life

ki·nun·kan \ǩi-núŋ-ǩaŋ\ *adv* : separately, between two, divided, each having a part < ~ *wicak'u* He gave them each a part, *i.e.* two things. *Hehan* ~ *kiciyuzapi* At that time each *i.e.* of the two women were married. > — **kinunkan·kiya** \ǩi-núŋ-kaŋ-ǩi-ya\ *adv* : separately < *Can k'un hena* ~ *iyaya* The two trees sprang apart, *i.e.* separated as the wind blew. > — **kinunkan·yan** *adv* : separately - D.27

ki·nun·ki·ci·ya·pi \ǩi-núŋ-ǩi-ci-ya-pi\ *v* : to tell each other - RH

ki·nun·wan \ǩi-núŋ-waŋ\ *vn* wa·kinunwan [fr *nunwan* to swim] : to swim home, to swim back again, to return swimming - Bl

kin *or* **ki** \ǩiŋ\ *def art* : the < *Tuwa ohiye ci toka hwo?* Was he first who won? > - Note: when "a" or "an" change to terminal "e" and precede *kin* or *ki*, the latter become "ci"
— *conj contrac* : if or when < *Ina iyeyakiye šni kin, niktepi kta* If you do not find my mother, you will be killed. > - Note:
a . at the beginning or first part of the sentence, "kin" seems to mean the Latin *cum temporale, i.e.* when... < *Oyate icagapi kin, tuweni t'e šni unpi* When people mature, no one is dying. >
b . at the end of the sentence or independent *cl*, it gives the idea: It is a sure thing. - Note: in a sense, the word functions as the terminal "yelo" or "epé kin" < *Niniveh otonwahe kin ihangyapi kte kin* The city of Niniveh will certainly be destroyed. *Miyeš tantan waceye kin* It's a fact, I cried well. >
— *adj* or perhaps *v* : having had its season < *Šahiyela tinpsila* the Cheyenne turnips grow spongy, puff out and turn bad in June. So formerly it was said: *Wanna kin yelo* It has now had its season, but today is said: *Wanna popópi* They now pop open. >
— *partic* signing and ending a rhetorical question < *Tokayelaka hecannon kin?* What was your reason for doing that? *Takuwe miniwicayakaštan kin?* Why was it you baptized them? >
— *adv cl* is to be substantivalized by "kin" accompanying various *adv*, thus:

kin hecel - B.H.85.21, 98.11
kin hehanl - B.H.15.11, 94.11
kin hehanyan - B.H.52.14
kin lehanl - B.H.55.1, 71.11, 76.1, 81.4, 86.12, 118.4, 122.23, 124.2, 14.11 Gramm.247s

---

\a\ father \e\ they \i\ machine \o\ smoke \u\ lunar \an, aŋ\ blanc Fr. \in, iŋ\ ink \on, oŋ, un, uŋ\ soon, conifier Fr. \c\ chair \ġ\ machen Ger. \j\ fusion \clusters: bl, gn, kp, ȟšl, etc...\ bᵉlo ... said with a slight vowel
See more in the Introduction, Guide to Pronunciation

kin·ca \k̇íŋ-ca\ *adj* : scraping – Note: the word is not used alone *See* yukínca

kin·ca·han \k̇iŋ-cá-haŋ\ *part* : bare, fallen off, as hair from a dead animal, or as scales

kin·han \k̇iŋ-háŋ\ *conj* : if, when – Note: after a word ending with "a" or "an" changed to "e", the word becomes cinháŋ

kin'·in \k̇iŋ-íŋ\ *vt* wa·kin'in ma·kin'in ni·cin'in : to throw at, to assail with something thrown < *inyan on* ~ to pelt with stones > — *vi* ma·kin'in : to assail – D.58 and 63 note 1

kin·ja \k̇íŋ-ja\ *vi* : to whine, as babies do when they want something – LT

kin·sko·ke·ca \k̇íŋ-sk̇o-k̇e-ca\ *adv* : so large — **kinskoskokeca** *adv red* : so very large

kin·sko·sko·ya \k̇íŋ-sk̇o-sk̇o-ya\ *adv red of* kinskoya : thus far way around

kin·sko·ya \k̇íŋ-sk̇o-ya\ *adv* : thus far around

kin·ška \k̇in-šk̇á\ *n* : a horn spoon

kin·šye·la \k̇iŋ-šyé-la\ *adv* : whizzing, as a bullet, a bird, a fast horse < ~ *ya* to go buzzing > – *Syn* ŠLIYELA Bl

kin·yan *or* **kinye** \k̇iŋ-yáŋ\ *vn* : to fly, as do birds < ~ *iyaya* It went away flying. *taku kinye cin* things that fly, *i.e.* birds > — **kinyan·pi** *n* : those that fly, birds

kin·ye·ki·ya·pi \k̇iŋ·yé-k̇i-ya-pi\ *n* : a kite, an air ship – P Bl

ki·on·pa \k̇i-óŋ-pa\ *v poss of* ónpa : to lay or place on one's own

ki·pa \k̇i-ṗá\ *v poss* wa·kipa [fr *pa* complain] : to blame one's self, to suffer in consequence of one's own course; to murmur, "kick" because somebody does not help one; to silence one by talking and having the last word < *Toš kipahci* Oh yes! He really blamed himself, *i.e.* he suffers for his own foolishness. > – *Syn* APAKSONLYA Bl

ki·pa·ble \k̇i-ṗá-ble\ *v* : to come to a halt, as in the course of flight, to stop and become immobile – Note: the word is used in speaking of horses when they stop run-ning and stand still – *Syn* KIPÁMNA Bl WHL

ki·pa·ci·ca \k̇i-ṗá-ci-ca\ *v poss* : to wear out or off by knocking or rubbing against, as the hair of a quiver that bumps against one while walking

ki·pa·hci \k̇i-ṗá-ȟci\ *v perhaps of* kipá : to bring misfortune on one's self < *Toš,* ~ Well yes, what he did fell back on him, as is said when something hard happened to a man through his own fault because he did not listen > – Note: *toš* and *ito* are close in meaning – Ba SB Bl

ki·pa·jin \k̇i-ṗá-jiŋ\ *va* wa·kipajin [fr *pajin* prevent] : to stand up against, oppose, resist — **kipajin·picašni** \k̇i-ṗá-jiŋ-ṗi-ca-šni\ *adj* : irresistible — **kipajin·yan** *adv* : opposing

ki·pa·kin·ta \k̇i-ṗá-k̇iŋ-ṫa\ *va* wa·kipakinta [fr *pakinta* to wipe] : to cleanse away for one, to wipe off

ki·pa·ki·ya \k̇i-ṗá-k̇i-ya\ *va* kipa·wa·kiya : to cause to blame one's self

ki·pa·mna \k̇i-ṗá-mna\ *v* : to halt, when coming to a place of safety, as do horses or buffalo in scattered places – Note: the word is related or the same as *kipable, i.e.* implying to a stand-still *Syn* KIPABLE Bl

ki·pa·na \k̇i-ṗá-na\ *v* wa·kipana : to make a little room for one by pressing closer to the other < ~ *po* Make room for him. *Lel cicipana, tahena le ku wo* I am making room for you, come back here on this side. > – Bl

ki·pan \k̇i-ṗáŋ\ *v* wa·kipan [fr *pan* call out] : to call to one < *Father Henry (Grotegeers, S.J.) wicoh'an wašte on Greenwood ekta makipan kin he lila iyomakipi* Father Henry was very well pleased with calling me to Greenwood because of good work. >

ki·pa·s'a \k̇i-ṗá-s'a\ *n* : a lazy person, who gets along with difficulty and blames himself much

ki·pa·š'i·ya·ya \k̇i-ṗá-š'i-ya-ya\ *v* : to evade, elude, to turn sideways, avoid, to dodge – *Syn* TANHMINKIYA IYAYA Bl B.H.68.12

[1]**ki·pa·ta** \k̇i-ṗá-ta\ *v poss of* patá : to join together *e.g.* skins in making one's own tent

[2]**ki·pa·ta** \k̇i-ṗá-ṫa\ *v poss of* páta : to cut up one's own *e.g.* meat – Note: the word may be more correct, *kpáta*

[1]**ki·pa·tan** \k̇i-ṗá-ṫaŋ\ *v* wa·kipatan [fr *patán* take care of] **a** : to keep for one, to save, esteem highly, to take care of **b** : to feel for by pushing with anything other than the hand — **kipatan·han** *part* : pushing against

[2]**ki·pa·tan** \k̇i-ṗá-taŋ\ *v* wa·kipatan [fr *patán* to mash up] : to mash up *e.g.* potatoes as food

ki·pa·ti·tan \k̇i-ṗá-ṫi-taŋ\ *va* wa·kipatitan [fr *patitan* to push, push against] : to push with all one's might

ki·pa·ye·hca \k̇i-ṗá-ye-ȟca\ *vn* : to rise up again, recover itself, as grass bent down – R Bl

ki·pa·zo \k̇i-ṗá-zo\ *v* wa·kipazo ma·kipazo [fr *pazo* to show, present] : to point to for one, to show to one

ki·pca \k̇i-pcá\ *v* : to swallow *e.g.* food or saliva < *Lowacin ca on tahna wakipcahe lo* Since I was hungry on that account I was swallowing my saliva. > – Bl WHL

ki·pe \k̇i-ṗé\ *va* : to fold over — **kipe·han** *va* : to roll up, perhaps, to fold one's own < *Tašina kin kipehe* She was folding her shawl. > — B.H.112.4

ki·pi \k̇i-ṗí\ *vn* ma·kipi **1** : to hold, contain, to carry as a vessel, to cart *etc* **2** : to be large enough for, as a coat, to be sufficient for < *Makipi* It is sufficient for me. > — **kipi·ya** *va* kipi·wa·ya : to cause to fit — *adv* : fittingly, properly enough for < ~ *kaga* to adapt, adjust to, ~ *ecamon* I did it properly, *nunpa can* ~ enough, *i.e.* of it, for two days, *Tkeiyutapi wanji* ~ One was aptly weighed. > – B.H.55.17, 237.4

ki·pi·za \k̇i-ṗí-za\ *v* wa·kipiza : to smack one's lips, to produce a sound at somebody, as might a baby – Bl

ki·psa·ka·he·šni \k̇i-psá-ka-he-šni\ *part perhaps* : uninterrupted, continuous < ~ *au welo* Uninterrupted they came. > – Bl

ki·psi·ca \k̇i-psí-ca\ *v* wa·kipsica : to jump down from, alight from, as from a horse

kis \k̇is\ *vn contrac of* kíza : to grate

ki·sa·gye \k̇i-sá-gye\ *vn* : to turn into a cane, rod – B.H.48.14

ki·san \k̇i-sáŋ\ *vn* ma·kisan [fr *san* whitish] : to become whitish for one

ki·sa·pa \k̇i-sá-ṗa\ *or* \k̇i-sá-ṗa\ *vn* [fr *sapa* black] : to become black, or bare again, as does the ground by the disappearance of snow — *n* : bare ground

ki·sin·c'i·ya \k̇i-síŋ-c'i-ya\ *v refl* : to ready one's self, to groom and tidy up one's self – *Syn* PIIC'IYA WHL

ki·sin·kpe \k̇i-síŋ-kṗe\ *v* wa·kisinkpe : to trick, deceive one into doing, to solicit < *Wakisinkpe na mak'u welo* I tricked him and he gave it to me, *i.e.* receiving what one wanted very badly. *Makisinkpe na ungnayelo* He bluffed me and it may have been so. > – Bl WHL

ki·sin·te \k̇i-síŋ-te\ *v* wa·kisinte : to solicit, deceive one into doing < *Wakisinte cik'a na mak'u welo* I deceived a bit and he gave it to me, *i.e.* when a person gets what he wanted very badly. > – Note: the word may really be *kisinkpe* Bl

ki·ska \k̇i-ská\ *vn* : to bleach, *fig* to recover common sense - *Syn* KIWAŠTE Bl

ki·ski·za \k̇i-skí-za\ *v red of* kiz : to grate or gnash *e.g.* the teeth, to squeak, as shoes might

ki·sli·pa \k̇i-slí-ṗa\ *v* we·slípa : to lick up one's own again, as a dog does its vomit

ki·sna·han \k̇i-sná-haŋ\ *vn* ma·kisnahan : to break and fall off, as beads from a strand, for one

ki·sni·ki·ya \k̇i-sní-k̇i-ya\ *va* kisni·wa·kiya : to cure one - Bl

ki·so \k̇i-só\ *v poss of* so : to cut a string from a hide, to cut up one's own

ki·son \k̇i-sóŋ\ *v poss* we·són *or* wa·kison [fr *son* to braid] : to braid one's own

ki·so·ta \k̇i-só-ṫa\ *vn* ma·kisota ni·cisota [fr *sota* to be spent] : to be used up for one

ki·spa·ya \k̇i-sṗá-ya\ *v* ma·kispaya [fr *spaya* become wet] : to be or become wet for one

ki·sye·la \k̇i-syé-la\ *adv* : with a grating sound < ~ *mani* to creak under foot, *i.e.* to make a grating noise in walking through snow in cold weather > - Bl

ki·s'in·s'in \k̇i-s'íŋ-s'iŋ\ *v* wa·kís'ins'in : to crane, jerk the head or move it up and down in quick motion - *See* kas'ins'in, and s'ins'inya Bl WHL

ki·ši·ca \k̇i-ší-ca\ *va* **1** : to check, oppose, put a stop to, to forbid, command to stop **2** : to drive or kick out *e.g.* a dog from a house, to cast away **3** : to be mean to, to order back < *tankakula kin ~ he c'un* who had been so mean to her younger sister > - D.120

ki·škan \k̇i-škáŋ\ *va* wa·kiškan [fr *škan* do, act] : to do to, act towards one

[1]**ki·ška·ta** \k̇i-šká-ṫa\ *va* wa·kiškata [fr *škata* to play] : to play to or with, to play for

[2]**ki·ška·ta** \k̇i-šká-ṫa\ *v perhaps pl* : to wrestle with others in fun, playfully, as also do horses at times - Bl

ki·šle·ya \k̇i-šle-ya\ *v* : to hold and feel, forcibly, to commit rape < *Kišléyaya* You raped her. > — *va* : to annoy, vex, continue to press or urge one, to make ashamed, to offend, dishonor - R

ki·špa·han \k̇i-špá-haŋ\ *or* \k̇i-šṗá-haŋ\ *v* wa·kišpahan : to break up and go < *Na hihanna el oyate kišpahanpi ca wazitakiya aya* And when they broke up the next morning they went in a northerly direction. >

ki·što *or* **kšto** \k̇i-štó\ *adv emph assertion* : It is a fact ...

ki·ta·la \k̇i-ṫá-la\ *adv* : close together, as one hole near the other < *Canku kin ~ guheya yunkelo* The road lies along a varied course with trails close on one another, *i.e.* many roads together. > - Bl

[1]**ki·tan** \k̇i-ṫáŋ\ *vn* wa·kitan : to stick to *e.g.* an opinion, continue to assert, to insist upon and not yield < *Nihinciye kin on sam lila kitanpi* Since there was fright, the more they stuck to their opinion, *i.e.* that the turtle be thrown into the water. *K'éyaš lila kitanpi* But they really did not yield. > - D.20, 117 B.H.49.21

[2]**ki·tan** k̇í'-ṫaŋ\ *adv* : scarcely, hardly — **kitan·ecinyan** *adv* : slightly, just able — **kitan·hci** \k̇í-ṫaŋ-ḣci\ *adv* : at last < ~ *migluštan* At last I am through, finished, *or* Scarcely am I through. > - D.262, 100 R Mi

ki·tan'·in \k̇i-ṫáŋ-iŋ\ *v* ma·kitan'in [fr *tan'in* appear] : to appear, be visible for — **kitan'inšni** *vn* ma·kitan'inšni : to be lost for one - D.268-9

ki·tan·ko·gna·gye·la·hci \k̇i-ṫáŋ-ko-gna-gye-la-ḣci\ *adv* : alienating one, pressing one's demands upon one < ~ *unpi* They are drifting apart, as is said of a disaffected couple thinking of divorce. ~ *oyaštanyelo* He put a stop to press-ing for divorce. > - Bl WHL

ki·tan·la \k̇í-ṫaŋ-la\ *adv* : a little, very little, in a slight degree < ~ *tokeca* a little different, ~ *oiyokpaza* a little dark, *Na wanna wicokanyan ~ sanpa hehanl wanna eyapaha onhe ake u.* And that announcer came again a little after noon. *Na hocoka kin ~ isam unkiyaglapi* We had gone back a little beyond camp center. *Wata kin ~ pacokab iyeye* He shoved the boat a little toward the middle. > - B.H.66.9, 186.445

ki·tan·pa·wo·sla·he·ye·la·kel \k̇i-ṫáŋ-ṗa-wo-sla-he-ye-la-kel\ *adv* : reposefully, pushed a bit upright, reclining < ~ *manke c'on nawajin yelo* I stood because I was reclining and resting. > - Bl WHL

ki·tan s'e \k̇í-ṫaŋ s'e\ *adv* : with difficulty, as though but a little achieved

ki·tan·yan \k̇i-ṫáŋ-yaŋ\ *adv* : continuously, insisting upon — **kitanyan·kel** \k̇i-ṫáŋ-yaŋ-k̇el\ *adv* : with the greatest difficulty, contrary to all expectation < ~ *ecamon* I did it, *i.e.* although I thought I was unable, *e.g.* as lifting a heavy weight which one though one could not lift. > - *Syn* YUS'ÓYAKEL

ki·tan·ye·hci \k̇i-ṫáŋ-ye-ḣci\ *adv* : with difficulty, hence not thoroughly < *Mini el iyayapi na minit'api, tka ~ glinapapi* They went into the water and drowned, but contrary to all expectations they came in sight coming home. > — **kitan·yel** *adv* : with difficulty < ~ *mikpanajinkelo* I was brought to a halt for all my own difficulties. ~ *otan'in* It is hardly, just a little, visible. > — **kitanyela·keleš** *adv* : being in a favorable attitude < ~ *emáca* I am well disposed to it. > - R Bl WE

ki·ta·ta *or* **kitata·la** \k̇i-ṫá-ta\ *adv* : near together, frequently, *i.e.* in close succession < ~ *Yutapi Wakan iwacu kte* I should receive Holy Communion frequently. > - *Syn* ÍCIKANYELA

ki·ti·yu·s'e·ya *or* **kitiyu·zeya** \k̇i-ṫí-yu-s'e-ya\ *adv* : barely, hardly < ~ *tan'inyan* barely visible, ~ *bluštan* I hardly finished it. > -Br

ki·ton·wa·ya \k̇i-tóŋ-wa-ya\ *v* : to ooze < *Tehan ~ lo* It seeped out for a long time. > - Bl

ki·ton·yan \k̇i-tóŋ-yaŋ\ *adv perhaps* : in an increasing manner, growing < *cehpi ~* flesh growing, *i.e.* my flesh growing > - B.H.44.15

ki·t'a \k̇i-t'a\ *vn* ma·kit'a [fr *t'a* to die] : to die or be dead for one, as one's child

ki·un \k̇i-úŋ\ *vn* [fr *k̇i* arrive home] : to return home, as a horse returns to its place on the range < *Tehan ~ na* Take it the long way home, *i.e.* it had gone far away. > - Bl WHL

ki·un'·un la·ke \k̇i-úŋ-uŋ la-k̇è\ *v* wa·kiun'un lake : to act foolishly < *Winyan nunb ataya cagu-iyuhpa wanicapelo* Two women are entirely lacking all their lungs. *Lena tuktel kiun'unpi lake lo* These [women] where did they get this foolish way of living, *i.e.* where did they grow up anyway. > - Note: the word, as we might say, means: "They must live some life!" *Ki* is a dative, *un* to be, exist, and is *red* , *pi* they, *la ref* to one who is open to mild ridicule

ki·un·yan \k̇i-úŋ-yaŋ\ *v* wa·kiunyan : to lose for one, to lose what belongs to another

ki·wa·kan·he·ja \k̇i-wá-kaŋ-he-ja\ *vn* wa·kiwakanheja : to desire to be with, to be on good terms with, to be

---

\a\ father \e\ they \i\ machine \o\ smoke \u\ lunar \an, aŋ\ blanc Fr. \in, iŋ\ ink \on, oŋ, un, uŋ\ soon, confier Fr. \c\ chair \ġ\ machen Ger. \j\ fusion \clusters: bl, gn, kp, hšl, etc...\ b[e]lo ... said with a slight vowel **See more in the Introduction, Guide to Pronunciation**

intimate with

ki·wa·kan·yeš \k̇i-wá-kaŋ-yeš\ *adv* : carefully < ~ *au wo* Bring it carefully. ~ *unkomanipelo* We traveled with care. ~ *eyoks'in yo* Carefully peep in on him. ~ *oyakilehan ca he cicu welo* I took you because you were searching for it with great care. ~ *woyakile s'elececa* It seems you search with sensitivity. >

ki·wa·ksa \k̇i-wá-ksa\ *va* kiwa·wa·ksa : to cut in two in the middle *e.g.* a stick

ki·wa·ni·ce \k̇i-wá-ni-ce\ *v* : to turn to nothing, vanish, *lit* there is nothing there whatsoever - Bl

ki·wan·ji·ca \k̇i-wáŋ-ji-ca\ *adj* : not one but all < *Taku ~ šni slolya* He understands [knows] everything thoroughly. > - Bl WHL

ki·wa·psa·ka \k̇i-wá-psa-k̇a\ *va* kiwa·wa·psaka : to cut a cord or string in two in the middle

ki·wa·sle·ca \k̇i-wá-sle-ca\ *va* kiwa·wa·sleca : to split or saw in the middle something soft — **kiwa·šleca** *va* : to saw in the middle something hard - Note: this latter word is perhaps not used

ki·wa·špa \k̇i-wá-šṗa\ *va* kiwa·wa·špa : to cut in two in the middle, as an apple

ki·wa·šte \k̇i-wá-šte\ *vn* ma·kiwašte : to become good, to convert, return to God, to be on good terms again - *Syn* KISKA — **kiwašte·šte** *adj red of* kiwašte : having become good [in *ref* to many] — **kiwaštešte·ka** *adj* : being good to one - WHL

ki·wa·š'a·gpi·ca šni \k̇i-wá-š'a-gpi-ca šni\ *adj* : acting wrong in spite of all good advice - Bl

ki·wa·š'a·ka \k̇i-wá-š'a-k̇a\ *adj* : strong, having strong muscles - Bl

ki·wi·ta·ya \k̇i-wí-ṫa-ya\ *vn* [fr *witaya* together] : to assemble < *Unkiwitayapi kte* We shall have a gathering. *Ptanyetu kinhan lel ake kiwitayapi kte* They will meet here again in the fall. > — *adv* : together, assembled together, *i.e.* of their own accord, spontaneously - Bl D. 225 B.H. 61a.4

ki·wi·tko·tko·ka \k̇i-wí-tko-tko-ka\ *v* : to be or become foolish - B.H.104.18

ki·wi·wi·la \k̇i-wí-wi-la\ *v* : to turn into a spring - B.H. 181.21

ki·wo·ksa \k̇i-wó-ksa\ *va* kiwo·wa·ksa : to shoot in two in the middle

ki·wo·psa·ka \k̇i-wó-psa-k̇a\ *va* : to shoot off in the middle *e.g.* a cord

ki·wo·špa \k̇i-wó-šṗa\ *va* kiwo·wa·špa : to shoot *e.g.* an apple in two

[1]**ki·ya** \k̇í-ya\ *v aux* : to cause, to make to be < *econkiya* to make it be done > - Note: the word is always affixed to the *v* end *etc*; whereas the *pron* is inserted before the "kiya"

[2]**ki·ya** \k̇í-ya\ *v aux poss* [fr *ya* to go] : to go for or for one — *adv* : towards < *tokatakiya* in future, *ektakiya* to or towards > — *adv* : separately, in different ways or in different places < *Oyate nunpakiya wicoti* People encamped in two separate places. *Na el taniga k'on he topakiya pahloka* And he had pierced four times into its paunch. >

ki·ya·gla \k̇í-ya-gla\ *v* wa·kiyagla ya·kiyagla un·kiyagla·pi : to have gone home < *Hecel waglinawapa na tona glinapapi kin hecena agla ca miš eya wakiyagla na tiyata wagli. Lecel totankaya eya: Unkiyaglapi kte lo, unkiyagni kte* So I came out and when those who emerged finally were on their way back, I too had gone home and arrived at home. Yes, this is what my younger sister said: We should have gone home, we shall go home. > - D.219

ki·ya·gla·pta \k̇i-yá-gla-pṫa\ *v poss* wa·kiyaglapta [fr *kiyakapta* to have passed over] : to have passed over *e.g.* a hill in going home

ki·ya·han \k̇i-yá-haŋ\ *vn* wa·kiyahan : to climb a hill *etc* and stand, to stand on top < *Yunkan paha el kiyahanpi* Then they climbed onto a hill. *Wanbli Kiyahe* Climbing Eagle, name of a North Dakota Lakota in the 1870's, *Yunkan paha wan etan u k'on ~ šni ecel atan'in šni iyaya* And then he went on, as it was, out of sight, not climbing the hill from which he had come. >

ki·ya·ka·pta \k̇i-yá-k̇a-pṫa\ *vn* wa·kiyakapta : to have passed over *e.g.* a hill in going home

ki·ya·ki·ju *also* **kiyokiju** \k̇í-ya-ki-ju\ *vn* : to unite — **kiyakiju·ya** *va* kiyakiju·wa·ya : to put together, cause to unite — *adv* : together, unitedly - R

Ki·ya·ksa \K̇i-yá-ksa\ *np* : a Dakota band, so called, it is said, for the inter-marrying of relatives among them - *See* kiyáksa

ki·ya·ksa \k̇i-yá-ksa\ *v* ki·bla·ksa [fr *yaksa* to bite] : to bite in two in the middle

ki·ya·mna \k̇i-yá-mna\ *v* wa·kiyamna [fr *yamna* to acquire by talking] : to acquire for another by talking

ki·ya·pa \k̇i-yá-pa\ *v* wa·kiyapa : to suck for, take in the mouth and suck, as the Dakota conjurers once did < *A k'un el ~* He had sucked in his armpit. > — **kiyapa·pi** \k̇i-yá-pa-ṗi\ *n* : a drawing, sucking with the mouth - D.59

ki·ya·tan'·in \k̇i-yá-taŋ-iŋ\ *va* wa·kiyatan'in [fr *yatan'in* declare] : to make manifest to or for

ki·ye \k̇i-yé\ *adv* : nearby < ~ *au wo* Bring it closeby. > - BT

ki·ye·la \k̇i-yé-la\ *adv* : near, near to < *Tokša nikiyelapi waun kte lo* I will sometime be near to you. > - Note: the word is used in *ref* to time and place. *See* ikíyela

ki·yo·kpe·ca \k̇i-yó-kpe-ca\ *v* wa·kiyokpeca : to have come back to one's home that is away < *Tokiyab kiyokpeci na u kapin yelo* He being tired out comes and had come back to one's home, *i.e.* does not care to come back. > - Cf gliyokpeca

ki·yo·na·ki·jin \k̇i-yó-na-k̇i-jiŋ\ *v* : to arrive and take refuge in with others < *Wanna napapi na paha wan el kiyonakijinpi* They now went out and came taking refuge on a hill with others. >

ki·yo·ta·ka \k̇i-yó-ṫa-k̇a\ *vn* wa·ki·blo·taka ya·ki·lo·taka [fr *ki* arrive back + *iyotaka* sit] : to arrive and remain at home - Note: the word is used by the person who arrives, or by another person when away from the place

ki·yu·a·ja·ja \k̇i-yú-a-ja-ja\ *va* : to explain to one — **kiyuajaja·ya** *va* : to explain to one < *Wowapi Wakan kin ~* He explained the Holy Bible to him. > - B B.H. 288.7, 301.3

ki·yu·gal \k̇i-yú-gal\ *v contrac of* kiyugata : to lift up one's arms, as in prayer < ~ *wacekiya* Extending his arms he prayed. > - B.H.55.28

ki·yu·gan \k̇i-yú-ġaŋ\ *va* wa·kiyugan [fr *yugan* to open] : to open for one, as a door — **kiyuga·ta** \k̇i-yú-ġa-ta\ *va* wa·kiyugata [fr *yugata* raise up hand and arm] : to open *e.g.* the hand, to stretch out the hand to, to implore as in worship, to hold out one's arms towards somebody, as a baby towards its mother - Bl

ki·yu·ha \k̇i-yú-ha\ *v* wa·kiyuha [fr *yuha* to have] : to have or keep for one < *Wowacinye kiyuhapi kin he Jesus iyokipi. Wakantanka wowacinye ~* Jesus is pleased with having confidence in him. He has trust in God. > - B.H. 187.8, 266.6

ki·yu·ȟa \k̇i-yú-ȟa\ *va* : to copulate as do animals

ki·yu·i·na·hni \k̇i-yú-i-na-ȟni\ *vt* : to hurry things for one < *Makiyuinahni yo. Wanagi el mahipelo* Hurry thinks up for me. A spirit has come to me. > – D.244

ki·yu·ja·ja \k̇i-yú-ja-ja\ *v* wa·kiyujaja [fr *yujaja* to wash] : to wash for another

ki·yu·ju·ju \k̇i-yú-ju-ju\ *va* : to repeal

ki·yu·kan \k̇i-yú-kaŋ\ *va* wa·kiyukan ma·kiyukan ci·ciyukan : to make room for, *e.g.* in a room, *fig* to be for one < *Catku el makiyukanpi* They made room for me in the honor place [that opposite the door]. *Makiyukan yo, hel waku welo* Get out of the way for me, I am coming there yonder. > — **kiyukan·yan** *adv* : as one making room for something or someone < *Tatuye ~ unyanpi kta* We should go giving room for the wind, *i.e.* to drop dust so as to know which way the wind blows, in order to get to the leeward of the buffaloes. > – Bl D.71 B.H. 224.17

ki·yu·ko \k̇i-yú-k̇o\ *v* ci·ciyuko : to make room for one between others by moving closely together – Note: the word is perhaps *kiyuoko*. *See* oko

ki·yu·ksa \k̇i-yú-ksa\ *v* ki·blu·ksa [fr *yuksa* break off by hand] : to break or cut in the middle < *Šunka wan cokan ~ na španšni yuta* He cut the dog in two and ate it raw. > — *va* : to break in two for one – Note: here the word is pronounced k̇iyúksa, but the 1st *pers singl* is doubtfully kiblúksa .

ki·yu·kse·ya *or* kiyušpeya \k̇i-yú-kse-ya\ *or* \k̇i-yú-šṗe-ya\ *adv perhaps* : separately < ~ *egle* to set it separately, *i.e.* by itself > – Fr

ki·yun·ka \k̇i-yúŋ-k̇a\ *vn* wa·ki·mun·ka : to go home and sleep at home < *Psunpsunkiya ~* He got home and lay down prostrate. > – B.H.81.8

ki·yu·še \k̇i-yú-še\ *va* wa·ki·blu·še : to hate one, do evil to one < *Lila ~* She severely maltreated her. > – D.270

ki·yu·ška \k̇i-yú-šk̇a\ *va* wa·kiyuška *and* waki·blu·ška [fr *yuška* untie] : to loose, untie, unharness, to release as from prison or confinement

ki·yu·špa \k̇i-yú-špa\ *va* and *vn* ki·blu·špa *and* wa·ki·blu·špa [fr *yušpa* break off, divide] **1** : to break into pieces, divide *e.g.* bread **2** : to deliver, free, as from a trap or evil of any kind < *Letanhan oyate kin nunpakiya ~ iyayapi kte* From now on the people will proceed in two ways. > — **kiyušpa·pi** \k̇i-yú-šṗa-ṗi\ *n* : a dividing, delivering — **kiyušpa·špa** \k̇i-yú-šṗa-šṗa\ *v red* : to divide often

ki·yu·špe·ya \k̇i-yú-šṗe-ya\ *adv* : separately < ~ *egle* to place separately > – *Syn* KIYUKSEYA Fr

ki·yu·te \k̇i-yú-ṫe\ *n* : a strait or channel, an isthmus

ki·yu·to·kan \k̇i-yú-to-k̇aŋ\ *va* : to remove for one < *Wošica mitawa kin oysi'in miyetanhan mayakilutokan kte* You will remove from me all my evil deeds. > – Pb.30

[1]**ki·yu·we·ga** \k̇i-yú-we-ġa\ *v* wa·kiyuwega : to break something belonging to another, to break to

[2]**ki·yu·we·ga** \k̇i-yú-we-ġa\ *v* wa·ki·blu·wega [fr *iyuwega* pass through, to cross] : to cross *e.g.* a stream in going home < *Na ake mini el kiyuwegapi na oyate kin napapi etkiya agla na etipi* And again they crossed at the stream, and the tribe fled to go toward home and set up camp. >

ki·yu·za \k̇i-yú-za\ *va* wa·kiyuza [fr *yuza* to grasp] : to hold to one < *Wacin ipaweh mayakiluzelo* You grasp my incorrect thinking, *i.e.* you don't mind me. >

ki·yu·za·mni \k̇i-yú-za-mni\ *va* wa·kiyuzamni [fr *yuzamni* to uncover] : to open to or for one, to uncover for one

[1]**ki·za** \k̇í-za\ *vn* : to creak, to grate

[2]**ki·za** \k̇í-za\ *va* wa·kiza : to fight, quarrel with

ki·zo·mi \k̇i-zó-mi\ *v* wa·kizomi : to covet, desire passionately < *Wakizomi na mak'u welo* I coveted it and he gave it to me, as is said when a man gets where he wanted. *Makizomi na magnayelo* He passionately desired me and so he deceived me. *Woyuha taku k'eyaš etkiya yakizomi kilo* Do not covet with respect to any one's property. > – B.H.57.26

ki·zu·ze·ca \k̇i-zú-ze-ca\ *vn* : to turn into a snake – B.H.48.12

[1]**ko** \k̇o\ *conj* : and, too, also < *Miye ~ kte* Me too it will be. *Wanna canpa na kanta ~ yutapi. Na iȟ'e wan lila zizipela ca ~ wicak'u po* They ate plums and chokecherries too. And give them as well very fine stones. >

[2]**ko** \k̇o\ *v* : to desire strongly, to be anxious for – Note: the word follows another *v* . < *oh'an* to act + *k̇o* to be anxious to do a thing, to be quick about it, *oh'anko* and *oh'an·wa·ko* to be quick at doing *and* I am quick in doing things, *wacinko* to pout, *ptehiko* and *ptehi·wa·ko* to ceremonialize to attract buffalo *and* I gestured to draw the buffalo, *maštek̇ola* to desire a bit of hot weather, and is also another name for *ištanica tanka* the horned lark, *gliwako* I am anxious to see him return, *Waglekšun bloka osniko s'e hu ȟolyéla* or *Osni kte cin* The wild gobbler's legs are grayish as though it were anxious for cold weather, *or* It wants the weather to become cold. *Hacila kin k̇ópi kayeš ópapi* The very children themselves had a great desire to join in it, *i.e.* the exercise of repentance. > – B.H.117.21 Bl

ko·a·ka·tan \k̇o-á-k̇a-ṫaŋ\ *adv* : over or across the river – *Syn* HUTASANPATA — **koakatan·han** *adv* : from beyond the river

kog \k̇og\ *n* or *v contrac of* kóka : to make a sound, to rattle < ~ *hingla* to suddenly sound a rattle >

ko·gin·gin *or* ogingin \ko-ǵíŋ-ǵiŋ\ *v* : to nod < *Tipi kin iyaza canunp' ~ omani* He traveled nodding and taking a smoke at one house after the next. ~ *nankahelo h'unyela wahiyelo* Your were sitting beckoning, I having hardly arrived. > — **kogingin·kel** *adv* : slow, being away long < ~ *yanka* to be so, being away long > — **kogingin·lag** *adv* : rather slow about going, being far away < ~ *nanka na hi na taku yaka he* You are rather slow and he has arrived so what do you have in mind? > – BT FB

ko·gla·mna \k̇o-glá-mna\ *adv* : around, over — **koglamnayan** *va* koglamna·wa·ya : to surround, restrain, cut off retreat

ko·gli \k̇o-glí\ *adj* : clear, translucent — **kogli·gli** *adj red* or *n* : flint corn, so called for its being translucent

ko·gna *or* kaogna \k̇ó-gna\ *adv* : on that side

ko·gna·gye·la \k̇o-gná-gye-la\ *adv* : just a little < *Kitan ~ ile* Scarcely just a little did it burn. > – Bl

ko·han \k̇o-háŋ\ *adv* : now, quickly, meanwhile, before something else is done < ~ *iyaya, tokša wau kte, Kola, ~ gla yo, lena mau kin na tokša ehakela waku kte lo* Meanwhile he went, soon I shall come, my Friend, go quickly home, here now I am surely coming, and soon I being the last shall return. *Wica kin ~ paha wan el eyokas'in.* ~

\a\ father \e\ they \i\ machine \o\ smoke \u\ lunar \an, aŋ\ blanc Fr. \in, iŋ\ ink \on, oŋ, un, uŋ\ soon, confier Fr. \c\ chair \ġ\ machen Ger. \j\ fusion \clusters: bl, gn, kp, hšl, etc...\ b^elo ... said with a slight vowel
See more in the Introduction, Guide to Pronunciation

mak'u wo The man meanwhile spied on a hill. Quickly give it to me! > — **kohan·ke šni** \ǩo-háŋ-ke šni\ *adv* : before the time comes, for the time being < ~ *iyaye ki yelo* to arrive home and in the time being went on > – *Syn* TOKŠA Bl

ko·hanš \ǩo-háŋš\ *adv* : since that, so that

ko·htin·lah \ǩo-ȟtíŋ-laȟ\ *adv* : lately, a little while ago – *Syn* LECÁLA WE

ko·i·ya·yu·hki·ya *also* **kaiyayuhkiya** \ko-í-ya-yu-ȟǩi-ya\ *adv* : meeting at a small angle < ~ *iyaya* to go meeting at a sharp turn, as is said of a road leading to and into another at a narrow angle > – Bl

ko·ja·gjal \ǩo-já-gjal\ *adv* [fr *jata* fork-like] : apart, spread < ~ *mani* to walk with the legs apart >

[1]**ko·ka** \ko-ǩá\ *n* : a keg, barrel < ~ *maza* a water tank >

[2]**ko·ka** \ǩó-ka\ *n* : the sound created by knocking

ko·kab \ǩo-ǩáb\ *adv* : before one, in the way of < ~ *inajin* to stand in the way of, so as to hold him > – *Syn* KUŠEYA NAJIN — **koka·bya** *v* or *adv perhaps* : to go before one, ahead of one

ko·ka·la \ǩo-ǩá-la\ *n dim of* koká : a small keg

ko·ka·mna \ǩo-ká-mna\ *v* : to get, to secure < *Palani ~ hi s'e lila owewakankan* He often lies as if he were a Pawnee Indian come to get something, as is said when a person tells lies. > – La

ko·ka·o·ju·ha \ǩo-ǩá-o-ju-ha\ *n* : an empty barrel

ko·ke·la \kó-ǩe-la\ *v* : to make noise, to rattle, *e.g.* dishes, to toll < *Cancan s'e škan yo: wi ohiyaye ~ yelo* Hurry with your work: the setting sun tolls, *i.e.* the sun will set soon. *Tawacin kokelapi šni yo* Do not rattle their minds! > — *adv* : quickly, rapidly – B.H.194.7

ko·ki·ca·špa \ko-ḱí-ca-špa\ *v* : to dig two holes into one, to shoot twice in the same place – Note: *ko·we·ca·špa* is a doubtful form *Syn* KOKIYUHCI R

ko·ki·ci·ya·s'in \kó-ǩi-ci-ya-s'iŋ\ *adv* : uniting, coming together and flowing on, as two streams in one, stuck or fastened together, as dogs after copulating, or as potatoes in a bunch – R Bl

ko·ki·jan·jan \ǩo-ḱí-jaŋ-jaŋ\ *vn* : to become thinner and lighter here and there, as clouds or the prairie – *Syn* KOKIWOTAN'IN Bl

ko·ki·ju \ǩó-ǩi-ju\ *vn* : to come together — **kokiju·ya** \ko-ḱí-ju-ya\ *or* \ko-ḱí-ju-ya\ *vn* : to cause to unite together – *See* óki-juya — *adv* : unitedly, together

ko·ki·pa \ǩo-ḱí-pa\ *va* ko·wa·kipa ko·ma·kipa ko·un·kipa·pi : to fear, be afraid of — **kokipa·pi** \ǩo-ḱí-pa-ṗi\ *part* : feared < *wokokipe* fear, the cause of fear > — **kokipe·kiya** \ǩo-ḱí-ṗe-ǩi-ya\ *va* kokipe·wa·kiya : to cause to fear — **kokipe·šniyan** \ko-ḱí-ṗe-šni-yaŋ\ *va* kokipešni·wa·ya : to render fearless < *Takuni kokipešniniyin kta cin* He wished that he might fear nothing from you. >

ko·ki·pe·ya \ǩo-ḱí-ṗe-ya\ *va* kokipe·wa·ya : to cause to fear, make afraid of — *adv* : timidly — **kokipeya·han** \ǩo-ḱí-ṗe-ya-haŋ\ *adv* : fearing, fearful, afraid

ko·ki·ptan \ko-ḱí-ptaŋ\ *v* : to feel, make unsteady < *Tawat'elwaye šni tka yelo, tka Lakota kin komayakiptanpi ca heon blelo* He might not be willing to do or suffer, but since you Lakotas make me feel unsteady, I am going. > – MS.532

ko·ki·wo·hci \ko-ḱí-wo-ȟci\ *v* kokiwo·wa·hci : to cut or tear through the skin – Bl

ko·ki·wo·tan'·in \ko-ḱí-wo-taŋ-iŋ\ *vn* : to become thinner and lighter, as clouds, or a prairie *etc* , to be transparent, as a moquito net – Bl

ko·ki·yu·hci \ǩo-ḱí-yu-ȟci\ *v* koki·blu·hci : to unite two holes that are close together into one, by tearing the separating material – *Syn* KOKICAŠPA

ko·ko \kó-ko\ *conj red* [fr *ko* also] : also – Note: the word is used in *ref* to more than one thing – B.H.39.12

ko·ko·gya \ǩo-ǩó-gya\ *adv* [fr *kokoka* to rattle] : rattling

ko·ko·ju·ha *or* **koka·ojuha** \ko-ǩó-ju-ha\ *n* [fr *koka* a barrel + *ojuha* an empty container] : an empty barrel

ko·ko·ka \ǩo-ǩó-ka\ *vn* : to rattle, as a stiff skin

ko·ko·ya·han·la *or* **kokoyah'anla** \ǩo-ǩó-ya-ȟaŋ-la\ *n* : a chicken, fowls, so called perhaps for their quick picking up < ~ *oti* a chicken coup > – Note: the rooster's song is: *Mató kawínge* Bear, turn back. *See* kóka Bl

ko·ko·ye·la \ko-kó-ye-la\ *adv* : hurrying, hastening a little, in quick succession

[1]**ko·kta** \ǩo-ǩtá\ *num adj* ; one hundred < ~ *šica* a million *or* billion > – Note: the word indicates everything beyond a million, *i.e.* *wóiyawa*

[2]**ko·kta** *or* **koktaya** \ǩó-kta\ *adv* : also, besides

ko·kto·pa·win·ge \ko-ǩtó-ṗa-wiŋ-ġe\ *adj* : a thousand — **koktopawinge·ge** *adj red* : a thousand often – B.H. 57.8

ko·la \ǩó-la\ *n* mita·kola nita·kola : a friend, the particular friend of a Lakota man < *takolaku* his particular friend > — **kola·kiciyapi** \ǩo-lá-ǩi-ci-ya-pi\ *n* : friendship — **kola·ya** \ǩo-lá-ya\ *va* kola·wa·ya : to have for a particular friend

ko·me·ya \ko-mé-ya\ *va* kome·wa·ya : to destroy – B.H.51.10, 72.20, 244.5

ko·mi \ko-mí\ *vn* : to melt, perhaps < *Wa kin ~ kta* The snow will melt. > – Bl

ko·na·tke \ǩo-ná-ṫke\ *adv* : high, tall < *Cincala ~ s'e micitonpi* A pretty tall colt was born to me. *Onzoge ~ s'e un elo* But he wears pants drawn in pretty high. > — **konatke·ya** *or* **konatke·yela** *adv* : high, as a high tree with a bushy crown and a thin trunk, *i.e.* < *can ~ hiyeya* a high tree become elevated, ~ *waókšupi* a high wagon loaded, *hlahla ~ otke* a big heavy bell hung on a thin stand, ~ *omani* a big heavy man walking on thin legs >

kon \ǩoŋ\ *v* wa·kon : to desire, to covet — **kon·la** \ǩóŋ-la\ *v dim* wa·konla : to desire < *Owaš'ag ~ taoglihpaye lo* Their fall was terrible so strong their desires. > – B.H.195.21

kons \ǩoŋs\ *v contrac of* kónza : to pretend < *Nah'on šni ~ hiyaye* Pretending not to hear he went along. > — **kon·sya** *and* **konsya·kel** \ǩoŋ-syá\ *adv* : pretending

kon·za \ǩóŋ-za\ *v* wa·konza : to pretend < *kahúŋ ~* to pretend to strike, *witko ~* to pretend to be ignorant, *Iyopteya ye ~* He pretends to go on. > — *va* wa·konze maya·konze wica·konzapi : to wish evil to one – B.H. 273.8, 148.28 B

ko·pe·gla \ǩó-ṗe-gla\ *vn* kope·wa·gla : to be afraid, be in fear

ko·pe·ya \ǩó-ṗe-ya\ *va* kope·wa·ya : to make afraid — *adv* : insecurely < ~ *waun* I live insecurely. >

kos \kos\ *va contrac of* kóza : to wave < ~ *hiyaya* to pass by waving, *Hupahu ~ iyuta* It tried to flap its wings. > – MS.145

ko·san \ǩo-sáŋ\ *adv* : onward, farther on than was intended < ~ *iyaya* He went on farther, *i.e.* traveling a little farther than was expected because the sun was still up high. *Na he ozuye kin hunh hetan namni agli na hunh ~ éyaya. ~ éyaya* And some from that warparty turned back to go home, and some went on farther. And they went onward, *i.e.* they kept on following the calling. > – Note: R gives *ákosan adv* : whilst, in the meantime

ko·ska \k̔o-ská\ *n* : gonorrhoea

ko·skos \k̔ō'-sk̔ōs\ *v contrac of* koskoza : to swing < *Hanpošpu hokšicala k'on wanna ~ najinpi* Now those little dolls stopped swinging. >

ko·sko·za \k̔ō'-sk̔o-za\ *v red of* kóza : to wave, beckon, to swing < *Na mila el ~ ške lo* And they say he beckoned for a knife. >

ko·sya \k̔o-syá\ *va* ko·swa·ya : to cause to wave or make a signal

ko·ška \k̔o-šk̔á\ *v* ko·má·ška : to be affected with venereal disease

ko·ška·la *or* **koškala·ka** \ko·šká-la\ *or* \k̔o-šk̔á-la-k̔a\ *n* ko·ma·škalaka : a youth, young man — **koška·škalaka** \ko-šká-ška-la-ka\ *n* : a boy turning, growing into manhood and acting like a man < ~ *mani* to act like a growing boy > - R Bl

ko·ška·un·ci·hi·ka·ca \ko-šká-uŋ-ci-hi-ka-ca\ *v* : to be or become a grandmother, as is said teasingly of a young woman not seeming to care to marry - Bl

ko·ya \k̔ó-ya\ *conj* : and, too, also < *Na wanna oyate kin tipi kin ojupila na tankal ~ . Wakanheja šunka ~ yuahwayela miyeciluzin kta* And now the house was full of people, and outside as well. You should gently hold for me child and dog too. > Bl

ko·yag \k̔o-yág\ *va contrac of* koyáka : to wear < ~ *waun* I am wearing it. ~ *un* It is hitched. > — **koya·gkiya** \k̔o-yá-gki-ya\ *va* koya·gwa·kiya : to cause to put on or wear — **koya·gya** \k̔o-yá-gya\ *va* koya·gwa·ya : to cause to put on, to attach to — *part* : clothed < *Hena tahca šunkala tahaya ~ el nihipelo* They come to you clothed in sheep's clothing. > - P

ko·ya·h'an \k̔o-yá-ȟ'aŋ\ *vn* koya·wa·h'an : to be quick in doing a thing, to hasten, hurry < *Koyamakih'an yo, nituwa heci* Hurry me along! if it is yours. Hurry me along! > — **koyah'an·na** *adv* : quickly, immediately — **koyah'an·yela** *adv* : quickly - *Syn* INAHNI D.90 R Bl

ko·ya·ka \k̔o-yá-k̔a\ *va* ko·bla·ka ko·un·yaka·pi : to put on or wear *e.g.* clothes — **koyaka·pi** *part* : clothed < *taku ~* what is put on, *i.e.* clothing >

ko·ya·ki·h'an \k̔o-yá-ki-ȟ'aŋ\ *v* : to be quick in doing perhaps one's own < *Taku ecanon kta heci ~ yo* If you are about to do something do your thing quickly. *Koyamakih'an yo, nituwa ka heci* Hurry up do mine. Does he intend yours? > - B.H.253.15

ko·ya·nun \k̔o-yá-nuŋ\ *adj* ma·koyanun : of quick growth, precocious - *See* hiyánun

ko·yan \ko-yáŋ\ *adv* : quickly < ~ *upi yo* Come quickly! > — **koyan·la** *adv* : quickly - R Bl

ko·ye·la \ko-yé-la\ *adv* : promptly, quickly

ko·za \k̔ó-za\ *va* : to shake, to wave *e.g.* a signal, to swing < *ȟupahu ~* to wave a wing, *šina ~* to wave a blanket, *nape kicoza* to wave the hand at >

[1]**kpa** \kpa\ *pref poss* - *v* that take "pa" as a *pref*, make the *poss* form by adding "k", thus: *pagan* to spare, *kpagan* to spare one's own

[2]**kpa** \kpa\ *vn* : to swell, as rice does in cooking — *adj* **1** : durable, lasting, not soon eaten up, as some kinds of food such as rice **2** : punched out < *nonge kpa* deaf, *išta kpa* blind >

kpa·bla \kpa-blá\ *v poss of* pablá : to spread flat by hand one's own - Bl

kpa·bla·za \kpa-blá-za\ *v poss of* pabláza : to burst or tear open one's own - Bl

kpa·ble·ca \kpa-blé-ca\ *v poss* wa·kpableca [fr *pableca* to crush] : to break in pieces one's own by pressure

kpa·gan \kpa-ǧáŋ\ *v poss* wa·kpagan [fr *pagan* to spare or part with] : to spare or part with one's own, to leave or separate from one's own

kpa·gmun \kpa-gmúŋ\ *v poss* wa·kpagmun [fr *pagmun* roll up by hand] : to twist or roll up one's own

kpa·ha·ha·pi·ka \kpa-há-ha-p̔i-k̔a\ *n* ma·kpahahapika : one who is put forward in company

kpa·hi \kpa-hí\ *v poss* wa·kpahi un·kpahi·pi : to gather or pick up one's own

kpa·hle·ca \kpa-ȟlé-ca\ *v poss* wa·kpahleca [fr *pahleca* pull or tear to pieces] : to make a hole in one's own, to lance

kpa·hpa \kpa-ȟpá\ *v poss* wa·kpahpa [fr *pahpa* put or throw off] : to lay down or put off one's own load - B.H.38.2

kpa·ja·ja \kpa-já-ja\ *v poss* wa·kpajaja [fr *pajaja* to wash or mop] : to wash out one's own, *e.g.* a gun

kpa·ju·ju \kpa-jú-ju\ *v poss* wa·kpajuju [fr *pajuju* to erase] : to rub out one's own

kpa·kin·ta \kpa-k̔íŋ-t̔a\ *v poss* wa·kpakinta un·kpakinta·pi : to wipe one's own < *Na wasé kic'unpi kin hena kpakintapi na glapi kte lo* And they will wipe off the red paint and go for home. >

kpa·kpas \kpa-kpás\ *adj red contrac* [fr *kpakaza* fr *kpaza* dark] : dark < *Ite ~ mahingle lo* My face suddenly became dark, *i.e.* I had a spell of dizziness. > - GA

kpa·kpi \kpa-k̔p̔í\ *v poss of* pakpí : to crack or break open one's own, as a chicken breaking its shell

kpa·kši·ja \kpa-kší-ja\ *v poss* wa·kpakšija [fr *pakšija* fold up] : to double up one's own

kpa·ku·ka \kpa-k̔ú-ka\ *v poss* wa·kpakuka [fr *pakuka* wear out by hand] : to wear out one's own by rubbing

kpa·man \kpa-máŋ\ *v poss* wa·kpaman [fr *paman* to file] : to file, to polish one's own < *Hekpamahan* That is what he was polishing. > - D.91

kpa·mni \kpa-mní\ *va poss* wa·kpamni [fr *pamni* distribute] : to divide out, distribute one's own < *Hecel wanna tipi iyohila kpamnipi* So they divided out each house. >, — **kpamni·pi** *n* : a distribution

kpa·na·jin·ka \kpa-ná-jiŋ-ka\ *v refl of* panajin : to get up from the ground on one's limbs, as do old people < *Kitanyel mikpanajinkelo* With difficulty did I get up with my own hands. > - Bl

kpan \kpaŋ\ *adj* : fine, as flour - Note: the word in Santee Dakota is *tpan* fine, and *wotpan* to grind fine — **kpan·kpanla** \kpaŋ-kpáŋ-la\ *adj red of* kpánla : fine, soft < *makoce ~ k'el* in the land that is soft, *i.e.* prairie with little elevations all over > - Bl

kpan·la \kpáŋ-la\ *adj* : fine, soft < *Taku ~ ota ca yawapica šni* Many fine things cannot be counted, as was stated by Bl when *ref* to the fact that Lakota has countless fine little words >

kpan·yan \kpaŋ-yáŋ\ *va* kpan·wá·ya : to tan, dress *e.g.* a skin < *Taha kpanyanpi kin ohomni waso.* After the skin was tanned he cut around a string. *Lila tanyan ~ yuštan.* He finished tanning very well. *Yunkan šina kpanyanpi wan el akahpa egnaka* Then she put throwing on him a tanned skin. > - Note: WI *ref* to the word as from *kpan* fine or soft, but that is doubtful

kpa·on·jin·jin·tka yan·ka \kpa-óŋ-jiŋ-jiŋ-tka yaŋ·kà\ *v* :

\a\ f<u>a</u>ther \e\ th<u>e</u>y \i\ mach<u>i</u>ne \o\ sm<u>o</u>ke \u\ l<u>u</u>nar \an, aŋ\ bl<u>anc</u> Fr. \in, iŋ\ <u>in</u>k \on, oŋ, un, uŋ\ s<u>oo</u>n, c<u>on</u>fier Fr. \c\ <u>ch</u>air \ǧ\ ma<u>ch</u>en Ger. \j\ fu<u>s</u>ion \clusters: bl, gn, kp, hšl, etc...\ <u>b</u>ᵉlo ... said with a slight vowel
See more in the Introduction, Guide to Pronunciation

to be in a stooping posistion out of sorrow, *i.e.* hiding one's face, as it were – Cf kpašinšin yanka Bl

kpa·o·wo·tan·ka \kpa-ó-taŋ-ka\ *v poss of* paowotan : to make one's self right, *i.e.* get things one needs badly and receives *e.g.* clothing, weapons *etc* < *Kitanyel mikpaowotankelo* With difficulty did I get the things I needed badly. > Bl

kpa·pson \kpa-psóŋ\ *v poss* wa·kpapson [fr *papson* to spill] : to spill over one's own *e.g.* blood – Pb.32

kpa·pta \kpa-pṫá\ *v* wa·kpapta : to leave one's company, escape, to leave before company breaks up, to free one's self and go away as from jail while others remain < *Tokel kpaptin kte cin iyukcan* He understood why he was going to escape. *Mišnala wakpapta ca hošicicagli* I arrived home with word for you since I alone escaped. *Mnit'e šni* ~ He escaped without drowning. ~ *iyaya* to free one's self and go away, or to go through breaking things, as cattle through a fence > *Hecel unkpaptapelo* We excaped in that way – B.H.42.27, 304.4 Bl

kpa·pu·za \kpa-ṗú-za\ *v poss* wa·kpapuza [fr *papuza* wipe dry] : to make one's own dry by wiping

kpa·smin·yan·yan \kpa-smíŋ-yaŋ-yaŋ\ *v* : to load a gun, hammering in the load with the rod – Bl

kpa·snon \kpa-snóŋ\ *v poss* wa·kpasnon [fr *pasnon* to roast] : to roast one's own meat

kpa·su·ta \kpa-sú-ṫa\ *v poss* wa·kpasuta [fr *pasuta* to stiffen by kneading] : to make hard by kneading one's own bread

kpa·šin·šin yan·ka \kpa-šíŋ-šiŋ yaŋ-kà\ *v* kpašinšin man·ka : to be in a sitting and stooping position, as once one did when in sorrow, to be silent out of sorrow – *Syn* KPAONJINJINTKA Note: *šinšin ref* to wrinkles, and *unjincala ref* to a fledgling bird with a round and short tail

kpa·špu \kpa-špú\ *v poss of* pašpú : to loosen one's own < *Hiyomayatake cin wakpašpu ktelo* I will loosen what is stuck between me teeth, *i.e.* will remove that piece of meat that got stuck between the teeth. > – Bl

kpa·ta \kpá-ṫa\ *v poss* wa·kpata [fr *pata* to butcher] : to cut up or carve one's own meat, to butcher one's own

kpa·tan \kpa-ṫáŋ\ *v poss* wa·kpatan [fr *patan* to save] : to take care of one's own, to save one's own, to think much of, so as to spare or not use up, to save *e.g.* money < *nih'kpatan* to avoid spoiling one's appetite, *i.e.* to eat little knowing that something better is coming > – Pb.26 B.H.214.13

kpa·tan·tan·kel *or perhaps* **kpatantan** \kpa-ṫáŋ-ṫaŋ-kel\ *adv red* : sparingly, using little by little, slowly < *Woeye ciscila bluha ca ~ oblakelo* I spoke sparingly because I had a quite short speech. > – Bl

kpa·t'a \kpa-t'á\ *v poss* : to kill one's own by pressure — **kpat'a·t'a** \kpa-t'á-t'a\ *vn* : to be numb or asleep < *Siha wakpat'at'a* I have my feet asleep. > – B.H.99.4

kpa·wa·š'a·ka \kpa-wá-š'a-ka\ *v poss of* pawaš'aka : to make one's own strong and secure – WHL

kpa·wi·ya·kpa \kpa-wí-ya-kpa\ *v poss of* pawíyakpa : to polish one's own < *sican kin* ~ to polish one's thigh > – D.1

kpa·za *also* **kpasa** \kpá-za\ *adj* : dark

kpa·zan \kpa-záŋ\ *v poss* wa·kpazan [fr *pazan* to part] : to part or separate one's own *e.g.* hair

kpa·zi·gzi·ca \kpa-zí-gzi-ca\ *v poss red* wa·kpazigzica [fr *pazigzica* roll or stretch out] : to stretch one's own < *Hel ota wohanpi ca nige ~ yo* Stretch your belly when there there are many feasting. > – Bl

kpa··zo \kpa-zó\ *v poss of* pazó : to show one's own < *ceji* ~ to show, stick out, one's tongue, *Hayapi kpazopi* They showed off their clothes. > – B.H.153.18, 290.16

kpe *or* **kpa** \kpe\ *pref poss* to *v* that have *pa* as a *pref*

kpe·han \kpe-háŋ\ *v poss* wa·kpehan [fr *pehan* fold up] : to fold up one's own

kpe·ya \kpé-ya\ *adv* : sounding < ~ *apa* to strike anything and make a sound > — **kpe·yela** \kpe-yĕ'-la\ *adv perhaps* : resounding, with a loud sound, report, as a gun shot off < *Na lila ~ iyeya* And it made a very loud report. >

kpi \kpi\ *syll* : suggesting the act of breaking open – *See pakpí* to crack open

kpu·kpa \kpu-kṗá\ *adj* : boiled up, mixed up, not clear, full of dirt, as is said of water slightly turbid, or of soup which contains floating particles — **kpukpe·ya** \kpu-kṗé-ya\ *adv* : mixed up, all kinds together

kpu·spa \kpu-sṗá\ *v poss* wa·kpuspa [fr *puspa* to glue, seal] : to glue or seal one's own

kpu·ta·ka \kpu-tá-ka\ *v poss* [fr *putaka* to touch as with the hand] : to touch one's own

ksa \ksa\ *adj* : separated – Note: the word is used with *pref* "ya, ..."

ksab \ksab\ *adj contrac of* ksápa : wise, prudent

ksa·bya \ksa-byá\ *va* ksa·bwa·ya : to make wise — *adv* : wisely, prudently < ~ *waun* He is wisely well-to-do. > — **ksabya·han** *adv* : wisely — **ksabya·kel** *adv* : wisely – B.H.45.7

ksa·han \ksá-haŋ\ *part* : broken in two of itself

ksa·ksa·pa \ksa-ksá-ṗa\ *adj red of* ksápa : quite wise

ksa·pa \ksá-ṗa\ *adj deriv* wa·ksapa : wise, prudent, having understanding

ksa·wa·han \ksa-wá-haŋ\ *part* : broken into

ksi·ze·ca \ksí-ze-ca\ *adj* ma·ksízeca : cross, grum, stern – Note: the word is used now more than and instead of *wóhinyanze,* and in *ref* to wild animals

ksi·ze·ke \ksí-ze-ke\ *adj* : to be good on, *i.e.* boastingly < *Maksizeke* I am a good one. >

ksi·ze·o·i·e \ksi-zé-o-i-e\ *or* \ksi-zé-o-ì-e\ *n* : a laughable word, a word that causes laughter

ksi·zi·c'i·la \ksi-zí-c'i-la\ *n* or *adj* : a bully < *Ksizmíc'ila* I am a bully. >

ksun·kah \ksuŋ-ḱáȟ\ *v* : to deceive, fool < ~ *kuwa* to make a fool of one, to treat one with deceit. >

ksu·ye·ya \ksú-ye-ya\ *va* ksúye·wa·ya : to hurt, injure, inflict pain on

kša *and* **kšan** \kša\ *adj* : bent, rolled — **kša-ka** \kšá-ḱa\ *adj* ma·kšáka : bent up, as an aged person, decrepit — **kša·la** \kšá-la\ *adj* : bent – Note: *kša* and *ksan* are probably the same root

kšan \kšaŋ\ *adj* – *See* kša

[1]**kšan·kšan** \kšaŋ-kšáŋ\ *adj red* : with many crooks – R

[2]**kšan·kšan** \kšáŋ-kšan\ *vn* : to wriggle, as does a fish

kšan·kšan·yan \kšaŋ-kšáŋ-yaŋ\ *adv* : crookedly

kšan·yan \kšaŋ-yáŋ\ *va* kšan·wá·ya : to make crooked, to bend — *adv* : crookedly

kši·ja \kší-ja\ *adj* : bent, doubled up – Cf yukšija — **kšija·han** \kši-já-haŋ\ *part* : bent up, doubled up

kši·kša \kši-kšá\ *adj* : numb, stiff with cold

kši·kšan \kši-kšáŋ\ *adj* : crooked

kši·kše *or* **kšikša** \kši-kšé\ *adj* : tired < *Makšikše s'elececa* I seem to be stiff, *i.e.* I am tired. > — **kšikše·ca** *adj* : numb < *Nape makšikšeca* My hands are numb. >

kši·kše·ya \kši-kšé-ya\ *vt* : to make tired, tire out < *Owekinaš kšikšeciyin ktelo* It may be I'll tire you out, *or* Perhaps I'll make you tired. > – Bl

kšiš \kšiš\ *adj contrac of* kšíja : bent up < *kšišic'ilaka* to regard one's self as bent up >

kšto *or* **kšt** *or* **kišto** \kšto\ *or* \k̇i-štó\ *suff* – It is affixed to *v* , to *emph* a fact about which others have a doubt or know nothing of. Thus: *Ecamon* ~ I certainly did do it, *Kepékšt* I most certainly stated that. "*Nakun lece šna waceye* ~ ," *eyin na*, "*Kuwa, kuwa*," *eye* "Besides I was clearly crying continually in this way," he said, and, "Come, come," he said

kšu \kšu\ *va* wa·kšú : to bead things < *ak'in kšupi* a beaded saddle blanket, *hanpa kšupi* beaded moccasins, *Na ilazatanhan can eya šayapi ca wiyaka kšupi* And on the back of some wood pieces made red they did quillwork. *Hena (i.e. wiyaka* quills*) wapaha na wahukeza ko el kšupi kte lo* These will be beaded: a headdress and a lance as well. > – MS.153

kšun·ka·hya·kel \kšuŋ-ká-ḣya-kel\ *adv* : in a deceiving manner – *Syn* ZOMIYANKEL KS

[1]**kta** \kta\ *partic* — indicates **futurity**, to be on the point of something when ... < *Hecel waglinawapin kta, yunkan eyapaha unhe leya ... Lepin kte hcin ehanl. Kta, yunkan ehanl, tka ecanl* So I shall show up on my way home, and then this is what the announcer says ... I shall say this very thing then. Will say, and so then: but just then, > — indicates **intention** also, to do something intended, expressed by the *fut* < *Yunkan anpetu wan el wicaša unpin omani iyayapi kta* And then one day they being men intended to go on a journey. >

[2]**kta** \kta\ *v* wa·ktá : to wait for, to neglect doing and expecting another to do — **kta·ka** \ktá-k̇a\ *v* wa·kta·ka : to wait, expect another to act – Note: it seems used is only the 1st *pers*

ktan \ktaŋ\ *adj* : crooked, curved – *See* yuktán — **ktan·ktan** \k̇taŋ-k̇táŋ\ *adj red* : crooked, as a tree – *Syn* ŠKOŠKÓPA

[1]**ktan·ktan·kiya** \ktaŋ-k̇táŋ-k̇iya\ *va* ktanktan·wa·kiya : to bend, to make somebody bend himself < *Cuwi ktanktankiyin na taku kakyela wakšica el ohinhpaya* Something fell into a dish with a clatter and bent its back. >

[2]**ktan·ktan·kiya** \ktaŋ-ktáŋ-k̇i-ya\ *adv* : crookedly, indirectly

ktan·ktan·yan *and* **ktan·yan** \ktaŋ-ktáŋ-yaŋ\ *and* \ktaŋ-yáŋ\ *adv* : crookedly

[1]**kte** \kte\ *va* wa·kte : to kill anything, to overcome one in a game < When two men were fighting, the one would say: *Mató wakte hce* I really beat Bear. The other, badly beaten, replied: *Mató makte hce* Bear really beat me. >

[2]**kte** \kte\ *partic of* kta – It indicates futurity or intention

kte·ki·ya \kte-k̇í-ya\ *va* kte·wá·kiya : to cause to kill

kte·la \kté-la\ *va* wa·ktela : to overcome, be victorious over, to win, beat

[1]**ku** \ku\ *vn* wa·ku un·ku·pi : to be coming home or back, to come towards home < *Unci, he ku wo. Ate, waku šni kinhan miye cekiya wicaša ki le wanji u kta. Leci u wo* Grandmother, come here. Father, if I do not come, I am a prayer man here who should come. Come here. >

[2]**ku** *or* **kul** \k̇u\ *n* : the lower parts of things < ~ *k'el tanyan šni* Something is wrong in the below, *i.e.* in the wagon's undercarriage. > – Bl

[3]**ku** \k̇u\ *pron suff* : his, hers, its *etc*

ku·ci·ye·la \k̇ú-ci-ye-la\ *adv* : low down, near the ground, low of stature, short < *Yunkan hinhan wan* ~ *h'anhiya kinyan iyaya. Wi* ~ *hcehanl* And then an owl came flying low with difficultly. Just then the sun was quite low. > – Note: the word in Dakota is *kúcedan* D.209 and 227

ku·ja \k̇ú-ja\ *adj* ma·kuja : sick

ku·ka \k̇u-ká\ *adj* : rotten, spoiled, as meat, tender, worn out, as clothes < *Hehé, haámakuke lo* Too bad, the clothes I have on are worn out. > — **kuke·ya** \k̇u-k̇é-ya\ *va* kuke·wa·ya : to make rotten, to wear out — *adv* : rotten, spoiled, decayed, fallen to pieces < ~ *špan* to be cooked too much >

ku·ku·še \k̇u-k̇ú-še\ *n* : a pig, hog, hogs, pork < ~ *šin* fat pork, pickled pork, ~ *wigli* hog's lard

kul \k̇ul\ *adv* : below, under, beneath, down < ~ *hpaya* to fall down > — **kul·kuciyela** \k̇ul-k̇u-ci-ye-la\ *adv red perhaps* : down under, low down < *Paha* ~ *yukelo* It is down under the hill. *Mahpiya* ~ *kahwog au welo* They came floating beneath a low cloud. > — **kul·kul** \k̇úl-k̇ul\ *adv red* : below, under, beneath, down < ~ *hpayapi* They fell beneath it. > — **kul·tkiya** \k̇úl-tki-ya\ *adv* : downwards

Kul·wi·ca·ša \Kúl-wi-ca-ša\ *np* : the Lower Brule band of the Lakota division of the Dakota peoples < ~ *iyak'oza wan yuhapi* The Lower Brule have a horse with swollen joints. >

[1]**kun** *or* **kon** \k̇uŋ\ *v* : to covet

[2]**kun** \k̇uŋ\ *n* ni·kun : mother-in-law — **kun·ku** \k̇úŋ-ku\ *n* : his or her mother-in-law,

kun·ši \k̇úŋ-ši\ *n* ni·kunši : a grandmother — **kun-kišitku** *or* **kun·kšitku** *or* **kun·šitku** \k̇úŋ-ki-ši-tku\ *n* : his or her grandmother – *Syn* UNCÍ R

kun·tkun·ta \k̇úŋ-tkuŋ-ṫa\ *adj* : grooved

kun·ya \k̇uŋ-yá\ *va* kun·wa·ya : to have for a mother-in-law

kun·za \k̇úŋ-za\ *v* – *See* kónza

ku·se \k̇u-sé\ *vn* : to leak, as a vessel – R Bl

kuš \k̇uš\ *adj contrac of* kúja : feeble, inactive < ~ *amayan* I am growing feeble. >

ku·še·ton \k̇u-šé-toŋ\ *va* kuše·wa·ton : to bar, stop < ~ *najin* to stand in the way of > – B.H.155.4

ku·še·ya \k̇u-šé-ya\ *va* kuše·wa·ya : to put in the way of, to stop something, *e.g.* a ball — *adv* : in the way of, obstructing < ~ *un, inajin, egnaka. Kušéciya* to be, to stand, to put in one's way. I am in your way. > – B.H. 78.12

ku·ši·pa·ton \k̇u-ší-ṗa-toŋ\ *v* : to give support to, to hold up < *Can kušipawaton kte lo* I shall support the post. > – Bl

ku·šle·ca *or* **hoyazela** \ku-šlé-ca\ *n* [fr *Kušleca Wakpa* the Split River, *i.e.* the Loup River] : the kingfisher

Ku·šle·ca Wa·kpa \Ku·šlé-ca Wa-kpà\ *np* : the name of the Loup fork of the Platte River in central Nebraska

ku·š'i·t'a \ku-š'í-t'a\ *v* kuš'i·ma·t'a [fr *kuja* sick + *it'a* to die for a cause] : to die or be dying of laziness, to be very lazy

ku·š'kon·za \k̇u-š'kóŋ-za\ *vn* : to pretend to be sick – Bl

ku·ta \k̇ú-ṫa\ *adv* : low down < ~ *gla yo* Be pretending you are going home. *Lel paha wan yanka ... yunkan* ~ *lila tatanka na pte otapi* Here there is a hill ... then many were the buffalo bulls and cows below it. *Oyate* ~ *unpi el lila cajeyatapi.* ~ *ahiwatonwan* When people lived down there, it was much spoken of. I came down to take a look around. > – MS.356, 355

ku·ta·gle·ya \k̇ú-ṫa-gle-ya\ *adv* : downward < *Pa* ~ *i-*

\a\ father \e\ they \i\ machine \o\ smoke \u\ lunar \an, aŋ\ blanc Fr. \in, iŋ\ ink \on, oŋ, un, uŋ\ soon, confier Fr. \c\ chair \ġ\ machen Ger. \j\ fusion \clusters: bl, gn, kp, hšl, etc...\ b^e^lo ... said with a slight vowel
See more in the Introduction, Guide to Pronunciation

hpeya to throw one down head foremost > – Bl

ku·ta·ki·ya \k̇ú-ṫa-ki-ya\ *adv* : downward < *Itokšan towicaya na pahte el ~ icazo na tapon kin anonkatan ecel econ na iku el oyasin hecel owicawa* He painted a blue stripe around their faces, and on the forehead he made a mark downward, he did so on both sides of the cheeks, and he painted them on all their chins. >

ku·tan·han \k̇ú-ṫaŋ-haŋ\ *adv* : under, as one under the other while wrestling, from below < *Ikce wicaša kin lila ~ ehakela ata nicagapi heon* The reason is that all of you were the last common men created very much underlings. >

ku·te \k̇u-ṫé\ *va* wa·kúte : to shoot anything with a gun or arrow

ku·tki·ya \k̇ú-ṫki-ya\ *adv* : downwards

[1]**ku·wa** \k̇ú-wa\ *va* wa·kuwa **1** : to follow after, chase, pursue, hunt **2** : to treat or act towards one evil or good **3** : to prosecute or execute a piece of work

[2]**ku·wa** \k̇ú-wa\ *v imper* : Come here – Note: the word is used only in the *imper*, thus: *~ yo* or *po*, or *Kúwi ye* – D.71 note 2

ku·wab \k̇ú-wab\ *adv* : downward < *Wi ~ ya ca na išta kin lemaceca yelo; aogi amayelo* My eyes are like the sun when it goes down; mine become blurred. > – Note: *kuwapa* as an expanded source of the word is doubtful – BT

ku·wa·cin \k̇u-wá-ciŋ\ *v* : to think of coming home

ku·wa·pi·ca \k̇ú-wa-ṗi-ca\ *adj* : manageable – P

ku·ya \k̇ú-ya\ *adv* : below, beneath, under, underneath, down — **kuya·tanhan** \k̇ú-ya-ṫaŋ-haŋ\ *adv* : from below

k'a \k'a\ *va* wa·k'a : to dig *e.g.* the ground < *ic'ic'a* to dig for one's self, *kicic'a* to dig for another, Wecic'a I dug for another. *Maka ekta ciscila wak'elo* I dug a bit into the ground. *Maka k'e k'on* There was a reason for digging the ground. > – B.H.108.17

k'a·na·jin \k'á-na-jiŋ\ *vn* : to refuse to do something – Note: the idea is, one would suppose, taken from a boy who while being pulled digs his feet in the ground for support

k'e *or* **k'a** \k'e\ *va* : to dig

k'e·ga \k'é-ġa\ *v* wa·k'ega : to grate, scrape

k'eh \k'e\ *v contrac of* k'ega : to scrape — **k'eh·k'ega** \k'eȟ-k'é-ġa\ *vn red* wa·k'éhk'ega : to have a rattling in the throat, as anything choking to death — **k'eh·k'eh** \k'eȟ-k'éȟ\ *vn red contrac* : to be choking — **k'ehk'e·hya** *adv* : in a scraping manner *etc*

k'el *or* **c'el** \k'el\ *contrac* [fr *kin* the + *el* in, at] : there < *Wanna ob toka iyayapi k'el glipi* They now arrived home there where strangers together went. *Na yuštan k'el lecel eya* And when he finished he said this. *Htayetu k'el eyapaha wan u* During the evening an announcer came. *Na koškalaka kin hpaye k'el okšan enajin* And there where the young man fell they stood around. >

k'e·leš \k'é-leš\ *express contrac* [fr *he é k'eš* that is my luck] : This is my luck!, as is said when recognizing something that one lost – Bl

k'es \k'es\ *adj contrac of* k'éza : trodden down, hard and smooth — **k'e·sk'eza** \k'e-sk'é-za\ *adj red of* k'éza : smooth, trodden down

k'eš \k'eš\ *adv conj* : if, even, as for me < *Hecon ~ wakasaksakin kte* If he did that, I shall whip him. *Ablezapi ~ koláƙiciyapi wašte kin heuncapi tka yelo* If they were sober and clear-sighted ours would be a fine friendship. *He é ~* That would be my luck!, as is said when recognizing something lost – *See* k'éleš P Bl B.H.68.20, 229.8 MS.649

k'e·ya \k'é-ya\ *pron adj* : some, that kind < *Canpá ~ etan hinhpaya* That kind of choke-cherries fell from it. *Yunkan tokeya pangi ~ wicakipazo* He then showed them some of the first artichokes. *Na inyan ~ šakpe agli* And he brought home six of that kind of stone. *Yunkan taku ~ cikcik'ala ca el (canwakšica) okala* Then he poured into (a wooden dish) some thing that was very tiny. >

k'e·yaš \k'é-yaš\ *conj contrac* [fr *ke eyaš* or *ke c'eyaš, ke* pretty much + *eyaš* nonetheless] : although, but < *Keya kin nunwan niun, ~ oyate kin iš t'a keyapi* They say the turtle lives swimming underwater, whereas the people themselves die doing so. >

k'e·za \k'é-za\ *adj* : hard, smooth, trodden down – R

k'e·ze \k'é-ze\ *adj* : short but hardy < *wicaša ~* a hardy small man>

k'in \k'iŋ\ *va* wa·k'in : to carry, bear, carry on the back < *kic'in* to carry one's own, *Šunkawakan wanji wawat'eca ca tohanl aya ca na k'in mawani kte lo* When they go I shall then travel with a gentle horse carrying a load.> – Note: BS indicates that *k'in* means to carry on one's shoulders, whereas *kic'in,* to carry on one's back. But this may be doubtful — **k'in·kiya** \k'iŋ-ḱí-ya\ *va* k'in·wa·kiya : to cause to carry – B.H.113.4, 102.6

k'in·na·pa \k'íŋ-na-pa\ *v* [fr *k'in* to carry + *napa* run away] : to run away, as a horse with a wagon, or a truck on a long steep road

k'o \k'o\ *n* : the noise created by making a hum or buzz, by bustling, talking together *etc* < *Na wanna k'o hingla* And suddenly now there was a stir of activity. >

k'o·ga \k'ó-ġa\ *vn* : to rattle, make a rattling noise

k'oh \k'oȟ\ *vn contrac of* k'oga : to rattle < *~ iyeya* to make a sudden rattling noise. > — **k'oh·k'oga** \k'oȟ-k'ó-ġa\ *vn red* : to keep rattling — **k'oh·k'oh** \k'oȟ-k'óȟ\ *vn contrac* : to rattle continually — **k'oh·k'ohya** \k'oȟ-k'ó-ȟya\ *v* k'ohk'ó·hwa·ya : to cause to rattle, to make a rattling noise — *adv* : rattling

k'on \k'oŋ\ *art contrac* – *See* c'on *and* k'un

k'o·sye·la \k'o-syē'-la\ *adv* : smoothly < *~ yunka* to lie smoothly, *i.e.* smooth as a floor >

k'o·s'e \k'ō'-s'e\ *adv* : apparently all gone, noisily perhaps < *~ éyaye k'on miyeš ehakela ble c'on tahca wan kanyela un k'on wao welo* Of those apparently all who had gone, I having gone last shot this deer nearby. >

k'o·ye·la \k'o-yē'-la\ *adv* : all, everything < *~ éwicayaya* They, *i.e.* the cattle, everyone of them were taken away, *i.e.* they disappeared, not one could be seen. *~ glasota* He exhausted everything, *i.e.* to his last word, or he eats up one's last. *Canli kin ~ henala* That is the last of all the tobacco, *i.e.* not a bit left. *~ akiyagle* All went straight home, *i.e.* all the thunderstorm clouds passed by. > – Bl

k'u \k'u\ *va* wa·k'u : to give anything to one – Note: *kicu* to give one his own — **k'u·kiya** \k'u-ḱí-ya\ *v* k'u·wa·kiya : to cause to give

k'un \k'uŋ\ *art def* or *dem pron* : that, in *ref* to the past, to something done or said before, to some person or thing mentioned in a previous sentence – Note: when the word immediately preceding changes *a or an* to *e*, *c'on* is used. The *pron* often takes the form *k'un he* that, *k'un hena* those, *k'un hehan* when < *Ehanl wikoškalaka k'on t'a* At that time the young woman had died. *Niye el taku econ mayaši k'on hena wanna waglušt an* What you bade me do for you, those are the things I finished. *Tokel yacin k'on ecel ecamon* I so did that as you wished it. *Hunhunhe, micinkši onšiwakila k'on* It's too bad, I had taken pity on my son. *Ake tokel econ k'on ecel econ* Again he so did as he had done. *Taku cinpi kin ecawicayecon kta kehe k'on* You had said that you would do for them what they wished. *Ate, ahitonwan yo, hóuciciye ca nayah'on kta kehe k'on* Father, come there and look, you had said that you would hear because I kept crying out to you. *Tokel wanbli wan amai k'on na tokel icimani wai k'on he ecel owaglaka* Why he brought me an eagle, and why I had gone on a journey I told as it was. *Taku wan tanke mak'u k'on he nape ogna bluha* I held in my hand something my older sister had given me. *Nitakola k'on miye* I am that friend of yours. > - Note: the word following a *v* seems to make the *v* past time, as "I did it," *or* "I have" ... thus: < *Lecaš ecamon k'on* I did it just a little while ago, *i.e.* someone asks a person a second time to do a thing which he already had done. *Heš, nila yeš wahteyalašni k'un* Why! He is the one you rejected when he wanted you. *Ehanni owakiyake k'on* I thought I told him long ago. *Monday k'on hehan wanciyankin kta wacin* I wanted to see you then last Monday. *Hehehe, he mitawa šni, owalote k'un, eye* He said: "O my goodness! That is not mine, I had borrowed it." *Hinún, ótaš k'in s'a k'un* How funny, he used to carry much more than that. > - Note also: while *k'un* generally stands as the past form of the *def art* , at times it furnishes the *"whereas"* in a compound sentence thus: Whereas you commanded me to take nothing, I took an owl. Cf k'on BD SI D.204, 115 B.H.116.4

k'un·han \k'uŋ-háŋ\ *adv* : when - Note: the word always *ref* to past time. It becomes *c'onhan* after terminal *e* which has taken the place of *a* or *an*

k'un he·han \k'uŋ hé-haŋ\ *adv* : when < *unkipi* ~ when we arrived home, *nahahci honikšila* ~ when you were yet a boy, *wicat'a hanhepi el wicayaȟa* ~ when you bury the dead at night, *niteca* ~ when you were young > - B.H.35.4, 271.1, 121.6, 127.20, 276.6

k'un he·han·yan \k'uŋ he-háŋ-yaŋ\ *adv coord conj* : so long, thus: < *Na tohanyan yugal un* ~ *Amalekites kin napewicayapi* And as long as he was extending his arms in prayer, just so long did they make the Amalekites flee > - B.H.56.1, 96.2, 156.1, 124.10, 129.20

k'un he·tan \k'uŋ he-ṫáŋ\ *adv conj* : from, as from a place < *Yunkan Wakantanka mahpiya šape* ~ *hotan'in na heye* God spoke raising his voice to be heard from a dark cloud. > - B.H.56.19

k'u·ši \k'ú-ši\ *v* k'u·wa·ši : to command to give

k'u·wa·cin \k'u-wá-ciŋ\ *v* k'u·wácanmi : to be disposed to give

L

[1]**la** \la\ *va* wa·lá **1** : to ask, demand < *kilá* to ask for one > **2** : to form an opinion of, whether good or bad, to think of or esteem in any manner, to take for – Note: the word is used *esp* with *wašte* and *šica* . < *Wakantanka la* to ask of God > – B.H.267.10

[2]**la** \la\ *suff* : very – Note: it seems to make a word a superlative < *šicela* very bad, *Kolapila, ungna nayapapi kilo* Dear friends, perhaps you ought not flee. *cepela* very fat, *h'anhila* very slow > — *suff dim* – It terminates *pron, adj, v,* and *adv* . When *suff* to *num adj, dem pron,* and *adv,* it signifies "only", thus: *wanjila* only one, *henala* only these

la·bya \la-byá\ *adv* : very much so, intensely, as working or giving something very good < *Labyelo* It is very much so. ~ *waecon* He is very much involved. >

lah \laḣ\ *suff abbrev* [fr perhaps *lahca* very much more] : more of indeed < *wacinlah* to want still more. *Hunhe, lote wašicunlah* Sad to say, he is one still more voracious. > — **la·hca** *and* **lah** \la-ḣca\ *suff* – *See* lah — **lahcaka** \la-ḣca-ka\ *suff partic* : very < *Tatanka ota ópilahcakelo* Many indeed were the buffalo that were shot. *Nonge can oyaglukse laka he wapanhelahcake c'on* It was I who was shouting out very much, when you as a deaf post cut short what you were saying. > – Note: the Santee Dakota, in order to express the superlative to a *v* , adds *hca* very. But the Teton Lakota inserts the *la* and *ka* so that we have added to the *v lahcaka* . – Bl BT D.57 note 1

[1]**la·ka** \la-k̇á\ *va* wa·laka : to have an opinion of < *Wašte walaka* I think well of him. *Hecetu laka* He figures that is just right. >

[2]**la·ka** *and* **lake** \la-ká\ *adv encl* : much, rather < *Wicaša tanka laka* The man is rather oldish. *Kakišyaye laka* You have rather punished him. > – Note: the word implies a question : "Why don't you?" < *Wankal étonwe lake* He looked up (without the others knowing it, to infer "Try"), or Look up, why don't you. *Tokiya egnaka laka* Where did you ever place it anyhow? *Nonge can oyaglukse laka he wapanhelahcake c'on* It was I who was shouting out very much, when you as a deaf post cut short what you were saying. *Omawani kta, kohan škan laka yo* Meanwhile, get a move on you, so I might travel. *Yugnayelaka* He must have missed him, or have evidently missed him. *Takowe miye heci wai ktelaka* How in the world could I go do such a thing [kill it] ? *Ie laka yo* Try speaking it. *Icimani k'un el ilaka can ayaštan iyeyi na heya ke* The instant the traveler reached him he then stopped shouting and nonetheless he said this. > – Note also: the word is an *encl* which, added to any *va* means: the instant one did so-and-so, and is always followed by *can* then

la·kaš \la-k̇áš\ *adv* : indeed, truly, of course

la·ke \la-k̇é\ *adv encl* [fr *laka* rather] : rather – Note: the word follows an *adj* < *Wicaša tankinkinyan* ~ *eya* He said things rather as a man of importance. ~ *ci* or ~ *cin* pretty much, rather, *ateca lake cin* the younger people, ~ *s'e* apparently pretty much, *Kaipazilya* ~ *s'e han* He stands a bit higher than the others. *Kaipazilya* ~ *s'e inyanka* He ran a little ahead of the others. *hotanka* ~ *s'e* a voice a bit louder than others', *kaoh'ankoya* ~ *s'e* in a bit greater hurry than others >

la·kel \la-kél\ *adv encl* [fr *laka* rather, pretty much] – It forms an *adv* of manner < *tokel okihilakel* how *or* as ably – B.H.83.3, 67.7, 134.18, 283.6, 108.5, 148.10 Gramm.187

La·kol \La-k̇ō'l\ *adjp* : Lakota < ~ *ia* to speak Lakota, ~ *iwaya* I speak Lakota. > — **lakol·kiciyapi** \la-k̇ól-k̇i-ci-ya-pi\ *n* : a Lakota confederacy

la·ko·lya \la-k̇o-lya\ *va* lako·lwa·ya : to be friendly with, to have for a friend

La·ko·ta \La-k̇ó-ṫa\ *np* : the Dakota peoples

la·pa \lá-ṗa\ *adj* : smooth, level — **lape·la** \lá-ṗe-la\ *adj* : level, as a floor, smooth, as a face without wrinkles < *Ite wicalapela k'el éceka yelo* Their faces only were smooth [fair]. > – Bl

la·ta·ku·wa·cin \la-ṫá-k̇u-wa-ciŋ\ *v* : to make much of a little thing, to exaggerate in jesting – *Syn* LWICOH'ANWACIN WE

la·wi·co·h'an·wa·cin \la-wi-có-ḣ'aŋ-wa-ciŋ\ *v* lawicóh'aŋwa·cami : to make much of a little thing, to exaggerate in jesting – *Syn* LATÁKUWACIN WE

la·za·ta \la-zá-ṫa\ *adv* : by the side of, behind — **lazata·kiya** \la-zá-ṫa-k̇i-ya\ *adv* : backward < ~ *mani* to walk backward > — **lazatan·han** *adv* : back behind < *Cokan hunh t'a hpayapi na nakun* ~ *hunh hpayapi* Some lay dead in the center, so lay back behind. *Oglala kin hunh waziyata aya na ake ḣe lazatanhan aya* Some Oglalas have gone north, and again they they retreated behind a ridge. > – B.H.9.14

[1]**le** \le\ *pron* : this – Note: the word may be placed before the *n* or after the *art* < *Le wicaša kin,* or *Wicaša kin le* This man > — *adv* : here, now < *Le na ti po* Live here. *Yunkan mini el nonwan, na le wanonwe lo, eya na le iyuha econ po* Then he swam in the water, and he said: "Here I swim," and "Now everyone do so." *Le kiyela unyanpi kte lo, hiyu po, eya* He said: "Let us go here closeby. Come along!" *Oyate wan le wicoti kin lena nitawa kta* The people here will belong to your camps. *Ate, le u kta keya, eya* He said Father stated that he would now come. *Le yaglapi na tanyan wol niglaštanpi hehanl ...* When you finish having a good meal, and here you are on your way home, then ... >

[2]**le** \lē\ *partic ending a statement with some emph* – the word is used by women, where men say "lo" < *Hinu, onapuza ca hanpi cola wówahe le* Oh-h-h, with it all gone dry, I've cooked it to being no-soup! > – BT

le·ca \lé-ca\ *pron* : such as this – B.H.171.17

le·ca·kca·la \le-cá-kca-la\ *adj* : new, as a new suit < *hayapi* ~ new clothes >

le·ca·ki·ci·on \lé-ca-ki-ci-oŋ\ *va* : to do such as this to < *Can teca kin el lecakicionpi kin, tokeške can šeca ecakicionpi kta hwo* If they do such as this to one in the green wood, just what will they do to one in the dry wood? > – B.H.265.17

le·ca·ki·con \lé-ca-ki-coŋ\ *va* leca·we·con leca·un·ki-con·pi : to do thus to – Note: the word may be the same as *lécakicion*

le·ca·ki·on \lé-ca-k̇i-oŋ\ *va* léca·wa·kion : to do this to

le·ca·la \le-cá-la\ *adv* : lately, a little while ago, soon perhaps — **le·caš** \le-cáš\ *adv* : just a little while ago < ~ *lel hi na iyaye* He arrived here just a little while ago and went on. >

le·ce *or* **lecel** \lé-ce\ *adv* : thus, in this way < *Nakun* ~ *šna waceye kšto, eyin na, Kuwa, kuwa eya* "Besides, I might well have kept weeping in this way," said he, and "Come, come!" he said. > — **lece·ca** *adv* le·ma·ceca lececa·pi : like this, such as < *He kin heca wan el wicowoyake wan* ~ The horn on such a one is like this that was told. *Ištinmapi na oikpaḣicapi kin* ~ *sehingle* When they were sleeping and woke up it happened to be like this. > – B.H.39.4

le·ce·gla \lé-ce-gla\ *adv* : close, as in standing close to < *Wópate wan ~ icicanyan hiyeye kin, eye ške* It is said he said: "A stack of all the trimmings came to be standing nearby." > — **lecegla·la** *adv* : only this close, this is all < *Na ungna tahenakiya hiyu na ~ katōnaunk hiyaya ca akiš'api* And I don't know but that he came this way, and when he went gallopping by only this close they cheered him. *Yunkan itaglahwetanhan šunkawakan ota au na ~ ahinajin na najinpi* Then many horses came downwind and halted and stood only so close. *Wana ~ ca waglustan kte* When this is all I shall have finished. > - MS.148 D.56

le·ce·kce·ca \lé-ce-kce-ca\ *adv red of* lececa : such as these

le·ce·kcel \lé-ce-kcel\ *adv red of* lecel : thus, after this manner — **lecekce·lya** *adv red of* lecelya : so, thus

le·cel \lé-cel\ *adv* : thus, after this manner

le·ce·la \le-cé-la\ *adv* : this alone

le·ce·lya \lé-ce-lya\ *adv* : so, thus

le·ce·tki·ya \le-cé-tki-ya\ *adv* : this way (as one points out the whole road) < *Oyate kin ~ igláka eyaya ca etkiya ungni kte lo* We shall go with them when the people go traveling. > - MS.54

le·ce·tu \lé-ce-ṫu\ *adv* : thus, so, right; this is right < *Oyate oyasin le ~ na hehantan waniyetu opawinge šni makoce le wanblaka* Now this is right for all tribes, and since that time I have seen here hardly a hundred winters. >

le·ce·ya \lé-ce-ya\ *adv* : this is so, right now, really, certainly < *~, kola, kapsintapi s'e škinmic'iye lo* Certainly, my friend, I busied myself as if he were being corrected. *~ cante matakuni šni yelo* Really my heart has not come to nothing. *Toke ~ cante iyuhpa niwanica hwo* Do you suppose right now you are lacking all heart? > - D.8 and 32 BT Bl

le·ci \lé-ci\ *adv* : here, in this place < *Na wanna ~ wakpala wan opaya ata akinajin el ake lecel eya*: And here all along a creek where he stayed, he again said this. >

le·cin \le-cíŋ\ *v* : to think that < *Hecel el iyotaka na ~ : Le wicaša kin takuwe isto sanni wanica how* So he sat down there and thought: "Why does this man lack his other arm?" > - MS.143

le·ci·ya \lé-ci-ya\ *adv* : here, about here — **leciya·tan** \lé-ci-ya-ṫaŋ\ *adv* : from this — **leciyatan·han** *adv* : from this place, on this side

le·ci·yo·tan *and* **leciyotan·han** \le-cí-yo-ṫaŋ\ *adv* : in this direction, this way

le·con \lé-coŋ\ *va* lecamon : to do this, act in this way < *Le inše oyate wowicak'u kta ca ~* . Now evidently he did this so he might give people food. *~ s'e* in this manner, *i.e.* like doing this, hence, or thus, *Topa akigle oblake cin ~ s'e econpi* This was done four times just as I have described it. > - D.199 and 106 MS.163

le·e \lé-e\ *v* : this is it - Note: *ee, lee, hee* each contains the substantive *v*

le·ga \lé-ġa\ *adj* : glittering - Bl

le·han *or* **lehanl** \le-háŋ\ *adv* : now, thus far, at this place

lehan·han \lé-haŋ-haŋ\ *adv red* : at this place < *Šunksi koška s'e šaké* A step-mother is like a horse with a swollen hoof, *i.e.* when nails are unusually long. >

lehanhan·keca \le-háŋ-haŋ-ke-ca\ *adv red of* lehankeca : so long, so high, so short

lehan·han·la \le-háŋ-haŋ-la\ *adv red of* lehanla : thus far, now

lehanhan·yan *adv red of* lehanyan : so far in space, so long in time < *Na hehantan wanna waniyetu ota itahena eša ~ nahahci yuhapi, i.e. wawakan* And from that time therefore, though, since many were the winters, they had yet kept them, *i.e.* the five Sacred Arrows. >

lehan·kalkatanhan \le-háŋ-ka-lka-ṫaŋ-haŋ\ *adv* : from there hence, thence, hither < *Oyate ~ ahipi* People from there came hither, *i.e.* people from other countries, foreigners.

lehanka·ta \le-háŋ-ka-ṫa\ *adv* : hither, from far away < *wicaša ~* a foreigner >

lehanke·ca \le-háŋ-ǩe-ca\ *adv* : so long, so high, so short

lehanl *or* **lehan** \le-háŋl\ *adv* : at this place, thus far, now

lehan·leš \le-háŋ-leš\ *adv* : nowadays < *~ héceca* It is like that nowadays. >

lehan·tanhan \le-háŋ-taŋ-haŋ\ *adv* : from this

lehan·tu \le-háŋ-ṫu\ *adv* : to this, thus far, now

lehantu·kel \le-háŋ-ṫu-ǩel\ *adv* : just so far, in this way, just now

lehantu·ya \le-háŋ-ṫu-ya\ *adv* : to this extent, on or in this wise

lehantuya·kel \le-háŋ-ṫu-ya-ǩel\ *adv* : just now, on this wise

lehan·yan \le-háŋ-yaŋ\ *adv* : so far, in space, so long, in time < *Na hehantan wanna waniyetu ota itahena eša ~ nahahci yuhapi, i.e. wawakan* And from that time therefore, though since many were the winters, they had yet kept them, *i.e.* the five Sacred Arrows. >

lehan·yank \le-háŋ-yank\ *adv* : away, somewhere else, apart < *~ iyaya* to go somewhere apart, *oyate ~ unpi kin* other people, people living in other places, *~ egnaka* to set somewhere else >

lehan·yela \le-háŋ-ye-la\ *adv* : thus far, just now - B.H.34.3, 27.30, 15.23, 102.15, 83.6, 123.2, 201.14 and 24, 271.14

le·hin·ci·ta \le-híŋ-ci-ta\ *adv* : so often, again and again, more than expected < *~ iyungahe* to be asking questions again and again, *~ iyunk yapi* They traveled often lying down. > - Note: the word is perhaps from *lehanic'ita* *Syn* KITATALA D.2 B.H.77.12

le·hin·ya·gle·ya \le-híŋ-ya-gle-ya\ *adv* [fr perhaps *lehan* thus far + *iyagleya* to reach to] : until this day

le·hle·ga \le-ȟlé-ġa\ *adj red of perhaps* lega : glittering often

le·i·c'i·ya \le-í-c'i-ya\ *v refl of* leyá : to say this to one's self, as at the beginning of a quotation - B.H.22.18

le·ja \lé-ja\ *vn* wa·leja : to urinate — **leja·pi šni** \lé-ja-pi šni\ *n* : inability to urinate, a sickness known to the Dakota

le·ki·ya \le-kí-ya\ *v* : to say this to one - Cf ekíya and hekíya - B.H.16.19, 169.9, 178.2

le·kši \le-kší\ *n* ni·lékši : one's mother's brother - Note: one's father's brother is called *até* — **lekši·tku** \le-kší-tku\ *n* : his or her uncle — **lekši·ya** \le-kší-ya\ *va* lekši·wa·ya : to have for an uncle

lel \lel\ *adv* : here, in this place

le·na \lé-na\ *pron pl of* le : these

le·na·gna·ke·ca \le-ná-gna-ǩe-ca\ *adv red of* lenákeca : so very many, so very much

le·na·ke·ca *or* **lenake** \le-ná-ǩe-ca\ *adv* le·má·nakeca

\a\ father \e\ they \i\ machine \o\ smoke \u\ lunar \an, aŋ\ blanc Fr. \in, iŋ\ ink \on, oŋ, un, uŋ\ soon, confier Fr. \c\ chair \ġ\ machen Ger. \j\ fusion \clusters: bl, gn, kp, hšl, etc...\ b[e]lo ... said with a slight vowel **See more in the Introduction, Guide to Pronunciation**

le·ún·nakeca·pi : so many, so much < *Lenake mic'iksape lo* That much I saved for tomorrow. *He waniyetu topa* ~ He is four years old. > – Pb.28

le·na·ke·hcin *or* **lenakehci** \le-ná-k̇e-ḣciŋ\ *adv* : all these

le·na·la \le-ná-la\ *adv* : only so many, so few

le·na·na \le-ná-na\ *pron red of* lena [fr Dakota for the Lakota word *lenála*] : only so many, so few – B.H. 62.10

le·na·os *or* **lenios** *or* **leniyos** \le-ná-os\ \le-ní-os\ \le-ní-yos\ *adv* : both these, these two

le·o·gna *or* **logna** \lé-o-gna\ *adv* : around here < *Hinhanna kin leogna u kta ca kokipe šni oyuspa po* Catch it without fear because it will come around here tomorrow morning. >

le·pca \le-pcá\ *v 1 pers singl* [fr *le* this + *epca* I thought] : I thought this – Note: no other form is used

leš \leš\ *vn contrac of* léja : to urinate < *leš wacintanka* one who is long-enduring and does not have to urinate often > — **le·šleja** \le-šlé-ja\ *vn red of* leja : to urinate often

le·tan *and* **letan·han** \le-ṫáŋ\ *adv* : from this place, from this time; after (the Latin *post*) < *Ca ~ wanna tuktogna iyonicipipi kin ogna iyaya po* Therefore go from this place in whichever direction you find convenient. *~ waniyetu topa kin oyate wan ahi kta keye lo* He stated that a tribe would arrive four winters from then. *~ topa can kinhan hehanl ...* After four days, then ... *Lemátanhan* I am from here. >

le·tka \lé-tka\ *adj* : having spent all < *Maletka* I am "broke". > – *Syn* WEGAHAN Bl

le·tki·ya \lé-tki-ya\ *adv* : this way, pointing towards one's self < *~ u wo* Come this way. >

le·tu \lé-ṫu\ *adv* : here, at this place or time, *lit* now — **letu·hca** \lé-ṫu-ḣca\ *adv* : just here

le·ya \le-yá\ *v* lepá lehá le·un·k̇eya·pi : to say this < *~ hoyekiya* He cried to him saying this. *~ hoyeya* He raised his voice to say this. *~ oštegla* He insulted him to say this. *~ owa* He noted to say this. *~ oyaka* He spoke saying this. *~ pan* He yelled to say this. *~ omani* He walked saying this. *~ wacekiya* He praying saying this. > – B.H.212.8, 86.7, 215.5, 95.4, 175.16, 69.8, 172.5, 100.20

li·gli·la \lí-gli-la\ *adv emph* : very < *~ lúzahan, húnkešni, ohitika, iyunka, inyanka, wowaši econ* He did work very fast, poorly, bravely, resting, and running. > – Bl

li·la \lí-la\ *adv* : very < *~ kahmi wan wašte* a very fine river-bend > — **lilah** *or* **lila·hci** \lí-laḣ\ \lí-la-ḣci\ *adv* : exceedingly — **lila·ka** \lí-la-k̇a\ *adj* ma·lílaka : being good on or at something, *i.e.* skillful *e.g.* in running *etc*

li·la·kel \lí-la-kel\ *adv* : very much – B.H.66.4

li·li·ta \li-lí-ṫa\ *n* : a child's word for white man < *~ unyanpi kte* We white men should go; whereas another would say to the children: You should go to town *Otonwahe ekta yapi ktelo.* >

li·ta·škan \li-ṫá-škaŋ\ *v* lita·wa·škaŋ : to get busy – Bl

[1]**lo** \lo\ *n* : food, soft, tender, moist stuff, as fresh meat or soft hide < *Tahálo saka kakšapi wacin šni, lo ca wacin yelo* He did not think the hide rolled up was dry, He thought it was moist. >

[2]**lo** *or* **yelo** \lo\ *partic for emph or euph by men* – the word is placed at the end of a sentence or phrase, and women rather say *ye* < *Na le tuwa hwo? ecannipi nacece lo* Now who was it? It may be you did it. >

lo·bya \lo-byá\ *adv* : in a tenderizing way < *~ špan* to cook tender > – Cf lolóbya

lo·cin \lo-cíŋ\ *v* lo·wa·cin lo·un·cin·pi : to want food, be hungry — **locin·pi** *n* : appetite — **locin·ya** *va* : to cause to feel hungry *e.g.* by speaking of good food

lo·gna \ló-gna\ *adv* : this way, in this manner < *~ yakagege kta* You should sew it this way. > – *Syn* HOGNA

lo·gu·te \lo-ǧú-ṫe\ *n* : the hollow of the flank of man or beast

lo·he \lo-ḣé\ *n* : the gills, the parts of the cheeks and throat which are loose and not fastened to the bones – B.H.122.26

lo·i·gni *or* **lo'igni** *or* **loligni** \lo-í-gni\ *v* loi·wa·gni : to hunt food < *Miniyušpala loiwagni yelo* I and hunting a puddle for food, *i.e.* perspiring I am looking for food. > – Bl

lol·hwa·ka *or* **lol'hwaka** \lol-ḣwa-k̇a\ *adj* lol·wa·hwa·ka : unable to eat much – Note: the word is used when a person wants to eat more than what he got – *Syn* LOLWAZAZE Bl

lo·li·cupi *or* **lol'icupi** \lo-lí-cu-pi\ *n* : an issuing food, rations

lo·li·gni *or* **lol'igni** \lo-lí-gni\ *v* : to look for food – B.H.181.5

lo·li·h'an *or* **lol'ih'an** \lo-lí-ḣ'aŋ\ *v* loli·wa·h'an : to prepare food, to cook < *Hanpa cicagapi nainš lolicicih'anpi kta ca wau we* I came so I might cook and make moccasins for you. >

lo·lo \lo-ló\ *adj red of* lo : soft, damp, fresh

lo·lo·bya \lo-ló-bya\ *va* lolo·bwa·ya : to boil soft *e.g.* meat, corn *etc*, to cook until tender — *adv perhaps* : tenderly, very tender, as is said of meat well cooked < *~ špan* to cook very tender > — **lolobya·pi** \lo-lō'-bya-pi\ *n* : meat, beans *etc* cooked so that they are very soft, overboiled — **lolobye·la** *adj* : soft, very soft – Bl D.12 Lhb

lo·lo·pa \lo-ló-ṗa\ *adj* : soft – Note: the word among the Tetons does not seem to carry the meaning: miry — **lolope·la** *adj* : too soft, flabby, as of over-ripe fruit

lo·lwa·na·gi *or* **lol'wanagi** \lo-lwá-na-ǧi\ *v* : to give food to a spirit < *~ yewaye c'un tanyan wíyewaye lo* I dine well when I give his spirit food, *i.e.* he has his full. > – Bl

lo·lwa·za·ze *or* **lol'wazaze** \lo-lwá-za-ze\ *adj* : being hindered from eating much, not able to eat, as is said when a man wants to eat more than what he got – *Syn* LOLHWAKA Bl

lol'·i·ji·ca·ya·kel \lol'-í-ji-ca-ya-kel\ *adv* : having many provisions < *~ un welo* He is having many supplies. > – Bl

lol'·i·yu·can *also perhaps* **lol'iyucan·ka** \lol'-í-yu-caŋ\ *v* : to have hardly anything to eat – Bl

lol'·o·pe·ton \lol'-ó-pe-toŋ\ *v* : to buy grub – B.H.208.2

lol'·o·pi·ye \lol'-ō'-ṗi-ye\ *n* : a leather pouch for meat *etc*

lo·pa \lo-ṗá\ *adj* : soft – Note: miry is doubtful

lo·te \lo-ṫé\ *n* : the throat < *~ ayáskabyapi* a neck-band *i.e.* in the manner of *wanap'in* neckware >

lo·te·o·gmus yu·za \lo-ṫé-o-gmus yù-za\ *v* : to throttle

lo·te o·na·hna·hna *or* **lotonahnahna** \lo-ṫé o-nà-ḣna-ḣna\ *v* lote ona·ma·hnahna : to have a rattling in the throat

lo·te·po·pi \lo-ṫé-ṗò-pi\ *n* : a swelling of the throat sickness known by the Dakota – Bl WE

lo·te wa·ši·cun \lo-ṫé wa-ši-cuŋ\ *n* : one who desires to eat very much, very often – Bl

lo·tku \lo-tk̇ú\ *n* : the throat of man and animals, the part under the jaw

lo·tkun·ke·šni \lo-ṫkuŋ-k̇e-šni\ *adv perhaps* : "Oh! I wanted to tell you ... - Note: the word corresponds to this *express* in English when while talking one forgets something and it comes to mind < ~ *wociciyakin kte* Oh! I should tell you. >

lo·to·gmus yu·za *or* **loteogmus yuza** \lo-ṫó-gmus yù-za\ *va* : to seize by the throat, to throttle

lo·wan \lo-wáŋ\ *vn* wa·lowan : to sing — **lowan·pi** \lo-wáŋ-ṗi\ *n* : hymns, songs, singing — **lowan·wan** *v red* : to sing over and over - B.H.140.1

lo·wi·ta·ya \lo-wí-ṫa-ya\ *adv* : all fresh, raw, as meat < ~ *icu, yuha iyohpeya yo* Take what is fresh, hold and throw it in. > - Bl

lo·ya \lo-yá\ *adj* : moist (not dry), fresh, as meat — **lo-ya·ke** \lo-yá-k̇e\ *adj* : fresh, not dried < ~ *un* to be fresh > — **loya·kel** \lo-yá-k̇el\ *adv* : in a moist condition

lu·glu·ta \lu-glú-ta\ *adj red of* lúta : red all over - Bl

lul \lul\ *adj of* lúta : red — **lu·luta** \lu-lú-ṫa\ *adj red* : red, as in speaking of leaves turning color — **lu·lya** \lu-lyá\ *va* lu·lwa·ya : to color or paint red or scarlet *e.g.* porcupine quills < *sinte lulyapi* the red-tail deer > - SI

lu·pi \lú-ṗi\ *adj perhaps* : dangling - Cf yulúpi šni, and walúpi šni *Syn* WOYÁ Bl

lus \lus\ *adv* : swiftly < ~ *ya* to go fast > — **lu·skiya** \lu-sk̇í-ya\ *va* : to cause to be swift

lu·slu·za·han \lu-slú-za-haŋ\ *adv red of* lúzahan : to be quite fast

lu·sma·ni \lu-smá-ni\ *v* lusma·wa·ni : to walk fast < ~ *po* Walk fast. - Note: this is in opposition to *Mani glapo* Walk slowly. >

lu·ta \lú-ṫa\ *adj* : red, scarlet

lu·za·han \lú-za-haŋ\ *vn* ma·lúuzahan ni·lúzahan : to be fast, fast running

M

[1]ma \mă\ *interj* : "Look here!", "Attention!" to call for one's attention - Note: the word is used by women D.78 note 2

[2]ma \ma\ *pron obj* : me - Note: it is used also with a class of *neut* and *adj v*, when it is translated by the *nom* case "I"; and with some *n* it is used as the *poss*, my or mine

ma·ca \ma-cá\ *n* : the coyote - *Syn* ŠUNKMANITU

ma·ga \ma-ġá\ *or* \ma-ȟ'á\ *n* : a goose, geese

ma·ga \má-ġa\ *n* : a cultivated spot or field

ma·ga·ga·i·c'i·ya \ma-ġá-ġa-i-c'i-ya\ *vn* : to be amused, amuse one's self — **magaga·kiya** \ma-ġá-ġa-ǩi-ya\ *va* magaga·wa·kiya : to amuse, comfort one — **magaga·ya** *va* magaga·wa·ya : to amuse, divert one < *magagaic'i-ya* to amuse one's self >

ma·ga·hu \má-ġa-hu\ *n* : cornstalks

ma·ga·ju \ma-ġá-ju\ *n* : rain —*vn* : to rain — **maga-ju·kiya** \ma-ġá-ju-ǩi-ya\ *va* magaju·wa·kiya : to cause to rain — **magaju·mini** *n* : rainwater — **maga-ju·ya** *va* magaju·wa·ya : to cause to rain, to cause rain

ma·ga·ki·ci·ya·pi \ma-ġá-ǩi-ci-ya-pi\ *n* : a pastime in which boys taking a swim will dive and grab somebody's leg and say: "*Maga nicinca tonakeca hwo* How many are you goslings?" while the aggressor will push the other under so many times. The game is announced by saying: "*Maga unyanpo!*" "Come on, you goslings!" Then all dive and try to grab somebody.

ma·ga·ksi·ca \ma-ġá-ksi-ca\ *n* : a duck, ducks < ~ *agli wi* the moon when the ducks come back, *i.e.* April > - Note: the ducks say: "*Magá, magá, magá.*" - Bl

ma·ga·ska *or* **magaska tanka** \ma-ġá-ska tàn-ka\ *n* : the swan < ~ *s'e ahiyaye* to pass by like a swan, *i.e.* dressed in white >

ma·ga·ša·pa \ma-ġá-ša-pa\ *n* : the common wild goose, the Canadian goose - Note: a woman teasing her brother-in-law would say while she goes: *Eyin nahan ~ ca mániye s'e kagle* Well then, being a wild goose he uncoils like as if walking, *i.e.* with a waddling gait, — **magašapa tanka** *n* : the black swan - Bl

ma·ga·še·kše·ca·la \ma-ġá-še-kši-ca-la\ *n* : the brant, a large white water bird with bill about three inches long, like that of a crane, and tall as it with legs two decimeters long < ~ *s'e ho wašte* He has a voice that of a brant, as they would say of a fellow with a good voice. > - Bl

ma·ga·šni·yan·la *or* **magašniyan·yanla** \ma-ġá-šni-yaŋ-la\ *n* : the red-headed duck, though the name is applied also to other ducks:

~ *ȟupáhu skaska* the red-headed duck
~ *ikcéka* the black duck
~ *ištóhlate ska* the blue winged teal
~ *nawáte to* the green winged teal
~ *pa to* the bald-pate duck
magašniyanyanla ȟota the gadwell duck, a wild duck about the size of the mallard

ma·ga·ta \ma-ġá-ṫa\ *adv* : at or in the field

ma·ga tan·ka \ma-ġá tàŋ-ǩa\ *n* 1 : a goose 2 : the swan - R

ma·ga·tan·ka u \ma-ġá-taŋ-ka u\ *n* : swellings on the back, or elsewhere with matter therein - EM Bl

ma·ga ta·šun·pe \ma-ġá ta-šùŋ-pe\ *n* : a swift, round and black waterbug, a long legged bug that walks on the water - Bl

Ma·ga Wa·kpa \Ma-ġá Wa-kpa\ *np* : the Laramie River

ma·ga wa·pa·ha \ma-ġá wa-pà-ha\ *n* : a headdress of goose feathers < " ~ *iwekcu ktelo* I shall take back my goose headdress." *Tiiyaza tiole ayin kte* So he'll go begging from house to house. > - Cf wapáha Bl

ma·ga·yu·šla \má-ġa-yu-šla\ *v* : to weed a field

ma·gi·ca·hin·te \ma-ġí-ca-hiŋ-ṫe\ *n* : a rake, a harrow - *Syn* MAGIYUHINTE

ma·gi·ca·mna \ma-ġí-ca-mna\ *or* \ma-ġ'í-ca-mna\ *n* : a hoe, hoes

ma·gi·yu·blu \ma-ġí-yu-blu\ *n* : a plow

ma·gi·yu·hin·te \ma-ġí-yu-hiŋ-ṫe\ *n* : a rake, a harrow - *Syn* MAGICAHINTE

ma·he *or* **mahel** \ma-hé\ *prep* : within, in into < *Maka ~ iyemayelo* He shoved me into the dirt. *can ~* in the woods, *Tipi kin ~ han* The house stood in it, *i.e.* in the snow pile. > — **mahe·lhel** *prep red of* mahehe : in and out and in again <~ *iyaya* to go up and down behind something so that the head disappears and appears again, as children do > - Note: the word is fundamentally from *mahél* *Syn* YUSNISNIS WE B.H.36.5

ma·he·lhe·tu·ya \ma-hé-lhe-tu-ya\ *adv red of* mahétuya : in deeper and deeper - Bl

ma·he·lo·gle \ma-hé-lo-gle\ *n* : an undershirt

ma·he·lun·zo·ge \ma-hé-luŋ-zo-ġe\ *n* : drawers, undershorts

ma·he·lwa·pa \ma-hé-lwa-pa\ *adv* : inward, towards the interior

ma·he·ta·ki·ya \ma-hé-ṫa-ǩi-ya\ *adv* : towards the inside, inwards < *Na ake wanji o, tatanka, ca na he hin kin ~ ihpeyapi.* And again he shot one, a bull buffalo, and then when it stood it was thrown towards the inside. *Hecel wanna oun wašteiciyapi* So conditions among them were improved. >

ma·he·tan·han \ma-hé-ṫaŋ-haŋ\ *adv* : on the inside, as is something lying a ways under or among other things < *timahetanhan* in the house, *minimáhetanhan* in the water > — **mahe·tatanhan** \ma-hé-ṫa-ṫaŋ-haŋ\ *adv* : from inside, from within

ma·he·tu \ma-hé-ṫu\ *adv* : within, inward, *i.e.* deep — **mahetu·ya** *adv* : deep in < *Yunkan ~ o* Then he shot it deep in. *Hecel taku on* (an arrow) *opi kin, lila ~ iyayin kta* So for some reason when (an arrow) was shot, it would go very deep into it. > - MS.481

ma·he·tu·ya·la·ke s'e \ma-hé-ṫu-ya-la-ke s'e\ *adv* : way into for a suitable place < ~ *hiyáya* to go into, *e.g.* a crowded room, and pass through all to find a place > - Bl

mah \maȟ\ *n contrac* 1 : a goose 2 : tilled ground

ma·ȟa·ka·ta \ma-ȟá-ǩa-ta\ *v* maȟa·wa·kata : to hoe *e.g.* corn

ma·hcin·ca \ma-ȟcíŋ-ca\ *n* : the young of geese and ducks

ma·hgla·gmi \ma-hglá-gmi\ *v* ma·hwa·glagmi : to clear off *e.g.* weeds from a field, to cultivate, to hoe

ma·ȟi·ca·hin·te *or* **magicahinte** \ma-ȟí-ca-hiŋ-ṫe\ *n* : a rake or harrow

ma·ȟi·yu·blu *or* **magiyublu** \ma-ȟí-yu-blu\ *n* : a plow

ma·ȟi·yu·hin·he \ma-ȟí-yu-hiŋ-he\ *n* : a harrow, a drag

ma·ȟi·yu·hin·te *or* **magiyuhinte** \ma-ȟí-yu-hiŋ-ṫe\ *n* : a harrow, a drag

ma·hka·šla \ma-ȟǩá-šla\ *v* : to hoe a field

ma·hki·can·yan \ma-ȟǩí-caŋ-yaŋ\ *v* : to work or till a field

ma·hpi·hpi·ya \ma-ȟpí-ȟpi-ya\ *n red of* mahpíya : scattering clouds

ma·hpi·o·han·zi \ma-ȟṗí-o-haŋ-zi\ *n* : a shadow caused by a cloud <~ *ahi* The cloud's shade came over. >

ma·hpi·ya \ma-ȟṗí-ya\ *n* 1 : the clouds 2 : the sky, the heavens 3 : Heaven
- ~ *ayáskapa n* an isolated cloud
- ~ *ayáskapa wanice* not one cloud is visible - Bl
- ~ *šápa n* black clouds
- ~ *šóka n* thick clouds
- ~ *špušpú n* long broken clouds
- ~ *tacéjiksica n* little white clouds scattered over a part of the sky. This looks like the thing layer of fat covering the paunch
- ~ *tan'in n* the northern lights, the aurora borealis. The Lakotas once when this sort of even took place would paint their faces, sit up all night, and burn leaves as incense
- ~ *to n* the blue sky
- ~ *tola n* the clear sky, blue sky

Ma·hpi·ya To \Ma-ȟṗí-ya To\ *np* : the Arapahoe Indian

ma·hpi·yo·han·zi·zi \ma-ȟṗí-yo-haŋ-zi-zi\ *n perhaps* : the passage of clouds at intervals obstructing the sunlight - Bl

ma·hta·ni \ma-ȟtá-ni\ *n* : an old field

ma·h'a·wan·gla·ke *or* **mah'awanglakela** \ma-ȟ'á-waŋ-gla-ǩe\ *n* : a cicada or harvest fly, the seventeen-year locust, so called because it is doing nothing but singing all day and apparently watching the fields

ma·h'o·win·je \ma-ȟ'ó-wiŋ-je\ *n* : a corn husk tick - Wi

ma·h'wa·pa·jin \maȟ'wá-ṗa-jiŋ\ *v* : to have the ducks against one's self, *i.e.* unable to kill any while others kill aplenty < *Mah'wamapajin yelo* Ducks have it against me, *i.e.* they seem to avoid me as when hunting them. >

ma·h'yu·šla \ma-ȟ'yú-šla\ *v* ma·h'blu·šla : to make a field bare, *i.e.* to pull weeds

[1]**ma·ka** *or* **manka** \ma-ǩá\ *n* : the skunk or polecat < ~ *cincala* a young skunk >

[2]**ma·ka** \ma-ǩá\ *n* : ground, the earth < ~ *namah'on* The earth hears me, as a person would say touching the ground in taking an oath. If one should then tell a lie, he was sure to stumble with his horse. ~ *nanih'on he* Did the ground hear you? *ómaka* a season of the year, winter or summer, a half-year season, *Omaka tahena Scili kin ake šunkawakan wicawakiyelo* This last season I again robbed the Pawnees of their horses. >

ma·ka a·li·šni·šni s'e ma·ni \ma-ǩá a-ȟi-šni-šni s'e má-ni\ *v* : to walk lightly and without noise - Bl BT

ma·ka·blu \ma-ǩá-blu\ *n* : dust

ma·ka·ca·hli \ma-ǩá-ca-ȟli\ *n* : coal

ma·ka·ca·na·hpa \ma-ǩá-ca-na-ǩpa\ *n* : the lady's slipper, a flower - Note: it is eaten BE

ma·ka·can·šin·hu \ma-ǩá-caŋ-šiŋ-hu\ *n* : the prairie pink, a rush-like lygodesmia, lygodesmia juncea, of the composite family. - Cf *canhlogan hu can swula* Note: it can be chewed, and a tea made of the whole plant is supposed to stop the diarrhoea of children - WE #143 BT

ma·ka·ce·ga \ma-ǩá-ce-ġa\ *n* : a pot, an earthen vessel

ma·ka·ce·ya·ka \ma-ǩá-ce-yà-ka\ *n* : lance-leaved sage, salvia lanceolata, of the mint family - #159

ma·ka·ce·ya·ka i·ye·ce·ca \ma-ǩá-ce-yà-ka i-yé-ce-ca\ *n* : lemon mint, monarda citriodora - Note: this was new to the State herbarium #289

ma·ka·gle *or* **makegle** \ma-ǩá-gle\ *adv* : end on the ground < *Cankpeška* ~ *inajin* He knelt upright on the ground. > - R

ma·ka gle·ška \ma-ǩá gle-ška\ *n* : the little spotted skunk, the civet cat

ma·ka·gle·ya \ma-ǩá-gle-ya\ *vn* : to fall down, as a long stick, endwise < *Cankpeška* ~ *inajin* He fell to his knees. >

ma·ka·gna \ma-ǩá-gna\ *adv* [fr *maka* earth + *ogna* in] : in the ground, as grass that has not yet shown itself growing < ~ *tehan yahi šni* You did not arrive in the country for a long time, *i.e.* you let us wait for you very long. *Inyankehanla ilale c'un* ~ *yaun welo* Although you went away running, you were there in the country, *i.e.* there very long. ~ *lake s'e* very slowly, late, *Kikta yo, kikta yo,* ~ *lake s'e tehan nunkelo* Get up! Get up! It seems you would lie around in the ground a long time, as is said when a person sleeps too long. > - Bl

ma·ka·he·ya \ma-ǩá-he-ya\ *va* : to accomplish finally what one has long desired < *Išpá kic'unyan makahewayelo* I elbowed my way through to get what I much wanted, *i.e.* I killed him. > - Bl

ma·ka·hli·hli·la *or* **makahlihli** \ma-ǩá-ȟli-ȟli-la\ *n* : mud

ma·ka·i·k'e \ma-ǩá-i-k'e\ *n* : a pick axe

ma·ka·i·yu·hlo·ke \ma-ǩá-i-yu-ȟlo-ke\ *n* : an auger to dig post holes - R Bl

ma·ka·i·yu·ksa·ksa \ma-ǩá-i-yu-ksa-ksa\ *n* : a cultivator

ma·ka·i·yu·pte \ma-ǩá-i-yu-pte\ *n* : a breaking plow - R Bl

ma·ka·i·yu·ta \ma-ǩá-i-yu-ta\ *v* : to measure land, to survey — **makaiyuta·pi** *n* : a surveyor's measuring chain for *e.g.* an acre of ground perhaps

ma·ka ki·ci·in·pi \ma-ǩá ki-ci-iŋ-pi\ *n* : the mud and willow game - Bl

ma·ka·k'a·k'a s'e \ma-ká-k'a-k'a s'e\ *adv* : pawing < ~ *najin* to stand shuffling with the feet, as it were pawing the ground. > - Bl

ma·kal \ma-ǩál\ *adv* : on the ground < ~ *hpaya* to lie on the ground >

ma·ka·ma·ni \ma-ǩá-ma-ni\ *n* and *v* makama·wa·ni : a pedestrian, one who travels on foot

ma·ka·ma·ni in·yan·ka \ma-ǩá-ma-ni ìŋ-yaŋ-ka\ *v* : to ride a bicycle

ma·ka·non·ge·ya \ma-ǩá-noŋ-ġe-ya\ *v* makanonge·wa·-ya : to know it al-ready, as if havng the earth as an ear < *Ehanni nawah'on welo; maka kin nongewayehcelo* Long ago I heard it; really I had as an ear the earth, as an old saying goes. > - EM

ma·ka·o·i·yu·te \ma-ǩá-o-i-yu-ṫe\ *n* : an allotment, a piece of surveyed land, *i.e.* a quarter, half, full section *etc.* Its size is defined by adding *šokela* a quarter part < *tamákaoiyute* his allotment > - *Syn* MAKAOWASPE

ma·ka o·k'e *or* **makok'e** \ma-ǩá o-k'e\ \ma-ǩó-k'e\ *n* : a dug-out, a pit — **maka o·ok'e** *n* : an old cistern - B.H.27.20

ma·ka·o·pa·špe \ma-ǩá-o-ṗa-špe\ *n* : a measured tract of land — **makao·špe** *n* : an acre of land - WI Bl

ma·ka·o·wan·ke *or* **makaowanke·la** \ma-ǩá-o-waŋ-ke\ *n* : the bobolink, a little bird so called because it has two white stripes over the back from head to tail like a skunk; otherwise the bird is black and lives near water among bulrushes - *Syn* MANKÁ ZINTKALA Bl

---

\a\ father \e\ they \i\ machine \o\ smoke \u\ lunar \an, aŋ\ blanc Fr. \in, iŋ\ ink \on, oŋ, un, uŋ\ soon, confier Fr. \c\ chair \ġ\ machen Ger. \j\ fusion \clusters: bl, gn, kp, hšl, etc...\ b[e]lo ... said with a slight vowel **See more in the Introduction, Guide to Pronunciation**

ma·ka·o·wa·špe \ma-k̇á-o-wa-šṗe\ *n* : a piece of measured, surveyed land, defining the size by adding *šokela, okise,* a quarter, a half, *etc* – *See* makopašpe *and* makowašpe *Syn* MAKAOIYUTE

ma·ka·pa \ma-k̇á-pa\ *n* : a skunk's head

ma·ka pte \ma-ká pte\ *n* : buffalos made of clay to play with as a pastime – Bl

ma·ka·san \ma-k̇á-saŋ\ *n* : a whitish or yellowish clay

ma·ka·san·pa \ma-k̇á-saŋ-pa\ *n* : next year, next season

Ma·ka·san Wa·kpa \Ma-k̇á-saŋ Wa-kpà\ *n* : The White River in southern South Dakota State

ma·ka·si·to·mni \ma-k̇á-si-ṫo-mni\ *n* : the whole world – **makasitomni·yan** *adv* : all the world over

ma·ka·su·hu·la \ma-k̇á-su-hu-la\ *n* : sandy soil

ma·ka·špan *or* **makašpan·yanpi** \ma-k̇á-špaŋ\ *n* : a brick

ma·ka šun·ka·wa·kan \ma-ká suŋ-ka-wa-kaŋ\ *n* : horses made of clay to play with

ma·ka·ta \ma-k̇á-ṫa\ *adv* : at or on the ground, on the floor < *Na wanna wahinkpe kin ~ glihan* And the arrow came down and stuck in the ground. > — **makata·kiya** \ma-k̇á-ṫa-ki-ya\ *adv* : towards the earth < *~ amayuta yo* Look upon me on the ground, as the Lakota are used to pray to God. >

ma·ka·ta·na·su·la \ma-ká-ta-na-su-la\ *n* : a kind of soil with whitish streaks, a clay perhaps that boys used for making clay horses – Bl

ma·ka·te·ca i·yu·blu \ma-ká-ṫe-ca i-yù-blu\ *n* : a breaking plow – EB

ma·ka ti·pi \ma-ká ti-pi\ *n* : a sod house, a cellar

ma·ka·to \ma-k̇á-to\ *n* : blue earth – Note: *Mankato,* a city in the state of Minnesota

ma·ka·to·mni·ca *or* **omnica** *and* **Lakota omnica** \ma-k̇á-to-mni-ca\ *n* : the trailing wild bean, strophostyles helvolva – #111

ma·ka to o·yu·ze \ma-ká to o-yù-ze\ *n* : a place east of the Powder River in Montana where the Lakotas got blue earth to paint with – Bl

ma·ka·wa·kši·ca \ma-k̇á-wa-kši-ca\ *n* : earthen dishes

ma·ka wa·na·ka·ja·ta *or* **maka wanakajatan·han** *or* **maka wana·kaš** \ma-ká wa-nà-k̇a-ja-ta\ *adv* : long ago – Bl

ma·ka·wa·se \ma-k̇á-wa-se\ *n* : red earth used as paint — **makawase ša** *n* : red earth used by the Dakotas as a paint instead of vermillion

ma·ka·yu·blu \ma-ká-yu-blu\ *v* : to plow

ma·ka·zi \ma-ká-zi\ *n* : brimstone, sulphur

ma·ka zin·tka·la \ma-ká ziŋ-tkà-la\ *n* : the bobolink – Cf manka owanke FR

ma·ke·gla·kin·yan \ma-ké-gla-kiŋ-yaŋ\ *adv* : across the earth < *~ omani* to travel from afar, *i.e.* from far away > – Note: only this form is used, although one would expect the form: *makáglakinyan* Sb

ma·ki·ci·ma \ma-k̇í-ci-ma\ *n* : a two-year-old horse, or a young horse a few years old, in opposition to one that is old, *i.e. gan*

ma·ki·ci·non \ma-kí-ci-noŋ\ *v* ma·we·cinon [fr *manón* to steal] : to steal anything from another

ma·ki·gla·ta \ma-k̇í-gla-ta\ *v* : to take much leave < *Tuwa ~ iyahe tokel iyayelo* A person stepped in only to take leave as he went on, as is said if a man came on foot and wanted to stay a few days, but then suddenly disappears. > – Bl

ma·ki·gle·ya \ma-k̇í-gle-ya\ *adv* : endwise, downwards perhaps < *pa ~* with the head downward >

ma·ki·glu·kšan \ma-k̇í-glu-kšaŋ\ *adv* : to go around the world, to go very far < *~ omawaniyelo* I traveled the whole world round. *~ owakawinge* I went around and around the world. > – *Syn* MAKÓKAWINH Bl

ma·ki·han·ke \ma-k̇í-haŋ-ke\ *n* : the end of the world

ma·ki·i·na·ski·lya \ma-k̇í-i-na-ski-lya\ *n* : a roller

ma·ki·ka·bla·ska gli·hpe·ya \ma-k̇í-ka-bla-ska gli-ḣpe-ya\ *va* : to beat flat to the ground – B.H.239.1

ma·ki·ka·co·co \ma-k̇í-ka-co-co\ *n* : a cement mixer to mix mortar

ma·ki·ka·špe \ma-k̇í-k̇a-šṗe\ *n* : a pick axe

ma·ki·kce·ka \ma-k̇í-kce-ka\ *n* : the land, as opposed to water, soil, as opposed to clay or gravel, the layer of good soil, as opposed to sand *etc* below the humus, loam < *~ ic'iun* to have the land for its use > — **makikce·ya** *adv* : on land

ma·ki·na·ksa·ksa \ma-k̇í-na-ksa-ksa\ *n* : a harrow

ma·ki·na·pte *or* **makinašpe** \ma-k̇í-na-pṫe\ *n* : a spade

ma·ki·non \ma-kí-noŋ\ *v* ma·wá·kinon [fr *manón* to steal] : to steal, take back secretly what one has given

ma·ki·pa·blu·ya \ma-k̇í-ṗa-blu-ya\ *adv* : raising dust *e.g.* by falling < *~ ihpeic'iya* to throw one's self into the dust > – B.H.64.10

ma·ki·pa·hla·la \ma-k̇í-ṗa-ḣla-la\ *adv* : brushing the earth, creeping along the ground, lingering along the horizon < *~ wakinyan ukiye lo* The thunderbird came brushing the earth's horizon, *i.e.* storm clouds were all along the horizon and coming towards one. > – Bl

ma·ki·pa·pte \ma-k̇í-ṗa-pṫe\ *n* : a shovel, spade – R

ma·ki·pa·si·se \ma-k̇í-ṗa-si-se\ *n* [fr *maku* breast] : a breast pin

ma·ki·pa·sto·ya \ma-k̇í-ṗa-sto-ya\ *adv* : in a fixed prone position on the ground < *~ ihpeic'iya* to throw one's self down prone > – B.H.215.7

ma·ki·pu·ski·ca \ma-k̇í-ṗu-sk̇i-ca\ *vn* [fr *maka* ground + *ipuskica* to press together] : to press on the ground, to lie flat on the ground — **makipuskil** *vn contrac* : to press flat on the ground < *~ ihpeic'iya* to throw one's self on the ground >

ma·ki·pu·sli \ma-k̇í-ṗu-sli\ *adv* : with the face on the ground, prone — **makipusli·ya** *adv* : bowed down to the ground

ma·ki·san·pa \ma-k̇í-saŋ-pa\ *n* : the next season

ma·ki·wan·yan·ke \ma-k̇í-waŋ-yaŋ-ke\ *n* : a compass, a surveyor

ma·ki·wo·hli·ya \ma-k̇í-wo-ḣli-ya\ *adv perhaps* : sticking tight in the ground < *Tawahunkeza kin on akigna ~ cawapin kte lo* With his spear I shall stab fixing him tight to the ground. > – B.H.89.13

ma·ki·ya·gle \ma-k̇í-ya-gle\ *v* : to place or hold on the ground < *~ yuzin na akan ihpeic'iya* he held it (the sword) on the ground and he threw himself on it. > — **makiyagle·ya** *adv* : to the ground, to the earth < *Ozan kin ~ okinahlece* He trampled the bed-curtains on the ground> – B.H.90.22, 268.7

ma·ki·ya·ka·san·ni \ma-k̇í-ya-k̇a-saŋ-ni\ *n* : a side or part of a country

ma·ki·ya·pa \ma-k̇í-ya-pa\ *va perhaps* makiya·wa·pa : to hit the ground, as in falling < *Ite makiyamapa* My face hit the ground. > – B.H.59.2

ma·ki·ya·p'o·ya \ma·k̇í-ya-p'o-ya\ *adv perhaps* : raising much dust < *~ upi* They came with a cloud of dust, *i.e.* they raise much dust as they are coming. > – Bl

ma·ki·ye·ya \ma-k̇í-ye-ya\ *v* : to shove aside onto the ground < *Wicaša ~ yunka* A man lies shoved aside onto the ground, *i.e.* sick and forsaken. > – *Syn* MAKÓKAHCIYELA

ma·ki·yo·ki·pi \ma-k̇í-yo-k̇i-ṗi\ *vn* : to be acclimated,

to like it in a certain country — **makiyokipi·ya** *va* : to acclimate - Bl WI
ma·ki·yu·blu \ma-k̇í-yu-blu\ *n* : a plow < ~ *iwoju* a lister > - EB
ma·ki·yu·hin·he \ma-k̇í-yu-hiŋ-he\ *n* : a cultivator
ma·ki·yu·hin·te \ma-k̇í-yu-hiŋ-te\ *n* : a harrow
ma·ki·yu·hlo·ke \ma-k̇í-yu-ḣlo-k̇e\ *n* : an auger to dig post holes
ma·ki·yu·pte \ma-k̇í-yu-ṗte\ *n* : a breaking plow, the wheel or cutter of a breaker
ma·ki·yu·tan \ma-k̇í-yu-ṫaŋ\ *n* [fr *maku* breast + *iyutan* to try] : a cinch, a saddle girth
ma·ki·yu·t'in·ze \ma-k̇í-yu-t'iŋ-ze\ *n* : a surcingle, girth
ma·ko·bla·ye \ma-k̇ó-bla-ye\ *n* : a plain
ma·ko·ca·je·ya·te \ma-k̇ó-ca-je-ya-te\ *n* : the direction on a letter
ma·ko·ce \ma-k̇ó-ce\ *n* : a country, a place
~ *átan'in* a mirage ~ *iwanyankapi* surveyors
~ *oihanke* a globe ~ *opašpe tanka* a country
~ *owapi* a map, maps - P Bl
ma·ko·gmi·gma \ma-k̇ó-gmi-gma\ *n* : a globe - P
ma·ko·hlo·ka \ma-k̇ó-ḣlo-k̇a\ *n* : a hole in the ground, a cave < ~ *wan el mahel iyaya* He went on deep into a cave. >
ma·ko·i·ca·go \ma-kó-i-ca-ġo\ *n* : a boundary line of land - B.H.39.18
ma·ko·ka·hci·ye·la \ma-kó-k̇a-ḣci-ye-la\ *adv* : floating about on the ground < ~ *hpaya* He lies around going from place to place, *i.e.* nobody looks after him. > - Bl
ma·ko·ka·winh \ma-k̇ó-k̇a-wiŋḣ\ *adv* : around the world - *Syn* MAKIGLUKŠAN WE
ma·ko·ko·can·ku \ma-k̇ó-k̇o-caŋ-k̇u\ *n* : a road with fences on each side - BT Bl
ma·ko·k'a·pi \ma-k̇ó-k'a-pi\ *n* : a bulwark, an intrenchment - P
ma·ko·k'e \ma-k̇ō'-k'e\ *n* : a dug-out, a pit - B.H.108.25
ma·ko·mni·ca hu \ma-k̇ó-mni-ca hu\ *n* : james' cristabella, the earth bean, cristatella jamesii, the caper family — **makomnica hu hlo·hlota** *n* : the silky sophora, sophora sericea, the pulse family - D.97 Bl #57, 301
ma·kon·ca·ge \ma-k̇óŋ-ca-ġe\ *n* : a season, the seasons
ma·ko·pa·špe \ma-k̇ó-ṗa-špe\ *n* [fr *maka* land + *opašpe* a piece cut off] : a section or so of land - *See* makáowašpe
ma·ko·p'o·ya *also* **makaop'oya** \ma-kó-p'o-ya\ *v* : to raise dust < ~ *upi* They come raising the dust. > - Bl
ma·ko·skan \ma-k̇ó-sk̇aŋ\ *adv* : for naught, in vain — *n* : a place where no one dwells
ma·ko·skanl \ma-k̇ó-sk̇anl\ *adv* : in the wilderness < *Yunkan hihanna el wicaša k'on išnala ~ aunyanpi ške.* And then in the morning, it was reported we brought that man who had been alone in the wilderness. *Wanna lila tehan išnala ~ unpi keye* And he says we were alone in the wilderness for a very long time. > - Note: the word doubtfully carries the meaning: "for naught or in vain"
ma·ko·skan·tu \ma-k̇ó-sk̇an-ṫu\ *adv* and *n* : desert-like, away from trees or dwellings — **makoskantu·ya** *adv* : away from any dwelling — **makoskantuya·kel** \ma-k̇ó-sk̇aŋ-ṫu-ya-k̇el\ *adv* : in a desert place - B.H.180.15
ma·ko·sma·ka \ma-k̇ó-sma-ka\ *n* [fr *maka* land + *osmaka*] : a ditch, any low place
ma·ko·ši·ca \ma-k̇ó-ši-ca\ *n* : bad land, desert
ma·ko·ši·ce peji ḣo·ta \ma-k̇ó-ši-ce pe-ǰi ḣo-ta\ *n* : the long-leaved mugwort, artemisia longifolia, the composite family - Note: it is found in the South Dakota Bad Lands - Bl #144

ma·ko·šla \ma-k̇ō'-šla\ *n* : bare ground - D.205
ma·ko·ta·he·na \ma-k̇ó-ta-hè-na\ *adv* : far from any dwelling - Bl
ma·ko·wa·ki·c'i·pa \ma-k̇ó-wa-k̇i-c'i-ṗa\ *n* : a place or little hollowing, a light hollow or depression in the prairie
ma·ko·wan·ca \ma-k̇ó-waŋ-ca\ *n* : all the earth — **makowanca·ya** *adv* : all over the world < *Makowancaya sitomniyan omawani* All over the world afoot I walk, as is the lyric of an old song. >
ma·ko·wa·pi \ma-k̇ó-wa-pi\ *n* : a map of a country, maps
ma·ko·wa·špe \ma-k̇ó-wa-špe\ *n* : surveyed land - *See* makáowašpe
ma·kte·ka \ma-kṫé-k̇a\ *express* ni·kteka [fr *ma* me + *kte* kill + *ka* one concerned]: "That kills me.", *i.e.* overcomes me, as is said by one loving irresistibly a person or catching a fancy for something - *Syn* IMÁCUKA
ma·ku \ma-k̇ú\ *n* : the breast
ma·ku·a·ka·hpe \ma-k̇ú-a-k̇a-ḣpe\ *n* : a bib, a napkin
ma·ku·hu \ma-k̇ú-hu\ *n* : the breastbone, the sternum
ma·ku·i·pa·ti·tan \ma-k̇ú-i-pa-ti-taŋ\ *n* : a breast strap, going between the forelegs of a horse
ma·ku·nu·snun·ja \ma-k̇ú-nu-snuŋ-ja\ *n* : the lower extremity of the breastbone
ma·ku·pin·kpa \ma-k̇ú-ṗiŋ-kṗa\ *n* : the end of the breast, the part just above the navel
ma k'e·ya \ma k'é-ya\ *interj express* : Rediculous!, as said in answer to a remark considered foolish or rediculous - Note: the *express* is used by women Cf wan k'eya B.H.43.25, 111.13
ma·k'e·ya·ke s'e \ma-k'é-ya-k̇e s'e\ *adv* : apparently unwilling < ~ *ayuštanpi* Evidently unwillingly did they stop it. >
ma·ma \má-ma\ *n* : a woman's breast
ma·ni \má-ni\ *vn* ma·wá·ni : to walk
ma·ni·ca \ma-ní-ca\ *vn 1st pers singl of* níca : I have none
ma·ni·han \má-ni-haŋ\ *part* : walking — **mani·kel** \má-ni-k̇el\ *adv* : walk-ing
ma·ni·ki·ya \má-ni-k̇i-ya\ *va* mani·wa·kiya : to cause to walk
ma·nil \ma-níl\ *adv* : abroad, away from the house, into the wilderness < ~ *ya* to go abroad, ~ *tehanl eihpeya wicaši* He told them to take and leave him far from his house. > - B.H.50.25
ma·ni·o·pa·wa·kin·ye·la \má-ni-ò-ṗa-wa-k̇iŋ-ye-la\ *n* : the sandpiper
ma·ni·ta·ki·ya \ma-ní-ṫa-k̇i-ya\ *adv* : disappearing from camp < ~ *iyaya* to go away from camp without notice, *Koškalaka k'on he (wanagi) ḣeyab iyaya na ~ gla* The young man (his spirit) went elsewhere and disappearing from camp he was on his way home, *.i.e.* he disappeared from camp without giving a reason why, for doing something wrong apparently. *Hece ~ tacejikšica k'u wo* So give him some paunch fat as he disappears from camp. > - Bl MS.166 and 55
ma·ni·tu·ka·la \ma-ní-ṫu-ka-la\ *n* : a little guardian spirit < "~ *sinte ónamašloke*" "The little guardian spirit's tail ran off with me", as children sing who are playing, running about zigzag and holding a shawl up behind

\a\ father \e\ they \i\ machine \o\ smoke \u\ lunar \an, aŋ\ blanc Fr. \in, iŋ\ ink \on, oŋ, un, uŋ\ soon, confier Fr. \c\ chair \ġ\ machen Ger. \j\ fusion \clusters: bl, gn, kp, hšl, etc... \ b[e]lo ... said with a slight vowel
See more in the Introduction, Guide to Pronunciation

sailing it > – Bl

ma·ni·yan \má-ni-yaŋ\ *adv* : walking < *Maka gi oyuze el wicoti na etanhan zuya yapi maka ~* They dwelt at the brown earth quarry and from there they went on the warpath, traveling afoot. *Hecel nupin ~ unpi* For that reason we both are walking. *Cokata ~ waun* I am walking in the midst. *maniye s'e* as though taking a walk, *Eyin nahan maga šapa ca maniye s'e kagle* "He had his say, and then as if ambling along he takes home a goose that is filthy," as a woman might say teasing her brother-in-law when he goes. > – Bl

ma·non \ma-nóŋ\ *va* ma·wá·non ma·ún·non·pi : to steal anything — **manon·pi** *n* : stealing, theft

man *or* **ma** \maŋ\ *interj* : Look here! < *Man le man!* Get a look at this!, as a woman says, as a man *Wan le Wan!* > – Bl

man·ka \maŋ-ká\ *vn* 1st *pers singl of* yanká : I am, or I sit — *n* : a skunk – Note: maká

man·ka zin·tka·la *or* **makaowanke** \maŋ-ká ziŋ-tkà-la\ *n* : a bobolink – FR

ma·pi·ȟa *or* **witapiȟa** *or* **matapiȟa** \má-ṗi-ȟa\ \wi-tá-pi-ȟa\ \ma-tá-hi-ȟa\ *n* : a toad – Note: R gives in two of these variations ...ȟa ; whereas Buechel gives a glottal stop in *mapih'a*

ma·sce·ga \ma-scé-ga\ *n* [fr *maza* iron + *ceġa* pot] : a kettle, a metal pot

ma·si·ca·špe \ma-sí-ca-špe\ *n* : a chisel

ma·si·wan·yan·ke \ma-sí-waŋ-yaŋ-ke\ *n* : a telescope, a field glass, a microscope

ma·ska·pe *or* **maskapa** \ma-sk̇a-ṗe\ *or* \ma-ská-ṗa\ *n* [fr *maza* iron + *kapa* to pound] : a blacksmith – Note: there is question of the ṗ B.H.302.9

ma·skin·ska *or* **mazakinska** \ma-sk̇íŋ-ska\ *n* : a metal spoon, a spoon

ma·s'a·hi \ma-s'á-hi\ *v* mas'a·wa·hi : to arrive with freight, as iron goods were often with what formerly was hauled to reservation agencies – IS

ma·s'a·pa·pi can \ma-s'á-pa-pi caŋ\ *n* : a telephone post – Bl

ma·s'can·wa·pa·i·ka \ma-s'cáŋ-wa-pa-i-ka\ *n* : a check strap

ma·s'can·ya·pa \ma-s'cáŋ-ya-pa\ *n* : a bridle < ~ *ikceka* a riding brikle > — **mas'canyapa iku swu** *n* : a bridle bit with dangling ornaments – LB

ma·s'i·ci·ca·ȟa·ȟa *or perhaps* **mas'icicagaga** \ma-s'í-ci-ca-ȟa-ȟa\ *n* [fr *maza* iron + *ici* together + *kagaga* or perhaps *kagege* sew] : a chain, iron made in links

ma·s'i·gmun·ke \ma-s'í-gmuŋ-ke\ *n* : a trap – Note: *cápa* is a *deriv* of the word *cap'igmunke* a beaver trap

ma·s'i·ku·še \ma-s'í-k̇u-še\ *n* : a buckle – P Bl

ma·s'i·yu·me \ma-s'í-yu-me\ *n* : a file to form wood or metal

ma·s'pe·pe \ma-s'ṗe-ṗe\ *n* : barbed wire

ma·s'wa·kši·ca \ma-s'wá-kši-ca\ *n* : tin plates

ma·s'wi·ca·ye·ge \ma-s'wí-ca-ye-ġe\ *n* : a sewing machine – Note: the *y* , instead of the *ġ*

ma·s'wi·con·pi \ma-s'wí-coŋ-pi\ *n* : a frying pan

ma·s'wi·yo·gli \ma-s'wí-yo-gli\ *n* : a steel on which to sharpen knives

ma·s'wi·yo-ka-tan \ma-s'wí-yo-ka-taŋ\ *n* : a nail

ma·s'wo·gna·ka \ma-s'wō'-gna-k̇a\ *n* : canned food

ma·še \ma-šé\ *n* : a man's brother-in-law, a title given if they are on good terms – Cf *wašé* a woman's sister-in-law *Syn* TANHÁN Sbj

ma·še·ya \ma-šé-ya\ *va* : to have for a *mašé* , a brother-in-law *Syn* TANHÁNYA

ma·ške \má-ške\ *n* : a friend; a word used by women as men say *kóla* — **maškeya** \ma-šké-ya\ *va* maške·wa·ya : to have, *i.e.* for a woman, for a female friend

ma·šle·ca *or* **mayašleca** \mā'-šle-ca\ \ma-yá-šle-ca\ *n* : a coyote

ma·šte \ma-šṫé\ *adj* : warm, hot, as applied to weather

ma·šte·a·gli·han \ma-šṫé-a-gli-haŋ\ *vn* maštea·ma·glihan : to get a sunstroke

ma·šte·can·han·pa \ma-šṫé-caŋ-haŋ-ṗa\ *n* : slippers, warm weather shoes

ma·šte·ko \ma-šṫé-k̇o\ *n* : a horned lark perhaps, a small grayish bird, who sing as they rise in flight: oosh-oosh-oosh – *See* maštékola BE

ma·šte·ko·la \ma-šṫé-k̇o-la\ *n* : the horned lark *ištanica tanka* – Note: the name is *deriv* from *mašteko,* and to desire warm weather. The Lakota called it that because there would be good weather (warm) whenever it went straight up into the air, singing: *Mašteko.* Cf ptehiko, oh'anko, osniko, and also the Handbook of Birds of the Western U. S. by Florence Meriman Bailey, pg. 247. Bs

ma·šte·na·pta·pta \ma-šṫé-na-pṫa-pṫa\ *n* : hot waving air, as on a hot day over a field, or over a stove

ma·šte·o·sni \ma-šṫé-o-sni\ *adj* : clear and cold, cold and bright

ma·šte·šte \ma-šṫé-šṫe\ *adj red of* mašte : warm and hot weather

ma·šte·t'a \ma-šṫé-t'a\ *vn* : to be killed by heat

ma·šte wa·po·štan \ma-šṫé wa-pò-staŋ\ *n* : a summer bonnet

ma·šte·ya \ma-šṫé-ya\ *adv* : in a warm state, warmly — **mašteya·kel** \ma-šṫé-ya-k̇el\ *adv* : warmly, hotly

ma·štin·ca *or* **maštinca·la** \ma-šṫíŋ-ca\ *n* : the rabbit

Ma·štin·ca·la Wi·ca·ša *or* **Maštincala Ha Šina In** \Ma-šṫíŋ-ca-la Wi-cà-ša\ \Ma-šṫíŋ-ca-la Ha Ši-nà Iŋ\ *np* : the Cree Indians, a neighbor to the Dakotas – Bl

ma·štin·ca pu·te \ma-šṫíŋ-ca pu-tè\ *n* : the buffalo berry or rabbit berry — **maštinca pute can** *or* **maštinca pute hu can** *n* : the buffalo berry bush bearing red edible berries, argentea oleaster family – Bl #223

ma·štin·sa·pa *or* **maštinsapc·la** \ma-šṫíŋ-sa-ṗa\ *n* : the common rabbit, the cotton-tail rabbit — **maštin·ska** *n* : the hare or jackrabbit, the prairie rabbit – Bl

ma·ta·pi·ȟa \ma-tá-ṗi-ȟa\ *n* : the toad – Note: D pronounces the word *matápeh'a* – D.47

ma·te·te \ma-ṫe'-ṫe\ *n* [fr Dakota *tete* the rim or edge of anything] : the side or rim, the edge of anything, *e.g.* of a creek, table, *etc* – Note: the Lakota for *tete* is *icéte*

ma·to \ma-tó\ *n* : the gray or polar bear < ~ *s'e sicuha ȟolyahci* Bear-like the soles of his shoes are hashed, as is said when the soles of one's shoes are worn out. > – Bl

ma·to cin·ca·la \ma-tó ciŋ-cà-la\ *n* : a bear's cub

ma·to ȟo·ta \ma-tó ȟò-ṫa\ *n* : the grizzly bear

ma·to·ki·ci·ya·pi \ma-tó-ki-ci-ya-pi\ *n* : a game played by boys: the boy acting the bear hides in the bushes while the hunters are outside holding switches. He goes for them *iyáhpaya,* to grab them, tickling them while they hit him with their switches. *Mato minišoše kin hehanyan unkuwapi* We hunted bears as far as the Missouri, as was said in former times – Bl

ma·to ta·span \ma-tó ta-spàŋ\ *n* : the round-leaved hawthorn, crataegus chrysocarpa; it is seen in the South Dakota Badlands – RO #256

ma·to ta·tin·psi·la \ma-tó ta-ṫìŋ-psi-la\ *n* : the large bracted psoralea, psoralea cuspidata, the pulse family – Note: Bl says it has the same qualities as the *aunyeyapi.* It is also a medicine Bl #217

Ma·to Ti·pi·la \Ma-tó Ṫi-p̣i-la\ *np* : the Gemini, Castor and Pollux being the prominent stars in a constellation of eight stars, as they say, standing in a circle - Note: BT denied the name applies to Gemini BT Mh

ma·tu·gna *or* **matuška** \ma-ṫú-gna\ *n* : the crayfish or crawfish < ~ *s'e ti šikšica* Like a crawfish it is a really a poor place in which one lives, as they say of one who has a poor house. ~ *ok'e unyin kte* Let's us go dig up crayfish, the reason being that their claws can be boiled and treated with grease, whereupon they turn red and were once used for ornaments. ~ *kinhan mniawakaštan ktelo* If they are crawfish I shall wash them with water, *i.e.* as if they were thirsty. > - Bl

ma·ya \ma-yá\ *n* : a bank, a steep place *e.g.* along a river

ma·ya·ca \má-ya-ca\ *n* : the coyote - *Syn* ŠUNKMANITU

ma·ya·gli·he·ya \ma-yá-gli-he-ya\ *n* : a steep bank < *Yunkan mni kin okigluslece na itannunk ~ s'e yunke, na ocokanyan ocanku kahya pusyela he. ~ kin ataya inyan* He split the water in two, and on both sides there lay it seemed a steep bank, and right in the middle there was lay a dried road. The sheer cliff was entirely rock. > - D.29

ma·yal \ma-yál\ *adv* : deep in the forest < *Ozuye tanka k'un ~ yewicaye* That large warparty had forced them deep into the forest. > - MS.563

ma·ya·šle \má-ya-šle\ *n* : the jackal, a small species of wolf

ma·ya·šle·ca \ma-yá-šle-ca\ *or* \má-ya-šle-ca\ *n* : a coyote < *Máyašlecala s'e ite šok'ínyan* His face is a midget like that of a coyote, as they say of a man with a small face. > - Bl

ma·za \má-za\ *n* : metal of any kind —

máza aglèhan *or* máza aglèhe *n* : an anvil
máza aglìheya *v* máza aglìhe·wa·ya : to print - Bl
mázablaska *n* : a flat iron
mázacah'ìcazo *n* : skates
mázacanku *n* : a train, a railroad
máza cánku p̣etìjanjan *n* : a conductor's lantern
mázacanku ṫìpi *n* : a railroad car - RH
mázacega *n* : a kettle, an iron pot
mázaceškìkan *n* : metal buttons
mázacola wìnah'on *n* : a radio - *Syn* IKAN COLA MAS'APAPI *or* TATÚYE ON WÍNAH'ON
máza eglè *v* **1** : to set a trap **2** : to put up a store - Bl
mázahlahla *n* : a bell
mázaìciyok̇ihe *n* : a chain
mázaiyòk̇aṫan *n* : nails
mázaiyòkatkuge *n* : a nut, iron nuts for bolts
mázak̇aga *n* : a worker in metal, a blacksmith - *See* maz'kape
mázakan *n* : a gun, rifle < *Tona ~ luhapi oyasin u po* All those who have a rifle come. >
mázakan i *n* : the muzzle of a gun, the barrel of a gun
mázakan i nùnpa *n* : a double-barreled gun
mázakan ìyopazan *n* : the tubes or ferrules which hold in the ramrod, the ramrod itself
mázakan iyòpuhli *n* : gun-wadding
mázakannawàte *n* : the plate of a gunlock, a gunlock
mázakannoge *n* : a gun lock, *esp* the pan, the nipple
mázakanpahu *n* : the breech of a gun
mázakan šup̣ùte *n* : the butt of a gun
mázakan ùta *v* : to shoot, fire off a gun
mázak̇insk̇a *n* : an iron spoon, a spoon
mázalowànk̇iyap̣i *n* : a loud speaker, a sound recorder a talking machine
mázamna *v* : to smell of iron < ~ *s'e woyaka* to speak smelling like iron, as is said when a person of his serious troubles and difficulties that are hard to listen to, as when using harsh words. > - BE
mázanapsìohli *n* : finger-rings
mázaocèṫi *n* : an iron fireplace, a stove
mazápa *v* mazá·wa·pa : to telephone
mázap̣ep̣e *n* : barbwire
mázap̣ošla *n* : a tack with a big round head, *e.g.* a thumbtack
mázapsonpsonla *n* : wire
mázasapa *n* : iron, black metal
mázasiìnahtake *n* : a spur
mázaska *n* **1** : money, a dollar **2** : white metal, silver
mázaska aònatake *n* : a safe
mázaska el ahìgle *v* : to bet - Bl P
mázaska ignì *or* mázaska kamnà *v* : to raise money
mázaska kpànla *n* : currency, change
mázaska ògnake *n* : a pocket book, a money bag
mazáskaognake *n* : a safe
mázaska omnàye *n* : the treasury
mázaska wanàp'in *n* : a silver medal
mázaska wanjìla *n* : one dollar
mázaskazi *n* : gold, yellow silver
mázasu *n* : a bullet, bullets, shots, cartridges
mázasu ìšloya *n* : something in which to melt lead
mázasu ìyokaštan *n* : bullet molds
máza sutà *n* : steel
mázaša *n* : copper, red metal
mázašala *n* : a penny - Note: the penny which once a person received who was appointed to collect money for the fourth of July celebration
mázaškanškan *n* : a clock, a watch
mázaškanškan ìkan *n* : a watch chain and fob
mázaškanškan tànka *n* : a clock
mázaškòpa *n* : a hook
mázašloyàpi *n* : pewter, so called because it is used for running on the bowls of Dakota pipes
mázašnkàkanyanka *n* : a bicycle
mázawakan *n* : a gun, a rifle
mázawakan šup̣ùte *n* : the butt of a gun
mázawakan ùta *n* : to shoot a gun, fire off a gun
mázawakšica *n* : tin or iron pans
mázawiyowa *n* : a pen - Note: *canwiyowa* a pencil
mázawiyùhomni *n* : a jack-screw - Bl
mázawiyuṫe *n* : a carpenter's square
máza wìyuwanka aya *n* : a jack-screw - Bl
mázawoyuspa *n* : pincers, tongs - Bl
mázayajopi *n* : brass instruments, a brass band
mázazazèca *n* : screen wire
mázazi *n* : copper, yellow metal

ma·zcan·ya·pa \má-zcaŋ-ya-pa\ *or* \má-s'caŋ-ya-pa\ *n* : a bridle

ma·zi·cu·ke·ya \má-zi-cu-ke-ya\ *n* : a chain

ma·zi·wan·ke \ma-zí-waŋ-ke\ *n abbrev of* maziwanyanke **a** : an opera glass **b** : a telescope < *Na ~ yeyapi* They extended a telescope. >

\a\ father \e\ they \i\ machine \o\ smoke \u\ lunar \an, aŋ\ blanc Fr. \in, iŋ\ ink \on, oŋ, un, uŋ\ soon, confier Fr. \c\ chair \ġ\ machen Ger. \j\ fusion \clusters: bl, gn, kp, hšl, etc... \ b^e^lo ... said with a slight vowel
See more in the Introduction, Guide to Pronunciation

ma·zi·wan·yan·ke \ma-zí-waŋ-yaŋ-ke\ *n* : any scope
ma·zi·ya·pa \ma-zí-ya-pa\ *n* : a hammer
ma·zi·yu·ho·mni \ma-zí-yu-hò-mni\ *n* **1** : a wrench **2** : a screw driver **3** : a drill with which to make holes
[1]**ma·zi·yu·hlo·ke** \ma-zí-yu-ȟlo-ke\ *n* : a can opener
[2]**ma·zi·yu·hlo·ke** \ma-zi-yú-ȟlo-ke\ *n* : a drill to make holes into iron
ma·zi·yu·ji·pe \ma-zí-yu-ǰi-ṗe\ *n* : tongs
ma·zi·yu·kce \ma-zí-yu-kce\ *n* : a trimmer's snip
ma·zi·yu·wi \ma-zí-yu-wi\ *n* : bridle bits
ma·zkin·ška \ma-zk̇íŋ-ška\ *n* : an iron spoon
ma·zo·pi·ye \ma-zó-ṗi-ye\ *n* : a store < ~ *wicaša* a trader, a merchant >
ma·zo·yu·spe \ma-zó-yu-spe\ *n* : a pliers
ma·z'i·ca·kse \má-z'i-ca-kse\ *n* : a chisel
ma·z'i·gmun·ke *or* **mas'igmunke** \ma-z'í-gmun-ke\ *n* : a trap
ma·z'i·pa·me \ma-z'í-ṗa-me\ *n* : a file with which to make smooth surfaces
ma·z'i·yo·ka·tan \ma-z'í-yo-k̇a-ṫaŋ\ *n* : a nail
ma·z'ka·pe \ma-z'k̇á-ṗe\ *n* [fr *maza* metal + *kapa* to pound] : a blacksmith, a worker of metal – *See* maskápe
ma·z'o·ce·ti \ma-z'ó-ce-ti\ *n* : a stove
mi \mi\ *pron poss in comp* : my or mine, me, for me or to me < *Mikte* He kills for me. > – *See* ni
[1]**mi·ca** \mi-cá\ *pron* and *prep in comp of* kicá : for me < *Opemicaton* He buys for me. >
[2]**mi·ca** \mi-cá\ *n* : the hip area < *tamíca* lean meat on the side of an animal near the rump, *tamícahu* the hipbone > – Cf R who renders the meaning of the word as meat from near the rump. But BD gave the Lakota as here illustrated – R BD
mi·ca·ga \mí-ca-ġa\ *v of* kicága : to make to or for one
mi·ca·hu *or* **micaki** \mi-cá-hu\ \mí-ca-k̇i\ *n* : the bone near the hip-bone – R Bl
mi·ca·ksi·ca \mí-ca-ksi-ca\ *n* : a small wolf – *See* míyaca *and* míyašleca
mi·ca·pe·ca \mí-ca-ṗe-ca\ *n* : porcupine grass, needle spear, or devil's grass, a grass armed with long sharp beard, stipa spartea, the grass family < ~ *ota kinhan, waniyetu wašme kte* When there is much porcupine grass the winter snow will be deep. > – WE RH #178
mi·ca·pe·ca on ki·ci·o·pi \mí-ca-ṗe-ca oŋ ki-cì-o-pi\ *n* : a mischievous pastime in which boys once would take a bunch of devil's grass, *micapeca*, and to hurt those without coats on, throw it on them – *Syn* WÍCAPECA
mi·ci \mí-ci\ *pron* with *prep* kici : for me, *not* with me < *mici un* in my stead, or for me, but *kici maun* with me, *Witanšna un num omak'u po; hena cannunpa miciyuhapi kte lo* Two virgins give me some food; they will hold the pipe for me. >
mi·ci·ca·ya \mi-cí-ca-ya\ *v* : to be with me – Cf kicícaya Pb.45
mi·c'i \mi-c'í\ *pron refl* : myself < *Mic'ikte* I kill myself, *i.e.* for myself. *Mic'icaga* I make for myself, or I make myself. > – Cf nic'í *and* ic'í
mi·gnag \mi-gnág\ *va contrac of* mignaka : to gird with < ~ *waun* I gird myself with it. >
[1]**mi·gna·ka** \mi-gná-k̇a\ *va* mi·wa·gnaka : to put in under the girdle *e.g.* a knife or hatchet, to wear around the loins < *Hohumila wan ~ ; canke ikikcu.* And so he took it back, and he wore the bone knife under his belt. *Ungna kapemniyan micignake ci* It may be a fact that I put it hanging under your belt, *i.e.* boasting. > – Note: the word seems to be used usually with *míla* or in *ref* to *míla* – D.33 Bl
[2]**mi·gna·ka** \mí-gna-ka\ *v of* kignaka : he lays up for me
mi·la \mí-la\ *n* : a big knife < *hohu* ~ a modern but old knife, *tablo* ~ a modern knife >
mi·la·han·ska \mí-la-haŋ-ska\ *n* **1** : a long knife **2** : an American
mi·la·ka·š'in \mí-la-ka-š'iŋ\ *n* : a sickle
mi·la·pa·ksa \mí-la-pa-ksa\ *n* : table knives, round-pointed knives, a case knife
mi·la·ya \mí-la-ya\ *va* míla·wa·ya : to have or use for a knife
mi·li·yu·ma \mí-li-yu-ma\ *n* : a grind stone
mi·ma *or* **mime** \mi-má\ *adj* : round, circular — **mi·me·la** \mi-mé-la\ *adj* : round as is a disk, but not as a ball, which is *gmigméla*
mi·me·la wa·hca·zi \mi-mé-la wà-ȟca-zi\ *n* : the stiff or hard-leaved goldenrod, solidago rigida – *Syn* TAL'AGNAKE, CANHLOGA MAKA AYUBLAYA, WAHPE APE BLASKASKA
mi·me·ya \mi-mé-ya\ *adv* : in a circle < ~ *najinpi* They stood in a circle. >
mi·me·ye·la \mi-mé-ye-la\ *adv* : round < ~ *yuktan* to bend round by hand > – Bl MS.349
mi·na \mí-na\ *n* : a knife – Note: this is the Santee form of the word which is used also by the Lakota who otherwise would use *míla*
mi·ni *or* **mni** \mi-ní\ *n* : water
mi·ni·ma·hel zu·ze·ca \mi-ní-ma-hel zu-zè-ca\ *n* : a water snake – Bl
mi·ni·o·hu·ta \mi-ní-o-hu-ṫa a-glà-gla wa-ȟcá-zi\ *n* : the stickseed, beggar's tick, beggar's lice, the stickseed sunflower, sticktight, pitchforks, bur marigold, bidens glaucescens, the composite family – BT #68
mi·ni·o·pa·kin·ye·la *or* **miniopa·wakinyela** \mi-ni-ó-pa-k̇iŋ-yè-la\ *n* : the spotted sand piper – Note: it flies on the water and teeters often as it roams the shore Bl
mi·ni·san·tu·hu \mi-ni-sáŋ-tu-hu\ *n* : schweintz cyperus, cyperus schweinitzii, the sedge family – LB #247
mi·ni·wi·ca·gna·ška can \mi-ní-wi-ca-gna-ška caŋ\ *n* : the water goose-berry bush
min·ska \míŋ-sk̇a\ *n* : a piece of tin with which to scrape hides – Note: there may be another name for this tool BD
mi·o·gla·s'in \mí-o-gla-s'iŋ\ *n* : a mirror
mi·o·gle *or* **miyogli** \mí-o-gle\ *n* [fr *mila* knife + *egle* or *ogle* to place] : a whetstone, a razor strop
mi·o·ju·ha \mi-ó-ju-ha\ *n* : a knife sheath
mi·ska \mí-ska\ *n* : a hide scraper to remove hair – *Syn* TAHÍNCACICE
miš \miš\ *pron* : I < ~ *miye* I myself >
mi·šna·ka \mi-šná-k̇a\ *pron* and *adv* : I alone < *mišnak̇es'e* as if I alone>
mi·šna·la \mi-šná-la\ *pron* : I alone < *mišnalakes'e* as if I alone >
mi·šna·san·ni·ca \mi-šná-saŋ-nì-ca\ *adv* : on my side
mi·ta \mi-tá\ *pron pref* : my, mine
mi·ta·he \mí-ta-he\ *n* : a tomahawk-like weapon, consisting of a wooden handle and a number of knives protruding from one side at the other end – *Syn* CANMÍLOKATANPI
mi·ta·wa \mi-tá-wa\ *pron adj* ni·tawa táwa : my, mine < *Nimitawa ktelo* You will be mine. *Unnitawapi kte lo* We will be yours. > – Note: doubtful are the *express, Manitawa kte* I will be yours, and *Niunkitawapi kte* You will be ours.
mi·wa·kan \mí-wa-kaŋ\ *n* : a sword < ~ *iyuze* the hilt

of a sword > – P

Mi·wa·tan·ni \Mi-wá-ṫaŋ-ni\ *np* : the Mandan tribe

mi·wo·šta·ke \mí-wo-šṫa-ḱe\ *n* [fr *mi* for me + *woštaka* what is soft like ice] : a blunt-pointed arrow, *i.e.* one all of wood with the head thicker than the shaft, and used to kill birds – Bl

mi·ya·ca \mí-ya-ca\ *n* : the prairie wolf – *Syn* MÍCAKSICA

mi·ya·pa·he \mí-ya-ṗa-he\ *n* : anything with which to cover the loins, such as was perhaps done for Jesus on the Cross had < ~ *kiton* to wear a loin cloth > — **miyapehe·kiya** \mí-ya-ṗe-he-ḱi-ya\ *va* : to use as a cover for the loins < *šiná* ~ to use a robe for a cover >

mi·ya·šle·ca \mí-ya-šle-ca\ *n* : the coyote, a small kind of wolf – *Syn* MÍCAKSICA

mi·ye \mí-ye\ *pron* : I, me

mi·ye·cin \mi-yé-ciŋ\ *pron abbrev of* miyécinka : I myself, I alone — **miyecin·ka** \mi-yé-ciŋ-ḱa\ *pron* : I myself, I alone – *Syn* MIYECUHCI

mi·ye·cu·hci \mi-yé-cu-ȟci\ *pron emph* : I my very self – *Syn* MIYECINKA

mi·ye·k'e \mi-yĕ'-k'e\ *pron emph* : even I, such a one as I — **miyek'eš** *pron emph superl* : I myself, of all people it should be me – R Bl

mi·yeš \mi-yéš\ *pron emph* : I

mi·yo·gla·s'in \mí-yo-gla-s'iŋ\ *n* : a mirror, looking-glass, round mirrors tastened to a sash called *ptanhá wanáp'i'* an otter skin necklace < ~ *hiyuya* to give a signal with mirror reflections > – Bl

mi·yo·gli *or* miogle \mí-yo-gli\ *n* : a whetstone

Mi·yo·gli·o·yu·ze \Mí-yo-gli-o-yù-ze\ *np* : the Whetstone Agency

mi·yo·ka·š'in \mí-yo-ḱa-š'iŋ\ *n* : the small of the back – *Syn* MIYOPAWEGA

mi·yo·kši·ja·pi *or* **miyukšija** \mí-yo-kši-ja-ṗi\ *n* : a pocket knife < ~ *opé* the blade of a pocket knife >

mi·yo·pa·we·ga \mí-yo-ṗa-we-ġa\ *n* : the small of the back, *i.e.* that part of the spinal column that is bent – Bl

mi·yu·gin·gin \mí-yu-ġiŋ-ġiŋ\ *adv* : disturbing one < *Agleška s'e ~ hingla mani* Like an alligator he walked suddenly disturbed, *i.e.* as in walking, the skin wrinkles as a lizard's; the comparison is in *ref* to old people. > – Bl WHL

mi·yu·ta·pa·pi mi·la \mi-yú-ṫa-ṗa-ṗi mì-la\ *n* : a kitchen knife, the upper part of which is missing – Bl

Mmla \M'm-la\ *np* : a fabulous being women once used when putting restless children to sleep < *Inila hpaya; Mmla wan úwe* Lie quiet; a Mmla is coming. > – Note: this is a very old word whose meaning is lost *Syn* CÍCIYE, ȞʼEYA PD

mna \mna\ *vn* : to swell < *Šupe mna la yelo* He took it that its guts were swollen. > – Cf yumná

mna·han \mna-háŋ\ *n* : a rip — *part* : ripped of itself — **mnahan·han** *part red* : ripping

mna·hca·hca \mna-ȟcá-ȟca\ *n* : the prairie lily – Note: the word is perhaps not used now

mna·i·c'i·ya \mna-í-c'i-ya\ *v* : to gather for one's self – B.H.193.25

mna·ki·ya \mna-ḱí-ya\ *va* : to take up a collection for one, to gather one's own < *Wahpaye mnakiyapi* They took up a collection for his expenses. > – B.H.260.20

mna·yan \mna-yáŋ\ *va* mna·wa·ya mna·ub·yan·pi : to gather together, collect — **mnayan·pi** *n* : a collecting, a collection — **mnaye·kiya** \mna-yé-ḱi-ya\ *va* mnaye·wa·kiya : to cause to collect < *Mazaska ota iye mnayewicakiye* He had them collect much money. >

[1]**mni** \mni\ *root syll* : suggesting a circular motion < *yumni* to turn round *e.g.* a crank by hand >

[2]**mni** \mni\ *n* : water — *va* wa·mni : to lay up to dry, spread out in the sun to dry — *v* 1st *pers singl of* ya < *mni kta* I will go. *Ni kta* You shall go. >

mni·a·gla·pe·pe·ya \mni-a-glá-ṗe-ṗe-ya\ or \mni-á-gla-ṗe-ṗe-ya\ *v* mniáglapepe·wa·ya : to make a flat stone skip on the water – Bl

mni·a·ka·štan \mni-á-ḱa-šṫaŋ\ *v* : to baptize, pour water on – Br WI

mni·a·li \mni-á-li\ *v* : to travel over the water < *Canhpan ~ inyanke* A loot, a mud hen travels over the water, *i.e.* using its wings. >

mni·a·pa·hta \mni-á-pa-ȟta\ *v* : to carry water in a skin — *n* : a skin bottle for water

mni·a·p'e·ye·la \mni-á-p'e-ye-la\ *n* : very shallow water – Bl

mni·ca·gla \mni-cá-gla\ *adv* : by the water

mni·ca·hmun \mni-cá-ȟmuŋ\ *n* : the noise made by a stream flowing over a rocky bed – *See* mnikáhmun – RTj

mni·ca·lu·za \mni-cá-lu-za\ *n* : rapid water

mni·ca·ški·lye·la \mni-cá-ški-lye-la\ *adv* : all wet, soaked, in the manner of pressing out water < ~ *unkomanipi* We traveled all soaked with water. > – *Syn* MNIH'EH'EYELA

mni·ca·šni·yan·yan·la \mni-cá-šni-yaŋ-yaŋ-la\ *adj* or *n* : rippling water < *Mni kin kašniyanyanla yunkelo* He lay along the rippling water. >

mni·ca·to·mni \mni-cá-to-mni\ *n* : a windmill

mni·ci·ya \mní-ci-ya\ *v* mni·mi·ciya mni·ni·ciya mni·un·ciya·pi *or* mni·unki·ciya·pi [fr perhaps *mni* I go] : to assemble *e.g.* a feast, to make a feast or call an assembly < *Taku on mniciyapi ca on inahni oyate kin witaya awicayau kte lo* You should hurry to bring the people together since there is some reason they are assembling. >

mni·co·co \mni-ćó-ćo\ *adj* : slushy

mni·c'a \mni-c'á\ *v* : to dig for water – Bl B.H.4920

mni·c'a·pi *or* **minic'api** \mni-c'á-pi\ *n* [fr *mni* water + *k'a* to dig] : a water well, a spring, a little hole made where the water gathers more plentifully – *Syn* WIWÍLA

mni·ga \mní-ġa\ – Cf yumníga Note: the word is not *deriv* from *mni* water

mni·hi·pi s'e \mni-hí-pi s'e\ *adv* : flooding, seeping in, as water into a house

mni·hi·ya·ya \mni-hí-ya-ya\ *n* : a flood of water

mni·ȟa·ȟa \mni-ȟá-ȟa\ *v* : to run with water < *Išta ~ manke* My eyes were running with water, *i.e.* water was running from my eyes. > – Bl

mni·ȟu·ha \mni-ȟú-ha\ *n* 1 : linen or cotton cloth, calico 2 : paper – Note: the word is not *deriv* of *mni* water

mni·ȟu·ha can·nun·pa \mni-ȟú-ha caŋ-nùŋ-pa\ *n* : a cigarette

mni·ȟu·ha i·pa·tin \mni-ȟú-ha i-pà-tiŋ\ *n* [fr *mniȟuha* cloth + *ipat'inza* to firm up by means of] : starch

mni·ȟu·ha i·yo·wa \mni-ȟú-ha i-yò-wa\ *n* : a pen, a pencil

\a\ father \e\ they \i\ machine \o\ smoke \u\ lunar \an, aŋ\ blanc Fr. \in, iŋ\ ink \on, oŋ, un, uŋ\ soon, confier Fr. \c\ chair \ġ\ machen Ger. \j\ fusion \clusters: bl, gn, kp, hšl, etc... \ b^e^lo ... said with a slight vowel **See more in the Introduction, Guide to Pronunciation**

mni·ȟu·ha ka·kan·ke \mni-ȟú-ha k̇ak̇àŋ-k̇e\ *n* : writing paper or newspaper
mni·ȟu·ha ma·za·ska \mni-ȟú-ha mà-za-ska\ *n* : paper money
mni·ȟu·ha ma·za·ska·i·i·cu \mni-ȟú-ha mà-za-ska-i-í-cu\ *n* : a bank check
mni·ȟu·ha o·gle \mni-ȟú-ha o-gle\ *n* : a shirt
mni·ȟu-ha o·han·zi \mni-ȟú-ha ò-haŋ-zi\ *n* : an awning, a shade
mni·ȟu·ha o·pe·mni can·nun·pa \mni-ȟú-ha o-pe-mni caŋ-nùŋ-pa\ *n* : a rolled cigaret
mni·ȟu·ha o·špu·la \mni-ȟú-ha o-šṗù-la\ *n* : pieces of *e.g.* calico *etc* – P Bl
mni·ȟu·ha o·wa·pi šni \mni-ȟú-ha o-wà-pi šni\ *n* : a blank, blanks
mni·ȟu·ha o·yu·šle·ce \mni-ȟú-ha o-yù-šle-ce\ *n* : a rag – R Bl P
mni·ȟu·ha pan·pan·la \mni-ȟú-ha paŋ-pàŋ-la\ *n* : silk
mni·ȟu·ha·ska \mni-ȟú-ha-ska\ *n* 1 : white cotton or muslin 2 : white paper, writing paper
mni·ȟu·ha·ska šo·ka \mni-ȟú-ha-ska šò-ka\ *n* : bed ticking
mni·ȟu·ha·ska zi·bzi·pe·la \mni-ȟú-ha-ska zi-bzì-pe-la\ *n* : fine muslin
mni·ȟu·ha to·hca \mni-ȟú-ha tò-ȟca\ *n* : blue cloth, as distinguished from green
mni·ȟu·ha wa·na·p'in \mni-ȟú-ha wa-nà-p'in\ *n* : a neckerchief
mni·ȟu·ha wa·pa·hla·te \mni-ȟú-ha wà-ṗa-ȟla-te\ *n* : crape
mni·ȟu·ha wi·yu·ma \mni-ȟú-ha wì-yu-ma\ *n* : sandpaper – P
mni·h'e·h'e·ye·la \mní-ȟ'e-ȟ'e-ye-la\ *adv* : with the water dripping from one < ~ *unkomanipelo* We trudged along the water dripping from us. > – *Syn* MNICAŠKILYELA Bl
mni·h'i·c'i·ya \mni-ȟ'í-c'i-ya\ *v refl* : to pay close attention to a certain thing < ~ *yanka* to be silent and thinking, *i.e.* while others talk, *i.e.* so to sit, drawn up in a stooping position, ~ *omani* to amble along quietly stooped thinking > – Note: an other way to express this attitude may be done with the use of *wákicokic'un* carefully. Moreover, perhaps *mnihya* is not used. Cf yumniga Bl
mni·i·ca·psin·psin \mni-í-ca-psiŋ-psiŋ\ *n perhaps* : the slashing rain < ~ *hinhelo* It rained a cutting rain. > – Bl
mni·i·wo·sli \mni-í-wo-sli\ *n* : a water spout
mni·i·yatke \mni-í-yatke\ *n* : a dipper with which to drink, a drinking vessel
mni·i·yo·ka·štan \mni-í-yo-ka-štaŋ\ *n* : a pitcher
mni·i·yo·sni·sni·ya·pi s'e \mni-í-yo-sni-sni-ya-pi s'e\ *adv* : in the manner of shrinking back from cold water < ~ *taku tokon* to do something at intervals, hesitatingly, as one not knowing much about it, *Lehanyan waun kinhan ~ waun* If I am so far I am wavering. ~ *hpaya* to lie down with hesitation > – Note: the word is doubtfully *mniyosnisniyanpi s'e*
mni·i·yu·ȟe·pe \mni-í-yu-ȟe-pe\ *n* : a sponge – B.H. 268.2
mni·i·yu·hlo·gya·pi \mni-i-yú-ȟlo-gyà-pi\ *n* : a flume
mni·i·yu·sli \mni-i-yú-sli\ *n* : a water faucet
mni·i·yu·sli \mni-í-yu-sli\ *n* : a squirt
mni·ka·a·ta·ja \mni-ká-a-ta-ja\ *n* [fr *mni* water + *taja* agitated] : waves
mni·ka·hmun \mni-ká-ȟmuŋ\ *n* : the roaring of waves
mni·ka·ki·ci·pe·han \mni-k̇á-k̇i-ci-ṗe-haŋ\ *n* : rolling waves – Note: the prefered form seems to be *mnikakicipehan* B.H.71.12, 203.6, 209.4
mni·kan'·o·ju *or perhaps* **mnikooju** \mni-k̇áŋ-o-ju\ *n* [fr *mni* water + *kanyela* near + *oju* a field] : a field near water
mni·ka·o·ško·kpa \mni-k̇á-o-ško-kpa\ *n* : a canyon made by floods
mni·ka·po·hya hi·yu·ta·ke \mni-ka-ṗó-ȟya hi-yò-ta-k̇e\ *n* : a blister
mni·ki·yu·pta \mni-kí-yu-pta\ *v* : to make a ditch — **mnikiyupta·pi** *n* : a ditch
Mni·ko·wo·ju \Mni-k̇ó-wo-ju\ *np* : a band of Teton Sioux in central South Dakota
mnil \mnil\ *adv* : in the water
mnil·t'a \mníl-t'a\ *vn* mnil·wa·t'a : to drown or be drowned — **mnilt'e·ya** *va* mnilt'e·wa·ya : to drown, cause to drown
mni·na·ka·poh hi·yu·ye *or* **mni·na·pas hi·yu·ye** \mni-na-ká-ṗoȟ hi-yù-ye\ \mni-ná-ṗas hi-yù-ye\ *n* : a blister
mni·na·ta·ke *or* **mninataka·pi** \mni-ná-ta-ke\ \mni-na-tá-ka-pi\ *n* : a dam
mni·o·gna·ke \mni-ó-gna-ke\ *n* : a water pitcher, tank, or reservoir – Note: *mnikóka* is Dakota for water pitcher
mni·o·hu·ta \mni-ó-hu-ta\ *n* : the shore, the edge of a river < *Hecel wakan k'on ~ el inajin na hanbloglaka* So then that strange one had stopped at the shore and told his dream. >
mni·o·hpa·ya \mni-ó-ȟpa-ya\ *va* : to rinse
mni·o·i·cu \mní-o-ì-cu\ *n* : a made well
mni·o·ka·bla·ya \mni-ó-k̇a-bla-ya\ *n* : an inundation, water spread out
mni·o·ško·kpa *or* **mniwoškokpa** \mni-ó-ško-kpa\ *n* : a gutter – Bl
mni·o·t'a \mni-ó-t'a\ *vn* mnio·ma·t'a : to die in the water — **mniot'e·ya** *va* mniot'e·wa·ya : to cause to die in the water < *mnit'eic'iya* to drown one's self > – D.45
mni·o·wa·mni·yo·mni \mni-ó-wa-mni-yo-mni\ *n* : an eddy
mni·o·wan·ca \mni-ó-waŋ-ca\ *n* : the ocean, water all over
mni·o·we \mni-ó-we\ *n* : a well or spring of water, a fountain of water < ~ *akínicapi k'el* at that contested spring, *i.e.* a certain spring near the Platte River in Nebraska > – Bl
mni·pa·sli \mni-pá-sli\ *n* : a pump for water
mni·pa·ta·ja·pi \mni-ṗá-ta-ja-pi\ *n* : a water faucet opening by pressure from a pump-jack, a pump perhaps – *Syn* MNIYUTAJAPI — **mnipataje** *n* : a pump – *Syn* MNIPASLI
mni·pe·ji \mni-ṗe-ji\ *n* : slough grass
mni·pi·ga \mni-ṗí-ġa\ *n* : beer, ale, seltzer or soda water – Bl
mni·sa·pa \mní-sa-ṗa\ *n* : ink — **mnisapa ipapuze** \mní-sa-ṗa i-ṗà-ṗu-ze\ *n* : an ink blotter — **mnisapa wicazo** \mni-sá-ṗa wi-cà-zo\ *n* : a penholder
mni·skan·mni \mni-skáŋ-mni\ *n* : water obtained by melting snow < ~ *ota kta lo* There will be much meltwater, as is said when much snow is expected to thaw. >
mni·sku·ya \mni-skū'-ya\ *n* : salt – Note: this word is pronounced slowly so as to make meaning differences clear. Hence, *mnĭ'skŭyă* vinegar, *mnī'skŭyă* lemonade, and *mni iskuya* mouth watering for water perhaps — **mniskuya ognake** \mni-skū'-ya ò-gna-ke\ *n* : a salt shaker — **mniskuya oyuze** \mni-skū'-ya o-yù-ze\ *n* : a salt lake — **mnisku·yeton** \mni-skū'-ye-toŋ\ *va* : to

salt - B.H.123.4

mni·sol i·ya·ya \mni-sō'l i-yà-ya\ *v* : to have gone never to return, as a man who went far away, or as horses lost, *etc* < *Toké tokiyab mnisol ilalehce c'on tohinni yagli so?* Where had you gone so far away that you never came back? > - BE

mni·ša \mni-šá\ *n* [fr *mni* water + *ša* red] : wine, cider, or ale

mni·šo·še \mní-šo-še\ *n* : turbid water

Mni·šo·še Wa·kpa \Mní-šo-še Wa-kpà\ *np* : the Missouri River that flows through the middle of the Dakotas

mni·š'e·š'e \mni-š'ē'-š'e\ *vn* : to sprinkle, to fall in drops as rain

mni·ta·can·ku \mni-tá-caŋ-ku\ *n* : a ditch, a channel

mni·ta·ga \mni-ṫá-ġa\ *n* : spittle, foam, froth

mni·tan \mni-ṫáŋ\ *vn* : to overflow, be flooded — *n* : a flood - Note: the word is not a *deriv* of *mnitanka* as R suggests

mni·tan·ya \mni-ṫáŋ-ya\ *va* mnitan·wa·ya : to cause to flood

mni·ta·te \mni-tá-ṫe\ *n* : waves, as caused by the wind - Bl

mni·t'a \mní-t'a\ *vn* mní·ma·t'a : to drown — **mnit'e-ya** *va* : to drown something

mni·wa·kan \mní-wa-kaŋ\ *n* : whiskey

mni·wa·kan ska \mni-wa-káŋ ska\ *n* : alcohol

mni·wa·mnu·h'a \mní-wa-mnù-ȟ'a\ *n* : a snail, snails, periwinkles, which are used as ornaments - Note: the ornament is otherwise said to be the *tunsla ognake* the snail's place or shelter R Bl

mni·wan·ca \mni-wáŋ-ca\ *n* : the sea, the ocean

mni·wan·ca o·ka·hmin \mni-wáŋ-ca o-kà-ȟmiŋ\ *n* : a bay, a gulf

mni·wan·ca·wa·ta \mni-wáŋ-ca-wa-ṫa\ *n* : a ship

mni·wan·ji·la pa·psun \mni-wáŋ-ji-la pa-psùŋ\ *v* : it rains unceasingly - B.H.8.2

mni·wa·šte·mna \mni-wá-šte-mna\ *n* : perfume

mni·wa·ta·ge \mni-wá-ta-ġe\ *n* : foam, perhaps - *Syn* MNIWATICOGA Bl

mni·wa·ti·co·ga \mni-wá-ṫi-co-ġa\ *n* : water-moss, or the scum on stagnant water

mni·wi·to·ye \mni-wí-to-ye\ *n* : a certain blue water dye

Mni Woblu \Mni Wo-blú\ *np* : Fall River that flows east from the southeast corner of the Black Hills

mni·wo·ȟa·ȟa \mni-wó-ȟa-ȟa\ *n* : a water falls - P

mni·wo·sli \mní-wo-sli\ *n* : a syringe

mni·wo·sli i \mní-wo-sli ì\ *n* : a nozzle

mni·wo·t'a \mni-wó-t'a\ *vn* mniwo·ma·t'a : to be drenched, soaked with water - Bl

mni·wo·zan \mni-wō'-zaŋ\ *n* : fine drizzling rain, a mist — *vn* : to drizzle - *See* R under *bózan*

mni·ya·pa·tan·han \mní-ya-pa-taŋ-haŋ\ *adv* : next to the river, by the river, by the water

mni·yo·hca·ya \mni-yó-ȟca-ya\ *adv* : full of water, as tears < *Išta ~ waceyakiye* You prayed with your eyes full of tears. > - B.H.127.18

mni·yo·hpan·yan \mni-yó-ȟṗaŋ-yaŋ\ *v* : to soak in water

mni·yo·sni·ya \mni-yó-sni-ya\ *v* : to make the water very cool, to cool water, to become cool water < *Mniyosnisnikiciyapi ktelo* The water will be made very cold for him. *Hiya, mni kinhan áp'eyela yunkelo* No, the water is very shallow. > - Bl

mni·yo·wan·ca *i.e.* **mniowanca** \mni-yó-waŋ-ca\ *n* : the sea

mni·yo·we *i.e.* **mniowe** \mni-yó-we\ *n* : a well, spring

mni·yo·we *i.e.* **mniowe** \mni-yó-we\ *n* : a well, spring — **mniyowe·glepi** *n* : a water well

mni·yu·pi·za \mni-yú-ṗi-za\ *v* mni·blú·piza : to drink noisely - Bl

mni·yu·špa·la \mní-yu-špà-la\ *n* : a puddle, a water hole < *~ loiwagni yelo* I went looking for food in a puddle, *i.e.* causing me to break out with a sweat. > — **mni·yu·špa·špa·ye·la** \mni-yú-špa-špa-ye-la\ *n* or *adv perhaps* : little water pools < *Magaju akisni; yunkan ~ ota* The weather recovered from the rain; and then many were the puddles. *Wakpa ~ opaya omawani yelo* I took a walk along the river bogs. > — **mniyušpa·ye** *or* **mniyušpaye·la** \mni-yú-šṗa-ye\ *n* : a pool < *temniyušpala* perspiring much > - Bl BD B.H.50.1

mni·yu·ta·ja \mni-yú-ta-ja\ *v* : to pump — **mniyutaja-pi** *n* : a faucet, a pump-jack, a pump perhaps - *See* mnipatajapi *and* taja

mni·zi \mni-zí\ *n* : bile, which is accumulated in the stomach; beer or whiskey perhaps

mni·zi·cin·ca \mni-zí-ciŋ-ca\ *n* [fr *mnizi* beer + *cin* to desire] : a drunkard - Mh

mnu·ga \mnú-ġa\ *v* : to crunch, as a horse does in eating corn

mnuh \mnuȟ\ *v contrac of* mnuga : to crunch — **mnu-hmnuga** \mnu-ȟmnú-ġa\ *v red* : to be crunching - Cf yamnumnuga

mnu·hye·la \mnu-ȟyé-la\ *adv* : in a crunching way

mnu·mnus \mnú-mnus\ *v* : to creak < *~ hingla* to creak suddenly, as a piece of wood when one breaks it in two > - LC

N

[1]**na** \na\ *pref to v* : indicates the action is done with the foot; less commonly it expresses the effects of frost, heat, *etc,* and it suggests rapid motions *e.g.* of machines or spontaneous motions – Cf náka, napcá

[2]**na** \na\ *v imper,* added to *v* and used with anything offered : Take it. < *Mak'u na* Take give it to me. *Wakalya na* Take heat it. > – Note: *Hohí* Take it, refers only to a burning pipe offered. In being added to *v* "na" is employed the same as "ye", except that it is used by everybody – R RF

[3]**na** \na\ *conj* : and, also, moreover – Note: people often say it twice in succession, one seemingly belonging to the first half of the sentence, the other to the second. < *Woligluštanpi na, na lecel eya* They finished eating and also he this is what he said. *Wanna can wakan el egle na na wankaltkiya yugal najin* Now he put him on the holy tree, as well as stood him with arms out-stretched upwards. > — *adv conj of purpose,* as the Latin "ut" : to, that – Note: this is expressed in two coordinated but not subordinated sentences < *Okiyaka yo na econ kte* Tell him to do it. *Wicaśa num wicakico na wihuta yujunpi* He called two men that they might pull out cattails. >

na·a·bla·ya \na-á-bla-ya\ *v* naa·wa·blaya : to make level by trampling on

na·a·gla·pšun *or* **naaglapšun·yan** \na-á-gla-pšuŋ\ *v* naa·wa·glapšun [fr *aglapšun* disjoint one's own] : to kick over < ~ *eihpeya* to throw away kicking something over, ~ *iyeya* to kick over a thing suddenly >

na·a·ka·hli·ye·ya \na-á-ka-ȟli-ye-ya\ *v* : to hang out < *ceji* ~ to let one's tongue hang out, as dogs do in hot weather >

na·a·ka·kci·ya \na-á-ka-kci-ya\ *v* : to bend or slant backwards – *Syn* NAÁKAŠ'IN Bl

na·a·ka·mni \na-á-ka-mni\ *v* : to cause to burst or spread out, as one's moccasins or shoes — **naakamni·ton s'e** *adv* : burst open < ~ *yanka* It was bursting at the seam, as is said when the moccasins or leggings burst open. > – Bl

na·a·ka·š'in \na-á-ka-š'iŋ\ *v* : to bend backwards, as the written letter "t" < ~ *iyaya* to go away bent over backward. > — **naakaš'in·yan** *adv perhaps* : bending backwards – *Syn* NAÁKAKCIYA R Bl

na·a·ka·winš \na-á-ka-wiŋš\ *v contrac of* naakawinja : to tread down < ~ *iyeya* to suddenly bend over by foot > – Bl

na·a·ki·ya·ta·gta·ke s'e \na-á-ki-ya-ta-gtà-ke s'e\ *adv* : as if the legs were crossed, in knock-kneed fashion <*Ya, heyin nahan ka ~ gle* Hey! She said this and meant that she was on her way home knock-kneed, *i.e.* her legs were in an "X" shape, as others might say of a woman who slanders someone and then goes home. >

na·a·o·kpa·ni \na-á-o-kpa-ni\ *vn* : to lack < *Tawowicala kin ~ šni* Her faith is not lacking. > – B.H.42.2

na·a·tan'·in·šni aya \na-á-taŋ-iŋ-šni à-ya\ *v* : to obliterate tracks with the foot – Bl

na·bkan \na-bkáŋ\ *n* [fr *nape* hand + *kan* sinew] : the sinews of the wrist

na·bla·bla·ga \na-blá-bla-ġa\ *v red of* nablaga : to pop *e.g.* corn — **nablablah** *v red contrac* : to burst open

na·bla·ga \na-blá-ġa\ *vn* : to pop or burst open *e.g.* corn — **nablah** \na-bláȟ\ *vn contrac* : to swell out, as corn in boiling < ~ *iyaya* to exceed swelling >

na·bla·hya \na-blá-ȟya\ *v* nablá·ȟwa·ya : to cause to burst open, as corn < *wagmeza nablahyapi* popcorn >

na·blas \na-blás\ *vn* or *va* : to burst or make burst by kicking < ~ *iyeya* suddenly to burst >

na·bla·ska \na-blá-ska\ *va* na·wa·blaska : to flatten with the foot

na·bla·ya \na-blá-ya\ *va* na·wa·blaya : to make level or smooth with the foot — *vn* : to become level, spread out

na·bla·za \na-blá-za\ *va* na·wa·blaza : to kick open, make burst by kicking *e.g.* a football — *vn* : to burst, as a kettle by freezing, to burst open, as hominy by boiling

na·ble·ble·ca \na-blé-ble-ca\ *v red of* nableca : to break by stepping on — **nableblel** *v red contrac* : to smash by foot – B.H.72.15

na·ble·ca \na-blé-ca\ *va* na·wa·bleca : to break *e.g.* glass by kicking or stepping on — *vn* : to blossom, unfold, as *wahca* flowers, to crack open as seeds do — **nablel** \na-blél\ *v contrac* : to break by foot < ~ *iyeya* suddenly to break a thing by foot > — **nable·lya** *va* nable·lwa·ya : to break with the foot

na·blu \na-blú\ *va* na·wa·blu : to pulverize with the foot — *vn* : to become dry and fine, as sugar stirred up — **nablu·blu** \na-blú-blu\ *v red* : to grind under foot

na·blu·ya \na-blú-ya\ *vn* : to be plain or manifest, as tracks not long since made

na·bu \na-bú\ *va* na·wa·bu : to drum with the foot, beat on the ground, to stamp — **nabubu** \na-búbu\ *v red* na·wa·bubu : to make a noise by stamping

na·ca \na-ćá\ *n* : a chief – Note: in former times there were only *nacá,* e.g. *naca okolakiciye* a political or social chief, moderator or coordinator. The *itancan* was later introduced by the white man – RF

na·can·can \na-ćáŋ-ċaŋ\ *vn* na·ma·cancan [fr *cancan* to tremble] : to shiver, tremble – Note: TT pronounces the word *nacáncan,* not *naćáṅcan* — *va* : to make shake with the foot — **nacancan·yeya** \na-cáŋ-caŋ-ye-ya\ *adv* nacancanye·ma·ya : to tremble <~ *heya* He said that trembling. > – B.H.289.2

na·can·ku·ton \na-cáŋ-ku-toŋ\ *v* nacanku·wa·ton : to make a track or path somewhere *e.g.* by going or riding repeatedly

na·can·te·ši·lya \na-cáŋ-te-ši-lya\ *adv* : with yet a glutonous feeling or desire for more < ~ *wipi* to be satisfied while desiring more, *i.e.* having eaten all one can take and being sorry for not being able to eat more > – Bl

na·can·ze \na-cáŋ-ze\ *va* na·wa·canze : to make angry by kicking or tapping with one's foot

na·ca·pcab \na-cá-pcab\ *vn contrac of* nacapcapa : to trot < ~ *ya* to go on a trot > — **nacapca·bya** *va* nacapca·bwa·ya : to cause to trot

na·ca·pca·pa \na-cá-pca-ṗa\ *vn* : to trot, as a horse

na·ce·ca \na-cé-ca\ *adv* : probably, perhaps, it may be < *Na le tuwe hwo? ecannipi nacece lo* And who is this? it may be you wonder. *Ake econpi na ake iyenakeca ~ wicaopi* Again they shot as many of them, and a second time they did. > – Note: the word is placed *after* the word to which it belongs – B.H.184.12 D.249

na·ceg \na-cég\ *va contrac of* naceka : to stagger with a kick — **nace·gceg** *va red contrac of* nacegceka : to stagger by kicking — **nacegce·ka** *v red of* naceka : to make stagger — **nace·gyeya** *v* nacegye·wa·ya [fr *naceg* to stagger + *iyeya* swift motion] : to make stagger by kicking

na·ce·ka \na-ćé-ka\ *va* na·wa·ceka : to make stagger by kicking, as in trying to kick down a fence post that will not yield

na·ce·ya \na-cé-ya\ *va* na·wa·ceya [fr *na* by foot + *ceya*

to cry] : to make cry by kicking
na·ci·k'a *or* **nacik'a·la** \na-cí-k'a\ *v* na·wa·cik'ala [fr *cik'ala* small] : to make small by trampling
na·ci·sci·la \na-cí-sci-la\ *va* na·wa·ciscila [fr *ciscila* tiny, quite small] : to make less by trampling on
na·co·co \na-cō'-ċo\ *v* : to make soft with the feet *e.g.* the mud < *Nawacoco ca hlihlila* It was quite muddy after I softened it with my feet. > – *See* cocó
na·ga \na-ġá\ *vn* : to gape open, as a wound < *Yamnipi k'on maya el yapi na ~ s'e hingla. Yunkan mahel iyayapi* It was suddenly as though the three began having gaping wounds, so they had gone to the river bank. And then they went in. > – *See* nagán R
na·gab \na-ġáb\ *va contrac of* nagápa : to skin < ~ *iyeya* suddenly to skin *e.g.* one's leg >
na·ga·ga \na-ġá-ġa\ *v red of* nagá : to spatter or fly out, as grease on the fire — **nagaga·ya** *adv* : partly molten, as is said of grease — **nagagaye·la** *adj* : partially
na·gal \na-ġál\ *vn contrac of* nagata : to extend the foot < ~ *iyeya* suddenly to put out one's foot > — **nagal·gata** \na-ġál-ġa-ta\ *v red* : to keep stretching out one's foot
na·gan \na-ġáŋ\ *vn* : to gape open, as a wound < *Na lila tehan tiyopa s'e maya kin nagahan* And it was as though the river bank were a door long gaping open. > – *See* nagá — **nagan·gan** \na-ġáŋ-ġaŋ\ *v red* : to be gaping open – B.H.293.11, 299.25
na·ga·pa \na-ġá-ṗa\ *va* na·wa·gapa : to strip off the skin of anything with the foot, as a horse might do to a man by kicking him, to skin *e.g.* one's knee
na·ga·ta \na-ġá-ṫa\ *vn* na·wa·gata : to stretch out the foot
na·gi \na-ġí\ *n* mi·nagi un·nagi·pi : the soul or spirit, the shadow of anything, *wicánagi*, as that of a man, or *tinági*, as that of a house < ~ *ekta iyaya* He has gone to the spirit world. *Opta hiyaye ka, ~ kin aiyohanswicaye kin on akisnipi kte* He meant to go through and on; they will recover their health by the spirit overshadowing them. > – B.H.283.4
na·gi a·kton·šya \na-ġí a-ktòŋ-šya\ *va* : to surprise *e.g.* wild game by stealing closeby – Bl
na·gi·ca \na-ġí-ca\ *va* na·wa·gica : to wake one up with the foot or by making a noise with the feet
na·gi·ha·ha \na-ġí-ha-ha\ *adj* : scared, nervous on hearing something – WE
na·gi·i·ya·ya \na-ġí-i-ya-ya\ *vn* : to yield up one's spirit, to die
na·gi·ksa·bi·c'i·la \na-ġí-ksa-bi-c'i-la\ *v refl* : to think one cannot be taken by surprise — **nagiksa·bya** *adv* : observantly < ~ *omani* to walk with open eyes, watching everything, ~ *opic'iya* to act watchfully, *i.e.* circumspectly > – Bl
na·gi·ksa·pa \na-ġí-ksa-ṗa\ *adj* : elated over one's fulfilled predictions, *esp* when one made a good guess and is now glad over it – MF
na·gil \na-ġíl\ *va contrac of* nagíca : to wake one with the foot < ~ *iyeya* to wake one quickly with the foot >
na·gi ni·i·c'i·ya \na-ġí ni-ì-c'i-ya\ *v* nagi ni·mi·c'iya : to save one's soul
na·gi·ton \na-ġí-toŋ\ *v* : to be haunted, *lit* to produce ghosts < *He* ~ The place is haunted. > – SH
na·gi·ye·ya \na-ġí-ye-ya\ *va* nagiye·wa·ya : to trouble, vex, bother one
na·gi·yu·wa·šte \na-ġí-yu-wa-šťe\ *adj* : salutary – P
na·gla \na-glá\ *vn* : to uncoil of itself < *Maza wikan* ~ A metal strap is not binding. > — *adj perhaps* : loose, not tied tight, untied
na·gla·gla \na-glá-gla\ *adj* : moving, *i.e.* as the ribs of a buffalo — **naglagla·ke s'e** \na-glá-gla-ǩe s'e\ *adv perhaps* : standing out, as the ribs of a poor animal, lean, very poor, as is said of animals whose ribs stand out
na·gla·ke \na-glá-ǩe\ *vn* na·má·glake : to stand out, as the ribs of a poor animal when lean, very poor — **naglake·ya** \na-glá-ǩe-ya\ *adv* : sticking out, as the ribs of an animal — **naglakeye·ya** *adv* : expanded, bloated, stretched outward < *Tucuhu ~ wimapi yelo* I'm so full my ribs are expanded, *i.e.* so overloaded with food that the ribs are stretched far apart. > – Cf nainyanyeya, nawizipanyeya Bl
na·gla·kin·yan \na-glá-ǩiŋ-yaŋ\ *adv* : set crosswise or turned out, as the foot < *si ~ iyeya* to turn the foot quickly outward >
na·gla·pšun·yan \na-glá-pšuŋ-yaŋ\ *v* : to turn bottom up with the foot
na·gla·ptus \na-glá-pṫus\ *vn contrac of* naglaptuza : to spring back
na·gla·ptu·za \na-glá-pṫu-za\ *vn* : to fly or spring back, as a bow that is bent or a tree that is pulled and let go
na·gle·gles \na-glé-gles\ *vn contrac of* naglegleza : to be checkered < ~ *aya* to become striped, staring > – D.275
na·gle·gle·za \na-glé-gle-za\ *vn* : to be checkered or marked
na·glo·ka \na-glō'-ǩa\ *va* na·wa·gloka : to knock and injure, as the joint of one's leg < *cankpe* ~ to injure the knee, *nagloke s'e* with as it were injured limbs, *Nagloke s'e waku* I came home as if with injured legs. >
na·gmi·gma \na-gmí-gma\ *va* na·wa·gmigma : to make round with the foot
na·gmi·yan·yan \na-gmí-yaŋ-yaŋ\ *va* na·wa·gmiyanyan : to make roll with the foot, as a football
na·gmu·gmun \na-gmú-gmuŋ\ *va red* [fr *nagmun* to curl] : to curl or crisp *e.g.* bark or burned leather – R
na·gmun \na-gmúŋ\ *vn* : to twist of itself, to curl or crisp, as bark or burnt leather — **nagmun·yan** *adv* : curled
na·gna \na-gná\ *va* na·wa·gna : to knock off with the foot, as fruit off a tree
na·gna·ka *or* **nagnanka** \na-gnáŋ-ǩa\ *v red* ma·nagnanka [fr *naka* or perhaps *nanka* to twitch] : to twitch, as the muscles of the eyes, mouth, *etc* cause the flesh. < When people once had presentiments that somebody was coming, they said: *Nónhmapan yelo, sicuha managnankelo, icimani ahi kte lo* My ears are ringing, the soles of my feet tingle, travelers will be coming. > – Note: the word also seems to be used for the beating of the heart
na·gna·yan \na-gná-yaŋ\ *va* na·wa·ġnayan : to stumble, to miss step, to miss trying to kick, to miss something partly, *i.e.* not meeting it right, with the foot, as in kicking a ball partly and so giving it a wrong direction
na·go·go \na-ġó-ġo\ *v* : to make scratches, as on the floor by walking, with the shoes *etc*
na·go·ya \na-ġó-ya\ *va* nago·wa·ya : to scratch out, erase with the foot *e.g.* something written in the sand
na·gu·ka \na-ǩú-ǩa\ *va* : to sprain *e.g.* one's ankle
na·gwag \na-gwág\ *vn contrac of* nagwaka : to kick out

the foot < *Si ~ iyeya makahlihlila nakintapi* They brushed off mud, kicking their feet abruptly — **nagwa·gwaka** *v red* : to kick out the foot repeatedly

na·gwa·ka \na-gwá-ka\ *vn* na·wa·gwaka : to kick out the foot, to struggle, *fig* to criticize *etc* – Note: the Dakota for the word is *nabaka* R

na·ha·ha \na-há-ha\ *adv* : slowly, carefully, putting down the feet carefully, stealthily, walking on the toes, tiptoeing < ~ *waimnakelo* I ran tiptoeing. > – Bl

na·ha·hci \na-há-ȟci\ *adv* : still, yet < *Le winyan kin ~ niun keyapi* It is said this woman is still living. *nahahci... šni* not...yet > — **nahahci·ke** *adv* : not really yet, a little time left

na·ha i·ye·ya \na-há i-yè-ya\ *v* : to kick out of the way – *Syn* NAȞEYAB IYEYA Bl

na·han \na-háŋ\ *conj* : and, then, also, besides < *Hokšila kin kici canpagmiyanpi kin el iyotaka ~ lila luziyayapi* He sat in the wagon with the boy, and they really made a dash for it. >

na·he·bye·la \na-hé-bye-la\ *adv* : in a squatting manner < ~ *mankelo* I sat squatting, ~ *iyotaka* to sit on one's haunches, ~ *yanka* to sit with one knee bent and the other almost touching the ground and resting on this lower leg > – RF

na·hinl \na-híŋl\ *va contrac of* nahinta : to scrape off with the foot < ~ *iyeya* to scrape off quickly, *Wa k'ecel ~ owale kte, wanjihci ektonjapi naceca ca wapahi ktelo* He should pick it up; I'll look for the snow to scrape off, since it may be some they forgot. > – Bl

na·hin·ta \na-híŋ-ṫa\ *va* na·wa·hinta : to scrape or wipe off with the foot

na·ho·ho \na-hó-ho\ *vn* na·wa·hoho : to shake or make loose with the foot

na·ho-mni \na-hó-mni\ *va* na·wa·homni : to turn round with the foot, as in the operation of a bicycle

na·ho·ton \na-hō'-toŋ\ *va* na·wa·hoton : to make howl *e.g.* a dog by kicking — *vn* : to sound by machinery, *e.g.* by any form of talk-reproducing machine

na·hun·huns \na-húŋ-huŋs\ *va contrac of* nahunhunza : to rock with the foot < ~ *iyeye* to rock fast >

na·hun·hun·za \na-húŋ-huŋ-za\ *va* na·wa·hunhunza : to shake or rock with the foot < *Makoce kin si on ~* She shook the countryside with her foot. >

na·ȟa \na-ȟá\ *vn* na·ma·ȟa **1** : to become rough, as one's hands when chapped by the wind, or as roads when thawing after the winter < *Maka kin ~* The ground became rough. > **2** : to stand up on end, as grains of corn when boiling, perhaps – A

na·ȟab \na-ȟáb\ *va contrac of* naȟápa : to scare, drive away by stamping — **naȟa·bhapa** \na-ȟá-bȟa-ṗa\ *va red* : to keep stamping to frighten away

na·ȟa·pa \na-ȟá-ṗa\ *va* na·wa·ȟapa : to scare away by stamping

na·hci \na-ȟcí\ *va* na·wa·hci : to tear off a piece by stepping, to break out a piece with the foot

na·hco \na-ȟcó\ *vn* : to lossen or untie, as do one's shoestrings or stockings — **nahco·hco** *vn red* : to get loose or untied continually < ~ *omani* to walk about with stockings down and open shoes, *hinyakon ~* to have slouchy stockings > — **nahco·ka** \na-ȟcó-ka\ *vn* : to come loose, as one's leggings — **nahco·ya** *adv* : loose, untied, as the strings that hold up one's leggings

na·ȟe·yab \na-ȟé-yab\ *v perhaps* : to kick out of the way – *Syn* NAHA IYEYA Bl

na·ȟe·ya·ta \na-ȟé-ya-ṫa\ *va* na·wa·ȟeyata : to kick off to one side

na·hla \na·ȟlá\ *vn* na·wa·hla : to ring, as a telephone bell – Note: R gives the word as *va* , to rattle with the foot

na·hla·gan \na-ȟlá-ġaŋ\ *vn* : to open, spread out, be enlarged

na·hla·hla \na-ȟlá-ȟla\ *vn red of* nahlá : to be ringing

na·hla·hlal \na-ȟlá-ȟlal\ *va contrac of* nahlahlata : to be scratching often < ~ *un* to be scratching > – D.98

na·hlal \na-ȟlál\ *va contrac of* nahlata : to scratch with the toes

na·hla·lmni·mni \na-ȟlá-lmni-mni\ *n* : a spring to which it is hard to approach because of steep banks

na·hlal mniowe \na-ȟlál mni-ò-we\ *n* : a spring scratched from the soil, or a climbing along a cliff next to the water – WHL

na·hlal un·kun·za \na-ȟlál un-kùn-za\ *v* : to pretend holding back – D.79 Bl

na·hla·ta \na-ȟlá-ṫa\ *va* na·wa·hlata : to scratch with the toes

na·hla·ya \na-ȟlá-ya\ *vn* : to peel off of itself, to fall off, as a scab – B.H.126.15

na·hle·ca \na-ȟlé-ca\ *va* na·wa·hleca : to rend or tear open with the foot

na·hle·ce·la s'e \na-ȟlé-ce-la s'e\ *adv perhaps* : almost bursting, as is said of very fleshy men or animals < ~ *un* to be all but bursting > – Bl

na·hle·hle·ca \na-ȟlé-ȟle-ca\ *va red of* nahléca : to tear

na·hlel \na-ȟlél\ *va contrac of* nahleca : to tear open

na·hli \na-ȟlí\ *vn* na·wa·hli : to step into mud — **na·hli·hli** \na-ȟlí-ȟli\ *vn* na·wá·hlihli : to trample in mud

na·hlog \na-ȟlóg\ *va contrac of* nahloka : to wear a hole with the foot < ~ *iyeya* to a hole in it quickly >

na·hlo·hlo·ka \na-ȟló-ȟlo-ka\ *v red of* nahlóka : to be making a hole in with the foot — **nahlohloke s'e** *adv* : noiselessly < ~ *mani* to walk lightly, without noise > – Bl

na·hlo·ka \na-ȟló-ka\ *va* na·wa·hloka : to make a hole with the foot, to wear a hole in the foot as by walking — **nahloke s'e** *adv* : noiselessly < ~ *mani* to tiptoe >

na·hma \na-ȟmá\ *va* na·wa·hma na·ci·hma : to hide, conceal < ~ *iyaya* to go into hiding, ~ *glapi* a return in scret, ~ *glipi* an arrival without commotion, ~ *icupi* a taking done under cover > — **nahma·hmala** *adv red of* nahmala : to keep doing covertly — **nahma·kel** *adv* : secretly

na·hma·la *or* **nahmala·kel** \na-ȟmá-la\ *adv* : secretly, slyly, covertly – B.H.164.7, 229.17, 35.9

na·hme \na-ȟmé\ *va* : to conceal — **nahme·yahan** *adv* : secretly

na·hmi·ȟa \na-ȟmí-ȟa\ *v* nahmi·wa·ȟa : to laugh slyly

na·hmin \na-ȟmíŋ\ *va* na·wa·hmin : to turn outward or make turn out, *e.g.* one's heels < *siyete ~* to turn the heels outward >

na·hni·ye·la \na-ȟní-ye-la\ *adv* : hurriedly

na·hni·ye·ye·la \na-ȟní-ye-ye-la\ *adv red* : hurrying, breaking into a run < *nahniyeyelahci omani* to travel walking and running in turns > – Bl

na·ȟol \na-ȟól\ *v contrac of* naȟóta : to wear < *Oyé ~ iyaya* He makes tracks as he goes. >

na·ȟo-ta \na-ȟó-ta\ *v* [fr perhaps *na* by foot + *ȟota* gray, *fig* beaten] : to wear or beat *e.g.* a track

na·hpa \na-ȟṗá\ *va* na·wa·hpa : to kick to make fall, throw down with the foot — *vn* : to be loose, fallen — **nahpa·hpa** \na-ȟṗá-ȟṗa\ *v red* : to be slovenly, untidy, as is said of one whose stockings are hanging down and hindering his gait < ~ *s'e omani* to walk in a slouchy way, as is said of an old man walking slowly like a heavy horse with its long-haired knuckles > - Cf napšapša s'e — **nahpahpa·ka** *n* : a slovenly, untidy person < *he nahpahpake c'un* that one, she is untidy. > - *See* yuhpahpa s'e - Bl D.9 WHL

na·hpan·yan \na-ȟpáŋ-yaŋ\ *v* na·wa·hpanyan : to moisten with the foot

na·hpe·ya \na-ȟpé-ya\ *va* nahpe·wa·ya : to kick, cause to make fall, as in kicking a box on which someone is sitting

na·hpi·hpi s'e \na-ȟpí-ȟpi s'e\ *adv perhaps* : slouchy - Note: the word is used in *ref* to little heavy horses with long hair at the ankles — **nahpihpi·ya** *adv* : slouchy in manner, unkempt, with things hanging down - Bl

na·hpu \na-ȟpú\ *va* na·wa·hpu : to knock off with the foot anything sticking — *vn* : to fall off of itself — **na-hpu·hpu** \na-ȟpú-ȟpu\ *vn red* : to fall off, as anything that has been struck

na·htag \na-ȟtág\ *va contrac of* nahtaka : to kick anything < ~ *iyeya* to kick something quickly >

na·hta·gya \na-ȟtá-gya\ *va* nahta·gwa·ya : to typewrite - LB

na·hta-·hta·ka \na-ȟtá-ȟta-ka\ *va red of* nahtaka : to kick something repeatedly < *Maka nahtahtakapi* They were pounding the ground with their feet. > - D.67

na·hta·ka \na-ȟtá-ka\ *va* na·wa·htaka : to kick anything

na·ȟu-ga \na-ȟú-ġa\ *va* na·wa·ȟuġa : to crack *e.g.* a nut with the foot or by knocking

Na·ȟu·ya Ho·hpi Wa·kpa·la \Na-ȟú-ya Ho-ȟpì Wa-kpa-la *np* : a creek south of the Niobrara River in Nebraska, *i.e.* Eagle Nest Creek, not be confused with that in South Dakota in Jackson County - Bl

na·hwa \na-ȟwá\ *va* na·wa·hwa : to put to sleep by rocking with the foot

na·h'an·hi·ya \na-ȟ'áŋ-hi-ya\ *adv* : slowly

na·h'e·h'e·ya·kel \na-ȟ'é-ȟ'e-ya-kel\ *adv* : unevenly, in a bitten-off manner, looking ragged and torn < ~ *nakseya* to cut unevenly, *i.e.* grass left uncut here and there > - *Syn* ONÁKIKIYAKEL Bl

na·h'on \na-ȟ'oŋ\ *va* na·wa·h'on **1** : to hear anything **a** : to listen to **b** : to attend to **2** : to obey — **nah'on-kiya** \na-ȟ'oŋ-ki-ya\ *va* nah'on·wa·kiya : to relate, to make or cause to hear — **nah'on·yan** *va* nah'on·wa·ya : to cause to hear

na·i·ca·bya *or* **naicabye·ya** \na-í-ca-bya\ *adv* : with the mouth wide open < *Hogan wan tanka ~ anatan* He attacked a great fish. > - B.H.122.24 D.104

na·i·co·ga *or* **nahcoka** \na-í-co-ġa\ *vn* : to come loose, to slip down *e.g.* one's leggings

na·i·coh \na-í-coȟ\ *vn contrac of* naícoga : to cause to come untied and slip down *e.g.* one's leggings; to loosen one's belt and drop one's pants; to kick one's quilt to the feet, as children do *etc* < ~ *iyeya* to make slip down what covers one, *Tanyan ecel iyunka ~ aya u we* He came bringing it (a quilt) along, dropped his pants, and lay down nicely as he was. > - Bl

na·i·c'i·hma \na-í-c'i-ȟma\ *v refl* na·mi·c'ihma [fr *nahma* to hide] : to hide one's self

na·i·c'i·hmin·yan \na-í-c'i-ȟmiŋ-yaŋ\ *vn* : to get out of gear, out of place, as a wheel *etc*, as is said of any vehicle and machinery *etc*.

na·i·c'i·jin \na-í-c'i-jiŋ\ *v* : to defend one's self, to speak for one's self, instead of having a lawyer or the like - Cf nakícijin

na·i·c'i·k'e·ga \na-í-c'i-k'e-ġa\ *v refl* : to scratch one's self - Bl

na·i·c'i·o·co·za \na-í-c'i-o-co-za\ *v* : to make one's self warm by running - Bl

na·i·c'i·šna·šna \na-í-c'i-šna-šna\ *v refl of* našnašna : to scratch one's self with the foot, perhaps - Cf našná *Syn* NAIC'IWAZA Bl MW

na·i·c'i·špa \na-í-c'i-špa\ *vn* : to get away from, avoid danger or trouble

na·i·c'i·wa·za \na-í-c'i-wa-za\ *v refl of* nawaza : to scratch one's self with the foot, as dogs do - Bl

na·i·kpi·ska \na-í-kpi-ska\ *v* [fr *na* with the feet + *ikpi ska* white belly] : to kick over, as a dog , on its back, belly up which is among animals often white, *ikpi ska*, < ~ *ehpeya* to throw itself over on the back >

na·i·le·ga *and* **nalega** \na-í-le-ġa\ *v* na·wa·ilega : to make shine, perhaps, by kicking, poking *e.g.* the fire with one's feet

na·i·leh \na-í-leȟ\ *v contrac of* nailega : to make sparks fly with the foot — **naile·hya** *v* : to make shine or sparkle with the foot - R Bl

na·inl \na-íŋl\ *vn* [fr *inila* silent] : to be or become silent < *Wagugeca kaga ca nainlpica šni* It was impossible for him to remain silent as crusted snow formed. > - Bl

na·inš \na-íŋš\ *conj altern* : or

na·in·yan·ye·ya \na-íŋ-yaŋ-ye-ya\ *adv* [fr *inyan* stone + *yeya* to cause to be] : having become like a rock, tight-packed and hard < *Nige ~ wipi* His belly was filled hard as a rock. > *Syn* NAWIZIPANYEYA, NAGLAKEYEYA

na·i·pa·weh \na-í-pa-weȟ\ *va contrac* [fr *na* by foot + *i* for a purpose + *pawega* to break] : to kick something out of one's way, to keep away with the foot

na·i·tun·kab \na-í-tuŋ-kab\ *v* : to go over backwards, as a horse when its head is pulled back < ~ *yanká* to go over backwards sitting, ~ *ehpeya* to kick over backwards, as a cow may one when being milked, ~ *iyeya* to turn over backwards >

na·i·yo·ja·he·ya·kel \na-í-yo-ja-hè-ya-kel\ *adv* : rattling by itself, as the loose spokes of an old wheel < ~ *naunkelo* He galloped with a clatter. > - *Syn* KAKAG HINGLE Bl

na·i·yo·was \na-í-yo-was\ *va contrac* [fr *naiyowaza* to make echo] : to create an echo < ~ *iyeya* to make an echo suddenly >

na·i·yo·wa·za \na-í-yo-wa-za\ *va* na·wa·iyowaza : to cause an echo by stamping

na·i·yo·ya·ȟe \na-í-yo-ya-ȟe\ *vn* : to evaporate by itself

na·ja \na-já\ *va* na·wa·ja : to crush by trampling on *e.g.* rice - R Bl

na·ja·ja \na-já-ja\ *va* na·wa·jaja : to wash out with the feet, trample out - Note: R gives the doubtful meaning, to wash out by boiling

na·ja·ka·ye·la \na-já-ka-ye-la\ *adv* : lying open < ~ *han* to stand open, as is said of a wound when the margin is swollen and showing a deep cut > - Bl

na·jal \na-jál\ *va of* najata : to spread or gape open, as a wound < ~ *iyeya* suddenly to gape >

na·ja·lya·kel \na-já-lya-kel\ *adv* : open, as a wound - P

na·jan·jan·ye·la·ye·ye \na-jáŋ-jaŋ-ye-la-yè-ye\ *vn* : to be ripe and shining, to come to a mature head, as is said

---

\a\ father \e\ they \i\ machine \o\ smoke \u\ lunar \an, aŋ\ blanc Fr. \in, iŋ\ ink \on, oŋ, un, uŋ\ soon, confier Fr. \c\ chair \ġ\ machen Ger. \j\ fusion \clusters: bl, gn, kp, hšl, etc...\ b[e]lo ... said with a slight vowel
See more in the Introduction, Guide to Pronunciation

of a boil that is ripe - Bl

na·ja·ta \na-já-ta\ *va* na·wa·jata : to make forked by kicking, to split

na·jib \na-jíb\ *va contrac of* najipa : to punch with the foot

na·ji·ca \na-jí-ca\ *vn* : to run away, to flee, retreat — **najil** \na-jíl\ *vn contrac* : to flee < ~ *iyaya* to go in retreat > - R Bl

na·jin \ná-jiŋ\ *vn* : to stand < *owanjila* ~ to stand still > - Note: *inájin* to rise to one's feet, and *ina·wa·jin* I stood up

na·jin·ca \na-jíŋ-ca\ *vn* na·wa·jinca : to run away, flee or retreat

na·jin·han \ná-jiŋ-haŋ\ *part* : standing < ~ *najin* to rise up and stand>

na·jin hi·ya·ya *also perhaps* **inajin hiyaya** \ná-jin hi-yà-ya\ *v* : to stand up, go get up < *Canke iheceglala najin hiyayapi* And so right at that moment they got to their feet. > - B.H.170.2, 273.15

na·jin·kiya \ná-jiŋ-ǩi-ya\ *va* nájin·wa·kiya : to cause to stand, to raise, to raise or lift up

na·jin·yan \ná-jiŋ-yaŋ\ *va* nájin·wa·ya : to cause to stand, to stop, to corner, to hold at bay, to cause to fight < *Na wanji najinyanpi ca etakpin na iyahpaya* And as one was stopped, he grabbed him while they attacked him. > - B.H.73.1 D.71 note 3

na·jin·ye·ya·pi \ná-jiŋ-ye-ya-pi\ *v pl* : they stand in a row, *i.e. ipahlalya inajinpi* they stand, from one thing to another, in rank formation like soldiers < *Letanhan hoanunk ataya* ~ *na ecel tipi he el anunk ihunniya po* They all stood in a row on both sides of center camp from this time on; and so make both sides reach to that tent. >

na·ji·pa \na-jí-pa\ *va* na·wa·jipa : to pinch or prick with the toes, to punch or touch with the foot

na·ju \na-jú\ *n* : the back part of the head - *See* najúte

na·ju·ju \na-jú-ju\ *va* na·wa·juju : to kick to pieces — *vn* : to come to pieces of itself

na·ju·ka·o·sni·sni s'e \na-jú-ǩa-o-sni-sni s'e\ *adv* : as if cooling the back of the head < ~ *inyanka* He runs cooling his head, as is said of a man who has but little hair left and this is waving in the wind while he runs. > - Bl

na·jun \na-júŋ\ *v* : to pull or kick out something with the foot

na·ju·te \na-jú-ṫe\ *n* : the back of the head, the occipital bone, the base of the skull < ~ *el apapa* to strike one at the base of the skull > — **najuto·škokpa** *n* : the hollow of the neck behind

na·ka \na-ká\ *vn* 1 : to twitch, as the eye or flesh at times does involuntarily < *Išta manáke* My eye twitches. *Sicuha manake* The sole of my foot twitches. > 2 : to ring as the ears might, this being taken as a sign that something happened < *Noge manake* My ears ring. >

na·kab \na-káb\ *va of* nakápa : to kick out of the way < ~ *iyeya* to give something a swift kick >

na·ka·ka \na-ká-ǩa\ *va* na·wa·kaka : to make rattle with the foot, as stiff hides might do

na·kan \na-káŋ\ *va* na·wa·kan : to thresh out *e.g.* corn *etc* with the feet by treading

na·ka·pa \na-ká-ṗa\ *va* na·wa·kapa : to kick *e.g.* a ball < *tápa nakapapi* a ball game played by girls >

na·ka·pas \ná-ǩa-ṗas\ *v* : to gather, bring, force together < *mninakapas hiyuya* to ooze *e.g.* droplets of water, as one does when scalded, ~ *hiyumayelo e.g.* my ear secretes wax, or I blistered. >

na·ka·po *or* **nakapo·ga** \na·ǩá-ṗo\ \na-ǩá-ṗo-ġa\ *vn* : to swell, rise like dough, or warp as wood of a door after a rain, or any body to swell *esp* a dead body

na·ka·poh \ná-ǩa-ṗoȟ\ *v* : to make swell up, come together < *Mini* ~ *hiyuya* Water gathered together making it swell, as is said of the drops of water that appear in the place where one scalded one's self. ~ *hiyumayelo* I blistered. > - *Syn* NÁKAPAS

na·ka·š'in \na-ǩá-š'iŋ\ *v* : to bend backwards < *nakaš'inc'iya* to bend one's self backwards, ~ *yeya* to make bend backwards, to cause *e.g.* a horse to rear, as a man riding it bends back and pulls back its head >

na·ka·tin \na-ǩá-tiŋ\ *va* na·wa·katin : to straighten with the foot — *vn* : to become straight of itself

na·ka·wa \na-ǩá-wa\ *vi* : to spring open, to shrink and not stay closed, as a door might — *vt* na·wá·kawa : to kick open

na·kca \na-kcá\ *v* : to be smooth of itself < *Pehin namakca* My hair is even. >

na·ke *or perhaps* **nakeš** \na-ǩé\ *adv emph* : at last, just now < *Osni, yunkan tiyo ceyati šni;* ~ *mašte, yunkan ceyati ehan on le heyónika yelo* It was cold, and so you did not build a fire indoors; just now it was hot and sultry, and so at the time you built a fire since here you are a heyoka. ~ *išta apiyin kte hcin eyaš wicala šni keye* At last, he would restore his sight to his eyes, but he stated that he did not believe him. > — **nake·hca** *adv* : at last, as one wanted — **nake·nula** *adv* : a short time, a little while < ~ *wani* I have lived but a little while. > - Note: this word seems to *ref* rather to a sudden death inflicted by an enemy; thus it is a saying, "*Nakenula ni waun welo* I am living but for a short time," ~ waniyelo, *i.e.* an excuse for leading a merry life, with the attitude: Be merry while you live. MS.96 Bl GA Ba

na·keš *also* **nake** \na-ǩéš\ *adv* : at last, just now < ~ *tiwahe wan tokata unkicu kte lo* At last, you and I shall receive the beginnings of a family. *Hihanna* ~ *wahi kte* At last I shall arrive in the morning. *Pte kin tukte ihankeya cepe kin iyuha awicunglepelo ca* ~ *tantan wayatin kte lo* You shall eat well at last, because we put up in the end all whichever were the fat buffalos. > -MS.95 B.H.58

na·ki·bla·ya \na-ǩí-bla-ya\ *v poss* na·wa·kiblaya [fr *nablaya* to level by foot] : to trample one's own level

na·ki·ble·ca \na-ǩí-ble-ca\ *v poss* na·wa·kibleca [fr *nableca* to break by foot] : to break one's own by treading on it

na·ki·ca \na-kí-ca\ *va* : to scrape with the foot, to paw, as a horse scraping towards one's self - Note: the word is not *natica*

na·ki·ca·pca \na-kí-ca-pca\ *v poss of* napca : to swallow down one's own spittle *e.g.*, or blood from a bleeding tooth

na·ki·ci·bla·ya \na-ǩí-ci-bla-ya\ *v* na·we·ciblaya [fr *nablaya* to level by foot] : to make level by trampling on for one

na·ki·ci·ble·ca \na-ǩí-ci-ble-ca\ *v* na·mi·cibleca : to break *e.g.* a plate with the foot for one; to break for one by freezing, *etc*

na·ki·ci·bu \na-ǩí-ci-bu\ *v* na·we·cibu [fr *nabu* to drum with the foot] : to drum with the foot for one

na·ki·ci·gmun \na-ǩí-ci-gmuŋ\ *v* na·mi·cigmun [fr *nagmun* to curl up] : to twist for one, to become twisted on

na·ki·ci·hun·hun·za \na-ǩí-ci-huŋ-huŋ-za\ *v* na·we·cihunhunza [fr *nahunhunza* to rock by foot] : to shake or rock for one — **nakicihunhunza·pi** *n* : see-sawing

na·ki·ci·hma \na-ǩí-ci-ȟma\ *v* na·we·cihma [fr *nahma* hide] : to conceal for one

na·ki·ci·hta·ka \na-ǩí-ci-ȟta-ka\ *v* na·we·cihtaka [fr *na-*

htaka to kick] : to kick for one

na·ki·ci·h'on \na-k̇í-ḣ'oŋ\ *v* na·we·cih'on [fr *nah'on* to hear, listen] : to hear for one < *Nakicih'onpi* They hear each other. >

na·ki·ci·ja \na-k̇í-ci-ja\ *v* na·we·cija [fr *naja* crush by foot, or *nakija* to tread out one's own] : to tread out for one, to hull for one *e.g.* rice by treading – R Bl

na·ki·ci·jin \na-k̇í-ci-jiŋ\ *va* na·we·ci·jin [fr *najin* to stand + *kici* with or for] : to stand for one, represent somebody as a delegate, to defend < *Tunkašila oyate kin nacicijin kte* Grandfather, I shall defend your tribe. *Namicijin* He defends me. *Nanicijin* He defends you. *Oyate kin lila nacicijinpelo* I really defend your tribe – Note: *Namic'ijin* I defend myself. *Nanic'ijin* You defend yourself. *Naic'ijin* He defends himself

na·ki·ci·jin·ka \na-k̇í-ci-jiŋ-ka\ *v* na·we·cijinka : to stand up for one, stand by one

na·ki·ci·ksa \na-k̇í-ci-ksa\ *v* na·we·ciksa [fr *naksa* to break off] : to break off with the foot for one

na·ki·ci·kšin \na-k̇í-ci-kšiŋ\ *v* na·we·cikšin [fr *nakikšin* defend self] : to stand up for one in danger, to stand by one – R Bl

na·ki·ci·ku·ka \na-k̇í-ci-k̇u-k̇a\ *v* na·we·cikuka [fr *nakuka* wear out with the feet] : to wear out with the foot for one

na·ki·ci·pa \nak̇í-ci-pa\ *v* na·we·cipa [fr *napa* to flee] : to flee from any person or thing < *Ḣcehánl pte kin taku nakicipapi iteya iyayapi* Just then the buffalo apparently went and fleeing from something. > – D.257 and 99

na·ki·ci·pan \na-k̇í-ci-paŋ\ *v* na·we·cipan [fr *napan* to tread out] : to trample or tread out *e.g.* grain for one

na·ki·ci·po·ta \na-k̇í-ci-ṗo-ṫa\ *v* na·we·cipota [fr *napota* wear out as shoes do] : to wear out *e.g.* moccasins for one

na·ki·ci·psa·ka \na-k̇í-ci-psa-k̇a\ *v* na·we·cipsaka [fr *napsaka* break by foot] : to break *e.g.* a cord with the foot for one

na·ki·ci·su·ta \na-k̇í-ci-su-ṫa\ *v* na·we·cisuta [fr *nasuta* trample hard] : to tread hard for one

na·ki·ci·špa \na-k̇í-cii-špa\ *v* na·we·ci·špa [fr *našpa* break off by foot] : to release one from trouble, as a lawyer his client – BD

na·ki·ci·špu \na-k̇í-ci-špu\ *v* na·we·cišpu [fr *našpu* to break off what sticks] : to kick off for one anything sticking

na·ki·ci·ta·ka \na-k̇í-ci-ta-k̇a\ *v* na·we·citaka [fr *nataka* to bolt or bar] : to fasten or lock for one

na·ki·ci·we·ga \na-k̇í-ci-we-ġa\ *v* na·we·ciwega [fr *nawega* to break by foot] : to break *e.g.* an axe handle for one by treading on it

na·ki·ci·wi·zi·pi \na-k̇í-ci-wi-zi-pi\ *v recip* na·un·kicizi·pi [fr *nawizi* to be jealous] : they are jealous of each other

na·ki·cun·ni·ni·yan·kel \na-k̇í-cuŋ-ni-ni-yaŋ-kel\ *adv red of* nakicunniyankel : cautiously – ***Syn*** NAT'ON-T'ONGYANKEL Bl

na·ki·cun·ni·yan·kel \na-k̇í-cuŋ-ni-yaŋ-kel\ *adv* : hesitatingly out of fear – ***Syn*** NAT'ONGYAKEL *or* NA-T'UNGYAKEL Bl

na·ki·gmun \na-k̇í-gmuŋ\ *v* na·ma·kigmun [fr *nagmun* curl up] : to become twisted of itself for one

na·ki·hma \na-k̇í-ḣma\ *v* na·wa·kihma [fr *nahma* conceal] : to hide or conceal one's own

na·ki·hta·hta·ka \na-k̇í-ḣta-ḣta-k̇a\ *v poss red* na·we·htahta-ka [fr *nahtahtaka* to kick anything] : to kick one's own *e.g.* horse

na·ki·h'on \na-k̇í-ḣ'on\ *v poss* na·wa·kih'on [fr *nah'on* to hear] : to hear one's own *e.g.* what one has said or is reported to have said

na·ki·ja \na-k̇í-ja\ *v poss of* najá : to tread out one's own *e.g.* rice – R Bl

na·ki·ksa \na-k̇í-ksa\ *v poss* na·we·ksa *or* na·wa·kiksa : to break one's own with the foot

na·ki·kšin \na-k̇í-kšiŋ\ *va* na·we·kšin na·un·kikšin·pi : to defend one's self < *yupin* ~ to work hard and hurriedly to finish a job in a certain time, to be anxious to finish a job. > – Bl

na·kin·ca \na-k̇íŋ-ca\ *va* na·wa·kinca : to scrape off *e.g.* hair with the foot

na·kinl \na-k̇íŋl\ *v contrac of either* nakinca *or* nakinta : to scrape off with the foot < ~ *iyeya* to scrape off > — **nakin·lkinl** \na-k̇íŋ-lk̇iŋl\ *v contrac red* : to scrape thoroughly < ~ *hpayelo* He slipped on his feet backwards and fell. > – Note: this can also be said, Nak'eh-k'eh hpayelo Bl

na·kin·ta \na-k̇íŋ-ṫa\ *va* na·wa·kinta : to brush off with the foot < *Canke si nagwag iyeya makahlihlila nakintapi* And so mud was brushed off in kicking out his feet. >

na·kin·tki·lya \na-k̇íŋ-tk̇i-lya\ *adj* : tender, as meat

na·ki·pa \na-k̇í-pa\ *v poss* na·wa·kipa [fr *napa* to flee] : to flee or retreat towards home, to turn back for fear

na·ki·pca \na-k̇í-pca\ *v poss* na·wa·kipca [fr *napca* to swallow] : to swallow down one's own *e.g.* spittle

na·ki·psa·ka \na-k̇í-psa-k̇a\ *v poss* na·wa·kipsaka [fr *napsaka* break in half a cord by foot] : to break with the foot one's own string

na·ki·pson \na-k̇í-psoŋ\ *v poss* na·wa·kipson [fr *napson* kick and spill] : to spill over one's own with the foot

na·ki·pu·ski·ca \na-k̇í-ṗu-sk̇i-ca\ *va* na·wa·kipuskica : to press close together with the feet

na·ki·šlo·ka \na-k̇í-šlo-ka\ *v poss of* našloka : to extricate one's self from, to kick off one's own moccasins

na·ki·šna \na-k̇í-šna\ *v poss* na·wa·kišna [fr *našna* to slip or miss one's footing] **1** : to miss one's footing, to slip, to miss while trying being in a hurry **2** : to put on one's shoes **3** : to neglect to mind, care about one's own < *Hehe, hunkake nawicakišna* Sad to say, he does not care about his closest relatives, *i.e.* he does not care for or look after his nearest relatives. > – Bl

na·ki·ta·ka \na-k̇í-ta-k̇a\ *v poss* na·wa·kitaka [fr *nataka* to close or stop] : to fence, fasten, bolt or bar one's own

na·ki·we·ga \na-k̇í-we-ġa\ *v poss* na·wa·kiwega [fr *nawega* break by foot] : to break or splinter one's own with the feet, or somebody else's stick with one's feet

na·ki·wi·zi \na-k̇í-wi-zi\ *va* na·wa·kiwizi *or* na·ma·kiwizi [fr *nawizi* to be envious] : to be envious or jealous of

na·ki·za \na-k̇í-za\ *v* : to make one's shoes or so creak < *Canhanpa nakizapi* His shoes creak. >

na·kog \na-kóg\ *va contrac of* nakoka : to tap with one's foot < ~ *iyeya* to knock by foot. >

na·ko·ka \na-kó-k̇a\ *va* na·wa·koka : to knock with the foot, and thus producing a noise — **nako·koka** \na-kó-ko-k̇a\ *v red* : to be knocking with the foot

na·kon·ta \na-kóŋ-ṫa\ *va* : to wear out partly with the

\a\ father \e\ they \i\ machine \o\ smoke \u\ lunar \an, aŋ\ blanc Fr. \in, iŋ\ ink \on, oŋ, un, uŋ\ soon, confier Fr. \c\ chair \ġ\ machen Ger. \j\ fusion \clusters: bl, gn, kp, hšl, etc...\ b[e]lo ... said with a slight vowel **See more in the Introduction, Guide to Pronunciation**

foot *e.g.* a rope, strap *etc*, *i.e.* make thinner, to fray - BD

na·kpa \na-kpȧ\ *n* : the external ear of animals and humans < *nakpala* large ears, ~ *sanni waglahomni kte lo* I shall turn an ear to him. ~ *okógna* between the ears > — **nakpa·hute** \na-kpȧ-hu-ṫe\ *n* : the root of the ear, where is grown to the head - Bl

na·kpa·kpa \na-kpȧ-kp̣-a\ *vn* : to crackle, pop, as wood burning

na·kpan \na-kpȧŋ\ *va* na·wa·kpan : to grind with the feet by treading

na·kpa·sto·gya \na-k̇pá-sto-gya\ *adv* : moving the ears to and fro, as does a horse

na·kpa wi·ca·hci \na-kpȧ wi-cȧ-ȟci\ *n* : a pointed piece of fat attached to a buffalo's heart - Bl

na·kpa yu·wo·slal i·ki·kca \na-kpȧ yu-wȯ-slal i-kí-kca\ *v* : to prick up the ears *e.g.* of a horse at anything

na·kpe·ye·ya \na-kpé-ye-ya\ *v* : to lift up one's ears to hear < *Nonh'nakpeyemaye* I am hard of hearing, or My hearing is dead. > - Bl

na·kpi \na-kp̣í\ *va* na·wa·kpi : to crack with the foot, as boys do with the eyes of butchered cattle — **nakpi·kpi** \na-kp̣í-kp̣i\ *v red* : to make successive sounds, as a gun sometimes does in hanging fire

na·kpi·šla·ya·tan·han \na-kp̣í-šla-ya-ṫaŋ-haŋ\ *n* [fr *nakpa* ear + *išlayatanhan* right *vs* left] : the right ear - B.H.256.18

na·kpo·ta \na-kpó-ṫa\ *v poss* na·wa·kpota [fr *napota* to wear out as shoes] : to wear out one's own moccasins *etc* - R Bl

na·kpu·kpa \na-kpú-kpa\ *vn* : to mix together, as in boiling stew - P

na·kpu·ta·ke \na-kp̣ú-ta-k̇e\ *n* [fr possibly *nakpa* ear + *putáka* to touch in falling] : a scarf, an ear wrapper

na·ksa \na-ksá\ *va* na·wa·ksa : to break off *e.g.* a stick in two with the foot — **naksa·ksa** *v red* : to be breaking with the foot — **naksa·ya** *v* naksa·wa·ya : to cause to break with the foot

na·kse·ya \na-ksé-ya\ *va* nakse·wa·ya : to cut *e.g.* hay

na·kša *or* **nakša·la** \na-kšá\ *va* : to coil, to roll up with the foot *e.g.* a rope < *Wikan nawakša* I rolled up the rope. > — *vn* : to coil, roll up, as anythng burnt

na·kšan \na-kšáŋ\ *va* na·wa·kšan : to bend with the foot *e.g.* a stick by two hands and bent with the foot — **nakšan·kšan** *va red* : to be bending with the foot

na·kše·ca·pi \na-kšé-ca-pi\ *n of* nakša : cramps, a sickness of the Dakotas, the limbs being contracted and leading to death - Bl

na·kši·ja \na-kší-ja\ *va* : to double up anything with the foot, to bend up the leg — *vn* : to double up on, as the stockings do in hanging down < *Hunyankon nawakšikšija* My stocking are slouched down. > — **nakši·kši·ja** *v red* : to double up *e.g.* with the foot — **nakšiš** *v contrac* : to bend up *e.g.* one's legs < ~ *iyeya* suddenly to bend up >

na·ktan \na-ktáŋ\ *va* na·wa·ktan : to bend with the foot by stepping on and giving permanent bend to — **naktan·ktan** *va red* : to bend with the foot — **naktan·yan** *va* naktan·wa·ya : to cause to bend with the foot

na·ku·ka \na-k̇ú-k̇a\ *va* na·wa·kuka : to wear out with the feet

na·kun \na-k̇úŋ\ *conj* : and, also < *Wicaša wan kaga na* ~ *winyan wan kaga* He created a man and he also created a woman. > - Note: the word is often preceded by *na* — **nakunš** *conj emph of* nakún : as well as, besides *etc*

na·k'e·ga \na-k'é-ġa\ *va* na·wá·k'ega : to scratch, using the spur upon a horse

na·k'eh *or* **nak'eȟk'ega, nak'eȟk'eȟ** \na-k'éȟ\ *va contrac of* nak'éga : to scratch < ~ *hpayelo* He slipped out with the feet backward, not finding a hold and falling. ~ *un* to be slipping or losing traction > - *Syn* NAŠLUŠLUL, NAKINLKINL

na·la \ná-la\ *adv* : alone, only < *mišnala* I alone, *nišnala* you only, *išnala* he alone, *unkišnala* we alone >

na·le·ga \na-lé-ġa\ *va* na·wa·lega : to make shine or sparkle, as in pushing up or kicking the fire with the foot — *vn* : to sparkle, scintillate - R Bl

na·leh \na-léȟ\ *va contrac of* nalega : to shine, sparkle < ~ *iyeya* to stir embers to fly or sparkle > — **nale·hlega** \na-lé-ȟle-ġa\ *v red* na·wa·lehlega [fr *nalega* to make sparks fly] : to kick or poke up the fire by stirring with the foot — **nale·hya** \na-lé-ȟya\ *va* : to make sparkle *e.g.* burning wood by kicking - *Syn* NAÍLEHLEGA R Bl

na·lo·lo·pa \na-ló-lo-p̣a\ *va* na·wa·lolopa : to trample and make limber - Bl

na·mna \na-mná\ *va* na·wa·mna : to rip *e.g.* the seam of a coat — *vn* : to rip of itself — **namna·mna** *v red* : to be ripping — **namna·yan** *va* namna·wa·ya : to cause to rip *e.g.* one's moccasins

na·mni \na-mní\ *vn* na·wa·mni : to turn back when going on a journey < *Na he ozuye kin hunh hetan* ~ *agli na hunh kosan eyaya* Some from the war turned back to arrive home, and some went on farther, *i.e.* coming back before one reached the destined place. ~ *gli* to turn back to get home, ~ *wagli* turned back to go home >

na·mni·ga \na-mní-ġa\ *vn* : to shrink, draw up, as cloth by washing

na·mnih \na-mníȟ\ *vn contrac of* namniga : to shrink < ~ *iyeya* to shrink > — **namni·hkiya** \na-mní-ȟki-ya\ *v* : to shrink, to full up — **namni·hya** *va* namni·hwa·ya : to cause to shrink

na·mni·mni \na-mní-mni\ *v red of* namni : to swing *e.g.* one's blanket

na·mnu·mnu·za \na-mnú-mnu-za\ *v red of* namnuza : to crackle, as green wood in fire or as a prairie fire - *Syn* PELNAKPAKPA R Bl

na·mnus \na-mnús\ *va contrac of* namnúza : to make creak < ~ *iyaya* to go making a creaking sound > - R Bl

na·mnu·za \na-mnú-za\ *va* na·wa·mnuza : to make creak or sound, as when one walks out on newly formed ice - R Bl

na·na \ná-na\ *conj red of* na : Take it, here it is - Note: the word is used by women in handing anything or telling people when others offer them something

na·ni \na-ní\ *va* na·wa·ni : to touch or jog with the foot, to rouse up — **nani·ni** *v red* na·wa·nini : to jog with the foot, to wake one up

na·ni·yan \na-ní-yaŋ\ *v* : to have sore feet < *Onahlokin kte laka* ~ *ca canku ipaweh ecé inyanka cin yelo* He wanted only to run across the road, would you know! so he might make a hole in the ground when his feet were sore. *Si* ~ His feet pain him. *Si nawaniya* My feet pain me. > - Bl WHL

nan·ka *or* **naka** \naŋ-ká\ *v* 2nd *pers singl of* yanká : you are — *vn* : to twitch, as the eye-lid < *Išta mananke lo, mitakuye ake wanji t'e* My eye-lid twitched, for again a relative of mine died. > - BA

na·o·blel \na-ó-blel\ *adv* : scattered, spread out in a line < ~ *aye s'e* It seemed they began to spread out their line of attack. *kaoblagaheya* spreading out a line from a central place, as is said of a line of men, *e.g.* soldiers when they move farther apart, thus lengthening the line and being less likely to be hit > - Bl

na·o·gla·pšun \na-ó-gla-pšuŋ\ *v* : to kick anything over < ~ *ihpeya* to kick anything over bottom up > — **naogla-pšunyan** *adv* : kicking over < ~ *iyeya* to kick over > - R Bl

na·o·glu·ta \na-ó-glu-ta\ *va* na·wá·ogluta : to close up or cover with the foot

na·o·gmi·gma *and* **naogmigme·ya** \na-ó-gmi-gma\ *va* na·wa·ogmigma : to roll anything with the foot *e.g.* downhill - D.217

na·o·gmus \na-ó-gmus\ *v contrac of* naogmuza : to close up < ~ *iyaya* to go covering up, with the foot, *Išta ~ amaya* My eyes began to close. > - Bl

na·o·gmu·za \na-ó-gmu-za\ *vn* : to close up of itself, to close or shut up, as a flower blossom — *va* nao·wa·gmuza : to close up or cover with the foot

na·o·hmin \na-ó-ȟmiŋ\ *vn* : to glance off sideways < ~ *iyaya* to go glancing off >

na·o·hpa \na-ó-ȟpa\ *vn* na·wa·ohpa : to press or sink down into *e.g.* mud or water, to break through ice

na·o·hpe·ya \na-ó-ȟṗe-ya\ *va* naohpe·wa·ya : to cause to sink down into, to make break through

na·o·h'an·ko \na-ó-ȟ'aŋ-ḳo\ *va* nao·wa·h'anko : to quicken one's movements by kicking him

na·o·ki·yu·ta \na-ó-ḳi-yu-ta\ *v* na·ma·okiyuta : to close up or heal *e.g.* a crack or a wound - B.H.65.8

na·o·ko \na-ó-ko\ *vn* : to open, split - B.H.157.8

na·o·ko·ton·ton·yan \na-ó-ḳo-toŋ-toŋ-yaŋ\ *adv red of* naokotonyan : making a crack, a split - B.H.65.6

na·o·ko·ton·yan \na-ó-ḳo-toŋ-yaŋ\ *adv* : making a crack or split < *Maka kin ~ nasleslece* The earth split making a crack. > - B.H.65.4

na·o·kpa·ni \na-ó-kpa-ni\ *va* nao·wa·kpani : to miss, be short of, to have lost < *Ehaka taku wanjila naoyakpani* One last thing you are missing. > - B.H.234.1, 254.4, 298.11

na·o·ksa \na-ó-ksa\ *v* nao·wa·ksa : to break through, as when walking on ice or crusted snow

na·o·ksa·ksa·la s'e \na-ó-ksa-ksa-la s'e\ *adv* : trippingly along < ~ *hiyaya* to pass by trippingly, as people with short legs > - Bl

na·o·kši·ja \na-ō'-kši-ja\ *va* nao·wa·kšija : to bend double, to double up in with the feet, as in bed sheets

na·o·ktan \na-ó-ḳtaŋ\ *va* nao·wa·ktan : to bend into with the foot — **naoktan·yan** *adv* : bent in

na·o·mnu·mnus *or* **naomnumnuza** *or* **naomnuza** \na-ó-mnu-mnus\ *va* [fr *naomnumnuza* and *naomnuza* make creak or sound] : to make creak or sound, as when one walks on newly formed ice or in a pile of potatoes < ~ *mani* to walk with a creaking, sloshing or other sound > - Note: the use of this word is doubtful

na on \na óŋ\ *adv conj* : and that is the reason - B.H. 79.10

na·on·zi·wo·sla \na-óŋ-zi-wo-sla\ *v* : to kick bottom upwards < ~ *iyeya* to kick upside down, ~ *iyeic'iya* to turn a somersault >

na·o·pe·mni \na-ó-ṗe-mni\ *va perhaps* : to prevent from moving, as in walking and getting entangled, twisted, wrapped around as a rag lying in a rut that gets around a wheel, or a too-long overcoat that flaps around the limbs and makes walking difficult < *Minihuha hugmiyan ~ , ~ s'e u* A rag prevented the wheel's motion. He came as though it prevented his progress. >

na·o·pi·je·la \na-ó-ṗi-je-la\ *adv* : loose fitting

na·o·po \na-ó-po\ *vn* : to warp, to draw together as a flower, to shut up

na·o·sin \na-ó-siŋ\ *va* : to make into a hard knot by kicking, as a horse its traces, or by using the foot — **na-osin·yan** *adv* : in the manner of a hard knot < ~ *iyeya* to make a knot hard by using the foot, as in closing a loop > - R Bl

na·o·swa \na-ó-swa\ *v* na·wa·oswa : to cut off, as from a bank or cliff - Bl WHL

na·o·sli \na-ó-šli\ *vn* : to press up around, as when one sits down in soft mud — **naošli·ya** *adv* : puffed up around < ~ *pō* to swell full up >

na·o·t'ins \na-ó-t'iŋs\ *va contrac of* naot'inza : to press down tight < ~ *iyeya* to press down, ~ *ayapelo* You waited to pack tight. — **naot'in·sya** *va* naot'in·swa·ya : to cause to press down tight in, as a horse's foot — *adv* : in the manner of pressing down tight in < *Ota aun wo, ite ecuhci ~ unyankapi kte lo* Put on much (*i.e.* wood on the fire), our faces at least we shall be pressing tight. > - Bl

na·o·t'in·za \na-ó-tiŋ-za\ *va* : to press in tight with the foot *e.g.* the ground around a fence post — *vn* : to become fat, as horses in the pasture - *Syn* CEPÁYA

na·o·wan·ca·ya \na-ó-waŋ-ca-ya\ *v* : to spread out < ~ *aya* to become spread out *e.g.* a heap of sand with the feet > - Bl

na·o·win·ga \na-ó-wiŋ-ġa\ *v* : to turn in the toes — **na-owinge s'e** \na-ó-wiŋ-ġe s'e\ *adv* : with turned in toes as it were < ~ *mani* to walk with the feet turned in > - *Syn* HMINHMIN perhaps - R

na·pa \na-pá\ *v* and perhaps *n* na·wa·pa : to run away, to flee *e.g.* from a fight < *Pel'ipimayala ca nacicipin ktelo* Since I am cold in your room, I shall leave you. > - Bl

na·pa·gle \na-ṗá-gle\ *va* napa·wa·gle [fr *nape* hand + *agle* place on] : to place the hand on, rest it on < *nata ~ ištinma* to sleep resting the head on one's hand > — **na-pagle·pi** *n* : a span, the distance from the end of the thumb to the end of the middle finger when stretched out - Bl

na·pa·hun·ka \na-pá-huŋ-ka\ *n* : the thumb < *Tuweni waépazo kin on epazo šni, ~ kin he on econpi* No one did he point at with the index finger, it was done with the thumb. >

na·pa·hpa·ga \na-ṗá-ȟṗa-ġa\ *vn* : to snap or crackle, as corn parching - Bl

na·pa·hpah \na-ṗá-ȟṗaȟ\ *vn contrac of* napahpaga : to snap or crackle < ~ *iyeya* to pop, crackle > — **napahpa-hya** \na-ṗá-ȟṗa-ȟya\ *va* napahpa·hwa·ya : to parch *e.g. corn* - Bl

na·pa·ka·ha \na-ṗá-ḳa-ha\ *n* : a wrist band, a piece of leather stretched over the left hand while shooting with arrows so as to protect it against friction, though R gives this to be the back of the hand, whereas for the latter we say *napitakaha*

na·pa·ka·za \na-ṗá-ḳa-za\ *n* : the five fingers of a hand, or claws of a foot < *Capa s'e ~ kaksa kaca* Like a beaver his fingers do not cut, as is said when a man's fingers are cut off. *Pehán s'e ~ hanskaska kaca* Like a crane his fingers are long. > - Bl

---

\a\ f<u>a</u>ther \e\ th<u>e</u>y \i\ mach<u>i</u>ne \o\ sm<u>o</u>ke \u\ l<u>u</u>nar \an, aŋ\ bl<u>a</u>nc Fr. \in, iŋ\ <u>i</u>nk \on, oŋ, un, uŋ\ s<u>oo</u>n, c<u>on</u>fier Fr. \c\ <u>ch</u>air \ġ\ ma<u>ch</u>en Ger. \j\ fu<u>s</u>ion \clusters: bl, gn, kp, hšl, etc...\ <u>b</u>[e]lo ... said with a slight vowel
See more in the Introduction, Guide to Pronunciation

na·pa·ko \na-ṗá-ko\ *vn* : to bend up of itself — **napa-ko·ya** *adv* : rounded up < ~ *po* swelled up >

na·pan \na-páŋ\ *va* na·wa·pan : to trample fine, to tread out *e.g.* grain — **napan·pan** *va red* : to tread out

na·pa·pa \na-pá-pa\ *v* : to make bark < *Waecakca nunkin na ~ umayaye* You lay ready to do things and so you get me started barking, as a father would say to his child or wife if they do wrong. ~ *taku econ mayayapelo* You start me barking over what he does, or You bother me unceasingly. > – Bl

na·pa·pa·zo \na-pá-ṗa-zo\ *v* : to shake the finger at one, as in scolding < *Napamayapazo yelo* You shook your finger at me. > – Bl

na·pa·ta \na-ṗá-ta\ *adv* : by the hand < ~ *yuza* to hold by the hand, ~ *yus áya* They go holding hands. *Tuwehci ~ yuzin kta atonwe* Someone took a look so as to get a hold on it with the hand. > – B.H.289.6, 295.2

na·pa·tu·ja \na-ṗá-ṫu-ja\ *va of* patuja : to kick and make bend — **napatuš** *va contrac* : to kick and make bend < ~ *iyeya* to kick suddenly and bend >

na·pca \na-ṗcá\ *va* na·wa·pca : to swallow *e.g.* food — **napca·pca** *va red* : to put in the mouth one piece after another

na·pce·ya \na-pé-ya\ *va* napce·wa·ya : to cause to swallow

na·pcin·yun·gyun·ka \na-pcíŋ-yuŋ-gyuŋ-k̇a\ *adj red of* napcinyunka : nine and nine, nine on both sides, by nines

na·pcin·yun·ka \na-pcíŋ-yuŋ-k̇a\ *adj num* : nine

na·pco \na-pcó\ *n* : the lean meat near the backbone, the tenderloin, the longissimus dorsi – Cf tanápco

na·pco·ka \na-pcó-k̇a\ *n* [fr *nape* hand + *cokanyan* in the middle] : the palm of the hand < *Waowešica s'e ~ kin yuh'iyela yankin na* It was as if a bear scratched the palm of his hand, as is said when a person's hands were scratched badly. > – Bl

na·pco·kan·yan \na-pcó-k̇aŋ-yaŋ\ *n* : the middle-finger

[1]**na·pe** \na-pé\ *v of* napá with *term* "a" changed to "e" : to flee from

[2]**na·pe** \na-pé\ *n* : the hand < *Manape on wakaga* I made it with my hands. >

na·pe·a·pa·ha \na-ṗé-a-ṗa-ha\ *v* napéa·wà·paha : to raise the hand to, to strike anything

na·pe·ce·šni \na-ṗé-ce-šni\ *adv* : slowly, perhaps, not being afraid or bashful *etc* < ~ *u, ištima, kul hpaya.* ~ *waun* He came unafraid, collapsed, and fell asleep. I am content, as they used to say, whereas we now say *Cantewašteya waun* I am glad. *Taku henun kin suksutaya pahta yo;* ~ *unkomanipi kte* What you tied up pack quite tightly; we shall be traveling slowly. > – RF

na·pe·gla·ska·pa \na-ṗé-gla-skà-ṗa\ *vn* : to clap the hands, to applaud

na·pe·glu·ja·ja \na-ṗé-glu-ja-ja\ *v* : to wash one's own hands

na·pe i·ci·ca·ška \na-ṗé ì-ci-ca-ška\ *v* napé ìci·wa·kaška : to tie somebody's hands together

na·pe·i·kpa·hin \na-ṗé-i-kṗà-hiŋ\ *v* napei·wa·kpahin [fr *nape* the hand + *ikpahin* to pillow head in one's own hand] : to lie pillowing the head on the hand

na·pe·ki·co·za \na-ṗé-k̇i-co-za\ *v of* napekoza : to beckon, gesticulate waving the hand(s)

na·pe·ko·za \na-ṗé-k̇o-za\ *v* : to beckon with the hand, wave the hand

na·pe·kši·kša \na-ṗé-kši-kša\ *v* nape·ma·kšikša : to have the hands numb or stiff with cold

na·pe·mni \na-ṗé-mni\ *vn of* pemni : to twist of itself

na·pe o·gle·ce·ku·te·pi \na-ṗé o-gle-cè-k̇u-ṫe-pi\ *n* : a game played by one man throwing a pronged stick as far as he can to make it stand upright, and others who try to win by having their's fall the nearest to his

na·pe·o·i·cu *or* **napoicu** \na-ṗé-o-i-cu\ *n* : handwriting < ~ *tokeca* a different handwriting > – NP

na·pe o·i·le·ki·ya·pi \na-ṗé o-ì-le-k̇i-ya-pi\ *n* : Indian hemp, the clasping-leaved dogbane, apocynum canbinum, hyperici folium, the dogbane family. – Note: it is so called because some people used to place the wooly seeds on their hands and light them. While they burn very rapidly, it does not hurt. *Nape oilekiyapi hu tanka un heca yelo: hanta po* The large dogbane bush is such to be of use: but watch out! *i.e.* snakes often hide under them – BT #105

na·pe·o·ju·la \na-ṗé-o-ju-la\ *n* : a handful

na·pe·on·wo·gla·ka \na-ṗé-oŋ-wò-gla-ka\ *v* : to use the sign language – *Syn* WÍYUTA

na·pe·o·štan *or* **napoštan** \na-ṗé-o-šṫaŋ\ *n* **1** : a thimble **2** : the coneflower

na·pe·pi·ca·šni \na-ṗé-ṗi-ca-šni\ *adj* : inevitable

na·pe·pin·kpa \na-ṗé-ṗiŋ-kṗa\ *n* : the tip of a finger

na·pe·wi·ca·špan \na-ṗé-wi-ca-špaŋ\ *n* : a thin layer of meat adhering to the small ribs on the inside – Bl

na·pe·ya \na-pé-ya\ *va* nape·wa·ya : to cause to flee, to drive or scare off or away

na·pe·ya·han \na-ṗé-ya-haŋ\ *adv* : carefully, watching out < *Takunl icu wacin po na ~ škan po* Think of receiving something, and move about on the lookout for it. >

na·pe·ye·ki·ya \na-ṗé-ye-k̇i-ya\ *v* : to stretch out the hand to — **napeye·ya** *v* : to stretch out one's hand – *Syn* ISTOYEYA Bl

na·pe·yu·pšun·ka \na-ṗé-yu-pšuŋ-ka\ *n* : the fist — *vn* : to clench the fist – Bl

na·pe·yu·za \na-ṗé-yu-za\ *v* : to shake hands

na·pi·ca·ška \na-ṗí-ca-šk̇a\ *v* [fr *nape* the hand + *kaška* to tie] : to tie to the hands of one < *Ptehe wan ~ ca ki* He robbed a buffalo horn that he tied to his hands. > — **napicaške·ya** *adv* : tied to the hand, *i.e.* always with one and following one about < ~ *un* to be tied to the hand, *i.e. fig* to accompany constantly >

na·pi·kce·ya·kel \na-ṗí-kce-ya-kel\ *adv* : by hand < ~ *icahya* to make grow by hand > – B.H.93.11

na·pin \na-ṗíŋ\ *adj* : tasty, satisfying, strong, rich, oily, as some kinds of food are – Note: one of the sayings of the meadow lark: "*Ptehincala pi napin* Calf's liver is rich"

na·pin·kpa \na-ṗíŋ-kpa\ *n* [fr *nape* hand + *inkpa* small end] : gloves < ~ *ot'oza* mittens, ~ *yugaga* gloves > – R Bl

na·pin·yun \na-ṗíŋ-yuŋ\ *adv* : without weapons, with the hands or arms alone

na·pi·škan \na-ṗí-šk̇aŋ\ *vn* : to put the hand to for evil, to lay hands on, to touch with evil design — **napiškan-kiya** \na-ṗí-šk̇aŋ-k̇i-ya\ *va* napiškan·wa·kiya : to cause to move the hands on, to caress

na·pi·škan·yan \na-ṗí-šk̇aŋ-yaŋ\ *va* napiškan·wa·ya : to hurt, destroy, kill anything *esp* what is not one's own < *Tokša tuwa cin kin, napiškanmayin kte* Sometime one who wishes will destroy me. > – Bl

na·pi·šla·ya·tan·han \na-ṗí-šla-ya-taŋ-haŋ\ *adv* : at the right hand – B.H.284.8

na·pi·štan *or* **napištan·ka** \na-ṗí-šṫaŋ\ *n* : one who is always active, one who accomplishes much — **napi-štan·yan** \na-ṗí-šṫaŋ-yaŋ\ *vn* napištan·wa·ya: to be active and accomplishing things — **napištan·kiya** \na-ṗí-šṫaŋ-k̇i-ya\ *va* napištan·wa·kiya : to keep one busy

and accomplishing things
na·pi·ta·ka·ha \na-p̣í-ta-ka-ha\ *n* : the back of the hand < *Nape okazonte kin ~ kin nupin iciyagleya iyakaškapi* The ordered pattern of the fingers on both the hands reaching back to back and tied. > - *See* siitakaha #340
na·pi·ya·gle·ya \na-p̣í-ya-gle-ya\ *v* : to lay hand on < *Napiyagle·maya·yapi šni* You did not lay hands on me. > - B.H.256.25
na·pi·ya·ya \na-p̣í-ya-ya\ *v* [fr *napá* to run away + *iyaya* went] : to go running away
na·pi·ya·yus \na-p̣í-ya-yus\ *adv perhaps* : held in the hands < ~ *yuha* to hold tight in one's hands > - B.H. 48.10
na·pi·ye·ya \na-p̣í-ye-ya\ *v* [fr *nape* hand + *iyeya* to put in] : to have a hand in something - B.H.122.26 SLB
na·pi·yun \na-p̣í-yuŋ\ *adv* - *See* napinyun
na·pi·yu·ski·ya \na-p̣í-yu-sḳi-ya\ *va* : to cause to capture one, in the sense: "He shall be delivered to the hands of the gentiles, *i.e.* they shall cause the gentiles to have power over him."
na·pi·yu·sya \na-p̣í-yu-sya\ *va* : to deliver into somebody's power, hand over, to make hold — *adv* : controlling < ~ *škan* to control by guiding others >
na·pi·yu·za \na-p̣í-yu-za\ *va* napi·blu·za napi·wica·yu-za·pi : to lay hands on, capture - Note: *napiyeya unyuzapi* we had a hand in grabbing him - B.H.163.9
na·pi·yu·ze·ca \na-p̣í-yu-ze-ca\ *v* napi·blu·zeca : to take things into one's own hands, to do it one's self
na·pi·za \na-p̣í-za\ *vn* : to make a creaking noise, as when one steps on a mouse and it creaks or squeaks, to creak
na·pkan \na-pkáŋ\ *n* [fr *nape* hand + *kan* tenden] : the sinews or tendons of the wrist
na·pka·win·te s'e \na-pḳá-wiŋ-ṭe s'e\ *adv* : as if wiping or fanning something away with the hand < ~ *škan* to steal, *sl* to swipe > - Bl
na·pki·co·za *or* **napekicoza** \na-pḳí-co-za\ *va* na·pwe·co·za : to wave the hand to — **napko·za** \na-pkó-za\ *v* na·pwa·koza : to wave the hand
na·po \na-p̣ó\ *vn* : to swell, as soaked corn
na·pob \na-p̣ób\ *vn contrac of* napopa : to burst with a noise < ~ *hingla* suddenly to burst, ~ *iyeya* to cause to burst and make a noise > — **napo·byapi** *n* : fire crackers
na·po·ga \na-p̣ŏ'-ġa\ *vn* : to swell, raise, as corn soaked or dough, to ferment - Note: the word is used in *ref* to a swelling hand — **napoga·pi** *n* : a swelling < ~ *kuja* one who has that disease bringing on swelling, *Aguyapi ~ šni* The bread failed to rise. > - HM
na·po·gle·ce·ku·te·pi \na-p̣ó-gle-ce-ku-te-pi\ *n* : a game of skill in shooting the bow and arrow - *See* oglecekutepi Bl
na·po·gmus \na-p̣ó-gmus\ *va contrac of* napogmuza : to close the hand on < ~ *icu na kul ihpeya* He took and grasped it and cast it down. ~ *oyuspa* to take hold on grasping it, *Napogmuzapi* He was laid hold on. > - B.H. 137.27
na·po·gmu·za \na-p̣ó-gmu-za\ *va* napo·wa·gmuza : to close the hand on
na·po·gna \na-p̣ó-gna\ *n* : what is in the hand, a handful < *Canhanpi ska ~ mak'u* He gave me a handful of white sugar. > — **napogna·ka** *va* napo·wa·gnaka : to put into the hand
na·poh \na-p̣óȟ\ *vn contrac of* napoga : to swell < ~ *iyeya* to quickly swell > — **napohya** *va* napo·hwa·ya : to cause to ferment, to leaven, make light — **napohyapi** *n* : leaven
na·po·i·cu *or* **nape·oicu** \na-p̣ó-i-cu\ *n* : handwriting
na·po·ka·ške \na-p̣ó-ḳa-šḳe\ *n* : cuffs, a bracelet < ~ *kšupi* beaded cuffs, but formerly metal bands, *i.e. napoktan*, were used > - *Syn* NAPOKTAN which cf
na·po·ka·zun·te \na-p̣ó-ḳa-zuŋ-te\ *n* : the fingers
na·po·ktan \na-p̣ó-ktaŋ\ *n* : a bracelet, an armband
na·pol \na-p̣ól\ *va contrac of* napota : to wear out < ~ *iyeya* to keep wearing out with the feet > — **napo·lpota** *v red of* napota : to wear out with the feet repeatedly
na·pon·yan \na-p̣óŋ-yaŋ\ *v* : to crush, to grind with the feet - Bl
na·po·pa \na-pó-p̣a\ *vn* : to burst, as a boiler, a gun, popcorn — *va* : to burst something
na·po·pa·we·ga \na-p̣ó-p̣a-we-ġa\ *va* napo·wa·pawega : to rub in the hands
na·po·po·pe·la \na-pop-ó-p̣e-la\ *n* : a motorcycle
na·po·šin \na-pó-šiŋ\ *vn* : to shrivel up while drying - Bl
na·po·štan *or* **napeoštan** \na-p̣ó-štaŋ\ *n* **1** : a thimble **2** : the prairie coneflower, the long-headed coneflower, lepachys colu-mnaris, the composite family. Also called *asanpi iyatke*, so called because of the shape of the fruit. - Note: BT was used to giving it to horses when they could not urinate. WE said a tea made from the coneflower is good against belly-ache. RV said a tea made from the tops is good for headache - #66
na·po·ta \na-p̣ó-ṭa\ *va* na·wa·pota : to wear out with the feet *e.g.* one's shoes
na·po·wa·ya \na-pó-wa-ya\ *v* na·wa·powaya: to fringe, perhaps - *Syn* NASWAYA
na·po·yu·bla·ya \na-p̣ó-yu-blaya\ *v* : to open the palm of the hand < *Letanhan napoyublayapi s'e yunka ca napecešni woimnankin ktelo* Since it lay as if with open hands, he should be unabashedly capable, *i.e.* the road is now level. > - Bl WHL
na·po·yu·ja·ja \na-p̣ó-yu-ja-ja\ *n* : a wash basin
na·psag \na-pség\ *va contrac of* napsaka : to break by foot < ~ *iyeya* to break in two by foot >
na·psa·ka \na-psá-ka\ *va* na·wa·psaka : to break *e.g.* a chord with the foot, to break something in two with the foot
na·psan·ni \na-psáŋ-ni\ *n* [fr *nape* hand + *sanni* on one side] : the hand on one side, one hand of a person
na·psa·psa·ka \na-psá-psa-ka\ *va red of* napsaka : to break in different places *e.g.* a string
na·psa·psa·ke·la s'e \na-psá-psa-ke-la s'e\ *adv* : breaking like rope tearing apart < ~ *mani* to walk tripllingly along, the *napsaka* suggesting the tearing of a cord with the foot > - B.H.77.1 Bl
na·psi·ca \na-psí-ca\ *vn* na·wa·psica : to skip, hop, jump around
na·psil \na-psíl\ *vn contrac of* napsica : to jump < ~ *iyaya* to go jumping > — **napsi·lya** *va* : to make jump, make dance
na·psi·psi·ca \na-psí-psi-ca\ *vn* na·wa·psipsica [fr *napsica* to jump about] : to dance about; *fig* to spatter out *e.g.* hot grease when water is dropped into it
na·psi·psil \na-psí-psil\ *vn contrac red of* napsipsica : to hop about < ~ *iyaya* to go about jumping > —napsipsi-

---

\a\ f<u>a</u>ther \e\ th<u>ey</u> \i\ mach<u>i</u>ne \o\ sm<u>o</u>ke \u\ l<u>u</u>nar \an, aŋ\ bl<u>an</u>c Fr. \in, iŋ\ <u>in</u>k \on, oŋ, un, uŋ\ s<u>oo</u>n, <u>con</u>fier Fr. \c\ <u>ch</u>air \ġ\ ma<u>ch</u>en Ger. \j\ fu<u>s</u>ion \clusters: bl, gn, kp, hšl, etc...\ <u>b</u>ᵉlo ... said with a slight vowel
See more in the Introduction, Guide to Pronunciation

lya *va* napsipsi·lwa·ya : to make skip or dance about
na·psi·yo·hli *or perhaps* **napsiyohle** \na-psí-yo-ȟli\ *n* : a finger ring, a ring
na·psi·yo·hli ku·te·pi \na-psí-yo-ȟli ku-tè-pi\ *n* : a game in which one person holds a stick carrying six rings and tosses them into the air to catch thereafter as many as possible on the same stick – Bl
na·pska·šni \na-pská-šni\ *adj* : of unclean hands; *fig* a sinner
na·pson *or* **napsun** \na-psón\ *va* : to kick spilling
na·psu \na-psú\ *n* mi·napsu : a finger
na·psu·han·ska \na-psú-haŋ-ska\ *n* : the middle finger
na·psu·hu *n* : a finger bone > – B.H.274.20
na·psu·hu o·ko \na-psú-hu o-kō'\ *n* : the spaces between the fingers
na·psu·ka·za *or* **napsu·okaza** \na-psú-ǩa-za\ *n* : the five fingers of the hand – Cf *napsuokihe* the knuckles
na·psun \na-psúŋ\ *va* na·wa·psun : to kick over and spill
na·psu·o·ka·za \na-psú-o-ǩa-za\ *n* : the fingers
na·psu·o·ki·he \na-psú-o-ǩi-he\ *n* : the knuckles of the fingers – Bl
na·pša \na-pšá\ *vn* : to be a hindrance to the motion of the feet – Note: the word is doubtfully used
na·pša·pša \na-pšá-pša\ *v red* : to be a hindrance to one's walking < ~ *s'e omani* to walk with difficulty, slowly as one hindered in doing so, as is said when an old man walks slowly. Similarly, *nahpahpa s'e omani* to walk as one tottering about to fall. *Wašicun tawa s'e ~ hiyayelo* A white man passes by with difficulty as though the place were his, as is said when a person walks with difficulty on account of too long clothing, pants or stockings hanging down, like Arabian horses with their hairy feet. > – Bl
na·pši·ja \na-pší-ja\ *v* : to ruin by stepping on – Bl WHL
na·pšun \na-pšúŋ\ *vn* : to break by kicking, to dislocate the foot or leg — *va* na·wa·pšun : to put out of joint *e.g.* the foot or leg
na·pšun·ka \na-pšúŋ-ǩa\ *n* : any round growth on one, a lump or swelling – Cf pšunka *n*
na·pta \na-ptá\ *va* na·wa·pta **1** : to throw over ground, as is done in using a spade **2** : to wear off or cut by foot < *makinapte* a spade >
na·pta·he·na \na-ptá-he-na\ *adv obsol* : forgetting < ~ *ecamon šni* I failed forgetting to do it. > – *Syn* LOTKUNKEŠNI RF
na·ptan·yan \na-ptáŋ-yaŋ\ *va* na·wa·ptanyan : to upset by kicking *e.g.* a coal bucket, to kick over — **naptanyan·kel** \na-ptáŋ-yaŋ-ǩel\ *adv* : in the manner of turning over
na·pte·ca \na-pté-ca\ *adv* : less – *Syn* AOPTECA
na·ptel *or* **naptelya** \na-ptél\ *adv contrac of* napteca : less – *Syn* AOPTEL *or* AOPTELYA — **naptelye·la** *adv* : less, diminished – *Syn* AOPTELYELA
na·pte·tu·ka \na-pté-tu-ka\ *adj* : a few < *wicaša* ~ a few men >
na·ptu·ga \na-ptú-ǧa\ *va* na·wa·ptuga : to break off a piece with the foot — *vn* : to break off of itself, as a piece of ice – BD
na·ptu·ja \na-ptú-ja\ *vn* : to crack, split of itself or by the action of heat or cold — **naptu·ptuja** *vn red* : to be splitting — **naptuš** *vn contrac* : to crack < ~ *iyaya* to go cracking >
na·p'a·ka·špe·ya \na-p'á-ǩa-šp̣e-ya\ *v* nap'a·ma·kašpeya : to let slip or drop from the hands because a thing is too heavy or too hot or *etc*
na·p'a·nunk yu·za \na-p'á-nuŋk yu-zà\ *v* : to take hold on something with both hands < *Nap'anunk ȟan* Both his hands are sore. >
na·p'in \na-p'íŋ\ *va* : to wear around the neck *e.g.* beads *etc* < *Nupin šiyotanka nap'inpi* Both large grouse wore it around their necks. > — **nap'in·kiya** \na-p'íŋ-ǩi-ya\ *va* nap'in·wa·kiya : to cause to wear on the neck — **nap'in·pi** *n* : a yoke < *ca* ~ an ox yoke >
na·p'i·ta·ka·ha \na-p'í-ṫa-ǩa-ha\ *n* : the back of the hand – *See* napitakaha
na·p'ku·wa·š'a·ka \na-p'ǩu-wa-š'à-ka\ *vn* nap'kuwa·ma·š'aka : to grasp firmly
na·p'o \na-p'ó\ *vn* na·wa·p'o : to raise dust with the feet, as horses do walking *etc*
na·p'o·mna \na-p'ó-mna\ *va* na·wa·p'omna : to cause to smell by stepping on
na·sa *or* **nase** \na-sá\ *va* na·wa·sa : to hunt buffalo, to surround and kill, as once they did in the buffalo hunt < *Lecetanhan taku ahinapa tka nasa s'e ahinapelo: iglakapi šni yelo: šunkakanyankapi s'elececa yelo* It was like riding horseback: they did not pitch their tents:afterwards, they came in sight of something but they came out as to a buffalo hunt. > — *vn* : to stand erect, as hogs' bristles
na·sa·tin \na-sá-ṫiŋ\ *v* : to stretch out, as an animal when dying, to become straight — **nasatin·tin** *v red* : to be straight < ~ *iyaya* to go straight, as *e.g.* a *hutanacute* a puck for ice hockey >
na·sa·ya \na-sá-ya\ *adv* : prickly, knobby, sharp < ~ *han* it is said to be sharp. > – Bl
na·seb \na-séb\ *vn contrac* [fr *nasepa* in Dakota, to leak out] : to go scraping along, cleaning off, brushing off
na·ska \na-sǩá\ *vn* : to bleach, get white
na·skeb \na-sǩéb\ *vn contrac of* naskepa : to leak out
na·ske·pa \na-sǩé-p̣a\ *vn of* skepa : to leak out, be empty – B.H.106.7
na·ski·ca \na-skí-ca\ *va* : to press down with the feet, as a man walking on a hay wagon to get it down — *vn perhaps* : to go down or become less of itself, to settle — **naskil** \na-sǩíl\ *vn* : to diminish, become less < ~ *iyaya* to abate, to go down, as a swelling does >
na·sla \na-slá\ *va* na·wa·sla : to grease with the foot
na·slal \na-slál\ *adv contrac of* naslata : without noise, stilly < ~ *ya* to go quietly, ~ *bla* I went noiselessly, *i.e.* to walk or crawl up without noise. > — **nasla·slal** *adv contrac red* : noiselessly < ~ *omani, ya* He went walking without a sound. > – D.272
na·sla·sla·ta \na-slá-sla-ta\ *v red* na·wa·slata : to make a quiet approach
na·sla·ta \na-slá-ṫa\ *va* na·wa·slata : to go softly up to anything, to crawl up to
na·sle·ca \na-slé-ca\ *va* : to crack or split — *vn* : to crack or split of itself, as a board or the earth in winter < *Maka kin* ~ The ground cracked. > – Bl D.67
na·slel \na-slél\ *v contrac of* nasleca : to crack or split; to saw < ~ *iyaya* to go cracking > — **nasle·lya** *va* nasle·lwa·ya : to cause to split or crack < *can* ~ to saw boards on the saw mill > — **nasle·sleca** \na-slé-sle-ca\ *v red of* nasleca : to crack or split
na·sli \na-slí\ *va* na·wa·sli : to crush with the foot *e.g.* a bug, *etc* — *vn perhaps* : to hiss, as wet wood in the fire — **nasli·sli** *v red* : to crush be foot — **nasli·ya** *adv* : oozing out, as sap from a tree
na·slo·han \na-sló-haŋ\ *va* : to make slide by kicking *e.g.* a dog
na·slu·ta \na-slū'-ṫa\ *va* na·wa·sluta : to kick out with

the feet, as from one's bed — *vi* : to slip out, as a foreign object from an ulcer - D.60

na·smin·yan \na-smíŋ-yaŋ\ *va* na·wa·sminyan : to scrape off with the foot — **nasminyan·yan** *v red* na-·wa·sminyanyan : to scrape or wear off with the feet and leave bare

na·sna \na·sná\ *va* na·wa·sna : to make a rattling noise with the feet, as with the spurs — *vn perhaps* : to fall off of itself, as rice when the tying breaks — **nasna·sna** *v red* : to rattle < ~ *mani* to make a tinkling sound as one walks >

na·sni \na-sní\ *va* na·wa·sni : to put out a fire with the foot

na·son *or* **nasun** \na-sóŋ\ *vn* na·wa·son : to stretch out the feet and legs — **nason·son** *or* **nasunsun** \na-sóŋ-soŋ\ *v red* na·wa·sonson : to struggle

na·son·spe *or* **nazunspe** \na-sóŋ-spe\ *n* : an axe

na·son·yan *or* **nasunyan** \na-sóŋ-yaŋ\ *adv* : in a manner struggling

na·so·ta \na-só-ṫa\ *va* na·wa·sota : to use up, to destroy with the feet

na·spa \na-sṗá\ *vn* : to get wet < *Yunkan hanpa kin naspapi* And then his shoes got wet. > — **naspa·ya** *va* na·wa·spaya : to wet the feet, the shoes, to wet with the feet < *Si namicispaya ca ito k'eyaš pusmic'iyin ktelo* Since he wet my feet for me, but come now, he should dry them for me. >

na·stan·ka \na-sṫáŋ-ka\ *va* na·wa·stanka : to moisten with the feet

na·su \na-sú\ *n* : the upper part of the head, the brain < ~ *kaosnisni s'e* He is like one keeping his head cool, as is said when a person has got little hair left and standing in all directions. > — **nasu·hu** *n* : the skull, the cranium - *Syn* NATAHU Bl

na·su·ka·za \na-sú-ka-za\ *n* : the knuckle

na·su·la \na-sú-la\ *n dim of* nasú : the brain, the cerebrum - Note: *nasú* is not used for this English meaning

na·sun·pa·kce \na-súŋ-ṗa-kce\ *n* [fr *nasu* upper head + *pakca* to comb] : a comb < ~ *swúla* a fine comb >

na·sun·sun *or* **nasonson** \na-súŋ-suŋ\ *v red* na·wa·sunsun : to struggle

na·sun·yan *or* **nasonyan** \na-súŋ-yaŋ\ *adv* : with the feet and legs stretched out < *Kat'eyetanka ~ yanka* to sit on the ground long and still with both legs stretched out. ~ *hpaya* He fell flat, *i.e.* stretched on the ground. > - RF

na·su·su·za \na-sú-su-za\ *v red of* nasuza : to snap, as ice forming

na·su·štin·ca s'e \na-sú-štiŋ-ca s'e\ *adv* : as if swept clean of hair on the head, as is said of a person who has very little hair left, thin and looking ragged - Bl

na·su·ta \na-sú-ṫa\ *va* : to trample hard

na·su·za \na-sú-za\ *vn* : to splinter or fly off, as a piece of a bone, to snap, as water freezing

na·swa \na-swá\ *vn* : to tear into fringes, to fray, rip - Note: the word is used to denote what is done when one steps *e.g.* on a silk dress and it stretches partly, the thread tearing one way

na·swa·ka \na-swá-ka\ *v* : to fall off, as feathers

na·swa·ya \na-swá-ya\ *v* na·wa·swaya : to fringe - *Syn* NAPOWAYA

na·s'a \na-s'á\ *vn* : to simmer, make a slight noise, as water before boiling; *fig* said of a fast horse - Bl

na·s'in·ye·la \na-s'íŋ-ye-la\ *adv* : stretched out < *Itunkab ~ yunka* He lay all stretched out on the back. >

na·s'o·s'o \na-s'ó'-s'o\ *vn* na·wa·s'os'o : to shuffle, to scrape the feet along as in dancing; to draw the feet over the floor as men once did to show their anger < ~ *mani* to walk with a shuffle >

naš \naš\ *conj emph of* na : and, and indeed - B.H.19.7, 123.5, and pages 92,99,108,124,133,135,136,145, *etc*

na·ša \na-šá\ *vn* [fr *na* and + *ša* red] : to blush, to become red < *Ite ~ hingla* His face suddenly blushed, *i.e.* his face colored up. >

na·šab \na-šáb\ *va contrac of* našapa : to soil < ~ *iyeya* to defile with the feet > — **naša·bya** *va* naša·bwa·ya : to cause to soil with the feet

na·ša·ka·ye·la \na-šä'-ka-ye-la\ *adv* : fresh, as a wound not yet closed up < *Oo kin ~ han na we hiyu* The wound stood open while blood issued. >

na·ša·k'o·ha·ye·ya \na-šá-k'o-ha-ye-ya\ *adv* : making a rattling sound as something grow red < ~ *ayugal waun welo, peta kin* I raised my hands it making a crackling sound, *i.e.* the fire. > - Bl

na·ša·pa \na-šá-pa\ *va* : to soil, blacken, defile with the feet

na·še·ca \na-šé-ca\ *va* na·wa·šeca : to make wither by trampling on *e.g.* grass — **naše·lya** *va* na·še·lwa·ya : to cause to trample on and make wither

na·šib \na-šíb\ *va contrac of* našipa : to bend by foot < ~ *iyaya* to go bending by foot > — **naši·bšib** *va red* : to sustain bending with the foot < ~ *iyeya.* ~ *mani* He quickly bent it. He walked bending it with his foot, as one does when the shoe laces are loose. >

na·ši·ca \na-ší-ca\ *va* na·wa·šica : to spoil or defile with the feet

na·ši·ca·ho·wa·ya \na-ší-ca-ho-wa-ya\ *va* na·wa·šicahowaya : to make howl by kicking *e.g.* a dog, and not a human being

na·šin·šin \na-šíŋ-šiŋ\ *vn* : to contract and wrinkle, as warm glue does when cooling off *etc*, or as a wet cloth when drying < ~ *aya* to begin to wrinkle, ~ *iyaya* to get to be wrinkled, as is said of something that has been stretched and cut in two, and then the two pieces crinkle, *i.e.* shorten > - Bl

na·ši·pa \na-ší-pa\ *va* na·wa·šipa : to bend *e.g.* a stick by stepping on

na·ška \na-šká\ *va* na·wa·ška : to untie with the foot — *vn* : to come untied of itself

na·ška·bya \na-šká-bya\ *va* naška·bwa·ya [fr *naškapa* to collide] : to make bump *e.g.* two tops spinning collide with each other

na·ška·han \na-šká-haŋ\ *part* : untied, loose, as a knot - R Bl

na·škan \na-škáŋ\ *va* : to jostle, jolt < *Tapon ~ s'e inyanke* He ran as if he was jostling his cheeks, *i.e.* the cheeks went up and down from the wagon jolting. > — **naškan·škan** *va* na·wa·škanškan : to shake or move about with the foot — *vn* : to move rapidly, as by a machine; to be shaking, trembling *i.e.* as an automobile when the engine starts - Note: *naškanškan* differs from *kaškanškan.* The former means a rapid motion, and the latter, a shaking from slow bumping or hitting or striking. For that reason "moving pictures" are called *itowapi naškanškan* - Bl

na·ška·pa \na-šká-ṗa\ *v* : to collide with, bump, rub

\a\ father \e\ they \i\ machine \o\ smoke \u\ lunar \an, aŋ\ blanc Fr. \in, iŋ\ ink \on, oŋ, un, uŋ\ soon, confier Fr. \c\ chair \ǧ\ machen Ger. \j\ fusion \clusters: bl, gn, kp, hšl, etc...\ b[e]lo ... said with a slight vowel
See more in the Introduction, Guide to Pronunciation

along against something - Bl

na·ška·wa·han \na-šká-wa-haŋ\ *part* : untied, loose, as a knot - R Bl

na·škí·ca \na-škí-ca\ *va* na·wa·škica : to press with the foot, to press out by trampling on — **naškil** \na-škíl\ *va contrac of* naškica : to press out with the foot *e.g.* the intestines after butchering < ~ *iyeya* to press out >

na·ški·ška \na-škí-ška\ *va* na·wa·škiška : to make rough *e.g.* the ground by trampling on it < *Canku naškiškapi ca canpagmiyanpi t'inzani mani šni yelo* Since the road was rough a wagon did not travel smoothly. > - Bl

na·ško·kpa \na-škó-k̇pa\ *va* na·wa·škokpa : to indent, make a hollow place with the foot

na·ško·pa \na-šk̇ó-ṗa\ *va* na·wa·škopa : to twist with the foot — *vn* : to twist or become crooked of itself — **naško·škopa** \na-šk̇ó-šk̇o-ṗa\ *v red* : to be twisting

na·šla \na-šlá\ *va* na·wa·šla : to make bare with the feet — **našla·ya** *vn* : to come off, as the hull from corn when boiled — **našla·ye** *adv* : peeling away, making bare < ~ *niktepi* They kill you peeling you away, *i.e.* they keep bothering you. *Šehanštuka tuweni ~ nikte šni hwo?* For once, at last, don't they leave you unbothered? > Bl

na·šle \na-šlé\ *va* : to divide, to split < *Cehupa namašle kinica* My jaw tried to split me in two, as a person might say who chewed suddenly into something very sour. > - Bl

na·šle·ca \na-šlé-ca\ *va* or perhaps *n* : to split something heavy or big with the foot and with effort — **našlel** *va contrac* : to make split < ~ *iyaya* to go splitting > — **našle·lya** *va* našle·lwa·ya : to cause to split — **našle·šleca** *v red* : to be splitting

na·šli \na-šlí\ *vn* na·ma·šli : to swell and form sores, to ooze out as sap from trees or juice from meat roasting

na·šlog \na-šlóg\ *v contrac of* našloka : to run or flee away suddenly, as horses do at times < ~ *glicu* to start off home suddenly, *kos hiyuya na ~ iyaya* to go running away and to send one off waving >

na·šlo·ka \na-šló-ka\ *va* na·wa·šloka : to kick off *e.g.* one's shoes — *vn* : to come off, escape, fly out, as the cork of a bottle

na·šlul \na-šlúl\ *vn contrac* : to slide < ~ *hpayelo* He slipped falling. > — **našlu·lya** *va* našlu·lwa·ya : to cause to slip — **našlu·šlul** *v contrac red* : to slip repeatedly, as horses do on ice — **našlušlu·ta** \na-šlú-šlu-ṫa\ *vn* : to slip often — *va* na·wa·šlušluta : to make smooth with the feet

na·šlu·ta \na-šlú-ṫa\ *vn* an perhaps *va* na·wa·šluta : to slip, slide, slip down

[1]**na·šna** \na-šná\ *vn* : to miss one's footing, to slip — *va* na·wa·šna : to miss something in kicking < *Canku naunšnapi, tka tanyan unkupelo* We missed the road, but we got home alright, *i.e.* in spite of one's missing one's road when coming home. >

[2]**na·šna** \na-šná\ *adv* : again and again, always < ~ *apapi* He was struck repeatedly. > - Note: there is some doubt about the use of *šna* compounded this way; cf šna

na·šna·šna \na-šná-šna\ *v red* : to miss one's footing repeatedly

na·šni·ja \na-šní-ja\ *va* na·wa·šnija : to trample on and and kill *e.g.* the grass — *vn* : to be withered, as after a frost

na·šo·ka \na-šõ'-k̇a\ *vn* na·ma·šoka : to thicken, swell, a piece of wood in water, to get a thick skin on one's feet from walking

na·šo·ša \na-šó-ša\ *va* na·wa·šoša : to make turbid or dirty *e.g.* water with the feet

na·špa \na-špá\ *va* na·wa·špa : to break off anything with the foot — **našpa·špa** *v red* : to break off many things with the foot

na·špe·ya \na-šṗé-ya\ *va* našpe·wa·ya : to cause to break off with the foot, *e.g.* by pushing somebody

na·špi \na-šṗí\ *va* na·wa·špi : to break off *e.g.* fruit with the foot

na·špu \na-šṗú\ *va* na·wa·špu : to break off with the foot something sticking, *e.g.* pumpkins, to knock off something with the foot — **našpu·špu** *va red* na·wa·špušpu : to break off pieces, to break in pieces with the foot *e.g.* tallow — *vn red* : to come to pieces, as meat in boiling

na·šta·šta· s'e \na-štá-šta s'e\ *adv* : as though tired out or exhausted < ~ *mani* to walk as if one's legs are weak > - WE

na·šu·ja \na-šú-ja\ *va* na·wa·šuja : to bruise or crush with the foot

Na·šun·ȟa·pe *or* **Natableca** \Na-šúŋ-ȟa-pe\ *np* : a Flathead Indian - SB

na·šuš \na-šúš\ *va contrac of* našuja : to bruise or crush by foot < ~ *iyeya* suddenly to crush >

na·šu·ška \na-šú-ška\ *va* : to make one tardy, *fig* to become a worthless fellow < *Tezi našuškayeya wimape nat'insya he kapi* They meant that in pressing tight my weapon to his belly caused to retard him. >

na·šu·šu·ja \na-šú-šu-ja\ *v red* na·wa·šušuja [fr *našuja* to bruise or crush by foot] : to bruise or mash by trampling on — **našušuš** *v contrac* : to mash or bruise - B.H.112.16

[1]**na·ta** \na-ṫá\ *n* : the human head - Cf *pa*

[2]**na·ta** \na-tá\ *v* : to kick up, to kick out of the way perhaps < ~ *aya* to begin kicking away, ~ *iyeya* to kick up things, ~ *ole* to look for kicking away things, as is said of a child who kicks its covers to the feet where they are heaped up > - Bl

na·ta·a·ka·hpe \na-ṫá-a-ka-ȟpe\ *n archaic* : a hat - WR

Na·ta·ble·ca \Na-ṫá-ble-ca\ *np* : a Flathead Indian — *n* : a square head

na·ta·co·ku·hpuhpu \na-ṫá-co-k̇u-ȟpu-ȟpu\ *n* : dandruff - P Bl

na·ta·ghan \na-tá-ghaŋ\ *va of* nataka : to stand fastened, as a closed up fence < ~ *iyeya* to fasten, as in a hurry perhaps >

na·ta·gu·gu \na-ṫá-ġu-ġu\ *n* : a curly head, as that of a Negro - Bl

na·ta·ha \na-ṫá-ha\ *n* : the skin of the head - Bl

na-ta-hu \na-ṫá-hu\ *n* : the skull, the cranium

na·ta·hpu·hpu \na-ṫá-ȟpu-ȟpu\ *n* : dandruff

na·ta·hton·yan \na-tá-ȟtoŋ-yaŋ\ *va* natahton·wa·ya : to beat *e.g.* eggs - P Bl

na·ta·ka \na-tá-k̇a\ *va* na·wa·taka : to bolt or bar *e.g.* a door, to close up, to fence up *e.g.* a field; to stop a leak

na·ta·ku·ni·šni \na-ṫá-k̇u-ni-šni\ *va* na·wa·takunišni : to destroy with the foot — *vi* : to turn into nothing by itself, to vanish by itself, to evaporate

na·ta·na·šun·pa·kce \na-ṫá-na-šuŋ-ṗa-kce\ *n* : a side comb, an ornament

[1]**na·tan** \na-táŋ\ *va* na·wa·tan : to touch with the foot, feel with the foot < *han natantan* to stand feeling with the foot >

[2]**na·tan** \na-ṫáŋ\ *va* na·wa·tan : to make an attack, to go after and rush upon *e.g.* the enemy < *Hecel ~ aglinajin* So they came home and stood to make an attack. >

na·tan·ka \na-táŋ-ka\ *vn* : to enlarge, become larger, as a shoe

na·tan'·onb \na-táŋ-oŋb\ *adv* : leaning, inclined — **na·tan'on·bya** *adv* : leaning < ~ *han* It stands leaning. >

[1]**na·tan·tan** \na-ṫáŋ-ṫaŋ\ *v red of* naṫan : to rush upon, perhaps repeatedly, or in great numbers < ~ *hiyupi* They came out in great numbers. >

[2]**na·tan·tan** \na-táŋ-taŋ\ *va red* na·wa·tantan [fr *natan* to feel by foot] : to feel one's way by foot < *Han* ~ He stood feeling his way with his feet. *Kenatantan kte s'e hanpokihe lo* He put on his shoes like a turtle about to feel his way along. > — **natantan·kel** *adv* : feeling one's way with the feet < ~ *iwaštegla yahe* He was going carefully feeling his way with his feet. > - D.223

na·ta·šla \na-ṫá-šla\ *adj* : bald-headed

[1]**na·ta·ta** \na-ṫá-ṫa\ *va* : to shake off *e.g.* dust from one's feet or blanket - Bl

[2]**na·ta·ta** \na-tá-ta\ *or perhaps* \na-ṫá-ṫa\ *va* : to heap up with the feet, as is done when boys wrestle and pile up ground with the feet, or as children kick down their bed clothing and heap it up at the feet

na·ta ya·zan·pi \na-ṫá ya-zàŋ-pi\ *n* : a head-ache, a sickness common among the Sioux peoples

na·teb \na-ṫéb\ *va contrac of* natépa : to wear off < ~ *iyeya* to wear away > — **nate·bya** *va* nate·bwa·ya : to cause to wear off *e.g.* one's horse's hoof

na·te·mni \na-ṫé-mni\ *v* na·ma·temni : to sweat from excitement, or perspire from heat or warm weather - B.H.255.19

na·te·pa \na-ṫé-ṗa\ *va* na·wa·tepa : to wear off with the foot *e.g.* one's shoes, to wear short, as a hoof or shoe — *adj* : worn off, worn out, as a shoe

na·tib \na-ṫíb\ *vn* [fr *natipa* to contract] : to draw up, as a person dying, or as a hide drying — **nati·bti·pa** \na-ṫí-bṫi-ṗa\ *vn contrac red* na·má·tibtipa : to have the cramps — **nati·bya** \na-ṫí-bya\ *va* nati·bwa·ya : to cause to draw up

na·ti·ca \na-ṫí-ca\ *va* : to scrape with the foot, *i.e.* away from one, but not pawing like a horse nor like a child kicking off the bed clothes

na·ti·kti·ca \na-ṫí-kṫi-ca\ *vn* : to thicken by boiling; to trample, make thick by tramping

na·til \na-ṫíl\ *va contrac of* natica : to scrape away with the foot < ~ *iyeya* to scrape away by foot >

na·tin \na-ṫíŋ\ *v* : to be in convulsions < ~ *hapaya* to fall into convulsions, as might a dying person or animal > — **natin·tin** \na-ṫíŋ-ṫiŋ\ *v red* : to be convulsing - Bl

na·ti·pa \na-ṫí-ṗa\ *vn* : to draw up, as does leather when put on the fire, to crisp, to cramp, contract the muscles < *He lecel eya ayaštan kin icunhan skayela (mahpiya) he k'on natipe s'e, wankatakiya kigla* While he finished speaking this too, as though a cloud had drawn him up gloriously, he returned toward the heavens. >

na·ti·pa·si·se \na-ṫí-ṗa-si-se\ *n* : hair pins

na·ti·tan \na-ṫí-ṫaŋ\ *va* na·wa·ti·tan : to pull backwards or forwards by bracing the feet, as a horse in pulling, as a person in using the brake on a wagon or in stretching something

na·ti·yu·ski·te \na-ṫí-yu-ski-te\ *n* [fr *naṫa* a person's head + *iyuskite* bind around] : a wreath or crown - Note: *wateślake* any wrapping around the head, and *nakputake* a scarf are both misnomers

na·tku·ga \na-tkú-ǧa\ *va* : to break square off with the foot — *vn* : to break square off of itself, to break by itself, as a mirror or window pane - BD

na·to·gye·ya \na-ṫó-gye-ya\ *v* : to make different, to give a strange appearance to the face *etc* < *Išta* ~ *yaun welo* Your eyes are giving a strange look, *i.e.* you look terrified. > - Bl

na·to·ki·in·yan·ke \na-ṫó-ǩi-iŋ-yaŋ-ke\ *n* [fr *nata* head + *okiinyanka* to run directly through the middle] : the sutures of the skull - EF

na·to·to \na-ṫó-ṫo\ *va* na·wa·toto : to knock at something, *e.g.* a door with the foot, to make a noise by knocking with the foot

na·tu·htuh \na-ṫú-ḣṫuḣ\ *va of* túga : to lift or pull and so becoming hunched over, to make horses pull hard < ~ *yeya* to cause pull or lift hunched over > - Bl

na·tu·ja \na-tú-ja\ *vi* na·ma·tuja : to have the itch - LT

na·tu·ka \na-ṫú-ǩa\ *va* na·wa·tuka : to stamp off and destroy *e.g.* fur

na·tu·ta \na-ṫú-ta\ *vn* : to smart, as one's feet by traveling much < *Si namatuta* My feet do smart. >

na·tu·tka \na-ṫú-tǩa\ *va* na·wa·tutka : to knock pieces off with the foot

na·t'a \na-t'á\ *va* na·wa·t'a : to kill by kicking

na·t'e·ki·ni·ca \na-t'é-ǩi-ni-ca\ *v* [fr *nat'a* to kill by kicking + *kinica* strive] : to beg to death, to annoy, vex, or worry

na·t'e·ya \na-t'é-ya\ *v* : to kill by running *e.g.* a wagon

na·t'in·hye·ya \na-t'iŋ-ḣye-ya\ *va* : to cause to grunt, as with medicine given to a woman in the throes of childbirth - FB

na·t'ins \na-t'íŋs\ *va contrac of* nat'inza : to press hard by foot < ~ *iyeya* to exert pressure by foot >

na·t'in·za \na-t'íŋ-za\ *va* na·wa·t'inza : to press hard with the foot

na·t'o·pe s'e \na-t'ó-ṗe s'e\ *adv* : in a tottering manner, when *e.g.* one walks a great distance and then is ready to drop < ~ *omani* to travel as one about to collapse >

na·t'un·gya·kel \na-t'úŋ-gya-kel\ *adv obs* : hesitatingly, carefully as though afraid - *Syn* KOKIPEYA

na·t'un·ka \na-t'úŋ-ka\ *vn* na·wa·t'unka : to refuse to go, hold back, hesitate, as a man not liking an order or such — **nat'un·kiya** *va* nat'un·wa·kiya : to make afraid, make hesitate — **nat'un·t'ungyakel** *adv red of* nat'ungyakel : hesitatingly as though afraid

na·ung \na-úŋg\ *vn contrac of* naúnka : to gallop, as a horse does < ~ *iyaya* to go galloping along > — **naun·gkiya** \na-úŋ-gǩi-ya\ *va* : to cause to gallop

na·un·ka \na-úŋ-ka\ *vn* na·wa·unka **1** : to gallop, as a horse does < *naunka u* or *naung u* to come galloping, *Pte na tahca ko naunkapi na šake icicašla naunkapi* Deer and the buffalo as well gallop and they gallop clicking their hooves together. > **2** : to kick and make fall, perhaps

na·wa·kan·kan·la \na-wá-kaŋ-kaŋ-la\ *adv* : carefully, quietly < ~ *mani* to walk with care > - Bl

na·wa·ni·ca \na-wá-ni-ca\ *va* na·wa·wanica : to trample to nothing, destroy by trampling on — *vi* : to turn into nothing by itself, to disappear or evaporate — **na·wanil** \na-wá-nil\ *va contrac* : to destroy or annihilate, to walk or run off sickness or fatigue

na·wan·kal \na-wáŋ-ǩal\ *v* : to rise upward < ~ *hiyu* to spring upon, as on the boards of a floor, ~ *iyeya* to blow up, as with powder, *Etanhan (cega) wicanape wan ~ hiyu ške* From the kettle they say a human hand rose to

---

\a\ father \e\ they \i\ machine \o\ smoke \u\ lunar \an, aŋ\ blanc Fr. \in, iŋ\ ink \on, oŋ, un, uŋ\ soon, confier Fr. \c\ chair \ǧ\ machen Ger. \j\ fusion \clusters: bl, gn, kp, hšl, etc...\ b[e]lo ... said with a slight vowel
See more in the Introduction, Guide to Pronunciation

the surface. > – D.54

na·wa·te \na-wá-ṫe\ *n* : the temples of the head < ~ *a-nunk mayazan* The temple on either side of my head pains me. >

na·wa·za \na-wá-za\ *va* na·wa·waza : to scratch with the foot as chickens do, to move the foot to and fro, as in crushing a bug or in putting out a fire < *naic'iwaza* to scratch one's self with the foot, as do horses and dogs >

na·we·ga \na-wé-ġa\ *va* na·wa·wega : to break by kicking, to break with the foot < *Šunkawakan namahtaka na namawega* My horse kicked me and broke loose from me. > — **naweh** \na-wéḣ\ *va contrac* : to break by foot < ~ *iyeya* to break kicking suddenly > — **nawe·hkiya** \na-wé-ḣk̇i-ya\ *va* : to cause to break with the foot — **nawe·hya** \na-wé-ḣya\ *va* nawe·hwa·ya : to cause to break with the foot

na·wi·ca·kše·ca \na-wí-ca-kše-ca\ *n obs* : the cramps, an old-time sickness that can lead to death, convulsions *Syn* NAWICATIPA, NAKŠECAPI

na·wi·ca·šli \na-wí-ca-šli\ *n* : the measles, a rash

na·wi·ca·ti·pa \na-wí-ca-ṫí-pa\ *n* : cramping, the cramps

na·wi·ci·te \na-wí-ci-ṫe\ *n* : the flesh or muscles on the upper arm near the shoulder < ~ *el mayazan* My shoulder aches. > – Bc

na·wi·gnu·ni \na-wí-gnu-ni\ *va* na·wa·wignuni : to destroy with the foot – R Bl

na·wi·lwi·te s'e \na-wí-lwi-ṫe s'e\ *adv* : as if scraping together with the feet < ~ *mani* to walk dragging the feet over the ground as if one gathered snow together > – Bl

na·win·ce·šni \na-wíŋ-ce-šni\ *adj* : immovable, by the feet perhaps, as a rock set firmly in the ground

na·win·ja \na-wíŋ-ja\ *va* na·wa·winja : to trample down *e.g.* grass, to mat down, to bend *e.g.* a fence wire by stepping on it

na·winl i·ye·ya \na-wíŋl i-yè-ya\ *va* 1 : to scratch one with one's foot 2 : to attract one's attention by touching him – Bl

na·winš \na-wíŋš\ *va contrac of* nawinja : to trample down — **nawin·škiya** *or* **nawin·šya** \na-wíŋ-šk̇i-ya\ *va* : to make one bend down with the foot, as a fence wire — **nawin·šwinja** *v red* : to make crooked or bent by stepping on repeatedly, to cause to trample down

na·win·ta \na-wíŋ-ta\ *v* : to clear space on the ground with the feet, scraping away things – P WHL

na·wi·zi \na-wí-zi\ *v* na·wa·wizi : to be jealous, envious

na·wi·zi·pan·ye·ya \na-wí-zi-paŋ-ye-ya\ *adv* : swollen, bloated, filled up, distended < *nige ~ wipi* the belly to be full and bloated with food, full as a bag > – *Syn* NAINYANYEYA, NAGLAKEYEYA

na·wi·zi·s'a \na-wí-zi-s'a\ *n* : a jealous person

na·wo·ho·lye·ya \na-wó-ho-lye-ya\ *adv* : taking or forming the shape of a tube < *Ila kin ~ matásakelo* The mouth of mine taking the shape of a tube, *i.e.* with my lips protruding, was stiff from the cold. ~ *po* to swell to a tubular shape >

na·wo·sa·ki·ya \na-wó-sa-k̇i-ya\ *vn* : to bristle up, to stand erect, as hair < *Hin ~* The hair stood on end. >

na·wo·sla i·ye·ya \na-wó-sla i-yè-ya\ *v* : to cause something to stand upward by stepping on, as a pile of wood

na·ye·i·c'i·ya \na-yé-i-c'i-ya\ *v refl* : to make one's self perspire, as in a sweat lodge – Note: the word is quite doubtful

na·za·mni \na-zá-mni\ *v* : to open by kicking away, as children kick away the bed clothes < ~ *s'e* like opening by kicking > – Bl

na·zan \na-záŋ\ *v* na·wa·zan : to hurt, to stun by kicking

na·ze·ya \na-zé-ya\ *v* naze·wa·ya : to filter

na·zi·ca \na-zí-ca\ *adj* : over-stretched, as a machine belt that becomes too wide — *va perhaps* : to stretch *e.g.* a rope by means of the knees or feet – Bl

na·zi·gzil \na-zí-gzil\ *adj* : pliant, flexible, flimsy < *Yunkan taku ~ iwahan waku* And then I came back and stood on something slimsy. > – MS.356

na·zon·spe \na-zóŋ-spe\ *n* : an axe < ~ *ihupa* an axe handle, ~ *opetanka* a broad-axe >

ni \ni\ *pron in comp* : you *pl* (thee), you *singl* (thou), your (thy), yours (thine) – *See* ma, mi

— *suff* – It converts a word into the contrary (šni), thus: *wanji* one, *wanjini* none; *hankeni* no part; *tukteni* nowhere, *Eyaš tostos hankeni wate šni ka, eye* But, Oh yes, he said he indicated he had eaten not a morsel. *icinunpani* not again, not a second time B.H.282.8

— *vn* wa·ni : to live

— *partic* – It is put after the *v* expressing a wish < *Toke he bluha ni (nunwe)* Oh I wish I had that. > – B.H. 84.4, 245.20

[1]**ni·ca** \ni-cá\ *v of* ka : He means you

[2]**ni·ca** \ní-ca\ *vn* ma·níca ni·níca un·nica·pi : to be destitute of, to have none of

ni·ca·o·le \ní-ca-o-le\ *v* nícao·wà·le : to look for poor people

ni·ci \ní-ci\ *pron + prep* : for you – Note: this does not mean "with you", although BD holds it means both for and with you Cf nicíca

ni·ci·ca \ni-cí-ca\ *prep + pron* : with you < *Tokša ~ waun kte lo* Soon I shall be with you. *Itancan kin ~ yaun* The Lord is with you. > — **nicica·ya** *v* : to cause to be with you < ~ *waun* I have you with me. > – B.H.48.2, 74.14 Pb.6

ni·c'i \ni-c'i\ *refl pers pron 2nd pers in comp* : yourself

ni·ge \ni-ġé\ *n* : the stomach, the paunch

ni·ge·san·la \ni-ġé-saŋ-la\ *n* : an antelope; the prairie antelope or gazelle – *Syn* TATOKALA

ni·ge·tan·ka a·u·pi \ni-ġé-taŋ-ka a-ù-pi\ *n* : a swelling of the abdomen with the arms and legs lean, such a sickness – Bl

ni·ge·tan·kin·yan \ni-ġé-taŋ-k̇iŋ-yaŋ\ *n* : a "Big Belly", a by-name for chiefs < ~ *wacipi kte lo* the Big Bellies will be dancing, *i.e.* each one carrying a hatchet. > – BT

ni·han \ni-háŋ\ *adj* ma·nihan : afraid — **nihan·yan** *va* nihan·wa·ya : to scare – R Bl

ni·hin·ci·ya \ni-híŋ-ci-ya\ *vn* nihin·mi·ciya nihin·unki·ciya·pi : to be frightened, scared, to hurry, cry, scream as in fright — **nihinciya·kel** *adv* : in fright

ni·hka·zi·lki·ya \ni-ḣká-zi-lk̇i-ya\ *v* [fr *nige* stomach + *kazilya* to stretch out] : to fast, *i.e.* to stretch one's stomach < *Nihkazilwakiyin kte* I shall do a fast. > – Bl

ni·h'kpa·tan \ni-ḣ'kpá-ṫaŋ\ *v* : to eat little, knowing something better is coming – Bl

ni·h'to·ka·ye·ya·šni \ni-ḣ'tó-ka-ye-ya-šni\ *v* nih'tokaye·wa·yašni : to fill one's self – Bl

ni·i·c'i·ya \ni-í-c'i-ya\ *v* : to make one's self live, to save one's self, to escape, have a narrow escape – Pb.35

ni·ka \ni-k̇á\ *n* : a former time or age < *Wicanike c'on hehan lena ocanku* In olden times there were these roads. > – BT

[1]**ni·ki·ya** \ni-k̇í-ya\ *va* ni·wa·kiya ni·ci·ciya : to prevent *i.e.* to stop – *Syn* ANAPTA WE

[2]**ni·ki·ya** \ni-k̇í-ya\ *va* ni·wa·kiya [fr *ni* to live] : to

cause to live – Pb.42

nil \nil\ *vn contrac of* níca : to have none of, to be destitute of

ni·ni \ni-ní\ *adj* **1** : curdled, coagulated, as is said of thick sour milk **2** : quivering, jelled < *asanpi* ~ cream, *canpá* ~ choke-cherry jelly, perhaps >

nin \niŋ\ *interj* : May it be, Would that it were < *Toke bluha nin* I wish I had it. > – *See* under toke...ni

ni·se·hu \ni-sé-hu\ *n* : the hip-bone, *Lat* os ilium < ~ *aglé* something soft *e.g.* bedding to put under one's back while resting, ~ *gli homni kte* Hip Bone will turn around and go back. > – BMj Bl

ni·sko \ní-sk̇o\ *adv* : so large — **nisko·keca** *or* **nisko·skokeca** \ní-sk̇o-k̇e-ca\ *adv* : so great or large — **nisko·la** *or* **nisko·skola** \ní-sk̇o-la\ *adv* : small, only so large, very little *i.e.* with the idea of derision or contempt < *Ptehincala wan* ~ *tonpelo* A puny calf was born. *He - owanjila eša ektana nake šni, niskole, takuwe yau ca?* Though like him, afterwards he did not twitch, you Twerp (a name used in contempt), why is it you come? *Wicaša nimaskola* I am a man only so big. *Tahca cincala s'e tahu kin* ~ *kagle* He being very little, like a fawn, he took it home by the nap of the neck. > — **nisko·sko** \ní-sko-sko\ *adv red* : being only so big < *Maštincala išta* ~ Rabbits' eyes are only so big. *Iyotan honiskosko panpanpi* They shouted out, a very faint voice. > — **ni-sko·tanka** \ní-sk̇o-taŋ-k̇a\ *adv* : so large — **nisko·ya** \ní-sk̇o-ya\ *adv* : so far around — **niskoye·la** *adv* : only so far around

niš \niš\ *pron* : you < ~ *niye* you yourself > – *See* iš, miš, unkiš

ni·šna·la \ni-šná-la\ *pron pers* : you *singl* alone *nišnala*, you *pl* alone *nišnapila* – *See* išnala, mišnala, unkišnala

ni·štu·šte \ni-štú-šte\ *n* : the rump, the heavy part near the tail, the lower part of the back – *Syn* NITE

ni·ta \ni-tá\ *pron adj in comp* : your, yours *singl* and *pl* – *See* ta, mita, unkita — *pron adj* : your, yours – *See* tawa, mitawa, unkitawa

ni·te \ni-ṫé\ *n* : the rump, the lower part of the back

ni·te·he·pi \ni-ṫé-he-ṗi\ *n* : a woman's skirt, a petticoat < ~ *okijata* a pair of pants, *archaic* > – WR

ni·to \ni-tó\ *imper partic* : Let me...for a second – Note: this is the woman's form used, *yetó* the man's B.H.137

ni·to·ški *or* **nitoške** \ni-ṫó-ški\ *n* : a woman's underskirt – R Bl

ni·un \ní-uŋ\ *v* ní·wa·un : to be living

ni·ya \ni-yá\ *vn* wa·niya : to breathe < ~ *šni* He does not breathe. ~ *kin šota s'e hemaceca yelo* When he breathes it is like as if I were smoking. — **niya·ke** \ni-yá-k̇e\ *adj* ma·niyake : alive < ~ *yuza* to take alive > — **niya·kel** \ni-yá-k̇el\ *adv* : alive, in a living manner – B.H. 99.19, 114.21

ni·yan \ni-yáŋ\ *va* ni·wa·ya [fr *ni* to live + *ya* causative] : to revive *e.g.* a sick person, to cause to live, make live; to let live, to miss or fail in killing *e.g.* wild game or an enemy — *vn perhaps* : to breathe, to take a breath, to inhale – Cf niyá Bl

ni·ya·šni·šni \ni-yá-šni-šni\ *adv red* [fr *niyá* to breathe] : all out of breath < ~ *kihunni* He arrived home breathless. > – D. 272, 120

ni·ya·šni t'e·ya \ni-yá-šni t'e-yà\ *va* : to choke to death < *Niyašni t'eyapi kte epcehce* I gave much thought to their being about to choke to death. > – BT

ni·ya·šo·ta s'e \ni-yá-šo-ta s'e\ *adv* : as though smoke were coming from the nostrils, as it seems with horses in the cold weather, *Šunkawakan kin* ~ *inyankelo* The horse ran as if smoke were coming from its nose – Bl

ni·ya·ya \ni-yá-ya\ *v red of* niyá : to blow out one's breath, exhale vigorously – D.208

[1]ni·ye \ní-ye\ *pron* : you *singl; níyepi* you *pl* – *See* íye, míye, unkíye

[2]ni·ye \ni-yé\ *v of* niyán : to cause to live

[3]ni·ye \ní-ye\ *v imper* : Take it – Note: the word is used by men

ni·ye·cu·hcin \ní-ye-cu-ḣciŋ\ *pron emph* : You at any rate

ni·ye·ka·leš *or* **niyekeš** *or* **iyekaleš** \ní-ye-k̇a-leš\ *pron emph* : Even you – P

ni·yeš \ní-yeš\ *pron emph* : you – *See* íyeš

no·ksu·hu-te \nó-k̇su-hu-ṫe\ *n* : the base of the ear – *See* nónhsuhute

non·ga *or* **nunga** \nóŋ-ġa\ *adj* : enlarged, lumpy, *i.e.* grown-out and hardened < *cuwi* ~ hunched back >

non·ge \nóŋ-ġe\ *n* : the ear, the sense of hearing — **nonge·kpa** \nóŋ-ġe-kṗa\ *adj* nónge·ma·kpa : deaf, hard of hearing — **nongekpe·ya** *va* nóngekpe·wa·ya : to make deaf — **nonge·ogmus gluza** \noŋ-ġé-o-gmus glu-zà\ *v* : to hold one's ears tight shut so as not to hear – B.H.286.3

non·ge·o·hlo·ka \nóŋ-ġe-o-ḣlo-ka\ *n* : the orifice of the ear

non·ge yu·za \nóŋ-ġe yù-za\ *v* : to listen to, heed, to obey < *El* ~ *šni* At the time, he did not listen. > – B.H.35.4

non·go·ptan \nóŋ-ġo-ptaŋ\ *v* nongo·wa·ptan [fr *nonge* ear + *ptan* to care about] : to attend to or listen, to turn the ear towards < *Tipi el opa lowan wicaši na "~ econ po" eya* He told them to follow singing in the house, and he said: "You do listening." *Hokšila kin ištinma; canke el* ~ The boy was asleep; and so there he attended to him. > — **nongoptan·ptan** *v red* : to listen < ~ *najin* to stand listening > – MS.97 D.19

non·hcan \noŋ-ḣcáŋ\ *adj* ma·nónhcan : deaf

non·hcan·ši·hu·ta \noŋ-ḣcáŋ-ši-hù-ṫa\ *v* nonhcán·ma·šihùta : to pretend not to hear — **nonhcanšihuta·yela** *adv* : pretending to be deaf or not to hear, *i.e.* because one does not care to hear < ~ *yanka* to sit making as if not hearing > – Bl

non·hka·ti·ya \noŋ-ḣká-ṫi-ya\ *v* : to awaken one by a sudden noise, to not hear well because of talking very loud < *Mištinma tka nonhkátimayayelo* I was asleep but you woke me. > — **nonhkatiye·ce** *va* : to hear suddenly < *Capunka nonhkatiwayece lo* Suddenly I heard a mosquito, *i.e.* its buzzing. > – Note: the word is not *nonhkat'iyece* Bl BT

non·hke·ci·ya \nóŋ-ḣk̇e-ci-ya\ *v* : to bend one's head sideways, trying to hear

non·hpan \nóŋ-ḣk̇paŋ\ *n* [fr *nonge* to hear + *pan* to yell] : the ringing of the ears < *Nónhmapan* My ears are ringing. > – R Bl

non·hpe·ki·c'un \noŋ-ḣpé-ki-c'uŋ\ *v* : to have a hissing sound in the ears < ~ *yankahe c'un taku wan ononhs'ake* He, one who actually is hearing something, had been sitting with a hissing sound in his ears. > — **nonhpeki-c'un·šniyan** *adv* : without anything disturbing one's hearing, hence not having need to use one's hands to

---

\a\ f<u>a</u>ther \e\ th<u>e</u>y \i\ mach<u>i</u>ne \o\ sm<u>o</u>ke \u\ l<u>u</u>nar \an, aŋ\ bl<u>an</u>c Fr. \in, iŋ\ <u>in</u>k \on, oŋ, un, uŋ\ s<u>oo</u>n, <u>con</u>fier Fr. \c\ <u>ch</u>air \ġ\ ma<u>ch</u>en Ger. \j\ fu<u>s</u>ion \clusters: bl, gn, kp, hšl, etc...\ <u>b</u>[e]lo ... said with a slight vowel
See more in the Introduction, Guide to Pronunciation

communicate – Bl WHL

non·hsu·hu·te *or* **noksuhute** \nóŋ-ȟsu-hu-ṫe\ *n* : the base of the ear

nonh'·s'a·ka \nóŋȟ'-s'a-ka\ *v obsol* : to be listening although one does not seem to < *Nónhmas'akelo* I am listening all signs to the contrary. > – *See* anagóptan – St

non·hwa·co·ka \noŋ-ȟwá-co-ka\ *n* [fr *nonge* ear + *wacoka* valley] : the outer ear cavities – Bl

non·hwa·za·za \noŋ-ȟwá-za-za\ *v* : to hear only snatches of what is said < *Nonhwámazaza tka nonhkatimayayelo* You did not hear me well for all the loud talk, on the other hand I heard little of what he said, as a man says when asked why he is silent while the other people talk much. > – Bl

non·hwi·ca·hlo·ke s'e \noŋ-ȟwí-ca-ȟlo-ke s'e\ *adv* : with ears open < ~ *ociciyakin kte* I shall speak, explain it, to you with your ears open. > – WHL

non·h'o·pa·ya \nóŋ-ȟ'o-pa-ya\ *adv* [fr *nonge* ear + *opaya* along] : in or accompanying one's hearing < ~ *yazan* to have an ear-ache >

non·wan *or* **nunwan** \noŋ-wáŋ\ *vn* wa·nonwan : to swim < *Yunkan mini el ~ na "Le wanonwan welo", eya; "na le iyuha econ po". ~ niun* And then he swam in the water, and he said: "Here I swim. And so do everything here." He lives swimming. >

num \num\ *num card contrac* [fr *nunpa* two] : two — **num·kaskaska** \nú·mka-ska-ska\ *adv* : by twos < ~ *ye wicaši* He told them to go by twos. > — **nu·mlala** \nú-mla-la\ *adj* : two alone, only two — **nu·mnum** \nú-mnum\ *adj* : two and two — **nu·mnun·pa** \nú-mnuŋ-ṗa\ *adj red of* nunpa : by twos

nu·mnu·za \nú-mnu-za\ *adj* : creaking or sounding, as a house does when shaken by the wind < *Tipi hanhepi ataya ~ he* The house was creaking the whole night through. >

nu·ni \nú-ni\ *v* wa·núni : to wander, to miss the road and wander about, to get lost; to be mistaken about a thing < *Hece canku yanuni kte šni* In this way you will not miss the road. > — **nuni·niyan** \nú-ni-ni-yaŋ\ *adv red of* nuniyan : lost — **nuni·ya** \nú-ni-ya\ *va* nuni·wa·ya : to cause to wander — **nuni·yan** \nú-ni-yaŋ\ *adv* : wandering, lost < ~ *mani* to blunder one's way >

[1]**nun** *or* **nunwe** \nuŋ\ \nuŋ-wé\ *fut* or *opt partic* used in place of *kta* : would that ... – Cf nunwé P Bl

[2]**nun** \nuŋ\ *v of* un *2nd pers singl* : you use

nun·bla·la \núŋ-bla-la\ *adj* : only two

nun·ga \núŋ-ġa\ *adj* ma·núnga : enlarged, swollen < *cuwi ~* a hunchback, *iškahu* a swollen ankle from a sprain >

nun·hcan \nuŋ-ȟcáŋ\ *vn* nun·hma·can : to be deaf, hard of hearing

nun·hnu·ga \nuŋ-ȟnú-ġa\ *adv* : with many lumps < *tacan ~* a lumpy body > *and* **nunhnun-·ga** \nuŋ-ȟnúŋ-ġa\ *adj red of* nunga : swollen up

nunh'·s'a \núŋȟ'-s'a\ *v* nun·hma·s'a : to hear well – WE

nun·ka \núŋ-ka\ *vn of* yunka *2nd pers singl* : you lie down

nun·pa \núŋ-pa\ *num ord adj* : two, twice — **nunpa·kiya** \núŋ-ṗa-ki-ya\ *adv* : twice, in two ways

nun·pe·gna·ka \núŋ-ṗe-gna-ka\ *vn* : to be placed in two places

nun·po·we·cin·han \núŋ-ṗo-we-ciŋ-haŋ\ *adv of* ówecinhan : in double file – B.H.293.9

nun·s'e \nuŋ-s'é\ *adv* : almost, nearly < *T'e ~ ake kini* He almost died, again he recovered. *ša ~* almost red, *waniyetu nuns'iyohakab* nearly after winter, *Tohanl kte ~ nicuwapi kin* When he almost killed it you were being chased as a fact. > — **nuns'e·lececa** \nuŋ-s'e-lé-ce-ca\ *adv* : almost, pretty near < *Tipi kin tiyo nawapa ~ yelo* I was pretty near to running away into the house. >

nun·šnun·ja·he·la \nuŋ-šnúŋ-ja-he-la\ *adj* : flexible, as bones of a child, tender, like fresh young leaves < *Can'inkpa kin ~* The tree top is pliant. >

nun·wan *or* **nonwan** \nuŋ-wáŋ\ *vn* : to swim

nun·we \nuŋ-wé\ *opt partic* : May it be so, Let it be so, Amen! *i.e.* expressive of desire < *Wakanheja otuyubleza* May children be awake; *maka iyokiseya tatanka ota nawah'on ca wakanheja wagluhika ~* when I heard half the country's many buffalo, the child hushed up. > – Bl

nu·pin \nu-ṗíŋ\ *adj* : both — **nupin·caska** *adv* : both together — **nupin·tu** \nu-ṗíŋ-ṫu\ *adv* : alike, equal, as two things — **nupin·yan** \nu-ṗíŋ-yaŋ\ *adv* : on both sides < ~ *zanniyan okan unkihunnipi kte* Let us reach old age in good health both here and hereafter – B.H. 124.25 WHL

O

[1]**o** \o\ *pref* to *v* : It forms *n*, thus: *kašpá* to cut loose from, *okášpe* a piece cut from — *prep contrac pref* to *v* **a)** [the *pref* being fr *ogná* in, into] : It forms the locative in "o", thus: *okáštan* to pour into **b)** [the *pref* being fr *oŋ* for] : It indicates purpose, for the purpose of; thus: *okuwa wašte, lit* It is good for following, *i.e.* easily followed

[2]**o** \o\ *va* wa·o un·k'o·pi : to shoot, to hit when shooting

o·a·ble *or* **oablel** \o-á-ble\ *adv archaic* : in a pile, as in placing pieces of beef in a pile

o·a·gle \o-á-gle\ *n* : a place *e.g.* a stand, shelf, hook for holding or resting something; the end of the stem that is inserted into the bowl of a pipe — **oagle·han s'e** *adv* : as a foundation – B.H.120.3

o·a·he \o-á-he\ *n* : something to stand on – *See* owáhe

o·a·he·ce·ca \o-á-he-ce-ca\ *adj* : better, pretty well, as is said of one sick < *Aliya kin ogna ~ kilo ca ogna unyanpi ktelo* Since it is by no better for him climbing hills, let us go along ridges, when the snow is not drifted – LB

o·a·hi·ya·ye \o-á-hi-ya-ye\ *n* [fr *ahiyaya* sing a tune] : a going or taking sound, a songful tune, the air of a tune

o·a·i·e \o-á-i-e\ *n* [fr *aia* to slander] : slander

o·a·ka·hpe \o-á-ka-ȟpe\ *n* : a cover *e.g.* for a bed *etc* – P Bl

o·a·kan·kan \o-á-kaŋ-kaŋ\ *n* : a seat < *~ hanska* a bench > — **oakanke** \o-á-kaŋke\ *n contrac of* oákanyanke : anything used for a seat, a wagon seat

o·a·ka·te \o-á-ka-te\ *n* : the drawing of a bow < *~ wašte* a bow easy to draw, *~ šica* a bow hard to draw > – Bl

o·a·ki·h'an \o-á-ki-ȟ'aŋ\ *n of* akih'an : starving

o·a·ki·ni·ca \o-á-ki-ni-ca\ *n of* akinica : a dispute, perhaps

o·a·ki·ye·co·kan \o-á-ki-ye-co-kaŋ\ *adv* : in the middle, before others < *Na ob econpi el ~ econ na ake tawa kin opi* And when they were at doing it with one another, he got in between, and a second time his own shot him, *i.e.* he was fighting in the middle, between two conflicting parties. >

o·á·ki·ye·la \o-á-ki-ye-la\ *adv of* akiyela : near, not far

o·a·kšu \o-á-kšu\ *n* : a load, an armful

o·a·le·tka o·mni·ci·ye \ó-a-le-tka o-mnì-ci-ye\ *n* [fr *aletka* a branch] : a branch assembly

o·a·li \o-á-li\ *n* : a step, as on a buggy or in a flight of stairs

o·an·pe·tu can *or* **oanpetu ka can** \o-áŋ-pe-tu caŋ\ *adv* : daily < *~ wacekiyapi kta* They should pray daily. *Oanpetu iyohi, ohinhanna oyasin. ~ na hinhannahci kikta na* Each day, every morning. Let a person rise daily in the morning. > – LP B.H.60.23, 185.3, 42.6, 29.2

oa·pe \oá-pe\ *n* [fr *apá* to strike] : beatings, strokes, stripes; the striking of the clock an hour

o·a·ši·ca \o-á-ši-ca\ *adj of* ašica : unpleasant, disagreeable, as the country, the weather, *etc* ; worried, in the sense that something does not stand well on something else — **oaši·lya** *adv* : not standing well on, not up to standard < *~ helo* It does not stand well. > — **oašilya·kel** *adv* : not mixing well, nor appear appealing, not presentable or pleasant – Bl

o·a·ška·ye·la \o-á-ška-ye-la\ *adv* : short, near – Bl

o·a·u \o-á-u\ *n* : access to – Bl

o·a·wan·yan·ke ši·ce \o-á-waŋ-yaŋ-ke ši-ce\ *adj perhaps* : hard to watch – *Syn* OYUHA ŠICE Bl

o·a·ye \o-á-ye\ *n of* aya : continuation, progressing thing < *Iyapi ~ etan unkagin kte* You and I shall set down something of a continuation of the language, *i.e.* we will continue finding words when I come again. *Taku ota tiwahe ~ na oigluha* A family is progressive in many things and towards its welfare. >

o·a·yu·štan \o-á-yu-štaŋ\ *n* [fr *ayuštan* to cease] : a stop or cessation from

ob \ob\ *prep* [fr *ópa*] : with, together with, in *ref* to more than one; *kicí* in *ref* to one < *Na ob tanyan upi, na ob tanyan unpi* And together they came in good shape, and together they are doing well. >

o·be \o-bé\ *n* : a divison, class, or sort

o·bi·c'i·ya *or* **opeic'iya** \ó-bi-c'i-ya\ *v refl* : to join, to conform self to < *Cankeš ~ wol iyotake* And so he sat to join the eating. > – B.H.3.13, 46.5, 65.10, 78.8, 273.10

o·bla·ska \o-blá-ska\ *n* [fr *blaska* flat in surface] : the flat side of anything — **oblaska·ya** \o-bla-ska-ya\ *adv* : on the flat side, flat

o·bla·ya \o-blá-ya\ *adj of* blaya : level — **oblaye** *n* : a valley, a plain, a level place — **oblaye·la** *adv* or *adj perhaps* : level — **oblaye·ya** *adv* : evenly

o·ble·ca \o-blé-ca\ *adj* : cornered, edged, as a board or a house (tent), hence < *tiyobleca* a square (cornered) tent > — *n* : the edge *e.g.* of a board or a blanket; the edge or bit of an axe *etc*

o·ble·ca·han \o-blé-ca-haŋ\ *part* : scattered, as a people, broken into fragments, as the bones of a dead animal — **oblecahe·ya** \ó-ble-ca-he-ya\ *adv* : scattered < *~ aya* to become scattered > **obleca·ya** \o-blé-ca-ya\ *adv* : on the side, with the sharp part up, not on the flat surface – B.H.254.8

o·blel \ó-blel\ *n* : an edge — *adj* : the edge — **oblelya** \ó-ble-lya\ *adv* : scattered < *~ nankapelo* You are all scattered *i.e.* you are not ready yet, although we will go now. > — **oblelya·kel** \ó-ble-lya-kel\ *adv* : in a scattered condition – Bl

o·bles \o-blés\ *vn contrac* : to be sober, clear-minded — **oble·sya** \o-blé-sya\ *adv* : clearly, soberly, brightly

o·ble·ton \o-blé-toŋ\ *adj* : square-edged – *See* oblóton

o·ble·za \o-blé-za\ *vn* o·ma·bleza [fr *bleza* clear] : to be sober, clear

o·blo·ton \o-blŏ'-toŋ\ *n* : an angle, a corner of anything — *adj* : cornered, having corners < *can na ~* any piece of wood with corners, *e.g.* 2" x 2" *etc*, but not a board which is *can blaska* > — **obloton·ton** *adj red* : having many corners, angular

o·blo to·pa son \o-blo tó-pa soŋ\ *v* : to braid, weave together four strings — **oblo yamnila son** \oble yá-mni-la soŋ\ *v* : to braid, weave together three strings – Bl

o·blu·la \ó-blu-la\ *n* or *adj* **a** : rain or wind-proof, as of the roof or walls of a house < *Tipi ~* The house is rain-proof. > **b** : calm, sheltered, protected < *Wanna ~* Now it is calm. *Le ~* This is a sheltered place. *~ wanice ca unkácanpi kte lo* Without being protected we shall be shivering. > – EM

o·bši·š'i·c'i·ya \o-bši-š'i-c'i-ya\ *v* : to have much but not giving anything away < *Ecaca ~ nankelo* You were having much but not giving something away. > – Bl BT

o·btu \ó-btu\ *prep* : with, *i.e.* in *ref* to more than one – B.H.41.7

\a\ father \e\ they \i\ machine \o\ smoke \u\ lunar \an, aŋ\ blanc Fr. \in, iŋ\ ink \on, oŋ, un, uŋ\ soon, confier Fr. \c\ chair \ġ\ machen Ger. \j\ fusion \clusters: bl, gn, kp, hšl, etc...\ b^e^lo ... said with a slight vowel **See more in the Introduction, Guide to Pronunciation**

o·ca·ga \o-cá-ġa\ *vn of* cága : to freeze or become ice in

o·ca·hsu \o-cá-ȟsu\ *v* : to be icy, to be frozen in *e.g.* articles of clothing < *Wakpala oguhan oyasin ~ ca oomani šice* It is a hard walk when all the creek trails are icy. > – Bl

o·ca·je \o-cá-je\ *n* : a kind, sort, or species; a name for < *Na wamakaškan ~ oyasin ahiyaya.* And every sort of creeping thing sings a song. *Na taku woyute ~ oyasin etanhan icu* And from every sort of food it takes something. >

o·can·ko·ze \o-cáŋ-ko-ze\ *n* : the swinging of a stick towards an object that is distrusted to keep it away < *Na oonakijin el ihunni na ~ k'on hecena iyawicahpayapi na wicaksotapi.* And he arrived at a shelter, and swinging a stick at them they seized and killed them off. *Na wana ekta ikiyela yapi; ehanl owicakiyapi; ehanl Tašunke Witko ekta tokeya okaȟ'ol iyeic'iyin na ocankoza* And they were going close to it; they then helped them; then swinging a stick he first threw himself away at Crazy Horse. > – MS.527

o·can·ku \o-cáŋ-k̇u\ *n* : a road, street, way — **ocanku s'e** *adv* : like a pathway — **ocanku·tonyan** *adv* : forming a road, perhaps — **ocanku·ya** *adv perhaps* or *n* : a path, in the manner of a road < *Ocankuyapi k'on ogna ihpeyapi* They had thrown it into the roadway. > – B.H.112.5, 54.14, 112.15 WHL

o·can·na·sle·ce \o-cáŋ-na-sle-ce\ *n* : a sawmill – P

o·can·na·tu·hci \o-cáŋ-na-ṫu-ȟci\ *adv* : in the middle of something, *cokata kapi* center camp is meant < *~ un welo* He lives in the very middle of it. > – Bl St

o·can·pa·ji·pe \o-caŋ-pá-ji-pe\ *n* : a carpenter shop

o·can·te·ši·lya \o-cáŋ-te-ši-lya\ *adv* : sadly — **ocantešilyakel** *adv* : in a saddened condition < *~ kigle* to go and arrive home sad > – B.H.89.9, 234.4

o·can·yu·ki·ze \o-cáŋ-yu-k̇i-ze\ *n* : a place or house where ther is an organ

o·can·ze \o-cáŋ-ze\ *vn* o·ma·canze o·un·canze·pi *or perhaps* ma·canze un·canze·pi : to anger easily — **ocanze·wakan** *adj* : hot-headed, ill-tempered — **ocanze·yakel** *adv* : in an angry manner < *~ heya* to say that angrily > — **ocanze·ze hingla** *v* : to become suddenly angry – P Bl B.H.5.19

o·ca·pe \o-cá-ṗe\ *n* : a wound – B.H.130.10, 274.21

o·ca·štan'·in \o-cá-štaŋ-iŋ\ *v* : to be famous – B.H.91.7

o·ca·šton *or* **ocašton·ka** \o-cá-štoŋ\ *v* oca·šma·ton : to make a name for one's self by doing something great < *Na wana lila ~* And he has now made a name for himself. > – MS.154

o·ce·on \o-cé-oŋ\ *part* : cooked < *~ wašte* something cooked easily >

o·ce·sli \o-cé-sli\ *v of* ceslí : to defecate in < *~ tipi* a privy, an outhouse >

o·ce·ti \o·cé-ṫi\ *n of* cetí : a fireplace, a chimney < *maza ~* a stove, *~ ipásotka* a coal stove, *i.e.* one that is high in the shape of a frustum, tapering to the top, in contrast to a wood stove, *~ sam iya* or *~ wóslahan* a stove pipe, *~ šol iyeya* a chimney, a flue > – EB

o·cib \ó-cib\ *adv* : one after another < *Na ohanketa ~ ota ayapi na šunkawakan kin heepi slolyapi* After awhile the brought along many one after another, for they knew those were the horses. > — **oci·bcib** \ó-ci-bcib\ *adv red* : with many things piled on one another, *i.e.* many flat and straight things — **oci·blagaheya** *and* **oci·blagan** \ó-ci-bla-ġa-he-ya\ *or* \ó-ci-bla-ġaŋ\ *adv* : abreast, in a row – P Bl

o·ci·hi·šni·šni \ó-ci-hi-šni-šni\ *vn* : not to be unanimous in judgment < *~ unhipi: unptayapila šni* We arrived at no unanimous judgment: we were not all together. > – *See* óciwašte, ócišica as to meetings together – Wwc Bl

o·ci·hi·šni·šni·yan *adv* : being strung out in a file, unequally spaced, as horses coming in to the finish line; unequal in size, as the children in a family < *~ econ* to do in a straggling manner > – Bl Wwc

o·ci·kan \ó-ci-kaŋ\ *adv* : having room, roomy

o·ci·kci·k'a·ya \o-cí-kci-k'a-ya\ *adj* or *adv red* [fr *ocik'aya* in space made small] : quite restricted, narrowed in space – *See* cik'aya B.H.194.26

o·ci·kpa·kpa·ni *or* **ocikpa·nini** \ó-ci-kpa-k̇pa-ni\ *adj red of* ocikpani : some longer and some shorter in *ref* to many – Note: more used perhaps is *ócikpanini* — **ocikpakpani·yan** *adv perhaps* : greatly varied in length or height – B.H.92.13

o·ci·kpa·ni \ó-ci-k̇pa-ni\ *adj* : unequal in length, *i.e.* one taller than the other, as the pipes of an organ, or boys lined up according to size – *See* aocikpani — **ocikpani·ni** *adj red of* ocikpani : some longer and some shorter, of varied length

o·ci·k'a·la \o-cí-k'a-la\ *adj of* cik'ala : small within < *ti ~* a small room > — **ocik'a·ya** \o-cí-k'a-ya\ *v* or *adj* : to make small in space, made to be small — **ocik'aye·la** *adj of* cik'ayela : small inside, of small dimensions < *Hehé, ~ ca teȟi iblotaka* Alas, it was quite narrow and uncomfortable for me to sit, *i.e.* by sitting tight between others. > – Bl

o·cin \o-cíŋ\ *va* o·wá·cin un·kó-ciŋ·pi : to desire, beg, ask for < *Mitakoja wakablapi wanji ~ u maši ye* He told me to come to ask a piece of *pápa* dried meat for my grandchild. *Itancan kin he ~ yelo* The chief himself asked for it. > – B.H.238.6

o·cin·ȟin·yan·pi \ó-ciŋ-ȟiŋ-yaŋ-pi\ *v recip of* oȟinyan : They feel slighted, offended at each other

o·cin·ki·wa·kan \o-cíŋ-k̇i-wa-kaŋ\ *vn perhaps* ocin·wa·kiwakan : to be unwilling to help out one; to so speak as to bring harm to another < *Ocínmayakiwakan yelo* You talk so as to bring harm on me, or You are unwilling to help me out, *i.e.* give me one. *Ocinmic'iwakan* I so speak as to bring harm on myself. >

o·cin·ši·ca \o-cíŋ-ši-ca\ *vn* ocin·ma·šica : to be cross, bad-tempered, ill-disposed — **ocinšica·ya** *or* **ocinši·lya** *adv* : evilly disposed < *He kici ~ waun* I am cross with that person. > – A

o·cin·wa·kan \o-cíŋ-wa-kaŋ\ *adj* ocin·ma·wakan : unwilling to help out; forgetful < *Ecakel ocinniwakan yelo* Purposely you were unwilling to help him out, *i.e.* you do not want to help one out. > Bl

o·cin·wa·šte·ya \o-cíŋ-wa-šte-ya\ *adv* : well disposed < *He kici ~ waun* I have a good feeling toward him. > – A

o·cin·yan *or* **ociyan** \ó-ciŋ-yaŋ\ *v* : to threaten < *Ociniyanpi kin hena wacewicakiciciya po* Pray for those who threaten you. > – B.H.191.17

o·ci·pte·ca \ó-ci-pte-ca\ *adj* : shorter than — **ociptel** *adv* : not equal to, lacking — **ocipte·ptel** *adv red* : unevenly < *~ econ* to do it unevenly > — **ocipte·tu** *adv* : unequal in length or otherwise – R Bl

o·ci·sci·la \o-cí-sci-la\ *adv* : for a little while, little — **ocisci·yela** \o-cí-sci-ye-la\ *adv of* cisciyela : for a little while

o·ci·ši·ca \ó-ci-ši-ca\ *adj* [fr *ocín* ask for + *šica* bad] : being on bad terms with, not getting along with – Fi

o·ci·tkons \ó-ci-ṫkoŋs\ *adj contrac of* ocitkonza : of the same size or length < *Wicaša ~ wacinpi* Men think alike. >

o·ci·tkon·za \ó-ci-ṫkoŋ-za\ *adj* : equal, alike, of the same size or length < *can* ~ trees of the same height >
o·ci·t'in·za \ó-ci-t'iŋ-za\ *vn* : to be crowded together -R Bl
o·ci·wa·šte \ó-ci-wa-šte\ *adj* [perhaps fr *ocín* beg for + *wašte* good] : reconciling with, making up with, being on good terms with < *Kici ~ yo* Be reconciled with him. > - Note: *ocišica* too is perhaps *deriv* from *ocín* — **oci-wašte·ya** \ó-ci-wa-šte-ya\ *adv* : on good terms with < *Ake kici ~ waun welo* I am again on good terms with him. > - B.H.88.27, 157.13 BD Bl
o·ci·yan \ó-ci-yaŋ\ *v* : to threaten < *Ociniyanpi kin hena wacewicakiciciya po* Pray for those who threaten you. > - *See* ócinyan
o·ci·yu·štan \ó-ci-yu-štaŋ\ *v of* oyuštan : to be one in another, as kettles or cups, to be doubled up, as a blanket — **ociyuštan·štan** *v red* : to be placed one inside of another, as kettles, cups, *etc* < ~ *egnag ayapi* It was taken and laid away. > - Bl
o·co·kab \o-có-k̇ab\ *adv of* cokab : in the midst
o·co·ka·ka \o-có-ka-ka\ *vn of* coka : there is room, to be empty, not full *e.g.* of persons in a house
o·co·kan·ya *or* **ocokanyan** \o-có-k̇aŋ-ya\ *adv of* cokanya : in the middle < *ti* ~ in the middle of the house, *tipi* ~ the tent in the middle of the other tents > - D.4 B.H.54.11
o·cos \o-cós\ *adj of* ocoza : warm < ~ *manka* I am in a warm place. > — **oco·sya** *adv* : in a warm condition < ~ *igluza* to put warm clothes on, to dress warmly > - ES
o·co·wa·sin \o-có-wa-siŋ\ *adj* : befitting all - Bu
o·co·za \o-có-za\ *adj* : warm, as a house that keeps warm because well built < *Macuwita ca yukšala munke; hecel omacoze* Since I felt cold I was bent up; so I was warm. > — *n* : warmth, heat
o·cu \o-cú\ *vn of* cu : to become damp in, to have drops of water inside
o·cun·wa·ni·ca \o-cúŋ-wa-ni-ce\ *n* : a vacant or free place with timber on both sides - *Syn* OTINTOSKA
o·cu·ya \o-cú-ya\ *va* : to dampen with dew < ~ *egnaka* to spread or set out *e.g.* a hide to have dew fall on it > - Bl
o·e·ce·ca \o-é-ce-ca\ *vn* : to be slow in coming to boil, as when something is at last boiling - Bl
o·e·ci·ye *or* **oekiye** \o-é-ci-ye\ *vn* or *n* : to convince one < *taku ~ šice: owahokonkiye šice, oyaksab šice wanagoptan šice* one hard to advise something, to instruct, to teach for lack of attention, one who is heedless of things > - Bl
o·e·con \o-é-coŋ\ *n of* ecón : doing, work < ~ *wašte* good to do, or easy to do > — **oecon·hca un** *v* : to do frequently at some place, to go often for a special purpose, as to go frequently to a bawdy-house - R Bl
o·e·con·la e·con \o-é-coŋ-la e-cóŋ\ *v* : to do things excitedly before others, in the center < *Na wanna oyate kin ḣaka unpi na hocokata oeconla econpi* And the people were ruffled and doing things excitedly in center camp. >
o·e·con·ši·lya \o-é-coŋ-ši-lya\ *va* : to cause one to do his work badly by bothering him too much < *Taku oeconšilunyayapelo* You caused us to botch some of our work. > - Bl
o·e·gle \o-é-gle\ *va* oe·wa·gle [fr *egle* to place] : to set or place in — *n* : a saying, a verse, a sentence, a setting down < *Ca ~ nisuksuta k'el blihic'iya yo* Therefore keep busy with your hard verses. >
o·e·gna·ka \o-é-gna-ka\ *n of* egnaka : a placing down, a stop, period - R Bl
o·e·ha·ke \o-é-ha-k̇e\ *n perhaps of* eháke : the last < *Na wanna ~ kin unkisakib ukiye ehanl ake ungnahela ouwicuntapi. Anpetu ~ kin* And as they were coming to our side, then suddenly they were again shot at. It was precisely the last day. > - B.H.44.14, 178.19, 229.12 Pb.34-35
o·e·ki·ye \o-é-k̇i-ye\ *vn* or *n* : to convince one of something, persuade one of < *taku ~ šica* hard to convince one of something > - Wwc
o·e·ti \o-é-ṫi\ *n of* eti : an encampment ahead < ~ *ataya coco welo* The encampment was entirely soft *i.e.* muddy. ~ *šicelo* The encampment has problems about it. *Hececa k'eyaš aliya ekta hinajin yo, tokeš opicakelo* But come stand climbing to a place like this, as it is perhaps not so bad a place after all > - Bl
o·e·ye \o-é-ye\ *n of* éya : a saying, verse, sentence < *Tuktunma le ~ wašte hwo* Is either one of these two verses good? *Yamni akigle ~* Three times it is a verse. > - Pb. 37 B.H.187.13
o·ge \ó-ġe\ *n* : clothes, covering, a sheath - Cf hayápi
o·ge·i·c'i·ton \ó-ġe-i-c'i-toŋ\ *v* : to clothe one's self < *Hena on ogenic'itonpi* You are clothed with these. >
o·ge·ju·ya \ó-ġe-ju-ya\ *v* : to take hold of *e.g.* one's clothes — *adv* : together with, among < ~ *yuza* to grasp together something with >
o·ge·ya \ó-ġe-ya\ *adv* : just as it is, whole, altogether, the whole thing < ~ *icu* to take it as it is, *Wicaša k'un he taoyunke ~ hiyohpeyapi* They had come and let down the man along with his entire bedding. > - B.H.187.7
[1]**o·gi** \o-ġí\ *n* : rust — *v* : to rust - B.H.193.12
[2]**o·gi** \o-ġí\ *adj perhaps* : brown < *Išta omagi* My eyes are brown. > - BT
o·gin \ó-ġiŋ\ *n* : a sheath, clothes covering
o·gin·gin \ó-ġiŋ-ġiŋ\ *vn* : to nod, be nodding, as in one's sleep < ~ *yanka* to sit nodding one's head >
o·gin·ki·ci·ton \ó-ġiŋ-ki-ci-toŋ\ *v* óge·we·citon : to clothe for one — **oginki·ton** \ó-ġiŋ-k̇i-toŋ\ *v poss* ó-ge·we·ton [fr *oginton* put on a cover or wrapping] : to put clothes on one's own
o·gin·ton \ó-ġiŋ-toŋ\ *va* óge·wa·ton : to put on a cover or a wrapping
o·gi·ya \o-ġí-ya\ *v of* gi : to paint yellow
o·glag \o-glág\ *v poss contrac of* oglaka : to tell of one's own < *He ~ wahi* I came to tell that. >
o·gla·hni·ga \o-glá-ḣni-ġa\ *v poss* o·wa·glahniga [fr *o-kahniga* understand] : to understand one's own affairs — **oglahnih** *v poss contrac* : to understand one's own < ~ *manka* I was understanding my own affairs. >
o·gla·ka \o-glá-ka\ *v poss* o·wa·glaka unko·glaka·pi : to tell of one's own < *caje* ~ to tell one's own name >
o·gla·kin·yan \o-glá-kiŋ-yaŋ\ *n* or perhaps *adv of* gla-kinyan : width, breadth < ~ *ópta* across the width > - B.H.60.10
o·gla·la \o-glá-la\ *v poss of* okala : to sow or pout out
O·gla·la \O-glá-la\ *np* O·ma·glala [fr *okála* scatter, *oglala* scatter one's own] : name of one of the southern clans of the Teton Lakota Sioux
o·gla·pšun \o-glá-pšuŋ\ *v poss* o·wa·glapšun [fr *glapšun* knock out one's own] : to break or twist or loosen one's own - Note: the word *ref* to the action of one when pulling off the bowl of a pipe and holding the stem in the mouth - Bl

o·gla·pta \o-glá-pta\ *v poss* o·wa·glapta [fr both *oyapta* have left over, and *okapta* be left over or lade out] : to leave some of one's own < *Ha ecela omiglapte* Skin only did I have left, *i.e.* you gave away everything but the skin. > – Bl

o·gla·ya \o-glá-ya\ *v* : to thrust into, as a stick into a tube — **oglaye·ya** *v* : to shove into

[1]**o·gle** \o-glé\ *va* o·wa·gle [fr *gle* put or place] : to set or place in

[2]**o·gle** \ó-gle\ *n* : a shirt, a coat < ~ *wakan* a Ghost Shirt, ~ *áhco wanice* a vest > – Bl

o·gle·ce·ku·te \o-gle-cé-k̇u-ṫe\ *v* : to play the game of *oglecékutepi* which consists in shooting arrows so as to come near as possible to where the first arrow stickls in the ground < *Ogleceunkutepi kte* Let us play oglecékutepi. > — **oglecekute·pi** \o-gle-cé-k̇u-ṫe-pi\ *n* **1** : the shooting off of arrows to see whose will stick closest to the first; also a gambling game with bow and arrow, by trying to strike the bowstring with one's arrow **2** : two bright stars standing opposite each other, one in the east and the other in the west sky – Bl Mh

o·gle ci·yu·ksa \ó-gle ci-yu-ksa\ *n* : a vest

o·gle han·ska \ó-gle haŋ-ska\ *n archaic* : wife as a title in the mouth of her husband < ~ *wan kici waun kin he* She is the long-shirt, *i.e.* my wife, with whom I live. > – WR

o·gle hin·šma \ó-gle-hiŋ-šmà\ *n* : a fur coat

o·gle i·yo·tke·ye \ó-gle i-yò-tke-ye\ *n* : a clothes peg – Bl

o·gle ka·un·ji·ca \ó-gle k̇a-ùŋ-ji-ca\ *n* : a short coat, as opposed to a one-time Prince Albert

o·gle pa·po·a \ó-gle pa-pò-a\ *n* : a clothes brush

o·gle ta·hu \ó-gle ṫa-hù\ *n* : a coat collar

o·gle u·pi han·ska \ó-gle ù-pi han-ska\ *n* : a Prince Albert coat

o·gle·za \o-glé-za\ *adj of* gléza : striped in, in ridges or rows in, streaked < *Ite onigleza* You have stripes on your face, *i.e.* have a dirty face. >

o·gle zi·gzi·ca \ó-gle zi-gzì-ca\ *n* : a sweater

o·gli·cu \o-glí-cu\ *v* : to get down into; to go down as from a table or high ground < *Wata kin etanhan mini* ~ He got from the boat into the water. *aohomni* ~ to travel downhill on a curved road > – B.H.209.4 Wwc RTj

o·gli·gla \o-glí-gla\ *vn* o·wa·gligla [fr *gligla* to pass by] : to go on a journey, to travel from place to place

o·gli·gle \o-glí-gle\ *part* : going from place to place < ~ *ya* to go from place to place > — *n* : messengers and guardsmen appointed for a meeting < ~ *wakan* a good angel >

o·gli·gle·ki·ya \o-glí-gle-k̇i-ya\ *va* ogligle·wa·kiya : to cause to go from place to place

o·gli·gle wa·kan \o-glí-gle wa-k̇àŋ\ *n* : a good angel

o·gli·gle·ya \o-glí-gle-ya\ *va* ogligle·wa·ya : to send hither and thither — *adv* : going from one place to another < ~ *waun* I am one going from place to place. > — **ogligleya·pi** *n* : those sent, messengers; apostles

o·gli·han \o-glí-haŋ\ *vn* : to fall in anything end-wise — **oglihe·ya** *va* oglihe·wa·ya : to cause to fall in end-wise — **ogliheya·kel** *adv* : causing to fall in end-wise

o·gli·hpa·ye \o-glí-ȟpa-ye\ *n* : a falling down on < *Ówaš'ag konla taoglihpaye lo* His fall was terrible, a bit of greed become strong. > – B.H.195.21

o·gli·ki·ya \o-glí-ki-ya\ *v* : to sharpen < *Kan iwapsake wan imicikinte šni ca ogliwakiyin kte lo* The tendon cutter that was too dull for me I will sharpen. > – *See* miogle, aglušlušluta Bl

o·gli·mni·ci·ye \ó-gli-mni-ci-ye\ *v coll pl* : they assemble in < *Na wanna* ~ *el wašicun k'on agla opawinge* And now when they assembled a hundred white men had gone home. >

o·gli·wi·ta·ya \ó-gli-wi-ṫa-ya\ *n* : a concourse, a place to which all roads lead or to which people return < *Lel ogliwitayelo* Here there is a junction, an intersection, as is said of many roads joining in one leading to some place. > – Bl

o·gli·ya \o-glí-ya\ *va* ogli·wa·ya : to hone *e.g.* a knife < *kaštaštag* ~ to hone by hammering > – *Syn* MIOGLE *or* MIOGLI

o·gli·yo·tke \ó-gli-yo-tke\ *n* : a screw eye

o·gli·yo·u \o-glí-yo-u\ *v* [fr *gliyou* bring home one's own] : to take home one's own < *Wana awicapa po, wanna* ~ *wašteyelo* Now give them a blow, it's good to take one's own home, *i.e.* now we are in sight of home, or any place one is called to. > – Note: BT gives the word as *oglíhiyou* Bl

o·glu \o-glú\ *n* : lluck, fortune < ~ *šica* bad luck, ~ *wašte* good luck > – P Bl

o·glu·ho·mni·mni \o-glú-ho-mni-mni\ *v* o·wa·gluhomnimni : to turn something to and fro constantly < *Yunkan wanji nakpa sanni* ~ And then he turned to and fro one of his ears. >

o·glu·ksa \o-glú-ksa\ *v refl* o·mi·gluksa : to stop abruptly in one's speech < *Nonge can oyaglukse laka he wapanhe lahcake c'on.* It was I who had been shouting out this very much, so try then to cut short hearing your talk. *Nonge can oyagluksa laka, taku oniciyakapi kinhan anayagoptan šni yelo* You do not listen when something is said to you, so try then to cut short hearing your talk. > – Bl

o·glu·ma·za \o-glú-ma-za\ *v poss* o·wa·glumaza [fr *oyumaza* strike the bull's eye] : to hit one's own mark

o·glun·ge *or* **ogluge** \ó-gluŋ-ġe\ *v poss* o·wa·glunge [fr *oyunge* a bed] : to put on, to wear one's own – Note: the word is the Dacota for the Lakota *ogic'iton* and *kic'un* R

o·glu·so·ta \o-glú-so-ta\ *vn* : to go off, to leave, be all gone, as ducks in the fall of the year

o·glu·spa \o-glú-spa\ *v poss* o·wa·gluspa un·kogluspa·pi [fr *oyuspa* to catch] : to catch, take a hold of one's own < *nonge ogmus* ~ to close one's ears with the hands >

o·glu·ta \ó-glu-ṫa\ *vn* : to be closed up, as a wound — **oglute·ya** *va* oglute·wa·ya : to close up

o·glu·ze \o-glú-ze\ *v poss* o·wa·gluze [fr *oyuze* to dip out] : to dip out from into one's own dish

o·gmun·he·ca \o-gmúŋ-he-ca\ *v* : to gurgle, as a bad egg – *Syn* OHLAGANLA, OKAĊOĊO, OKAĊO

o·gmus \ó-gmus\ *vn contrac of* ogmuza : to be closed < *I* ~ *waun* My mouth is shut. *nonge* ~ *ogluspa* to close one's ears with the hands > — **ogmu·sya** *v* or *n* ógmu·swa·ya : to shut, cause to shut

o·gmu·za \ó-gmu-za\ *vn* : to be shut or closed < *Išta* ~ His eyes are shut. >

o·gna \o-gná\ *or* \ó-gna\ *prep* : in, in the direction of (place), in the way of, in one's speech < *nape* ~ *taku yuha* to hold something in the hand, *Tokel onnispepi k'on* ~ *onspewicakiya po* Teach them in how you do it. *Itancan kin he tokel iyukcan na oniciyakapi ca* ~ *unpo* Be the leader in how to understand and speak to you. *Na u k'on* ~ *gla ca oyate wanyankapi* And people saw he was going home in the direction he came. ~ *nuns'e* in about that way, *tipi* ~ in a house, *Tokel econ wicaši k'un* ~ *econpi* It was done the way in which he told them to do it.

Woope ~ according to the Law – R B.H.45.13, 124.15, 136.18, 118.4, 137.26, 154.1, 242,2

o·gnag \o-gnáġ\ *va contrac of* ognáka : to place in

o·gna·gna \o-gná-gna\ *prep red of* ogna : in the way of, in the way of one's speech < *Ungna toka ška yaitešla ciyuzin na ~ acipe cin* I do not know but that still at the first, I as a fact in a way waited for you and caught hold on you, your face made bare. *Iye iapi kin ~ wowicakiya-kapi* They spoke to them each in his own language. > – B.H.278.7

o·gna·gna·ka \o-gná-gna-ka\ *v red of* ognáka : to keep putting in — **ognagnaka·pi** \o-gná-gna-k̇a-pi\ *n* : a thing in which other things are put or laid away, a chest

o·gna·ka \o-gná-ka\ *va* o·wa·gnaka un·kognaka·pi : to place in < *Na ake hunh el ~ na ota španyan* And again she put in some and cooked a great amount. > — **ognaka·pi** \o-gná-k̇a-pi\ *n* : a deposit, a placing in — **ognake** \ó-gna-k̇e\ *n* : a place to keep things in < *wakšica ~* a cupboard. *miniógnake* a water pitcher, a water tank, *mi-niskuya ~* a salt-shaker >

o·gna·la \o-gná-la\ *adv* : in, *i.e.* holding only a little < *napognala* only a handful >

o·gna·yan \o-gná-yaŋ\ *adv* : accordingly < *Tokel wica-šayatapi kin econ niši kin ~ oyate kin awanwicalakin kta* You shall look after the people accordingly as the chief bade you do. >

o·gna·ye·hci \o-gná-ye-ḣci\ *adv* : nearly, closely, about, approximately < *Taku oyasin ~ owicakiyake* He told them just about everything. > – P Bl

o·gna·ye wa·šte \o-gná-ye wa-štè\ *adj* : easy to fool – D.71

o·gu \o-ġú\ *vn of* ġu : to burn in, as in a kettle < *Ite kin ~ s'e* It was as if his face was burnt, as is said when the face has not been washed. > — *n* : scraps, dregs, *e.g.* coffee grounds, but not the sediment of dirty water

o·gu·gu·ye \o-ġú-ġu-ye\ *n* : a brand, a mark burnt in

o·gu·han \o-ġú-haŋ\ *n* : tracks, a trail < *Wakpala ~ oya-sin ocahsu ca oomani šice* All creek trails that are frozen over are hard to walk on, *i.e.* roads through valleys are icy. >

o·gun·ga \o-ġúŋ-ġa\ *vn* o·ma·gunga : to doze or to be drowsy, to be half asleep or awake, to slumber < *Yun-kan omagunga na wacipi el cokam munka ena wekta na lila cantemašica* And then I became drowsy, so I sat in the center during the dance and woke up feeling sad. >

o·gu·ya \o-ġú-ya\ *va* ogu·wa·ya : to cause to burn in, as meat

[1]**o·gu·ye** \o-ġú-ye\ *n* : a brand, as on cattle

[2]**o·gu·ye** \o-gú-ye\ *n* : a handful < *~ wanji mak'u ye* Please give me a handful. >

o·gwa·han \o-gwá-haŋ\ *part* : fallen to pieces in a hole

o·gwu \o-gwú\ *vn* : to curdle, become rather cheesy, as milk — **ogwu·gwu** *adj* : curdled in *e.g.* a jar

o·ha \ó-ha\ *vn* ó·ma·ha : to stick or adhere to, as do feathers or paint < *Yunkan hucan cokanyan hehanyan ataya we ~* And then blood adhered as far as to the middle of the arrow's shaft. *Si kin makahlihlila ohapi* Mud stuck to his feet. *Iya kico ska ówahehcelo* I really stuck to him to speak inviting him to the white way, as a man says trying to help another who is being lazy. > – Bl

o·ha·kab \ó-ha-k̇ab\ *adv* : afterwards, after < *Na le ~ Hlihlila Wakpala el tate ahi* And afterwards they arrived here for hunting at Muddy Creek. *Hecel le heconpi na ~ wanna wacinksapapi* So here they did so and afterwards they thought it a good idea. > — **ohaka·bya** *adv* : after

o·ha·ka·pa·tan·han \ó-ha-k̇a-pa-ṫaŋ-haŋ\ *or* \o-há-k̇a-pa-ṫaŋ-haŋ\ *adv* : afterwards – R B.H.37.9

o·ha·mna \o-há-mna\ *adj* : smelling of skin

[1]**o·han** \ŏ-háŋ\ *interj* : Oh, yes.

[2]**o·han** \o-háŋ\ *va* o·wa·han : to boil *e.g.* meat

[3]**o·han** \o-háŋ\ *va* o·wa·han un·kohan·pi : to wear, to put on *e.g.* socks < *Na wanna he hanpa ~ omani i* And he went walking and wearing a pair of shoes. >

[4]**o·han** \ó-haŋ\ *v* ó·wa·he : to try, attempt, to apply one's self, to study

[5]**o·han** \ó-haŋ\ *n* : a straight place in a river between two bends – R Bl

[6]**o·han** \ó-haŋ\ *prep* : among, within or in *e.g.* the woods, fire, or water < *Wa ~ iyaye* He went out in the snow. *Can ogu ~ iyaye* He went in the burnt forest. *Wicota ~ iyaye* He went among the crowd. *Wicohan opa. ~ wicaunpi* He followed in their company. They were among them. > – B.H.55.11, 90.4, 116.7, 118.1 226.1

o·han·gle \ó-haŋ-gle\ *v* : to follow about – Cf ohangle-ya

o·han·gle·la *or* **ohangleyela** \ó-haŋ-gle-la\ *adv* : through the middle, through all — **ohangle·gleya** *adv red of* ohangleya : continually through – B.H.51.9

o·han·gle·ya \ó-haŋ-gle-ya\ *va* ohangle·wa·ya : to keep near one, follow about, as a colt its mother — *adv* : right through, walking through a city — **ohangleye·la** *adv* : in the middle, through the middle

o·han·han \ó-haŋ-haŋ\ *prep red of* óhan : among, within, through < *Peta kin okšan psilya na ecel peta k'un ~ iyayapi* He jumped around the fire, and as it was they had gone through the fire. >

o·han·he·pi \o-háŋ-he-pi\ *n perhaps* : a given night < *~ el* on a certain night >

o·han·ke·ta \ó-haŋ-ke-ṫa\ *adv* : at the end, finally, at length, after a while < *Lila wanyankapi na oyuspapi na lila kuwapi na wanna ~ oyate el un* They looked and looked, they took hold on, they hunted for, and in the end he was among the tribe. >

o·han·pi \o-háŋ-pi\ *part* : boiled

o·han·ska \o-háŋ-ska\ *n of* hanská : length — **ohan-ske·ya** \o-háŋ-ske-ya\ *adv* : in length < *~ epin kte* I shall say at length. > – B.H.7.8, 60.10

o·han·zi \ó-haŋ-zi\ *n* : shade, a shadow, a defense against the heat < *Can wegna ~ el ištinma* He slept in the shade among the trees. > — **ohanzi·glepi** \ó-haŋ-zi-gle-ṗi\ *n* : a bower made of branches, something set up for a shade, *e.g.* tree branches, an arbor, a porch — **ohanzi·zi** \ó-haŋ-zi-zi\ *n red perhaps* : shadow < *Ke-nági paha ~ yukelo, he kapi* There is the hill's shadow, meaning that is the turtle's spirit, > – Bl

o·he \o-hé\ *n* mi·tóhe nitóhe : a place, a niche, a bed, the old or former place < *k'in ~* the collar mark > – B.H. 110.14, 238.9

o·he e·ce \o-hé e-cè\ *adv* : without, empty < *Canke ~ wahukeza kin glihpaye, šunšunla kin ~ iyaye* And so the spear fell again, the mule went away empty, *i.e.* the spear did not hit anything. *~ hinajin, wahinawajin* to arrive at a dead end, I came to a dead end, *i.e.* to come to a place and find it deserted. > – B.H.88.9, 95.24 Bl

o·he·gle *or* **oheglepi** \o-hé-gle\ *n* : a camp site, a good

---

\a\ f<u>a</u>ther \e\ th<u>e</u>y \i\ mach<u>i</u>ne \o\ sm<u>o</u>ke \u\ l<u>u</u>nar \an, aŋ\ bl<u>anc</u> Fr. \in, iŋ\ <u>in</u>k \on, oŋ, un, uŋ\ s<u>oo</u>n, c<u>on</u>fier Fr. \c\ <u>ch</u>air \ġ\ ma<u>ch</u>en Ger. \j\ fu<u>s</u>ion \clusters: bl, gn, kp, hšl, etc...\ <u>b</u>[e]lo ... said with a slight vowel
See more in the Introduction, Guide to Pronunciation

place for camping, resting *etc* – WE Bl
o·he·gle·pi \o-hé-gle-pi\ *n* : a bedstead, a bed
o·he·yun \o-hé-yuŋ\ *n* : a wrapper — *va* ohe·mun ohe·nun : to wrap up in
o·hi \ó-hi\ *va* o·wa·hi o·ma·hi : to be able to reach to, to be tall enough to reach up to, to be long enough to reach down to, to reach to one, be large enough for < *o-hipicašni* to be unable to reach or get across to, as very deep snow, where one cannot get through >
o·hi·i·c'i·ya \o-hí-i-c'i-ya\ *v refl* : to gain for one's self < *Waonšila ohiic'iyapi kte* They will gain being merciful for themselves. > – B.H.189.6
o·hi·i·c'i·ya wi·co·h'an \o-hí-i-c'i-ya wi-cò-ḣ'aŋ\ *n* : a pension
o·hi·ki·ya \o-hí-ki-ya\ *v poss* ohi·wa·kiya [fr *ohiya* win] : to win back one's own, to give something to another of what one has won, to win for another
o·hi·mni·ci·ye \ó-hi-mni-ci-ye\ *v coll pl* : they come together for a meeting < *Ake lel ohinimniciyepi kte lo* Again here you should come together for a meeting. >
o·hi·na·pe \ó-hi-na-ṗe\ *n of* hinapa : a place of egress
o·hin·han·na *also* **ohinhanni** \o-híŋ-haŋ-na\ *n* : the morning, during the forenoon < ~ *iyohila* every morning, ~ *kin iyohila tankal hinajin* He came and stood outside each morning. ~ *oyasin wowaši econ* Every morning he did work. > – Bl D.113 B.H.86.6, 105.15
o·hin·hpa·ya \o-híŋ-ḣpa-ya\ *vn* o·ma·hinhpaya [fr *hinhpaya* to fall] : to fall into, to fall from; to forsake < *Yunkan gnugnuška wan i etan nape el* ~ And then a grasshopper fell from its mouth into its hand. *Na taku kakyela wakšica el* ~ And something fell with a noise into a dish.>
o·hin·ni \ó-hiŋ-ni\ *adv* : always < *Na hetan* ~ *can mahel ecé tipi* And since then they always lived only in the woods. > **ohinni·kiya** \ó-hiŋ-ni-k̇i-ya\ *or* \ó-hiŋ-ni-k̇i-ya\ *va* ohinni·wa·kiya : to finish, cease from – Note: the word is Dakota for *ikihunnikiya* — **ohinni·yan** \ó-hiŋ-ni-yaŋ\ *adv* : always, all along, all through < *Zintkala maka* ~ *unpi kin iyuha awicagli* The bird brought back all those that live always throughout the earth. > – R B.H.69.13
o·hin·yan·sye·la \o-híŋ-yaŋ-sye-la\ *adv* : in bad humor < ~ *omawani ška winkcekce nanka yelo.* ~ *tak'takamna welo* You sat unconcerned, but I walked along in bad humor. He earned in poor grace something his. > – BT
o·hin·yan·ze·ca *also* **ohinyanzeke** \o-híŋ-yaŋ-ze-ca\ *vn* o·wa·hinyanzeca : to be stern, cross < *Wicaša wan cinca wahokonkiye šni laka wamanon ohinyanzekelahcak* The man must not have advised his son very sternly not to steal. > — **ohinyanze·ka** *adj* : cranky < *Winyan wan tokiyatanhan* ~ *hi yelo* A cranky woman from somewhere arrived. > – Bl
o·hi·pi·ca šni \ó-hi-ṗi-ca\ *v* : to be unable or impossible to be reached, *e.g.* because something is too high – Bl
o·hi·ti·ka \o-hí-ṫi-k̇a\ *vn* o·ma·hitika : to be furious, terrifying, to be brave — **ohiti·la** *va* ohiti·wa·la : to consider brave or furious — **ohitila·ka** \o-hí-ṫi-la-k̇a\ *n* : a brave person — **ohiti wacin** *v* : to mean to be brave — **ohiti·ya** *adv* : furiously, terribly < *Tona* ~ *o-h'anyanpi kin hena ecel ewicaglepi* So those who acted bravely they had stand in place. > – Bl MS.521
o·hi·wi·ta·ya \ó-hi-wi-ta-ya\ *v coll pl perhaps* : they assemble – *Syn* ÓHIMNICIYE Bl
[1]**o·hi·ya** \o-hí-ya\ *va* ohi·wa·ya : to win, to get the better of one in any way, as in a game, to acquire < *Wanna tipi he ohiyayelo. Ecel okicize kin ohiyapi* You have won that house. As it was they won the fight. > – B.H.56.4
[2]**o·hi·ya** \ó-hi-ya\ *va* ohi·wa·ya : to cause to reach — *adv* : reaching to, hanging over, as hair
o·hi·ya·ye \o-hí-ya-ye\ *n* : a setting, an arrival, a term, conclusion < *Cancans'e škan yo; wi* ~ *kokela yelo* Be quick about your work; there tolls the sun's setting, *i.e.* Hurry up with your work, the sun will set soon. > – Bl
o·hi·ye \ó-hi-ye\ *n* : one length of anything, as a line in a book < ~ *yamni* three lines, when speaking of fence wires; ~ *num zi,* ~ *yamni zi* two yellow stripes, three yellow stripes, *i.e.* the police or soldier arm stripes, *Ikan kin tablokan ca* ~ *num pagmunpi* The shoulder sinew, that of a buck, is rolled up in two lines [rolls, skeins]. > – MS.481 D.92
o·hi·ye·ki·ya *or* **ohiye·ya** \o-hí-ye-k̇i-ya\ *va* ohiye·wa·kiya ohiye·wa·ya : to cause to win
o·hi·ye za·ptan \ó-hi-ye za-ptàŋ\ *n* : a tent 10' x 12' < *óhiye tòpa* a tent 8' x 10' >
o·hi·yo·u \o-hí-yo-u\ *n* : a port of arrival, a nesting place, home-sweet-home, as may be said < ~ *wašte* a comfortable place (room), a niche, as is said when one comes near the place of his destination, a place not his own > – Cf ogliyou Bl KE
o·hi·yu \o-hí-yu\ *v* [fr *hiyu* come out of] : to come through, as water through a roof, to leak, to come into, come through on, to pass through on, to pass through, as through a crack < ~ *šica* a bad place to pass through >
o·ho·hpa \o-hó-ḣṗa\ *va* oho·wa·hpa [fr *hohpa* to cough] : to cough and spit into
o·ho·ka \ó-ho-k̇a\ *n* : one who is respected while in reality he should be punished
o·ho·ki·la \o-hó-k̇i-la\ *v poss of* ohola : to honor one's own
o·ho·la *also* **ohola·ka** \o-hó-la\ \o-hó-la-k̇a\ *va* oho·wa·la oho·un·la·pi oho·wa·laka : to respect, honor, worship — **ohola·ya** *adv* : with respect, honorably
o·ho·mni \o-hó-mni\ *adv* : around, round about < *Ḣe ki* ~ *lapi kte* You should go around the mountain, but it is also said: *Ohomni yo, i.e.* Go around that, *i.e.* since the road is bad or there is a carcas lying on it. *Omahomni po* God around me, *i.e.* avoid me. > – Bl
o·ho·mni·ku·wa \o-hó-mni-k̇ù-wa\ *v* ohomni·ma·kuwa : to hint at, to go round about in regard to
o·ho·mni·yan \o-hó-mni-yaŋ\ *adv* : around, round about, evasively
o·ho·wa·kan·yan·kel \o-hó-wa-kàŋ-yaŋ-kel\ *adv* : weeping in sorrow < ~ *inyan on iglašpašpa ounye* Weeping in grief he dwelt there bruising himself with stones. > – B.H.203.6
o·hun·ka·kan \o-húŋ-k̇a-k̇aŋ\ *n* : a fable, myth, story
o·hun·ke·šni \ó-huŋ-k̇e-šni\ *vn* : to be weak, not strong — **ohunkešni·ya** *va* : to cause one to be weak, to weaken one — **ohunkešni·yan** *adv* : poorly < ~ *kuwa* to treat one poorly >
o·hun·ni·ca·ta \o-húŋ-ni-ca-ta\ *n* : a stone hammer – Note: the word and the word *ihunicata* are both misspellings of the word *ihonicata* which cf
o·hun·we·la \o-húŋ-we-la\ *interj expressing* doubt – B.H.26.16
o·hu·ta *or* **ohute** \ó-hu-ṫa\ *n* : the shore or edge, the place where the water meets the feet — **ohuta·pa** \ó-hu-ṫa-pa\ *adv* : at the edge or shore — **ohuta·ta** \ó-hu-ṫa-ta\ *adv* : at the shore — **ohutata·henatanhan** \ó-hu-ṫa-ta-he-na-ṫaŋ-haŋ\ *adv* : on this side of the shore or water – *Syn* MNI KIN ITAHENA, HUTÁTA-HENATANHAN B.H.45.21 D.37 FB
o·hu·te \o-húṫe\ *n of* húte : the root, the bottom

o·hu·te·ta·na·jin \o-hú-te-ta-na-jin\ *adv* : in the very beginning - Wh

o·hu·tkan \o-hú-tkaŋ\ *n* : the beginning of things - B.H.1.1

oh \oȟ\ *interj expressing* disbelief - B.H.44.1

[1]**o·ȟa·ka** \o-ȟá-k̇a\ *vn* o·ma·ȟaka : to be surfeited, stuffed with food, to be made sick or injured with food

[2]**o·ȟa·ka** \o-ȟá-k̇a\ *adj* : forked, as a stream — *n* : the forks of a stream — **oȟaka·yakel** \o-ȟa-k̇a-ya-k̇el\ *adv* : in many ways - B.H.70.9

o·ȟa·pe \o-ȟá-p̣e\ *v* : to overlook, not find < ~ *tan'inšniyan yankelo* He sat unseen and overlooked, *i.e.* a man sitting between others is overlooked. *Omniciye tipi el tuweni ~ eša un šni* In the meeting hall he failed to find anyone, though he was there, *i.e.* one finds nobody at home. *Hanhepi ~ tan'inšni wakiyagle* I had gone home at night unseen and not found, *i.e.* went home in the evening without anybody knowing it. > - NP Bl

o·ȟa-ya \o-ȟá-ya\ *va* : to fill up *e.g.* a hole with brush wood - P Bl

o·hci \o-ȟcí\ *v* : to dangle, or hang perhaps — **ohci·hci** \o-ȟcí-ȟci\ *adv* : hanging, dangling — **ohcihci·kes'e** *adv* : dressed carelessly and raggedly, not having washed one's self — **ohcihci·ya** *v* : to make dangle

o·ȟin·yan \o-ȟíŋ-yaŋ\ *v* o·wa·ȟinyan un·koȟinyan·pi : to pout, to be out of humor about, to be dissatisfied with one's portion or treatment; to slight or refuse < *Šunšunla ca wak'in oȟinye s'e* I carried the load as though I were a dissatisfied mule, as is said when a man does not care to do even a little job, because mules are slow with a light load but fast with a heavy one. > - Bl

o·hla·gan \o-ȟlá-ġaŋ\ *adj* : not fitting, loose, as is said of a small thing in a large place — **ohlagan·la** *adj* or *adv* : loosely, not fitting, loose as a small bolt in a large hole, too small *e.g.* for a form, frame *etc* ; gurgling, as may be said of a bad egg — **ohlagan·yela** *adv* : loosely < ~ *mun welo* I wear it loosely, *or* It [a coat] is too large for me. > - Bl

o·hla·hla·ye·la \o-ȟlá-ȟla-ye-la\ *adv* : loosely, as knitting, not stretched, as a cord — **ohla·hyela** *adv* : loosely, as in too big clothes - B.H.87.4

o·hla·in \o-ȟlá-iŋ\ *v* : to work loose < ~ *manice,* or ~ *wanil waškan* I am without getting slack, *or* I am always busy. > - Bl LHB

o·hla·te \o-ȟlá-t̄e\ *adv* : under, beneath < *Maya ~ canku iyaya* The road goes under the hill (bank). *Wanna Wizipan Paha kin ~ wakpala el iyotakapi* They sat down at the creek beneath Satchel Hill. *Pa gegéya otkeyapi na ~ cetipi* The head was hung swinging and beneath they set a fire. > — **ohlate·tanhan** \o-ȟlá-t̄e-taŋ-haŋ\ *adv* : from beneath — **ohlate·ya** *adv* : beneath, under < *Unkiš hunh le maya kin ~ unyanpi ktelo* Some of us will go beneath the bank [hill]. *Can kin le ~ unyankapi kte* Under this tree let us rest. > - Bl

o·hli \o-ȟlí\ *adj* : filthy in or within, as unwashed dishes < *Omahli* I am not clean. *Ištohli* His eyes are filthy, *or* He has a dirty look. > - Bl

o·hli·s'e \o-ȟlí-s'e\ *adv* : crowded about, as people around a tent to see a dance < *Na isam winyan wan ena wicaša wan kici yankahanpi ca ~ hinglewicakiyapi.* There was a man with a woman who were sitting beyond there suddenly crowded about them. *Yunkan tipi wan el ~ han ca tima iyaya* Then at one tent he who remained crowded about went inside. *Ehanl ~ makuwapi* They then chased me about the crowd. >

o·hli·ya \o-ȟlí-ya\ *adv* : in a filthy manner < *Wakšica kin ~ han* The dishes remain unwashed. > - Bl

o·hlo·ge·ca \o-ȟló-ġe-ca\ *adj perhaps* : covered with < *we ~* all bloody >

o·hlo·hlo·ka \o-ȟló-ȟlo-k̇a\ *n red of* ohlóka : holes < *Nakeš wa k'on ~ yelo* At last there were many holes in the snow, *i.e.* there were dry spots visible here and there. > - Bl

o·hlo·ka \o-ȟló-k̇a\ *n* : a hole

o·hmi·hmin·yan *also* **ohminyan** \ó-ȟmi-ȟmiŋ-yaŋ\ *adj* : crooked

o·hmun·ye·ce \o-ȟmúŋ-ye-ce\ *v* : to give attention to < *Ohmunyayece lo* You paid attention to him, *i.e.* when you passed him. *waóhmunyece* a talkative fellow >

o·ȟo·lya \o-ȟó-lya\ *adv* : grayish < *Wa ~ hinhpeya* Snow is strewn, *i.e.* when it snows the snow remains only here and there > - Bc

o·ȟo·pa \o-ȟǒ'-p̣a\ *adj* : looking well in *e.g.* a suit, attractive < *Hayapi kin omáȟopa* My clothes are winsome. > - Cf ǵópa

o·hpa \o-ȟpá\ *vn* : to drop < *Pa ~ hingni* The head suddenly dropped. > - B.H.268.6

o·hpan \o-ȟp̣áŋ\ *vn* : to be wet or moist in

[1]**o·hpan·ki·ya** \o-ȟp̣áŋ-k̇i-ya\ *vn* : to dabble, splash gently

[2]**o·hpan·ki·ya** \o-ȟp̣áŋ-k̇i-ya\ *va* ohpan·wa·kiya : to dip into, sop or soak in, to wet or soak *e.g.* so as to take off the hair

o·hpan·yan \o-ȟp̣áŋ-yaŋ\ *va* ohpan·wa·yan : to soak *e.g.* a wash in water

o·hpa·ye ti·pi \o-ȟpá-ye t̄i-pi\ *n* : a dormitory quarters

o·hpu·hpu·ya \o-ȟpú-ȟpu-ya\ *adv* : in rags, poorly dressed, peeling off, perhaps < ~ *aya* to become in rags, as is said when a wound is healed and the skin or scab is coming off >

o·hta·hta \ó-ȟt̄a-ȟt̄a\ *adj* : loose, not stretched tight, as a slackened bowstring — **ohtahta·yela** *adv* : loosely, not stretched

o·hta·ni \o-ȟt̄á-ni\ *v perhaps* : to be laboring < *Zintkala ~ šni kas'a kinyanpi* Birds fly gliding without laboring. > - Bl

o·hta·te·ya \o-ȟt̄á-te-ya\ *adv* : being or becoming weak and languid for some reason < *Ake hel asnikiyin kta iyukcan na el ~ ya. Yunkan el tiyopa s'e han* Again he understood there he should get a long rest, and there he went all tired out. There then he went at night as if it were a doorway. > - MS.142

o·hta·ye·tu \ó-ȟt̄a-ye-t̄u\ *n of* htayetu : the evening < ~ *iyohila* every evening > - B.H.86.6, 105.15

o·hya \ó-ȟya\ *adv* : obliquely, from corner to corner, sloping, as the characters in writing

o·h'a \o-ȟ'á\ *adj* : gray, black and white specks on a black ground

o·h'a·bye·la \ó-ȟ'a-bye-la\ *adv* : not quite full, almost full - Bl

o·h'a·ka \o-ȟ'á-k̇a\ *adj* : gray, black appearing through the white, all colors intermingled

o·h'a·mna \o-ȟ'á-mna\ *vn* : to smell moldy, to stink - Cf h'a *Syn* ONȞYEMNA Bl

[1]**o·h'an** \o-ȟ'áŋ\ *v* o·wa·h'an : to do, to work < *Tokel ~ kin hena slolwaya* I know how they work. > — *n* : work

---

\a\ father \e\ they \i\ machine \o\ smoke \u\ lunar \an, aŋ\ blanc Fr. \in, iŋ\ ink \on, oŋ, un, uŋ\ soon, confier Fr. \c\ chair \ġ\ machen Ger. \j\ fusion \clusters: bl, gn, kp, hšl, etc...\ b[e]lo ... said with a slight vowel
See more in the Introduction, Guide to Pronunciation

or action, custom, artifices < *Mioh'an oyasin cic'u kte* I shall give you all my work. ~ *witonpešni oyah'an he* Do you do your work fearlessly? *Teȟiya omicih'an yelo* He works for me with difficulty, as one would say if his companion had plenty without letting him share. *Unk'oh'anpi* We are in for it, *or* We've done noisy things. *Šikšica oyah'an ca hece* So you are the wicked one who did it. *Le t'in kte iyecel oh'an yelo* Now he will die as he acted. > – MS. 354 B.H.38.7, 68.19, 258.12

[2]**o·h'an** \ó-ȟ'aŋ\ *vn* ó·ma·h'an : to be slow, perhaps; to be long in doing < ~ *ekta akibleza* He thought about the treatment he had given him (David). > – B.H.90.14

o·h'an·e·cin·šni·yan \o-ȟ'áŋ-e-ciŋ-šni-yaŋ\ *adj* : impolite – P

o·h'an·gla·wa \o-ȟ'áŋ-gla-wa\ *v poss perhaps* : to call something one's own work, to say to have worked when in reality it does not amount to much < *Taku ecanon kin ~ ecanon we* If you do something, do it calling it your own work, so a woman would say to her husband who thought he did much work. ~ *tak'tokanon* What you do she calls it her own work. >

o·h'an·han·han *also* **oh'anhanhan·ka** \o-ȟáŋ-haŋ-haŋ\ *vn* oh'an·wa·hanhan : to do odd things, to play pranks, cut capers, to do badly < *Na ungna ~ s'e wahinkpe wan ekta egle* And suddenly as if in fun he set an arrow in place. ~ *sicápsanpsan mankelo* I was wagging my feet in cutting a caper. > – D.26 Bl

o·h'an·hi \o-ȟ'áŋ-hi\ *vn* : to be slow in < *Wicalapi kte kin el onih'anhipi* You are slow at belief in the future. > — **oh'anhi·ya** *va* : to cause to be slow

o·h'an·ki·han·han \o-ȟ'áŋ-ki-haŋ-haŋ\ *v* oh'an·wa·ki-hanhan : to play pranks upon one, to do badly to

o·h'an·ko \o-ȟ'áŋ-ǩo\ *vn* o·ma·h'anko o·ni·h'anko un-koh'anko·pi : to be quick in doing anything — *n* : a minute, 60 seconds < *Walehantu ca šunkawakan hunkešni oh'ankopelo* It is at this time (the spring) that sickly horses are fast. > — **oh'anko·ya** *adv* : quickly — **o-h'ankoya·kel** \o-ȟ'áŋ-ǩo-ya-ǩel\ *adv* : rather quickly — **oh'anko·yela** *adv* : quickly, suddenly

o·h'an·o·pte·li·c'i·ya *also* **o·h'optelic'iya** \o-ȟ'áŋ-o-pte-li-c'i-ya\ *v* : to slacken and give up one's work

o·h'an·pi \o-ȟ'áŋ-p̣i\ *vn* [fr *oh'an* to do + *pi* sign of *pl*] : to be generous, liberal < *Oh'anmapi* I am generous. > — **oh'anpi·ya** *adv* : generously, liberally

o·h'an·sin·kpe·kpe \oȟ'áŋ-siŋ-kpe-kpe\ *v* : to be fearless in one's doings, muskrat-like – BT

o·h'an·sla·ta \o-ȟ'áŋ-sla-ṫa\ *vn* oh'an·ma·slata [fr *oh'an* to act + *slata* slow] : to be slow in one's movements, to work slowly and deliberately

o·h'an·ši·ca \o-ȟ'áŋ-ši-ca\ *vn* oh'an·ma·šica : to be ill-behaved, to be stingy, to be of a mean or cross disposition — **oȟ'anšica·ya** *adv* : badly

o·h'an·ši·lya \o-ȟ'áŋ-ši-lya\ *va* oh'anši·lwa·ya : to make stingy, make bad — *adv* : badly, wickedly

o·h'an·šun·ke·ca \o-ȟ'án-šun-ǩe-ca\ *va perhaps* : to give up hope, to be helplessly lost, as one who will die, to act disastrously — *vn* o·wa·h'anšunkeca : to act disastrously < *Wanji únyan el oyapapi kin oyah'anšunkecapi kte lo* You will be hopelessly lost if you join up with one when he has dropped out of sight. > – Bc ED D.58 note 2

o·h'an·te·han \o-ȟ'áŋ-ṫe-haŋ\ *vn* oh'an·ma·tehan [fr *o-h'an* to do + *tehan* for a long time] : to be long in doing a thing

o·h'an·to·ke·ca \o-ȟ'áŋ-to-ke-ca\ *adj* : to be queer in one's way – BD

o·h'an·wa·kan·kan·yan \o-ȟáŋ-wa-kàŋ-kaŋ-yaŋ\ *adv* : acting like a wayward person, remarkable in operating < *Kukuše s'e ~ wakita* Like a pig he keeps on the watch in a remarkable way, *i.e.* to see everything as boys have clear eyes. > – Bl WHL

o·h'an·wa·ši·cun \o-ȟ'áŋ-wa-ši-cuŋ\ *n* : one who can make all sorts of things, like a white man –EB

[1]**o·h'an·wa·šte** \ó-ȟ'aŋ-wa-šte\ *n* : order, courtesy, etiquette, protocol — *adj* : well-behaved, good, generous, good-humored, open-hearted, orderly

[2]**o·h'an·wa·šte** \o-ȟ'áŋ-wa-šte\ *vn* oh'an·ma·wašte : to behave well, be good and generous

o·h'an·wi·ȟa \o-ȟ'áŋ-wi-ȟa\ *adj* : funny, cute < *hokšila ~* a funny boy >

[1]**o·h'an·yan** \o-ȟ'áŋ-yaŋ\ *vn* o·wá·h'anya o·ya·h'anya un-koh'anyan·pi : to do work, to act < *Tona ohitiya oh'anyanpi kin hena ecel ewicaglepi* Thus they had stand those who acted with great bravery. >

[2]**o·h'an·yan** \ó-ȟ'áŋ-yaŋ\ *v* o·wá·h'anbla *and* o·wá·h'an-yan un·koh'anyan·pi : to do, habitually work, be active < *Tona wakan óh'anyayanpi k'on oyasin hocokata hiyaya po* All you holy ones who have been active go past the center. > – Note: though BD says óh'anyan is not used, still we have *óh'anyayanpi*

o·h'an·ye \o-ȟ'áŋ-ye\ *n* : the doings of a person < ~ *ci wanyankapi, heon lila cajeyatapi* They saw his deeds, so his name was much spoken. >

o·h'an·ye·ya \o-ȟ'áŋ-ye-ya\ *va* oh'anye·wa·ya : to cause to do

o·h'a·ya \o-ȟ'á-ya\ *adv* : in a grayish or mixed manner, as is said of putting paint on the face – Cf ȟ'a

o·h'e·h'e \o·ȟ'é-ȟ'e\ *v* : to be drooping, dangling < *Šunka aze ~ s'e wahanpi waštelake* He likes soup much as a dog an udder drooping, as is said when someone likes broth very much. > – KE WHL

o·h'e·ya \ó-ȟ'e-ya\ *vn* : to have but little in

o·h'i·ton·ki·pa *or* **oh'an'itonkipa** \o-ȟ'í-toŋ-ki-p̣a\ \o-ȟ'áŋ-i-toŋ-ki-p̣a\ *v* : to do something against orders and have bad luck but not showing it

o·h'o·kpa·ya \o-ȟ'ó-kpa-ya\ *vn* : to be sunk and ringed around with circles < *Wanagi s'e išta ~* Like a ghost, his eyes are deep-set. > – Bl WHL

o·h'o·pte·li·c'i·ya *or* **oh'an'optelic'iya** \o-ȟ'ó-pte-li-c'i-ya\ *v* oh'opte·lmi·c'iya : to slacken and give up one's work < *Oh'optelmic'iyešni na pilamic'iyelo* I am glad I did not give up. > – Bl

o·i·a·li \o-í-a-li\ *n* : stairs, as in a house

o·i·ca·ga \o-í-ca-ġa\ *vn* oi·ma·caga [fr *icaga* grow] : to grow in anything, to grow up — **oica·ge** *n* : a growing, a generation, creation, interest taken on money lent <*cunwiyapehe ~* a crop of grapes > – Note: there is some doubt as to the use of *wicoicage* – A B.H.62.12

o·i·ca·hi·ton \o-í-ca-hi-toŋ\ *va* oicahi·wa·ton [fr *icahi* to mix] : to mingle, mix together in, as tobacco and bark, in anything — **oicahi·ye** *n* : a mixture, a mixing

o·i·cah \o-í-caȟ\ *vn contrac of* oicaga : to grow up, in < ~ *kokela* of quick growth, ~ *tehan* of slow growth > — **oica·hwan·ka·la** *adj* : growing easily — **oica·hya** *va* oica·hwa·ya : to produce a yield, to yield, to make grow, to cause to produce – B.H.157.8

o·i·ca·zo \o-í-ca-zo\ *n* [fr *icázo* a drawn mark or line] : a giving credit, a marking, taking things and giving things on credit, credits

o·i·ci·ma·ni \o-í-ci-ma-ni\ *n of* ícimani : traveling, a company of many travelers – Note: *icimani* has *ref* to one < *Iyotiyeyakiyapi heon ~ kin le cic'upi* I gave you this trip because you had troubles. ~ *waŝte yuhapi kte kin he Wakantanka icekiye* He prayed to God that they might have a good journey. > – B.H.36.7

o·i·ci·pa \o-í-ci-pa\ *v* – *See* oic'ipa

o·i·co·ga \ó-i-coǧa\ *n* : wood drifted ashore – WHL

o·i·cu \o-í-cu\ *n* [fr *icu* take or receive] : a quarry or pit, a place where one finds or receives things, as when one goes for *e.g.* gravel, rocks *etc* < ~ *ŝica* a poor mine or source, ~ *ŝilyá* to spoil a resource, ~ *ŝilya yankelo* He was ruining a dig. > — **oicu-·waŝte** \o-í-cu-wa-ŝte\ *adj* : good to take, acceptable

o·i·c'i·gla·ka \o-í-c'i-gla-ka\ *or* \o-í-ci-gla-ka\ *v* [fr *oi-glaka* to tell of one's self] : to say to one's self concerning one's self < *woic'iconze* ~ to make a vow > – B.H. 22.18

o·i·c'i·gmi·gme·la \ó-i-c'i-gmi-gme-la\ *adv* or *adj* : with one's self rolled up < ~ *munkelo* I lay all rolled up, *i.e.* to lie with knees drawn towards the body. > – *Syn* ÓIC'I-PŠUNPŠUNKEL LC

o·i·c'i·hi \o-í-c'i-hi\ *v refl of* okíhi : to be selfish, to be able for one's self, to be rich, to get for one's self < *omic'ihi* to be able to accomplish things, to profit > – R

o·i·c'i·h'an \o-í-c'i-ȟ'aŋ\ *v* : to do injury to one's self < *Woteȟi omic'ih'an* My affliction did me injury. > – Bl WHL

o·i·c'i·kpa·ni \o-í-c'i-kp̣a-ni\ *v refl* o·ma·c'ikpani : to be poor, to be unable to take care of one's self or family

o·i·c'i·ma·ni \o-í-c'i-ma-ni\ *n* : a trip – *See* oicimani P

o·i·c'i·pa *also* **oicipa** \o-í-c'i-pa\ *v* : to act as a tributary to < *Canku oic'ipe* The road served as junction, *i.e.* a side road tributary to a main road. > – Bl

o·i·c'i·pšun·pšun·kel \ó-i-c'i-pšuŋ-pšuŋ-ḳel\ *adv* : curled up < ~ *munkelo* I lay curled up, *i.e.* with knees drawn towards the body. > – *Syn* ÓIC'IGMIGMEYELA

o·i·c'i·wa \o-í-c'i-wa\ *v refl of* owá : to write one's self < *caje* ~ to sign one's own name >

o·i·c'i·ya \ó-i-c'i-ya\ *v refl of* ókiya : to help one's self – B.H.290.6

o·i·c'o·ni·ca \o-í-c'o-ni-ca\ *v* o·mi·c'onica o·un·kic'onica-·pi : to control one's self, not giving in to one's temper

o·i·e \o-í-e\ *n of* iá : a word, a saying or speech < *Wicaŝa wan ~ owotanla ehantanš he eca kahnigapi.* ~ *yušpica šni* If a man's speech is honest really he is appointed. He is not one that picks words. > – Bl

o·i·e·ki·ca·ton\o-í-e-ḳi-ca-toŋ\ *vn* oie·we·caton : to use language

o·i·e·ki·c'un \o-í-e-ḳi-c'uŋ\ *vn* oie·we·c'un : to command, enforce obedience

o·i·e·ki·ton \o-í-e-ḳi-toŋ\ *vn* oie·we·ton : to use language, words < *Wašagyela oieyetonpi kin mitaakicita ob wamayalakapi kte lo* You should ask me when you use words easily with my officers. > – ST

o·i·e pe·pe·ka \o-í-e p̣e-p̣e-ka\ *n* : sharp talk, bitter words < *oie pepekelahcaka i.e. taku eye cin oyasin canzéka ecé ca heon heyapelo* His words were very bitter, *i.e.* that was said because everything he said was angry. > – Bl WHL

o·i·e ta·tu·ye·ye·ke *also simply* **tatuyeke** \o-í-e ta-ṫù-ye-ye-ḳe\ *adj* : changing one's views often < *Oie ma·tatuyeyeke* I change my views often. > – Bl

o·i·e wa·ši·cun \o-í-e wa-šĭ-cuŋ\ *n* : one who is a noisy and sassy person – WHL

o·i·e wa·ši·kši·cun \o-í-e wa-šĭ-kši-cuŋ\ *n red* [fr *oie wašicun* a sassy person] : one who talks without let, a garrulous person < *Oie niwašikšicun welo* You are one who talks far too much. > – BT WHL

o·i·e·ya *or* **oieye** \o-í-e-ya\ *vn* oie·wa·ya : to use words, to speak < *Wóiȟa oieyaye lo* You spoke something laughable. *Itancan tuwe kaca he oieye nawah'on* Who is Lord that I listen not to what he says? > – B.H.49.4

o·i·gla·gya \o-í-gla-gya\ *adv* : traveling in – B.H.63.20, 165.7

o·i·glak \o-í-glak\ *v contrac of* oíglaka : to be moving < ~ *unpi* They are moving. *Na oyate kin ~ unpi* And the people are on the move. *Wi yamni ~ yapi* They went traveling for three months. > – B.H.56.1

o·i·gla·ka \o-í-gla-ḳa\ *v* : to move, be moving, as a family or camp traveling – Note: BD believed the word in this sense is not used — *v refl* o·mi·glaka [fr *oyaka* to tell] : to tell one's own name, to confess, to make one's self known – B.H.127.10, 174.19, 221.14

o·i·gla·ke \o-í-gla-ḳe\ *n* [fr *igláka* to travel] : an expedition, journey, excursion < *Wana maštešte, ~ kte taniga wanji pusya yuha yo* It is quite hot and sultry, so carry along a dry buffalo paunch for the journey. > – Bl

o·i·gla·pta \o-í-gla-pta\ *v* o·mi·glapta : to take all that is left when things are distributed; to pour out for one's self, perhaps – D.66

o·i·glo·ni·ca \o-í-glo-ni-ca\ *v* : to be stubborn about moving away out or away – B.H.165.7

o·i·glo·ye \o-í-glo-ye\ *n* : progressing, making progress or getting along well < *Onigloye ekta tokeca,* or *Oigloye nitawa tokeca he* Is there any change in your getting along? *or* Is there any difference in your progress? *i.e.* How are you getting along? > – BD

o·i·glu·ble·ca \o-í-glu-ble-ca\ *v refl* : to scatter, as a crowd of people do – B.H.10.2

o·i·glu·ha \o-í-glu-ha\ *v poss* o·mi·gluha : to be well off, to have one's self < *Wicaša ksapapi lena wawiyaksapapi ca oyate kin ogna ~ yapi* These wise men who spoke wisely went well-off among the people. > – BM.483

o·i·glu·ki·ki \o-í-glu-ḳi-ḳi\ *v* o·mi·glukiki : to enter a complaint, to be dissatisfied *etc.* and finally speak against those who seem to be against us < *Oiglukikipišni* They did not complain, as is said of a man so people would get along with each other well. > — **oiglukiki·ya** *va* : to cause to quarrel with each other by back biting *etc.* – Bl

o·i·glu·ši·ca \o-í-glu-ši-ca\ *v refl* o·mi·glušica : to spoil one's own reputation

o·i·glu·škan \o-í-glu-šḳaŋ\ *vn* : to have a relapse, become sick again

o·i·glu·ze \o-í-glu-ze\ *n of* igluza : clothing, what one puts on

o·i·han·ke *or* **owihanke** \o-í-haŋ-ke\ *n* [fr *ihanke* end or border] : the end of time, space *etc.*, the end of a story — **oihanke·ya** *va* : to make an end of, to destroy

o·i·he·ya \o-í-he-ya\ *va* oihe·wa·ya [fr *iheya* to discharge] : to shoot into — **oiheye** *n* : the place where the shot is sent — **oiheye tipi** \o-í-he-ye ṫi-pi\ *n* : a toilet – R

o·i·hun·ni \ó-i-huŋ-ni\ *va* oi·wa·hunni [fr *ihunni* to reach, finish] : to land in or at — *n* : a landing < *tipi kin ~ waŝte* to be easy to reach the house > – D.251

o·i·ȟa-ȟa \o-í-ȟa-ȟa\ *va* : to ridicule, laugh at, to scorn

\a\ father \e\ they \i\ machine \o\ smoke \u\ lunar \an, aŋ\ blanc Fr. \in, iŋ\ ink \on, oŋ, un, uŋ\ soon, confier Fr. \c\ chair \ǧ\ machen Ger. \j\ fusion \clusters: bl, gn, kp, hšl, etc...\ b^e^lo ... said with a slight vowel **See more in the Introduction, Guide to Pronunciation**

— **oiȟaȟa·ya** *adv* : in a mocking manner < ~ *ia* to speak scorning > — **oiȟaȟaya·kel** *adv* : mockingly - B.H.77.22, 57.11, 108.5, 111.13, 263.8

o·i·hpe·hpe·ya \o-í-ȟpe-ȟpe-ya\ *v red of* oihpeya : to throw into often < *oihpehpeyapi s'e wicoti* a camp as though being tossed into, as said when a few tents are scattered over a valley > - *Syn* YAWAWAPILAS'E Bl

o·i·hpe·ya \o-í-ȟpe-ya\ *va* oihpe·wa·ya : to throw into < *Na mini šma cin el (keya kin) oihpeyapi* And it (the turtle) was thrown into the deep water. >

o·i·kca·pta \o-í-kca-pta\ *v poss perhaps* : to talk angrily to one's self - B.H.44.8

o·i·kpa·ġi·ca \o-í-kpa-ġi-ca\ *v* : to awake, come awake < *Hecel ~ na lila wiyuškin* So he awoke and was very glad. > - Cf oikpaȟica MS.152

o·i·kpa·hun·za·pi \o-í-kṗa-huŋ-zà-pi\ *n* : a rocking-chair

o·i·kpa·ȟi·ca \o-í-kpa-ȟi-ca\ *vn* o·mi·kpaȟica un·koi-kpaȟica·pi : to wake up, awake

o·i·kpa·ptan·ši·lya \oí-kpa-ptaŋ-ši-lya\ *adv* : hard to roll around in, as in a bed < ~ *mayakuwapelo* You chased me with difficulty rolling around in *e.g.* a bed. ~*ic'iya* to be hard to roll one's self around, ~ *tipi* hard to roll about in a tent >

o·i·kpa·ptan·wa·šte·ya \o-í-kpa-ptaŋ-wa-šte-ya\ *adv* : easy to roll from side to side in < ~ *epelo* I said truthfully, as is said when somebody doubts a statement. > - Bl

o·i·kpa·sya \o-í-kpa-sya\ *adv* : in darkness < ~ *han* to be, stand, in darkness > - B.H.1.2

o·i·kpa·t'a \o-í-kpa-t'a\ *vn of* ikpí : to be stillborn, to die within on account of pressure from outside — n : an abortion, as of a child < *Omikpat'a* I aborted, as the mother says when it happens to her child. > — *v refl* : to have an abortion accidentally, by pressure as while digging with the *hunpe* stick with which to dig turnips < *Onikpat'in ktelo* You might abort. >

o·i·kwa \o-í-kwa\ *v poss* o·mi·kwa un·koikwa·pi : to write one's own name, paint or draw one's own *e.g.* name or picture < *caje, ite ~* to write/draw one's own name, *Ite omikwa* I drew my face. *Omic'ikwa* I wrote my own name. *Caje ~ yo* Write your name. > — **oi-kwaya** *va* oikwa·wa·ya : to cause one to write his/her name

o·i·le \o-í-le\ *vn of* ilé : to blaze in, to burn within < *Peta kin ~ ecetu šni* The fire didn't burn just right. > — *n* : a flame - Bl B.H.273.14

o·i·le·le·ka \o-í-le-le-ka\ *n* : a fool, a good-for-nothing person - Note: oí·ma·leleka *or* omáileleka may perhaps be used. *oílelepi* is used to *ref* to more than one - WE

o·i·le·ya \o-í-le-ya\ *va* : to set on fire - B.H.241.6

o·i·mni·ci·ye \ó-i-mni-ci-ye\ *v coll pl* : they go to a meeting < *Oyate kin ataya hocokata wicakico au na hecel wanna ~* The enite tribe came and called them to center camp, and so they went to the meeting. >

o·i·na·hme \o-í-na-ȟme\ *n* : a hiding place - *See* inahmekiciciyapi, the playing of hide-and-seek - P

o·i·na·jin \o-í-na-ǰiŋ\ *n of* inajin : a standing place, a starting place — **oinajin·ta** *n* : a goal, the place of standing - Note: the word is the name applied to the town of Valentine, Nebraska

o·i·na·pe \o-í-na-ṗe\ *n* : a place of coming out, a doorway

o·i·ni·ka·ga \o-í-ni-ġa\ *n* : a sweat lodge or house < *Hihanna el ~ wan lila tanka ca etipi na hel tima iyayapi šni* In the morning a very large sweatlodge was set up, but they did not enter it. ~ *tipi* a sweat house, a sauna > - MS.344, 349

o·in·kpa \ó-iŋ-kṗa\ *n* : the end of anything < *Ḣemakoskantu kin he itahena na Cahli Wakpa ~ kin ogna unkiyayapi. Wakpala ~ kin guhéheya yunkelo* On that side of the wilderness and to the head of Powder River we went. The creek head lay diverting in many directions. > — **oinkpata** *adv* : in the very beginning, *e.g.* of ancestry, *etc.* < ~ *oyate toká icagapi hehanl* At that time in the beginning, they became a first tribe. > - Bl

o·in·yan·ka \ó-iŋ-yaŋ-ka\ *vi* : to run about in - D.35

o·in·yan·ke \o-íŋ-yaŋ-ke\ *n* : a race track

o·i·pa·kšan \o-í-ṗa-kšaŋ\ *n* : a bend, a crook, an angle

o·i·pa·ktan \o-í-ṗa-ktaŋ\ *n* : a bend in a stream

o·i·pa·sli·ya \o-í-ṗa-sli-ya\ *adv* : squeezing out into, pressing out against something

o·i·pe·ya \o-í-ṗe-ya\ *n* : a shelter from the wind, which faces the sun east or west, a sheltered place, a warm place out of the wind < *Tipi ~ el manka* I sat in the shelter of a house. ~ k'el oluluta helo It was hot and sultry in the shelter. ~ *eciyatanhan puza oh'anko welo* Because of the shelter it quickly became dry. > - *Syn* ÓBLULA Bl

o·i·pi·ya·ke \o-í-ṗi-ya-ke\ *n of* ipiyaka : the waist, the place around which a girdle is put

o·i·pu·ta·ke \o-í-ṗu-ta-ke\ *n of* iputaka : a kiss

o·i·pu·za \o-í-pu-za\ *vn* : *vn* : to thirst after - B.H. 189.4

o·i·sa \o-í-sa\ *n* : the outer corner *e.g.* of a house < ~ *yamni* three corners, *i.e.* a triangle, as the Lakota call it >

o·i·šta·gle·wan·ji·la \o-í-šta-gle-waŋ-ǰi-la\ *n* : a steady gaze, a fixed look

o·i·štin·me \o-í-štiŋ-me\ *n of* ištinma : a bedroom < *Ikpaptanptan ihpeic'iyelo, ~ šica ca* He threw himself down and tossed about, since it was a bad bedroom, *i.e.* bad in sleep. > - Bl

o·i·tan·can \o-í-taŋ-caŋ\ *n* : a head man < *Na oyate el ~ unpi kin.* And in the tribe there are head men. *ti el ~ kin he* the head man in a home, *i.e.* the head servant > — **oitancan·yan** *adv* : at the head < ~ *unpi* They are at the head, ~ *waawanyanka* The foreman watched over the work. > - B.H.100.8,11

o·i·to·mni \o-í-to-mni\ *v* : to be dizzy, as from looking downward from a high place - Bl

o·i·wa·wan·yan·gwa·ci \o-í-wa-waŋ-yaŋ-gwa-ci\ *n* : a place where there has been held a sundance - RTj

o·i·wi·ta·ya \ó-i-wi-ta-ya\ *v* : to assemble < ~ *welo* They came together. > - *Syn* KIWITAYA, ÓKIMNICIYE Bl

o·i·ya·cin·yan \o-í-ya-ciŋ-yaŋ\ *adv* : in the same manner as somebody else, after the same pattern *etc.* < ~ *ecunkonpi kte kaga* He made it so we would do it after the same pattern, *i.e.* as a pattern of beadwork. > - Bl WE

o·i·ya·gle \o-í-ya-gle\ *n* : a road leading to - B.H.194.24

o·i·ya·han \o-í-ya-haŋ\ *vn of* iyahan : to alight down in - R Bl

o·i·ya·he \ó-i-ya-he\ *n* : a reaching the top, as of a hill

o·i·ya·hpe·ya \o-í-ya-ȟpe-ya\ *v* : to hold up the pipe, as the Dakotas do, to the Creator before smoking

o·i·ya·hpe·ye \o-í-ya-ȟpe-ye\ *n* : a load, what can be thrown over the back of a horse < ~ *wanjila* one load >

o·i·ya·ka·pe·ya \ó-i-ya-ka-pe-ya\ *adj* : steep, as a road, going upward < *canku ~* a steep road *i.e.* where the road leads up it is steep >

o·i·ya·ka·ška \o-í-ya-ka-ška\ *va* oiya·wa·kaška : to tie into — **oiyakaške** *n* : a knot, a tying into

o·i·ya·ni·ca \o-í-ya-ni-ca\ *vn* oiya·ma·nica : to be prevented in, to be unable to get through for one reason or another : snow, quarantine, *etc.* < *Oiyamanica* I cannot get through. *Inikagapi tima ~ kin...* When he was not able to get through a sweat... > — **oiya·nil** *vn contrac of* oiyanica : to be prevented in — **oiyani·lya** *va* : to prevent, be the cause of prevention, to clog - D.51 MS.351

o·i·ya·pa \ó-i-ya-pa\ *or* \o-í-ya-pa\ *v* : to hit, beat on the side of — *n* : the hitting side, as the drum head - WHL

o·i·ya·ye \o-í-ya-ye\ *n* : a getting through *e.g.* over a bad road or through deep snow < ~ *wanice* A way through is lacking, *or* It is impossible to get through. ~ *šilya nawicatakapi* A way through was badly closed off to them. > — **oiyaye·šilya** *v* : to prevent one from leaving, as by speaking to him, although he is anxious to go < *Oiyayešilmayayelo* You prevented me from leaving, and the use of the *Syn oúnc'onnilmayayelo* He held me back from leaving. > - *See* oiyanica B.H.118.7 Bl

o·i·ye·ki·ye \o-í-ye-k̇i-ye\ *n* [fr *iyekiya* find or recognize one's own] : recognition < ~ *šicapi* They were hard to recognize. ~ *wašteya* easily recognized, easy to find out, ~ *wašteya wiyaskabtonpi* a seal easily found > - D.224 B.H.269.22

o·i·ye·ye \o-í-ye-ye\ *n* : a wound, a hole made by a shot

o·i·yo·blu·la \o-í-yo-blu-la\ *n* : a shelter, such as brush, a hill, *etc.* — **oiyoblu·ya** *also* **oiyoblu·yela** *adj* or *n* : calm

o·i·yo·gnag \o-í-yo-gnag\ *n contrac of* oiyognaka : a mouthful < ~ *tonala* a few mouthfuls >

o·i·yo·gna·ka \o-í-yo-gna-ka\ *n* [fr *iyognaka* to put in the mouth] : a mouthful, very little

o·i·yo·han·zi \ó-i-yo-haŋ-zi\ *n* : a wagon umbrella

o·i·yo·hpa·ya \o-í-yo-ȟṗa-ya\ *v* oiyohpa·bla : to fall into — \ó-i-yo-ȟpaya\ *adj* : steep, *i.e.* downward < *canku* ~ a steep road >

o·i·yo·hpa·ye \ó-i-yo-ȟpa-ye\ *n* : a ford or crossing - *Syn* ÓIYUWEGE P Bl

o·i·yo·hpa·ye·ya \o-í-yo-ȟpa-ye-ya\ *v* : to make fall, perhaps, into, to go into < *Taku epe cin, nonge oiyohpayeyayešni yelo* What I say you do not take seriously, *i.e.* make fall into your ears. > - BT

o·i·yo·hpe·ya \o-í-yo-ȟṗe-ya\ *va* oiyohpe·wa·ya : to throw or cast into, to go into *e.g.* a river at a ford

o·i·yo·ki·pi \o-í-yo-ki-ṗi\ *vn* oiyo·ma·kipi : to be pleased with — *adj* : pleasant, agreeable - Note: this is not said of persons, but of places and of the weather < *Wanna lila mašte, lila ~* It is now very sultry, very pleasant. *hanwiyanpi ~* a pleasant moon-light > — *n* : attracktion < ~ *t'a nuns'e* The attraction just about died, as is said when the crowd has a very jolly time. ~ *tajontka* A buffalo kidney is a delight, *i.e.* good to eat, as an old saying goes. > — **oiyokipi·ya** *adv* : pleasantly, agreeably < ~ *oyate ounkijupi* Pleasantly the people met, greeted us. > - P GT

o·i·yo·ki·ši·ca \o-í-yo-ki-ši-ca\ *adj* oiyo·ma·kišica : disagreeable, as the weather, unhappy, feeling badly < ~ *ahi* It storms, *i.e.* is unpleasant weather. *Hecel wanna wakanheja wanjigji wola ceyapi na lila ~* So each child cried begging food and was feeling very bad. >

o·i·yo·ki·ši·lya \o-í-yo-k̇i-ši-lya\ *adv* : being a sad thing to say or see < *Tipi kin ~ he* The house is a sad sight, in great disorder. ~ *yaceya yelo* How sad to see you weep! > — **oiyokišilye·la** *adv* : disagreeably - Bl D.122 WHL

o·i·yo·kpas *or* **oiyokpaz** \o-í-yo-kpas\ *n contrac of* oiyokpaza : darkness < ~ *hingla* There was suddenly darkness, *i.e.* it suddenly turned dark. > — **oiyikpa·sya** *va* : to make dark — *adv* : darkly, in darkness < ~ *han* He stands in darkness. > - B.H.52.2, 54.7

o·i·yo·kpa·za \o-í-yo-kṗa-za\ *n* : darkness < *Tohanl ~ aya ca na wicaša lila waš'aka* When it becomes darkness then a man is really strong. >

o·i·yo·kši·ca \o-í-yo-kši-ca\ *adj* : ill-matched - P

o·i·yo·pa \o-í-yo-pa\ *vn* oiyo·ma·pa : to be affected, to have a swelling *etc.* resulting from a sore in another part of the body - *Syn* SNIYOPA WE

o·i·yo·pe·ye \o-í-yo-ṗe-ye\ *n of* iyopeya : a scolding

o·i·yo·ta·ke \o-í-yo-ṫa-ke\ *n of* iyotaka : a seat, a sitting place

o·i·yo·ti·ye·ki·ya \o-í-yo-ti-ye-k̇i-ya\ *v*: to have, endure hard times < *Oiyotiye·wa·kiya* I am having a hard time. > - B.H.104.20

o·i·yu·ktan \o-í-yu-k̇taŋ\ *n of* yuktan : a bend

o·i·yu·ski·lya \o-í-yu-ski-lya\ *adv* : oppressed in, as from smoke in a room < ~ *mankelo* I am oppressed in here. > - BT

o·i·yu·ski·te \o-í-yu-ski-te\ *n of* iyuskita : a place where a band goes around *e.g.* around the arm or wrist

o·i·yu·spe \ó-i-yu-spe\ *n* : the handle, *i.e.* that part of a handle which is grasped, like the wooden part of a bucket handle

o·i·yu·te \o-í-yu-ṫe\ *n* : a dimension, a rate < ~ *ciscila* an inch, ~ *wanji* one section, ~ *okise* a half section, ~ *šokela* a quarter section, ~ *canku* a section road >

o·i·yu·we·ge \o-í-yu-we-ġe\ *n* : a ford, crossing, a place of crossing a stream

o·i·zi·lya \ó-i-zi-lya\ *v* : to smoke in the tanning process < *Itóizilwayin kte lo* I shall smoke its face. > - WHL

o·i·zi·ta \o-í-zi-ṫa\ *vn* : to smoke, as might a stove

o·jan·jan \o-jáŋ-jaŋ\ *n* : a light — *v perhaps* : to light < *Tohanl oiyokpaz aya ca na wicaša lila waš'aka, na ~ ca na hunkešni. Na tuktel ~ ca na natakapi* When it become dark, then a man is very strong, and when light, weak. *Na tuktel ~ ca na natakapi* And where it is light, he is fenced in. > - MS.351

o·jan·jan·gle·pi \o-jáŋ-jaŋ-gle-pi\ *n* : a window, windows — **ojanjanglepi akahpe** *n* : a shade, curtain, shutter - P Bl

o·ja·te \o-já-ṫe\ *n of* ja : a fork, the forks of a road or stream

o·ji \o-jí\ *va* o·wa·ji o·wicawa·ji : to whisper about < *Okicijipi* They whisper to one another. >

o·ji·ca·ka \o-jí-ċa-ka\ *adj* : rich in goods *etc.* < ~ *ca wawicak'u we* You rich give to them. > - Bl

o·ji·ji \o-jí-ji\ *v red of* ojí o·wa·jiji : to whisper about, to whisper to — **ojiji·ya** *adv* : in a whispering manner, secretly — **ojijiha·han** *adv* : whispering

o·ji·la·ka \ó-ji-la-ka\ *n perhaps* : the offspring, the young one's of both men and animals < ~ *ko óimniciye* All the children too were in the meeting. >

o·ju \o-jú\ *va* o·wa·ju : to plant, put in the ground, one by one as in planting corn — *n* : a growth, a field *etc.*, *e.g.* of weeds *etc.* < *Hehanl unkcela oju wan el awicai. Na onjinjintka oju wan el awicai. Wagacan oju.* He then took them into a cactus patch. And he brought them

---

\a\ father \e\ they \i\ machine \o\ smoke \u\ lunar \an, aŋ\ blanc Fr. \in, iŋ\ ink \on, oŋ, un, uŋ\ soon, confier Fr. \c\ chair \ġ\ machen Ger. \j\ fusion \clusters: bl, gn, kp, hšl, etc...\ blo ... said with a slight vowel
See more in the Introduction, Guide to Pronunciation

into a rose garden. So he planted cotton-wood trees. >

o·ju·gju·la \o-jú-gju-la\ *adj red of* ojula : full, filled

o·ju·ha \o-jú-ha\ *n* : a sheath, a case for anything, an empty bag < *Wímakan nitawa ~ el iyekiya yo* Put my straps in your bag. >

o·ju·ju \o-jú-ju\ *vn* : to fall to pieces in any place — **o-juju·wahan** *part* : fallen to pieces in, as an old wagon or a house

o·ju·ki·ci·ton \o-jú-k̇i-ci-toŋ\ *v* oju·we·citon [fr *ojuton* to fill into sacks] : to fill a bag for one — **ojuki·ton** *v poss* oju·wa·kiton : to fill up one's own bags *etc.*

o·ju·la *or* **ojuya** \o-jú-la\ *adj* o·má·jula o·ní·jula : full, filled — **ojula·ya** *va* ojula·wa·ya : to fill full

o·ju·mi·ni·ya·tke \o-jú-mi-ni-ya-tke\ *n* : a tank, a place filled for drinking water – Note: *ošunminiyatke* a place for horses to drink water, and *šunminiyatka* to water horses, *i.e.* to give horses water to drink

o·ju·pi \o-jú-pi\ *part* : filled, planted — *n* : seed for sowing, something to plant or sow

o·ju·ton \o-jú-toŋ\ *va* oju·wa·ton : to fill up into sacks *etc.* — **ojuton·pi** *n* : filled bags

o·ju·ya \o-jú-ya\ *va* oju·wa·ya : to cause to fill or plant < *Woptuh'a ojumayayelo* You got the scraps all over me.> — *adj* : full, filled < *Apamagleya u na isam lila ošota ~ han* (or perhaps *ojuyahan*) He came downhill and the more the place was filled getting very smoky. >

[1]**o·ka·bla** \o-k̇á-bla\ *n of* kablá : a slice, a piece cut off broad and flat, as meat cut for drying

[2]**o·ka·bla** \ó-k̇a-bla\ *adj* or *adv* : spread out on, or perhaps over, enlarging as the foot of a stand < ~ *aya* to begin to spread, *i.e.* as water spilled > – *Syn* ÓKASKE

o·ka·bla·ya \o-k̇á-bla-ya\ *adv of* kabláya : peacefully without obstruction, expanded, plain, level, freely as in discoursing, *fig* having good luck < ~ *mayuhapelo* I had good luck. ~ *munkin ktelo* I'll have the whole room to myself. *Tuweni nagiyewicaye šni ca ~ unpi* No one is free who is troubled. ~ *wicaša* a free man, ~ *iglušt̄an kte* He will finish easily, *i.e.* without trouble. > — **okablaya·kel** *adv* : in a conveniently open place < ~ *yanka* to be or sit in a comfortably large place, as opposed to *ícipiyela* what is sufficient for one's self, ~ *unyankapelo* We get along with one another. >

o·ka·bla·ye *also perhaps* **okablaya** \o-k̇á-bla-ye\ *n* : a level place, a plain

o·ka·ble·ble·ca \o-k̇á-ble-ble-ca\ *v red of* okableca : to be breaking to pieces in – B.H.303.14

o·ka·ble·ca \o-k̇á-ble-ca\ *va* o·wa·kableca [fr *kableca* to break by striking] : to break in pieces in anything — **okableca·han** *part* : broken in — **okablece** *n* : a breaking in — **okablel** *va contrac of* okableca : to break or crush to pieces in < ~ *iyeya* to crush suddenly >

o·ka·blu \o-k̇á-blu\ *vn* : to blow into, as the wind does — **okablu·ya** *v* okablu·wa·ya : to cause a draft in the room, by opening the door < *Tiyopa yugan s'a ye, ~ tka* Keep opening the door, it should create a draft. > – Bl

o·ka·ca·gla \o-k̇á-ca-gla\ *v perhaps* : to be too large for one, as a coat, a shoe, *etc.* < *Hanpa omákacagla* My shoes are too big for me. > — **okacagla·yela** *adv* : as it is when *e.g.* one's coat is too large for one < ~ *un, mun, o-hlaganyela mun welo* to wear a coat too big, I wore it, I wore it with a loose fit. > – Bl

o·ka·co \o-k̇á-ċo\ *vn* : to make a noise in, as in a bad egg, gurgling — **okaco·co** *v* : to make noise in, to gurgle — **okaco·ya** *adv* : producing a gurgling sound < *Pagé ~ omawani* I traveled with my stomach growling, *i.e.* with an empty stomach. > — **oka·c'oya** *adv* : making a noise in, as fluid in a partly filled bag when shaken < *Iwanyank wawatin na page ~ wagni kte* I shall go home with my stomach growling and so look to my eating, *i.e.* to go home with almost an empty stomach, like a horse when it has drunk only water. > – Bl

o·ka·ga \o-k̇á-ġa\ *va obsol* : to copy, to make a model, to add to — *n* : creation < *Maka ~ eciyatanhan* since creation of the world > — **okaga·pi** *n obsol* : a copy, a model, image – Pb.195

o·ka·ga·ya *also* **okaḣaya** \o-k̇á-ġa-ya\ *va* : to stick into, as something sharp like an arrow, *fig* to use cutting words

[1]**o·ka·ge** \ó-k̇a-ge\ *v* : to float – B.H.8.6, 116.8

[2]**o·ka·ge** \o-k̇á-ġe\ *n* : creation, things made in the same manner, kinds of things as a bundle or bundles of arrows made alike < *wicaša ~* a class of people, *maka ~* creation of the world > – B.H.245.27

o·ka·ge·ge \o-k̇á-ġe-ġe\ *n of* kaġége : a seam, a place where anything is sewed < *Wakeya ~ owoblu* It blew in a seam of the tipi, as is said when in a blizzard the fine snow is blown into the tent through the seam. > – M

o·ka·gla·la \o-k̇á-gla-la\ *adv* : by the side of — **okagla-yela** *adv* : near to, close by – R Bl

o·ka·glo·glo·ka \o-k̇á-glo-glo-ka\ *v red* : to rattle, as a car might – Br

o·ka·hi \o-k̇á-hi\ *vn* : to hang over, as grass over the road, or hair over the forehead — *n* : hair bangs — **o-kahi·ka** \o-k̇á-hi-k̇a\ *n* : one who wears hair bangs – P

o·ka·hin·han \o-k̇á-hiŋ-haŋ\ *v* : to precipitate, rain or snow *etc.* < *Wa okahinhe ca oye kin tanyan ablespica šni* It snowed so the track could not be well seen – Bl WHL

o·ka·hi·ya \o-k̇á-hi-ya\ *va* okahi·wa·ya : to cause to hang over, to comb the hair over the face — *adv* : hanging over

[1]**o·kah** \o-k̇áḣ\ *n contrac of* okága : a make < ~ *wašte* of good form >

[2]**o·kah** \ó-k̇aḣ\ *adv* : floating < ~ *u* to come floating, *ya* to float down, as a song, *Mihakab ~ u wo* Come float after me. > – D.32

o·kah gle·pi \ó-k̇aḣ gle-pi\ *n* – *See* hokah glepi

o·kah hi·ya·ya \ó-k̇aḣ hi-yà-ya\ *v* : to float by

o·ka·hle·ca \o-k̇á-ḣle-ca\ *va* o·wa·kahleca [fr *kahleca* to split open] : to tear a hole in, tear in pieces, to fracture — **okahlece** *n* : a rend, a fracture — **okahlel** *adv contrac* : tearing in pieces < ~ *iyeya* to rend suddenly >

o·ka·hlog \o-k̇á-ḣlog\ *va contrac of* okahloka : to seep through < ~ *iyeya* to pass through quickly >

o·ka·hlo·hlo·ka \o-k̇á-ḣlo-ḣlo-ka\ *v red* : to seep through < *Mahpiya ahi k'on mahpiya tola okahlohloke* The cloud that came had passed through a very blue sky. > – Bl

o·ka·hlo·ka \o-k̇á-ḣlo-k̇a\ *va* o·ma·kahloka : to make its way through *e.g.* water through cloth, to come through < *cogin ša oyakahloke ehantanš* if you make a way through red pith, *i.e.* when you strike a tree with red pith > — **okahloke** *n of* kahloka : a hole, a gash, made by striking – D.12 B.H.274.20

o·ka·hmin \o-k̇á-ḣmiŋ\ *n* : a bay, a corner as made by houses

o·ka·hni·ga \o-k̇á-ḣni-ġa\ *va* o·wa·kahniga un·kokahni-ga·pi : to understand, comprehend — **okahnih** *va contrac* : to understand < ~ *šica* hard to understand, abstruse, ~ *wašte* easy to understand > — **okahni·hkiya** \o-k̇á-ḣni-ḣki-ya\ *va* okaḣni·ḣwa·kiya : to cause to understand — **okahnihpicašni** *adj* : incomprehensible < ~ *woglakelo* It was an incomprehensible talk. > —

okahni·hya *va* okahni·hwa·ya : to explain to one, to make comprehend

o·ka·ḣo \o-k̇á-ḣo\ *vn* : to soar, sail, glide in the air as do hawks *etc.* - *Syn* OKÁS'A Bl

o·ka·hpa \o-k̇á-ḣṗa\ *va* o·wa·kahpa [fr *kahpa* strike down] : to make fall into by striking

o·ka·hpu \o-k̇á-ḣpu\ *va* o·wa·kahpu [fr *kahpu* to knock off] : to knock or brush off into

o·ka·htan \o-k̇á-ḣṫaŋ\ *vn of* kahtan : to soak in, become soaked *e.g.* from water, grease, *etc.* — **okahtan-yan** *va* okahtan·wa·ya okahtan·un·yan·pi : to dip in, sop up, to absorb, to sponge, to soak in — **okahtanye** *n* : a sponge

o·ka·hto·gto·gye \o-k̇á-ḣto-gto-gye\ *adv* : variously made

o·ka·hto·gye \o-k̇á-ḣto-gye\ *adv* : made in a different manner < *Tuwa ... ungna wakuwapi el wahinkpe wanjila on pte num wicao na wahinkpe kin ~ kagapi* I suppose the arrow was constructed differently, so that in hunting with a single arrow a person shot two buffaloes. > - MS.482

o·ka·hwan·ji·la \o-k̇á-ḣwaŋ-ji-la\ *n* : the same form - BD

o·ka·hwo·ka \o-k̇á-ḣwo-k̇a\ *vn* o·wa·kahwoka : to float in the air, to travel around much, as is said of a man who travels much - HC

[1]**o·ka·hya** \o-k̇á-hya̜\ *v* : to set something afloat, *fig* to bring to birth < *Šungwinyela wan cincokahya* The mare set a colt afloat, *i.e.* she brought to birth more than one colt, which one wished. > - Bl

[2]**o·ka·hya** \ó-ka-ḣya\ *va* : to cause to float downstream — *adv* : floating < ~ *u* to come floating down >

o·ka·h'ol i·ye·ya \o-k̇á-ḣ'ol i-yè-ya\ *v* : to throw away into < *Na šna nonge ~ iyewicaya* He was constantly deaf to them. > — **okah'ol iyeya econpi** *n* : a game played on ice - Bl

o·ka·ja·ya \o-k̇á-ja-ya\ *adv* : between, in the forks of

o·ka·kab \o-k̇á-k̇ab\ *va contrac of* okakapa : to hit into, as a ball into a room < *Mniyokakab iyemayayin kte lo* You will knock me into the water. > - D.33

[1]**o·ka·kan** \o-k̇á-kaŋ\ *va of* kakan : to shake into, as buffalo berries into a pail

[2]**o·ka·kan** \o-k̇á-kaŋ\ *va* o·wá·kakan [fr *k̇ak̇án* to notch a hard surface] : to hew in anything — *vn* : to be broken to pieces, as a wagon during a runaway

o·ka·ka·pa \o-k̇á-ka-ṗa\ *va* o·wa·kakapa : to hit into, as a ball into a room

o·ka·kin \o-k̇á-k̇iŋ\ *vn* o·wa·kakin : to peep in < *Taku oyasin ~ inajin slolye* He knows everything by standing to peep in. > - *See* aókaki Bl

o·ka·ki·šya \o-k̇á-k̇i-šya\ *adv* : abusively

o·ka·ko·sko·za \o-k̇á-k̇o-sko-za\ *v red of* okakoza : to dangle - D.273

o·ka·ko·za \o-k̇á-k̇o-za\ *vn* : to dangle - P Bl

o·ka·kpan \o-k̇á-kṗaŋ\ *vn* : to be broken up in < ~ *yanke nawah'on welo* I was hearing it all broken up, *i.e.* I did not hear or understand it very well. > — **okakpan-yankel** *adv* : broken up in, dimly < ~ *wanyanka* to see it unclearly, *i.e.* just a little bit of it, ~ *nah'on* to hear it poorly, ~ *wayakita hwo* Do you watch carelessly? > - *Syn* CISCILA OTAN'IN, KITANYEL OTAN'IN Bl WE

o·ka·ksa \o-k̇á-ksa\ *va* o·wa·kaksa [fr *kaksa* to split or cut off] : to cut down a tree or root that is in the way < *okakse šica* hard or difficult to cut > — **okakse** *n* : a notch cut in, cuttings, pieces cut out

o·ka·kse·ya *or perhaps* **okakšeya** \o-k̇á-kse-ya\ *adv* : hard to unwind or untangle, as a rope strewn in a pile - WHL

o·ka·kšan *also* **okakšan·yan** \o-k̇á-kšaŋ\ *adv* : round about, by a round-about way < ~ *iblabla* I am going by a round-about way. > - Cf akakšan, aokakšanyan EE

o·ka·kše \o-k̇á-kše\ *n of* kakša : a roll of thread, or of ribbon, or a skein of yarn, or roll of cloth

o·ka·la \o-k̇á-la\ *va* o·wa·kala un·kokala·pi : to sow or plant *e.g.* grain, to scatter in or on, to pour out into < *Yunkan taku k'eya cikcik'ala ca el ~ i.e. canwakšica el* Then he poured on something that was very small, *i.e.* on a wooden plate. >

o·ka·la·i·he·ya \o-k̇á-la-i-he-ya\ *v* okalaihe·wa·ya : to load a gun in haste without a wad

o·ka·la·la \o-k̇á-la-la\ *v red of* okála : to be sowing

o·ka·li·c'i·ya \o-k̇á-li-c'i-ya\ *v refl* : to warm up, warm one's self in - B.H.258.6 Bl

o·ka·ltki·ya \o-ká-ltk̇i·ya\ *adv* : towards a warm place < *cuwi ~ hpaya* to lie with one's back to the fire >

o·ka·lus \o-k̇á-lus\ *n contrac of* okaluza : wind or draft < *Lila ~ hiyu* There came forth a sudden wind. > **okalu·-sya** *adv* : airy

o·ka·lu·za \o-k̇á-lu-za\ *n* : a draft of wind, air in motion — *vn* o·ma·kaluza : to blow through or into, to blow on one — *adj* : airy < ~ *šni* close, as a room > - P

o·ka·lya \o-k̇á-lya\ *va* : to make hot in

o·ka·ma \o-k̇á-ma\ *v* o·wá·kama : to hit the center, as in shooting - Bl

[1]**o·ka·mna** \o-k̇á-mna\ *v* : to avoid, go around, go out of the way - *Syn* AYUKŠANYAN, AOKAMNA

[2]**o·ka·mna** \o-k̇á-mna\ *n* [fr *kamna* to earn] : earnings, wages, pay < ~ *wašte* good pay >

o·ka·mna·yan \o-k̇á-mna-yaŋ\ *adv* : going round, avoiding, taking care, picking one's steps as in walking < ~ *mani* to walk circumspectly > - R Bl

o·ka·mni·mni \o-k̇á-mni-mni\ *v* : to whirl around, as snow or sand around houses < *Okamnimniyelo* It was swirling around. > - Bl

[1]**o·kan** \o-k̇áŋ\ *vn* o·ma·kan : there is room, room for, not crowded; to be at the disposal of others

[2]**o·kan** \o-k̇áŋ\ *n of* kan : old age, one's youth when spoken of by old men < ~ *kin ektab* unto his old age, ~ *ihunni* to reach old age > — **okan·ke** \o-k̇áŋ-k̇e\ *adv* : at old age, at the last, at the end < ~ *ektab wašte* good to the end >

o·kan·šni·yan \o-k̇áŋ-šni-yaŋ\ *adv* : having no time < ~ *un* to be without time, ~ *mayukuwapelo* They had no time to chase after me. *Blaye kin ataya ~ pte hiot'inza ške* They say there was no time that they found the entire prairies crowded with buffalos. > - B.H.200.3 Bl WE D.204

o·kan·te·han *also* **okante·ḣike** \o-k̇áŋ-ṫe-haŋ\ \o-k̇áŋ-ṫe-ḣi-k̇e\ *vn* [fr *kan* old age + *tehan* long in time] : to be long becoming old, bear old-age well, to retain a youthful appearance, being old one looks young

o·kan·yan \o-k̇áŋ-yaŋ\ *adv* : roomy - B.H.225.3

o·kan·ye·la \o-k̇áŋ-ye-la\ *adv* : near, nearby < *Wana letan ~* From here it (the house) is nearby. > - B.H.69.10

o·ka·pa \o-k̇á-pa\ *vn* : to be spoiled by standing in a vessel

---

\a\ father \e\ they \i\ machine \o\ smoke \u\ lunar \an, aŋ\ blanc Fr. \in, iŋ\ ink \on, oŋ, un, uŋ\ soon, confier Fr. \c\ chair \ǧ\ machen Ger. \j\ fusion \clusters: bl, gn, kp, hšl, etc...\ b[e]lo ... said with a slight vowel
See more in the Introduction, Guide to Pronunciation

o·ka·pan \o-k̇á-paŋ\ *v* o·wa·kapan [fr *kapan* to beat] : to pound or beat in

o·ka·pa·za \o-k̇á-pa-za\ *v* o·ma·kapaza : to make smart as pepper does the mouth, to bite as also do onions, tobacco, *etc.* < *Ceji owicakapa* It bit their tongues. > – A

o·ka·po \o-k̇á-ṗo\ *v* : to make swell by striking

o·ka·pol \ó-k̇a-ṗol\ *vn contrac of* ókapota : to float on < ~ *iyaya* to go floating, ~ *hinápa* to come up from the bottom of, say, a creek or lake, as fish, or a piece of wood thrown in and coming up again, to float in water, *Can wan ~ u welo* A stick of wood came up to float (on water). > — **okapol·ya** *va* ókapo·lwa·ya : to cause to float on – BD Me

[1]**o·ka·po·ta** \ó-k̇a-ṗo-ṫa\ *vn* : to be borne upon, float on water

[2]**o·ka·po·ta** \o-k̇á-ṗo-ṫa\ *vn* : to be torn by shaking, as a pocket by keys carried in it

o·ka·psi·ca \o-k̇á-psi-ca\ *v* : to rise up, leap us, as water into tall waves < *Hecel mini kin ota ~* So the water rose up in many tall waves. > – B.H.203.7

o·ka·pta *or* **okapte** \o-k̇á-pṫa\ *va* o·wa·kapta : to dip out into, lade out; to take out one's wages gradually < *Na wanna mini ~ na glicu kte ehanl* He then bailed out water when he was about to start for home. *Wacowak'inla k'un écuhciš omiyecapta caš* Well at least what I had roasted in the coals you surely then left for me. *Zuzeca k'un hecela okaptapi* The snake alone they had left him. > — *vn perhaps* : to be left < *Tuweni ~ šni* No one left, *i.e.* all are here. *Mišnala omakapta ca hoši cicahi yelo* I brought you to tell the news that I alone am left. *Wicaša wakan kin mišnala okaptapi lel waun welo* I am the only priest left here. > — **okapta·pi** *n* : what is left, leavings, remnants – D.22, 59 B.H.43.3, 107.12

o·ka·pte \o-k̇á-pṫe\ *va* – *See* under okapta

o·ka·sa·ke·ci·ya·tan \o-k̇á-sa-ke-ci-ya-taŋ\ *n* : the right horse, the one whipped < ~ *k'inkiya yo* Make the right horse take the load. > – P Bl

o·ka·ske \o-k̇á-sk̇e\ *n* : a bunch or lump of things sticking together, as candy, sugar *etc.* < *canhanpi ~* a lump of sugar, *canhanpokaske* a sugar lump, *wowapi ~* a book with many leaves > — **okaske·ske** *n red* : a bunch sticking together — **okaskeske·ya** *adv red of* okaskeya : sticking together in a bunch — **okaske·šilya** *adv perhaps* : gathered together < ~ *oṗíic'iya* to conduct one's self in a way gathering together, as is said when men and animals are mixed up in a bunch > – Bl

o·ka·ske·ya \o-k̇á-sk̇e-ya\ *adv* : sticking together in a lump, as candy

o·ka·sla·ta \o-k̇á-sla-ṫa\ *vn* : to stick in, as a splinter

o·ka·sle·ca \o-k̇á-sle-ca\ *va* o·wa·kasleca [fr *kasleca* to split] : to split within anything that can be split easily without effort

o·ka·slo·han \o-k̇á-slo-haŋ\ *va of* kaslohan : to make slide in — *vn* : to make a trail by being dragged along in — **okaslohe** *n* : a mark of anything dragged along, a trace or trail

o·ka·slo·slo \o-k̇á-slo-slo\ *va* o·wa·kasloslo : to bruise, mash or crush in or into

o·ka·slu·ta \o-k̇á-slu-ṫa\ *v* : to hit the center, as in shooting and knocking out a piece perhaps – *Syn* OKAMA, OKAT'INZA

o·ka·sni \o-k̇á-sni\ *v* : to get cold from a draft entering in < *Omakasni yelo* I am getting cold from a draft, as is said when the wind comes in through the sleeves *etc.* >

o·ka·sol \o-k̇á-sōl\ *v contrac of* okasota : to use up

o·ka-so·ta \o-k̇á-so-ṫa\ *v* o·wa·kasota : to use up, destroy

o·ka·spe·ya \o-k̇á-sṗe-ya\ *v* : to make sink, immerse

o·ka·stag \o-k̇á-sṫag\ *va of* okastaka : to throw or stick on *e.g.* mud < ~ *iyeya* to make stick, ~ *ihpeya* to throw to stick on >

o·ka·sta·ka \o-k̇á-sṫa-ka\ *va* o·wa·kastaka [fr *kastaka* throw on] : to throw on or in, make stick on, as in daubing a house

o·ka·sto \o-k̇á-sṫo\ *adv of* kastó : making or leaving a trail in the grass, as that made by another < ~ *ya* to go leaving a trail > – Note: R gives the word as a *n*

o·ka·su *or* **okaswu** \o-k̇á-su\ *n of* kaswú : a fringe

o·ka·swu \o-k̇á-swu\ *n* [fr *kaswú* to cut into small strips] : a fringe < *šiná okaswupi* a shawl with fringe >

o·ka·s'a \o-k̇á-s'a\ *vn* : to sail, soar, glide in the air as do birds

o·ka·s'a·ya·kel \o-k̇á-s'a-ya-kel\ *adv* : proudly < ~ *ayuta* to look at with pride >

o·ka·s'in \o-k̇á-s'iŋ\ *v* : to look into

o·ka·ška \o-k̇á-ška\ *va* o·wa·kaška [fr *kaška* to tie] : to tie into, as a scalp into a loop, to fasten up, as green hide to dry

o·ka·škan \o-k̇á-škaŋ\ *vn* o·ma·kaškan : to be injured internally, as a woman during pregnancy – *See oígluškan* to hurt one's self inwardly — **okaškan·ton** *va* okaškan·wa·ton : to bring forth before its time — **okaškanton·pi** *n* : an abortion

[1]**o·ka·ške** \ó-k̇a-šk̇e\ *adj* : tapering, large at one end and small at the other — *n* : the large end of a thing < *Tašnaheca bloka s'e pa ~* Like the male striped ground squirrel, his head is tapered, as is said of a man with a big nose. > – Bl

[2]**o·ka·ške** \o-k̇á-šk̇e\ *n of* kaška : a place to tether, picket, or moor, as horses, ships, *etc.*, a hitching post < ~ *najin* to stand tied or bound to, as a horse to a post >

o·ka·ški \o-k̇á-šk̇i\ *vn* : to be mashed in or become jelly as berries carried in a vessel, to pound or mash in — **okaški·ce** *vn* : to be mashed in, made jelly of < *Wojuha zizipela ca canpa iyuha okaškicelo* He mashed all the chokecherries that were in a thin bag. > – Bl

o·ka·šle·ca \o-k̇á-šle-ca\ *va* o·wa·kašleca [fr *kašleca* to split] : to split within anything that requires effort

o·ka·šna \o-k̇á-šna\ *va of* kašna : to miss, to pass over *e.g.* a day

o·ka·špa \o-k̇á-šṗa\ *va* o·wa·kašpa [fr *kašpa* cut loose from] : to strike a piece off in, to spit, expectorate in perhaps — **okašpe** *n* : a piece struck off, those people living in on district

o·ka·špe·ton·ton·yan \o-k̇á-špe-toŋ-toŋ-yaŋ\ *adv red* : by or in groups — **okašpeton·yan** *adv* : by or in a group – B.H.208.9 OS Bl

o·ka·šta·ka \o-k̇á-šṫa-k̇a\ *va* o·wa·kaštaka [fr *kaštaka* to smite] : to smite one in a place, as in a house — **okaštake** \o-k̇á-šṫa-k̇e\ *n* : a punishment, smiting < *Kikta hiyayin na lolih'an onspic'iya yo* Wake up and go on learn to cook; *lecanon kin tuktel hignayaton kin ~ hca yaun kte lo* if you do this where you are married, your punishment will be there; *he wicawake lo* that is the truth I speak. > – GA

o·ka·štan \o-k̇á-šṫaŋ\ *va* o·wa·kaštan [fr *kaštan* pour out] : to pour into, spill into, as is said of liquids

o·ka·šu·šu·je \o-k̇á-šu-šu-je\ *n* : bruises – B.H.130.10

o·ka·š'a·gya \ó-k̇a-š'a-gya\ *adv* : prevented, hindered, as by having too much clothing on < ~ *un* to be encumbered > – R Bl

[1]**o·ka·ta** \o-k̇á-ta\ *or* \o-k̇a-tá\ *v* [fr *katá* assemble toge-

ther] : to fill in or cover up *e.g.* holes or a fire in a stove < ~ *aya* to bring to cover up, as is said when things are brought into a heap by sweeping together, ~ *kuwa* to stop, to prevent > - Bl

²**o·ka·ta** \o-k̇á-ṫa\ *vn* : to be warm inside < *tiókata* a warm house > — *n* : heat

o·ka·ta·kin \o-k̇á-ta-k̇iŋ\ *va of* katákin : to strike and cause to lean in place < *Anpetu wan* ~ *wanica ca iyablagyela helo* The day was calm without a stir. > - Bl

o·ka·tan \o-k̇á-ṫaŋ\ *va* o·wa·katan : to drive in *e.g.* a nail or pin, to nail, make fast with nails < *Na can pteptecela on ecel* ~ And so he made fast with nails a tiny piece of wood. *Ptehan kin he lila yat'ins okatanpi* That cow stanchion was nailed down very firmly. > - MS.482

o·ka·t'a *or* **okat'e** \o-k̇á-t'a\ *va* : to kill by striking in, to beat to death *e.g.* a cat in a sack, or young animals in their mother's womb

o·ka·t'ins \o-k̇á-t'iŋs\ *va of* okat'inza : to pound in tight < ~ *iyeya* to fill in tightly >

o·ka·t'in·za \o-k̇á-t'iŋ-za\ *va* o·wa·kat'inza **1** : to pound in tight, make tight, fill up **2** : to hit the "bull's eye", the center in shooting - Bl

o·ka·wa·ton \o-k̇á-wa-toŋ\ *v* : to be recovered, to be alright — **okawaton·yan** *adv* : without hindrance or obstruction, as also applied to the weather

o·ka·win·ga \o-k̇á-wiŋ-ġa\ *vn* o·wa·kawinga [fr *kawinga* to return] : to go round and round at a distance < *Na wanna okšan hoton okawingapi* And they now went round and round crying out round about. *Lila wanbli ota okawingapi wanyanka* He saw many eagles circling superbly. > - MS.148

o·ka·winh \o-k̇á-winḣ\ *vn contrac of* okawinga : to circle round about < ~ *ya* to go round and round, as the sun does. *Wamakaškan ocaje oyasin ahihunni na wanna ataya* ~ *au na oyate kin okšan au na wicakat'api* Every sort of creature arrived, and now they all came circling about so the people came round for they were stunned. >

o·ka·win·ḣe·la \o-k̇á-wiŋ-ḣe-la\ *n* : a merry-go-round

o·ka·win·hya \o-k̇á-wiŋ-ḣya\ *adv* : round and round

o·ka·ye·ge \o-k̇á-ye-ġe\ *n* : seams < ~ *wanice* It is without seams. > - B.H.266.2

o·ka·za \o-k̇á-za\ *n of* kazá : the articular bones of the arms and feet < *takan* ~ thread of sinew *i.e. takán* >

o·ka·za·pa \o-k̇á-za-ṗa\ *v* o·wa·kazapa : to cut up and spread nicely, to cut the meat *e.g.* of deer along the spinal column into long strips - *Syn* TAKÁHLOKA Bl

o·ka·ze \o-k̇á-ze\ *va* o·wa·kaze [fr *kaze* dip out] : to dip out into

o·ka·ze·ze \ó-ka-ze-ze\ *vn* : to swing, as something suspended from a cord — **okazeze·ya** *adv* : swinging, dangling

o·ka·zon·te \o-k̇á-zoŋ-ṫe\ *n* : a design, pattern-work < *napokazonte* the ordered pattern of fingers on the hand, *Nape* ~ *kin napitakaha kin nupin iciyagleya iyakaškapi* The hand design was tied to the back of both hands back to back. *siokazonte* pattern-work of the foot, *i.e.* of the toes. > - MS.340

o·ki \o-k̇í\ *pref to v* [fr *ogna* in + *ki* to] : through the middle - Note: the word is composed of two *prep*, and means the action of the *v* is done through the middle

o·ki·bli·he·ca \o-k̇í-bli-he-ca\ *vn* o·wa·kibliheca [fr *bliheca* to be industrious] : to be smart in doing anything

o·ki·blo·ton·ton \í-k̇i-blo-toŋ-toŋ\ *adj of* oblóton : angular, having many corners

o·ki·ca·bla·za \o-k̇í-ca-bla-za\ *va* oki·wa·kablaza [fr *kablaza* make burst] : to cut or rip open in the middle, *e.g.* anything soft, as a melon

o·ki·ca·ble·ca \o-k̇í-ca-ble-ca\ *va* oki·wa·kableca [fr *kableca* break by striking] : to break in two in the middle, *e.g.* a plate or a piece of wood *etc.* by striking

o·ki·ca·ḣa \o-k̇í-ca-ḣa\ *v* oki·wa·kaḣa : to pull a knot very tight, to tie one thing to another, to tie a knot — **okicaḣa·ḣapi** *adj* : knotty, full of knots

o·ki·ca·hni·ga \o-k̇í-ca-ḣni-ġa\ *va* oki·wa·kahniga [fr *okahniga* understand] : to understand, to comprehend

o·ki·ca·ksa \o-k̇í-ca-ksa\ *va* oki·wa·kaksa [fr *kaksa* to cut] : to cut in two in the middle, as a stick with an axe

o·ki·can·ye \o-k̇í-caŋ-ye\ *n of* kicanyan : work, tillage, cultivation < ~ *ota* complicated, as a piece of mechanism >

o·ki·ca·pta \o-k̇í-ca-pta\ *va* [fr *okapta* to dip or leave] : to dip or deal out for one — *vn* : to be left for, remain for < *Hecel Chanaan kin he Abraham okicaptapi* So the land of Canaan was left to Abraham, *i.e.* he left behind Canaan. > - B.H.11.15

o·ki·ca·ptu·ga \o-k̇í-ca-pṫu-ġa\ *va* oki·wa·kaptuga : to split in two in the middle, as with a chisel

o·ki·ca·sle·ca \o-k̇í-ca-sle-ca\ *va* oki·wa·kasleca : to split something light with little effort in two in the middle - Note: where *sleca* and *šleca* are used, the former is used to indicate splitting when no effort is needed — **okica·slel** *va contrac* : to split in two in the middle < ~ *iyeya* to split in half, ~ *ihpeya* to throw down to break in half, ~ *unkaglipi kte* Divided half of us shall arrive home. > - Bl

o·ki·ca·ška \o-k̇í-ca-ška\ *va* oki·wa·kaška : to tie into, to knot, tie knots in

o·ki·ca·šle·ca \o-k̇í-ca-šle-ca\ *va* oki·wa·kašleca : to split in the middle, as a log - Note: *šleca* refers to hard splitting; *sleca*, to easy splitting of — **okica·šlel** \o-k̇í-ċa-šlel\ *va contrac* : to split what is hard < ~ *iyeya* to split >

o·ki·ca·špa \o-k̇í-ċa-špa\ *v* oki·wa·kašpa [fr *kašpa* separate from] : to smite in two in the middle

o·ki·ca·štan \o-k̇í-ċa-štaŋ\ *va* o·we·caštan [fr *okaštan* to pour into] : to pour one's own into, to pour into for one

o·ki·ci·ca·štan \o-k̇í-ci-ċa-štaŋ\ *v* o·we·cicaštan [fr *okaštan* to pour into] : to pour into for one, as into a vial *etc.*

o·ki·ci·cin \o-k̇í-ci-ciŋ\ *v* o·we·cicin [fr *ocin* beg or desire] : to desire or beg of one for another

o·ki·ci·ci·ya \o-k̇í-ci-ci-ya\ *v* [fr *ok̇iya* to court] : to talk together, as in courting

o·ki·ci·co \o-k̇í-ci-co\ *n of* kicó : an inviting each other, as to feasting

o·ki·ci·cu·wa·pi \o-k̇í-ci-cu-wa-pi\ *v* [fr *okuwa* chase after] : they follow or run after each other, as children do in playing a game

o·ki·ci·gna·ka \o-k̇í-ci-gna-k̇a\ *va* o·we·cignaka [fr *ognaka* to set in] : to put or place in for one

o·ki·ci·han \o-k̇í-ci-haŋ\ *v* o·we·cihan [fr *ohán* to boil] : to boil anything <u>for</u> another

o·ki·ci·in co·kan \o-k̇í-ci-iŋ co-k̇àŋ\ *n* : a no-man's-land - *Syn* OWÁKIHE COKÀN Co

o·ki·ci·ji \o-k̇í-ci-ji\ *v* : to whisper to one another — oki-

ciji·ji *v red* : to keep whispering — **okiciji·pi** *n* : whispering — **okiciji·ya** *adv* : whisperingly - B.H.210.17
o·ki·ci·ju \o-ki-ci-ju\ *va* o·we·cijua [fr *oju* to fill or to plant] **1** : to fill for another **b** : to plant for another
o·ki·ci·le \o-ki-ci-le\ *v* o·we·cile [fr *ole* to seek something] : to seek anything for another
o·ki·ci·lo·ta \o-ki-ci-lo-ta\ *v* o·we·cilota [fr *olóta* to borrow] : to borrow of one for another
o·ki·cin \o-ki-ciŋ\ *v* o·wa·kicin unko·kicin·pi : to ask or desire of one, beg something of one < *El yin na wakablapi wanji omakicin yo* Go there and ask a piece of dried meat for me. >
o·ki·ci·pa \o-ki-ci-pa\ *v* o·we·cipa [fr *opa* join in with] : to follow for anything, to obey *e.g.* commands
o·ki·ci·štan \ó-ki-ci-štaŋ\ *vt* [fr *óštan* put on or in] : to put in *e.g.* a cork for another < *Hinhan išta k'eya el okicištanpi* They put in for him that pair of owl eyes, *i.e.* in place of the ruined ones. > - D.220
o·ki·ci·wa \o-ki-ci-wa\ *v* o·we·ciwa [fr *owá* to write] : to write for one
o·ki·ci·wa·ša·ka·la \o-ki-ci-wa-ša-ka-la\ *adj* : easily purchased for one - Bl
o·ki·ci·wa·šte \o-ki-ci-wa-šte\ *adj* [fr *wašte* good] : good together, as two things eaten together, advantageous
o·ki·ci·ya \ó-ki-ci-ya\ *v* [fr *ókiya* to help one] : to help another - Note: perhaps forms, *ókici·ci·ya* and *ókiciciyapi* for the meaning: to help each other
o·ki·ci·yak a·u·pi \o-ki-ci-yak a-ù-pi\ *n* : tradition - B.H.305.11
o·ki·ci·ya·pta \o-ki-ci-ya-pta\ *v of* oyapta : to have leftovers, to leave *e.g.* a part of one's food for one
o·ki·ci·ya·s'in \o-ki-ci-ya-s'iŋ\ *vn* : to unite, to come together and flow, as two streams, to cling to each other as several potatoes hanging together, to be fastened together as two dogs in copulation — *adv perhaps* [fr *yaš'in* to copulate] : together in copulation < *kokiciyaš'in* to copulate striving together >
o·ki·ci·yu·sin·pi \o-ki-ci-yu-siŋ-pi\ *v recip of* oyusin : to quarrel, to fall out with another
o·ki·ci·yu·štan \o-ki-ci-yu-štaŋ\ *v* o·we·ciyuštan [fr *oyuštan* to finish within or to put one into another] : to put one into an-other for one, as one kettle into another
o·ki·ci·yu·štan·štan \ó-ki-ci-yu-štaŋ-štaŋ\ *adv* : placing one in with the other < *Oyé ~ unyanpi ktelo* We will go placing our feet in our footprints, *i.e.* will follow in each other's footsteps. *Oyé óciyuštanštan ciu ktelo* I will come putting my steps in yours, *i.e.* follow your footsteps. > - Bl
o·ki·ci·yu·ze \o-ki-ci-yu-ze\ *n* [fr *yuzá* to take] : to marry one, a taking each other, as in marriage < *~ wan unkagapi ktelo* We shall have a marriage. *~ wašte wan kagapi* They had a fine marriage. >
O·ki·ci·yu·ze Wa·kan \O-ki-ci-yu-ze Wa-kàŋ\ *np* : Matrimony, one of the seven christian Sacraments - D.232
o·ki·ci·ze \o-ki-ci-ze\ *n* [fr *kicize* fight together] : fighting a battle, a war
o·ki·c'u \o-ki-c'u\ *va* : to restore, to take back for a purpose < *Yu! iye kayeš iyoha sanni ~ šni wote* See here! he did not himself restore the side of his jaw to eat, *i.e.* he chews only on the one side. > - Bl
o·ki·c'u·ni·ca \o-ki-c'u-ni-ca\ *vn* : to be made angry, to be offended < *Cante owec'unica* I am angry at heart. > — **okic'uni·lya** *va* okic'uni·lwa·ya : to provoke to anger, to offend
o·ki·gla·ha \o-ki-gla-ha\ *v poss of* okicaha : to tie, perhaps, one's own together tight *e.g.* one's string - Bl
o·ki·gla·hni·ga \o-ki-gla-hni-ga\ *v refl* o·we·glahniga : to know or understand what pertains to one's self
o·ki·glu·sle·ca \o-ki-glu-sle-ca\ *v refl* : to split in the middle — **okiglusle·lya** *adv* : split in the middle - B.H.54.9,15
o·ki·gna·gton·ton *or* **okignagtonton·yan** \ó-ki-gna-gtoŋ-toŋ\ *adv* : in layers, having many layers or groups < *~ ahiyaye* to pass by in smaller groups > - R Bl
o·ki·gna·ka \o-ki-gna-ka\ *v poss* o·we·gnaka [fr *ognaka* to place in] : to place one's own in < *Na cahli k'on na wahinša k'on hena ecel owegnaka na lila wakanwala* And my gunpowder and guncaps I put in and I reckoned it very marvelous >
o·ki·gnun·ka \o-ki-gnuŋ-ka\ *vn of* kignunka *or* kignuka : to dive or put one's head under the water in a vessel or bath
[1]**o·ki·han** \o-ki-haŋ\ *v poss* o·wa·han [fr *ohán* to put on, wear] : to put on, wear one's own *e.g.* moccasins < *Kenatantan kte s'e hanpokihe lo* He wore moccasins like a turtle about to make attacks, as is said when shoes are too wide. >
[2]**o·ki·han** \o-ki-haŋ\ *v poss* o·wa·kihe [fr *ohán* to boil *e.g.* meat] : to boil for one
[3]**o·ki·han** *or* **okihe** \ó-ki-haŋ\ *or* \ó-ki-he\ *va* o·wa·kihan : to follow or be after one in travelling, to follow in years, be younger than < *Waniyetu yamni omayakihan* You are three years younger than I. *Icagla omakihan po* Follow after me closely. *Waniyetu wanjila ócicihe* I am but one year younger than you. > — *adj* : next to, following, second < *Wicaša omakihe kin he inajin waun ktelo* That man next to me will be standing. >
o·ki·he \ó-ki-he\ *n* : a joint, as of a finger
o·ki·he·ya \ó-ki-he-ya\ *adv* : secondly, after
o·ki·hi \o-ki-hi\ *va* o·wa·kihi unko·kihi·pi **1** : to be able, able to accomplish **2** : to win over, to overcome *etc.* < *Tehan omakihi šni* It did not overcome me for a long time. *Na wasu nakun ~ šni* And hail as well could not destroy it. > — **okihi·ic'iya** *v* : to enable one's self < *Taku wašte yacin kin he okihinic'iyin kte na wicakeya ceya yo* What good you desire will make it possible for yourself, and so in truth pray. > — **okihi·ka** *vn* : to be able — **okihi·kiya** \o-ki-hi-ki-ya\ *va* okihi·wa·kiya : to make able for — **okihi·la** *v dim of* okihi : to be a bit able - Note: this form of the word is used by children MS.350
o·ki·hi·pi·ca \o-ki-hi-pi-ca\ *adj* : possible, that can be done < *~ šni* impossible >
o·ki·hi·šni·ya \o-ki-hi-šni-ya\ *va* okihišni·wa·ya : to disable, to thwart — **okihišniyan** *adv* : disabling, thwarting < *Oic'iya ~ kuš hpaye* He lay feeble disabled helping himself. > - B.H.290.6
o·ki·hi·ya \o-ki-hi-ya\ *va* okihi·wa·ya : to render able, to cause to be able for — *adv* : according to ability
o·ki·hpa·ya \o-ki-hpa-ya\ *vn* o·wa·kihpaya unko·kihpaya·pi : to rest, not to remove, remain in the same place < *Le icunhan oyate kin okihpayapi kta keyapi* They stated that here meanwhile the people would remain. *Can ota eyaku wo, okihpayapi kte lo* Take up many trees, they will be remaining in the same place. > — **okihpaye·kiya** \o-ki-hpa-ye-ki-ya\ *va* okihpaye·wa·kiya : to cause to lie by or rest - B.H.122.21, 171.12
o·ki·hyan \o-ki-hyaŋ\ *n* : a bird flying or hovering about - Bl WHL
o·ki·h'an \o-ki-h'aŋ\ *v* o·wa·kih'an [fr *oh'án* do or act] : to do to one < *Iyotanla omayakih'an yelo* You did me

well. *Tehiya onicih'an ca unyak'upi kte lo* You should give to us since he has with difficulty done things for you, *i.e.* the wolf said, and when one's companion would not let one share of his plenty, one would say: "*Tehiya omayakih'an yelo. Tanyan ~ kin atkuku kin okiyake. Šica ocicih'an šni. Wicaša owotanla kin he tuktognani ~ šni ye* You have done things hard for me to do. When he did him well he spoke to his father. I have done you no wrong. Do in no way anything to that just man. > - B.H.126.23, 235.16, 262.19

o·ki·h'an šun·ke·ca \o-ǩí-ȟ'aŋ šuŋ-ǩē'-ca\ *va* o·wa·ki-h'an šunkeca unko·kih'an šunkeca·pi : to do badly to, to treat like a dog, to destroy what one has depended on, *e.g.* food, hence not to give food to < *Kicunniyan wilukcan kinhan oyate kin owicakih'an šunkeca kte lo* If you understand poorly, he will treat the people badly. >

o·ki·h'an·yan \o-ǩí-ȟ'aŋ-yaŋ\ *v* o·wa·kih'anyan [fr *oh'anyan* do work, act] : to do, to act towards others

o·ki·ja·ta *or* **okijate** \o-ǩí-ja-ṫa\ *n* : the dividing of two rivers with one river dividing into two, a river fork < ~ *el* in a river fork > — *adj* : forked < *Hehan can ~ tob waksa agli* At the time, they arrived back bringing four forked trees cut. >

o·ki·je·ya \o·kí-je-ya\ *adv* : together < *ataya* ~ entirely together >

[1]**o·ki·ju** \ó-ǩi-ju\ *vn* : to be united, to meet as two parties might < *Blokecokanyan ehanl oyate yamni ~ . Oiyokipiya oyate ounkijupi* At mid-summer then three tribes met. Happily our people were united. >

[2]**o·ki·ju** \o-ǩí-ju\ *v of* ojú 1 : to sow or plant one's own, to plant for one 2 : to fill up *e.g.* a bag

o·ki·ju·ya \ó-ǩi-ju-ya\ *va* okiju·wa·ya : to cause to unite — *adv* : unitedly, together

o·ki·ka·ȟa \o-ǩí-ka-ȟa\ *v* oki·wa·kaȟa : to tie a knot

o·ki·ka·hni·ga \o-ǩí-ǩa-ȟni-ǧa\ *v* : to understand one's own perhaps < *Na tokel eonpi kin okiwakahnige šni ca eya wacipi kin el owapa eša el ewacanmike šni* And as I did not give much thought to the burial which I did not understand, still I joined in the dance. >

o·ki·ka·šle·ca \o-ǩí-ǩa-šle-ca\ *va* : to split in the middle - B.H.99.22

o·ki·kcan·pte \o-ǩí-kcaŋ-pte\ *v* [fr *kikcanpta* console] : to seek to console, comfort for some reason < ~ *nišicelo* You are no consolation, as is said when two are disputing, another butts in, and so they say this to him. > - Bl

o·ki·ki·ya·kel \o-ǩí-ǩi-ya-ǩel\ *adv* : covered with scrofulous sores, *fig* in a run-down problematic condition of a meeting < ~ *un* to be afflicted with scrofula, ~ *inyanka* to run a sickly meeting >

o·ki·kpa·ni \o-ǩí-kṗa-ni\ *va* o·wa·kikpani : to be impotent, unable for a thing — **okikpani·ya** *va* okikpani·wa·ya : to render unable — **okikpani·yan** *adv* : incompetently < ~ *waun* I am being incompetent. >

o·ki·ksab \o-ǩí-ksab\ *vn contrac of* okiksapa : to be wise in some regard — **okiksa·bic'iya** *v refl* : to make one's self wise — **okiksa·bya** *va* okiksa·bwa·ya : to cause to experience or know — *adv* : wisely

o·ki·ksa·he \o-ǩí-ksa-he\ *n* : an abyss

o·ki·ksa·pa \o-ǩí-ksa-ṗa\ *vn* o·wa·kiksapa [fr *ksapa* wise or prudent] : to be wise in repect to, to have gained wisdom by experience

o·ki·ksu·ye \o-ǩí-ksu-ye\ *va of* kiksuya : to remember < ~ *wašte* easy to remember > — *n* : a remembrance

o·ki·kšu \o-ǩí-kšu\ *v poss* : to fill one's own, to put into one's own, *e.g.* into one's pocket

o·ki·le \o-ǩí-le\ *v poss* o·wa·kile [fr *olé* to search for] : to seek for one's own

o·ki·li·ta·ton \o-ǩí-li-ṫa-toŋ\ *vn* : to make a great show of activity and cheer < ~ *škan* to work excitedly, *Kangi wicaša toya najinwicayapi na* ~ Crow Indians were had to stand in a blue manner, so as to make a show of enthusiasm. > - *See* owílita, owólutaton MS.526 Bl

o·ki·lo·ta \o-ǩí-lo-ṫa\ *v* o·wa·kilota unko·kilota·pi o·ma·kilota oci·ci·lota [fr *olota* borrow] : to borrow anything of one

o·ki·me \ó-ǩi-me\ *n* : a seam or joint — *vn* : to join, meet, to encircle, go round, to circle — **okime·ya** *va* ókime·wa·ya : to encirdle, enclose, to cause to go round — *adv* : encircling

o·ki·mni·ci·ye \ó-ǩi-mni-ci-ye\ *v* : to come together < *Oyate kin witaya ecicaskaya ~ kta keyapelo* They said the people will be coming together from all over. > - *Syn* KIWÍTAYA, ÓWITAYA LHB

o·ki·na·bla·ga \o-ǩí-na-bla-ǧa\ *vn of* nablaga : to burst open, as corn in boiling

o·ki·na·bla·za *or* **okinablaga** \o-ǩí-na-bla-za\ *vn of* nablaza : to burst open, as corn in boiling

o·ki·na·ble·ca \o-ǩí-na-ble-ca\ *va* okina·wa·bleca : to break in two *e.g.* a plate *etc.* by trampling on — **okinablel** *va contrac* : break in two < ~ *iyeya* to break by trampling on >

o·ki·na·han \ó-ǩi-na-haŋ\ *adv* : perhaps - Note: the word occurs at the beginning of a clause

o·ki·na·hle·ca \o-ǩí-na-ȟle-ca\ *vn* : to tear in the middle - B.H.268.7

o·ki·na·ksa \o-ǩí-na-ksa\ *va* okina·wa·ksa [fr *naksa* break off by foot] : to break anything in two in the middle with the foot

o·ki·na·sle·ca \o-ǩí-na-sle-ca\ *vn of* nasléca : to split or burst open lengthwise, being so done very easily

o·ki·na·špa \o-ǩí-na-šṗa\ *va* okina·wa·špa [fr *našpa* break off something by foot] : to divide in the middle, to break off

[1]**o·ki·ni** \o-ǩí-ni\ *va* o·wa·kini unko·kini·pi : to share, receive a part in a division, to obtain a share, in any way where there is a small amount < *Kal ótkeya yo* (the *táblo,* at the door) *hecel ptejincala ake unkokinipi kte lo* Over there hang it up *i.e.* the shoulder, at the door, so we might share a buffalo calf again, a superstitious old saying. *Tabló wan ecela ai ške. Heceglahci ~ ca* They say he took only a buck. Only so much is it that he shared. > - D.119

[2]**o·ki·ni** \ō'-ǩi-ni\ *adv* : perhaps, possibly - Note: the word is used at the beginning of a clause

o·ki·ni·ca \o-ǩí-ni-ca\ *v* : to try, attempt, to strive for some purpose - Bl

o·ki·ni·han \o-ǩí-ni-haŋ\ *va* o·wa·kinihan : to single out, select for praise — *adv* [fr *kinihan* reverence] : honorably, honorable

o·ki·ni·ki·ya \o-ǩí-ni-ǩi-ya\ *va* okini·wa·kiya : to give a share of, cause to partake - Pb.30

o·ki·ni·yan \o-ǩí-ni-yaŋ\ *vn of* niyá *and coupled with* cuwí : to gasp, breathe as one dying, to breathe deeply, to heave a deep sigh < *cuwí ~* to gasp, *Ehanl cuwi owakiniyan keyapi* They said at the time I heaved a deep sigh. > - D.88, 90

\a\ father \e\ they \i\ machine \o\ smoke \u\ lunar \an, aŋ\ blanc Fr. \in, iŋ\ ink \on, oŋ, un, uŋ\ soon, confier Fr. \c\ chair \ǧ\ machen Ger. \j\ fusion \clusters: bl, gn, kp, hšl, etc...\ b°lo ... said with a slight vowel **See more in the Introduction, Guide to Pronunciation**

o·kin on ši·ca \o-ǩíŋ oŋ ši-ca\ *adj* : being stubborn - Note: this *express* is used of a man or horse that refuses to obey - Bl

o·kin·yan \o-ǩíŋ-yaŋ\ *vn of* kinyan : to fly in, to fly about overhead < *Zitkala iyuha okinyanpi na okawinh au na kiyela okinyanpi. Icunhan piško k'eya okinyanhanpi* All birds fly, they come round, and fly in near. Meantime some night hawks were out flying about. > — *adj in comp with* wašté : docile, gentle - D.73

o·kin·yan·ke \o-ǩíŋ-yaŋ-ke\ *n* [perhaps fr *oki* through the midst + *inyanka* to run] : an arena for racing, a gathering for competitive sports < *Okinyanke onspic'iya yo* Get acquainted yourself with the arena racetrack. > - GA

o·ki·pa \o-ǩí-pa\ *v poss* o·wa·kipa [fr *ópa* join in] : to follow or obey one's own, follow *e.g.* the habits or trade of one's father < *Le hiyu ca oye ~ gle lo* He went home following the same track, road, he came on. > - Bl

o·ki·pa·gi \o-ǩí-pa-ǧi\ *v* : to fill the pipe for - D.249

o·ki·pa·ta \o-ǩí-p̣a-ta\ *va* oki·wa·pata [fr *patá* to patch] : to patch on, join one to the other — **okipata·pi** \o-ǩí-p̣a-ta-p̣i\ *n* : patchwork

o·ki·pe \o-ǩí-p̣e\ *v* : to follow one's own - *See* okípa — **okipe·ca** *vn* o·wa·kipeca : to do as one has been accustomed to — **okipe·kiya** \o-ǩí-p̣e-ǩi-ya\ *va* oki-pe·wa·kiya : to cause to follow one's own, carry on a tradition

o·ki·pe·mni \o-ǩí-p̣e-mni\ *v poss* o·wa·kipemni [fr *opemni* wrap around] : to wrap around one's own

o·ki·pe·ya \o-ǩí-p̣e-ya\ *va* okipe·wa·ya : to cause to follow one's own — *adv* : following < ~ *waun* I am following or to be following >

o·ki·pi \o-ǩí-p̣i\ *v* o·má·kipi o·ni·kipi unko·kipi·pi [fr *kipí* to contain] : to hold, admit, receive, be large enough < *Pa kin lila tanka canke ~ šni* His head was very large and so it was not big enough. > - D.28

o·ki·sa·bya \o-ǩí-sa-bya\ *adv* : blackish, barren < *Maka ~ yunkelo* The land lay barren, as is said when there is but little snow in winter. > - Bl

o·ki·sa·pa \o-ǩí-sa-p̣a\ *vn of* kisápa : to become bare, black, as a spot of ground while the snow remains around

o·ki·se \o-ǩí-se\ *n* : a part, the half of anything — **oki-se·la** *n dim* : a bit of something < *Maza ša ~ mun* I use a bit of copper. > — **okise·ya** *or* **okiseye·la** *adv* : half < *Tašunkepi kin ~ wicunktepi* We killed half his horses. >

[1]**o·ki·so·ta** \o-ǩí-so-ṭa\ *vn of* sóta : to be all gone, used up

[2]**o·ki·so·ta** \ó-ǩi-so-ṭa\ *v coll of* yusota : they are all gone - *See* ósota B.H.71.16

o·ki·sta·ka \o-ǩí-sṭa-ǩa\ *vn* : to be enfeebled by or on account of

o·ki·sya·kel \o-ǩí-sya-kel\ *adv* : is used to, is only fighting < ~ *un* to be used to fighting > - Note: *owicakisyakel* is doubtfully used - B.H.86.22

o·ki·s'a·s'a \o-ǩí-s'a-s'a\ *v* : to hush or hiss one < *Ištinma unkokis'as'a* He hushed us both to sleep. > - Bl

o·ki·ši·li·a \o-ǩí-ši-li-a\ *v* : to speak entirely bad language - Bl

o·ki·štan \ó-ǩi-štaŋ\ *v poss perhaps* [fr *oštan* put on or in] : to put in place of, to put in one's own < *Yunkan isto k'on ecel ikikcu na ecel ~ na ku* Then as it was he had taken back his arm, and so he put in his own and came back. > - MS.147

o·ki·šya·kel \o-ǩí-šya-kel\ *adv* : in a manner belligerent, or unsociable, or uncooth < ~ *nanke lo* You are in the habit of being belligerent, as is said by a visitor who is received in silence as though he were not welcome. - *Syn* OT'INHYAKEL Bl

o·ki·tan'·in \o-ǩí-taŋ-iŋ\ *vn* : to appear, be conspicuous, as a hill — *n* : manifestation, clarity of the understanding, perspecuity < ~ *wašte* easy understanding > — **o-kitan'in·yan** *adv* : manifestly, gloriously < ~ *unpi* they are become famous. > - D.258

o·ki·ti \o-ǩí-ṭi\ *vn* : to live in some place, to have a residence < *Ḣe ihanke ca el Šahiyela okitipi* The Cheyennes live in the foorhills of the mountains. >

o·ki·t'a \o-ǩí-t'a\ *vn* : to be tired, fatigued or worn out by, to be made sick by < *Wamatuka yelo, taku iyuha owakit'e lo* I was exhausted, I was tired of everything, as one would say when he did not care for anything any more. >

o·ki·t'e·ya \o-ǩí-t'e-ya\ *va* **1** : to prevent, obstruct in < *canku ~* to put a limit to a roadway, or to put a hindrance in a road, as is said of a narrow road, *~ unyankapi* We sat crowded together because room is small. > **2** : to tire out, to bother unceasingly — *adv* : silent from exhaustion < ~ *manke lo* I sat exhausted and silent > - B.H.58.6, 137.25, 238.24

o·ki·t'e·ya·kel \o-ǩí-t'e-ya-kel\ *adv* : obstructing, preventing - *Syn* PATAGYA, PATAGYAKEL

o·ki·t'e·ye·la \o-ǩí-t'e-ye-la\ *adv* **a** : too large, bulky **b** : tired out - R Bl

o·ki·un ši·ca \o-ǩí-uŋ ši-ca\ *adj* : hard to handle, as a lively horse or child on account of its tossing - Bl

o·ki·wa \o-ǩí-wa\ *v* *o·wa·kiwa* [fr *owa* write or draw] : to write for one

o·ki·wa·bla·za \o-ǩí-wa-bla-za\ *va* okiwa·wa·blaza : to rip open in the middle

o·ki·wa·ble·ca \o-ǩí-wa-ble-ca\ *va* okiwa·wa·bleca [fr *wableca* to break with a knife] : to break through the middle *e.g.* of a plate by cutting on it

o·ki·wa·ksa \o-ǩí-wa-ksa\ *va* okiwa·wa·ksa [fr *waksa* to cut off] : to cut with a knife through the middle

o·ki·wan·ji·la \ó-ǩi-waŋ-ji-la\ *adv* : always, continually; alike, uniform < ~ *nahmala kigla.* He always got home in secret. *Hecel wicitawokšan unyanpi na ~ unkutapi* So we went around and fired off our guns alike. >

o·ki·wa·ptu·ga \o-ǩí-wa-p̣ṭu-ǧa\ *va* : to cut in two with a knife in the middle, as pemmican, anything crusted or half frozen

o·ki·wa·sle·ca \o-ǩí-wa-sle-ca\ *va* okiwa·wa·sleca [fr *wasleca* to saw up or split] : to slit or rip down something soft, *e.g.* an apple in the middle with a knife or saw < *Na ake tatanka wan o na on ha kin ~* And a second time he shot a bull buffalo and so ripped the hide. > — **oki-waslel** *va contrac* : to slit or rip down

o·ki·wa·šle·ca \o-ǩí-wa-šle-ca\ *va* okiwa·wa·šleca [fr *wašleca* to saw] : to split or rip down *e.g.* a log or board in the middle with a saw

o·ki·wa·špa \o-ǩí-wa-šp̣a\ *va* okiwa·wa·špa [fr *wašpa* to scalp] : to cut into halves, in two in the middle *e.g.* an apple with a knife

o·ki·wa·špu \o-ǩí-wa-šp̣u\ *va* okiwa·wa·špu [fr *wašpu* cut up into pieces] : to halve *e.g.* a potato with a knife

o·ki·wa·š'ag ši·ca \o-ǩí-wa-š'ag ši-ca\ *adj* : wrongheaded, unable to be advised or to receive advice - Bl

o·ki·win·ja \o-ǩí-wiŋ-ja\ *v* : to bind down thoroughly < *Na wana lel yanka ye, eyin na pteha okise wan ~* And now sit here, he said and bound down entirely half a buffalo hide. > - MS.143

o·ki·wi·ta·ya \ó-ǩi-wi-ṭa-ya\ *adv perhaps* : gathering about something

o·ki·wo·šle·ca \o-k̇í-wo-šle-ca\ *va* oki·wa·wošleca : to split by shooting

[1]**o·ki·wo·ta·he·na** \o-k̇í-wo-ta-he-na\ *adv* : by mere chance < ~ *wankiciyankapi* By mere coincidence they saw one another. >

[2]**o·ki·wo·ta·he·na** \o-k̇í-wo-ṫa-he-na\ *adv* : between two places, things, or persons < ~ *ti* to live in the inbetween, *i.e.* alone away from the crowd, ~ *iblotake* I sat in between, ~ *egnaka* to put it in between >

[1]**o·ki·ya** \o-k̇í-ya\ *va* o·wa·kiya : to talk with, court, as a man courts a woman; to make peace with – D.51,269

[2]**o·ki·ya** \ó-k̇i-ya\ *va* ó·wa·kiya : to help, assist one in anything

o·ki·yag \o-k̇í-yag\ *va contrac of* okiyaka : to tell to < *He ~ wahi* I came to tell this to him. >

o·ki·ya·ka \o-k̇í-ya-k̇a\ *va* o·wa·kiyaka unko·kiyaka·pi, *but also* o·wa·kiblaka o·ya·kilaka [fr *oyaka* to tell, relate] to tell anything to one

o·ki·ya·pta \o-k̇í-ya-pṫa\ *v* o·wa·kiyapta [fr *oyapta* to leave over] : to leave *e.g.* food for one

o·ki·ya·sin \o-k̇í-ya-siŋ\ *vn* : to stick together, as potatoes growing on the same root

o·ki·ya·ska·pa \o-k̇í-ya-sk̇a-ṗa\ *vn* 1 : to stick on, stick together, cleave to 2 : to fall or cave in and so become flat, as an animal that is poor

o·ki·ye·ki·ya \ó-ki-ye-k̇i-ya\ *va* : to make one help – B.H.265.9

o·ki·yu·slel \o-k̇í-yu-slel\ *v* [as fr *okiyusleca, oki* in the middle + *yusleca* to split by hand] : to divide < *Woyuha ... okimakiyuslel ši yo* Tell him to divide my belongings for me. *Talo kin hena ~ icupo, eya ke* He wished to say: Take, divide up these pieces of fresh meat. > – B.H.224.2 MS.96

o·ki·yu·ta \ó-k̇i-yu-ṫa\ *vn* : to heal up *e.g.* a wound, to grow over, as bark of a tree

o·ki·zi \o-k̇í-zi\ *vn* o·ma·kizi : to heal up, recover from a hurt or wound — **okizi·kiya** \o-k̇í-zi-k̇i-ya\ *va* okizi·wa·kiya : to cause to heal up — **okizi·ya** *va* okizi·wa·ya : to cause to heal, make well, to cause to take a rest

o·ko \o-k̇ŏ'\ *n* : a crack, hole, aperture, a space, as in a house, a location, or as in perhaps a space of time < ~ *wanjica* one week, ~ *oyate ob mayani kte* You will travel with the people for a time, as the chief is told when he is inaugurated. > — *adv* : between < *Can kin he ~ kin ogna iblable* I am going in between the trees. *Le September 25-30 oko el St. Francis Mission ekta wai ktelo* In the time between September 25 and 30, I shall go to St. Francis Mission. *Yunkan makoce kin owancaya wašicunpi na Lakota kin ~ oyasin ceya unpi* And then they are all everywhere in the country crying between the white men and the Lakotas. > – *See* sióko space between toes, *napsúhu* space between fingers MS.355

o·ko·gna \o-k̇ŏ'-gna\ *adv* : between

o·ko·gna·gna·ka \o-k̇ó-gna-gna-ka\ *v* : to put between others, *e.g.* a child between a number of persons so that it cannot fall *etc.* – Bl

o·ko·ki·pe \o-k̇ó-k̇i-ṗe\ *n* : danger, fear — **okokipe·ya** *adv* : in fear

o·ko·la·ki·ci·ye \o-k̇ó-la-k̇i-ci-ye\ *n* : a fellowship, a society, a league, a community

o·ko·la·ya \o-k̇ó-la-ya\ *v* : to have as a friend < *Ake hokšila wan ~* Again she had a boyfriend. >

O·ko·mi \O-kó-mi\ *np* – *See* Hokomi *and* Yokomi

o·kon \o-k̇óŋ\ *n* : a desire

o·kon·ze \o-k̇óŋ-ze\ *n* : a law, a rule

o·ko·pe \o-kó-ṗe\ *n* : fear

o·ko·pe·ya \ó-k̇o-ṗe-ya\ *adv* : seen through a hole, as one seen through an opening in the bushes < ~ *wanblaka* to see through a hole, ~ *owojun wan tan'inyan he lo* A garden, a field, is just a little visible between the hills. > – BT

o·ko·šni·yan \o-k̇ó-šni-yaŋ\ *adv* : there being no space < ~ *han* There was no room. > – B.H.130.9

o·ko·ton \o-k̇ŏ'-toŋ\ *v* : to be a crack, a hole — **okoton·yan** *n* : an opening or communication; an expanse, of space, of the heavens, the firmament — *adv perhaps* : with free spaces < ~ *ayuštan* to leave space free, as in putting boards on a wall and leaving a space for windows >

o·ko·wa·ni·lya \o-k̇ó-wa-ni-lya\ *adv* : with no room between < ~ *yankapi* They sat close together, and in the obverse sense, They sat all over. > – *Syn* ÍCIPAT'INS B.H.50.4

o·ko·ya \o-k̇ŏ'-ya\ *adv* : between < ~ *ayuštan* to leave a space free between rows >

o·kpa·gi \o-kṗá-ġi\ *v poss* o·wa·kpagi [fr *opagi* fill a pipe] : to fill one's own pipe with one's own tobacco

o·kpa·ni \ó-kṗa-ni\ *vn* : to be lacking, less than, *i.e.* lacking to what one already has, as money *etc.*

o·kpan·kpan \ó-kpaŋ-kpaŋ\ *vn* : to become crumbly < *Šunk'hinša wicahcala s'e ite san ~* The sorrel horse's white face became crinkled like that of an old man. > — *n* : crumbs or decay – Bl WHL

o·kpan·la \o-kpáŋ-la\ *adj* : crumbled, as coal, bread *etc.* < *aguyapi ~* crumbled bread > – B.H.213.7

o·kpas \ó-k̇pas\ *vn contrac of* okpaza : to be dark < ~ *icu* to become dark >

o·kpa·spa \o-kpá-spa\ *v* o·wa·kpaspa : to repress, suppress one's own reaction, *i.e.* actions, feelings *etc.* < *wacin ~* to suppress one's own thoughts, as is said of a person who keeps silent inspite of his own anger > – Bl

o·kpa·sya \ó-kṗa-sya\ *va* okpa·swa·ya : to darken, make dark — *adv* : in the dark, darkly < *Wanagi s'e ištokpasya* Like a spirit it darkens its eyes. *Šunk'ite pšunka s'e poge kin ~* Like a puckered-up face of a horse he darkened his nose, as is said when a man's nose points upwards. > – Bl

o·kpa·za \ó-kṗa-za\ *vn* : to be dark — *n perhaps* : darkness, night

o·kpa·zan \o-kpá-zaŋ\ *v refl* : to slip one's own in and under, to weave one's own in between things

o·kpe \ó-kṗe\ *v* : to meet and assist in carrying a load, or in taking a part of one's load, to offer an assist < ~ *ya* to go help, *Tanke, ciye okpewicani kte lo, teȟiya kupi ca iya yo* Big sister, big brother will lend a hand to carry life's load, speak up when it is hard to come home. ~ *šni heyáhe* He kept on saying that without helping. > – MS.74 D.71

o·kpi·kpi \o-kpí-kpi\ *adj* : very small, slender, slit-like < *Maka cincala s'e išta cikcik'aya išta ~ kaca* Like a skunk cub its eyes are very slender, eyes properly slit-like, *i.e.* having very small eyes. > – Bl

o·kpu·kpa \o-kṗú-kṗa\ *adj of* kpukpá : full of dirt, not clear, as water, soup *etc.* — **okpukpe** *n* : dregs, lees

---

\a\ father \e\ they \i\ machine \o\ smoke \u\ lunar \an, aŋ\ blanc Fr. \in, iŋ\ ink \on, oŋ, un, uŋ\ soon, confier Fr. \c\ chair \ġ\ machen Ger. \j\ fusion \clusters: bl, gn, kp, hšl, etc...\ b^e^lo ... said with a slight vowel **See more in the Introduction, Guide to Pronunciation**

o·ksa \ó-ksa\ *vn* : to break off *e.g.* a stick in a hole — **oksa·han** *or* **oksahe** \o-ksá-haŋ\ *part* : broken off in, fallen in *e.g.* in a corn hole

o·ksa·pe wo·te·ȟi \o-ksá-ṗe wò-ṫe-ȟi\ *adj phr* : stupid, hard to teach – *Syn* TEHAN KSAPEŠNI

o·kse \ó-kse\ *n* : anything broken off short

o·kšan \ō'-kšaŋ\ *prep* and *adv* : around, round about < ~ *kinyan* to hover, *Na wanna hanhepi el ataya tipi kin ~ enajin* And they now stood around the house the whole night through. >

o·kšan'·i·pa·ta \ó-kšaŋ-i-ṗa-ta\ *v* : to put edging around *e.g.* quill-work

o·kšan·kšan \ó-kšaŋ-kšaŋ\ *adv red* : round about < *Wekta na ~ ewatonwan na lila cantemašica* I awoke, looked around, and became very sad. ~ *wakita* He looked out round about. *Išnala pahata ~ etonwan* He took a look round about the lone hill, *i.e.* he viewed the country round about. > – B.H.234.5 D.120 MS.162

o·kšan·tan *or* **o·kšan·tan·han** \ó-kšaŋ-ṫaŋ\ *adv* : from all around, from all directions < *Tohanl letanhan ble ci hehanl ~ awicaupi kte lo* When I go from here they will be brought from all around. >

o·kšu \o-kšú\ *v poss* o·wé·kšu [fr *ojú* put in *e.g.* the ground] : to load *e.g.* one's gun, to load a wagon < *Cahli ecel okšupi kin iyecel uwata na takuni šni* Thus when it was loaded, I so fired it, and there was nothing. *Hohu ~ wo* Pile in the bones, *i.e.* in a kettle. *Kola, omicikšu wo; omani mni ktelo* Friend, fill it for me; I shall be going on a journey. >

o·kte \o-kté\ *n perhaps* : a killing, in regard to killing < *Zintkala owe oyasin kinyanpi na okte šicapi* All sorts of birds fly, so killing them is difficult. > – MS.479

o·ku·ja \o-ǩú-ja\ *vn* o·ma·kuja [fr *kuja* to be sick] : to be sick on account of — **okuje** *n* : a sickness < ~ *tipi* a sickroom > – Note: the word is doubtfully interpreted to mean sickness – R

o·kun \o-kúŋ\ *adj in comp* : in regard to desire < ~ *on wašte* gentle, mild >

o·ku·te \o-ǩú-ṫe\ *n of* kuté : a shooting, a shot

o·ku·wa \o-ǩú-wa\ *va* o·wa·kuwa [fr *kuwa* follow after] : to chase, run after < *Taku ~* She worked with something. > – D.272

o·k'a \o-k'á\ *va* o·wa·k'a unko·k'a·pi [fr *k'a* to dig] : to dig into, dig through, out, up < *Šunkmanitu wan hi na omak'in na imacu welo* A coyote came, picked me us, and took me. *Itaokšan maka kin ok'in na* Take it and dig up the ground all around. > — **ok'a·pi** *n* : a digging into — **ok'e** *n* : a mine, a digging

o·k'in \o-k'íŋ\ *v* o·wa·k'in : to carry in — *n* : a pack, load, something to carry or pack in, *e.g.* in a blanket or sack < ~ *wanji kage* He prepared a pack. > – D.66

o·k'i·pe \o-k'í-ṗe\ *n* : the prize, something staked

[1]**o·k'o** \ó-k'o\ *v* ó·wa·k'o ó·ma·k'o 1 : to stick to or on, as feathers or down or flour dust 2 : to gather around for something to eat < *Eceš lila ómak'onpi kelah* Of course they really crowded around me ever more, *i.e.* fearfully for myself. > – Bl

[2]**o·k'o** \o-k'ó\ *n* : a noise, hum, buzz, bustle, a disturbance < ~ *hingla. Lila wakiyan ukiye na lila wasu ko hihanna wakangli makata iheyapi na lila ~ na ecel anpa el akisni* Suddenly there was noise. The thunder is really coming, really the hail too, in the morning the lightning flash on the earth, and really there is a noise and thus at dawn it recovers . ~ *unkagin ktelo* We shall create a noise. *Icunupa, icunonpa, ~ kta wacin šni* Off to the side I do not want that there should be a disturbance. > — **ok'o·ka** *or* **ok'o·s'e** \o-kō'-ǩa\ *n* [fr *ok'o* noise + *ka* adding emph] : noise, disturbance, tumult < *Na wanna lila ~* And there was a really noisy disturbance. > — *va* : to cause disturbance < *Ho hanpatanhan taku ok'oke; yunkan el gli* Well, something from moccasins was making noise; then he arrived at home. > – Bl BM MS.164

o·k'o·s'e \o-k'ó-s'e\ *n* : disturbance, tumult

o·k'o·ya \o-k'ó-ya\ *vn* ok'o·wa·ya : to make a noise or bustle < *Na wana oyate k'un oimniciye na lila ~ škanpi* And the people had gone to a meeting, and they were making a great fuss. > — *adv perhaps* : noisely < ~ *yanka* to sit making noise. *Na cokata lila wicotapi na taku ~ škanpi* And in the midst there was a real crowd and they were noisely bustling about. > — **ok'oya·kel** \o-k'ō'-ya-kel\ *adv* : noisely < *Na wanna ok'oyakel škanpi* They were now busy noisely making an ado. > – MS. 577, 342 B.H.205.5 R

o·k'u \o-k'ú\ *va* o·wa·k'u [fr *k'u* give] 1 : to lend anything to one 2 : to give to, *e.g.* food, to give a portion to < *Canke šunk ok'upi na lila wicota ko ekta wanyank ahi* And so they came to the place to see them give him and a great crowd dog (to eat). > 3 : to share with – D.97 note 3

o·la·bya \o-lá-bya\ *va* ola·bwa·ya ola·bci·ya : to cheer up, make glad by giving

o·la·bya *or* **olabyakel** \o-lá-bya\ \o-lá-bya-ǩel\ *adv* : exceedingly, gratifyingly, very much – P LHB Bl

o·la·kol \o-lá-kol\ *n contrac of* olakota : friendship, alliance, fraternity < ~ *kaga* to make a friend > – P

o·la·ko·lki·ci·ya·pi \o-lá-ǩo-lki-ci-ya-pi\ *n* : friendship, peace < *Wakanpi ~* the Communion of Saints >

o·la·ko·lwi·ca·ye šni \o-lá-ko-lwi-ca-ye šni\ *adj* : without care for relatives and natural affection

o·la·ko·lya \o-lá-ko-lya\ *v* : to have for a friend — *adv perhaps* : as friends < ~ *unpi kte kin oihanke wanicin kte* There will be no end if they should be friends. > –B.H. 129.8

o·la·kot *or* **olakol** \o-lá-koṫ\ *n contrac of* olakota : friendship < *olakotkaga* making of peace, of friendly association >

o·la·ko·ta \o-lá-ǩo-ṫa\ *n* : friendship, fraternity, alliance

o·la·nun·s'e \ó-la-nuŋ-s'e\ *adv* : almost, nearly – Bl

o·le \o-lé\ *va* o·wa·le unko·le·pi : to seek for, to hunt for anything

o·le·ja \o-lé-ja\ *v* o·wa·leja [fr *leja* to urinate] : to urinate in anything — *n* : the bladder perhaps, a chamber-pot

o·lol \o-lól\ *va contrac of* olota : to borrow

o·lo·lo·bya \o-ló-lo-bya\ *va ololo·bwa·ya* : to over-boil something in

[1]**o·lo·ta** \o-ló-ṫa\ *va* o·wa·lota : to borrow anything

[2]**o·lo·ta** \ó-lo-ṫa\ *adj red of* óta : much of various kinds < *lila ~* being largely of various kinds, *Hecel top zuya ipi kin iyuha ~ waontonyanpi* So all four who went on the warpath suffered a variety of injuries. >

o·lo·ta·pi \o-ló-ṫa-pi\ *n* : a hireling, anything borrowed from others – P Bl

o·lo·wan \o-ló-waŋ\ *n* : a song, hymn, a tune

o·lu·lu·ta \o-lú-lu-ṫa\ *n* : heat — *adj* : warm, hot, as a room or the weather, sultry – P

o·lu·te \o-lú-ṫe\ *n* : the large muscle or flesh on the thigh or legs < *Wana ~ kin icah ayapelo* His muscles began to grow, *i.e.* get fat from grass in the spring. > – Bl

o·lu·za·han \o-lú-za-haŋ\ *n of* luzahan : swiftness

O·ma·ha \O-má-ha\ *np* : an Omaha Indian

o·ma·ka \ó-ma-ka\ *n* : a year, a season < ~ *opta tawo-*

econ wowapi a book of one's deeds through the years, *i.e.* an History book, a record > – B.H.147.25

o·ma·ni \o-má-ni\ *v* oma·wa·ni oma·un·ni·pi unko·ma-ni·pi [fr *máni* to walk, travel] : to walk in or according to, as in a road, to travel — *n* : a walk — **omani·yan** *v* oma·wa·niyan : to go on a walk < *Wanna ake omaniyanpi kta* They will now go on a second walk. > — **omaniyankel** *adv* : walking < ~ *waun* I am walking. >

o·ma·ska·pe *or* **omas'kaġe**\o-má-sk̇a-ṗe \ *n* : a blacksmith shop, a blacksmith – P

o·ma·šte \o-má-šte\ *n* : heat, warmth, the sunshine, where the sun shines — *vn* [fr *mašte* hot or sultry] : to be hot in

o·ma·wa·hi·ton \o-má-wa-hi-toŋ\ *n* omawahiton mitawa *or* nitawa [fr *unmawaton* or *omawaheton* enriched by the other] : the title applied to each other by the two fathers of husband and wife; and by the mothers as well – Note: this is a term of direct address, used regardless of sex between the parents, aunts, uncles, and grandparents of a person when speaking either of or to that person's spouse's parents, uncles, aunts and grandparents — **omawahiton·kiciya** *v refl* : to have each other for *omáwahiton* — **omawahiton·ya** *or* **omawahetonya** *va* omawahi-ton·wa·ya : to have for a *omáwahiton*

[1]**o·ma·za·pe** \o-má-za-pe\ *n* : a graphophone

[2]**o·ma·za·pe** \ó-ma-za-pe\ *n* : a telephone

o·mi·me·ye·la \o-mí-me-ye-la\ *adv* : encircling

o·mi·ni·o·we \o-mi-ní-o-we\ *n* : a made well – *Syn* MINIOICU

o·mna \ó-mna\ *va* ó·wa·mna ó·un·mna·pi : to smell something, such as whiskey, burnt herbs *etc.* — *n* : a smell < *Cinca k'on azilya. Yunkan* ~ *na akisni* He had incensed the child. Then he smelled it and recovered. > — **omna·kiya** \ó-mna-k̇i-ya\ *v* : to give a smoke to < *Omnamakiyi ye* Please give me a smoke. >

o·mna·yan \o-mná-yaŋ\ *v* omna·wa·ya [fr *mnayan* to collect] : to gather into < *Wicawe wanjila el omnaunyanpelo* We were gathered into only one man's blood. >

o·mni·ca \o-mní-ca\ *n* : beans; also the *mak̇átomnica* the earth bean or Lakota omnica, the trailing wild bean, strophostyles helvola; also falcata comosa, the pulse family, *wahpe wakan heca ota yelo* there are many leaves that are quite special. – Note: as a medicine, you pulverize the leaves and put them on swellings together with any salve; *lila wašte* they are very effective — **omnica gmigmi** *or* **omnica gmi·gmela** \o-mní-ca gmi-gmì\ *n* : peas — **omnica·hu** *n* : the legumen, strophostyles pauciflora — **omnica tankinyan** \o-mní-ca taŋ-kìŋ-yaŋ\ *n* : large beans – BT Bl # 111, 292

o·mni·ci·ye \o-mní-ci-ye\ *n* [fr *mniciya* assemble] : an assembly < ~ *econ* to hold a meeting >

o·mni·mni \o-mní-mni\ *v* : to sprinkle into

o·mni·ya·tke \o-mní-ya-tke\ *n* : a place to drink water – Pb.31

o·mni·ye·la \ó-mni-ye-la\ *adv perhaps* : in a manner of setting something out to dry, *fig* applied to acting stingily < ~ *wayatapelo* They chew away laid out to dry, *i.e.* selfishly, as they say when some ate sitting with others and without sharing with them. *Ena* ~ *ayuhel wicakuwi* Come right here after them waiting around to be aired, as horses wait in a small place. > – BT GA

o·na \o-ná\ *n* : a fire, a prairie fire – *See* onikušeya, oninatake, words for a fireguard

o·na·blu \o-ná-blu\ *v* ona·wa·blu : to raise dust by walking through sand

o·na·cu \o-ná-cu\ *v* : to be damp or chilly as to the feet < *Hanpa kin onawacu welo* My moccasins are frosty inside. > – Bl

o·na-glo \o-ná-glo\ *vn* : to rattle in the throat — **onaglo·glo** *v red* : to snort, have a rattling in the throat, as one about to die – Note: the word is applied to things boiling and rattling in the kettle – D.272

o·na·gu \o-ná-ġu\ *n* : scorched earth, a place where a prairie fire burned everything < *Ataya* ~ *pte kin au welo* The buffalo came, the whole a scorched earth, *i.e.* so full of buffalos that the prairie looked black. >

o·na·gu·mna \o-ná-ġu-mna\ *v perhaps* [fr *ona* a fire + *ġumna* smelling burnt] : to smell like a prairie fire

o·na·gwu \o-ná-gwu\ *vi* : to curdle in, as milk in a pot

o·na·hla·te \o-ná-ḣla-ṫe\ *n* [fr *nahlata* to scratch] : a scratch

o·na·hle·ca \o-ná-ḣle-ca\ *va* ona·wa·hleca : to tear a hole in a hole, to rent — **onahlece** *n* [fr *nahleca* to tear] : a rent, a tear

o·na·hlo·ka \o-ná-ḣlo-k̇a\ *va* ona·wa·hloka : to make a hole either in the ground with the foot, or in the foot by walking

o·na·hna *also perhaps* **onaglo** \o-ná-ḣna\ *n* : the death rattle of a dying person

o·na·hta·ka \o-ná-ḣta-k̇a\ *v* ona·wa·htaka [fr *nahtaka* to kick] : to kick in — **onahtake** *n* : a wound made by kicking

o·na·h'on \o-ná-ḣ'oŋ\ *v* ona·wa·h'on [fr *nah'on* to hear] : to hear what is reported, to hear of or concerning — *n* : hearing < ~ *wašte* good hearing > — **onah'on·kiya** \o-ná-ḣ'on-k̇i-ya\ *va* onah'on·wa·kiya : to communicate to concerning, to cause to hear of — **onah'on·pi** *n* : hearing — **onah'on·ya** *va* onah'on·wa·ya : to cause to hear, communicate to, to announce

o·na·ja·ja \o-ná-ja-ja\ *vn of* najaja : to cleanse or wash out *e.g.* clothes by boiling

o·na·jin \o-ná-jiŋ\ *v* ona·wa·jin [fr *najin* to stand] : to stand in, to take refuge in or at < *P'osyakel* ~ *k'on* for being out of humor he had taken refuge > Bl

o·na·ju·ju \o-ná-ju-ju\ *vn* : to come apart, to go to pieces – Note: the word is applied to a wagon when its wheels are broken – BT

o·na·kab \ó-na-k̇ab\ *v contrac* [fr *nakapa* to kick something] : to kick into < ~ *iyeya* to be kicking in, *Si on can kin peta ekta* ~ *iyeya škan* With his foot he made a sudden movement kicking the log into the fire. >

o·na·kan \o-ná-kaŋ\ *va* ona·wa·kan : to tread off in, to strike and knock off into — *vn* : to be kicked to pieces, as the teeth of one's mouth < *Hi ataya onamakan* My teeth were entirely kicked to pieces. >

o·na·ki·ci·tan·pi \o-ná-k̇i-ci-taŋ-pi\ *v recip of* onatan : to kick each other, as boys in play < *Onaunkicitanpi* We kicked each other. >

o·na·ki·jin \o-ná-k̇i-jin\ *vi* ona·wa·kijin : to take shelter or refure in or behind, as behind a tree in a battle < *Hecena ataya hepiya el onakijinpi* Finally they took refuge altogether on the side of a hill. >

o·na·ki·ki·ya·kel \o-ná-k̇i-k̇i-ya-kel\ *adv* : unevenly < ~ *nakseya* to cut (grass) unevenly, *i.e.* leaving some here and there > – *Syn* NAH'EH'EYAKEL Bl

---

\a\ father \e\ they \i\ machine \o\ smoke \u\ lunar \an, aŋ\ blanc Fr. \in, iŋ\ ink \on, oŋ, un, uŋ\ soon, confier Fr. \c\ chair \ġ\ machen Ger. \j\ fusion \clusters: bl, gn, kp, hšl, etc...\ b[e]lo ... said with a slight vowel **See more in the Introduction, Guide to Pronunciation**

o·na·ki·kšin \o-ná-k̇i-kšiŋ\ *va* ona·we·kšin [fr *nakikšin* defend self] : to take shelter or refuge in or behind, as behind a tree in battle

o·na·ki·šo·še \o-ná-k̇i-šo-še\ *v* : to stir up water with the foot, so that others cannot use it, *fig* to spoil somebody's chance to buy things that someone else wants *etc.*, to spoil things for another that he wanted to do < *Onamayakišoše* You spoiled matters for me. >

o·na·kpa \o-ná-kṗa\ *vn* [fr *o* within + *na* by foot + *kpa* to swell] : to burst within something

o·na·kpan \o-ná-kṗaŋ\ *n* : a mill < *aguyapi* ~ a flour mill > — *v perhaps* [fr *na* by foot + *kpan* fine] : to make fine in, as by machinery

o·na·ksa \o-ná-ksa\ *va* ona·wa·ksa : to break into or through, as in walking on ice < *Siyete ošoke k'el unkcela onawaksa* I broke a cactus through (the thick skin of) my heel. > — **onakse** *n* : a breaking in - Bl

o·na·kšan \o-ná-kšaŋ\ *n of* nakšan : to bend, a crook

o·na·ktan \o-ná-k̇taŋ\ *vn* : to bend into of itself - Cf naktan, naoktan — *n* : a bend

o·na·k'e·ga \o-ná-k'e-ġa\ *v* : to scratch around at or on < *Ite pšunka wan onamak'ega helo* He was scratching around on my chubby face, as is said when desiring a smoke. > - BT

o·na·k'e·sk'e·za \o-ná-k'e-sk'e-za\ *v red of* onak'eza : to make smooth by stomping on

o·na·k'e·za \o-ná-k'e-za\ *va* ona·wa·k'eza : to make smooth by stamping on

o·na·k'os \o-ná-k'os\ *vn contrac of* onák'oza : to stamp making hard — **onak'o·sk'oza** *v red* : to make hard by stamping

o·na·k'o·za \o-ná-k'o-za\ *vn* ona·wa·k'oza : to trample on and make hard

o·na·mni·mni \ó-na-mni-mni\ *v* : to be on one's way < ~ *icu* to take off on one's way somewhere repeatedly but go back again > - Bl

o·na·mni·ye·ta \o-ná-mni-ye-ta\ *adv* : being off on one's own way < ~ *éihpeic'iyaya* You betook yourself back, being off on your own way, or You went on in a crowd somewhere, but returned when someone else had caught up. ~ *eihpeic'imayayapelo* You left me while I was off on my own way. > - Bl

o·na·pa \o-ná-ṗa\ *va* ona·wa·pa [fr *napá* leave, run away] : to flee to, to take refuge in

o·na·pce \o-ná-pce\ *n* 1 : a bite, the act of swallowing < *Pusya španyayapi ca* ~ *omašicelo* It is hard for me to swallow because you cooked it dry. > 2 : the esophagus, *perhaps* — **onapce·šilya** *adv* : hard to swallow - LHB

[1]**o·na·pe** \o-ná-ṗe\ *n* : a refuge where enemies cannot do harm to one

[2]**o·na·pe** \o-ná-ṗe\ *n* or *adv* : in hand < *Miye kayeš* ~ *el able šni wak'u welo* I myself not carrying it in hand gave it to him, *i.e.* gave him something new, something never handled. >

o·na·pi·ga \o-ná-pi-ġa\ *vn* 1 : to foam, froth 2 : to spoil, as spoiling meat

o·na·po·hya \o-ná-ṗo-ḣya\ *vn* : to swell out, puff up

o·na·po·hye \o-ná-ṗo-ḣye\ *n* : leaven

o·na·po·pa \o-ná-po-ṗa\ *vn of* napó-pa : to burst within something

o·na·pu·za \o-ná-ṗu-za\ *v* : to dry up, evaporate < *Hinu,* ~ *ca hanpi cola wowahete* Good grief! I cooked it without soup because it evaporated, as a woman might be surprised. > - BT

o·na·se \o-ná-se\ *n* : the buffalo chase

o·na·sla·ta \o-ná-sla-ta\ *v* : to make one's way slowly by foot < *Canku onaslatapi* They advance slowly on a road, *i.e.* as slow horses. > - Bl

o·na·sto \o-ná-sto\ *v* : to tramp down, make hard with the feet in < *Peji* ~ *ehpeya.* They left grass tramped down. *Hopo, wanna wahpe wokeya ekta owanka* ~ *lapi kte lo.* Alright, they will ask to tramp a place for a leaf peace shelter. *Tokel owanka onastopi he onspewicakiya* He taught them how a site is tramped. >

o·na·s'a·mna \o-ná-s'a-mna\ *v* : to give off a bad odor, to stink - Bl LHB

o·na·s'e·ya \o-ná-s'e-ya\ *vn* : to begin to boil, simmer in, as water in a pot - Bl

o·na·škan \o-ná-škaŋ\ *vn* ona·wa·škan : to become sick again, to relapse

o·na·šla·šla \o-ná-šla-šla\ *v red* ona·wa·šlašla [fr *našla* make bare by foot] : to bare or make bare with the feet < *Na hin ko onašlašlapi* And hair too was bared. >

o·na·šlog \ó-na-šlog\ *vn* [fr *onašloka* leave behind] : to leave something behind < ~ *iyaya* to go leaving behind *Waun letan okanyela ca aškinyankapila* ~ *unkihunnipi kte lo* We shall arrive leaving from a short distance because I am but a little distance from here. > - Bl

[1]**o·na·šlo·ka** \ó-na-šlo-k̇a\ *vn* óna·wa·šloka [fr *našloka* come off, fly out] : to leave behind, run off and leave

[2]**o·na·šlo·ka** \o-ná-šlo-k̇a\ *va* oná·wa·šloka : to pull off in, as shoes in the mud <*Wicaša wan nata kin ataya* ~ *ca išta kin akahpeya hiyu* A man's scalp he pulled entirely off hung down covering the eyes. > - D.224

o·na·s'o \o-ná-s'o\ *vn* : to pace, as a horse — **onas'o·la** *n* : a pacing horse — **onas'o·s'o** *v red* : to do pacing

o·na·tag \ó-na-tag\ *va contrac of* nataka : to fasten, lock < ~ *iyeya* to quickly fasten>

o·na·ta·ka \ó-na-ta-k̇a\ *va* óna·wa·taka [fr *nataka*]: to fasten, bar, bolt, lock *e.g.* a door, to fasten *e.g.* a fence, to fasten or lock up in

o·na·take \o-ná-ta-k̇e\ *n* : a cage, a pen

o·na·tan *also* **onatan·yan** \o-ná-taŋ\ *va* ona·wa·tan ona·ci·tan : to kick, to crush open; *fig* to use harsh words - D.215

o·na·t'ins \o-ná-t'iŋs\ *va contrac of* onat'inza : to pack by foot < ~ *iyeya* to pack firmly by foot >

o·na·t'in·za \o-ná-t'iŋ-za\ *va* ona·wa·t'inza [fr *nat'inza* pack firmly by foot] : to make firm by treading on

o·na·t'os \o-ná-t'os\ *v contrac of* onat'oza : to make smooth by foot stamping

o·na·t'o·za \o-ná-t'o-za\ *v* : to make smooth by stamping on

o·na·ya \o-ná-ya\ *v* ona·wa·ya : to start a prairie fire

o·na·zon *or* **ona·son** \o-ná-zoŋ\ *v* : to braid together, to sew or weave < *tatamni* ~ to sew together the womb > - Bl

o·ni \o-ní\ *n* : life < ~ *mitawa kin wakpagan yelo* My life I give away. > - B.H.254.2

o·ni·ku·še·ya \o-ní-k̇u-še-ya\ *n perhaps* [fr *ona* fire + *ikušeya* blocking, hindering] : a fireguard - *See* oninatake

o·ni·na·ta·ke *also* **onainatake** \o-ní-na-ta-ke\ \o-ná-i-na-ta-ke\ *n* : a fireguard

o·ni·sko·ke·ca \o-ní-sk̇o-ke-ca\ *adj* : so large

o·ni·ya \o-ní-ya\ *v* o·wa·niya [fr *niya* to breathe] : to breathe into, to breathe out of < ~ *šica* to have bad breath > — **oniyan** *n* : breath <~ *hanska* a long breath>

o·ni·ya·šni t'e \o-ní-ya-šni t'e\ *v* : to choke to death - WE

o·ni·ye \o-ní-ye\ *n* : breath — **oniye·mna** *v* : to have a foul breath, to smell bad – Bl Pb.34

o·ni·ye·ton \o-ní-ye-toŋ\ *vn* oniye·wa·ton : to be affected by some internal hurt or disease, to have the lungs affected, as in pulminary consumption

o·non·hho·ye·ya \o-nóŋ·ȟho·ye·ya\ *v* onónhhoye·wa·ya : to hear with one's ears < *Miš eya onónhhoyewayelo* I too hear with my ears. > – Bl

o·nu·ni \o-nú-ni\ *vn* o·wa·nuni [fr *nuni* get lost] : to wander in — **onuni·šniyan** *adv* : to the point, not at all wandering < *Taku oyasin ~ waĥelo* You speak everything to the point, asthey say to a joker. > — **onuni·ya** *va* onuni·wa·ya : to cause to wander in a place — **onuni·yan** *adv* : wanderingly, lost — **onuni·yata** *adv* : wandering – R Bl

o·nun·we \o-núŋ-we\ *n* : a bath tub

on \oŋ\ *prep* : for, on account of; of, by means of, with *i.e.* when used with cause or instrument < *Maza on kagapi* It was made of iron. *Si on can kin peta ekta onakab iyeya* With his foot he kicked suddenly a log into the fire. *Maka hlihlila on'iic'iyun* He smeared himself with dirt turned muddy. *Nazonspe cannunpa wan on, huhu! kin kawehweh apa ške lo* Good heavens! It was with an axe, they say, that he gave a blow breaking to pieces a pipe. *Tona išta on wanlakapi kin hena kokipa po* Fear those who see with their eyes. *Hena on onnitonpi kta* On their account you will be injured. *Taku mitawa on owicakiyapi kta* With what is mine they will be helped. *Taku tona cic'upi owasin on miksuya po* Remember me with what I have given all of you. > – Note: when used alone, *on* means "with". < *Na taha kpanyanpi kin ohomni waso na on tušu kin hena pahta* And she cut around in strips a tanned hide, and with it she bound the tent poles. *Tatanka pizi wan ota latkan ca on aiyahanble lo* With you drinking up much buffalo bull gall, you had dreams. > — *prep contrac of* on'etanhan – at the end or at times within the sentence, what has just been said is : the reason, that is why – B.H.96.8,11

on'·a·zin·pi \óŋ-ziŋ-pi\ *n* : a nipple – *See* azín

on·ca·blu o·ju \óŋ-ca-blu o-jù\ *n* : a pile of snow or rubbish carried together by the wind, the place where snow *etc.* are so piled – Bl

on·ci \oŋ-cí\ or \uŋ-cí\ – Cf the following under "un" úncihi, úncihiya, uncíši, uncíšicala, *etc.*

on·c'i·kpa·ni \óŋ-c'i-kpa-ni\ *vn* ón·mi·c'ikpani and perhaps ón·ma·-c'ikpani : to be poor, not able to sustain one's self — **onc'ikpani·yan** *adv* : in a destitute condition < ~ *waun* I am very much in need. >

on·c'un·ni·ca \óŋ-c'uŋ-ni-ca\ *vn* on·ma·c'unnica : to be delayed, be prevented, to wait until the thing cannot be done — **onc'unni·lya** *va* onc'unni·lwa·ya : to stop, keep from doing, to prevent, hinder

on'·e·ci·ya·tan·han \ó-e-ci-ya-taŋ-haŋ\ *adv* : by means of, on account of

on'·e·tan·han \óŋ-e-taŋ-haŋ\ *adv* : therefore, for that cause

on·gla·kca·pi \óŋ-gla-kca-pi\ *n* : the narrow-leaved cone flower – Note: this plant grows in the hills; it is used as a tooth-ache medicine *See* icáhpe hu

on·glo·ge \óŋ-glo-ǧe\ *n* : a shirt

on·glo·hpe *or* **ongluhpe** \óŋ-glo-ȟpe\ *n* : one's occupation, work to be accomplished, burden to carry and disposed of < ~ *maota* Many are my burdens to carry, *i.e.* much work and not time. > – MO

on·glu·ze \óŋ-glu-ze\ *n* : things attended to, matters in hand < ~ *maota kaca* It is fitting I have much to attend to. > – Bc

on·gna·wi·ca·ške \óŋ-gna-wi-ċà-ške\ *n* : *archaic,* a bed – *See* oyúnke HM

on·gna·ye \óŋ-gna-ye\ *adv* : under pretense < ~ *kaȟkaȟ ahitipelo* They came and coughing under pretense pitched their tents. > – Bl

on hun·ka·lo·wan·pi i·ye·ce·ca \oŋ huŋ-ká-lo-waŋ-pi i-yè-ce-ca\ *n* : the slender beard-tongue, so called because the plant resembles somewhat the *hunkatacanunpa,* the wand used in *hunkalowanpi* ceremonies. Its leaves are opposite, their position reminding one of the strains of horse hair attached to the *hunkatacannunpa* at intervals – Bl #5

on'·i·glu·ja·ja·pi \óŋ-i-glu-ja-ja-pi\ *n* : a wash basin

on·jin·jin·tka \óŋ-jiŋ-jiŋ-tka\ *n* : the rose, roses, rosebuds < ~ *hu* rosebushes, ~ *mazognaka* canned tomatoes >

On·jin·jin·tka Wa·kpa \On-jiŋ-jíŋ-tka Wa-kpà\ *np* : the Rosebud River in south central South Dakota, or also Montana

on·ki·ci·ška·ta·pi \óŋ-ki-ci-škà-ta-pi\ *v recip of* ónškata : to jest, joke or banter each other, as persons within a certain degree of affinity are at liberty to do among the Dakotas – R

on·ki·ška·ta \óŋ-ki-ška-ta\ *va archaic* on·wa·kiškata [fr *onškata* brag, jest] : to boast, brag, joke with one, to talk as one pleases with – Note: to boast *etc.* is a privilege in Siouan society allowed only between brothers-in-law and sisters-in-law – R

on·na·pe wa·to·gya \óŋ-na-ṗe wa-tò-gya\ *adv* [fr *oŋ* the reason being + *napé* to flee + *watogya* to ruin or to take vengence] : as a threat, being a dangerous person, *i.e.* one with weapons < ~ *mazawakan, mazaska bluha kte* I should have a rifle and money for emergency's sake, *i.e.* to be prepared for anything.> – Bl WHL

on·na·ptan \óŋ-na-ptaŋ\ *adj* : sloping < *ȟeónnaptan* a side-hill >

on·pa *or* **unpa** \óŋ-ṗa\ *va* wa·onpa : to lean, place or lay away any long object in a reclining attitude < *Wayaka kin tima pahta onpapi* The captive was placed tied up inside >

on·spe \o-spé\ *vn* on·ma·spe unkon·spe·pi : to know how to do a thing < *Onmaspe wanji glahniga po* Select one thing of your own that I know how to do. > — **onspe·ka** \oŋ-spé-ka\ *vn* at times *neg* : to know how to do a thing – Note: sometimes the "ka" introduces the *neg* sense of *onspešni* not to know how — **onspe·kiya** \oŋ-spé-ki-ya\ *va* onspe·wa·kiya onspe·ma·kiya onspeci·ci·ya : to teach, to cause to know how < *onspeic'iciya* to learn >

on·s'co·ka·la·ka \oŋ-s'co-ka-la-ka\ *n* : a loafer, one who loafs on horseback a great deal and thus has lean horses <~ *canke* That is why he is a loafer, as is said of a loafer's lean horse. > – Bl

on·s'ha·ha \oŋ-s'há-ha\ *adj* : sitting restlessly, wishing to get away < *Ungnahela ons'mahaha yelo* All at once, I had a desire to travel. > – BT Bl

on·ši \óŋ-ši\ *adj* : miserable, poor < *Na wanna kéya ~ íyahan* And now a poor old turtle stepped on it. > — **on·ši·c'i·ya** *or* **onši·ic'iya** \óŋ-ši-c'i-ya\ *v refl* onši·mi·c'iya : to make one's self miserable, to pretend to be

---

\a\ father \e\ they \i\ machine \o\ smoke \u\ lunar \an, aŋ\ blanc Fr. \in, iŋ\ ink \on, oŋ, un, uŋ\ soon, confier Fr. \c\ chair \ǧ\ machen Ger. \j\ fusion \clusters: bl, gn, kp, hšl, etc...\ b[e]lo ... said with a slight vowel **See more in the Introduction, Guide to Pronunciation**

in misery <*Hecena keya ceya iyaya na lila onšiic'iya* Finally the turtle went weeping and making himself as if really poor. >

on·ši·h'an \óŋ-ši-ȟ'aŋ\ *vn* óši·wa·h'an [fr *onši* miserable + *h'an* to act] : to be humble, to act humbly — **onših'an·ka** *vn* onši·wa·h'anka : to be humble, to try to excite compassion, to fawn — **onših'an·pi** *n* : humility

on·ši·i·c'i·ca·hya \óŋ-ši-i-c'i-ca-ȟya\ *adv* : humbling self deeply < ~ *pasto* with knees or face to the ground to humble one's self > - B.H.43.11

on·ši·ka \óŋ-ši-ka\ *adj* on·ma·šika on·un·ši·pika : poor, destitute, miserable

on·ši·ki·h'an \óŋ-ši-ki-ȟ'aŋ\ *va* onši·wa·kih'an [fr *onših'an* act humble] : to humble one's self to another, act humble towards

on·ši·ki·la *also* **onšikilaka** \óŋ-ši-ki-la\ *v poss* onši·wa·kila : to have mercy on one's own < *Ate ... oyate kin onšiwicakila ye* Father, ... have mercy on your people. > - Pb.35

on·ši·la \óŋ-ši-la\ *va* onši·wa·la onši·ma·la : to have mercy on, to pity < *Kola, onšiunlapo* Friend, take pity on us. > — *interj* : Poor thing! - Note: the word is said by women to infants — **onšila·ka** \óŋ-ši-la-ka\ *va* ónši·wa·laka : to have mercy, to pity

on·ši·ši·ya \óŋ-ši-ši-ya\ *adv red of* onšiya : dolefully, pitifully < ~ *ceyaya* to sob dolefully > - B.H.35.3, 117.20

on·ši·ya \óŋ-ši-ya\ *adv* and perhaps *adj* : poorly, miserably < *Tuwa ~ wanyankapi kin onšila wicaši* He told them to pity the one they see in misery. Micinkši, ~ miye ekta iyotiyekiya mayahipi Nephew, in your misery you all have come to me with your troubles. *Hokšicala ~ hpaya cin wanyanka* I saw the little lad lying in misery. >

on·ši·ya·ca *or* **onši·yeca** \óŋ-ši-ya-ca\ *adj* ónši·ma·yaca : wretched, miserable

on·ši·ya·kel \óŋ-ši-ya-kel\ *adv* : pitifully, sadly < ~ *yanka* to sit in a wretched state >

on·ška·ta \óŋ-ška-ta\ *vn* on·wa·škata : to brag, boast, jest, to talk as one pleases, as brothers and sisters-in-law are priveleged to do among the Dakotas

on·špa \oŋ-špá\ *n* : a piece or part of anything < ~ *oniwaja* It concerns you partly, or you are concerned in it. > — **onšpa·la** *n dim* : a little piece

on·štin·ma kpa·t'a \óŋ-štiŋ-ma kpa-t'à\ *v* : to kill one's own by lying on in one's sleep - B.H.99.4

on·štin·ma ni·hin·ci·ya \óŋ-štiŋ-ma ni-hìŋ-ci-ya\ *v* : to feel scared in one's sleep - B.H.31.10

on·štin·ma·pi·hin \óŋ-štiŋ-ma-pi-hiŋ\ *n* [fr *on* with + *ištinmapi* they sleep + *hin* hair] : the eye-lashes < *Onštinmapihinpi acahsusu iwayayelo* I spoke of forming droplets of ice on the eye-lashes. > - Bl

on·štin·ma·t'a \óŋ-štiŋ-ma-t'a\ *v* : to die in one's sleep, or to be very sound asleep — **ónštinmat'a·ya** *va* : to cause one to sleep very soundly - B.H.2.15

on·šun·k'na·sa·pi hu \óŋ-šuŋ-k'na-sa-pi hu\ *n* : the wolf berry - *Syn* zuzeca tawote #10

on·šun·k'o·yu·spa·pi \óŋ-šun-k'o-yù-spa-pi\ *n* : the wild honeysuckle, *tatawabluška tacanhlogan* - Note: the wild honeysuckle is used by chewing and rubbing on the hands - #8

on·tan·tan·han \oŋ-táŋ-taŋ-haŋ\ *prep* and *adv* : for the sake of < *Wakantanka caje kin ~* for the sake of God's name > - B.H.49.2, 117.9

on·ton \óŋ-toŋ\ *vn* ón·ma·ton ón·un·ton·pi : to be injured < *Hena on onnitonpi kta* You will be hurt by these. > — **onton·ic'iya** *v refl* ónton·mi·c'iya : to injure one's self — **onton·šniyan** *adv* : without being hurt < *Daniel igmu tanka egna ~ yankahe* Daniel was sitting unharmed among lions. > — **onton·yan** *va* onton·wa·ya : to hurt, wound, injure < *Ota ontonniyanpi šni* Many of you failed to be wounded. > - B.H.145.2

on·t'e·wa·cin \óŋ-t'e-wa-ciŋ\ *v* : to intend to die on account of < *Tokeš'unlaka wayatkanpi kin ~* It being as it was, she intended to die on account of your drinking. > - *Syn* IT'ÉWACIN Bl

on·wa·hin·yun·ton·pi \óŋ-wa-hìŋ-yuŋ-toŋ-pi\ *n* : annual erigeron - Note: so called because it was mixed, its blossoms with *nasula* brain, *tapí* liver, *tapišleca* spleen, and rubbed into the hides of animals to bleach them *Hecel skayela kpanyanpi* So they were dressed in bleaching. *See* more under *iniyan pejuta* WC.61 Bl #54

on·we·o·ju·ton·pi \oŋ-wé-o-ju-toŋ-pi\ *n* : fourth cavity of a ruminant's stomach - *Syn* tašoka Bl

on·we·ya \oŋ-wé-ya\ *n* : provisions < *Le ~ tehan bluha ktelo* Here I shall have supplies for a long time, *i.e. papa* dried meat. >

On·we·ya Wa·kan \Oŋ-wé-ya Wa-kàŋ\ *np* : Viaticum, the Eucharist received by a person in danger of dying - Pb.44

on·wi·yu·ta·pi \oŋ-wí-yu-ta-pi\ *n* [fr *on* by means of + *iyuta* to measure] : something to weigh or measure with, a standard measuring tool

on·wo·han·pi o·ce·ti \óŋ-wo-haŋ-pi o-cè-ti\ *n* a cooking range

on·ze \oŋ-zé\ *n* : the rump, anus

on·ze·hu \oŋ-zé-hu\ *n* : to copulate

on·ze·kte \oŋ-zé-kte\ *v* : to give birth to another child while still nursing one

on·ze·o·ka·štan·pi \oŋ-zé-o-ka-štaŋ-pi\ *n* : an injection

on·ze·pi·ja \oŋ-zé-pi-ja\ *v* : to be the older of two infants, one of which was born before the other was weaned - Bl

on·ze·slo·han \óŋ-ze-slo-haŋ\ *vn* : to slide on the buttox, as do some dogs or mules that sit and drag their rump by the front feet - WE Bl

on·ze·š'a·š'a·ki·ya \oŋ-zé-š'a-š'a-ki-ya\ *v* : to yelp, as wolves and coyotes do - Bl

on·ze·yu·gmu·za \oŋ-zé-yu-gmu-za\ *va* : to shut up or hold shut the anus

on·zi·na·tan \oŋ-zí-na-taŋ\ *n* : the tail strap

on·zi·wo·sla *or* **onziwoslal** \oŋ-zí-wo-sla\ *adv* : head over heels < ~ *najin, yanka* to stand with the heels up, to turn a summersault, *fig* to be in a flurry not to know what one is about >

on·zo·ge \oŋ-zo-ǧe\ *n* [fr *onze* the rump + *oge* a cover] : pants < ~ *pteca* knickerbocker pants, ~ *to* overalls, or blue jeans >

o·o \ő-ő'\ *n* : a wound, a place where one is shot

o·o·gna·ke \o-ó-gna-ke\ *n* : a holder < *petijanjan ska ~* a candlestick >

o·o·he \o-ó-he\ *n* [fr *ohán* to boil *e.g.* meat] : a boiling, enough to boil at once < ~ *wašte* something easily cooked, or *fig* something that fits or wears well, as shoes or clothes > - Bl

O·o·he·nun·pa \O-ó-he-nuŋ-pa\ *np* : the Two Kettles, a clan among the Teton Sioux < *Tatahpa kin le ~ he awagli ktelo* I shall bring the Two Kettles this buffalo breast. >

o·o·hi·ye \o-ó-hi-ye\ *n* [fr *ohíya* to win] : a victory

o·o·ju \o-ó-ju\ *v* oo·wa·ju [fr *ojú* to plant] : to plant in

o·o·ka·hni·hte·hi·ke \o-ó-ka-ȟni-ȟte-ȟi-ke\ *adj* : obscure - P Bl

o·o·ka·hnih wa·šte \o-ó-ka-ȟniȟ wa-štè\ *adj* : easily understood, obvious < *Ookahnih niwašte* You are easily understood. > - Bl B.H.259.10

o·o·ka·štan \o-ó-ǩa-štaŋ\ *va* [fr *okaštan* to pour *i.e.* liquids into] : to pour perhaps non-liguids into, as grain, salt, *etc.*

o·o·ki·hi \o-ó-ki-hi\ *v* : to be able to be helped < ~ *šica* hard to be able to be helped, *Hecel le wicoh'an kin ~ šica* It is so hard to be able to maintain this custom. > - MS. 489

o·o·ki·ye \o-ó-ki-ye\ *n* [fr *ókiya* to help] : an assistant, a servant

o·o·kšu \o-ó-kšu\ *n* : a load

o·o·k'e \o-ó-k'e\ *n* : a digging, as a mine < *maka* ~ an old cistern >

o·o·ma·ni \o-ó-ma-ni\ *n* : a walking on, a sidewalk < *Wakpala oguhan oyasin ocahšu ca ~ šice* It is hard walking on all the valley trails when covered with ice. ~ *tehike* It is a difficult treck. > - Bl D.200

o·on·pa \o-óŋ-ṗa\ *v* o·wa·onpa o·un·k'onpa·pi [fr *onpa* to put or place] : to put or place in

o·on·ši·la \o-óŋ-ši-la\ *n* or *adj* : hard to please perhaps < ~ *nišicelo* You are a hard one to please. > - BT D.33

o·o·pe·ton \o-ó-pe-toŋ\ *n* : a fare < *tiyopa* ~ a toll gate >

o·o·tan'·in \o-ó-taŋ-iŋ\ *vn* [fr *otan'in* to become manifest] : to be manifest through

o·o·wa \o-ó-wa\ *n* : a letter or character, as the letters of the alphabet, a figure or mark of any kind < *Šina ~ ša nainš to nainš gi ... kahpapi* A shawl marked in red or blue or brown ... was knocked down. > - D.113

o·o·wa·pta·ya \o-ó-wa-pta-ya\ *n* [fr *oowa* a character + *ptaya* together] : the alphabet

o·o·ya·ke \o-ó-ya-ke\ *n* [fr *oyaka* to tell, relate] : the act of telling a story, a narrative, relation

o·o·yu·hpa *or* **oeyuhpa** \o-ó-yu-ḣpa\ *n* : a rest area, a place of resting or throwing down burdens - R Bl

o·o·yu·spe \o-ó-yu-spe\ *n* : the handle of anything < *Itazipa ... ~ wašteya econpi* The bow handle ... was well done. > - MS.481

[1]**o·pa** \ō'-ṗa\ *va* ó·wa·pa ó·un·pa·pi : to go with, follow, to be present at, take part in < *Oyate kin lila oimniciye ca el owapa.* I joined up with the people who had really attended a meeting. *Miye kin el omapa šni* When I did so he failed to join me. > - B.H.301.7

[2]**o·pa** \o-pá\ *adv* : in or along in < *Yunkan wakpala wan ~ canku ca opaya aya ewicunkiglegapi* And then we overtook them going along a creek in a ravine that served as a road. > - *Syn* EL UN

o·pa·gi \o-ṗá-ġi\ *va* o·wa·pagi unko·pagi·pi : to fill or cram a pipe with tobacco < *Cannunpa wan opagipi na wicitokab eonpapi* A pipe was filled and carefully placed before them. *Omáyakipagi šni, toka?* How is it you did not pack it for me? as they would say when on visiting the pipe was not offered. > — *n* : a pipeful of tobacco

o·pa·ha *also* **maya opaha** \o-ṗá-ha\ \ma-yá o-pà-ha\ *v* o·wa·paha : to push over a bank - R

o·pa·hi \o-pá-hi\ *v* o·wa·pahi [fr *pahi* to collect] : to gather or pick up into

o·pa·hci \o-pá-ḣci\ *n* : a ravine, a hollow, the hollow among the hills where creeks head, a gully with or without water

o·pa·hle·ca \o-ṗá-ḣle·ca\ *v* o·wa·pahleca [fr *pahleca* pull to pieces] : to tear in — **opahlece** *n* : a rent

o·pa·hlo·ka \o-ṗá-ḣlo-ka\ *v* o·wa·pahloka [fr *pahloka* to pierce] : to pierce in, to wear holes in, as a sick man's bones do when they come through the flesh — **opahloke** *n* : a hole < *ceškikan* ~ a button hole, *Na taha k'on hena on wihuta ~ el cel ikanyan na can pteptecela on ecel okatan* And he fixed fast the deer skins by means of small wooden pegs and thus having handle holes in the bottom edge. >

o·pa·hta \o-pá-ḣṫa\ *v* opa·wa·hta [fr *pahta* to bind] : to tie or bind in < *Šina wanji tanka opahtapi kte* In a large blanket it will be tied up, *i.e.* a turtle. > — **opahta·hta** \o-ṗá-ḣta-ḣta\ *v red* : to tie all up in — **opahte** \o-pá-ḣṫe\ *n* : a package, a bundle, a bale of blankets, a bunch of beads - B.H.35.13, 201.15

o·pa·kin·sla·sla \o-ṗá-ǩiŋ-sla-sla\ *adv* : wiping the dirt away < *Išta kin ~ iyewakiyelo* In wiping the dirt from my eyes, I recognized it. > - Bl

o·pa·mna \o-ṗá-mna\ *vn* : to rip *e.g.* a seam — *n* : a rip or rend

o·pa·na·kse·ye \o-pá-na-kse-ye\ *n* : a gibbet - B.H. 147.22

o·pan·ga \o-ṗáŋ-ġa\ *vn* o·ma·panga : to be bulky, to hinder or impede one, as cumbersome clothes do — **opange·ca** *vn* o·ma·pangeca : to be hindered by bulky articles, to be bulky — **opangece** *adj perhaps* o·ma·pangece : to have on too many clothes - Bl

o·pan·hya \o-ṗáŋ-ḣya\ *va* opan·hwa·ya : to hinder, impede — *adv* : bulky, not compressed — **opanhyakel** \o-ṗáŋ-ḣya-ǩel\ *adv* : bulkily — **opanhye·la** : not well arranged, bulkily

o·pa·pa \o-pá-ya\ *adv perhaps red* [fr *opá* along in] : many along in, as a herd of cattle grazing along a creek — **opapa·ya** *adv perhaps red of* opaya : along in < *Canku ~ ewicaglepi* They were placed along in the road. > - B.H.283.3

o·pa·pin·sla·sla i·ye·ya \o-pá-ṗiŋ-sla-sla i-yè-ya\ *v* : to wipe or rub clean < *išta kin* ~ to rub impurities out of the eyes > - Note: the more correct form of the word is *opakinslasla* Bl

o·pa·pon *or* **opapun** \o-ṗá-ṗoŋ\ *n* : the border or edge of anything, the stripe of a blanket, the edge of a book, the stripes or points that are put into which blankets to show their size < *Canke (wikan) ihanke on winyan tašina ~ el iyakaška* And so with the end of a leather thong the woman bound her blanket to the stripe. > - MS.353

o·pa·pson *or* **opapsun** \o-pá-psoŋ\ *v* o·wa·papson [fr *papson* pour out] : to pour out into, to spill into

o·pa·ptan \o-pá-ptaŋ\ *v* [fr *paptan* to turn over] : to turn over < ~ *iyeya* to roll over quickly > — **opaptanptan** *vn* : to roll over and over in anything — **opaptanyan** \o-pá-ṗtaŋ-yaŋ\ *va* o·wa·paptanyan : to roll anything on or into

o·pa·pun *or* **opapon** \o-ṗá-ṗuŋ\ *n* : and edge - Cf opápon

o·pa·pun·tan·han \o-ṗá-ṗuŋ-ṫaŋ-haŋ\ *adv* : from under the bottom edge of a tent

o·pa·seb \o-ṗá-seb\ *va contrac of* opasepa : to keep with care < ~ *gnaka* to lay away with care >

o·pa·se·pa \o-ṗá-se-ṗa\ *va* o·wa·pasepa : to keep with care

o·pa·si \o-ṗá-si\ *v* o·wa·pasi [fr *pasi* to escort] : to follow after in, as in a road

o·pa·ska \o-ṗá-ska\ *vt* : to press down and flatten *e.g.* dough in a bread pan < *aguyapi* ~ to press or perhaps

---

\a\ father \e\ they \i\ machine \o\ smoke \u\ lunar \an, aŋ\ blanc Fr. \in, iŋ\ ink \on, oŋ, un, uŋ\ soon, confier Fr. \c\ chair \ġ\ machen Ger. \j\ fusion \clusters: bl, gn, kp, hšl, etc...\ b[e]lo ... said with a slight vowel
See more in the Introduction, Guide to Pronunciation

knead bread > - Note: *wópaska* a bread pan for baking *Syn* YUT'INZA
o·pa·skan \o-ṗá-skaŋ\ *v* : to melt by lying on < *Unkopaskanpi eti ktelo* They will camp with us giving a melt, *i.e.* camp here at the snow, > - Bl
o·pa·sla·ta \o-ṗá-sla-ta\ *v* : to stick in, as a sliver or splinter < *Can ómapaslata* I ran a splinter into *e.g.* my hand. >
o·pa·sle·ca \o-ṗá-sle-ca\ *va* : to split, slice, cut *e.g. wasna* in something — **opasle·sleca** *v red* : to cut up < *Na wasna wan icu na can wakšica wan el ~ na k'u* And she took some for pemmican, pulverized it in a wooden dish, and gave it to him. > - MS.143
o·pa·spa \o-ṗá-ṡpa\ *v* o·wa·paspa : to push under in the water, to press down into the water — **opaspa·spa** *v red* : to keep pressing down into the water - Bl
o·pa·šni·ya \ó-pa-šni-ya\ *va* ópašni·wa·ya : to except, exempt, exclude
o·pa·šu·šu-ja \o-ṗá-šu-šu-ja\ *v* : to mash up in
o·pa·šwo·ka \o-ṗá-šwo-ka\ *v* : to push in *e.g.* a stick and splash
o·pa·tan \o-ṗá-taŋ\ *va* o·wa·patan : to push into, to mash up in — **opatan·tan** *v red* : to be mashing up in
o·pa·ti·ca \o-ṗá-ṫi-ca\ *va* o·wá·patica : to stick or push in or under, as a handspike — **opatil** \o-ṗá-ṫil\ *va contrac* : to push under, as a crowbar
o·pa·tkons \ó-ṗa-tkoŋs\ *va contrac of* opatkonza : to put even with, make flush with — **opatkon·syela** *adv* : in line, fronting one way, facing one way - *Syn* ÁKIYEHAN WE
o·pa·tkon·za \ó-ṗa-tkoŋ-za\ *va* : to make flush, even with
o·pa·t'a \o-ṗá-t'a\ *va* : to kill by pressure in, as a cat in a sack, or young animals in their mother's womb
o·pa·wa·ga \o-ṗá-wa-ġa\ *va* o·wa·pawaga [fr *pawaga* roll or twist in hand] : to roll over anything in the hand, to rub in the hands
o·pa·win·ge \o-ṗá-wiŋ-ġe\ *adj* : one hundred — **opawinge·ge** *or* **opawin·hwinge** *adv* : by hundreds
o·pa·wi·wi \o-ṗá-wi-wi\ *adv* : tangled together in a mass, many, *e.g.* a great many magots, or a great many people — **opawiwi·s'e** *adv* : shaking, as a mass of anything
o·pa·wi·ya \o-ṗá-wi-ya\ *adv* : many together, as a herd
o·pa·ya \o-ṗá-ya\ *adv* : along in < *canku ~* along in the way, *Na wanna wakpa cik'ala kin ~ akicita kin akiyunka* The soldier spent the night along in the small creek. *Wakpala kin ~ ya po* Go along in the creek. > — **opayaya** *adv red* : along in < *Babylon makoce kin el wakpala kin ~ Sion unkiksuyapi can unyankapi* We were in the land of Babylon along a stream when we recalled you O Sion. > - B.H.135.17
o·pa·ye·ya \o-ṗá-ye-ya\ *v* [fr *ópa* join] : to include, add to, to cause to join - WHL
o·pa·zan \o-ṗá-zaŋ\ *va* o·wa·pazan : to push into or under, as into a sheath or belt, to push under and over, to interlace, as in making baskets — **opazan·yan** *adv* : running under — **opazan·zan** *v red* o·wa·pazanzan : to weave into - B.H.55.11
o·pa·zo \o-ṗá-zo\ *n* : a protuberance
o·pa·zon·ta \o-ṗá-zoŋ-ṫa\ *va* o·wa·pazonta : to wrap around, wind up in, as a dead body in a winding sheet, or a spool with thread
o·pce·bye·la \o-pcé-bye-la\ *adv* : for a short time < *~ ob ye* She went together briefly. *~ wowicala yuhapi* They believed for awhile. > - B.H.14.2, 200.21, 244.14

o·pe \o-ṗé\ *n* : a blade as of a knife, a plow share, the edge, the sharp part of anything < *miyokšijapi ~* a pocketknife blade, *nazonspe ~* an axe blade > - B.H. 116.3
o·pe·han \o-ṗé-haŋ\ *v* o·wa·pehan [fr *ṗehán* to fold] : to fold up in — **opehe** *n* : a fold, a bolt of cloth
o·pe·i·c'i·ya \ó-ṗe-i-c'i-ya\ *v refl* : to side with, to follow - Note: the fast form of the word is *óbic'iya* - B.H.3.9
o·pe·ji ka·šla k'el \o-ṗé-ji ka-šlà k'el\ *n perhaps* : a certain place somewhere near the Platte River in Nebraska where a Lakota saw hay cut for the first time - Bl
o·pe·ki·ca·ton \o-ṗé-ki-ca-toŋ\ *v* ope·we·caton ope·un·kicaton·pi [fr *opeton* to purchase] : to buy for one with one's own money — **opeki·citon** *v* ope·we·citon : to buy in place of another — **opeki·ton** *v poss* ope·wa·kiton ope·un·kiton·pi : to buy or purchase one's own — **opeki·tonpi** *part* : redeemed, redeeming — **opekitonyan** *va* opekiton·wa·ya : to cause to redeem
o·pe·mni \o-ṗé-mni\ *va* o·wa·pemni unko·pemni·pi : to wrap around, as a garment; to be wrapped in — **opemni·yan** *adv* : wrapped around < *~ un* to be wrapped around >
o·pe·sto \o-ṗé-sto\ *n* : a point
o·pe·ton \o-ṗé-toŋ\ *va* ope·wa·ton ope·un·ton·pi : to buy, purchase, to hire
o·pe·ya \ó-pe-ya\ *adv* : with, together with < *Anpetu 60 niopeyapi waun kte lo* I shall be with you all for 60 days. *Wakantanka niopeya un ni* May God be with you. *winyan wicópeya* among women > — *va* ópe·wa·ya : to cause to go with
o·pe·ya un \ó-ṗe-ya uŋ\ *n* : a member, adherent, one belonging to a gang - Bl
[1]**o·pi** \o-ṗí\ *v perhaps* : to be pleased < *~ šni* to be displeased, *Takuku ~ šni on t'in kta awacin* He figured he would die since he was displeased with trifles, *i.e.* he was not contented. > - B.H.86.14, 109.5
[2]**o·pi** \ó-ṗi\ *n* or *part* : a wound, wounded, one wounded - B.H.112.3
o·pi·ca·ka \o-ṗí-ca-ka\ *v* : to be good, a little better than another < *Ataya coco welo,* It is entirely soft, *i.e.* soft ground after the melting of snow, *oeti šicelo* it was a bad place to be camped; *hececa k'eyaš aliya ekta hinajin yo, tokeš opicakelo* such though as it is come and stand climbing here, as it is a little better place, *i.e.* perhaps it is not so bad after all. > - Bl
o·pi·c'i·ye \o-ṗí-c'i-ye\ *n* and *v perhaps* : a good place for resting, a camping site *Syn* OHEGLE WE — *v refl* : to act < *tawacinhinyansyakel ~* to act in a melancholic way > - *See* opiic'iya
o·pi·i·c'i·ya \o-ṗí-i-c'i-ya\ *v refl* : to form an opinion and act for one's self, on one's own responsibility, to conduct one's self, to ready one's self < *Ptanškiška iyecel opinic'iyelo, škinnic'iyelo* Like the up and down, right and left movement of the otter, so is your movement and conduct. > - D.2, and 35
o·pi·je·ca \o-ṗí-je-ca\ *adj* : wrinkled, as an old person
o·pi·ki·la *or* **opikilaka** \o-ṗí-ki-la\ *vn* opi·wa·kila : to be satisfied with *e.g.* food < *~ unkomanipi; šikigla unkomanipi* We are travelling well enough, *i.e.* making headway; we are getting on pretty well. > - Bl
o·pi·šye·la \o-ṗí-šye-la\ *adv* [fr *pija* wrinkled] : wrinkled in < *~ un* to be wrinkled in face >
o·pi·ya \o-ṗí-ya\ *v* : to tie with, be alike, to renew, mend - BD
o·pi·ye \o-ṗí-ye\ *n* : a box or chest, a place wherein are put away and kept things — *vn* [fr *piya* to renew] :

to mend or make well < ~ *šica* bad to doctor, or hard to make well >

[1]o·po \ó-ṗo\ *vn* : to be warped, to be shrunken

[2]o·po \o-ṗó\ *vn* o·ma·po : to be swelled

o·po·gan \o-ṗó-ġaŋ\ *va* o·wa·pogan : to blow in upon, to blow out from — **opoh** \o-ṗóḣ\ *va contrac* [fr *opogan* blow in or out] : to blow away, blow from the mouth < ~ *iyeya* to cause to blow >

o·po·po \ó-po-po\ *v red of* ópa : to be warped, shrunken < *Capa s'e šake ~ kaca* His fingernails are so shrunken as to be similar to a beaver's claws, as is said when a person has long fingernails. > – Bl

o·po·po·ya \o-pó-ṗo-ya\ *vn red of* oṗó : to be made open and swollen, as a sore or wound < *ocape kin ~* the wounds gaping > – B.H.130.10

o·psun·psun \ó-psuŋ-psuŋ\ *va* : to rinse, to draw back and forth in the water

o·psun·wa·he *or* **opšunwahe** \o-psúŋ-wa-he\ *n* : small things broken off, like the teeth of a comb – Bl

o·pšun·pšun·ye·la \ó-pšuŋ-pšuŋ-ye-la\ *adv* : making use of little things, in a slack way < ~ *ic'ignaka po* Set aside for yourself the use of little things, *i.e.* Be ready, for we will go soon > – Bl

o·pšun·wa·he \o-pšúŋ-wa-he\ *n* – *See* opsúnwahe

o·pta \ó-pṫa\ *adv* or *prep* : through, across (locally) < *Yunkan blaye wan ~ ya ške. ~ ya* It is said he went across the lake. Across he went. > — **opta·pta** \ó-pṫa-pṫa\ *adv red* : through and through – B.H.54.3, 283.4 Bl

o·pta·ye \o-ptá-ye\ *n* : a herd of animals — *adv perhaps* : in a bunch < ~ *yankapi* They sat together in a bunch. *Pte ~ kin etan aglinapapi* They brought out some of the buffalos in a bunch. >

o·pte \ó-pṫe\ *n* [fr *yupta* to cut from or out] : what is left over, leavings

o·pte·bye·la \o-pté-bye-la\ *adv* : a little while or distance < ~ *el waun kta* I shall be in after awhile. *Letanhan na owakpamni ~* It is a little ways from here to Pine Ridge. ~ *tankal aye wicaši* He told them to go out-side for awhile. > – B.H.284.13

o·pte·ca \o-pṫé-ca\ *adv* : less

o·pte·he·ca \ó-pṫe-he-ca\ *adv* : almost empty, as is said of vessels

o·pte·kte \o-pṫé-kte\ *n* : a slaughter house

o·pte·li·c'i·ya \o-pṫé-li-c'i-ya\ *v refl* opte·lmi·c'iya : to cease from, as from anger or strife, to become gentle – *See* aópteca

o·pte·lye·la *or* **optébyela** \ó-pte-lye-la\ *adv* : for a little while, for a short time < ~ *ocic'u welo* I loan it to you for a short time. ~ *tatóheya unglapi ktelo* We shall head for home upwind for a short while. > – Bl

o·ptu·ḣa·ḣa·la \o-ptú-ḣa-ḣa-la\ *n* : crumbs, leavings < *Winuhcala, pápa ~ eša igni yo; wanagi el mahipelo* Old woman, go hunt for some scraps of *papa* dried meat; the spirits have come to me. > – *Syn* ÓPTE Bl

o·pu·gi \o-ṗú-ġi\ *va* o·wa·pugi : to stuff, fill, to push into, as hay into moccasins — **opugi·pi** *n* : a stuffing — **opugi·ton** *va* opugi·wa·ton : to put in stuffing, to do the art of taxidermy in stuffing and mounting a bird or animal for display — **opugiton·yan** *adv* : in a stuffed manner

o·pu·hli \o-ṗú-ḣli\ *va* : to stuff anything into, as an old coat into a broken window — **opuhli·yahan** *adj* : stopped up, clogged – Note: *iyopuhli* gun wadding B.H. 129.19

o·pu·htin·yan·kel \o-ṗú-ḣtiŋ-yaŋ-kel\ *adv* : angrily < ~ *ia* to speak with anger, ~ *iwaya* I talked angrily. > – Bl

o·pu·ske·bya \o-ṗú-ske-bya\ *adv* : filtered – Bl

o·pu·ski·ca \o-ṗú-sk̇i-ca\ *va* o·wa·puskica : to press down in — **opuskil** \o-ṗú-sk̇il\ *va contrac* : to press in

o·pu·sya \o-ṗú-sya\ *adv* : teeming with, infested with *e.g.* vermin in something < *Tehmunga ~ yankapi* It was teeming with flies. > – RA

o·pu·š'in \o-ṗú-š'iŋ\ *n* : a curve, as of the outer side opposite the string of a bow – *Syn* IPÚŠ'IN Bl

o·pu·ta·ka \o-ṗú-ta-ka\ *v* o·wa·putaka [fr *putaka* to touch by hand] : to touch in < *Oyate el tuwa wayazan kin le oputakin kta, eya* He said he would touch one of the people feeling this pain. >

o·pu·tkan \o-ṗú-tk̇aŋ\ *va* o·wa·putkan : to dip into, put or lay in *e.g.* the fingers, to sop, as with bread < *Ninape kin uyin na micuwi kin el ~ yo* Put your fingers and send your hand on my back. >

o·pu·za \o-ṗú-za\ *vn* : to be covered with *e.g.* vermin *etc.*, being dry as it were < *Oko wanilya opuzapi* There was no place without being infested. >

o·pu·ze \o-ṗú-ze\ *n* : the shore, the dry edge of a river or sea < ~ *kin el inajin* He stepped on the shore. > – B.H.50.4, 175.8, 275.17

o·p'o \o-p'ó\ *n* : fog, steam; a dust cloud < *Pte otapi k'on ataya mak'op'o na egna tan'inšniya iyayapi.* Many were the buffalos that had traveled together and in a dust cloud that caused them to be invisible. *Na el op'o wan iwankab han wanyankapi* And in it they saw a cloud hovering above. >

o·p'o·sa *or* **op'oza** \o-p'ó-sa\ *adj* : clear and cold, with particles of snow in the air — **op'o·sya** *adv* : clear and cold

o·p'o·ya \o-p'ó'-ya\ *adv* : in a cloud, as of dust, *i.e. mak'op'oya*, snow *wa op'oya, etc.* < *Yunkan taku wan, heya, mak'op'oya naunk u* And then something, a swarm of lice, came gallopping. *Yunkan wa ~ inyankin na glinajin* And he ran into a snow cloud and stopped when he got home. *Kiyela kupi ecel ataya okšan mak'op'oya han na wanna glihunnipi* They have now reached home having come back recently with a dust cloud hovering all about. *Na lila tehan maka ~ han ecel wiyaya tka* And for a very long time the dust cloud remaining would thus move on. *Yunkan etanhan wanna maka ~ han* And then on that account the dust cloud now stayed. >

o·p'o·za \o-p'ó-za\ *adj* – *See* op'osa

o·san·ka·ya·kel \o-sáŋ-k̇a-ya-kel\ *adv* : void of game, such as deer *etc.* < ~ *yunkelo* It lies devoid of game, as is said of a creek. >

o·san·san·ke s'e \o-sáŋ-saŋ-ke s'e\ *adv* [fr *san* white] : as one who is white all over, as to hair and beard – Bl

o·sin·kpe·kpe·ya·kel \o-síŋ-kpe-kpe-ya-kel\ *adv* [fr *sinkpe* the muskrat] : in a sneaky way, sneaking, snooping around as does the muskrat < ~ *taku ecannon welo* You did something in a sneaky, covert way. > – *Syn* IYUPSEYAKEL Bl

o·sin·sin \o-síŋ-siŋ\ *vn* o·má·sinsin : to leave a mark, as tears drying on one

o·skab \ó-sk̇ab\ *va contrac of* óskapa : to adhere to, to climb — **oska·bya** *adv* : adhering, sticking to

o·ska·ka \o-sk̇á-k̇a\ *adj* : bare, as a tree whose leaves are fallen off; open, as a country without thickets

---

\a\ father \e\ they \i\ machine \o\ smoke \u\ lunar \an, aŋ\ blanc Fr. \in, iŋ\ ink \on, oŋ, un, uŋ\ soon, confier Fr. \c\ chair \ġ\ machen Ger. \j\ fusion \clusters: bl, gn, kp, hšl, etc...\ b^{e}lo ... said with a slight vowel
See more in the Introduction, Guide to Pronunciation

o·ska·pa \ó-sk̇a-ṗa\ *va* ó·wa·skapa **1** : to climb up or in *e.g.* a tree, a pole **2** : to adhere to perhaps, to stick in – B.H.223.2

o·ska·pi \ó-sk̇a-pi\ *n* : ornamental work, such as is put on pipe stems < *Pehin on wikan wan iyapehanpi, he ~ eciyapi.* They call ornamental work the cord wound up with a lock of hair. *waké ~* a curio or memento, ornaments attached to the walls of a tent. *~ s'e woyaka* to give a nice, clear talk > – Bl

o·ski·ca \ó-sk̇i-ca\ *adj* [fr *yuskica* press tight] : tight, drawn around, as a garment — **oskice·la** *adj* : tight, well-fitting

o·ski·ske \o-skí-ske\ *n* : a draw < *~ wan el unglicupi* We came back in a draw and headed for home, *i.e.* we got into a hollow in the countryside. > – Bl

o·ski·ski·ta \ó-sk̇i-sk̇i-ṫa\ *v red of* oskita : to bind up

o·ski·ta \ó-sk̇i-ṫa\ *v* : to bind up in, as a child

o·sku·mna *or* **oškumna** \o-skú-mna\ *adj* : having a fetid smell, a bad sour odor, as of a dirty scalp – Bl

o·sku·ya \o-sk̇ū'-ya\ *adj* : sour, *e.g.* as milk – Note: *skuya* sweet

o·slo·han \o-sló-haŋ\ *vn* o·ma·slohan : to slide, slip, slide down to the ground < *~ kic'un* to slide on *e.g.* a board, sled, or one's feet, *~ wec'un* I slid on my feet. > — *n* : a drawing or sliding in – D.247

o·slo·lya \o-sló-lya\ *va* oslo·lwa·ya : to know of < *Canku ~* He knew about the road. *Wakantanka oslolyapi šni* pagans, *Takuni oslolye šni* He knew nothing of it, *i.e.* of what had happened. > — **oslolya·pišniyankel** *adv* : unnoticed, not recognized – B.H.121.8, 283.7

o·slo·lye \o-sló-lye\ *n* : knowledge

o·sma·ka \ó-sma-ka\ *n* : a ditch, ravine, gulch, hollow, valley – B.H.172.6

o·smi·smi·ka \o-smí-smi-k̇a\ *adj* : without leaves, bare, as big-leaf trees in the cold of winter

o·sna·ze *or* osnazeca \o-sná-ze\ *n* : a scar

o·sni \o-sní\ *n* : cold weather, winter, year < *~ tanka wan hi* A deep cold winter occurred. > — *adj* : cold in < *Ti ~* It is cold in the house. > – Note: the word *špan* is used for frozen or frost-bitten *e.g.* fingers — **osni·ka** *or* **osni·ke** \o-sní-k̇a\ *adj* : cold

o·sni·ko \o-sní-k̇o\ *n* [fr perhaps *osni* the cold + *k̇o* to desire] : the screech owl – *Syn* PAGLA, POPOTKA Is

o·sni·sni \o-sní-sni\ *n red* [fr *osni* cold] : very cold weather

o·sni·ta·wa·na·p'in \o-sní-ta-wa-nà-p'iŋ\ *n* : a necktie, scarf, cape, or tippet

o·so \o-só\ *v* o·wa·so : to cut open *e.g.* the skin of an animal in preparing to skin it

o·son \o-sóŋ\ *va* [fr *son* to braid] : to braid, plait *e.g.* the hair — *n* : a braid of hair < *Winyan wan ~ k'el oyuspe, hecena mina icu na ~ nupin owaksa* A woman took hold of her braids, took a knife thus, and cut off both the braids. > – MS.560

o·so·ta \ō'-so-ṫa\ *v coll* [fr *yu* to cause + *sota* used up, made an end of] : they are all gone, used up, killed < *Wanna ~* Now all are gone. > – B.H.71.14

o·span·span·he·ca \o-ṡpáŋ-ṡpaŋ-he-ca\ *adj* : swelling and becoming doughy < *Omaspanspanheca* I am thawing >

o·spa·ya \o-ṡpá-ya\ *v* [fr *spaya* to dampen] : to become damp in — **ospaye** *n* : moisture

o·spe·ya \ó-spe-ya\ *va* : to sink, make sink

o·stag \ó-sṫag\ *v contrac of* óstaka : to be enfeebled — **osta·gya** *va* osta·gwa·ya : to make stick on

[1]**o·sta·ka** \o-sṫá-k̇a\ *v* [fr *staka* feeble, weary] : to be feeble, debilitated on account of

[2]**o·sta·ka** \ó-sṫa-k̇a\ *vn* o·ma·staka : to stick on or in *e.g.* dirt on a plow or mud in a house, to stick on as flesh

o·su·kan·lyu·za \o-sú-k̇aŋ-lyu-za\ *v* osunkan·lblu·za : to take one's choice, to take the best – R Bl

o·su·ta *or* **osute** \o-sú-ṫa\ *adj* : hard, tough in < *Hankeke waksapi na ~ ece yuzapi s'e* He was cut half and half, and it seemed hard in thus laying hold of him, as is said when a man, although little himself, has fleshy arms and legs, the word being applied also to a horse with short legs. > – Bl

o·su·ta·ya \o-sú-ṫa-ya\ *adv* : for good < *Ho lena ~ yuha yo, na ektonje šni yo* Well, hold onto these for good, and do not forget it. >

o·su·ton·yan \o-sú-toŋ-yaŋ\ *adv* : ripening, fit for use; *fig* fairly well < *~ econ* He did it fairly well. >

o·swa·han \ó-swa-haŋ\ *part perhaps* : caving in, as sand, coal, *etc.* when some is taken from below < *Na paha okise maya óswahe kin heca wanyanka* And he saw half the hill's river bank was caving in. > — **oswa·swaya** *also perhaps* **oswaya** *part* : sinking in, as feet in soft snow or soil – MS.563 Bl

o·s'a·mna \o-s'á-mna\ *adj* : sour smelling, smelling like stale or rancid meat, tainted < *si ~* feet that stink > – *Syn* H'AMNA

o·s'i·ca \ó-s'i-ca\ *n* : misfortune, bad luck, which suggests a sudden craning, throwing a person on his back. < *Hecel yaun kin, ~ ayakipa kte lo* So if it is you, misfortune will befall you, *i.e.* you will meet with bad luck for not listening to good advice. *~ akipe kin naké miyeksuyin kte* When bad luck comes to him, only then will he remember me, as an old lady once said. > – *Syn* WOTEḢI, TAKU ŠICE BE BT

o·s'i·c'i·ya *or* oziic'iya \o-s'í-c'i-ya\ *vn* [fr *s'i* or *zi* to rest, refresh] : to rest and refresh one's self < *Ungnahelahci anpetu wanji ~ yaun welo* All of a sudden one day I am taking a refreshing rest. > – BT

o·ša·pa \o-šá-pa\ *vn* : to be dirty in *e.g.* one's face <*Ištihuku maka unkošapapelo* Below our eyes dirt, dust, gathered. > – Bl

o·ši·ca \o-ší-ca\ *adj* : bad with, as one kind of food with another, not agreeing as sweet and sour < *Wabluška mayuta yelo, ~ kta secelo* Insects are eating me, it is like it should be a bad mix, as they would say when on account of a headache or kneeache or rheumatism they felt that a storm was coming. >

o·ši-ca-mna \o-ší-ca-mna\ *adj* : becoming spoiled, giving off a bad odor – Bl LHB

o·ši·ce·ca \o-ší-ce-ca\ *adj* and *n* : stormy, a storm < *Wi u k'on cetiyelo ca ~ kte lo. ~ ahiyelo* It will be stormy when the sun has come to start a fire. A storm arrived. > – Bl

o·ši·ce·ca·ke \o-ší-ce-ca-ke\ *adj* : unpleasant, as rainy weather, not pleasing, as certain country

o·ši·ce·ca·ki·ksu·ya \o-ší-ce-ca-ki-ksu-ya\ *v* : to know by one's feelings when bad weather is coming

o·ši·gla \o-ší-gla\ *adj* : irritable

o·ši·kši·ce·la \ó-ši-kši-ce-la\ *n* and *adj perhaps* : worthless things < *~ ece mayak'u welo, waštešte kin yakpahi na* You gave me only worthless things, take a bite out of the really good. > – Bl

o·ši·kši·lo·h'an·ka *and* **oši·lh'anka** \o-ší-kši-lo-ḣ'aŋ-ka\ *vn* oši·lwa·h'anka : to act badly, wickedly

o·ši·lya \o-ší-lya\ *adv* : in disorder < *Tipi kin ~ he lo* The room or house stands in or shows great disorder. > – Bl D.125

o·ši·lye o·h'an \o-ší-lye o-ḣ'àŋ\ *vn* ošilye o·wa·h'an : to act badly

o·ši·pa \ó-ši-ṗa\ *n* : clusters - B.H.62.14

o·ši·tki·gla \o-ší-tk̇i-gla\ *vn* [fr *šitkigla* to be angry with] : to be angry with — **ošitkigla·ya** *va* ošitkigla·wa·ya : to make angry, cause to suffer

o·škan \ó'-šk̇aŋ\ *n* : motion, movement < *Tka migluške k'on hehan ~ ewatonwe* But I observed movement when I had untied myself. >

o·škan·ši·lya \ó-šk̇aŋ-ši-lya\ *va* : to impede one's progress, to prevent from moving freely

o·ška·ta \o-šk̇á-ṫa\ *v* o·wa·škata [fr *škata* to play] : to play in — **oškate** *n* : play, diversion < *~ tipi* a playroom >

o·ški \o-šk̇í\ *n* : poor land, with hills and canyons < *wazi ~* a forest wilderness, *oblaye ~* a desert wilderness >

o·ški·i·ya·za o·can·ku \o-šk̇í-i-ya-za o-càŋ-ku\ *n* : a road from hill to hill as hidden after a heavy snowstorm - FB

o·škin·c'i·ye \o-šk̇íŋ-c'i-ye\ *n* : an occupation < *Le anpetu kin iyamatagle ca heon ~ mašicelo* Today is too much for me so that my job is no good for me. > — **oškin'·i·c'i·ya** *vn* oškin·mi·c'iya : to busy one's self about, be busy < *Tokel wicaša oškinc'iyapi he slolye wacinpi* They were anxious to know how men occupy their time. >

o·ški·ška \o-šk̇í-ška\ *adj* [fr *škiška* rough] : abrupt, rough in word, intricate

o·ški·ške·lya \o-šk̇í-šk̇e-lya\ *adv* : confusedly — **oškiške·ya** *also perhaps* **oškiškiya** *va* oškiške·wa·ya : to make complicated or confused, to create difficulties, to perplex — *adv* : with difficulty, crookedly

o·ški·ški *or* **oškiške** \o-šk̇í-šk̇i\ *n* : broken land, bad country, *i.e.* land with hills and canyons — **oškiški·ic'i·ya** *v refl* : to confuse one's self, as in disputing points - Bl

o·ško·kpa \o-šk̇ó'-kṗa\ *n* : a concavity, a hollow place < *Tawicu k'un lel ~ mahel kiglapi, i.e. hokšila kici* His wife had gone home here in a hollow, *i.e.* with her boy. >

o·šku·mna *or* **oskumna** \o-šk̇ú-mna\ *adj* : sour, spoiled, as food

o·šla \o-šlá\ *n perhaps* : an open place < *Makošla yunke el* when open country lay before him, *i.e.* bare and grassless ground, *šlayá* without covering > - *Syn* O-TINTOSKA

o·šlo·ka·han \o-šló-k̇a-haŋ\ *part* : peeling or coming off as a scab — **ošlokahe** *part in past time* : having come off or peeled — **ošlo·šlokahan** *part red* : continually peeling off

o·šme \o-šmé\ *n* : depth

o·šna·pi \ó-šna-pi\ *n* : crumbs, scraps - R Bl

o·šni·yan·yan \o-šní-yaŋ-yaŋ\ *vn* : to move about, as worms in the stomach

o·šo·gya \o-šó-gya\ *adv* [fr *šoka* thick] : thickly

o·šo·ka \o-šó-k̇a\ *adj* or *n* : thick — **ošoke** *n* : thickness

o·šo·še \o-šó-še\ *v* : to become turbid, mirky, muddy - Bl

o·šo·ta \o-šō'-ṫa\ *adj* [fr *šota* to smoke as does fire] : smoky, filled with smoke, as a tent — *n* : smoke < *Hecena mahpiya eciyatanhan ~ s'e hiyu na iyowotan'in šni* There was no vantage point, so in the end as if it were smoke a cloud came from there. *~ mat'in kte, misun, eya ške. ~ yelo, wipipaha egle po* My brother, I'll die of the smoke, they say he said. It is smoke, Set open the vent flaps. >

o·šo·ta·mna \o-šó-ta-mna\ *n* : the smell of smoke < *Na tatiye kin canli šota nainš ~ eša hena slolye wacinpi* And they thought they knew about the direction of the tobacco smoke or some smell of smoke. >

o·so·ta o·gna i·ya·ya \o-šō'-ṫa o-gna i-yà-ya\ *n* : a chimney - B.H.51.3

o·šo·ta t'a \o-šó-ta t'a\ *v* : to suffocate from smoke - D.196

o·šo·ta·ya \o-šō'-ṫa-ya\ *adv* : smoky < *Yunkan oyate wan wicoti ca lila wicomani na ~ wicoti* Then a group who set up camp did much traveling and their camp was smoky. > — *va* ošota·wa·ya : to make smoke

o·šo·ti·ya·ye \o-šō'-ṫi-ya-ye\ *n* : a chimney - *Syn* OŠO-TA OGNA IYAYE

o·špa·špa·ye \o-šṗá-šṗa-ye\ *adv red of* ošpaye : by groups < *~ ecel ipahlahlalya au* They came by groups as it was row by row. >

o·špa·ye \o-šṗá-ye\ *n* : a herd, a drove consisting of different kinds of animals, a company separated from the main body < *Šunkakanyanka ~ wanji ehakela manipelo* A group horseback traveled last. > — **ošpaye·tontonyan** *adv red* : in groups - Bl

o·špe \o-šṗé\ *n* a : a verse, a sentence, a saying - Note: in *ref* to Sacred Scripture *oégle* is used b : a piece or part of a section of land - Cf yušpa

o·štan \ó-šṫaŋ\ *va* : to put on, put in, as a cork, a handle into an axe *etc.* < *ogle, wapoštan, hanpa ~* to put on a coat, a hat, a pair of shoes > — *vn* : to be on *e.g.* a hoop, or in *e.g.* as is a stopper; to be in agreement with; to be in place of — *prep perhaps* : in place of, on, at — *adv perhaps* : on, at < *mazaškanškan wanjila ~* at one o'clock sharp, *Tunkašila taanpetu he ~ matonpi* I was born on Washington's birthday. *Wismahi ca el, i.e.* arrow, *oštanpi* It was the point that was fitted on *i.e.* the arrow. *Tooštan mankelo* I am in a rented house. > - Bl MS.481

o·štan·han \o-šṫáŋ-haŋ\ *part* : being in or on — *n* : a running watering sore — *vn* : to ooze out *e.g.* water from a sore

o·štan'·i·yo·ta·ka \o-šṫáŋ-i-yo-ṫa-ka\ *vn* : to take one's place as *e.g.* a temporary superior

o·štan·na·jin \o-šṫáŋ-na-jin\ *vn* : to take one's place, to be a substitute, a stand-in person - *Syn* OŠTANIYO-TAKA

o·šte \o-šté\ *adj* : deformed < *Omašte* I am misshapened. > - *See* ošteka

o·šte·gla \o-šté-gla\ *va* ošte·wa·gla [fr *ošte* grotesque + *gla* detest] : to mock, call names, revile, abuse, insult, defy < *Wakantanka ~* to blaspheme > — **oštegla·pi** *n* : contempt, opprobrious language

o·šte·ka \o-šté'-k̇a\ *adj* o·ma·šteka : ugly, deformed, crippled - *Syn* TANŠICA

o·šte·ka·ya \o-šté-k̇a-ya\ *va* : to unmold, spoil *e.g.* a good horse — **ošteke·kiya** \o-šté-ke-k̇i-ya\ *va* : to cripple, deform

o·šte·ke·šni \o-šté-ke-šni\ *adj* : inviolate, immaculate

o·šte·la \o-šté-la\ *adj* : misshapen

o·šte·šte·ya \o-šté-šte-ya\ *adv* : imperfectly, clumsily < *~ wicakuwapi* They teased them disagreeably, pestered them. > — **oštešteya·kel** *adv red of* ošteyakel : unpleasantly - D.45

o·šte·ya \o-šté-ya\ *adv* : imperfectly, clumsily; acciden-

\a\ father \e\ they \i\ machine \o\ smoke \u\ lunar \an, aŋ\ blanc Fr. \in, iŋ\ ink \on, oŋ, un, uŋ\ soon, confier Fr. \c\ chair \ǧ\ machen Ger. \j\ fusion \clusters: bl, gn, kp, hšl, etc...\ b[e]lo ... said with a slight vowel
See more in the Introduction, Guide to Pronunciation

tally, by chance — **ošteya·kel** \o-šté-ya-kel\ *adv* : deformedly

o·šti \o-ští\ *interj of strong disappointment and regret* : Oh alas! – Note: it would seem to be taken good-naturedly. It indicates sudden and unlooked for disappointment – *Syn* HUŠTÍ D.28 note 2

o·štu·lya \o-štú-lya\ *adv* : soft, not frozen < ~ *yanka* to remain soft, as meat buried in the snow > – Bl

o·šung i·hpe·ya \o-šúng i-hpè-ya\ *va* [fr *ošung* overly much + *ihpeya* to do violence] : to maltreat

o·šun·gšun·gye \o-šúŋ-gšun-gye\ *adv red* : very much, violently < ~ *ihpeya* to destroy things >

o·šun·gye \o-šúŋ-gye\ *adv* : too much, more than one can take care of, very much, violently < ~ *wo mak'u* He gave me more food than I could eat. ~ *ihpeya* to destroy or spoil things, *i.e.* breaking windows, tearing up things *etc.* *Lila anunk ~ ihpekiciyapi* They really spoiled things for both parties. *Hihanna kin honunpinyanwayin na wihpewayin kte* Tomorrow morning I shall make a surround and will do damage, *i.e.* kill many buffalos. *Wasna na papa ko ~ kin* It was a sure thing there was more than enough pemmican and dried meat, *i.e.* in great abundance. > — **ošun·gye·la** *or* **wošungya** *adv* : violently, very, *slang* lots < *Talo ~ yuhpa* He lay down more fresh meat than he was able to care for. > – R Bl D.271

o·šun·ka·yan·kel \o-šúŋ-ka-yaŋ-kel\ *adv archaic* : in a miserable condition < ~ *hapya* He lay in a pitiable state. > – Bl

o·šun·ke·ca·la·ka \o-šúŋ-ke-ca-la-ka\ *n* **1** : a very little thing **2** : a very sick person

o·šun·ko·wo·te \o-šúŋ-ko-wo-te\ *n* : a manger

o·šun·ko·yu·spe \o-šúŋ-ko-yu-spe\ *n* : a corral

o·šun·k'o·gle·ši·ca \o-šúŋ-k'o-gle-ši-ca\ *adj perhaps* : there being no room for large crowds

o·š'a·ka \o-š'á-ka\ *vn* : to become hard, as gravy in a kettle

o·š'e \o-š'é\ *n* : a drop *e.g.* of water — *vn* : to drop into — **oš'e·š'e** *vn red* : to drip into — **oš'e·ya** *va* : to make drop in, as water

o·ta \ó-ta\ *adj* : much, many < *Unkotapi* We are many. *wicota* a great company, crowd, *Išta mini maota* Many are my tears. *waniyetu maota* Many are my winters, years. *He ~ šunkmanon* He stole many horses. > – MS. 487

o·tab \o-táb\ *v of* otápa : to follow after one, as in a road < ~ *glau* to come following after one on one's way home, *oyé ~* to follow after one's track, *taku oye ~ omani* to walk following after something's track, *i.e.* to follow the track as of game > — **ota·btab** *v red* : to be tracking — **ota·bya** *v* : to trail, follow tracks

o·ta·can *also perhaps* **otancan** \o-tá-caŋ\ *n* : the principal part of anything, something very prominent and very good — **otacan·ke** *and perhaps* **otancanke** \o-tá-caŋ-ke\ *n* : something very good, very nice, the greatest, as giving something very nice

o·ta·he·la \ó-ta-he-la\ *adv perhaps* : many or much piled up

o·ta·he·na \ó-ta-he-na\ *adv* : on this side, as in meeting one suddenly on this side of the place where one was looking for him < ~ *iapi* They spoke of a former unsettled matter, as is said when coming back to something that was talked about but not settled. > – Bl

o·ta·he·pi \o-tá-he-pi\ *adv* : between places — **otahepi·yela** *adv* : by the way, between places

o·ta·ja \ó-ta-ja\ *n* : one of the four marks seen on the hoop used in the game *painyankapi*, a hoop game

o·ta·ka \ó-ta-ka\ *adj* : many, much – Note: the word also can mean *óta šni*, not much, nor many. *See* ^{3}ka Mi

o·ta·ki·ya \ó-ta-ki-ya\ *adv* : in many places, times, ways; often < *Otonwahe ~ wahokonwakiyin kte* I must give advice in many towns, *i.e.* cities in different directions. > – B.H.186.4

o·ta·ku·ye \o-tá-ku-ye\ *n* : brotherhood, relationship, relations, kinsfolk, kinship < *Palani ~* a Pawnee brotherhood > — **otakuye·ya** *v* : to form a relationship < *Hel Raguel eciyapi wan nitošpaye kin otakuyewicaya ca un welo* There one who is called Raguel who is of your kin with whom to form a relationship. > – D.220 B.H.123.3

o·tan·can \o-táŋ-caŋ\ *n* [fr *tancan* the body] : the chief, the greatest – *See* itáncan — **otancan·ke** \o-táŋ-caŋ-ke\ *n* : the greatest in numbers, as the greatest herd, the largest warparty — **otancanke·ya** *adv* : in the greatest numbers

o·tan·gla·kin·yan \o-táŋ-gla-kiŋ-yaŋ\ *n* : breadth – *Syn* OGLÁKINYAN

o·tan'·in \ó-táŋ-iŋ\ *vn* [fr *tan'ín* to be visible] : to be manifest, visible < *Tankaya ónitan'in kte lo* To a great extent you were visible. ~ *hecel slolwaya ca tanyan oblaka* He was visible so I spoke well that I knew him. *Si ecela otan'inpi* His feet alone showed. *Peji inkpa ecel ~ yelo* Tops of grass alone were visible, *i.e.* the snow was deep. > — **otan'in·ka** \ó-taŋ-iŋ-ka\ *vn* : to appear, be manifest – Note: this form is used at times in the sense of *otan'in šni*, to be invisible — **otan'in·šniyan** *adv* : not manifestly < *Na lowan wacipi kin ~ han na tokša tan'inšni* And when they danced the song he stood not clearly seen, so after sometime he disappeared. > — **otan'in·yan** \ó-taŋ-iŋ-yaŋ\ *adv* : manifestly, openly < *Wanna ~ kupi* They now came home openly. >

o·tan·ka \o-táŋ-ka\ *n* [fr *tanka* large] : greatness, largeness — *adj* : large, broad

o·tan·ka·la \o-táŋ-ka-la\ *va* otanka·wa·la : to have in greatest, highest esteem — **otankala·ka** \ó-taŋ-ka-la-ka\ *va* ótanka·wa·laka : to esteem most highly

o·tan·kan \o-táŋ-kaŋ\ *adv* : singling one out – *Syn* Á-PATONYELA WE

o·tan·ka·ya \o-táŋ-ka-ya\ *adj* : spacious, largely, extensive < *Kahmi wan lila ~ ca el etipi* They encamped in a very spacious river bend. > — *adv* : largely, extensively < *Oyate ota hocoka ~ wicoti ške lo* It is said many tribes set up camp largely about a center area. *Wanna lila hocoka ~ oimniciye* They now largely have meetings very much in center camp. *Hocoka kin lila ~ na cokata lila wicotapi* Center camp is quite large, and really large crowds are in the center. *Wakpa wan ~ na šma ca el iyohloke* The confluence in a river is large and deep. > — **otankayaka** \o-táŋ-ka-ya-ka\ *n* : greatness – R D. 198 and 37

o·tan·kin·kin·yan \o-táŋ-kiŋ-kiŋ-yaŋ\ *adv* : in a big circle < *Oyate iglak omanipi na wanna hocoka ~ wicoti* They traveled about camping out and camped with a big center area. >

o·tan·ktan·ka·ya \o-táŋ-ktaŋ-ka-ya\ *adv red of* otankaya : extensively – D.225

o·tan·la \o-táŋ-la\ *vn* o·ma·tanla : to be proud, vain — *va* : to treasure, consider valuable, as one's clothes *etc.*

o·tan·ton \o-táŋ-toŋ\ *adj* : abundant — **otanton·ka** \o-táŋ-toŋ-ka\ *adj* : large, prodigious — **otanton·yan** *adv* : very lively, zealously, excitedly, as in playing, fighting *etc.* < ~ *econpi* It was done with gusto. > — **otantonyankel** \o-táŋ-toŋ-yaŋ-k̇el\ *adv* : exaggeratedly < ~ *ia* to speak in a dissatisfied way >

o·tan·yan \o-ṫáŋ-yaŋ\ *vn perhaps* o·ma·tanyan : to be well, feel no pain < *Minit'eyapi kin he ~ kte tka* It were better for him to be drowned. > - B.H.215.12

o·ta·pa \o-tá-pa\ *v* ota·wa·pa ota·maya·pa·pi ota·un·pa·pi *or* unko·tapa·pi unkoni·tapa·pi *or* unko·ta·ni·pa·pi [fr *tapá* follow after] : to follow after one *e.g.* on a road < *oye ~* to follow tracks > ; *fig* to imitate, follow after *e.g.* in imitation of Christ — **otape·ya** \o-tá-ṗe-ya\ *adv* : following - B.H.107.3, 103.4, 58.4, 199.7, 234.5, 234.2, 63.2, 66.15, 301.9

o·ta·pi·ka \o-tá-ṗi-ka\ *n* : one who is "tops", the "best" - RE

o·ta·pi s'e \ó-ta-pi s'e\ *adv perhaps* : in large numbers < ~ *ahiyaye* to pass by in large numbers >

o·ta·sa·gya \ó-ta-sa-gya\ *v* : to keep hard, stiff, frozen - MS.483

o·ta·šo·ša \o-tá-šo-ša\ *v* otá·wa·šoša : to spit in — **otašoše** *n* : a spittoon

o·ta·te \o-tá-ṫe\ *n* : a clime, climate

o·ta·tkon·za \ó-ta-ṫk̇oŋ-za\ *adj* : equal to, parallel

o·ta·wan·ji·la \o-tá-waŋ-ji-la\ *n* : two alike, a pair of one kind

o·ta·wa·t'e·lši·ca \o-tá-wa-t'e-lši-ca\ *adj* : unendurable, unbearable < *Otáwat'elnišicelo* You are unsufferable. > — **otawat'elši·lya** *adv* : exceedingly bad

o·ta·wa·t'e·lya \o-tá-wa-t'e-lya\ *v* otawat'e·lwa·ya : to be willing, willing to do

o·ta·wa·t'e·ši·ca \o-tá-wa-t'e-ši·ca\ *adj* : great, fearful, numberless, awesome

o·te·bya \o-ṫé-bya\ *v* : to gnaw on or into, as a mouse does on cheese, or a wolf to a carcass < *mahel ~* to gnaw into >

o·te·han \o-ṫé-haŋ\ *adv* : far, a long distance

o·te·han·ya \o-ṫé-haŋ-ya\ *va* otehan·wa·ya : to hinder, cause to be long about a thing, to let one wait long for a thing < *Taku ecamon tka otehanmayayelo* I did the thing, but you delay me. > — **otehanyalaka** \ó-te-haŋ-ya-la-ka\ *adv perhaps* : a little while, in *ref* to the future < *Hótan'inpi tka ka ótehanyalake on oyate kin tanyan nah'onpi šni* The people did not hear well because their voices would be heard yonder with delay. > - *Syn* TEHAN Bl

o·te·ḣi \o-ṫé-ḣi\ *n* : misery, difficulty, as a thicket of bushes presents when one cannot pass through without difficulty — **oteḣi·ka** *adv* : very hard to endure, trying, difficult; expensive < *Taku ~ hiyagle* Some difficulty came upon him. > - B.H.42.1

o·ti \o-ṫí\ *vn* o·wa·ti unko·ti·pi : to dwell in — *n* : a house, dwelling < *Tunkašila oti* the White House > — **oti·kiya** \o-ṫí-k̇i-ya\ *v* : to make camp < *Lel otiwakiyehcelo* Here is where we make camp. > - Bl

o·tin·to·ska \o-ṫíŋ-ṫo-sk̇a\ *n* : an open place in the woods - *Syn* OCÚNWANICE — **otintoska·skaya** *adv* : with open places in the woods here and there - Bl

o·ti·wo·ta *also* **otiwota·ta** \o-ṫí-wo-ṫa\ *n* : an old encampment — **otiwo·tanl** \o-ṫí-wo-ṫaŋl\ *adv* : at the old camping ground - MS.67

o·ti·yo·hi *also* **otoiyohi** \o-ṫí-yo-hi\ *adj* : each one, every one < *Šunkawakan šaglogan wicaša itancanpi hena iyuha ~ wicawak'u welo* All the leading men I gave each eight horses. > - BT

o·tka *or* **otke** \o-tk̇á\ *vn* : to hang from, be suspended from anything, as from a tree < *Wikankan num el ~* He hung from a double rope. > - *See* otké

o·tka·bya \o-tk̇á-bya\ *va* otka·bwa·ya : to make stick on, to daub

o·tkan \o-tk̇áŋ\ *v* : to storm perhaps < *Wana ~ hwo* Is there now a storm? *Hanótkan k̇telo* There will be a night storm. > - Bl

o·tka·pa \o-ṫk̇á-ṗa\ *vn* : to clog

o·tke \o-tk̇é\ *vn* : to hang from, to be hung up, as a coat — **otke·ya** \ó-tk̇e-ya\ *va* ótke·wa·ya : to hang up, suspend anything; to advertise — **otkeya·han** *part* : hanging up — **otkeya·piya** *va* : to have one hung < *Eca le yuakagal otkeniyanpiwayin nainš ciyuška wowaš'ake bluha kin slolyaye šni yelaka* Truly I now have you hung with arms outstretched, or indeed did you not know I have the power to release you? > - B.H.264.12

o·tke·yu·te \o-tk̇é-yu-ṫe\ *n* : a weight

o·tkin \o-tk̇íŋ\ *vn* : to become damp in

o·tkons \ó-tk̇oŋs\ *adj contrac of* ótkonza : even, equal < ~ *yuksa* to break off even, *Wicaša wan tawicu kici tawacin kin ~ wakiksapelo* The man and his wife are of one mind on everything. > — **otkon·sela** *or* **otkon·sye·la** *adv* : evenly < ~ *wana henámala* Now I am even having nothing anymore. > Bl

o·tkon·za \ó-tk̇oŋ-za\ *adj* : even, equal, parallel

o·to·gmun \o-tó-gmuŋ\ *v* : to appear kept, orderly, straight < *Tipi kin ~ šni he* His room looks very disorderly. > - Bl

o·to·han·yan \o-ṫó-haŋ-yaŋ\ *adv* : for a short time or distance < ~ *oholaya kuwa* to treat honorably one briefly > — **otohanyan·kel** *adv* : for some time < ~ *lel mankin ktelo* I shall be here for some time. > - B.H.206.2 D.67 Bl

o·to·i·yo·hi \o-ṫó-i-yo-hi\ *adj* : each one, every one < *Na taku wašpanka econpi kinhan hena ~ etanhan icupi* And And they took from each one what food was cooked. > — **otoiyohi·hi** *adj red perhaps* : some of each, perhaps < *Oyate ~ ahi yelo* Some of each tribe arrived. > — **otoiyohi·la** *adj perhaps* : each one, every one - *See* otoiyohi BD B.H.195.5

o·to·ka·he \o-ṫó-k̇a-he\ *n* : the beginning, that which goes first < ~ *kin le unhpayapi kin isam akiyagle kin hehanl ouwicuntapi kte lo, eya* He said we would then shoot them if they started to go further home when we were first to lie down. ~ *le waku welo* I am now the first to come back. *Wagli ~ ku welo* He was first to come back bringing home game. > — **otokahe·ta** *adj* : at the head — **otokahe·ya** *n* : the first, the beginning — *adv* : at the beginning < ~ *oyanke* the first place > - BD B.H.242.9

o·to·ka·ta \o-ṫó-k̇a-ṫa\ *adv* : before, foremost

o·to·ke·tu \o-ṫó-k̇e-ṫu\ *interrog adv* : How is it?... As things go... < *Owicatoketu tan'inšni* It is not clear how they are, as is said when somebody did not do well and others did not care to hear about it. > - WE

o·to·ki·yo·tan \o-ṫó-ki-yo-taŋ\ *n perhaps* : a way - *Syn* OCANKU B.H.254.20

o·to·kšu \o-ṫó-kšu\ *v* oto·wa·kšu oto·un·kšu·pi [fr *tokšu* to transport] : to haul or transport in *e.g.* a cart — *n* : hauling, transporting < ~ *wašte* It is good hauling. >

o·ton \o-ṫóŋ\ *va* o·wa·ton : to wear, put on *e.g.* leggings or pantaloons < *Hunskoweton kta* I shall put on

---

\a\ father \e\ they \i\ machine \o\ smoke \u\ lunar \an, aŋ\ blanc Fr. \in, iŋ\ ink \on, oŋ, un, uŋ\ soon, confier Fr. \c\ chair \ǧ\ machen Ger. \j\ fusion \clusters: bl, gn, kp, hšl, etc...\ b[e]lo ... said with a slight vowel
See more in the Introduction, Guide to Pronunciation

my pants, *i.e.* Lakota pants. *Wizi wan kazazapi ca oton* He wore stripped pieces of an old tipi. > – D.36

o·ton·wa·he \o-tóŋ-wa-he\ *n* : a cluster of houses, a village, town, city; Washington, D.C. — **otonwahe·tu** \o-tóŋ-wa-he-ṫu\ *prep* and *n* : at or to the city of Washington, D.C. < ~ *yin kte* He will go to Washington. >

o·ton·wan \o-ṫóŋ-waŋ\ *v* o·wa·tonwan unko·tonwan·pi [fr *tonwan* to look, spy] : to look into

o·ton·we \o-ṫóŋ-we\ *n* : sight, eye-sight – B.H.236.9

o·ton·yan \o-ṫóŋ-yaŋ\ *adv* [fr *tonyan* to yield pus] : suppurating

o·to·pi ka *or* **otapi ka** \ó-ṫo-ṗi ka\ *interrog express* : Is it a crowd over there? < ~ *nunke* Are you crowded there? > – Note: the word is used by boys

o·to·sa \o-ṫó-sa\ *adj* **1** : blunt, round < *Cap'sto s'e ite kin ~ kaca* His face is like that of a fat beaver, *i.e.* when the face is big. > **2** : not cut up < ~ *špan* cooked whole > — **oto·sya** *adj* : blunt, round

o·to·tan·han *or* **ototanhan·han** \o-ṫó-ṫaŋ-haŋ\ *prep perhaps* : from every kind, as taking some away from each kind < *Na oyate ~ Omaha tipi el zuya ai* And the Omahas went to war in homes from every kind of tribe. > – MS.520

o·to·to·la *or* **totola** \o-ṫó-ṫo-la\ *adj perhaps* : clear of brush, long grass *etc.*; thinly as grass – *Syn* OWANKE WAŠTE, ŽAZECALA ET Bl

o·to·ya·sin \o-ṫó-ya-siŋ\ *adv* [fr *otoiyohi* each + *oyasin* all] : every single one, all – BD

o·to·za \o-ṫó-za\ *adj* : blunt, round, round and long as a stick; not split < *can ~* a round stick >

o·tu·hci *also* **ituhci** \o-ṫú-ȟci\ *adv* : in vain, for nothing, gratis < ~ *peji opetonpi* Grass was bought in vain, *i.e.* they bought it for your horses but you did no come for it. >

o·tu·h'an \o-ṫú-ȟ'aŋ\ *v* otu·wa·h'an : to give away, to make a present — **otuh'an·pi** *n* : the giving away things **otu·kih'an** \o-ṫú-ki-ȟ'aŋ\ *va* otu·wa·kih'an : to make a present of to, to give to one

o·tu·ma·ko·skanl \o-ṫú-ma-ko-skaŋl\ *adv* : without cause

o·tu·tka *also* **tutka** \o-ṫú-tka\ \ṫu-tká\ *n* : small articles, trinkets, crumbs, a little to eat < *Takunl onitutka ka hwo* Did he ask for something of your bit to eat? *i.e.* at least a little to eat. *Hiya, takunl omatutka šni ye* No, there was nothing of my little crumbs. > — **otutka·la** \o-ṫú-tka-la\ *adj* : only a very little of < ~ *eša tuweni el un šni yelo* Though it was only a very little, there was no one present there, *i.e.* nobody is in. > – Bl KE

o·tu·tu·ya·cin \o-ṫú-ṫu-ya-cin\ *adv red of* otuyacin : at random, in vain, for nought – Bl

o·tu·wo·ta *also* **otiwota** \o-ṫú-wo-ṫa\ *n* : an old deserted camping place < *Wantanyeyela tawicu kicila ~ ena unpi* A sharp-shooter along with his wife lived there in an old deserted camp site. > – MS.100

o·tu·ya \o-ṫú-ya\ *adv* : in vain, groundlessly, for nothing < ~ *iyaya* to have gone to no use > — **otuya·cin** *also* **otuyacin·yan** *adv* : at random, in vain, for nought < *Hanhepi ca ~ utapelo* When it was night they fired their guns at random. *Wakantanka ~ wacinyanpi kte šni* They will not trust God for nought. > – B.H.120.19

o·tu·ya·un \o-ṫú-ya-uŋ\ *v* : to be in a wild state

o·tu·yu·ble·za \o-ṫú-yu-ble-za\ *v* : to wake up, arouse, perhaps by shaking, *yuhi* < *Wakanyeja ~ ; maka iyokiseya tatanka ota nawah'on ca wakanyeja wagluhika nunwe* She woke up the children; let the children keep silent because I hear half the neighborhood in many buffalos, as an old man would call out before going on a buffalo hunt. > – Bl

o·t'a \o-t'á\ *vn* o·ma·t'a [fr *t'a* to die] : to die in any place, to have the stomach overloaded, to die of surfeit, to be sick from eating or drinking too much < ~ *hpaya* to lie dying from eating too much. > – B.H.133.19, 133.20

o·t'e \o-t'é\ *v* or *perhaps n* : to die, be dying < ~ *teȟi* hard to die, tenacious of life, *Wi s'e ot'e yuha un ke* He just kept on dying pretty much as though it were a month, *i.e.* when a person faints often. > – B.H.40.2

o·t'e i·ki·ci·hun·ni *or* **ot'ikicihunni** \o-t'é i-kì-ci-huŋ-ni\ *v* : to be about to die, to be near death – B.H.255.19

o·t'e i·ya·gle·ya *or* **ot'iyagleya** \o-t'é i-yà-gle-ya\ *adv perhaps* : unto death < *Minagi kin ot'iyagleya iyokišice* My spirit is sorrowful unto death. > – B.H.255.7

o·t'e kpa·gan \o-t'é kpa-ġaŋ\ *v* : to give up one's life – B.H.223.19

o·t'i·ki·ci·hun·ni \o-t'í-ki-ci-huŋ-ni\ *v* – *See* ot'e ikicihunni – B.H.255.19

o·t'in \o-t'íŋ\ *va perhaps* o·wa·t'in : to drink much and greedily

o·t'in·h'ya·kel \o-t'íŋ-ȟ'ya-kel\ *adv* : uncooth, hard, cold, unsociable < ~ *nanke lo, okišyakel nanke lo* You are unsociable, you are belligerent, as is said by a visitor who is received silently by the person he came to see, as though he were not welcome. > – *Syn* OKIŠYAKEL Bl

o·t'ins \o-t'íŋs\ *vn contrac of* ot'inza : to choke < ~ *yanka* to be choking, *Iyuhinta kin ataya i etkiya na ~ amau* He brought me with him and choking where he went raking everything. ~ *ahiyotake* They came choking and sat down. *Maku ~ ape* He struck him on the chest when choking. > – D.111, 248,58

o·t'ins·t'in·za \o-t'íŋs-t'iŋ-za\ *vn red of* ot'inza : to be tight

o·t'in·sya *or* **otinsyakel** \o-t'íŋ-sya\ \o-t'íŋ-sya-ḱel\ *adv* : tightly, firmly

o·t'in·t'in \o-t'íŋ-t'iŋ\ *v red of* ot'in : to gulp down

o·t'in·za \o-t'íŋ-za\ *vn* o·ma·t'inza : to be tight or fast in *e.g.* clothes that are too small, and food that sticks in the throat; to be too small for so many, as a church may be

o·t'i·ya·gle·ya \o-t'í-ya-gle-ya\ *adv* – *See* ot'e iyagleya

o·t'o·gnag \o-t'ó-gnag\ *vn contrac of* ot'ognaka : to risk one's life < ~ *lowanpi* a death song, *i.e.* one in which a person cares nothing whether he lives or dies > — **ot'o·gna·gya** *adv* : at the risk of life

o·t'o·gna·ka \o-t'ó-gna-ḱa\ *vn* ot'o·wa·gnaka : to risk life, to be foolhardy, to be willing to die — **ot'ogna·kel** *adv* : although unwilling – B.H.147.11

o·t'o·ja *i.e.* **ot'oza** \o-t'ó-ja\ *adj* : hard, as of a surface

o·t'o·za *or* **ot'oja** \o-t'ó-za\ *adj* : hard, as a mud floor of a house or as a road < *Wa ca canku ~ kinhan paslohanpi unk'onpi kte* We shall use a Dakota skid if there is a hard track when it snows. > – Bl

o·tun·yan·kel \o-t'úŋ-yan-kel\ *adv* : contrary to one's liking < ~ *ecamon* I did it contrary to his liking. >

o·un \o-úŋ\ *vn* o·wa·un [fr *un* to be] **a** : to be, to be in **b** : a condition, a state, a place, room, one's ways < *Nitaoun kin ogna manipi šni. Hecel wanna ~ wašteiciyapi* In your condition they do not travel. So now they make for themselves a good place. > — *n* [fr *un* to use] : a load of a gun, a dose of medicine, what is used at once, ammunition – B.H.7.6, 83.5, 175.1,

o·un·ca·ge \o-úŋ-ca-ġe\ *n* oun·ma·cage : likeness, form, kind, growth < *Lehanl ~ tokel imacage cin ociciyakin kte* *lo* At this time I shall tell you about growing up, how I grew up. *Unkouncagepi kin iyecel unkagapi kte* We shall bring it about in the way of a likeness. > – B.H.1.20

o·un·c'on·ni·lya *also perhaps* **unc'onnilya** \o-úŋ-c'oŋ-ni-lya\ *v* : to hold one back by speaking to him, as he is anxious to leave < *Ihacikta na ounc'onnilmayayelo* I guarded you while you held me back by your talking > – *Syn* OIYAYEŠILYA Bl

O·un Le·ca·la *also* **Ounteca** \O-úŋ Le-cà-la\ *np* : The New Deal, a series of reform programs inspired by President Franklin Delano Roosevelt (1933-1945) to promote economic recovery and social reform during the United States' great depression of the 1930's

o·un·pa \o-úŋ-ṗa\ *va* o·wa·unpa : to lay in and bind up *e.g.* an infant on a board < *wan ounpapi s'e ocanku* a road straight as an arrow, *Wanna micicau, hokšicala, owaunpin kte* Now he brought it, the baby, for me to wrap it. > — **ounpa·pi** *n* : one bound in, an infant child < *hokšiounpapi* an infant boy or girl when wrapped on a cradle board >

o·un·ši·la \o-úŋ-ši-la\ *adj* : showing of kindness and pity toward others < *Kawicaša ~ wašte* That man there finds it easy to be kind, *i.e.* he is always ready to help. > – Bl

O·un Te·ca \O-úŋ Tè-ca\ *np* : The New Deal – Cf Oún Lecàla

o·un·yan \o-úŋ-yaŋ\ *vn* o·wa·unyan : to be or stay habitually, perhaps in a certain district, to live somewhere, to live – B.H.9.18, 39.4, 86.12, 173.1, 203.6 Bl

O·un·ye \O-úŋ-ye\ *n* : Nature, one's being, one's home < *Toke eša nitounye kin he nunpa iyakigleya bluha ni* I wish to have twice your share of spirit. *Iye taounye ogna yapi* He went on in his own power. *Jerusalem el ounye kin* It was his home in Jerusalem. >

o·un·ye·ki·ya \o-úŋ-ye-k̇i-ya\ *va* ounye·wa·kiya : to cause to dwell in or rule over — **ounye·ya** *va* ounye·wa·ya : to cause to dwell in, make a place one's home, to give power to < *Tuktel ounyeye kin okiyakapi* He was told where he resided. *Makata ~* He dwelt on earth. *Jerusalem el ounyeye kin* It was in Jerusalem he made his home. *Hena ~ yo* Make your home there. > – B.H.112.8, 200.22, 278.6, 62.21, 89.5, 101.1, 169.5, 170.4 Pb.31

o·u·ta \o-ú-ṫa\ *va* ou·wa·ta : to shoot, as with a gun, not a bow < *Hanhepi kin ouwicuntapi kte lo* Tonight we shall shoot them. *Wakangli kin outapi* The lightning is striking. *Tipi kin outa* He shot into the house. > – MS. 564 B.H.56.15

o·u·ye \o-ú-ye\ *n* [fr *uya* to start] **1** : the coming, the springing up, as of grass **2** : a quarter or direction of the heavens < *tateouye topa* the four quarters, directions, of the wind >

o·wa \o-wá\ *va* o·wa·wa : to paint, sketch, write, figure < *Wanna glinapapi na oic'iwapi* Now after painting themselves they came from their home. *Wokpan owa wayupikapi* They were skilled in fine-flour painting. > – MS.482

o·wa·ce·ki·ya \o-wá-ce-k̇i-ya\ *v of* wacekiya : to pray in < ~ *owayawa* a denominational school > — **owacekiye** *n* : a church building or the Church – B.H.306.17, 18, 213.11

o·wa·ci \o-wá-ci\ *n* : a dance hall

o·wa·cin·ksab \o-wá-ciŋ-ksab\ *adj contrac of* owacinksapa : intelligent — **owacinksa·bya** *adv* : intelligently

o·wa·cin·ksa·pa \o-wá-ciŋ-ksa-ṗa\ *adj* owacin·ma·ksapa [fr *wacinksapa* wise, having presence of mind] : intelligent, wise, understanding

o·wa·go \o-wá-ġo\ *va* o·wa·wago : to score

[1]o·wa·he \o-wá-he\ *n* [fr *o* on + *wa* absolutizes + *han* to stand] : something to stand on

[2]o·wa·he \o-wá-he\ *vn* : to have cooked something < *Lila škankapi ca iyowakteke ca heon owahehce* Since they were very lazy and I scolded him he got "boiling", *i.e.* he spoke to him with harsh words, so went to "boiling". >

o·wa·he·ce·lya *or* **owahecelya·kel** \o-wá-he-ce-lya\ *adv* : prudently, far-seeingly, circumspectly < ~ *econ* to do circumspectly, ~ *kaga* to bring about prudently, *i.e.* to know something about what one could not do for a long time, *Kitanyel ~ bluštan yelo* I carefully perfected it a bit, *i.e.* improved something a little. > – *Syn* AIYACINYAN, KAIWANYANGYA Bl

o·wa·he·gle \o-wá-he-gle\ *n* : a platform, a foundation

o·wa·he·gle·pi \o-wá-he-gle-pi\ *n* : a foundation – Bl

o·wa·hi·na·pe \o-wá-hi-na-ṗe\ *n of* ahinapa : the springing up of vegetables, water, *etc.* — **owahinape·ya** *va* owahinape·wa·ya : to cause to spring up

o·wa·ho·kon·ki·ye \o-wá-ho-k̇oŋ-k̇i-ye\ *n* : a pulpit < ~ *šica* one hard to advise > – Bl

o·wa·hun \o-wá-huŋ\ *n* : a gash – Bl

o·wa·ḣa·bya \o-wá-ḣa-bya\ *v* owaḣa·bwa·ya [fr *oyasin* all + *ḣabya* away] : to scare all away — *n* : one who scares away

o·wa·hla·gan \o-wá-ḣla-ġaŋ\ *v* : to enlarge, as by cutting a hole with a knife

o·wa·hla·ye \o-wá-ḣla·ye\ *n* [fr *wahlaya* to pare off] : parings, as of an apple, something to peel off in, perhaps

o·wa·hlo·ka \o-wá-ḣlo-k̇a\ *va* o·wa·wahloka : to cut a hole in when shaving, as in making a dish — **owahloke** *n of* wahloka : a knife with which to cut a hole in

o·wa·hpa·ni·ca \ó-wa-ḣṗa-ni-ca\ *adj* o·ma·wahpanica [fr *wahpanica* poor] : poor

o·wa·hpa·ni·ya \o-wá-ḣṗa-ni-ya\ *va* o·wa·hpani·wa·ya : to make poor — **owahpani·yan** *adv* : poorly, miserably

o·wa·hwa·ya·kel \o-wá-ḣwa-ya-kel\ *adv* : peacefully, quietly – B

o·wa i·cu \o-wá i-cù\ *v* : to make a memorandum of something, to note, take note of

o·wa·i·hpe·ye \o-wá-i-ḣṗe-ye\ *n* : a dump, a dumping place

o·wa·i·zi·lye \o-wá-i-zi-lye\ *n* : a vessel in which to put incense, a censer – B.H.64.14

o·wa·ja \o-wá-ja\ *vn* o·ma·waja o·ni·waja : to be concerned in – *See* iyowaja

o·wa·ka·hla \o-wá-k̇a-ḣla\ *n* : a belfry, bell tower, a steeple

o·wa·ki·he co·kan \o-wá-k̇i-he co-k̇àŋ\ *n* : a "no man's land", a place of danger to life and limb – Co

o·wa·ki·ta \o-wá-k̇i-ṫa\ *v* : to look for, look about < *Owakitapi s'e lemaceca* I am like those who seem to be gawking around, as old people say when they cannot see well anymore. > – Bl

[1]o·wa·ki·ya \o-wá-k̇i-ya\ *va* o·wa·wakiya owa·ci·ciya [fr *okíya* to speak for peace] : to speak to or with one, to offend, to speak harshly, to reprimand

[2]**o·wa·ki·ya** \o-wá-k̇i-ya\ *va* o·wa·wakiya [fr *owá* to paint or write] : to cause to write

o·wa·kon·ze \o-wá-k̇oŋ-ze\ *n of* konza : determination

o·wa·kpa·mni \o-wá-kṗa-mni\ *n* : an Indian Agency, a place of distribution

o·wa·ksa \o-wá-ksa\ *va* : to cut within < *Ceji kin ~ icupi* They took and cut out his tongue. *Mina icu na oson nupin owakse* He took a knife and cut both his braids. > — **owakse** *n* : a cut - B.H.153.8 MS.560 Bl

o·wa·kta \o-wá-kta\ *va* owa·wa·kta owa·ci·kta : to look out for, wait for one < *Mišna owamaktapelo* They were looking out for me alone, *i.e.* they want me alone for work. > — **owakta·yakel** *adv* : looking out for < ~ *waun* I am looking out for him. > - Bl

o·wa·ma·non \o-wá-ma·noŋ\ *v* owama·wa·non [fr *manon* to steal] : to steal in or from any place — *n* : a thief

o·wa·mni·o·mni \o-wá-mni-o-mni\ *n* : an eddy, whirlpool, a cyclone - Note: It is said fish are found where there is a whirlpool

o·wa·na·h'on \o-wá-na-ḣ'oŋ\ *n* : hearing < *Mnitate ca ~ šice* It is hard to hear because of the waves. > - Bl

o·wa·na·sa·pi \o-wá-na-sa-pi\ *n* : a place for chasing buffalo — **owana·se** \o-wá-na-se\ *n* [fr *nasa* to hunt buffalo] : a place of chasing buffalo, the buffalo chase < ~ *Wakpala iyohloke* the mouth of Slaughterhouse Creek or Canyon > — **owanase·ta** \o-wá-na-se-ṫa\ *adv* : at or on the buffalo hunting place < *Na le ohakab Hlihlila Wakpala el tate ahi na owanaseta akicita ... natan ahi ...* And after this they arrived for hunting in Muddy Creek, and the head warriors came attacking at the buffalo hunting grounds. >

o·wa·na·tan·ye \o-wá-na-taŋ-ye\ *n* : a grinding mill - BD

o·wa·ni·ye·tu \ó-wa-ni-ye-ṫu\ *n* : winter, wintertime

o·wan *or* **owanka** \o-wáŋ\ *n* : a place to lie on

o·wan·ca *or* **owanca·ya** \ó-waŋ-ca\ *adv* : all over, everywhere, all together < *Yunkan lila makoce kin ~ pte ojula* And then the countryside was absolutely everywhere filled with buffalos. *Maka ~ cah'owancaya* The land everywhere was was covered with ice. > - Bl

o·wang *or* **owan** \o-wáng\ *n contrac* [fr *owanka* a bed] : a place to lie down

o·wan·gki·ci·ya \o-wáŋ-gki-ci-ya\ *v* : to infect one another < *Wicokuje šikšica on owangkiciyapi kte* They will infect one another with a serious sickness. > - B.H. 245.10

o·wan·gya \o-wáŋ-gya\ *va perhaps* owan·gwa·ya : to imitate, resemble, to follow the example of to take lessons from < *Owangkiciyapi* They are similar to one another, as sick like another. > - B.H.63.12

o·wan·g'i·c'i·ya \o-wáŋ-g'i-c'i-ya\ *v* : to be in the habit of — *adj* : habitual - P

o·wan·ji \o-wáŋ-ji\ *adv* : at rest, at leisure < ~ *yanka* to be at rest > — **owanji·gjila** *adv red of* owanjila : being at rest < *Iyótahena ~ yanka yo* Take your forgotten rest

[1]**o·wan·ji·la** *adv* : at rest, unemployed, disengaged < ~ *yanka* to be unemployed > - Cf iyotahena

[2]**o·wan·ji·la** \ŏ'-waŋ-ji-la\ *adj* : the same, alike < ~ *igluzapi* They dress alike. *Ateyapi na Cinhintku na Woniya Wakan ki ówanjilapi* The Father, Son, and Holy Spirit are the same [God]. *Kici we ounwanjilapi* We are of one blood with him. > - B.H.28.4

o·wank *or* **owan** *or* **owang** *and* **owanka** \o-wáŋk\ *n contracs of* owanka : a place to lie down, a floor, a place for pitching a tent, the ground < ~ *kahinta* to sweep a floor, *Hopo, wanna wahpe wokeya ekta ~ onasto lapi kte lo. Cokata ~ yakagin kta* Alright, they will now ask to tramp down the ground to the Sundance leaf lodge. You should make a site in center camp. > - MS.349

o·wan·ka·i·ca·hin·te *or* **owank'icahinte** \o-wáŋ-k̇a-i-ca-hiŋ-ṫe\ *n* : a broom, something to sweep with

o·wan·ke \o-wáŋ-ke\ *n perhaps* [perhaps fr *owanyanke* a vision, the looks of something] : likeness, size perhaps < *Íya tanka ~* like unto a big Íya, *omawanke* my size, my looks, šunka ~ a dog's likeness, *Wicat'e owankepi* They have the likeness of dead men, *i.e.* they look like corpses. > - B.H.95.6, 231.6

o·wan·ki·yu·hin·te \o-wáŋ-ki-yu-hiŋ-ṫe\ *n* : a rake

o·wank ka·ga \o-wáŋk k̇à-ġa\ *v* : to prepare a place - B.H.92.9

o·wan·k'i·ca·hin·te \o-wáŋ-k'i-ca-hiŋ-ṫe\ *n* : a broom

o·wan·k'i·pa·kin·te \o-wáŋ-k'i-pa-kiŋ-ṫe\ *n* : a mop, a floor-cloth

o·wan·yag \o-wáŋ-yag\ *va contrac of* owanyanka : to look upon < ~ *wašte* easy to look at, good-looking, beautiful, ~ *šica* ugly >

o·wan·yan·ka \o-wáŋ-yaŋ-k̇a\ *va* owan·bla·ka [fr *wanyanka* to see] : to look upon — **owanyanke** *n* : a sight or show, a vision, appearance, one's looks — **owanyankešniyan** *adv* : invisibly < ~ *winyan wan wowakan lapi* A woman was thought unseen to be something sacred. > - B.H.302.11

o·wan·ye·ye \o-wáŋ-ye-ye\ *n* : a place to look out at, a porthole, a loophole — **owanyeye·ton** *v* : to have portholes, as for shooting - R Bl

o·wa·pa·hlo·ke·han \o-wá-ṗa-ḣlo-k̇e-haŋ\ *part* : being bruised or skinned < *Išpa ha ~ owakihi yelo* I was able with the skin of my elbow bruised, *i.e.* although they bruise the skin of my elbow, held up for protection, I will carry it out. > — *v* : to execute - GA WHL

o·wa·pa·te \o-wá-ṗa-ṫe\ *n* : heaped up matter, things pushed aside — *v* : to fill in a hole, to stuff - KE

o·wa·pi \o-wá-pi\ *part* : written, figured, calculated

o·wa·pšun \o-wá-pšuŋ\ *va* : to disjoint - B.H.153.10

o·wa·sa·bgle·pi \o-wá-sa-bgle·pi\ *n* [fr *wasablepi* a sighting pole] : a footing, foundation < *tipi ~* something for a tower, a tower, a high monument > - B.H.9.4

o·wa·sku \o-wá-sku\ *v* owa·wa·sku : to pare in anything — *n* [fr *wasku* to peel or shave off] : a paring

o·wa·sle·ce \o-wá-sle-ce\ *n* [fr *wasleca* to split] : a split or splitting — **owaslel** *v contrac of* wasleca : to split < ~ *wašte* good to split, easy to split >

o·wa·smin \o-wá-smiŋ\ *n* [fr *wasmin* to cut, clean off] : something to shave off into

o·waš \o-wáš\ *vn contrac of* owaja : to be concerned in < ~ *waun šni* I am not affected by, not concerned in >

o·wa·ša·ka·la \o-wá-ša-k̇a-la\ *adj* : cheap, easily purchased

o·wa·škan·ye·la \o-wá-škaŋ-ye-la\ *adv* : near, not far < ~ *tipi* They live nearby. > - Bl

o·wa·špan·ye \o-wá-špaŋ-ye\ *n* : an oven

o·wa·špe \o-wá-špe\ *n* [fr *wašpa* to scalp] : a piece cut off

o·wa·šte \o-wá-šte\ *adj* : pleasant, wholesome, as weather *etc.* < *Htayetu ~ ca etanhan aglihunni* They arrived straight back on account of the pleasant evening. > — **owašte-ca** *or* **owašteca·ka** \o-wá-šte-ca-ka\ *adj* : pleasant, as a place, weather *etc.* < *Anpetu wan lila ~* It was a very pleasant day. *oblaye ~* a pleasant open plain > - B.H.156.9 D.216

o·wa·šte·kal \ó-wa-šte-kal\ *adv* : picking, choosing < ~ *icu* to take choosing, or to take the pick of > - *Syn* OTANKAN, APATONYELA WE

o·wa·šte·ya \o-wá-šte-ya\ *vn* : to feel good, pleasant, comfortable - KE

o·wa·šya \o-wá-šya\ *va* [fr *owaja* to be concerned about or in] : to bring near to, cause to be near < *Okíyapi keš, wikoškalaka kin, owašyapi šni* Although they courted her, the young woman, she had no interest, *i.e.* they did not succeed. > - Note: the word is commonly used with the *neg,* as *owašwaye šni yelo* I failed to accomplish it, *e.g.* because of unfavorable weather - D.51 Bl

o·wa·š'ag \ó-wa-š'ag\ *vn contrac of* owaš'aka : to be strong for doing < *Na ~ konla taoglihpaye lo* Their fall was awful so strong their desires. His desire was feeble to be strong enough to accomplish it, hence his fall was terrible. > - B.H.195.21

o·wa·š'a·ka \o-wá-š'a-ka\ *vn* owa·ma·š'aka [fr *waš'aka* strong to do] : to be strong for the accomplishment of anything < *Taku kin oyasin okiciwaš'akapi* Together they are strong to accomplish all things. > - B.H.218.15

o·wa·tan·ka·ya \o-wá-taŋ-ka-ya\ *va* : to cut larger, as in cutting a hole - *Syn* OYUTANKAYA, YUTANKAYA P Bl

o·wa·to·han·tu ka wan \o-wá-to-haŋ-tu ka waŋ\ *n phr* : some times past < ~ *el wokcan wicaša cinca koškalapi eya ... ipi* He said in times past a prophet's sons were young men ... he was content. > - B.H.116.1

o·wa·to·han·yan *or* **owatohanyankel** \o-wá-to-haŋ-yaŋ\ *adv* : for a short time < ~ *yewicašipi* They were sent for a short span of time. ~ *šni* but a little time afterwards, a short time after > — **owatohanye·la** *adv* : soon afterwards < *Woyute wan ~ takuni kte šni kin he* It is a thing certain that soon afterwards there will not be food, nothing at all. > - B.H.290.1, 132.1, 205.16, 132.11, 209.5, 205.16

o·wa·un·yan \o-wá-uŋ-yaŋ\ *v perhaps* : to sacrifice in any place — *n* : an altar, a place of sacrifice

o·wa·u·ye \o-wá-u-ye\ *n* [fr *uya* to grow, spring up] : the growing, springing up of things

o·wa·wo·pte \o-wá-wo-pte\ *n* [fr *wopta* to dig] : the place from which *tinpsila* turnips have been dug

o·wa·ya·kpan \o-wá-ya-kpaŋ\ *n* [fr *yakpan* to chew fine] : what is chewed fine, as is the muskrat's food - R Bl

o·wa·ya·šla \o-wá-ya-šla\ *n* : a pasture < *Peji ~ kin wanil aye* They went without any of the pasture grass. > - B.H.11.2, 223.14

o·wa·ya·wa \ó-wa-yà-wa\ *n* : a school, a schoolroom

o·wa·yu·ja·ja \o-wá-yu-ja-ja\ *n* : a laundry, a bathtub, anything in which to wash

o·wa·yu·kpan \o-wá-yu-kpaŋ\ *n* [fr *yukpan* to grind] : what is ground up fine

o·wa·yu·šna \o-wá-yu-šna\ *v* owa·blu·šna [fr *yušna* to miss, mistake] : to sacrifice in any place — *n* : an altar, a place of sacrifice - *Syn* OWAUNYAN

o·we \o-wé\ *n* : a kind, a class, division, order < *Zintkala owe ota* many kinds of birds, *owe toktokeca* a different sort >

o·we·ce·ya \o-wé-ce-ya\ *vn* : to cry over one, as in praying for one < *Jerusalem cunwintkupi, owemaceyapi šni yo* Women of Jerusalem, do not weep for me. > - B.H. 265.12

o·we·cin·han \ó-we-ciŋ-haŋ\ *adv* : in succession, in Indian file, *i.e.* one behind the other < *Lakota ehanna tokel icagapi kin wicahcala ehanna ~ oyak aupi.* The Lakota old men once upon a time were used to come to tell how once they grew up. ~ *Wicakico* He called on them one after the other. > — **owecinhan·han** *adv red* : continually one after the other < ~ *yankapi* They sat in a long file. — **owecinhan·yan** *adv* : in Indian file > - D.248

o·we·con·kel \o-wé-coŋ-kel\ *adv* : with something doing or going on - *See* wóeconkel KE

o·we·han·han \ó-we-haŋ-haŋ\ *vn* ówe·wa·hanhan : to jest, make fun — **owehanhan·ka** *n* : a jester, a comedian — **owehanhan·kel** *adv* : in jest < ~ *econ* to do it meaning no harm > — **owehanhan·kešniyan** *adv* : in earnest, not fooling — **owehanhan·yan** *adv* : jestingly

o·we·han·ke·ta \o-wé-haŋ-ke-ta\ *adv* : at the end

o·we·he·ca \o-wé-he-ca\ *n* : an arrow thrown for a mark for others to shoot at

o·we·hca \ó-we-hca\ *n* : something said or done to one < *Ya, ~ makihanhan ye* Yah! I have arrived at a stand in what has been said, as a woman says refusing an offer of marriage. > - Bl KE

o·we·ki·ce·ya \o-wé-ki-ce-ya\ *vn* owe·wa·kiceya : to cry over the loss of one's own, as when someone died < *Nitakuyepi tona tewicayahilapi heci hena owicakiceyapi po* If you are those who dearly love your relatives weep over their loss, *i.e.* doing the Ghost Dance. > -B.H.41.4, 91.1, 170.13 D.28

o·we·ki·na·hanš \o-wé-ki-na-haŋš\ *adv* : lest, so you may not < ~ *wahtanipi* lest they sin > - P B.H.42.8

o·we·ki·naš \o-wé-ki-naš\ *adv* : perhaps — **owekiš** *adv* : perhaps, it may be, lest < *Hecon šni ye ~ anip'api nainš niktepi kte* Please do not do that, lest you should be struck or be killed. > - MS.51 B.H.58.3

o·we·ki·wa·kan \o-wé-ki-wa-kaŋ\ *v* owe·wa·kiwakan [fr *owewakan* to lie, tell untruth] : to lie about one - Pb.23

o·we·na·pe \o-wé-na-pe\ *n* : a place of shelter, as against rain *etc.* - R Bl

o·we·šle·ke \o-wé-šle-ke\ *n* : a war award, prize, such as a feather, a decoration - *See* iwešleke

o·we·šte \o-wé-šte\ *vn* owe·wa·šte : to use a by-word, a well-known phrase, as: "*Icin niyeš ehe kin, etc.* It was because you said it ... — **owešte·ka** *n* : a by-word — **owešte·pi** *n* : by-words, cant phrases — **owešte·ya** *adv* : in the manner of a by-word, a saying < ~ *ia* to speak in catchwords, or slogans, butts >

o·we·šun·ke·ca \o-wé-šuŋ-ke-ca\ *vn* owe·wa·šunkeca : to be unable to do a thing - R Bl

o·we·wa·kan \o-wé-wa-kaŋ\ *vn* owe·ma·wakan : to lie, tell and untruth — **owewakan·kan** \o-wé-wa-kaŋ-kaŋ\ *vn red* owe·ma·kankan owe·ni·kankan owe·un·wakankan·pi : to persist lying

o·wi·ca·he \o-wí-ca-he\ *n* : a graveyard, cemetery

o·wi·ca·hko·ke·la \o-wí-ca-hkò-ke-la\ *adj* : precocious, as a child who walks early, or as plants *etc* that grow early or quickly

o·wi·ca·hte·han \o-wí-ca-hte-haŋ\ *adj* owica·hma·tehan : of slow growth or development, as applied to all living things - R Bl

o·wi·ca·ka·ške \o-wí-ca-ka-ške\ *n* : a jail

o·wi·ca·ku·ja \o-wí-ca-ku-ja\ *n* : an unhealthy locality or house

o·wi·ca·k'o·la hu \ó-wi-ca-k'o-la hu\ *n* : western vir-

\a\ father \e\ they \i\ machine \o\ smoke \u\ lunar \an, aŋ\ blanc Fr. \in, iŋ\ ink \on, oŋ, un, uŋ\ soon, confier Fr. \c\ chair \ǧ\ machen Ger. \j\ fusion \clusters: bl, gn, kp, hšl, etc...\ b^{e}lo ... said with a slight vowel **See more in the Introduction, Guide to Pronunciation**

gin's bower, traveler's joy, the old man's beard; clematis ligustici folia, of the crowfoot family - BT #125

o·wi·ca·wa·pi \o-wí-ca-wa-pi\ *n* : a list, as of names

o·wi·han·ke \o-wí-haŋ-ke\ *n* : end, term - *See* oíhanke — **owihanke·šniyan** *adv* : endlessly, eternally — **owihanke·ta** \o-wí-haŋ-ke-ta\ *adv* : at the end < *Tokša ~ ate ijehan oniciyapi kta* Soon in the end my Father will assist you forever as time goes along. > — **owihanke·wanica** *adj* : endless — **owihanke·wanil** *adv* : ever, always, interminably — **owihanke·ya** *va* owihanke·wa·ya : to bring to an end, to destroy

o·wi·he s'e \ó-wi-he s'e\ *adv* : in a large number < *~ ahiyaye* They pass by in great numbers. > - Bl

o·wi·h'an \o-wí-h'aŋ\ *n* : an occupation, the being busy about many things

o·wi·ke·šni \o-wí-ke-šni\ *vn* o·ma·wikešni : to be strong, not to fail as might the strength of a person, to accumulate without being used, as property — *adv* : staying together, not scattering, as cattle, not scattered, not spent < *~ najinpi* They stood staying together. > - MG Bl

o·wi·li·ta *also* walita \o-wí-li-ta\ *adj* or *adv* : official and cheerful in going about one's appointed task < *~ škan* to work in good spirits > - Bl KE

o·win \o-wíŋ\ *vn* o·wa·win o·un·win·pi : to wear *e.g.* an ornament, as earrings, or a pinned ensignia on the dress or lapel — *n* : an earring, or other ornament

o·win·ga \ó-wiŋ-ga\ *adj perhaps* : crooked, as a road

o·win·ge \ó-wiŋ-ge\ *n* : a curl, as of hair

o·win·hya \ó-wiŋ-hya\ *adv* : curved, curled < *Pehin ~ waglakca. ~ wakaga* I combed curling my hair. I made it turn out with curls, *i.e.* trying to bend something straight and getting it curled. >

o·win·ja \o-wíŋ-ja\ *n* : something spread to lie down or sit on, as a bed, a floor < *can ~* a wooden floor > — *va* o·wa·winja unko·winja·pi : to make a bed, use for a bed < *Na tatanka ha wan owinjapi ca el itunkam iyunka na hecena t'a. Peji hota owinjapi* After he lay down on his back on a buffalo robe hide, he finally died. They used gray grass (or sage) for a bed. >

o·win·ja a·ka·hpe \o-wíŋ-ja a-ka-hpe\ *n* : a bed quilt

o·win·ja po·po·pa \o-wíŋ-ja po-pò-pa\ *n* : a quilt

o·win·ki·ya \o-wíŋ-ki-ya\ *va* : to cause to wear jewels

o·win·la \o-wíŋ-la\ *n* : ear jewels

o·win·pi \o-wíŋ-pi\ *n* : earrings, jewels

o·winš \o-wíŋš\ *n contrac of* owinja : a bed or mat — **owin·škiya** \o-wíŋ-ški-ya\ *va* owin·šwa·kiya : to make a bed of, to strew or spread down for a bed — **owin·šton** *va* owin·šwa·ton owin·šun·ton·pi : to make a bed of < *Šina hin šma tonakel nakun opemnipi hena kuya ~* He made a bed of a heavy hair blanket, and he was wrapped underneath in it. > - D.229

[1]**o·win·šya** \o-wíŋ-šya\ *va* owin·šwa·ya : to make a bed of

[2]**o·win·šya** \ó-wiŋ-šya\ *adv* : bent downward, as a tree

o·wi·pi \o-wí-pi\ *n* : one filled up < *~ woteħi* a trouble of one getting full, as is said when one does not stop eating. > - Bl KE

o·wi·tko \o-wí-tko\ *vn* o·ma·witko [fr *witko* crazy] : to be drunk with — **owitko·tko** \o-wí-tko-tko\ *adj* : foolish — **owitkotko·ya** *adv* : foolishly — **owitkoya** \ó-wi-tko-ya\ *adv* : acting foolishly by choice, playing the fool — **owitkoya·kel** \ó-wi-tko-ya-kel\ *adv* : foolishly - Note: above the change of accent to the first *syll*

o·wi·wi·la \o-wí-wi-la\ *adj* : soft, mushy, flabby, as if stored with water < *~ s'e un* to be it seems flabby, as is said of a very fleshy man or animal > — **owiwi·yela** *adv* : in a swampy place < *Psa owoju ~ han* A patch of rushes stood in a swampy area. > - B.H.31.5

o·wi·yu·škin·yan \o-wí-yu-škiŋ-yaŋ\ *adv* : with joy < *Wakantanka oholaya ~ wotapi* They ate enjoyably honoring God. > - B.H.125.16

o·wo·blu \o-wó-blu\ *vi* : to blow in, as fine snow does through cracks *etc.* < Wokeya okagege ~ It [the snow] blows through the tent seams, *i.e.* during a blizzard. > - M

o·wo·gla·ke \o-wó-gla-ke\ *n* : a place of council, a parlor; a council, consultation < *Na wanna otonwahetanhan agli,* Now they arrived home from town [Washington], *i.e.* the dele-gates, *na ~ na Mahpiya Luta lecel woglake* and there was a consultation, where Red Cloud thus gave a speech. *~ tipi* a council house, chamber >

o·wo·he \o-wó-he\ *n* : a kitchen, a place where a feast is to be < *~ unkahnigapi kta* They should select a dining-room. > - B. Ed

o·wo·hi·ti·ka \o-wó-hi-ti-ka\ *adj* owo·ma·hitika [fr *ohitika* courageous] : brave on or in something

o·wo·he·šma \o-wó-he-šma\ *adj* [fr *wóhešma* thick] : thick in, as in weeds within a garden or field of corn *etc.*

o·wo·hlo·ke \o-wó-hlo-ke\ *n* [fr *wohloka* make a hole by shooting] : a hole made by punching

o·wo·i·ci·šlok \o-wó-i-ci-šlok\ *vt contrac of* owošloka : to fling < *Wanjila eša i ~ wacin šni* Someone failed to try to go shoot together into it, *i.e.* he too should get one. > - Bl

O·wo·ju A·wa·ce·ki·ya·pi \O-wó-ju A-wà-ce-ki-ya-pi\ *n* : Praying for the Fields, the name for the procession held on one of the spring Rogation Days

o·wo·ju wa·šte \o-wó-ju wa-štè\ *adj* : fertile - P Bl

o·wo·kšan \o-wó-kšaŋ\ *n* : a curve - P

o·wo·lu \o-wō'-lu\ *vn* : to blow in, as the wind does through a hole causing a draft < *lila ~* to blow heavily in, *~ hiyu welo* It came blowing in. > - Note: the word may more properly be, *owoblu*

o·wo·lu·ta·ton \o-wó-lu-ta-toŋ\ *vn* owo·wa·lutaton : to make a noise or bustle — *n* : noise, bustle, clamor — **owolutaton·yan** *adv* : clamorously < *~ yanka* to be making noise > - B.H.205.3

o·wo·po·ta \o-wó-po-ta\ *va* owo·wa·pota [fr *wopota* destroy by shooting] : to shoot to pieces in anything

o·wo·pte \o-wó-pte\ *n* : the place from which a turnip is dug - Note: this word is rarely used, but rather, *owawopte,* which Cf

o·wo·ski·ca \o-wó-ski-ca\ *va* owo·wa·skica [fr *woskica* to pound tight] : to punch or ram hard in a hole — **owoskil** *va contrac* : to pound tight in < *~ iyeya* to cause to pound in tight >

o·wo·slal \o-wó-slal\ *adv* : straight up < *~ hiyaye* to come and go straight up, *i.e.* to pass by going straight up > - B.H.53.2

o·wo·sla·ta \o-wó-sla-ta\ *n* : height, perpendicularity

o·wo·šlo·ka \o-wó-šlo-ka\ *vt* : to throw, sling, fling into < *Tinpsila wotapi kin wanjila eša i owomic'išlokin kte,* Some one will go shoot into for me an edible turnip. *Wanjila eša i owounkicišlokapi kte* Someone of us will go shoot a hole in each other, as women would say going to dig turnips. > - Bl

o·wo·špe \o-wó-špe\ *n* [fr *wošpa* shoot or punch off a piece] : a piece shot or punched off

o·wo·ta \o-wó-ta\ *v* : to drift < *~ aya* to begin to drift, as is said when snow or sand *etc.* is drifting to a certain place and heaping up > - Bl KE

o·wo·tan \o-wó-taŋ\ *v* owo·wa·tan [fr *wotán* pound tight in] : to pound hard or ram in a hole

o·wo·tan'·in \o-wó-taŋ-iŋ\ *adj* : clear, manifest < ~ *šni* hazy, foggy, smoky > — *n* : clearness, appearance < ~ *šni* haziness, *Na wicaša wan najin k'on el owotan'inšni* And it was not clear where the had stood. > — **owotan'·inka** \o-wó-taŋ-iŋ-ka\ *adj* : clear, manifest — **owotan'inyan** *adv* : clearly < *Taku owotan'inšniyan han* What remained was unclear. > - MS.570

o·wo·tan·la \o-wó-taŋ-la\ *adj* owo·ma·tanla owo·un·tanla·pi : just, right, upright, straight, not crooked — **owotanlakel** \o-wó-taŋ-la-ke\ *adv* : justly — **owotanla·šniyan** *adv* : unjustly — **owotan·tanla** *adj red* : being upright - B.H.241.22 Pb.26 MS.351

o·wo·te \o-wó-te\ *n* [fr *3 pers singl of wáta* to eat] : a place to eat in < *Tuktel ~ otiyaye so* Where do you have a place to eat? ~ *tipi* a dining room, a hotel > — **owoteya** \o-wó-te-ya\ *va* : to use for a dining room - B.H.251.11, 251.12

o·wo·t'in·za \o-wó-t'iŋ-za\ *v* owo·wa·t'inza [fr *wot'inza* to tighten, inflate] : to pound in hard and tight

o·wo·un·ka \o-wó-uŋ-ka\ *adj* : lying knocked down or killed in, as in a house, valley *etc.* - *Syn* TIKAUNKA

o·wo·wi·ca·k'u \o-wó-wi-ca-k'u\ *n* : a distribution or issue station

o·wo·za·ka \o-wó-za-ka\ *v* : to rush, be in a hurry

[1]**o·ya** \o-yá\ *vn* and *va* o·má·ya **1** : to stick to, to stain or sully **2** : to come off one, as white-wash — *n* : the arms, legs, the limbs

[2]**o·ya** \o-yā'\ *adj* : spoiled, moldy, as meat may become < *Talo oya yuta* He ate a piece of spoiled meat. >

[3]**o·ya** \ó-ya\ *n* : a start, a proceeding < ~ hunkešni a slow start >

o·ya·gi \o-yá-ġi\ *va* o·bla·gi : to impede, as tall grass does in walking, to scratch, to affect the throat, as do choke-cherries < *omayagi* to affect me, *i.e.* to cause me trouble > — **oyagi·ya** *va* oyagi·wa·ya : to cause to impede, as by sending one into the brush, to pierce right through — **oyagiye·la** *adv* : impeded by < ~ *capá* to stab right through > - B

o·ya·glo·glo \o-yá-glo-glo\ *vn* : to rattle, gurgle, as water in a pipe - *Syn* ONAGLOGLO MG R

o·ya·gpi·ca·šni \o-yá-gpi-ca-šni\ *adj* : unspeakable, beyond expression - P

o·ya·gwa \o-yá-gwa\ *v* o·bla·gwa : to chew on and thus to spoil - Bl

o·ya·he \o-yá-he\ *vn* : to evaporate, to dry up *e.g.* water, to fall or diminish *e.g.* water in a stream or pond, or vessel when a little is taken out < *Casmu ca mini oyasin aóyahe iyaye* It was sand where all the water went and dried up. > - Bl B.H.108.26

o·ya·he·ko·ke·la \o-yá-he-ko-ke-la\ *adj* : boiling away fast, as is said of a pot or kettle - *Syn* KOKELA

o·ya·he·ya \o-yá-he-ya\ *va* oyahe·wa·ya : to cause to boil away or evaporate

o·ya·hlo·hlog \o-yá-hlo-hlog\ *va contrac of* oyahlohloka : to bit into < ~ *eya* to talk like a baby, or like one wh does not know what he is talking about, ~ *ia* to babble, gibber, chatter > - R

o·ya·hlo·hlo·ka \o-yá-hlo-hlo-ka\ *v* o·bla·hlohloka : to begin to speak, as does a very young child

o·ya·hlo·ka \o-yá-hlo-ka\ *va* : to bite a hole in anything, to make a mark with the teeth, to bit in — **oyahloke** *n* : a hole bitten in

o·ya·h'u \o-yá-h'u\ *n* : a stump or stub < *Canli ~ munpa yelo* I am smoking a cigar stump. > - Bl

o·ya·ka \o-yá-ka\ *va* o·bla·ka unko·yaka·pi : to tell, report, relate *e.g.* a story to somebody or a person his name < *Ociyakin kte* I will report you. *Omayaka* He told on me. >

o·ya·ke ti·pi \o-yá-ke ti-pi\ *n* : a conference room, a parlor

o·ya·ksa \o-yá-ksa\ *va* o·bla·ksa [fr *yaksa* to bite off] : to bite anything off in

o·ya·ksab ši·ca \o-yá-ksab ši-ca\ *adj* : one hard to teach because he or she pays no attention - Bl

o·ya·ksa·ksa \o-yá-ksa-ksa\ *v red of* oyaksa : to keep biting off in — **oyaksaksa·yakel** *adv* : biting off in

o·ya·kse \o-yá-ske\ *n* : a biting off

o·ya·k'o·ga \o-yá-k'o-ġa\ *v* : to bite, gnaw off in

o·ya·k'o·za \o-yá-k'o-za\ *va* : to bite off short, as do horses grazing

o·ya·ma \o-yá-ma\ *v* o·bla·ma o·la·ma **1** : to guess, as when one holds something hidden and lets others figure what it is < *Heca sece; hiya, olame šni* It seems to be that. No! You are not guessing. > **2** : to gnaw in or on

o·yan·ka \o-yáŋ-ka\ *vn* : to be, to be in a place < *Tioyankapi kin nahunhuns hingle* Suddenly the room rocked. > - B.H.278.2, 282.3

o·yan·ke \o-yáŋ-ke\ *n* : a room, a seat, a place of residence - B.H.293.10

o·ya·pe \o-yá-pe\ *v* bla·pé lapé oyápapi : to put or take in the mouth *e.g.* a pipe - Note: the peculiar changes in the principal parts of this *v* — *n* : the mouth piece or small end of a pipe stem which is taken in the mouth

o·ya·pta \o-yá-pta\ *va* o·bla·pta o·un·yapta·pi : to leave, have over and above what one eats — **oyapta·pi** *n* : crumbs, remnants, *i.e.* of a meal - B.H.112.18

o·yas \o-yás\ *adj contrac of* oyas'n : all, everyone

o·ya·sa·ka \o-yá-sa-ka\ *adj* : dried hard or withered on or in

o·ya·sin \o-yá-siŋ\ *adj contrac of* oyas'in : all

o·ya·ska \o-yá-ska\ *va* o·bla·ska : to clean off, *i.e.* by passing through the mouth

o·ya·smin·yan \o-yá-smiŋ-yaŋ\ *adv* : being gnawed at, as by wolves < *Inše le šunkmanitu ~ munkin kta ca waun welo* Well now, it is I who will be lying here being munched upon by coyotes. > - MS.486

o·ya·s'in \o-yá-s'iŋ\ *adj* : all, every one

o·ya·ši·ca \o-yá-ši-ca\ *va* o·bla·šica [fr *yašica* to curse, speak ill of] : to speak ill of, give bad impressions of, to character assassinate

o·ya·ški·ška \o-yá-ški-ška\ *v* o·bla·škiška [fr *yaškiška* to create difficulties by talk] : to speak unintelligibly

o·ya·špa·špa \o-yá-špa-špa\ *v red of* oyašpa : to tear off with the mouth from, as birds do with meat *etc.* - B.H. 51.6

o·ya·š'in·š'in \o-yá-š'iŋ-š'iŋ\ *vn* o·ma·yaš'inš'in : to feel an itch, to itch, feel as if something wanted to be rubbed, itched < *Poge omayaš'inš'in hecel on wapšahelo* I sneezed since my nose was so prickled. > - Bl

o·ya·tag \o-yá-tag\ *vn contrac of* oyataka : to stick or drag heavily — **oyata·gya** *va* oyata·gwa·ya : to cause to stick or drag heavy, as a sled on bare ground

---

\a\ father \e\ they \i\ machine \o\ smoke \u\ lunar \an, aŋ\ blanc Fr. \in, iŋ\ ink \on, oŋ, un, uŋ\ soon, confier Fr. \c\ chair \ġ\ machen Ger. \j\ fusion \clusters: bl, gn, kp, hšl, etc...\ b[e]lo ... said with a slight vowel
See more in the Introduction, Guide to Pronunciation

o·ya·ta·ka \o-yá-ta-ka\ *vn* : to stick or drag heavily < *Locin wawata tka hiyomayatake* I was hungry and ate, but pieces got stuck between my teeth, *i.e.* in *ref* to tough meat. > - Bl

o·ya·tan \o-yá-taŋ\ *va* o·bla·tan : to bite, press on with the teeth

o·ya·tan'in \o-yá-taŋ-iŋ\ *vn* o·bla·tan'in : to show, manifest, testify

o·ya·tan·tan \o-yá-taŋ-taŋ\ *v red of* oyatan : to bite

o·ya·tan·yan \o-yá-taŋ-yaŋ\ *v* : to stick, be sticking within, so as to hold and keep — *adv* : sticking in - Bl KE

o·ya·te \o-yá-te\ *n* : a people, nation, tribe, or band

O·ya·te·nun·pa \O-yá-te-nuŋ-pa\ *np* : the Omaha tribe - Note: this tribe was said to have camped in two concentric circles - R Bl

o·ya·te·ya \o-yá-te-ya\ *adv* : as a people < ~ *unpi* They live as a people or nation. > - B.H.118.8

O·ya·te·ya·mni \O-yá-te-ya-mni\ *np* : a name attributed to the Ponca tribe by the Dakotas - *See* Oyatenunpa R Bl

o·ya·tkan \o-yá-tkaŋ\ *va* o·bla·tkan [fr *yatkan* to drink] : to drink in anything — **oyatkan·kan** \o-yá-tkaŋ-kaŋ\ *v red* 1 : to drink repeatedly 2 : to come to a head, as a sore

o·ya·tka·pa \o-yá-tka-pa\ *vn* [fr *otkapa* to clog] : to stick on or in anything

o·ya·tke \o-yá-tke\ *n* : a drink, draft, of anything

o·ya·to·to \o-yá-to-to\ *v* : to eat off clean, as a horse does the grass

o·ya·t'a \o-yá-t'a\ *va of* yat'a : to bite to death in

o·ya·t'a·ge \o-yá-t'a-ġe\ *adj* : rough, roughened, as a screw so it does not work *etc.*, or as one's tongue by medicine

o·ya·t'e \o-yá-t'e\ *n* : a biting to death

o·ya·wa \o-yá-wa\ *va* o·bla·wa o·un·yawa·pi : to read or count in, to read, to count; to go to school < ~ *tipi* a schoolhouse >

[1]**o·ya·ya** \o-yá-ya\ *v red of* oyā' : to be musty, moldy

[2]**o·ya·ya** \o-yá-ya\ *n* : the limbs of the body, or those of a horse, arms and feet < *Yunkan taku wan ~ topa ca u na cokam hinajin ~ kin yuakagal iyuzigzil okatanpi* And then something came that had four limbs, and it came to a stand still in their midst, his limbs were outstretched and nailed up. > - B.H.265.22

[3]**o·ya·ya** \o-yá-ya\ *n* : a string, a bunch, a skein, as of beads < ~ *topa* four strings, as of beads >

o·ya·ya·mna \o-yá-ya-mna\ *v of* oyá : to smell moldy

o·ya·ya·to·pa \o-yá-ya-to-pa\ *adj* : four-footed, on all four - *Syn* HUHÁ-TOPA Bl

o·ya·za \o-yá-za\ *va* o·bla·za : to string *e.g.* beads < *pšito oyazapi* strings of beads > - Note: the word is used only of past time — *n* [fr *yaza*, but this form is not used] : things strung on together, as a string of beads - Cf iyaza, *va* — **oyaza·han** \o-yá-za-haŋ\ *v* o·bl·zahan : to continue to string beads

o·ya·zan \o-yá-zaŋ\ *vn* o·ma·yazan : to be sick for, sick in consequence of — **o·ya·zan'·i·c'i·ya** \o-yá-zaŋ-i-c'i-ya\ *v refl* : to be sick one's self < *Taku on oyazanmic'iye* For some reason I am sick. > - Bl

o·ya·za·za \o-yá-za-za\ *v red of* oyaza : to string together

o·ye \o-yé\ *n* ma·oye : a track or tracks of something, footprints, marks left by anything < *Yunkan ake pte ca oye akiyagla ške* And then again they said they were cattle tracks that went straight home. *Ate, tohanl yau kin oye kin tanyan omale yo* Father, when you come be sure to look for my tracks. > — **oye·han** *v* : to leave tracks < *Wan lel oyemahelo* See, here I left my track, or Here are my tracks. *Hecel el ipi na el oyehanpi na hetanhan wana glicupi* So they went there, there they left their tracks, and from there they came arriving home. > - MS.157

o·yo·pta *or* **iyopta** \o-yó-pta\ *v* oyo·ma·pta : to pass, to begin through something < *Katinyeya oyoptin kta* He will start directly through, *i.e.* will go straight. > - Bl KE

o·yu·bla·ya \o-yú-bla-ya\ *va* : to spread out in < *Nap'oyublayapi s'e yunkelo* He lies as though he were spread out as flat as his hand, *i.e.* the ground being level as one's hand. > - Bl

o·yu·bla·ye \o-yú-bla-ye\ *n* : a page in a book

o·yu·ble·ca \o-yú-ble-ca\ *va* o·blu·bleca [fr *yubleca* to crush] : to break to pieces within something, to divide out, scatter — **oyublece** *n* : a breaking in — **oyublel** *va contrac* : to divide out, scatter, or crush within < ~ *iyeya* suddenly to scatter, ~ *egnaka* to open out, ~ *ihpeya* to cause disorder, confusion, as in a room > - *Syn* OYUGLAGLAYA Bl

o·yu·blu tan·ka \o-yú-blu tàŋ-ka\ *n perhaps* : a field perhaps large to plow

[1]**o·yu·co·ka·ka** \o-yú-co-ka-ka\ *v* : to take all out of, as the load of a gun - Cf wayucokaka

[2]**o·yu·co·ka·ka** \o-yú-co-ka-ka\ *v* : to produce a hoise, as by squeezing somebody's arm and making the bones jar

o·yu·gla·gla·ya \o-yú-gla-gla-ya\ *v* : to tangle < ~ *ihpeya* to tangle up, confuse *e.g.* ropes *etc.* > - *Syn* OYUBLEL Bl

o·yu·ha \o-yú-ha\ *v* [fr *yuha* to have or hold] - a word used in connection with *wašte* and *šica etc.* < ~ *wašte* good to have, ~ *šice* hard to watch, look after, handle, manage *etc.* > - Note: the word is used in *ref* to persons and things *Syn* OÁWANYANKE with ŠICE

o·yu·hi \o-yú-hi\ *v* : to scatter about, to spread *e.g.* hay for horses to eat — **oyuhi·hi** *v red* : to continue spreading < ~ *ihpeya yo* Keep scattering it about. >

o·yu·hin·han *or* **oyuhi** \o-yú-hiŋ-haŋ\ *v* o·blu·hinhan : to scatter about

o·yu·hla·gan šni \o-yú-ȟlo-ġaŋ šni\ *vn* : to stay or remain in the same place

o·yu·hla·ta \o-yú-ȟla-ta\ *va* o·blu·hlata [fr *yuhlata* to scratch or claw] : to scratch in — **oyuhlate** *n* : a scratch

o·yu·hle·ca \o-yú-ȟle-ca\ *va* o·blu·hleca [fr *yuhleca* to tear] : to tear in, as in an old hole — **oyuhlece** *n* : a rent

o·yu·hlo·ka \o-yú-ȟlo-ka\ *va* o·blu·hloka [fr *yuhloka* to bore a hole] : to bore or make a hole in, to make holes in *e.g.* as hard snow does in horses' legs — **oyuhloke** *n* : an opening

o·yu·hpa \o-yú-ȟpa\ *va* o·blu·hpa o·un·yuhpa·pi [fr *yuhpa* pull or throw down, release] : to put or pull down in — **oyuhpe** *n* : a throwing down

o·yu·h'e·h'e·ya·kel \o-yú-ȟ'e-ȟ'e-ya-kel\ *adv* : going and coming from *e.g.* one's work or occupation < ~ *e ayuštan* to quit one's work, *i.e.* work that one has done only in part, in places here and there and not done well > - KE

o·yu·h'i \o-yú-ȟ'i\ *n* [fr *yuh'i* to pimple] : a pimple, pimples, *fig* a rough place

o·yu·ju·ju \o-yú-ju-ju\ *va* : to pull asunder *e.g.* a package of letters - P

o·yu·jun·kjun·ta·pi \o-yú-juŋ-kjuŋ-ta\ *v red* o·blu·jun-kjunta [fr *oyujunta* thrust *e.g.* the hand into] : to thrust into, as the hand into a pail repeatedly < *Canke a oyujunkjuntapi* And so they thrust their hands between the legs of the turtle, *i.e.* so as to tickle her. >

o·yu·jun·ta \o-yú-juŋ-ṫa\ *v* o·blu·junta : to thrust into, as the hand into a pail; to lay or put in < *Na cega wan pihya he k'on ekta ~ na šunka pa k'on icu* And he had thrust his hand into a bucket of boiling water, and taken out a dog's head. *Na maku el ocape k'un he oblujunte šni kin* And certainly unless I put my hand into the wound in his side ... > - B.H.274.21

o·yu·ka·ka \o-yú-ka-k̇a\ *vn perhaps* : to rattle in, as a pebble in a rattle — *va* : to rattle in a place

o·yu·ki·ki·ke *or* **oyukiki** \o-yú-k̇i-k̇i-k̇e\ *va* : to interfere with one's planned work < *Omayukiki* He interrupts my work. > - Bl

o·yu·kpu·kpa \o-yú-kṗu-kṗa\ *va perhaps* : to crumble in, to crumble and scatter about in

o·yu·ksa \o-yú-ksa\ *va* o·blu·ksa [fr *yuksa* break off by hand] : to break off *e.g.* a stick in a hole — **oyukse** *n* : a broken off piece < *aguyapi ~* to break off a piece of bread > - B.H.253.14

o·yu·kša \o-yú-kša\ *adv* : in a little closed-in place or area < *~ imunkelo* I lay down in a garret. > - Bl KE

o·yu·kšan \o-yú-kšaŋ\ *n* : a link - P Bl

o·yu·ktan \o-yú-kṫaŋ\ *va* o·blu·ktan [fr *yuktan* to bend by hand] : to bend anything into something else — *n* : a bend or crook — **oyuktan·yan** *adv* : bent into

o·yu·kun·ta \o-yú-k̇uŋ-ṫa\ *v* : to pick in *e.g.* the nose or ears

o·yul \o-yúl\ *va contrac of* yuta : to eat < *~ wašte* good to eat >

o·yu·ma \o-yú-ma\ *v* : to confirm < *oyumapi s'e oyake lo* He spoke as if he were confirmed, *i.e.* he says the same thing another said, thus he confirms. *Oyume lo* He confirmed him. > - *Syn* OYUŠLATA Bl

o·yu·ma·za \o-yú-ma-za\ *vt* o·blu·maza : to make a hit, as in hitting a target in the center, or to hit something in the intended place

o·yu·mni \o-yú-mni\ *v* o·blu·mni : to rove, wander about, to roam aimlessly < *Oblumni kte lo* I'll walk around, *i.e.* here or there. *Maka tanka oblumni* I roamed aimlessly a large country, *i.e.* went very far. > — **oyu-mni·mni** *adv* : round and round - Bl D.100

o·yung \o-yúŋg\ *v contrac of* oyunka : to lie down in

o·yun·ka \o-yúŋ-k̇a\ *v* o·munka : to lie down in — **o-yunke** *n* : a bed, a place to lie down < *~ hu* a bedstead, *óyunke hugmìya* a bed caster >

o·yun·k'a·kan·yan·ka·pi \o-yúŋ-k'a-k̇aŋ-yaŋ-ka-pi\ *n* : a lounge

o·yu·pe·mni \o-yú-ṗe-mni\ *v* : to whirl < *Tate wan oyupemnipi s'e hinyankelo* He did hold on as though a wind was being whirled, *i.e.* like one caught in a whirlwind. > - Bl

o·yu·pon·wa·ya \o-yú-ṗoŋ-wa-ya\ *v* o·blu·ponwaya : to scatter and thus waste *e.g.* some sugar - Bl

o·yu·po·ta \o-yú-ṗo-ṫa\ *va* : to tear to pieces in, as a cat sticking her paw into a hole and grabbing a mouse, or an eale grabbing a rabbit - *See* yupota — **oyupote** *n* : a rent, a torn place

o·yu·pson·pson \o-yú-psoŋ-psoŋ\ *v* : to spill or sprinkle *e.g.* water on a floor

o·yu·pta \o-yú-pṫa\ *va* o·blu·pta : to cut out in or of, as clothes — **oyupta·ptapi** \o-yú-pṫa-pṫa-pi\ *n* : scraps or remnants such as cloth — **oyupte** *n* : pieces left in cutting out a garment, scraps, remnants

o·yu·ptu·h'a·ya·kel \o-yú-ptu-ḣ'a-ya-kel\ *adv* : in small quantities < *~ egnaka* to lay away in small portions, as of tobacco > - *Syn* OYUTUTKAYAKEL Bl

o·yu·sin·ka \o-yú-siŋ-k̇a\ *v* o·blu·sinka unko·yusinka·pi : to hate — **oyusin·yan** \o-yú-siŋ-yaŋ\ *adv* : out of humor with

o·yu·ski·ski·ta \o-yú-ski-ski-ṫa\ *v red* o·blu·skiskita unko·yuskiskita·pi [fr *yuskita* to bind, to package] : to wrap up in, as a baby in its blankets, to bind tightly in < *Yunkan ataya omayuskiskitapi ca wekta kta k'on owakihi šni* And then I had been unable to wake up because I was entirely wrapped up. *Ptehinšma wan ataya oyuskiskitapi* They tied up hand and foot a long-haired buffalo. > - D.245

o·yu·ski·ta \o-yú-sk̇i-ṫa\ *va* o·blu·skita [fr *yuskita* to tie, to package] : to wrap up in, as a babe in its blankets

o·yu·slo·han \o-yú-slo-haŋ\ *va* : to make slide in — *vn perhaps* : to slide - Cf oslohan

o·yu·slo·he \o-yú-slo-he\ *n* : a mark left by dragging anything along, a trace, a trail - *Syn* OKASLOHE

o·yu·sni \o-yú-sni\ *v* : to cool, as by placing *e.g.* a pipe, a freshly baked pie < *~ ewegnakin kte* I shall place it up to cool off. >

o·yu·spa \o-yú-sṗa\ *va* o·blu·spa : to take hold of, to hold, to catch < *napóyuspa* to hold by hand >

o·yu·spa·ya \o-yú-sṗa-ya\ *va* o·blu·spaya [fr *yuspaya* to wet or sponge] : to make wet with the hands in anything

o·yu·spe·ki·ya \o-yú-sṗe-k̇i-ya\ *va* oyuspe·wa·kiya : to cause to lay hold of one

o·yu·sya \o-yú-sya\ *adv* : laying hold of

o·yu·s'o \o-yú-s'o\ *v* : to swim one's way underwater < *~ un* to be swimming underwater, as one does in deep water without touching the bottom > - Bl

o·yu·ši·ca \o-yú-ši-ca\ *v* o·blu·šica : to quarrel, have a fall-out with one < *Oblušica na lila howayelo* I quarreled with him and there was yelling. > — **oyušica** *v* o·ma·yušica unko·yušica·pi : to do wrong in respect of — **oyušice** *n* : that which injures - Bl

o·yu·škan \o-yú-škaŋ\ *v* o·mi·gluškan : to relapse, to become restless

o·yu·ške·ya \o-yú-ške-ya\ *adv* : lively in movement, being on the alert < *~ un* to be lively, *~ econ* to be lively doing, *~ he lo* He remains on the alert. >

o·yu·ški·ca \o-yú-ški-ca\ *va* : to press out, as juice from grapes - B.H.30.20

o·yu·šla·ta \o-yú-šla-ta\ *v* o·blu·šlata : to make something smooth, as a wall being plastered; *fig* to confirm what another said

o·yu·šna \o-yú-šna\ *va* o·blu·šna unko·yušna·pi : to let drop or fall into — *n* : something dropped — **oyu-šna·šna** *n* : many things dropped, as crumbs or scraps *etc.* - D. 37-38 BD

o·yu·štan \o-yú-šṫaŋ\ *va* o·blu·štan [fr *yuštan* to perfect, finish] : to finish within, as a house; to put one into another, as buckets, or as a cork into a bottle

o·yu·š'e \o-yú-š'e\ *va* o·blu·š'e : to make drop in, *e.g.* into a glass when pouring medicine

o·yu·tan \o-yú-taŋ\ *va* o·blu·tan unko·yutan·pi : to

\a\ father \e\ they \i\ machine \o\ smoke \u\ lunar \an, aŋ\ blanc Fr. \in, iŋ\ ink \on, oŋ, un, uŋ\ soon, confier Fr. \c\ chair \ġ\ machen Ger. \j\ fusion \clusters: bl, gn, kp, hšl, etc...\ b[e]lo ... said with a slight vowel
See more in the Introduction, Guide to Pronunciation

touch, feel < *Tohanyan* i.e. *wagmeza šeca šni kin hehanyan tuweni ~ kte šni* As long as it, *i.e.* corn is not dry, so long should no one touch it. >

o·yu·tan·ka·ya \o-yú-taŋ-ka-ya\ *va* [fr *yutankaya* enlarge] : to enlarge in – *Syn* **OWATANKAYA**

o·yu·tan·tan \o-yú-taŋ-taŋ\ *v red* o·blu·tantan [fr *oyutan* to feel, touch] : to feel

o·yu·tan wan·ka·la \o-yú-taŋ waŋ·kà-la\ *n* : a two-barreled muzzled-loader, a powder loader – Bl

[1]**o·yu·te** \o-yú-te\ *n* : eating, food

[2]**o·yu·te** \o-yú-te\ *n* : the parts just above the hips, the sides < *Na tatanka kin ~ el kute wicaši. ~ kin yuogmuza ye, keya s'e oyute kin hpuhpuya* And he told them to shoot the buffalo in the side. Please close up the tear in the side [of your dress], as is said when the dress is torn on the side near the hip. Like a turtle your sides are crumbling away. *~ el apin na yugicin na ...* He, *i.e.* the angel, struck him, namely Peter, on the side and woke him, and ... > – B.H.293.4

o·yu·te·pa \o-yú-te-pa\ *v* : to wear off, as by rubbing against something < *Cecá kin izuza oyutepe s'e* It is like a grindstone that ground off the thigh, as is said when a man or horse is very lean. *Sicán kinhan izuza oyutepe s'e* It is like a grindstone that wore off the outer thigh, as is said when the hips are lean as a whetstone. > – Bl

o·yu·tkon·za \o-yú-tkoŋ·za\ *va* o·blu·tkonza : to make equal, to break off and make equal with something else — **oyutkonze** *n* : something that makes equal

o·yu·tku·ga \o-yú-tku-ga\ *va* o·blu·tkuga unko·yutku-ga·pi : to fasten *e.g.* a horse in a stall; to lock a door — **oyutkuga·han** *part* : fastened, locked – B.H.77.6

o·yu·tu·tka·ya·kel *or* **oyuptuh'ayakel** \o-yú-tu-tka-ya-kel\ *adv* : in small quantities < *~ egnaka* to put in in small quantities, in small bits > – Bl

o·yu·t'a \o-yú-t'a\ *va* o·blu·t'a [fr *yut'a* to choke to death] : to kill in

o·yu·t'in·za \o-yú-t'iŋ·za\ *va* o·blu·t'inza [fr *yut'inza* tighten] : to make firm in — **oyut'inze** *n* : a strengthener

o·yu·wi \o-yú-wi\ *adj* : vine-like

o·yu·zan \o-yú-zaŋ\ *va* : to spread out, as a curtain

o·yu·ze \o-yú-ze\ *va* o·blu·ze [fr *yuzé* to dip out, itself fr *yúza* take hold of, to take] : to take or dip out food into — *n* : a catching, a taking, a place where one finds or takes much or many < *mini-skuya ~* a salt mine, deposite, *Maka gi ~ el wicoti* They were encamped at a brown earth deposite. *Inyan to ~ el ewicoti* They set up camp at a blue rock quarry. *miogli ~ el* in a whetstone quarry >

o·za \ó-za\ *adj* : both < *lenioza* both these, *heniyoza* them both >

o·zan \ó-zaŋ\ *n* : a curtain < *ozanpi* bed curtains > – B.H.268.7

o·zan·ni·yan·kel \o-záŋ-ni-yaŋ-kel\ *adv* : in good health or in a healthy way < *~ piunkiyin kta na unkištinma ktelo* We, you and I, should rearrange it, then we shall go to sleep. > – Bl WHL

o·zan·ye·la \o-záŋ-ye-la\ *adv* : remaining visible < *Ikpá-h'ozànyela inyangya* The [arrow] was run deep leaving *e.g.* only the notch visible. > – Bl

o·ze \ó-ze\ *v of* yúza : to catch < *~ wašte* good to catch, to get, take >

o·ze·ze·ya \o-zé-ze-ya\ *adv* : swinging

o·zi \ó-zi\ *vn* o·ma·zi unko·zi·pi : to rest

o·zi·ca \ó-zi-ca\ *vn* o·wa·zica : to stretch out arm and body to reach or get something

o·zi·i·c'i·ya \o-zí-i-c'i-ya\ *vn* ozi·mi·c'iya : to refresh or rest one's self – Note: the idea of stretching one's self seems to underlie the root *zi*

o·zi·ki·ya \o-zí-ki-ya\ *vn* ozi·wa·kiya : to rest, to take a brief rest or stretch – Note: to take a long rest is *asnikiya*

o·zi·lya \o-zí-lya\ *va* ozi·lwa·ya : to make a smoke; to fumigate

o·zi·wa·nil \ó-zi-wa-nil\ *adv* : without rest continually

o·zi·ya \o-zí-ya\ *v* [fr *ózi* to rest] : to rest, take a rest < *oziic'iya* to rest one's self, *ozimic'iya* to rest myself >

o·zu·ye \o-zú-ye\ *n* [fr *zuyá* to make war] : war, a warparty, an army

P

[1]**pa** \ṗa\ *pref to v* – it indicates the action is done by pushing or drawing, rubbing or pressing with the hands or arms. Note: *pron* are inserted before the *pref*

[2]**pa** \pa\ *n* **1** : the head of man or animal, *fig* the principal part of anything < *pte pa* a buffalo head, *mato pa* a bear's head > **2** : the nose < *Pa we hiyu* The nose is bleeding. > **3** : the beak or bill of birds

[3]**pa** \ṗa\ *va* : to push, urge perhaps; to complain, murmur < *Mayapa šni kinhan, wašte yelo, kola* If you do not pressure me, well and good, my friend. > – BT

[4]**pa** \pa\ *vn* : to fall, as does snow – P

[5]**pa** \pa\ *va* : to bark – Note: the word is not used as a root word. *See* pápa

[6]**pa** \pa\ *adj* : bitter to the taste < *pejuta pa* bitter medicine >

pa·a·gla·pšun \ṗa-á-gla-pšuŋ\ *adv* : turning bottom upward < ~ *ihpeya* to leave something turning bottom up by pushing *etc.* > — **paaglapšun·yan** *adv* : bottom upwards, overturned by pushing < ~ *iyeya* to turn bottom upwards >

pa·a·los \ṗa-á-los \ *v* : to make one start up suddenly as by stinging < ~ *iyeya* to start suddenly > – Bl

[1]**pa·bla·ska** \ṗa-blá-ska\ *va* wa·pablaska [fr *blaska* flat] : to press out flat, to flatten

[2]**pa·bla·ska** \pá-bla-ska\ *n* : the broad bill of a duck

pa·bla·ya \ṗa-blá-ya\ *va* wa·pablaya [fr *blaya* level, plain] : to spread out *e.g.* dough, to make level; to iron *e.g.* clothes, to make smooth

pa·bla·za \ṗa-blá-za\ *va* wa·pablaza : to burst or tear open *e.g.* a bag by sitting on it

pa·ble·ble·ca \ṗa-blé-ble-ca\ *v red of* pableca : to crush

pa·ble·ca \ṗa-blé-ca\ *va* wa·pableca : to break or crush *e.g.* brittle ware, glass *etc.* by pressing, pushing or sitting on — **pablel** *va contrac* : to break something brittle suddenly < ~ *iyeya* to break quickly, suddenly > — **pable·lya** \ṗa-blé-lya\ *va* pable·lwa·ya : to cause to break something brittle

pa·blu \ṗa-blú\ *va* wa·pablu : to crush, pulverize by pushing, as hogs do running their snoots through the ground, to flatten — **pablu·ka** \ṗa-blú-k̇a\ *v* : to become crushed or routed

pa·bu \ṗa-bú\ *va* wa·pabu : to drum on with the fingers — **pabu·bu** *v red* : to be drumming with the fingers — **pabu·ya** *va* pabu·wa·ya : to cause to make a drumming noise with the hand

pa·can·can \ṗa-caŋ-caŋ\ *va* wa·pacancan : to push and make tremble *e.g.* one's arm by hard pushing

pa·can·gle·ya hi·yu·ya *or* **kacangleya hiyuya** \pa-cáŋ-gle-ya hi-yù-ya\ *v* : to roll toward one *e.g.* a hoop *tahuka cangleška* – D.198-199

pa·can·nanl \ṗa-cáŋ-naŋl\ *adv* : shoved off < ~ *iyeya* to shove out *e.g.* a boat from the shore, ~ *aya* to push ahead >

pa·can·ši·hu·ta \pá-caŋ-ši-hu-ṫa\ *n* : the English sparrow, short, thick billed

pa·ceg \ṗa-cég\ *va contrac* [fr *paceka* make stagger by a push] : to push aside and make stagger < ~ *iyeya* to make stagger by pushing > — **pace·gceg** *va red contrac* [fr *pacegceka* to be pushing staggering one] : to keep pushing staggering one

pa·ce·gce·ka \ṗa-cé-gce-ka\ *v red* wa·pacegceka [fr *paceka* push and make stagger] : to make stagger — **pace·gyeya** *va* : to make one stagger suddenly by pushing – Bl

pa·ce·ka \ṗa-cé-ka\ *va* wa·paceka : to push and make stagger

pa·ce·te \pa-cē'-ṫe\ *n* : the nostrils

pa·ci·ca *or* **ipacica** \pa-cí-ca\ *va* : to mix up, to muss *e.g.* the hair by rubbing

pa·ci·k'a·la *and* **pacik'ala** \ṗa-cí-k'a-la\ *va* wa·pacik'ala [fr *cik'ala* small] : to make small by rubbing – Bl

pa·ci·sci·la *and* **pacisci·yela** \ṗa-cí-sci-la\ *v* wa·pacisci-la : to make small by rubbing or pressing – Bl

pa·co·co \ṗa-có-co\ *va* [fr *coco* soft] : to rub soft *e.g.* mortar, paint *etc.*

pa·co·kab \ṗa-có-kab\ *v* : to push into the middle < ~ *iyeya* to push suddenly into the midst > – B.H.186.5

pa·co·ka·ka \ṗa-có-ka-ka\ *va* wa·pacokaka : to empty, to push or draw out entirely

pa·co·la \pa-có-la\ *adv* : without a head

pa·co·za \ṗa-có-za\ *va* wa·pacoza [fr *coza* comfortably warm] : to make warm by rubbing

pa·e \ṗa-é\ *va* wa·páe : to inflict punishment in order to prevent future lapses – Ww

pa·e·ce·ca \ṗa-é-ce-ca\ *va* wa·paececa : to make something go the way it ought to by pushing *etc.*, as a flashlight

pa·e·ce·tu \ṗa-é-ce-ṫu\ *va* wa·paecetu : to adjust as it was or should be, to push into the right place *e.g.* a dislocated joint

pa·e·šya \ṗa-é-šya\ *adv* : being against < ~ *un* to be against > – Bl

pa·e·za \ṗa-ē'-za\ *va* wa·paeza : to be against, to work against – Bl

pa·e·ze \ṗa-é-ze\ *va* : to rival, seek to supplant

pa·gab \ṗa-ġab\ *va contrac of* pagapa : to skin or to be skinned < ~ *iyeya* to skin quickly >

pa·gan \ṗa-ġáŋ\ *va* wa·pagan **1** : to be able to spare, *i.e.* for the giving away, to part with, to give away, to spare **2** : to open by pushing, to open up *e.g.* land of the tribal reservation — **pagan·gan** *v red* : to be sparing — **pagan·ya** *va* pagan·wa·ya **1** : to cause to give away **2** : to cause to open — **paganya·han** *part* : habitually inclined to part with things < ~ *un* to be liberal in giving > — **paganyan** *adv* **1** : parting with **2** : opening

pa·ga·pa \ṗa-ġá-ṗa\ *va* wa·pagapa : to push off with the hand *e.g.* the skin of an animal; to get skinned, wounded while pushing or thrusting

pa·ge \pa-ġé\ *n* : the diaphragm, abdomen, belly < ~ *hákakša omawani yelo* I traveled on an empty stomach, *i.e. walk around with an empty stomach.* > – Bl

pa·ge·ya \ṗa-ġé-ya\ *va* page·wa·ya : to make flee, run away — *adv* : troublesome, threatening < ~ *akinajin* They went back and stopped. *Anunkatanhan upi na ~ najinpi canke hehanl wana tokicikpapi* They came from both sides and stopped making him run away, so they then enemy-like readied to attack their own, *i.e.* stood ready to charge and then they began to fight. ~ *akinajin* They got back and stood to make them flee. > – D.267 KE

pa·gin·ge šni \ṗa-ġíŋ-ġe šni\ *adv perhaps* : going without stopping < ~ *iyaya* to go without stopping in any place > – WL MS.105

pa·gin·gin \ṗa-ġiŋ-ġiŋ\ *va* : to wrinkle or make wrinkles *e.g.* on cloth by rubbing in one direction – Bl

---

\a\ f<u>a</u>ther \e\ th<u>e</u>y \i\ mach<u>i</u>ne \o\ sm<u>o</u>ke \u\ l<u>u</u>nar \an, aŋ\ bl<u>an</u>c Fr. \in, iŋ\ <u>in</u>k \on, oŋ, un, uŋ\ s<u>oo</u>n, c<u>on</u>fier Fr. \c\ <u>ch</u>air \ġ\ ma<u>ch</u>en Ger. \j\ fu<u>s</u>ion \clusters: bl, gn, kp, hšl, etc...\ <u>b</u>[e]lo ... said with a slight vowel **See more in the Introduction, Guide to Pronunciation**

pa·gin·gin \ṗa-ġiŋ-ġiŋ\ *va* : to wrinkle or make wrinkles *e.g.* on cloth by rubbing in one direction - Bl

pa·gla \ṗa-glá\ *n* : an owl that is small and whose call is first to be heard in spring - Note: it is said to be the same as the *cehúpaglagla* brown thrasher or catbird, not the screech owl. Also it is very tame and small and seems to live in tree holes, and hence hardly ever seen. The word is also an *archaic* name for any kind of woodpecker < ~ *wan can štuta iyutelo; wana wetu welo* It is an owl that eats warm wood; it is now spring. Nobody knows what kind of bird it is, or perhaps animal. But its call in the evening is a sign of spring. It may be a bird, a little owl with ears, the same as the *cehupaglagla* and the *ungnágicala* the screech owl. It is also the same as the *popótka* and the *osníko*, names for the screech owl. The bird is so named for its snapping of the bill, snapping mandibles, and its wavering call. It goes by the names: *cehupaglagla, ungnagicala,* and *poptka, i.e.* the saw-whet. > - WF HH Wc RF

pa·gla·ȟu·ga \pá-gla-ȟu-ġa\ *v* pá·wa·glaȟuga : *v refl* : to break or deform the head - Bl

pa·gla·kin·yan \ṗa-glá-ķiŋ-yaŋ\ *adv* : pushing or crowding to one side

pa·gla·ptus i·ye·ya \pa-glá-ptus i-yè-ya\ *v* : to tip over < *Apajeje iblotaka ca paglaptus iyewayelo* While sitting on the edge I suddenly toppled over, *i.e.* was sitting at one end of the bend and so tipped over. > - *Syn* PAÓNZE WOSLA IYEYA

pa·gle·ga \ṗa-glé-ġa\ *va* : to mark off *e.g.* the names on a list

pa·gle·za \ṗa-glé-za\ *va* wa·pagleza [fr *gleza* stiped or made in rows] : to make spotted or ringed by rubbing

pa·glo·glo \ṗa-gló-glo\ *v* : to throttle or choke a person - Bl WHL

pa·glo·ka \ṗa-gló-ķa\ *va* wa·pagloka : to dislocate, put or push out of joint

pa·gmi·ca *va* blu·gmica : to pull one's hair — *va* : wa·pagmica : to press the head and hair - Bl WHL

pa·gmi·gma \ṗa-gmí-gma\ *va* wa·pagmigma : to make round *e.g.* like a ball with the hands, to roll *e.g.* a barrel with the hand, pushing against it — **pagmi·yan** *and* **pagmiyan·yan** *va* wa·pagmiyan wa·pagmiyanyan : to roll with the hand *e.g.* a barrel, to roll by pushing against < *wa pagmiyanpi* rolling snow >

pa·gmun \ṗa-gmúŋ\ *va* wa·pagmun [fr *gmun* twisted] : to twist with the hand, to roll up something with the hand < *Tablokan ca ohiye num pagmunpi* It was a buck that was twisted in two strings of wire. > — **pagmun·pi** *n* : anything rolled up, as a skein of yarn, a hide, blanket *etc.* - MS.481

pa·gna \ṗa-gná\ *va* : to shake off *e.g.* fruit with the hand, to shell off *e.g.* corn with the hands by rubbing, to make fall off by rubbing, as by rubbing two ears of corn together to remove the kernels

pa·gna·gya \pá-gna-gya\ *adv* : doing something with one's head set, not losing sight of it, not giving up, going straight for it - WE

pa·gna·ka \pá-gna-ka\ *v* : to have resolved upon something, set one's head towards a thing < *Takomni etkiya pawagnakelo* Nevertheless, I was resolved, *i.e.* to go there. > - Bl

pa·gna·škin·yan \ṗa-gná-škiŋ-yan\ *va* wa·pagnaškinyan [fr *gnaškinyan* to be wild, frantic] : to make furious by pushing about

pa·gna·yan \ṗa-gná-yaŋ\ *va* wa·pagnayan [fr *gnayan* deceive, cheat] : to miss something partly trying to rest on something and thus fall down *e.g.* from a chair, to miss in pushing - R

pa·go \ṗa-ġó\ *va* wa·pago : to carve, engrave; to mark *e.g.* by a line for a race, to pace ground — **pago·go** \ṗa-ġó-ġo\ *va red* wa·pagogo : to mark, scribble, as a baby does with a lead pencil — **pago·kiya** \ṗa-ġó-ķi-ya\ *va* pago·wa·kiya : to cause to carve or engrave

pa·gon·ta \pa-ġóŋ-ṫa\ *n* : ducks, the common tame duck, the mallard duck, the loon
~ *nawate ska* the hooded merganser
~ *pa to* the shoveller
~ *pa sapa* the pin-tail and the lesser scaup duck
~ *išta ša* the wood duck, said to be *wakan selececa* seeming to be mysterious on account of its head feathers. There is a saying when a woman is always with her husband: "~ *s'e wiyuhlagan šni* Like a duck his wife traipses after her husband." For, the mallard duck is monogamous in its wild state, but becomes polygamous in captivity.

pa·go·pa·ti·ca \pa-ġó-ṗa-ṫi-ċa\ *v* [fr *pagé* abdomen + *opatica* to push under] : to put in under the girdle *e.g.* a knife — **pagopatil** *v contrac* : to stick and put under < ~ *iyeya* to put and thrust under >

pa·go·ptan \pa-ġō′-ptaŋ\ *adv perhaps* [fr *pagé* the abdomen] : around the waist < ~ *yuza* to hold a person about the waist >

pa·go·ya \ṗa-ġó-ya\ *va* pago·wa·ya : to cause to mark, to make carve *etc.*

pa·gug \ṗa-ġúg\ *va contrac of* paguka : to sprain < ~ *iyeya* to cause a sprain >

pa·gu·ka \ṗa-ġú-ka\ *va* wa·paguka : to sprain by rubbing *etc.*, to rub down as in dressing skins

pa·gun·ta *or* **pagonta** \ṗa-ġóŋ-ṫa\ *n* : a duck

pa·gwes \ṗa-gwés\ *va contrac of* pagweza : to roughen by rubbing < ~ *pahpa* to remove the meat from a hide, scraping with a *wahintka* a hoe-like scraper and doing so in the same parallel direction, this being done when the hide is to be used for a tipi > - Cf gwegwes

pa·gwe·za \ṗa-gwé-za\ *va* wa·pagweza : to make somewhat rough by rubbing

[1]**pa·ha** \ṗa-há\ *n* : a hill, a mound

[2]**pa·ha** \ṗa-há\ *va* **1** : to raise to strike, be ready to strike < ~ *najinpi* They stood ready to strike. > **2** : to push onward, push aside; to oppose; to reject < ~ *ihpeya, iyeya* to throw aside, to cause to reject, *Mapaha ye* Please push me, as on a swing. > - *Syn* PATOKANL IYEYA Bl

[3]**pa·ha** \pá-ha\ *n* : the hair of the head, the scalp < ~ *icu* to take a scalp, *Wanna koškalaka wan ~ zizi ca šina hin akatanhan ca hinajin na lecel eya* ... A young man with a head of bright yellow hair came and stood while his robe had its hair on the outside, and this he said ... >

pa·ha·ha \ṗa-há-ha\ *v red* [fr *ṗahá* to abandon] : to be rejecting < *Ungna toka ška ~ ihpeciye ci* Perhaps it was reported why it was I opposed rejecting you; or Perhaps it was reported why it was I threw you down and was about to strike. > Bl

pa·ha·ha·yela \pa-há-ha-ye-la\ *adv red of* pahayela : abundantly, in great numbers < ~ *tebwicaye* He devoured them in great numbers. > - D.106

pa·han·ske·ya \ṗa-háŋ-ske-ya\ *va* : to make bigger by rubbing or rolling *e.g.* a cake - Bl

pa·ha·o·han·zi \ṗa-há-o-haŋ-zi\ *n* : dusk - Note: *mahpiohanzi* a shadow cast by by a cloud. Here, one cast by a hill perhaps. - Bl

pa·ha·pa·jo·la \ṗa-há-ṗa-jo-la\ *n* : a prominent or conspicuous hill

pa·ha·ta \ṗa-há-ta\ *adv* : at or on a hill < ~ *mni kte* I shall go on the hill. ~ *iyotakapi* They sat down on the hill. >

pa·ha·ya \ṗa-há-ya\ *adj* : projecting, prominent, piled up — **pahaye·la** *adv* : in a pile; abundantly < ~ *egle* to put in a pile, *Can kašlešlecapi ota ~ eglepi* Much split wood was stacked. >

pa·hi \ṗa-hí\ *va* wa·pahi : to pick up, gather up, to collect *e.g.* words — **pahi·higla** \ṗa-hí-hi-gla\ *v* : to pick up things on the way home < ~ *toki ipi* They went somewhere picking up things on their way back, *i.e.* they went alone there, nobody else. > — **pahihilag** *adv* or *adj* : having picked or pushed one's way to < ~ *óhimic'iye* a meeting having got through to, *i.e.* for once I was there first > Bl WHL

pa·hi·ȟa·ȟa \ṗa-hí-ȟa-ȟa\ *va* : to strike one in the face, so that his face, *hi* teeth, looks twisted and crooked - Bl

pa·hin \pa-híŋ\ *n* : the porcupine, or its quills

pa·hinl \ṗa-híŋl\ *va contrac of* pahinta : to brush or wipe off quickly and completely < ~ *iyeya* to whisk clean > - Bl

pa·hin na·sun·pa·kce \pa-híŋ na-sùŋ-ṗa-kce\ *n* : the part of the porcupine tail used as a comb

pa·hin·pa·bla \pa-híŋ-pa-bla\ *n* : a tool with which to flatten porcupine quills used in ornamenting

pa·hin·ska·ye·la \ṗá-hiŋ-sk̇a-ye-la\ *adv* : by way of making manifest, disclosing, revealing; debriefing, letting go < *Hena ~ omayakilaka wacin* I want you to tell me these matters in debriefing, *i.e.* tell me all you know about it. *Wocin yahi ca cic'u; yunkan ~ cic'u yacin yelo* Since you came to ask I gave it to you; then you wanted it to be clear I gave it to you. *Canli kin ~ unglasotapi* We let it be clear that we used up all our tobacco, *i.e.* used up the last bit. ~ *akiyagle* They all went in clear weather straightway home, *i.e.* all the storm clouds passed by. > - Bl HC Yh

pa·hin·ta \ṗa-híŋ-ṫa\ *va* wa·pahinta : to rub, brush, or wipe off

pa·ho·ho \ṗa-hó-ho\ *va* wa·pahoho : to shake or move, to make loose by pushing *e.g.* a tooth, a fence post — **pahoho·šniyan** *adv* : immovably

pa·ho·mni \ṗa-hó-mni\ *va* wa·pahomni : to push anything round < *Cantepi kin ake wicayapahomni kin akiblezapi kte* They should think about the hearts you again upset. > - B.H.108.22

pa·ho·ton \pa-hó-toŋ\ *va* wa·pahoton [fr *hoton* to cry out] : to cause to make a noise, as iron by filing, or an animal by stabbing

[1]**pa·hu** \pa-hú\ *n* : the large part or head of anything, as the *cannunpa* ~ the bone of the pipe; *blo* ~ the root of a Dakota potato; *tinpsinla* ~ the upper part of the wild turnip; *wagmeza* ~ the butt-end of a corn cob

[2]**pa·hu** \pá-hu\ *n* : the skull bone

pa·hu·kul \ṗa-hú-k̇ul\ *adv* : with head down < ~ *iyeya* to bow somebody's head, to push one's head down, to push or shove down >

pa·hun·huns \ṗa-húŋ-huŋs\ *va contrac of* pahunhunza : to shake by hand < ~ *iyeya* to cause to shake of a sudden > — **pa-hunhun·sya** *va* pahunhun·swa·ya : to cause to shake with the hand

pa·hun·hun·za \ṗa-húŋ-huŋ-za\ *va* wa·pahunhunza : to shake, make shake by pushing, as a tree

[1]**pa·hu·te** \pa-hú-ṫe\ *n* : the place where the head and neck meet, or the ridge of the nose at the base between the eyes - R

[2]**pa·hu·te** \pá-hu-ṫe\ *n* : the upper hard part of the nose - Bl

pa·hu·zi \pa-hú-zi\ *n* : an old-time pistol, so named on account of the yellow handle

pa·ȟa \ṗa-ȟá\ *va* wa·paȟa : to make rough by rubbing — **paȟa·ȟa** *vn* : to be rough, as ice sometimes is

pa·hci \ṗa-ȟcí\ *va* wa·pahci : to tear out a piece, pick out a piece — **pahci·hci** *v red* : to be tearing or picking out

pa·ȟe·yab \ṗa-ȟé-yab\ *v of* paȟeyapa : to push aside quickly < ~ *iyeya* to thrust aside >

pa·ȟe-ya-pa \ṗa-ȟé-ya-pa\ *v* wa·paȟeyapa : to shove aside — **paheya·ta** \ṗa-ȟé-ya-ṫa\ *v* : to push aside < ~ *iyeya* to push back or out to one side >

pa·hgla·jin·ca \pa-ȟglá-jiŋ-ca\ *v* pa·hwa·glajinca : to snivel, perhaps - Bl

pa·ȟin hi·yu·ki·ya *or* **paȟin iyekiya** \ṗa-ȟíŋ hi-yù-ki-ya\ *v* : to excell one, do better than another < *Paȟin hiyumakiyelo* He did better than I, as a man, to whom one had talked and then yet another very urgently, would say. > - Bl

pa·hla·gan \ṗa-ȟlá-ġaŋ\ *va* wa·pahlagan : to enlarge, to cause to lengthen out

pa·hla·jin·ca \pa-ȟlá-jiŋ-ca\ *v* : to sniff or snuff the nose

pa·hla·ta \ṗa-ȟlá-ṫa\ *va* wa·pahlata : to scratch or scrape along

pa·hla·te \pa-ȟlá-ṫe\ *n* : the internal parts of the nose, the nasal fossae, the root of the nose; the holes in the skull communicating with the nostrils

pa·hla·ya \ṗa-ȟlá-ya\ *va* : to rub or roll off something sticking, as a piece of wet paper; to pull off *e.g.* the skin of a potato — *vn* : to peel off of itself

pa·hle·ca \ṗa-ȟlé-ca\ *va* wa·pahleca : to tear to pieces, pull to pieces, to tear something by pushing or leaning against it — **pahle·hleca** *va red* : to tear or shred by pushing — **pahlel** *v red contrac* : to tear to pieces < ~ *iyeya* to cause something a sudden tearing apart, as a wild horse running into a tent >

[1]**pa·hli** \ṗa-ȟlí\ *va* wa·pahli : to stick in the ground *e.g.* a stake or stick

[2]**pa·hli** \pa-ȟlí\ *n* : the excretion of the nasal fossae

pa·hli·hli \ṗa-ȟlí-ȟli\ *v red of* ṗahlí : to put in the ground

pa·hli i·yo·ka·ski·ca \pa-ȟlí ì-yo-ka-ski-ca\ *v* : to clog, to be stuffed, as the nose with matter < *Pahli iyomakaskica* My nose is stuffed. >

pa·hli·pa·kin·te \pa-ȟlí-ṗa-k̇iŋ-ṫe\ *n* : a handkerchief

pa·hli·ya \ṗa-ȟlí-ya\ *va* pahli·wa·ya : to cause to push into the ground

pa·hlog \ṗa-ȟlóg\ *va contrac of* pahloka : to pierce, or bore, break through - Note: ~ *iyeya* to pierce quickly — **pahlo·hlo·ka** \ṗa-ȟló-ȟlo-ka\ *v red* : to make many holes

pa·hlo·ka \ṗa-ȟló-k̇a\ *va* wa·pahloka : to pierce, run through, to pierce *e.g.* the ears by pushing or exerting pressure; to bore, break through *e.g.* ice; to make a hole in < *Num cante pahlokapi kta* Two hearts will be broken. *Na maka el pahlokin na el mahel egnaka* He made a hole in the ground, and in it he placed it. >

pa·hni·hpi·lpi·ca·šni \ṗa-ȟní-ȟpi-l̇pi-ca-šni\ *adj* : hard-

\a\ father \e\ they \i\ machine \o\ smoke \u\ lunar \an, aŋ\ blanc Fr. \in, iŋ\ ink \on, oŋ, un, uŋ\ soon, confier Fr. \c\ chair \ġ\ machen Ger. \j\ fusion \clusters: bl, gn, kp, hšl, etc...\ b[e]lo ... said with a slight vowel
See more in the Introduction, Guide to Pronunciation

ly worth wanting or choosing, worthless indeed <~ *wawapahi* I gathered up all sorts of things, the good and worthless as well. > - Bl

pa·hpa \ṗa-ȟṗá\ *va* wa·pahpa 1 : to throw, as a horse its rider 2 : to take down *e.g.* something hanging up 3 : to lay down or put off *e.g.* one's load 4 : to scrape off *e.g.* the flesh sticking to a hide

pa·hpe·ya \ṗa-ȟṗé-ya\ *va* pahpe·wa·ya : to cause to throw down

pa·hpu \ṗa-ȟṗú\ *va* wa·pahpu : to break or pick off in small pieces, as with a chisel — **pahpu·hpu** *va red* : to whittle away at — **pahpu·ya** *va* pahpu·wa·ya : to cause to pick off

pa·hta \ṗa-ȟtá\ *va* pa·wá·hta : to tie up, to hobble < *hu* ~ to hobble a horse *na on* and with *e.g.* straps, *Si nupin pahtapi* His both feet were tied. *Iyujipa pakihte cin etulahci kute* He shot just at the clip that bound his forelock. > — **pahta·hta** *va* wa·pahtahta : to tie and make into bundles — **pahta·pi** *n* : a bundle, a pack - D.88

pa·hte \pa-ȟté\ *n* : the forehead, the space on the brow directly above the bridge of the nose < *Itokšan towicaya na ~ el kutakiya icazo na tapon kin anunkatan ecel econ* He made them a blue stripe around their faces, drew a line downward on the forehead, and did the cheeks so on both sides. > — **pahte·yukokiya** \pa-ȟté-yu-kò-ḱi-ya\ *or* \pa-ȟté-yu-ko-ḱi-ya\ *v* pahte·blu·kokiya : to frown or grimace

pa·ȟu·ga \ṗa-ȟú-ġa\ *va* wa·pahuga : to break or push a hole in *e.g.* an egg — **paȟuh** *va contrac* : to crack < ~ *iyeya* to crack or crush quickly > — **paȟu·ȟuga** *v red* : to crack or crush something continually

pa·hwa·ya·ška·bya \pa-ȟwá-ya-ška-bya\ *va* : to make one gasp from exhaustion, as from laughing heartily < *Lila iȟat'emayayapi na pahwayaškabmayayapelo* You really made me laugh so hard you wore me out gasping for breath. > - Bl

pa·hwa·ya·ška·pa \pa-ȟwá-ya-ška-pa\ *vn* pahwaya·ma·škapa : to gasp from exhaustion, as from laughter, *i.e.* the peritoneum contracts - Bl

pa·hyu·ti·bya \pa-ȟyú-ti-bya\ *v* pahyuti·bwa·ya : to cause one to laugh very heartily <*Lila iȟat'emayayapi na pahyutibmayayapelo* or *pahwayaškabmayayapelo* You really made me laugh hard, and you made me laugh very heartily, *or* so you made me wear myself out and gasping for breath. >

pa·i·ca·ksa *or* **paicakša** \ṗa-í-ca-ksa\ *or* \ṗa-í-ċa-kša\ *v* : to carry a bedroll over the shoulders < ~ *éyaye* to take one's bedroll carrying it over the shoulders > - Note: *ṗaíċakša* is perhaps more properly the pronunciation, the root of the word being , *kakša* to roll up - Bl WHL

pa·i·ci·san·ni·ca \pa-í-ci-saŋ-ni-ca\ *v* : to pull to the opposite side < ~ *iyeya* to pull quickly to the opposing side > - Bl WHL

pa·i·kpi·ska \ṗa-í-kpi-ska\ *adv* [fr *pa* by hand + *ikpi* belly + *ska white*] : with belly up < ~ *ihpeya* to throw over on the back, belly up as a dog >

pa·i·le \ṗa-í-le\ *v* : to rekindle a fire < ~ *iheya yo, oteȟike* Strike a light to rekindle a fire, it is a difficult matter, *i.e.* when it is cold. > - Bl WHL

pa·i·le·ga \ṗa-í-le-ġa\ *v* wa·pailega : to make a fire shine or sparkle by poking it - Bl

pa·i·le·pi \ṗa-í-le-pi\ *n* : a flashlight

pa·in·lpi·ca \ṗa-íŋ-lṗi-ca\ *v* : to be able to bear or concentrate upon < *Cante kin ~ šni* He was unable to focus his heart, *i.e.* he cannot make an impression on him, persuade him. > - Bl KE

pa·in·yan·ka \ṗa-íŋ-yaŋ-ḱa\ *va* wa·painyanka *perhaps* [fr *ínyanka* to run] : to shoot or throw a stick through a hoop when rolling; to push through by hand

pa·in·yan·ka·pi \ṗa-íŋ-yaŋ-ḱa-ṗi\ *n* : the hoop game, a game played by two or any number of two's. Each one has two sticks connected by a strap. A hoop with four marks is rolled on, and when it stops and tips sideways, each player throws his pair of sticks under it. The position of the sticks with respect to the marks decides the game < ~ *un* to play the hoop game > - D.2

pa·i·pu·ski·ca \ṗa-í-ṗu-ski-ca\ *va* wa·paipuskica [fr *ipuskica* to be close to or touch] : to press down on with the hand — **paipuskil** *va contrac* : to touch, to be close to < ~ *iyeya* to make touch >

pa·i·tkons \ṗa-í-tḱoŋs\ *va contrac of* paitkonza : to make even

pa·i·tkon·za \ṗa-í-tḱoŋ-za\ *va* wa·paitkonza : to make even by pressing, to strike off level, as a measure of grain

pa·i·wa·šte·la \ṗa-í-wa-šte-la\ *adv* [fr *iwaštela* carefully] : slowly < ~ *iyeya* to shove along slowly > — **paiwašteya** *adv* : slowly, gently

pa·i·ya·pa·t'o \ṗa-í-ya-ṗa-t'o\ *vn* [fr *iyapat'o* to butt against] : to be pushed by < ~ *ihemic'iye* I hit myself butting against it. ~ *iyeya* to push *e.g.* a door to make it catch and be fully closed > - Bl

pa·i·yo·tag \ṗa-í-yo-tag\ *adv* : down < ~ *ihpeya* to make sit down, to set one down, ~ *egnaka* to set something down, *Akicita najinpi k'on el hihunni na wanji ~ ihpeya* He made sit down one of the warriors, and he came to the place where they were standing. >

pa·i·yo·wa·za \ṗa-í-yo-wa-za\ *va* wa·paiyowaza : to make echo by striking with the hand

pa·i·yu·wi·ya \ṗa-í-yu-wi-ya\ *adv* : tangling < ~ *ihpeya* to tangle up, mix up *etc.*, by rolling on, as buffalo do while rolling in weeds >

pa·ja \ṗa-já\ *adv* : through < ~ *capá* to stab through >

pa·ja·ja \ṗa-já-ja\ *va* wa·pajaja : to wash *e.g.* a floor, to mop

pa·jal \ṗa-jál\ *va contrac of* pajata : to make forked < ~ *iyeya* to make forked > — **pajal·jata** \ṗa-já-lja-ṫa\ *v red* : to keep thrusting into to make forked

pa·ja·ta \ṗa-já-ṫa\ *va* wa·pajata : to make forked by punching or thrusting something into

pa·je·je *or* **pajeje·ya** \ṗa-jé-je\ *vn* : to be in danger < ~ *najin* to stand or be at the edge of something, and so be in danger of falling or following > - A

pa·jib \ṗa-jíb\ *va contrac of* pajipa : to prick or sting < ~ *iyeya* to sting quickly or suddenly, ~ *kuwa* to be after one for something > — **paji·bjipa** \ṗa-jí-bji-ṗa\ *v red* : to keep stinging - Bl

pa·jin \ṗa-jíŋ\ *v* : to prevent - R Bl

pa·jin·ca \ṗa-jíŋ-ca\ *va* wa·pajinca : to make croak by shaking up — **pajin·gjinca** *v red* : to make croak - Bl

pa·ji·pa \ṗa-jí-ṗa\ *va* wa·pajipa : to prick with a pin, to press against and make penetrate; to sting

pa·jo \ṗa-jó\ *n* : the common or expected trait of a thing or expected manner of action < *Šunšunla s'e ituhu ~ kaca* His forehead is aptly his common trait that of a mule, as is said of a man whose forehead is very convex, bill-like. > — **pajo·jo** *n red* : a quite common trait < *Šunšunla ikpi san s'e ištahe ~ kaca* His eyebrows are aptly the quite common trait of the white belly mule, as is said of a man with heavy eyebrows. > — **pajo·ke s'e** \ṗa-jó-ḱe s'e\ *adv* : in a way opposite in expectation < ~

cankoze to swing a stick as if to hit, but with the left hand, *i.e.* he whips with the left hand, not the right > - Bl

pa·jo·la \ṗa-jó-la\ *n* : a high knoll, hill, or peak — *adj* : hill, as in "hill country" perhaps < *paha pajola* a prominent, conspicuous hill > — **pajo·ya** *adv* : hill-like, swelled up, as pimples get < ~ *kaga* to hill up creating a ditch, *i.e.* as a road in the middle so that the water may run off >

pa·ju·ju \ṗa-jú-ju\ *va* wa·pajuju **1** : to rub out, cross out, erase < *Wase kic'unpi k'on hena peji ȟota on wicakicipajuju* He rubbed out for them with wild sage the red paint they had been wearing. > **2** : to get out of joint by pressure, as a box loosening where the nails hold the corners

pa·jun \ṗa-júŋ\ *va* wa·pajun : to push down and pry up *e.g.* roots, to pull up, as ducks do grass roots under and in water

pa·jun·ta \ṗa-júŋ-ta\ *va* : to touch, as a bunch of hair the eyes < *Išta mapajunta* It touched, got in, my eyes. > - Bl

pa·ka \ṗa-k̇á\ *va* : to split or cut a slit in for an arrowhead — **paka iyeya** *v* : to push down, or break down *e.g.* ribs of an animal

pa·kab \ṗa-káb\ *va of* pakapa : to throw or toss *e.g.* a ball, to run against one < ~ *iyeya* to throw or toss, ~ *iyeciyin kte lo* I'll drive and throw you, so the bull calf has said. >

pa·ka·hun·ghung \pa-k̇á-huŋ-ghuŋg\ *v red of* pakahunka : to nod or bow the head < ~ *iyeya* to nod, as horses do constantly when chasing away flies > - *Syn* PAMAGLEGLE IYAYA Bl

pa·ka·hun·ka \pa-k̇á-huŋ-k̇a\ *va* pa·wa·kahunka : to bow or nod the head to one, as in assenting - *See* pómnamna

pa·ka·i·c'i·cu·ya \pá-k̇a-i-c'i-cu-ya\ *n* : the American red crossbill - Note: it is otherwise named ~ *hanpi*, or *pakȟic'icuyela*. They are said to breed in mid-winter - FH

pa·ka·ksa \pa-k̇á-ksa\ *va* pa·wa·kaksa : to strike off a man's head

[1]**pa·kan** \ṗá-k̇aŋ\ *vn* : to prevent < *mini* ~ to be prevented by water, as in making a journey >

[2]**pa·kan** \ṗa-k̇áŋ\ *va* wa·pakan : to rub off dirt, rub clean *e.g.* a dirty window - Bl

pa·kan·yan \ṗa-k̇áŋ-yaŋ\ *adv* : alongside, along < ~ *ya* to go alongside *e.g.* a lake, or as a horse along a fence trying to get away, *Mini kin šica ca ~ blelo* I go along the lake that is foul. > - *Syn* AGLAGLA

pa·ka·pa \ṗa-ká-ṗa\ *va* wa·pakapa : to toss; to strike a ball that is thrown and send it back, to push away; to strike or stab before falling - *Syn* KAKAPA

pa·ka·s'in \pa-k̇á-s'iŋ\ *vt* or *vn* pa·wa·kas'in : to be with one's head raised, to raise one's head < *Yunkan ake ~ na wancala eyi na ake t'a* And then again he raised his head, he spoke once only, and again he passed out. > - D.13, 28

pa·ka·tin \ṗa-k̇á-tiŋ\ *va* wa·pakatin [fr *katin* straightened] : to straighten out *e.g.* the arm when bent at the elbow

pa·ka·wa \ṗa-k̇á-wa\ *va* : to make a split, to split

pa·kca \ṗa-kcá\ *va* wa·pakca : to comb, disentangle, to untie

pa·ki·ca·hun·ka \pa-kí-ca-huŋ-ka\ *v* pa·we·cahunka [fr *pakahunka* to bow or nod the head to one] : to bow or nod the head to one

pa·ki·gni \ṗa-kí-gni\ *v* : to pull home, draw behind one homeward < *Hupákignipi* They tied up the legs, *i.e.* the two long tent poles to the vehicle. > - BT

pa·ki·gnung \ṗa-k̇í-gnuŋg\ *v of* pakignunka : to push under water < ~ *iyeya* to cause being pushed under water >

pa·ki·gnun·ka \ṗa-k̇í-gnuŋk̇a\ *v* wa·pakignunka : to push under water, to make dive

pa·ki·hta \pa-k̇í-ȟta\ *v poss* pa·wa·kihta [fr *pahta* to bind up] : to tie up or bind together one's own, to pack up < *Iyujipa pakihte cin etulahci kute* He shot just at the clip that bound his forelock. > - D.88

pa·kin \ṗa-k̇íŋ\ *vn* : to stand leaning, stooping < ~ *iyaya* to go, *i.e.* walk, stooping down > - *Syn* TAK̇IN, PAKINYAN Bl

pa·kinl \ṗa-k̇íŋl\ *va contrac of* pakinta : to wipe < ~ *iyeya* to wipe off all quickly >

pa·kin·ta \ṗa-k̇íŋ-ṫa\ *va* : to wipe *e.g.* dishes, to rub off; to cleanse, to clean *e.g.* a gun barrel by rubbing up and down < *Peji ȟota on wicapakinta* He wiped them off with wild sage. >

pa·kin·yan \ṗa-k̇íŋ-yaŋ\ *vn* : to walk stooping — *adv* : with the upper part of the body leaning forward, as one who has a backache < ~ *mani* to walk with a forward lean > - Bl

pa·ki·paš \ṗa-k̇í-ṗaš\ *v* : to strike and make bend, *i.e.* where one was hit - Bl

pa·ki·pu·ski·ca \ṗa-k̇í-ṗu-sk̇i-ca\ *vn* : to be pressed tight together — **pakipuskil** *vn contrac* : to be pressed together < ~ *iyeya* to press together, ~ *egnaka* to lay or set on for the purpose of pressing down > — **pakipuski·ta** \ṗa-k̇í-ṗu-sk̇i-ṫa\ *vn* : to be pressed together

pa·kis \ṗa-k̇ís\ *va contrac of* pakiza : to make creak

pa·ki·ški·za \ṗa-k̇í-šk̇i-za\ *v red of* pakiza : to be making creak by rubbing

pa·ki·ya *or* **pakiya·kel** \pa-k̇í–ya\ *or* \pa-k̇í-ya-k̇el\ *adv* : leading < *Inyan wan tiihanke el ~ he lo* The stone at the corner stands in a capitular, leading, role. ~ *yanka* to sit in a leading role or position, heading up > - B.H.240.10, 281.14

pa·ki·za \ṗa-k̇í-za\ *va* wa·pakiza : to make creak by rubbing

[1]**pa·ko** \ṗa-k̇ó\ *va* - *See* pakol

[2]**pa·ko** \ṗa-k̇ó\ *adj* : crooked, bent around

pa·kol \ṗa-k̇ól\ *va contrac of* pakota : to dig out

pa·ko·na·tke \ṗa-k̇ó-na-tke\ *va* : to press together and make bulky - Bl

pa·kon·ta \ṗa-k̇óŋ-ṫa\ *va* : to wear out partly *e.g.* a rope or strap *etc.* by pressure or rubbing *etc.* - BD

pa·ko·ška·la \ṗa-k̇ó-šk̇a-la\ *n* : the whippoorwill, also the *johótonla* bobwhite; a bird like the *hinhan kap'ipila* long-eared owl, but not an owl, living in the woods < ~ *s'e i kin nisko* Like the bobwhite his mouth is just so big, as they say of a man having a big mouth. > - Bl Is

pa·ko·ta \ṗa-k̇ó-ṫa\ *va* wa·pakota : to dig or take out *e.g.* marrow from a bone, to probe

pa·ko·za \ṗa-k̇ó-za\ *va* wa·pakoza : to swing, push back and forth

pa·kpa \ṗa-kṗá\ *va* wa·pakpa : to pierce, gouge out *e.g.* an eye

---

\a\ father \e\ they \i\ machine \o\ smoke \u\ lunar \an, aŋ\ blanc Fr. \in, iŋ\ ink \on, oŋ, un, uŋ\ soon, confier Fr. \c\ chair \ǧ\ machen Ger. \j\ fusion \clusters: bl, gn, kp, hšl, etc...\ b^e^lo ... said with a slight vowel
See more in the Introduction, Guide to Pronunciatio

pa·kpan \ṗa-kṗáŋ\ *va* wa·pakpan : to crush, make fine by pressing — **pakpan·kpan** *v red* : to be crushing
pa·kpi \ṗa-kṗí\ *va* wa·pakpi : to crack open, to mash *e.g.* a louse or flea — **pakpi·kpi** *v red* : to prick holes in *e.g.* bread before baking, to dot all over
pa·ksa \ṗa-ksá\ *va* wa·paksa : to break something with the hand by pushing or using pressure, or by sitting *e.g.* on a board and breaking it — **paksa·ksa** *v red* : to break or smash by hand — **paksa s'e** *adv* : cut short in manner < ~ *najin* to stop or cease walking, as when one is tired or when it is very warm > - *Syn* WOTÓKA S'E Bl
pa·kša \ṗa-kšá\ *v* : to fold *e.g.* a blanket — *adj* : bent down, like an old person
pa·kšan \ṗa-kšáŋ\ *va* wa·pakšan : to bend, make bend by pushing — **pakšan·kšan** *v red* : to keep making bend by pushing — **pakša·yela** *adv* : in a bent condition
pa·kši·ja \ṗa-kší-ja\ *va* : to double up anything, *e.g.* folding chairs, beds to put them away — *vn* wa·pakšija : to sit down, in the fashion of old people < *Unpakšijin kte lo* Let us sit down. *To eyaš unpakšijapi kte lo* Yes but let us sit down, *i.e.* and rest. > - Bl
pa·kší·kšan \ṗa-kší-kšaŋ\ *adj* : crooked, zigzag
pa·kši·kši·ja \ṗa-kší-kši-ja\ *v red of* pakšija : to double up or fold — **pakšiš** *v contrac* : to fold up < ~ *iyeya* to make fold up quickly >
pa·ktan \ṗa-ktáŋ\ *va* wa·paktan : to bend around with the hand — **paktan·ktan** *v red* : to bend continuously — **paktan·yan** *va* : to cause to bend — *adv* : bent around
pa·ku·ci·ye·la \ṗá-ǩu-ci-ye-la\ *adv* : head down < ~ *yuza* to hold the head down > - R Bl
pa·ku·ka \ṗa-ǩú-ka\ *va* wa·pakuka : to wear out by handling, as the knees of one's pants by rubbing them often with the hand
pa·ku·ta·gle·ya \pa-ǩú-ta-gle-ya\ *adv* : with head down < ~ *ihpeya* to throw one down head foremost > - Bl
pa·k'e·ga \ṗa-k'é-ǧa\ *va* wa·pak'ega : to scrape with the hand and with glass — **pak'eh** *v contrac* : to scrape by hand < ~ *iyeya* to scrape suddenly > — **pak'e·k'ega** *v red* : to scrape much - Note: the word is not *pak'ehk'ega* - R
pa·k'es \ṗa-k'és\ *va contrac of* pak'eza : to make a raspy noise < ~ *iyeya* to cause a grating sound > — **pak'e sk'eza** *v red* : to keep making an irritating noise
pa·k'e·za \ṗa-k'é-za\ *va* wa·pak'eza : to scrape, make smooth by scraping, to make a noise by rubbing, as in filing
pa·k'os \ṗa-k'ós\ *va contrac of* pak'oza : to make smooth < ~ *iyeya* to cause to make smooth quickly > — **pak'osk'oza** *v red* : to file smooth
pa·k'o·za \ṗa-k'ó-za\ *va* wa·pak'oza : to rub and make smooth and hard
pal \ṗal\ *v contrac of* páta : to cut up *e.g.* meat < ~ *iyuta* to try to cut up, ~ *yuštan* to finish cutting up > - D.199
pa·la \ṗá-la\ *n dim* : a little nose, a "poor" little nose, *i.e. yaonšiyakel eyapi* they say speaking with pity < *Pala kin hanke kin kaksapi s'e* It is as though part of the nose were cut off, as is said when the nose is very short. > - Bl
Pa·la·ni \Pa-lá-ni\ *np* : the Pawnee Indians — *n* : a liar, as the Pawnee were known to be liars < *Mapálani kéyeh* He claims I am a liar. > - Mh
Pa·la·ni ta·zin·tka·la \Pa-lá-ni ta-ziŋ-tkà-la\ *n* : perhaps the upland plover *šlošlola*, a bird looking somewhat like it, *ȟolȟotapi* mostly gray, its bill is thin and about an inch long. It lives in prairie dog holes, but is not an owl - Bl
pa·la·pa \ṗa-lá-ṗa\ *va* : to smooth off *e.g.* a rough road - B
pa·le·ga \ṗa-lé-ǧa\ *va* : to poke and stir a fire, *fig* to encourage during an intermission, as by fighting between two other conflicts; thus to threaten a fight asking foolish questions - WHL KE
pa·le·han·yank \pa-lé-haŋ-yaŋk\ *vn* : to be separated from others < ~ *yuza* to hold one's self apart from others > - B.H.297.13
pa·le·hle·ga \ṗa-lé-ȟle ǧa\ *va* : to poke or stir a fire — **pale·hya** *va* : to make shine by poking
pa·lob \ṗa-lō'b\ *va contrac of* palopa : to push into the mud — **palo·blob** \ṗa-lō'-blōb\ *v red* : to keep pushing into mud < ~ *iyeya* to cause to bemire suddenly >
pa·lo·pa \ṗa-lō'-ṗa\ *va* wa·palopa [fr *lopa* soft] : to push into the mud, to bemire
pa·ma·gle \pa-má-gle\ *adv* : with head bowed down < ~ *yanka* to sit bowing one's head, ~ *inajin* to stand with head bowed > — **pamagle·gle** *adv red* : nodding < ~ *iyaya* to go about nodding constantly, as horses do in the summer chasing away flies > - *Syn* PAKÁHUNGHUNG IYEYA Bl
pa·ma·gle·la *or* **pamagle·yela** \pa-má-gle-la\ *adv* : with head bowed down, prone
pa·ma·he *or* **pamahel** \ṗá-ma-he\ \ṗá-ma-hel\ *adv* : with the head covered as by a shawl < ~ *inajin* to stand up with head covered, *Pamahe yaun kin, ite kazamni; hece wicaša iyecel wowiyukcan tanktanka luha kte* When you have your head covered, uncover your face; thus men likewise will have great consideration. > - Note just below: *pamáhel* pushing in,
pa·ma·he·he \ṗa-má-he-he\ *v* : to push under water repeatedly < ~ *iyeya* to thrust repeatedly one's head under water > - Bl
pa·ma·hel \ṗa-má-hel\ *adv* : by way of pushing in < ~ *iyeya* to push in *e.g.* a person in or under water >
pa·man \ṗa-máŋ\ *va* wa·paman : to file, as in making smooth a piece of wood or metal < *Lila peya pamanpi* It was filed very smooth. > — *adj perhaps* : filed, made smooth - MS.481
pa·me *or* **paman** \ṗamé\ *va* wa·pame : to file, *i.e.* by rubbing
pa·mi \pa-mí\ *vn* : to move away slowly < *Kaektawapaya laka ca kohan miye wapami ktehce lo* Since he must be closeby there (whereas it is far), I should indeed quickly move slowly away. >
[1]**pa·mi·ma** \ṗa-mí-ma\ *va* wa·pamima : to make round, *i.e.* flat and round like a coin, by filing
[2]**pa·mi·ma** \ṗá-mi-ma\ *adj* [fr *pa* head or end + *mimá* round] : round and pointed
pa·mna \ṗa-mná\ *va* wa·pamna : to rip *e.g.* one's coat-sleeve — **pamna·mna** *v red perhaps* : to keep ripping
pa·mni \ṗa-mní\ *va* wa·pamni : to divide, distribute < *Wagmeza kin he wakšica ogna pamnipi* The corn was distributed in a dish. > - Note: used quite usually is the form, *kpamni* distribute one's own - BD
pa·mnis'e u \pa-mnís'e ù\ *v* : to have a cold, a catarrh, *i.e.* water running from the nose < *Pamnis'e mau, makaluza* I have a cold, a runny nose. *Pamnis'e hiyu. Pamnis'e kaluza* He has developed a cold. He has a streaming nose. > - Bl
pa·mnu·mnu·ga \pa-mnú-mnu-ǧa\ *n* : the gristle or cartilage in the end of the nose, the end of the nose

pa·nag \ṗa-nág\ *v* : to start, jump, startle < ~ *iyeya* to make start suddenly, as by pinching or stinging > Bl

pa·na·jin \ṗa-ná-jiŋ\ *v* : to stand with the help of the hands

pa·na·kse·ya \ṗá-na-kse-ya\ *va* pánakse·wa·ya : to hang somebody

pa·ni \ṗa-ní\ *va* wa·pani : to push or jog one with the elbow, to touch one secretly as a sign to come along — **pani·ni** *va* wa·panini : to push or jog with the elbow or hand, to wake one out of sleep by jogging – Bl

pa·nun·ga \ṗa-núŋ-ġa\ *va* wa·panunga : to sprain *e.g.* the arm or hand

[1]**pan** \paŋ\ *n* : a woman's work-bag – D.229

[2]**pan** \paŋ\ *vn* wa·páŋ : to yell, call, halloo

pan·ga \ṗáŋ-ġa\ *adj perhaps sl* : drunk

pan·ge·ce \ṗáŋ-ġe-ce\ *adj* ma·pangece : bulky, puffed out – R Bl

pan·gi \paŋ-ġí\ *n* : the artichoke, helianthus tuberosus < ~ *hu* the artichoke stalk (which is edible) >

~ *hanska* the parsnip
~ *pepe* the raddish
~ *šaša* the beet
~ *zizi* the carrot

Pan·gi Tan·kin·kin·yan \Paŋ-ġí Taŋ-kȟŋ-kiŋ-yaŋ Wa-kpa-la\ *np* : the Great Artichoke Creek, a little creek tributary to the Powder River near its mouth in Montana – Bl

pan·hpan·hya *or* **panhya·kel** \ṗaŋ-ȟṗáŋ-ȟya\ *adv* : breaking out < ~ *hinape* an eruption, ~ *yanke* a breaking out > – Bl

pan·ja \ṗáŋ-ja\ *adj* : puffed up and soft, bunchy — **panje·la** *adj* : puffed out, bulky

pan·ke·ska \paŋ-ḱé-ska\ *n* **1** : crockery, chinaware < ~ *hokšicala* a doll > **2** : celluloid **3** : large shells

Pan·ke·ska Wa·kpa \Paŋ-ḱé-sḱa Wa-kpa\ *np* : name of the Platte River, *lit* Shell River, a major tributary to the Missouri in the states of Nebraska, Wyoming, and Colorado

pan·nun·pa·la \paŋ-núŋ-pa-la\ *n* : the showy milkweed, asclepias speciosa, of the milkweed family – Note: it is a medicine, being eaten – *Syn* WAHCAHCA #76

pan·pan \ṗaŋ-ṗáŋ\ *v red* wa·panpan [fr *pan* to yell] : to yell, make a noise, shout, as children do – D.244

pan·pan·la *or* **panpan·yela** \paŋ-páŋ-la\ *adj* : soft as a deer skin, tender like meat < *hayapi* ~ velvety apparael >

pan·ša \paŋ-šá\ *n* : a suitcase

pan·špan·ja \paŋ-špáŋ-ja\ *adj* : soft, bunchlike — **pan-španje·la** *adj* : soft as furs, cotton, or wool; bulky, puffed up like bread with yeast — **pan·šya** \ṗáŋ-šya\ *adv* : bulky, bunched

pan·wa·k'in \ṗáŋ-wa-k'iŋ\ *n* : a saddle of a sort consisting of a piece of leather and two stirrups only – Bl Bs

pan·wi·yo·pe·ya \ṗáŋ-wi-yo-pe-ya-pi\ *n* : an auction sale EB

pan·wo·tu·ka \paŋ-wó-ṫu-ka\ *n* : a woman's bag in which she keeps her sewing utensils, a work-bag

pan·yan \ṗáŋ-yaŋ\ *adv* : crying out — **panyan·han** *adv* : crying out, yelling < ~ *eya* to speak yelling >

pa·o·ble·lya \ṗa-ó-gle-lya\ *va* : to spread by rubbing – Bl

pa·o·gla \pa-ó-gla\ *vn* : to be set up or arranged in order, lined up in order < ~ *iyeya* to cause to be set in order expeditiously > — **paogla·ya** *adv* : singly, one by one in a row far apart < ~ *yankapi* They sat singly in a row far apart. >

pa·o·glu·ta \ṗa-ó-glu-ta\ *va* wa·paogluta [fr *ogluta* closed up] : to close up or over *e.g.* a hole by rubbing — **paoglute·ya** \ṗa-ó-glu-ṫe-ya\ *va* paoglute·wa·ya : to cause to close up by rubbing – Bl

pa·o·gmus \ṗa-ó-gmus\ *va contrac of* paogmuza : to shut or close by hand <*Wipá kin ~ egle yo* Set and shut the vent flaps. > – Bl

pa·o·gmu·za \ṗa-ó-gmu-za\ *va* wa·paogmuza : to shut or close with the hand, as a door < *Wanna wipa tiyepa ko paogmuzapi* Now the flaps and the door too are closed by hand. >

pa·o·ha \ṗa-ó-ha\ *va* wa·paoha : to push one into, *e.g.* into a creek or a hole < *Mini ~* He pushed him into the water. > — **paoha·ha** *v red* wa·paohaha : to turn around *e.g.* meat in a frying pan, < ~ *yo, ázeya un welo* Push the whole thing in, it is going aground, *i.e.* push the thing and everything on it in. > – Bl

pa·o·hmin \ṗa-ó-ȟmiŋ\ *v* : to shy from, jump sideways as some horses do when an automobile passes by – Bl

pa·o·hpa \ṗa-ó-ȟṗa\ *va* : to stick through with something < ~ *iyewaya* He shoved and stuck through it with something. *Yunkan maka kin ~ iyeya na kutakiya hinhpaya, i.e. hunpe on* And then she suddenly stuck through the ground with it, *i.e.* with a stick to dig turnips, and she plummeted downward. >

pa·o·ka·ga \ṗa-ó-ḱa-ġa\ *adv* : exceedingly, extravagantly < *Hokšicala wan wašte ~* The baby was extraordinarily pretty. > – B.H.46.1

pa·o·kan·šni·yan \ṗa-ó-kaŋ-šni-yaŋ\ *v* or *adv perhaps* : to crowd out – B.H.200.6

pa·o·ki·he \pa-ó-ḱi-he\ *n* [fr *pa* nose + *ókihe* joint] : the bridge or ridge of the nose, bone and cartilage

pa·o·ki·ju \ṗa-ŏ'-ḱi-ju\ *v* : to put together *e.g.* a deck of playing cards – *Syn* ÓKIJU

pa·o·ki·ya·ska·pa \ṗa-ó-ḱi-ya-sḱa-ṗa\ *vn* : to be bent in, jammed in

pa·o·ko·gna i·ye·i·c'i·ya \ṗa-ó-ḱo-gna i-yè-i-c'i-ya\ *v* : to squeeze one's self into a row of men – Bl

pa·o·ko·ton \ṗa-ó-ḱo-toŋ\ *v* : to make a split so as to insert something < ~ *o* to shoot to make a split for an insertion > – *Syn* PAKAWA

pa·o·ksa \ṗa-ó-ksa\ *va* wa·paoksa : to make cave in *e.g.* a ditch *etc.*, so as to fill the cavity and level the ground

pa·o·na \ṗa-ŏ'-na\ *va perhaps* wa·paona : to push on *e.g.* a ring on a stick, to shove on – Bl

pa·on·ze wo·sla i·ye·ya \ṗa-óŋ-ze wo-sla i-yè-ya\ *v phr* : to tip over < *Apajeje iblotaka ca paonze wosla iyewayelo* I suddenly tipped over when I sat down on the edge. > – *Syn* PAGLAPTUS IYEYA Bl

pa·o·po \ṗa-ó-po\ *vn* : to warp, to push and make a hollow place – *Syn* NAOPO

pa·o·pu·ski·ca \ṗa-ó-ṗu-ski-ca\ *va* : to press down into — **paopuskil** *va contrac* : to pack in tight by hand

pa·o·ski·ca \ṗa-ó-sḱi-ca\ *va* wa·paoskica : to cram in

pa·o·spa \ṗa-ó-sṗa\ *va* wa·paospa : to push under, as in water

pa·o·šlog \ṗa-ó-šlog\ *va contrac of* paošloka : to push in and break through < ~ *iyeya* to break through suddenly, as through ice, to get suddenly into deep water,

---

\a\ father \e\ they \i\ machine \o\ smoke \u\ lunar \an, aŋ\ blanc Fr. \in, iŋ\ ink \on, oŋ, un, uŋ\ soon, confier Fr. \c\ chair \ġ\ machen Ger. \j\ fusion \clusters: bl, gn, kp, hšl, etc...\ b°lo ... said with a slight vowel **See more in the Introduction, Guide to Pronunciatio**

to break through *e.g.* ground that is undermined >
pa·o·šlo·ka \ṗa-ó-šlo-k̇a\ *va* wa·paošloka : to make go in by pressure, as a stick into the ground, or a nail into a hollow wall where, unexpectedly, it suddenly goes in
pa·o·tkons \ṗa-ó-tk̇oŋs\ *va contrac of* paotkonza : to make level full
pa·o·tkon·za \ṗa-ó-tk̇oŋ-za\ *va* wa·paotkonza : to press in full, to strike off level as in measuring grain
pa·o·tku·ga \ṗa-ó-tk̇u-ġa\ *va* : to push and thereby lock *e.g.* a door with a night latch
pa·o·t'ins \ṗa-ó-t'iŋs\ *va of* paot'inza : to press tight *e.g.* a half-closed door < ~ *iyeya*, or *iyotaka* He slammed it tight, he sat tight. *Hena papa na wašin icicahi ~ ognakapi* Therein they stored dried meat and fat mixed together and pressed tight. > – MS.483
pa·o·t'in·za \pa-ó-t'iŋ-za\ *va* wa·paot'inza : to press in hard and tight with the hand
pa·o·wan·ca·ya \pa-ó-waŋ-ca-ya\ *v* : to disperse by – Bl
pa·o·wo·tan *or* **paowotan·la** \ṗa-ó-wo-taŋ\ *va* wa·pa-owotan : to make straight, make stand upright < ~ *hi-yuic'iya* to make one's self sit up, having been on one's back > – Bl
pa-o-ze-ze \ṗa-ó-ze-ze\ *vn* : to swing, dangle, hang as berries do on a bush – *Syn* KAOZEZE
pa·o·ze·ze·ya \ṗa-ó-ze-ze-ya\ *adv* : swinging, dangling – *Syn* KAOZEZEYA
[1]**pa·pa** \pa-pá\ *v* : to bark, as dogs do < *Šunka mapapa* A dog barked at me. *Šunka wan ska ca u na papa* A dog that is white came and barked at it. > – MS.573 SI
[2]**pa·pa** \ṗá-ṗa\ *n* : dried meat, *i.e.* ~ pápa sàka < *Wi-nuhcala, ṗápala wan cik'ala yegnake c'on hanpi kaga yo; hanp'miglatkanpi ktelo* Old lady, make soup where you have had a little bit of jerky put in it; they should drink my own soup delicacy. > – Bl
pa·pa·ga \ṗa-ṗá-ġa\ *vn* : to pop *e.g.* corn or meat in parching – R Bl
pa·pa·hya \ṗa-ṗá-ḣya\ *va* : to parch *e.g.* corn, meat *etc.* — **papahya·pi** *n* : dried intestines that are filled with fat and then roasted like sausage – Note: *tašupa can iya-pehanpi* the intestines are wound around a stick of wood – *Syn* TALIPA R Bl
pa·pa·la \pá-pa-la\ *adj red* [fr *pa* bitter] : bitter, biting as pepper
pa·pin·kpa \pá-piŋ-kpa\ *n* : the point of the nose
pa·pi·spi·za \ṗa-ṗí-sṗi-za\ *va red of* papiza : to make creak
pa·pi·za \ṗa-ṗí-za\ *va* wa·papiza : to make creak by pressure or by sitting on – Bl
pa·pob \ṗa-ṗób\ *va of* papopa : to burst < ~ *iyeya* to make burst >
pa·po·pa \ṗa-ṗó-ṗa\ *va* wa·papopa : to make burst or pop by squeezing or pressing
pa·po·ta \ṗa-ṗó-ṫa\ *va* : to pierce and open up, as with a knife < *Wapepeka on pa kin unpapotapi* We disfigured his head, piercing it with thornes. > – Pb.27 WHL
pa·po·wa·ya \ṗa-ṗó-wa-ya\ *va* wa·papowaya [seem-ingly fr *powaya* which is not used] : to rub, to brush up *e.g.* fur or nap on a hat or blanket
pa·psag \ṗa-pság\ *va contrac of* papsaka : to break or tear in two < ~ *iyeya* to break a rope or wire in two, and the like, by one's quick and sudden pressure > — **pa-psa·gya** *va* papsa·gwa·ya : to cause to break or snap *e.g.* a cord *etc.* by use of pressure — *vn* : to break away as a horse from a rope, to break loose or through
pa·psa·ka \ṗa-psá-ka\ *va* wa·papsaka : to break or tear in two by pressure or by sitting *e.g.* in a swing < *Hokšila hohotela* ~ The boy's swng broke in two. >
pa·psi·psi·ca \ṗa-psí-psi-ca\ *v red* [fr *papsica*, which seems *obsol*] : to push and make fly as chips – *See* psíca
pa·pson *or* **papsun** \ṗa-psúŋ\ *va* wa·papsun : to spill – Cf kpapson *refl*
pa·psun·psun·la \ṗa-psúŋ-psuŋ-la\ *v* wa·papsunpsunla : to rub and make smooth and round, as an arrow shaft
pa·pšun \ṗa-pšúŋ\ *va* wa·papšun : to put out of joint or to dislocate *e.g.* one's arm, to sprain one's own – Note: *kpapšun* is the *refl* form of the word to dislocate one's own; hence, *wa·kpapšun* I put mine out of joint. *Nape kin* He threw it spraining his own hand, *i.e.* that of *Waziya* Santa Claus
pa·pšun·ka \ṗa-pšúŋ-k̇a\ *va* wa·papšunka : to make blunt *e.g.* a pointed stick, needle *etc.* – *See* pšunk̇á
pa·pšun·pšun \ṗa-pšúŋ-pšuŋ\ *v red of* papšun : to sprain *e.g.* an arm often < *Tokel owanaseta nape* ~ *kin on kokipe* He was afraid because it was where the buffalo hunt was on that he sprained his arm. >
pa·pta \ṗa-ptá\ *adv* : through < *Tipi kin ~ unkiyaglapi. Wanna can kin ~ iblabla* We had gone through the house home. Now I am going through the forest. >
pa·ptan \ṗa-pṫáŋ\ *va* wa·paptan : to turn over — **pa-ptan·ptan** *vn red* wa·paptanptan : to roll over, to writhe; to wallow about — **paptanptan·yan** *adv* : rolling or wallowing about — **paptan·yan** *va* wa·pa-ptanyan : to cause to turn over, upset or turn over by pushing < *Paptanyepica šni* He was unable to push and topple it. > — *adv* : rolling about
pa·pte·hin·ca·la \ṗá-pte-hiŋ-ca-la\ *n* : a buffalo cow with a head similar to that of a calf – Bl
pa·ptu·ga \ṗa-ptú-ġa\ *va* wa·paptuga : to break off a piece by pressure – BD
pa·ptu·ja \ṗa-pṫú-ja\ *va* wa·paptuja : to split, to crack by working with the hands — **paptu·ptuja** *v red* : to continuously crack
pa·ptus \ṗa-pṫús\ *vn contrac perhaps of* paptuza : to be stooped over — *adv* : in a stooping position < ~ *iyunka* to lie down stooped > – R
pa·ptuš \ṗa-pṫúš\ *va contrac of* paptuja : to crack by hand < ~ *iyeya* to make split >
pa·ptu·šya \ṗa-pṫú-šya\ *va* paptu·šwa·ya : to cause to crack or split
pa·ptu·za \ṗa-ptú-za\ *vn perhaps* : to stoop, bend over
pa·pus \ṗa-ṗús\ *va contrac of* papús : to wipe dry
pa·pu·za \ṗa-ṗú-za\ *va* wa·papuza [fr *púza* dry] : to rub dry, wipe dry
pa·p'o·h'a \ṗa-p'ö'-ḣ'a\ *va* wa·pap'oh'a : to make the hair stand straight up with the hand
pa·seb \ṗa-séb\ *va contrac of* pasepa : to rub off < ~ *iyeya* to cause continually to rub off > — **pase·bsepa** *v red* : to be rubbing off
pa·se·pa \ṗa-sé-ṗa\ *va* wa·pasepa : to rub off *e.g.* whitewash – R Bl
pa·si \ṗa-sí\ *va* : to inquire about something secretly, to escort somebody, as a prisoner to jail, to march one on < ~ *agla* They escorted him on. > – D.105, 270
pa·si·sa \ṗa-sí-sa\ *va* wa·pasisa : to pin together, to stick in, as a needle or pin
pa·si·ya·kel \ṗa-sí-ya-kel\ *adv* : watching, following up – B.H.258.6 Lh
[1]**pa·ska** \pá-ska\ *adj* : white-headed
[2]**pa·ska** \ṗa-ská\ *va* wa·paska : to bleach or rub and make white
pa·ske·pa *and perhaps* **paškepa** \ṗa-sk̇é-ṗa\ *va* : to rub off or move away water or any fluid with the hand, as

from a table - R
pa·ski·ca \ṗa-sḱí-ca\ *va* : to press down on with the hand; *sl* to swipe, *i.e.* steal — **paskil** *va contrac* : to press down on < ~ *iyeya* to press on suddenly >
pa·sla \pá-sla\ *adj* : bald-headed
pa·slal \ṗa-slál\ *va contrac of* pasláta : to set a pole or stake < *Na can eya okijata ca ~ he k'on hena icu* He took some of those forked poles he had set. >
pa·sla·lye·la *or perhaps* **pasla·yela** \ṗá-sla-lyē'-la\ *adv* : steadily < ~ *econ* to do, *i.e.* work, slowly but steadily > - Bl
pa·sla·ta \ṗa-slá-ṫa\ *va* wa·paslata : to set up a pole in the ground, to drive in *e.g.* a stake
pa·sla·ye·la \ṗá-sla-ye-la\ *adv* : slowly < ~ *un* to keep quiet and do nothing, to take it easy, *~hci omawani* I sauntered, ambled along. > - *See* páslalyèla
pa·sle·ca \ṗa-slé-ca\ *va* wa·pasleca : to split *e.g.* a hide or sack *etc.* with a knife — **paslel** *va contrac* : to split < ~ *iyeya* to split suddenly > — **pasle·sleca** *v red* : to be splitting continually
pa·sli \ṗa-slí\ *va* wa·pasli : to squeeze out by use of pressure
pa·slo·han \ṗa-sló-haŋ\ *va* : to push or shove along *e.g.* a sled — **paslohan·han** *va red* : to push along — **paslohan·pi** *n* : a long stick with a large head once made for sliding on the snow or ice
pa·slu·ka \ṗa-slú-ka\ *n* : masturbation, onanism
pa·slul \ṗa-slúl\ *v contrac of* pasluta : to push out of — **paslu·sluta** *v red* : to be pushing out of
pa·slu·ta \ṗa-slú-ṫa\ *v* wa·pasluta : to push out of, as dirt from a pipe stem
pa·smag \ṗa-smág\ *va contrac of* pasmaka : to indent < ~ *iyeya* to hollow out >
pa·sma·ka \ṗa-smá-ka\ *va* wa·pasmaka : to make a hollow in by pushing, to indent
pa·smin·yan *or* **pasminyan·yan** \ṗa-smíŋ-yaŋ\ *va* wa·pasminyanyan : to rub or scrape off, to make smooth or clean
pa·sna \ṗa-sná\ *va* wa·pasna : to make rattle or ring by pushing *e.g.* a doorbell
pa·sni \ṗa-sní\ *va* wa·pasni : to extinguish a firebrand or a light, by sitting on it or pushing it into the ashes
pa·snon *or* **pasnun** \ṗa-snóŋ\ *va* wa·pasnon : to roast *e.g.* meat on a spit or stick
pa·so·ta \ṗa-só-ta\ *va* wa·pasota : to use up by rubbing with the hand, as soap < *Haipajaja wapasota* I used up soap. >
pa·spa·ya \ṗa-spá-ya\ *va* wa·paspaya : to make wet, to sponge; *vulg* to have sexual intercourse. In this sense the word *tawinton* is also used
pa·stan·ka \ṗa-stáŋ-ḱa\ *va* : to moisten; *vulg* to have coitus. In this sense the words *tawinton* and *paspaya* are used
pa·stan·ki·ya \ṗa-stáŋ-ḱi-ya\ *va* pastan·wa·kiya : to cause to take off the hair, as in dressing a skin
pa·sto \ṗa-stó\ *va* wa·pasto : to smooth or brush down *e.g.* the hair - *Syn* KASTO
pa·sto i·hpa·ya \ṗa-stó i-ȟpà-ya\ *vn in comp* : to fall on one's hands and knees, or on one's face < *Pasto iwahpaya* I fell on my face. ~ *iyunka* He lay fallen on his hands and knees. *Makata pasto ihpeic'iye* He threw himself prone on the ground. > - B.H.43.11, 133.9
pa·sto·sto \ṗa-stó-sto\ *vn red of* pasto *in comp* < ~ *ihpeic'iyapi* They got on their knees with heads on the ground. ~ *iwahpaye* I was fallen face-down on the ground. > - Bl B.H.109.1
pa·sto·ya \ṗa-stó-ya\ *va* pasto·wa·ya : to cause to brush down — *adv* : brushing down
pa·su \pa-sú\ *n* : the human nose, the beak or bill of birds
pa·su·bla·ska \pa-sú-bla-ska\ *n* : a broad-billed duck
pa·su·ta \ṗa-sú-ṫa\ *va* wa·pasuta [fr *sutá* hard, stiff] : to make stiff and hard by kneading, as dough
pa·swu \ṗa-swú\ *v* **1** : to push into, bury, as in a barrel of corn < ~ *iyeya* to make rattle, as corn by pushing into it > **2** : to cut into strings < *taha* ~ to make fringes on a skin >
pa·swu·i·c'i·gle \ṗa-swú-i-c'i-gle\ *v* paswu·mi·c'igle : to squeeze one's self in, to be important, obtrusive - Bl
pa·swu·pi \ṗa-swú-pi\ *n* : fringe or fringes
pa·swu·swu \ṗa-swú-swu\ *v red of* paswu : to be constantly rattling — **paswu·ya** *va* : to rattle by pushing — *adv* : rattling
pa·ša \ṗa-šá\ *va* wa·paša [fr *ša* red] : to make red
pa·ša·pa \ṗa-šá-ṗa\ *va* : to defile something by rubbing
pa·šib \ṗa-šíb\ *va contrac of* pašipa : to bend or form — **paši·bšib** *va red* : to be giving a new form — **paši·bšipa** \ṗa-ší-bši-ṗa\ *va red of* pašipa : to be giving a form by bending
pa·ši·ca \ṗa-ší-ca\ *va* wa·pašica [fr *šica* bad] : to spoil with the hands or by rubbing, to soil or injure
pa·ši·ca·ho·wa·ya \ṗa-ší-ca-ho-wa-ya\ *va* wa·pašicahowaya [fr *šicahowaya* to moan or scream] : to make cry out by pushing with the hand, to push or punch and make cry out
pa·ši·htin \ṗa-ší-ȟtiŋ\ *v* : to make badly, to do a thing incorrectly
pa·ši·pa \ṗa-ší-ṗa\ *va* wa·pašipa : to bend something giving it another form
pa·ška \ṗa-šká\ *va* : to loosen by pressure, as in untieing a knot - Bl
pa·škan·gle \ṗa-škáŋ-gle\ *v* : to take as a sign, perhaps - Note: perhaps only the form used is *wípaškanglepi* - Bl
pa·ška·pa \ṗa-šká-ṗa\ *v* wa·paškapa : to make a noise with one's hands in water - *Syn* KAŠKAPA
pa·škeb \ṗa-škéb\ *va contrac of* paškepa : to rub off with the hand < ~ *iyeya* to rub off quickly with the hand > - Bl
pa·ške·han \ṗa-šké-haŋ\ *v* : to push or toss away < ~ *iyeya* to push sideways with the head, to toss away, ~ *kuwa* to chase pushing away > - *Syn* PAKAB IYEYA
pa·ške·pa *or* **paskepa** \ṗa-škē'-ṗa\ *va* : to squeegee away, *e.g.* water, with the hand from a surface - R
pa·ški·ca \ṗa-škí-ca\ *va* wa·paškica : to wring, press out with the hand, but not by twisting - Note: *yuškica* to wring by twisting. *See* paškita
pa·ški·ška \ṗa-šķí-šķa\ *va* wa·paškiška : to disarrange by rubbing
pa·ški·ta \ṗa-škí-ṫa\ *va* wa·paškita : to press, squeeze out by pressing
pa·ško·kpa \ṗa-škō'-kṗa\ *va* wa·paškokpa : to make a cavity or ditch by pressing with the hands, or by sitting
pa·šku \ṗa-škú\ *va* : to shell corn, by pressing a stick between the rows of kernels and thus prying them off - Bl
[1]**pa·šla** \ṗa-šlá\ *va* wa·pašla [fr *šla* bare or bald] : to

---

\a\ f<u>a</u>ther \e\ th<u>e</u>y \i\ mach<u>i</u>ne \o\ sm<u>o</u>ke \u\ l<u>u</u>nar \an, aŋ\ bl<u>anc</u> Fr. \in, iŋ\ <u>in</u>k \on, oŋ, un, uŋ\ s<u>oo</u>n, c<u>on</u>fier Fr. \c\ <u>ch</u>air \ġ\ ma<u>ch</u>en Ger. \j\ fu<u>s</u>ion \clusters: bl, gn, kp, hšl, etc...\ <u>b</u>ᵉlo ... said with a slight vowel
See more in the Introduction, Guide to Pronunciation

make bare, rub off *e.g.* hair

[2]**pa·šla** \ṗa-šlá\ *adj* : bald-headed – Note: the word is used only of animals such as turkeys

pa·šla·ya \ṗa-šlá-ya\ *va* pašla·wa·ya : to cause to make bare

pa·šla·ye·la \ṗá-šla-ye-la\ *adv* : making bare the head < ~ *s'e woyaka yo* Speak as though making bare your head, *i.e.* tell the full truth. > – *Syn* HE PAŠPUPI *i.e. lit* lice being washed out La

pa·šle·ca \ṗa-šlé-ca\ *va* wa·pašleca : to split something hard or heavy by pressure — **pašlel** *va contrac* : to split < ~ *iyeya* to make split > — **pašle·šleca** *v red* : to keep splitting

pa·šlo·ka \ṗa-šló-ḳa\ *va* wa·pašloka : to push or shove off *e.g.* one's coat sleeve

pa·šlu·šlu·ta \ṗa-šlú-šlu-ta\ *v* : to keep popping up < *Na hucan kin lila pašlušlutapi* And the arrow's shaft just kept popping up. > – MS.481

pa·šlu·ta \ṗa-šlú-ta\ *v* : to loom up < ~ *hinapa* to come looming up, *i.e.* before one suddenly as when passing through a draw unseen and thence coming up and into sight > – WE

pa·šna \ṗa-šná\ *va* wa·pašna : to miss while thrusting or pushing

pa·šni·ja \pa-šní-ja\ *v* : to push or blow air out – Bl WHL

pa·špa \ṗa-šṗá\ *v* : to cut or break a piece off with a knife pressing hard — **pašpa·špa** *v red* : to break off continually

pa·špe·ki·ya \ṗa-šṗé-ḳi-ya\ *va* pašpe·wa·kiya : to cause to break off; to cause to come out, perhaps as does a stain — **pašpe·šni** *adj* : indelible — **pašpe·ya** *va* pa-špe·wa·ya : to cause to come out, as a stain *etc.* – Bl

pa·špu \ṗa-šṗú\ *va* wa·pašpu **1** : to break off, as a bulb or excrescence, to loosen and make fall off by pushing **2** : to wash out, as a stain < *Hepašpupi* [*he* lice + *pašpupi* were washed out] *s'e woyaka yo*, *lit* Tell it as though the lice were washed out of one's hair, *i.e.* Tell all about it. >

pa·špu·špu \ṗa-šṗú-šṗu\ *va red* wa·pašpušpú [fr *pašpu* to cut into pieces] : to cut or break off into pieces *e.g.* a cake

pa·štan \ṗa-štáŋ\ *va* wa·paštan : to soak and take the hair off, as from a hide

pa·štu·ta \ṗa-štú-ta\ *v* : to rub, as perhaps the feet with snow – ED

pa·šu·ja \ṗa-šú-ja\ *va* : to crush with the hand, to break or mash by punching — **pašuš** \ṗa-šúš\ *va contrac* : to be mashing < ~ *iyeya* to crush quickly > — **pašu·šuja** \ṗa-šú-šu-ja\ *v red* wa·pašušuja : to mash up, break in pieces *e.g.* bones

pa·šwo·ka \ṗa-šwó-ka\ *vn* : to overflow, come over

pa·š'a·ka \ṗa-š'á-ḳa\ *va* wa·paš'aka : to push or strike with too little force to penetrate, to dent

[1]**pa·ta** \ṗa-tá\ *adv* : together, crowded < ~ *iheya* They crowd together. >

[2]**pa·ta** \ṗa-tá\ *va* wa·pata : to cut out and sew up, as in making a tent

[3]**pa·ta** \ṗá-ṫa\ *va* wa·páta : to cut up, butcher meat < *Nupin wicao, pte, na wicapata* He shot them both, cows, and butchered them. >

[4]**pa·ta** \ṗá-ṫa\ *n* : a grove of timber – *Syn* HINTA, CANPATA R MG Bl

pa·tag \ṗa-tág\ *v* [fr *pataka* to run about] : to come to a stop after running, as horses do, to stop short < ~ *inajin* to stand having come to a stop > — **pata·gtag** *v contrac red* : to stop now and then < ~ *inyanka* to run stopping now and then > – D.19, 77, 271 Bl

pa·ta·gya \ṗa-tá-gya\ *va* : to scare, prevent < *Patagmayayelo, okit'emayayelo* You prented me, putting obstructions in my way. > — *vn* : to stop short — *adv* : haltingly – *Syn* NAT'UNGYAKEL, KOKIPEYA

pa·ta·gya·kel \ṗa-tá-gya-kel\ *adv* : bringing to a stop – *Syn* OKIT'EYAKEL Bl

pa·ta·ka \ṗa-tá-ḳa\ *v* : to dodge about, run here and there, to come to a stand as a horse does < ~ *inajin* It came to a stop from running about. *Patake šni keš katinyeya iyaya po* Go non-stop, but do not take stops. > — **pata·ktaka** *v* : to stop < *Tanyan unkomanipi; yunkan kal ecela unpataktakapi* We traveled well; and then only over there did we make a stop. > – R Bl

[1]**pa·tan** \ṗa-ṫáŋ\ *va* wa·patan : to esteem highly, to take care of, to save < *Miniša waštehce kin lehan yapatan yelo* You saved for now the good wine. ~ *najin* to resist, ~ *maunpi s'elececa* They seemed to be against me, seem to push me away, ~ *iyeya* to save things > – B.H. 178.20

[2]**pa·tan** \ṗa-ṫáŋ\ *va* wa·patan **1** : to mash up *e.g.* potatoes **2** : to feel for, by pushing with anything other than the hand

pa·tan·han \ṗa-ṫáŋ-haŋ\ *part* : pushing against

pa·tan'·in \ṗa-ṫáŋ-iŋ\ *va* wa·patan'in : to rub and make appear — **patan'in·šni** *vn* wa·patan'inšni : to rub off, to obliterate

pa·tan·ka \ṗa-ṫáŋ-ka\ *va* wa·patanka : to push out, make larger by pushing — **patan·kal** *v contrac* : to enlarge < ~ *iyeya* to cause to be enlarged, ~ *hiyuya* to come to be enlarged by pushing > – B.H.52.15, 130.9

[1]**pa·tan·tan** \ṗa-ṫáŋ-ṫaŋ\ *v red of* patan : to push one on < *Patantanpi s'e mayani hwo* Do you walk as though they they were pushing you onward? > – Bl

[2]**pa·tan·tan** \ṗa-ṫáŋ-taŋ\ *v red of* patan : to push into, as a stick into the sand in hunting for tortoise eggs, feeling around with the stick < *kepatantan* to stick in search of turtle eggs > — **patantan·yan** *adv* : pushing *e.g.* for turtle eggs in the sand < ~ *kuwa* to hunt using a stick to search in the sand >

pa·tan·wan·ji·la \ṗá-ṫaŋ-waŋ-ji-la\ *adv* : directly, in one path, with one purpose, unchangeably

[1]**pa·tan·yan** \ṗa-ṫáŋ-yaŋ\ *adv* : reserving, keeping

[2]**pa·tan·yan** \ṗa-ṫáŋ-yan\ *adv* : pushing against

pa·ta·pi \ṗá-ṫa-pi\ *n* : a cutting up of meat, a butchering

pa·te·ca \ṗa-ṫé-ca\ *va* wa·pateca : to make new, rub up and make new again, to furbish

pa·te·pa \ṗa-ṫé-ṗa\ *va* wa·patepa : to wear off by rubbing, to wear out by pressure, as the spring on a wagon

pa·ti *or* **patil** \ṗa-ṫí\ *va contrac of* patica : to work up by pressing on *e.g.* dough when sticky and soft; to shove, push < *pati mahel iyeya* to shove into the house > — **pati·ca** *va* : to scrape off by hand — **patima** \ṗa-ṫí-ma\ *v* : to push into a room < ~ *iyeya* to push one into a room, ~ *hiyuya* to make one go into a room, *i.e.* to thrust or force into > – D.44 FE

pa·tin \ṗa-ṫíŋ\ *adj* ma·patin : stiff, as a new ribbon; firm, not springing or yielding; stiff with the cold – *See* katin, satin — **patin·yan** *va* patin·wa·ya : to cause to become stiff

pa·ti·tan \ṗa-ṫí-ṫaŋ\ *va* wa·patitan : to push against, to push *e.g.* a wheelbarrow — **patitan·yan** \ṗa-ṫí-ṫaŋ-yaŋ\ *adv* : pushing against

pa·tka·ša *and* **patkaša·la** \pa-ṫká-ša\ *n* : a turtle of a small species, living in the water – Note: *keglezela*

pa·tku·ga \ṗa-tḱú-ġa\ *va* wa·patkuga : to break in square pieces by pushing or punching — **patkuh** \ṗa-tḱúḣ\ *va contrac* : to punch squares < ~ *iyeya* to punch out square pieces > — **patku·tkuga** *v red* : to break or punch out squares continually - BD

pa·to·ka·he·ya \ṗa-tó-ḱa-he-ya\ *va* : to push to the front - B.H.93.2

pa·to·kanl i·ye·ya \ṗa-tó-kanl i-yè-ya\ *or* \ṗa-ṫó-kaŋl i-yè-ya\ *v* : to push aside - *Syn* PAHÁ IYÉYA

pa·ton·wan·wan \ṗa-ṫóŋ-waŋ-yaŋ\ *adv* : rubbing clear for seeing < ~ *iyeya* to rub to clear for vision, *Išta kin ~ iyewakiyelo* Rubbing my eyes I recognized it, *i.e.* to rub one's eyes in order to see better. ~ *iyeyin na tanyan ables wacin yo* Try to see well rubbing your eyes to clearify your vision. > - Bc Bl

pa·tu·ja \pa-tú-ja\ *vn* wa·patuja : to bend over, lean forward, stoop down to get something — **patuš** \ṗa-ṫúš\ *vn contrac* : to be bent over < ~ *inajin* to stand bent over forward, ~ *hotonkel škan* to move about bent over groaning. > — **patu·štuš** \ṗa-ṫú-šṫuš\ *v red* : to be continually bent over < ~ *iyaya* to pass on stooping > — **patu·šya** \pa-ṫú-šya\ *va* patu·šwa·ya : to cause to bend forward or stoop, to make bow down

pa·t'a \ṗa-t'á\ *va* wa·pat'a : to kill by pressure, as by lying on — **pat'a·t'a** *vn red* : to be numb or asleep, as a limb

pa·t'e·ca \ṗa-t'ẽ'-ca\ *va* wa·pat'eca : to make soft by pressing *e.g.* fruit

pa·t'i·hpe·ya \ṗa-t'í-ḣpe-ya\ *va* [fr *pat'a* to kill by pressing + *ihpeya* to throw down] : to cast or throw down to kill under pressure, as by pressing or stepping on

pa·t'ins \ṗa-t'íŋs\ *va contrac of* pat'inza : to knead, to press down tight < ~ *iyeya* to press quickly > — **pat'in·st'inza** *v red* : to keep pressing tight

pa·t'in·za \ṗa-t'íŋ-za\ *va* wa·pat'inza : to make stiff by kneading, as in mixing up bread, to press down tight

pa·un·ka \ṗa-úŋ-ka\ *va* wa·paunka : to push and make fall down; *colloq,* to eat one out of grub (push down), one who gives a feast - CG

pa·wa·ga \ṗa-wá-ġa\ *va* wa·pawaga : to roll or twist in the hand

pa·wa·ksa \ṗá-wa-ksa\ *va* pá·wa·waksa : to behead

pa·wa·k'in \ṗá-wa-k'iŋ\ *n* : a saddle, a pack-saddle

pa·wan·kal \ṗa-wáŋ-ḱal\ *adv* : upward < ~ *iyeya* to shove up, to raise, ~ *yuza* to hold up high > - Pb.17 B.H.244.10

pa·wa·š'a·ka \pa-wá-š'a-ka\ *v* : to put to a test of strength, to strengthen - WHL

pa·wa·za \ṗa-wá-za\ *va* wa·pawaza : to push and rub, as one cow does to another, hence to annoy or vex by pushing - Note: *ikpawaza* to rub one's self against one thing or another - R

pa·we \ṗá-we\ *v* : to bleed at the nose

pa·we·ga \ṗa-wé-ġa\ *va* wa·pawega : to break with the hand, but not entirely off, or by pushing, falling, sitting *etc.* < *Hehé kola locin wapáwegehcelo* Too bad friend, I broke my hunger indeed, *i.e.* when wanting food very badly. > - Bl

pa·we·hi·yu \ṗá-we-hi-yu\ *or* \ṗa-wé-hi-yu\ *v* pawe·ma·hiyu : to bleed at the nose

pa·weh \ṗa-wéḣ\ *va contrac of* pawega : to break by hand < ~ *iyeya* to break with the hand *e.g.* a stick suddenly or quickly > — **pa·we·hwe·ga** \ṗa-wé-ḣwe-ġa\ *v red* : to break continually

pa·we·hya \ṗa-wé-ḣya\ *va* pawe·hwa·ya : to cause to break by pushing against

pa·we·ka·lu·za·pi \ṗá-we-ḱa-lu-za-pi\ *n* : a violent bleeding of the nose, a sickness in former days - Bl

pa·we·we \ṗa-wé-we\ *va* wa·pawewe : to make bleed < *Mikpawewe* I made myself bleed. >

pa·wi \ṗa-wí\ *v* : to hover about, move about slowly and quietly, as a bird over carrion or an old person who is yet able to move about; *fig* to be old but still moving - *See* wápawi

pa·wi·ce·gna \ṗa-wí-ce-gna\ *n* : one, *e.g.* a horse, that has returned to its group < ~ *hiyuya* to cause to come back to the herd > - BT LHB

pa·wi·gnu·ni \ṗa-wí-gnu-ni\ *va* wa·pawignuni : to become unable to figure out or understand what has happened, to become confused - R Bl LHB

pa·wi·ka \ṗa-wí-ḱa\ *vn* wa·pawika : to be still strong, have some vitality left, as is said of a person who will die < *Nahahci* ~ He still has some vitality. > - *See* owikešni, *or possibly* owik'ešni — *adv* : with many staying on for naught - BD

pa·win·hya \ṗa-wíŋ-ḣya\ *adv* : turning out of a straight direction

pa·win·ja \ṗa-wíŋ-ja\ *va* wa·pawinja : to bend or press down *e.g.* grain by one's weight, as in sitting on a branch, or a knife while cutting with it — **pawinš** *va contrac* : to bend or press down < ~ *iyeya* to bend or press down swiftly > — **pawin·šwinja** *va red* : to bend down, to make shake

pa·win·ta \ṗa-wíŋ-ṫa\ *va* wa·pawinta : to rub

pa·wi·s'e \ṗa-wí-s'e\ *adv* : crowded together, as cattle or sheep *etc.*, moving about as maggots do < ~ *inyanka* to run over others > - Note: the word seems to carry the idea of crawling over each other as a moving mass - R Bl

pa·wi·ta·ya \ṗa-wí-ṫa-ya\ *va* wa·pawitaya [fr *witaya* together] : to gather with the hand, as in gathering crumbs

pa·wi·ta·ye·la \ṗá-wi-ta-ye-la\ *adv* : sticking the heads together, as when crowding around a messenger to hear the news < *Taku kápelaka: wozá hinglapelo* He excels in something: they started up all at once; *wána el yucik'ayela el ahiyayelo; wana ~ el ahiyayelo* he sang a tune there in a crowded area; there he sang a tune there where he pressed in around. > - Bl

pa·wi·wi \ṗa-wí-wi\ *adv red of* pawi : in crowds — **pawiwi·s'e** *adv* : crowded together and moving en masse; shaking — **pawi·ya** *adv* : teeming with *e.g.* flies on something - R Bl RA

pa·wi·ya·kel \ṗa-wí-ya-kel\ *adv* : still strong, as is said of a person who will die < ~ *hpaya* to be lying as one still strong > - BD

pa·wi·ya·kpa \ṗa-wí-ya-kṗa\ *va* wa·páwiyakpa [fr *wiyakpa* to shine] : to make shine, to polish, brighten by rubbing

pa·wo·sla·he·ye·la·kel \ṗa-wó-sla-he-ye-la-kel\ *adv* [fr *pawoslata* to push up straight] : pushing up to stand properly straight < *Kitan ~ manke c'on nawajin yelo* I stood since I had been scarcely sitting pushing it up straight. >

pa·wo·slal \ṗa-wó-slal\ *v contrac* [fr *pawoslata* push up straight] : to straighten up by pushing < ~ *iyeya* to

---

push up *e.g.* a tent to make it stand, ~ *egle* to put something up, such as a pole, *wowapi* ~ *iyeya* to hoist the flag, *Natahe kpanyanpi kin ohomni waso na on tušu kin hena pahta na* ~ *eglepi* He cut thongs from the dressed skin around the head, for the purpose of then tying up the tent poles and pushing them up to set them. *Na wana canwákan kin* ~ *eunglepi* And now the flag pole we set pushing it up straight. > – B.H.163.5

pa·wo·sla·ta \ṗa-wó-sla-ta\ *v* : to push up straight

pa·ya·pa \pa-yá-pa\ *vn* : to be of the upper part of something – LHB

pa·ya pe·ju·ta \pa-yá ṗe-jù-ṫa\ *n* : Geyer's spurge – Cf canhlogan wapoštan, *lit* hollow stalk cap or hat – BT #24

pa·ya·ta \pa-yá-ṫa\ *adv* : in or at the head

pa·ya·ya·la \pá-ya-yà-la\ *n* : a pliant nose or beak

[1]**pa·za** \ṗa-zá\ *va* wa·paza : to stick up bushes for a shelter, as once was done to sleep under, or to put up *e.g.* sticks in a row closely together as a fence < ~ *egle* to set up a fence, *húpaza* with knees folded and legs drawn against one's chest, a way of gaining some shelter against the cold >

[2]**pa·za** \pá-za\ *adj* : bitter, as gall

[1]**pa·zan** \ṗa-záŋ\ *va* wa·pázan 1 : to part or separate *e.g.* the hair 2 : to hurt or kill by striking

[2]**pa·zan** *or perhaps* **pasan** \pa-záŋ\ *adv* : with the head concealed, as a hen in the bushes, *i.e.* with the head invisible < ~ *hpaya* to lay with head unseen, ~ *egle* to conceal *e.g.* a stick in deep water, and so out of sight >

[1]**pa·zan·yan** \ṗa-záŋ-yaŋ\ *adv* : dividing, parting < *Taté* ~ , *i.e. tatoheya, unglipi ktelo* We shall arrive back with the wind parting, *i.e.* against the wind. >

[2]**pa·zan·yan** \pa-záŋ-yaŋ\ *or perhaps* \ṗa-záŋ-yaŋ\ *adv* : under the brush, but without the idea of concealment < ~ *iyunka* to lie down, sleep under the brush >

pa·ze·ca \pá-ze-ca\ *adj* : bitter; *fig* bitter, as in one's remarks – Bl

pa·ze·ze *or* **pazezela** *or* **pazezeya** *or* **pazezeyela** \pá-ze-ze\ *adv* swinging, nodding the head, letting the head drop as in sleep < ~ *manka* I sat with my head nodding. ~ *ištinma* to sleep with head dropped >

pa·zi \ṗa-zí\ *va* wa·pazi : to push into, as a stick into the sand in hunting turtle eggs – R Bl

pa·zi·ca \ṗa-zí-ca\ *va* wa·pazica : to roll out or stretch with the hand, to stretch by pressing against — **pazi·gzica** *v red* : to stretch continually

pa·zo \ṗa-zó\ *va* wa·pazo : to show, present anything in view < ~ *yetó* Let me see, *or* Now show me. > — **pazo·kiya** \ṗa-zó-ki-ya\ *v* pazo·wa·kiya : to cause to show

pa·zunl \ṗa-zúŋl\ *va contrac of* pazunta : to sew or run up

pa·zun·ta \ṗa-zúŋ-ṫa\ *va* wa·pazunta : to sew or run up at the sides some distance from the edge *e.g.* of leggings; to lace – D.228

pa·zu·ya \pa-zú-ya\ *v* : to crack, *e.g.* a bone, to break < *Hu mapazuye* I cracked my bone. > – Cf zuya Ka

pce·ce·la \pcé-ce-la\ *adj* : short

pce·lye·la \pce-lyé-la\ *adv* : awhile, for a short time, briefly

pce·pce·ce·la \pce-pcé-ce-la\ *adj red of* pcecela : short, implying many are short — **pcepce·lyela** *adv red* [fr *pcelyela* for a short time] : at short intervals

[1]**pe** \ṗe\ *n* : the top of the head < *Pe awicaputaka na oyasin asnipi* Everybody got well when he imposed his hand on the top of their heads. >

[2]**pe** \ṗe\ *adj* : sharp, as edged tools; pointed

[3]**pe** \ṗe\ *partic indicating the precatory pl imper terminationof v* < Econpe Do it, *or* You are to do it. > – Note: this *partic, pe,* is used by women where men use *po*

[4]**pe** \ṗe\ *adv* – the modal *pl* ending, the old form for *pi* and used by women only

pe·a·gla·ta·ta \ṗe-á-gla-ṫa-ṫa\ *v* pea·wa·glatata : to use all up, to exhaust one's supply by giving to others

pe·a·gna·gki·ya \ṗe-á-gna-gki-ya\ *va* : to make settle upon, to put on or apply something from the outside; hence to shine upon < *Anpetu wanji towanjica ca peagnagwicakiyin ktelo* A day that is all blue, *i.e.* a clear blue sky, will shine on them. > – LP

pe·co·kan \ṗe-có-ǩaŋ\ *n* : the scalp lock that some used to grow on the back of the head, a round tuft

Pe·co·kan Han·ska \Ṗe-có-ǩaŋ Haŋ-skà\ *np* : a Chinaman, *i.e.* the big and long scalp lock

pe·co·kan·yan *or* **pecokanyan·kisonpi** \ṗe-có-ǩaŋ-yaŋ\ \ṗé-co-ǩaŋ-yaŋ-ki-sòŋ-pi\ *n* : the scalp lock < ~ *Hanska* a Chinaman >

pe·gna·gki·ya \ṗé-gna-gǩi-ya\ *va of* pégnaka : to cause to wear in the hair or on the head < *Na tatanka hin pahpa wan k'on na* ~ And he had him wear a tuft of buffalo bull's hair that he had put off. >

pe·gna·ka \ṗé-gna-ǩa\ *v* : to wear in the hair on the head *e.g.* a *wótawe,* a battle charm, a bunch of buffalo hair *etc.* — **pegnaka·pi** *n* : ornaments worn in the hair or on the head, *e.g.* feathers *etc.*

[1]**pe·han** \ṗe-háŋ\ *n* : the crane < ~ *s'e napakaza hanskaska kaca* Its claws (fingers), so it seems, are quite long like those of a crane. > — **pehan·gila** *n* : the gray or sand-bill crane — **pehan san** *n* : the large white crane — **pehan ska** *n* : the heron — **pehan ša** *n* : the little blue heron — **pehan to** \pe-háŋ ṫo\ *n* : the great blue heron

[2]**pe·han** \ṗe-háŋ\ *va* wa·pehan : to fold up anything < ~ *egnaka* to fold up and put away > — **pehan·han** *v red* : to fold up much or all < ~ *egnake* to fold up all and lay away >

pe·hin \pe-híŋ\ *n* ma·péhin : the hair of the head

pe·hin·ci·ci·la \ṗe-híŋ-ci-ci-la\ *n* : the killdeer, a plover

pe·hin'·i·ca·sto \ṗe-híŋ-i-ca-sṫo\ *n* : a hair brush – *Syn* PEHINPAPOA

pe·hin'·i·sla·ye \ṗe-híŋ-i-sla-ye\ *n* : hair oil

pe·hin'·i·yo·sto·la \ṗe-híŋ-i-yo-sto-la\ *n* : a hair net

pe·hin·pa·po·a \ṗe-híŋ-pa-po-a\ *n* : a hair brush

pe·hin·pa·si·se \ṗe-híŋ-ṗa-si-se\ *n* : hair pins

pe·hin·tu·ta \ṗe-híŋ-ṫu-ṫa\ *adv* pehin·ma·tuta : dishevelled, unkempt – Bl

pe·hni·ga \ṗe-ȟní-ǧa\ *adj* : red hot — *vn* : to be red hot — *n* : that which is heated to a red heat – *See* pešnija

pe·hnih \ṗe-ȟníȟ\ *vn contrac of* pehniga : to be red hot — **pehni·hniga** \ṗe-ȟní-ȟni-ǧa\ *vn* : to be red hot consistently — **pehni·hya** *va* pehni·hwa·ya : to make red hot

pe·ji \ṗe-jí\ *n* : grass, hay, herbs

~ *blaskaska* blue grass, perhaps
~ *icape* or *pejícape* a pitch fork, a hay fork
~ *icašla* or *pejícašla* a scythe
~ *icašla opé* or *pejícašla opé* a mowing sickle
~ *hánskaska psi iyececa* Hungarian or awnless brome grass, bromus inermis, the grass family – BT #41
~ *hinkṗíla* moss, a short grass growing in light-green,

mat-like patches
pejíhcaka slender wheat grass, agropyron occidentalis, of the grass family; also called salt grass. When it is abundant and tall it was said the coming snow would reach to its head, and horses *etc.* would eat just that - Bl #185
~ *ȟóta* dark-leaved mugwort, of the composite family; a herb of whitish or grayish appearance; wild sage, artemisia ludoviciana. The genus of five plants well known and frequently used, all having characteristics of gray grass or sage - #77
~ *ȟóta apé blaskaska* prairie mugwort, the western or cudweed mugwort; white sage, artemisia gnaphalodes, sagebrush, wormwood, artemisia natroninsia, the composite family - BT Bl #63,146
~ *ȟóta pepè* a prickly herb that has but one use and may be used only once - LHB
~ *ȟóta skùya* one of the five kinds of gray medicinal herbs frequently found in the Bad Lands
~ *ȟóta swùla* silvery wormwood, aremisia filifolia, the the composite family; a medicine - Bl #287
~ *ȟóta šicàmna* rabbit brush, the rayless goldenrod, chrysothamnus graveolens - Bl #188
~ *ȟóta tanka* big sage brush, a medicine
~ *ȟóta totó* blue sage brush, a medicine
~ *ȟóta waštèmna* pasture sage brush, wormwood sage, artemisia frigida, the composite family - Bl #64
~ *icášla* [fr *kašla* to mow] : a scythe
~ *ináksе* a mowing machine
~ *inkpá* oats; also *wayáhota* wild rice, oats
~ *ipáhte* a baler, a bundle
~ *ité on ašníyakiyapi* fox-tail grass, a grass that tickles the face - Cf ité ašnìyanpi, pejijiji - #186
~ *itókšu* a hay rack
~ *iwícakoyaka* dark-green bulrush, scirpus atrovirens, of the sedge family; buffalo grass, buchloe dactyloides of the grass family. Also, *sipáwicaše* that has two specimens, one male, the other female - BM #69,182
~ *iyúhinte* a hay rake
~ *iyúwanka àya v* : to unload a wagon into a barn
pejíjiji squirrel-tail grass - Cf peji ite on ašniyakiyapi, *i.e.* a grass that tickles the face - #186
pejíkašla v peji·wa·kašla : to cut hay or grass, to mow
~ *mícapeca* devil's grass - *See* mícapeca
pejínakse or *peji inakse* a mowing machine
~ *oákšu* a wisp of hay, what hay one can hold in the arms or on a fork - P Bl
~ *ojúpi* a lawn - P
~ *okášla* hay ground, a meadow, a place to cut hay
~ *ókihe totó* a grass growing along rivers
~ *okíjata* grama or mesquite grass, boutelous oligostachya of the grass family. Most specimens of these plants have two spikes. But for the sake of sport some youngsters once hunted for those with three. Spikes one and three are gray - YW #224
~ *onákseyapi* hay land
~ *owínja* a tick
pejípaha a hay stack
pejípata àye a hay stacker
~ *psunpsúnla* heavy sedge, carex gravida, the sedge family - Bl #184
pejíptaptahan n : in stacks

~ *skúya* cockspur or barnyard grass, water grass, echinochloa crusgali, the grass family - Bl #230
~ *suksúta* alkali grass, salt or marsh spike grass, distichlis spicata; the plant cannot be eaten - Bl #175
~ *swùla* or *wanyéca swùla* horsetail - BT
~ *swula cík'ala* the low milkweed, asclepias pumila, the milkweed family - Note: it is also called *cešlošlo pejuta* or *ȟante iyececa*, a tea is made with it for children who have diarrhoea Bl BT #89
pejíšaša a grass that cattle do not eat
~ *šaša inkpa jiji* Indian grass, sorghastrum nutans, of the grass family - B. #243
~ *šaša ókihe tankínkinyan* blue stem, forked beard grass, andropogon furcatus, of the grass family - Bl #240
~ *šaša swula* beard grass, little blue stem, broom beard grass, andropogon scoparius, the grass family - Bl #242
~ *šicámna* June grass, spear grass, Kentucky blue grass, poa prattensis - Bl #293
~ *takán* sand dropseed, rush grass, sporobolus cryptandrus, the gray grass family, so called for the sheath is as tough as *takan* deer sinew - Bl #85
~ *takàn kazá* the three-awned bemch grass, wire grass, aristida purpurea, the grass family - Lhb #201
pejítokšu a hay rack - Cf peji itokšu
~ *unkcékcela* sand burs
~ *unkcéla* the sand bur, small burr-grass, cenchrus carolinianus, the grass family - #23
~ *wabluška* the walking stick, an insect - WE
~ *wacánġa* sweet grass
~ *wakán* scribner's panic grass, panicum scribnerianum, - Note: horses die eating it WE Bw BH #9
~ *Wokéya Oti kin* the Shoshone Indians, otherwise called *Súsuni*
pejíyuhìnta v : to rake hay
~ *yuskíta kutèpi* a pastime for boys, a game played with grass - Cf yuskíta
~ *zizi* gutierrezia, broomweed, gutierrezia sarothrae, the composite family - Note: a tea is made with it using the whole plant, boiling it, for coughing and colds - WE BT #59

pe·jo·gnake \pe-jó-gna-ke\ *n* : a hay loft
pe·ju·ta \pe-jú-ta\ *n* [fr *peji* grass + *húte* roots] : medicine

~ *gmigméla* pills, a round medicine
~ *ha sápa* red-root - *See* pejuta wah'e ša
~ *huókihetonton* a tall medicinal herb with many roots, and used for sore joints -LHB
~ *ȟáka* a medicinal herb root, an herb having many roots - KE
~ *icú ši v* : to prescribe a medicine
~ *janjan s'ele* alum
~ *níġe tànka* the bush morning glory, ipomoea leptophylla, the morning glory family - Note: BS

\a\ father \e\ they \i\ machine \o\ smoke \u\ lunar \an, aŋ\ blanc Fr. \in, iŋ\ ink \on, oŋ, un, uŋ\ soon, confier Fr. \c\ chair \ġ\ machen Ger. \j\ fusion \clusters: bl, gn, kp, hšl, etc...\ b^e^lo ... said with a slight vowel
See more in the Introduction, Guide to Pronunciation

heard from his grandmother that in days when there were no matches they used to start fire in the roots, wrap them up and hang them outside. Fire would keep seven months as *petaga, i.e.* as burning coals. As a medicine the root is used; the kernel of the large root is eaten raw. Old CD used to scrape some off the big root to eat when he had stomach trouble - BS Bl CD HM #18

~ *sápa* coffee

~ *sapsápa* the narrow-leaved puccoon, lithospermum angustifolium, the borage family, a medicine - Bh #155

~ *ska hu* locoweed, milk vetch, or tragacanth, a plant like astragalus recemosus or canadensis - Note: Ho called it *pejuta zi*, the root being so colored. The roots were BT's big medicine for pains of the chest and back. The roots are pulverized and chewed and can be used with another herb against spitting blood. A tea of the roots is taken for coughing - Ho BT

~ *skúya* the slender milkweed, astragalus parviflorus, the pulse family; the roots are medicinal, mothers chew the roots when they have no milk

~ *swúla* horsetail, scouring rush - Bw

~ *tínpsila* a turnip plant with medicinal properties for the cure of the wounded

~ *totó* a plant quite common on the prairie. It is applied perhaps to the medicinal preparation of *pejuta ṗa* and used for abdominal pains

~ *wahínheya iṗíye* or *canhlogan makatola* purple fritillaria

~ *wah'é ša* or ~ *ha sápa* red-root, the hairy puccoon, hairy gromwell, lithospermum gmelini, of the borage family, having a black, *sápa*, skin that covers the red root. A powder is made of the roots, and people take it when they are wounded in the chest. A girl who had been shot through the chest was treated with this powder as a medicine and recovered in spite of a doctor's prediction of death - L

~ *wicáša* a physician, a medicine man

pe·ju·ta·ya \pe-jú-ṫa-ya\ *va* : to use as a medicine

pel \ṗel\ *n contrac of* péta : fire

pe·la·ki·gle \ṗe-lá-k̇i-gle\ *v* pela·wa·kigle : to place pith on one's arm, to light it and let it thereon burn up. To endure it was a sign of bravery - Cf akígle *v poss*

pe·li·ca·gla \ṗe-lí-ca-gla\ *adv* : near or by the fire

pe·li·cu \ṗe-lí-cu\ *n* : a little coal shovel

pe·li·jan·jan \ṗe-lí-jaŋ-jaŋ\ *n* : a lamp, a torch < ~ *ihupa* a candlestick, ~ *inkpa* a lamp chimney > — **peli·janjan ska** *n* : a candle — **pelijanjan wigli** *n* : lamp oil, kerosene — **pelijanjan·pi** *n* : a torch — **peli·janjan·ye** *n* : a lamp - B.H.75.22, 247.1

pe·li·kce·ya \ṗe-lí-kce-ya\ *adv* : over fire < ~ *ceonpa* to roast over fire > - B.H.53.1

pe·li·le·ya·pi \ṗe-lí-le-ya-pi\ *n* : kindling, something with which to light a fire

pe·li·mna šni \ṗe-lí-mna šni\ *v* : to be unafraid of fire, not satisfied with extreme heat - LB LHB

pe·li·po·gan \ṗe-lí-ṗo-ġaŋ\ *n* : bellows

pe·li·škan \ṗe-lí-škaŋ\ *vn* peli·ma·škan : to draw near the fire, to warm one's self

pe·li·ya·gla·šya·han \ṗe-lí-ya-gla-šya-haŋ\ *v* : to keep the fire low < *Peliyaglašyahelo* He keeps the fire, *i.e.* glimmering under the ashes. > - Bl

pe·lkan·ye *or* **pelkanye·la** \ṗe-lkáŋ-ye\ or \ṗe-lkáŋ-ye-la *adv* : near the fire

pe·lko·ki·pa \ṗe-lkó-ki-pa\ *v* : to be afraid of fire < *Kimimila ska s'e pelkokipe šni yelo* Moths it seems have no fear of fire. > - Bl

pe·lmna \ṗe-lmná\ *vn* : to smell of fire — *adj* : smelling burnt, having the smell of fire < *Pelmnašni nankahanpelo* You were sitting having no smell of being burnt, *i.e.* when there is no heat in the house. > — **pelmna·mnaya** *v red of* pelmnaya : to roast beef, turning it around all the time

pe·lmna·ya \ṗe-lmná-ya\ *v* : to make smell of fire < *Pelmnayan po, hecel wašte yelo* Make it smell of fire, then you are getting somewhere with it, *i.e.* start a fire! >

pe·lna·kpa·kpa \ṗe-lná-kpa-kpa\ *vn* [fr *peta* fire + *nakpakpa*] : to crackle, as fire - *Syn* NAMNUMNUZA

pe·lwi·yu·škin \ṗe-lwí-yu-škiŋ\ *v* : to sparkle, crackle, spit, as does fire when certain resinous woods are burned, and sparks fly from little explosions < ~ *yelo* The fire sparkles. > - Bl

pel'·i·yu·can·yan·kel \ṗel'-í-yu-caŋ-yaŋ-kel\ *adv* : with the fire getting low for lack of wood < ~ *nanka* hwo Is your fire in need of wood? > - Bl LHB

pel'·ki·ton·kel \ṗel'-k̇í-toŋ-kel\ *adv* : absorbing the effects of fire, its warmth *etc.* < ~ *nanka hwo* Are you soaking up the fire's heat, *i.e.* staying near the fire? > - Bl

pe·ma·ki·wo·to \ṗé-ma-k̇i-wo-ṫo\ *v perhaps* : to strike the ground with one's head < ~ *glihpeya* to throw a person down his head striking the ground > — **pemakiwo·to·ya** *adv* : the head striking the ground - B.H.184.25, 112.14

pe·mni \ṗe-mní\ *adj* : warped, twisted, crooked — *vn* : to warp, twist, become crooked or entangled — **pe·mni·mni** *v red* : to warp much — **pemni·yan** *adv* : perversely, in a twisted manner

pe·o·wi·wi·la \pe-ó-wi-wi-la\ *n* : the soft spot in the top of an infant's cranium

pe·o·zan \pe-ō'-zaŋ\ *n* : the line where the hair of the head is divided, parted

pe·pe \ṗe-ṗé\ *adj red of* ṗe : prickly, jagged < *maza* ~ barbed wire, *unkcela* ~ burgrass or sandbur > — **pepe·ya** *adv* : prickly, sharp or rough as a frozen roadway < ~ *hiyeya* to become rough. >

pe·sle·te \pe-slé-te\ *n* : the top of the head < *Na* ~ *el awicaputaka* He imposed his hands on the top of their heads. ~ *ówinge* the crown of the head, ~ *owamniomni* the top of the head where hair forms an eddy >

pe·sle·te·ša \pe-slé-te-ša\ *n* : the red comb of a cock chicken

pe·sto \ṗé-sṫo\ *adj* : sharp-pointed < *šunkitepesto* a grayhound >

pe·sto·la \ṗé-sṫo-la\ *adj* : sharp-pointed; *fig* the diamond in a deck of playing cards — **pesto·stola** \ṗe-sṫó-sṫo-la\ *adj red* : bristling with points — **pestosto·ya** *adv red of* péstoya : in the manner of much bristling - D.67

pe·sto·ya \ṗé-sṫo-ya\ *adv* : in a sharp-pointed manner — *adj perhaps* : pointed < *Tokala s'e ite cik'aya, ite ~, cehupa cikcik'a kaca* Like the small gray fox, its snout is pointed, its lower jaw is just right, as is said when a man has a very small face. > — **pestoye·la** *adv* : in a sharp-pointed manner < *Yunkan inyan wan icu zizipela ca na he ~ kaga* And then he took a thin stone and made it in a way sharp-pointed. >

[1]**pe·ša** \ṗé-ša\ *n* : the headgear used in the Omaha dance, and made of porcupine skin, the Omahas being

the first to use it

[2]**Pe·ša** \Pé-ša\ *np* : the Kwapa Indians

[3]**pe·ša** \pe-šá\ *n* : the comb of the domestic rooster or hen, the fleshy crest of caruncle on the head of a domestic cock or hen – *Syn* PESLETEŠA FR

[4]**pe·ša** \ṗé-ša\ *n* : the Jack in playing cards

pe·ška \ṗe-šká\ *n* : the air bladder of a fish – Note: at one time it was used for making glue, and hence the name, *cunpeška* or *conpeška*

pe·šni \ṗé-šni\ *adj* : dull, as a knife

pe·šni·ja \ṗe-šní-ja\ *n* : sparks of fire < *Peta ca kahwoka canna* ~. ~ *akáhwogmayayelo* It was fire carried away by the wind when there were sparks. Fire laden sparks you let fly over me, *i.e.* while smoking. > – Bl

pet \ṗeṫ\ *n contrac of* péta : fire – Note: as in the word *petijanjan* a lamp

pe·ta \ṗé-ṫa\ *n* : fire

pe·ta·ga \ṗe-ṫá-ġa\ *n* : burning coals — **petaga kicin'inpi** *n* : a pastime practiced by boys to test one's bravery by throwing burning pieces of wood at each other – Bl

pe·ta·ga·i·ce·on·pa \ṗe-ṫá-ġa-i-ce-oŋ-pa\ *v* petagaice·wa·onpa : to broil on the coals

pe·ta·ki·gle \ṗe-ṫá-ki-gle\ *v* : to test bravery with burning pith – Cf pelákigle

pe·tanl \ṗe-ṫáŋl\ *adv* [fr *peta* fire + *akanl* on] : on the fire < ~ *ihpeya* to throw on or in the fire > – B.H.195.9

pe·ta yu·ha·la \ṗé-ṫa yu-hà-la\ *n* : the walking fire, night fire; will-o'-the-wisp, in Latin: ignis fatuus – Note: this is well known to the Lakotas who see all sorts of colors. It is sometimes near the ground, but also high up. They know that it may come from rotten wood, but do not know it originates in swampy places, *esp* along the upper White River in Southwest South Dakota and the Northwest Panhandle of Nebraska

pe·ti·jan·jan \ṗe-ṫí-jaŋ-jaŋ\ *n* : a lamp

~ *agléhan* a candle-stick
~ *ġeġéya* a lantern
~ *ihúpa* a candle-stick
~ *iyókaštan* a funnel to pour oil into a lamp
~ *iyúkse* a candle snuffer
~ *janján woslàhan* a lamp chimney
~ *oštán* a candle-stick
~ *ska* a candle
~ *ska oognake* a candle-stick
peṫíjanjanye a lamp, perhaps
~ *yuha omànipi* a lantern – Bl R B.H.60.25

pe·ti·le·ya·pi *or* **petileye** *or* **pelileye** \ṗe-ṫí-le-ya-pi\ *n* : kindling < *wazizi* ~ pine wood kindling, ~ *winyeya gnakapi canke yuile icupi* Prepared kindling was put aside and so it was taken to start a fire. > – LB D.275

pe·ti·škan \ṗe-ṫí-škaŋ\ *vn* peti·ma·škan : to draw near the fire, warm one's self

pe·tka·gla \ṗe-tká-gla\ *adv* [fr *peta* fire + *kagla* nearby] : near the fire, by the fire

pe·tka·i·le s'e \ṗe-tká-i-le s'e\ *adv* : in the manner of fanning a fire < ~ *yainankelo* You run as though fanning a fire, *i.e.* with swinging arms. >

pe·tki·ye·la \ṗe-tkí-ye-la\ *adv* : near the fire

pe·to·ka·li·c'i·ya \ṗe-ṫó'-ka-li-c'i-ya\ *v refl* : to warm one's self at a fire — **petokalya** *va* petoka·lwa·ya : to warm up the fire

pe·to·wa·ya·ke *or* **petowoyake** \ṗe-ṫó-wa-ya-ke\ *n* : a piece of wood laid in a stove to keep up the fire overnight < *Can tanka ileya ayanpa kta iyececa; sni okihi šni* It is a good idea to start a large piece of wood afire to hold through the night; it cannot then get cold. >

pe·tu·spe \ṗe-ṫú-sṗe\ *n* : a firebrand — **petu·ste** \ṗe-ṫú-sṫe\ *n* : a firebrand with which to start another fire < *Can hanke ȟugnage šni yanke kin* ~ *eciyapi* It was said to him that not half a firebrand was being consumed. > – R

pe·wi·wi·la \ṗé-wi-wi-la\ *n* : the soft spot in the cranium of infants – Note: more often used is *peówiwila*

pe·ya \ṗé-ya\ *adj* or *adv* : sharp, as edged tools < *Wahinkpe k'on he yuman* He had sharpened his arrows. *Hecel lila* ~ *kaga na nakun pestola* So they were made very sharp and as well very pointed. ~ *pamanpi* They were filed sharp. > – MS.481

pe·yo·han *or* **pehohan·la** \ṗe-yó-haŋ\ *n* : the line running over the middle of the head from the forehead, the parting of the hair

pe·yo·zan \pe-yó-zaŋ\ *n* : the place that is left on the head by separating the hair, a part

pe·zi \ṗe-zí\ *n* : the King in playing cards

[1]**pi** \ṗi\ *n* ma·pí wicá·pi : the liver

[2]**pi** \ṗi\ *v aux abbrev* [fr *píca* to be able, possible] : to be able, or possible

[3]**pi** \ṗi\ *suff* – the common *pl* termination of *v*, *n*, *adj*, and sometimes *adv*, and *prep*. It often becomes *"pe"* before *"yelo"*, when the *"ye"* is lost, *e.g.* *heconpelo* for *heconpi yelo*

[1]**pi·ca** \ṗi-cá\ *adj* : good < *Taku* ~ *yuha šni ic'ikte* She killed herself not having something good. > – Bl

[2]**pi·ca** \ṗí-ca\ *v aux* : to be able, possible; it has the force of "can" and conveys the idea of power or possibility < *Econpica* That can be done. *Na taku econpicašni econ keyapi* It was stated that he did what is impossible to do. *Opta iyayepica šni wan el kušeya najin* He stood inhibiting the way where there was no possible way through. *Wakantanka tawoope ateunyanpi etanhan unkicupi kin hena kicaksaunpicapi šni* We must not break God's commandments we received from our Father. *Mapica šni* I cannot. *Painlpica* One can consider it (*i.e.* be tempted). *Kicaksaunpicapi šni* We should not disobey. *Woope kin kicaksaunpicapi šni* The customs we cannot violate. *Taku slolyepica šni k'un* It is something one ought not to know. *Iyaunpemapica šni* I cannot be blamed. *Ehpeye pi* They are able to hit it. (Here *pi* is the *abbrev* or *píca*). > — **pica·ka** \ṗi-cá-ka\ *v aux* [fr *píca* able or possible to + *ka* a sign of *emph*, or a sign of *interrog*] : to be able or possible, or the *interrog* sign — *adj* : a little good, a little better than some other — **pica·lake** *adj* : more perfect than some other < ~ *cin he icu yo* Take the better or best one. > — **pica·šni** \ṗi-cá-šni\ *v* : it cannot be, it is impossible — **pica·ya** *adv* : well – B.H.68.14, 153.6, 139.12 and 16 RA

pi·ga \ṗí-ġa\ *vn* : to boil, *i.e.* foaming, bubbling, as heated water *etc.* < *Na wanna inyan k'eya kate k'on can okijata on icu na el ognaka na oyasin el ognaka na lila* ~ And now with a forked stick he took a sort of rock that had been heated, placed it in, put everything in, and it (*e.g.* the water) really boiled. > — **pige·s'e** *adv* : bubbling with a noise, as a swimmer but with a bubbling noise, with bubbles rising – Cf píga

\a\ father \e\ they \i\ machine \o\ smoke \u\ lunar \an, aŋ\ blanc Fr. \in, iŋ\ ink \on, oŋ, un, uŋ\ soon, confier Fr. \c\ chair \ġ\ machen Ger. \j\ fusion \clusters: bl, gn, kp, hšl, etc...\ b[e]lo ... said with a slight vowel
See more in the Introduction, Guide to Pronunciation

pi·hya \ṗi-ȟyá\ *adv* : boiling < ~ *han* to stand boiling, *Na cega wan pihyáhe k'on ekta oyujunta* And he thrust it into a kettle that had been boiling. >

pi·i·c'i·ya \ṗi-í-c'i-ya\ *v refl* [fr *pi* good + *ya* to cause] : to prepare one's self, get ready < *pimic'iya* to ready myself > – *Syn* ḰISÍNC'IYA Bl

pi·ja \ṗí-ja\ *adj* ma·pija : wrinkled

pi·ki·ci·la \ṗi-ḱí-ci-la\ *v* pi·we·cila : to be glad or thankful with or for another, to take part with one in his thankfulness

pi·ki·ci·ya \ṗi-ḱí-ci-ya\ *v* : to make one well – Bl

pi·ki·la \ṗi-ḱí-la\ *vn* pi·wa·kila : to be thankful, glad

pi·ki·ya \ṗi-ḱí-ya\ *vt* pi·wa·kiya : to mend, repair, reset, rearrange one's own – D.22

pi·ki·ya \ṗi-ḱí-ya\ *or* \ṗi-kí-ya\ *v* pi·wa·kiya : to get one's bed ready < *Wanna piyakiyin na inunkin kte* Now you should ready your bed and lie down, *i.e.* now you make ready to go to sleep, don't you? > **2** : to doctor, treat; to conjure as after the Lakota way of doctoring – Sa Bl D.59, 226 ES

pi·la \ṗi-lá\ *vn* pi·wa·la pi·ya·la pi·un·la·pi : to rejoice, be glad — **pila·ic'iya** *v refl* : to make one's self thankful — **pila·kiya** \ṗi-lá-ḱi-ya\ *va* pila·wa·kiya : to make glad, make thankful — **pila·ya** *va* pila·wa·ya pila·ma·ya : to make glad — *adv* : gladly — **pili·c'iya** \ṗi-lí-c'i-ya\ *v refl* : to make one's self thankful – Pb.29

pi·lya \ṗi-lyá\ *v* : to use up, consume < *Pilyapelo* They ate up all *e.g.* the grass. > – Bl

pin·ja \ṗíŋ-ja\ *adj* : destitute of hair

pin·kpa \ṗíŋ-kpa\ *n* : the top, as of a tower *etc.* – B.H.9.4

pin·ksi·hu \ṗíŋ-ksi-hu\ *n* : tall marsh grass in water – Note: it the same as *santuhu tanka* Bl

pin·špin·je·la \ṗiŋ-šṗíŋ-je-la\ *adj* : thin scattering, as of hair or grass

pin·ze·ce \ṗíŋ-ze-ce\ *adj perhaps* : becoming small, little, dwindling down, as snow, or a crowd < *Wa kin ~ cinhe. Wana ~ lo* The fact is the snow was becoming less. It now was dwindling. > – Bl

pi·pi·ya \ṗi-ṗí-ya\ *adv red of* ṗíya : well, anew; again and again, thoroughly < ~ *kipanpi* Again and again they called to him. ~ *iyunka* Again and again he settled down *i.e.* in a lying position. > – D.20, 52, 81

pi·san·san o·h'an·ke \ṗí-saŋ-saŋ o-ȟ'aŋ-ke\ *v phr* : to carry on with a wild idea, a dangerous and ill-considered course of thought – Note: the *phr* is used when a man gets an idea of doing something and starts at once doing it without considering it and thinking it over first. One is said to have had a *písan* and died from it. Sb

[1]**pi·spi·za** \ṗi-sṗí-za\ *n* : the prairie dog, or the ground squirrel

[2]**pi·spi·za** \ṗí-sṗi-za\ *v red* [fr *píza* to creak] : to squeal as a ground squirrel when caught, to make a noise with the lips, as in whistling for a dog

pi·spi·za ta·wo·te \ṗi-sṗí-za ta-wȯ-te\ *n* : the fetid marigold, the false dog-fennel, dyssodia papposa, the composite family – Note: this is one of BT's medicines; he pulverizes the leaves and gives them to people when they find breathing difficult BT #34

pi·ško *or* **piš** \ṗi-ško\ *n* : the night hawk < ~ *wašin aglipi hehanl* Then night hawk brought home the fat. ~ *s'e hokšiyuha wóšikšiceke* Like the night hawk she gives birth to ineptitude, as is said of a woman who loses her children through carelessness. > – Note: the *píško* returns last of all the birds. At that time the grass is in good condition and the buffalo are fat. So *píško* brings on the fat. *Píško* is said to lay her eggs in any place, having no nest. < *Piško ca wanigle s'e unglahanpi* We were returning, the way it is with the night hawk migrating to the South, as is said when we cannot get on fast going home; Night hawks do much flying around in the fall while other birds go south directly, *i.e. wanigla* return to the South for the winter. > – RA

pi·šle·ca \ṗi-šlé-ca\ *n* : the spleen

pi·špi·ja \ṗi-šṗí-ja\ *adj red* ma·pišpija [fr *píja* wrinkled] : many-wrinkled < ~ *hiyeya* to shrivel > — **pispije·la** *adj* ma·pišpijela : wrinkled or shriveled, as one's hands from being in water, withered — **pišpiš** *adj contrac* : much wrinkled or withered < ~ *hingla* to become wrinkled > – Bl

[1]**pi·ya** \ṗi-yá\ *va* pi·wa·ya [fr *pi* good] : to make anew, mend up, repair; to conjure the sick

[2]**pi·ya** \ṗí-ya\ *adv* : well anew, again < ~ *kaga* to mend, make anew, *Tokata ~ inicagapi ktelo* In the time to come you will be made anew. > – MS.355 D.22

pi·ya i·yo·ta·ke \ṗi-yá i-yȯ-ta-ke\ *v* : to move away in a sitting position – WE

pi·ya i·yu·kcan \ṗí-ya i-yu̇-kcaŋ\ *v* : to take another view, to change one's mind

pi·ye \ṗi-yé\ *va of* piyá : to make anew, to repair

pi·ye·leš \ṗi-yé-leš\ *adv* : notwithstanding, heedlessly – Note: the word is used of one who does not listen to what is said to him, but is now not used – Bl WE

pi·ye·pi·ca \ṗi-yé-ṗi-ca\ *adj* : reparable < *Piyepicašni* That cannot be repaired. >

pi·za \ṗí-za\ *vn* : to creak, as one's shoe in walking – *Syn* ḰÍZA

pi·zi \ṗi-zí\ *n* ma·pizi : the gall < *Inše he tatanka ~ wan ota latkan ca on aiyahanble lo* Know that since you drank much of a buffalo bull's gall, you had dreams of it. >

pi·zo \ṗi-zó\ *n* : a clown, contrary person or dancer < ~ *wan u welo* A clown came. > – Bl

po \ṗȯ\ *vn* ma·pó : to swell, puff out

po \ṗo\ *suff* – the *pl* termination of *v* in the *imper* mood [fr perhaps *pi* sign of *pl* + *wo* sign of the *imper*]

pob \ṗȯb\ *vn contrac of* pópa : to burst < ~ *iyaya*, ~ *hingla* to go pop, *i.e.* burst out, to snap suddenly > — **pobya** \ṗo-byá\ *adv* : snapping, popping with a sudden noise, as when hitting a table with one's knuckles < ~ *awaṗelo* I struck popping it. >

po·gan \ṗȯ'-ġaŋ\ *va* wa·pogan : to blow, as with the mouth — *vn* : to spread out, as a balloon when blown into < *Le pejuta wan tatuye topa oyasin wapogan kta.* ~ *na yatkan yo* I shall blow this medicine in all four directions. Draw and blow it, *i.e.* when things are hot. > – Bl

po·ge \ṗó-ġe\ *n* ma·poge, perhaps : the nose < ~ *glujinca* to blow the nose >

Po·ge Hlo·ka \Ṗó-ġe Ḣlȯ-ka\ *np* : the Nez Percé Indians — *n* : the nostrils

po·gin·jo \ṗo-ġíŋ-jo\ *v* : to sniff, as when breathing causes a whistling sound in the nose – Bl

po·go \ṗo-ġó\ *n archaic* : a leading man who makes decisions for travel, *wicaša itancan wakiconza* < ~ *unyankapelo* We are leading men, as they might say to a new-comer. > – GS Lc A

po·ha \ṗó-ha\ *adj* : having much hair and all unkempt, standing and flying about, as long hair < *Pehin mapóha* My hair was all unkempt. > — *va* wa·póha : to make the hair stand up by running the fingers through it

po·ha·ha·s'e \ṗó-ha-ha-s'e\ *adv red* : shaking, as a buffalo shaking its head — **poha·s'e** *adv* : having an abundance of hair on the head that stands out disorderly

po·hcan·te \pó-ȟcaŋ-ṫe\ *n* : the wings of the human nose - Bl

po·hwo·mnan·kel \po-ȟwó-mnaŋ-kel\ *adv* : getting a scent - *Syn* PÓJANJAN

po·i·pi·ye \ṗo-í-ṗi-ye\ *n* : the name for any medicine good for swellings, *e.g.* the *sunkcankahupiye* the western false gromwell and the *hitunkala nakpala* white plantian - WE BT RT #21, 115, 158

po·jan·jan \ṗó-jaŋ-jaŋ\ *v* : to snuff up, as an animal does the wind; to snuff, sniff, scent, as a dog does - *Syn* PÓŠIN

po·ki·mna·mna \ṗó-k̇i-mna-mna\ *va* po·wa·kimnamna [fr *pomnamna* shake the head at] : to shake the head continually at one

po·ksan \ṗó-ksaŋ\ *v* wa·poksan : to shake the head to the right and left — **poksan·s'e** *adv* : shaking the head to the right and left

pol \ṗol\ *adj contrac of* póta : worn out, spoiled — **po-lpota** \ṗo-lṗó-ṫa\ *adj red* : much worn out — **polpo-tanhan** \ṗo-lṗó-ṫaŋ-haŋ\ *part red* [fr *potáhan* worn out] : worn full of holes, torn, ragged, as a worn out garment

po·mna·mna \ṗó-mna-mna\ *v* wa·pomnamna : to shake the head, as in refusing or denying a thing - *See* pakáhunka — **pomnamna·kiya** \ṗó-mna-mna-k̇i-ya\ *or* \ṗó-mna-mna-k̇i-ya\ *v* pómnamna·wa·kiya : to shake or wag the head at; to cause to wag the head

po·nu·nu·je \ṗó-nu-nu-je\ *n* : the lower part of the nose - Bl

pon·pon *or* **ponpon·la** \ṗoŋ-ṗóŋ\ *adj* : rotten or soft, as wood

po·o·wa·šte \po-ó-wa-šte\ *n* : the false boneset - Note: it is otherwise called *wahpe pa* - BT #228

po·pa \ṗō'-ṗa\ *vn* : to burst

po·po \ṗo-ṗó\ *or* \po-pó\ *vn red of* ṗo : to swell, puff out

po·po·pa \po-pó-ṗa\ *adj* : full of pith — *n* : cotton < *owinja* ~ a quilt > — **popope·s'e** *adv* : resembling cotton, with a downy or hairy surface, as is said of nap on a blanket or fine fur on a robe

po·po·tka *or* **popotka·la** \ṗo-ṗó-ṫka\ *n* : a screech-owl, *hinhan* an owl - Note: its call is: Hohí, hohí. It may be the same owl as the *paglá, osníko,* and *ungnágicala*

po·po·tka·ki·ya \ṗo-ṗó-ṫka-k̇i-ya\ *vt* : to silence one by one's argument or saying, for the *popotka* screech-owl is said not to move when shot - Is

po·ptan \ṗó-ptaŋ\ *v* : to turn one's head, in one direction perhaps < *Hinhán makotila s'e ~ wašicun* The white man rotated his head around like that of the burrowing screech owl, the *hinhán makòtila,* as is said of a person who is rubber-necked. > - Bl

po·ptan·ptan *or* **pomnamna** \ṗó-ptaŋ-ptaŋ\ *vn* pó·wa·-ptanptan : to shake the head signifying dissent — **po-ptanptan·kiya** \ṗó-ptaŋ-ptaŋ-k̇i-ya\ *v* póptanptan-·wa·kiya : to shake the head at, and \ṗó-ptaŋ-ptaŋ-k̇i-ya\ *va* poptanptan·wa·kiya : to cause to wag the head

po·ski *or* **poskil** \ṗō'-ski\ *adv contrac of* poskica : by the neck < *Na ~ omayuspa* He held onto my neck. ~ *mayuza* He took me by the neck. >

po·ski·ca \ṗó-sk̇i-ca\ *v* : to clasp around the neck

po·skil \ṗō'-skil\ *adv contrac of* poskica : to hug one about the neck

~ *iyakaška va* : to tie around the neck, *e.g.* a halter

~ *kte v* poskil·wa·kte : to kill by choking

~ *yut'a v* : to put to death by hanging < ~ *mayalut'e kinica yelo* He tried to have you put me to death by hanging >

~ *yúza v* ~ bluza : to clasp about the neck, to hug putting the arms around one's neck, to embrace, to hold in one's arms - Cf póski Bl D.222

po·ski·ski \ṗō'-sk̇i-ski\ *adv red of* póski : holding, squeezing by the neck < ~ *mayuza* He squeezed my neck. >

po·šin \ṗó-šiŋ\ *vn* pó·wa·šin **1** : to sniff, snuff up the nose **2** : to make a face at — **pošin·šin** \ṗó-šiŋ-šiŋ\ *v red* pó·wa·šinšin : to make faces at

po·šla \ṗó-šla\ *adj* : rounded off at one end < *maza ~* a piece of metal with a rounded end, *nata ~* a head rounded on top > - WE

po·šli·co·ma \ṗó-šli-co-ma\ *adj* or *v perhaps* póšli-·wa·coma : to have the head covered *e.g.* with a blanket - Bl BD

po·šli·šli \ṗó-šli-šli\ *v* : to have one's face always covered, *i.e.* out of bashfulness < ~ *un* to live with one's face covered > — **pošlišli·ka** *or* **pošlišlis'a** \po-šlí-šli-ka\ *or* \ṗó-šli-šli-s'a\ *n* : one who keeps his face covered with his blanket

po·štan \ṗó-štaŋ\ *v* pó·wa·štan : to wear *e.g.* a hat or head covering — *n* : a hood, a child's cloak with a hood < ~ *ipatapi* a hood-like ornamented quill-work, a piece of leather in which little babies are tied up, a bonnet-like baby cradle >

po·ta \ṗō'-ṫa\ *adj* : worn out, spoiled, as shoes *etc.* — **pota·han** \ṗo-ṫá-haŋ\ *part* : wearing out < *Hanpa potáhe lo* His shoes were wearing out. > — **potahe·ya** \ṗo-ṫá-he-ya\ *va* potahe·wa·ya : to make wear out

po·wa·ya \po-wá-ya\ *n* : nap, fur — *adj* **a** : having nap, fur-trimmed **b** : rough, made rough **c** : flaking off, coming off, as dry paint — *va* : to brush *e.g.* a coat < *Unkcela heca waksin na on apawinta, i.e.* the painted hide, *ca he tohinni jajahe šni nainš powayešni* It was a cactus he cut off, and so he rubbed on it, *i.e.* on the painted hide, and he neither brushed it nor was it in need of washing. > — **powaye·la** *adj* : having nap - MS.482

po·wi·wi·la *or* **peowiwila** \pó-wi-wi-la\ *n* : the soft spot in the top of an infant's cranium

psa \psā\ *n* : a kind of rush or water-grass — **psa·cinca** \psa-cíŋ-ca\ *n* : pithy grass or rush, which are edible - *Syn* PSASWULA, PSAPÓPOPELA WE Bw Bc

psa·ka \psá-k̇a\ *adj* : broken - *See* yupsáka — **psaka-han** \psá-k̇a-haŋ\ *or* \psa-k̇á-haŋ\ *part* : broken, as a string, or as in broken-hearted - Note: *psákahe* is used in *ref* to past time — **psaka·heca** \psa-k̇á-he-ca\ *adv* or *part* : broken, as a way through < *Tuweni psakahece šni niunpi k'on hehan lena ocanku* These were roads in past days which none of you had been breaking a way. > - BT

Psa·lo·ka \Psá-lo-ka\ *np* : the Crow Indians

psan·psan·ka \psaŋ-psáŋ-ka\ *adj* : easily changing one's views < ~ *canke* That's why he is vacillating. > - *See* sintónpsanpsan — *n* : a fool - GV

psa·o·blo·ton *or simply* **oblotonton** \psa-ó-blo-toŋ\ \ó-blo-toŋ-toŋ\ *n* : a swamp grass that is edible, having four corners to each leaf - L LHB

\a\ father \e\ they \i\ machine \o\ smoke \u\ lunar \an, aŋ\ blanc Fr. \in, iŋ\ ink \on, oŋ, un, uŋ\ soon, confier Fr. \c\ chair \ġ\ machen Ger. \j\ fusion \clusters: bl, gn, kp, hšl, etc...\ b^elo ... said with a slight vowel
See more in the Introduction, Guide to Pronunciation

psa·o·ju \psa-ó-ju\ *or* \psá-o-ju\ *n* : a growth of rush - B.H.45.21

psa·o·win·ja *or* **psao·yunke** \psá-o-wiŋ-ja\ *n* : rush mats - P

psa·psa·ka·han \psa-psá-ka-haŋ\ *part red of* psakáhan : broken, hurt emotionally

psa·swu·la \psá-swu-la\ *n* : pithy grass or rush - *Syn* PSACÍNCA, PSAPÓPOPELA

Psa·wa·ci·pi \Psa-wá-ci-pi\ *np* : the Crow Indian Dance

psa·wa·po·štan *or* **psa·poštan** \psá-wa-po-štaŋ\ *or* \psá-po-štaŋ\ *n* : a straw hat

psa·wo·gna·ke \psa-wó-gna-ke\ *n* : a basket - Note: the Dakota for the word is *wakíškokpa*

pse \pse\ *n* : a very nervous water bird, *i.e.* a very restless bird that never remains sitting or standing for any length of time in the same place, hence the saying: < *Pse kinyanpi eša ekta opa iyececa yelo* It is like joining up with a water bird though they fly, as is said of people who never stay at home long, but go to every gathering there is anywhere. > - EM

pse·hte *or* **psehtin** \psé-ȟte\ *n* : the ash tree, *colloq* a pipe, since pipe stems are made of ash wood < ~ *icu wo, okihe kahya unyankapi kte lo* Take a pipe, we shall sit to have one made. > - WE

pse·htin *or* **psehte can** \psé-ȟtiŋ caŋ\ *n* : the green ash tree, fraxi-nus lanceolata, the olive family - Note: the wood was used for bows - MS.481 #120

psi·ca \psí-ca\ *adj* : jumping - Cf yupsíca, ipsíca

psi·ca·la \psí-ca-la\ *n* : a flea

psil \psil\ *adj contrac of* psíca : jumping < ~ *iyaya* to jump or hop away > — **psi·lya** \psi-lyá\ *adv* : jumping

psin \psiŋ\ *n* : rice, wild rice < ~ *ská* white rice, barley >

psin un·wo·han·pi \psiŋ úŋ-wo-haŋ-pi\ *n* : a double boiler, so named since it once was used to cook rice

psi·psi·ca \psi-psí-ca\ *v red of* psíca : to jump much, to skip

[1]**psi·psi·ca·la** \psi-psí-ca-la\ *n* : the grasshopper

[2]**psi·psi·ca·la** \psí-psi-ca-la\ *n* : the jumping mouse — **psipsicala sapa** \psi-psí-ca-la sà-pa\ *n* : the jumping mouse or the field cricket

psi·psil \psí-psil\ *v red contrac of* psipsíca : to bump or skip < ~ *ya, inyankapi* He went jumping, they ran skipping. ~ *itkobwicaye* He went jumping forward to meet them. > - D.120

pso·han·pa \pso-háŋ-ṗa\ *n* : Indian snow shoes

pson·pson·ki·ya \psoŋ-psóŋ-ǩi-ya\ *or* \psoŋ-psóŋ-ki-ya\ *adv* : with the face down < ~ *gliyunka* to lie down on arriving home, *i.e.* to lay face downward >

pson·pson·la *or* **psonpson·yela** \psoŋ-psóŋ-la\ *adj* : supple, lithe, bendable, as is said of a willow stick or a wire that can be moved in all directions

psun·psun·ki·ya - *See* psonpsónkiya

psun·psun·la - *See* psonpsónla

psun·psun·ye·la - *See* psonpsónyela

pša \pša\ *vn* wa·pša : to sneeze, as from a cold < *Poge omayaš'inš'in hecel on wapšahelo* My nose itched so I was sneezing. *apšá* to sneeze on *e.g.* on a handkerchief > — **pša·pša** \pša-pšá\ *v red perhaps* : to sneeze constantly — **pšapša s'e** *adv* : appearing disorderly < ~ *un* to look disorderly, *i.e.* in ragged clothes and dishevelled hair, ~ *glepa* to vomit in a careless way, *itúpšapša s'e un* to be seemingly disorderly > — **pša·ya** \pša-yá\ *va* pša·wa·ya : to cause to sneeze - Bl

pši·ca *or* **pšinca** *or* **icapšinpšincala** \pši-cá\ *n* : a swallow, or the flying squirrel < ~ *kinyékiyehcelo* A swallow made a graceful flight, as they say of him who is riding (a horse) fast. > - R BT

pšin \pšiŋ\ *n* : onions, leeks

pšin·ca *or* **pšica** \pšiŋ-cá\ *n* : a swallow < ~ *kinyé s'e* to be like swallows flying "up and away", as is said when a crowd disbands suddenly, like a bunch of swallows > - LC

pšin hu·blo·ka \pšiŋ-hu-bló-ka\ *n* : an onion or onion-like plant poisonous to man

pšin ši·ca·mna \pšiŋ ši-cá-mna\ *n* : the edible wild onion, allium reticulatum, the lily family - #265

pšin tan·ka \pšiŋ-táŋ-ka\ *n* : the mariposa lily, calochortus nuttallii, the lily family - Bl #300

pši·to \pši-tō'\ *n* : beads

pši·to·la hu \pši-tó-la hu\ *n* : the broad-leaved arrow head, sagittaria latifolia, so called because of the roots that are edible and eaten as a medicine - *Syn* HINHANTAHANPE WE Bl #126

pši·to·la·hu i·ye·ce·ca \pši-tó-la-hu i-yè-ce-ca\ *n* : the black bindweed (the leaves), polygonum convolvulus - Bl #296

pši·to·su·hu·la \pši-tó-suhù-la\ *n* : very small beads — **pšito·šuhula** *n* : intermediate size beads

pšu·ke \pšú-ǩe\ *n* : a deformed thing, crushed, twisted < *Pa ca* ~ *kaca yankin na* Take it to be not a thing deformed, namely his nose, as is said of one with a short, crooked nose. > - Bl

pšun \pšuŋ\ *adj* : shed, fallen off, as horns; drawn out - Cf kapšún, yupšún — **pšun·han** \pšuŋ-háŋ\ *part* : fallen off, dislocated

pšun·ka \pšuŋ-ǩá\ *adj* : round, short, and thick < *paha* ~ a round mound > — *n perhaps* : a bulge, a knot as on a tree; a pill — **pšunka·ka** *n* : pills, tiny round things — **pšunka·la** *n* : any tiny round thing

pšun·ka·ya \pšuŋ-ǩá-ya\ *adv* : in a bunch, in a heap, as an animal curled up < ~ *yanka* to sit curled up. > — **pšunkaya·kel** \pšuŋ-ǩá-ya-ǩel\ *adv* : in a bunch, drawn up together — **pšunkaye·la** *adv* : in a bunch, as rags and not animate things

pšun·pšun·wa·han \pšuŋ-pšúŋ-wa-haŋ\ *part red* [fr *pšunpšunwahe* fr *pšunwahan* fallen off] : with many little things fallen off or dropped out — **pšunpšunwahela** *adj perhaps* : being dropped out or fallen off, as in little things being dropped out — **pšun·wahan** \pšuŋ-wá-haŋ\ *part* : dropped out or fallen off < *Awicakehan mapšunwahelo* Truly I am fallen off, *i.e.* sore broke. > - *Syn* ŠIBSIPAHAN Bl

pta \pta\ *root* : signifying to cut < *yupta* to cut out or off > — **pta·han** \pta-háŋ\ *part* : to cut off, to cut out — **ptahan·han** *part red* : cut up in many places <*Mini maptahanhan, heon anatokelyakel mawani* I was all cut up, water running down from sores, so I walked in a lame way. ~ *yelo* He is all cut up indeed, *i.e.* all his clothes are ragged and torn everywhere. > - Bl

ptan \ptaŋ\ *n* : the otter < ~ *s'e tan lehan hu pteptecela kaca* Like an otter, his legs are very short compared to his body. > - Note: in the sacred dialect the otter is called *hepán* — **ptan·ha** \ptaŋ-há\ *n* : the otter's skin

ptan·ptan \ptaŋ-ptáŋ\ *adj* : unsteady, rocking, as a canoe — **ptanptan·la** *adj* : unsteady in mind - Note: the word is not defined as tottering

ptan·ški·ška \ptaŋ-škí-ška\ *adj perhaps* : up and down and right and left, as is the way of a mole < ~ *iyecel omani yelo; miš eya owale yelo* I too searched; in like manner, in nearly every direction it traveled. ~ *iyecel opinic'iyelo, škinnic'iyelo* In like manner up, down, right, and left, did you move, conduct yourself. > - Bl BT

ptan·ta·can·ku \ptáŋ-ta-caŋ-k̇u\ *n* : an otter's trail, the trail of small animals in general

Ptan'·un·pi Wa·kpa·la \Ptáŋ-uŋ-pi Wa-kpà-la\ *np* : Pumkin Creek, a little creek entering the Tongue River near its mouth - Bl

ptan·yan \ptaŋ-yáŋ\ *adv* : excited, flurried, as is said of animals

ptan·ye·tu *or* **ptanyela** \ptaŋ-yẽ'-tu\ *n* : autumn, the fall season < ~ *kin, kinhan* The autumn, when it is fall. >

pta·pta·ya \ṗtá-ṗta-ya\ *adv red of* ptáya : together, collectively < ~ *unkomani;* ~ *eglepi* We traveled; doing the shocking of *e.g.* grain. > - Note: a similar expression, *wilwitaya eglepi* doing shocking

pta·ya *or* **ptaye·la** \ptá-ya\ *or* \ptá-ye-la\ *adv* : together, collectively < ~ *unyanpi kta* Let us go together. *Hokšila* ~ *najinpelo* Boys stand together. > - BT

pte \pte\ *n* : the female buffalo

pte·a·san·pi \pte-á-saŋ-ṗi\ *n* : a cow's milk — **pteasanpinini** *n* : thick, curdled milk — **pteasanpi·wasna** *or* **pteasanpi·wigli** *n* : butter

pte·blo·ka \pte-bló-ka\ *n* : a steer

pte·ce \pte-cé\ *n* : buffalo dung <~ *pahi unyin kte* Let us two go collect buffalo dung. > - Bl MW

pte·ce·la \ptẽ'-ce-la\ *adj* : short < *Maptecela* I am short. >

pte·ga \pté-ġa\ *n* : the dense marsh grass around a lake - *See* ptégaglonìca

pte·ga·glo·ni·ca \pté-ġa-glo-nì-ca\ *n* : a small gray bird living on the prairie in swampy places and able to alight on weeds. Its call: (smacking) tch, tch, tch—s s s s (hissing) - Note: while *ptega* is a marsh, the word is not used alone. *Zintka šlila* a hissing bird, and *zintka tanagila* a humming bird may be the intended small bird R Bl

pte·gle·ška \pte-glé-ška\ *n* : tame cattle

Pte·gle·ška Can·li \Pte-glé-ška Caŋ-li\ *np* : Bull Durham Tobacco

pte·go·pe·ca \pte-ġó-ṗe-ca\ *n* : the marsh hawk, a kind of hawk so called because it frequents marshes, its *nité* rump white, its feet yellow < ~ *ša* the red marsh hawk, ~ *ska* the white marsh hawk > - R Bl

pte·gu·ya \pte-ġú-ya\ *va* : to brand cattle

pte·ha·hin·šma \pte-há-hiŋ-šma\ *n* : a buffalo robe, a buffalo skin with thick hair

pte·ha·šla \pte-há-šla\ *n* : a buffalo hide from which the hair has been removed - *See* tehpí

pte·he \pte-hé\ *n* : a buffalo or cow's horn

pte·he·cin·ška \pte-hé-ciŋ-ška\ *n* : a spoon, one made of cow's horn

pte·he·cu·ti·c'in \pte-hé-cu-ti-c'iŋ\ *n* : a powderhorn carried at one's side

pte·he·šte \pte-hé-šte\ *n* : a sort of puck in a game where men throw it sliding it over the ice. It is a thin short stick fastened to one end of a short cow's horn

pte·he wa·pa·ha \pte-hé wa-pà-ha\ *n* : a horned headdress

pte·hi·ko \pté-hi-ko\ *v* ptehi·wa·ko : to hold a ceremony to locate buffalo < *"Kipazo Ptehiko"* "Locating Buffalo Ceremony", taken from a wintercount for 1871-1872 > - RB

pte·hin·ca·la \pte-híŋ-ca-la\ *n* : a calf

pte·hin·ci·ciòla \pte-híŋ-ci-ci-la\ *n* [doubtfully fr *ptehinca + ic'ila*] : the killdeer, the American ring plover; its call: *Tiblō, tibló, tiblo:* or *Tiblo wewe, tiblo wewe.* The Lakota answers: *Hau!*

pte·hin·pa·hpa \pte-híŋ-ṗa-ȟṗa\ *n* : tags of buffalo hair, old matted hair shed and fallen from buffalo - D.36

pte·hin·šma \pte-híŋ-šma\ *n* : a thick or long-haired buffalo — **ptehinšma·ha** *n* : a buffalo robe - *See* pte-háhinšma

pte·hi·ya·pa \pte-hí-ya-ṗa\ *v* : to chase buffalo into a large bunch - La WHL

pte·i·ca·ȟa·pe \pte-í-ca-ȟa-pe\ *n* : a blacksnake whip

pte·i·ci·yu·ȟa un·ma \pte-í-ci-yu-ȟa uŋ-ma\ *n* : the blossoms (*inkpa zizi* a yellow top) of this plant boiled with *pispiza tawote* fetid marigold make a good tea for the spitting of blood - Note: the given name of this plant in Lakota may suggest its name in English, "the other buffalo curled up together". - Ti

pte·i·šta \pte-í-šta\ *n* : a buffalo's eye - Bl

pte·hu ka·še \pte-hú ka-še\ *express* : He struck against a buffalo's leg

pte·jin·ca·la \pte-jíŋ-ca-la\ *n* : a new-born buffalo calf < *Kal otkeya yo* Hang it up over there, *i.e.* the *táblo* shoulder, at the door, *hecel* ~ *ake unkokinipi ktelo* so we might again share a new calf -- which is an old superstitious saying. > - Bl

pte·ki·ci·ya·pi \pté-ki-ci-ya-pi\ *n* : a boys' pastime

pte·lye·la \pte-lyé-la\ *adv* : for a short time < *Hehanl ehake* ~ *wauncipi na enaunkiyapi* Then we danced a bit for the last time and stopped. > - Note: the word seems not to be used by the *Titonwan* Titons

pte·ma·ki·ci·ma \pte-má-k̇i-ci-ma\ *n* : a heifer

pte·ma·ko·ka·wa·ze \pte-má-k̇o-ka-wa-ze\ *n* : a buffalo wallow - WF

pte·mna·yan·pi \pte-mná-yaŋ-pi\ *n* : a gathering cattle, a roundup

pte·na·kpa \pte-ná-kpa\ *n* : a buffalo's ear - Bl

pte·nun·we·ki·ya·pi \pte-núŋ-we-k̇i-ya-pi\ *n* : a dipping of cattle

pte·o·ki·ca·ška *or* **pteakicaška** \pte-ó-k̇i-ca-ška\ *n* : work-oxen, a span of oxen, perhaps

pte·o·na·jin \pte-ó-na-jiŋ\ *n* : a cow barn

pte·o·pta·ye \pte-ó-pta-ye\ *n* [fr *pte* a buffalo + *optaye* a herd] : a buffalo herd

pte·o·wa·ci \pte-ó-wa-ci\ *n* : a buffalo wallow - *Syn* PTEMÁKOKAWAZE D.207 note 4

pte·pa·ka·h'e·pi s'e \pte-pá-ka-ȟ'è-pi s'e\ *adv* : with great care < ~ *econ, oyake* to do, say *etc.* something very carefully > - Bl

pte·pa·pa·la \pte-pá-pa-la\ *n* [fr *pápala* a bit of dried meat] : a small amount of dried buffalo meat; *fig* the main news, whatever is new - Br

pte·pte·ce·la \pte-ptẽ'-ce-la\ *adj red of* ptécela : short in *ref* to more than one thing - Note: any *red* suggests *pl*

pte·san \pte-sáŋ\ *n* : a white buffalo cow, a rarity whose hide is used in religious ceremonies

pte·ta·ma·ka \pte-tá-ma-ka\ *n* : a lean cow

pte·tan \pte-táŋ\ *n* : buffalo meat cut perhaps from the middle of the back - Bl

pte·ta·wa·na·p'in \pte-tá-wa-na-p'iŋ\ *n* : an ox-yoke

pte·ta·wo·te \pte-tá-wo-ṫe\ *n* [fr *pte* buffalo + *tawote* its food] : the ground plum, astragalus caryocarpus, the pulse family. It is a prairie plant that bears juicy berries. As a medicine it is good for horses - L RT #154

pte·wa·k'in \pte-wá-k'iŋ\ *n* : work-oxen < ~ *akikaška* to hitch work-oxen, ~ *ícicaškapi* a span of work-oxen >

\a\ father \e\ they \i\ machine \o\ smoke \u\ lunar \an, aŋ\ blanc Fr. \in, iŋ\ ink \on, oŋ, un, uŋ\ soon, confier Fr. \c\ chair \ġ\ machen Ger. \j\ fusion \clusters: bl, gn, kp, hšl, etc...\ b^{e}lo ... said with a slight vowel
See more in the Introduction, Guide to Pronunciation

– *Syn* PTEÓKICAŠKA B.H.110.15, 42.11 R Bl

pte·wa·ni·yan·pi \pte-wá-ni-yaŋ-pi\ *n* : tame cattle

pte·wa·to·gla \pte-wá-to-gla\ *n* : a wild cow

pte·win·kte \pte-wíŋ-kte\ *n* : a fat and dry buffalo cow – Bl

pte·win·ye·la \pte-wíŋ-ye-la\ *n* : a cow

pte·wo·ya·ke \pte-wó-ya-ke\ *n* 1 : the large grasshopper without wings. It is an insect found along sand, roads; it is brown and the upper legs are very wide, and is really not a grasshopper. It would seem they tell of buffalo 2 : the fifth bone in the *tasiha unpi* a women's game played with a string of five deer bones, some loops, *etc.*

pte·ya·ȟo·ta \pte-yá-ȟo-ta\ *n* : wild rye, nodding white rye, elymus canadensis, of the grass family – BT #86

pte·ya·hpa \pte-yá-ȟpa\ *n* : the cowbird – *Syn* WAHPA HOTA Bl

ptin·han *or* **ptinhanna** \ptíŋ-haŋ\ *n* : last autumn < ~ *heconpelo* It was done last autumn. > – Note: *ptanyetu* the autumn or fall; so, *han* and *hanna* seem both to refer to the night BT HM

ptu·h'a \ptu-ȟ'á\ *vn* : to crumble down – *Syn* KAÓKSA — **ptuh'a·h'a** *v red* : to be crumbling down — **ptuh'ah'a·yakel** *adv* : in small crumbs *etc.* < *Anpetu wan takušniŝni ~ pahi unkomani yelo* One day we walked gathering up little trifling crumbs. > – Bl

ptu·ja \ptú-ja\ *adj* : cracked, split < *yuptuja* to make split or crack > — **ptuja·han** \ptu-já-haŋ\ *part* : cracked of itself

pu \ṗu\ *v 1 pers singl* [*archaic*, meaning *waú* I come] : I am coming – *See* šku

pu·can·can i·ya·ya \ṗu-cáŋ-caŋ i-yà-ya\ *v* : to pass under, stooping – Bl

pu·ga \ṗú-ġa\ *vn* : to snort, as a horse frightened

pu·lki·cin·kel \ṗu-lkí-ċiŋ-kel\ *adv* : with the lips drooping < ~ *un* to let the lips hang down, because of being greatly displeased with something > – Bl

pun·pun *or* **ponpon** *or* **punpun·la** \ṗuŋ-ṗúŋ\ *vn* : to decay, rot, as is said of wood *etc.*, but not of animal matter — *adj* : rotten, as wood

pu·sa \ṗú-sa\ *adj* – *See* púza

pu·skeb \ṗu-skéb\ *va contrac of* pusképa : to empty < ~ *okaštan* to pour emptying into >

pu·ske·pa \ṗu-ské-ṗa\ *va* wa·puskepa : to pour all out, to empty – R

pu·ski·ca \ṗu-skí-ca\ *vn* : to be very heavily burdened < *Cantemašice na cuwimapuskica mat'e* Sorrowful and heavily burdened I died. > — **puskica·t'a** *vn* : to tire out from suppressing one's feelings of sorrow, to suffer great tension – KE WHL

pu·ski·ya \ṗu-ski-ya\ *va* pu·swa·kiya : to dry or cause to dry, as wet clothes

pu·spa \pu-spá\ *va* wa·puspa : to stick on, to glue, seal < *Yunkan tankšitku conpeška wan on išta ~ keye; canke ištagonga keye* And then his younger sister stated that she sealed his eyes with a paste; and so she said he is blind. > — **puspe·kiya** \ṗu-spé-ki-ya\ *va* puspe·wa·kiya : to cause to glue on or to seal — **puspe·ya** *va* : to cause to seal or glue

pu·spu·za \ṗu-spú-za\ *adj red of* púza : dry

pu·stag \ṗu-stág\ *vn contrac of* pustáka : to squat down < ~ *iyunka* to squat down, *or* to lie low, ~ *ehpeic'iya* to get down so as to hide, bow down, squat down > — **pusta·gtukel** \ṗu-stá-gtu-kel\ *adv* : squatting

pu·sta·ka \ṗu-stá-ka\ *vn* wa·pustaka : to squat down < *Pustake s'e emaonpi kte* Let me be laid to rest as one squat down. > – *Syn* PATUJA Bl

pu·sta·kel \ṗu-stá-kel\ *adv* : into a squat position < ~ *ihpeya* to make one squat down, to put down > – Bl

pu·sta·sta·ka \ṗu-stá-sta-ka\ *v* : to stoop < ~ *iyaya* to pass below something, stooping > – Bl

pu·sya \ṗ-syá\ *va* pu·swa·ya : to dry, cause to dry — *adv* : in a drying manner < ~ *henamala* I have nothing more drying. > — **pusya·kel** \ṗu-syá-kel\ *adv* : in a drying manner

pu·sya·špan \ṗu-syá-špaŋ\ *adj* : cooked dry — **pusyašpan·yan** *v* : to cook cry, to cook too long — **pusye·la** *adv* : dry < ~ *han* to remain dry > — **pusye·ya** *v* : to dry one out < *Wanagoptanpi c'on caka na pusyemayelo* Having been listening with mouth wide open I dried myself out. *Fig* I did too much listening to talk, or I was dumb-struck. > — *adv* : in the manner of drying up < ~ *anagoptan manke* I was listening to him drying up. > – Bl B.H.54.10, 112,5

pu·ški \ṗu-škí\ *adv* : in a bunch, as rags and not cattle – *Syn* PŠUNKAYELA

pu·ški·ca \ṗu-škí-ca\ *va* wa·puškica : to press or rub out with the hand

pu·škil \ṗu-škíl\ *va contrac of* puškica : to press or rub out < ~ *yanka* to sit crowed together > — **puški·lya** *adv* : pressed, squeezed

pu·š'in·š'in \ṗu-š'íŋ-š'iŋ\ *adj* : bent, curved – Cf opúš'in, ipúš'in Bl

pu·tag \ṗu-tág\ *va contrac of* putáka : to touch by hand < ~ *ihpaya* to fall down with the hands on the ground >

pu·ta·ka \ṗu-tá-ka\ *va* wa·putaka : to touch, as with the hand when one falls

pu·tan·la s'e \ṗu-táŋ-la s'e\ *adv* : short, small and thick, as might be a man, horse, wagon *etc.* – Bl

pu·tan·ye·la \ṗu-táŋ-ye-la\ *adv* : being cold and wrapped up in a bundle < *Itoceš ~ mic'ignakin kte* Alright, being wrapped in a bundle I shall set it aside for myself *fig* speaking, I shall hold my tongue. > – Bl LHB

pu·te \ṗu-té\ *n* **a** : the upper lip, the lower lip is *ihá* **b** : the nose and mouth of animals, *e.g.* of horses

pu·te·hni·yan·yan \ṗu-té-ȟni-yaŋ-yaŋ\ *vn* pute·ma·hniyanyan : to have the lips quiver with cold or in anger

pu·te·o·ki·cu *or* **putokicu** \ṗu-té-o-ki-cu\ *n* : the elephant

pu·tin·hin \ṗu-tíŋ-hiŋ\ *or* \ṗu-tíŋ-hiŋ\ *n* : the beard, *esp* what grows on the upper lip, the mustache < ~ *icášla* a razor, ~ *ipájaja* a shaving brush >

pu·to·ki·cu *or* **puteokicu** \ṗu-tó-ki-cu\ *n* [fr *pute* upper lip + *wokicu* what one restores] : an elephant

pu·t'in·ge·la \ṗu-t'íŋ-ġe-la\ *v* : to give a little grunting sound < *Wakinyela maku kaca ~ s'e yankin na* Be sitting giving something of a little grunt sound like that of a mourning dove's breast, as is said of a proud, short and fleshy person. > – Bl

pu·za \ṗú-za\ *adj* : dry, as wood – Note: the word is *not* púsa

pu·zal \ṗu-zál\ *adv contrac if* puzáta : on dry land < ~ *iyayeya* to make go or run one ashore; *fig* to show that one has told a falsehood >

pu·za·la \ṗú-za-la\ *n* : a cat – Note: old women use the word

pu·zanl *or* **puzal** \ṗu-záŋl\ *adv contrac of* puzáta : on dry land < ~ *yeya* to prove one is a liar, ~ *yeciyin kte.* ~ *ni kte lo* I will drive you ashore. On dry land he will live. > – BT

pu·za·ta \ṗu-zá-ta\ *adv* : on dry land; *fig* caught in a lie < ~ *glicu* to reach shore > – Bl

S

pu·ze·la \ṗú-ze-la\ *adj* : shallow, as a stream of water nearly dry

p'e \p'e\ *n* : the elm tree — **p'e·can** *n* : the white elm, ulmus Americanus, of the elm family — **p'e tuntunpa** \p'e ṫuŋ-ṫúŋ-pa\ *n* : the slippery elm — **p'e·ikceka** \p'e-í-kce-ka\ *n* : the common elm - #127

p'o \p'o\ *n* : fog, mist — *adj* : foggy, misty < ~ *yelo* It is foggy, so they say and thus indicate that it will be warm, whereas the oldtimer said: *Cuhanzi yelo* It is a day wrapped in a heavy wet fog. ~ *wakitapi s'elececa* It is as though they watched the fog, as they used to say when they could not see well, for the fog it seems. > — **p'o·p'o** \p'ó-p'o\ *adj red* : very foggy - Bl

p'o·sya·kel \p'o-syá-kel\ *adv* : out of humor, displeased < ~ *unk'un winhahakelo* We had been displeased, we now are in good spirits, or After we did not like it in the beginning, we are now in good spirits. > - Bl

p'o·wa·ki·ta \p'ó-wa-ki-ṫa\ *v* : to see in only a blurred and indistinct way < *Išta kin p'owakitapi s'elemaceca yelo* My eyes seem to see in only an indistinct way, *i.e.* they do not see well, blurred and foggy. *P'owakitapi s'e waun* My vision is blurred. > - Bl

p'o·ye·la \p'o-yé-la\ *adj* : steaming < *Na wanna cega kin el u na wanna* ~ *han* And now it comes in the kettle, while now it remained steaming. >

p'o·ze·ca \p'ó-ze-ca\ *vn* ma·p'ózeca : to be out of humor

sab \sab\ *adj contrac of* sápa : black

sa·bsa·pa \sa-bsá-pa\ *adv red of* sápa : quite black — **sabsa·pya** *adv perhaps, red of* sápya, *i.e.* sábya : black, dark

sa·bya \sa·byá\ *va* sa·bwá·ya : to blacken, as one's shoes — *adv* : darkly, in a black way — **sabya·han** *adv perhaps* : dark, blackish, as water seen at a distance — **sabya·kel** *or* **sabyela** *adv* : blackish, in sight far-off < *Yunkan i etan taku wan sabyela nape el ohinhpaya* And then something blackish fell from his mouth into his hand. >

sa·gsa·ka \sa-gsá-ḳa\ *adj red of* sáka : raw, uncooked, or hard, dried - Note: the word is used in *ref* to many things — **sa·gya** \sa-gyá\ *va* sa·gwa·ya [fr *sáka* dry or hard] : to make hard or stiff - *Syn* YUSÁKA

sa·gye \sa-gyé\ *n* : a cane, a staff — **sagye·kiton** \sa-gyé-ki-toŋ\ *v* sagye·we·ton : to use a staff in walking, as an old person might — **sagye·ton** *v* sagye·wa·ton : to make use of a cane — **sagye·ya** *va* sagye·wa·ya : to use anything for a staff

sak \sak\ *adj contrac of* sáka : hard, stiff, dried, as an old hide < *pápa sáka* > — **saka** \sá-ka\ *adj* : dried stiff

sa·ka·la \sa-ká-la\ *adj* : green, limber < *can* ~ a switch >

sa·kib \sa-kíb\ *adv* : together < *nupin* ~ two side by side, *Cansákib unkaškin kte* We will tie it to a tree. *Heciyatanhan le wau ca* ~ *ungni kte lo* I just now came from there; so we two shall go home together. > - *Syn* ISAKIB D.102 Bl

sa·ki·btu \sa-kí-bṫu\ *adv* : two together — **sakibtu·kel** \sa-kí-bṫu-kel\ *adv* : both together

sam \sam\ *adv contrac of* sánpa : more, more than, beyond < *sam iyaya* to go beyond, surpass, *sam iyeya* to make one go over or beyond, *Sam taku ota slolyayapi kte lo* You will know something much more. *Sam kiyela ya po* Go closer. *Sam tahenakiya u* He came more towards him. *Tuwa yuha kin sam toketu kin slolyin kta* One who has will know more as it is. *sam iyaye* more than, *Tipi opawinge sam iyaye yawapi* More than a hundered houses were counted. > — **sam-sam** \sam-sám\ *adv red* : much more — **sam·san·pa** \sam-sáŋ-pa\ *adv red of* sánpa : more, more than, over or beyond — **sam·ye s'e** \sam-yé s'e\ *adv* : more, at it were, increasingly < ~ *iyotan šica ayapi* They became increasingly very evil. >

san \saŋ\ *adj* : gray, whitish or yellowish < *pehin* ~ gray hair, *maka* ~ white earth >

san a·ya \saŋ á-ya\ *v* : to fade

sanb \saŋb\ *adv contrac of* sánpa : more than, beyond < ~ *econ* to do more > - B.H.287.14

san·ni \saŋ-ní\ *adj* : or one side, on one side < *Nakpa kin* ~ *wagluhomni kte lo* I'll turn the other ear. *Na nape* ~ *pejuta wanji ca yuha* And his hand on one side held just a single medicine. > — **sanni·ca** *adv* : on one side, sideways < *Wapoštan* ~ *kic'un* He wore his hat sideways. > — **sanni·la** *adv* : of only one side < *Na ake nape* ~ *taku icu na ake el okala* And again his hand on only one side took something, and in it again he poured. >

san·o·kpu·kpa \saŋ-ó-kpu-kpa\ *adj* : gray, black and white mixed, as hair

---

\a\ father \e\ they \i\ machine \o\ smoke \u\ lunar \an, aŋ\ blanc Fr. \in, iŋ\ ink \on, oŋ, un, uŋ\ soon, confier Fr. \c\ chair \ġ\ machen Ger. \j\ fusion \clusters: bl, gn, kp, hšl, etc...\ b^e^lo ... said with a slight vowel **See more in the Introduction, Guide to Pronunciation**

san'·o·pa·pa \sáŋ-o-pa-pa\ *adj* : gray hairs here and there on one's head, turning gray – *See* san'ókpukpa

san·pa \sáŋ-pa\ *adv* : more, more than, beyond, over < *Lena ~ taku tona onnispepi kte wacin* He thought you would know how to do a number more than these. *Wanna wicokanyan ~ ehanl ungna wanna u* He came now perhaps at a time a little past noon-time. >

san·pa·tan·han \sáŋ-pa-taŋ-haŋ\ *adv* : from beyond — **san·psan·pa** \sáŋ-psaŋ-pa\ *adv red* : repeatedly more

san·san \saŋ-sáŋ\ *adj red of* san : whitish — **sansan'·o-papa** \ *adj red of* sán'opapa : continually graying – P B.H.35.19

san·tu·hu \saŋ-ṫú-hu\ *n* : a species of red grass with a hard round stalk and strong blade; it not *pejišaša* the puccoon — **santuhu hcaka** *n* : sand grass, long-leaved reed grass, calamovilva longifolia, of the grass family. – Note: it is used for pipe cleaning. Chief Crazy Horse wore the top of this plant as a *wotawe* charm on his head instead of a feather — **santuhu okiheton** \saŋ-ṫú-hu ò-ki-he-toŋ\ *n* : perhaps related to blue grass or forked beard grass – Cf pejí šaša ókihe tankinkinyan — **santuhu tanka** *n* : tall marsh grass, spartina cynosuroides, of the grass family – Bl BT #145, 240, 281

san·yan \saŋ-yáŋ\ *va* san·wa·ya : to whiten, white-wash — *adv* : whitish < *Anpo ~ hinapa* The dawn appears brightly. >

san·ye·la \saŋ-yé-la\ *adj* : grayish < *makoce ~* a drab countryside >

sa·pa \sá-ṗa\ *adj* : black < *Masápa* I am black. >

sa·pa tan·ka \sá-ṗa tàŋ-ka\ *n* : the spade in playing cards

Sa·pa Wi·ca·ša \Sá-pa Wi-cà-ša\ *np* : a Ute Indian

sa·pa yu·ġa·ġa \sá-pa yu-ġà-ġa\ *n* : the club in playing cards

sa·ta \sā'-ṫa\ *n* : a forked stick – *Syn* HÚNṖE OKÍJATA

sa·tgla·kin·yan *or* **cansata** \sa-ṫglá-kiŋ-yaŋ\ *n* : the horizontal stick resting on two others with forked ends, a stick to dry meat on – Note: the "t" in *satglakinyan* is made liquid in sounding it Cf húnpe okíjata — *v perhaps* : to hang out, as in drying something

sa·tin \sa-ṫíŋ\ *adj* : stretched out straight, as in death — **satin·s'e** *adj* : stretched out, as it were; tall < *Hanska he kapi* "That is what long means." > — **satin·tin** *adj red* : stretched out — **satin·yela** *adv* : stretched out, as one dead < *~ hpaya* to lie stretched out > – Bl

sa·ti·ya·ka·ške \sa-ṫí-ya-ḱa-šḱe\ *n* : that which ties up the *sáta*, the stick on which meat is dried

sa·tka·ksa \sa-tká-ksa\ *v* : to cut poles used in the tent to hang things on < *Satkakse unyanpi kte* We shall go cutting poles for hanging things. > – Bl

sa·zu \sa-zú\ *n* : an old name for the cross-sticks of the *ḣaká*, a shooting instrument in a game; in later days *tu-cuhu* ribs may have been used in shooting

sce·pan \sćé-paŋ\ *n* : a woman's sister-in-law — **scepan·ku** *or* **šcepanku** *n* : her sister-in-law — **sce-pan·ši** *n* : a woman's female cousin; my female cousin or perhaps her husband's brother's wife < *Niscepanši* she is your female cousin. > — **scepanši·tku** *n* : her female cousin; her husband's brother's wife — **scepanši·ya** *va* scepanši·wa·ya : a woman to have for a female cousin, to have for a husband's brother's wife — **scepan·ya** *va* scepan·wa·ya : a woman to have for a sister-in-law

Sci·li \Sćí-li\ *np* : a Pawnee Indian perhaps – Note: it is said they have almost the same language as the Lakota. Grinnell, in "The Story of the Indians", on pages 127, 128, 132, calls them the Skídi

scu \scu\ *v* : to make one's self important, as by dressing up, to attract attention to one's self < *Na tokel okihi scu* And he drew attention as hard as he could. > – *See* wawáscuscuke MS.104

se·ca *or* **sece** \sé-ċa\ *adv* : as though, seemingly; I thought so < *Na Lakota akicita ~ ehakela nakun manipelo* And the last ones seemed to be Lakota warriors and they were also afoot. *Ungnayehci unkiyepi na niyepi koya ikipi kte šni seca ca, eyaš heca wiyopeye kin ekta yapi na ...* Perhaps we and you it seems to me will not have enough, but then such people go to the merchant and ... *sece k'un* seemingly that > – B.H.247.13, 69.4, 93.15, 175.4

se·ce·la·ka \sé-ce-la-ka\ *vn* séce·wa·laka : to have an opinion, to think < *Ho le hecel slolwaya na lila wakanyan econpi secewalaka* Well, this is as I know it, with the idea that they were acting in a very sacred way. > – *Syn* WICALA, HECETULAKA

se·hin·gla \sē'-hiŋ-gla\ *adv* : so happening < *wanlaka sehingle cinhan* if you happen to see him, *Ištimapi na oi-kpaḣicapi kin lececa sehingle* It happened like this that they slept and awoke, *i.e.* as though they awoke from a deep sleep. *Wanun eša tokel omayaluspe sehingle cinhan yatonwan kte* You will see him though accidentally if somehow you happen to catch me. *Tiwegna glicu canke k'o ~ ške'* It is said he happened to start coming back among the houses, and then there was a commotion. > – R B.H.39.5 D.35.49

se·kse *or* **s'elececa** \sé-kse\ *adv* : as it were, as if, it seems so < *Yublaya ~ hinhpaye* It fell seemingly to level out things, as is said when snow falls here and there in large flakes. *Yunap'iyeyapi ~ inyankelo* It ran as if describing a curve as it moved, as is said of a horse running off in a curved track. *Tinpsila kin itka nahca ca wa-gacan hiyeyelo* There occurred cottonwood trees and the wild turnips as big as an egg. *wagmu apapi ~ apa* to strike a pumpkin as though struck, *i.e.* so it sounds, *Lena suta k'eš akinye ~ unkiyayapi tka yelo* If these (roads) were hard (smooth), we would as it were go flying over them. > – Bl

se·ksel \sē'-ksel\ *adv* : like

se·mni \sē'-mni\ *n* : a loafer, a bum; an unmarried young man – *Syn* SINTÉ, KOŠKALAKA Bl Cl

se·wi·mna \se-wí-mna\ *adj* : rancid, as fat that stood long — **sewi·ye** *adj* : spoiled, rancid, as rotting meat

si \si\ *n* : the foot

si·a·kša \si-á-kša\ *adj* sia·ma·kša : pigeon-toed, the toes turned in, in opposition to *sihahmin* with toes pointed outward — **siakša·kša** *adj red* : with toes persistently turned in

si·can \si-cáŋ\ *n* : the outer side of the thigh <*~ kan namatipelo* The tendon of my thigh cramped. > – Bl D.1

Si·can·gu \Si-cáŋ-ġu\ *np* Sican·ma·gu : the Brule Indians, those of the Rosebud Reservation, *lit* the Burned Thighs

si·can·o·pi·ye \si-cáŋ-o-ṗi-ye\ *n* [fr *sican* thigh + *opiye* a place to keep things] : a side pocket, as in one's pants or coat, any pocket

si·ca·psan \si-cá-psaŋ\ *v* si·wa·kapsan : to shake the foot – *Syn* KAPSANPSAN — **sicapsan·psan** *v red* : to move one's feet right and left, like a god wagging its tail < *Oh'anhanhan ~ nankahelo* You were shaking your feet back and forth playing pranks. > – Bl

si·co·co·la \si-có-co-la\ *adj red of* sicóla : bare-footed — **sico·kakala** *adj red of* sicokala : many bare-footed

si·co·ka·la \si-có-ka-la\ *adj* sico·ma·kala : bare-footed

si·co·la \si-cō'-la\ *adj* : bare-footed

si·cu·ha \si-cú-ha\ *n* : the sole of a shoe, or of the foot — **sicuha·ton** *v* : to sole, put a sole on a moccasin - Bl

si·cun \si-cúŋ\ *n* : *(philosophy)* that in a person or thing which is spirit or spirit-like and guards one from birth against evil spirits, and thereafter one may derive other *sicunpi* through the *ton* power of other beings, *esp* animals. - Note: the shaman's *sicun*, his implements, *etc.* are kept in his *wakan* spiritual bag called a *wasícun*, just as the medicines *etc.* and *sicunpi* are kept in a spiritual bag by the *pejuta wicaša* medicine man. Such *sicunpi* can be lent to others, while other and evil *sicunpi* are derived through bad and similar means - WJR.158-9

si·gla·psan·psan \sí-gla-psaŋ-psaŋ\ *or* \si-glá-psan-psan\ *v* si·wa·glapsanpsan : to swing the feet - *Syn* KAPSANPSAN, SICAPSAN

si·glu·ha \sí-glu-ha\ *vn* sí·wa·gluha : to escape, to get out of the way, *i.e.* having a bad conscience

si·ha \si-há\ *n* : the sole of the foot, the skin of the feet; the feet of horn-footed animals (horses *etc.*), a hoof

si·ha·hmin \si-há-ḣmiŋ\ *adj* siha·ma·hmin : the toes pointed side-ways, as in walking, in opposition to *sinkšakša* toes pointing inward, pigeon-toed - Bl

Si·ha·sa·pa \Si-há-sapa\ *np* : the Blackfeet Sioux

si·hu \si-hú\ *n* : the bones of the foot, the toes

si·hu·kan \si-hú-kaŋ\ *n* - *See* sihutkan

si·hu·tkan *or* **sihukan** \si-hú-tkaŋ\ *n* : the place on the leg just above the heel, *i.e.* the muscle or tendon of the heel, the foot ligament - D.92 Bc

si·ḣa·pe *or* **si·oḣape** \si-ḣá-ṗe\ *n* : the hollow of the foot

si·i·c'i·ya·pa \si-í-c'i-ya-pa\ *v* : to strike the feet together in walking — **siic'iyapa·pa** *v red* : to knock the feet together continually in walking

si·i·na·tan \si-í-na-ṫaŋ\ *n* : stirrups < ~ *akáhpe* a covered stirrup > - Cf ínatan

si·i·ta·ka·ha *or* **siitaka** \si-í-ṫa-k̇a-ha\ *n* : the top of the foot, the instep

si i·to·kab e·gle \si i-tó-kab é-gle\ *v phr* : to make one fall over one's foot while wrestling with him - Bl

si·i·yo·ti·ye·ki·ya \sí i-yo-ṫi-ye-k̇i-ya\ *v*: to have pains in one's feet for lack of good shoes < *Siiyotiyewakiye, tuweni makagege šni ca* I have pains in my feet for lack of good shoes, because no one sewed mine. > - Bl GA

si·i·yu·te \si-i-yú-te\ *n* : a foot measure

si ka·kab i·ye·ya \si k̇a-káb i-yè-ya\ *v phr* : to make one fall by holding the foot in one's way while he is running - Bl

si·ko·ška·pi \si-kó-ška-pi\ *n* : a sickness of horses swolen hooves - Bl

si·ksa \si-ksá\ *adj* : club-footed

si na·ni·yan \si na-ní-yaŋ\ *or* \sí-na-nì-yaŋ\ *v* si na·wá·niya : the feet to hurt

sin·kpe *or* **wasinkpe** \siŋ-kṗé\ *n* : the muskrat — **sinkpe·icuwa** *n* : spears, traps, axes, *etc.* used in killing muskrats — **sin·kpe·la** \siŋ-kṗé-la\ *n* : the muskrat

sin·kpe·on·ze·mna \siŋ-kṗé-oŋ-ze-mna\ *n* : musk

sin·kpe·ta·wo·te \siŋ-kṗé-ta-wo-ṫe\ *n* : calamus, sweet-flag, the acorus calamus - Note: a medicine used for cramps of the arms and legs. The roots are pulverized, mixed with gun powder and given as a drink in water

sin·kpe·ya·kel \siŋ-kṗé-ya-kel\ *adv* : in the manner of a muskrat < ~ *lila wota, wipiic'iya* He fills himself with very much eating, the way the muskrat does. >

sin·sin \siŋ-síŋ\ *adj* : besmeared, slimed, as with fish; dried on, glued or glazed over

sin·te \siŋ-ṫé\ *n* **1** : the tail of an animal; *fig* a young man *i.e.* koškalaka; < *He sinte yelo* He is no baby any longer. > **2** : the bait accompanying a purchase, *e.g.* a sale's bonus

sin·te·han·ska \siŋ-ṫē'-han-ska\ *n* : the Virginia white-tailed deer; *fig* a young buck, a rowdy - *Syn* CANTAHCA

sin·te·hla \siŋ-té-ḣla\ *n* : a rattle snake

Sin·te·hla Wi·ca·ša \Siŋ-té-ḣla Wi-cà-ša\ *np* : the Snake Indians, or the Comanches

sin·te·lu·lya·pi \siŋ-ṫé-lu-lya-pi\ *n* : the red-tailed deer - IS St

sin·te·sa·pe·la \siŋ-ṫé-sa-ṗe-la\ *n* : the mule-deer, or the black-tailed deer

sin·te·wa·ksa·pi \siŋ-ṫé-wa-ksà-pi\ *n* : the bob-tail deer

sin·te·win·yan \siŋ-ṫē'-wiŋ-yaŋ\ *n* : an unmarried young woman - Cf sinté, koškálaka - Bl

sin·ton·psan·psan *or* **sintupsanpsan** \siŋ-ṫóŋ-psaŋ-psaŋ\ *v red* : to wag the tail - Note: these two words seem to be used often *fig* , whereas *psanpsanka* and *kapsanpsan* use the *lit* meaning B.H.126.11 P Bl

si·o·co·kan \si-ó-co-k̇aŋ\ *n* : the middle toe

si·o·ḣa·pe *or* **siḣape** \si-ó-ḣa-ṗe\ \si-ḣá-ṗe\ *n* : the hollow of the foot

si·o·ka·za \si-ó-ka-za\ *n* : the toes - Cf siókazunte

si·o·ka·zun·te \si-ó-k̇a-zuŋ-ṫe\ *n* : the toes, all taken together or taken singly perhaps < ~ *wanji* a toe > - Note: *siō'ko* the space between the toes

si·o·ki·ci·ya·hla·lya·pi \si-ó-k̇i-ci-ya-ḣla-lya-pi\ *n* : a pastime for children

si·o·ko \si-ō'-k̇o\ *n* : the spaces betweem the toes

si·o·štun·ka·la \si-ō'-šṫuŋ-ka-la\ *n* : the soft claws of a buffalo calf - Bl

si·pa \si-pá\ *n* : the front part of the foot a person steps on; the toes, the end of the big toe — **sipa·hunka** \si-pá-huŋ-k̇a\ *n* : the big toe

si·pa·gna·gya \si-pá-gna-gya\ *adv* : at the tip of the toes < ~ *éyayelo* They have gone at the tip of his toes, *i.e.* to the end or perhaps beginning of its tracks. > - BT LHB

si·pa·ha i·ye·ya \sí-ṗa-ha i-yè-ya\ *v* : to kick away sideways - Bl

si·pa·i·yo·ki·he \si-pá-i-yò-k̇i-he\ *n* : the second toe

si·pa·ksi·ze \si-ṗá-ksi-ze\ *n* : the lower part of the leg of animals

si·pa·wa·ka·še \si-pá-wa-k̇a-še\ *vn* sipawa·ma·kaše : to stumble < *Sipawamakaše hena maḣica yelo* There it was I stumbled over a hoe. > - P Bl

si·pa·wi·ca·ka·še \si-pá-wi-ca-ka-še\ *n* : buffalo grass, buchloe dactyloides, of the grass family - *Syn* PEJI IWICAKOYAKE #182

si·pa·wi·ca·ya·ksa \si-pá-wi-ca-ya-ka-še\ *n* : a black beetle that snaps - Note: when people have pain in the tips of the toes, they use this word to denote it, assuming that this beetle has bitten them - EM

si·pin·kpa \si-ṗíŋ-kṗa\ *n* [fr *sipa* the toes + *inkpa* the top point] : toes — **sipinkpa·kpala** *adv* : on the toes < ~ *mani* to walk on tiptoes > - *Syn* NASLASLAL

si·san·ni \si·sáŋ-ni\ *n* : one foot, the foot on one side

Si·si·ton·wan \Si-sí-toŋ-waŋ\ *np* : the Sisitons. a band of an eastern group of the Dakotas

---

\a\ father \e\ they \i\ machine \o\ smoke \u\ lunar \an, aŋ\ blanc Fr. \in, iŋ\ ink \on, oŋ, un, uŋ\ soon, confier Fr. \c\ chair \ġ\ machen Ger. \j\ fusion \clusters: bl, gn, kp, hšl, etc...\ b^e^lo ... said with a slight vowel
See more in the Introduction, Guide to Pronunciation

si·ša·šte \si-šá-šte\ *n* : the little toe < ~ *iyókihe* the toe next, *i.e.* the fourth toe >

si·šta·ȟe \sí-šta-ȟe\ *n* : the two little bones, claws, on the feet of cows and horses

si·to·mni \si-tó-mni\ *adv* : all over, throughout < *Wanna maka ~ eyapaha* Now he proclaimed it throughout the world. *Maka ~ wakinyan agli* They all returned flying all over the world. > — **sitomni·yan** *adv* : all over < *Maka akanl ~ omawani* I walk the world over. > - MS.101

si·tu·pi \si-tú-pi\ *n* : a bird's tail feathers - Cf sitúpsan

si·tu·pi a·h'a·ye·ton·pi \si-tú-p̣i a-ȟ'à-ye-toŋ-pi\ *n* : the lark sparrow, the tips of whose tail feathers are white, otherwise it is gray, and hence its name. Its breast is whitish and head *gleglega* speckled. The white tips appear as white feathers glued to the tips of the eagle feathers used in warbonnets *etc.* Hence, *ah'ayeton* to decorate

si·tu·pi wan·bli·la \si-tú-p̣i waŋ-bli-la\ *n* : the magnolia warbler - Bl

si·tu·psan *or* **sintonpsan** \si-tú-psaŋ\ \siŋ-tóŋ-psaŋ\ *v* : to wag the tail < ~ *iyeya* to switch the tail > — **situpsan·psan** *vn red* : to wag the tail, as do dogs or birds - Cf kapsánpsan

si·t'a·t'a \sí-t'a-t'a\ *adj* : asleep, numb, as the foot

si·ya·pa·ya·kel \si-yá-pa-ya-kel\ *adv* : with the feet wet or pained, hurting < ~ *iyotiyekiye* to suffer troubles, with feet wet and hurting > - Bl

si·ye \si-yé\ *interj* : Take it from me, as a warning to a person not to do a certain thing because one is sure he cannot do it < *Hiya, oyakihi šni siyé.* > — **siye epe** \si-yé e-pè\ *v* : to tell the truth, as is said when one is asked about one's statement < *Siyé epin kte* I shall tell the truth. *Siye epe lo* I told the truth, *or* I am telling the truth. >

si·ye·mi·la \si-yé-mi-la\ *interj* : I warn you < ~ , *wakinyan maktepi, maka niye šni ška* Beware, thunder birds kill me, they say do not take Land. > - Sb

si·ye·te \si-yé-te\ *n* : the heel < ~ *mayazan* My heel pains me. > — **siyete iyahe** \si-yé-te ì-ya-he\ *n* : the ball and heel of the foot - Note: the word *íyahe* alone does not seem to be used — **siyete oškoke** *n* : the thick skin of the heel < ~ *k'el unkcela onawaksa tka oteȟike* My heel skin got stuck with a cactus, but it was troublesome. > - Bl

si·yo·ka·ja *or* **siokaza** \si-yó-ka-ja\ *n* : the toes

Si·yo·ko \Si-yó-ko\ *np* : a mythical wicked man whose name is used to scare children < ~ *u* Siyoko comes. >

si·yo·ko \si-yō'-ko\ *n* : the spaces between the toes - *See* sióko

si·yo·na·ti·ca \si-yó-na-ti-ca\ *v* : to be sticky and stinking as to the feet, to have unclean feet < *Siyonawatica* My feet are stinking wet. > — **siyonati·ktica** *v red* : to have one's feet continually wet and fetid - Bl LHB

si·yu·ha \sí-yu-ha\ *v* : to go to die < *Hena tanyan wakagin kte hcin yelo, ungna unyan siwicabluha hehantanš iye hena slolyapi kte* There I shall indeed make out well, perhaps if I have them go to die dropping from sight, there he will be known, *i.e.* if I should die. > - Bl

ska \ska\ *adj* : white, clear — **ska·ka** \skā'-ka\ *adj* : doubtfully white or gray, as a house seen from a distance < *ti ~* a dingy appearing house, seen from afar > — **ska·la** \ská-la\ *adj dim of* ska : a little bit white

ska·ni·ya·ka \ská-ni-ya-ka\ *interj in comp with tunwehca* : That is a lie, I doubt that very much, Who indeed knows? < *Tuwehca ~* Indeed who knows (the truth)?, *i.e.* That is a lie. > - Note: the word is *wiciyela,* in use by the Yankton tribe *Syn* ŠKÉKA *or* SKÉKA Bl LHB

skan \skaŋ\ *vn* : to melt, as snow and not as butter, metal *etc.,* to dissolve - *See* šlo — **skan·yan** \skaŋ-yáŋ\ *va* skan·wa·ya : to melt < *Mini yatkanpi šni, wa ece skanyanpi na yatkanpi* They did not drink water, only snow did they melt and drink. >

skan·ye·ca \skaŋ-yé-ca\ *adj* : blue < ~ *s'e* bluish, *Pejihcaka ~ s'e yunke* He lay on the bluish slender wheat grass, *i.e.* very blue or green. > - Bl

ska·ska \ska-ská\ *adj red of* ska : quite white < ~ *hingla hiyaya* to turn away one's eyes in passing so as not to notice one, *i.e. fig* the white of his eyes > — **skaskala** \ska-ská-la\ *adj red of* skála : white a bit

[1]**ska·ya** \ska-yá\ *va* ska·wa·ya : to whiten

[2]**ska·ya** \ská-ya\ *adv* : white

ska·ya·kel \ska-yá-kel\ *adv* : purely, undefiled — *adv perhaps* : white, whitish, purely < *Yunkan taku wan ~ mahpiya eciyatan u na yuzukapi s'e han* And then something whitish came from the heavens and straightway stood. >

ska·ye·la \ska-yé-la\ *adv* : brightly - Note: the word is Dakota

ske·bya \ske-byá\ *va* ske·bwa·ya : to draw all out, as a fluid, to exhaust

ske·ka *or* **škeka** \skē'-ka\ *interj of doubt as to the truth of what one says who lies* : I don't believe it < *Túnwehca ~* Who in-deed? *i.e.* doubting a person's word. > - MG

ske·pa \ské-p̣a\ *vn* : to leak out slowly, to escape, pass away by evaporation, as do fluids — **ske·skepa** \ske-ské-p̣a\ *v red* : to escape continually

ski·ca \skí-ca\ *vn* : to settle, press, pack

ski·ca·han \ski-cá-haŋ\ *part* : pressed down, close

ski·ska \ski-ská\ *n* **1** : a rough way, as a bad road **2** : the wood duck - *See* pagonta išta ša LHB

ski·ski·ca \ski-skí-ca\ *vn red of* skíca : to be settling — **skiskica·han** *part* : all pressed together

ski·ski·ta \ski-skí-ta\ *vn* : to be marked, as a log by worms under the bark - Cf yuskiskita, yuskíta R

ski·ta \skí-ta\ *adj* : tied, bound as a baby to a board R

sko·ko·gli \sko-kó-gli\ *adj* : clear as a crystal < *Taku ~* Just what is clear as a crystal? *i.e.* I do not believe it. >

sko·we \sko-wé\ *adv perhaps* and *archaic* : wrong < *Taku ~ ecanon he* What did you do wrong? > - BT

sku \sku\ *adj* : broken out a little

sku·mna \sku-mná\ *adj* : sourish, smelling badly or sour, as the scalp when dirty - Bl

sku·sku \sku-skú\ *adj red of* sku : shaved off < *Pa ~* His head is shaved. >

sku·sku·ya \sku-skú-ya\ *adj red of* skúya : very sweet

sku·ya \skú-ya\ *adj* : sweet - Note: *oskuya* sour

sku·ye·la \sku-yē'-la\ *adj* : delicious - P

sku·ye·ya \skú-ye-ya\ *va* skuye·wa·ya : to make sweet

sla \sla\ *n* : oil, grease, ointment, salve < *Sla Wakan* the Holy Anointing, one of the seven Christian Sacraments > — **sla·kiya** \sla-kí-ya\ *va poss* sla·wa·kiya [fr *slaya* to anoint one] : to anoint or grease one's own — **slakiya·pi** *n* : ointment, grease for greasing — **sla·o·ju·ha** *or* **islaye ojuha** \slá-o-ju-ha\ *n* : an oil bag

sla·sla·ta \sla-slá-ta\ *adj red of* slata : being slow or feeble < *oie ~* slow of speech >

sla·ta *or* **slate·ca** \slá-ta\ *adj* ma·slateca : slow, feeble < *toh'an ~* slow at his work, *oie ~* slow of speech >

sla·ya \sla-yá\ *v* sla·wa·ya : to anoint, grease

sle·ca \slé-ca\ *v* : to split, as with an axe - *See* kasléca

sle·ca·han \sle-cá-haŋ\ *part* : split of itself

sli \sli\ *adj* : tapering — *vn* : to ooze, as gum from a tree - P

slib \slib\ *va contrac of* slípa : to lick, lick up anything < ~ *iyeya* to make lick up > — **sli·bki·ya** *or* **slibya** \sli-bḱí-ya\ *va* sli·bwa·kiya *and* sli·bwa·ya : to cause to lick

sli·hin·gla \slí-hiŋ-gla\ *v* sli·wa·hingla : to fire a shot — **slihingle** *adv* : with the loud report of a gun - Cf hinglá — *n* : the report of a gun < *Lena* (a medicine man's powder and shots) *on taku wakute kin lila ~ šni, iwaštela iyaya na taku wakute kin wancag wicawao* By means of these (a medicine man's powder and shots) what he shot there was really no report, it went slowly, and what he shot hit them at once. >

sli·pa \slí-ṗa\ *va* wa·slipa : to lick, lick up anything

sli·sli \sli-slí\ *adj red of* sli : tapering - Bl

sli·sli·pa \slí-sli-ṗa\ *v red of* slípa : to keep licking up

sli·sli·ya \sli-slí-ya\ *adv red of* sliya : with a swishing or hissing sound < ~ *apa* to strike with a swish, *Ungna toka ška yupatuš icicu na ~ acipe ci* I warn you, there is something said, that I'll have you bend down and will hit you with a swish; *i.e.* Watch out, I will hit you. > - Bl

sli·ya \sli-yá\ *adv* : hissing, swishing, the sort by a rapidly moving switch < *Canke šiyo k'un iyuha ~ wacipi* And so all those prairie chickens danced aswishing, *i.e.* as they do with a booming caused by beating their wings against the air >

slo·han \slo-háŋ\ *vn* wa·slohan : to crawl < ~ *ku* to come back crawling, ~ *omani* It traveled at a crawl, as is said of horses. > — **slohan·han** *v red* wa·slóhanhan : to crawl along, as one does in getting near ducks < *Slohanhanhca wagliyelo* I was on the way home at a crawl, as is said of one who drags his feet when he is very tired. > — **slohan·s'e** *or* **slohes'e** \slo-hã'ŋ-s'e\ *adv* : slowly - BT

slo·he·s'e \slo-hĕ'-s'e\ *adv* : slowly, as if crawling along

slo·li·c'i·ya \slo-lí-c'i-ya\ *v refl* : to know one's self, to feel - P

slo·lki·ci·ya \slo-lḱí-ci-ya\ *v* : to know one another < ~ *unkicagapelo* We made sure we knew each other. > - Bl

slo·lki·ya \slo-lḱí-ya\ *v poss* slo·lwa·kiya [fr *slolya* to know] : to know one's own < *Tokeške waȟ'an kin slolwakiye šni* How am I not to know the way I am to deal with my own? > — **slo·lki·ye·ya** *va* : to alarm, to put on one's guard, to cause one to know something that pertains to himself

slo·lya \slo-lyá\ *va* slo·lwa·ya : to know, have knowledge of anything or person < *Slolwicakiciyapi* They knew it of them. > - B.H.282.6

slo·lye·i·c'i·ya \slo-lyé-i-c'i-ya\ *v* : to make one's self known — **slolye·kiya** \slo·lyé·ḱi·ya\ *va* slolye·wa·ki·ya : to cause to know

slo·lye·šni kon·za \slo-lyé-šni kòŋ-za\ *v* slolyešni wa·konza : to disown, disavow - B.H.253.19, 254.13

slo·lye·wa·cin \slo-lyé-wa-cin\ *va* : to inquire; *fig* to beat the bush

slo·lye·ya \slo-lyé-ya\ *va* slolye·wa·ya : to cause to know - Pb.28

slo·slo·la \slo-sló-la\ *adj* : turning soft, as meat *e.g.* bacon and other foodstuffs such as ice cream when it begins to melt - BS A

slo·ta \sló-ṫa\ *adj* : aware of things < *ieslota* one who tells the truth, *iemaslota* I am one who tells the truth > - Note: the word seems to be *v contrac* of *slolyá* to know Bl LHB

smag \smag\ *adj contrac of* smáka : hollow — **smagsmagya** \sma-gsmá-gya\ *adv red of* smagyá : in a way indented or concave

sma·gya *or* **smagya·kel** \sma-gyá\ \sma-gyá-ḱel\ *adv* : indented, concave

sma·ka \smá-ka\ *adj* : hollow, concave — *n* : a hollow, a sunken place

smi \smi\ *adj* : stripped clear, as a tree of limbs - Cf smismí

smin \smiŋ\ *adj* : bare, clean < *wasmin* cut clean, as meat from bones > — **smin·yan** \smíŋ-yaŋ\ *adj* : bare or smooth - Cf sminyányan

smin·yan·yan \smiŋ-yáŋ-yaŋ\ *adj* : clean, bare, smooth as a worn blanket, nothing extraneous or sticking to

smi·smi \smi-smí\ *adj* : stripped clear of limbs, as a tree - *See* smiyan — **smismi·yan** *adv* : destitute, deprived of everything

smi·yan \smí-yaŋ\ *adj* : bare or smooth - Cf smínyan

sna *or* **kasna** \sna\ *vn* : to ring, sound < *wahácanka ~* ringing shield > — **sna·han** \sna-háŋ\ *part* : ringing, rustling, as leaves falling in autumn — **snahan·han** *part red* : falling off, rustling

snan·za *or* **snaza** *or* **snas'a** \snáŋ-za\ *vn* : to draw up, as burnt skin, to be scarred — *n* : a scar - R

sna·sna \sna-sná\ *vn red of* sna : to ring, rattle

sna·sna·la \sna-sná-la\ *adj* : bare, as a tree when its leaves have all fallen off

sna·s'e \sná-s'e\ *adv* : tinkling, ringing - *Syn* HLAYELA Bl

sna·ye·la \sna-yé-la\ *adv* : ringing < ~ *iyaya* to ring, sound, to go ringing as iron *etc.* do when struck, ~ *iyeya* to cause to ring >

sna·za *or* **snanza** \sná-za\ *vn* : to draw up, to crisp, as burnt skin, to be scarred — **sna·ze** \sna-zé\ *n* : a scar - P

sni \sni\ *adj* : cold, as the weather or as ice; gone out, as in *peta sni* fire has gone out < *talo sni* cold meat (after cooking), *petijanjan sni* The lantern went out. > — *n* : cold < *Sni mákat'elo* The cold is killing me. >

sni·ca·t'a \sni-cá-t'a\ *v* sni·ma·kat'a : to feel sleepy from heat or cold < *Htayetu sniunkat'api ca lila unkištinmapi* In the evening we feel sleepy from the cold so we feel very much like sleeping. > - BT

sni·sni \sni-sní\ *adj red* : cold < *han ~* cold nights >

sni·ya \sni-yá\ *va* : to cool < *Miceji kin sniyin kte lo* My tongue will cool, *or* It will cool my tongue. > — **sniyahota** \sni-yá-ho-ṫa\ *vn* sni·bla·hota : to take cold, to draw in the cold by breathing - B.H. 228.3

sni·yan \sni-yáŋ\ *v* : to become cold, as the weather < ~ *uya* It is becoming cold. >

sni·yan·ka·t'a \sni-yáŋ-ka-t'a\ *v* : to knock somebody senseless

sni·yan·t'a \sni-yáŋ-t'a\ *v* : to faint

sni·yo·pa \sni-yó-pa\ *adj* : frostbitten, as might be the limbs, affected by the cold - Cf oíyopa - WE LHB

[1]**so** \so\ *va* wa·so : to cut into strings < *Na taha sópi k'on hena on wihuta opahloke el cel okatan* And with these deer hide strings he made fast the tipi pierced at approximately the lower edge >

[2]**so** \so\ *interrog partic* - Like to *hwo* and *he*, except that *so* implies one is expecting an affirmative answer,

---

\a\ father \e\ they \i\ machine \o\ smoke \u\ lunar \an, aŋ\ blanc Fr. \in, iŋ\ ink \on, oŋ, un, uŋ\ soon, confier Fr. \c\ chair \ǧ\ machen Ger. \j\ fusion \clusters: bl, gn, kp, hšl, etc...\ b[e]lo ... said with a slight vowel **See more in the Introduction, Guide to Pronunciation**

but *he* one is leaving the answer to the addressee < *Hokšila kin le waniyetu tona ilukcan so* How many years old you figure this boy is? *Kola, tohanl wanasapi kte so* Friend, when will they be hunting buffalo? > – F

so·kso·ta \so-ksó-ṫa\ *adj red of* sóta : hazy < *išta ~* blurred, *i.e.* bad eyes >

sol \sol\ *adj perhaps contrac of* sóta : vacated, gone, hazy < ~ *iyeya* or *aya* to disappear, die off gradually >

so·lki·ya \so·lk̇í-ya\ *va* so·lwa·kiya [fr *sóta* expend, spend, destroy] : to use up, expend, spend, destroy for one – *Syn* KASOTA, YUSOTA

so·lya \so·lyá\ *va* so·lwa·ya : to have used up *e.g.* one person's wood supply – Bl

son \soŋ\ *va* wa·són : to plait, braid *e.g.* the hair, or thin cords into a rope < *wikansónpi* a lasso with which to catch horses, *Šupé wason kte* I'll plait *lit* his guts, *i.e.* will call him to order. > — **son·pi** \sóŋ-pi\ *n* : braids, strings of corn

so·so \só-so\ *va* wa·sóso : to cut into strings, as a hide < *Tahalo k'on he hanke ~* She had fringed part of that hide. > — **soso·pi** \só-so-ṗi\ *n* : a strip or string cut from hide

so·ta \só-ṫa\ *adj perhaps* 1 : used up, gone < *Iyuha sotapi* All are dead. > 2 : hazy – *Syn* KASOTA, SOLKIYA, YUSOTA

so·tka \so-tká\ *adj* : outstanding, as one tall thin tree standing among smaller ones

span \sṗaŋ\ *v* : to thaw, perhaps < *Anpetu wan span s'e wašte he yelo* That was a pleasant day, a quiet pleasant day in winter, a balmy winter day. > — **span·la** \sṗáŋ-la\ *vn* : to become soft, to melt, as snow < *wa ~* snow melts > — **spanla·ya** \sṗáŋ-la-ya\ *va* spánla·wa·ya : to cause to thaw, as snow — **span s'e wašte** *adj* : tender and good to eat – Bl LHB

spa·spa·ya \spa-spá-ya\ *vn red of* spáya : to be wet

spa·ya \spá-ya\ *vn* ma·spaya : to be wet, as in one's clothes — **spaye·ya** \spá-ye-ya\ *va* spaye·wa·ya : to wet, cause to wet or moisten

stag \stag\ *adj of* stáka : feeble, weary, sick — **stagya** \sta-gyá\ *va* sta·gwa·ya : to make feeble — *adv* : feebly, languidly — **stagya·kel** *or* **stagye·la** *adv* : feebly

sta·ka \stā'-k̇a\ *adj* ma·staka : feeble, weary, not able to walk, sick and lying down from exhaustion < *Cankahu mastaka* My backbone is weary. *Cuwístaka* His back is worn out. *Hupahu staka* The travois pole is feeble. *Ungnahahci le anpetu kinhan išta mastaka s'elececa* It may be today my eyes seem to be weary. > – MS.145 Bl

stan \staŋ\ *adj* 1 : moist, wet 2 : purple, grape-colored < *ša ~* dark red, *ha ~* dark complexioned >

[1]**stan·ka** \staŋ-ká\ *adj* : moist < *can ~* soaked wood >

[2]**stan·ka** \stáŋ-k̇a\ *adj* : purple

sta·sta·la \sta-stá-la\ *adj* : pliable < ~ *s'elececa* to seem pliable, as is said of a bow when it bends well, or of a gun when the hammer works well, *i.e.* oiled *etc.* *Itazipa kin ~ s'e* (or *lolopela s'e*) *awakate lo* I drew the bow that seemed pliable (or seemed too soft, weak). > – Bl

sto \sto\ *adj* : smooth, lying smooth, as hair < *Cap'sto s'e nakpa cikcik'a* Like the beaver, his ears are quite small. > – Cf kastó

sto·la \stó-la\ *adj* ma·stola : neat and small

sto·sto \sto-stó\ *adj red of* sto : smooth, lying flat

sto·ya \sto-yá\ *va* sto·wa·ya : to make smooth, to smooth down *e.g.* the hair

sto·ya·kel *or* **stoye·la** \sto-yá-k̇el\ *adv* : smoothly

stu \stu\ *adj* ma·stú un·stú·pi : proud

stu·i·c'i·la \stú-i-c'i-la\ *v refl* stu·mi·c'ila : to think much of one's self, to be proud

stu·sta \stu-stá\ *adj* ma·stusta : tired, weary, unable to move < *Cankahu mastusta* My backbone is unable to move. > — **stuste·ya** \stu-sté-ya\ *adv* : wearily, tired out, in an exhausted condition < ~ *waglihunni* I arrived exhausted. > — *va perhaps* : to weaken – P

su \su\ *n* : the seed of anything < *maza su* a bullet, *wasu* hail >

su·kpan·la \su-kṗáŋ-la\ *n* : a shotgun, shot – R

su·ksu·ta \su-ksú-ṫa\ *adj red of* súta : hard, strong — **suksuta·ya** *adv red of* sutáya : firmly, hard – Bl

[1]**sun** \suŋ\ *n contrac of* súnka mi·sun : a younger brother – Note: men and women use the word in addressing him

[2]**sun** \suŋ\ *v* : to braid – *See* son\soŋ\

sun·ka \súŋ-ka\ *n* mi·sunka : a younger brother of a man or a woman – Note: certain cousins are likewise so called

sun·ka·ki·ci·ya·pi \suŋ-k̇á-k̇i-ci-ya-pi\ *n* sunka·un·kiciya·pi : those related as brothers, thus brethren

sun·ka·ku \suŋ-ká-ku\ *n* : a younger brother of him or her

sun·ka·ya \suŋ-ká-ya\ *va* sunka·wa·ya : to have for a younger brother

su·o·ju·ha \su-ó-ju-ha\ *n* : a pod

su·pe·sto·la *or* **suzizila** \su-ṗé-sto-la\ *n* : a muskmelon

su·su \su-sú\ *n* : the testicles — **susu icu** \su-sú i-cu\ *v* : to castrate – Bl

Su·su·ni \Sú-su-ni\ *np* : the Shoshone people – Note: they are also known as Pejí Wokéya Otí kin, *i.e.* the Grass Hut Dwellers

su·ša·ša·la \su-šá-ša-la\ *n* : a 22-caliber rifle

su·ta \su-ṫá\ *adj* ma·súta : hard, not yielding to the touch, capable of endurance, strong — **su·ta·ka** \su-ṫá-k̇a\ *adj* : tough, hardy — **suta·ya** *adv* : firmly, hard — **sutaya·kel** \su-ṫá-ya-k̇el\ *adv* : firmly

su·to \su-tó\ *n* : a metal cartridge filled < *Na mazasu wan ~ ikoyaka* And he stuck a bullet in a filled metal cartridge. >

su·ton \su-tóŋ\ *vn* : to ripen, have seed, to be ripe, fit for use, as corn

su·zi·zi·la *or* **supestola** \su-zí-zi-la\ *n* : muskmelon

swa \swa\ _– *See* yuswá

swa·han \swa-háŋ\ *part* : raveled

swa·ka \swa-ká\ *adj* : ragged, as an old flag, fringed — **swa-swaka** \swa-swá-k̇a\ *adj red* : tattered

swu·la \swú-la\ *adj* : small, fine, as beads *etc.* — **swuswula** \swú-swu-la\ *adj red* : many being fine

swu·wa·ya \swu-wá-ya\ *adj* : soft and fine, as snow in warm weather < *Wa kin ~ ca tanyan oomani waštеyelo* The walking on the fine snow is well and good. > – Bl

s'a \s'a\ *vn* wa·s'a : to hiss, as a serpent or angry people do; to splash, as does water

s'a \s'a\ *aux suff* to *v* signifying frequency of action < *Wai s'a* I keep going. >; or gives the *v* the force of a *n* of agent < *wamanon ~* a thief >

s'a·mna \s'a-mná\ *adj* : smelling sour, stinking

s'e *or* **s'e·céca** *or* **s'e·lé** \s'e\ *adv* : like, as though < *Hecel he hinhan s'e wacinpi on heconpi* So did it because they wanted to be like the owl. *Na makoce wan peji to ca akanl maglihe s'ececa na mani iblabla* It was as if I came down standing on a land of blue grass, so I went walking. > – Note: *s'ecéca* may be Yankton Sioux *Syn* S'ELECECA B.H.149.8, 150.19

s'e·le·ce·ca \s'e-lé-ce-ca\ *adv* : as if, it seems as if, it seems so, it appears so < *Unyanpi kin slolyyapi* ~ It seems as if they knew us coming. *Atkuku toki iyayapi s'e s'elemaceca* It appears to me as though their father went off somewhere, as is said at the departure of one who was like a father. > - Bl

s'e·wa·can·mi \s'ē'-wa-caŋ-mi\ *v 1 pers singl of* s'ewacin : I think it is so - Note: this form of the word is used when one is speaking of something that is not distinctly recollected

s'e·wa·cin \s'ē'-wa-ciŋ\ *v* : to think it to be so < *Canke tibloku kin he cinca ~ na ceya iyayin na icu keye* And so she stated that she took him, went away crying, and thought the child to be her older brother. > - MS.96

s'in \s'iŋ\ *adv* : craning one's neck, or stretching one's throat, or swallowing with difficulty < ~ *napca. Ahiyoka-s'in* He swallowed craning his neck. He came and peeped in. ~ *s'e inyanka* He ran as though craning his neck, *i.e.* as a horse throwing up its head while running, thus *Yukós'inpi s'e inyanka* He ran as a horse with its head thrown high. > - *Syn* EYOKAS'IN — **s'in·s'in** *or* **s'ins'in·ya** *or* **s'ins'in·yan** \s'íŋ-s'iŋ\ *adv red* : in the manner of craning the neck < *Canke akih'an t'in kta ca cehupa kin akiyataka ca ~ iyaye wota ške* And so it is said that it (a wolf) went away eating, trying hard to swallow while its legs were cramped and about to die from starvation. ~ *iyaya wanapca* It was swallowing and going on in a way craning its neck. *Tokiyatan taákih'an wahi yelaká ~ wanawapce lo* I ate craning my neck since I came from a place where there is starving. > - *Syn* KA-S'INS'I, KIS'INS'IN Bl

š \š\ *suff* to words to give them *dem emph*, and for that reason it is like *hci* < *wancakeš* at once, *hecenaš* finally, *éhaš* undoubtedly, *miyeš* I myself, *wannaš* right now >

ša \ša\ *adj* : red, crimson < *We ša* Blood is red. > - P

ša-a-ya·ska·pa \šá-a-ya-ska-pa\ *n* : a patent in fee, so named perhaps because of the red seal attached - HH

šab a·ya ku·ja \šab á-ya kù-ya\ *v phr* : to have consumption, *i.e.* of the bones

ša·bša·bya \ša-bšá-bya\ *adv red of* šabya : to soil < *Mahpiya ~ kahwokelo* A cloud of dirt was carried away by the wind. > - Bl

ša·bya \ša-byá\ *va* ša·bwa·ya [fr *šapa* dirty, blackened] : to soil, defile — *adv* : dirtily

ša·gi \ša-ǵí\ *adj* : auburn, sandy - P

Ša·gla·ša \Ša-glá-ša\ *np* : an Englishman

ša·glo·gan \ša-glō'-ġaŋ\ *num card adj* : eight — **šaglo-gan·la** *adv* : only eight — **šagloglogan** *adv* : by eights

ša·hin·gla \šá-hiŋ-gla\ *vn* : to glow < *Ite* ~ A face glowed. > - P Bl

Ša·hi·ya \Ša-hí-ya\ *np* : a tribe of western Indians (perhaps a group with a lesser spelling difference from that of the Šahiyela) - Bl

Ša·hi·ye·la \Ša-hí-ye-la\ *np* : the Cheyenne Indians

ša·hi·ye·la ta·tin·psin·la \ša-hí-ye-la ta-tìŋ-psiŋ-la\ *n* : the white-flowered parsley, cogswellia orientalis, the parsley family - Note: the roots are eaten — **šahiyela huzizi** *n* : the yellow-flowered parsley, cogswellia montana, the parsley family - Note: it is also called *wahcazi iyawicaskapa* a plant that is sticky perhaps when young #263, 262 Bc

ša·i·c'i·ya \ša-í-c'i-ya\ *v refl of* šayá : to paint one's self red, to dress well - P B.H.112.9

ša·ke \ša-ké\ *n* : the nails of the fingers and toes, the claws of birds and beasts, the hoofs of animals

ša·ke·han·ska \ša-ké-haŋ-ska\ *n* : the grizzly bear

ša·ke·hu·te s'e hin·gla \ša-ké-hu-ṫe s'e hiŋ-gla\ *v* : to become very angry, *i.e.* like a bear - Bl

ša·ke ta·pa \ša-ké tà-ṗa\ *n* : a sickness of the fingertips swelling - Bl

ša·ki·ya \ša-kí-ya\ *va* ša·wa·kiya : to paint red one's own or for one, to redden as once did the Dakotas to scalps, to make glad by gifts < *Nupin giic'iyapi na itokšan šakiyapi* Both painted themselves brown and they had their own faces painted with a red circle. >

ša·ko·win \ša-kó-wiŋ\ *num card adj* : seven — **šako-win·la** \ša-kó-wiŋ-la\ *adv* : only seven — **šakowin-win** *adv* : by sevens

ša·kpe \šá-kpe\ *num card adj* : six — **šakpe·kpe** \šá-kpe-kpe\ *or* \ša-kpé-kpe\ *adv* : by sixes — **šakpe·la** \šá-kpe-la\ *adv* : only six

ša·kton s'e \ša-któŋ s'e\ *adv* : as if a funny sort of man - Bl WHL

ša·k'o·ya·zan \ša-k'o-ya-zaŋ\ *vn* : to have pains under the finger nails because of cold weather

ša·mna \šá-mna\ *adj* : dark brown - Bl

[1]**šan** \šaŋ\ *n* : the vagina

[2]**šan** *or* **e·šan** \šaŋ\ \e-šáŋ\ *adv placed at the end of the sentence* : also < *Unšila wan leciš manke* ~ Poor little one, and here I sit, as is said of him who was kind to your grandfather sits over here! > - D.116

šan·ke \šaŋ-ké\ *n* : a step-mother, a father's other wife — **šanke·ya** \šaŋ-ké-ya\ *va* šanke·wa·ya : to have for a step-mother - R Bl

šan·ku \šáŋ-ku\ *n* : one's mother, *archaic* form for *húnku* - Mh

ša·pa *or* **šape** \šá-ṗa\ *adj* ma·šapa ma·šape : dirty, defiled, blackened < *Nape mašapa* My hands are really dirty. >

ša·pe·sto·la \ša-pé-sto-la\ *n* : the diamond in cards

ša·pša·pa *or* **šapšape** \ša-pšá-ṗa\ *adj red of* šápa : many black

ša·p'a·ya·pi \ša-ṗ'á-ya-pi\ *n* : consumption, a sickness that causes one to refuse to eat after having tasted food - Bl EM

šaš *or* **ešaš** *or* **eša** \šaš\ *conj emph* : also - B.H.28.4

ša·ša \ša-šá\ *adj red of* ša : red — **šaša·ya** *va* šaša·wa·ya : to dye or paint red — *adv* : redly, in a red way

ša·šte \ša-šté\ *n* : the little finger — **šašte·iyokihe** \ša-šté-i-yò-ki-he\ *n* : the third finger, the ring finger, *i.e.* that next to the little finger

Ša·wa·la \Ša-wá-la\ *np* : the Shawnee Indians (*Tóka ca kapi* It is an enemy that is meant.) - R

ša·ya \ša-yá\ *va* : to paint red, *i.e.* to clothe one, to give clothes to somebody — *adv* : redly, in a celebrative way

ša·ye·la \ša-yé-la\ *adv* : reddest < *Maštincapute ~ ota* Many are the reddest rabbit, buffalo, berries. >

še \še\ *interj* used by men : Hist!, Hark!, Hey!

še·ca \šé-ca\ *adj* : dry, dead, as wood, rotten

še·han *or* **šehanš** \še-háŋ\ *interj of* impatience : Good heavens!, For heaven's sake!

He, kola, kola tatuye
Ṭopakiya natan hiyuye
Šehan tamunka šni ye.

\a\ f<u>a</u>ther \e\ th<u>e</u>y \i\ mach<u>i</u>ne \o\ sm<u>o</u>ke \u\ l<u>u</u>nar \an, aŋ\ bl<u>anc</u> Fr. \in, iŋ\ <u>in</u>k \on, oŋ, un, uŋ\ s<u>oo</u>n, <u>con</u>fier Fr. \c\ <u>ch</u>air \ġ\ ma<u>ch</u>en Ger. \j\ fu<u>s</u>ion \clusters: bl, gn, kp, hšl, etc...\ <u>b</u>[e]lo ... said with a slight vowel
See more in the Introduction, Guide to Pronunciation

Look here, friend, friend, in this directions
Four he comes to make his attack,
Hist! Heavens! do not take your rest! - MS.101 RT

še·han·leš \še-háŋ-leš\ *adv interrog* : how much more, how much less < *Niciye epi kayeš iyeyapi šni k'un, ~ le hanikakta kin taku oyakihi kte laka* Even your elder brothers have not found her, then how much less will you who are the youngest have any luck? >

še·hanš \še-háŋš\ *adv interj of* impatience : for heaven's sake! < *Micopi ca el wai na lila wicotapi tka ~ wana slolwaya* I went there since I was invited, and there was a great crowd, but for the life of me, I knew of it. *Na nakun sunkakupi kin heciya ~ tehilapi heci henana on Benjamin lila apatonyela kuwa* And besides, he pursued Benjamin their younger brother really singling him out, alas, in that way for the fact that he was loved dearly. > - B.H.43.3

še·han·ška *or* **šehanška·laka** \še-háŋ-ška\ *adv* : at any rate, nontheless - R Bl

še·ha·štu·ka \še-háŋ-štu-ka\ *adv* : well, but, this time for sure, at last < *Anbwašte ca ~ hlahla kin tehan hotan'in ktelo* This time for sure was a pleasant day so that long the bells might ring, might have their voices heard. *~ ecamon kta* At last, I will not forget to do it, *i.e.* as I did before in spite of my resolutions. *~ okata heci wašteyelo* This time for sure it is good to have the place warm, as a man says coming into and finding the room warm for once. *~ tuweni našlaye nikte šni hwo* At last, for once, did no one bother you? *i.e.* not one is after to get you. *~ akipa ca* Finally, he was really punished. > - R Bl FB SHB B.H.68.14

še·kše·ca \še-kšé-ca\ *adj red of* šéca : dry, dead, rotten

še·lya \še-lyá\ *va* še·lwá·ya : to make dry, to lay up to season, to make wither — *adv* : seasoning, withered — **šelya·kel** *adv* : in dry condition < *~ yanka* It rested in dry condition. > - B.H.65.20

še·na *or* **jena** \šẽ'-na\ *adj* ma·šéna : having used up, spent, sold, *etc.* everything and hence having nothing < *Mazaska mašena* I am out of money. > - Cf yuíjena

še·ya·ka \še-yá-ka\ *n* : peppermint, but not the medicinal mint *ceyáka*, a water plant, from which a tea is prepared with its leaves especially when one is entertaining visitors

[1]**ši** \ši\ *interj* to call attention privately : Hist! Hist! Heh! - Note: the word is used by women

[2]**ši** \ši\ *va* wa·ší : to command, bid < *Econ ši* He told him to do it. > - Note: the word is always preceded by another *v*

ši·bši·pa·han \ši-bší-pa-haŋ\ *part red of* šipahan : dropped out, fallen off - *Syn* PŠUNPŠUNWAHAN

ši·ca *or* **šice** \ší-ca\ *adj* ma·šíca : bad, ugly, wicked

ši·ca·ho·wa \ši-cá-ho-wa\ *vn* šicaho·wa·wa : to cry out — **šicahowa·ya** *vn* šicahowa·bla šicahowa·la šicahowa·un·yan·pi : to moan, to scream < *Na ataya akicita k'on šicahowayapi na Lakota ko* And altogether the soldiers, and the Lakotas too, moaned. >

ši·ca·ki·ci·la·pi *or* **šilkícilapi** \ší·ca·ki·ci·la·pi\ *v recip* : They were hating each other — **šicaki·la** *or* **šilkíla** \ší-ca-ki-la\ *v poss* šica·wa·kila [fr *šicela* to hate] : to hate one's own

ši·ca·ki·ya *or* **šilkíya** \ší-ca-ki-ya\ *va* šica·wa·kiya : to think low of

ši·ca·mna \ši-cá-mna\ *adj* : bad smelling < *Nišicamna ca gni na yaki kin ikpakintin na u wo* Come, and wipe yourselves when you go and return home because you get bad smelling. >

ši·ca·wa·cin \ši-cá-wa-ciŋ\ *vn* : to be frightened and to hurry overmuch; to scream out - B.H.112.9 — *adv* : frantically < *~ wau* I came bersek. > - D.194 and 4

ši·ca·ya *or* **šicaya·kel** \ši-cá-ya\ \ši-cá-ya-kel\ *adv* : badly, not well < *~ kuwa* to treat meanly >

ši·ce·ca \ši-cẽ'-ca\ *n* : a child, little children - Note: the word is doubtfully used by the Tetons - R. Bl

ši·ce·la \ší-ce-la\ *va* šíce·wa·la : to hate, esteem as bad - *Syn* WAHTÉLAŠNI, ŠILLÁ

ši·ce·lah \ší-ce-lah\ *adj dim of* šica : funny, cute, as applied as an endearing name to babies *etc.*

ši·ce·la·ka \ší-ce-la-ka\ *v* šíce·wa·laka : to think bad, to hate

ši·ci·t'e \ší-ci-t'e\ *adj* [fr *šica* bad + *it'a* die for] : worthless, very bad, *lit* dead of badness

ši·ci·ya \ši-cí-ya\ *vn* šici·wa·ya : to talk angrily

ši·co·ki·ya \ši-có-ki-ya\ *va* [fr *šica* bad + *okíya* to court] : to speak evil to one's spouse - Bl

ši·cun *or* **sicun** \ši-cúŋ\ *n* : the group of powers, possessed by nature or attained by effort peculiar to each being

ši·c'e \ši-c'é\ *n* : a woman's brother-in-law and mine, *i.e.* her husband's brother and her sister's husband < *nišic'e* your brother-in-law > — **šic'e·ku** *n* : her brother-in-law, *i.e.* her husband's brother and sister's husband

ši·c'e·ši \ši-c'é-ši\ *n* : a woman's male cousin and my male cousin < *nišic'eši* your male cousin > — **šic'eši·tku** *n* : her male cousin — **šic'eši·ya** *va* šic'éši·wa·ya : to have for a male cousin

ši·c'e·ya \ši-c'é-ya\ *va* šic'e·wa·ya : a woman to have for a brother-in-law, *i.e.* her husband's brother and sister's husband

ši·gla \ši-glá\ *vn* ši·lwa·gla ši·lya·gla ši·lun·gla·pi : to be or become angry, to take offense at < *Tuwa ~ ca kat'api* One who was angry was struck dead. > - Note: the "l" is introduced before the *pron* — **šigla·pi** *n* : anger, wrath

ši·gla·ya \ši-glá-ya\ *va* šigla·wa·ya : to make angry, provoke to anger

ši·htin \ši-htíŋ\ *adj* : bad, poorly made, imperfect — **šihtin·yan** *adv* : poorly made, imperfectly

ši·ka \ši-ka\ *interj* : Pitiful one! - Note: the word has no accent and can stand or be omitted without affecting the sense of the sentence. It is something of an aside by the person telling the story to stir pity in the hearers for a character in the tale < *~ onšiyehci omašte wan el anpetu ataya hpayelo ke* They say: Poor fellow! What a pity, he lay in a hot and sultry place for a whole day on end, *i.e.* the helpless animal sought out a sunny spot and lay there all day. *Tima lekšitkula k'un wayaka s'e tisanpatanhan pa icu šni yanka* There sat his uncle, like a pitiable captive, on the opposite side of the tipi, never once raising his head. > - Note: in this last example we see the omission of *šika* from its place immediately after *k'un* - D.123, 110

ši·ki·gla \ši-kí-gla\ *v* : to be satisfied with < *~ unkomanipelo* We are satisfied with our travel, *i.e.* are making good headway. > - *Syn* OPIKILA Bl

ši·kši·ca \ši-kší-ca\ *adj red of* šíca : really bad — **šikšicaya** *adv* : badly < *~ mani* to be hard walking, *Ota ~ econ* Much was very hard to do. > — **šikši·cela** *adj* : bad, hard, difficult — **šikšil** *adj red contrac* : badly < *~ ia* to talk badly, *~ iwaya* It was hard for me to speak. > — **šikši·loh'an** *v* : to act badly, to do wickedly

— šikšiloh'an·ka \ši-kší-lo-ȟ'aŋ-ka\ *n* : one who does badly — **šikšilya** *adv of* šilyá : badly - B.H.199.6
ši·la·ptan·ye·ya \ši-lá-ptaŋ-ye-ya\ *va* : to curse, to cause to have bad luck - B.H.67.9
ši·la·wa·cin \ši-lá-wa-ciŋ\ *v* : to think bad of, have bad desires for - B.H.191.7
ši·le·con a·pe \ši-le-cóŋ a-pè\ *v* : to solicit <*Wicoh'an šica econ ape* He expected her to work a bad habit. > - B.H.29
ši·lgla *or* **šigla** \ši-lglá\ *v* ši·lwa·gla : to detest, not wishing to see it — **šilgla toie** \ši-lglá tò-i-e\ *v* : to curse < *Šilwicagla toie* He cursed them. *Šilwagla mitoie* I cursed. > - Cf glatóie B.H.113.12
ši·lh'an \ši-lȟ'áŋ\ *vn* ši·lwá·h'an : to behave badly — šilh'an·ka *n* : one who acts badly — **šilh'an·yan** *adv* : behaving badly - Bl
ši·lki·ci·la·pi *or* **šícakicilapi** \ši·lkí-ci-la-pi\ *v recip* : hating each other
ši·lki·la *or* **šícakila** \ši·lkí-la\ *v poss* : to hate one's own
ši·lki·ya *or* **šícakiya** \ši-lkí-ya\ *va* : to think low of
ši·lla \ši·llá\ *v* ši·lwá·la : to esteem bad
ši·lo·h'an \ši-ló-ȟ'aŋ\ *v* šilo·wa·h'an : to do wrong < ~ *ape* She expects to do wrong. > - B.H.94.3, 137.20
ši·lo·i·e·pi \ši-ló-i-e-pi\ *n* : bad talk - B.H.103.7
ši·lwa·e·con \ši-lwá-e-coŋ\ *v* : to commit wrong deeds, act badly < ~ *šni yunš tohanni unnicahipi šni tka yelo* If he had not committed wrong, we would never have brought him to you. > - B.H.260.16
ši·lwa·ki·pa \ši-lwá-ki-pa\ *v* : to have bad luck - B.H. 44.3
ši·lwa·na·ki·h'on \ši-lwá-na-ki-ȟ'oŋ\ *v* : to listen to something bad < *Šilwanakih'onpi s'e inila mankehe lo* I was standing silent as if they heard something bad, *i.e.* I am silent. >
ši·lwi·ya·un·pa \ši-lwí-ya-uŋ-pa\ *v* : to slander, accuse one falsely of evil - B.H.164.6
ši·lwi·yu·kcan \ši·lwí·yu·kcan\ *v absol* šilwí·blu·kcan : to plan evil - D.258
ši·lwo·ka·hni·hya \ši-lwó-ka-ȟni-ȟya\ *va* : to scandalize *e.g.* children, to teach evil to the young - B.H.215.10
ši·lwo·ya·ka \ši-lwó-ya-ka\ *v* : to talk bad about others
ši·lya \ši-lyá\ *va* ši·lwá-ya : to spoil - *Syn* YUŠICA — *adv* : badly — **šilya·kel** \ši-lyá-kel\ *adv* : badly — šilye·hci \ši-lyé-ȟci\ *vn* : to spoil rather badly < ~ *hlogeca it'eyela* He died thin for some reason spoiled rather badly, as is said when a man is very lean. > - Bl D. 273 WHL
šil'·a·na·go·tan \šil'-á-na-ġo-ptaŋ\ *v* : to hear bad stories about others and spread them
ši·na \ši-ná\ *n* : a blanket, shawl, robe

šina apáhlate ribbon, ferret
šina apahlate zibzípela silk ribbon
šina cankóhan the center beaded back part of a shawl, a blanket beaded across the middle - R
Šinágleglega *np* the Navajo tribe
šináhinšma a buffalo robe
šináhota the common white blanket
šináikceka a buffalo robe
šináipatapi a robe ornamented with quillwork
šinájanjan a red blanket
šiná kasúpi a fringed shawl
šiná okásu the fringe of a shawl
šináokipata a quilt made of pieces
šináopapun ciscila a blanket with a small border, save list cloth
šináopapun hóta gray list cloth
šináopapun ska white list and stroud
šináopehe a bale of blankets
šinásan a light colored blanket
šináša a red blanket
šináto a blue or green blanket, blue skirt cloth
šináto zibzípela blue broad cloth
šinázibzipela broad cloth
šinókasu or *šina okasu* the fringe of a shawl

šin \šiŋ\ *n* : the fat part of animals, *esp* fat meat; the sappy part of wood, thus *canšin*
šin·kcin·yan \šiŋ-kcíŋ-yaŋ\ *adv* : cranky < ~ *un* to be angry always and cranky > - Note: *Wawohilhitikin kte hcin ca hecel kapi* So they mean that one would be superactive, almost terrifying - Bl
šin·kpan·ka·hu *or* **šinkpanka** \šiŋ-kpáŋ-ka-hu\ *n* : food roots, the name for an edible root that grows in low lands - D.97
šin·šin \šiŋ-šíŋ\ *adj* : wrinkled
šin·ta·to ce·gna·ke \šiŋ-tá-to ce-gnà-ke\ *n* : a loin cloth made of blue or black cloth
ši·pa \ši-pá\ *v* : to strip or cut off - *Syn* KAŠIPA, YUŠIPA — **šipa·han** *or* **šipa·wahan** *part* : broken off close, as the limbs of a tree, the teeth of a comb - *Syn* PŠUNWÁHAN
ši·šo·ka \ši-šó-ka\ *n* : the robin - R FR
ši·tki·gla \ši-tkí-gla\ *vn* : to be angry, to be afflicted < ~ *un* to be angry > - R
ši·ya·gla \ší-ya-gla\ *n* : a duck
[1]**ši·ya·ka** \ši-yá-ka\ *n* : the teal duck, the American eared grebe, and the mud hen (duck) - D.130 WHL
[2]**ši·ya·ka** \ši-yá-ka\ *n* : a boil < ~ *upi* boils come up, *i.e.* a little hard swelling containing hard matter > - EM
ši·ya·ta·ka·la \ši-yá-ta-ka-la\ *n* **1** : the American dipper **2** : the water ouzel, a small black bird that lives near water - Bl
ši·ya·ta·kan·la \ši-yá-ta-kaŋ-la\ *n* : a small bird that frequents rice lakes - R Bl
ši·yo *or* **šiyoka** \ši-yó\ *n* : the grouse, the prairie hen - Note: the male heralds forth the morning: Wíja bū ... and the female answers: Mabú, mabū ... Male prairie chickens inflate their neck sacs as sounding boards and sen their "oom-boom-boom" often two miles across the prairie. *Šiyo wacipi* The prairie chicken dances. < ~ *s'e pa canšihuta laka ca yankin na* Stay around when your head like a grouse finds it rather difficult to understand, as is said of a person with a little nose. >
ši·yo ci·k'a·la *or* **cánšiyo** \ši-yó cì-k'a-la\ *n* : the quail, the bob-white - FR
ši·yo i·što·hca·pi wi \ši-yó i-štò-ȟca-pi wi\ *np* : the month of March
ši·yo·ka \ši-yó-ka\ *n* : the prairie chicken - WHL
ši·yo·šun·ka \ši-yó-šuŋ-ka\ *n* : a bird dog
ši·yo·tan·ka \ši-yó-taŋ-ka\ *n* : the large grouse < ~ *yajo* The large grouse plays on its instrument. >
ši·yo·to \ši-yō'-to\ *n* : the muscle in the front side of the upper part of a man's leg; in times past, men always died when that muscle was hurt badly - Gv
ši·yo wa·ci·pi \ši-yó wa-cì-pi\ *n* : the drumming per-

\a\ father \e\ they \i\ machine \o\ smoke \u\ lunar \an, aŋ\ blanc Fr. \in, iŋ\ ink \on, oŋ, un, uŋ\ soon, confier Fr. \c\ chair \ġ\ machen Ger. \j\ fusion \clusters: bl, gn, kp, hšl, etc...\ b[e]lo ... said with a slight vowel
See more in the Introduction, Guide to Pronunciation

formed by the grouse during the spring mating season
ši·yu·ta·ka·hpe \ši-yū'-ṫa-ḱa-ȟṗe\ *n* [fr *šiyute* the lap + *akahpe* a covering] : an apron
ši·yu·te \ši-yū'-ṫe\ *n* : the lap, the front part of the legs < ~ *akahpe* an apron >
[1]**ška** \ška\ *conj* : but, and yet < *Nikuja ška tankal ilala* You are sick and yet you went outside. *Inše he tokašni ška hepelo* Well that does not matter and yet I said it. > – B.H.181.10
[2]**ška** *or* **ške** \šk̇a\ *vn impers* : they say, it is said, reported – Cf ške
ška·bye·la *or* **škab hinglá** \ška-byē'-la\ *adv* : with a noise such as is made by a rock *etc.* thrown into water
škal \škal\ *vn contrac of* škáta : to play < ~ *iya* He spoke playing. > — **ška·lki·ya** \ška-lḱí-ya\ *va* ška·lwa·kiya : to cause to play — **škalwa·yupika** \škálwa-yu-ṗi-ka\ *adj* : skillful at games
škan \škaŋ\ *vn* wa·škán : to do, act, move about < ~ *hinglá* to be quick of movement > – D.217
škan·hin·gle·ki·ya \škáŋ-hiŋ-gle-ḱi-ya\ *v* : to make one start up – Bl
škan·ka·pin \škaŋ-ḱá-ṗiŋ\ *adj* : lazy, unwilling to move about — **škankapin·pi** \škaŋ-ḱá-ṗiŋ-ṗi\ *n* : laziness
škan·ki·ya \škaŋ-ḱí-ya\ *va* škan·wá·kiya : to cause to move about
škan·škan \škaŋ-škáŋ\ *v red* wa·škanškan : to stir, move about, to change place < *mázaškanškan* a clock >
škan·škan o·ki·le \škaŋ-škáŋ o-ḱí-le\ *v* : to make things comfortable for one's self – Bl
škan·škan wa·ši·cun \škaŋ-škáŋ wa-ši-cuŋ\ *n* : a restless person – *Syn* WANAPTONKA cf woslotonšni – Bl
škan·škan·yan *or* **škanyan** \škaŋ-škáŋ-yaŋ\ \škaŋ-yáŋ\ *va red* škanškán·wa·ya : to cause to move about — *adv* : moving, in motion
ška·ta \šká-ṫa\ *vn* wa·škáta : to play
ške *or* **ška** *or* **ške'** *or* **ke** *or* **keyapi** \ške\ \šk̇e'\ \ké-ya-pi'\ *vn impers* : it is said, they say, it is reported < *Hecel wicakte* ~ So it was reported he killed them. > – Note: all these word entries are used in non-eye-witness narration D.1 note 1
ške·ca \ške-cá\ *n* : an otter or animal similar to an otter < ~ *ha* the pelt of an otter or little black animal used in ornamenting ladies' winter coats > – R Bl KE
ške·han *or* **ške·he** \šké-haŋ\ *adj* : wild, prancing as a horse, ambitious — **škehan·han** \ške-háŋ-haŋ\ *adj red* : frolicsome, jumpng around
ške·he·ca \ške-hé-ca\ *n* : an animal that is wild or unsteady — **ške·he·šni** \šké-he-šni\ *adj* : gentle
[1]**ške·he·ya** \ške-hé-ya\ *va* škehé·wa·ya : to make wild, make prance about
[2]**ške·he·ya** \šké-he-ya\ *adv* : ambitiously
ške·ka \škē'-ḱa\ *interj* : so he says – Cf tunwehca
ške·lo *or* **ške'** \šké-lo\ *vn impers* : it is reported that ...
ške·lu·ta \šk̇e-lú-ṫa\ *n* : the oriole, or perhaps an audubon — **škeluta tanka** *n* : the Baltimore oriole — **škeluta cik'ala** *n* : the orchard oriole < *Škeluta s'e ahiyaye* He went and passed by dressed more or less as it were in yellow with a little black and white. > – Bl
ške' \šk̇e'\ *vn impers* : it is said, they say – Note: the *e'* in the word signifies a vowel stop, rare compared to the number of consonant stops as *k'in, p'o, t'a, c'i, nah'on* – D. explained the subtle pronunciation of this vowel stop is begun with the vowel as usual and suddenly concluded without any delay.
ški·ca \ški-cá\ *va* : to press or wring – Cf yuškica
ški·ca·han \ški-cá-haŋ\ *part* : squeezing, pressed
škin·c'i·ya *or* **škinciya** \škíŋ-c'i-ya\ \škiŋ-cí-ya\ *v* škín·mi·c'iya : to move one's self < *Hehanl wícat'e k'un* ~ Then that instrument of death moved. > – R
ški·pi·pi *or* **škipipi·la** *or* **škibibila** \škí-ṗi-ṗi\ *n* : the chickadee – Note: the bird is said to have a seven-cleft tongue. It begins to split in October; the seventh split occurs in April when it heals up again. Then it asks of the buzzard, *hecá* : *Gli hwō* Did he get home? Upon a person answering: *Gli yelo* He's arrived home, the bird is satisfied and remains silent for a long time. When the buzzard is back, there will be no cold weather anymore, so it is said. – *Syn* WIYÁWALA, GUGÚYA ŠKÚLA BS D.88
ški·ška \ški-šká\ *adj* : rough, not smooth and level, as a road
ški·ške·ya \ški-šké-ya\ *va* škiške·wa·ya : to make rough — *adv* : roughly
ški·ški·ta \ški-škí-ṫa\ *adj* : rough, not smooth and level
ški·ški·ta hu \ški-škí-ṫa hu\ *n* : the cut-leaf nightshore – *See* canhlogan škiškita Bl #236
škob \škob\ *adj* : crooked, warped — **ško·bya** \ško-byá\ *va* ško·bwa·ya : to make crooked — *adv* : crookedly
ško·gin·gin·lak yan·ka \ško-ġíŋ-ġiŋ-lak yaŋ-kà\ *v archaic* : to sit idle – BD
ško·kpa \ško-ḱpá\ *adj* : hollowed out, concave, as a shell
ško·pa \škō'-ṗa\ *adj* : crooked, warped, concave < *pa* ~ a crooked nose >
ško·pe·la *or* **zizi škopela** \škó-ṗe-la\ *n* : a banana
ško·ško·pa \ško-škó-ṗa\ *adj red of* škópa : crooked, warped, concave; curled, as hair – RF
[1]**šku** \šku\ *vn* ma·škú : to be roasted wholly or partially, *i.e.* red from the heat, to be covered with red spots, as one who lies too close to the fire in cold weather < *Ikpi nišku* You roasted your belly. > – R HC
[2]**šku** \šku\ *v archaic phr* : you come, *i.e. yau* – Note: *ṗu* I come. A man would say on seeing and recognizing another: *Hepela niye yo, tokiyatan šku hwo* Revive him is all I said, where do you come from? Our visitor would then answer: *Heciyatanhan ṗu welo* I am coming toward that place. Cf škípipi
Šku·ta·ni \Škú-ta-ni\ *np* : the Kootenai Indians
šla \šla\ *adj* : bald, bare
šla e·gna \šla é-gna\ *adv* : openly, exposed , in full view, uncovered; without a house, defenseless < ~ *han* standing in full view, unsheltered, standing out > – Cf šlaégnag
šla·e·gnag \šla-é-gnag\ *adv* : in a barren place, where nothing grows, *šla* < *Can* ~ *han* A tree stands in a barren country, *i.e.* nothing else is growing. >
šla·šla \šla-šlá\ *adj red of* šla : bare in different places, as a pasture or doze (a place of fallen timber)
šla·ya \šla-yá\ *va* šla·wa·ya : to make bare — *adv* : nakedly, without covering < *maka* ~ *yunke kin* bare and grassless ground, but now we would say: *maḱóšla* fr *maka ground* + *ošla* a barren place, *Makošla yunké el* he lay in a place where the land was barren. >
šle·ca \šlé-ca\ *v* : to split, divide < *kašleca* to split as with an axe >
[1]**šli** \šli\ *adv* : hissing, fizzing, as two persons whispering to each other
[2]**šli** \šli\ *vn* : to ooze out, as gum < *Nawicašli* They broke out with swelling and sores. > — **šli·yela** \šli-yē'-la\ *or* \šlí-ye-la\ *adv* : making the noise of rain or

whizzing like a bullet through the air — **šliyela·han** *part* 1 : making noise of a rain < *Magaju kin ~* The rain was making noise. > 2 : whizzing, as a bullet in the air - Note: *konšyéla* is a *comp* with *kons* to pretend, and seems weak in denotation - R

[1]**šlo** \šlo\ *vn* : to melt, as butter, grease, metal, ice < *Mini ~ ayelo* Snow is begun to melt, *or* the snow is melting. > - Bl

[2]**šlo** \šlo\ *v* : to lisp - IS

šlo·ka \šló-ka\ *v* : to come out or off < *kašloka* to knock or fall out > — **šloka·han** \šlo-ka-haŋ\ *part* : out of place, as an axe head off the handle, or an eye out of its socket

šlo·šlo \šlo-šló\ *v red of* šlo : to melt — *adj* : soft, melted, as fat

šlo·šlo·ka·han \šlo-šló-ka-haŋ\ *part perhaps* : falling off < *Šake kin ~* Its hoofs were falling off. > - B.H.231.5

[1]**šlo·šlo·la** \šló-šlo-la\ *n* : the upland plover - Note: its rolling sound in its nocturnal flights (migrating) to and from the pampas of South America is a forelorn sound < *~ ca ikpakpi s'e* It is the upland plover, like a bird that hatches out its own, as they say when a man has greased his hair, like a bird fresh from the shell. *~ s'e hu cikcik'aya hu okihe tankinkinyan kaca* Like an upland plover, its legs are slim, its leg joints properly very big. as is said of a person who has thing legs but thick knees. > - Bl IS

[2]**šlo·šlo·la** \šlo-šlō'-la\ *n* : slush; the soft fat parts in an animal perhaps - R

šlo·ya \šlo-yá\ *va* šlo·wa·ya [fr *šlo* to melt] : to make melt, as butter or grease < *wašin šloyapi* fried bacon > — **šloya·gnaka** *va* : to place near the fire to soften or melt - *See* tasagyagnaka — **šloya·pi** *n* : that which is melted

šlu·šlu·ta \šlu-šlú-ṫa\ *adj* : slippery, as a road, smooth, as ice or a horn *etc.* < *He ~* A horn is smooth. *Fig* penniless, "broke", having spent everything, *Wanna mašlušluta* I am broke. *Nonge nišlušluta* Your ears are slippery, *i.e.* you do not listen. > - Bl BT

šlu·ta \šlú-ta\ *adj* : to be slippery - Cf našluta, yušluta

šma \šma\ *adj* : deep, as water or snow, dense, as foliage, thickly set, as hair — **šma·šma** *adj red* : much that is deep

šme \šme\ *adj of* šma : deep, dense, thick — **šme·ya** \šmé-ya\ *adv* : deeply, densely < *Wa ~ hinhpeya ca* It was a heavy snowfall. > — **šmeya·ta** \šme-yá-ta\ *adv* : in the deep

šmi \šmi\ *adj* : bare — **šmi·šmi** \šmi-šmí\ *adj red* : much that is bare — **šmišmi·ka** \šmi-šmí-ka\ *adj perhaps* : hairless, bald < *Nasu ~* His head is bald. > - Bl

[1]**šna** \šna\ *v* : to miss - Cf yušna

[2]**šna** \šna\ *adv* 1 : again and again, continually, in *ref* to something that so occurs < *~ apápi* They kept striking it. *Le on ~ wocekiye yakagapi kta* For this reason you should keep having prayers for him. *Can ~ yanka* Wood is always there, here, now. > 2 : sometime, sometimes < *anpetu ~* sometimes at day, *Le wahinkpe kin, tohanl amicih'anpi ca oyate kin witaya ~ lapi na yeyayapi kte lo* When my own were starving, the people together kept pleading that you should launch this arrow. *Koškalaka k'on he omani i na ~ tahca na pte na heȟaka hecel ~ wagli ca tawicu k'on wakabla* This young man had gone on a trip, and continually there were deer, buffalo, and elk, so since he brought in game again and again, his wife had sliced meat. *Waunyanpi el ~ ihpeyapi* When an offering was made, it kept being left there. *Hena wi wanji can okašpe wanji el ~ omniciye econpi* They continually held a meeting for a day a month in a district. *Na ~ unkcepi na ~ kawankal kiglahanpi* And they kept breaking wind, while they continued going on up toward home. > - Note: the word seems to be placed ante *pos* to indicate much continuity, post *pos* to indicate sometimes - R B.H.61.6, 178.19, 265.5, 257.4 MS.73, 143, 158, 344, 106

šna·šna·ye·la \šná-šna-ye-la\ *adv* : at times, a little < *Wa ~ hinhpayelo* At times there is a snowfall. > - LB

šni \šni\ *adv neg partic* : not - Note: the word follows *v, n, pron, adj, adv, etc.* - Cf D.9 note 2 Gramm.352, 289

šni·ja \šní-ja\ *adj* a : withered, dead, dried up, as leaves by the sun b : blurred, indistinct < *Ištómašnija* My eyes are blurred. >

šni pu·te ya \šní ṗu-ṫè ya\ *v* : to play a game in throwing a bow - Bl

šniš \šniš\ *adv neg emph* : no, not < *I šniš gliyelo* He is not going to his home. *I šni kayes gliyelo* Clearly he did not go to his home, as is said when one returns after nobody knew of his whereabouts. > - Note: *i šniš* may more properly be written *išníš* Bl

šni·šni \šní-šni\ *adv neg red* : no, not < *Maka ali ~ s'e mani* He walked as if he were definitely not stepping on the ground, *i.e.* he walked lightly, inaudibly. > - Bl

šni·šni·ja \šni-šní-ja\ *adj red of* šnija : withered, dried up

šni·šya \šni-šyá\ *va* šni·šwa·ya a : to make wither or dry up b : *fig* to disappoint one, to shrink < *Šnišmaya* He disappointed me, *i.e.* by not coming or giving praise. > — *adv* : withered - B.H.200.6 WW

šni·yan \šni-yaŋ\ *suff converting v and n to neg adv* < *Na iye el unšniyan taku wokage keša wokage šni* And in him whatever creature is not in being is no creature. *Wowica-kešniyan waayatan'in kta eya awicakitapi* Some were sought out so as to testify falsely. > - MS.279

šni·yan·yan \šni-yáŋ-yaŋ\ *adv* : very rapidly, in *ref* to the motion of *e.g.* the wings *etc.* < *~ kinyan, ~ inyanka* to fly with rapidity, to speed run > - *Syn* HUKPANKOS, HNIYANYAN — **šniyanyan·la** *n* : the rapid moving of wings < *kašniyanyanla* to ripple along, as water in a stream > - Bl

šni·ye·ca \šní-ye-ca\ *v* : to fade away, reduce to nothing < *Wa ~* Snow was reduced to nothing, as is said when snow melts on touching the ground. > - Bl

šun·šun·je·la \šun-šúŋ-je-la\ *adj* : pliant - *Syn* KCAN-KCANLA, WINŠWINJAHELA Bl

šog \šog\ *adj of* šóka : thick or dense — **šo·gšogya** \šo-gšó-gya\ *adv red of* šogyá : densely

šo·gya *or* **šogyeh** \šo-gyá\ *adv of* šóka a : strongly, firmly < *Ito le icinunpa wicoh'an econ eša lila ~ econ yawapi* Well, they considered very firmly him doing it though now he does the second ceremony. > b : seriously, badly, greatly, much < *~ awacin, sutaya awacin* He gave it much thought, gave it some tough thinking. *~ kaga* to make badly, *~ opi* He was seriously wounded > c : thickly, piled as clothes heaped on each other, *etc.*

šo·ho·ton·la \šo-hó-toŋ-la\ *n* : the black-billed cuckoo

šo·ka \šō'-ka\ *adj* : thick, as applied to solids such as cloth, board wood; dense, as woods < *Na can ~ etkiya ya* He goes towards a dense forest. >

šo·ke·la \šó-ke-la\ *n* : a quarter of a dollar, a quarter

\a\ father \e\ they \i\ machine \o\ smoke \u\ lunar \an, aŋ\ blanc Fr. \in, iŋ\ ink \on, oŋ, un, uŋ\ soon, confier Fr. \c\ chair \ġ\ machen Ger. \j\ fusion \clusters: bl, gn, kp, hšl, etc...\ b[e]lo ... said with a slight vowel
See more in the Introduction, Guide to Pronunciation

section of land - Cf šóka
šo·kšo·ka \šo-kšõ'-ka\ *adj red of* šóka : much, dense < *Can kasleslecapi ota pahayela eglepi na canha ~ ko na lila ota ileyapi* Much split wood was set in a pile, much bark too, and very much was burned. >
šo·k'in \šo-k'íŋ\ *v* : to resemble a small but odd, humorous or absurd person < *Tahca cincala s'e ite kin ~ laka ca yankin na* Take a seat, for his face rather resembles so it seems that of a fawn, as is said of a man with a little face. > — **šok'in-yan** *adv* : having an unusual human appearance < *Mayašlecala s'e ite ~* His strangely human face resembles that of a midget coyote, as is said of a man with a strikingly small face. > - Bl LHB
šol \šol\ *n contrac of* šóta : smoke — **šo·lanini** \šo-lá-ni-ni\ *n* : soot, smut — **šola·šapa** \šo-lá-ša-pa\ *vn* : to become dirty from smoke — **šo·lki·ya** \šo-kí-ya\ *v* : to make smoke < *Pute mayukan ca šolwakiyin kte* I shall make smoke when my lip is put to it, as a man may say when he is ready to smoke a pipe. > — **šo·lya** \šo-lyá\ *v* : to make smoky
šon·šon i·kpi·san *or* **šonšon ikpiska** \šóŋ-šoŋ i-kpì-saŋ\ *n* : a donkey — **šonšonkpisan** *n contrac* : a donkey
[1]**šon·šon·la** \šóŋ-šoŋ-la\ *adj* : long-eared, hanging down, as the ears of many dogs do
[2]**šon·šon·la** \šóŋ-šoŋ-la\ *n* : a mule
šo·ša *or* **šoše** \šo-šá\ *adj* : turbid, muddy, as water — **šoše·ya** \šo-šé-ya\ *va* šoše·wa·ya : to make turbid or muddy, to stir up — *adv* : turbidly
šo·ta \šó-ta\ *n* : smoke — *vn* : to smoke, as does fire
šo·ta sam i·ya·ye \šó-ta sam i-yà-ye\ *n phr* : a chimney, one built on the roof
šo·ti·ya·ski·lya \šó-ti-ya-ski-lya\ *adv* : envoloped by smoke < *~ nankahanpelo* You were sitting swamped with smoke, as is said when people sit in a smoky room. > - *Syn* ŠOTIYOWOTAN'INŠNIYAN
šo·ti·yo·wo·tan'·in·šni·yan\šó-ti-yo-wò-taŋ-iŋ-šni-yaŋ\ *adv* : invisible from smoke, surrounded by smoke < *~ mankelo* I am sitting in the smoke. > - *Syn* ŠÓTIYUSKILYA Bl
šo·tka·zi \šo-tká-zi\ *n* : soot — *adj* : smoked black, sooty
šo·to·ju \šo-tõ'-ju\ *adj* : smoky, full of smoke, hazy, as the atmosphere < *Tak wanyangpica šni ohinniyan ~* It was always full of smoke, impossible to see anything. > — **šotoju·ya** *v* šotoju·wa·ya : to make smoky, to fill with smoke
špa \špa\ *v* : to break off, divide - Cf yušpá
špa·han \špa-háŋ\ *part* : broken off — **špahan·han** *part red* : broken off, crumbling away < *Wayakayah'u špahanhanpi* There is leprous breaking off of skin. > - B.H.114.21, 184.21
špan \špaŋ\ *adj* : cooked, burnt or frozen, as parts of the body by heat or cold < *Talo ~* Meat is cooked. *Nonge mašpan* My ears are frozen. — *vn perhaps* : to be cooked, burnt or frozen < *Na tehan hecel ~ el icu na ake hunh el ognaka na ota španyan* And when it was thus cooked, he took it, again put some in, and cooked a big mess. *Canke wanji icu* (a hot dog's head) *tka nape ~* And so he took (one dog's head) but his hand got burnt. *maka španpi* a brick, *Yupiyela wana wapasnon k'un ~* Now it *e.g.* meat on a spit had been nicely, just about done roasting. > - D.22
špan·i·c'i·ya \špaŋ-í-c'i-ya\ *v refl of* španyán : to get burned or frozen - Note: *guic'iya* to get one's self burnt
špan·ka·ga·pi \špaŋ-ká-ga-pi\ *n* : green corn dried
špan·ki·ci·ci·ya \špan-kí-ci-ci-ya\ *va* špan·we·ciciya : to cook for one — **španki·ya** *va poss* špan·wa·kiya : to cook one's own food, to cook for another
špan·la s'e i·a \špáŋ-la s'e i-á\ *v* : to speak excitedly, angrily < *~ ielo* He spoke with excitement. > - Bl
špan·šni \špáŋ-šni\ *adj* : raw, not cooked < *~ yutapi* raw food, *i.e.* what is eaten raw, *e.g.* melons, cucumbers *etc.* >
špan·šni·yu·ta·pi i·ye·ce·ca \špaŋ-šní-yu-ta-pi i-yè-ce-ca\ *n* : the buffalo burr, sandburr, solanum rostratum, the nightshade family - Bl #222
špan·yan \špan-yáŋ\ *va* špan·wa·ya : to cook *e.g.* food
špe *or* **špa** \špe\ *va* : to break off, divide
špi \špi\ *v* : to pick, gather < *yušpi* to pick *e.g.* berries >
špu \špu\ *v* : to pull off < *yuspu* to pull off what is on tight >
špu·ke·šni \špú-ke-šni\ *adj* : a very lively character < *Hokšila-hakaktala wan ~ , yunkan he e* The boy, the little youngest one was of a lively disposition, and he is so, *i.e.* wide awake. > - *Syn* BLIHECA D.14 WE
špu·la \špú-la\ *adj perhaps dim* : nicknacks, trifles, little things torn from something < *taku ~* some trifle, *Taku ~ kin oyas'in tehila, kpagan šni* He treasures every little nicknack, parting from none, *i.e.* to be attached to all sorts of little things such as nicknacks. > — **špu·špula** \špu-špú-la\ *adj red* : many trifling things < *taku ~ keci* pretty much all sorts of little things > - Bl Bc
špu·wa·han \špu-wá-haŋ\ *part* : fallen off of itself, shed as anything that adhered, *e.g.* a telephone wire
štag \štag\ *adj contrac of* štáka : soft
šta·gya \šta-gyá\ *va* šta·gwa·ya : to mash up, to make preserves — *adv* : mushy, as said of soft ice
šta·ka \štá-ka\ *adj* : soft, as ice < *kaštaka* to beat, whip >
štan \štaŋ\ *v* : to finish, settle - Note: *kaštan* to pour out, *yuštan* to finish, settle, complete >
šta·šta \šta-štá\ *adj* : weak or brittle
šta·šta·ka \šta-štá-ka\ *adj red of* štaka : soft, as ice
šta·šta·la \šta-štá-la\ *adj* : brittle — **štašta·ye·la** *adj* : soft, tender, as skin may be
šte·i·c'i·la \šte-í-c'i-la\ *v refl* : to think much of one's self
šte·la \šte-lá\ *v* šte·wa·la : to rate high, admire — **štelapi** \šte-lá-pi\ *n* : admiration — **štela·ka** \šte-lá-ka\ *v* šte·wá·laka : to rate high
štu·lya \štu-lyá\ *va* štu·lwa·ya : to thaw out, as anything frozen
štun·ka \štuŋ-ká\ *adj* : unripe, as fruit, green, as we say — **štunka·la** \štuŋ-ká-la\ *adj* : soft, mellow, not ripe, as corn in the milk
štu·šta \štu-štá\ *adj* : soft, as the flesh of animals when hard chased and wanting flavor — **štušte la** \štu-šté la\ *adj* : tender, tired out in *ref* to man < *Maštušte la hcakelo* I am very much tired out. > — **štušte·ya** \štu-šté-ya\ *va* štušte·wa·ya : to chase and so weary and render the meat flavorless
štu·ta \štú-ta\ *adj* : thawed, warmed < *Nape maštuta. Pagla wan ca ~ iyutelo* My hands were warmed. It was a catbird he tried warmed. > — *vn* : to be thawed, warmed < *Wana unštutapelo* We are now thawed out. > - HH
šun \šuŋ\ *n* : the large feathers of birds' wings
šung \šuŋg\ *n contrac of* šúnka : a horse, the four-footed animal that becomes as familiar as does a dog
šun·ga·k'in \šuŋ-gá-k'iŋ\ *n* : a saddle blanket
šun·gblo·ka \šuŋ-gbló-ka\ *n* : the male of horse or dog
šun·ghu·la \šun-ghú-la\ *n* : a pony, a shetland pony, a small horse, a short-legged horse
šun·gi·la \šuŋ-gí-la\ *n* : the fox

šun·gle·ška \šuŋ-glé-ška\ *n* : a spotted horse
šun·gma·ki·ci·ma \šuŋ-gmá-ki-ci-ma\ *n* : a young horse
šun·gma·ni·tu \šuŋ-gmá-ni-tu\ *n* : a wolf
šun·gnan·kpo·gi \šun-gnáŋ-kpo-ġi\ *n* : a brown-eared horse
šun·gni·ni \šuŋ-gní-ni\ *n* : a wild horse - Bl
šun·gnu·ni s'e yan·ka \šuŋ-gnú-ni s'e yaŋ-kà\ *v* : to be silent and sad, as if one had lost one's horses - WE
šun·gwin·ye·la \šuŋ-gwíŋ-ye-la\ *n* : a mare horse
šun·g'i·ca·kce \šuŋ-g'í-ca-kce\ *n* : a horse curry
šun·g'i·ca·psin·te \šuŋ-g'í-ca-psiŋ-te\ *n* : a horse whip
šun·g'i·ca·ške \šuŋ-g'í-ca-ške\ *n* : a picket-pin, anything with which to fasten a horse
šun·g'i·kan \šuŋ-g'í-kaŋ\ *n* : a strap to tie a horse
šun·g'i·kte \šuŋ-g'í-kte\ *n* : poison, *lit* that by means of which a wolf is killed
šun·g'i·na·hta·ke *or* **šung'ina·jipa** \šuŋ-g'í-na-ȟta-ke\ *n* : a spur
šun·g'i·pa·hte \šuŋ-g'í-pa-ȟte\ *n* : a bridle
šun·g'o·han·pi \šuŋ-g'ó-haŋ-pi\ *n* : dog soup - LHB
šun·g'o·na·jin \šuŋ-g'ó-na-jin\ *n* : a stable, horse barn
šun·g'o·na·š'o \šuŋ-g'ó-na-š'o\ *n* : a pacing horse
šun·hpa·la \šuŋ-ȟpá-la\ *n* : a puppy, little dog
šun·ka \šúŋ-ka\ *n* : a dog
šun·ka·ce *or* **šunkcé** \šúŋ-ka-ce\ *n* : the root of the calamus plant, a bulbous esculent root that grows in the swamps and whose leaves are called *hohwá*
šun·ka ce-mi-la \šúŋ-ka cè-mi-la\ *n* : a knife with a crescent-like blade which is used in butchering, the cutting edge being along the outer side - Bl
šun·ka·ho \šuŋ-ka-hó\ *v* : to howl like a dog
šun·ka·hlo·wan·pi \šuŋ-ká-ȟlo-waŋ-pi\ *n* : a parade with singing made by those who are on the point of going to war - Bl
šun·ka·in *or* **šunka·k'in** *or* **šunga·k'in** \šuŋ-ká-iŋ\ *n* : a horse blanket < ~ *hlohloka* a fly cover >
šun·ka i·te·pšun·ka \šúŋ-ka i-tè-pšun-ka\ *n* : a bull dog
šun·ka·kan·yanka \šuŋ-ká-kaŋ-yaŋ-ka\ *n* : a rider, a person on horseback — *v* šunkakan·man·ka : to ride horseback < ~ *ošpaye wanji ehakela manipelo* A group going horseback traveled last. >
šun·ka·na·gi·hlo špan·wa·ge·hce \šúŋ-ka na-ġì-ȟlo špaŋ-wá-ġe-ȟce\ *express* : a dog's growling attitude makes one shiver
šun·kan \šuŋ-káŋ\ *n* [fr *šun* the large wing feathers + *kan* old and worn out] : *fig* an old man
šun·kan·yan \šun-káŋ-yaŋ\ *adv* **a** : shooting and missing game **b** : *fig* cheaply, after striking a bargain < *Talo wan ~ iyayelo* The fresh meat got away cheaply, *i.e.* one missed in shooting, as is said when one fails to catch a rabbit *etc.* for food. *Lecala taku wan oye iyaya, tka ~ oye iyayelo* A little while ago something's track went by, on the other hand the track went on paying no price, *i.e.* it seems to be a fresh track, > — **šunkanyan·kel** *adv* : poorly, cheaply, thin < ~ *igluza* to have poor clothing on that does not protect, ~ *mak'u* He gave me only a very little. *Tulá, šunkanya yaun welo, mato wayakita yelo* Shame on you, you are getting by cheaply, you are looking out for a bear, *i.e.* meeting one who did not notice one's coming and was afraid. *Le pahin s'e ~ mani tka tanktankaya omani yelo* Now like a porcupine, he walks when striking a bargain, but he travels in a big way. > - BT Bl LHB
šun·ka·šta·ka \šuŋ-ká-šta-ka\ *va* : to abuse a horse by striking - B.H.68.10
šun·ka·wa·kan \šúŋ-ka-wa-kan\ *n* : a horse
šun·ka·wa·kan ta·pe·ju·ta \šúŋ-ka-wa-kan ta-pe-jù-ta\ *n* : silvery groundsel, senecio canus, the composite family - Bl #94
šun·ka·wa·kan ta·wa·na·p'in \šúŋ-ka-wa-kaŋ ta-wa-nà-p'in\ *n* : a horse collar
šun·ka wi·ca·ša \šúŋ-ka wi-cà-ša\ *n* : a monkey
šun·kcan·ka·hu·i·pi·ye \šuŋ-kcáŋ-ka-huu-i-pi-ye\ *n* : the western false gromwell, onosmodium occidentale, the borage family - Note: the roots and seeds are used for horses as a tea and for rubbing in. It is also used for swellings on men BS #115
šun·kce *or* **šun·kace** \šuŋ-kcé\ \šuŋ-ká-ce\ *n* : the root of the calamus plant, the leaves being called *hohwá*
šun·kce·ca·hu·šte \šuŋ-kcé-ca-hu-šte\ *n* : a horse lame in the hip - Bl
šun·kcin·ca \šuŋ-kcíŋ-ca\ *n* : a young coyote
šun·kcin·ca·la \šuŋ-kcíŋ-ca-la\ *n* : a colt
šun·kcin·ca o·ti \šuŋ-kcíŋ-ca o-ti\ *n* : a wolf's den
šun·khin·ša *or simply* **hinšá** \šuŋ-khíŋ-ša\ *n* : a sorrel horse < ~ *wicahcala s'e ite san okpankpan* Like an old man's the sorrel horse's white face became wrinkled. ~ *gleška* a spotted sorrel horse > - Bl MS.561
šun·khu·la *or* **šunghula** \šuŋ-khú-la\ *n* : a horse or pony with short legs < ~ *s'e huwakiš'ake* Like a short-legged horse, he is agile on his feet, as is said of a man with short legs who is good at running. >
šun·khu·šti·pi·ye \šuŋ-khú-šti-pi-ye\ *n* : wooly white hymenopappus, hymenopappus tenuifolius, the composite family - Note: from the plant are made tea and salve to treat horses' hoofs - Bl #268
šun·ki·ca·kca \šuŋ-kí-ca-kca\ *n* : a horse curry
šun·ki·ca·po·wa \šuŋ-kí-ca-po-wa\ *n* : a horse brush
šun·ki·ca·psin·te \šuŋ-kí-ca-psiŋ-te\ *n* : a horse whip
šun·ki·ca·ške \šuŋ-kí-ca-ške\ *n* : a picket-pin, a stick, pin to tie a horse to
šun·ki·co·co \šuŋ-kí-co-co\ *v* : to call one's dogs - Bl
šun·ki·gmun·ke \šuŋ-kí-gmuŋ-ke\ *n* : poison, anything to use in trapping wolves
šun·ki·te·pe·sto \šuŋ-kí-te-pe-sto\ *n* : a greyhound
šun·kko·ya·kya \šuŋ-kkó-ya-kya\ *v* suŋkkóya·kwa·ya : to rope a horse
šun·kle·ja hu \šúŋ-klé-ja hu\ *n* : racemose milk vetch, astragalus racemosus, the pulse family - Bl #39
šun·klu·za·han \šuŋ-klú-za-haŋ\ *n* : a race horse
šun·kma·ni·šni·ki·ya \šuŋ-kmá-ni-šni-ki-ya\ *adv* : walking in the manner of a played-out horse - Bl
šun·kma·ni·tu \šuŋ·kmá-ni-tu\ *n* : a coyote
šun·kma·ni·tu·ho \šuŋ-kmá-ni-tu-ho\ *vn* šunkmanitu·wa·ho : to howl like a wolf
šun·kma·ni·tu·tan·ka \šuŋ-kmá-ni-tu tàŋ-ka\ *n* : a wolf
šun·knon·ge·kpa s'e \šuŋ-knóŋ-ġe-kpa s'e\ *adv* : in the manner of a stupid person, one purposely not listening < *Hunhé, wokiyakapi kin el ewacin šni ~* It's too bad, he failed like a stupid person to think over what was said to him. *Roboam ~ wokiyakapi k'un el ewacin šni* Roboam as a stupid fellow failed to give attention to things said to him. > - B.H.103.10
šun·knu·ni \šuŋ-knú-ni\ *n* : a wild horse
šun·knu·ni·ki·ci·ya·pi \šuŋ-knú-ni-ki-ci-ya-pi\ *n* : a boys' game in losing horses - LHB

\a\ father \e\ they \i\ machine \o\ smoke \u\ lunar \an, aŋ\ blanc Fr. \in, iŋ\ ink \on, oŋ, un, uŋ\ soon, confier Fr. \c\ chair \ġ\ machen Ger. \j\ fusion \clusters: bl, gn, kp, hšl, etc...\ b^e^lo ... said with a slight vowel
See more in the Introduction, Guide to Pronunciation

šun·kon·pa *or* **šun·onk'onpa** \šúŋ-koŋ-pa\ \šuŋ-óŋ-k'oŋ-pa\ *n* : a pony drag

šun·ko·wa·ša·ka·la \šuŋ-kó-wa-ša-ka-la\ *n* : the Canadian milk vetch, the Canadian rattleweed, astragalus canadensis, the pulse family – Note: the seeds are an eating delight to horses – BT #118

šun·ko·wo·te \šuŋ-kó-wo-te\ *n* : a nosebag

šun·ksi·ko·ška \šuŋ-ksí-ko-ška\ *n* : a horse with a swollen foot – Bl

šun·ksi·ma·za \šuŋ-ksí-ma-za\ *n* : a horse shoe

šun·kša·ki·yu·ksa \šun-kšá-ki-yu-ksa\ *n* : a hoof trimmer

šun·kšan \šuŋ-kšáŋ\ *n* : an old worn-out horse < *Šunkšánhca yeš peji k'in yelo* The good old plug however carried a load of hay, as an old horse may be used on occasion for hauling hay, so also a lazy man works once in a while, or works for once. > – Bl

šun·kta·can·gle·ška \šuŋ-ktá-caŋ-gle-ška\ *n* : the basket-like hoop laid over the two poles of the *šúnkonpa* pony drag in which loads and children are packed

šun·kta·han·pa \šuŋ-ktá-haŋ-pa\ *n* : real horse shoes, as once were used, made of leather to protect the hoofs

šun·kta·hu wa·š'a·ka \šuŋ-ktá-hu wa-š'à-ka\ *n* : a horse with a very strong neck, so that it cannot be guided easily – Bl

šun·kta·ma·ka \šuŋ-ktá-ma-ka\ *n* : a lean horse or dog – Cf támaka

šun·kta·pe·ju·ta \šuŋ-ktá-pe-ju-ta\ *n* : stemless locoweed, crazy-weed, colorado loco vetch, oxytropis lamberti, the pulse family – Note: horses eat this plant and even dig out the roots Cf FD.257 L #4

šun·kta·wa·na·p'in \šuŋ-ktá-wa-na-p'iŋ\ *n* : a horse collar

šun·kta·wo·te *or* **šunktapejuta** \šuŋ-tá-wo-te\ *n* : false indigo, bastard indigo, and river locust, one of these three kinds of *zitkatacan* wild tea, lead plant, or shoe strings; amorpha practicosa, the pulse family; also branched eriogonum, eriogonum multiceps, the buckwheat – BT WE Bl #4, 130, 288

šun·k'i·šta·kpa s'e \šun-k'í-šta-kpa s'e\ *adv* : walking or going about in the manner of a blind horse, fearlessly when it should fear, wandering as certain women do < ~ *omani* to travel about fearlessly not knowing where one is going > – Bl

šun·k'i·yo·pe·ya \šuŋ-kí-yo-pe-ya\ *va* šunk'iyope·wa·ya : to make a poor and cheap exchange for, to give a mean price for < *Wahanpi šunk'iyopewayelo* I paid a "pretty" price for soup, *i.e.* now that I have no teeth anymore and eat no meat but soup only. > – Bl

šun·k'lo·te \šuŋ-k'lō'-te\ *adj perhaps* šun·k'má·lote : slow because one is tired or not able to care for one's self < *Tuwa úncihišni he kapi* One is not able to take care of one's self is meant here. >

šun·k'na·sa·pi \šuŋ-k'ná-sa-pi\ *n* : a boys' pastime shooting arrows through a *waléġa* bladder in which worms get water – Bl

šun·k'nu·ni·ki·ci·ya·pi \šuŋ-k'nú-ni-ki-ci-ya-pi\ *n* : a boys' pastime in which they try to lose one another

šun·k'o·i·ya·ki·lsu·ta s'e \šuŋ-k'ó-i-ya-ki-lsù-ta s'e\ *adv* : in the manner of a horse that slackens again and again in spite of all urging and whipping < ~ *kagišnišni nagwaka* He criticized like a stubborn horse, without regard for others, as is said of a man who continues to criticize in spite of all explanations. > – Bl

šun·k'o·kah \šuŋ-k'ó-kaȟ\ *adv* : in or having the form of a horse < ~ *wanjica nunb wicayuha* He has two horses perfectly alike. > — **šunk'oka·hwog** *n* : a horse that wanders all over < ~ *un ca šicelo* It is bad that a horse be one wandering all over, *i.e.* as is said of a horse that changes its owners very often. > – Bl

šun·k'o·ka·sa·k'su·ta \šuŋ·k'ó-ka-sa-k'su-ta\ *n* : a horse that does not react to urging or whipping – Bl

šun·k'o·na·š'a·ke \šuŋ-k'ó-na-š'a-ke\ *n* : an old, worn out horse – Bl

šun·k'o·na·š'o·la *or* **šung'onaš'o** \šuŋ-k'ó-na-š'o-la\ *n* : a pacing horse

šun·k'on·jin·ca \šuŋ-k'óŋ-jiŋ-ca\ *n* : a horse that defecates < ~ *s'e yusniza s'a ye* Like a horse defecating, he keeps going breaking wind. > – Bl

šun·lu·ta \šúŋ-lu-ta\ *n* : the red-shafted flicker, the woodpecker – Note: the under-side of its wings and tail is red. They sing when good weather is coming – RF

šun·mní·ya·ta aya \šuŋ-mní-ya-ta à-ya\ *v* : to water the horses

sun'·on·k'on·pa *or* **šun'unk'onpa** \šuŋ-óŋ-k'oŋ-pa\ *n* [fr *šunka* pony or dog + *on* by means of + *k'inpi* bearing a load] : a pony or dog travois, drag, the original vehicle of the Dakotas displaced by the wagon, the former consisting of two poles, one pair of ends fastened together and placed on the back of the pony or dog with a strap around the breast, the other pair of ends dragging over the ground. The baggage rested on the *šunktacangleška* baggage basket which is tied across the poles behind the tail of the horse or dog – *Syn* HUPAWAHEYUNPI

šun·pa \šuŋ-pá\ *vn* : to shed, moult, as birds do their feathers, to be in moulting

šun·pa·hli·hli \šuŋ-pá-hli-ȟli\ *v* : to have the feathers partly groan, as geese

šun·pe·la \šuŋ-pé-la\ *adj perhaps* : moulting, shedding – Bs

šun·šun i·kpi·san *or* **šunšunkpisan** *or* **šunšun ikpi·ska** \šúŋ-šuŋ i-kpi-saŋ\ \šúŋ-šuŋ-kpi-saŋ\ \šúŋ-šuŋ i-kpi-ska\ *n* : a donkey

šun·šun·la \šúŋ-šuŋ-la\ *n* : a mule < ~ *ikpi san ištahe pajojo kaca* His eyebrows are aptly the common trait of the white belly mule, as is said of one with heavy eyebrows. > – Bl

šun·to·to \šuŋ-tó-to\ *vn* : to have the feathers partly grown

šun'·un·k'on·pa *or* **šunkunk'onpa** \šuŋ-úŋ-k'oŋ-pa\ *n* : a pony or dog travois – BS

šun·zi·ca \šuŋ-zí-ca\ *n* : the northern flicker, a woodpecker, and it is colored brown. – Note: what it says is: "*Anpētu waštē, anpētu waštē* Good day, good day." < *Hunhé, ~ s'e šaké hanskaskalah* How sad, like the woodpecker, Oh so long are his fingernails, as is said when a person has very long fingernails. > – Bl

šu·pe \šu-pé\ *n* : intestines, the guts

šu·pe·o·ši·ca \šu-pé-o-ši-ca\ *adj* : hard to digest, disagreeing with one — *n* : anything hard to digest

šu·ptan·ka \šu-ptáŋ-ka\ *n* [fr *šupe* intestines + *tanka* large] : the large intestines

šu·pu·te \šu-pú-te\ *n* 1 : the pit of the stomach, *i.e.* below the navel 2 : a gun stock

šu·ška \šu-šká\ *adj* ma·šuška : slow, tardy; worthless, good for nothing — **šuška·ka** *n* : a worthless fellow

šu·šuš hin·gla \šú-šuš hiŋ-gla\ *v* : to come crashing down with a loud noise – Bl LHB

šu·ta \šu-tá\ *v* šu·wa·te : to miss as in shooting, fail of, to be unable to obtain < *Ehanl wanji kiyela šumata* At the time he was unable to get me one nearby. >

T

šu·ta·ka·hpe \šú-ta-k̇a-ḣpe\ *n* [fr *šiyute* the lap + *akahpe* a covering] : an apron

šu·te·ya \šu-ṫé-ya\ *va* šute·wa·ya : to cause to fail or miss

šwe·ka \šwẽ'-k̇a\ *adj* : having used up everything, "broke" < *Wanna mašweka* I am no broke. > - Bl

šwo·šwo·ke s'e \šwõ-šwõ'-ke s'e\ *adv* : extraordinarily fleshy, as a man or his nose, lips *etc.* - *Syn* WAŠOŠO S'E, KAYOYO S'E

šwu \šwu\ *vn* : to drop, as water or any other liquid — **šwu·šwu** \šwu-šwú\ *vn red* : to drip repeatedly - *See* kašwú R Bl

š'a \š'a\ *vn* wa·š'a : to shout

š'a·gi·c'i·ya \š'a-gí-c'i-ya\ *v refl* : to sustain one's self, have command over one's self, to be resolute

š'a·gš'a·ka \š'a-gš'á-k̇a\ *adj red of* š'aka : strong - Bl

š'a·gya \š'a-gyá\ *v* : to sustain one, have command over, to steady, give support to one — **š'agya·kel** *adv* : steadily < *Tate wan ~ u* A wind came, blowing steadily. > - B.H.278.3

š'a·ka \š'á-k̇a\ *adj* ma·š'áka : strong < *nap'kuwa ~* to grasp firmly, *miwankab ~* to be stronger than I > - Note: waš'aka, yuš'aka - Bl B.H.174.7

š'a·ke·ca \š'á-k̇e-ca\ *adj* **a** : mighty, powerful **b** : hard to deal with, severe, austere < *Maš'akece* Mighty am I, *Unš'akapi* We are powerful. > - *See* waš'áka

š'a·s'e \š'ā'-s'e\ *n* : noise caused by a large gathering of men *etc.* < *S'as'ehe yankapi* They were sitting making noise. > - Note: in the word *s'as'ehan*, *s'a* seems to act as a *part*

š'e \š'e\ *vn* : to drop, as water — **š'e·š'e** \š'é-š'e\ *v red* : to trickle, as water < *miniš'eš'e* to sprinkle, fall in drops as rain > — **š'e·ya** \š'e-yá\ *va* š'e·wa·ya : to make fall or drop as in drops — **š'eya·pi** *n* : drops

[1]ta \ta\ *pref* to *n* signify members of the body, limiting them to the corresponding parts in ruminating animals; thus: *ceji* the tongue *tacéji* a buffalo tongue. Hence *ta* may properly be considered as the generic term for all ruminating animals, since it enters into *comp* of the names of most of them, *tatánka* the bull buffalo, *tahcá* the deer

[2]ta \ta\ *adj* : one of a pair < *tawanjila* a pair, *tanunpa* two pairs >

[3]ta \ta\ *pron in comp* : his, hers, or its; theirs *i.e.* with *pi* at the end of the *n*

[4]ta \ta\ *prep suff in comp* affixed to *n* gives them the force of *adv* : at, to, on < *makata* on earth, *ata(ya)* entirely, *tiyata* at home > - Cf ata, yata

ta·a·jun·tka \ta-á-juŋ-tka\ *n* : a buffalo's kidneys — **ta-ajuntk'ognake** *n* : cow kidney fat - Bl WHL

ta·a·ki·h'an \ta-á-k̇i-ḣ'aŋ\ *vn* [fr *tan* very + *akih'an* to be hungry] : to be very hungry, man or animal < ~ *wahiyelo* I came being very hungry. > - Bl WHL

tab \tab\ *n contrac of* tápa : a ball to play with

ta·bi·ca·ka·pe \ta-bí-ca-ka-ṗe\ *n* : a ball club, a bat

ta·bi·ca·psi·ce \ta-bí-ca-psi-ce\ *n* : a ball club, shinny stick

ta·bi·ye·ya \ta-bí-ye-ya\ *v* : to throw a ball

ta·bi·yu·ka·pe \ta-bí-yu-ka-pe\ *n* : a catching glove

ta·bka·kab \ta-bk̇á-kab\ *v of* tabkakapa : to play ball by striking and knocking < ~ *iyeya* to bat a ball > — **ta-bkakabkab** \ta-bk̇á-ka-bkab\ *v red* : to be batting a ball

ta·bka·psi·ca \ta-bká-psi-ca\ *v* ta·bwa·kapsica : to play ball by taking up the ball in the club and throwing it, as in shinny — **tabkapsica·pi** *n* : the game of shinney - Cf kapsíca

ta·blas *or* **tanblas** \ta-blás\ *adv contrac of* tanblaza : on the side - Note: *tanblaza* seems not to be used

ta·ble·ca·ki·ya *or* **tanblecakiya** \ta-blé-ca-k̇i-ya\ *v* : on the side - Cf tanblécakiya

ta·blo \tá-blo\ *n* : the shoulder of cattle and horses — **tablo·hu** \ṫá-blo-hu\ *n* : the shoulder blade of animals <*Na wanna tablo wan ake inyan on kašleca yuman* And he now sharpened splitting again with a stone a cow's shoulder blade >

ta·blo·ka \ṫa-bló-k̇a\ *n* : a buck, the male of the common deer

ta·blo·kan \tá-blo-kaŋ\ *n* : the sinew of the shoulder blade

ta·bu·bu \ta-bú-bu\ *n* : a monster, such as a bigfoot, something very large but unknown and talked of by the old people < ~ *kaga* to create a monster, as in having a boy stand with back bent and other children pile robes on him, and so he would become something big > — **ta-bubu s'e** *adv* : tabúbu-like, in *ref* to something round and big that no one ever saw - Bl Bt

Tab Wan·ka·ye·ya·pi *or* **Tapa Wankayeyap** \Tab Waŋ-k̇á-ye-ya-pi\ *np* : the Throwing of the Ball, a Dakota religious ceremony in which the giftgiving is in favor of orphans - BR.127

ta·ca·gu \ta-cá-ġu\ *n* : lungs, of man or animal

ta·ca·ka \ta-cá-k̇a\ *n* : the roof of a buffalos mouth - Bl

ta·can \ta-cáŋ\ *n* : the body

ta·can·ḣa·ḣa·ka wa·pa·ha \ta-cáŋ-ḣa-ḣa-ka wa-pá-ha\ *n* : a headdress, made from the upper end of the buffalo's spinal column

ta·can·ḣa·ḣa·ke \ta-cáŋ-ḣa-ḣa-ke\ *n* : the first bones of the forward end of the buffalo's spinal column - Bl

ta·can·hpi \ṫa-cáŋ-ḣṗi\ *n* : his war club

ta·can·ka·hu \ta-cáŋ-ka-hu\ *n* : the middle part of the spinal column - Bl

ta·can·ka·slu·ta \ṫa-cáŋ-k̇a-slu-ṫa\ *n* : the white nerve running over the back of animals and going to the brain

ta·can·ko·han·han·ke \ṫa-cáŋ-k̇o-haŋ-haŋ-k̇e\ *n* : the parts along the spinal column of a buffalo; *fig* parts of a thing well ordered, straight < *Oie* ~ The parts of his speech were well ordered, *i.e.* his speech was straight talk, as is said of a man who talks nicely and does not use harsh words. >

ta·can·ko·ye \ta-cáŋ-ko-ye\ *n perhaps* : extra thick layers of fat covering a buffalo - St

ta·can·kpe o·gna·ke *or* **tacankpognake** \ta-cáŋ-kṗe ò-gna-k̇e\ *n* : the meat above the knees of cattle

ta·can·ksa \ṫa-cáŋ-ksa\ *n* : his club

ta·can·pa·hmi·yan \ṫa-cáŋ-ṗa-ḣmi-yaŋ\ *adv* : with the body bent to right or left, crooked

ta·can·ta \ṫa-cáŋ-ṫa\ *n* **1** : the heart of the buffalo, the ox *etc.* **2** : the hearts in playing cards **3** : **tacanta inkpa** \ṫa-cáŋ-ṫa íŋ-kpa\ *n* : the top of the buffalo's heart — **tacanta·mnumnu·ga** \ṫa-cáŋ-ṫa-mnu-mnu-ġa\ *n* : fleshings hanging on a buffalo's heart — **tacanta ogin** *or* **tacantogin** \ṫa-cáŋ-ṫa o-ġíŋ\ *n* : the membranous bag that surrounds and protects the buffalo's heart, the pericardium - Note: it was used as a glove in mixing greasy foodstuffs — **tacanta·su** \ṫa-cáŋ-ṫa su\ *n* : buffalo heart dribblings, perhaps — **tacanto·pazan** \ṫa-cáŋ-ṫo-ṗa-zaŋ\ *n* : a piece of fat attached to the buffalo's heart - Bl BD MS.483

ta·ce·ji \ṫa-cé-ji\ *n* : the tongue of ruminating animals — **taceji inkpa** \ṫa-cé-ji ìŋ-kpa\ *n* : the point of a buffalo tongue — **taceji okaslute** \ṫa-cé-ji o-k̇à-slu-te\ *n* : the cutting out of a cow's tongue - Bl LHB

ta·ce·ji o·zi \ṫa-cé-ji ò-zi\ *vn* : his tongue to be at rest, *fig.* to be less talkative, reticent, perhaps - Bl

ta·ce·ji su \ṫa-cé-ji su\ *n* : dribblings of the cow's tongue, mouth perhaps - Bl LHB

ta·ce·sli \ta-cé-sli\ *n* : the dung of ruminating animals, *esp* that of the buffalo

ta·ce·ši·kši·ce *or* **tacejikšica** *or* **tacejigjica** \ṫa-cé-ši-kši-ca\ *n* : the thin layer of fat covering the paunch, the lumps of white fat that surround the paunch < ~ *wanji na wašin wanji kici unyak'upi kte lo* You might give us a piece of paunch fat and one of fresh pork. *mahpiya* ~ cloud lumps, as they say of the heavens covered with balls and patches of white clouds > WE

ta·ce·ška ha \ta-cé-ška ha\ *n* : part of the buffalo hide near the collar bone — **taceška ha šunk'ak'in** \ta-cé-ška ha šuŋ-k'à-k'iŋ\ *n* : the hide part of the buffalo *ceška* breast near the collar bone used as a saddle blanket; *taceška ha* is used *fig* meaning: one who sticks to his job, does not give up, thus: *tacéška·ma·ha* I do not give up < *Tacéškamaha keyapelo* Look here! They stated that I did not quit, as is said of one who is very brave in battle. > - Es Bl

ta·ce·ton·te \ta-cé-ṫoŋ-ṫe ò-štaŋ\ *n* : the place where the legs join the body, the crotch - Bl

ta·cin·ca·la \ta-cíŋ-ca-la\ *n* : a fawn, the young of deer

ta·cu·pa·la s'e \ta-cú-ṗa-la s'e\ *adv* : as one easily losing self-control, in ways flighty or impetuous, having no understanding of self < ~ *un* to be a health scrupler, to lose one's self-control easily > - Cf tacúpe Bl

ta·cu·pe \ta-cú-ṗe\ *n* : marrow < *Ehanni tacupala s'elemaceca, fig* I used to be like one highly sensitive, hence weak. > - Bl

ta·ga *or* **tage** \tá-ġa\ \ta-ġé\ *n* : an issuance, a coming out: froth or foam, scum, spittle < *minitaga* froth or foam, in water >

ta·gi·ca \ta-ġí-ca\ *n* : a lean buffalo - Bl

ta·glo·glo·ska \ta-gló-glo-sk̇a\ *n* : the windpipe in animals

ta·gu·ha \ta-ġú-ha\ *n* : a scabby, singed or old bull - GA

ta·ha \ta-há\ *n* : a deerskin

ta·ha·i·yo·ka·tan \ta-há-i-yò-ka-taŋ\ *v* tahaiyo·wa·katan [fr *iyokatan* to pin or nail down] : to stretch out *e.g.* a hide with pins

ta·ha·ka·la·la \ta-há-k̇a-la-la\ *n* [fr *kalala* to sow, scatter] : a woman's buckskin dress, usually fringed *etc.*

ta·ha·kpan·yan \ta-há-kpaŋ-yaŋ\ *v* tahakpan·wa·ya : to tan a hide, *i.e.* by rubbing it on a pole until it is soft and pliable

ta·ha·lo \ta-há-lo\ *n* : a hide < ~ *saka kakšapi* a stiff rolled-up hide >

ta·ha·o·pa·hlo·ke \ta-há-o-ṗa-ḣlo-k̇e\ *n* : the slits cut in a hide by which it is stretched

ta·ha·pe \ta-há-ṗe\ *n* : a tanned hide

ta·ha·pe na·pin·kpa \ta-há-ṗe na-pìŋ-kpa\ *n* : mittens made of buffalo fur with the hair outside - Bl

ta·ha·pe wa·po·štan \ta-há-ṗe wa-pò-štaŋ\ *n* : a cap made of buffalo fur with the hair outside - Bl

ta·ha·sa·ka \ṫa-há-sa-k̇a\ *n* **a** : dried skin, parchment **b** : a skin with the hair taken off but not yet dressed

ta·ha·so·pi \ṫa-há-so-pi\ *n* : leather strings

ta·ha·ya \ṫa-há-ya\ *n* : leathern clothing - B.H.195.2

ta·ha·yu·šta·šta \ṫa-há-yu-šta-šta\ *v* taha·blu·štašta : to soak a hide *e.g.* for one night after it has been treated with gall, brain and marrow

tahe·ca·šun·wi \ta-hé-ca-šuŋ-wi\ *n* : the month of December, *i.e.* the moon in which deer shed their horns - R Bl

ta·he·gle \ta-hé-gle\ *n* : a stick one end fastened to a buffalo or deer horn and used in the game or pastime, *paslohanpi*, sliding on ice - Note: when the horn is fixed perpendicularly, the instrument is used as a weapon *Syn* TAHEZEZE

ta·he·ja·ta \tá-he-ja-ṫa\ *n* : a two-year old male deer, or elk perhaps, *i.e.* one with two prongs, one fork on either horn - Bl

ta·he·na \ṫa-hé-na\ *adv* : on this side, in *ref* to time and place < *anpetu* ~ before the evening, *Anpetu* ~ *wanblakin kta hwo* Will I see him before evening? > — **tahena·kiya** \ṫa-hé-na-ki-ya\ *adv* : this way, towards one < *Le wašicun kin* ~ *waktepi kta ca le ohomni unyanpi* At the moment we are going around, before this white man should be killed. *Na ungna* ~ *hiyu* And perhaps he is coming out this way. *Tehanl ye šni ecel wicaša wan lila hanska ca* ~ *u* As it was, he did not go far before there came a very tall man. > — **tahena·tanhan** \ṫa-hé-na-ṫaŋ-haŋ\ *adv* : from this side - D.102

ta·he·pi \ta-hé-ṗi\ *adv* : by the way, on the road, between one place and another < *Iglag* ~ *wanaunsapi ktelo* We shall go on a buffalo hunt traveling about on the road. > — **tahepi·ya** *adv* : on the side of, on the side of a wall < *Wicaša šunkawakan* ~ *otka* A man hung on the side of his horse. *Na paha kin* ~ *hpayapi* And they fell on the side of the hill. > - B.H.7.10 Bl

ta·he·ze·ze \ta-hé-ze-ze\ *n* [fr *tahe* an animal horn + *zeze* hanging down] : a stick with a horn fastened to it perpendicularly at one end and used originally to kill smaller animals; in some cases the horn was fixed to swing at the end of the stick

ta·hin \ta-híŋ\ *n* : buffalo or deer hair — **tahin·cacice** *n* : an instrument made from tin to scrape hair off skins — **tahin·paguke** \ta-híŋ-ṗa-ġu-k̇e\ *n* [fr *paguka* to rub down] : the knee bone used as a pemmican stone and as a tool to scrape hair from hides, and thus the name - Note: another name for the hair scraper is *ptehcaka hinyete* a shoulder of very much a buffalo

ta·hin pa·kin·ce *or* **tahca tahin pakince** \ta-híŋ ṗa-k̇iŋ-ce\ *n* : a scraper for work on hides

ta·hin·špa \ta-híŋ-šṗa\ *n* : an awl, a needle made from the upper part of an elk horn — **tahinšpa cik'ala** *n* : a needle — **tahinšpa cik'ala ipasisapi** *n* : a pin cushion — **tahinšpa ipasise** *n* : a pin

Ta·hin Wi·ca·ša \Ta-híŋ Wi-cà-ša\ *np* : the Cheyenne Indians, living in south central, as contrasted with those in north central United States who are known as the *Šahiyela* Coming Red; in the south, *Tahin Wicaša* Buffalo Hair Men < *Mašte maka el unpi, itokaga* In the South, they live in a land of humid heat. >

ta·hin·ye·te \ta-híŋ-ye-ṫe\ *n* : the shoulder of animals < ~ *oštan* the place where the arms join the shoulder > - Bl

ta·ho·gmi \ta-hó-gmi\ *n* : the hoop on which a scalp or hide is stretched < ~ *kahyá* the figure: four curves forming a four-sided object with the concave sides outward, painted on that part of a robe which covers the back; ~ *kagapi hanpa* a moccasin with a hoop-like design on the upper side > - Bl

ta·ho·ka·ške \ta-hó-ka-šk̇e\ *n* : the cross bars inside a tent on which a skin is fastened to dry — **tahoka·tan** \ta-hó-k̇a-ṫaŋ\ *v* taho·wa·katan : to stretch out a hide on pickets for tanning - Bl

ta·hu \ṫa-hú\ *n* : the back of the neck — **tahu·akahpe** \ta-hú-a-k̇a-ḣṗe\ *n* : a cape for the neck — **tahu·cehkiya** \ta-hú-ce-ḣkí-ya\ *v* : to shrug the shoulders, draw up the shoulders - *Syn* TAHUŠLIKIYE

ta·hu·hu·te \ta-hú-hu-ṫe\ *n* : the nape of the neck, the prominent articulation of the neck behind— **tahu·icosya** *n* : a scarf or comforter

ta·hu·i·yu·ti·tan \ṫa-hú-i-yu-ti-taŋ\ *n* : the check strap

ta·hu·ji·pa ki·cun \ta-hú-ji-ṗa ki-cuŋ\ *v* : to somersault on the neck

ta·hu·ka \ta-hú-k̇a\ *n* : the hide of a buffalo, a green hide < ~ *cangleška* a hoop with leather straps drawn over it, thus making it like a sieve for use in the game *tahuka cangleška;* ~ *wacipi* jumping rope, as children do, ~ *wata kagakpi* a hoop with a hide stretched over it and serving as a boat for things to be placed on while swimming across a river, a bull-hide boat > - D.198 Bl

ta·hun·sa·pa wi·kan \ta-húŋ-sa-pa wì-k̇aŋ\ *n* : a rope made of hair from the horse's mane

ta·hun·ska \ta-húŋ-ska\ *n* **1** : leggings made of deer skin **b** : a shirt collar

ta·hu·sli·ye·ya \ta-hú-sli-ye-ya\ *v* : to gallop loudly, to speed < *Tahusliyeyapi s'e unkupelo* We came home as though in a clatter of hoofs, *i.e.* we sped in coming like galloping horses. > - EB

ta·hu·šli·ki·ya \ṫa-hú-šli-kì-ya\ *v perhaps* : to draw up or shrug the shoulders - *Syn* TAHUCEHKIYA

ta·hu·wa·na·p'in \ṫa-hú-wa-na-p'iŋ\ *n* : a horse collar

tah \taḣ\ *n* : saliva, foam, lather - WHL

ta·hca \ṫá-ḣca\ *n* : the common deer, cervus capreolus < ~ *taló* mutton > - Note: in Dakota the word is *taḣínca* and when *contrac* becomes *táhca* in Lakota - R

ta·hca i·to·pta sa·pa \ṫá-ḣca i-ṫò-pta sa-pa\ *n* : a deer with a black streak across the face - Note: such specimens were once considered *wakán* mystery-bearing - Bl

ta·hca na·kpa·la \ṫa-ḣca na-kpà-la\ *n* : the mouse ear deer - Cf hitúnkala nakpála Bh #158

ta·hca šin šlo u kte \ṫá-ḣca šiŋ šlo u kte\ *express* : a fat deer will come and melt, as is said when the weather is to be very warm

ta·hca šun·ka·la \ṫá-ḣca šùŋ-ka-la\ *n* : a sheep

ta·hgla·ho·ta \ta-ḣglá-ho-ta\ *v* ta·hwa·glahota : to swallow the wrong way — **tahgla·škape** \ta-ḣglá-šk-ṗe\ *v* ta·hwa·glaškape : to have one's saliva go the wrong way and so feel choked

ta·hin·ca \ṫá-ḣiŋ-ca\ *n* : the common deer - *See* táhca

ta·hna \ṫa-ḣná\ *n* : running saliva < *Lowacin ca on* ~ *wakípcahe lo* Since I was hungry I was swallowing my saliva. > - Bl WHL

ta·hpa \ta-ḣṗá\ *n* : the lower part of the neck and breast of animals, the part between the shoulders of a man, the muscle across the abdomen

ta·hpi·yo·gin \ta-ḣpí-yo-ġiŋ\ *n* : a muscle below the *tatahpa* buffalo's breast, which is thrown away - Bl

ta·hton \ta-ḣtóŋ\ *v of* tagé : to have scum

ta·hu·ha \ta-ḣú-ha\ *n* : the scrapings of hides or skins, which are used when food is scarce

ta·hu·wa·pa·hpa \ta-ḣú-wa-ṗa-ḣṗa\ *n* : the thin layer of flesh that sticks to a hide, near the ribs on both sides

ta·ja \ṫā'-ja\ *n* : waves — *adj* : rough, as agitated water

ta·ji \ta-jí\ *n* : a red, *šašá*, buffalo calf, whereas it is usually black when young < *Yunkan pte san wan* ~ *wan kici ištinmapi el gli* And then a white buffalo along with a red one arrived home when they were asleep. >

ta·jon·tka \tá-jóŋ-tk̇a\ *n* : the kidneys in animals

ta·ju·ška *or* **tašuška** \ta-jú-ška\ *n* : the ant, ants

ta·ka \tá-k̇a\ *va* wa·taka : to roast off the hull, as of rice, to roast *e.g.* coffee

ta·ka·hlo·ka \ta-k̇á-ḣlo-ka\ *v* ta·wa·kahloka : to cut the meat of deer along the spinal column so as to get long slices, to cut up and spread nicely - *Syn* OKAZAPA, but *onakazapa* seems *obsol* Bl

ta·kan \ta-k̇áŋ\ *n* : sinew taken from the back of deer, buffalo, or cow, which is used for thread < ~ *okáza* a string or thread of *takán* > - Cf *kazá* to pick apart

ta·kan·gi \ta-k̇áŋ-ġi\ *n* : the tails of the *wakinyan* thunder-bird < ~ *toki hilu we? yau we?* Thunder-bird Tail, whence did you ever emerge? did you really come? as they say to a fellow who would not go with the bunch but would want his own ways and left, but finally came back to them, ~ *taku yaka hwo* Thunder-bird Tail, what do you intend? > - Bl WHL

ta·kan·he·ca·hu *or* **takanhecalahu** \ta-k̇áŋ-he-ca-hu\ *n* : the raspberry bush, the American wood strawberry bush, fragaria Americana, the rose family, so called because of its *kan* string-like runners. - Cf *wahpe skuya* veined dock

ta·kan·he·ca·la *or* **takan·yecala** \ta-k̇áŋ-he-ca-la\ *n* : the black raspberry, also known as the American wood strawberry

ta·kan·he·ca·la hu \ta-k̇áŋ-he-ca-la hu\ *n* : the black raspberry, black cap, scotch cap thimble berry bush, rubus occidentalis, the rose family - Ba #129, 261

ta·kan'·i·ta·zi·pe \ta-k̇áŋ-i-ta-zi-pe\ *n* : a bow, the back

---

\a\ father \e\ they \i\ machine \o\ smoke \u\ lunar \an, aŋ\ blanc Fr. \in, iŋ\ ink \on, oŋ, un, uŋ\ soon, confier Fr. \c\ chair \ġ\ machen Ger. \j\ fusion \clusters: bl, gn, kp, hšl, etc...\ b°lo ... said with a slight vowel **See more in the Introduction, Guide to Pronunciation**

of which is overlaid with sinews

ta·kan·ye·ca·la \ta-káŋ-ye-ca-la\ *n* : raspberries – Cf takánhecala

ta·ki·kpe \ta-k̇í-kpe\ *v poss perhaps of* takípa : to pursue one to recover one's own that was stolen < ~ *unglapi ktelo* We shall go recover ours that was stolen. > – Bl

ta·kin \ta-k̇íŋ\ *vn* : to lean sideways < ~ *iyaya* to go leaning sideways, *pakin iyaya* to walk stooped over >

ta·kin·ta·zi·pa \ta-k̇íŋ-ta-zi-pa\ *n* [fr *takan* sinew + *itazipa* a bow] : a bow to whose one side are glued sinews

ta·kin·wa·psa·ke \ta-k̇íŋ-wa-psa-ke\ *n* : a knife to cut off the *takán sinew* when one is finished with sewing

ta·kin·yan \ta-k̇íŋ-yaŋ\ *adv* : leaning, not perpendicular

ta·ki·pa \ta-k̇í-pa\ *v* ta·wa·kipa [fr *tapa* follow] : to follow one and take one's own from him, *i.e.* what he has stolen – Bl

ta·ki·yu·ha \ta-k̇í-yu-ḣa\ *n* : any bull of cattle, deer, *etc.* — **takiyuḣa wi** \ta-k̇í-yu-ḣa wi\ *n* : November, the month when deer copulate

ta·ko·ja \ta-kó-ja\ *n* mi·tákoja *or* mi·takoš : a grandchild — **takoja·kpa** *or* **takojakpa·ku** \ta-k̇ó-ja-kpa\ \ta-k̇ó-ja-kpa-k̇u\ *n* : his or her grandchild < *Winuhcala wan ~ wan kici ti* An old woman and her grandchild live together. > — **takoja·ya** *va* : to have for a grandchild

ta·ko·la·ki·ci·ya·pi \ṫa-k̇o-la-k̇i-ci-ya-pi\ *n* : particular friends — **takola·ku** \ta-k̇ó-laku\ *n* : his special friend — **takola·ya** *va* takola·wa·ya : to have one for a particular friend

ta·ko·mni \ṫa-k̇ó-mni\ *adv* **1** : nevertheless, still **2** : always, ever, at any time < ~ *niyašicin kte sece lo* Still he will certainly curse you to your face. > – B.H.42.19

ta·ko·mni ... šni \ṫa-k̇ó-mni ... šni\ *adv* : at no time ~ *el owapa kte šni yelo* At no time will I join in with him, *i.e.* although I advised not to do so. > – MS.103

ta·koš \ta-kóš\ *n* mi·tákoš ni·tákoš : a son or daughter-in-law — **tako·šku** *n* : his or her son or daughter-in-law — **tako·šya** *n* tako·šwa·ya : to have for a son or daughter-in-law

ta·kpe \ta-kṗé\ *va* ta·wa·kpe : to come upon, attack < ~ *ya* to go to attacking > — **takpe·ya** \ta-kṗé-ya\ *adv* : attacking

ta·ku \ṫá-k̇u\ *n* : something < ~ *hutopapi* something two-footed > — *pron interrog* : what? — *pron* : that, in *ref* to a relative < *takuye* a relative > – B.H.291.15

ta·ku ca \ṫá-k̇u ca\ *pron interrog* : what?, what is it that?

ta·ku·e·ya *or* **taku eya** \ṫá-k̇u-e-ya\ *pron* : something < *Yunkan ~ ceonpahan* And so he was roasting something. >

ta·ku i·c'i·h'an \ṫa-kú i-c'i-ḣ'aŋ\ *v in comp* : what does he do for himself?

ta·ku i·h'an \ṫa-kú i-ḣ'aŋ\ *v in comp* : what does he do for him? < ~ *yahi* what have you come to do for him? > – R Bl

ta·ku ke c'e·yaš \ṫá-k̇u ke c'e-yaš\ *pron indef* : anything, whatever – Note: the alternate forms:

táku ke ešá	táku kešá
táku ke éyaš	táku k'éyaš

< *Tawoyuha taku k'eyaš etkiya yakizomi kilo* Do not covet possessions whatever the purpose. > – B.H.57.26

ta·ku·ki·ci·ya·pi \ṫa-k̇ú-ki-ci-ya-pi\ *n* : relationship or relations

ta·ku·ki·ya \ṫá-k̇u-ki-ya\ *va poss* : to value one's own – B.H.153.19

ta·ku·ku \ṫa-k̇ú-k̇u\ *n red of* táku : trinkets, small articles, one thing or another < *Misun, eš ~ koyakipe sece lo* My little brother, it seems you fear indeed one thing or another. ~ *kounkipapi kin hena unkoglakapi kte* We shall for sure tell of those things we fear. > — **takuku·kel** \ṫa-k̇ú-k̇u-k̇el\ *adv* : of everything, all sorts of things < ~ *itancan kin kaaye wicaši.* ~ *el onah'on* The chief bade them bring him everything. He heard reported to him all sorts of things about him. > – D.103 B.H.36.4

ta·ku·la \ṫá-ku-la\ *pron interrog* : what? – Note: *He ~ hwo* Just what is that? – R Bl

ta·ku·mna \ṫa-kú-mna\ *vn* : to have taste or smell < ~ *šni* to be without smell, taste, or aroma >

ta·ku·ni \ṫá-k̇u-ni\ *n generally followed by šni* : nothing <~ *ota epin kte šni* I shall say nothing much. *Lena ecamon kin ~ šica slolyayin kte šni* You will learn nothing bad of these things I have done.> — **takuni·kel** *adv* : in no way < ~ *toka šni* Nothing's happened. ~ *akipa šni* There was no trouble, *i.e.* it was an uneventful journey > — **takunišni** *n* : nothing — *vn* : to come to nothing, to fail, to perish < *Matakunišni* I failed. > — **takunišni·yan** *adv* : gone or come to nothing, perishing – MS.481 D.269

ta·kunl \ṫa-k̇úŋl\ *n* : something, anything < ~ *yulpica eša yaglepi hwo* Did you put out something it is able to eat? *Na wanna on* (a bow) ~ *kute iyuta* and now he tried to shoot anything with (a bow). *Tanyan econ po na ~ icu wacin po na napeyahan škan po. Hecena ištogmus wawaci kin ~ slolwaye tka iblukcan* Do it well, aim taking anything, and move about on the look out. In the end if I dance with eyes shut I learn about something, but I understand. ~ *aiyoptemayaye ci hignaciyin kte* I shall marry you who are something of a match for me. ~ *onitutka k'u hwo* Did he give you a bit of something to eat, *i.e.* something little to eat? > – Bl B.H.147.16

ta·ku on \ṫá-k̇u oŋ\ *n* : the why, the reason why < ~ *kin he* That is the reason why. > – B.H.81.23

ta·ku·ša·ša \ṫá-k̇u-ša-ša\ *n* : any red thing

[1]**ta·ku·ša·ša·la** \ṫá-k̇u-ša-šà-la\ *n* : jelly

[2]**ta·ku ša·ša·la** \ṫá-k̇u ša-šà-la\ *n* : swamp smart weed, polygonum emersum, the buckwheat family; or the foxglove, which is edible < ~ *ececa unma inkpa šaša un he* The smart weed is like another that has a red top, the lady's thumb, the pink knot weed, the joint weed, polygonum pennsylvanicum, as well as ~ *hu iyececa* like the smart weed bush, the tall dock and the peach-leaved dock, rumex altissimus. > – Note: this is Bl's medicine, an effective remedy for stomach cramps, diarrhea or hemorrhage – Bl #303, 226, 229 BT

ta·ku ša·ša·la hu swu·la \ṫá-k̇u ša-šà-la hu swúla\ *n* : lady's thumb, heart weed, polygonum persicaria, the buckwheat family — **taku šašala hu wínyela** *n* : the dock-leaved or pale knotweed, polygonum lapatifolium, the buskwheat family – DE Bl #304, 302

ta·ku·škan·škan \ṫá-k̇u-škaŋ-škaŋ\ *n* : a Power working or moving things secretly, one of the powers in a *Wakan Wicoh'an* sacred ceremony, that which causes everything to move – WJR.154

ta·ku·šni \ṫá-k̇u-šni\ *n* : nothing — **takušni·šni** *n* : small articles, trifles

ta·ku·we *or* **takowe** \ṫá-k̇u-we\ *pron interrog* : why?, what for? < *Kola, ~ migluze k'on iyecel ecannon hwo* Friend, why is it you did as I had dressed, painted, myself? ~ *ca* just why?, why is it that? > – Bl B.H.30.10

ta·ku·ya \ṫa·kú-ya\ *va* taku·wa·ya : to have one for a relation — **takuye** \ṫa-kú-ye\ *n* mi·tákúye unki·taku-

ye·pi : a relative
ta·k'e·ya \ṫá-k'e-ya\ *v* tá·k'e·pa tá·k'un·keya·pi [fr *éya* to say] : to say something < *Yunkan glakinyan inajin na ~ . Yunkan ... ták'epa.* And then he stood up facing on and said something. Then ... I said something. > — **ta·k'eyaya** \ṫá-k'e-ya-ya\ *v red* tá·k'eṗa·ṗa tá·k'un·keyaya·pi : to say often, repeat – Cf eyáya
ta·k'o·le \ṫá-k'o-le\ *v* : to look for something < ~ *yahi he* What have you come looking for? >
ta·le·ja \ta-lé-ja\ *n* : urine
ta·li·ca·kse \ta-lí-ca-kse\ *n* : a butcher saw
ta·li·pa \ta-lí-ṗa\ *n* [fr *talo* fresh meat + *ipá* the high end of a ridge] : sausage of a sort, prepared with long slices of beef cut and put into gut casings, tied and cooked that way < ~ *eciyapi wakagin ktelo* I shall make sausage they say, or I shall make what is called sausage. > – Bl
ta·lo \ṫa-ló\ *n* : fresh meat < ~ *wanji* a piece of meat > — **talo iyukpan** \ṫa-ló i-yu-kpaŋ\ *n* : a meat chopper — **talo·yukpanpi** \ṫa-ló-yu-kṗaŋ-pi\ *n* : cut meat, as sold in stores
ta·l'a·gna·ka i·ye·ce·ca \ta·l'á-gna-ka i-yè-ce-ca\ *n* : the western iron weed, veronia fasciculata, the composite family — **tal'agnake** *n* : the stiff or hard-leaved goldenrod, solidago rigida, the composite family, the leaves of which are laid under meat – Note: this goldenrod is also called *canhlogan* or *maka ayublaya*, or *waphe ape blaskaska*, or *mimela wahcazi* – Bl #147, 25
ta·ma·he·ca \ṫa-má-he-ca\ *adj* ma·támaheca : poor, lean, not fat
ta·ma·hel \ta-má-hel\ *adv* : in the body, within
ta·ma·he·lhe·ca \ta-má-he-lhe-ca\ *adj red of* tamaheca : poor, lean — **tamahe·lya** *adv* : poorly, not in a fat state
ta·ma·ka \tá-ma-ḱa\ *adj* : poor, lean < *ptetamaka* a lean cow
ta·ma·ko·yun·ka \ta-má-ko-yuŋ-ka\ *n* : a deer, one that contrary to habit used to stay in the same place and hence became fat < ~ *s'e leniceca yelo* You are like a deer that stays at home, as is said of a man who sleeps unduly long. > – Note: the word is applied to a deer that leaves the impression in the ground where it has been lying around for a long time – Bl
ta·ma·ku·hu \ta-má-ḱu-hu\ *n* : the breast bone of animals
ta·ma·ške·ku \ta-má-ške-ku\ *n* : her female friend
ta·mi·ca \ta-mí-ca\ *n* **a** : the short sharp bone ends in the single parts of the spinal column **b** : the lean meat on the sides near the animal rump, the small of the back **c** : the lean meat of the thigh – Bl
ta·mi·ca·ho·hu \ta-mí-ca-ho-hu\ *n* : the bone near the hip-bone
ta·mna \ṫa-mná\ *n* : a swelling on a buffalo
ta·mna·tkan \ta-mná-tkaŋ\ *n* : the meat on the front side below the knee of the buffalo – Note: the corresponding part in other animals is called *tasícogin* – Bl
ta·mni \ṫa-mní\ *n* : the womb, or the afterbirth, sack that envelopes the foetus
ta·mni·o·hpi can \ta-mní-o-ḣpi caŋ\ *n* : the fig tree
ta·mni·o·hpi hu \ta-mní-o-ḣṗi hu\ *n* : the clammy ground-cherry, physalis heterophylla, the night shade family, and it grows about a foot high with green berries that turn yellow, looking like little bags filled with yellow grease when frozen – Note: give three to five, one after the other, to one who has no appetite. Children eat them. The word may also be the word used for **fig** – B.H.177.23, 225.15 BT #131
ta·na·gi·la \ta-ná-ġi-la\ *n* : the hummingbird < *Zitka ~ s'e iniwašicun welo* You are talkative as a hummingbird, a little bird, as is said of a little person. > – Bl
ta·na·ji·ca \ta-ná-ji-ca\ *v* : to flee — **tanaji·lhi** *v* tanaji·lwa·hi : to come fleeing – Bl
ta·na·pco \ta-ná-pco\ *n* : the lean meat near the backbone, the longissimus dorsi of an animal – *See* napcó
ta·na·pkan *or* **tanakpan** \ta-ná-pkaŋ\ *n* : the fleshy part on the leg below the knee of an animal, the cords in the leg of animals – *Syn* TASICOGIN R
ta·na·su·la \ta-ná-su-la\ *n* : the brain of animals
ta·na·wi·ci·te \ta-ná-wi-ci-ṫe\ *n* : the little bulbous piece of meat on the foreleg
ta·ni·ga \ṫa-ní-ġa\ *n* : the paunch of a buffalo or cow
ta·ni·ga mi·ni·ya·ye \ṫa-ní-ġa mi-ni-ya-ye\ *n* : a paunch for carrying water, made of the buffalo paunch
ta·ni·ga šin \ṫa-ní-ġa šiŋ\ *n* : the fat covering the paunch – Bl
ta·ni·hyu·sku \ta-ní-ḣyu-sku\ *v* : to empty the paunch of a buffalo
ta·ni·h'o·hin·šma *or* **tanih'o·škokpa** \ta-ní-ḣ'o-hiŋ-šma\ *n* : the curved half of the paunch proper, used for various purposes < ~ *oškokpa* the concavity of the curved half of the paunch > — **tanih'o·šla** *n* : the other half of the paunch proper which is smooth inside, while the other half is called *tanih'ohinšma, etc.* – Bl
ta·ni·ka \ṫa-ní-ḱa\ *adj* : old, worn out – Cf tanníka
ta·ni·štu·šta \ta-ní-štu-šta\ *n* : the meat in the quarters of an animal < *ništušte* the rump > – Bl
ta·ni·ta·hu \ta-ní-ṫa-hu\ *n* : the backbone of the buffalo < *Na ~ ko aku wacinpo* And the backbone too plan to bring home. > – Bl
ta·ni·tko·hlo·ke \ta-ní-tko-ḣlo-ke\ *n* : the meat inside the thigh bones of a buffalo – Bl
ta·ni·ya \ta-ní-ya\ *n* : his or her breath or life – *Syn* WÓNIYA
ta·num *or* **tanunb** \ta-núm\ *adj num card contrac* : his or her two < *ogle ~* his two coats > — **tanu·mnum** \ta-nú-mnum\ *adj num card red* : in two sets < *wokoyake ~* two sets of suits > – B.H.115.15, 206.4
ta·nun·h'šin *or* **tanunh'suhute** \ta-núŋ-ḣ'šiŋ\ *n* : the fat behind the ears – HC
[1]**tan** \taŋ\ *adj contrac of* tánka *usually pref to other adj* : very < *tanwankatuya* very high, *Wahinkpe kin tanwankatuya ya* The arrow went very high. *Tan naké unhipelo* At last! we are here, *i.e.* we ought to have come sooner. > – *Syn* TANTÁN
[2]**tan** \taŋ\ *n contrac of* tancán : the body < *mitancan* my body, *tánhanska* tall of stature >
[3]**tan** \taŋ\ *n* : a side of the beef, including the bones < ~ *wanjila* one side or half the animal cut down the middle of the backbone >
[4]**tan** \taŋ\ *root e.g. yután* to touch, or to honor
[5]**tan** \taŋ\ *prep* or *adv suff* used in the formation *esp* of *adv* < *heciya·tan* from that place >
tan'·a·ko·tan·han \taŋ-a-ḱó-ṫaŋ-haŋ\ *adv* : beyond a person or animal, *i.e.* something with a body
tan'·a·ta·ye·la \taŋ-á-ṫa-ye-la\ *adv* : towards a person
tan·blas \taŋ-blás\ *adv contrac of, archaic* tanbláza : on the side < ~ *yunka* to lie on the side, as do animals > – *Syn* TANBLECAKIYA

\a\ father \e\ they \i\ machine \o\ smoke \u\ lunar \an, aŋ\ blanc Fr. \in, iŋ\ ink \on, oŋ, un, uŋ\ soon, confier Fr. \c\ chair \ġ\ machen Ger. \j\ fusion \clusters: bl, gn, kp, hšl, etc...\ b^e^lo ... said with a slight vowel
See more in the Introduction, Guide to Pronunciation

tan·ble·ca·ki·ya \taŋ-blé-ca-ki-ya\ *or* \táŋ-ble-ca-ki-ya\ *adv* : on the side < ~ *yunka* to lie on the side, *Cankahu mastake ca ~ munke.* I lay on my side since my backbone is weak. ~ *hiyu* to come walking sideways, *i.e.* with the side towards something >

tan·can *or* **tacan** \taŋ-cáŋ\ *n* mi·tancan un·tancan·pi : the body — **tancan oyuze** \taŋ-cáŋ o-yù-ze\ *n* : the exterior, the looks of a person – ***Syn*** ITEOYUZE

tan·can·ton \taŋ-cáŋ-toŋ\ *v* : to have a body, to be ripe or full-grown – B.H.85.5

tan·ca·tka·ya·tan·han \taŋ-cá-tka-ya-taŋ-haŋ\ *adv* : at the left side of the body < ~ *iyayin na ake el iyeya* (shot) *na ake wounka* It went at its left side, again he shot at it and again made it fall. > – B.H.265.24

tan·co·co·la \taŋ-có-co-la\ *adj red of* tancola : all but naked — **tanco·kala** *adj* tanco·ma·kala : naked, without clothing

tan·cola \taŋ-có-la\ *adj* : nearly naked, poorly clad, naked – ***Syn*** HACÓCOLA

tan·gla·kin·yan \taŋ-glá-kiŋ-yaŋ\ *adv* : crosswise, across something else

tan·glu·sa·sa·se·ca \taŋ-glú-sa-sa-se-ca\ *v* tan·ma·glusasaseca : to be frightened, as at a ghost or at anything, to be made sick by seeing anything — **tanglusasa·ya** *adv* : in a state of fright

tan·glu·za·za \taŋ-glú-za-za\ *v* : to be an awful thing, such as to be a murder < *Tanwicagluzaza s'e oyah'an ye* You act as if they were awful people. > – Bl KE

[1]**tan·han** \taŋ-háŋ\ *prep suff usually* : from < *heciya·tanhan* towards that time or place >

[2]**tan·han** \taŋ-háŋ\ *n* ni·tanhan : my brother-in-law, a man's brother-in-law, a wife's brother, and a man's sister's husband — **tanhan·kiciyapi** \taŋ-háŋ-ki-ci-ya-pi\ *n* : brothers-in-law — **tanhan·ku** *n* : his brother-in-law

tan·han·ši \taŋ-háŋ-ši\ *n* ni·tanhanši : my male cousin, a man's male cousin – Note: this does not include a father's brother's sons who are brothers — **tanhanši·tku** *n* : his male cousin – Cf tanhánši — **tanhanši·ya** *va* tanhánši·wa·ya : to have for a male cousin

tan·han·ya \taŋ-háŋ-ya\ *va* : a man to have for a brother-in-law

tan·hmin·ki·ya \taŋ-hmíŋ-ki-ya\ *adv* : bending one's body away, as a horse does when passing something it fears, shying away < ~ *iyaya* to go shying from > – ***Syn*** KIPAŠ IYAYA

tan'·i·ca·tka·ya·tan·han *or* **tan·catkayatanhan** \taŋ-í-ca-tka-ya-taŋ-haŋ\ *adv* : at the left side of somebody

tan'·in \taŋ-íŋ\ *vn* ma·tan'in un·tan'in·pi : to appear, be manifest, be visible < *Tokel ecamon kta ~ šni* It is not clear how I should do it. > — **tan'in'in** *vn red* : to appear occasionally, as one passing under a hill, or as the sun through the clouds, to flicker — **tan'in'in·yan** *adv red* : appearing occasionally < ~ *iyaya* to go on appearing every now and then > – P

tan'·in·šni \taŋ-íŋ-šni\ *vn* ma·tán'inšni : to be lost, to have disappeared — **tan'inšni·yan** *adv* : out of sight, lost from view < *Ataya mak'op'o na egna ~ iyaya* There was a dust storm into the midst of which he went on entirely out of sight. >

tan'·in·yan \taŋ-íŋ-yaŋ\ *adv* : manifestly, openly, without concealment

tan'·in·yun·la \táŋ-iŋ-yuŋ-la\ *adv perhaps* : being deprived of what is necessary for life, or for a certain kind of work < ~ *éyotakin kte* They should sit down helpless, as is said of a meeting when the books are missing. > – TB

tan'·i·pa \taŋ-í-pa\ *n* : the meat along the spinal column of a buffalo – Bl

tan'·i·šla·ya·tan·han *or* **tan'išleyatan** \taŋ-í-šla-ya-taŋ-haŋ\ *adv* : at the right side of somebody, *tan* < *Našlog hiyu na ~ iyayin na el iyeya* (shot) It bolted and came forward, went to the right side, and there he shot it. > – B.H.265.23

tan'i·ya·ta·ye·la \taŋ-í-ya-ta-ye-la\ *adv* : individually, directly, in person < ~ *glajuju* each one to pay for himself > – ***Syn*** TAN'ÁTAYELA

tan'·i·yo·hi·la \taŋ-í-yo-hi-la\ *pron indef* : each one, every one

tan'·i·yu·pse \taŋ-í-yu-pse\ *v* : to turn one's body to the side in order to see something — **tan'iyupse·ya un** *v* : to be turned sideways and look – Bl

tan'·i·yu·t'in·ze \taŋ-í-yu-t'iŋ-ze\ *n* : a corset

[1]**tan·ka** \táŋ-ka\ *adj* ma·tanka : large, great in any way

[2]**tan·ka** \taŋ-ká\ *n* : a woman's younger sister < *Mitan, toké wicahpi wan lila ilege cin he waštewalaka* My little sister, would that I loved a star that really shines. > – Note: *mitán* my younger sister, *nitán* your younger sister

tan·ka·ki·ci·ya·pi \taŋ-ká-ki-ci-ya-pi\ *n* : they who are sisters

tan·ka·ki·ya \táŋ-ka-ki-ya\ *adv* : largely < *ho ~* with a loud voice >

tan·ka·ku \taŋ-ká-ku\ *n* : her younger sister

tan·kal \taŋ-kál\ *adv contrac* : out of doors, without < ~ *iyaya* to go out, ~ *iyeya* to turn or put out of doors — **tankal iya** *v* : to go to the toilet

tan·ka·la \táŋ-ka-la\ *v* : to consider great

tan·ka·ta \taŋ-ká-ta\ *adv* : out of doors – *See* tankál — **tankata·han** *adv* : outside or from the outside < *Na oyate kin el ~ wanyank najinpi* And they stood looking outside at the people. >

[1]**tan·ka·ya** \taŋ-ká-ya\ *va* : a woman to have for a younger sister

[2]**tan·ka·ya** \táŋ-ka-ya\ *adv* : greatly, to a great extent < ~ *onitan'in kte lo* You will be visible to a great extent. > – B.H.194.24

tan·ke \taŋ-ké\ *n* mi·tanke ni·tanke : a man's older sister — **tanke·ku** *n* : his older sister — **tanke·ya** *va* tanke·wa·ya : to have for an older sister

tan·kin·kin·yan \taŋ-kíŋ-kiŋ-yaŋ\ *adj red pl* [fr *tanka* large + *tankinyan* very great] : very large or important, as men in authority – B.H.67.7

tan·kin·yan \taŋ-kíŋ-yaŋ\ *adj* : very great, large — **tankinyan·yan** *adj red* : many very great

tan·kši \taŋ-kší\ *n* mi·tánkši ni·tankši : a man's younger sister — **tankši·tku** *n* : his younger sister — **tankši·ya** *va* : to have for a younger sister

tan·ktan·ka \taŋ-ktáŋ-ka\ *adj red of* tánka : very great — **tanktanka·ya** \taŋ-ktáŋ-ka-ya\ *adv red of* tánkaya : largely < *Maka ~ omani ye* Travel the greater part of the country. > – Bl B.H.62.14

tan·ku \taŋ-kú\ *or* \táŋ-ku\ *n contrac of* tankéku *archaic* : his older sister

tan·la *or* **tanla·ka** \taŋ-lá\ *or* \taŋ-lá-ka\ *va* tan·wa·la **a** : to love, honor, respect **b** : to be patient with

tan·ma·hel \táŋ-ma-hel\ *adv* : in the body, within — **tanmahe·ltanhan** \táŋ-ma-he-ltaŋ-haŋ\ *adv* : from within the body

tan·na·ke·ki·ya \taŋ-ná-ke-ki-ya\ *adv* : on the side, with the head on one side < ~ *yunka* to lie on one side > — **tannake·ya** *or* **tanna·kiciya** \taŋ-ná-ke-ya\ \taŋ-ná-ki·ci·ya\ *adv* : on the side, with the head turned to one side, as a drowsy person — **tanna·kinc'i·ya** \taŋ-ná-k̇íŋ-c'i-ya\ *v refl* or *adv contrac of* tannákan'ic'iya : to shy from, bow one's body away, as a timid horse does while passing by something it is afraid of - Note: very doubtful is the word *tannakiociya* *Syn* TANHMINKI-YA Bl

tan·na·pa \táŋ-na-pa\ *v* : to be scared, frightened, as by sudden motion, and to flee, to jerk involuntarily, to move sideways, as when one is frightened — **tannapa-pa** *v red* : to dodge something — *adv* : dodging, avoiding, bending one's body to the right or left while passing through something lest one touch something or tear one's clothes < ~ *ya* to go sidestepping, ~ *un* to be avoiding, to be timid or hesitating out of fear while going to some place > — **tannapekiya** \táŋ-na-pe-k̇i-ya\ *v* : to bend one's body sideways so as to avoid being hit - Bl

tan·ni \ṫaŋ-ní\ *adj* : old, worn out — *adv* : of old, before, already < ~ *kta s'e oyaka* to tell something hurriedly, *i.e.* lest it become old > - Note: the example is not construed: ~ *kte šni s'e oyaka; sni* is not used - Bl

tan·ni·ca·la *or* **tannicela** \táŋ-ni-ca-la\ *n* : tiny flies or insects, gnats that pester horses *etc.* during the hot weather

tan·ni·ka \taŋ-ní-k̇a\ *adj* : old, worn out, ancient, archaic

tan-ni kta s'e \taŋ-ní kta s'e\ *adv phr* : in great haste, sooner than expected, before others < ~ *oyaka, econ, tebya.* ~ *womakiyakelo* to devour, to act, to speak very hurriendly, He spoke to me in great haste. > - Bl B.H.273.16

tan·ni·la \taŋ-ní-la\ *adj* : old, ahead of others, before others — *adv* : long ago < *Yunkan šunka najinpi atayela unkihunnipi na* ~ *Tašunke Luzahan el un* And then horses directly stopped while we went on across, and for a long time Fast Horse was there. *Yunkan giic'iya wan* ~ *t'a hpaya* Then one who painted himself brown fell dead. *Yunkan* ~ *slolya na leya* And she knew it before others and this she said ... > - *Syn* EHANNI

tan·ni·ni \taŋ-ní-ni\ *adj red of* tanní : worn out

tan·niš \taŋ-níš\ *adv emph* : already, *i.e.* sooner than expected, later than expected < ~ *hi* to have arrived already, ~ *luštan so* Did you finish already? *Hinȟota akanyanka wan ena kinajin tka* ~ *Cantku Wankatuya kte* He rode a gray horse and recovered his position, but High Breast killed it. > - Note: word is opposed to *aškans'e*, later than expected, rather late MS.530 Bc

tan·ni·špan \ taŋ-ní-špaŋ\ *n* : red earth used for painting one's self - *Syn* WASE, WASE ACETIPI

tan'·o·han·gle·gle·ya \taŋ-ó-haŋ-gle-gle-ya\ *adv* : parting the body in two < ~ *yusleslel kte* to kill splitting the body in two > — **tan'o·kikašleca** \taŋ-ó-k̇i-ka-šle-ca\ *va* : to split in two in the middle — **tan'oki·sese** \taŋ-ó-k̇i-se-se\ *n* : the halves of the body or any body - B.H.76.12, 99.16

tan·o·kšan \taŋ-ó-kšaŋ\ *adv* : around about, surrounding, *lit* around the body < *unkitan'okšanpi* around us > - D.74

tan·onb \taŋ-óŋb\ *v contrac* [fr *tan* body + *onpa* to lean] : to be leaning to one side — **tan'on·-bya** *v* tan'ón-bi·blabla : to walk with the body leaning to one side — **tan'onbyan·ka** *v* tan'ón·bmanka : to sit with the body leaning to one side — **tan'onpa** *v* : to be leaning

tan·pa \taŋ-ṗá\ *n* : a little basket in a woman's game, *cunwiyawa kansu kutepi*, in which plum pits are shot

tan·sag \taŋ-ság\ *v* [fr *tansaka* which is not used] : to frighten < ~ *t'a* to die of great fright, to faint > — **tan-sa·gt'eya** \taŋ-sá-gt'e-ya\ *va* tansagt'e·wa·ya : to frighten very much

tan·san·ni \táŋ-saŋ-ni\ *but pronounced* \ta-sáŋ-ni\ *n* : one side of the body < ~ *awagli kte lo* I shall bring back a side (of game). > — **tansanni t'a** \taŋ-sáŋ-ni t'a\ *v* : to be paralyzed on one side

tan·si·to·mni \taŋ-sí-ṫo-mni\ *n* : the whole body — **tan-sitomni·yan** *adv* : all over the body

tan·smin·yan·yan \taŋ-smí-yaŋ-yaŋ\ *adv* : alone, deprived of everything — **tansmiyanyan·ka** *n* : one who is alone, without relatives

tan·ši·ca \taŋ-ší-ca\ *adj* tan·má·šica : ugly, deformed

tan·šin \ṫaŋ-šíŋ\ *n* : the fat on the ribs

tan·šna \ṫaŋ-šná\ *adj* : alone, single, unmarried < *wicá-tanšna* an unmarried man, *witánšna* an unmarried woman, a virgin > — **tanšna·la** \taŋ-šná-la\ *adj* : alone, without one's family

tan·tan \ṫaŋ-ṫáŋ\ *adv* : very good, very well, very nicely < ~ *wayatin kte lo* You should eat very well. ~ *ceye* She cried very nicely. > - Cf [1]tan MS.95

tan·tan·han \táŋ-ṫaŋ-haŋ\ *adv* mitántanhan unkítantan-han·pi : for the sake of one < *Nitantanhan ecamon* I did it for your sake. *Le nitantanhan iyopemayanpi* I was punished now for your sake. *David* ~ *on* the reason being for Davi's sake, *he on* ~ because of that for his sake >

tan·tan'·in·šni·yan \táŋ-taŋ-iŋ-šni-yaŋ\ *adv* : in a way unnoticed < ~ *econ* to do things unnoticed > - Bl

tan·tan·yan \ṫaŋ-ṫáŋ-yaŋ\ *adv red of* tányan : quite well — **tantanyan·kel** *adv red of* tanyankel : in a way well

tan·ton·šni \taŋ-tóŋ-šni\ *vn* : to be unsubstantial, as are some kinds of food *e.g.* *wójapi* a fruited pudding; or as a thrown-off calf that may be only a month or two old, *i.e.* still formless — **tantonšni·yan** *va* tantónšni·wa·ya : to spoil meat *etc.*, as by negligence while cooking — *adv* : unsubstantially, destitute — **tanton·ya** *v* : to let *e.g.* vegetables or other edibles spoil because one has too much — **tantonyan·kel** \taŋ-tóŋ-yaŋ-k̇el\ *adv* : excessively, intemperately < ~ *oh'an, ohitiya oh'an* to work excessively, to work furiously > - Bc BT Bl

tan·t'a·t'a \táŋ-t'a-ṫ'a\ *adj* : paralyzed - B.H.187.1,4

tan·wa·šte \taŋ-wá-šte\ *adj* tan·ma·wašte : handsome, of fine form

tan·yam \taŋ-yám\ *adv* : in behalf of one < ~ *ia* to speak for one, in one's behalf; to take one's part, as when a few are disputng, *He* ~ *iwaye* I went in his behalf, or perhaps I spoke in that one's behalf. > - R Bc

tan·yan \ṫáŋ-yaŋ\ *adv* : well < ~ *un, econ, slolya* to be, do, or to know well > — **tanyan·kel** \ṫáŋ-yaŋ-k̇el\ *adv* : as if, in a way, well - B.H.99.6 D.81

tan·ya·ta·ki·ya \taŋ-yá-ṫa-k̇i-ya\ *adv* : towards one < ~ *hiyu* to come towards one >

tan·ye·hci \ṫaŋ-yé-ȟci\ *adv* : very well, exceedingly well

tan·ye·kel \ṫaŋ-yé-k̇el\ *adv* : whole, without injury

tan·ye·la \ṫaŋ-yé'-la\ *adv* : well < ~ *wanblake* I see well. ~ *ȟugnahye* He had it burning well. > - B.H.108.23

tan·ye·ni \ṫaŋ-yé-ni\ *adv* : not well < ~ *ištinme šni* He does not sleep well. > - B.H.111.11

\a\ father \e\ they \i\ machine \o\ smoke \u\ lunar \an, aŋ\ blanc Fr. \in, iŋ\ ink \on, oŋ, un, uŋ\ soon, confier Fr. \c\ chair \ġ\ machen Ger. \j\ fusion \clusters: bl, gn, kp, hšl, etc...\ b[e]lo ... said with a slight vowel **See more in the Introduction, Guide to Pronunciation**

tan·yu·tkan·la *or* **tanyutkanlak** \tán-yu-tkan-la\ \tán-yu-tkàn-lak\ *adj* : much of something as food < ~ *onweya yuha unyanpi* We go carrying a great plenty provisions, *i.e.* go with much grub. *Canli kin ~ yuha* He has a plentious amount of tobacco. > – Bl

tan·za·ni \tan-zá-ni\ *adj* tan·ma·zani : healthy, sound in health, not injured in body — **tanzani·ke** \tan-zá-ni-ke\ *adv* : well, in good health — **tanzani·yake** \tan-zá-ni-ya-ke\ *adv* : without injuring, as in killing an animal without injuring its hide < ~ *kat'e* to kill it uninjured > — **tanzaniyan** *adv* : whole, not wounded

ta·o \ta-ó\ *va* ta·wá·o : to wound by shooting, wound but not kill – B.H.112.3

ta·o·ka·ške \ta-ó-ka-ške\ *n* : its tether, prison – Cf iktómi taókaške

ta·o·ki·ye \ta-ó-ki-ye\ *n* mi·taokiye : his disciple or assistant — **taokiye·ya** *va* : to have for one's servant or helper

ta·o·pi \ta-ó-pi\ *n* : a wound — *part* : wounded, a wounded person < *Na hel ~ k'on he wanji akignaka iyeyapi ca he t'a ca ena hapi* And there they quickly placed a casualty who had died and right there he was buried. > – Note: they wound *taniyopi* perhaps fr *taniya* his life + *opi* they wound *or* wounded – Pb.36

ta·o·un·ye \ta-ó-un-ye\ *n* : his dwelling

ta·o·ya·te \ta-ó-ya-te\ *n* mita·oyate : his people

[1]**ta·pa** \tá-pa\ *n* : a ball < *Šaké nitapa kte* Your fingertip will be your ball, as mothers would tell their children when they point at a rainbow, *i.e.* their fingertips would be as round as a ball, which was to say they should not do it. > – *See* šaké tápa Bl

[2]**ta·pa** \ta-pá\ *va* ta·wa·pa : to follow after one who has gone, to follow *e.g.* game, to pursue *e.g.* an enemy < *Na tawicapa* And he followed after them. > – MS.352

ta·pa·ga \ta-pá-ga\ *n* : the diaphragm of man or animal

ta·pa·kšin \ta-pá-kšin\ *n* : the fat that sticks to the kidneys – R Bl

ta·pa na·ka·pa·pi \tá-pa na-ká-pa-pi\ *n* : a game for girls

ta·pa·pa \ta-pá-pa\ *v* : to hit a ball

ta·pe·te *or* **tapeto** *or* **tapetu** \ta-pé-te\ *n* : the back, the upper part of the back – BD

ta·pe·to·gna·gya \ta-pé-to-gna-gya\ *adv* : placed on the back

ta·pe·to·gna·ka \ta-pé-to-gna-ka\ *v* : to put or place on the back – LB

ta·pe·to·ka·tki·ya \ta-pé-to-ka-tki-ya\ *adv* [fr *tapeto* the back + *kata* hot + *kiya* make one's own] : with the back against the fire

ta·pe·to ska \ta-pé-to ska\ *n* : white spotted shoulders, as on a mature buffalo – Cf the Song of Hiawatha by Longfellow Bt LHB

ta·pe·to·ta *or* **tapetuta** *or* **tapetotanhan** \ta-pé-to-ta\ *adv* : on the back – R Bl-

ta·pe·tu \ta-pé-tu\ *n* : the back, the upper part of the back < *Wanbli wan ~ el owawa* I painted an eagle on the back (on the Ghost Shirt). > – Cf tapéte

ta·pe·ya \ta-pé-ya\ *va* ta·wa·peya : to go after, follow *i.e.* in order to catch

ta·pi \ta-pí\ *n* : the liver of animals

ta·pi·šle·ca \ta-pí-šle-ca\ *n* : the spleen or animals

ta·pi·ye·ya \ta-pí-ye-ya\ *v* : to throw a ball

ta·pi·zi \ta-pí-zi\ *n* : gall

ta·po \ta-pó\ *n* : the duodenum, one of the stomachs of ruminating animals, the crop of fowls

ta·pon \ta-pón\ *n* : the cheek — **tapon·hu** *n* : the cheekbone

ta·po·po·ska \ta-pó-po-ska\ *n* : anything nicely round – R Bl

ta·psi·psi·za \ta-psí-psi-za\ *v red of* tapsiza : to bubble up — **tapsiš** *v contrac* : to bubble < ~ *hingla* suddenly to bubble up, as water when anything is thrown in, or spontaneously >

ta·psi·za *or* **tapšija** \ta-psí-za\ *v* : to bubble up, come up, as bubbles in water — **ana·tapšija** *vn* : to bubble up onto water

ta·pun *or* **tapon** \ta-pún\ *n* : the cheek

ta·p'i·ca·ka·pe *or* **tap'ica·psice** *or* **tap'icapsi·te** \ta-p'í-ca-ka-pe\ \ta-p'í-ca-psi-te\ *n* : a bat with which to hit a ball *etc.*, a shinny stick, a baseball bat – Cf icápsinte

ta·p'i·yu·ka·pe \ta-p'í-yu-ka-pe\ *n* : a catching glove for baseball

ta·sa·gya \ta-sá-gya\ *va* : to cause to harden — *adv* : in a hardened state < ~ *gnaka* to lay away to harden >

ta·sa·ka \ta-sá-ka\ *adj* : stiff, hard, as tallow; frozen, hardened by cooling, whether at a temperature above or below the freezing point; cold, as *nape matasaka* my cold hands

ta·san·ni t'a \ta-sán-ni t'a\ *v* : to be paralyzed on one side – Note: *tansanni t'a* is the correct spelling of the word here presented however as it is said

ta·se \ta-sé\ *interj, an express of contradiction or discredit, followed by ka, kakeca,* or *kacaš* : of course not! < ~ , *le ciciyuha kacaš, hunke cic'u ka eye* Of course I did not give it to you to keep. He said he meant that I a relative gave it to you. ~ , *wanagi wan cehpi na hohu ikoyake ka* Of course a ghost does not have flesh and bone. > – B.H.274.1

ta·si·co·gin \ta-sí-co-gin\ *n* : the fleshy part on the leg below the knee of an animal on the rear side. – Note: meat on the front side is called *tamnátkan. Tasicogin* itself is a piece of meat in the lower leg of ruminants and is full of sinew and a most undesirable part of the meat. Hence the *fig* something better than nothing – D.116 Bl

ta·si·co·ska \ta-sí-co-ska\ *n* : the white meat on the thigh bone perhaps of the buffalo – Bl

ta·si·ha un·pi \ta-sí-ha un-pi\ *n* : a game played mostly by women, a string of five deer bones, a few beaded loops, and a pin to catch them on while swinging the bones

ta·sin·ta \ta-sín-ta\ *n of* sinté : the tail of the buffalo – D.37

ta·si·tu·pa·hu \ta-sí-tu-pa-hu\ *n* : the lump of fat above the tail of a fat buffalo – Bl

ta·ska·kpa \tá-ska-kpa\ *n* : the wood tick

ta·span \ta-spán\ *n* **1** : the apple **2** : the red haw

ta·span·han·pi \ta-spán-han-pi\ *n* : cider, as apple cider

ta·span·hin·šma \ta-spán-hin-šmà\ *n* : the peach

ta·span·hu \ta-spán-hu\ *n* : the hawthorn, the common hawthorn, white thorn, the scarlet-fruited thorn, the red haw, thorn apple, mayflowers, crataegus sheridana, the rose family – Note: the berries are mixed with medicines and thus taken – Bl #218

ta·span·hu can \ta-spán-hu can\ *n* **a** : the hawthorn **b** : an apple tree

ta·span on·wo·han·pi \ta-spán òn-wo-han-pi\ *n* : a sauce pan, *i.e.* in which to boil sweets

ta·span o·pe·mni·pi \ta-spán o-pè-mni-pi\ *n* : a pie

ta·span pe·sto·sto·la \ta-spán pe-stò-sto-la\ *n* : a pear – HL

ta·span pu·zya·pi \ta-spán pu-zya-pi\ *n* : dried apples

ta·span·slo·slo·la \ta-spán-slo-slo-la\ *n* : the dwarf red haw - R Bl

ta·spi·ca·hi·ye *or* **taspincahiye** \ṫa-spí-ca-hi-ye\ *n* [fr *icahiya* to mix together] : lemon extract

ta·sp'o·pe·mni·pi \ta-sp'ó-pe-mni-pi\ *n* : an apple pie - P BD

ta·su·su \ta-sú-su\ *n* : the narrow-leaved American vetch, vicia linearis, the pulse family, so called because of its little beans — **tasusu canhlogan** \ta-sú-su caŋ-ḣlò-ġaŋ\ *n* : long-leaved milk vetch, astragalus longifolius, the pulse family - B #156, 252 Bl

ta·su·ta·pa·hu *or* **tasu·tupahu** \ta-sú-ṫa-ṗa-hu\ *n* [fr *tasúsu* vetch + *ṫapahu* its upper stalk] : the vetch bush head - Bl

ta·ši·šake \ta-ší-ša-ke\ *n* : the nails or hoofs of animals - Note: the Dakotas once used them for rattles - R Bl

ta·ši·ya·gnun·pa \ta-ší-ya-gnuŋ-pa\ *n* : the meadow lark - Note: the spelling of the word is doubtfully *tajiyagnunpa*. The meadow lark is a friendly bird to the Dakotas, with its elaborate lingo:

Scepán, mícakca Sister-in-law, comb my hair
Šic'é, mícakce Brother-in-law, comb my hair
He túwa, ti hwo? Whose is it, does he live there?
Kiktápo, wánna ánpa yelo Get up, it's now daylight
Ptehíncala, pí napin Buffalo calf, the liver is tasty
Kóla, ptehíncala wacín yelo Friend, the calf is trying
Kóla, wakínyan ukíyelo, tíyo napá po Friend, thunder is is coming, rush indoors
Kóla, Kiyáksi kiglág aú welo Friend, the Kiyaksi circle are come home - Note: the circle among the Oglala who closely intermarry
Héci cíye t'elo Over there my older brother died
Míye imátancan yelo I am in charge
Íṫoye cik'a tiblo My older brother is of a slight appearance
Wówaglakin kte lo He will give a talk - Bl

- Note: they say two meadow larks meet; the one says: *Tašiyagnunpa, nitákoja wan gli yelo, iwakici yo* Meadow lark, your grandchild got home, dance for him. Whereupon the other dances and sings: *Hahé, híhohó,* or *Híye, ahéye hi* Ha-héy hée-ho-hó *or* Hée-yey a-héy-yey hee

ta·ši·ya·ka \ta-ší-ya-ka\ *n* : the pylorus or lower orifice of the stomach of ruminating animals, the large intestine < ~ *imnáhanhan* the smallest manyple of the large intestine > - Bl

ta·šna·he·ca \ṫa-šná-he-ca\ *n* : the striped ground squirrel — **tašnaheca sinte** \ta-šná-he-ca siŋ-ṫè\ *n* : millet

ta·šo·ka *or* **onweojutonpi** \ta-šō'-ka\ *n* : the fourth cavity of a ruminant's stomach called seed or rennet, abomasus - Bl

ta·šo·ša \ta-šó-ša\ *v* : to spit

ta·špu \ta-šṗú\ *n* **1** : the stem, as of a pumpkin < *unkcela* ~ the cactus berry, *Hehan unkcela* ~ *wicakipazo* He show-ed them the cactus berry at that time. > **2** : a knob, a door-knob

ta·šun·šin \ta-šúŋ-šiŋ\ *n* : the fat on both sides of the neck of a buffalo - Bl

ta·šu·pa *or* **šupe** \ta-šū'-ṗa\ \šu-ṗé\ *n* : intestines, guts < ~ *wašin* fat of the intestines, ~ *can iyawapehan na cewaonpin ktelo* I shall wrap the intestines around a stick and roast them. > - Note: *tašupa can iyapehanpi* dried intestines, casings, filled with fat *etc.* wrapped around a stick and roasted to become sausage *papahyapi*, or *talipa* **2** : a hose, *i.e.* in as much as *tašupe* is applied *fig* to water for a garden *e.g.* or gasoline *etc.*; a hose, because intestines convey the fluids from one place to another

ta·šu·p'kšan·kšan \ta-šú-p'kšaŋ-kšaŋ\ *n* : the intestines — **tašup'o·kahmi** \ta-šú-ṗ'o-kà-ḣmi\ *n* : the gut cavity of a body — **tašup'o·wotanla** *n* : the colon - Bl D.197

ta·šu·ška *or* **tajuška** \ta-šú-ška\ *n* : a common ant < ~ *kinyán* the flying ant, ~ *sápa* the black ant, ~ *šašá* the red ant, which ants are mashed and mixed with other medicines for people to drink when shot > - Bl

ta·ta \ta-tá\ *adj* : dull, blunt, bruised up as the point of a stick *etc.* - R Bl

ta·ta·hu \ta-tá-hu\ *n* : the back of the neck of cattle, the neckbone of animals

ta·ta·hpa \ṫa-tá-ḣpa\ *n* : the breast of young animals where the hair droops over the head and breast of the buffalo, hence the buffalo neck just behind the head < ~ *payápa* being of the upper part of the animal breast, meat on the top of the neck > - Bl KE

ta·ta·mni \ta-tá-mni\ *n* : the womb of animals, that which surrounds the foetus < *Cega wan ile ca* ~ *ota kte lo* "Many will be the kettles ablaze", an old superstitious saying, ~ *onazon* to sew together the womb > - Bl

ta·tan·ka \ta-táŋ-ḱa\ *n* : the male buffalo < ~ *héšlušluta* a buffalo bull with exceptionally smooth horns, ~ *winkte* a buffalo whose testicles are exceptionally small > - Bl

ta·ta·pa \ta-tá-ṗa\ *adj* : almost dry, as laudry, or meat *etc.* hanging in the wind — **tatape·šni** *adj* : still quite wet, as one's wash or meat

ta·ta·po \ta-tá-po\ *n* : the third stomach of ruminating animals, the omasum or manyplies or psalterium - Note: the *tapó* is the fourth stomach, the duodenum

ta·ta·psin \ṫa-ṫá-psiŋ\ *n* : buttons of fat, varied in size and adhering to the inner surface of the chorion membrane which carries the unborn calf, the sweet meat in the *taniga*, the pancreas section of the buffalo cow, the most tasty part of the animal, prepared as a sausage and boiled - Bl KE WHL

ta·ta·wa·blu·ška \ta-tá-wa-blu-ška\ *n* : the horsefly < ~ *ḣóta* the gray horsefly, ~ *sápa* the black horsefly >

ta·ta·wa·blu·ška ta·can·hlo·gan *or* **ónšunkoyušpapi** \ta-tá-wa-blu-ška ta-càŋ-ḣlo-ġaŋ\ *n* : wild honeysuckle, scarlet gaura, gaura coccinea, the evening primrose family - Bl BT #8

ta·te \ta-ṫé\ *n* : wind, *i.e.* in motion

ta·te \ṫá-ṫe\ *or* \ṫá-te\ *n* : hunting, chasing < ~ *ai, ahi* They went or came hunting, *Na le ohakab* ~ *ahi* And after this they came hunting. *Manil tatetipi* They lived alone while he was deer-hunting. > - D.271

ta·te·i·yu·mni \ta-ṫé-i-yu-mni\ *n* : a whirlwind - R Bl

ta·te ka·hwo·gya·pi \ta-ṫé ka-ḣwo-gya-pi\ *n* : a toy for little boys, made so as to sail or float in the wind

ta·te ka·jo \ta-ṫé ka-jò\ *vn* : to storm and make things creak

ta·te·ka·s'a \ta-ṫé-ḱa-s'a\ *v* : to whistle, as the wind

ta·te·o·u·ye \ta-ṫé-o-u-ye\ *n* : a quarter of the heavens < ~ *tópa* the four quarters of the universe >

Ta·te·ta·can·ku \Ta-ṫé-ta-caŋ-ku\ *np* : the Wind River perhaps, a tributary to the Platte River near the center of the State of Wyoming - Bl

ta·te·ya \ṫá-ṫe-ya\ *v* : to hunt < *ṫáṫe aya* to go on a hunt with a large party > - Note: *ṫáṫe* the *n,* hunting

---

\a\ father \e\ they \i\ machine \o\ smoke \u\ lunar \an, aŋ\ blanc Fr. \in, iŋ\ ink \on, oŋ, un, uŋ\ soon, confier Fr. \c\ chair \ġ\ machen Ger. \j\ fusion \clusters: bl, gn, kp, hšl, etc...\ b^{e}lo ... said with a slight vowel **See more in the Introduction, Guide to Pronunciation**

ta·te·yan·pa \ta-ṫé-yaŋ-ṗa\ *n* : a blast of wind — *v* : to blow as the wind, the wind blows < ~ *hi* A heavy wind set in. ~ *kte* There will be a wind storm. > - Cf B.H.43.8 Bl

ta·tin·gle·ska \ta-ṫíŋ-gle-ska\ *n* : intestinal worms

ta·ti·po·gan \ta-ṫí-ṗo-ġaŋ\ *n perhaps* : a wind storm - B.H.195.16

ta·ti·wo·ki·ta·he·na \ta-ṫí-wo-k̇i-ta-he-na\ *adv* : being homeless < *Ito he hecel econpi šni kinhan, oyate ~ iyotiyekiya un tka yešan* Come now, if she does not do things in this way, people in being homeless would be having troubles nonetheless. > - Cf tiwókitahena Bl WHL

ta·ti·ye *or* **tatuye** \ta-ṫí-ye\ *n* : a quarter of the heavens

ta·tka·ša *or* **patkaša** \ta-ṫk̇á-ša\ *n* : a kind of turtle - KE

ta·to·he·ki·ya *or* **tatoheya** \ta-ṫó-he-k̇i-ya\ *adv* : against the wind or current, upstream < ~ *unglapi kte lo.* ~ *yapi* We shall be on our way home upstream. Upstream they went. > - Bl B.H.208.22

ta·to·ka \ta·tó-k̇a\ *n* : the big-horned antelope

ta·to·ka·he cin·ška \ta-tó-k̇a-he ciŋ-škà\ *n* : a spoon or dipper made of the horn of a mountain sheep

ta·to·ka·la \ta-tó-k̇a-la\ *n* : the gazelle or prairie antelope - *Syn* NIGESANLA

ta·to·na *or* **tona** \ta-tó-na\ *n* : a pair < *Hanpa ~ yacin hwo* How many pairs of moccasins do you want? *Na wanna oyate ~ oimniciye k'on he etanhanyan na wanna waci au* And now a pair of tribes who had come for a meeting were from different places, and they came now to dance. >

ta·to·wab \ta-ṫó-wab\ *adv contrac of* tatowapa : upstream, against the wind < ~ *unyanpi* We are going upstream. >

ta·to·wal \ta-ṫó-wal\ *adv contrac of* tatowata : on the windward side of anything < *Mitátowal iyaya* He went on the side where the wind strikes me. >

ta·to·wa·pa \ta-ṫó-wa-pa\ *adv* : up-stream, up the river, against the wind — **tatowapa·tanhan** \ta-ṫó-wa-pa-ṫaŋ-haŋ\ *adv* : from above, *i.e.* perhaps from up stream — **ta·to·wa·ta** *or* **tateowa·tanhan** \ṫa-ṫó-wa-ṫa\ *adv* : with the wind against one < *Komakipapi na mitátowata ece ahiyaya* I was feared while with the wind coming from my direction only sang a tune. > - *Syn* ITATOWATA

ta·tu \tā'-tu\ *n* : a root used as a liniment when boiled, taken as a tea or chewed, to check the spitting of blood - Bl BD

ta·tu·cu·hu \ta-ṫú-cu-hu\ *n* : cutlets, the ribs of cattle < ~ *wapáha* a headdress of ribs >

ta·tun·kce \ta-ṫúŋ-kce\ *n* : manure < ~ *ptaya glepi* a dung hill, ~ *tankálhiyuya* to clean out a stable >.

ta·tu·ye *or* **tatiye** \ta-ṫú-ye\ *n of* tateouye : a quarter of the heavens, as north, east, *etc.* < ~ *tópa* the four quarters, always honored in religious ceremonies by directing the Sacred Pipe *etc.* in these directions, *Le pejuta wan ~ oyasin wapogan kta* I shall blow this medicine here in all directions. >

ta·tu·ye·kta·šni·yan \ṫa-ṫú-ye-kta-šni-yaŋ\ *adv* : with the wind coming sideways, right or left, as in walking

ta·tu·ye on wi·na·h'on \ṫa-ṫú-ye oŋ wi-na-ȟ'oŋ\ *n* : a radio - *Syn* MAZACOLA WINAH'ON, IKANCOLA MAS'ÁPAPI

ta·t'e·ca \ta-t'é-ca\ *n* [fr *ta* a ruminant animal's + *t'eca* a carcass] : the carcass of a ruminant beast - Bl B.H. 246.11

ta·t'e·can·nu·ga \ta-t'é-caŋ-nu-ġa\ *n* : the snakeroot — **tat'ecannunga hu** *n* : the dotted button snakeroot, the blazing star, liatris punctata, the composite family - Note: the plant is said once to have been found in the intenstines of a deer all the contents (excrement) hardened into balls like the bulbous roots of this plant, and hence its name. The roots are pulverized and taken when one does not have an appetite — **tat'ecannunga huiyececa** *n* : the large button snakeroot, the blue blazing star, rattlesnake master, devil's bite, ligulistylis, the composite family - *Syn* WAZIMNINKPA IYECECA BT HM #17, 102 Bl

ta·un·ka·šni \ta-úŋ-ka-šni\ *v* ta·mun·kašni ta·nun·kašni : to be unwilling to do

> < *He ... kola, kola, tatuye*
> *topakiya natan hihu ye*
> *šehan tamunkašni ye.*
> Look here, friend, friend, in directions
> Four he comes to make his attack.
> Hist! Heavens! do not take your rest! - MS.101
> RT >

< *Leconpi tamunkašni* I am unwilling this be done. > - *Syn* TAWAT'ELYEŠNI Bl RT LP

ta·wa \ṫá-wa\ *pron adj* mi·tawa ni·tawa : his, hers, its, *etc.*

ta·wa·cin \ṫa-wá-ciŋ\ *n* mi·tawacin : the mind, will, understanding; disposition, purpose, thought

ta·wa·cin ha·ha·la \ta-wá-ciŋ ha-hà-la\ *adj* : fickle, unsteady - P Bl

ta·wa·cin·han·ska \ta-wá-ciŋ-haŋ-skà\ *adj* : patient, long-suffering — **tawacinhanske·ya** *adv* : patiently

ta·wa·cin·hin·yan·sya·kel \ta-wá-ciŋ-hiŋ-yaŋ-sya-kel\ *adv* : melancholicly — **ta·wa·cin·hin·yan·za** \ṫa-wá-ciŋ-hiŋ-yaŋ-za\ *adj* : morose

ta·wa·cin·ki·c'un \ta-wá-ciŋ-ki-c'uŋ\ *vn* tawacin·we·c'un : to be resolute, obstinate, to have a mind of one's own — **tawacinkic'un·yan** *adv* : resolutely

ta·wa·cin ki·ksu·ya \ta-wá-cin k̇i-ksù-ya\ *v* : to become reasonable again, to assume reason - Bl

ta·wa·cin·ki·ton·yan \ta-wá-ciŋ-k̇i-tòŋ-yaŋ\ *adv* : promisingly, holding great promise - B.H.123.17

ta·wa·cin pan·pan·la \ta-wá-cin pàŋ-paŋ-la\ *adj* : weak minded, credulous, easy to fool - Bl

ta·wa·cin·su·ta \ta-wá-ciŋ-su-ṫa\ *adj* : firm, resolute, not easily influenced — **tawacinsuta·ya** *adv* : resolutely

ta·wa·cin·ši·ca \ta-wá-ciŋ-ši-ca\ *adj* tawacin·ma·šica : of a bad disposition

ta·wa·cin·ši·lwo·te \ṫa-wá-ciŋ-ši-lwo-ṫe\ *vn* tawacinši·lwa·wate : to eat greedily, not wishing to share with others

ta·wa·cin to·ke·ca \ta-wá-ciŋ tò-k̇e-ca\ *adj* : whimsical — *n* : a whim - P

ta·wa·cin t'a·t'a·ka \ta-wá-ciŋ t'a-t'à-ka\ *adj* : stupid - Note: *Waéktanjašni he kapi* Lacking docility is meant P Bl

ta·wa·cin·wan·ka·la \ta-wá-ciŋ-waŋ-ka-la\ *adj* : fickle, easily influenced — **tawacin wašakala** \ta-wá-ciŋ wa-šà-k̇a-la\ *adj* : venal, easily seduced or fooled - *Syn* KAT'INSYA WIYUKCANŠNI, TAWACIN PANPANLA Bl

ta·wa·cin·wa·šte \ta-wá-ciŋ-wa-šte\ *adj* tawacin·ma·wašte : of a good disposition

ta·wa·gan \ta-wá-ġaŋ\ *n* : a step-son or step-daughter, any step relation — **tawagan·ku** \ta-wá-ġaŋ-k̇u\ *n* : his step-son < ~ *winyan* his step-daughter > — **tawagan·ya** *va* : to have for a step-son or step-daughter

ta·wa·i·c'i·ya \tá-wa-i-c'i-ya\ *v refl* : to own one's self, to be free — **tawaic'iya·pi** \tá-wa-i-c'i-ya-pi\ *n* : freedom, liberty

ta·wan·ji \ta-wáŋ-ji\ *n* : a pair, one of anything < *tanúnpa* two pairs, *tayámni* three pairs >

ta·wa·pšun·ka·kan \ta-wá-pšuŋ-k̇a-k̇aŋ\ *n* : the glands on both sides of the throat or neck. - Note: they are so called because they break out on the surface looking like gopher hills which suggest another name, *wahinheya opi*

ta·wa·še \ṫá-wa-še\ *n* mi·tawaše [*mita·waše* is perhaps fr *waše* a woman's female friend, or simply from *tawaše*] : a woman's female friend < *Mitawaše* My friend, is said by women, — **tawaše·tku** *n* [this form too seems to be fr *waše*] : her friend *i.e.* a female friend ~ *kin okiyapi. Na wanna unkitawašetku kin lila ahiyu* Her woman friends are courting him. And now our women friends are really on their way home. > — **tawaše·ya** *v* : to have for a female friend

ta·wa·t'e·lki·ya \ta-wá-t'e-lki-ya\ *va* tawat'e·lwa·kiya : to allow, be willing to have such a thing happen to one — **tawat'e·lya** *va* tawat'e·lwa·ya : to endure, be willing for anything, desirous to do or suffer

ta·wa·ya \ṫá-wa-ya\ *va* ta·wa·waya : to possess anything, have for one's own — **tawe·kiya** \tá-we-k̇i-ya\ *va* : to cause to own - Pb.34 B.H.111.22

ta·we·la·ha \tá-we-la-ha\ *n* : a kind of summertime robe one without hair and so used - R Bl

ta·wi·cu \ṫa-wí-cu\ *n* mita·wicu nita·wicu : his wife — **tawicu·ton** *v* tawicu·wa·ton : to have a wife, to be married

ta·wi·na·pce \ta-wí-na-pce\ *n* : the gullet of animals

ta·win \ta-wíŋ\ *n* mi·tawin ni·tawin : a wife - Note: the word is used only with the *pron, mi* or *ni* — **tawinton** \ta-wíŋ-toŋ\ *va* tawin·wa·ton : to have sexual intercourse with a woman — **tawin·ya** \ṫa-wíŋ-ya\ *va* tawin·wa·ya tawin·ma·ya : to have coitus with a woman

ta·wi·ye·la \ṫa-wí-ye-la\ *n* : a doe or hind, the female of the common deer

ta·wo·e·con \ṫa-wó-e-coŋ\ *n* : his work, business, doing

ta·wo·gmun·ke ka·hya \ta-wó-gmuŋ-k̇e ka-ȟyà\ *express* : He made it to be like a spider's web, as is said *e.g.* of a *tahuka cangleška* a hoop with leather strips criscrossing to make it like a sieve, or say like a pattern in beadwork

Ta·wo·hi·ya·ye Wi·ca·wo·te *or* **Wicawotapi** \Ta-wó-hi-ya-ye Wi-cà-wo-te\ *np* : the Paschal Lamb < ~ *unniciyawinyeyapi* We are preparing for you the Paschal Lamb. > — **Tawohiyaye Wotapi** \Ta-wó-hi-ya-ye Wó-ta-pi\ *np* : the eating of the Paschal Lamb - B.H.251.4, 6, 12, 14, 16, 251.20

ta·wo·kon·ze \ta-wó-k̇oŋ-ze\ *n* nita·wokonze : his influence or purpose - Note: the word is used for the Spirit of God, *e.g. Wakantanka Tawokonze* - R

ta·wo·sa \ta-wō'-sa\ *n* : a lump of fat found on both sides of a cow's neck below, and ordinarily boiled for use

ta·wo·ši·tku \ta-wó-ši-tku\ *n* : his or her helper, one that sides with him or her - Bl

ta·wo·wa·ši \ta-wó-wa-ši\ *n* : an assistant, helper or servant < ~ *kin inahni canpagmiya ikoyagyapi* His assistants tied up the wagon in a hurry. > — **tawowaši·ya** \ṫa-wó-wa-ši-ya\ *va* : to have for a helper, an assistant

ta·wo·yu·te \ta-wó-yu-te\ *n* : his food

ta·wo·ze \ta-wó-ze\ *n* : the fat found behind the ears of buffalo and cattle - Bl

Ta·ya·mni \Ta-yá-mni\ *np* [fr *ta* his + *yamni* three] : a constellation of stars composed of the stars of Orion and the Pleiades of Taurus: the seven stars of the Pleiades in Taurus, ~ *pa* the head of Tayamni; ~ *cankahu* its backbone, *i.e.* the belt or girdle of Orion; ~ *tucuhu* its ribs, *i.e.* the two flanking stars, Betelgeuse and Rigel, each on the opposite side of the studded girdle in Orion; ~ *sinte* the tail of Tayamni, *i.e.* the last of the other large stars of Orion lying off from the tip of Orion's sword - Bl BT

ta·za \tá-za\ *n* : the inner fleshy part of a cow's udder, which is a good dish

te·bki·ci·ci·ya \ṫe-bk̇í-ci-ci-ya\ *v* : to eat up for one — **tebkici·ya** *v* te·bwé·ciya [fr *tebya* to devour] : to eat up provis-ions of any kind for another — **tebkiciya·pi** *v pl* : they eat each other up — **tebki·ya** \ṫe-bk̇í-ya\ *v poss* : to eat up one's own — *va* te·bwá·kiya : to eat up another's for another

te·bte·pa \ṫe-bṫé-ṗa\ *adj red of* tépa : many worn off

te·bya \ṫe-byá\ *va* te·bwa·ya : to eat all up, to devour

te·ca \ṫé-ca\ *adj* : new, young < *niteca k'un hehan* when you were young > — **teca·ya** *va* : to make new, to renew — *adv* : newly — **tecaya·kel** \ṫé-ca-ya-k̇el\ *adv* : newly, in a way freshened - B.H.276.6

te·han \ṫé-haŋ\ *adv* : far, long, *i.e.* in *ref* to time and place < ~ *wote šni* He did not eat for a long time. > — **tehan·han** \ṫé-haŋ-haŋ\ *adv red* : very long < *Hecel lila ~ yanipi kta* You will live a really very long time. >

te·hanl \té-haŋl\ *adv* : far, long < *Lila ~ yapi* They went very far. >

te·han la·ke *or* **tehanlake ci** \té-haŋ la-ke\ *adv* : after a little while < ~ *u wo* Come after a little while. >

te·han·tan *or* **tehantanhan** \té-haŋ-taŋ\ \ṫé-haŋ-taŋ-haŋ\ *adv* : from afar < ~ *teȟiya unkupelo* We came back with difficulty from a long way away. >

te·han·tu *or* **tehantu·ya** *or* **tehantuya·kel** \ṫé-haŋ-ṫu\ \ṫé-haŋ-ṫu-ya-k̇el\ *adv* : far off, to or at a great distance

te·han·wan·kal \ṫé-haŋ-waŋ-k̇al\ *adv* : high up — **tehanwankan·tu** *or* **tehanwankatu·ya** \ṫe-háŋ-waŋ-k̇aŋ-ṫu\ *adv* : very high — **tehanwankatuya·kel** \ṫe-háŋ-waŋ-k̇a-ṫu-ya-k̇el\ *adv* : high up, loftily

te·han·yan \té-haŋ-yaŋ\ *adv* : far away < *Hena yamni ~ yapi* Those three went far away. *Na tokeya šunkakanyanka ~ manipelo* And they were the first to travel far away horseback. *Na taku okiyaka, tka ~ ; heon nawah'on šni* And he said something to him, but he was far away; so I did not hear him. >

te·ȟi \ṫe-ȟí\ *adj* : difficult, hard to be done, hard to be endured — **teȟi·ȟika** \ṫe-ȟí-ȟi-k̇a\ *adj red of* teȟíka : very difficult — **teȟiȟi·ya** *adv red of* teȟiya : hardly, badly, with difficulty — **teȟi·ka** \ṫe-ȟí-k̇a\ *adj* ma·teȟika : hard to do or hear, difficult; *fig* dear, costly, valuable; hard to get along with; unreasonable

te·ȟi·ke·ki·la *or* **teȟikekila·ka** \ṫe-ȟí-k̇e-k̇i-la\ \ṫe-ȟí-k̇e-k̇i-la-k̇a\ *v poss* teȟike·wa·kila [fr *teȟikela* think it hard, of great value] : to value one's own — **teȟikela** *or* **teȟikela·ka** \ṫe-ȟí-k̇e-la\ *va* teȟike·wa·la : to think hard or difficult; to value very much

te·ȟi·la \ṫe-ȟí-la\ *va* te·wa·ȟila : to love, value very highly; to be unwilling to part with

---

\a\ father \e\ they \i\ machine \o\ smoke \u\ lunar \an, aŋ\ blanc Fr. \in, iŋ\ ink \on, oŋ, un, uŋ\ soon, confier Fr. \c\ chair \ġ\ machen Ger. \j\ fusion \clusters: bl, gn, kp, hšl, etc...\ b[e]lo ... said with a slight vowel **See more in the Introduction, Guide to Pronunciation**

te·ȟi·slo·lye·ki·ya \ṫe-ȟí-slo-lya-k̇i-ya\ *v* : to punish, to cause to suffer

te·ȟi-ya *or* **teȟiya·kel** \ṫe-ȟí-ya\ \ṫe-ȟí-ya-k̇el\ *adv* : hardly at all, with diffiiculty, badly < ~ *econ* to do with difficulty, to do badly, ~ *owah'an yelo, omakih'an yelo, waku welo* I came back, he worked for me, I did the work badly. > - Bl

te·ȟi·ya·ku·wa \ṫe-ȟí-ya-k̇u-wa\ *va* : to follow after for evil, to persecute, to treat badly

te·hmi·so·ha \ṫe-ȟmí-so-ha\ *n* : a tanned hide - *Syn* TEHPICEHA — **tehmiso·pi** *n* : a leather strap - WR

te·hmun·ga \ṫe-ḫmúŋ-ġa\ *n* : the horsefly, flies - *Syn* TATAWABLUŠKA

te·hpi \ṫe-ḫṗí\ *n* : a skin with the hair removed and worn as a blanket - *Syn* PTEHAŠLA — **tehpi·ceha** *n* : a tanned hide - *Syn* TEHMISOHA — **tehpi hanpa** *n* : moccasins with the roughsurface of the skin outside - Bl

te·hpi·wi·kan \ṫe-ḫṗí-wi-k̇aŋ\ *n* : a strap cut from a dry hide

te·ki·ci·ȟi·la \ṫe-k̇í-ci-ȟi-la\ *v* : to value, hold precious for one, as a mother values her child or does things for it in the name of her child - B.

te·ku·i·yu·ta·pi \ṫe-k̇ú-i-yu-ṫa-pi\ *n* : a pound measure

te·mni \ṫe-mní\ *vn* te·ma·mni te·un·mni·pi : to sweat, to pant, give out — **temni·t'a** *vn* temni·ma·t'a : to sweat profusely, to die of sweating < *Šunka temnit'api ktelo* Dogs will die sweating, as is said when predicting a warm day. > — **temnit'e·yela** *adv* : perspiring profusely < ~ *wowaši econ* to do one's work, dripping with sweat. > — **temni·yan** *adv* : sweating < *Ite ~ wayatapi ktelo* They will chew with faces sweating. > - B.H.235. 15 Bl BT

te·pa \ṫé-ṗa\ *adj root* : worn off < *katépa* to wear out by striking > — **tepa·han** \ṫe-ṗá-haŋ\ *part* : worn off

te·šlag \ṫe-šlág\ *v contrac of* tešlaka : to wear, have on —**tešla·gkiton** \ṫe-šlá-gk̇i-toŋ\ *v* : to put on or wear *e.g.* a crown or fillet on the head; to don a so-called Lakota hat, which has no roof but only a rim — **tešla·gkiya** \ṫe-šlá-gk̇i-ya\ *va* : to make one wear on the head, as a wreath *etc.* — **tešla·gton** *v* tešla·gwa·ton : to put on or wear a fillet around the head - Pb.38

te·šla·ka \ṫe-šlá-ka\ *v* te·wa·šlaka : to wear, as a crown or fillet, around the head < *Ha kin le hanke tewašlakin kte* I shall wear a part of this hide, as a head-piece. > - D.23

te·wa·pa \ṫe-wá-pa\ *n* : an esculent root that grows in the water, which is taken, boiled, and eaten - R Bl

te·wi·ca·mni \ṫe-wí-ca-mni\ *n of* temní : one's sweating

te·ya \ṫé-ya\ *n* : one who has more than one wife — **teya·kiciyapi** \ṫé-ya-k̇i-ci-ya-pi\ *n pl* : those who stand in the relation of *téya* to each other — **teya·ku** \ṫé-ya-k̇u\ *n* : her *téya* — **teya·ya** *va* teya·wa·ya : to have one for a *téya* a sort of consort

te·zi \ṫe-zí\ *n* : the stomach < ~ *natiptipa* stomach cramps >

ti \ṫi\ *vn* wa·tí : to live, dwell, abide — *n* : a house - *Syn* TÍPI

ti·a·ka·sta·ka \ṫi-á-ka-sta-k̇a\ *v* : to daub a house - IS

ti·a·ka·šlu·ta \ṫi-á-k̇a-šlu-ṫa\ *n* : a trowel - P Bl

ti·a·nun·ka·tan·han \ṫi-á-nuŋ-k̇a-taŋ-haŋ\ *adv* : in both sides of the house

ti·a·pi·ya \ṫi-á-ṗi-ya\ *v* : to repair a house

ti·a·wan·yan·ka \ṫi-á-waŋ-yaŋ-ka\ *v* : to stand guard about a house, to stay at home and watch the house

ti·blo \ṫi-bló\ *n* ni·tíblo : a woman's older brother, my elder brother, as used by women — **tiblo·ku** *n* : her elder brother — **tiblo·ya** \ṫi-bló-ya\ *va* tiblo·wa·ya : to have for an elder brother

ti·ca \ṫí-ca\ *v root* : scraping < *patica* to scrape off by hand >

ti·ca·ga \ṫi-cá-ġa\ *v* ti·wa·kaga [fr *ti* house + *kaga* to make] : to put up a tent, to build a house

ti·ca·han \ṫi-cá-haŋ\ *part* : scraped off, falling off of itself

ti·ca·ni·ca \ṫí-ca-ni-ca\ *n* : the long-billed curlew, having a long thin bill < ~ *s'e pasu kin lehanhci* Like the curlew, his nose is really this long, as is said of a man with a long nose. > - Note: its whistle goes: *Mnišwū, mnišwū* Water-splash, water-splash...(trembling sound) The *ticanica tanka* sings: *Optepteptecela, optepteptecela.* The sound seems built on the *red* word pteptecela really short - FR Bl LT IS

ti·ca·ni·ca hu \ṫí-ca-ni-ca hu\ *n* : the psoralea, a plant growing on the prairie, similar to the wild turnip, but not hairy like it. Its tough stems when green once were made into a sort of basket to carry meat in the home. It is also used as a medicine — **ticanica hu ȟolȟota** *n* : the silver-leaf psoralea, the psoralea argophylla, the pulse family - Note: its root is fed to horses when they are tired — **ticanica hu tanka** *n* : the large few-flowered psoralea , psoralea tenuiflora, the pulse family - Note: a tea is made from the root as a remedy for headache; a smudge made from the plant is specially good against mosquitoes — **ticanica tinpsila** *n* : wild alfalfa, psoralea digitata, the pulse family - BT #3, 13, 187 Bl Lhb

ticankahu \ṫi-cáŋ-ka-hu\ *n* [fr *ti* house + *cankahu* spine, backbone] : the long cross beam of a roof against which both sides rest

ti·ca·tka·ya·ta·han \ṫi-cá-tka-ya-ta-haŋ\ *adv* : at the left side of a tent, to the left of the *catku* chest — *n* : the left part of the tent or house opposite the door, *i.e.* the place of honor — **ticatku·ta** \ṫi-cá-tk̇u-ṫa\ *adv* : opposite the door

ti·ce \ṫi-cé\ *n* : the roof, the ceiling; the top of a tent or house, the smoke hole vent — **tice·inkpa** *or* **ticeška** \ṫi-cé-iŋ-kṗa\ \ṫi-cé-šk̇a\ *n* : the top of a tent, the ridge of a house — **ticeška·ohloka** \ṫi-cé-ška-o-ȟlo-ka\ *n* : the hole at the top of the tent by which smoke escapes — **tico·hloka hukutahan** \ṫi-có-ȟlo-ka hu-kú-ta-haŋ\ *n* : the part just below the tent hole, in the front and above the *wicéška* vent hole — **ticohloke** *n* : the vent hole at the tent top — **tico·pa** \ṫi-có-pa\ *n* : the center hole of a tent

ti·gi·ya·pi \ṫi-ġí-ya-pi\ *n* : a tipi painted brown

ti·gle \ṫi-glé\ *v* ti·wa·gle ti·un·gle·pi : to make a home, to have a family, to be married

ti·gli·yo·ya \ṫi-glí-yo-ya\ *v* : to come and camp at the place of hunting and butchering buffalo < *Toketu keš yukpanhan po, ota yaopi kin na tigliyounyanpi ktelo* No matter what, do the grinding, and when you shoot many we shall come and camp at the butchering site. > - Bl

ti·glo·ni·ca \ṫi-gló-ni-ca\ *v* ti·wa·glonica : to forbid one's house, to prevent others from coming in

ti·glu·hla·gan šni \ṫi-glú-ȟla-ġaŋ šni\ *v* : to always stay at home

ti·glu·ju·ju \ṫi-glú-ju-ju\ *v poss of* yujuju : to fold up one's tent - B.H.12.4

ti·hu·ȟa \ṫi-hú-ȟa\ *n* : the poles of a tent left standing, the skeleton of a tent or of a log house — **tihuȟa·ka** *n* : the skeleton of a tent, an unfinished log house - R Bl

ti·ȟa·ha *or* **tiȟamnamna** \ṫí-ȟa-ha\ *n* : the second of the stomach cavities, the reticulum - Cf R under iȟa-ha Bl

ti·ȟa-mna·mna \ti-ȟa-mna-mna\ *n* : the second of the stomach cavities in ruminants, the honey comb or reticulum, next in size to the *taniga* paunch < ~ *wan ena tacupe wan hecel mak'u ca iwacu na wawata* So when she gave me some honey-comb and marrow, I took and ate it. >

ti·i·ca·ska·pi \ti-í-ca-ska-pi\ *n* : a trowel

ti·i·han·ke \ti-í-haŋ-ke\ *n* : a house nearly completed; the corner of a house, perhaps - B.H.240.10, 281.13

ti·i·ȟe·ya·pa·ya \ti-í-ȟe-ya-pa-ya\ *adv* : out on the prairie

ti·i·kce·ya·kel \ti-í-kce-ya-kel\ *adv* : in tents < ~ *ti* to live in tents > - B.H.6.6

ti·i·pa·sla·te *or* **tipaslate** \ti-í-pa-sla-te\ *n* : a brace with which to support a roof, a pillar - B

ti·i·pa·so·tka \ti-í-pa-so-tka\ *n* : a tower - B.H.239.3

ti·i·san·ye \ti-í-saŋ-ye\ *n* : paint

ti·i·šla·ya·ta·han \ti-í-šla-ya-ta-haŋ\ *n* : the right side of a tent, the right of the *catku* place of honor opposite the door

ti·i·ya·za \ti-í-ya-za\ *adv* : from house to house < ~ *tiole ayin kte* He will begin hunting for a place from house to house. > - Bl

ti·i·yo·ka·hmi \ti-í-yo-ka-ȟmi\ *n* : a corner of a room < ~ *ke'l* or *tiúngnaga k'el* in the corner or a rooom > - Bl

ti·i·yu·pah \ti-í-yu-paȟ\ *adv perhaps* : "bag and baggage", "of the whole bunch" - B.H.39.2

ti·ka·i·te·pa \ti-ká-i-te-pa\ *n perhaps* : a pent house, a shed or little house with a roof only on one side and built onto another, a lean-to - Note: *kaitepa* to cut diagonally, *kaitebya* slanting

ti·ka·un·ka \ti-ká-uŋ-ka\ *n perhaps* [fr *kaunka* to fell] : a tent or house knocked down by the wind - *Syn* OWANKA

ti·ki·ci·i \ti-kí-ci-i\ *v* ti·we·cii ti·mi·cii : to visit one another - Bl

ti·kte \ti-kté\ *va* ti·wa·kte : to commit murder - D.249

ti·kti·ca \ti-ktí-ca\ *or* \ti-ktí-ca\ *adj* : thick, as hair, stiff, as mush, sticky - R BD

til \til\ *adv phr contrac* [fr *ti* house + *el* in, into] : in the house < *Til hiyu* He came in the house. >

ti·la \tí'-la\ *v of* ti wa·tla : to dwell, live < *kici* ~ to take sides with >

ti·le·hang \ti-lé-haŋg\ *v contrac* tilehanyang : to pay a visit < ~ *iyayelo* He went visiting. > — **tilehanyang ya** *v* : to go visiting < *Tilehanyang yešni waun* I am not going visiting. > - Bl FE

ti·ma·hel *or* **timahe** \ti-má-hel\ *adv* : inside the house, within < ~ *iyayapi, i* He, they went indoors. > — **timahetakiya** \ti-má-he-ta-ki-ya\ *adv* : toward the interior — **timahe·tanhan** \ti-má-he-taŋ-haŋ\ *adv* : from within — **timahe·tu** \ti-má-he-tu\ *adv* : within

ti·ma·ma i·ya·ya \ti-má-ma i-yà-ya\ *v* : to go in to more than one thing - B.H.50.3

tin·gle·ška \tíŋ-gle-ška\ *n* : a fawn — **tingleška·la** *or* **takingleškala** \ta-kíŋ-gle-ška-la\ *n* : the young of deer, so called because they are spotted *i.e. gleška* < *Nige kinhan ~ s'e leniceca yelo* Your belly is much like that of this young deer's, as was once said of the old men whose abdomens became spotted from exposure when they did not wear clothing that covered that part. > - Bl

tin·psi·la \tíŋ-psi-la\ *n* : the wild turnip, the prairie apple, pomme blanche, psoralea esculenta, the pulse family < ~ *kin wicapahli s'e hinapelo* The turnip rises as do sniffles. ~ *kin itka na hcá yelo ca wagacan sekse hiyeyelo* When the turnip seedpods blossom they start out like the cottonwoods. >

tin·psi·la pe·ju·ta \tíŋ-psi-la pe-jù-ta\ *n* : the narrow-leaved milkweed, acerates angustifolia, the milkweed family - Note: the root is given to children when they have no appetite CH #257

tin·psin·la i·tka·hca wi \tíŋ-psiŋ-la i-tkàk-ȟca wi\ *n* : the month of June, when the seedpods of the wild turnip blossom

tin·psin·la ska·ska \tíŋ-psiŋ-la ska-ska\ *n* : the white turnip

tin·psin·la ša·ša \tíŋ-psiŋ-la ša-ša\ *n* : the raddish, the beet

tin·psin·la zi·zi \tíŋ-psiŋ-la zi-zi\ *n* : the carrot

tin·sko \tíŋ-sko\ *adv interrog* : how large? - Note: the word is used *esp* as a rhetorical question — **tinskokeca** \tíŋ-sko-ke-ca\ *adv interrog* : how big, large? - R Note: *hinskokeca adv* : so large, so great — **tinskoskokeca** \tíŋ-sko-sko-ke-ca\ *adv red interrog* : how big?

tin·sko·sko·ya \tíŋ-sko-sko-ya\ *adv red interrog of* tinskoya : how far around? how extensively? < *Ka ~ anikpablaye* How far around there did you spread youself?, *i.e.* you certainly spread your ignorance over a great area. > - D.72, 75

tin·ško·la \tíŋ-ško-la\ *adv interrog* : of what size, how small? - Note: *hinskola* is a direct *adv,* so small

tin·tin·yan \tiŋ-tíŋ-yaŋ\ *adj perhaps* [fr *t'int'in* to dry up] : lean, beginning to dry up < *Tahu kin* ~ The back of his neck is lean. > - *Syn* TAMAHECA

tin·yan·ka *or* **tóhinyanka** \tíŋ-yaŋ-ka\ *v imper* : Hold off!, Wait a minute!

ti·o·ki·ta·he·na \ti-ó-ki-ta-he-na\ *n* : the space in between farms and ranches - Br

ti·o·ko \ti-ó-ko\ *n* : a house yard

ti·o·kšan \ti-ó-kšaŋ\ *adv* : around the house, inside or outside < ~ *wawakita* I took a look around the house, inside and out. >

ti·o·kšu \ti-ó-kšu\ *va* tio·wa·kšu : to carry into the house < *Na woyute tokel hokšicala kin yutin kte cin* ~ And she brought food into the house, as the baby was about to eat. >

ti·o·kte \ti-ó-kte\ *v* : to commit homicide, murder, to kill in the house, in distinction from killing in war

ti·o·le \ti-ó-le\ *v* : to hunt a house for lodging or for a meal < ~ *mni kta* I shall go hunt a house for lodging. >

ti·o·na·blu \ti-ó-na-blu\ *v* tiona·wa·blu : to raise dust with the feet in the house

ti·o·na·ki·pa \ti-ó-na-ki-pa\ *v* : to flee to the house

ti·o·na·pa \ti-ó-na-pa\ *v* tiona·wa·pa : to flee to, take refuge in the house < *Ikce wicaša tipi kin tionawapa nuns'elececa yelo* It was just about like my taking refuge in an unruly man's house. >

ti·o·sni \ti-ó-sni\ *adj* : cold in the house

ti·o·špa·ye \ti-ó-špa-ye\ *n* : a party under one chief, a clan, a band

ti·o·wa \ti-ó-wa\ *n* : a painted tipi or tent < *witiowapi* a tipi with a picture of the sun painted above the door > - Note: *tišayapi* a red painted tipi

ti·o·wan·ji·la \ti-ó-waŋ-ji-la\ *adj perhaps* : living with others < ~ *ti* to live in one house with others, living in

\a\ father \e\ they \i\ machine \o\ smoke \u\ lunar \an, aŋ\ blanc Fr. \in, iŋ\ ink \on, oŋ, un, uŋ\ soon, confier Fr. \c\ chair \ġ\ machen Ger. \j\ fusion \clusters: bl, gn, kp, hšl, etc...\ b^{e}lo ... said with a slight vowel **See more in the Introduction, Guide to Pronunciation**

one house > - B.H.99.2

ti·o·yan·ka·pi \ti-ó-yaŋ-k̇a-pi\ *n* : a room - Bl

ti·pa \ṫí-ṗa\ *v* : to draw up, cramp - Cf yutípa

ti·pa·hin \ṫí-ṗa-hiŋ\ *n of* ipahin : his or her pillow

ti·pa·kel \ṫí-pa-k̇el\ *n* : the meat behind the head over the spinal column of buffalo - HH Bl

ti·paòsla·te \ṫi-ṗá-sla-ṫe\ *n* : a pillar of a house < *tiípa-slate* a brace or support > - B.H.77.23

ti·pi \ṫí-ṗi\ *n* : a tent, house, dwelling < ~ *wakan* a church, a place of prayer and ceremony >

ti·pi i·pa·so·tka·ya \ṫí-ṗi i-pà-so-tka-ya\ *n* : a church tower, as it seems to suggest a *wahukeza* spear when ornamented, thin and tapering to about six or seven feet in height

ti·pi i·yo·ki·he \ṫí-ṗi ì-yo-k̇i-he\ *n* : a house next to

ti·pi i·yo·ki·he·ya *or* **ti·pi·yo·ki·he·ya** \ṫí-ṗi i-yò-k̇i-he-ya\ \ṫí-ṗi-yò-k̇i-he-ya\ *n* : a council tent, constructed by joining a number of tents and capable of seating about 500 persons at once - D.3, 225, 246, 3 note 3

ti·pi·la \ṫí-pi-la\ *n* : a little house < *Mato Tipila kin hetan ilalapi kte lo* You all will go from the Bear's Lodge.>

ti·pi wa·kan \ṫí-pi wa-kàŋ\ *n* : a church, a sacred house

ti·pi·yo·ki·he \ṫí-pi-yo-k̇i-he\ *n* : a council tent - *See* ti-pi ìyokihe

ti·sam \ṫi-sám\ *adv* : beyond the tent or house, on the other side of the house - Note: *hosám* beyond the camp

ti·san·pa·ta·han \ṫi-sáŋ-pa-ta-haŋ\ *n* : the side wall of a tent, *i.e.* inside

ti·sa·pa \ṫi-sá-ṗa\ *n* : the top of a buggy

ti·sto co·ni·ca \ṫí-sto ċo-nì-ca\ *n* : a part of the meat on the shoulder blades of a buffalo - *Syn* IYUH'EYAYAPI HH Bl

ti·ša·ya·pi \ṫi-šá-ya-pi\ *n* : a tipi painted red

ti·ška·kan \ṫí-ška-kaŋ\ *n of* iškakan : the large sinew or muscle in the neck < ~ *kajalya yanka* The neck muscles were stretched apart, as when the two muscles are very prominent with lean persons and form a cavity between them. > - Bl

ti·šta·šin \ṫí-šta-šiŋ\ *n* : the fat behind the eyes at the temples of buffalo and cattle - Bl

ti·ta·he·pi·ya \ṫi-ṫá-he-ṗi-ya\ *n* : the middle part of a tent between the *wipá* vent flaps and the *wihuta ša* lowest part of the tent where it is pinned and usually painted red < ~ *kaȟol yeya* to make go gray the mid-part of the tent sides > — *adv* : on the tent wall - D.247 B.H. 140.5

ti·ta·ku·ye \ṫí-ṫa-k̇u-ye\ *n* : the immediate relatives - D.230

ti·tan \ṫi-ṫáŋ\ *v* : to pull to or in a certain direction < *Cante kin nahahci wakan wicoh'an etkiya ~ yelo* His heart was yet drawn toward a sacred ceremony. *Isam yatitan kte šni* You should not bother one, *i.e.* for something. ~ *šni s'e mani* It walks without seeming to pull. > - Bl BT

ti·tan wa·ya·wa \ṫí-ṫaŋ wa-yà-wa\ *v* : to attend a day school

ti·ta·zi·pe \ṫi-ṫá-zi-pe\ *n of* itazipa : his bow

ti·to·kanl \ṫi-ṫó-kaŋl\ *adv* : as a guest < ~ *un, i, hi* to be a guest, to go as a guest, to arrive as a guest > - P

Ti·ton·wan \Ṫí-ṫoŋ-waŋ\ *np* [fr *tinta, obsol* + *tonwan* arrows] : the Tetons, those bands of the Dakotas living on and beyond the Missouri River west, in the states of North and South Dakota. - Note: they probably represent the majority of the entire Sioux Nation. Their language differs from the the dialects of the other bands in their use of "l" for "d" - R

ti·tu·tu·ka \ṫí-ṫu-ṫu-k̇a\ *v* : to spoil or tire of visiting < ~ *wímapi yelo* I am full up and tired of visiting, as is said when one comes from other houses where he got his fill. > - Bl

ti·un·gna·ga \ṫi-úŋ-gna-ġa\ *n* : the corner of a room < ~ *k'el* in the corner > -*Syn* TIÍYOKAHMI Bl

ti·un·ma k'el ya \ṫi-úŋ-ma k'el ya\ *v phr* : to go visiting < ~ *mni kte lo* I shall go visiting. > - Bl

ti·un·na·ptan·yan \ṫi-úŋ-na-pṫaŋ-yaŋ\ *n of* unnaptan : the sides of a house, sides of the roof

ti·wa·he \ṫi-wá-he\ *n* un·tiwahe·pi : a household, *i.e.* including persons as well as things

ti wa·kpa·la el *or* **tipi wakpala el** \ṫí wa-k̇ṗà-la el\ *phr* : a house or houses standing on a creek

ti·wan·ka·ta \ṫi-wáŋ-ka-ṫa\ *adv* : upstairs

ti·wi·ca·kte \ṫí-wi-ca-k̇te\ *n* : a murderer — *va* tiwica·wa·kte : to commit murder < *Na wanjini ~ heca kte šni* And a murderer should not kill anyone. > — **tiwicakte·pi** *n* : murder

ti·wo·han \ṫi-wó-haŋ\ *adv* : between, among the tents < ~ *omanipi* They walked among the tents. > - Cf égna — **tiwohan·han** *adv red* : many among the tents < *Wanna ihinhana yunkan tatanka kin ~ ahiyu* Now it was the next day and the buffalos came out among the tents. > - B.H.89.9 D.209

ti·wo·ki·ta·he·na *or* **tiyokitahena** *or* **tatiwokitahena** \ṫi-wó-k̇i-ta-he-na\ *adv* : away from houses, being homeless, from a woman not being willing and ready to confront her own motherhood and the problems attendant upon it < *Ito he hecel econpi šni kinhan, oyate ~ iyotiyekiya un tka yešan* Come now, if that is not done, people homeless would nonetheless be having troubles. > — *n* : the wilderness < ~ *onápeya un* to be a fugitive, ~ *ounye* He lives in the wilderness. > - B.H.6.3, 173.1

ti·wo·sla·ta \ṫi-wŏ'-sla-ṫa\ *n* : a miner's tent, without side walls and roof-like

ti·ya·ki·hpe·ca \ṫi-yá-ki-ȟpe-ca\ *adj* : having fallen in with one, *i.e.* one of the household because of the close environment, as is said of a young man wanting to marry a relative - *See* ómniyela HH

ti·yan·ka yo \ṫí-yaŋ-k̇a yo\ *interj* [perhaps fr *ito* come now + *hi* arrive + *yanka* to be] : Wait!, Hold on!, as is said interrupting one in his speech or action *etc.* - Note: the word is not a *deriv* of *ṫo* and *inyanka*

ti·ya·pa kte \ṫi-yá-ṗa kte\ *va* : to massacre — **tiyapa wicaktepi** *n* : a massacre - B Bl

ti·ya·ta \ṫi-yá-ṫa\ *adv* : at the house, at home

ti·ya·ta·ki·ya \ṫi-yá-ṫa-k̇i-ya\ *adv* : toward the house, home < ~ *inyanke* He ran toward home. >

ti·ya·ta·na \ṫi-yá-ṫa-na\ *adv* : at home - B.H.34.8, 115.5

ti·ye·pa \ṫi-yé-ṗa\ *n* : the door of a tent, consisting of a piece of leather < ~ *canyúktan* the two flaps which the upper part of a tent can be closed or opened, *i.e.* the *wipípaha,* ~ *hukútahan* the part of a tent below the door and corresponding to a door sill > — **tiyepa·ta** \ṫi-yé-ṗa-ṫa\ *adv* : at the door

ti·ye·ya·ke \ṫi-yé-ya-k̇e\ *adv* : in camp, as for the winter < ~ *wicayuš'inyeya* He frightened them in camp, *i.e.* surprising them in their winter quarters. > - Bl

ti·yo \ṫi-yó\ *adv root* : inside, within, the same as the *root, timá*

ti·yob \ṫi-yób\ *n contrac of* tiyopa : door, an entrance

ti·yo·bco·ka·ton \ṫi-yó-bco-k̇a-ṫoŋ\ *v* : to clear the middle by raising the pole opening the top of a tipi from within — *n* : the middle part of a tipi - Bl KE WHL

ti·yo·ble·ca \ṫi-yó-ble-ca\ *n* : a square tent, with corners *obleca,* not a Dakota tent

ti·yo·ble·ze šni s'e škan \ti-yó-ble-ze šni s'e škaŋ\ *v phr* : to move about, *i.e.* to stir excitedly in the house without accomplishing anything – Bl

ti·yo·bya \ti-yó-bya\ *va* tiyo·bwa·ya : to have or use for a door

ti·yo·gna·ka \ti-yó-gna-ka\ *n* : the household

ti·yo·gna·škin·yan s'e škan \ti-yó-gna-škiŋ-yan s'e škaŋ\ *v phr* : to hustle and bustle about the house accomplishing nothing – *Syn* TIYOBLEZE ŠNI S'E ŠKAN Bl

ti·yo·han·ko·ki·pa *or* **tiohankokipa** \ti-yó-haŋ-ko-ki-pa\ \ti-ó-haŋ-ko-ki-pa\ *v* : *fig* to be hungry, *i.e.* to be afraid of the ghosts in the night < *Tiyohankowakipelo* I am hungry! *wanagi el mahipelo* ghosts have come to me! > – Note: this may be said in daytime too, and it is also said of one who comes first for a big meeting but remains alone for a long time and so uses up his provisions

ti·yo·he \ti-yó-he\ *n* : a household, a place where a house once stood, a deserted house – Note: *tiwahe* a house well inhabited

ti·yo·hi·yu·kša \ti-yó-hi-yu-kša\ *v* : to remain or wander about in the house < ~ *nankahe* You just sit and remain in the house. > – Bl WHL LHB

ti·yo·ȟa \tí-yo-ȟa\ *n* [fr *ta* buffalo + *iyoȟa* cheek] : the cheek of a buffalo < *Lel tiyoȟaš wicoti* Here there dwelt a village of buffalos (cheeks). > – Bl

ti·yo·ȟe·yun·ka \ti-yó-ȟe-yuŋ-ka\ *n* [fr *ti* house + *ȟeyunka* frost] : frost settling on the inside wall of houses or tents < *Can ota anpo* ~ *au welo* At dawn frost settled on many trees. > – BT

ti·yo·ȟe·un·ka wi \ti-yó-ȟe-uŋ-ka wi\ *np* : the month of February, when there is frost inside the house < *Can ota anpo* ~ *au welo* In February frost settles for many days at dawn. > – BT

ti·yo·hwa·i·c'i·ya \ti-yó-ȟwa-i-c'i-ya\ *v* : to rest – Bl

ti·yo·ka·lya \ti-yó-ka-lya\ *v* tiyoka·lwa·ya : to warm up a room < ~ , *hececa kin mabliheca kte lo* It warms up the room; when it is such, I'll be busy.> – Bl

ti·yo·ka·ška·pi s'e škan \ti-yó-ka-ška-pi s'e škaŋ\ *v phr* : to move away from somebody, disliking him, as far as one can in a room, thus acting like a timid horse *etc.* that is tied but tries to get away when someone comes near – Bl

ti·yo·ka·winh \ti-yó-ka-wiŋȟ\ *v contrac* [fr *ti* house + *okawinga* go around in] : to go around in a circle in the house < ~ *omani* to travel in a circle in the house >

ti·yo·ki·ta·he·na *or* **tiokitahena** *or* **tiwokitahena** \ti-yó-ki-ta-he-na\ *adv* : between houses — *n* : spaces between farms or ranches – Br

ti·yo·ki·ti \ti-yó-ki-ti\ *n* : one who lives in his own tipi < ~ *wan* Even he is one who lives in his own tipi, as is said of one who, owning a tipi, is buried in it, *i.e.* resting on a scaffold. Once one who had no tipi was placed on the scaffold without a tent around it. > – D.227 Cf MS.487

ti·yo·ko \ti-yõ'-ko\ *adv* : between houses – Note: tióko

ti·yo·ku·ta \ti-yó-ku-ta\ *adv* : downstairs

ti·yo·lo·lya \ti-yó-lo-lya\ *v* : to go and rent a house – Bl

ti·yo·mna·ki·ya \ti-yó-mna-ki-ya\ *va* : to gather one's own in the bin, to store up – B.H.174.10

ti·yo·pa \ti-yó-pa\ *n* : a door, the place of entrance
~ *gmigmá* or ~ *gmigméla* a door knob, a small door knob
~ *iyókatkuge* a nail, nails, screws, *i.e.* such as are used in connection with a door
~ *oyútkogi* a door lock, a padlock

ti·yo·pa·ta \ti-yó-pa-ta\ *adv* : at the door

ti·yo·pa wi·ši·mna·ye \ti-yó-pa wi-ši-mna-ye\ *n* : a publican, a toll collector – B.H.232.1

ti·yo·pe·ya·pi \ti-yó-pe-ya-pi\ *n* : the camping around a herd of buffalo – Note: it is said this was done in days past when this animal was gentle – Bl

ti·yo·p'i·ku·še \ti-yó-p'i-ku-šè\ *n* [fr *tiyopa* door + *ikúše* to block] : the bolt of a door on the inside – Note: *ikušeya* in the way of

ti·yo·p'i·na·ta·ke \ti-yó-p'i-na-ta-ke\ *n* : a door lock

ti·yo·p'i·pa·ta·ke \ti-yó-p'i·pà-ta-ke\ *n* : a stick to hold the door of a tent tight from within – Bl

ti·yo·šlo·la \ti-yó-šlo-la\ *adj* : with a kind of rolling sound in the house < *wabluška* ~ a cricket >

ti·yo·špa·ye *or* **tiošpaye** \ti-yó-špa-ye\ *n* : a community, a band, a division of a tribe

ti·yo·ta·he·na *or* **tiwotahena** \ti-yó-ta-he-na\ *adv* : away from any house < ~ *owanjigjila yanka yo* Stay at home. > – *See* iyótahena and its sense – RF

ti·yo·ta·te·šni \ti-yó-ta-te-šni\ *n* : a close, warm room – P Bl

ti·yo·ti \ti-yó-ti\ *v* tiyo·un·ti·pi : to set up a soldiers' lodge — **tiyoti·pi** *n* : a soldiers' lodge, one set up for the purpose of making laws generally to regulate the buffalo chase and to provide for their being carried into effect

ti·yo·ton·wan \ti-yó-toŋ-waŋ\ *v* [fr *ti* house + *otonwan* to look in] : to look into a house

ti·yo·t'e·ble·ze šni s'e škan \ti-yó-t'e-ble-ze šni s'e škaŋ\ *v phr* : to move about excitedly in the house without accomplishing anything – *Syn* TIYOGNAŠKINYAN S'E ŠKAN Bl

ti·yo·wo·sla·ta \ti-yó-wo-sla-ta\ *n* : a wall in a house – P

ti·yu·kan \ti-yú-kaŋ\ *v of* yukán : to leave the house, as is said when the women and children leave the tent for the men to feast in it – *Syn* KIYUKAN

ti·yu·ktan hpa·ya \ti-yú-ktaŋ ȟpà-ya\ *vn* : to sleep in a *tiyuktan wakeyapi* a round lodge like a sweatlodge — **tiyuktan wakeyapi** *n* : a round lodge like a sweatlodge – Note: when a person had no tent while travelling, he would take any sticks, bend and slip them in the ground and cover them with hides. *See* wakéya, [3]kéya 1

tka \tka\ *conj contrac* [fr *tuká*, in the *wiciyela* Dakota dialect] : but < *Mni el iyayapi na minit'api,* ~ *kitanyehci glinapapi* They went into the water and drowned, but at last they came out. > – B.H.174.15, 182.3 — *partic* : – the sign of the subjunctive — *va* wa·tka : to scrape the hair off a hide — *adj* matka : heavy

tka·bya \tká-bya\ *adv* : stiffly

tka kin *or* **tka k'un** \tka kiŋ\ *partic* in *comb contr* to fact < *Tawa tka k'un. Jesus oyusinka tka k'un* He would have owned it. He would have hated Jesus. > – B.H.204.15, 109.10, 114.4, 115,23, 119.1,6, 14 0.4, 157.19, 289.27, 271.3 278.9

tka·pa \tká-pa\ *adj* : adhesive, clammy, as rice when there is hardly any water in it

tkaš \tkaš\ *part emph of* tka : on the other hand < *Yuš'inyemaya* ~ On the other hand he frightened me. >

tke *or* **tka** \tke\ *adj* : heavy — **tke·iyuta** \tke-i-yú-ta\ *va* tkei·blu·ta *or* tkeiyu·wa·ta : to take up and feel the

---

\a\ father \e\ they \i\ machine \o\ smoke \u\ lunar \an, aŋ\ blanc Fr. \in, iŋ\ ink \on, oŋ, un, uŋ\ soon, confier Fr. \c\ chair \ġ\ machen Ger. \j\ fusion \clusters: bl, gn, kp, hšl, etc...\ b[e]lo ... said with a slight vowel
See more in the Introduction, Guide to Pronunciation

weight, to weigh anything — **tke·tke** \tke-tké\ *adj red* : many heavy — **tke·uta** \tke-ú-ta\ *va* tkeu·wa·ta : to weigh anything — **tke·ya** \tk̇é-ya\ *adv* : heavily

tke·ya·wa·k'in·ki·ya \tké-ya-wa-k'iŋ-k̇i-ya\ *v* : to load heavily, to overload

tkon·ski·ya \tkoŋ-sk̇í-ya\ *v* : to finish a job, be done < *Wana tkonswakiyelo* I am finished now. >

tkon·sya *or* **tkonsyela** \tkoŋ-syá\ *adv* : evenly

tkon·za \tkóŋ-za\ *adj* : even, square with, just, exactly — **tkonze·la** \tkóŋ-ze-la\ *adj* : even, in numbers, as twenty, thirty, *etc.*

tku·ga \tkú-ġa\ – *See* katkuga

tku·ga·han \tku-ġá-haŋ\ *part* : broken off

tku·tku·ga \tku-tkú-ġa\ *red of* tkuga – *See* katkuga — **tku·tku·ga·han** *part red* : broken off in several places

[1]to \ṫo\ *n* : the noise made by a blow delivered < *katoto* to rap, knock, as on a door >

[2]to *or* **ito** \to\ *interj* : Come now, Well

[3]to \ṫo\ *interj of affirmation* : Yes.

[4]to \to\ *adj* : blue or green

[5]to \to\ *pron adj* : his, hers, theirs – *See* canníyan Note: the word is used in some cases for *ta* when the *n* begins with *wo*, thus: *wocanniye* or *tocanniye* his being angry with her.

tob \ṫob\ *num card of* tópa : four < *Tob kin* The Four Winds; the messenger of all the world Powers > — **to·bla·la** \ṫó-bla-la\ *adv* : only four — **tob·tob** \ṫo-bṫó'\ *adv red* : by fours, four and four — *n* : four by four, four times four < *Tobtob kin* the Four general world Powers related, multiplied by four other relations thus to the product of sixteen relations: *Wikan-Hanwikan; Taku Škanškan-Tatekan; Tob kin-Yumnikan; Makakan-Wohpe; Inyankan-Wakinyan; Tatankakan-Hununpakan; Wanagi-Waniya; Nagila-Wašicunpi* Aged Sun-Aged Moon; What Moves-Aged Winds; The Four-Aged Turn; Aged Earth-To Shoot Down; Aged Rock-To Fly; Aged Buffalo Bull-Aged Two Leggeds; Spirits-To Make Live; Souls-Powers > – WJR 153

to·can·ni·ye \ṫó-caŋ-ni-ye\ *n of* wocanniye : his wrath against his wife

to·el \ṫó-èl\ *conj* : but before, but first < *Talo k'un ataya tebmakiyapelo eyin na locin canke ~ woyute owekiceya ške* He said they had eaten up all the meat and he was hungry, and so but first they said he mourned over his own. *Wacinhin k'un he ataya ikoyaka canke ena ~ glušpuhin na wana wicaša sapa k'un he glihunni kta hanl* He fixed the entire headdress, and so it was, but first he pulled it off and a black man was about to arrive back directly at the time. > – Note: the word indicates that time is taken before doing something important, to do something else first, but the speaker is impatient with the delay, does not approve of it. But, using *tóéyaš* would show that the speaker approves of the delay – D.109, 28 note 1

to·e·yaš *or* **toel, tok'eyaš, itok'eyaš, itoeyaš** \ṫó-è-yaš\ \ṫó-èl\ *conj* : but first, but before < *Inše le ociciyapi kta tka ~ waunšiyalapi hecinhan he slolwayin kta wacin ye* Well, I will now help you, but first his purpose is that I should know he was thinking you take pity on us. *Hecel ~ okuwa šni ca ayuštan. Na wanna anpetu wan el kipi kte ci iyehantu wicokanyan ~ asnikiyapi* So first however he quit because he did not go hunting. And now on one day when they were about to arrive home at the moment of noon, but first they took a rest. *Hehanl wanna wauncipi na ~ hunh ececapi ehanl asnikiyapi* At that time we went dancing, but before when some were indisposed they then took a rest. *Lecel eya: ~ hena najin po.* He spoke this way: But first stand you there. *Ungnahela leya: ~ asnikiya po, eya* All at once he said this, he said: Take a rest! *Yunkan: ~ ena najin po, eya* And then he said: But first you too stand. *Na wanna oyate kin kiblecahanpi na ~ wol akiyagla* And now the people went their separate ways going home to eat, *i.e.* as they were told to do. *Oyate kin lel amapepi kte lo; ~ paha ekta mni na wicokan hiyaye kin wagli kta* The people will expect me at this time; but first I shall go to the hill and when it is afternoon I shall start home. > – D.67

to·gan·gan o·ki·wa·sle·ca·pi \tó-ġaŋ-ġaŋ o-k̇i-wa-sle-ca-pi\ *n* : a very fat cow – HH Bl

to·gmon·šni \to-gmŋóŋ-šni\ *adv* : topsy-turvy, disorderly – Bl

to·gmun s'e \tó-gmuŋ s'e\ *adv* : being organized but little, confusedly < *~ un* He lives in a mess, as is said of a man who has poor property and has troubles with relatives. *~ yaun welo* You are cluttered. > – Bl

to·gto·ka \to-gtó-ka\ *adv* : in another way, otherwise < *Can kin ~ aon po tiyoḣeyunka au welo* Put the log on otherwise, February is come, *i.e.* put more wood on the fire. > – Bl

to·gye \ṫo-gyé\ *adv* : in a different manner, differently, a little different, in a different set of many ways, as one word is a little different from another < *Oglala ciscila ~ eyapi* The Oglalas speak a very little different. *Heon ecanna ~ iwanblakin kte lo na ecel ecamon kte lo ca oyaka yo* For that reason I should soon see differently, and when I shall have done so, say so. *~ kaga* to make different >

to·g'i·a \to-g'í-a\ *v* tog'i·wa·ya : to talk a strange language

to·han \ṫó-haŋ\ *adv indef* : sometime < *Ake ~ wanciyankin kte* Sometime again I shall see you. > — *adv interrog* : when, at what time or place?

~ ... kinhan < If ... sometime ... >
< If it be sometime ... >

~ ... hecetu kta? < When ... will it be alright? >
< When ... will it be alright? >

~ ... hehan < When ... then ... >
< *~ gnaška hinhan uyapi kin hehan hecetu kta he?* When the owl starts the frog going, will it then be alright? *i.e.* good weather. >

~ ... ca na, < Whenever ... then ... >
< *~ iglakapi ca na eyapaha wanji el un* Whenever they pitched camp there was then an announcer in it. >

tohán ... hehán ..., as long as ... then ...
< *~ yani eša hehán* as long as any of you live, then ...>

tóhan ... héhan ... < until > (subordinated)
< *Na tonweya k'on hena ena najinpi kte lo ~ unkupi šni hehan, eya* And those scouts will have stood right there until we come back. *Na hel tohanyan glipi šni* (the delegates*) hehan hel wicoti* (the people) And the delegates there did not go home then until the people stayed there. >

to·han·han \ṫo-háŋ-haŋ\ *adv red interrog of* tohan : at what time or times or places? how far? **tohanhan·keca** \ṫo-háŋ-haŋ-ke-ca\ *adv red interrog* : how long? (*esp* as to space)

to·han·han·yan \ṫo-háŋ-haŋ-yaŋ\ *adv red of* tohanyan : as long or far as — *adv red interrog* : for how long?

to·han·hun·ni·yan *or* **tohun·hunniyan** \ṫo-háŋ-huŋ-ni-yaŋ\ *adv* : as long as – Bo

to·han·hci \ṫó-haŋ-ȟci\ *adv indef* : at some other time in the future perhaps < ~ *wounglakin kte* You and I will talk at some other future time. >
to·han·ke·ca \ṫo-háŋ-ke-ca\ *adv interrog* : how long? - Cf lehankeca, hehankeca, Note: the word usually is used in *ref* to space
to·hanl *or* **tohan** \ṫo-háŋl\ \ṫo-háŋ\ *adv conj* and *interrog* : when, when? < *Na ~ wanna akisnipi lila wiyuškinpi* And when they were now rested they rejoiced. ~ *oiyokpaz aya ca na wicaša lila waš'aka. Kola, ~ wanasapi kte so?* When it grows dark a man is very strong. Friend, there will be a buffalo chase when? > - Cf *tóhan* to see further considerations
~ ... *ca na* or *can* or *eša*, whenever ...
~ ... *kin hehanl* ... , when ... then ...
- B.H.80.19, 120.5, 61.6, 94.11
to·han·ni \ṫó-haŋ-ni\ *adv* : never - B.H.48.8, 68.24, 98.17, 138.5, 222.10 Pb.29
to·han·šna \ṫó-haŋ-šna\ *adv* : sometime
to·han·tan \ṫo-háŋ-taŋ\ *adv* or *n* : for all the past time < ~ *kin iyotiyewakiye* All my life I have had a hard lot. > - D.269
to·han·tu \ṫo-háŋ-ṫu\ *adv interrog* : when? < ~ *kin takpe ayin kta ška hwo* At what time did they say they should begin to attack? > - D.91
to·han·tu·ka wan \ṫo-háŋ-ṫu-ǩa waŋ\ *adv* : at a certain time < *Wana ~ lila tiyata gla cin* At a specific time he wanted to go home. *Itohantuka yunkan leya ške* They say he said this and so at this precise moment. > - D.60, 91
to·han·tu ke c'e·yaš *or* **tohantu ǩeš** *or* **tohantu ǩešà** *or* **tohantu k'e èyaš** \ṫo-háŋ-ṫu ke c'è-yaš\ *adv indef* : whenever, at any time - R Bl
to·han·yan \ṫo-háŋ-yaŋ\ *adv* : as long or as far as < ~ *oyakihipi ȟupahu koza po* As long as you all are able wave a wing. *Letanhan tohinni iyopemaye šni ye, ~ unni hehanyan* (~ ... *hehanyan*) From now on please never correct me, as long as you and I live. ~ *ištayeyapi hehanyan pte au* (~ ... *hehanyan*) Buffalo came on as far as the eye can see. ~ *ye šni hci* He had not gone far yet. *Na ~ mahpiya kin he owanjila hecel han ca hehanyan oyate kin owanjila tipi; na tohanl mahpiya kin ȟeyab iyaya can na iš eya iglakapi* And as long as this same cloud so stood, the people alike then remained camped; and whenever the cloud went on away they too moved camp. - Note: ~ *šni hanni* in no time, ~ *yapi; yunkan* They went for some time; a while, ~ ... *iyehanyan* as far as ... the same distance > B.H.55.15, 249.18, 256.20, 121.3,61.11, 98.17, 100.22, 267.11 D.157
to·han·yan·kel \ṫo-háŋ-yaŋ-kel\ *adv* : how far, to where
to·han·yan šni hanni \ṫo-háŋ-yan šni haŋ-nì\ *adv* : with no measures lacking, with promptness - B.H.256.20 LHB
to·he \ṫó-he\ *n* : his place, his camp, his office or position - B.H.218.3
to·hin·gla \ṫó-hiŋ-gla\ *vn of* ṫo : to resound
to·hin·ni \ṫó-hiŋ-ni\ *adv* : never - Note: the word is used usually as a *coord* with *šni*, thus: ~ ... šni < ~ *ecamon šni yelo* I never did it. >
to·hin·yan·ka yo \ṫó-hiŋ-yaŋ-ka yo\ *v imper interj* : Hold on!, Wait a minute! < ~ *po, wicaša wanji t'in kta keš ehake hotan'in na t'e lo* Hold on! though the man was about to die, at last his voice was heard, and he died. > - Note: this word is used by a speaker who does not wish to be interrupted *Syn* TOEYAŠ, TÍNYANKA YO
to·hun·hin·ni·yan *or* **tohunhunniyan**\ṫo-húŋ-hiŋ-ni-yaŋ\ *adv* : always, forever < *He wicaša kin ~ cajeyatapi kte* That man's name will forever be spoken. > - B.H.152.21, 12.1 Bl
to·hca \ṫó-ȟca\ *adj* : blue, *i.e.* as distinguished from green
to·h'an \ṫó-ȟ'aŋ\ *n of* oh'án : his acts, deeds, works < *Wicaša iyecel toyah'an* A man likewise (is pleased with) his works. > - B.H.134.22
to·i \ṫó-i\ *interj of affirmation* : Yes - Note: the word is used by women; *han*, by men
to·i·a \ṫo-í-a\ *v* toi·wa·ya : to criticize, to knock
to·i·e \ṫó-i-e\ *n* : his word
to·i·e·han·pi \ṫo-í-e-haŋ-pi\ *n pl* : critics - Cf toies'a
to·i·e·s'a \ṫo-í-e-s'a\ *n* [fr *ṫo* noise made by a blow + *ie* to speak + *s'a* repeating] : a critic, a crank, knocker - Note: the word is used for one person; for more than one, *toiehanpi*.
to·i·yo·ki·tan'·in \ṫó-i-yo-ki-taŋ-iŋ\ *n* : his manifestation
to·jan \ṫo-jáŋ\ *n* mi·tojan ni·tojan : a niece, my niece, when she is addressed - Note: this form is used by women; men use *tonján* — **tojan·ku** \ṫo-jáŋ-ǩu\ *n* : her niece — **tojan·ya** *va* tojan·wa·ya : (a woman) to have for a niece
to·je·la \ṫo-jé-la\ *adj* : short - *Syn* PTECELA
[1]**to·ka** \ṫó-ǩa\ *n* : one of a foreign or hostile nation, an enemy
[2]**to·ka** \ṫó-ka\ *adv interrog* : why, how is it, what is up? < ~ *hwo* What is the matter? *Ina, ~ ca ate ihpeya ungni kte he?* Mother, why is it that you and I are going home and leaving father? *Tuwa ohiye ci ~ hwo?* What is matter that a person gets the better of one? *Tunkašila, ~ ca he yagluman hwo?* Grandfather, why is it you are grinding that (axe)? *Taku ~ hwo?* What is up? *or* What is the news? *Taku ~ kin nah'onpi?* What news have they heard, *i.e.* what is the matter? *Tomáka* There is nothing the matter with me. > - Cf tokeca; *tomákeca šni* nothing the matter, *e.g.* not sick - D.224 B.H.278.6, 45.23, 81.7
[3]**to·ka** \ṫo-ǩá\ *adv* : at the first < *Tuwa ~ hi na wawanyanka cana išta hca yelo* One first arrived, and when he looked he had obscure vision. *Na hehanl wanna ob ~ iyayapi k'el glipi* And at that time now, they went home where they had first gone together. >
to·kab \ṫo-ǩáb\ *n contrac of* tokápa : before, first < ~ *ya* to go before >
to·ka·ca \ṫó-ka-ca\ *adv* [fr *tóka* why + *ca* and] : why, wherefore?
to·ka·he \ṫo-ǩá-he\ *n* : the first, the beginning — *v* : to be first, to go before — **tokahe·kiya** \ṫo-ǩá-he-ǩi-ya\ *va* tokahe·wa·kiya : to cause to go before — **tokahe·ya** *adv* : at the first, before, in the beginning, the Latin prímo < ~ *oyate tona lel yaunpi kin hihanna kin wo cic'upi kte lo* If a number of you are here beforehand, I shall give you food tomorrow. > — *n* : the first - B.H. 30.15, 215.3, 126.5,
to·ka·hu \ṫó-ǩa-hu\ *n* : the thistle, carduus lanceolatus — **tokahu wahinkpe on ziyápi** *n* : the prickly poppy, argemone intermedia, the poppy family - Note: the name indicates with it they dye arrows - R K #294
to·ka·hci \ṫo-ǩá-ȟci\ *adv* : at the first, the very first
to·ka·hta·ye·tu \ṫo-ǩá-ȟta-ye-tu\ *n* : the first of the night - R Bl
to·ka·h'an \ṫó-ka-ȟ'aŋ\ *vn* or *adj* or *adv* toka·ma·h'an

\a\ father \e\ they \i\ machine \o\ smoke \u\ lunar \an, aŋ\ blanc Fr. \in, iŋ\ ink \on, oŋ, un, uŋ\ soon, confier Fr. \c\ chair \ġ\ machen Ger. \j\ fusion \clusters: bl, gn, kp, hšl, etc...\ b[e]lo ... said with a slight vowel
See more in the Introduction, Guide to Pronunciation

: to lose, suffer loss, to be gone, lost < A person says: What has become of it? And I say: *Tokah'an* It is gone, *i.e.* I do not know how it happened. *Ogle na hunska, na šina ko el un na tacan kin tokah'an* A shirt and leggings, and a blanket as well are on him, and the body is gone. *Na ake ungnahela ~ na ake pte pa šeca k'on eca yanka* And again of a sudden it was gone, and again it had really been a cow's skeleton head. > *Yunkan tokah'anpi na wikoškalaka k'on el unpi* Then they were gone when young women had been there. *Hecel oyate ištapi kin etanhan ~* So he somehow was lost from the people's sight. *Yunkan ~ ca, el etonwan po, epa* And then since he was gone, I said: Look there! *Yunkan ~ na mišnala ena nawajin* Then while I stood right there myself alone, he was gone. >

to·ka·i·a·pi \tō'-ka-i-à-pi\ *n* : a foreign language, an enemy's language

to·ka·i·c'i·gna·ka \to-ka-i-c'i-gna-ka\ *v* toka·mi·c'ignake šni toka·ni·c'ignake šni : to make note of, write down for one's self *e.g.* a word or two – Note: the *abbrev*, tokíc'ignake – Bl

to·ka·ka·la in·yan·ka \to-ká-ka-la iŋ-yaŋ-ka\ *v* : to run like a horse, with body bent as when the head is pulled back and sideways – Bl

to·ka ka·ta \to-ká ka-tà\ *v* : to throw a bow on the ice, but then strike the ice at once because one does not know how to do it, *i.e.* the trick in throwing – Bl

to·ka·ka ye šni *or* **tokani ye šni** \tó-ka-ka ye šni\ *v* : to be unable to go any place, having no horses *etc.*

to·ka·ki·ci·ya·pi \tó-ka-ki-ci-ya-pi\ *n* : enemies

to·ka·ki·ci·yu·t'a·pi \to-ká-ki-ci-yu-t'a-pi\ *n* : perhaps a choking game played by boys – Bl

to·ka·ki·con \tó-ka-ki-coŋ\ *v of* tókon : to do to or for one

to·ka·ki·h'an \tó-ka-ki-h'aŋ\ *v* toka·ma·kih'an : to suffer injury or loss, to lose something – B.H.77.17, 53.14

to·ka kin he·han·na \to-ká kiŋ he-hàŋ-na\ *adv phr* : at the first, formerly < ~ *pejuta k'upi kinhan akisni kta iyecana tka yelo* It he had been given medicine in the begining of the sickness he would have got well soon. > – Bl

to·ka kte \tó-ka kte\ *express* : "Something may happen." or "It ought to be something." < *Owekiš ~ sece* It seems there may be something to happen. >

to·ka·k'e·han *or* **tokak'unhèhan** \to-ká-k'e-haŋ\ *adv* : at the first

[1]**to·ka la** \tó-ka la\ *v* toka wa·la : not to be influenced by – B.H.241.27

[2]**to·ka·la** \to-ká-la\ *n* : a small gray fox, and very fast

to·ka·la·hci \to-ká-la-hci\ *adv* : for the very first time

to·ka·la ta·pe·ju·ta hu blo·ka \to-ká-la ta-pe-jù-ta hu blò-ka\ *n* : white prairie clover, petalostemum candidum, the pulse family — **tokala tapejuta hu wìnyela** *n* : the violet or purple prairie clover, petalostemum purpureum, the pulse family. – Note: it is a medicine; the root is chewed as a gum – Bl #249, 176 L

to·ka·la wa·ci·pi \to-ká-la wa-cì-pi\ *n* : the fox dance

to·ka·mon \tó-ka-moŋ\ *va* 1*st* *pers singl of* tókon : I misplaced it

to·ka·ni \tó-ka-ni\ *adv* usually followed by a *v* with *šni* : in no way, having no means or way < *Mni kin el ~ hiyu šni kin heon* The reason is that it had no way of coming to the water, *i.e.* no way of crossing the river. *~ ble šni* No way did it go, *i.e.* no way of going: no horses, no wagon, no nothing. *Hecel toeyaš ~ okuwa šni ca ayuštan* So first since he had no way of chasing after it he let it alone. *Canke ~ akiyuwege šni* And so it had no means for it to cross, *i.e.* the Platte River in the fall. *Ca heon ~ tak'epe šni yelo* And for that reason it had no way of saying anything. *~ tak'epe šni kin on lila cantemašice* Since I had nothing to say I was very sad, or I would not say anything, and that is why I am very unhappy. *~ glicu šni* It had no way to start coming home, *i.e.* had no way of coming out. > – D.132, 278, 28, 32

to·ka·non \tó-ka-noŋ\ *va* 2*nd* *pers singl of* tókon : You misplaced it

to·kan *or* **tokanl** \to-káŋ\ \to-káŋl\ *adv* : in another place, elsewhere, another *i.e.* a different way < *Letanhan nihun kici ~ unyanpi kte lo* We shall go by a different way from here along with your mother. > — *n* : another, as another person < ~ *tawa* to belong to another person. *Wanna ake iglakapi na ~ yapi* They are going another way and now are traveling about again. *Ho hehanl ~ iblabla na wi num ece ~ waun* Well then I went elsewhere, and after only two months I am in another place doing well. > — **tokanl·kanl** *adv red* : in quite a different place — **tokanl·tanhan** *adv* : from another source, place, or person < *Jerusalem el ~ yahi yelaka?* You came to Jerusalem from somewhere else, did you not? > – R Bl B.H.5.5, 272.7, 223.2, 232.3, 260.24

to·ka·pa \to-ká-pa\ *n* toka·ma·pa to·un·kapa·pi : the first, first born, the eldest — **tokapa·tanhan** \to-ká-pa-taŋ-haŋ\ *adv* : ahead, before — **tokapa·ya** *adv* : leading < ~ *škan* to lead > – D.1 B.H.61.24

to·kaš \to-káš\ *adv* : maybe, perhaps, possibly < ~ *kigle sece* It seems he possibly arrived home. *~ éciciya owakihi kte séce* It is just possible I shall be able to speak for you, *i.e.* be able to help you. > – B.H.174.15, 182.21, 222.3, 242.2 D.270

to·ka ška \tó-ka ška\ *express* : there is something said < *Ungna ~ pahaha ihpeciye ci* Perhaps there is something said about my leaving to abandon you. >

to·ka·šni \tō'-ka-šni\ *adv* : it does not matter, indifferently < *Lila wanasapi na lila wawicašeca na ~ unpi* It mattered not they were well off, they energeticly went on the buffalo chase and very abundantly made provisions. > — **tokašni·kiya** \tó-ka-šni-ki-ya\ *va* tokašni·wa·kiya : to make light of — **tokašni·yan** *adv* **a** : without any trouble < ~ *wawanyanke* He saw without any trouble. > **b** : with no resistance, more or less willing but reluctantly < *Takuni ~ unpi* They get on without friction, *i.e.* are all right with one another. *~ niwicayuzapi* You took them with little resistance, *i.e.* took them alive without much resistance on their part. > – B.H.135.7, 80.3

to·ka·ta \to-ká-ta\ *adv* : in the future, in future, yet to come < ~ *anpetu wakan* Sunday is yet to come. > — *n* : the future

to·ka·ta·han can·bla·ska \to-ká-ta-haŋ caŋ-blà-ska\ *n* : a dashboard

to·ka·ta·ki·ya \to-ká-ta-ki-ya\ *adv* : in the future — **tokata·yab** *adv* or perhaps *adj* : future, ahead – Pb.27

to·ka un šni \to-ká un šni\ *adv interrog* : why?, how is it?, What is up? < *Wiši ca wacanmi na wok'in toka waun šni yelo* It was pay I thought about, and how I was doing with my pack, *i.e.* I got more than I expected and could hardly take care of it. > – Bl

to·ka·ya \tó-ka-ya\ *va* toka·wa·ya : to have for an enemy – B.H.201.4

to·ka·ye·la·ka *or* **tokayelakaš** \tó-ka-ye-la-ka\ *adv interrog* : why? for what reason? what for? – Note: at times *kin* is added to the word. *See* yelakaš. < ~ *hecanon kin?* Why did you do that?, implying you should not have done it. *Ito le wounptin kta; ~ heyapi kin? eya* Now then you and I should dig here; she said: what reason did they have for saying that?, *i.e.* they were told not to dig turnips. *Iho, oh'an emacetu šni eša; takoja, taku woteȟi ota tka ~ nitunkašila lehan amahi yelo* Behold, I broke my contract to do some work; grandchild, there will be many troublesome things why your grandfather has brought me to this place. > – MS.477 D.198

to·kcel *or* **tokicel** \ṫŏ'-k̇ċel\ \ṫŏ'-k̇i-cel\ *adv* or *interj of* doubt or ignorance, as in answer to a question of the whereabouts (of place only) of something : somewhere, I don't know where, perhaps – P

to·kcin·cin·yan *or* **tokecincinyan** *or* **tokcinkinyan** \ṫó-k̇ciŋ-ciŋ-yaŋ\ *adv* : anyhow, as pleases

To·kcin·ka Wo·ta \Tó-kciŋ-ka Wò-ta\ *np* [fr *tokcinka* thoughtlessly + *wota* to eat] : the Cheyenne Indians living on the Tongue River Reservation

to·kcin·kcin·ka \ṫó-kciŋ-kciŋ-ka\ *adv* : thoughtlessly, as one pleases < ~ *waihpeyelah* to throw everything anywhere away into any place *etc.* > – Bl

[1]**to·ke** \ṫo-k̇é\ *interj* said on hearing a noise unexpectedly: Listen!

[2]**to·ke** *or* **toki** \ṫó-k̇e\ *interj* : I suppose, of course < ~ *ota icazo, eyaš kicipajuju k'un he ecel* I suppose he was in much debt, but it must be he had paid it off. >

[3]**to·ke** \ṫo-k̇é\ *opt mood signs and "ni"*

toke ešá ... ni, I wish I ...
toke ... laká, Would that ... (implying a wish)
toke ... ni, Oh that, *or* I wish ... (that something may be) < *Toke he bluha ni* I wish I had it. *Toke mat'a ni* I wish I was dead. *Toke Itancan taogligle wakan kin yecicapi ni* May the angel of the Lord be with you. > – Note: "*... ni.*" simply is often used
toké ... so?, really ... ? < *Toke yagli so?* Did you really come back? (as I was afraid you would not). *Toke ti šni yešan etiyoyankahe so?* Really, wasn't he living in a tent though he had no residence? *Mitan, toke wicahpi wan lila ilege cin he waštewalaka ca kici waun* My little sister, really I suppose I live with a star that burns very bright because I love him, *i.e.* really I suppose. > – B.H.199.15, 221.12, 84.4, 112.7, 122.10,14, 55.4, 125.6, 157.8, 264.4 MS.1

[1]**to·ke·ca** \ṫó-k̇e-ca\ *adj* : different, another < *wicaša ~* another man, *Matókeca* I am different. > – R

[2]**to·ke·ca** \ṫó-k̇e-ca\ *adj* tó·ma·keca to·ni·keca : unwell, sick – Note: *tokecašni* to be well, Cf tokécela

to·ke·ca·ca *or* **toke ècaca** \ṫo-k̇ĕ'-ca-ca\ *adv* : unconcernedly, without specific purpose, at random < ~ *omani* to travel without any concern, ~ *omanihan* He was traveling without a destination in mind. > – *Syn* WINKCEKCEYA

to·ke·ca·e \ṫó-k̇e-ca-e\ *adv* : why? – R Bl

to·ke·ca·ka·cel \ṫó-k̇e-ca-k̇a-cel\ *adv* : for no reason – R Bl

to·ke·ca·kel \ṫo-k̇é-ca-kel\ *adv* : in case of need < ~ *owinja luha* Have you got an extra blanket, *i.e.* on to spare? > – *Syn* WANÚNTOKAYAKEL S

to·ke·ca·šni \ṫŏ'-k̇e-ca-šni\ *adj* : well, recovered, there being nothing the matter < *Hecel wanna kuje k'on tipi k'on etan ~ aglinapa na tiyatakiya glapi* So he who had been sick had come from the house recovered, and they were on their way homeward. > – Cf tokécela

to·ke·ce·la \ṫo-k̇é-ce-la\ *adv* : weakly, from weakness, gradually, slowly < ~ *hpaye* He fell gradually. *Ake mini el iyayapi kta, tka ~ aglagla inajinpi. ~ glihunni* Again they were about to go to water, but they gradually stood up alongside it. They slowly reach their home. *Anpa eciyatan ~ ayanpa* Gradually it became light a little before daytime. ~ *hoyekiya* to call out softly to one, ~ *manila* barely walking > – D.67, 219

to·ke·cin *or* **tokecin·cin** \ṫó-k̇e-ciŋ\ *adv* : anyhow, as one pleases < ~ *waun* I do as I please. > — **tokecin·cinyan** *or* **tokecin·yan** *adv* : as one pleases < ~ *un* to live one's own way > – MS.485

to·ke e·ca·ca *or* **toke·caca** \ṫo-k̇é e-cà-ca\ *adv* : without caring, carelessly, at random – D.19

to·ke·hci \ṫó-k̇e-ȟci\ *adv* : howsoever

to·ke·ke·kel \ṫo-k̇é-k̇e-kel\ *adv of* toké : with ripe concernedness < ~ *tokiyatanhan yaku welo* Where do you come back from with great concern?, as is said when one returns hurriedly as though something had happened or he was bringing a message. ~ *nayajinpi s'elececa* You seem to stand there listening and talking about something. > – Bl

to·kel \ṫŏ'-k̇el\ *adv* or *interrog* : somewhere, to some place; why; as, how, in what way < ~ *iyaya* to go somewhere, disappear, ~ *on wibluškin kta hwo?* Why should I be glad? ~ *okihi* as hard, loud, strong as one can, ~ *eya ca na ecel econ po* As he said do so, *tokel ... ca na ecel,* as ... so. ~ *h'an* how to act, ~ *h'anpìca šni* as nothing can be done about it. > – B.H.225.8, 122.4, 45.7, 58.14, 225.8, 252.5, 152.17 D.221 Gramm.191

to·ke·lke·ltu \ṫó-k̇e-lk̇e-lṫu\ *adv* : in whatever way — **tokelkeltu·ya** *adv* : in what way soever – R Bl

to·ke·lki·ya·tan·han \ṫó-k̇e-lk̇i-ya-ṫaŋ-haŋ\ *adv* : from where, from what direction; on what side – B.H.118.9

to·kel o·ki·hi·ka \ṫó-kel o-k̇ì-hi-ka\ *adv phr* [fr *okihi* to be able + *laka* rather] : as able as one can be — **tokel okihi·lakel** *adv phr* : by all means, in every way, with all might – *See* tókel B.H.125.3, 139.19, 95.22, 119.10, 140.1, 105.3

to·ke·na yanka \ṫó-k̇e-na yaŋ-kà\ *v* : to remain while others move, to stay partly the way they were < *Na ena lila tehan manka icunhan tanke ena ate kici tokena yankapi k'on hecetu wanjica yankapi* And while I stayed there a very long time, his older sister and their father who remained stayed without a change. >

to·ke·ni \ṫó-k̇e-ni\ *interj* : by no means of course < *Wan, ~ wowahtani el nitonpi tka waohola šni waonspeunyakiyapi wacanniyelo* Look now! By no means are you born in sin to aim without respect to teach us! *Tokeniš nawicah'on šni iyecel iye kapi šni s'e hiyaya ke* Hold it! As he did not listen to them, so he went on by as if they pretty much did not mean him, *i.e.* he paid no attention as if they did not mean him. > – B.H.222.13 D.29.

to·keš \ṫó-k̇eš\ *adv emph of* tokel : as < ~ *he niye s'e wacanmi* I thought that was you. > – R Bl

to·ke·ša \ṫó-k̇e-ša\ *adv* : after a little while, at any rate – Note: the word is used as a word of assent to word or action *Syn* TOKŠA

to·ke·ške \ṫó-k̇e-šk̇e\ *adv* : how, how in the world?; in whatsoever way < *Takoja, ~ yah'an hwo* Grandchild, what in the world have you been doing? *He kigna yo* Caress him! ~ *naka he?* How did he react? said he. ~ *yah'an na hecel nanka hwo?* How did you do, and did you

---

\a\ father \e\ they \i\ machine \o\ smoke \u\ lunar \an, aŋ\ blanc Fr. \in, iŋ\ ink \on, oŋ, un, uŋ\ soon, confier Fr. \c\ chair \ġ\ machen Ger. \j\ fusion \clusters: bl, gn, kp, hšl, etc...\ b[e]lo ... said with a slight vowel **See more in the Introduction, Guide to Pronunciation**

thus sit? ~ *wah'an kin slolwaye šni* I don't know how I was doing. ~ *yahilu hwo?* How did things turn out for you? ~ *econ ciši k'un hecehci econ wo* Do it just so how I told you to do it. > — **tokeške·ške** *adv red* : how in various ways < ~ *waunyeyapi nainš ... hena okiyake* How sacrifice is made *etc*... he told him of them. > — **toke-ške unpi s'e omani** *v* : to travel over very bad roads or on no roads at all, as in hilly country - *Syn* TEḢIḢIYA OMANI, PTANŠKIKA S'E OMANI B.H. 241.15, 60.6, 80.22, 184.11, 211.7

to·ke·tkel \ṫó-ke-ṫkel\ *adv red* or *interrog of* tókel : how, in what way, why? — **toke·tkiya** \ṫó-ke-tki-ya\ *adv* : in whatever way < ~ *mni kta hwo?* Which way should I go? > - R Bl B.H.28.3, 298.4

to·ke·tu \ṫó-ke-ṫu\ *adv* or *interrog* : as it is, how is it? < ~ *kin ecel oblakin kta.* ~ *he?* I shall tell it as it is. How is it? *or* What is the matter? *Toniketu?* How is it with you? *or* How are you? ~ *tan'in šni* As it is it was not visible. ~ *kakeš* as it happens >

to·ke·tu ke·c'e·yaš \ṫó-kě-ṫu ke-c'e-yaš\ *adv* : however, in whichever way < *Toketu kec'eyaš* No matter what happens. > - D.12

to·ke·tu keš \ṫó-ke-ṫu keš\ *adv perhaps* : no matter what, all the same < *Le yacin niš yacin šni, šice nacece; hiya,* ~ *mak'u wo* This you want this you don't want, it's probably bad; no, no matter what give it to me. > - Bl

to·ke·tu·ya ka·keš \ṫó-ke-ṫu-ya ka-kèš\ *adv* : in whatever way, at random perhaps

to·ke·wa·cin·šni un \ṫó-ke-wa-ciŋ-šni uŋ\ *v* to pretend to be unaware of something, as when somebody comes who has wronged one long ago and acts as if nothing ever happened. < *Tokewacinšni waun, wowaglaka. Yunkan isam lila wicoti na lila oiyokipi ca el tokawacinšni bla* I put on a good front, I spoke. And then I went pretending to be unaware while he was being really agreeable, and beyond that there were many encamped. >

to·ke·ya \to-ke-ya\ *adj* or *n* : the first, in opposition to others following

to·ke·ya ... ca he·hanl \ṫó-ke-ya ... ca he-hàŋl\ *adv coord* : before ... then < *Tokeya wicoh'an wanji, num, yamni econpi, ca hehanl tawicutonpi* Before there were one, two, three customs, there was then marriage, *i.e.* marriage was. >

[1]**to·ki** \ṫŏ-kĭ'\ *interj of* admiration for something beautiful : Oh how beautiful! - Note: the word is used by women

[2]**to·ki** *or perhaps* **tóke** \ṫó-ki\ *adv* : where, somewhere < *Wanna* ~ *iblabla tan'in šni* It is not apparent where I am going now. ~ *wi wikcemna ecetu* It has has been accomplished in ten months somewhere. > - B.H.232.2

to·ki·ci·c'on *or* **tokicic'un** \to-kí-ci-c'oŋ\ *v* [fr *tokic'on* to take revenge on] to·we·cic'on to·un·kicic'on·pi : to take vengeance on for one

to·ki·ci·kšu \to-kí-ci-kšu\ *v* to·we·cikšu [fr *tokšu* to transport] : to transport for one

to·ki·con·ze \ṫó-ki-coŋ-ze\ *n of* wokiconze : his law or determination

to·ki·c'un *or* **tokic'on** \to-kí-c'uŋ\ *va* to·we·c'un : to revenge, take revenge on < ~ *wacinhanpi* They were thinking of taking revenge. > - B.H.135.9

to·ki e·i·hpe·ya \ṫŏ'-ki é-i-ḣpe·ya\ *v* : to misplace something — **toki ihpekiya** \ṫó-ki i-ḣpè-ki-ya\ *va* toki ihpe·wa·kiya : to lose one's own, misplace one's own — **toki ihpe·ya** *v* : to lose, misplace, drop - Bl

to·ki i·ya·ya s'a \ṫó-ki i-yà-ya s'a\ *n* : a tramp, one who is gone much < ~ *tan'in šni* The tramp did not appear. > - D.81

to·ki·na·hanš *or* **tokinaš** \ṫó-ki-na-haŋš\ *adv* : maybe < *Ya!* ~ *taku otaka ca ekitan wamašipi kte hcin* Oh my God! Maybe they will very well employ me anyhow when there isn't much of anything. > — **tokinaš** *interj* : maybe < ~ *yacin šni s'elececa* Maybe, it seems you do not want it. ~ *he niye s'e wacanmi* Maybe, it seems I think that is you. > - *Syn* SECA, TOKÁŠ

to·kin ... ni *or* **toké ... ni** \ṫo-kíŋ ... ni\ *opt signs* : Oh that ... , I wish ... - Note: *konpi s'e eyapi* It is said as if it was coveted, much desired perhaps out of greed

[1]**to·kinš** \ṫó-kiŋš\ *adv* : well, implying that one was mistaken in one's assumptions < ~ *he niye s'e wacanmi* Oh well, I thought that was you. ~ *wašicun wakan kin hi kte sece, i.e. yunkan hi šni* Anyhow, the white-man doctor it seems will arrive, *i.e.* and then he did not come. ~ *le wapoštan s'elececa; yunkan heca šni* Well, it seemed as if this was the hat. ~ *el mahi* Well, he came to me. > - B.H. 115.3 Rf

[2]**to·kinš** \ṫo-kíŋš\ *adv* : carelessly, wrong < ~ *ecanon, yakage* You did it carelessly, you made it. *Tohinni* ~ *wote šni* Never did he eat carelessly. > - D.120-121

to·kin·še·šeš \ṫo-kíŋ-še-šeš\ *adv* : luckily enough, almost too good to be true < ~ *oyakihi keci (kecin)* He thought that nonetheless you are lucky enough to be able, as is said when encouraging one, knowing that he "can" do it. ~ *iyowinyan ce* Is it not so, almost too good to be true, he allowed it? > - D.160 note 3

to·kin·škinš \ṫo-kíŋ-škiŋš\ *adv red* : anyhow, anyway < ~ *anátakinyece* anyhow surreptitiously > — **tokinš·ya·kel** \ṫo-kíŋ-šya-kel\ *adv* : carelessly, without care - Bl LHB

[1]**to·ki·ya** \to-kí-ya\ *va* to·wa·kiya : to paint blue < *Itokšan tokiyapi* He had a blue stripe painted around his face. >

[2]**to·ki·ya** *or* **tóki** \ṫó-ki-ya\ *adv interrog* : where? in what place? where did he go? — **tokiyab** *adv of* tokiyapa : where, in what direction? <~ *tuwa can katoto hwo?* Where does one knock on wood? ~ *omani ye ši* Where did he say to go take a walk. *Yunkan* ~ *cancega nah'on ke* And then pretty much in what direction did he hear a drum? > — **tokiya·la** *cl v* 2nd *pers singl of* ya : where are you going? - Note: the word does not just mean "where" — **tokiya·ni** *adv* : nowhere, to no place < ~ *ya* to go nowhere, ~ *yin kte šni* He will go nowhere. > - Cf tókani — **tokiya·pa** *adv interrog* : where? — **tokiya·tan** \ṫó-ki-ya-ṫaŋ\ *adv interrog* : whence? from what place? < ~ *hi* Where did he come from? *Na tuwepi nunpapi kin* ~ *šunkahopi ca na aiyopteya yapin na ake hopi* Come now! And again, where are the two persons who howl like dogs and are a match at biting? *Wicaša wan hi* ~ Where does the man come from? *Wan! hokšila wan* ~ *waohola šni yahi yelo* Behold! Whence comes the boy you come not to honor? > — **tokiya·tan-han** \ṫó-ki-ya-ṫaŋ-haŋ\ *adv* : whence, from what place? from some place < *Yunkan wicaša wan koškalaka wan kici* ~ *glipi* A man with a young man from somewhere were on their way home. *Tonikiyatanhan hwo?* Are you from some place? > - *See* leciyatanhan *etc.* — **tokiya·wapa** *adv* : where, in what place

to·ki·yo·pe·ki·ci·ya·pi \to-ki-yó-ṗe -ki-ci-ya-pi\ *n* : barter, exchange — **tokiyope·kiya** *va* tokiyope·wa·kiya tokiyope·ci·ciya : to barter, exchange one thing for another with one - Cf iyopekiya

to·ki·yo·pe·ya \to-ki-yó-ṗe-ya\ *va* tokiyope·wa·ya [fr *toki* where + *iyopeya exchange, sell*] : to barter, exchange one thing for another

to·ki·yo·tan *or* **tokiyotan·han** \ṫo-k̇í-yo-taŋ\ *adv* : somewhere, in some direction, towards somewhere at once < *Yunkan hakela ~ iyaya keye* And then he stated that the youngest child went somewhere. > - *See* leciyotan, heciyotan, kakiyotan

to·kon \ṫó-k̇oŋ\ *va* tóka·mon tóka·non tó·un·k'on·pi : to do, to misplace, thus being unable to find < *Inyan k'on he tokanon hwo* Had the rock been lost? *Mazaska wikcemna tókanonpelo* You all lost ten dollars. *Tokamayanon oyakihi šni tka* You would not be able to find me. *Anpetu kin lena el taku tokonpi kin hena slolyaye šni yelaka?* In these days you evidently did not know what were the things misplaced. > - PD B.H.264.14, 272.7

to·kon·pi·ca \ṫo-k̇oŋ-ṗi-ca\ *adj* : useful, good for something

to·ko·štan \to-kó-štaŋ\ *vn* [fr *tokan* elsewhere + *oštan* put in] : to sprain, dislocate one's own < *Cankpe tokomaštan* My knees are sprained, *i.e.* they do not work well. *Cecá tokomaštan* My thigh is cramped. > — **toko·yu·štan** \ṫo-kó-yu-štaŋ\ *va* tokó·blu·štaŋ : to displace, dislocate, to put one in the place of another - R Bl

to·ksa·pe \tó-ksa-ṗe\ *n of* wóksape : his wisdom < *nitoksape* your wisdom >

to·kša \tō'-kša\ *adv* : presently, by and by, before long, yes < *Le miye hca ca ~ oyate el unki kte eya keya* He stated that he said you and I will arrive home to the tribe soon since I myself am here. *~ óhinni awanciyankapi kte lo* Soon I shall always behold you. >

to·kšu \to-kšú\ *va* to·wa·kšu to·un·kšu·pi : to carry, draw, transport; to go back and bring < *Hecel towicakšupi* So they were transported, *or* They went back and brought them, *i.e.* they picked up the wounded. >

to·ktog \to-ktō'g\ *adj* : another < *wanji ~* by turns, *Wanji ~ asanpi yuslipi* They milk by turns, *i.e.* every morning another boy does the milking. *únma ~* by turns, in *ref* to two persons, thus also the *adv*, *itoktog* alternately > - R

to·kto·gye *or* **toktogye·kel** \to-któ-gye\ \to-któ-gye-k̇el\ *adv red of* ṫogyé : in different ways - B.H.277.5, 278.4

to·kto·ke·ca \ṫo-kṫo-k̇e-ca\ *adj red of* tókeca : different - D.250

to·ktu \ṫó-kṫu\ *adv interrog* : how is it? < *Hanska nainš ptecela, ~ ?* How is it, short or long? *Tuwa le yuha kin sam ~ kin slolyin kta* He should know more how it is when a person has this. *Tokata ~ kte cin ob gluštanpi kte lo* They will finish together how the future will be. *~ ke c'éyaš* however, in whichever way >

to·kyab \ṫó-k̇yab\ *adv* : - *See* tókiyab

to·k'e·yaš \ṫó-k'è-yaš\ *conj* : but, but first - Cf tóèyaš

to·la·hca·ka \tō'-la-ȟca-k̇a\ *adj* : very blue - Cf hcáka

to·la·s'e \ṫó-la-s'e\ *adj* [fr *to* blue + *s'e* like] : blue-like < *Išta ~ ayuta* His eyes looked blue-like, *i.e.* He looked at him angrily. > - Cf under ištá

to·lu·te \to-lú-ṫe\ *adj* : purple < *Tahayapi kin ~ ece koyakapi* They put on him only a purple cloak. > - B.H. 91.23, 263.9

to·ma·wa·hi·ton *or* **tomawaheton** \tó-ma-wa-hi-toŋ\ *n* [fr perhaps *unma* the other + *hi* come + *ton* to have] : his or her in-laws in general - Note: this is the word it seems for addressing in-laws, *See* omáwahiton

to·na \ṫō'-na\ *adv interrog* : how many?, which? < *Taku ~ onnispepi kta wacin* How many things did he think you were going to know how to do? *Ake lel wicoh'an ~ econ kta ca ake u wo* Come again when he will again do here a number of works. > — **tona·can** *adv interrog* : how many days? — **tona·gna** *or* **tonagnag** *or* **tonagnakeca** \ṫó-na-gna-k̇e-ca\ *adv interrog* : how many? - *See tónakeca*

to·na·gna·la \ṫó-na-gna-la\ *adv red of* tonala, *i.e.* tonana : a few, how few

to·na·ke·ca \ṫó-na-ke-ca\ *adj interrog* : some, a few; how many? how much? < *Pejuta wan icu na tonakecapi oyasin wicak'u* He took a medicine and he gave them all some. *Wanna hokšila kin waniyetu ~ na wanna mani luzahan* Now the boy is a few years old, and now he walks fast. *Oniye tonamakeca heci hena oyas'in cic'u* I give you all some of my spirit. > - *See* lenakeca *etc.* — **tona·kec'e·yaš** *adv* : how many soever — **tona·kel** *adj* : a few, some, a few times; several, a fair number < *Na el wicaša ~ yankapi* And there there were several men sitting. *~ ewicunktepi* Several we killed. *Na ikiyela maya ca ~ ob waun* And it was near a bank a few were together doing well. *~ owicakaptapi* A few were left. *Hinšma ~ owinšton* A few spread out a bed of fur. > - Pb.34 MS.535 B.H.135.9 D.229

to·na·ki·ya \ṫó-na-ki-ya\ *adv* : how many? how many times? in how many ways < *Hecel oyasin ~ wapatapi kin ptepa olepi eša tancan econpi* So when in how many ways they butchered everything, they did the carcass though they sought the buffalo heads. >

to·na·na \ṫó-na-na\ *adv* : a few; how few < *Lena wanwicayanka po; ~ wicaopi kin wanyanka po* See these; see how few were shot! >

to·nan·gnang \ṫó-naŋ-gnaŋg\ *adv red* : how many? - *See* tónagnag

to·ni \tō'-ni\ *n* : his or her life

ton \toŋ\ *va* wa·ton : to have, give birth to; to acquire, possess < *cinca ~* to bear a child, *Onzoge weton kte; ogle weton kte* I shall acquire a pair of pants; I shall acquire a shirt. > — *n* **1** : a spiritual or quasi-spiritual power or quality that makes a person of thing *wakan.* Thus the *wicaša wakan* is one who has the power to make wakan other things, as an ordained priest blesses things, and even persons **2** : matter, pus - WJR.152

ton·han *or* **ton·heca** \tóŋ-haŋ\ *va archaic* ton·wa·han : to be afraid of - R Bl

ton·hli·hli \toŋ-ȟlí-ȟli\ *v* : to loosen the phlegm in the throat by coughing - Bl

ton'·i·ka·špa \toŋ-í-k̇a-šṗa\ *v* ton'i·wa·kašpa : to expectorate, spit

ton·jan \toŋ-jáŋ\ *n* : a man's niece - Note: *tojan* a woman's niece, *tonjanku* his niece, *tonjanya* to have for a niece. Cf *tunjan, tunjanku, tunjanya,* alternative spelling

ton·ka·špa \toŋ-ká-šṗa\ *v* ton·wa·kašpa : to spit out phlegm - Bl

ton·kce \ṫóŋ-kce\ *n* : excrement

ton·la \ṫóŋ-la\ *adj* : weak < *Ehanni ~ s'elemáceca, tacúpala s'ele·ma·ceca* In the past it seemed I was weak, It seemed I was losing my self-control. > — **tonla s'e un** *v* : to be idle on account of not feeling well, to be too much, to be too much afraid for one's health < *~ waun welo* I am weak and not feeling good. > - Bl BT

ton'·o·gna·ga·gya \toŋ-ó-gna-ġa-gya\ *adv* : with matter on sores here and there < *~ ȟáŋpi* scabs with pus running here and there > - B.H.231.4

\a\ father \e\ they \i\ machine \o\ smoke \u\ lunar \an, aŋ\ blanc Fr. \in, iŋ\ ink \on, oŋ, un, uŋ\ soon, confier Fr. \c\ chair \ġ\ machen Ger. \j\ fusion \clusters: bl, gn, kp, hšl, etc...\ b^e^lo ... said with a slight vowel **See more in the Introduction, Guide to Pronunciation**

ton·ška *or* **tunška** \toŋ-šká\ *n* mi·tonška : a nephew, my nephew - Note: women use *tunšká* — **tonška·ku** *n* : his nephew — **tonška·ya** \toŋ-šká-ya\ *va* : to have for a nephew

ton·ton \tóŋ-toŋ\ *v red of* ton : to come forth steadily — *n* : that which has physical properties, hence: *tontonšni* that which is without physical properties — **tonton·ya** *adj* : visible from its properties, hence: *tontonšniyan* invisible because of properties - WJR.153

ton·t'e \toŋ-t'é\ *n* : his death - Cf wicont'e B.H.229.2

[1]**ton·wan** \toŋ-wáŋ\ *n* mi·tonwan : an arrow of any kind < ~ *šikšica, tka mak'u welo* The arrows were poor ones, but he gave them to me. ~ *waštešte* good arrows > - R Bl

[2]**ton·wan** \ṫoŋ-wáŋ\ *vn* wa·tonwan un·tonwan·pi : to look, to see < *Hecel pamagle iblotake na ištogmus iblotake na wanna watonwan* So I sat with head bowed, sat with eyes shut, and I saw. *Ištogmus ece wayacipi na yatonwanpi kte šni* Just dance shutting your eyes and you will not see. > — **tonwan·han** *part* : looking, seeing

ton·wan·ye·ca \toŋ-wáŋ-ye-ca\ *vn* tonwan·wa·yeca : to dwell at a place, to live there - Bl

ton·wel *or* **tunwel** *or* **ehanni** \ṫóŋ-wel\ *adv* [fr *tohan* sometime + *el* at] : once upon a time < *tónwěl* or *tó nwě wétu ká wǎn* long ago in springtime, ~ *ptanyétu ká wan* long ago in fall, ~ *waniyetu ka wan* long ago in wintertime, *Cosya igluze omani yo* Travel dressed to keep warm; *tuwa* ~ *šunkmanitu cuwita kacaš* What then, is one to feel cold like a coyote? ~ *wetuka wicahcala* Long ago in the spring-time he was an old man, as is said of a young man or boy who acts or talks like an old man or who grew up very fast. > - Note: the word is doubtfully a *deriv* of *ṫonwán*

ton·we·ni \ṫóŋ-we-ni\ *adv* [perhaps fr *tóhunweni* but not used] : when? < *Hunhunhé* ~ *yahi hwo?* How sad! When did you come? *i.e.* when I knew nothing about it. > — **tonweni ... šni** \ṫóŋ-we-ni ... šni\ *adv* : never < *Nilekši tonwenihcinš hi šni* Your uncle definitely never came. > - Note: LP said *tonweni* is a *deriv* of *tonwel* + *ni* the *neg* sign Bc Bl D.154, 81

ton·we·ya \ṫoŋ-wé-ya\ *n* : a spy, a guide — *vn* tonwe·bla perhaps, tonwe·un·yan·pi : to go to see, to go as a spy — *va* tonwe·wa·ya : to cause one to see, give sight to

ton·yan \toŋ-yáŋ\ *vn* : to suppurate, form or run pus

to·o·pe \tó-o-pe\ *n* mi·toope [fr *wóope* law] : his law

to·pa *or* **tob** \ṫó-ṗa\ *adj num card* : four < *Wicaša untopapi* We are four men. > — **topa·kiya** \ṫó-pa-ki-ya\ *adv* : in four ways, four times

to pe·sto·la \to ṗé-sto-la\ *n* : hoary or mullein-leaved vervain, verbena stricta, the vervain family - BT #27

to·pto·pa \ṫó-ṗto-ṗa\ *adj red of* tópa : by fours, four and four - *See* tóbtob

to·san \to-sáŋ\ *adj* : light blue — **tosan·ya** *va* : to make light blue - B.H.60.14

to·sa·pa \to-sá-ṗa\ *adj* : grape-colored

to·ska·la \ṫo-ská-la\ *n* : the downy and hairy woodpecker < *Ya!* ~ *akoecon* Oh no! Do get away from here, woodpecker. > - Note: the bird has on the head a red spot FR

toš \toš\ *interj of affirmation* by women only : Yes, Yea - *See* ṫo *and* han

to·ša \to-šá\ *adj* : purple - B

to·še \to-šé\ *adj* : dull, blunt — **toše·yakel** \to-šé-ya-ḳel\ *adv* : bluntly

to·ška \ṫo-šká\ *n* mi·toška ni·toška : a nephew, my nephew < *Mitoška yuha mankin kta* I shall be having my nephew. > - Note: this form of the word is used by women only; men will use **tonšká** *or* **tunška** — **toška·ku** \to-šká-ḳu\ *n* : her nephew — **toška·ya** \to-šká-ya\ *va* toška·wa·ya : to have for a *toška*

to·škin·ci·ye \tó-škiŋ-ci-ye\ *n of* škinciye : his or its work, his field, his occupation, as is said on seeing trees felled in a creek and concluding that beavers are at work there - Bl

to·štoš \tō-štō'š\ *adv red of* toš : Yes, Yea < *Eyaš* ~ *hankeni wate šni eye* But he said Yea, he ate not a part. >

to·tin·yan·ka yo \ṫo-ṫíŋ-yaŋ-ka yo\ *interj for* to halt : Wait a little, Hold it < ~ *yo* Wait a bit! > - *Syn* ITÓ

to·to \to-tó\ *adj red of* to : many blue or green

[1]**to·to·la** \to-tó-la\ *n* : blue or green beads

[2]**to·to·la** *or* **o·tótola** \ṫo-tō'-la\ *adj* : bare - Cf yutóto *va* ET

to·to·pa \tō-tō'-ṗa\ *adj* ma·tótopa : soaked, all wet, as moccasins from rain or snow < *Mak'éya, nitotopin kte* Rediculous! You will be drenched, *i.e.* you will be wet from dew or fog. > — **totope·la** \to-tó-ṗe-la\ *adj* : dripping or sopping wet < *Hokši* ~ *iyeniceca yelo* You are like a child sopping wet, *i.e.* you act like a child, or are childish. > - Bl

to·to·ya \to-tó-ya\ *adv red of* toyá : to dye or paint blue or green - MS.340

to·wa·kan \tó-wa-kaŋ\ *n of* wówakan : his *wakán* or spirit

to·wan·ji·ca \to-wáŋ-ji-ca\ *adj* : blue entirely, all blue < *Anpetu wanji* ~ *ca peagnagwicakiyin kte lo* A clear blue day (sky) is to shine, settle upon them. > — **towanji·la** *n* : the blue sky, all blue - LP

to·wa·on·ši·la \tó-wa-oŋ-ši-la\ *n* ni·towaonšila [fr *wówaonšila* mercy] : his mercy

to·wa·šte \tó-wa-šte\ *n* ni·towašte [fr *wówašte* goodness] : his goodness

to·wa·š'a·ke \tō'-wa-š'a-ḳe\ *n* ni·towaš'ake [fr *wówaš'ake* strength] : his strength or power

to·we·ni *or* **tonweni ... šni** \ṫó-we-ni\ *adv* : never < *Koškalaka kayeš* ~ *taku emakiye šni yelo* Never did that young man say a thing to me. > - Bl

to·wi·ca·ke \tó-wi-ca-ḳe\ *n* ni·towicake [fr *wówicake* truth] : his truth < *Na* ~ *ca tan'inšni* And it was not apparent his truthfulness, *i.e.* although he might have spoken the truth. >

to·win·je \tó-wiŋ-je\ *n* mi·towinje [fr *owinja* a bed] : his bed

to·ya \to-yá\ *va* to·wa·ya : to dye or paint blue or green — **toya** \tó-ya\ *adv* : in a blue or green manner — **toya·kel** *adv* : in a blue or green form — **toye·la** *adj* : bluish, a bit blue, greenish

to·zi \to-zí\ *adj* : light green — **tozi·tka** \ṫó-zi-tka\ *adj* : greenish - Note: *zi* is not always placed in *comp* and carrying the meaning "yellow", as in : *canhpán pizi* a loot's gall

tu·cu·hu \ṫu-cú-hu\ *n* : a rib, or the ribs

tu·cu·šte \ṫu-cú-šte\ *n* : the flank, the side below the ribs

tu·ga \ṫū'-ġa\ *adj* ma·túga: hunch-backed, as a man or a camel — *n* : a hump or hunch

tu·hma·ga *or* **tuhmunga** \ṫu-ȟmá-ġa\ *n* : a bee or wasp < ~ *ȟota* a gray bee or wasp > - Bl

tu·hmun·ga \ṫu-ȟmúŋ-ġa\ *n* : bees, wasps, hornets — **tuhmunga canhánpi** *or* **tuhmunga tùnkce** *n* : honey — **tuhmunga tánka** *n* : the bumblebee — **tuhmunga wigli** *n* : bees' wax

[1]**tu·ka** \ṫu-k̇á\ *conj* : but - Note: the word seems to be used only in *compos*, thus: *Eyaš ~ unkicante kin unkoile s'elececa* But on the other hand, our hearts seemed to be on fire. *Šehanš ~, miyeš ~.* But good heavens! Though nobody else acts, I will. - B.H.273.14 D.71 note 4

[2]**tu·ka** \ṫú-k̇a\ *va in comp* as in *katuka* : to knock off, to destroy — **tuka·han** *part* : scabby, having lost one's hair, as a dog or horse *etc.* might; hence spoiled or destroyed, as said of fur - R

tu·ka·ka \ṫu-ká-k̇a\ *part* : tired < *Miyeš ~ , wanagi el mahipelo* I was tired, spirits came to me. > - BT

tu·kaš \ṫu-k̇áš\ *adv* : but - R Bl

[1]**tu·ki** \ṫu-k̇í\ *interj* : Is that so? < *~ yahi so?* Is it so you came? > - Note: the word is used by women - D.115

[2]**tu·ki** \ṫu-k̇í\ *n* : a clam — **tuki·ha** *n* : a shell, without the animal — **tuki·pšito** \ṫu-kí-pši-tō\ *n* : a pearl — **tuki·winunkal** *n* : a large shell, or a small round clam shell - Bl

tu·kte \ṫu-kṫé\ *pron interrog* : which? when? < *unma ~* which of the two? *~ ehan* when? *~ e* which is it? *Ho, nicinca kin ~ ehe ci ikikcu wo* Well then, take back which it was your child said. *~ oyate ca enitanhan hwo?* From which tribe are you? *Wicaša nitukte wanjipi* Which of you men are one? > - B.H.121.26, 224/9

tu·kte e k'e·yaš *or* **tukte e·ke e·yaš** \ṫu-kṫé e k'è-yaš\ *pron indef* : anybody < *tukte ... ke c'eyaš* whichever, *tukte anpetu k'eyaš* whichever day > - B.H.52.10

tu·kte·han \ṫu-kṫé-haŋ\ *adv* : at some time to come < *Iškanškan amayakita ye, ~ akih'an t'emayayin kte* You look at me with a hungry look; sometime you will make me die of hunger, as a woman would say to grandchildren who want to eat along with her. > - Bl

tu·kte i·han·ke·ya \ṫu-kṫé i-hàŋ-ke-ya\ *adv* and *adj* : where or which from the ground up, from first to last < *~ can otehike kin on kage* With difficulty he made it which in its entirety was of expensive wood, *i.e.* the best of wood. > - B.H.60.9

tu·kte·kte \ṫu-kṫé-kṫe\ *pron red interrog of* tukté : which?

tu·kte·ktel \ṫu-kṫé-kṫel\ *adv red of* tuktel : sometimes, once in a while, now and then; in some places

tu·kte·kte·tan·han \ṫu-kṫé-kṫe-ṫaŋ-haŋ\ *adv red interrog* : from what or which place? < *Hecel ~ cehpi opawinge nainš wikcemna zaptan nainš aokpaniyan na wana gluštanpi* So from which place did they finish with a hundred bits of flesh, or fifty, or less. > - MS.343

tu·kte·kte·tu \ṫu-kṫé-kṫe-ṫu\ *adv red interrog of* tuktetu : at what place? where? < *~ k̇ak̇éš* anywheres, *~ ke s'e* It is pretty much somewhere, *i.e.* hard to choose. *Oyasin wašte s'elececa.* Every one seems good. *Na wanna lila oiyokipi koškalaka k'on ~ ke s'e wanna enajin na wanna lowanpi* And the young man had now been very pleased, it seemed with where he was, so they stood and now sang. > - B.H.108.10

tu·ktel \ṫu-kṫél\ *adv interrog* : where?, in what place?; somewhere < *Ake ~ ištinma* Again he slept somewhere. *Wanna tipi he ohiyayelo, ca ~ kagapi yacin hwo?* He now reached a house, so where do you want it to be made? *Le hihanna kin mat'in kta ca ~ paha wanji el tanyan emaonpa po* Since I am about to die this morning, bury me nicely somewhere on a hill. > — **tuktel ... hel** *adv coord* : where ... there < *Tuktel wicaȟapi kin hel woyute eša égnakapi* Where the grave is there some food is placed. >

tu·kte·na \ṫu-kṫé-na\ *pron interrog* : which one of these? < *~ Israel oyatepi tka k'un otan'inpi šni* Which one of the tribes of Israel would not have appeared? > - B.H.119.1 LHB WHL

tu·kte·ni \ṫu-kṫé-ni\ *adv* in *compos* with *šni* : nowhere < *Huhu ece ca na tukteni talo ikoyake šni yelo* Yumyum, so it is when nowhere does meat stick. >

tu·kte·o·gna·gna *or* **tukteogna** \ṫu-kṫé-o-gna-gna\ *adv red interrog* : in what direction?, where? - Cf tuktogna B.H.88.25

tu·kte·tan·han \ṫu-kṫé-ṫaŋ-haŋ\ *adv* : from what place?

tu·kte·tu \ṫu-kṫé-ṫu\ *adv interrog* : at what place? < *~ ȟapi tan'in šni* It is not apparent where he is buried. > — **tuktetu kakeškeš** *or* **tuktetu kakeš** \ṫu-kṫé-ṫu k̇à-k̇e-šk̇eš\ *adv* : at most any place < *Wakantanka ~ waunyekiyapi* They made offerings to God most any place. *~ iyomakipi* I am pleased with him most anywhere. > - *See* kakéškeš — **tu-ktetu k'eyaš** *or* **tuktetu ke c'eyaš** *adv* : in any place, everywhere, wherever - B.H.50.3, 154.2

tu·kto·gna *or* **toktéogna** *or* **toktogna·gna** \ṫu-kṫó-gna\ *adv interrog* : in what direction? where? which way? < *~ unyin kte he?* Which way shall you and I go? *Letan wanna ~ iyonicipipi kin ogna iyaya po* Now after this go in the way you are pleased to go. *~ oti iwašte kin he ogna kahnigapi* They chose where there was a better place in which to live. *~ ktepi kta tan'in šni* It was not clear which way they might kill it. > — **tuktogna ke c'èyaš** *adv* : however in whichever way

tu·kto·gna·kel \ṫu-kṫó-gna-kel\ *adv* : in no way < *~ iwayupiya gnaye iyunh šipi* He was told to question cheating nicely in no way. *~ waayupte šni* In no way did he give an answer. > — **tuktogna·ni** *adv* : in no way < *~ napa okihi šni* In no way could he run away. > - B.H.45.6,12, 46.2, 266.13, 88.25,137.25, 266.3, 77.11, 261.21, 262.18, 292.7

tu·ktu·ka·han \ṫu-kṫú-ka-haŋ\ *adj* : spoiled, as furs when the hair is off - R Bl

tu·ktun·ma \ṫu-kṫúŋ-ma\ *adv* : either one of two - B.H. 199.14, 187.13

tu·la \ṫu-lá\ *interj exclam of* surprise or protest : For shame!

tum \ṫum\ *n* : a whistling or whizzing sound of *e.g.* a bullet's ricochet

tun·jan \ṫuŋ-jáŋ\ *n* mi·tunjan ni·tunjan : a man's niece, a man's brother's children, and a woman's sister's children are considered as children and are not *tunška* nephews or *tunjan* nieces — **tunjan·ku** *n* : his niece — **tunjan·ya** *va* tunjan·wa·ya : he to have for a niece

[1]**tun·kan** \ṫuŋ-k̇áŋ\ *n* mi·túnkan ni·túnkan : a sacred stone spoken in the sacred language, supposed to have great power, and used in the *oinikage tipi* sweatlodge . This stone is called a *tunkan wašicun*, and also the *yuwipi wašicun* - *See* wašicun HM FD.204

[2]**tun·kan** \ṫuŋ-k̇áŋ\ *n* tunkan·ši *or* mi·túnkan ni·túnkan : a father-in-law — **tunkan·ku** \ṫuŋ-k̇áŋ-k̇u\ *n* : his or her fath-er-in-law — **tunkan·ši** *n* : my father-in-law — **tunkanši·ya** *or* **tunkan·yan** *va* tunkan·wa·yan : to have for a father-in-law

tun·ka·ši·la \ṫuŋ-k̇á-ši-la\ *n* ni·tunkašila : a grandfather, my grandfather — **Tunkašila** *np* **1** : the president of the United States of America **2** : God, the Godhead, the Supreme Being

Tun·ka·ši·la O·ti \Ṫuŋ-k̇á-šila O-ṫì\ *np* : the White

\a\ father \e\ they \i\ machine \o\ smoke \u\ lunar \an, aŋ\ blanc Fr. \in, iŋ\ ink \on, oŋ, un, uŋ\ soon, confier Fr. \c\ chair \ġ\ machen Ger. \j\ fusion \clusters: bl, gn, kp, hšl, etc...\ b°lo ... said with a slight vowel
See more in the Introduction, Guide to Pronunciation

House, the current United States President's residence

tun·ka·ši·la·ya \ṫuŋ-k̇á-ši-la-ya\ *n* tunkaši·lwa·ya : to have for a grandfather — **tunkaši·tku** *n* : his or her grandfather

tun·kce \ṫúŋ-kce\ *n* : excrement, faeces; a breaking wind

tun·sla \ṫuŋ-slá\ *n* : the snail, the leech

tun·ška \ṫuŋ-šká\ *n* mi·tunška ni·tunška : a nephew, *i.e. tankeku cinca hokšila* the boy child of his older sister — **tunška·ku** *n* : his nephew — **tunška·ya** *va* tun-ška·wa·ya : to have for a nephew

tun·tun·pa \ṫuŋ-ṫúŋ-pa\ *adj* : slippery, slimy, ropy < *p'e* ~ the slippery elm > - R Bl

tun·we·hca \ṫúŋ-we-ḣca\ *express of disbelief or doubt* : so you say < ~ *škeka, lila on'iwakankan ye* Indeed so you say, you are really a babbler. > - Note: but the word is used usually with *škė'ka* as when a man makes a statement who is known to be a liar - B.H.99.10

tun·wel \ṫúŋ-wel\ *adv* : once upon a time - *See* tónwel — **tunwel·wel** *adv red* : in past time often - Bl

tun·wi·cu \ṫuŋ-wí-cu\ *n* : his or her aunt on the father's side — **tunwicu·ya** *va* tunwicu·wa·ya : to have for one's aunt

tun·win \ṫuŋ-wíŋ\ *n* ni·túnwin : an aunt, my aunt, on the father's side, an uncle's wife - Note: a mother's sisters are called *ina* — **tunwin·ya** *va* tunwin·wa·ya : to have for an aunt on the father's side

tu·sla \tu-slá\ *n* : a blood sucker < *Mni el ~ unpi. Si el ~ imakoyake* Blood suckers live in water. A sucker fastened to my foot. > - KE WHL

tu·sla wa·ya·ska·pe s'e \tu-slá wá-ya-ska-pe s'e\ *adv* : sticking in the manner of a leech < *tusla wáyaskape s'e kuwa* to be intent upon speaking to a person and hence come again and again while the other knows nothing about this and does not ask either. > - Bl

tu·swe·ca \ṫu-swé-ca\ *n* : a dragon fly — **tusweca ša** *n* : the red dragon fly — **tusweca tanka gleglèġa** *n* : the large speckled dragon fly — **tusweca tanka zizi** *n* : the large yellow dragon fly — **tusweca to** *n* : the blue dragon fly - Bl

tu·šu \ṫu-šú\ *n* : a tent pole, tent poles, a lodge pole

tu·šu·he·yun·pi \ṫu-šú-he-yuŋ-pi\ *n* : a travois, a drag, *i.e.* tent poles tied together to pack things on - *Syn* HU-PÁHEYUNPI

tu·šu in·kpa \ṫu-šú iŋ-kpa\ *n* : the upper, visible ends of tent poles - *Syn* TICÉ INKPA

tu·šu i·pa·tan·ton \ṫu-šú i-pà-ṫaŋ-toŋ\ *v* : to brace the inner wall of a tent lest it shake too much during a storm — **tušu iyutanton** *v* : to put a rope around the tent poles above and fasten it inside to the ground so as to hold it tightly together while a heavy wind blows - Bl

tu·ta \ṫu-tá\ *adj* : smarting, chapped by the wind < *Ite matúte* My face is chapped. >

tu·tka \ṫu-tká\ *n* : small articles, trinkets (but not insects) — **tutka·la** *n dim* : little trinkets — **tutka·tka** *n* : small, trifling articles or trinkets — **tutkatka·yakel** *or* **tutka·yakel** \ṫu-tká-tka-ya-k̇el\ *adv* : in bits, small quantities < ~ *wawakamna* I earned money in small quantities at a time > - *Syn* YUH'EH'EYAKEL, PTU-H'AH'AYAKEL Bl

tu·wa \ṫú-wa\ *pron rel* : who < ~ *ohíye ci toka hwo* Why is it that one won? > — **tuwa ... ca na** *or* **ca he** *pron rel* : who *or* whom ... he *or* him; if one ... he < *Tuwa nahmala wanasa ca na akicita ktepi* One who goes buffalo hunting in secret him warriors kill. > — **tuwa ... eša** *pron indef* : anyone, someone < *Tuwa icimani eša* Anyone goes on a tour. > - B.H.57.17

tu·wa e ka·ga \ṫú-wa e kà-ġa\ *v* : to take for, mistake for - B.H.221.16

tu·wa ka ke·ša *or* **tuwa ka kešaš** *or* **tuwakakša** *or* **tuwa akakeša** *or* **tuwekakeša** *or* **tuwe kakša** \ṫú-wa ka k̇e-šà\ \ṫú-wa ka k̇è-šaš\ \ṫú-wa-kakša\ \ṫú-wa a-k̇á-ke-ša\ \ṫú-we-ka-ke-ša\ \ṫú-we-ka-kša\ *interj* : It is impossible, *or* never heard of!, Preposterous!, Absurd! - R D.160 B.H.179.18, 29.10, 179.26

tu·wa ta·wa \ṫú-wa tà-wa\ *pron* : whose?

tu·wa·tu \ṫu-wá-ṫu\ *interrog pron rel of* túwa : who here? < ~ *lúza* Whom do you suppose you have here? > - Bl LHB WHL

tu·we \ṫu-wé\ *pron interrog* : who?, which? (rarely) - Note: *tuwe ... ca* who ... ? B.H.148.20

tu·we ce e·yaš *or* **tuwe ke eyaš** \ṫu-wé ce è-yaš\ *pron indef* : anybody, whoever — **tuwehci k'eyaš** *or* **tuwe ke c'eyaš** *pron indef* : everybody, all < *Tuwe ke c'eyaš slolyapi na miš slolwaya* Whomever they know I too know. *wicaša tuwe ce eyaš* any man > - B.H.236.11

tu·we·hca \ṫú-we-ḣca\ *pron interrog* : who indeed? < ~ *škéka* You really tell lies who indeed says Who really are those that say it? ~ *škeka lila oweniwakankan* Who indeed are those who say you are a real liar? > - B.H.99.10

tu·we·ka·leš \ṫú-we-k̇a-leš\ *pron* : whoever - R

tu·we ke·ša \ṫu-wé k̇e-šà\ *pron* : whoever - B.H. 190.23 261.7

tu·we·la \ṫu-wé-la\ *pron* : who < *He ~ hwo?* Just who is he? ~ *wanwicayanke šni* Who is it that did not see them? > - R Bl

tu·we·ni \ṫu-wé-ni\ *pron* : nobody < ~ *un šni* It was nobody. *Cinkši, nitankšila manil ~ un šni ekta kici ti na awanyanka yo* My son, your little sister does not live in the wilderness where there is nobody to live with, and so look after her. *Tehanl ~ un šni wan ekta etipi keye* He said they set up camp at a place where for a long time there was nobody. >

tu·we·ška \ṫu-wé-ška\ *interj* : Who is this? < ~ *hwo?* Who is this said to be? > - Bl

t'a \t'a\ *vn* : to die, to faint away, lose consciousness temporarily < *Mat'a* I fainted. >

t'a·ga \t'á-ġa\ *adj* : rough, as a floor on account of sand strewn over it; bitter or astringent, as oak bark

t'a·ġe·la hu \t'á-ġe-la hu\ *n* : alum root - *See* wahpe t'aga - BT #267

t'a·hi·yu·ya \t'á-hi-yu-ya\ *vn* : to be stillborn

t'a·ht'a·ga \t'a-ḣt'á-ġa\ *adj red of* t'aga : rough, not smooth < *Ocanku ~ kin hena yualapapi kte* They should smoothen those rough roads. > - B.H.172.8

t'a·nun·s'e \t'á-nuŋ-s'e\ *adv* : about dead

t'a·t'a \t'a-t'á\ *adj* : numb, asleep as a limb < *Hu mat'á-t'a* My leg is numb. > — **t'at'a·ka** \t'a-t'á-k̇a\ *adj* mat'át'aka : numb, palsied

t'e *or* **t'a** \t'e\ *vn* : to die

t'e·ble·ze šni \t'e-blé-ze šni\ *v* : to be frantic, wild < *Hokšila k'un ~ na ceye* The boy had cried and got frantic. ~ *wawiyahpahpaya ayahilala* You sang a tune for fun making an attack and getting wild, *i.e.* wrestling for fun. > - Bl

[1]**t'e·ca** \t'e-cá\ *adj* : lying dead < *pte* ~ a dead cow >

[2]**t'e·ca** \t'é-ca\ *adj* : warm, lukewarm, tepid, as water — **t'eca·ya** *ot* **t'ecaya·kel** \t'é-ca-ya\ \t'é-ca-ya-k̇el\ *adv* : still a little warm, in a dead state - Note: the word is used in *ref* to fluids, as coffee

t'e·gna·škin·yan s'e \t'e-gná-škiŋ-yaŋ s'e\ *adv* : franticly, in very great excitement < ~ *ole* to look for one everywhere in utter distress > – Bl

t'e·ho·wa·ya \t'e-hó-wa-ya\ *vn* wa·t'ehowa·bla : to cry out badly, to scream for fear, as is said of men and animals — **t'ehowaye·ya** *va* t'ehowaye·wa·ya : to cause to cry out badly

t'e·i·ca·kiš *or* **t'eicaki·šya** \t'e-í-ca-kiš\ \t'e-í-ca-ki-šya\ *adv* : in a dying state

t'e·ki·ni·ca \t'e-kí-ni-ca\ *vn* t'e·ma·kinica : to contend with death, to be doubtful whether one dies or lives < *Hecel yankahe c'on he ceya lila iyokišica on ~ ške'* So as he was sitting there, they say that he was contending with death because he was utterly sad and crying, *i.e.* he felt as though he must die of grief. > – D.225

t'e·ki·ya \t'e-ǩí-ya\ *va* t'e·wa·kiya : to cause to die

t'e·kon \t'e-ǩóŋ\ *v* t'e·wa·kon : to wish to be dead — **t'ekon·za** *v* : to curse, wish one dead

t'e·la nu·we *or* **t'ela nuwe·la** \t'é-la nu-wè\ *n* : a lizard of a smaller sort found in the hills, the sand lizard – S Bl

t'e·šni·yan·kel \t'e-šni-yaŋ-kel\ *adv* : not dying < *Elias ~ wankatakiya eyayapi* Elijah without dying was taken up (to heaven). > – B.H.113.5

t'e·ya \t'e-yá\ *va* t'e·wa·ya : to cause to die < *Ota t'ewicayaya* You brought about the death of many. > — **t'eya·su** \t'e-yá-su\ *v* : to condemn to die – Note: this is a new word — **t'eyasu·pi** \t'e-yá-su-pi\ *part* : condemned to die

t'in \t'iŋ\ *vn of* t'a : to die – Note: this form is used when followed by *kta*, the sign of the *fut*

t'in·ga \t'íŋ-ġa\ *vn* wa·t'inga : to snivel, to grunt, as a woman in childbirth

t'in·si·c'i·ya \t'íŋ-si-c'i-ya\ *va* : to restrain one's self, to brace up — *adv* : firmly, without fear

t'in·sya \t'íŋ-sya\ *va* t'in·swa·ya : to make firm — **t'insya·kel** \t'iŋ-syá-ǩel\ *adv* : firmly, bravely

t'in·t'in \t'iŋ-t'íŋ\ *adj perhaps* : beginning to dry < *Tatunkce nunb wanblaka; yunkan unma puza na ~ yelo* I saw two dung hills; and then another dry and beginning to dry. > – *Syn* PÚZA ÁYA Bl

t'in·za \t'íŋ-za\ *adj* : hard, stiff, as mud; firm, brave < *wowaši ~* a hard worker, *cante ~* a brave heart >

t'in·za·ni \t'iŋ-zá-ni\ *adv* : stilly, smoothly, calmly < *Canku naškiškapi ca canpagmiyanpi ~ mani šni yelo* Since the road was rough the wagon did not travel smoothly, *i.e.* rough roads and unpleasant riding. *~ najin okihi šni* He was unable to stand calmly still. > – Bl

t'o·ja \t'ó-ja\ *adj* : dull, pointless — **t'ošya** \t'ó-šya\ *adv* : bluntly < *~ kaga* to make bluntwise >

t'un·gya \t'uŋ-gyá\ *va* t'un·gwa·ya : to suspect, have a suspicion about a thing — **t'ungya·kel** *adv* : unwillingly < *~ econ* to do something unwillinglly, *i.e.* hesitating perhaps out of suspicion > — **t'ungye·šni** *adv perhaps* : not unwillingly – B.H.5.16

t'un·ka \t'úŋ-ka\ *v contrac* ma·t'únka [fr *t'unkeca* to be suspected] : to be suspicious — **t'unke·ca** \t'úŋ-ke-ca\ *vn* ma·t'unkeca : to be suspected, suspicious — **t'unkiya** \t'uŋ-kí-ya\ *v* : to suspect concerning one's self

U

u \u\ *vn* wa·u un·ku·pi : to come, be coming – R

U·c'i·ta A·u *or* **Uc'ita Nataupi** *or* **Uc'ita Au Inyankapi** \Ú-c'i-ta A-ù\ *np* : the morning parade on Independence Day, July 4th — *v* [fr *uic'ita, uta* to fire off one's own, to try a gun by firing it] : to march in celebration the 4th of July < *Uc'ita unkaupi kte lo* Let us bring on the 4th of July march. *Hinhanna el wana Uc'ita ayin kta ca toka ktepi hena oh'anpi k'un ecel ewicaglepi* In the morning when the March is about to begin, they had them stand such that those who were generous kill an enemy. *Na wana Uc'ita ahiyaya* And now the March passes by (the reviewing stand). > – MS.565

u·ka \u-ǩá\ *n* : the skin, hide, *esp* the skin of a living animal, the skin without hair, in opposition to *ha* which is a hairy hide – R Bl

[1]**u·ki·ya** \u-kí-ya\ *vn coll pl* : they are coming, on their way home, *i.e.* where the speaker is – Note: the word is used in *ref* to many, whereas *ku* is said of one < *Wana agli yelo* They have arrived home, *i.e.* where the speaker is. *Wakinyan ukiye lo* Thunder is coming. *Na wanna iyehantu k'on hehan ukiya na wanna ake zaptan ca el owakpamni el agli* And now it being the time, then they were on their way home, and in fifteen days they arrived back to the distribution center. > – Note: *Wana glapelo* Now they are on their way home, *i.e.* the speaker being absent. *Wana tiyata kipelo* Now they have arrived at their house, *i.e.* the speaker is absent. *Wagli ukiyelo* They were on their way home successful bringing in game. – LB D.3

[2]**u·ki·ya** \u-ǩí-ya\ *va* u·wa·kiya : to cause to come

u·man *or* **unma** \u-máŋ\ *adj* : the one, the other

[1]**un** \uŋ\ *vn* wa·ún ya·ún un·k'un·pi : to be — *va* mun nun unk'unpi : to use aything, have for use, to wear < *Nupin tatanka wapaha unpi* Both wear a buffalo headdress. *sapun* to wear black, *skaun* to wear white > – Note: here *un* is the same as *in* to wear. *Sapun* is the title for a catholic priest, *Skaun* for the episcopalean priest — *va* : to play < *Haka unpi* They play Haka. > — *pron in compos* with unk'unpi : we, us

[2]**un** *or* **on** *and* **un·pi** \uŋ\ \úŋ-pi\ *partic perhaps* : being, *i.e.* perhaps the Latin *ens*. – Note: *un* seems to take the place of the *art* *"kin"*, or is the same as *"k'un"* or *"k'on"*. < *Canke kangi un lila onšic'iya* And so the crow pretended to be very miserable. *Na pte unpi kin el egna iyaya* He went among the buffalo that were there. *Hehan wicaša hin šma un hiyu* Then there came out a man with a heavy head of hair. > – B.H.190.20, 85.7, 14.11, 15.16

un·a·zi·pi *or* **onazinpi** \úŋ-a-zi-pi\ *n* : a nipple for sucking

un·ca \úŋ-ca\ *va* ún·wa·ca ún'·un·ca·pi : to mock, imitate, to ridicule one

un·ca·blo·ju \úŋ-ca-blo-ju\ *n archaic* [fr *uncablu* + *oju*] : deep snow, *esp* drifts along fences – Bl

un·ci \uŋ-cí\ *n* ni·kunši : a grandmother, my grandmother – Note: a woman calls her mother-in-law *uncí*. *See* kúnši — **Unci** \Uŋ-cí\ *np* : Mother Earth, Earth, a term so applied by the Dakotas in former times as a subject of concern in their prayers

un·ci·hi \úŋ-ci-hi\ *vn* ún·ma·cihi ún'·un·cihi·pi : to have attained one's growth, to be able to take care of one's self — **uncihi·ya** *va* úncihi·wa·ya : to cause to sustain one's self, to raise, train up to manhood

un·ci·la \uŋ-cí-la\ *n dim of* uncí : dear little grandmother

un·ci·ši \uŋ-cí-ši\ *n* : a mother-in-law, my mother-in-law < ~ *nitawa* your mother-in-law >

un·ci·ši·ca·la \uŋ-cí-ši-ca-la\ *n* : the crow, crows, the corvus Americanus, and the little crow, and perhaps also what R calls *ungnagicala*, a bird like a small owl. < ~ *s'e ho šica tka lowan* He would sing like a crow with its croaking voice, as they say of a fellow who has a bad voice. > – Note: *kangi* is a raven Bl

un·ci·ši·la \uŋ-cí-ši-la\ *n dim of* unciši : a mother-in-law — **uncišiya** *va* unciši·wa·ya : to have for a mother-in-law

un·ci·ya \uŋ-cí-ya\ *va* unci·wa·ya : to have for a grandmother

un·c'on·ni·ca \úŋ-c'oŋ-ni-ca\ *vn* ún·ma·c'onnica : to give up, yield, not try to escape; to be prevented, penned up; to be stage-struck, be frozen on the spot < ~ *hingla* Suddenly she was stage-struck, *i.e.* words stuck in her throat and she could not utter them. > – D.271 note 1, 244

un·c'on·nil \úŋ-c'oŋ-nil\ *vn contrac of* unc'onnica : to be prevented — **unc'onni·lya** *va* unc'onni·lwa·ya : to obstruct, prevent, disarm < *Hecon kin on* ~ Since he did that she disarmed him. > — *adv* : prevented

un·c'un·ni·ca *and* **unc'unnil** *and* **unc'unnilya** – *See* under *unc'onnica* and *unc'onnil etc.*

un·gna \uŋ-gná\ *interj of* caution : perhaps, my guess is, I do not know but that < *Na ~, nitakuye wanji nikiyela apa glihpaya eša, el eyatonwe kiló* So, though perhaps one of your close relatives struck him, he got home and lay down, so don't you go look at him. *Kolapila, ~ nayapapi kilo na wipe kin kiksuya po.* Remember, dear friends, the weapons and do not flee. *Na wanna wicokanyan sanpa ehanl ~ wanna u.* And in the afternoon it was perhaps at this time he came. ~ *ṫóka ška pahaha ihpeciye ci* How is it they say that perhaps I opposed rejecting you? ~ *kapemniyan mic'ignake cin* I don't know but that he set it handily aside for me. > – Bl B.H.81.1

un·gna·ga·ta \uŋ-gná-ġa-ṫa\ *adv* : at or in the *ungnage* the corner behind the door

un·gna·ge \uŋ-gná-ġe\ *n* : the places on both sides of the tent door inside, the corner of a room and as such is an *okahmin* a corner behind the door, the place fenced off on each side of the door of a lodge – R LO

un·gna·gi·ca·la \uŋ-gná-ġi-ca-la\ *n* : a screech owl, a bird like a small owl that wails in the night while perched in a tree; women imitate it in a certain dance – Note: it is also called the *popotka*, and the *pagla*; ~ *hotonpi* they sound off as do women in the dance: "lilili ... ", *hohnágicala hotonpi* the screetch owl's sound.

un·gna·ha·hci \uŋ-gná-ha-ḣci\ *adv* : possibly, it may be so < ~ *le anpetu kinhan išta mastaka s'elececa* It may be it seems my eyes are tired today. > – Bl

un·gna·han·la \uŋ-gná-haŋ-la\ *adv* : suddenly, immediately — **ungnahanš** *or* **ungnahan·šna** *adv* : every now and then, at certain times < *Cante pahlokapi kin henayos ~ yutitanpi* Now and then they pull on these two perforations of the heart, as is said in the Sundance. > — **ungnahe·la** *or* **ungnahe·lake** *adv* : all at once, suddenly < *Yunkan ~ wekta* And then all at once I awoke. *Yunkan ~ taji nunp cokab hiyupi* And suddenly two red buffalo calves came into the center. > — **ungnahela·ya** *va* ungnahela·wa·ya : to surprise one – B.H. 76.6

un·gna·h'i·ca·ške \úŋ-gna-ḣ'i-ca-ške\ *n* : a tripod of three sticks to which are fastened the *cankázontapi* bed matting over which robes to sleep on were spread – GA Bl

un·gna·kah *or* **ungnayekah** \úŋ-gna-ḳaḣ\ *adv* : easing one's way simultaneously towards < ~ *econ* to do it easing one's way toward, *Makoce ataya cah'owancaya; yunkan ~ skan ayelo.* The whole countryside was ice-covered; and then at the same time it began to melt. *Hena wana ~ ablezapi* They now progressively understood things. > – Bl LHB WHL

un·gnaš \uŋ-gnáš\ *interj emph of* ungná : perhaps!, maybe! < ~ *ecanna nit'api kte lo* Maybe you will die soon enough! > — **ungna·yehciš** *interj emph* : perhaps! possibly! – B.H.34.27, 117.4

un·gna·ye·ka·hkah \úŋ-gna-ye-ḳa-ḣḳaḣ\ *adv* : easing one's way forward at the same time < ~ *econ* to work one's way forward with others, ~ *peji uya ayelo* Grass began gradually to sprout. > – Bl

un·he *or* **unhéna** \uŋ-hé\ *pron dem* : that < *Na eyapaha ~ tankal hinapin na lecel eya* And that announcer came out and this is what he said. *Ehanl eyapaha k'un he eyapaha au na lecel eya* At the moment that announcer who had made an announcement came to announce further saying this. *Unkoniciyakapi unhe le anpetu kin e yelo* This is that day about which we talked to you. *Wakantanka aguyapi eya iwaktaniyanpi unhe lena e yelo* This is bread of God and for that you are on the look-out. *Yunkan Juda hokšila eya topapi k'un hena ceb ayapi na tanyan unpi na unmapi unhena hececapi šni* And then some four Jewish boys got fat and were doing well, while those others did not do that well. > – MS.71 B.H.55.14, 136.22

un·hce·gi·la \uŋ-ḣcé-ġi-la\ *n* : a mastodon perhaps, or other large animals whose petrified remains are found in the Dakota Territory < ~ *s'e kagišnišni wala yelo* Like a mastodon, I asked as I pleased. > — **unhcegila·hu** *n* : the bones of the *unhcegila* that were once used for the making of medicines

un·hce·la \uŋ-ḣcé-la\ *n* : the mescal bean

un·hce·la bla·ska \uŋ-ḣcé-la bla·ska\ *n* : the flat cactus

un·hce·la ka·ga·pi \uŋ-ḣcé-la ḳà-ġa-pi\ *n* : the feather disk attached to the back of a dancer, so called because of the central part appears like a cactus; a dance bustle

un·hce·la pte \uŋ-ḣcé-la pte\ *n* : a toy for boys

un·hce·la tan·ka \uŋ-ḣcé-la tàŋ-ka\ *n* : the tall cactus

un·hce·la ta·špu \uŋ-ḣcé-la ta-šṗu\ *n* : the cactus berry

un·hce·la yu·ta ta·wo·hta·te \uŋ-ḣcé-la yú-ta ṫa-wó-ḣta-te\ *n* : the paraphernalia used in the Peyote Service of the Native American Church – LTf

un·i·glu·ja·ja·pi \úŋ-i-glu-ja-ja-pi\ *n* : a wash basin

un·jin·ca·la \uŋ-jíŋ-ca-la\ *n* : a fledgling bird before the tail has grown, any bird with a short tail < ~ *iblotakelo* I sat down a mere fledgling, as a man says when in sitting down he almost tips over in a forward direction. > – Bl

un·jin·jin·tka \uŋ-jíŋ-jiŋ-tḳa\ *n* : a tomatoe

un·jin·jin·tka hu \uŋ-jíŋ-jiŋ-tḳa hu\ *n* : a rosebush — **unjinjintkahu can** *n* : the wild rosebush – #29

un·kanš \uŋ-kčáŋš\ *adv* : at some time – *Syn* TOKŠÁ

un·kce \úŋ-kce\ *vn* ún·wa·kce ún·un·kce·pi : to defecate with sound, to break wind < ~ *hingla* suddenly to break wind > — *n* : a breaking wind — **unkce·kce** *v red* ún·wa·kcekce : to break wind repeatedly – D.73 BT

un·kce·ki·ha \uŋ-kcé-ḳi-ḣa\ *n* : the magpie – Note: its call or song is: "Halháta, halhata, hal, hal, hal". < ~ *s'e wašin waštelake* Like the magpie he like fat meat. > – Bl RF Rl

un·kce·la \uŋ-kcé-la\ *n* : the cactus – Note: the *altern* spelling, *unhcela* < ~ *tašpú* the cactus berry, ~ *blaska* the flat cactus, ~ *kagapi* an ornament of feathers and looking like a blossom which is attached to the seat of a man in the Omaha dance, a dance bustle. ~ *tanka* the tall cactus > - Note: the roots of the *unkcela blaska* in being boiled make a tea good for people who cannot urinate. < *Lakota maka sapa na wase ocaje oyasin on owa na yuštan ca nahahci spaye ci el piya yuspaya na ~ heca waksin na on apawinta ca he tohinni jajahe šni nainš powaye šni.* The Lakota painted with every sort of black and red earth, and when he finished if it is still wet he dampened it again, and it is the flat cactus he cuts, and when he rubs on with it it never washes off, nor does it flake. > - MS.482

un·kce·la pe·pe \uŋ-kcé-la ṗe-ṗè\ *n* : burgrass, the sandbur, cenchrus carolinianus, the grass family - BT #23

un·kce·pa·gmi·gma *or* **unkcepagmiyanyan** \uŋ-kcé-pa-gmi-gma\ *n* : the tumble bug

un·ki...pi \uŋ-kí...pi\ *pers pron in compos* : we, us — **unkiš** \uŋ-kíš\ *pron emph* miš niš iš : we ourselves < *Unkiš hunh le maya kin ohlateya unyanpi kte lo* Some of us will go below this bank. > — **unkišna·la** *pron dual* : we two alone — **unkišna·pi·la** *pron dual pl* : we two and others perhaps

un·ki·ta \uŋ-ḱí-ta\ *pron poss in compos with* "pi" *to end the word* : ours — **unkita·wa** *pron dual* : ours, *i.e.* yours and mine — **unkitawa·pi** *pron dual pl* : ours, *i.e.* yours and mine and others

un·ki·ya \uŋ-ḱí-ya\ *va* [fr *un* to use + *kiya* to cause] : to cause one to use or wear *e.g.* a coat, to help one on with something as a coat < *Unmíciciya yo* Help me putting it on. > - Pb.31

un·ki·ye \uŋ-kí-ye\ *pron* : we two, us — **unkiye·pi** *pron pl* : we, myself and others, us - Cf miye, niye, iye

un·kto·mi *or* **iktomi** \uŋ-ḱtó-mi\ *n* : the spider, a fabulous creature like the fox in western European folklore — **unktomi taokaške** \uŋ-ḱtó-mi ta-ò-ḱa-ške\ *n* : a spider's web

un·k'un·pi \uŋ-k'úŋ-pi\ *v pl* : we are

un·la \úŋ-la\ *v dim* : to be or to use

un·ma \uŋ-má\ *adj* : the one, the other < ~ *tukte?* which of the two?> — **unma·ciyatan** \uŋ-má-ci-ya-taŋ\ *adv* [fr *unma* the other + *eciyatan* from, thence] : from the other side, on the contrary — **unma·eciyatanhan** *adv* : from the other side, on the contrary

un·ma·gma \uŋ-má-gma\ *adj* : one or the other, either of two < *Le ~ icupo* Take anyone of the two (you may wish). >

un·ma·la ... šni \uŋ-má-la ... šni\ *adj* : neither — **unma·ni** *adj* : none of two, neither < ~ *wašte šni* Both are bad. ~ *unyuha kte šni* Neither of us should have it. *Heceš ~ o šni* Thus he shot neither one. > - Bl B.H.99.21 D.111

[1]**un·ma to·ktok** \uŋ-má ṫò-kṫok\ *adv* : by turns, one after another < ~ *econpi* They did it by turns. ~ *išta wankal yekiyapi* One after the other they raised their eyes up. >

[2]**un·ma·to·ktok** \úŋ-ma-ṫo-kṫok\ *adv* : two by two in turns, only two by turns < ~ *econpi* It was done two by two in turns. >

un·na·han *or* **unnihan** \úŋ-na-haŋ\ *adv* : at last, soon, shortly

un·na·ptan \úŋ-na-ptaŋ\ *adj perhaps* : inclined to one side, sideling - *Syn* HEPÍYA — **unnaptan·yan** \úŋ-na-ṗtaŋ-yaŋ\ *adv* : slanting

un·ni·han \úŋ-ni-haŋ\ *adv* : at last, soon, shortly < ~ *šak'ómayazan yelo* At last my finger tips pained me. *Wana ~ ataya tebye sece c'un* Surely he seemed at last to have eaten everything. > - BT D.96, 194, 74

[1]**un·pa** *or* **onpa** \úŋ-ṗa\ *va* wa·unpa : to place

[2]**un·pa** \úŋ-ṗa\ *vn* múŋ·pa núŋ·pa úŋ·kunpa·pi : to smoke *e.g.* tobacco < *Cannunpa kin le nunpapi kta* You should smoke this pipe. >

un·pan \uŋ-páŋ\ *n* : the female elk — **unpan·ha** *n* : elk skin — **unpan·hinske** \uŋ-páŋ-hiŋ-sḱe\ *n* : elk teeth — **unpan tawote** \uŋ-páŋ ta-wò-ṫe\ *n* : the smaller red-root, ceanothus ovatus, the buckthorn family - Note: the leaves are used for drinking tea. The eastern variety, ceanothus americanus was used by American troops during their Revolution - BT #52

un·pi \úŋ-ṗi\ *v pl of* un : they are

un·pši·ja *or* **unpšiš** \uŋ-pší-ja\ *n* : mud < ~ *s'e* like mud, as is said of a large herd of buffalo, ~ *eyala s'e wagli yelo* He brought home game apparently nothing but mud, *i.e.* all bespattered with mud. > - Note: the word applies to thin mud, while *hlihlila* is applied to light mud — **un-pšišya** *adv* : muddy

un·sin \uŋ-síŋ\ *n* : the small end of a porcupine quill; the large quills in the porcupine's tail

un·štin·ma·pi·hin *or* **onštinmapihin** \úŋ-štiŋ-ma-ṗi-hiŋ\ *n* : the eyelashes

un·što \uŋ-štó\ *suff* when affixed to *v* : the said act has already been said or done < *Heṗéunšto, hehéunšto* I already said that, that you already said. >

un·š'ke·ya·pi·ka *or* **unškeyapika** \úŋ-š'ḱe-ya-ṗi-ḱa\ *adv* : "But getting back to our topic", as is said in coming back to our subject when forgetting all about the subject or point of one's conversation < *Wan, ~ he woyak maši, ewaktonje* You see, but getting back to our topic, I forgot he charged me to tell that. > - Note: *lotkunkešni* "Oh, I should tell you" is *archaic.* Cf tonwel *Syn* INŠEYAPIKA, INŠKEYAPIKA LP BT SI

un·š'un·ma·ke·ci *or* **inš'unmakeci** *or* **išunmakeci** \úŋ-š'un-ma-ḱe-ci\ *interj* [fr *iš* as for one + *unma* the other one of two + *ka* in a manner of speaking + *kin* the] : Oh, yes; just because ..., as one man explains something to another who in turn tries to explain the same thing to a third party but asks questions continually because he did not understand in the first. Then the first man says to the second: "Unš'unmakeci kiyuieska ye Oh yes, please explain it to him, *i.e.* speak bluntly for another." < ~ *eya ca heon hecon* Oh yes, he did that just because he said it. ~ *woglakahapi na awektonje* Oh yes, just because they were saying it I forgot it. > - Note: the parts of the word when brought together mean something like: then he, the other one of a pair. In other words, this second person that comes up for consideration is instantly labelled as being exactly as stupid, silly, ridiculous, as the other just mentioned — **unš'unmake·c'un** *interj* : Oh yes, just because ..., *i.e.* in *ref* to something mentioned before - MN

un·we·ya \uŋ-wé-ya\ *n* : provisions for a journey

un·wo·han·pi o·ce·ti \úŋ-wo-haŋ-pi o-cè-ti\ *n* : a cooking range

un·yan \úŋ-yaŋ\ *va* wa·ún·bla ya·ún·la un·k'unyan·pi wa·un·mni kta : to lose, to drop out of sight < *Taku wan únyanpi k'on he ole* He looked for something that had been lost. ~ *kigle* to drop from sight arriving at

---

\a\ father \e\ they \i\ machine \o\ smoke \u\ lunar \an, aŋ\ blanc Fr. \in, iŋ\ ink \on, oŋ, un, uŋ\ soon, confier Fr. \c\ chair \ġ\ machen Ger. \j\ fusion \clusters: bl, gn, kp, hšl, etc...\ b[e]lo ... said with a slight vowel **See more in the Introduction, Guide to Pronunciation**

home, ~ *kiglapi* They got lost on their way home. ~ *imayayapi* You said I was lost. *Hena ~ unkinapapi kte šni.* We shall not take our chances there in getting lost. *Hopo, wanjini ~ napapi šni po; ~ inawicapin.* Alright, do not run away any of you and get lost; he took shelter with them out of sight. *Hena (i.e. inyan gmigmela) ~ okicize el yapi kte šni* They (the Round Rocks) will not get into a fight and drop out. ~ *iwicayayapi* You exceded them and got lost. ~ *kigla* to forsake > – B.H.237.3, 166.15, 239.14, 80.14 MS.353, 351 P

u·pi \u-ṗí\ *n* : the lower border of a garment, the hem < *situpi* the tail of a bird >

u·pi·gle·ga \u-ṗí-ġle-ġa\ *n* : a Balmoral skirt

u·pi·ja·ta \u-pí-ja-ṫa\ *n* : the swallow, the generic name by reason of their forked tail – Note: its nest is made in banks along streams and it is the same as the *icapšinpšincala* barn swallow. The *upijata* is black, other are white, a large bird with a two-inch bill. < *Hena iš eya zuzeca yutapi* They eat the snake too. >

u·ši \u-ší\ *va* u·wa·ši [fr *u* to come + *ši* to command] : to command to come, to send one

[1]**u·ta** \u-tá\ *va* : to try, as a gun by firing it, to fire off < *Tokša anpa ca wicocanlwanka yelo, na hanhepi ca otuyacin utapelo, eya.* He says when it is sun-up he is a coward, and when night, in vain is he tried. *He utapelo* He is tried, as in giving one much more food than he can eat. > – Bl

[2]**u·ta** \ú-ṫa\ *n* : the hazelnut, acorns

u·ta·hu *or* **ituhu** \ú-ṫa-hu\ \i-ṫú-hu\ *n* : the oak tree

u·ta·hu can \ú-ṫa-hu caŋ\ *n* : oak wood; the burr oak, the scrub oak, the mossy cup oak, quercus macrocarpa, the beech family – #114

u·ta·hu can·hlo·gan \ú-ṫa-hu caŋ-ȟlò-ġan\ *n* : the flour-of-an-hour, the venice mallow, the modesty, so named from its shape of leaf, the hibiscus trionum, the mallow family – B. #307

u·wa \ú-wa\ *v imper* : Come!, as women say; men say *Uwa yo!* < *Takoja, uya ye, ungni kte* Grandchild, please come, let us go home. > Jairus said: *Uwi na ninape kin aputaki ye* Come and touch your hand. *Misun uwi ye, Iktomi ekiya* Little brother, please come, Iktomi said to him – B.H.204.24 D.117

u·ya \u-yá\ *va* : to send, start, to cause to go — *vn* **a** : to come, to become < *Sniyan ~* It is becoming cold > **b** : to spring up, grow as does grain < *Tokiyatanhan ~ hwo?* Whence does it come? *i.e.* where does the wind come from? *Tate wan waš'agya uye lo* The wind grew strong. > — **uye·kiya** \u-yé-ḱi-ya\ *va* uye·wa·kiya : to cause to grow or spring up – Bl

u·ye·ya \u-yé-ya\ *va* uye·wa·ya : to cause to come

W

wa \wa\ *pref* to:
v usually puts the *v* into the absolute or intransitive sense, *i.e.* the *v* is changed into an *adj neut* or a *v pass*; thus, *ónšila* to have mercy upon, becomes *waónšila* merciful. In some cases, it forms of them *n* denoting the agent or actor; indeed the absolute forms may all be so used, as in *Wanikiye* the Savior — R
n it makes their meaning more general; moreover it indicates in some action words that the action is done by a sawing motion, as with a knife or saw

wa \wa\ *pron in compos* with *v*, *1st pers singl* : I ... < *He na·wa·h'on* I hear that. > – I

wa \wa\ *n* : snow

wa·a·bles \wa-á-bles\ *v contrac of* waableza : to be clear-sighted, be observing < ~ *hingla* suddenly to observe > — **waable·sya** *v* : to make one observe — *adv* : aware

wa·a·ble·za \wa-á-ble-za\ *v* waa·wa·bleza : to be observing, be clear-sighted, to have use of one's senses

wa·a·can·kšin \wa-á-caŋ-kšiŋ\ *v* waacan·wa·kšin [fr *acankšin* pass or jump over] : to step over *e.g.* kettles and dishes standing on the floor - Bl

wa·a·can·ze \wa-á-caŋ-ze\ *v of* ocanze : to be angry at others, ill-tempered — **waacanze·ka** \wa-á-caŋ-ze-ka\ *vn* : to be ill-tempered, cranky — **waacanze·ya** *adv* : in a surly manner

wa·a·gla \wa-á-gla\ *v* waa·wa·gla [fr *agla* to be going carrying home] : to take home

wa·a·gla·he·ya \wa-á-gla-he-ya\ *v* : to be slipping out or dripping - *Syn* WAÁHINHPAYA Bl

wa·a·gle·ca \wa-á-gle-ca\ *v* waa·wa·gleca : to take home - *Syn* WAÁGLA R Bl

wa·a·gli *or* **wágli** \wa-á-gli\ *v of* aglí : to bring home

wa·a·gli·he·ya \wa-á-gli-he-ya\ *v of* agliheya : to come down and smite, as lightning - B.H.129.24 - B.H. 60.22

wa·a·gna gle·pi \wa-á-gna glè-pi\ *n* : a table

wa·a·han·na·jin \wa-á-haŋ-nà-jiŋ\ *v* : to come to stand < ~ *kuwa* to come again and again trying *e.g.* to speak to one but finding him busy > - Bl

wa·a·hin·hpa·ya \wa-á-hiŋ-ȟpa-ya\ *v* : to be fallen on something, *i.e.* we were the lucky ones - Bl KE LHB

wa·a·ho·tan·ka \wa-á-ho-taŋ-ka\ *n* waaho·wa·tanka : one who bawls out, one who vociferates

wa·a·ho·ton \wa-á-ho-toŋ\ *n* : something that makes a noise, as does thunder *etc.*

wa·a·ho·ye·ya \wa-á-ho-ye-ya\ *v of* hoyeya : to reprove, to scold - Note: the form of the *1st pers singl* is not used

wa·a·i·a \wa-á-i-a\ *v* waai·wa·ye waai·un·yan·pi [fr *aia* to slander] : to talk about, to slander; to try a case in court — **waaiya·pi** *n* : a talking against, slander; a consultation, a trial in court — **waaie·s'a** *n* : a slanderer

wa·a·ja·ja \wa-á-ja-ja\ *va* waa·wa·jaja : to take off clean, as meat from bones - Bl GA

wa·a·ka \wa-á'-ka\ *n* : a prisoner of war

wa·a·ka·ga \wa-á-ka-ġa\ *v* waa·wa·kaga [fr *akaga* to add on] : to add to, to make a lie on — **waakaga·pi** *n* : a making on, a blasphemy perhaps

wa·a·ka·hpa \wa-á-ka-ȟpa\ *v* waa·wa·kahpa [fr *akahpa* cover up, conceal] : to cover — **waákahpe** *or* **wóakahpe** *n* : a covering — **waakahpe·tonpi** *n* : a cover, a lid, as of a basket - B.H.46.1

wa·a·kanl \wa-á-kaŋl\ *adv* : on, on top of the snow < ~ *yanka* to sit on the snow > - Bl KE LHB

wa·a·ka·ta \wá-a--ka-ta\ *v* : to cover with snow

wa·a·ki \wa-á-ki\ *v* waa·wa·ki [fr *aki* bring home] : to have taken home, which is away from the speaker - B.H.36.12

wa·a·ki·ca·ga \wa-á-ki-ca-ġa\ *v* : to play jokes on, make sport of

wa·a·ki·ci·ya·tan'·in \wa-á-ki-ci-ya-taŋ-iŋ\ *n of* kiciyatan'in : a manifestation

wa·a·ki·kton·ja \wa-á-ki-ktoŋ-ja\ *v* wa·we·ktonja [fr *akiktonja* forget] : to forget — **waakiktonja·pi** *n* : forgetfulness

wa·a·kil \wa-á-kil\ *v contrac of* waakita : to seek, look for

wa·a·ki·ni·ca \wa-á-ki-ni-ca\ *v* waa·wa·kinica [fr *akinica* to contend over ownership] : to dispute — *n* : one who disputes — **waakinica·pi** *n* : a dispute over something — **waaki·nil** *v contrac of* waakinica : to dispute < ~ *unpi* they are disputing. > — **waakini·lya** *adv* : in the way of disputing

wa·a·ki·ta \wa-á-ki-ta\ *v* waa·wa·kita [fr *akita* to seek or hunt for] : to hunt, seek for

wa·a·ki·ye·ce·tu \wa-á-ki-ye-ce-tu\ *adj* : equal, equal in size, number, or age < *Waakiyeuncetupi* We are equal *e.g.* in number. > - WHL

wa·a·kši·ja \wa-á-kši-ja\ *v of* akšija : to take or retain what is claimed by another

wa·a·ku \wa-á-ku\ *v* : to bring home - Bl

wa·a·na·go·ptan \wa-á-na-ġo-ptaŋ\ *v* waána·wa·goptan [fr *anagoptan* to listen to, obey] : to listen to, obey — **waanagoptan·yan** *adv* : obediently < ~ *waun* I am listening closely. >

wa·a·na·i·c'i·pta \wa-á-na-i-c'i-pta\ *v refl* waana·mi·c'i-pta : to stop, forbid one's self

wa·a·na·ki·ci·go·ptan \wa-á-na-ki-ci-ġo-ptaŋ\ *n* : a listener, an audience

wa·a·na·ki·kšin \wa-á-na-ki-kšiŋ\ *v* waana·we·kšin [fr *anakikšin* to defend one in danger] : to expose one's self for others, to take the place of one in danger — **waanakikšin·yan** *adv* : exposing self for others

wa·a·na·pta \wa-á-na-pta\ *v absol* waana·wa·pta [fr *anapta*] : to stop, forbid people

wa·a·na·ša·pa \wa-á-na-ša-pa\ *n* waana·wa·šapa [fr *a on* + *na* by foot + *šapa* soiled, defiled] : to defile or soil by trampling upon

wa·a·na·šlo·ka \wa-á-na-šlo-ka\ *n* : something that flies out or refuses to stay in, as a cork in a bottle *etc.*

wa·a·na·tan \wa-á-na-taŋ\ *v* waana·wa·tan [fr *anatan* to make an attack on one] : to rush on, make an attack

wa·a·ni·ca \wa-á-ni-ca\ *v* waa·wa·nica [fr *anica* withhold, oppose] : to refuse to give up, surrender something

wa·a·o·ki·ya·pi \wá-a-o-ki-ya-pi\ *n* : a mutual plan - Bl WHL

wa·a·pa \wa-á-pa\ *v* waa·wa·pa [fr *apá* to strike one] : to strike one

wa·a·pe \wa-á-pe\ *v* waa·wa·pe [fr *apé* to wait] : to wait, be in waiting < ~ *yankahanpi* They were sitting waiting. > - D.194, 219, 251

wa·a·skab \wa-á-sk̇ab\ *vn contrac of* waaskapa : to stick on — **waaska·bya** *va* waaska·bwa·ya : to cause to stick on, make adhere — **waaskabya·pi** *n* : sticking plaster

wa·a·ska·pa \wa-á-sk̇a-ṗa\ *vn of* Dakota *áskapa* : to stick on or to

wa·a·ska·pe \wa-á-sk̇a-ṗe\ *n* : something that sticks, a sticking plaster

wa·a·sni·yan \wa-á-sni-yaŋ\ *v* waasni·wa·ya [fr *asníya* to cure] : to heal, make well — *n* : a healer, or a healing - B.H.184.13

wa·a·s'in \wa-á-s'iŋ\ *v* waá·wa·s'in [fr *as'ín* to long for, covet] : to covet, desire what is another's, to stay where others are eating expecting to share - Note: the word is used only in *ref* to food, perhaps

wa·a·ša·pa \wa-á-ša-ṗa\ *vn* waa·ma·šapa [fr *ašapa* to become black or dirty] : to be defiled — **waašape** *n* : dirt, as on soiled hands, grease *etc.;* a blotter, perhaps

wa·a·šla·ya \wa-á-šla-ya\ *v* waa·wa·šlaya [fr *šlaya* to make bare, without cover] : to skin an animal

wa·a·šlu·šlu·ta \wa-á-šlu-šlu-ta\ *vn* : to be smooth and slippery from dirt, as a boy's sleeves sometimes become - Bl

wa·a·š'a·ka \wa-á-š'a-ka\ *vn* : to be loaded with or coated, as the tongue in sickness - Note: waš'aka

wa·a·š'a·ke·ce \wa-á-š'a-ke-ce\ *n* : a noisy person - *Syn* WAÓHMUNYECE

wa·a·š'a·pi \wa-á-š'a-pi\ *n* : applause by acclamation - Bl

wa·a·ta·ya \wa-á-ṫa-ya\ *v* waata·wa·ya [fr *atáya* to go directly to] : to be fortunate, lucky — **waataye·s'a** *n* : a fortunate one, as a good hunter - Bl

wa·a·ton·wan \wa-á-toŋ-waŋ\ *v* waa·wa·tonwan [fr *atonwan* to look on or at] : to be observing — **waatonwe** *n* : an observer

wa·a·un·ye·ya \wa-á-un-ye-ya\ *v* : to scare away *e.g.* game by one's coming - Bl

wa·a·wa·cin \wa-á-wa-ciŋ\ *v* waa·wa·cánmi [fr *awacin* to think, consider] : to think about, consider, be thoughtful < *Waawacanmi šni yelo* I did not have my wits about me, as they would say when persons did not intend to stay, having their thoughts somewhere else. > — *n* : an interest — *adj* : devout, sincere - BT P

wa·a·wa·cin·yan \wa-á-wa-ciŋ-yaŋ\ *va* waawacin·wa·ya : to cause to think or consider — *n* : one who makes others think

wa·a·wan·glag \wa-á-waŋ-glag\ *v contrac of* waawanglaka : to oversee one's own

wa·a·wan·gla·ka \wa-á-waŋ-gla-k̇a\ *v* waawan·wa·glaka [fr *awanglaka* to oversee one's own] : to watch over one's own — **waawanglake** *n* : a shepherd, one who watches over *etc.*

wa·a·wan·yan·gki·ya·pi \wa-á-waŋ-yaŋ-gk̇i-ya-pi\ *n* : a steward, one who is employed to observe

wa·a·wan·yank \wa-á-waŋ-yaŋk\ *v contrac of* waawanyanka : to oversee < ~ *unpi* They are giving surveillance or supervision. > - B.H.270.7

wa·a·wan·yan·ka \wa-á-waŋ-yaŋ-k̇a\ *v* waawan·bla·ka [fr *awanyanka* to watch over] : to oversee, watch over *etc.* — **waawanyanke** *n* : a watchman - B.H.293.10

wa·a·ya \wa-á-ya\ *v* waá·bla [fr *áya* to bring] : to take or bring to

wa·a·ya·ška·he·ye·la *or* **waayaškaṫuyela** \wa-á-ya-ška-he-ye-la\ *v* waá·bla·škaheyela [fr *ayaškaheyela* [speak of a near] : to speak of as near - Bl

wa·a·ya·štan \wa-á-ya-štaŋ\ *v of* ayáštan : to finish or complete with the mouth, as eating or speaking

wa·a·ya·ta \wa-á-ya-ṫa\ *v* waá·bla·ta [fr the Dakota, *ayáta* to predict] : to guess, predict, foretell - R

wa·a·ya·tan'·in \wa-á-ya-taŋ-iŋ\ *v* waa·bla·tan'in [fr *ayatan'in* to reveal for by speaking] : to proclaim, testify or bear witness, to make manifest — *n* : a witness — **waayatan'inyan** *adv* : testifying - Cf ayáta

wa·a·ya·te \wa-á-ya-ṫe\ *n* : a prophet

wa·a·yu·pta \wa-á-yu-pṫa\ *v* waa·blu·pta [fr *ayupta* to respond] : to answer

wa·a·yu·ptan·yan \wa-á-yu-ptaŋ-yaŋ\ *v of* ayuptanyan : to turn back on one, to redound on one's self or one's relatives

wa·a·yu·pte \wa-á-yu-pṫe\ *n* : one who answers or gives an account

wa·a·yu·s'o \wa-á-yu-s'o\ *v of* the Dakota, *ayús'o* to wade in : to wade after

wa·a·yu·ta \wa-á-yu-ṫa\ *v* waa·blu·ta waa·un·yuta·pi : to look at

wa·a·zi·lton \wa-á-zi-ltoŋ\ *v* waazi·lwa·ton [fr *azilton* to incense] : to burn incense to or for - B.H.159.9

wa·bla \wa-blá\ *va* wa·wa·bla: to cut in slices, as bread, meat *etc.* — **wabla·bla** *v red* : to be slicing

wa·bla·bla·za \wa-blá-bla-za\ *v red of* wablaza : to rip open

wa·blas \wa-blás\ *v contrac of* wablaza : to rip open < ~ *iyeya* suddenly to rip open, ~ *iyewaya* I suddenly ripped it open. > — **wabla·sblaza** *v red of* wablaza : to rip continually

wa·bla·ska \wa-blá-sk̇a\ *va* wa·wa·blaska [fr *blaska* flat] : to make dull or flat on the edge, as a knife by shaving

wa·bla·ya \wa-blá-ya\ *va* wa·wa·blaya [fr *blaya* level] : to make flat with a knife, to shave off lumps *etc.*

wa·bla·za \wa-blá-za\ *va* [fr the Dakota *bamdaza*, the Lakota *blaza* to rip open] : to rip open lengthwise, as in butchering an animal, cutting open a watermelon or boil *etc.*

wa·ble·ble·ca \wa-blé-ble-ca\ *v red of* wableca : to break, shatter

wa·ble·ca \wa-blé-ca\ *va* wa·wa·bleca : to shatter, break *e.g.* brittle ware with a knife — **wablel** \wa-blél\ *v contrac of* wableca : to break, shatter < ~ *iyeya* to break suddenly >

wa·ble·ni·ca \wa-blé-ni-ca\ *n* wa·ma·blenica : an orphan, one without relatives

wa·bles \wá-bles\ *v contrac of* wableza : to understand < ~ *kic'un* to try and understand, *Yunkan ~ hinglapi* Their eyes were then opened. > — **wable·sya** *v* wable·swa·ya : to see, be seeing, *i.e.* with the eyes < *Ištagonge kin wablesyapi* The blind men saw. *Tanyan ~ ške* They say he was seeing well. > — **wablesye·hci** *or* **wablesyehca** *adj* : sharp-sighted, clear-sighted < ~ *blihel hingle* to suddenly become active seeing clearly > - Bl B.H.273.11, 39.5, 69.7 LWOW.177 D.35 Wh

wa·ble·za \wá-ble-za\ *vn* wa·wa·bleza : to see clearly, to understand — *n* : an inspector

wa·blo·ska \wá-blo-ska\ *n* : the lark bunting, calamospiza melanocorys; the white-winged black bird - Note: when it takes to flight it sings:

Ska, ska, ska;	White, white, white;
to, to, to;	Blue, blue, blue;
ša, ša, ša;	Red, red, red;
zi, zi, zi;	Yellow, yellow, yellow;
ḣol, ḣol, ḣol.	Gray, gray, gray.

And while alighting:

Wil, wil, wil. In a flock, in a flock, in a flock. - Bl R

wa·blo·ša \wá-blo-ša\ *n* : the red-winged black bird, whose songs are:

Tōke, mat'ā nī. Oh! that I might die.
Nakun miyē. And me.
Miš eyā. Me too!
Cap'cehlī. A beaver's running sore.

- *See wapagica* the yellow-headed black bird - Bl RF

wa·blu·ška \wa-blú-ška\ *n* : a bug, an insect

wa·blu·ška hinšma iyececa \wa-blú-ška hiŋ-šma i-yè-ce-ca\ *n* : the blue lettuce, the large-flowered blue lettuce, lactuca pulchella, the composite family - Note: it is cut-leaved and reminds one of a beetle or other hairy insect - Bl #254

wa·blu·ška hu·ha o·ta pe·ji *or* **peji wabluška iyececa** \wa-blú-ška hu-ha ò-ta pe-ji\ *n* : crab grass, schedonuardus paniculatus, the grass family - Note: it reminds one of the insect called the "walking stick" - Bl #282

wa·blu·ška ti·yo·šlo *or* **wabluška tiyošlo·la** \wa-blú-ška ti-yò-šlo\ *n* : a cricket

wa·ca·je·ki·ya·ta \wa-cá-je-ki-ya-ta\ *va* wacaje·wa·ki·mbla·ta : to mention the names of deceased relatives to one and beg for their sakes < *Wakantanka ni un kin on wacajeciciyate* By the living God, tell us your family line.> — **wacajeyata** *v* wacaje·bla·ta [fr *cajeyata* to name] : to ask for or beg in the name of the dead; to make a parlimentary motion — **wacajeyata·pi** *n* : a petition, a motion — **wacajeyal** *v contrac of* wacajeyata : to ask in one's name, to make a motion - WHL KE

wa·can·ga \wa-cáŋ-ġa\ *n* : a species of sweet-smelling grass, sweet-grass - Note: it is burnt in religious ceremonies

wa·can·ȟin-yan \wa-cáŋ-ȟiŋ-yaŋ\ *v absol of* canȟinyan : to be attached, devoted to others < *Atayeš wacanȟinye šni un* He is not attached at all to others, *i.e.* he has no use at all for his relatives, always avoiding them. > - LB

wa·can·kšu \wa-cáŋ-kšu\ *v* wacan·wa·kšu : to dry things on a stick

wa·can·lki·ya *or* **wacantkiya** \wa·cáŋ-lki-ya\ *v* : to be kind and generous in loving - Pb.36

wa·can·mi \wa-cáŋ-mi\ *v defect* : I thought

wa·can·ši·lya \wa-cáŋ-ši-lya\ *v* : to make sad

wa·can·te·i·yo·ki·šica \wa-cáŋ-te-i-yò-ki-ši-ca\ *adj* : sad - B.H.85.18

wa·can·te·ši·ca \wa-cáŋ-te-ši-ca\ *adj* wacante·ma·šica [fr *cantešica* sad, heart-broken] : unhappy — **wacante·ši·lya** *va* wacanteši·lwa·ya : to make sad

wa·can·ti·yo·ki·ši·ca \wa-cáŋ-ti-yo-ki-ši-ca\ *adj* : displeased, vexed, provoked, as when many bother one - *See* wacánteiyokišica

wa·can·tki·ya \wa-cáŋ-tki-ya\ *v* wacan·lwa·kiya wacan·lun·kiya·pi [fr *cantekiya* to have an affection for] : to be gracious, kind, benevolent, generous in giving love — **wacantkiya·pi** *n* : benevolence

wa·can·to·gna·ka *or* **wacanteognaka** \wa-cáŋ-to-gna-ka\ *v* wacanto·wa·gnaka [fr *cantognaka* to love] : to be generous, affectionate — *adj* : generous, affectionate — **wacantognaka·pi** *n* : generosity, affection

wa·can·to·kpa·ni \wa-cáŋ-to-kpa-ni\ *v* wacanto·wa·kpani [fr *cantokpani* to long for] : to desire much, long for, to be impatient for

wa·can·ze·ya \wa-cáŋ-ze-ya\ *v* wacanze·wa·ya [fr *canzeya* make angry] : to make angry — **wacanze·zeka** *n* : one easily angered, susceptible, easily irritated - Pb.26

wa·ca·pe \wa-cá-pe\ *v* waca·wa·pe : to stab

wa·ca·šton \wa-cá-štoŋ\ *v* wa·wa·cašton [fr *cašton* to gain a name, reputation] : to name, give a name — *n* : the namer, one who names

wa·ce·i·c'i·ci·ya \wa-cé-i-c'i-ci-ya\ *v refl* : to pray privately, within one's self, to pray in one's behalf perhaps - B.H.232.5

wa·ce·ki·ci·ci·ya \wa-cé-ki-ci-ci-ya\ *v* : to pray for one

wa·ce·ki·ya \wa-cé-ki-ya\ *v* wace·wa·kiya [fr *cekiya* to pray to] : to pray

wa·ce·on·pa \wa-cé-oŋ-pa\ *v* : to roast - *See* waceunpa

wa·ce·t'un·gla \wa-cé-t'uŋ-gla\ *v* wacet'un·wa·gla [fr *cet'ungla* to doubt] : to doubt, disbelieve — *n* : one who always doubts — **wacet'ungla·pi** *n* : unbelief, doubting — **wacet'ungla·ya** *adv* : doubtingly

wa·ce·un·pa *or* **waceonpa** \wa-cé-uŋ-pa\ *va* wace·wa·unpa [fr *ceonpa* to roast] : to roast *e.g.* meat — *n* : one who roasts anything

Wa·ce·un·pa \Wa-cé-uŋ-pa\ *np* Wa·ma·ceunpa : the *Yankton* the Border Guardians and the *Sicangu* the Burnt Thigh bands of the Sioux

wa·ce·ya \wa-cé-ya\ *va* wa·wa·ceya [fr *ceya* to cry] : to make cry by cutting

wa·ci \wa-cí\ *vn* wa·wa·ci : to dance

wa·ci·k'a·la \wa-cí-k'a-la\ *va* wa·wa·cik'ala [fr *cik'ala* small] : to shave small

wa·ci·k'a·ye·la \wa-cí-k'a-ye-la\ *n* : a little < ~ *áya yo.* Bring a little. > - Bl

[1]**wa·cin** \wa-cíŋ\ *v* 1st *pers singl of* cin : I want, wish it.

[2]**wa·cin** \wa-cíŋ\ *vn* wacan·mi wacan·ni wa·un·cin·pi : to think, to aim at, to purpose or try to, to be anxious to < *Ni ~ yo* Aim to live! *Mazawakan kin icu ~ po* Take and aim your guns. *Icu ~* Try to get, take it. *ohiye ~* to try to win, *Yus-inyankmawacin yo* Try to get a hold of me, *i.e.* by running after me. > - Note: this word requires another *v* in the *infin* mood to precede it - D.35, 34, 28

wa·cin·ble·za \wa-cíŋ-ble-za\ *vn* : to be clear headed, to be smart, quick to comprehend

wa·cin·ci·k'a·ye·la *or* **wacincisciyela** \wa-cíŋ-ci-k'a-ye-la\ *adj* wacin·ma·cik'ayela wacin·ma·cisciyela : fickle-minded

wa·cin'·e·kta·yu·za \wa-cíŋ-e-kta-yu-za\ *vn* wacinekta·blu·za : to be kind, forebearing, longsuffering

wa·cin·gnu·gnu·ni \wa-cíŋ-gnu-gnu-ni\ *adj red* wacin·ma·gnugnuni [fr *wacin* to think + *gnugni* to wander] : wandering in mind, bewildered, oblivious — **wacingnuni** *vn* : to be wandering or bewildered < *Hehanl wacingnunipi kte lo* Then they will be bewildered. > — *adj* : bewildered — **wacingnuniya** *va* wacingnuniwaya : to bewilder, confuse, distract, puzzle — **wacingnuniyan** *adv* : confusedly - P Bl

wa·cin·ha·he·la *or* **wacinhahàla** \wa-cíŋ-ha-hè-la\ *adj* wacin·ma·hàhela wacin·ma·háhala : easily excited or alarmed < *tawacinhahàla* fickle, unsteady > - BD

wa·cin·hin \wá-ciŋ-hiŋ\ *n* : the headdress of a Dakota man, anything standing up on the head, *e.g.* feathers, down or soft feathers, *etc.* - P Bl
wa·cin·hin sa·psa·pa \wá-ciŋ-hiŋ sa-psà-pa\ *n* : black plumes, ostrich feathers
wa·cin·hin·ya \wá-ciŋ-hiŋ-ya\ *va* wácinhin·wa·ya : to use for a plume
wa·cin·hin·yan·za \wa-cíŋ-hiŋ-yaŋ-za\ *adj* wacín·ma·hinyanza : cruel, morose
wa·cin·hun·ke·šni \wa-cíŋ-huŋ-ke-šni\ *adj* wacin·ma·hunkešni : impatient, irascible — **wacinhunkešni·ya** *va* : to irritate, provoke - B.H.45.12
wa·cin'·i·c'i·ya·pi \wa-cíŋ-i-c'i-ya-pi\ *n* : self-reliance - P Bl
wa·cin'·i·ha·la \wa-cíŋ-i-hà-la\ *adj* : easily excited to an-ger < *Cekpa s'e ~ yanke* Like a twin he was easily excited to anger. > - Bl
wa·cin'·i·wo·š'ag \wa-cíŋ-i-wo-š'ag\ *vn contrac of* waciniwoš'aka : to be discouraged, let down — **wacin'iwoš'agya** *v* : to discourage one — **wacin'iwoš'ak** *vn contrac of* wacin iwoš'aka : to be discouraged < *~ hingla* to suddenly become discouraged > - B.H.62.24, 209.5
wa·cin'·i·wo·š'a·ka \wa-cíŋ-i-wo-š'a-ka\ *vn* wacin'iwo·wa·š'aka [fr *iwoš'aka* to be struck, hit] : to be discouraged, to be out of heart
wa·cin'·i·yo·ki·pi \wa-cíŋ-i-yo-ki-ṗi\ *vn* wacin'iyo·ma·kipi : to be contented, satisfied with — **wacin'iyokipi·ya** *adv* : contentedly
wa·cin'·i·yo·ki·ši·ca \wa-cíŋ-i-yo-ki-ši-ca\ *vn* wacin'iyo·ma·kišica : to be displeased with; to be sad on account of, to regret — **wacin'iyokiši·lya** *adv* : displeased with
wa·cin·ja·ta \wa-cíŋ-ja-ṫa\ *adj* wacin·ma·jata : hesitating, undecided, forked mind
wa·cin·ka *or* **wacin** \wa-cíŋ-ka\ *vn* : to think
wa·cin·ki·ci·ya·pi \wa-cíŋ-ki-ci-ya-pi\ *n* : confidence - Bl
wa·cin·ki·ci·yu·za·pi \wa-cíŋ-ki-ci-yu-za-pi\ *v recip* : having regard for each other - *See* wacinkiyuza
wa·cin·ki·ksu·ya \wa-cíŋ-ki-ksu-ya\ *v* wacin·we·ksuya : to remember all things well < *Yunkan heceglala wacinweksuye* And then I remembered only so much. >
wa·cin·ki·ya \wa-cíŋ-ki-ya\ *v poss* wacin·wa·kiya [fr *wacinyan* to trust, depend on] : to trust in, as in anything laid up for one's own use, to trust to or have confidence in *e.g.* a friend
wa·cin·ki·yu·za \wa-cíŋ-ki-yu-za\ *va* wacin·wa·kiyuza : to think of, hold in mind, either for good or for evil
wa·cin·ko \wa-cíŋ-ko\ *adj* wacin·wa·ko wacin·un·ko·pi [fr *wacin* think + *ko* desire stongly] : ill-natured, pouting — **wacinko·kela** \wa-cíŋ-ko-ke-la\ *adj dim* : pouting a bit — **wacinko·pi** \wa-cíŋ-ko-ṗi\ *n* : passionateness — **wacinko·ya** *adv* : passionately, crossly
wa·cin·ksab \wa-cíŋ-ksab\ *adj contrac* : wise, intelligent < *Tanyan ~ kic'un wo* Wear it well with presence of mind. > — **wacinksa·bic'iya** *v refl of* wacinksabya : to act discreetly in one's own regard — **wacinksa·bya** *adv* : discreetly - Bl Pb.33 D.215 note 1
wa·cin·ksa·pa \wa-cíŋ-ksa-ṗa\ *adj* wacin·ma·ksapa wacin'·un·ksapa·pi : intelligent, wise, conscious, with presence of mind < *Na miš icunhan wacinmaksapa na wacipi kin asnikiya yankapi* And they were getting a long rest while I was conscious and they danced. > — *vn perhaps* : to be aware. < *~ yo* Be alert. >
wa·cin·nun·pa \wa-cíŋ-nuŋ-ṗa\ *adj* wacin·ma·nunpa : hesitating, undecided as to doing or not doing — **wacinnunpašniyan** *adv* : honestly, truthfully < *~ iyuha tanyan ociciya ktelo* Truly I shall help you all in a way convenient. > - Bl
wa·cin'·o·a·ye \wa-cíŋ-o-a-ye\ *n* : inclination < *~ manica* I am without inspiration, am discouraged. >
wa·cin'·o·yu·ze \wa-cíŋ-o-yu-ze\ *n* [fr *wacinyuza* to have one's own thought in a matter] : thought or one's thinking
wa·cin·ši·ca \wa-cíŋ-ši-ca\ *adj* : bad dispositioned
wa·cin·tan·gya \wa-cíŋ-taŋ-gya\ *adv* : patiently - B.H. 201.1, 227.2
wa·cin·tan·ka \wa-cíŋ-taŋ-ka\ *adj* wacin·ma·tanka : patient, magnanimous, long-suffering, enduring long < *Na wacinnitanka kin heon wicašayatapika oyapa kte lo* And if you are patient, then you will fall in with a head chief. > — **wacintank kic'un** *v* : to have patience - BD
wa·cin·te·ȟi \wa-cíŋ- ṫe-ȟi\ *v* : to take interest in nothing — *adj perhaps* : indifferent - Bl
wa·cin·ton \wa-cíŋ-toŋ\ *v* wacin·wa·ton : to have understanding, have a mind of one's own, to be wise
wa·cin·ton·gna·gya \wa-cíŋ-toŋ-gna-gya\ *va* wacintongna·gwa·ya : to comfort, usually by giving to the afflicted, to cause to have a different view — **wacintongnake** *or* **wakicanpte** *n* [fr *wacin* thought + *ton* to issue from + *gnaka* to place] : a comforter
wa·cin·ton·šni \wa-cíŋ-toŋ-šni\ *vn* wacin·wa·tonšni : to be foolish
wa·cin·t'a *or* **wacint'a·t'a** \wa-cíŋ-t'a\ *vn* wacin·ma·t'a wacin·ma·t'at'a : to be forgetful — **wacint'at'ake** *n* : one who is weak-minded and forgetful
wa·cin·wa·ša·ka·la \wa-cíŋ-wa-ša-ka-la\ *v* : to be poised and ready to act toward one, to be inclined *e.g.* to help one < *Ungna wacinniwašakala ki* Perhaps he is ready to rob you, *i.e.* Beware, he is ready to steal you blind. > - MS.350 LHB
wa·cin·wi·ki·c'un·šni \wa-cíŋ-wi-ki-c'uŋ-šni\ *vn* : to be indifferent about
wa·cin·yan \wa-cíŋ-yaŋ\ *va* wacin·wa·ya wacin·ci·ya wacin·ma·ya : to trust in, depend upon, to need one; to believe in — *adj* : confiding — **wacinyan·pi** *n* : trust, confidence, faith, trustiness; responsibility perhaps — **wacinye·hci** *adv* : very confidently — **wacinye·kiya** \wa-cíŋ-ye-ki-ya\ *va* wacinye·wa·kiya : to cause to trust in — **wacinye·pica** \wa-cíŋ-ye-ṗi-ca\ *n* : what can be trusted in, depended upon, faithful, reliable — **wacinye·ya** *v* : to purpose, set the mind to; to cause to trust in < *Wacinyewaya šni* I am discouraged, lost hope in one> — **wacinye·yešni** *v* : to object to, to lose hope in < *Wacinyeyapišni* They lost hope in it. > - Pb.35 P B.H.220.9, 66.3 D.221
wa·cin·yu·sya \wa-cíŋ-yu-sya\ *va* : to cause one to have a certain opinion, to persuade one < *Tokel Jesus el wacinluze kin iyecel ohinniyan Jesus el wacinyusmayiye* As you intended to be in Jesus, so in Jesus you always intended me to be. > - Pb.10
wa·cin·yu·za \wa-cíŋ-yu-za\ *v* wacin·blu·za : to have an opinion, to be inclined < *Hel wacinblluza waun* That is my mind. *Nahmakel kiiglušpin kta wacinyuze* It was his intention that he would divorce her secretly. > — **wacinyuze** *n* : the intention < *Tokata hecel econ kte ~ iyukcan* He understood that his intention was that in the future he was to do it this way. > - B.H.164.7 P Bl
wa·ci·pi \wa-cí-ṗi\ *n* [fr *waci* to dance] : dancing, a dance
wa·ci·sci·la \wa-cí-sci-la\ *va* wa·wa·ciscila [fr *ciscila* small] : to make small by cutting

wa·co·ka \wa-cō'-ka\ *n* : level land, a river bottom with hills on both sides, low land near a river or lake without timber < ~ *el iyotan wa šmelo* Snow was very deep in the bottoms. > - R Bl

wa·co·kon \wa-có-koŋ\ *v* waco·wa·kon [fr *cokon* to plot evil against one] : to desire to take life — **waco-kon·pi** *n* : a desire of taking life

wa·co·k'in \wa-có-k'iŋ\ *v absol* wico·wa·k'in [fr *cok'in* to roast on spits] : to roast something on coals < *Wacounk'inpi kte lo* Let us do some roasting, roasting potatoes *etc.* in fire. > - Note: D spells the word: cok'ín

wa·co·ni·ca \wa-có-ni-ca\ *n* [fr *conica* flesh, meat] : wild meat of any kind, fresh or dry, venison — **waconi-caka** *n* : wild meat dried

wa·co·sya \wa-cō'-sya\ *v* waco·swa·ya : to cause to warm, to put out to dry, as cooked victuals, to dry and smoke, as meat — **waco·sya·pi** \wa-có·sya·pi\ *n* : smoked pork; a paunch half-boiled and hung out to dry

wa·cu·ti·c'in \wá-cu-ti-c'iŋ\ *n* : anything carried diagonally over the chest from the left shoulder to the right hip < ~ *wakan* a certain *wotawe* charm > - *See* cutic'in BT

wa·e·ca·kca \wa-é-ca-kca\ *adj* : ready to do things at will, from caprice < ~ *nunkin na napapa umayaye* You lay ready at will so you get me to come barking, as a man would say to a child or wife when they did foolish things. > - Bl LHB

wa·e·ca·ki·on \wa-é-ca-ki-oŋ\ *v* waeca·wa·kion : to treat - B.H.63.11

wa·e·con \wa-é-coŋ\ *v* waeca·mon : to do things or make preparations, as for a feast — *n* : an actor < *Te-hiya waecamon* I have done a tragic deed. > - B.H.64.3, 88.25, 90.14, 57.20, 305.9 D.249

wa·e·con·con·ka \wa-é-coŋ-coŋ-ka\ *n* waeca·monmon·-ka *or perhaps* waeca·munmun·ka : a jack of all trades, a handy man, one who does all sorts of things - WE

wa·e·con·hca i·c'i·la \wa-é-coŋ-hca i-c'ì-la\ *v* : to brag, boast, make much of one's own little actions, exaggerate < *Hecon na* ~ That is what he did and bragged about it. > - Bl

wa·e·con·ki·ya \wa-é-coŋ-ki-ya\ *v* : to tax one's strength - P Bl

wa·e·ki·cin·cin·ke \wa-é-ki-ciŋ-ciŋ-ke\ *n* : one who persists asking for, one who wants a thing very badly and often asks for it - ED

wa·e·ki·gna·ka \wa-é-ki-gna-ka\ *v* : to lay something away < *wanagi* ~ , to put something, *i.e.* some of one's food, away for souls before eating, as a sort of grace before meals > - BT

wa·e·ki·ya \wa-é-ki-ya\ *v* wae·wa·kiya : to speak to one - Bl B.H.47.7, 157.9, 184.16, 186.3

wa·e·ktan·ja·šni \wa-é-ktaŋ-ja-šni\ *adj* : unpliable, lacking docility, not educable

wa·e·kta·šni·yan \wa-é-kta-šni-yaŋ\ *adv* : improperly, falsely < ~ *iyeya* to bring about deceptively > - *Syn* WAÍPAWEH

wa·e·lhi·ya·ya·ke \wa-é-lhi-ya-ya-ke\ *n* : a friendly not hostile person < ~ *takuni onspe šni tka* A friendly person would not know how to do anything, *i.e.* he wants to help work but knows nothing about it. > - Bl KE

wa·e·lho·ye·ya \wa-é-lho-ye-ya\ *v* : to make fun of persons < *Bluskaka, yunkan waelhoyeyin kte hcin* I equipped him with a new set of clothes, and then he made fun of it, *i.e.* gave him a new suit but he was ungrateful. > - Bl KE

wa·e·lon'·on·ke \wa-é-loŋ-oŋ-ke\ *n* : a careless person - KE

wa·e·pa·zo \wa-é-pa-zo\ *n* **1** : the index finger or forefinger < *Tuweni* ~ *kin on epazo šni, napahunka kin he on econpi* No one pointed with his finger, they did it with the thumb. ~ *kin on wojapi kin cokayelahci palob egle na yazoka ke* He pretty much sampled it, with his index finger putting and sticking it well into the middle of the pudding. > **2** : a pointed piece of meat on the shoulder blades of buffalo - D.121 Bl HH

wa·e·ya \wa-é-ya\ *v* wa·epa [fr *éya* to say] : to speak < *Taku oyasin onunišniyan waehelo* You spoke everything right to the point, as they might say to a habitual joker. *Tokel* ~ *kinhan oblakin kta wacin* I want to tell it as he said. *Niciye Aaron waeyin kta okihi* Your brother Aaron is able to speak. > - B.H.48.24, 55.6, 68.27, 139.14, 166.12, 242.4, 199.7

wa·e·ya·ku \wa-é-ya-ku\ *v* wae·bla·ku wae·un·yaku·pi [fr *éyaku* to take away] : to take, carry away by force

wa·e·ye·ca \wa-é-ye-ca\ *v* : to tell or speak facts, the truth < *Wicaša wan* ~ *šni un k'un héye lo* A man who had not told the truth said that. > - Cf waíečešni BE Bl WHL LHB

wa·ga·can *or* **canyah'u** \wá-ġa-caŋ\ *n* : the western cottonwood tree, populus sargentii, the willow family - #193

wa·ga·lga·ta \wa-ġá-lġa-ta\ *v red* wa·wa·galgata [fr *wagata* to mark or cut] : to make marks, each cut or sawed in anything

wa·ga·pa \wa-ġá-pa\ *va* wa·wa·gapa [fr *gapa* as in *nagapa* and *pagapa* to skin] : to take off *e.g.* the skin of an animal with a knife, to skin, to open with a knife

wa·ga·ta \wa-ġá-ta\ *va* wa·wa·gata [fr *gata* as in *kagata* and *nagata* to stretch open] : to make marks, to mark or cut with a knife, to carve or hack

wa·gla \wa-glá\ *va* wa·wa·gla **1** : to take off, as tallow from entrails, with a knife, to shave off with a knife **2** : *fig* to sicken one — **wagla·gla** *v red* : to strip off - F D.202

wa·gla·gla·ka \wa-glá-gla-ka\ *v* wa·wa·glaglaka : to criticize food, to find nothing good enough — **wagla-glake** *n* : a crank, one who is dissatisfied with the food offered, who does not find it tasty enough; hence is finicky, very particular, exacting, easily excited - B

wa·gla·mni \wa-glá-mni\ *v* : to go after what one has left - Note: *glamna* perhaps is meant here, not *glamni*

wa·gla·šlo·šlo \wa-glá-šlo-šlo\ *v* wa·wa·glašlošlo : to whistle, *i.e.* with one note < *Yunkan el u na šiyotanka* ~ And then a grouse whistled and here it comes. >

wa·gla·š'a·pi \wá-gla-š'a-pi\ *n* : the shout that children once made when meat *etc.* was brought into camp, they met the man returning, and when the women heard them shout, they said: *Wanna* ~ Now to our business; and they get busy starting a fire. The shout was: Uká hu, hu, hu! - Cf hu

wa·gle \wa-glé\ *n* : provisions, a storehouse, storage < *hitunktanka* ~ the provisions of rats carried together > — *v* [fr *gle* to put or place] : to put into storage - B.H. 107.21

wa·gle·kšun \wa-glé-kšuŋ\ *n* : the wild turkey < ~ *s'e nape pepe kaca* Like a wild turkey his hands are jagged, as is said when pieces of skin hung on one's hands. > - Bl

wa·gle wo·šna·pi \wá-gle wò-šna-ṗi\ *n* : an altar

wa·gle·za \wa-glé-za\ *n* : the garden snake, the garter snake - D.273

[1]**wa·gli** \wa-glí\ *v* 1st *pers singl of* gli : I arrived at home

[2]**wa·gli** \wá-gli\ *v* wá·wa·gli wá·un·gli·pi : to bring home game, meat *etc.* < *Pte nainš wamakaškan hecekce wawicaglipi* Buffalo or other animals they brought home, *i.e.* as game. > — *n perhaps* : hunted game < *Wágli otokahe kuwelo* He was the first to come back with hunted game. > - MS.557 BT

wa·gli·gla \wa-glí-gla\ *v of* gligla : to travel, to go about from place to place < ~ *waun* I am touring. >

wa·gli·gle·ca \wa-glí-gle-ca\ *n* : one who is always travelling - R Bl

wa·gli·gli \wá-gli-gli\ *v red of* wágli : to arrive at home with meat < *Taku wagliglipi* They got home with some game. > — **wagli·ku** \wá-gli-ku\ *v* wágli·wa·ku : to bring home meat < *Wicaša wan ~ ca wahanpi unyatkanpi kte* When a man brings home meat, we shall be drinking soup, as they say when a man bring meat home. > - Bl D.273

wa·gli·na·wa·pa \wa-glí-na-wa-pa\ *v* 1st *pers singl of* gli-napa *with a double inseparable pron* : I came in sight arriving home < *Hecel waglinawapin kta, yunkan eyapaha un he leya* And then that announcer said this so I might come in sight on the way home. > - Cf wahínapa

wa·gli·u·ki·ya \wá-gli-u-ki-ya\ *v* : to come home with a packhorse loaded with meat - KE

wa·gli·yo·ya \wá-gli-yo-ya\ *or perhaps* *wa-glí-yo-ya*\ *v* : to go after one's own — **wagliyoya·pi** *n* : a pastime for children - Note: it was played in former times in imitation of camp life with a boy as chief, they needed provisions, so the chief let a certain number of the children bite into a stick and those had to go home and get from their parents whatever these wanted to give. Thus was created an imitation of *wágliku* bringing home meat - Bl

wa·glu·ha \wa-glú-ha\ *v* wa·wá-glu-ha [fr *gluha* to have one's own] : to have one's own, to keep — **wa-gluha·haka** \wa-glú-ha-ha-ka\ *adj* : saving, frugal, parcimonious < *Wagluhahake lo miye tka pilamic'iye lo* He is frugal, but for my part I made myself thankful. > — **wagluhahakeci** \wa-glú-ha-ha-ke-či\ *n* : a parsimonious person — **wagluhaha·kteca** *adj* : going to become a parsimonious person, giving promise of so becoming - BT

wa·glu·hi·ka \wa-glú-hi-ka\ *v* [fr *wayuhi* to scare away] : to hush, keep silent by threats *etc.* — *adj perhaps* : keeping quiet < *Maka iyokiseya tatanka ota nawah'on ca wakanyeja ~ nunwe* May children keep silent because I hear many, half of the earth's buffaloes. > - Cf wayuhi, wayuhika B. BT

wa·glu·he \wá-glu-he\ *vn* wa·wa·gluhe : to live with one's wife's relatives, to be a hanger-on

Wa·glu·he \Wá-glu-he\ *np* : the Loafer band of the Oglalas

wa·glu·hta·ta \wa-glú-hta-ta\ *v* wa·wa·gluhtata : to offer one's own

wa·glu·la \wa-glú-la\ *n* : worms, maggots, tapeworm

wa·glu·šna \wa-glú-šna\ *v* : to drop one's own

wa·glu·ta·pi \wá-glu-ta-pi\ *n* : a table < ~ *akáhpe* a table cloth >

wa·glu·za \wa-glú-za\ *v* wa·wá·gluza : to take back what one has given

wa·gme·za \wa-gmé-za\ *n* : corn ...
wagmezahu corn stalks
wagmeza icàkse a corn sickle
wagmeza nablàġa or *wagmeza nablahyapi* popcorn

wa·gmu \wa-gmú\ *n* : a squash, a pumpkin or gourd *etc.* — **wagmu blu** *n* : a squash — **wa·gmu·ha** \wa-gmú-ha\ *n* : a rattle, as used in the *wapiyapi* a conjuring ceremony — **wagmuhu** *n* : pumpkin vines

wa·gmung \wa-gmúŋg\ *v or* wagmunka : to trap < ~ *bla* I am going trapping. >

wa·gmun·ka \wa-gmúŋ-ka\ *v* wa·wa·gmunka : to trap, hunt with traps — *v* 1st *pers singl of* gmunka : I am trapping — **wagmunka·pi** *n* : trapping

wa·gmu·ško·pa \wa-gmú-ško-pa\ *n* : the Japanese pumpkin

wa·gmu·špan·šni yutapi \wa-gmú-špaŋ-šni yù-ta-pi\ *n* : a watermelon

wa·gna \wa-gná\ *va* wa·wa·gna : to cut off *e.g.* corn from the dried ear which is call *waštunkala,* to make fall off by cutting, as fruit from a tree

wa·gnag \wá-gnag\ *v contrac of* wágnaka : to place, lay away < ~ *cola* without putting a thing away > — **wagna·gton** *n* : something put with another thing < ~ *k'u* to give *e.g.* a blanket with a gun, or *e.g.* to furnish a pad on a horse's sore back >

wa·gna·ka \wa-gná-ka\ *v* 1st *pers singl of* gnaka : to lay away

wa·gna·ka \wá-gna-ka\ *v* wa·wa·gnaka [fr *agnaka* to place on anything] : to place on, put on *e.g.* poultices on sores *etc.* - Cf wakicignaka

wa·gna·škin·yan \wa-gná-škiŋ-yaŋ\ *va* wa·wa·gnaškin-yan [fr *gnaškinyan* to be wild, franctic] : to make crazy or frantic by cutting or stabbing — *n* : a lunatic - P

wa·gna wo·pe·ton·pi \wá-gna wò-ṗe-toŋ-pi\ *n* : a store counter

wa·gna wo·šna·pi \wá-gna wò-šna-pi\ *n* : an altar of sacrifice

wa·gna·wo·ta·pi \wá-gna-wo-ta-pi\ *n* : a table on which to eat

wa·gna·yan \wa-gná-yaŋ\ *va* wa·wa·gnayan [fr *gnayan* to deceive] 1 : to miss in attempting to strike with a knife 2 : to deceive *or* 1st *pers singl of* gnayan : I deceive one — **wagnaye** *n* : an imposter - P

wa·gna·yu·ta·pi \wá-gna-yu-ta-pi\ *n* : a table

wa·gnu·ka *or* **wagnuka ṗe ša** \wa-gnú-ka\ *n* : the red-headed woodpecker - FR D.38

wa·go \wa-ġó\ *va* wa·wa·go : to make marks or gashes in the flesh, to mark, carve or engrave with a knife in wood — **wago·kiya** \wa-ġó-ki-ya\ *va* wago·wa·kiya : to cause to carve — **wago·pi** *n* : one of the four marks seen on the hoop used in the *painyankapi* game

wa·gu·ge·ca \wa-ġú-ġe-ca\ *n* : hardened, crusted snow < *Wašpanla ca wakašloyakel maunnipelo; ~ kinhan tehiya unkupi tka yelo* You traveled in the melting snow when it was hot weather; if the snow gets crusted we would have trouble coming home. > - Cf *waišnaheca* soft snow

wa·gu·gu·ya \wa-ġú-ġu-ya *va red* wagugu·wa·ya : to cause to burn, scorch — **waguya** \wa-ġú-ya\ *va* wagu·wa·ya : to scorch

wa·gwe·za \wa-gwé-za\ *va* wa·wa·gweza [fr *gweza* ragged] : to carve, make rough with a knife

wa·ha \wa-há\ *n* : hides, in opposition to anything else - Bl

wa·ha·can·ka \wa-há-caŋ-ka\ *n* : a shield

wa·ha·can·ka ki·c'in \wa-há-caŋ-ka ki-c'ìŋ\ *n* : a snail, one who carries his shield on his back; also perhaps a kind of lizzard - Bl

wa·ha·can·ka wan ska(san) k'in \wa-há-caŋ-ka waŋ ska (saŋ) k'iŋ\ *v phr* : to be generous, liberal, benevolent - Note: this is a *phr* used in the winter; in summer is used: *wahacanka wan šayapi k'in* to carry a shield made red, *i.e.* to be festal, convivial, hospitable, recreational - R Bl BT

wa·han·gya \wa-háŋ-gya\ *v* wahan·gwa·ya : to destroy — **wahangye·ca** *n* : one who destroys everything - D.216

wa·han·pi \wa-háŋ-pi\ *n* : broth, soup of any kind < *Wicaša wan wagliku ca ~ unyatkanpi kte* When a man comes home bringing game, we shall drink soup. > - Bl

wa·ha·pa·hpa \wa-há-pa-hpa\ *v* waha·wa·pahpa : to flesh a robe or skin while the hide is still fresh - Cf wahátka, wahíŋtka R Bl

wa·ha·šla \wa-há-šla\ *n* : a tanned hide

wa·ha·tka \wa-há-tka\ *va* waha·wa·tka : to scrape a dry hide, taking off any meat there may yet be on it < *Hohe un winyan ~ ca tiyopa el kat'iyewaye lo* I shot and killed the woman at the door, she being an Assiniboin Indian who scraped a dry hide. > - Cf wahintka BT

wa·he·ce·kce·tu \wa-hé-ce-kce-tu\ *adv perhaps red of* wahecetu : about < *Wiyute nunpa nainš yamni ~ ca he* That measured about two or three yards. > - B.H.178. 12

wa·he·cel \wa-hé-cel\ *adv* : about that time < *Omaka yamni ~* It was about that time three years ago. > - SLB B.H.225.1

wa·he·ce·tu *or* **wahecetuya** \wa-hé-ce-tu\ *adv* : about < *Opawinge ~* It was about a hundred. > - *Syn* SECE B.H.82.6

wa·he·han \wa-hé-haŋ\ *adv* : betimes, in good time — **wahehanl** *adv* : about at that time, *i.e.* past and future < *Na wana lila lowanpi ~ tice ekta šiyotanka k'on he yajopi* And now around that time those grouse sounded off toward the smoke vent, really singing. *Hancokanyan ~* It was about noon. > - *Syn* IYÉHANL MS.340 B.H.247.7, 17.12, 77.7, 137.8

wa·he·ki·c'un \wa-hé-ki-c'uŋ\ *v poss* wahe·we·c'un : to pack up or tie one's own - Cf wahéyun

wa·he·yun \wa-hé-yuŋ\ *v* wahe·mun wahe·nun : to pack up in bundles — **waheyun·pi** *n* : packing up < *Šunkawakan wan hupa ~ wan k'inkiyapi na ekta hipi* And they came to where they loaded a horse with packing up the travois poles. >

wa·hi·bu \wa-hí-bu\ *v 1st pers singl of* hibú : I arrived

wa·hi·na·wa·pa \wa-hí-na-wa-pa\ *v 1st pers singl with a double pron of* hinápa : I came into sight. - Cf waglinawapa

[1]**wa·hin** \wa-híŋ\ *n* : hairs

[2]**wa·hin** \wa-híŋ\ *n* [fr *wan* arrow + *hi* teeth] : a flint, flints — **wahin·cola** *n* : an arrow when the head (*wismahin*) came off - Bl

wa·hin·he \wá-hiŋ-he\ *v* [fr *hinhan* to precipitate, as rain] : It snows < *Wáhinhin kta* It will snow. >

wa·hin·he·ya \wa-híŋ-he-ya\ *n* : the pocket gopher

wa·hin·he·ya hu blo·ka *or* **wahcahca hu bloka** \wa-híŋ-he-ya i-pì-ye\ *n* : roots - Bl #250

wa·hin·he·ya o·pi \wa-híŋ-he-ya ò-pi\ *n* : glands open and swollen, frequently occurring among American Indians, hence the name because they appear as gopher hills

wa·hin·he·ya·pa·blu \wa-híŋ-he-ya-pa-blu\ *n* : gopher-hills

wa·hin·kpe \wa-híŋ-kpe\ *n* : an arrow, arrows < *~ hinájin* the jaws of an arrow which hold the point (*wismahin*), *~ kin'inyeyapi* a bow-shot > - Bl

wa·hin·pa·hpa \wa-híŋ-pa-hpa\ *n* : a fleshing knife or chisel used in preparing green hides for drying

wa·hin·pa·spa *or* **wihinpaspa** \wa-híŋ-pa-spa\ *n* : tent pins

wa·hin·ske \wa-híŋ-ske\ *n* : the long-grained or southern corn, so called because the grains resemble the canine teeth of animals

wa·hin·ša \wa-híŋ-ša\ *n* : gun caps

wa·hin·šma \wa-híŋ-šma\ *n* : furs - B.H.60.13

wa·hin·tka \wa-híŋ-tka\ *n* : a scraper used on hides, once made of a bit of steel fixed to an elk-horn handle and handled as a hoe on the hide's fleshy side, making the hide the same thickness

wa·hin·ya·ji·ce \wa-híŋ-ya-ji-ce\ *n* : down, fur, such as was once used by the Dakotas in sacred ceremonies

wa·hin·yun·ton \wa-híŋ-yuŋ-toŋ\ *v* [fr *iyúnton* to apply grease to a skin] : to rub *tanasula* brains, marrow, gall on hides to prepare them for tanning - Bl

wa·hi·šna·he·ca \wa-hí-šna-he-ca\ *n* : soft new snow, whereas *waíšnaheca* is used in speaking of snow that will fall tomorrow - Pa

wa·hi·yo \wa-hí-yo\ *v absol of* hiyo : to come for something - *See* hiyó — **wahiyo·hi** *v* wahiyo·wa·hi *or* wa·wa·hiyohi wa·un·hiyohi·pi : to come for or after but without mentioning what — **wahiyo·i** *v* wahiyo·wa·i : to have gone after

wa·hi·yu \wa-hí-yu\ *v 1st pers singl of* hiyú : I come out

wa·ho·co·ka *or* **hocoka** \wa-hó-co-ka\ *n* : an inner courtyard - P

wa·ho·gnu·gnu \wa-hó-gnu-gnu\ *v* : to warble, quaver as one's voice may do when singing, to make a certain gutteral sound in singing for some sacred ceremonies - WHL LHB

wa·ho·hpi \wa-hó-hpi\ *n of* hohpí : nests - Note: *zintkala hohpi* a bird's nest

wa·ho·ki·ya \wa-hó-ki-ya\ *va* waho·wa·kiya : to send word to < *Mato waglamna wahokiye lo* Bear sent word to bring together help, *or* The Bear sends for extra help. > - D.115

wa·ho·kon·ki·ya \wa-hó-koŋ-ki-ya\ *va* wahokon·wa·kiya : to instruct, counsel, advise one — **wahokonkiyapi** *n* : instructions, counsel, advice — *adj* : counselled

wa·ho·ši \wa-hó-ši\ *v of* hoší : to carry word, to bring or carry news, to be an apostle < *~ wan ... David okiyak šipi* The messenger ... was bade to speak to David. > - Note: this word is always used with *i, hi, ya, etc.* B.H.96.1, 189.2

wa·ho·ši gli \wa-hó-ši gli\ *v* : to bring home news — **wahoši hi** *or* **wahoši kahi** *v* : to arrive somewhere with a message — **wahoši·yapi** \wa-hó-ši-ya-pi\ *n* : one sent with a message — **wahoši·ye wakan** *n* : an apostle - B.H.62.18, 43.7, 262.18 SLB Pb.42

wa·ho·ya \wa-hó-ya\ *va* waho·wa·ya : to send for one, to send word to one, to promise something to one, to order something by mail < *Leciya wacipi kta ški na wahomayanpi ca le inahni omawani* They say there will be

---

\a\ father \e\ they \i\ machine \o\ smoke \u\ lunar \an, aŋ\ blanc Fr. \in, iŋ\ ink \on, oŋ, un, uŋ\ soon, confier Fr. \c\ chair \ǧ\ machen Ger. \j\ fusion \clusters: bl, gn, kp, hšl, etc...\ b[e]lo ... said with a slight vowel
See more in the Introduction, Guide to Pronunciation

a dance here, and when I was informed I now traveled in a hurry. > — **wahoya·pi** *n* : a sending word to - R D.20

wa·hu·a·pa \wa-hú-a-p̣a\ *n* : corn, an ear of corn

wa·hu·a·ta·ya \wa-hú-a-ṫa-ya\ *vn* wahuata·wa·ya : to find one's self all at once unable to proceed, to be unable to escape for fright or some other cause — **wahuataye·ya** *va* wahuataye·wa·ya : to frighten or in some way make unable to escape

wa·hu·hni·ye s'e škan \wa-hú-ȟni-ye s'e škaŋ\ *v* : to work hurriedly - Cf huhniyeya, inahni Bl

wa·hu·ke·za \wa-hú-ḳe-za\ *n* : a spear

wa·hu·nun·pa \wa-hú-nuŋ-pa\ *n* : a biped, an appellation also for man - R Bl

wa·hun \wa-húŋ\ *va* wa·wá·hun : to cut across, *i.e.* in one's flesh or in meat of any kind, to slash or gash or cut the flesh as once the Dakotas were accustomed to do in behalf of the dead — **waic'ihun** \wa-í-c'i-huŋ\ *v* : to cut or gash one's self - D.33

wa·hun·ca·la *or* **wauncala** \wa-húŋ-ca-la\ *v* : to ape, do monkey-ish tricks, as some do when aping clown tricks — *n* : a monkey, one who acts like a monkey < ~ *s'e wainakihnihnike; wána kakena iyayelo* Monkey-like, he is always in a great hurry about himself, as is said when one of a crowd is in a great hurry and goes on while the others are rather slow in getting ready. > - ED WHL LHB

wa·hun·hun *or* **wahonhon** \wa-húŋ-huŋ\ *va red of* wahún : to cut loose, to cut off *e.g.* ropes in different places < *Inahni wicin kin wohohopi* When the womanizer was in a hurry they shot him loose. >

wa·hu·ta·kta·ya·kel \wa-hú-ṫa-ktà-ya-kel\ *adv* : at the end, lastly < ~ *mni kte* I shall go last, *i.e.* when all others have gone. > - Bl

wa·hu·te \wa-hū'-ṫe\ *n* : a stump of anything, stumps < *canhute* the stump of a tree > - Note: the word implies stumps in opposition to anything else

wa·hu·to·pa \wa-hú-ṫo-p̣a\ *n* : quadrupeds, the generic term for four-footed animals; the dog or wolf in the sacred or philosophic terms - R

wa·hu·wa·pa \wa-hú-wa-p̣a\ *n* : an ear of corn, corn unshelled < ~ *ağón* cornsilk > - Bl

wa·hu·wa·ta·ya \wa-hú-wa-ṫa-ya\ *v* : to flail one's arms as in running, so as to cause that impression for the enemy, instead of fleeing - *See* wahúataya — **wahuataye·ya** *va* : to cause to flail one's arms as in running - *See* wahuatayeya

wa·ȟa \wa-ȟá\ *v* wa·wá·ȟa [fr *ȟa* to bury] : to bury many things or in many places — *v 1 pers singl of* ȟa : I bury it

wa·ȟa·bya \wa-ȟá-bya\ *v* waȟa·bwa·ya [fr *ȟabya* to frighten away] : to frighten or scare away, as game by one's coming - Bl

wa·ȟa·pi \wa-ȟá-pi\ *n* : a burying, something buried

wa·hca \wa-ȟcá\ *n* : flowers, their generic name < ~ *nableca* to blossom, unfold > — **wahca·hca** *n* : flowers or blossoms; the showy milkweed, asclepias speciosa, the milkweed family - Note: the blossoms boiled and mixed with flour make a very good dish. Eating flowers is not a modern idea. North American Indians used the floral bud clusters of the milkweed to thicken soups and stews, and cut up the full-blown flowers for a sort of preserve. *See* pannúnpala BT #76

wa·hca·hca hu bloka \wa-ȟcá-ȟca hu blo-ka\ *n* : swamp milkweed, asclepias incarnata, the milkweed family - Bn #250

wa·hca pe·pe·la \wa-ȟcá p̣e-p̣è-la\ *n* : trumpet weed, purple thoroughwort, the Joe Pye weed, gravel or kidney root, the tall or purple boneset, eupatorium purpureum, variety maculatum, the composite family - BT #117

wa·hca wa·ste \wa-ȟcá wa-šṫè\ *n* : the closed or blind gentian, the bottle gentian or barrel gentian, cloistered heart, gentiana andrewsii, the gentian family - BT #133

wa·hca·zi·blu \wa-ȟcá-zi-blu\ *n* : the rock goldenrod, solidago canadensis, the composite family - BT #28

wa·hca·zi ci·k'a·la \wa-ȟcá-zi cì-k'a-la\ *n* : the yellow prairie mallow, tooth-leaved primrose, oenothera serrulata, the evening primrose family BT #7

wa·hca·zi kan·ta mna unma hu tanka \wa-ȟcá-zi káŋ-ta mna unma hu tàŋ-ka\ *n* : the golden parosela, parosela aurea, the pulse family - BT #275

wa·hca·zi su·ta \wa-ȟcá-zi sù-ṫa\ *n* : sage brush - Note: the same as *peji ȟota waštemna* BT #64

wa·hca·zi ši·ca·mna \wa-ȟcá-zi ši-cà-mna\ *n* : yellow flox - Note: the same as *canhlogan pa* LB #150

wa·hca·zi tan·ka \wa-ȟcá-zi tàŋ-ka\ *n* : the sunflower, having medicinal use - Note: *canhlogan wahcazi panšpanjela*

wa·hca·zi wa·šte \wa-ȟcá-zi wa-šṫè\ *n* : white prairie aster, aster commutatus, the composite family. < ~ *ota yelo, hiyu po* Come, there is much white prairie aster. *Hu paksa ayapi Lakota waštelakapi* Lakotas like bringing them, breaking the stem. > - BT #137

wa·hca·zi wa·šte·mna *also* **canhlogan pepela** \wa-ȟcá-zi wa-štè-mna\ *n* : the cut-leaved sideranthus spinulosus, the composite family - BT #100

wa·hca·zi·zi \wa-ȟcá-zi-zi\ *n* : yellow flowers, the sunflower

wa·hci \wa-ȟcí\ *va* wa·wa·hci [fr *hci* a gap] : to cut or break out notches by cutting

wa·hcin·ca \wa-ȟcíŋ-ca\ *n* : the small and thin poplar tree < ~ *oju* to plant a poplar tree > - Bl

wa·ȟe·ya·ta i·ye·ya \wa-ȟé-ya-ta i-yè-ya\ *v* : to push back — *n* : one who pushes others back

wa·hla \wa-ȟlá\ *va* wa·wa·hla [fr *hla* to rattle] : to make rattle with a knife

wa·hla·gan \wa-ȟlá-ġaŋ\ *va* wa·wa·hlagan [fr *hlagan* loose] : to enlarge *e.g.* a hole by cutting around

wa·hla·hla \wa-ȟlá-ȟla\ *va* wa·wa·hlahla [fr *hlahla* to rattle] : to make rattle by cutting

wa·hla·ya \wa-ȟlá-ya\ *va* wa·wa·hlaya **1** : to pare off < *ha* ~ to peel > **2** : to circumcise

wa·hle·ca \wa-ȟlé-ca\ *va* wa·wa·hleca : to cut or break in pieces with a knife, to rend in cutting — **wahle·hleca** *v red* : to break or cut in pieces — **wahlel** \wa-ȟlél\ *va contrac of* wahleca : to break in pieces < ~ *iyeya* to cut in pieces >

wa·hlog \wa-ȟlóg\ *va contrac of* wahloka : to cut a hole in < ~ *iyeya* to cut a hole in >

wa·hlo·hlo·ka \wa-ȟló-ȟlo-ka\ *n* : lace

wa·hlo·ka \wa-ȟlō'-ḳa\ *va* wa·wa·hloka [fr *hloka* full of holes] : to cut a hole in anything with a knife

wa·hna \wa-ȟná\ *v* : to groan — **wahna·hna** *v red* : to be groaning - Bl

wa·hna·hna·he·ca \wa-ȟná-ȟna-he-ca\ *n* : the wild cucumber, the mock apple, echinocystis lobata, the gourd family - CR #225

wa·hpa \wa-ȟp̣á\ *va* wa·wa·hpa : to cut off anything and let it fall

wa·hpa ȟo·ta *or* **pteyáhpa** \wá-ȟpa ȟò-ta\ *n* : the cowbird, which is accustomed to sitting on cattle and horses - R Bl FR

wa·hpa·ka \wa-ḣpá-ka\ *n perhaps* : one who being sickly has not put his clothes on well < *Hehe, he wana wahpakelo* How sad! He is one sick and half dressed. > - Bl

wa·hpa·ni·ca \wa-ḣṗá-ni-ca\ *adj* ma·wahpanica un·wahpanicapi : poor, destitute, having nothing — **wahpani·kiya** \wa-ḣṗá-ni-ḳi-ya\ *v poss* : to make self poor < *Ite wahpaniwakiye* I made my face appear that I was penniless, *i.e.* made my face look sorrowful, so as to attract sympathy. > — **wahpani·la** *va* wahpani·wa·la : to consider poor — **wahpani·ya** *va* wahpani·wa·ya : to make poor, cause to be poor — **wahpani·yan** *or* **wahpaniyan·kel** *adv* : poorly, in a destitute way < ~ *hakiton* to dressed as if destitute. ~ *wahi* I arrived in a way destitute. > - B.H.133.8 R

wa·hpan·yan \wa-ḣṗáŋ-yaŋ\ *v* wahpan·wa·ya : to soak anything, to soak and take the hair off - R

wa·hpa tan·ka \wá-ḣpa tàŋ-ka\ *n* : the common black bird

wa·hpa·ye \wa-ḣṗá-ye\ *n* **1** : movable goods, baggage **2** : paying for a living somewhere **3** : taxes < ~ *mnakiyapi* They took up a collection to pay his expenses. ~ *glajuju* to pay tax >

wa·hpa·ye·ca \wa-ḣṗá-ye-ca\ *n* : baggage

wa·hpe \wa-ḣṗé\ *n* **1** : a leaf, leaves **2** : tea

~ *akikaškapi* \a-ḳí-ka-škapi\ : common hop, humulus lupulus - *Syn* WINAKAPO BT #74

~ *ape blaskaska* or *tal'ágnake* \a-ṗé bla-ska-ska\ : hard-leaved goldenrod - *Syn* MIMELA WAHCAZI Bl BT #25

~ *blaskaska* \bla-ská-ska\ : winter-greens

~ *canli* \caŋ-lí\ : a leaf used for tobacco, a small vine that runs on the ground as the winter-green, the leaf of which serves as a tobacco

~ *cansakala* or *wapepeka* \caŋ-sá-ka-la\ : thorns - BT #33

~ *ceyaka* or *icikoyagyaka* \ce-yá-ka\ : Virginia mountain mint, pycnanthemum, the mint family; a tea made from it is used for coughing - BT #121

~ *hcahca* \ḣca-ḣcá\ : Texas croton, skunk weed, croton texensis, a female plant, the male has no blossoms; tea of the leaves is good for stomach pains - Bl BT #208

~ *hla* \ḣla\ : the clammyweed, polanisia trachysperma, the caper family - Bl #309

~ *h'eh'e* \ḣ'e-ḣ'é\ : pink cleome, common bee plant, stinking clover, cleome serrulata, the caper family - BT #20

~ *icikoyagyaka* or *ceyaka* \í-ci-ko-ya-gya-ka\ : mint BT #121

~ *inkpa jiji* \iŋ-kpá ji-jì\ : strong-scented lettuce, lactuca virosa, the composite family - WE #110

~ *inkpa pepe* or *wókahtan blaskaska* \iŋ-kpá ṗe-ṗè\ : the showy tick trefoil - BT #119

~ *Kute* \Ḳu-ṫe\ *np* : the Leaf-shooters, a band of Dakotas among the Nebraska Santees

~ *maka ayublaya* \ma-ká a-yù-bla-ya\ : prostrate ameranth, ameranthus blitoides; or the small-flowered verbena, verbena bipimatifida, the vervain family - BT #274

~ *pa* \pa\ : the false boneset, kuhnia eupatorioides, the composite family - WE #228

~ *peji* \pe-jí\ : alfalfa

~ *pepe* \ṗe-ṗé\ : the Douglas phlox, phlox douglasii andicola, the phlox family - Bl #266

~ *pepela* \ṗe-ṗé-la\ : knotgrass, doorweed, goosegrass, dooryard weed, polygonum aviculare, the buckwheat family - BT #35

~ *popa* \pó-ṗa\ : a species of willow

~ *popa can* \po-ṗá caŋ\ : a large species of willow - L

~ *skuya* \skú-ya\ : veined dock, rumex venosus, the buckwheat family; its leaves are sour, and tea of the roots is given to women when an after-birth does not come in time; also : lady's sorrel, upright yellow wood sorrel, oxalis stricta, of the sorrel family - Bl BS #235

~ *swula* \swú-la\ : yellow melilot, sweet clover, millet, the balsum flower, king's clover, king's crown, melilotus officinalis, the pulse family - Bl #279

~ *šica* \ší-ca\ : the burweed marsh elder, iva xantifolia, the composite family. *Wahpe šica ota yelo; ungna el lapi kilo* There is much burweed; don't get into it, I warn you. - Note: the seeds cause irritation on the bare skin BT

~ *šlušluta* \šlu-šlú-ta\ : entire-leaved groundsel, senecio perplexus, the composite family - HH #151

~ *tinpsila* \tíŋ-psi-la\ : the whorled milweed, asclepias verticillata, the milkweed - Note: mothers use it when they have no milk - ŚG #220

~ *to* \to\ : the prairie violet , viola pedatifida, the violet family - HH #152

~ *Tonwan* \Toŋ-waŋ\ *np* : a band of Dakotas on the Lake Traverse Reservation

~ *t'aga* \t'á-ġa\ : alum root, rough heuchera, heuchera hispida, the saxifrage family, having tuberous roots used for making a medicinal tea for diorrhoea; when powdered and thrown into water it makes it turn red; this powder is also used on sores - Cf *canhloh snasnala, t'agela hu* BT Bs #267

~ *wacanga hu bloka* \wa-cáŋ-ġa hu blo-ka\ : cleavers, goose-grass, cleaver-wort and is not sweet-scented, galium aparine, the madder family - Cf *wahpe wacanga hu winyela* Bl #305

~ *wacanga hu winyela* \wa-cáŋ-ġa hu wìŋ-ye-la\ : the sweet-scented bedstraw, galium trifolium, the madder family - Cf the non-scented *hu bloka* L #172

~ *waštemna* \wa-šté-mna\ : wild bergamont, horse-mint, menthalfolia monarda, the mind family - Note: it is known for its fragrance and is similar to *heȟaka tapejuta* the slender dalea; the leaves are often chewed while singing and dancing - FD.178, 270 Bl #209

~ *wizilya* \wi-zí-lya\ : the sandbar willow, salix fluviatilis; the *cohwáŋjica* the smaller willow - BT #104

~ *wokeya* \wo-ḳé-ya\ : a bower

~ *yatapi* \ya-tá-ṗi\ : fragrant giant hyssop, agastache foeniculum, the mint family - Note: it has the aroma of anise and hence is also called lophantus anisatus; as a tea for drinking, it is very good and as a herb grows in the canyons about Pine Ridge in South Dakota, and serves as a substitu-

---

\a\ f<u>a</u>ther \e\ th<u>e</u>y \i\ mach<u>i</u>ne \o\ sm<u>o</u>ke \u\ l<u>u</u>nar \an, aŋ\ bl<u>anc</u> Fr. \in, iŋ\ <u>in</u>k \on, oŋ, un, uŋ\ s<u>oo</u>n, <u>con</u>fier Fr. \c\ <u>ch</u>air \ġ\ ma<u>ch</u>en Ger. \j\ fu<u>s</u>ion \clusters: bl, gn, kp, hšl, etc...\ <u>b</u>ᵉlo ... said with a slight vowel
See more in the Introduction, Guide to Pronunciation

te for other teas. - BS #206
~ *yatapi iyececa* \ya-tá-ṗi i-yè-ce-ca\ : the tumble weed amaranthus graecizans, the amaranth family; also the western figwort, scrophularia occidentalis; also the false dragon head, obedient plant, lion's heart, physostegia viginiana; also lopseed, phryma leptostachya - BT #32, 199, 237,138 Bl
~ *yazokapi* \ya-zŏ'-ƙa-pi\ : downy painted cup, castilleja sessiliflora, the firwort famly; the honey is sucked fro its blossoms - Bl #264

wa·hpe·yu·ta·pi \wa-ȟpé-yu-ṫa-ṗi\ *n* : cabbage

wa·hpo·ki·ja·te \wa-ȟpó-ƙi-ja-te\ *n* : the few-flowered psoralea, psoralea tenuiflora, the pulse family - BT #13

wa·hpu \wa-ȟṗú\ *va* wa·wa·hpu : to cut off in small pieces — **wahpu·hpu** *v red* : to be cutting into small pieces

wa·hta·ni \wa-ȟtá-ni\ *v* wa·wá·htani [fr *ahtani* to sin, to work at] : to transgress a law, to sin — **wahtani-c'iya** \wa-ȟtá-ni-c'ì-ya\ *v refl* : to make one's self commit sin — **wahtani·s'a** *n* : a transgressor, a sinner — **wahtani·ya** *va* wahtani·wa·ya : to cause to transgress or sin - Pb.13

wa·hte·ka \wa-ȟtĕ'-ƙa\ *adj* : no good for the purpose designated, as a bad cigar — **wahteka·ca** \wa-ȟté-ka-ca\ *adj* : bad

wa·hte·ke·šni \wa-ȟtĕ'-ƙe-šni\ *adj* wa·ma·htekešni : skillful, good in something < *Wowaši econ* ~ He was skillful at his work. *Iapi econ* ~ He gave good talks. >

wa·hte·la·šni \wa-ȟté-la-šni\ *va* wahte·wa·lašni : to dislike, to abominate

wa·hte·šni \wa-ȟté-šni\ *adj* ma·wahtešni : bad, worthless, wicked < ~ *kin!* The worthless one! ~ *šicapi kin unci míktepi* The worthless bad ones my grandmothers kill. ~ *šicapi kin* the worthless who are bad, ~ *šica* To be worthless is bad. > - D.16, 57, 56, 105

wa·hte·šni·i·t'a \wa-ȟté-šni-i-t'a\ *interj cursing* : Damned be you! *or* Go to hell! *more lit,* You are practically dead, for today I will kill you - Note: when *ref* is made to more than one, they say *wahtešniit'api* < *Wahtešniit'api kin anpetu tahena iyuha wicawakte kte šan, eya keya* He stated that he said "Damn them! And I'll kill them all before eveningtime!" *Wahtešni imat'e, mni kta tka* I am sick and tired of it, I should be going, *i.e.* I'm sorry I missed my good luck or chance, because I was absent when things were distributed. >

wa·hte·šni t'a \wa-ȟté-šni t'a\ *n perhaps* : one who gets away with misdeeds < *Wahtešni t'e kin magnaye yelo* The rascal deceived me! >

wa·htin·ki·ya \wa-ȟtíŋ-ki-ya\ *v poss* wahtin·wa·kiya [fr *wahtinyan* to be fond of] : to be fond of one's own

wa·htin·yan \wa-ȟtíŋ-yaŋ\ *va* : to be fond of, to care for or about, to love, as in expressing love of any members of the family < *Wahtinkiciyapi* They care about one another, as is said of a married couple, *Wahtinmaye kacé* He does not care about me. *Wahtinciye šni* I want nothing to do with you, which is akin to cursing one.>

wa·ȟu·gna·hya wa·un·yan·pi \wa-ȟú-gna-ȟya wa-ùŋ-yaŋ-pi\ *n* : a holocaust, a totally burnt sacrifice - B.H.61.8

wa·ȟu·hna·hya \wa-ȟú-ȟna-ȟya\ *v* waȟuhna·hwa·ya : to burn up, as rubbish

wa·ȟun·win·ye \wa-ȟúŋ-wiŋ-ye\ *v of* ȟunwinye : to smell, stink, as meat does in the hot weather

wa·ȟu·pa·ko·za \wa-ȟú-ṗa-ƙo-za\ *n* : fowls, domestic fowls, *lit* wing-flappers - MS.477

wa·hwa \wá-ȟwa\ *adj* : gentle, mild — **wahwa·ka** *or* **wahwake·ca** \wá-ȟwa-ka\ \wá-ȟwa-ƙe-ca\ *adj* ma·wáhwaka : mild, gentle — **wahwa·kiya** \wá-ȟwa-ƙi-ya\ *adv* : gently, noiselessly < ~ *tima hiyu welo* He came indoors quietly. > — **wahwakiya·kel** \wá-ȟwa-ƙi-ya-ƙel\ *adv* : gently with *ref* to one's own < *Ho ~ ake hewicakiye* Yes, he said it again to them. ~ *iyopewicaye* He gently corrected them. > — **wahwakiye·la** *adj perhaps* : gentle - R Bl B.H.38.6, 80.23, 238.9

wa·hwa·la \wá-ȟwa-la\ *adj* ma·wáhwala : gentle, mild < *oh'an* ~ mild action, *or* His actions are gentle. >

wa·hwa·ya \wá-ȟwa-ya\ *adv* : mildly, gently, peacefully < *David wicaša kin ~ unpi kin heca* It was David's men who conducted themselves peacefully. > — **wahwaya·kel** *or* **wahwaye·la** \wá-ȟwa-ya-ƙel\ *adv* : mildly, peaceably - B.H.96.1, 198.12

wa·h'an·hi·ya \wa-ȟ'áŋ-hi-ya\ *adv of* h'anhiya : slowly, as in cutting perhaps

wa·h'an·h'an·i·c'i·la \wa-ȟ'áŋ-ȟ'aŋ-i-c'i-la\ *v refl* wah'an-h'an·mi·c'ila : to be self-sufficient, self important - Cf *wah'an'ic'iya* to pretend doing work — **wah'anh'an'ic'i-ya** *v red of* wah'an'ic'iya : to keep pretending work — **wah'an'ic'ila** *v refl* wah'an·mi·c'ila [fr *wah'anla* to esteem] : to think highly of one's self, to be proud — **wah'an'ic'ilapi** *n* : pride - EM Bl

wa·h'an'·i·c'i·ya \wa-ȟ'áŋ-i-c'i-ya\ *v* : to pretend to do much work while very little is done - Bl

wa·h'an·ka \wa-ȟ'aŋ-ƙa\ *v* wa·wa·h'anka : to find it hard to work, to do difficult things well < *Han wánji amayanpa canna wawah'anke lo* I find it difficult to do the work when I am up the whole night. >

wa·h'an·ksi·ca \wa-ȟ'áŋ-ksi-ca\ *n* : the marten - WH

wa·h'an·la \wa-ȟ'áŋ-la\ *va* wah'áŋ·wa·la : to esteem, think highly of one

wa·h'e·ca \wa-ȟ'é-ca\ *n* : round white hail, like to shot

wa·h'u \wa-ȟ'ú\ *va* wa·wa·h'u : to peel, cut the hull or rind off *e.g.* an orange with a knife by scraping — **wa-h'u·h'u** *v red* wa·wá·h'uh'u : to keep peeling

wa·h'un·t'e·ya \wa-ȟ'úŋ-t'e-ya\ *v* [fr *h'unt'a* to get exhausted from working] : to tire one out

wa·i·ca·ga \wa-í-ca-ġa\ *v of* icága : to grow, produce, as a field or plants < *Yunkan wagmeza kin lila ~* And then the corn produced abundantly. *Tamaka el lila waicage* On his land there was a bumper crop. > — **waicahya** *v absol of* icahya waica·hwa·ya : to produce, to raise things, as horses, children, *etc.*, to create — **waicahya·pi** *n* : produce, a crop, that which is raised or produced - B.H.225.2 D.257

Wa·i·ca·hye \Wa-í-ca-ȟye\ *np* : the Creator

wa·i·ca·skan \wa-í-ca-skaŋ\ *v* : to melt snow - Bl

wa·i·ci·ȟa·ȟa \wa-í-ci-ȟa-ȟa\ *n* : a jester, and insolent fellow, one who does evil to others and laughs at the mischief he has done — **waiciȟaȟapi** *n* : insolence

wa·i·ci·kšu·kšu \wá-i-ci-kšu-kšu\ *v* wá·mi·cikšukšu : to decorate, cover one's self with all sorts of ornaments, *i.e. pahayela wakoyake* to wear them piled on - Bl

wa·i·ci·šni·yan *or* **wawicišniyan** \wa-í-ci-šni-yaŋ\ *v* : to run the knife out of the right course in cuttng < ~ *iyeya* to swerve from the mark when cutting. > - R

wa·i·ci·ya \wa-í-ci-ya\ *v of* iciya : to assist, to take one's part - R Bl

wa·i·cu \wa-í-cu\ *v* wai·wa·cu [fr *icu* to take, receive] : to take < *Kagišnišni waiculah* He takes as it pleases him without the least hindrance, *or* He helps himself unceremoniously. > - Bl B.H.236.12

wa·i·cu·cu·ka \wa-í-cu-cu-ka\ *n* : a pilferer — **waicu-cu·kteca** *v* : to be going to be a pilferer

wa·i·cu·cu·kte hcin \wa-í-cu-cu-kte ȟciŋ\ *v* : to covet – P

wa·i·c'i·glu·hta·ta \wa-í-c'i-glu-ȟta-ta\ *v* : to offer a sacrifice for one's self, *e.g.* parts of one's flesh, as once was a custom — **waic'iglu·šna** *v refl* wa·mi·c'iglušna [fr *wayušna* to offer sacrifice] : to sacrifice one's self, to let one's self fall

wa·i·c'i·hon *or* **waic'ihun** \wa-í-c'i-hoŋ\ *v refl* wa·mi·c'ihon [fr *wahun* to gash one's flesh] : to cut or gash one's self

wa·i·c'i·hta·ni \wa-í-c'i-ȟṫa-ni\ *v refl* wa·mi·c'ihtani : to sin against one's self – Cf awaic'ihtani

wa·i·e·ce·šni \wa-í-e-ċe-šni\ *v* wai·wa·yecešni : to tell lies < *Tuwe ca hoši gli hwo?* Who is it that came home with news? *Akšaka he ~ k'on* Oh, that is an old liar.> – Bl

wa·i·e·lgle \wa-í-e-lgle\ *n of* íelgle : an accuser, one who casts up to another — *v* : to accuse – P

wa·i·gla·mna \wa-í-gla-mna\ *v of* iglámna : to make a for one's self – B.H.171.1

wa·i·glu·hta·ta \wa-í-glu-ȟṫa-ṫa\ *v* : to offer one's self in sacrifice as did Christ

wa·i·glu·šna \wa-í-glu-šna\ *v refl* wa·mi·glušna [fr *wayušna* to offer something as a sacrifice] : to sacrifice one's self

wa·i·glu·štan \wa-í-glu-štaŋ\ *v refl* wa·mi·gluštan [fr *yuštan* to finish] : to finish what pertains to one's self – B.H.268.5

wa·i·ha·kta \wa-í-ha-kta\ *v* : to make one wait and follow — *adj* : fond

wa·i·hpe·ya \wa-í-ȟpe-ya\ *v* **1** : waihpe·wa·ya [fr *aihpeya* to dispose of] : to throw away or give to others **2** : to give as sacrifice to departed souls

wa·i·ka·le·le·pa·ke \wa-í-k̇a-le-le-ṗa-ke\ *n* [fr perhaps *kalepa* to cut a notch in, a nitch] : a domineering person, one who acts as if he knows all and issues commands to everyone < *Waikalelepakelahcake* He is one who rather acts as if he knows everything and bosses everywhere he goes. > – Bl

wa·i·kce·ya \wa-í-kce-ya\ *adv perhaps* [fr *ikceya* commonly, ordinarily] : instead of something else < *~ k'u* to give something other instead of the article asked for, *~ mnayan* to have received, *i.e.* at a collection tour, all sorts of things, as calico *etc.*, instead of money which was asked for >

wa·i·ki·cu \wa-í-k̇i-cu\ *v* wai·wa·kicu : to take from others by magic, as some medicine men once pretended to do — **waiki·kcu** *v of* ikíkcu : to take one's own – B.H.245.22

wa·i·le·ya \wa-í-le-ya\ *v* waile·wa·ya [fr *ileya* to set fire to] : to burn, set fire

wa·i·na·ki·hni \wa-í-na-ki-ȟni\ *v* : to be always in a hurry about one's self — **wainakihni·hnike** *n* : one who is continually super-active in all he does < *Wahuncala s'e ~ ; wana kakena iyayelo* He is one super-active, as though he were aping clown tricks; now he is gone off somewhere, as is said when one in a crowd is in a great hurry and goes on while the others are slow in departing. > – ED

wa·i·pa·te \wa-í-ṗa-ṫe\ *n* : a snow plow – An Gr

wa·i·pa·weh i·ye·ya \wa-í-ṗa-weȟ i-yè-ya\ *adv* : improperly, falsely – *Syn* WAĖKTAŠNIYAN Bl

wa·i·pi·la \wa-í-ṗi-la\ *n* [fr *ipila* to withhold] : one who forbids or refuses to part with what he has

wa·i·ška·hu \wa-í-ška-hu\ *n* : the knuckles < *~ nunga* swollen knuckles of a horse, *~ nunga wan yuha yelo* It (his horse) has a swollen knuckle. > – Bl

wa·i·šna·he·ca \wa-í-šna-he-ca\ *n* : soft new snow – *See* the differences in *wahišnaheca* and *wagugeca*

wa·i·šte·ca \wa-í-šṫe-ca\ *adj* : bashful

wa·i·šte·lya \wa-í-šte-lya\ *va* waište·lwa·ya : to put to shame

wa·i·te·bya \wa-í-ṫe-bya\ *adv* : cut shorter on one side – Cf watépa

wa·i·ya·ka·pe·ya \wa-í-ya-k̇a-ṗe-ya\ *v* [fr *íyakapeya* to overcome] : to give one no chance to speak while one is talking angrily – Bl

wa·i·ya·pa·t'o·ya \wa-í-ya-ṗa-t'o-ya\ *v* waiyapat'o·wa·ya : to obstruct, bear down on – Bl

wa·i·ya·pe \wa-í-ya-ṗe\ *v of* íyape : to lie in wait — **waiyape·pi** \wa-í-ya-ṗe-ṗi\ *n* : an ambush

wa·i·ya·ta·gle \wa-í-ya-ta-gle\ *v* waiya·ma·tagle : to have exceeding much *e.g.* work and hence cannot do it — **waiyatagle·ic'iya** *v refl* : to overdo, overtax one's self, to fail by having overtaxed one's strength — **waiyatagle·ya** *v* waiyatagle·wa·ya : to urge on over-much

wa·i·ye·ki·ya \wa-í-ye-ki-ya\ *v* waiye·wa·kiya : to find one's own

wa·i·ye·ya \wa-í-ye-ya\ *v* waiye·wa·ya [fr *iyeya* to find] : to find

wa·i·ye·ye·ca \wa-í-ye-ye-ca\ *n* : one who finds much

wa·i·yo·jan·jan \wa-í-yo-jaŋ-jaŋ\ *v* [fr *iyojanjan* light] : to dazzle, blind < *Išta waiyomajanjan yelo* It (light) dazzles my eyes, as when one has sore eyes. > – Bl

wa·i·yun·ga \wa-í-yuŋ-ġa\ *v* : to inquire – B.H.96.2

wa·ja·gja·ta \wa-já-gja-ṫa\ *v red of* wajáta : to make forked

Wa·ja·je \Wa-já-je\ *np* : the Wajáje, a clan among the Oglalas and Sicangu bands of the Lakotas – GA

wa·jal \wa-jál\ *va contrac of* wajata : to make forked — **waja·lja·ta** \wa-já-lja-ṫa\ *v red* : to be making forked — **waja·lya** *va* waja·lwa·ya : to cause to cut forked, make forked

wa·ja·ta \wa-já-ṫa\ *va* wa·wa·jata : to make forked by sawing or cutting, as one end of an arrow notched for the string, to cut into a fork

wa·ju \wa-jú\ *v* 1st *pers singl of* ju : I am doing rooting

wa·ju·ju \wa-jú-ju\ *va* wa·wa·juju [fr *júju* to pay off] : to quarter, to cut up beef, to cut it into pieces, to butcher *e.g.* an animal – B.H.107.15 GA

wa·ka \wa-k̇á\ *va* wa·wa·ka : to cut or strip, as the feather from a quill, to cut off *e.g.* the ribs of an animal, to split a quill in the middle

wa·ka·a·ja·ja *or* **wakaa·šlaya** \wa-k̇á-a-ja-ja\ *v* : to lay bare, to uncover, as by sweepng

wa·ka·bla \wa-k̇á-bla\ *v* wa·wa·kabla [fr *kabla* to slice up] : to slice — *v* 1st *pers singl of* kablá : I am doing slicing up (the beef) — **wakabla·pi** *n* : meat cut up for drying, dried meat – *Syn* ṖAṖA D.271

wa·ka·bla·ya \wa-k̇á-bla-ya\ *v* wa·wa·kablaya [fr *kablaya* make level] : to make level, to spread out, to cut in thin slices, as meat for drying — *v* 1st *pers singl of* kabláya : I made it level, *or* I sliced *e.g.* meat for drying

wa·ka·bla·za \wa-k̇á-bla-za\ *v* wa·wa·kablaza [fr *kablaza* to make rip open] : to rip open — *v* 1st *pers singl of* kablaza : I caused it to burst

wa·ka·ble·ca \wa-k̇á-ble-ca\ *v* wa·wa·kableca [fr *kableca* break to pieces] : to dash to pieces — *v* 1[st]*pers singl*

\a\ father \e\ they \i\ machine \o\ smoke \u\ lunar \an, aŋ\ blanc Fr. \in, iŋ\ ink \on, oŋ, un, uŋ\ soon, confier Fr. \c\ chair \ġ\ machen Ger. \j\ fusion \clusters: bl, gn, kp, hšl, etc...\ b[e]lo ... said with a slight vowel
See more in the Introduction, Guide to Pronunciation

of kableca : I dashed it to pieces

wa·ka·blu \wa-k̇á-blu\ *v* wa·wa·kablu [fr *kablu* pulverize] : to pulverize — *v 1 pers singl of* kablú : I pounded it fine

wa·ka·bu \wa-k̇á-bu\ *v* : to drum - P

wa·ka·ga \wa-k̇á-ġa\ *v* wa·wa·kaga [fr *kaga* to make] : to make — *v 1 pers singl of* káġa : I made it — **wakaga·pi** *n* : an image, picture, idol, something made < *wicaša* ~ a man's image, a scarecrow > - Note: they say the Pawnee had a scarecrow called *cuwáculùza* and that *cuwaculuza wan apapi kin hehan* at the time they struck their scarecrow - BL

wa·ka·ge·ge \wa-k̇á-ġe-ġe\ *v* wa·wa·kagege [fr *kagege* to sew] : to sew — *v 1st pers singl of* kagege : I did sew it

wa·ka·gi \wa-k̇á-ġi\ *v* wa·wa·kagi [fr *kagi* to stop one's course] : to hinder or prevent by one's presence, so as to keep one from speaking or from doing something to be feared, to be revered — *v 1st pers singl of* kagí : I am preventing him — *n* : one who restrains by his presence — **wakagi·ya** *va* wakagi·wa·ya : to hinder, obstruct, to keep others from going fast — *adv* : preventing, slowly, detaining

wa·ka·gmi·gma \wa-k̇á-gmi-gma\ *v* wa·wa·kagmigma [fr *kagmigma* to round by striking] : to make round — *v 1st pers singl of* kagmigma : I rounded it by striking

wa·ka·gmi·yan·yan \wa-k̇á-gmi-yaŋ-yaŋ\ *v* wa·wa·kagmiyanyan [fr *kagmiyanyan* make roll by striking] : to roll — *v 1 pers singl of* kagmiyanyan : I made it roll

wa·ka·gmun \wa-k̇á-gmuŋ\ *v* [fr *kagmun* to spin with the extended hand] : to spin, twist — *v 1st pers singl of* kagmun : I spun it — **wakagmun·pi** *n* : a spinning

wa·ka·han \wa-k̇á-haŋ\ *part* : split, as the feather end of a quill

wa·ka·hanl \wa-k̇á-haŋl\ *adv* : sometime in the future - Bl

wa·ka·hi \wa-k̇á-hi\ *v* wa·wa·kahi [fr *kahi* to stir] **1** : to rummage in or through, as children might do in trunks *etc.* — *v 1st pers singl of* kahí : I rummaged in **2** : to bring < *wa·ma·kahi* he brings to me >

wa·ka·hi·ka \wa-k̇á-hi-k̇a\ *n* : one who rummages

wa·ka·hin·hpe·ya \wa-k̇á-hiŋ-ȟpe-ya\ *v* wakahinhpe·wa·-ya : to knock down and run over one or something, as a horse over-running a child

wa·ka·hin·ta \wa-k̇á-hiŋ-ṫa\ *va* wa·wa·kahinta wa·un·kahinta·pi [fr *kahinta* to sweep *e.g.* a floor] : to sweep — *va 1st pers singl of* kahinta : I swept it

wa·ka·ho·ho \wa-k̇á-ho-ho\ *v* wa·wa·kahoho [fr *kahoho* to loosen by striking] : to loosen, to shake to make loose — *v 1st pers singl of* kahoho : I made it loose

wa·ka·ho·mni \wa-k̇á-ho-mni\ *v* wa·wa·kahomni [fr *kahomni* to spin by striking] : to make turn round — *v 1 pers singl of* kahomni : I twirled or spun a thing

wa·ka·hun \wa-k̇á-huŋ\ *v* wa·wa·kahun [fr *kahun* to make a mark by striking] : to make marks, cuts, by striking with an axe or knife

wa·ka·hun·hun·za \wa-k̇á-huŋ-huŋ-za\ *v* wa·wa·kahunhunza [fr *kahunhunza* to shake] : to shake by striking — *v 1 pers singl of* kahunhunza : I shook it with a blow

wa·ka·ȟa·pa \wa-k̇á-ȟa-ṗa\ *v* wa·wa·kaȟapa [fr *kaȟapa* to drive or ride herd] : to drive along — *v 1st pers singl of* kaȟapa : I drove them along

wa·ka·ȟe·pa \wa-k̇á-ȟe-ṗa\ *v* wa·wa·kaȟepa [fr *kaȟepa* to bail] : to bail out *e.g.* water — *v 1 pers sing of* kaȟepa : I bailed it out

wa·ka·ȟi·ca \wa-k̇á-ȟi-ca\ *v* wa·wa·kaȟica [fr *kaȟica* to waken one] : to waken up by striking — *v 1 pers singl of* kaȟica : I did waken him - Note: an *altern* spelling, k̇aġíca

wa·ka·hla \wa-k̇á-ȟla\ *v* wa·wa·kahla [fr *kaȟla* to rattle or rummage] : to rattle or rummage — *v 1st pers singl of* kahlá : I rattled it — **wakahla·ka** *n* : one who pilfers much

wa·ka·hle·ca \wa-k̇á-ȟle·ca\ *v* [fr *kahleca* to split open] : to break open, to fracture — *v 1st pers singl of* kahleca : I broke it open

wa·ka·hli·hli \wa-k̇á-ȟli-ȟli\ *v* : to become mired in mud < ~ *wau welo* I came mired in mud, *i.e.* waded through deep mud. > — **wakahli·ya** *v* wakáhli·wa·ya [fr *kahliya* to cause one to mire in mud] : to make mire in mud - Cf kahlihli Bl

wa·ka·hlo·ka \wa-k̇á-ȟlo-k̇a\ *v* wa·wa·kahloka [fr *kahloka* to break a hole in something] : to make a hole in — *v 1st pers singl of* kahloka : I made a hole in it

wa·ka·hni·ga \wa-k̇á-ȟni-ġa\ *v* wa·wa·kahniga [fr *kahniga* to choose, select] : to choose — *v 1st pers singl of* kahniga : I selected it

[1]wa·ka·hpa \wa-k̇á-ȟṗa\ *v* wa·wa·kahpa [fr *kahpa* make fall] : to throw down — *v 1st pers singl of* kahpa : I threw it down

[2]wa·ka·hpa \wá-ka-ȟṗa\ *v* wá·wa·kahpa [fr *akahpa* to cover, conceal] : to cover

wa·ka·hpu \wa-k̇á-ȟṗu\ *v* wa·wa·kahpu [fr *kahpu* to scale off] : to tear down, to strike and make fall down, to strike and loosen from its fastenings — *v 1 pers singl of* kahpu : I tore it down

wa·ka·hta·ka \wa-k̇á-ȟta-k̇a\ *vn* wa·ma·kahtaka : to be easily hurt, touchy, nervous — **wakahtake·ca** *n* wa·ma·kahtakeca : one who is made sick by a little matter, one who is nervous — **wakahtake·ke** \wa-k̇á-ȟta-ke-k̇e\ *n* : a grumbler, one who is nervous, fretful, dissatisfied with almost everything - Bl

wa·ka·ȟu·ga \wa-k̇á-ȟu-ġa\ *v* wa·wa·kaȟuga [fr *kaȟuga* to break in] : to break *e.g.* the skull, kettles *etc.* — *v 1st pers singl of* kaȟuga : I cracked it in

wa·ka·ȟun·ta \wa-k̇á-ȟuŋ-ṫa\ *v* [fr *kaȟunta* to wear out gradually] : to fray, make rough, as birds do tearing open husks of corn

wa·ka·h'o \wá-ka-ȟ'o\ *vn* : to linger about something, as buzzards do about a carcass

wa·ka·h'u \wa-k̇á-ȟ'u\ *v* wa·wa·kah'u [fr *kah'u* to skin] : to peel off *e.g.* bark — *v 1st pers singl of* kah'u : I stripped it off

wa·ka·i·le \wa-k̇á-i-le\ *v* wa·wa·kaile [fr *kaile* to fan a flame] : to make blaze

wa·ka·ja·ja \wa-k̇á-ja-ja\ *v* wa·wa·kajaja [fr *kajaja* to wash something away] : to wash by drawing back and forth in the water, and so to see well — *v 1st pers singl of* kajaja : I splashed on water to wash it clean

wa·ka·ji·pa \wa-k̇á-ji-ṗa\ *v* wa·wa·kajipa [fr *kajipa* to shave, plane] : to shave, to plane

wa·ka·ju·ju \wa-k̇á-ju-ju\ *v* wa·wa·kajuju [fr *kajuju* to knock off, pay off] : to pay off, erase, forgive — *v 1st pers singl of* kajuju : I paid it off, *or* I forgave it — **wakajuju·kiya** *v* : to tax, impose a tax - P

wa·ka·jun \wa-k̇á-juŋ\ *v* [fr *kajun* to knock or pull out] : to tear or pull up by the roots

wa·ka·kab i·hpe·ya \wa-k̇á-kab i-ȟpè-ya\ *v* [fr *kakab ihpeya* to knock or bat away] : to push out of the way - Bl

wa·ka·kan \wa-k̇á-kaŋ\ *v* wa·wa·kakan [fr *kakan* to make marks or notches in] : to hew, to harvest, beat or strike off *e.g.* berries or grain, to hammer on or strike as in shaping a stone < ~ *unyanpi kte* Let us go to harvesting. > - Bl B.H.201.14

wa·ka·kca \wa-ǩá-kca\ *v* wa·wa·kakca [fr *kakca* to comb, straighten] : to comb, to disentangle — *v 1st pers singl of* kakca : I combed (my hair)

wa·ka·kin·ca \wa·ǩa·ǩin·ca\ *v* wa·wa·kakinca [fr *kakinca* scrape off] : to scrape — *v 1st pers singl of* kakinca : I scraped it off

wa·ka·ki·šya \wa-ǩá-ki-šya\ *v* wakaki·šwa·ya : to cause to suffer, to give trouble - D.268

wa·ka·ko·ka \wa-ǩá-ko-ǩa\ *v* wa·wa·kakoka [fr *kakoka* to thump, knock] : to make rattle — *v 1st pers singl of* kakoka : I made it rattle

wa·ka·kpan \wa-ǩá-kṗaŋ\ *v* wa·wa·kakpan [fr *kakpan* to beat fine] : to pound fine — *v 1st pers singl of* kakpan : I mashed it fine

wa·ka·ksa \wa-ǩá-ǩsa\ *v* [fr *kaksa* to split, cut off] : to cut off with an axe — *v 1st pers singl of* kaksa : I cut it off

wa·ka·kša \wa-ǩá-kša\ *v* wa·wa·kakša [fr *kakša* to coil, roll up] : to roll up

wa·ka·kšan \wa-ǩá-kšaŋ\ *or* \wá-ǩa-kšaŋ\ *v* wa·wa·kakšan [fr *kakšan* to bend] : to bend — *v 1st pers singl of* kakšan : I bent it - Bl

wa·ka·kši·ja \wa-ǩá-kši-ja\ *v* wa·wa·kakšija [fr *kakšija* to bend, double up] : to double up, as a pocket knife

wa·ka·ktan \wa-ǩá-ktaŋ\ *v* wa·wa·kaktan [fr *kaktan* to put a bend in] : to make bend — *v 1st pers singl of* kaktan : I made a bend in something

wa·ka·ku·ka \wa-ǩá-ku-ka\ *v* wa·wa·kakuka [fr *kakuka* wear out] : to pound to pieces, to destroy — *v 1 pers singl of* kakuka : I destroyed it

wa·ka·lya \wa-ǩá-lya\ *v* waka·lwa·ya [fr *kalya* to heat] : to boil — **wa-kalya·pi** \wa-ǩá-lya-ṗi\ *n* : anything boiled - Note: the word is commonly used for coffee

wa·ka·mna \wa-ǩá-mna\ *v* wa·wa·kamna [fr *kamna* to gather, earn] : to collect, gather, to earn, make money, to merit — *v 1st pers singl of* kamna : I earned it - Pb. 30 — **wakamna·ka** \wa-ǩá-mna-ǩa\ *n* : one who collects, a collector — **wakamnan·pi** *n* : a collecting, an earning

wa·kan \wa-ǩáŋ\ *adj* : sacred, holy, consecrated, incomprehensible, special, possessing or capable of giving *ton* a spiritual quality received or transmittable to beings for making what is specially good or evil < *Ma·wakan* or *Wa·ma·kan* I am holy. *Taku iyahanbla ca wanikan keha he? eya* He said, Did you state you are holy because you dreamt something? *Miš eya heon mawakan yelo* I too for that reason am holy. > - WJR.152-153 MS.244

wa·kan'·e·con \wa-ǩáŋ-e-coŋ\ *v* wakan'eca·mon : to do triks *e.g.* of jugglery — **wakan'econ·pila** \wa-ǩáŋ-e-coŋ-ṗi-la\ *n* : magic, tricks of jugglery

wa·kan·gli \wa-ǩáŋ-gli\ *n* : the lightning < ~ *makata iheyapi* Lightning is discharged on the ground. > - MS. 258

wa·kan·he·ja *or* **wakanyeja** \wa-ǩáŋ-he-ja\ *n* [fr Dakota *kanheja* poor, feeble, distressed] : a child, children — *adj* : poor, feeble, distressed < *Waníkanheja šni* You are not distressed, feeble. > - Note: the *adj* does not seem to be used in Teton

wa·kan·h'an \wa-ǩáŋ-ȟ'aŋ\ *v* : to court a woman, as by playing a flute *etc.* - Bl

wa·kan i·a *or* **wakinya** \wa-ǩáŋ i-a\ *v* wakan i·wa·e : to foretell - B.H.67.4, 145.2

wa·kan'·i·c'i·con·za \wa-ǩáŋ-i-c'i-coŋ-za\ *v* : to profess *e.g.* faith - P

wa·kan'·i·c'i·la \wa-ǩáŋ-i-c'i-la\ *v refl* wakan·mi·c'ila [fr *wakanla* to think of as holy, to worship] : to esteem one's self *wakan* holy, to be proud — **wakanic'ila·pi** *n* : pride

[1]**wa·kan·ka** \wa-ǩáŋ-ǩa\ *n* [fr *ǩan* aged] wa·ma·kanka : an old woman

[2]**wa·kan·ka** \wa-ǩáŋ-ǩa\ *adj* wa·ma·kanka : doubtfully mysterious, *i.e.* if a person or thing is said to be *wakan* holy

wa·kan·ka·ga \wa-ǩáŋ-ǩa-ǧa\ *v* wakan·wa·kaga : to make *wakán* holy or consecrated, to perform acts of worship according to ideas of the Dakotas

wa·kan·ka·la \wa-ǩáŋ-ǩa-la\ *n dim of* waǩanǩa : a little old lady

wa·kan·kan·pi \wa-ǩáŋ-kàŋ-pi\ *n* : spirits engaged to persons - LHB

wa·kan·kan·yan \wa-ǩáŋ-kaŋ-yaŋ\ *adv red* [fr *wakanyan* in a sacred manner] : in a holy, mysterious way < ~ *mioh'an* the miracles I wrought > - B.H.63.17, 114.22

Wa·kan·ki·ci·yu·za·pi \Wa-ǩáŋ-ki-ci-yu-zà-pi\ *np* : the sacrament of Matrimony, marriage, *i.e.* a love union in which a man and a woman who both are free to marry publicly and mutually promise to share their lives in a permanent exclusive union that may prove fruitful in the fostering and the having and raising of children

wa·kan·ki·la \wa-ǩáŋ-ǩi-la\ *v poss* wakan·wa·kila [fr *wakanla* to think of as sacred, to worship] : to regard one's own as sacred

wa·kan·la *or* **wakanla·ka** \wa-ǩáŋ-la\ *va* wakan·wa·la : to reckon as holy or sacred, to worship < *Na cahli k'on na wahinša k'on hena ecel owegnaka na lila wakanwala* And I really had reckoned it as sacred when I put in that gunpowder and guncaps. >

wa·kan·la s'e un \wa-ǩáŋ-la s'e uŋ\ *v* : to be a health scrupulant - Bl

Wa·kan·ši·ca \Wa-ǩáŋ-ši-ca\ *np* : Satan, a devil, the bad spirit

Wa·kan·tan·ka \Wa-ǩáŋ-taŋ-ǩa\ *np* : God, the Creator of all things, the Great Spirit, *in philosophy:* all *wakan* beings because they are all as one - WJR.152

wa·kan wa·ci·pi \wa-ǩáŋ wa-cì-pi\ *n* : a sacred dance

wa·kan·wo·han \wa-ǩáŋ-wo-haŋ\ *v* wakanwo·wa·he : to make a sacred feast — **wakanwohan·pi** *n* : a sacred feast

wa·kan·yan *or* **wakanyan·kel** \wa-ǩáŋ-yaŋ\ *adv* : in a sacred, holy, or wonderful, or even a mysterious way < *Winyan kin le otuyacin u šni yelo, ~ u welo* This woman did not come to no purpose, she came in a wonderful way. ~ *wóha nanké* You are property in a sacred manner, as is said of one who travels with much luggage. ~ *wóecon* wonderful deeds done, *or* to do wonderful deeds > - Bw B.H.290.9,20

wa·kan·ya wo·wan·yan·ke \wa-ǩáŋ-ya wò-waŋ-yaŋ-ke\ *n* : a sacred vision - B.H.291.13

wa·kan·ye·ja *or* **wakanheja** *or* **kanyéja** \wa-ǩáŋ-ye-ja\ *n* : a child, children < ~ *otuyubleza* She woke up the children. >

wa·kan·ye·lak *or* **wakanyelakel** \wa-ǩáŋ-ye-lak\ \wa-ǩáŋ-ye-la-kel\ *adv* : with great difficulty, only by over-

---

\a\ father \e\ they \i\ machine \o\ smoke \u\ lunar \an, aŋ\ blanc Fr. \in, iŋ\ ink \on, oŋ, un, uŋ\ soon, confier Fr. \c\ chair \ǧ\ machen Ger. \j\ fusion \clusters: bl, gn, kp, hšl, etc...\ b[e]lo ... said with a slight vowel **See more in the Introduction, Guide to Pronunciation**

coming almost insurmountable obstacles < ~ *icu* He took it with greatest difficulty. >

wa·kan·yu·za \wa-k̇áŋ-yu-za\ *v* wakan·blu·za : to take a wife after the manner of Christians

wa·ka·o·hpa \wa-k̇á-o-ḣṗa\ *v* wa·wa·kaohpa [fr *kaohpa* to break through] : to smash through — 1st *pers singl of* kaohpa : I broke through it

[1]**wa·ka·pa** \wa-k̇á-pa\ *v* waka·wa·pa [fr *kapá* to surpass or win as in a race] : to excel, exceed, surpass, to win in a race

[2]**wa·ka·pa** \wa-k̇á-pa\ *v* wa·wa·kapa [fr *k̇apá* to pound up] : to pound off — *v* 1st *pers singl of* k̇apá : I beat it off

wa·ka·pan \wa-k̇á-paŋ\ *v* wa·wa·kapan [fr *kapán* to pound off] : to pound off *e.g.* corn — 1st *pers singl of* kapán : I beat it off — **wakapan·pan** *v* wa·wa·kapan-pan [fr *kapanpan* to beat soft] : to pound soft — *1 pers singl of* kapanpan : I beat it soft

wa·ka·pa·pi \wa-k̇á-pa-pi\ *n* : pemmican, meat mashed up and mixed with marrow

wa·ka·pce·ce·la *or* **wakaptecela** \wa-k̇á-pce-ce·la\ *v* : to cut off shorter

wa·ka·pe \wá-k̇a-ṗe\ *n* : a piece of leather on which to mash beef, cherries *etc.* < *Na ~ wan ogna wakapapi ojula ahimigle* He came and set before me pemmican in a leather that was full. >

wa·ka·pe·mni \wa-k̇á-ṗe-mni\ *v* [fr *kapemni* to make crooked] : to twist, to swing *e.g.* a lasso — *v* 1st *pers singl of* kapemni : I tossed swinging it

wa·ka·pe·sto \wa-k̇á-ṗe-sṫo\ *v* wa·wa·kapesto [fr *kapesto* to cut to a point] : to sharpen, point — *v* 1st *pers singl of* kapesto : I sharpened it

wa·ka·pe·ya \wa-k̇á-ṗe-ya\ *v* wakape·wa·ya : to excel, to cause to excel

wa·ka·po·pa \wa-k̇á-po-ṗa\ *v* [fr *kapopa* to make pop] : to make burst — *v* 1st *pers singl of* kapopa : I made it burst with a pop

wa·ka·po·po *or* **wa kapopa** \wa-k̇á-po-pa\ *v* : to crunching noise in deep snow by walking and compressing the snow < ~ *wau welo* I come crushing snow with my feet. > - Bl

wa·ka·po·ta \wa-k̇á-ṗo-ṫa\ *v* wa·wa·kapota [fr *kapota* to tear by beating] : to pound to pieces — *v* 1st *pers singl of* kapota : I beat it to pieces, as clothes torn by flapping in the wind

wa·ka·psa·ka \wa-k̇á-psa-k̇a\ *v* [fr *kapsaka* cut or break *e.g.* a string or wire] : to break in two, as a string — *v* 1st *pers singl of* kapsaka : I broke it in two

wa·ka·psi·ca \wa-k̇á-psi-ca\ *v* wa·wa·kapsica [fr *kapsica* make jump by striking] : to make hop — *v* 1st *pers singl of* kapsica : I made it jump by striking

wa·ka·psin·psin·ta \wa-k̇á-psiŋ-psiŋ-ṫa\ *v* wa·wa·ka-psinpsinta [fr *kapsinpsinta* to flog, whip] : to whip — 1st *pers singl of* kapsinpsinta : I whipped it

wa·ka·pson \wa-k̇á-psoŋ\ *v* wa·wa·kapson [fr *kapson* to spill by striking] : to spill — 1st *pers singl of* kapson : I spilled it

wa·ka·pšun \wa-k̇á-pšuŋ\ *v* wa·wa·kapšuŋ [fr *kapšun* to knock out, as a tooth being struck] : to dislocate — *v* 1st *pers singl of* kapšun : I dislocated it

wa·ka·pta \wa-k̇á-pṫa\ *v* wa·wa·kapta [fr *kapta* to lade or bail out] : to dip out — *v* 1st *pers singl of* kapta : I dipped it out < *Wana ~ po* Dish it out, as they say when ready to eat. > - LO

wa·ka·pte·ce·la \wa-k̇á-pṫe-ce-la\ *v* wa·wa·kaptecela [fr *ka* striking + *ptecela* short] : to cut off shorter — *v* 1st *pers singl of* kaptecela : I cut it off shorter

wa·ka·pu·s'ki·ya \wa·k̇á-ṗu-s'k̇i-ya\ *v* wakapu·swa·-kiya : to hang up to dry - Bl

wa·ka·sa \wa-k̇á-sa\ *v* wa·wa·kasa [fr *kasa* cover over with snow] : to bury in the snow

wa·ka·se \wa-k̇á-se\ *n* [fr *kasan* to turn white] : a thing growning old and white - Bl

wa·ka·ska \wa-k̇á-sk̇a\ *v* : to whiten — *v* 1st *pers singl of* kaska : I bleached it white

wa·ka·ska \wá-k̇a-ska\ *v* wa·wa·kaska [fr *akaska* to be greedy] : to eat greedily, eat long < *Toki etonwe šni waunkaskapi* We were long eating where he did not look. > - R Bl

wa·ka·ske·pa \wa-k̇á-sk̇e-ṗa\ *v* [fr *kaskepa* to empty out] : to bail out

wa·ka·ski·ca \wa-k̇á-sk̇i-ca\ *v* wa·wa·kaskica [fr *kaskica* to pack by striking] : to press or pound tight

wa·ka·sle·ca \wa-k̇á-sle-ca\ *v* [fr *kasleca* to split *e.g.* wood] : to split without effort — *v 1 pers singl of* kasleca : I easily split it

wa·ka·sli \wa-k̇á-sli\ *v* wa·wa·kasli [fr *kasli* to strike and force out] : to strike and make fly out, to make spirt out by striking, as matter from a sore

wa·ka·slo·han \wa-k̇á-slo-haŋ\ *vn* : to drive along, as the wind does a boat

wa·ka·sma·ka \wa-k̇á-sma-k̇a\ *v* wa·wa·kasmaka [fr *kasmaka* to indent] : to indent by pounding

wa·ka·smin·yan·yan \wa-k̇á-smin-yaŋ-yaŋ\ *v* : to make bare, as the wind does the ground driving off the snow

wa·ka·sna \wa-k̇á-sna\ *v* [fr *kasna* to strike making a ringing sound] **1** : to make ring **2** : to shake off, as the wind does leaves from a tree — *v* 1st *pers singl of* kasna : I made it ring, *or* I shook it off

wa·ka·šni \wa-k̇á-šni\ *v* wa·wa·kašni [fr *kasni* to beat out a fire, or to cool what is hot] : to extinguish — *v 1 pers singl of* kasni : I put out (the fire)

wa·ka·so·ta \wa-k̇á-so-ṫa\ *v* wa·wa·kasota [fr *kasota* to use up certain things, as trees, water, game, soldiers *etc*] : to use up, expend, make an end to — *v* 1st *pers singl of* kasota : I destroyed *e.g.* the forest — **wakasote·ka** \wa-k̇á-so-te-ka\ *n* : a spendthrift - B.H.226.1

wa·ka·sto \wa-k̇á-sṫo\ *v* [fr *kasto* to smooth down by hand, as the hair] : to smooth down

wa·ka·swu \wa-k̇á-swu\ *v* wa·wa·kaswu [fr *kaswu* to cut into dangles] : to cut dangles, cut in strips — **wa-kaswu·pi** \wa-k̇á-swu-ṗi\ *n* : dangles, fringes

wa·ka·ša·pa \wa-k̇á-ša-ṗa\ *v* wa·wa·kašapa : to make black, dirty by smiting

wa·ka·še·ca \wa-k̇á-še-ca\ *v* [fr *kašeca* to deaden by cutting] : to deaden — 1st *pers singl of* kašeca : I dead-ened it by cutting around it

wa·ka·še·ya \wa-k̇á-še-ya\ *v* wakaše·wa·ya [fr *kašeya* to fend off] : to obstruct

wa·ka·ši·ca·ho·wa·ya \wa-k̇á-ši-ca-ho-wa-ya\ *v* wa·wa·-kašicahowaya [fr *kašicahowaya* to cry out, scream] : to cause to cry out by smiting

wa·ka·ši·pa \wa-k̇á-ši-ṗa\ *v* wa·wa·kašipa [fr *kašipa* to knock or cut off close] : to break off, as limbs from a tree — *v* 1st *pers singl of* kašipa : I trimmed close

wa·ka·ška \wa-k̇á-šk̇a\ *v* wa·wa·kaška [fr *kaška* to tie or bind] : to bind — *v* 1st *pers single of* kaška : I bound him, handcuffed him

wa·ka·ški·ca \wa-k̇á-šk̇i-ca\ *v* wa·wa·kaškica [fr *kaški-ca* to beat or pound out] : to press, pound or beat out — *v* 1st *pers singl of* kaškica : I pounded it

wa·ka·ško·kpa \wa-k̇á-ško-kṗa\ *v* wa·wa·kaškokpa [fr

kaškokpa to hollow out, cut concave] : to hollow out *e.g.* a trough — *v* 1st *pers singl of* kaškokpa : I hollowed it out

wa·ka·ško·pa \wa-k̇á-ško-ṗa\ *v* wa·wa·kaškopa [fr *kaškopa* to make crooked, twisted] : to cut crookedly — *v* 1st *pers singl of* kaškopa : I cut it crookedly

wa·ka·šle·ca \wa-k̇á-šle-ca\ *v* wa·wa·kašleca [fr *kašleca* to split by striking hard] : to split with a knife or axe by striking making real effort — *v* 1st *pers singl of* kašleca : I split it with effort

wa·ka·šlo·ka \wa-k̇á-šlo-k̇a\ *v* wa·wa·kašloka [fr *kašloka* to knock off or out] : to knock off *e.g.* the head of an axe handle

wa·ka·šlo·ya·kel \wa-k̇á-šlo-ya-kel\ *adv* : in a way causing melting < *Waspanla ca ~ maunnipelo* When it was slushy we traveled. > - Bl

wa·ka·šlu·ta \wa-k̇á-šlu-ṫa\ *v* wa·wa·kašluta [fr *kašluta* to glance off] : to make glance, as an axe — *v* 1st *pers singl of* kašluta : I made it glance off

wa·ka·šna \wa-k̇á-šna\ *v* wa·wa·kašna [fr *kašna* to miss attempting to hit] : to miss in striking — *v* 1st *pers singl of* kašna : I missed trying to hit it

wa·ka·šo·ta \wa-k̇á-šo-ṫa\ *adj* [fr *šota* to smoke] : blackened with smoke — **wakašote·šni** *adj* : clean, undefiled, pure, virgin - *Syn* WOTIYEMNAŠNI — **wakašotešni·yan** *adv* : purely, undefiled - ED R Bl

wa·ka·špa \wa-k̇á-šṗa\ *v* wa·wa·kašpa [fr *kašpa* to cut loose from] : to expectorate; to cut off a piece — *v* 1st *pers singl of* kašpa : I spat it out

wa·ka·šta·ka \wa-k̇á-šṫa-k̇a\ *v* wa·wa·kaštaka [fr *kaštaka* to beat, whip] : to smite — *v* 1st *pers singl of* kaštaka : I struck him

wa·ka·štan \wa-k̇á-šṫaŋ\ *v* wa·wa·kaštan [fr *kaštan* to pour out] : to pour out — *v* 1st *pers singl of* kaštan : I poured it out

wa·ka·šu·ja \wa-k̇á-šu-ja\ *v* wa·wa·kašuja [fr *kašuja* to] : to crush by striking — *v* 1st *pers singl of* kašuja : I crushed, smashed it

wa·ka·š'a·ka \wa-k̇á-š'a-ka\ *v* wa·wa·kaš'aka [fr *kaš'aka* to hit, cuff, bump] : to strike with too little force to penetrate — *v* 1st *pers singl of* kaš'aka : I bumped it

wa·ka·tan·ni \wa-k̇á-taŋ-ni\ *v* [fr *katan* to pound on + *ni i.e. šni* not] : to wear out by striking — *v* 1st *pers singl of* katan : I wore it out striking it

wa·ka·ta·ta \wa-k̇á-ta-ṫa\ *v* wa·wa·katata [fr *katata* to shake off] : to shake out *e.g.* a bed or blanket — *v* 1st *pers singl of* katata : I shook (the dust) out

wa·ka·te·pa \wa-k̇á-ṫe-pa\ *v* wa·wa·katepa [fr *tepa* of root form] : to cut to a stump — *v* 1st *pers singl of* katepa : I reduce it to root form by cutting

wa·ka·ti·ca \wa-k̇á-ti-ca\ *v* [fr *katica* to stir in mixing] : to scrape off, to mix up *e.g.* mortar - R

wa·ka·tin \wa-k̇á-ṫiŋ\ *v* wa·wa·katin [fr *katin* straight, straightened] : to straighten with a knife, to cut straight

wa·ka·tka \wa-k̇á-tka\ *v* wa·ma·katka [fr *katka* to choke or be choked] : to choke

wa·ka·tku·ga \wa-k̇á-tk̇u-ġa\ *v* [fr *katkuga* to strike off square pieces] : to cut up short

wa·ka·tkun·za \wa-k̇á-tk̇uŋ-za\ *v* wa·wa·katkunza [fr *katkunza* to cut off square, to square off] : to cut off square

wa·ka·to·to \wa-k̇á-ṫo-ṫo\ *v* : to knock *e.g.* on a door — *v* 1st *pers singl of* katoto : I knocked - Note: the meaning, to clear land for plowing, is doubtful

wa·ka·tu·ka \wa-k̇á-tu-k̇a\ *v* wa·wa·katuka [fr *katuka* to knock off fur] : to spoil by striking *e.g.* furs

wa·ka·tu·tka \wa-k̇á-ṫu-tk̇a\ *v* wa·wa·katutka [fr *katutka* to break up fine] : to break into small pieces

wa·ka·t'a \wa-k̇á-t'a\ *v* wa·wa·kat'a [fr *kat'a* to stun or kill] : to kill by striking

wa·ka·t'in·za \wa-k̇á-t'iŋ-za\ *v* wa·wa·kat'inza [fr *kat'inza* to pound tight or firm] : to pound in tight

wa·ka·t'o·za·pi \wa-k̇á-t'o-za-pi\ *n* : a stone hammer - *Syn* IHONICATA WR

wa·ka·un·ka \wa-k̇á-uŋ-k̇a\ *v* wa·wa·kaunka [fr *kaunka* to fell] : to fell, chop down *e.g.* timber, to blow down as the wind does trees — *v* 1st *pers singl of* kaunka : I chopped it down

wa·ka·we·ga \wa-k̇á-we-ġa\ *v* wa·wa·kawega [fr *kawega* to break, crack] : to break, fracture

wa·ka·wi·gnu·ni \wa-k̇á-wi-gnu-ni\ *v* wa·wa·kawignuni [fr *kawignuni* to break, destroy by striking] : to destroy - R Bl

wa·ka·win·ja \wa-k̇á-wiŋ-ja\ *v* wa·wa·kawinja [fr *kawinja* to beat down] : to bend down by striking

wa·ka·zan \wa-k̇á-zaŋ\ *v* wa·wa·kazan [fr *kazan* to hurt, make feel pain] : to make sick by striking

wa·ka·ze \wa-k̇á-ze\ *v* wa·wa·kaze [fr *kaze* to lade out] : to lade or dip out *e.g.* food from a kettle

wa·ka·zon·ta *or* **wakasonta** \wa-k̇á-zoŋ-ṫa\ *v* wa·wa·kazonta [fr *kazonta* to weave, *son* to plait, braid] : to weave — *v* 1st *pers singl of* kazon-ta : I wove it

wa·kcan·yan \wa-kcáŋ-yaŋ\ *v* : to observe and report < *~ waku welo* I returned to report what I observed. > — **wakcanye·ya** *va* wakcanye·wa·ya : to cause to go, send and spy out - R Bl

wa·kce·ya \wa-kcé-ya\ *va* wakce·wa·ya : to roast, hang over a fire — **wakceya·pi** *n* : the ribs of an animal, the roasting piece, because the ribs are generally so prepared - Cf kceya

wa·ke·ya \wa-k̇é-ya\ *va* wake·wa·ya : to have for a tent — *n* : a round skin Lakota tent — **wakeya·ska** *n* : a canvas tent — **wakeya·ton** *va* : to make a tent of, *i.e.* to form a *wakéya* - D.246 B.H.61.3

wa·ke·za *or* **wakiza** \wa-k̇ĕ'-za\ *v* wa·wá·keza [fr *kiza* to fight] : I fight — *va* 1st *pers singl of* kíza : I fought him - Cf wak'eza Bl KE

wa·ki \wa-k̇í\ *v* wa·wa·ki [fr *ki* to rob] : to rob — *v* 1st *pers singl of ki* to arrive back : I arrived at my home, *i.e.* where I live

wa·ki·ble·ca \wa-kí-ble-ca\ *v poss* wa·wa·kibleca [fr *wableca* to break] : to break one's own, *i.e.* by attempting to cut with a knife

wa·ki·ca·ga \wa-kí-ca-ġa\ *n* : a sacred ceremony < *~ lowanpi* the singing of sacred song >

wa·ki·ca·mna \wa-kí-ca-mna\ *v* [fr *kamna* to earn] : to earn money for one < *Wawicakicamna* He earned money for them. > - B.H.299.16

wa·ki·ce·pa *or* **wakicipa** \wa-kí-ce-ṗa\ *n* : a fat animal < *Wamicipa* My animal is fat, *~ mini wohlecelo* A fat animal tore through the water, as is said when just a few drops of rain do fall. *Hehlokeca tanka wakinašleca ~* It is a fat buffalo long and hollow-horned that split its horns, as is said of fat buffalo. > - Bl BT KE

wa·ki·ci·bla·za \wa-k̇í-ci-bla-za\ *v* wa·we·ciblaza : to cut open or cut lengthwise for one - *See* wakiciksa

---

\a\ father \e\ they \i\ machine \o\ smoke \u\ lunar \an, aŋ\ blanc Fr. \in, iŋ\ ink \on, oŋ, un, uŋ\ soon, confier Fr. \c\ chair \ġ\ machen Ger. \j\ fusion \clusters: bl, gn, kp, hšl, etc...\ b^{e}lo ... said with a slight vowel
See more in the Introduction, Guide to Pronunciation

wa·ki·ci·glu·hta·ta \wa-kí-ci-glu-ȟta-ṫa\ *v* : to offer something of one's own as a sacrifice for another, as God gave his Son for the whole world

[1]**wa·ki·ci·gna·ka** \wa-ḱi-ci-gna-ka\ *v* wa·we·cignaka [fr *gnaka* to place or lay away] : to lay away for one

[2]**wa·ki·ci·gna·ka** \wá-ḱi-ci-gna-ka\ *v* wa·we·cignaka [fr *agnaka* to apply on] : to lay on for one, apply a poultice to one

wa·ki·ci·go \wa-ḱi-ci-ġo\ *v* wa·we·cigo [fr *wago* to etch or carve] : to cut or carve for one

wa·ki·ci·hon *or* **wakicihun** \wa-ḱi-ci-hoŋ\ *v* wa·we·cihon [fr *wahon* to gash, slash] : to cut or gash for one — **wakicihon·hon** *v red* : to cut across, gash

wa·ki·ci·h'u \wa-ḱi-ci-ȟ'u\ *v* wa·we·cih'u [fr *wah'u* to peel] : to cut the rind or hull off for another

wa·ki·ci·kpan \wa-ḱi-ci-kṗaŋ\ *v* wa·we·cikpan [fr *wakpan* to cut up fine] : to cut off fine, *e.g.* tobacco for one

wa·ki·ci·ksa \wa-ḱi-ci-ksa\ *v* wa·we·ciksa [fr *waksa* to cut off crosswise] : to cut off for one — **wakiciksa·ksa** *v red* wa·we·ciksaksa : to cut off for one often

wa·ki·ci·pa \wa-ḱi-ci-ṗa\ *n* : a fat animal < *Wamicipa* My animal is fat. > - BT

wa·ki·ci·pta \wa-ḱi-ci-pṫa\ *v* wa·we·cipta [fr *wapta* trim off the edge of] : to cut off or trim for one

wa·ki·ci·sku \wa-ḱi-ci-sḱu\ *v* wa·we·cisku [fr *wasku* to pare or shave off] : to peel or pare for one

wa·ki·ci·sle·ca \wa-ḱi-ci-sle-ca\ *va* wa·we·cisleca [fr *wasleca* to saw up or split] : to split with a knife, to rip with a saw for one

wa·ki·ci·šla \wa-ḱi-ci-šla\ *v* wa·we·cišla [fr *wašla* shave or scrape off] : to cut or shave off with a knife for one

wa·ki·ci·šlo·ka \wa-ḱi-ci-šlo-ka\ *v* wa·we·cišloka [fr *wašloka* to cut out] : to cut out, cut a hole for one, to take out a piece for

wa·ki·ci·špa \wa-ḱi-ci-špa\ *v* wa·we·cišpa [fr *wašpa* to scalp, cut off] : to cut off a piece for one — **wakicišpa-špa** \wá-ḱi-ci-špa-špa\ *v red* : to cut off pieces for one < *Taku oyasin ~ kte hcin* He will cut up everything in very many pieces, *i.e.* he makes big deeds of all his little actions. > - Bl

wa·ki·ci·špu \wa-ḱi-ci-špu\ *v* wa·we·cišpu [fr *wašpu* to cut or rip up into pieces] : to cut off something that was stuck on, for another

wa·ki·ci·un·yan \wa-ḱi-ci-uŋ-yaŋ\ *v* : to offer sacrifices for one

wa·ki·co·ki·c'un \wá-ḱi-co-ki-c'uŋ\ *adv* : carefully < ~ *aya yo* Lead it carefully. > - Bl

wa·ki·con·za *or* **wakicunza** *or* **wakiconze** \wa-ḱi-coŋ-za\ *n* : a leader or a sort of magistrate in a traveling group of Indians, one who determines or decides; in earlier days older men used to go in formation ahead of the others < *Na wicahcala top ~ wicabluha na ob wati kin hena tehan nipi kta* And I had as leaders four older men, and those with whom I lived would live a long time. > — *va* wa·we·conza : to purpose, determine for one, to resolve to do to or for one — **wakiconze** *n* : a delegate - D.225, 262

wa·ki·co·ya \wá-ḱi-co-ya\ *adv* : slightly, just a little < ~ *wanblakelo* I saw just a little. ~ *wao* I wounded it slightly. > — **wakicoya·kel** \wá-ḱi-co-ya-ḱel\ *adv* : well done, well finished < ~ *kagelo* He made it well done. > - Bl

wa·ki·cu·wa *or* **wakicuwaya** \wa-ḱi-cu-wa\ *v* [fr *kicuwa* to pursue, follow up] : to follow up < ~ *yahi hwo?* Did you come following up on it, *i.e.* come for lease *etc.* and money? > - BT

wa·ki·c'un·pi \wa-ḱi-c'uŋ-pi\ *n* : common property, what is taken and used by all; a gift or alms perhaps - Bl

wa·ki·gla·ka \wa-ḱi-gla-ka\ *n* : dressed skin, leather such as is used to make and mend moccasins

wa·ki·gle \wa-ḱi-gle\ *n* : a store, stores, what one has laid up, supplies, inventory

wa·ki·glu·hta·ta \wa-ḱi-glu-ȟta-ṫa\ *v* : to sacrifice one's own

wa·ki·gna \wá-ki-gna\ *n* : newborn animals < *Wana wetu ca ~ ota ktelo* There will be many newborn animals when it is now springtime. > - Bl

wa·ki·gnag \wa-ḱi-gnag\ *v contrac of* wakignaka : to store up < ~ *wahi* I came for supplies. >

wa·ki·gna·ka \wa-ḱi-gna-ka\ *v* wa·we·gnaka [fr *kignaka* to lay up for one, to adjourn] : to store away one's own — **wakignaka·pi** *n* : laid up things, as money *etc.*

wa·ki·go \wa-ḱi-ġo\ *v poss* wa·wa·kigo [fr *wago* to mark or gash] : to cut or carve one's own; to engrave

wa·ki·hi·ye·ce \wa-ḱi-hi-ye-ce\ *n perhaps* [fr *kihiya* raise or train *e.g.* children] : one who raises up children < *Wakihiyecelah* He is considered an educator of children, as is said of a man who brought up many children. > - Bl

wa·ki·hon \wa-ḱi-hoŋ\ *v poss* wa·wa·kihon [fr *wahon, i.e. wahun* to cut, slash, gash] : to cut or gash one's own — **wakihon·hon** *or* **wakihunhun** *v red* wa·wa·kihonhon : to make slight cuts or indentations in the surface of anything one's own < *Itazipa ikan kin ~* He cut nicks in his own bowstring. > - Cf wahunhun D.111

wa·ki·hta·ni \wá-ki-ȟta-ni\ *v* [fr *wahtani* to transgress, sin] : to sin against - *See* awahtani

wa·ki·h'an·ke \wa-ḱi-ȟ'aŋ-ke\ *n perhaps* : a hair stylist perhaps, one who does all sorts of hair work - Bc

wa·ki·ja·ni·gni·cašni \wa-ḱi-ja-ni-gni-ca-šni\ *v* : to be elusive, unable to be grasped — *n* : greediness, as is said when one wants to have everything - Cf kijanicašni Bl LHB

wa·ki·kcan·pta \wa-ḱi-kcaŋ-pṫa\ *va* wa·we·kcanpta : to comfort, console — *adj* : compassionate — **wakikcanpte** *n* : a comforter — **Wakikcanpte** *np* : the Holy Spirit

wa·ki·ksa \wa-ḱi-ksa\ *v poss* wa·wa·kiksa *or* wa·we·ksa [fr *waksa* to cut off] : to cut off one's own with a knife or saw — **wakiksa·ksa** *v red* : to cut off one's own frequently

wa·ki·ksa·pa \wa-ḱi-ksa-pa\ *v* : to consult, be wise < *Wicaša wan tawicu kici tawacin kin otkons wakiksapelo* The man along with his wife consult equally their mind in matters of concern, as is said when a couple is of one mind. > - Bl

wa·ki·ksu·ya \wa-ḱi-ksu-ya\ *v* [fr *kiksuya* to remember] **1** : to remember or recall **2** : to hold communion with or receive communications from supernatural beings **3** : to call to remembrance a dead friend **4** : to see and be afraid of signs of enemies — **wakiksuya·pi** *n* remembering the past, having dreams and visions

[1]**wa·ki·kšu** \wa-ḱi-kšu\ *v* wa·wa·kikšu [fr *wakšú* to do or make beadwork] : to do beadwork ornaments — **wakikšu·kšu** *v red* : to hang many ornaments on one's own as children do - Bl

[2]**wa·ki·kšu** \wá-ki-kšu\ *v* [fr *wákšu* to pile on, load] : to pile or load on for one - *See* wákšu KE

wa·ki·kton·ja \wá-ki-ḱtoŋ-ja\ *v* wá·we·ktonja [fr *akiktonja* to forget] : to forget, not remember

wa·kil \wá-ḱil\ *v contrac of* wakita : to look, watch

< *Tanyan ~ ble c'on išta gmus makilowahce lo* I who had gone to watch, with eyes shut, sang my very self a song. *Wankatakiya ~ ši* He told him to look up above. > - BT B.H.13.10

wa·ki·la \wa-ǩí-la\ *v* wa·wa·kila [fr *kila* to ask of one] : to ask or beg of one - Pb.36 B.H.120.11

wa·ki·lki·tan \wa-ǩí-lǩi-ṫaŋ\ *v red* wa·wa·kilkitan [fr *wakitan* to insist, persist] : to do things wrong and defend them anyhow — **wakilkitan·yan** *adv red* : obstinately, perseveringly

wa·ki·na·šle·ca \wa-kí-na-šle-ca\ *v* : to split with the foot < *Héhlokeca tanka ~ wakicepa* A fat animal splits its long hollow horns, as is said of fat buffalo. > - Bl WHL

wa·ki·ni·ca \wá-ǩi-ni-ca\ *v* wá·wa·kinica wá·ci·kinica [fr *akinica* to dispute over a matter] : to dispute, argue < *Wacikinil wahiyelo* I came to argue with you. > - Note: this example and the one under *wakinil* — **wakinica·pi** *n* : a disputation, contest - Bl B.H.285.13

wa·ki·ni·han \wa-ǩí-ni-haŋ\ *v* 1st *pers singl of* kiníhan : I respect one

wa·ki·nil \wá-ǩi-nil\ *v contrac of* wákinica : to argue < *~ waun* I was arguing. *~ wahiyelo* I came to dispute with you. >

wa·ki·ni·ya \wa-ǩí-ni-ya\ *vn* wa·wa·kiniya : to be sensitive, touchy, to get out of humor

wa·kin'in \wa-ǩíŋ-iŋ\ *v* wa·wa·kin'in [fr *kin'in* to throw at, assail] : to throw at, to stone — 1st *pers singl of* kin'in : I threw at him

wa·kin·ya \wa-ǩíŋ-ya\ *v contrac* wakin·wa·ya [fr *wakan ia* to speak a subtlety, an enigma] : to say something that comes true, to foretell - Note: *He ~ ške* They say he foretold it. But in Santee Dakota: *He waayata ške* They say he predicted it.

wa·kin·yan \wa-ǩíŋ-yaŋ\ *n* [fr *kinyan* to fly] : thunder, the cause and source of thunder and lightning, once supposed by the Dakotas to be a great bird. Philosophy: one of the 16 *wakan* mystery beings *Wakantanka* Great Mystery that are associated with the west and which is never a carrier of our prayers, but rather is defied by them. Hence the *wakan* being is usually counter-posed to *Inyan* Rock as *Wi* Sun is to *Han* Night. Thus the winged *Wakantanka* < *Na ecel lila ~ agli* And as it really is thunder comes back. *~ namah'on* Thunder hears me, which was formerly used for an oath. It was once believed that whoever would say this and lie anyhow was sure to die or be killed by lightning. Similarly *Maka namah'on* Earth hears me, was used. > — *v* : to fly, as does a bird

~ ha n the sharp-shinned hawk. *Cetan iyececa* It is like a hawk

~ hotón n the thunder, *lit* the thunder uttered its voice

~ hoton s'e adv : with a thunder-like noise, thunderingly < *Can kin ~ hoton s'e yunkahe* The tree was lying down with thundering. > - WJR.152.6 MG

wa·kin·yan·la pa·hli·hu \wa-ǩíŋ-yaŋ pa-ȟli-hu\ *n* : water plantain, alisma plantago-aquatica - Bl #298

wa·kin·yan o·na·yan·pi \wa-ǩíŋ-yaŋ o-nà-yaŋ-pi\ *n* : a prairie fire started by lightning

wa·kin·yan·pi \wa-ǩíŋ-yaŋ-pi\ *n* [fr kinyan to fly] : birds, those that fly - R Bl

wa·kin·yan·pi \wa-ǩíŋ-yaŋ-pi\ *n* [fr *wakinya* to foretell] : the coming true of something foretold by a medicine man - BD

wa·kin·yan ton·wan·pi \wa-ǩíŋ-yaŋ ṫoŋ-wàŋ-pi\ *n* : sheet lighning, summer lightning, hence heat lightning; *lit* the thunderbird's look — **wakinyan tonwanpi** \wa-ǩíŋ-yaŋ ṫòŋ-waŋ-pi\ *n* : an X-ray machine, electric lights, *i.e.* an electrical apparatus where sparks are seen — **wakinyan tonwanpi peti-jajan** \wa-ǩíŋ-yaŋ ṫòŋ-waŋ-pi ṗe-tí-ja-jaŋ\ *n* : a flash-light

wa·kin·ye·la \wa-ǩíŋ-ye-la\ *n* : the mourning dove - Note: its song is: M ..., m ... , and when early in the morning she goes to sounding this dolefull wail, children say: < *Hínyankaga hoton welo* The owl is hooting, *i.e.* there is a ghost there. *~ s'e hupteptecela kaca* He is like the mourning dove built stockily and having short legs, as is said of a person having a heavy body but short legs. *~ s'e cantku kin nisko nankin na* You are so large in the chest, like that of a mourning dove, *i.e.* in having a broad chest. > - Bl

[1]**wa·ki·pa** \wa-ǩí-ṗa\ *n* : misfortune, ill-fortune, adversity, bad luck — *v* : to allow envy, jealousy - KE WHL

[2]**wa·ki·pa** \wá-ǩi-ṗa\ *v* [fr *akípa* to occur, befall] : to befall, happen to one, to have an accident - B.H.35.1, 58.5

wa·ki·pa·jin \wa-ǩí-pa-jiŋ\ *v* wa·wa·kipajin wa·un·ki-pajin·pi [fr *kipajin* oppose, resist] : to oppose — *v 1 pers singl of* kipajin : I resisted it

wa·ki·pa·pi \wá-ǩi-ṗa-pi\ *n* : an accident, casualty — **wakipa·ya** \wá-ǩi-ṗa-ya\ *va* : to cause one to have bad luck - B.H.106.4

wa·ki·pi \wa-ǩí-ṗi\ *n* : robbery, a spoiling

wa·ki·pi·ka \wa-ǩí-ṗi-ǩa\ *adj* : roomy, as anything that can contain much - Bl

wa·ki·pša·pša \wa-ǩí-pša-pša\ *adv* : close together, thick - R Bl

wa·ki·pta \wa-ǩí-pṫa\ *v poss* wa·wa·kipta [fr *wapta* to cut off or trim] : to pare, cut off or trim one's own

wa·ki·pu·ski·ca \wa-ǩí-ṗu-sǩica\ *v* wa·wa·kipuskica : to clap together and make fit or adhere by shaving — **wakipuskil** *v contrac* : to make join together < *~ iyeya* to make join suddenly together >

wa·kis \wa-ǩís\ *v contrac of* wakiza : to cause a squeaking sound with knife or saw < *~ iyeya* suddenly to make squeak >

wa·ki·scu *or* **wakisca** \wa-kí-scu\ *v* wa·we·scu [fr *scu* to make one's self important] : to exhibit one's self by laying claim < *He miye wawescu* This will be mine, *i.e.* let me shoot this bird. > - *Syn* GLONICA Bl KE

wa·ki·ski·za \wa·ǩí-sǩi-za\ *v red of* wakiza : to make a continuous squeaking noise

wa·ki·sku \wa-ǩí-sǩu\ *v poss* wa·wa·kisku [fr *wasku* to peel, pare] : to pare one's own *e.g.* an apple or potato — **wakisku·sku** *v poss of* waskusku : to slice off one's own < *Wawapasnon k'on waweskusku ktelo* I shall slice up what I had roasted. > - Bl

wa·ki·sle·ca \wa-ǩí-sle-ca\ *v poss* wa·wa·kisleca [fr *wasleca* to saw, slit, rip, split] : to split or rip *e.g.* a board or stick with a knife or saw — **wakisle·sleca** *v red* : to saw many

wa·ki·ški·ta \wa-ǩí-ški-ṫa\ *v poss* wa·wá·kiškita [fr *waškita* to notch] : to cut across on one's own, to gash

wa·ki·šla \wa-ǩí-šla\ *v* wa·wa·kišla [fr *wašla* to shave or scrape off] : to cut off and make bare, as in cutting one's own grass, with a knife — **wakišla·šla** *v red* : to

---

\a\ father \e\ they \i\ machine \o\ smoke \u\ lunar \an, aŋ\ blanc Fr. \in, iŋ\ ink \on, oŋ, un, uŋ\ soon, confier Fr. \c\ chair \ġ\ machen Ger. \j\ fusion \clusters: bl, gn, kp, hšl, etc...\ b[e]lo ... said with a slight vowel
See more in the Introduction, Guide to Pronunciation

shave or cut off bare

wa·ki·špa \wa-k̇í-šṗa\ *v poss* wa·wa·kišpa [fr *wašpa* to scalp, cut off a piece] : to cut off a piece from one's own — **wakišpa·špa** *v red* : to keep cutting off pieces from one's own

wa·ki·špu \wa-k̇í-šṗu\ *v poss* wa·wa·kišpu [fr *wašpu* to cut into pieces] : to cut up one's own in pieces, as potatoes for planting — **wakišpu·špu** *v red* : to be cutting up in pieces one's own

wa·ki·š'ag \wa-k̇í-š'ag\ *adj contrac of* wakiš'aka : capable of endurance — **wakiš'a·gya** *va* wakiš'a·gwa·ya : to make endure

wa·ki·š'a·ka \wa-k̇í-š'a-ka\ *adj* wa·ma·kiš'aka wa·ni·ci·š'aka : capable of endurance, strong to endure hardship or suffering, not easily exhausted or overcome, indefatigable — **wakiš'ake** *n* : strength

wa·ki·ta \wá-k̇i-ta\ *v* wá·wa·kita wá·un·kita·pi [fr *akita* to seek, look for] : to look out for, to watch - Note: the word *akita* seems not to be used < *Ipá k'el akanl iyotaka yo: hecon na tanyan ~ yo* Sit down on the ridge at the high end; do that and watch well. > - Pb.47

wa·ki·tan \wa-k̇í-ṫaŋ\ *v* wa·wa·kitan [fr *kitan* to insist] : to insist upon, to persist in doing — *v 1st pers singl of* kitan : I insist upon it — **wakitan·ka** \wa-k̇í-ṫaŋ-k̇a\ *n* : one who insists upon

wa·ki·ton·ton·ka \wa-k̇í-toŋ-toŋ-k̇a\ *vn* wa·wa·kitontonka : to be frugal, economical < *Le hokšila wakitontonke lo* This boy is frugal. > *Syn* WAGLUHAHAKA — *n* : one who is frugal *etc.*, who saves everything, tries to save and have things

wa·ki·un·yan \wa-k̇í-uŋ-yaŋ\ *v* wa·wa·kiunyan wa·ci·unya wa·ni·ciunya waic'iunyan wa·wa·kiun·mni kte : to sacrifice or make an offering to one, to sacrifice one's own < *Wakantanka cekiyapi na wakiunyanpi* They pray to God and offer sacrifice to Him. > - Cf waunyan B. Pb.12, 43

wa·ki·ya \wá-k̇i-ya\ *v* wá·wa·kiya : to talk about, discuss; to try *e.g.* a case in court — **wakiya·pi** *n* : a trial — **wakiya·tipi** \wá-k̇i-ya-ṫi-pi\ *n* : a courthouse, a council house

wa·ki·ya·zan \wa-k̇í-ya-zaŋ\ *v poss* wa·ma·kiyazan wa·ni·ciyazan [fr *wayazan* to feel unwell] : to become sick for one, as one's child

wa·ki·ye·la *or* **wakinyela** \wa-k̇í-ye-la\ *n* : the mourning dove

wa·ki·ye wi·ca·ša \wá-k̇i-ye wi-cà-ša\ *n* : a lawyer

wa·ki·yu·še \wa-k̇í-yu-še\ *v* wa·wa·kiyuše [fr *kiyuše* to act out of hate toward one] : to oppose, to hate

wa·ki·yu·ška \wa-k̇í-yu-šk̇a\ *v* wa·wa·kiyuška *or* wa·wa·ki·blu·ška [fr *kiyuška* to loose, release] : to loosen, release — *1st pers singl* : I set it loose

wa·ki·yu·šna \wa-k̇í-yu-šna\ *va* wa·wa·kiyušna **1** : to drop for one, as for a dog **2** : to sacrifice to, offer to in sacrifice - R

wa·ki·yu·wa·ni·ce \wak̇í-yu-wa-ni-ce\ *adj* : deprived of property < *Wakiyuwanicelah* He is much more deprived of things, as is said perhaps of one who had nothing yet received much from others. > — *v* : to squander one's holdings - Bl KE

wa·ki·yu·za \wa-k̇í-yu-za\ *v* wa·wa·kiyuza [fr *kiyuza* to hold to one] : to gesture holding to or towards one, to hold up the pipe towards heaven *etc.* as is done before smoking

wa·ki·za \wa-k̇í-za\ *va* wa·wa·kiza [fr *kíza* to creak or grate] : to make a scraping, squeaking noise with a knife or saw

wa·ko \wa-k̇ó\ *n* : a horse with its tail cut short - *Syn* WAÚNJINCA Bl

wa·ko·gla \wa-k̇ó-gla\ *n* : a gully, gulch, a ravine made by water

wa·ko·ki·pa \wa-k̇ó-k̇i-ṗa\ *v* wako·wa·kipa [fr *kokipa* to fear] : to be afraid, fearful — **wakokipe·kicaga** \wa-k̇ó-k̇i-ṗe-k̇i-ca-ġa\ *v* wakokipe·we·caga : to make afraid, frighten into a measure — **wakokipe·wicakicah wawicaki** \wa-k̇ó-k̇i-ṗe-wi-ca-k̇i-ca-ȟ wa-wì-ca-k̇i\ *n* : a robber, a hold-up man - B.H.128.4, 174.2, 223.3, 282.7

wa·ko·ki·pe·ya \wa-k̇ó-k̇i-ṗe-ya\ *adv* : timidly - B.H. 209.4

wa·kon \wa-k̇óŋ\ *v* [fr *kon covet*] : to desire — *v 1st pers singl of* kon : I desire it — **wakon·la** *v* : to covet

wa·kon·ni·yan \wa-k̇óŋ-ni-yaŋ\ *v* wakonni·wa·ya : to have done much, performed much - Bl

wa·kon·ni·ye·ya \wa-k̇oŋ-ni-ye-ya\ *v* : to destroy everything - Bl

wa·kon s'e \wa-k̇óŋ s'e\ *adv* : forging the future beforehand, by plan; like a dream < *Wakonpi s'e nankapi* You are planning ahead, *i.e.* are in good spirits. > - BT KE

wa·kon·ta \wa-k̇oŋ-ṫa\ *va* wa·wa·konta [fr *konta* to wear away, weaken] : to dig out with a knife, to hollow or groove; to wear out a rope or strap *etc.* partly with a knife, *i.e.* making it weaker — **wakon·tkonta** \wa-k̇óŋ-tkoŋ-ṫa\ *v red* wa·wa·kontkonta : to make in grooves or ridges

wa·kon·za \wa-k̇óŋ-za\ *v* wa·wa·konza [fr *konza* to pretend] : to influence, determine, decree — *v 1st pers singl of* konza : I influenced him — **wakonze** *n* : an influence

wa·ko·ya·gki·ca·ton \wa-k̇ó-ya-gki-ca-toŋ\ *v* : to clothe — **wakoyagya** *v* wakoya·gwa·ya : to put on, clothe, to cause to put on - B.H.194.6

wa·ko·ya·ka \wa-k̇ó-ya-k̇a\ *v* wako·bla·ka wako·un·ya·ka·pi [fr *koyaka* put on, wear] : to put on clothes — **wakoya·keca** \wa-k̇ó-ya-k̇e-ca\ *n* wako·ma·yakeca : one who puts on clothes, one who dresses up

wa·kpa \wa-k̇ṗá\ *n* : a river, a stream of water — *va* wa·wa·kpa : to cut off, cut from, to cut out or cut into — **wakpa·la** *n* : a creek, a small stream

wa·kpa·mni \wa-k̇ṗa-mni\ *v* wa·wa·kpamni *or 1st pers singl of* kpamni [fr *kpamni* distribute one's own] : to distribute, serve out one's own < *Na hehanl yul wicaši. Canke oyate kin wakpamnipi na cantewašteya wotapi* And then he told them to eat. And so it was served out to the people and they ate with joy. > — **wakpamni·pi** *n* : a distribution

wa·kpan \wa-k̇ṗáŋ\ *va* wa·wa·kpan [fr *kpan* fine] : to cut up fine with a knife *e.g.* tobacco — **wakpan·kpan** *v red* : to shred

Wa·kpa Ši·ce \Wa-k̇ṗá Šì-ce\ *np* : the city Pierre in South Dakota, so-named from the Bad River, a western tributary to the Missouri there

wa·kpa·tan·ka \wa-k̇pá-ṫaŋ-k̇a\ *n* [fr *kpatan* to conserve] : one who is economical

wa·kpi \wa-k̇ṗí\ *va* wa·wa·kpi : to cut open *e.g.* a nut with a knife, to crack with a knife

wa·kpi·ca·gla \wa-k̇ṗi-ca-gla\ *adv* : by the side of a stream

wakpi·kpi \wa-k̇ṗí-kpi\ *v red of* wakpi : to be cracking open *e.g.* a nut

wa·kpo·gna \wa-k̇ṗó-gna\ *adv* : on the stream

wa·kpo·pta \wa-k̇ṗó-pta\ *adv* : across the stream

wa·kpu·kpa \wa-k̇ṗú-k̇ṗa\ *n* : dust, motes, particles of dust — **wakpukpe·ca** \wa-k̇ṗú-k̇ṗe-ca\ *n* : dust or anything scattered about

wa·ksa \wa-ksá\ *va* wa·wa·ksa [fr *ksa* separated] : to separate anything by cutting crosswise, to cut off *e.g.* a stick with a knife or saw — **waksa·ksa** *v red* wa·wa·ksaksa : to cut off in several places, cut in pieces with a knife or saw < *Na wanna talo k'on he hanke ~ . Wansak ~* He had cut part of the fresh meat in several pieces. He cut arrow shafts to size. > – D.40

wa·kši *or* **wakši·ca** \wa-kší\ *n abbrev of* wakšica : a dish, plate, bowl, or pan < ~ *egle, yujaja, tanka* to set dishes, to wash dishes, a large dish >
~ *blaská* a plate
~ *ógnake* a cupboard
~ *opíye* a cupboard – B.H.207.10

wa·kši·ja \wa-kší-ja\ *va* wa·wa·kšija [fr *kšija* doubled up] : to shut up *e.g.* a knife blade when in the act of cutting

wa·kši·o·pi·ye \wa-kší-o-ṗi-ye\ *n* : a cupboard – R Bl

wa·kši·sko·kpa \wa-kší-sko-kṗa\ *n* : soup plates, saucers

wa·kšiš \wa-kšíš\ *va contrac of* wakšija : to shut up *e.g.* a knife < ~ *iyeya* suddenly to make fold up >

wa·kši·ta·pe·la \wa-kší-ṫa-ṗe-la\ *n* : a flat plate

wa·kši·ya·ta·bla \wa-kší-ya-ta-bla\ *n* : a plate

[1]**wa·kšu** \wá-kšu\ *v* wá·wa·kšu [fr *akšu* to load on] : to pile, load, or lay on – Bl

[2]**wa·kšu** \wa-kšú\ *v* wa·wa·kšu : to make beadwork, do beading — **wakšu·pi** *n* : beadwork

wa·kta \wa-kṫá\ *v absol* wa·wa·kta : to look out for, watch for, to be on one's guard < *Zuya itancan kin lila waktapi* The war chiefs are very much on their guard. *Waktašnihca hanl ite kin cahli onapobyapi ške* They say when one does not watch out for his face then gunpowder explodes. > — *n* : a mark, a sign

wa·kta·kel \wa-kṫá-k̇el\ *adv* : on the look out for, guardedly, expecting it – D.12

wa·ktan \wa-kṫáŋ\ *va* wa·wa·ktan [fr *ktan* crooked, curved] : to make crooked by shaving — **waktan·ktan** *v red* : to shave crooked

wa·kta·ya \wa-kṫá-ya\ *va* wakta·wa·ya wakta·un·yan·pi — *adv* : on one's guard, warily, prudently — **waktaya·kel** \wa-kṫá-ya-k̇el\ *adv* : on the lookout < ~ *waun* I am on the lookout. > – Bl

wa·kte \wa-kṫé\ *v* wa·wa·kte [fr *kte* to kill] : to kill, to have killed or scalped, to triumph < ~ *hi* to come in triumph, ~ *agli* They come home in triumph, ~ *gli* to arrive back in triumph, ~ *gla* to be on the way home in triumph, ~ *ku* to come back in triumph, ~ *ki* to arrive at one's own home in triumph, *etc. Wakte agli ca ite sabkiyapelo* When they arrived home in triumph their faces were disfigured. > — *v* 1st *pers singl of* kte : I killed it – D.9 B.H.88.16

wa·kte·a·gli \wa-kṫé-a-gli\ *v* 3rd*pers pl* : They returned having killed enemies – Bl

wa·kte·ka \wa-kṫé-ka\ *n* : one who kills much

wa·kto·glag \wa-kṫó-glag\ *v poss contrac of* waktoglaka : to recount one's own exploits — **waktogla·gkiya** \wa-kṫo-gla-gk̇i-ya\ *va* waktogla·gwa·kiya : to cause to tell how many scalps one has taken

wa·kto·gla·ka \wa-kṫó-gla-k̇a\ *v poss* wakto·wa·glaka [fr *wakte* to kill + *oglaka* to tell of] : to tell over one's own war-like exploits, to tell how many scalps one has helped to take

wa·kto·ki·ci·ya·ka \wa-kṫó-k̇i-ci-ya-k̇a\ *v* wakto·we·ci·yaka [fr *wakte* to kill + *okiciyaka* to tell for another] : to tell, recount to one the war-like deeds of another for him

wa·kto·ki·ya·ka \wa-kṫó-k̇i-ci-ya-k̇a\ *v* wakto·wa·kiyaka [fr *wakto* to kill + *okiyaka* to tell to one] : to tell one of war-like exploits

wa·kto·ya·ka \wa-kṫó-ya-k̇a\ *v* wakto·bla·ka [fr *wakte* to kill + *oyaka* to tell about] : to tell what one has done in killing enemies

wa·ktu·ki·ye \wa-kṫú-k̇i-ye\ *v* [fr *wakte* to kill + *ukiya* to come] : to come in triumph — *n* : a triumph celebration < *Yunkan ~ el oyate kin David tawicoh'an kin nah'onpi* And then at the triumph celebration the people heard of David's deeds. > – B.H.88.1

wa·ku·ni *or* **wakonniyan** \wa-k̇ú-ni\ *v* : to have done much < *Maka ohinniyan lila ~ yelo* The earth always accomplishes very many things. > – MS.659

wa·kun·za \wa-k̇úŋ-za\ *v* – *See* wakonza

wa·ku·te \wa-k̇ú-ṫe\ *v absol* wa·wa·kute [fr *kute* shoot something] : to shoot, to be shooting < *Miye štunka wawakute kte. ~ onspekiya* I who am green should shoot. He taught him to shoot. > — *va* 1st *pers singl of* kuté : I shot it — **wakute·pi** *n* : a shooting – D.71

wa·ku·wa \wa-k̇ú-wa\ *v* wa·wa·kuwa [fr *kúwa* to chase] : to hunt, hunt *esp* for furs < *Na wanna ~ na lila cepa wan o keya* And now he stated that he hunted and shot a really a fat one. > — *v* 1st *pers singl of* kúwa : I hunted — *n* : a manager – P

wa·ku·wa·pi \wa-k̇ú-wa-pi\ *n* : hunting *e.g.* furs

wa·k'a \wa-k'á\ *v* wa·wa·k'a [fr *k'a* to dig] : to dig — *v* 1st *pers singl of* k'a : I dug it

wa·k'e·ga \wa-k'é-ġa\ *v* **a** : to butcher < *Kohan ~ yo* Hurry up to butcher. > **b** : to choke, strangle – Bl

wa·k'e·sya \wa-k'é-sya\ *part* : cutting off < ~ *aya* He began to strip off clean *e.g.* meat from bones. ~ *abla* I started to strip clean (the bones). >

wa·k'e·za \wa-k'é-za\ *v* wa·wa·k'eza [fr *k'eza* trodden down] : to smooth over by shaving – Cf yuk'eza

wa·k'in \wa-k'íŋ\ *v* wa·wa·k'in [fr *k'in* to bear a load] : to pack, carry on one's back — *v* 1st *pers singl of* k'in : I packed a load — *n* : a pack, a burden, luggage, baggage < *Yunkan ~ k'on ena pahpa ekignaka na akanl iyotaka. ~ yuha yankapi* And then he had taken down and put away a pack and sat on it. They sat holding luggage. > — **wak'in·kiya** \wa-k'íŋ-k̇i-ya\ *va* : to cause to pack or carry, *i.e.* on the back, as on a horse — **wa·k'in·k'inla s'e** *or* **wak'ink'inlas'e** *n* : something like a pack, *i.e.* a square or cube — **wak'in·pi** *n* : a burden, a pack – B.H.298.4 D.251

wa·k'u \wa-k'ú\ *v* wa·wa·k'u [fr *k'u* to give] : to give < *Wakantanka wawicak'u kin he mazaska on opetonpica kecanni* You thought that he was able to purchase with money what God gave them. > –B.H.287.6

wal \wal\ *n contrac of* wáta : a boat

wa·la \wa-lá\ *v* wa·wa·la [fr *la* to ask or beg] : to ask or beg < *wakíla* to ask or beg of one > — **wala·kel** \wa-lá-kel\ *adv* : begging < ~ *yankahe* He was sitting begging> – B.H.98.14, 236.2

wa·la·ko·ta·šni \wa-lá-ko-ṫa-šni\ *adj* wala·ma·kotašni : not caring, having no regard for one's own people, as Indians for Indians < *ite ~* a disagreeable face, *i.e.* in *ref* to an angry face > – *See* olákolwicaye šni

wa·la·la \wa-lá-la\ *v red of* walá : to ask, beg — **wala-**

\a\ father \e\ they \i\ machine \o\ smoke \u\ lunar \an, aŋ\ blanc Fr. \in, iŋ\ ink \on, oŋ, un, uŋ\ soon, confier Fr. \c\ chair \ġ\ machen Ger. \j\ fusion \clusters: bl, gn, kp, hšl, etc...\ b^{e}lo ... said with a slight vowel
See more in the Introduction, Guide to Pronunciation

laka *n* wa·ma·lalaka : a beggar
wa·lce·te \wa-lcé-ṫe\ *n* : the keel or bottom of a boat
wa·le·ga \wa-lé-ġa\ *n* : the bladder — **walega miniyaye** *n* : a water jug - Bl
wa·le·han *or* **walehanl** \wa-lé-haŋ\ *adv* : by this time - B.H.37.9
wa·le·han·tu \wa-lé-haŋ-ṫu\ *adv* : at this time < *Wanyang omani po; ~ ca šunkawakan hunkešni oh'ankopelo.* See them travel; it is at this time (the spring) sickly horses are fast. > - Bl
wa·le·le·pa \wa-lé-le-ṗa\ *v red of* walepa : to cut rounded notches *e.g.* on a feather - *Syn* WAŠKIŠKITA Bl
wa·lhe·ktab \wa-lhé-kṫab\ *adv contrac of* walhektapa : at the stern
wa·lhe·kta·pa \wa-lhé-kṫa-ṗa\ *n* : the stern of a boat — **walhektapa·tanhan** *n* : the stern of a boat — *adv* : at the stern
wa·li·ta \wa-lí-ṫa\ *adj* wa·ma·lita : brave — **walitagya** \wa-lí-ṫa-gya\ *adv* : bravely < ~ *kipajin* to resist bravely > — **walita·ke** *adj* wa·ma·litake : brave, active and courageous < *Walitakelo* He is involved and brave. > — **walita·ya** *adv* : actively, bravely together with others < ~ *škan* He gets around and involved. > - *Syn* WAŠ'AGYA Note: this is a word said to be Sissiton - Bl
wa·lo·gna·ka *or* **waloh'egnaka** \wa-ló-gna-ka\ *n* : a bag, a cow bladder fromerly used like a paper bag - Bl
wa·lo·lo·bya \wa-lō'-lo-bya\ *va* walolo·bwa·ya : to boil until tender, or to over-boil and thereby turn things into mush or meat, beans *etc.* - D.54
wa·lo·lo·pe·la \wa-lō'-lo-ṗe-la\ *n* : slush, half-molten snow
wa·lo·o·gna \wa-ló-o-gna\ *n* : a bag to keep dried meat
wa·lo·pe·la \wa-lō'-ṗe-la\ *n* : over-boiled and mushlike meat, beans, *etc.* - Cf walolopela
wa·lo·te·te·ke \wa-ló-ṫe-ṫe-ke\ *n* wa·ma·loteteke [fr *loté* the throat] : one who is hungry often, is fond of food < *Inahni unglapi k'un ~* We who were hurrying home are people fond of food. *Wamaloteteke caš slolyaye c'un* It is you who have known that I have indeed been always hungry. > - Note: *caš* is ca *emph* D.12
wa·lo·wan \wá-lo-waŋ\ *v absol* : to be sung, to be music sung or played — **walowan·pi** *n* : the *hunkalowanpi*, a rite by which we establish a relationship on earth which is a reflection of that real relationship which always exists between man and God, *Wakantanka.* It is sometimes said it is one of the seven Dakota religious rites. - Bl BD BR.101
wa·lpa \wa-lpá\ *n* : the bow of a boat
wa·lsin·te \wa-lsíŋ-ṫe\ *n* : a steering oar, the helm, the rudder of a boat — **walsinte yuhomni** \wa-lsíŋ-ṫe yuhò-mni\ *v* : to pilot or steer a boat of any kind — *n* : a helmsman
wa·ltu·cu·hu \wa-ltú-cu-hu\ *n* : the ribs of a boat
wa·lu·lya \wa-lú-lya\ *v* walu·lwa·ya [fr *lulya* to paint red] : to dye red or scarlet — **walulye** *n* : a dyer of scarlet
wa·lu·pi šni \wa-lú-ṗi šni\ *n* : that which is intact, still whole, where nothing has been cut off as yet, as fresh ham *etc.* < ~ *wanji ikikcu wo* Take back a whole one. > - *Syn* YULUPI ŠNI Bl
wal'i·ca·ške \wal'í-ca-ške\ *n* : an anchor < ~ *ehpeya* to cast anchor >
wal'i·ca·špe \wal'í-ca-špe\ *n* : a form of adze used for hollowing out a canoe
wal'i·to·pe \wal'í-ṫo-ṗe\ *n* : an oar, paddle
wal'i·ya·cin \wal'í-ya-ciŋ\ *va* wal'í·bla·cin : to adopt a child in place of one that died, because it has the same looks and features - Note: this was an old custom among Indian peoples where such children received goods but not real estate. D.269
wal'i·yo·pe·ya \wal'í-yo-ṗe-ya\ *va* wal'iyope·wa·ya : to accuse one of doing what another has done
wal'i·yo·wa·lya \wal'í-yo-wa-lya\ *v* wal'iyowa·lwa·ya : to excuse one's self, *i.e.* let someone else do what one was supposed to do
wal'o·i·huni *or* **wal'óinajin** \wal'ó-i-huni\ *n* : a boat landing
wa·ma el i \wa-má el i\ *express* : There it goes, *i.e.* making their presence seen and heard < *Wama el ipi s'e* It was as though all creation went to it, *i.e.* sounding off, as is said of a flock of birds in confusion and making a great noise. > - Bl
wa·ma·he·tu·ya·kel \wa-má-he-ṫu-ya-ḳel\ *adv* : by one's self < ~ *econ, oyaka* to do or say something on one's own, *i.e.* something great without advice from anyone >
wa·ma·ka ma·ni šni \wa-ṁá-ka mà-ni šni\ *adv* : suddenly and without being noticed, not having one's footsteps heard < ~ *hi.* ~ *tehan yahi so?* He arrived unnoticed. Did you come unnoticed for a long time? ~ *tak eya* He said something that was not expected, and hence ceases doubts. > - Bc OS
wa·ma·ka·škan \wa-má-ḳa-škaŋ\ *n* [fr *maka* earth + *škan* to move] : the animal kingdom in general, all things that move on the earth, creeping things
wa·ma·ka·škan s'e \wa-má-ḳa-škaŋ s'e\ *adv* : brutally, like wild animals
wa·ma·ka te·han·tu·la·ke s'e \wa-má-ka ṫe-hàŋ-ṫu-la-ḳe s'e\ *adv* : from afar < ~ *yahi* You came from afar. > - BS
wa·ma·ki·non \wa-má-ki-noŋ\ *v* wama·wa·kinon [fr *makinon* to steal what one has given] : to steal from one
wa·ma·ko·gna·ka \wa-má-ḳo-gna-ka\ *n* : Creation, the contents of the world, the whole of creation - R Bl
wa·ma·ni·ka \wa-má-ni-ka\ *n* : a visitor, a good visitor < *wicaša ~* a person who visits or sees people much, but not to pass the time, but for business of any kind, one who is industrious and does not loaf, ~ oyamani hwo? Did you come alone to visit? ~ *agli yelo* to arrive home from visiting > - UW Bl
wa·ma·non \wa-má-noŋ\ *v* wama·wa·non wama·uŋ·noŋ·pi [fr *manon* to steal anything] : to steal — **wamanon·pi** *n* : stealing, theft — **wamanon·s'a** *n* : a thief
wa·ma·yal \wa-má-yal\ *adv contrac of* wamayata : toward a bank *mayá* < ~ *i s'e yankapi* They were as it were going toward a bank, as is said when a meeting is full of much talking by many present at once, the *ref* is made to a bank where there come echoes. >
wa·mi·ni \wá-mi-ni\ *n* : snow water
wa·mna \wa-mná\ *va* wa·wa·mna : to rip *e.g.* a seam with a knife
wa·mna·i·c'i·la \wa-mná-i-c'i-la\ *v refl* wamna·mi·c'ila [fr *wamnala* to respect, honor one] : to be proud of one's self — **wamnaic'ila·pi** *n* : pride
wa·mna·la \wa-mná-la\ *va* : to honor, respect, fear; to consider brave or energetic; to think little of one - Bl
wa·mna·mna \wa-mná-mna\ *v red of* wamna : to rip
wa·mna·yan \wa-mná-yaŋ\ *v* wamna·wa·ya wamna·un·yan·pi [fr *mnayan* to gather, collect] : to gather, collect — *n* : a collector — **wamnayan·pi** *n* : a gathering, a collection — **wamnaye·kiya** *v* : to take up a

collection for
wa·mni \wa-mní\ *v* wa·wa·mni [fr *mni* to lay up to dry] : to dry by spreading out *e.g.* shelled corn — *v 1st pers singl of* mni : I laid it out to dry
wa·mni·a·ka·štan \wa-mní-a-ka-štaŋ\ *n* : a baptizer, one who baptizes, *e.g.* John the Baptist — *v* wamnia·wa·kaštan : to baptize - B.H.176.8
wa·mni·mni \wá-mni-mni\ *v* wá·wa·mnimni [fr *amnimni* to sprinkle on anything] : to sprinkle — *n* : one who sprinkles
wa·mni·o·mni \wa-mní-o-mni\ *n* **1** : a whirlwind, tornado, hurricane; a whirlpool **2** : a caccoon a small worm or puppa - Bl D.218
wa·mni·pi \wa-mní-pi\ *n* [fr *wamni* to spread out to dry] : fruit *etc.* spread out thinly
wa·mni·tu \wa-mní-ṫu\ *n* : a whale or hippopotamus
wa·mnu·h'a \wa-mnú-ȟ'a\ *n* : a cowry, a small shell used as an ornament on dresses < ~ *cuwignaka* a woman's cowry dress > — **wamnuh'a·la** *n dim of* wamnuh'a : the dress ornamented with very small shells, or perhaps a small dress so ornamented
wa·mun·lmun·ta \wa-múŋ-lmuŋ-ṫa\ *adj red of* wamunta : short and rounded < *Si kin* ~ Its nails are short, as is said when the nails are off a bird's foot. >
wa·mun·ta \wa-múŋ-ṫa\ *adj* : short and rounded off when it should be long, as a horse's tail < *Šunkawakan wan sinte* ~ A horse's tail is short. > — *n* : an ear of corn well filled and flat at the end - R
wa·na *or* **wanna** \wa-ná\ *adv* : now, already
wa·na·bla·ska \wa-ná-bla-ska\ *v* wana·wa·blaska [fr *nablaska* to flatten] : to flatten with the foot
wa·na·bla·ya \wa-ná-bla-ya\ *v* wana·wa·blaya [fr *nablaya* to level, smoothen] : to spread out with the feet
wa·na·bla·za \wa-ná-bla-za\ *v* [fr *nablaza* to burst by kicking it] : to burst open
wa·na·ble·ca \wa-ná-ble-ca\ *v* wana·wa·bleca [fr *nableca* break by foot] : to break in pieces with the foot
wa·na·bu \wá-na-bu\ *v* wána·wa·bu [fr *anábu* to stamp the foot] : to make a drumming noise with the foot on the ground, to drum the foot on the ground — **wánabubu** *v red* : to keep drumming the foot on the ground
wa·na·can·can \wa-ná-caŋ-caŋ\ *v* wana·wa·cancan [fr *nacancan* tremble, shiver] : to shake with the foot
wa·na·ce·kce·ka \wa-ná-ce-kce-ka\ *v* wana·wa·cekceka [fr *nacekceka* to make stagger] : to make stagger by kicking
wa·na·ce·ya \wa-ná-ce-ya\ *v* wana·wa·ceya [fr *naceya* make cry by kicking one] : to kick and make cry — **wanaceye·s'a** *n* : one who kicks and makes cry
wa·na·gi \wa-ná-ġi\ *n* [fr *nagí* a soul or spirit] : the soul when separated from the body; spirits of the departed; a shadow — **wanagi okaške** *n* : Purgatory — **wanagi ktepi** *n* : a stroke, an illness resulting in a distortion of the face to one side
Wa·na·gi Ta·can·ku \Wa-ná-ġi Ta-caŋ-ǩù\ *np* : the Milky Way, *lit* the Spirit Road
wa·na·gi·ta·ki·mi·mi·la \wa-ná-ġi-ta-ki-mi-mi-la\ *n* : a miller or moth - Bl
wa·na·gi·ta·ma·ko·ce \wa-ná-ġi-ta-ma-ǩo-ce\ *n* : the world of spirits
wa·na·gi·ta·šo·ša \wa-ná-ġi-ta-šo-ša\ *n* : heavy dew, a ghost spittle, cuckoo spittle, a kind of exudative found around some plants
wa·na·gi tin·psi·la \wa-ná-ġi tìŋ-psi-la\ *n* : the prairie larkspur, delphinium virescens, the crowfoot family - Bl #180
wa·na·gi·ti·pi \wa-ná-ġi-ti-pi\ *n* : abode of the dead, Hades, *lit* house of spirits
wa·na·gi·ya \wa-ná-ġi-ya\ *vn* : to go to the spirit land — **wanagiya·ta** \wa-ná-ġi-ya-ṫa\ *adv* : in the land of spirits < ~ *i* to go to the spirit land, an expression used in the former Ghost Dance toward the end of the nineteenth century and following the visions of Wavoka. >
wa·na·gi·ye·ya \wa-ná-ġi-ye-ya\ *v* wanagiye·wa·ya [fr *nagiyeya* to cause one trouble] : to annoy, trouble, vex
wa·na·gmun \wa-ná-gmuŋ\ *v* [fr *nagmun* to curl up] : to curl or twist
wa·na·gna \wa-ná-gna\ *v* wana·wa·gna : to kick off *e.g.* fruit from a bush
wa·na·gnan·ka *or perhaps* **wanagnunka** \wa-ná-gnaŋ-ka\ *v red* : to shake, twitch — **wanagnanke** *n* : one's possessions, what is retrieved after shaking - Cf wanagnunka - WHL
wa·na·gna·yan \wa-ná-gna-yaŋ\ *v* : to slip, slide; to deceive — **wanagnaye** *n* : a deception; a slipping
wa·na·gnun·ka \wa-ná-gnuŋ-ka\ *v* : to have something in one's possession < ~ *šni s'e tak eyé* He said something as though he were not in possession of himself, *i.e* he does not tell the truth. > - RF WHL
wa·na·go·ptan \wá-na-ġo-ptaŋ\ *v* : to listen, heed, as in listening to a sermon < *Wánagoptanpi c'on ca ka na púsyemayelo* He considered what they had been listening to and it dried me up, *i.e.* I got nothing out of it. > — **wanagoptan šica** *n* : one hard to advise, a heedless person - Bl WHL
wa·na·gu·ka \wa-ná-ġu-ka\ *v* wana·wa·guka [fr *naguka* to sprain an ankle] : to sprain
wa·na·gwa·gi·ye·ya \wa-ná-gwa-ġi-ye-ya\ *v* [fr *nagwaka* kick out the foot] : to kick away, kick out the foot, *fig* to criticize
wa·na·gwa·ka \wa-ná-gwa-ka\ *v* [fr *nagwaka* to kick] : to kick out the foot - Cf wanagwagiyeya
wa·na·hinl \wa-ná-hiŋl\ *v contrac* [fr *nahinta* scrape off by foot] : to scrape with the foot < ~ *iyeya* to scrape away with the foot > - Bl
wa·na·hin·ta \wa-ná-hiŋ-ṫa\ *v* wana·wa·hinta [fr *nahinta* scrape off by foot] : to scrape off with the foot
wa·na·ho·ho \wa-ná-ho-ho\ *v* wana·wa·hoho [fr *nahoho* to shake loose by foot] : to make loose with the foot
wa·na·ho·mni \wa-ná-ho-mni\ *v* wana·wa·homni [fr *nahomni* to turn round, to peddle] : to turn round with the foot
wa·na·ho·ton \wa-ná-ho-toŋ\ *v* wana·wa·hoton [fr *nahoton* make howl] : to cause to make a noise by kicking
wa·na·hun·hun·za \wa-ná-huŋ-huŋ-za\ *v* wana·wa·hunhunza [fr *nahunhunza* shake or rock by foot] : to shake with the foot
wa·na·ȟa·pa \wa-ná-ȟa-pa\ *v* wana·wa·ȟapa [fr *naȟapa* scare away by stomping] : to scare away by walking — *n* : one who frightens game
wa·na·hca \wa-ná-ȟca\ *n* : flowers, *esp* cultivated ones
wa·na·hca to·to *or* **canhlogan hlahla** \wa-ná-ȟca to-tò\ *n* : the sharp-leaved beard tongue - BN #157
wa·na·hci \wa-ná-ȟci\ *v* [fr *nahci* break out a piece by foot] : to beak out a piece with the foot, to break out a piece *e.g.* from a horse's hoof

---

\a\ father \e\ they \i\ machine \o\ smoke \u\ lunar \an, aŋ\ blanc Fr. \in, iŋ\ ink \on, oŋ, un, uŋ\ soon, confier Fr. \c\ chair \ġ\ machen Ger. \j\ fusion \clusters: bl, gn, kp, hšl, etc...\ b^e^lo ... said with a slight vowel
See more in the Introduction, Guide to Pronunciation

wa·na·ȟe·ya·ta \wa-ná-ȟe-ya-ṫa\ *v* [fr *naȟeyata* kick to the side] : to kick out of the way < ~ *iyeya* to give a kick to hit out of the way > - R Bl

wa·na·ȟi-ca *or* **wanaǧica** \wa-ná-ȟi-ca\ *v* wana·wa·ȟica [fr *naȟica* or *naǧica* to awaken one by foot] : to waken up with the foot

wa·na·hla \wa-ná-ȟla\ *v* wana·wa·hla [fr *nahla* to ring] : to rattle with the foot

wa·na·hla·ta \wa-ná-ȟla-ta\ *v* wana·wa·hlata [fr *nahlata* to scratch with the toes] : to scratch with the foot — *n* : one that scratches with the foot, as a cat may do

wa·na·hle·ca \wa-ná-ȟle-ca\ *v* wana·wa·hleca [fr *nahleca* to rend by foot] : to tear with the foot — *n* : one who tears open

wa·na·hlo·ka \wa-ná-ȟlo-ka\ *v* wana·wa·hloka [fr *nahloka* make a hole by foot] : to wear holes in the feet by means of something

[1]**wa·na·hma** \wa-ná-ȟma\ *v* wa·wa·nahma *or* wana·wa·hma [fr *nahma* to conceal] : to conceal, hide

[2]**wa·na·hma** \wá-na-ȟma\ *v* wa·wá·nahma *or possibly* wána·wa·hma [fr *anahma* to conceal, hide] : to conceal; to deny a charge

[1]**wa·na·hpa** \wa-ná-ȟp̣a\ *v* wana·wa·hpa [fr *nahpa* kick to make fall] : to knock or shake down, as on may do by walking on an upper floor

[2]**wa·na·hpa** \wá-na-ȟp̣a\ *v* : to kick or cast about snow with the feet, as buffalo and horses do

wa·na·hpu \wa-ná-ȟp̣u\ *v* [fr *nahpu* knock off by foot what is sticking] : to kick off pieces

wa·na·hta·gya \wa-ná-ȟta-gya\ *v* wanahta·gwa·ya [fr *nahtaka* to kick anything] : to typewrite

wa·na·hta·ka \wa-ná-ȟta-ḳa\ *v* wana·wa·htaka [fr *nahtaka* kick anything] : to be in the habit of kicking

wa·na·h'on \wa-ná-ȟ'oŋ\ *v* wana·wa·h'on [fr *nah'on* to hear] : to hear, hearken, obey - *See* anagoptan — *adj* : hearkening, obedient — **wanah'on·pi** *n* : the act of listening, hearkening — **wanah'on·šni** *vn* wana·wa·h'onpišni : to be disobedient — **wanah'onšni·yan** *adv* : heedlessly

wa·na·i·c'i·hma \wa-ná-i-c'i-ȟma\ *n* : a hypocrite, one who conceals himself

wa·na·i·ye·ya *or* **wanahaiyeya** \wa-ná-i-ye-ya\ *v* : to kick down with the foot, to kick aside

wa·na·ja·ja \wa-ná-ja-ja\ *v* [fr *najaja* to wash out by trampling] : to wash *e.g.* clothing by boiling — **wanajaja·ya** *va* wanajaja·wa·ya : to cause to wash out or come clean by boiling

wa·na·ji·ca \wa-ná-ji-ca\ *n* : a run-away, a truant - P Bl

wa·na·ji·pa \wa-ná-ji-p̣a\ *v* wana·wa·jipa [fr *najipa* to pinch, punch] : to pinch or scratch with the toes

wa·na·ju·ju \wa-ná-ju-ju\ *v* wana·wa·juju [fr *najuju* to kick to pieces] : to kick down, kick to pieces — *n* : one who kicks to pieces

wa·na·ka·ka \wa-ná-ka-ḳa\ *v* wana·wa·kaka [fr *nakaka* make rattle by foot] : to make rattle with the foot *e.g.* icicles, stiff hides *etc.* — **wanakaka·ka** \wa-ná-ka-ka-ḳa\ *v red* : to rattle with the foot

wa·na·kan·yan \wa-ná-kaŋ-yaŋ\ *v* [fr *nakan* to thresh out as corn] : to thresh *e.g.* wheat

wa·na·ka·tin \wa-ná-ḳa-ṫiŋ\ *v* wana·wa·katin [fr *nakatin* to straighten by foot] : to stretch out with the foot

wa·na·ki·hma \wá-na-ki-ȟma\ *v* wána·wa·kihma [fr *anakihma* to conceal, refuse to tell] : to conceal — **wanakihman·pi** \wá-na-ki-ȟmaŋ·pi\ *n* : hypocrites

wa·na·ki·kšin \wá-na-ki-kšiŋ\ *v* wána·we·kšin wána·mi·kšin [fr *anakikšin* to interject one's self] : to interpose and defend one by taking his place in danger

wa·na·ko·ka \wa-ná-ko-ḳa\ *v* wana·wa·koka [fr *nakoka* to bash with the foot] : to rattle with the foot

wa·na·ksa \wa-ná-ksa\ *v* wana·wa·ksa [fr *naksa* break off by foot] : to break off with the foot — **wanaksa·ksa** *v red* : to break off many things

wa·na·kse·ya \wa-ná-kse-ya\ *v* : to mow grass, to harvest grain — **wanakseye** *n* : a harvester, one who cuts grain - B.H.201.14

wa·na·kši·ja \wa-ná-kši-ja\ *v* wana·wa·kšija [fr *nakšija* to bend or double up] : to double up with the foot

wa·na·ktan \wa-ná-ḳtaŋ\ *v* wana·wa·ktan [fr *naktan* to put a bend in] : to bend with the foot

wa·na·ku·ka \wa-ná-ku-ka\ *v* wana·wa·kuka [fr *nakuka* to wear out] : to wear out with the feet

wa·na·ku·ke·ca \wa-ná-ku-ke-ca\ *n* : one who wears out moccasins badly

wa·na·mna \wa-ná-mna\ *v* wana·wa·mna [fr *namna* to rip] : to rip with the foot, as moccasins

wa·na·mna·ka \wa-ná-mna-ka\ *n* : on who rips his moccasins much

wa·na·o·hpa \wa-ná-o-ȟp̣a\ *v* wana·wa·ohpa [fr *naohpa* to sink or break into] : to break into with the feet

wa·na·o·ksa \wa-ná-o-ksa\ *v* wana·wa·oksa [fr *naoksa* to break through, as when walking on ice to kill muskrats] : to break through

wa·na·o·ktan \wa-ná-o-ḳtaŋ\ *v* wana·wa·oktan [fr *naoktan* to bend into] : to bend into with the foot

wa·na·o·t'in·za \wa-ná-o-t'iŋ-za\ *v* wana·wa·ot'inza [fr *naot'inza* press in tight by foot] : to tread in tight

wa·na·pa \wa-ná-pa\ *v* wana·wa·pa [fr *napa* to flee] : to run away, flee

wa·na·pan \wa-ná-paŋ\ *v* wana·wa·pan [fr *napan* to tread out *e.g.* grain] : to tread out, to crush out with the feet — **wanapan·pan** *v* wana·wa·panpan [fr *napanpan* to soften by treading] : to make soft by treading

wa·na·pca \wa·ná·pca\ *v* wana·wa·pca [fr *napca* to swallow] : to swallow, or a general word for eating perhaps < ~ *iyeya* to commence eating, *Oyanke wanji wakahnigin na hel wakanheja tanyan ištinmapi na tanyan wanapcapi kte lo* "I shall choose a place and there children will sleep and eat well," the saying of Sitting Bull. ~ *yuha kte* He will have something to eat, *i.e.* to live on. > - MS.540

wa·na·pe i·ca·ge yu·ha *or* **wanapicageyuza** \wa-ná-p̣e i-cà-ǧe yu-há\ *v* : to have power over all, being feared by all - R BD

wa·na·pe·ya \wa-ná-p̣e-ya\ *v* wanape·wa·ya : to drive off, cause to flee — *n* : one who makes flee

wa·na·pi·ca·ge \wa-ná-p̣i-ċa-ǧe\ *n* : a feeling of self-importance, expecting to control everything and issuing commands < ~ *yuha* to have the expectation to control most everything, as is said of an angry person who bosses others while the rest remain quiet, ~ *yuha wacin* He wants to boss everyone. > - *Syn* WAUNKEIC'ILA - LC

wa·na·pi·škan·yan \wa-ná-p̣i-šḳaŋ-yaŋ\ *v* **1** : to play with, as children do with toys **2** : to perform, exhibit as in a circus or demonstration

wa·na·pi·štan·yan \wa-ná-p̣i-šṫaŋ-yaŋ\ *v* [fr *napištanyan* to be industrious] : to destroy or injure everything

wa·na·po·bya \wa-ná-po-bya\ *v* wanapo·bwa·ya : to cause to burst — *n* : fire-crackers

wa·na·po·gna·ka \wa-ná-p̣o-gna-ka\ *v* : to put or hold in the hands

wa·na·po·hya \wa-ná-ṗo-ȟya\ *v* wanapo·hwa·ya : to leaven, cause to rise — **wanapohya·pi** *n* : a balloon

wa·na·po·pa \wa-ná-po-ṗa\ *vn* [fr *napopa* to burst] : to burst

wa·na·po·ta \wa-ná-ṗo-ṫa\ *v* wana·wa·pota [fr *napota* to wear something out] : to wear out with the feet — **wanapote·ca** *n* wana·wa·poteca : one who wears out with the feet

wa·na·psa·ka \wa-ná-psa-ka\ *v* wana·wa·psaka [fr *napsaka* to break in two by foot] : to break *e.g.* a string with the foot

wa·na·pson \wa-ná-psoŋ\ *v* wana·wa·pson [fr *napson* to kick something spilling it] : to spill by kicking, to kick over

wa·na·pton·ka \wa-ná-ptoŋ-ḱa\ *n* : a restless person - *Syn* WOSLOTON ŠNI, ŠKANŠKAN WAŠICUN Rl

wa·na·ptu·ja \wa-ná-pṫu-ja\ *vn* [fr *naptuja* to crack] : to split or crack

wa·na·p'in \wa-ná-p'iŋ\ *n* : a necklace of beads, a medal; a handkechief, anything worn around the neck, a comforter *etc.* < ~ *blaska* a necklace of beads interwoven >

wa·na·p'in·ki·ca·ton \wa-ná-p'in-ḱi-ca-toŋ\ *va* wanap'in·we·caton : to put on as a *wanap'in* a piece of neckware, to cause to wear a necklace *etc.* — **wanap'in·ya** *va* wanap'in·wa·ya : to have or use for neckware

wa·na·sa \wa-ná-sa\ *v* wana·wa·sa wana·un·sa·pi [fr *nasa* to hunt buffalo] : to hunt by a surround and shooting *e.g.* buffalo, to do a buffalo chase < *Tohanl pte ota ca wanasapi* They took to the buffalo hunt when buffalo were plenty. *Maka kin tan'inšniyan owanjila yunka škelo* They say (the fall of buffalo) lay giving the appearance of the earth being invisible, *ca ikanyela euntipi na akašpa icu wanaunsapi kte lo* and so we shall set up camp nearby and hunt buffalo taking a cut from the herd. > — **wanasa·pi** *n* : the buffalo chase — **wanase·ya** *v* : to go on a buffalo hunt, to make a surround - Bl

wa·na·sla·ta \wá-na-sla-ṫa\ *v* wána·wa·slata [fr *anaslata* to stalk, pursue stealthily] : to crawl up to

wa·na·sle·ca \wa-ná-sle-ca\ *v* [fr *nasleca* to crack, split] : to split light things

wa·na·sna \wa-ná-sna\ *v* wana·wa·sna [fr *nasna* to rattle with the feet] : to make ring with the feet

wa·na·sni \wa-ná-sni\ *v* [fr *nasni* put out a fire by foot] : to trample out *e.g.* fire

wa·naš \wa-náš\ *adv emph of* waná : now

wa·na·ša·pa \wa-ná-ša-ṗa\ *v* wana·wa·šapa [fr *našapa* to soil, defile, blacken] : to defile with the feet

wa·na·še·ca \wa-ná-še-ca\ *v* wana·wa·šeca [fr *našeca* to trample and make wither] : to trample and make dry, as grass

wa·na·ši·ca \wa-ná-ši-ca\ *v* wana·wa·šica [fr *našica* to defile with the feet] : to injure with the feet

wa·na·ši·pa \wa-ná-ši-ṗa\ *v* wana·wa·šipa [fr *našipa* to bend by foot] : to break off with the feet

wa·na·ški·ca \wa-ná-ški-ca\ *v* wana·wa·škica [fr *naškica* to press by foot] : to press with the foot — *n* : one who presses with the foot

wa·na·ški·ški·lya \wa-ná-ški-ški-lya\ *v* : to ruffle, as a dress

wa·na·šla \wa-ná-šla\ *v* [fr *našla* make bare by feet] : to make bare with the feet

wa·na·šle·ca \wa-ná-šle-ca\ *v* [fr *našleca* to split what is large by foot with force] : to split heavy things and with effort

wa·na·šlo·gya \wa-ná-šlo-gya\ *v* wanašlo·gwa·ya : to hull corn, *i.e.* with ashes as once it was done, to make hominy < *Wagmeza cahota on wanašlogyapi* Corn is hulled by means of ashes. > - *Syn* CATANAŠLOGYA

wa·na·šlo·ka \wa-ná-šlo-ka\ *v* wana·wa·šloka [fr *našloka* to kick off] : to pull off *e.g.* pantaloons

wa·na·šni·ja \wa-ná-šni-ja\ *v* wana·wa·šnija [fr *našnija* trample down] : to trample down *e.g.* grass and make it wither

wa·na·šo·ša \wa-ná-šo-ša\ *v* wana·wa·šoša [fr *našoša* to stir dirt by foot into suspension] : to foul, befoul *e.g.* water with the feet

wa·na·špa \wa-ná-šṗa\ *v* wana·wa·špa [fr *našpa* break off] : to break off with the feet

wa·na·špu \wa-ná-šṗu\ *v* wana·wa·špu [fr *našpu* knock off by foot] : to break off, as in trampling on pumpkins

wa·na·šu·ja \wa-ná-šu-ja\ *v* wana·wa·šuja [fr *našuja* to bruise or crush by foot] : to bruise with the feet

wa·na·ta·ka \wa-ná-ta-ḱa\ *v* wana·wa·taka [fr *nataka* to close up, lock up] : to fasten up

wa·na·tan \wá-na-ṫaŋ\ *v* wána·wa·tan [fr *anatan* flee to or rush on one] : to run upon, to attack

wa·na·te·pa \wa-ná-ṫe-ṗa\ *v* wana·wa·tepa [fr *natepa* to wear off or out] : to wear off short with the foot

wa·na·ti·ca \wa-ná-ṫi-ca\ *v* wana·wa·tica [fr *natica* to scrape by foot] : to scrape away *e.g.* snow, to paw as do horses

wa·na·ti·pa \wa-ná-ṫi-ṗa\ *v* [fr *natipa* to crisp, to cramp as muscles may do] : to cramp

wa·na·ti·tan \wa-ná-ṫi-ṫaŋ\ *v* wana·wa·titan [fr *natitan* pull by bracing the feet] : to pull of push against

wa·na·tu·ka \wa-ná-ṫu-ḱa\ *v* wana·wa·tuka [fr *natuka* to stamp off, destroy] : to stamp to pieces *e.g.* furs — *n* : one who destroys by stamping

wa·na·t'a \wa-ná-t'a\ *v* wana·wa·t'a [fr *nat'a* to kill by kicking] : to kick to death

wa·na·un·gya \wa-ná-uŋ-gya\ *v* : to scare away *e.g.* game by one's coming near - Bl

wa·na·un·ka \wa-ná-uŋ-ḱa\ *v* [fr *naunka* to kick and make fall] **1** : to kick and make fall down **2** : to start off on the gallop, as a herd of buffalo

wa·na·we·ga \wa-ná-we-ġa\ *v* wana·wa·wega [fr *nawega* to break by foot] : to break with the foot

wa·na·win·ja \wa-ná-wiŋ-ja\ *v* wana·wa·wiŋ-ja [fr *nawinja* trample down] : to bend down with the foot *e.g.* grass, to mat down

wa·ni \wa-ní\ *va* wa·wa·ni **a** : to shake in cutting, as jelly **b** : to cut off *e.g.* the fastenings of a skin stretched out, to rip

wa·ni·ca \wa-ní-ca\ *adj* ma·nica ni·nica un·nica·pi [fr *nica* destitute, having none of] : none, without any

wa·ni·co·kan wi \wa-ní-co-ḱaŋ wi\ *n* : December, the mid-winter moon — **wanicokan·yan** *n* : the mid-winter

wa·ni·gla \wa-ní-gla\ *v* : to go home on account of the winter, to go south as do birds < *Piško ca ~ s'e unglahanpi* We were going home, it being like the night hawk going south for the winter, as is said when one's horses or cattle cannot make headway, being too slow. > - Note: the night larks do much travelling, but it stays in the same place while other birds go on fast. The same

---

\a\ father \e\ they \i\ machine \o\ smoke \u\ lunar \an, aŋ\ blanc Fr. \in, iŋ\ ink \on, oŋ, un, uŋ\ soon, confier Fr. \c\ chair \ġ\ machen Ger. \j\ fusion \clusters: bl, gn, kp, hšl, etc...\ b^{e}lo ... said with a slight vowel **See more in the Introduction, Guide to Pronunciation**

is true when they begin to leave for the South - RA
wa·ni·gni·ca \wa-ní-gni-ca\ *adj red of* wanica : without in *ref* to a number of things
wa·ni·han \wa-ní-haŋ\ *n* : last winter - Note: *blokéhan* last summer
wa·ni·ȟe·yun·ka \wa-ní-ȟe-yuŋ-ka\ *n* : winter frost when wintertime begins < ~ *iwahunni* I made it through to wintertime. > - Cf ȟeyúnka, aȟéyunka
wa·ni·ki·ya \wa-ní-ḱi-ya\ *v* wani·wa·kiya [fr *nikiya* to cause to live] : to save, cause to live — *n* : one who makes live, a savior — **Wanikiye** *np* : the Savior, *i.e.* Jesus Christ of Nazareth in Israel
wa·ni·k'a·la \wá-ni-k'a-la\ *n* : a very little < *Wana ~ ihelo* Now very little remains, *i.e.* very little is left. > - Bl
wa·nil \wa-níl\ *adj contrac of* wanica : lacking, without < *owihanke* ~ endless, ~ *aya* to become extinct, die out > — **wani·lya** *adv* : in a way lacking, without - Cf opuza
wa·ni·ni \wa-ní-ni\ *v red of* waní : to cut loose, as when a skin is cut loose from stretching mounts
wa·ni·ti \wa-ní-ṫi\ *v* : to spend the winter, to winter — **waniti·pi** \wa-ní-ti-pi\ *n* : a winter encampment
wa·ni·un \wa-ní-uŋ\ *v* : to winter, spend the winter
wa·ni·yan \wa-ní-yaŋ\ *v* wani·wa·ya [fr *niyan* to make live] : to cause to live — **waniyan·pi** *or* **waniyanpipi** \wa-ní-yaŋ-pi-pi\ *n* : domestic animals
wa·ni·ye·tu \wa-ní-ye-ṫu\ *n* : winter; a year — **waniyetu okisapa** \wa-ní-ye-ṫu o-ḱi-sa-ṗa\ *n* : an open winter, *i.e.* little snow here and there — **Wani-yetu wi** *np* : November, the winter moon - Bl
wa·non·hka·ti·ye·ce \wa-nóŋ-ȟka-ṫi-ye-ce\ *v* [fr *nonhkatiyece* to hear suddenly] : to hear the buzzing of things, to suddenly catch sound of - Bl
wa·nu·hci \wa-nú-ȟci\ *adv* : all of a sudden, all at once - *Syn* UNGNAHELA, WANNA BT
wa·nun \wa-núŋ\ *adv* : accidentally, by chance < ~ *econ* to do by accident, as killing, not purposely, ~ *kta šni epe* I said I did not, would not mean it. > - Note: the *express* : *wanun kta šni* means perhaps "not to intend" — **wanun·hci** *adv* : by accident
wa·nun·ke·ca \wa-núŋ-ḱe-ca\ *v archaic* : to escape < ~ *gle lo* He escaped and went home. > - BT
wa·nun·kel \wa-núŋ-ḱel\ *adv* : accidentally
wa·nun·kta šni \wa-núŋ-kta šni\ *adv* : not purposely < ~ *epe* I said I did not mean it. >
wa·nun·to·ka·he·ya \wa-núŋ-ṫo-ka-he-ya\ *adv archaic* : prudently < ~ *lena hepa* I said these things with prudence. > - *Syn* WAKTAYA
wa·nun·to·ka·ka·ya·kel \wa-núŋ-ṫo-ka-ka-ya-ḱel\ *adv red of* wanuntokayakel : for an emergency, a spare < *Ten dollars ~ blušpušpu* I set aside ten dollars for an emergency, *i.e.* to use it for any emergency in any way not known as yet, or as in taking more blankets along than one needs, thinking that one might need them. ~ *waun* I am waiting, expecting perhaps, looking for one, watching for one. > - Bl
wa·nun·to·ka·ya·kel \wa-núŋ-ṫo-ka-ya-ḱel\ *adv* : for any emergency < *Akan ogle wan ~ yuha mni kte lo* I shall go with an overcoat for an emergency, as in summertime one takes a heavy overcoat along. > - Bc
wa·nun·wa·a·ta·ye·la \wa-núŋ-wa-à-ṫa-ye-la\ *v* : to strike it well by chance - Bl
wa·nun·wa·ki·pa \wa-núŋ-wa-ki-pa\ *v* : to have bad luck or a bad accident - Bl
wa·nun·wo·a·ki·pa \wa-núŋ-wo-a-ki-pa\ *n* : an accident
[1]**wan** \waŋ\ *interj* an introductory expletive : Why! *or* Look! *or* See! < *Wan! Hokšila wan tokiyatan waohola šni yahi yelo* See! You came not to honor where the boy was from. *Hoh, wan, kola nikunši ... wahtemalašni* Oh-h-h, look, friend, your grandmother dislikes me. *Wan! kakiya ka Ikto wak'in na hiyaye* See! Look at that, Iktomi carrying a load and he passes on by. > - B.H.123.5 D.97, 20, 78 Gramm.266-267
[2]**wan** \waŋ\ *n contrac of* wahínkpe *or* wanhínkpe : an arrow < *wanju* a quiver, *Na šunkawakan tawa wanyámniyanpi nainš wannúnpayanpi* And his horse was hit with three or two arrows. *Wan on o* He hit it with an arrow. *Wan on t'eya* It died from an arrow shot. *Wantanyeya* He is skilled in shooting an arrow. >
[3]**wan** \waŋ\ *art indef* : a, an - Note: the word applies to the modification of its own substantive word, or even of the whole sentence < *Nic'iya yo wan* Save yourself, why don't you? *Niunyanpi ye wan* Please save us, will you? *Teȟislolyin kta wan ikicihunni* He arrived at his going to know trouble, *i.e.* a time of suffering. *Mnilatke cinhan mayalušna kte lo wan* If you drink water you will catch me will you not? *Ma, zuya hila seca wan* Notice, it is possible he has really come to war. *Kola, wan tanka s'e mak'u ye wan* Friend, give me a larger portion, would you. > - D.97, 78, 33 B.H.98.14, 182.21, 183.7, 248.21, 266.4, 267.4, 294.4 Gramm.328-329
wan ka wan \waŋ ka waŋ\ *exclam* of surprise on seeing something at a distance : Look at that! — **wan le wan** *exclam* by men, of surprise on seeing something nearby : Look over here! — **man le man** *exclam* by women, of surprise on seeing something nearby : Oh see this!
wan'·a·pa·ya·pi \waŋ-á-pa-ya-pi\ *n* : an arrow that hits and sticks in the wound - A
wan·bli \waŋ-blí\ *n* : the royal war eagle - Note: there were known to be four kinds of eagles: *wanbli gleška* the spotted eagle, *anunkiyan* a cross-breed with white tail feathers black tipped , *anunkasan* the bald white-head eagle, and *ȟuyá* the common eagle
wan·bli gle·ška \waŋ-blí gle-ška\ *n* : the spotted eagle — **Wanbli Gleška** *np* : the epitome of powers of the North < ~ *s'e išta bleze lo* Like the Spotted Eagle his eyes are clear-sighted, as is said of a man with sharp eyes. > - Bl
wan·bli·ta·he·ya \waŋ-blí-ta-hè-ya\ *n* : the American goldfinch
wan·blu·pi \waŋ-blú-ṗi\ *n* [fr *wanbli* eagle + *upi* the hem, lower border of a garment; *situpi* tail feathers] : eagle tail feathers
wan·ca \wáŋ-ċa\ *adv* or *adj num* : once — **wan·ca·eš** *adv* : at once — **wancag** *adv* : at once < ~ *wicakuwapi* Immediately they set in pursuit of them. > — **wancagcala** *adv* : a few times, now and then once, once apiece — **wanca·gna** *adv* : at once, immediately - R Bl B.H.147.5 D.105
wan·ca·hci \wáŋ-ca-ȟci\ *adv* : just once, for once, at least once < ~ *he bluha kte* Just once shall I hold that, as a man would say as he grabbed for something, whereas others received plenty and he got nothing. *Ho, iló, ~ Ikto wawapilaya ške* Yes, alright, come now, for once Ikto, they say, does a favor. > - D.5
wan·ca·kca·la \wáŋ-ca-kca-la\ *adv* : a few times, seldom or once apiece - P
wan·ca·keš \wáŋ-ca-keš\ *adv* : at once < *Hokšila kin he ayaupi šni ehantanš, ~ yaupi kte šni* If you do not bring that boy, you will not come right away. > - B.H.36.5
wan·ca·la \wáŋ-ca-la\ *adv* : only once — **wancale·ša** *adv* [fr *wancala* only once + *eša* further possibility] : at least once < ~ *ecamon kta* I shall do it at least once. >

wan·ca·yeš *or* **wancaeš** \wáŋ-ca-yeš\ *adv emph* : at once

wan·ci \wáŋ-ċi\ *adj* : one, as used in counting

wan·gla·ka \waŋ-glá-k̇a\ *v poss* wan·wa·glaka [fr *wanyanka* to see] : to see one's own

wan·gle·gle·ga \wáŋ-gle-gle-ġa\ *n* : the bull snake

wan·hi \waŋ-hí\ *n* [fr *wan* arrow + *hi* teeth] : a flint, flints, so called perhaps from the fact that arrowheads were formerly crafted from flint stone – R

wan·hin·kpe *or* **wahinkpe** \waŋ-híŋ-kpe\ *n* : an arrow

wan·hi o·štan·pi \waŋ-hí o-štaŋ-pi\ *n* : a gun once distributed at the *wakpamni tanka* great distribution with which no caps as yet were used but only powder – Bl

wan'·i·gla·ka \waŋ-í-gla-k̇a\ *v refl* wan·miglaka wan'·un·kiglaka·pi [fr *wanyanka* to see, look at] : to look at one's self

wan'·i·pa·me \waŋ-í-pa-me\ *n* : a grinding tool to make arrows round and smooth, consisting of two rocks each with a groove to match the other and drawn to and fro with the arrow inserted

wan'·i·ya·hpe·ya \wáŋ-i-ya-ḣpe-ya\ *va* : to shoot arrows

wan'·i·yu·go·la \waŋ-í-yu-ġo-la\ *n* [fr *wanyugo* to make marks or furrows on arrows] : a tool to incise arrows with crooked lines

wan'·i·yu·ke·ze \wáŋ-i-yu-k̇e-ze\ *n* : a scraper used in the making of arrows

wan·ji \waŋ-jí\ *adj num card* : one

wan·ji·ca \waŋ-jí-ca\ *adj num card* : one — *adv* : in one way < *hecetu* ~ in the same state, without change >

wan·ji·gji \waŋ-jí-gji\ *adj red of* wanji : one apiece, each one one; some < *Tahca ~ ataya k'inpi* They carried the entire load one deer apiece. > – B.H.115.15, 235.11

wan·ji·gji·la *or* **wanjikjila** \waŋ-jí-gji-la\ *adj red of* wanjila : one by one, one apiece, singly < *Oyasin ~ tima yaupi kte lo ca tohanl cicopi ca u po* All should come inside one by one, and when I call for you, come. >

wan·ji·la \waŋ-jí-la\ *adj num card* wa·wánjila : one < *Wanjipila* They are one. >

wan·ji·la·kel \waŋ-jí-la-k̇el\ *adv* : in one manner — **wanjila·kiya** \waŋ-jí-la-k̇i-ya\ *adv* : in one way – B.H. 32.3

wan·ji·la·k'in \waŋ-jí-la-k'iŋ\ *n* : a body cart with two wheels

wan·ji·ni \waŋ-jí-ni\ *pron* : none < *Hopo, ~ unyan napapi šni po* All right! Do not run away and get lost. >

wan·ji·to·ktok \waŋ-jí-ṫo-k̇tok\ *adv* : one after the other *i.e.* by turns < *~ econpi* They did it by turns, *or* It was done one after the other. > – B.H.159.7

wan·ju \wáŋ-ju\ *n* : a quiver < *~ pute* the lower end of a quiver where it is sewn together giving the appearance of lips. > – Bl

wan·kab \waŋ-k̇áb\ *adv* mi·wankab [fr a supposed root: *wankapa* above] : above < *Na wi ~ u kin hehan šunkawakan ota wicawaki yelo* And when the sun was up, I then robbed many horses. *Wicaša wan ataya ska igluza ca miwankab hinajin* A man who was dressed entirely in white came and stood above me. > – MS.645, 355

wan·ka·ga \waŋ-k̇á-ġa\ *va* wan·wa·kaga : to make arrows — **wankah** \waŋ-k̇áḣ\ *va contrac* : to manufacture arrows < *~ wicašipi* They ordered arrows to be made. *~ wayupika* skillful in making arrows > – Bl

wan·kal \waŋ-k̇ál\ *adv* : above, up high < *~ otkeyapi* He was hung up high. *Le lowanpi kin oyasin ~ etonwan po* Now, all you who sing, Look above! >

wan·ka·la \waŋ-ká-la\ *adj* ma·wankala : weak, tender, soft; brittle, easily broken or torn

wan·ka·lka·tu·ya \waŋ-k̇á-lka-ṫu-ya\ *adv* : high < *Cunkaške ~ han* The fence stood high. > – B.H.72.2

wan·ka·lti·pi \waŋ-k̇á-lti-pi\ *n* : an upper room, the upstairs

wan·kal·tki·ya \waŋ-k̇ál-tk̇i-ya\ *adv* : upwards, uphill < *~ yugal najin na hoyeya* He stood with his hands extended upwards and cried out. > – P

wan·ka·pa \waŋ-k̇á-ṗa\ *adv* : above – Note: the word is not used in Lakota, *wankáb* its *contrac* being prefered

wan·ka·pa·ya \waŋ-k̇á-pa-ya\ *adv* : high up, in a high position < *Tuwa ehakela hci eyaš ~ un kte* He who is the very last however will be the first. *Taakicita itancan wankapayehce kin kico* He called the commander of his troops in a high position. > – B.H.92.27

wan·ka·ta·han \waŋ-k̇á-ṫa-haŋ\ *adv* : from above

wan·ka·ta·ki·ya \waŋ-k̇á-ṫa-k̇i-ya\ *adv* : high upwards < *~ kigla* It went high upwards. *Na wanna wahinkpe kin ~ iyeya* And now he sent the arrow high upward. >

wan·ka·ta·tan·han \waŋ-k̇á-ṫa-ṫaŋ-haŋ\ *adv* : from above < *Miyeš ~ wahi yelo* I myself have come from above. >

wan·ka·tki·ya \waŋ-k̇á-ṫk̇i-ya\ *adv* : upward

wan·ka·tu \waŋ-k̇á-ṫu\ *adv* : up above, high up — **wankatu·ya** *or* **wankatuyakel** \waŋ-k̇á-ṫu-ya-k̇el\ *adv* : high up < *Wahinkpe kin tanwankatuya ya* The arrow went gliding high up. >

wan·ka·ye·i·c'i·ya \waŋ-k̇á-ye-i-c'i-ya\ *v refl of* wankayeya : to make one's self go high, as in a swing — **wan·ka·-ye·ki·ci·ya e·con·pi** \waŋ-k̇á-ye-ki-ci-ya e-còn-pi\ *n* : a pastime done by going high together – Bl

wan·ka·ye·la \wáŋ-ka-ye-la\ *adv* : loose, free to turn

wan·ka·ye·ya \waŋ-k̇á-ye-ya\ *v* wankaye·wa·ya : to throw *e.g.* a ball high up < *Wicaša kin keya icu na tice etkiya ~* The man took a turtle and threw it up high toward the smoke vent. >

wan·ki·ci·yan·ka·pi \waŋ-k̇í-ci-yaŋ-k̇a-pi\ *v recip of* wanyanka : to see each other — *n* : a visit

wan·ki·pa·ksa \wáŋ-k̇i-ṗa-ksa\ *n* : a lizzard, a four-legged creature that can separate off it tail — **wankipaksela** *n* : a small lizzard – Bl BH

wan·k'e·ya \waŋ-k'é-ya\ *interj* at seeing one do something wrongly, or when one says but does not do : But the fact is! *or* It is ridiculous! < *~, miyehca ca pte kin hena wicawao welo* Why, the fact is it is I who shoot all the beef, game. > – Note: the word is used by men TT BT D.114 B.H.108.5, 188.15, 279.7

wan·li·la \waŋ-lí-la\ *interj* of surprise at the great quantity or quality of things : Get a load of that! Wow!

wan·lwan·ca·la \wáŋ-lwaŋ-ca-la\ *adv red of* wancala : for once< *~ oie wašte šte* At last, there is some right speech, *or* For once he spoke right. > – Bl

wan·lwan·lwan·ca·šni·yan \waŋ-lwáŋ-lwaŋ-ca-šni-yaŋ\ *adv* : many different articles but all of one kind, as differently shaped pipes < *~ yuké* There is one kind of article but of many shapes. >

wan·na \waŋ-ná\ *adv* : now, already

wan·nun·pa·ya \waŋ-núŋ-ṗa-ya\ *v* wannunpa·wa·ye : to hit *e.g.* game with two arrows

wan'·o·ta·ya \waŋ-ó-ṫa-ya\ *v* : to hit one with arrows in many places – Bl

wan o·un·pa·pi·s'e o·can·ku \wáŋ o-un-pa-pi-s'e o-càŋ-ku\ *n express* : a road as straight as an arrow – BT

\a\ f<u>a</u>ther \e\ th<u>e</u>y \i\ mach<u>i</u>ne \o\ sm<u>o</u>ke \u\ l<u>u</u>nar \an, aŋ\ bl<u>an</u>c Fr. \in, iŋ\ <u>in</u>k \on, oŋ, un, uŋ\ s<u>oo</u>n, c<u>on</u>fier Fr. \c\ <u>ch</u>air \ġ\ ma<u>ch</u>en Ger. \j\ fu<u>s</u>ion \clusters: bl, gn, kp, hšl, etc...\ <u>b</u>ᵉlo ... said with a slight vowel
See more in the Introduction, Guide to Pronunciation

wan·sa·ka \waŋ-sá-ka\ *n* : arrows before they are ready for use, *i.e.* dry sticks cut to size *etc.* < *Wansák-waksaksa hiyaye* He passed by dry-cut arrows. *Wakinyan hotonpi šni k'el wansak'kaksa unyanpi ktelo* Let us go cut arrow material where the Thunderbird's voice has not been sounded. > - D.40 Bl

wan·tan·ye·ya \waŋ-táŋ-ye-ya\ *v* wantanye·wa·ya : to be skillful in shooting — **wantanyeye·la** *n* : an archer, one who shoots (arrows) well - B.H.19.5 MS.97

wan·to \wáŋ-to\ *n* : the blue racer snake

wan·wan·ca šni \waŋ-wáŋ-ca šni\ *adj* : uneven as to size or to kind, to character *etc.* - Note: the word is used in *ref* to many, as a crowd - WE

wan·wan·yan·ka \waŋ-wáŋ-yaŋ-ka\ *n* : a spectator < *Winyan wanwanyankapi kin šicahowaya eyaya* The women spectators have gone screaming. *Na ake ~ k'on kiyela au na wanyank inajinpi* And again the spectators had come near and they stood up to see. >

wan·yang \waŋ-yáŋg\ *v contrac of* wanyanka : to see < ~ *he* to stand or come to see > — **wanyan·gki·ya** \waŋ-yáŋ-gki-ya\ *va* wanyan·gwa·kiya : to cause to see anything

wan·yan·gpi·ca \waŋ-yáŋ-gpi-ca\ *adj* : visible

wan·yan·gya \waŋ-yáŋ-gya\ *va* wanyan·gwa·ya : to cause to see or perceive

wan·yan·ka \waŋ-yáŋ-ka\ *va* wan·bla·ka : to see, perceive anything

wan·ye·ca \waŋ-yé-ca\ *n* **1** : rushes **2** : the fire fly, the lightning bug

wan·ye·ca·hu tan·ka \waŋ-yé-ca-hu tàŋ-ka\ *n* [fr *wan* arrow + *iyececa* alike] : the scouring rush, pipe stem, equisetum hyemale, the horsetail family - Note: horses are said to get fat on it - Bl BT #122

wan·ye·ca swu·la \waŋ-yé-ca swu-la\ *n* : horsetail, scouring rush, equisetum variegatum, the horsetail family - L

wan·ye·ya \waŋ-yé-ya\ *va* wanye·wa·ya : to shoot arrows, to shoot in the sacred dance - *See* wantányeya

wan·yu·go \waŋ-yú-ġo\ *va* wan·blu·go [fr *wan* arrow + *yugo* to etch or groove] : to make the croooked marks or furrows on arrows, such being considered essential to a good arrow

wan·yu·gu·ka \waŋ-yú-ġu-ka\ *v* : to draw an arrow out of the quiver

wan·yu·kpan·han \wáŋ-yu-kpaŋ-haŋ\ *v* wan·blu·kpanhan : to shoot arrows one after another

wan·yu·za \waŋ-yú-za\ *v* : to be able to handle bow and arrow, as is said of a boy < *Wana wanjuze* He can now handle bow and arrow. > - TT

wa·o \wa-ó\ *v* wa·wa·o : to hit in shooting — *v* 1st *pers singl of* o : I shot and hit it.

wa·o·ho·la \wa-ó-ho-la\ *v* wa·wa·ohola [fr *ohola* to pay honor, respect] : to honor, worship < *Hokšila wan tókiyatan ~ šni yahi yelo* You came not to honor where the boy came from. > — **waohola·šniyan** *adv* : irreverently - B.H.63.10, 80.21

wa·o·hmun·ye·ce \wa-ó-ȟmuŋ-ye-ce\ *n* : a very talkative person, on who makes much noise wherever he is - Bl

wa·o·ka \wa-ó-ka\ *n* wa·wa·oka: a marksman, a good hunter, to be one such one — *n pl* : waopika - D.64

wa·o·ka·hni·ga \wa-ó-ka-ȟni-ġa\ *v* wao·wa·kahniga : to be smart, intelligent, to be skillful in finding game < *Waokahnigelo, wigni wayupikelo* He is smart, keen at hunting for provisions. *Wicaša ksapa na waokahnigehce* He is a smart and wise man. > - B.H.32.7

wa·o·ka·hwan·ji·ca \wa-ó-ka-ȟwaŋ-ji-ca\ *n* or *adj* : one "make", one style; all *e.g.* arrows made in the same manner - Bl

wa·o·ka·la \wa-ó-ka-la\ *v* [fr *okala* to sow as grain] : to sow, plant - B.H.248.17

wa·o·ki·ca·hni·ga \wa-ó-ki-ca-ȟni-ġa\ *v* waoki·wa·kahniga : to have understanding, be wise - B.H.121.2 Bl BH

wa·o·ki·hi \wa-ó-ki-hi\ *v* wao·wa·kihi [fr *okihi* to be able] : to be able, to have ability — **waokihi·ka** \wa-ó-ki-hi-ka\ *n* wao·wa·kihika : one who is able — **waokihi·ya** *va* waokihi·wa·ya : to make able — *adv* : ably, powerfully - Bl

[1]**wa·o·ki·ya** \wa-ó-ki-ya\ *v* [fr *o* to shoot + *kiya* to make or allow] : to let one do the shooting *etc.* while hunting - Bl

[2]**wa·o·ki·ya** \wá-o-ki-ya\ *v* : to command - R Bl

wa·o·k'u \wa-ó-k'u\ *v* wao·wa·k'u [fr *ok'u* to lend] : to lend

wa·o·mani \wa-ó-ma-ni\ *v* : to travel in snow -WHL

wa·on·spe \wa-óŋ-spe\ *v* waon·ma·spe [fr *onspe* to learn] : to know how < *wicaša* ~ a learned man > - B.H.172.1

wa·on·spe·i·c'i·ya \wa-óŋ-spe-i-c'i-ya\ *n* : a scholar - P

wa·on·spe·ki·ya \wa-óŋ-spe-ki-ya\ *v* waonspe·wa·kiya [fr *onspekiya* to teach] : to teach — **waonspekiye** *n* : a teacher - B.H.177.5

wa·on·spe·wi·ca·ki·ye \wa-ó-spe-wi-ca-ki-ye\ *n* : a disciple, an apostle - B.H.177.1

wa·on·ši·la \wa-óŋ-ši-la\ *adj* waonši·wa·la : merciful, gracious

wa·on·ton·ki·ya \wa-óŋ-toŋ-ki-ya\ *v poss* : to ruin, spoil one's own — **waonton·yan** *va* waonton·wa·ya : to spoil, miss; injure - Bl

wa·on·ze \wa-óŋ-ze\ *n* : a nickname for a bear, *lit* the rump

wa·o·po \wa-ó-po\ *va* wa·wa·opo : to push in with a knife, to make a hole in

wa·o·p'o \wa-ó-p'o\ *n* : light snow flying in the sunlight

wa·o·šte·gla \wa-ó-šte-gla\ *v* waošte·wa·gla [fr *oštegla* to mock, revile, insult] : to slander, revile, to speak evil of, to call bad names

wa·o·ta \wa-ó-ta\ *n* : much of anything < ~ *luha yelo* You have a great number of things, *i.e.* things aplenty. > - B.H.32.25

wa·o·ta·pe s'e \wa-ó-ta-pe s'e\ *adv* [fr *otapa* to follow after one] : following a certain plan unintentionally - B.H.157.20

wa·o·we·ši·ca \wa-ó-we-ši-ca\ *n* : a bear, in general < ~ *s'e napcoka kin yuh'iyela yankin na* It was as if a bear scratched the palm of his hands ..., as they say when a person has many scratches on his hands. > - Bl

wa·o·ya·tan \wa-ó-ya-taŋ\ *v* wao·bla·tan : to backbite, slander, disparage; to talk bad secretly about somebody, to spoil one's reputation; to bite unawares, as a dog or animals do - *See* wayatawawacinhinyanza

wa·o·ye \wa-ó-ye\ *n* : foot tracks < ~ *ótalahcake* Many are the tracks. > - Bl

wa·o·ze·ze \wa-ó-ze-ze\ *va* wa·wa·ozeze : to cut nearly off with a knife and let swing — **waozeze·ya** *va* waozeze·wa·ya : to cause to cut in strips or dangles

[1]**wa·pa** \wa-pá\ *n of* pa **a** : the head of anything, *e.g.* a dog's head used as a headdress for dancing **b** : the source of locomotion, as the engine or locomotive of a train **c** : anything placed at the lead position

[2]**wa·pa** \wa-pa\ *adv suff to the word it develops* : towards, upwards < *tokatawapa* forward, toward the future, *ektawapa inajin* to stand farther on >

wa·pa·a·gla·pšun·yan \wa-ṗá-a-gla-pšuŋ-yaŋ\ *v* [fr *paaglapšunyan* head down] : to turn bottom upwards < ~ *iyeya* to go suddenly bottom up >

wa·pa·bla *or* **wapablaya** \wa-ṗá-bla\ *v* wa·wa·pabla : to spread out, make level or smoothen; to iron *e.g.* clothes

wa·pa·bla·ska \wa-ṗá-bla-ska\ *v* wa·wa·pablaska [fr *pablaska* to flatten] : to flatten — *v* 1st *pers singl of* pablaska : I made it flat

wa·pa·bla·ya \wa-ṗá-bla-ya\ *v* wa·wa·pablaya [fr *pablaya* to spread out and smoothen] : to make smooth; to iron *e.g.* clothes — *v* 1st *pers singl of* pablaya : I ironed it

wa·pa·bla·za \wa-ṗá-bla-za\ *v* wa·wa·pablaza : to make burst by pressing — *v* 1st *pers singl of* pablaza : I squeezed it to bursting

wa·pa·ble·ca \wa-ṗá-ble-ca\ *v* wa·wa·pableca [fr *pableca* to crush by hand] : to crush to pieces — *v* 1st *pers singl of* pableca : I crushed it

wa·pa·blu \wa-ṗá-blu\ *v* wa·wa·pablu [fr *pablu* to pulverize; to root up or dig in] : to pulverize — *v* 1st *pers singl of* pablu : I dug in it

wa·pa·bu \wa-ṗa-bu\ *v* wa·wa·pabu [fr *pabu* to drum on with the fingers] : to drum, beat — *v* 1st *pers singl of* pabu : I drummed or beat on with my fingers

wa·pa·can·can \wa-ṗá-caŋ-caŋ\ *v* [fr *pacancan* to shake] : to make shake — *v* 1st *pers singl of* pacancan : I made it shake

wa·pa·can·nal i·ye·ya \wa-ṗá-caŋ-nal i-yè-ya\ *v* : to shove toward the middle or center - R Bl

wa·pa·ce·ka \wa-ṗá-ce-k̇a\ *v* : to push one off balance - *See* wapacekceka

wa·pa·ce·kce·ka \wa-ṗá-ce-kce-k̇a\ *v* [fr *pacekceka* to knock or push off balance] : to push and make stagger — *v* 1st *pers singl of* paceckceka : I staggered him

wa·pa·e·ze *or* **wapayezaha** \wa-ṗá-e-ze\ *n* : a rival, a jealous person, one who does not like everybody - R

wa·pa·gan \wa-ṗá-ġaŋ\ *v* wa·wa·pagan [fr *pagan* to push open] 1 : to part with 2 : to push open — *v* 1st *pers singl of* pagan : I pushed it open

wa·pa·ga·pa \wa-ṗá-ġa-ṗa\ *v* wa·wa·pagapa [fr *pagapa* to skin or get skinned] : to skin an animal, push off — *v* 1st *pers singl of* pagapa : I skinned it

wa·pa·ge·ya \wa-ṗá-ġe-ya\ *v* wapage·wa·ya [fr *pageya* to frighten away] : to scare away a crowd of men or animals — **wapageye·ca** *v* [fr *pageya* to frighten into flight] : to conquer — *part* : conquering; causing some trouble to others - KE WHL

wa·pa·gi·ca \wá-pa-ġi-ca\ *n* : the yellow-headed blackbird < ~ *s'e oie cantet'inst'inzelo* His words are courageous like those of the yellow-headed black bird, as is said when a man speaks angrily. > - *See wabloska* the lark bunting Bl FR

wa·pa·gmi·gma \wa-ṗá-gmi-gma\ *v* wa·wa·pagmigma [fr *pagmigma* to make round or roll by hand] : to make round — *v* 1st *pers singl of* pagmigma : I made it round **wapagmi·yanyan** *v* wa·wa·pagmiyanyan [fr *pagmiyanyan* to make something roll by hand] : to roll — *v* 1st *pers singl of* pagmiyanyan : I rolled it

wa·pa·gmun \wa-ṗá-gmuŋ\ *v* wa·wa·pagmun [fr *pagmun* to twist or roll up by hand] : to twist — *v* 1st *pers singl of* pagmun : I twisted it by hand — **wapagmun·ke** \wa-ṗá-gmuŋ-ke\ *n* : a spinner, one who twists — **wapagmun·pi** *n* : twisted thread, yarn

wa·pa·gna·škin·yan \wa-ṗá-gna-škiŋ-yaŋ\ *v* wa·wa·pagnaškinyan [fr *pagnaškinyan* to push and infuriate one] : to make crazy — *v* 1st *pers singl* : I made him furious

wa·pa·gna·yan \wa-ṗá-gna-yaŋ\ *v* [fr *pagnayan* to miss, escape] : to miss, as in attempting to stab — *v* 1st *pers singl* : I missed trying to hit

wa·pa·go \wa-ṗá-ġo\ *v* wa·wa·pago [fr *pago* to carve, sculpt] : to carve — *v 1 pers singl of* pago : I carved it — *n* : a carver, an engraver — **wapago·ya** *va* : to cause to carve

wa·pa·gwe·za \wa-ṗá-gwe-za\ *v* wa·wa·pagweza [fr *pagweza* to roughen by hand] : to make rough

[1]**wa·pa·ha** \wa-pá-ha\ *n* : a headdress of feathers < *Nupin Tatanka ~ unpi* The Two Bulls are wearing feathered headdresses. >

[2]**wa·pa·ha** \wá-ṗa-ha\ *n* : the staff or pole on which are tied feathers of farious colors and used in the Dakota dances; a standard, banner, flag

wa·pa·ha he·ton·pi \wa-pá-ha he-tòŋ-pi\ *n* : a horned headdress — **wapaha héyuga** *n* : a branch-horned headdress

wa·pa·ha i·ye·ya \wa-ṗá-ha i-yè-ya\ *v* [fr *paha* to push aside + *iyeya* to cause it] : to push down - R Bl

wa·pa·ha i·yu·slo·he·ton \wa-pá-ha i-yù-slo-he-ton\ *n* : a warbonnet with one tail that falls in a train

wa·pa·ha ka·mni·mni·la pe·ji \wá-ṗa-ha ka-mnì-mni-la ṗe-jí\ *n* : tall grama grass, bouteloua curtipendula, the grass family; also called anthers vermillion or cinnamon red - Note: the plant is so called because of the sharp upper end (*wapaha* a staff) of the grass blades - Bl #221

wa·pa·ha mi·ma *or* **wapaha mimela** \wa-pá-ha mi-mà\ *n* : a round war-bonnet without a tail

wa·pa·ha o·ki·ja·ta \wa-pá-ha o-k̇ì-ja-ta\ *n* : a warbonnet with two tails

wa·pa·ha pa·yu·ktan \wá-ṗa-ha pa-yù-ktaŋ\ *n* : a staff, a sort of spear looking almost like a bishop's staff and used by the *Wic'inska* the White Meat Strap and the *Ihoka* the Badger *Okolakiciye* Societies, military societies among the Oglala Lakotas - FD.313

wa·pa·ha yu·slo·he \wa-pá-ha yu-slò-he\ *n* : the trailer, the lower part of a warbonnet

wa·pa·hi \wa-ṗá-hi\ *v* wa·wa·pahi [fr *pahi* to pick up] : to gather or pick up — *v* 1st *pers singl of* pahi : I picked things up

wa·pa·hinl \wa-ṗá-hiŋl\ *v contrac of* wapahinta : to rub or brush off < *Sunkawakan ~ wota yelo* The horse ate rubbing it off, *i.e.* scratched snow away and ate the grass. > — **wapahinta** *v* : to brush or scratch away - LB

wa·pa·hi·pi \wa-ṗá-hi-pi\ *n* : a gathering or picking up of things

wa·pa·ho·ho \wa-ṗá-ho-ho\ *v* [fr *pahoho* to shake and loosen] : to shake and make loose

wa·pa·ho·mni \wa-ṗá-ho-mni\ *v* wa·wa·pahomni [fr *pahomni* to push anything round] : to turn around — *v* 1st *pers singl of* pahomni : I pushed it around

wa·pa·ho·ton \wa-ṗá-ho-toŋ\ *v* wa·wa·pahoton [fr *pahoton* to cause to make an outcry] : to make cry out — *v* 1st *pers singl of pahoton* : I made it cry out

---

\a\ father \e\ they \i\ machine \o\ smoke \u\ lunar \an, aŋ\ blanc Fr. \in, iŋ\ ink \on, oŋ, un, uŋ\ soon, confier Fr. \c\ chair \ġ\ machen Ger. \j\ fusion \clusters: bl, gn, kp, hšl, etc...\ b^e^lo ... said with a slight vowel **See more in the Introduction, Guide to Pronunciation**

wa·pa·hun·hun·za \wa-ṗá-huŋ-huŋ-za\ *v* wa·wa·pahunhunza [fr *pahunhunza* to make shake by hand] : to shake with the hand, shake by pushing against — *v* 1st *pers singl of* pahunhunza : I shake it by pushing

wa·pa·ȟa·tka \wa-ṗá-ȟa-tka\ *v* [fr *paȟa* to rub + *tka* contrarily] : to rub against the grain — *v* 1st *pers singl of* paȟatka : I rubbed against his or its grain

wa·pa·hci \wa-ṗá-ȟci\ *v* [fr *pahci* to tear or pick out a piece] : to tear out pieces — *v* 1st *pers singl of* pahci : I tore or picked out a piece

wa·pa·ȟe-ya *or* **wapaġeya** \wa-ṗá-ȟe-ya\ *v* wapaȟe·wa·ya : to scare away a crowd of men or animals - Bl

wa·pa·hla·gan \wa-ṗá-ȟla-ġaŋ\ *v* [fr *pahlagan* to enlarge] : to enlarge or lengthen — *v* 1st *pers singl of* pahlagan : I enlarged it

wa·pa·hla·lton \wá-ṗa-ȟla-ltoŋ\ *v* wapahla·lwa·ton : to work with ribbon, to embroider — **wapahla·ta** \wá-ṗa-ȟla-ṫa\ *v* [fr *apahlata* to embroider] : to embroider

wa·pa·hla·ta·pi \wa-ṗá-ȟla-ta-pi\ *n* : the burying of meat in snow < *Hecel talo kin oštulya yankin kte, tasakin kte šni yelo* So that the fresh meat might remain unfrozen it will have not to be frozen. > - Bl

wa·pa·hla·te \wá-ṗa-ȟla-ṫe\ *n* : a ribbon, ribbons

wa·pa·hle·ca \wa-ṗá-ȟle-ca\ *v* wa·wa·pahleca [fr *pahleca* to pull to pieces] : to tear, rend — *v* 1st *pers singl of* pahleca : I tore it to pieces

wa·pa·hli \wa-ṗá-ȟli\ *v* [fr *pahli* to stick in the ground] : to push into the ground or mud

wa·pa·hlo·ka \wa-ṗá-ȟlo-ka\ *v* wa·wa·pahloka [fr *pahloka* to pierce] : to pierce, make holes in — *v* 1st *pers singl of* pahloka : I pierced it

wa·pa·hmin \wa-ṗá-ȟmiŋ\ *v* [fr *hmin* crooked] : to make crooked

wa·pa·hpa \wa-ṗá-ȟpa\ *v* wa·wa·pahpa [fr *pahpa* to throw off or down] : to throw down — *v* 1st *pers singl of* pahpa : I threw him down

wa·pa·hpu \wa-ṗá-ȟṗu\ *v* wa·wa·pahpu [fr *pahpu* to pick off in small pieces] : to pick off — *v* 1st *pers singl of* pahpu : I chipped away at it

wa·pa·hta \wa-ṗá-ȟṫa\ *v* wa·wa·pahta [fr *pahta* to tie up or hobble] : to tie in bundles — *v* 1st *pers singl of* pahta : I did packing

wa·pa·hta \wá-ṗa-ȟṫa\ *n* : a pack, a bundle < *Canli ~ etan kagapi* They made some tobacco ties. >

wa·pa·ȟu·ga \wa-ṗá-ȟu-ga\ *v* wa·wa·paȟuga [fr *paȟuga* to break or push a hole in] : to break holes in — *v* 1st *pers singl of* paȟuga : I cracked holes in

wa·pa·hwu·hwu \wa-ṗá-ȟwu-ȟwu\ *adv* : in deep snow < ~ *waimnankelo* I ran in deep snow, *i.e.* through snow and falling over on one's hands. > - Note: *pahwuhwu* seems more proper, though that itself seems either not to exist or to be *archaic* - Bl KE

wa·pa·ja·ja \wa-ṗá-ja-ja\ *v* wa·wa·pajaja [fr *pajaja* to wash or mop] : to wash — *v* 1st *pers singl of* pajaja : I mopped it

wa·pa·jin\wa-ṗá-jiŋ\ *vn* wa·ma·pajin : to be prevented or not to be able to accomplish

wa·pa·ji·pa \wa-ṗá-ji-pa\ *v* wa·wa·pajipa [fr *pajipa* to prick, to sting] : to pinch — *v* 1st *pers singl of* pajipa : I pinched her

wa·pa·ju·ju \wa-ṗá-ju-ju\ *v* wa·wa·pajuju [fr *pajuju* to erase, rub out] : to erase, demolish — *v* 1 *pers singl of* pajuju : I erased it, demolished it

wa·pa·jun \wa-ṗá-juŋ\ *v* [fr *pajun* to reach and pry up] : to dig up with the bill, as ducks do under water

wa·pa·ka·tin \wa-ṗá-ka-ṫiŋ\ *v* [fr *pakatin* extend the arm] : to straighten out

wa·pa·ka·wa \wa-ṗá-ka-wa\ *v* [fr *pakawa* to split] : to open out

wa·pa·kca \wa-ṗá-kca\ *v* [fr *pakca* to comb, untangle] : to comb — *v* 1st *pers singl of* pakca : I combed him

wa·pa·kin·ta \wa-ṗá-kiŋ-ṫa\ *v* wa·wa·pakinta [fr *pakinta* to wipe or clean] : to wipe — *v* 1st *pers singl of* pakinta : I wiped it

wa·pa·ki·za \wa-ṗá-ki-za\ *v* [fr *pakiza* make creak by rubbing] : to make creak — *v* 1st *pers singl of* pakiza : I made it creak by rubbing

[1]**wa·pa·ko** \wa-ṗá-ko\ *v contrac* wa·wa·pako [fr *pakota* or *pakol* to dig out] : to make room for somebody by pushing away from each other - Bl

[2]**wa·pa·ko** \wa-ṗá-ko\ *v* wa·wa·pako [fr *pako* crooked] : to cut or saw crooked

wa·pa·ko·ta \wa-ṗá-ko-ṫa\ *v* : to probe or dig out — *v* 1st *pers singl of* pakota : I dug it out

wa·pa·kpa \wa-ṗá-kṗa\ *v* wa·wa·pakpa [fr *pakpa* piece or gouge] : to pierce — *v* 1st *pers singl of* pakpa : I pierced it

wa·pa·kpi \wa-ṗá-kṗi\ *v* wa·wa·pakpi : to pick open *e.g.* eggs — *v* 1 *pers singl of* pakpi : I picked it open

wa·pa·ksa \wa-ṗá-ksa\ *v* wa·wa·paksa [fr *paksa* break] : to break off with the hand — *v* 1st *pers singl of* paksa : I broke it off by hand

wa·pa·kši·ja \wa-ṗá-kši-ja\ *v* wa·wa·pakšija [fr *pakšija* to double or fold up] : to make double up — *v* 1st *pers singl of* pakšija : I folded it up

wa·pa·ktan \wa-ṗá-kṫaŋ\ *v* wa·wa·paktan [fr *paktan* to bend around] : to crook, make crooked — *v* 1st *pers singl of* paktan : I bent it around

wa·pa·k'e·ga \wa-ṗá-k'e-ġa\ *v* wa·wa·pak'ega [fr *pak'ega* to scrape by hand] : to scratch — *v* 1st *pers singl of* pak'ega : I scratched, scraped

wa·pa·k'e·za \wa-ṗá-k'e-za\ *v* wa·wa·pak'eza [fr *pak'eza* scrape smooth] : to make hard and smooth — *v* 1st *pers singl of* pak'eza : I scraped it smooth

wa·pa·man \wa-ṗá-maŋ\ *v* wa·wa·paman [fr *paman* to file by rubbing] : to file using a tool — *v* 1st *pers singl of* paman : I filed it

wa·pa·mi·ma \wa-ṗá-mi-ma\ *v* wa·wa·pamima [fr *pamíma* to make round] : to make round — *v* 1st *pers singl of* pamíma : I made it round

wa·pa·ni·ni \wa-ṗá-ni-ni\ *v* 1st *pers singl of* panini : I jogged him *e.g.* with my elbow

wa·pan·ge·ye·ca *or perhaps* **wapageyeca** \wa-ṗáŋ-ġe-ye-ca\ *v* : to make burdensome, bulky; to overcome, conquer, to frighten into flight; to cause trouble to others - Cf pángece KE WHL

wa·pa·o·glu·ta \wa-ṗá-o-glu-ta\ *v* [fr *paogluta* to close up by rubbing] : to close up < ~ *iyeya* to make it close suddenly > — *v* 1st *pers singl of* paogluta : I closed it up

wa·pa·o·ksa \wa-ṗá-o-ksa\ *v* wa·wa·paoksa [fr *paoksa* to make cave in so as to fill in] : to push or break through — *v* 1st *pers singl of* paoksa : I broke through

wa·pa·o·spa \wa-ṗá-o-sṗa\ *v* wa·wa·paospa [fr *paospa* to push under] : to push under *e.g.* water — *v* 1st *pers singl of* paospa : I pushed him under

wa·pa·o·t'in·za \wa-ṗá-o-t'iŋ-za\ *v* wa·wa·paot'inza [fr *paot'inza* to pack in tight by hand] : to press in tight — *v* 1st *pers singl of* paot'inza : I pressed it in tight

wa·pa·o·wo·tan *or* **wapaowotan·la** \wa-ṗá-o-wo-taŋ\ *v* wa·wa·paowotan [fr *paowotan* to make straight, make stand upright] : to make straight — *v* 1st *pers singl of* paowotanla : I made it straight

wa·pa·pa \wa-pá-pa\ *v of* papá : to bark as does a dog < *Šunka ~ ota ktelo* A dog will do much barking. >

wa·pa·pa·hya \wa-ṗá-ṗa-ȟya\ *v* wapapa·ȟwa·ya [fr *papahya* to parch] : to parch *e.g.* corn, fat, *etc.* - R Bl

wa·pa·po·pa \wa-ṗá-po-ṗa\ *v* : to parch, burst open, as corn — *v 1st pers singl of* papopa : I parched it

wa·pa·psa·ka \wa-ṗá-psa-ka\ *v* [fr *papsaka* to tear or break in two] : to break *e.g.* cords — *v 1st pers singl of* papsaka : I broke it in two

wa·pa·pson \wa-ṗá-psoŋ\ *v* wa·wa·papson [fr *papson* to spill] : to spill *e.g.* water — *v 1st pers singl of* papson : I spilled it

wa·pa·ptu·ja \wa-ṗá-ptu-ja\ *v* : to take out a piece as with a chisel, to crack or split — *v 1st pers singl of* paptuja - R BD

wa·pa·pu·za \wa-ṗá-ṗu-za\ *v* wa·wa·papuza [fr *papuza* to wipe dry] : to make dry by wiping — *v 1st pers singl of* papuza : I wiped it dry

wa·pa·ska \wa-ṗá-ska\ *v* wa·wa·paska : to make white by rubbing — *v 1st pers singl of* paska : I bleached it

wa·pa·sla·ta \wa-ṗá-sla-ta\ *v* wa·wa·paslata : to set up *e.g.* a pole in the ground — *v 1st pers singl of* paslata : I set or drove in a stake

wa·pa·sle·ca \wa-ṗá-sle-ca\ *v* wa·wa·pasleca [fr *pasleca* to split with a knife] : to split — *v 1st pers singl of* pasleca : I slashed it in half

wa·pa·sma·ka \wa-ṗá-sma-ka\ *v* wa·wa·pasmaka : to indent — *v 1st pers singl of* pasmaka : I indented it

wa·pa·smin·yan·yan \wa-ṗá-smiŋ-yaŋ-yaŋ\ *v* : to make bare and clean — *v 1st pers singl of* pasminyanyan : I stripped it clean

wa·pa·snon \wa-ṗá-snoŋ\ *v* wa·wa·pasnon [fr *pasnon* to roast meat on a spit] : to roast *e.g.* meat — *v 1st pers singl of* pasnon : I roasted it - D.22

wa·pa·stan·ka \wa-ṗá-staŋ-ka\ *v* wa·wa·pastanka [fr *pastanka* to moisten] : to moisten; *vulg* to have coitus

wa·pa·ša·pa \wa-ṗá-ša-ṗa\ *v* wa·wa·pašapa [fr *pašapa* to defile] : to defile

wa·pa·ši·pa \wa-ṗá-ši-ṗa\ *v* wa·wa·pašipa [fr *pašipa* to bend, reshape] : to break off close *e.g.* the limbs of a tree — *v 1st pers singl of* pašipa : I broke it off close

wa·pa·ški·ca \wa-ṗá-ški-ca\ *v* wa·wa·paškica [fr *paškica* to wring out] : to press, squeeze

wa·pa·ški·ška \wa-ṗá-ški-ška\ *v* [fr *paškiška* to disarrange by rubbing] : to make rough

wa·pa·ško·kpa \wa-ṗá-ško-kṗa\ *v* [fr *paškokpa* to make a cavity or ditch by hand or by sitting] : to make hollow, to cut or dig out

wa·pa·ško·pa \wa-ṗá-ško-ṗa\ *v* [fr *škopa* crooked, warped] : to make twist, become warped

wa·pa·šle·ca \wa-ṗá-šle-ca\ *v* wa·wa·pašleca [fr *pašleca* to split what is hard or heavy] : to split with an effort — *v 1st pers singl of* pašleca : I split it with a hard blow

wa·pa·šna \wa-ṗá-šna\ *v* wa·wa·pašna [fr *pašna* miss] : to miss

wa·pa·špa \wa-ṗá-špa\ *v* wa·wa·pašpa [fr *pašpa* break or cut off a piece] : to push away, break off; to wash out *e.g.* stains — *v 1st pers singl of* pašpa : I scrubbed it out — *n* : that which is washable, cleaned out

wa·pa·špu \wa-ṗá-špu\ *v* wa·wa·pašpu [fr *pašpu* loosen and make fall] : to break off

wa·pa·šu·ja \wa-ṗá-šu-ja\ *v* wa·wa·pašuja [fr *pašuja* to smash by hand] : to crush — *v 1st pers singl of* pašuja : I crushed it

wa·pa·š'a·ka \wa-ṗá-š'a-ka\ *v* wa·wa·paš'aka [fr *paš'aka* to dent, score] : to stab or push with too little force — *v 1st pers singl of* paš'aka : I struck scoring it

wa·pa·ta \wa-ṗá-ṫa\ *v* wa·wa·pata [fr *pata* to butcher] : to butcher, cut up an animal < *Hecel miš num wicawao na wawapata* So I shot two and butchered them. > — *v 1st pers singl of* páta : I butchered it

[1]**wa·pa·tan** \wa-ṗá-ṫaŋ\ *v* wa·wa·patan [fr *paṫán* to take care and save] : to be saving of — *v 1st pers singl of* I took care of him

[2]**wa·pa·tan** \wa-ṗá-taŋ\ *v* wa·wa·patan [fr *ṗatan* to push or mash] : to mash up, as potatoes — *v 1st pers singl of* ṗatán : I mashed it

wa·pa·tan·ka *or* **wakpatanka** \wa-ṗá-ṫaŋ-ka\ *n* : one who is saving, economical

wa·pa·ta·pi \wa-ṗá-ṫa-ṗi\ *n* : meat cut up, or the act of cutting up meat

wa·pa·ti·ca \wa-ṗá-ṫi-ca\ *v* wa·wa·patica [fr *patica* to knead with the hands, Dakota] : to work up by pressing on *e.g.* dough when sticky and soft; to shove, push — *v 1st pers singl of* patica : I kneaded it

wa·pa·ton·yan \wa-ṗá-toŋ-yaŋ\ *v* wapaton·wa·ya : to make flee, put to flight — **wapatonye·ce** *n* : one who makes all flee, puts all to flight - Bl

wa·pa·t'i·hpe·ya \wa-ṗá-t'i-ȟpe·ya\ *v* [fr *pat'ihpeya* cast down to kill with pressure] : to push hard out of the way - Bl

wa·pa·t'in·za \wa-pá-t'iŋ-za\ *v* wa·wa·pat'inza : to press hard *e.g.* dried wash — *v 1st pers singl of* pat'inza : I pressed it hard

wa·pa·wa·ga \wa-ṗá-wa-ġa\ *v* [fr *pawaga* to roll in hand] : to roll or twist — *v 1st pers singl of* pawaga : I rolled it in or by hand

wa·pa·we·ga \wa-ṗá-we-ġa\ *v* wa·wa·pawega : to break or fracture — *v 1st pers singl of* pawega : I fractured it

wa·pa·wi \wa·ṗá-wi\ *or* \wá-ṗa-wi\ *v* : to gather about, as buzzards do about a carcass < *Tuhmunh ~ s'e nicuwapelo* The bees went after you as if gathering about a carcass, *i.e.* many wasps buzzing about one. > — **wapawi·ya** *adv* : yet moving about - Bl KE

wa·pa·wi·gnu·ni \wa-ṗá-wi-gnu-ni\ *v* wa·wa·pawignuni [fr *pawignuni* to become confused] : to destroy amid turmoil — *v 1st pers singl of* pawignuni : I became confused amid turmoil and distress - R Bl

wa·pa·win·ja \wa-ṗá-wiŋ-ja\ *v* [fr *pawinja* to bend pushing down] : to bend down *e.g.* grass — *v 1st pers singl of* pawinja : I bent it down

wa·pa·win·ta \wá-ṗa-wiŋ-ṫa\ *v* wa·wa·pawinta [fr *apawinta* to rub on it or one] : to rub on; to plaster — *n* : an application, as plaster in plastering

wa·pa·ya·la·ke s'e \wa-pá-ya-la-ke s'e\ *adv* : as one would have expected to the top or head of < *Na wana ka ekta ~ kupi* And they came toward home not yet as one might have expected. > - MS.150

wa·pa·ye \wá-ṗa-ye\ *n* : seasoning of any kind, grease, meat — **wapaye·ya** *va* wapaye·wa·ya : to use for seasoning

wa·pa·zan \wa-ṗá-zaŋ\ *v* wa·wa·pazan : to part, to separate *e.g.* the hair — *v 1st pers singl of* pazan : I parted his hair, *i.e.* killed so by striking

---

\a\ father \e\ they \i\ machine \o\ smoke \u\ lunar \an, aŋ\ blanc Fr. \in, iŋ\ ink \on, oŋ, un, uŋ\ soon, confier Fr. \c\ chair \ġ\ machen Ger. \j\ fusion \clusters: bl, gn, kp, hšl, etc...\ b[e]lo ... said with a slight vowel **See more in the Introduction, Guide to Pronunciation**

wa·pa·zo \wa-ṗá-zo\ *v* wa·wa·pazo [fr *pazo* to show] : to show — *v 1st pers singl of* pazo : I showed it — **wapazopi** *n* : a show, an exhibition

[1]**wa·pe** \wa-pé\ *v* wa·wa·pe [fr *pe* sharp or pointed] : to sharpen with a knife

[2]**wa·pe** \wá-ṗe\ *n* : leaves, *obsol* < *canwape* foliage >

wa·pe·gna·ka \wa-pé-gna-ka\ *n* : a headdress, one wearing full regalia and decked with a feather in his hair - WHL KE

wa·pe·han \wa-ṗé-haŋ\ *v* wa·wa·pehan : to fold — *v 1st pers singl of* pehan : I folded it up

wa·pe·mni \wa-ṗé-mni\ *va* wa·wa·pemni [fr *pemni* warped, twisted, crooked] : to make twisted or crooked by shaving — **wapemni·yan** *part* : shaved twisting

wa·pe·pe \wa-ṗé-ṗe\ *n* : the Russian thistle, Russian tumbleweed, salsola tenuifolia, the goosefoot family; also called *wapepeka* and *wahpe cansakala* - BT #33

wa·pe·pe·ka \wa-pé-pe-ḱa\ *n* : thorns, briers, prickles

wa·pe·sto \wa-ṗé-sto\ *va* wa·wa·pesto [fr *pesto* sharp-pointed] : to shave to a point

wa·pe·to·gto·gya \wá-ṗe-to-gto-gya\ *adv* : marvelously, miraculously

wa·pe·to·gto·ke·ca \wá-ṗe-to-gto-ḱe-ca\ *n* : wonders, miracles, signs, marks

wa·pe·to·gton \wá-ṗe-to-gtoŋ\ *va* wápeto·gwa·ton : to have a sign, to mark anything — **wapetogton·pi** *n* : signs, marks — **wapetogton·yan** *adv* : marked, signed < *He ~ ayaskabton* He sealed that with his signature. > - B.H.6.10, 209.8

wa·pe·to·gya \wá-ṗe-to-gya\ *adv* : marvelously — **wapetogya·kel** *adv* : distinctively, peculiarly < *Tuktogna ~ yapazo* In what way did you show it peculiar You showed in what way it was distinctive, *i.e.* a sure sign. > - B.H.209.12 SLB

wa·pe·to·ke·ca \wá-ṗe-to-ḱe-ca\ *n* : a sign, a mark, a boundary or limit; a miracle

wa·pi \wă'-ṗi\ *adj* wá·ma·pi : fortunate, lucky — **wapika** \wă'-ṗi-ḱa\ *adj* wá·wa·pika : fortunate — **wapi·ke** *n* : one who is fortunate - B.H. 27.29 Bl

wa·pi·ki·ya \wa-ṗí-ḱi-ya\ *v* wapi·wa·kiya : to put up and lay away things well, to rearrange < *Wapikiye-kons taku okuwa* She worked with something pretending to rearrange things. > - D.272

wa·pi·ki·ye·ce šni \wa-ṗí-ḱi-ye-ce šni\ *adv* : having prepared one's self well, provided one's self with everything before starting on a journey *etc.* - *Syn* IŠITUTEĆE ŠNI LC

wa·pi·la \wă-pí'-la\ *vn* wa·wa·pila : to be thankful — **wapila·pi** \wa-ṗí-la-pi\ *n* : gratitude — **wapilapi šni** *n* : ingratitude — **wapila·šni** *vn* wa·wa·pilašni : to be unthankful, ungrateful - Pb.33

wa·pi·šni \wă'-ṗi-šni\ *adj* : unfortunate

[1]**wa·pi·ya** \wa-ṗí-ya\ *v* wapi·wa·ya : to conjure the sick; *fig* to powwow in the Indian way

[2]**wa·pi·ya** \wá-ṗi-ya\ *va* wapi·wa·ya : to make fortunate — *adv* : fortunately - D.260

wa·pi·ya·pi \wa-ṗí-ya-pi\ *n* : conjuring

wa·pi·ye·hci \wa-ṗí-yeȟci\ *adv* : sound and well < ~ *waki ehantanš* if I arrive home sound. > - B.H.22.19

wa·pi·ye·ki·ya \wa-ṗí-ye-ḱi-ya\ *va* : to cause one to apply Indian medicine - Pb.24

wa·po·ble·ca \wa-pó-ble-ca\ *n* [fr *wapaha* headdress + *obleca* cornered, edged] : a headdress with corners

wa·pol \wa-ṗól\ *va contrac of* wapota : to destroy by cutting < ~ *iyeya* to rip or destroy with a knife > — **wapo·lpota** \wa-ṗó-lṗo-ṫa\ *v red* wa·wa·polpota [fr *wapota* destroy by cutting] : to cut to pieces

wa·po·štan \wa-pó-šṫaŋ\ *n* : a hat, bonnet < ~ *gmigma* or *gmigmela* a cap, ~ *gmigmela hinšma* a fur cap > — **wapoštiyut'inze** \wa-ṗó-šti-yù-t'iŋ-ze\ *n* : a hat band

wa·po·ta \wa-ṗó-ṫa\ *va* wa·wa·pota : to destroy by cutting, to cut to pieces as in cutting up a tent, to make holes while cutting as in taking off the hide of an animal

wa·psag \wa-pság\ *va of* wapsaka : to cut or saw in two < ~ *iyeya* to cut off suddenly *e.g.* a string with a knife, *Yamni šunk wápsak iwacu welo* I took three horses to break. > - RC D.92

wa·psa·ka \wa-psá-ḱa\ *va* wa·wa·psaka : to cut off *e.g.* string or cord with a knife, to saw or cut something in two — **wapsa·psaka** \wa-psá-psa-ḱa\ *v red* : to cut off in pieces

wa·psi·ca \wa-psí-ca\ *v* : to make chips fly — **wapsipsica** *v red* : to cut and make the chips fly off - Bl

wa·pšun \wa-pšúŋ\ *va* wa·wa·pšun [fr *psun* fallen off, shed] : to cut round a joint, to cut or saw asunder as when two bones are tightly joined — **wapšun·pšun** *v red* : to disjoint by cutting

wa·pta \wa-pṫá\ *va* wa·wa·pta : to cut off a piece, trim off the edge of anything, to cut out *e.g.* a garment; to cut through < ~ *iyeya* to trim off with a stroke >

wa·ptan·yan \wá-pṫaŋ-yaŋ\ *adj* or *vn* : lucky, to be fortunate < *Canke Juda oyate kin wáptanyanpi ka woyuha olota yuha glipi* And so was not the tribe of Judah lucky? They arrived in their own country with a great variety of properties. - B.H.134.17

wa·pta·pta \wá-pṫá-pṫa\ *v red of* waptá : to cut off or trim much

wa·pta·ya·hu·ji·ji \wa-pṫá-ya-hu-ji-ji\ *n* : the snake root - Note: it and all its forms are medicines — **waptayahla** *n* : a form of snake root — **waptaya ȟota** *n* : snake root

wa·pta·ye \wa-ptá-ye\ *n* : any weed, snake root - WHL

wa·pte·ce·la \wa-pṫé-ce-la\ *va* wa·wa·ptecela [fr *ptecela* short, *i.e.* small] : to cut short or too short

wa·ptu·ga \wa-ptú-ġa\ *va* wa·wa·ptuga : to cut or saw off a piece — **waptuh** *va contrac* : to cut off a piece < ~ *iyeya* to cut off a piece quickly > — **waptu·ptuga** *v red* : to cut off pieces - BD Bl

wa·pu·ske·pa \wá-pu-ske-ṗa\ *v* : to empty — *v 1st pers singl of* puskepa : I emptied it

wa·pu·spa \wá-ṗu-sṗa\ *v* wá·wa·puspa [fr *puspa* to glue, seal] : to glue, seal — *v 1st pers singl of* puspa : I sealed it

wa·pu·sta·ka \wá-ṗu-sṫa-ḱa\ *v* wá·wa·pustaka [fr *pustaka* to squat] : to stoop down — *v 1st pers singl of* pustaka : I squat down - Bl

wa·pu·sya \wa-ṗú-sya\ *v* wa·wa·pusya [fr *pusya* to dry out] : to dry *e.g.* clothes

wa·pu·ta·ka \wá-ṗu-ta-ka\ *v* wa·wa·putaka [fr *aputaka* to lay on hands] : to touch with the hand, press upon

wa·sa·bgle \wa-sá-bgle\ *v* wasa·bwa·gle [fr *sapa* black + *gle* to set up] : to place for a landmark, to set up signs, to set up a stick in the ground (*can pakin* a stick leaning) to point the way one is going, to place something black for a sign, to place "ducks" (little rock stacks) to mark a trail — **wasabgle·pi** *n* : the mark or boundary, a stake *etc.* as is used in playing baseball < *Inahni ~ wanji kagapi na ilazatanhan enajin* Hurry! They made a mark and they are standing back of it. > — **wasabgle·ya** *adv* : in the manner of a sign

wa·sa·bya \wa-sá-bya\ *v* wasa·bwa·ya [fr *sabya* to make black] : to blacken

wa·san·ni·ca·ya \wa-sáŋ-ni-ca-ya\ *va* : to assist one, *fig* to be one's "right-hand" man; *sl* to be for one a "side-kick" < *Tokel išna wasannicayapi kta he iyukcanpi* Why he is alone they understood, namely that he might assist you. > - MS.214

wa·san·yan \wa-sáŋ-yaŋ\ *v* wasan·wa·ya [fr *sanyan* to make white] : to whiten

wa·sas \wa-sás\ *adj contrac* : protected, guarded well from evil and hardship

wa·sa·ski·ya \wa-sá-ški-ya\ *v* wasa·swa·kiya wasa·sma·kiya wasa·sci·ye : to care for tenderly < *Haun, haun, wasaswakiye c'on* Oh! ... Oh! ... I had cared for you so tenderly, as one might wail at a child dead. >

wa·sa·sye·la \wa-sá-sye-la\ *adv* : mildly, gently

wa·sa·s'i·c'i·ya \wa-sá-s'i-c'i-ya\ *v refl* : to take more care of one's self than is right - Bl

wa·sa·za \wa-sá-za\ *adj* wa·ma·saza : well guarded and protected from evil and hardship

wa·sa·ze·ca \wa-sá-ze-ca\ *n* : one who is easily made sick, or one who is getting well

wa·se \wa-sé\ *n* : red earth, vermillion < ~ *kic'unpi kin hena kpakintapi na glapi kte lo* Since they were wearing red, they should wipe it off themselves and go home. >

Wa·se·ca Wa·kpa \Wa-sé-ca Wa-kpà\ *np* : the Vermillion River, a tributary to the Missouri River in eastern South Dakota

wase acetipi *n* : flat pieces of clay burned in fire, pulverized, and then used for painting one's self - *Syn* TANNIŠPAN Bl

wa·se·ki·c'un \wa-sé-ki-c'uŋ\ *v* : to paint red, to put on vermillion

wa·se·yan·ka \wa-sé-yaŋ-ka\ *vn* wase·ma·yanka : to have a spot on one's face — *n* : a pimple

wa·sin·kpe \wa-siŋ-kpe\ *n* : the muskrat - Cf sinkpe *and* wašinkpe

wa·ska·ska \wa-ská-ska\ *n* : white things - Bl

wa·ska·ya \wa-ská-ya\ *v* : to whitewash — *Syn* WA-SANYAN

wa·ski·ca \wa-ški-ca\ *va* wa·wa·skica : to press out with a knife

wa·skil \wa-škíl\ *va contrac of* waskica *and* waskita : to press with a knive

wa·ski·ta \wa-ški-ṫa\ *va* wa·wa·skita : to press upon with a knife

wa·sku \wa-škú\ *va* wa·wa·sku : to pare, peel, shave off *e.g.* the skin of a potato or apple or flesh from the hide < *blo wasku* to peel potatoes > — **wasku·sku** *v red* : to be paring

wa·sku·ye·ca \wa-skú-ye-ca\ *n* : fruit of all kinds

wa·sla·ya \wa-slá-ya\ *v* wasla·wa·ya [fr *slaya* to anoint] : to oil or grease

wa·sle·ca \wa-slé-ca\ *va* wa·wa·sleca : to saw, split, rip up by sawing, to split something with a knife — **waslel** *va contrac* : to split with a knife or saw — **wa·sle·sleca** *va red* wa·wa·slesleca [fr *wasleca* to saw or rip by sawing] : to saw up *e.g.* a log into boards, to cut into small strips — **wasleslel** *va red contrac* : to saw into strips as of lumber

wa·sli \wa-slí\ *va* wa·wa·sli : to press out with a knife or by cutting

wa·sli·pa \wa-slí-ṗa\ *v* wa·wa·slipa [fr *slipa* to lick up] : to lick with the tongue — *v* 1st *pers singl of* slipa : I licked it up < *Watage ota yelo, ~ po; unnihan akahtan yelo* There was much foam, lick it up; shortly it overflowed. > — **wasli·sli** *v red* : to lap something up - BT

wa·slo·han \wá-slo-haŋ\ *v* wá·wa·slohan : to crawl - Bl

wa·slo·lya \wa-sló-lya\ *v* waslo·lwa·ya [fr *slolya* to know] : to know < *Hunh t'api na waslolmayapi* Some died and some knew me. > — **waslolya·pi** *n* : knowledge — **waslolyapi·šni** *n* : ignorance — **waslolye** *n* : one who knows — **waslolye·wacin** *v* waslolyewa-can·mi : to be eager to learn — **waslolye·ya** *v* waslolye·wa·ya : to cause to know

wa·slo·slo·tki·ya *vn* : to be well informed and able to speak and tell of things — **wasloslotkiye·ce** *n* : one who knows everything and is able to inform others - *See* wašlošlotkiya Bl KE

wa·sma·ka \wa-smá-ḱa\ *va* wa·wa·smaka [fr *smaka* to hollow out] : to indent or make a hollow place by cutting with a knife

wa·smin \wa-smíŋ\ *va* wa·wa·smin : to cut or shave off clean, as meat from a bone < *hohu wasminpi* a soup made of the backbones > — **wasmin·smin** *v red* wa-·wa·sminsmin : to pare or trim the meat off clean from the bones — **wasmin·yan** *part* : cutting off very smoothly - P

wa·sna \wa-sná\ *n* **a** : lard, grease, tallow **b** : a mixture of pounded beef and marrow and kept in a powdered state < *wagmeza* ~ a mixture of corn and marrow, *canpa* ~ a mixture of cherries and marrow > - R

wa·sna·sna·he·ca \wa-sná-sna-he-ca\ *n* : the kingbird
~ *ikpíska* the white breasted kingbird
~ *ikpízi* the yellow-breasted kingbird
- Note: *"Hokšicala, hokšicala, hokšicala" eyapi* They say: "Baby, baby, baby." ~ *cincala s'e ipahlala unyankapelo* We sit together in a row formation like kingbird chicks

wa·sna·ta·sa·ka \wa-sná-ṫa-sa-ka\ *n* : tallow, hardened grease

wa·so \wa-só\ *v* wa·wa·so : to cut a strip or string as from a hide < *Na taha kpanyanpi kin ohomni waso na on tušu kin hena pahta na pawosla eglepi* And when deer hide is tanned he cuts around strips, and with them he ties together tent poles, and they are set erect. >

wa·son \wa-sóŋ\ *v* wa·wa·son [fr *son* to braid] : to braid in strings, as corn or hair — *v* 1st *pers singl of* son : I braided his

wa·so·so \wa-só-so\ *v red of* waso wa·wa·soso : to cut into strips or strings

wa·span·la \wa-spáŋ-la\ *n* : melting snow, slush < ~ *ca wakašloyakel maunipi yelo* When it was slushy we traveled. > — *adv* : slushy - Bl R

wa·spa·ye·i·c'i·ya \wá-spa-ye-i-c'i-ya\ *v refl* : to perspire, make one's self wet < *Wáspaye·mi·c'iyelo* I perspired, as they say after eating plenty. > - Bl

wa·stan·mi \wa-stáŋ-mi\ *interj archaic* : Welcome! - *Syn* AKO, CANNAKO

wa·stu·ste·ya \wa-stú-ste-ya\ *v* wastuste·wa·ya : to weary one - Cf waštušteya

wa·su \wa-sú\ *n* : hail — **wasu·hinhan** *v* : to hail

wa·su·hu·la \wa-sú-hu-la\ *n* : a necklace in Iroquois - R

wa·su·ki·ya \wa-sú-ḱi-ya\ *va* wasu·wa·kiya **a** : to decree or make a decree **b** : to judge, condemn **c** : to hold sacred < *Na akicita kin hena oyate wasuwicakiyapi na omani šni wasuyapi.* And the people judged these

---

\a\ f<u>a</u>ther \e\ th<u>ey</u> \i\ mach<u>i</u>ne \o\ sm<u>o</u>ke \u\ l<u>u</u>nar \an, aŋ\ bl<u>an</u>c Fr. \in, iŋ\ <u>in</u>k \on, oŋ, un, uŋ\ s<u>oo</u>n, <u>con</u>fier Fr. \c\ <u>ch</u>air \ǧ\ ma<u>ch</u>en Ger. \j\ fu<u>s</u>ion \clusters: bl, gn, kp, hšl, etc...\ <u>b</u>ᵉlo ... said with a slight vowel
See more in the Introduction, Guide to Pronunciation

warriors and made a decision not to travel. *Ate hecel wasuunkiyapelo* So Father judged us. >

wa·su·la \wa-sú-la\ *n contrac of* wasuhula : a necklace < ~ *cuwignaka* a woman's dress with a neckpiece, ~ *wabluška* an insect necklace >

wa·su·sna·ka \wa-sú-sna-ka\ *n* : the narrow side of a feather, or the narrow barbs on one side of the shaft or quill that are used on the notch end of arrows < ~ *hena iyagya yo, hecena kin oh'anko ktelo* Fit these barbs on the notch end of the arrow, the result being it will be fast. > - Bl

wa·su·ton \wa-sú-ṫoŋ\ *v* [fr *suton* to be ripened] : to get ripe, ripen as does grain or fruit — **wasuton·pi** \wa-sú-toŋ-pi\ *n* : the harvest — **Wasuton Wi** *np* : the month of August, *i.e.* the Harvest Moon — **wasuton·yan** *v* : to bring forth fruit - B.H.240.12

wa·su·ya \wa-sú-ya\ *v* wasu·wa·ya **a** : to make a law **b** : to judge or condemn

wa·s'in \wá-s'iŋ\ *v* : to look at greedily - Bl KE

wa·s'o·ju·ha \wa-s'ó-ju-ha\ *n* : a bag in which to keep the *wasé* vermillion paint

wa·ša·gki·ci·ya \wa-šá-gki-ci-ya\ *va* : to render weak for one - B.H.75.6

wa·ša·gla \wa-šá-gla\ *v* waša·gwa·la waša·gci·la waša·gmaya·la : to consider one not very intelligent - Bl

wa·ša·gya \wa-šá-gya\ *va* waša·gwa·ya : to beat one easily - Cf wašakala *and* waš'aka

wa·ša·gye·la \wa-šá-gye-la\ *adv* : easily, cheaply < *Šunkawakan ~ wak'u* I gave a horse cheaply, *i.e.* for a little money. ~ *oieyetonpi kin mitaakicita ob wamayalakapi kte lo* You will be begging me along with my warriors when they utter words easily. > - B ST

wa·ša·ka·la \wa-šá-ka-la\ *adj* : cheap, easy < *Šunka wašakalapi* A horse is easily got, *i.e.* easy to get. > — **wašaka·yela** *adv* : easily, cheaply — **waša·kšakala** \wa-šá-kša-ka-la\ *adj red* : cheap, easy

wa·ša·šte *or* **šašte** \wa-šá-šte\ *n* : the little finger < ~ *wapáha* Little Finger's headdress > - KE

wa·še \wa-šé\ *n* : a woman's female friend corresponding to *kóla*; a woman's sister-in-law, thus a word used if persons are not on very good terms - Note: *mašé* a brother-in-law - Sb

wa·še·ca \wa-šé-ca\ *adj* wa·ma·šeca : rich, *esp* in provisions — **wašeca·ya** *adv* : richly *esp* in provisions < *Lila talo ota yuhapi na ~ tipi* They live well off and have very much fresh meat. > - D.116

wa·še·ki·ci·ya \wa-šé-ki-ci-ya\ *v* : to have each other for special friends - Note: a word used only by women

wa·še·pa \wa-šé-ṗa\ *adj* : unclean - BT

wa·še·ya \wa-šé-ya\ *v* waše·wa·ya : to have for a friend - Note: the word is used of women only

wa·ši \wa-ší\ *va* wa·wa·ši : to employ < *Yun! Tokinahanš taku otaka ca wamašipi kte hcin* Oh! Maybe they will just hire me when there is something *not* much to do. *Le winyan kin tuktel wašipi ca hel wokajuju k'upi* This woman was given a reprieve there where she was hired. *Wamašipi šni yelo* I am not hired, as once was said by a medicine man. > - MS.482

wa·šib \wa-šíb\ *va contrac of* wašipa : to prune < ~ *iyeya* to trim back > — **waši·bšipa** *v red* : to cut off

wa·ši·ca \wa-ší-ca\ *va* wa·wa·šica [fr *šica* bad or evil] : to spoil by cutting

wa·ši·ca·ho·wa·ya \wa-ší-ca-ho-wa-ya\ *va* wa·wa·šicahowaya [fr *šicahowaya* to cry out] : to cause to cry out by cutting, to cry out badly, moan, groan

wa·ši·ce·la·ka \wa-ší-ce-la-ka\ *v* wašice·wa·laka [fr *šícelaka* think bad, to hate] : to dislike — *n* : one who dislikes

wa·ši·cun \wa-ší-cuŋ\ *n* **1** : the white man, as used *esp* disparagingly **2** : any person or thing that is *wakan* wrapped in mystery, as *tunkan ~* or *yuwipi ~* a power stone used in the sweatlodge or *yuwipi* ritual - Note: A person or thing may be characterized by special powers resident in the universe and be looked upon as a container or carrier of *ton*, that by which the person or thing is *wakan*. The *wašicun* may also be any object into which has been put *ton* by a person such as a *wicaša wakan* holy man for his ceremonies and carried about by him in a bag, but not the *wašicunpi* medicine bag. The white man seemed to be *wakan*, so the Dakotas called this new-comer among them *wašicun*, one coming from across the *mni ~* ocean, while later others met the *pusyata wašicun* white man in the central part of the United States. Buechel speculated that the word may be *wa* one + *šica* bad or short + *un* wearing, *i.e.* one wearing inappropriate clothes (to the Indian eye), as is said: *sapun* wears black, the Catholic priest; *skaun* wears white or the Episcopalean priest - WJR.153

wa·ši·cun cin·ca \wa-ší-cuŋ ciŋ-cà\ *n* : a mixed blood person — **wašicun hokšila** *n* : a white man's boy — **wašicun pteòle** *n* : the American cowboy — **wašicun wakàn** *n* : the white man's doctor — **wašicun wicincala** *n* : a white man's girl - BBB

wa·ši·cu·ta \wa-ší-cu-ta\ *adv phr* : at or to a white man's town < ~ *wai na wašicun šakowin el mahipelo* I went to a white man's town and seven white men came to me. *Otonwaheta yin kte* He will go to Washington D. C. >

wa·ši·gla \wa-ší-gla\ *v* waši·wa·gla : to mourn for the dead, painting one's self or wearing black — *n* : mourning habiliments < *Micinca on wašiwagla* I mourned for my child> - B.H.71.1

wa·ši·gla·gla \wa-ší-gla-gla\ *v red of* wašigla : to get angry often — **wašiglaka** *or* **wašiglake** *n* : one who get angry at everything

wa·ši·gla·ya \wa-ší-gla-ya\ *adv* : mourning

wa·ši-htin \wa-ší-ḣtiŋ\ *va* wa·wa·šihtin [fr *šihtin* done poorly] : to enfeeble by cutting, to do poorly with saw or knife

wa·ši·kši·ca \wa-ší-kši-ca\ *v red of* wašica : to spoil by cutting

wa·ši·lh'an \wa-ší-lḣ'aŋ\ *v* waši·lwa·h'an [fr *šilh'an* to behave badly] : to act wickedly - R Bl

wa·ši·lki·gla \wa-ší-lki-gla\ *v* : to be angry

wa·ši-lki·gla·ya \wa-ší-lki-gla-ya\ *va* [fr *šilkiglaya* make one angry] : to distress or make one angry — *n* : one who makes another angry

wa·ši·lkte \wa-ší-lkte\ *n* : pulmonary consumption, a lingering disease, failing health — *vn* : to be covered with scrophula - R Bl

wa·šin \wa-šíŋ\ *n* : fat not dried out, fat meat, pork — **wašin cosyàpi** *n* : smoked ham or bacon, plain bacon — **wašin šloyàpi** *n* : fried bacon

wa·šin·kce·ka \wa-šíŋ-kce-ka\ *n* [fr *ikceka* common] : tallow

wa·šin·kpe *or* **sinkpe** \wa-šíŋ-kpe\ *n* : the muskrat - Note: the word is *wiciyela* Yankton Dakota for muskrat - KE

wa·šin·kpe·kpe·ka \wa-šíŋ-kpe-kpe-ka\ *n* : one who acts in a way like a busy muskrat < *Óh'an ~ tak tokon welo* He was long busy as a muskrat having lost something. > — **wašinkpekpe·yakel** *adv* : in the manner of a muskrat < *Wicaša wan ~ waículahcaka* The man like a muskrat unceremoniously took things, *i.e.* stole. > – Bl

wa·šin·lo \wa-šíŋ-lo\ *n* : a fresh and juicy piece of fat or fat meat – Bl

Wa·šin Wa·kpa \Wa-šíŋ Wa-kpà\ *np* : the south fork of the Platte River in the States of Colorado and Nebraska

wa·ši·pa \wa-ší-ṗa\ *va* wa·wa·šipa : to prune, cut off *e.g.* a branch from a tree, to cut off *e.g.* a pin with a knife

waš i·ye·ya \waš i-yé-ya\ *va* : to find one to be weaker than one's self – B.H.25.1

wa·ši·yu·ta \wa-ší-yu-ta\ *adv phr* [fr *wašicuta* at or to a white man's town] : at or to a place where white men live < ~ *mni kte* I shall go to the white man's home. ~ *wai* I went to the white man's town. > – Note: this was the first name for an Agency, and perhaps the first attempt to name Washington D.C.

wa·škan·škan·yan \wa-škáŋ-škaŋ-yaŋ\ *v* waškanškan·wa·ya [fr *škan* to move] : to cause to move — *n* : one who causes to move or live

wa·ške \wá-ške\ *v* : to present little demand for things, to offer what is not on demand < *Wáyaškehelo* You were offering what is not needed, as is said when there is much on hand but little brought, so the remark is made when in cutting what tobacco I brought I dropped some. > – Bl

wa·ški·ca \wa-škí-ca\ *va* wa·wa·škica : to squeeze by cutting, to press out *e.g.* water from a cloth with a knife, to scrape out

wa·škil \wa-škíl\ *v contrac of* waškica *and* waškita : to press or to cut

wa·ški·ški·ca \wa-škí-ški-ca\ *v red of* waškica : to press out or scrape out

wa·ški·ški·ta \wa-škí-ški-ṫa\ *v red* wa·wa·škiškita [fr *waškita* to gash or cut across] : to cut much, to gash, to make an edge toothed, as a feather – *Syn* WALELEPA R Bl

wa·ški·ta \wa-škí-ṫa\ *v* wa·wa·škita : to cut across, to gash, to make notches

wa·šku \wa-škú\ *va* wa·wa·šku : to shell, cut off *e.g.* corn from the cob — **wašku·šku** *v red* : to strip off by cutting

wa·šla \wa-šlá\ *va* wa·wa·šla [fr *šla* bare, bald] : to make bare by cutting with a knife, to shave or scrape off *e.g.* hair from a hide — **wašla·šla** *v red* : to shave clean

wa·šlog \wa-šlóg\ *va contrac of* wašloka : to cut out a part < ~ *iyeya* to cut out a piece >

wa·šlo·ka \wa-šló-ka\ *va* wa·wa·šloka [fr *šloka* to come out or off] : to cut a hole in, cut out a piece or part *e.g.* an eye, to cut loose something that is fast in *etc.* — **wa-šlo·šloka** *v red* : to cut out, or cut loose

wa·šlo·šlo·tki·ya \wa-šló-šlo-tki-ya\ *v* : to have a good memory — **wašlošlotkiye·ce** *v* : One with a good memory – Cf wasloslotkiya *and* wasloslotkiyece KE

wa·šlo·ya \wa-šló-ya\ *v* wašlo·wa·ya : to melt, smelt *e.g.* metal

wa·šni·ja \wa-šní-ja\ *adj* [fr *šnija* dried up] : withered — **wašni·šya** *v* wašni·šwa·ya : to cause to wither — *n* : one who causes to wither

wa·šon *or* **wašun** \wa-šóŋ\ *n* : a den or hole

wa·šo·še \wa-šó-še\ *n archaic* : a daring warrior

wa·šo·šo s'e *or* **šwošwoke s'e** *or* **kayoyo s'e** \wa-šó'-šo s'e\ *adv* : very fleshy, as to the whole or part

wa·špa \wa-šṗa\ *va* wa·wa·špa [fr *špa* to break off, divide] : to scalp, to cut off a piece, to cut up < ~ *iyeya* to scalp in one stroke, ~ *yusota* to make an end of one by scalping, ~ *kte* to kill and scalp > – MS.100, 102

wa·špan·ka \wa-špáŋ-k̇a\ *n* : cooked food < *Na hehanl taku ~ econpi kinhan hena otoiyohi etanhan icupi* And then something was taken from each of them when the cooked food was done. ~ *ognake* a case for dried meat, a grub box, ~ *ognake k'on tanyan iyojuwakiyelo* That grub box of mine I made chuck-full, *i.e.* my stomach. *Wašpank'ognake kin matasake* My cooked food grub box is cold, *i.e.* my stomach. > – B.H.31.19 Bl

wa·špan·ki·ya \wa-špáŋ-ki-ya\ *v* : to cook for one – B.H.31.11 KE

wa·špan·šni \wa-špáŋ-šni\ *adj* : raw, not cooked

wa·špan·yan \wa-špáŋ-yaŋ\ *v* wašpan·wa·ya [fr *španyan* to cook *e.g.* food] : to cook, as food, to make a feast

wa·špa·špa \wa-šṗá-šṗa\ *v red* wa·wa·špašpa [fr *wašpa* to cut up] : to cut into many pieces *e.g.* meat < *Canke tancan kin ~ ayapi* And so they began to cut up the carcass. > – MS.101

wa·špi \wa-šṗí\ *va* wa·wa·špi : to cut off *e.g.* fruit from a tree — **wašpi·špi** *v red* : to be cutting off

wa·špu \wa-šṗú\ *va* wa·wa·špu : to cut up, cut into pieces, to rip *e.g.* a seam, to rip up, cut as in ripping, to cut off a piece — **wašpu·špu** \wa-šṗú-šṗu\ *v red* wa·wa·špušpu : to cut up into small pieces

wa·šte \wa-šté\ *adj* ma·wašte : good, pretty

wa·šte·ca *or* **wašteca·ka** \wa-šté-ca\ \wa-šté-ca-k̇a\ *adj* : good, well-disposed

wa·šte·hca \wa-šté-ȟca\ *adj* : very good

wa·šte·i·c'i·la \wa-šté-i-c'i-la\ *v refl* wašte·mi·c'ila [fr *waštela* to esteem good] : to love one's self, to be selfish, to be proud

wa·šte·ka \wa-šté-k̇a\ *adj* : good-hearted, good, little good, doubtfully good, sort of good < *Waštekelo* He is a fine (ironically) fellow. > – Note: the word is like to *wakanka* doubtfully holy or mysterious, where "ka" is a *suff* – D.194 note 1

wa·šte·ki·ci·la·pi \wa-šté-ki-ci-la-pi\ *v recip* : loving each other

wa·šte·ki·la *or* **waštekila·ka** \wa-šté-ki-la\ *v poss* wašte·wa·kila wašte·wa·kilaka [fr *waštela* to esteem good] : to love one's own

wa·šte·la \wa-šté-la\ *va* wašte·wa·la : to esteem good, to love < *wašteic'ila* to love one's self > — **waštela·ka** \wa-šté-la-k̇a\ *va* wašte·wa·laka : to love — **waštelakapi** *n* **a** : love **b** : one who is loved

wa·šte·mna \wa-šté-mna\ *adj* [fr *omna* to smell something] : sweet-smelling, odoriferous — **waštemna·ya** *va* waštemna·wa·ya : to perfume, to embalm

wa·šte·šte \wa-šté-šte\ *adj red of* wašte : many good — **waštešte·ya** *adv red* : to make good — **wašte·ya** *va* wašte·wa·ya : to make good < *Hecel wanna on wašteiciyapi* So now for good reason they perfected themselves. > — *adv* : well, in a good manner < *Ooyuspe ~ econpi* The bow handle was well done. > — **wašteyakel** \wa-šté-ya-k̇el\ *adv* : in a good manner – MS.487

wa·štu·lya \wa-štu-lya\ *v* wašu·lwa·ya [fr *štulya* thaw out] : to thaw, to cause to thaw things that are frozen

wa·štun·ka·la \wa-štúŋ-ka-la\ *n* : corn on ears boiled and dried, a favorite Indian provision

wa·štu·šte·ya \wa-štú-šte-ya\ *v* waštušte·wa·ya [fr *štušteya* to chase and render meat flavorless] : to weary

wa·šun \wa-šúŋ\ *n* : the den or hole of small animals,

\a\ father \e\ they \i\ machine \o\ smoke \u\ lunar \an, aŋ\ blanc Fr. \in, iŋ\ ink \on, oŋ, un, uŋ\ soon, confier Fr. \c\ chair \ǧ\ machen Ger. \j\ fusion \clusters: bl, gn, kp, hšl, etc...\ b^elo ... said with a slight vowel
See more in the Introduction, Guide to Pronunciation

of snakes and bugs, any hole in the ground - BD

wa·šun·ka·jun \wa-šúŋ-ka-juŋ\ *v* : to moult, shed feathers - *Syn* WAŠUNKAŠLOKA Bl

wa·šun·ka·šlo·ka \wa-šúŋ-ka-šlo-ka\ *v* : to moult, shed feathers - Bl

wa·šu·ta \wa-šú-ta\ *v* : to shoot and miss < *Wašutešni* Never Misses a Shot, a family name>

wa·š'ag \wa-š'áġ\ *adj contrac of* waš'aka : strong < ~ *hingla* to become strong > — **waš'a·gic'iya** *vn* : to strengthen one's self

wa·š'a·ka \wa-š'á-k̇a\ *adj* wa·ma·š'aka : strong

[1]**wa·ta** \wá-ṫa\ *n* : a boat

[2]**wa·ta** \wá-ṫa\ *v* wa·wá·ta wa·yá·ta wa·ún·ta·pi [fr *yúta* to eat] : to eat — *v* 1st *pers singl of* yúta < *Talo watin kte lo* I shall eat fresh meat. >

wa·ta·ge \wa-tá-ġe\ *n* : froth, foam, as in a boiling kettle < ~ *ota yelo, waslipa po; únnihan akahtan yelo* There is much foam, lick it! Shortly it boiled over. > - BT

wa·ta·kpe \wa-ṫá-k̇pe\ *v* wata·wa·kpe [fr *takpe* to come upon, attack] : to attack or to attempt to seize

wa·ta·ku·ni·šni \wa-ṫá-k̇u-ni-šni\ *va* wa·wa·takunišni [fr *takunišni* come to nothing] : to destroy by cutting, to cut to pieces

wa·ta·ku·ya·pi \wa-ṫá-ku-ya-pi\ *n* : relatives - B.H. 171.12

wa·ta·ma·he·lhe·ca \wa-tá-ma-he-lhe-ca\ *adj* : lean - Bl

wa·tan \wa-ṫáŋ\ *n* : bait, as used in fishing < ~ *ikoyagya* to fasten on a bait, *i.e.* bait a hook, *Hoye, hoapeša wan mini céteta ape kahihiya nunke, ~ šašala yeciciye* Very well, you red-fin lying at the bottom of the water wafting along your fins, I extend to you a nice little red bait. >

wa·tan·can \wa-táŋ-caŋ\ *n* : the appearance of material things < ~ *iwanyankapi šni yo* Do not keep your eyes on the appearance of material things, *i.e.* judge not. ~ *iwanyanke* He watched after material things. Thus *waoholašni* he did not respect her. > - B.H.194.13

wa·tan'·in·šni \wa-táŋ-iŋ-šni\ *adj* : lost

[1]**wa·tan·ka** \wa-táŋ-ka\ *va* wa·wa·tanka [fr *tanka* big] : to cut large

[2]**wa·tan·ka** \wa-táŋ-ka\ *n* : one who is great or rich — **watanka·ic'ila** *v refl* : to esteem one's self highly, to be proud — **watankaic'ila·pi** *n* : pride, haughtiness — **watanka·la** *va* watanka·wa·la : to esteem great

wa·tan·kanl \wa-ṫáŋ-kaŋl\ *adv* : trying to be wise or of some reputation < ~ *oye un welo* It is a fresh track, *i.e.* after snowing. ~ *unhpayapi kte lo* We shall spend the night here, *i.e.* will scrape the snow away and camp here for the night. > - Bl

wa·tan·ki·c'i·la \wa-ṫáŋ-ki-c'i-la\ *v* : to think one's self wise, or in some way great - *Syn* WAH'ANIC'ILA LHB WHL

wa·tan·ni \wa-ṫáŋ-ni\ *n* : old things < *Hena* ~ Those are old things. >

wa·tan·ton·šni \wá-taŋ-toŋ-šni\ *v* wá·ma·tantonšni : to be poor, destitute in consequence of sickness *etc.*; to have lost everything — **watantonšni·yan** *adv* : having lost everything, become poor - Bl

wa·tan·ya \wa-táŋ-ya\ *va* watan·wa·ya : to us a thing for bait

wa·ta·pa \wa-tá-pa\ *v* wata·wa·pa [fr *tapá* follow after] : to pursue

wa·ta·pe·ta \wá-ta-ṗe-ṫa\ *n* : a steamboat

wa·ta·ta·bki·ya \wa-tá-ta-bki-ya\ *v* watata·bwa·kiya : to hang up, to dry - *Syn* WAKÁPUSKIYA Bl

wa·ta·wa·t'e·lya \wá-ta-wa-t'e-lya\ *v* wátawat'e·lwa·ya [fr *tawat'elya* to be ready to endure willingly] : to be willing to do or suffer

wa·te \wá-ṫe\ *v absol* wá·wa·te wá·un·ta·pi [fr *yúta* to eat] : to eat something - Note: *wóta* is the 1st *pers singl of* wáte *and* yúta

wa·teb \wa-ṫéb\ *v contrac of* watépa : to cut shorter < ~ *iyeya* to cut short >

wa·te·bki·ci·ci·ya \wa-ṫé-bki-ci-ci-ya\ *v* wate·bwe·ciciya [fr *tebya* devour] : to eat up for one — **watebki·ya** *v poss* wate·bwa·kiya [fr *watebya* eat up all] : to eat up one's own, to eat up for one

wa·te·bya \wa-ṫá-bya\ *v* wate·bwa·ya [fr *tebya* eat all up] : to eat all up, to devour, as does a wolf

[1]**wa·te·ca** \wa-ṫé-ca\ *n* : a part of one's food, *esp* which one takes home from a feast

[2]**wa·te·ca** \wá-ṫe-ca\ *n* : snow lately fallen

wa·te·ḣi·ka \wa-ṫé-ḣi-k̇a\ *adj* : difficult, hard, as a man in his dealings; dear, as goods *etc.* - R Bl

wa·te·ḣi·la \wa-ṫé-ḣi-la\ *v* wate·wa·ḣila [fr *teḣila* to value highly, to love] : to be stingy, withhold what one has, not to give away — *n* : a miser — **watehila·pi** *n* : parsimony

wa·te·pa \wa-ṫé-ṗa\ *va* wa·wa·tepa : to shorten by cutting off at the end with a knife, to cut short — *v* [fr *tepa* worn off] : to wear off short, be worn out

wa·te·šla·gki·ca·ton \wa-ṫé-šla-gki-ca-toŋ\ *va* : to crown one — **watešlagkiton** *v* watešla·gwe·ton [fr *tešlagkiton* put on or wear *e.g.* a crown of fillet on the head] : to wear a fillet or garland around the head — **watešlagkiya** *v* : to make wear a crown — **watešla·gton** *v* watešla·gwa·ton [fr *tešlagton* put on, wear a crown or fillet] : to have or wear a garland or civic crown - Pb.38

wa·te·šla·ke \wa-ṫé-šla-k̇e\ *n* : a fillet, wreath, a civic crown, anything wrapped around the head

wa·te·zi \wa-ṫé-zi\ *n* : the stomach, belly < *Ituhu ~ kaca yankin na* His forehead is like his belly, take it and sit, as they say when a man has a prominent, balding forehead. > - Bl

wa·tka \wa-tká\ *v* wa·wa·tka [fr *tka* to scrape hair on a hide] : to scrape, as one does to hides

wa·to \wa-ṫó\ *n* : grass, green grass; weeds

wa·tob \wa-ṫób\ *v contrac of* watopa : to paddle a canoe < ~ *bla* I am going paddling a canoe. >

wa·to·gcin \wa-tó-gciŋ\ *v* wato·gwa·cin : to desire another kind of food - BT

wa·to·gla \wa-tó-gla\ *adj* wa·ma·togla [fr *watoka* what grows wild as weeds and grasses] : wild, hostile, untrained, skittish

wa·to·gya \wa-tó-gya\ *va* wato·gwa·ya : to spoil, ruin; to take vengeance, retaliate, to kill - Note: *tóka* an enemy or stranger — **watogya·pi** *n* : **reprisal**

wa·to·han·hanl *or* **watohanl** \wa-tó-haŋ-haŋl\ *adv red* [fr *watohanl* sometime] : sometime < ~ *šna oh'an waštepi šni* Some-time they are not good at continually keeping busy. *watohanl šna* time and again > - B.H. 128.2, 81.1

wa·to·han·tu·ka wan \wa·ṫó-haŋ-tu-ka waŋ\ *adv* : rather at a certain time, or sometime rather - B.H.12.6

Wa·to·ḣta·ta \Wa-ṫó-ḣta-ṫa\ *np* : the Otoe tribe that once lived near the Missouri River in the state of Nebraska about 45 miles south of the city of Omaha - R Bl

wa·to·i·huni \wa-ṫó-i-hu-ni\ *n* : a boat landing place

wa·to·ka \wa-tó-ka\ *n* : vegetation - B.H.51.19

wa·to·kan·kan \wa-tó-kaŋ-kaŋ\ *adv* : evasively < ~ *woglaka* to speak avoiding a topic, to dodge, to talk of something else when others talk to us > - Bl

wa·to·ka·pa \wa-tó-k̇a-pa\ *n* wato·ma·kapa [fr *tokapa* the first, eldest] : the first born, the birthright - R Bl

wa·to·ke·ca \wa-ṫó-ke-ca\ *n* [fr *tókeca* different] : a different thing, a contrast, *e.g.* a kind of food other than what one has been accustomed to such as fruits, vegetables < *Le maka akanl ~ nakun ca tanyan yaunip kta* There is a difference on this land and you will live well as too. > - P

wa·to·ke·lke·tu·ya \wa-ṫó-k̇e-lk̇e-ṫu-ya\ *adv* : in certain amounts - B.H.79.6

wa·to·ke·tu·ka \wa-ṫó-k̇e-ṫu-ka\ *adv* : being pretty good-sized - B.H.171.2

wa·to·ki·c'on \wa-tó-ki-c'oŋ\ *v absol* [fr *tokic'on* to take revenge on] : to take vengeance — *n* : an avenger — **watokic'on·pi** *n* : the reprisal made, retaliation - P

wa·to·ki·kšu \wa-ṫó-ki-kšu\ *v* : to haul one's own things

wa·to·ki·ya \wa-ṫó-k̇i-ya\ *adv interrog* : what is his concern? < *Iwatokiya* it is a matter of concern for him. > - BT LHB WHL

wa·to·ki·yo·pe·ya \wa-tó-k̇i-yo-pe-ya\ *v* [fr *tokiyopeya* to sell, exchange] : to trade - B.H.179.11

wa·to·kšu \wa-tó-kšu\ *v* wato·wa·kšu wato·un·kšu·pi [fr *tokšu* to transport] : to carry, transport — **watokšu·pi** *n* : transportation

wa·ton·ka *or* **watanka** \wa-tóŋ-k̇a\ *n* : one who is rich

wa·ton·šni \wa-tóŋ-šni\ *v* wa·wa·tonšni : to be poor, to own nothing - WE

wa·to·pa \wa-ṫó-pa\ *v* wato·wa·pa : to paddle a canoe

Wa·to·pa·hla·te *or* **Watopala** \Wa-ṫó-pa-ḣla-ṫe\ *np* : the Nez Perce tribe of northern Indians who live on the other side of the *Ḣeska* Rocky Mountains from the high plains of the midwest United States - Bl

wa·to·pa·pi \wa-ṫó-pa-ṗi\ *n* : rowing, paddling — **watope·kiya** \wa-ṫó-ṗe-k̇i-ya\ *va* watope·wa·kiya : to make paddle or row — **watope·ya** *or* **watopeya·kel** *adv* [fr *wata* boat + *opeya* along with] : by boat < *~ gle wicaši* He told them to go by boat. *~ iyaya* He went by boat. > - B.H.208.20, 294.8, 303.10

wa·to·to·ka \wa-tó-to-k̇a\ *n red of* watoka : vegetation < *Taku ~ ojupi kin heca ecela yutapi* What is planted vegetation only is eaten. > — **watoto·ya** *adv* : grass-like, green - B.H.136.14

wa·to·ya \wa-tó-ya\ *adv* : greenly

wa·tu·cu·hu \wa-ṫú-cu-hu\ *n* [fr *tucuhu* ribs] : ribs

wa·tu·ka \wa-ṫú-k̇a\ *adj* wa·ma·tuka : faint, weary, exhausted — *va* wa·wa·tuka : to cut off *e.g.* hair or fur, to destroy *e.g.* furs by cutting — **watuka·ya** \wa-ṫú-ka-ya\ *v* : to make tired, to weary

wa·tu·kte \wa-ṫú-kte\ *pron of* tukte : which, whichever < *Wanna watukte he slolye* Now he knows which. > - BT

wa·tu·še·kše·ca \wa-ṫú-še-kše-ca\ *n* : dust, dirt, sweepings, *e.g.* manure

wa·tu·še·tka \wa-ṫú-še-tka\ *n* : withered old weeds - OS

wa·tu·tka \wa-ṫú-ṫka\ *va* wa·wa·tutka [fr *tutka* trinkets] : to cut up into crumbs, into bits and scraps, to whittle — *n* : little things, as scraps, shavings, crumbs and bits *etc.* — **watutka·la** *n* : very small things — **watutka·tka** *n red* : trifles, trinkets - R

wa·t'a \wa-t'á\ *va* wa·wa·t'a [fr *t'a* to die] : to kill with a knife

wa·t'un·gya \wa-t'úŋ-gya\ *v* [fr *t'ungya* to suspect] : to suspect, have an indistinct knowledge of

wa·un \wa-úŋ\ *v* wa·wa·un [fr *un* to be] : to be well-off — *v 1st pers singl of* un : I am

wa·un·ca *or* **waunca·la** \wa-úŋ-ca\ *v* waun·wa·ca [fr *únca* to mock] : to mock, to imitate one — *n* : one who mocks, makes fun of one

wa·un·jin·ca \wa-úŋ-jiŋ-ca\ *n* : a horse whose tail is cut short - *Syn* WAKÓ Bl

wa·un·ka \wa-úŋ-ka\ *va* : to fell by sawing *e.g.* a tree - Bl

wa·un·ke·i·c'i·la *or* **waunkaic'ila** \wa-úŋ-k̇e-i-c'i-la\ *v refl* : to be proud, to think one as all "it" - B.H.3.5, 151.2, 101.2, 232.13 D.49

wa·un·ke·šni \wa-úŋ-k̇e-šni\ *v* : not to stay or be present, to lack right consideration or respect for others, to display a poor way of living < *~ tka heye lo* He did not stay around but he says that, *i.e.* he is lying. > - BE

wa·un·ki·c'i·la *or* **waunkeic'ila** \wa-úŋ-k̇i-c'i-la\ *v* : to think much of one's self, to be proud

wa·un·un·ka \wa-úŋ-uŋ-k̇a\ *n* : a tramp, vagabond, one who wanders about

wa·un·yan \wa-úŋ-yaŋ\ *va* waun·wa·ya *or* wa·wa·un·ya : to offer sacrifice, as in the form of money *etc.*, to lose < *Taku waunyepica* He is able sacrifice something. > - Cf wakiunyan — **waunyan·pi** \wa-úŋ-yaŋ-ṗi\ *n* : sacrifices, things offered < *Oyate kin tipi iyohila waunyanpi au po* Each home of the tribe bring an offering. *Can wan paslatapi na el ~ kin eglepi* They set up a post and on it they placed their offering. *Hel ~ econpi* There the offering is made. > - Note: the word seems to imply the offering of something promised before, something hung up and not edible *Syn* WAYUHTATAPI B.H. 5.6, 61.4, 108.23 MS.351

wa·un·yan·pi i·tan·can \wa-úŋ-yaŋ-ṗi i-ṫàŋ-caŋ\ *n* : a high priest - B.H.146.6

wa·un·ye \wa-úŋ-ye\ *n* : the act of offering — **waunye itancan** \wa-úŋ-ye i-ṫàŋ-caŋ\ *n* : a priest of the Jewish tradition < *~ tanka* a high priest > - B.H.8.1, 97.11, 259.19, 262.16

wa·un·ye·ki·ya \wa-úŋ-ye-ki-ya\ *v* : to make offerings to < *Waunyewicakiciciyapi* Offerings were made to him for them. > — **waunye·ya** *v* : to offer sacrifices < *~ itancan* a priest > - B.H.11.20, 39.9, 49.23, 156.6, 60.6, 61.1, 260.26

wa·u·ta \wa-ú-ta\ *v* : to give to eat < *Wautapi* They give away much food. *Waumatapi* They give me much to eat. > - Bl

wa·wa·bla \wa-wá-bla\ *v* wawa·wa·bla [fr *wabla* to slice] : to slice, cut in slices

wa·wa·bla·bla·za \wa-wá-bla-bla-za\ *v red of* wawablaza : to rip — **wawabla·za** *v* wawa·wa·blaza [fr *wablaza* rip open lengthwise] : to rip open or rip up

wa·wa·ble·ca \wa-wá-ble-ca\ *v* wawa·wa·bleca [fr *wableca* to shatter with a knife] : to cut up or break to pieces with a knife

wa·wa·can·li·li·ke \wa-wá-caŋ-li-li-k̇e\ *n* : one who is always smoking - Bl

wa·wa·ga·pa \wa-wá-ġa-ṗa\ *v* wawa·wa·gapa [fr *wagapa* to skin an animal] : to skin animals, to be in the habit of taking off skins

wa·wa·gla \wa-wá-gla\ *v* wawa·wa·gla [fr *wagla* to shave off] : to make uncoil by cutting

wa·wa·gna \wa-wá-gna\ *v* wawa·wa·gna [fr *wagna* to shell] : to cut off, as in shelling corn with a knife, to

---

\a\ father \e\ they \i\ machine \o\ smoke \u\ lunar \an, aŋ\ blanc Fr. \in, iŋ\ ink \on, oŋ, un, uŋ\ soon, confier Fr. \c\ chair \ġ\ machen Ger. \j\ fusion \clusters: bl, gn, kp, hšl, etc...\ b^e^lo ... said with a slight vowel **See more in the Introduction, Guide to Pronunciation**

make fall by cutting

wa·wa·gna·yan \wa-wá-gna-yaŋ\ *v* wawa·wa·gnayan [fr *wagnayan* to miss in trying to strike with a knife] : to miss trying to cut

wa·wa·go \wa-wá-ġo\ *v* wawa·wa·go [fr *wago* make marks or gashes] : to carve, engrave

wa·wa·gwe·za \wa-wá-gwe-za\ *v* wawa·wa·gweza [fr *wagweza* to carve roughly] : to make rough, to haggle

wa·wa·ha \wa-wá-ha\ *n* : furs or peltries, the generic name

wa·wa·he·ye šni \wa-wá-he-ye šni\ *adv* or *adj* : pretending; frank and open, not hesitating to speak out < ~ *mani* to move about as though one knew the country although one is a stranger. > - BE WHL

wa·wa·hi·yan·ska·la·ka \wa-wá-hi-yan-sk̇a-la-k̇a\ *adj* : morose, cross — **wawahiyan·syakel** *adv* : roughly, crossly — **wawahiyan·zeca** *n* : a morose person

wa·wa·ho·kon·ki·ya \wa-wá-ho-koŋ-ki-ya\ *v* [fr *wahokonkiya* advise one] : to exhort, advise - B.H.173.1, 252.1

wa·wa·ho·ya \wa-wá-ho-ya\ *v absol* : to order things — **wawahoya·pi** \wa-wá-ho-ya-p̣i\ *n* : things ordered by mail

wa·wa·hun \wa-wá-huŋ\ *v* wawa·wa·hun [fr *wahun* to gash or slash] : to cut, gash — **wawahun·hun** *v red* : to cut *e.g.* a piece of meat nearly off in many pieces < ~ *wak'u* I gave it to him to cut in many pieces. >

wa·wa·hu·te·la \wa-wá-hu-te-la\ *v* wawa·wa·hutela [fr *wahutela* a small stump] : to wear off to a stump, as a knife

wa·wa·hla·gan \wa-wá-ȟla-ġaŋ\ *v* wawa·wa·hlagan [fr *wahlagan* to enlarge by cutting] : to make large, to cut so that a thing becomes larger, as in enlarging a hole

wa·wa·hla·ya \wa-wá-ȟla-ya\ *v* wawa·wa·hlaya [fr *wahlaya* to pare off, to circumcize] : to pare, cut off the rind or skin — **wawahlaye·la** *n* : parings, peelings

wa·wa·hle·ca \wa-wá-ȟle-ca\ *v* wawa·wa·hleca [fr *wahleca* cut or break in piece] : to tear in attempting to cut

wa·wa·hlo·ka \wa-wá-ȟlo-ka\ *v* wawa·wa·hloka [fr *wahloka* cut a hole in] : to cut holes - Cf wawašloka

wa·wa·ȟo·bȟo·pe·ce \wa-wá-ȟo-bȟo-p̣e-ce\ *n* : one who is proud of his wearing apparel, while he does not look good otherwise - Bl

wa·wa·hpa·ni·yan \wa-wá-ȟp̣a-ni-yaŋ\ *v* wawahpani·wa·ya [fr *wahpaniyan* in a poor, destitute way] : to make poor

wa·wa·h'u \wa-wá-ȟ'u\ *v* wawa·wa·h'u [fr *wah'u* to peel] : to peel, pare

wa·wa·ju·ju \wa-wá-ju-ju\ *v* [fr *wajuju* to butcher an animal] : to cut into pieces, butcher < ~ *nišipi* You were told to butcher it. >

wa·wa·kan \wa-wá-k̇aŋ\ *n* : the sacred Arrow, the *Wahinkpe wakan* that the Cheyenne tribe are supposed to have received

wa·wa·kan·kan \wa-wá-kaŋ-kaŋ\ *n* or *v* : one who does wonderful things < *Wawakankanpi ke ci* Wonderful things were done nonetheless. > — **wawakankan·ka** \wa-wá-kaŋ-kaŋ-k̇a\ *adj* : acting in a mysterious way, soothsaying < *Wicaša wawakankanpika* Men are soothsaying. > - B.H.67.6, 49.11

wa·wa·ki·ci·špa·špa·ke \wa-wá-ki-ci-špa-špa-ke\ *n* : one who has been generous in giving away and yet sacrifices more - Bl

wa·wa·ki·pa·jin \wa-wá-k̇i-p̣a-jiŋ\ *vn* wawa·wa·kipajin : to rebel against, oppose, to be a rebel — **wawakipajin·pi** *n* : opposition, rebellion — **wawakipajin·yan** *adv* : rebelliously

wa·wa·kon·ta \wa-wá-k̇oŋ-ṫa\ *v* wawa·wa·konta [fr *wakonta* to hollow, groove] : to cut or notch — **wawakon·tkonta** \wa-wá-k̇oŋ-tk̇oŋ-ṫa\ *v red* : to whittle out

wa·wa·kpan \wa-wá-kp̣aŋ\ *v* wawa·wa·kpan [fr *wakpan* to cut up fine] : to cut up fine — **wawakpan·šni** *adj* wawa·ma·kpanšni : fine, active, stirring as a man; nervous, quick-stepping as a horse; fleet as a dog - Note: this word is used in the *neg* form only

wa·wa·ksa \wa-wá-ksa\ *v* wawa·wa·ksa [fr *waksa* to cut off] : to cut off *esp* crosswise

wa·wa·kta·ka \wa-wá-kṫa-ka\ *v* [fr *wakta* watch for] : to look for < *Wawaktakešni unhipelo* We arrived not being expected, *or* Our coming was a surprise to them. > - Bl

wa·wa·ktan \wa-wá-kṫaŋ\ *v* wawa·wa·ktan [fr *waktan* to make crooked by shaving] : to cut so as to make crooked

wa·wa·kta·ya·pi \wa-wá-kta-ya-pi\ *n* : something or someone expected, as a child - SLB

wa·wa·k'e·za \wa-wá-k'e-za\ *v* wawa·wa·k'eza [fr *wak'eza* to smoothen by shaving] : to make smooth by cutting — **wawak'eze** *n* : a board on which to trim feathers or to shave wood

wa·wa·k'on·šni \wa-wá-k'oŋ-šni\ *adj* : active - *Syn* ŠPUKEŠNI, BLIHECA WE

wa·wa·mna \wa-wá-mna\ *v* wawa·wa·mna [fr *wamna* to rip] : to rip with a knife

wa·wa·mna·la \wa-wá-mna-la\ *v* wawamna·wa·la [fr *wamnala* to respect, fear] : to respect, honor, to have a high opinion of — *n* : one who respects < *wawamnalašni* one who respects nothing >

wa·wa·ni·ce \wa-wá-ni-ce\ *v* or *n* : to be nothing — *n* : a dearth, a lack, scarcity < *Wawanicin ktelo* There will be a scarcity. > — **wawanice·ca** *v* : there is nothing or very little

wa·wan·ke \wá-waŋ-k̇e\ *n* [fr *waawanyanke* oversee] : a watchman

wa·wan·yank \wa-wáŋ-yaŋk\ *v contrac of* wawanyanka : to look in, see < ~ *mni kta* I shall go see. > - B.H. 269.21

wa·wan·yan·ka \wa-wáŋ-yaŋ-k̇a\ *v* wawan·bla·ka [fr *wanyanka* to see, perceive] : to look in, see < *Tuwa toka hi na ~ ca na išta hca yelo* Some stranger arrived so that when he saw him then his eyes got very sore. >

[1]**wa·wan·yan·ke** \wa-wáŋ-yaŋ-k̇e\ n : a spectator, a looker-on

[2]**wa·wan·yan·ke** \wá-wan-yank-k̇e\ *n* : an overseer, a policeman

wa·wa·pe·sto \wa-wá-p̣e-sto\ *v* wawa·wa·pesto [fr *wapesto* shave to a point] : to shave to a point

wa·wa·pi·la·ki·ya \wa-wá-p̣i-la-ki-ya\ *v* wawapila·wa·kiya [fr *pilakiya* make glad, thankful] : to make glad — *n* : one who makes glad

wa·wa·pi·la·ya \wa-wá-p̣i-la-ya\ *v absol* : to give cause for gratitude, to do a favor - D.25

wa·wa·po·ta \wa-wá-p̣o-ṫa\ *v* wawa·wa·pota [fr *wapota* destroy by cutting] : to destroy by cutting *e.g.* a tent

wa·wa·psa·ka \wa-wá-psa-ka\ *v* wawa·wa·psaka [fr *wapsaka* to saw or cut off] : to cut off *e.g.* a cord

wa·wa·pta \wa-wá-pta\ *v* wawa·wa·pta [fr *wapta* cut off, trim] : to cut out, pare around

wa·wa·pte·ce·la \wa-wá-pṫe-ce-la\ *v* wawa·wa·ptecela [fr *waptecela* cut short or cut too short]\: to cut off short

wa·wa·ptu·h'a *or* **wawaptuga** \wa-wá-ptu-ȟ'a\ *v* [fr *waptuh'a* to cut or saw off a piece] : to scrape off crumbs, as from a medicine root - Bl

wa·wa·scu·scu·ke \wa-wá-sċu-sċu-ke\ *n* : one who dresses well in order to be noticed by the women folk - Bl

wa·wa·sku \wa-wá-sku\ *v* wawa·wa·sku [fr *wasku* peel off] : to pare *e.g.* potatoes

wa·wa·smin \wa-wá-smiŋ\ *v* wawa·wa·smin [fr *wasmin* to cut off clean] : to make bare with a knife

wa·wa·s'in \wá-wa-s'iŋ\ - perhaps *obsol* Bl

wa·wa·ša·gya \wa-wá-ša-gya\ *v* : to spoil, to render worthless - B.H.34.18

wa·wa·ši·cun·ke \wa-wá-ši-cuŋ-ke\ *n* : one who imitates or tries to be like a white man, as in playing the part — **wawašicun·yan** *adv* [fr *wašicun* a white man] : like a white man — **wawaši·kšicunke** *n* : one who imitates or tries to be like a white man

wa·wa·ši·lki·gla \wa-wá-ši-lki-gla\ *vn* : to be angry, vexed — *n* : one who is angry — **wawašilkigla·ya** *v* wawašilkigla·wa·ya [fr *šilkiglaya* to make angry with one] : to make angry

wa·wa·ški·ta \wa-wá-ški-ta\ *v* wawa·wa·škita [fr *waškita* to gash, cut across] : to cut, gash

wa·wa·šla \wa-wá-šla\ *v* wawa·wa·šla [fr *wašla* to shave or scrape] : to shave off

wa·wa·šlo·ka \wa-wá-šlo-ka\ *v* wawa·wa·šloka [fr *wašloka* to cut a hole in] : to cut out of

wa·wa·šp̣a \wa-wá-šp̣a\ *v* wawa·wa·šp̣a [fr *wašp̣a* to scalp] : to cut off pieces

wa·wa·šp̣u \wa-wá-šp̣u\ *v* wawa·wa·šp̣u [fr *wašp̣u* cut or rip into pieces] : to cut in pieces — **wawašp̣u·šp̣u** *v red* wawa·wa·šp̣ušp̣u : to cut up in pieces *e.g.* tallow

wa·wa·ta·ku·ni·šni \wa-wá-ṫa-ku-ni-šni\ *v* wawa·wa·takunišni [fr *watakunišni* to destroy by cutting] : to destroy

wa·wa·te·pa \wa-wá-ṫe-p̣a\ *v* [fr *watepa* to cut short] : to wear off to a stump, to cut off short - R

wa·wa·t'a \wa-wá-t'a\ *v* [fr *wat'a* kill with a knife] : to kill with a knife

wa·wa·t'e·ca̧ \wa-wá-t'e-ca\ *adj* or perhaps *adv* : gentle, mild < *Šunka-wakan wanji ~ k'in mawani ktelo* I shall walk, the gentle horse bearing a load. > — **wawat'eca·ka** *n* : one who is kind, as a gentle horse

wa·wa·yu·šna \wa-wá-yu-šna\ *v* wawa·blu·šna [fr *wayušna* to offer sacrifice] : to sacrifice — *n* : a priest, one who sacrifices

wa·we·ce·ya \wa-wé-ċe-ya\ *v absol* wawece·wa·ya [fr *weceya* to be congenial, good-natured, on good terms with *e.g.* one's relatives] : to have confidence in people — **waweceye·šni** *v* wawece·wa·yešni : to distrust — **waweceyešni·šni oiekiton** \wa-wé-ċe-ye-šni-šni o-ì-e-ki-toŋ\ *v* : to slander, bring forward speech to spoil another's good name -Bl

wa·wi·ca·hya \wa-wí-ca-ȟya\ *v* [fr *icahya* raise, train, rear] : to cause to grow, to form or create — **wawicahye** *n* or *np* : a maker, a former; the Creator

wa·wi·ca·k'u \wa-wí-ca-k'u\ *v* wawica·wa·k'u : to donate, make a donation — **wawicak'u·pi** *n* : a gift - P Bl

wa·wi·ce·ki·ya \wa-wí-ce-ki-ya\ *v* wawice·wa·kiya : to solicit help, support

wa·wi·ci·ȟa·ȟa \wa-wí-ci-ȟa-ȟa\ *n* : one who commits adultery, one who sins against others and makes light of it — **wawiciȟaȟa·pi** *n* : adultery, a laughing stock - B.H.233.14

wa·wi·ci·ya \wa-wí-ci-ya\ *n* [fr *iciya* take sides in a dispute] : an advocate, one who helps and assists one against another, supposing two are fighting - *Syn* WANICIYE *See* under *wanikiya*

wa·wi·gni \wa-wí-gni\ *v* wawi·wa·gni : to search for something, to hunt

wa·wi·han·gya \wa-wí-haŋ-gya\ *v* wawihan·gwa·ya [fr *ihangya* to destroy, bring to an end] : to destroy — **wawihangye** *n* : a destroyer - B.H.14.12, 50.17

wa·wi·ȟa \wa-wí-ȟa\ *v* wawi·wa·ȟa [fr *iȟa* to laugh or laugh at] : to laugh at — **wawi·ȟa·ȟa** *v red* : to be laughing at

wa·wi·ȟa·ka \wa-wí-ȟa-ka\ *n* : a jester, one who makes sport — **wawiȟa·pi** *n* : a jesting, making sport

wa·wi·ȟa·t'e·ya \wa-wí-ȟa-t'e·ya\ *v* : no to understand one's business, *i.e.* to do it wrong, to make others laugh at one's ignorance - Bl

wa·wi·ȟa·ya \wa-wí-ȟa-ya\ *va* wawiȟa·wa·ya : to cause to laugh at — *adv* : wittily

wa·wi·hpe·ya \wa-wí-ȟp̣e-ya\ *v* wawihpe·wa·ya : to give away

wa·wi·h'an·ka \wa-wí-ȟ'aŋ-ka\ *n* : a hustler, one who is always doing something

wa·wi·ko·ya·ka \wa-wí-ko-ya-ka\ *n* : the showy tick trefoil, sticktights, *i.e. wokahtan blaskaska* - Bl #119

wa·wi·ma·ga·ga·ye·ca \wa-wí-ma-ġa-ġa-ye-ca\ *n* : one who encourages, cheers up others by his talk - Bl

wa·wi·mna·šni·yan \wa-wí-mna-šni-yaŋ\ *adv* : haughtily, considering others weaklings - B.H.86.13

wa·wi·na·hni \wa-wí-na-ȟni\ *v* [fr *inahni* to hurry] : to be in a hurry, in haste — **wawinahni·yan** *v* wawinahni·wa·ya : to hasten, cause to hurry < *Wawinahniwaya tka wablahlokešni* I hurried him but I failed to get through to him, *or* I tried to get them busy but I made no impression on them. > - Bl

wa·wi·na·ki·hni \wa-wí-na-ki-ȟni\ *v* wawina·wa·kihni : to be in haste, in a hurry, to do beforehand — **wawinakihni·ka** *n* : one who is in haste

wa·wi·ni·han \wa-wí-ni-haŋ\ *adj* [fr *inihan* to be frightened] : fearful, afraid, inspiring fear, excited < ~ *manka* I sat fearful. > — **wawinihan·yan** *v* wawinihan·wa·ya : to make afraid

wa·wi·pi·i·c'i·la \wa-wí-p̣i-i-c'i-la\ *v refl* [fr *wawipila* not to give, to refuse] : to be self-centered, to think more of one's self than of anyone else

wa·wi·pi·la \wa-wí-p̣i-la\ *v* [fr *ipila* refuse to give, to withhold] : to refuse, not to give < *Iyeš waonšila na taku yuha kin tohinni ~ šni na tuwa onšika ca taku yuha kin on okiya keya okiyaka* He is merciful, and what he has he never withholds, and he said that he stated that one who is miserable helps with what he has. > - D.214, 53 note 2

wa·wi·štan·ye·ca \wa-wí-štaŋ-ye-ca\ *n* : a comedian, one who can cheer up others by his funny talking - Bl

wa·wi·šte·ca \wa-wí-šte-ca\ *adj* : modest, ashamed - Note: the better form is *wišteca*

wa·wi·šte·lya \wa-wí-šte-lya\ *v* wawište·lwa·ya : to make ashamed — *adv* : ashamedly, bashfully

wa·wi·tko·ya \wa-wí-tko-ya\ *v* wawitko·wa·ya [fr *witkoya* to make foolish] : to make drunk

wa·wi·ton·pa \wa-wí-toŋ-pa\ *v* wawiton·wa·pa [fr *iton-*

\a\ father \e\ they \i\ machine \o\ smoke \u\ lunar \an, aŋ\ blanc Fr. \in, iŋ\ ink \on, oŋ, un, uŋ\ soon, confier Fr. \c\ chair \ǧ\ machen Ger. \j\ fusion \clusters: bl, gn, kp, hšl, etc...\ b^e^lo ... said with a slight vowel **See more in the Introduction, Guide to Pronunciation**

pa to wonder, praise] : to praise one — **wawitonpa·pi** \wa-wí-toŋ-pa-p̣i\ *n* : praising — **wawitonpapišni** *n* : not praising

wa·wi·wa·ho·ya \wa-wí-wa-ho-ya\ *v* : to issue orders — **wawiwahoye** *n* : one who gives orders - B.H.231.1

wa·wi·wa·kta·ya \wa-wí-wa-kta-ya\ *v* : to give one notice, cause one to expect or wait for something, as for a call - B.H.157.12, 242.2 SLB

wa·wi·ya·cin \wa-wí-ya-ciŋ\ *v* wawi·bla·cin [fr *iyacin* compare with] : to liken to, to use parables — **wawiya-cin·yan** *adv* : figuratively

wa·wi·ya·hpa·hpa·ya \wa-wí-ya-ȟpa-ȟpa-ya\ *v red* [fr perhaps *wawiyahpaya* to seize one] : to seize or make an attack on < *T'ebleze šni ~ ayahilale* You sang a tune to seize getting wild, *i.e.* to wrestle for fun. > - Bl WHL

wa·wi·ya·hta·gi·ya \wa-wí-ya-ȟta-gi-ya\ *v* wawiyahta-gi·wa·ya : to find fault, criticize one - Note: there is some question as to the spelling of the word's end, *-giya* — **wawiyahta·ka** *v* [fr *yahtaka* to bite one] : to find fault with

wa·wi·ya·ka·pe·i·c'i·ya \wa-wí-ya-ka-p̣e-i-c'i-ya\ *v refl* [fr *wawiyakapeya* to do beyond moderation, to overdo] : to exceed one's self, to be intemperate

wa·wi·ya·ka·pe·ya \wa-wí-ya-ka-p̣e-ya\ *v* : to exceed, go beyond moderation

wa·wi·ya·ksa·pa \wa-wí-ya-ksa-pa\ *v* wawi·bla·ksapa [fr perhaps *iyaksapa* to make wise by talking] : to say wise words < *Wicaša ksapapi lena wawiyaksapapi ca oyate kin ogna oigluhayapi* These wise men who spoke wise words are well-to-do among the people. *Na tokel okihi scu na taku eyaš wawiyaksapin na tanyan kinye wicaši* He drew their attention as he was able, but on the other hand with what wise words he spoke he told them to fly well. > - WH MS.483, 104

wa·wi·ya·pe *or* **waiyape** \wa-wí-ya-p̣e\ *v* wawiya·wa·pe [fr *iyape* to lie in ambush] : to lie in wait — *n* : an ambush — **wawiyape·pi** *or* **waiyapepi** \wa-wí-ya-p̣e-p̣i\ *part* : lying in wait, in ambush

wa·wi·ya·yuh \wa-wí-ya-yuȟ\ *v contrac* [fr *wawiyayuha* to follow, stay with] : to be following, as a colt its mother — **wawiyayuha** *v* [fr *iyayuha* to have an attachment to] : to follow, be attached to — *n* : a follower, one who follows — **wawiyayu·hya** *adv* : following - B.H.290.10

wa·wi·ye·ke s'e \wa-wí-ye-ke s'e\ *adv* : as one who dines upon < *Šunka ~ gliyankin kte lo* He will return to be at home as one who dines upon dog, as was said of the priest Father Westropp on the Pine Ridge Reservation in the State of South Dakota during the first quarter of the 20th century. *šunkpala ... wowiyuškin* a puppy ... delight > - Bl

wa·wi·ye·ki·ya \wa-wí-ye-ḳi-ya\ *v* wawiye·wa·kiya [fr *iyekiya* to recognize] : to recognize something one's own

wa·wi·ye·ya \wa-wí-ye-ya\ *v* wawiye·wa·ya [fr *iyeya* to find] : to find — **wawiyeye·ca** *n* : one that finds much, as does a good dog

wa·wi·yo·hi \wa-wí-yo-hi\ *v* wawiyo·wa·hi [fr *iyohi* to reach to, arrive at] : to reach to, extend too, to be sufficient for — **wawiyohi·ya** *va* wawiyohi·wa·ya : to cause to reach to — *adv* : reaching to

wa·wi·yo·ki·pi \wa-wí-yo-ḳi-p̣i\ *v* wawiyo·ma·kipi [fr *iyokipi* to please another] : to be pleased with — **wawi-yokipi·ya** *adv* : joyfully, gladly, pleasantly — **wawi-yokipi·ye** *n* : an attractive person, one liked by others at first sight - B.H.85.14

wa·wi·yo·ki·ši·ca \wa-wí-yo-ḳi-ši-ca\ *v* wawiyo·ma·ki-šica [fr *iyokišica* to be sad, grieved] : to be sad — **wawiyokišil** *v contrac* : sad, to be sad < *~ waun* to be sad > — **wawiyokiši·lya** *v* wawiyokiši·lwa·ya : to make sad < *Wawiyokišilwaya iyecel wahi yelo* I made him sad in same way I arrived. > — *adv* : sadly, sorrowfully - Bl BT

wa·wi·yo·ki·šni \wa-wí-yo-ḳi-šni\ *v* : to forbid - B.H. 111.8, 260.20

wa·wi·yo·pa·šta·ka \wa-wí-yo-p̣a-šta-ḳa\ *v* [fr *iyopašta-ka* to incite, encourage, urge] : to encourage, urge on

wa·wi·yo·pe·ki·ya \wa-wí-yo-p̣e-ḳi-ya\ *v* wawiyope-·wa·kiya [fr *iyopekiya* to reprove, scold, punish, to sell perhaps] : to reprove

wa·wi·yo·pe·ya \wa-wí-yo-p̣e-ya\ *v* wawiyope·wa·ya [fr *iyopeya* to exchange, sell] : to reprove

wa·wi·yo·win·yan \wa-wí-yo-wiŋ-yaŋ\ *part* : accomodating - Bl

wa·wi·yu·ka·ki·ja \wa-wí-yu-ḳa-ḳi-ja\ *v* wawi·blu·kaki-ja [fr *yukakija* cause to suffer] : to make suffer

wa·wi·yu·kcan \wa-wí-yu-kcaŋ\ *v* wawi·blu·kcan [fr *iyukcan* to have an understanding, judge] : to judge, examine — **wawiyukcan·ka** *n* : a judge, one who examines and judges

wa·wi·yun·ga \wa-wí-yuŋ-ġa\ *v* wawi·mun·ga wawi-·un·yunga·pi [fr *iyunga* to ask a question of one] : to ask questions, inquire of one — **wawiyunga·pi** *n* : an inquiry — **wawiyunge s'a** *adj* : inquisitive — **wawi-yunh** *v contrac of* wawiyunga : to ask questions < *~ bla* I go to ask him questions. > — **wawiyun·htukel** \wa-wí-yuŋ-ȟtu-ḳel\ *adv* : in an inquiring, quizzing manner < *~ omani* to walk quizzing him > — **wawi-yun·hya** *adv* : inquiringly - B.H. 236.3 P R Bl

wa·wi·yu·pi·ya \wa-wí-yu-p̣i-ya\ *adv* : expertly, well

wa·wi·yu·ta \wa-wí-yu-ta\ *v* [fr *iyuta* to measure] : to measure, *e.g.* weigh, try - B.H.194.14

wa·wi·yu·tan \wa-wí-yu-ṭaŋ\ *n* : solicitation, temptation, what solicits as to temptation < *~ awakipa kin, Jesus onšimala ye* Jesus, take pity on me when I meet with temptation. > — **wawiyutan·yan** *v* wawiyutan·wa·ya [fr *iyutanyan* to try or tempt] : to tempt — **wawiyu-tanye** *n* : a tempter, one who tempts, tries others < *~ oyas'in kowakipin kte* I should fear all who tempt others. > - Pb.34, 27 SLB

wa·wo·bla·ya \wa-wó-bla-ya\ *v* wawo·wa·blaya [fr *wo-bláya* spread out by punching] : to make spread out by shooting or punching

wa·wo·bla·za \wa-wó-bla-za\ *v* wawo·wa·blaza [fr *wobláza* tear open by shooting] : to tear open by shooting *etc.*

wa·wo·ble·ca \wa-wó-ble-ca\ *v* wawo·wa·bleca [fr *wo-bléca* shoot or break to pieces] : to break in pieces by shooting or punching

wa·wo·blu \wa-wó-blu\ *v* wawo·wa·blu [fr *woblú* to crush fine] : to pound fine, to pulverize

wa·wo·blu \wá-wo-blu\ *v* : the snow flies < *Iwaštegla tate yešan, wáwoblu welo* Though the wind was slight the snow was flying. > - Bl

wa·wo·ceg \wa-wo-ceg\ *v contrac of* wawoceka : to make unsteady on the feet by shooting < *~ iyeya* to make stagger by shooting >

wa·wo·ce·ka \wa-wó-ce-ḳa\ *v* : to make stagger by shooting

wa·wo·c'o \wa-wó-c'o\ *v* wawo·wa·c'o [fr *woc'ó* to churn] : to churn

wa·wo·gna \wa-wó-gna\ *v* wawo·wa·gna [fr *wogná* to

shoot off, as fruit from a tree] : to knock off, as fruit by shooting

wa·wo·gna·škin·yan \wa-wó-gna-š;kiŋ-yaŋ\ *v* wawo·wa·gnaškinyan [fr *wognaškinyan* make furious by shooting] : to make crazy by pounding, punching, or shooting

wa·wo·gna·yan \wa-wó-gna-yaŋ\ *v* wawo·wa·gnayan [fr *wognayan* partly to miss in shooting] : to miss in shooting

wa·wo·ha·i·ye·ya \wa-wó-ha-i-ye-ya\ *v* [fr *wohá iyeya* suddenly to shoot punch over] : to make tumble over by shooting

wa·wo·hi·lhi·ti·ka \wa-wó-hi-lhi-ti-ka\ *adj red perhaps* : to be very active, awesomely energetic < *Wawohilhitikin kte hcin* She is indeed marvelously active. *Sinkpela s'e ónšika tka wawohilhitikece* Like a muskrat she is pitiful but she is awfully busy, as is said when an old woman, in spite of her helplessness, takes care of her husband and household. > — **wawohilhitike·ca** *adj* : determinedly active - Bl

wa·wo·hin·ta \wa-wó-hiŋ-ṫa\ *v* wawo·wa·hinta [fr *wohinta* sweep off clean by shooting] : to sweep all off by shooting

wa·wo·ho·ho \wa-wó-ho-ho\ *v* wawo·wa·hoho [fr *wohóho* to shake or loosen by shooting] : to make loose by shooting

wa·wo·hun·hun·za \wa-wó-huŋ-huŋ-za\ *v* wawo·wa·hunhunza [fr *wohunhunza* to shake something by shooting] : to make shake by shooting

wa·wo·hci \wa-wó-ȟci\ *v* wawo·wa·hci [fr *wohci* to break out a piece by punching] : to shoot or punch out pieces

wa·wo·ȟin·yan \wa-wó-ȟiŋ-yaŋ\ *v* wawo·wa·ȟiŋyaŋ [fr oȟinyan] : to be dissatisfied with

wa·wo·hlo·ka \wa-wó-ȟlo-ka\ *v* wawo·wa·hloka [fr *wohloka* to shoot or punch a hole in] : to shoot or punch holes

wa·wo·hmin \wa-wó-ȟmiŋ\ *v* wawo·wa·ȟmiŋ [fr *wohmin* make a gun crooked shooting] : to make crooked by shooting

wa·wo·hpa \wa-wó-ȟpa\ *v* [fr *wohpa* make fall by shooting] : to shoot on the wing

wa·wo·hta·ka \wa-wó-ȟta-ka\ *v* : to knock with the end of anything - Bl

wa·wo·ja·ja \wa-wó-ja-ja\ *v* wawo·wa·jaja [fr *wojája* to wash] : to wash out by punching

wa·wo·ji \wa-wó-ji\ *v* wawo·wa·ji [fr *oji* to whisper about] : to tell secretly — **wawoji·ji** *v red* wawo·wa·jiji [fr *ojiji* to whisper] : to whisper — *n* : a whisperer

wa·wo·ka·htan·yan \wa-wó-ka-ȟṫaŋ-yaŋ\ *v* wawokahtan·wa·ya [fr *okahtanyan* absorb, soak in] : to have much influence over < *Oyate... wawokahtanwaye* I wield a great influence over people. >

wa·wo·ki·ca·hni·ga \wa-wó-k̇i-ca-ȟni-ġa\ *adj* : of quick understanding

wa·wo·ki·hi \wa-wó-k̇i-hi\ *v* wawo·wa·kihi [fr *okihi* to be able] : to be able — **wawokihi·ka** \wa-wó-k̇i-hi-k̇a\ *n* : one who is able — **wawokihi·ya** *v* wawokihi·wa·ya : to make able

wa·wo·ki·ya \wa-wó-k̇i-ya\ *v* wawo·wa·kiya [fr *ókiya* to help one] : to help, to be with, to accompany < *Takomni wawowicakiyapi wan yuk̇e* Nevertheless he was one of those who were helped. > — **wawokiye** *n* : a helper, one who helps, a help or help, those who help

wa·wo·kpa·ni \wa-wó-kpa-ni\ *v* [fr *okpani* to be lacking] : to be unsuccessful, unlucky - Bl

wa·wo·kpan \wa-wó-kṗaŋ\ *v* wawo·wa·kpan [fr *wokpan* to grind *e.g.* grain] : to pound fine

wa·wo·ksa \wa-wó-ksa\ *v* wawo·wa·ksa [fr *woksá* to break off by shooting] : to break off by shooting or punching

wa·wo·ktan \wa-wó-k̇ṫaŋ\ *v* wawo·wa·ktan [fr *woktán* to bend or make bend by punching] : to bend by shooting or pounding

wa·wo·ku·ka \wa-wó-ku-ka\ *v* wawo·wa·kuka [fr *wokuka* to punch or shoot all to pieces] : to destroy by pounding or shooting

wa·wo·ku·wa \wa-wó-k̇u-wa\ *v* wawo·wa·kuwa [fr *okuwa* to chase, go after] : to follow after constantly, to chase

wa·wo·k'o·ya \wa-wó-k'o-ya\ *n* : excitement, tumult < ~ *tanka* a great tumult, riot > — *vn* : to be clamorous, noisy, to make noise - *Syn* OWÓLUTATON B.H. 303.3

wa·wo·k'o·ye·ce \wa-wó-k'o-ye-ce\ *n* : a clamor and dispersal of a crowd of people as they do in all directions on noticing a snake loose among them - Bl

wa·wo·lwi·ca·ye·šni un \wa-wó-lwi-ca-ye-sni un\ *v* : to be tactful, unassuming < ~ *yaun* You are tactful. > - Bl

wa·wo·pan \wa-wó-paŋ\ *v* wawo·wa·pan [fr *wopán* to pound fine] : to pound fine *e.g.* hominy — **wawopanpan** *v red* : to make soft by pounding — **wawopan·pi** *n* : cornmeal, or anything pounded fine

wa·wo·pe·mni \wa-wó-ṗe-mni\ *v* wawo·wa·pemni [fr *wopemni* turn aside or twist by shooting or by blowing] : to twist by shooting

wa·wo·po·ta \wa-wó-ṗo-ṫa\ *v* wawo·wa·pota [fr *wopota* to destroy shooting and making many holes] : to shoot or pound to pieces

wa·wo·psa·ka \wa-wó-psa-ka\ *v* wawo·wa·psaka [fr *wopsáka*] : to shoot off *e.g.* strings

wa·wo·pta \wa-wó-pṫa\ *v* wawo·wa·pta : to cut out *e.g.* turnips, to dig up by striking with a stick endwise, as in digging *tinpsinla* the wild turnip - D.243

wa·wo·pte·ca \wa-wó-pte-ca\ *adj* : sluggish, lazy < ~ *šni* active, energetic, *wicaša* ~ a lazy > - Pb.21 KE

wa·wo·sla·ta \wa-wó-sla-ṫa\ *n* : hollow gones used for ornaments, a kind of long bead and large in the middle, worn by the Dakotas; ~ *wanap'in* an ornamental breast piece made of hollow bones - R

wa·wo·sle·ca \wa-wó-sle-ca\ *v* wawo·wa·sleca [fr *wosléca* to split by shooting or punching] : to split by shooting

wa·wo·sni \wa-wó-sni\ *v* wawo·wa·sni [fr *wosni* to cool by blowing, to extinguish fire] : to blow out, extinguish

wa·wo·so·ta \wa-wó-so-ṫa\ *v* wawo·wa·sota [fr *wosota* to kill off all] : to exterminate by shooting

wa·wo·ški·lya \wa-wó-ški-lya\ *v* : to make trouble - KE

wa·wo·ški·ške·ye·ce \wa-wó-ški-ške-ye-ce\ *n* : one who dominates a discussion, butting in and causing confusion - Bl

wa·wo·šla \wa-wó-šla\ *v* wawo·wa·šla [fr *wošlá* make

\a\ father \e\ they \i\ machine \o\ smoke \u\ lunar \an, aŋ\ blanc Fr. \in, iŋ\ ink \on, oŋ, un, uŋ\ soon, confier Fr. \c\ chair \ġ\ machen Ger. \j\ fusion \clusters: bl, gn, kp, hšl, etc...\ b^e^lo ... said with a slight vowel
See more in the Introduction, Guide to Pronunciation

bare] : to shoot off bare

wa·wo·šlo·ka \wa-wó-šlo-ka\ *v* wawo·wa·šloka [fr *wo-šloka* fire off a gun] : to shoot or punch out, as an eye

wa·wo·šna \wa-wó-šna\ *v* wawo·wa·šna [fr *wošná* to miss the mark in shooting] : to miss in shooting

wa·wo·špa \wa-wó-špa\ *v* wawo·wa·špa [fr *wošpa* to knock off a piece by shooting] : to shoot off a piece

wa·wo·šte·gla \wa-wó-šte-gla\ *v* wawošte·wa·gla [fr *o-štegla* to revile, insult] : to call bad names — *n* : a slanderer, one who speaks evil of another

wa·wo·šu·ja \wa-wó-šu-ja\ *v* [fr *wošúja* to crush, mash] : to shoot to splinters as a bullet does to bones

wa·wo·š'a·ka \wa-wó-š'a-ka\ *v* wawo·wa·š'aka [fr *wo š'áka* to shoot with little force; *fig* to give little impression by way of word] : to shoot or punch with too little force to penetrate; *fig* to impress others little

wa·wo·ta i·han \wa-wó-ta i-haŋ\ *n* : a snow drift – *Syn* WAWÓTA IHEYA

wa·wo·ta·ku·ni·šni \wa-wó-ta-ku-ni-šni\ *v* wawo·wa·takunišni [fr *wotakunišni* destroy by shooting all to pieces] : to shoot to pieces, destroy

wa·wo·ti·ca \wa-wó-ti-ca\ *n* : a snow drift – Bl KE

wa·wo·ti·ye·ki·ya \wa-wó-ti-ye-ki-ya\ *v* : to plead for < *Oyate kin wawotiyewicakiyapi kta on* It is because they would plead for the people. > – B.H.49.9

wa·wo·t'a \wa-wó-t'a\ *v* wawo·wa·t'a [fr *wot'á* to kill by shooting, to strike so as to endanger one's life] : to kill by punching

wa·wo·t'in·za \wa-wó-t'iŋ-za\ *v* wawo·wa·t'inza [fr *wo-t'ínza* to make tight punching, to blow up, inflate] : to pound tight

wa·wo·we·ga \wa-wó-we-ġa\ *v* wawo·wa·wega [fr *wo-wéga* to break, crack] : to break, fracture by shooting or punching

wa·wo·ya·ka \wa-wó-ya-ka\ *v* wawo·bla·ka [fr *oyaka* to tell] : to relate — *n* : a narrator, one who relates

wa·wo·yu·sin \wa-wó-yu-siŋ\ *v* : to hate, to be out of humor with — **wawoyusin·ke** \wa-wó-yu-siŋ-ke\ *n* : one who hates

wa·wo·yu·spa \wa-wó-yu-spa\ *v* wawo·blu·spa [fr *oyu-spa* seize, catch] : to seize, arrest as a prisoner — *n* : a policeman — **wawoyuspa·pi** *n* : the making of arrests

wa·ya·a·gla·pšun·yan \wa-yá-a-gla-pšuŋ-yaŋ\ *v* [fr *aya-pšunyan* to uproot] : to root over one's own, as a hog does anything < ~ *iyeya* to root over *e.g.* its pen >

wa·ya·a·šla·ya \wa-yá-a-šla-ya\ *adv* [fr *yaášlaya* to explain, talk about what was said] : explaining, unfolding

wa·ya·tan'·in \wa-yá-taŋ-iŋ\ *v* wa·bla·tan'in [fr *yaatan'-in*] : to proclaim, make manifest — *n* : a prophet – B.H.197.11

wa·ya·bla·ska \wa-yá-bla-ska\ *v* wa·bla·blaska [fr *ya-blaska* flatten with the mouth] : to make flat with the mouth — **wayablaska·ska** *v red* : to talk about unimportant thing per-longum-et-latum, to make much of a little thing, to add details, to thrash out

wa·ya·bla·ya \wa-yá-bla-ya\ *v* wa·bla·blaya [fr *yablaya* to level with the teeth] : to make level with the mouth

wa·ya·bla·za \wa-yá-bla-za\ *v* wa·bla·blaza [fr *yablaza* to tear open with the teeth] : to bite or tear open with the teeth

wa·ya·ble·ca \wa-yá-ble-ca\ *v* wa·bla·bleca [fr *yableca* break, crush with the teeth] : to break, crush, tear to pieces with the teeth

wa·ya·ble·za \wa-yá-ble-za\ *v* wa·bla·ble·za [fr *yableza* to cheer, enlighten, to sober by talking to] : to cheer up by speaking

wa·ya·blu \wa-yá-blu\ *v* wa·bla·blu [fr *yablu* make fine by chewing] : to chew fine — **wayablu·blu** *v red* : to do much chewing

wa·ya·can·can \wa-yá-caŋ-caŋ\ *v* wa·bla·cancan [fr *ya-cancan* make shake with the mouth, as a dog does with its prey] : to make shake with the mouth

wa·ya·can·ze \wa-wá-caŋ-ze\ *v* wa·bla·canze [fr *yacan-ze* to talk and make angry] : to anger others by talking out of habit

wa·ya·ca·ske·ske·ke \wa-yá-ca-ske-ske-ke\ *v* wa·bla·caskeskeke : to eat slowly — **wayacaškeškeke** *v* wa·bla·caškeškeke : to eat a small ration of food slowly so as to make it last longer – Bl

wa·ya·ce·kce·ka \wa-yá-ce-kce-ka\ *v* wa·bla·ce·kce·ka [fr *yacekceka* to bite and make stagger] : to make stagger by biting *etc.*

wa·ya·ce·ya \wa-yá-ce-ya\ *v* wa·bla·ceya [fr *yaceya* cry being bitten] : to make cry by scolding

wa·ya·ci·k'a·la \wa-yá-ci-k'a-la\ *v* wa·bla·cik'ala [fr *ya-cik'ala* to speak of as small] : to underrate,

wa·ya·ci·sci·la \wa-yá-ci-sci-la\ *v* wa·bla·ciscila [fr *yaci-scila* count as little or few] : to underrate

wa·ya·co·co \wa-yá-co-co\ *v* wa·bla·coco [fr *yacoco* to chew up fine] : to chew, making soft by biting

wa·ya·co·co·ka \wa-yá-ċo-ċo-ka\ *n* : an opiniated person, one who always gives his own opinion – R Bl

wa·ya·co·za \wa-yá-co-za\ *v* wa·bla·coza [fr *yacoza* to make warm with the mouth, to call warm] : to make warm by biting *etc.*

wa·ya·c'o \wa-yá-c'o\ *v* : to smack the lips while eating < *Šunkwícahcala s'e walac'o* While eating you smack your lips like an old horse, *or perhaps* an old monkey. > – Bl

wa·ya·e·ce·ca \wa-yá-e-ce-ca\ *va* [fr *yaececa* to talk into doing something] : to persuade one, to talk someone into something – IS WE

wa·ya·e·ce·tu \wa-yá-e-ce-tu\ *v* wa·bla·ecetu [fr *yaecetu* to correct a misstatement, to tell as it ought to be told] : to accomplish or bring to pass by speaking

wa·ya·ga \wa-yá-ġa\ *v* [fr *yagá* to peel off with the teeth] : to bite off *e.g.* husks — **wayaga·pa** \wa-yá-ġa-pa\ *v* [fr *yagapa* to bite off skin or husk] : to bite off skin or husk — *n* : one who bites, as a horse

wa·ya·gi·ca \wa-yá-ġi-ca\ *v* wa·bla·gica [fr *yagica* to waken one by using the mouth] : to waken up, cause a person to awaken by speaking

wa·ya·gla \wa-yá-gla\ *v* [fr *yagla* bite off, as does a dog] : to draw out or uncoil, as a dog does when eating the fat from entrails

wa·ya·gla·kin·yan \wa-yá-gla-kiŋ-yaŋ\ *v* wa·bla·glakinyan [fr *yaglakinyan* to contradict, go across in one's speech] : to create intrigue, to set at variance, to make mischief between others < ~ *na heyahelo* He said that to start mischief. > – Bl

wa·ya·glo·ka \wa-yá-glo-ka\ *v* [fr *yagloka* to put out of place with the mouth] : to disjoint, put out of joint with the teeth

wa·ya·gmi·gma \wa-yá-gmi-gma\ *v* wa·bla·gmigma [fr *yagmigma* make round with the mouth] : to round a thing with the mouth

wa·ya·gmi·yan *or* **wayagmiyan·yan** \wa-yá-gmi-yaŋ\ *v* wa·bla·gmi·yan [fr *yagmiyan* to roll by mouth] : to roll with the mouth

wa·ya·gna·škin·yan \wa-yá-gna-škiŋ-yan\ *v* wa·bla·gnaškinyan : to make crazy by talking to

wa·ya·gna·yan \wa-yá-gna-yaŋ\ *v* wa·bla·gnayan : to deceive, tell a falsehood, to miss with the mouth
wa·ya·ha·ha·ke \wa-yá-ha-ha-ke\ *n* : to bite and cause one to waver — **wayahaha·yela** *v* wa·bla·hahayela : to one unstable, to make waver by biting
wa·ya·ga i·ye·ya \wa-yá-ha i-yè-ya\ *v* : to throw down by biting, as one horse does another
wa·ya·hin·ta \wa-yá-hiŋ-ṫa\ *v* wa·bla·hinta [fr *yahinta*] brush away or eat all up with the mouth : to brush away with the mouth — *n* : who names every point of his speech, and thus brushes it away
wa·ya·ho·ho \wa-yá-ho-ho\ *v* wa·bla·hoho [fr *yahoho* shake or loosen with the mouth] : to make loose by biting
wa·ya·ho·mni \wa-yá-ho-mni\ *v* wa·bla·homni [fr *yahomni* make change one's view] : to persuade one to change his opinions, to turn one around by talking
wa·ya·ho·ta \wa-yá-ho-ṫa\ *n* : wild rice, oats — **wayahota blaska** *n* : the name for spelts — **wayahota hinšmašma** *n* : barley – P
wa·ya·ho·ton \wa-yá-ho-ṫoŋ\ *v* wa·bla·hoton [fr *yahoton* to bite and cry out] : to make cry out by biting
wa·ya·hun·hun·za \wa-yá-huŋ-huŋ-za\ *v* wa·bla·hunhunza [fr *yahunhunza* to weaken one's resolution by talking to] : to shake with the mouth
wa·ya·ȟa·pa \wa-yá-ȟa-ṗa\ *v* wa·bla·ȟapa [fr *yaȟapa* to scare up by talking] : to scare up *e.g.* game by talking
wa·ya·hci \wa-yá-ȟci\ *v* wa·bla·hci [fr *yahci* tear out a little piece with the teeth] : to bite out a piece
wa·ya·ȟe·pa \wa-yá-ȟe-ṗa\ *v* wa·bla·ȟepa [fr *yaȟepa* to drink up, empty] : to drink all up
wa·ya·ȟe·ya·ta \wa-yá-ȟe-ya-ta\ *v* wa·bla·ȟeyata [fr *yaȟeyata* to reject or put aside in speaking] : to get others away by talking – R Bl
wa·ya·hla \wa-yá-ȟla\ *v* [fr *yahla* make rattle with the mouth] : to make rattle using the mouth
wa·ya·hla·ta \wa-yá-ȟla-ta\ *v* [fr *yahlata* speak as one dying, gasping] : to scratch with the teeth
wa·ya·hla·ta \wa-yá-ȟla-ta\ *v* wa·bla·hleca [fr *yahleca* to tear from something] : to tear with the teeth
wa·ya·hlo·ka \wa-yá-ȟlo-ka\ *v* wa·bla·hloka **a** : to bite a hole in **b** : to persuade, make an impression by talking < *Wawinahniwaya tka wablahloka šni* I was in a hurry, yet I did not impress him with talk. > – Bl
wa·ya·hpa \wa-yá-ȟpa\ *v* wa·bla·hpa [fr *yahpa* to pull or throw down with the mouth] : to throw down with the mouth
wa·ya·hpu \wa-yá-ȟpu\ *v* wa·bla·hpu [fr *yahpu* to bite off something sticking] : to bite off anything glued on
wa·ya·hta·gi·a \wa-yá-ȟta-gi-a\ *v* [fr *yahtaka* to bite + *ia* to speak] : to find fault
wa·ya·hta·ka \wa-yá-ȟta-ka\ *v* wa·bla·htaka [fr *yahtaka* to bite and hold on] **a** : to bite **b** : to abuse by speaking evil of — *n* : one that bites, as a dog
wa·ya·ȟu·ga \wa-yá-ȟu-ġa\ *v* wa·bla·ȟuga [fr *yaȟuga* to chew, or crack with the mouth] : to crush with the teeth
wa·ya·ȟu-gna·ga \wa-yá-ȟu-gna-ġa\ *v* [fr *yaȟugnaga* to destroy, burn up another's character] : to slander spoil-ing another's good name – Bl
wa·ya·hwa \wa-yá-ȟwa\ *v* wa·bla·hwa [fr *yahwa* make sleepy by talking to] : to make doze talking to
wa·ya·h'an·hi·hi·ke \wa-yá-ȟ'aŋ-hi-hi-ke\ *v red* wa·bla·ȟ'aŋ-hi-hi-ke [fr *yah'anhike* eat slowly] : to eat quite slowly — **wayah'anhike** *v* : to eat very slowly
wa·ya·ȟ'u \wa-yá-ȟ'u\ *v* wa·bla·h'u [fr *yah'u* to peel with the teeth] : to peel off with the teeth
wa·ya·i·ȟa \wa-yá-i-ȟa\ *v* [fr *yaiȟa* make laugh by talk] : to make laugh by talking — *n* : a comedian, a jester, one who makes others laugh
wa·ya·i·i·yo·wa·ja \wa-yá-i-i-yo-wa-ja\ *v* [fr *yaiyowa-ja* to speak to the point] : to speak pertaining to, as near
wa·ya·i·je·na \wa-yá-i-je-na\ *v* wa·bla·ijena [fr *yaije-na* to speak confusedly] : to create rumors, cause trouble between others by talking < ~ *na heyahelo* He said that to create rumors, to cause trouble. > – Bl
wa·ya·i·na·hni \wa-yá-i-na-ȟni\ *v* wa·bla·inahni : to hasten one, make hurry along by talking to — **wayainahni·ya** *va* : to hasten one by speaking to him
wa·ya·i·ni·la \wa-yá-i-ni-la\ *v* wa·bla·inila [fr *yainila* to put to silence by speaking to] : to silence one by speaking to him — **wayaini·lya** *adv* : putting to silence < ~ *ia* to speak silencing one >
wa·ya·i·šte·ca \wa-yá-i-šte-ca\ *v* : to make ashamed by talking to
wa·ya·i·yo·ya \wa-yá-i-yo-ya\ *v* [fr *ya* of the mouth + *iyoya* to gape] : to make yawn by talking
wa·ya·ja·ja \wa-yá-ja-ja\ *v* [fr *yajaja* to lick washing with the mouth] : to wash or clean with the mouth, as a wolf of dog does by licking bones
wa·ya·ja·ta \wa-yá-ja-ta\ *v* wa·bla·jata [fr *yajata* seduce one] : to seduce, making others give up their good views or resolutions – WE
wa·ya·ji·pa \wa-yá-ji-ṗa\ *v* [fr *yajipa* bite or sting as do certain insects] : to bite as do mosquitos
wa·ya·jo \wa-yá-jo\ *v* wa·bla·jo [fr *yajo* to blow or play on a musical instrument] : to blow an instrument — **wayajo·pi** *n* : a horn, a cornet, *etc.* – B.H.75.22
wa·ya·ju·ju \wa-yá-ju-ju\ *v* wa·bla·juju [fr *yajuju* tear to pieces with the mouth, or to refute an argu-ment] : to demolish *e.g.* an argument by counter argument; to tear to pieces as a dog does anything with it mouth — *n* : a destroyer, one who demo-lishes with this mouth
wa·ya·ka \wa-yá-ka\ *n* : a captive taken in war, a prisoner < ~ *oyupapi* A captive was seized. >
wa·ya·ka·ka \wa-yá-ka-ka\ *v* [fr *yakaka* to champ on] : to champ, as does a horse on the bit
wa·ya·ka·pa \wa-yá-ka-ṗa\ *v* wa·bla·kapa [fr *yakapa* to catch with the mouth what is tossed] : to catch in the mouth
wa·ya·ka·tin \wa-yá-ka-tiŋ\ *v* : to straighten with the mouth
wa·ya·ka·wa \wa-yá-ka-wa\ *v* [fr *yakawa* to open with the mouth] : to open with the mouth
wa·ya·ka·ya·h'u wi·co·ku·je \wa-yá-ka-ya-ȟ'u wi-cò-ku-je\ *n* : leprosy, something like eczema, white < ~ *španhanhanpi* Leprosy was breaking out. > – B.H. 114.20, 129.23, 184.21
wa·ya·ki·za \wa-yá-ki-za\ *v* : to grit or grind the teeth, as cows do
wa·ya·ko·ko·ka \wa-yá-ko-ko-ka\ *v* wa·bla·kokoka : to make rattle the teeth
wa·ya·kon·tkon·ta \wa-yá-koŋ-tkoŋ-ta\ *v red* wa·bla·kontkonta : to indent or notch with the teeth
wa·ya·kpan \wa-yá-kpaŋ\ *v* wa·bla·kpan [fr *yakpan* to chew fine] : to masticate, chew fine

---

\a\ father \e\ they \i\ machine \o\ smoke \u\ lunar \an, aŋ\ blanc Fr. \in, iŋ\ ink \on, oŋ, un, uŋ\ soon, confier Fr. \c\ chair \ġ\ machen Ger. \j\ fusion \clusters: bl, gn, kp, hšl, etc...\ b[e]lo ... said with a slight vowel **See more in the Introduction, Guide to Pronunciation**

wa·ya·kpi \wa-yá-kpi\ *v* wa·bla·kpi [fr *yakpi* to crack with the teeth] : to crack with the teeth, as a louse

wa·ya·ksa \wa-yá-ksa\ *v* wa·bla·ksa [fr *yaksa* to bite off] : to bite off — **wayaksa·ksa** *v red* : to bite off a number of pieces

wa·ya·ksa·pa \wa-yá-ksa-pa\ *v* wa·bla·ksapa [fr *yaksapa* to make wise by speaking to] : to make wise by instruction, to teach

wa·ya·kšan \wa-yá-kšaŋ\ *v* [fr *yakšan* to bend with the mouth] : to bend with the mouth - Bl

wa·ya·kši·ja \wa-yá-kši-ja\ *v* wa·bla·kšija [fr *yakšija* to double up with the teeth] : to double up with the teeth

wa·ya·ktan \wa-yá-kṫaŋ\ *v* wa·bla·ktan [fr *yaktan* to bend with the mouth] : to bend with the teeth — **wayaktan·yan** *adv* : bending with the teeth

wa·ya·ku·ka \wa-yá-ku-ka\ *v* wa·bla·kuka [fr *yakuka* to bite to pieces, destroy] : to bite to pieces

wa·ya·k'e·ga \wa-yá-k'e-ġa\ *v* wa·bla·k'ega [fr *yak'ega* to grate with the teeth] : to gnaw with a grating noise

wa·ya·k'e·za \wa-yá-k'e-za\ *v* wa·bla·k'eza [fr *yak'eza* to make smooth with the teeth and a grating sound] : to bite smooth with a grating noise

wa·ya·k'o·ga \wa-yá-k'o-ġa\ *v* wa·bla·k'oga [fr *yak'oga* to bite or gnaw off] : to gnaw

wa·ya·mi·ma \wa-yá-mi-ma\ *v* wa·bla·mima [fr *yamima* to make round with the mouth] : to round in the mouth

wa·ya·mna \wa-yá-mna\ *v* wa·bla·mna [fr *yamna* rip with the mouth] **1** : to rip with the teeth **2** : to gain by talking

wa·ya·mnu·ga \wa-yá-mnu-ġa\ *v* wa·bla·mnu-ġa [fr *yamnuga* to crush or grind] : to grind as in eating parched corn — **wayamnu·mnuga** *v red* : to graw as a dog does a bone

wa·ya·o·hin·yan·ze \wa-yá-o-hiŋ-yaŋ-ze\ *v* [fr *yaohinyanze* to dissuade] : to dissuade by representing the thing as bad - Bl

wa·ya·o·h'an·ko \wa-yá-o-ȟ'aŋ-ko\ *v* wa·bla·oh'anko [fr *yaoh'anko* to hasten by talking to one] : to make quick by speaking to

wa·ya·o·ji·gji·ca \wa-yá-o-ji-gji-ca\ *v* : to brag; to be quite rich in, to be made rich in < *Tašiyagnunpa s'e* ~ Like the meadow lark he is made rich, as is said when a man desires meat. > - Bl WHL

wa·ya·o·kpa·ni·yan \wa-yá-o-kṗa-ni-yaŋ\ *v* : to speak of as unequal, to make unequal

wa·ya·o·ksa \wa-yá-o-ksa\ *v* wa·bla·oksa [fr *yaoksa* bite through] : to bite through

wa·ya·o·ktan \wa-yá-o-kṫaŋ\ *v* wa·bla·oktan [fr *yaoktan* to bend in with the mouth] : to bend into with the teeth

wa·ya·o·l'o·ta·ke \wa-yá-o-l'o-ta-ke\ *v* : to eat slowly so as to make a small ration last long - Bl

wa·ya·o·ni·han \wa-yá-o-ni-haŋ\ *v* wa·bla·onihan [fr *yaonihan* to honor, praise] : to honor, to praise one — **wayaonihan·yan** *adv* : praising

wa·ya·o·pte·lya \wa-yá-o-pṫe-lya\ *v* : to make less with the mouth

wa·ya·o·tan \wa-yá-o-ṫaŋ\ *v* : to exhort, urge one - P

wa·ya·o·tan'·in \wa-yá-o-taŋ-iŋ\ *v* [fr *yaotan'in* to proclaim, make manifest] : to make manifest — *n* : one who reveals or makes manifest

wa·ya·pa \wa-yá-ṗa\ *v* wa·bla·pa [fr *yapá* to bite, take and hold *e.g.* a pipe in the mouth] : to hold in the mouth — *n* : something edible taken home - NP

wa·ya·pe·mni \wa-yá-ṗe-mni\ *v* wa·bla·pemni [fr *yapemni* twist or turn crooked with the mouth] : to twist with the teeth

wa·ya·pe·sto \wa-yá-ṗe-sṫo\ *v* wa·bla·pesto [fr *yapesto* to make sharp pointed with the mouth] : to bite to a point

wa·ya·pi \wa-yá-ṗi\ *v* wa·bla·pi [fr *ya* by mouth + *pi* to be good] : to declare to be good - Cf wayapika

wa·ya·pi·ka \wa-yá-ṗi-ka\ *vn* wa·bla·pika : to be fluent or eloquent, to speak a language well

wa·ya·ṗin·ṡpin·ze·ce \wa-yá-ṗiŋ-ṡpiŋ-ze-ce\ *v* wa·bla·pinspinzece : to eat very slowly, because the ration is very small - Bl

wa·ya·pi·ya \wa-yá-ṗi-ya\ *adv* : fluently

wa·ya·pi·za·pi \wa-yá-pi-za-pi\ *n* : a mouth organ

wa·ya·po·pa \wa-yá-po-ṗa\ *v* wa·bla·popa [fr *yapopa* to make pop] : to make burst by biting

wa·ya·po·ta \wa-yá-ṗo-ṫa\ *v* wa·bla·pota [fr *yapota* to tear in pieces with the mouth] : to rend, to be ravenous, to tear to pieces with the mouth — *n* : one that tears in pieces with the teeth, as does a dog

wa·ya·psa·ka \wa-yá-psa-ka\ *v* wa·bla·psaka [fr *yapsaka* to tear in two with the mouth] : to bite off *e.g.* cords

wa·ya·psi·ca \wa-yá-psi-ca\ *v* wa·bla·psica [fr *yapsica* to make skip or jump by biting] : to make hop by biting

wa·ya·pson *or* **wayapsun** \wa-yá-psoŋ\ *v* wa·bla·pson [fr *yapson* to spill with the mouth] : to spill by mouth

wa·ya·pšun \wa-yá-pšuŋ\ *v* [fr *yapšun* to cast off, shed *e.g.* its teeth] : to shed, as a horse its teeth

wa·ya·ptan·yan \wa-yá-ptaŋ-yaŋ\ *v* wa·bla·ptanyan [fr *yaptanyan* to turn over with the mouth] : to turn over with the mouth, to roll over

wa·ya·pte·ce·la \wa-yá-pte-ce-la\ *v* [fr *yaptecela* to make short by biting] : to bite off short

wa·ya·ptu·ja \wa-yá-ptu-ja\ *v* wa·bla·ptuja [fr *yaptuja* to crack or split with the mouth] : to split *e.g.* a tooth

wa·ya·ska·pa *or* **wayaškapa** \wa-yá-ska-pa\ *v* : to smack one's lips; to kiss < *howáyaskapa* fish sound a kiss, as is said of the noise made by fish when they break the surface of the water, or as in kissing itself > - Note: the play on the word: *Ho wayáskapa* Alright, he smacked her a kiss, and *howáyaskapa* a fish smacked kiss

wa·ya·ske·pa \wa-yá-sǩe-ṗa\ *v* [fr *yaskepa* to drink up] : to drink all out

wa·ya·ski·ca \wa-yá-ski-ca\ *v* wa·bla·skica [fr *yaskica* to suck or lick on] : to press on with the mouth

wa·ya·ski·ta \wa-yá-ski-ta\ *v* wa·bla·skita : to press on with the mouth, make tight

wa·ya·sku \wa-yá-sku\ *v* wa·bla·sku [fr *yasku* to bite or peel off with the teeth] : to peel off with the teeth, to bite off the skin or rind — **wayasku·sku** *v red* wa·bla·skusku [fr *yasku* to bite or peel off] : to bite off the rind or hull

wa·ya·sle·ca \wa-yá-sle-ca\ *v* [fr *yasleca* to split with the teeth] : to split with the teeth

wa·ya·slo·han \wa-yá-slo-haŋ\ *v* [fr *yaslohan* to drag along with the mouth] : to drag along with the mouth as a wolf or other animal does its prey

wa·ya·slu·ta \wa-yá-slu-ta\ *v* : to pull out with the teeth, as does a dog

wa·ya·sma·ka \wa-yá-sma-ka\ *v* [fr *ya* bite + *smaka* a sunken place] : to bite and make indentations

wa·ya·smin \wa-yá-smiŋ\ *v* [fr *yasmin* to gnaw or make bare] : to gnaw off, as dogs do — **wayasmin·yanyan** *v* : to be eaten off smooth

wa·ya·sna \wa-yá-sna\ *v* wa·bla·sna [fr *yasna* to make ring with the mouth, to ravel with the teeth] **a** : to

make ring using the mouth **b** : to ravel with the teeth
wa·ya·sni \wa-yá-sni\ *v* [fr *sni* cold] : to talk until the fire goes out, to make go out by talking
wa·ya·so·ta \wa-yá-so-ta\ *v* wa·bla·sota [fr *yasota* to use all up with the mouth] : to eat all up *e.g.* food; *fig* to use up words — **wayasote·ca** *n* : a voracious person, one who eats up much
wa·ya·spa·ya \wa-yá-spa-ya\ *v* wa·bla·spaya [fr *yaspaya* wet with the mouth] : to make damp or wet with the mouth
wa·ya·stan·ka \wa-yá-sṫaŋ-ka\ *v* [fr *yastanka* to use the mouth to moisten] : to moisten with the mouth
wa·ya·sto \wa-yá-sṫo\ *v* [fr *yasto* to lick smooth] : to lick down, as one cow does the hair of another
wa·ya·su \wa-yá-su\ *v* wa·bla·su [fr *yasu* to judge or decree, set things right by speaking] : to judge, condemn — *n* : a judge
wa·ya·su·ta \wa-yá-su-ṫa\ *v* wa·bla·suta [fr *yasuta* to make firm with the mouth] : to establish or decree
wa·ya·su·ya \wa-yá-su-ya\ *adv* : in the manner of judging
wa·ya·swa·ka \wa-yá-swa-ka\ *v* wa·bla·swaka [fr *yaswaka* to make fringed trying to bite off] : to make fringed by trying to bite off a piece of tough meat, *i.e.* not getting off much - Bl
wa·ya·sya·zan·ka \wa-yá-sya-zaŋ-ka\ *adj* : sickly — *n* : ill health - WE KE
wa·ya·ša·pa \wa-yá-ša-ṗa\ *v* [fr *yašapa* to soil with the mouth] : to defile with the mouth
wa·ya·ši·ca \wa-yá-ši-ca\ *v* wa·bla·šica [fr *yašica* to curse, speak evil of one] : to curse or speak evil of one
wa·ya·ši·gla \wa-yá-ši-gla\ *v* [fr *yašigla* to insult one] : to make angry by talking to
wa·ya·ši·htin \wa-yá-ši-ȟtiŋ\ *v* [fr *yašihtin* to enfeeble by biting] : to enfeeble by biting or talking to perhaps; to spoil or make bad with the mouth, to talk badly about or to find fault with — **wayašihtin·ka** *n* : a complainer, controller, one who always finds fault
wa·ya·ši·pa \wa-yá-ši-pa\ *v* [fr *yašipa* to bite off close] : to bite off close, as do animals to small twigs of trees
wa·ya·ška \wa-yá-ška\ *v* [fr *yaška* to untie with the mouth] : to untie with the mouth
wa·ya·škan·škan \wa-yá-škaŋ-škaŋ\ *v* [fr *yaškanškan* to make move about by talking to] : to cause to move using the mouth
wa·ya·ška·pa \wa-yá-ška-pa\ *v* : to make the noise of lapping water < *Howáyaškapa* The fish sounds its kiss in breaking the water, as is said of the noise made by splashing water-grass. > - *See* wayaskapa
wa·ya·ški·ca \wa-yá-ški-ca\ *v* [fr *yaškica* to chew] : to chew and press with the mouth, as in chewing tobacco
wa·ya·ški·ška \wa-yá-ški-ška\ *v* wa·bla·ški·ška [fr *yaškiška* to object, make difficulty, to create dissention] : to get into difficulty by talking, to misrepresent
wa·ya·ško·kpa \wa-yá-ško-kpa\ *v* wa·bla·škokpa [fr *yaškokpa* to bite out a hollow] : to gnaw out a hollow place
wa·ya·ško·pa \wa-yá-ško-ṗa\ *v* [fr *yaškopa* to make crooked or twisting with the mout] : to make warp or twist with the mouth
wa·ya·šla \wa-yá-šla\ *v* [fr *yašla* to graze off, make bare] : to graze, browse, to make bare as do cattle do by grazing < *Iyupaga po, tokša hantahena wayašlapi kte lo* Get along, soon before night they will have it grazed. > - Note: the word is used in the present time of their doing it now BT B.H.42.25
wa·ya·šla·ki·ya \wa-yá-šla-ki-ya\ *va* : to herd - B.H. 85.11
wa·ya·šlo·ka \wa-yá-šlo-ka\ *v* [fr *yašloka* to pull out with the teeth] : to bit out *e.g.* a cork
wa·ya·šna \wa-yá-šna\ *v* wa·bla·šna [fr *yašna* to blunder in speaking] : to make mistakes in talking, to stammer, to miss or let fall from the mouth
wa·ya·špa \wa-yá-špa\ *v* wa·bla·špa [fr *yašpa* to bite or break off a piece with the mouth] : to bite off pieces
wa·ya·špi \wa·ya·špi\ *v* [fr *yašpi* to pick or pluck off] : to pick off fruit, as do birds
wa·ya·špu \wa-yá-špu\ *v* [fr *yašpu* to bite off what is stuck] : to pick off with the mouth something that has been stuck on
wa·ya·šu·ja \wa-yá-šu-ja\ *v* [fr *yašuja* to crush or mash with the mouth as a dog does to bones] : to crush with the mouth
wa·ya·ta \wa-yá-ta\ *v* wa·bla·ta [fr *wóta* to eat] : to chew — **wayata** \wa-yá-ṫa\ *v* 2nd *pers singl of* wóta : You chewed something
wa·ya·ta·ku·ni·šni \wa-yá-ṫa-ku-ni-šni\ *v* wa·bla·takunišni [fr *yatakunišni* to eat up, destroy with the mouth, *fig* to speak contemptuously of one] : to destroy with the mouth
wa·ya·tan \wa-yá-ṫaŋ\ *v* : to praise - Bl
wa·ya·tan'·in \wa-yá-taŋ-iŋ\ *v* wa·bla·tan'in [fr *yatan'in*] : to make manifest, make evident
wa·ya·tan·ka \wa-yá-taŋ-ka\ *v* wa·bla·tanka [fr *yatanka* to speak of as large] : to speak of as great
wa·ya·ta·ta \wa-yá-ta-ta\ *v red* : to chew
wa·ya·ta·wa·cin·hin·yan·za \wa-yá-ta-wa-ciŋ-hiŋ-yaŋ-za\ *vn* : to take others habitually to be morose persons
wa·ya·te·han \wa-yá-ṫe-haŋ\ *v* : to speak of as far — **wayatehan·han** *v* wa·bla·tehahan : to speak slowly
wa·ya·te·ȟi·ka \wa-yá-ṫe-ȟi-ka\ *v* [fr *yateȟika* to speak of as difficult] : to speak of as a difficulty
wa·ya·te·kon·za \wa-yá-ṫe-koŋ-za\ *v* [fr *wayata* to chew + *konza* to pretend doing] : to chew the cud as do cows, *lit* to pretend to chew
wa·ya·te·pa \wa-yá-ṫe-ṗa\ *v* wa·bla·tepa [fr *yatepa* to bite, wear off short, as the teeth] : to wear off the teeth
wa·ya·ti·ktil i·he \wa-yá-ti-ktil i-hè\ *v* wayatiktil i·wa·he : to nag, to find fault with others when there is no reason for it; to get off meat on a bone as dogs do - LB
wa·ya·ti·tan \wa-yá-ṫi-ṫaŋ\ *v* wa·bla·titan [fr *yatitan* to pull with the mouth, as a dog holding a bone under foot and pulling meat off] : to pull with the teeth
wa·ya·tkan *or* **wayatke** \wa-yá-tǩaŋ\ *v* wa·bla·tkan [fr *yatkan* to drink] : to drink — **wayatke·kiya** \wa-yá-tǩe-ǩi-ya\ *va* wayatke·wa·kiya : to cause to drink, to give medicine to
wa·ya·tkon·za *or* **wayatkunza** \wa-yá-tkoŋ-za\ *v* wa·bla·tkonza [fr *yatkonza* to bite off even] : to make equal
wa·ya·to·gto·gya \wa-yá-to-gto-gya\ *v* [fr *yatogtogya* to tell lies as one narrates an event] : to lie while narrating something < *wayatogtog ià* to speak while fabricating, perhaps >
wa·ya·to·kan \wa-yá-to-kaŋ\ *v* wa·bla·tokan [fr *yatokan* to speak of as being in another place] : to speak of as in

---

\a\ father \e\ they \i\ machine \o\ smoke \u\ lunar \an, aŋ\ blanc Fr. \in, iŋ\ ink \on, oŋ, un, uŋ\ soon, confier Fr. \c\ chair \ǧ\ machen Ger. \j\ fusion \clusters: bl, gn, kp, hšl, etc...\ $b^{e}lo$ ... said with a slight vowel
See more in the Introduction, Guide to Pronunciation

another place
wa·ya·to·ke·ca \wa-yá-to-ke-ca\ *v* wa·bla·tokeca [fr *yatokeca* to speak of as different] : to alter, change, speak of as different
wa·ya·tu·ka \wa-yá-tu-ka\ *v* wa·bla·tuka [fr *yatuka* to nibble off and so spoil] : to nibble off *e.g.* hair *etc.*
wa·ya·tu·ta \wa-yá-tu-ta\ *v* wa·bla·tuta : to make smart by biting
wa·ya·t'a \wa-yá-t'a\ *v* wa·bla·t'a [fr *yat'a* to bite to death] : to bite something to death
wa·ya·t'in·za \wa-yá-t'iŋ-za\ *v* [fr *yat'inza* to affirm] : to establish, declare, make firm with the mouth
wa·ya·un·ka \wa-yá-uŋ-ka\ *v* wa·bla·unka [fr *yaunka* to pull or throw down with the mouth, as do beavers to trees] : to bite and make fall - R Bl
wa·ya·wa \wa-yá-wa\ *v* wa·bla·wa [fr *yawá* to read, count, consider, say over again] : to read, count, to go to school
wa·ya·wa·hin·yan·za *or* **wayuwahinyanza** \wa-yá-wa-hiŋ-yaŋ-za\ *v* : to make morose or ill-disposed
wa·ya·wa·ja \wa-yá-wa-ja\ *v* [fr *yawaja* to split or make a noise with the mouth]: to bite or gnaw at, as dogs do
wa·ya·wa·kan \wa-yá-wa-kaŋ\ *v* wa·bla·wakan : to speak of as sacred
wa·ya·wa·pi \wa-yá-wa-pi\ *n* : arithmetic, numeration, reading
wa·ya·wa·ša·ka·la \wa-yá-wa-ša-ka-la\ *v* wa·bla·wašakala : to speak of as easy or cheap
wa·ya·wa·šte \wa-yá-wa-šte\ *v* wa·bla·wašte [fr *yawašte* to bless, declare good] : to bless
wa·ya·wa·š'a·ka \wa-yá-wa-š'a-ka\ *v* wa·bla·waš'aka : to call strong
wa·ya·wa·za \wa-yá-wa-za\ *v* [fr *yawaza* to bite or gnaw, to bite in play, as dogs do] : to bite, as dogs do in playing with one another
wa·ya·we·ga \wa-yá-we-ġa\ *v* wa·bla·we·ga [fr *yawega* to fracture, break *e.g.* a stick with the mouth] : to break partly off with the mouth
wa·ya·wi·ca·ka \wa-yá-wi-ca-ka\ *v* wa·bla·wicaka : to call true
wa·ya·wi·ca·ša·šni \wa-yá-wi-ca-ša-šni\ *v* wa·bla·wicašašni : to speak of as wicked
wa·ya·wi·gnu·ni \wa-yá-wi-gnu-ni\ *v* wa·bla·wignuni [fr *yawignuni* to talk bad, destroy with the mouth] : to confuse by butting in and saying hard words - R Bl
wa·ya·win·ja \wa-yá-wiŋ-ja\ *v* wa·bla·winja : to bend down with the mouth
wa·ya·wi·ya·kpa \wa-yá-wi-ya-kpa\ *v* [fr *yawiyakpa* to interpret, make shine with the mouth] : to give an interpretation
wa·ya·za·mni \wa-yá-za-mni\ *v* [fr *yazamni* to expose, open, uncover with the mouth] : to uncover with the mouth
wa·ya·zan \wa-yá-zaŋ\ *v* wa·ma·yazan [fr *yazan* to feel pain] : to feel unwell, to have pains — **wayazan·gla** *v* wayazan·wa·gla : to feel pain — **wayazan·ka** \wa-yá-zaŋ-ka\ *v* wa·ma·yazanka : to be sick — *n* : one who does not feel right - Cf yazán
wa·ya·ze \wa-yá-ze\ *v* [fr *yaze* to retrieve] : to take out food with the mouth, as does a dog
wa·ya·zi·ca \wa-yá-zi-ca\ *v* wa·bla·zica : to stretch anything with the mouth
wa·ya·zo·ka \wa-yá-zo-ka\ *v* wa·bla·zoka [fr *yazoka* to sip or draw a fluid to taste] : to suck *e.g.* candy or sugar
wa·ya·zon·ta *or* **wayazunta** \wa-yá-zoŋ-ta\ *v* [fr *yazonta* to praise one who should be reproved] : to praise an undeserving person
wa·ye \wa-yé\ *va* : to hunt for edibles and game; to look for money, as once it was gotten at the Agency < ~ *omani, i, ya iyaya, mni kte* He went afoot hunting, He went hunting, He goes hunting, He went on hunting, I shall go hunting. *Waye ya coka ukiye s'elececa* He goes hunting as if he would come back empty-handed. ~ *wai tka coka wagli yelo* I had gone hunting but arrived home with nothing. ~ *coka kau welo* He looked for money and came home emptyhanded, as is said when a man returns without having found anything. ~ *i na wana hlayetu hanl watuka gli* He went hunting and now by nightfall he arrived home exhausted. > - LT Bl Ja D.232
wa·yu·a·bla·ya \wa-yú-a-bla-ya\ *v* [fr *yuablaya* to spread on the level] : to make level
wa·yu·a·gla·pšun·yan i·ye·ya \wa-yú-a-gla-pšuŋ-yaŋ i-yè-ya\ *v* : to turn upside down, *i.e.* bottom up
wa·yu·a·ki·h'an \wa-yú-a-ki-ȟ'aŋ\ *v* [fr *yuakih'an* to cause to starve] : to make starve - *See* akih'an *vn* to be starving
wa·yu·a·ki·pab \wa-yú-a-ki-ṗab\ *adv* : separately - Note: how we say "to divide" or "to separate" : ~ *egnaka; akipab egnaka* is rendered "divided" or "separate"
wa·yu·a·pa·ko \wa-yú-a-ṗa-ko\ *v* [fr *yuapako* to make crooked] : to make crooked - *See* apako
wa·yu·a·ška·ye·la \wa-yú-a-ška-ye-la\ *v* [fr *yuaškayela* to make or bring near] : to make near - Cf *aškatuyela* lately, a short time ago R Bl
wa·yu·a·šla·ya \wa-yú-a-šla-ya\ *v* wa·blu·ašlaya [fr *yuašlaya* to uncover, expose a secret] : to uncover, make manifest — **wayuašlaya·pi** *n* : an interpretation - Cf ašlaya B.H.30.13
wa·yu·a·zi \wa-yú-a-zi\ *v* [fr *yuazi* to pull ashore] : to run aground, as a boat - *Syn* ÁZE
wa·yu·bla·ska \wa-yú-bla-ska\ *v* [fr *yublaska* to flatten] : to make flat - Cf blaska
wa·yu·bla·ya \wa-yú-bla-ya\ *v* wa·blu·blaya [fr *yublaya* to unfold, spread out, level] : to spread out, make level
wa·yu·bla·za \wa-yú-bla-ya\ *v* [fr *yu* to cause + *blaza* to burst] : to rip open - Cf blazahan
wa·yu·ble·ca \wa-yú-ble-ca\ *v* wa·blu·bleca [fr *yu* to cause + *bleca* to get more sick] : to crush, break in pieces, to have broken health - Cf blecahan
wa·yu·blu \wa-yú-blu\ *v* wa·blu·blu [fr *yu* to cause + *blu* to pulverized] : to plow, make mellow
wa·yu·bu \wa-yú-bu\ *v* [fr *yu* to cause + *bu* to cause a noise by beating *e.g.* a drum] : to make a drumming noise — **wayubu·bu** *v red* : to beat a drum
wa·yu·can \wa-yú-caŋ\ *v* wa·blu·can [fr *yu* to cause + *can* or *cancan* to shake] : to sift — **wayucan·can** *v red* : to shake, sift
wa·yu·ce·ka \wa-yú-ce-ka\ *v* wa·blu·ceka : to stagger one — **wayucekce·ka** *v* wa·blu·cekceka [fr *yu* to cause + *cekceka* to stagger] : to make stagger or reel
wa·yu·ce·ya \wa-yú-ce-ya\ *v* [fr *yu* to cause + *ceya* cry] : to make cry
wa·yu·ci·k'a·la *or* **wayuciscila** \wa-yú-ci-k'a-la\ *v* wa·blu·cik'ala [fr *yu* to cause + *ci-k'ala* little] : to compress, to make small
wa·yu·co \wa-yú-co\ *adv* [fr *ayuco* excellently, well] : neatly, well — **wayuco·co** *adv red* : superbly, well
wa·yu·co·ka·ka \wa-yú-co-ka-ka\ *v* wa·blu·cokaka [fr *yu* to cause + *coka* empty] : to take out or empty *e.g.* the

load from a gun

wa·yu·co·ya \wa-yú-co-ya\ *adv* : excellently – *Syn* AYUCOYA

wa·yu·co·za \wa-yú-co-za\ *v* wa·blu·coza [fr *yucoza* to make comfortable, warm] : to make warm by kindling a fire – Cf coza

wa·yu·e·ce·lya \wa-yú-e-ce-lya\ *v* wa·blu·e·ce·lya [fr *yuecelya* to make something correctly] : to make a thing as it ought to be, as prescribed – Bl

wa·yu·e·ce·tu \wa-yú-e-ce-ṫu\ *v* wa·blu·ecetu [fr *yu* to cause + *ecetu* just so] : to make right, to accomplish, fulfill, to do as prescribed

wa·yu·e·ci·ya \wa-yú-e-ci-ya\ *v* wa·blu·eciya [fr *ayueciya* to turn inside out] : to turn the wrong side out

wa·yu·e·kta·šni·yan \wa-yú-e-kta-šni-yaŋ\ *v* wa·blu·ektašniyan [fr *yu* to cause + *ektašniyan* not according to] : to act wrongly – B.H.82.6

wa·yu·ga \wa-yú-ġa\ *v* wa·blu·ga [fr *yuga* to husk] : to pull off, open out, as in husking corn, to husk corn

wa·yu·gan \wa-yú-ġaŋ\ *v* wa·blu·gan [fr *yugan* to open]

wa·yu·ga·pa \wa-yú-ġa-pa\ *v* wa·blu·gapa [fr *yugapa* to skin an animal] : to skin, flay an animal, to take off the skin

wa·yu·ga·ta \wa-yú-ġa-ta\ *v* wa·blu·gata [fr *yugata* to extend the hand and arm upward] : to spread out *e.g.* the hands

wa·yu·gla \wa-yú-gla\ *v* wa·blu·gla [fr *yugla* to unroll, to stretch] : to untwist, uncoil

wa·yu·glo·ka \wa-yú-glo-ka\ *v* wa·blu·gloka : to dislocate

wa·yu·gmi·gma \wa-yú-gmi-gma\ *v* wa·blu·gmigma [fr *yugmigma* to make round, *i.e.* into a ball] : to make round, to roll, as in making a ball – Bl

wa·yu·gmi·yan·yan \wa-yú-gmi-yaŋ-yaŋ\ *v* wa·blu·gmiyanyan [fr *yugmiyanyan* to make roll with the hand]

wa·yu·gmun \wa-yú-gmuŋ\ *v* wa·blu·gmun [fr *yugmun* to twist] : to twist

wa·yu·gna \wa-yú-gna\ *v* [fr *yugna* to shake and make *e.g.* fruit fall off from the tree] : to shake off *e.g.* fruit

wa·yu·gna·škin·yan \wa-yú-gna-škiŋ-yaŋ\ *v* wa·blu·gnaškinyan [fr *yugnaškinyan* to be possessed, to rave] : to make crazy

wa·yu·gna·yan \wa-yú-gna-yaŋ\ *v* : to deceive; to miss trying to take a hold on, to grasp

wa·yu·go \wa-yú-ġo\ *v* wa·blu·go [fr *yugo* to make scratches] : to make crooked marks

wa·yu·gu·ka \wa-yú-ġu-k̇a\ *v* wa·blu·guka [fr *yuguka* to draw out or unfold *e.g.* an arrow or a knife] : to stretch, strain, sprain

wa·yu·gwe·za \wa-yú-gwe-za\ *v* [fr *yugweza* to roughen] : to make rough

wa·yu·ha \wa-yú-ha\ *v* wa·blu·ha [fr *yuha* to have] : to have things, possess things, to have or own property < ~ *iyeya* to come suddenly into possession of > — **wayuhaha·ka** *n* wa·blu·hahaka : one who possesses much

wa·yu·ha·ha·ye·la \wa-yú-ha-ha-ye-la\ *v* wa·blu·hahayela [fr *yuhahayela* to shake, make unstable] : to make unsteady

wa·yu·hi \wa-yú-hi\ *v* wa·blu·hi [fr *yuhi* to startle and drive off game] : to drive off *e.g.* game, to arouse or startle *etc.* < *Mato Wayuhi* Bear Stops, the name of Bear Shirt's old father > — **wayuhi·ka** \wa-yú-hi-ka\ *adj* : disturbing, troublesome

wa·yu·hinl \wa-yú-hiŋl\ *v contrac of* wayuhinta : to sweep off < *Šunkawakan ~ wotapelo* Horses eat after sweeping it away, *i.e.* after scratching away the snow to eat the grass. > – LB

wa·yu·hin·ta \wa-yú-hiŋ-ta\ *v* wa·blu·hinta [fr *yuhinta* to rake away] : to sweep off

wa·yu·ho·ho \wa-yú-ho-ho\ *v* wa·blu·hoho [fr *yuhoho* to shake or move what should be firm] : to catch and hold loosely, as something too large to grasp

wa·yu·ho·mni \wa-yú-ho-mni\ *v* [fr *yuhomni* to turn, to turn around anything] : to turn round on

wa·yu·ho·ton \wa-yú-ho-toŋ\ *v* : to cause to make noise

wa·yu·hun·hun·za \wa-yú-huŋ-huŋ-za\ *v* wa·blu·hunhunza [fr *yuhunhun-za* to shake by hand *e.g.* a tree] : to shake

wa·yu·ȟa·tka \wa-yú-ȟa-tka\ *v* [fr *yuȟatka* to ruffle *e.g.* the hair or feathers] : to make rough

wa·yu·ȟe·pa \wa-yú-ȟe-pa\ *v* [fr *yuȟepa* to empty, lading out] : to drain off, to absorb

wa·yu·ȟe·ya·ta \wa-yú-ȟe-ya-ta\ *v* [fr *yuȟeyata* to reject and put back] : to shove aside, push back

wa·yu·ȟi·ca *or* **wayuġica** \wa-yú-ȟi-ca\ *v* wa·blu·ȟica [fr *yuȟica* or *yuġica* to awaken one] : to waken one up, cause to awaken

wa·yu·ȟi·ya·ya *or* **wayuh'iyaya** \wa-yú-ȟi-ya-ya\ *v* wa·blu·ȟiyaya [fr *yuȟiyaya* or *yuh'iyaya* to do badly, to bungle] : to be awkward, to bungle — **wayuȟiyayaka** *n* : a bungler

wa·yu·hla \wa-yú-ȟla\ *v* [fr *yuhla* to ring or rattle] : to make rattle

wa·yu·hla·gan \wa-yúu-ȟla-ġaŋ\ *v* [fr *yuhlagan* to enlarge, to separate and leave] : to make larger, to enlarge

wa·yu·hla·ta \wa-yú-ȟla-ta\ *v* [fr *yuhlata* to scratch as does a cat] : to scratch, to dig under

wa·yu·hle·ca \wa-yú-ȟle-ca\ *v* wa·blu·hleca [fr *yuhleca* to tear in pieces by hand] : to tear

wa·yu·hlo·ka \wa-yú-ȟlo-ka\ *v* wa·blu·hloka [fr *yuhloka* to make a hole by hand] : to make a hole, *fig* to open

wa·yu·hmi \wa-yú-ȟmi\ *v* : to make crooked

wa·yu·hmin \wa-yú-ȟmiŋ\ *v* [fr *yuhmin* to disjoint, to sling, to make go crooked sideways] : to throw off sideways

wa·yu·hmun \wa-yú-ȟmuŋ\ *v* [fr *yuhmun* to make whizz] : to buzz or make buzz

wa·yu·hpa \wa-yú-ȟpa\ *v* [fr *yuhpa* to loosen, let down or fall] : to lay or throw down

wa·yu·hpu \wa-yú-ȟpu\ *v* [fr *yuhpu* to pick off a piece] : to pick off pieces

wa·yu·hta·ta \wa-yú-ȟta-ṫa\ *v* wa·blu·htata [fr *htata* weak or languid] : to offer sacrifices, to kill in sacrifice – Note: the word is used generally of animate objects, whereas *waunyan* is used of inanimate ones

wa·yu·hta·ta·pi \wa-yú-ȟta-ṫa-pi\ *n* : sacrifices, animals or things offered in sacrifice, *esp.* to avoid some evil, but also to express one's community with departed spirits. Thus pieces from one's meal are offered to a *wanagi* before one sets to eating, by dropping them on the ground, so that animals and birds may pick them up. Non-edible sacrifices are generally termed, *waunyanpi*

wa·yu·ȟu·ga \wa-yú-ȟu-ġa\ *v* wa·blu·ȟuga [fr *yuȟuga* to crack by hand] : to break holes in

wa·yu·ȟun·ta \wa-yú-ȟuŋ-ṫa\ *v* wa·blu·ȟunta [fr *yu*-

\a\ father \e\ they \i\ machine \o\ smoke \u\ lunar \an, aŋ\ blanc Fr. \in, iŋ\ ink \on, oŋ, un, uŋ\ soon, confier Fr. \c\ chair \ġ\ machen Ger. \j\ fusion \clusters: bl, gn, kp, hšl, etc...\ b^e^lo ... said with a slight vowel
See more in the Introduction, Guide to Pronunciation

ȟunta to make soft by rubbing] : to make soft or pliant *e.g.* a skin by rubbing
wa·yu·ȟun·win \wa-yú-ȟuŋ-wiŋ\ *v* [fr *yuȟunwin* to make putrify, as flesh] : to cause to putrify - R Bl
wa·yu·h'an·hi \wa-yú-ȟ'aŋ-hi\ *v* : to retard, make slow — **wayuh'anhi·ca** *v* : to play out, exhaust a horse by not knowing how to handle it — **wayuh'anhi·hike** *n* : a laggard, slowpoke, one who is slow in his actions
wa·yu·h'i·ya·ya·ka \wa-yú-ȟ'i·ya·ya·ka\ *vn* wa·blu·h'i-yayaka : to be inexperienced, to be a greenhorn - KE
wa·yu·h'u \wa-yú-ȟ'u\ *v* wa·blu·h'u [fr *yuh'u* to peel, pull off little pieces] : to peel
wa·yu·i·ci·ca·hi \wa-yú-i-ci-ca-hi\ *v* [fr *yuicicahi* to mix together] : to mingle, mix together
wa·yu·i·e·ska \wa-yú-i-e-ska\ *v* : to translate — *n* : an interpreter — **wayuieska·pi** *n* : an interpretation - B.H.30.13
wa·yu·i·le \wa-yú-i-le\ *v* [fr *yuile* to start a fire, to kindle a fire] : to make blaze
wa·yu·i·na·hni \wa-yú-i-na-ȟni\ *v* wa·blu·inahni [fr *yuinahni* to hurry, hasten one] : to cause to hasten
wa·yu·in·yan·ka \wa-yú-iŋ-yaŋ-ka\ *v* wa·blu·inyanka : to hurry along, getting ahead of others by hurrying - IS
wa·yu·i·šte·ca \wa-yú-i-šte-ca\ *v* [fr *yuišteca* to shame a person] : to make ashamed
wa·yu·i·yo·wa·za \wa-yú-i-yo-wa-za\ *v* [fr *yuiyowaza* to make echo, resound] : to cause an echo
wa·yu·ja \wa-yú-ja\ *v* wa·blu·ja [fr *yuja* to mash and make mush, to stir such] : to stir up, make mush or a hasty pudding
wa·yu·ja·ja \wa-yú-ja-ja\ *v* wa·blu·jaja [fr *yujaja* to wash things] : to wash *e.g.* clothes, to do a washing
wa·yu·ja·ka \wa-yú-ja-ǩa\ *v* wa·blu·jaka [fr *yujaka* to pull or strain open a person's eyes] : to pull open
wa·yu·jin·ca \wa-yú-jiŋ-ca\ *v* wa·blu·jinca [fr *yujinca* to blow or pull the nose] : to pull or blow *e.g.* the nose
wa·yu·ji·pa \wa-yú-ji-pa\ *v* [fr *yujipa* to pinch] : to pinch — *n* : one who pinches
wa·yu·ju·ju \wa-yú-ju-ju\ *v* wa·blu·juju [fr *yujuju* to deface, pull to pieces, to undo, open] : to tear down, demolish
wa·yu·jun \wa-yú-juŋ\ *v* wa·blu·jun [fr *yujun* to uproot or pull out] : to pull out by the roots, to uproot
wa·yu·ka·ki·ja \wa-yú-ǩa-ǩi-ja\ *v* [fr *yukakija* to cause to suffer] : to make suffer
wa·yu·kan \wa-yú-kaŋ\ *v* [fr *yukan* to shake off] : to shake off *e.g.* the dew
wa·yu·ka·pa \wa-yú-ka-ṗa\ *v* wa·blu·kapa [fr *yukapa* to catch *e.g.* a ball in the hand] : to catch in the hand *e.g.* a ball
wa·yu·ka·tin \wa-yú-ka-ṫiŋ\ *v* [fr *yukatin* to straighten out by hand] : to straighten out
wa·yu·ka·wa \wa-yú-ǩa-wa\ *v* wa·blu·kawa [fr *yukawa* to open a wound, a sore, a person's mouth] : to open out, push back
wa·yu·kca \wa-yú-kca\ *v* wa·blu·kca [fr *yukca* to loosen or untie, unwrap] : to untie, unbraid
wa·yu·kcan \wa-yú-kcaŋ\ *v* wa·blu·kcan [fr *yukcan* to know, guess, understand, comprehend] : to examine, investigate
wa·yu·ke·ca \wa-yú-ǩe-ċa\ *vn* [fr *yuǩan* to be, there is] : there is some
wa·yu·kin·ca \wa-yú-ǩiŋ-ca\ *v* [fr *yukinca* to scrape off by hand] : to scrape
wa·yu·ki·pa·ja \wa-yú-ǩi-ṗa-ja\ *v* [fr *yukipaja* to bend around, double over, to hem] : to double or fold up — **wayukipe·han** *v* [fr *yukipehan* to fold, lay in folds] : to fold up
wa·yu·ki·za \wa-yú-ǩi-za\ *v* wa·blu·kiza [fr *yukiza* to make creak] : to make creak
wa·yu·ko·ka *or* **wayukokoka** \wa-yu-ko-ǩa\ *v* [fr *yukoka* to ring or rattle] : to rattle, giving a dull sound
wa·yu·kpan \wa-yú-kṗaŋ\ *v* wa·blu·kpan [fr *yukpan* to grind *e.g.* corn] : to grind fine, to pulverize
wa·yu·ksa \wa-yú-ksa\ *v* wa·blu·ksa [fr *yuksa* to break off by hand] : to break off, cut grain — **wayuksa·ksa** *v red* : to reap - B.H.79.2
wa·yu·ksa·pa \wa-yú-ksa-pa\ *v* [fr *yuksapa* to make wise] : to make wise — *n* : an instructor, one who makes wise
wa·yu·kse \wa-yú-kse\ *va* : to harvest, break off *e.g.* ears of corn - B.H.183.6
wa·yu·kša \wa-yú-kša\ *v* [fr *yukša* to double up] : to roll up *e.g.* a blanket — **wayu·kša·la** \wa-yú-kša-la\ *v* [fr *yukšala* bent up, crooked] : to bend up
wa·yu·kšan \wa-yú-kšaŋ\ *v* [fr *yukšan* to bend something] : to bend
wa·yu·kši·ja \wa-yú-kši-ja\ *v* [fr *yukšija* to double up *e.g.* a knife, the arm] : to double up
wa·yu·ktan \wa-yú-kṫaŋ\ *v* wa·blu·ktan [fr *yuktan* to bend by hand] : to bend
wa·yu·ku·ka \wa-yú-ku-ka\ *v* [fr *yukuka* to pull to pieces, make rotten, destroy] : to spoil, wear out
wa·yu·k'e·ga \wa-yú-k'e-ġa\ *v* [fr *yuk'ega* to scratch where it itches] : to scratch with a grating noise
wa·yu·k'e·za \wa-yú-k'e-za\ *v* [fr *yuk'eza* to shear off close] : to make smooth with a grating noise
wa·yu·k'o·ga \wa-yú-k'o-ġa\ *v* [fr *yuk'oga* to scratch and make rough with the nails] : to scratch making rough with a grating noise
wa·yu·k'o·za \wa-yú-k'oza\ *v* [fr *yuk'oza* to make hard and smooth by taking off hair or grass] : to make smooth by scraping away
wa·yu·ma·hel i·ye·ya \wa-yú-ma-hel i-yè-ya\ *v* : to put or push into
wa·yu·man \wa-yú-maŋ\ *v* wa·blu·me [fr *yuman* to sharpen, by grinding, filing, whetting] : to grind, file, whet *e.g.* edged tools
wa·yu·mi·ma \wa-yú-mi-ma\ *v* wa·blu·mima [fr *yumima* to make round, as a wheel] : to make round by grinding
wa·yu·mna \wa-yú-mna\ *v* [fr *yumna* to rip a seam] : to rip
wa·yu·mni \wá-yu-mni\ *v* [fr *a* on + *yumni* to turn round] : to turn round on
wa·yu·mni·ga \wa-yú-mni-ġa\ *v* [fr *yumniga* to shrink] : to make shrink or draw up
wa·yu·na·jin \wa-yu-na-jin\ *v* wa·blu·najin [fr *yunajin* to raise, lift up, make stand] : to cause to stand up
wa·yu·na·ke·ya *or* **wayunankeya** \wa-yú-na-ǩe-ya\ *v* [fr *yunakeya* to turn partly as on one side] : to turn on one side
wa·yu·ni·ya·šni \wa-yú-ni-ya-šni\ *v* wa·blu·niyašni [fr *yuniyašni* to put out of breath] : to strangle or suffocate
wa·yun·ka \wá-yuŋ-ka\ *v* : to watch and stay with the buffalo kills < *Waunyunkapi kte lo* We shall stand watch, as some men would say when they wanted to stay with the buffalos killed, while others went off to call the people. > - Bl
wa·yu·o·ble·ca \wa-yú-o-ble-ca\ *v* wa·blu·obleca [fr *yuobleca* to disperse, divide, as a crowd of people] : to scatter abroad, disperse

wa·yu·o·ci·kpa·ni \wa-yú-o-ci-kṗa-ni\ *v* [fr *yuocikpani* to make unequal] : to make unequal

wa·yu·o·cin·ši·ca \wa-yú-o-ciŋ-ši-ca\ *v* [fr *yuocinšica* to make cross, angry] : to make cross

wa·yu·o·hmin \wa-yú-o-ȟmiŋ\ *v* [fr *yu* to cause + *o* a purpose + *hmin* crooked] : to miss, to throw on one side of the mark

wa·yu·o·hpa \wa-yú-o-ȟṗa\ *v* [fr *yuohpa* to break off or pull through and into] : to break through and into

wa·yu·o·h'an·ko \wa-yú-o-ȟ'aŋ-ko\ *v* wa·blu·oh'anko [fr *yuoh'anko* to make hasten] : to make hurry along

wa·yu·o·ka·hwo·ka \wa-yú-o-ka-ȟwo-ka\ *v* [fr *yuokahwoka* to make wave in folds, as a flag] : to cause to float in the air

wa·yu·o·ki·ni·han \wa-yú-o-ki-ni-haŋ\ *v* [fr *yuokinihan* to make honorable] : to make honorable

wa·yu·o·ki·wan·ji·la \wa-yú-o-k̇i-waŋ-ji-la\ *v* [fr *yuokiwanjila* to make alike or similar] : to unite, to make into one

wa·yu·o·ni·han \wa-yú-o-ni-haŋ\ *v* wa·blu·onihan [fr *yuonihan* to honor, treat with attention] : to honor, to be respectful — **wayuonihan·yan** *adv* : respectfully

wa·yu·o·pe·ša \wa-yú-o-ṗe-ša\ *n* : one who has respect for others — *adj* : respectful < ~ *nahahci ni waun* He who respects others still lives, *i.e.* he insists on having something, though he does not understand it so well. > - BT KE

wa·yu·o·pe·ša sni \wa-yú-o-ṗe-ša šni\ *n* : one who disrespects others < ~ *nahahci ni waun* He yet lives who disrespects others, *i.e.* he insists on having something though he does not understand it so well. > - BT KE

wa·yu·o·ptel \wa-yú-o-ptel\ *v contrac of* wayuopteca : to shorten — **wayuopte·tu** *or* **wayuptecela** *v* : to shorten - Bl

wa·yu·o·se·ya \wa-yú-o-se-ya\ *v* [fr *yuoseya* to knot tight] : to tie in a fast knot

wa·yu·o·ta \wa-yú-o-ṫa\ *v* wa·blu·ota [fr *yuota* to multiply] : to multiply

wa·yu·o·tan'·in \wa-yú-o-taŋ-iŋ\ *v* wa·blu·otan'in [fr *yuotan'in* to spread news, make manifest or appear] : to make manifest

wa·yu·o·tkon·za \wa-yú-o-tkoŋ-za\ *v* [fr *yuotkonza* to make of equal length, to finish] : to make equal

wa·yu·o·t'in·za \wa-yú-o-t'iŋ-za\ *v* wa·blu·ot'inza [fr *yuot'inza* to press in firm or tight] : to make tight in

wa·yu·o·wo·tan *or* **wayuowotan·la** \wa-yú-o-wo-taŋ\ *v* wa·blu·owotan [fr *yuowotan* to make or set up straight] : to straighten, to make upright

wa·yu·pan·ga \wa-yú-ṗaŋ-ġa\ *v* [fr *yupanga* to tie loosely, make a large bundle, *fig* to make one drunk,] : to multiply - *Syn* WAYU-OTA Bl

wa·yu·pan·pan *and* **wayupanpan·la** \wa-yú-paŋ-paŋ\ *v* wa·blu·panpan [fr *yupanpan* to soften *e.g.* a hide by rubbing] : to make soft

wa·yu·pa·tu·ja \wa-yú-ṗa-ṫu-ja\ *v* [fr *yupatuja* to cause to stoop or get down] : to bend down

wa·yu·pce·ce·la *or* **wayuoptecela** \wa-yú-pce-ce-la\ *v* [fr *yupcecela* to make short] : to shorten

wa·yu·pe·han \wa-yú-ṗe-haŋ\ *v* [fr *yupehan* to fold up] : to fold up

wa·yu·pi \wa-yú-ṗi\ *vn* wa·blu·pi : to be skillful, ingenious — **wayupi·ka** \wa-yú-ṗi-k̇a\ *vn* wa·blu·pika : to be skillful, expert — **wayupi·ya** *or* **wayupiya·han** *or* **wayupiya·kel** \wa-yú-ṗi-ya-k̇el\ *adv* : expertly, skillfully, well < *Oh'an ~ tak tokon* He is missing something he took long doing expertly. >

wa·yu·po·pa \wa-yú-po-ṗa\ *v* [fr *yupopa* to cause to burst or snap] : to cause to burst

wa·yu·po·ta \wa-yú-ṗo-ṫa\ *v* wa·blu·pota [fr *yupota* to tear to pieces, with the beak as a hawk does] : to wear out, cut up — **wayupote·ca** *n* : a consumer, one who wears out or uses up much

wa·yu·po·wa·ya \wa-yú-po-wa-ya\ *v* [fr *yupowaya* to roughen up *e.g.* fur or nap] : to brush up

wa·yu·psa·ka \wa-yú-psa-ka\ *v* wa·blu·psaka [fr *yupsaka* to break of pull in two, as a string] : to break *e.g.* a cord

wa·yu·psi·ca \wa-yú-psi-ca\ *v* wa·blu·psica [fr *yupsica* to make jump or toss] : to make jump

wa·yu·pson \wa-yú-psoŋ\ *v* wa·blu·pson [fr *yupson* to spill by pulling] : to spill out

wa·yu·pšun \wa-yú-pšuŋ\ *v* wa·blu·pšun [fr *yupšun* to pull out sideways, to pull and break] **a** : to pull out by the roots **b** : to dislocate

wa·yu·pta \wa-yú-pta\ *v* wa·blu·pta [fr *yupta* to cut out a garment with a pattern] : to cut out *e.g.* clothes

wa·yu·ptan·yan \wa-yú-ptaŋ-yaŋ\ *v* wa·blu·ptanyan [fr *yuptanyan* to turn over by pulling] : to turn over

wa·yu·pta·ye·la \wa-yú-pta-ye-la\ *v* wa·blu·pta [fr *yuptayela* to collect, put together] : to put together, to collect - Bl

wa·yu·pte·ce·la *or* **wayupcecela** \wa-yú-pte-ce-la\ *v* : to shorten

wa·yu·ptu·ȟ'a *or* **wayuptuġa** \wa-yú-ptu-ȟ'a\ *v* [fr *yuptuȟ'a* to pick to pieces] : to pick to pieces

wa·yu·ptu·ja \wa-yú-ptu-ja\ *v* [fr *yuptuja* to make crack or split] : to crack, to split

wa·yu·san \wa-yú-saŋ\ *v* [fr *yusan* to make fade, to make whitish or brownish] : to whiten, to whitewash

wa·yu·sa·pa \wa-yú-sa-pa\ *v* [fr *yusapa* to blacken] : to make black, to blacken

wa·yu·se·pa \wa-yú-se-pa\ *v* wa·blu·sepa [fr *yusepa* to deface, to rub or wear off] : to rub off *e.g.* dirt or paint - R Bl

wa·yu·ska \wa-yú-ska\ *v* wa·blu·ska [fr *yuska* to make white] : to whiten, make white; to acquit, clear one who has been charged with a crime — **wayuska·pi** *n* : a defendant acquitted of charges laid against him

wa·yu·ske·pa \wa-yú-sk̇e-ṗa\ *v* [fr *yuskepa* to evaporate or cause to escape or drain off] : to exhaust, to draw all out

wa·yu·ski·ca \wa-yú-sk̇i-ca\ *v* wa·blu·skica [fr *yuskica* to tighten, to press] : to be neat and tidy, surpassing all others, one who is feared by others or restrains others

wa·yu·ski·ta \wa-yú-ski-ṫa\ *v* : to bind, press - *Syn* WAYUSKICA

wa·yu·sku \wa-yú-sk̇u\ *v* wa·blu·sku [fr *yusku* to peel or pare away] : to shear off close, to shave, pare off — **wayusku·sku** *v red* : to shear off many

wa·yu·sla·sla·ta \wa-yú-sla-sla-ta\ *v red* : to do something slowly, deliberately

wa·yu·sla·ta \wa-yú-sla-ṫa\ *v* : to do a thing slowly

wa·yu·sle·ca \wa-yú-sle-ca\ *v* wa·blu·sleca [fr *yusleca* to split or tear *e.g.* meat by hand] : to split

wa·yu·slo·han \wa-yú-slo-haŋ\ *v* wa·blu·slohan [fr *yuslohan* to draw, pull, drag] : to draw along

---

\a\ father \e\ they \i\ machine \o\ smoke \u\ lunar \an, aŋ\ blanc Fr. \in, iŋ\ ink \on, oŋ, un, uŋ\ soon, confier Fr. \c\ chair \ġ\ machen Ger. \j\ fusion \clusters: bl, gn, kp, hšl, etc...\ b^e^lo ... said with a slight vowel
See more in the Introduction, Guide to Pronunciation

wa·yu·slu·ta \wa-yú-slu-ta\ *v* wa·blu·sluta [fr *yusluta* to pull out from under] : to pull out
wa·yu·sma·ka \wa-yú-sma-ka\ *v* [fr *yusmaka* to hollow out] : to indent, to hollow out
wa·yu·smin \wa-yú-smiŋ\ *v* [fr *yusmin* to pull or pick off what is not tight] : to pick off, make bare
wa·yu·sna \wa-yú-sna\ *v* wa·blu·sna [fr *yusna* to ring, tinkle; to ravel out] 1 : to ring, to rustle, as leaves a-falling 2 : to ravel out, to pull off *e.g.* beads on a string
wa·yu·sni \wa-yú-sni\ *v* [fr *yusni* to extinguish a fire, turn out a light] : to make cold, to extinguish
wa·yu·so·ta \wa-yú-so-ta\ *v* wa·blu·sota [fr *yusota* to use up] : to consume, to spend or use up
wa·yu·sto \wa-yú-sto\ *v* wa·blu·sto [fr *yusto* to smooth down *e.g.* one's hair] : to groom or smooth down one's hair — **wayusto·ka** *n* : a beautician perhaps, one who makes the hair smooth
wa·yu·su \wa-yú-su\ *v* wa·blu·su [fr *yusu* to make things right and ready] : to get things ready
wa·yu·su·ta \wa-yú-su-ta\ *v* wa·blu·suta [fr *yusuta* to make firm] : to establish, to make strong
wa·yu·swa \wa-yú-swa\ *v* [fr *yuswa* to ravel out, pick to pieces] : to pick to pieces
wa·yu·swu \wa-yú-swu\ *v* [fr *swu* to cause a rattling noise] : to make a noise, that of handling shelled corn
wa·yu·s'o \wa-yú-s'o\ *v* [fr *yus'o* to trim the edge of something] : to cut off a strip at the edge *e.g.* of paper
wa·yu·ša \wa-yú-ša\ *v* [fr *yuša* to make red by rubbing or touching] : to make red
wa·yu·ša·pa \wa-yú-ša-pa\ *v* wa·blu·šapa [fr *yušapa* to blacken, defile] : to soil
wa·yu·še·ca \wa-yú-še-ca\ *v* : to make dry up or wither
wa·yu·ši·ca \wa-yú-ši-ca\ *v* wa·blu·šica [fr *yušica* to injure, spoil] : to spoil, make bad
wa·yu·ši·htin \wa-yú-ši-ȟtiŋ\ *v* [fr *yušihtin* to enfeeble, to debase] : to injure in any way, to make bad
wa·yu·ši·kši·ca *or* wayušikšice·ca \wa-yú-ši-kši-ca\ *n* *red of* wayušica : a clumsy person, lacking dexterity, who does nothing well, spoils things because he does not know how
wa·yu·ši·pa \wa-yú-ši-pa\ *v* [fr *yušipa* to bend *e.g.* wire *etc.*] : to break off close
wa·yu·ška \wa-yú-ška\ *v* [fr *yuška* to loosen, untie] : to untie
wa·yu·škan·škan \wa-yú-škaŋ-škaŋ\ *v* wa·blu·škanškan [fr *yuškanškan* to make or shake up some person or something, make move about] : to cause to move or stir about
wa·yu·ške·han \wa-yú-ške-haŋ\ *v* [fr *yuškehan* to make wild] : to make wild or unsteady, to cause to prance
wa·yu·ški \wa-yú-ški\ *v* wa·blu·ški [fr *yuški* to plait] : to plait
wa·yu·ški·ška \wa-yú-ški-ška\ *v* wa·blu·škiška [fr *yuškiška* to make rough, to cut notches] : to make difficult or confused, to make mischief, to make rough
wa·yu·ško·kpa \wa-yú-ško-kpa\ *v* [fr *yuškokpa* to hollow out] : to hollow out, form a concavity
wa·yu·ško·pa \wa-yú-ško-pa\ *v* [fr *yuškopa* to bend to make crooked or twisting] : to make twisting
wa·yu·šla \wa-yú-šla\ *v* wa·blu·šla [fr *yušla* to make bare, bald] : to make bare, to cut off
wa·yu·šle·ca \wa-yú-šle-ca\ *v* [fr *yušleca* to split by hand] : to split with an effort
wa·yu·šlo·ka \wa-yú-šlo-ka\ *v* [fr *yušloka* to pull off *e.g.* a garment, or pull out *e.g.* a cork] : to pull out
wa·yu·šlu·šlu·ta \wa-yú-šlu-šlu-ṫa\ *v red* [fr *yušlušluta* to make slippery, to slip from one] : to make slippery
wa·yu·šna \wa-yú-šna\ *v* wa·blu·šna [fr *yušna* to miss catching] : to drop, let slip, thus making a mistake — *va* : to sacrifice or offer sacrifice — *n* : a sacrifice, a sacrificing
wa·yu·šni·šni \wa-yú-šna-šni\ *adj* : accurate
wa·yu·šo·ša \wa-yú-šo-ša\ *v* [fr *yušoša* to make *e.g.* water muddy] : to make turbid
wa·yu·špa \wa-yú-špa\ *v* wa·blu·špa [fr *yušpa* to break off, divide] : to break off pieces
wa·yu·špi \wa-yú-špi\ *v* wa·blu·špi [fr *yušpi* to pick off, as fruit from a tree or from a bush] : to pick off, as berries – *Syn* WOŠPI
wa·yu·špu \wa-yú-špu\ *v* wa·blu·špu [fr *yušpu* to pull off by hand what is tight] : to pick off what is stuck on
wa·yu·štan \wa-yú-štaŋ\ *v* wa·blu·štan [fr *yuštan* to finish, perfect, settle *e.g.* a question] : to finish — **wayuštan·ka** *n* : one who finishes, is thorough
wa·yu·šu·ja \wa-yú-šu-ja\ *v* [fr *yušuja* to crush, break into splinters] : to crush
wa·yu·š'a·gya \wa-yú-š'a-gya\ *va* wayuš'a·gwa·ya : to overload *e.g.* an animal
wa·yu·š'a·ka \wa-yú-š'a-ka\ *v* wa·blu·š'aka [fr *yuš'aka* to be heavily laden] : to be overloaded
wa·yu·š'in·š'in \wa-yú-š'iŋ-š'iŋ\ *v* wa·blu·š'inš'in : to tickle
wa·yu·š'in·ye·ya \wa-yú-š'iŋ-ye-a\ *v* wayuš'inye·wa·ya [fr *yuš'inyeya* to frighten] : to frighten, scare – D.215
wa·yu·ta \wa-yú-ṫa\ *v* wa·wá·ta [fr *yúta* to eat something] : to eat up — *n* : one who eats all up – *See* wó ta R Bl
wa·yu·tan \wa-yú-taŋ\ *v* [fr *yutan* to touch or feel] : to touch
wa·yu·tan·co·la \wa-yú-taŋ-co-la\ *v* [fr *yuṫancola* to make naked] : to make naked
wa·yu·tan'·in \wa-yú-taŋ-iŋ\ *v* wa·blu·tan'in [fr *yutan'in* to make manifest, clear, visible] : to expose
wa·yu·tan·ka \wa-yú-taŋ-ka\ *v* [fr *yutanka* to enlarge] : to make large
wa·yu·tan·ni \wa-yú-taŋ-ni\ *v* wa·blu·tanni [fr *yutanni* to wear our, make old] : to make old, wear out — **wa-yutanni·ka** \wa-yú-taŋ-ni-ka\ *n* : one who wears out
wa·yu·tan·tan \wa-yú-taŋ-taŋ\ *v red* [fr *yutantan* to feel about, to grope] : to feel all over
wa·yu·tan·yan \wa-yú-taŋ-yaŋ\ *v* [fr *yutanyan* to make good] : to make things well – Bl
wa·yu·te·ca \wa-yú-ṫe-ca\ *v* wa·blu·teca [fr *yuteca* to renew, make new] : to make new, to renew
wa·yu·te·han \wa-yú-ṫe-haŋ\ *v* [fr *yutehan* to make slow, to prolong, retard] : to make long, to be slow
wa·yu·te·han·han·ka \wa-yú-ṫe-haŋ-haŋ-ka\ *v* wa·blu·tehanhanka : to be always long in doing a thing
wa·yu·te·ȟi·ka \wa-yú-ṫe-ȟi-ka\ *v* wa·blu·teȟika [possibly fr *yuteȟika* to cause difficulty] : to make difficult
wa·yu·te·pa \wa-yú-ṫe-ṗa\ *v* [fr *yutepa* to wear off short] : to wear off
wa·yu·ti·ca \wa-yú-ṫi-ca\ *v* [fr *yutica* to scrape away] : to scrape away, as a horse does snow by pawing
wa·yu·ti·pa \wa·yu·ṫi-ṗa\ *v* [fr *yutipa* to cramp or draw up] : to cramp, draw up
wa·yu·ti·tan \wa-yú-ṫi-ṫaŋ\ *v* [fr *yutitan* to pull, stretch] : to pull, tug
wa·yu·tkon·za \wa-yú-tkoŋ-za\ *v* wa·blu·tkonza [fr *yutkonza* to cut off even, as with a shears] : to make even
wa·yu·tku·ga \wa-yú-tku-ġa\ *v* [fr *yutkuga* to break off square] : to break off – R Bl

wa·yu·to·kan \wa-yú-to-kaŋ\ *v* wa·blu·tokan [fr *yutokan* to remove or reject] : to remove, put in another place
wa·yu·to·ke·ca \wa-yú-to-k̇e-ca\ *v* wa·blu·tokeca [fr *yutokeca* to alter, revoke] : to alter, to make different
wa·yu·tu·ta \wa-yú-tu-ta\ *v* wa·blu·tuta [fr *yututa* to make smart, have a stinging cutting pain] : to make smart by rubbing
wa·yu·tu·tka \wa-yú-ṫu-tk̇a\ *v* [fr *yututka* to break in little pieces] : to break into small pieces
wa·yu·t'a \wa-yú-t'a\ *v* wa·blu·t'a [fr *yut'a* to choke to death] : to kill, choke to death
wa·yu·t'in·za \wa-yú-t'iŋ-za\ *v* wa·blu·t'inza [fr *yut'inza* to draw tight, to tighten] : to make firm
wa·yu·un·ka \wa-yú-uŋ-ka\ *v* [fr *yuunka* to make lie or throw down, to demolish] : to throw down
wa·yu·wa·cin·ton \wa-yú-wa-ciŋ-toŋ\ *v* [fr *yuwacinton* to make intelligent] : to make intelligent - R Bl
wa·yu·wa·hin·yan·za *or* **wayawahinyanza** \wa-yú-wa-hiŋ-yaŋ-za\ *v* : to make morose or ill-disposed

- Note:
wayatawacinhinyanza vn to take by habit as morose
yatawacinhinyanza va to make surly or cross by talking
wacinhinyanza adj cruel, morose - R

wa·yu·wa·ḣa \wa-yú-wa-ḣa\ *v* : to conciliate - B.H. 129.7
wa·yu·wa·hpa·ni·ca \wa-yú-wa-ḣṗa-ni-ca\ *v* wa·blu·wahpanica [fr *yuwahpanica* to make poor] : to make poor
wa·yu·wa·hwa·la \wa-yú-wa-ḣwa-la\ *v* wa·blu·wahwala [fr *yuwahwala* to make gentle] : to make mild, gentle
wa·yu·wa·kan \wa-yú-wa-kaŋ\ *v* wa·blu·wakan [fr *yuwakan* to consecrate, make holy, make special] : to make sacred, to consecrate - B.H.66.17
wa·yu·wan·kal i·cu \wa-yú-waŋ-k̇al i-cù\ *v* : to lift up — wayuwankal iyeya *v* : to raise or pry up
wa·yu·wa·ša·ka·la \wa-yú-wa-ša-k̇a-la\ *v* wa·blu·wašakala [fr *yuwašakala* to make cheap or easy] : to make cheap or easy
wa·yu·wa·šte \wa-yú-wa-šte\ *v* wa·blu·wašte [fr *yuwašte* to bless, make good] : to improve, make good
wa·yu·wa·š'a·ka \wa-yú-wa-š'a-k̇a\ *v* wa·blu·waš'aka [fr *yuwaš'aka* to strengthen] : to invigorate, make strong — **wayuwaš'ake·šni** *v* wa·blu·waš'akešni : to make weak
wa·yu·wa·za \wa-yú-wa-za\ *v* [fr *yuwaza* to twist and turn as the hands in running, *fig* to vex or tease] : to cause one to be annoyed - Bl
wa·yu·we·ga \wa-yú-we-ġa\ *v* wa·blu·wega [fr *yuwega* to break *e.g.* a stick by hand but not entirely off] : to break partly off
wa·yu·wi \wa-yú-wi\ *v* [fr *yuwi* to bind up, bandage] : to wrap around
wa·yu·wi·ca·ka \wa-yú-wi-ca-ka\ *v* [fr *yuwicaka* to prove or convince] : to make true
wa·yu·wi·ca·ša·šni \wa-yú-wi-ca-ša-šni\ *v* wa·blu·wicašašni [fr *yuwicašašni* to make mean, excited] : to debase, corrupt, make bad
wa·yu·wi·gnu·ni \wa-yú-wi-gnu-ni\ *v* [fr *yuwignuni* to destroy, cause to perish] : to make wander - R Bl
wa·yu·win·ja \wa-yú-wiŋ-ja\ *v* [fr *yuwinja* to bend or break down] : to bend down
wa·yu·win·ta \wa-yú-wiŋ-ṫa\ *v* wa·blu·winta [fr *yuwinta* to wipe in gesture] : to stroke
wa·yu·win·ye·ya \wa-yú-wiŋ-ye-ya\ *v* wa·blu·winyeya [fr *yuwinyeya* to get ready, prepare] : to make ready - *Syn* WAYUSU
wa·yu·wi·tan·tan \wa-yú-wi-ṫaŋ-ṫaŋ\ *v* : to make proud by giving good things - R Bl
wa·yu·wi·ta·ya \wa-yú-wi-ṫa-ya\ *v* wa·blu·witaya [fr *yuwitaya* to collect or assemble] : to gather together, to collect
wa·yu·wi·tko \wa-yú-wi-tko\ *v* [fr *yuwitko* to make foolish] : to make naughty — **wayuwitko·tkoka** *v* : to make foolish
wa·yu·wi·ya·kpa \wa-yú-wi-ya-kpa\ *v* [fr *yuwiyakpa* to make shine, *fig* to interpret] : to radiate, interpret
wa·yu·wo·sla·ta \wa-yú-wo-sla-ṫa\ *v* [fr *yuwoslata* to set upright] : to set upright
wa·yu·za \wa-yú-za\ *v* [fr *yuza* to catch, take hold of] : to take, to take the clothes of those who come home in triumph - R Bl
wa·yu·za·mni \wa-yú-za-mni\ *v* wa·blu·zamni [fr *yuzamni* to uncover or open] : to uncover
wa·yu·zan \wa-yú-zaŋ\ *v* [fr *yuzan* to part *e.g.* the hair on the head] : to part, to separate
wa·yu·ze \wa-yú-ze\ *v* wa·blu·ze [fr *yuze* to dip, lade, or skim] : to lade or dip out from a kettle
wa·yu·zi·ca \wa-yú-zi-ca\ *v* wa·blu·zica [fr *yuzica* to stretch, as a rubber band] : to stretch
wa·yu·zon·ta \wa-yú-zoŋ-ṫa\ *v* wa·blu·zonta [fr *yuzonta* to make a person honest, make them better men] : to make honest, better men - R Bl
wa·zab \wa-záb\ *va contrac of* wazapa : to skin or to cut off, as meat for drying < ~ *iyeya* to cut off *e.g.* strips of meat > — **wazab·zapa** \wa-zá-bza-ṗa\ *v red of* wazapa : to cut off meat
wa·zan·zan \wá-zaŋ-zaŋ\ *n* : a fine snow mist < ~ *u welo* A snow mist came, as is said when a few snow flakes, very little, drop here and there. > - Note: *mniwozan* a drizzle — *adv* : lying thin, as snow on things
wa·za·pa \wa-zá-ṗa\ *va* wa·wa·zapa : to skin, cut off *e.g.* meat for drying
wa·za·za \wa-zá-za\ *va* : to cut into fringes < *Ogle, hunska wawazaza* I cut shirt and legging fringes. > — *vn* : to be fringed or dangled - *See* kazaza — *adv* : in dangles — **wazaza·pi** \wa-zá-za-ṗi\ *n* : fringes or dangles
wa·zi \wa-zí\ *n* : the pine tree, pines
wa·zi can \wa-zí caŋ\ *n* : the western pine tree, pinus scopulosum, ponderosa; the common pine tree
wa·zi·hca·ka \wa-zí-ḣca-ka\ *n* : the Black Hills spruce
wa·zi·lya \wa-zí-lya\ *vn* and perhaps *va* wazi·lwa·ya [fr *zilya* to smoke, fumigate] : to burn as does incense < *Hehanl tatiye topa kin iyuha wazilyapi. Hecel ~ na azilwicaya* Then all the four directions were incensed. So he burned incense for him to give the *azilyapi* to them. > - B.H.64.17
wa·zi·mna *or* **wazi·mninkpa** \wa-zí-mna\ *n* : the tall meadow-rue of the crowfoot family
wa·zi·mnin·kpa \wa-zí-mniŋ-kpa\ *n* [fr *wazimna* meadow-rue + *inkpa* the summit top] : the tall meadow-rue, thalictrum polygamum, cornuti, the crowfoot family. - Note: the seeds have a pleasing odor and are given to

---

\a\ father \e\ they \i\ machine \o\ smoke \u\ lunar \an, aŋ\ blanc Fr. \in, iŋ\ ink \on, oŋ, un, uŋ\ soon, confier Fr. \c\ chair \ġ\ machen Ger. \j\ fusion \clusters: bl, gn, kp, hšl, etc...\ b^{e}lo ... said with a slight vowel
See more in the Introduction, Guide to Pronunciation

horses to make them lively. When the seeds are chewed and rubbed on the hands, they serve as a pleasant lotion Bl WE Bc Bn BH #194

wa·zi·mnin·kpa i·ye·ce·ca \wa-zí-mniŋ-kpa i-ye-ce-ca\ *n* : the large button snake root, the blue blazing star, the rattle snake master, devil's bite, liatris ligulistylis – Note: another name for the devil's bite is *tat'ecannunga hu iyececa,* and also the maple-leaved goosefoot, chenopedium hybridum – Bl #153

wa·zi·pin·kpa \wa-zí-ṗiŋ-kṗa\ *n* : the pine cone, cones

wa·zi s'e \wa-zí s'e\ *adv* : pine-like, very tall – R Bl

wa·zi ši·yo \wa-zí ši-yo\ *n* : the spruce grouse

wa·zi·ške·ca *or* **waziškecala** \wa-zí-šk̇e-ca\ *n* : the strawberry, fragaria Americana

wa·zi·ta·ki·ya \wa-zí-ṫa-k̇i-ya\ *adv* : towards the north < *Hihanna el oyate kišpahanpi ca ~ aya* In the morning when the people went their separate ways, they went towards the north. >

wa·zi·wi·ca·gna·ška \wa-zí-wi-cà-gna-šk̇a\ *n* : pine berries

Wa·zi·ya \Wa-zí-ya\ *np* : the Santa Claus – Note: this is the name for and personification of the power or powers , the nature characteristics of the North, as *e.g.* Tate, the Winds; Wašicunpi, *esp* the Bearers of Powers that make it possible to walk in a sacred way

wa·zi·ya ce·ka·ga \wa-zí-ya cè-k̇a-ga\ *n* : a pastime of children who dip a branch into water and then place it upright in very cold weather; it would freeze and then they would suck it as it were a piece of stick candy – Bl

wa·zi·ya·pa \wa-zí-ya-pa\ *adv* : at or to the north — **waziyapa·tanhan** \wa-zí-ya-pa-ṫaŋ-haŋ\ *adv* : northwards, from the north — **waziya·ta** \wa-zí-ya-ṫa\ *n* : the north, at the pines — **waziyata·kiya** \wa-zí-ya-ṫa-k̇i-ya\ *adv* : towards the north — **waziya·tanhan** *or* **waziyata·tanhan** \wa-zí-ya-ṫaŋ-haŋ\ \wa-zí-ya-ṫa-ṫaŋ-haŋ\ *adv* : at or from the north

Wa·zi·ya·ta Wi·ca·ša \Wa-zí-ya-ṫa Wi-cà-ša\ *np* : a branch or group of the Assiniboins tribe

wa·zi·zi \wa-zí-zi\ *n* : pieces of pine < ~ *pet'ileye* pine kindling wood > – LB

wa·zi·zin·tka·la \wa-zí-ziŋ-tka-la\ *n* : the pine siskin, or the pine finch

wa·z'o·ju \wa-z'ó-ju\ *n* [fr *wazi* pine + *oju* a growth] : a growth where many pine trees grow as in canyons

[1]**we** \we\ *n* : blood —*adj* : bloody —*vn* : to bleed

[2]**we** \we\ *pron insep 1st pers singl* – compounded of "wa" and "ki" Cf Gramm.45

[3]**we** \we\ *imper singl partic* used by women < *Mihakab u we* Come after me. *Iwacu we na cicu we* I must take it, and so I must return it to you. *Israel el woitancan tanka yaun we* You be commander-in-chief in Israel. > – Cf ye B.H. 111.13

we·ce·ya \wé-ce-ya\ *va* wéce·wa·ya : to be on good terms with one's relatives, have regard for them; to have confidence in a person or thing, trust, believe in the ability of one or of a thing < *Hécon kta keye, eyaš wecewaye šni* He said he would do it, but I do not believe he will, *i.e.* I do not believe he can or will do it. *Wécekiciyapi* They trust one another. >

we·ce·ye·pi·ca \wé-ce-ye-ṗi-ca\ *adj* wéceye·ma·pica : trustworthy, reliable, as is said of persons and things

we·ce·ye·šni \wé-ce-ye-šni\ *va* wéce·wa·yešni : to disregard, to slight; to have a grudge against a relative, not looking at him or her; to have no confidence in, to doubt about the ability of somebody or an animal doing something, as in distrusting a poor horse making a long trip *etc.* – *Syn* WÓIMNA ŠNI B B.H.115.4

we co·la·kel \we có-la-kel\ *adv* : unbloody – B.H.61.5

we e·ya·la s'e \wé e-yà-la s'e\ *adv* : all bloody < ~ *gli ye* Get home in a real bloody condition. > – Bl

we·ga \wé-ġa\ *adj* : broken – Cf yuwega *etc.* — **we·ga·han** *part* : broken but not entirely off < *Isto mawegahan. Mawegahe yelo* My arm was broken. I was really "broke". >

we·gna \wé-gna\ *prep* : among < *Paha Can ~ Yanka,* Hill In The Woods, the name of a hill in the White River valley some ten miles north of Oglala, South Dakota. >

we·han \wé-haŋ\ *n* : last summer < ~ *hecamon welo* I did that last summer. >

we·i·c'i·ya \we-í-c'i-ya\ *v refl* : to bleed one's self

we·i·glak \we-í-glak\ *v contrac of* iglaka : to travel camping along the way < *Wanáka ~ ayin ktelo* He will presently begin a journey camping out. >

we·ka·lu·za·pi \wé-k̇a-lu-za-pi\ *n* : hemorrhage, an unnatural flow of blood, a sickness of women – *Syn* WE-NÁPOPAPI

we·ki·ci·ya \we-kí-ci-ya\ *va* : to bleed each other

we·la·ka *or* **yelaka** \wé-la-ka\ *adv* : indeed since < *Le wicaša taku ~* What indeed is this man? > – B.H.203.13, 68.18, 161.8

we·la s'e \wé-la s'e\ *adv* : all bloody < ~ *škanpi* They were busy bleeding, *i.e.* got all bloody cutting themselves. >

we·na·po·pa·pi \we-ná-po-ṗa-ṗi\ *n* : hemorrhage typical of women – Cf wékaluzapi

we·o·špan \wé-o-šṗaŋ\ *vn* wé·ma·ošpan : to dry up, cease to flow as does blood in a critical point of afterbirth

we·o·ta \wé-o-ṫa\ *n* : a blood clot – Note: *wéyota* is the Santee Dakota form of the word WW D113

weš *or* **weša, wešan** *or* **yeš, yeša, yešan** \weš\ *adv conj of concession* : though or although – B.H.123.6

we·šle·ka·pi \we-šlé-k̇a-pi\ *n* : the wearing of honors, *esp* feathers as signs of honorable wounds – R Bl

we·tu \wé-ṫú\ *n* : the spring of the year – Note: *iwétu* next or following spring

we-we-we \wĕ'-wĕ'-wĕ'\ *interj* : – women use the *express* in calling dogs

we·we \we-wé\ *adj* : bloody

We Wi·ca·ša \We Wi-cà-ša\ *np* : the Blood Indian, a Sioun band in Canada north of the State of Montana

we·ya \we-yá\ *va* we·wa·ya : to shed blood, make bleed, hence to put to death – B.H.263.6

we·yo·hlo·ge·lya \we-yó-ȟlo-ge-lya\ *adv* : all bloody – Bl

we·yo·ta *or* **weota** \wé-yo-ta\ *n* : a clot of blood

we yu·ke·ya \wé yu-k̇è-ya\ *adv* : bloody – B.H.61.3

[1]**wi** \wi\ *pref* to some *v* commencing with *i* make the *absol* form by a *pref w,* instead of *wa* , thus *iyúkcan* becomes *wíyukcan*

[2]**wi** \wi\ *n* : the sun or the moon; a month; a personification of the most immense power in creation, for it determines all seasons < *anpetu wi* the sun, *hanhepi wi* the moon, *wi hinapa* the sun to rise, *wi mahel iyaya* the sun has set > – FD.86 WJR.153

[3]**wi** \wi\ *n contrac of* winyan : woman < *wiinahma* to commit fornication >

wi·a·ce·i·c'i·ti *or* **wiacic'iti** \wí-a-cè-i-c'i-ṫi\ *n* [fr *wi* sun + *aceti* set a fire to or on] : sundogs, a ring around the moon —*v* : there are sundogs; there is a ring around the moon – Note: it is said the sun does this because it will be cold or stormy – Fr

wi·a·hi·na·pa \wí-a-hi-na-pa\ *v* : to have the sun rise on one

wi·a·tan'·on·mya \wí-a-taŋ-oŋ-mya\ *adv* [fr *atan'onpa* to lean as the sun is said to do in the afternoon] : when the sun is leaning, in the afternoon

[1]**wi·ca** \wi-ca\ *pref to v* to make them *pl* , and used when one is speaking of a unit, a certain crowd of people, or all people in general < *Lila wicištinmelo* They are deep in sleep, as is said of a family, or visitors, of members of a meeting, *etc.* > – Note: *Ištinmapi* They are asleep, is said in *ref* to individuals singly and not belonging together

[2]**wi·ca** \wi-cá\ *n* wi·ma·ca : a man, a male of the human species

[3]**wi·ca** \wi-cá\ *pron in compos with v* to represent the *3rd pers pl obj* : them < *Wicawakte* *wicá-wa-ktè* them-I-killed\ *i.e* I killed them. And when it is used with *neut v* and *adj* it generally forms what may be regarded as abstact *n* , *e.g. cancan* to shake: *wicacancan* the ague >

[4]**wi·ca** \wi-cá\ *adj pref* to *n* that have *ref* to Man : human, male, pertaining to sex – Note: when the *n* begins with a vowel, the *a* of *wica* is dropped, thus: *išta* an eye, *wicišta* the human eye

[5]**wi·ca** *or* **wiciteglega** \wi-ċá\ *n* : the raccoon – R Bl D.36

wi·ca·a·ki·h'an \wi-cá-a-k̇i-ȟ'aŋ\ *n* : famine, starving < *Oyate wicoti na lila ~ na anpetu wan el wanasapi* Many were the tibes and accute was starvation, so one day they went hunting buffalo. *Waniyetu zaptan ~ kte* In five years there would be famine. >

wi·ca·a·tku·ku \wi-cá-a-tk̇u-k̇u\ *n* : a father, their father

wi·ca·ba·pi *or* **wicaṗapi** \wi-cá-ba-pi\ *n* : blame – R

wi·ca·ble·ce \wí-ca-ble-ce\ *n* [fr *kableca* to break] : a sledge hammer, an instrument used to break in pieces

wi·ca·bwo·ta·pi \wí-ca-bwo-ṫa-ṗi\ *n* : a table fork — **wica·byutapi** \wí-ca-byu-ṫa-pi\ *n* : a meat fork

wi·ca·ca·je \wi-cá-ca-je\ *n* : names, names of persons < *~ wowapi* a catalogue, a list of names >

wi·ca·can *or* **wiyucan** \wí-ċa-caŋ\ *n* [fr *kacan* shake or sift] : a sieve

wi·ca·can·can \wi-cá-caŋ-caŋ\ *n* : the ague, shivering

wi·ca·can·pi \wí-ċa-caŋ-pi\ *n* : a measure

wi·ca·can·te \wi-cá-caŋ-te\ *n* : the human heart — **wicacante·oyuze** *n* : the thought of the heart

wi·ca·ce \wi-cá-ce\ *n* : the human penis

wi·ca·ce·hpi \wi-cá-ce-ȟṗi\ *n* : human flesh

wi·ca·ce·ji \wi-cá-ce-ji\ *n* : the human tongue

wi·ca·ce·pa \wi-cá-ce-ṗa\ *n* : obesity, human fatness

wi·ca·ce·pa·ha·la \wi-cá-ce-ṗa-ha-la\ *n* : a certain high but not wide mountain – Bl

wi·ca·ce·sli \wi-cá-ce-sli\ *n* : human or raccoon excrement

wi·ca·ceya *or* **wicaceye** \wi-cá-ce-ya\ *n* : weeping, crying < *Oyate kin wanna ~ ayaštan* The people are now finished weeping. >

wi·ca·ci·ce \wí-ċa-ci-ce\ *n* : a clothes brush, one to brush up the fur of skins

wi·ca·cin·ca \wi-cá-ciŋ-ca\ *n* : offspring, children, posterity

wi·ca·co·kon \wi-cá-ċo-k̇oŋ\ *n* [fr *cokon* desire to do evil to one] : threatening, intending evil

wi·ca·cu·wi·ta \wi-cá-cu-wi-ṫa\ *n* : the feeling of coldness, the sense of cold as experienced by human beings

wi·ca·gan·gan \wi-cá-ġaŋ-ġaŋ\ *adj* : not crowded — *n* : a sprinkling of people – Br

wi·ca·ge \wí-ċa-ġe\ *n* : a tool with which to make something

wi·ca·ge·ge \wí-ċa-ġe-ġe\ *n* : anything to sew with, as thread or lace < *mas'wicagege* a sewing machine >

wi·ca·gla·ta \wi-cá-gla-ṫa\ *n* : the women who follow the men in singing at the war dance or other like dances – Cf aglata

wi·ca·gna·ka·pi \wi-cá-gna-k̇a-ṗi\ *n* : dead bodies laid on top of the ground or scaffolds, or the scaffold itself on which a dead person is placed < *Yunkan ~ wan tima otka* And then he erected a scaffold indoors. >

wi·ca·gna·ška \wi-cá-gna-šk̇a\ *n* : the goose berry — **wicagnaška·hu** *n* : the goose berry bush, the golden, the buffalo, the flowering currant, ribes longiflorum, the saxifrage family – Note: the branches were once used for the making of arrows < *Wicaša wanji na yamni na tob oyate el wahinkpe kaga wayupikapi ca hena wankah wicašipi, wišiyukeya. ~ hena cogin tanka heon* Since there was one man in three and four tribes who were skilled in making arrows, they were given orders to make arrows for a price. The reason for the use of goose berry wood was its large pith. > — **wicagnaška tanka** *n* : the large goose berry – MS.481 Bl OF Bh #163

wi·ca·gna·ye \wi-cá-gna-ye\ *n* [fr *gnayan* to deceive one] : a cunning, crafty, art-ful person, one who deceives, or deception itself < *~ s'a* treacherous, wily person, hence a trickster >

wi·ca·go \wí-ċa-ġo\ *n* : a marking instrument

wi·ca·gu·ke *or* **wicacice** \wí-ċa-ġu-k̇e\ *n* : a clothes brush

[1]**wi·ca·hi** \wi-cá-hi\ *n* : human teeth

[2]**wi·ca·hi** \wí-ċa-hi\ *n* : a spoon or other instrument to mix with

wi·ca·hi ka·ge \wi-cá-hi kà-ġe\ *n* : a dentist

wi·ca·hin·te \wí-ċa-hiŋ-ṫe\ *n* [fr *kahinta* to sweep off or up] : a broom, or a rake

wi·ca·hi·ya \wí-ċa-hi-ya\ *v* wicahi·wa·ya [fr *icahiya* to mix together] : to mingle

wi·ca·hi·yu·ta·pi *or* **wicáhiyayutapi** \wí-ċa-hi-yu-ṫa-pi\ *n* : spices, seasoning, sauce, *etc.* – P

wi·ca·hi·yu·ta·pi to·to \wí-ċa-hi-yu-ṫa-pi to-tò\ *n* : salad

wi·ca·hi·yu·ta·pi zi \wí-ċa-hi-yu-ṫa-pi zi\ *n* : mustard

wi·ca·ho \wi-cá-ho\ *n* : the human voice < *~ wan nawah'on* I hear a voice. >

wi·ca·ho·hu \wi-cá-ho-hu\ *n* : human bones

wi·ca·ho ka·hwo·gya·pi \wi-cá-ho ka-ȟwo-gya-pi\ *v* : to radio broadcast

wi·ca·ho·o·yu·spa *or* **wicaho oyuspe** \wi-cá-ho-o-yù-sṗa\ *n* : a voice or sound recorder

wi·ca·hu·ha \wi-cá-hu-ha\ *n* : limbs of the body

wi·ca·hu·hu \wi-cá-hu-hu\ *n* : the human skeleton

wi·ca·hun·ka·ke \wi-cá-huŋ-k̇a-ke\ *n* : ancestors

wi·ca·hun·ku \wi-cá-huŋ-k̇u\ *n* : a mother, mothers

wi·ca·ȟan·ȟan \wi-cá-ȟaŋ-ȟaŋ\ *n* : the small pox

wi·ca·ȟa·pi \wi-cá-ȟa-pi\ *n* [fr *ȟa* to bury] : graves, tombs, bodies interred — **wicaȟapi ognake** *or* **canwognake** *n* : a coffin

wi·ca·hca \wi-cá-ȟca\ *n* : an old man, a father-in-law — **wicahca·la** *n* : an old man of any kind

wi·ca·ȟe·pa \wí-ca-ȟe-ṗa\ *n* [fr *kaȟepa* to bail out *e.g.*

\a\ father \e\ they \i\ machine \o\ smoke \u\ lunar \an, aŋ\ blanc Fr. \in, iŋ\ ink \on, oŋ, un, uŋ\ soon, confier Fr. \c\ chair \ġ\ machen Ger. \j\ fusion \clusters: bl, gn, kp, hšl, etc...\ b^e^lo ... said with a slight vowel
See more in the Introduction, Guide to Pronunciation

water] : a ladle - R Bl
wi·ca·hle·ce \wí-ca-ȟle-ce\ *n* [fr *kahleca* to split open, to fracture] : an instrument with which to tear or bruise
wi·ca·hlo·ke \wí-ċa-ȟlo-k̇e\ *n* [fr *kahloka* to strike, breaking a hole in] : a tool with which to make holes, *e.g.* a gimlet
wi·ca·hmun·ga \wi-cá-ȟmuŋ-ġa\ *v* : to shoot or send by magic something, *e.g.* a knife, nail, or bullet, into one as some Dakota wizards pretend to do; to remove such things by magic, *i.e.* *wokabiyeya* — *n* : a magician who practices such shooting < *wicáhmungas'a* a magician >
wi·ca·hpe \wí-ċa-ȟpe\ *n* [fr *kahpa* to make something fall] : an instrument with which to throw something down, *e.g.* a sling
wi·ca·hpi \wi-cá-ȟṗi\ *n* : a star < *Wicahpi Hinhpaya* Falling Stars, *i.e.* a title applied to the year 1833 when there occurred the falling of stars (perhaps meteors), ~ *sintéton* a comet, ~ *ša* a planet, perhaps Mercury > - BT
wi·ca·hpu \wí-ċa-ȟṗu\ *n* [fr *kahpu* to scale off] : a tool with which to pick something off
wi·ca·hu·ge \wí-ċa-ȟu-ġe\ *n* [fr *kahuga* to break in] : something with which to break in
wi·ca·hun·win \wi-cá-ȟuŋ-wiŋ\ *n* [fr *hunwin* to become putrid] : putrifaction
wi·ca·hwa \wi-cá-ȟwa\ *n* [fr *hwa* drowsy] : drowsiness, sleepiness
wi·ca·i \wi-cá-i\ *n* : the human mouth
wi·ca·i·ha \wi-cá-i-ha\ *n* : the human lips
wi·ca·ji·pa \wi-cá-ji-pa\ *n* : a wasp < ~ *mayajipa* You cleared a wasp off me. >
wi·ca·ji·pe \wí-ċa-ji-ṗe\ *n* [fr *kajipa* to plane] : a plane, a tool with which to smooth or shave
[1]**wi·ca·ka** \wi-cá-ka\ *v* [fr *ka* to mean] : to mean, or he means them
[2]**wi·ca·ka** \wi-ċá-ka\ *vn* wica·wa·ka : to speak truth, to be true
wi·ca·ka·hi·ya·ya \wi-cá-k̇a-hi-ya-ya\ *v* [fr *kahiyaya* sing a tune] : to carry round to them, to sing to them
wi·ca·ja·hun·hun·za·pi \wi-cá-k̇a-huŋ-huŋ-za-pi\ *n* : a cradle
wi·ca·ka·ha·pa \wi-cá-k̇a-ȟa-ṗa\ *n* [fr *kahapa* drive along as in riding herd] : a driver, one who drives
wi·ca·kanl \wi-cá-k̇aŋl\ *adv* [fr *wica* them + *akanl* on] : behind them < ~ *waun welo* I am behind them. > - Syn WICILAZATE Bl
wi·ca·ka·pi·hca \wi-cá-ka-pi-ȟca\ *adj* : absolutely certain, dead sure - P
wi·ca·kca \wí-ċa-kca\ *n* [fr *kakca* to comb] : a curry comb
wi·ca·ke·la \wi-ċá-k̇e-la\ *va* wicake·wa·la [fr *wicaka* to be true + *la* esteem] : to esteem true, to believe one < *wicakeic'ila* to believe one's self true, continue to affirm, *Yunkan wicaša kin Jesus eye kin ~ na ekta gla* And then the man believed what Jesus said, so he to his home. >
wi·ca·ke·la·ki·ya \wi-ċá-k̇e-la-k̇i-ya\ *va* : to convince - P
wi·ca·ke·ya \wi-cá-ke-ya\ *adv* : in truth < *Taku wašte yacin kin he okihinic'iyin kta na ~ ceya yo* What good you desire will make it possible for you, so pray in truth. > - MS.350
wi·ca·ki·ca·šla \wi-cá-k̇i-ca-šla\ *n* : a barber
wi·ca·ki·ci·ca·ju·ju·pi \wi-cá-k̇i-ci-ċa-ju-ju-pi\ *n* : forgiveness
wi·ca·ki·ci·la \wi-cá-ki-ci-la\ *v* : to comply — *adj* : positive - P
wi·ca·ki·ci·lo·wan \wi-cá-k̇i-ci-lo-waŋ\ *v* [fr *lowan* sing] : to wail or sing for, as for those who have gone on the warpath *etc.*
wi·ca·ki·co·pi \wi-cá-k̇i-co-pi\ *n* [fr *kico* to invite] : a calling, an invitation
wi·ca·ki·h'an *or perhaps* **wicaakih'an** \wi-cá-ki-ȟ'aŋ\ *v* [fr *akih'an* to starve] : to go hungry - B.H.106.2
wi·ca·ki·je \wí-ċa-k̇i-je\ *n* [fr *icakija* affliction] : distress, suffering — **wícakije·šniyan** *adv* : lacking nothing - D.64
wi·ca·ki·kcan·pte \wi-cá-k̇i-kcaŋ-ṗte\ *n* [fr *kikcanpta* to console or comfort one] : a comforter; the Holy Spirit
wi·ca·ki·ni \wi-cá-k̇i-ni\ *n* : resurrection - B.H.229.12
wi·ca·kin·ce \wí-ċa-k̇iŋ-ce\ *n* [fr *kakinca* to scrape] : a scraper
wi·ca·ki·pi \wi-cá-k̇i-pi\ *n* : robbery
wi·ca·ki·šya \wí-ċa-k̇i-šya\ *v* wícaki·šwa·ya : to make suffer — *adv perhaps* : in need < ~ *unkunpi* in our necessities >
wi·ca·ki·ya·pa \wi-cá-k̇i-ya-pa\ *v* [fr *kiyapa* to suck into for, to take in the mouth and suck] : to suck into the mouth, as conjurers once did for one who was ill - R
Wi·ca·ki·yu·ha·pi \Wi-cá-k̇i-yu-ha-pi\ *np* : *lit* The Keeper, or the Great Bear, a constellation in the northern sky - Note: another name is *Cinškásinteyukan* The Dipper, or the Big Dipper, *lit* Being a Spoon with a Tail - IS
wi·ca·ko·ka \wí-ċa-ko-k̇e\ *n* [fr *kakoka* to thump on] : a rattle, a rattler
wi·ca·kpe \wí-ċa-kṗe\ *n* : a lancet
wi·ca·ksa·pa *or* **wicaoksape** \wi-cá-ksa-ṗa\ *n* : wisdom
wi·ca·kse \wí-ċa-kse\ *n* [fr *kaksa* to split or cut off] : an instrument with which to cut off
wi·ca·kte·pi \wi-cá-kte-pi\ *n* : a killing
wi·ca·kte·pi·s'a \wi-cá-kte-pi-s'a\ *n* : a killer, one who kills
wi·ca·k'u·pi \wi-cá-k'u-pi\ *n* : a giving, a donation or contribution
wi·ca·la *or* **wicala·ka** \wi-ċá-la\ \wi-cá-la-k̇a\ *va* wica·wa·la wica·wa·laka : to believe, put confidence in, to agree to
wi·ca·la·pe·la \wi-cá-la-ṗe-la\ *adj* : trusting in one < *Ite ~ k'el ėcela yelo* It is only right when relying on a face, as they once said encouragingly to a war party or to one going off to war. > - Bl KE
wi·ca·la·pi \wi-ċá-la-pi\ *n* : a belief, believing, a faith — **wicala·pica** \wi-ċá-la-ṗi-ca\ *adj* : worthy of belief
wi·ca·la·ya \wi-ċá-la-ya\ *va* wicala·wa·ya : to persuade or cause one to believe < *Wicake s'elececa yelo, wicalamaye lo, epa* He seemed to speak the truth, I said he persuaded me. >
wi·ca·le·ja \wi-cá-le-ja\ *n* : human urine
wi·ca·lu \wí-ca-lu\ *n* : a fan
wi·ca·lu·za·he \wi-cá-lu-za-he\ *n* [fr *luzahan* swift] : speed, swiftness, rapidity
wi·ca·na·kše·ca·pi \wi-cá-na-kše-ca-pi\ *n* [fr *nakšecapi* the cramps] : the cholera
wi·ca·nan·ka \wi-cá-naŋ·k̇a\ *n* [fr *nanka* or *naka* to twitch] : tremor
wi·ca·na·pe \wi-cá-na-ṗe\ *n* : the human hand - B.H. 140.6
wi·ca·na·su *or* **wicanasula** \wi-cá-na-su\ *n* : the human brain
wi·ca·na·ta·šlo·ka \wi-cá-na-ṫa-šlo-k̇a\ *n* : a dry human skull

wi·ca·ni \wi-cá-ni\ *vn 3rd pers pl* : they live — *n* : life, prosperity - Note: *wicani* is used in *ref* to many; *wiconi* in *ref* to one
wi·ca·ni·te \wi-cá-ni-ṫe\ *n* : the loins
wi·ca·no·ge \wi-cá-no-ġe\ *n* : the human ears
wi·ca·o·h'an·ko \wi-cá-o-ȟ'aŋ-ko\ *n* [fr *oh'anko* quick at doing things] : dexterity
wi·ca·pa·ha \wi-cá-pa-ha\ *n* : the human scalp
wi·ca·pa·hu \wi-cá-pa-hu\ *n* : the human skull
wi·ca·pa·hli \wi-cá-pa-ȟli\ *n* : excretion of the human nose < *Tinpsila kin ~ s'e hinapelo* The wild turnip emerged as though it were from a running nose. > - Bl
wi·ca·pa·pta·pta *or* **wicapaptanptan** \wi-cá-pa-pta-pta\ *n* : a wallowing, rolling about < *~ iyaye olé* He went looking for a person, as one goes rolling about, *i.e.* among a throng. > - LHB
wi·ca·pe \wí-ca-ṗe\ *n* [fr *capa* to stab, pierce] : a fork, a table fork, a spit
wi·ca·pe·ca *or* **micapeca** \wí-ca-ṗe-ca\ *n* [fr *capa* to pierce] : a grass armed with a long sharp beard
wi·ca·pe·hin·ka·ga·pi \wi-cá-ṗe-hiŋ-ka-ġa-pi\ *n* : a wig, false hair
wi·ca·pe·la \wí-ca-ṗe-la\ *n dim of* wicape : a small table fork
wi·ca·pi \wi-cá-ṗi\ *n* : the human liver
wi·ca·po \wi-cá-ṗo\ *n* : a swelling
wi·ca·po·ge \wi-cá-ṗo-ġe\ *n* : the human nose
wi·ca·po·te \wí-ċa-ṗo-te\ *n* [fr *kapota* to be weather-beaten] : an instrument with which to rend something
wi·ca·psi·ce \wí-ċa-psi-ce\ *n* [fr *kapsica* to make jump by striking] : anything used to make jump
wi·ca·psin·te \wí-ċa-psiŋ-ṫe\ *n* : a whip
wi·ca·ski·ce \wí-ċa-sḱi-ce\ *n* [fr *kaskica* to settle or press down] : a press
wi·ca·sle·ce \wí-ċa-sle-ce\ *n* [fr *kasleca* to split] : a wedge, something with which to split
wi·ca·so·te \wi-cá-so-ṫe\ *n* : the decease of many, a general dying, loss of life - Bl
wi-ca-sto \wí-ċa-sṫo\ *n* [fr *kasto* to smooth *e.g.* the hair] : a brush, anything with which to smooth
wi·ca·ša \wi-cá-ša\ *n* : Man, a man, mankind < *Wimacaša* I am a man. > - Note:

~ akántu *n* : one of human kind, a mortal as distinguished from the dead and spirits
~ ha *n* : a term for a lazy man < *Iyotiyewakiye, ~ ha wan kici waun ca* I had troubles, since I am with a lazy man, as a woman would say of her lazy husband. > - GA
~ igláwa *n* : a chief, one who counts himself a man
~ ikté *n* : a poison
wicášake *n* : human nails of the toes or fingers
~ lehánkaia *n* : a foreigner - B.H.27.30 HH Bl
~ šin *n* : the meat on the buffalo's breast, the brisket
~ šni *adj* : prankish, mean, wicked, tricky, deceptive, crooked in dealings; mischievous, waggish as a woman or man - D.25 SLB
wicašašniyan *adv* : wickedly
~ tánka *n* : a middle-aged man < *Yunkan ~ kin he wicahpi wan lila ilege cin hée* And then it was that middle-aged man who was the glistening star. > - MS.1
~ wakán *n* : a priest, formerly the native shaman
wicášayaiapi or *wicašayatapi* or *wicašayatapika* *n* [fr *yatan* to speak well of] : a chief, a ruler, king — *wicašayatapi·ya* *va* : to have for a king - B.H. 263.9, 264.24

Wi·ca·ša Yu·ta \Wi-cá-ša Yu-ṫa\ *np* : the Ute tribe of western United States, so named for possibly having been cannabalistic - Bl
wi·ca·ške \wí-ċa-ške\ *n* : a bond, something with which to tie
wi·ca·ški·ce \wí-ċa-šḱi-ce\ *n* : a press
wi·ca·škin \wí-ċa-šḱiŋ\ *n* : a hammer with which to pound cherries - W
wi·ca·šla \wí-ċa-šla\ *n* [fr *kašla* to shave or mow] : a scythe
wi·ca·šni \wi-cá-šni\ *v* wica·mi·cašni wica·ni·cašni : to tell a falsehood < *~ s'e gnayan* deceptively as if telling a lie, hence in a childish manner > - WE Bl
wi·ca·ta·ku·ni·šni \wi-cá-ṫa-ku-ni-šni\ *n* : destruction
wi·ca·tan·can \wi-cá-ṫaŋ-caŋ\ *n* : the human body - Pb.35
wi·ca·tan·ka·ga·pi \wi-cá-taŋ-ka-ġa-pi\ *n* : a tipi with figures representing ribs and hearts seemingly, painted somewhat horizontally around the outer surface of the tipi
wi·ca·tan·ka·la \wi-cá-taŋ-ka-la\ *n* : the gull, a white bird, its breast blackish, legs short, bill short and not broad as that of pigeons; it lives near lakes and flies always over water - Note: it is also named: *winyan tazintkala* a woman's bird
wi·ca·tan·šna \wi-cá-taŋ-šna\ *n* : a single man < *~ s'e tawak'in tanka* Like a single man his luggage is much. >
Wi·ca·ta·wi \Wi-ċá-ta-wi\ *np* : the month of February, *i.e.* the raccoon moon - R Bl
wi·ca·tku·hye \wí-ca-tku-ȟye\ *n* : the nut of a hub
wi·ca·to·ka \wi-cá-to-ka\ *n* : a male captive
wi·ca·to·ke·ca \wi-cá-to-ḱe-ca\ *n* : differences, things different — **wicato·ktokeca** *n red* : many differences
wi·ca·tu·te \wi-cá-ṫu-ṫe\ *n* : roughness as of the hands, but not chapping, *wicayuh'i*
wi·ca·t'a \wi-cá-t'a\ *n* : the dead
wi·ca·t'e \wí-ca-t'e\ *n* : an instrument with which to kill
wi·ca·t'in·ze \wí-ċa-t'iŋ-ze\ *n* : a screw driver or hammer, something to make tight with screw or nail
wi·ca·we·ge \wí-ċa-we-ġa\ *n* : something with which to break
wi·ca·wi·wa·zi·ca \wi-cá-wi-wa-zi-ca\ *n* : a widower
wi·ca·wo·ha \wi-cá-wo-ȟa\ *n* : a son-in-law, my son-in-law; a man who lives with his relatives, being attracted to a family among them < *~ nitawa* your son-in-law > - D.14 note 4
wi·ca·wo·ha ta·ta·hca \wi-cá-wo-ȟa ta-tà-ȟca\ *n* : a small sized antilope, *nige sanla* - Bl
wi·ca·wo·haya \wi-cá-wo-ȟa-ya\ *va* wicawoȟa·wa·ya : to take or have for a son-in-law
wi·ca·wo·ta \wi-cá-wo-ṫa\ *n* : a feast, a banquet < *~ tanka kte. ~ kagapi* The feast will be large. They put on the feast. > - B.H.77.21, 178.17
wi·ca·ya \wi-cá-ya\ *adv* : manly, with firm decision
wi·ca·ya·ji·pa \wi-cá-ya-ǰi-ṗa\ *n* : a bee, bees - Note:
~ zi *n* : the yellow bee
~ tacanhanpi *n* : honey bee
~ hinšma *n* : a fuzzy bee larger than the honey bee

\a\ father \e\ they \i\ machine \o\ smoke \u\ lunar \an, aŋ\ blanc Fr. \in, iŋ\ ink \on, oŋ, un, uŋ\ soon, confier Fr. \c\ chair \ġ\ machen Ger. \j\ fusion \clusters: bl, gn, kp, hšl, etc...\ b^e^lo ... said with a slight vowel
See more in the Introduction, Guide to Pronunciation

~ *zi* *n* : the yellow bee – B.H.173.4 BI

wi·ca·ya·su·pi \wi-cá-ya-su-pi\ *n* : condemnation, pronouncing sentence
wi·ca·ya·tan·pi \wi-cá-ya-ṫaŋ-pi\ *n* : praise, compliments
wi·ca·ya·zan \wi-cá-ya-zaŋ\ *n* : sickness, a being sick
wi·ca·yu·he \wi-cá-yu-he\ *n* : a master
wi·ca·yu·h'i \wi-cá-yu-ȟ'i\ *n* : chapping of the hands – Cf wicatute
Wi·ca·yu·ska·pi *or* **Peta Cik'ala** \Wi-cá-yu-sǩa-ṗi\ *n* : Purgatory *or lit* Little Fire
wi·ca·yu·š'in·yan·yan s'e \wi-cá-yu-š'iŋ-yaŋ-yaŋ s'e\ *adv* : in sudden surprise seeing something I never saw be-fore I had an accident – KE
wi·ca·yu·wa·hpa·ni·ca \wi-cá-yu-wa-ȟṗa-ni-ca\ *n* : making poor
wi·ca·yu·win·ta·pi \wi-cá-yu-wiŋ-ta-pi\ *n* : an honoring salutation, as the Dakotas do at feasts, calling the host by some signifying relationship or title of friendship, or the gesture of stroking in or before the face in token of respect or friendly greeting and saying: "*Haiye, haiye.* What good news!"
wi·ca·zo \wí-ċa-zo\ *n* : a pen or pencil
wi·ce·ki·ya *or* **wicekiye** \wí-ce-ki-ya\ *n* : a prayerbook or missalette, something to pray with — *v* wice·wa·kiya : to solicit help with *e.g.* a printed prayer, or with a petition for help with signatures, to apply for help
wi·ce·ška \wi-cé-ška\ *n* : the vent hole in the top of a tipi or tent; the two flaps overlap between the upper part (the *wipá*, the large flaps), and the entrance and held together with pins, the pins that hold these two ends together < *Na wanna tipi k'on he ~ iyusna iyeyapi* And suddenly they pulled out the tent pins in the tipi's vent hole. *Yunkan leya ~ kin ogna kute kte sece c'un* And then he said this that it had seemed as though he might have shoot into the vent. *~ ipasise* the pins that hold the *wiceška* opening in the top together and the overlapping ends above the entrance togethere. *wiceškipasise* tent pins *or* a badge, *~ ohloke* pin holes for the holding of the *wiceška* together > – R RF SI D.111
wi·ce·ti *or* **wiaceic'iti** \wí-ce-ti\ *n* : sundogs
wi·ce·un·pe \wí-ce-uŋ-ṗe\ *n* : a frying pan – B.H.153.7
wi·ci·ble·za \wi-cí-ble-za\ *n* : pleasantness, clearness
wi·ci·ca·ške \wi-cí-ċa-šǩe\ *n* : strips of blanket or ornamented strips of anything worn over the shoulders and trailing on the ground as a *wicicaške wapaha* a headdress so ornamented
wi·ci·lo·wan \wi-cí-lo-waŋ\ *vi* : to serenade < *~ upi kte* They will come to sings songs. *~ mni kte lo* I shall go to serenade. > — *vt* : to perform a serenade for one – WHL
wi·ci·na·pci·yun·ka \wi-cí-na-pci-yuŋ-ka\ *adj num ord* : the ninth
wi·ci·nun·pa \wi-cí-nuŋ-pa\ *adj num ord* : the second
wi·cin \wi-cíŋ\ *v* wi·wa·cin : to hunt after women, to desire women
wi·cin·ca \wi-cíŋ-ca\ *n* : a girl — **wicinca·la** *n* wi·má·cincala : a little girl
wi·cin·pi \wi-cíŋ-pi\ *n* : the desiring women
Wi·cin·ska O·ko·la·ki·ci·ye *or* **Wiciska ...** \Wí-ciŋ-ska O-kò-la-ki-ci-ye\ *np* : the Wait-a-Minute Society, a one-time military society among the Oglala Lakotas < *Wicinska waci ahiyaye* They went on by doing the Wícinska dance. >

wi·cin·škan \wi-cíŋ-škaŋ\ *v* : to do flirting or courting while busy at some kind of work
wi·ci·ša·glo·gan \wi-cí-ša-glo-ġaŋ\ *adj num ord* : eigth
wi·ci·ša·ko·win \wi-cí-ša-ko-wiŋ\ *adj num ord* : seventh
wi·ci·ša·kpe \wi-cí-ša-kpe\ *adj num ord* : the sixth
wi·ci·šna·la \wi-cí-šna-la\ *adj* : alone, none with one
wi·ci·špa \wi-cí-šṗa\ *n* : a cubit, the forearm, *i.e.* the distance from the elbow to the end of the middle finger
wi·ci·šta \wi-cí-šṫa\ *n* : the human eye
wi·ci·štin·me \wi-cí-šṫiŋ-me\ *n* : sleep; they are asleep
wi·ci·te \wi-cí-ṫe\ *n* : the human face, countenance
wi·ci·te·gle·ga \wi-cí-ṫe-gle-ġa\ *n* : the raccoon
wi·ci·te·i·ya·ska·bye \wi-cí-te-i-ya-ska-bye\ *n* : a postage stamp
wi·ci·te o·wa·pi \wi-cí-ṫe o-wa-pi\ *n* : a photograph, the picture of a face
wi·ci·ti·ye·ki·ya·pi s'e \wi-cí-ṫi-ye-ki-ya-pi s'e\ *adv* [fr *wica* a human + *ite* face + *iyekiya* to recognise] : as if they recognized one another after a long time < *~ wanblakelo* I saw him as if not having seen him for a long time, as is said when greeting one another very heartily as though one did not meet for some time. > – BF
wi·ci·to·ka·pa \wi-cí-to-ǩa-pa\ *n* : the eldest born
wi·ci·to·pa \wi-cí-ṫo-ṗa\ *adj rum ord* : the fourth
wi·ci·to·wa \wi-cí-ṫo-wa\ *va* wicito·wa·pa : to photograph — **wicitowa·pi** *n* : a pictured postcard
wi·ci·wi·kce·mna \wi-cí-wi-kce-mna\ *adj num ord* : the tenth
wi·ci·ya·mni \wi-cí-ya-mni\ *adj num ord* : the third
Wi·ci·ye·la \Wi-cí-ye-la\ *np* : the Yankton Dakota, a name applied by the Teton to the Yanktons and Yanktonais – R
wi·ci·yo·ki·pi \wi-cí-yo-ǩi-ṗi\ *n* : pleasantness, excellence, beauty
wi·ci·yun·ka \wi-cí-yuŋ-ka\ *n* : bedtime
wi·ci·za·ptan \wi-cí-za-ptaŋ\ *adj num ord* : the fifth
wi·co·a·ho·pe \wi-có-a-ho-ṗe\ *n* [fr *ahopa* to keep, observe] : law, custom, ceremony
wi·co·a·i·e \wi-có-a-i-e\ *n* [fr *aia* to slander] : slander
wi·co·a·yu·štan \wi-có-a-yu-štaŋ\ *n* [fr *ayuštan* to cease, stop] : the leaving off, a stop
wi·co·bli·he·ca \wi-có-bli-he-ca\ *n* [fr *bliheca* to be active] : activity
wi·co·ca·je·ya·te \wi-có-ca-je-ya-te\ *n* [fr *cajeyata* to name or call by name] : traditions in honoring by name
wi·co·can·lwa·kan \wi-có-caŋ-lwa-ǩaŋ\ *n* : a coward < *Tokša anpa ca ~ yelo, na hanhepi ca otuyacin utapelo* Soon when daylight they are cowards, and when night they fire off their guns at random. >
wi·co·can·ni·ye \wi-có-caŋ-ni-ye\ *n* [fr *canniyan* to be angry at women] : anger, malice of husband towards wife
wi·co·can·ta·gle \wi-có-caŋ-ṫa-gle\ *n* [fr *cantagle* to set the heart on *esp* evil] : evil intention, malice
wi·co·can·te \wi-có-caŋ-ṫe\ *n* : the human heart
wi·co·can·te·i·yu·tan·ye \wi-có-caŋ-ṫe-i-yù-ṫaŋ-ye\ *n* : temptation
wi·co·can·te·o·yu·ze \wi-có-caŋ-ṫe-o-yu-ze\ *n* : disposition, thought, purpose, wish
wi·co·can·te·ši·ca \wi-có-caŋ-ṫe-ši-ca\ *n* : sadness
wi·co·can·te·wa·šte \wi-có-caŋ-ṫe-wa-šte\ *n* : gladness
wi·co·can·ti·he·ye \wi-có-caŋ-ti-he-ye\ *n* : covetousness or excessive desire
wi·co·can·ti·ya·gle·ya \wi-có-caŋ-ti-ya-gle-ya\ *n* : that which is desired

wi·co·can·ze·ka \wi-có-caŋ-ze-ka\ *n* [fr *canzeka* angry] : anger, malice

wi·co·e·ce·tu \wi-có-e-ce-ṫu\ *n* [fr *ecetu* to be as a person or thing ought to be] : uprightness

wi·co·e·ki·ce·tu·ye \wi-có-e-k̇i-ce-tu-ye\ *n* [fr *ekicetuya* to restore, make right again] : restoration, reestablishment

wi·co·gli·gle \wi-có-gli-gle\ *n* : traveling

wi·co·han \wi-có-haŋ\ *adv* [fr *wica* people + *ogna* into] : into the crowd – R

wi·co·hta·ni \wi-có-ḣṫa-ni\ *n* [fr *htani* being poor, miserable] : work, labor

wi·co·h'an \wi-có-ḣ'aŋ\ *n* [fr *oh'an* to do, to work at] : custom, habit, work

wi·co·h'an·ya \wi-có-ḣ'aŋ-ya\ *va* : to have for a custom – B.H.262.11

wi·co·h'un·ka \wi-có-ḣ'uŋ-ca\ *v* [fr *wicoh'an* a custom + *únca* to mimic] : to ape, mimic < *Wicoh'an únwaca* I aped the custom. > – BT

wi·co·i·ca·ge \wi-có-i-ca-ġe\ *n* [fr *icaga* to grow, become] : a generation

wi·co·i·e \wi-có-i-e\ *n* [fr *oie* a word, saying, speech] : a word, speech, story, legend, *etc.*

wi·co·i·gla·tan \wi-có-i-gla-ṫaŋ\ *n* [fr *iglatan* to boast of one's self] : boasting

wi·co·i·na·hni \wi-có-i-na-ḣni\ *n* [fr *inahni* to hurry] : hurrying, haste

wi·co·i·štin·me \wi-có-i-štiŋ-me\ *n* [fr *ištinma* to sleep] : sleep

wi·co·i·ton·pe \wi-có-i-toŋ-ṗe\ *n* [fr *itonpa* to praise in wonderment] : carefulness

wi·co·i·yo·ki·ši·ce \wi-có-i-yo-k̇i-ši-ce\ *n* : sorrow

wi·co·i·yo·pe·i·c'i·ye \wi-có-i-yo-ṗe-i-c'i-ye\ *n* : repentence

wi·co·ji·ce \wi-có-ji-ce\ *n* [fr *jica* rich] : riches

wi·co·ju·la \wi-có-ju-la\ *n* [fr *ojula* full] : fullness, full of people

wi·co·ka·gi \wi-có-ka-ġi\ *n* [fr *kagi* to obstruct one's way] : a hindrance —**wicokagi·ye** *n* : an obstruction

wi·co·ka·ki·je \wi-có-k̇a-k̇i-je\ *n* [fr *kakija* to suffer] : suffering

[1]**wi·co·kan** \wi-có-k̇aŋ\ *n* : age < ~ *unkitawa k'un tasagye kin iyacu* You have taken the staff of our old age (and sent him away). > – B.H. 122.13

[2]**wi·co·kan** \wí-co-k̇aŋ\ *n* [fr *wi* sun + *cokan* middle] : noon < *Na wanna ~ kiyela hehanl inajin na wankal etowan najin na lowan. Na wanna ~ sanpa hehanl eyapaha k'on he ake u* And now when it was near noon, he then stood up and while he stood looking up he sang. And when it was afternoon the announcer had come then a second time. >

wi·co·kan·hi·ya·ya *or* **wicokan sam iyaya** \wí-co-k̇an-hi-ya-ya\ *n* : afternoon < *Le wicaša kin hihanna ~ šni ecel kigni kta* This man should go home, as it was morning and not afternoon. >

wi·co·kan·hi·yu·i·c'i·ya \wi-có-k̇aŋ-hi-yu-i-c'i-ya\ *v* [fr *wica* certain people + *cokan* middle + *hiyuic'iya* to have one's self come] : to come unasked

wi·co·kan·yan \wí-co-k̇aŋ-yaŋ\ *n* : noon < *Na wanna ~ sanpa ehanl ungna wanna u* And now he is to come presently perhaps after noon. *Na wanna ~ kitanla sanpa hehanl wanna eyapaha onhe ake u* And now when it was a little after noon, that herald came then a second time. >

wi·co·ka·ške \wi-có-ka-ške\ *n* : a prison – P Bl

wi·co·kco·ta \wi-có-kco-ta\ *n red of* wicota : a multitude – B.H.82.19

wi·co·ki·ca·mna \wi-có-k̇i-ca-mna\ *v* : to be stirred up, going to and fro, as people in turmoil < *Le anpetu kin ~ yelo* Today there was much turmoil. > – Bl KE

wi·co·ki·ci·yu·wa·šte \wi-có-ki-ci-yu-wa-šṫe\ *n* : a blessing, a peace

wi·co·ki·ci·ze \wi-có-k̇i-ci-ze\ *n* [fr *kiciza* to fight] : fighting

wi·co·ki·pa·jin \wi-có-k̇i-pa-jiŋ\ *n* [fr *kipajin* to resist] : opposition

wi·co·kon·ze \wi-có-k̇oŋ-ze\ *n* : an influence, a law, a kingdom or government, a political system

wi·co·ksa·pe \wi-có-ksa-ṗe\ *n* [fr *ksapa* wise] : a wisdom

wi·co·ku·je \wi-có-k̇u-je\ *n* [fr *kuja* to be sick] : a sickness

wi·co·mni·ci·ye \wi-có-mni-ci-ye\ *n* [fr *mniciya* gather, assemble] : an assembly

wi·co·na·wi·zi \wi-có-na-wi-zi\ *n* : jealousy – Bl

wi·co·ni \wi-có-ni\ *n* [fr *wica people* + *oni* life] : life, *i.e.* of the present, but *esp.* of that to come; a lifetime < ~ *owihanke wanica* everlasting or eternal life >

wi·co·ni·hin·ci·ye \wi-có-ni-hiŋ-ci-ye\ *n* : a general fear, or turmoil, panic as in a great deluge or flood – Bl

wi·co·ni·yan·pi \wi-có-ni-yaŋ-pi\ *n* : salvation < ~ *kte kin he Juda oyate kin etanhan kte lo* Salvation that will be will be from the Jewish people. > – B.H.182.10

wi·con·t'e \wi-cóŋ-t'e\ *n* [fr *wica* people + *on* on account + *t'a* to die] : death < *Hehanl ~ kin hi kta* Death will then come. >

wi·co·on·ši·ke \wi-có-oŋ-ši-ke\ *n* [fr *onšika* pitiful, miserable] : poverty

wi·co·o·we·wa·kan *or* **wicoowewakankan** \wi-có-o-we-wa-kan\ *n* [fr *owewakan* to tell an untruth] : a lie, a falsehood, a deceit

wi·co·o·wo·tan·la \wi-có-o-wo-taŋ-la\ *n* [fr *owotanla* just or right] : righteousness

wi·co·pe·ya \wi-có-pe-ya\ *prep phr* [fr *wica* them + *opeya* among] : among them < *Iktomi ~ , i.e. Piško, iyaya ške* Spider, *i.e.* Night Hawk, they say went among them. > – MS.1-5

wi·co·su·ta \wi-có-su-ṫa\ *n* [fr *suta* hard, firm] : firmness, strength

wi·co·ši·ce \wi-có-ši-ce\ *n* [fr *šica* bad] : evil

wi·co·ši·htin \wi-có-ši-ḣṫiŋ\ *n* [fr *šihtin* imperfect, badly made] : debility

wi·co·škan·škan \wi-có-škaŋ-škaŋ\ *n* [fr *škanškan* move about] **1** : motion, moving **2** : rule, government, governance – R

wi·co·ška·te \wi-có-ška-te\ *n* [fr *škata* to play] : play

wi·co·ški·ške \wi-có-ški-ške\ *n* [fr *oškiška* rough, abrupt] : difficulty; distraction

wi·co·špi *or* **wicošpe** \wi-có-šṗi\ *n* : a wart

wi·co·ta \wi-có-ṫa\ *n* : a multitude, many people < *Wiúncotapi* We are a multitude of people. >

wi·co·ta·ku·ni·šni \wi-có-ṫa-k̇u-ni-šni\ *n* : destruction

wi·co·ta·ku·ye \wi-có-ṫa-k̇u-ye\ *n* [fr *takuye* a relative] : relationship, brotherhood

wi·co·ta·la s'e \wi-có-ta-la s'e\ *adv* : rather many < ~ *yahipi kin icanlmawašte* I am glad for rather many of you

---

\a\ father \e\ they \i\ machine \o\ smoke \u\ lunar \an, aŋ\ blanc Fr. \in, iŋ\ ink \on, oŋ, un, uŋ\ soon, confier Fr. \c\ chair \ġ\ machen Ger. \j\ fusion \clusters: bl, gn, kp, hšl, etc...\ b[e]lo ... said with a slight vowel **See more in the Introduction, Guide to Pronunciation**

having come. > – Bl

wi·co·ta·pi·šni·yan·kel \wi-có-ta-pi-šni-yaŋ-kel *adv* : away from a crowd – B.H.251.1

wi·co·ta·wa·cin \wi-có-ta-wa-ciŋ\ *n* : disposition

wi·co·te·ca \wi-có-ṫe-ca\ *n* [fr *teca* new] : newness

wi·co·ti \wi-có-ṫi\ *n* : a village, a camp — 3rd *pers pl of* oti : They are encamped < *Na htayetu hehanl ~ kin kiyela glapi* And when it was evening they were then on their way home near the camp. >

wi·co·to·ke·tu \wi-có-ṫo-k̇e-ṫu\ *adv interrog* : how is it? < *~ tan'in šni* How it is is not apparent. >

wi·co·un *or* **wicotakuye** \wi-có-uŋ\ *n* **a** : a family, all who are related by blood **b** : a place where men live **c** : a covenant under which men live in union – R Bl

wi·co·wa·cin·ko \wi-có-wa-ciŋ-ko\ *n* [fr *wacinko* pouting, ill-tempered] : a bad temper

wi·co·wa·hwa·la \wi-có-wa-ḣwa-la\ *n* : gentleness

wi·co·wa·šte \wi-có-wa-šte\ *n* [fr *wašte* good] : goodness

wi·co·wa·š'a·ke \wi-có-wa-š'a-k̇e\ *n* : human strength

wi·co·we *or* **wicowepi** \wi-có-we\ *n* [fr *owe* a kind, class, division] : relationship between brothers, sisters, cousins; these and their aunts and uncles; a generation, *i.e.* son-father-grandfather *etc.* < *Na wanna anpa ca na hehanl ~ nainš owapate nainš šunkawakan ceslipi nainš tokel wicaša oškinc'iyapi hena slolya wacinpi* And now when it was daylight, they wanted to know about the generations, or things pushed aside, or the horse dung, or how men occupied their time. >

wi·co·wi·ca·ša·šni \wi-có-wi-ca-ša-šni\ *n* : villainy – B.H.31.1

wi·co·wo·gla·ke \wi-có-wo-gla-k̇e\ *n* : relating stories, biography < *~ k'u* to let one make a speech >

wi·co·wo·ya·ke \wi-có-wo-ya-k̇e\ *n* [fr *oyaka* to tell, relate] : a narration, declaration, chapter, doctrine

wi·co·yu·ta·ku·ni·šni \wi-có-yu-ṫa-k̇u-ni-šni\ *n* : that which causes destruction

wi·co·zan·ni \wi-có-zaŋ-ni\ *n* : health – Pb.38

wi·cun·ke·šni \wi-cúŋ-ke-šni\ *n* : one who knows nothing or does not care to do anything, is incompetent even to keep house < *Lila tanyan loliyah'an šni yelo* You don't cook very well at all; *~ ca lolih'an s'e* since she is incompetent she only seems to prepare food, as they would say of a woman whose cooking was very poor, intimating that for this reason she had many husbands. > – Note: the word is applied only to women – BA

wi·cun·ksu \wi-cúŋ-ksu\ *n* : the pole on which meat is dried – Bm

wi·cuns i·a \wí-cuŋs i-a\ *v* : to make a wrong statement unintentionally < *Hehehé wicuns iwayelo* Too bad! I stated it wrong. > – BT

wi·cun·ska·ye·šni \wí-cuŋ-ṡka-ye-šni\ *v* wicunska·wa·yešni – Note: *wicunskaye* is not used *Syn* EL ETONWANŠNI EM

wi·cun·šni \wí-cuŋ-šni\ *v* : to be very incompetent in women's work – Cf wicunkešni. This word is used only of women who can neither cook nor keep house La KE

wi·c'i·ca·ge *or* **wic'oncage** \wi-c'í-ca-ġe\ *n* : a growth of men, a gener-ation – SHB

wi·c'in \wí-c'iŋ\ *n* [fr *k'in* to carry a load] : the strap the Dakotas once used to carry meat < *Inahni, ~ kin wahunhunpi* Hurry! The strap was cut loose. >

wi·e·ya·ku \wi-é-ya-k̇u\ *va* wie·bla·ku : to take away a woman

wi·gla·hpa \wi-glá-ḣpa\ *v poss* wi·wa·glahpa : to strike or take down one's own tent

wi·gla·šta·ka \wi-glá-šta-k̇a\ *v poss* wi·wa·glaštaka : to beat one's wife

wi·gla·wa \wí-gla-wa\ *v* wi·wa·glawa [fr *iglawa* to count or esteem one's self] : to count one's self; to figure, settle – B.H.248.3

wi·gli \wí-gli\ *n* [fr *igli* grease, soft fat of animals] : oil or grease

wi·gli·gla \wí-gli-gla\ *v* wí·wa·gligla : to travel to and fro away from one, as does the sun – WE

wi·gli on ka·ga·pi \wí-gli oŋ kà-ġa-pi\ *n* : Indian bread

wi·gli za·ze·ca·la \wí-gli za-zè-ca-la\ *n* : the drops of grease floating on a good soup, seemingly like floating eyes – Bl

wi·glo·ce·ti \wí-glo-ce-ṫi\ *n* : an oil stove

wi·glu·kcan \wí-glu-kcaŋ\ *v* wí·wa·glukcan [fr *iglukcan* to understand one's self] : to understand one's own or one's self, to form an opinion, to judge one's self – Pb.23

wi·gmun·ke \wí-gmuŋ-ke\ *n* : the rainbow < *mas'í-gmunke* a trap, or snare > – Note: according to some people of past generations, the rainbow is not the result of rain, but rather it stops further rain

wi·gna·gna·ye \wí-gna-gna-ye\ *n* or *adv* : giving things to others to make them forget, giving something step by step in a progression < *~ tonpi s'e amaupelo* I was brought step by step to birth. > – Cf ignagnaye s'e Bl KE

wi·gni \wí-gni\ *v* wi·wa·gni [fr *igni* hunt for game, provisions] : to look for provisions, to hunt *e.g.* deer to provide < *He écuhciš tanhánka na hankaku wiwicakigni kte* He will at least hunt supplies for his brother and siste-in-law. > – Pb.24 D.12

wi·gnu \wí-gnu\ *v* wí·wa·gnu [fr *ignu* to blame] : to reproach, murmur, be displeased with — **wignu·pi** *n* : a murmuring, complaining

wi·gu·ye \wí-ġu-ye\ *n* : a branding iron, as is used in the branding of cattle, horses, *etc.*

wi·ha·ka·kta \wi-há-k̇a-kta\ *n* : the fifth child, if a daughter, so called probably from its usually being the last. In the month of March the Dakotas would say: *Ištawicaniyanpi wi tan'in yelo; wihakakte iyuha wiyuškin po; ake wigli luzapi kte lo* There appear sore eyes in the month of March; all you fifth child girls, be glad; oil will again go fast – Note: *hoihákakta* the youngest of a man's wives – BT

wi·ha·ka·kta ce·pa·pi \wi-há-ka-kta cè-pa-pi\ *n* : the month of April – Note: the youngest wife had to crack bones; for, on the marrow they would get fat – Bl

wi·han·bla·pi \wí-haŋ-bla-pi\ *n* : a dreaming

wi·han·ble *or* **ihanbla** \wí-haŋ-ble\ *v* : to dream

wi·han·ble·s'a \wí-háŋ-ble-s'a\ *n* : a dreamer

wi·hi·gna·ton \wi-hí-gna-toŋ\ *n* : a married woman – Pb.25

wi·hi·na·pa \wí-hi-na-ṗa\ *n* : the east, the sun rising

wi·hin·pa·spa *or* **wahinpaspa** \wi-híŋ-ṗa-ṡpa\ *n* : tent pins, picketpins < *~ kasa* to cut tent pins > – Bl

wi·hi·ya·la *or* **wihiyayela** \wí-hi-ya-la\ *n* : the passing of the sun, the measure of clock time, the hour of the day < *~ tonakeca* What time is is? > – FN LHB

wi·hu·ta \wi-hú-ṫa\ *n* : the lower border of a tent < *~ iyuha kahoho po* Knock loose your lower borders, as is announced before breaking up camp. > – BT

wi·hu·ta hu \wi-hú-ṫa hu\ *n* : the broad-leaved cattail, typha latifolia, the cattail family; a water plant three or four feet tall with thin broad leaves and one round stalk bearing fruit which is called *hantkán* – Bl #231

wi·hu·ta hu i·ye·ce·ca \wi-hú-ṫa hu i-yè-ce-ca\ *n* : the eastern plantain, healing blade, plantago major – B. #181

wi·hu·ta hu swu·la \wi-hú-ta hu swu-la\ *n* : the great bulrush, scirpus validus – BT #70

wi·hu·ta i·na·ta·ke \wi-hú-ta i-na-ta-ke\ *n* : something as grass used to fasten up around the bottom of a tent

wi·hu·ta ša \wi-hú-ta ša\ *n* : the lowest part of the tent, the border that is usually painted red — **wihuta ša ohloke** \wi-hú-ta ša o-ȟlò-ke\ *n* : the holes made in the lowest part of a tent through which tent pins go

wi·hmun·ge \wí-ȟmuŋ-ġe\ *n* : witch-medicine

wi·hpan·yan·pi \wí-ȟpaŋ-yaŋ-pi\ *n* : dried meat, *pápa*

wi·hpe·ya \wí-ȟpe-ya\ *va* wihpé·wa·ya : to give away things, to give as after a death in a family < *Hihanna kin honunpinyanwayin na ošungye wihpewayin kte* Tomorrow I shall do a full surround and with more force than needed put on a give-away, *i.e.* intending to kill many buffalos. > — **wihpeya·pi** *n* : a give-away, a practice of giving away property on the death of a member of the family, things being laid out for giving away < ~ *bluha kte* I shall hold a give-away. > – R Bl GA

wi·ȟu·pa **wipipa** \wi-ȟú-pa\ *n* : tent flaps – Note: *wipipaha* the two smoke vent flaps at the top of a tipi

wi·h'an \wí-ȟ'aŋ\ *v* wi·wa·h'an [fr *ih'an* to be busy with] : to be busy with many things — **wih'an·pi** \wí-ȟ'aŋ-pi\ *n* : a being busy about many things

wi·i·ca·hta·ke·šni \wi-í-ċa-ȟta-ke-šni\ *adj* : not having known women, as by contacting, touching

wi·i·ci·gni \wi-í-ci-gni\ *v* wií·we·cigni *or* wii·wa·kigni : to scold or whip a woman

wi·i·c'i·glu·kcan \wí-i-c'i-glu-kcaŋ\ *v* wí·mi·c'iglukcan : to make a vow, to promise or resolve to do a certain thing – Bl

wi·i·c'i·gni \wi-í-c'i-gni\ *v abol* [fr *wigni* look for provisions] : to provide for one's self, by way of good food *etc.*, to look out for things one's self – MS.557

wi·i·glu·kcan \wí-i-glu-kcaŋ\ *v* : to form one's opinion

we·i·hpe·ya \wi-í-ȟpe-ya\ *va* wiihpe·wa·ya : to divorce one's wife, to leave one's wife, to throw away a woman

wi·i·na·hma \wi-í-na-ȟma\ *v* wiína·wa·hma : to fornicate, to take off with a woman, to conceal a woman

wi·i·ya·glu·ȟa \wi-í-ya-glu-ȟa\ *v* : to be a constant companion of one's wife – Bl

wi·i·ya·hpa·ya \wi-í-ya-ȟpa-ya\ *v* : to rape, force a woman

wi·i·ya·na·jin·ce \wi-í-ya-na-jin-ce\ *v* : to run away holding a woman

wi·i·ya·on·pa·pi *or* **wiiyaunpapi** \wi-í-ya-oŋ-pa-pi\ *n* : a charging with infidelity, or with having illicit intercourse

wi·i·ya·pa·ȟi·ce \wí-i-ya-pa-ȟi-ce\ *n* : the tent fittings, fastenings for the top of a tent

wi·i·ya·pe \wi-í-ya-pe\ *v* : to court a woman, waiting to talk to her

wi·i·ya·ya \wí-i-ya-ya\ *v* : the sun sets — *n* : sundown

wi·i·ya·yuȟ \wi-í-ya-yuȟ\ *adv* : in the path of the sun, *i.e.* from east to west < ~ *ya* to go with the sun > – R Bl

wi·i·ya·yu·ȟa \wí-i-ya-yu-ȟa\ *v* wiiya·blu·ȟa : to leave home and take a wife in another locale and live with her friends

wi·i·yu·hla·te \wi-i-yú-ȟla-te\ *n* : a pipe wrench

wi·ji·ca \wi-ji-ca\ *adj* wi·ma·jica [fr *ijica* to be rich in goods] : rich < *Lila wak'upi canke wijica ke* He meant that he was very gifted and therefore rich. > — *n* : riches < *wíjica* the rich > — **wijica·ya** \wí-ji-ca-ya\ *va* : to enrich – P

wi·ji·mna \wí-ji-mna\ *vn* : to smell of something burning, such as fat, bones, *etc.*

wi·ka·lye \wí-ka-lye\ *n* : a tea or coffee pot

wi·kan \wí-kaŋ\ *n* : a leather cord, a packing strap < ~ *sonpi* a lasso, *i.e.* strands of thin cord twisted into thick cord > – D.257

wi·kan·gi·gi·ke \wí-kaŋ-ġi-ġi-ke\ *n* wí·ma·kangigike : one who is very anxious to acquire things as he has nothing – Bl

wi·kan·kan \wí-kaŋ-kaŋ\ *n* : a double rope < *Na ~ num el otka* And he was suspended on two double ropes, *i.e.* as in the Sundance. >

wi·ka·wan·ka·p'u \wí-ka-waŋ-ka-p'u\ *n* : the hour about 7:00 or 8:00 AM – *See* kawánkalwapa

wi·ka·ze \wí-ka-ze\ *n* : a gravy strainer

wi·kce·mna \wi-kcé-mna\ *adj num card* : ten < ~ *nunpa* twenty, ~ *yamni* thirty, *etc.* > — **wikcemna·mna** *adj num card* : ten by ten – P

wi·ki·can·yan·pi \wí-ki-caŋ-yaŋ-pi\ *n* : a tool, tools

wi·ki·ca·ye *or* **wikicanye** \wí-ki-ca-ye\ *n* : tools, implements – R

wi·ki·ci·yun·ga·pi \wí-ki-ci-yuŋ-ġa-pi\ *n* [fr *iyunga* to ask of one] : a mutual inquiry, a questioning of one another

wi·ki·c'un \wí-ki-c'uŋ\ *adv* : with a concern < *wacin ~ šni* one who is indifferent >

wi·ki·kšan \wi-kí-kšaŋ\ *v* wi·wá·kikšan : to love-play, to play with one's wife — **wikikšan·pi** *n* : a playing with one's wife – BD

wi·ki·ni·ca \wí-ki-ni-ca\ *v* wí·wa·kinica : to pick up, grabbing what others drop < *Akicita k'on wanna ti unyan éyaya na lila wiunkinicapi* That soldier now had taken and lost his house, so we really grabbed to pick up what others had dropped. >

wi·ki·ška·ta \wi-ki-ška-ta\ *v* [fr *wi* woman + *kiškata* to wrestle playfully] : to love-play with one's wife – *Syn* WIKIKŠAN

wi·ki·šle·ya \wi-kí-šle-ya\ *va* wikišle·wa·ya : to offer insults to a woman — **wikišleya·pi** *n* : rape

wi·ki·yu·ta \wí-ki-yu-ta\ *v* wi·wa·kiyuta : to beckon to, to talk by signs < *Nape on ~* He talks by hand. > – B.H.160.6

wi·ko·pa \wí-ko-pa\ *v* wiko·wa·pa [fr *ikopa* to fear something] : to be afraid, to bear with — **wikope·ca** \wí-ko-pe-ca\ *n* : one who is afraid — **wikope·šni·yan** *adv* : without fear, securely

wi·ko·ška \wi-kó-ška\ *n* : a veneral disease of women

wi·ko·ška·la·ka \wi-kó-ška-la-ka\ *n* : a young woman

wi·ko·ška ta·pe·ju·ta \wi-kó-ška ta-pe-jù-ta\ *n* : the small western poison ivy, rhus rydbergii, the sumac family – Note: when touched it causes irritations, hence the name. It is not a medicine plant. – *See* wikoška BT #92

wi·kpi zi \wí-kpi zi\ *n* : the yellow-breasted chat, which sings at night – FR

wi·ksa·pa \wí-ksa-pa\ *v* wi·wa·ksapa[fr *iksapa* to be wise about anything] : to comprehend well, to have experience looking after a thing intelligently < ~ *iyaye cin he wašte tka yelo* He who exceeds in being wise about

---

\a\ father \e\ they \i\ machine \o\ smoke \u\ lunar \an, aŋ\ blanc Fr. \in, iŋ\ ink \on, oŋ, un, uŋ\ soon, confier Fr. \c\ chair \ġ\ machen Ger. \j\ fusion \clusters: bl, gn, kp, hšl, etc...\ b[e]lo ... said with a slight vowel **See more in the Introduction, Guide to Pronunciation**

things would be good. > - Bl
wi·kte \wi-kté\ *v* : to beat one's wife
wi·ku·ci·ye·la \wí-ǩu-ci-ye-la\ *n* : late afternoon, time towards sunset — **wiku·wabya** *n* : mid-afternoon, time about 3:00
wi·le·ca·la \wí-le-ca-la\ *n* : the crescent of the moon between New Moon and First Quarter - LB
wi·lu·lye \wí-lu-lye\ *n* : red dye, cochineal
wi·lu·te \wí-lu-te\ *n* : red, scarlet dye, *i.e.* a fluid with which to dye something *e.g.* porcupine quills scarlet
wi·lu·zi·gna·gton \wi-lú-zi-gna·gtoŋ\ *v* : to make a tent tight around the lowest part, the border, by pins or by putting hay *etc.* all around < *Osni kte lo, ~ wo* Insulate around the bottom, it will get cold, as they say when a storm is coming, thus to cover up the tipi at the bottom all around so the wind may not blow in. > - BT
wi·lu·zi·gna·ke \wi-lú-zi-gna-ke\ *n* : Insulation - Bl
wi·lwi·ta \wí-lwi-ta\ *adv* : in groups, in bunches < *Peji šaša ~ han* A red grass stands in patches. > — **wilwitaya** *adv red* [fr *witaya* together] : in groups, assembled in different places < *~ eglepi* shocked grain > - Bl
wi·ma·hel i·ya·ye \wí-ma-hel i-yà-ye\ *n* : the setting of the sun < *Wimahel iyayetkiya etonwe* He looks towards the setting sun. >
wi·ma·ka·he·ya \wí-ma-ka-he-ya\ *n* : vitality, initiative, enterprise, vigor, energy, *i.e.* that which enables a person to earn or accomplish much
wi ma·ka·tan·han \wi ma-ká-taŋ-haŋ\ *n* [fr *wi* moon + *maka* earth + *etanhan* from] : the moon between Full Moon and Third Quarter < *~ u* The Full Moon is coming, *i.e.* it rises late and "from the earth". > - LB
wi mi·ma \wi mi-má\ *n* : the Full Moon — **wi mima·kanyela** \wi mi-má-ǩaŋ-ye-la\ *n* : the moon between First Quarter and Full Moon, *i.e.* when it is gibbous *i.e.* humpbacked - LB
wi·mna šni \wí-mna šni\ *v* : to have little confidence, to be doubtful of one's ability - **Syn** WÉCEYEŠNI B
wi·na·gi·ye·ya \wí-na-ġi-ye-ya\ *adv* : annoying a person, as in seeking from a woman the sexual act - WHL
wi·na·hta·gye \wí-na-ȟta-gye\ *n* : a typewriter - LB
wi·na·h'on \wí-na-ȟ'oŋ\ *v* wína·wa·h'on [fr *nah'on* to hear] : to hear, to be able to hear
wi·na·ja·ja \wí-na-ja-ja\ *n* : a washing machine
wi·na·kan·ye \wí-na-kaŋ-ye\ *n* : a threshing machine
wi·na·ka·po \wí-na-ǩa-ṗo\ *n* : common hop, humulus lupulus, the nettle family - Note: it is also called *wahpe akicaškapi* and is used as baking powder, hops, yeast, in making bread - R BT Bl #74
wi·na·ki·wi·zi \wí-na-ǩi-wi-zi\ *v* wina·wa·kiwizi : to be jealous or envious of
wi·na·pce \wí-na-pce\ *n* : the esophagus < *~ mahel popi* a swelling in the throat, *i.e.* swollen toncils >
wi·na·pin·škan·ye *or* **winapiškanye** \wí-na-ṗiŋ-ška-ye\ *n* : a toy, toys, playthings
wi·na·po·hye \wí-na-ṗo-ȟye\ *n* [fr *pogan* to inflate, swell] : yeast, leaven
wi·na·p'i·la \wi-na-p'í-la\ *or* \wí-na-p'iŋ-la\ *n* : the large grouse, so-called because it appears to wear a yoke about its neck
wi·na·ta·ke \wí-na-ta-ǩe\ *n* [fr *inátake* a fastener] : a lock, a fastening
[1]**wi·na·wi·zi** \wi-ná-wi-zi\ *n* : the cockle or clot burr < *~ hu* the cockle burr plant, *Ate, nata catkayatan ~ wan imakoyakin kte lo* Father, a cockle burr will be sticking on the left side of my head. >
[2]**wi·na·wi·zi** \wí-na-wi-zi\ *vn* wína·wa·wizi : to be jealous or envious - Note: *wínakiwizi* is the *vt* form
wi·na·wi·zi ci·k'a·la \wi-ná-wi-zi cì-k'a-la\ *n* : wild liquorice *or* licorice, burr legume, buffalo burr, glycyrrhiza lepidota, the pulse family - Note: as a medicine BT used the root by mixing it with *pejuta ska* milk vetch; the root is bitter when chewed and often used during the time of the flu - BT #78
wi·na·wi·zi hu tan·ka·hca \wi-ná-wi-zi hu tàŋ-ka-ȟca\ *n* : the cockle or clot burr, xanthium echinatum, the composite family - Note: as medicine it is used as *šilyapi* what is spoiled in ceremonies - MS.356 BT #108
wi·na·wi·zi·pi \wí-na-wi-zi-pi\ *n* : jealousy
wi·na·wi·zi·s'a \wí-na-wi-zi a'a\ *n* : a jealous person — *adj* : of a jealous disposition
wi·na·ze \wí-na-ze\ *n* : a strainer, filter - Note: *nazéya* to filter, strain
wi·nu·hca \wi-nú-ȟca\ *n* : a man's mother-in-law < *~, cuiyohe wanji micah yuha yo* Mother-in-law, make for me and keep a pair of old-tent moccasins. > **winuhca·la** *n* wi·ma·nuhcala : an old woman - Bl
wi·nu·hca·la ta·can·pe·ti·pi·ye *or* **winuhcala tacanpelipiye** \wi-nú-ȟca-la ta-càŋ-ṗe-ti-ye\ *n* [fr *caŋ* wood + *peta* fire + *apiya* revive a fire] : an old lady's poker, *Can tukte on peta apiyapi he e lo* That is, any piece of wood with which to poke a fire - Note: *cantetipiye* is a misspelling
wi·nun·ka·la *or* **winuhcala** \wi-núŋ-ka-la\ *n* : an old woman - Bl
win \wiŋ\ *adj* : female, of a woman or wife - Note: the word is commonly a *suff* to the name of a woman, much the same as Mrs *or* Ms is *pref* to a woman's name
win·ga \wíŋ-ġa\ *v* : bend - Note: this is a root word
win·ha·ha \wíŋ-ha-ha\ *adj* : jovial, good-natured — **winhaha·ka** *n* : one who is pleased with trifles < *P'osyakel unk'un winhahakelo* We are displeased, he is quite pleased. > — **wínhaha·kel** *or* **wíhahayakel** *or* **wínhahayakel** *adv* : in good spirits < *~ un* to be in good spirits, *Cantewašte kapi* Its mean-ing is to be glad or joyful. > - SE D.278
win·ha·ha·ya \wíŋ-ha-ha-ya\ *adv* : easily pleased < *~ icu* to take trifles gladly > — **winhahaya·kel** *or* **wihahayakel** *adv* : apparently in good spirits, happily - Note: the latter spelling seems to be Santee Dakota Cf kel D.278
winh \wiŋȟ\ *v root contrac of* wínga : bend — **win·hya** *adv* : in a bent manner
win·ja \wiŋ-já\ *v root* : bend < *yuwinja* to bend > — **winja·han** *part* : bent down, as grass may be
win·kce·kce \wíŋ-kce-kce\ *adv* : unconcerned, not in a hurry, not concerned or minding anything < *~ mani* to walk without the slightest concern, *Iye amawicawani šni s'e ~ yankahanpelo* They were sitting unconcerned, as if I had not walked on them. *Takuni onah'on ~ nankahelo* You were sitting in no any hurry to hear about anything. > — **winkcekce·ya** *adv* : to no purpose - *Syn* TOKÉCACA BT D.4 Bl R
win·kte \wíŋ-kte\ *n* : a hermaphrodite, a plant or animal having both male and female reproductive organs
winš \wiŋš\ *v root contrac of* winjá : bend — **win·škiya** \wiŋ-šǩí-ya\ *va* : to make bend, bend down — **winšwinja** \wiŋ-šwíŋ-ja\ *adj red* : flexible — **winšwinjahela** *or* **winšwinjela** *adj red* : limber, pliant, not stiff; tender < *maza winšwinjahela* a pliant piece of iron >
win·yan \wíŋ-yaŋ\ *n* and *adj* : the Queen in playing cards, a woman < *Winmáyan* I am a woman. >
win·yan·cin \wíŋ-yaŋ-ciŋ\ *v* : to buy a wife

win·yan co·kab ti win \wíŋ-yaŋ co-kab ti wiŋ\ *n* : a virgin - *Syn* WITANŠNA UN Bl

win·yan ta·pe·ji·ĥo·ta \wíŋ-yaŋ ta-pe-ji-ĥo-ta\ *n* : silvery wormwood, a woman's medicine - HM #287

win·yan ta·wi·ya·ka \wíŋ-yaŋ ta-wi-ya-ka\ *n* : the gull - Note: it is otherwise known as *winyan tazintkala, lit* women's bird - BT

win·yan ta·zin·tka·la \wíŋ-yaŋ ta-zíŋ-tka-la\ *n* : the gull, the American avocet, so-called because women used its feathers for quill-work and on account of its belly; also perhaps the *ptehincicila.* One species has red legs, the other green. It is a water bird with wings and back white, black wingtips, the bill like that of the *šlošlola* the upland plover, tail white and its legs about 2 dm long. Its call: "Tibló wewé," and the male answers: "Úhu, úhu." - Bl Rl

win·yan ton·wi·ya·ka \wíŋ-yaŋ toŋ-wì-ya-ka\ *n* : the gull, otherwise known as the *winyan tazintkala* - BT

Win·yan Wa·kpa·la \Wíŋ-yaŋ Wa-kpà-la\ *np* : Woman Creek, a creek south of the Niobrara River in northwestern Nebraska State, perhaps the Loup River or one of its tributaries

win·yan·ya·ta·pi \wíŋ-yaŋ-ya-ṫa-pi\ *n* : a queen

win·ye·la \wíŋ-ye-la\ *n* : a female animal

win·ye·ya \wíŋ-ye-ya\ *adv* : ready, prepared < ~ *nakapi hwo?* Are they prepared to ring or twitch? *Wanna tipi wan ~ eglepelo* A tipi is now set up and ready, *i.e.* for religious ceremonies. *Hihanna kin wocic'upi kte lo ca ~ un po* Tomorrow be ready I shall have breakfast for you. >

win·yu·pin *or* **wiyupi** *or* **wiyunpi** \wíŋ-yu-ṗiŋ\ *n* : house paint, as is used on walls *etc.*

wi·o·can \wi-ō'-caŋ\ *n* : a dumb woman < *iéšni* a dumb man >

wi·o·co·kan·yan \wi-ó-co-kaŋ-yaŋ\ *n* : the month of January and of July, namely the "middle moon" - R Bl

wi·o·hi·na·pa·tan·han \wí-o-hi-na-ṗa-ṫaŋ-haŋ\ *adv* : from the east

wi·o·ki·ci·ci·ya e·con·pi \wi-ó-ki-ci-ci-ya e-còŋ-pi\ *n* [fr *okíya* to talk with] : an innocent pastime practicing courting between boys and girls

wi·o·ki·se·ya \wí-o-ki-se-ya\ *n* : the First Quarter of the moon, *i.e.* approaching Half Moon

wi·o·ki·ya \wi-ó-ki-ya\ *v* wio·wa·kiya [fr *okíya* to talk with] : to court or talk with a woman, to enjoy converse with a woman — **wiokiya·pi** *n* : courting

wi·o·pta·sa·bya·pi \wi-ó-pta-sa-byà\ *n* : a tent with a black ring painted all around in the middle - Bl

wi·o·ša·ya \wí-o-ša-ya\ *n* : the aurora, dawn, or light moving in streams high in the night sky

wi·o·te·ĥi·ka \wi-ó-ṫe-ĥi-ka\ *n* : January, the "hard moon

wi·o·kte·ye \wí-o-tke-ye\ *n* : a hook or string *etc.* on which to hang up things - Bl

wi·o·wa \wi-ó-wa\ *n* : a painted tent

wi·o·we·šte lo·wan·pi *or* **wioyešte lowanpi** \wi-ó-we-šte lo-wàŋ-pi\ *n* : night or love songs - IS

wi·o·yu·spa \wi-ó-yu-spa\ *v* : to stop and detain a woman in order to court - D.52 note 1

wi·pa \wi-pá\ *n* : a windflap, the upper part of a tent with the vent flaps, painted red or black on a given kind of tent - D.4

wi·pa·bla *or* **wipablaye** \wí-ṗa-bla\ *n* : a flatiron or sadiron; anything with which to flatten or to smooth things - Cf pabláya

wi·pa·gu·ke \wí-ṗa-ġu-ke\ *n* [fr *paguka* to rub down] : a scraper, bone or iron, used for scraping down skins in the process of dressing

wi·pa·hte \wí-pa-ĥte\ *n* : a string or anything used for tying

wi·pa·ja·ja *or* **haípajaja** \wí-ṗa-ja-ja\ *n* [fr *pajaja* to mop] : soap

wi·pa·jin \wí-ṗa-jiŋ\ *v* wi·ma·pajin : to be prevented from succeeding in what one attemps to do by having lost a friend *etc.*

wi·pa·ju·ju \wí-ṗa-ju-ju\ *n* : a rubber eraser

wi·pa·me \wí-ṗa-me\ *n* : a file, a tool to make smooth

wi·pa·pi·ya \wi-ṗá-ṗi-ya\ *v* : to open the flaps of a tent < ~ *po, ošota yelo* Open the flaps, it is full of smoke. *Išta jotomakte yelo, ~ po* My eyes are suffering from the smoke, open the flaps! > - Bl

wi·pa·po·wa·ya \wí-ṗa-ṗo-wa-ya\ *n* : a clothes brush - P

wi·pa·sa·bya·pi \wi-ṗá-sa-byà-pi\ *n* : a tent whose upper and lower ends are painted black - Bl

wi·pa·si·se \wí-ṗa-si-se\ *n* : a safetypin

wi·pa·slo·han \wí-ṗa-slo-haŋ\ *n* : a wheelbarrow

wi·pa·snon \wí-ṗa-snoŋ\ *n* : a spit, a stick with which to roast meat - Bl

wi·pa·spe \wí-ṗa-spe\ *n* : tentpins

wi·pa·ša·ya·pi \wi-ṗá-ša-yà-pi\ *n* : a tent whose upper and lower ends are painted red - Bl

wi·pa·škan·gle·pi \wí-ṗa-škaŋ-gle-pi\ *n* : fires made by a returning warparty as a sign of their returning - Bl

wi·pa·ški·ce *or* **wipaškite** *or* **wipaškiškite** \wí-ṗa-šk-ce\ \wí-ṗa-ški-ṫe\ *n* [fr *paškica* to wring by hand] : a washboard, a sort of press

wi·pa·ta \wí-ṗa-ṫa\ *v* wi·wa·pata [fr *ipata* to work quills] : to ornament, work with pocupine quills — **wipata·pi** *n* : quill-work, embroidery < ~ *eyalas'e* covered entirely with quill-work. > - D.51 note 2

wi·pa·tin \wí-ṗa-ṫiŋ\ *n* : starch

wi·pa·zu·kan *or* **wipazokan** \wí-ṗa-zu-kaŋ\ *n* : the service or June berry, a species of red berry growing in small bunches and excellent eating - Note: it is used in making a *tahuka cangleška* a bull-hide boat not easily broken to float things across water < *wipazuka wašte wi* the month of June > — **wipazuka·hu** *n* : this shrub was once used in making the *tahuka cangleška,* the *canpahu* chokecherry, and the *wicagnaškahu* gooseberry or buffalo berry bush were used for the making of arrows - *See* tahuka cangleška Bl

wi·pa·zu·tkan *or* **wipazuka** \wí-ṗa-zu-tkaŋ\ *n* : the June berry, ser-vice or May berry, amelanchier canadensis, the rose family; the shad bush - RT #161

wi·pe \wí-ṗe\ *n* [fr *pe* sharp, pointed] : weapons or arms of any kind, fire-arms, sharp instruments < *wípenica* without weapons, *Kolapila, ungna nayapapi kilo na ~ kin kiksuya po. Na tanyan ~ yuha* Dear friends, remember your weapons, I have a feeling you ought not come out. Keep your weapons well out of the way. > - MS.352

wi·pe·ki·ton \wí-ṗe-ki-toŋ\ *v* wipe·we·ton : to equip one's self with *e.g.* gun, ammunition, *etc.* - Bl

wi·pe·mna·šni \wí-ṗe-mna-šni\ *adv* : dead without apparent cause, dead but not wounded — **wipemna·yan** *adv* : wounded, with a wound < ~ *t'a* to die from an arrow or gunshot, *Tuwa ~ hpaya ca wašte yelo* It is good

---

\a\ father \e\ they \i\ machine \o\ smoke \u\ lunar \an, aŋ\ blanc Fr. \in, iŋ\ ink \on, oŋ, un, uŋ\ soon, confier Fr. \c\ chair \ġ\ machen Ger. \j\ fusion \clusters: bl, gn, kp, hšl, etc...\ b^{e}lo ... said with a slight vowel
See more in the Introduction, Guide to Pronunciation

for one to fall with a wound. > – MS.486

wi·pe·o·hlo·ka \wí-ṗe-o-ȟlo-ǩa\ *n* : a wound from a spear

wi·pe·ya \wí-ṗe-ya\ *v* : to sell a woman or girl in marriage, as once was done

wi·pi \wí-ṗi\ *vn* wí·ma·pi [fr *ipi* to be sated, satisfied in eating] : to be full of food, be satisfied < *Wanna wimapi* Now I am full eating. *wipit'a* to gorge one's self >

wi·pi·pa \wi-ṗí-ṗa\ *n* : tentflaps — **wipipa·ha** *n* : the two vent flaps on the top of a round tent, tipi < *Ošloka yelo; ~ egle yo* If they are come off, set them in. *~ oštanpi* The flaps are put on them, *i.e.* on the two supporting pole ends which fit into the two flap pockets. >

wi·pi·ya \wí-ṗi-ya\ *va* wipi·wa·ya : to fill or cause to be filled or full < *wipiic'iya* to satisfy one's self with eating > — *adv* : full

wi·pu·sye *or* **ipusye** \wí-ṗu-sye\ \i-ṗú-sye\ *n* [fr *pusya* to dry] : something to dry on or with *e.g.* a dryer

wi·p'o·sya·kel \wí-p'o-sya-kel\ *adv archaic* : cross, morosely < *~ un* to be cross, *Tawacin šica na inila un* His disposition is wrong and unchanging. > – *Syn* HÍN-YANZEKE, P'OSYAKEL

wi·sa·bye \wí-sa-bye\ *n* : blacking, that which gives a black hue

wi·san·ye \wí-saŋ-ye\ *n* : whiting

wi·sku·ye \wí-sǩu-ye\ *n* : that which sweetens or sours other things

wi·slo·lye \wí-slo-lye\ *n* : a meter, something to know by *e.g.* a thermometer, a barometer, *etc.* – B.H.127.17

wi·sma·hin \wi-smá-hiŋ\ *n* : an arrowhead < *~ íkceka* an arrowhead in the exact form of a triangle and without a neck for tying > – *Syn* KEHUKA, KESTON Bl

wi·šan \wi-šáŋ\ *n* : the vagina and inner and outer lips, the woman's mons veneris

wi·ša·šla·ye·la a·ye \wí-ša-šla-ye-la à-ye\ *vn* : the sun becomes clear and distinctly seen

wi·ša·ye \wí-ša-ye\ *n* : that which is used to color red

wi·ši \wí-ši\ *n* : pay for work, remuneration, hire < *~ nic'u kte lo* He will give you pay for work. >

wi·ši·ka·hya \wí-ši-ka-ȟya\ *adv* : instead, in lieu of wages – B.H.266.1

wi·ši·mna·ye \wí-ši-mna-ye\ *n* : toll collector, a publican – B.H.173.23, 191.23

wi·ši·ton o·lo·ta·pi \wí-ši-toŋ o-lò-ta-pi\ *n* : a hireling – B.H.223.22

wi·ši·ton·yan \wí-ši-toŋ-yaŋ\ *adv* : for wages < *~ olota* There is a great variety of work for wages. > – B.H. 223.19

wi·ši yu·ke·ya \wí-ši yu-ǩè-ya\ *adv* : for payment – B.H. 100.3

wi·špan \wí-špaŋ\ *n* : iodine – OS

wi·šte·ca \wí-šťe-ca\ *adj* wi·ma·šteca : modest, bashful

wi·šte·lki·ci·ya·pi \wí-šťe-lǩi-ci-ya-pi\ *n* : the being ashamed of each other

wi·šte·lki·ya \wí-šťe-lǩi-ya\ *va* wište·lwa·kiya : to be bashful or reserved, to be ashamed of, as a man is of some of his wife's relations, *esp* the males — **wištelkiya·pi** *n* : the habit of being ashamed or reserved in the presence of one's spouse's relatives *esp* of the opposite sex

wi·šte·lya \wí-šťe-lya\ *va* wište·lwa·ya : to cause to be ashamed

wi·šte·šte·ca \wí-šťe-šťe-ca\ *adj red of* wišteca : modest

wi·šu·te *or* **wišuta**\wí-šu-ťe\ *v* wišu·wa·te : to fail doing or miss < *Mazawakan kin le tohantan bluha kin wiwognaye wanicelo. Yunkan lehantu kin wišuwatelo* This gun for all the time I have had this gun it did not miss its aim; and then to this time I do not miss. > – Bl

wi·šwe e·pi *or* **wišwi eyepi** \wi-šwé e-pi\ *interj* : Oh!, Almost!, Nearly!

wi·šwi e·ye·pi i·he·ya \wi-šwí e-yè-ṗi i-hé-ya\ *v* : Whew! He just missed, *i.e.* in shooting < *Wišwí eyepi okapta* Man! He is down almost to the last bit. > – Note: *wišwí eyépi* is an idiomatic *express,* and indicates a very close accident or dangerous circumstance has been avoided. *wišwí* serves as an *interj* , calling suddenly to attention – Bl D.141 note 1 and note 3

wi·š'o·š'o \wí-š'o-š'o\ *adj* wí·ma·š'oš'o : quick, hasty — **wiš'oš'o·ka** *n* : one who is lively — *adj* wí·ma·š'oš'oka : ready for work, wishing to work < *Taku icaniniyuha yelaka winiš'oš'okelo* You were set and ready for action since you were wanting to work. > – CG Bl

wi·ta \wí-ṫa\ *n* : an island — *v* : to gather < *Wíuntapi kte* We shall gather. >

wi·ta·ke \wí-ta-ǩe\ *n* : a frying pan

wi·ta·kin·yan·yan·ka \wí-ta-ǩiŋ-yaŋ-yaŋ-ka\ *n* : the afternoon

wi·ta·ki·ya \wí-ṫa-ǩi-ya\ *adv* : together, en masse

wi·tan \wí-ṫaŋ\ *adj* wí·ma·tan : proud, elated

wi·tan·šna un \wi-táŋ-šna uŋ\ *n singl* and *pl* [fr *wi* woman + *tanšna* alone + *un* to live] : a virgin or maiden, one who is without a husband, one who lives alone

wi·tan·šna·hu \wi-táŋ-šna-hu\ *n* : the fig tree – Note: the name was given by Renville

wi·tan·tan \wí-ṫaŋ-ṫaŋ\ *v red* wí·ma·tantan [fr *witan* proud] : proud, vain — **witantan·ka** \wí-ṫaŋ-ṫaŋ-ǩa\ *n* : one who is proud, as one may be in having on good clothes — **witantan·pi** *n* : vainglory, pride – Pb.25, 24 Bl

wi·tan·tan·ya \wí-ṫaŋ-ṫaŋ-ya\ *va* : to make one proud — **witantan·yan** *adv* : glorying

Wi·ta·pa·ha *or* **Witapahatu** \Wí-ta-ṗa-ha\ *np* : the Kiowa or Osage tribe – R M

wi·ta·pi·ha \wi-tá-pi-ȟa\ *n* : a toad

wi·ta·wa·t'e·lya \wi-tá-wa-t'e-lya\ *v* : to be willing – *See* tawat'elya

wi·ta·ya \wí-ṫa-ya\ *adv* : together, in company < *~ tipi* They live in the house together. *~ wicakico* He invited them together. *Oyate kin ~ awicayau kte lo* You ought to bring the people together. *Wanna hihanna el oyate kin ~ aya na oimniciye* Now in the morning the people came together and went to a meeting. >

wi·ta·ya·i·he·ya \wí-ṫa-ya-i-he-ya\ *v* witayaihe·un·yan·pi : to assemble together

wi·ta·ye·la *or* **witaya** \wí-ṫa-ye-la\ *adv* : together, in company < *~ ihanpi, au* They came and remained together. *Wanna owasin lel ~ ku po* Now all of you come back together here. *Oyate kin ataya ~ tipi* The entire tribe live together. *Wanna pa ~ el ahiyaye lo* Now they came by with their heads together, *i.e.* sticking their heads together to listen as they gather around a messenger. > – D.225 Bl

wi·ti·o·wa·pi \wí-ṫi-o-wa-pi\ *n* : a tipi with the picture of the sun painted above the door – Bl

wi·tka \wí-ṫka\ *n* : an egg — **witka·ton** *v* : to lay eggs, as fowl do

wi·tke·yu·te *or* **witkeute** \wí-ṫke-yu-ṫe\ *n* : a scale and weights of measure, one pound *etc.*

wi·tko \wi-ṫkó\ *adj* wi·ma·tko : foolish

wi·tko·ka·ga \wi-ṫkó-ǩa-ġa\ *n* : the fool-maker, an imaginary being said to visit one in one's dreams

wi·tko·kon·za \wi-ṫkó-ǩoŋ-za\ *vn* witko·wa·konza : to

pretend to be foolish

wi·tko·pi \wi-tḱó-p̣i\ *n* : foolishness

wi·tko·tko \wi-tḱó-tḱo\ *adj red* wi·ma·tkotko wi·un·tkotko·pi [fr *witko* foolish] : foolish — **witkotko·ka** \wi-tḱó-tḱō-ka\ *vn* wi·ma·tkotkoka : to act foolishly — *n* : a fool — **witkotko·pi** *n* : foolishness — witkotko·ya *adv* : foolishly

wi·tko·win *or* **witkowin·la** \wi-tḱó-wiŋ\ *n* : a harlot, a foolish woman — **witkowin waštelaka** *n* : a lewd fellow

wi·tko·ya \wi-tḱó-ya\ *va* witko·wa·ya : to make foolish — *adv* : foolishly < ~ *oh'an* to act foolishly > — **witkoya·han** *or* **witkoya·kel** \wi-tḱó-ya-ḱel\ *adv* : foolishly, sillily < ~ *oyah'an yelo* You acted foolishly. > - Bl

wi·to·ka \wi-tó-ḱa\ *n* : a female captive

wi·ton·pe·šni \wí-toŋ-p̣e-šni\ *adv* : without fear or regard for anything, not honoring - *See* itonpa

wi·to·ye \wí-to-ye\ *n* : that which dyes blue or green, green or blue blanketing

wi·t'e \wi-t'é\ *n* : the New Moon - LB

wi·t'in·kta kan·ye·la \wi-t'iŋ-kta kaŋ-yè-la\ *n* : the moon between Third Quarter and New Moon - LB

wi·wa·ho·ya \wí-wa-ho-ya\ *v* wíwaho·wa·ya [fr *iwahoya* to warn] : to warn, order < *Wiwahoyapi un ektonjin na* Take and forget he was warned. *Wiwahociyapi kin hena ecanonpi šni* You did not do the things I warned you about. > — **wiwahoye** *n* : an order to do something - B.H.15.16, 101.15, 16.7

wi·wa·kon·za \wí-wa-koŋ-za\ *va* wí·wa·wakonza wí·wicaya·wakonza : to wail for those who have gone out in a warparty

wi·wan·ka·tu·ya \wí-waŋ-ḱa-ṫu-ya\ *n* : the hour of about 9:00 A.M. < ~ *u, hiyu* He came out when the sun got to be well up. >

wi·wan·yan·ka \wí-waŋ-yaŋ-ka\ *v* : to observe, judge - B.H.63.10, 85.5, 224.3

Wi·wan·yank Wa·ci·pi \Wi-wáŋ-yank Wa-cì-p̣i\ *np* : the Sundance, a Dakota tribal celebration of endurance in behalf of relatives and friends

wi·wa·šte \wi-wá-šte\ *n* : a fine woman — **wi·wa·šte·ka** \wi-wá-šte-ḱa\ *n* : a beautiful woman, a lady

wi·wa·ya·ka \wi-wá-ya-ḱa\ *n* : a woman captive from another people

wi·wa·zi·ca \wi-wá-zi-ca\ *n* : a widow

wi·wi·ca·gnu·pi \wí-wi-ca-gnu-pi\ *n* : accusation, a blaming

wi·wi·ca·ji·ca \wí-wi-ca-ji-ca\ *n* : riches

wi·wi·ca·yun·ga·pi \wí-wi-ca-yuŋ-ġa-pi\ *n* : questions

wi·wi·la *or* **minic'api** \wi-wí-la\ *n* : a water spring

wi·wi·la ka·pa·pa \wi-wí-la ḱa-pà-pa\ *n* : a swamp, when the earth's surface lies in water

wi·wi·la ta·pe·ji \wi-wí-la ta-p̣e-ǰi\ *n* : swamp grass

wi·wi·ye·la \wi-wí-ye-la\ *adj* : boggy, marshy from the presence of springs - BT KE

wi·wo·gna·ye \wí-wo-gna-ye\ *n* : no missing of the aim < *Mazawakan kin le tohantan bluha kin ~ wanicelo; yunkan lehantu kin wišuwatelo* All the time I had this gun it missed nothing; and then now I miss my aim. > - Bl

wi·wo·ha \wi-wó-ḣa\ *n* : a woman who lives with her husband's relatives < ~ , *wakšu nišipi kin tokeške yah'an kte hwo* Woman, when you were told to do beadwork, in what way will you do work? *Wawiḣayayin kte lo* You will make him laugh at it. > - Note: *wicawoḣa* a man who lives in on his relatives GA

wi·wo·šta·ke *or* **miwoštake** \wí-wo-šta-ḱe\ *n* : a blunt arrow, such as boys once used to kill birds with, the shaft tapering large at the point end

wi·wo·ti·ki·ya \wi-wó-ṫi-ḱi-ya\ *v* [fr *wi* woman + *wotikiya* to beg of one for another] : to ask for a wife for another man

wi·ya·cin \wí-ya-ciŋ\ *v* wi·bla·cin [fr *iyacin* to compare with] : to liken to, compare to or with — **wiyacin'·iapi** *n* : parables, similitudes — **wiyacin·pi** *n* : a likeness, resemblance, similitude — **wiyyacin·yan** *adv* : parabolic, in the form of a similitude - B.H.246.1

wi·ya·gya·ta \wi-yá-gya-ta\ *adv* : looking at or towards the sun < ~ *inahme s'e eyatonwe lo* You looked towards the sun as if secretly. > - BT

wi·ya·hlo·ka \wí-ya-ḣlo-ka\ *v* wi·bla·hloka : to make an impression upon in saying something < *Cehupa wiblahloke šni s'elececa* It seemed my jaw made no impression on him, *i.e.* apparently though I told him repeatedly. > - Bl

wi·ya·ka \wí-ya-ḱa\ *n* : a quill, a feather of the wing or tail of geese; or also the two feathers fastened to the *peša* the headgear worn in the Omaha dance, and called *peša ogle lit* to place on a crest for headgear

wi·ya·ka·hpe \wí-ya-ḱa-ḣpe\ *n* : a cover - B.H.60.13

wi·ya·ka·pan \wí-ya-ḱa-paŋ\ *n* : a flat bag in which to keep tools or cherries *etc.* < *tahasaka* ~ a deer skin tool bag > - Note: *pan* a woman's work bag

wi·ya·ka·ške \wí-ya-ka-ške\ *n* : a band with which to tie something

wi·ya·ko \wí-ya-ḱo\ *vn* wi·bla·ko : to feel nausea, feel like vomiting on seeing or smelling something bad - Bl

wi·ya·ko·ju·ha \wí-ya-ko-ju-ha\ *n* [fr *wiyaka* a quill + *ojuha* a bag] : the fullet, esophagus of ruminating animals and so called because it was used to fill with air and so to dry. Then feathers as well as grease were kept in this sausage-like bag - Bl BD

wi·ya·kpa *or* **wiyakpa·kpa** \wi-yá-kpa\ *vn* : to reflect, shine, glisten — *adj* : bright, glistening < *Pšito* ~ Beads shine, as do metal beads. *pšito janjanla* transparent glass beads > — **wiyakpakpa·yela** *adv red* : brightly — **wiyakpa·pi** *n* : brightness — **wiyakpaya** \wi-yá-kp̣a-ya\ *adv* : brightly — **wiyakpaye·la** *adv* : brightly, flashing < ~ *ku, iyojanjan* He came back, his face flashing, giving light. > - B.H.270.9, 59.20, 100.18 D.209

wi·ya·ksa·pa \wí-ya-ksa-pa\ *v* wi·bla·ksapa : to make clear to, to tell intelligently to - Bl

wi·ya·na·jin·ce \wí-ya-na-ǰiŋ-ce\ *v* wiyana·wa·jince : to hurry away with what one has received - GA

wi·yan·ke·ca \wi-yáŋ-ḱe-ca\ *vn* : to remain at home and keep one's self busy with something - Bl

wi·ya·pa·hi·ca \wí-ya-pa-ḣi·ca\ *n* : the one pole in the middle of the rear wall of a tent < ~ *hinhpaya ehantanš wakeya ataya hinhpaye* If the one pole falls, the whole tent falls, hence, one of the three main tent poles that stands at the rear and with it stands or falls the tent itself. > - Note: *wiiyapaḣice* tent fittings, fastenings for the top of a tent

wi·ya·pe \wí-ya-p̣e\ *v* wiya·wa·pe [fr *iyape* lie in wait for] : to lie in wait, as for game < *Hanhepi el ~ iyaya ške* They say at night he went on and lay in wait . ~ *kute ya*

\a\ father \e\ they \i\ machine \o\ smoke \u\ lunar \an, aŋ\ blanc Fr. \in, iŋ\ ink \on, oŋ, un, uŋ\ soon, confier Fr. \c\ chair \ġ\ machen Ger. \j\ fusion \clusters: bl, gn, kp, hšl, etc...\ b°lo ... said with a slight vowel
See more in the Introduction, Guide to Pronunciation

He went to shoot, lying in wait for it. > – Bl

wi·ya·ska·bton \wí-ya-ska-btoŋ\ *va* : to seal < *Inyan tanka k'un he* ~ He sealed that large rock. > — **wiya·ska·bye** *n* : mucilage or solder – R B.H.269.22 Bl

wi·ya·špa·pi \wí-ya-špa-pi\ *n* : the Third Quarter of the moon – LB

wi·ya·ta \wi-yá-ta\ *adv* : at the sun or the moon – BS

wi·ya·ta·gle \wí-ya-ta-gle\ *v* wiya·ma·tagle : to have exceeding much — **wiyatagle·ya** *adv* : having much, surpassingly

wi·ya·tan'·on·mya \wí-ya-taŋ-on-mya\ *n* : the sun leaning, the afternoon – *See* wiatan'onmya

wi·ya·ta·pi·ka wa·ci·pi \wi-yá-ṫa-ṗi-k̇a wa-cì-ṗi\ *n* : a single women's dance, one performed by single young women only, and two young men do the drumming and singing – Bl

wi·ya·tke \wí-ya-tke\ *n* : a drinking cup

wi·ya·tke a·gle·he \wí-ya-tke a-glè-he\ *n* : a saucer

wi·ya·un·pa *or* **wiyaonpa** \wí-ya-uŋ-ṗa\ *v* wiya·wa·unpa wiya·un·kunpa·pi [fr *iyaunpa* accuse or blame] : to charge with slander — **wiyaunpa·pi** *or* **woiyaunpa** *n* : an accusation, a charge

wi·ya·un·pe·pi·ca šni \wí-ya-uŋ-ṗe-ṗi-ca šni\ *adj* : blameless < ~ *un* to be or walk blamelessly > — **wiyaunpepicašni·yan** *adv* : perfectly, without possibility of blame < ~ *un* to live perfectly > – B.H.159.4, 192.1

wi·ya·wa·la \wi-yá-wa-la\ *v* : to ask the month count

wi·ya·wa·pi \wi-yá-wa-pi\ *n* : a calendar, a month

wi·ya·yu·ski·ta \wí-ya-yu-ski-ṫa\ *v* wiya·blu·skita : to bind around — **wiyayuskite** \wí-ya-yu-ski-ṫe\ *n* : a bandage

wi·ye·ya \wí-ye-ya\ *v* : to dine well < *Tanyan wiyewaye lo* I ate well. *Lolwanagi yewaye c'un tanyan wiyewaye lo* I dined well when I had fed his spirit. >

wi·yo·han \wí-yo-haŋ\ *v* [fr *iyohan* to boil with] : to boil < *Cega cik'ala (cegiscila)* ~ *popa* The small (tiny) kettle burst into boiling. *Cegiscila wiyohanpi popa* Tiny kettles burst into boiling. > – Bl

wi·yo·hi \wí-yo-hi\ *v* [fr *iyohi* go and arrive at a place] : to reach to, to be sufficient for

wi·yo·hi·yan·pa \wi-yó-hi-yaŋ-ṗa\ *n* : the east, the sun rising — **wiyohiyanpa·ta** \wi-yó-hi-yaŋ-ṗa-ṫa\ *n* : the east < ~ *eciyatanhan* from the east > — *adv* : at the east, eastward — **wiyohiyanpata·han** *adv* : from the east

wi·yo·hpa·ya \wí-yo-ḣpa·ya\ *v* [fr *iyohpaya* go down from a hill] : to come down from < *Išta wiyo·ma·hpaya* I lowered my eyes, *i.e.* something got into my eyes. > – Bl

wi·yo·hpe·ya \wí-yo-ḣpe-ya\ *va* wiyohpe·wa·ya [fr *iyohpeya* throw into] : to put or throw into, as meat into a kettle to boil < *Yunkan tima cega wan ogna wiyohpeyapi na lila kalyahan na wicaša ota tima yankapi* And then indoors there were many men sitting, and inside they threw into a kettle while it was getting very hot. > – MS.145

wi·yo·hpe·ya·ta \wi-yó-ḣpe-ya-ṫa\ *n* : the west, where the sun sets, at the west — **wiyohpeyata·kiya** \wi-yó-ḣpe-ya-ṫa-k̇i-ya\ *adv* : the west, towards the west < *Yunkan lila wankatuya* ~ *kinyan gla* Then it went back flying very high towards the west. > — **wiyohpeya·tan·han** *adv* : from the west

wi·yo·jan·jan \wí-yo-jaŋ-jaŋ\ *v* [fr *iyojanjan* light or to shine on] : to shine

wi·yo·ka·tku·gye \wí-yo-ka-tku-ġye\ *n* : a wood screw

wi·yo·ki·he \wí-yo-k̇i-he\ *n* : a flag, a banner

wi·yo·ki·he·he·la \wí-yo-k̇i-he-he-la\ *n* : wampum, like the *wasuhula* the Iroquois necklace

wi·yo·pe·ki·ya \wí-yo-ṗe-k̇i-ya\ *v* wiyope·wa·kiya [fr *iyopekiya* to scold, reprove] : to sell something or one's own – B.H.179.6

wi·yo·pe·ya \wí-yo-ṗe-ya\ *v* wiyope·wa·ye wiyope·un·yan·pi [fr *iyopeya* to exchange, sell] : to sell, to trade — **wiyopeye** *n* : a merchant, an entrepreneur, a seller; merchandise for trade

wi·yo·tke·ye \wí-yo-tke-ye\ *n* : a hook or peg

wi·yo·wa \wí-yo-wa\ *n* : ink, paint, something to mark or write with < *maza* ~ a pen, *can* ~ a pencil >

wi·yu·can *or* **wicacan** *or* **wiyucancan** \wí-yu-caŋ\ *n* : a sieve

wi·yu·hin·te \wí-yu-hiŋ-te\ *n* : a common rake

wi·yu·ho·mni \wí-yu-ho-mni\ *n* : a wrench

wi·yu·hla·gan šni \wi-yú-ḣla-ġaŋ šni\ *v* : to have one's wife with one all the time, wherever one goes < *Pagonta s'e* ~ He has his wife with him, like a common duck everywhere he goes. > – Bl

wi·yu·hlo·ka \wí-yu-ḣlo-ka\ *v* wi·blu·hloka : to get hold, to hold with the view to opening < *Matasaka ca nape kin wibluhloka šni* Since my hands were stiff I did not get a hold, *i.e.* cannot take a good hold of it, as one's hands are stiff. *Tok̇é, nape kin wiyuhloke šni so?* Really, did he not get a hold with his hands? as they say when someone drops things. > — **wiyuhloke** *n* [fr *iyúhloke* something with which to make a hole in] : an opener, a key

wi·yu·ḣon·te \wí-yu-ḣoŋ-ṫe\ *n* : a rope made of sinew on which they make a hide pliant by pulling it over to and fro – Bl

wi·yu·ja·ja \wí-yu-ja-ja\ *n* : something in which to wash *e.g.* corn, a colander, a basket, a tub

wi·yu·kcan \wí-yu-kcaŋ\ *v* wí·blu·kcan wí·un·yukcan·pi [fr *iyukcan* to understand] : to understand, to have an opinion — *n* : one who forms an opinion — **wiyu·kcan·pi** *n* : forming an opinion — **wiyukcan·yan** *adj* : judicious

wi·yu·ke·ze *or* **wiyukezepaha** \wí-yu-k̇e-ze\ \wí-yu-k̇e-ze-ṗa-ha\ *n* : an incisor, a tool for making the zigzag or winding marks on arrows – R Bl

wi·yu·kin·ce \wí-yu-k̇iŋ-ce\ *n* : a scraper

wi·yu·kpan \wí-yu-kpaŋ\ *n* : a mill to grind with, as a coffee mill, *etc.*

wi·yu·kse \wí-yu-kse\ *n* : a knife or scissors *etc.*, anything with which to cut off < ~ *luha he?* Do you have something to cut with, as a man asks when he wants to cut off a string? > – Bl

wi·yun \wí-yuŋ\ *v* wí·wa·yun [fr *íyun* to rub or apply on] : to anoint – B.H.183.5

wi·yun·ga \wí-yuŋ-ġa\ *v* wi·mun·ge wi·nun·ge wi·un·yuga·pi wi·mayanun·ge [fr *iyunga* to question one] : to ask questions or inquire < *Ho le wimunge k'on hecel amayupta* Come now, this was the question I asked so he answered me. > — **wiyunga·pi** *n* : questions

wi·yunh \wí-yuŋḣ\ *v contrac of* wiyunga : to ask questions < ~ *wahi* I came to inquire. > — **wiyun·hya** *va* wiyun·hwa·ya : to cause to inquire

Wi·yun·pi Wa·kan \Wí-yuŋ-pi Wa-kàŋ\ *np* : the sacrament for the Anointing of the Sick, a sacramental rite of the Catholic Church – Pb.44

wi·yu·ski·te \wí-yu-ski-ṫe\ *n* : a bandage, a press

wi·yu·slo·han *or* **wíyuslohe** \wí-yu-slo-haŋ\ *n* : a sled, a sleigh

wi·yu·ški·ce \wí-yu-ški-ce\ *n* : a wringer, a press

wi·yu·škin \wí-yu-škiŋ\ *v* wí·blu·škin [fr *iyuškin* to be glad, to rejoice in] : to rejoice, be glad — **wiyuškin-**

kiya \wí-yu-škiŋ-ki-ya\ *va* : to cause to rejoice — **wi-yuškin·pi** *n* : rejoicing — **wiyuškin·škin** *v red* : to keep rejoicing < *Hecena keya šina kin etanhan ikpahloke na mini mahel* ~ Finally the turtle cut a hole through the blanket and plunged rejoicing into the water. > — **wi-yuškin·yan** *va* wiyuškin·wa·ya : to cause to rejoice — *adv* : gladly, rejoicingly

wi·yu·šla \wí-yu-šla\ *n* : a shears - Note: *iyušla* only seems to be used

[1]**wi·yu·ta** \wí-yu-ta\ *v* wí·blu·ta [fr *yúta* to eat something] : to eat one thing with another

[2]**wi·yu·ta** \wí-yu-ta\ *v* wí·blu·ta [fr *iyúta* to measure] **a** : to measure, weigh **b** : to make signs, to use a sign language, to motion to < *Wiyutab* They talk in signs. *Wanyanka yo, wíniciyutelo* See! I make signs for you. > — **wi·yu·ta·pi** \wí-yu-ta-pi\ *n* : a measure — **wiyute** \wí-yu-te\ *n* : a measure, a measuring tape, a steel yard - Bl B.H.295.8w

wi·yu·wi \wí-yu-wi\ *n* : a bandage *etc.*, something tied around < *can* ~ a vine >

wi·yu·za \wí-yu-za\ *v* : to hold or take things with one's left hand *catka* < *Wíyuzapi wakute ktelo* They took hold of it so I might shoot it. > - MS.483

wi·zi \wi-zí\ *n* : an old smoky tent, or part of one

wi·zi·han·pa \wi-zí-haŋ-pa\ *n* : moccasins made of an old tent hide

wi·zi·la \wi-zí-la\ *n dim* : a little old and smoky tent

wi·zi·lya \wí-zi-lya\ *v* wízi·lwa·ya : to offer incense — **wizilye** *n* : incense, such as herbs, grasses *etc.* < *Na wanna wizilye eya icu na izilya* And now he took some incense and made it smoke. >

wi·zi·pan \wi-zí-paŋ\ *n* : a rawhide sack or satchel, a trunk or carpet bag (round) made from untanned hide, but not a suitcase which is *panšá;* a container in which to gather berries < ~ *sapa* a satchel >

wi·zi·ye \wí-zi-ye\ *n* : varnish, or something with which to color yellow

[1]**wo** \wo\ *pref to v* : signifies the action is done by shooting, punching, pounding with end of a stick, or by blowing - Note: the *pref* is used when the action of rain falling is expressed. Also, the *insep pron* is placed after the *pref*

[2]**wo** \wo\ *n* : food, as in *wo·yute* something to eat < *Šunkawakan tawocola awaniyetupi ca ota t'api* Many horses died since winter came on catching them destitute. > - BT

[3]**wo** \wo\ *partic* : sign of the *imper singl* used by men instead of *yo* , the more common form. *wo* is used when an *u* sound precedes, similarly as *yelo* and *welo* when preceded by an *u* sound < *Canksa kin le icu wo* Take this club. *Itancan kin ayuta wicaun wo* Lord be watching them. *Le atonwan wo* Look on this. *Ake u wo* Come again. *Wicakico wo* Invite them. > - Note: *Ektonje šni wo* Do not look at it.

wo·a·can·kšin \wó-a-caŋ-kšiŋ\ *n* [fr *acánkšin* to step or pass over] : a stepping over — *np* : the Jewish Passover < *Yunkan ~ Juda oyate taanpetu wakan wan he wanna ikiyela ihan* And then the Passover, a Holy Day for the Jewish people, was now closely approaching. >

wo·a·gla \wó-a-gla\ *n* : a taking home

wo·a·gli \wó-a-gli\ *n* : a bringing home

wo·a·ho·pe \wó-a-ho-pe\ *n* : a commandment, a reverence or ceremony, a custom, rule, regulation, a law - P

wo·a·hta·ni \wó-a-hta-ni\ *n* [fr *ahtani* to sin, break a law] : a sin, a transgression

wo·a·i \wó-a-i\ *n* : the act of taking to a place

wo·a·i·e \wó-a-i-e\ *n* : a slandering, a talking about

wo·a·i·hpe·ye \wó-a-i-hpe-ye\ *n* [fr *aihpeya* to bequeath] : a will, testament, legacy, a leaving to; that which is left to one; responsibility for things entrusted to one < ~ *kin miye wak'in kte* I shall carry the burden of responsibility. > - B.H.36.3

wo·a·ka·ge \wó-a-ka-ge\ *n* : blasphemy, a making on

wo·a·ka·ge·ge \wo-á-ka-ge-ge\ *n* : lace-work *etc.* , things sewed on ladies' dresses for decoration

wo·a·ka·hpe \wó-a-ka-hpe\ *n* [fr *akahpe* a spread, a bed covering] : a covering

wo·a·kan·hi·yu·ya \wo-á-kaŋ-hi-yu-ya\ *va* woakanhiyu·wa·ya : to cause to rise to the top, as scum or froth, by shooting in, as in water

wo·a·ke·ye \wó-a-ke-ye\ *n* : a curtain, screen, something thrown up around like a tent < *awakeyapi* a shade, a booth, shelter >

wo·a·ki·kton·je \wó-a-ki-ktoŋ-je\ *n* [fr *akiktonja* forget] : forgetfulness

wo·a·ki·ni·ce \wó-a-ki-ni-ca\ *n* : a competition, a dispute, a row — **woakini·lya** \wó-a-ki-ni-lya\ *v* : to dispute - P Bl B.H.297.1, 168.19

wo·a·ki·pa \wó-a-ki-pa\ *n* [fr *akipa* to befall one] : misfortune, fortune, an event < ~ *kin le unhiyaglepi* This misfortune was brought upon us. > - B.H.35.4, 81.5

wo·a·kta \wó-a-kta\ *n* [fr *akta* have respect for] : regard - Note: this word is always used with *šni,* thus: *wóaktašni* disregard

wo·a·kton·je \wó-a-ktoŋ-je\ *n* : forgetfulness - Bl

wo·a·na·go·ptan \wó-a-na-go-ptaŋ\ *n* [fr *anagoptan* to listen to] : obedience — **woanagoptan·yan** *adv* : obediently

wo·a·na·hma *or* **woanahme** \wó-a-na-hma\ *n* : concealment, a secret - B.H.164.4

wo·a·na·pte \wó-a-na-pte\ *n* [fr *anapta* to hinder one] : a restraint, a stopping, something astringent

wo·a·ni·ce \wó-a-ni-ce\ *n* : detention - P

wo·a·o·ki·ye \wó-a-o-ki-ye\ *n* : a promise - *Syn* WÓIWAKTA, WÓIWAHOYE WE

wo·a·pe \wó-a-pe\ *n* [fr *ape* to await one] : a waiting for , an expectation, hope

wo·a·sni \wó-a-sni\ *n* [fr *asni* recover, get well] : recovery from sickness — **woasni·kiye** \wó-a-sni-ki-ye\ *n* : a lasting rest - Pb.18, 30

wo·a·ša·pe \wó-a-ša-pe\ *n* [fr *ašapa* to become dirty on anything] : defilement

wo·a·šla·ya \wo-á-šla-ya\ *va* [fr *ašlaya* openly, plainly] : to lay open, expose by shooting in, to make bare < ~ *iyeya* suddenly to lay it open >

wo·a·ta·ku·ni·šni \wó-a-ta-ku-ni-šni\ *n* [fr *takunišni* to destroy] : destruction

wo·a·wa·cin \wó-a-wa-ciŋ\ *n* [fr *awacin* consider] : a thinking on, cares, thought, faith - B.H.156.9, 200.23

wo·a·wan·yan·ke \wó-a-waŋ-yaŋ-ke\ *n* : care, protection - P

wo·a·yu·pte \wó-a-yu-pte\ *n* [fr *ayupte* to answer one] : an answer

wo·blas \wo-blás\ *va contrac of* wobláza : to tear open by shooting < ~ *iyeya* to rip open suddenly >

wo·bla·ska \wo-blá-ska\ *va* wo·wá·blaska [fr *blaská* to

\a\ father \e\ they \i\ machine \o\ smoke \u\ lunar \an, aŋ\ blanc Fr. \in, iŋ\ ink \on, oŋ, un, uŋ\ soon, confier Fr. \c\ chair \ġ\ machen Ger. \j\ fusion \clusters: bl, gn, kp, hšl, etc...\ b[e]lo ... said with a slight vowel **See more in the Introduction, Guide to Pronunciation**

flat as a board] : to flatten by shooting, as in shooting a bullet against a stone

wo·bla·ya \wo-blá-ya\ *va* wo·wá·blaya [fr *blaya* level, plain] : to spread out by blowing or punching

wo·bla·za \wo-blá-za\ *va* wo·wa·blaza : to tear open by shooting *e.g.* the bowels of an animal

wo·ble·ble·ca \wo-blé-ble-ca\ *v red of* wobléca : to batter

[1]**wo·ble·ca** \wó-ble-ca\ *va* **a** : to break open *e.g.* a trunk **b** : to scatter things, as is done by a child in searching a trunk

[2]**wo·ble·ca** \wo-blé-ca\ *va* wo·wá·bleca : to break in pieces by striking with a pestle, or by shooting, to shoot something to pieces, to shatter - D.30

wo·ble·ce s'a \wó-ble-ce s'a\ *n* : one who breaks open trunks and while searching scatters things

wo·blel \wo-blél\ *va contrac of* wobléca : to break in pieces by striking < ~ *iyeya* to smash to pieces >

wo·bli·he·ca \wó-bli-he-ca\ *n* : industry, activity

[1]**wo·blu** \wo-blú\ *va* wo·wá·blu [fr *blu* pulverized] **1** : to crush, pound up fine — *vn* : to blow in fine parti-cles, to drift as does snow, to blow about as dust, to boil up as does water in a spring < *Iwaštegla tate icaluza ca maka ~ welo* Wind that overly flows makes dust drift in a pattern. *cañota ~ iyeya* to make ashes blow about. > - D.77

[2]**wo·blu** \wó-blu\ *v* wa·yublu [fr *yublu* to plow] : to plow, pulverize the ground — **woblu·blu** *v red of* wo-blu : to plow — **woblu·ya** *part* : blowing up as the wind blows dust or snow — *v* woblu·wa·ya : to spit on, to blow < *Maka ša ~ i etanhan* On that account he went and spat on red ground. >

wo·ca·je·ya·lya \wó-ca-je-ya-lya\ *va* : to give expres-sion to < *Cante mahel wokiksuye yuhapi kin hena lecel wocajeyalyapi* When those who hold a memory thus in their hearts, they give expression to it. > - Note: the words of a song: *wócajeyate*. This is derived from the custom of naming a man, to sing his praises in song; *wocajeyalya* is used for the words of the song of one man's praises B.H.135.16 D.261 note 2

wo·ca·je·ya·te \wó-ca-je-ya-ṫe\ *n* : the words of a song in praise of the name of another - D.261 note 2

wo·can·can \wo-cáŋ-caŋ\ *va* wo·wa·cancan [fr *cancan* to tremble] : to make trouble by shooting

wo·can·ȟin·yan \wó-caŋ-ȟiŋ-yaŋ\ *v* [fr *canȟinyan* to be to one a fast friend] : to be very much attached to one - BD

wo·can·kšu \wó-caŋ-kšu\ *n* : a long stick on which to hang meat for drying

wo·can·lwan·ka \wó-caŋ-lwaŋ-ka\ *n* : cowardice

wo·can·ni·ye \wó-caŋ-ni-ye\ *n* [fr *canniyan* to be angry at a woman] : a man's anger against his wife

wo·can·ši·ce \wó-caŋ-ši-ce\ *n* : sorrow

wo·can·ta·gle \wó-caŋ-ṫa-gle\ *n* [fr *cantagle* to set the heart upon] : malice, an evil intention against; the ob-ject of evil purpose

wo·can·te·ha·ha·ye·la \wó-caŋ-ṫe-ha-ha-ye-la\ *n* : over-sensitiveness, timidity, a divided heart - P KE

wo·can·te·i·ya·pa·ya \wó-caŋ-ṫe-i-ya-pa-ya\ *adv* : with a beating heart < ~ *na teȟiya unkinyanpi* We flew with difficulty and with heart beating. > - MS.103

wo·can·te·i·yo·ki·ši·ce \wó-caŋ-ṫe-i-yo-ḱi-ši-ce\ *n* : sad-ness < *Iwašicun ca ~* Since he used bad talk there was sadness. > - Bl

wo·can·te·i·yu·tan \wó-caŋ-ṫe-i-yu-ṫaŋ\ *n* : temptation — **wocanteiyutan·ke** *n* : that which tempts - B.H.92.2

wo·can·te·i·yu·tan·ye \wó-caŋ-ṫe-i-yu-ṫaŋ-ye\ *n* tempta-tion

wo·can·te·ka·ptan·yan \wó-caŋ-ṫe-ḱa-pṫaŋ-ya\ *n* : irri-tation, the becoming upset, anger < ~ *yuha* to hold anger > - Bl

wo·can·te·ki·ya \wó-caŋ-ṫe-ki-ye\ *n* : love - *See* wocan-tkiye

wo·can·te·o·yu·ze \wó-caŋ-ṫe-o-yu-ze\ *n* : character, mature personality, infatuation, the state of having a high or low esteem or regard for a person - KE WHL

wo·can·te·ši·ce \wó-caŋ-ṫe-ši-ce\ *n* : sorrow, adversity < ~ *wanice* He lacked adversity > - Pb.47

wo·can·te·wa·šte \wó-caŋ-ṫe-wa-šte\ *n* : gladness

wo·can·ti·he·ye \wó-caŋ-ṫi-he-ye\ *n* : ardent desire

wo·can·ti·yu·tan *or* **wocanteiyutan** \wó-caŋ-ṫi-yu-ṫaŋ\ : temptation

wo·can·tki·ye *or* **wocanṫekiye** \wó-caŋ-tki-ye\ *n* : love, benevolence - Pb.36

wo·can·to·gna·ke \wó-caŋ-ṫo-gna-ḱe\ *n* : compassion, pity - Pb.31

wo·can·to·kpa·ni \wó-caŋ-ṫo-kṗa-ni\ *n* : a longing for

wo·can·ze \wó-caŋ-ze\ *n* : anger — **wocanze·ka** \wó-caŋ-ze-ka\ *n* : rage

wo·ca·s'a·ya \wó-ca-s'a-ya\ *n* : that which is note-worthy, prominent, known < *Makoce wan ~ kaca* It is hardly a noteworthy land, *i.e.* a prominent and well-known country. > - B.H.62.13

wo·ca·s'a·ya·kel \wó-ca-s'a-ya-kel\ *adv* : very famous < *Iyotan ~ un. Solomon ~ cajeyatapi* He is very famous . They spoke of as very famous Solomon's name. > - B.H. 88.17, 102.4

wo·ceg \wo-cég\ *va contrac of* woceka : to make stag-ger < ~ *iyeya* to make stagger, as by a sudden blow > — **woce·gya** *adv* : staggeringly

wo·ce·ka \wo-cé-ka\ *va* wo·wá·ceka : to make stagger by shooting or punching — **wocekce·ka** *v red* : to cause to stagger

wo·ce·ki·ye \wó-ce-ki-ye\ *n* [fr *cekiya* to pray to] : prayer, a crying out

wo·ce·t'un·gla \wó-ce-t'uŋ-gla\ *n* [fr *cet'ungla* to dis-believe] : unbelief, doubt < ~ *yuhašniyan oholapi* He was honored in not possessing doubts. > - B.H.169.20

wo·ce·ye *or* **wicaceya** \wó-ce-ye\ *n* [fr *ceya* to cry] : crying

wo·cin \wō'-ciŋ\ *v* wó·wa·cin [fr *ocin* to desire, beg] : to beg, ask for, to be begging < ~ *yahi ca cic'u yacin yelo* When you came to beg, you wanted me to give to you. > - Bl

wo·cin·la \wó-ciŋ-la\ *n* : a beggar — **wocin·pi** *n* : begging, hunger, craving - P

wo·co·kon \wó-co-ḱoŋ\ *n* [fr *cokon* to purpose to do evil to another] : a threat, a curse

wo·c'u *or* **woc'o** \wo-c'ú\ *va* wo·wá·c'u : to churn — **woc'u·c'u** *va red* : to do churning

wo·e·ce·tu \wó-e-ce-ṫu\ *n* [fr *ecetu* to be accompished, fulfilled] : fulfillment, simplicity - P

wo·e·con \wō'-e-coŋ\ *n* : a doing, a work < ~ *ota woitonpeya econpi* They performed in a wonderful way many good works. > - B.H.66.17, 156.2, 192.10

wo·e·con·ka \wó-e-coŋ-ka\ *n* : work or endeavor often neglected

wo·e·con·kel \wó-e-coŋ-ḱel\ *adv* : with something ado-ing

wo·e·con·la \wó-e-coŋ-la\ *v* : to consider something hard work whereas it is not

wo·e·con·la·ka \wó-e-coŋ-la-ka\ *n* : a difficult work

- BD

wo·e·con·yan \wó-e-coŋ-yaŋ\ *v* woecon·wa·ya : to do — *n* : one who is always doing, a self-motivated person, a busy person

wo·e·ki·ce·tu \wó-e-k̇i-ce-tu\ *n* : a renewal, resurrection — **woekicetu·ye** *n* : restoration

wo·e·kton·je \wó-e-ktoŋ-je\ *n* : forgetfulness

wo·e·ye \wó-e-ye\ *n* : a saying, a speech < *Yunkan ~ kin le slolyapi šni* And then this saying was not known. > - *See* *wóie* a word

[1]**wo·ga** \wo-ġá\ *adv* : straddling, sprawling, spreading out < ~ *s'e najinpi* They stood as though straddling it. >

[2]**wo·ga** \wó-ġa\ *v* wa·blu·ga wa·un·yuȟa·pi [fr *wayuga* to husk] : to husk *e.g.* corn

wo·ga·ga *or* **yugaga** \wo-ġá-ġa\ *vn* : to shoot out in different directions, as rays of light or the branches of a tree - R

wo·ga·ga·ya \wo-ġá-ġa-ya\ *adv* : spreading, as a tree top when cut down, its branches shooting out from a center

wo·ga·pi \wó-ġa-pi\ *n* : the act of husking corn

wo·ga·ya *or* **yugaya** \wo-ġá-ya\ *adv* : shooting out from a point - R

wo·gi \wó-ġi\ *n* [fr *ġi* brown] : brownness

[1]**wo·gla** \wo-glá\ *va* wo·wá·gla : to shell off by shooting or punching

[2]**wo·gla** \wó-gla\ *n* : that which is detested < *Woglapi, mihakab iyaya po* Depart from me, you who are detested, *i.e.* ye cursed, despised. > - B.H.249.21

wo·gla·gla·ka \wó-gla-gla-ka\ *v red of* woglaka : to chat

wo·gla·ka \wó-gla-k̇a\ *v* wó·wa·glaka [fr *ogláka* to tell of one's own] : to converse of one's own affairs, to talk, counsel — **woglaka·pi** *n* : a telling of one's own affairs < *Woglakapi Wakan* the sacramental confession of one's own sins, otherwise titled the Sacrament of Confession, of Penance, or of Reconciliation >

wo·gla·kin·yan \wo-glá-kiŋ-yaŋ\ *v* [fr *glakinyan* transversely] : to cause to glance, as a bullet

wo·gla·wa \wó-gla-wa\ *n* : something bitter or disagreeable - B.H.191.24

wo·gla·ya \wó-gla-ya\ *v* : to consider a thing a detestable thing < *Tona woglawicayaye kin hena teȟiya unpi kta* Those whom you count detestable will hardly do well, *i.e.* those whom you curse. *Cain woglayapi un kte lo* Cain will be under a curse. > — **woglaya·pi** *n* : a thing detestable, cursed < ~ *yaun kte* You will be held under a curse. > - Cf gla *va* B.H.4.16, 6.1, 9.16, 67.11

wo·gli·gle·ye *or* **wogligleya·pi** \wó-gli-gle-ye\ *n* : a pattern, design, as for beadwork - IS

wo·glo·glo *or* **wogloka** \wo-gló-glo\ *v red* : to grunt, as do pigs or buffalo - Bl

wo·gmun·ke \wó-gmuŋ-k̇e\ *n* [fr *gmunke* a trap] : a place where trapping is done < *Iktomi tawogmunke* a spider's web > - BD

[1]**wo·gna** \wo-gná\ *va* wo·wá·gna : to shoot off *e.g.* fruit from a tree

[2]**wo·gna** \wó-gna\ *prep* [fr *ogna* in, where *wogna* is an *altern* spelling for *euph* sake] : in

wo·gna·ka \wó-gna-ka\ *v* wo·wa·gnaka [fr *ognaka* to place in] : to put or place in — **wognaka·pi** *n* : a basket, a receptacle

wo·gna·škin·yan \wo-gná-škiŋ-yaŋ\ *va* wo·wá·gnaškinyan [fr *gnaškinyan* to be wild, crazy] : to make crazy or furious, as an animal by shooting it — **wognaškinye** \wó-gna-škiŋ-ye\ *n* : lunacy, madness - P

wo·gna·yan \wo-gná-yaŋ\ *va* wo·wá·gnayan [fr *gnayan* to deceive] : to miss partly in shooting or striking with the end of a stick, *i.e.* not hitting *e.g.* an animal well so that it can get away - Note: *wošná* to miss the mark completely

wo·gna·ye \wó-gna-ye\ *n* [fr *gnáyan* to deceive] : deceit, delusion

wo·gu \wó-ġu\ *n* : scraps, as of tallow dried out

[1]**wo·ha** \wó-ha\ *n contrac of* woyuha : property < *Lecel ~ na Wakantanka lila ohola kin on iš eya oyas'in oholapi* Since God honors highly even property in this way, everyone honors him. > - B.H.42.13

[2]**wo·ha** \wo-há\ *v* : to shoot or punch over < ~ *iyeya* to cause to shoot over > — **woha·hayela** *v red* : to make totter by shooting or pushing

wo·ha·i·hpe·ya \wo-há-i-ȟpe-ya\ *va* : to shoot or make fall, and thus to punch over

wo·ha·ka·kta \wó-ha-ka-kta\ *n* : the youngest, the last

wo·han \wó-haŋ\ *v* wó·wa·han wó·un·han·pi [fr *ohán* to boil, cook] : to cook, boil, to make a feast — **wohanpi** \wó-haŋ-ṗi\ *n* : a feast, a boiling < ~ *kaga* to make a feast >

[1]**wo·he** \wo-hé\ *n* : a horse with big knuckles < ~ *ešan lila luzahan* Though a big-knuckled horse it is very fast. > - Cf iyanunga *Syn* IYÁK'OZA Bl

[2]**wo·he** *or* **wohan** \wó-he\ *v* : to boil, cook — **wohe·la** \wó-he-la\ *n* : a cook — **wohe·kiya** \wó-he-k̇i-ya\ *va* wóhe·wa·kiya : to cause to cook, to have for a cook — **wohekiya·pi** *n* : a cook - *See* wóhela

wo·he·yun \wó-he-yuŋ\ *n* [fr *heyun* to pack] : a package, parcel, bundle, as of dried meat < ~ *top yanka ca wanji tokeya yajuju* While there were four packages, it tore open the first of them. >

wo·hil \wo-híl\ *va contrac of* wohínta : to sweep all off, as men on a battlefield, to blow away

wo·hin·hpa·ya \wo-híŋ-ȟpa-ya\ *va* : to make fall by shooting or punching

wo·hin·ta \wo-híŋ-ta\ *va* wo·wa·hinta : to sweep off by shooting *e.g.* men in a battlefield, to blow away

wo·hin·yan·sya \wó-hiŋ-yaŋ-sya\ *adv* [fr *hinyansya* to provoke] : sternly, crossly — **wohinyansya·kel** *adv* : in a cross or stern manner, like quite unpleasant or stormy weather < ~ *un* to be ornery, fierce-looking like a bull, ~ *magaju* a fierce rain storm > - Cf ohinyansyela

wo·hin·yan·sye·la \wó-hiŋ-yaŋ-sye-la\ *adv* : sternly - Bl B.H.34.17

wo·hin·yan·ze \wó-hiŋ-yaŋ-ze\ *adj* : stern, cross, as at times could be said of a mean man or animal, *e.g.* as a mean horse < ~ *h'an* to act sternly > - Note: the word is less usually used, rather preferred is *ksízeca* — **wohinyanze·ke** *n* : a stern man, one who is feared

wo·hi·ti \wó-hi-ṫi\ *adj* : terrible, furious — **wohiti·gla** *n* [fr *hitigla* to deeply dislike] : something loathed

wo·hi·ti·gya \wó-hi-ti-gya\ *adv* : bravely < ~ *un* He is brave. > - B.H.62.9

wo·hi·ti·ka \wó-hi-ti-ka\ *adj* wó·ma·hitika wóhiti·pi·ka, the *pl* form : terrible, furious, violent, energetic < *Na okicize el wohítipikè ci hena wicaka* It is true they were violent in war. >

wo·hi·ti·la *or* **wohitilaka** \wó-hi-ṫi-la\ \wó-hi-ṫi-la-k̇a\

\a\ father \e\ they \i\ machine \o\ smoke \u\ lunar \an, aŋ\ blanc Fr. \in, iŋ\ ink \on, oŋ, un, uŋ\ soon, confier Fr. \c\ chair \ġ\ machen Ger. \j\ fusion \clusters: bl, gn, kp, hšl, etc...\ b[e]lo ... said with a slight vowel
See more in the Introduction, Guide to Pronunciation

va : to regard as terrifying

wo·hi·ti·ya \wó-hi-ti-ya\ *adv* : violently, furiously, energetically

wo·hi·ya·ye \wó-hi-ya-ye\ *n* : a passage, as of the sun going from east to west — **Wóhiyaye** *np* : Passover, the chief annual Jewish celebration of liberation - B.H. 61.2, 171.8, 179.2

wo·ho·ho \wo-hó-ho\ *va* wo·wá·hoho : to shake or loosen by shooting

wo·ho·ta \wo-hó-ta\ *adj* : chubby, short and thick

wo·ho·tan'·in \wo-hó-taŋ-iŋ\ *va* wo·wa·hotan'in [fr *hotan'in* to have one's voice heard] : to make cry out by punching

wo·ho·ton \wo-hó-toŋ\ *va* wo·wa·hoton [fr *hoton* to sound the voice] : to make bawl by shooting or punching

wo·hun·huns \wo-húŋ-huŋs\ *va contrac* [fr *wohunhunza* to] : to shake by shooting something — **wohunhunsya** *part* : shaken by shooting or punching

wo·hun·hun·za \wo-húŋ-huŋ-za\ *va* wo·wá·hunhunza : to shake *e.g.* a tree by shooting it

wo·ȟa \wó-ȟa\ *n* [fr *ȟa* to bury] : a place in which to bury, a place of deposit in the ground, a cellar, pit, a cache, or something buried < *miniwóȟa* a cistern >

wo·ȟa·ka \wó-ȟa-ka\ *n* [fr *oȟaka* to be sick from eating food] : something eaten that does not agree with the stomach, hence poison; *fig* a job with much incidental work, *oécon ota* — *vn* wó·ma·ȟa-ka : to be poisoned, to feel bad after eating something - R Bl WE

wo·hci \wo-ȟcí\ *va* wo·wa·hci : to break out a piece by punching, as from the end or edge of a chisel — **wohci·hci** *v red* : to break out many pieces

wo·hci·hci·ya *or* **wohci·ya** \wo-ȟcí-ȟci-ya\ *adv* : in dangles, dangling

wo·ȟe·šma \wó-ȟe-šma\ *adj* : thick, as grass of underbrush

wo·ȟe·ya·ka \wó-ȟe-ya-ka\ *n* : presents, for one having been cured - B.H.115.9

wo·ȟin·yan \wó-ȟiŋ-yaŋ\ *v* wó·wa·ȟinya [fr *oȟinyan* to pout, be dissatisfied] : to pout, be dissatisfied with, to take offense at — **woȟinyan·pi** *n* : dissatisfaction, offence

wo·hla \wo-ȟlá\ *va* wo·wá·hla : to make rattle by shooting — **wohla·gan** \wo-ȟlá-ǧaŋ\ *va* wo·wa·hlagan [fr *hlagan* loose] : to make loose by shooting — **wohla·hla** *va red* : to make rattle by shooting

wo·hla·ya \wo-ȟlá-ya\ *va* wo·wa·hlaya : to peel off by shooting, as the bark of a tree

wo·hle·ca \wo-ȟlé-ca\ *va* wo·wa·hleca : to tear through by shooting or running into something, *e.g.* a wagon tongue into a tent < *Waȟicepa mini wohlece lo* A fat animal tore into the water, as is said when just a few drops of rain fell. > — **wohle·hleca** *v red* : to go tearing into or through something — **wohlel** \wo-ȟlél\ *v contrac* : to tear or run through < ~ *iyeya* to run suddenly into or through > - Bl

wo·hle·pe s'e \wo-ȟlé-ṗe s'e\ *adv* : standing upright, as hair < *Itoye kin ~ he c'on* His forelock had been standing upright. > - Bl

wo·hli k'el \wó-ȟli k'el\ *adv phr* [fr *ohli* filthy, dirty within] : filthy, confusedly within < ~ *ahiyaya* to sing with much discord, as in all trying to sing together > — *n* : filth or confusion that is within - Bl LHB

wo·hlog \wo-ȟlóg\ *va contrac of* wohloka : to shoot or punch a hole < ~ *iyeya* to cause to make a hole >

wo·hlo·hlo·ka \wo-ȟló-ȟlo-ka\ *v red of* wohloka : to make many holes *etc.*

wo·hlo·ka \wo-ȟló-ka\ *va* wo·wá·hloka [fr *hloka* hollowed] : to shoot or punch a hole, thus to make a hole

wo·hlo·ka·pi šni pe·ju·ta \wo-ȟló-ka-pi šni ṗe-ǰù-ta\ *n* : waxwork or the climbing bitter-sweet, celastrus scandens, the stafftree family - Note: the red roots are chewed and smeared over all the body, as once it was thought then one would be impervious to wounding - BT #46

wo·hmin \wo-ȟmíŋ\ *va* wo·wa·hmin [fr *hmin* crooked] : to make a gun crooked shooting — **wohmin·yan** *part* : crooked in shooting

wo·hpa \wo-ȟpá\ *va* wo·wa·hpa : to make fall by shooting, to shoot down, as a bird on the wing — **wohpa·hpa** *v red* : to shoot down - MS.100

wo·hpa·ni \wó-ȟpa-ni\ *n* : something perhaps to mix in *e.g.* paint

wo·htag \wo-ȟtág\ *va contrac of* wohtaka : to pound with the end of anything

wo·hta·ka \wo-ȟtá-ka\ *va* wo·wa·htaka [fr *htaka* take a hold on with perhaps] : to pound or punch or knock with the end of anything

wo·ȟu·ga \wo-ȟú-ǧa\ *va* wo·wa·ȟuga : to break in or break open by shooting or punching, to crack something by shooting or running against something like a rabbit's head by a shot — **woȟuȟ** *va contrac* : to crack open — **woȟu·ȟuga** *v red* : to break in or open

wo·h'an *or* **woh'anka** \wō'-ȟ'aŋ\ *n* : something hard to do, a hard proposition

wo·h'an·hi *or* **óh'an** \wō'-ȟ'aŋ-hi\ *vn* wó·ma·h'anhi wó·un·h'anhi·pi : to be slow or long doing something, to take much time at doing - R Bl

wo·h'an·ka \wó-ȟ'aŋ-ka\ *n* : a hard proposition

wo·h'an·yan·kel \wó-ȟ'aŋ-yaŋ-kel\ *adv* : with difficulties of all sorts, unnecessarily burdening *esp* one's self with an extra load, charge or duty; doing things the hard way < ~ *canli iyátan* He had many difficulties lighting tobacco, or It took quite a while to light his cigaret. > - WHL LHB

wo·h'i·ya·ya \wó-ȟ'i-ya-ya\ *v* wó·ma·h'iyaya : to do a thing poorly, badly — **woh'iyaya·ka** *v* : to do one's work not well at all, yet pretending to be very busy and know all about it < *Akšaka he ~* He did not in fact do work well. > - Bl

wo·h'u \wo-ȟ'ú\ *va* : to peel off *e.g.* bark by shooting, to strike and scrape along - R

wo·i·ca·ge \wó-i-ca-ǧe\ *n* [fr *icaga* to grow] : a growth, a generation — **woica·hye** *n* : the produce - P

wo·i·ca·je *or* **wóicaje·ka** \wó-i-ca-je\ *adj* : many, very many, many kinds, a great variety

wo·i·can·ši·ca \wó-i-caŋ-ši-ca\ *n* : sadness, a cause of sadness

wo·i·ca·šye·la \wó-i-ca-šye-la\ *adv* [fr *caje* a name] : wonderfully much < *Blo ~ mak'u welo* He wonderfully gave me an abundance of potatoes. > - BS

wo·i·ca·zo \wó-i-ca-zo\ *n* [fr *icazo* a line drawn] : credit, debt

wo·i·ci·ȟa·ȟa·ya \wó-i-ci-ȟa-ȟa-ya\ *adv* : in a mocking way or manner < ~ *eya* to say mocking, jeering one > - B.H.57.10

wo·i·cu \wó-i-cu\ *n* [fr *icu* to take, receive] : a receiving, acceptance, a reception

wo·i·c'i·con·ze \wó-i-c'i-coŋ-ze\ *n* : a resolution, a binding one's self by oath or resolve < ~ *oic'iglaka* to make a vow > - B.H.284.16

wo·i·c'i·gle \wó-i-c'i-gle\ *n* : one who lays up, saves for himself, one's substance

wo·i·e \wó-i-e\ *n* : a word < *wóeye* a saying > - B B.H.69.13, 103.9

wo·i·e·lgle \wó-i-e-lgle\ *n* : a casting up, a charging with

wo·i·gla·ka \wó-i-gla-ka\ *v refl* wó·mi·glaka [fr *woglaka* to tell] : to vow, declare one's self, to declare one's purpose < *Na hihanna el tona cante pahloka woiglakapi heci hena wanna hocokata ai* And in the morning those who promised a piercing of the heart went there now to center camp. >

wo·i·gla·tan \wó-i-gla-taŋ\ *n* [fr *iglatan* to boast] : boasting

wo·i·glu·ze·ze \wó-i-glu-ze-ze\ *n* [fr *igluzeze* to cling to] : a support, a hope, a clinging to < *Tunkašila tahokšila yaunpi kin niš eya he ~ slolyayapi; icin he unkokiyakapi kin tóki* If you are sons of God you too have come to know that hope; for you know somewhere it was declared to us. > - MS.648

wo·i·gnu \wó-i-gnu\ *n* : a murmuring

wo·i·ha·kta \wó-i-ha-kta\ *n* : the regard, respect, one has for another

wo·i·ha·mna·yan \wó-i-ha-mna-yaŋ\ *adv* : generously, richly < ~ *kajuju* to pay off generously > - B.H.13.3

wo·i·han·ble \wó-i-haŋ-ble\ *n* : a dream

wo·i·han·gye \wó-i-haŋ-gye\ *n* : destruction - P

wo·i·han·ke \wó-i-haŋ-ke\ *n* : a conclusion, an end or loss - P B.H.13.18

wo·i·ȟa \wó-i-ȟa\ *n* [fr *iȟa* to laugh] : that which is laughable < ~ *oieyaye lo* You say things funny. >

wo·i·ȟa·ȟa \wó-i-ȟa-ȟa\ *n* : raillery, banter, jest

wo·i·ȟa·ka \wó-i-ȟa-ka\ *v* : to laugh at, to jest < ~ *lo* He laughed at it. > — *n* : something funny — *adj* : such as to cause laughter - KE WHL

wo·i·ȟa·la \wó-i-ȟa-la\ *n* : that which causes laughter

wo·i·ȟa·ya *or* **woiȟaya·kel** *or* **wowiȟaya** \wó-i-ȟa-ya\ \wó-i-ȟa-ya-kel\ *adv* : laughably, ludicrously, funny, queer < *Woškatela wan oh'an woiȟaya econhanpi* They were carrying on ludicrously putting on a little skit. *Taku oh'an wowiȟaya zuya hila ye* Your should go come to war putting on a funny act. *Wócin hi ca k'upi yešan ~ iyuha k'upi cin* They gave to him when he came begging, but it was a strange fact he was given everything. > - D.33, 78 Bl

wo·i·ȟo·i·e \wó-i-ȟo-i-e\ *n* : a laughable word

wo·i·hpe·ki·ci·ye \wó-i-ȟpe-ki-ci-ye\ *n* : a divorce - B.H.232.20

wo·i·hpe·ye \wó-i-ȟpe-ye\ *n* [fr *ihpeya* to throw or put away] : a putting or throwing away

wo·i·ja·ja·pi \wó-i-ja-ja-pi\ *n* : a tub

wo·i·jan·jan \wó-i-jaŋ-jaŋ\ *n* : a light - B.H.164.14

wo·i·ji·ca \wó-i-ji-ca\ *n* : wealth, riches, with *ref* to or in terms of < *He ~ unglawa ye* Count him our wealth. > - B.H.122.16

wo·i·ka·zo *or* **woicazo** \wó-i-ka-zo\ *n* : debts - B

wo·i·ki·ksa·pe \wó-i-ki-ksa-pe\ *n* [fr *ikiksapa* to be wise for one's own] : experience

wo·i·ko·pe \wó-i-ko-pe\ *n* [fr *ikopa* to be afraid] : fear, anything frightful or discouraging - B.H.45.6

wo·i·kpi·ska \wo-í-kpi-ska\ *v* : to shoot or punch and knock over on its back < ~ *ehpéya* They knocked it over and threw it down. >

wo·i·ksa·pe *or* **woiksapeca** \wó-i-ska-pe\ *n* : something difficult. that which is difficult

wo·i·ku·še \wó-i-ku-še\ *n* : an impediment, obstacles, resistance

wo·i·la·gi·c'i·ya \wó-i-la-ġi-c'i-ya\ *v refl* : to serve, to make one's self a servant < *El ~* There he made or had himself be a servant. > - B.H.243.11, 44.1

wo·i·la·gya \wó-i-la-gya\ *v* : to employ - P

wo·i·la·ke \wó-i-la-ke\ *n* wói·ma·lake : an employment, a person or thing made to serve for a definite purpose to which each one is put < *Onšikilake kin heon kici woinilake kin niš eya onšiyalakin kta iyececa šni hwo?* Is it not right that you too should show favor, a favor for one's own when you are employed together? >

wo·i·le \wo-í-le\ *va* wa·wá·ile [fr *ile* to light a fire] : to blow and make blaze, as a fire — **woile·ya** *va* woile·wa·ya : to cause to make blaze by blowing

wo·i·ma·ga·ga \wó-i-ma-ġa-ġa\ *vn* wóima·ma·gaga [fr *imagaga* to be cheered by] : to be cheerful or merry — *n* : an amusement, entertainment, something cheering < ~ *woškate* an amusing play >

wo·i·mna \wó-i-mna\ *adj* : famous, popular, well known — **woimna·mna** *adj red* : popular, capable, strong < *Ituyahcin woimnamnapi na takuni okihipi šni* They are capable of nothing and popular for no reason at all. > — **woimnan·ka** *adj* : powerful, strong, capable — **woimna·yan** *adv* [fr *ímnayan* filled, satisfied] : ably, capably with satisfaction — *n perhaps* : ability - WE B.H.160.13

wo·i·na·hme \wó-i-na-ȟme\ *n* [fr *inahma* to keep secret] : concealment

wo·i·na·hni \wó-i-na-ȟni\ *n* [fr *inahni* to hurry] : haste

wo·i·na·ki·wi·zi \wó-i-na-ki-wi-zi\ *n* [fr *inakiwizi* to be envious, jealous of one's own relations] : jealousy

wo·i·na·pe \wó-i-na-pe\ *n* [fr *inapa* to take shelter or refuge] : a refuge, a retreat — **woinape·ka** \wó-i-na-pe-ka\ *n* : harm, that which is threatening < *Takuni ~ ecacicion kte šni yelo* Nothing of harm will I do to you. > — **woinape·ya** \wó-i-na-pe-ya\ *va* : to use or have for a refuge - B.H.90.15 Pb.26

wo·i·na·pi·škan·ye \wó-i-na-pi-škaŋ-ye\ *n* : a toy, that which is to be played with < *Lena ~ ca cic'u welo* These that are toys I give to you. > - MS.356 KE

wo·i·na·wi·zi \wó-i-na-wi-zi\ *n* [fr *inawizi* to be jealous of] : jealousy, envy, or the cause of envy

wo·i·ni·han \wó-i-ni-haŋ\ *n* [fr *inihan* to be frightened] : fear or something frightful — **woinihan·yan** *adv* : fearfully - D.215

wo·i·pu·ta·ke \wó-i-pu-ta-ke\ *n* : a kiss - B.H.256.6

wo·i·štin·ma *or* **woištinme** \wó-i-štiŋ-ma\ *n* [fr *ištinma* to sleep] : sleep

wo·i·tan \wó-i-taŋ\ *n* : a thing of honor < *Taku wanji ~ yala hwo?* What one thing do you figure to be a mark of honor? ~ *wašte kagelo* He performed a good deed. > - Bl

wo·i·tan·can \wó-i-taŋ-caŋ\ *n* : leadership, government, authority, power < ~ *tanka yaun we. Wicaša ~ yuha kin hemaca* You be in authority. I am the man who has the authority. > - B.H.111.13, 196.15

wo·i·tkon \wó-i-tkoŋ\ *va* wo·wa·itkon [fr *itkon* to burn or blaze] : to kindle, to make burn by blowing

wo·i·ton·pe \wó-i-toŋ-pe\ *n* woi·ma·tonpe : a surprise, a cause for wonder < *waš'aka ~* a wonder of strength > — **woitonpe·peya** \wó-i-toŋ-pe-pe-ya\ *adv red* : in or with great astonishment — **woitonpe·ya** *v* : to be a

---

\a\ father \e\ they \i\ machine \o\ smoke \u\ lunar \an, aŋ\ blanc Fr. \in, iŋ\ ink \on, oŋ, un, uŋ\ soon, confier Fr. \c\ chair \ġ\ machen Ger. \j\ fusion \clusters: bl, gn, kp, hšl, etc...\ b^e^lo ... said with a slight vowel
See more in the Introduction, Guide to Pronunciation

surprise < *Tawoonspe kin woitonpeyapi na imnapi* His learning they were surprised at, and they were satisfied. > — *adv* : wonderfully, surprisingly, abundantly < *Wagmeza kin ~ yuke* There existed surprisingly an abundance of corn. > - B.H.76.10, 222.8, 135.2, 171.19, 178.1 Bl

wo·i·t'in·ze \wó-i-t'iŋ-ze\ *n* : a support, a supporter < *Maza kin takuni ~ šni* The iron (fence posts) was no support at all, *i.e.* the iron being soft. > - Bl

wo·i·t'un·gye \wó-i-t'uŋ-gye\ *n* : a suspicion - P

wo·i·wa·ho·ye \wó-i-wa-ho-ye\ *n* : a promise - *Syn* WÓIWAKTA, WÓAOKIYE P WE B.H.7.14

wo·i·wa·kta \wó-i-wa-kta\ *n* : a promise - *Syn* WOAOKIYE, WOIWAHOYE WE B.H.13.17

wo·i·wan·yan·ke \wó-i-waŋ-yaŋ-ke\ *n* : an example, a fair proposition, a review - P B.H.107.22, 252.15

wo·i·wa·pe·to·gye \wó-i-wa-pe-to-gye\ *n* : a signal, a sign or mark < *Taku ~ eša on yau kte* You should come with something as a signal. > - B.H. 245.2

wo·i·ya·ksa·pe \wó-i-ya-ksa-pe\ *n* : advice useful and wise < *~ on woglak wicaši kte* He told them to speak with useful advice. > - Bl MS.482

wo·i·ya·pa·t'o·ye \wó-i-ya-pa-t'o-ye\ *n* : a hindrance

wo·i·ya·un·pa *or* **woiyaunpe** \wó-i-ya-uŋ-pa\ *n* : an accusation - Bl B.H.36.14, 174.3

wo·i·ya·wa \wó-i-ya-wa\ *n* : a million - Note: a count beyond this number is called: *kokta šica* - *Rac*

wo·i·ye·ce·tu \wó-i-ye-ce-tu\ *n* : uprightness, fulfillment - *See* wóecetu

wo·i·yo·ki·pi \wó-i-yo-ki-pi\ *n* : pleasure, satisfaction - P Pb.40

wo·i·yo·ki·ši·ce \wó-i-yo-ki-ši-ce\ *n* : sorrow, sadness - Pb.40

wo·i·yo·pa·šta·ke \wó-i-yo-pa-šta-ke\ *n* : pressure - P

wo·i·yo·pe·ye \wó-i-yo-pe-ye\ *n* : a scolding, punishment

wo·i·yo·ti·ye·ki·ya \wó-i-yo-ti-ye-ki-ya\ *n* : suffering, adversity - P R Bl

wo·i·yo·wa·ja \wó-i-yo-wa-ja\ *n* : a share of, an inheritance, a business - P B.H.240.3, 261.1

wo·i·yo·was \wo-í-yo-was\ *va contrac* [fr *woiyowaza* to echo a sound] : to make an echo

wo·i·yo·wa·za \wo-í-yo-wa-za\ *va* wo·wa·iyowaza : to make an echo by shooting

wo·i·yo·win·ki·ye \wó-i-yo-wiŋ-ki-ye\ *n* : a permission

wo·i·yu·kcan *or* **wowiyukcan** \wó-i-yu-kcaŋ\ *n* : understanding

wo·i·yun \wó-i-yuŋ\ *n* : an anointing, anointment - B.H.83.22

wo·i·yunge wo·wa·pi \wó-i-yuŋ-ge wò-wa-pi\ *n* : a catechism

wo·i·yu·škin \wó-i-yu-škiŋ\ *n* : gladness — **woiyuškinya** *v* : to make something the occasion for much rejoicing - B.H.88.2

wo·i·yu·tan·ke \wó-i-yu-taŋ-ke\ *n* : that which tempts - Bl

wo·ja \wō'-ja\ *v* wó·wa·ja *or* wablúja [fr *yuja* to mash] : to mash, to stir as a mush, to make mush

wo·ja·gja·ta \wo-já-gja-ta\ *v red of* wojata : to make forked

wo·ja·ja \wo-já-ja\ *vn* : to wash, as rain does the road — *n* : a washtub — **wojaja·pi** \wó-jajapi\ *n* : washing - P

wo·ja·pi \wō'-ja-pi\ *n* : that which is mashed and stirred up, a mush or stew of any kind mixed, thus: *canpa ~* choke-cherry wojapi, *kanta ~* plum wojapi

wo·ja·ta \wo-já-ta\ *va* wo·wá·jata [fr *játa* forked] : to make forked by punching, as is done to a turnip digger

wo·ji·ce \wó-ji-ce\ *n* [fr *jica* rich] : riches

wo·ju \wó-ju\ *v* wó·wa·ju wó·un·ju·pi [fr *oju* to plant, or a field] : to sow, to plant — *n* : a sower

wo·ju·ha \wó-ju-ha\ *n* : an empty bag, a sack, a case

wo·ju·ha·gla·ta·ta \wó-ju-ha-gla-ta-ta\ *va* wojuha·wa·glatata : to exhaust, use all up, *e.g.* one's supply by giving to others

wo·ju·ha·la \wó-ju-ha-la\ *n* : a small bag

wo·ju·i·yu·ta·pi \wó-ju-i-yu-ta-pi\ *n* : an acre < *~ 40* a 40 acres >

[1]**wo·ju·ju** \wo-jú-ju\ *va* wo·wa·juju [fr *juju* to break up] : to break to pieces or destroy by shooting, to knock or punch to pieces, to break as rain does ice or as a flood does a bridge

[2]**wo·ju·ju** \wó-ju-ju\ *v* wó·wa·juju *or* wa·blu·juju [fr *yujúju* to tear down, destroy] : to take to pieces, to demolish, to unpack — **wojuju·pi** \wó-ju-ju-pi\ *n* : a taking to pieces, a dismantling

wo·ju·pi \wó-ju-pi\ *n* : a sowing or planting a field or garden — **wojupi wi** *np* : May, the moon of planting

wo·ju·ti \wó-ju-ti\ *n* : a farmhouse or a farmer

wo·ju·ton \wó-ju-toŋ\ *v* woju·wa·ton : to fill up into bags or sacks — *n* : a filled sack — **wojuton·pi** *n* : a bag or sack filled < *aguyapi ~* a sack filled with bread >

wo·ju·wi·ca·ša \wó-ju-wi-ca-ša\ *n* : a farmer

wo·ka·bi·ye·ya \wo-ká-bi-ye-ya\ *va* wokabiye·wa·ye : to remove what has been sent into another's body by magic - *Syn* WICAHMUNGA

wo·ka·bkab \wo-ká-bkab\ *v* : to issue < *ton ~ hiyuya* to expectorate freely, to spit out phlegm freely > *Syn* WOŠLOŠLOG

wo·ka·ge \wó-ka-ge\ *n* [fr *kaga* to make] : creation, anything made; forms < *Maka ~ kin hetanhan* On that account was the creation of the world. > - B.H.165.14

wo·ka·ge ti·pi \wó-ka-ge tì-pi\ *n* : a factory

wo·ka·gi \wó-ka-gi\ *n* [fr *kagi* to stop one's progress] : a hindrance — **wokagi·ye** *n* : one who obstructs

wo·ka·hni·ga \wó-ka-hni-ga\ *v* wo·wa·kahniga [fr *okahniga* to comprehend] : to understand

wo·ka·hni·ge *n* [fr *kahniga* to make a choice] : a choice, a selection or election - B.H.107.9

wo·ka·htan \wó-ka-htaŋ\ *n* : small grass burs that easily stick to one's clothing

wo·ka·htan bla·ska·ska \wó-ka-htaŋ bla-skà-ska\ *n* : the showy tick trefoil, sticktights, desmodium canadense, the pulse family - WE #119

wo·ka·ki·je \wó-ka-ki-je\ *n* [fr *kakija* to suffer] : suffering, misery — **wokaki·šye** \wó-ka-ki-šye\ *n* : the cause of suffering

wo·ka·la \wó-ka-la\ *v* wo·wa·kala [fr *kala* to sow] : to scatter, to sow - B.H.248.21

wo·ka·mna \wó-ka-mna\ *n* : salary, wage, income, livelihood

wo·kan \wo-káŋ\ *va* wo·wa·kan : to shoot or punch off

wo·ka·pa \wó-ka-pa\ *n* : something pungent < *Taku éye cin oyasin ~ ececa* He was affected by something pungent in everything he said, *i.e.* all his words were cutting. *Taku wanji epe cinhan hena ~ ca epe s'elececa* When I said something, it seemed I said things that were cutting. > - Bl

wo·ka·pan *or* **wokapa** \wó-ka-paŋ\ *n* : pounded meat or a meat-block

wo·ka·pa·za \wó-ka-pa-za\ *n* : pungency, anything

pungent as is pepper

[1]**wo·ka·pe** \wó-ka-pe\ *n* 1 : a hide on which to pound cherries, meat, *etc.*, the hide from the head of the buffalo, a rawhide container 2 : a going beyond, an excelling, a win, a transgression - R

[2]**wo·ka·pe** \wó-ka-pe\ *n* : a catcher, one who catches a ball

wo·ka·se \wó-ka-se\ *n* [fr *kasa* to bury in snow] : a deposit in the snow - R Bl

wo·ka·sla·te \wó-ka-sla-te\ *v* wó·ma·kaslate [fr *okaslata* to stick in as a splinter] : to stick *e.g.* in the finger - R

wo·ka·so·te \wó-ka-so-te\ *n* : the using up of a thing

wo·ka·swu \wó-ka-swu\ *n* : fringes < *Hena pan ipatapi na anung ~ heca ipatapi* Those work-bags were embroidered and it was on both sides fringes ornamented them. > - MS.483 IS

wo·ka·še·ya \wó-ka-še-ya\ *n* : a hindrance, that which opposes

wo·ka·tin \wo-ká-tiŋ\ *va* wo·wa·katin [fr *katin* straightened out] : to make stretch or straighten out by punching

wo·kcan \wó-kcaŋ\ *n* : a seer — *v* : to see for one's self, with one's own eyes < ~ *ya* to go and find out for one's self, ~ *i* to have gone to learn for one's self > - Note: the word *wokcan* is used with another word, generally speaking

wo·kcan·ka \wó-kcaŋ-ka\ *n* : a person who understands things

wo·kcan wi·ca·ša \wó-kcaŋ wi-cà-ša\ *n* : a prophet

wo·ke·ya \wo-ké-ya\ *n* : once an Indian dwelling made of *psa* straw or *peji* grass, *etc.* < *wahpe ~* a bower of leaves, a special lodge used in the Sundance > - B.H. 9.15

wo·ki·ble·ble·ca \wo-kí-ble-ble-ca\ *v red of* wokibleca : to break one's own — **wokibleca** *v poss* wo·wa·kibleca [fr *wobleca* to break in pieces] : to break one's own by pounding or shooting — **wokiblel** *v contrac of* wokibleca : to break one's own < ~ *iyeya* to break by pounding suddenly >

wo·ki·ca·hni·ga \wó-ki-ca-hni-ġa\ *v* : to detect or perceive or understand, to see through *e.g.* the deception or untruthfulness of another - Cf okicahniga

wo·ki·ci·ble·ca \wo-kí-ci-ble-ca\ *va* wo·we·cibleca [fr *wobleca* to break in or up] : to break for another by shooting or punching

wo·ki·ci·c'o \wo-kí-ci-c'o\ *v* wo·we·cic'o [fr *woc'o* to churn] : to churn for one

wo·ki·ci·hlo·ka \wo-ki-ci-hlo-ka\ *v* wo·we·cihloka [fr *wohloka* to make a hole as by shooting or punching] : to make a hole for another by shooting or punching

wo·ki·ci·hpa \wo-kí-ci-hpa\ *v* wo·we·cihpa [fr *wohpa* to shoot down] : to shoot down for another something on the wing or that is hanging up

wo·ki·ci·ju \wó-ki-ci-ju\ *n* wó·we·ciju [fr *woju* to sow or plant] : to sow or plant for one

wo·ki·ci·kpan \wo-kí-ci-kpaŋ\ *v* wo·we·cikpan [fr *wokpan* to shoot to pieces] : to pound for one

wo·ki·ci·ksa \wo-kí-ci-ksa\ *v* [fr *woksa* to break off] : to shoot or punch off *e.g.* a limb or an arm from one — **wokiciksa·ksa** *v red* : to break off limbs

wo·ki·cin \wó-ki-ciŋ\ *n* : an entreaty - P

wo·ki·ci·pa·si \wó-ki-ci-pa-si\ *n* : a military evolution, a maneuver - P

wo·ki·ci·pta \wo-kí-ci-pta\ *v* wo·wé·cipta [fr *woptá* to dig with a stick's end] : to dig or pry up for one, as in digging a turnip

wo·ki·ci·sni \wo-kí-ci-sni\ *v* wo·we·cisni [fr *wosni* to blow out *e.g.* a candle, to cool by blowing] : to blow out for one, to cool by blowing *e.g.* hot food for one

wo·ki·ci·so·ta \wo-kí-ci-so-ta\ *v* wo·we·cisota [fr *wosota* to use or kill off all, to waste all] : to kill off for one by shooting *e.g.* cattle

wo·ki·ci·šlo·ka \wo-kí-ci-šlo-ka\ *v* wo·wé·cišloka [fr *wošloka* to fire off a gun] : to shoot off a gun for one

wo·ki·ci·šna \wo-kí-ci-šna\ *v* wo·wé·cišna [fr *wošna* to miss the mark shooting] : to miss shooting for one

wo·ki·ci·špa \wo-kí-ci-špa\ *v* wo·we·cišpa [fr *wošpa* to knock off a piece] : to shoot off a piece for one, to shoot or kill for one and relieve from danger, as from a wild animal

wo·ki·ci·we·ga \wo-kí-ci-we-ġa\ *v* wo·we·ciwega [fr *wowega* to break, fracture by falling] : to break but not entirely off for one by shooting or punching

wo·ki·ci·ze \wó-ki-ci-ze\ *n* [fr *kiciza* to quarrel with one] : fighting, a fight

wo·ki·con·ze \wó-ki-coŋ-ze\ *n* [fr *konza* to pretend, *kiconza* to determine in regard to] : authority, dominion, government, law, a kingdom, state *etc.* < ~ *yuha* to have jurisdiction or authority > - B.H.173.8

wo·ki·hin·ta \wo-kí-hiŋ-ta\ *v poss* [fr *wohinta* to sweep clear a place] : to make clear a place, as is said of rain clouds that pass by with only a few drops of rain falling - *Syn* WOKÍŠLOKA

wo·ki·hye \wó-ki-hye\ *v* wo·wa·kihye : to regret, to have missed something good by not being there and so being sorry for it < *He ~* He regretted that. > - IS

wo·ki·ja \wó-ki-ja\ *v* wó·wa·kija [fr *woja* to mash and make mush] : to make hasty-pudding for one

wo·ki·ka·hni·ga \wó-ki-ka-hni-ġa\ *v* [fr *okikahniga* to understand one's own perhaps] : to have understanding - B.H.273.3

wo·ki·kcan·pte \wó-ki-kcaŋ-pte\ *n* [fr *kikcanpta* to comfort, take sides with one] : comfort, consolation - Pb.44

wo·ki·ksa \wo-kí-ksa\ *v poss* wo·wa·kiksa [fr *woksa* to break off] : to break in two one's own by shooting or punching — **wokiksa·ksa** *v red* : to break many in two

wo·ki·ksu·ye \wó-ki-ksu-ye\ *n* [fr *kiksuya* to remember] : a remembrance or commemoration < ~ *anpetu* an anniversary > — **wokiksuye·ya** *va* : to have for a remembrance, to remember by - B.H.237.16, 253.7

wo·ki·kšan \wó-ki-kšaŋ\ *n* : friendly teasing, such as between males and females

wo·ki·kta \wó-ki-kta\ *n* [fr *kikta* to awaken from sleep] : waking, watching

wo·ki·ktan \wo-kí-ktaŋ\ *v poss* wo·wá·kiktan [fr *woktan* to make bend] : to crook, bend, one's own by shooting, as one's arrow

wo·ki·la·pi \wó-ki-la-pi\ *n* : the act of requesting

wo·ki·mnan·ka \wó-ki-mnaŋ-ka\ *adj* : wise, honored, good, large, liberal - R Bl

wo·ki·ni \wō'-ki-ni\ *v* wó·wa·kini [fr *okini* to share] : to get a share, to be lucky in getting something < *Lila tanyan wowakini yelo; šunkawakan mak'u welo* I was lucky doing very well; he gave me a horse. >

wo·ki·ni·han \wó-ki-ni-haŋ\ *n* : one's part, respect, honor < *Wicaša iyuha niyawaštepi kte na ~ luha kte* All

---

\a\ father \e\ they \i\ machine \o\ smoke \u\ lunar \an, aŋ\ blanc Fr. \in, iŋ\ ink \on, oŋ, un, uŋ\ soon, confier Fr. \c\ chair \ġ\ machen Ger. \j\ fusion \clusters: bl, gn, kp, hšl, etc...\ b[e]lo ... said with a slight vowel
See more in the Introduction, Guide to Pronunciation

men will bless you, and you should carry your own part. >

wo·ki·nun·kan \wo-k̇í-nuŋ-k̇aŋ\ *va* [fr *kinunkan* divided as between two] : to separate by shooting < ~ *iyeya* to cause to separate >

wo·kin·ca \wo-k̇íŋ-ca\ *va* : to scrape or scratch in shooting, to make sting or smart by shooting — **wokinlkinca** *or* **wokin·tkinca** \wo-k̇íŋ-lk̇iŋ-ca\ *v red* : to make sting by shooting – R

wo·ki·pa·jin \wó-k̇i-ṗa-jiŋ\ *n* : opposition, rebellion

wo·ki·po·wa·ya \wo-k̇í-ṗo-wa-ya\ *v poss of* wopowaya : to make *e.g.* nap or fur soft for one by blowing up or by striking it with the fingers

wo·ki·pu·ski·ca \wo-k̇í-ṗu-sk̇i-ca\ *va* wo·wa·kipuskica [fr *puskica* to be heavily burdened] : to drive up close together by punching or shooting; to rain on — **wokipuskil** *va contrac* : to drive close together < ~ *iyeya* to cause to crowd together quickly >

wo·ki·sa·pa \wó-k̇i-sa-ṗa\ *v poss of* wosapa : to make one's self black by shooting; to rain on as snow and make the ground bare

wo·ki·šla \wo-k̇í-šla\ *v poss* wo·wa·kišla [fr *wošla* to make bare by shooting] : to injure or lay bare by shooting — **wokišla·ya** *va* wo·wa·kišlaya : to make bare or expose by shooting

wo·ki·šle·ca \wo-k̇í-šle-ca\ *v poss* wo·wa·kišleca [fr *wošleca* to split off a small piece] : to split off a piece from one's own by shooting or punching

wo·ki·šlo·ka \wo-k̇í-šlo-k̇a\ *v poss* [fr *wošloka* to fire off a gun] : to shoot or punch a hole in one's own, shoot off one's own gun, to blow out and make clear, as a tube – Note: it is also said of rain clouds that pass by with only a show of a few rain drops – *Syn* WOKIHINTA Bl

wo·ki·šna \wo-k̇í-šna\ *v poss* wo·wa·kišna [fr *wošna* to miss the mark shooting] : to miss attempting to shoot one's own

wo·ki·špa \wo-k̇í-šṗa\ *v poss* wo·wa·kišpa [fr *wošpa* to knock off a piece by shooting] : to shoot off a piece from one's own

wo·ki·tan \wó-k̇i-ṫaŋ\ *n* : a little of anything < *Wanciglakapi kte hcin ca ~ hci wau na wahi yelo* I am coming and have arrived so I might see a little of your own. *Wokitanhci teȟiya* A very little is hardly at all. > – Bl

wo·ki·tan'·in \wó-k̇i-taŋ-iŋ\ *n* [fr *okitan'in* to be conspicuous] : renoun, popularity; manifestation — **wokitan'in·yan** *adv* gloriously

wo·ki·t'a \wó-k̇i-t'a\ *v* wo·wa·kit'a wo·ma·kit'a [fr *okit'a* to be worn out, tired out] : to be tired out — *n* : weariness, exhaustion < ~ *wanice* to be inexhaustible, energetic, unflagging > – Bl

wo·ki·ya \wó-k̇i-ya\ *v* wo·wa·kiya [fr *okíya* to make peace] : to speak or talk with, to make peace – R Bl

wo·ki·yag \wó-k̇i-yag\ *v contrac of* wokiyaka : to tell to < ~ *wahi* I have come to announce to one >

wo·ki·ya·ka \wó-k̇i-ya-k̇a\ *v* wo·wa·kiyaka *or* wo·wa·ki·bla·ka [fr *okiyaka* to tell to one] : to speak to, to tell or declare to < *Lila tanyan womakiyakelo* He spoke to me very well. >

wo·ki·ya·ka·ki·ya \wó-k̇i-ya-k̇a-k̇i-ya\ *va* : to make speak to < *Niye wounkiyakapi ye ... tka Wakantanka wounkiyakapikiye šni ye* You make him speak to us ... but do not have God speak to us. > – B.H.58.2

wo·ki·ya i·ya·ya \wŏ'-k̇i-ye i-yà-ya\ *v* : to go to buy, trade at a store < ~ *mni kte* I shall go shopping. *Tehan wokiye wahi* I came a long way to shop. >

wo·ki·yu·ȟe \wó-k̇i-yu-ȟe\ *n* [fr *kiyuȟa* to copulate as animals do] : copulation

wo·ki·yu·ške \wó-k̇i-yu-ške\ *n* [fr *kiyuška* to release one] : deliverance, a setting free

wo·ki·zi \wó-k̇i-zi\ *n* [fr *okizi* to recover from a hurt] : the scar left after healing, a healing, salve – R

wo·ko·ka \wo-k̇ó-k̇a\ *va* wo·wa·koka : to make rattle by shooting or punching

wo·ko·ki·pa·pa·ka \wo-k̇ó-k̇i-pa-pa-ka\ *vn* : to be timid, scared of things < ~ *šni mani* He walks without being scared. > — **wakokipapake** *n* : timidity – Bl KE

wo·ko·ki·pe \wó-k̇o-k̇i-ṗe\ *n* [fr *kokipa* to fear] : fear, or the cause of fear < *Maka hlihlila on iic'iun nata ko. Canke lila puza ca ~* He also rubbed his own head with mud. And so when it was very dry he was a cause of fear. > — **wokokipe·ya** \wó-k̇o-k̇i-ṗe-ya\ *adv* : fearfully < ~ *magaju* fearfully hot weather > – *Syn* WOHINYANSYAKEL B.H.120.5

wo·kon \wó-k̇oŋ\ *n* [fr *kon* covet] : desire, or something desirable — **wokon·ka** \wó-k̇oŋ-k̇a\ *n* : something desired

wo·kon·ze \wó-k̇oŋ-ze\ *n* [fr *konza* to wish evil to one, to threaten] : an influence, a law, a decree

wo·ko·ya·ke \wó-k̇o-ya-k̇e\ *n* [fr *koyaka* to wear *e.g.* a coat] : clothing

wo·ko·ze \wó-k̇o-ze\ *n* [fr *koza* to wave] : a swinging or waving, a brandishing

wo·kpa \wo-kṗá\ *va* wo·wá·kpa [fr *kpa* punched out] : to shoot or punch out < ~ *iyeya* to cause to shoot out >

wo·kpa·mni \wó-kṗa-mni\ *n* : a pile, a share, a distribution

[1]**wo·kpan** \wo-kṗáŋ\ *v poss* wo·wá·kpan [fr *wopan* to pound fine] : to shoot to pieces

[2]**wo·kpan** \wó-kpaŋ\ *v* wa·blú·kpan [fr *yúkpan* to grind, pulverise] : to grind *e.g.* grain

wo·kpan·kpan \wo-kṗáŋ-kṗaŋ\ *v red of* wokpán : to shoot to pieces

wo·kpi \wo-kṗí\ *va* wo·wá·kpi : to crack with the thumb

[1]**wo·ksa** \wo-ksá\ *va* wo·wá·ksa [fr *ksa* separated] : to break off by punching or shooting *e.g.* a stick, a limb *etc.*, to break while running, as a team of horses running against a tree and breaking the neckyoke *etc.*

[2]**wo·ksa** \wó-ska\ *v* wa·blu·ksa wa·un·yuksa·pi [fr *yuksa* to break off by hand] : to pull *e.g.* corn < *Yunkan wagmeza kin lila waicaga. Hecel oyate kin woksapi* And then the corn really grew. So the people picked or husked it. >

wo·ksa·ksa \wo-ksá-ksa\ *v red* wo·wá·ksaksa [fr *woksá* to break off] : to break off in many places by shooting

wo·ksa·pe \wó-ksa-ṗe\ *n* [fr *ksapa* wise] : wisdom

wo·ksa·pi \wó-ksa-pi\ *n* : a harvest, pulling or husking corn; reapers, those engaged in harvesting

wo·kše·ca \wo-kšé-ca\ *va* wo·wá·kšeca : to shoot and make keel over, to shoot and make double up — **wokšel** \wo-kšél\ *va contrac* : to shoot and make fall over < ~ *iyeya* to cause to keel over suddenly >

wo·kši·je \wó-kši-je\ *n* : that which is bent or folded up < ~ *topa c'un: wanji eyé lo* There had been four folded up: he said it was one, as is said when someone tells a big lie. > – Bl

wo·ktan \wo-ktáŋ\ *va* wo·wá·ktan [fr *ktan* crooked or curved] : to bend or make bend by punching

[1]**wo·kte** \wo-kṫé\ *va* wo·wa·kte [fr *kte* to kill] : to kill

by punching
[2]**wo·kte** \wó-kṫe\ *n* [fr *kte* to kill] : a massacre, a slaughter, a killing
wo·ku·je \wó-ku-je\ *n* [fr *kuja* sick, ill] : sickness, indisposition
wo·ku·ka \wo-k̇ú-k̇a\ *va* [fr *kuka* rotten, worn out] : to shoot or punch al to pieces
wo·k'e \wō'-k'e\ *n* [fr *k'a* to dig] : a pit, a digging, a place dug to bury in < *ḣoká wok'e* a heap of soil before a badger's hole, or perhaps the hole itself > - Bl
wo·k'e·ġa \wo-k'é-ġa\ *va* wo·wa·k'ega : to misfire as in firing a gun, to snap as a gun, to scrape as a gun misfiring < *Mazawakan kin šice c'eyaš ~ šni un kin owanjila yuha un wo* Though the gun is poor, when it is not misfiring, be holding it unengaged. > — **wok'eh** \wo-k'éḣ\ *va contrac* : to go off after a long time < ~ *hingla. ~ iyaya* Suddenly it snapped. Then it went and fired, *i.e.* went on to hang fire, as with a gun. > — **wok'ehya** *part* : missing fire, as a gun
wo·k'in \wó-k'iŋ\ *n* [fr *k'in* to carry a load] : a pack, a carrying < ~ *mayut'e lo* A pack was choking me to death, as is said when the burden is very heavy. > - Bl
wo·k'in·yu·t'e·ya \wó-k'iŋ-yu-t'e-ya\ *va* : to overload
wo·k'u \wó-k'u\ *v* wó·wa·k'u **1** : to give food to **2** : to lend — **wok'u·pi** *n* : a lending, a giving to
wol \wol\ *v contrac of* wóta : to eat < *Le yaglapi na tanyan wol niglaštanpi, hehanl ... Wol eyotake* While you are now on your way home and you are pretty well finished eating, then ... they sat down to eat > - B.H. 124.3
wo·la \wó-la\ *v* wó·la wó·un·la·pi : to beg food < *Hecel wanna wakanheja wanjigji ~ ceyapi* So now children cried each one begging for some food. > — *n* : begging
wo·la·ko·lki·ci·ya·pi \wó-la-k̇o-lk̇i-ci-ya-pi\ *n* : friendship, amity, cordiality, mutual esteem; peaceful mutual relations — **wolakota** \wó-la-k̇o-ṫa\ *n* : peace, friendship < ~ *kagapi* They made peace. > - B.H.189.7
wo·la·s'a \wó-la-s'a\ *n* : a beggar
wo·le \wó-le\ *v* wo·wa·le [fr *ole* to look for] : to seek for
wo·li·glu·štan \wo-lí-glu-štaŋ\ *v refl* : to finish eating - B.H.37.6
wo·lki·ya \wo-lk̇í-ya\ *va* wo·lwa·kiya [fr *wota* to eat] : to feast, to cause to eat
wo·lol \wó-lol\ *v contrac of* wó-lota : to borrow < ~ *wahi* I have come to borrow. > — **wolota** \wó-lo-ṫa\ *v* wó·wa·lota [fr *olota* to borrow something] : to borrow, to hire — *n* : a borrowing < *Wólota kin inakinlmaya upelo* They came conning me into their borrowing, *i.e.* but I would not. > — **wolota·pi** *n* : a borrowing - Bl
wo·lu·ta \wó-lu-ṫa\ *n* : the round of a beef animal when dried < ~ *šapa* a dirty beef round > - Cf olúte Bl
wo·lu·za·he *or* **wicaluzahe** \wó-lu-za-he\ *n* : speed, swiftness, one who is swift - Note: *wicoluzahe* is perhaps also used
wo·lwi·ca·ya·pi \wo-lwí-ca-ya-pi\ *n* : a feast, a banquet - P
wo·lwol \wó-lwol\ *v contrac of* wólwota : to be eating < ~ *wounglakapi kte* We shall talk over our affairs while eating. > - Me
wo·lwo·ta \wó-lwo-ṫa\ *v* : to eat, be eating
wo·lya \wo-lyá\ *va* : to make a feast - P B.H.93.15
wo·mi·me \wó-mi-me\ *n* : a circle - P
wo·mna \wó-mna\ *v* wo·wa·mna [fr *omna* to smell an odor] : to smell, perceive a smell — *n* : an odor — **wo·mna·ka** \wó-mna-ka\ *n* : a person or animal that perceives easily a scent, as a bird, dog, *etc.*, *esp* a bird dog - P
wo·mna·šni \wó-mna-šni\ *n* : one who does not perceive, smell
wo·mna·ye \wó-mna-ye\ *n* [fr *mnayan* to collect] : a collection
wo·mni·ci·ye \wó-mni-ci-ye\ *n* : an assembly - R Bl
wo·na·gi·yeye \wó-na-ġi-ye-ye\ *n* : a bother, a trouble, inconvenience
wo·na·h'on \wó-na-ḣ'oŋ\ *n* : information
wo·nan·ke \wó-naŋ-ke\ *n* [fr *nanka* or *naka* to twitch] : a tremor, an omen
wo·na·pe \wó-na-ṗe\ *n* [fr *napa* to flee] : flight for fear of something - Bl
wo·na·se \wó-na-se\ *n* [fr *nasa* to hunt buffalo] : a hunting of buffalo - D.113
wo·na·sun·sun \wo-ná-suŋ-suŋ\ *v* : to make struggle by shooting < ~ *iyeya* to make struggle suddenly >
wo·na·ta \wó-na-ta\ *v* : to excel or exceed, get far ahead of others leaving them far behind; *fig* to be unsuccessful in everything while others are < *Wónamatapelo* They left me far behind, or I was quite unsuccessful. > - B. EM
wo·na·te \wó-na-te\ *v* wona·wa·te : to beat, as in a race, to excel < *Inahni škan yo. Wonanitapi ktelo* Get a move on you. You'll get beat, *i.e. fig* the enemies will catch you if you stay behind. > - P Bl
wo·na·tan \wó-na-ṫaŋ\ *n* : a military maneuvre - P
wo·na·wi·zi \wó-na-wi-zi\ *n* : jealousy < *Hehanl oyate kin ~ on wanjigji kuwapi* Then the people followed after each one out of jealousy. > - MS.525 B.H.37.1, 65.11
wo·ni \wo-ní\ *va* wo·wa·ni [fr *ni* to live] : to resuscitate by blowing < ~ *iyeya* suddenly to recover >
wo·ni·hin·ci·ye \wó-ni-hiŋ-ci--ye\ *n* [fr *nihinciya* to be frightened] : fright - B.H.76.7 Pb.22
[1]**wo·ni·ya** \wo-ní-ya\ *va* wo·wa·niya [fr *niya* to breathe] : to resuscitate by blowing
[2]**wo·ni·ya** \wó-ni-ya\ *n* : breath, life, spirit
Wo·ni·ya Wa·kan \Wó-ni-ya Wa-kàŋ\ *np* : the Holy Spirit, third Person in the divine Trinity of Persons
wo·o·gla·ke \wó-o-gla-ke\ *n* [fr *oglaka* to tell of one's own] : a declaring of one's own rights or intentions < *Sinte Gleška ~ el opa* Spotted Tail joined in declaring his intentions. > - MS.525
wo·o·hi·ti·ke \wó-o-hi-ti-ka\ *n* : hardihood, courage, bravery, fury
wo·o·ho·la \wó-o-ho-la\ *n* [fr *ohola* to honor one] : a respecting, an honor - Pb.33
wo·o·hpa \wo-ó-ḣṗa\ *va* wo·wá·ohpa : to break in *e.g.* the skull by shooting or punching
[1]**wo·o·h'an·ko** \wo-ó-ḣ'aŋ-ko\ *va* wo·wá·oh'anko [fr *oh'anko* to be quick in doing] : to make lively by punching or shooting
[2]**wo·o·h'an·ko** *or* **wooh'anka** \wó-o-ḣ'aŋ-ko\ *n* : speed
wo·o·i·yo·ki·pi \wó-o-i-yo-ki-pi\ *or* \wó-i-yo-ki-pi\ *n* : pleasure, satisfaction - B.H.155.9
wo·o·ka·hni·ge \wó-o-k̇a-ḣni-ġe\ *n* [fr *okahniga* to understand, comprehend] : the understanding of things, comprehension
wo·o·ki·hi \wó-o-ki-hi\ *n* [fr *okihi* to be able] : ability,

---

\a\ father \e\ they \i\ machine \o\ smoke \u\ lunar \an, aŋ\ blanc Fr. \in, iŋ\ ink \on, oŋ, un, uŋ\ soon, confier Fr. \c\ chair \ġ\ machen Ger. \j\ fusion \clusters: bl, gn, kp, hšl, etc...\ b[e]lo ... said with a slight vowel
See more in the Introduction, Guide to Pronunciation

power

wo·o·ki·tan'·in \wó-o-k̇i-taŋ-iŋ\ *n* : a manifestation

wo·o·ki·ye \wó-o-k̇i-ye\ *n* [fr *ókiya* to assist] : help

wo·o·ksa \wó-o-ksa\ *vn* : to break off in, as the bank of a river < ~ *iyeya* to break and slide off suddenly > — **wookse** \wo-ó-kse\ *n* : an erosion, a washout made in a bank by water flowing in the stream - Bl

wo·o·ktan \wo-ó-ktaŋ\ *va* wo·wa·oktan : to bend into by punching — **wowoktan·yan** *vn* to become crooked, as an arrow by being shot into anything < ~ *iyeya* to become crooked suddenly >

wo·o·lo·ta \wó-o-lo-ta\ *n* : rental, lease

wo·on·spe \wó-oŋ-ṡpe\ *n* [fr *onspe* to know how to do something] : a lesson, a precept — **woonspe·kiye** *n* [fr *onspekiya* to teach] : teaching < *Jerusalem otonwahe kin ~ nitawapi kin on ojuwicayayapelo* You have filled the city of Jerusalem with your teaching. > - B.H.284.3

wo·on·ši·la \wó-oŋ-ši-la\ *n* : mercy - B.H.63.14

wo·o·pe \wó-o-ṗe\ *n* [fr *opa* to observe] : custom, law

wo·o·ški·ške \wó-o-ški-ške\ *n* [fr *škiška* rough like a road] : confusion, difficulty, complexity

wo·o·tan'·in \wó-o-taŋ-iŋ\ *n* [fr *otan'in* to be visible] : a manifestation, news

wo·o·t'in·za \wo-ó-t'iŋ-za\ *va* woó·wa·t'inza : to press tight, as with a pole the ground around a fence-post — *vn* : to be tight < *Caga* ~ The ice is firm. >

wo·o·wo·gla·ke \wó-o-wo-gla-ke\ *n* : an oration, an address, a speech

wo·o·wo·tan·la \wó-o-wo-taŋ-la\ *n* [fr *owotanla* just, upright] : righteousness, uprightness

wo·o·yu·sin·ke \wó-o-yu-siŋ-ke\ *n* : hatred - B.H.97.4

wo·o·ze·ze \wo-ó-ze-ze\ *va* wo·wá·ozeze : to shoot almost off and let swing — **woozeze·ya** *adv* : shot almost off and swinging < ~ *egle* to set up to shoot off >

wo·o·zi·ki·ye \wó-o-zi-k̇i-ye\ *n* : a brief rest, a siesta - Note: *asnikiyapi* a long rest

wo·pa·gi \wó-ṗa-ġi\ *n* : a percussion, the noise made by a drum stick — **wopagi·kiya** \wó-ṗ-ġi-k̇i-ya\ *v* : to drum, to make rhythmic noise < *Wahinkpe wan ena itazipa wan hecel yuha na wanna itazipa el wopagikiyin na lowan* An arrow and a bow thus he held, and he now sang and drummed on the bow. > - R Bl

wo·pa·hta \wó-pa-ḣta\ *n* : a bale or bundle - P

wo·pa·jin \wó-ṗa-jiŋ\ *vn* wo·ma·pajin [fr *pajin* to prevent] : to be prevented by, be made unsuccessful

wo·pa·kan \wó-ṗa-k̇aŋ\ *vn* wo·ma·pakan [fr *pakán* to dust clean as a window] : to be honored - R Bl

wo·pa·kin·te \wó-ṗa-k̇iŋ-ṫe\ *n* [fr *pakinya* to wipe clean or dry] : a wiping

wo·pa·ko \wo-ṗá-k̇o\ *va* wo·wa·pako [fr *pako* crooked, bent around] : to knock crooded by shooting or punching

wo·pa·mna·yan \wó-ṗa-mna-yaŋ\ *adv* : collected together

wo·pa·ni *or* **wawopani** \wó-ṗa-ni\ *v* : to nudge, give a sign or signal - Note: *wapani* doubtfully exists, but cf *wapanini* Bl KE WHL

wo·pan \wo-páŋ\ *va* wo·wa·pan : to pound fine, as corn in a mortar — **wopan-pan** *v red* : to grind as with a mortar — **wopan·pan·la** *va* wo·wa·panpanla [fr *panpanla* tender like meat] : to pound soft with the end of a stick

wo·pa·ska \wó-ṗa-sk̇a\ *n* : a bread pan, one for baking

wo·pa·ska tan·ka \wó-ṗa-ska tàŋ-ka\ *n* : a dis pan, one for mixing flour or for washing dishes

wo·pa·smi \wó-ṗa-smi\ *n* [fr *pa* to complain + *smi* stripped clear] : anger, spite - R

wo·pa·snon \wó-ṗa-snoŋ\ *n* [fr *pasnon* to roast on a spit] : a roast, a roasting of meat

wo·pa·ta \wó-pa-ṫa\ *n* [fr *páta* to butcher] : a butcher shop, the act of cutting up meat

wo·pa·tan \wó-pa-taŋ\ *n* : the saving of things

wo·pa·te \wó-pa-ṫe\ *n* : the scraps, things thrown away in butchering when meat is plentiful: the head, intestines, backbone *etc.*, the heap of such things < *Ito ~ ekta šunkmanitu kuwa unyanpi ktelo* Now then, let us go after the coyote to a heap of butcher scraps. > - Bl

wo·pa·t'in·ze \wó-pa-t'iŋ-ze\ *n* : a pressure - P

[1]**wo·pe·mni** \wo-ṗé-mni\ *va* wo·wa·pemni [fr *pemni* warped, twisted, entangled] : to turn aside or twist by blowing or shooting

[2]**wo·pe·mni** \wó-ṗe-mni\ *n* : an accumulation, a rolling up — **wopemni·kagapi** \wó-ṗe-mni-k̇a-ġa-pi\ *n* : something made into a roll, a pie, pies

wo·pe·mni·yan \wo-ṗé-mni-yaŋ\ *part* : twisting or turning aside by blowing or shooting

wo·pe·sto \wo-ṗé-ṡto\ *v* wo·wá·pesto [fr *pesto* sharp-pointed] : to shoot or punch to pieces, to destroy by shooting

wo·pe·ton \wó-ṗe-toŋ\ *v* wope·wa·ton [fr *opeton* to buy or hire] : to buy, to buy and sell, to trade — *n* : a merchant, a trader

wo·pe·ton i·ka·zo·pi \wó-ṗe-toŋ i-kà-zo-pi\ *n* : a bill, an account or debt - Note: *ikazopi* is perhaps more properly pronounced \i-ċá-zo-pi\ - Cf icázo P

wo·pe·ton·pi \wó-ṗe-toŋ-pi\ *n* : commerce

wo·pi·ka \wó-ṗi-k̇a\ *adj* : skilled in making anything - Cf wayupika

wo·pi·la \wó-ṗi-la\ *n* [fr *pila* to rejoice or be glad] : thanks, joy, gladness < ~ *k'u, eciya* He said to him he gives thanks. > — **wopila·kiye** \wó-ṗi-la-k̇i-ye\ *n* : something that makes glad — **wopila·ye** *n* : that which makes glad, an advantage - P

wo·pin·spin·za \wo-ṗíŋ-ṡpiŋ-za\ *v* wo·wa·pinspinza : to inflict light wounds < *Wan'otayapi, tka wopinspinzapelo* They struck one with many arrows, in many places, but they inflicted light wounds. > - Bl

wo·pin·ta \wó-piŋ-ṫa\ *part* : causing trouble to one - *Syn* wóškiška

wo·pi·ye \wó-ṗi-ye\ *n* [fr *opiye* a box or chest] : a case, box, or bag, a medicine bag, any place in which things are kept — **wopiye·ya** *va* wopiye·wa·ya : to have for a *wopiye* a place to keep things - D.229

wo·po·lpo·ta \wo-ṗó-lṗo-ṫa\ *v red of* wopóta : to shoot and destroy

wo·po·ta \wo-ṗó-ṫa\ *va* wo·wá·pota [fr *póta* worn out or spoiled] : to shoot or punch to pieces, to destroy thereby, to make holes by shooting

wo·po·wa·ya \wo-pó-wa-ya\ *va* wo·wa·powaya [fr *powaya* to brush *e.g.* a coat] : to make soft by blowing upon *e.g.* nap or fur, or by striking with the fingers

wo·psag \wo-pśág\ *va contrac of* wopsaka : to cut in two < ~ *iyeya* to break off or cut off suddenly >

wo·psa·ka \wo-psá-k̇a\ *va* wo·wa·psaka [fr *psaka* broken] : to break off *e.g.* a cord by shooting or punching, to cut something in two by shooting — **wopsa·ksaka** *v red* : to be breaking off or cutting in two

wo·pšun \wó-pšuŋ\ *v* : to break something by dropping or by falling

[1]**wo·pta** \wo-ptá\ *v* wo·wa·pta wo·ya·pta wo·un·pta·pi : to punch or dig with the end of anything, as in digging wild turnips < *Tinpsila wopte yapi* They went out to dig

turnips. >

[2]**wo·pta** \wó-pta\ *v* [fr *yupta* to cut out from a pattern] : to tear in two *e.g.* a blanket – R Bl

wo·ptan·yan \wo-pṫáŋ-yaŋ\ *va* wo·wa·ptanyan [fr *ptanyan* excited as are some animals] : to make glance off as in shooting, to make turn over by shooting *e.g.* into a boat

wo·pta·pta \wo-pṫá-pṫa\ *v red of* woptá : to dig or punch in

wo·pte·ca·šni \wó-pte-ca-šni\ *adj* : immeasurable, not a little – Cf optéca R

wo·ptu·ga \wo-pṫú-ġa\ *va* wo·wa·ptuga : to shoot off a piece – BD

wo·ptu·h'a \wō'-pṫu-ȟ'a\ *n* : litter, rubbish, scraps, leavings, remnants, as in a room < *can* ~ wood chips, ~ *ojumayayelo* You filled me with scraps, *or* You got the scraps, *i.e.* splinters, little bits of things as stickseeds *etc.* all over me. > — **woptu·ptuga** *v red of* woptuga : to shoot off chips of wood *etc.* – Bl

wo·ptu·za \wo-pṫú-za\ *va* wo·wa·ptuza : to make a man fall on his knees by shooting

wo·pu·ski·ca \wo-ṗú-sḱi-ca\ *va* wo·wá·puskica [fr *puskica* to be heavily burdened] : to ram in tight

wo·pu·skil \wo-ṗú-sḱil\ *va contrac of* wopuskica : to jam in tight < ~ *iyeya* to make drive in tight >

wo·pu·tkan \wó-pu-tkaŋ\ *v* [fr *oputkan* to dip into with the fingers] : to dip in < *Aguyapi wan on woputkanpi* They dipped in with a piece of bread. > – B.H.253.13

wo·san·ka·ya·kel \wo-sáŋ-ka-ya-kel\ *adv* : desolate, as a country void of everything, with nothing there to be obtained, *esp* no game *etc.* – R Bl

wo·sa·pa \wó-sa-ṗa\ *n* [fr *sápa* black] : blackness

[1]**wo·ska** \wo-ská\ *va* : to wash off, as rain does white-wash

[2]**wo·ska** \wó-ska\ *n* **a** : one who makes white **b** : ornamental work — **woska·ka** *n* : one who makes white, or who works moccasins

wo·skan \wo-sḱáŋ\ *vn* : to cause to melt and flow off, as rain does snow

wo·ska·pa \wo-sḱá-ṗa\ *va* wo·wa·skapa : to make a noise, as one might with a pop-gun or toy pistol, to miss fire as when the cap explodes but does not ignite the charge — **woskapa·pi** \wo-sḱá-ṗa-ṗi\ *n* : the pop of a toy gun

wo·ska·pi \wó-sḱa-pi\ *n* : quill-work, quill design

wo·ski·ca \wo-sḱí-ca\ *va* wo·wa·skica : to press down tight by pounding — **woskil** *va contrac* : to press down with force of pounding < ~ *iyeya* to make press down tight > — **woski·lya** \wó-sḱi-lya\ *or perhaps* \wo-sḱí-lya\ *va* : to crush < *Woskilmayayelo* You press, crush me. > – Bl

wo·sku·ye \wó-sḱu-ye\ *n* [fr *skuya* sweet] : taste, savor

wo·sla \wo-slá\ *adv* or *adj* : upright, straight up < *Yunkan šina ikceka heca wan* ~ *yanke s'elececa wanyanke. Tehan* ~ *inawajin owakihi šni* And then he saw what seemed to be straight up one such common blanket. For a long time I was not able to stand upright, as says a man with back-aches. > — **wosla·han** *adv* : upright, up — **woslal** *or* **woslá·lhan** *or* **wosla·sla** *adv contrac of* woslata : upright, straight up < ~ *najin* to stand straight up, *Inyan* ~ *han. Šota kin* ~ *han* The rock stood upright. The smoke stood straight up. > – P MS.71

wo·sla·sla·te \wó-sla-sla-te\ *n* : one slow and good *e.g.* at working – *Syn* WAYUH'ANHIHIKE Ww

wo·sla·sla·te·ke \wó-sla-sla-te-ke\ *n* : that which stands erect

wo·sla·ta *or* **woslatu** \wo-slá-ṫa\ *adv* : erect, perpendicularly, on end

wo·sle·ca \wo-slé-ca\ *va* wo·wa·sleca : to split by shooting or punching

wo·slel \wo-slél\ *va contrac of* wosleca : to split < ~ *iyeya* suddenly to split something, as by shooting or punching > — **wosle·sleca** *v red of* wosleca : to be at splitting

wo·sli \wo-slí\ *va* wo·wa·sli **a** : to push down in as in churning **b** : to squirt

wo·slo·han e·hpe·ya \wo-sló-haŋ e-ȟpé-ya\ *v* : to make cattle *e.g.* slide shooting them

wo·slo·he \wó-slo-he\ *n* : a drag, a sled

wo·slo·lye \wó-slo-lye\ *n* [fr *slolya* to know] : knowledge

wo·slo·ton šni \wó-slo-toŋ sni\ *v* woslo·wa·ton šni : to be careless, always jumping at first impressions and not showing planned caution < *woslotonpi šni* carelessness, impetuosity > – Cf wanaptonka, škanškán wašicun Rl PD

wo·sna \wo-sná\ *va* wo·wa·sna [fr *sna* to ring or sound] : to make ring by shooting, to make a bell ring and thus try shooting at it — *n* : the noise of leaves falling when they are shot from trees — **wosna·sna** \wo-sná-sna\ *v red of* wosna : to toll a bell

wo·sni \wo-sní\ *va* wo·wa·sni [fr *sni* cold] : to blow out *e.g.* a candle, to cool by blowing — *vn* : to put out as rain does fire, to stanch a fire — **wosni·sni** *v red* : to smother a fire

wo·sol \wo-sól\ *va contrac of* wosota : to kill off all < ~ *iyeya* to kill off all quickly > — **woso·lsota** \wo-só-lso-ṫa\ *v red of* wosota : to exterminate

wo·so·so \wó-so-so\ *n* : jerky, meat cut in strips or strings < ~ *hanskaska kaga yo;* Make jerky in long strips; *wiunpipi ktelo* We'll be satisfied eating. ~ *k'un yuha kinyan iyaye* He went on flying carrying that jerky. > – Cf soso Bl D.73

wo·so·ta \wo-só-ṫa\ *va* wo·wa·sota [fr *sota* all used up] : to kill off all, use up all by shooting, to use up all one's shot, to shoot all the game such as ducks < *Su iyuha wowasota* I used up all the seed. >

wo·spa·ya \wo-sṗá-ya\ *vn* [fr *spaya* to be wet] : to get wet, by raining on — **wospaye** \wó-sṗa-ye\ *n* : wetness

wo·stan·ka \wo-sṫáŋ-ḱa\ *v* [fr *stanka* moist] : to moisten by raining on

wo·su·ki·ye \wó-su-ki-ye\ *n* : the law's fulfillment or completion perhaps

wo·su·ksu·ta \wo-sú-ksu-ṫa\ *v red of* wosuta : to make hard

wo·su·ta \wo-sú-ṫa\ *v* wo·wa·suta wo·un·suta·pi [fr *suta* hard, firm] : to make hard by punching or ramming, to harden by raining on

wo·s'i·cu \wó-s'i-cu\ *va* : to take by force

wo·ša \wó-ša\ *n* [fr *ša* red] : redness

wo·ša·pe \wó-ša-pe\ *n* [fr *šapa* defiled, dirty] : filth, anything that defiles

wo·šib \wo-šíb\ *va contrac of* wošipa : to shoot off a branch or anything projecting from another body < ~ *iyeya* to cause to knock off projections > — **woši·bšipa**

\a\ father \e\ they \i\ machine \o\ smoke \u\ lunar \an, aŋ\ blanc Fr. \in, iŋ\ ink \on, oŋ, un, uŋ\ soon, confier Fr. \c\ chair \ġ\ machen Ger. \j\ fusion \clusters: bl, gn, kp, hšl, etc...\ b[e]lo ... said with a slight vowel **See more in the Introduction, Guide to Pronunciation**

\wo-ší-bši-ṗa\ *v red* : to break off many by shooting

[1]**wo·ši·ca** \wo-ší-ca\ *va* wo·wa·šica [fr *šica* bad, evil] : to injure or spoil by shooting of punching, to commit evil deeds

[2]**wo·ši·ca** \wó-ši-ca\ *v* wó·wa·šica wó·un·šica·pi : to commit evil deeds < *Tona wošicapi s'a kin hena tanagi kin tokakiyapi* The spirits of those who are evil doers make enemies. > – B.H.127.16

wo·ši·ca·ho·wa·ya \wo-ší-ca-ho-wa-ya\ *va* [fr *šica* bad + *howaya* to cry out, to groan] : to make cry out by shooting or punching

wo·ši·ce \wó-ši-ce\ *n* [fr *šica* bad] : evil, badness, the cause of disease – Pb.39

wo·ši·gla \wó-ši-gla\ *n* [fr *šigla* to become angry, take offense at] : anger

wo·ši·htin \wó-ši-ḣtiŋ\ *n* [fr *šihtin* poorly made, imperfect] : feebleness, debility

wo·ši·h'an \wó-ši-ḣ'aŋ\ *n* [fr *ših'an* to behave badly] : wickedness

wo·ši·kši·ce·ke \wó-ši-kši-ce-ke\ *n* awkwardness, ineptitude — *adj* : unaware, troublesome, not able to see or solve according to usual practice – WHL LHB

wo·šil i·ya·gle \wó-šil i-yà-gle\ *v* wóšil iya·ma·gle : to meet with bad luck, to be cursed – B.H.4.25

wo·ši·pa \wo-ší-ṗa\ *va* wo·wa·šipa : to shoot off *e.g.* a branch or anything projecting from another body

wo·ši·tki·gla \wó-ši-tki-gla\ *n* [fr *šitkigla* to be angry, afflicted] : affliction, displeasure — **wošitkigla·ya** *v* : to make angry, to afflict

wo·škan·ka·pin \wó-škaŋ-ka-ṗiŋ\ *n* : laziness, sloth – P

wo·ška·te \wó-ška-te\ *n* [fr *škata* to play] : play

wo·ške·han \wó-šk̇e-haŋ\ *v* or perhaps *part* : making totter and fall by shooting < *tokeya* ~ one who on the warpath kills the first enemy > – Cf paškehan

wo·ški \wo-šk̇í\ *va* wo·wá·ški : to pound *e.g.* corn not well dried

[1]**wo·ški·ca** \wo-šk̇í-ca\ *va* wo·wa·škica : to squeeze out by ramming

[2]**wo·ški·ca** \wó-ški-ca\ *v* [fr *yuškica* to squeeze or wring] : to press — **woškil** \wo-šk̇íl\ *v contrac of* woškica : to press < ~ *iyeya* to cause to press suddenly > — **wo·ški·lya** \wó-šk̇i·lya\ *va* : to crush, compress with great force – *See* wawoškiškeyece, wawoškilya – KE WHL

wo·škin·ci·ye \wó-škiŋ-ci-ye\ *n* : action, work, occupation – Bl B.H.57.13

wo·ški·ška \wó-ški-ška\ *part* : causing trouble to many < ~ *ḣeóški* Rough country was causing trouble > – *Syn* WOPINTA

wo·ški·ške \wó-ški-ške\ *n* [fr *oškiške* broken up land with steep hills and draws] : trouble, confusion – Note: *ḣeóški* rough countryside

wo·ško·pa \wó-ško-pa\ *n* : the curve of something – P

wo·šla \wo-šlá\ *va* wo·wa·šla [fr *šla* bare, bald] : to make bare by shooting, to shoot off *e.g.* hair *etc.* — **wo·šla·šla** *v red of* wošlá : to make bare

wo·šla·šla·te·ke \wó-šla-šla-te-ke\ *n* : the pulling out of weeds, feathers and such like – KE

wo·šle·ca \wo-šlé-ca\ *va* wo·wa·šleca : to split off a little piece by shooting or punching — **wošlel** *va contrac* : to split off a small piece < ~ *iyeya* to cause to split off a piece > — **wošle·šleca** \wo-šlé-šle-ca\ *v red* : to spit off a small piece by shooting

wo·šle·šle·ca·pi \wō'-šle-šle-ca-ṗi\ *n* : hominy

wo·šlog \wo-šlóg\ *va contrac of* wošloka : to fire off a gun

wo·šlo·ka \wo-šló-k̇a\ *va* wo·wa·šloka : to fire off a gun, to shoot out a load, to blow out, clear out by blowing through a tube

wo·šlo·šlog \wo-šló-šlog\ *v contrac of* wošlošloka : to clear out by blowing < *ton ~ hiyuya* to expectorate, spit out phlegm freely > – *Syn* WOKABKAB Bl

wo·šlo·šlo·ka \wo-šló-šlo-k̇a\ *v red of* wošloka : to clear out by blowing

wo·šlul \wo-šlúl\ *v contrac of* wošluta : to make glance as a bullet < ~ *iyeya* to make something glance >

wo·šlu·ta \wo-šū'-ta\ *vn* [fr *šluta* to be slippery or let drop] : to glance, as a bullet

wo·šme \wó-šme\ *n* : depth – P

[1]**wo·šna** \wo-šná\ *va* wo·wa·šna : to miss in shooting, to miss the mark

[2]**wo·šna** \wó-šna\ *v* wo·wa·šna [fr *yušna* to let slip or drop] : to sacrifice, to drop something in offering — *n* : an offering, something offered to God in sacrifice

wo·šna·ka·ga \wó-šna-k̇a-ġa\ *n* : a priest, one who offers sacrifice – Note: the word in Teton: waunyan·kaga *and* wayuhtata·kaga

wo·šna·ki·ya \wó-šna-k̇i-ya\ *va* wóšna·wa·kiya : to cause to sacrifice

wo·šna·pi·ka·ga *or* **wošnakaga** \wó-šna-ṗi-k̇a-ġa\ *n* : a priest

wo·šna·šna \wo-šná-šna\ *v red of* wošná : to miss the mark repeatedly

wo·šna·ya \wo-šná-ya\ *va* wošna·wa·ya [fr *wošná* miss the mark] : to cause to miss

wo·šo·ka \wo-šó-k̇a\ *adj* : enlarged, puffed out, ending in a knob

wo·šo·šo s'e \wo-šō'-šo s'e\ *adv* : extraordinarily thick or fleshy, as is said of a man or his nose or his lips – *Syn* ŠWOŠWOKE S'E Bl

wo·špa \wo-šṗá\ *va* wo·wa·špa : to knock off, punch or shoot off a piece

[1]**wo·špi** \wo-šṗí\ *va* wo·wa·špi : to shoot off *e.g.* fruit

[2]**wo·špi** \wó-šṗi\ *v* wa·blu·špi wa·lu·špi un·wošpi·pi [fr *yušpi* to pick, gather] : to pick *e.g.* berries < ~ *eyaya* They have gone picking. >

wo·špi·pi \wo-šṗí-ṗi\ *v red of* wošpí : to shoot off *e.g.* fruit — **wošpipi kaġapi** *n* : once the distribution of Christmas presents from the tree

wo·špu·špu \wo-šṗú-šṗu\ *v red* wo·wa·špušpu [fr *wošpu* to punch or pull away a piece] : to punch to pieces, as a cake of tallow

wo·šta·ka \wo-šṫá-k̇a\ *va* [fr *šṫáka* soft, as ice] : to soften by punching or shooting – Bl

wo·štan \wó-šṫaŋ\ *va* or *vn* [fr *óštan* to put on or fit in] : to put or fit on or in < *wóštanpi* a stopper >

wo·šte \wo-šṫé\ *interj* : Horrible!

wo·šte·pi \wó-šṫe-pi\ *n* : trite phrases – *See* oweštepi — **woštepi iyeya** *v* : to throw, as it were a bow onto ice – Bl

wo·šu·ja \wo-šú-ja\ *va* wo·wa·šuja [fr *šuja* which seems to stem from *ošungye* violently, very or too much] : to crush by punching, to crush or mash up as a bullet does bones — **wošuš** \wo-šúš\ *va contrac* : to mash up < ~ *iyeya* to cause suddenly to be crushed > — **wošušuja** *v red* : to be crushing

wo·š'a \wó-š'a\ *adj* : overloaded < ~ *ku welo* He returned overloaded. > – Bl

wo·š'ag \wo-š'ág\ *va contrac of* woš'áka : to shoot with little force — **woš'a·gš'a·gya** \wo-š'á-gš'a-gya\ *part red of* woš'ágya : shooting with too little force — **woš'a·gš'a·ka** *v red of* woš'áka : to make but an impression

— **woš'a·gya** *part* : shooting with too little force
wo·š'a·ka \wo-š'á-k̇a\ *va* wo·wa·š'aka : to shoot with too little force to penetrate; *fig* to make no impression with one's words < *He wowaš'ake lo, woyaš'ake lo, woš'a-ke lo* I did not impress it, you did not impress it, he did not impress it. > - Bt
wo·š'a·kel \wó-š'a-kel\ *adv* : overloaded < ~ *omawani* I traveled with too much of a load. > - Bl
wo·š'in \wó-š'iŋ\ *n* : a bull frog - Bl
wo·š'in·š'in·ki·ye \wó-š'iŋ-š'iŋ-k̇i-ye\ *n* : that which invites interest or curiosity < ~ *wognake yagle yelo* You placed there an attractive box. ~ *k'el* where there is a curiosity > - BT Bl
wo·š'in·ye·ye \wó-š'iŋ-ye-ye\ *n* : a surprise, a scare
[1]**wo·ta** \wo-tá\ *v* : to press against < ~ *iyeya* to blow off > - B.H.71.12
[2]**wo·ta** \wō'-ta\ *v* wa·wá·ta wa·ún·ta·pi *or* wa·ún·yuta·pi [fr *yuta* to eat] : to eat - B.H.226.23
wo·ta·ka \wo-tá-k̇a\ *v* : to stop suddenly, give up or desist - B.H.10.4, 107.9
wo·ta·kpe \wó-ta-kṗe\ *n* [fr *takpe* to assault] : an attack or assault
wo·ta·ku·ni·šni \wo-tá-k̇u-ni-sni\ *va* wo·wa·takunišni [fr *takunišni* nothing] : to destroy by shooting or punching, shoot all to pieces; to carry off as rain does snow
wo·ta·ku·ye \wó-ta-ku-ye\ *n* : consanguinity - P
[1]**wo·tan** \wo-táŋ\ *va* : to pound, as in washing clothes
[2]**wo·tan** \wó-taŋ\ *v* [fr *yutan* to touch] : to touch, feel; anything that feels about for food as does the raccoon
wo·tan·glu·sa·sa·ya·kel \wó-taŋ-glu-sa-sa-ya-kel\ *adv* : as if getting into everything < ~ *magaju* with rain getting into everything, *i.e.* it rains terribly > - *Syn* WOKOKIPEYA, WOHINYANSYAKEL Bl
wo·tan'·in \wó-taŋ-iŋ\ *v* [fr *otan'in* to be visible] : to be apparent — *n* : news
Wo·tan'·in Wa·šte \Wó-taŋ-iŋ Wa-štè\ *np* : the Gospel - P
wo·tan'·in wo·wa·pi \wó-taŋ-iŋ wò-wa-pi\ *n* : a newspaper
wo·tan·ka \wó-taŋ-ka\ *n* : largeness or anything large < *Wotankahci mak'u welo* He gave me much, meaning *i.e.* very little. *Pangi sinte kayeš ~ yelo* Especially the *sinte* tail or root end of the artichoke is a large thing, as a person said when he gave half of the little he had. *Hena yuta yo, pangi sinte yeš, ~ yelo* Eat these, it's something large though it be the tail of the artichoke, as is said when giving only a little food because there is not much on hand. > - Bl
wo·tan·ki·ya \wo-táŋ-k̇i-ya\ *va* wotan·wa·kiya : to cause to pound
wo·tan·ton \wó-taŋ-toŋ\ *n* : abundance - Bl
wo·ta·pi \wó-ta-pi\ *n* : eating
wo·ta·ta \wo-tá-ta\ *va* : to make dull, as a pestle by pounding it in a mortar, or as an arrow by shooting
wo·ta·wa·cin \wó-ta-wa-ciŋ\ *n* : desire, ambition < ~ *wašte. Takuwe ~ kin le nicante mahel luha hwo?* Ambition is good. Why do you hold this desire in your heart? > - B.H.13.10, 283.3
wo·ta·we \wó-ta-we\ *n* : weapons and armor consecrated by religious ceremonies; a charm relied upon in war
wo·teb \wo-ṫéb\ *va contrac of* wotepa : to wear off < ~ *iyeya* to wear off, as the point of an arrow >
wo·te·ca \wó-ṫe-ca\ *n* : newness
wo·te·hi \wó-te-h̔i\ *n* : that which is hard to be endured a difficulty, trouble < *Lila aiapi ca ~ akipapi* Hardships befell them because they seriously slandered him. >
— **woteh̔i·h̔iya** *adv* : with great difficulty - B.H.94.2
wo·te·h̔i·ke \wó-ṫe-h̔i-k̇e\ *n* : hardship, difficulty
wo·te·kte·gla \wó-ṫe-kte-gla\ *vn* wotekte·wa·gla : to be hungry — **wotektegla·pi** *n* : hunger
wo·te·pa \wo-té-pa\ *va* wo·wa·tepa [fr *tepa* worn off] : to wear off short, as an arrow by shooting
[1]**wo·ti·ca** \wo-tí-ca\ *vn* wo·wa·tica : to make spatter out *e.g.* mud by shooting
[2]**wo·ti·ca** \wó-ṫi-ca\ *n perhaps* [fr *tica* to scrape] : scraping or pawing as a horse does snow - R Bl
wo·ti·ki·ci·ci·ya \wó-ṫi-ki-ci-ci-ya\ *v* : to petition for - B.H.212.11
wo·ti·ki·ya \wó-ṫi-k̇i-ya\ *v* woti·wa·kiya : to beg of one for another - Note: in Dakota the word is *ikicituka*
wo·tin \wo-ṫíŋ\ *vn* : to take a stiff position, become stiff or be stiff as a dead person; to stand erect, upright — *adj* : stiff, standing up as horses' ears — **wotin·kiya** \wó-ṫiŋ-k̇i-ya\ *adv* : stiffly < *tahu ~* being stiff-necked > — **wotin·tin** \wo-ṫíŋ-ṫiŋ\ *adj red* : stiff, standing up — **wotintin·yan** *adv red of* wotinyan : in a stiff manner — **wotin·yan** *adv* : stiffly - B.H.285.21
wo·ti·tan \wo-ṫí-ṫaŋ\ *v* : to pull a load
wo·ti·ti \wo-ṫí-ṫi\ *adv* : irresolutely, unsteadily < ~ *mani* to walk unsteadily, *i.e.* as a blind man, ~ *econ* to do it hesitatingly, ~ *inajin* to stand undecided, ~ *un* to be or use without determination > — **wotiti·kel** \wó-ṫi-ṫi-kel\ *adv* : unsteadily, in a shaky manner < *Ištamagonga ca ~ wahi yelo* I came in a shaky manner because I am blind. > - Bl
wo·ti·ye \wó-ṫi-ye\ *v* : to plead < ~ *waun* I am pleading. > - Cf iyotiyekiya — **wotiye·kiya** \wó-ṫi-ye-k̇i-ya\ *v* : to plead with one for a favor, for deliverance from trouble - B.H.147.4
wo·ti·ye·mna·šni \wó-ṫi-ye-mna-šni\ *adj* : clean, pure, as a person or a house *etc.* - B.H.8.16
wo·ti·ye·ya \wo-ṫí-ye-ya\ *adv* : idle, because of lack of ability < ~ *waun welo* I was idle. > - *Syn* WOTITI BT
wo·tku·ga \wo-tkú-ġa\ *va* wo·wa·tkuga : to shoot off square *e.g.* a stick, to shoot and break partly off, to strike and crack *e.g.* a plate — **wotkuh** \wo-tk̇úh̔\ *va contrac of* wotkuga : to shoot and crack something
wo·to \wo-ṫó\ *vn* **a** : to misfire, as a gun because of faulty loading or a poor cartridge, **b** : to knock with the end of anything < *Mazawakan ~ yelo* He knocked the gun. ~ *inawajin* I stood up and it misfired, *i.e.* I found the door closed. *Wountopi kte* Let us shake a leg, *i.e.* Let us dance. >
wo·to·gye \wó-to-gye\ *va* : to do things in a different way - Bl
wo·to·ka \wo-ṫó-k̇a\ *adj* : pounded off short, short < *He ~* That is short. >
wo·to·ka·pa wo·i·yo·wa·ja \wo-ṫó-ka-pa wò-i-yo-wa-ja\ *n* : the first birthright - B.H.19.12
wo·to·ka s'e *or* **wotoka·sekse** \wo-ṫó-ka s'e\ *adv* : immovably, like a post < ~ *inajin* to stop walking and stand still, as in warm weather or when one is tired > - Bl
wo·to·ke·ca \wo-ṫó-k̇e-ca\ *va* [fr *tokeca* different] : to alter and make different by punching or shooting

---

\a\ father \e\ they \i\ machine \o\ smoke \u\ lunar \an, aŋ\ blanc Fr. \in, iŋ\ ink \on, oŋ, un, uŋ\ soon, confier Fr. \c\ chair \ġ\ machen Ger. \j\ fusion \clusters: bl, gn, kp, hšl, etc...\ b[e]lo ... said with a slight vowel
See more in the Introduction, Guide to Pronunciation

wo·to·ki·c'on \wó-to-ki-c'oŋ\ *n* [fr *tokic'on* to revenge] : *n* : revenge
wo·to·to \wo-ṫó-ṫo\ *v red of* wotó : to knock with an end of something
wo·tu·ka \wo-ṫú-ka\ *va* wo·wa·tuka : to spoil *e.g.* the fur of a small animal by shooting — **wotuka·ka** *v red* wo·wa·tukaka : to spoil or hurt by shooting, to make smart by shooting
wo·tu·tka \wo-ṫú-ṫka\ *va* wo·wa·tutka [fr *tutka* trinkets] : to shoot or punch off pieces
[1]**wo·t'a** \wo-t'á\ *va* wo·wa·t'a [fr *t'a* to die] : to kill by punching or shooting, to stun, strike so as to endanger life < ~ *iyeya* suddenly to stun, *woic'it'a* to stun one's self by shooting, to shoot and kill one's self, *mini* ~ to drown one, to drench, as when the water leaks on one through the roof >
[2]**wo·t'a** \wó-t'a\ *v* wo·ma·t'a : to be dead of food, to have eaten too much, to be surfeited — **wot'e** *n* : death caused by food — **wot'e·ic'iya** *v* : to over-eat one's self, even to becoming sick — **wot'e·ye** *n* : the cause of death
wo·t'ins \wo-t'íŋs\ *va contrac of* wot'inza : to tighten < ~ *iyeya* suddenly to draw up tight > — **wot'in·st'inza** *v red of* wot'inza : to tighten — **wot'in·sya** *adv* : tightly
wo·t'in·za \wo-t'íŋ-za\ *va* wo·wa·t'inza [fr *t'inza* stiff, firm] : to tighten, make tight by punching, to blow up tight as a bladder, to inflate
wo·t'o·ga \wo-t'ó-ǧa\ *adj* : rasping, hackling, with point blunted – WHL
wo·t'o·ja \wo-t'ó-ja\ *va* wo·wa·t'oja : to make short or blunt by shooting — **wot'oš** *va contrac* : to shorten
wo·un·ka \wo-uŋ-ka\ *va* wo·wa·unka : to make fall, to fell *e.g.* an animal when shot < *Yunkan lila kpeyela iyeya na ogna ~ na psunpsunkiya gliyunka* And then suddenly there was a very loud report and it fell in and it retreated and collapsed face-down. >
wo·un·ye·ya \wó-uŋ-ye-ya\ *va* : to have for a victim – B.H.130.5
wo·wa \wó-wa\ *v* wó·wa·wa wó·ya·wa [fr *owa* to mark, write, paint] : to mark, write, paint < *Winyan wan ~ wayupike ci he* That is a woman who is skilled in painting. > – MS.482 B.H.198.17
wo·wa·a·i·hpe·ye \wó-wa-a-i-ȟpe-ye\ *n* : a written legacy
wo·wa·ci \wó-wa-ci\ *n* [fr *waci* to dance] : a dance, dancing
wo·wa·cin \wó-wa-ciŋ\ *n* : faith, confidence < *Cisciyela wowacin luhapi kin* You certainly have a very little bit of faith. > – B.H.203.12
wo·wa·cin·gnu·ni \wó-wa-ciŋ-gnu-ni\ *n* : delirium – P
wo·wa·cin·ko \wó-wa-ciŋ-ko\ *n* [fr *wacinko* pouting, ill-natured] : irascibility
wo·wa·cin·tan·ka \wó-wa-ciŋ-taŋ-ka\ *n* : patience, perseverance
wo·wa·cin·yan *or* **wowacinye** \wó-wa-ciŋ-yaŋ\ *n* [fr *wacinyan* to trust] : trusting in, reliance upon, faith
wo·wa·cin·ye *or* **wowacinyan** \wó-w-ciŋ-ye\ *n* : that which one needs badly, a necessity < ~ *kin ojumaye* I was filled with my necessities. ~ *wašte* an interest *i.e.* what is interesting > — **wowacinye·ya** *v* wowacinye·wa·ya : to depend on, rely on < *Itazipa na wahinkpe kin hena wowacinyeyapi na on woyute icupi* They relied on bow and arrow and so with them they took something to eat. > – Pb.34 D.259, 106
wo·wa·cin·yu·ze \wó-wa-ciŋ-yu-ze\ *n* : emotion, inclination, tendency, propensity – P
wo·wa·he·con *or* **wowahicon** *or* **wowahicun** \wó-wa-he-coŋ\ *n* mita·wowahecon : kindred, relationship < *Winyan kin le iyuha wowahicun unkiyuhapi* All these women keep relationships for us. We all have a relationship to this woman, *i.e.* she is some relation to us all. ~ *tonakeca kin iyuha cajeyate* She named all how much was the relationship. > – D.57, 220
wo·wa·ho·kon·ki·ye \wó-wa-ho-koŋ-ki-ye\ *n* [fr *wahokonkiya* to instruct] : advice, counsel, instruction
wo·wa·hpa·ni·ca \wó-wa-ȟpa-ni-ca\ *n* [fr *wahpanica* destitute, poor] : poverty
wo·wa·hta·ni *or* **woahtani** \wó-wa-ȟta-ni\ *n* : sin, a transgression
wo·wa·htc·la·šni \wó-wa-ȟte-la-šni\ *n* [fr *wahtelašni* to dislike, abominate] : dislike, abhorrence — **wowahtelašni·ya** *va* : to dislike — **wowahtelašniyan** *adv* : not pleased with – B.H.93.26, 216.1
wo·wa·hwa \wó-wa-ȟwa\ *n* : peace — **wowahwa·la** *n* [fr *wahwala* gentle, mild] : gentleness, meekness – B.H.166.14
wo·wa·kan \wó-wa-kaŋ\ *n* [fr *wakan* sacred] : something supernatural < *Hecel ~ kin le slolwaya* So I know about this mystery. > – *See Wawákan* the Sacred Arrow
wo·wa·ki·š'a·ke \wó-wa-ki-š'a-ke\ *n* : endurance – P
wo·wa·ki·tan \wó-wa-ki-taŋ\ *n* [fr *wakitan* to persist or insist upon] : that which is contended for — **wowakitan·ye** *n* : determination, resolution, that which causes obstinacy
wo·wa·kon·ze \wó-wa-koŋ-ze\ *n* [fr *wakonze* an influence] : justice, determination, rule, law
wo·wa·kta \wó-wa-kta\ *n* [fr *wakta* to watch for] : a mark or sign, circumspection — **wowakta·ya** *v* : to make a mark or sign
wo·wa·la \wó-wa-la\ *n* : a petition – Pb.34
wo·wa·ma·non \wó-wa-ma-noŋ\ *n* : theft, secretly to steal
wo·wa·na·h'on \wó-wa-na-ȟ'oŋ\ *n* : obedience < *wowanah'onšni* disobedience, insubordination > – P
wo·wa·ni·ca \wo-wá-ni-ca\ *va* [fr *wanica* without any, none] : to shoot or punch to nothing — **wowanice** \wó-wa-ni-ce\ *n* : the state of nothingness – B.H.1.1
wo·wa·ni·ki·ye \wó-wa-ni-ki-ye\ *n* [fr *wanikiya* to save, cause to live] : salvation < *Wakantanka towanikiye kin wanyankapi kte lo* They shall see the salvation of God. > – B.H.172.9
wo·wa·nil \wo-wá-nil\ *va contrac of* wowánica : to reduce to nothing < ~ *iyeya* to shoot to pieces, destroy by shooting >
wo·wan·ke \wó-waŋ-ke\ *n* : a wonder to see, as once it was said when a woman had twins, or when a meadow lark was found in the stomach of a deer, or when even an old woman was found in the belly of a deer! An admirable object, what attracts attention. That which is contagious as are some diseases or sicknesses – Bl KE
wo·wan·yan·ke \wó-waŋ-yaŋ-ke\ *n* : a vision, a sight, a show < ~ *yukeya* publicly a show > – B.H.300.14, 289.9
wo·wa·on·spe \wó-wa-oŋ-spe\ *n* [fr *waonspe* to know how] : an instruction, a precept — **wowaonspekiye** \wó-wa-oŋ-spe-ki-ye\ *n* : instruction
wo·wa·on·ši·la \wó-wa-oŋ-ši-la\ *n* : pity, kindness, mercy < *Le na ~ ca ecamonpi na tehanhan yanipi kta* At this time it is possible I should do what is kindness, while you should be able to live a very long time. >
wo·wa·pe·to·gton \wó-wa-pe-to-gtoŋ\ *n* [fr *wapetogton* to mark, have a sign] : a mark or sign

wo·wa·pe·to·ke·ca \wó-wa-pe-ṫo-ke-ca\ *n* : a wonder, miracle, sign — **wowapeto·ktokeca** \wó-wa-ṗe-ṫo-kṫo-ke-ca\ *n red* : signs - B.H.70.5

wo·wa·pi \wó-wa-ṗi\ *n* [fr *owa* to paint, write, figure] : a picture, letter or book, a flag < ~ *paósla* (of *paslata*) *iyeya* to hoist a flag > - Note the following:

~ *icáge* *n* : a pen or pencil, what is used to paint or write with
~ *ináhtagye* *n* : a typewriter
~ *káġa* *v* : to write, make a book < *Wowapi wakaga* I wrote a book. > — *n* : a scribe, a clerk
~ *naškánškanye* *n* : a moving picture projector
~ *oh'ánko* *n* : a postcard
~ *oíhpeya* *v* : to cast a vote
~ *okíjata* *n* : a flag of truce

Wo·wa·pi Wa·kan \Wó-wa-ṗi Wa-kàŋ\ *np* : the Holy Bible

wo·wa·su·ki·ye \wó-wa-su-ḱi-ye\ *n* : a regulation, rule, a law < ~ *oholapi* Law is honored. ~ *wanjila ahounpapi kte* We should observe a rule or law. > - D.20, 231

wo·wa·ša·gya \wó-wa-ša-gya\ *v* : to overcome easily - B.H.123.14

wo·wa·ši \wó-wa-ši\ *n* a : work, labor b : a hired man, an employee — **wowaši·ya** *va* : to make work, have for a hired man - B.H.81.17, 86.23, 45.12

wo·wa·špe \wó-wa-špe\ *n* [fr *wašpa* to cut off a piece, to scalp] : a piece cut off, a scalp-lock

wo·wa·šte \wó-wa-šte\ *n* [fr *wašte* good] : goodness

wo·wa·šte·la·ke \wó-wa-šte-la-ke\ *n* : love, complacency

wo·wa·šte·mna \wó-wa-šte-mna\ *n* : a pleasing odor - Pb.33

wo·wa·š'a·gya \wó-wa-š'a-gya\ *adv* : strongly

wo·wa·š'a·ke \wó-wa-š'a-ḱe\ *n* [fr *waš'aka* strong] : strength

wo·wa·tu·ka \wó-wa-ṫu-ka\ *n* : weariness - P

wo·wa·un·ye \wó-wa-uŋ-ye\ *n* : a sacrificial victim, the gift that serves as a sacrifice < *Wakinyela wan hece šna* ~ *aipi* Therefore a dove did they sometimes bring in sacrifice. *Wakinyela nunblala šna wowaunyin kta aipi* They brought sometimes for sacrifice only two doves. > - B.H.16.20, 167.5, 6, 168.3 Pb.16

wo·wa·un·ye·i·c'i·ye \wó-wa-uŋ-ye-i-c'i-ye\ *n* : self-immolation, the offering of one's self - Pb.34

wo·wa·wo·ki·ye \wó-wa-wo-ḱi-ye\ *n* [fr *wawokiya* to help, assist] : help

wo·wa·wo·yu·štan \wó-wa-wo-yu-štaŋ\ *n* : finishing, completion, perfection

wo·wa·ya·zan \wó-wa-ya-zaŋ\ *n* [fr *wayazan* to have pains] : sickness, disease

wo·wa·yu·pi·ke \wó-wa-yu-pi-ke\ *n* : art, adroitness, cleverness - P D.205

wo·we·ga \wo-wé-ġa\ *va* wo·wa·wega : to break but not off by shooting, to break something by falling < *Tahu* ~ He broke his leg. > — **woweh** \wo-wéȟ\ *va contrac* : to fracture < ~ *iyeya* to fracture suddenly > — **wowe·hwega** \wo-wé-ȟwe-ġa\ *v red* : to break often — **wowe·hya** *part* : broken by shooting, but not breaking entirely off < ~ *yanka* to sit breaking it >

wo·wi·ca·gi \wó-wi-ca-ġi\ *n* : an impediment, a difficulty, obstacle

wo·wi·ca·gna·ye \wó-wi-ca-gna-ye\ *n* : deception - Note: *wognaye* deceit in process, deception been done

wo·wica·hta·ke wa·ni·ca \wó-wi-ca-ȟta-ke wa-nì-ca\ *vn* wowicahtake ma·nica : to be unwilling to be touched, to be irritable, easily provoked

wo·wi·ca·ke \wó-wi-ca-ḱe\ *n* [fr *wicaka* to be true] : truth, fact, reality < ~ *šni ca ayuštan yo* Leave the matter alone because there is no truth to it, *i.e.* there is no truth in it. > — *adj* : serious, genuine - P

wo·wi·ca·ke·šni·yan \wó-wi-ca-ḱe-šni-yaŋ\ *adv* : falsely < ~ *waayatan'in* a false witness > - B.H.257.19

wo·wi·ca·ke·ya \wó-wi-ca-ḱe-ya\ *adv* : truthfully - B.H. 129.14

wo·wi·ca·ke·ya·tan·han \wó-wi-ca-ḱe-ya-ṫaŋ-haŋ\ *adv* : truly, of a truth

Wo·wi·ca·ki·gna \Wó-wi-ca-ḱi-gna\ *np* : the Holy Spirit *i.e.* the Comforter — *n* : a comforter - B.H.254.22,

wo·wi·ca·k'u·pi \wó-wi-ca-k'u-pi\ *n* : an offering, an issue, distribution, an allowance - P

wo·wi·ca·la \wó-wi-ca-la\ *n* [fr *wicala* to believe] : faith and belief — **wowicala·ya** *va* wowicala·wa·ya : to cause to believe, to persuade

wo·wi·ca·ša·šni \wó-wi-ca-ša-šni\ *n* : spite, mischief, meanness - B.H.245.15

wo·wi·gnu \wó-wi-gnu\ *n* [fr *ignu* to blame or charge with] : murmuring

wo·wi·han·ble *or* **woihanble** \wó-wi-haŋ-ble\ *n* : a dream

wo·wi·ȟa *or* **woiȟa** \wó-wi-ȟa\ *n* [fr *iȟa* to laugh at] : the laughable — **wowiȟa·ȟa** *n* : laughing, making fun, as perhaps in adultery < *Na lena kohan taku* ~ *ece econpi* And meanwhile these did just what he laughed at. *Wowiȟa oyah'an yelo* You did the laughing, as is said when a man acts badly. > — **wowiȟaȟa·kiya** *v* wowiȟaȟa·wa·kiya : to laugh at one's own - R Bl

wo·wi·ȟa·ȟa·ya \wó-wi-ȟa-ȟa-ya\ *adv* : shamefully - D.33

wo·wi·ȟa·la \wó-wi-ȟa-la\ *n* : fun, something laughable

wo·wi·ȟa·ya *or* **woiȟaya** \wó-wi-ȟa-ya\ *v* : ludicrously, funny — **wowiȟaya·kel** *or* **woiȟayakel** *adv* : laughably

wo·wi·h'o·i·ye·ya \wó-wi-ȟ'o-i-ye-ya\ *v* [fr *ȟ'a* to smell bad + *o* in place + *iyeya* to put] : to back-bite, to say something evil about a person thinking he or she is not present whereas he is and hears - Bl

wo·wi·ji·ca \wó-wi-ji-ca\ *n* : wealth < ~ *yuhakiyin kta* Let him have his wealth. > - B.H.86.16

wo·wi·ji·ca wa·cin \wó-wi-ji-ca wa-cìŋ\ *n* : avarice, overly ambitious desire

wo·wi·ji·ce \wó-wi-ji-ce\ *n* [fr *wijica* rich] : riches

wo·wi·lag \wó-wi-lag\ *n contrac of* wowilake : a hired person, an employee — **wowila·gya** *va* wowila·gwa·ya : to make or have as an employee or servant of, to cause to serve < *Wamakaškan wan hutopa ca cic'upelo ca he wowilagyayapi kta* So you might have as a servant I have given you a four-legged animal. >

wo·wi·la·ke \wó-wi-la-ḱe\ *n* : an employee, a hired man, a servant

wo·wi·ma·ga·ga *or* **woimagaga** \wó-wi-ma-ġa-ġa\ *vn* : to be merry or cheerful

wo·wi·na·hni *or* **woinahni** \wó-wi-na-ȟni\ *n* : a hurry, haste

---

\a\ father \e\ they \i\ machine \o\ smoke \u\ lunar \an, aŋ\ blanc Fr. \in, iŋ\ ink \on, oŋ, un, uŋ\ soon, confier Fr. \c\ chair \ġ\ machen Ger. \j\ fusion \clusters: bl, gn, kp, hšl, etc...\ b^e^lo ... said with a slight vowel
See more in the Introduction, Guide to Pronunciation

wo·wi·na·ki·wi·zi *or* **woinakiwizi** \wó-wi-na-ki-wi-zi\ *n* : jealousy or envy toward one's own

wo·wi·na·pe *or* **woinape** \wó-wi-na-ṗe\ *n* : a refuge, a retreat — **wowinape·ya** *n* : to have or use for a refuge

wo·wi·na·wi·zi *or* **woinawizi** \wó-wi-na-wi-zi\ *n* : jealousy toward others, or the cause of jealousy - D.260

wo·wi·ni·han *or* **woinihan** \wó-wi-ni-haŋ\ *n* : fear, or that which is fearful — **wowinihan·yan** *or* **woinihanyan** *adv* : fearfully

wo·win·ye \wó-wiŋ-ye\ *n* : little packets (ties) of tobacco offered as a sacrifice < ~ *kaga* to make ties > - Note: canwówinye may be a variation of the tie because *canli wapahte sece* it is like to the tobacco tie

wowinyeya wó-wiŋ-ye-ya\ *va* wowinye·wa·ya : to use as an instrument — **wowinyeya·pi** *n* : tools, instruments - R Bl

wo·wi·šte·ca \wó-wi-šte-ca\ *n* [fr *išteca* to be ashamed] : shame

wo·wi·šte·lya \wó-wi-šte-lya\ *va* : to consider disgraced — *adv* : disgracefully, shamefully — **wowištelye** *n* : the cause of shame - B.H.101.19

wo·wi·tan \wō'-wi-ṫaŋ\ *n* [fr *itan* to be proud] : pride, honor, glory — **wowitan·yan** *va* wowitan·wa·ya : to glory in — *adv* : honorably, gloriously

wo·wi·ton·pe \wó-wi-toŋ-ṗe\ *n* [fr *itonpa* to be astonished, to wonder] : that which one thinks great or strong

wo·wi·ya·kpa \wó-wi-ya-kpa\ *n* : a reflexion, splendor - P Bl B.H.166.5

wo·wi·yu·kcan \wó-wi-yu-kcaŋ\ *n* : a thought

wo·wi·yun ka·ga·pi \wó-wi-yuŋ kà-ġa-pi\ *n* : a ceremony had before a buffalo hunt, thus when many buffalo were seen, they did an anointing, *i.e.* they put down red blankets which were sacrifices for *Wakantanka* God - BT

wo·wi·yu·škin \wó-wi-yu-škiŋ\ *n* [fr *iyuškin* to be glad] : gladness, rejoicing < *Wicaša kin lila ~ anpetu kin he el ojula keyapi* It was stated that one that day Man's joy was complete, full. > **wowiyuškin·yan** \wó-wi-yu-škiŋ-yaŋ\ *adv* : gladly, rejoicingly

wo·wi·yu·tan \wó-wi-yu-ṫaŋ\ *n* [fr *iyutan* to be tried, to tempt] : temptation < ~ *on iniyute* He tries you with temptation. ~ *oyas'in kipajin* He stood up against every temptation. > - B.H.127.2 Pb.46

wo·wi·yu·tan·pi \wó-wi-yu-ṫaŋ-pi\ *n* : probation

wo·wi·yu·tan·ye \wó-wi-yu-ṫaŋ-ye\ *n* : temptation

wo·wo·t'in·za \wo-wó-t'iŋ-za\ *va* : to ram down tight in

wo·ya *or* **woya s'e** \wo-yá\ *adv* : ragged, dangling - *Syn* LÚPI

wo·yag \wó-yag\ *v contrac of* wóyaka : to tell, relate < ~ *wahi* I have come tell about something. >

wo·ya·gki·ya·pi \wó-ya-gki-ya-pi\ *n* : a witness, a person made to testify — **woya·gya** \wó-ya-gya\ *va* : to talk about things everywhere < *He makoce kin hel woyagyapi* That was talked about everywhere in that country. > - LWOW, 23 Pent

wo·ya·ka \wó-ya-ka\ *v* wo·bla·ka wo·un·yaka·pi [fr *oyaka* to tell, report] : to tell, relate, declare, publish < *Yunkan lecel woyakapi* And then in this way it was told. > — **woyaka·pi** \wó-ya-ka-ṗi\ *n* : a narration, declaration — **woyake** \wó-ya-ke\ *n* : a report, an indication - P B.H.306.1

wo·ya·o·ni·han \wó-ya-o-ni-haŋ\ *n* : a eulogy - P

wo·ya·pta·pi *or* **woyapte** \wó-ya-pṫa-pi\ *n* [fr *oyapta* to have left-overs] : leavings, fragments of food

wo·ya·su \wó-ya-su\ *n* [fr *yasu* to judge, decree, make things right through speaking] : judgment, condemnation

wo·ya·ši·ca \wó-ya-ši-ca\ *n* : a curse < *Ungna ~ iyoyewicayaya kilo* Beware of uttering a curse at them. > - B.H.67.16

wo·ya·tan \wó-ta-ṫaŋ\ *n* [fr *yatan* to praise one] : praise - B.H.239.3

wo·ya·tke \wó-ya-tke\ *n* [fr *yatkan* to drink] : a drink

wo·ya·t'a·ge \wó-ya-t'a-ġe\ *n* [fr *yat'aga* to make rough by biting] : that which is puckery, astringent, acrimony

wo·ya·wa \wó-ya-wa\ *n* [fr *yawa* to read, count] : a counting < ~ *tanka* a million >

wo·ya·wa·šte \wó-ya-wa-šte\ *n* [fr *yawašte* to bless, decalare good] : blessing, praise - B.H.102.11

wo·ya·wa·tan·ka \wó-ya-wa-taŋ-ka\ *n* : a great count, a million

wo·ya·ya \wó-ya-ya\ *n* : a string of beads - Note: the form *oyáya* is preffered - BD

wo·ya·zan \wó-ya-zaŋ\ *n* : infirmity, an ache, a disease - P Pb.47

wo·yu·a·šla·ye \wó-yu-a-šla-ye\ *n* : things now revealed that should have been kept secret - B.H.168.20

wo·yu·e·ce·tu \wó-yu-e-ce-ṫu\ *n* [fr *yuecetu* to fulfill, correct one] : a reconciliation, a making right

wo·yu·ha \wó-yu-ha\ *n* [fr *yuha* to have, hold] : property, a possession, one's goods < *Nita ~ kin uncinpelo* We want some of your property. >

wo·yu·ha o·i·ca·ge \wó-yu-ha o-ì-caġe\ *n* : income, revenue - P

wo·yu·ha·ya \wó-yu-ha-ya\ *va* : to own, to have for property, to consider one's property or one's own - Pb.22

wo·yu·hta·ni \wó-yu-ḣta-ni\ *n* : difficulties created, mistakes made - Bl

wo·yu·hu·pton·yan·kel \wó-yu-ḣu-pṫon-yaŋ-kel\ *adv* : making a display of being brave < ~ *omawani* I walked around strong and bravely. > - *Syn* **WOŠ'AKEL**, TÁNYUTKANLAK, TÁNYUTKANLA

wo·yu·kcan \wó-yu-kcaŋ\ *n* [fr *yukcan* to understand, know] : opinion, judgement

wo·yu·o·ni·han \wó-yu-o-ni-haŋ\ *n* : an honor, honor

wo·yu·ptin·na·pe \wó-yu-ptiŋ-na-ṗe\ *v* : to come and explain or ask for help by explaining what one is charged with - Bl

wo·yu·ska \wó-yu-ska\ *n* : ornamental work, such as the cutting strips into skins and winding them with quills - R

wo·yu·so·te \wó-yu-so-ṫe\ *n* : expense

wo·yu·su \wó-yu-su\ *n* [fr *yusu* to make right or ready] : a finishing, a making right

wo·yu·su·ta \wó-yu-su-ta\ *n* [fr *yusuta* to make firm] : a making firm

wo·yu·ši·ce \wó-yu-ši-ce\ *n* : a bad quality, that which makes bad, harm

wo·yu·ši·htin \wó-yu-ši-ḣtiŋ\ *n* : that which makes feeble, which injures or makes bad

wo·yu·ške \wó-yu-ške\ *n* : absolution - B.H.241.3

wo·yu·ški·ške \wó-yu-ški-ške\ *n* [fr *yuškiška* to roughen with notches] : that which causes difficulty

wo·yu·šla·ye·gnak \wó-yu-šla-ye-gnak\ *adv* [fr *šlaégnag* in a barren place] : in a place stripped and barren < ~ *najin* to stand in an arid place >

wo·yu·šna \wó-yu-šna\ *n* [fr *yušna* to let slip, to miss] : the sacrificing of something, a missing something, letting fall — **woyušna·šnapi** \wó-yu-šna-šna-ṗi\ *n* : things dropped or left < ~ *pahi* to pick up *etc.* things that were dropped or lost > - Bl

wo·yu·štan \wó-yu-štaŋ\ *n* [fr *yuštan* to finish, perfect] : a finishing, completion, perfection, a putting one in another < *Na hel woyajupi na nicincapi hel wayawapi kte lo, tka cuwignaka sapa un ca Tunkašila wakila ca. "How" eyelo "ca he ~ heca yelo."* And there will you root and there your children will go to school, but the President even asked for you the black robe (the catholic priest who wore a black cassock). "Yes," said he, "and that was it," he said. > -RC

wo·yu·š'in·ya·ye \wó-yu-š'iŋ-ya-ye\ *n* : terror -P

wo·yu·š'in·ye \wó-yu-š'in-ye\ *n* : wondering, astonishment -P

wo·yu·ta·ku·ni·šni \wó-yu-ṫa-ḱu-ni-šni\ *n* : ruin

wo·yu·tan'·in \wó-yu-taŋ-iŋ\ *n* : evidence, disclosure

wo·yu·te \wó-yu-ṫe\ *n* [fr *yuta* to eat] : food, something to eat

wo·yu·te·han \wó-yu-ṫe-haŋ\ *n* : duration -P

wo·yu·te·ya \wó-yu-ṫe-ya\ *va* woyute·wa·ya : to have or use as food

wo·yu·ti·tan \wó-yu-ṫi-ṫaŋ\ *n* : tension -P

wo·ya·su \wó-ya-su\ *n* [fr *yasu* to judge, decree, make things right through speaking] : judgment, condemna-

wo·yu·tkon·ze \wó-yu-tḱoŋ-ze\ *n* [fr *yutkonza* to cut off even, as with a shears] : a making equal

wo·yu·wa·šte \wó-yu-wa-šte\ *n* [fr *yuwašte* to bless, to make good] : that which makes good

wo·za \wo-zá\ *v* : to start, to respond < ~ *hingla* to start up of a sudden, as a company on hearing some startling intelligence from a messanger around whom all suddenly gather >

[1]**wo·zan** \wo-záŋ\ *va* wo·wa·zan : to hurt or feel pain by shooting, as with a pop-gun — *vn* : to get hurt by running against something

[2]**wo·zan** \wó-zaŋ\ *n* : a curtain < *miniwozan* a mist, a slow rain >

wo·zan·ni \wó-zaŋ-ni\ *n* [fr *zanni* not sick] : health

wo·ze \wó-ze\ *n* [fr *yuze* to dip, lade out] : lading *i.e.* taking out, as of a kettle < *Le hihanna kin ~ kta ca tona el oyapapi kte ci hena el ya po* This morning when there will be a dishing out, go to a number of those with whom you should join. > — **woze·pi** \wó-ze-pi\ *part* : laded out

wo·zi \wó-zi\ *n* : yellow color

wo·zun·te \wó-zuŋ-ṫe\ *n* : honesty, the doing things rightly -PD

Y

[1]ya \yā\ *interj exclam of* fear or indignation, used by women; whereas men would simply utter the "*hnahna*", a bear-like expression to make himself brave < *Ya! toskala akoecon* Oh no! Get away from here, woodpecker. > – D.52 note 1 B.H.46.3

[2]ya \ya\ *pref* affixed to a large classes of —
v and signifies that the action of the *v* is done with the mouth by biting, talking. Thus: *yaksa* to bite off
adj and sometimes to *n* to make of them *v* meaning to speak of as such, or to make so with the mouth. Thus: *yawašte* to call good, *yawicaša* to speak of as a man – Note: in these cases, the different persons are formed as in *ya* to go

[3]ya \ya\ *pron in compos* : you, or you *pl*

[4]ya \ya\ *suff causa* : to make, to have for, to regard as. Affixed to —
v, adj, etc., thus: *econya* to have it done, *sabya* to make something black, *ateya* to have for a father; the *insep pron* is placed before, as in *ate·wa·ya* I have for a father

[5]ya *or* **yakel** *or* **yan** \ya-kél\ *adv suff* –
terminations of *adv* made from *adj* ;
terminations of *adv* and *part* made from *v* . Thus: *šicaya* badly, *yuktanyan* bending, crookedly

[6]ya \ya\ *vn* bla la unyanpi; *singl fut* mni kte ni kte yin kte : to go, start, proceed < *Ake hocokata lapi kte lo* You should again go in the center. >

ya·a·ja·ja \ya-á-ja-ja\ *v* : to speak plainly in detail – Bl

ya·a·los i·ye·ya \ya-á-los i-yè-ya\ *va contrac* : to hurt the feelings of someone – *Syn* YAÍYOYAGIYEYA

ya·a·lo·slo·za \ya-á-lo-slo-za\ *v red of* alosloza : *fig* to singe < ~ *s'e iyeya* to injure one's feelings, to say something that makes another feel uncomfortable. >

ya·a·o·pte·ca \ya-á-o-pṫe-ca\ *va* bla·aopteca [fr *aopteca* little, less] : to underrate, to speak of as being small — **yaaoptel** *va contrac* : to speak pejoratively < ~ *iyeya* to belittle > — **yaaopte·lya** *adv* : in a depreciating manner

ya·a·o·pte·tu \ya-á-o-pṫe-ṫu\ *va* bla·aoptetu [fr *aoptetu* less in size] : to underrate, speak of as less — **yaaopte·tu·ya** *adv* : underrating

ya·a·pa·ko \ya-á-ṗa-ko\ *v* [fr *pako* bent around] : to bend or twist with the mouth

ya·a·ška·la \ya-á-ška-la\ *va* bla·áškala [fr *aškala* to say a little, perhaps of *ška* they say] : to speak of as near – **yaaška·škala** \ya-á-ška-ška-la\ *v red* : to speak much of as near — **yaaška·ya** *or* **yaaškaya·kel** *adv* : speaking of a near — **yaaška·yela** *adv* and *va* bla·aškayela : to speak of as near

ya·a·šla·ya \ya-á-šla-ya\ *va* bla·ašlaya : to explain or talk about what somebody has said

ya·a·tan'·in \ya-á-taŋ-iŋ\ *va* : to prove – B.H.257.16

ya·blas \ya-blás\ *va contrac of* yablaza : to tear open with the teeth < ~ *iyeya* to rip open >

ya·bla·ska \ya-blá-sḳa\ *va* bla·blaska [fr *blaská* flat] : to flatten with the mouth

ya·bla·ya \ya-blá-ya\ *va* bla·blaya [fr *blaya* level] : to make level with the teeth

ya·bla·za \ya-blá-za\ *va* bla·blaza [fr *blazá* rip open] : to tear open with the teeth

ya·ble·ble·ca \ya-blé-ble-ca\ *v red* [fr *yableca* crush with the teeth] : to shake up with the mouth, as a dog does something it caught

ya·ble·ble·za \ya-blé-ble-za\ *v red* bla·blebleza [fr *yableza* to enlighten, to cheer by talking to] : to make one sober by talking to

ya·ble·ca \ya-blé-ca\ *va* bla·bleca : to break or crush with the teeth, to break *e.g.* a bottle or one's teeth with the mouth — **yablel** *v contrac* : to break < ~ *iyeya* to break or crush suddenly with the mouth >

ya·ble·sya \ya-blé-sya\ *adv* : cheeringly < ~ *ia* to speak cheeringly >

ya·ble·za \ya-blé-za\ *va* bla·bleza [fr *bleza* clear-sighted] : to make sober by talking to, to enlighten or cheer

ya·bli·he·ca \ya-blí-he-ca\ *va* bla·bliheca : to make active by talking

ya·blu \ya-blú\ *va* : to make fine by chewing — **ya·blu·blu** *v red* : to be making fine

ya·bu \ya-bú\ *va* [fr *bu* to make a distinct sound, as a drum] : to make a loud but distinct sound, or some disagreeable noise, as children might do with horns *etc.* — **yabu·bu** *v red* : to make *e.g.* a drumming sound

ya·bu·ya \ya-bú-ya\ *adv* : hoarsely < ~ *ia* to speak with a hoarse voice >

ya·can·can \ya-cáŋ-caŋ\ *va* [fr *cancan* to tremble, shake] : to make shake with the mouth, as a dog does its prey

ya·can·ga *or* **canhcanga** \ya-cáŋ-ġa\ *vn* bla·canga : to make a noise in chewing anything hard, *e.g.* corn, to crunch

ya·can·le·ce·ca \ya-cáŋ-le-cè-ca\ *va* bla·canlececa : to make one downcast by saying things – Bl

ya·can·li·ya·pa i·ye·ya *or* **yacantiyapa iyeya** \ya-cáŋ-li-ya-pa i-yè-ya\ *and* \ya-cáŋ-ṫi-ya-pa i-yè-ya\ *v* : to say something to hurt another's feelings

ya·can·ze·ka \ya-cáŋ-ze-ka\ *va* bla·canzeka : to make angry by talking to

ya·ca·ške·ške·ke *or* **wayacaškeškeke** \ya-cá-ške-ške-ke\ *v* : to eat up slowly

ya·ce·g i·ye·ya \ya-ċéġ i-yè-ya\ *v* : to make stagger with the mouth – Bl

ya·ce·ka \ya-ċé-ḳa\ *va* : to make stagger by biting

ya·ce·kcek \ya-ċé-kcek\ *va contrac of* yacekceka : to bite and make stagger < ~ *icu* Taking his breath he jerked *Ikto* towards him. > — **yacekce·ka** \ya-ċé-kce-ka\ *va* bla·cekceka : to bite and make stagger as a dog jerks a boy around by his clothes – D.1 WHL

ya·ce·ya \ya-cé-ya\ *vn* bla·ceya : to cry for having been bitten, or to make cry by talking or biting – R

ya·ci·k'a·la \ya-cí-k'a-la\ *va* bla·cik'ala [fr *cik'ala* small] : to count small, to make small with the mouth, *fig* to undervalue

ya·ci·sci·la \ya-cí-sci-la\ *va* bla·ciscila [fr *ciscila* quite small] : to speak of as small, to count as little or few

ya·co·co \ya-ċó-ċo\ *va* bla·coco : to mash, chew up fine

ya·co·ka·ka \ya-có-ka-ka\ *va* : to empty by eating out the side, as do dogs a dead animal

ya·co·na·la \ya-có-na-la\ *va* : to speak of as few

ya·co·za \ya-có-za\ *va* bla·coza : to call warm, or to make warm with the mouth

ya·e·ce·ca \ya-é-ce-ca\ *va* bla·ececa : to persuade, talk somebody into something, to make one believe a thing to be so

ya·e·ce·la \ya-é-ce-la\ *va* bla·ecela : to speak of as right, to make right with the mouth — **yaece·lya** *adv* : rightly told < ~ *oyaka* to tell a thing as it ought to be told > – Cf yaecetu

ya·e·ce·tu \ya-é-ce-tu\ *va* bla·ecetu : to correct a statement, to tell a thing as it ought to be told — **yaecetuya** \ya-é-ce-ṫu-ya\ *adv* : speaking correctly

ya·ga \ya-ġá\ *va* bla·ga : to peel off with the teeth, to husk with the mouth

ya·gab \ya-ġáb\ *va contrac of* yagapa : to bite off *e.g.* skin or bark < ~ *iyeya* to peel, husk, shell by mouth >

ya·ga·ga \ya-ġá-ġa\ *v red of* yaga : to peel, husk < ~ *iyeya* to peel quickly >

yu·ga·lga·ta \yu-ġá-lġa-ṫa\ *va red* bla·galgata [fr *yagata* make forked with the mouth] : to prevaricate, invent, fabricate, to lie

ya·gan \yaġáŋ\ *va* bla·gan : to open with the mouth

ya·ga·pa \ya-ġá-ṗa\ *va* bla·gapa : to bite off *e.g.* the skin or bark from anything

ya·ga·ta \ya-ġá-ta\ *v* : to lie – Cf yagalgata

ya·ge \ya-ġé\ *va* bla·ge : to drink up *e.g.* water from a spring, or to gather grass with the mouth as cattle do — **yage·ge** *va* : to gather with the mouth as cattle do grass

ya·gi·ca \ya-ġí-ca\ *va* bla·gica : to waken one, arouse with the mouth or by talking — **yagil** *va contrac of yagica* : to awaken one < ~ *iyeya* to cause to waken >

ya·gi·ta *or* **hogita** \ya-ġī'-ṫa\ *v* : to become hoarse < *hóyagita* to make the voice hoarse by speaking >

ya·gla \ya-glá\ *va* : to bite off, as a dog does the fat from entrails — **yagla·gla** *va red* : to bite off repeatedly

ya·gla·he·ya \ya-glá-he-ya\ *adv* : explaining < ~ *ia* to set in order, to lay open, explain >

ya·gla·kin·yan \ya-glá-k̇iŋ-yaŋ\ *va* bla·glakinyan [fr *glakinyan* transversely] : to go across in one's speech, to contradict one's self, to tell what is false

ya·gla·pi·s'e \ya-glá-pi-s'e\ *adv* : fluently, plainly < ~ *oyaka* to tell about it plainly >

ya·glo·ka \ya·gló-ka\ *va* bla·gloka : to put out of place by means of the teeth

ya·gmi \ya-gmí\ *va* : to clear off, to bite, graze off as cows do grass

ya·gmi·ca \ya-gmí-ca\ *v* bla·gmica : to catch by the hair, using the mouth

ya·gmi·gma \ya-gmí-gma\ *va* bla·gmigma : to make round with the mouth

ya·gmi·pi s'e \ya-gmí-pi s'e\ *adv* : rounded off, as a bunch of grass or weeds whose tops have been bitten off

ya·gmi·yan·yan \ya-gmí-yaŋ-yaŋ\ *va* bla·gmiyanyan : to roll in the mouth and perhaps with the mouth

ya·gmun \ya-gmúŋ\ *v* : to twist *e.g.* thread with the mouth and hand

ya·gna \ya-gná\ *va* : to drop something from the mouth while breaking it, as does a horse when eating a cob of corn, to shake off *e.g.* fruit with the mouth – R

ya·gna·yan \ya-gná-yaŋ\ *va* : to miss something partly with the mouth in attempting to catch, *fig* to tell a falsehood – R

ya·gnu·ni \ya-gnú-ni\ *va* bla·gnuni [fr *gnuni* to wander or to be lost] : to cause to wander in the wind by talking to, to confuse

ya·go \ya-ġó\ *va* bla·go : to make a mark with the teeth

ya·gob \ya-ġō'b\ *va contrac of* yagopa : to gobble < ~ *iyeya* to cause to draw in one's breath noisely, ~ *yatkan* to sip *e.g.* water or other liquid noisesomely >

ya·go·pa \ya-ġó-ṗa\ *va* bla·gopa : to suck, to draw in one's breath with a noise, to sip making noise trying to get the remnants of a fluid, as once did the old *pejuta wicaša* medicine man, or to make feel proud by talking – *Syn* YATITAN

ya·gu·gu·ga·pi can *or* **yamnumnugapi** \ya-ġú-ġu-ġa-pi caŋ\ *n* : the American nettle, the hackberry or sugar berry tree, celtis occidentalis, the nettle family – WE #227

ya·gu·ka \ya-ġú-k̇a\ *va* bla·guka : to strain *e.g.* one's neck by biting something

ya·gwa \ya-gwá\ *va* bla·gwa : to shell with the mouth or to bite off – R Bl

ya·gwe·za \ya-gwé-za\ *va* bla·gweza : to bite and make rough

ya·ha·ha·la \ya-há-ha-la\ *va* bla·hahala : to persuade, to shake or move with the mouth, to move one in his purpose by talking to — **yahaha·yela** *va* bla·hahayela : to shake in one's purpose, to move by talking to

ya·ha·i·ye·ya \ya-há-i-ye-ya\ *va* : to throw down or turn aside with the mouth – *Syn* YACEG IYEYA R Bl

ya·han \ya-háŋ\ *vn* ma·yáhan : to prick or stick or run into one, as a splinter, thorn *etc.* < *Yunkan wicaša wanjila unkcela wan ~ keyapi* And then they said a cactus stuck the man. >

ya·hinl \ya-híŋl\ *va contrac of* yahinta : to eat all up < ~ *iyeya* to devour >

ya·hin·ta \ya-híŋ-ṫa\ *va* bla·hinta : to devour, eat all up, to brush away with the mouth

ya·ho·gi·lya \ya-hó-ġi-lya\ *adv* : hoarsely

ya·ho·gi·ta \ya-hó-ġi-ta\ *vn* : to become roarse from much singing

ya·ho·ho \ya-hó-ho\ *va* bla·hoho : to shake or make loose with the mouth — **yahoho·ya** *adv* : shaking with the mouth

ya·ho·lya \ya-hó-lya\ *va* yaho·lwa·ya [fr *yahota* inhale] : to cause to inhale and thus cough

ya·ho·mni \ya-hó-mni\ *va* : to be converted or to convert someone else, for which it is said *winyan ša* red or Indian women are well known; to make one change his views, to turn one round by arguments — *vn* : to believe anything at once and go to talking as old women might do

ya·ho·mni·pi·ca·šni·yan \ya-hó-mni-ṗi-ca-šni-yaŋ\ *adv* : unchangeably < ~ *canzeka* constantly angry > – B.H.89.7

ya·ho·ta \ya-hō'-ṫa\ *v* bla·hota : to inhale, to draw in with the breath, *e.g.* cold air, dust, water into the wrong pipe and thus to cough, to smoke and thus cough, having inhaled, *etc.* — **yahote** \ya-hó-ṫe\ *n* : inhalation

ya·ho·ton \ya-hó-toŋ\ *va* bla·hoton [fr *hoton* to cry out] : to bite and cry out

ya·hun·huns \ya-húŋ-huŋs\ *va contrac of* yahunhunza : to shake with the mouth

ya·hun·hun·za \ya-húŋ-huŋ-za\ *va* bla·hunhunza : to shake with the mouth, to shake ones resolution by talking to

ya·ȟab \ya-ȟáb\ *v contrac of* yaȟapa : to frighten off < ~ *iyeya* to scare away *e.g.* game by talking >

ya·ȟa·pa \ya-ȟá-ṗa\ *v* bla·ȟapa : to frighten or scare up *e.g.* game by talking

ya·hci \ya-ȟcí\ *va* bla-hci : to tear out a little piece with the teeth — **yahci·hci** *v red* : to tear out pieces with the teeth

ya·ȟeb \ya-ȟéb\ *v contrac of* yaȟepa : to drink up < ~ *iyeya* to drink up at once >

ya·ȟe·bȟe·pa \ya-ȟé-bȟe-pa\ *v red of* yaȟepa : to drink

\a\ f<u>a</u>ther \e\ th<u>e</u>y \i\ mach<u>i</u>ne \o\ sm<u>o</u>ke \u\ l<u>u</u>nar \an, aŋ\ bl<u>anc</u> Fr. \in, iŋ\ <u>in</u>k \on, oŋ, un, uŋ\ s<u>oo</u>n, c<u>on</u>fier Fr. \c\ <u>ch</u>air \ġ\ ma<u>ch</u>en Ger. \j\ fu<u>s</u>ion \clusters: bl, gn, kp, hšl, etc...\ <u>b</u>ᵉlo ... said with a slight vowel
See more in the Introduction, Guide to Pronunciation

to empty

ya·he·pa \ya-hé-pa\ *va* bla·hepa : to drink, to empty *e.g.* water *etc.* < *Yunkan (tatanka) opi ca he pizi kin blahepa* And then I drank up the gall of the buffalo bull that was shot. >

ya·he·yal \ya-hé-yal\ *v contrac* bla·heyata : to reject in speaking, put aside with the mouth < ~ *iyeya* to reject abruptly when speaking >

ya·he·ya·ta \ya-he-ya-ta\ *v* bla·heyata : in speaking to reject, put aside with the mouth

ya·hla \ya-hlá\ *va* bla·hla : to make rattle with the mouth

ya·hla·gan \ya-hlá-ġaŋ\ *va* bla·hlagan : to enlarge with the mouth

ya·hla·hla \ya-hlá-hla\ *v red of* yahla : to make rattle by mouth

ya·hlal \ya-hlál\ *v contrac of* yahlata : to speak gasping for life < ~ *ia* to speak as one does who is starving to death >

ya·hla·ta \ya-hlá-ta\ *v* bla·hlata : to speak as one dying

ya·hla·ya \ya-hlá-ya\ *va* bla·hlaya : *fig* to tell a lie, to bite or peel off the skin or rind of anything with the teeth - R Bl

ya·hle·ca \ya-hlé-ca\ *va* bla·hleca : to tear with the mouth a part of something, as a piece from a newspaper — **yahle·hleca** *v red* : to tear out things — **yahlel** *va contrac* : to tear from < ~ *iyeya* to rip from >

ya·hlog \ya-hlóg\ *v contrac* bla·hloka [fr *yahloka* to bite a hole in] : to bite open < ~ *iyeya* to gnaw at a hole, *Papa blahloka owakihi šni. Hitunkala kin wak'in hiyeye cin mahel* ~ I was unable to bite open the dried meat. The mouse bit a hole to carry in the whole load. > - *Syn* YAS'AKA

ya·hmin \ya-hmíŋ\ *va* bla·hmin : to distort, to crook or turn aside with the mouth — **yahmin·yan** *adv* : turning aside with the mouth < ~ *egnaka* turning to lay something down >

ya·hmun \ya-hmúŋ\ *v* : to make a humming or rattling noise with the mouth < *Yahmuns'e yatapi* They ate as though humming. >

ya·hmun·hmun·he·la *or* **yahmunhmunhla** \ya-hmúŋ-hmuŋ-he-la\ *v red* bla·hmunhumhela : to lick and lap noisely as one sucks dissolving a piece of hard candy in his mouth

ya·hpa \ya-hpá\ *va* : to pull something with the mouth so as to make it come down, as a dog jumping at a piece of beef; to throw anything down with the mouth — **ya-hpa·hpa** *v red* : to be throwing down with the mouth - R

ya·hpan \ya-hpáŋ\ *va* bla·hpan : to moisten or soak in the mouth, to dissolve in the mouth *e.g.* pills — **ya-hpan·hpan** *v red* : bla·hpanhpan : to soften with the mouth *e.g.* a quill or sinew (thread)

ya·hpe·ya \ya-hpe-ya\ *va* yahpe·wa·ya : to cause to throw down with the mouth

ya·hpu \ya-hpú\ *va* bla·hpu : to bite off in little pieces *e.g.* of pine gum, to bite off off something sticking on another — **blahpu·hpu** *v red* bla·hpuhpu : to bite off what is sticky or sticking

ya·htag \ya-htág\ *v contrac of* yahtaka : to bite to hold something — **yahta·gkiya** \ya-htá-gki-ya\ *va* yahta-gwakiya : to cause to bite anything — **yahta·gya** *va* yahta·gwa·ya : to cause to bite — *adv* : biting

ya·hta·ka \ya-htá-ka\ *va* bla·htaka : to bite, to take a hold of with the mouth < *Capunka mayahtaka* A mosquito bit me. >

ya·hu·ga \ya-hú-ġa\ *va* bla·huga : to bite into, to crush or crack something as a nut with the teeth, to chew — **yahuga·pi** *n* : peanuts, nuts *i.e.* because they are cracked with the teeth

ya·hu·gna·ga \ya-hú-gna-ġa\ *va* bla·hugnaga [fr *hugnaga* to be consumed, burt up] : to speak evil of, to destroy one's character, as if one were being consumed or as if one's character were burnt up

ya·huh \ya-húh\ *v contrac of* yahuga : to bite or chew < ~ *iyeya* to crush or crack suddenly > — **yahu·hkiya** *va* yahu·hwa·kiya : to cause to bite into or to crush — **yahu·huga** *va red of* yahuga : to crack open - D.70

ya·hu·hya \ya-hú-hya\ *va* yahu·hwa·ya : to cause to crush with the teeth

ya·hun·lhun·ta \ya-húŋ-lhuŋ-ta\ *v red of* yahunta : to draw through the mouth as a treatment for sinews

ya·hun·ta \ya-húŋ-ta\ *va* bla·hunta : to draw through the mouth to make pliable, as sinews for sewing and bark for tying

ya·hwa \ya-hwá\ *va* bla·hwa : to make sleepy by talking to

ya ·hwu \ya-hwú\ *vn* : to make a crunching noise as in chewing snow or ice

ya·h'a·kpa \ya-h'á-kpa\ *va* bla·h'akpa : to bite and make rough

ya·h'an·hi·ke \ya-h'aŋ-hi-ke\ *v* : to eat quite slowly

ya·h'an·hi·ya \ya-h'aŋ-hi-ya\ *adv* [fr *h'anhi* to advance rather leisurely] : making slow by talking to

ya·h'i·ya·ya \ya-h'í-ya-ya\ *v* bla·h'iyaya : to be awkward with the mouth as in speaking *etc.*

ya·h'u \ya-h'ú\ *va* bla·h'u : to peel off *e.g.* a rind or hull with the teeth, or a piece of skin with the mouth *etc.*

ya·i \yaí'\ *interj of* doubt and surprise when something funny has been stated : Oh no!, That can't be true! - Note: this is a word girls alone seem to use

ya·i·gnu·ni \ya-í-gnu-ni\ *va* : to confuse by interrupting *etc.* - Bl

ya·i·ha \ya-í-ha\ *v* bla·iha [fr *iha* to laugh at, make fun of] : to make laugh by talking to

ya·i·je·na \ya-í-je-na\ *v* [fr *ijena* mixed, of a variety] : to speak confusedly

ya·i·kce·ya \ya-í-kce-ya\ *va* bla·i·kceya [fr *ikceya* commonly] : to speak of as worth little - WE B.H.291.20

ya·i·ki·yuta \ya-í-ki-yu-ta\ *va* : to taste drinking - B.H. 265.20

ya·i·kpi·ska i·hpe·ya \ya-í-kpi-ska i-hpè-ya\ *v* [fr *ikpi* belly + *ska* white + *ihpeya* throw down] : to make turn over on the back as a dog by speaking to or biting

ya·i·le \ya-í-le\ *va* bla·ile [fr *ile* to burn] : to make blaze by blowing with the mouth

ya·i·na·hni \ya-í-na-hni\ *va* bla·inahni [fr *inahni* to hurry] : to make haste, hurry by speaking to — **yainahni-ya** *adv* : hastening by speaking to

ya·i·nil \ya-í-nil\ *va contrac of* yainila : to put to silence by speaking to < ~ *iyeya* to cause to be silent, ~ *ehpeya* to put to silence by argument >

ya·i·ni·la \ya-í-ni-la\ *va* bla·inila [fr *inila* to be silent] : to put to silence by speaking to

ya·in·ce·šni \ya-íŋ-ce-šni\ *v* bla·incešni : to be unable to eat up anything given, to leave over much - *Syn* YAOWIŠNI Bl

ya·i·o·ya·ya *or* **yaiyowa** \ya-í-o-ya-ya\ *va* bla·iyoya [fr *iyoya* to yawn, gape] : to make yawn by speaking to

ya·i·pa·weh i·ye·ya \ya-í-pa-weh i-yè-ya\ *v* : to work a fraud, to represent something different from what it is

ya·i·šte·ca \ya-í-šte-ca\ *va* bla·išteca [fr *išteca* to be ashamed] : to make ashamed by speaking to — **yaište·lya** *va* : to shame one by speaking to — *adv* : making ashamed by speaking to

ya·i·to·kan \ya-í-to-kaŋ\ *va* bla·itokan : to reject, put aside

ya·i·yo·wa \ya-í-yo-wa\ *va* bla·iyowa [fr *iyowa* or *iyoya* to yawn] : to make yawn by speaking - Cf iyoya

ya·i·yo·wa·ja \ya-í-yo-wa-ja\ *va* bla·iyowaja [fr *iyowaja* concerned in, near to] : to speak to the point, to speak of as near — **yaiyowaja·šni** *va* bla·iyowajašni : to speak beside the point

ya·i·yo·was \ya-í-yo-was\ *va contrac of* yaiyowaza : to make echo < ~ *iyeya* to cause an echo >

ya·i·yo·waš \ya-í-yo-waš\ *va contrac of* yaiyowaja : to speak to the point < ~ *ie šni* He does not speak to the point. >

ya·i·yo·wa·za \ya-í-yo-wa-za\ *va* bla·iyowaza : to make echo by speaking — *n* : an echo

ya·i·yo·yag i·ye·ya \ya-í-yo-yag i-yè-ya\ *v* : to make sad by speaking to - *Syn* YAALOS R Bl

ya·i·yo·ya·ka \ya-í-yo-ya-k̇a\ *va* [fr *iyoyaka* to be offended] : to make sad by speaking to

ya·ja·ja \ya-já-ja\ *va* : to lick or wash with the mouth, as does a cat

ya·ja·ta \ya-já-ta\ *va* : to seduce one, to persuade to give up one's good resolutions - WE

ya·jib \ya-jíb\ *va contrac of* yajipa : to bite or sting < ~ *iyeya* to pinch with the teeth, to bite as does a mosquito> — **yaji·bjipa** \ya-jí-bji-ṗa\ *v red of* yajipa : to bite or pinch with the teeth — **yaji·byela** *adv* : nibbling < ~ *yahtaka* to chew something very small with the incisors, the front teeth > - Bl

ya·ji·ca \ya-jí-ca\ *v* : to speak of one as rich - *See* iglajica

ya·jin·ca \ya-jíŋ-ca\ *va* bla·jinca : to snuff up the nose < *canli* ~ to take snuff >

ya·ji·pa \ya-jí-ṗa\ *va* bla·jipa : to bite or to pinch with the teeth, to bite as do bugs or mosquitos, to sting as do wasps

ya·jo \ya-jó\ *va* bla·jo : to blow on a musical instrument, to play on a fife or flute < *Šiyotanka yajo* The big grouse honks. > — **yajo·jo** \ya-jō'-jo\ *v red* bla·jojo : to play a tune on a musical instrument — **yajo·kiya** \ya-jó-k̇i-ya\ *va* yajo·wa·kiya : to cause to blow on an instrument

ya·jo·pi hu \ya-jó-pi hu\ *n* : the hemlock water parsnip, sium cicutaefolium, the parsley family - Note: the stems are streaked with purple if it is hemlock; the roots are used for medicine to treat the stomach; the fleshy roots of the poison hemlock contain a deadly poison; children use the stems for whistles — **yajo-pi hu cik'ala** *n* : the small water hemlock - BT #128

ya·jo·ya \ya-jó-ya\ *va* yajo·wa·ya : to make one blow a fife or flute

ya·ju·ju \ya-jú-ju\ *va* bla·juju : to tear down or tear to pieces with the mouth, *fig* to refute or demolish an argument

ya·jun \ya-júŋ\ *v* bla·jun : to uproot, pull up by the roots with the mouth as birds do corn < *Ašakagleyela peji to yajunpelo* The blue grass was pulled up by the roots in spots here and there. >

ya·ka \ya-k̇á\ *va* bla·ka : to split with the mouth, as the feather end of a quill

ya·kab \ya-k̇áb\ *va contrac of* yakapa : to catch in the mouth something tossed < ~ *iyeya* to make catch in the mouth >

ya·ka·ka \ya-k̇á-k̇a\ *va* : to champ, as does a horse its bit

ya·ka·ki·ja \ya-k̇á-k̇i-ja\ *va* bla·kakija [fr *kakija* to suffer] : to make suffer by scolding or by biting

ya·kan·ye·la \ya-k̇áŋ-ye-la\ *v* : to speak of as near, *i.e.* not talking loud - M

ya·ka·pa \ya-k̇á-ṗa\ *va* bla·kapa : to catch in the mouth anything that is tossed

ya·ka·tin \ya-k̇á-ṫiŋ\ *va* bla·katin : to straighten or bend out straight with the mouth

ya·ka·tin·tin \ya-k̇á-ṫiŋ-ṫiŋ\ *va* : to criticise, to set right, to straighten by talking < *Tokša nihu yakatintinpi kte* Soon your leg bone will be set right, as is said when one says or does many things wrong. Similarly: *Tokša niyásminpi kte* Soon your bones will be eaten bare. > - Bl

ya·ka·wa \ya-k̇á-wa\ *va* bla·kawa : to open or push back anything with the mouth

ya·kca \ya-kc̣á\ *va* bla·kca : to untie with the mouth, to disentangle

ya·kel \ya-k̇el\ *adv suff* - < *yus'oyakel* : *yus'o* exhausted + *yakel* in a way > - Cf ya *suff*

ya·ki·pa·ja \ya-k̇í-ṗa-ja\ *va* bla·kipaja : to double or fold up with the mouth so as to make the ends meet — **yakipaš** \ya-k̇í-ṗaš\ *va contrac of* yakipaja : to double up < ~ *iyeya* to make fold up >

ya·ki·pe·han \ya-k̇í-ṗe-haŋ\ *va* bla·kipehan [fr *pehan* to fold up] : to double or fold up with the mouth, so as to make ends meet - *Syn* YAKIPAJA

ya·ki·pu·ski·ca \ya-k̇í-ṗu-ski-ca\ *va* bla·kipuskica : to press close together with the mouth — **yakipuski·lya** *adv* : putting close together with the mouth

ya·kis \ya-k̇ís\ *va* : to make creak with the teeth < ~ *iyeya* to make a sharp creaking sound with the teeth >

ya·ki·ski·za \ya-k̇í-ski-za\ *v red of* yakiza : to gnash, make a grating sound with the teeth

ya·ki·ye·la \ya-k̇í-ye-la\ *v* : to speak of as near in place or time - Note: *yakanyela* refers to near in place only — **yakiyela·kel** \ya-k̇í-ye-la-kel\ *adv* : near

ya·ki·za \ya-k̇í-za\ *va* bla·kiza : to gnash the teeth, to make a grating or creaking noise with the teeth

ya·kog \ya-kóg\ *va contrac of* yakoka : to rattle the teeth < ~ *iyeya* suddenly to chatter the teeth >

ya·ko·ka \ya-kó-k̇a\ *va* bla·koka : to gnash or chatter or rattle the teeth

ya·ko·ke·la \ya-kó-k̇e-la\ *va* bla·kokela [fr *kokela* to make noise rattling things] : to make active by talking to one

ya·ko·ki·pa \ya-kō'-k̇i-pa\ *va* bla·kokipa [fr *kokipa* to fear] : to make afraid by talking to

ya·ko·kog \ya-kó-kog\ *va red contrac of* yakoka : to chatter the teeth — **yakoko·gya** *va* yakoko·gwa·ya : to cause to make a chattering with the teeth — *adv* : chattering

ya·ko·ko·ka \ya-kó-ko-k̇a\ *va* bla·kokoka [fr *yakoka* to rattle with the teeth] : to rattle the teeth, to chatter or gnash the teeth

ya·ko·na·tke \ya-k̇ó-na-tke\ *adv* : with high words < ~ *makuwapi* They are after me with high words, as is said by one who does not get a chance to defend himself and his case because others always counter-attack with high-

---

\a\ father \e\ they \i\ machine \o\ smoke \u\ lunar \an, aŋ\ blanc Fr. \in, iŋ\ ink \on, oŋ, un, uŋ\ soon, confier Fr. \c\ chair \ǧ\ machen Ger. \j\ fusion \clusters: bl, gn, kp, hšl, etc...\ b^elo ... said with a slight vowel
See more in the Introduction, Guide to Pronunciation

sounding words. Thus similarly : *Yawankal makuwapi, kul k'u šni maktepi* They are after me with highfalutin words, they kill me, not giving a chance to an underdog. > – Bl

ya·kon·pi \ya-k̇óŋ-pi\ *v defect* [fr perhaps *yanka* to be] : they are – Note: the word is Dakota

ya·kon·ta *or* **yakunta** \ya-k̇óŋ-ṫa\ *va* : to wear out partly with the mouth a rope or strap *etc., i.e.* making it thinner and less strong – BD

ya·ko·pe·gla \ya-kó-ṗe-gla\ *va* bla·kopegla [fr *kopegla* to be in fear] : to make afraid by talking to

ya·kpa \ya-k̇ṗá\ *va* bla·kpa : to bite out or through — *adj* : hard of hearing on account of noise < *Noge mayákpa* I am hard of hearing. > — **yakpa·kpa** *v red* : to bite frequently

ya·kpan \ya-k̇ṗáŋ\ *va* bla·kpan : to chew fine, to masticate — **yakpan·kpan** *v red* : to chew much — **yakpan·yan** *adv* : chewing fine

ya·kpi \ya-k̇ṗí\ *va* bla·kpi : to crack with the teeth, *e.g.* lice — **yakpi·kpi** *v red* : to crack with the teeth

ya·kpu·kpa \ya-k̇ṗú-k̇ṗa\ *va* bla·kpukpa : to bite in small pieces, to crumble with the teeth

ya·ksa \ya-ksá\ *va* bla·ksa : to bite off *e.g.* a stick — **yaksa·ksa** *v red* bla·ksaksa : to bite off often — **yaksaksa·yakel** *adv* : biting off

ya·ksa·pa \ya-ksá-ṗa\ *va* bla·ksapa : to make wise by talking to

ya·ksa·ya \ya-ksá-ya\ *va* yaksa·wa·ya : to cause to bite off — *adv* : biting off

ya·kša \ya-kšá\ *va* bla·kša : to bend up with the mouth — **yakša·kša** *v red* : to bend up by mouth — **yakša·la** *va* bla·kšala : to bend up somewhat with the mouth

ya·kšan \ya-kšáŋ\ *va* bla·kšan : to bend by mouth — **yakšan·kšan** *v red* bla·kšankšan : to bend or curl up

ya·kši·ja \ya-kší-ja\ *va* : to double up with the teeth — **yakši·kšija** *v red* : to fold up with the teeth — **yakšiš** *va contrac of* yakšija : to double up < ~ *iyeya* to make fold up >

ya·ktan \ya-ktáŋ\ *va* bla·ktan : to bend with the mouth — **yaktan·ktan** *v red* : to bend in several places with the mouth — **yaktan·yan** *va* yaktan·wa·ya : to cause to bend with the mouth — *adv* : bending with the mouth

ya·ku·ka \ya-kú-ka\ *va* bla·kuke : to destroy with the teeth, to bite to pieces

ya·kun·tkun·ta \ya-k̇úŋ-tkuŋ-ṫa\ *va* bla·kuntkunta : to bite notches in

ya·k'e *or* **šunkmanitu tanka** \ya-k'é\ *n* : a wolf

ya·k'e·ga \ya-k'é-ġa\ *va* bla·k'ega : to make a grating noise with the teeth — **yak'eh** *va contrac* : to make a grating noise < ~ *iyeya* to be grating one's teeth > — **yak'e·hk'ega** *v red* : to make much grating the teeth

ya·k'eš \ya-k'éš\ *va contrac of* yak'eza : to make smooth with the teeth < ~ *iyeya* to cause to make smooth > — **yak'e·sk'eza** *v red* : to make many smooth

ya·k'e·za \ya-k'é-za\ *va* bla·k'eza : to make smooth with the teeth and making a grating noise doing so

ya·k'o·ga \ya-k'ȯ́-ġa\ *va* bla·k'oga : to bite or gnaw off *e.g.* something hard < *Hitunkala wan taku yak'ogahan ca nah'on* He heard a mouse that was gnawing at something. > — **yak'oh** *va contrac* : to gnaw at < ~ *iyeya* to cause gnawing > — **yak'o·hk'oga** *v red* : to be doing gnawing

ya·k'os \ya-k'ós\ *va contrac of* yak'oza : to make smooth < ~ *iyeya* to make smooth > — **yak'o·sk'oza** *v red* : to make smooth

ya·k'o·za \ya-k'ó-za\ *va* bla·k'oza : to make smooth with the mouth, to crop, to eat all off smooth, *i.e.* the grass

yal \yal\ *prep contrac in compos* : in, at, to, by < *cajeyata* when *contrac* becomes *cajeyal, i.e.* in the name of >

ya·le·ble·pa \ya-lé-ble-pa\ *va* : to bite notches in – R Bl

ya·le·ca·kca·la \ya-lé-ca-kca-la\ *va* bla·lecakcala [fr *lecakcala* new] : to speak of as new or near perhaps – *Syn* YAAŠKAŠKALA WE

ya·le·ca·la \ya-lé-ca-la\ *va* bla·lecala [fr *lecala* lately] : to speak of as near in time

ya·le·han·yang \ya-lé-haŋ-yaŋg\ *va* [fr *lehanyank* away, apart] : to speak of as away somewhere else < ~ *iyeya* to make speak of as away > – Bl

ya·lus i·cu \ya-lús i-cù\ *v* yalus i·wa·cu : to draw in the smoke of one's pipe through the mouth

ya·lus ya·tkan \ya-lús ya-tkàŋ\ *v* : to sip in – Bl

ya·lu·za·han \ya-lú-za-haŋ\ *va* bla·luzahan : to call swift < *Nakun le, i.e.* a played-out horse, *šunšunla ikpi ska k'eyaš ~ iyececa yelo* And also this played-out horse is still a match for him to call fast a white bellied mule. > – Bl

ya·ma \ya-má\ *va* bla·ma : to gnaw, bite off *e.g.* a thread sticking out of a coat *etc.*

ya·ma·he e·ya·ya \ya-má-he è-ya-ya\ *va* : to snatch with the mouth as a dog does < *Yamahe iwacu, iyewaya* I found it, and took it snatching it with the mouth. *Tuwa mini hiyo i ca wamnita wan mini mahetanhan yamahe ewicayaya keyapi* They stated some whale that came for water took them along snatching them from in the water. *Ito, miš eya waniya na yamahe eciyayin kta eya* Come now, he said, I too breathe and will snatch you away. > – B.H.127.1

ya·ma·he·li·ye·ya \ya-má-he-li-ye-ya\ *va* yamaheliye·wa·ya : to push into the mouth

ya·me·ca \ya-mé-ca\ *va* bla·meca : to graw, to chew < ~ *yo* Set to chewing, *i.e.* eat all you can, there is much on hand. > – Bl

ya·mi·ma \ya-mí-ma\ *va* bla·mima : to make round *e.g.* a wheel with the mouth

ya·mna \ya-mná\ *va* bla·mna 1 : to rip with the mouth, as a dog or horse might do to one's coat 2 : *fig perhaps* to gain, to win over by talking, to acquire by talking or in any other way with the mouth – R Bl

ya·mna·ki·ya \ya-mná-k̇i-ya\ *va* yamna·wa·kiya 1 : to cause to gain by talking *etc.* 2 : to cause to rip – R

ya·mna·yan \ya-mná-yaŋ\ *va* yamna·wa·yan : to cause to rip as a dog by making it go after somebody

[1]**ya·mni** \ya-mní\ *v* 2nd *pers singl of* mni : you laid up to dry

[2]**ya·mni** \yá-mni\ *adj num card* : three

ya·mni·ga \ya-mní-ġa\ *va* bla·mniga : to make shrink by biting, as some big bite of food through chewing – *Syn* YAPIŠITKA

ya·mni·ki·ya \yá-mni-k̇i-ya\ *adv* : in three different ways or places < ~ *wai* I went to three different places. >

ya·mni·la \yá-mni-la\ *adv* : only three

ya·mni·mni \yá-mni-mni\ *adv red* : by threes < ~ *manipi* They walked in threes. *Witka ~ icupi* They each received three eggs. >

ya·mni·ye·ya \ya-mní-ye-ya\ *va* yamniye·wa·ya : to turn or change the course or plan of one by speaking to or with – Bl

ya·mnu·mnu·ga \ya-mnú-mnu-ġa\ *va* bla·mnumnuga : to crunch, crush, grind, champ, or make noise with the teeth as in eating

ya·mnu·mnu·ga i·ye·ce·ca \ya-mnú-mnu-ġa i-yè-ce-ca\ *n* : the great ragweed, the horseweed, bitterweed *etc.*, ambrosia trifida, the composite family, and otherwise called *canhlogan panšpanjela* - Note: its seeds are medicinal - B #48

ya·mnu·mnu·ga·pi \ya-mnú-mnu-ġa-pi\ *n* : black pepper

ya·mnu·mnu·ga·pi can *or* **yagugugapi can** \ya-mnú-mnu-ġa-pi caŋ\ *n* : the hackberry tree, so called because animals crunch its berries

ya·na·jin \ya-ná-jiŋ\ *va* bla·najin [fr *najin* to stand] : to cause to stand by speaking

ya·nang \ya-náŋg\ *va* : to make one jerk sideways *etc.* suddenly by biting, as a bee does a person, or as one horse another < ~ *iyeya* suddenly to jerk sideways > - Bl

yan \yaŋ\ *suff* for *adv* and *part; causa suff* for *v*

yan·ka \yaŋ-ḱá\ *vn* manká nanka unyankapi : to be, or to sit < *el* ~ to be at home > - D.96 note 3

ya·o·ci·kpa·ni \ya-ó-ci-kṗa-ni\ *va* bla·ocikpani [fr *ocikpani* unequal in length] : to make unequal with the mouth

ya·o·ci·pte·ca \ya-ó-ci-pte-ca\ *va* bla·ocipteca : to count less, make less, to underestimate — **yaociptel** *va contrac* : to underestimate — **yaocipte·lya** *adv* : speaking of as less or unequal — **yaocipte·tu** *va* bla-ociptetu : to count less — **yaociptetu·ya** \ya-ó-ci-pṫe-ṫu-ya\ *adv* : speaking of as less, as unequal — **yaociptetuya·kel** \ya-ó-ci-pṫe-ṫu-ya-ḱel\ *adv* : speaking as unequal - R Bl

ya·o·gla·pšun \ya-ó-gla-pšuŋ\ *v* : to turn over or twist with the mouthholding *e.g.* a pipe stem while turning the bowl < ~ *ihpeya* to leave twisted, loose > — **yaoglapšunyan** *adv* [fr *oglapšunyan* turning loose] : turning over with the mouth < ~ *iyeya* to make turn or loosen >

ya·o·gmus \ya-ó-gmus\ *adv* [fr *ogmus* shut or closed] : with mouth shut < ~ *s'e ia* to talk with the mouth full >

ya·o·gwa \ya-ó-gwa\ *v* : to speak stiffly, mouthing one's words < *Lila s'e eyi ye laogwu welo* You mouth your words, please say them as well as you can, *i.e.* doing the way you sip *e.g.* hot soup. >

ya·o·ha \ya-ó-ha\ *va* : to make fall over with the mouth - *Syn* YACEG IYEYA, YAHA IYEYA Bl

ya·o·hin·yan·ze \ya-ó-hiŋ-yaŋ-ze\ *v* bla·ohinyanze : to persuade one to give up by representing the thing as bad

ya·o·hlo·ka \ya-ó-ȟlo-ka\ *va* : to bite a hole in

ya·o·hmin \ya-ó-ȟmiŋ\ *v* bla·ohmin : to hint or insinuate, to say anything sideways < ~ *iyeya* to hint at >

ya·o·hpa \ya-ó-ȟṗa\ *va* bla·ohpa : to bite into

ya·o·h'an·ko \ya-ó-ȟ'aŋ-ḱo\ *va* bla·oh'anko [fr *oh'anko* to be quick at] : to hasten one by speaking to

ya·o·ki·ni·han \ya-ó-ḱi-ni-haŋ\ *va* bla·okinihan [fr *okinihan* to select for praise] : to praise, to honor with the mouth - R Bl

ya·o·ksa \ya-ō'-ksa\ *v* bla·oksa : to bite through — **yaoksa·ksa** *v red* : to bite through much

ya·o·ktan \ya-ó-kṫaŋ\ *va* : to bend in with the mouth — **yaoktan·yan** *adv* : bending with the mouth

ya·o·l'o·ta·ke *or* **wayaol'otake** \ya-ó-l'o-ta-ke\ *v* : to eat slowly to make a small ration last long

ya·o·ni·han \ya-ō'-ni-haŋ\ *va* bla·onihan : to praise or honor one — **yaonihan·yan** *adv* : praising

ya·on·ši·ya·kel \ya-óŋ-ši-ya-kel *adv* : speaking meekly < *Pála ~ eyapi* Little Nose is said to speak meekly. > - Bl

ya·o·po \ya-ó-po\ *va* : to compress by biting

ya·o·pon \ya-ó-ṗoŋ\ *v* bla·opon : to spread *e.g.* news by telling it; *lit* to bite off and blow away, as flowers < ~ *iyeya* to make spread *e.g.* news more and more and to exaggerate > - *Syn* AKAHAYA R Bl

ya·o·šlog i·ye·ya \ya-ó-šlog i-yè-ya\ *v* : to swallow something inadvertently that one should not, *e.g.* to swallow one's toothpick

ya·o·ta \ya-ō'-ṫa\ *va* bla-ota : to multiply, to speak of as many

ya·o·tan'·in \ya-ō'-taŋ-iŋ\ *va* bla·otan'in [fr *otan'in* to be visible] : to proclaim, make manifest — **yaotan'in·yan** *adv* : declaring

ya·o·te·hi·ka \ya-ó-ṫe-ȟi-ḱa\ *va* bla·otehika [fr *otehika* trying, difficult] : to make difficult with the mouth, to speak of as difficult < *Nitunkašila kin taku tob yaotehikapi tka* ... Four things were spoken of as difficult for your grandfather, but ... >

ya·o·t'ins \ya-ō'-t'iŋs\ *va contrac of* yaot'inza : to get something caught between teeth < ~ *iyeya* to cause to get something caught between teeth >

ya·o·t'in·za \ya-ó-t'iŋ-za\ *va* : to get something as meat into a hollow tooth or between teeth, to press in tight with the mouth < *Talo blaot'inza* I got a piece of fresh meat between my teeth. > - R

ya·o·win·ga \ya-ó-wiŋ-ġa\ *va* bla·owinga : to bite or pull round with the teeth, as in the making of moccasins — **yaowinh** *va* : to bite or pull with the teeth < ~ *iyeya* to bite and pull with the teeth > — **yaowin·hwinga** *v red* : to pull biting with the teeth

ya·o·wi·šni \ya-ó-wi-šni\ *v* bla·owišni : to be unable to eat up everything given, to leave overmuch - Bl

ya·pa \ya-pá\ *va* bla-pa : to bite, to take in the mouth *e.g.* a pipe in smoking or in the *wapiyapi* conjuring; to hold in the mouth as a dog does a bone < *Wašin wan ~ kagli ške* They say it came home holding in its mouth a piece of fat. *Toeyaš blapin kta* But first I shall take a bite, as they say taking a few puffs on the pipe in a hurry. > - BlW

ya·pan·pan \ya-páŋ-paŋ\ *va* bla·panpan : to make limber or pliable by biting, as in making moccasins — **yapanpan·la** *va* bla·panpanla [fr *panpanla* soft, as a skin treated] : to make soft with the mouth

ya·pa·pa \ya-pá-pa\ *va red of* yapá : to take in the mouth, as in smoking a pipe - Bl

ya·pce·ce·la \ya-pcé-ce-la\ *va* : to speak of as short, to shorten with the mouth

ya·pe \ya-ṗé\ *va* bla·pe : to bite sharp — **yape·šni** *va* bla·pešni : to make dull *e.g.* the teeth by biting

ya·pe·han \ya-ṗé-haŋ\ *v* bla·pehan [fr *pehan* to fold and put away] : to fold up with the teeth

ya·pe·mni \ya-ṗé-mni\ *va* bla·pemni [fr *pemni* twisted, crooked, warped] : to twist, turn, of make crooked with the mouth — **yapemni·yan** *adv* : twisting with the teeth

ya·pe·sto \ya-ṗé-sṫo\ *va* bla·pesto : to make sharp-pointed with the teeth

[1]**ya·pi** \ya-ṗí\ *va* bla·pi [fr *pi* possible, able, good] : to declare good

[2]**ya·pi** \yá-ṗi\ *v* 3[rd] *pers pl of* ya : They go

\a\ father \e\ they \i\ machine \o\ smoke \u\ lunar \an, aŋ\ blanc Fr. \in, iŋ\ ink \on, oŋ, un, uŋ\ soon, confier Fr. \c\ chair \ġ\ machen Ger. \j\ fusion \clusters: bl, gn, kp, hšl, etc...\ b[e]lo ... said with a slight vowel
See more in the Introduction, Guide to Pronunciation

ya·pin·ja \ya-ṗíŋ-ja\ *va* bla·pinja [fr *pinja* destitute of hair] : to pull out long hairs from a skin with the teeth
ya·pin·spin·ze·ce *or* **wayapinspinzece** \ya·ṗíŋ-ṡpiŋ-ze-ce\ *v red of* yapinzece *obsol* : to eat very slowly because the ration is small - Bl
ya·pis \ya-ṗís\ *v contrac of* yapiza : to squeak with the mouth < ~ *yatkan* to drink slowly, sip, to drink in draughts, to drink carefully as though something bad was floating on the fluid > - Bl
ya·pi·ši·tka \ya-ṗí-ši-tka\ *va* : to reduce in size by chewing, as a big lump of food < ~ *wota* to eat with repugnance and therefore little >
ya·pi·za \ya-ṗí-za\ *v* bla·piza [fr *piza* to creak] : to make squeak with the mouth — **yapiza·pi** *n* : a mouth organ
ya·pi·za·pi hu \ya-ṗi-za-pi hu\ *n* : wild spikenard, false Solomon's seal, smilacina racemosa, the lily family - Note: it is so called because it was used to produce musical tones with its leaves. It is also called *zuzeca tawote hu iyececa* BT SH #1
ya·pi·za·pi i·ye·ce·ca \ya-pí-za-pi i-yè-ce-ca\ *n* : the sand lily, the little white lily, mayflower, lencocrinum montanum, the lily family; the prairie false dandelion, agoseris cuspidata, the composite family - BT #276 Bl #278
ya·po \ya-ṗó\ *va* bla·po : to compress by biting
ya·pob \ya-pŏ'b\ *va contrac of* yapopa : to make pop < ~ *iyeya* to cause a sudden pop >
ya·po·lpol \ya-ṗó-lṗol\ *v red contrac* yapolpota : to tear in pieces with the mouth - B.H.114.2
ya·po·lpo·ta \ya-ṗó-lṗo-ṫa\ *v red of* yapota : to tear to pieces by mouth
ya·po·pa \ya-pŏ'-ṗa\ *va* bla·popa [fr *popa* to burst] : to make pop, as in blowing a leaf
ya·po·ta \ya-ṗŏ'-ṫa\ *va* bla-pota [fr *pota* worn out] : to tear in pieces with the mouth
ya·po·wa·ya \ya-pó-wa-ya\ *v* bla·powaya [fr *powaya* to blow and roughen *e.g.* fur] : to blow up or make rough, as nap or fur
ya·ptag \ya-pśág\ *va contrac of* yapsaka : to bite < ~ *iyeya* to bite *e.g.* a thread suddenly, quickly in two > — **yapsa·gya** \ya-psā'-gya\ *va* yapsa·gwa·ya : to cause to bite in two — *adv* : biting off *e.g.* cords
ya·psa·ka \ya-psá-ḱa\ *va* bla·psaka [fr *psaka* broken] : to tear a thing as a string in two with the mouth — **yapsake šni eye** *v* : to speak of something again and again - *Syn* HOKUNPE ŠNI EYE LC
ya·psa·psa·ka \ya-psá-psa-ḱa\ *v red of* yapsaka : to tear often in two
ya·psi·ca \ya-psí-ca\ *va* bla-psica [fr *psica* jumping] : to cause to skip or jumb by biting — **yapsil** *va contrac* : to make skip or jump < ~ *iyeya* to cause to jump by biting at >
ya·pson *or* **yapsun** \ya-psóŋ\ *va* : to turn over and spill with the mouth — **yapson·pson** *v red* : to turn over and over with the mouth
ya·pša \ya-pšá\ *vn* 2nd *pers singl* wa·pša [fr *pša* to sneeze] : You sneeze - Note: someone is said to sneeze when a lover mentions the name of his beloved. *Tuwa cajemayate laka mayapša yelo* Of course someone mentioning my name I sneezed - Bl
ya·pšun \ya-pšúŋ\ *va* bla·pšun : to case off or shed *e.g.* teeth, to pull and break with the mouth - Cf yupšun BD
ya·pta \ya-pṫá\ *va* bla·pta : to bite off around
ya·ptan·yan \ya-ptáŋ-yaŋ\ *va* bla·ptanyan [fr *ptanyan* excited, agitated] : to turn over with the mouth
ya·pte·ce·la \ya-pté-ce-la\ *va* bla·ptecela [fr *ptecela* small] : to bite off short, to shorten with the mouth
ya·ptu·ga \ya-ptú-ǧa\ *va* bla·ptuga : to bite off a piece < *Hi waglaptuga* I bit off a piece of my tooth. > — **yaptuh** \ya-ptúȟ\ *v contrac* : to bite off a piece < ~ *nape el okignake* It bit off a piece depositing it in its hand, *i.e.* the mouse had bitten it off into his palm. > - BD D.97
ya·ptu·ja \ya-pṫú-ja\ *va* bla·ptuja [fr *ptuja* cracked, split] : to crack of split with the mouth — **yaptu·ptuja** *v red* : to crack or split much — **yaptuš** *v contrac* : to split < ~ *iyeya* to make crack or split > — **yaptu·šya** *va* yaptu·šwa·ya : to cause to crack with the mouth
ya·pu·za \ya-ṗú-za\ *v* : to dry with the mouth - Bl
ya·p'o \ya-p'ó\ *v* bla·p'o [fr *p'o* fog, mist] : to make steam with the mouth, as in breathing in cold air
ya·san \ya-sáŋ\ *va* bla·san : to whiten with the mouth — **ya·san·ka** \ya-sáŋ-ka\ *v* : to make white
ya·ska \ya-ská\ *va* bla·ska : to make clean with the mouth
ya·skan \ya-sḱáŋ\ *va* bla·skan : to let dissolve in one's mouth
ya·ska·pa \ya-sḱá-ṗa\ *va* bla·skapa : to make a noise as in kissing
ya·skeb \ya-sḱéb\ *va contrac* bla·skepa : to drink up < ~ *iyeya* to have one drink up >
ya·ski·ca \ya-sḱí-ca\ *va* bla·skica : to suck or lick *e.g.* bones, to press with the mouth — **yakil** *v contrac* : to lick < ~ *iyeya* to have lick or suck >
ya·ski·ska \ya-sḱí-sḱa\ *v* : to make teeth marks, to press together with the teeth
ya·ski·ski·ta \ya-sḱí-sḱi-ṫa\ *va* bla·skiskita : to bite and make soft *e.g.* a hard string
ya·sku \ya-sḱú\ *va* bla·sku : to bite off or peel off with the teeth, as the skin from an apple — **yasku·sku** *v red* : to peel, bite off
ya·sku·ya \ya-sḱú-ya\ *v* bla·skuya : to act by a certain noise as though something is sweet, and so by chewing it induce children to take it
ya·sla \ya-slá\ *va* : to grease with the mouth, as a dog does anything
ya·sle·ca \ya-slé-ca\ *va* bla·sleca : to split with the teeth — **yaslel** *va contrac* : to split < ~ *iyeya* to split with one's teeth suddenly, quickly > — **yasle·sleca** *v red* : to split repeatedly
ya·sli \ya-slí\ *va* bla·sli : to bite and press out, as grease from a bag
ya·sli·tka \ya·slí·tḱa\ *va* bla·slitka [fr Dakota *sdidka*, Lakota *slitka* tapering, rounded off] : to taper with the teeth, to make knobbed
ya·slo·han \ya-slŏ'-haŋ\ *va* bla·slohan [fr *slohan* to crawl] : to drag along with the mouth, as does a dog — **ya·slohan·han** *part* and *v red* : to drag along < ~ *inyanka* to run dragging something in its mouth > - R
ya·slul \ya-slŭ'l\ *va contrac of* yasluta : to pull out with the teeth < ~ *icu* to take and extract it with the teeth >
ya·slu·ta \ya-slū'-ṫa\ *va* bla·sluta : to pull out with the mouth
ya·smin \ya-smíŋ\ *va* : to bite off *e.g.* meat from a bone, to gnaw, to eat the meat off, to make bare with the mouth — **yasmin·kiya** \ya-smíŋ-ki-ya\ *va* yasmin·wa·kiya : to cause to eat off, make bare with the teeth — **yasmin·smin** *v red* : to eat at, gnaw — **yasmin·yan** *va* : to cause to make bare with the teeth — **ya·sminyan·yan** *va red* : to make bare with the mouth, to eat off close and smooth - D.14 R

ya·sna \ya-sná\ *va* bla·sna : to cause to ring with the mouth, to ravel, raddle, break up with the teeth

ya·sni \ya-sní\ *va* bla·sni [fr *sni* cold] : to blow, cool by blowing

ya·sol \ya-sŏ'l\ *va contrac of* yasota : to eat all up < ~ *iyeya* to consume > —**yaso·lya** *adv* : eating up

ya·so·ta \ya-sŏ'-ṫa\ *va* bla·sota [fr *sota* to use up] : to use up with the mouth

ya·spa·ya \ya-spá-ya\ *va* bla·spaya [fr *spaya* to be wet] : to wet with the mouth

ya·stan·ka \ya-sṫáŋ-ǩa\ *va* bla·stanka : to moisten with the mouth

ya·sto \ya-sṫŏ'\ *va* bla·sto : to lick smooth *e.g.* the hair —**yasto·sto** \ya-sṫó-sṫo\ *v red* : to lick and groom *e.g.* the hair

ya·su \ya-sú\ *va* bla·su : to judge, decree, make right by speaking < *wayasu wicaša* a man serving as judge, *Na wanna mini mahel ayapi kta yasupi* It was settled that they should go about in water. >

ya·su·ksu·ta \ya-sú-ksu-ṫa\ *v red of* yasuta : to establish or make firm by word of mouth

ya·su·pi \ya-sú-pi\ *n* : condemnation

ya·su·pi·šni·yan \ya-sú-pi-šni-yaŋ\ *adv* : with a hearing < ~ *kasaksaka* to scourge one without a hearing > - B.H. 300.14, 303.4

ya·su·ta \ya-sú-ṫa\ *va* bla·suta [fr *suta* to make firm, to establish] : to establish, make firm by word of mouth

ya·su·ya \ya-sú-ya\ *adv* : judging, condemning

ya·swa \ya-swá\ *va* bla·swa : to pick in pieces with the teeth —**yaswa·ka** *va* : to make fringed by trying to bite off a piece from a tough piece of meat and so getting much —**yaswa·swa** *v red* : to keep at biting off

ya·swu \ya-swú\ *v* : to take in small bead-like pieces with the mouth < ~ *s'e yuta* to eat as if in taking, biting off, *swula* in small pieces >

ya·sya·zan \ya·syá-zaŋ\ *v red* ma·yasyazan [fr *yazan* to feel pain] : to be lame or sick all over, as from hard labor

ya·s'a \ya-s'á\ *va* bla·s'a [fr *s'a* frequency of action] : to make a ringing or roaring noise in speaking

ya·s'a·ka \ya-s'á-ka\ *v* bla·s'aka : to be unable to bite of chew *e.g.* tough meat - Bl

ya·s'o·s'o \ya-s'ó-s'o\ *vn* : to be stiff from the cold < *Nakpa kin mayas'os'ohcelo* My ears are stiff from the cold. > - Bl

ya·šab \ya-šáb\ *va contrac of* yašapa : to soil by mouth < ~ *iyeya* to cause to soil >

ya·ša·pa \ya-šá-ṗa\ *va* bla·šapa [fr *šapa* blackened, dirty] : to soil with the mouth

ya·šib \ya-šíb\ *va of* yašipa : to bite off close < ~ *iyeya* to have bite off close >

ya·ši·ca \ya-ší-ca\ *va* bla·šica [fr *šica* bad, evil] : to curse, make bad with the mouth, to speak evil of

ya·ši·gla \ya-ší-gla\ *va* bla·šigla : to insult by talking

ya·ši·htin \ya-ší-ȟtiŋ\ *va* bla·šihtin : to make feeble by biting

ya·šil \ya-šíl\ *va contrac of* yašica : to talk badly < ~ *ši* to give orders with bad talk > - B.H.69.3

ya·ši·lpi·ca·šni \ya-ší-lṗi-ca-šni\ *adj* : faultless, blameless - P

ya·ši·pa \ya-ší-ṗa\ *va* bla·šipa : to crop, bite off close as an animal does branches or twigs of a tree

ya·ška \ya-šká\ *vn* bla·ška : to untie with the mouth

ya·škan·škan \ya-škáŋ-škaŋ\ *va* bla·škanškan : to make move about by talking to

ya·ške·pa *or* **yaskepa** \ya-šké-ṗa\ *va emph* : to suck dry, as a calf does all the milk - Bl KE

ya·ške·ške·ke \ya-šké-ške-ke\ *v* : to untie with the teeth - WHL

ya·ške·ške·pa \ya-šké-ške-ṗa\ *v* : to suck and spit out - KE

ya·ški·ca \ya-škí-ca\ *va* bla·škica : to chew, press with the teeth or mouth < *canli* ~ to chew tobacco > —**ya·škil** *va contrac* : to chew < *canli* ~ *un* to be chewing tobacco >

ya·ški·pa \ya-škí-ṗa\ *v* : to bite and make full up - R

ya·ški·ška \ya-škí-ška\ *va* bla·škiška : to make difficulty, raise objections, to disarrange by talking to, make rough with the mouth

ya·škob \ya-škób\ *va of* yaškopa : to make crooked by mouth < ~ *iyeya* to make twisted by mouth >

ya·ško·kpa \ya-škó-kṗa\ *va* bla·škokpa : to bite out and make concave

ya·ško·pa \ya-škó-ṗa\ *va* bla·škokpa : to make crooked or twisting with the mouth

ya·šla \ya·šlá\ *va* : to have been grazed, cropped, to bite or graze off, to make bare as cattle do a pasture - Cf wayašla —**yašla·šla** *v red* : to be cropped short —**yašla·ya** *adv* : grazing off

ya·šla·ye·gnag \ya-šlá-ye-gnag\ *v* : to put away talking about what one said - Cf yaášlaya

ya·šlog \ya-šlóg\ *va contrac of* yašloka : to pull out < ~ *iyeya* to make pull out with the teeth > —**yašlo·gya** *adv* : pulling out with the teeth

ya·šlo·i·a \ya-šló-i-a\ *v* yašloi·wa·ya : to speak with much saliva in the mouth, to make a whistling or hissing sound with the teeth in talking

ya·šlo·ka \ya-šlŏ'-ǩa\ *va* bla·šloka : to pull out with the teeth *e.g.* a cork

ya·šlo s'e \ya-šló s'e\ *v* : to whistle as the upland plover, not producing any sound but as they do when they both go and come back again - CO

ya·šlul \ya-šlúl\ *va contrac of* yašluta : to let slip from the mouth < ~ *iyeya* to cause to let slip > —**yašlu·šluta** \ya-šlú-šlu-ṫa\ *va* bla·šlu-šluta : to make slippery with the mouth

ya·šlu·ta \ya-šlú-ṫa\ *va* bla·šluta : to let slip from the mouth, to have the teeth slip off from anything

ya·šna \ya-šná\ *va* bla·šna : to blunder in speaking, to miss while trying to catch with the mouth —**yašna·kiya** \ya-šná-ǩi-ya\ *va* yašna·wa·kiya : to cause to miss with the mouth —**yašna·šna** *v red* : to stammer, falter

ya·šna·ya \ya-šná-ya\ *va* yašna·wa·ya : to make stammer, to cause to miss with the mouth

ya·šna·yan \ya-šná-yaŋ\ *adv* : blundering with the mouth, mistaking

ya·šni·ja \ya-šní-ja\ *va* bla·šnija : to make wither by biting —**yašniš** \ya-šníš\ *va contrac of* yašnija : to wither by biting < ~ *iyeya* to cause to wither >

ya·šni·šni·ja \ya-šní-šni-ja\ *v red* : to shrink at biting < *Cante mayašnišnijelo heon howahpahelo* My heart withered at its biting me so I was coughing. > - Bl

ya·šo·ško·pa \ya-šó-ško-ṗa\ *va red of* yaškopa : to make crooked, twisting with the mouth repeatedly

ya·špa \ya-špá\ *va* bla·špa : to bite off a piece, to break off a piece with the mouth

---

ya·špa·pi \ya-šṗá-ṗi\ *part* : bitten off, as is said of the moon when it has commenced waning

ya·špa·špa \ya-šṗá-špa\ *v red* bla·špašpa [fr *yašpa* to bite off a piece] : to bite off a piece in different places

ya·špe·ki·ya *or* **yašpeya** \ya-šṗé-k̇i-ya\ *va* yašpe·wa·kiya : to cause to bite off a piece

ya·špi \ya-šṗí\ *va* : to pick off, as do birds berries

ya·špu \ya-šṗú\ *va* bla·špu : to bite off anything stuck on — **ya·špu·špu** *v red* : to bite in pieces *e.g.* candy, ice *etc.* — **yašpu·ya** *v* ma·yašpuya : to bite as do lice, to make itch or to itch < *Išta mayašpuya* My eyes itch. > — *adj* : itching — **yašpuya·ya** *v red* : to itch < *Iš eya waci kinica na sicuha kin yašpuyaye* He too tried to dance when the sole of his foot itched. > - D.43

ya·štan \ya-šṫáŋ\ *v* bla·štan : to finish speaking, to keep quiet < *oyak* ~ to cease speaking >

ya·šu·ja \ya-šŭ'-ja\ *va* bla·šuja : to crush, as a dog does a bone, to mash up — **yašuš** *va contrac* : to crush or mash up < ~ *iyeya* to make crush suddenly >

ya·šu·ška \ya-šú-šk̇a\ *va* ma·yašuška [perhaps fr *šuška* slow, worthless] : to belittle, not to appreciate a favor < *Mayašuška* He did not appreciate what I did for him. > - Note: the word may be *archaic* - BD

ya·šu·šu·ja \ya-šú-šu-ja\ *v red of* yašuja : to crush or mash

ya·š'a·ka \ya-š'á-k̇a\ *va* bla-š'aka : to make no impression with the mouth < *Ia* ~ to make no impression in speaking >

ya·š'in·š'in \ya-š'íŋ-š'iŋ\ *v* bla·š'inšin : to strain in the peak of copulation

[1]ya·ta \ya-tá\ *va* bla·ta : to chew, to try by taste

[2]ya·ta \yā'-ṫa\ *prep in compos* : at, by, to < *ȟeyata* at a mountain > — *v* 2nd *pers singl of* yuta : You ate — *v* : to speak, utter < *cajeyata* to mention one's name, *wicašyatanpi* one spoken of as a chief, a leading man >

ya·ta·kin \ya-tá-k̇iŋ\ *va* : to make lean with the mouth, as a dog in trying to pull down a stick — **yatakin·yan** *adv* : making lean with the mouth

ya·ta·ku \ya-ṫá-k̇u\ *va* bla·taku [fr *taku* something] : to make something of in relating, make up a story about

ya·ta·ku·ka \ya-ṫá-k̇u-k̇a\ *va* bla·takuka : to overestimate, to make something of nothing in narration

ya·ta·ku·ni·šni \ya-ṫá-k̇u-ni-šni\ *va* bla·takunišni : to speak contemptuously of, to destroy by mouth, *fig* to eat up — **yatakunšni·yan** *adv* : destroying by mouth

ya·ta·ku·šni \ya-ṫá-k̇u-šni\ *va* bla·takušni : to speak of as being of no value, to depreciate

ya·ta·ku·ya \ya-ṫá-k̇u-ya\ *adv* : speaking of as if it were something < ~ *oyaka* to tell something as if it were something great or important >

[1]ya·tan \ya-ṫáŋ\ *va* bla·tan : to praise, speak well of

[2]ya·tan \ya-ṫáŋ\ *va* bla·tan : to touch with the mouth, to pull as in sucking

ya·tan'·in \ya-ṫáŋ-iŋ\ *va* bla·tan'in [fr *tan'in* to be visible] : to declare anything, make manifest or clear — **yatan'in·yan** *adv* : manifestly - B.H.137.21

ya·tan·ka \ya-ṫáŋ-k̇a\ *va* bla·tanka : to speak of as large or great - Pb.41

ya·tan·ni \ya-ṫáŋ-ni\ *va* bla·tanni : to wear out or make old with the mouth

ya·tan·tan \ya-ṫaŋ-ṫaŋ\ *v red* bla·tantan [fr *yatan* to praise] : to praise < *Ake oyate kin Wicahpi Hinhpaya yatantanpi* Again the people paid high praise to Fallen Star. > — **yatan·yan** *adv* : praising

ya·ta·ta \ya-tá-ta\ *v red* bla·tata [fr *yatá* to chew, try by taste] : to chew for a while < *Na pejuta wan* ~ *najin* He stood for a while chewing the medicine. > - D.257

ya·ta·wa·cin·hin·yan·za \ya-tá-wa-ciŋ-hiŋ-yaŋ-za\ *v* blatawacinhinyanza : to speak of one as a morose person, to make cross or surly by talking to

ya·teb \ya-ṫéb\ *va contrac of* yatepa : to bite or wear off with one's teeth < ~ *iyeya* to bite off short >

ya·te·han \ya-ṫé-haŋ\ *va* bla·tehan [fr *tehan* long in time] : to speak long, to speak of as long or as far in the future — **yatehan·han** *v red* : to speak on and on

ya·te·pa \ya-ṫé-ṗa\ *va* bla·tepa : to wear off with one's teeth, to bite off short, wear off, as the teeth

ya·ti·ca \ya-ṫí-ca\ *va* : to scrape away with the mouth *e.g.* snow

ya·ti·kti·tan \ya-ṫí-k̇ti-ṫaŋ\ *vt* bla·tiktitan : to draw breathing in, perhaps inhaling, repeatedly, to draw smoke as in smoking - D.103

ya·til \ya-ṫíl\ *va contrac of* yatica : to scrape away < ~ *iyeya* to make scrape away with the mouth >

ya·ti·ma·he·li·cu \ya-ṫí-ma-he-li-cu\ *va* yatimaheli·wa·cu : to call one into the house where one is

ya·ti·tan \ya-ṫí-ṫaŋ\ *va* bla·titan : to pull with the mouth, as a dog holding a bone under foot and pulling meat off — **yatitan·yan** *va* yatitan·wa·ya : to cause to pull with the teeth — *adv* : pulling with the teeth

ya·tkan \ya-ṫk̇áŋ\ *va* bla·tkan : to drink — **yatkan-ktan** *va red* : to guzzle, gulp < *Wakalyapi* ~ *k'el na wolwol wounglakapi kte lo* Let us talk when eating and while drinking coffee. > — **yatkan·yan** *adv* : drinking - Me

ya·tka·pa \ya-ṫk̇á-ṗa\ *va* bla·tkapa : to eat *e.g.* something that is viscid or sticks in the mouth

ya·tke·ki·ya \ya-ṫk̇í-k̇i-ya\ *va* yatke·wa·kiya : to cause to drink

ya·tku·ga \ya-ṫk̇ú-ġa\ *va* bla·tkuga : to pite or pull and break with the mouth

ya·tkuns \ya-ṫk̇úŋs\ *va contrac of* yatkunza : to bite off even < ~ *iyeya* to bite off even suddenly >

ya·tkun·tkun·ta \ya-ṫk̇úŋ-ṫkuŋ-ṫa\ *v* - *See* yakuntkunta

ya·tkun·za \ya-ṫk̇úŋ-za\ *va* bla·tkunza : to bite off even

ya·tku·tku·ga \ya-ṫk̇ú-ṫku-ġa\ *v red of* yatkuga : to bite and break with the mouth

ya·to·gto·gya *or* **yatogtog ia** \ya-tó-gto-gya\ *va* : to tell lies while narrating something

ya·to·gye \ya-tó-gye\ *adv* : telling differently < ~ *oyaka* to relate a thing differently >

ya·to·kan \ya-tó-kaŋ\ *va* bla·tokan : to put in another place with the mouth, to speak of as being in another place

ya·to·ke·ca \ya-tó-ke-ca\ *va* bla·tokeca [fr *tokeca* different] : to alter with the mouth, to speak of as different

ya·to·to \ya-ṫó-ṫo\ *va* bla·toto : to eat up, as a horse does grass < *pejuta wan* ~ to champ on the medicine. >

ya·tu·ka \ya-ṫú-k̇a\ *va* : to nibble off, spoil, as mice do on furs

ya·tu·tka \ya-ṫú-ṫk̇a\ *va* bla·tutka : to bite into little pieces

ya·t'a \ya-t'á\ *va* bla·t'a : to bite to death

ya·t'a·ga \ya-t'á-ġa\ *va* bla·t'aga : to make rough by biting

ya·t'ins \ya-t'íŋs\ *va contrac of* yat'inza : to affirm < ~ *oyaka* to speak firmly and with authority > — **yat'insya** *adv* : firmly < *Hena imanunga ca iyuha* ~ *ociciyakelo* I tell you for sure of all this that I be enlarged. > - Bl

ya·t'in·sya·kel \ya-t'íŋ-sya-kel\ *adv* : well and clearly < ~ *ia* to speak well, correctly, pronouncing the words well > - Bl

ya·t'in·za \ya-t'íŋ-za\ *va* bla·t'inza : to affirm, make firm with the mouth - Cf wicáka
ya·un·ca \ya-úŋ-ca\ *v* bla·unca : to ridicule with one's speech - Bl
ya·ung \ya-úŋg\ *va contrac of* yaunka : to fell using the mouth
ya·un·ka \ya-úŋ-ka\ *va* bla·unka : to throw down, pull down with the mouth, *e.g.* trees as beavers do
ya·wa \ya-wá\ *va* bla·wa : to read, say over, to count, to consider < *Tipi tonakeca yawa po* Count how many houses there are. *Tipi opawinge sam iyaye yawapi* They counted more than a hundred houses. *Le pejuta kin lila wakan yawapi* They considered this medicine very sacred. >
ya·wa·cin·hin·yan·za \ya-wá-ciŋ-hiŋ-yaŋ-za\ *v* : to make morose, ill-disposed and cross - *See* wayuwahinyanza
ya·wa·cin·ko \ya-wá-ciŋ-ko\ *va* bla·wacinko : to make angry by talking
ya·wa·cin·ton \ya-wá-ciŋ-toŋ\ *va* bla·wacinton : to instruct, make intelligent
ya·wa·hwa·ka \ya-wá-hwa-ka\ *va* bla·wahwaka : to make gentle, to pacify by talking kindly to
ya·wa·hwa·la \ya-wá-hwa-la\ *va* bla·wahwala : to make gentle by talking to, to soothe, to make one sleepy by talking
ya·wa·ja \ya-wá-ja\ *va* bla-waja : to make a noise with the mouth, to split fork-like with the mouth - *Syn* YAHÓTON WE
ya·wa·kan \ya-wá-kaŋ\ *va* bla·wakan : to consider *wakan*, or consider supernatural
ya·wan·kal \ya-wáŋ-kal\ *v* : to raise, elevate the voice < ~ *iyeya, yeya* to make one raise his voice, to send raising one's voice, ~ *makuwapi* They are after me with high-sounding arguments. > - *Syn* YAKONATKE Bl
ya·wa·pi·ca·šni \ya-wá-pi-ca-šni\ *adj* : innumerable — **yawapicašni·šniyan** *and* **yawapicašni·yan** *adv red* : numberless < *Šiyo cik'ala kin ~ mahpiya kin tan·inšniyan kinyan au* A countless number of quail came flying as the sky was lost from sight. > - B.H.50.2, 55.10
ya·was \ya-wás\ *va contrac of* yawaza : to gnaw, bite
ya·wa·ša·ka *or* **yawašaka·la** \ya-wá-ša-ka\ *v* bla·wašakala : to count cheap or easy, to underrate
ya·wa·šte \ya-wá-šte\ *va* bla·wašte : to bless, declare good
ya·wa·š'ag \ya-wá-š'ag\ *va of* yawaš'aka : to encourage — **yawaš'a·gya** *adv* : in a strenghtening manner
ya·wa·š'a·ka \ya-wá-š'a-ka\ *va* bla·waš'aka : to encourage, strengthen by talking to
ya·wa·š'a·ke·šni \ya-wá-š'a-ke-šni\ *va* bla·waš'akešni : to make weak by talking to < *Šunka kici ~ s'e ake lehanl wakinicahanpelo* They were disputing now again, like dogs quarrelling with one another, *i.e.* done quit quarrelling like fighting dogs. > - Bl
ya·wa·wa \ya-wá-wa\ *v red* [fr *yawa* to count] : to be easily counted, being distinctly separated < *Yawawapila s'e unpelo* They are very easily counted. *Yawawapila s'e wicoti* The camp was very easily counted, *i.e.* when the tents of a camp are rather scattered. > - *Syn* OIHPEHPEYA Bl
ya·wa·za \ya-wá-za\ *va* : to bite or gnaw, as a horse does wood, to bite in play as do horses or dogs
ya·wa·ze·ca \ya-wá-ze-ca\ *va* : to gnaw at, *fig* to annoy or pester by begging - P Bl
ya·we·ga \ya-wé-ġa\ *va* bla·wega : to break, crack a stick with the mouth, but not entirely off — **yaweh** \ya-wéh\ *va contrac* : to break by mouth < ~ *iyeya* to make crack with the mouth >
ya·we·hki·ya \ya-wé-hki-ya\ *va* yawe·hwa·kiya : to cause to break with the mouth
ya·we·hwe·ga \ya-wé-hwe-ġa\ *v red of* yawega : to break with the mouth — **yawe·hya** *va* yawe·hwa·ya : to cause to break with the mouth
ya·wi·ca \ya-wí-ca\ *va* bla·wica [fr *wica* a man] : to call a man, to call brave
ya·wi·ca·ka \ya-wí-ca-ka\ *v* bla·wicaka [fr *wicaka* speak the truth] : to speak of as true, to affirm to be true
ya·wi·ca·ke·ya s'e \ya-wí-ca-ke-ya s'e\ *adv* : deceptively, ironically < ~ *oyaka* to tell a thing not at it is, to make a statement of which the very reverse is true. >
ya·wi·ca·ke·ye·hci \ya-wí-ca-ke-ye-hci\ *adv* : making appear as true < ~ *oyaka* to tell under appearance of truth, *i.e.* to try to make a thing appear true by telling it as true >
ya·wi·ca·ša \ya-wí-ca-ša\ *va* bla·wicaša [fr *wicaša* man] : to call a man — **yawicaša·šni** *va* bla·wicašašni : to corrupt, to make one mischievous by talking to, to call bad or make bad by talking to - R
ya·wi·gnu·ni \ya-wí-gnu-ni\ *va* : to destroy with the mouth, to talk bad - R Bl
ya·wi·nu·hca·la \ya-wí-nu-hca-la\ *v* bla·winuhcala [fr *winuhcala* an old woman] : to call a woman, to speak of as a woman
ya·win·ja \ya-wíŋ-ja\ *va* bla·winja [fr *winja* bend] : to bend something with the teeth, as a fork in the mouth, to bend down with the teeth - R
ya·winš \ya-wíŋš\ *va contrac of* yawinja : to bend with the teeth < ~ *iyeya* to cause to bend > — **yawin·škiya** \ya-wíŋ-ški-ya\ *va* yawin·šwa·kiya : to cause to bend down with the mouth — **yawin·šwinja** *v red of* yawinja : to bend with the teeth
ya·win·yan \ya-wíŋ-yaŋ\ *va* bla·winyan [fr *winyan* a woman] : to call a woman, to speak to as a woman
ya·wi·ta·ya \ya-wí-ta-ya\ *va* bla·witaya [fr *witaya* together] : to collect together with the mouth
ya·wi·ya·kpa \ya-wí-ya-kpa\ *va* bla·wiyakpa : to interpret, to make shine with the mouth
ya·wo·sla \ya-wó-sla\ *v* [fr *wosla* upright] : to set up with the mouth
ya·ya *or* **yayaya** \yá-ya\ *adv* : undecided, bewildered < ~ *najin* to stand bewildered > - WE
ya·ya·la \ya-yá-la\ *adj* : pliant, limber, not stiff - *Syn* WINŠWINJA
ya·ya·ya *or* **yaya** \yá-ya-ya\ *adv* : bewildered, confused, undecided, stubborn < ~ *najin* to stand undecided, *Taku ociciyake cin namayah'on šni na ~ inayajin yelo* You stood up confused and when I said something to you you did not hear me. > - Sb Bl
ya·za·he s'e \ya-zá-he s'e\ *adv* : bead-like - *Syn* OWECINHAN Bl
ya·za·mni \ya-zá-mni\ *va* bla·zamni : to open or uncover with the mouth, *fig* to lay bare or expose by argument
ya·zan \ya-záŋ\ *vn* ma·yazan : to feel pain < *nata* ~ to have a headache > - Cf wayazan
ya·zan·gla \ya-záŋ-gla\ *vn* ma·yazangla *or perhaps* ya-

zan·wa·gla : to feel pain and be touchy about it, *i.e.* not wanting anybody to touch the suffering limb

ya·zan·hin·gla \ya-záŋ-hiŋ-gla\ *vn* : to become sick suddenly

ya·zan·ya \ya-záŋ-ya\ *va* yazan·wa·ya : to make one sick

ya·ze \ya-zé\ *va* bla·ze : to take out with the mouth from something, as food from a kettle the way a dog does, or a killed duck from a pond

ya·ze·ze \ya-zé-ze\ *va* : to make swing with the mouth

ya·zi·ca \ya-zí-ca\ *va* bla·zica : to stretch anything with the teeth — **yazil** \ya-zíl\ *va contrac* : to stretch with the teeth < ~ *iyeya* to cause to stretch > — **yazi·lya** *adv* : slowly drawing out < ~ *lowan* to sing slowly, drawling the notes > – NP

ya·zo·ka \ya-zō'-ka\ *va* : to draw or sip a fluid to see what it tastes like – Note: the word *yagopa* is a sucking of the honey from a blossom; whereas *azin* is a baby's sucking in nursing the breast

ya·zo·ka·pi hu \ya-zó-ka-pi hu\ *n* : the white-flowered gilia, gilia longiflora, the flox family – Note: when fresh the flowers appear a little purple – BT #83

ya·zon·ta *or* **yazunta** \ya-zóŋ-ta\ *va* : to flatter, adulate or blandish, to praise one who ought to be reproved

[1]**ye** \ye\ *pron 2nd pers in compos, ya + ki; e.g. ye·ksuya* fr *kiksuya* to remember, instead of *yaki·ksuya*

[2]**ye** \ye\ *partic* 1 : the word often follows at the close of a sentence to give *emph* to what is said; it is used by women, as is *yelo* by men; moreover, it seems that after a "u" sound the *y* is changed to *w* 2 : a sign for a precatory form of the *imper singl,* used by women and men, but chiefly by women < *Komakipe šni ye* (a woman speaker) Please do not fear me. *Ate, oyate kin onšiwicakila ye* (a man speaking) Father, I entreat you, take pity on them. > – B.H.78.12

ye·a·pe \ye-á-pe\ *va* yea·wa·pe : to wait for one, to come along – Bl

ye·ka·pin un \ye-ká-piŋ uŋ\ *v* : to linger – P

[1]**ye·ki·ya** \ye-kí-ya\ *va* ye·wa·kiya : to bet, stake anything – B.H.117.4

[2]**ye·ki·ya** \ye-ki-ya\ *va* [fr *ya* to go] : to send, cause to go, to drive, to extend to *e.g.* one's hand < *Icokab u; canke kute yekiyapi, na ake ataya ihunni* He came up front; and so they had him shoot it and a second time completely finish it off. >

ye·ki·ya·pi \ye-kí-ya-pi\ *n* : a bet, a gambling stake – *Syn* AHIGLE P Bl

ye·la \yé-la\ *suff* to *adj* makes them *adv* < *sab·yela* blackish, *to·yela* greenish, *hol·yela* grayish > – Note: as *adv* these forms tend to shift toward *adj* again

ye·la·ka *or* **yelakaš** \yé-la-ka\ \yé-la-kaš\ *adv* : indeed, truly; as, since, because < *Tokeške pte kin cepapi šni ~ wašin cola šna wawatelo ca awicaku po, eya ke* He pretty much said: Bring them back, for somehow the buffalo were not fat while he kept stabbing to death those without fat. *Toka ~ ecamon kin?* Indeed, why did I do that? *Hehe takoš, eya, wanikau ~ hehelo* Alas son-in-law, said he, because I brought you home you said that. *Taku icanliniyuha ~ , winiš'oš'okelo* You are one who is ready to work because you have what is needed. *Tokiyatan taakih'an wahi ~ s'ins'inyan wanamapce lo* Since I came from somewhere starving, I ate craning my neck. *Nišnala tokeca niglawa ~* Evidently you regard yourself as different, in a different class by yourself. > – Bl MS.144, 94 D.53 note 3 B.H.142.10, 1 85.6, 204.2, 235.19, 259.22, 272.7,8, 276.11,14

ye·le \ye-lé\ *partic emph* : It's a fact ... – Note: the word is used by women to indicate the real fact of the statement preceding, whereas men use *yelo*

ye·lo \ye-ló\ *partic emph* : It's a fact ... – Note: the word is used to terminate a statement with *emph* stressing the fact. Hence, often a brief pause precedes the *patic.* After a *pl* termination *pi,* the *ye* is often dropped and the *pi* become *pe* . *Hecel econpelo* Thus it is done. Cf *ye* above

ye·ma \ye-má\ *partic,* an *imper* form of *ye* and used by women < *T'a ~* May he die. > – B.H.43.26

yeš \yeš\ *conj contrac of* yeša : but, although < *Zintkala wan iye wipe yuha šni ~ cinca awicakikšija* Though he did not carry a weapon he it was who gathered in the chicks. *Tipi ocoza bluha ~ waniyetu cokanyan* Though it was mid-winter I had a warm house. *Lena cikciscipila ~ t'api šni yelo* Though these dear little ones were quite small they did not die. > – B.H.95.9

ye·ša *or* **yešan** *or* **eša** \ye-šá\ *conj* : although < *Wocin hi ca k'upi ~ woihayakel iyuha k'upi cin* Though he was given it when he arrived, he wanted to be given everything just for fun. *Ito ehaš tanyan wowak'u kte šni ~ , eya ke* He said: "Now then, on the other hand, I surely shall not be doing well giving her food." > — **yešaš** *conj emph* : although, though, even if < *Tuwé wankatuic'iya (iglawankatuya) ~ kul glicu kte* Though one make himself go high (make one's own go high), he will return down > – B.H.66.9, 194.15, 30.1 BT

ye·ši \ye-ší\ *va* ye·wa·ši : to send, command to go

ye·to *or* yo \ye-tó\ *partic imper* < *Ku ~* Come home. *Pazo ~ , to pazo* Show it to me, or Let me see it for a second. *Ito hinyanki ~* Well now, wait. > – B.H.20.26, 43.17

ye·ya \ye-yá\ *va* ye·wa·ya ye·un·yan·pi : to send, cause to go, to extend to < *Na wanna wawakan kin le yeyin kta* And now let him send this sacred arrow. >

ye·ye \ye-yé\ *v* : to be, continue, to last, perdure < *Hecel wanase kin paha kin tohan yeye kin* (as long as it lasts), *hehan ipahlalya aya, na kakel enape kin hecena ptaptaye wan opawinge wahecetu ca ayapya kulkul hpayapi* So as long as the buffalo hunt attack lasts, they continue in formation, and when they fled they kept in a herd of about a hundred with all falling down one after the other. *Na wakpala kin tohan yeye kin hehan aglagla wicoti na tipi kin oyasin akilececa na ošota šni* And as far as the creek extended there alongside it was an encampment, with all the houses the same and no smoke. >

yo \yo\ *partic,* sign of the *imper singl,* used by men – Cf wo Note: when there are two *imper* in one sentence (*e.g.* Go and see.) only the second one has the *yo* ; whereas the ending of the first is *in* instead of *a,* supposing the *v* does end in *a* . < *Iyayin na nape nupin el oyuspa yo* Go and grasp it in both hands. *Blihec'iyapi na tokel econ cišipi kin iyecel econ po* Keep yourselves busy and do as I gave you orders to do. *Paha skan kin hel akanl emaonpipi na ih'e omakšu po* There on the slope of the hill lay me carefully to rest and put a stone over me. >

Yo·ko·mi \Yo-kó-mi\ *np* : the name of a Zuni chief who was also associated with the Comanche tribe – Cf Hokomi or Okomi

[1]**yu** \yu\ *exclam* when a woman protesting scolds one : How can you do such a thing! < *Yu! tokinahanš taku otaka ca ekitan wamašipi kte hcin* How can you! Yes, they will employ me anyhow since many are the things to do. > – Note: the woman's *excĺam* in prefacing a reprimand is in a rather high pitched voice, but the same is

true of a declaration of disapproval

[2]**yu** \yu\ *pref* : – it expresses the idea of causation in some way not conveyed by *ka, pa, wa, wo, ya* . Thus: *yunajin* to cause to stand or to lift up. Sometimes it conveys the idea of pulling. As a *pref* to an *adj* or to a *n*, it forms *v* of them and means to make or cause to be. Thus: *yuwašte* to make good

yu·a·bla·ya \yu-á-bla-ya\ *va* blu·ablaya : to make level on, to spread something, as a rug, on level ground – B.H. 172.7

yu·a·gla·pšun·yan i·hpe·ya \yu-á-gla-pšuŋ-yaŋ i-ȟpè-ya\ *v* : to upset *e.g.* a kettle – Bl

yu·a·hwa·ye·la \yu-á-ȟwa-ye-la\ *v* : to cause gently < *Šunka yuinila miciyuza, šunka ~ miciyuza* He held a dog and kept it quiet for me; he held a dog for me and made it gentle. *Taku aškatuyela ~ hošimakaglipi* They arrived back lately with a sensitive message for me. >

yu·a·ja·ja \yu-á-ja-ja\ *va* blu·ajaja : to explain, make clear *e.g.* a doctrine – Hh

yu·a·ka·gal \yu-á-ka-ǧal\ *adv* : with arms out-stretched crosswise < ~ *otkeya* to crucify, ~ *okatan* to nail down with arms out-stretched > – MS.100 B.H.262.23 RT

yu·a·ka·hpa \yu-á-ka-ȟpa\ *v* [fr *akahpa* to cover up] : to cover, to conceal < ~ *icu* to draw anything over one, as a blanket turned down >

yu·a·kan \yu-ā'-ǩaŋ\ *v* [fr *akan* on, upon] : to cause to come up < ~ *hiyuya* to cause to come up, as a fish on a line, ~ *ehpeya* to cause to come up and be thrown back, as a fish >

yu·a·kanl i·cu \yu-á-ǩaŋl i-cù\ *v* : to pull up from on something, as from a hole < *Ehaš hogan ota yuakanl awicaupi* Indeed, many fish were brought and drawn up. *Nape ~ icupica šni yelo* A hand was not available to pull it out, *i.e.* it is very cold. > – Bl

yu·a·ka·za·mni \yu-á-ǩa-za-mni\ *va* blu·akazamni [fr *akazamni* to open upon one] : to open out, uncover <! *iyeya* to make open out, to uncover >

yu·a·ki·h'an \yu-á-ǩi-ȟ'aŋ\ *va* blu·akih'an [fr *akih'an* to starve, be without food] : to cause to starve

yu·a·ki·pab \yu-á-ǩi-ṗab\ *adv* [fr *akipab* divided, shared equally] : to separate, divide

yu·a·ki·pa·ja \yu-á-ǩi-ṗa-ja\ *va* blu·akipaja [fr *akipaja* to fold or double over] : to place across — **yuakipaš** *va contrac* : to cross each other, as in bows < ~ *icu* to tie in a bow-knot >

yu·a·ko·wa·pa \yu-á-ko-wa-pa\ *adv* : further on, beyond < ~ *egnakelo* He prolonged it. *Cunkaške ~ egnake* He moved the fence a little back. >

yu·a·la·pa \yu-á-la-ṗa\ *va* : to smooth off *e.g.* a rough road < *Ocanku t'aht'age kin hena yualapapi kte lo* Those rough roads should be smoothed. > – *Syn* PALÁPA B.H.172.8

yu·a·los \yu-á-los\ *v* : to scare < ~ *iyeya* to make one scared > – Bl

yu·a·lo·slo·za s'e i·y·e·ya \yu-á-lo-slo-za s'e i-yè-ya\ *va* : to injure one's feelings in any way

yu·a·o·kpa·ni \yu-á-o-kpa-ni\ *va* : to lessen, reduce, cut down – B.H.150.21

yu·a·o·pte·ca \yu-á-o-pte-ca\ *va* blu·aopteca : to make less — **yuao·ptel** \yu-á-o-ṗtel\ *va contrac* : to lessen < ~ *iyeya* to make less, as in making a price lower > — **yuaopte·tu** \yu-á-o-ṗte-ṫu\ *va* blu·aoptetu : to make less, lessen — **yuaoptetu·ya** *adv* : lessening – R Bl

yu·a·pa·ko \yu-á-ṗa-ǩo\ *va* blu·apako : to make crooked — **yuapako·ya** *adv* : making crooked, twisting

yu·a·sni \yu-á-sni\ *v* blu·asni : to quiet down, to soothen *e.g.* a person excited or sad — **yuasni·yan** *va* : to console – B.H.229.6

yu·a·ša·pa \yu-á-ša-ṗa\ *va* blu·ašapa [fr *ašapa* become black or dirty on] : to defile

yu·a·ška s'e \yu-á-ška s'e\ *adv* : near, nearby, in a sense < ~ *tan'inyan yunkelo* It seems to appear near, *e.g.* a hill – or even to be afar off, *tehantu.* > – Bl

yu·a·ška·yela \yu-á-ška-ye-la\ *va* blu·aškayela : to bring or make near – R Bl

yu·a·šla·ya \yu-á-šla-ya\ *va* blu·ašlaya : to expose, uncover, to reveal what one should not tell, *i.e.* secrets *etc* — **yuašlaye·la** *adv* : explaining, clearly, plainly < ~ *oyaka* to speak plainly > – B.H.60.7

yu·a·tan'·in \yu-á-taŋ-iŋ\ *v* : to manifest – B.H.213.9

yu·a·taš \yu-á-taš\ *va* : to absorb – P

yu·a·ta·ya \yu-á-ṫa-ya\ *va* : to cure, make whole or complete – B.H.232.4

yu·a·zi \yu-á-zi\ *va* blu·azi [fr Dakota *ázi* , the Lakota *áze* to run aground] : to run aground or pull ashore *e.g.* a boat

yu·bla·bla·ya e·gna·ka \yu-blá-bla-ya è-gna-ǩa\ *v* : to lay out and spread *e.g.* a blanket – Bl

yu·bla·ga \yu-blá-ǧa\ *va* : to spread out *e.g.* an umblella, or the toes, as of a duck < *Oiyohanzi ~ . Maga siha ~ po!* Spread out your goose toes! Open out your wagon umbrella. *i.e.* Use your brain, think! > — **yublah** *va contrac* : to spread out < *Maga siha ~ mankelo* I sat and spread out my goose feet, *fig* I am thinking. > – Bl

yu·bla·pi·se·kse \yu-blá-pi-se-kse\ *adv* : openly, distinctly < ~ *hinhpaye* Individually snow fell, as is said when snow falls in heavy flakes here and there. *Ehanna ~ wawakita* I saw things well when time was. > – Bl

yu·blas \yu-blás\ *va contrac of* yublaza : to burst open < ~ *iyeya* to make burst open suddenly, ~ *egnaka* to open out, as in dressing a cow > – D.247

yu·bla·ska \yu-blá-ska\ *va* blu·blaska : to make flat

yu·bla·ya \yu-blá-ya\ *va* blu·blaya : to unfold, open and spread out, to make level < *Na oyate najinpi etkiya, i.e. šina kpanyanpi kin, ~ pazo* She displayed it, *i.e.* a blanket when tanned, and people stood with it. *Šina wan yuha hinapa na ~ egnaka* She came out with the blanket and placed it unfolded. >

yu·bla·za \yu-blá-za\ *va* blu·blaza : to burst open

yu·ble·ble·ca \yu-blé-ble-ca\ *v red* : to burst open repeatedly

yu·ble·ca \yu-blé-ca\ *va* blu·bleca lu·bleca : to break to pieces or crush *e.g.* brittle ware by pressing with the hands — **yublel** *va contrac* : to crush by hand < ~ *iyeya* suddenly to smash > — **yuble·lkiya** *va* yuble·lwa·kiya : to cause to break to pieces

yu·ble·za \yu-blē'-za\ *va* blu·bleza : to make clear

yu·bli·he·ca \yu-blí-he-ca\ *va* blu·bliheca : to make active or lively, to activate

yu·blu \yu-blú\ *va* blu·blu : to pulverize, to plow, make mellow — **yublu·blu** *va red* blu·blublu : to plow thoroughly — **yublu·kiya** \yu-blú-ǩi-ya\ *va* yu-blu·wa·kiya : to cause to plow — **yublu·ya** *va* yu-blu·wa·ya : to cause to pulverize

---

\a\ father \e\ they \i\ machine \o\ smoke \u\ lunar \an, aŋ\ blanc Fr. \in, iŋ\ ink \on, oŋ, un, uŋ\ soon, confier Fr. \c\ chair \ġ\ machen Ger. \j\ fusion \clusters: bl, gn, kp, hšl, etc...\ b^{e}lo ... said with a slight vowel **See more in the Introduction, Guide to Pronunciation**

yu·bu \yu-bú\ *va* blu·bu : to make a drumming sound —**yu·bu·bu** *v red* : to drum —**yubu·ya** *adv* : in a manner of drumming

yu·cab \yu-cáb\ *v contrac of* yucapa : to make trot —**yuca·bcabkiya** \yu-cá-bca-bki-ya\ *v red* : to cause to trot —**yucabca·pa** \yu-cá-bca-ṗa\ *v red of* yucapa : to trot —**yuca·bkiya** *va* yuca·bwa·kiya [fr *yucapa* to trot] : to cause to trot —**yuca·bluzahan** *v* : to trot rapidly —*adj* : fast trotting, as a horse

yu·can \yu-cáŋ\ *va* blu·can : to sift, shake in a sieve; *fig* to be without, not to have < *Canli mayucan* I have no tobacco. > —**yucan·can** *va* blu·cancan : to make shake, in sifting

yu·can·la·sni \yu-cáŋ-la-sni\ *va* blu·canlasni [fr *cante* heart + *asni* to soothen, to quiet] : to quiet down, recover, to soothen - B.H.170.13, 255.21

yu·can·lwa·hte·šni \yu-cáŋ-lwa-ȟte-šni\ *va* blu·canlwahtešni : to make angry - Bl

yu·can·nal i·ye·ya \yu-cáŋ-nal i-yè-ya\ *v* : to push into the middle of a room *etc.* - R Bl

yu·can·pi·s'e \yu-cáŋ-ṗi-s'e\ *adv* : shivering < ~ *inajin* He stood up shivering. >

yu·can·te·wa·šte \yu-cáŋ-ṫe-wa-šte\ *va* : to cheer up - B.H.85.22

yu·can·to·gla \yu-cáŋ-ṫo-gla\ *v* blu·cantogla : to settle on going another, one's own, way; to be unwilling to change one's mind

yu·can·to·gna·gya \yu-cáŋ-ṫo-gna-gya\ *v* yucantogna·gwa·ya : to apply one's self wholeheartedly, to set one's mind directly toward the issue

yu·can·to·gna·ya \yu-cáŋ-ṫo-gna-ya\ *v* yucantogna·wa·ya : to circumvent, skirt, avoid; to compromise —*adv* : skirting the issue, avoiding something

yu·can·ze \yu-cáŋ-ze\ *v* : to cause to become angry, to make angry —**yucanze·ka** *va* blu·canzeka : to make angry - Bl

yu·ca·pa \yu-cá-ṗa\ *v* : to trot, as a horse - *Syn* IKACANCAN trotting

yu·ceh \yu-céȟ\ *v contrac* : to hold, as in holding a bucket < ~ *naunka* to gallop with the head (of the horse) drawn towards the breast >

yu·ce·ka \yu-ċé-ḳa\ *va* blu·ceka : to pull in vain, *i.e.* what cannot be pulled out, to make stagger - *Syn* YUTITAN —**yucekceka** \yu-ċé-ḳċe-ḳa\ *va* blu·cekceka : to make stagger

yu·ce·ya \yu-cé-ya\ *va* blu·ceya ma·yuceya : to make cry

yu·ci·k'a·la \yu-cí-k'a-la\ *va* blu·cik'ala : to make small or compress *e.g.* a coat that is too baggy —**yucik'a·yela** *adv* : in a small space, pressed together, compactly < *Wana el ~ el ahiyaye lo* Now there they, *i.e.* a crowd, passed by in a compact space. > - Bl

yu·cin·kta·kta \yu-cíŋ-kta-kta\ *va* blu·cinktakta [perhaps *lit* fr *yu* causing + *ceyin* to cry + *kta will* + *kta* would] : to make one cry or sob by catching him, a runaway; meaning: he will cry if I catch him!

yu·ci·sci·la \yu-cí-sci-la\ *va* blu·ciscila : to make small

yu·co·co \yu-ċō'-ċo\ *va* blu·coco : to make soft as mortar, *i.e.* by pouring in water

yu·co·ka \yu-có-ka\ *va* blu·coka : to empty, make empty

yu·co·kab \yu-có-ḳab\ *adv contrac of* cokapa : making centrally located < *Ošota yelo, wipipaha egle yo inš eša tiyopa kin ~ icu wo* It is filled with smoke, set the vent flaps or also take up the door at the center. > - BT

yu·co·ka·ka \yu·có-ka-ka\ *v red of* yucoka : to empty —**yucokaka·ya** *v* : to make empty, by setting all in order —*adv* : setting all in order < *Tipi wan tanka iticagi na timahel ~ egle* He set up a large tipi and he set the inside all in order, *i.e.* he erected it and arranged things attractively inside. > - D.15

yu·co·ka·la \yu-có-ka-la\ *va* : to keep free for work, *e.g.* a horse, by letting it rest -*Syn* ĖĊECOLA P

yu·co·na·la \yu-cō'-na-la\ *va* blu·conala : to make few, lessen in number of quantity - B.H.45.17

yu·co·sco·za \yu-có-sco-za\ *v red of* yucoza : to make comfortably warm *e.g.* a room

yu·co·ya \yu-có-ya\ *adv* : finished, well done < ~ *kagelo* He made it a fine finish. > - *Syn* WAKICOYAKEL R Bl

yu·co·za \yu-có-za\ *va* blu·coza [fr *coza* comfortably warm] : to make comfortably warm, as a room

yu·e·ce·ca \yu-é-ce-ca\ *va* blu·ececa : to start, make go or act the way it ought to, as one does in winding a train or cranking an automobile —**yuece·lya** *v* blu·ecelya : to make a thing as it ought to be, to make a correction in something —*adv* : rightly, correctly —**yuecelya·kel** *adv* : correctly, rightly - Bl

yu·e·ce·tu \yu-ē'-ce-ṫu\ *va* blu·ecetu [fr *ecetu* to be fulfilled, accomplished] **a** : to fulfill, to accomplish **b** : to correct a wrong statement < *gluecetu* to straighten *e.g.* one's house > —**yuecetu·ya** *va* yuecetu·wa·ya : to cause to fulfill —*adv* : fulfilling, making right

yu·e·ci·ya \yu-é-ci-ya\ *va* blu·eciya : to turn wrong side out *e.g.* a garment or a bag

yu·e·kta·šni *or* **yuektašniyan** \yu-é-kta-šni\ *v* : to do a thing in a wrong way < *Luektašniyanpi kin, wayahtanipi kta* When you do a thing in a wrong way, you might sin. > - *Syn* IPAWEH ECON

yu·ga \yu-ġá\ *va* blu·ga lu·ga un·yúga·pi : to husk *e.g.* corn

yu·gab \yu-ġă'b\ *va contrac of* yugapa : to strip off *e.g.* the skin < ~ *iyeya* to skin >

yu·ga·ga \yu·ga·ga\ *vn* : to display, spread or open out —*adv* : spread out, to open

yu·gal \yu-ġál\ *v contrac of* yugata : to lift a hand or arm out-stretched < ~ *iyeya* to raise one's arms, to stretch out one's arms upwards, ~ *najin, un.* ~ *yanka nape nupin on. Na wankalkiya ~ najin na hoyeya.* ~ *iwahoya* He stood his arms being outstretched. He sat with both his hands raised. And he stood with arms raised aloft and cried out. He gave a warning with arms outstretched. > - B.H.56.1, 163.8, 276.7

yu·ga·lga·ta \yu-ġa-lġa-ta\ *v red* [fr *yugata* to reach out one's arms] : to stretch out or raise the arms, as do babies *etc.*

yu·gal i·c'i·con·za \yu-ġál i-c'i-coŋ-za\ *v* : to promise under oath —**yuga·lki·ya** \yu-ġá-lḳi-ya\ *va* : to administer an oath, make one swear, saying: *Ho yugata yo* Well then, raise your hand to swear. > - P

yu·ga·lya \yu-ġá·lya\ *v* : to speak out to, to worship —**yugalya·pi** *n* : worship, worshipping

yu·gan \yu-ġáŋ\ *va* blu·gan : to open *e.g.* a door —**yugan·ganla** *va* : to make open or flimsy —**yugan ihpeya** \yu-ġáŋ i-ȟpè-ya\ *va* : to fling open, to uncover *e.g.* a sleeping person < *Yunkan tiyopa kin yugan ihpeyapi* And then the door was flung open. > - *Syn* YUZAMNI IHPEYA, AKAZAMNI IHPEYA

yu·gan·yan \yu-ġáŋ-yaŋ\ *va* yugan·wa·ya : to cause to open

yu·ga·pa \yu-ġá-ṗa\ *va* : to skin, to strip or pull off *e.g.* the skin from an animal < ~ *s'e mahingle lo, fig* It

was by the skin of my teeth. > - GA
yu·ga·ta \yu-ġá-ṫa\ *v* blu·gata : to swear an oath, to stretch out the hand and arm upwards < *wankatuya* ~ to reach out the hand upwards > - B.H.52.2
yu·ge \yu-ġé\ *va* blu·ge : to take out or remove with the hand — *n* : a part or portion, some < ~ *icu wo* Take a part. ~ *unyuhapi kte lo* Let us carry, or have, some. > - Note: the word is probably *archaic*
yu·ge·ge \yu-ġé-ġe\ *va* : to gather up in the hand, to take up by handfuls < ~ *icu* to take up by handfuls > - Bl
yu·ge·ki·ca·ga \yu-ġé-ḱi-ca-ġa\ *v* : to bait
yu·ge·ki·cah \yu-ġé-ḱi-caȟ\ *v contrac of* yugekicaga : to tempt, to hold out tempting things < ~ *au* to lead on by holding out tempting with *e.g.* oats for a horse, holding it before its face and making it come along > - *Syn* A-YUSLOHAN AU WE Bl
yu·ge·la \yu-ġé-la\ *n* : a large quantity, much - Bl
yu·gi·ca \yu-ġí-ca\ *va* blu·gica : to wake one up, to a-rouse one from sleep — **yugil** *va contrac* : to awake one < ~ *iyeya* to cause one to awake suddenly >
yu·gi·mna·mna \yu-ġí-mna-mna\ *v* : to make brown a little - Bl
yu·gi·pa·ye·la \yu-ġí-pa-ye-la\ *adv* : closely, as when one wound is inflicted near to the first one < ~ *opi* He was wounded closely where the first was. >
yu·gla \yu-glá\ *va* blu·gla : to uncoil, unroll, untwist; to stretch — **yugla·gla** *va red* : to unwind, to stretch out < ~ *aya* to go in single file, *i.e.* one after another, following in Indian file > - D.54
yu·gla·ke·ke \yu-glá-ḱe-ḱe\ *adj* : standing separately, somewhat in isolation < *Tucuhu* ~ *hingla yaun welo* Your ribs were suddenly standing out, drawing side-wise, *i.e.* you are getting thin. > - Bl WHL
yu·gla·kin·yan \yu-glá-kiŋ-yaŋ\ *adv* : transversely, a-cross or athwart < ~ *icu* to pull or put something so that it is transverse to one >
yu·gla·ki·ya \yu-glá-ḱi-ya\ *va* yugla·wa·kiya : to cause to stretch out, or uncoil
yu·gla·kšin·kšan \yu-glá-kšiŋ-kšaŋ\ *adv* : in a zigzag line < *Makasan on* ~ *owa* to paint a zigzag line with white earth, ~ *kinye* It flew in a zigzag line. >
yu·gla·kšin·kšin \yu-glá-kšiŋ-kšiŋ\ *adj* : zigzag or in all kinds of ways, as children might make a mark on the snow - B.H.172.7
yu·gla·kšin·kšin·ya \yu-glá-kšiŋ-kšiŋ-ya\ *adv* : in a zig-zag line < ~ *mani* to walk zigzag >
yu·gla·ya \yu-glá-ya\ *va* yugla·wa·ya : to cause to un-coil
yu·glo·glo \yu-gló-glo\ *va* blu·gloglo : to make grunt *e.g.* a buffalo calf by catching it; perhaps to hit hard in anger and make howl - Bl
yu·glo·ka \yu-gló-ka\ *va* blu·gloka : to sprain badly, dislocate a joint
yu·gmi \yu-gmí\ *va* blu·gmi : to clear off *e.g.* grass *etc.* from a field, to rake or perhaps to till
yu·gmi·ca \yu-gmí-ca\ *va* blu·gmica : to catch by the hair of the head, to pull one's hair < *Miciglugmica* I pulled my own hair. *Iciglugmica* He pulled his own hair. >
yu·gmi·gma \yu-gmí-gma\ *va* blu·gmigma : to make into a ball, *e.g.* a bunch of paper, but not a snow ball; to make round
yu·gmil \yu-gmíl\ *va contrac of* yugmica : to catch or pull one's hair < ~ *yuza* to grasp the hair of the head >
yu·gmi·yan·yan \yu-gmí-yaŋ-yaŋ\ *va* blu·gmiyanyan : to make roll with the hand
yu·gmi·yus \yu-gmí-yus\ *adv* : holding by the hair < ~ *yupocancan* to take one by the hair and pull the person to and fro > - Bl KE
yu·gmun \yu-gmúŋ\ *va* : to twist *e.g.* string or tobacco < *canli yugmunpi* cigars > — **yugmun·gmun** *v red* : to be twisting
yu·gna \yu-gná\ *va* : to shake *e.g.* fruit from a tree, to make fall off, as corn in shelling it
yu·gna·gna·yan \yu-gná-gna-yaŋ\ *v* [fr *yugnayan* to miss in trying something] : to take a loose hold of < ~ *wakuwa* to try and miss getting a hold of something >
yu·gna·škin·yan·yan \yu-gná-škiŋ-yaŋ-yaŋ\ *v red* [fr *yu* causing + *gnaškinyan* to be frantic, wild] : to cause to rave, be possessed - B.H.185.21
yu·gna·yan \yu-gná-yaŋ\ *va* blu·gnayan : to miss, as in trying to grasp something - D.84
yu·gnu·ni \yu-gnú-ni\ *va* blu·gnuni : to cause to wan-der
yu·go \yu-ġó\ *va* blu·go : to make scratches — *vn* : to be tired, fatigued, as is said of Man and animal — **yugo·go** \yu-ġó'-ġo\ *v red* blu·gogo : to make marks by scratching
yu·go·ya·kel \yu-ġó-ya-kel\ *adv* : in an exhausted con-dition
yu·gu·ka \yu-ġú-ḱa\ *va* blu·guka : to draw from the pocket and open a knife; to stretch, strain, to pull out *e.g.* an arrow from the quiver < *mila* ~ to draw a knife out of something >
yu·gwa \yu-gwá\ *v* : to make soften or spoil by hand - Bl
yu·gwa·yan \yu-gwá-yaŋ\ *va* : to drop while holding - BD
yu·gwe·za \yu-gwé-za\ *va* blu·gweza : to make rough
yu·gwo·gwog \yu-gwó-gwog\ *adv red* : drawing or paddling water toward one's self < ~ *hpaya* He reclined paddling himself afloat, as is said of a person unable to swim but keeps himself above water by moving. > - Bl KE
yu·ha \yu-há\ *va* 1 : to have, own, possess 2 : to lift, be able to carry (with this meaning, the terminal *a* is not changed to *e* < *Bluha šni* I am not able to carry it. > — *part* : carrying with one, where the word is almost a *prep* meaning: with < *Šina wan yuha hinapa na yublaya egnaka. Tahca ha wan yuha najin* She came out with a shawl and set it up unfolded. She stood and held a deer skin. > 3 : to have given birth to a child
yu·ha·ha \yu-há-ha\ *adv* : spreading out like a tree with many branches < *Šunkawakanla k'on unšilapica šni ~ yuzapi s'e naunke* as is said when a played-out horse comes on trotting. > We had no pity for that colt that went gallopping as if it were spread out everywhere. > - Bl KE
yu·ha·ha·la \yu-há-ha-la\ *va* blu·hahala : to make not firm, to unsettle
yu·ha·ha·pi·ka \yu-há-ha-ṗi-ka\ *adj* : probably worth the begging < *Ungnahahci ~ lowacin yelo* It may be worth the begging for food, as a hungry visitor would say who, being told that there is nothing in the house, thinks they have still something hidden away. > - Bl

\a\ father \e\ they \i\ machine \o\ smoke \u\ lunar \an, aŋ\ blanc Fr. \in, iŋ\ ink \on, oŋ, un, uŋ\ soon, con-fier Fr. \c\ chair \ġ\ machen Ger. \j\ fusion \clusters: bl, gn, kp, hšl, etc...\ b^{e}lo ... said with a slight vowel
See more in the Introduction, Guide to Pronunciation

KE

yu·ha·ha·ye·la \yu-há-ha-ye-la\ *va* blu·hahayela : to move, shake, make unstable

yu·ha i·ya·ya \yu-há i-yè-ya\ *v* : to find or receive something unexpectedly - Bl

yu·ha·ki·ya \yu-há-k̇i-ya\ *va* : to cause one to have, to make one have

yu·han·ska \yu-háŋ-sk̇a\ *va* blu·hanska : to lengthen out, make longer, to prolong

yu·ha·pi \yu-há-pi\ *part* : owned, held < ~ *cin* He wants to be hired. >

yu·ha·šni·yan \yu-há-šni-yaŋ\ *adv* : without, perhaps < *Wocet'ungla* ~ *oholapi* He was honored for lacking doubts. > - B.H.169.20

yu·ha·ya \yu-há-ya\ *adv* : in the manner of having, having < ~ *un* to wear in the way of having things >

yu·hel·hel \yu-hél-hel\ *adv red* : bewildered, confused < *Yáyaya,* ~ *, wotiti najin* Bewildered, confused, he stood still and bewildered, not knowing what to do, ~ *nawajin* or *bluhehel waun* I stood bewildered *or* I am bewildered. > - Sb

yu·hi \yu-hí\ *va* blu·hi : to drive off *e.g.* game; to arouse, startle

yu·hi·ka \yu-hí-k̇a\ *va* blu·hika : to shake up, as in waking one up, to arouse one from sleep < *Mayaluhike lo* You shook me up. *Unma nahahci luhike šni hwo* Yet the other one did you not wake him up? > - Bl

yu·hin·han \yu-híŋ-haŋ\ *va* blu·hinhan : to tease, provoke one so as to get him angry - Bl

yu·hinl \yu-híŋl\ *va contrac of* yuhinta : to rake away < ~ *iyeya* to make rake *e.g.* one's yard >

yu·hin·ta \yu-híŋ-ṫa\ *va* blu·hinta : to rake away, to rake a field or yard

yu·ho·ho \yu-hó-ho\ *va* blu·hoho : to move, shake anything not firm, to loosen — **yuhoho·la** \yu-hŏ'-ho-la\ *va* blu·hohola : to shake, as something not solid — **yuhoho·picašni** *adj* : immovable — **yuhoho·ya** *adv* : shaking — *va* : to cause to shake - Pb.34

yu·ho·mni \yu-hó-mni\ *va* blu·homni : to turn around anything, to turn *e.g.* a grindstone < ~ *taciyotanka* He turned it around, *i.e.* his flute. > — **yuhomni·mni** *v red* : to turn something around frequently

yu·hon·hon·za \yu-hóŋ-hoŋ-za\ *va* : *See* yuhunhunza

yu·ho·tan·ke \yu-hó-ṫaŋ-ke\ *va* blu·hotanke : to make one cry - *Syn* YUCEYA

yu·ho·ta·pi s'e \yu-hó-ṫa-pi s'e\ *adv* : clearing away obstacles < ~ *iyeya* He went on, as though there were no obstacles. > - R Bl

yu·ho·wa·ya \yu-hó-wa-ya\ *va* blu·howaya : to make whine, as dogs do < *Ayuštan na luhowayahe* Let it alone, *i.e.* the dog, you make it whine. > - Bl

yu·hu·kul i·ye·ya \yu-hú-k̇ul i-yè-ya\ *v* : to cast down, to humble < ~ *iyewaya* I caused him to be humbled. > — **yuhuku·ya** *va* blu·hukuya [fr *hukuya* at the lowest place] : to humble, to bring down

yu·hun·hun \yu-húŋ-huŋ\ *va* blu·hunhun : to shake, move something not firm < *Pa* ~ *na inajin* He shook his head and stood up. > — **yuhunhuns** *va contrac of* yuhunhunza : to shake, move < ~*un* He is moving it. > — **yuhunhun·sya** *va* yuhunhun·swa·ya : to cause to shake and move — *adv* : shaking, moving

yu·hun·hun·za \yu-húŋ-huŋ-za\ *va* blu·hunhunza : to shake *e.g.* a tree with the hands

yu·ȟa \yu-ȟá\ *vn* : to curl, branch out — *adj* : curled, frizzled < *Nata* ~ His head is curled. >

yu·ȟa·ȟa \yu-ȟá-ȟa\ *vn red of* yuȟa : to become curled or branched — *adj* : curly, having many branches or prongs < *Hanp yúȟaȟa kšupi* A moccasin beaded with a design on the upper side and lines going in all directions > - Bl

yu·ȟa·tka \yu-ȟá-tka\ *va* blu·ȟatka : to ruffle *e.g.* the hair or feathers

yu·ȟeb \yu-ȟéb\ *va contrac of* yuȟepa : to lade out < ~ *iyeya* to empty by lading out >

yu·ȟe·bȟe·pa \yu-ȟé-bȟe-ṗa\ *v red of* yuȟepa : to lade out — **yuȟe·bya** *va* : to imbue - P

yu·ȟe·ki·cah a·u *or* **a·ya** \yu-ȟé-ki-caȟ a-u *or* a-ya\ *v* : to decoy, coax one on, lure against one's will, in order to entrap by going ahead and showing a small number -WE Bl

yu·ȟe·pa \yu-ȟé-ṗa\ *va* blu·ȟepa : to empty a vessel by lading out

yu·ȟe·yab \yu-ȟé-yab\ *va contrac of* yuȟeyab : to set aside < ~ *iyeya* to have something put aside, ~ *icu* she took and put aside > - B.H.46.1

yu·ȟe·yal \yu-ȟé-yal\ *va contrac of* yuȟeyata : to put aside or back, reject < ~ *iyeya, icu* She took and had it put aside. >

yu·ȟe·ya·pa \yu-ȟé-ya-pa\ *va* blu·ȟeyapa **1** : to put a little back, put aside **2** : to get out of the way — *vn* : to make room < ~ *yo* Get away from here. > — **yuȟeyapa·ya** *va* : to leave one alone, to get away from one < *Mayuȟeyapaya yo* Leave me alone. *Tipi wakan kin yuȟeyapaye šni* He did not leave the Temple. > - R B.H.52.10, 168.23

yu·ȟe·ya·ta \yu-ȟé-ya-ṫa\ *va* blu·ȟeyata : to put back, to reject

yu·hla \yu-ȟlá\ *va* blu·hla : to ring *e.g.* a bell, to rattle

yu·hla·gan \yu-ȟlá-ġaŋ\ *va* blu·hlagan **1** : to enlarge **2** : to leave, separate from < *Ti gluhlagan šni She* does not leave her own home, *i.e.* she always stays at home. *Wiyúhlagan šni* The woman does not separate from, *i.e.* he is always in company with his own wife. *Pagonta s'e wiyuhlagan šni* Duck-like, a woman does not leave her husband. > - Bl

yu·hla·hla \yu-ȟlá-ȟla\ *v red of* yuhla : to ring or rattle

yu·hla·hla·ta \yu-ȟlá-ȟla-ṫa\ *v red of* yuhlata : to claw or scratch

yu·hla·hla·ya \yu-ȟlá-ȟla-ya\ *v red of* yuhlaya : to pull or peel off

yu·hlal \yu-ȟlál\ *v contrac* blu·hlata [fr *yuhlata* to scratch or claw] : to scratch, as does a cat < ~ *iyeya* to make one scratch >

yu·hla·ya \yu-ȟlá-ya\ *va* blu·hlaya : to pull or peel off *e.g.* paper or plaster sticking on the wall

yu·hle·ca \yu-ȟlé-ca\ *va* blu·hleca : to tear in pieces with the hands — **yuhle·hleca** *v red* : to tear off

yu·hlel \yu-ȟlél\ *v contrac of* yuhleca : to tear in pieces < ~ *iyeya* to cause to tear in pieces, ~ *icu* to receive a partial payment, as on a lease *etc.* > — **yuhle·lkiya** \yu-ȟlé-lk̇i-ya\ *va* yuhle·lwa·kiya : to cause to rend — **yuhle·lya** *va* yuhle·lwa·ya : to cause to tear up

yu·hli·hli \yu-ȟlí-ȟli\ *va* : to make dirty, slimy, slippery - Bl

yu·hlo \yu-ȟló\ *va* blu·ȟlo : to make growl

yu·hlog \yu-ȟlóg\ *va contrac of* yuhloka : to make a hole by hand < ~ *iyeya* to cause a hole to be made, ~ *han* to stand open > — **yuhlo·gkiya** *va* yuhlo·gwa·kiya : to cause to open

yu·hlo·he·la s'e \yu-ȟló-he-la s'e\ *adv* : seemingly burdened or unwell < ~ *mani* to walk slowly, as though one carried a heavy burden or were sick > - Bl

yu·hlo·hlo·ka \yu-ȟló-ȟlo-ǩa\ *v red* blu·hlohloka [fr *yuhloka* to make a hole by hand] : to make holes in

yu·hlo·ka \yu-ȟló-ǩa\ *va* blu·hloka : to make a hole, using the hand

yu·hmin \yu-ȟmíŋ\ *va* blu·hmin 1 : to twist out of joint 2 : to sling *e.g.* a stone sideways, to make go crooked — **yuhmin·hmin** *v red* : to sling — **yuhmin·yan** *adv* : off sideways, crookedly, as a ball might go; sliced, as in golf - R B.H. 294.17

yu·hmun \yu-ȟmúŋ\ *va* blu·hmun : to make whizz, as in throwing a stone from a sling — **yuhmun·hmun** *v red* : to make whizz — **yuhmun·yan** *adv* : making whizz

yu·hni·ga \yu-ȟni-ǧa\ *va* blu·hniga : to dress one up nicely < *Migluhniga* I am dressed up. > - Cf igluhniga

yu·hni·yan \yu-ȟní-yaŋ\ *vn* : to quiver, to shake badly < *Pute yuhniyanpi s'e najin yankelo* He was standing as one with quivering lips, *i.e.* with quivering lips as from fear. > — **yuhniyan·yan** *v red* : continually quivering < *Pute yuhniyanyanpi s'e nanke hwo* Did you sit like one with quivering lips? > - Bl KE

yu·ȟon·ta *or* **yuȟunta** \yu-ȟóŋ-ṫa\ *va* blu·ȟonta : to make soft *e.g.* flax in dressing it, to rub soft *e.g.* a hide by pulling the hands back alternately

yu·hpa \yu-ȟpá\ *va* blu·hpa : to pull something so as to make it fall, to loosen the bow string after use, to throw down or shake off one's load — **yuhpa·hpa** *v red* : to relax or rest something < ~ *s'e kinyan* to fly slowly, perhaps leisurely, *i.e.* as a big bird dragging something as it were >

yu·hpan \yu-ȟpáŋ\ *va* blu·hpan : to soak and make soft *e.g.* a piece of leather — **yuhpan·hpan** *v red* bluhpanhpan : to soak and make a little soft *e.g.* a piece of leather-work

yu·hpe·ya \yu-ȟpé-ya\ *va* yuhpe·wa·ya : to cause to throw down, shake off < *Misun, (šiyo kin) miciyuhpeye* Little brother, (the prairie chicken) caused me to throw it down. > — **yuhpi·hpeya** *va* : to throw down - MS.98

yu·hpu \yu-ȟpú\ *va* blu·hpu : to pick off a piece < *canšin* ~ to pick off a piece of tree resin > — **yuhpuhpu** *v red* blu·hpuhpu : to pick off pieces from *e.g.* trees or shrubs

yu·hta·ka \yu-ȟtá-ka\ *va* : to loosen < *Ehaš maka kin yuhtakin kte s'e inyankelo* For sure, it ran as if the ground were about to let it loose, as is said of a horse that holds the head down while running. > - Bl LHB

yu·htan *or* **yuhtan·yan** \yu-ȟtáŋ\ *va* blu·htanyan : to make rough, to whet or do a rough edge

yu·htu·te šni i·cu *or* **k'u** \yu-ȟtú-ṫe šni i-cù *or* k'ù\ *v* [fr *yuhtute* to have in use] : to take *or* give the whole leaving nothing - Note: to give the whole thing, such as a box of cigars, without keeping anything back - Et

yu·ȟu·ga \yu-ȟú-ǧa\ *va* blu·ȟuga : to crack something, the hand

yu·ȟu·gna·ga \yu-ȟú-gna-ǧa\ *va* blu·ȟugnaga : to cause to burn up

yu·ȟuh \yu-ȟúȟ\ *va contrac of* yuȟuga : to crack by hand < ~ *iyeya* to make crack > — **yuȟu·ȟuga** \yu-ȟú-ȟu-ǧa\ *v red* : to crack by hand

yu·ȟun·lhun·ta \yu-ȟúŋ-lȟuŋ-ṫa\ *v red of* yuȟunta : to soften

yu·ȟun·ta *or* **yuȟonta** \yu-ȟúŋ-ṫa\ *va* blu·ȟunta : to make soft *e.g.* a piece of thread, to rub soft *e.g.* a skin

yu·ȟun·win \yu-ȟúŋ-wiŋ\ *va* blu·ȟunwin : to make putrify *e.g.* flesh

yu·hwa \yu-ȟwá\ *va* blu·hwa : to make drowsy

yu·h'a·kpa \yu-ȟ'á-kṗa\ *va* blu·h'akpa : to make curved *e.g.* an edge of a knife that has been long in use

yu·h'an·hi \yu-ȟ'áŋ-hi\ *va* blu·h'anhi : to make slow — **yuh'anhi·ka** \yu-ȟ'áŋ-hi-ǩa\ *adj* : slow

yu·h'e·h'e \yu-ȟ'é-ȟ'e\ *adv* : tearing *e.g.* a cloth by twisting, tearing to shreds — *n* : drippings, drooling, drivel — **yuh'eh'e·yakel** *adv* : in bits, in small quantities < ~ *wawakamna* I earn money in small quantities at a time. > - *Syn* TUTKAYAKEL Bl LHB

yu·h'i \yu-ȟ'í\ *vn* : to pimple, be pimpled or rough, to be chapped, as the hands; to be broken out full of pimples < *Nape mayuh'i* My hands broke out in pimples. *Ite mayuh'i* My face broke out in pimples. > — **yuh'ih'i** *v red* : to be pimpled, rough

yu·h'i·s'e \yu-ȟ'í-s'e\ *adj* : chapped-like

yu·h'i·ya \yu-ȟ'í-ya\ *v* : to be made rough < *Nape kin yujaja kangi tanka nape s'e nape kin sabyela* ~ He washed his hands, which were hands like a raven's, hands made rough and blackish, as is said when a person's hands are rough from dirt. *Mato s'e siyete* ~ His heels are made rough as those of a bear. > - Bl

yu·h'i·ya·ya \yu-ȟ'í-ya-ya\ *va* blu·h'iyaya : to bungle, to do badly

yu·h'i·ye·la \yu-ȟ'í-ye-la\ *adv* or *adj* : pimpled, marked and rough, as by scratches or gouging < *Waowešica* (bear) *s'e napcoka kin* ~ *yankin na* Take let the palm of his hand be markedlike the foot of a bear, as when a person's hands are scratched. > - Cf waowešica

yu·h'u \yu-ȟ'ú\ *va* blu·ȟ'u : to peel off *e.g.* bark with the hand, to take off the hull or rind, to pull off a little piece of skin

yu·i·ca·pa \yu-í-ca-ṗa\ *va* blu·icapa : to open somebody's mouth, as a horse's

yu·i·ci·ca·hi \yu-í-ci-ċa-hi\ *va* blu·icicahi : to mix together, to mingle — **yuicicahi·ya** *adv* : mingling < ~ *iyeya* to cause to mix together >

yu·i·ci·ca·win \yu-í-ci-ċa-wiŋ\ *va* blu·icicawin : to make turn back on the same way

yu·i·c'i·c'u·ya \yu-í-c'i-c'u-ya\ *va* blu·ic'ic'uya : to make overlap each other, to cause to pass by over or alongside of each other, as the two ends of anything

yu·i·e·ska \yu-í-e-ska\ *va* blu·ieska : to interpret, explain *e.g.* a piece of the Holy Scriptures

yu·i·ȟa \yu-í-ȟa\ *va* blu·iȟa : to make laugh

yu·i·je·na \yu-í-je-na\ *v* blu·ijena : to stir or mix together, *fig* to confuse, mix up things < *Mayaluijena* You confuse me. *Ciyuijena* I confuse you. > - BT

yu·i·kpi·ska i·hpe·ya \yu-í-kṗi-ska i-ȟpè-ya\ *v* : to turn anything over on its back, as a dog

yu·i·le \yu-í-le\ *va* blu·ile : to kindle a fire, cause to blaze < *Ehanl izigzita na ungna yuile* At the time there was smoke and probably the cause for the blaze. > — **yuile·pi** *n* : a match to start a fire

yu·i·na·hni \yu-í-na-ȟni\ *va* blu·inahni : to make one hurry, to hasten one < *Makiyuinahni yo; wanagi el mahipelo* Hurry it up for me; the spirits are come to me, as an Indian might say when he is very hungry. > — **yui-nahni·kiya** \yu-í-na-ȟni-ǩi-ya\ *va* : to cause one to hasten — **yuinahni·yan** *or* **yuinahni·yela** *adv* : hastening < ~ *škan* to move with haste > - Bl

---

\a\ father \e\ they \i\ machine \o\ smoke \u\ lunar \an, aŋ\ blanc Fr. \in, iŋ\ ink \on, oŋ, un, uŋ\ soon, confier Fr. \c\ chair \ǧ\ machen Ger. \j\ fusion \clusters: bl, gn, kp, hšl, etc...\ b^elo ... said with a slight vowel
See more in the Introduction, Guide to Pronunciation

yu·i·ni·la \yu-í-ni-la\ *va* blu·inila [fr *inila* silent, quiet, still] : to put to silence, to make still < ~ *yuza* to caress and make still, as a mother does her child > — **yu-ini·lya** *adv* : putting to silence – Bl

yu·in·yan·ka \yu-íŋ-yaŋ-k̇a\ *va* blu·inyanka : to make run — **yu·in·yan·k'in·yan·ka** \yu-íŋ-yaŋ-k'iŋ-yaŋ-k̇a\ *vn* yuinyan·k'wa·imnanke : to run dragging one along, to make one run along

yu·i·pa·htu \yu-í-ṗa-ḣtu\ *va* blu·ipahtu : to reverse a thing, to undo a thing – B.H.20.11

yu·i·šte·ca \yu-í-šṫe-ca\ *va* blu·išteca : to make one ashamed

yu·i·što·gmus \yu-í-šṫo-gmus\ *va contrac* blu·ištogmuza [fr *ištogmuza* to close the eyes] : to make shut the eyes, *fig* to deceive one

yu·i·tan·nunk \yu-í-taŋ-nuŋk\ *adv* : on both sides < ~ *iyakaška* to tie on both sides *e.g.* a horse on both sides of one's team >

yu·i·te·šla \yu-í-ṫe-šla\ *adv* : uncovering the face < *Ungna tóka ška ~ ciyuzin na ognagna acipe ci* They said perhaps it was an enemy, I grabbed hold of you uncovering your face, and accordingly I waited to rob you. > – *See* tešlaka – Bl LHB

yu·i·to·kan \yu-í-to-kaŋ\ *va* blu·itokan : to to put out of the way, to reject, remove one

yu·i·to·mni \yu-í-to-mni\ *va* blu·itomni : to make one dizzy by turning him around and around

yu·i·ya·ki·pab *or* **yuiyakipapab** \yu-í-ya-k̇i-ṗab\ *adv* : dividing, separating

yu·i·yo·tag \yu-í-yo-ṫag\ *v contrac of* iyotaka : to sit down : to make sit < ~ *ehpeya* to push one down, to make sit down *i.e.* by force. >

yu·i·yo·wa·ja·šni \yu-í-yo-wa-ja-šni\ *v* : to place afar off

yu·i·yo·was \yu-í-yo-was\ *v contrac of* yuiyowaza : to make echo

yu·i·yo·waš \yu-í-yo-waš\ *v contrac of* yuiyowaja : to make near, have concern for < ~ *iyeye šni* to cause to have no concern for > – Cf yuiyowajašni

yu·i·yo·wa·za \yu-í-yo-wa-za\ *va* blu·iyowaza : to make echo, make resound

yu·i·yo·yag \yu-í-yo-yag\ *v* [fr *oyaka* to tell] : to scare and get a person excited < ~ *iyeya* to make one excited > – Bl

yu·i·yu·pse i·cu \yu-í-yu-pse i·cu\ *v* : to close a tent door very tight from within – Bl

yu·ja \yu-já\ *va* blu·ja : to mash, make mush, to stir up *e.g.* mush < *Taḣuha bluja kte pangi icahi.* She mixted together artichokes so I might make a mush of hide scrapings. *Wa kin yujapi s'e yunkelo* The snow lay like a mush, as is said of snow when thawing. > – Bl

yu·jag \yu-jág\ *va contrac of* yujaka : to strain open, < ~ *iyeya* to make strain open the eyes >

yu·ja·han \yu-já-haŋ\ *va* blu·jahan : to make a jarring noise — *adj* : sounding — **yujahe·ya** *adv* : sounding harshly

yu·ja·ja \yu-já-ja\ *va* blu·jaja : to wash *e.g.* clothes

yu·ja·ka \yu-jä'-k̇\ *va* blu·jaka : to pull open or strain open somebody's eyes

yu·ja·pi \yu-já-pi\ *part* : mixed up, as mush

yu·jib \yu-jíb\ *va contrac of* yujipa : to pinch < ~ *iyeya* to make pinch > — **yuji·bjib** *v* : to pinch < ~ *kuwa* to bother, treating roughly > – SLB

yu·ji·bji·pa \yu-jí-bji-pa\ *v red* : repeatedly to pinch

yu·ji·bye·la \yu-jí-bye-la\ *v* blu·jibyela : to pinch up with the fingers, as in pinching the skin — *adv* : pinching up with the fingers < ~ *yuza* to take hold on and pinch >

yu·jin·ca \yu-jíŋ-ca\ *va* blu·jinca : to pull or blow *e.g.* the nose

yu·ji·pa \yu-jí-ṗa\ *va* blu·jipa : to pinch

yu·jo \yu-jó\ *va* blu·jo : to whistle to — **yujo·jo** *v red* blu·jojo : to whistle to, again and again perhaps

yu·ju·ju \yu-jú-ju\ *va* blu·juju : destroy, tear down, deface; to pull in pieces, to undo, to open *e.g.* a bundle; to make void *e.g.* an agreement *etc.*

yu·jun \yu-júŋ\ *va* blu·jun : to pull up with the roots something that is tight, pulling up straight < *Wicaša num wicakico na wihuta yujunpi* She called two men who raised the lower border of the tent. >

yu·jun·ta \yu-júŋ-ṫa\ *va* : to thrust into < *išṫa* ~ to thrust something into the eye, to strike the eye >

yu·ka \yu-k̇á\ *va* blu·ka : to strip off *e.g.* the feather part of a quill

yu·kab \yu-k̇ä'b\ *va contrac of* yukapa : to jerk < ~ *iyeya* to suddenly jerk >

yu-ka-gal *or* **yuakagal** \yu-ká-ġal\ *adv* : with arms out-stretched < ~ *otkeyapi* crucifixion > – MS.102

yu·ka·ka·ka \yu-ká-ka-k̇a\ *v* : to shake, one at a time < *Otutkala eša tuweni el un šni yelo; ca tiyopa blukakakin na wagliyacu welo* There was no one there though small things were; so he shook the door while I was on my way home. > – Bl KE

yu·ka·ki·ja \yu-k̇á-ki-ja\ *va* blu·kakija : to cause to suffer < *Oyate eya wicalukakije na ota t'ewicayaya* Some people you caused to suffer, and many you made to die. >

[1]**yu·kan** \yu-k̇áŋ\ *vn* unkanpi lukanpi yukanpi : to be, there is – Note: lacking are forms for the 1st and 2nd *pers singl*. It is often used with a *pl* meaning, as in : *Tahca yukan. Hu mayukan.* There are deer. They are my legs. *Pute mayukan ca šolwakiyin kte* I shall make smoke when they are my lips, as a man says when he fills a pipe — *va* : to give room < *kiyúkan* to make room for one >

[2]**yu·kan** \yu-káŋ\ *va* blu-kan : to shake off *e.g.* the dew < *Cuglukan* He shook the dew off himself. >

[3]**yu·kan** \yu-k̇áŋ\ *va* blu·kan [fr *k̇an* old in age] : to make old

yu·kan·kan \yu-káŋ-kaŋ\ *v red of* yukan : to shake off

yu·kan·na·kša i·kan·ton \yu-káŋ-na-kša i-kàŋ-toŋ\ *v* : to keep a firm hold on something and not letting it go < ~ *hcelo* He did indeed keep a firm hold on it. > – Bl

yu·ka·pa \yu-kā'-ṗa\ *va* blu·kapa : to catch *e.g.* a ball in the hand < *tabyúkapa* to catch, field a ball >

yu·ka·po·je·la \yu-ká-po-je-la\ *va* : to lighten – P

yu·ka·ta \yu-ká-ṫa\ *va* blu·kata [fr *káta* hot] : to make warm by rubbing

yu·ka·tin \yu-k̇á-tiŋ\ *va* blu·katin : to straighten out with the hand

yu·ka·wa \yu-k̇á-wa\ *va* blu·kawa : to open *e.g.* a wound, a sore, or somebody's mouth, implying effort being made in so opening — **yukawa·kiya** \yu-ka-wa-k̇i-ya\ *va* yukawa·wa·kiya : to cause to open a sore, a wound, *etc.* – B

yu·kca \yu-kcá\ *va* blu-kca : to loose a knot, to untie, unwrap; to open what is tangled

yu·kcan \yu-kcáŋ\ *va* blu·kcan : to comprehend anything, to understand; to know, guess, have an opinion, to judge — **yukcan·yan** *adv* : comprehending, guessing

yu·ke \yu-k̇é\ *vn* [fr *yuk̇an* to be] : to be — **yuke·ya** *adv* : being, having, possessing < *Peta* ~ *waun kte* I shall be well off having fire. *Hena wankah wicašipi wiši* ~ They were given orders for those arrows to be made, there being pay. > - MS.481

yu·ki·ca·hi·pi s'e \yu-k̇í-ca-hi-pi s'e\ *adv* [fr *kicahi* to rummage for one] : there being no real search for one < ~ *wiyukcan* to understand there being an unsteady character to one's actions, ~ *wiblukcan yelo* I have an uncertainty about the way he acts. > - BT

yu·ki·ki·ke \yu-k̇í-k̇i-k̇e\ *va* : to pull *e.g.* a tree at its top towards the ground - Bl

yu·ki·kta \yu-k̇í-k̇ta\ *v* blu·kikta : to cause to wake up < *Isto el yuzin na* ~ He grabbed onto his arm and made him wake up. >

yu·ki·ni \yu-k̇í-ni\ *va* blu·kini : to cause to live again, to make recover < *Na wanna yukinipi na wota okihi* And He recovered and was now able to eat. >

yu·ki·nu·kan \yu-k̇í-nu-k̇aŋ\ *va* blu·kinukan : to divide between, as apples *etc.* between those present, to separate *e.g.* cattle < ~ *wicayus-wacin* He planned to hold them apart, *i.e.* two trees. > — *adv* : divided < ~ *egnaka* to place out separately > — **yukinukan·kiya** \yu-k̇í-nu-kaŋ-k̇i-ya\ *va* : to part in two, to separate — *adv* : divided, separately < ~ *unpi* They are divided. > — **yukinukan·yan** *adv* : separately

yu·kin \yu-k̇íŋ\ *va* blu·kin : to give room to pass, to lean to one side

yu·kin·ca \yu-k̇íŋ-ca\ *va* blu·kinca : to scrape off with the hand or finger, to clean *e.g. taniga* paunch by pulling it through two fingers

yu·kin·ja \yu-k̇íŋ-ja\ *v* [fr *kinja* to whine as children may do] : to make whine < *Tate wan yukinjapi s'e u welo* There came a wind as though made to whine, *i.e.* howling. > - Bl

yu·kin·kin \yu-k̇íŋ-k̇iŋ\ *adv* : to and fro, from side to side

yu·kinl \yu-k̇iŋl\ *va contrac of* yukinca : to scrape or clean with hand or fingers < ~ *icu* to take and clean *etc.* by hand >

yu·ki·pa·ja \yu-k̇í-ṗa-ja\ *va* blu·kipaja : to hem as in sewing, to bend anything around or double over *e.g.* a piece of paper, a blanket, a string, so as to make the ends meet — **yukipaš** *va contrac* : to double or bend over < ~ *iyeya* to cause to double over, making the ends meet, ~ *yuza* to double around and hold, ~ *iyakaška* to tie a knot with a loop > - Cf yušinyan icu Bl

yu·ki·pe·han \yu-k̇í-ṗe-haŋ\ *va* blu·kipehan : to fold, to lay in folds < ~ *egnaka* to place in folds >

yu·ki·pu·ski·ca \yu-k̇í-ṗu-sk̇i-ca\ *va* blu·kipuskica : to press, put close together — **yukipuskil** *va contrac* : to put close together < ~ *yuza* to hold one thing close to another > — **yukipuski·lya** *adv* : pressed close to

yu·kis \yu-k̇ís\ *va contrac of* yukiza : to make creak < ~ *iyeya* to cause something to creak > — **yuki·skiza** \yu-k̇í-sk̇i-za\ *v red of* yukiza : to make creak

yu·ki·ye·la \yu-k̇í-ye-la\ *va* blu·kiyela : to make near

yu·ki·yu·te·ya \yu-k̇í-yu-ṫe-ya\ *adv* : crisped, drawn up

yu·ki·za \yu-k̇í-za\ *va* blu·kiza : to make creak < *can'iyukize* an organ >

yu·ko \yu-k̇ō'\ *va* blu·ko : to make a hole larger with the hand

yu·kog \yu-k̇ō'g\ *va contrac of* yukoka : to ring or rattle < ~ *iyeya* to cause to ring or rattle >

yu·ko·ka \yu-k̇ō'-k̇a\ *va* blukoka : to ring, to rattle as an old kettle

yu·ko·ke·la \yu-k̇ó-k̇e-la\ *va* blu·kokela : to stimulate, to make active

yu·ko·ki·ya \yu-k̇ó-k̇i-ya\ *va* : to make wrinkle < *ite* ~ to frown or scowl >

yu·ko·ko·ka \yu-k̇ō'-ko-k̇a\ *v red of* yukoka : to ring continually

yu·kon·ta \yu-k̇óŋ-ṫa\ *va* blu·konta : to wear out partly by handling *e.g.* a strap or rope, *i.e.* to make it thinner - BD

yu·ko·s'in \yu-k̇ó-s'iŋ\ *v* : to throw high craning one's neck < *yukos'inpi s'e inyanka* to run as with head thrown high up, *i.e.* like a horse craning > - Cf s'in s'e

yu·ko·ya·h'an \yu-k̇ó-ya-ḣ'aŋ\ *va* blu·koyah'an : to cause to be quick, to hasten

yu·kpa \yu-kṗá\ *va* blu·kpa : to stifle, quench, crush, ruin < *išta* ~ to make blind > — **yukpa·kpa** *va* : to ruin - P

yu·kpan \yu-kṗáŋ\ *va* blu·kpan : to grind *e.g.* corn *etc.*, to make fine, to pulverize — **yukpan·kpan** *v red* blu·kpankpan : to grind — **yukpan·pi** \yu-kṗáŋ-ṗi\ *n* : grinding — **yukpan·yan** *va* yukpan·wa·ya : to cause to grind

yu·kpi \yu-kṗí\ *va* blu·kpi : to crack or burst *e.g.* a louse — **yukpi·kpi** *v red* : to crack often

yu·kpu·kpa \yu-kṗú-kṗa\ *va* blu·kpukpa : to crumble up and scatter about, to make fine

yu·ksa \yu-ksá\ *va* : to break off *e.g.* a stick with the hand < *hu yuksa* to break a leg > — **yuksa·ksa** *v red* blu·ksaksa : to break off

yu·ksa·pa \yu-ksá-pa\ *va* blu·ksapa [fr *ksapa* wise, understanding] : to make wise

yu·ksa·pi \yu-ksá-ṗi\ *n* 1 : monthly payments, as on deposits *etc.* 2 : a breaking off

yu·kse·kse·ya \yu-ksé-kse-ya\ *v red of* yukseya : to break off

yu·kse·ya \yu-ksé-ya\ *va* yukse·wa·ya : to cause to break off, as in trapping — *adv* : broken off, as iff straight down, cliff-like, as is a bluff shore where the water is deep and the bank appears broken off

yu·kša \yu-kšá\ *va* blu·kša : to bend or double up *e.g.* a blanket — **yukša·kša·la** *adj red of* yukšala : bent or crooked - MS.104

yu·kša·la \yu-kšá-la\ *adv* : bent up, crooked < ~ *icu* He received it in a bent over way. *Macuwita ca ~ munke; hecel omacoze* Since I am cold I lay all bent up; so I am warm and comfortable. *Wi k'on ~ yankelo, wioteḣi kte lo* For that month he was out of shape, it (January) will be a hard month. > - BT

yu·kšan \yu-kšáŋ\ *va* blu·kšan : to bend — **yukšan·kiya** *va* yukšan·wa·kiya : to cause to bend — **yukšan·kšan** *v red* : to bend and make crooked — *adv* : in a crooked line, in a manner zigzag < ~ *mani* to walk zigzag > — **yukšan·ya** *adv* : curved < ~ *iyaya* He went in a curved line. > — **yukšan·yan** *va* yukšan·wa·ya : to cause to bend — **yukšanye·ya** *adv* : bent around, in a circle

yu·kša·ye·la \yu-kšá-ye-la\ *adv* : bent, with the knees drawn up, in a bent position < ~ *hpaya* to lie in a bent up position >

yu·kši·ja \yu-kší-ja\ *va* : to double up *e.g.* a knife or one's arm < *glukšija* to double up one's own > — **yukši·kšija** *v red* : to double up — **yukšiš** *v contrac* :

\a\ father \e\ they \i\ machine \o\ smoke \u\ lunar \an, aŋ\ blanc Fr. \in, iŋ\ ink \on, oŋ, un, uŋ\ soon, confier Fr. \c\ chair \ġ\ machen Ger. \j\ fusion \clusters: bl, gn, kp, hšl, etc...\ b^e^lo ... said with a slight vowel
See more in the Introduction, Guide to Pronunciation

to double up < ~ *iyeya* to make double up > —**yukši·šya** *va* yukši·šwa·ya : to cause to double up

yu·ktan \yu-ktáŋ\ *v* blu·ktan : to bend with the hand

[1]**yu·ktan·ki·ya** \yu-k̇táŋ-k̇i-ya\ *va* yuktan·wa·kiya : to cause to bend anything

[2]**yu·ktan·ki·ya** \yu-k̇táŋ-k̇i-ya\ *adv* : crookedly

yu·ktan·ktan \yu-k̇táŋ-k̇taŋ\ *v red* : to bend, to crook —*adj* or *adv* : bent, zigzag —**yuktanktan·kiya** \yu-k̇táŋ-k̇taŋ-k̇i-ya\ *adv red* : crookedly

yu·ktan·ktan·yan \yu-k̇táŋ-k̇taŋ-yaŋ\ *adv red of of* yuktanyan : crookedly

yu·ktan·yan \yu-k̇táŋ-yaŋ\ *adv* : crookedly — **yuktanye·ya** *adv* : not in a straight line, crookedly

yu·ku·ka \yu-kú-ka\ *va* blu·kuka : to pull to pieces, to make rotten, to destroy

yu·kun·ta *or* **yukonta** \yu-kúŋ-ta\ *va* : to wear out

yu·k'e·ga \yu-k'é-ġa\ *va* : to scratch, as after itching - Cf yuhlata

yu·k'eh \yu-k'éȟ\ *va contrac* : to scratch < ~ *iyeya* to cause to scratch, after itching > — **yuk'ehk'ega** \yu-k'e-ȟk'e-ġa\ *v red of* yuk'ega : to scratch —**yuk'e·ȟya** *va* yuk'e·hwa·ya : to cause to scratch or scrape —*adv* : scratching, scraping —**yuk'ek'ega** \yu-k'é-k'e-ġa\ *v red of* yuk'ega : to scratch from itching

yu·k'es \yu-k'ěs\ *va contrac* blu·k'esk'eza [fr *yuk'eza* to shear the head close] : to shave off close and smooth *e.g.* the hair of the head

yu·k'e·za \yu-k'é-za\ *va* blu·k'eza : to shear, clip off close *e.g.* the hair of the head, perhaps to make hard and smooth

yu·k'o·ga \yu-k'ō'ġa\ *va* blu·k'oga : to scratch up, make rough with the nails —**yuk'oh** \yu-k'ō'ȟ\ *va contrac* : to scratch up < ~ *iyeya* to cause to scratch up > —**yuk'o·hkoga** \yu-k'ó-ȟko-ġa\ *v red* : to scratch and make rough

yu·k'os \yu-k'ō's\ *va contrac of* yuk'oza : to make hard and smooth < ~ *iyeya* to make smooth and hard by taking off the grass or hair > —**yuk'o·sk'oza** \yu-k'ō'-sk'o-za\ *v red of* yuk'oza : to make smooth and hard

yu·k'o·za \yu-k'ō'-za\ *va* bluk'oza : to make hard and smooth by removing the grass or hair *etc.*

yul \yul\ *va contrac of* yuta : to eat < ~ *Wicaša* There was a Ute tribal member (in an area of the southwest United States). *Na hehan ~ wicaši, canke oyate kin wakpamnipi na cantewašteya wotapi* And at that time he told them to eat, so the people had a distribution of goods and cheerfully feasted. >

yu·lab \yu-láb\ *va contrac of* yulapa : to make smooth < ~ *iyeya* to cause to make smooth > —**yula·blapa** *v red of* yulapa : to smooth or smoothen

yu·la·ko·ta \yu-lá-ko-ta\ *v* : to do a thing in the way of a Lakota, to change things so that they suit a Lakota - PB

yu·la·pa \yu-lā'-ṗa\ *va* blu·lapa : to make smooth

yu·le·ble·pa \yu-lé-ble-ṗa\ *va* : to make notches in, to make a jagged edge, as with a scissors, to produce a serrate margin, edge

yu·le·na \yu-lé-na\ *v* : to make distance in a brief time, to make or anticipate a date before that on which something is expected, as the time of one's arrival < ~ *s'e yaglihunni yelo* You came and straightway arrived home as though it took no time. > - Hm WHL

yu·le·šle·ja \yu-lé-šle-ya\ *v red* [fr *leja* to urinate] : to make urinate — Bl

yu·lki·ya \yu-lk̇í-ya\ *va* yu·lwa·kiya [fr *yúta* to eat] : to feed, cause to eat

yu·lo·lo·pi *or* **ota** \yu-ló-lo-ṗi\ \ó-ṫa\ *adj* : many < *Heheḣé, oyate ~ lel ohimniciye na oiyokipilahcake el wanweglaka, yunkan cantemašice* Oh my! All the people once met here, and while it was most pleasant for me to see it, I then became sad, as was said on seeing a place where big gatherings used to take place in times of old. >

yu·lpi·ca \yu-lpí-ca\ *adj* : edible < *Takunl ~ eša yaglepi hwo* Did you set out some of anything edible? > - B.H. 274.4

yu·lu·pi šni *or* **walupi šni** \yu-lú-ṗi šni\ *n* : that which is whole, intact, not opened, as a fresh bag of tobacco untouched by "human hands" < ~ *hca wanji ahigle yo* Set before him one that is definitely untouched. > - Bl

yu·lu·za·han \yu-lú-za-haŋ\ *va* blu·luzahan [fr *luzahan* to be fast, as at running] : to make swift, fast

Yul Wi·ca·ša \Yúl Wi-ca-ša\ *np* : the Yute tribe, of the southwest United States

yu·lya \yu-lyá\ *va* yu·lwa·ya : to feed, cause to eat

yu·lyul \yú-lyul\ *v contrac red of* yul *and* yuta : to eat appreciatively, to eat hastily on the way —*adv* : eating hastily along the way < *Hena tokeya ~ waku kte lo* Before this I shall come back and eat up. > - D.54

yu·ma·hel i·ye·ya \yu-má-hel i-yè-ya\ *va* yumahel iye·wa·ya : to insert, to push one thing into something else, to hold in < ~ *icu* to draw back, to hide under one's clothes > - D.39, 114

yu·man *or* **yume** \yu-máŋ\ *va* blu·man : to sharpen by grinding, filing or whetting *e.g.* an axe

yu·mi·ma \yu-mī'-ma\ *va* blu·mima : to make round *e.g.* a wheel

yu·mi·me·ya \yu-mí-me-ya\ *adv* : in a circle, circular-wise < ~ *yanke* It was circular. ~ *iyotaka po* All sit in a circle. > - D.34

yu·mna \yu-mná\ *va* blu·man : to rip a seam with a scissors or by pulling —**yumna·kiya** \yu-mná-k̇i-ya\ *va* yumna·wa·kiya : to cause to rip —**yumna·mna** *v red* : to rip up

yu·mni \yu-mní\ *va* blu·mni : to turn round *e.g.* a crank < *Na unma pestola k'on he el icapa na on ~* And the other that was sharp stuck into it and with it he turned it round. >

yu·mni·ga \yu-mní-ġa\ *v* : to shrink, draw up

yu·mni·ja \yu-mní-ja\ *adj* : ruffled, as hair on a hide

yu·mni·mni \yu-mní-mni\ *vn* and *va* : to turn round and round, to whirl

yu·mni·mni·ga \yu-mní-mni-ġa\ *v red of* yumniga : to shrink, draw up

yu·mni·mni·ja \yu-mní-mni-ja\ *va* : to curl —*adj red of* yumnija : curled, ruffled, as hair on a hide —**yumnimniš** *va* or *adj red* : to curl, curled, ruffled < ~ *iyeya* to cause to curl, or be ruffled > — **yumnimni·šya** *va* yumnimni·šwa·ya : to cause to curl —*adv* : curly — **yumnimni·yan** *adv* : turning round and round < ~ *otke* suspended and turning round and round, *i.e.* as a flag in the wind >

yu·mnu·mnu·ga \yu-mnú-mnu-ġa\ *va* blu·mnumnuga : to make a noise, as in handling corn

yu·na·jin \yu-ná-jiŋ\ *va* blu·najin : to cause to stand, to raise or lift up —**yunajin·kiya** \yu-ná-jiŋ-k̇i·ya\ *va* : to make stand < *Na unma wanna tokeya ~* And now he makes the other stand up first. *Nape el oyuspin na ~* He grasped her by the hand and helped her to her feet. > - B.H.290.19

yu·na·ke \yu-ná-k̇e\ *v* : to turn or tip —**yunake·ya** *va* blu·nakeya : to tip, turn anything partly, to turn on one side

yu·nan·ke \yu-náŋ-ke\ *v* *2 pers singl* [fr *yu* to cause + *yanka* to be, to sit] : to cause you to be present, you become or come present < *Nuns'e unkanipepi* We waited for you in expectation, *i.e.* waiting long thinking you would come soon, but you did not. > – Bl

yu·na·p'i·ye·ya \yu-ná-p'i-ye-ya\ *v* : to describe a curve by one's motion, gesture < *Yunap'iyeyapi sekse inyankelo* It ran as if describing a curve with its motion, as is said of a horse that runs off in a curve. > – Bl KE

yu·na·s'a \yu-ná-s'a\ *va* : to try the *hutanacute* a rib-like puck by making it hop in one's right hand above one's head before slinging it, to see if it balances well – Note: *nas'a* to simmer with a slight noise when about to boil; the word may be used *fig* of a fast horse – Bl

yu·na·ya \yu-ná-ya\ *v* yuna·wa·ya : to pass something along — **yunaye·kiya** \yu-ná-ye-ki-ya\ *va* : to pass on, give to someone else — **yunaye·ya** *v* : to get and then give to others – Bl KE

yu·ni \yu-ní\ *va* blu·ni : to touch one, so as to call his attention to something – *Syn* PANÍ

yu·ni ku·wa \yu-ní kù-wa\ *v* yuni wa·kuwa : to bother, annoy by pulling or touching — **yuni·ni** \yu-nī'-ni\ *v red* blu·nini [fr *yuni* to touch one to draw attention] : to touch so as to arouse one or call his attention to anything

yu·ni·ya·šni \yu-ní-ya-šni\ *va* blu·niyašni : to put out of breath, to strangle

yu·nun·ga \yu-núŋ-ġa\ *va* blu·nunga : to make a hard or callous place, by strain or otherwise

yu·nun·pa \yu-núŋ-pa\ *va* : to divide in two – B.H. 60.15

yun \yuŋ\ *interj exclam* on feeling pain : Oh! ... , Oh dear me! – Note: the word is used by women R

yun·gyun·ka \yuŋ-gyúŋ-ka\ *v* : to rock or sway from side to side — **yungyunka·han** \yuŋ-gyúŋ-ka-haŋ\ *v* ma·yungyunkahe : to rock or sway from side to side, as a sailor does in walking < *Canke wikoškalaka yamnipi k'on hinhan kin kuwa eyayapi na ~ hpayapi na wanji oyuspa. Na ecel yungyunkahanpi* And so there had been three young women who were saying they had been gone after an owl, and they lay swaying while oy grabbed one of them. And in a way they swayed to the side> — **yungyunke s'e mani** *v* : to walk as a sailor, swaying from side to side – P Bl

yun·ka \yuŋ·ká\ *v* mun·ka un·yunka·pi : to lie along < *Hecel miš wiyeya munka* So I myslelf lay along the way dining. *Yunkan isanpatanhan makoce wan lila canwape to na makoce kin toyela yunka* And from beyond, there lies a land very much in green leaves, and the land lies there quite green. >

yun·ka·han \yuŋ-ká-haŋ\ *vn* ma·yunkahe : to lie down or fall down — **yunkahe** *adv* : lying prone, *i.e.* face down, as a tree cut down, or as a whole fence — **yunkahe·ya** \yuŋ-ká-he-ya\ *va* yunkahe·wa·ya : to throw down, cause to fall — *adv* : obliquely, devious, neither perpendicular nor parallel, as might be said of characters in writing < *~ ówa* to write confusedly >

yun·kan *or* **unkan** \yúŋ-kaŋ\ *conj* : and, also, then

yun·kanš \yúŋ-kaŋš\ \yuŋ-káŋš\ *conj* : if – Note: but by far more commonly used is *k'eš*

yun·ka·pi \yuŋ-ká-pi\ *n* : an encampment, a lying down

yunš \yuŋš\ *conj* : if, provided that < *Hecon šni ~* If he had not done it, *Šilwaecon šni ~* If he had not done wrong, *Okiwaš'agnišicelo, ahoyasotkamayayelo, cehupa aciyawehwega kta ~ , aciyawega ye* You are simply wrong-headed, taking no good advice, and expressing your anger toward me; if I should break you, you chatterbox, I am pleased to break you, *i.e.* when a person does not listen to advice. > – Note: *yunš* is used when only the speaker knows or claims to know the fact indicated in the conditional clause; whereas *k'eš* is used when both the speaker and the person addressed are aware of it – B.H.260.16 Gramm.284

yu·o·ble·ca \yu-ó-ble-ca\ *va* blu·obleca : to divide, disperse, break into pieces, to scatter abroad, as does a people — *vn* : to be with the narrow or sharp part up < *~ yuza* to hold the sharp part up, as the edge of a board > — **yuobleca·han** *part* : in a dispersed state, scattered — **yuoblel** *va contrac* : to disperse < *~ iyaya* to go off and disperse, *~ iyeya* to cause to disperse, scatter abroad >

yu·o·ci·kpa·ni \yu-ō'-ci-kpa-ni\ *va* blu·ocikpani : to make unequal

yu·o·cin·ši·ca \yu-ō'-ciŋ-ši-ca\ *va* blu·ocinšica : to make cross, angry

yu·o·ci·pte·ca *or* **yuociptel** \yu-ó-ci-pte-ca\ *va* blu·ociptela : to make one shorter than another, to make a difference, to diminish — **yuocipte·lya** *adv* : diminishing by degrees – R Bl

yu·o·ci·pte·tu \yu-ó-ci-pte-tu\ *va* blu·ociptetu : to make a different size, to lessen — **yuociptetu·ya** *adv* : lessening — **yuociptetuya·kel** *adv* : of different sizes – R Bl

yu·o·ci·tkun·za \yu-ō'-ci·tkun·za\ *va* blu·ocitkunza : to make equal, even

yu·o·co·sco·za \yu-ó-co-sco-za\ *v red* [fr *yuocoza* to make one feel warm and comfortable] : to make one feel warm by, let him wear much clothing

yu·o·co·za \yu-ó-co-za\ *va* blu·ocoza : to make one feel warm and comfortable, *e.g.* by rubbing his hands and putting good clothing on him – Bl

yu·o·gla \yu-ó-gla\ *adv* : lined in a row < *~ icupo* Take to lining up, to formation, as is said to a group to line up in a row abreast. > *Syn* OCIBLAGAHEYA – Bl

yu·o·gla·pšun \ yu-ó-gla-pšuŋ\ *v* : to turn something over < *~ ihpeya* to turn and throw over > — **yuogla·pšun·yan** *adv* : turning over

yu·o·gmus \yu-ō'-gmus\ *v contrac of* yuogmuza : to wrap or close up < *~ icu* to close up *e.g.* a door, to button *e.g.* one's coat. *~ icu yo* Take and close it. *Na ake tiyopa kin ~ icupi* And again the door was shut. >

yu·o·gmu·za \yu-ó-gmu-za\ *v* : to wrap up in, to close up or button closed < *Wakanheja wicayuogmuza yo, hinhanna iglakapi kte lo* Button up the children, in the morning they will be moving camp, as a herald once said on the day before moving away. > – Note: the word also *ref* to the mending of children's moccasins < *Oyute kin ~ ye* Close up that hole (tear) in your side (dress). > – Bl

yu·o·gna i·cu \yu-ó-gna i-cù\ *v* : to open *e.g.* the barrel of a gun in order to put in a cartridge – Bl

yu·o·ha \yu-ó-ha\ *va* blu·oha : to push one into *e.g.* a hole or a water hole

yu·o·ho·ho \yu-ó-ho-ho\ *va* blu·ohoho : to shake something in a tight place, as a tree stump around which is made a hole but none is able to pull it out – WE

\a\ father \e\ they \i\ machine \o\ smoke \u\ lunar \an, aŋ\ blanc Fr. \in, iŋ\ ink \on, oŋ, un, uŋ\ soon, confier Fr. \c\ chair \ġ\ machen Ger. \j\ fusion \clusters: bl, gn, kp, hšl, etc...\ b°lo ... said with a slight vowel
See more in the Introduction, Guide to Pronunciation

yu·o·ȟan·ko·ya \yu-ō'-ȟaŋ-ǩo-ya\ *adv* : hastening
yu·o·ȟan·ši·ca \yu-ó-ȟaŋ-ši-ca\ *va* blu·oȟanšica : to make act badly
yu·o·hla·gan \yu-ō'-ȟla-ġaŋ\ *va* or *vn* : to loosen, make loose, *e.g.* a nut on a bolt; to become loose — **yu-oȟlaȟ** *va* or *vn contrac* : to loosen; to become loose < ~ *icu* to take loose > - R
yu·o·hpa \yu-ō'-ȟp̣a\ *va* blu·ohpa : to break off into and through, to pull through and into
yu·o·hpe·ya \yu-ó-ȟp̣e-ya\ *va* yuohpe·wa·ya : to cause to break through
yu·o·hya \yu-ó-ȟya\ *adv* : obliquely, indirectly, neither perpendicularly nor horizontally, as characters might be placed in writing < ~ *egnaka* to put obliquely >
yu·o·h'an·ko \yu-ō'-ȟ'aŋ-ǩo\ *va* blu·oh'anko : to make hasten
yu·o·ka·hwo·ka \yu-ó-ǩa-ȟwo-ka\ *va* blu·okahwoka : to make wave in folds, as does a flag *etc.*
yu·o·ka·po·ta \yu-ó-ǩa-p̣o-ṫa\ *v* : to float, to cause to be borne, lifted up as in water
yu·o·ki·ni·han \yu-ó-ǩi-ni-haŋ\ *va* : to make honorable
yu·o·ki·wan·ji·la \yu-ō'-ǩi-waŋ-ji-la\ *va* blu·okiwanjila : to make alike or similar
yu·o·ki·yu·ta \yu-ó-ǩi-yu-ta\ *va* [fr *okiyuta* to heal up] : to heal over, to close up by drawing together *e.g.* a wound for healing < *Tiyopa kin ~ yo, kazamnimni iyayelo, tanyan iyakaška yo* Close the door, it goes opening and shutting, tie it down well, *i.e.* the tent door is flapping to and fro. > - Bl
yu·o·ko \yu-ō'-ǩo\ *va* blu·oko : to make a hole
yu·o·ksa \yu-ō'-ksa\ *va* blu·oksa : to break off into, to pull through into
yu·o·ktan \yu-ó-ǩtaŋ\ *va* blu·oktan : to bend into
yu·o·ni·han \yu-ó-ni-haŋ\ *va* blu·onihan : to honor, treat with attention — **yuonihan·yan** \yu-ō'-ni-haŋ-yaŋ\ *adv* : honoring, treating politely
yu·on·jin·ca·ye·la \yu-óŋ-jiŋ-ca-ye-la\ *adv* : making short < ~ *pahta* to tie up short *e.g.* a horse's tail, ~ *iyaglaška* to tuck up *e.g.* one's robe or dress > - Bl KE
yu·on·ši \yu-óŋ-ši\ *adj perhaps* : reducing to weakness, humble < *Osni wan ~ unyuzapelo* The cold weather had a grip on us to weaken us, or A cold wave hit us mercilessly. > — **yuonši·ka** *va* : to reduce to littleness, to humble - Bl B.H.232.13
yu·o·pe·ja šni \yu-ó-p̣e-ja šni\ *v* : to interfere with or disturb one < *Ciyuopeja šni s'elececa. To, mayaluopeja šni yelo* I do not seem to disturb you. No, you do not interfere with or disturb me, *i.e.* you do not come in. > - Bl KE
yu·o·po \yu-ó-po\ *va* blu·opo : to press out of shape, press in at the sides *e.g.* a kettle, to make warp
yu·o·pte·ca \yu-ó-p̣te-ca\ *va* blu·opteca : to make less — **yuoptel** *va contrac* : to make less — **yuopte·lya** *adv* : making less — **yuopte·tu** \yu-ó-p̣te-ṫu\ *va* blu·opte-tu : to make less — **yuoptetu·ya** *adv* : lessening
yu·o·se·kse *or* **yuos'e** \yu-ó-se-kse\ *n* : one who misses shooting at something
yu·o·se·ya \yu-ō'-se-ya\ *v* : to get into a hard knot — *adv* : tightly, in a hard knot < ~ *iyakaška* to tie tightly to something, ~ *iyaya* a knot to become very tight, *i.e.* *yuškepicašni* unable to be loosed, ~ *icu* to tie in a bow knot, ~ *kagege* to tuck > - P
yu·o·smag \yu-ó-smag\ *va contrac of* yuosmaka : to indent, make a hollow place — **yuosma·gsmaka** *v red* : to make a dent in
yu·o·sma·ka \yu-ó-sma-ka\ *va* blu·osmaka : to make a hollow place or indent
yu·o·spe i·cu s'e ma·ni \yu-ó-spe i-cu s'e mà-ni\ *v* : to limp, to go with a catching gait
yu·o·swa \yu-ó-swa\ *v* : to pull down with gentle force, as in pulling hay down from the top of a stack, to pull down *e.g.* sand or soil from a bank with a tool - Cf *óswahan* caving in, as sand or coal does when some is taken from below - WHL
yu·o·s'e \yu-ó-s'e\ *n* : one who shoots but fails to hit - Note: seemingly the word is used ironically
yu·o·šin \yu-ó-šiŋ\ *v* : to tie in a bow knot or loosely — **yuošin·šin** *v red* : to make loose ties — **yuošin·yan** *adv* : loosely, tied in a bow knot - Bl
yu·o·ta \yu-ō'-ṫa\ *va* blu·ota : to multiply
yu·o·tan *or* **yuówotan** \yu-ó-taŋ\ *v* : to make straight *e.g.* a crooked road with many bends
yu·o·tan'·in \yu-ō'-taŋ-iŋ\ *va* blu·otan'in : to spread news, to make appear or manifest — **yuotan'in·yan** *adv* : celebrating, making manifest
yu·o·tan·ka·ya \yu-ó-taŋ-ǩa-ya\ *va* : to make larger *e.g.* a road by removing things
yu·o·ta·pi \yu-ó-ṫa-pi\ *n* : a multiplying, multiplication
yu·o·te·ȟi·ka \yu-ó-ṫe-ȟi-ǩa\ *va* blu·oteȟika : to make hard or difficult to be endured
yu·o·tkon·za \yu-ō'-tǩoŋ-za\ *va* blu·otkonza : to cut off evenly, make of equal length, to finish
yu·o·tku·ga \yu-ó-tǩu-ġa\ *va* : to lock a door with a key or by hand - BD
yu·o·t'ins \yu-ó-t'ins\ *va* : to press in tight, to make firm < ~ *icu* to draw in tight, ~ *iyeya* suddenly to become tight > — **yuot'inst'inza** *v red* : to press in tight
yu·o·t'in·za \yu-ó-t'iŋ-za\ *va* blu·ot'inza : to press in tight, to make firm in
yu·o·wan·ca·ya \yu-ó-waŋ-ca-ya\ *v* : to circulate or spread out over an area, to make or cause all over, everywhere - Cf ówancaya - Bl
yu·o·wan·ji·la \yu-ó-waŋ-ji-la\ *va* : to unite - Pb.35
yu·o·we·cin·han \yu-ō'-we-ciŋ-haŋ\ *v* blu·owecinhan : to place in a row, one behind the other
yu·o·wi·šni \yu-ó-wi-šni\ *v* : to be unused, to accumulate without being drawn upon, as provisions - R Bl
yu·o·wo·tan \yu-ó-wo-taŋ\ *va* blu·owotan : to make straight, to make upright, to justify < ~ *icu* to set up straight what fell or was upset > - Bl
yu·o·wo·tan·la \yu-ō'-wo-taŋ-la\ *v* blu·owotanla : to make straight or right
yu·o·ya·ȟe \yu-ō'-ya-ȟe\ *va* blu·oyaȟe **1** : to absorb, to cause to absorb, as with a blotter **2** : to empty *e.g.* a well by pumping — *vn* : to evaporate, as water being gone
yu·o·ya·tan·yan \yu-ó-ya-taŋ-yaŋ\ *v* : to stick and hold - Cf oyatanyan Bl KE
yu·pa \yu-pá\ *va* blu·pa : to make bitter
yu·pa·ga \yu-p̣á-ġa\ *va* blu·paga : to grasp tightly — **yupah** \yu-p̣áȟ\ *va contrac* : to grasp tightly < ~ *yuza* to grasp and hold tightly >
yu·pan·ga \yu-p̣áŋ-ġa\ *va* blu·panga : to make somebody drunk; to tie up loosely, make a large bundle - R
yu·panh \yu-p̣áŋȟ\ *va contrac of* yupanga : to tie up loosely < ~ *iyeya* to cause to tie a bundle loosely > — **yu-pan·hya** *adv* : loosely, as in a large bundle
yu·pan·ja \yu-p̣áŋ-ja\ *va* blu·panja : to seize something soft *e.g.* hair, wool
yu·pan·pan \yu-páŋ-paŋ\ *va* blu·panpan : to make soft by rubbing < *maka ~* to soften the ground, *Inyan na can on yupanpanpi* They, *i.e.* ten hides, were rubbed soft

by means of a piece of stone and a piece of wood. > — **yupanpan·la** *va* blu·panpanla : to make soft *e.g.* leather

yu·panš \yu-ṗáŋš\ *va contrac of* yupanja : to seize something soft, as hair or wool < ~ *iyeya, oyuspa* to seize suddenly something soft, to hold onto it. >

yu·pa·tu·ja \yu-ṗá-ṫu-ja\ *va* blu·patuja [fr *patuja* to stoop to get] : to cause to stoop down, to get or bend down

yu·pa·tuš \yu-ṗá-ṫuš\ *va contrac of* yupatuja : to make stoop down < ~ *iyeya* to make stoop, *Ungna toka ška ~ icicu na slisliya acipe ci* Watch out, how is it that still I took you stooped down, and having arrived home, with a swish I struck you. > - Bl

yu·pce·ce·la \yu-pcé-ce-la\ *va* blu·pcecela : to make short, to shorten — **yupce·lyela** *v* blu·pcelyela : to make short, to shorten — *adv* : shortening, fastening

yu·pe \yu-ṗé\ *va* blu·pe : to make sharp

yu·pe·han \yu-ṗé-haŋ\ *va* blu·pehan : to fold up

yu·pe·mni \yu-ṗé-mni\ *va* blu·pemni [fr *pemni* twisted, warped, crooked] : to twist, make warp, as a board < *Wociciyaka; yunkan ~ mazakiyelo* I spoke to you; then he made the iron piece crooked. > — **yupemni·mni** *v red* blu·pemnimni : to warp, crook, twist — **yupemni·yan** *adv* : crookedly - Bl

yu·pe·sto \yu-ṗé-sto\ *va* blu·pesto : to make pointed, as in shaping a hat

yu·pi \yu-ṗí\ *va* blu·pi : to make good

yu·pi·ka \yu-ṗí-ḱa\ *va* blu·pika : to clothe one well, to make look well — *n* : one who dresses well, who does things neatly

yu·pin na·ki·kšin \yu-ṗíŋ na-ḱi-kšin\ *v* : to work hard and hurriedly in order to finish a job in a certain time, to be anxious to finish a job by working hard - Cf kapin, škankapin Bl

yu·pin·ja \yu-ṗíŋ-ja\ *va* blu·pinja : to pull out the coarse hair from a skin, to pull off the hair or fur

yu·pin·pin·ta·pi s'e \yu-ṗíŋ-ṗiŋ-ṫa-pi s'e\ *adv* : seemingly growing or becoming smaller < ~ *inyanka* It runs seemingly getting smaller, as is said of little animals running. ~ *wapaha* a headdress seemingly gets smaller > - Bl

yu·pinš \yu-ṗíŋš\ *va contrac of* yupinja : to pull out hairs from skins < ~ *iyeya* to make pull out hairs from hides > — **yupin·špinja** *v red* : to pull out hairs

yu·pi·pi·ya \yu-ṗí-ṗi-ya\ *adv red* [fr *yupiya* beautifully done] : nicely < ~ *iglutanpi* They were well dressed. > — **yupipiye·hci** *adv red of* yupiyehci : neatly well done - B.H.108.1, 227..5

yu·pis \yu-ṗís\ *va contrac of* yupiza : to make creak < ~ *iyeya* suddenly to make creak > — **yupi·spiza** \yu-ṗí-sṗi-za\ *v red of* yupiza : to make creak

yu·pi·ya *or* **yupiya·kel** \yu-ṗí-ya\ *adv* : well, nicely, finely, beautifully < ~ *igluza* to dress one's self becomingly > - *Syn* TANYEHCI — **yupiye·hci** *adv* : very nicely, pleasantly < ~ *aiyohansya hpaye* He lay pleasantly in the shade. > — **yupiye·la** *adv* : gracefully < *Tap'ḱápsicapi* They played ball gracefully, beautifully. > - Pb.44 B.H.118.2 D.3

yu·pi·za \yu-ṗí-za\ *va* blu·piza : to make creak

yu·po \yu-ṗṓ'\ *va* blu·po : to make swell, as by scratching often

yu·pob \yu-pṓ'b\ *va contrac of* yupopa : to burst, snap < ~ *iyeya* to cause to snap, burst >

yu·po·can·can \yu-pó-caŋ-caŋ\ *v* : to shake one up < *yugmiyus* ~ to take by the hair and shake one up to and fro > - Bl KE

yu·pol \yu-ṗŏ'l\ *va contrac of* yupota : to tear to pieces < ~ *iyeya* to cause to tear apart > — **yupo·lpota** \yu-ṗŏ'-lṗo-ṫa\ *v red* : to tear apart piece by piece

yu·po·pa \yu-pṓ'-ṗa\ *va* blu·popa : to cause to burst or snap

yu·po·ta \yu-ṗó-ta\ *va* : to tear to pieces, as does an eagle a rabbit with the bill and not by scratching, to wear out, to tear to pieces *e.g.* a garment to use up < *Maštincala hin yupotehcelo* It is tearing to pieces rabbit fur, as they say of only a few snow flakes falling. > - Bl

yu·po·wa·ya \yu-pṓ'-wa-ya\ *va* blu·powaya : to roughen up *e.g.* fur or nap

yu·psag \yu-psā'g\ *va contrac of* yupsaka : to break in two < ~ *iyeya* to cause to break or pull in two, *e.g.* a string > — **yupsa·gya** \yu-psā'-gya\ *va* yupsa·gwa·ya : to cause to break *e.g.* a string — *adv* : breaking, a cord

yu·psa·ka \yu-psá-ka\ *va* blu·psaka : to break or pull in two *e.g.* a string

yu·psan·psan \yu-psáŋ-psaŋ\ *va* : to wag *i.e.* the tail, to cause to move back and forth

yu·psa·psa·ka \yu-psá-psa-ḱa\ *v red of* yupsaka : to break or pull in two

yu·psi·ca \yu-psī'-ca\ *va* blu·psica : to toss, to make jump — **yupsil** \yu-psī́l\ *va contrac of* yupsica : to make jump < ~ *iyeya* to cause to make jump >

yu·psin·psin·ta \yu-psíŋ-psiŋ-ta\ *v* : to whip

yu·psi·psi·ca \yu-psí-psi-ca\ *v red of* yupsica : to make jump — **yupsipsil** *v contrac of* yupsipsica : to make jump < ~ *iyeya* to cause one to jump > - B.H.203.7

yu·pson *or* **yupsun** \yu-psóŋ\ *va* blu·pson : to turn over and spill *e.g.* water, to spill something by pulling

yu·pson·la \yu-psóŋ-la\ *va* blu·psonla : to move something limber, as a willow or a piece of wire - Cf *adj* psonpsonla

yu·pson·pson \yu-psóŋ-psoŋ\ *va red* [fr *yupson* to spill by pulling] : to wag, cause to move back and forth, as in sprinkling a lawn - Note: *glupsunpsun* to wag one's own, as a cow or horse its tail

yu·pson·pson·la \yu-psóŋ-psoŋ-la\ *va* blu·psonpsonla : to make round, to take off the corners

yu·psun \yu-psúŋ\ *va* : - *See* yupsón

yu·pšun \yu-pšúŋ\ *va* blu·pšun : to pull out sideways, to pull and break, *i.e.* to pull not by the roots, which is *yujún*

yu·pšun·ka \yu-pšúŋ-ka\ *va* blu·pšunka : to double up in a round bunch < *nape* ~ to clench the fist > — **yupšunka·ya** \yu-pšúŋ-ḱa-ya\ *adv* : doubled up < *Nape ~ gluza* He struck him in the face with closed fists. > - B.H.258.15

yu·pšun·pšun \yu-pšúŋ-pšuŋ\ *v red* blu·pšunpšun [fr *yupšun* to pull out and break] : to roll into a wad < ~ *ihpeya* to roll and throw awau, to make round like a ball with the hands > - D.2 B.H.271.14 Bl

yu·pta \yu-ptá\ *va* blu·pta : to cut out *e.g.* a garment after a pattern, to cut off as in making two shawls out of one big one

yu·pta·e·gnag \yu-ptá-e-gnag\ *adv* : all together, collectively < ~ *našlog iyayapi* They bolted and went on

---

\a\ father \e\ they \i\ machine \o\ smoke \u\ lunar \an, aŋ\ blanc Fr. \in, iŋ\ ink \on, oŋ, un, uŋ\ soon, confier Fr. \c\ chair \ġ\ machen Ger. \j\ fusion \clusters: bl, gn, kp, hšl, etc...\ b^e^lo ... said with a slight vowel **See more in the Introduction, Guide to Pronunciation**

together. > – R Bl

yu·ptan·pi·la s'e \yu-ptáŋ-pi-la s'e\ *adv* : quickly and in disorder, disorderly as opposed to *katkanheya* slowly and soundly < ~ *wiyukcan* to form an opinion in a disorderly way, *katkanheya wiyukcan* to form an opinion with care, ~ *pimic'iye lo* I prepared myself quickly in a disorderly way, *škeheya pimic'iyelo* I readied myself ambitiously, *Pa ~ yanka* He sat turning his head from side to side, as it were, *i.e.* as one confused over what to think and do. > – D.5 BT

yu·ptan·ptan \yu-ptáŋ-ptaŋ\ *va* blu·ptanptan : to rock, to turn or roll back and forth with the hand < ~ *wanyanka* to see *e.g.* a kernel of corn roll back and forth, *Nape ~ cewec'ipchcelo, peta kin oile ecetu šni ca* Since the fire did not break into flames, I prepared meat for myself rolling it over with my hand. *makiyuptanptan* to plow, *ciciyuptanptan* I am rolling it for you. > — **yuptanptan·yan** \yu-ṗtáŋ-ṗtaŋ-yaŋ\ *va* blu·ptanptanyan : to roll back and forth, to roll over and over — **yuptan·yan** \yu-ṗtáŋ-yaŋ\ *va* blu·ptanyan : to turn over by pulling < *yuptanyepicašni* immovable being rolled >

yu·pta·pta \yu-ptá-pta\ *v red* blu·ptapta [fr *yupta* to cut out or off] : to throw over or down in lumps, as in plowing hard ground

yu·pta·ya \yu-ptá-ya\ *adv* [fr *ptaya* together] : together, collectively < ~ *egnaka* to set or put together > — **yuptaye·la** *va perhaps* : to collect, to put together -Bl

yu·pte·ce·la \yu-pté-ce-la\ *va* blu·ptecela : to shorten — **yupte·lyela** *or* **yupcelyela** *adv* : shortening, fastening

yu·pti·na·pa \yu-ṗtí-na-pa\ *v* yuptina·wa·pa : to take shelter, hide < *Yuptiṅamapa yo* Hide behind me. > — **yuptinape·yakel** \yu-ṗtí-na-ṗe-ya-kel\ *adv* : shielded, protected from as in shielding one's self from the wind, or in carrying a stick for frightening off animals *etc.*, or shielding one's self by hiding < ~ *mun kte lo* I shall use it to frighten off *e.g.* dogs. > – Bl WHL

yu·pto·ka·kin \yu-ṗtó-ka-kiŋ\ *v* : to look around, look for < *Paha hiyeye kin na wakpala yunke kin hena ~ oškin'ic'iye* All those who stayed in the hills and creeks put themselves to work looking about, *i.e.* hunting buffalo. *Makoce lena ~ onicage tuktel iyayahin na tatanka oškinci'ye wanlake heci pilamayakiye* These lands he looked around in, your creation where he was going, and you saw buffalo busy, so I am grateful to you. *Taku sitomni ~ slowayelo* I know what he looked for everywhere around. > – Cf *okakin* to peek in BT Bl

yu·ptu·ga \yu-ṗtú-ġa\ *va* blu·ptuga : to pick to pieces – Note: perhaps otherwise written: yuptúh'a

yu·ptu·ja \yu-ṗtú-ja\ *va* blu·ptuja : to make crack or split *e.g.* a board by boring — **yuptu·ptuja** \yu-ṗtú-ptu-ja\ *v red* : to make crack, split

yu·ptu·ptu·ta \yu-ptú-ptu-ta\ *v* : to scatter in bits here and there, like heavy snowflakes – Bl

yu·ptuš \yu-ptúš\ *va contrac of* yuptuja : to make crack < ~ *iyeya* to make split suddenly > — **yuptu·škiya** \yu-ptú-ški-ya\ *va* yuptu·šwa·kiya *or* yuptu·šwa·ya : to cause to split

yu·pu·hpu·ga \yu-ṗú-ḣṗu-ġa\ *v* : to hit hard in anger – Bl

yu·pu·za \yu-ṗú-za\ *v* : to make dry, to wipe dry

yus \yus\ *v contrac of* yuzá : to grasp or hold < ~ *najin* to hold one standing, ~ *aya* to lead one, ~ *kaška yus aya* to lead on a bridle or such, *yus iyeya* to throw away > – Pb.19, 29 D.208

yu·sa·ka \yu-sá-k̇a\ *va* : to whip, snapping, to make a stiff hide soft by bending it to and fro – Note: *kasáka* to whip somebody or some thing

yu·sa·kib *or* **yusakibtu** \yu-sá-k̇ib\ \yu-sá-k̇i-bṫu\ *adv* : both together < ~ *unpi* They both stay together. >

yu·sa·ksa·ka \yu-sá-ksa-ka\ *v* : to hit from a distance, as horses, with a long whip

yu·san \yu-sáŋ\ *va* blu-san : to make brownish or whitish, to make fade

yu·san·pa \yu-sáŋ-pa\ *va* blu·sanpa [fr *sanpa* more, more than] : to make more, cause to increase

yu·sa·pa \yu-sá-ṗa\ *va* blu·sapa : to blacken

yu·scu \yu-scú\ *va* blu·scu lu·scu ma·scu : to have captured some young man or woman's affection or attention and to be elated over it, *esp* in *ref* to future marriage < *Mascu* I am captured. > – *See* ascú

yu·seb \yu-séb\ *va contrac of* yusepa : to rub off, deface < ~ *iyeya* to cause to rub off or deface >

yus e·na·pa \yus é-na-pa\ *v* : to lead out of doors < *Yus enawicape* They led them out. > – B.H.283.8

yu·se·pa \yu-sé-ṗa\ *va* blu·sepa : to rub off *i.e.* paint, to deface, to wear off e.g. the skin from the hand

yus i·cu \yús i-cù\ *va* : to grasp and take along

yu·sin·c'i·ya yan·ka \yu-síŋ-c'i-ya yaŋ-kà\ *v* : to be apparently asleep, to say nothing < *Hankeya ~ mankelo* I sat apparently half asleep, *i.e.* to look hostile at one. > – Bl

yus in·yan·ka \yús ìŋ-yaŋ-ka\ *va* : to run and catch < *Sinte kin ~ yo* Run and catch its tail. > – B.H.48.13, 217.12

yu·ska \yu-sk̇á\ *va* blu·ska : to whiten, cleanse; to gather with the fingers

yu·ska·ka \yu·ská-k̇a\ *va* blu·skaka : to equip one with new clothes – Bl

yu·ska·ki·ya \yu-sk̇á-k̇i-ya\ *va* yuska·wa·kiya : to cause *e.g.* linen to bleach

yu·ska·pa \yu-ská-pa\ *v* : to crack a whip, *i.e.* but without striking < *Icapsinte ~* He cracked his whip. >

yu·ska·pi·la s'e \yu-ská-ṗi-la s'e\ *adv* : neatly, clearly, as a job done

yu·ska·pi·s'a \yu-sk̇á-ṗi-s'e\ *adv* : close together

yu·skeb \yu-sk̇ĕ'b\ *v contrac of* yuskepa : to make escape, evaporate < ~ *iyeya* to make it evaporate >

yu·ske·pa \yu-sk̇é-ṗa\ *va* blu·skepa : to cause to escape, to drain off, to evaporate

yu·ski·ca \yu-skí-ca\ *va* blu·ski·ca : to press, make tight — **yuskil** \yu-skíl\ *va contrac of* yuskica *and* yuskita : to press and make tight — **yuski·skil** *va contrac of* yuskiskica *and* yuskiskita : to press tight

yu·ski·ski·ta \yu-skí-ski-ṫa\ *v red* blu·skiskita [fr *yuskita* to bind or tie *e.g.* a package] : to wrap around and round as in fastening a child on a board

yu·ski·ta \yu-skí-ṫa\ *v* blu·skita : to bind or tie something hard with a string or so, as a bundle or package, to bind or bandage, to hoop *e.g.* a barrel

yu·ski·ya \yu-skí-ya\ *va* yu·swa·kiya [fr *yúza* to take hold on] : to cause to marry

yu·sku \yu-skú\ *va* blu·sku : to peel off the skin with the hand < *Canke kangi na halhata kici wašinlo kin yuskupi na manil etokšupi keye* And so he stated that they went back on foot to get it, and the crows along with the magpies had peeled off pieces of the skin with their claws. > — **yusku·sku** \yu-skú-sk̇u\ *v red* : to peel away *e.g.* the skin – MS.96

yu·sku·ya \yu-sk̇ú-ya\ *va* blu·skuya : to make sweet or sour *etc.*, to flavor

yu·sle·ca \yu-slé-ca\ *va* blu·sleca : to split with one's hands, to tear *e.g.* meat —**yuslel** \yu-slél\ *va contrac* : to split or tear by hand < ~ *iyeya* to tear suddenly > —**yusle·lki·ya** \yu-slé-lki-ya\ *va* yuslé·lwa·kiya : to cause to split —**yusle·lya** *va* yusle·lwa·ya : to make split

yu·sle·sle·ca \yu-slé-sle-ca\ *v red of* yusleca : to split or tear by hand —**yusleslel** *va red contra* : to plit by hand < ~ *kte* He killed it (a lion) splitting it in two. > - B.H.76.12

yu·sli \yu-slí\ *va* blu·sli : to squeeze out, as matter from a sore, to milk at the utter

yu·sli·tka \yu-slí-tka\ *va* blu·slitka : to make taper, to make small by pinching

yu·slo·han \yu-sló-haŋ\ *va* blu·slohan : to pull a sled, to drag or draw along < ~ *aya* to tow, ~ *icu* to pull off on, as bark on a tree > - Cf ayuslohelaka —**yuslohanhan** *v red* blu·slohanhan : to pull, draw, to pull off —**yuslohan·yan** *adv* : dragging along —**yuslohe·kiya** *va* yuslohe·wa·kiya : to cause to draw along

yu·slo·slo \yu-sló-slo\ *va* blu·sloslo : to make soft by pressing with the hand, as an apple

yu·slul \yu-slúl\ *va contrac of* yusluta : to pull or slip or draw out from under < ~ *icu* to take and slip out from under, ~ *iyeya* to make slide from under >

yu·slul i·cu·pi \yu-slúl i-cù-pi\ *n* : a drawer

yu·slul o·gna·ke \yu-slúl ò-gna-ke\ *n* : a bureau with drawers

yu·slu·ta \yu-slú-ta\ *va* blu·sluta : to pull out, to draw out from under, as a splinter from under a fingernail, or a book from a shelf < *Hecel okahi na heyata ~ ške* They say, it (his hair) hung over (his forehead) and so he pulled it (the hair) out from under the ridge (of his head). > - B.H.122.26

yu·smin \yu-smíŋ\ *va* blu·smin : to pull off or pick off what is not tight < *Hintkala ~* She picked off nits. > —**yu·smin·yanyan** *va* blu·sminyanyan : to pick off *e.g.* meat from a bone - Note: R gives the meaning: to make smooth or bare, to wear off smooth, the root being *yusmismi* it seems rightly so, and not *yusminsmin*

yu·smi·smi \yu-smí-smi\ *v red* blu·smismi [fr *yu causing* + *smi* stripped clear] : to shave off short *e.g.* the hair —**yusmi·smin** \yu-smí-smiŋ\ *v red* blu·smismin [fr *yusmin* to pick off] : to pick off what is tight - Note: in the *red* of *smin* the *smi* is preferred to the *smin* in the first syllable

yu·sna \yu-sná\ *va* blu·sna 1 : to ring or tinkle, as with little bells 2 : to pull off anything being on a string, as beads, to ravel out *e.g.* a stocking - *Syn* YUSWÁ

yu·sna·sna \yu-sná-sna\ *v red* blu·snasna : to ring a bell

yu·sni \yu-sní\ *va* blu·sni : to put out, extinguish *e.g.* a fire; to turn out a light or lamp; to make cold < *petijanjan ~* to turn out a lamp > —**yusni·sni** *v red* blusnisni : to turn out the lights

yu·sni·snis i·cu \yu-sní-snis i-cù\ *v* : to take, not take, then take again - Note: *mahelhel* or *mahehe iyaya* to go in, out, then in again - Cf yusnis'

yu·snis' \yu-snís'\ *v* : to become invisible < ~ *iyaya* to be visible with one's head and then invisible, as children do hiding their head behind something by lowering themselves. If this is done repeatedly, we say: do hiding their head behind something by lowering themselves. If this is done repeatedly, we say: Yusnisnis' icu. > - WE

yu·so \yu-só\ *va* blu·so : to cut in strings or strips *e.g.* a hide

yu·sol \yu-sól\ *va contrac of* yusota : to use up, to make and end of < ~ *iyeya* to bring a sudden end to > —**yuso·lkiya** *va* yuso·lwa·kiya : to cause to use up, expend —**yuso·lya** *va* yuso·lwa·ya : to cause to use up

yu·so·so \yu-só-so\ *v red of* yusoso blu·soso : to cut in strips of hide

yu·so·ta \yu-só-ta\ *va* blu·sota : to make an end of, to use up, expend

yu·spa·ya \yu-spá-ya\ *va* blu·spaya : to make wet, to sponge

yu·stan·ka \yu-stáŋ-ka\ *va* blu·stanka : to moisten

yu·sto \yu-stó\ *va* blu·sto : to smooth down *e.g.* the hair, to make smooth

yu·sto·ki·ya \yu-stō'-ki-ya\ *va* yusto·wa·kiya : to cause to make smooth —**yusto·sto** \yu-stō'-sto\ *v red* [fr *yusto* to smooth down by hand] : to stroke - D.257

yu·sto·ya \yu-stó-ya\ *va* yusto·wa·ya : to cause to make smooth —*adv* perhaps : making smooth < *Iyake kin ~ tanyan econ wo* Do well making smooth the feather end of an arrow. > - MS.481

yu·su \yu-sú\ *va* blu-su : to make right, to make things ready < ~ *egle* to put things ready, so as to have them ready at hand when needed > - *Syn* YUECETU, YUWINYEYA

yu·sus *or* **yusyus** \yú-sus\ *v* or *adv contrac* [fr *yúsyus* to affect or touch one, itself fr *yúsyuza*] : to impress deeply with the importance of something, impressively < ~ *iwahoya etc.* to instruct one impressively, *i.e.* taking hold of his arm repeatedly, to be sure to instruct, ~ *iwahowicaya yo na tanyehci eonpi kte lo* Instruct them with assurance, and so you will indeed do well. > - EM Bl

yu·su·ta \yu-su-ta\ *va* blu·suta : to make firm

yu·su·ya \yu-sú-ya\ *va* yusu·wa·ya : to cause to make ready —*adv* : ready < *Taku oyasin ~ he* He was having everything made ready. ~ *egle* He set it just right. > - B.H.241.1, 251.7

yu·swa \yu-swá\ *va* blu·swa : to ravel out *e.g.* a stocking, to pick to pieces *e.g.* wool - *Syn* YUSNÁ —**yuswa·swa** \yu-swá-swa\ *v red* blu·swaswa : to ravel out —**yuswa·ya** *v* or *adv* : to pick to pieces

yu·swu \yu-swú\ *va* blu·swu : to make a rattling noise as in taking hold of shelled corn —**yuswu·pi s'e** *adv* : as though running smoothly along, rustling as falling grains or leaves, or the tolling of a bell < *Léceya taku au tka ~ au welo, i.e. iglaka au šni, he kapi. ~ icagapelo* Really they brought something, but they brought a delightful sound, *i.e.* they meant that they did not come to travel. They grew up with a pleasant sound, as is said when all the children of a family do grow up well. > —**yuswu·swu** *v red* : to give off a pleasant sound - Bl

yu·syus *or* **yusus** \yú-syus\ *v* or *adv contrac of* yusyuza : to impress one, affectively

yu·syu·za \yú-syu-za\ *v* or *adv* : impressively, for certain

yu·s'o \yu-s'ó\ *va* 1 : to cut off a strip at the edge of something 2 : to swim as does a duck or muskrat, *i.e.* to come up for air, as a muskrat brings its head above water and so gulps air < ~ *nunwan* to swim duck-wise,

---

i.e. to swim coming up for air > - Note: perhaps the idea of exhaustion is suggested from the apparent *compos* : *yuza* to hold + *o i.e. on* on account of —**yus'o·ki·ya** \yu-s'ó-ki-ya\ *va* yus'o·wa·kiya : to cause to swim duck-like, to come to the surface

yu·s'o·la·s'e \yu-s'ō'-la-s'e\ *adv* : in an exhausted manner, as one tired < ~ *iglušṫan* to finish coming up for air > —**yus'o·s'e** \yu-s'ō'-s'e\ *adv* : almost, hardly, scarcely < ~ *t'a* He almost died. >

yu·s'o·s'o \yu-s'ó-s'o\ *v red of* yus'o : to swim duck-like —**yus'o·ya** \yu-s'ó-ya\ *adv perhaps* : all tired out < *Kitanyel ~ wawatelo* Exhausted, I ate very little, *i.e.* have eaten but little. > —**yus'oya·kel** *or* **yus'oye·hci** \yu-s'ó-ya-ḱel\ *adv* : in an exhausted manner, all tired out, contrary to all expectation < ~ *ecamon.* ~ *waglihunni yelo* I did it all worn out. Contrary to all expectation I reached home. < ~ *wahi* I arrived utterly exhausted. > - *Syn* KITANYANKEL Bl BT

yu·ša \yu-šá\ *va* blu·ša : to make red by rubbing or touching

yu·šab \yu-šáb\ *va contrac of* yušapa : to soil, blacken < ~ *iyeya* to cause to soil > —**yuša·bya** *va* yuša·bwa·ya : to cause to soil

yu·ša·pa \yu-šá-ṗa\ *va* blu·šapa : to soil, to defile or blacken anything

yu·še·ca \yu-šé-ca\ *va* blu·šeca : to make dry, to deaden — **yuše·kšeca** *v red* : to make dry, dead dry —**yu·šel** \yu-šél\ *va contrac* : to make dry, wither < ~ *iyeya* to cause to wither >

yu·šib \yu-šíb\ *va contrac of* yušipa : to bend, as wire *etc.* < ~ *iyeya* to make bend > —**yuši·bšipa** \yu-ší-bši-ṗa\ *v red of* yušipa : to bend

yu·ši·ca \yu-ší-ca\ *va* blu·šica : to injure, spoil, to make bad

yu·ši·gla \yu-ší'-gla\ *va* blu·šigla : to make angry

yu·ši·htin \yu-ší-ȟtiŋ\ *va* blu·šihtin : to enfeeble, to debase — **yušihtin·pi** *n* : feebleness —**yušihtinyan** *adv* : feebly

yu·ši·lh'an \yu-ší-lȟ'aŋ\ *va* blu·šilh'an [fr *šilh'an* to act badly] : to make act badly —**yušilh'an·yan** *adv* : causing to do badly —**yuši·lya** *adv* : treated badly < ~ *ecaniconpelo* They wronged you. > - Bl

yu·ši·na i·hpe·ya \yu-ší-na i-ȟpè-ya\ *v* : to take away one's shawl < *yušina tancocola ihpeya* to take away a shawl and render naked > - Bl

yu·šin \yu-šíŋ\ *vn* : to wrinkle *e.g.* the forehead —**yušin·kiya** *va* yušin·wa·kiya : to wrinkle < *Pahte yušinwakiya* I wrinkled my forehead. *ite* ~ to frown at one > —**yušin·pi** *n* : wrinkles —**yušin·šin** *v red* : to wrinkle —**yušin·yan** *adv* : wrinkled, folded < ~ *iyakaška* to tie a knot in such a manner (with a loop) that it can be loosened by pulling, otherwise said *yukipaš iyakaška* to tie a knot with a loop > - Bl

yu·ši·pa \yu-ší-ṗa\ *va* blu·šipa : to bend *e.g.* wire *etc.*

yu·ška \yu-šká\ *va* blu·ška : to loosen, to untie

yu·škan·škan \yu-škáŋ-škaŋ\ *va* blu·škanškan : to cause to move about, to shake up somebody or something

yu·ška·ška \yu-šká-ška\ *va red of* yuška : to loosen, untie - B.H.38.2

yu·ške·han \yu-šké-haŋ\ *va* blu·škehan : to make wild < *Bluškehin kta* Let me make it wild. > —**yuškehan·han** *v red* bluškehanhan : to make prance about, to stir up *e.g.* people - B.H.261.13

yu·ške·pa \yu-šké-pa\ *va* : to wring out *e.g.* water from wet clothes - Bl

yu·ške·ya \yu-šké-ya\ *adv* : free, loose, *i.e.* on the loose < ~ *napapi unpi* They are on the loose running away. >

yu·ški \yu-škí\ *va* blu·ški : to plait, braid *e.g.* the hair

yu·ški·ca \yu-škí-ca\ *va* blu·škica : to press, squeeze or wring *e.g.* clothes, to press out water by twisting, to wring *e.g.* a washrag —**yuškil** *va contrac* : to wring < ~ *iyeya* to make wring >

yu·ški·pi \yu-škí'-ṗi\ *part* : plaited, braided, or gathered in folds

yu·ški·ška \yu·škí-ška\ *va* blu·škiška : to make rough, make notches

yu·ški·ške·ya \yu-škí-ške-ya\ *va* yuškiške·wa·ya : to cause to make difficult

yu·ški·ški·ca \yu-škí-ški-ca\ *v red of* yuškica : to wring or squeeze, to press

yu·škob \yu-škō'b\ *v contrac of* yuškopa : to bend or make twisted < ~ *iyeya* to make bend or get twisted >

yu·ško·kpa \yu-škō'-kṗa\ *va* blu·škokpa : to hollow out *e.g.* a trough —*adj* or *adv perhaps* : hollowed out, in a concave way < *Šiná ~ yuza yo, el ognakin kte* Hold out the blanket, so he might put things in, *i.e.* hold the blanket in such a way as to make a concavity for things to be poured in. >

yu·ško·pa \yu-škō'-ṗa\ *va* blu·škopa : to bend, to make crooked or twisting —**yuško·škopa** *v red* : to bend making things crooked

yu·šku \yu-škú\ *va* blu·šku : to shell off *e.g.* corn by hand —**yušku·šku** *v red* : to shell off *e.g.* corn

yu·šla \yušlá\ *va* blu·šla : to cut off the hair, to shear *e.g.* sheep, to pull out weeds, to make bare or bald —**yušla·kiya** *va* yušla·wa·kiya : to cause to pull, to pluck or shear off —**yušla·šla** *v red* : to pull out < *pejiȟota* ~ to pull up quantities of sage brush > —**yušla·ya** *va* yušla·wa·ya : to cause to make bare, bald *etc.* - D.112

yu·šle·ca \yu-šlé-ca\ *va* blu·šleca : to split by hand

yu·šli \yu-šlí\ *va* blu·šli : to press or squeeze by hand —**yušli·ya** *adv* : pressing < ~ *iyakaška* to squeeze up and tie tight >

yu·šlog \yu-šlóg\ *va contrac of* yušloka : to pull off or out < ~ *iyeya* to make pull out > —**yušlo·gki** \yu-šlō'-gḱi\ *va* yušlo·gwa·ki : to snatch away —**yušlo·gya** *va* yušlo·gwa·ya : to cause to pull off or out

yu·šlo·ka \yu-šlō'-ḱa\ *va* blu·šloka : to pull off *e.g.* a garment, to pull out *e.g.* a cork —**yušlo·šloka** \yu-šló-šlo-ḱa\ *v red* : to pull off or out

yu·šlul \yu-šlúl\ *v contrac of* yušluta : to slip out or let slip < ~ *iyeya* to cause to slip from > —**yušlu·šluta** \yu-šlú-šlu-ṫa\ *v red* blu·šlušluta [fr *yušluta* to let slip out, to slip from] : to let slip from one, to make slippery or smooth

yu·šlu·ta \yu-šlú-ṫa\ *va* blu·šluta : to slip out, to let slip from one, as a fish

yu·šma *or* **yušme** \yu-šmá\ *va* blu·šma : to make deep *e.g.* by pouring water —**yušme·ya** *adv* : deeply

yu·šna \yu-šná\ *va* blu·šna : to drop anything, to let slip, or to miss while trying to catch

yu·šna·kon·za \yu-šná-koŋ-za\ *v* yušna·wa·konza : to pretend to make a mistake

yu·šna·pi \yu-šná-pi\ *n* : a mistake

yu·šna·šna \yu-šná-šna\ *v red* blu·šnašna < fr *yušna* to miss while trying > : to try to catch and fail often, to miss

yu·šna·šni \yu-šná-šni\ *adv* : accurately —**yušnašni e·conpi** *n* : accuracy - Bl

yu·šni·ja \yu-šní-ja\ *va* blu·šnija : to cause to wither

— **yušni·šnija** *v red* blu·šnišnija : make wither much

yu·šo·ša \yu-šó'-ša\ *va* blu·šoša : to make muddy *e.g.* water

yu·špa \yu-špá\ *va* blu·špa : to divide, to break off < *iglušpa* to free one's self, *Wicaša kin le ~ šni ca eniyayin kte* This man who is not honest will carry you away (he has no good intentions, so stay away from him). > — **yušpa·špa** \yu-špá-špa\ *v red* blu·špašpa : to break into pieces *e.g.* a loaf of bread, to scratch off pieces - *Syn* YUKSAKSA — **yušpašpa wiyopeya** *v* : to retail — **yušpašpa·ya** *adv* : in parcels, pieces < *Makoce kin ~ iwicakiyute* He measured out the land for them in parcels. > - FP Bl B.H.73.13

yu·špi \yu-špí\ *va* blu·špi : to pick or gather *e.g.* berries, to pull or pick off *e.g.* cherries from a tree — **yušpí·ka** \yu-špi-ka\ *adj* : worth buying or keeping < *Iogmus ~ waeye eyelo* He said as to speaking it is worth keeping the mouth shut. > - Bl

yu·špi·špi \yu-špí-špi\ *v red of* yušpi : to pick, gather

yu·špu \yu-špú\ *va* blu·špu : to pull off with the hand what is tight

yu·špu·la o·ta \yu-špú-la ò-ta\ *n* : redroot, green amoranha, amaranthus retroflexus - BT #22

yu·špu·špu \yu-špú-špu\ *v red* blu·špušpu [fr *yušpu* to to pull off what is tight] : to strip off what is on tight

yu·špu·špu·pi \yu-špú-špu-pi\ *n* a : coin money, change b : pieces broken off

yu·štan \yu-štáŋ\ *va* blu·štan a : to perfect or finish anything b : to settle *e.g.* a question in a meeting, to have decreed < *Zitkala tanka oyasin kiinyankapi kta gluštanpi* All the big birds were finished with their own so that they might have a race. >

yu·šta·šta \yu-štá-šta\ *v* blu·štašta : to soak a skin, a hide, as a preparation for dressing it, to moisten one's skin < *tahayuštašta* to soak a hide for one night >

yu·štu·ta \yu-štú-ta\ *v* : to rub or soak the feet as with snow - Ed

yu·šu·ja \yu-šú-ja\ *va* blu·šuja : to crush *e.g.* bones, to break in slivers, *e.g.* by twisting a tough piece of wood

yu·šun'·on·pa *or* **yušun'unk'onpa** \yu-šúŋ-oŋ-pa\ *n* : the shape or form of a "V", like that made by the poles of a travois on the back of a dog, or that made by cranes travelling either way off and back, from the wing tips of the leader < *~ kahya* in the form of a "V" > - MS.104 BS

yu·šuš \yu-šúš\ *va contrac of* yušuja : to crush < *~ iyeya* to crush into splinters > — **yušu·šuja** *v red* : to crush in splinters by twisting

yu·š'ag \yu-š'ág\ *vn contrac of* yuš'aka : to be heavily burdened — **yuš'a·gya** *va* yuš'a·gwa·ya : to overburden, loverload — *vn* : to have much of a thing considered a burden < *He tuwa šunhpala yuš'agye, yuš'ag ble lo* Someone overloaded that puppy, I too go overloaded, *i.e.* then somebody has plenty puppies. > - Bl

yu·š'a·ka \yu-š'á-ka\ *vn* blu·š'aka : to be heavily laden, to have has much as one can carry

yu·š'e \yu-š'é\ *va* blu·š'e [fr *š'e* to trickle, to drip] : to make drip, trickle, to cause to fall in drops, *e.g.* drops of medicine — **yuš'e·š'e** *v red* blu·š'eš'e : to make trickle as water - Cf š'eš'e

yu·š'in·š'in \yu-š'íŋ-š'iŋ\ *va* : to tickle, *e.g.* under the arm

yu·š'in·ya·ya \yu-š'íŋ-ya-ya\ *vn* ma·yuš'iŋyaya : to be afraid, frightened, to be surprised < *Wicayuš'inyaye s'e taku wanblaka, nawah'on* I heard, I saw something as if they were afraid, *i.e.* unexpectedly something very beautiful. > - BE D.215

yu·š'in·ye·ya \yu-š'íŋ-ye-ya\ *va* yuš'inye·wa·ya : to frighten, scare one

yu·ta \yũ'-ta\ *va* wáta yáta unyútapi : to eat anything

yu·ta·e·gle \yu-tá-e-gle\ *v* : to sweep together in a heap *e.g.* of hay, rubbish *etc.* - GA BT

yu·ta·he·na \yu-tá-he-na\ *va* blu·tahena : to make nearer, to put towards < *~ icu* to draw it this way or towards himself >

yu·ta·kin \yu-tá-kiŋ\ *va* blu·takin : to cause to lean < *Toki ~ šni lecel mankahelo* What wonder! I was sitting motionless. > - Bl

yu·ta·kin·yan \yu-tá-kiŋ-yaŋ\ *adv* : leaning

yu·ta·ku \yu-tá-ku\ *va* : to make a thing to be something - B.H.70.4

yu·ta·ku·ni·šni \yu-tá-ku-ni-šni\ *va* blu·takunišni : to destroy — **yutakunišni·yan** *adv* : destroying — **yutaku·šni** *va* blu·takušni : to bring to naught, to frustrate

[1]**yu·tan** \yu-táŋ\ *va* blu·tan : to touch, to feel

[2]**yu·tan** \yu-táŋ\ *va* blu·tan : to honor, glorify - *Syn* YATAN

yu·tan·co·la \yu-táŋ-co-la\ *va* blu·tancola : to make naked

yu·tan'·in \yu-táŋ-iŋ\ *va* blu·tan'in : to make manifest, to reveal — **yutan'in·yan** *adv* : manifestly, openly

yu·tan·ka \yu-táŋ-ka\ *va* blu·tanka : to make great or large

yu·tan·kal ki·co \yu-táŋ-kal ki-cò\ *va* : to call one outside < *yutankal iyeya* to take one outside >

yu·tan·ka s'e \yu-táŋ-ka s'e\ *adv* : seemingly made big, made wide or broad - Bc KE

yu·tan·ka·ya \yu-táŋ-ka-ya\ *va* : to enlarge something, as by adding *e.g.* a picture made larger or a house given an addition - *Syn* YUOTANKAYA — *adv* : largely, greatly < *~ kaga* to make bigger, *i.e.* in scale >

yu·tan·ni \yu-táŋ-ni\ *va* blu·tanni : to make old, wear out — **yutanni·ka** \yu-táŋ-ni-ka\ *va* blu·tannika : to wear out *e.g.* clothes, to make old

yu·tan'·om \yu-táŋ-om\ *adv* : leaning < *~ egle* to place leaning, *~ han* It is leaning. > - BD

yu·tan'·on·pa \yu-táŋ-oŋ-pa\ *vn* : to lean - P

yu·tan·tan \yu-táŋ-taŋ\ *v red* blu·tantan [fr *yutan* to touch or feel] : to touch much — **yutantan·kel mani** *v* : to grope, as a blind person does - Bl

yu·tan·yan \yu-táŋ-yaŋ\ *va perhaps* : to make good — *adv* : praising — **yutanyan·kel** \yu-táŋ-yaŋ-kel\ *adv* : for good, really, in earnest < *~ ecamon kta* I shall be in earnest to do it. >

Yu·ta·pi Wa·kan \Yú-ta-pi Wa-kaŋ\ *np* : Holy Communion

yu·ta·ta \yu-tá-ta\ *va* blu·tata : to shake off *e.g.* dust from a garment, to scrape or brush off with the hand

yu·ta·wa·cin·hin·yan·za \yu-tá-wa-ciŋ-hiŋ-yàŋ-za\ *va* blu·tawacinhinyanza : to make cross, disgruntled

yu·teb \yu-té'b\ *va contrac of* yutepa : to wear off short < *~ iyeya* to cause to wear off > — **yute·bte·pa** \yu-té-bte-pa\ *va red of* yutepa : constantly wearing off short

yu·te·ca \yu-té-ca\ *va* blu·teca : to make new, to renew - Pb.35

yu·te·han \yu-té-haŋ\ *va* blu·tehan : to prolong, to put off, to make slow or retard — **yutehan s'e** *adv* : de-

---

\a\ father \e\ they \i\ machine \o\ smoke \u\ lunar \an, aŋ\ blanc Fr. \in, iŋ\ ink \on, oŋ, un, uŋ\ soon, confier Fr. \c\ chair \ǧ\ machen Ger. \j\ fusion \clusters: bl, gn, kp, hšl, etc...\ b°lo ... said with a slight vowel **See more in the Introduction, Guide to Pronunciation**

laying – Bc
yu·te·lya \yu-ṫé-lya\ *va* [fr *yuteca* to make new] : to renew – LP
yu·te·pa \yu-ṫé-pa\ *va* blu·tepa : to wear off short, as a bolt on a wagon – R
yu·tib i·ya·ya \yu-ṫíb i-yà-ya\ *vn* : to draw up, as does leather when it is near a fire — **yuti·bya** *adv* [fr *yutipa* to cramp] : drawn up, as burned leather, or as a muscle cramp < ~ *yanka* to sit cramped up > – Bl
yu·ti·ca \yu-ṫí-ca\ *va* blu·tica : to scrape away, *e.g.* to slide snow away with the hand, to paw away as does a horse — **yutil** *va contrac* : to scrape away with the hand < ~ *iyeya* to make slide away with the hand >
yu·ti·ma·hel \yu-ṫí-ma-hel\ *adv* : into the house < ~ *icu* to take into the house > – Bl B.H.249.11
yu·ti·pa \yu-ṫí'-ṗa\ *va* : to cramp *e.g.* the muscles, to make crisp, draw up *e.g.* burned leather < *siyutipa* to have cramps in the feet, *simayutipa* I have cramps in my feet, *teziyutipa* to have stomach cramps, *tahuyutipa* to have a cramp in the neck >
yu·ti·tan \yu-ṫí-ṫaŋ\ *va* blu·titan : to pull < ~ *icu* to get by pulling, as in a tug-of-war, or as in treating a stubborn horse > – Note: *yuzica* to pull, in the sense of to stretch something — **yutitan·yan** \yu-ṫí'-ṫaŋ-yaŋ\ *va* yutitan·wa·ya : to cause to pull at
yu·tkab o·ma·ni \yu-tkáb o-mà-ni\ *v* : to walk with difficulty, as through gumbo – Bl
yu·tkan·la \yu-tkáŋ-la\ *adj* : plenty, plenteous, abundant, much – *Syn* YUGÉLA P Bl
yu·tke·ya \yu-tk̇é-ya\ *adv* : deeply, as is said of a bluff shore where the water is deep
yu·tkons \yu-tk̇óŋs\ *va contrac of* yutkonza : to cut off even < ~ *iyeya* to cause to cut off even >
yu·tkon·za \yu-tkóŋ-za\ *va* blu·tkonza : to cut off even, as with a shears
yu·tku·ga \yu-tk̇ú-ġa\ *va* blu·tkuga : to break off square — **yutkuh** *va contrac* : to break off < ~ *iyeya* to cause to break off square >
yu·tkun·za \yu-tkúŋ-za\ *va* : – *See* yutkonza
yu·tku·tku·ga \yu-tkú-tk̇u-ġa\ *v red* [fr *yutkuga* to break off square] : to break or divide in several pieces
yu·to·gye \yu-tó-gye\ *va* : to make different < ~ *econ* to do it and make it different >
yu·to·kan \yu-tó-kaŋ\ *va* blu·tokan : to put in another place, to remove or reject — **yutokan·kan** *v red* : to scatter < ~ *iyeya* to make scatter abroad >
yu·to·kanl \yu-tŏ'-k̇aŋl\ *adv* : in another place < ~ *iyeya* to remove, push away, ~ *yuza* to lead away, ~ *unkiciyuzapi ye* Lead us together away. > – Pb.18
yu·to·kan·yan \yu-tó-kaŋ-yaŋ\ *adv* : in another place, removed < ~ *iyeya* to make move away >
yu·to·ke·ca \yu-tŏ'-ke-ca\ *va* blu·tokeca : to alter, to revoke
yu·to·to \yu-ṫó-ṫo\ *va* blu-toto : to clear off *e.g.* a field
yu·to·to·bya \yu-tó-to-bya\ *va* yutoto·bwa·ya [fr *yutotopa* to become soft] : to soak and make soft
yu·to·to·pa \yu-tó-to-ṗa\ *vn* : to become soft, as leather by soaking
yu·tu·gtu·ka \yu-ṫú-gṫu-k̇a\ *v red of* yutuka : to pick to pieces *e.g.* furs
yu·tu·hye·la \yu-ṫú-ḣye-la\ *adv* : bent, doubled up, stooped as an old man < ~ *hiyaya, mani* He walked, going by stooped. >
yu·tu·ka \yu-ṫú-k̇a\ *va* blu·tuka : to pull, spoil, or destroy *e.g.* furs
yu·tun·tun·pa \yu-ṫúŋ-ṫuŋ-pa\ *va* : to make slimy or slippery – R Bl
yu·tu·ta \yu-ṫú-ta\ *va* blu·tuta : to make smart
yu·tu·tka \yu-tú-tka\ *va* blu·tutka : to break in small pieces — **yututka·yakel** *adv* : in parts, pieces, in small amounts < ~ *econ, eya* to say and do something only partly, hence imperfectly > – LP
yu·tu·tu·ka \yu-ṫú-ṫu-k̇a\ *v red of* yutuka : to pull or spoil *e.g.* furs
yu·t'a \yu-t'á\ *va* blu·t'a : to choke to death — **yut'a-t'a** *v red* : to benumb – P
yu·t'ins \yu-t'íŋs\ *va contrac of* yut'inza : to tighten < ~ *iyeya* to cause to tighten > — **yut'in·st'inza** *va red* : to draw up tight
yu·t'in·za \yu-t'íŋ-za\ *va* : to draw tight, to tighten *e.g.* a saddle-girth < *Kola, ~ yo* Friend, draw up tight, as a visitor would say who wanted to smoke the pipe. >
yu·ung \yu-úŋg\ *va contrac of* yuunka : to make lie or throw down < ~ *iyeya* suddenly to cause to lie down >
yu·un·ka \yu-úŋ-ka\ *va* blu·unka : to make lie down or throw down, to demolish < *Ciyuunke kin wakan kte lo, na mayaluunke kin pilaniciyin kte lo, eya* He said: If I throw you down it will be a wonder, if you throw me down it will make you glad. >
yu·un·zi \yu-úŋ-zi\ *va* blu·unzi : to take one around the waist and pull backwards < *Na wanna cante pahloke el can eya ikoyagya na ~ hekta pagopta yuzin na icu na topa lila yutitan* And when he now pierced the heart, he also fixed it to a tree; and last he took and grabbed around the waist and four he pulled very hard. > – *Syn* YUTITAN
yu·wa·cin·ko \yu-wá-ciŋ-ko\ *va* blu·wa·cinko : to make angry
yu·wa·cin·ksa·pa \yu-wá-ciŋ-ksa-pa\ *va* blu·wacinksapa : to make wise
yu·wa·cin·tan·ka \yu-wá-ciŋ-taŋ-ka\ *va* blu·wacintanka : to make magnanimous, or to make stubborn
yu·wa·cin·ton \yu-wá-ciŋ-toŋ\ *va* blu·wacinton : to make intelligent
yu·wa·ga \yu-wá-ġa\ *va* blu·waga : to twist, roll, turn as the hands in running
yu·wa·hpa·ni·ca \yu-wá-ḣpa-ni-ca\ *va* blu·wahpanica : to make poor
yu·wa·hwa·ka *or* **yuwahwala** \yu-wá-ḣwa-k̇a\ *va* blu·wahwaka : to make mild, gentle
yu·wa·kan \yu-wá-k̇aŋ\ *va* blu·wakan : to make holy, to consecrate or make special — **yuwakan·yan** *adv* : consecrating, keeping holy, piously < ~ *econpi* it was done devoutly. > – B.H.57.12, 73.7
yu·wa·ni·ca \yu-wá-ni-ca\ *va* **a** : to annihilate, destroy **b** : to spend one's money < *Taku wowaš'ake luhapi kin ko niyuwanicapi cinpi* They wanted you to spend your money and what strength you have. > — **yuwanil** *va contrac* : to destroy < ~ *aya* to bring to naught >
yu·wan·ji·la \yu-wáŋ-ji-la\ *va* : to unite, to make into one – B.H.233.9
yu·wan·kal \yu-wáŋ-k̇al\ *v* : to cause to move upward < ~ *icu* to lift or raise up, ~ *iyeya* suddenly to rise up, ~ *aya* to raise, put on a high place, to honor, *nakpa ikikcu* to prick up one's ears >
yu·wan·ka·la \yu-wáŋ-ka-la\ *va* blu·wankala : to make soft or tender
yu·wan·ka·tu \yu-wáŋ-k̇a-ṫu\ *va* : to exalt, raise up — **yuwankatu·ya** *va* **a** : to raise *e.g.* a curtain, *i.e.* to let it go up **b** : to promote — *adv* : upwards, above – B.H.232.14
yu·was \yu-wás\ *va contrac of* yuwaza : to twist or

turn < ~ *iyeya* to cause to twist or turn > — **yuwas kte** *va* : to bother, annoy by pulling one here and there < *Yuwas wakte* I kill him bothering him. >

yu·wa·sla \yu-wá-sla\ *va* blu·wasla : to grease, by rubbing salve on one's hands

yu·wa·sna \yu-wá-sna\ *va* blu·wasna : to make any food very tasty < *He luwasna* You made that tasty. > – Note: *wasna* was always a very much sought-after dish

yu·wa·swa·za \yu-wá-swa-za\ *v red of* yuwaza : to twist or turn the hands in running — **yuwa·sya** *adv* : in a twisting manner, vexing

yu·wa·ša·ka·la \yu-wá-ša-k̇a-la\ *va* blu·wašakala : to make cheap or easy

yu·wa·šte \yu-wá-šte\ *va* blu·wašte : to bless, to make good

yu·wa·š'ag \yu-wá-šag\ *va contrac of* yuwaš'aka : to strengthen < ~ *iyeya* to cause to make strong > — **yu-waš'a·gya** *va* yuwaš'a·gwa·ya : to cause to make strong

yu·wa·š'a·ka \yu-wá-š'a-k̇a\ *va* blu·waš'aka : to make strong, to strengthen

yu·wa·š'a·ke·šni \yu-wá-š'a-k̇e-šni\ *va* blu·waš'akešni : to make weak or feeble, to weaken

yu·wa·za \yu-wá-za\ *va* **a** : to twist or turn, as the hands do in running **b** : to vex, tease, annoy and continue to do so **c** : to throw up dirt with the foot and let it down on the back, as a bull does < *maka yuwaza* to throw up dirt by the feet, *igluwaza* to throw on one's own >

yu·we \yu-wé\ *v* : to make bleed – Bl

yu·we·ga \yu-wé-ġa\ *va* blu·wega : to break *e.g.* a stick with the hands, but not entirely off — **yuweh** *va contrac* : to break partly < ~ *iyeya* to cause to break > — **yuwe·hwega** \yu-wé-ḣwe-ġa\ *va* blu·wehwega : to break something in different places — **yuwehweh** *va contrac* : to break < ~ *iyeya* to cause to break > — **yuwe·hya** *va* : to cause to break

yu·wi \yu-wí\ *va* blu·wi : to bandage, bind up, to wrap around – R

yu·wi·ca·ka \yu-wí-ca-k̇a\ *va* blu·wicaka : to make true to prove or convince, to show that a cause is true and to establish it < *Tokša bluwicakin ktelo* In time I shall prove it. > — **yuwicake·hca** *adv* : truthfully < ~ *oyaka* to tell a thing not as it is, to make a thing appear true by telling it as true > – *Syn* YAWICAKEYEHCI

yu·wi·ca·ke·ya *or* **yuwicakeya s'e** \yu-wí-ca-k̇e-ya\ *adv perhaps* : telling a thing as true – B.H.70.4

yu·wi·ca·ša \yu-wí-ca-ša\ *va* : to make manly

yu·wi·ca·ša·šni \yu-wí-ca-ša-šni\ *va* blu·wicašašni : to make mean, to get excited

yu·wi·co·h'an \yu-wí-co-ḣ'aŋ\ *va* : to turn a trifling affair into something big – EE

yu·wi·gnu·ni \yu-wí-gnu-ni\ *va* blu·wignuni : to cause to perish, to destroy — **yuwignuni·ya** *va* yuwignuni·wa·ya : to cause to destroy – R Bl

yu·wi·lwi·ta·ya \yu-wí-lwi-ta-ya\ *adv* : make to be grouped in different places < ~ *ahiyaye* a big crowd together but then smaller parties and persons about nearby > – Bc

yu·wi·nu·hca·la \yu-wí-nu-ḣca-la\ *va* blu·winuhcala : to make a woman of, to render effeminate

yu·win·ga \yu-wíŋ-ġa\ *va* blu·winga : to turn around, to turn back — **yuwinh** *va contrac* : to turn back < ~ *iyeya* to turn suddenly back > — **yuwin·hwinga** *v red* : to turn around often — **yuwin·hya** *adv* : coming around < ~ *glicu* to come back coming around and arriving home > – Bl

yu·win·ja \yu-wíŋ-ja\ *va* **1** : to bind down *e.g.* with a piece of wire **2** : to make limber or pliant — **yuwinš** *va contrac* : to make pliant < ~ *iyeya* to cause to make limber > — **yuwin·šwinja** *va* blu·winšwinja : to make limber — **yuwin·šya** *va* yuwin·šwa·ya : to cause to bend down

yu·win·ta \yu-wíŋ-ṫa\ *va* : to salute with the hand < *ite* ~ to salute as once was a Dakota custom to express a desire for peace *etc.*, wiping the face of the other with the hands, not actually, but in gesture, as a sign of friendly relations >

yu·win·yan *or* **yuwinuhcala** \yu-wíŋ-yaŋ\ *va* : to make a woman of one, to render effeminate — **yuwinyan·ke s'e** *adv* : being a bad woman < ~ *un* one who is a bad woman but wishes to be thought good >

yu·win·ye·ya \yu-wíŋ-ye-ya\ *va* blu·winyeya : to get ready, make ready, prepare

yu·wi·pi \yu-wí-pi\ *n* : stones that are transparent and found on ant hills and used in the *wakan wicoh'an* mystery or trick custom called *yuwípi* in which one is tied all round and loosed by magic — **yuwipi wašicun** *n* : a particular round hard stone that is supposed to have power in the hands of those who have dreamed, *i.e.* ~ *iwicawahanble* I had a vision of them, the *yuwipi* power stones – Note: the stones are also titled *tunkan wašicun* *See* wašicun

yu·wi·tan \yu-wí-ṫaŋ\ *va* blu·witan : to honor, glorify

yu·wi·tan·tan \yu-wí-ṫaŋ-ṫaŋ\ *va* : to make proud by giving good things

yu·wi·ta·ya \yu-wí-ṫa-ya\ *va* blu·witaya : to collect together, to assemble *e.g.* horses — *adv* : all together, assembled

yu·wi·tko \yu-wí-tko\ *va* blu·witko : to make foolish — **yuwitko·tko** *or* **yuwitkotko·ka** *va* blu·witkotko : to make foolish – B.H.102.16

yu·wi·wi·he s'e \yu-wí-wi-he s'e\ *adv* : in large numbers < ~ *ahiyaye* to pass by in crowds > – Bl

yu·wi·ya·kpa \yu-wí-ya-k̇pa\ *va* blu·wiyakpa : *fig* to interpret, to make shine

yu·wo·hol \yu-wó-hol\ *v* : to cause to move upward < *nakpa kin* ~ *ikikcu* to prick up one's ears > – *Syn* IWOSLA, YUWANKAL Bl

yu·wo·o·tan·la \yu-wó-o-taŋ-la\ *va* : to adjust – P

yu·wo·slal \yu-wō'-slal\ *v* [fr *woslal* upright] : to make upright < ~ *egle, iyeya, icu* to set up on end > – B.H. 280.10 Pb.44

yu·wo·sla·ta \yu-wō'-sla-ṫa\ *va* blu·woslata : to set upright *e.g.* a flag pole

yu·za \yū'-za\ *va* blu·za **1** : to take hold of, to catch **2** : to take a wife < *Cannunpa ciciyuzin kte* I will hold the pipe for you, *i.e.* I will pray, as a person would say to *Wakantanka* God. > – BT

yu·za·han \yu-zá-haŋ\ *va* blu·zahan : to make a noise, one made by tearing cloth

yu·za hi·yan·ka \yú-za hì-yaŋ-ka\ *va* : to grab running < *Tašina el yuza hiyanke* She ran grabbing at his cloak. > – B.H.29.14

yu·za·mni \yu-zá-mni\ *va* blu·zamni : to uncover, to

\a\ father \e\ they \i\ machine \o\ smoke \u\ lunar \an, aŋ\ blanc Fr. \in, iŋ\ ink \on, oŋ, un, uŋ\ soon, confier Fr. \c\ chair \ġ\ machen Ger. \j\ fusion \clusters: bl, gn, kp, hšl, etc...\ b[e]lo ... said with a slight vowel **See more in the Introduction, Guide to Pronunciation**

Z

open by pulling something away, as in uncovering a bed by pulling away the blankets *etc.*, to find one by pulling away a screen or curtain, to spread out < *Tiyopa kin ~ hiyeya* He pulled the door opened. > — **yuzamni-han** *adv* : standing open < *~ egle* to put or place it ajar > — **yuzamni·mni** *v red* : to pull open — **yuzamni-yan** *adv* : open < *Mahpiya tatiyopa kin ~ han* The door of heaven was standing open. > – B.H.286.2

yu·zan \yu-záŋ\ *va* blu·zan : to part or separate *e.g.* tall grass, to push aside, to raise up *e.g.* a curtain

yu·za·za \yu-zá-za\ *v* : to pick to pieces *e.g.* sinew or a piece of cloth

yu·ze \yu-zé\ *va* blu·ze : to dip or lade out *e.g.* food from a kettle, to skim

yu·zi·ca \yu-zí-ca\ *va* blu·zica : to stretch *e.g.* a skin or a rubber band < *Amagaju nahan cu kin(han) yuzicapi s'e u ktelo* It will come as though rain and dew stretch it, *i.e.* it will grow fast (as grain) when it rains and dews. > **yuzi·gzica** \yu-zí-gzi-ca\ *v red* blu·zigzica : to stretch, to make pliable — **yuzil** \yu-zíl\ *va contrac of* yuzica : stretching < *~ icu* to stretch > – Bl

yu·zon·ta \ya-zóŋ-ta\ *va* : to make honest, to make them better men – Bl

yu·zug \yu-zúg\ *va contrac* [fr *yuzuka* to stretch out] : to stretch out from one

yu·zu·ka \yu-zú-k̇a\ *va* blu·zuka : to stretch out from one

yu·zu·ka·pi·s'e \yu-zú-k̇a-pi-s'e\ *adv* : moving in a straight direction up or down, or in any other direction < *Yunkan taku wan skayela mahpiya eciyatan u na ~ han na tipi kin iwankal ikiyela hinajin* And then something came brightly from out the sky, and it stood moving up and down, while a tipi above came and stood nearby. >

yu·zu·ze·ca \yu-zú-ze-ca\ *va* : to turn into a snake – B.H.49.2

za \za\ *root* : – *See* yuzá

za·han \za-háŋ\ *adj* : ragged – Cf zazáhan

za·mni \za-mní\ *va* : to uncover – Cf yuzamni

za·mni·mni s'e \za-mní-mni s'e\ *adv* : as though uncovering — **zamni·yahan** *part* : uncovered — **zamni-yan** *adv* : uncovered < *~ un* to be uncovered > – Bl

zan·kel \záŋ-kel\ *adv* : with a whimpering cry < *~ ie* to speak with a whining, crying voice to as to call for pity >

zan·ni \zaŋ-ní\ *adj* : well, not sick < *Mazanni* I am well. > — **zanni·ka** \zaŋ-ní-k̇a\ *adj* : healthy, sound, well < *Mazannika* I am healthy. > — **zanni·yan** *or* **zan-niyankel** \zaŋ-ní-yaŋ-k̇el\ *adv* : in good health, well

zan·zan·la \zaŋ-záŋ-la\ *n* : gauze, mosquito netting *etc.* — *adv* : scattered, standing far apart – R

zan·zan·ye·la \zaŋ-áŋ-ye-la\ *adv* : unprotecting, thinly covering < *~ igluza* to have very light clothing on that does not protect > – *Syn* ŠUNKANYANKEL Bl

za·ptan \zá-ṗtaŋ\ *adj num card* : five — **zaptan·kiya** \zá-ṗtaŋ-ki-ya\ *adv* : in five ways, in five places — **zaptan·la** \zá-ptan-la\ *adv* : only five — **zaptan-·ptan** \zá-ptan-ptan\ *adv* : by fives, five apiece

za·za·han \za-zá-haŋ\ *adj* : ragged

za·ze·ca \zá-ze-ca\ *adj* : here and there, few, as trees standing about, or the few hairs on a person's head – Note: *huzazeca* the spokes in a wheel

za·ze·ca·la \za-zé-ca-la\ *adj dim* [fr *zazeca* few here and there] : thinly, thinly strewn and the like < *Peji kin~ yunkelo* The grass lay scattered thinly. > –*Syn* OTOTO-LA — **zazeca·yela** *adv* : scattered here and there as shocks of grain < *~ hiyeyelo* It is quite scattered. > — *Syn* GLAKEYELA Bl

ze \ze\ *adj* : disturbed – *See* canzé — **ze·ka** \zé-k̇a\ *adj* : shaken, disturbed < *canzeka* angry. > — **ze·ya** \zé-ya\ *va* zé·wa·ya : to make angry < *canzeya* to make angry >

ze·ze \ze-zé\ *adv perhaps* : hanging, dangling < *~ iko-yake* to wear hanging downward, dangling as a lap rope does on the sides > – BT

ze·ze·ya \zé-ze-ya\ *adv* : swinging, dangling < *~ otka* to hang dangling, *~ otkeic'iya* to hang dangling one's self >

zi \zi\ *adj* : yellow

zi·bzi·pe·la \zi-bzí-ṗe-la\ *adj* : thin, fine as is silk or fine cloth

[1]**zi·ca** \zi-cá\ *n* : the reddish gray squirrel

[2]**zi·ca** \zí-ca\ *adj* : stretching < *yuzica* to stretch *e.g.* a rubber band >

zi·ca·ho·ta \zi-cá-ḣo-ta\ *n* : the common gray squirrel – R Bl

zi·gzi·ca \zi-gzí-ca\ *adj* : flimsy, not firm, elastic — *n* : a rubber hose < *ogle ~* a sweater >

zi·lya \zi-lyá\ *va* zi·lwa·ya : to smoke, fumigate < *Pe-juta kin he ~ ye* Please smoke that medicine. >

zin·lye·i·c'i·ya \zíŋ-lye-i-c'i-ya\ *v refl* zinlye·mi·c'iya : to have spent everything – Bl

zin·tka·can·hpaŋ·la \ziŋ-tká-caŋ-ḣpaŋ-la\ *n* : a small water bird with a large bill, perhaps the spotted sandpiper or the willet – R Bl

zin·tka·la *or* **zitkala** \ziŋ-tká-la\ *n* : the generic name for small birds

zin·tka·la i·pa·ta·pi \ziŋ-tká-la i-ṗà-ta-pi\ *n* : a bird's ornamental work, *i.e.* the thin moss, mold, growing in figures on rocks, said to be ornaments made by birds – Bl

zin·tka·la o·gna·ke \ziŋ-tká-la ò-gna-ke\ *n* : a bird cage

zin·tka·la si·tu·pi han·ska \ziŋ-tká-la si-tù-pi háŋ-ska\ *n* : a peacock, *i.e.* a bird with long tail feathers - Bl

zin·tka·la sli·la \zíŋ-tká-la slí-la\ *n* : a small bird identified by its perculiar song - Cf ptegaglonica *Syn* ZINTKA TANAGILA

zin·tka·la ta·can \ziŋ-tká-la ta-càn\ *n* : the false or bastard indigo, the river locust, amorpha practicosa, the pulse family; *mini aglagla unpi* they grow along, near water and it seems to be a shrub and not a weed like the other kinds of *zintka tacan*, so called because birds alight on it in the prairie where there are no trees, and its stalks were once used in making arrows - *Syn* ŠUNKTAWOTE

zin·tka ta·na·gi·la \ziŋ-tká ta-nà-ġi-la\ *n* : the humming bird

zin·tka·to \zin-tká-to\ *n* : the blue bird

zin·tka·to gle·gle·ga \ziŋ-tká-to gle-glè-ġa\ *n* : the blue jay

zin·tka·to i·kpi ska \ziŋ-tká-to i-kpì-ska\ *n* : the blue bird, or the jay, both common in the Black Hills of South Dakota

zin·tka·zi·la \ziŋ-tká-zi-la\ *n* : the warbling vireo

zin·tka·zi·la ci·k'a·la \ziŋ-tká-zi-la cì-k'a-la\ *n* : the yellow-billed fly catcher

zin·tki·sci·la \ziŋ-tkí-sci-la\ *n* : the tree sparrow

zi·pan \zi-ṗáŋ\ *n* : a youngster about ten years old or younger, boy or girl

zi·pe·la \zí-ṗe-la\ *adj* : thin, fine < *aguyapi* ~ a pancake > - Note: the difference from *zibzipela*

zi·ša \zi-šá\ *adj* : reddish

zi·ta \zí-ṫa\ *vn* : to smoke, as from things burning - Cf izita

zi·tka·la *also* **zintkala** \zi-tká-la\ *n* : a bird

zi·tka·la ta·wo·te \zi-tká-la ta-wò-te\ *n* **1** : the prairie bird's foot trefoil, hosackia americana, the pulse family **2** : pepper grass, lepedium apetalum - Note: it in the form of a tea is good for kidneys

zi·tka·la wi·pa·ta·pi \zi-tká-la wì-ṗa-ta-pi\ *n* : two kinds of thin moss growing on rocks, a third kind is *inyan wakšupi* - Bl

zi·tka·ta·can *or* **zintkalatacan** \zi-tká-ta-caŋ\ *n* : wild tea, lead plant, shoe strings, amorpha canescens, the pulse family; also called *šunktawote, blaye ~ hu stola* the stalk of the lead plant of the plains is neat and small, *na ~ mini aglagla unpi* and the lead plant grows along the water (shore) - HM BT Bl # 11, 130, 136

zi·tka·to ci·k'a·la \zi-tká-to cì-k'a-la\ *n* : the small blue bird, a corn eater, and in April the Dakota once would say: *Wanna zitkato agli yelo, winyeya unpo igluwinyeya po* The blue bird has now come back, be ready, prepare yourselves. For after its return there occur cold rains that kill many horses because they have shed their winter hair < ~ *s'e ahiyaye* The blue bird passed by, as it were, *i.e.* it passed by dressed in blue. > - Bl

zi·tka·to gle·gle·ga *or* **zitkato tanka** \zi-tká-to gle-glè-ġa\ *n* : the blue jay - Note: it is said of the blue jay that *iwašikšicun* it really talks bad - FR

zi·tka·zi ci·k'a·la \zi-tká-zi cì-k'a-la\ *n* : the yellow-billed fly catcher

zi·tka·zi·la \zi-tká-zi-la\ *n* : the warbling vireo

zi·ya \zi-yá\ *va* zi·wa·ya : to dye or paint yellow — *adj* : yellowish

zi·ya·to \zi-yá-to\ *adj* : green

zi·ye·la \zi-yé-la\ *adj* : yellowish — **zi·zi** \zi-zí\ *adj red* [fr *zi* yellow] : yellow - Bl

zi·zi·bye·la \zi-zí-bye-la\ *adv* : thinly, finely < ~ *opi* He was wounded slightly, *i.e.* not a dangerous wounding. >

zi·zi·pe·la \zi-zí-ṗe-la\ *adj* : fine, thin < *Yunkan inyan wan icu ~ ca na he pestoyela kaga* And then he took a stone that was thin and he made it sharp-pointed. >

zi·zi ško·pe·la *or* **škopela** \zi-zí škò-ṗe-la\ *n* : a banana

zo·he·la \zo-hé-la\ *adv* : very slowly, as in going < ~ *bla* I went very slowly. >

zo·mi \zo-mí\ *adj* : trying to get things from others by pretending to be poor, attempting to swindle, manipulate, cajole, conning one < *Mazomi* I tried to con him. > — **zomi·ka** \zo-mí-ka\ *n* : one who tries to manipulate others to get things by pretending to be poor — **zo·mi·yankel** \zo-mí-yaŋ-kel\ *adv* : in a tricky or deceptive manner < ~ *icu* to get things in a sly way by pretense of being poor >

zon·lya·kel \zoŋ-lyá-kel\ *adv* [fr *zónta* trustworthy] : right, honestly < ~ *econ wo* Do it right. > - Bt B.H.155.17

zon·ta \zóŋ-ṫa\ *adj* : honest, trustworthy < *Wan! nizonte šni yelo* Look now! You are not doing it right. > - Cf zúnta

zon·ta·he·ca \zóŋ-ṫa-he-ca\ *n* : an honest person - R Bl

zon·ta·he·ya \zoŋ-ṫá-he-ya\ *adv* : in close succession, connectedly

zu·han *or* **zuhan·han** \zu-háŋ\ *adj* or *adj red* : striped — **zuhe·ya** *adv* : in a striped manner

zun·lya *or* **zunlya·kel** \zuŋ-lyá\ *adv* : correctly, joined, well

zun·mi·yan·kel \zuŋ-mí-yaŋ-kel\ *adv* : in the way a muskrat does < ~ *lila wota wipiic'iya* In the way a muskrat eats much he fills himself. >

zun·ta \zúŋ-ṫa\ *adj* : braided, woven together, connected — **zunte·šni** \zúŋ-ṫe-šni\ *adj* : incorrect, disjoined as in trying to use a language

zu·ya \zu-yá\ *vn* wa·zuya un·zuya·pi : to go out with a war party, to make war, to lead out a war party < ~ *iyaya, kupi* He went out to make war, and they came back. >

zu·ze·ca \zu-zé-ca\ *n* : a snake

zu·ze·ca bla·ska \zu-zé-ca bla-skà\ *n* : a flat-looking snake

zu·ze·ca ho·gan \zu-zé-ca ho-ġàŋ\ *n* : an eel - *Syn* HOKÁ

zu·ze·ca kin·yan·pi \zu-zé-ca kiŋ-yàŋ-pi\ *n* : a flying snake

zu·ze·ca lu·za·han \zu-zé-ca lù-za-haŋ\ *n* : a fast-moving snake

zu·ze·ca ta·pe·ju·ta \zu-zé-ca ta-pe-jù-ta\ *n* : the slender beard-tongue, penstemon gracilis, the figwort family - Note: the roots are used against snake-bite - BT #5

zu·ze·ca ta·wo·te \zu-zé-ca ta-wò-te\ *n* : the wolf berry, buckbrush, buckbush, symphoricarpos occidentalis, the honeysuckle family - *Syn* ÓNŠUNK'NASAPI HU, so called because arrows were once made from the bush and shot at dogs in play - Bl RT #10

zu·ze·ca ta·wo·te hu tan·kin·yan he·ca \zu-zé-ca ta-wò-ṫe taŋ-kíŋ-yaŋ\ *n* : true Solomon's seal, polygonatum commutatum, the lily family - BT #132

zu·ze·ca ta·wo·te pta·pta i·ko·ya·ka \zu-zé-ca ta-wò-te-

\a\ father \e\ they \i\ machine \o\ smoke \u\ lunar \an, aŋ\ blanc Fr. \in, iŋ\ ink \on, oŋ, un, uŋ\ soon, confier Fr. \c\ chair \ġ\ machen Ger. \j\ fusion \clusters: bl, gn, kp, hšl, etc...\ b[e]lo ... said with a slight vowel **See more in the Introduction, Guide to Pronunciation**

ptá-pta i-kò-ya-ka\ *n* : the carrion flower, Jacob's ladder, smilax herbacea, the lily family – Note: the name means *lit* snake's food that sticks together WE #140

zu·ze·ca ta·wo·te un·ma a·pe to·to he \zu-zé-ca ta-wò-te uŋ-má a-ṗè to-tó he\ *n* : the great lobelia, the blue cardinal flower, lobelia syphilitica, the bell flower family – Note: this name means *lit* snake's food is the other green leaf there BT #84

ENGLISH–LAKOTA

A ENGLISH–LAKOTA

a *or* **an** *art indef* : wan
abandon *v* : ihpeya *~ by throwing away* — aonasloka *~ by deserting* — oh'optelic'iya *~ one's work* – Cf leave
able *v* : okihi *have power to...* – wawokihi *to be ~* – wawokihika *an ~ person* – okihiya *to make ~* — pica *or* picaka *v aux* : *to have power or ability* – picašni *to be impossible, cannot be* — oic'ikpani *v refl* : *not ~ to care for one's own, i.e. to be very poor* — heyapikešni *they think one not ~, or one so thought of* — pawi *to be yet ~ to move about* – *See* iyokihi, oic'ihi
abominate *va* : wahtelašni
abort *va* : okaškanton – okaškantonpi *an abortion* — oikpat'a *to be stillborn, to have an abortion* – Cf pregnancy
about *or* **approximately** *adv* : cetu *or* cel – *See* ecelya, wahecetu
above *adv* : wankata *up high* – *See* awankata, iwankata, wankapa, iwankapa, iwankabtu
abreast *adv* : ociblagan
abroad *adv* : manil *from home*
absolution *n* : wóyuške
absorb *va* : yuataš — ayuȟepa *vn to ~* on
abstain *v* : kicunni *to ~ from* – Cf leave off
abundant *adj* : otanton *or* otantonka *prodigious* – wótanton *an abundance* – otantonya *superabundantly* — wiyatagle *to have in superabundance*
abusively *adv* : okakišya
abyss *n* : okiksahe *vastness*
acceptable *adj* : oicuwašte – Cf get
access *n* : oau *~ to*
accident *n* : wakipapi *bad luck* – wakipaya *va* : *to make one have bad luck* — ošteya *adv* : *accidentally, by chance* — wanun *adv* : *accidentally* – wanunwoakipa *an accident*
acclimate *vn* : makiyokipi *be acclimated*
accomodate *part* : wawiyowinyan *accomodating*
accompany *v* : wawokiya *be accompanying, of some help* — icinakšinpi *they ~ one another* — nicicaya *to make ~*
accomplish *va* : makaheya — oh'anye *n* : *accomplishments* — wakonniya *to have accomplished much* — wayaecetu *v* : *to accomplish by speaking*
according *adv* : ektašniya — ognayan *adv* : *accordingly*
accumulation *n* : wópemni — yuowišni *v* : *to accumulate things not drawn on by others*
accurately *adv* : yušnašni — yušnašni econpi *n* : *accuracy*
accuse *v* : šilwiyaunpa *to ~ one of evil* — wiwicagnupi *n* : *an accusation*
acquire *v* : kiciyamna *~ by talking for one* — ton *va* : *to get, possess, or give birth to*
acrimony *n* : wóyat'age
across – *See* opposite
act *or* **do** *or* **move** *v* : econ *do* – lecon *do it in this way* – šilwaecon *do badly, wrong* — oh'an *act* – toh'an *n* : his acts – yuoh'anšica *va* : *to make act badly* — opiic'iya *or* opic'iya *v refl* : *to move on one's own, conduct one's self* — škan *va* : move – kiškan *move towards, do to one*
active *or* **lively** *adj* : bliheca – bliheca *also vn* : *to be ~* – bleheya *va* : *to make ~* – blihelya *adv* : *actively* — iš'oš'o *hasty* — iwalitake *or* wawak'onšni *or* špukešni *active* — yakokela *va* : *to make ~ by talking* — h'anlita *vn* : *to progress in work*
actor *n* : waecon
add *or* **overdo** *va* : aegnaka *v* : *to add to* – aokignaka *va* : *to help ~* — akaga *va* : *to ~ an untruth* — akicaga *va* : *to overdo* – aokaga *vn* or *va* : *to ~ more* – aokageca *va* : *to add too much to* — aopeya *va* : *~* with — aoyaka *v* : *to ~ to in talking*
address *n* : makocajeyate
adhere *vn* : ayaskapa *~ to* – waaskabya *va* : *to make ~* — tkápa *adj* : adhesive
adjacent *adv* : yugipayela *closely* — icipatkuh *to be ~ to*
adjourn *va* : kignaka
adjust *va* : iyuteya *a measure* — paecetu *~ rightly, set in place* — yuwootanla *adjust*
admire *or* **rate** *v* : štelaka *rate high* – štelapi *n* : *admiration*
admit *adv* : tokinš *admittedly*
adopt *va* : wal'iyacin *~ a child*
adorn *v* : waicikšukšu *~ one's self*
adultery *n* : – *See* intercourse
advise *va* : econši – econšipi *n* : *advice* — owahokonkiyešica *n* : *one hard to ~* — wanagoptanšica *n* : *one who fails to listen to advice* — wóiyaksape *n* : *good ~*
affected *vn* : oiyopa *be badly ~ with a sore* — oniyeton *vn* : *to be ~ by*
affection *adv* : olakolwicayešni *without natural ~*
affirm *va* : yat'inza
afraid *vn* : nihinciya *to be ~* — nihanyan *va* : *to frighten* – wawinihan *adj* : *fearful* – wawinihanyan *v* : *to make one afraid* — kópegla *vn* : *to be afraid* – kópeya *va* or *adv* : *to make one fear* — wokókipapaka *to be afraid, timid*
after *adv* : ektana *there behind, after* — étulake *after a while* — ihakab *after* – ihakapa *after, behind* – iyakapatanhan *afterwards, behind* – iyatabyela *soon ~* – íyohakab *~ in time, subsequent to* – óhakab *afterwards, ~* — ítehanlake *~ a while* — letan *after (the Latin* post*) from this time or place* — óhanketa *~ a while*
again *or* **often** *adv* : ake *or* akeš – akeececa *vn* : *to recur* – akeiyenakeca *adv* : *~ as much* – akešnašna *repeatedly* – iake *~, so many more* – icima *ever ~* – icinunpa *~ a second time* — iciyokiheya *or* lehincita *or* pipiya *adv* : *~ and ~* — itkob *back again*
against *adv* : kicipaesya *being ~ each other* — ipustan *pushing up ~* — iyapatan *right up ~*
age *or* **old** *or* **worn out** *adj* : kan *aged as opposed to youthful* — kicicawota *n* : *one of the same age* — wakase *n* : *a thing growing old and white* — nika *a former age or era*
agency, Indian reservation *n* : owakpamni – Miyogli-oyuze *the Whetstone Agency*
ago *adv* : – *See* late
agree *or* **disagree** *adj* : ošica *incompatible, as sour vs. sweet* — wicoun *n* : *a covenant, agreement*
aground *v* : áze *run ~* – yuazi *to make run aground*
ahead *or* **before** *adv* : kaipsilyalake s'e *a little ~* – kaiyakapeya *adv* : *a little more than* — tannila *adj* : *~ of others, before others* — tokapatanhan *adv* : *before*
aimlessly *adv* : oyumnimni *round and round*
airplane *n* : kinyekiyapi *an air ship*
alarmed *adj* : wacinhahela *or* wacinhahala *easily ~*
alert *or* **lively** *adv* : oyuškeya *on alert*
alight *vn* : oiyahan *jump down in*
align *v* : – *See* flush
alike *adv* : yupintu — ówanjila *adj* : *identically or alike* – otawanjila *n* : *two alike, a pair* – Cf equal
all *adv* : átaya – atayakinil *nearly all* — ecaoyankeya *all by groups* — eyala s'e *seemingly all* – *See* huteiyuhpa,

hutipak'oh, hutipak'oyela, iyuhpa, kinil, k'os'e *all those buzzing about,* k'oyela *all, everything* — ošpašpaya *all by groups,* oyasin *or* oyas'in *adj* : *all* — kiwanjica *not one but all* — sitomniyan *or* alata *or* ecaowancaya *all over* — éšeš *partic* : *alright* - howe *or* howo *or* hoye *O.K.*

allow *or* **permit** *v* : iyowinkiya — wowicak'upi *n* : an allowance, an issue — iyokišni *v* : encourage

ally *n* : wawiciya *or* wawiciye *taking sides with*

almost *or* **nearly** *or* **scarcely** *adv* : nuns'elececa *or* olanuns'e *or* ognayehci *or* yus'o s'e

alone *or* **only** *v* : ecaun *be* ~ — ece *adv* : *only* - hecegla *or* hecela *only that, only so* — iatayela *pron adj* : *that alone* - icuhca *adv* : *the only one* — išnala *pron* or *adj* : *a lone one,* or *alone* - išnalati *vn* : *to live alone* - kicišnala *v* : *to be alone with* - wicišnala *adj* : *alone* - nala *adv in compos with pron* mišnala nišnala *etc.* : *alone* — tanšnala *adj* : *without one's family* — tansmiyanyan *adv* : *deprived of all* - tansmiyanyanka *n* : *one so deprived* — katoyeyapi s'e *adv* : *going alone*

along *adv* : aglagla *or* hoaglagla ~ *side* — pakanyan *alongside, beside* — opaya ~ *in*

already *adv* : ehantan *ever since* — tanniš *adv* : *sooner than expected*

also *conj* : ko - kokta *or* koktaya *adv* : *besides* — eša *or* ešaš *or* šaš *conj* : *also, some (when placed after a n or v)*

altar *n* : wagle wošnapi *or* wagna wošnapi

alter *va* : wotokeca

alternately *adv* : itoktog, itoktogye, itoktokanl - itoktokeca *adj* or *adv* : *alternately, or alternate*

although *or* **but** *adv conj* : eša *or* ešaš *or* šaš *(ending the sentence)* - keš *adv conj* : *but* - Cf keeyaš, c'eyaš, weš, weša, wešan, yeš, yeša, yešan, yešaš, *all conj*

always *or* **ever** *adv* : óhinni *or* ohinniyan — ókiwanjila *continually, alike* — tohunhunniyan kin *adv* : *forever* — takomni *adv* : *at any time*

amateur *n* : wayušikšica

amazement *n* : inihanpi - inihanyan *adv* : *in* ~

ambitious *adj* : škehan - škeheya *adv* : *ambitiously*

among *prep* : egna *or* wegna — íjehan *adv perhaps* : *in the midst* — ópeya *adv* or *prep phr* : *together with* - wicopeya *with them*

amplify *v* : iyoja *to* ~ *sound*

amputate *v* : - Cf cut

amuse *v* : bleblesya — imagaga *vn* : *to be amused* - imagagaya *va* : *to* ~ *others*

ancestor *n* : hunka, hunkake - hunkakeya *or* hunkaya *va* : *to have as an* ~ *, a relative* - hunkayapi *n* : *one called a relative* - wicahunkake *ancestors*

ancient *adj* : tannika *old, worn out* - Cf old

and *or* **also** *or* **too** *conj* : na, naš, nahan, nakun(š) — yunkan(š) *also, then* — ko *as well as* (ko *follows the word it joins)*

angel *n* : ogliglewakan

angle *n* : oipakšan — okiblotonton *adj* : *many-cornered* - *See* corner

anger *or* **wrath** *va* : ahniyan *make angry* — ahokšiwinkte *get angry* — ahoyasotkaya *express anger* — akašpeya *provoke to* ~ — canlniyan *angry at women* - canniyekiciyapi *with one another* - cantehahala *quick-tempered* - canteokic'unica *offended* — canteptanyan *passionately angry* - cantewahinyanšica *irascible* — cantiyagle *vengeful* — canze *be angry* - canzeka *angry* - nacanze *make angry* - wayacanze *talking into anger* — icinkcin *angrily* — igluhinhan *to lose temper* — ikcapta *talking badly* — išigla *angry about* — opuhtinyankel *angrily* - ošitkigla *angry with* — šakehute s'e hingla *angry as a bear* — šicia *talk angrily* - šiglapi *wrath* - šiglaya *provoke* wašiglagla *be irritable* - wašilkiglaya *n* : *one who makes others angry*

animal, rodent, reptile *n* :

1. IN GENERAL : wamakaškan

2. PARTS OF : (*pref* ta-)

waloh'egnaka *bladder,*
tanasula *brain,*
tatahpa *the breast,*
tašup'owotanla *colon,*
tucušte *flank,*
tahuwapahpa *flesh (near the knee),*
tanakpan *flesh (below the knee,*
tanawicite *flesh (foreleg),*
tapizi *gall,*
tawinapce *or* wiyakojuha *the gullet,*
tašupa *intestines,*
tajontka *kidney,*
tapakšin *kidney fat,*
tapi *liver,*
tahpiyogin *muscle,*
tatahu *neck (the back of),*
kan *and* tacankasluta *(over the back)* *nerve,*
taniga *paunch,*
tucuhu, kceya, *or* wakceyapi *rib,*
tablo *or* tahinyete *shoulder,*
tablohu *shoulder blade,*
tablokan *shoulder sinew,*
tapišleca *spleen,*
tapo *stomach,*
kan *or* tanakpan *(leg) or* tasicogin *tendons,*
taceji. *tongue,*
táza *the udder,*
taglogloska *windpipe,*
tatamni *womb.*

3. NAMES : of animals -

heton cik'ala *antilope,*
nigesanla *gazelle,*
tatoka *big-horned antilope,*
tatokala *prairie antilope,*
wicawoȟa tatahca *small white bellied antilope,*
ȟoka *badger,*
matoȟota *gray bear,*
šakehanska *or nicknamed* waonze *the grizzly bear,*
waowešica *a bear in general,*
cápa *or* cap'... *beaver,*
takiyuha *bull (in general),*
ptehincala *or* hitobuye *calf,*
igmu *cat,*
ptegleška *or* ptewaniyanpi *cattle,*
pte *or* hohetapte *cow,*
mašleca *or* mayašleca *or* miyašleca *or* šunkcinca *or* šunkmanitu *coyote,*
matocincala *bear cub,*
tahca *deer,*
hekaza *a yearling deer,*
tawiyela *doe of the red deer,*
šunka *dog,*
waniyanpi *a domestic animal,*
sonson-ikpisan *a white-bellied donkey,*
puteokicu *or* putokicu *elephant,*
heȟaka *or* heslatkala *or* unpan *elk,*
itopta sapa *the black ferret,*
šungila *or* tokala *fox,*

animal Names continued:
waš'in *bull frog,*
nigesanla *gazelle,*
itignila *gopher,*
wahinheya *pocket gopher,*
pesto *grayhound,*
pispiza *or* tašnaheca *ground squirrel,*
ptemakicima *heifer,*
šunkawakan *horse,*
mayašle *jackal,*
igmu tanka *or* igmuwatogla *lion,*
agleška *or* wankipaksa *lizard,*
t'elanuwe *sand lizard,*
wah'anksica *marten,*
unhcegila *mastodon,*
ikusan *the mink,*
šunkawicaša *monkey,*
itunkala *or* hitunkala *mouse, mice,*
itunpsicala *field mouse,*
psipsicala *the jumping mouse,*
sonsonla *mule,*
sinkpe *muskrat,*
ptan *or* škeca *otter,*
kukuše *pig,*
pahin *porcupine,*
pispiza *prairie dog,*
maštinca *rabbit,*
wiciteglega *raccoon,*
itungtanka *or* hitunktanka *rat,*
cinškayapi *or* hecinškayapi *or* tahcašunkala *sheep,*
maka *skunk,*
hetkala *squirrel,*
zica *the red squirrel,*
zicahota *the gray squirrel,*
ptebloka *a steer,*
mapih'a *or* witapiha *or* witapih'a *the toad,*
itunkasan *or* hitunkasan *the weasel,*
šunkmanitu tanka *wolf, variously titled :* caksi, yak'e, huhatopa, maca, mayaca, mayašle, micaksica

annihilate *va* : nawanil - *See* destroy
annoy *or* **vex** *v* : kišleya *continue to urge, make ashamed, to pet, rape* — nat'ekinica *beg to death* — wanagiyeya *to trouble one* — yawazeca *beg one* — yunikuwa *pull or touch* — yuwas kte *va : to pull one here and there*
anoint *va* : iyun - iyunpi *or* wiyunpi *n : an unction* — slaya *v : to grease*
another *adv* : tokan *or* tokanl *in ~ place, or in ~ way* — *n : ~ person* - tokantanhan *adv : from ~ source* - tokanyan *in ref to ~ place* — toktog *adj : another*
answer *va* : aglata *respond in song* — aitoheya *~ accusations* - aitohikiciyapi *~ sharply* — ayupta *respond to* - eciyupta *~ one another* — iyokakišya *~ sharply*
anticipate *v* : wawinakihni *do in anticipation of* - Cf expect, hurry
anxious *adv* : tokekekel *most anxiously* — hahake *spurred on to move*
any *adv indef* : kakeš *or* tokinškinš *any way, Latin cumque whenever* - kaš *or* keša *adj indef* : - ke c'eyaš ... *makes a pron universal, as* taku ke c'eyaš *anything whatever, and* takunl *anything, something, and* tukte e k'eyaš *anybody, and* tuktektetu *anywhere, and* tuktektetanhan *from anywhere* - Cf all, every
anyhow *adv* : ecakaleš *at any rate, or* ékitan - Cf please
apart *adv* : icitehan *or* kicitehanyanlake s'e *a little ~* — icitohanyan *how far ~ ?* — kakinunkan *~ or forced apart* — kojagjal *spread, ~* — oyujuju *pull asunder* - onajuju *to come ~* — zanzanla *standing scattered ~*
apostle *n* : wahošiye *or* wahošiyapi *or* wahošiyapi wakan — ogligleyapi *messenger*
apparent *va* : kaotan'in *make ~* - *See* appear
appear *vn* : tan'in *or* atan'in *be visible, manifest* - akitan'inšnišni *appear now and then* - tan'in'in *~ occasionally* — hinajin *~ standing* — hiyahan *~ on a hill* — hinapa *~ fleeing* - glinapa *~ going home*
appearance *or* **looks** *or* **countenance** *n* : iteoyuze — kahyakel *in ~* — tancan'oyuze *the exterior of a person* - watancan *~ of material things*
appetite *adv* or *adj* : lolhwaka *without ~* — yaincešni *unable to eat all that was served* - yaowišni *to have leftovers from eating*
applause *n* : waaš'api
apply *va* : agnaka *put on* - peagnagkiya *to ~ to* - wakicignaka *to ~ a medicine poultice to one*
apportioned *or* **divided** *adv* : akipab *in allotments*
approve *v* : hecetula - hecetulakapi *approval*
arena *n* : okinyanka
argue *n* : hinskekagya *to be ready to rebut, be argumentative*
arithmetic *n* : wayawapi - Cf read
arm *n* : napoktan *an armband* — oakšu *n* : an armful — pagopatica *to arm one's self with* — wipekiton *to arm with weapons*
around *adv* : ahocokaya *or* aitkob *or* akimeya — aokime *go ~ something* — aohanktonyan *encircle* — ayukan *go ~ , give place to* — iyoglamna *circuitously* — hinskoya *so far ~* — *honunpinyan ya v* : to surround — kaokokab *go ~* — ayukšanyan *v* or *adv* : to go ~ , out of the way — hookšan *or* howokšan *or* iglukšan *or* itan'iglukšan *or* itan'okšan *or* itaokšan *or* iyayukšan *(these latter adv serve as prep adv* - okšantan *from all ~* - okakšanyan *by a ~ about way* - taokšan *surrounding* — ohomni *or* aohomni *~ about* — akawinga *circle about* - aokawinga *encircle* - hookawinga *~ camp inside* - yuwinga *turn ~ , back, coming around*
arrange *v* : paogla
arrest *v* : kaškapiya *or* kaškeya *have one arrested* - Cf tie
arrive *v* : kigli *to ~ at home* - kihan *to ~ and stand* - iyakitan'in *to ~ in the daylight* - *See* come
arrow *n* : wahinkpe *or* wanhinkpe - wan *n contrac* : an arrow - wahincola *an ~ with no head* - wahin-hinajin *jaws of an ~ head* - wahinkin'inyeyapi *a bow-shot* - wanju *quiver* - tonwan *any ~* - wan'apayapi *~ stuck in a wound* - wankaga *make arrows* - wannunpaya *strike with two arrows* - wan'otaya *strike with many arrows* - wansaka *an ~ in the making* - wantanyeya *be a good shot* - wantanyeyela *one good at shooting arrows* - wanyeya *to shoot arrows* - wanyugo *incise an ~ well* - wanyuguka *to draw an ~* - wanyukpanhan *let fly many arrows* - wanyuze *handle bow and arrow* — wismahin *~ head* - wiwoštake *or* miwoštake *a blunt ~* — kehuku *an arrowhead* — keston *a barbed arrowhead* — Wawakan *np : a Sacred Arrow in the tradition of the Cheyenne tribe*
article *adj* : kin *or* ki *or* ci *or* ka *the (def)* — wan *a (indef)* — un *or* unpi *the* — kin *or* k'un *or* on *or* k'on (being)
as *adv* : tókel *or* tókeš *as ... as one can* - tóketu *as it is* — sékse *or* s'elececa *as it were* — iyena *pron* : so many - iyenaka *so many as* - iyenakeca *adj* or *pron : as many, as much* - iyenangnakeca *adv red : as many, as much* — séca *or* s'elececa *adv : seemingly* - s'e *adv : like, as if, as though*

B

ascend *va* : ali – aliagla *climb over a hill* — aiyakapteya *adv* : *sloping up* — itawankagle *adv* : *up a very steep hill* – Cf alí *etc.*
ashame *v* : oh'itonkipa *do without shame having disobeyed* — wištelya *va* : *to make ashamed* – wištelkiciyapi *n* : *ashamedness*
ashes *n* : caȟota *or* canlogu – cahlišniyanpi *coal ashes*
aside *adv* : kaȟeyata *to one side, back* — kaitokanl *push to one side*
ask *or* **desire** *v* : cin *want, ask for* – ocin *beg for* – okicin *as something of one* – waekicinke *n* : *one anxiously asking to get* — kila *va* : *to beg of one*
assemble *v* : aokiya *come together* — égeju *they assembled* — hiheya *they came together* — ignagnaya s'e *coming one at a time* — katá *va* : *to assemble persons or things* — mníciya *v* : *to assemble, gather together* – amniciyapi *they assembled* – Cf imniciya, oglimniciya, ohimniciya, oimniciya *to go to a meeting*, okimniciya, omniciya *an assembly* — wítaya *adv* : *together* – ewitaya *or* ohiwitaya *v* : *to assemble there or they assembled* – oiwitaya *or* witayaiheya *assemble together*
asset *or* **substance** *n* : woic'igle *one who saves, one's ~*
assist *or* **serve** *n* : ókiye – ookiye *n* : *an assistant or servant* – taokiye *n* : *his assistant, disciple* — okpe *v* : *to give an ~* — wawakicišpašpake *one who helps or gives to others, as by cutting up or sacrificing in small pieces*
assure *va* : ayuwicaka
astonishment *n* : wóyus'inye
at *adv* : écuhci *at least* — ekta *or* el *prep* : *to* or *in* – etulahci *adv* : *just to, in, at* — yata *prep in compos* : by, to
attach *v* : ikoyaka *or* iyak'inton *or* iyakiciyuha *or* iyayuha *adhere to*
attack *v* : ékicipa *meet and ~* — natan *rush at* – anatan *assault* – anatanpi *an assault* — takpe *make an assault*
attempt *or* **try** *va* : akoza — iglutata *try or test one's own* — óhan *try to apply one's self to study*
attend *v* : ecewakta *~ to* — mnih'ic'iya *give attention to* — ohmunyece *to ~ to* — oyaksab šica *adj* : *inattentive* — titanwaya *v* : *to ~ school* — wicunskayešni *to pay no attention* — el étonwanšni *distracted, not to look at one*
attractive *adj* : iwicayutan — oiyokipi *n* : *attraction*
auction *n* : panwiyopeyapi *~ sale*
audition *n* : wanah'onpi
autumn *n* : ptanyetu – ptinhan *last autumn*
available *adj* : icupica
avarice *n* : wowijica wacin *avarice* — wikangligike *an avaricious person*
avenge *v* : watokic'on – *n* : an avenger
avoid *or* **evade** *or* **elude** *v* : kipaš'iyaya — okamna *avoid* — tanhminkiya iyaya *to shy from* — ayukšanyan *to circumvent*
awake *v* : oikpagica *to come ~* — han'ištinma *to lie ~ at night* – Cf sleep
aware *v* : tokewacinšni un *pretend to be unaware of* – wacinksapa *be aware* — ieslota *speaking aware of the situation*
away *adv* : alehanyank *far removed* – kalehanyank *divide away* – lehanyank *somewhere else* — ȟeyab *or* ȟeyapa *adv* : *away* – iȟeyab *~ from* — hlahya *to a distance* — icišniyan *~ off* — ihehanyan *so far from*
awkward *v* : wayuȟiya *be ~* — yah'iyaya *be ~ speaking* — wóšikšiceke *ineptitude, or awkward*

babbler *n* : íwakan – *adj* : *talkative* – íwakanyan *adv* : *babbling* — oyaškiška *talk unintelligibly*
back *or* **backwards** *adv* : hektakiya *returning back* – kahektakiya *backwards* – lazatakiya *backward* — itunkab *on the back* — katanblablas *on both sides of the back* — kaitkob *~ again* — tapete *the upper back* – tapetegnagya *adv* : *placed on the ~* – tapetegnaka *v* : *to place on one's back* — katkiya *adv* : *with the ~ to the fire* – tapetota *or* tapetotanhan *adv* : on the back
bad *or* **wicked** *or* **ugly** *adj* : šica – kicišica *vn* : become ~ to or for one – oh'anšicaya *adv* : badly, wickedly – šicaya *or* šicayakel *badly, not well* — osikšiloh'anka *or* ošilye oh'an *act badly* – šicit'e *very bad* – šilya *badly*
badge *n* : ipasise *a pin* – cantkuipasise *a breast pin* – wicešipasise *tent pins, or a badge*
baffle *va* : ištelic'iyeya
bag *n* : lol'opiya *for meat* — ojuha *a bag* – was'ojuha *to keep paints* — pan *a woman's work bag* – panwotuka *a sewing bag* – wiyakapan *tool bag, or for cherries* — walo-ogna *a meat bag* — wópiye *a medicine bag*
baggage *n* : wahpayeca
bail *va* : kaȟepa *empty out* — kapta *lade or bail out*
bait *n* : watan – watanya *va* : to use for ~
balance *va* : yunas'a *try the ~ of a hutanacute (puck)*
bald *or* **bare** *adj* : šla *or* natašla (bald headed) — nasuštinca s'e *balding*
balk *v refl* : iglonica *to refuse to go*
ball *n* : tápa – tapapa *v* : hit a ball – tapaicakape *n* : a ball bat – tapaicapsice *n* : a shinny stick – tapaiyeya *v* : to pitch a ~ – tapaiyukape *n* : a catching glove – tapakakab iyeya *bat a ~* tapakapsica *bat out a ~* – tapaicapsice *n* : *a ball bat by one*
band *n* : ȟantkunza *an arm band* — oiyuskite *n* : *a place for a band to be fit* — wiyakaške *a band with which to tie something*
bandage *n* : iyukite – wiyayuskita *v* : *to bandage* – wiyayuskite *or* wiyuskite *n* : *a bandage*
bank (*earthen*) *n* : maya – mayagliheya *a steep ~* – wamayal *adv* : toward a ~ – Cf money
banquet *n* : – *See* dine
baptizer *n* : wamniakaštan *one who baptizes* – Cf below under sacrament
bar *n* : iyonatake *that used to close up*
barb *n* : keze *a sharp point* — pepe *adj* : *barbed, jagged, prickly, rough* — keston *vn* : *to be barbed* – *va* : *to barb*
barber *n* : wicakicašla
bare *adj* : cokala *naked* – sicokala *bare-foot* – hacola *naked* — kak'oza *or* kak'os *va* : *to make bare* – icak'oza *vn* : *to be bare* – kak'eza *v* : *leave bare* — kincahan *fallen off bare* — oskaka *bare of tree leaves, open* – otintoska *n* : *an open place* — ayusmin *va* : *to pick bare* — snasnala *adj* : *bare as a tree* — kasmin *to trim off* — šla *bald* – aošla *a bare place tred* – ašla *bare on* – ašlalyeta *or* ašla-ya *openly, bare* – awošla *va* : *to make bare on by punching* – icicašla *making each other bare striking* – kicašla *or* onašla *or* našlaye *or* pašlaya *make bare* – pašlayela *making bare* – ošla *an open place* – wošla *to shoot bare* — šmi *bare* — totola *bare* – ototola *thin of grass and shrubs*
bark *va* : papa *or* wapapa *to bark at one or something*
barn *n* : pteonajin *a cow ~* – šung'onajin *horse ~, a stable*
barrel *or* **keg** *n* : koka – kokaojuha *an empty ~*
barren *adv* : šlaegnag *in ~ country*
basin *n* : un'iglujajapi *wash basin*
basket *n* : psawognake

bat *va* : kakapa *bat a ball* - pakapa *bat a ball back*
batter *v* : woblebleca
bawl *v* : hotonton - hotonkel *bawling* - hotonkiya *to make cry* - howaya *be bawling*
bayonet *n* : iwahukeza
bay *n* : okahmin
be *or* **exist** *or* **be well** *v* : eca ... laka *he is ... there is* - ececa *vn* or *adv* : *affected with, thus, so ...* - *See* ecehci, ecekcel, ecel, ecetu — lee *this is,* hee *that is* — hiyeya *vn* : *to become or cause to be* — oun *vn* or *n* : *to be a condition or state, a place, a room; one's ways or being* - unk'unpi *we are,* unpi *they are,* waun *be well-off* — yanka manka nanka *vn* : to be - ayanka *be in a condition or on* - kiciyanka *be for one* - oyanka *be in* — yukan *or* wayukeca *vn* : *there is some* - yukeya *adv* : *being, having, possessing*
bead(s) *va* : kšu *to bead things* — pšito *n* : bead(s) - pšitosuhula *very small ~* - pšitošuhula *medium size ~* — totola *blue or green ~* — oyáya *a string of ~* (the prefered word) - wóyaya *a string of ~* — yazahe s'e *bead-like, i.e.* ówecinhan *one after another* - Cf Hokomi
beard *n* : putinhin *also mustache*
beat *or* **thresh** *va* : akapota *or* aglapota *~ to pieces on* — ihubloya *to flog on the legs* — eiyapat'o *~ against* — icicašnašna *clash, striking one against another* — icigni *to maltreat* — iglat'a *to pummel or strike dead one's own* — ikaskapa *~ slapping the mouth* — kabu *~ a drum* — katakunišni *~ to pieces* — akoza *try to ~* - cankoza *swing a stick to ~* — kte *or* ktela *va* : to ~, win in a game — makiblaska glihpeya to *~ flat* — natahtonyan *whip eggs etc.* — akapa *thresh off on* - akicipa *~ for* - akipa *~ one's own* - apa *smite* - apapa *a blow* - ekicipa *to mince blows* - iakipapa *strike on the mouth, to whoop* - iyapa *the heart ~ against* - kapa *~ off* - wó pagi *a drum-beat* - wópagikiya *make a rhythmic ~* — aka-pan *or* aglapan *to thresh* - icapan *to thresh to pieces* - kapan *thresh off* - akaštaka *or* aglaštaka *~ one on another* - kaštaka *to whip* - wiglaštaka *to ~ one's wife* — oiyapa *to ~ on the side of*
beau *or* **dandy** *n* : wawascuscuke
beautiful *adj* : gópa *or* ȟópa *or* gópeca - igluȟopa *v refl* : make self ~ - owanyangwašte *~ to the eye*
because *or* **indeed** *adv conj* : ca *or* caheca — welaka yelaka *adv* : *indeed since*
beckon *or* **wave** *or* **signal** : kóza *or* kos *to wave or signal* - koskos *to swing* - koskoza *wave, beckon* - napekoza *wave, beckon with the hand* - kosya *make a signal* — wikiyuta *talk to with sign language*
become *vn* : akihececa *~ so on arriving home* — áya - uya
bed *n* : ohe *or* oheglepi *or* oyunke — cuwiogle *or* mah'owinje *(cornhusks) or* nisehuogle *bedding* — oištinme *bedroom* - oyunke hu *bed-stead* - ungnah'icaške *a tripod support for robes* –oyunke hugmiya *bed caster* - peji winja *tick,* towinja *his tick* - mniȟuhaskašoka *ticking* — aowinskiya *make a bed on for* - owinja *use for a bed* - owinjaakahpe *or* owinjapopopa *a bed quilt* - owinškiya *make a bed of* — wiciyunka *n* : bed-time — kihpaya *to bed down*
befall *v* : wákipa *have an accident, to ~ one*
before *adv* : hanni — ikokab *or* icokab *in time or place* - kokab *in the way of* — ihtahepi *n* : the before evening — ikanyetanhan *from in front of* — ikoglamnaya *go or get ahead of* — itetanhan *face to face* — itoka *or* aitokab *or* itokabtu *or* itokaya *or* itokamna *adv* - itokapa *vn* : *to be before in birth, i.e. older* — ahankeyela *adv* : *just before*
beg *or* **ask** *v* : la *or* wala - lakel *begging* - walalaka *a beggar* — wocinla *beggar* - wocinpi *a begging, craving, hungering* — wola s'a *begging i.e. for food*
begin *adv* : ohutetanajin *in the very beginning* - ohutkan *n* : *the beginning of things* — oinkpata *in the beginning* — otokahe *n* : *the beginning, the first* - otokaheta *at the head* - otokaheya *n* : *the first* - *adv* : *at the beginning*
behalf *or* **part** *adv* : tanyam *in ~ of*
behave *vn* : šilh'an *act badly* - šilh'anka *n* : *behavior*
behead *va* : pakaksa *or* pawaksa
behind *or* **back** *n* : hekta - *adv* : behind, back - hektab *adv* : *behind, back* - hektapatan *adv* : *at the rear* - iȟektapa *adv prep* : *behind or after one* — iȟeyata *adj prep* : *back from, behind* — iyokapatanhan *adv* : *after, younger* — iyagna *prep* : *after, following, together with* — lazata *behind* - ilazata *by the side of or behind it* - wicilazate *beside them* — wicakanl *adv* : *behind them*
belch *vn* : apablu — blokasak *n* : a ~
believe *or* **agree to** *va* : wicala - wicalapi *faith* - wicalapela *adv* : *believing* - wicalapica *worthy of belief* - wicalaya *to make ~*
belittle *va* : yatakušni
bell *n* : hlahlatanka - owakahla *a belfry or bell steeple*
belly *n* : ikpi - paikpaska *adv* : *with the ~ up*
below *adv* : kuya *underneath, beneath* - kuyatanhan *from ~*
bend *or* **crook** *or* **angle** *va* : akata *draw a bow* — huwoga *adj* : *bent* — kahmin *to ~ something* - tanhminkiya *adv* : *bending the body away* — kaš'in *v* : *to bend concave* - naakaš'in *or* nakaš'in *to ~ backward* — apakpan *va* : *to make fine* — kša *adj* : *bent over, decrepit* - ayukša *fold, double up on* - pakša *bent, aged* - yukšayela *in a bent posture* - ipakšan *a fold, bend of a river* - istoglukšan *to ~ one's own arm* - istopakšan *the ~ of the arm* - kiciyukšan *to ~ for one* - nakšan *to ~ by foot* - oipakšan *a crook, angle* - pakša *to fold, or bent down* — akakšija *to ~ into, or ~ round* - akikšija *or* anakšija *or* ayukšija *bend down* — istopakšija *or* istoyukšija *to ~ the arm* — akaktan *va* : *to bend around or onto* - Cf anaktan, ayuktan, kaktan, kaoktan, naktan, naoktan, oipaktan, oiyuktan, onaktan, oyuktan, paktan, wooktan, yuoktan — pako *bent around* - nako *vn* : *bent up* — naakakciya *v* : *bend backward* — napatuja *va* : *bend by kicking* — našipa *va* : *to bend by stepping on* — pakipaš *bend by striking* — paokiyaskapa *be bend in* — agluwega *~ upon one's own* — winga *or* winh *be bending* - winhya *in a bent manner* — anawinja *to ~ down by foot* — gluptuza *to ~ one's self over* - kaptuza *to ~ with a blow* - Cf ayuwinja, nawinja, owinšya, pawinja, winjahan
benefit *v* : iyuwašte *make good by*
benevolence *n* : - *See* gracious
beset *v* : kicamna *to be overwhelmed*
beside *adv* : isakib
besmirched *adj* : ohlogeca *covered with*
bet *va* : ahigle - ahikicigle *vn* : *to bet* — yekiya *va* : *to stake something on* - yekiyapi *n* : *a stake*
better *vn* : ahececa *recover, get ~* - ahececake *adj* : *rather ~* — awašte *vn* : *become ~ than* - awašteya *adv* : *well, ~ than* - iwašte *vn* : *to be benefited by* - iwašteya *adv* : *better* — opicaka *to be ~*
between *adv* : okogna *or* iokogna *in the midst* - okognaka *v* : *to put ~ others* — otahepi *adv* : ~ places - iyotahepi *on the way this side of destination* - iyotahepiya *~ one place and another, on this side*

beverage *alcoholic etc.* *n* : mni *water* — mnipiga *beer, ale, soda water* - mniša *wine, cider, ale* - mniwakan *whiskey* - mniwakanska *alcohol* - mniiskuya *or* mniskuya *lemonade etc.*
bewail *va* : kiciceya
bewildered *or* **oblivious** *or* **wandering** *adj* : wacingnuni — yaya *adv* : *undecided* — yuhelhel *confused* — iwacingnuniyan *causing bewilderment*
bewitch *enchant, sicken* *va* : hmunga - kicihmunga *v* : *to enchant each other*
beyond *adv* : ainatagya — akab *prep* : *over, beyond, upon* — ako *on the other side of* - akokiya ~ *away from one* - akotanhan ~ *as to place, time, and things, from* ~ - akowapatanhan *from* ~ — hosam ~ *the camp* - isampa ~ *that place or time, more than* — iyakapeya *va* : *to go beyond, to overcome* — iyakapta *va or adv* : *to pass over and* ~ - iyako ~ *anything* - iyakotanhan *from* ~ — iyokopeya ~ *in sight, opposite to.* — anawab *over* ~ - inamni ~ *over*
Bible *np* : Wowapi Wakan
bicycle *n* : mazašunkakanyanka - makamani inyanka *run or ride a bicycle*
bier *n* : can'agnakapi
big *adj* : - *See* large
bill *n* : pa *beak* - pablaska *a duck's* ~ - pasu *beak or nose* — wopeton icazopi *one's debt*
bind *v* : oskita *tie or bind up a child on a board* - aski-ta *adj* : *tied, bound, fastened as a child on a board* — iyakicaška *to* ~ *together* — iyayustaka *to hold one firmly to another* — wipahte *string for tying* — yuwinja *va* : tie down - okiwinja *to bind down well*
bird *n* : -
1 : **IN GENERAL** :
anpaohotonla *a domestic* ~
wakinyanpi *winged creatures*
zintka(la) *bird in general*
unjincala *a fledgling bird*
2 : **SOME PARTS** :
pa *or* pasu *beak*
wíyaka *feather*
situpi *tail-feather*
pa *head*
sinte *tail*
ape *wing*
hokamanipila *a crane's nesting place*
3 : **PARTICULAR BIRDS** :
hupakiglake *bat*
wabloša *red wing blackbird*
wahpatanka *common blackbird*
wapagica *yellow-headed blackbird*
zintkato *bluebird*
makaowanke *or* manka zintkala *bobolink*
magašekšecala *the brant*
wabloska *the lark*
heca *buzzard*
wikpizi *the chat*
škipipi *or* wiyawala *chickadee*
kokoyaȟanla *a chicken*
huntka *a comorant*
cantipan *or* hinlhincala *coot*
pteyahpa *or* wahpakaȟota *cowbird*
pehan *or* pehanska *crane or white crane*
pakaic'icuya *the red crossbill*
kangi *a crow or crows,* Cf uncišicala
cepela tanka *or* šohotonla *or* coka sapa *the cuckoo*
ticannica *curlew*
wakinyela *morning dove*
magaksica *or* pagonta *a duck*
magašniyanla *the red-headed duck*
pasublaska *broad-bill duck*
šiyagla *or* šiyaka *teal*
mahcinca *duckling*
anunkasan *bald eagle*
ȟuya *common or old eagle*
wanbligleška *the spotted eagle*
wanblitaheya *the gold finch*
wazizintkala *pine finch*
šunluta *red-headed flicker*
šunzica *brown wood flicker*
zintkazila cik'ala *yellow-billed flycatcher*
maga *goose*
maga sapa the black *wild goose*
canwahpa tanka *the bronze grackle*
šiyo *or* canšiyo *wood grouse*
wazišiyo *the spruce grouse*
wicatankala *or* winyan-tazintkala *the gull*
canška *red-legged hawk*
cetan *common hawk*
piško *a night hawk*
ptegopeca *marsh hawk*
wakinyaha *sharp-shinned hawk*
hokagica *heron*
hokato *blue heron*
pehanska *white heron*
pehangila *sand-bill heron*
okihyan *a birth that hovers*
tanagila *hummingbird*
zintkatogleglega *blue jay*
cantu sapela junco
pehincicila *or* ptehincicila *the killdeer*
wasnasnaheca *kingbird*
ohyazela *or* oyazela cik'ala *or* hupucansakala *or* kušleca *kingfisher*
ištanica tanka *lark*
maštekola *horned lark*
winap'inla *meadow lark*
bles *or* bleza *or* bloza *or* blega *a loon*
halhate *or* unkcekiȟa *magpie*
jialepa *or* tašiyagnunpa *meadow-lark*
zintkala canhpanla *mud hen*
škeluta *oriole*
ši-yatakala *the water ousel*
hinhan *owl*
hinyankaga *the hoot owl*
osniko *or* pagla *or* popotka *or* ungnagicala *screech owl*
zintkala situpi hanska *peacock*
bleza *pelican*
šlošlola *plover*
Palani tazintkala *or* pse *the upland plover*
šiyo cik'ala *quail*
kangi tanka *raven*
canpiško *or* kansu zintkala *the red-start*
šišoka *robin*
maniopawakinyela *or* miniopawakinyela *sand-piper*
pagla *saw-whet*
cetan watapela *the shrike*
ginlgincala *or* hokagica *snipe*
hupuwanblila *snow bunting*
iȟuȟaotila *sparrow*
pacanšihuta *English sparrow*
situpi ah'ayetonpi *the lark sparrow*

zintkalaslila *grasshopper sparrow*
zinkiscila *tree sparrow*
hokaȟica *stork*
hupucansakala *or* igugaotila *cliff swallow*
icapšinpšincala ikpiska *tree swallow*
icapšinpšincala ikpiša *barn swallow*
ipšincala *adj* : in the likeness of a small swallow
upijata *the swallow in general*
magaska *swan*
cehupaglagla *thrasher*
canguguyaša *thrush*
canguguyagleška *towhee*
wagleksun *wild turkey*
zintkazila *the warbling vireo*
situpiwanblila *warbler*
miniopakinyela *a water bird*
pakoškala *whippoorwill*
kankeca *woodcock*
skiska *woodduck*
toskala *woodpecker*
canšinkahpu *downy woodpecker*
wagnuka *red-headed woodpecker*
canheyala *the wren*
hlahla iyognaka *the marsh wren* - HT

birth *v* : hokšiyuha *give ~ to* - hokšitokapa woiyowaja *or* wotokapa woiyowaja *n* : *first birthright* — onzekte *give ~ when nursing* - onzepija *be unweaned at ~ of another* - t'ahiyuya *vn* : *to be stillborn* - Cf pregnancy
bit *n* : wókitan *a little ~ of anything* - yuh'eh'eyakel *adv* : *in bits*
bite *va* : ayakšan *bend by mouth* - ayaktan *bend* - oyatan *~ down on* - onapce *a bite or wound* - kiciyahtaka *~ for one* - glajata *~ a fork in* - ayakpi *~ cracking* - ayahloka *or* oyahloka *~ a hole in* - wayasmaka *~ indenting* - pápala *biting as pepper* - ayapota *~ in pieces* - yakpukpa *~ in small pieces* - yaȟuga *or* yaohpa *~ into, crack, chew* - kiyaksa *~ in two* - kalkalya *adv* : bitingly out of anger - ayapsaka *or* yašpu *~ off* - yapta *bite off around* - yatkunza *~ off even* - kiciyapsaka *or* kiciyašpa *~ off for* - ayahpu *or* ayaksa *or* oyaksa *or* ayawaja *~ off on* - yaptuga *or* yašpa *~ off a piece* - yašpaya *part* : bitten off - ayašpa *~ off a piece on* - oyak'oza *~ off short* - ayak'oza *~ off smooth* - ayašpu *~ off what sticks* - ayahtaka *~ one on another* - ayakpa *~ out on* - ayajipa *~ pinching* - ayakca *~ untying* - yagmipi s'e *bitten off* - ayawega *break, fracture in biting* - ayaškica *chew* - ayakšija *double up by mouth* - ayak'oga *gnaw off on* - ayak'ega *gnaw on* - ayašuja *mash* - iglašna *miss with the mouth* - ayahlaya *or* yagapa *peel* - yaowinga *pull about with the teeth* - ayatitan *pull by mouth* - ayapšun *pull out by teeth* - ayasleca *split* - ayasmin *or* yagla *strip off, clean* - glapa *or* yapa *or* yahtaka *take hold of by mouth or teeth* - ayakuka *tear in pieces* - ayahleca *tear on* - ayapemni *or* ayaškopa *twist by mouth*
bitter *adj* : pa *or* páza - pázeca *~ in word* - íwokokipeke *fig a sharp-tongued person* - t'ága *astringent, rigid* - wóglawa *a ~ thing*
black *adj* : sápa - cehnagila *one dressed in ~* - itisabye *the blacking used for the face*
black eye *va* : išta otoya *give one a ~*
blacksmith *n* : maskape *or* maz'kape *or* mazakage *a smithy* - omaskape *or* omas'kage *a ~ shop*
bladder *n* : peška *a fish air ~* — walega *a ~ water-jug*
blade *n* : ope - Cf edge
blame *v* : íelgle — ignu *charge one* — iyaunpa *accuse one* - iyaunpapi *an accusation* - iyaunpapicašni *adj* : *blameless* - iyaunpapicašniya *blamelessly* — kipa *blame one's self or one's own* - kipakiya *to make ~ self* - wicapapi *they ~ others, or the ~ of others* — yašilpicašni *adj* : *blameless*
blanket *or* **quilt** *or* **shawl** *or* **robe** *n* : šina — witoye *n* : *blue blanketing*
blasphemy *n* : wóakage
blaze *or* **flame** *n* or *vn* : ile - kaile *va* : *to make or fan a flame* - oile *vn* : *to blaze in* - *n* : *a flame*
bleach *or* **clear** *n* : onwahinyuntonpi *for hides* — kaska *become clear* - kiska *vn* : *to bleach* - naska *vn* : *to get white* - paska *va* : *to bleach something*
bleed *vn* : iwe *or* iwehiyu - iwehiyupi *a bleeding* - iwehiyuya *to make bleed* - iweyošaya *with a bloody mouth* - kawewe *strike and make bleed* - pawe *or* pawehiyu *to bleed at the nose* - pawewe *make ~*
bless *va* : ayawašte - glawašte *bless one's own*
blind *n* : ištaakahpe *blinds for horses* - ištakakpa *put out an eye* - ištaglakpa *put out one's own eye* - ištahca *to have poor vision* - ištajotokte *to ~ with smoke* - ištakpa *to be blind, an eye put out* - ištakpeya *make blind* — ištagonga *not able to see well, blind* - ištagongapi *blindness* - ištagongaya *blindly* - ištagonge *blindness* — iyošnija *be blinded as by the sun* - ištaiyošnija *the eyes be dazzled by light* - ištawaiyojanjan *snow-blindness*
blink *v* : kap'i
blister *n* : kanna *or* mnikapohya hiyotake *or* mninapas hiyuye
bloated *v* : naglakeyeya — nawizipanyeya *swollen, distended*
block *va* : ikušeton *to set to blocking something* — wókapan *n* : *a meat pan*
blood *n* or *adj* or *vn* : we *blood, bloody, to bleed* - wecolakel *adv* : *unbloody* - we eyala s'e *or* eyawela s'e *or* wela s'e *in a bloody condition* - weyóhlogelya *in a bloody way* - awe *to bleed on* - weic'iya *bleed self* - weki-ciya *bleed each other* - wéošpan *to cease the ~ flow as in afterbirth* - wéota *or* weyota *bloodclot* - wewe *or* wéyukeya *bloody* - weya *shed ~*
blossom *or* **bloom** *n* : itka — kawa *to bloom, open* — nableca *to blossom, unfold*
blow *va* : ataeyanpa *wind to ~* — iwoblu *or* owoblu *blow in* — icamna *be blowing as a storm* — jinca *~ the nose* - yujinca *pull or ~ the nose* — glajo *~ a musical instrument* — kak'es *~ off as the wind does* — kalu *brush away* - owolu *~ in* — pogan *~ by mouth* - aikpogan *to ~ on self* - aipogan *~ upon* - aopogan *~ on* - apogan *or* apohpogan *~ something on* - opogan *~ in upon, or out from* — iwoslohan *~ along* — wosni *~ out, extinguish* — wosloka *~ out, clear, empty* — kazamnimniyela *blowing open and flapping*
blowout *v* : hunapobya *have a ~*
blunder *v* : wawiȟat'eya *in one's business* — yašna *in speaking*
blunt *va* : katata *or* papšunka *make ~* — tata *dull or bruised* — toše *dull* - tošeyakel *bluntly* — wot'oja *make ~ by shooting*
blurry *adj* : aogi *blurred* - aoginton *make indistinct, hide* - aoginyan *in a blurred manner* — p'owakita *to see in a blurred manner* — šnija *blurred, indistinct*
blush *v* : itešahingle *or* itewe s'e hingle
board *n* : wawak'eze *a work board for cutting*
boast *va* : onkiškata *brag playfully* - Cf brag, jest
boat *n* : canyuwipi kagapi *a float* — wáta *or* wal *a boat* - canwata *a log canoe, a skiff* - mniwancawata *a ship*

– watapeta *a steamship* – wataopeya *by ship* – watahektab *at the stern* – watasinteyuhomni *to pilot* or *the helmsman* – wal'oihuni *a landing* – wal'oinajin *a dock* – walhektapa *the stern* – walcete *the keel, bottom* – walpa *the bow* – walsinte *the helm, rudder* – waltucuhu *ribs* – wal'icaške *anchor* – wal'icašpe *canoe router* – wal'itope *oar* or *paddle*

body *n*
1. **IN GENERAL :** tancan, tacan, *or* tan *body* – Cf bone
2. **PARTS :**
ceyohe *abdomen*
ikpi *belly*
pagé *diaphragm*
šupute *lower abdomen*
tamni *afterbirth*
iškahu *ankle*
ah'co *upper arm*
isto *lower arm*
cuwi *back*
cuwinunge *a camel's back*
míyo-kaš'in *small of the back*
míyopawega *lower bent small of the back*
tapete(o, u) *upper part of the back*
nasu *brain*
ceška *the upper breast*
maku *the breast*
iyujipa *the brow*
itehohu *or* tapon *the cheek*
cantku *chest*
tahpa *upper chest*
iku *chin*
tapaga *diaphragm*
nonge *ear or the sense of hearing*
išpa *elbow*
winapce *the esophagus*
išta *eye*
šašte *the little finger*
cehpi *flesh*
nawicite *flesh of the upper arm*
si *foot*
ituhu *forehead*
pahte *brow*
pahlate *fossae, nasal passages*
pizi *gall*
tawapšunkahan *a throat gland*
caná *or* cannopa *or* logute *the groin*
glogleska *gullet*
hin *hair*
nape *hand,* Cf fingers
pa *head*
peslete *top of head*
naju *or* najute *back of head*
natableca *a square head*
natagugu *curly head*
iyuhinte *a rake to remove intestines*
iyuhota *intestines and guts*
šupe *intestines*
cehupa *jaw*
iyoȟa *upper jaw*
ókihe *finger joint*
ajuntka *or* asunkta *kidneys*
cankpe *knee*
huokahmi *back of the knee*
nasukaza *knuckle*
yute *one's lap*
hu *leg*
huha *limb*
iha *lips*
wišán *vagina lips*
pi *liver*
cagu *or* tacagu *lungs*
i *mouth*
wicašake *nails*
cekpa *the navel*
tahu *or* najutoškokpa *back of neck*
pahute *nap of the neck*
tiškankan *neck muscle*
kan *nerve*
pa *or* pála *or* pasu *or* poge *nose*
pahute *or* paokihe *bridge of the nose*
pacete *nostrils*
caká *palate*
ce *penis*
tucuhu *rib*
ništušte *or* nite *rump*
onze *the anus*
nataha *scalp*
ablo *or* hinyete *shoulder*
cuwipaha *the side below the arms*
oyute *side above the hips*
nasuhu *or* natahu *sutures of the skull*
peowiwila *or* pewiwila *the soft spot at the top of an Infant's cranium*
tacanȟaȟake *first vertebrae of the spine*
tacankahu *middle vertebrae*
pišleca *spleen*
nige *stomach, paunch*
tezi *stomach*
nawate *temples*
kan *tendon*
itka *or* susu *the testes*
thigh *ceca* or *olute*
sican *outer thigh*
šiyoto *front of thigh*
ceškohloke *lower throat*
lote *throat*
lotku *throat under the jaw*
ceji *tongue*
winapce *tonsils*
šan *vagina*
kan *vein or artery*
oipiyake *the waist*
glogloska *windpipe*
tamni *womb*
nabkan *wrist*
napkan *sinews*
3. **SOME EXPRESSIONS :**
aloksohan *vn* : *to carry under the arm*
cankpeska *adv* : *on the knees*
huhaton *vn* : *to have limbs*
huhaya *va* : *to have for legs*
ikpignaka *va* : *to put about the belly*
istoyukan *vn* : *to have arms*
onzeyugmuza *va* : *to hold the anus shut*
tacanpahmiyan *adv* : *with the body bent*
tamahel *or* tánmahel *adv* : *in or within the body*
tan'akotanhan *adv* : *with a body, beyond flesh*
tancanton *v* : *to have a body, to be full-grown*
tan'ohanglegleya *or* tan'okikašleca *adv* : *dividing the body in two*
tan'okisese *n* : *halves of the body*

tánsanni *n* : *a side of the body*
tansitomni *n* : *the whole body*
tansitomniyan *adv* : *all over the body*

boil *vn* : anahlohlo *as a goose bubbles up under water* — oececa *be slow to ~* — ohan *va* : to ~ *e.g. meat* - ohanpi *part* : *boiled* - iyohan *to boil something* - okicihan ~ *anything for one* - okihan *~ for one* - oohe *n* : *a boiling* — ololobya *va* : *to overboil in* — onas'eya *vn* : *to simmer in* — oyaȟeya *va* : *to make ~ away* — piga *vn* : *to boil* - piga s'e *or* pihya *adv* : *boiling noisely* - ipiga *vn* : *to boil, to foam* — anapšapša *or* iyopšapša *to be bubbling* — wakalya *to ~ something* — šiyaka *n* : *a boil, a sore*
boisterous *n* : waohmunyece *a talkative, garrulous person* — yas'a *va* : *to roar in speaking*
bold *adj* : iohitika
bolt *or* **fasten** *or* **lock** *va* : nataka *to bar inside* — tiyop'ikuše *n* : *a door bolt or lock* - tiyop'inatake *or* tiyop'ipatake *a door bold inside*
bond *n* : inatake

bone *n*
1 : IN GENERAL :
hohu *bones*
gugeca *or* guyeca *or* cupe *marrow*
wicahuhu *the human skeleton*
2 : PARTICULARS :
cankahu *or* cankohan *or* cankahohu *or* cankaslute *the spine*
caukpepajo *patella ~*
ceblo-hu *collar ~*
cecahohu *femur*
cecaoakle *pelvis*
cehu-oagle *jaw joint*
cetunte *thigh*
cetuntoštan *femur head*
hohušunkakan *astroyolus ~*
hutanacute *rib*
huwa-k'ipe *an outer extremity ~*
išpahu *~ of the lower arm*
tamakuhu *breast ~*
mica *hip area*
micahu *or* micahi *or* micaki *or* nisehu *hipbone*
tamicahohu *part near the hip*
okaza *arm, foot*
pahu *skull*
tatahu *neck-bone*
tamica *the spinal end*
taponhu *cheek bone*

húicignuniyan *adv* : *with bones nexed together*

bonus *n* : *fig* sinte *a sale's ~*
book *n* : wówapi - Cf picture, flag
booth *n* : awakeyapi - awakeya *va* : *to make a ~*
bore *or* **drill** *va* : oyuhloka *or* pahloka *pierce*
born *vn* : t'ahiyuya *be stillborn* - wakigna *n* : *a newborn animal*
borrow *va* : olota - olotapi *what is borrowed* - okicilota *to ~ of for* - okilota *to ~ anything of one*
both *adj* : nupin - nupincaska *adv* : *~ together* — óza *adj* : both - leniyoza *or* heniyoza *~ these, ~ those* - yusakib *or* yusakibtu *adv* : *~ together* — nupinyan *on ~ sides*
bother *va* : icagiya *or* iwanagiyeya — ahannajin kuwa *or* akuta kuwa — aok'o *vn* : to bother - aok'oya *va* : *to bother another* — kahtakeke *to irk one*
bottom *n* : cete *of a vessel* - coka *a place of lakes and marshes* — kaaglapšin *adv* : ~ up — kaonze woslal *heels up* - Cf more under dish
bounce *v* : iyakicihpaya
bow *va* : ayukipatuja *or* ayukipatušya *make or cause to bow down*
bower *n* : wahpewokeya
box *n* : can'ognaka *or* canwognaka — wópiye *container for medicines esp*
brace *v* : ipataka *or* ikpataka *to support* - ipatagton to *~ out or stretch* - ipatagya *to ~ out, reinforce* - ipatake *or* ipatan *a support or ~* - ipatangle *to ~* — owaš'aka *to be braced for* — oyut'inze *n* : *a ~ strengthener*
brag *v* : waeconhcaic'ila *or* wayojigjica
braid *va* : ason - kicison *~ for* - sonpi *braids* - kicon *to ~ one's own*
brake *n* : huinak'ehye — huinat'ahton *to put on the ~* - huinat'age *a ~* - huinat'ahya *to ~ or with the ~ on* - huinat'ahye *a ~ on a vehicle*
branch *adv* : ahutkanyan *branching* — aletka *n* : *a limb of a tree* — can'apakan *a crooked, hanging ~* - can'apakinyan *a ~ growing down* - can'inkpa *~ ends* - can'inkpata *at a top ~* — ȟáka *or* ȟákaya *adj or adv* : *branching* - yuȟa *vn* : *to ~ out, to curl* - yuȟaȟa *v* or *adj* : *many-pronged, curly*
brand *n* : cangugu *by hot iron* - oguguye *one burnt in* - oguye *a ~* - pteguye *va* : *to ~ cattle* - wiguye *a branding iron*
brave *vn* : cantet'inza *to be ~* - cantet'ns kic'un *take courage* - cantet'nsya *encourage or encouragingly* — ilitaka *be ~ for e.g. a game* - walita *brave* - walitagya *bravely* - walitake *active, courageous* - walitaya *actively* — waš'aglitaya *courageously* — owohitika *~ on or in* - t'inza *firm and ~* — wóyuȟuptonyankel *bravely* — wóš'akel *overloaded*
bread *n* : aguyapi *wheat ~* - blopahi aguyapi *potato ~* - kiaguyapi *v* : to turn into ~ - aguyapi wigli on kagapi *Indian ~, i.e. fried bread* - *See* aguyapi
break *v* : yubleca *to ~ open by hand* — hukawegapi *a fractured limb* — panhyakel *breaking out, swelling* — wópšun *to ~ letting fall* — wowéga *to ~ in falling* — yuohpeya *make ~ through* — yušpa *to ~ in pieces* — paksa s'e *adv* : *breaking off*
breast *n* : askan *veins of the ~* — aze *the female ~ or udder* - azeinkpa *the nipple* - azepinkpa *the teat* - on'azinpi *or* un'azipi *the nipple* — maku *the ~* - makuhu *the ~ bone* - makunusnunja *extremity of the ~ bone* - makupinkpa *pit of the stomach* — máma *a woman's ~* — tatahpa *the ~ of animals, the flanks, meat left on a hide*
breathe *vn* : niya - aniya *to make ~* - gobgobniya *to ~ hard* - iniya *to ~ from* - niyašnišni *without breathing* - niyaya *to ~ out vigorously* - oniya *~ into, out of* - oniye *a breath, breathing* - oniyemna *to have foul breath* - ge-bniyan *to ~ in a choking way* - gemniyan *or* gepa *to gasp for breath* - oniya *a breath* — yus'o *to duck under water and then come up for air* - yus'okiya *to make surface*
breed *n* : anunkiyan
brick *n* : makašpan *blocks*
bridge *v* : ceakton *or* ceyakton *to make a ~* - ceaktonpi *a bridge*
bright *or* **intelligent** *or* **alert** *or* **shine** *vn* : wacinbleza *to be intelligent* — wiyakpapi *brightness* - Cf glisten
bring *va* : áya *also v coll pl: they brought* - ayakiya *or* ayaya *make ~* - ecinic'iciya *va* : *to ~ one's self to do*

— eke s'e *bringing something better* — kagli *to ~ home* - kícicagli *~ home for* - wagli *~ home meat* - ahi *to ~ there* - ahigle *or* ahiunpa *to ~ and place* - ahik'u *to ~ and give* - ahignaka *to come or ~ and set down* - ahiyagle *to ~ home and place on* - ahiyu *to be coming and bringing* - glohi *to ~ one's own to a place* - hiyoya *to ~ or fetch* kahi *to ~ to one* - kiciglohi *to ~ one's own to another* — aigluhpa *to ~ on one's self* - kai *to go in bringing something to one* — aku *to ~ back something* - kaku *to start to ~ home* — au *to ~ something towards* - glou *to come bringing one's own* - kau *to come bringing to*
briskly *adv* : kátka
bristly *adj* : jijiya *or* jila *as hair standing on end* - anasa *to bristle up* - nawosakiya *make bristle up*
brittle *adj* : štašta *~ and weak*
broadcast *v* : wicaho kahwogyapi *e.g. via radio etc.*
broil *v* : petagaiceonpa *to ~ on coals*
brood *vn* : hpeyunka
broom *n* : icahinte *or* owanka icahinte *or* owank'icahinte - wícahinte *a ~ or rake*
broth *n* : hanpi — hohuwasminpi *a soup made from bone*
brotherhood *or* **fellowship** *n* : otakuye - *See* relative
brown *adj* : gi - giyá *to make, dye ~ , or appearing ~*
bruise *or* **batter** *v* : ikasli *or* kagwa *or* kaošpa *or* kaošpa *or* kašuja *or* okasloslo — okašušuje *a bruise* - našuja *to ~ one by foot* — wicahlece *that used to tear or ~*
brush *va* : ayahinta *to ~ off* - pahinta *rub, wipe, comb off* - yahinta *to ~ away by mouth* — ipaho *to ~ up* — okahpu *va* : to ~ off into — kapoya *or* papowaya *or* powaya *to ~ e.g. lint from a coat* - powayapi *a brush* — pasto *va* : to ~ down, smoothen — yutata *~ off something by hand* — pazayan *adv* : *under the ~*
brutally *adv* : wamakaškan s'e *animal-like*
bubble *v* : anahlohlo — *vn* : anapšapša *or* apablublu — tapsiza *or* anatapšija *or* katapšija *to ~ up*
buck *va* : pahpa *to throw off one, as by a horse*
bud *n* : cán'inkpa

buffalo *n*
1 : IN GENERAL :
tatanka *or* ta *the buffalo,*
pteoptaye *a buffalo herd*
2 : KINDS :
cehinka tapte *a large cow*
hehutela *an old bull*
hehlogeca *a horned cow*
hinhpihpila *an animal that shed old hair (buffalo, horse, or etc.)*
pte *a cow*
ptehincala *a calf*
ptejincala *a newborn calf*
ptesan *a white cow*
ptewinkte *a fat dry cow*
tagica *a lean ~*
taguha *an old scabby ~*
3 PARTS :
hinhantahanpe *part of the heart*
huwicayutipa *leg meat*
iškakan *a tendon*
nakpawicahci *part of the heart*
nige *the paunch*
ptece *dung*
pteišta *an eye*
pte-nakpa *the buffal's ear*
ptetan *a cut of the back*
taajuntka *kidney*
tacaka *roof of the mouth*
tacankoye *fat layers*
tcanta *the buffalo's heart*
tacantamnumnuga *flesh about the heart*
tacantaogin *the heart membrane*
tacantopazan *heart fat*
taceji inkpa *the tongue tip*
tacešikšice *paunch fat*
taceška ha šunk'ak'in *saddle hide*
tacetonte oštan *trunk of the body*
tamnatkan *leg meat*
taniga *paunch*
tanigašin *the fat*
tanihyusku *to empty the paunch*
tanih'ohinšma *the curved part of the paunch*
tanih'ošla *the smooth half of the paunch*
tanitahu *the backbone*
tanitkohloke *the inner thigh meat*
tanipa *meat along the spine*
tasicoska *thigh white meat*
tasinta *the tail*
tasitupahu *tail fat*
tašunšin *neck fat*
tipakel *meat from the back of the head*
tísto conica *or* iyuh'eyayapi *shoulder meat*
tiyoħa *cheek*
wicašašin *the breast*

buffalo chase *n* : onase - owanase *the place of the ~* - owanaseta *at or on the place of the ~* - owanasapi *a ~ run* - wanasapi *the ~* - wanaseya *go on a ~*
buggy *n* : aokiye — tisapa *the ~ top*
bulge *or* **protuberance** *n* : opazo — ipazica *adv* : *bulging*
bulky *adj* : pangece *puffed out* - pakonatke *to make ~ in packing* - panšya *in a bunchy way*
bully *n* or *adj* : ksizic'ila
bump *vn* : íciyapa *to ~ into one* - íciyapapi *a bump, collision* - iyoto *to ~ against* — naškapa *to ~ something* - naškabya *to make ~ against something* — naškan *to jolt* — pajo *a pointed bump, as a ripe pimple*
bunch *adv* : iyupah *in a ~* — kawilwita *to ~ e.g. things together that are scattered*
bundle *or* **bunch** *va* : pahtahta *to tie up in bundles* - pahtapi *or* wapahta *n* : *a pack* — puški *adv* : *in a ~* - Cf heap
bungle *v* : wayuħiyaya *to be awkward* - wayuħiyayaka *a bungler* - yuh'iyaya *va* : *to do something badly* - Cf awkward
burden *n* : itannunkwak'inkiyapi *a load carried on both sides of a horse* — puskica *to be burdened* — wóh'anyankel *unnecessarily burdening, with difficulties of all sorts* — wapangeyeca *to make burdensome* — yuhlohela s'e *seemingly burdened*
burgeon *n* : ouye *burgeoning* - owauye *the growing of*
burn *vn* : ogu *to ~ in* - špan *adj* : *burnt from heat or cold* - španic'iya *v refl* : *to get one's self burnt or frozen*
burst *v* : nablaga *or* okinablaga *to ~ open* — kablaza *to rip open* - nablaza *to ~ by foot* - pablaza *rip open by hand* - ayublaza *va* : *to ~ open on* - inablablaza *~ open in some way* — nahlecala s'e *adv* : bursting — onakpa *to ~ within* — naakamni *to make ~ open* — napopa *va* or *vn* : *to explode* - onapopa *~ within* - apapopa *va* : ~ on - papopa *to ~ by squeezing, pressing* — kapta iyaye *v* : *to go bursting* — okinablaza *vn* : *to ~ open*
bury *va* : éħa *to ~ there* - kiciħa *to ~ for* - ħa ai *va* : *to*

C

bring for burial - waȟapi *a burial* — wakasa *to ~ in snow*
bush *n* : canȟaka *bushes in general* - canȟotka *a ~ used for arrows* - canȟun'aptan *a group of bushes* - can'icahpe hu *nettles* - canptayahan *a ~ in general* - cunȟaka *a brush of bushes* — gánka *bushy* — hpíka *shaggy* — paza *to make bushes erect, for sleeping under*
business *vn* : iwatokiyašni *be none of one's ~* — tawoecon *his work, doing, his ~* — wóiyowaja *inheritance*
busy *vn* : oh'anyan *be active* - wíh'an *be ~ with much* - wih'anpi *an occupation* - owih'an *an occupation, the being ~ about* — wiyankeca *vn* : *to ~ one's self at home* — kihe laka *to keep ~ , to stick to it*
but *conj contr* : k'eyaš *although* — ška *or* tka *or* tuka *yet* — toel *or* toeyaš *but first, but before* — éyaš tuka(š) *but as you should ...* — šehanš tuka *well ... but at last*
butcher *v* : wak'ega
butt *va* : pawaza *to push or rub so to annoy one*
butter *n* : - *See* milk
button *n* : mazaceškikan *a metal ~*
buy *or* **hire** *or* purchase *v* : opeton - opekiton *to purchase one's own, to redeem* - opekiciton *to ~ in place of* — opekicaton *to ~ for* - wókiye iyaya *to go to ~ or trade*
buzz *vn* : hmun - ayuhmun *to make a noise at a crowd murmuring* - hmuns'e *or* hmuns'ekse *or* hmunsececa *in a buzzing way* - hmunya *to cause to hum, buzz* - hmunyan *or* hmunyela *buzzing* - icahmun *to make a ~ with* - kahmun *to make ~* — k'o *the sound of ~ people* - k'ós'e *with the ~ apparently gone* — š'ás'e *the ~ of a crowd of men* — nonhpekic'un *to have a buzzing sound in the ears*
by *prep* : - Note: in Lakota the agent exists only as the subject of the action, thus: *The boy was killed by an enemy* Toka wan iyohlogya hokšila kin he ktepelo. - "by means of", instrumentality, as in *mila on* by or with a knife

cabinet *n* : yuslul icupi *drawers* - yuslul ognake *a bureau* - Cf drawer
cache *n* : wókase *a ~ made in snow*
cactus *n* : unhcela *or* unkcela *a mescal ~ bean* - unhcelablaska *the flat ~* - unhcelatanka *the tall ~* - unhcelatašpu *the ~ berry*
cage *or* **pen** *n* : onatake — zintkala ognake *a bird ~*
calculate *va* : owa *or* wayawa *to count*
calendar *n* : wiyawapi
call *or* **cry out** *v* : kican *to ~ to the dead* - kico *~ or invite* - ekico *to ~ through* — pan *vn* : to ~ out, yell - ikipan *to ~ to one* - kicipan *to ~ for* - kipan *to ~ to* - panyan *adv* : *calling out* — wawoštegla *to ~ bad names* — yatimahelicu *va* : *to ~ into the house* — Hei ... uyeto *Hey, stop there, wait!*
callous *vn* : iyanungah *be callous* - iyanungahya *to cause to be ~* - yununga *to make ~* — iyak'oza *a swollen ~*
calm *adv* : ablagyela *peacefully* - ablakela *n* : a ~ - ablak hingla *to turn ~* - ablak hingla *still, without a wind* - iyablagyela *calmly* — cantiyozikiya *to be ~* — oiyobluya *or* oiyobluyela *a calm* - *adj* : *~ or quiet*
camera *n* : itocicacu
camp *v poss* : gliyunka *make one's own ~* — hoiyokise *a half a ~* — aiglagya *to make move one's own ~* - aiglagcankuya *to break ~* — ohegle *or* opic'iye *a good place to ~* — ati *to be encamped* - ahiti *they came and pitched their tents* - eti *to encamp at* - etikaga *to ~ at a certain place* - etikel *traveling and camping overnights* - etiyoyanka *to live or ~ in a tent* - ewicoti *they encamped* - oti *to make ~* - otiwota *or* otuwota *an old encampment* - otiwotanl *at an old encampment* - tigliyoya *to ~ at the hunting area* - oeti *an encampment ahead* - tiyopeyapi *a camping about the herd* — tiyeyake *encamped*
can *n* : mas'wognake *canned food*
candid *adv* : ašlaya *or* ašlayala
candidate *n* : icajeyatapi
candle *n* : pelijanjan ska *or* petijanjan ska - pelijanjan ihupa *or* pelijanjan oštan *or* pelijanjan ska oognake *or* petijanjan ska aglehan *a ~ stick* - pelijanjan iyukse *a ~ snuffer*
cane *n* : sagye *or staff* - kisagye *turn into a ~* - sagyeton *or* sagyeya *use for a staff in walking*
canyon *n* : mnikaoškokpa *a draw or gulch*
capable *v* : okihi *be ~ or able* - okipi *be ~ to hold, admit, receive* — owešunkeca *vn* : incapable of — mnayan *capably* - wóimnanka *i.e. strong* - wóimnanyan *ably, capably* or *capability* - Cf unable and *okihišni*
capricious *adj* : waecakca *inclined to do from caprice*
capture *va* : gmunka *to trap* - gmunk wacin *to plot trapping one* - ahioyuspa *have come and captured* — napiyuskiya *cause others to capture one* - napiyuza *lay hands on one* - wicatoka *or* witoka *a male* or *female captive* - wiwayaka *a captive from another people*
carcass *n* : tat'eca *of a ruminant animal*
care *or* **keep** *v* : awanyanka *or* awanyanglaka *look after* - awankiciyanka *watch over* — cucic'in *keep some things with one's self* — ekicignaka *to keep for one* - ahopa *take good care of* - ahokipa *take good care of one's own* — óngluze *things attended to* — aki-cikšija *to keep for one* - akšija *retain what is claimed by another* — akicinica *retain for one* — ekicionpa *lay away for another* — ipatan *a prop for one* - kicipatan *take ~ of for one* — atantonyan *to have one save* — walakotašni *not caring for one's own* — wasaza *well guarded from hard-ship* - wasaskiya *to ~*

for tenderly — wóawacin *one's cares* — ikiciyuštan *to take ~ of e.g. a sick person*
carefree *n* : waelon'onke *a ~ person, a busy-body*
carefully *adv* : ikpatanyan *taking care carefully of one's self* — iktahela *gently* — kaiwanyangya *prudently* - kaiyacinyan *or* kaslala *carefully, juggling, slowly* — kiwakanyeš *~ with babies* - nawakankanla *quietly* — napeyahan *watching out* — ptepakah'epi s'e *with great care* — wákicokic'un *putting on with a bit of care*
careless *adj* : ah'anh'anka - ah'anh'an *va* : *to do carelessly* — aškehan *vn* : *not to care* — hlete *a very ~ person showing no responsibility, carelessness* — tokinš *carelessly, wrongly* - tokinšyakel *without care*
caress *va* : kigna - Cf fondle
carpenter *n* : canpajipe - ocanpajipe *a carpenter's shop*
carry *va* : agla *bring home* - áya *take or ~ along* — gloaya *go carrying one's own* - glogla *to ~ one's own back home* — ai *to ~ to a place* — ahiyaya *take and carry around something* — akiyuhapi *they together ~ something back* — akiyuhpa *~ home and throw down* — au *to carry bringing towards* — cutic'in *to ~ at one's side* - cutikic'in *to ~ at the side for one* — hošikaya *~ or take word to one* — k'in *to ~ a load, to pack* - ok'in *to ~ in, or a load, a pack* — atokšu *to transport, to ~ off, away, or pick up* - etokicikšu *to haul for another* — wotákunišni *to ~ off as by rain*
cart *n* : wanjilak'in *a two-wheeled ~* - Cf wagon
cartilage *or* **gristle** *n* : pamnumnuga *of the nose*
carve *va* : apago — ipago *a carving tool* - kicipago *to ~ for one* — wagata *to ~ by knife* - wago *to ~ or engrave* - wagokiya *to have something carved* - wagopi *an etched mark on a game hoop* - wakicigo *to ~ for* - wakigo *to ~ one's own* — wagweza *to roughen with a knife*
castrate *v* : susu-icu
catch *v* : icaštinyanka *to ~ up with* — iciyahpaya *to infect others* — wókape *a catcher* - yakapa *to ~ in one's mouth* - yukapa *to ~ a ball* — oze *to ~ or to get* — yagmica *to ~ the hair by the mouth* - oyuspa *to ~, to take hold of* - Cf hold
catechism *n* : wóiyunge wowapi
caterpillar *n* : azewicahinšma
cattail *n* : psaobloton, *more properly an edible swamp grass*
cause *v aux* : kiya *make be or do etc.* — on *prep* : *(means, reason, purpose)* - on'eciyatanhan *adv* : *by means of, because of* - onetanhan *adv* : *for that reason* — otumakoskanl *adv* : *without cause*
caution *va* : ah'inh'inciya *to make one's way with ~* — a-h'inlh'inlciyelakel *slowlly painfully with great care* — anahaha *slowly, carefully in ref to one* — han'iyagnaka s'e *cautiously, as one who follows with others at night travelling*
cave *n* : makohloka — oswahan *part* : caving in — paoksa *to make ~ in*
cease *v* : yaštan *stop talking*
celebrations *np by name* : Jesus Tonpi *Christmas* — Kini Anpetu *Easter* — Wiwanyangwacipi *Sundance* — Wóacankšin *Passover*
cellar *n* : maka tipi *a sod house*
cellophane *n* : pankeska
cement *n* : inyan maka
cemetery *n* : owicahe
censer *n* : owaizilye
center *n* : cogin - cókab *adv* : *in the midst* - hocokata *n* and *adv* : *center-camp, at the camp ~* — ikanye *towards the ~ as towards the fire* — icisannica *to ~ something* - icisannicab *to ~ half-way* - tiyobcokaton *the ~ of a tipi, or to clear the ~ of the house*
ceremony *n* : wakicaga *a sacred rite* — wakanwicoh'an *a special ceremony, as* Cannunpa Wakan *the Ceremonial Pipe,* Hanbleceyapi *the Vision Quest,* Hokšicankiyapi *Releasing the Soul,* Hunkapi *or* Hunkalowanpi *or* Wawlowanpi *Making Relatives,* Inipi *Purification Bath,* Išnata Awicalowan *Maiden Becomes Woman,* Tapa Wanyankap *or* Tab Wankayeyapi *Throw the Ball,* Wiwanyank Wacipi *Sundance.* Ceremonial needs : ptehiko *to do a ~ for buffalo,* wahinyajice *fur for a special ~ ,* wanyeya *to shoot arrows in a sacred dance,* wówiyunkàgapi *a ~ just before a buffalo hunt*
certain *adv* or *interj* : cintok *or* cintoka *certainly* — ecaš *or* éeš *indeed,* ecašni *indeed not* — ehaš *undoiubtedly* — ehankec'un *or* ehank'un *really, indeed* - hantuk'e *for once indeed* — hécehan *or* héceya *really, certainly* — hunše *surely, doubtless* — wicakapihca *adj* : *absolutely certain*
chair *or* **seat** *or* **bench** *n* : can'akanyankapi *or* canhankayankapi *or* cankankapi *a place to sit* — oikpahunzapi *a rocking chair*
champ *va* : yakaka *as a horse on its bit*
chance *adv* : okiwotahena *by mere ~*
change *or* **alter** *adj* : cantekaptanyan *changeable in one's own views* - canteyušlog *to have a ~ of mind* — hoakab hiyuya *make one ~ what he said* — piya iyukcan *to ~ one's mind* — itokeca *to be changed, affected* - itokecašni *it makes no difference to him, or to be unchanged* - ayatogya *to ~ in the telling* - ayutogyakel *unchanging on* — ya-mniyeya *to alter course by speaking to*
channel *or* **strait** *or* **isthmus** *n* : kiyute
chap *vn* : yuh'i *to be chapped* — yuh'i s'e *adj* : chappedlike - wicayuh'i *n* : chapping — tuta *adj* : chapped
charm *n* : izuyapi *a palladium carried as a ~ for those gone to war* — wótawe *a personal ~ carried in war* — wiciyokipi *beauty, excellence*
chase *va* : okuwa - wawokuwa *pursue*
chatter *v* : hiyakiglegle *or* yakoka *the teeth to ~*
cheap *adj* : awašaka *or* awašakala *or* oawašakala *easily purchased, cheap* - wašagyela *adv* : easily done — šunkányan *cheaply, with little effort*
check *n* : ipashan *a trip, trigger, latch* — iyopazan *what is used to hold in position* — paglega *va* : to ~ off a list
cheer *vn* : akiš'a — canlwašteya *to ~ up one* - canteyat'inza *to comfort one* - canteyawašte *to use encouraging words* - cantopeya *or* kacanlabiyeya *to ~ up* - icanlkaspeya *to ~ one's self* — olabya *to ~ up by giving gifts* — wawimagagayeca *a cheery person* — wawištanyeca *one who is able to cheer others with funny things said* — owilita *cheerful in doing* — yableza *to enlighten others, make them sober*
cheese *n* : - *See* milk
cherish *va* : patan
chew *va* : ayableca *or* ayablu *or* ayagwa *using front teeth* - oyagwa *~ on and spoil* - iyata *to ~ together* - wayata *to ~* - yata *to ~ tasting* — yas'aka *to be unchewable* — yaškica *to ~ on*
chief *n* : itancan *president, chairman* — naca *an able voice of the community* - Note: Nigetankinyan *Big Belly, a nickname for a chief* Cf government, lord, military
child *n* : cinca *offspring, little children* - wakanheja *or* wakanyeja — zipan *a youngster ten or less years old*
chilly *adj* : iyosniyan
chimney *n* : ošota ogna iyaye *or* ošotiyaye *or* šota sam iyaye
chisel *v* : kape - *See* tool

choice *adv* : watankanl *being choicely, trying to seem able*
choke *v* : katka *to ~ or be choked* — niyašnit'eya *to ~ one to death* - oniyašnit'e *to ~ to death* — s'in *adv* : craning — pagloglo *vn to choke*
choose *or* **elect** *v refl* : apiic'iya *revive as in electing new officers of a society* — kahniga *elect or appoint* - icahniga *to pick one* - glahniga *to ~ one's own* - iglahniga *to ~ for one's self, or to ~ one's self as the object* - kicahniga *~ for* — osukanlyuza *to take or make one's choice* — owaštekal choosing, picking
chunky *adj* : pšunka - wohota *chubby*
church *n* : owacekiya *place of prayer* — tipi wakan *holy house* - ipasotkaya *~ tower*
churn *n* : iwoc'u — woc'o to churn *something e.g. butter*
cider *n* : taspanhanpi *fruit juice*
cinder *n* : cata - catanašlogya *to hill up corn with ashes*
circle *adv* : hocokatonyan *or* kaowinh *or* mimeya *in a ~* - okimeya *to encircle something or to enclose or encircling* - omimeyela *encircling* - wómime *a circle* - yumimeya *in a ~, circular*
circulation *v red* : guheheya *to take from ~*
circumcise *va* : wahlaya
circumvent *v* : aoglakšan *to go around*
circumspect *or* **careful** *adv* : kicunniyankel *or* owahecelya *or* aiyacinyan *or* kaiwanyangya *with cirumspection* — wówakta *circumspection*
circumvent *v* : aoglakšan *to go around*
citizen *v refl* : aigluha *to be a ~, provide for one's self*
claim *v* : eic'icaga *to ~ to be* — glogliyacu *to get back what one lent* — oh'anglawa *to ~ something to be one's own work, lay ~ to something not one's own*
clamor *n* : - *See* noise
clamp *v* : anagipa *to be held or pinned down* - anagibya *to ~ or hold fast, to pin something*
clap *v poss* : glaskapa *to clap, applaud* - napeglaskapa *to ~ one's hands*
clash *vn* : ícipa *to meet with force*
clasp *v* : kaskita *to ~ in the arms*
class *or* **sort, kind, division, species** *n* : obe *or* owe, okage, ocaje
clatter *va* : ayakoka
claw *va* : oyupota *to ~ to pieces* - oyupote *a ~ mark* — šioštunkala *a buffalo calf ~* — sištaȟe *a little ~ on the foot of cow or horse*
clean *v refl* : iglatata *shake off one's self* — pakan *to rub off* — pasluta *push out* — waajaja *take off clean*
clear *vn* or *adj* : ables - ablesya *make ~, visible* - blézela *~, as water* — cah'owata *transparently* — gangan-yela *clearing up* — gmi s'e *or* yugmi *to ~ off, to crop* - icagišniyan *without obstacles* — iglatokan *to ~ self of a charge* — iyašlaya *plainly, clearly* — iyusotka *~ weather* — jajaya *plainly* — janjanla *transparent* — kahmin *to ~ off e.g. a field* — owotan'in *to ~ off as weather, or ~ to sight* - kaskaya *make ~ up* - ska *clear* - kask'iyaya *to ~ up* — kasota *to ~ up, i.e. use up* — katan'in *to ~ off, make apparent* — kogli *translucent* — ototola *~ of brush* — owankewašte *easy to look on* — patonwanyan *clearing one's eyes* — zazecala *all but clear of*
clearing *n* : ocunwanice *or* otintoska *a ~ in the woods*
clerk *n* : wówapikage *a scribe*
clever *n* : wówayupike *cleverness*
climb *v* : iyali *to ~ up on* - iyakili *to ~ onto one's own* — kiyahan *to ~ a hill and stand* — oskapa *to ~ up, shinny up*
cling *vn* : kaayaskab *or* okiyaskapa *be clinging to, to cleave to* — kiyuza *to ~ to* — okiyasin *to ~ together*
clock *or* **watch** *n* : mázaškanškan - mazaškanškanikan *a fob* - mazaškanškan tanka *a large clock*
clog *vn* : otkapa — pahli iyokaskica *to clog* - Cf stick
close *adv* : akipšaya *~ together* — akiptan *together joined* — akišoka *thick standing* - akišogya *thickly* — akit'eya *crowded together* — akiš'agya *growing thickly* - akiš'aka *thick, as weeds in a patch* — aogluta *vn* : *to ~ or fill up e.g. a hole* — aogluteya *to ~ up to heal, closing up* — aoyutkuka *to shut up* - kaotkuh *to ~ and shut behind* — naogluta *to ~ or cover by foot* - ógluta *to be closed* - pao-gluta *to ~ up, rub over* — ištogmuza *to ~, shut the eyes, with the eyes shut* - paogmuza *to shut a thing by hand* — yuiyupseicu *to shut e.g. a tent tight* — kitala *close toge-ther* - nakitaka *to shut in one's own* — ektawapa *~ by facing one* — gonga *the eyes gently closed* — ícaštan *~ up to one* — icipasiseya *put close one another* — icišleca *to be or stand ~ together* — ipuskica *or* ipusli *to be ~, to press or touch one* — itagna *with close observation* — íyokašeyela *closely, ~ to* — lécegla *adv* : *close, as in standing close*
cloth *n* : mniȟuha *linen or cotton ~* - mniȟuhaošpula *pieces of ~* - mniȟuha oyuhlece *a rag* - mniȟuha panpanla *silk* - mniȟuhaska *muslin* - mniȟuhaska zibzipela *fine muslin* - mniȟuhatohca *blue mkuslin* -mniȟuhawapahlate *crape* — opehe *a bolt of ~* — šinaopapun *list ~* — šinazibzipela *broad ~* — šina apahlate *ribbon* - Cf mniȟuha
clothe *va* : oginton — wakoyagkicaton *to put on or ~ one* — yupika *to ~ one well, one who dresses well*
clothing *n* : (in general) oigluze — maštewapoštan bonnet — óglekaunjica *a short ~* - óglehinšma *a fur coat* - ógletahu *a coat collar* - mniȟuha ógle *a light coat* - ógleupihanska *a Prince Albert coat* — ainkicaton *to put on or wear a coat* — mahelunzoge *drawers, shorts* — napinkpa *gloves* — wapoštan *hat* — miyapahe *a loin cover* — mniȟuhawanap'in *a neckerchief* —nite okijata *or* onzoge *a pair of pants* — nakputake *a scarf* — ainkitan *to wear a shawl* — ógle *a shirt* — nitehepi *a skirt* — hinyakon *or* hunyakon *or* iyohe — óglezigzica *a sweater* — mahelogle *or* nitoški *an undershirt* — kahlogoštanpi *or* ogleciyuksa *a vest* — ógle papoa *a clothes brush* — ógle wiyotkeye *a clothes peg or hanger*
cloud *n* : mahpiya *the sky, heavens, Heaven* - amahpiya *cloudy, or to ~ over* - cumahpiya *to be cloudy* - mahpihpiya *scattered clouds* - mahpiohanzi *a ~ shadow* — op'oya *in a ~ of dust or snow*
clover *n* : blaye zitkatacan hu stola - Cf herbs
clown *n* : heyoka *or* pizo *one who flaunts by his antics the faults and unreasonableness of men* — Šakton s'e *clownishly*
club *n* : canhpi *or* canksa — hohucanhpi *a ~ with a sharp horn fixed on one end with which to kill animals* — icat'e *a ~ with which to kill*
clumsy *adj* or *adv* : aoh'anhanšniyan *without skill*
cluster *or* **bunch** *or* **pack** *n* : iyagegnag *as of a group of grapes* - iyageya *in clusters* — óšipa *clusters*
coal *n* : cahli *charcoal* - makacahli *common coal*
coated *vn* : aš'aka *to get ~* - aš'agya *in a way ~*
coffee *n* : wakalyapi *or* pejuta sâpa
coffin *n* : wicaȟapi ognake *or* canwognaka
cohabitate *v* : wiinahma - Cf intercourse
coil *va* : akakša — wawagla *to make uncoil by cutting*
cold *vn* : cuwitaiglazan *to be affected by the ~* - cuwita *cold* - acuwita *to be ~ upon* - cuwitagla *to tremble with the ~* - op'oza *or* op'osa *~ and frosty clear* — pamni s'e u *v* : *to have a cold* — sni *adj* or *n* : *cold or a cold*

- htaosni *adj* : *cold in the evening* - iasni *to grow ~ in* - osni *n* : *~ weather, winter, or year* - osnika *adj* : cold - okasni *to get cold* - sniyaȟota *vn* : to take ~ , to breathe in ~ - sniyan *to become cold i.e. weather*

collapse *v* : kakšan *to bend up* — kakšikšija *to collapse* - Cf zigzag

collect *v* : wakamna *to gather* - wakamnaka *or* wamnayan *n* : *a collector of things* - wópamnayan *adv* : *collected together* — yuptaegnag *adv* : *collectively* - yuptaya *adv* : *together* - yuptayela *va* : *to put together*

color *n* or *adj* : híntokeca *~ in general* — **Black** *sápa*, or *šápa* - san'okpukpe *gray* - san'opapa *turning gray* - wisabye *blacking* - wósapa *blackness* - asapa, ašapa, ayašapa, ayušapa, isabye, isapa *to blacken or defile* - kiciyusapa *to blacken for* - kisapa *to become black or bare, i.e. the ground* - sabya *va* : *to blacken* - *adv* : *darkly* - wakašapa *make ~ by striking* - wasabya *to blacken* — **White** : san *gray, whitish, yellowish* - sanyela *adj* : grayish — ska *white, clear* - skaya *to whiten* - skáya *adv* : *white* - skayakel *purely, undefiled, in a clear manner* - šanšan *whitish* - asan *to become whitish* - aska *to become white on* - icasan *to whiten or make fade by striking* - ipasan *to put on white paint by daubing* - isanyan *to make white by rubbing* - kasan *to turn white* - kasansan *to scrape white* - kisan *become white for* - sanyan *va* : *to whiten* - *adv* : *whitish* - waskaska *white things* - waskaya *to whitewash* - wisanye *a whiting.* — **Red** : luta, lul *scarlet* - ša *red* - šayela *reddest* - ziša *reddish* - takušaša *a reddish thing* - wišaye *red coloring* - wóša *redness* - aša *or* naša *to become red* - paša *rub red* — **Yellow** : zi *or* zizi - ziya *to dye or paint ~* - ziyela *yellowish* - hohusan s'e *light ~* - aziya *to make ~* ogiya *to paint ~* - ziya *to dye or paint ~* — **Blue** *or* **Greem** : to *blue or green* - toto *green* - skanyeca *or* tóhca *blue* - tólahcaka *very blue* - tosan *light blue* - towanjica *all blue* - tozi *light green* - tózitka *greenish* - pezi *white-beaked as is a mudhen* - watoya *adv* : *grass-like green* - ziyato *green* - witoye *a blue or green dye or paint* - ato *to become blue or green on, or to tatoo* - ito *or* itoto *to become blue by means of* - tokíya *or* toya *to dye or paint blue or green* — **Miscellaneous** : ástan *to be or become purple on* - kaȟota *to make gray by striking* - hinzi *cream* - gi *brown* - gleška *spotted, striped* - glagleglega *to be of or changed to different colors* - wógi *brownness* - yugicala *to make a little ~* - ȟota *gray* or *brown* - ȟo-lya *in a gray or mixed manner* - oȟolya *grayish* - ogi *rust brown* - oh'a *gray, black and white speckled* - oh'aka *gray and all colors mixed* - stan *dark purple* - stánka *purple* - šagi *auburn, sandy* - šámna *dark brown* - tolute *or* toša *purple* - tosapa *grape-colored*

comb *v poss* : glakca *to ~ one's own* - kakca *to ~, disentangle* - kicicakca *to ~ for* - kicipakca *to ~ out* - nasunpkca *a comb* - pahinnasunpakca *a ~ of the porcupine tail* - pakca *to disentangle* — kaswa *to curry* — pesleteša *a cock's ~*

come *or* **arrive** *vn* : aun *to ~ with the wind* — gli *arrive home* - agliyohpaya *they came down from a hill* - glicu *to start to come ~* - gliyohi *to come for one's own* - gliyohpaya *to have ~ down from* — gloki *to arrive ~ with one's own* — hannatantan u *to ~ in the night, feeling one's way* — ahi *to arrive at* - ahignaka *to ~ and put down* - ahiicu *to have ~ and taken* - ahimniciya *to ~ and assemble* - ahinapa *to ~ out on* - ahioyuspa *to have ~ and captured* - ahitebya *to ~ and devour* - ahiti *to ~ and live, pitch one's tent* - ahiwitaya *to have ~ together* - ahiwota *to come and press against* - ahiyagle *to bring ~ and place on* - ahiyahan *to ~ home and stand, alight on* - ahiyanka *to ~ and stay around* - ahiyohpaya *to ~ down a hill* - ahiyokakin *to ~ and peep in* - ahiyu *to ~ bringing* - ahiyukan *to ~ and make room* - ahiyunka *to ~ or bring and lie down* - ahiyuslohan *to ~ dragging along* - ahiyuštan *to ~ and finish* - ahiyuwega *they cross, or came and broke it* — *hi arrive* - hibu ~ - hiayanpa *to come morning on* - hiheya *to ~ and enter as a bullet* - hihunni *to reach, ~ at a place* - himniciya *they ~ assembling* - hiyakapta *to ~ over a hill or stream* - hiyunka *to ~ and stop for the night* - iglohi *to bring one's self to a place* — hiyo *to ~ for* - hiyohi *to ~ for* - hiyohikiya *or* hiyohiya *to cause one to ~ for* - hiyohpaya *to ~ down from* - hiyohpeya *to ~ and let down* - hiyo u *or* hiyoya *to ~ and fetch, get* — hiyu *to ~ from out of* - aohiyu *to leak or ~ out on* - iglohiyu *to betake one's self to a place* - hiyukiya *to cause something to ~ to, to send* - hiyuya *to cause to ~ to, to send to* - ohiyu *to ~ through, to leak* — wicokanhiyu'ic'iya *to ~ unasked* — hoši *to tell the news, take word* - hošihi *to ~ with word* - hošii *to have gone to, to carry word* - hošikahi *to ~ with word for one* - hošikai *to go bringing word to one* - hošikaku *or* hošiu *to ~ with a message* — i *to have gone to* - ainapa *to have come is sight of or upon* - igloi *to betake one's self* or *one's own to* - icagejuya *to ~ up and accompany* - iglagyake *being loaded down with some of one's own luggage* - iglonica *to balk, refuse to go* - iyagle *to lead or reach to* — aki *prep in compos* : for - akinajin *to return and stay* - akinatan *to rush for one's own* - kiyokpeca *to have ~ back to one's home away* - akiyugo *to arrive worn out* — okahloka *to ~ its way through something* — pašpeya *to make come out* — u *to be coming* - ukiya *to make ~ , they coming home* - uyekiya *to make ~* - úwa yo *(a man's word)* or úwi ye *(a woman's word) Come!!* - au *to ~ on*, or *they ~* - gliu *to ~ to one's own home* — gliyagli *to go and ~ back* — oya *to ~ or wash off, to stick to* — igloya *v refl* : *to betake one's self to, to take to one's self*

comfort *n* : wacintongnake *or* wicakikcanpte *or* wówicakigna *a comforter* - wacintongnagya *to ~ one* — owašteya *to be comfortable*

comical *or* **funny** *or* **cute** *adj* : oh'anwiȟa - Cf laugh

command *va* or *n* : iwakiconza *or* iwakiconze — oiekic'un *to enforce obedience* — ši *to bid one to do something* — wáokiya *to ~* - Cf imperatives

commerce *or* **trading** *n* : wópetonpi

common *adv* : hécetuke *commonly, usually* — ikce *commonly* - ikceka *common* - ikceya *or* ikceyakel *commonly* — kiska *to recover ~ sense* — wakic'unpi *~ property*

commotion *n* : wawok'oyece *a fracas, an uproar*

compare *v* : wiyacin *~ to or with* - Cf figure, parable

compassion *v* : ionšila *to have ~ on in ref to something* - ionšilaya *pitifully* — ounšila *or* wakikcanpta *adj* : compassionate — wócantognake *n* : *pity* - Cf pity

complain *va* : acicahlo — anagwag *or* anagwaka *to murmur against* — ígle *grumble, whine, protest* — pa *va* : to bark - wayašihtinka *a complainer*

complete *v* : iyuhpa *be all finished* — akigna *really completely* — ékihunni *to finish the course*

complexity *n* : wóoškiške *confusion, difficulty*

complicated *adj* : oškiška *confused, abrupt* - oškiškiic'iya *v refl* : *to get confused* — canšihuta *complicated*

compliment *n* : wicayatanpi *praise*

comply *v* : wicakicila - *adj* : *positive*

comprehend *va* : yukcan *to know, have an opinion, guess*

compress *or* **bite** *va* : yapo *or* yaopo — ícipat'ins *to push tightly together* — wóškilya *to ~ with great force*
concave *n* or *adj* : smaka *hollow or a hollow* — oškokpa *a concavity, a sunken place*
concealment *n* : wóinahme - *See* hide
concern *vn* : itoka *to be without ~* - iwatokiya *to be much concerned* - iyowaja *in a concerned way* - owaja *to be concerned in* — wikic'un *with a concern* — wacinwikic'unšni *one unconcerned*
conciliate *v* : wayuwaȟa
condemn *va* : ayasu - glasu *to ~ one's own* - wasuya *to judge one* - wasuyapi *a condemnation*
condiment *or* **sauce** *n* : iyulkiton *or* iyulton *a sauce* — mniskuya *salt* — yamnumnugapi *black pepper*
condition *adv* : kayunš *under such conditions*
cone *n* : wazipinkpa *a pine ~*
confer *or* **council** *v* : woglaka - owoglake *a conference room, a council chamber*
confess *v refl* : oiglaka *to make self known*
confidence *n* : wacinkiciyapi - wacinyehci *very confidently* - wacinyekiya *to make one have ~* - wacinyepica *a source of ~* - wacinyeya *to cause to take ~* - wówacin *faith, confidence* — ícimna *or* íc'imna *to have ~ in one's self*
confirm *or* **corroborate** *v* : oyuma *or* oyušlata
confuse *adj* : hoka ca hanye kinye s'e *confused* — akinahanhan *confusedly* - hokiiyokpaza *having come into darkness* — wóškiška *causing trouble or confusion, or one's trouble or bewilderment* — yaignuni *to ~ by interruptions*
congest *v* : iyokaskica *to clog*
conglomerate *adv* : igleglehya *with a whole conglomeration*
conjure *v* : kiciyapa *to ~ by sucking for as if drawing off poison* — píya *to repair something* - wapiya *to renew the sick, powwow* - wapiyapi *a conjuring*
connect *va* : ayazunta *to speak manipulating one* — iciyokihe *adjoining* - iciyokiheya *to join, connect things*
consanguinity *n* : wótakuye - Cf relative
conscious *va* : kiksuya *to remember, be conscious of* — hangnagya *being semi-conscious*
consecutively *adv* : iyaza
consider *vn* : akiya *give attention to* — akibleza *to think about* - iyubleza *make clear for one* — canteyuza *to form an opinion* - ecin *or* epca, ecinka, hecin, epcapca, epceca, hepcapca *to think, to come to mind* — ecankin *or* hecankin *to think so of* — hecetulaka *to think, form an opinion* — heceyala *~ certain* — ayuhete *to ~ intently* — awiyukcan *to form an opinion on* — ic'ila *to ~ one's self* — awacin *to think on, meditate on* - awacinkel *reflecting upon* - awacinpi *a consideration* - awacinya *to influence one* - awacinyakel *in a way thinking on* - awakicin *to give one's attention to* - éwacin *or* éwacinka *to think concerning and to turn one's affections to* - íwacin *to thing of going to* — igluwitaya *to concentrate on one's own* — yawa *va* : *to consider*
consistently *or* **congruously** *or* **connectedly** *adv* : zontaheya - Cf weave
console *or* **comfort** *va* : kikcanpta *or* okikcanpte *or* wakikcanpta *to comfort, console* - wakikcanpte *a comforter, consoler* — yuasniyan *to console one*
conspicuous *adj* : ipasotka - ipasotkaya *conspicuously* — okitan'in *to be noticeable*
constrict *adv* : oikpaptanšilya *in a constricted way*
consult *vn* : kiksapa *to become wise*
consume *v* : pilya *to eat up all e.g. grass*
contagious *n* : wówanke *that which is ~*
contain *vn* : kipi *to hold or carry or sufficient for* — ógnake *a container for keeping things*
contemn *va* : iwakiniya *to get out of humor with* — kat'apt'apa (said with a gesture of contempt)
content *vn* : wacin'iyokipi *to be contented*
contention *n* : wówakitan *a point of ~ as of a resolution set* - wówakitanye *a resolution disputed*
continue *v* : yeye *to last*
continually *adv* : ahtatešniya *without stopping or resting* — glaheya *~ without interruption* — h'unwištan šni *persistent, incessant, never quitting* — katintinyeya *with no stop* — kipsakahešni *uninterrupted* — oaye *continuation* — oziwanil *without rest* — šna *again and again*
contract *or* **shrink** *vn* : našinšin *to ~ and wrinkle* — natipa *to draw up, curl or cramp*
contradict *va* : yaglakinyan *to ~ one's self*
contrary *adv* : ot'unyankel *~ to liking* — unmaciyatan *on the ~, from the other side* - unma ecetkiya *or* unma eciyatanhan *on the contrary* — yus'oyakel *~ to all expectations*
control *va* : ilaka *to govern, rule over* — napiyusya *controlling* — oic'onica *to ~ self* — s'agic'iya *to ~ one's self, to be resolute* — tacupala s'e *easily losing self-control* — iwanjica *to ~, check e.g. one's anger*
convalescent *adj* : kibleza
convenient *adv* : wicakiješniyan *convenienced*
convert *or* **persuade** *or* **change** *va* : yahomni *to turn one around by arguments*
convex *adv* : ipazilya
convince *v poss* : glahomni *to change one's own views by persuasion* — oekiye *to be convinced, or a conviction* — wicakelakiya *to ~ one* — painlpica *to be able to ~, to bear or concentrate upon*
convulse *vn* : natin *to be in convulsions*
cook *vn* : alo *to be cooked* - aloza *short of being cooked* - alesabya *or* alosabya *hardly cooked, all but cooked* - alosya *to scorch in a flame, fig to touch one's feelings of anger* — kceya *to ~ hanging over fire* — akceya *to ~, roast and then leave to dry* — apapson *to roast on or over* — špan *cooked, to be cooked* - ašpan *to be cooked* - španyan *to ~ anything* - špankiciciya *to ~ for* - špankiya *to ~ one's own* - wašpankiya *to ~ for one* — lolih'an *to prepare food* — oceon *cooked* — wóhan *to make a feast* - wóhela *or* wóhe-kiyapi *a cook* - wóhankiya *to have for a cook* - owahe *to have cooked* — ikih'an *to ~ for one*
cooking utensils *n* : psin'unwohanpi *a boiler* - wiyujaja *a colander* - miyutapapi míla *a kitchen knife* - wópaska *bread pan* - wópaska tanka *dish pan* - mas'wiconpi *or* wíceunpe *or* wítake *frying pan* - céga *a pot or kettle* - onwohanpi oceti *a cooking range* - icancan *or* wicacan *or* wiyucancan *a sieve* - ipuskepa *a strainer* - wíkaze *a gravy strainer*
cool *adj* : cusni - htacusni *~ or the evening* - icicasni *to ~ e.g. a hot cup of coffee* - iyosniyaya *to ~ something* - kaosni *to refresh* - osniya *to make ~* - oyusni *to ~ by placing* - wosní *to extinguish, put out a flame by blowing on or cooling it* — najukaosnisni s'e *as if cooling the back of the head*
coordinate *conj adv* : tóhan, tohanl, tohanyan ... ca na *whenever ... then* — tóhan, tohanhunniyan, tohunhunniyan ... hehan *as long as, until, as far as ... then* — tó hinni ... šni *never ... ever* — tókel ... cana ecel *as ... so* — tókeya ... ca hehanl *before ... then* — tuktel ... hel *where ... there* — unma ... unma *the one ... the other* — unmagma *one or the other*

copy *va* : okaga – okagapi *a model or image*
cord *n* : – *See* string
cordial *n* : wólakolkiciyapi *cordiality, amity*
corner *adj* : oblece *cornered* — kaobloton *to make or form a ~* – obloton *a ~, or cornered* — kahmin *an inside ~* – okahmin *a house ~* — najinyan *to ~, hold at bay* — oisa *the outer ~* — ungnagata *in the ~ behind the door* – ungnage *corners within either side of the door* – Cf bend
corral *n* : ošunkoyuspe
correct *va* : gleton *to ~ a mistake* — iyokteka *to reprove* — iyopeya *to punish, scold* – iyopekiya *to reprove, chide* — pašihtin *to do incorrectly* — yaecetu *to ~ a statement* — zunlya *correctly, joined*
corrupt *va* : iyušica *to make bad, injure*
cotton *n* : popopa – Cf pith
cough *vn* : hohpa *to have a spell of coughing* – hohpah'an hanska : whooping ~ – hohpapi *a ~* — kahkaga *to ~ up* — tonhlihli *to ~ up phlegm*
council *n* : owoglake *a ~ chamber* – Cf consult, confer
count *v* : glaota *to ~ many of one's own* — glatonana *to ~ one's own* — yawa *to ~ some things* – glawa *to ~ one's own* – iciyawa *to ~ up together* – kiciyawa *to account for one* – oyawa *to ~ in, to matriculate* – iyawa *to figure with* – hanglawakel *counting the days and nights*
courage *n* : – *See* terrible
court *n* : wakiya-tipi *a ~ house* – okiya *to talk to one* – okiciciya *to discuss together* — wakanh'an *v* : to court a woman with music — wíyape *to lie in wait for* – wíokiya *to talk flirtingly* – wiokiyapi *courting* — wíoyuspa *to detain a woman*
cover *or* **cloth** *n* : cegnake *a breachcloth* – cegnakekiton *or* cegnakiton *to wear a loincloth* — cekpiyuskite *a baby's swaddling band* — ceškasansan kšupi *a woman's beaded dress* – ceškikan *a button above the breast* – ceškipazize *a breast pin* – ceškiyutan *suspenders* — cuwignagya *to use for a gown* – cuwignaka *a non-Indian woman's dress* – cuwiyuskite *a vest, or corset* — aiglahpa *v refl* : to ~ one's self — aiglušla *to cut and ~ one's self with* — aiglutan *to besmear one's self with one's own emission* — aigluza *to dress up for an occasion* – igluza *to dress up* – iyogluze *wearing apparel* — hakiton *to be dressed* – hakiya *to dress one* – haya *to have for clothing* – hayake *or* hayapi *clothes* — igluhniga *to dress up one's self* — inkiya *to cause one to wear* — ištoyuha *an eye cover* — akahpa *to ~ up* – akahpe *a bed ~* – akahpekiton *to ~ up one* – akahpeton *to throw over* – akahpeya *covering* – akahpihpeya *to ~ over* – iteakahpe *a veil* – iyakahpe *a lid used to ~* – wiyakahpe *a ~* – iyakahpeya *serving as a ~* – oakahpe *a bed ~* – wakahpa *to cover* — kasa *to ~ with snow* — naatan'inšni aya *to begin to cover over tracks* — aognaka *to put a ~ on* – aokata *to ~ with earth* — iyaopemni *to ~ and enclose* — pošlicoma *to have the head covered* – pošlišli *to have the face covered* — aunyeya *to ~ put on e.g. a patch* — ayuta *to ~ with dirt, to cultivate* — naogluta *to ~ with the foot* — ayuwinta *to ~, overlay* — iyocošyakel *with added cover on*
covet *v* : kizomi *or* kon *or* waicucuktehcin *to desire passionately*
cow *n* : pte *a ruminant* – ptegleška *domesticated cattle* – ptewanap'in *oxen* – ptemakicima *a heifer* – ptewatogla *a wild ~* – ptewinyela *a female cow* — toganganokiwaslecapi *a very fat ~*
cowardice *n* : – *See* fear
cowboy *n* : wašicunpteole *a non-Indian who looks after cows*
crack *or* **deform** *v* : kaȟuga *to break* – naȟuga *va* : *to crack something and break by foot* – paȟuga *to break by pushing on* – yaȟuga *to crush and open* – yuȟuga *to crack something by hand* — pelnakpakpa *vn red* : to crackle — kakpi *to pierce and open* – kpakpi *to pierce one's own and open, to shell* – nakpi *to break open by foot* – pakpi *to mash something* — ptuja *adj* : cracked or split – kaptluja *to cause to be cracked* – naptuja *to be cracked* — nasleca *to crack or split, or to do so of itself* — kiciyuwega *to fracture or break for one* — pazuya *to crack e.g. one's bone*
crackle *adv* : našak'oȟayeya *making ~, growing red, as fire might glow*
cradle *n* : can'ic'ik'onpa *or* wicakahunhunzapi
cram *va* : paoskica
cramp *va* : ayutipa *to make draw up on* – hunatipa *vn* : to have a ~ in the leg – huyutipa *to have cramps in the calves of the leg* – kannatipa *to cramp nerves or muscles* – yutipa *to draw up as muscles etc, to fold up, to crisp*
crane *v* : kis'ins'in *to strain* – yukos'in *to draw up the neck*
cranky *adv* : šinkcinyan — toies'a *a person who is ~, a crank, a critic*
crash *va* : iwokpan *to ~ to pieces* — šušuš hingla *to come crashing down*
crawl *vn* : slohan — aslohan *to ~ along on* — ašniyanyan *vn* or *adv* : *to crawl around as do worms in a crawling manner* – ošniyanyan *to ~ about within* — ayuȟab *creeping toward*
crazy *vn* : kignaškinyan *to turn ~* – wayagnaškinyan *v* : to talk one ~ – Cf fool
creak *vn* : cankakiza *as trees do in the wind* – kakiza *to make ~ by rubbing* – nakiza *to make e.g. shoes ~* – pakiza *to make ~ by rubbing* — namnuza *to make ~ as in walking on ice* – naomnuza (an *archaic* word) – numnuza creaking – mnumnus *to sound when breaking* — napiza *vn* : *to creak or squeal in a high pitch voice* – papiza *to make ~*
cream *n* : – *See* milk
create *v* : wawicahya – wawicahye *or* waicahye *the Creator, Maker* – oicage *or* okage *or* wamakognaka *creation, the universe*
credit *n* : icazopi – aicazo *or* ikicazo *or* oicazo *to take ~ on account for a time*
credulous *adj* : tawacinpanpanla *weakminded, naive*
creep *va* : naslata *to ~ or move up to noiselessly* — makipahlala *creeping along the ground*
crest *or* **comb** *n* : peša
crinkle *vn* : kakeca
crippled *adj* : ošteka *or* tanšica – Cf deformed
crisp *adv* : yukiyuteya *drawn up*
criticize *vn* : *fig* nagwaka *to kick* — toia *to knock* — waglaglaka *to ~ food, to be finnicky* — yakatintin *va* : to set right by talking — iyoglušt'eya *to ~ badly* — wayazazaka *to take to pieces with the mouth, to ~ or one who criticizes much*
croak *va* : pajinca *to make ~ or shake*
crooked *adj* : cinhtin — glakinkinyan *adv red* : in a zigzag manner — hmi(n) *adj* : misshapen – ayuhminyan *or* hminyan *or* icihmninyan *adv* : done crookedly – wapahmin *or* yuhmin *to make crooked* — kšikšan *or* ktan *or* owinga *~, bent* — kapemni *to strike and make bend ~* — škopa *~, bent* – aškobya *in a ~ way* – aškopa *to be ~ on or arched-over* – ayaškopa *to twist by biting* – škobya *to make ~*, or in a ~ manner — wapako *to cut or saw ~*
crop *va* : yagmi *to bite off grass etc.* — wak'eza *to shave off to make smooth*
cross *v* : akokabya *to go across by a near way* — canwici-

paga *n* : *a cross* — hinyanza *to be stern,* ~ - hinyanzeca *sulky* - ohinyanzeca *to be stern, cranky* — ksizeca *stern* — hukaicicawinyan yanka *to sit with legs crossed* kaicic'uya *with legs crossed* — kaiciopteya *intersecting* — ocinšica *to be bad-tempered* - ocinšicaya *evilly disposed* — ahiyuwege *they came and crossed or broke it* - akiyuwega *a fording place, a ford* - can'icipawega *the cross, crucifix* - hiyuwega *to* ~ *a stream* - ícipawega *to* ~ *or lie across* - iyuwega *to pass through or ford* - kiyuwega *to ford a stream* — aiglagcankuya *to* ~ *on one's own path*
cross-eyed *adj* : ištahmin - ištakšin *to be* ~
crosswise *adv* : naglakinyan *set* ~ , *turned outward* - tanglakinyan *across* — kaiteb *diagonally* — aiciyopteptya *set* ~ , *each at the four quarters about a point of reference* - ícipawehweh *or* ícipaweh *or* ícipawehya *in* ~ *fashion*
crouch *adv* : putanyela *crouched, as when one is cold and wrapped in a bundle*
crowd *adv* : gangansni *or* gangansniyan *crowded together* — hooyaza s'e *close packed* — icata *to* ~ *together* — kaigejuya *crowding in* — kaipustagya *crowding against* — ohli s'e *crowded about* — paglakinyan *crowding to one side* — ahipani *to push and* ~ *against* - épani *to elbow one's way through* — paokanšniyan *to* ~ *out* — pata *or* icata *crowded together* — akit'eya *in a tight and stacked manner as books on a shelf* - icit'eya *crowding one another badly* — aot'insya *to* ~ *things, or in a crowded manner* - hiyot'inza *to come and* ~ - ocit'inza *to be crowded* — wicohan *into the* ~ — wicotapišniyankel *away from a* ~ — ahiwi-coti *a* ~ *oncoming*
crown *or* **fillet** *v* : tešlagkiton *to put on a* ~
crumble *va* : ayuhpu - hpuphu *crumbled* - hpuwahan *crumbled, come apart* - hpuya *crumbling off* — kaoksa *to* ~ *down* - kaoksaya *to make* ~ *down* — oyukpakpa *to* ~ *in* — okpankpan *to crumble, or crumbs, decay* - okpanla *crumbled* — ptuh'a *to be crumbling down* — špahanhan *crumbling away*
crumbs *or* **leavings** *n* : otutka
crunch *vn* or *adj* : canhcanga *to* ~ *in the mouth noisily, crunching* — mnúga *or* mnuh *to chew as a horse does eating corn* — yacanga *to make a noise in chewing what is hard* — yahwu *to make a crunching noise*
crush *v* : kpableca *to* ~ *one's own* - pableca *to* ~ *something with weight from above* — pakpan *to* ~ *fine by pressing* - icakpan *crushed, ground* — wóskilya *or* woskíIya *to* ~ *by pounding* — nasli *to* ~ *by foot* — onatan *to* ~ *upon, or fig to use harsh words* — napšija *to* ~ *by foot* - pašnija *to crush by pushing e.g. the air out of* — yašuja *to* ~ *by mouth* - yušuja *to* ~ *to slivers* - naja *to* ~ *by trampling on* - Cf grind
crutch *n* : canhuapi
cry *or* **moan** *vn* : céya - waceya *to* ~ *something* - naceya *to make* ~ *by kicking* - oweceya *to* ~ *over one* — šicahowa *to* ~ *out* - šicahowaya *to moan* - kahoton *to make* ~ *out* - Cf pout, sob, shout
crystalline *adj* : skokogli
cube *n* : wak'inlas'e *a pack* - Cf pack
cubit *n* : wicišpa
cultivate *or* **till** *or* **work** *va* : mahglamni *to clear off for cultivation* — okicanye *cultivation* - Cf hoe
cumbersome *vn* : opanga *to be* ~ - opangeca *to be encumbered* - Cf hinder
cupboard *n* : wakšica ognake
curdle *v* : kagwu *to make* ~ *by beating* - ogwu *to become cheesy* - onagwu *to* ~ *in* — nini *adj* : *coagulated, curdled*
cure *or* **heal** *va* : akisniya - akisniyepicašni *incurable* — aogluta *to heal over* - asniya *or* asnikiya *to make heal* - asnikiyekiya *to cause to get well* - asnikiyeya *to make well* - asnipica *curable* - asniya *to cure* - kisnikiya *to* ~ *a person*
curiosity *n* : wóš'inš'inkiye *what attracts one's interest*
curl *vn* : ayumnimnija *to ruffle* — glaȟa *to* ~ *or knot one's own* — gugula *curled or ruffled* — iyuwi *to twist, or a vine* — nagmugmun *to crips something* - nagmun *to be crisped* — ówinge *a hair curl* - ówinhya *to make curls, or in a manner curled or curved* — škoškopa *crooked or warped, curled* — yuȟa *vn* : to curl and branch out - yuȟaȟa *curly*
current *adv* : tatohekiya *or* tatoheya *against the* ~
curse *v* : glatoie *or* šilaptanyeya *to cause to have bad luck* - šilgla toie *to* ~ , *use curse words* — wayašica *to speak evil of* - wóšiliyagle *to be cursed, meet bad luck*
curtain *n* : ózan *or* wózan
curved *adv* : apahaya *convexly* — opuš'in *an arc, arch, a convex line* — owokšan *a curve* — wóškopa *the curve of something*
custom *or* **ceremony** *or* **law** *n* : wicoh'an *a habit of doing something* - oh'anya *to have for a* ~ — wicoahope *a ceremony* - wóope *a law*
customarily *adv* : kikiyakel *not customarily*
cut *or* **break** *va* : waicišniyan *to* ~ *crooked* — kagmipi s'e *as if cut all down* — kokiwohci *to cut through the skin*
cute *adj dim* : šícelah *funny*
cutting board *n* : awawapte — canlawakpan *or* canliawakpan *a* ~ *for cutting tobacco*
cyclone *n* : owaomniomni - Cf eddy

D

Dakota *np* : Lakota *and* Nakota *and* Dakota are the names of the three larger Siouan peoples living generally in the north-central United States of America. They differ in the dialect of a Siouan language. Dakota and Sioux are terms used occasionally to designate the three groups as a whole. Dakota, as Lakota and Nakota, means *Alliance*, an allied people. The word Sioux is said to be derived from Nadouessioux, *Enemy*, attributed to them by neighboring tribes as the Iroquois of the West. Over time the title shortened to Sioux. - Cf nation
dam *n* : capceyakton *a beaver's* ~ — mninatake *any* ~
damaged *adv* : tanzaniyake *undamaged*
damp *or* **moist** *vn* : ocu *become* ~ *in* - ocuya *to make* ~ — ospaya *to become* ~ *in* - ospaye *dampness* — otkin *to become* ~ *in* — tatapa *adj* : almost dry - tatapešni *adj* : still wet - Cf wet, dew
dance *v* : waci *to* ~ - wacipi *a dance* - awaci *to* ~ *on or in honor of* - iwakici *to* ~ *for one* - owaci *a* ~ *hall* — DANCES : Han Wacipi, *the Night* ~ - Howi Wacipi *the Ghost* ~ - Iwakici Wacipi *the Scalp* ~ - Kayola Wacipi, a Isanbati Wacipi, a Santee ~ - Omaha Wacipi *the Omaha* ~ - Maštinca Wacipi *the Rabbit* ~ - Psa Wacipi *the Crow* ~ - Tokala Wacipi *the Fox* ~ - Wakan Wacipi *a Sacred* ~ - Wiwanyank Wacipi *the Sundance* - Wiyatapika *a Young Woman's* ~ — **REGALIA** : huiyakaske *ankle ornament for the Sundance* - kangiha mignaka *a feather bustle* - peša *Omaha Dance headgear* - ptehe wapaha *horned headgear* - unhcelakagapi *a bustle fixed to the rear* - wacinhin *a headdress* - wacinhin sapsapa *black plumes* - wacinhinya *to use as a plume* - wapaha *a headdress*
dandruff *n* : natacokuhpuhpu *or* natahpuhpu

danger *n* : okokipe *fear of* - okokipeya *in fear* — pajeje *to be in danger*

dangle *vn* : okakoza *or* okakoskoza — kapemnimniyan *adv* : *dangling* — lupi *adj* : *dangling* — wóhciya *adv* : *in dangles* — izezeya *dangling* - aozeze *to be dangling* - paozezeya *dangling*

dare *vn* : aotognaka *or* aot'ognaka

dark *vn* : aiyokpaza *to be* ~ - aokpaza *to be* ~ *on* - oiyokpaza *n* : *darkness* - ókpaza *vn* or *n* : to be ~ , or *darkness or night* - akpasya *to darken*, or *in ignorance* - aokpas *to be* ~ *on* - aokpasya *to make* ~ *upon* or obscurely - oikpasya *in darkness* - oiyokpas *to turn* ~ — okisapa *to become bare and* ~ - okisabya *blackish as after the snow melt* — aotan'in *to be approaching dusk or growing dim* - awatan'inšni *adj* : *dark as at dusk*

date *n* : - *See* day, time

daub *va* : icatantan *daubing along, smudged* otkabya *to make stick on* — tiakastaka *to* ~ *a house* - Cf to stick

dawn *n* : anpo - anpakableza *at daybreak* - anptaniya *the first glimmer of morning* — kajanjan *vn* : *to become light* - "anpo wicahpi *the dawn of a new day*"

day *n* : ánpa *daylight, daytime* - anpahan *in daylight* - anpakableza *daybreak* - anpecokanya *noontime* - anpehan *adv* : *today as past* - anpetu *a day* - anpetuhankeyela *before noon* - anpetula *a lovely day* - anpetutahena *before the day is done* - Anpetuwakan *Sunday* - ianpetu *the same or next day* - oanpetu can *daily* - anpešiceca *an unpleasant, rainy day* - anbwašte *a pleasant day* - anpo *to dawn* - anpokableze *daylight* - anposkanl *or* anposkantu *by day, in the daytime* - anptaniya *the very first glimmer of morning* — can *day, date* - ihinhanna *the next day or morning* — iyotan'inlake *daylight* — iwacintokankangnagnahan *day-dreaming*

dazzle *vn* : ištiyošnija *to have eyes blinded by light* - ištiyošnijaya *to blind one with light* — ištiyowalya *to* ~ *one's eyes* — ištiyojanjanya *to* ~ *one* - waiyojanjan *to* ~ *one with light, to blind one*

deaden *v* : itoyuha t'ekiya *to make a deadened expression on the face*

deaf *adj* or *vn* : nonhcan *or* nunhcan *hard of hearing* - nonhcansihutayela *pretending not to hear*

debase *va* : yušihtin *to enfeeble one* - Cf feeble

debility *n* : wóšihtin

debt *n* : wóikazo

decay *n* : okpankpan — *v* : *to decay* - *See* rot

deceive *vn* : iyugnayan *to be deceived* - wanagnayan *to* ~ *one* - wanagnaye *deception* - wayugnanya *to miss taking hold on* - wówicagnaye *deception* — cejijalya *deceitfully* — kšunkahyakel *in a deceptive manner*

decide *v* : - *See* plan

declare *v* : yatan'in *to manifest* - kiciyatan'in *to* ~ *for* — wóyakapi *a declaration*

decoration *n* : owešleke *a war prize*

decoy *v* : yuȟekicah au *to coax into a trap*

decree *or* **judge** *or* **condemn** *v* : wakonza *to determine* — wasukiya *to make a* ~ *or condemnation*

deep *or* **below** *or* **beheath** *adv* : hukutakiya *downward* — šma *deep or dense* - ašma *deep on* - ašmeya *or* yutkeya *deeply* - awašma *piled* ~ - ošme *or* wóšme *depth*

deer *n* : sintehanska *the white-tailed* ~ - sintelulyapi *the red-tailed* ~ - sintesapela *the black-tailed* or *mule* ~ - sintewaksapi *the bob-tailed* ~ - tabloka *the buck* - tacincala *the fawn* - tahejata *a two-year old* ~ - tahca *the common* ~ - tahca itopasapa *the black-faced* ~ - tamakoyunka *a fatted* ~ - tingleška *a fawn*

deface *va* : yusepa *to wear off*

defame *vn* : ilega *to shine, glitter* — iglaonšika *to speak of one's self as miserable* — glašica *to speak evil of one's own* - iglašica *to blame one's self* - oyašica *to speak ill of* — ašilwoyaka *to speak evil of*

defecate *vn* or *n* : unkce *to break wind, a fart* (often considered vulgar)

defect *or* **fault** *vn* : ašihtin *or* ipinta *to be defective, to be not usual*

defend *v refl* : naic'ijin *to* ~ *one's self by speaking* — nakikšin *to* ~ *self*

defile *va* : ayašapa *to* ~ *by mouth* - iglušapa *to* ~ *one's self* - kiciyušapa *to* ~ *or blacken for* - šábya *in a dirty way, or to soil* - wapašapa *to defile* - iglušica *to make or get one's self in trouble*

deformed *adj* : oštela *misshapen* - ošteya *imperfectly, clumsily, accidentally, by chance* — pšúke *something deformed* — apaȟakayayapi *a deformation*

degree *suff to adj* or *adv dim* : ...la *very or only* ... — *compar adv in compos* : sam, isam, isanpa *more* ... — *superl postp* : iyotan or lila ... *most* ...

delay *va* : kagiya *to hinder* or *hindering* — hankignaka *to defer to the next morning* — našuška *to delay* — oiyayešilya *to prevent one leaving* — ónc'unnica *to be prevented* - oúnc'unnilya *to* ~ *one by talking to him* — oh'antehan *to* ~ *in doing* - kiciyutehan *to make* ~ *for* - otehanya *to cause* ~

delegate *n* : wakiconze *a leader, representative*

deliberately *adv* : wayuslaslata *to do slowly, deliberately*

delirium *n* : wówacingnuni

deliver *va* : kašpa

deluge *v* : - *See* inundate

demolish *va* : yuunka *to make or throw down* - Cf yutakunišni

demonstratives *or* **intensifiers** *pron postp* : miye kayeš *I myself* — *postp* : *as in* wicaša unhe *that man*

den *n* : šunkcinca oti *a wolf's den* — wašun *a hole*

dense *adj* : šma *thick* — wóȟešma *dense as grass or underbrush*

dent *or* **indent** *v* : kaosmaka *to make a* ~ - kasmaka *to make a track or path* - pasmaka *to indent* — paš'aka *to push or strike without penetrating*

dentist *n* : wicahikage

depart *v* : glušniyanyaan

depend *va* : wacinyan *to believe, trust on or in, to need one* - iwacinyehci *to* ~ *on others*

deploy *adv* : nablel *spread out*

deposit *n* : ognakapi - Cf place

descend *v* : glicuya *to make start home or to make camp* — apamagle *or* apamagleya *descending, downhill*

design *or* **pattern** *n* : wógligleye *or* wógligleyapi — okazonte *a pattern*

desirable *adj* : asinhte *very desirable* — as'in *to long for* - as'inyan *longingly* — canmihce *I want it very badly* — cantagle *to set the heart upon* - cantaglepi *the deciding evil against one* - cantiheya *covet, yearn for* - cantiheye *self-control, a want or desire* - cantokpani *to long for* - cantokpanipi *a longing for* - cantokpaniyan *to cause to long for, longing for* - icantokpani *to long for in ref to* — cin *to desire, wish, want* - aocin *to desire some* - cinka *to wish, desire* - cinkiya *to persuade, cause to desire* - cinpica *desirable* - cinya *to persuade* - cinyankel *desiringly* - icin *to desire something more for another* - icinya *to entice one* - ikicin *to desire a return gift* - kicin *to desire one's own, desire for or of one* - okicicin

- wicin *to desire and look for women* - wicinpi *the desiring women* — ikcan *to want to do only what another tried* — kónla *to desire with a passion* - okon *to covet* — šilawacin *to have bad desires for* — wotawacin *ambition*
desist *v* : wotáka *to stop suddenly*
desolate *adv* : wosánkayakel *void*
despair *v refl* : cantihang'ic'iya *to give up incomplete work* — oh'anšunkeca *to be helplessly lost, to give up hope*
despondently *adv* : ilenilyakel
destination *n* : ohiyou
destitute *adj* : keyecola *having nothing, entirely ~* — nica *to be ~ of* - wahpanica *poor, having nothing* — wahpanila *to consider poor* - wahpaniya *to cause to be poor* - wahpaniyan *in a ~ way* — watantonšni *to be ~ of everything* - watantonšniyan *having lost all*
destroy *v* : wahangya *to ruin* - wahangyeca *one who destroys* - wawihangya *to bring to an end* - wawihangye *a destroyer* — komeya *to ~ things* — napiškanyan *to ~ or injure esp not one's own* - wanapištanyan *to ~ everything* — okih'anšunkeca *to ~ one's necessities* — kaatakunišni *to ~ by striking* - kiciyutakunišni *to ~ for another* - wicatakunišni *destruction* - wotákunišni *to ~ by shooting* — katuka *to ~ by smiting* - watuka *to ~ by cutting to pieces* — wakonniyeya *to ~ everything* — kawignuni *to ~, break in pieces by striking* - kicawignuni *to ~ for one, as a toy* - wapawignuni *to ~ amid turmoil* — wopesto *to ~ by shooting* — yakuka *to bite to pieces*
determine *v* : kicunza *to ~ in regard to* - owakonze *a determination*
detest *adv* : cinšniyankel *detestingly* — wogláya *to consider detestable* - woglayapi *a destable thing* - šigla *to take offense at one*
detour *v refl* : igluipawehtu *to leave the straight road*
devil *n* : wakanšica *an evil spirit, a satan*
devour *v* : wayuta *to devour, or one who devours all*
dew *vn imperf* : acu *to ~ on, bedew* - acuya *to cause ~ upon* - cumni *dewdrops* - cumni š'e *dewdrops standing* - cuya *to cause dew* — katatabya *to make dry by shaking* — wanagitašoša *heavy ~* - Cf damp, wet
dexterity *n* : wicaoh'anko
diarrhoea *v* : kajo *to have ~*
die *adv* : ot'e iyagleya *unto death* - ot'e kpagan *to part with one's own life* — kih'anyan *to be likely to ~ for* — itamye *to die* — kašeca *to deaden something* — síyuha *to go to ~* — t'a *or* t'e *to die* - akih'an-t'a *to starve to death, ~ of hunger* - akit'a *to arrive home and ~* - it'ewacin *to intend to die purposefully* - it'a *to die for a reason* - kan'it'a *to ~ of old age* - kit'a *to ~ or be dead for* - maštet'a *to ~ from the heat* - onštinmat'a *to ~ in one's sleep* - ont'ewacin *to intend to ~ for* - it'ewacin *to intend death for* - t'a *to be dead* - it'a *to die for a reason* - kicit'a *to ~ for* - ot'a *to ~ in a place, or from gluttony* - ot'e *to be dying* - ot'e ikicihunni *to be about to die, to be near death* - ot'e iyagleya *adv* : *unto death* - temnit'e *to ~ of sweating* - t'a *to faint away, lose consciousness* - t'anuns'e *adv* : *being about dead* - t'eca *lying dead* - t'eicakiš *in a dying state* - t'ekinica *to be in the throes of death, contending with death* - t'ekiya *of* t'eya *to cause to die* - tont'e *his death* - t'ekon *or* t'ekonza *to wish to be dead* - t'ešniyankel *adv* : *not dying* - t'eyasu *to condemn to ~* - wicat'a *the dead* - wicont'e *death* - wót'a *to die of food* - wot'e *death caused by overeating* - wóic'iya *to get sick eating* — yahla-ta *to speak as one dying*
different *express* : etanhanš toka *or* etanštokaka *or* hetanhaš tokaka *what difference does it make?* - togye *in a ~ manner* - okahtogye *made differently* - toktogye *or* toktogyekel *in ~ ways* - wotogye *to do in a ~ way* - yatogye *telling differently* — tokeca *adj* : different - atokeca *to become ~* - icitokeca *~ from each other* - iglutokeca *to disguise one's self* - kiciyutokeca *to make ~ from for* - wicatokeca *a difference*
difficulty *adv* : kitan s'e *with ~* - kitanyankel *with greatest ~* — napšapša s'e *with ~* — iyus'oya *exhausted, reluctantly, hardly* — teȟi *difficult, hard to endure* - teȟika *hard to do or bear, costly, unreasonable* - teȟikela *to think it hard or difficult* - wayateȟika *to speak of as difficult* - wayuteȟika *to make difficult* - wóteȟi *a ~ or trouble* - wóteȟiya *with ~* - wóteȟike *hardship* — wakanyelakel *with great ~* — wóyuškiške *the source of a ~* — wóyuhtani *a ~ that is made*
diffident *v* : wímna šni *to be ~, with little confidence* — weceyešni *to have no confidence in something*
dig *v refl* : ikpahloka *to make a hole for one's self* — k'a *to ~ in the ground* - ak'a *to ~ on or in making a mark* - ok'a *to ~ into or through, or out or up* - ok'api *a digging into* - ok'e *a mine or digging* - kic'a *to ~ one's own for* — pakota *to ~ something out, to probe* — iyupta *to spade up* - owawapte *a dug hole for a turnip* — ayuswa *to ~ under and let collapse*
digest *adj* : šupeošica *hard to ~* - *n* : *what is hard to ~*
diligent *or* **attentive** : aic'ikita *to be concerned with one's own* - aic'ikiya *to be ~ and industrious* - aic'iktašni *to give little care and concern for others*
dim *n* : htaojanjan *a dimming* — aotan'in *to grow dim as at dusk*
diminish *adv* : yuociptelya *diminishing by degrees* - Cf less
dine *n* : owohe *a dining room or hall* - owote *a place in which to ~* - owote típi *a dining room, cagé, restaurant* - owoteya *to use for dining* — wíyeya *to ~ well*
dinner *adv* : ípaga *before dinnertime*
dip *v* : kapta icu *to take and ladle out* - iyokapte *a dipper or ladle* — mniyatke *a dipper* — ipagmunka *to be able to dip with e.g. a bucket* — oputakan *to dip into with the fingers* — ptenunwekiyapi *the dipping of cattle* — wó putkantkan *to ~ in* — ayuze *to ~ or skim off on* - glaze *to lade out one's own* - ogluze *to lade from into one's own dish* - okaze *to dip out into*
direct *vn* : atáya *to go straight towards* - atayela *directly* — eciaiyopteya *directly by, in the direction of* — ecetkiya *in some direction or other* - íciiyopta *in the same direction* - íciiyopteya *in that direction across or through* — katinyan *directly, immediately, off-hand* — ktanktankiya *indirectly* — patanwanjila *directly without veering*
direction (geographic) *n* : wiyohpeyata *the west* — waziyata *the north* — iwiyohiyanpata *the east* — itokaga *the south* — wiyohpeyatanhan *from the west* - iwaziyapa *northward* - wazitakiya *or* waziyatakiya *toward the north* - waziyapa *at or to the north* - waziyapatanhan *northward, from the north* - waziyatanhan *at or from the north* — wiyohinapatanhan *from the east* - wiyohiyanpa *the east* — kaakokiya *in another ~* — kákel *or* kákena *in some ~* - kakiyotan *in that ~*
dirt *n* : anablu *to kick dirt on* — anini *a dust that settles on* — ohli *dirty in or within* — okpukpa *full of ~, mirky* — apašica *to soil by rubbing on something* — aiglap'o *to get one's self dusty by moving about* - kaop'o *or* kap'o *to raise dust as by sweeping* — aš'aka *to get dusty* - aš'akeca *to accumulate dirt, refuse, grease etc.* — šápa *dusty, blackened* - ašabya *to soil, make dirty, tarnish* - *adv* : *in a dirty manner* - ašapa *to become dirty on* - ošapa *to be dirty in* - waašapa *dirty hands*

disable *va* : okihišniyan *to thwart one*
disaffected *vn* : icanlšica *to be ~*
disagree *va* : apoptanptan *to dissent from* — ocihišnišni *not to be unanimous* — oiyokišica *disagreeable* - *Cf quarrel*
disappear *adv* : manitakiya *to ~ from camp* — tan'inšni *to be lost, have disappeared* - tan'inšniyan *our of sight, lost* — kacel *partic postp* : to be lost or disappeared
disappoint *v* : šnišya *to wither, fig to ~* — kagal hingle *to be disappointed, throw up one's hands*
disapproval *n* : ówehca
disarm *va* : ónc'unnilya *to stop, prevent, or hinder one from doing*
disband *vn* : kibleca — kišpahan *to break up and go*
discharge *v* : kauta *to fire a gun by accident*
disciple *n* : waonspewicakiye *a pupil, student, apostle*
disclosing *adv* : pahinskayela
disconsolate *v* : wípajin *to be prevented from succeeding in what one tries to do, all because of sadness*
discourage *vn* : wacin'iwoš'aka *to be discouraged*
discuss *v* : wákiya *to talk about*
disease *n* : - *See* sickness
disentangle *v* : ayukca *to ~ and unite on*
dish *n* : wakšica *tableware in general* — wíyatke *cup* - ognake *or* opiye *cupboard* — mniiyokaštan *or* mniognake *pitcher* — wakšica blaska (flat) *or* canwakšica (wood) *or* makawakšica (clay) *or* mas'wakšica (tin) *plates* — ognake skokpa *or* wíyatke aglehe *saucer or soup plate* — mniskuya ognake *a salt shaker* — cete *the bottom of a vessel* - ceteiyaskabyela *sticking to the bottom* - cetekanyela *little being in the bottom* - cetesapa *suet in the bottom* - ceteta *at or on the bottom* - mni ceteta *at the bottom of a stream* - ceteyela *having little in the bottom* - Cf bottom
dishevel *va* : pacica *to mix up* — gan *dishevelled*
disjoin *adj* : zuntešni *disjoined, incorrect language* Cf weave
disjoint *v* : - *See* joint
dislike *va* : hitiglaya *to loathe e.g. certain food* — iwahtelašni *to dislike something in one* — wašicelaka *to ~*, - *n* : one that dislikes
dislocate *v* : ipagloka *to be disjointed by* - pagloka *to put or push out of joint* - yugloka *to sprain badly* — anapšun *or* apapšun *to put out of joint on* - kapšun *to ~ a joint by striking* - napšun *to be dislocated* - *va* : to ~ a leg - papšun *to ~ the arm, put out of joint*
dismantle *v* : wojúju *to disassemble, take to pieces* - wojujupi *a disassembly*
disobey *va* : kicaksa *lit, to cut in two; to ~ a law* — wanah'onšni *to be disobedient*
disorderly *adv* : itupšapša s'e — ošilya *in disorder* — paškiška *to disarrange by rubbing* — togmunšni *topsyturvy* — yuptanpila s'e *disorderly* — katkanheya *or* kaskiglag *orderly*
disorganized *adv* : togmun s'e *little organized*
disown *v* : slolyešni konza *to disavow*
disperse *v* : paowancaya *to ~ by* — yuobleca *to scatter, divide* - yuoblecahan *dispersed*
displace *va* : tokoyuštan *to put in place of another, dislocate*
display *v* : okilitaton *to make a great ~*
displeased *adj* : canlwahtešni - canteelai *to be ~* - cantiyokišice *to be outrage at* - iyucantešica *to feel bad* — wacin'iyokišica *to be ~* — hinyanzeke *unpleasant, stern* — ip'ozeca *to be out of humor with, i.e. ~ i*
disposed *adv* : ocinwašteya *well ~* - óciwašte *being on good terms with, making up with* — ocinšicaya *evilly ~* - ócišica *ill-disposed towards* — ohinyansyela *in bad humor* — tawacinšica *of a bad disposition* — tawacinwašte *of a good disposition* — wašteca *~ well, good*
dispute *va* : akinica *to ~ about* - oakinica *a dispute* - waakinica *to ~ or one who disputes, a disputant* - waakinicapi *a ~ over something* - wákinica *to argue* - wákinicapi *a contest*
disregard *va* : iyaktašni
disrespectful *adj* : glugluka *saucy*
disrupt *va* : oyakikike *to break up e.g. a gathering*
dissatisfy *v refl* : iwaic'iniyan *to be dissatisfied with one's self*
dissolve *vn* : skan *to melt or dissolve; thus water is drunk, but snow melts and is drunk*
distant *adv* : itohanyan *or* kaiyuzeya *a little distance away*
distemper *express* : šunkanagihlo španwagehce *to feel as a growling dog*
distinctly *adv* : yublapisekse *openly* — kablesglepi s'e *in a clear and distinct way*
distort *va* : iyuhmin *to deform* - Cf twist
distraction *n* : wicoškiške *a difficulty or what distracts* — wígnagnaye *distracting, as in changing the topic of conversation*
distress *n* : wícakije *suffering*
distribute *va* : pamni *to divide* - kikpamni *to divide one's own* - kpamnipi *an issue, distribution* - wakpamni *to ~ one's own* - wakpamnipi *a distribution* — owowicak'u *an issue station, center*
district *n* : okašpe *a piece struck off*
disturb *vn* : cantehniyanyan *to be disturbed* — canteihala yanka *to be irascible* — canteiyapa *to be flurried or excited* - canteiyapaya *in an excited manner* - canteiyapapi *excitement, a beating heart or a disturbance* — cantekazan *to be distressed esp when thirsting or eating or swallowing what is heady* — it'enihan *bothered by someone or thing* — míyugingin *disturbing one* — ok'os'e *a tumult* — zéka *disturbed, shaken*
ditch *or* **trench** *or* **bulwark** *n* : makok'api *an entrenchment* — makosmaka *a low ~* — mnikiyupta *to make a ~* - mnikiyupta *a ~ or channel* — mnitacanku *a channel or strait*
dive *vn* : glucega *to ~ head foremost* — kignun *to dive* — okignunka *to ~, put one's head under water as in a bath or a vessel* - pakignunka *to make ~, or push under water*
divert *v* : kawinga *to turn one's course*
divest *v refl* : iyušlok *to divest one* - iglušloka *to pull or put off one's own, as one's clothes* — iglušpa *to tear off one's own, as a scab; to tear one's self loose*
divide *va* : apamni *to ~ out on* — kalehanyank *to ~ away, to separate parts* - kicikpamni *to ~ among themselves* — kicašpa *to ~ for* - iyokicašpa *to ~ in the middle* - okinašpa *to break off in the middle* — okiyuslel *to divide* — yuiyakipab *dividing* — yununpa *to ~ in two*
divorce *n* : wóihpekiciye
dizzy *v* : kaitomni *to be struck ~* - oitomni *to be ~*
do *v* : canteokic'unya *to do in a stirring manner* — ecakicion *to do for one* - ecakicon *to do to one* - ecakion *to do against* - ecaic'ion *to do for one's self* - econkiya *to cause to do anything* — hécakici-on *to do that for one* - hécakicon *to do thus to one* - hécakion *to do that to one* — hécon *to do that* - lécon *to do this* - kécon *to do that* — lécakicon *to do thus to* - lécakion *to do this to* - lécakicion *to do this* — tókakicon *to do to or for one* — gluh'eh'e *to do one's job only partly* — h'an *to work at*

- h'anpica *to be able to work* - oh'an *to work, or work* - okih'an *to do to one* — akiptan *to do together* — oweconkel *with something doing*
docile *adj* : okinyanwašte *gentle* - Cf fly
doctor *n* : pejuta wicaša (in the Dakota sense) *a medicine man* — wašicun wakan (in the non-Indian sense) *one with high and special skills in care of the sick* — pikiya *to ~ or treat, to conjure*
dodge *v* : pataka *to run about here and there*
dog *n* : šúnka - šungnaškinyan *a mad dog* - šiyošunka *a bird dog* - šunhpala *a puppy* - šunkaitepšunka *a bull dog* - šunkitepesto *a grayhound* - šunkicoco *to call one's dog* — keca *a long-haired dog*
doll *n* : amonmonla *or* hanpošpu hokšicala
domination *n* : wanapicage *control* — waunkec'ila *to be proud and demanding* — kitankognagyelahci *in a domineering manner*
donate *v* : wawicak'u - wawicak'upi *a gift, donation*
door *or* **entrance** *n* : tiyopa - tiyopagmigma *or* tiyopagmigmela *a ~ knob* - tiyopaiyokatkuga *~ nails and screws* - tiyopaoyutkogi *a ~ lock, a padlock* - tiyopata *at the entrance*
dormitory *n* : ohpaye tipi
double *adv* : jagjalya *doubly* — yakipaja *to double up by mouth and with ends meeting* - yukipaja *or* yukipaš *to double over* — kšija *to bend up* - kakšija *to bend up* - kpakšija to bend up one's own - nakšija *to bend up by foot with ends meeting, to be doubled up* - naokšija *to bend double with the feet* — iglununpa *to have two jobs at one time* — ínunpa *two-mouthed, as a gun* — yušunka *to ~ up in around, to bunch* - yupšunkaya *doubled up* — icipašpaš *doubled backward and foreward*
doubt *va* : cet'ungla *to ~ something*
doughy *adv* : ospanspanheca *becoming ~*
down *v* : iyohpeya *to throw down into* - aiyohpeya *down-hill, or a declivity* - kaaiyohpeya *steeply down-hill* — kah'ol *to throw or get ~* — kuta *or* kahukul *low ~* - ikuta *downstream* - kutkiya *or* kuwab *downward* — makigleya *downward endwise* — kaiyohpeya *downward*
downcast *va* : yacanlececa *to make ~ by talking*
downstream *adv* : hutawab *further down* - hutawabkiya *downstream* - hutab *below* - ihutawab downstream beyond - hutabkiya *~ towards* - hutabya *or* hutabyakel *~ as opposed to toward the stream head* - ihuta *~ of, below*
dowry *va* : šunk'iyopeya *to give a ~*
doze *vn* : ogunga *to be drowsy or to slumber* — yusinc'iyanka *seemingly asleep to say nothing*
draft *va* : to cause a ~ - okabluza *a ~ of wind, or to blow somewhat, or drafty*
drag *va* : yuslohan *to ~ along by mouth pulling* - iyuslohan *to ~ along* - iyuslohe *something to ~ along*
draw *vn* : ipaka *to ~ back* — ipašloka *to ~ off over, to divest* — oakate *the ~ of a bow* — oyuzan *to ~ a curtain* — yalusicu *to take a ~ on a pipe* — yalusyatkan *to take a draft of* — yatan *to suck* — yatiktitan *to ~ in smoking* — yuguka *to ~ a knife or arrow* — yuslohan *to ~ or drag or pull* - yuslohanyan *pulling* — yusluta *to pull out* — yuglakeke *drawing separately across* — yuoswa *to ~ down* — iteowa *to sketch* — oikwa *to write or draw one's own* - owa *to ~ or sketch or paint* - Cf pull, sketch
drawer *n* : yuslul icupi
dream *vn* : hanble *to fast to reap a vision* - aihanble *to ~ about* - hanbleceya *to pray for vision* - hanbloglagia *to tell one's dreams and visions* - hanbloglagyakel *disclosing one's own visions and dreams* - hanbloglaka *to tell one's dreams or visions* — ihanbla *to have dreams or visions* - wíhanblapi *a dreaming* - wíhanblas'a *a dreamer* — wakon s'e *as a dream or wish*
dregs *or* **scraps** *n* : ogu — okpukpe *the lees, sediment*
dress *n* : wahpaka *one poorly dressed* — wakoyakeca *a well dressed person* — wawahobhopece *a prim dresser* — yuhniga *to ~ up nicely* — yupika *a good dresser* — holwanca *dressed in gray* — iyošala s'e *dressed in red* — kicanyan *to ~ meat* — okazapa *to cut up and spread nicely* — kipata *or* kpata *to cut up, butcher one's own* — pastankiya *to dehair, ~ a skin*
drift *v* : kahwoka *to ~ off, be carried away* — oncablu oju *a pile of snow or rubbish carried together by the wind* — wáwotica *a snow drift* - wawótica *any sort of drift* - owota *to drift* — oicoga *driftwood*
drink *va* : ayahepa *to ~ up on* - glahepa *to ~ up one's own* - kiciyahepa *to ~ up for one* — ot'in *to ~ much greedily* — mniyupiza *to ~ quietly* — yage *to ~ up* — yatkan *to ~* - ayatkan *to ~ something on or after eating* - glatkan *to ~ one's own* - omniyatkan *a drinking place* - oyatkan *to ~ in, or a drinking place* - wíyatke *a drinking cup* — yaskepa *to ~ up*
dripping *adj* : totopela *dripping wet*
drive *va* : ipaspa *to pound in* — nahapa *to ~ away by stamping* — okatan *to ~ in a nail or pin* — wicakahapa *a driver* — yuhi *to ~ off e.g. game* — hutipašpu *to ~ back or away e.g. an enemy*
drool *n* : imništan *drivel* — ískuya *the mouth watering for* - ískuyagla *to have one's mouth water* - ískuyeya *to make the mouth water* — kas'ins'in *to drivel*
droop *v* : oh'eh'e *to hang low, dangle or droop*
drop *vn* : ohpa — ayuptuja *to let slip ahead something while shooting an arrow etc.* — ayušna *to drop something* - oyušna *to fall or waste* - oyušnašna *crumbs fallen* — nap'akašpeya *to let slip from the hands* — šwu *to precipitate* - ašwu *to fall* - ašwuya *to cause to precipitate on* — š'e *to fall in drops of water* - ayuš'e *to make drops on, or to fall on in drops* - ayuš'eya *in a dripping manner* - š'eya *to make fall as in drops* - oš'e *a ~ as of water, or to drop into* - oyuš'e *to make ~ in* - š'eš'e *to trickle* - š'eyapi *drops as of water*
drown *vn* : mnilt'a *to ~ in water* - mnilt'eya *to cause to ~* - mniot'a *to die in water* - mniot'eya *to cause one to die in the water* - mnit'a *to ~* - mnit'eya *to ~ something*
drum *n* : cancega — icabu *or* kat'ela *a drumstick* - nakicibu *to ~ with the foot for one* - pabu *to ~ on with the fingers*
drunk *adj* : itomni *intoxicated* - itomniic'iya *to get one's self ~, to revel, carouse* - itomnimni *dizzy from sickness* - itomnipi *drunkenness* - itomnis'a *a drunkard* - itomniya *to make one ~* — mnizicinca *a drunkard* — pánga *drunk, slang* — iwitko *to be ~, crazy* - iwitkotkoka *to become foolish by means of* - iwitkoya *to make one ~ with* - owitko *to be ~ with* - wawitkoya *to make ~*
dry *va* : akceya *to cook and let dry* — ašeca *to become ~ on* — at'ahya *to make ~ having been wet* — ayuskepa *to make evaporate on or from* — blublu *~ as fruit or vegetables* - nablu *to become ~ and fine* — gluhepa *to ~ up, soak up* — hemakoskanl *in a desert, dry place* - hemakošikšica *badlands* — katapa *to ~ by shaking as in the wind* —kat'aga *to shake ~* — mni *to lay up to ~ in the sun* — oyahe *to dry up or evaporate or go ~* - aoyahe *to ~ up on* — apapuza *to wipe ~ on* - apuspuza *to ~ on* - apusya *to make ~ on* - iyupuza *to make ~ with* - kapuza *to make ~* - wakapus'kiya *to hang up to ~* - kpapuza *to wipe ~ one's own*

E

- opuza *to be ~ all over* - opuze *a ~ land* - papuza *to rub ~* - puskiya *to make ~* — pusyašpanyan *to cook too long ~* - wakapus'kiya *to hang up to ~* - pusyeya *to ~ out* - pus aya *to begin to ~* - wípusye *a drier* — sáka *dried, stiff* - asaka *to be dry and stiff* - oyasaka *dried hard on or in, withered* — satglakinyan *to hang out to dry* — šelya *to lay out to ~ and season, or seasoning* — šnija *dried up* — t'int'in *be-ginning to ~* — wacankšu *to ~ on a stick* - wicunksu *a pole on which meat is dried* — watatabkiya *to hang and ~*

due *adv* : - *See* timely

dull *vn* : icaš'aka *not to penetrate as an axe* — ikinta *to be defective* — ik'ege šni *~ as a knife can be* — kajapa *or* kat'oza *to make ~* — péšni *blunt* — wotata *to make blunt by pounding*

dumb *n* : iešni *a man who is mute* - wiocan *a woman who is mute*

dump *n* : owaihpeye

duration *n* : wóyutehan

dusk *n* : pahaohanzi *of the evening*

dust *v* : katata *to shake off ~* — makablu *dirt in the air* - makipabluya *to raise ~* - makiyap'oya *raising much ~* - makop'oya *to raise ~* - nap'o *to raise ~ with the feet* — onablu *to raise ~ in walking* — wakpukpeca *anything scattered about, dust etc.*

dwell *v* : éun *to go and ~* — išnati *to ~ alone, or a woman to have her menses* - išnatipi *a dwelling alone during menstruation* - oti *to ~ in, or a dwelling place* — ounyan *to ~ as a regular thing* - aounyan *to be or abide on* - taounyan *his or her dwelling* — tonwanyeca *to dwell or live at*

dwindle *adj* : pínzece *dwindling down, becoming small, lessening*

dye *or* **stain** *n* : mniwitoye *blue ~* — walulya *to dye or stain red or scarlet* - walulye *a dyer of scarlet* — wílulye *anything with which to color red, red dye stuff* - wílute *red or scarlet dye*

each *adj* : itiyohila *every one* - otiyohi *or* otoiyohi *~ or every one* - otoiyohihi *some of ~, perhaps* — tan'iyohila *pron* : *~ one, every one* — ototanhan *prep* : *from or away from ~ kind* — otoyasin *adv* : *every single one*

eager *adj* : ipuhniya

ear *n* : nakpa - nakpahute *root of the ~* - nakpaokogna *between the ears* - nakpastogya *moving the ears* - nakpa yuwoslal ikikca *to prick up the ears* - nakpišlayatanhan *the right ~* — nonge *the ~ or the sense of hearing* - nongekpa *deaf* - nongekpeya *to cause one to be deaf* - nongeogmusgluza *to hold one's ears* - nongeohloka *an ~ hole* - nonhwicahloke s'e *with ears open* — nonhcan *deaf* - nonhkeciya *to bend one's ~* - nonhpan *ringing ears* - nonhsuhute *the base of the ~* - nonhwacoka *the outer ~ cavity* — šónšonla *long-eared, drooping ears; or a mule*

earn *vn* : iwešleka *to do something worthy of honor* — kamna *to ~ or get* - kicamna *to ~ or get for* - wakicamna *to make money, to ~ merit* - wakicamnanpi *an earning of money*

earnest *adv* : yutanyankel *in ~, for good*

earth *n* : maka *the planet, clay, soil, ground, land, country, world* — kamakatakiya *earthward* - maka glakinyan *across the earth* - makagle *with the end set on the ground* - makata *on the ground* - maka san *light-colored clay* - makasuhula *sandy soil* - maka to *blue earth* - makatooyuze *a blue earth quarry* - makasitomni *the orb of the earth, the world* - makatanasula *moulding clay* - makawase *red earth, paint* - makawase ša *vermillion paint* - makikceka *land, loam, soil* - makaikceya *on land* - makaipusli *on the ground, touching ground* - makaiyagleya *to the ground* - makaiyakasanni *part of the country* - makaiyapa *to hit the ground* - makoce *country, place* - makoce oihanke *a world globe* - makohloka *a cave* - makokawinh *around the world* - makošica *badlands, desert* - makošla *bare ground* - makowanca *all the earth* — tannišpan *or* wase *red earth or paint* — *fig* Unci *Mother Earth*

ease *v* : úngnakah *to ~ one's way towards*

easy *adv* : paslayela *slowly, going ~* - paslayela un *to take it easy* — wašakala *cheap, ~* — šunkanyankel *got easily, i.e. got cheap*

eat *va* : ayaštan *or* aglaštan *to stop speaking or eating* — cak'iglaska *or* wákaska *to eat up fast* - caic'ipa *fig, to eat one's self full* — glajipa *to bite or nibble at one's own food* - išpukiton *to eat little of the little available* — nihkpatan *to ~ little* - nihtokayeyašni *to eat one's fill* — ahitebya *to come and devour* - atebya *to cut up or devour on* - tebkiciciyapi *they eat each other up* - tebkiciya *to ~ up provisions* - tebkiciyapi *they eat each other* - tebkiya *to ~ one's own, or to eat up another's* - tebya *to devour* — wáte *to eat something* - watebya *to eat all up* - wóta *to ~* - wóta igluštan *to finish eating* - wolkiya *to have someone eat, to feast* - wólwota *to be eating* - lolwazaze *not able to eat* — ya-caškeškeke *to eat up slowly* — yaowišni *to be unable to eat up all* — ayasota *to eat all up* - glasota *to eat one's own all up* — yatoto *to eat up e.g. grass* — yúta *to eat* - ayuta *to eat on* - agluta *to eat one's own on* - iyuta *to eat with* - kiciyuta *to eat with, for* — wauta *to give to eat* - wiyuta *to eat with* — wagliukiya *to bring home the "bacon"*

echo *va* or *n* : kaiyowaza *to make ~ with the hand* - naiyowaza *to make ~ with the foot* - paiyowaza *to make ~ with the hand* - woiyowaza *to make ~ by shooting* - yaitowaza *to make ~ with the voice*

economical *adj* : wakpatanka *an ~ person*

edible *adj* : yulpica — spans'e wašte *easily edible*
eddy *n* : owamniomni *whirlpool, cyclone, tornado*
edge *or* **border** *n* : agleyela — apajeje *at the ~ or brim* — kaobloton *to make edged* — matete *the ~ or rim, shore* — obleca *edged or cornered, or an ~ of a board or a bit of an axe* — obleton *square edged* — okšan'ipata *to put an ~ on* — opé *the ~ or sharp part of anything* - opapon *the border or stripe or ~ on anything* - opapuntanhan *from under the bottom ~ of a tent*
effeminate *vn* : kaigluwinyan *to become ~*
effort *n* : akitapi *a research, an ~ put forth* — kihe *to put in effort, make effort*
egg *n* : itka *the, blossom, seed, the testicles* - itkaska *the white of an egg* - itkazica *the yolk of an egg* - witka *an egg* - witkaton *to lay eggs*
either *adv* : tuktunma *~ of two*
elaborate *vt* : kah'e *to explain, lit to work out something*
elastic *adj* : zigzica *flexible, pliable*
elated *adj* : wítan *proud* — nagiksapa *gleeful*
elbow *n* : išpakic'unyan *using the elbows* - išpazihin *a buffalo's elbows*
elder *or* **eldest** *n* : wicitokapa *the eldest son or daughter born*
elect *v* : - Cf choose, kahniga
eloquent *or* **fluent** *vn* : awayapika *or* wayapika *to be~* - wayapiya *eloquently*
elsewhere *adv* : atokan
elusive *vn* : kijanicašni *to be ~, unable to be grasped*
emaciate *vn* : okiyaskapa *to be emaciated*
embrace *v* : poskilyuza *to hold in one's arms*
embroider *v* : ipata *to ~* - ipatapi *embroidery* — wapahlalton *to work with ribbon or embroidery*
emergency *adv* : wanuntokayakel *for or in any urgency*
emphasis *suff to v to the fact of* : -kšto *or* -kšt, *or to end a sentence* : ... yelo *or* lo, ye *or* le
employ *adv* : owánjila *unemployed* — waši *to hire one* — wóilake *an employee, a hireling* - wóilagya *to ~ one*
empty *adj* : coka - sicokala *bare-footed* - glucokaka *to ~ one's own barrel* — haece *~ or blank* - ohe ece *without* — ópteheca *almost empty* — kaoyaȟe *to ~ something* — yuȟepa *to lade out* — iyokala *to ~ or pour into, a measure used in emptying it* — hloka *hollow* — kaskepa *to ~ by drinking* - puskepa *to pour all out* — awošloka *to ~ a gun by shooting*
enchant *v* : - *See* bewitch
encircle *v* : - *See* around
end *adv* : hocatkayatanhan *atthe left ~ of the open camp circle* — hoisleyatanhan *at the right ~ of the open camp circle* — hinhanke *an end, ending this way; or to come to an end, to a stop* - hoihanke *either ~ of the camp circle* - ihanke *an ~, a border, to ~ or to come to an end* - ihanketa *at the ~* - ihangya *to destroy or come to an ~* - makihanke *the ~ of the world* - owihankešniyan *eternally, without an ~* - owihankeya *to bring to an end* - oihanke *an end* - oihankeya *to make an ~ of* - owihanke *an end* - owehanketa *at the ~* — wahutaktayakel *at the ~, lastly* — inkpa *an ~ point, a tip* - oinkpa *the ~ of anything*
endure *v* : akpaspa *to suffer patiently* — haiyotiyekiya *to suffer poorly clad* - oiyotiyekiya *to endure* — icakišya *to make one suffer, to afflict or in a suffering manner, inadequately* — iyowinyan *to consent to bear or endure* — otawat'elšica *unbearable* — oteȟika *hard to ~, trying, excessively* — wakiš'aka *long-suffering* - huwakiš'aka *having stamina, enduring* - wakiš'agya *to make ~* - wakiš'ake *strength, endurance* - wówakiš'ake *endurance*
enemy *n* : tóka - tókakiciyapi *they are enemies to one another* - Cf foreign
energetic *n* : wiš'oš'oka *an ~ person, one ready for work*
enfeeble *va* : wašihtin *to ~ by cutting, to do poorly with a knife or saw*
enforce *vn* : oiekic'un *to ~ obedience*
engage *vn* : iksapa *to be heavily preoccupied, engaged with matters*
engrave *va* pago *to mark with a line, to scribble* - wago *to carve* - wakigo *to ~, to carve one's own*
engulf *vn* : naosli *to be engulfed, as in mud, being pressed up around*
enlarge *v* : yutankas'e *enlarged* - *See* large
enlighten *n* : iwicableza *an enlargement* — iyoyanbya *to instruct*
enslave *va* : ilaka *to have and use as a servant*
entangle *v* : - *See* ravel
entertain *n* : wóimagaga *entertainment*
entice *v* : inakihma *to solicit, subvert* - Cf intercourse
entrance *n* : húnkpa *the ~ to the camp circle or hollow square always to the west*
envy *va* : nawizi *to be jealous of one* - inakiwizi *to be evious of one's own* - inawizi *to be jealous of* - inawizipi *envy* - nawizi s'a *a jealous person* - inawiziya *to make one envious; or envious* — wakípa *to allow ~, jealousy*
equal *adj* : akilececa *~ to* — waakiyecetu *~ in* - akilecel *like to* - akilecelya *equally* - akilehan *just as far* - akilehanyan *equally far* - akilehankeca *or* akilehanwankatuya *of the same or ~ height or length* - akilehanyan *equally far* - akilenagnakeca *alike* - akilenakeca *many of ~ number* - akilenana *few alike, or not all alike* - iyakilehankeca *of the same length with* - iyakilehanyan *of ~ distance* - iyakilenakeca *of ~ number* - iyakilenala *as few as* — ákinskokeca *or* ákinskoya *of the same or ~ size* - íyakiniskokeca *of the same size* — ecitapa *all of the same length, or fitted together* — iyehankeca *two being of the same length* - iyehanyan *to be even, of the same size, length, height, etc.* — *tkonza even, exactly* - ócitkonza *alike in size, and length* - ótatkonza *~ to, parallel* - otkonza *even, parallel* - oyutkonza *to make or break off another ~, to equalize* - *n* : *an equalizer* - paitkonza *to equalize* - igluotkonza *to equalize one's own*
equip *va* : yuskaka *to ~ with new clothes*
erase *va* : nagoya *to scratch out by foot* — glajuju *to ~ one's own* - kicipajuju *to ~ for* - pajuju *to rub or cross out* - wípajuju *a rubber eraser*
erect *v* : jin *to be or stand ~* — wóslaslateke *that which stands erect*
err *or* **mistake** *v* : wícuns ia *to ~ speaking*
erupt *adv* : panhpanhya *erupting*
escape *v* : hannapa *to ~ at night* - napa *to flee* — inašloka *to ~ danger* — iyaglupta *to ~ breaking or slipping away* — sígluha *to get out of the way from having a bad conscience* — wahuataya *to be unable to ~ out of fright* — yuskepa *to ~, drain off, or evaporate*
escort *va* : pasi *to ~ or march one as to jail* — iyawanyangkiciya *to escort one*
esteem *suff* : ...la, ...kila, ...laka, *as in* wašte·la *to ~ good, to love one;* wah'an·la *to think highly of one;* wašte·kila *to ~, love one's own;* iyotan·laka *to ~ or value most highly;* otanka·la *to ~ greatest (singling him or her out);* šil'la *to consider one bad*
estrange *adj* : kitankognagyelahci *alienating one by putting unreasonable demands on him or her, estranged*
eulogy *n* : wóyaonihan *an honoring speech*
evaporate *vn* : naiyoyaȟe *to ~ on its own* — natakunišni

vi : *to vanish, to ~ on its own* — nawanica *vi* : *to turn to notheing, to disappear of itself* — onapuza *to dry*

evasive *adv* : watokankan *evasively*

even *adv* : itkonza *or* itkónsya *~ with* - ítkonsya *to make ~ , or fig to have accomplished one's task* - ítkonzela *even with, coming up to the mark as in a measuring cup* — oblayela *evenly*

evening *adv* : htakiyaka *toward ~* - htamakiyokpaza *to grow dusk* - htaotan'inšni *dusk* - htáyetamna *at dusk* - htáyetu *the ~* - óhtayetu *the ~* - íhtayetu *the following or next ~*

event *n* : wakinyanpi *a foretold eventuality* — wóakipa *a fortune or misfortune, an ~*

every *adv* : ówanca *everywhere* — tuktetu kakeš *everywhere, wherever, in any place* — tuwe cc eyaš *everybody or anybody* - Cf each, all, any

everywhere *adv* : écicaskaya *coming from everywhere*

evil *v refl* : ecaic'ion *or* ecokon *to determine and do evil to one's self* — hinyansela *or* hinyanziyela *wickedly, badly* — icantagle *to plot ~ against one* — wakonza *to wish ~ to one* — išilaya *to be or become bad on account of* — šicokiya *to speak ~ to* — wóšica *to commit ~ deeds* - wóšice *evil, badness*

exact *adj* : tkonza *just exactly*

exaggerate *n* : aokicageca *an exaggeration* — otantonyankel *exaggeratedly* — yatakuka *to ~ the unimportant* — latakuwacin *to ~ in jesting* — yuwicoh'an *to ~ a trifle into a big thing*

exalt *v refl* : iwankabic'iya *to ~ one's self* - Cf honor, praise

examine *va* : iciyunga *to ~ with cross-questioning* — iwanyanka *to look at* - iwanyangyehci *looking intently at* — wawiyukcan *to ~ for judgement* - wawiyukcanka *a judge*

example *vn* : iyowanke *to set an ~* - iyowangya *to follow the ~ of* - wóiwanyanke *an ~, review, fair proposition*

exceed *adv* : kaiyakapeya *by a little more, ahead of* — olabyakel *exceedingly* — acokata *going too far* - Cf more

excel *v* : pahinhiyukiya *lit to attract a porcupine* - pahin'iyekiya *lit to recognize a porcupine* — wónata *to get far ahead of others*

exchange *va* : íciiyopeya *to barter* - iciiyopeyapi *an exchange* - tokiyopekiciyapi *barter* - tokiyopekiya *to barter* - tokiyopeya *to barter or exchange one thing for another*

excite *vn* : ikik'o *to be excited by tumult* — iyopaštaka *to ~ and urge one* — otantonyan *very lively* — ptanyan *flurried as are animals* — canteiyapa *to be excited* - wócanteiyapaya *with a beating heart*

exclamations : - *See* interjection

exclude *adv* : áecela *exclusively* — ópašniya *to except or exempt*

excrete *va* : aleja *to urinate on; a diaper* — cesli *dung of animal and man; to dung* - acesli *to urinate on* - ocesli *to defecate in* - oceslitipi *an outhouse, a toilet room* - tacesli *dung* — kaswu *urine* — pahli *nose excretion* — tónkce *excrement* - túnkce *breaking wind* - tatunkce *manure*

excuse *vn* : kicunni *to be discouraged* — wal'iyowalya *to ~ one's self doing what was supposed to be done, to leave to others to do; to abstain from doing* — iyowalya *to have an excuse*

exercise *or* **drill** *vn* : kicipasi *to drill as do soldiers*

exhale *vn* : ipogan *to breathe out* - ipohya *to cause to ~ , or exhausting*

exhaust *adv* : yus'olas'e *in an exhausted manner* - yus'oya *tired all out* - yus'oyakel *or* yus'oyehci *all tired out, contrary to all expectation*

exhibit *or* **display** *or* **perform** *v* : wanapiškanyan *to play with toys; to perform as in a circus*

exhort *or* **encourage** *v* : wayaotan

exit *n* : óhinape *or* oínape *a place of egress*

expand *va* : akamna *to acquire in addition to*

expect *n* : wawaktayapi *one expected, a baby*

expend *n* : wóyusota *an expense*

experience *n* : wóikiksape *an ~*

expert *vn* : wayupika *to be ~* - wayupiya *skillfully* - wayupiyahan *or* wayupiyakel *with expertise* - wawiyupica *expertly*

explain *v* : wóyuptinnape *to come to ~ or ask for help* — yuajaja *to make clear* - kiyuajaja *to ~ to one*

expose *adv* : šla egna *in full view, exposed* — yazamni *to open, uncover, ~ by arguments*

expression *vn* : owešte *to use a by-word, a well known pet ~* - owešteka *a pet or nickname ~* — oyagpicašni *unspeakable, beyond ~*

extend *v* : kcékiye *to hold or hang over* — otankaya *extensive, large, spacious* — yekiya *to ~ (the hand) to* — yaya *to ~ something to*

extinct *vn* : atakunišni *to be ruined or ~*

extinguish *va* : akasni *to ~ (fire) on* - kasni *to ~ by beating a fire* - kicicasni *to put out (a fire) for another* - nasni *to put out fire by foot* - pasni *to snuff out fire*

extract *va* : skebya *to ~ or exhaust fluid* — yaze *to take out, retrieve with the mouth*

extravagant *adv* : aokahya *extravagantly as in speaking from a wild imagination* — paokaga *as in exceedingly beautiful*

eye *n* : išta - išta su *the eye ball* - ištihanke *the outer corners of the eyes* - ištogna *in the eyes* - ištognake *the eye socket* - ištaha *the eyelid* - on'ištimapihin *eyelashes* - ištahe *the eyeridge* - ištahin *the eyebrow* - ištahepihin *the eyelashes* — skaska *the white of the eyes* - ištaiyohiya *as far as the ~ can see* - ištamaza *eyeglasses* — ištanatogyeya *with an unnatural eye expression* - ištasankiya *a snap of the eye*

F

fable *n* : ohunkakan *a story*
fabulous beings *np* : cíciye *a bogeyman* – íya *an eater* – mmla *a giant* – iktomi *a trickster* – siyoko *the wicked man* – tabubu *the monster* – waziya *a santa claus*
face *v* : apošin *to make faces at* — íkšinkiya *to make faces at* — ite *one's ~* – iteanung *on both sides of the ~* – itešinšin *a wrinkled ~* – iteyukšilkiya *to cut faces* – itešniyopa *to freeze the face* – iteyušinkiya *to make faces at, to grimace at* – itogna *in the ~* – itognake *one's countenance* – itokšan *around the ~* — kaitkobya *facing, fronting* — ópatkonsyela *facing one way* — psonpsonkiya *with face down*
fact *or* **emphasis** *partic* : lo, yelo, *used by men;* le, yele, *used by women, in concluding a sentence to give emph to the fact just stated*
factory *n* : wókage tipi
fade *v* : san áya *to be or have faded*
fail *vn* : išuta *to ~ doing or accomplishing a task, to miss as in shooting* – išuteya *to cause failing to do* — ayatakuni-šni *to fail by destroying with talk* — kicih'anyan *to fail or get worse i.e. sick for one* — mah'wapajin *to ~ getting some ducks when others are hunting them*
faint *n* : cúniyant'a *a ~* — ȟpécaka *weak, as a ~ sound* – iyoniyan *just audible* — sniyant'a *to ~ , lose consciousness*
faith *n* : awacinpi a ~ or trusting in — wówicala *belief* – wówicalaya *to cause to believe, to persuade one*
fall *vn* : aglakšiš *to ~ on top of one another* — aglapta *to stop falling as the rain* – kaptapta *to ~ to pieces* — aglihan *to ~ on, descend upon* – aglihpaya *to ~ , hitting the ground* – oglihpaye *a falling down on* — aȟicahan *to stumble and ~ on* — ašwu *to drop water to ~ on* – ašwuya *to make ~ on by dropping* — ayašna *to let ~ on from the mouth* — glihan *to ~ and stand* – glihpa *to ~ down* – glihpaya *to ~ and lie down* — agnahan *of itself fallen off in* — ahinhan *to ~ i.e. as rain on* – ahinhpaya *to ~ on* – hinhan *to ~ , i.e. rain* – hinheya *to make it rain* — hinhpaya *to ~ or ~ down* – waahinhpaya *to ~ on or to* — aigluhpa *to bring upon one's self* — awohpa *to make ~ on by shooting* – ikpahpa *to throw one's self of e.g. a horse* – kahpa *to make ~ , or to fell* – okahpa *to make ~ into by striking* – yuhpa *to fell by pulling, to loosen, drop* — ágan'ihpaya *to ~ or jump into water with a splash* — aglaptus ihpaya *to ~ flat on the ground* – aiyahpaya *to ~ upon* – aihpaya *to ~ on* – apaglihpaya *to ~ on one wounded* – ihpaya *to ~ down* – oiyohpaya *to ~ into* – pasto ihpaya *to ~ prostrate on one's hands and knees, to ~ on one's face* — nahpeya *to make ~ with the foot* – wohái-hpeya *to shoot or make ~* — jujuwahan *fallen to pieces* – ojuju *to ~ to pieces* – ojujuwahan *fallen to pieces in* — kanhan *falling off or out as hair, fruit etc.* — kaoswa *to ~ or cave in when undercutting* — kimnahan *to ~ off* — makagleya *to ~ down end-wise* — nahpu *to make ~ off by striking* — naswaka *to ~ off as do feathers* — oglihan *to ~ in endwise* — ogwahan fallen to pieces — opšunwahe *that which falls out or off, as teeth, horns, etc.* — pa *to ~ as does snow* — si itokab egle, *or* si kakab iyeya to make trip over one's feet — šlošlokahan *falling off, shedding* — špuwahan *fallen off* — ayuunka *to make fall on* – paunka *to push to make ~* — wanaunka *or* woúnka *to fell* — yaoha *to make ~ over by mouth*
falls *n* : iyoȟaȟa *or* mniwoȟaȟa *waterfalls*
false *v* : wicašni *to tell a falsehood* — yatogtogya *to falsify* – Cf lie

Family *n* :

IN GENERAL :
tiwahe *a household*
takuye *or* hankeya *a relative*
ahan *to be related*
tigle *to make a home*
wicotakuye *a ~ residence*
IN PARTICULAR :
tunwicu *his or her aunt on the father's side*
tunwin *an aunt, my aunt on the father's side*
hokšicala *a baby*
ciyé *a man's older brother, my brother*
hakakta *the youngest child*
maše *a man's brother-in-law*
šic'e *a woman's brother-in-law, my brother-in-law*
tanhan *a man's or my brother-in-law*
cinca *or* cincala *a child, offspring*
icinca *a child in ref to*
cinhintku *his or her stepchild*
cinkši *a son, a man's brother's son, or a woman's sister's son* – Cinkš *My son! as is said by fathers to their children*
hokšicantkiyapi *the beloved son*
kanyeja *a child*
takoš *a son or daughter-in-law*
wakanheja *or* hacila *children*
scepanši *a woman's female cousin*
hankaši *a man's female cousin*
šic'eši *a woman's male cousin, my male cousin*
tanhanši *his or my male cousin*
cunwitku *his or her daughter* — Cunkš! *My daughter!*
tiblo *her elder brother*
ciye *his or my elder brother*
cuwe *her elder sister*
tanke *his elder sister*
ate *father*
atkuku *his father*
tunkan *a father-in-law*
wicinca *or* wicincala a girl
takoja *grandchild*
tunkašila *grandfather*
unci *or* kunši *grandmother*
hanka *his sister-in-law*
omawahiton *a title applied to the fathers of husband and wife, perhaps like: Dad, or Dads*
hakakta *his or her youngest child, boy or girl*
wiha-kakta *the youngest or fifth girl child*
ina *my mother* — hunku *his or her mother*
kun *mother-in-law*
unciši *a mother-in-law, my mother-in-law*
winuhca *his mother-in-law*
tonška *his nephew* – toška *her nephew*
tojan *her niece* — tonjan *his niece* – Cf elder in *ref* to older
cuwe *a woman's older sister* – cuweku *her older sister* – hakata *man's or woman's older or younger sister, or her brothers*
tankakiciyapi *sisters*
scepan *her in-laws*
hanka *his sister-in-law*
cinca *one's child, offspring* — Cinkš! *My child!*
wicawoȟa *a son-in-law, or my son-in-law*
šanke *a stepmother*
tawagan *a step relation*
lekši *an uncle, one's mother's brother*
tawicu *or* tawin *his wife* – mitawin *my wife*
sunka *or* sunkaku *his or her younger brother* Misun, ...

My younger brother, ...
tanka *hers or my younger sister*
tankši *his younger sister*
hake *the youngest child*
kaka *a baby's name for grandfather*

famous *vn* : ocaštan'in *to be ~ , well-known* — wóimna *to be ~*
fan *v* : kalulu *to ~ something* - ic'iglalu *or* iglalu *to ~ one's self* - kaoluic'iya *to ~ one's self* — guheya *to fan out from, to spread out from a single point or place*
far *adv* : ílehan *so far off* — ítehan *far from* - katehan *at a distance* - kaitehanlake *a little farther in time or place* - kaotehehan *distantly in time* — kahan *thus far, to this* — kaektawapaya *at a distance* — kasan *farther on* — kaohlahyalaka *not far from* — lehantukel *just so far, or just now* — lehantuya *to this extent; on or in this wise* - lehanyan *so far in space, so long in time* — lehanyela *thus far, just now* — makotahena *far from any habitation* — otehan *at a long distance* - tehantan *or* tehantanhan *from afar* - tehantu *far off, at a great distance* - tehantuya *or* tehantuyakel *to or at a great distance* - tehanyan *far away* — wamakatehantulake s'e *from afar*
fare *n* : icajuju *or* oopeton *toll*
farm *n* : wójuti *a ~ house* - wójuwicaša *a farmer*
fast *n* : kaluluka *the fastest* - kalusyalakes'e *swift so it seems* — akih'anic'iya *to have one's self go hungry, or starving* — hanble *to fast seeking a vision* — nihkazilkiya *to fast, to stretch the stomach*
fasten *or* **bar** *or* **lock** *va* : okaška *to fasten or latch, to lock, to tie as to a hitching post, or to tie into so as to hide* — ónataka *to bar, bolt, to ~ a fence* — oyutkuga *to tie as a horse in a stall, to lock* - oyutkugahan *tied up, locked*
fat *n* : cešikšice *the ~ covering the paunch* — talipa *a sausage* — tašupa can papahyapi *intestines in which to pack fat* — tanunh'šin *the ~ between the buffalo's ears* - tanšin *the ~ on the ribs* - tawosa *the ~ on the lower neck* — tawoze *the ~ behind the ears* — tištašin *the ~ at the temples* — tatapsin *buttons of fat* — wakicepa *a too fat animal or person* - Cf fatten
fatigue *vn* : yugo *to be fatigued* - yugoyakel *in an exhausted condition*
fatten *vn* : acebya *to make fat for* - cépa *fat, as a fat cow* - acebyakel *in a state of fattening for* - acepa *to be or get fat for* - cebkiya *to ~ one's own* - cebya *to ~* , or fatly, liberally - cebyapi *fattened, fatted* - cebyela *fat* - icebya *to ~ by means of* - icepa *fat by reason of* — hóapašin *the hard fat on the taniga, on the paunch*
fault *v* : wawiyahtaka *to find ~ with* - wawiyahtagia *or* wayahtagia *to find fault, to bite, fig to abuse one by speaking evil of another*
favor *adv* : kitanyelakeleš *in a favorable mind*
fear *vn* : canlwanka *to be a coward fearing everything* - canlwankala *cowardly* - canlwankan *weak-hearted, or cowardliness, cowardice* - cantewakanheja *to be weak of a child-like heart* — hinyansgla *to fear on seeing what is terrible* — inagihaha *to feel scared at seeing something* — inihan *to be frightened or astonished* - woinihanyan *fearfully* - inihinciya *to be alarmed on seeing or hearing something* — hankokipa *to ~ the night, or fearing the night* - ikopa *to be afraid of, to ~ something* - ikopegla *to be in the state of ~* - ikopekiya *to make one fearful* - kokipa *to ~ something* - okokipeya *in fear* - okope *fear* -
fearlessly *adv* : inihanšni *or* inihinciyešniyan — napecešni *unabashedly, not being bashful* — oh'ansinkpekpe *to be fearless in doing* — šunk'ištakpa s'e *going about ~*

feast *va* : awašpanyan *to feast for a person or event* — cekitipi *a ~ said to be partaken of by virgins and men who have had sexual intercourse with women* — kicico wótapi *a public ~* - wicawota *or* wólwicayapi *a banquet or ~* - wólya *to make a feast* — šunk'ohanpi *a dog ~* — wakanwohan *to make a sacred ~* - wakanwohanpi *a sacred ~*
feather *n* : aopazan *eagle feathers* — iyake *the ~ end of a quill, or the ~ on an arrow* - wíyaka *a wing or tail ~ of geese* - iyagton *to put a ~ on an arrow* — situpi *a tail ~* - šun *the large wing feathers* — šunpahlihli *or* šuntoto *to have feathers partly grown* — wanblupi *eagle tail feathers* — wasusnaka *the narrow side of a ~*
feeble *v* : kahtata *to make ~* — kuja *to be weak, sick* — ostaka *to be ~ because of* - okistaka *to be weakened by* — yašihtin *to make weak by biting* - yušihtin *to enfeeble* - yušihtinpi *feebleness* - yušihtinyan *feebly* — iš'ake hunkešni *slow and feeble as sick old men* - yuwaš'akešni *to make ~*
feed *va* : iognaka *to put into the mouth* - iognagkiya *to ~ another* - iognagya *to have another eat, to cause eating* — lolwanagi *to ~ the spirits* — yulkiya *or* yulya *to ~ one*
feel *v* : aluslus *to have a feeling the body over caused by a grating sound* - yualosloza s'e iyeya, *fig to injure one's feelings* — ayutan *to touch, feel* - iyutantan *to touch to ~ in different places* - oyutan *to touch, feel* - patan *to ~ about for with by pushing* - wotan *a touch, or one that feels*
feisty *v* : wawolhilhitika *to be testy or quarrelsome*
fell *v* : kaunka *to cut* - waunka *to saw down, to ~*
female *n* : win *of woman or wife* - winyela *~ animals*
fence *va* : acankaškaya *to make a ~ , to enclose* - acan'iglaška yanka *to ~ fence in one's own, to be fortified* - aconkaška *or* acunkaška *and* acunkaške *or* aconkaške *to fortifiy, or a fortress; stronghold* — inatake *a lock, a ~ , a fort*
ferment *or* **leaven** *va* : napohya *to cause to ~* - napohyapi *leaven*
fertile *adj* : owojuwašte
fetch *or* **get** *v* : kicihiyohi *to go and fetch for one*
few *adv* : conala - cogconala *several* - conalaka *many, or a few* — iyakilenala *as few as* — naptetuka few — tónala *or* tonana *or* tonagnala *a few, or how few?* - tónakeca *some* - tónakel *several of times or in number*
fickle *or* **whimsical** *n* : kcánka *one who is ~* - kcankcanla *false in making promises* — tawacinhahala *changeable* - tawacin tokeca *whimsical* - tawacinwankala *easily influenced* - wacincik'ayela *fickle-minded*
field *n* : mága *a cultivated ~* - magáta *in the ~* - mahtáni *an old ~* — oju *a ~ or patch* - owoju *a garden, a planted ~* — oyublu tanka *a ~ for plowing*
fight *va* : kíza *to quarrel with, to fight* - kiciza *to ~ or quarrel with* - kicizapi *a quarrel* - okisyakel *being used to fighting*
figure *adv* : wawiyacinyan *figuratively* — wiglawa *to calculate, settle*
file *or* **rasp** *va* : ayuman - paman *to ~ or grind to sharpen, or filed* - kpaman *to ~ or polish one's own* - kícipame *to ~ for one* — ówecinhan *in single ~ succession*
fill *vn* : awoblu *to ~ up or inflate quickly* — hokapta *to ~ up* — oȟaya *to ~ up a hole* — ipic'iya *to ~ one's self up with* - ípiya *to fill up, make full* - owipi *one who is filled up* — iyojuya *to ~ to the brim* - juton *to ~ one's self with food* - ojukiciton *to ~ a bag for* - ojukiton *to ~ up one's own bags* - ojula *filled* - ojupi *something or seed to sow* - ojuton *to ~ in sacks* - ojutonpi *filled bags* - ojuya *to cause to ~ or plant* - okici-ju *or* okiju *to ~ up for*

- okikšu *to ~ one's own* — owapate *to stuff* — aopagi *to ~ a pipe again* - aokicipagi *to ~ a pipe again for one* - opagi *to ~ or cram one's own pipe with tobaccco* — okata *to ~ or cover over a hole* — átaja *to be filled to the brim*

filter *va* : ayucan *to sift on or over* - ikacan *to sift by shaking* - iyucan *to sift something* — apuskepa *to ~ out on* - apuskebya *in a filtering manner* - opuskebya *filtered* — nazeya *to ~*

filth *n* : wóšape — wóhlik'el *filthy inside*

final *adv* : óhanketa *finally* — ehakeke *for the very last time*

find *va* : iyeya *to go and ~* - iyeyaya *to keep finding* - waiyeyaca *one the finds much* - wawiyeya *to ~* - yuha iyeya *to ~ or receive something unexpectedly*

fine *adj* : swula *small as are beads* - swuwaya *soft and small*

finger *n* napsu - napapazo *to shake the finger at one* - waepazo *the index or forefinger* — šak'oyazan *to pain under the fingernails* — šašte *the little ~* - šašteiyokihe *the middle ~*

finish *v poss* : gluco *to ~ one's own* - yucoya *finished* - wakicoyakel *finished or done well* — h'unhikiya *to ~ or perfect something, or in a finished way, perfected* - h'unhiya *to perfect something* - h'unhiyela *exhausted, played out* — óhinnikiya *to ~ and cease from* — ahiyuštan *to come and ~* - iglaštan *to ~ speaking or eating one's own* - iyuštan *to ~ inside or for* - oyuštan *to ~ within* - yuštan *to perfect something* — tkonskiya *to ~ a job, to be done* — yupinnakikšin *to be huried to ~ work*

fire *va* : aun *or* aon *to put on the ~* - cantakse ya *to fell a large tree by setting ~ to its roots* - ceti *to build a ~* - aceti *to make a ~ on or at* - akiceti *to arrive home and start a ~* - cekicati *to make a fire for me, perhaps* - cekicati *or* cekiciti *to make a ~ for one* - éceti *to build a ~* - iceti *to start a ~ to or at* - oceti *a fireplace* - mázaoceti *a stove* — gu *to burn, singe, scorch* - agu *to burn on something for a reason* - aguya *to make to burn on* - cegugu *burnt black* - ceguguya *to burn black, to fry meat* - gugnagya *to destroy by ~* - gumna *smelling burnt* - gušica *burnt, hence worthless* - *guya* to cause to burn - iyaguya *to burn as food in the bottom of a pan* — hingnu *to singe off* - hingnupi *singed off* — ȟugnaga *to burn up, consume* - ȟugnahya *to cause to burn up* - ȟugnaya *to burn down, to destroy by ~* — ile *to burn, or a blaze* - aile *to burn on* - ailešašaya *in the red flame* - aileya *to set ~ to, or setting fire to* - cankaile *to make blaze by rubbing* - haileyapi s'e *as one coming close to a ~* - ileya *to set ~ to* - oileya *to set on ~* — itkon *to burn or blaze* - itkonyahan *burning, alive as coals* - itkonyan *to make burn, blaze* — aleleya *to char a stick* - alesab *to burn by frostbite* — alo *scorched, cooked* - aloza *scortched but not cooked* - alosabya *to let food get black while roasting it* - aloshingle *to get black suddenly while roasting* - aloslosyeca *to sense a burning sensation when becoming angry* - alosloza *to be scorched but not cooked* - alosya *to scorch something in the flame* — anatipa *to shrivel, to be burned* - inatibya *to roast on coals making meat curl up* — ona *prairie ~* - onagu *burnt prairie* - onagumna *the smell of a prairie ~* - onaya *to start a prairie ~* - onikušeya *or* oninatake *a fireguard* — aon *or* aun *to stoke a ~* - ceonpa *to roast esp meat* - pelakigle *to burn pith on the arm as a test of bravery* - pelicagla *near the ~* - pelikceya *over the ~* - pelileyapi *kindlings* - pelimna šni *to be unafraid of fire or extreme heat* - peliškan *to draw near ~ to warm one's self* - peliyaglašyahan *to bank a ~* - pelkanye *near ~* - pelkokipa *to be afraid of ~* - pelmna *to smell of ~, or smelling of ~* - pel'iyucanyankel *with the fire getting low for lack of firewood* - pel'kitonkel *having or absorbing enough heat from the fire* — péta *a ~* - petkagla *or* petkiyela *near or by the ~* - petaga *coals* - petanl *in or on the ~* - péta yuhala *walking fire, night fire, will-o-the-wisp* - petkaile s'e *fanning the ~* - petowayake *chunks of wood to bank a ~* - petuspe *a firebrand* - petuste *a firebrand with which to start another ~* — ašpan *to be burnt or cooked on or by anything* — aizita *to burn as incense etc.* — wakinyan onayanpi *a prairie fire started by lightning* — wípaškanglepi *fires started along the return from a triumph*

firesteel *n* : canka *or* cankognake

firm *adv neg* : ahahayela *or* aheheyela *not firmly* — aiyasaka *to stiffen or become hard* — apasuta *to stiffen by kneading on* - asuta *to become hard or strong on* - ayusuta *to make ~ on* - cantesuta *to be strong of heart, to be brave* - iglusuta *to establish one's self* - osutaya *firmly, for good* — šogya *firmly* — anat'insya *to tramp down firmly* - aput'inst'insya *firmly pressed upon* - ipat'inza *to strengthen, make ~, solidify; sustenance, nourishment* - it'insya *to make ~ by means of* - it'inza *to be ~ by reason of* - it'inze *a fastener or tightener* - kat'inza *to make ~, to pound tight* - onat'inza *to make ~ by tredding on* - oyut'inza *to make ~, strengthen, to brace* - t'insya *to brace up; firmly, bravely*

first *adv* : aotanhci *before all else* - toká *at the ~* - tokaci *at the very ~* - tokahe *the beginning; to be ~, go before* - tokahekiya *to go ahead of others* - tokaheya *at the ~, first, the ~* - tokahtayetu *at the beginning of night* - tokak'ehan *or* tokak'unhehan *at the ~* - tokalahci *for the ~ time* - tokapa *~ born, eldest* - tokaya *~, or the ~*

fish *n* : hogan *~ and marine life in general* — hoiwotka *or* hosan *carp* - howasapa *catfish* - tuki *clam* — matuška *crawfish* - matugna *crayfish* — hoka *or* zuzecahogan *eel* — gnaška *frog* — tunšla *leech* — hogansanla *or* hoganscila *minnow* - hogleglega *the grass pike, or perhaps also the rainbow trout* - hoapeša *the red-fin* - holaska *shad* — mniwamnuh'a *or* tunšla *or* wahacankakic'in *the snail* — hopepe *the stone-roller* — matapiȟa *or* matapeȟa *toad* — ke *or* keya *turtle* — hogantanka *or* wamnitu *a whale* — **SOME PARTICULARS** : hoape *a fin* - hocaka *a gill* - hocešpu *or* hopašku *a scale* - hot'eca *dead fish* — hokuwa *to go fishing* - homnayan *to collect fish* - hopatan *to spear ~* - hoganmna *or* homna *or* hosamna *or* hosewimna *fishy in ref to smell or taste* — cakiyuhlate *or* hoicuwa *or* hoipate *or* hoiyupsice *a fish-hook*

fit *or* **able** *or* **suited to** *vn* : aecetu *to be able* — kipiya *to make fit; properly enough for* — wakipuskica *to fit closely, tightly together*

flabby *adv* : kayoyo s'e *with one's fleshy parts shaking* — lolopa *soft and ~ as of over-ripe fruit*

flag *n* : wiyokihe *a banner* — wówapi *a ~* - wówapiokijata *a truce ~*

flame *v* : kaȟaȟa *to ~ up, lick* — oile *a ~*

flap *or* **beat** *or* **quake** *v* : kaozeze *to beat in the wind* — šniyanyan *with wings flapping* — hpihpi s'e *flapping* — hníyanyan *quaking from fear*

flash *or* **spark** *n* : pailepi *a ~ of light* — wakinyan tónwanpi petijanjan *a flashlight* - wakinyan tónwanpi *sparks that are given off*

flat *adj* : blaska - blaskaya *flat-wise* - icablaska *to be flattened* - iwoblaskayela *made flat* - kablaska *to make ~ by striking* - nablaska *to flatten by foot* - oblaska *the ~ side* - oblaskaya *on the ~ side* - pablaska *to press out ~*

— wípablaye *a flatiron* — opaska *to press out and flatten* — ipustaka *to be ~ , defective*
flatter *va* : yazonta *to ~ a person*
flatten *v* : yaskiska *to ~ with the teeth, as quills*
flavor *va* : yuskuya *to make sweet or sour* — štušta *lacking ~* - štušteya *to make lose ~*
flax *n* : atašošapina nablaga *the yellow ~*
flay *v* : wayugapa *to strip off an animal's skin*
flee *va* : napa - anakipa *to ~ from* - anapa *to ~ to for refuge* - aonapa *to take refuge in or on or at* - ikpiyonapa *to ~ toward a shelter* - nakipa *to retreat homeward* - napeya *to make ~* - onapa *to take refuge in* — pageya *to make flee* — iyanajica *to run off with something* - najinca *to ~ or retreat* — nakicipa *to ~ from one or from some thing* - tanajica *to flee* - tanajilhi *to come fleeing* - naic'išpa *to ~ from danger or trouble* — pageya *to make ~* — wapatonyece *a person who makes one ~ , a threat* — ozanyela *taking to flight* - Cf refuge
flesh *or* **meat** *vn* : akicepa *to become fleshy* — coku *the skin* - cokukiton *to take on flesh* — conica *meat of any kind* — ȟuwapahpe *~ sticking to the hide* — šwošwoke s'e *or* wašošo s'e *or* kayoyo s'e *being very fleshy*
flexible *or* **pliant** *or* **fresh** *or* **tender** *va* : yupsonla *to move something limber* — nunšnunjahela *or* nunšnunja *tender or pliant* — psonpsonla *supple, lithe* — winšwinje *or* winšwinjahela *or* winšwinjela *limber, pliant, tender, not stiff*
flimsy *adj* : zigzica *or* nazigzil *elastic, rubbery*
flinch *v* : - Cf shy
flirt *vn* : wicinškan *to be flirting while at work*
float *v* : ókage *to ~* - aokahwoka *to ~ and drift downstream* - okahwoka *to ~ in the air* - ókahya *to make ~ downstream, or floating* — aokapota *to rise to the water's surgace, to ~* - aokapolya *to make something ~* - ókapota *to be borne on upon, to ~ on water* - aglapota *to ~ upon*
flood *or* **overflow** *vn* : mnitan *to be flooded* - imnitan *to ~ ; or a flood* - imnitanyan *to cause a ~* - mnítanyan *to be flooded*
floor *n* : canwinja *a ~* - canwowinge *matted flooring* — owanka *or* owang *or* owank *a floor, the ground, a place to lie down or set up a tent*
flour *n* : owayukpan *what is ground up fine*
flow *vn* : amnitan *to ~ on or over* - amnitanya *to make ~ on or over, to irrigate* - amnitanyan *in an overflowwing manner* — kaluza *to ~ rapidly* - kalusya *to cause to ~ ; or flowing swiftly* - icaluza *to flow over*
flower *or* **weed** *n* : **In General** : wahca *the genus* - wanahca *or* hca *a blossom* - hcaya *to blossom* — waptaye *a weed* — canhlogan *a hollow stalk* - Cf grass, medicine — **In Particular** : wahpe maka ayublaya *amaranth* — hitunkala tunkce *anemone* — canhlogan pepela *a dense aster* - wahcazi waštemna *the prairie aster* — canhlogan hašlušluta *or* canhlogan hlahla *or* hanpinatopi *the beard-tongue* — wahpewacanga huwinyela *bedstraw* - wahpe h'eh'e *the bee-plant* — miniohuta aglagla wahcazi *beggar's lice* — kimimila tawanahca *or* psitola hu iyececa *blindweed* — wohlokapišni pejuta — zuzecatawote apetotohe *the blue cardinal ~* — wahpe pa *boneset* — canhlogan hutkan *a species of buckwheat* — wihuta huswula *bullrush* — španšniyutapi iyececa *the sand burr* — wahpešica *burweed* — sinkpetawote *calamus* — hantkan *or* hintkan *or* wihutahu *cat-tail* — wahpehla *clammyweed* - wahpewacanga hubloka *cleavers* — tokalatapejuta hubloka *or* wahpeswula *clover* — winawizi *cockle-burr* — napoštan *the coneflower* — canhlogan wicagnaške *a species of crowfoot* — minisantula *cyperus* — hupteptecala *the daisy* — canhlogan suta *dalea* — napeoilekiyapi *dogbane* — wahpe pepela *doorgrass* - wahpeyazokapi *downy painted cup* — onwahinyun tonpi *erigeron* — canhlogan nablaga *lupine flax* — canhlogan waštemna iyececa *fleabane* — canhlogan ištewiyowicahpaya *froelichia* — kapopapi *or* wahcewašte *gentian* — yazokapihu *the gilia* — canhlogan makaayublaya *or* cannungahu pteptecela *or* mi-mela wahcazi *the goldenrod* - tal'agnake *the stiff golden-rod* - wahcaziblu *the rock goldenrod* — šunkcanka huipiye *the gromwell* — šunkawakantapejuta *or* wahpešlušluta *groundsel* — matotaspan *the hawthorn* — tatawabluška tacanhlogan *or* onšunkoyušpapi *honeysuckle* — wahpeakikaškapi *hops* — tal'agnaka iyececa *ironweed* — wikoškatapejuta *poison ivy* — zuzecatawote ptaptaikoyaka *Jacob's ladder* — takušašala huwinyela *knotweed* - takušašala huswula *lady's thumb* — wanagitinpsila *larkspur* — makacanakpa *lady's slipper* — can-hlogan mah'awanglakela *or* mnahcahca *the prairie lily* - kewapa *the water lily* — pšintanka *the mariposa lily* — yapizapi iyececa *the little white sand lily* — šunktawote *the loco-weed* — canhlogan kcankcanla *the looking-glass* — canhlogan wahcazi *loosestrife* — utahu canhlogan *or* wahcazi cik'ala *mallow* — panunpala *or* wahcahca *or* tinpsila pejuta *milkweed* — hantepepe iyececa the *mimosa* — makaceyaka iyececa *the lemon mint* — ceškikan iyececa *the monkey flower* — canhlogan huwanjila *or* hitunkalanakpala *or* tahcanakpala *mouse ear* — makošice pejiȟota *mugwort* — canhlogan wabluškahu *the tumble mustard* — can'icahpe *nettle* — ih'e makaceyaka *penny-royal* — canhlogan apepepe *oreocarya* — hokšicekpa *the Pasch flower* — canhlogan inkpagmi-gmela *or* owicak'o *or* canhlogu *pigweed* - canhlogan wapoštankagapi *or* wakinyanla pahlihu *or* wihutahu iyececa *plantain* - canhlogan hucanswula *or* makacan-šihu *prairie-pink* — tokahuwahinkpeonziyapi *prickly poppy* — huhla *or* husansan *primrose* — matotatinpsila *or* ticanicahu *or* wahcazi kantamna unmahutanka *or* wahpokijate *psoralea* — wahca pepela *pyeweed* — canhlogan onzipakinte *ragweed* - canhlogan sotka *ragwort* — unpantawote *or* yušpulaota *red-root* — onjinjintka *the rose* — makaceyaka *sage* — wahcazi waštemna *sideranthus* — takušašala *smartweed* — tat'ecannuga *or* wazimnikpa iyececa *snakeroot* - wazimninkpa *the button snakeroot* — makomica *sophora* — yapizapihu *or* zuzecatawote hutankinyan heca *Solomon's seal* — canhlogan panpanla *spiderwort* - canhlogan wapoštan *or* apelatapišlecala iyececa *spurge* — hupepe *stickweed* — wahcazi tanka *or* wahcazizi *sunflower* — tokahu *the thistle* — wahpepeka *the Russian thistle* — ih'eh'e canhlogan *townsendia* — hutkanhanska *or* wahpeyatapi iyececa *the tumbleweed* — canhlogan ókiheton *umbrella-wort* — topestola *vervain* — šunklejahu *milk vetch* - šunkowa-šakala *the Canadian vetch* - šunktapejua *the loco vetch* — tasusu *the American vetch* — wahpeto *the prairie violet* — owicak'olahu *virgin's bower* — canhlogan pa *wallflower* — wahpeblaskaska *winter-greens* — onšunk'nasapihu *or* zuzecatawote *the wolfberry*
fluently *adv* : yaglapi s'e *plainly*
fluff *n* : - Cf soft
flush *or* **level** *or* **align** *va* : kaotan *to make ~* — paotkonza *to make level with*
fly *vn* : kinyan - okinyan *to ~ in or about* - okinyanwašte *docile or gentle* - akinyan *to ~ over or on* — našloka *to ~ off or out* - waanašloka *what persists in flying off or*

out — akahwogya *to let ~ and scatter over one* — papsipsica *to make ~ by pushing* — ínasaka *to let fly as a limb sprung and released, or a bow drawn and released to shoot an arrow*

foam *n* : ipiga — kataga *to make ~* - mniwataga *foam* - mniwaticoga *scum*

fog *or* **steam** *or* **dust** *n* : p'o *a mist, or misty* - anap'o *to be ~ on one* - ap'o *to be ~ on things* - op'o *a fog or mist* - iyap'osp'os *fog, or turbulent cloud formations*

fold *adv* : aicitakigna *doubled* — iciyahlal *folding* - apako *to be bent over* — ayukša *to bend, double up on* - oyukša *folding up, in a ~ or bend* - hákakša *folded up after use* - pakša *to ~ e.g. a blanket* — apakšija *or* pakšija *to double up* — akipaja *to ~ on or double up* — pehan *to ~ up anything* — ayapehan *to ~ up with the mouth on* - ayupehan *to ~ up on* - glapehan *to ~ up one's own* — íciyahlah *to ~ e.g. the hands and cross and lock the fingers in praying* - iyapehan *to ~ or wrap around* - iyapehanyan *folding, winding or wrap-ping around* - kicipehan *to ~ up for one* - kpehan *to ~ up one's own* - opehan *to ~ up in* - opehe *a ~, a bolt of cloth*

follow *vn* : ecaeconka *to ~ a business or occupation* — ahankeya *immediately following* - ohangleya *to ~ about* — ícihaktaya *following each other* - ihakabya *to ~ one* — ioglamniyan *following around the curves as of a stream* — iokawinh *following around the circle* — iyayuhkiya *following* — iyayuhya *following something* - iyagluȟa *to ~ along after one's own as a colt its mother* — ékuwa *to ~ one then and there* - kicuwa *to ~ up after* — wawiyayuȟa *to tag along, or one who tags along* wawiyayuhya *tagging along* — ókihan *to ~ being after one in travelling* - ókihe *to ~ one travelling, or following, next* — ópa *to ~, going with* - opasi *to ~ after in e.g. a road* - aopa *to ~ with* - aopeya *to cause one to ~ with* - akicipa *to ~ for, to obey* - okipa *to ~ the ways or trade of others, to obey* - okipeca *to ~ and do as one is accustomed* - okipekiya *to make one ~ one's own* - okipeya *to make ~ one's own, or following* — apasi *to ~ after or on* - pasiya-kel *following up, watching* - atapa *to ~ after on* - atapaya *to cause to ~ up* - otapa *to ~ after one; fig to imitate* - waotape s'e *following unintentionally*

fond *or* **caring** *v poss* : wahtinkiya *to be ~ of one's own* - wahtinyan *to be ~ of* - wahtinciye šni (*cursing*) *I don't care about you!*

fondle *or* **hold** *v* : katakoha *to hold in one's arms* — kignayan *to caress*

food *n* : lo *soft stuff* - walopela *~ overboiled and become mushy* — wóta *to eat ~* - wótapi *or* wol *or* wo *what is for eating* — heȟakatawote *~ for elk* — wóla *to beg for ~* — wateca *part of one's ~ taken home from a feast* — watogcin *to desire other ~* — yúte *or* oyute *the eating* - tawoyute *his or her ~* - wóyuteya *to have or use as ~*

fool *v refl* : aikpajuju *or* aikpablaya *to make a ~ of one's self by talking or acting foolishly* — eceyanuniya *to lead astray* — ecinšni *thoughtless* — glezezeka *making a ~ or one's self* — caguka *foolishness* - igluguka *to expose one's self and so to make a ~ of one's self* - guguhan *crazy* — heyoka *a clown* — iglagleglega *to paint one's self so as to appear a ~* — iȟaȟake *a jesting ~* - iic'iȟaȟa *to jest making a ~ of ones self* — kiun'unlake *to act a ~* — oileleka *a good-for-noth-ing, a ~* — ot'ognaka *to be foolhardy, to risk one's life* — psanpsanka *a ~* — caske *to take by mistake* — wacintonšni *to be foolish* — witko *foolish* - kiwitkotkoka *to be foolish* - owitkotko *foolishly* - witkokaga *the Fool-Maker* - witkokonza *to pretend to be foolish* - witkopi *foolishness* - witkotkoka *a fool, or to act foolishly* - witkotkopi *foolishness* - witkotkoya *foolishly* - witkoya *to make a ~ of, or foolishly* - witkoyahan *foolishly, in a silly manner*

foot *v* : kpanajinka *to get to one's feet* — anatitan *to push on by foot* — anatokelyakel *using the feet unusually* — anatuka *to wear off by ~* - anat'a *to kill with the ~ on something* — si *the foot* - siakša *pigeontoed, fig in opposition to* - sihahmin *toes pointing out* - sicapsan *to shake the ~* - siglapsanpsan *to swing the feet* - sicola *bare-footed* - sicuha *the sole of the ~ or shoe* - siha *the sole or hoof* - sihutkan *or* sihukan *a ~ ligament* - siȟape *or* sioȟape *the hollow of the ~* - siic'iyapa *to strike the feet together when walking* - siitakaha *the instep* - siiyotiyekiya *to pain one in the ~* - siksa *club-footed* - sínaniyan *the ~ to hurt* - sipa *the front of the ~* - sisanni *one is a set of feet* - siyete *the heel* - siyeteoškoke *the skin of the heel* - isi *at or on the foot* — oyayatopa *four-footed, or on all four* — huhatopa *a quadruped* - huiyun *on foot*

for *prep in compos* : ...kica... *or* ...kici...

forbid *va* : kišica *to oppose, check, stop one* — wawiyokišni *to ~*

force *va* : kasli *to ~ or press out*

ford *n* : óiyohpaye *a crossing* — gliyuwega *to return across by fording* - oiyuwege *a fording place*

foreign *n* : tóka *a foreigner, a hostile, an enemy* — wicaša lehankata *a foreigner*

foremost *adv* : otokata *before* - Cf begin

forest *n* : cannahmela k'el *a concealed woods* - can'owancaya *or* cunwanca *a dense forest, a jungle perhaps* - can'owoju *an orchard* - canwita *a little grove of trees* - cónteȟi *thick ~* - cúnšoke *dense woods* - cúntanka *a timber, groves of trees* - cunwinziye oyuze *a place where a yellow resin is extracted from pine trees to make a yellow dye* - cúnwohešma *dense woods* — mayál *deep in the forest* - Cf timber

foretell *v* : wakan iya *or* wakinya - Cf predict

forget *adj* : ocinwakan *purposely forgetful* — wacint'a *to be forgetful* — akiktonja *not to remember* - aktonja *or* aktonktonja *forgetful, absent-minded* - aktonšya *to make forget* - aktonyan *forgetfully* - éktonja *to forget something* - wákiktonja *to forget* — naptahena *forgetting* — pawignuni *to become forgetful of*

forgive *va* : kicicajuju - wicakicicajujupi *foregiveness* - akiciktonja *to forgive one*

fork *adj* : játa *forked* - akijata *or* jagjata *forked* - okijata *or* ojate *a fork as in a road or stream* - okajaya *between or in the forks of* - kajata *to cut making forked* - najata *to make forked by foot* - pajata *to make forked by thrusting into* - wajata *to make forked by cutting or sawing* - wojáta *to split by punching as into the ground* — oȟaka *forked, or a fork* - oȟakayakel *in many ways* — koiyayuhkiya *forking, meeting at a small angle*

form *or* **kind** *n* : ouncage *a likeness* — okahwanjila *one of the same form or style* — kaskiska *to make rough or wavy by pounding* - kaskiskaska *to ~ by pounding*

formerly *adv* : itokehan *at the first* - itok'ehan *of old* - itola kin *or* k'on hehan *long ago*

forsake *vn* : ohinhpaya *to fall from* — ayuhlagan *to leave one*

fortune *adj* : wapi *or* wapika *fortunate, lucky* - wapike *a fortunate person* - wapišni *unfortunate* - wapiya *to make lucky, or fortunately*

foundation *n* : oagle *or* owaheglepi *a foundation, a place on which something is put to rest*

fowls *n* : ánpaohotonla *or* waȟupakoza *domestic fowls, wing-flappers* - Cf birds

fracture *v* : kawega *to break* - kicawega *to ~ for* — okahleca *to tear in pieces, to ~*
fragment *n* : owošpe *a piece shot or punched off*
frame *va* : agle *to place or make stand on* - aglehan *a ~ or foundation* - aglehiyeya *placed one after the other*
frank *adj* : wawaheyešni *open, not hesitating to speak out*
frantic *vn* : šicawacin *to be frightened hurrying and screaming; or frantically* — t'ebleze šni *to be ~ , wild* — t'egnaškinyan s'e *frantically, in great excitement*
fray *adj* : swaka *frayed* - naswa *to fray, wear out by ripping* — wakaȟunta *to make ~ , i.e. peel off or tear open*
free *va* : igluha *to possess one's self, to act well* — išicola *without remuneration* — ituhci *gratuitously* — kiiglušpa *to wrestle and ~ one's self* — kpapta *to ~ one's self and leave* — nakišloka *to extricate one's self* — tawaic'iya *to be ~ , own one's self* - tawaic'iyapi *freedom, liberty* — yuškeya *on the loose* — éke šni *to be freed from, to get out and free without effort*
freeze *adj* : acahšlaya *covered with ice* - cága *ice* - acaga *to ~ in, or on, or upon* - acahsu *to ~ droplets* — aȟeyunka *to be frost on* — anap'in *frost-bitten and stiff* — ȟeyunka *frost* — hanyagu *a robe freeze-dried* — ótasagya *to keep frozen, hard or stiff*
freight *v* : mas'ahi *to arrive with ~*
frequent *v* : oeconhca un *to ~ a place purposefully*
fresh *adj* : lolo *~ and soft* - loya *moist, ~ as meat*
friction *v* : - Cf rub
friend *n* : kóla (*used by men*) - kolakiciyapi *friendship* - kolaya or takolakiciyapi *to have as a special or particular ~* - okolaya *to have as a friend* - takolaku *his particular ~* - lakolya *to be friendly with* - olakolya *to have as a friend, or as friends* - olakolkiciyapi *friendship, peace* - olakota *friendship, alliance, fraternity* - wólakota *friendship, peace* — táwaše *a woman's female friend* - táwašetku *her female friend* — kicuwa *a ~*
frighten *adj* : nagihaha *frightened* — onštinmanihinciya *to be frightened in sleep* — owaȟabya *to scare all away, or one who scares away all* — itangluzaza *to have a fearful scare* — tanglusasaya *in a state of fright* - tanglusasaseca *to be frightened sick at seeing* - tansag *to frighten* - itansak t'e *to be frightened to death* - tansagt'eya *to frighten one very much* — yu-š'inyeya *to cause one to fear*
fringe *v* : napowaya *or* naswaya *to fringe with furs etc.* — okasu, okaswu, paswupi *a fringe or fringes* — waozezeya *to cut in fringes* — wazaza *to cut fringes, or in fringes* - wazazapi *dangles*
frog *n* : gnaška - gnaškacanli *a tree frog* - gnaškawakan *the bull frog* — honagila *or* honawitkala *tadpoles*
frolic *adj* : škehanhan *frolicsome*
from *adv* : eciyatan *thence, hence* - eciyatanhan *of, on account of, concerning, hence* - heciyatan *from that place, thence* - heciyatanhan *therefore* — iheciya *in that way from* - iheciyatan *in that direction from* - iheciyotan *in that direction from* — ehantanhan *from that time or place* — etan *adv or prep* : from - *pron* : some, somewhat — etanhan *or* etantan *prep* : from - etanhanhan *prep* : from different places or kinds - íkahan *or* íkahanyan *so far from* — k'un hetan *from something* — ...tan *or* ...tanhan *prep suff* : from (in some sense)
front *adv* : kahyapayalake s'e *towards the front* - kaipatkuhya *fronting* — kanyeta *in ~ of* - Cf before
frost *n* : waniȟeyunka *the first ~* — sniyopa *frost-bitten*
froth *or* **foam** *vn* : onapiga *to foam or ~*
frown *v* : itešinkiya *to ~ , or to grin* - iteyukokiya *to give a scowl* - pahteyukokiya *to grimace*
frugal *adj* : wagluhahaka *saving, parsimonious* — wakitontonka *economical*
fruit *esp* **berries** *n* : taspan *apple* (of the haw) - taspanpuzapi *dried apple* — pangi *artichoke* — škópela *or* ziziškopela *banana* — aunyeyapi *the sand or ground berry* — capceyazala *the wild black currant* — háza *huckleberry* — maštincapute *the buffaloberry* — canpa *chokecherry* — tamniohpi hu *the groundcherry* — tamniohpi *the fig* — wicagnaška *the gooseberry* — cunwiyapehe *or* cunyapehe *the grape* — taspicahiye *lemon extract* — supestola *or* suzizila *muskmelon* — taspanhinšma *the peach* — taspanpestostola *the pear* — waziwicagnaška *pineberry* — kánta *plum* - kansu *the plum pit* — ptetawote *the ground plum* — takanhecala *the black raspberry* — taspansloslola *the red haw* — aunyeyapi *the sandberry* — wípazukan *or* wípazokan *or* wípazutkan *the Juneberry or serviceberry or May berry* — waziškeca *strawberry* — wasutonyan *to bring forth fruit*
fry *v* : cekipa *to prepare meat for one* - cekipapi *meat that is prepared for one, as pápa or a roast*
fulfil *vn* : ecetu *to be accomplished or fulfilled* - ayuecetu *to ~ or accomplish on* - ecetukiya *to make so fulfilled or accomplished* - ecetuya *to bring about* - wóecetu *an accomplishment, fulfilment; simplicity* — enakiya *to finish* — glaheyapi s'e *doing or saying without interruption*
full *adj* : ojula - íojula ~ to the brim - ojuya *to cause to fill, or plant* - iyojukiya *to make one's own full* - iyujibyela *brimful* — ípi *or* wípi *to be ~ , satisfied eating* - íyapahayela *or* íyapašnišyela *brimful, much of anything* - íyatagle *~ and running over* — kazan *to feel full eating* — kicunskehan *half-full* — oh'abyela *almost ~* — yaškipa *to bite and make ~ up*
fume *va* : kaginlginca *to make ~* — ozilya *or* zilya *to smoke, fumigate*
fun *adv* : ecaca *as a diversion, for or in fun* — íȟanhan *in fun, jestingly* - wóiȟaka *a funny thing, or to jest*
funnel *n* : iyokaštan pestola
funny *adj* : - *See* fun
fur *or* **nap** *n* : powaya - *adj* : trimmed - powayela *having nap* — wahinšma *a fur*
furious *va* : pagnaškinyan *to make one ~ , terrifying by pushing one about*
future *adv* : tokata *in the ~ , or the future* - tokatakiya *in the ~* - tokatayab *ahead, future as in: future days* — wakahanl *sometime in the ~* — tuktehan *in the future*
futurity *opt partic* : ... kta *or* ... kte, ... nun *or* ... nunwe

G

gain *va* : ohiya *to acquire, win, get the better of* — yamna *to ~ by talking* - yamnakiya *to cause to ~ by talking* - Cf win

gallop *vn* : naunka - katonaunka *to ~ slowly* - wanaunka *to start off on a ~* — tahusliyeya *to speed*

[1]**game** *adv* : osankayakel *being void of hunted ~*

[2]**game** *n* : SOME PASTIMES : hanpakutepi *a ~ for young men* — hinyankahwaciyapi *a ~ for boys, Believing the Owl* — hitunk'nahabyapi *a ~ in which boys scare up mice by stamping* — iyopsilkakicipa econpi *a ~ in which boys do jumping down* — pejiyuskitakutepi *a ~ with grass tied in bundles* — petagakiciinpi *a ~ to test one's bravery by throwing at each other pieces of burning wood* — tokakiciyut'api *a ~ of choking an enemy* — tápanakapapi *a girl's ~ somewhat like soccer* — tasihaunpi *a woman's ~ with bones, beads, and a pin* — SOME DETAILS : cunwiyawa kansukutepi *a counting stick in playing with plum pits* — hánpapeconpi *a hand guessing ~* — hutanacute *a cow bone ~* — kignunkacicipapi *an underwater race* — magakiciyapi *water ducks* — makakiciinpi *mud and willow* — matokiciyapi *a tickling ~* — micapeca onkiciopi *a mischievous ~* — napeoglece *or* napoglecekutepi *stick-throwing* — napsiyohli kutepi *a stick and ring ~* — oglece kutepi *arrow-shooting* — okah'oliyeya econpi *an ice ~* — painyankapi *the hoop ~* - otaja *a mark on one of the four hoops* — paslohanpi *the tahegle for sliding on snow or ice* — petagakiciinpi *testing with coals* — ptewoyake *the bones girls use in the* tasihaunpi — sazu *the cross-sticks of the ȟaka, a shooting instrument in the ~* — šnipute ya *to throw the bow* — šunk'nasapi *shooting arrows through a* walega, *a bladder* — šunk'nunikiciyapi *a ~ in losing horses* — tabkapsicapi *shinny* — tanpa *the little basket used in the ~ , cunwiyawa kansukutepi* — tate kahwogyapi *a little boy's toy made to sail or float in the wind* — toka kata *throwing a bow on ice* — wiokiciciya econpi *a ~ to practice courting* — wóohiye *an inning* — inahmekiciciyapi *hide-and-seek* — siokiciyahlalyapi *and* wankayekiciya econpi *children's games* — waziyacekaga *a pastime where sticks are dipped into water and placed in the cold to freeze and then sucked on as though it were candy*

gap *adj* or *n* : hci *broken out in gaps, or a gap* - hcihci *gapped or notched* - hcihciya *gapped, in gaps* - hciwahan *broken out in gaps* - kahci *to make a gap*

gape *v* : kagapa *to spread out, to lay open by cutting* — naga *or* nagan *or* najal *to make or ~ open as a wound* — najakayela *lying open*

garbage *n* : wóyaptapi - Cf leave, leavings

garment *n* : - *See* clothing

garrulous *adj* : íyaška *or* iyáška *loose-tongued, blatherous* - oie wašikšicun *a ~ person* - Cf boisterous

garter *n* : húncaje - hlahla húncaje *garters with bells attached* - hunskicaȟe *garters*

gash *n* : owahun — wago *to mark or ~ the flesh* — waic'ihon *to ~ one's self* - wakihon *to ~ one's own, to cut nicks* - wakicihon *to ~ for* — waškita *to ~ , to cut across*

gasp *vn* : okiniyan (*used with* cuwí) — onaglo *to rattle in the throat* — onahna *a dying breath* — pahwayaškabya *to make one ~*

gather *va* : canle *to ~ firewood* — aicoga *to ~ on anything* - kaicoga *to bunch* — gluge *to pick up scraps from one's floor* - ogejuya *to ~ up one's clothes* - yage *to collect something by mouth* — akimnamnaic'iya *to ~ everyone his own supply* - akimnayan *to consolidate some things* - amnanyan *to ~ together to* - glamna *to collect one's own* - imnayan *to ~ together by means of* - mnaic'iya *to collect for one's self* - mnakiya *to take a collection, to ~ one's own* - mnayan *to ~ or collect something* - mnayekiya *to cause to or make one ~* - omnayan *to ~ into* — aimniciya *they assemble* - okimniciye *to come together* — akpahi *to ~ up one's own on* - nakpas *gathering, or to force together* - apahi *to pick up and ~ on anything* - kicipahi *to ~ for one* - kpahi *to one's own* - opahi *to ~ into* — wíta *to ~* - okiwitaya *gathering about* — owikešni *staying together, not scattered* — pawitaya *gathered by hand* - pawitayela *collecting heads together* — wapawi *to ~ about, to swarm, flock about*

gauze *n* : zanzanla - Cf net

gaze *n* : oištaglewanjila *a steady ~*

gear *vn* : naic'ihminyan *to get out of ~, out of place*

generation *n* : iwicacaga *or* wic'icage *or* oicage *or* wóicage *a ~ or growth*

generous *vn* : canlyuha *to be charitable* - canteyukan *to be benevolent* — oh'anpi *to be ~* — wóihamnayan *richly*

gentle *adv* : asasya *or* asasyela *or* wasasyela *gently, slowly, mildly* — iktahela *carefully* — okun'onwašte *mild* — wahwa *quiet* - awahwayela *quietly* - wówahwala *gentleness* — paiwašteya *slowly, gently* — wawat'eca *being ~ as a ~ horse* - wawat'ecaka *one who is like a ~ horse* - Cf mild

geometry *n* : oisa *an angle* - oisa yamni *a triangle* — opesto *a point* — óhiye *a line* — ótatkonza *parallel or equal* — owokšan *a curve* — opuš'in *a convex curve* — owoslata *perpendicularity, height*

get *v* : aiglaptanyan *to ~ unexpectedly* — ayamna *to gain for one* — cank'inyan *to ~ firewood* — icu *to ~ or take* - icukiya *to cause one to receive and maintain self-control* — ikicicu *to take for one* — ikinica *or* ikinil *to try and ~ grabbing for something* - akicikta *to ~ or accept from another* - akta *or* ihakta *to ~ respect for* - oigloye *one's getting along, progress* - oiyaye *one's getting through e.g. a bad road*

get ready *v* : - *See* prepare

ghost *n* : nagi - nagiton *to make ghosts, i.e. to be haunted* - wanagi *a departed soul, a ghost*

gibbet *n* : opanakseye

gift *n* : wakic'unpi — wošpípikagapi *gift-giving at the Christmas tree*

gill *n* : iyoȟa *or* loȟe *the gills of fish*

gimlet *n* : - Cf drill under tool

girdle *va* : ipiyagkiton *or* ipiyagton *to be girded*

give *v* : ȟetkoza *to ~ as if rich but in fact poor* — hiyukiciya *to ~ handing to one his own* — iglat'e *to give one's self away* — iyahpekiya *to give or hand one e.g. a pipe* — wihpeya *to give away things* - wihpeyapi *a give-away* — akpagan *to ~ away one's own for some benefit* - akpaganyan *giving away for* - paganya *to cause to give away* — k'u *to give to one* - haok'u *to ~ , loan ones clothes* - ok'u *to ~ a portion, to lend* - k'uši *to command to ~* - k'uwacin *to be disposed to ~* - wók'u *to ~ food to , to lend* - wók'upi *a lending, giving away to* - wówicak'upi *an allowance, issue, offering* — akimnimniciyapi *each one's little bit they brought to give away, to make a present, a give-away* — anamni *to ~ way under foot* — otuh'an *to give a present* - otuh'anpi *a give-away* - otukih'an *to ~ to one a present* — ayukan *to yield to, give way to*

glad *va* : canteyawašte *to gladden one* - icanlwašte *to be ~ for* - icanlwašteya *gladly for* — wawapilakiya *to make ~ , or a good angel*

glance *v* : kagnayan *to strike and ~* — kaiyab *or* kašluta

to ~ off — wošluta *to make ~* — naohmin *to ~ off* — woglakinyan *to cause to ~* — woptanyan *to make ~ off, to ricochet*
glass *n* : janjan *a vial, a bottle, a drinking ~ , a pane of ~*
glaze *adj* : sinsin *glazed over*
glisten *adj* : léga *glittering* — wiyakpa *to glisten, shining* - wiyakpapi *brightness* - wiyakpayela *flashing* - awiyakpa *to glisten on anything*
glory *vn* : iwinkte *to be proud of* - iwinktepi *the taking of pride in something* - iwinkteya *to cause to ~ in, or glorying in* — yutan *to glorify one* — okitan'inyan *gloriously*
glow *vn* : ša hingla *to ~ as one's face*
glue *n* : ah'ayeton *to glue* — apuspapi *or* wíyaskabye *mucilage or solder* - kpuspa *to ~ one's own* — cúnpeška *or* conpeška *glue* - Cf solder
glut *v* : iyot'inst'ins *to glut* — nacantešilya *with yet a gluttonous feeling*
glutton *n* : iyaka *or* iyas'e *or* lotewašicun - waloteteke *gluttony* — wót'a *to die from gluttony, to glut one's self*
gnash *va* : yakiza *to grate one's teeth* - kiskiza *to ~ the teeth with a squeak* — yak'ega *to make a grating sound with the teeth*
gnaw *v* : otebya *to ~ on or into or at* — yak'oga *to bite off* - oyak'oga *to ~ off in* — yasmin *to ~ off, eat off* - yasminkiya *to cause to bite off e.g. meat from a bone* - oyasminyan *being gnawed at* — yak'eza *to ~ smooth* — yama *to bite off* - yameca *to chew* — yawaza *to nip one* - yawazeca *to ~ at* — wayawaja *to nip at playfully*
[1]go *v imper* : Akoecon *Go! Get away!* — Hánta *Get away! Begone!*
[2]go *v* :
gla *to go home*
akiyagla *they go home*
kiyagla *to have gone home*
glaši *to bid go home* - gligleyakel *going hither and yon*
gliyagla *to go from and return*
gliyoi *to go and get one's own*
gliyoya *to go take one's own home*
iyagle *to go or come to, to extend or reach to*
kigla *to have gone home*
kikigla *to go home and leave one*
oglicu *to go down in or from*
ogligle *going from place to place*
hošiai *to go there with a message*
hošihi *to arrive with a message*
hošii *to have been at to carry word*
hošiiyaya *to have gone there with word*
hošiya *to go to take a message*
hlahyeca *to ~ off a distance*
i *to have gone to or been at*
aihan *they go stand on something*
aitkob *adv* : *around* < aitkob i *or* u *to go or come around* >
akiwanyaka *to go and see one's own*
akiyagle *to go home, or they go or went straight home*
éokiyaka *to go there and tell*
iheya *to go or pass through*
íhca *to be sure to have gone to*
ímani *to go home*
itohekiya *to go on home*
itoheya *to go on to any place*
iyahan *to go up a hill and stand*
wahiyoi *to go for or after*
kigli *to go directly home*
kigni *he goes home,* wagni *I go home,* yagni *you go home*
makiglukšan *to go far, around the world*
iyaya *to have gone*
akil iyaya *to go hunting*
iyayekiya *to pretend to go away*
iyayeya *to send, to cause to go*
iyayuh *to go closely behind another*
iyohpaya *to go down from a hill, away from the speaker*
kahayeya *to go away, to leave*
timama iyaya *to go into more than one thing*
ya, bla, la, mni kte (*fut*) *to go to, to start for, to proceed*
kiciya *to go in place of another*
aohomni *to go around*
onamnimni *to be on the way*
waglamni *to go for, or after*
yekiya *to make go*

goad *or* **quicken** *va* : naoh'anko *to ~ by kicking*
goal *n* : oinajinta *the place of standing*
gobble *v* : yagob iyeya *to slurp eating or drinking*
go-cart *n* : hokšipaslohe
God *np* : Wakántanka - Tunkašila Wakantanka *the God-Head* — Ateyapi *the person of God the Father* - Ateunyanpi *our Father* — Cinca, Cinhintku *the person of the Son, the Father's Son* — Wóniyawakan *or* Wicakikcanpte *the person of the Holy Spirit* - Tawokonze Their Influence, by the three persons in God - Wówicakigna *Comforter, a title of the Holy Spirit, for a chief influence had upon all Creation*
good *adv* : ayuco *goodly, well, excellently* - ayucoya *or* ayucoyakel *well-done* — lilaka *good at or on, skilled* — picá *good* — picaka a *little ~ , little more good, better* — wašte *good* - awašte *to be ~ on or for, become better than* - awašteka *to be fit, be good for* - awašteya *well or better than* - awašteyakel *in a better manner* - ayuwašte *to make ~ on or for* - canlwašte *to be good, contented, to be happy* - canlwašteya *to make good of heart, to cheer one up* - iciwašte *to be ~ with or for* - igluwašte *to make reparations for one's own wrongs* - kiciwašte *to be ~ for* - kiciyuwašte *to make ~ for* - kiwaštešteka *being good to one* - waštehca *very good* - kiwašte *to become ~ , to convert to God* - okiciwašte *~ together, advantageous* - towašte *his or her goodness* - wašteka *good-hearted, a little ~* - wašteya *to make ~ , or doing well* - wówašte *goodness, grace* — yapi *to declare good* — yupi *to make ~* — šilyehci *a no-good thing* - Cf wakanka
goose-berry *n* : miniwicagnaška can *the water gooseberry bush*
gopher-hills *n* : wahinheyapablu
gorge *adv* : zunmiyankel *gorging one's self* — wípit'a *to ~ one's self* - Cf muskrat
Gospel *np* : Wótan'in Wašte *the Good News of Jesus Christ*
gossip *v* : oiglukiki *to backbite, complain* — šil'anagoptan *to spread ~* — yahomni *to believe anything on hearing and to carry on gossiping*
gouge *va* : pakpa *to ~ out, to pierce*
government *n* : wókiconze *governance* — wicoškanškan *rule, government* — itancan *a chairman or chairperson, a president, a chief*
grab *v* : wawiyahpaya *to attack or grip one, to seize one*
gracious *or* **benevolent** *v* : wacantkiya *to be ~ and generous with one's love* - wacantkiyapi *benevolence*
gradually *adv* : tokecela *~ out of weakness*
grain *n* : wayahota hinšmašma *barley, a spelt* — wagmeza *corn* — wagmeza nablaga *popcorn* — wahinske *Southern corn* — wahuapa *or* wahuwapa *or* wamunta *an ear of corn* — magahu *stalks* — waštunkala *dehydrated corn* — tašnaheca sinte *millet* — wayahota *oats or wild rice* — pteyaȟota *rye* — wayahota blaska

spelt — aguyapi su *wheat*
grandmother *n* : koškaunćihikaca *to be a ~* - *See* family
grape *n* : cunwiyapejiji *the yellow grape* - cunyapehe *the common grape*
grasp *va* : napogmuza - nap'kuwaš'aka *to ~ firmly* — yugnayan *to ~ at something*
grass *n* : peji *grasses in general* — wato *green grasses and weeds* — psa *pithy grasses* - Cf grain — wahpepeji *alfalfa* — psiska *barley* — hupestola *bayonet ~* — pejiša-ša swula *beard ~* — pejiblaskaska *ble ~* — pejišaša okihetankinkinyan *blue-stem ~* — pejihanskaskapsi iyececa *brome ~* - sipawicakaše *buffalo ~* — pejiiwicakoyaka *bullrush, or buffalo ~* — hohwa *calamus or watergrass* — pejiskuya *cockspur* — wabluškahuota peji *crab ~* — pejiȟota šicamna *goldenrod* — pejiokijata *or* wapahakamnimnila *grama ~* — pejišaša inkpajiji *Indian ~* — pejišicamna *June ~* — ptéga *lake-side ~* — pejisuksuta *or* santuhu *or* pinksihu *marsh ~* — pejiswula cik'ala *milkweed* — pejihinkpila *moss ~* — zintkala wipatapi *bird quill-work, a moss* — pejiinkpa *or* wayahota *oats* — pejiwakan *panic ~* — micapeca *or* wicapeca *porcupine ~* — psin *rice* — pejiokihetoto *river ~* — pejiswula *milkweed rush* — wanyecaswula *the horsetail rush* — pejitakan *rush grass* — psacinca *or* psaswula *the pithy rush or ~* — wanyecahutanka *scouring rush, pipe stem* — perjiȟota waštemna *pasture sage* — pejihcaka *salt ~* — unkcelapepe *sandbur* — santuhuhcaka *sand ~* — pejipsunpsunla *sedge* — celi *seed-grass* — mnipeji *slough ~* — iteašniyanpi *squirrel or fox-tail ~* — wó kahtan *sticktights, a small burr* — wiwilatapeji *swamp ~* — wa-canga *sweet ~* — hohwa *or* psa *water or rush ~* — peji-takankaza *wire ~* — iteawicašniyanhu *witch ~* — **Some Particulars** : pejiyuhinte *a hay rake* — pejiptaptaha *in stacks* — pejipaha *a hay stack* — pejioakšu *a whisp of hay* — pejioju *a lawn* — pejiokašla *or* pejionakseyapi *hay land, a meadow* — wiwila tapeji *spring grass* — pejognake *a hayloft*
grate *vn* : kiza *to creak* - kisyela *with a grating sound* - k'éga *to scrape* — kak'ega *to make grate*
grateful *adj* : canl'ope - canl'opeya *in a thankful manner* - olabya *gratifyingly* — wapila *to be ~* - wapilapi *gratitude* - wapilapišni *or* wapilašni *to be ungrateful* - wawapilaya *to give cause for gratitude, to do a favor*
gratuitous *adv* : ituya *or* ituyakel *gratuitously* - Cf free
gravel *n* : iswula
graying *adv* : osansanke s'e
graze *v* : oyatoto *to crop* — kanwinla iyeya *to brush by*
grease *vn* : asla *to apply lard* - aslaya *to ~, with ~* - nasla *to ~ by foot* - osla *to be greased in* - ihaislaye *lip ointment* — iyuton *or* iyunton *to add ~ or lard* — igli *or* wigli *oil*
great *adj* : iyutepicašni *immense, large* — šogya *or* šogyeh *greatly* — tánka *big* - otanka *greatness, or large, broad* — iyotanyan *greatly* — otancan *the greatest* - otancanke *the greatest in number* - otancankeya *in greatest numbers* - otankayaka *greatness* - tankakiya *largely* - tankala *to consider ~* - tankaya *to a ~ extent* - tankinyan *very great or large, important* - tanktanka *very great* - watanka *a great and rich person* - watankala *to esteem ~*
greed *vn* or *adj* : akaska *to be greedy, greedy* — amnanyan *to gather and add something to* — išicawacin *to want more, to be greedy* - tawacinšilwote *to eat greedily* — wakijanignica šni *greediness*
greeting *n* : hoakicipapi *a salutation*
grid *n* : - Cf network
grim *or* **serious** *v* : kaiteyešni *to make ~*
grimace *v* : natogyeya *to frown at one*
grin *v* : itešinkiya to frown
grind *va* : ahiglahtaka *to ~ one's teeth or with the teeth* — ayak'ega *to gnaw on something* — higlakiskiza *to grate the teeth* - higlakokoka *to gnash or shatter the teeth* — ikabluya *crushing fine, to crush to dust* — inakuka *or* inasli *to crush or destroy with the feet* — apakpan *or* ayukpan *to ~ and make fine on* - kiciyukpan *to ~ (as corn) for* - yukpanpi *a grinding* - yukpanyan *to make ~* - nakpan *to ~ under foot* — naponyan *to crush, grind by foot* — owanatanye *a grinding mill* — agluman *to ~ one's own upon* - ayuman *to ~ something on* - akiciyuman *to ~ e.g. an axe for* - Cf pulverize
grip *v* : wiyuhloka *to take a ~ on* — yupaga *to ~ something tightly*
groan *va* : wašicahowaya *to cry out something*
groom *v* : iglasto *to ~ one's self* — kisinc'iya *to tidy up one's self*
groove *va* : paškokpa *to make a ~, a cavity, by hand, sitting* — wakonta *to rout something* - wakontkonta *to make in ridges* - kuntkunta *grooved*
grope *v* : yutantankel mani *to ~ as does a blind man*
ground *v* : tokakayešni *or* tokaniyešni *to be grounded, without means of travel* — makiyagle *to hold to the ~* - makiyeya *to push aground* - makokahciyela *floating about on the ground* - Cf earth
group *n* : cannunge *a bunch, a lump on a tree* — cincoga *bunches, clumps as driftwood along a stream* - cincopamna *a bunch of children with their parents* — kaiȟeya *grouping in bunches* — okašpetontonyan *by or in bunches* - ošpašpaye *or* wilwita *in or by groups*
grow *or* **growth** *n* : haoyuh'u — icaga *to ~* - oicaga *to ~ in or up* - oicage *a growing, a generation, creation* - icahkiya *or* icahya *to raise, rear, train up* — kaowanya *to develope, increase* - ikicicaga *to to ~ for one* - wawicahya *to form or create, cause to grow* - ikicaga *to ~ to be, to become* — koyanun *of quick growth, precocious* — oju *a growth, a field* — uya *to ~ or spring up* - uyekiya *to cause to ~ or spring up*
growl *va* : ayabu — hlo *to ~* - hlokiya *to make ~* - hloya *to make ~, or growling* - kihlo *to ~ over something*
gruff *adj* : jahan *harsh of voice* - jahe s'e *harshly, noisily, unpleasantly*
grumble *v poss* : oikcapta *to talk angrily to one's self* — wakahtakeke *a grumbler* — oie pepeka *a person's grumbling, sharp or bitter words*
grunt *v* : glo *the frequent ~ of buffalo* — hna *to ~ or snort as one might do when angry* — t'inga *to snivel and ~ as a woman in labor* - kat'inhya *to grunt on collapsing* - nat'inhyeya *to cause to ~ as in the throes of childbirth*
guage *n* : - Cf meter, measure
guard *n* : iwakta *to be on the lookout* - iwaktaya *to put on one's ~, to admonish, or guardedly, expecting* - waktaya *to put on ~, or being on ~*
guardian *n* : cannakseyuha *a policeman* — iawanyanka to watch over — manitukala *a little ~ spirit, commonly called a guardian angel*
guess *v* : oyama *Take a guess.* — yukcanyan *guessing*
guest *adv* : titokanl *as a guest, ~ u* to come as a guest
guillemot *n* : hoka *the thick billed ~, Brunnich's murre*
guilt *v* : awaic'ihtani *to sin and so abuse one's self with ~*
gully *n* : wakogla *a ravine*
gum *n* : canšinkahpu *pine gum, sap* - siyonatica *to be gummy, sticky*
gun *n* : hútela *a pistol* — mázawakan *or* mázakan *a*

rifle – mazakan'i *a muzzle* – mazakan'inunpa *a double-barreled ~* – mazakan'iyopazan *a metal sleeve for a gun, i.e. ferrules* – mazakan'iyopuhli *gun-wadding* – mazakannawate *a gun lock* – mazakannoge *the pan or nipple* – mazakanpahu *the breech* – mazakanšupute *the butt* – mazakan'uta *to fire a gun* — wanhioštanpi *a flintlock* — cahli *gunpowder*
gurgle *v* : ogmunheca *fitting loose and suggesting a gurgling sound* — okaco *to make a gurgle* — oyagloglo *to ~ as water in a pipe* — yugwoggwog *with a stifled sound*
gut *n* : tašup'okahmi *a gut cavity*

H

habit *vn* : ayaic'iya *to have a ~ of doing* — owangic'iya *to be in the ~ of, or habitual*
hackling *adj* : wot'óga *rasping*
hail *n* : wasu – *v* : to hail — wah'eca *shot-like hail*
hair *n* : aške *a tuft of ~ grown on the side of the head* – heašketon s'e *with the braids standing out sideways* — hin *the general word for hair* – hinhte *thick ~* – hínjijila *thin ~ as on arms and hands* – hinkaciceyela *with ~ matted* – hinkpila *short hair as on hides taken* – hinnasakiya *to have hair standing on end when a dog is about to attack* – hinoškušku *to shed old hair* – hinpahla *a bunch of old thrown buffalo ~* – hinyajice *down, swan's down* – iyoȟahin *whiskers* – itecinhin *facial ~* — hpihpi s'e *flapping in the wind* — iškogin *a sheath of ~ on a horse's ankle* — ítoye *or* ítowe *or* ítoe *the forelock* — ítoewoblu *or* ítoeyuh'o *to have the ~ stand up on the head* – okahi *~ bangs* – okahika *one wearing bangs* – okahiya *to make bangs* — páha *~ of the head* — paštan *to de-hair a hide* – pehin *hair of the head* — pínja *hairless* — ptehinpahpa *tags of buffalo ~* — tukahan *losing its hair, scabby* – tuktukahan *having lost the spoiled hair* — wakih'anke *a hair stylist, a worker in hair* — GROOMING : aškiyuwi *or* hehute *a hairband* – waške *a ~ string or fastener* — natipasise *a hairpin* – pehin'icasto *a hairbrush* – pehin'islaye *hair-oil* – pehin'iyostola *a hair- net* – pehinpapoa *a hairbrush* – pehinpasise *a hairpin* — gugukašla *with hair hacked* — yugmiyus *holding the ~ or held by the hair*
half *n* : hanke *a part of* – wócantehahayela *half-heartedly* – hankeya *to halve, divide something* — icisannicab *to have made over a half of one's way* – iyakasanni *one side or a ~ of something* — iyokise *~ of what is cut in two* – okise *~ or anything* – okiseya *in half* — okiwašpa *or* okiwašpu *to cut something in two*
halt *v refl* : ogluksa *to stoop abruptly in one's speech* — patagya *haltingly* — nat'ungyakel *hesitatingly as if afraid* — kokipeya *timidly* — kipable *to come to a halt as in flight*
hand *n* : nape – napagle *to put a ~ on* – napaglepi *a span* – napakaha *a ~ guard put on the left wrist* – napata *by the ~* – napeapaha *to raise the ~ to strike* – napaglujaja *to wash one's own hands* – napeicicaška *to tie one's hands* – napeikpahin *to lie pillowing the head on the ~* – napekicoza *to beckon, gesticulate waving the hand(s)* – napekoza *to beckon, waving the hand* – napekšikša *to have the hands numb with the cold* – napeoicu *handwriting* – napeojula *or* napogna *a handful* – napeyekiya *or* istoyeya *to stretch out the hand to* – napeyupšunka *the fist or to clench the fist* – napeyuza *to shake hands* – napikceyakel *by hand* – napiškan *to put the ~ to evil* – napiyagleya *to lay a ~ on* – napiyayus *held in the ~* – napiyeya *to have a ~ in* – napiyusya *to ~ over, to make hold* – napiyuzeca *to take into one's own ~* – napkicoza *to wave the ~ to* – napkoza *to wave the ~* – napognaka *to put into the ~* – napsanni *the ~ on one side* – onape *hand, or in hand* — pastoihpaya *to fall on hands and knees* — yuge *to take a handful* — PARTS OF THE HAND : napahunka *the thumb* – napakazan *fingers, claws* – napcoka *the palm* – napcokanyan *the middle finger* – napepinkpa *the tip of the finger* – napeyupšunka *the fist, or to clench the fist* – napitakaha *or* nap'itakaha *the back of the hand* – napokazunte *fingers* — napsu *a finger* – napsuhu oko *the spaces between the fingers* – *also* napsuokaza *fingers, claws* – napsuokiha *the knuckles* — oguye *or* yuge *a handful*
handkerchief *n* : pahlipakinte
handle *n* : ihupa *a bail* ihupakiton *to ~ one's own* – ihupakiciton *to put in a ~ for one* – ihupaton *to have a ~ to anything* — iyuhomni *a knob* – iyuze *a holder* – oiyuspe *or* ooyuspe *a ~ of any sort*
handsome *adj* : oȟopa *attractive* — tanwašte *of fine form*
hang *or* **suspend** *v* : hpi *to ~ down, or hanging down* — naakahliyeya *to ~ out* — kamnimni *to dangle, to swing, to ~ loosely as a blanket* — kceya *to ~ over and cook* — ohci *to dangle* – ohcihci *dangling* – ohcihcikes'e *raggedly* – ohcihciya *to make dangle* — okahi *to ~ over* – aokahi *to ~ over on* – aokahiya *through hanging hair* – okahiya *to make ~ over e.g. the face* — otka *to ~ from* – otke *to be hung up* – ótkeya *to ~ up something, to advertise* — panakseya *to hang a person* — paozeze *to be hanging as berries on a bush* — zeze *hanging* – zezeya *swinging* – Cf dangle
hanger *or* **poles** *v* : satkaksa *to cut poles* — wiotkeye *a hook or cord ~*
hanger-on *vn* : wagluȟe *to be a ~*
hanker *v* : was'in *to hanker for* – wawas'in *one who hankers for things*
happen *va* : akipaya *to cause to occur, befall one* — séhingla *so happening, ~ to* — tóka kte *something may ~*
happily *adv* : kan'iyeyapi s'e *cheerfully, without difficulties*
harangue *v* : waiyakapeya *to spout off*
hard *adj* : kamasya *hard as iron* — kašpepipicašni hard to chip — nainyanyeya *become rock-like* — osuta *hardened* — ayuk'oza *to make hard and smooth on* – onak'oza *to harden by tramping on* — ot'oza *hard packed* – ot'oja *hard, said of a surface* — sáka *dry, stiff* – asaka *to become dry and hard on* – sagya *to make ~ or stiff* – yusaka *to make a stiff hide soft by flexing it* – tasakaya *to stiffen, or hardened* – tasaka *stiff, frozen* — oš'aka *to get stiff* — súta *hard* – aglasuta *to make one's own firm* – kicisuta *to become ~ for* – nasuta *to trample ~* – wosúta *to harden by ramming* – wateȟika *~, difficult in dealings, dear or treasured* — ayuk'eza *to make ~ and smooth by shaving off hair* – Cf firm
hardly *adv* : kitiyus'eya *or* ecinyan *barely*
hardware *n* : iyopazan *a bushing, a ferrule* — iyokatkuge *a nail, a screw, bolt and nut* – mazaiyokatkuge *a metal nut for a bolt* – wíyokatkugye *a wood-screw* – wícatkuhye *a hub-nut* — mázahlahla *a bell* – máziciyokihe *or* mázicukeya *a chain* – mázapepe *or* más'apepe *barbed wire* – mázapošla *a tack* – mázapsonpsonla *wire* – mázazazeca *wire screen* – más'iyume *a file* – ógliyotke *a screw-eye* — aokatan *to nail on* – mázaiyokatan *or* máz'iyokatan *or* was'wiyokatan *a nail, nails* – íokatan *to nail one thing on another*

hardy *adj* : - Cf sturdy
harlot *n* : witkowinla
harm *v* : ocinkiwakan *to speak bringing ~* - Cf injure, hurt
harvest *n* : wasutonpi *the grain ~* — wóksapi *the ~ husking of corn*
haste *va* : húhniyeya *to hasten one* - hníyeye s'e *with ~* — tannikta s'e *in great ~* — wíš'oš'o *hasty* — yuoȟankoya *hastening*
hat *n* : wapoštan - wapoštiyut'inze *a hat-band*
hatch *vn* : ikpakpi
hate *v* : oyusinka *to be out of humor with* - oyusinyan *being out of humor with* - wawoyasin *to be out of humor* - wawoyasinke *one who hates* — šícakila *to ~ one's own* - šícakiya *or* šilkiya *to think low of* - šillá *to esteem bad*
haughty *n* : watankaic'ilapi *haughtiness* — wawimnašniyan *haughtily* - Cf wimna šni
haul *v* : otokšku *to transport, or hauling, transportation* - watokikšu *to ~ one's own*
haunt *vn* : nagiton
have *va* : yuha *to possess, lift, having, carrying with one, to give birth to* - kiyuha *to keep or have for one* - yuhakiya *to make one ~* - yuhaya *having* — iyoyas'in *with, wearing, bearing*
hay *n* : - *See* grass
he she it *pron* : íye *he/she, or emph* iš, iyéš, íyeeš - iyékaeš *even he/she* - íyeškalaka *he himself/she herself* - kae *that is he/she* — iyéštuka *he\she who ought*
head *n* : pa *the generic name for the top end of something, and for the nose and beak* - pe *or* peslete *the top of the head* - ipesletanhan *from the ~ end* - oitancan *a head man* - oitancanyan *at the head* — oyatkankan *to come to a head* — SOME SPECIFICS : pacola *without a ~* - págnagya *headed right for* - pahu *the ~ of anything* - pahukul *with ~ down* páhute *the junction of ~ and neck* - pakas'in *to raise one's ~, or to be with ~ raised* - pákuciyela *or* pakutagleya *with head down* - pamagle *with bowed ~* - pámahel *with ~ covered* - páska *white headed* - pásla *bald-headed* - pašlá *to make bare, to rub off* - payata *in or at the ~* - pazán *or* pasán *with ~ concealed* — pókimnamna *to shake the ~ contin-ually at* - póksan *to shake the ~ to right to left* - pómnamna *to shake the ~ in denial* - pómnamnakiya *to wag the ~ at, or to cause one to wag the ~* - póptanptan *to shake the ~ in dissent* - póšlicoma *to have the ~ covered with a blanket* - tannakekiya *with the ~ to one side*
headdress *n* : wapaha - wapahahetonpi *a horned headdress* - wapahaheyuga *a branched-horned ~* - magawapaha *a ~ of goose feathers* - wapaha iyušloheton *a warbonnet with one tail* — wapegnaka *a ~ of any sort*
heal *vn* : ókiyuta *to heal up* - naokiyuta *to close up e.g. a wound* — okizi *to recover from hurt or wound* - okiziya *to cause to make well*
health *n* : owicakuja *an unhealthy local or house* — tanzani *in health and sound* - tanzanike *in good ~* - zanni *well, sound* - tanzaniyan *whole* - ozanniyankel *or* zanniyan *in good health* - wózanni *health* - zannika *healthy*
heap *adv* : pšunkaya *in a ~* - pškunkayakel *in a bunch, drawn together*
hear *va* : anagoptan *to listen to or obey* - anakicigoptan *to listen for one* - anakigoptan *to listen to one's own, to obey* - anongoptan *to listen to one* - anonhkeciya *to try to listen to something* - nonhkatiyece *to hear suddenly* - nonhpekic'unšniyan *with hearing unimpeded* - nonhwazaza *to ~ only snatches* - nonh'opaya *in one's hearing* - ononh'hoyeya *to listen with one's own ears* - nunh's'a *to listen well* — gluiyupse *to take a hold of one's own (ears)* — hóinkpala *being barely audible at a distance* - hótan'in *to have one's voice heard* - Iho! *Listen now!* — nah'on *to hear something* - nakicih'on *to listen for* - nakih'on *to ~ one's own* - onah'on *to ~ a report, to hear of, or a hearing* - nah'onya *to announce to* - wanah'onpi *a hearing* - owanah'on *that which causes one to hear* - šilwanakih'on *to hear bad said of one* — yakpa *hard of hearing* — yasupišniyan *without a hearing*
heart *n* : cante - cantehuta *the aorta* — cantekiciciyapi *love of each other* - cantekiya *to have an affection for* - cantekiyapi *benevolent love* - cantekiyuza *to hold a given disposition* — canteogin *or* cantogin *the heart's pericardium* - canteokihidšniya *to have ~ failure* — canteonšika *low-spirited* — canteoyusya *with the whole ~* - cantewašte *to be glad* - cantewašteya *cheerfully, or to make glad* — canteyazan *heartsick* — cantihangya *to cause heartache* — cantiyokipiya *hearty, or heartily* — cantognagya *to place in the ~* - cantognawaya *in a loving manner* — canyanka *to be heartsick, to groan* - icante *in or at the ~* — icantognaka *purposely to put in the heart*
heat *v* : kátkiya *or* kálkiya *to ~ one's own* - kalya *to ~ e.g. rocks* — ololuta *sultry, or muggy atmosphere in* — omašte *to be hot in, or styfling hot air in*
heaven *n* : mahpiya *the heavens, the cloud(s), the afterlife of mankind* — CELESTIAL BODIES AND PHENOMENON : anpetu wi *or* anpawi *the sun* - anpowicahpi *the morning star* - hanhepiwi *the moon* - hohetamahpiya *the northern lights* - mahpiya *the heavens, clouds* - wi *sun or moon* wicahpi *a star* - wiyošala *the aurora borealis, the northern lights* — CONSTELLATIONS : Matotipila *the eight stars about Gemini* - Tayamni *Orion and the Pleiades* - Wanagitacanku *the Milky Way or the Spirit Road* - Wiaceic'iti *the Sundogs* - Wicakiyuhapi *the Big Dipper*
heavy *adv* : kahluhlata *hanging in abundance* - kasabyela *heavily in weight or fatigue* — tka *heavy* - tkeya *heavily*
heed *v poss* : akikta *to give ~ to* — wanagoptan *to heed* - anakicigoptan *to give ~ to for one* - anakigoptan *to listen to one's own, to obey* — kiwaš'agpica šni *one who acts heedlessly* — piyeleš *heedlessly, notwithstanding* — wanah'onšniyan *not hearing or listening to another, not heeding advice offered*
height *n* : - Cf high
help *v* : anakicikšin *to come to one's aid* — ekiciyaku *to ~ one load on the back* - ékiciglaku *to ~ load one another* — ícinakšin *to help standing up for others* — ic'ih'an *to ~ extricate one's self* — iic'ikçu *to ~ take what one is to have* - ikiya *to aid taking another's side* - iciya *to take sides with* - oic'iya *to ~ one's self* - okiciya *to ~ another* — ókiya *to ~ one* - wawokiya *to ~ accompanying another* — wice-ya *to apply for ~* — ocinkiwakan *to be unwilling to ~* - ocinwakan *unwilling to help out* — oókihi *to be able to help* — tawowaši *a helper or servant*
hem *n* : upí
hence *adv* : iwatukte *from hence* — lehankalkatanhan *or* lehankata *hither*
herb *n* : blayezitkatacan hustola *clover* — ceyaka *or* heȟakatapejuta *a mint* — hiiyat'inze *cloves* — peji ȟota *gray grass, wild sage* - Cf medicine, grass
herd *v* : kaȟapa *to ride herd* — opawiya *in a ~* - *optaye* a herd, or in a bunch - ptehiyapa *to herd* — ošpaye *a mixed ~* - ošpayetontonya *in groups, droves* — wayašlakiya *to drive a ~*
here *adv* : éna - enanakiya *here and there* - enanatanhan *from here and there* - gligleyake *here and there* — le

here – léci *here in this place* – léciyatan *from this place, from here* – léciyatanhan *from here, on this side* – lel *in this place* – létu *at this place or time, now* – léogna *around here*

hermaphrodite *n* : winkte *a living thing with a complete reproductive system*

hesitate *adv* : kokipeya *hesitatingly* — nat'ungyakel *carefully as though fearful* – nat'unka *to hold back, hesitate* — wotíti *or* wotitikel *unsteadily, irresolutely, in a shaky manner*

hew *v* : kakan – kicicakan *to ~ for* – okakan *to ~ in* — kataptapa *to ~ rocks*

hiccough *or* **hiccup** *vi* : blokaską

hide *adv* : aisinyan *out of sight* — nahma *to conceal anything* – oinahme *a place to ~* – nakicihma *to conceal for one* – nakihma *to ~ one's own* – anahma *to hide something* – anahmanpi *a concealment* – anahmeya *in a hidden manner* – anahmneyahan *secretly* – ínahma *to seduce, fornicate, or commit adultery* – inahmekiya *to hide from one* – anakihma *to conceal one's own, refuse to tell* – anakihmanpi *a concealing, a denial, or concealed* – anakihmeya *to cause to conceal, or covertly* – anakihmeyahan *privately, stealthily* — anawinyan *stealing up secretly taking a round-about route, fig concealing by circumlocution* — aoginton *to ~ making things indistinct* — inabya *or* inakikšin *taking refuge in* — inapa *to take shelter* — ioblula *or* iyoblula *a sheltered place, or in a sheltered way* — yuptinapeyakel *shielded from as in hiding* — ptehašla *a buffalo ~ (skin or hide)* – taha *deerskin* – tahakalala *a buckskin dress* – tahalo *a hide* – tahaopahloke *slit holes for stretching ~* – tahape *tanned ~* – tahapenapinkpa *fur mittens* – tahapewapoštan *a fur cap* – tahasaka *dried skin, parchment* – tahasopi *leather strings* – tahahin *hair of buffalo or deer* – tahuka *green buffalo ~* — uka *skin, ~ without hair* – ha *skin or ~ with hair* — tehpi *skin used as a blanket* – ptehašla *buffalo ~ without hair* — tahaiyokatan *to stretch a ~* — tahincacice *or* tahinpaguke *also* ptehcaka hinyete *(a very handy buffalo shoulder) or* tahinpakince *also* tahcatahinpakince *a tool used to remove hair* — tahokške *a ~ stretcher* — tahokatan *to stretch for tanning* — tahmisoha *or* tehpiceha *or* wahašla *a tanned ~* — wahapahpa *to flesh a ~ when yet fresh* – wahatka *to scrape a dry ~* — tahakpanyan *to tan a ~* — tahayuštašta *to soak a ~* — wahinyuton *to rub gall, marrow etc. on a ~*

high *adj* or *adv* : gliheya *steep, or steeply* — ȟuhcincayela *very ~ or far away* — kaipazilya *highly* — konatke *~ or tall* — owoslata *height* — pajola *~ in the center* e.g. of the hoad — tehanwankatu *~ up, very high* – wankalkatuya high in stature – wankapaya *~ up, in a ~ position* – wankatakiya *~ upwards* – wankatu *or* wankatuya *~ up*

hill *n* or *adj* : apableca *a small ~ next to another thus forming a ridge* – apaha he *on a low ~, or fig on the one side of the rump* – apahalaka *a low ~, hill-like* – apajola *a little rise of the ground* – akicipa *a flat tableland* — hepiya *the side or flank of a ~* — ȟe *a mountain* – ȟébloka *a hilltop or ridge* – ȟehukul *the bottom or foot of a ~* – ȟeinkpa *the brink or brow of a hill* – ȟeipa *the brow of a hill* – ȟekpankpanla *hilly land* – ȟeku *the foot of a hill back from a river* – ȟémayacan *a wooded ~* – ȟenagi *a hill's shadow* – ȟeohlate *the foot of a big ~* – ȟeunnaptan *a hillside* – ínyanȟe *a rocky ~* – ȟehepiya *partway up a hill* – ȟétakiya *toward the hills* –ȟeyatanhan *on top of a ~* — paha *a mound, hill* – pahapajola *a prominent ~* – pahata *at or on the hill*

hinder *v* : kagi *to stop progress, be in one's way* – kagišni *without hindrance* — ókaš'agya *prevented* — onc'unnilya *to stop or ~ one from doing* — opanhya *to impede one for something being bulky* – opanhyela *being bulky for things poorly arranged*

hint *or* **insinuate** *v* : ikuteka *to throw (shoot) hints* — ohomnikuwa *to ~ at* — yaohmin *to insinuate*

hippopotamus *n* : wamnitu – animal

hire *n* : olotapi un *a hireling* — yuhapi *held, owned* – Cf borrow, own

his hers its *pron adj pref* or *suff* : ta... , *as in* táwa – ...ku, *as in* atkúku – Note: *ta* is ante-positive, whereas *ku* is post-positive

hiss *or* **fizz** *vn* : nasli *to ~ as wet wood in the fire* — šli *hissing* — s'a *to ~ like a snake might do* – kas'a *to make ~*

hit *vn* or *n* : iwohtaka *to strike or bump against, or a hit* — iwowanka o *to glance off and strike, hit another* — íyapat'ola *to butt against or to be cramped by* – íyapat'oya *to run against, to prevent one* – íyapat'oyakel *cramping together* – iyapaya *to run, be thrown against* – iyab *to strike or collide against something* — okakapa *to hit something into* — okama *or* okasluta *to hit the center, as in shooting* — oyumaza *to make a hit on target* – oglumaza *to hit one's own mark* – yusaksaka *to ~ from a distance while whipping*

hitch *n* : okaške *a place to tether, moor*

hoarse *adj* : hógita – hoglagita *to make one's self ~ by talking* – hoiglagita to make one's self ~ by speaking – iglahogita *to become ~ from speaking* – yagita *to become ~* – hoiyóhpaya *to become ~ from wind blowing on one* – hójahan *raucously, hoarsely*

hobbles *n* : huipahte

hoe *va* : akata – aglata *to hoe one's own* – akateya *to cause to hoe* – akicicata *to hoe for one* — maȟakata *to hoe e.g. corn* – mahkašla *to ~ a field*

hold *v* : yúza *or* yus *to catch, take ~ of, to take a wife* – agleyuza *to ~ against or near to, to come near to* – akiyuza *to seize* – akiyuzapi *to hold or seize anything* – igluzeze *to ~ up one's self by, to cling to* – igluzezeya clinging to – iyayus *or* iyayuza *to ~ to, or a holder* – iyuza *to ~ on or to by hand* – kiciyuza *to ~ for* — nap'anunk yuza *to take ~ with both hands* — oyuzapekiya *to make lay ~ of, catch* – oyuzaya *laying ~ of* — akinica *to ~ for one* – ayuha *to ~ or lift on* — anahlata *to ~ on carefully as a man to a horse* — ayugata *or* ayugal *to ~ up, raise the hands and arms extended* — ognala *holding only a bit* – oognake *a holder* — wa-yuhoho *to ~ loosely, awkwardly* — yugnagnayan *to take a loose ~ on* — yukannaksa ikanton *to keep a firm ~ on*

hole *va* : ayuhloka *to make a ~ on or open on* – gluhloka *to make a ~ in one's own* – hlohloka *full of holes* – hlohlokahan *perforated with holes* – kahlokaya *to make a ~* – kiciyuhloka *to open a ~* – nahloka *to make or wear a ~ with the foot* – ohloka *a hole* – okahloke *a cut or gash made by striking* – onahloka *to make a ~ by or in the foot* – opahloke *a hole* – owahloka *to cut a ~ in* – owohloke *a ~ made by punching* – oyahloke *a ~ bitten in* – wahloka *to cut a ~ in* — ayuȟuga *to break a ~ in* — ganganla *full of holes* — kakpa *to make a ~ , i.e. pluck out* – kicakpa *to strike into making a ~ for one* – ikpakpi *to pick a ~ , to hatch* – okpikpi *slit-like* — kaoksa *to cut a ~* — kokicašpa *to dig two holes into, or to shoot twice in some place* — oko *a crack, an aperture, a space* — wopóta *to make holes by shooting*

holler *v* : hokiton *to use the voice, as in drawing attention to a person afar off*

hollow *v* : jipa *to smoothen, clear off* — kah'akpa *to ~ out* — škokpa *hollowed out* - kaškokpa *to ~ out* — makowakic'ipa *a shallow depression in the prairie land* — opahci *a gully* — oskiske *a draw* — smáka *a sunken place* - osmaka *a sink, a ditch, a ravine or valley* - wasmaka *to make an indent or ~ with a knife* - wayusmaka *to indent or ~ out* — paopo *to push up to make a ~ place*

holocaust *n* : wahugnahya waunyanpi *a burnt sacrifice*

home *v* : to come or bring ~ — aglekiya *to make take ~* — agli *to arrive at ~, or they came back* - agliceti *to come ~ and start a fire* - aglihunni *to take straight back ~, or they arrived coming straight back* - aglihpeya *to leave on the way ~* - agliiyape *to await their coming ~* - aglinajin *they came ~ and stood there* - aglinapa *to bring out one's own* - aglipsica *they come ~ and dismount* - agliti *they come ~ and stay (camp)* - aglitokicikšu *to bring along for one coming ~* - agliwanyanka *they come back ~ to see their own* - agliwota *to stop for a meal on the way ~* - agliyacu *to be on one's way bringing something, or they are on their way ~* - agliyagla *to pass by with something to a place or they passed by* - agliyaglahan *they continue to pass by going ~* - agliyahan *they came up a hill in sight of their ~* - agliyaku or agliyacu *to come ~ with something, or they come ~ together* - agliyohi *they reach ~ on returning* - agliyotaka *they stopped somewhere on the way ~* - agliyugo *to arrive ~ tired* - agliyuhpa *to come ~ and unload* - agliyukan *they come ~ and stay* - agliyunka *to come ~ and sleep, or they camped on the way ~* — aglogla *to carry ~* — ahiyagle *to bring ~ and place on, or to be brought and set on, or to come and go on toward ~* — aki *to arrive ~ carrying something, or they reached ~* — gligni *to come or go along towards one's ~* - glihunni *to reach ~ coming straightway* - glinunwan *to arrive ~ swimming* - glitan'inka *to arrive ~ suddenly* - gliu *to be coming ~* - glicu or gliyacu *to be on one's way back ~* - gliyahan *to show up on a hill in sight of my ~* - gliyahpaya *to come ~ and fall upon one* - gliyaku *to start to come ~, to return ~* - gli-yokpeca *to return ~ from somewhere* - gliyotaka *to sit down on the way ~* - gliyou *to come to take one's own ~* — glogli *to arrive ~ with one's own* - glokiyagla *to go ~ taking one's own* — akiceti *to arrive ~ start a fire* — aku *to come bringing ~* — gloku *to come ~ with one's own* — hošigla *to go ~ carrying news* - hošigli *to arrive ~ with news* - hošiglicu *to be on the way ~ with news* - hošiglihunni *to reach ~ with a message* - hošikagla *to be on the way home with word to one* - hošikagli *to arrive ~ with a message to one* - hošikaki *to arrive back somewhere with word to one* - hošikaku *to bring a message ~ to one* - hoši-ki *to have reached ~ with a message* - hošiku *to be coming ~ with a message* — ignigla *to go ~ for* — tiglonica *to forbid entrance to one's ~* — tigluhlaganšni *to stay always at home* - títika or títutuka *to feel at home* - tiyohiyukša *to stay indoors most of the time* - tatiwokitahena or tiwokitahena *homeless*

hoop *n* : tahogmi *a ~ on which a hide is stretched*

holy *adj* : wakan *sacred, special* - awakan *to be sacred or incomprehensible on some account, or a supernatural being* - ayuwakan *to consecrate, make sacred for* - iwakanyan *supernaturally*

hominy *n* : wóšlešlecapi - Cf vegetable

honest *adv* : wacinnunpašniyan *honestly* — zonta *trustworthy* - zontaheca *an ~ person* - zonlyakel *honestly* - wózunte *honesty, a doing rightly*

honor *va* : ohola *to respect, ~, or worship one* — okinihan *honorably, or to select for praise* - wókinihan *one's share or part* — wešlekapi *the wearing of honors* — wicayuwintapi *the giving a title of ~* — wópakan *to be honored* — wówitan *pride, glory* - wowitanyan *proudly, or to glory in* — yaonihan *to ~ one, or praising* - yuonihan *to treat one with honor, attention, politeness*

hoof *n* : - Cf nail

hook *v* : iyuhlata *to catch hold with e.g. a ~* - kahlata *to catch with a sharp ~ or as a hawk with its claws* — kacangle iyeya *to ~ a hoop* — wíyotkeye *a peg*

hoot *vn* : hinhanhoton *to ~* - hinhankaga *to ~ as an owl*

hop *v* : hóšnašnakic'un *to ~ on one leg, as in a game* - Cf jump, skip

hope *va* : ape *to ~ for*

horn *n* : he *an animal ~* - héhlogeca *hollow-horned* - hepola *a buffalo bull's ~* - heton *horned* - heyuha *animals with branching horns* - heyuktan *bent-horned, or an animal with bent horns*

horse *n* : šúnkawakan

NAMES and DESCRIPTIONS :

hecenicala *a yearling colt*
hínhpihpila *a buffalo or horse having shed its winter hair*
hín'ikceka or hinkceka *a dark bay horse*
hínpahin *a mouse-eared ~*
hinštan *a chestnut-colored ~*
hinša or hinšaša *a sorrel ~*
hinto *a gray ~*
hínzi *a buckskin ~*
hínziša *orange ~*
hinum uya or makicima *a two-year old colt, or a young horse*
itewatogla *a ~ sensitive to its head*
iwaglamna *a spare ~*
iyak'oza *a large-knuckled ~*
okasakeciyatan *the right, the whipping ~ to bear the load*
onaš'ola or šung'onaš'o *a pacing ~*
šungbloka *a stud ~*
šunghula *a pony, a shetland pony*
šungleška *a spotted ~*
šungmakicima *a young ~*
šungnankpogi *a brown-eared ~*
šungnini *a wild ~*
šungwinyela *a mare*
šunkcecahušte *a ~ lame in the hip*
šunkcincala *a colt*
šunkhinša *a sorrel ~*
šunkhula *a short-legged ~*
šunkluzahan *a race ~*
šunknuni *a wild ~*
šunksikoška *a swollen-footed ~*
šunkšan *an old worn-out ~*
šunktahuwaš'aka *a strong-necked ~*
šunktamaka *a lean ~*
šunk'okah *horse-shaped*
šunk'okasak'suta *a stubborn ~*
šunk'onaš'ake *a worn-out ~*
šunk'onaš'ola *a pacing ~*
šunk'onjinca *a bob-tail ~, or rich in horses*
wako or waunjinca *a ~ with a cut tail*
wohe or iyak'oza *a large-knuckled ~*
apeyohan *the horse's mane*
sinte *the tail*
šunkmanišnikiya *to walk as a played out ~*
šunkkoyakya *to rope a ~*
šunkaštaka *to abuse a ~*
šunmniyata áya *to water the horses*
HARNESS : ic'in *a harness*

cakipatan *a bit*
ic'in'ikan *the lines*
ic'inpasu *the hame*
ic'inyuhlate *a snap*
ikiyuwi *or* ípahte *a bridle*
iteha *halter*
iyutitan *a tug, or double-tree*
makiyutan *a cinch*
makiyut'inza *a surcingle*
makuipatitan *a breast strap*
mas'canwapaika *a check strap*
mas'canyapa *a bridle*
mas'ikuše *a buckle*
ázasiinahtake *a spur*
mázcanyapa *a bridle*
maziyuwi *a bit*
nap'inpi *the yoke*
onzinatan *the tail strap*
páwak'in *a brief saddle, or a pack saddle*
šungak'in *or* šunkain *or* šunkak'in *a saddle blanket*
šung'inahtake *or* šung'inajipa *a spur*
šung'ipahte *a bridle*
šunkawakan tawanap'in *the harness collar*
tahuiyutitan *or* ceškiyutan *the martingale or check strap*
tahuwanap'in *the collar*
šung'icakce *or* wícakca *a curry comb*
šung'icapsinte *a whip*
šung'icaške *a hitch*
šung'ikan *a hitching strap*
šunkicapowa *a curry brush*
šunksimaza *or* šunktahanpa *a horse shoe*
šun-kšakiyuksa *a hoof trimmer*
šunkowote *a nose-bag*

hot *adj* : káta *or* kal — mašte *~ weather* — pehniga *red-hot, to be very ~, the heat*

house *n* : típi *or* ti *or* oti *a dwelling, a house, room, tipi (teepee), tent* – tiwahe *or* tiyognaka *or* tiyohe *a household* — KINDS : heyoka oti *the heyoka's place of works* – tikaitepa *a pent-house, a lean-to* – tikaunka *a ~ knocked down* – típila *a small ~* – ti wakpala el *a ~ on a creek* – tiyohe *a deserted ~* – tiyuktan wakeyapi *improvised shelter* – wokeya *a straw ~* — PARTS : ticatku *the place opposite the door or entrance* – tice *or* ticeška *the roof, ceiling, or top of a ~* – ticopa *a center tent pole* – tiihanke *the corner of a ~* – tiiyokahmi *a corner of a room* – tioko *the yard about a ~* – tioyankapi *a room* – tipaslate *a pillar, a brace* – tiunnaptanyan *the roof and sides of a ~* – tiyopa *an entrance, door, gate* – tiyowoslata *a wall* — SOME SPECIFICS : tianunkatanhan *in both sides of the ~* – tiapiya *to repair a ~* – tiawanyanka *to watch a ~, to give surveillance over a ~* – ticaga *to build a ~* – ticatkayatahan *at or to the left side of the ~* – tiihanke *a ~ short of completion* – tiiyaza *from ~ to ~* – tiiyupah *with all one's belongings* – til *or* timahel *or* tiyo *inside, within or in the ~* – tiokšan *arouind, in, out of the ~* – tiokšu *to transport, carry into the ~* – tiokte *to kill in the ~, commit homicide* – tionablu *to raise dust in the ~* – tionakipa *or* tionapa *to flee to the ~* – tiosni *cold in the ~* – tisam *beyond the ~* – tiwankata *upstairs, as in going* – tiwokitahena *or* tiyotahena *away from homes* – tiyata *or* tiyatana *at the ~ or home* – tiyatakiya *toward the ~ or home* – tiyobleze šni s'e škan *to move about purposely with excitement* — tiyognaškinyan s'e škan *or* tiyobleze šni s'e škan *to move about excitedly but getting nothing done* – tiyobya *to use for a door* – tiyokawinh *to go around in a circle in a ~* – tiyokuta *downstairs, as in going* – tiyololya *to rent a ~* – tiyošlola *with a rolling sound in a ~* – tiyotonwan *to look into a ~* – tiyukan *to leave the ~* – yutimahel *into the ~*

how *adv conj* : – Cf manner

however *adv expl* : únš'keyapika *or* ínšeyapika *or* únškeyapika *coming back to the subject*

howl *v* : kagloglo *or* kahoton *or* kahowa *to hit an animal and make it ~* – nahoton *or* našicahowaya *to make an animal ~ by kicking it* – pašicahowaya *to make one cry by pushing or punching by hand* – šunkahó *to ~ like a dog* – šunkmanituho *to ~ like a wolf* –

hull *v* : wanašlogya *to ~ e.g. corn*

humble *v refl* : igluhukuciyela *to lower one's self* – igluhukuya *or* iglukuya *to be humble* – hukul iyeya *to bring one down, to humble one* — ónših'an *to be ~, to act pitifully* – ónših'anka *to excite compassion* – ónših'anpi *humility* – ónšikih'an *to ~ one's self before others* – yuonši *reducing to weakness* – yuonšika *to ~ one*

humor *adv* : p'osyakel *out of ~* – p'ózeca *to be out of ~* – Cf displease, hate

hump *n* : canȟaȟake *a vertabra, a buffalo's ~* – canȟaȟaketon *to be humped, to have a ~* – túga *hunch-backed, a ~ or hunch* – Cf hunch

hunch *va* : natuhtuh *to lift or pull and so becoming hunched over* – túga *hunch-backed*

hundred *adj* : kaunhye *one ~*

hungry *v* : locin *to be hungry* – ilocin *to be ~ for a reason* – kalocin *to be ~ for being shaken up* — tiyohankokipa *to be afraid of ghosts at night, fig to be hungry* — wócinpi *hunger, a craving, begging food* – wótektegla *to be ~* – wó tekteglapi *hunger* — kahlogeca *hungry*

hunt *v* : igni *to stalk game* – iic'igni *to ~ game for one's self* – ikicigni *to ~ for one* – ikigni *to ~ for one's own* – loigni *to ~ food* – loligni *to look for food* — akita *to search for what is lost* – akicicita *to ~ a thing for another* – akicita *to ~ for another* — akitonwan *to search for a thing lost* — kúwa *to chase, pursue in hunting* – icuwa *something with which to catch or trap* – wakuwapi *trapping or hunting* — mázaegle *to set a trap* — nasa *or* anansa *to hunt buffalo* — táte *hunting, chasing* – táteye *to hunt* – táteaya *to go on a ~* – waye *to ~ for edibles, supplies, money*

hurricane *n* : wamniomni *cyclone, tornado*

hurry *vn* : inahni *to be in a ~* – inahnikel *in a ~* – inahnikiya *to make one ~* – inahnipi *a ~* – inahniyan *or* inahniyela *or* nahniyela *hastily* – kainahni *to be busier, to ~ up in working* – kiyuinahni *to ~ things for one* – wainakihni *to be always hurried* – wawinahni *or* wawinakihni *to be in a ~* — iyakita *to urge one on, as is done to slow horses* — kaoh'ankoya *with a great ~* – kokoyela *hurrying a little in quick succession* – koyah'an *to be quick in doing* – koyakih'an *to be quick in doing one's own* — owozaka *to rush, be in a ~*

hurt *va* : apaguka *to sprain by rubbing on* – apašica *to soil or injure rubbing on* – išica *to be ~, harmed, injured* — hunapta *to have injured one's self and so becoming lame* — icama *to ~ or prick, as something in the eye or elsewhere* – icabheya *right through as pain the chest* — iglušihtin *to enfeeble one's self* — iyoyagya *to ~ one's feelings* — ksúyeya *to injure, to inflict pain on one* — wakahtaka *to be easily ~* — wozan *to ~ or feel pain by shooting, or to get ~ running against* — yacanliyapa iyeya *or* yacantiyapa iyeya *to ~ one's feelings* — siyapayakel *with wet or paining feet*

husband *n* : anungkison *obsol* — higna *one who is a ~*

– hignaku *her ~* – hignaton *or* hignaya *to have a ~ , to be married*
hush *v* : wagluhika *to keep silent (used in a threat context)* — okis'as'a *to hush one, as to sleep* – Cf silent
husk *va* : ayuga – kiciyuga *to ~ for* — wóga *to ~ esp corn* – wógapi *the husking*
hypocrite *n* : óhoka *one who is respected yet deserving of punishment* — wakanic'ila *to be hypocritical* – wakanic'ilapi *hypocrisy* — wanaic'ihma *a hypocrite, one who conceals himself* – wánakihmanpi *hypocrites*

I

I *or* **me** *1st pers pron* : miye, miyeš, miš — miyecinka *I myself, I alone* — miyecuhci *I my very self* — miyek'e *I myself, even I* — mišnaka *or* mišnala *I alone* — wa *I (in subj compos)* — we *I...to (wa...ki in subj compos)* — ci *I...you (wa...ni in compos)* — ma *or* mi *me (in obj compos)* — mic'i *myself (in compos)* — mitawa, mita *my or mine* — ma, mi *I (in subj compos)* — mica, mici *for me (in obj compos)* — unkiyepi *or* unkiš *we or us* — unkišnapila *we alone* — un... *or* unki...pi *we or us* — unkitawapi *our*
ice *n* : cága – cágata *at or on ~* – cágatakiya *out on the ~* – cágoti *an ice-house* – caȟágleyela *standing on ~ seen from afar* – cahkáhloka *to make a hole in the ~* – cahkat'a *to be stunned or killed by a fall on ~* – cahkazo *to slide with the feet on ~* – cahnajuju *an ice breakup* – cahsu *smooth or bare ~* – ocahsu *icy* – cahswula *thin ~* – cah'owancaya *ice all over* cah'panpanla *ice to be soft* – cah'suta *ice to be hard or thick* — kicaga *to become ice again*
identity *v refl* : eic'ila *to esteem one's self as*
idle *adv* : wotíyeya *idle for lack of ability*
if *adv conj* : ehantanš — kinhan *or* cinhan *~ when* — k'eš *or* yunkanš *if* — yunš *provided that, or if*
ignorance *n* : waslolyapišni
ill-health *n* : wayasyazanka
image *n* : wakagapi *a picture, an idol*
imbue *va* : yuȟebya *to instill in one*
imitate *va* : iaunca *to mimic on* — kigmaic'iya *to make one resemble another, to ~* — otapa *to follow after one, to ~* — wahuncala *to ape or do monkeyish tricks*
immeasurable *adj* : wóptecašni
immediately *adv* : agna *at once, at one notice* — ecahankeya *right after, ~, continuously, completely* — ihecegla *at once, ~* — ungnahanla *~ , suddenly* – ungnahelake *all at once, suddenly*
immolation *n* : wówaunyeic'iye *self-immolation*
immovable *adj* : hohopicašni – hohopicašniyan *immovably* — igluhtanikapin *or* igluškanškankapi *to be unable to move one's self, as when sick* — nawincašni *~ , as feet set firmly* — wotóka s'e *or* wotókasekse *immovably* — paksa s'e *in a manner cut short*
impatient *vn* : iwacinko *to be ~ about, to be out of sorts about* – wacinhunkešni *or* wacin'ihala *irascible, easily excited*
impede *va* : oyagi *to hinder one, to cause one trouble, to ~ one's walking, to scratch or affect one* — ikuše *to block the way* — kan'iyeyapi s'e *unimpeded, without hindrance*
imperfectly *adv* : iyututkayakel *partly, unsuitably* — šihtin *poorly made*
imperitive mood signs : (ending the statement)

	Singular	Plural	Beckoning
Men:	yo *or* wo	po	yeto *or* to
Women:	ye *or* we	pe	nito
		yema	

important *i.e. principal, very good, nice* *n* : otacan *the principal part of anything* – otacanke *the finest thing* — scu *to make self ~*
impose *va* : ipajunta *to force upon one*
impossible *adv* : kewoyuspa s'e *doing the impossible*
imposter *n* : wagnaye *a deceiver*
impoverishment *n* : wicayuwahpanica
impress *v* : wayahloka *to make an impression talking* – wiyahloka *to ~ one* — woš'áka *to make no impression on* – yaš'aka *to make no impression talking*
improperly *adv* : waektašniyan — waepaweh *to speak at cross purposes*
improve *v refl* : itanic'iya *to ~ one's self*
in *prep* : iyo... *in or into* — el *in a place* — mahel *or* mahe *within, in, into* – ímahel *within* — ogna *in a direction or manner* – wógna *in* — aglagla *alongside, in front of*
incense *n* : iwizilye *frankincense* – wizilye *grass or herb incense* – iyazilya *to burn ~* – iyazita *to burn to give off smoke for its odor* – wízilya *to offer incense*
incidentally *adv* : išunmakeci
incite *va* : palega *to ~ a riot, to stir up, ignite*
incline *n* : wacin'oaye *an inclination, a slope up or down*
income *n* : wókamna *salary, wage, livelihood* — wóyuhaoicage *revenue*
incompetent *n* : wicunšni *one who is ~, as in doing work suited to women*
inconsiderately *adv* : tokcinkcinka *thoughtlessly*
incorrectly *adv* : iyektašni – Cf mistake
incorrigibly *adv* : šunk'oiyakilsuta s'e *in the manner of a horse that slackens more and persistently in spite of whipping*
increase *vn* : iyakic'u *to be on the increase, or much more than one needs* — kitonyan *in an increasing manner*
incurable *adj* : asniyepicašni
indecision *vn* : iwacinjata *to be undecided about anything*
indeed *adv* : itušeš — ecah'eke *truly (a woman's express of impatience)* — lakaš *truly, of course* – wélaka *or* yélaka *indeed since* – Cf because
indelible *adj* : pašpešni
indent *va* : naškokpa *to make a hollow place by foot* – Cf dent
indicative mood stressed *partic postp* : yelo *or* lo *stressing the fact of what is stated*
indifference *v express* : ítokašni *It makes no difference* — wacinteȟi *indifferent* – wacinwikic'unšni *to be indifferent about*
indisposed *or* **tired** *adv* : – Cf unwilling, tired
indistinct *v* : ayaogwu *or* ayogwugwu *to do or speak indistincly*
individually *adv red* : iyagyatayela *personally, self alone* – iyatayela *personally, or it alone* – tan'iyatayela *directly or in person*
induce *va* : inapeya *to cause to come out, to appear*
industrious *vn* : abliheca *to be ~ in some way* – ablihelic'iya *to make one's self ~, busy in the good sense* – ablihelya *to cause one to be ~ , or industriously, stirringly* – bliheya *to make one active* – bliheic'iya *to make one's self active, or actively* – bliheca *to be active, or active* – blihel'heca *to be lively or active* — aigluškehan *to bestir one's own self* — napištan *one active who is busy and does much* — wímakaheya *industry, initiative, enterprising*
inept *adj* : wahteka *no good for the designated purpose* – Cf skillful

inexperienced *vn* : wayuh'iyayaka *to be ~*
infatuation *n* : wócanteoyuze
infect *or* **infest** *adv* : opusya *infested with, teeming with* — kašikšil *infected*
infidelity *n* : wiiyaonpapi *a charging with ~, having illicit sexual intercourse*
inflate *vn* : pógan *to blow to fill with air*
influence *va* : awacinyan *to ~ another's thinking, or in thinking upon* — tóka la *not to be influenced by* — wakonza *to determine, decree* - wakonze *an ~* — wawokahtanyan *to have great ~ over e.g. one's philosohy of life* — ton *the act of a thing by which knowledge of the thing comes to be known in itself and in its own characteristics*
inform *or* **communicate** *va* : iwahoya *to send word, to grant, permit, to warn, to let one know* — heyecešni *not informed about* — wasloslolkiya *to be well informed*
ingenious *or* **expert** *vn* : wayupi *to be skillful, to be ~*
inhale *va* : yaholya *to cough* - yahote *an inhalation* - Cf intake
inheritance *n* : wóiyowaja *a share in an ~*
injure *v* : kiiglaksa *to ~ one's self* — okaškan *to be injured internally* — ónton *to be injured* - óntonyan *to ~ or hurt one* — oyušice *a misunderstanding* — kiciyušinhtin *to ~ or enfeeble for one* — wanapištanyan *to ~ or destroy everything* — oic'ih'an *to injure one's self*
ink *n* : wíyowa *marking or writing material*
inquire *or* **question** *va* : pasi *to investigate, to question secretly* — slolyewacin *to inquire* — wiyunga *or* wawiyunga *to ask questions* - wawiyunge s'a *inquisitive* - wawiyunhya *in an inquiring way* - wíkiciyungapi *a mutual inquiry*

insect *n* : wabluška *bugs and butterflies in general*
tajuška *or* tašuška *ant*
hálablaska *bedbug*
tuhmunga *a bee* - tuhmunga tanka *bumble bee*
tuhmunga canhanpi *or* tuhmunga túnkce *honey bee*
sipawicayaksa *the black beetle*
kimimila *butterfly*
mah'awanglaka *cicada, locust*
psipsicala *or* wabluškatiyošlo *cricket*
hála *or* psícala *a flea*
tánnicala *or* tánnicela *small flies, gnats*
tusweca *a dragon fly*
gnugnuška *the grasshopper*
anpetacagu *the large grasshopper*
apeša *a grasshopper whose inner wings are red*
apezi *a grasshopper whose inner wings are yellow*
psipsicala *the grasshopper*
ptewoyake *the large grasshopper without wings*
tatawabluška *or* tehmunga *a horsefly*
wanyeca *the fire fly, the lightning bug*
héya *the louse*
waglula *a maggot, a tapeworm*
capunka *the mosquito*
wanagitakimimila *a miller*
iktomi *or* unktomi *a spider*
táskakpa *the wood tick*
unkcepagmigma *or* unkcepagmiyanyan *a tumble-bug*
pejiwabluška *the walking stick*
wicajipa *or* wicayajipa
maga tašunpe *a water bug*
tatingleska *the intestinal worm* - Cf maggot

inseparable *adj* : pahnihpilpicašni *worthless indeed*
insert *va* : yumahel iyeya *to hold in*
inside *va* : ayueciya *to make a thing inside-out* — kanyetanhan *on the ~* - kanyewapa *within, toward the center* — mahetanhan *on the ~* - mahetu *deep within* - mahetuya *deep in*
insist *adj* : íhiti *insistent* — kitanyan *insistently, continually*
insolence *n* : waiciȟaȟapi
inspector *n* : wábleza
instance *adv* : ínšešelakeš *for instance* - *n* : *an instance*
instead *adv* : e *rather* - ecanleha *but ~* - éekiya *to substitute for, or ~ of* - éha *~ on the contrary* - iyeha *~ rather he or she*
instep *n* : itakaha *the ~ or top of the foot*
instigate *v* : wawoškilya *to devise, get started, usually what is unjust or violent*
instruct *va* : wahokonkiya *to advise* - wahokonkiyapi *instructions, counsel, or advised* - iwahokonkiyapi *to advise, or instruction* — iyaksapa *to make wise talking* - wayuksapa *to make wise, or an instructor* — wówaonspe *instruction* - wówaonspekiye *an instruction or precept* — yawacinton *to ~ to make intelligent* — yusus *or* yu-syuza *earnestly to ~*
instrument *n* : icage
insufficient *vn* : icakija *to be lacking or in need* — ikipi *to need for one's self* — ókpani *to be lacking* - aokpani *to be lacking, in need* - aokpaniyan *insufficiently, less than* - iyokpani *to be insufficient, wanting* - naokpani *to lack*
insult *va* : aikšinkiya *to make faces at one held in contempt* — oštegla *to revile one* - ošteglapi *scolding one* — yašigla *to insult one in talking*
insure *or* **make firm** *v* : kiciyusuta *to ~ for one* - Cf firm
intake *v* : yahota *to draw in air and water with breathing*
intelligent *v* : iwacinton *to be ~ by reason of* — waokahniga *to be ~, skillful* — wašagla *to consider not ~*
intemperate *adv* : tantonyankel *excessively* — wawiyakapeic'iya *to be one's self ~* - wawiyakapeya *to exceed*
intend *n* : canteoyuze *one's intention or intent* — wacin *to try, to think, or to be anxious to* - wacinyuze *one's intention* - wacinyeya *to set one's mind to, to purpose*
intensely *adv* : labya *very much so*
intercede *v* : wótikiya *or* wótikiciciya *to beg or petition for another*
intercourse *n* : anakicison *to have sexual intercourse* — wawiciȟaȟa *an adulterer* - wawiciȟaȟapi *or* wówiȟaȟa *adultery, what is shameful* - yaš'inš'in *to come to climax in coitus* - kaogna iyeic'iya *or* kaokajaya *or* kiyuȟa (animal) *or* onzehu (human) *or* paspaya (vulgar) *or* pastanka *or* tawinton *or* tawinya *coitus* — onzeokaštanpi *to deposite seed, to ejaculate* — pasluka *masturbation, onanism* - iwicahupi (vulgar) *sodomy*
interest *n* : waawacin *to think about, consider* - wacinteȟi *to take an ~ in nothing*
interfere *v* : yopepeja šni *to ~ with* — iškiškeyece *interference*
interior *adv* : timahetakiya *toward the ~* - Cf within

interjections : exclamations and some expressions -
ACCUSATION : Okin on šíca! *How stubborn he (it) is!* — Tula! *For shame! (in protest)* — Yu! *You are a bad one! (said by a woman protesting and scolding)* —
AFFIRMATION : Hu! *Good!* — Itoleš! *Really now!* — Otapika! *You are the best!* — To. *or* Tói. *or* Toš. *Yes (used by women)* — Han. *or* Ohan. *Oh Yes.* — Skániyaka. *They say.* — Šehanš! *For heaven's sake! (impatience) or Most certainly!* — Šehanštuka! *Finally, to be sure!* — Tóka ška. *There is something said.* — Unš'unmakeci!

or Onš'unmakec'un *Oh yes! just because ...* — Wank'eya. *Why, the fact is ....*
ATTENTION : Haho! *Look at this!* or *Hey, Look here!* — Ma! *or* Man! *Look! (as women say)* — Še! *or* Š' *(men say, and)* Ši! *(women say) Hist!* — Toke! *Listen!* — Wan, wan ka wan! *Look, see!*
BIDDING : Níye! *Take it! (used by men)* — Huyi! *or* Hoiye! *or* Huya! *Come along!*
CONTRARY : šehanška *nonetheless, at any rate*
DENIAL : eceš *No sir.* or *Of course no. (unwillingness, used by women only)* — Híya! *No!* — Hoh! *Don't give me that!* — tase ... ka *of course not!*
DISAPPOINTMENT : Hohub! *Rats! What do you know*
DOUBT : Ama! *or* Apa *Bosh! or Nonesense! or Who can believe that?* — Hoħeceš! *Who will believe that!* — Iyešnica! *You don't say so!* — Ohunwela! *or* Oh! *I have my doubts! Oh?* — Séca. *Maybe.* — Skéka. *I have my doubts.* — tokaš *or* tókinaš *or* tókinahanš *Maybe, possibly, perhaps, maybe* — Túnwehca škeka. *So you say.* or *There are doubts about this.* — Túwakakeša! *or Túwakakša! Impossible! or Preposterous! or Absurd!* — ungnaš *or* ungnayehciš *maybe or possibly* — Yai! *Oh no, that can't be! (a girl's reaction)*
FEAR : Ya! *(women say),* — Hnahna! *(men say)*
GREETINGS : Cannako! *Welcome!* — Co Co! *Hello, Hello!* — Hau. *Greetings.*
HOPE : Nin. *May it be so.*
IMPATIENCE : Haš! *Nuts! or Why! or Well!* — Heš! *Well!* — Hin! *Rats! or Whoops!* — icinyunškaš *or* iyuwinškaš! *For heaven's sake!* — Wahtešniit'a *I'm sick and tired of ...! or Damn you! or Go to hell!*
JOY : Haiye! *A great day is here!*
NARROW MISS, ESCAPE : Wišwepi! *or* Wišwi! *Whew!*
PAIN : Yun! (women say) *Oh! Dear me!* — Makteka! *or* Imacuka! *That gets me! or That kills me!*
PATIENCE : Itok'eyaš. *Let me see. or Wait a bit* — Tíyanka yo. *or* Tóhinyanka yo. *or* Tótinyanka yo *Wait a little.*
COMPASSION : Ece. *Sorry. or Oh no.* — Hehehé. *or* Hunhunhé. *Alas, too bad. or Such is the case.* — Ónšila. *Poor thing.* — Šika. *Pitiful one. or Poor fellow.*
PRAISE : Ahahé ... *Three cheers for ...*
QUESTION : Tuweška? *Who is this?*
READINESS : Iyohob. *Ready, here I come!*
REJECTION : Inš hécel! *Who cares!* — Šehan! *Good heavens!* — Wošté! *Horrible!* — Ma k'éya! *Rediculous!*
SADNESS : Itoceš! *Oh my! What good does it do.* — Ošti! *or* Hošti! *Alas, that is bad!*
SILENCE : Hacíb! *Hush up! or Sh-h-h- !*
SOUND, CALL : Cu! (a gun report) — Š-š-š- *Leave!* — We-we-we- ! *Come! (women say in calling a dog)*
THOUGHT : Ínska in. *Let me see now.*
WARNING : Ahán! *Be careful! or Look out!* — Eyá lécel. *Try as you will, you know what I mean (you cannot).* — Hinahina. *Well, well, well. or* Óh oh — Hošti! *That's bad!* — Húhu Húhu Húhu ... ! *Hey Hey Hey! (the Lakota represents the sound boys make, like a coyote's, as the people bring home the beef)* — Iyuwinškalake s'e! *How frightful!* — Siye! *Watch out! or Be on your guard!* — Siyemila *I warn you!*
WONDER : Hinu hinu ... *How grand! or What a surprise to see you!* (used by women) — Hohub! *What do you know!* — Hojilá! *How beautiful! or Simply splendid!* — Lotkunkešni *i.e. Oh! I wanted to tell you...* — Tokí! *How wonderful! (used by women)* — Tuki! *Is that so! (used by women)* — Wanlila! *Get a load of that! or Wow! or Tremendous!*

intermittent *adv* : gnangnan s'e *in an ~ manner*
interpret *v* : wayuašlaya *to expose a secret, make manifest, to ~* - wayuašlayapi *an interpretation* — wayuieska *to translate, or an interpreter* - wayuieskapi *a translation* — yawiyakpa *to interpret something*

interrogatives : PARTICLES : kacaš *(postp, doubt or hesitation) What then? or What of it?* — kin *(postp, rhetorical question)* — so *or* ce *(postp, a question with an affirmation expected)* — hwo *or* hwe *or* huwé *or* he *(postp, with information expected)* — ka *(postp, with one's consent expected)* — PRONOUNS : túwa *or* tuwátu *who* - tuwe *who, or* tuwe ... ca *who is it that,... or* tuwela *just who, or* túwehca *who indeed* — tóna *how many, which* — tukte *which* — unma tukte *which of two* — táku *what* — táku ... ca *what is it that* — tákula *just what* — túwa táwa *whose* — ADVERBS : tókel *how, or why* — tókeške *how, how in the world* — tóketu *or* tóktu *or* otoketu *or* wicotoketu *how is it* — tínskoya *how large, how extensively* — itohan *how far, or long, from* — tohanhan *at what time or place, how far* — tohanyankel *how far, to where* — tínskokeca *how large or big* — tínskola *how small, of what size* — tohankeca *how long (as to space)* — ítona *of how many, which number* — icitona *how many* — tóna *of what quantity, how many* — tónakiya *how many, how many time, in how many ways* — tónagnag *how many* — tónakeca *of how many* — ítonaka *of how many* — ítonakeca *of what number* — šehanleš *how much more, how much less* — tóhan *or* tóhanl *when, at what time or place* — tohanhan *at what time or place* — tohantu *at what time, when* — tónweni *when* — tókiyatanhan *or* tuktetanhan *from what place, whence* — tohanhan *where, at what place or time, how far* — tókiyab *whither, where, in what direction* — tókiyawapa *where, in what place* — watokiya *whence* — tuktogna *which way, in which direction, where* — tuktetu *in or at which or what place* — tuktel *where, in what place* — tukte ihankeya *which, from the ground up, i.e. from start to finish* — tuktena *which one of* — tókaca *or* tókayelakaš ... kin *what reason is there for ..., why* — tókecae *why* — tókel *how, why*

interrupt *n* : wawoškiškeyece *one who interrupts* — ícisanb *or* ícisam *interruptingly*
intersect *vn* : ipawega - ipawehya *to make ~ , or intersecting*
intimate *v* : kiwakanheja *to be on good terms with, to desire to be on good terms*
introduce *n* : kpahahapika *one who is put forward in company*
inundate *adv* : kaokic'uya *flooding, inundating*
investigate *or* **examine** *v* : wayukcan
invisible *v* : yusnis' *to become ~* - Cf visible
invite *v* : kico *to call one* - ikico *to ~ to* - kicošniyan *uninvited* - okicico *the invitation of each other*
inward *adv* : maheta *or* mahel - imáhelwapa *inwards inside* - imahetuya *inward, within* - mahelwapa *inward, toward the interior* - mahetakiya *toward the inside, inward* — kanye *inward, toward the center*
irascible *n* : wówacinko *irascibility*
iron *n* : mázasapa — wapabla *to press clothes* - akan wapablapi *an ironing board*
irrespectfully *adv* : wítonpešni

irresponsible *n* : wicunkešni *usually an ~ woman* - wícunšni *a woman to be very ~ , incompetent in women's work*
irritate *or* **excite** *adj* : ošigla *irritable* — wacinhunkešniya *to ~ or provoke* — wówicahtake wanica *to be unwilling to be touched, to be irritable, easily provoked*
island *n* : wíta
isolated *adv* : okiwotahena *in an ~ place, alone, apart*
issue *n* : **tage** *an issuance, a froth, spittle, scum* — wokábkab *to issue* — wóšlošlog *to clear out by blowing the nose* — ton *to issue forth (philosophy), to come forth, as in birth*
itch *n* : awicayaspuya *an ~ or an itching* - yašpuya *to make ~ , or itchy, itching*

J

jack-of-all-trades *n* : waeconconka
jam *v* : naopemni *to get entangled and prevented moving* — paokiyaskapa *to be bent and jammed in*
jar *v* : iyonaniyan *to be jarred or shaken by a foot*
jaunt *v* : kaceslisli *to walk along with a bounce and a sway*
jealous *or* **envious** *v* : nawizi *to be ~ or envious* - nakiciwizipi *they are ~ of one another* - nakiwizi *to be ~ of*
jelly *n* : tákušašala
jerk *va* : yanung *to make ~ sideways* — yacekceka *to pull with the teeth and with a sudden forceful pull*
jest *vn* : ónškata *to brag or boast* - ónkiciškatapi *to ~ , joke or banter* — ówehanhan *to ~ , make fun* - ówehanhanka *a comedian* - aowehanhan *to ~ , make sport* — iyowinȟala *injest* - wayaiȟa *a joker, a comedian*
jewelry *n* : napokaške *or* napoktan *a cuff or bracelet* — natanaškunpakce *a comb ornament* — owinkiya *to wear ~* - owinla *ear jewels* - owinpi *earrings or jewels* — napsiyohli *a ring for the finger* *See* ornaments
jingle *or* **tinkle** *va* or *vn* : nasna
join *v* : kicicakiya *to ~ one's own* — zunlya *joined well*
joint *n* : ókihe - huokihe *a leg ~* - iyokihe *a joint* — kagloka *to put out of ~* — wapšun *to cut a ~* - owapšun *to disjoint* - apapšun *to put out of ~ on* - aglapšun *to put one's own out of ~*
jolt *vn* : kaunkaka *to be jostled, bounced up and down*
journey *vn* : aicimani *to be on a ~* — han'iglaka *to travel by night* - oiglake *an expedition*
jovial *adj* : wínhaha *good-natured* - wínhahaka *a ~ person* - wínhahakel *in good spirits* - wínhahaya *easily pleased, happily*
joy *adv* : owiyuškinyan *with joy* - wówiyuškin *gladness, joy or rejoicing* - Cf rejoice
judge *va* : yasu *to ~ or condemn one* - iyasu *to condemn one for, on account of* - kiciyasu *to ~ one for* - kiciyasupi *to ~ each other* - wóyasu *judgement, condemnation* - iglasu *to ~ one's own* — wiyukcanyan *judicious* - ikiciyukcan *to ~ for another on other evidence*
jump *vn* : ágan ihpaya *to fall or ~ into water with a splash* - akan iyeic'iya *to mount a horse* — psíca *jumping* - akapsica *to make something jump* - glipsica *to alight at home* - hipsica *to ~ down, to dismount* - iglupsica *to ~ about, to prance about* - ipsica *to ~ down from or to ~ over* - ipsipsica *to hop, as a grasshopper* - iyopsica *to hop or ~ down* - kapsica *to make something ~* - kipsica *to alight, ~ down* - psipsica *to skip*
junction *n* : ógliwitaya *a road intersection, a conjunction of many roads*
just *adv* : ínše *only* — owotanla *right, upright* - yuowotan *to make upright, to justify one*

K

keep *v* : kiciyuha *to reserve for* — yuhahapika *worth keeping* — kignaka *to ~ or lay up for* — opasepa *to ~ with care* — patanyan *reserving*
kettle *n* : céga - cehcíscila *a small ~ or bucket* - cehkáhloka *a bucket or kettle with a handle on either side* - cehhuhatan *a ~ having legs* - ceȟikan *a ~ handle* — ceȟiyokaske *the support from which the ~ is hung* - cehnigeton *a ~ that bulges at the middle* - cehpšunka *a pail with small top and large bottom* - cehp'o *steam from a ~* - cehska *a tin can* - cehtankinkinyan *a large ~* - cehwohota *a low wide ~* - ceh'iha *a cover for a ~ or bucket* - ceh'ihupa *a frying pan* - ceh'ihupa hanska *a long-handled kettle* - ceh'ihupaton *a bucket with a handle* - cehnaga *soot or black that accumulates of a ~ bottom* - ceh'okiyeton *a tea ~* - kannacega *that which suggests having the shape of a kettle* - mázacega *or* mascéga *a metal ~*
key *n* : iyuhloke *or* iyušloke — iyutkuge *a lock or key*
kick *va* : nahpa *to be kicked off or out* - anahpa *to ~ down on* - anahtaka *to ~ one on* - anaic'ipson *to ~ and spill on one's self* - anaha *to ~ a ball in a ball game* - anapsaka *to break by foot on* - anapson *to ~ over and spill on* - anaptuja *to crack or split with the foot* - anašloka *to ~ off e.g. one's shoes* - anata *to scrape dirt in and bury with the foot* — naglapšunyan *to ~ over bottom up* - naha iyeya *to ~ out of the way* - naȟeyab *to ~ away to one side* - naȟeyata *to ~ off to one side* - naipaweh *to ~ out of one's way* - nahpa *to ~ down* - nahtaka *to ~ anything* - naikpiska *to ~ over on one's back* - najipa *to nudge with the foot* - najuju *to ~ to pieces, or to come to pieces* - najun *to pull and ~ out* - nakapa *to ~ a ball* - nakawa *to ~ open* - nakici-htaka *to ~ for one* - nakicišpu *to ~ off for* - nakihtahtaka *to ~ one's own e.g. horse* - naoglapšun *to ~ over* - naonziwosla *to ~ bottom up* - nasluta *to ~ out* - na-šloka *to ~ off* - nata *to ~ up, away* — onahtaka *to ~ in* nahtake *injury done by kicking* - nakab *to ~ into* - nakan *to ~ off in, or to be kicked to pieces* — nakicitanpi *to ~ each other* — sípaha iyeya *to ~ away sideways* — wanaiyeya *or* wanahaiyeya *to ~ down or aside*
kidney *n* : tajontka — tapakšin *or* taajuntk'ognake *the kidney fat*
kill *va* : kte - ahikte *to ~ in battle* - ašunkt'eya *to ~ for misdemeanor* - icikte *to commit suicide* - ikte *to ~ with anything* - kiciktepi *they ~ each other* - kikte *to ~ one's own, or to ~ for one* - okte *a killing* - wakteka *one who kills, a killer* — akih'ant'eya *to cause one to die of hunger* — pat'a *to ~ by pressure as in lying on* - kpat'a *to ~ by lying on* - apat'a *to ~ by applying pressure on* - awot'a *to ~ on by punching* - cahkat'a *to die from a fall on ice* - glat'a *to ~ one's own by striking, or to bite one's own to death* - iglut'a *to kill one's self* - kat'a *to ~ or stun by striking* - kat'iyeya *to ~ by shooting* - nat'a *to ~ by kicking* - nat'eya *to ~ by running e.g. a wagon* - okat'a *to ~ by striking in, to beat to death* - onštinma kpat'a *to ~ one's own by lying on* - opat'a *to ~ by applying pressure or by biting* - oyut'a *to ~ in* - pat'a *to die under pressure* - wat'a *to ~ by knife* - wot'á *to ~ or stun by punching or shooting* - wosóta *to ~ off all*
kin *n* : otakuye *kinfolk* - Cf relative
kindle *n* : petileyapi *or* petileye *kindling* - glailega *to ~ again*

king *n* : wicašayatapika — wicokonze *a kingdom*
kink *n* : kaowotan *to straighten out a ~*
kiss *va* : iputaka *or* iiputaka - iikputaka *to ~ one's own* - oiputake *a kiss*
kitchen *n* : owohe
knead *v* : kicipasuta *to ~, to make stiff for* — pat'inza *to stiffen by kneading*
knee *vn* : makagleinajin *to kneel* — woptúza *to make fall on one's knees by shooting* - Cf body
knife *n* : míla *a large ~* - mílapaksa *a round-pointed ~* - mílaya *to have the use of a ~* - hohumila *a bone ~* - šúnka cémila *a crescent-bladed ~* - icapsake *a cutter for cutting strings* - ipapsake *a ~ to cut porcupine quills* — takinwapsake *a sinew ~* - hopeška s'e *a long blade, a short handle (an express implying a comparison)* - Cf míla
knob *n* : tašpu *a door ~*
knock *v* : glapšun *to ~ or bite out one's own* - glašpa *to ~ or bite off a piece from one's own* - glatata *to ~ or shake off* - glatoto *to ~ at one's own door* - glaunka *to fell or ~ down one's own* - iyaic'ipa *to ~ e.g. one's head against a wall* — kabuya *knocking or striking* - kakab *to bat e.g. a ball* - kakan *to ~ off e.g. fruit from a tree* - kašipa *to ~ or cut off e.g. limbs from a tree* - kašloka *to ~ off or out* - kašpu *to chip away at* - katoto *to ~ or beat on a door* - katuka *to ~ or beat off* - kicapšun *to ~ off or out for one* - kóka *a knocking* — sniyankat'a *to ~ cold or senseless* — nagloka *to ~ e.g. out of joint, so injuring one* - nagna *to ~ off with the foot* - nahpu *to ~ off by foot* - nakoka *to ~ with the foot impacting* - natoto *to ~ with the foot* - natutka *to ~ off pieces by foot* - onakan *to ~ off into* — to *a blow sounded with the fist etc.* — awošpu *to ~ off what is stuck on* - owounka *knocked down, killed* — wohá *to shoot or punch over* - woíkpiska *to shoot or punch and ~ over* - wojúju *to shoot or punch to pieces* - wošpá *to ~ off by shooting* - wóšpi *to knock off, pick e.g. berries* - wotútka *to ~ or shoot off pieces*
knock-kneed *adv* : naakiyatagtake s'e *in a cross-legged manner*
knot *v* : kaȟa *to curl* - okicaȟa *to pull a ~ very tight* - okicaȟaȟapi *knotty* — naosin *to tighten a ~ by kicking* — oiyakaške *a knot* - okicaška *to tie knots in* — pšunka *a tree ~* - yuoseya *to get into a ~, or into a hard knot*
know *v* : slolya - islolya *to ~ by means of* - oslolya *to ~ of or about* - oslolye *knowledge* - waslolye *one who knows* - waslolyapi *knowledge* - waslolyeya *to make one ~* — makanongeya *to ~ already* — onspé *to have know-how, savoir faire* - onspekiya *to teach something*

L

labor *or* **work** *v* : ahtani *to ~ for one, to work at something* - ohtani *to work, or working* — awowaši econ *to do work*
lace *va* : hanpí okaškeya *to ~ a moccasin* — pazunta *to ~ up* — wahlohloka *a ~, as a shoe ~*
lack *vn* : ókpani *to be lacking* — yucan *to sift, fig to be without, to be lacking in* - Cf wanting, sift
ladder *n* : can'oiali *or simply* oiale *stairs*
lade *v* : kaȟepa *to ~ out, to empty* — okapta *or* oyuze *to ~ out into* — kaze *to ~ out* - Cf utensil
laden *vn* : yuš'aka *to be heavily ~*
lake *n* : bléla *a pond, a little ~* - blekiyute *a ~ channel, a strait* - bleoškokpa *a ~ basin* - bleyata *at the lake*
lame *adj* : hušte - huštekel *with a limp* - hušteya *to cause one to be ~, or with a limp* - aglušte *to be ~ in* - anaglušte *to limp* - apaglušte *to be ~*
lamp *n* : pelijanjan *or* petijanjan *a ~* - pelijanjan inkpa *a chimney ~* - pelijanjanwigli *~ oil, kerosene* - pelijanjanye *a lamp* - pelijanjangegeya *a lantern* - pelijanjan iyokaštan *an oil funnel* - pelijanjanpi *a torch* - pelijanjan (inkpa) woslahan *a ~ chimney* - pelijanjanyuha omanipi *a lantern*
land *n* : makaoiyute *or* makaowašpe *a piece of surveyed ~* - makaopašpe *a tract of ~* - makowašpe *surveyed ~* - makaopašpe tanka *a country* - makaošpe *or* wóju-iyutapi *an acre of ~* - makopašpe *a section or so of ~* - šokela *a quarter section* - makaowapi *a map* - makowapi *a map of a country* - makogmigma *the globe* - makoicago *a boundary* — óihunni *a boat landing, or to land a boat* - watoihunni *a boat landing place* — okiciin cokan *a no-man's-land* — oški *poor ~, a hilly wilderness*
language *vn* : ie *or* ia, iye *or* iya *to speak* - oie *a word or speech* - oiekicaton *or* oiekiton *to use ~* - tog'ia *to speak a strange ~* - tókaiapi *a foreign ~* — oowa *a letter or word character* - oowaptaya *an alphabet* — zuntešni *incorrect ~* — ieska *the English language*
languid *adv* : ohtateya *being, or becoming weak*
lantern *n* : hanhepi petijanjan *a night lamp* - petijanjan yuha omanipi *a lantern*
large *adv* : ákapa *larger some* — apahlagan *to make ~ on* - ayuhlagan *to make ~ upon* - owahlagan *to enlarge e.g. a hole by cutting* - pahlagan *to enlarge, lengthen out* - wahlagan *to cut larger* — atanka *to be larger* - atankala *to be very little larger* - atankaya *extensively* - iglutanka *to make one's self great* - katanka *to beat out large* - natanka *to become larger, as a shoe might* - kiciyutanka *to enlarge for one* - owatankaya *to cut larger* - oyutankaya *to enlarge in* - yutankaya *to enlarge* - patanka *to enlarge by pushing out* - wótanka *an enlargement* — bubu *chunky like a drumhead* — hínsko *being so big* -hínskokeca *so big* - hínskotanka *so great* - hínskoyela *that big* - ínskokeca *or* kínskokeca *so big* - ínskokinica *to be doubtful which is largest* - nísko *or* oniskokeca *so ~* — núnga *enlarged, grown-out* — okacagla *to be too big for* — ókaške *large at one end, bauble, knob-like* — wošóka *large, ending in a knob, enlarged* — pahanskeya *to make bigger by rolling or rubbing* — yuko *to enlarge a hole by hand*
last *n* : ehake *or* ehakela *the ~ one, yet to come, a last time* - oehake *the last* - hakakta *last or latest* - hékta *the ~ one, the one behind* — hankeya *at ~, finally* — kitanhci *at ~, soon* — nakeš *or* nakehca *at ~, just now* — únnahan *or* únnihan *at last, shortly, soon* — kpa *lasting, durable*
latch *n* : ipashan *a trip, trigger*
late *adv* : áškans'e *rather ~* - aškatula *lately, not long since* - aškatuya *not long ago* - aškatuyela *or* áškatuyela *lately, but a short time ago, or near (in proximity)* - hantehan *~ in the night* - lecala *awhile ago, lately*
laugh *va* : iȟa - aiȟat'a *to ~ at one* - iȟaȟaya *to cause to ~ at, or jestingly* - iȟake *to ~, jest* - iȟakiya *to make one ~* - íȟanhan *in jest, in fun* - iȟat'a *to ~ hard* - iȟaya *to cause laughter* - iciciȟaȟapi *of* ikiciȟaȟa *they ~ at each another* - ikiȟa *to laugh at one's own* - kiciȟapi *they ~ at each other* - nahmiȟa *to ~ slyly* - wawiȟa *to ~ at* - wawiȟat'eya *to ridicule* wawiȟaya *to make one ~ at, or wittily* - wóiȟaka *to ~ at or to jest, or* something funny - wóiȟaya *ludicrously* - wóiȟoie *a laughable word* - wówiȟaȟakiya *to ~ at one's own* - wowiȟala *fun* — ksizeoie *a word that causes laughter* — pahyutibya *to make ~*

heartily — anapša *to break suddenly into laughter*
laundry *n* : owayujaja *a ~ , a bathtub, a place in which to wash*
law *n* : okonze *a rule* - wókonze *a ~ or decree* - wósukiye *a law's fulfillment* - tókiconze *his or her rule or influence* — tóope *his or her ~* — wasuya *to make a ~*
lawyer *n* : wakiye wicaša - Cf discuss, try
lay *v* : mígnaka *to ~ up for me, or note:* mignáka *to pack a knife or hatchet under one's belt* — kionpa *to ~ on one's own* — pahpa *to ~ down a load* - kpahpa *to ~ down one's own load*
layer *adv* : iyakigna *in layers, one on another* - ókignagtonton *in many layers or groups*
lazy *v* : glas'ic'iya *to be very ~* — škankapin *unwilling to move about, to be ~* - iškankapin *to be ~ by reason of* - škankapinpi *laziness* — kánhtal *with muscles totally and lazily relaxed* — kipa s'a *a ~ person who gets along with difficulty and keeps blaming himself* — kuš'it'a *to die from laziness*
lead *or* **reach** *vn* : aiyagle *to ~ to* - aiyagleya *to bring on one's self, to deserve, or leading to* — akagal *stretching out to* — glohinapa *to ~ out one's own* - yus enapa *they came in sight leading him out of doors by the hand* — pakiya *leading* - tokapaya *in a leading manner* - tokapayaškan *to be on the move leading the way*
leader *n* : aitancan *a ruler over* - wóitancan *leadership* — blotahunka *a ~ of a warparty and perhaps a chief*
leaf *n* : ape *a tree leaf, a blade of grass* - canwape *leaves or small branches* - wahpe *a leaf or leaves*
leak *or* **escape** *v* : ohiyu *to come through* - aohiyu *to ~ on* — sképa *to ~ out, evaporate* - askepa *to ~ out on* - naskepa *to leak out all, to empty*
lean *adv* : apakinyan *leaning over* - atakinyan *leaning on, slanting* - kaatakinyan *or* katakinyan *leaning* — takin *to ~ sideways* - katakin *to strike and make lean sideways* - takinyan *leaning* — tan'onpa *leaning to one side* - tan'onbya *to walk leaning sideways* - tan'onbyanka *to sit leaning to one side* - atan'onm *to ~ over, to incline* - atan'onmya *in a leaning manner* - katan'onpa *to lean* - katan'onb *leaning at a 45 degree angle* - natan'onb *leaning, inclined* — ícanyan *or* kaicanyan *leaning against* - ikakein *to ~ on* — ikpataka *to ~ on, brace one's self* - iyušinktinyan *leaning one way or another* — kaohya *leaning, sloping, twisting* — yukin *to ~ something to one side to give passage* — gwéza *thin, lean, ragged, poor* — huȟaka *nothing but skin and bones* - huh'a *~ , boney* - huh'as'e *with a ~ look* - huiyata *boney* - husangmi *very thin* — kan'akalaya *very lean or thin* — tamaheca *thin* - tamahelya *poorly* - tamaka *poor* - watamahelheca *very poor* — tintinyan *beginning to dry up and grow thin*
learn *v* : slolyewacin *to be eager to ~*
leather *n* : wakape *~ for mashing on* - wókape *a hide on which to pound cherries* — wakiglaka *dressed skin, hide* - Cf hide
leave *v* : ayuštan *~ alone* — yuhlagan *to ~ , separate from* - ayuhlagan *to forsake one* — Hánta *Get away!* — iglasto *to be left out* — iglutitan *to tear one's self away from* — iglutokan *to remove one's self to another place* — aglukan *to ~ unmolested, leave alone* — kicunni *to ~ off, to excuse* — oyapta *to have left-overs* - oglapta *to ~ some of one's own, to have one's own leftovers* - okiciyapta *or* okiyapta *to have leftovers, to ~ part of one's own food for another* - okicapta *to be left for* — oglusota *all to go and leave for* — ónašloka *to run off and ~ behind* — ópte *leavings* — optuȟaȟala *crumbs* — ošnapi *scraps* - Cf omit
leaven *n* : onapohye *or* winapohye — winakapo *hops* — wahpe akicaškapi *baking powder, yeast*
left *n* : catka *the ~ hand* - camatka *I am left-handed* - catkayatan *at the ~ side* - icatkayatan *to the ~ of* - kaiyocatka *a left-handed performance* - tancatkayatanhan *at the ~ side of the body* - tan'icatkayatanhan *at the ~ side of a person*
leg *n* : hu - huakiš'aka *strong in one's legs, not easily tired* - hublo *the shin bone or lower part of the ~* - hubloyunke *the front muscle of the lower human ~* - hucogin *the calf, the muscle, of the ~* - húhohu *the leg bones* - huiyut'inze *leggings* - hunska *leggings* - hunskaya *to have for leggings* - husanni *one of a pair, as one ~* - husli *the ankle* - hutokapatan *the front legs* - hutopa *the four-leggeds, or four-legged* - huwakiš'ake *to be good on one's legs, strong legged* - huyá *have as a staff* - huyakel *using as a ~ , as in using a spare horse to travel* - huyata *as the leg* — sipaksize *the lower part of the legs of animals* — šunkmanišnikiya *leg-wearied*
legacy *n* : wówaaihpeye *a written ~*
leisure *or* **rest** *adv* : kat'eyakel *leisurely* — owánjila *at rest, unemployed*
lend *va* : ok'u *to ~ to*
length *v* : kiciyuhanska *to lengthen out for* - ohanska the *~ of some thing* - ohanskeya *in length* — kahlagan *to lengthen, extend*
less *adv* : aiyopteca *~ than* - aiyoptel *or* aiyoptetu *or* aiyoptetuya *~ , towads or in the direction of* — aokpaniyan *wanting in* — aopteca *~ , little* - aoptel *~ than* - aopteutu *less in size* - aoptelya *to diminish, or ~* - aoptelyakel *~ , or ~ than* - aoptelyela *~ , diminished* — gluaoptetu *to make one's own ~* - kaaopteca *to do less* - kaaoptetu *to lessen, diminish* — napteca *or* naptelya *or* opteca *~* - wayo-ptelya *to make ~ by the mouth*
lesson *n* : waonspe — owangya *to take a ~ from, follow the example of one*
lest *adv* : owekinahanš *so you may not*
letter *n* : wówapi *written discourse*
level *adj* : blaska - ablaskabtonyan *aside of one another, ~* - ablaskaya *~ without ridges* - apablaska *to make flat on* - ayablaska *to flatten with the mouth on* - ayublaska *to make flat on* - blaskaya *on a flat side, flat-wise* — bláya *~ , plain* - ablaya *level on* - apablaya *to make ~ on* - ayablaya *to make ~ on with the teeth* - ayublaya *to spread or unroll on* - bláyela *plain, level-wise* - bláyeya *evenly* — glablaya *to make level one's own by beating* - kablaya *to beat level* — naablaya *to make level by foot* - nablaya *to make ~ or smooth by foot* - nakiblaya *to trample ~ one's own* - nakiciblaya *to trample ~ for one* - oblaya *level*
lever *n* : can'ipaptanye — iyupseya *crookedly, zigzag (when the ~ and fulcrum operate)*
lewd *n* : witkowinwaštelaka *a ~ person*
liberal *adj* : generous - wókimnanka *honored, wise* - *See* wahacanka wan ...
lick *va* : slípa - aslipa *to ~ on* - kislipa *to ~ one's own* — ayaspaya *to wet with the mouth on* - ayastanka *to moisten with the mouth on* - ayasto *to ~ smooth on* - oyaska *to ~ clean* - yajaja *to wash by mouth* - yaskica *to ~ or suck e.g. bones or what is eaten*
lid *n*: iha *the lower lip, fig a cover of anything, a lid*
[1]lie *v* : itonšni *to tell an untruth, a falsehood* - itonpišni lies - itonšniyan *falsely* - aitonšni *to tell lies on* — ajuton *to tell a little ~ in narrating* — akaga *to lie about, speak evil of* - akagapi *an addition that exaggerates or strains the truth* - aokicaga *to deal falsely* - aokicagapi *a falsehood* — gna-

yan *to deceive, to cheat* - ayagnayan *to tell a falsehood about one* - ic'ignayan *to deceive one's self* - igna-gnayan *to deceive by* - iwicagnayan *a deception* — cakala *a liar* — eyáyalaka *to lie* - heyáyalaka *to tell lies* — glaglegle-ga *one's self to be spotted, as is said of a person who tells lies* - iyagleglega *to tell lies* — glahlaya *to tell a lie* — ie-yašna *to talk as one pleases lying* — íjata *forked, double tongued* — íyašlata *to be found guilty of lying* — puzata *fig to be caught in a ~* — waiecešni *to tell lies* — íyašlalya *to prove one a liar* — owekiwakan *to ~ about one* - owewakan *to tell an untruth* — Palani *a liar, a name given to the Pawnee tribe once living in the central part of the state of Nebraska*

[2]lie *v* : yunka *to ~ along* — aglakšunyan yunka *to ~ prone or prostrate, i.e. on one's belly* - ahiyunka *to bring and ~ down* - akanyunka *to ~ upon* - ayungya *to cause to ~ on or for* - ayunka *to ~ on or in wait, or spend the night* - iyung *to ~ hidden* - iyunka *to ~ down in bed* - ki-yunka *to go home and ~ down* - oyunka *to ~ down in* - yunkahan *to be lying down along* - yunkahe *lying prone* - yunkapi *an encampment* - yuunka *to make ~ down* — akaunyan *to ~ over or across* — akiglaskil *to press or lie or sit down on* — aokihpa *to rest or ~ by for* — han-gnagya hpaya *to ~ down ready to get up early* - hpayeya *to cause to ~ down, to kill in battle* — ic'imnikel *sprawled out* — kazilya *to stretch or straighten out* — makipuskica *to ~ flat on the ground*

life *n* : oni - tóni *his or her ~* - wiconi *the present life*

lift *va* : yuha *to have, hold, lift* — kiyugata *to ~ or raise one's arms in prayer* - Cf raise

[1]light *vn* : aojanjan *to be ~ on* - aojanjanya *to light something* - aojanjanyan *in an illuminating manner* - ijanjan *to give ~ , or a light, e.g. a candle* - ijanjanya *to ~ e.g. a candle* - ijanjanyan *giving ~ for* - iyojanjan *a light, to shine or shine ~ into, to give ~ to* — hóhetamahpiya *the northern lights* — iyatan *to ~ e.g. a pipe* — iyoyanpa *or* iyoyam *to give light, to shine* — wakangli *lightning* — wakinyan tonwanpi *sheet lightning* - wakinyan tónwanpi *electric lights* — wakinyan tónwanpi petijan-jan *a flashlight*

[2]light *adj* : gmika *~ and small in weight* — kap'oja *not heavy* - icap'ošya *to lighten* - kapoš kic'un *to walk lightly* - yukapojela *to ligh-ten e.g. a load* — tókašni *not mattering, indifferently, lightly* - tókašnikiya *to make ~ of*

lightning *n* : wakinyan tonwanpi - Cf flash

like *adj* or *adv* : héceca *~ , such as* - hécetuwanjica *always the same* - léceca *~ or such as this* - lécekceca *such as these* — íakihehankeca *alike in length* - íakihehanyan *alike in distance* - íakihenakeca *of equal number with* - ía-kilececa *alike, equal to, of one kind* - íakilecel *like to, equal to* - íakilehankeca *equal to in length* - íakilehanyan *alike in distance, as far as* — icahya *made ~ , conformed to* — í-yakilececa *or* íyakilecel *~ , alike* — íciyacin *to compare several things to each other, to think equal* - íciyacinyan *likening to one another* — iglácin *to liken one's own, or one's self to* - iyacin *to compare with* - iyácinkel *by way of comparison* - iyacinpi *likeness* - eyeceleš *likewise a long time ago he said it* - iyacinyan *in ~ manner* - iyacinyankel *somewhat ~* - wíyacinpi *a likeness, resemblance, similitude* — iyececa *to be ~ to, to be fitting or proper* - iyecehci *being just ~* - iyecekceca *~ , such as* - i-yecekcelya *a bit ~ , less, much* - iyecelya *~ , a little less, not much* - iyecel *~ , in ~ manner, conformed to, consistent with, imitating* — owanke *a likeness* — seksel *likened to*

limb *n* : oya *or* oyaya *an extremity of the body, the limbs, arms and legs*

limber *va* : nalolopa *to make ~ by foot* — sakála *green*

limit *n* : wapetokeca *a boundary* — sabglepi *a stake marker*

limp *adv* : anahuštešteyakel *with a ~* - anaglušte *to be ~* — anaglegleyakel *or* anagleyakel *limping slowly, step-by-step* — anapoksanyankel *in a limping manner* — ópšunpšunyela *limply, in a slack way with little things* — yuospe icu s'e mani *to limp going with a catching gait* — kazewie s'e *limping*

line *n* : óhiye *~ of fence, print, etc., a length of*

linger *vn* : wakah'o *to ~ about, hover over* — yekapin un

liniment *n* : tátu *a root used for the making of ~ by boiling*

link *n* : oyukšan

lip *n* : ehahatun *chapped lips* — iha *the ~ of the mouth* - ihahpi *hanging lips* - íhaton *to have chapped lips* - iha-hpiya *with hanging lips* - ihnahan *to have the under ~ hanging down* — íjoka *to purse or pucker the lips* - íjokiya *to twist the mouth e.g. to whistle* — íkawawa *to move the lips repeatedly opening the mouth* — inangnanke s'e *as if moving the lips* — íšokšokapila *thick lips* — íšpašpa *to move the lips as some do when reading* — pulkicinkel *with hanging lips as though sad* - pute *the upper lip*

liquidate *v* : kajuju *to pay or knock off, to efface*

lisp *v* : šlo

list *n* : owicawapi *a ~ i.e. of names*

listen *v* : nóngeyuza *to obey or heed* - nóngoptan *to attend to*

little *adv* : iyucanyankel *a ~ , a very ~ of* — kitanla *very ~* — kognagyela *just a little* — ociscila *with ~ i.e. time* - wacik'ayela *a ~ bit e.g. of food* - wánik'ala *a very ~* — óh'eya *to have a ~ in* — ošunkecalaka *a very ~ thing* — wamnala *to think ~ of* — optebyela *a ~ while or distance* - óptelyela *for a short time* — otutkala *only a very ~ of* — šnášnayela *a ~ at times* — téhanlake *after a ~ while*

live *vn* : ni - ani *to ~ on or for* - kini *to ~ again* - kini-kiya *to make ~ again* - kiniya *to raise to life* - niic'iya *to make self ~* - nikiya *to cause to ~* - níun *to be living* - niyake *living, alive* - niyakel *in a living manner* - ni-yan *to inhale, breathe, to ~* - wicani *they live, or their lives* - wiconi *one's life* — ti *to dwell* - okiti *to ~ in, to have for a residence* - tíla *to dwell, to take sides* - tiowanji-la *living with others* - típi *a dwelling place* — waiglamna *to make a livelihood for one's self* — špúkešni *a very lively person* — bliheca *to be lively, active*

load *va* : akšu *to ~ on, pile up* — iglagyake *or* igla-gyakel *loaded down with luggage* - okšu *to ~ one's own gun, or wagon etc.* - ookšu *a load* - wakšu *to ~ on, pile on* — íyopazan *to put into the mouth, to ~* — kpa-sminyanyan *to ~ a gun* — okalaiheya *to ~ a gun in haste* — oun *a ~ of a gun* — tkéyawak'inkiya *to overload a gun, to ~ heavily* — oyucokaka *to unload* — peji iyu-wanka aya *to unload a wagon into a barn*

loaf *n* : ons'cokalaka *one who loafs on horseback* — wa-gluhe *to be a hanger-on* — sémni *a bum, an unmarried young man*

lock : akiyataka *to be locked or cramped, as a horse's legs* — aonakitaka *to fasten or lock a door on one* - aonataka *to lock up* - nakicitaka *to fasten for one* - aoglatan *to nail or lock up one's own* — kaotkuga *to close and be locked of itself* - paotkuga *to push closed and locked* - yuotkuga *to close a door and lock it by hand*

long *adj* : hanska - hanskeya *a ~ ways, extending far or ~* — hehanhankeca *each so ~ , so ~* - hehanyan *so far, so long a time* - hehanyela *only so ~ or so far* — íciyehan-yan *equally ~* — makagna *very ~* — téhan *far or long,* *in distance or time*

long ago *adv* : ehank'ehan *formerly* – ehanni *or* ehanna *a long time ago* – ehannitanhan *from a long time ago* — hanbleblekel *or* kilelekel *or* maka wanakajata *or* tannila *long ago*

long-winded *vn* : h'anhanska

look *va* : ableza *to ~ into, to notice* — aištacelya *to catch a glimpse of* – aištagnaka *to ~ at intently* – aištagnagyakel *in a closely observant manner, intently looking at* – ištaiyotapa *or* ištiyotapa *to ~ in the same direction another is looking* – ištayeya *to ~ into the distance* – ištokšin *to close one eye and ~ with the other* — aoglakin *to peep around at one's own* – aokakin *to peep into* eyokakin *to ~ round into* – okas'in *to ~ into* – aeyokas'in *to peep in at* – áyoka *to take a ~* – áyokas'in *to peep into* – éyokas'in *to peep in* — hakikta *to ~ back* — nakišna *to ~ after one's own* — nicaole *to ~ for poor people* – tak'ole *to ~ for something* — ascu *to ~ at others apparently to marry them* — akikta *to give heed to* – iškanškan akikta *to ~ at with a hungry mouth* — tonwan *to see, to take a ~* – ahitonwan *to take a ~ at or toward* – akicitonwan *to take a ~ for one* – akitonwan *to ~ for something lost* – atonwan *to ~ or at* – atonwanyan *to cause to look at* – waatonwe *an observer* – étonwan *to ~ to or toward* – itónwan *to ~ or see with* – otonwan *to ~ into* — awanyanka *to see or look on, to have oversight* éwanyanka *to ~ there* – iawanyanka *to keep eyes on one, to watch or guard* – iciwanyanka *to ~ at together, to compare* – owanyanka *to ~ upon* – owányanke *a show, vision, appearance, a sight, one's looks* — owanyeye *a place for a lookout* – iwan'ic'iglaka *to guard, watch over one's self, to set a guard* – wan'iglaka *to ~ at one's self* — iyowotan'in *a lookout* – iyowotan'inšniyan *invisibly* — ayuta *to ~ steadily at* – agluta *to ~ carefully at one's own* – akiciyukyuta *to ~ at one another* akiciyuta *face-to-face* – ayukyuta *or* ayul *to ~ at* — owakita *to ~ about, to examine*

loom *v* : pašluta *to ~ up, or pop up*

loop *n* : jojoyagton *to make a loop or noose*

loose *adv* : apajejeya *loosely, not securely* — ašakagle *holding loosely* — glugla *to loosen one's own e.g. hair* — hahala *easily moved* – hahayela *~ , free-moving* – inahahaya *loosely as wood badly corded, piled* — hlagan *loose* – gluhlagan *to loosen one's own bond* – hlahan *or* hlahlayel *not securely, loosely* – kaohlagan *to get loose or loosened* – kaohlakala *loosened* – ohlagan *not fitting, ~* – ohlahyela *loosely, not tight-fitting* – ohlain *to work ~* — kahoho *to knock ~* – glahoho *to knock ~ ones own* – hohola *~ , able to be shaken or moved* – nahoho *to shake or loosen by foot ~* – pahoho *to shake, move, or make ~ by pushing* – wohóho *to loosen by shooting* — aiyuhtata *to let ~ on, to give rope to* – ayuhtata *to loosen the lines on a horse to let it run* – ayuohtalya *in a ~ manner* – ayuohtata *to loosen e.g. a noose* — igluška *to untie, unloose one's self* – kiciyuška *to loosen for one* – kiyuška *to ~ , untie, unharness, release as from prison* – paška *to loosen by pressure as in untying a knot* — iglašpa *to bite or break one's self ~* — kableya *to loosen one's hair* — kca *straight, untangled, ~* — kpašpu *to loosen one's own* — nagla *~ , not tied tight, untied* — nahco *to become ~* — naopijela *~ fitting* — wahunhun *to make ~ by slashing* — wankayela *loosely and free to turn* — yuhpa *to loosen e.g. a bowstring* – yuhtaka *to lossen something* — yupanhya *loosely, in a large bundle*

loquacious *adj* or *n* : íwakan *talkative, tattling, gabbing, or a babbler*

lord *n* : itancan *a ruler, master, chieftain, chairman or chairperson* – itancanka *the chief person, ~ or master* – itancankiya *in a lordly manner, or to make a lord, a chief* – itancanya *to have or acknowledge as lord, master, chief* – itancanyan *with authority, as a chief* – itancanyankel *in the manner of a chief which one is not* — itognagya *with the appearance of a chief or of a lord* – Cf chief

lose *v refl* : aikpagan *to be able to spare, part with* — onuniyan *wandering lost* – onunišniyan *not lost* – gnuni *to be lost, or to ~* — hánpohya *losing one's way* — únyan *to ~ , drop from sight* – kiunyan *to ~ what belongs to another* — tókah'an *to ~ , suffer loss, to be gone, lost* – tókakih'an *to suffer injury or loss* – tóki éihpeya *to misplace* — watan'inšni *lost*

loud *adj* : – Cf noise

lounge *n* : oyunk'akanyankapi

louse *n* : héya – hejánjan *or* hintká *an unhatched ~* — heyokicile *to rid one of lice* — heyopuza *lousy, or to be lousy*

love *va* : canȟinyan *to be attached to one as one's mate, a lovng couple* – cantkiya *to love one, to make a sweetheart* – cantognaka *to place in the affections* – cantognakapi *love* — ic'ic'uya *being devoted, giving self up* — kicikšan *to wrestle with, to make love-play with one's wife* – wikikšan *to have love-play with one's wife* — wikiškata *to make love, have love-play* — teȟila *to value one highly* — waštelaka *to love one* – waštelakapi *the love of benevolence, or the beloved* – wówaštelaka *the love of complacency*

low *adv* : kuciyela *~ down, short*

lower *n* : ku *or* kul : the lower parts

luck *n* : oglu *fortune* — šilwakipa *to have bad ~* — tokinšešeš *luckily enough* — waataya *to be fortunate* – waatayes'a *a lucky one* — wanunwaatayela *to strike it well* — wanunwakipa *to have bad luck or an accident* — waptanyan *lucky, or to be lucky*

luggage *n* : panša *a suitcase, bag, baggage* – wizipan *a satchel*

lump *n* : cannunge *a ~ on a tree* — okaske *a ~ of things stuck together*

lunch *v* : icaska *to eat a light lunch*

lungs *n* : cagu – caȟuwayazan *or* hohpawayazan *tuberculosis of the ~*

lurk *adv* : iyapekel *lurking about*

M

magic *n* : wicahmunga *a magician* — wokábiyeya *to remove from the body by means of ~* – Cf bewitch

magistrate *n* : wakiconza *a sort of ~ in a traveling group* – wakicunze *a delegate or representative*

maiden *n* : witanšna un – Cf virgin

make *va* : kága – aic'icaga *to ~ e.g. a sign on one's self* – akicaga *to make on or add to, togo too far* – ékaga *to ~ something at a place* – ic'icaga *to ~ one's self or for one's self* – kahkiya *to cause to ~* – kahtutešni *poorly made* – kahya *a make, a kind or sort, or made like* – waokahwanjica *one make or style, all made in the same way* – kicaga *to ~ for* – kicicaga *to ~ for* – mícaga (of kicaga) *to ~ to or for one* — íksabya *to ~ anything do anythhing*

male *n* : bloká *the ~ of animals* — wica *a man, or human*

man *n* : wicaša *or* wica *a man* — hacila *children* — hokšinigešla *a pretentious adolescent* – hokšila wicahca *a lazy boy* — hununpa *the two-legged, biped* – wahununpa *Man in the sacred language* — ikcewicaša *the common man*

— koškalaka *a young ~ , fig sinté* — wicahcala *an old ~* - wicašaakantu *a living ~* - wicašaha *a lazy ~* wicašaiglawa *a ~ counting himself a ~ and perhaps a chief* - wicašatanka *a middle-aged ~* - wicatanšna *a single ~* wicaya *in a way manly* — wašicun *the white ~* - wašicun cinca *a mixed-blood person* - wašicun hoksila na wicincala *a white man's boy and girl* - wawašicunke *an imitator of the white ~* - wawašicunyan *like a white ~* - wawašikšicunke *an aper of the white ~* - Cf family

manage *adj* : kuwapica *manageable* — oyuha (*in compos with* wašte *or* šica) oyuha wašte *easy to manage;* oyuha šice *hard to manage*

manger *n* : ošunkowote

maniac *n* : onnapewatogya *a dangerous person, one out of his or her mind*

manifest *vn* : nablaya *to become open and plain, clear and visible* — tan'in *to appear* - kiciyaotan'in *to make it clear for one* - kiciyutan'in *to ~ for one* - kiyatan'in to *make visible to or for one* - okitan'inyan *gloriously* - ootan'in *to be visible through* - otan'in *to be clear* - tóiyokitan'in *his manifestation* - waakiciyatan'in *a manifestation* - wayaatan'in *to make clear, to proclaim*

manner *v* : óh'anwašte *order, courtesy, etiquette, protocol,* or *well-behaved, open-hearted, generous, orderly* - oh'ánwašte *to behave well, to be good and generous* — oiyacinyan *in the same manner, mode, pattern* — tókehci *howsoever* - tókelkeltu *in whatever way* - tókeške *howsoever* - tóketkiya *in whatever way* - tóketu kec'eyaš *however, in whichever way* - tóketu keš no matter what

many *adj* : óta — henagnakeca *so ~ of each* - henakeca *just ~ enough* - hénakel *only so ~ or so much* - henakiya *in so ~ ways* - henala *only so ~ or so much* - henalapila *only so ~ , with all gone* - henangnakeca *so ~ each* - iakehenakeca *so ~ more than ten* - iakelenala *only so ~ more than ten* — icaja *to think there are ~* - wóicaje *very ~ , great variety* — kanake *so ~ , all these* - lenake *so ~* - lenala *only so ~ , so few* — pawika *with ~ staying on for naught* — tonakec'eyaš *howmanysoever* — yulolopi *many*

marble *n* : icaslohe *marbles, or billiards*

mark *va* : ayugo *to make marks on* - glugo *to make marks in one's own* - gogo s'e *leaving a ~ with one's foot* - icago *a ~ or line drawn, or to make a ~ , draw a line, to sketch* - icagopi *a line, a mark* - icagoya *to cause to ~ , by way of marking* - kago *to draw a line on land, to ~ with cuts* - pago *to carve, engrave, to pace ground, or to mark off ground, a line for a game* - pagoya *to make a ~ , or to carve* - yago *to ~ with the teeth* — icázo *to draw a mark or line, or to take credit, to owe one, to be in debt, or a ~ or line drawn* - icazokiya *to take on credit, or to give credit* - iglazo *to ~ one's self or one's own* — iwapetokeca *or* iwapetog *what is marked, a sign* - iwapetogton *to ~ or to brand with* - wapetokeca *a sign, i.e. a miracle* — kaglega *to ~ across* - naglegleza *to be marked, striped* - owasaglepi *a bench mark* - wasabgle *to ~ one's way, or a boundary* — kahun *to make a ~ by striking with an axe, to chip* — kaškiškita *to ~ in equal lengths* — nahota *to wear or beat e.g. a track* — iwakta *or* wówakta *a ~ , a sign or pledge* - wówaktaya *to make a ~ or sign*

marksman *n* : waoka - Cf arrow, shoot

marry *v recip* : kiciyuzapi *to take each other, a man and a woman, as man and wife, i.e. marriage* - okiciyuze *a marriage* — tawicuton *to be married* — téya *a polygamous man* — wípeya *to sell a woman or girl in marriage* — yuskiya *to cause to marry* — tiyokitahena *between houses; throwing tent over tent, and lit hence wanting intermarriage within the degrees of affinity*

marshy *adj* : owiwila

marten *n* : wah'anksica

mash *va* : apašúja *to crush by hand on anything* - ayašuja *to bite or ~ up on with the teeth* - opašušja *to ~ up in* - pašuja *to crush by hand, to break or ~ by punching* - wošúja *to crush or ~ up by shooting* — patan *to ~ up e.g. potatoes* - bloipatan *a potato masher* - kipatan *to ~ up e.g. potatoes* - opatan *to ~ up in* - ipatan *to ~ up one thing on another* — inahuga *to ~ by stepping on* — kakpan *to beat* - owayakpan *what is ground up or chewed fine* — okaški *to pound or ~ in* - woškí *to pound e.g. corn partly dried* — štagya *to ~ up as in making preserves, or mushy* — wója *to ~ , to make as a mush* - wójapi *a stew* — yuja *to ~ or make mush, to stir up*

mask *n* : iteha

massacre *va* : tiyapa kte - tiyapa wicaktepi *a massacre*

master *n* : wicayuhe

masturbation *n* : pasluka

mat *n* : owinja - kawinja *to ~ down*

match *n* : hoišta *or* yuilepi *a ~ with which to start a fire* — aiyopteya *to ~ with what another contributes* — ícihloka *a matching suit or number, i.e. a pairing* - ícihlogya *to match, to follow suit* — oiyokšica *ill-matched*

mate *v* : kahtanka *to be a mate*

maturity *vn* : uncihi *to have attained maturity*

meal *n* : wawopanpi *cornmeal*

mean *va* : ka *to consider, ask for, signify* - kica *to ~ one's own* - nica *he means you* — kaocinšica *to make one mean by striking* — oh'anšica *to be ill-behaved, to be cross*

means *adv* : tókani ... šni *with no ~ to*

meanwhile *adv* : kohan *now, quickly, before* - kohanke šni *before the time comes*

measure *v* : iyuta *to weigh, to try, attempt* - iyutapi *a measure, e.g. an acre, a mile, a poound* - iyutekiya *to cause to ~ , adjust, arrange* - iyuteya *by measure* - oiyute *a dimension or rate* - oiyute císcila *an inch* - oiyute wanji *a section of land* - oiyute okise *a half section* - oiyute canku *a section road* - onwiyutapi *a standard for ~* - canwiyute *a cord stick* - igluta *to ~ one's own or one's self* - ikiyuta *to ~ out to* — iyakatin *to ~ by means of e.g. a yardstick* - akatinpi *a standard of ~ from fingertip to fingertip* — otkeyue *a weight* - siiyute *a foot measure* - witkeyute *a scale, weights, a pound* - wíyutapi *a ~* - wíyute *a measure, a measuring tape or rod etc.* — wícacanpi a measure

meat *n* : patapi *butchering, dressing ~* — kabla *to cut ~ for drying* — taloiyukpan *a ~ chopper* - taloyukpanpi *cut meat for sale* - meat parts :

PARTS :

iyuh'eyayapi *the buffalo shoulder*
napco *tenderloin*
napewicašpan *~ under the small ribs*
tacankpe ògnake *or* tacankpognake *~ above the knees*
tamica *the thigh*
tamnatkan *~ below the knee on the front side*
tasicogin *~ below the knee on the rear side*
tanapco *~ near the spine*
taništušta *beef quarters*
tan *a half beef*
tatucuhu *cutlets, the ribs of cattle*
wóluta *a round of beef*

KINDS :

pápa *or* pápasaka *dried ~*
šin *the fat parts*
šlošlola *soft fat parts*

talo *fresh ~*
talipa *sausage*
wakapapi *pemmican*
wasna *pounded beef and marrow etc.*
wašinlo *juicy fat parts*
wíhpanyanpi *dried ~* , pápa
wócankšu *a stick on which to hang ~ drying*
wókapan *pounded ~*

medal *n* : mázaskawanap'in *a silver ~* - Cf necklace
mediate *v* : - Cf friend
medicine *n* : pejuta — pšunka *a pill* — pejuta wicaša *a medicine man or, a Lakota medical doctor* - Note: the word medicine man is commonly applied by non-tribal people to tribal men who lead ceremonies whether or not they are involved with medicines and treatments. Doctor, an M.D., is the term the Lakota apply to the non-Lakota's medicine man who deals chiefly with medicines, treatments and operations. The doctor of the non-Lakota is then termed *wašicun wakan* - pejutaya *to use medicines* — wapiyekiya *to have one apply Indian medicine* — pejuta ȟáka *a medicine root*

REMEDIES :
aches : icahpehu or napoštan *or* ónglakcapi *purple coneflower, for tooth or belly ache* - pejuta huokihetonton, for sore joints - wahpataya ȟota *snakeroot or coneflower, for soreness*
appetite : tínpsila pejuta *milkweed*
breath : pispizatawote *fetid marigold*
chest : pejutaskahu *the loco-weed*
childbirth : canhlogan waštemna *or* yumnumnuga iyececa *ragweed, or* hupestola *the yucca plant or soapweed*
afterbirth : wahpeskuya *dock*
colds *or* **coughs** : heȟaka pejuta *mint* - pejizizi *broomweed* - wahpeceyaka *mountain mint* - wahpeicikoyagyaka *mint*
cramps : tákušašala hu iyececa *tall dock* - Cf diarrhoea
diarrhoea : hucinška *green milkweed* - pejiswula cík'ala *low milkweed* - tákušašala hu iyececa *tall dock*
excretion : canhlogan waštemna *ragweed*
head : matotatinpsila *or* ticanica hu tanka *psoralea*
hemorrhage : tákušašala hu iyececa *tall dock* — pteiciyuȟa unma *for spitting blood*
horses' hooves : ptetawote *ground plum* - šunkhuštipiye *hymenopappus*
kidneys : zitkala tawote *bird's root*
lotions for skin : pejiȟotaswula tánka *or* toto *sages or gray grass* - wazimninkpa *meadow-rue* - pejuta huokihetonton *a liniment for sore joints*
mother's milk : hucinška *green milkweed* - pejutaskuya *tender milkweed* - wahpetinpsila *milkweed*
mouth : íniyan pejuta *or* íniyanpi *or* ónwahinyuntonpi *erigeron*
poison : pejiwakan *panic grass* - yajopi *water hemlock*
snake-bite : zuzecatapejuta *beard-tongue*
sores : pejutajanjan s'ele *alum* - wahpet'aga *alumroot* - wíšpan *iodine*
stomach : hupestola *or* stóla *yucca or soapweed* - pejutanigetanka *the bush morning-glory* - wahpehcahca *croton or skunkweed* - canhloganškiškita *night-shore* - pejuta totó *or* pejuta pa
swelling : canhlogan makatola *purple fritillaria* - hitunkala nakpala *mouse ear* - oipiye *white plantain* - omnica *beans* - šunkcankahuipiye *false gromwell*
wound : pejutawah'e ša *hairy pucoon* - pejuta tínpsila *a turnip used for wounds*

meditate *va* : awacin *to think on or over*
meet *v* : akipa *to happen to one* - akicikipapi *they met each other* - akicipapi *they came upon one another* - écipa *to meet together, to confront one* - écipeya *to cause to meet together* — átaya *to meet one* - átayeya *to meet* — icitkokipapi *they met face to face* - itkokib *meeting face to face* - itkokipa *to meet coming from opposite directions* — kiciatakiciya *to meet face to face, i.e. squarely*
mellow *adj* : štúnka *soft, not ripe, green*
melon *n* : wagmu *a gourd, pumpkin, squash, etc.* - wagmublu *squash* - wagmuhu *a pumpkin vine* - wagmuškopa *the Japanese pumpkin* - wagmušpanšni yutapi *the watermelon*
melt *vn* : askan s'e *seemingly melting on* — aspan *to become soft or melting* — ašla *to be melted or bare* — ašloya *to cause to melt on, as in soldering or welding* - šloyapi *melted matter* - wakašloyakel *in the manner of melting* — komi *to be melting, perhaps* — opaskan *to ~ from lying on* - waicaskan *to ~ snow*
member *or* **adherent** : ópeya un *one belonging to a gang*
memory *n* : wakiksuyapi *memories, dreams, visions* — wašlošloltkiya *to have a good ~*
mend *v* : opiya *to renew, make alike*
menses *n* : išnatipi - išnati *to have a menstrual flow*
merchant *n* : mazopiye wicaša - wíyopeye *an entrepreneur* - wópeton *to trade, buy and sell, or a ~ , a trader*
mercy *v* : ónšila *to have ~ on, to pity* - ónšilaka *to pity one* - ónšikila *to pity one's own* - ónšiya *miserably, pitifully* - wóonšila *mercy* - tówaonšila *his compassion*
messenger *n* : ogligle - ogligleyapi *those sent as a messenger, an apostle* - wahošiyapi *one sent with a message*
mess *adj* : gan *messed* - ganic'iya *or* ganganic'iya *to muss e.g. one's own hair or clothes, to make one's own hair stand on end* - gáns'e *with the hair untidied or disarrayed* - ganyéla *with hair dishevelled*
metal *n* : máza - mázamna *smelling of ~ , iron* - mázaskazi *gold* - mázasuta *steel* - mázaša *copper* - mázašloyapi *pewter* - mázazi *copper*
meter *n* : wíslolye *as a thermometer or a barometer etc.*
middle *adv* : cókab *in the midst, central* - ahocoka *in the midst of camp* - iyocokaya *all swallowed up in, in the midst of* - cokán *the middle place* - cokanl *the middle, or in the midst* - cokangnagya *placed in the ~ half* - cokanyan *in the ~* - icokanyan *in the ~ between* - ocokanya *in the ~* - oakiyecokan *in the ~ before others* - cokapa *in the center or midst* - hócokab *or* hocokam *in the ~ of the camp circle* - ocokab *in the midst* - cokata *the ~ , or in the ~* - cokal *in the midst* - acokata *too far, exceeding the middle* - cokatakiya *toward the center* - cokatawapa *out in the ~ as in a stream* - icokata *in the ~ of* — égna *amidst* — hoaiciyopteya *through the ~ of e.g. the tent* - ocannatuhci *in the ~ of something* — yucannal iyeya *to push into the ~ of*
midnight *n* : hancokan *or* hanyecokan
migrate *v* : wanigla *to ~ southward because of the winter*
mild *adv* : ahwaya *or* ahwayela *mildly*
military *adj* : - Cf itáncan and personnel, rank, etc.
milk *n* : asanpi - pteasanpi *cow's ~* - pteasanpinini *~ curdled* - pteasanpiwasna *or* pteasanpiwigli *butter*
mimic *or* **mock** *or* **ridicule** *va* : unca *to mock, to imitate* - wicoh'unca *to ape another*

mind *n* : tawacin *disposition, thought, understanding*
mine *n* : ok'e - Cf dig
minor *n* : ah'eca *things of ~ or less importance, as in opposition to important matters* - Cf unimportant
mint *n* : can pejuta cík'ala *a mint for headaches or for a common tea*
minute *adj* : gwula• *small*
miracle *adv* : wakanyan *miraculously, in a sacred manner* - wakanyan wicoh'an *to perform miracles* — wówapetokeca *a sign, a wonder*
mirage *n* : makoceatan'in *a desert ~*
mire *v* : kahli *to ~ down, to get stuck in mud* — kajunhe s'e *knocked fast into mud, getting mired* — kalopa *or* kalob *to hit a soft spot* - palopa *to push into the mud, to bemire one*
mirror *n* : mioglas'in *or* miyoglas'in
mischief *v* : wayuškiška *to make ~*
miser *v* : obšiš'ic'iya *to be miserly*
misery *n* : otehi *difficulty, trouble*
misfire *va* : awok'ega *to ~ on trying to shoot* - awoskapa *or* awosna *to ~ on* - wotó *to ~ a gun* - awoto *to ~ on*
misfortune *n* : oš'ica - Cf luck
misplace - Cf lose
miss *v* : šuta *to fail, miss hitting e.g. a target* - ašuta *to ~ hitting something* — ayašna *to let fall on from the mouth, to ~ with the mouth* - kašna *to ~ batting* - okašna *to ~ a day* - pašna *to ~ pushing, thrusting* - wošná *to ~ the mark shooting* - yašna *to ~ with the mouth* — ayugnayan *to ~ in trying to grasp* - pagnayan *to fail to keep one's hold or one's seat* - wagnayan *to ~ with a knife* - wíwognaye *shooting accuracy* - wognáyan *to fail shooting, striking* - yagnayan *to ~ with the mouth* — íwonas'iyaya *to go over the target and up into the air, as a shot arrow* — aokamna *to go around, to avoid, miss* — naokpani *to fail, be short of* — wayuohmin *to ~ in throwing*
missle *n* : iwona s'a *a slice as in golf*
misstep *v* : kagloka *to put out of joint, to strike and stumble twisting* — kaošlok iyaya *to make a misstep and have a near fall*
mistake *va poss* : aglašna *to make a ~ in speaking* - aglušna *to make a ~ over* - glašna *to miss trying to strike one's own, to blunder in speaking, to miss putting food into the mouth* - glašnašnayan *blunderingly, incorrectly talking* - kiciyušna *to make a ~ for* - yušnakonza *to pretend to make a ~* — iyaglašna *to blunder in speaking* - yašna *to blunder in speaking* - yušna *to let drop, to miss* - yušnapi *a mistake* — ecaicišniyan *wrong, entirely wrong* — iigluge *to blunder* — ipawehya *incorrectly* — túwa e kaga *to ~ for*
mistress *v* : wíiyayuha *to go to one's ~*
misunderstanding *v* : oyušica *to have a falling out with*
mix *adv* : icahihiya *mixed together with* - icahikiton *to ~ together one's own* - icahiton *or* icahiya *to ~ together* - ícicahi *to be mingled with one's own* - ícicahiya *to ~ or stir together, to mingle, or mingled* - oicahiton *to ~ together in* - oicahiye *a mixture, blend* - wícahi an instrument with which to stir - wícahiya *to mingle* — ecáicijenaya *to mix together* — ijena *mixed up* - icaijena *to ~ up* — ícijehan *or* ícijena *mingled, mixed up* — kaijena *to confuse, to ~ up* - iyuijena *to ~* - icašoša *to ~ by shaking together* - icicašoša *to ~ to cool off a hot liquid, by pouring from one cup to another* — ícicaskaya *to ~* - ícignuni *to be mixed up and left indistinguishable* - ícignuniya *to cause not to be distinguished* - ícignuniyan *mixed up during that time* — ícikpukpeya *scattered and mixed up* - ikpukpa *mixed up, as people of a variety of nations dwelling together* — ipacica *to mix by rubbing* - iyukpukpa *broken up fine and mixed together* - nakpukpa *to ~ together* — iyupšaya *mixed both good and bad* — kacoco *to beat together e.g. eggs* — wóhpani *something in which to ~ e.g. paint* — gluja *to stir one's own*
moccasins *n* : cuiyohe ~ *made of old tent hides* — hanmwitka *fool moccasins, i.e. those with no design in the beadwork* — hánpa *moccasins* - hánpaitake *or* hanpítake *the face of the ~* - hanpákiglake *the sole of shoe or ~* - hánpa kšùpi *beaded ~* - tehpi hànpa ~ *with the rough side out* - wizihanpa ~ *made from old tent hides* - hanpikceka *common ~* - hanpiškaton *to sew an upper part to ~* - hanpitake *the face, upper part of ~* - hanpohan *to put on, wear ~* - hanpohekiciciya *to put ~ on one* - hanpohekiya *to have ~ put on one* - hanpokihan *to put on one's own ~* — hanpšišica *an old worn out pair of ~* - hanptanni *an old shoe or ~* - hanp'ceyaka ~ *with porcupine quill-work* - hanp'hinšma ~ *made of buffalo hide with the fur inside* - hanp'ipata ~ *covered with quill-work* - hanp'titinyanka *a pair of house ~* — iškahuton *to put tops on ~* - wóskaka *a worker of ~*
mock *n* : waunca *to ~, or one who makes fun of one* — wóicihahaya *in a mocking manner*
moderately *adv* : iktahela *or* kaihakteya *carefully, gently*
modest *adj* : wíšteca *bashful, ashamed* - wíštelkiya *to be reserved with respect to*
moist *v* : pastanka *to moisten* - wostánka *to ~ by rain* — alowitaya *not well dried*
moldy *v* : oyaya *to be ~, musty* - oyayamna *to smell ~*
money *n* : mázaskašala *a penny* - kašpapi *a dime* - šókela *a quarter of a dollar* - mázaska *a dollar* - yušpušpupi *coins, change* - mázaskakpanla *currency* - mnihuha mázaska *paper money* - mnihuha mázaskaiicu *a bank check* - ohiic'iya wicoh'an *a pension* - oicage *interest* - mázaska aonatake *a safe* - mázaska ògnake *a pocketbook* - mázaska omnaye *a treasury* — mázaska igni *or* mázaska kamna *to raise ~* - mázaska el ahigle *to bet*
month *n* : wi *a moon, month* - wiyawapi *a calendar, or a month count* :

wiocokanyan *or* wiotehika : January
cannapopa *or* tiyoheyunka *or* wicata wi : February
ištawicayazan *or* šiyo ištohcapi wi : March
wihakakta cèpapi : April
canwapto *or* wójupi wi : May
tínpsinla itkahca wi *or* wípazuka wašte: June
canpasapa wi *or* wiocokanyan : July
wasuton wi : August
canwape gi wi : September
canwape kasna wi : October
takiyuha *or* waniyetu wi : November
tahecapšun *or* wanicokan wi : December

moon *n* : hanhepi wi - hanwiyanpa *moonlight* - hanyetuwi *or* hanyewi *the moon* — hokeluta *full moon in the morning* - hokemi *or* hokemila *or* hokewin *the man in the moon* — wílecala *a crescent ~* — wi mima *full ~* - wi makatanhan *full third quarter* - wíyašpapi *the third quarter* - wi mimakanyela between *first quarter and full moon* - wíokiseya *the first quarter, i.e. approaching the half moon* - wit'é *the new moon* - wiyata *at the ~ or the sun* - Cf heaven
moor *n* : hokahglepi *or* okahglepi *something moored*
mop *n* : owank'ipakinte *a floor ~* — pajaja *to wash e.g. a floor with a mop*

more *v* : aiyakapa *to exceed, surpass* - ícapeya ~ *than that* - ikapeya ~ *than, beyond* - íyakab *in addition, more than what is needed, or to spare* - íyakabtu *surpassingly* - íyakapeic'iya *to be intemperate* - íyakapeya *to persuade or overcome, to go beyond, or* ~ *than surpassingly* — aiyotan ~ *or greater than* — ákta *again, over again* - akton ~ *than* — aotala s'e *more* - kaotalake s'e *a few* ~ — ipagoya *in passing exceeding in speed* — sanpa ~ *than, over, beyond* - isamyeš ~ *than before, all the* ~ - isanpa ~ *than, beyond that place or time* - isanbtu *or* isanbya ~ , *increasingly* — iyakawin *to go beyond bounds, to overflow* — iyakic'unc'unka *one who does* ~ *than usual, or who keeps on begging* — kaiyakic'uya *a little* ~ — ...lah *or* ...lahca *more of ... (it)*

morning *adv* : anpetuhankeyela *before noon* — hinhanni *or* hinhanna *the morning* - ohinhanna *the forenoon* - hihannahci *early in the* ~

morose *adj* : wacinhinyanza ~ *or cruel* - tawacinhinyanza *morose* - wayuwahinyanza *to make morse or ill-disposed* - wawahiyanskalaka *cross, bad-tempered* - wawahiyanzeca *a* ~ *person*

mortality *n* : wicasota

mosquito *n* : capunka - capunkwokeya *a* ~ *net* - capunk'i-cuwa *a* ~ *bar*

motion *n* : óškan *movement* - óškanšilya *to prevent, impede free movement* — wacajeyatapi *a* ~ *made for discussion etc.*

motorcycle *n* : napopopela

moult *vn* : šunpá *to shed feathers* - šunpela *moulting* - wašunkajun *or* wašunkašloka *to shed feathers*

mount *v* : akiyotaka *to* ~ *e.g. a horse* — okapsica *to* ~ *up*

mountain *n* : ȟe - ȟéta *on, to, in the mountains* — wicacepahala *a high wide* ~ *a high but not wide* ~ — Ȟe Sápa *or* Paha Sápa *The Black Hills* - Ȟeska *the Big Horns and the Rocky Mountains*

mourn *va* : aceya - akiceya *to* ~ *one's own* - owekiceya *to* ~ *over* — wašigla *to* ~ *for the dead, or mourning, grief garments etc.* -wašiglaya *grieving*

mouth *n* : i *the mouth* - icap'tanktanka *or* naicabya *with* ~ *wide open* — ielaya *to put things in the* ~ — iiyuwi *a halter for the* ~ — iniyanpi *sickness of the* ~ — iyognaka *to put into the* ~ - oiyognaka *a mouthful* — iyohloke *the* ~ *of a river or delta* — oyape *to take in the* ~ — yašloia *to mouth words*

move *adv* : ahiyuslohan *to come dragging along, moving out* — iglaka *to* ~ *camp* - aiglagya *to make* ~ *camp* — naglagla *moving* — akatin mani *to walk with arms outstretched* - škan *moving about* - škankiya *to cause to* ~ *about* - škanškan *to stir,* ~ *about* - aškanyan *in motion* - aškanškan *to* ~ *about on anything* - aškanškanyan *moving about on* - naškanškan *to shake or move about with the foot, or move rapidly, shaking or trembling* — waaškanškanyan *to make* ~ *or one causing to live* — glapsanpsan *to sway back and forth one's own* — glugweza *moving fast* — ínangnanka *to* ~ *the lips when reading* - iokpakpas *moving the lips* - íonwiyuta *to gesture with the mouth* — kacanl *to* ~ *the heart* — pahohošniyan *immovably* — pami *to* ~ *away slowly* — piyaiyotake *to* ~ *away to sit* — škinc'iya *to* ~ *one's self*

movie *n* : wówapi škanskan - wówapi naškanškanye *a movie projector*

mow *va* : kašla *to cut* - pejikašla *to mow*

much *adv* : akaecon s'e *over-much* — akeiyenakeca *as much again* — henakehci *so many, enough, finished, all gone* - lenake *or* lenakeca *so much, or so many* — akic'unc'unka *to do repeatedly or over-much* — akic'uya ~ *or plentifully* - iakic'uya ~ , *sufficent* — icajapi *very* ~ - icakiješniyan *plentifully, not in want of* — ícat'a *very e.g. big* — wóicašyela *wondefully* ~ — ihamnapi s'e *appealing much to one's appetite* — íyatagle *surpassing, excessive, or full, running over* - íyatagleic'iya *to be immoderate, to surfeit* - íyatagleya *to cause to be intemperate, or doing too much* — ka *and* laka *suff* : *rather* ~ — óta ~ *or many* - ólota ~ *of various kinds, of great variety* - ótaka *much, or not much* - ótahela *many or* ~ *piled up* — ošungye *too* ~ , *more than one can manage, very violently* — tányutkanla ~ *of something, e.g. food, provisions*

mud *n* : makahlihli, *a thin* ~ — unpšija, *a light* ~

mudhen *n* : šiyaka

muffle *adv* : iyopša s'e *muffled*

mule *n* : šónšonla

multiply *va* : yuota - íciyuota *to* ~ *together* - igluota *to* ~ *one's self, to do many things at one time, to* ~ - kiciyuota *to* ~ *for* - yuotapi *a multiplication*

munch *v* : yúlyul *to eat rapidly along the way, but with appreciation,*

murder *va* : tikte *to commit* ~ - tiokte *to commit homicide, to kill in the house* - tíwicakte *a murderer, or to commit* ~ - tíwicaktepi *murder*

murky *v* : ošoše *to become obscure, dim, indistinct*

murmur *v* : kipa *to blame one's self, to complain against one, to rebel*

mush *v* : yuja *to make* ~ - kiciyuja *to make* ~ *for one*

musical instruments *n* :

drum *cancega*
flute *ciyotanka* or *hokagapi*
harmonica *yapizapi* or *wayapizapi*
harp *cankicaton*
horn, brass horns *wayajopi*, *mázayajopi*
organ *can'iyukize* or *canyukizapi*, perhaps also a piano
organ pit *ocanyukize*, or the place where an organ is mounted
piano *canpakizapi*
violin *can'ipakize* - to play the violin *canpakiza*

musk *n* : sinkpeonzemna - Cf perfume

my *adj pron* : mitawa *my or in compos* ...ma... *or* ...mi... *me or I* - Cf I

mysterious *adj* : wakanka *doubtfully* ~ - wawakankanka *of a* ~ *activity, acting the part of a soothsayer*

N

nag *v* : wayatiktil ihe *to find fault with others for no reason*

nail *n* : šake *nails of fingers and toes,* also *claw or hoof* - tašišake *a hoof*

naked *adj* : šla - šlaya *in a* ~ *way* — tancola *poorly clad* - tancokala *stark naged*

name *n* : caje - acaje íglata *to praise one's self, to mention one's own name, to give a* ~ *to one's self* - cajeglal *to call, identify one's self* - cajeglata *to call one's own by* ~ - cajeiglata *to speak one's own* ~ - cajekaga *to* ~ *or make a* ~ *for one* - cajekiyata *to mention or speak of to one* - icaje *in the* ~ *of* - icajeka *to be named for or on account of* - icajeyata *in the* ~ *of, in speakib the* ~ *of* - ocaje *a kind or species* - wacajekiyata *to* ~ *one's deceased relatives* - caškiton *to give a* ~ *to one's own* - cašton *to make a* ~ *for one's self* - caš'tan'inyan *having a great* ~ - éyacašton *to* *give a ~ to one* - ocašton *to make a great ~ for one's self* - eciyapi *or* ekiyapi *called, named* — glawakan *to call one's own sacred or holy*

napkin *n* : iikpakinte — makuakahpe *a bib or ~*

nation : oyate *a people or the people or a tribe or a clan* - oyateya *as a nation.* Some tribes of the high plains tribes of central United States of America :

American *Mílahanska*
Apache *Cincakize*
Arapahoe *Mahpiyato*
Arickaree *Hewaktokta*
Assiniboin *Hohe* or *Waziyata Wicaša*
Blackfoot *Sehasapa*
Brule *Sicangu* or *Hinhanšunwapa* or *Kul Wicaša*
Cheyenne *Sáhiyela, Šahiya* or *Tahin Wicaša* or *Tokcinkawota*
Chinese *Picokanhanska*
Chipewa *Hahatonwan*
Comanche *Sintehla Wicaša, the same name as the Snakes*
Cree *Maštincala Wicaša*
Crow *Kangi Wicaša* or *Psáloka*
Dakota *Dakota Oyate* with *e.g.* a band: *Kiyaksa*
English *Šaglaša*
Eskimo *Cáh'otila*
Flathead *Natableca* or *Našunhape*
Ghost Dance Group *Howí Wicaša,* among the *Oglalas*
Hohwoju *and* Hunkpapa *Teton bands*
Kootenai *Škutani*
Kwapa *Peša*
Leaf Shooter *Wahpekute* or *Wahpetonwan*
Lakota a band of the *Dakota Titonwan*
Loafer a group of *Oglalas : Wagluhe*
Mandan *Miwatanni*
Mnikowoju *a Teton band*
Nez Perce *Pogehloka or Watopahlate or Watopala*
Northern Tribe : the Bloods *We Wicaša*
Oglala *a southern Teton band. Wajaje were a group of Oglalas and Sicangu of the Rosebud*
Omaha *Omaha* or *Oyatenunpa*
Osage *Witapahatu and Kiowas*
Oto *Watohtata*
Pawnee *Palani or Scili*
Ponka *Oyateyamni*
Santee *Isan'ati*
Shawnee *Šawala*
Shoshone *Susuni or Pejiwokeya Oti Kin*
Sicangu *Brule of the Rosebud*
Sioux *Dakota Oyate*
Sisseton *Sisitonwan or Hangeokute*
Snake *Sintehla Wicaša*
Teton *Titonwan esp the Ihoka, Oglala, and Mnikowoju etc.*
Two Kettle *Oohenunpa*
Ute *Sápa Wicaša or Wicaša Yuta*
Winnebago *Hótanke*
Yankton *Húnkpati* (the Lower Yanktonai), *Ihanktonwan, Waceunpa, and Wiciyela*

nausea *vn* : wíyako *to feel ~*

near *adv* : kiyé *nearby* - kiyela *~ to in time or place* - akiyela *near* - icikiyela *or* icikikiyela *close or ~ to each other* - ikiyéla *nearly* - ikinyela *near to in time or space* - itankiyela *~ to one* - oakiyela *not far* — atignagya *nearby* — kagla *nearby* - icagla *or* icaglaya *by the side of, near to* - okaglala *by the side* - okaglayela *near to, close by* — kanyela *near* - icikanyela *~ together* - ikanyela *~ to* - okanyela *nearby* - owaškanyela *not far* — inak'esya *alongside* — isiyatanhan *~ the feet of* — iyokal *holding ~ to as to a fire* — išnikaleš *nearly, pretty ~* — itiyopa *~ the door* — íyape *close or ~* — íyapela *close at hand* — kitata *in close succession, ~ together* — owasya *to bring and cause to be ~* — yaaskala *to speak of as ~* - yaaskayela *speaking of as ~ , or to speak of as ~* — yuaška s'e *nearby, in a sense*

neat *adj* : stola *small and neat* — wayaco *nearly* — yuskapila s'e *in a ~ way*

necessity *or* **need** *v* : kpaowotanka *to get necessities for one's self* — napepicašni *inevitable* — tan'inyunla *deprived of necessities i.e. of life, work, etc.*

neck *adj* : hlúte *long-necked* - hlute s'e *of a sort long-necked* — poskica *to clasp about the ~* - poskil *by the ~* - poskiski *squeezing by the ~* — tahu *the back of the ~* - tahuhute *the nape of the ~*

necklace *n* : wanap'in *a kerchief, a medal, etc.* - wanap'inblaska *a medallion as of beads* - wanap'inkicaton *to wear as a ~* - wanap'inya *to use as a ~*

need *adv* : tokecakel *in case of ~*

neglect *v* : aištagnakešni *not to look after e.g. one's child* — iwakiniya *to get out of humor with, out of contempt* — iyušpeyeya *with work being neglected* — wišute *to ~ doing, to miss doing*

neither *adj* : unmala ... šni, *said of one* — unmani ... šni, *said of two*

nervous *n* : wakahtakeca *a ~ person who is very sensitive* - wakahtakeke *a fretful person*

nest *n* : hecayunkapi *or* hohpi - hohpiya *to have or make a ~*

net *n* : zanzanla *netting*

network *or* **grid** *v* : tawogmunkekahya *to make a web of, a pattern of*

neurology *n* : éteiyokiseyazan

never *adv* : tóhanni - tónweni ... šni *or* tóweni ... šni

nevertheless *adv* : hécac'unš - hécaeša *though it is such, not withstanding* - hecašká *still, nonetheless* - héceca eša *or* héceca k'éyaš *or* hé eca éyaš *or* héecaška *nevertheless* — itušeka *by all means, by perseverance* — nahahci *yet, still* — takomni *nonetheless*

new *adj* : téca *young* - ateca *to become ~ on* - ayuteca *to renew on* - igluteca *to make one's self new* - kiciyuteca *to make new for* - pateca *to rub up and make new again* - wóteca *newness* - tecaya *to renew or newly* — lecakcala *brand new*

news *n* : ptepapala *the main ~* — wahoši *to bring ~* — wótan'in *the ~*

newspaper *n* : mnihuhakakakanka *newspaper or writing paper* — wótan'inwowapi *a news paper*

next *vn* : íyokihe *to be ~ to, to be second* - ókihe *following, second*

nibble *v* : oyak'oza *to bite short* — wayaol'otake *to ~ on* — yahpu *to ~ on what sticks* — yajipa *to bite as do insects* — yatuka *to ~ off as do mice*

nicely *adv* : yupiya *finely, pleasantly, with grace and skill*

nick *va* : wohci *to ~ using a tool*

nicknack *n* : špúla *a trifle, bits of things, or trifling*

night *vn* : akpaza *to come ~ on one* — ayungya *to go and spend the ~ at* — han *or* hanyetu *or* hanhepi *the night* - ohanhepi *a certain ~* - han'iyanpa *a moon-lit ~* - hanmšicelahcake *being a very windy ~* - hannatantankel *feeling one's way through the ~ with the feet* - han'oiyokipi *a pleasant ~* - han'oluta *a warm ~* - han'opta *through the ~* - han'otkan *a hot and sultry ~* - hántahena *before ~* - hantehan *late in the ~* - hanwahehantu *an appoint-*

ed time at ~ - hanwakan *mysterious in regard to a goings-on at ~* - hanwatohanlšna *again and again at ~ , anytime at ~* - hanwatohantu *at some time during the ~* - hanyagug *to spend the ~ in the cold* - hanyetu *night* - hehanpi *last ~* — htahepiyela *before retiring at ~* — ihan'iyupta *through most of the night*

no *adv* : híya — hánšni *decisively not!*

nobody *pron neg* : tuweni ... šni

nod *vn* : kogingin *to give a nod* - ógingin *to ~ in sleep* — pakahunka *to ~ to one* - pakicahunka *to bow to one* — pazeze *nodding, swinging*

noise *va* : ahmun *to drown one in ~* - waohmunyece *a talkative and very noisy person* — ah'a *to make ~* - h'ayela *with the ~ of rain or hail* — bu *to be drumbeating* - anabu *to stamp with the feet* - ayubu *to drumbeat on anything* - buya *noisily, as one lowing* - buyakel *in a noisy manner* - buyehci *with a loud noise* - buyel *noisily* — apakiza *to make ~ by rubbing, filing* — ayuswu *to make a rattling ~ on or over* — ginlgica *to make a choking ~* — hohnagicala hotonpi *the sound of a trill* — hokitanyankel *noisily as in making an attack* — hošpeyela *loudly of voices* — waaoton *a ~ maker* - wayuhoton *to make ~* — ȟuȟugahe s'e *with a thundrous ~* — inapša *to slosh about* — kakyela *with ~* — k'o *the bustling of people* - nahloke s'e *noiselessly* - ok'o *a buzz of voices* - ok'oya *with a buzzing ~ or to be buzzing* — owolutaton *to make a ~ or a bustle, clamor* - owolutatonyan *in a clamoring manner* — oyucokaka *to make crunch by squeezing* — pak'eza *to make a rasping or a filing sound* — waaš'akece *a noizy person*

none *adj* : wanica *without any or anything* — wanjini *pron* : none

nose *n* : pa - pacete *the nostrils* - paglaȟuga *to break one's own nose* - pahute *the upper part of the nose* - pahlate *the ~ fossae* - pasu *a beak or bill* - papinkpa *the tip of the ~* — póge *the nose* - póhcante *the wings of the ~* - pónunuje *the lower part of the ~ , the snoot*

not *neg suff postp* : kaca — kilo, *i.e.* šni yo — šni *or* šniš

notch *n* : ikpage - kakan *to make notches into something* — okakse *pieces cut out* — kaleblepa *to ~ by cutting* –kalepa *to cut a ~ in* - walepa *to cut round notches* - yaleblepa *to bite notches in* - yuleblepa *to make notches in*

note *v* : owaicu *to take ~ of* — tokaic'ignaka *to take ~ of, to write down for one's self*

nothing *n* : níca *to be destitute of* - wanica *lacking in, or to have ~ or none* - anica *to retain what is claimed by ananother* - wawanice *there to be ~ , or a dearth, scarcity* - wawaniceca *there is ~ or little* - wówanice *the state of nothingness* — tákuni ... šni *to come to ~ ,* or tákunišni *nothing* — éyapi ecehce *nothing but talk, nothing to it*

nourishing *adj* : iwicamna *satisfying* - iwicawašte *noutritious*

now *adv* : iyehantu *at the time* — lehanleš *nowadays* - lehantuyakel *just ~* — ungnahanšna *~ and then, at certain times* — wana *or* wanaš *or* wanna *now, in present time*

nudge *va* : pani *or* panini - wópani *to nudge one*

null *adj* : ecetušni *void* - ecetušniya *to make a breach, a contract, to rescind*

numb *adj* : glušte — kšikša *stiff with cold* - kšikšeca *numb* — t'at'a *~ as a limb asleep* - kpat'at'a *asleep* - pat'at'a *to be asleep, as might one's leg or arm* - sit'at'a *a foot asleep* - t'at'aka *palsied*

number *adv* : kicamnayan *in an overwhelming way* — ótapi s'e *in large numbers* — ówihe s'e *in a large ~* — pahayela *in a pile, abundantly* — yuwiwihe s'e *in large numbers* — otáwat'ešica *numberless, awesome* — yawapicašni *numberless, countless*

CARDINAL NUMBERS :

wanji, wánci, wan	*one*	1
núnpa, numb, num, núnp	*two*	2
yámni	*three*	3
tópa, tob, top	*four*	4
záptan	*five*	5
šákpe	*six*	6
šakowin	*seven*	7
šaglogan	*eight*	8
napciyunka	*nine*	9
wikcemna	*ten*	10
(wikcemna) ake wanji *	*eleven*	11
(wikcemna) ake núnpa	*twelve*	12
(wikcemna) ake yámni	*thirteen*	13 *etc.*

* wikcemna is omitted 11-19

wikcemna núnpa	*twenty*	20
wikcemna núnpa ake wanji	*twenty-one*	21
wikcemna núnpa ake núnpa	*twenty-two*	22 *etc.*
opawinge	*one hundred*	100
opawinge sam wanji	*one hundred one*	101
opawinge sam núnpa	*one hundred two*	102 *etc.*
opawinge sam wikcemna	*one-hundred ten*	110
opawinge sam ake wanji	*one hundred eleven*	111
opawinge sam ake núnpa	*one hundred twelve*	112 *etc.*
opawinge sam wikcemna núnpa		120
opawinge sam wikcemna núnpa ake wanji		121
opawinge sam wikcemna núnpa ake núnpa		122 *etc.*
opawinge núnpa sam wikcemna núnpa		220
opawinge núnpa sam wikcemna yámni ake wanji		231
opawinge yámni sam wikcemna tópa ake núnpa		342 *etc.*
opawinge wikcemna **		1000
opewinge wikcemna sam wanji		1001
opawinge wikcemna sam wikcemna		1010
opawinge wikcemna sam ake núnpa		1012
opawinge wikcemna sam opawinge		1100
opawinge wikcemna sam opawinge núnpa sam yámni		1203
opawinge wikcemna kin núnpa sam opawinge yámni sam wikcemna tópa ake záptan		2345 *etc.*
opawinge wikcemna kin wikcemna		10000
opawinge wikcemna kin wikcemna núnpa		20000
opawinge wikcemna kin wikcemna núnpa sam opawinge wikcemna kin yámni sam opawinge tópa sam wikcemna záptan ake šákpe		23456

The preferred way of counting follows this skema :

10	wikcema
100	opawinge *or* kaunhye *or* kawinhye
1000	opawinge wikcemna *or*

** koktopawinge

2000 opawinge wikcemna kin núnpa *or* koktopawinge núnpa

10000 opawinge wikcemna kin wikcemna *or* koktopawinge wikcemna

100000 opawinge wikcemna kin opawinge *or* koktopawinge opawinge

Thus for 987654:

opawinge wikcemna kin opawinge napciyunka
sam opawinge wikcemna kin wikcemna
šaglogan ake šakowin
sam opawinge šákpe
sam wikcemna záptan ake tópa

BY GROUPS:

by two's	numnunpa
by nine's	napcinyungyunka
by hundred's	opawingege

ALTERNATES:

every second one	inumnunpa
every third one	iyamnimni
every fourth one	itobtopa
every tenth one	iwikcemnamna

LIMITS:

only two	nunblala
his or her two	tanum
in two sets	tanumnum
in two different ways or places	numkiya

ORDINALS:

First	tokeya
second	inunpa *or* (w)icinunpa
third	iyamni *or* (w)iciyamni
fourth	itopa *or* (w)icitopa *etc.*
tenth	iwikcemna *or* iciwikcemna
twentieth	iwikcemna nunpa *etc.*
hundreth	iyopawinge
thirteenth	iakeyamni
thirty-third	wikcemna yamni iake yamni
the hundred third	opawinge sam iake yamni

nut *n* : yuȟugapi — uta *the hazelnut, or an acorn*

O

oar *n* : – Cf paddle

oath *va* : yugalkiya *to administer an oath, a public promise*

obey *va* : anagoptan *or* anongoptan *to lend an ear to, to listen to* – anakigoptan *to listen, obey one's own e.g. father* – waanagoptanyan *obediently*

object *v* : wacinyeyešni *to ~ to, to lose hope in* — yaškiška *to raise objections to*

obliquely *v* : kaohmin *to move ~* — óhya *slanting* – yuohya *obliquely*

obscure *adj* : ookahnihteȟike

observe *va* : iwanyanka *to examine* – iwanyankapi *an observation* – owanyeye *a place to ~* – wósukiye *observance e.g. of law*

obstacle *n* : wówicagi *a hindrance* — yuhotapi se *removing obstacles*

obstinate *adj* : okiwaš'ag šica *wrong-headed, obstinate, taking no advice, opiniated* – waektanjašni *wanting docility* — wakilkitanyan *obstinately*

obstruct *va* : unc'onnilya *to prevent one, to disarm one, or prevented* — wawopteca *obstructing, sluggish, lazy, hindering* — wóikuše *obstacles*

obtrusive *v* : paswuic'igle *to be ~, to be important* – Cf fringe

obvious *adj* : ookahnihwašte

occupy *adv* : kcanptepte *being occupied with thought* — oškinc'iye *an occupation, a job* – oškin'ic'iya *to busy one's self* – wóškinciye *an occupation, a work*

odd *n* : iyušna *one with no mate*

odor *n* : wówaštemna *a pleasing ~*

of course *adv* : tókeni *of course by no means*

offend *va* : iyoyaka *to displease one, make sick of* — okic'unica *to be made angry* — šigla *to take offense at, to be angry*

offer *v* : wagluhtata *to ~ one's own* – wakicigluhtata *to ~ a price, a sacrifice for* — waunye *an act of offering* – waunyekiya *to make offers to* — wówicak'upi *an offering*

often *adv* : ijehan *or* ijehanyan *often, repeatedly* – ijehanyankel *frequently, right along* — ótakiya *in many times, or places or ways, ~*

oil *n* : wiglizazecala *floating droplets of ~* – Cr grease

ointment *n* : sla *or* islaye *salve* – slaojuha *an oil bag*

old *v* : akan *to be ~* — hokšiunke *older, old enough* – kanhi *to live to be ~* – okan *~ age* – okanke *at old age, at the last* – okantehan *to bear old age well* — tanika *~ and worn out* – tanni *of old, already, before* – watanni *~ things*

omit *v* : agluštan *to let alone one's own*

on *or* **upon** *or* **at** *prep insep* : akan(l) – iakanl *upon or on top of* – iakatanhan *on top of, outside* – waákanl *on, or on top of the snow* — áta *suff* to *n*: *to, at, on* — aunyan *to be ~ or over* — iyagleton *to have on or over as in knitting* – iyagletonyan *being on or over* — óštan *to put on or in, to be on or in e.g. agreement, to be in place of, on or at* – oštánhan *being in or on*

once *adv* : tónwel *~ upon a time* — ehanni *long ago* — wánca *once* – wáncaeš *or* wáncayeš *or* wáncakeš *at ~* – wáncag *or* wáncagna *immediately* – wáncagcala *~ in awhile* – wáncahci *for, just, at least ~* – wáncaleša *at least ~* – wáncakcala *only ~ in awhile, seldom, or ~ apiece* – wáncala *only ~ or ~ only* — watohantuka wan *rather at a certain time, sometime rather, ~ upon a time*

one *adj num* : wanji – wanjica *one, or in ~ way* – wanjigji *~ apiece, i.e. some* – wanjigjila *~ by ~, singly* – wanjila *one* – wanjipila *they are ~* – wanjilakel *in ~ manner*

- wanjilakiya *in ~ way* - wanjitoktok *~ after the other, i.e. in turns*

only *adv* : ecela *only once* - Cf alone

ooze *vn* : au *to suppurate* — sli *to ~ as sap from a tree* - nasliya *oosing out* - šli *or* našli *to ~ out* — oštanhan *to ~ out* — kitonwaya *to ~ or seep out* - otonyan *suppurating* - tonyan *to form or run puss*

open *vn* : ama blága *Nonsense! It is opened out* — iyublah *to open out e.g. a tent* —kablaya *to ~ e.g. one's eyes* - okablaya *a level place, a plain, or without obstruction* — anablaza *to tear or burst open with the foot* — glubleca *to ~ out, take in pieces one's own* — gangan *open, as is thin cloth* - ayugan *to ~, e.g. a door on anything* - glugan *to ~ out one's own e.g. one's blanket* - kagan *to spread out* - kiyugan *to ~ for* - paganya *to make ~, to part with* - paganyan *parting with* - yagan *to ~ with the mouth* - yugan *to ~ e.g. a door* — aglugata *to ~ out or extend e.g. one's hands or arms* - galgata *open, as a piece of cloth* - kíciyugata *to open out and extend the hand for one* — ayuhloka *to make a hole ~ on* - igluhloka *to ~, unbosom one's self* - oyuhloke *a hole, an aperture* - wíyuhloke *an opener, a key* — kajahan *to press ~* - kajaka *to squeeze ~* - glujaka *to pull ~ one's own* — ínajalyeya *to keep the mouth ~* — aikapa *to ~ the mouth on, to scold one* - icapa *to ~ the mouth* — aglukawa *to ~ up one's own e.g. wound* - ayukawa *to cause to ~ on* - iglukawa *to ~ one's own mouth* - kakawa *to make ~ by striking* - wapakawa *to ~ out* — kpi *breaking ~* — našakayela *opening e.g. a wound* — yuogna icu *to take and ~ e.g. a gun* — naoko *to split* — anapopa *to burst ~ on anything* — tan'inyan *openly, not concealed* — iyuwicola *open as a sore, not bandaged or dressed* — akazamni *to ~ upon or throw ~* - ayazamni *to open or reveal by speaking* - ayuzamni *to set ~ on e.g. a door* - kiyuzamni *~ to or for* - glazamni *to ~ or uncover one's own* - nazamni *to ~ by foot* - yuzamniyan *opened*

opinion *va* : la *or* laka *to form or have an ~ of* — wacinyuza *to have an ~* — wayacocoka *one ever giving his own ~* — kitan *to insist upon one's own ~, to be opiniated or obstinate*

opportunely *adv* : ecekce *or* ecelkce *in the proper place or way* — cokehanl *or* étukehanl *at the proper time*

oppose *v* : pajin *to prevent* - kicipajinpi *they opposed each other* - kipajin *to stand up against* — paesya *against*

opposite *adv* : akasanpa - akasanpatanhan *on the other side e.g. of the river* — akokab *straight across by a near way* — hoopta *across center camp, through the camp* icitkokib *meeting face to face* — iyotatkons *~ to, over against, even* - iciyotatkons *~ to each other, equal to, even with* - iciyotatkonza *~ each other, even with, equal to*

oppressed *adv* : oiyuskilya *oppressed in*

optative mood *partic in compos* : toke *I suppose of course,* — tóki *adv* : *where or somewhere,* — toke eša ... ni *I wish I,* - toke ... laka *I wish that,* - toke ... ni *Oh that,* - tokin ... ni *Oh that* or *I wish that* - toke ... so? *Did you really want ... ?*

or *conj* : nainš

order *v* : kahši *or* wawahoya *to ~ things, to place an order* — wawahoyapi *things ordered esp by mail* - wíwahoye *an ~ to do something* — kaskiglag *to spread or do without ~ or system* — katkanheya *in an orderly way* — otogmun *to appear orderly, to be well kept* — tacankohanhanke *an orderly form*

ornament *n* : óskapi *or* wóska *or* wóyuska *ornamental work done on e.g. a pipe* — owin *to wear jewelry, or a personal ~* — pegnakapi *a hair ~* — wakikšukšu *to hang ornaments on one's own* — wamuh'a *a cowry shell* — wasuhula *necklace in Iroquois* - wasula *a necklace* — wawoslata *bone beads* — wicicaške *strips of blanket worn over the shoulders, or ornamented strips trailing on the ground*

orphan *n* : wablenica

oscillate *va* : ogluhomnimni *to vibrate or turn something to and fro constantly* — yupsonpson *to ~ as in sprinkling*

ostentaciously *adv* : pajoke s'e *in an ~ way*

other *adj* : unma *or* uman *the one ... the other ...* - unmaciyatan *from the one side* - unmagma *one or the ~* — itokanl *in an ~ place away from, as opposed to side by side, i.e. together* — togtoka *otherwise, in another way*

otter *n* : škecá *an otter or animal like an ~* - Cf animals

out *v* : kajun *to knock, or pull, or fall out*

outside *adv* : akapatanhan *on the ~, exteriorly* - akabhan *standing on the ~ of* — akantuya *or* akantuyela *on the ~, without, on the surface* - ákatanhan *on the ~* — holazata *~ the camp circle* — tankata(l) *or* - itankal *out of doors, outside, without* - itankatanhan *or* itankatahan *from the ~*

outstanding *adj* : sotka *as a tall tree among small ones*

oval *v* : šok'in *to have a small, odd but humorous face*

oven *n* : owašpanye *a baking ~*

over *adv* : íyakapatanhan ~ or *on top*

overflow *vn* : pašwoka *to ~, or to come over* - apašwoka *or* apašwog *to come up on or over*

overlap *va* : yuic'ic'uya *to make ~*

overload *adv* : hukitanla *overloaded* — wók'inyut'eya *to ~ something* — wóš'a *overloaded*

overlook *v* : oȟape *overlooked and not found*

overseer *n* : wawanyanke *a policeman or policewoman*

overshadow *v* : - Cf shade

overtake *v* : églega *or* ékiglega *or* íyakigleh *or* kiglega *to ~ one* - íyakiglega *to go on and ~*

overturn *adv* : paaglapšun *turning bottom-up, toppling*

own *v* : watonšni *to ~ nothing, to be poor* — yuhapi *owning, owned, held*

ox *n* : pteokicaška *or* pteakicaška *or* ptewak'in *work-oxen* - ptetawanap'in *an ox-yoke*

P

pace *vn* : onaš'o *to ~ as a horse does* — kaipsilyalake s'e *keeping pace ahead of one*

pack *v* : inapan *to be packed as a road after rain* — kaot'inza *to ~ tight* - naot'inza *to press in tight with the foot* — kic'in *to ~ one's own load* - kicic'in *to carry or ~ for one* — wahekic'un *to ~ one's own* — wak'in *baggage* - wak'inpi *a pack* — oiyahpeye *a horse ~* — opahte *baggage, a bundle or bunch, a bale* — pakigni *to ~ home, to carry home* - pakihta *to tie up one's own, to ~ up* — owotan *to ram in, to ~ in* — wopúskica *to ram tight* — waheyun *to ~ in a bundle*

paddle *v* : watopa *to ~ a canoe* - watopapi *the rowing or a boat* - iwatopekiya *an oar or ~ etc.*

page *n* : oyublaye *the ~ of a book*

pain *va* : kazan *to hurt one, to make feel ~* - yazan *to feel ~* - yazangla *to be touchy, painful*

paint *va* : owa — tiisanye *paint* — wínyupin *house or wall ~*

pair *n* : otawanjila *a ~ one of a kind* — ta *one of, a ~ of* - tatona *or* tóna *a ~* - tawanji *a ~, one of anything*

- tanunpa *two pairs*

palm *v* : napoyublaya *to open the ~ of the hand, esp as a gesture that something became level* - Cf hand

pan *n* : taspan onwohanpi *a sauce pan, a cooking pan*

pander *v* : wiwotikiya *to ask for a wife for another man*

paper *n* : mniȟuha - mniȟuhaowapi *~ blanks* - mniȟuhaska *writing ~*

parable *n* : wiyaciniapi - wiyacinyan *by way of a ~, parabolicly* - wawiyacin *to use parables* - Cf figures

parade *n* : šunkahlowanpi *an off-to-war ~* - Úc'ita Au *the 4th of July ~, Independence Day in the United States*

paralyze *v* : tansanni t'a *to be paralyzed on one side of the body* - tánt'at'a *paralyzed*

parch *va* : papahya *to ~ e.g. corn, meat, etc.*

parent *n* : wakihiyece *one who raises children* - Cf family

parlor *n* : oyake tipi - Cf confer

part *adv* : kazanyan *parting* - kpazan *to ~ one's own e.g. hair* - yuzan *to separate things* - pazan *to ~ the hair* - pazanyan *dividing* - peozan *or* peyozan *a part in the hair* — pagan *to ~ with* - kicipagan *to ~ with for* - kicipaganpi *they ~ with each other i.e. from each other* - kpagan *to ~ with one's own* - paganyahan *ready to ~ with* — kpapta *to leave one's own, to ~ with, separate from one's company* — okise *a ~ of, half of anything* — onšpa *a ~ or piece of anything* — ópa *to take a ~ in, to join up with*

participate *v* : ilita *to take part in*

particles *interj* or *exclam* : - Cf according to each purpose to which they are put, *e.g. Ho!* Alright! *or* Yes!, so as to affirm or allow

particular *n* : wayuskica *a very squeemish person*

Paschal Lamb *np* : Tawohiyayewicawote, *or* Wicawotapi *the Eating of the Paschal Lamb, in the Jewish celebration of the* Wóacankšin *Passover to memorialize their liberation from slavery in Egypt, during the time of Moses*

pass *v* : abluhehahaka *to ~ over quickly* — acankšinya *to step or jump over something* - acankšinyan *passing over* — acankuya *to make a road on, or pass through on, or lying on a road way through* - acankukiya *to ~ by a certain place on one's way somewhere* — gligla *to ~ by some thing or person* - wigligla *to come and ~ by* — hiyaya *to arrive and ~ on* — ícic'uya *coming in opposite directions and passing each other* — inašloka *to pass on beyond, to wear through or out* — inapiškanyan *to pass away time, to kill time* — iyopta *to ~ through or between* - iyoptiyeya *to cause to ~ through* — kinapa *to have passed through in going home* — kiyaglapta *to have passed over e.g. one's own land on one's way home* - kiyakapta *to have passed over e.g. a hill on the way home* — pucancan iyaya *to ~ under stooping* — yunaya *to ~ something along* - yunayekiya *to have one ~ along something to another*

passion *n* : wacinkopi *a craze, desire, infatuation* - wacinkoya *passionately*

pasture *n* : owayašla

patch *v* : iyopata *to sew on a piece* - okipata *to put on a ~ to join one to the other* - okipatapi *patchwork*

patent *n* : ša ayaskapa *~ in fee*

path *n* : canku - ocanku s'e *like a pathway*

patient *adj* : tawacinhanska *long-suffering* - tawacinhanskeya *patiently* - wacinektayuza *to be fore-bearing* - wacintanka *longanimous* - wacintank kic'un *to have patience*

patter *v* : ȟaȟaya *to ~ on, as rain on a tin roof, or feet on a kitchen floor*

pattern *n* : - Cf network

paw *va* : kawaza *to throw up dirt* - yuwaza *to ~ the ground* — makak'ak'a s'e *pawing the ground* — wótica *a pawing, scraping as a horse might do*

pay *v* : iši *to ~ wages* - išikicin *to want ~* — iyunwinton *to have the means to ~* — kicicajuju *to ~ for something for another, to forgive one* — yuksapi *monthly payments*

peace *n* : wówahwa — okiya *to make ~ with, as in courting a woman* — ablagyela *or* owahwayakel *peacefully, quietly*

peak *n* : pajola *a high hill, or prominent* - pajoya *humped, hill-like*

pedestrian *n* : makamani

peel *va* : ayugapa — yaga to peel off with the teeth — gluhlaya *to ~ one's own* - iyuhlahlaya *peeling* - nahlaya *to peel off of itself* - owahlaye *parings* - pahlaya *to ~ rolling off, or to peel off of itself* - wahlaya *to pare off, to circumcise* - wohláya *to ~ off by shooting* - yahlaya *to ~ with the teeth* - yuhla-ya *to ~ off* — ayuh'u *to ~ off e.g. bark* - cankah'u *to ~ bark off trees* - glah'u *to ~ with the teeth* - kah'u *to ~ by striking, as a potato on a rough surface* - wah'u *to ~ by cutting off the hull or rind* - woh'ú *to peel by shooting, strike and scrape along* - yah'u *to peel by mouth* - yuh'u *to ~ off e.g. bark by hand* — ayusku *to ~ or pare off on* - glasku *to bite or ~ off one's own* - hánasku *to crack and peel off* - hánaskuya *to crack and cause to ~ off* - kasku *to strike to crack and ~ off e.g. with an axe* - owasku *to ~ into, or the parings* - wakicisku *to ~ for* - wakiscu *to peel* - wasku *to ~ or shave off* - yusku *to ~ off or pare by hand* — canhapašlotanhan *to take off the inner bark of trees when the sap is up* - canhayušlotanhan *to take off the inner bark of cottonwood trees* — ošlokahan *peeling off* - ošlokahe *having peeled off*

peep *vn* : okakin *to ~ in*

pellet *n* : su *seed, hail, shot, bullet* - sukpanla *shotgun shot*

pen *n* : mázawiyowa - canwiyowa *a pencil* — wícazo *pen or pencil* — onatake *a cage or pen for animals or birds*

penetrate *va* : paošloka

peninsula *n* : izo *an upland plain that is a ~*

penniless *adj* : šlušluta *fig destitute*

people *n* : oyate *a tribe or nation*

perceptive *adj* : slóta

perch *adv* : guh'cincanyela *perching*

perfect *adj* : picalake *more ~ than* — wówawoyuštan *a finishing, completion, perfection*

perform *v* : oeconla econ *to do, perform excitedly* — wanapiškanyan *to exhibit, to play*

perfume *n* : mniwaštemna - waštemna *sweet-smelling* - waštemnaya *to put on ~*

perhaps *adv* : naceca — ókinahan *or* ókini (each begins a *cl*) *possibly* - owekinaš *or* owekiš *lest, it may be, possibly, perhaps, probably* — tokaš *possibly* — ungna *there is some probability that*

perish *vn* : atakunišni *to be ruined, come to naught, to become extinct* - atakunišnipica *perishable* — yuwignuniya *to cause to ~, to destroy*

persecute *va* : teȟiyakuwa *to bedevil, harass, molest*

perseverance *n* : wówacintanka *patience*

persevere *part* : owapahlokehan *perseveringly*

persist *v* : ipajin — inihanšniyan *persistently*

person *adv* : iyunkala *personally* — tan'atayela *towards a ~* - tan'iyatayela *individually, in ~*

perspicuity *n* : okitan'in *awareness*

perspire *v* : iglutemni - natemni *to sweat for e.g. the heat* — nayeic'iya *to make one's self ~, as in a sweatlodge*

persuade *va* : wicalaya *to cause one to believe* — yahahala *to convince by talk* - yahahayela *to shake one in his or her purpose* — yaohinyanze *to ~ to give up*

perversely *adv* : pemniyan, crooked, twisted
perstle *n* : iwopan
pet *n* : ihaktapila
petition *n* : wacajeyatapi *a motion*
petulant *n* : oie wašicun *a ~ person, on who is rude in speech*
peyote *n* : unhcela - unhcela yuta tawohtate *the gear for conducting a ~ cult ceremony*
phonograph *n* : omazape
photograph *n* : iteowapi - itoic'ikowa *to have one's picture taken* - wicitowa *to take another's picture*
pick *v refl* : ikpahi *to ~ up one's own things* - pahi *to ~ up, to collect* - pahihigla *to ~ up on the way* - pahihilag *having picked up one's own way to* — pahci *to tear or ~ out* — apahpu *to ~ or chip off on* - pahpu *to ~ or chip off in small pieces* - yuhpu *to ~ off a piece* — icahnih *to select and ~ out* — oyukunta *to ~ at or in the nose or ears* — yuptuga *or* yuptuh'a *to ~ to pieces* — ayasmin *to ~ off with the teeth* - yusmin *to ~ off something loose by hand* - yusmiyanyan *to ~ pick off e.g. meat from a bone* — yaswa *to ~ to pieces with the teeth* - yuswaya *to pick to pieces* — iyušpa *to ~ , pluck corn, etc.* — ayušpi *to ~ e.g. fruit on* - kašpi *to knock e.g. berries off* - kiciyušpi *to pick for one* - wóšpi *to ~ e.g. berries* - yašpi *to ~ off as birds do berries* - yušpi *to gather berries* — apašpu *to pull or ~ off one stuck on another* - ayušpu *to ~ or pull off on* - iyušpu *to pluck, ~ e.g. corn* — kaza *to ~ to pieces* - yuzaza *to ~ to pieces, as sinew or cloth*
picketpin *n* : wihinpaspa
picture *n* : itowapi - itowapognake *or* itowapojuha *a ~ frame* - Cf book, wówapi
pie *n* : taspan opemnipi *or* tasp'opemnipi *apple ~* - wópemni *a ~ or roll*
piece *n* : ošpe - Cf part
pierce *va* : icapcab *or* okagaya *to stab* - icapepeya piercing — pahloka *to ~ something* - opahloka *to ~ in* - wapahloka *to make holes in* — pa-ohpa *to ~ through* — waopa *to make a hole as with a knife*
pile *va* : ahiju *to bring and ~ up* — aošma *to heap up in or on* — ékšu *to lay up in a ~* — íciglapšunpšunyan *piled on top of each other* — ícipahaha *piled up, men and things* - íciyaglaskiskiya *piled on top of each other as flat things* — pahaya *piled up, prominent*
pilfer *n* : waicucuka *a pilferer, a thief* - waicucukteca *to become a thief* — wakahlaka *a pilferer*
pillow *vn* : ipahin *to lean the head against as for a ~ ,* or *a pillow* - ipahinya *to use for a ~* - tipahin *his or her ~*
pimple *vn* : yuh'i *to be pimpled, rough, chapped* - oyuh'i *a ~ or pimples, fig a rough place* — waseyanka *to have a spot on the face, or one having facial pimples*
pin *n* : heyopašpu *or* hiyopašpu *or* hiyopatake *or* ipasise *a pin* - ipasisa *to pin, stick and fasten with a pin* - makipasise *a breast-pin* - wipasise *a safety-pin* - pasisa *to pin together* — wípaspe *tent-pins*
pinch *va* : anajipa *to ~ with the feet* - apajipa *to ~ by putting pressure on as in sitting on* - wapajipa *to ~ or sting* - ayujipa *to ~ on with the hand* - glujipa *to ~ one's own* - yujipa *to ~ something or someone* - waiciya *to ~ hit, i.e. to assist and take one's place in accomplishing a task*
pine *n* : wazi *a ~ tree* - wazizi *pieces of ~* - waz'oju *a ~ timber*
pipe *n* : cannunpa - cannunpa pahin iyapehanpi *a ~ wrapped around with quill-work* - cannunpa wosláta *a ~ made from a hollow and straight deer bone with an erect end* — opagi *a tobacco-filled ~* - cannunp'ȟaka *a wand, imitative of the ~* — icašloke *a poker for a ~* - iglayeya *a pipe-stem cleaner* - oyape *the mouth-piece of a ~ stem* - pahu *a ~ bowl* - sinte *a ~ stem* - oagle *the stem insert for the bowl* - óskapi *the ornamental work for the ~ stem* — opagi *to fill a ~* - okipagi *to fill a ~ for* - oiyahpeya *to gesture with the ~* - wakiyuza *to gesture with the ~ , holding up the ~*
pit *n* : makaok'e *or* makok'e *a dugout* — oyuze *a quarry of sand, rock, etc.*
pitcher *n* : - *See* dish
pith *adj* : popopa *pithy, fluffy,* or *a type of cotton*
place : —
akeya *to ~ a roof on*
aloksohan *to carry placed, tucked under the arm*
aon *or* aonpa, *or* aun *or* aunpa, *or* onpa *or* unpa *to put or ~ on i.e. wood on a fire* - agliyaonpa *to come and ~ on* - ahiunpa *to bring and ~* - aklon *to ~ on for one* - éonpa *to ~ carefully* - hinyetaonpa *to ~ or put on the shoulder*
awinyeya *to put on, to wear* - glówin *to put around one one's own*
canpaslata *to ~ and set posts*
éekiya *to take the ~ of another*
ehantulahci *at a set time or ~ only*
glastokan *to put or smooth down the hair*
gle *to ~ , put, set on* - agle *to ~ on* - aglehiyeya *placed one after another* - ahigle *to set, to bring and place* - ahiyagle *to bring home and ~ on* - égle *to ~ or make stand in a ~* - ékicigle *to ~ for one* - ic'igle *to set aside for one's self* - ic'igleka *on who always accumulates* - ékigle *to ~ or lay away for one's own*
gnáka *to ~ or lay up* - ahignaka *to come and set down in* - aitagnagya *placing something on top of another* - aitagnaka *to ~ one on top of another* - akignagya *placed on* - akignaka *to ~ one's own on* - aognaka *to set or ~ e.g. a cover on* - égnaka *to ~ or lay away* - ic'ignaka *to ~ or locate one's self* - ékignaka *to lay away one's own* - ognaka *to ~ in* - okignaka *to ~ one's own in*
ihpeya *to throw down* - aihpeya *to throw or ~ on* - éyuhpa *to take and put down* - iyahpekiciciya *to put on for one* - iyahpekiya *to put on or throw over*
iyomnaya *to ~ much in the mouth*
ohe *a ~ or niche, a bed* - otahepi *in between places*
óštan *in ~ of* - oštán'iyotake *to take one's ~* - oštán'najin *a stand-in person*
šlokahan *out of place*
tuktetu kakeškeš *at most any ~* - tuktetu k'eyaš *in any ~*
yagloka *to put out of place, i.e. with the teeth*
plain *n* : bláye *or* makoblaye - oblaye *a valley* - okablaye *a level place, a ~* - blablata *an upland plain, a prairie or table* — blowanjila *an upland ~ between two streams, a divide, the top of a ridge* — ášlašlayela *adv* : *plainly, clearly*
plait *va* : yuški *to pleat or braid* - yuškipi *braided or pleated and gathered in folds*
plan *v* : aokiya *mutually to ~* - waaokiyapi *a planning of things together* — ic'iconza *to determine for one's self* — iglukcan *to have an opinion of one's self*
plane *n* : can'icajipe *or* can'iyujipa *a drawing knife or ~* - can'ipajipa *a plane*
plant *va* : oju - ojupi *planted* - ojuya *to cause to ~* - o-oju *to ~ in* - okiciju *to ~ for one* - okiju *to sow, ~ one's own or for another* - Cf chew, flower, grass, medicine, tea
plaster *n* : waaskabyapi *or* waaskape *an adhesive*

plateau *n* : iyoblaye
platform *n* : owahe *something to stand on* - owahegle *a ~ or foundation*
play *vn* : škáta - aškata *to ~ on or at* - iškata *to ~ to or for anything* - kiškata *to ~ to or for* - kiciškata *a playmate* - oškata *to ~ in* - oškate *a diversion* - škalkiya *to make ~* — wanapiškanyan *to ~ with toys* - awanapiškanyan *to ~ with as babies do with dolls* — ecaca *in fun, for diversion* — un *to be at playing* — kicikšan to have *love-play*
playing cards *n* : kansu - kansukute *to ~ cards*

The Cards and Suits of a Playing Deck :

Cóka *Joker*
Pezi *King*
Wínyan *Queen*
Peša *Jack*
Sápatanka *Spades*
Tacanta *Hearts*
Pestola *or* Šapestola *Diamonds*
Sápayugaga *Clubs*

plead *v* : wótiye - wótiyekiya *to ~ with for one*
pleasant *va* : iyokipi *to please one* - aiyokipi *pleasant, agreeable* - aiyokipiya *agreeably* - oiyokipi *pleasant* — owašte *wholesome* — wicibleza *~ weather*
please *v* : iyokipi *to be pleasant* - oiyokipi *or* wawiyokipi *to be pleased with* - wawiyokipiya *gladly* - wawiyokipiye *a pleasant appearing person* - opi *or* pila *to be pleased* — oonšila *one being sympathetic toward* — tókcincinyan *or* tókecincinyan *or* tókcinkinyan *or* tókecin *as one pleases, anyhow*
pleasure *v* : pila *to be pleased* - ipilaye *something that gladdens*
pleat *n* : - Cf ruffle
pledge *n* : iwakta *a sign*
plenty *n* : waota, *or plentiful* — yutkanla *much, abundant* — yugela *a large quantity, much*
pliable *va* : yuwinja *to make limber* — winšwinjahela *or* winšwinjela *or* winšwinja *or* yayala *pliant, tender, flexible* — yahunta *to make pliable with the mouth* — šnunšnunjela *or* štaštayela *pliant, soft* — kcankcanla *unsteady* — yapanpan *to make limber*
plot *va* : cokon *a desire to murder* — šilwiyukcan *to ~ evil*
plow *adj* : blu *pulverized* - aglublu *to ~ one's own upon* - ayublu *to pulverize or to make mellow on* - glublu *to ~ one's own* - kiciyublu *to ~ for one* - makayublu *to break up the ground, to plow*
plug *va* : nataka *to stop a leak*
plunge *v* : kaškapa *to make the noise of one striking water* - škabyela *with a plunge*
plural *suff to v, n, adj* : ...pi — *pron pl in compos, as in* wicopeya [fr wica *them* + *opeya among*] *among them*
pocket *n* : sicanopiye
point *v* : pazo *to cause to show* - akpazo *to ~ at one's own* - apazo *to ~ at something on* - ékicipazo *to ~ at for one* - ékipazo *to ~ to or for one* - épazo *to ~ to or at* - kicipazo *or* kipazo *to ~ to for one* — iyokahmin *a ~ of land* — íyokiwin *to ~ somewhere with the mouth* — íinkpata *at the ~ of anything* — pésto *or* péstola *sharp-pointed* - opesto *a point* - péstoya *in pointed manner, or sharp-pointed* — t'ója *pointless, dull* - t'óšya *bluntly* — yaiyowajašni *to speak beside the point*
poison *n* : šung'ikte - šunkigmunke *anything used in trapping wolves* - wicašaikte *poison to kill a person*
poke *va* : palehlega *to ~ a fire, stir a fire*
poker *n* : icašloke *a ~ used to stir and clean e.g. a pipe*
pole *n* : canwakan *a flag ~* - paslata *to set a ~* - hupaheyunpi *tent-poles used for a travois* - hupawaheyun k'inpi *a travois, an early vehicle for transporting things* - hupawanjila *a pony drag*
police *n* : cannakseyuha *a guardian of the people* — wawoyuspa *a policeman* - Cf seize
polish *n* : iyušlušluta *a polisher* - kašlušluta *to planish* — kpaman *to ~ one's own* — pawiyakpa *to ~ and make shine*
pool *n* : bleiyoka *small pools alongside a creek where weeds grow* - bleiyute *a lake channel, a strait* - bleiyoškokpa *a buffalo wallow* - blela *a pond* - bleokahmi *a bog, a beach*
poor *v* : atantonšni *to have nothing of one's own* — awahpanica *to become ~ on account of* — oic'ihpani *to be ~ and unable to care for one's self or family* - on'ic'ihpani *to be destitute* - owahpanica *or* wahpanica *~, without means to care for one's self* - owahpaniya *to make one ~ or destitute* - wówahpanica *poverty* — cóla *destitute, without anything* — hlogeca *~ and sickly or thin* — kagmipi s'e *entirely destitute* — wóh'iyaya *to do a thing poorly or badly* — ónšika *destitute* — létka *having spent all, fig gone "broke"* — htani *being poor, having difficulties*
pop *v* : kapopa *or* kapob *to make pop* - napopa *to explode* — nakpakpa *or* namnumnuza *to crackle and pop as wood burning* — napahpaga *to pop i.e. parch as corn* — woskápa *to make pop e.g. a toy gun* - woskápapi *a pop*
positively *adv* : wicakicila *believing for one, being positive*
possess *va* : yuha - ayuha *to have or ~ on, to hold or lift on* - gluha *to have one' own* - yuhakiya *to make one have* — táwaya *to have for one's own* - táwekiya *to cause to own* - itawacin *possession of mind or property* — tiiyupah *with "bag and baggage", i.e. all one's belongings* — ignaškinyan *to be possessed with a bad spirit* — wanagnanka *or* wanagnunka *to retrieve one's possessions from a shakedown*
possessives : - some words have a syllable that changes to convert to the possessive form of the word :

ka *and* ya *become* gla
pa *becomes* kpa
glo *and* gliyo *are simply inserted*
ki *sometimes is inserted in the v*
ta *prefixed to* wo *becomes* to
yu *becomes* glu

possible *v* : econpica *it is possible to do, or it can be done* - econpicaka *it is possible to do,* <u>or</u> *it is impossible to do* - econpicašniyan *impractically* — okihipica *possibly* - Cf perhaps
post *n* : mas'apapi can *a telephone ~*
postage *n* : wiciteiyaskabye *a ~ stamp*
postcard *n* : wówapi oh'anko
pottery *n* : makacega *an earthen pot* — pankeska *crockery, Chinaware*
pound *v* : katan *to ~ e.g. meat before it is dry* - iyokatan *to ~ a nail etc.* - wotán *to ~ as in washing clothes* - wotánkiya *to cause to ~* — kaona *to ~ or hammer on* - kapa *to ~ up meat* - kapán *to beat up meat* - okapan *to ~ or beat in* — kaški *to grind* - kaškica *to ~ out* — kakuka *to ~ to pieces* - kicakuka *to ~ to pieces for* — okat'inza *to ~ in tight* — wohtáka *to ~ or knock with the end of something*
pour *v refl* : aiglaštan *to ~ or spill on one's self* - akaštan

to ~ out on one - glaštan *to ~ out one's own, to spill from the mouth* - kaštan *to pour out* - okaštan *to ~ into* - okicaštan *to ~ one's own into for* - okicicaštan *to ~ for one* — kala *to ~ out* - akala *to ~ out on* - kicicala *to ~ out for* - anableca *to spread out in pouring out grain etc.* - ayupson *to ~ or spill out on* - kicipapson *to ~ out for* - opapson *or* opapson *to ~ out into*

pout *adv* : aitku *pouting* — ayaceya *to make one cry by talking* — inap'ibiyeya *or* inap'ip'iyeya *to be about to cry and drop the lower lip* — íwošo *pouting lips* - íwošoka *pouting with the mouth pushed up* - íwošokiya *to push out the lips when pouting* — ohinyanzeka *to be cranky* — wacinko *pouting*

powder *adj* : blu *fine as ~* - bluyela *in a ~ condition* - cahli *gunpowder*

power *n* : Ounye *Nature* - ounyekiya *to cause to dwell in or have ~ of rule over* - ounyeya *to give ~ to* — š'ákeca *mighty, powerful* - tówaš'ke *his or her ~, strength* - waš'akece *to be stout* - wówaš'ake *strength* — tákuškanškan *resident ~ to cause and set in motion, movement, as in Lakota philosophy* — sicunpi *holders of ~* — ton *an endowed or communicable ~ of spiritual quality able to manifest its presence* — wanape icage yuha *to have ~ over all* - wanapicageyuza *domination* — Wanbligleška *the Epitome of ~ of the north* — Waziya *the ~ power of the North* — wóokihi *~* or ability

prairie *adv* : tiiȟeyapapaya *out on the ~*

prairie chicken *n* : šiyoka

praise *v refl* : aiglatan *to ~ one's self for some ability* - ayatan *va* : to praise for - glatan *to ~ one's own* - iglatan *to boast, brag of one's own* — íitkopatanhan *returning the compliment fitting to be said to the one alone i.e. in private* - íitkob *in reply* — kíciyatan *to ~ for one* - yatan *to speak well of one* — ayaonihan *to ~ on or for* - glaonihan *to ~ or honor one's own* - iglaonihan *to honor one's self* — igluonihan *to honor one's self* — iyokinihan *honored* - kiciyaonihan *to ~ for one* - yuonihan *to ~ or honor one, to treat with attention* — caš'aya *to praise one's bravery* — glazunta *to speak well and unjustly of one's own* - glazunta *to ~ one's self* — ikiciyuškin *to congratulate one* — ilowan *to sing the praises of* — iwocajeyalya *to sing one's praises because of* — wawitonpa *to ~ one* - wawitonpapi *the praising*

prance *va* : škeheya *to make ~ about, to make wild*

prank *or* **caper** *vn* : oh'anhanhan *to play a ~* — waicihaȟa *a prankster* - Cf insolent

pray *v* : cékiya *to ~ to* - cekíyaya *to implore one, or pleadingly* - éya cèkiya *to have said praying* - icekiya *to ~ to one for something* - cékiciya *to ~ for another* - owacekiya *to ~ in a place* - owacekiye *a place or building in which is held public prayer, or the Church* - waceic'iya *to ~ within one's self* - wícekiye *a prayerbook or other assist to praying, any printed prayer* - wacekiya *to pray* - wócekiye *a prayer*

preceding *adv* : kaitokab *ahead of*

precipitate *vn* : wóslotonšni *to be careless* — okahinhan *to fall as rain or snow*

precisely *adv* : igleglehyakel *imprecisely, without a clear distinction between things*

precocious *adj* : koyanun *or* owicahkokela *of quick growth or maturation*

predict *v* : waayata *to foretell, guess*

prefer *v* : akiic'iya *to ~ one's self* - akiya *to consider, give thought to*

pregnant *v* : hokšihiyukiya *to cause an abortion* - hokšihiyuya *to have an abortion* - hokšiikpignaka *to be ~* - hokšikaga *to impregnate, beget* - hokšiksuya *to be in travail, in labor of childbirth* - hokšiyuha *to give birth* — igluš'aka *to be ~* — tamni *the womb or afterbirth* — ton *to bear* - tónpi *birth* - kíciton *to bear or have a child for one*

prepare *v* : aigluza *to dress up for an occasion* — apikiya *to get one's own ready* - piic'iya *to get one's self prepared* - wapikiyece *with one's self prepared well as for a journey* — icanliyuha *to be poised* — iglusuyakel *in the state of being ready* — igluwinyeya *to get one's self ready* — išitutece šni *with self well prepared* — loliȟ'an *to ~ food* — owank kaga *to ~ a place* — yusuya *or* yusu *to make right, i.e. make things ready* - wóyusu *a making things right, preparations* — isitutece *unprepared, lacking the necessities*

prescribe *v* : icuši *to ~ a medicine*

present *v* : oyanka *to be ~ in* — wacinksapa *having presence of mind* — wóȟeyaka *gifts, a ~*

preserves *va* : štagya *to make ~*

president *n* : - Cf chief

press *vn* : gnaškinyanyan *to be franticly oppressed* — aglaskica *to lie pressing down on one's own* - agluškica *to ~ out one's own on* - akaskica *to be pressing down* - akiglaskica *to ~ down on one's own by sitting on* — apuskica *or* apuskil *to ~ down tight upon* - ayuskica *to ~ down tight on* - glaskica *to ~ one's own with the mouth* - icaskica *to be pressed down* - icaskice *a press* — ayuškica *to ~ or wring out on* - iyaglaskica *to lie on, to ~ on or cover* - iyaglaskilya *to cause to ~ upon* — iyuškica *to ~ on and accidentally cut, to wring out e.g. water from clothes* - kaskica *to ~ down* — napipuskica *to ~ together* - naskica *to ~ down with the feet* - naškica *to ~ out by trampling* - opuskica *to ~ down in* - oyuskica *to ~ out e.g. juice* - paipuskica *to ~ down* - pakipuskica *to be pressed tight together* - paopuskica *to ~ down into* - paskica *to ~ on* - paškica *to ~ out* - puskica *to be heavily burdened* - skicahan *pressed down, close* — apaskita *to ~ on hard* - waskica *or* waskita *to ~ out with a knife* - woskíca *to ~ out by pounding* - yakipuskica *to ~ close together by mouth* - yukipuskica *to press close together* — wíyuskite *a press* — ipasli *to crush by pressing against something* - ipasliya *to ~ one against the wall* - wasli *to ~ out with a knife* — ínatan *to ~ upon to gain support* — apat'a *to kill by applying pressure on anything* - íyapat'o *to be pressed on or cramped in* - íyapat'oyakel *or* íyapat'oyela *pressed against or together, cramped close together* — akat'inza *to ~ down tight as with a weight* - anat'inza *to tramp down tight and hard* - aokat'insya *pressed in or on tight* - aokat'inza *to ~ or pound in or on tight* - aot'insya *to ~ in all about, to besiege* - apat'inza *or* aput'inza *to ~ tight on, as in making a thumb mark* - at'inza *to ~ on, to be tight on* - nat'inza *to ~ hard by foot* - paot'inza *to ~ in tight* — apaunka *to push down on anything* - apawinja *to bend or press down as grass* — wotá *to ~ against* - wotá iyeya *to blow off* - ahiwota *to arrive and ~ against*

pressure *n* : wópat'inze

pretence *or* **pretense** *adv* : ongnaye *under pretence*

pretend *v refl* : aiic'ila *to act as if one had brought in* — ecaeconka *or* ecaheconka *to feign, pretend to do* — iyayekiya *to ~ be going away* — kónza *to ~ to strike* — wawaheye šni *pretending*

prevaricate *va* : yagalgata *to fabricate a falsehood*

prevent *v refl* : ikušic'iya *to block the way for one* — oiyayešilya *to ~ one leaving* — inapteca *to be prevented by* — iyanapta *to detain* — pajin *to prevent* - ipajin *to be prevented and come to a stand-still* - ipajinyan *obstructing*

— iyanica *to be detained or hindered by, to be prevent-ed* - oiyanica *to be prevented in doing for some reason* — íyapat'oya *to run against, to hinder or ~* — iyokišni *to forbid, ~ or hinder* — nikiya *to stop one* — okit'eya *to obstruct in, to put a limit in e.g. a roadway* — pákan *to prevent, as flood waters one's travel*

previous *or* **former** *adv* : toká kin héhanni *then at the first*

price *n* : - Cf sell

prick *adj* : icama *pricking, rough, as certain cloth or as a man's beard, to hurt as when something gets in the eye* - icameca *to be pricked, fig to have one's feelings injured by something small* - icameya *pricked, injured in feelings* — pajipa *to sting one* - ipajipe *that which pricks or stings* — pakpikpi *to ~ holes in* — nakpeyeya *to ~ up the ears*

prickle *vn* : apaga *to be beset with prickles, sharp stickers* - apagaya *to cause to be assailed with prickles, e.g. by throwing devil's grass or cactus etc. on one* — nasaya *in a way of being prickly or affecting sharply*

pride *va* : iyotanla *to show ~* - watankic'ila *to think one's self great*

priest *n* : wicaša wakan *or* **wacekiye wicaša** — waunyanpi itancan *a High Priest as is known in Jewish tradition; the presider at a sacrifice, as a priest in the celebration of the Sacraments of Christian Tradition* — wóšnakaga *the person who offers sacrifice* - wóšnapikaga *a priest*

print *v* : mázaagliheya *to print*

prison *or* **jail** *va* : kaška *to imprison* - wókaške *a jail or prison* - owicakaške *a jail* — waaka *a prisoner of war*

prize *n* : wóokiye *merit* — ok'ipe *what is staked, a wager*

probably *adv* : iteyakel *apparently, likely, it stands to reason*

probation *n* : wówiyutanpi

probe *va* : pakota - pakote *a probe, to dig out* — pazi *to ~ into*

proclaim *v* : éyapaha *to proclaim aloud* - iéyapaha *or éyapaha a crier, an announcer* — iglaotan'in *to proclaim one's self* - wayaatan'in *to make manifest*

produce *va* : oicahya *to make grow or yield* — wakuni *to produce many things* - wóicahye *a growth, or the produce*

profess *v* : wakan'ic'iconze *to profess one's own faith*

prolong *v* : wayutehanhanka *to protract, be long in doing*

prominent *adj* : pahaya *projecting* — wócas'aya *a noteworthy thing* - wócas'ayakel *famously, well known*

promise *va* : wahoya *to ~ to* - iwahoya *to send word to concerning, to grant or permit, to promise* - iwahokiciyapi *they promise to each other* — tawacinkitonyan *holding great promise* — waokiya *to let another do the shooting* — yugalic'iconza *to ~ under oath*

prompt *n* : iš'óš'oka *a ~ person* - iš'oš'oya *promptly* — tohanyanšni hanni *with promptness* — ítab *soon after, quickly*

prone *adv* : pamaglela *in a ~ way* — makipastoya *in a prone position*

proof *adj* : óblula *weather-proof*

prop *va* : paza *to ~ up bushes for a shelter*

proper *vn* : ececa *to be ~* - yuececa *to make do properly* — yusu *to make ~, i.e. things ready* — yuecetu *to make proper*

property *n* : wóha *or* wóyuha *possessions*

prophet *n* : waayate *one who foretells or predicts* - wayaatan'in *one who proclaims or bears witness*

proposition *n* : wóiwanyanke *a fair ~*

prosper *v* : itányan *to be well off by reason of*

protect *va* : awanyanka - wóawanyanka *protection*

protrude *vn* : naglake *to stand out, as ribs on a thin horse* - naglaglake s'e *like something standing out*

proud *adv* : gúngagaya *proudly* — igluwankatuya *to elevate or raise up one's self i.e. over others* — ítan *to be ~* - ítanpi *vainglory, pride* - ítantan *to glory in, to be vain* - ítantanpi *arrogance, glorying, pride* - ítanyan *to be ~ by reason of* - wítan *~ elated, vain* - wítantanka *a ~ person* - wítantanpi *vainglory, pride* - wítantanya *to make one ~* - wítantanyan *glorying* — iwah'an'ic'ila *to be ~* — kas'ala *to put on airs* - okas'ayakel *proudly* — stu *proud* - stuic'ila *to think much of one's self, to be ~* — wamnaic'ila *to be ~ of one's own* - wamnaic'ilapi *pride* — yagopa *to sip noisily, fig to make feel ~ by talking*

prove *v poss* : glasuta *to confirm one's own words*

provide *v poss* : agluha *to ~ for some occasion, to have or take one's own on account of* - aigluha *to ~ for one's self, to have for one's own use* — lol'ijicayakel *having many provisions* - lol'iyucan *to be low on provisions* - lol'opeton *to buy provisions* — onweya *or* unweya *provisions* — wagle *a storehouse for provisions* — wiic'igni *to ~ for one's self*

provoke *va* : hinyansya *to ~, or sternly, crossly* — iwakuwa *or* iwawikuwa *to ~ and make one angry* — kamato *to ~ resistance, to anger or incite one*

prudently *adv* : aiyacinyan

prune *or* **pare** *v* : can'akansmiyan *to ~ trees* — wakipta *to trim back one's own* - Cf cut

pry *va* : opatica *to push under and ~* — waelhiyayake *a prying person* - Cf twist

pucker *va* : oyagi *to make wrinkle or fold up*

pudding *v* : wókija *to make hasty ~ for one*

puff *adj* : pánja *puffed up* — popo *to be puffed out, to swell*

pull *v* : titan *to ~ to or in a certain direction* - aglutitan *to stretch one's own upon* - akiyutitanpi *they pull different ways* - ayutitan *to ~ or stretch upon* - iyutitan *to ~ by* - natitan *to brace the feet for* — ákagal stretching out to — anazica *to stretch with the use of one's foot* - ayuzica *to draw or stretch on* - igluzica *to stretch one's self as on tiptoe* — apašloka *to ~ or shove off on, as one's coat* - ayušloka *to ~ out on* - onašloka *to ~ off in* - yašloka *to ~ out with the teeth* - yušloka *to ~ off and out* — ayapšun *to ~ out by the roots with the teeth on* - ayupšun *to extract by the roots e.g. teeth* - icapšun *anything with which to pry out or pull up by the roots* - kiciyupšun *to extract for* — ayasku *to peel or pull off on with the teeth* — ayuguka *to sprain on, i.e. draw out as one's sword from the scabbard* — ayuslohan *to drag or draw along on, fig to tempt by holding out alluring things* - ayuslohelaka *to ~ off something on, as hide on an animal or bark on a tree* — ayusluta *to ~ out on* — ayašluta *to slip pulling on with the teeth* - ayu-šluta *to draw or slip out on anything* — ayušpu *to pick or ~ off on* - yušpu *to ~ off by hand* — ayut'ins *to squeeze tight together* — gluceka *to try to ~ out one's own, as from being mired* — gluh'u *to ~ off one's own, as bark with one's hands* — glujinca *to ~ or blow one's nose* — huyukša *drawing up one's legs when in pain, cringing* — iyusna iyeya *to ~ out, as pins from a tent* — oyuhpa *to ~ down in* - yahpa *to ~ down by mouth* - yuohpa *to ~ through and into* — yaunka *to ~ down by mouth* — yuakan *to ~ or lift out* — yuakanl icu *to ~ up from* — yuceka *to ~ in vain* — pagmica *or* yugmica *to ~ one's hair* — wošlášlateke *the pulling out* — yujuju *to ~ to pieces, to void something* — yukikike *to ~ over and down* — yutuka *to ~ to pieces, destroy e.g. furs* — yuunzi *to ~ backwards*

pulpit *n* : owahokonkiye

pulverize *adj* : kpan *to pound fine* - iyukpan *to mill* - onakpan *to ~ fine in* — wopán *to pound fine* — blu *finely pulverized* - kablu *to pound fine as powder* - nablu *to ~ by foot* - pablu *to flatten* — katutka *to break in small pieces, to pound up fine*

pump *n* : mniyutaja - mniyutajapi *a ~ jack* — nahomni *to ~ by foot*

punch *va* : awobleca *to ~ and break in pieces* — awohleca *to punch on and split* — awohloka *to ~ a hole in one thing on another* — awoksa *to break off by punching on* — awokuka *to ~ to pieces on* — awopta *to ~ off a piece as in striking with the end of a stick* — awošla *to make bare on by punching* — awošleca *to split off on by punching* — kpa *punched out* — wohlóka *to ~ or make a hole* — owoskica *to ram in a hole* — wokán *to ~ off* — wošpúšpu *to ~ to pieces*

puncture *va* : papota *to pierce and open as with a knife*

pungent *n* : wókapa a ~ thing — wókapaza *pungency, as has pepper, or a ~ thing* - iokapaza *or* iyokapza *to be ~ in the mouth, to make smart as does pepper in the mouth*

punish *va* : pae *to inflict punishment* — teȟislolyekiya *to ~ , make one suffer, to correct*

purchased *adj* : okiciwašakala *easily ~ for one* - Cf buy

pure *adj* : oštekešni *inviolate, undefiled* — skayakel *in a ~ way, innocently, whitish, white, purely* — wakašotešni *clean, virgin-pure* - wakašotešniyan *undefiled, purely* — wótiyemnašni *immaculate, as a person or house*

purgatory *n* : wicayuskapi

purge *v* : kajo *to have diarrhoea, or to pass wind*

purpose *n* : tawokonze *his or her ~ , influence* - Wakantanka Tawokonze *the Holy Spirit, third person of the Holy Trinity in God* — eca *purposely* - wanunktašni *not purposely*

pursue *va* : kúwa *to follow or go after* — tapá *to ~ one* - tapeya *to go after something*

push *v* : ahipani *to ~ or crowd against* — aiyotan'ic'ila *to ~ one's self ahead of others* — akinyeic'iya *to ~ or thrust one's self upon or in upon* — aokpazan *to ~ into, as an arrow into a quiver or a feather into one's hair* - opazan *to ~ into or under, to interlace* — aopatica *to ~ or stick in or under or on, as a quill under the tick* — pahomni *to ~ around* - apahomni *to ~ on or shove around on anything* — apaunka *to ~ down on something* — pašloka *to shove off* - apašloka *to shove off e.g. one's coat on* — apatan *to ~ against* - iyopatan *to impel* - patanhan *or* patanyan *pushing against* - patitan *to ~ against* - apatitan *to ~ or brace against* - ikipatitan *to ~ one sideways, as during a race so as to win* - ikpatitan *to ~ along to steer e.g. a boat* - kipatitan *to ~ with all one's might* — ayuȟeyata *to ~ back on, or ~ on one side* - waȟeyata iyeya *to push back* — ayutokan *to shove away, put aside a little* — glaya *to ~ e.g. a wire down a pipestem* - iglayekiya *to ~ e.g. a straw down one's pipestem to clear it* — paceka *to ~ abruptly, to stagger* - ípaceka *to ~ and make stumble* — ipagan *to ~ aside e.g. a flap to look out* — pagapa *to ~ off by hand* — kakab *to ~ away* — pakapa *to bat away e.g. a pitched ball* - wakakab iȟpeya *to ~ out of the way* — paicisannica *to ~ away to the side* — paha *to swing, push aside, oppose or reject* - opaha *to ~ over a bank* - paoha *to ~ into, topple in* - wapaha iyeya *to ~ down* - yuoha *to ~ into* — pacannanl *shoved off and out e.g. a boat from shore* - wapacannanl iyeya *to ~ to the center, off shore* — pacokab *to ~ into the midst* - pacokaka *to ~ out, to empty some thing* — paececa *to guide anything by pushing* — paiyapat'o *to be pushed by* — pamahel *pushing in* - yapamahel iyeya *to ~ into the mouth* — paospa *to ~ under, to submerge* — paswu *to ~ into* — patica *to shove or ~ in or into* — wapahli *to ~ into the ground, into the mud* — wapat'iȟpeya *to ~ out of the way* — woslí *to ~ down in, to squirt*

puss *n* : ton *matter issuing from a wound, an infection*

put *v* : koyaka *to put on clothes* — okihan *to wear one's own* — oegnaka *a placing down, a stop, a period* — okicignaka *to place down for* — óštan *to ~ on or in, to be ~ in as a cork in a bottle, or as a handle in an axe head* - okicištan *to place in* - ókiciyuštanštan *placing one in with another* - ókištan *to ~ in place of, to ~ in one's own* - oyuštan *to ~ one into another, to cork* — oonpa *to place in*

putrid *v* : waȟunwinye *to smell ~* - wicaȟunwin *putrifaction*

Q

quadruped *n* : wahutopa

quantity *adv* : oyuptuh'ayakel *or* oyututkayakel *or* tutkatkayakel *or* yututkayakel *in small quantities, in small bits, parts, or pieces* — watokelketuya *in certain quantities* — yugela *a large quantity or amount*

quarrel *n* : ahoyekiciyapi — aigluhomni *to throw one's self at as in battle, fighting* — akinica *to dispute claiming one's own* - aicikinica *to dispute among themselves* - akinilkiya *to cause to debate* - akinilya *to cause to dispute about, or in a quarreling manner* — apaksonlya *to have the last word in a quarrel, to win by talking* - apaksontkiciyapi *some quarreling* — ékiza *to fight them there* — hépa *to fight* — hóhotela akiciyapi *a sham fight between two groups of boys using only their legs* — aikapa *to scold one* - íkapa *to talk loud to* - íkapaka *one who scolds* - íkapas'a *a scold* — ikipajin *to quarrel with one for or on account of* — oiglukikiya *to start a quarrel with back-biting* — okiciyusinpi *to fall out with one another*

quarry *or* **pit** *n* : oicu *or* oyuze

quarter *n* : ouye *a ~ of the heavens* - tatéouye tópa *the four quarters of the universe* - tatuye *a ~ , as the West, North, East, or South* - wajuju *a ~ of an animal that is butchered in four pieces*

quaver *v* : wahognugnu *to warble*

queen *n* : - *See* woman

queer *adj* : oh'antokeca

quench *va* : yukpa *to stifle, ruin*

question *v* : iyunga *to ask a ~* - wíwicayungapi *or* wíyungapi *questions* -wíyunhya *to cause to inquire* — iyakanwinlake s'e *questioningly, going beyond bounds*

quickly *or* **rapidly** *adv* : íšinl — kókela *or* koyanla *quickly* - koyela *promptly* — oh'anko *to be doing ~ , to be handy* - oh'ankoya *quickly*

quietly *adv* : iwahwayela *quietly, peacefully*

quill *n* : pahin *the porcupine, or its quills* — unsin *the small end of a ~ , or the large tail ~* — wípata *an ornament in quills* - wípatapi *quill-work or embroidery* — wóskapi *quill-work, quill design*

quilt *n* : owínja popópa - Cf bed

quit *vn* : íyakicunni *to give up, be tired and leave off* - íyakicunniya *to cause one to ~* - íyakicunniyan *leaving off, quitting* — iyénayan *to give up, to be tired of*

quiver *vn* : putehniyanyan *to have one's lips quivering* - yuhniyan *to quiver, shake* — *n* : wánju *an arrow pouch*

R

race *v* : ínyanka *to run* - kiinyanka *to race* - oinyanka *a ~ track* - okinyanka *a racing arena* — kakicipapi *a contest*
rack *n* : can'itokšu *a ~ with which to transport wood* — howiwotka *a ~ on which to dry fish* — hunkatacan *a ~ on which a cannunpa, pipe, is set*
radiate *vn* : wogága - wogáya *radiating from a center*
radio *n* : ikancola mas'apapi *or* mázacola wínah'on *or* tatúye on wínah'on *a radio, a wireless ~*
ragged *adj* : h'eh'é *droopy* - ah'eh'eya *or* ohpuhpuya *in rags raggedly* - haah'eh'e *having on ~ clothes* - haah'e-h'eya *in torn clothes* - h'eh'eya *slobbering, driveling* - woyá *~ and dangling* - zazahan *ragged*
railroad *n* : mázacanku *the train rails, or the train itself* — petijanjan *a lantern* — mázacanku tipi *a railroad car*
rain *vn* : aglapta *to cease to ~ on* — hinhan *to fall, i.e. to ~* - ahinhan *to ~ upon, to fall as ~ or snow* — magaju *to rain, or some rain* - amagaju *to ~ on something* - amagajukiya *or* amagajuya *to cause to ~ on* - imagajuya *to cause to rain by some means* — anbšiceca *an unpleasant, rainy day* — icaȟolȟota *or* icaȟota *drops of ~ or flakes of snow* - mniicapsinpsin *slashing ~* - mniwanjilapapsun *it rains ceaselessly* — mniwozan *fine drizzling ~ , mist* — šliyela *making the sound of falling ~* — wígmunke *a rainbow*
raise *va* : apaha *to ~ on or over to strike one* - ipaha *to ~ or hoist* — ayugata *or* ayugalgata *to ~ up hands and arms as in prayer or blessing* — ayuha *to hold or lift on* — hupagluza *to ~ the pipe in prayer* - hupakiyuza *to ~ the pipe in prayer toward the heavens* — kihiya *to ~ and train a child up to adulthood* — yuzan *to ~ a curtain*
rake *v* : ayuhinhan *to ~ or harrow over* — ayuhinta *to ~ or sweep off on* - hinte s'e *as though swept or raked away* - yuhinta *to ~ away*
ram *v* : iyopaskica *to pack in* — iyopuskice *a ramrod* ipasminyan *a ramrod for a gun*
rancid *adj* : sewimna *or* sewiye
range *adj* : ptanškiška *ranging about*
rank *n* : tóhe *his or her place, camp, office or position*
rap *or* **tap** *v* : kato - katohan *to ~ as does a woodpecker*
rape *va* : kikšan *to violate a woman's person* - kikšanpi *the crime of ~* — kišleya *to hold and feel a person* — wiiyahpaya *to commit ~* — wikišleyapi *a form of ~ by touch*
rascal *n* : wahtešni t'a *one who gets away with misdeeds*
rash *v* : ȟan'it'a *to be covered with a rash* — písansan oh'anke *to act rashly*
rather *adv* : laka - ...laka *why don't you?*
ration *n* : lolicupi *an issue*
rattle *v* : asnasna *to rattle or ring* - acahsnasna *to ~ as icicles formed on something* — hla *to rattle* - hlahla *a rattle* - hlahlaya *rattling, loosely* - akahla *to ~ by striking* - ayuhla *to ~ or ring over* - kahlahla *to ring or ~* — ayuswu *to make a rattling noise on or over* - paswuya *to make ~ by pushing something into a barrel of corn* - yuswu *to make a rattling noise as in taking hold of shelled corn* — hunkatawagmuha *a kind of ~ once used in the Making Relative ceremony* - wagmuha *a ~ used in the wapíyapi, a conjuring ceremony* — ícicašlašlayela *with a smash or clatter* — nakaka *to make ~ with the foot* - oyukaka *to ~ in, or to ~ in a place* - yukakaka *to rattle* — iyoglagla *rattling* — kagyela *rattling like an old wagon or car* — kó kela *to ring or toll* - kokóka *to ~ as does an old hide* — okaglogloka *to ~ as an old car might* — wakakoka *to make ~* - wicakoke *one who is a rattler* - wokóka *to make ~ by shooting* — k'óga *to make a rattling noise* — lote onahnahna *to have a rattle in the throat* — naiyojaheyakel *rattling of itself, as loose parts of an old wheel*
ravel *vn* : glahan *to untwist* - glahe *unrolled of itself* — íciyuwi *to entangle one's self* — swahan *ravelled*
ravine *n* : - Cf gully
raw *or* **fresh** *adv* : lowitaya *all fresh as meat* — sagsaka *or* španšni *not cooked, raw*
reach *vn* : ihunni - ihunnikiya *to cause to ~* - ihunniyan *to cause to ~ , or entirely, clear through* - kihunni *to ~ home or the goal* — hiyagle *to ~ to as a road, to happen upon* - hiyagleya *to cause to ~ to, or leading to* - íciyagle *to ~ one to another* - íciyagleya *to cause one to ~ to another i.e. to cause to meet, or reaching one to another* - iyagleya *to cause to ~ to, to lead or bring one to as a man into trouble, or leading somewhere as does a road, reaching even to, on top of something as a house on a foundation* — óhi *to be able to ~ to, as to height, depth, size* - óhipicašni *to be unable to be reached because of height* - óhiya *to cause to ~ , or reaching to, hanging over* — iyohi *to ~ to, to be sufficient for, to get to, to arrive at a place* — óiyahe *a reaching the top e.g. of a hill* — aozica *to ~ out after something* - aozigzica *to stretch up after something* - ozica *to ~ out straining for* — istihohiya *to ~ with the arm, or within arm's ~* — istoglukatin *to stretch out one's arms* - istoiyohiya *to ~ with the arm, or within arm's ~* - istokatinkiya *to cause to stretch out the arm*
read *v* : yawa - oyawa *or* *wayawa to read in or count, to go to school* - wayawapi *reading, arithmetic*
ready *v* : kenun'ic'iya *to get ~* — kican'ic'iya *to get ~ for* - kicinciya *to get one's self ~* - kiciic'iya *to make one's self ~* — wanagnanka *to have ready* — wínyeya *prepared* — yuze *to grab hold on, prepare things*
really *adv* : leceya *certainly, this being so*
ream *v* : iyuk'o *to ~, enlarge a hole by reaming*
rear *n* : catku *the back e.g. of a tent* - catkul *or* catkuta *at the rear or back of a tent or house, at or in the place of honor* - catkutanhan *or* icatkutanhan *to or at the back part of a tent from one* — héktapatan *by or at the rear*
reason *adj* : canteyukeya *reasonable* — taku on *the why of* — tawácinkiksuya *to become reasonable again, to assume reason*
rebellion *n* : wawakipajinpi - wawakipajinyan *rebelliously*
rebound *vn* : awoštaka *to bounce away, as an arrow not piercing*
recall *adv* : éyaš tukà *as you should recall*
receive *v* : - Cf get
recently *adv* : kalecalake s'e
receptacle *n* : wógnakapi
reckless *adj* : blézešni *desperate*
recline *adv* : kaitunkab *reclining on one's back* — ónpa *or* únpa *to lean, lay away in a reclining attitude, to stack*
recognize *va* : iyekiya *to ~ one's own* - oiyekiye *recognition* - wawiyekiya *to ~ one's own* - wawiyeke s'e *recognizing delightedly* - wicitiyekiyapi s'e *coming to ~ one a little* - Cf find
reconnoiter *v* : wakcanyan
record *n* : wicahooyuspa *a sound recorder, or a sound ~*
recover *vn* : asni - akisni *to get well, to ~ from anger* - canlakisni *to ~ from anger or sorrow, to become composed* - canlasniyan *to cause to ~ from sorrow* - canlasnikiya *to ~ from sorrow* - asniyakel *getting well, in the way of recovering* — ekícetu *to ~ , to become as before* - ekicetuya *to make right again, to restore, to ~ as from death* - ekicicetu *to become as before to or for one* — ahececa *to be rather*

better, to ~ a little - ahecel *a bit better* — blézic'iya *to restore one's health* — gincela *recovering* — kipayehca *to rise up, to ~ itself* — okawaton *to be recovered* — takipa *to ~ what is stolen*
recreate *v refl* : imagagaic'iya *to amuse one's self*
recruit *v* : blézic'iya
recur *v* : - Cf again
redound *v* : waayuptanyan *to ~ to one's self, to have an effect on one's self*
reduce *va* : yamniga *or* yapišitka *to shrink by chewing*
reflection *n* : wówiyakpa *splendor*
refrigeration *n* : wapahlatapi
refuge *v* : kiyonakijin *to arrive and take shelter in* - onakijin *to take ~ in or behind* — onakikšin *or* onajin *to take shelter or refuge behind, in or at, to stand in* — onape *a place of refuge where an enemy can do one no harm* — wamá el i *to take ~ in or on*
refuse *v* : akiciktašni *to reject when offered* — glonica *or* glonil *to ~ to give up what one claims, to forbid the use of one's own, to withhold* - kiciglonica *to ~ to give up for one, to ~ to give away one's own* — k'ánajin *to ~ to do, as is said of "dragging one's feet"* — wawipila *to ~, not to give*
regard *v poss* : iwanglaka *to have ~ for one's own* - iwan'ic'iglaka *to guard or watch after one's self* — wócanteoyuze one's ~ for, to have a regard for a person
regret *v* : wókihye *to be sorry for not being present for something good*
reinforce *va* : ipatagya
reject *va* : paha *to oppose, to puch onwards* — yaȟeyata *to ~ by speaking* - yuȟeyata *to put back* — yaitokan *to put aside, reject* - Cf refuse
rejoice *v* : iyuškin - Cf glad
rekindle *v* : paile *to ~*
relapse *vn* : oigluškan *to have a ~* - onaškan *to become sick again* - oyuškan *to get restless, to have a ~*
relative *va* : takúya *to have one for a ~* - watakuyapi *relatives, or relationship* - takukiciyapi *relationship or relations* - takuye *a person of kin* - titakuye *immediate relatives* - otakuye *kinsfolk, brotherhood, relationship* - otakuyeya *to form a relationship* — wicowe *relationship between e.g. brothers and sisters etc. , a generation* — wówahecon *relationship, words expressing it*
relax *adv* : kánhtal *relaxed, with a loss of tension*
release *v* : kiyuška *to ~ or loose from* — kiyušpa *to ~ from a trap* - nakicišpa *to ~ from trouble*
religion *n* : Kacegu Un *a member of the Congregationalist Church* — Sapun *a Catholic priest, a member of the Catholic Church* — Skaun *an Episcopal minister, a member of the Episcopal Church* — Ogleptecela *a Presbyterian minister, a member of the Presbyterian Church* — wócekiye *a prayer, the word used for religion*
rely *va* : wacinyan *to ~ on, to trust, or confiding in*
remain *vn* : ahiyanka *to come and stay* — blogyanka *to ~ home as during the hunt* — hiyanka *to stay where one has arrived* - tokena yanka *to ~ while others move, to ~ partly the way they were* — awiyaya *to stay away over night* — ecayaukeca *to ~ in one place, or a fixture* — hanyunka *to spend the night* — ihan *to stand at, to ~* — ihekiya *to have remaining, i.e. little of one's own* — ikicihan *to ~ for one* - kícihan *to be or ~ for one* — okapta *to be left* - okaptapi *remnants*
remember *v* : iksuya - ic'iksuya *to recall one's self* - kiciksuya *to recollect for* - kiksuya *to ~ something* - okiksuye *to ~, or a remembrance* - wacinkiksuya *to ~ all well*
remit *v* : kicahpa *to settle or pay for one*
remnant *or* **leavings** *n* : wóptuh'a *litter, rubbish, scraps*
remove *v* : kaponya *to ~ rough places, to smoothen* — kiciyutokan *or* kiyutokan *to ~ for one* - yuitokan *to ~ from, to reject* — waikikcu *to take, remove one's own* - waikicu *to ~ from by magic*
render *v* : kahiyaya *to ~ or give a rendition of a song*
renew *va* : yutelya
rent *v* : tiyololya *to ~ a house* - wóolota *rental, lease*
repair *va* : aglukaka *to ~ one's own, to refurbish* - gleton *to mend, repair, correct mistakes* — piyá *to mend something* - píya *well, anew* - ipíye *something with which to do a ~* - pikíya *to mend, reset, rearrange, to make one's bed* - piyépica *reparable*
repeal *va* : kiyujuju
repeat *adv* : iyakiglegle *repeatedly* — yapsake šni éye *to ~ saying again and again*
repent *v refl* : igluecetu *or* igluekicetu *to right one's self as before* — iyopeic'iya *to reprove one's self, to ~*
report *vn* : ške *it is reported, they say* — wakcanyan *to observe, prepare, and give a ~* — wóyake *an indication, a ~*
repose *adv* : kitanpawoslaheyelakel *reposefully, a bit upright*
represent *va* : nakicijin *to act as a delegate for one*
repress *v* : okpaspa *to suppress one's own reaction*
reprimand *va* : owakiya — waahoyeya *to reprove or scold* — wawiyopeya *to reprove one*
reprisal *n* : - Cf vengeance
reptiles *n* : - Cf animal
repute *v refl* : oiglušica *to spoil one's own ~ , i.e. one's good name*
research *n* : akitapi
resemble *vn* : kigma — owangya *to imitate* — wíyacinpi *a resemblance*
resent *v* : kaitececašni *to assume a resentful face* — hanliyáyapi s'e *leaving resentfully, indignantly as in having been offended*
reserve *v refl* : aikpatan *to ~ for one's self and duties* - aikpatanyan *reserving one's self for* - apatan *to ~, to take care of for some purpose* - kícipa *to keep for one, to ~, espouse, to hold in ~* — anica *to withhold* - akinil *to hold for one*
reservoir *n* : mniognake *a water tank*
reside *vn* : ounyan *to have a residence* - ounye *a home* - ounyekiya *to cause to dwell in, or to rule over* - ounyeya *to make a place home* — oyanke *a residence*
resolve *v* : akiconza *to make a resolution* - wóic'iconze *a resolution* — págnaka *to have resolved upon, to set one's face towards* — coic'icon *to be resolute in doing evil to one's self* — tawacinkic'un *to be resolute, obstinate* - tawacinkic'unyan *resolutely* — tawacinsuta *firm, constant* - tawacinsutaya *firmly, with determination*
resound *vn* : tóhingla — yuiyowaza *to make a sound or echo*
respect *v poss* : ahokipa *to value and ~ what is one's own, to honor, reverence or fear* — aktá *to have ~ and regard for, to welcome others* — canteelyuza *to hold one dear, to esteem* — wacinkiciyuzapi *to have a mutual regard for* — cantiyap'ic'iya *to feel scared at as one having done something unintentionally* — iglawa *to esteem or count one's self* — igloaya *to attend to one's self and get along well* — kinihan *to honor and respect, to have confidence in* - igluokinihan *to make one's self honorable* — ihakikta *to have regard for one's own* — tanla *or* tanlaka *to love, honor, be patient with* - wamnala *to honor for bravery* - wawamnala *to have a high regard for, or one who respects others* — wayuopeša *one who respects others, or respectful*

respond *v* : wozá *to start at, to ~*
responsibility *v* : igloeyaya *to take up or go on one's own* — ónglohpe *or* óngluhpe *work to be accomplished, burden to be carried and disposed of, one's occupation, profession*
rest *vn* : asnikiya *to take a long ~* - asniya *to cure e.g. a wound, to make get well* - asnisnikiya *to take a ~ often* — atans'ela yanka *to sit restfully motionless* — htanišni *without moving much, motionless* — icoga *to lodge on, to ~ on* — ózi *to ~* - ozíic'iya *to ~ one's self* - ozíkiya *to take a brief ~* - iyozi *a ~, a repose* - okiziya *to make take a ~* - oziya *to take a ~* - oziwanil *without ~* — kableblesic'iya *to ~ one's mind* — okihpaya *to remain at ~ in the same place* — ooyuhpa *a resting place* — škanškanokile *to make one's self comfortable* — tiyohwaic'iya *to ~ quietly making one's self at home*
restless *adj* : ons'háha *sitting restlessly* — škanškanwašicun *or* wanaptonka *a ~ person* — wóslotonšni *to be careless, always jumping at first impressions, not showing planned caution*
restore *v* : kicu *or* okic'u *to take back*
resurrection *n* : wicakini
retract *v poss* : gluecetu
return *v* : kiun *to ~ home*
revelation *n* : wóyuašlaye
revenge *n* : - Cf vengeance
reverently *adv* : oholaya - waoholašniyan *irreverently*
reverse *v poss* : glueciya
review *n* : wóiwanyanke *a commentary*
revive *va* : apiya *to mend, recoup* — kawacinksab *to restore, bring about conscious awareness*
ribbon *n* : wapahlate
rich *adj* : jíca - iglajica *to speak of one's self as ~* - iglajicaka *one who counts him or herself ~* - ijica *to be ~ in this world's goods* - ojicaka *rich in goods* - wíwicajica *wealth* - wijica *~ or riches* - wijicaya *to enrich* — ijilya *to cause to be ~, or richly* - jilya *to make ~* - wójice *riches* - wówijica *wealth* — iwašeca *to be ~ in provisions* — watonka *a ~ person*
ricochet *v* : ícana s'a *or* íwopsil *or* woglákinyan *to ricochet, to make glance off in shooting*
ride *v* : akanyanka *to sit upon* — anaunka *to gallop on* — šunkakanyanka *a rider horseback, or to ~ horseback*
ridge *n* : blo - bloáliya *along the ~* — ȟeyáta *on or to the ~, bluff, plateau*
ridicule *va* : iȟaȟa *to laugh at one* - oiȟaȟa *to ridicule, to scorn* - wówiȟaȟa *laughter, the making fun of one* — waelhoyeya *to make fun of persons*
right *adv* : išlayapatanhan *from the right side* - išlayatanhan *at of to the right hand* - itanišlayatanhan *at the right side of a person* - napišlayatanhan *at the right hand* - tanišlayatanhan *or* tan'išleyatan *at the right side of a person* — iyuecetu *to make right* - wóyuecetu *a righting* - kaecetu *to make right* - lécetu *this is right* — écela *correct*
righteousness *n* : wóowotanla
rim *n* : hugmiya ayut'inzela *the ~ of a wheel* — icete *the ~ or lip of a kettle*
ring *va* : ayasna *to make ~ with the mouth* - ayusna *to ~ on or over, as a bell* - pasna *to ~ by pushing* - snás'e *ringing, tinkling* - snáyela iyaya *to go ringing, as a strip of iron* — ayuhla *to ~ or rattle over* - gluhla *to ~ one's own bell* - hlayéla *ringing, tinkling* - hlahla *to rattle or ~, or a crier* - nahla *to be ringing as a telephone* — mázanapsiohli *a ring worn on the finger* - Cf jewelry
rip *n* : mnahan *a rip or tear, or ripped of itself* - awamna *to ~ on as with a knife* - ikamna *to ~ by striking* - kamna *to come apart as at a seam, to ~ by striking e.g. a ball-cover* - kimnahan *to rip off for* - namna *to ~ of itself at a seam* - opamna *a ~ or rend at a seam* - pamna *to ~ e.g. a sleeve* - wamna *to ~, open with a knife* - yamna *to ~ with the mouth* - wamnayan *to take a collection, fig to ~ off others* - anamna *to ~ open* - awabáza to ~ or cut open - awoblaza *to tear open by shooting* - ayablaza *to tear open with the teeth* - blazahan *ripping* - okiwablaza *to ~ open in the middle* — ayahleca *to tear with the teeth on* - apahleca *to tear with e.g. the hand shoved into the sleeve* - ayuhleca *to rend on one, as a garment* - haaigluhlehleca *to tear up one's clothing* - haakanhanheyela *in torn clothes* - haakuka *to be wearing worn-out clothes* - okiwašleca *to ~ down e.g. a log* - wakicisleca to ~ with a saw - wakisleca *to split or ~ with a saw or knife* — yuzahan *to make a ripping sound*
ripe *vn* : asuton *to become ~ on* - suton *to ripen, bear seed fit for use* - wasuton *to get ~* - suton áya *to begin to ripen* — gwáhan *over-ripe, become soft* — štunka *green, not ~, soft* — tancanton *to be ~, full-grown* — najanjanyelayeye *to be ~ and shining*
ripple *v* : kašniyanyan *to break up, toss about*
rise *v* : nawankal *to ~ upward* — woákanhiyuya *to make rise to the top, as scum* - Cf stand
risk *v* : iyot'ognaka *to ~ or endanger one's life*
river *n* : wakpa - wakpala *a creek* — kaokatan *over the ~* — óhan *the river's straight course between two bends. Some rivers the Lakota bands were familiar with are :*

Wakpašice *Bad River*
Heȟaka Wakpa *Elk* or *Yellowstone River*
Mniwoblu Wakpa *Fall River*
Maga Wakpa *Goose* or *Laramie River*
Kušleca Wakpa *or* Winyan Wakpala *Woman Creek or Split* or *Loup River*
Mnišoše Wakpa *the Missouri River*
Pangi Tankinkinyan *the Great Artichoke Creek* or the *Mizpah Creek*
Naȟuga Hohpi Wakpala *the Niobrara River*
Hokiyohloka Wakpala *Pass Creek*
Pankeska Wakpa *the Platte River*
Tátetacanku *or* Wašin Wakpa *the South Platte tributaries, the Wind River* or *Pork River*
Ptan'unpi Wakpala *Pumpkin Creek*
Onjinjintka Wakpa *the Rosebud River*

road *n* : canku - cankunaptan *a tilted or slanting ~* - cankuya *to have for a ~* - makokocanku *a fenced ~* - ocanku *a street, a way* - ocankuya *a path, or in the likeness of a ~* - ocankutonyan *forming a ~* - wan ounpapi s'e ocanku *a way that lay wrapped straight as an arrow, i.e. a very straight ~* — hocete *a direct ~ to the buffalo* — oiyagle *a ~ leading to* — oškiiyaza ocanku *a ~ drifted in and low*
roast *va* : cok'in *to ~ on spits* — pasnon *or* pasnun *to ~ on* - kicipasnun *to ~ for one* - kpapasnon *to ~ one's own* — pelmnamnaya *to ~ on a spit* — šku *to be roasted, all or parts* - táka *to ~ off the hull as of oats* — waceunpa *to ~, or one who roasts meat etc.* - Cf fire, burn
rob *n* : wakipi *or* wicakipi *robbery*
robe *n* : ptehahinšma *a buffalo ~ for winter wear having heavy fur* - ptehinšma tawelaha *a buffalo ~ without the heavy hair for summer wear*
rock *va* : yuptanptan *to oscillate, vibrate back and forth* — yuptanptanyan *to rol* — nainyanyeya *to become rock-hard* - *See* stone

rod *or* **hanger** *n* : satglakinyan *a drying rod* - Cf hanger

Rogation *np* : Owoju Awacekiyapi *the ~ Day procession and blessing of crops*

roll *v* : gmigma *to go around as a wheel does* - kagmigma *to ~ along* - kaogmigma *to make ~ into* - oic'igmigmela *with one's self rolled up* - naogmigma *to ~ something with the foot* - pagmigma *to ~ something by hand* — kagmiyayan *to make something ~* - nagmiyanyan *to make e.g. a football ~ with the foot* - pagmiyan *to make ~ by hand and pushing* — kipehan *to ~ or fold up one's own* — nakša *to coil or curl* - okakše *a ~ of ribbon, of cloth or thread, a skein of yarn* — opaptan *to turn or ~ over* - paptanyan *to upset one, or rolling about* - yuptanptanyan *to ~ something over and over* - yuptanyan *to turn or ~ over, or turning or rolling over* — oic'ipšunpšunkel *rolled or coiled up* - yupšunpšun *to ~ into a wad* — pablaya *to spread out e.g. some dough* — pacangleya hiyuya *to ~ e.g. a hoop toward one* — pagmun *to ~ up by hand* - pagmunpi *anything rolled up, e.g. a skein of yarn, a hide, a blanket etc.* — pawaga *to twist something in the hand* — wópemnikagapi *a roll*

roof *n* : aokiye *a wagon or buggy top* — awokeya *or* kéya *a flimzy roof* — kéya *to make a ~ over one* — keinyanhan *roof-like, sloping* — ticankahu *the beam in the peak of a gable* - tiipaslate *a pillar or other support*

room *v* : kipana *to make ~ for another* — iyokan *or* ocikan *roomy* - okan *there is room* - okanyan *roomy, there being ~* — ošunk'oglešica *being no ~ for many* — oyanke *a room or place of residence* — tiungnaga *or* tiiyokahmi *the cor-ner of a ~* — tiyokalya *to warm a ~* — tiyotatešni *a close, warm ~* — wakipika *roomy* — wankaltipi *an upper ~* — wapako *or* yukan *to make ~ for* — ahiyukan *to come and make ~* - kiyukan *to make ~ for* - Cf reside, house

root *n* : húte - ohute *a ~, the bottom* - canhuta *a tree stump* - canhutkan *or* hutkán *a tree root* - šinkpankahu *food roots* — huokihe hanskaska *umbrella wort, a medicine* — ju *to root a piece of a plant* - pajun *to push down and pry up the roots, to spade and pull up the roots* - yajun *to ~ up* - yujun *to ~ up by hand* — šúnkace *or* šunkcé *the ~ of calamus* — tátu *a medicinal ~* — tewapa *an esculent root that grows in water*

rope *n* : wíkan *a leather cord* - tahunsapa wíkan *a ~ made from hair that grows on a horse's mane* - wíkansonpi *a lasso* - wíkankan *a double ~* — wíyuhonte *a sinew ~*

rot *adj* : kuka *rotten* - ikuka *to rot* - ikukeya *in a rotting manner* - kukeya *to make ~* - akuka *to get rotten on* — kimaka *to ~, turning into soil* — ponpon *or* punpun *to decay, or rotten, soft* — šéca *dry and rotten*

rough *adj* : anaȟa *roughened up* - apaȟatka *~ against the grain* - apaȟatkaya *roughly against the grain* - ȟapa *~, as the wind or voice* - ȟeoški *roughness of the land* - naȟa *to become chapped, break the surface of* - paȟa *to rub ~* - paȟaȟa *to be ~* — ataja *to be ~ or in waves on one* - ataštaja *to be ~ e.g. on one in waves of water* - taja *~ in agitated water* — t'ága *~ and gritty, as a floor with sand on it* - at'ahya *to make dry and ~ on some surface* — ayugweza *to make ~ on* - kagweza *to roughen* - pagweza *to rub rather ~* - yugweza *to make ~* — cica *~ or frizzled as tightly curled hair* - iyacica *ruffled up, as feathers* — ecayuh'i *~ and uneven on the surface* - yuh'iya *to be made ~* — yuh'is'e *~ as when chapped* — ah'akpa *not level and a bit ruffled* — icama *~ as a beard, prickly* — kaglega *to mark, to make ~* — kaskiska *to make ~ by pounding* - kaškiška *to make ~ by striking e.g. with an axe* - naškiška *to make ~ by trampling on* - škiškeya *to make ~, or roughly* - škiškita *~ and not smooth* - skiska *a ~ thing* — pepeya *with a sharp and ~ surface, as on a frozen roadway* — wicatute *roughness of the hands not chapped* — yuhtan *to make rough in doing a rough edge*

round *adj* : gmiyan *~ as a wheel* - apagmiyanyan *to make ~ on* - gmigmiyan *~ like a ball* - gmiyanyanla *any little ~ things* — apagmon *or* apagmun *to twist or roll on anything* — mima *or* mimela *circular, as is a disk, not as a ball* - mimeyela *circularwise* - pamíma *to make ~ and flat, as a coin* - pámima *~ and pointed* — gmigma *to go around, turn as a wheel* - ayugmigma *to make ~ on* - gmigmela *~ as a wheel* - gmigmeya *going round* - kagmigma *to make ~* - pagmigma *to make ~ by hand* — cangleška *a hoop, a wheel* — icakša *to gather around the neck* — kapšunka *to make ~, nob-like* - pšunkaka *pills, tiny ~ things* — napako *to bend up or ~ of itself* — okawinga *to go ~ and ~* — otosa *blunt and ~*, filled out — pošla *rounded off at one end* — tapoposka *ball-shaped things*

round-up *n* : ptemnayanpi *the gathering of the cattle etc.* - Cf napako

rouse *va* : nani *to touch or jog to awaken, rouse one*

rout *v* : iyayeya *to turn away, to hew* — pabluka *to become crushed or routed*

row *n* : cankoye - cankoyeton *to be in rows or furrows* - cankoyetontonyan *in rows* — íciyaza *in rows from one to another* — ipahlala *in a row facing one way, as soldiers in rank formation* — yuogla *lined in a ~*

rowdy *n fig* : sintehanska

rub *va* : apacoza *to warm by rubbing* — apajaja *to wash by rubbing, mopping on* — apajuju *to wash by rubbing* — apakinta *to wipe or ~ off on* — apakiza *to make a noise rubbing on* — apakuka *to rub to pieces on* — apak'ega *to ~ smooth by hand* — apak'oza *to ~ and make smooth on* — apaman *to ~, file, polish on* — apasleca *to slit by rubbing on* — apawaga *to pulverize by rubbing with the hands* — apawinta *to ~ on* — napopawega *to ~ in the hands* — opawaga *to ~ over and over in the hands* — pacica *to ~ together, mix up* — pasepa *to ~ off* — pašla *to ~ off, make bare* — paštuta *to ~ with snow* — patan'in *to ~ clear, clean* - patan'inšni *to ~ off, obliterate* — pawinta *to ~ by hand* — wapaȟatka *to ~ against the grain* — ikpakinta *to wipe one's own* — ikpak'ega *to ~ one's self against something to stop an itch* — ikpawaza *to ~ one's self against something as do cattle* — inakinlya *to rub e.g. mud off the feet* — ipakinja *to ~ e.g. one's eyes with the hands* — ipaman *to ~ on, as with a file or rasp* - ipame *a tool to ~ or file with* — ipaskica *to ~ e.g. clothes on a washboard* — ipawinta *to ~ on with* — ayuȟunta *to ~ on to soften* — iyun *to apply on* - iic'iyun *to ~ and apply on one's self* - ikiyun *to ~ on one's self* — kalapa *to ~ smooth or level* — iyupan *to break or ~ up in the hand* — puskica *to ~ out* — yusepa *to ~ off, deface*

rubbish *n* : watušekš *dirt, sweepings*

rude *adj* : oh'an'ecinšniyan *impolite*

ruffle *adj* : yumnija *ruffled* - ayumnimnija *to ~, or a ruffle or pleat* - yumnimnišya *to curl* — ȟaká *ruffled, made rough* — yuȟatka *to ~ e.g. the hair or feathers* — wanaškiškilya *to ~ e.g. a dress*

ruin *va* : atakunišni *to come to naught, to be ruined, destroyed, become extinct, to wither away* - atakunišniyan *to reduce to naught, to ~* - awotakunišni *to destroy by shooting* - ayutakunišni *to destroy, bring to naught on* - iglutakunšni *to destroy one's self* — awanil *in a destructive manner* — ayujuju *to destroy, take to pieces* — ayuwignuni *to cause to perish on* — ihangya *to destroy, bring* *to an end* - ihangkiya *to destroy one's own* or *for one* — inajabjapa *to ruin, wear out e.g. one's shoes* — waontonkiya *to ruin or spoil one's own* — watogya *to spoil, to take vengeance on*

rule *n* : wówakonze *a law, determination, the ~ of justice*

rummage *va* : kahi or kicahi *to ~ for, to stir*

rumminate *v* : wayatekonza

run *vn* : ínyanka - ainyanka *to ~ on, to ~ for, to ~ to get* — hunkpan kos inyanka *to ~ waving toward the camp entrance* — kainyang iyaye *to go on making it ~* - kainyankelaka *to shuffle along* - oinyanka *to ~ about in* — napa *to ~ away, to flee, or a flight* - anakipa *to flee from* - anapa *to ~ to for refuge* - k'innapa *to ~ away with* — hanpohya *losing one's way* — ícacan or íkacan *to trot, as does a horse, or to adjust something carried on one's back* — íciwotopi *they ~ their heads together, as do rams* — íkato *to gallop, as do horses* — kahinhpeya *to ~ over something, to overthrow, to make fall over or down* — okicicuwapi *they ~ after each other* — tokala inyanka *to ~ with head and body bent* - yuinyank'inyanka *to ~ along*

ruse *adv* : zomiyanke *using a ruse*

rush *n* : - Cf grass

rust *n* : ogí *rust, to rust, or brown* - agí *to be covered with ~, or to have a rusty, brown stain*

rustle *vn* : ȟápa *to be making a rustling sound, to ~ as in leaves of bushes* - ȟabȟapela *with a rustling sound, or a rustle* - icaȟabȟapela *to ~, making a sound* - icicaȟabȟapa *to make a rustling sound* - kaȟabȟapa *to beat against and make a rustling noise, as wind blowing against grass* - ȟabȟabya *in a rustling manner* — snahan *rustling* — yumnumnuga *to ~, as corn blowing in the wind*

S

sacrament *n* : wóeconwakan - Note: the following being the seven celebrated sacraments of the Catholic Church :

Mniakaštanpi *Baptism* - mniakaštan *to baptize one*
Wicayusutapiwakan *Confirmation*
Yutapiwakan *Eucharist*
Wóglakapiwakan *Penance or Reconciliation*
Wíyunpiwakan *Anointing the Sick*
Wicašawakankagapi *Ordination*
Wakankiciyuzapi or Okiciyuzewakan *Matrimony*

sacred *adj* : wakan *holy, special i.e. notably, particularly* - wakankila *to regard one's own ~* - wakanla *to reckon ~*

sacrifice *v* : owaunyan *to ~ in, or a place of ~, an altar* - wakiciunyan *to ~ for, offer ~ for* - wakiunyan *to ~ or offer to* - waunyan *to offer ~* - waunyanpi *sacrifices* - waunyeya *to offer sacrifices* - wówaunye *the sacrificial gift* — owayušna *to ~ in or on, or an altar* - waic'iglušna *to ~ one's self, to let one's self fall* - waglušna *to ~ self* - wakiyušna *to ~ to, or to drop for one* - wayušna *to offer sacrifice* - yušnapi *a sacrifice* - wóšna *to drop and offering in, or an offering in* - wóšnakiya *to cause one to ~* — waic'igluhtata *to offer ~ for one's self* - waigluhtata *to offer self in ~* - wakigluhtata *to ~ one's own* - wayuhtata *to offer in ~, to kill in ~* - wayuhtatapi *a sacrifice*

sadly *adv* : ašilya unpleasantly - šilyakel *badly* — wawiyokišica *to be sad, grieved* — canksiksizeca *saucy, morose* - canpsis un *to be sad because of being neglected* - canšilya *to make one sad, or sorrowfully* - canšilyakel *sorrowfully* - cantehunkešniyan *discouraged* - cantemniskan'ojula deep in sorrow because of suffering - cantešica *to be sad or sorrowfull* - cantešicaya sadly - cantešilic'iya *to repent one's self* - cantešilyakel *sadly* - canteyašica *to dishearten by talking* - cantihanke - sad worrying - ocantešilya *sadly* - wacanteiyokišica *sad* - wócanteiyokišice sadness - icanšica or icanšil *to be sad over or for one who died, sorrowingly*

sad *adv* : oiyakišilya *being a sad saying or sight*

saddle *v poss* : akinglotaka *to ~ one's own, e.g. horse* — ak'in *a ~ blanket* - canwak'in *a wooden ~* — anungwakicaška *~ bags*

sage *n* : pejiȟota - pejiȟota pepe *prickly ~* - pehiȟota skuya *sweet ~, a Bad Land's sage*

saint *n* : wakanpi *saints* - wakanpi olakolkiciyapi *the communion of the saints*

sake *prep postp* : ontantanhan *for the ~ of* - tántanhan *for the ~ of one*

saliva *n* : tah *foam* - tahna *running saliva*

salt *n* : cak'iglaska *to get just a taste of something, or salts* — mniskuya *common salt* - mniskuyaoyuze *a salt mine* - mniskuyeton *to apply ~*

salutary *adj* : nagiyuwašte

salute *v* : kalabiyekiya

salvation *n* : wówanikiye or wiconicanpi

same *adv* : itkonza *even with* — okahwanjila *the ~ form*

sand *n* : casmu - casmuikacoco *a trowel* — mniȟuha wíyuma *sandpaper*

sap *n* : šin *sap from wood*

sarcasm *v* : ihe *to use ~, cutting words*

satisfy *v* : canlicaspekiton *to ~ one's self, as by eating* - canlicaspekiya *to ~ one* - canlicaspeya *to ~ desires of the heart whether good or evil* - canlimna *to be pleased with, to judge one to be up to standard* — canticaspeya *to gratify one's desires* — ímna *to be satisfied, to have enough of* - ímnahan *sufficiently, to satisfaction* - ímnahanhan *more than sufficiently, awfully* - ímnahanyan *sufficiently* - ímnahanyankel *being a great deal, very much, sufficiently* - ímnaic'iya *to ~ one's self with* - ímnayan *to fill, ~ one, or filled, satisfied* - íwicamna *satisfying, furnishing much nourishment* — iwakanyeja *easily satisfied* — opikila or šikigla *to be satisfied with e.g. food*

save *va* : atantonyan *to have one ~ and accumulate property* — ic'iksapa *to ~ for one's self, to have gained experience, to be wise* — patan *to take care of, to ~* - wapatan *to be saving of* - wapatanka *one who saves* - wópatan *the saving of things* — Wanikiye *the Savior, i.e. Jesus Christ* - Cf live

savor *adv* : ihamnapi s'e *savoring, appealing to the taste*

saw *n* : can'inaslelye *a sawmill* - can'iwakse *a cross-cut ~* - cannaslelya *to ~ logs* - canwaksa *to ~ wood* - canwasleca *to ~ lengthwise, i.e. with the grain, to rip-saw* - canwaslecapi *wood sawed lengthwise, the sawing of planks and boards* - cínwakse *a saw* — wakiksa *to ~ off one's own* — hugmiya pepela *a circular ~* — kiwasleca *to ~ in the middle what is soft* - kiwašleca *to ~ what is hard* — ocannaslece *a saw-mill*

say *v* : ékekiya *to ~ of one* - éya *to say* - ke *it is said* ške' they say - kéya *to ~ that* - keyapi *they say* - kéciya or kékiya *to ~ to one that it is so* — léya *to ~ this* - léic'iya *to ~ this to one's self* - lékiya *to say this to one* - tak'eya *to ~ something*

scab *vn* : háyuhpu *to be scabbed* — hocošpu *a ~ or wart* - ȟan *a scab* - ȟan'apaha *to have a thick ~ on a wound* - ȟanȟan *scabby* - ȟanȟanpi *sores* - ȟanȟanyan *to make scabby, or like a ~* - ton'ognagagya *with matter on scabs* *or sores here and there*

scale *vn* : kahpu *to ~ off i.e. fall off* — našlaya *to come off as the hull off boiled corn* — powaya *to flake off as paint when dried under intense heat*

scalp *vn* : iwaktegla *to go home in triumph with scalps* - iwaktegli *to come home in triumph with scalps* — páha *the hair of the head, the scalp* — pecokan *or* pecokanyan *the scalplock* - wašpa *to take one's scalp*

scandalize *va* : šilwokahnihya *to teach evil to the young*

scar *n* : osnaze

scarcely *adv* : h'únyela *or* iyus'eya *hardly* — kítan *barely, slightly* - kitan'ecinyan *just able*

scare *va* : ahabya *to ~ wild game* — inihan *to be frightened or amazed* - inihanya *to frighten or astonish one* - inihanyan *in amazement* - ainihan *to be frightened for some reason* - ainihanyan *fearfully, excitedly* — cuwaculuza *a scarecrow, a spirit pest* — waaunyeya *to ~ away* — wanaungya *to scare away e.g. wild game by one's presence* — yualos iyeya *to scare* — yuiyoyag *to get excited*

scatter *adv red* : ábebeya *or* ábekiya *separately, spreading out* - kaabeya *scattered as horses* - kaiyabebeya *in all directions* — ablecahan *scattered in falling off* - anableca *to spread out on, as grain when poured on a floor* - obleca-han *scattered as a people living apart* - oiglubleca *to ~ as a crowd of people do e.g. after a meeting* - oyubleca *to divide out and ~* — glegle *scattered here and there* - acaglegle *scattered with things far apart* - glegleka *scattered, one here and there* - ícigleglega *few scattering* — aglala *to ~ one's own on* — kala *to sow e.g. seed* — akipaptapi *they dispersed* — iyabya *scattering about, as those on the hunt* — kablesglepi s'e *scattered* — oyuhi *to ~ e.g. feed* - oyuhinhan *to ~ about* — yuptuptuta *to ~ in bits here and there*

scepter *n* : wakeza *a sort of staff symbolic of power and authority* - Cf wahukeza

scholar *n* : waonspeic'iya

school *n* : owyawa *a school or schoolroom* - gliowayawa *a day school* - glišniowayawa *a boarding school* - oyawa *to read or count, to go to ~*

scolding *n* : oiyopeye *a reproving* — wiicigni *to whip a woman*

scoop *v* : hutipak'oga *to use a shovel to pick up e.g. grain*

score *va* : owago *to score something*

scramble *vn* : iyahpahpaya

scrap *va* : watutka *to cut up and make scraps or crumbs* — wógu *scraps, as of tallow dried out*

scrape *v* : anawinta *to ~ the foot on* — tíca *to ~ off* - patica *to ~ off by hand* - ticahan *scraped off, falling off of itself* — aokatica *to draw of ~ snow on anything* - apatica *to ~ off e.g. snow from the ground* - natica *to ~ off with the foot* - **kinca** *adj* : ayukinca *to ~ something off onto* - kakinca *to ~ off hair from a hide* - nakinca *to ~ off with the foot* - kicakinca *to ~ e.g. fish for someone* - kicicakinca *to ~ for one* — ayuwaza *to scratch off with the fingernail on something* — ayuk'éga *to scrape or scratch the hand on something* - inak'ehya *to make a scraping sound, as of a brake on a wheel* - pak'ega *to ~ with the hand using glass* — huha *scrapings* — tahuha *scraps* — kak'oga *to ~ off e.g. paint, dirt, etc.* - icak'oge *a scraper* — kašku *to ~ off e.g. scales or corn* — nahinta *to scrape or wipe off* — nasepa *to ~ along, to clean* — nasminyan *to ~ off by foot* — nawilwita s'e *scraping together by foot* - nawinta *to scrape away thing e.g. on the ground, to clear a space by foot* — pahlata *to ~ along* — pahpa to ~ off — pak'eza *to ~ smooth* — tka *to ~ hair off a hide* — wawaptuh'a *to ~ off crumbs, chips etc.*

scratch *va* : ayuhlata *to ~ or claw on* - igluhlahlata *to scratch one's own* - kahyuhlata *to make a ~* - nahlata *to ~ with the toes* - onahlate *a scratch* - oyuhlata *to ~ in* - oyuhlate *a scratch* - wayahlata *to ~ with the teeth* - yuhlata *to ~ with the claws* - ayuwaza *to ~ off with the fingernails on something* - ikpawaza *to rub against something, as do cattle rubbing themselves on a tree* - naic'iwaza *to ~ one's self* - nawaza *to ~ with the foot* — ayuk'ega *to scrape or scratch the hands on anything* - iyuk'ege *something e.g a piece of wood with which to ~* - igluk'ega *to itch one's self* - ikpak'ega *to rub one's self against something to stop from itching* - naic'ik'ega *to ~ one's self* - nak'ega *to ~ e.g. a horse by foot using a spur* - onak'ega *to ~ around at* — ayuk'oga *or* yuk'oga *to ~ up and make rough with the nails or claws* — ikpakiskija *to make sore by scratching* — iyuhlahlel *being scratched* — nagogo *to score, make scratches as by walking with shoes on a new floor* - nagoya *to ~ out, erase with the foot e.g. something written in the sand* - yugo *to make scratches* — naic'išnašna *to ~ one's self* — nawinl iyeya *to ~ one with one's foot* — oyagi *to impede one, as in walking through tall grass or through what scratches, to affect the throat's normal activity*

scream *vn* : t'ehowaya *to ~ for fear*

screen *n* : wóakeye *something thrown up around to shelter one, like a tent forming a booth or curtain or shade*

screw *n* : - Cf nail

scrub *v* : ipawaga *to rub, scour e.g. a dirty floor*

scruple *v* : wakanla s'e un *to be a health scrupulant, a person who worries much about his or her own health*

scum *v* : tahton *to have ~* — hpo *esp ~ afloat on lakes* - Cf foam

seal *va* : puspa *to stick on something, to glue, to ~* - puspeya *to cause to ~ or to glue* — wíyaskabton *to ~ something*

seam *n* : hupeyozan *an outer ~, as on a legging* — okagege *the place where something is sown together* - okayege *seams* — ókime *a ~ or joint, or to join, meet, encircle, to circle, go around*

season *n* : makoncage - makasanpa *or* makisanpa *the next year or ~. Thus the seasons of the year* :

waniyetu *winter*
wétu *spring* - wéhan *last spring* - iwétu *next spring* - awétu *to become spring on one*
bloketu *summer, this or next summer* - blokecokanyan *mid-summer* - blokehan *last summer* - abloketu *to have lived until summer, to come summer*
ptanyetu *or* ptanyela *autumn or fall* - ptinhan *last fall*

seasoning *n* : ápaye *or* wápaye *grease or meat* - ápayeya *to use for ~, i.e. use grease or meat* — ašeca *to become dry or seasoned on anything* — šelyá *to dry and lay up to season, or in the manner of ~* — wicahiyutapi *spices or sauce* : wicahiyutapi toto *sauce for salads* - wicahiyutapi zi *mustard* — mniskuya *salt* — yamnumnugapi *peper* — canhanpi *sugar*

seat *v* : iyotaka *to sit* - kaiyotaka to be seated - oiyotake *a place to sit, a seat* — oyanke *a ~, a room, a place of residence* — oakankan *a bench* - oakanke *anything used for a seat* - Cf sit

secret *va* : ináhma *to hide, keep ~, or to conceal* - ínahma *to seduce, commit fornication or adultery with a person* - ínahmanpi *seduction* - ináhmayakel *secretly, unknown to others* - ináhmekiciciyapi *the game of hide-and-seek.*

- ináhmeya *secretly, covertly, silly* - ináhmeyahan *in secret, secretly* — wawoji *to tell secretly with a whisper*
secure *v* : kokamna *to get ~*
seduce *n* : ínahma *to ~ another* - ínahmanpi *seduction* — tawacinwašakala *credulous* — tawacinpanpanla *venal, weak-minded, easily persuaded* — kat'insya *to cause to be content, accepting, or at rest* — wíyukcanšni *to be credulous* — yajata *to ~ one into giving up his or her good resolve* - Cf credulous, intercourse
see *va* : wanyanka *to perceive something* - iwányanke something with which to see, e.g. a set of binoculars, a gun telescopic sight - wanglaka *to ~ one's own* - wankiciyankapi *the see each other* - wanyangkiya *to make one ~* - wanyangya *to cause one to ~ anything*
seed *n* : co *the kernel* — su *the ~ of anything* — itka *the ~ of anything, the egg, the testicles*
seek *va* : olé *to look for something* - okicile *to look for something for another* - okile *to look for one's own* - aole *to ~ for something more* — akuta kuwa *to go after again and again* — igni *to ~ for, to hunt, to follow after, to stalk* - íikiya *to ask back what one has given*
seem *v express* : éke šni *it seems not* — éke s'e *that seems yet to become better*
seep *adv* : wótanglusasayakel *as getting into everything, seeping in* — mnihipi s'e *seeping in*
seer *n* : wókcan *to see with one's own eyes* - wókcanka *a person of great insight, a prophet, a wise person with great understanding* - Cf understanding
seize *vn* : iyahpaya *to fall upon, to grab* - iyakihpaya *to grab e.g. one's own gun* — iyupaga *to gather up, to arrest* — wawoyuspa *to arrest* - wawoyuspapi *an arrest*
seldom *adv* : - Cf once
self *adv* : iyecinkala *on one's own, freely acting* — kihi *to be fledged, to be on one's own, to be self-supporting* - oic'ihi *to be rich and selfish* — tan'iyupse *to turn one's self to the side to see* — wacin'ic'iyapi *self-reliance* — wah'an'ic'ila *to be self-important* - wanapicage *the feeling of ~ importance* - wah'an'ic'ilapi *pride* — wamahetuyakel *by one's self* — wawipic'ila *to think self-centeredly*
sell *va* : ahiwiyopeya *to have come and sold something* - iyopeya *to exchange or sell, or a price*
semen *n* : hiyaye
send *va* : yeyá - iyayeya *to cause to go or turn away, to ~ away* — kigleya *to ~ off home* - ogligleya *to ~ here and there, or going from one place to another* — yekiya *to send driving e.g. a herd of cattle* — uší *to command to come, to ~ one* - uyá *to send, make go, to start one* — wahokiya *to ~ word for or to one, to promise or order something*
sense *n* : tónton *to come forth steadily, (philosophy) that which has sensible properties* - tóntonya *visible from its properties*
sensitive *adv* : oh'anwakankanyan *sensitively* — wacinwašakala *to be sensitive*
sentence *n* : oegle *a setting down e.g. a saying, a verse in writing* — wicayasupi *a condemnation, a sentence*
separate *adv* : ábebeya *scattered, singly spreading* - ábekiya *scattered, separately* - ábeya *separately and scattering* — acaglegle *scattered with things being far apart, with a motion this way and that* — ákamni iyaya *to separate with a splash* — ákipaptapi *they break up and go in different directions* — palehanyank *to ~ , part from* - ayukipab *separately, divided* - gluakipab *to divide or separate one's own* — glake *standing apart* - glakekeyela *separately* - glakeya *separately, at a distance from each* - glakeyela scattered about *here and there, as shocks of grain in a harvest field* — kašpa *to separate by striking* - kiyušpeya *separately* — kinunkan *separately, divided between two* — ksa *separated* — kiyukseya *separately* — yaksa *to bite off* - yuksa *to break off*
seriously *adv* : **šogya**
serve *n* : ookiye *a servant, assistant* — taokiye *his disciple or assistant* - taokiyeya *to have for a servant or helper* — wówilake *a servant, a hired man*
set *va* : ogle *to ~ or place in* - oegle *to ~ or place in, or a setting down in writing, as a saying, verse, or sentence* — paecetu *to ~ e.g. a broken bone* — yaȟeyata *to ~ aside, in speaking to reject, put aside by the mouth*
settle *vn* : ayumniga *to ~ , shrink, as does a fall of snow when melting* — kaskica *or* kaskil *to ~ down* - naskica *to ~ under foot by walking on something* — yuštan *to ~ a question*
severe *adj* : š'akeca *austere, mighty, hard to deal with*
sew *v* : kagege *or* kayege *to ~ , stitch* - kicicagege *to ~ for one* - aglagege *to ~ on something one's own* - akiglagkiciton *to patch for one* - akiglagkiton *to patch one's own* - akiglagton *patched* - akiglagya *to put on or use for a patch* — apasisa *to stitch on, patch* — pata *to cut out and ~ up e.g. a tent* - apata *to cut out and ~ on as in patching pants* - kipata *to join one thing to another* — mas'wicayege *a sewing machine* — napoštan *a thimble* — tahinšpa *an awl* - tahinšpa cik'ala *a needle*
shade *vn* : ahanzi *to be shady, over-shadowed* - aohanzi *to be ~ on* - aohanziya *to cause ~ upon, overshadow* - iyohanzi *a shadow* - óhanzi *the ~ , a shadow* - óhanziglepi *a bower or shade set up to provide against the heat of the sun* - óhanzizi *the shadow* - mniȟuha óhanzi *an awning, a shade* — aiyohansya *to overshadow, or in the ~* — amahposantagleya *silhouetted* — awakeya *to make a ~ of*
shake *vn* : acancan *to tremble* - akiyucanpi *they ~ anything when several things hit together, they hit off together* - apacancan *to make tremble by pushing on* - ayucancan *to make ~ or tremble* - glucancan *to cause one's own to ~ , to sift one's own repeatedly* - icancan *to tremble on account of or for* - kiciyucan *to ~ for one* - nacancan *to shiver, or to make ~ with the foot* - yupocancan *to ~ up by the hair* — ahiyukan *to come and ~ off* — cuglukan *to ~ off one's own the dew* - okakan *to ~ into* - yukan *to ~ off* — hunhunza *to ~ , tremble* - hunhunsya *to make tremble, or trembling* - hunhunzahela *shaking* - apahunhunza *to ~ on anything* - ayuhunhunza *to make ~ on something* - gluhunhunza *to ~ one's own e.g. one's own tree* - kahunhunza *to make ~* - kiciyuhunhunza *to ~ for one* - nahunhunza *to rock by foot* - pahunhunza *to rock by hand* - wohúnhunza *to ~ by shooting* — apomnamna *to ~ or wag the head about* — apoptanptan *to ~ the head about to dissent from* — ayuhoho *to ~ on, as something that is loose* - gluhoho *to ~ one's own, as one's teeth* - yuohoho *to ~ in a tight place* — cehupaglagla *to chatter, as one's teeth for the cold* — ic'iblebleca *to ~ one's self, as a horse does itself* — iglat'a *to ~ and have convulsions* — ikoze *to ~ and move with the hand* — iyokaniyan *to be jarred* — wani *to ~ in cutting e.g. jelly* — kaglogloka *to ~ and rattle* — kagna *to ~ off* - pagna *to ~ off e.g. fruit by hand, to shell* - yugna *to ~ and make e.g. fruit fall* — kaiyoyagya *to quiver* — kaškanškan *to be shaken* - naškan *to ~ by foot* — natata *to ~ off e.g. dirt from one's feet* - yutata *to brush off dust* — opawiwis'e *shaking as a mass of anything* — yuhaha *shaking up to spread out* — yuhika *to ~ one so as to arouse a person from sleep*
shallow *adj* : áp'eyela *so ~ that one can walk through water and scarcely get one's feet wet* — kázela *not very*

deep, as water through which a person can walk without swimming – púzela ~ as a stream nearly dry

shame *vn* : išteca *to be bashful, ashamed* – ištelkiya *to make one ashamed, to disappoint one* – ištelya *to make ashamed, to dishonor one* – iwicašteca *or* wówicašteca *shame, embarrassment, bashfullness* – wówicaštelya *to be ashamed of, or shamefully*

shape *or* **form** *v* : pašipa *to reshape, to bend to another form or shape*

shapeless *v* : put'ingela *to be ~ and pudgy*

share *va* : *apagan* to ~ or give away to a purpose – okíni *to share, receive, in a division of things* — yunaya *to pass to one* – yunayeya *to pass along to another*

sharpen *va* : yuman *or* yume *to sharpen by grinding* – ayuman *to grind or file off on, to sharpen by grinding* – pe *sharp as edged tools, or as the a point of an awl* – pěya *sharp as edged tools, or pointedly* – iwape *to make sharp or sharp-pointed* – kape *to ~ by pounding* – kapesto *to make sharp-pointed by employing the use of an axe* — kazanpeya *to ~ an end of a smooth stick* — wapé *to ~ with a knife* – yapesto *to ~ with the teeth* — iyogli *a razor strap, a steel hone* – iyogliya *to rub back and forth in whetting or strapping a razor* – mas'wiyogli *a sharpener* – oglikiya *to sharpen* – ogliya *to hone e.g. a knife* — okagaya *to stick e.g. arrows into one, fig to use cutting words*

shatter *v* : kahpahpa *to strike making pieces fly*

shave *v* : kajipa *to ~ clean* – akajipa *to shave with a knife* – can'okajipe *or* can'opajipe *wood shavings* – canpajipa *to ~ or plane wood* — awablaya *to ~ off lumps on* — wagla *to shave off* – awagla *to ~ off with a knife* — awašla *to ~ off with a knife on* – ayušla *to ~ off on* – glašla *to ~ or mow off one's own* – yašla *to graze* – kicašla *to cut low, to shave* – wašla *to ~ or scrape off e.g. hair* – putinhin'icašla *a razor* – putinhin'ipajaja *a shaving brush* – wakicišla *to cut or ~ off with a knife* — wayuk'eza *to shear off entirely and smoothly* — cankagiȟaȟa *shavings* — ihanceti *shavings etc. for kindling a fire in the morning* – skusku *shaved off*

shear *va* : yuk'eza *to clip e.g. hair close* — naoswa *to shear off* – Cf cut, shave

sheath *n* : ógin *or* ojuha — aokpazankiton *to be shiethed*

shed *adj* : hinska *~ off* — pšun *fallen off* – pšunhan *fallen, dislocated* – pšunwahan *dropped out, fallen off*

shell *va* : apagna *to shell e.g. corn* – ayugna *to shell, or shake off e.g. fruit on* – pagna *to shake or shell off* — ínyanha *a sea-shell* — kanhe *to shell out e.g. corn* — pange ska *large marine shells* — pašku *to ~ corn* – yušku *to ~ off* – wašku *to cut from or ~ off* — woglá *to ~ off by punching* — tukiha *a clam ~ alone* – tukipšito *a pearl* – tukiwinunkala *a large ~* — yagwa *to ~ with the mouth, to bite off to ~*

shelter *v* : iyonapa *to take ~ or refuge in* – owenapa *a place of refuge* – tionapa *to flee to, to take refuge in the house* — óblula *rain or wind-proof* – oiyoblula *a ~ as some brush, a hill, etc.* — oipeya *a wind or cold weather ~*

shepherd *n* : waawanglaka *an overseer*

shield *v* : kašeya *to fend off* — yuptinapeyakel *shielded* – wahacanka *a shield*

shine *va* : agliheya *to ~ on* — aiyojanjan *to ~ on* – aiyojanjanic'iya *to be illuminated by, to have lighted one* – aiyojanjanya *to throw light on, to illumine* – iyowicajanjan *an attraction* — ilega *to ~, glitter* – ilehlega *to ~, to twinkle* – ilehya *in a way shining, or to make something shine* – kalega *to make ~* – palehya *to make ~ by*

shingle *n* : canblaska zibzipela *a thin board*

shinny *n* : – Cf ball, game

shiver *v* : kacanhe *to shake with the cold* – yucanpi s'e *shivering*

shock *v* : tanglusasa *or* tangluzaza *to be shocked*

shoe *n* : hánpa *moccasins* – akanhanpa *overshoes* – cánhanpa *shoes* – hankpán *a shoestring* – hankpan ohloka *~ string holes* – hanponašloke *or* hanp'onašloke *slippers* – maštecanhanpa *slippers, warm weather foot-wear* – psohanpa *the Indian snowshoe* – hanpisabye *~ blackening*

shoo *adv* : nakpawinte s'e *as if shooing, chasing away*

shoot *v contrac* : agleyus kuté *to ~ holding the gun against* — aiglutan *to pull the trigger of a gun on one's self* — awošpa *to ~ a piece off on* – awošpu *to ~ and knock off what is stuck* – awoblaza *to ~ and tear open on* – awobleca *to ~ and break in pieces* – awohleca *to ~ and split on* – awohpa *to ~ and make fall* – awoksa *to ~ and break off* – awokuka *to ~ to pieces on* – awopota *to ~ and riddle to pieces on* – awopsaka *to ~ and break off e.g. a cord on* – awoptuja *to ~ e.g. an arrow against something hard making it crack or split* – awosleca *to shoot and split something* – awosota *to use up all by shooting* – awošla *to make bare by punching or shooting* – awošleca *to ~ and split a piece off on* – awošloka *to ~ off emptying a gun* – wogná *to ~ off* – wohpá *to ~ and bring down* – wokpá *to ~ out* – wokšéca *to ~ and make keel over* – woózeze *to ~ and let swing* – woptúja *to ~ off a piece* – wošípa *to ~ off a protuberance* — kuté *to shoot something* – okute *a shot* – cankute *to ~ at a target* – icute *something with which to ~* – kícicute *or* kikute *to ~ something for one* – wakutepi *a shooting* — iwópan *to ~ to pieces* — kiwoksa *or* kiwošpa *to ~ in two* – kiwopsaka *to ~ off in* — owopota *to ~ to pieces on* — kat'iic'iya *to ~ one's self* — kiinyeya *to ~ an arrow* — o *to ~ and strike* – oiheya *to ~ into* — utá *to try firing a gun* – outa *to try and fire with a gun* — slihingla *to fire a shot* – slihingle *a report of gun-fire* — wán'iyahpeya *to ~ arrows* — waokiya *to let one do the shooting* — wicahmunga *to ~ in or into by magic* — yuó s'e *one who misses in shooting (spoken ironicly)*

shore *adv* : hútawapa *at the water by the ~* – ohuta *the water's edge* – ohutapa *at the edge or ~* – ohutahenatanhan *on this side of the ~* — ȟel *ashore when the water retreats* — mniohuta *the ~, the edge of a river* — opuze *a dry ~* – puzata *on shore*

short *adv* : aškahayela *shortly, for a little time* – aškatula *lately, not long since* – aškatuya *not long ago* – aškatuyela *a ~ time ago, lately, near in distance* – aškinyankapila *in a short time, soon, from a short distance* – aškiyankel *at a ~ distance* – oaškayela *nearby* — otohanyan *for a ~ distance or time* – owatohanyan *for a ~ time* — ptécela *or* pcécela *short in length* – ocipteca *shorter than, not equal to* – akaptecela *or* wakaptecela *or* yulena *to shorten* – yuonjincayela *making short* — tojéla *short* — waitebya *cut shorter on one side* – watepa *to cut or wear ~* — wotóka *pounded off ~* — íyaȟagyela *too ~, too little left* — kapinja *to shorten e.g. a tail* — naokpani *to be ~ of* — iyucan *to be ~ of things* — katku *lacking a sufficiency*

shot *n* : oun *a gun load, ammunition, a dose as of medicine*

shoulder *v* : paicakša *to carry over the shoulders* — tapetoska *white-spotted shoulders, as on a mature buffalo*

shout *vn* : akiš'a to ~, to cheer – aš'a *to ~ at* – awicaš'a *the shouting* – iaš'a *to halloo* – íyakiš'a *to ~ at one's own* – íyaš'a *to ~ at or against* íyaš'api *an acclamation* – waglaš'api *children's shouting over food* — ašicahowaya *to cry out on accont of* — houya *to acost, to ~ at one*

— hoyekiya *to cry out to pray to* - hoyeya *to call or cry out* — ipanhoyeya *in a way screaming* - ayuceya *to make cry on*

shove *va* : iyeya *to ~ at* - iyeyaya *to keep putting in, to be finding* — pal̄eyapa *to ~ aside*

show *va* : pazo *to present to view* - apazo *to point at or show* - kpazo *to point at one's own, to show off* - ikpazo *to show one's self* — ayaotan'in *to make manifest on or for* - ayutan'in *to make manifest upon* - glaotan'in *to manifest or declare one's own* - igluotan'in *or* iglutan'in *to manifest one's self* - iyokitan'in *a manifestation* — owanyanke *or* wówanyanke *a vision, a sight, a show*

shred *v* : kaswaka *to make ragged, to shred*

shrink *v* : ayumniga *to ~ or settle on as does snow* - yumniga *to ~ , to draw up* — mniiyosnisniyapi s'e *shrinking as from cold water* — napošin *to shrivel up when drying* — ópo *to be shrunken* — snanza *or* snaza *or* snas'a *to be shriveled up* — tiyokaškapi s'e škan *to ~ from one*

shrub *n* : canl̄otka *small shrubs used for making arrows*

shrug *v* : tahucehkiya *or* tahušlikiya *to ~ the shoulders*

shuck *v* : wakicih'u *to cut the rind or husk away*

shuffle *vn* : nas'os'o

shut *v refl* : aeceliyeic'iya *to ~ one's self up* — awakšija *or* awakšiš *to close upon one* — kakšišya *to fold , double up* — ayuhpa *to throw down on, to ~ e.g. a window* — gmuza *closed, shut* - ayugmuza *to ~ the eyes on* - gmusya being shut up - íogmuza *a closed mouth, or to have the mouth closed* - iogmusya *to close the mouth* - naogmuza *to close up of itself, as a blossom* - ógmuza *to be ~ or closed* — naopo *to ~ up, as a flower*

shy *v* : paohmin *to ~ from* — tannapa *to ~ from, at, or to flinch*

sick *v* : yazan *to feel pain* - ayazan *to be sick on* - iwayazan *or* iyazan *to be sick as a result of* - iyazi *to be convalescent* - iglasyakel *in a sickly manner* - oyazan *to be ~ because of* - wakiyaza *to get sick for* - wayazanka *to be ~ , one feeling ~* - yasyazan *to be ~ all over* - yazanya *to make one ~* — cešlošlo *to have diarrhoea* — glaja *to be ~ or diseased in a state of confinement* — l̄múnga *to cause sickness, to bewitch* — kúja *to be ~ , affected with sickness* - ikuja *to be ~ or indisposed on account of* - kicikuja *to be ~ for* - kikuja *to have one ~ , as one's child* — kuškonza *to pretend to be ~* — okuja *to be ~ on some account* - okuje *sickness* — okit'a *to be exhausted and make ~* — ošunkecalaka *a very ~ person* — tokeca *unwell* — wasazeca *one easily made ~ , or one getting well*

sickness *n* : okuje *or* wicayazan *or* wóyazan
Some sicknesses are :

wicacancan *ague*
wicanakšecapi *cholera*
šap'ayapi *or* wašilkte *consumption* — šab áya kúja *to have consumption*
natin *to have convulsions*
nakšecapi *or* nawicakšeca *or* nawicatipa *cramps*
ištawicaniyan *an epidemic of sore eyes*
ištawakaške *a disease of the eyes*
koška *affected with a venereal disease* - koska *gonorrhoea*
natayazanpi *a headache*
ewehiyu *to hemorrhage* — pawekaluzapi a *nose-bleed*
wékaluzapi *or* wenápopapi *an unnatural vaginal bleeding*
wayakayah'uwicokiye *leprosy*
nawicašli *measles*
ipaswayazan *pleurisy*
cajunokapoja *pneumonia*
cakapo *pyorrhoea*
hohuyazanpi *rheumatism*
kikika *scrofulous* - okikiyakel *in a rundown manner*
wanagiktepi *stroke*
nigetanka aupi *a swelling of the belly*
šaketapa *a swelling of the fingertips*
wahinheya *swelling of a gland*
sikoškapi *swelling of a horse's hoofs*
lotepopi *swelling of the throat*
wicananka *tremor*
cal̄uwayazan *or* hohpakujapi *or* hohpawayazan *tuberculosis*
léjapišni *inability to urinate*
wikoška *a woman's venereal disease*

side *adv* : anung *on both sides* - anunkatanhan *on or from both sides* - hoanunk *on two sides within the camp circle* — hoitokagatahan *at the South ~ of the camp* — sanni *of or on one ~* - sannica *sideways* - sannila *of only one ~* - hasanni *one of a pair, a mate* — mišnasannica *on my side* — hounma *one of the sides of a surround in a buffalo hunt* — icionbya *or* icun'onpa *off to the side and out of the way* - hutasanpata *on the other side of* - hutatahenatanhan *on this ~ of a creek or lake* — íišlayatanhan *to the right ~ of* — íkakiya *on that ~ of* - íkakiyatanhan *in that way from, on that ~* - íkakiyotan *in that direction from* — íleciya *on this ~ of* - íleciyatanhan *from this ~ of, or in this way from* - léciyatanhan *from this place, or on this ~* — itahena *on this ~ of, in time or place* - itahenatanhan *on this ~ , in time or place* - itaokšan *round about on all sides, all around something* — itatowapatanhan *to the windward ~ , or on this ~ of* — tahena *on this ~ in time or place* - ótahena *on this ~* - tahenatanhan *from this side* - tahenakiya *towards one, this way* — itan *on the ~* - itan'anunk *or* itannunk *or* itan'anunkatanhan *on both sides* - itan'okšan *on all sides* — tanblas *or* tanblecakiya *on the ~* — yuitannunk *on both sides* — tan'iyupse *to turn sideways* — kaglala *by the ~ of* - kaglakinyan *sticking sideways* — kaicisannica *by or in striking sideways* — kahepiya *along the ~* - iyotahepiya *on this ~* - tahepi *by the wayside* - tahepiya *on the ~ of e.g. the wall* — kicicaic'iya *to take sides with one* — kikcanpta *to take sides with to comfort one* — kogna *on that ~* — ópeic'iya *to take sides with and follow* - óbic'iya *to join and conform one's self to another* — tawošitku *his or her help, one taking his or her ~* — kicitila *to ~ with* - Cf live

sift *v* : kacan *to ~ by shaking* - kícicacan *to ~ for one* - yucan *to ~ with a sieve* - Cf lack

sigh *vn* : cuwiokini - cuwiokiniya *to gasp as when dying*

sight *vn* : ištableza *to be clear-sighted* - ištablesya *to make one clear-sighted* — iyuziya *in sight* — otonwe *eyesight* - tonweya *to give ~ to* — owanyanke *an appearance, a sight* - wówanyanke *a show* — sabyakel *or* sabyela *in sight far off*

sign *v* : napeonwoglaka *to use ~ language* — cajeoic'iwa *to ~ one's own name* — wakta *a mark* — wapetokeca *a mark or ~ , a miracle*

signal *va* : kosya *to cause to wave and make a ~ , to beckon*

signature *v* : wícekiye *to solicit signaatures for help with a printed prayer or with a petition*

silent *adj* : inila - inilaya *to make still, quiet* - ainila *or* atans'e *stilly or silently for, as in making the approach to game* - nainl *to grow ~* — atans'ela yanka *to sit motionless, restfully* - atans'in *at a standstill* — hohošni *silent* — iyušpešni *mute* — popotkakiya *to ~ one by*

argument — šungnuni s'e yanka *to be ~ and sad as if he lost his horses*
silverware *n* : - Cf utensil, fork
similarly *adv* : aiyecelya — owangya *to imitate, resemble, to be similar or alike*
simmer *vn* : nas'a
simplicity *n* : wóecetu *fulfillment*
simultaneous *v* : iyokignag *to put in one's own and to act together*
sin *v* : wahtani *to transgress a law, to sin* - wahtaniya *to cause to transgress, sin* - awahtani *to transgress a custom or law, to sin, to fail to carry out a vow* - wahtanis'a *a sinner* - waic'ihtani *to sin or offend against one's self* - wákihtani *to sin against one*
since *adv* : kapiyehan *ever since* — kohanš *~ that, so that*
sincere *adj* : waawacin *devout, thoughtful*
sinew *n* : takan - Cf string
sing *v* : lowan - alowan *to ~ in praise of one, to ~ for* - canlowankiya *to play a musical instrument* - éya lowan *to ~ saying* - gloglolowan *to ~ with a hoarse voice* - gnagnalowan *to ~ a grunting song* - hanlowanpi *a night-song* - ikicilowan *to ~ to one in praise for another* - ilowan *to ~ to or for one, to ~ one's praises* - kilowan *to sing to as to a child* - lowanpi *songs, hymns* - olowan *a song* — hóšišipa *this word children once used as a word in a playful song* — ȟ'oká *to ~ with the drum* — kahiyaya *to sing through a tune or melody*
single *adj* : okinihan *to ~ out one for praise* — ápatonyela *singling out one thing from others, as a horse from a herd* — íciyakigle *one by one, or one after another* — iyabya *singly, scattered separately as in hunting* — paoglaya *singly, one by one in a row far apart*
sink *va* : áspeya *to cause to ~ as an anchor in water* - okaspeya *to ~ into* - óspeya *to make ~* — h'anyan *or* h'anyeca *to fail, decline, to ~ away, as in sickness or approaching death* — naohpa *to ~ into* - naohpeya *to cause one to ~ into, to break through* — óswaswaya *sinking in as feet into soft snow or soil*
sip *va* : yazoka *to draw or ~ in trying the taste* — yagopa *the sucking bees do in blossoms to get the nectar*
sit *v* : íyotaka - híyotaka *to arrive and stop, sit* - paiyotag *down, i.e. sitting* — yanka *to be seated, be present* — akiglaski *or* akiglaskin *to press down by sitting, standing, lying on* — akigna *to sit, as a hen on eggs, or as a person one's children* — awajal *to be astride* — húpazagle *to squat, sit with knees drawn up* — pakšija *to ~ down as old people might* - Cf bend
size *adv* : watoketuka *sizably, good sized*
skate *n* : cah'ícazo *ice skates* - cah'icazo kic'un *to wear ice skates* - mázacah'icazo *skates*
skein *n* : oyaya *a ~ of yarn* - Cf bunch, string
skill *vn* : iwayupika *to be skilled, handy* - iwayupiya *handily, nicely, well* — iyopteya *to become skilled*
skillful *adj* : ah'okaka *adept* — akiȟoka *skillful, skilled in* — aoh'anhanhankel *very skillfully* — awayupika *to be ~ about, more ~ than* - awayupiya *skillfully, well* — hlainšni *capable, skillful* — ksízeke *good on (a boast)* — okibliheca *to be ~* — škálwayupika *skilled at games* — wópika *skilled in making anything* — wahtekešni *good at doing something as doing good talks*
skim *v* : kagé *to ~ off*
skin *n* : ha - haoyasaka *with the ~ shriveled* - hápahlaya *to shed ~* - hapašloka *to pull off ~, to chafe the ~* — haton *to have chapped ~ as on the hands* — háyuza *to ~, to take off the skin of anything* — hastan *of a dark complexion* — huka *the skin* — hanpsicu *prepared moccasin skin* — nagapa *to strip off the skin as a horse might do kicking one with its foot* - pagapa *to get skinned pushing something* — ohamna *smelling of ~* — osó *to cut open in preparing to skin an animal* — waašlaya *to ~ an animal* — wagapa *to ~ with a knife* — glazapa *to cut off the fat with the ~ in skinning an animal* - wazapa *to ~, to cut off the meat for drying*
skip *v* : cah'aglapepeya *to make skip or bound as a flat stone thrown on the ice* - mniglapepeya *to make a flat stone skip when thrown on the water* — kaškehan *to make skip about by striking*
skull *n* : páhu *the ~ bone*
sky *n* : towánjila *the blue sky* - Cf heaven
slack *adj* : óhtahta *stretched not tight as a bowstring*
slander *n* : oaie - waaie s'a *a slanderer* — waweceyešnišni olekiton *to bring forward talk of things to spoil another's reputation* — wicoaie *defamation* — wal'iyopeya *to accuse one of doing what another has done* — waoyatan *to backbite, disparage, slander* — wawoštegla *to use or call one bad names* — wówih'oiyeya *to slander a person present to hear it*
slant *adv* : óhya *slanting as written characters, sloping*
slap *v* : kaskapa *to strike slapping one* — pahíȟaȟa *to strike one in the face and teeth*
slash *va* : kazaza *to cut in fine strips to hand down*
slate *n* : ínyan sápa *black rock*
slaughter *n* : optekte *a ~ house*
sled *n* : can'iyuslohan *or* can'iyuslohe *or* canwoslohan *a wooden sled* — hohukazunta on oslohe kic'onpi *a sled made for use with buffalo bones* — wíyuslohe *a ~ or sleigh* - wóslohe *a drag or sled*
sleep *adj* : hwa *sleepy, drowsy* - hwáka *sleepy, mild, gentle* - hwáya *drowsily, or to make sleepy* - hwáyela *slowly, softly, gently* - ahwaic'iya *to make one's self sleepy* - ahwayela *patiently, gently, easily* - kahwa *to put to ~* - nahwa *to put to sleep by rocking with the foot* — ahiyunka *to come and ~, or to bring and lie down* - éyunka *to go and ~ at* — ištinma *to sleep* - aištinma *to ~ on* - ónštinmat'a *to ~ soundly* — ayugin *to slumber, to nap* - ayugiic'iya *to take a nap one's self* — iyoyalal *in a sleeping manner* — snicat'a *to feel sleepy from heat or cold*
slice *n* : kablapi *something cut up into slices* - okabla *a ~ cut broad and thin for drying* - wabla *to cut in slices* — opasleca *or* yus'o *to slice* — wakiskusku *to ~ off one's own* — wazapa *to cut off meat for drying*
slide *v* : kaslohan *to make ~* - okaslohan *to make ~ in, or to make a trail with something dragging* - kaslohanhan *to ~ repeatedly* - naslohan *to make ~ by kicking* - onzeslohan *to ~ on the buttox* - oslohan *to ~ down* - oyuslohan *to make ~ in* — aglahan *to slip or ~ out as a pole from a travois* — aȟicahan *to stumble and fall on* — ašlulya *to make slip on* — ašlušluta *to be slippery on* - ayašluta *to have the teeth to slip on something* — cahkazo *to ~ on ice in moccasins or shoes* — cégya *to stumblingly* — gicahe *to have slipped and fallen* - gicaheya *to cause to slip and fall* — ikpasloka *to slip or take off a garment, esp one too large* — kaoswa *to ~ down an incline*
slight *va* : waceyešni *to make cry by cutting e.g. remarks* - ocinȟinyanpi *they feel slighted* — wakicoya *slightly, just a little*
sling *va* : ayuhmin *to throw on one side e.g. a stone* — ínyan'onyeyapi *a ~, a kind of rope weapon with which to throw stones at some distance*
slip *or* **slide** *vi* : nasluta *to ~ out* — našluta *to ~ or slide down* - šlušluta *slippery, fig penniless* - yašluta *to let ~ from the mouth* - yušluta *to ~ out, or let ~ from* — naki-

šna *to miss one's footing, to slip when being in a hurry* - našna *to miss one's footing* — naicoga *to loosen or to ~ down e.g. one's pants* — paona *to push on and slide something* — tuntunpa *slippery, slimy*

slit *v* : okiwasleca *to ~ or rip down what is soft* - pasleca *to split or slit e.g. a hide or sack* — paka *to split or cut a ~ in to fit an arrowhead*

sliver *va* : ayušuja *or* ayušušuja *to ~ up on by twisting and turning, to keep meandering*

slobber *adv* : h'eh'eya *slobbering*

slope *n* : ȟenake *a declivity* — kaapamagle *sloping down* - ónnaptan *sloping*

sloth *n* : wóškankapin *laziness* — éhuwehweganhan, *to be slothful, inert*

slovenly *adj* : cógeca *~ esp in dress* — ȟcóka *slatternly* - ȟcóya *or* hcóyakel *in a slovenly manner* — ȟlohán clothes not well put on - ȟloheca *slovenly* — ȟnahan *not tidy, hanging down as a horse's lip* - ȟnaheya *loosely or ~* — iyuhaya *slovenly* — nahpahpa *to be ~* — nahpihpi s'e *slouchy in dress*

slow *v* : aslohan *to crawl along on* - aslohankel *or* slohe s'e *slowly* — aspayeic'iya *to inhale ~ , deeply* — hún-kešni *~ in walking or working, sickly* — hpáka *very ~* — hwáyela *slowly, gently* - íhwahwa s'e *slowly, gradual-ly* — h'anhi *to be ~ at work, to advance leisurely* - h'anhika *one who does things leisurely or is incapable of* - h'anhikiya *slowly, carefully, as in putting the finishing touches on a work* - h'anhila *very ~* - kah'anhiya *in a labored way, a bit slower as in walking, reading, speaking etc.* - nah'anhiya *in a ~ way* — óh'an *to be ~ or long in doing* - oh'ánhi *to be ~ in* - oh'anslata *to work deliberately* - wah'anhiya *slowly as when cutting* - wayuh'anhihika *a ~ person* — icunsya *to be dilatory, to have no mind to work, to work only for pay* - icunsyakel *not heartily* - icunsyeca *one who is not faithful and does not do his duty well* — iwaštela *slowly, moderately, carefully* - iwaštegla *carefully* - paiwaštela *slowly* — kilyakel *slowly but surely, steadfastly, with firm determination* — koginginkel *slowly* — owicahtehan *of ~ development* — sláta *~ at doing, and feeble* - wayuslata *to do slowly* — šunk'lote *from utter weariness* — zohela *very slowly in going about* - Cf crawl

slush *adj* : mnicoco *slushy* — šlošlola *slush* — walolopela *half-melted snow*

smack *v* : kipiza *to ~ the lips at one to draw attention* — wayac'o *to ~ the lips when eating* — yaskapa *to ~ the lips when kissing* - pahwayaškapa *to smack the lips*

small *or* **little** *or* **tiny** *adj* : cík'ala - cík'alakel *for a little while, a little* - cík'aya *in a ~ way, or a ~ bit* - cík'ayela *in a ~ place, small-wise* - címcila *quite small* - císcīyela *narrow or pent up* - kacik'ala *to make ~ by chopping off, to cut ~* - nacik'ala *to make ~ by trampling on* - naciscila *to make less by trampling on* - ocik'ala *~ within* - pacik'ala *or* paciscila *to make ~ by rubbing* - wacik'ala *to shave or cut ~* — aopteca *less or little* — ašunšiye *or* ašunšiyeca *a little bit only, a ~ amount only* — hínskola *being so small* - nískola *only so large (said in derision), or very small* — hiyanun *puny, ~ and unable to grow*

smart *vn* : natuta *to ~ as one's feet may do by much travel* - wayatuta *to make ~ by biting* — okapaza *to ~ as pepper does the mouth* — okibliheca *to be smart in doing*

smear *va* : apašluta — sinsin *besmeared, slimed*

smell *va* : akanmna *or* aomna *to ~ something* - ecamna *having ~ or taste, fragrant or savory* - hámna *a rotting rancid ~ as meat does* - ijimna *to ~ like burning fat or bones* - nap'omna *to make ~ by stepping on* - ómna *to ~ something e.g. whiskey or burning herbs, or an odor* - os'amna *smelling rancid or tainted, esp in ref to sour or stale meat* - šicamna *bad smelling* - takumna *to have a taste or aroma* - azilkiya *to burn incense* - azilton *to incense, to give a good odor by burning* — gmunza *or* gmúnsmna *strong smelling like slimy fish, or spoiled meat* — ȟunwin *or* ȟuin *to putrify or stink* - ȟunwinmna *stinking, smelling putrid* - ȟunwinya *to cause to ~ badly, make ~ putrid* - iȟunwin *to ~ of, to stink, or a bad odor* — ȟwin *to become putrid* - ȟwínmna *smelling putrid* - h'amna *smelling like tainted meat*

smile *vn* : hih'akiya *to grin*

smoke *vn* : únpa *to ~ tobacco* - acannunpa *to ~ on or after, as after a meal* - cannumkiya *to cause to ~* - cannunpa *a pipe* - cánnunpa *to ~ tobacco* - cannunpa pahu *a pipe bowl* - cannunpa sinte *the pipe stem* - cannunpa iglaye *a pipe stem cleaner* - cannunpa hahin iyapehanpi *a quill-decorated pipe* — hokšišniyan cánnunpa *to send the ~ through the nose* - wawacanlilike *one who smokes always* — jotokte *to suffer from ~* — šóta *smoke, or to smoke as does a fire* - ašota *to be smoky on or at* - išota *a ~ cloud, atmosphere* - ošota *smoky, or ~* - niyašota s'e *as if breathing ~ in cold weather* - ošotamna *the smell of ~* - ošota t'a *to suffocate from ~* - ošotaya *in smoke, smoky* - šotiyowotan'inšniyan *enveloped and invisible in ~* - šotiyaskilya *enveloped in ~* - šotoju *smoky, hazy* - šotojuya *to fill with ~* - wakašota *blackened with ~* - šolašapa *to become dirty with ~* - šolkiya *to make ~* - šolya *to make smoky* — zíta *to ~ as from things burning* - azilic'iya *to ~ one's self* - azilkiya *to burn incense* - azilton *to make a pleasant smell with burning incense* - azilya *to ~ something as meat* - azita *to ~ upon, to burn e.g. incense* - izita *to ~ something holding it in ~* - oizita *to ~ as does a stove* - oizilya *to ~ in the tanning process* — gluskahcin *to ~ in clouds of ~* — kaop'ošya *to cause a stove to ~ by opening a room door* — ómnakiya *to give a smoke i.e. a cigaret to one*

smolder *vn* : wazilya

smooth *adj* : aglusto *to ~ one's own e.g. hair on* - akasto *to ~ down e.g. one's hair on* - kícasto *to ~ down for one* - aokasto *to ~ down e.g. a trail in the grass* - apasto *to make ~ , to brush down on something* - ástoya *to ~ down upon* - ayusto *to smoothen one's hair* - iyusto *to ~ down e.g. the hair* - kiciyusto *to smoothen for one* — k'éza *~ and trodden down* - anak'eza *to make ~ by tredding on* apak'eza *to make ~ by scraping on* - ayak'eza *to make ~ with the teeth* - ayuk'eza *to make ~ and hard, to shave off close* - onak'eza *to make ~ by stamping on* - wak'eza *to smooth over by shaving* - apak'ega *to rub ~ by hand, as with a tool on* - apak'oza *to rub and make ~ on* - ayuk'oza *to make hard and ~ on* - k'osyela *smoothly* - pak'oza *to rub ~ and make hard* - yak'oza *to make ~ with the mouth, to crop, eat all off* - yuk'oza *to make ~ and hard by removing grass or hair* — lápa *~ , level* - apalapa *to make or plane ~* - palapa *or* yualapa *to ~ off e.g. a rough road* — apaman *to file ~* — awablaya *to ~ over, shaving off lumps with a knife* — ayušlušluta *to make ~ on, to sharpen* — iyaskiska *to ~ down, as the hair on an animal swimming in water* — nakca *to be ~ of itself* — onat'oza *to make ~ by stamping on* — oyušlata *to make e.g. a wall ~ , fig to corroborate* — pablaya *to smoothen* — papsunpsunla *to rub ~ and round* — pasminyan *to rub or scrape ~ or clean* — t'inzani *smoothly, calmly*

smudge *v* or *n* - Cf smoke

snake *n* : sintehla *a rattle-snake* — wagleza *a garden-snake* — wangleglega *a bull-snake* — wánto *the blue racer snake* — zuzeca *a snake* - zuzecakinyanpi *the fly-*

ing snake - mnimahel zuzeca *a water snake* - kizuzeca *to turn into a snake*

snap *v* : nasusuza *to expand as in ice forming* - nasuza *to splinter off or fly off* - Cf splinter

snare *n* : igmunke

snatch *va* : yamahe éyaya *to take and go, taking something in the mouth* — yunap'iyeya *to snatch away by hand*

sneak *va* : anaslata *to creep up to carefully* - anaslatapi *a creeping up to wild game, to stalk* — aokamna *to ~ around stealthily* — apustag *to crouch up to*

sneeze *vn* : pša - apša

sniff *v* : pojanjan *to scent* - Cf snivel

snivel *v* : pahglajinca *to snivel* - pahlajinca *to sniff or snuff the nose* — poginjo *to sniff with a whistling sound in the nose* — pójin *to sniff or snuff up the nose* — t'ínga *to snivel and grunt as a woman in childbirth*

snore *v* : gópa - góbištinma *to ~ in one's sleep* - góbya *in a snoring manner*

snort *vn* : púga *to ~ as does a frightened horse*

snout *n* : puté *the nose and lips*

snow *n* : wa - awa *to ~ on* - awahinhe *to snow upon* - awahinheya *to cause a snowfall upon, or snowing upon* - wáakata *to cover with ~* - wagúgeca *crusted ~* - wáhinhe *it snows* - wahíšnaheca *soft new ~* - waišnaheca *soft new ~ tomorrow* - wakapopo *to crush e.g. snow* - wámini *snow-water* - waop'o *snow dust in the sunlight* — wapahwuhwu *running in crusted ~* - wáteca *new ~* - wawoblu *the ~ flies* - wázanzan *a fine ~ mist, a trace of ~* — awosoksolya *being all gone but the snow* - hinhan *to snow, i.e. precipitate* - íyapa *a ~ storm*

so *conj* : k'unhehanyan *as long as ... just so long* - lehankeca *as long, or high, or short as ... so long, high, short* — ehan'un *just so, according to some criterion*

soak *va* : hpanyan - mniyohpanyan *to ~ in water* — kahtan *to ~ up or in* - okahtan *to ~ in* — kazuksugyela *sopping wet* — mniwot'a *to be drenched with water*

soap *n* : haipajaja *or* wípajaja

soar *vn* : okaȟo *or* okas'a *to glide, sail in the air as a bird*

sob *va* : ceya *to cry* - ceyaokit'a *to sob as do children* - glaceya *to make one cry* - igluceya *to do something such that tears arise* — caokit'a *to sob* - caokit'at'aya *in a sobbing manner* - caiglat'e *to sob short of crying* — cínktakta *to cry sobbingly* — comniglazanzan *to sob esp before crying* — gínca *to snivel, grunt, sob* — hówakan *to wail* — ícilowan *to wail alone* — ic'ícan *to cry over one's own self*

sober *vn* : kibleza *or* obleza *to be ~ and clear*

society *n* : okolakiciye, *a league, fellowship, community* — Íȟoka *name of a band of Teton Sioux* — Wícinska *onetime Oglala military societies* — Íyuptala *a ~ like to the Omaha Dance Society*

soft *adj* : cocó *or* cocola *~ as mud* - cocoya *made or left soft* - nacoco *to make soft as mud using the feet* - pacoco *to rub soft* — hpan *softening as corn in water* - gluhpanhpan *to make ~ one's own by soaking in water* - kpánla *fine and ~* - kpankpánla *fine and soft as a piece of land* — hihi *~ as fur or down* - hihila *mellow as ground or mud* — kacica *to soften and smoothen* kapanyan *to soften by pummeling* — sloslola *turning ~* — štáka *mushy* - iyuštaka *to soften* — lopá *soft* - lolobya *to boil ~* — oštulya *~ and not frozen* — panpanla *~ as deer skin, tender like meat* - panšpanja *fluffy* — pat'eca *to soften by pressing* — wopówaya *to soften by blowing on* — yugwa *to soften by hand* — yuȟunta *or* yuȟonta *to rub ~ e.g. a skin, a thread* - ayuȟunta *to rub making ~ on* — yusaka *to soften by bending e.g. a stiff hide* - Cf bulky

soil *va* : našapa *to dirty with the feet* - waanašapa *to soil by trampling upon* — pašica *to soil and spoil by rubbing with the hands*

solder *va* : apuspa *to make stick on* - apuspapi *mucilage or solder* — ašlo *to fuse or melt as metal* - ašloya *to make melt and fuse* — wíyaskabye *mucilage or solder or other heavy metals*

soldier *n* : akicita - Cf akicita

sole *n* : sicuha - sicuhaton *the ~ of a shoe* — akiglake *the ~ of a shoe or moccasin, the ~ sewed on*

solicit *v* : šilecón apé *to lay in wait for one to do evil* — zomí *soliciting i.e. acting with deception or pretense* - zomika *one who solicits, such as a womanizer* — ignagnaye s'e *soliciting* — kisínkpe *or* kisinte *to ~ one, trick one into doing* — winagiyeya *making solicitations, i.e. alluring a woman or a man*

some *n* : hunh *a part of* - húnhlala *on a part, partly* — táku *or* tákueya *or* takúnl *something, anythhing* — enana *sometimes, here and there* - enagnala *sometimes, now and then* — watohanl *sometime* - íwatohanl *or* íwatohantu *sometime, one day in ref to something* - tóhan *sometime* - tóhanhci *at some other time in the future* - tóhanšna *sometime* — tókcel *or* tókicel *somewhere* - tokíyotan *or* tokíyotanhan *somewhere in some direction* — tókša *sometime, by-and-by* — tuktektel *sometimes, once in a while* — túwa ... eša *someone* — unkcanš *at some time, by-and-by*

somersault *v* : glukše *to turn a ~* — tahujipakicun *to ~ on the neck*

sometimes *adv* : watukte

song *n* : olowan *a tune or hymn* — wiowešteloawanpi *or* wioyeštelowanpi *night or love songs*

soon *adv* : áetulake el *rather quite soon* - aétulakeci *in a little while* — áškanyela *promptly* — ecana *soon* - ecakcana *soon in ref to several events* - íyecana *~ after* — ehakelakecinhan *soon, at the very last* — lecala a little while ago - kalecala *pretty soon* — ótehanyalaka *a little while, for a little time in ref to the future* — tókša *sometime, by-and-by*

soot *n* : šotkazi *soot or sooty* - šolanini *soot or smut*

sore *n* : hli *a sore, or to break out in sores* - hlihli *breaking out in sores, or miring in mud* - íhli *a sore mouth, or being sore* - ihlí *to have a sore breaking out as a consequence of* — ikpakiškija *to make sore by rubbing e.g. one's eyes* — ištaniyan *to have sore eyes* - ištaniyanpi *a disease of the eyes* - ištohli *bleary-eyed* — kaiȟeju *or* katuta *sore from riding* — naniyan *to have ~ feet* — našli *to swell, form a sore* — oštanhan *a running sore, or being in or on*

sorrow *vn* : acantešica *to be sad on account of* - acantešilyakel *or* acantešilya *sadly, sorrowfully* — cuwipuskica *or* cuwipuskicat'ekinica *to be oppressed or dying with esp pent-up ~, and not anger* — icakije *affliction* — icanšicapi *tribulation* - wócanšice *sorrow* — iyokišica *to be sad, grieved* — iyoyakeca *to be distressed*

soul *n* : hokšicankiya *the spiritual seed or influence, the root of the nation's hoop*

sound *va* : ahotan *to make a noise around one* — ahoton *to cry out for, as a bird for food* - nahoton *to reproduce ~* — ahlo *to growl over e.g. a bone* — kahla *to ring or ~ by striking e.g. a bell* - kahlayela *causing to ring* — káka *sounding dull* - kakaka *to make dull ~ by beating, pounding e.g. a kettle* - kakoka *or* kakog *to make a dull ~ by striking, but not drumming, to rattle or thump* — sna *to ring or rustle* - kasna *to make ~* — kpéya *sounding* - kpeyéla *resounding, i.e. with a loud ~ or report* — okaco *to ~ within e.g. one's empty stomach* — katkanheya

thoroughly, soundly
soup *n* : šung'ohanpi *a pot of dog soup*
sour *adj* : skumna *spoiled* – asunp skumnazi ~ *milk or cream* – oškumna *or* s'amna *spoiled, smelling badly, sour* — íciskuya *alike ~ or sweet* – oskuya ~ *as milk* – wískuye *that which sweetens or sours other things*
sow *va* : okala *to plant*
space *n* : iyoko *the ~ between the heavens and the earth* – okošniyan *being no ~* – okoton *there is a ~, a crack, or a hole* – okotonyan *an opening, a vista, or with free spaces* – okowanilya *with no ~ between all over* – okoya *spacing between* – tiyoko *with ~ between houses* – tiokitahena *or* tiyokitahena *between houses, open spaces between farms and ranches in the countryside* — cejaka *walking suchwise that there is much ~ between one's legs, pigeon-like*
sparce *adv* : jiyela *thinly, as hair on the hands* — zazeca *here and there* – zazecala *thinly strewn* – zazecayela *scattered here and there as shocks of grain* — glakeyela *here and there*
spare *adv* : akapeca *or* akapeya *having something to ~* — éce cola yuhà *to keep a horse free, a ~, e.g. for work* — pagan *to be able to part with something* – paganya *to make one give away* – ikpagan *to spare one's self, to yield up one's self* — kpatantankel *sparingly, using little by little, slowly*
spark *v* : kaȟaȟa *to curl up as a flame, to sparkle or send up sparks* — nailega *to make sparkle* – nalega *to make sparkle as in kicking the fire with the foot* – palega *to make sparkle by poking to stir a fire* — peliyaglašyahan *to keep the fire low, i.e. glimmering beneath ashes* — pešnija *a ~ of fire*
sparkle *v* : pelwiyuškin *to dance as do flames*
spatter *vn* : nagaga — wotíca *to make ~ out e.g. mud*
speak *vn* : iyá *to speak* – iyagnaškinyan *to say foolish things in anger* – iyata *to say what one intends* – iyayahan *talking, chatting* — ia *to speak* – iahan *speaking* – iapi *a talk, speech, or language* – iawayapika *to speak nicely* – iekapin *to be tired of speaking, or to unwilling to ~* – iekiya *to make a speaker of, to have as an interpreter* – ieksapa *to be eloquent* – ieska *an interpreter, to be fluent in a language* – ieskakiya *to have for an interpreter* – iešni *to be dumb, i.e. unable to speak* — íoyakšan *to get one to talk* — ayasuta *to confirm in speaking* — ayaškaheyela *and* ayaškatuyela – Note: *these two words are of doubtful use* — aglašna *to make a mistake in one's own speech* – ayaštan *to cease from speaking or eating* – aglaštan *to stop one's own speaking or eating* — ayazamni *to make clear or reveal in speaking* — ayazunta *to connect or weave together in speaking* — aia *to slander one* – aiapi *a slander, consultation* – aiekiya *to talk about another for good or bad, to consult with* – aikia *to talk about or against what concerns one's self* – caia *to talk crying* – aicapa *to speak against* – aiwancayapi *they ~ bad about each other* – aikapa *to scold one* – aikcapta *to reprove or scold one* — éya *to say anything* – eciya *to say to one* – eic'iya *to say to one's self* – ekiciyapi *they say to each other* – ekiya *to say or have said to* – éya hingla *to commence or burst out saying* – éya hóyekiya *to yell out to one, saying* – éya hóyeye *to say in a loud voice* – éya icekiye *to beseech one, saying* – éya iwahoya *to ask of me, saying* – éya iwaktaya *to expect, saying* – eyáke *you don't say!* éya kico *to call, saying* – eyákipan *to yell at one saying* — éyakpaha *to announce one's own* – éyaštan *they finished speaking or eating or singing* – eyéceleš *he said that long ago* – eyé le *he said so, said when doubting a statement made by men, by women:* eyé ke ... keyapi *he means to say ... it is said* – eyéya *to make say something* — heyá *to say that or this* – heyaya *to keep saying, to say much* – hecíya *to say that to one* – hehéla *you said so!* – heic'iya *to say that to one's self* – hekíya *to say that or this to one* – heyekiya *to cause to say that* – éoyaka *to tell there, as a messenger would* – éwoyaka *to tell there* – oglaka *to tell of one's own* – aoglaka *to tell in regard to, in addition to, to appeal to* – išnawoglaka *to talk to one's self* – iwoglaka *to speak in ref to one's own* – iwoyaka *to tell or relate something in ref to* – oic'iglaka *to talk to one's self* – wóowoglake *a speach, a lecture, an address* — glatokeca *to speak of one as different* — ajiji *to whisper about one* — ak'oka *to talk to one incessantly* – ayuhmun *to speak about something without let* – iwašicun *garrulous or to speak badly* – owakiya *to speak harshly to or with one* – yáta *to speak, utter e.g. one's name* — yugalya *to ~ out to* — hoakicipa *to ~ for one* – hobukiya *to ~ gruffly* – hohniyanyan *to whimper* – hokunpešni *babbling on* – hóokihipicašni *to be unable to get a chance to ~* – hoší *to tell the news, to take word* — okišilia *to use bad language*
speaker *n* : mázalowankiyapi *a record player*
species *n* : – Cf class
speckled *adj* : ícigleška ~ *as corn of different colors*
spectator *n* : wanwanyanka *or* wawanyanke
speed *n* : oluzahan — glukinyan *to ~ up* – Cf fast, swift
spend *adj* : šéna *or* jena *having used up, spent or sold* — létka *having spent all* — wakasoteka *a spend-thrift* — yuwanica *to ~ one's money* — zinlyeic'iya *to have spent everything*
spill *v* : kaštan *to pour* – akaštan *to pour out on* – aiglaštan *to pour or ~ on one's own or one's self* — anaic'ipson *to ~ on one's self by kicking* – apapson *to ~ on anything* – ayapson *to ~ with the mouth on* – ayupson *to pour or ~ on* – glapson *to ~ one's own by striking* – kapson *to ~ by striking* – kicapson *to knock over and ~ out* – napson *to ~ by kicking* – kpapson *to ~ one's own, e.g. one's own blood* – nakipson *to ~ with the foot* – papson *to ~ or pour out* – yapson *to ~ with the mouth* – yupson *to turn over and ~* — kicala *to ~ or pour grain for* – Cf pour, papsón
spin *v* : kagmun *to ~ or twist by hand* – wapagmunke *a spinner* — kahomni *to make something turn around by striking* – glapemni *to make one's self spin* – iglapemni *to spin one's self* — kawaci *to make ~ and dance e.g. a top by whipping* – glawaci *to make e.g. one's own top dance by striking*
spine *n* : tacanȟaȟaka wapaha *a bone, in the upper end of the buffalo's spina column, used for a headdress ornament*
spirit *n* : nagi *a soul* – nagi iyaya *to yield up the spirit* – naginiic'iya *to save one's own soul* – wanagi *the ~ separated from the body* – wanagi tamakoce *the ~ world* – wanagitipi *souls' home* – wanagiya *to go to the ~ land* – wanagiyata *in the land of the spirits* — wóniya *life breath, spirit* – Wóniya Wakan *the Holy Spirit in God* – towakan *his wakán, i.e. his spirit* — wakankanpi *the spirits engaged to men* – Cf shadow
spit *v* : aglaškica *to ~ out on something of one's own* — atašoša *to ~ on something* – itašoša *to ~ out* – otašoša *to ~ in* – otašoše *a spittoon* – tašoša *to spit* — mnitaga *spittle, foam, froth* — ohohpa *to cough and ~ into* — ton'ikašpa *to expectorate* tonkašpa *to ~ out phlegm* — wípasnon *a roasting spit, a stick used to hold what is being roasting*
spite *n* : wópasmi — wówicašašni *spiteful mischief*
splash *n* or *v* : š'a — paškapa *to ~ with the hand* – wayaškapa *to make the noise of lapping water* — apašwoka *to push in and ~*
splinter *vn* : nasuza *to fly off as a piece of wood or bone, to*

snap as water freezing

split *va* : awajata *to make a ~ on* - kaja *to ~ a little, to make gape, to hit and ~ somewhat* - pajata *to make forked, divided* - yawaja *to ~ fork-like with the mouth* — awaka *to cut or ~ e.g. the feather from the quill* - wakahan *split, as the feather end of a quill* — yaka *to ~ with the mouth e.g. the feather end of a quill* — pakawa *to make ~ and insert* — awasleca *to ~ on* - awosleca *to ~ by shooting upon* — ayusleca *to ~ on* - kasleca *to ~ as with an axe* - kícasleca *to ~ in two for one something soft or light* - kícicasleca *to ~ for one something in two in the middle and light* - okicasleca *to ~ something light in two in the middle and with little effort* - okiglusleca *to ~ in two one's own* - okinasleca *to ~ or burst open easily* - owaslece *a ~ , or a splitting* - slecahan *to ~ of itself* - wakicisleca *to rip by knife* - wakinašleca *to ~ by foot* - wosléca *to ~ by shooting or punching* - yusleca *to tear something* - awohleca *to ~ by shooting or punching on* — awoptuja *to ~ or crack when an arrow is shot against something* - paptuja *to crack by working* - okicaptuga *to ~ in two in the middle, as done with a chisel* — awošleca *to ~ off a piece on by shooting or punching* - kašleca *to ~ as wood with an axe* - kicašleca *to ~ e.g. wood for one, to cut with effort* - našleca *to ~ something heavy or big with the foot and with effort* - okašleca *to ~ within anything that requires effort* - okiwošleca *to ~ by shooting* - pašleca *to ~ something hard or heavy by applying pressure* - wošléca *to ~ off a little piece by shooting* — kaksa *to ~ open, to ~ up* - kícaksa *to cut or ~ in two for one* - kaksihpeya *to chop, sever* — kih'anka *to have rather stormy, a break in the weather; or to ~ e.g. wood* — naokotonyan *splitting, cracking, making a crack*

spoil *va* : ayušica *to ~ or make bad on* - kašica *to ~ e.g. a table by striking it with an axe* — kašikšil *spoiled* - kíciyušica *to ~ for one* - našica *to ~ or defile with the feet* - oiglušica *to ~ one's own reputation* - ošicamna *becoming spoiled* — šilya *to spoil, or badly* — wašica *to ~ by cutting* - wosíca *to shoot injuring or spoiling* — ayukuka *to make rotten on* — okapa *to be spoiled by standing in a vessel* — onapiga *to ~ as does meat* — oštekaya *to deform, ~ e.g. a good horse* — oya *spoiled, moldy* — tantonšniyan *to ~ through neglect, as in over-cooking* - tantonya *to let ~ from over-supply* — wakipi *a spoiling* — wotúka *to ~ from shooting*

spoke *n* : huzazeca *spokes of a wheel*

sponge *n* : iyuȟepe *an absorber* - mniiyuȟepe *or* okahtanye *a sponge* — okahtanyan *to sop up, to sponge, absorb* — atiole *Slang, to sponge off others*

sport *v* : waakicaga *to make ~ of, to jest* — wawiȟaka *a jester* - wawiȟapi *a jesting, making ~*

spotted *adj* : gleglega - gleška *speckled or ~* — pagleza *to rub to make ~ or ringed*

sprain *v* : hunašte *to ~ one's leg* — iyuguka *to sprain, injure by a hard pull* - naguka *to ~ one's ankle* - paguka *to ~ by rubbing* — panunga *to ~ the arm or hand* — tokoštan *to ~ or dislocate one's own*

sprawl *adv* : ic'imnikel *sprawled out* — nas'inyela *sprawling*

spray *v* : ícanah'o *to ~ as is done in watering a garden*

spread *vn* : akablaga - kablaga *to ~ out, to unfurl, to ~ open* - iyublah *to ~ , open out* - ókabla *~ out on, or in a ~ out manner* - wapabla *to ~ out and smoothen* - kaoblagaheya *centrifugally, spreading out in all directions from a central point* - ákablaja *to straddle, to go astride* - ákablas *to tear open* - ákablaya *to ~ out over, as with one's wings* - kíciyublaya *to ~ out for one* - oyublaya *to ~ out in* — ákipsonwaheya *spreading out into a line* — amni *to ~ out to dry on* - imnitan *to inun-date, or a flood* - kimni *to ~ out one's own to dry in the sun* - wamnipi *fruit etc. ~ out thinly* — ayublaya *to ~ out or unroll on* - gluglaya *to have one's own spread or unrolled on* — anableca *to ~ out on, as when grain is poured out* — glugata *to ~ out e.g. one's hands as in prayer* - kagata *or* kagalgata *~ out as the hands or fingers* — kahtanyan *to make ~ out* — kaobleya *to ~ apart* - paobleya *to ~ by rubbing* — nahlagan *to open out, to enlarge* — naowancaya *or* yuowancaya *to ~ out* — pazica *to roll or ~ out* — yaopon *to ~ news or rumors* — akaȟaya *to ~ news all the while exaggerating it*

spring *n* : wiwila *or* minic'api - iyowiwila s'e *as if springing water* - kiwiwila *to turn into a ~* - nahlal mniowe *a ~ scratched from the soil* — naglaptuza *to recoil* — owahinape *a springing up of* — uya *to ~ up* - uyekiya *to make sprout*

sprinkle *va* : amnimni *or* amnimniya *or* ayumnimni *or* iyamnimni *to ~ on anything* - omnimni *to ~ into* - wamnimni *a sprinkler* — mniš'eš'e *to ~ as in a light rain* - oyupsonpson *to spill or ~ onto*

sprout *n* : camni *a germ or bud* - acamni *to ~ on*

spy *n* : tonweya *a guide, or to go as a ~* — wakcanyeya *to send one to reconnoiter*

squander *adj* : wakiyuwanice *deprived of property*

square *v* : katkuga *to cut ~ pieces* - katkunza *to cut off pieces* — obleton *~ edged*

squat *or* **stoop** *adv* : kameyakel *squatting down* — húpaza *squatting* — nahebyela *on the haunches* — pustaka *to be ~ down*

squeal *or* **squeak** *v* : kapiza *to make ~ or squeak* - píspiza *to ~ as a ground squirrel when caught* - kiskíza *to squeak as one's shoes might* — pahoton *to make ~ , cry out*

squeegee *va* : paskepa *to ~ by hand*

squeeze *va* : apašli *to ~ out on* - apašliya *squeezing out on by hand* - pasli *to ~ out* — at'insya *in a squeezed way, tightly* - ayut'inza *to ~ something* — paokogna iyeic'iya *to ~ one's self in* — paškita *to press, ~ out anything* — škicahan *squeezing, pressed* — waškica *to scrape out* — wóškica *to press and ~ out, to wring*

squint *v* : ištokšinkiya *to look at with one eye closed* - ištokšin *to close one eye and look with the other* - ištakšin *to be squint or cross-eyed* - ištakšinka *a squint-eyed person* - ištakšinkšin *to be squint-eyed*

squirrel-tail *n* : pejijiji

squirt *v* : kaškepa *or* kaškeb *to ~ by striking and pressing out* — woslí *to push down and cause to ~* - iwosli *a ~ or a ~ gun, or a syringe*

stab *va* : capá - acapa *to stick in, to take stitches in* - aicapa *to stab one thing through or on another* - cakicipa *to pierce e.g. a boil for another* - cakipa *to pierce one's own* — acejiya *to stick out the tongue* — aopatica *to stick or push in or under* — apahloka *to pierce or make a hole in on anything* — cahkahloka *to make a hole in ice by striking it* — ikpahloka *to make a hole for one's self as does the muskrat* - ipahloka *to punch a hole through* — awašloka *to cut a hole in or on anything*

stack *v* : okiciyuštan *to put one into another* - ociyuštan *to be one in another* — paokiju *a deck or ~ of playing cards*

stage-struck *or* **freeze** *vn* : unc'onnica *to be ~*

stagger *vn* : céka - cégya *staggering* - cekcéka *to be staggering* - kacekaya *staggering* - naceka *to make ~* - yaceka iyeya *to cause to ~ when biting* — katakinkin *to be shaky and staggering* — yahaiyeya *to turn or throw down, aside with the mouth*

stain *vn* : osinsin *to leave a mark as by tears* — oya *to sully one, to be sullied, spoiled*
stair *n* : can'alipi *stairs, a ladder* - oiali *a stair well* — hokuta *downstairs*
stake *va* : paslata *to drive or set a ~* - Cf pole
stamp *v* : iteiyaskabya *to ~ an evelope* - iteiyaskabye *postage* — nabu *to stamp somethinng with the foot* — natuka *to ~ off e.g. snow from the feet*
stand *vn* : han *to ~ upright or remain, stay* - ahan *to ~ or rest on* - ahekiya *to cause to stand or step on* - ahiyahan *to come and alight on, as a flock of birds on a field* - aihan *they go and ~ on* - éhan *they ~ in or at* - éyahan *they go up on a hill and ~ there* - ihan *to ~ in or at, to remain* — nájinhan *standing* - nájinhiyaya *to ~ up* - nájinkiya *to make stand, to raise or lift up* - nájinyan *to cause to stop and ~, having cornered something* - nájinyeyapi *they stood in a row* - nakícijin *to ~ up for* - nakicijinka *to ~ up for one* - nakicikšin *to ~ by one in danger* - oinajin *a place to ~ or start* - oinajinta *a goal, the place of standing* - onajin *to ~ or take refuge in* - ayunajin *to cause to ~ on* - elnajin *to ~ at a place* - elnajinya *to have one ~ at* - énajin *to ~ at a place, or they ~* - glinajin *to return and ~* - iglunajin *to rise by one's self* - inajin *to rise or stop* - inajinkiya *to cause one to rise or to ~ up* - kinajin *to reach home and ~, to recover one's position* - kpanajinka *to get up on one's own feet* — akojalya *astride* — apatuza *to ~ stooping or crouching down on or over* — h'o *to ~ as hair on end* — ic'icanyan *standing or planted firmly as a post, a stack, a person* — igluowotanla *to straighten one's self up* — paowotan *to ~ something erect* — jíya *standing up as hair, bristling* — nawosla iyeya *to make ~ up by stepping on, as a pile of wood* — owahe *a platform* — pap'oh'a *to make the hair ~ on end with the hand* — wohlepe s'e *standing upright*
standard *or* **banner** *or* **flag** *n* : wápaha - wápaha payùktan *the one-time staff carried by Oglala military societies*
star *n* : wicahpi - wicahpihinhpaya *meteorite showers* - wicahpisinteton *a comet* - wicahpi ša *a planet*
starch *n* : mniȟuha ipatin *or* wípatin
stare *v* : ayuta — išta kte nuns'e *as with piercing eyes* - ištanagleskiya *to look sternly at one, eyes opened wide* - ištanatogkiya *to look sternly at one, with a change in the eyes* - ištatolas'e ayuta *to look at angrily*
start *n* : oinajin *a starting place* — uyá *to ~ one, cause something to go* - óya *a start* — škánhinglekiya *to make ~ up* — paalos *to make one ~ up suddenly e.g. at having been stung* — panag *to ~, jump, startle*
starve *vn* : akih'an - oakih'an *starvation* - taakih'an *a starving person*
state *n* : oun *a condition* - Oun Lecala *the New Deal* - Oun Téca *the Great Society*
stay *vn* : oyuhlagan šni *to ~ in the same place* — waunke šni *to ~ a short time only* - Cf remain
steadfast *adv* : kilyakel *steadfastly, with firm determination*
steady *adv* : paslalyela *steadily* — š'agyakel *giving support* — wóslaslate *one who is good and ~ at work* — kokiptan *to feel unsteady*
steal *or* **theft** *va* : manon - awamanon *to ~ from one* - makicinon *to ~ anything from another* - makinon *to ~ taking back secretly what one had given* - manonpi *theft* - owamanon *to ~ in or from, a thief* — paskica *sl to swipe*
stealthily *adv* : nahaha
steam *n* : ip'o - p'oyela *steaming* — ini *to ~* - inikaga *to take a ~ bath* - iniopa *to take a vapor bath with others, or to ceremonialize prayerfully, to make a sweat, as is said* - inipi *a steam bath* - iyašota *to make steam with the breath* - initi *a sweat lodge, or to be in a sweat lodge* — wokéya *a temporary shelter*
steep *adj* : oiyakapeya *~ up* - oiyohpaya *~ down*
stem *n* : hucán *like that of an arrow shaft* — tašpu *a ~ like that of a pumpkin*
step *n* : ca *one step's distance* - caegle *to tak a ~* - caeglepi *a step* - caglawa *to count one's steps* - caglegle iyutapi s'e mani *to make big steps* - caglepi *a pace* - icahli *or* nahli *to ~ into mud* — íyahan *to ~ on anything* — kinaksa *to hurt the foot* — oali *a stair or stairway* — yupinpinta *to take short steps or movements*
stern *adj* : wóhinyanze *cross* - hinyanza *to be ~*
steward *n* : waawanglakiyapi
stick *vn* : aikoyaka *to cleave to* - aikoyagya *to make something ~ to* — akastaka *to throw or daub on* - akastagya *or* akastagyakel *sticking on or in, clinging to* - okastaka *to daub or make ~ on* - ostaka *to ~ to, on, or in* — apuspa *to ~ or make ~ on* - apuspapi *a glue* - apuspeya *sticking* - iciyapuspa *to ~ together* - ipuspa *to ~ something to* - ipuspe *anything that sticks to* - iyapuspa *to glue on* - iyapuspeya *to glue, sticking to* — ayaskakpa *to adhere to* - ayaskabton *to ~ something to, as postage to an envelope* - ayaskabya *to ~ on, to seal* — íciyaskapa *to ~ one thing to another* - iciyaskabya *to ~ one to another, or adhering* - iyaskapa *to be stuck on* - iyaskabya *to make ~ to, or sticking to* - iyaskabye *a paste or glue* - óskabya *adhering to* - óskapa *to adhere in or to* - waaskapa *to ~ on* — okaskeya *lumped, sticking together* — ayuha *to have on* — katunp *sticky* — oyatanyan *to stick* - yuoyatanyan *to stick in* — can *a stick* - canot'oza *a round ~* - canpeti-piye *a wooden poker* - canwipasnon *a wooden spit for roasting meat etc.* - canwiyuze *a sharp ~ to get e.g. meat from the pot* - cunwiyawa *a ~ used for counting* - canjata *a forked ~* - cankujipa *two short wooden poles placed under the bedding to keep bedding from spreading out* - cankazontapi *or* cankazuntapi *reeds woven together for use as bed matting* — hiyoyatake *that which sticks between the teeth* — hunkatacannunpa *a pipe-like wooden wand* — húnpe *a ~ used in digging wild turnips* - húnpe okijata *a forked ~ used to brace tent poles inside* — icapa *to ~ in e.g. a thorn or ~* - icape *a splinter of wood* — icašloke *a pipe poker* — makiwohliya *to ~ tight in the ground* — pahli *to ~ something in the ground* — óha *to ~ to as does paint* — okaslata *to ~ in as might a splinter* - opaslata *to run e.g. a sliver into* — oyá *to stick, adhere, or to ~ to something* - oyatkapa *to ~ on or in* — sáta *a forked ~* - satiyakaške *that which ties on the sáta* — tiktica *sticky* — tuslawayaskape s'e *sticking as a leech* — yahan *to be stuck with as with a splinter*
stiff *vn* : atasaka *to be ~* - iyatasaka *to be ~* - iyatasagya *in a ~ manner or condition* — pasuta *to make ~, to knead* - kpasuta *to stiffen by kneading* — patin *rigid, frozen* — wotín *to taka a ~ position, to be ~, standing erect* - wotínkiya *to beg of one for another* - wotínyan *stiffly* — t'ínza *hard, firm as mud* - pat'inza *to stiffen* — tkábya *stiffly* — yas'os'o *to be ~ from the cold*
still *vn* : iyasni *to become ~ as a noise ceasing, to recover from* - iyasniya *to pacify, as in giving to one unexpectedly* — t'inzani *calmly, smoothly*
sting *va* : pajipa *to penetrate as in stinging* - yajipa *to bite or sting*
stingy *adv* : aponponyela *singily* — oh'anšica *to be ~* — omniyela *acting stingily* — wateȟila *to be ~, or a miser* - wateȟilapi *parsimony*
stink *va* : oh'amna *to smell badly* - onas'amna *to stink*

- oniyemna *to have bad breath*

stir *v* : kahi kahihiya *to move* - kahihiyela *to flow* — katica *to ~, mix* — onakišoše *to ~ up water by foot* — wawakpanšni *stirring, alert as a man* — wicokicamna *to be stirred up*

stitch *adv* : ipahna *stitching*

stoke *va* : aon *or* aonpa *to ~ a fire*

stomach *n* : tapó *the crop* - tatapo *the third cavity of the ~ of ruminants* - tiȟaha *or* tiȟamnamna *the second cavity of ruminants* - tašoka *the fourth stomach cavity* - tašiyaka *the mouth of the stomach* — itezi *the stomach* - watezi *the belly*

stone *n* : ínyan — icutu *a ~ for grinding* — iguga *or* ihe ih'e swula iswu iswula kangitame *black shale* — wahin *or* wanhin *flint stone* - yuwipi *transparent stones* - yuwipi wašicun *the yuwipi power ~ of a dreamer*

stoop *vn* : patuja *to ~ over, bow down* - apatuja *to ~ down or over* - apatuš *to stoop down or over* - ayukipatuja *to cause to ~ or bow down on* — apatuza *to stand stooping down on* - paptuza *to ~ or bend over* - apustag *to crouch* - apustagya *crouching* — kpaonjinjintka yanka *or* kpašinšin yanka *to be stooped in sorrow* — pakin *to stand stooping over* - pakinyan *to walk stooping over* — pustastaka *to stoop* — yutuȟyela *stoooped*

stop *v* : akiyunka *they stopped overnight* — akiti *to ~ somewhere for the night* — anapta *to stop, hinder, forbid* - anakipta *to bring to a stop* - anaptapi *stopping* - anapteton *to prohibit* - inapta *to wear out e.g. a shoe* — aoyutkuga *to shut out* — ayuštan *to cease, finish, stop* - ayuštankiya *to make an end of, put a stop to* - apa ayuštan *Stop? certainly not!* or *Quit?* - oayuštan *a stop or cessation from* — apat'o *to obstruct, to prevent progress* - apat'oya *to place a hindrance in one's way* — íakicunni *to desist from, to tire and leave off* — icagi *to be hindered by an obstacle* — icaše *something rubbing causing a hindrance* - icašeya *to hinder by means of, to make a hindrance of* — iglajata *to contradict one's self* — igluhika *to quit to care for an emergency* — ikipajinyan *opposing* — kušeton *to bar, to stop, stand in the way of* — oegnaka *a placing down, a stop, a period* — paginge šni *going nonstop* — pataka *to come to a ~, to ~ short, to halt, to bring to a ~* — okit'eyakel *obstructing, preventing*

stopper *n* : iyoštan *or* iyoštanpi *or* ioštanpi *a cork or ~*

store *va* : ju *to place or lay up* — opiye *a place for storage* - mazopiye *a store* — tiyomnakiya *to gather and ~ up, to engage in business* — kigle *to lay up a store* - wakigle *a supply* - wagle *a storehouse, storage*

storm *vn* : aicamna - icapogan *a blowing storm* — otkan *to be stormy* — ošiceca *stormy, or a storm* — kih'an *stormy weather, a storm*

story *n* : ohunkakan *an oldtime ~* — ooyake *story-telling, narrative* — yataku *to make up a ~ about*

stove *n* : mazaoceti *or* maz'oceti - wiglioceti *an oil ~*

straddle *v* : kablašya *to cause to ~* — wogá *straddling or sprawling*

straight *v* : katin *to straighten out* - akatin *straighten e.g. the arms to measure* - ayukatin *to straighten out on with the hand* - kakatin *to straighten out by striking* - nakatin *to straighten by foot, or to become ~ of itself* - nasatin *to stretch out or become ~* - pakatin *to straighten out* — owotanla *upright, ~ i.e. not crooked* - kaowotanla *to make ~* - kiciyuowotanla *to make right for* — pawoslata *to push upright* — yuotan *to make ~, as a new road construction* - yuowotan *to make ~, upright, to justify* — yuzukapi s'e *moving in a ~ line in any direction*

strain *v* : jáka *to roll or ~ the eyes* — yuguka *to ~ or stretch to pull out*

strap *n* : tehmisopi *a leather ~* - tehpiwikan *a ~ cut from a dry hide* — wíkan *a packing ~* — wíc'in *a meat ~*

straw *n* : - Cf grass

stray *n* : pawicegna *a ~ that has returned* — šunk'okahwog *a ~ horse*

streaked *or* **striped** *adj* : ogleza *~ in, in ridges or rows*

stream *adv* : wakpicagla *by the side of a ~* - wakpogna *on the ~* - wakpopta *across the ~*

strength *n* : wówaš'ake - pawaš'aka *to strenthen* - Cf strong

stretch *v* : iyutanyan *to ~ out* - iyutitanyan *to be stretched by* — kajalya *with things spread or stretched out* — kpazigzica *to ~ one's own* - nazica *to over-streth* - yazica *to ~ with the teeth* - yuzica *to ~ a skin or rubber band* — nagata *or* nagal *to ~ out the foot* - yugata *to ~ out the arms* — nasunyan *stretched out* — satin *stretched out straight* — yuglagla *to ~ out, unwind* — yuguka *to draw out* — yuzuka *to ~ out from* - Cf pull

stride *v* : kacanglegleya *to make strides such as cart-wheels*

strike *or* **smite** *va* : apa *to smite* — itokicile *to try to ~ the face* — kahunkunza *to pretend to ~* - kamakal iyeya *to strike down* - kaskapa *to slap or clap* - kasmin *to ~ off, to make bare* - kaš'aka *to ~ lightly* - kaštaka *to smite* - okaštaka *to ~ in a place* - okaštake *punishment by striking* - okašpa *to ~ off a piece* - okicašpa *to smite in two* — pahá *to be ready to ~* - pakapa *to toss or ~ back e.g. a thrown ball, to retaliate* - pazán *to hurt or kill by striking* - pémakiwoto *to ~ the ground by hand* — waagliheya *to come down and ~ like lightning* — yupuhpuga *to ~ in anger*

string *n* : kan *or* ikan *a ~, a cord, a rope* - ikankiciton *to tie on a ~ with which to carry things* - ikanton *to put a string on to carry it by* - ikanyan *to have for a ~ or handle* - heikan *a ~ for tying up the hair ends* — oyaya *a ~ of beads* — oyaza *to ~ beads, a ~ of beads* — so *to cut into strips* - sósopi *~ cut from hide* - waso *to cut a ~ from hide*

strip *v* : kanica *to ~ off clean* — kaswu *to cut into strips* — oyašpašpa *to ~ off by mouth* — smismi *or* sminyan *stripped clean, bare, smooth* — waká *or* yuka *to cut or ~ e.g. the feather from the quill* — yugapa *to ~ or pull off e.g. an animal hide* — yuso *to cut in strips* — yus'o *to cut off a ~ at the edge something* — kiciyušloka *to ~ or pull off for one e.g. one's clothes*

stripe *v* : iglagleglega *to put colored stripes on one's self, to make a fool of one's self*

striped *adj* : glegleza *or* glezela — gwegweza *thin, lean* — kagleza *to make in stripes or figures* - kaglezela *to stripe, make striped* — zuhan *striped* - zuheya *in a striped manner*

strive *v* : kinica *to try to, to be anxious to*

stroke *n* : mašteagliȟan *sun-stroke* — oape *a striking or stroking of the hour by a clock* — wayuwinta *to ~ the face* — yuswupi s'e *running the hand smoothly over*

strong *adj* : igluwaš'aka *to strengthn one's self* - iwaš'aka *to ~ by reason of* - iwaš'agya *to strengthen by means of* - waš'aka strong - kawaš'aka *to be made ~ by carrying heavy loads* - kiciyuwaš'aka *to make strong for* — kiwaš'aka *having ~ muscles* - kpawaš'aka *to make one's own ~ and secure* - š'agš'aka *strong* — owikešni *to be ~, not to fail* — pawika *to be yet ~, to have some strength* - pawiyakel *yet ~* — asuta *to become ~ on* — ȟupinyun *by main strength*

struggle *vn* : nasunsun — nagwaka *to ~ kicking out the foot*

stubbornly *adv* : yayaya
stubby *adj* : wamunta *short and rounded off by trimming*
study *va* : óhan *to apply one's self, to try, attempt*
stuff *v* : katica *to be stuffed up* — opugi *to fill, push in* - opugipi *a stuffing* - opugiton *to put in stuffing* - opugitonyan *to ~ , do the art of taxidermy, to ~ and mount* — opuhli *to ~ into* - opuhliyahan *clogged, obstructed*
stumble *v* : kaišuta *to ~ once, make a misstep, to slide, slip* — kalektehan *stumbling or tottering* — kaše *to strike against, stumble* — nagnayan *to miss a step or part of a step, to miss trying to kick* — sipawakaše *to ~ over*
stump *n* : oyah'u *a ~ or stub* — putanla s'e *stubby*
stun *v* : kaitokpaza *to ~ by striking, to bring darkness momentarily* — kat'a *to kill or ~ by striking* — nazan *to ~ by kicking, to hurt one*
stupid *adj* : oksape woteȟi *hard to teach* - tehan ksape šni *very slow coming to any understanding* — šunknongekpa s'e *stupidly* — tawacint'at'aka *simply ~ , as it were being one dead*
sturdy *adj* : k'éze *short by hardy*
stutter *v* : iaounc'unica *to ~ or stammer* — ieglašna *or* ieglašnašna *to blunder in speaking, to stammer, to speak falsely of one's own, e.g. one's visions* - ieglašna s'a *a blunderer*
style *n* : - Cf a form, a make
subjunctive mood *partic* : tka *or* tkaš - Note: tka is placed after the verb of the principal clause. Cf Gramm. #180 2)
submerge *v* : opaspa *to push under waer, to immerse* — oyus'o *submerged* — pakignunka *to push or dive under water* — pamahehe *to push under water repeatedly*
substitute *va* : heekiya *to count that to be put in the place of another* - *adv* : *in the place of* — hoyá *to have another sing in one's place*
successively *adv* : gliglekiya — ócib *or* ówecinhan *one after another*
such as *adj* : héca *such as that* - hécecaka *such a one, as a mean fellow* - hécekcecaka *always such, being this character* — léca *such as this*
suck *va* : ayagopa *to ~ up on* - yagopa *to ~ up, to nurse the breast* — ayazoka *to ~ out on* - glazoka *to ~ on one's own e.g. finger* — azin *to suck the breast* - azinkiya *to give suck, suckle, to nurse as a mother her child* — iyaskica *to press or suck one thing on another, as corn on the cob* - iyaskilya *pressing sucking on* — yapá *to bite taking in the mouth e.g. a pipe in smoking* - kiyapa *to ~ for, to take in the mouth and suck* — yaškepa *to ~ dry* - yaškeškepa *to ~ and spit out*
sucker *n* : tusla *a blood-sucker*
sudden *vn* : hingla — wanuhci *suddenly* — ungnahela *all of a sudden, all at once*
suffer *vn* : kakija *to be afflicted* - iyukakija *to make ~* - wawiyukakija *to make endure* - wícakišya *to make ~ , or in one's needs*
sufficiently *adv* : ícipiyela *~ for one's self*

suffix — some common ones appended to words:
...etu *or* ...el *suff to a n makes it a n of time*
...han *or* ...he *suff to a v makes it a participle, indicating repeated or occasional action*
...han *or* ...he *suff to a v gives the meaning:* ške *they say, or it is reported*
...hca *or* ...hce *or* ...hci *or* ...hcin *suff to words intensifies their meaning : very*
...ka *suff to n or v emphasizes the word*
... ka *post-positive can be equivalent to* šni, *or mean: almost*
...kel *suff to adv means: as it were*
...kiya *suff to v makes it causative, or makes it an adv of manner*
...ko *suff to v gives it the meaning: anxious to do*
...ku *suff to family relatives makes them poss, his or hers*
...la *suff to words makes them dim or superl*
suff to num or dem means: only ...
...laka *or* ...lah *suff to v and implies the question: Why don't you ... ?*
...lakel *suff to v makes it an adv of manner*
... ni *suff to words to change the word to its contrary*
...pi *suff for the pl form of words as such, but suff to v makes the v a n*
... s'a *suff to v indicates frequent action; suff to a n makes of it a n of agent*
... s'e *or* ...s'e *suff to words makes them adv of manner*
...ta *or* ...ata *or* ...yata *suff to n makes an adv phr :* at *or* on *or* to ...
...tan *suff to adv devolops the adv*
...tanhan *suff to adv means: from*
...tu *or* ...l *suff to words makes it an adv of time*
...unšto *suff to v means: all is said and done*
...wapa *suff to words to develop a word with the meaning: towards, forward in the future, upwards*
...ya *suff to v, adj, etc. makes a v of cause, or possession, or of regard*
...ya *or* ...yakel *or* ...yan *suff to adj converts the word to an adv* — *suff to a v makes it an adv or part*
...yan *suff to words make it a causative v*
...yela *suff to adj makes it an adv*
...yetu *is the euph* etu

sugar *n* : canhanpi
suitable *vn* : iyekicihantu *to be ~*
suitcase *n* : panša - Cf bag
sulfur *n* : makazi
summersaulting *adv* : onziwosla *turning head-over-heels*
sun *n* : wi - wíahinapa *to have the sun rise on* - wíhinapa *the rising sun, or the east* - wíiyaya *sundown, or the sun sets* - wíiyayuh *in the path of the sun* - wímahel iyaye *the setting of the sun* - wíšašlayela áye *the sun becomes clear and distinct* — wiyagyata *at or towards the sun* - wiyóhiyanpa *the sun rising, the east*
sunk *v* : oh'okpaya *to be sunken*
sunshine *n* : omašte - Cf heaven
supernatural *n* : wówakan *something that is ~* - Cf holy
supervisor *n* : waawanglake, *or* a shepherd
supplant *or* **displace** *or* **rival** *va* : paeze *to rival*
supple *adj* : psonpsonla *lithe* - psonpsonyela *in a supple way*
supply *or* **provision** *adj* : wašeca *rich in supplies* - wašecaya *well provided with or for*
support *n* : iyagluza *to have for a ~* — kušipaton *to hold up one* — wóit'inze *a support or supporter*
suppress *v* : ínapcapca iyeya *to ~ one's anger*
surface *adv* : gagaya *on the ~* — haakapa *on the outside*
surfeit *or* **stuffed** *vn* : oȟaka *to be surfeited*
surly *n* : waikalelepake *a ~ person*
surpass *vn* : iyakapa *to ~ , be larger* - iyokapa *to surpass* - kakipa *to excel* - kapeya *to go or pass beyond* — iyakigle *to overlap, to reach beyond the times* - iyakigleya *to make ~ , or surpassing*
surprise *v* : apablehiyuya *to take one by surprise* — itonpa *to be astonished, to praise one* - iton'ic'ipa *to be astonished at one's self, to praise one's self to, to wonder at one's*

self or one's own – itonkipa *to wonder at or praise one's self* – itonkipeya *to be astonished at or praise one's self* – itonpeyahan *surprisingly, praiseworthily, wonderfully* – íyapaštaka *to be taken by surprise* – iyapaštagya *to cause to be surprised* — íyatagle *to be speechless from surprise, awed* — iyuš'inyaya *to be surprised at, or frightened at* – wóš'inyeye *a scare* – yuš'inyaya *to be frightened* – wicayuš'inyanyan s'e *in sudden surprise* — nagiaktonšya *to ~ e.g. wild game by stealing closeby* — ungnahelaya *to ~ one*
surrender *va* : únc'onnica *to yield, give up*
surreptitiously *adv* : anatakinyece
surround *va* : koglamnayan *to restrain one* – Cf around
survey *v* : makaiyuta — maka-iwanyankapi *land surveyors*
survive *vn* : inapa *to live through* — ipašloka *to make it through e.g. the winter*
suspect *vn* : t'unkeca *to be suspicious* – it'unkeca *to be suspected of, to be unwilling to do* – t'ungya *to have suspicions* – it'ungya *to ~ one* – t'unkiya *or* it'ungkiya *to ~ concerning one's self* – kat'unkeca *to ~ one* — kenunyan *to know partly, to ~*
suspend *or* **dangle** *v* : iyukoltkeyela *hanging without touching down, e.g. hanging on a wire* — ceškiyutan *a pair of suspenders* — iyukoltkeyela *suspended*
suspense *v* : akicons *of* akiconza *to keep one in ~*
swallow *va* : napca – anapca *to ~ on or after* – atahnakipca *to ~ one's saliva* – kipca *to ~ saliva or food* – nakicapca *to ~ one's own* – nakipca *to ~ down one's own e.g. spittle* – onapce *the act of swallowing* – onapcešilya *to be hard to ~* — tahglahota *to ~ the wrong way, and hence to choke* – tahglaškape *to choke* — yaošlog iyeya *to ~ something inadvertently*
swamp *n* : wiwila kapapa – owiwiyela *in a swampy place* – wiwiyela *boggy*
swarm *or* **throng** *adv* : pawis'e *close-packed*
sway *adj* : kcankcanla *very movable* — yungyunka *to rock or ~ from side-to-side*
sweat *vn* : onacu *to be sweaty, to be perspiring* — temni *to sweat, pant, or give out* – temnit'a *to perspire profusely* – temnit'eyela *sweating profusely* – temniyan *perspiring* – tewicamni one's sweating — inikagapi *a sweat done in a sweatlodge at times ceremonially* – oinikaga *a sweat-house*
sweep *or* **brush** *v* : ayuhinta *to ~ or rake off on* – kahinta *to ~ off or out* – kahintu ska *sweeping or swept clean* – kícicahinta *to ~ for one* – wohínta *to ~ off by shooting as men on a battle field* — yutaegle *to ~ together in a heap*
sweet *or* **delicious** *adj* : skúya *or* skuyéla – wískuye *a sweetener or that which makes sour* – Cf sour
swell *vn* : po *to puff up, bloat, rise* – apo *to ~ on* – napo *to ~ as corn does when soaked* – kapo *to ~ as one's flesh* – nakapo *to rise as dough, or warp as wood* – nákapoh *to make swell* — oiyopa *to ~* – okapo *to make ~ by striking* – opo *to be swelled* – opopoya *to be swollen* — napoga *to ~ or raise as corn soaked* – kapogan *to puff out, to ~* – nakapoga *to swell, rise, warp* – napogapi *a swelling* – onapohya *to puff up or ~ out* – ipo *a swelling* – iwicapo *a swelling or inflation* – kpa *to ~ as rice in cooking it* – mna *to ~* – tamna *a swelling* – napšunka *a growth* – našoka *to thicken or to swell*
swerve *v* : iyukšan *to curve off, deviate from*
swift *vn* : luzahan *to be fast* – Cf fast
swim *vn* : nonwan *or* nunwan – anonwan *to ~ on or for* – inonwan *to swim* – kinonwan *to ~ back home*
swing *vn* : cankakiza *to ~ and creak as trees do in the wind* — gegeya *swinging, dangling* — hóhote *a hammock* – hóhotela *a swing* – hóhotela kic'un *to get on a ~* – hótela kaška *to make a swing* — kapsanpsan *to sway back and forth* — namnimni *to swing e.g. a blanket in the wind* — ókazeze *to ~, as something suspended from a cord* – ozézeya *swinging* – yazeze *to make ~ with the mouth* — pakoza *to ~, to push back and forth* — yuwaga *to move the arms as in running*
swirl *v* : okamnimni *to whirl around, as snow or sand around houses*
swish *adv* : sliya *swishing*
swivel *v* : póptan *to ~ the head, i.e. to rotate it left or right*

T

table *n* : ágnawotapi *anything on which to eat* – wágnawotapi *a ~ on which to eat* — wágnayutapi *a table for eating* – waglutapi *a table for one's eating* – waagnaglepi *any table* – wagnawopetonpi *a store counter* – wágnawòšnapi *an altar table*
tactful *v* : wawolwicayešni *to be ~*
tag *v* : wiyuhlagan šni *to have one's wife ~ along always i.e. follow after her husband*
tail *n* : situpi *a bird's ~ feathers* — sinte *an animal's ~* — *fig a young man*
tailwind *adv* : itaglahwe *with the wind, the wind to the back* – itaglahwekiya *with the wind* – itaglahwetanhan *from the direction whence comes the wind* – itaglahweya *with the wind at one's back*
take *va* : icu *to ~, accept, receive* – icucu *to ~ and have* – ahiicu *to have come and taken* – ahiyaya *to ~ and carry or hand around e.g. the pipe* – éyaya *to ~ or to have taken with one* – gloeyaya *to ~ or to have taken e.g. one's own child when going somewhere* — akinapa *to ~ out and go home* – akiyagla *to carry or ~ home* – kagla *to take home to one* – waagleca *to take home* — akšija *to ~ or retain what is claimed by another* — églaku *to ~ back again, to ~ up one's own* – éyaku *to ~ away* – wieyaku *to take away a woman* — yúza *to take hold of, to take a wife* – ékicigluza *to overtake and take one's own from another* – éyuza *to go and ~, to seize and hold at or on the way, to hold to or at* – okiciyuze *the taking of one another as in marriage* — épahpa *to ~ to and lay down at* – gluhpa *to ~ down one's own that was hanging* – pahpa *to take down* – wigláhpa *to take down one's own, i.e. tent* — éyawa *to take for, consider to be* – gloi *to ~ or have taken one's own to some place* –kícicai *to take to a place for one* — kícigloi *to take one's own to* — kícigloya *to take one's own to* — gluguka *to take out, to draw a knife* – gluȟeyapa *to ~* away one's own — hohi *Take it!* — icage *to ~ or skim off* — igluk'o *to ~ it all, as in a game that is staked* — ikipemni *to wrestle and ~ from* — ikpašloka *to slip or ~ off* — áya *to ~ or carry along* – kaaya *to be taking, bringing, carrying to one* — ki *to take from, to rob* — kicu *to take home or elsewhere to, to restore to one* — kícicai *to take to a place for one* — kícicagla *to take to one's home for him* — makiglata *to take much leave* — Na! *or* *Nána! Take it!* — ogluspa *to take hold on one's own* — oiglapta *to take leftovers* — okapta *to take, lade out e.g. wages by stages* — wóze *the dipping out* – wózepi *laded out* – yaze *to take out by the mouth* — yapa *to take into the mouth e.g. a pipe*
tale *n* : ohunkakan *a fable, a story*

talk *v* : kihowaya *to ~ loud to* — kiyamna *to acquire for another by talking* — oyahlohloka *to begin to talk, as a child just learning, to babble* — yawignuni *to ~ bad, to destroy by ~* — oiglukiki *to gossip or back-bite* — okiciciya *to ~ together as in courting* — šilwoyaka *to ~ bad of one* - Cf speak
tall *adv* : hanska, wazi s'e *tall like a pine tree, very tall*
tallow *n* : wašinkceka — wasnatasaka *hard grease*
tan *va* : kpanyan *to dress* - akpanyan *to tan, dress a hide*
tangled *adv* : iyuwiya *in a snarl, enmeshed* - paiyuwiya *tangling* - opawiwi *~ in a mass* — kaiyapehan *to get ~* - kaiciyapehan *~ up, folded* — oyuglaglaya *to tangle*
tank *n* : ojuminiyatke *a place used to hold drinking water* - Cf reservoir
tap *v* : kalope s'e *to give a love-tap* — apapa *to ~ one or some thing*
taper *v* : katepa — sli *tapering* - yaslitka *to make tapering with the teeth* - yuslitka *to make tapering by pinching*
tardy *adj* : šuška *worthless, slow*
target *n* : oweheca *a thrown arrow* - Cf goal
tasty *adj* : napin *rich* - anapin *to be ~* — glata *to taste one's own, to ruminate* — iyuta *to try* — oskuya *sour* - skúya *sweet* - wóskuye *savor* — takumna *to have taste or smell*
tattered *adv* : kanhan *falling off or out* - kanhanhan *ragged, dangling, old* - kanheca *ragged or ~ as one's clothes*
tattoo *v poss* : akito *to ~ one's own* - akitopi *a ~* - ato *to do a tattoo*
tax *or* **toll** *n* : tiyopa wíšimnaye *a toll collector* — waeconkiya *to ~ one's strength* — wahpaye *taxes* — wakajujukiya *to impose a ~*
tea *n* : cankalyapi — wahpe *tea leaves* — canhlogan wakalyapi *garden tickseed tea* — šeyaka *peppermint for a tea with visitors; ceyaka is the medicinal mint* — unpantawote *the smaller red-root* — wahpeyatapi *giant hyssop* — wahpewaštemna, Bergamont, *which is chewed* — zitkatacan *a wild tea made from the lead plant*
teach *v* : waonspekiya - waonspekiye *a teacher*
team *n* : hasánni *a mate, one of a pair, a ~* - *See* fellowship
[1]**tear** *or* **rend** *vn* : akablaza *to ~ open on* — kapota *to ~ by striking, as clothes by the wind* - kíciyapota *to ~ up with the mouth* - okápota *to be torn by shaking* - aiglupota *to rend one's own garment* — kíciyahleca *to ~ to pieces for one with the mouth* - kíciyuhleca *to ~ for one* - nahleca *to ~ a hole in, in pieces, to fracture* — napsapsakela s'e *tearing apart* - okahlece *a rent* - okinahleca *to ~ in the middle* - onahleca *to ~ a hole in* - onahlece *a rent or tear* - opahleca *to ~ in* - opahlece *a rent* - oyuhleca *to ~ in* - pahleca *to ~ by pushing against* — oyuh'eh'eyakel *slovenly, done only in bits and parts* - wohléca *to ~ through by shooting or running against* - yahleca *to from by mouth* - yuhleca *to ~ in pieces by hand* aigluhleca *to ~ one's own* — kíciyujuju *to ~ down or to pieces for one* - yajuju *to ~ down or to pieces by mouth* — wakajun *to ~ or pull up by the roots* — wópta *to ~ in two e.g. a blanket* — yusleca *to ~ by hand* — yuh'eh'e *tearing in shreds, in bits*
[2]**tear** *adv* : ištamnigaga *in tears, with tearful eyes running* - ištamnihanpi *tears* - ištamniošlo *with water standing in the eyes* - ištamniyan *running at the eyes*
tease *va* : íškanyan *to bring one to talk by teasing* — wókikšan *friendly teasing as between man and woman* — yuhinhan *to provoke one* — yuwaza *to ~ or annoy*
teem *adv* : pawiwi *teeming, in crowds* - Cf swarm
telephone *va* : mazapa - ómazape a telephone
tell *v* : oglaka *to ~ of one's own* - oyaka *to report, relate* - okiyaka *to ~ to* — kinunkiciyapi *they ~ each other*
temporary *adj* : - Cf short, as in time
tempt *v* : iyutan *to try* - wawiyutan *solicitation* - wawiyutanyan *to ~ one* - wawiyutanye or wócanteiyutanke *or* wócantiyutan *or* wówiyutan *a temptation* — yugekicaga *to hold out for, to bait, tempt* — ayuslohan *to drag along, fig to lead one on, to tempt, to bait*
tender *adj* : nakintkilya *as ~ meat* — štaštayela *as ~ skin*
tense *vn* : puskicat'a *to be tense*
tension *n* : wóyutitan
tent *n* : típi *or* ti - iticaga *to set up a special service ~* — iticicaške *the three main ~ poles* — ohiyezaptan *a ten by twelve foot ~* — wakeya *to have for a ~ , or a round skin ~* - wakeya ska *a canvas ~* - wakeyaton *to make a ~ of*
term *n* : ohiyaye *a setting, an arrival, a term, a conclusion* — waceya *to be on good terms with one*
terrible *vn* : ohitika *to be terrifying, furious, brave* - ohitikala *to consider brave* - ohitilaka *a brave person* - ohitiwacin *to intend to be brave* - wóhitika *terrifying*
test *vn* : íkutkuteka *to make a trial run, a pilot project*
testify *vn* : oyatan'in *to manifest, show*
thank *vn* : pila *to rejoice, be glad and thankful* - pikicila *to be glad, thankful with or for* - pikila *to be thankful, glad*
that *pron dem* : he *or* hena *or* cin *or* k'un *or* k'on *or* taku *something, i.e. in rel to an other* — he eca *that person there* — kae *or* kaeš *That is he (that one)* — kana *those yonder* — k'éya *that kind* — hógna *in that manner* — éyešan *That is he* — k'eleš *or* he e k'eš *That is it!*
thaw *adj* : štuta *thawed out, or to be thawed* - štulya *to ~ out something* - aštuta *to ~ or warm on anything* - aštulya *to cause to ~ on* — cuhanzi *It is a day wrapped in heavy wet fog* — span *to soften* - spanla *to melt as snow*
the *art def* : kin *or* cin - Note: *cin* is used when in the previous syllable there is an "e" or "i"
them *pron in compos* : ...wica...
then *adv* : ahankeya *immediately following or behind or then* — caš *but then* — cetu *then just so, so much* — ecanl *just then, at that instant* — ehan *at that time or place* - ehanl *then, at that time* - ehantu *at that time* - ehantuke *just then indeed* — éyaš *but then* — éya šna *every now and then* — héehan *at that time* - héhan *then at that time* - hehánhca *then and not until then* - hehanl *at that place then* - hehantu *at that time then* - hehantula *then, or just then* - hétu *at that place there* - hétulahci *just at that place or time* — icanl *but just then* - icunhanlahci *just then* — wahecel *about then*
thence *adv* : letanhan *from there*
there *adv* : he *or* hel *or* héna - hétu *at that place* - hétula *there then* - hétulahci *just at that place or time* - héci *in or at that place* - héciya *there at that place* - hecíyotan *in that direction* — ka *or* káki *or* kal *there yonder* - kákika *or* kákiya *over there yonder* — k'el *in that place there* — opá *there being there, in or along in*
therefore *adv conj* : ca *or* canke *or* cankeš *or* cankelaka — héce *or* hécel *so in this way* — héceca *so, always so* — héceca cankeš *therefore since that is the case* — héciyatan *from that place* - héciyatanhan *therefore from that place* — hehántan *from that time therefore* — héon *on that account therefore* - héon'etanhan *therefore* — hetán *or* hetanhan *from that place or time therefore*
thick *or* **dense** *adj* : šóka - šogyá *strongly, firmly, seriously, greatly* - akišogya *close together* - akišoka *dense or thick on* - ašoka *to be thick on* — ošokaya *thickly* - ošoka *thick* - ošoke *a thickness* - wošóšo s'e *extraordinarily thick, as the nose or lips etc.* — akiš'aka

thick, as grain or weeds growing in a field - akiš'agya *growing densely* — tiktica *stiff* - katiktica *to make ~ by stirring* - natiktica *to make ~ by boiling or trampling* — owoȟešma *~ in or with* — wakipšapša *densely, close together*

thief *n* : wamanon s'e - Cf steal

thin *adj* : atabyela *as a ~ slice of bread* — awe *to become lean, as cattle in the spring* — cikcik'aya *slenderwise* — híh'ayela *emaciated, showing one's teeth* — kokiwotan'in *to become ~, as clouds may do* — pinšpinjela *~ or sparse, as hair or grass* — zanzanyela *thinly covering* — zípela *thin as a fine pancake*

think *v* : iyukcan — kcáma *I thought* — s'éwacanmi *I think it is so, or It seems to me to be so* - wacanmi *v defect* : I thought — kécankin *to ~ of as such, to regard as* — kécin *or* lecín to think that — wacin *to think or purpose, aim at, try to, be anxious to* - kuwacin *to ~ of coming home* - s'ewacin *I think it is so* - wacinkiyuza *to ~ of, to keep in mind* - wacin'oyuze *a thought, one's thinking* — képca *I thought that* - lepcá *I thought this* — séca *seemingly, I thought so* - sécelaka *to think, have an opinion* — hecétulaka *to think having an opinion* — waunkic'ila *to ~ much of one's self* — šicelaka *to ~ bad* - Cf wicala

thirst *vn* : ipuza - oipuza *to ~ after* - ipuzapi *one's thirst* - ípuzat'a *to die or be dying of ~, to be very thirsty* - íwicapuza *thirst*

this *pron dem* : le *this*, léna *these* - lenákehcin *all these* - lenáos *or* lenίos *or* leníyos *both these, these two* — lehantanhan *from this* - lehan *thus far, at this place, afterwards* — lógna *in this manner*

thoroughly *adv* : katkanheya *soundly, i.e. ~* — kat'insya *slowly, soundly, well*

those *pron dem* : henake

thought *n* : wówiyukcan

thrash *v* : wayablaskaska *to ~ out in every detail*

thread *n* : haȟunta *~ or cord or twine* — iyoyaza *to string or thread a needle or a number of beads etc.* — wícagege *anything with whcih to sew*

threaten *v* : ócinyan — wóinapeka *harm that threatens* — iwohinyansyakel *in a threatening or irate manner*

thresh *va* : nakan *to ~ by foot, by trampling* — wahuwataya *to ~, beat the arms in decoying*

throng *adv* : wicapaptapta *among a vast crowd of people, as one rolling about in a ~*

throttle *v* : loteogmus yuza *to ~ a person*

through *or* **across** *adv* : ikapta *as to fall ~* — iyopta *to pass ~ or across* — iyopte *prep* : *through or across something* - iyopteya *straight ~, passing on* - ópta *across or ~* - papta *through* — ipaseya *or* ipazeya *right or clear ~* — óhanglela *~ all, ~ the midst of* — paja *~*, as in stabbing — sitomni *throughout, all over* - Cf all

throw *v* : aglahpa *to ~ to cover one's own* - akahpa *to ~ over to cover* - ayahpa *to ~ down with the mouth on* - ayuhpa *to ~ down on, to shut e.g. a window* - hpahan *fallen or thrown down* - hpawahan *thrown off and down* - ikpahpa *to ~ one's self off as from a horse* - pahpa *to buck one off* - yuhpa *to ~ down or shake off a load* — aiyahpeya *to ~ over in roping e.g. a horse* - akahpeton *to cover up, throwing a cover over to conceal* - akahpihpeya *to ~ a cover over* - éihpekiya *to ~ away at another place* - éihpeya *to dispose of somewhere* - éihpeic'iyaya *to ~ one's self over or out* - glihpeya *to ~ one down as in wrestling* - hinhpeya *to ~ down what is in one's hands* - hiyahpeya *to ~ over to one* - ihpekiciciyapi *a divorce* - ihpekiciya *to forsake, to leave one's own* - ihpeya *to ~ down or away* - iyahpeya *to ~ over or on* - iyohpeya *to cast into e.g. meat into the pot* - oihpeya *to ~ into e.g. the water* - oiyohpeya *to ~ or go into a ford* - oyuhpe *a toss* - pahpeya *to ~ down or put off a load* - yahpeya *to ~ down with the mouth* - yuhpeya *to make ~ down or shake off* - yuhpihpeya *to make ~ down* — aglaštan *to ~, spill e.g. water on one's self* — akazamni *to ~ open, as one's blanket* — akastaka *to ~ or daub on e.g. plaster* - kastaka *to ~ in e.g. the mud* — ayaunka *to ~ with the mouth on* — ayuhmin *to ~ or sling e.g. stones to one side* — kin'in *to ~ at, to assail* - icin'in *to ~ at or strike with* - kicin'in *to assail e.g. with stones one'own* — iȟeyatiyeya *to thrust forward* — iyowata *to cast rays* — kajojoyeya *to make whiz by throwing* — okah'ol iyeya *to ~ away into* — owošloka *to fling at* — painyanka *to ~ sending it through a hoop* — wankayeya *to ~ high up* — wayaha iyeya *to ~ down* — woštepi iyeya *to cast down* — yunkaheya *to cast down, or obliquely*

thrust *or* **shove** *va* : iȟeyatiyeya — oglaya *or* oyujunta *or* yujunta *to ~ into*

thunder *n* : wakinyan *the thunderbird, so titled for the natural world of space the bird shares with thunder and lightning* - wakinyan hoton *the sound of thunder* — takangi *the tail feathers of the thunderbird*

thus *or* **so** *adv* : hécegla *only so far or little, that's all* - hécehci *just so, only so, altogether* - hécekce *in this manner, so thus* - hécekceca *or* hécekceka so, always so - hécekcecaka *always such, bearing this character* - hécekcel *in this manner, so, thus, just as* - hécekcetu *so, in this manner* - hécel *so, in this way, hence, therefore* - hécelkiya *in that way* - hécelya *so, thus, in that manner* - hécena *thus, consequently, finally* - hécetkiya *in that direction* - hécetuya *to cause to be so, right, or so, thus, in showing one how* — hécina *thus, so it is* — lécel *thus, in this way, after this manner* - lécetu *thus, so, right, or this is right* — lehan *now, thus far, at this place* - lehantu *to this, thus far, now* — iyecetu *to be or become so, to be as expected, to take place, thus, so, right* - iyecetuya *so* - iyecetuyakel *in this manner* — hogna *in that manner, in that way or direction* — kákeca *in this manner* - kakétu *in this way, so, thus*

tickle *va* : yuš'inš'in *to ~ one under the arms* — ašniyakiya *to tickle one*

tie *va* : aheyun *to ~ a pack on* — kaška *to tie, bind, or to imprison* - aiyakaška to tie one thing on another - aiyakaškeya *bound together* - akaška *to tie onto* - akikaška *to tie two together* - akikiglaška *to tie one's own together, to hobble e.g. one's own horse* - akiglaške *to ~ one's self together with another* - glaška *to bind one's own* - icaške *something with which to bind around, e.g. a cincture* - icaškeya *to tie one with* - ícicaška *to bind together* - ícicaškeya *tied, united together* - ic'icaška *or* iglaška *to bind one's self, or to surrender one's self for punishment* - iyaglaška *to tie one's own to* - iyaiglaška *to tie one's self or give self up to be bound* - iyakaška *to tie one thing to or on another* - iyokaške *something with which one connects or binds* - iyokicaška *to tie together e.g. two strings or ropes* - kaškapi *to cause one to be bound, to have one arrested* - oiyakaška *to bind into* - oiyakaške *a knot* — akiyuskica *to tie or fasten together* — apahlata *to embroider* - apahlate *ribbon, tape, something for binding* — pahta *to bind in, bind up* - apahta *to bind or tie on* - opahta *to bind in* — ayuskita *or* ayuskiskita *to bind or bandage on* - kiciyuskita *to tie up for one* — can'iyuȟuge *to tie a tree for felling* — okikaȟa *to tie a knot* - okiglaȟa *to bind tight together* — yuošin *to tie loosely* - yuošinyan

loosely tied, tied in a bow knot
tight *adj* : oskica *drawn around* ~ - oskicela *well-fitting* - woskíca *to pound tight* — aot'inza *to be ~ on one, as a shirt on one* - at'insya *tightly, in some way squeezed* - át'insyakel *in a forced way* - glat'inza *to make one's own ~ by driving or by using the teeth* - it'inze *a garter, a supporter* - ot'inza *to be ~ or fast in, to be too small for one* - owot'inza *to pound ~* — iyotitanla *too small, tight fitting*
till *v* : kicanyan *to ~ the soil* - mahkicanyan *to work the soil* — napta *to spade* - yuptapta *to ~ the soil*
tilted *adj* : unnaptan *inclined, tipped, slanted, sideling* — ikakein *to knock into a tilt*
timber *n* : páta *a grove of trees, a timber* — hínta *a ~ of the bass, linden, or lime-wood trees*
time *adv* : akigle *once again, times, as in* yamni akigle *three times* - iyakigle *times, or to surpass, reach beyond the time* — iyehan *or* iyehanl *at the appointed time* - iyehantulahci *exactly at the time* - iyehantušni *being not time yet* - iyehantula *just at the time* - iyehanwapa *towards the time* — okanšniyan *having no time* — opcebyela *for a short time* — otóhanyankel *for some time* — takomni *always, ever, at any time, or nevertheless* - tohantan *for all past time* - tohantuka *at a certain time* - tohantuke c'eyaš *at any time, whenever* - owatohantuka wan *some times past* — wahecel *about that time* — wahehan *in good time, about that time* — walehan *by this time* - walehantu *at this time* — wihiyala *a time measure, the passing of the sun, clock time, hour of the day, etc.*

PERIODS :
anpetu *or* ánpa *or* can *day or daytime*
iope *an hour*
oh'anko *a minute*
okowanjila *a week*
ómaka *a year, a season*
waniyetu *a year, a winter*
wíatan'onmya *in the afternoon* — wícokanhiyaya *or* wícokan sam iyaye *or* wítakinyanyanka *the afternoon*
wícokan *or* wícokanyan *noon*
wíkawankap'u *the hour about 7:00 or 8:00 AM*
wíkuciyela *late afternoon, time towards sunset*
wíkuwabya *time about 3:00 PM*
wíwankatuya *time about 9:00 AM*

timely *v* or *adv* : iteka *it is time for, due, timely, timely indeed*
tip *v* : paglaptus iyeya *to tip over* — paonze wosla iyeya *to over-turn, to turn bottom-up*
tipi *or* **teepee** *or* **tent** *or* **lodge** *n* : tipi *a house*

KINDS :
hunkatacannum tiowapi *a tipi with a pipe painted and bearing four figures on it*
tigiyapi *a brown tipi* - tiowa *a painted tipi* - tišayapi *a red tipi* - tiwoslate *a miner's tipi* - tiyobleca *a square tipi*
típi iyokiheya *a council tipi*
wicatankagapi *a specially painted tipi*
wioptasabyapi *a tipi with a black circle around its outer surface*
wiowa *a painted tipi*
wipasabyapi *a tipi painted black on top and bottom*
wipašayapi *a tipi red on top and bottom*
wítiowapi *a tipi painted with the sun above the door*
wíyapaȟica *a main tipi*
wizi *an old smoky tipi*

PARTS :
tiislayatahan *the right side of a tipi*
tisanpatahan *a tipi wall*
titahepiya *a tipi's middle wall*
tiyopa *the door*
wiceška *the vent flaps, overlapping ends of a tipi cover*
wihuta *the lower border of a tipi*
wihutaša *the lowest edge of the tipi*
wiȟupa *the flaps of a tipi*
wipa *the windflaps in the upper part of a tipi*
wipipa *the tipi flaps* - wipipaha *the vent flaps*

ACCESSORIES :
tušu *tent poles*
wahinpaspa *or* wihinpaspa *tent pins*
wihuta inatake *or* wiluzignake *insulation*
wiiyapaȟice *tipi fastenings*

ODDS & ENDS :
tiglujuju *to fold up one's own tipi*
tiikceyakel *in tipis*
tiwohan *between or among tipis*
tiyepata *at the tipi door*
tiyokiti *one who lives in his own tipi*
tiyoti *to erect a soldier's tent*
wiluzignagton *to insulate the tipi bottom*
wipapiya *to open tipi flaps*

tire *vn* : okit'a *to be tired, fatigued* - blókit'a *to be very tired, weary, exhausted* - blókit'eya *to make weary, tire out* — watuka *faint, weary, exhausted* - iwatuka *to be tired of or on some account* - kawatuka *tired out riding as in a wagon or on horseback* - tukaka *exhausted, tired out* — kapin *to be tired* - econkapin *to be tired of doing, to be unwilling to do* — apablaya *to make level on, fig to play one out, to fatigue one* — aoš'agya *tired out with difficulty* — cán'opatinyanpi s'e *tired and stiff* — hánt'eya *wearily* — ȟ'únkpani *to play out, to be unable to accomplish, to be in an unfinished state* - ȟ'únt'a *to give out at work, to be laid up at work, be exhausted* - ȟ'únt'eya *to cause to give out, exhaust one's strength, to oppress one with work* - ȟ'únyan *to tire one* — icašloka *knocked out, colloq to be all in, played out* — istostaka *tired in one's arms* — kajabjapa *to be tired riding, to be made dull* — kakšikša *tired out* - kšikšeya *to make tire out* — naštašta s'e *as though exhausted, tired out* — kaštušta *to be tired from riding* — štuštelahcaka *tired out* — štušteya *to chase and so make weary* — wayuh'anhica *to play out, exhaust a horse by not knowing how properly to handle it*
to *or* **towards** *adv* : aiyoptetu *in the direction of, towards* - aiyopteya *to match with what one contributes, or in a straight-line direction* — akoitoheya *towards but with the face turned away from* — *prep suff* : ...ata *to, at, or on* — étkiya *towards, to, with* - hétkiya *towards that place* - ecetkiya *in one direction or another* — eciyapatanhan *towards e.g. evening* - héciyapatanhan *towards that time or place* — ektakiya *to or towards* — *prep* : el *in, on, at* — étu *to, at, in there* — *prep in compos* : ...ki... *to, of, for* — *prep in compos* : ...kici... *to each other* — akšankšan *to and fro, across and back* — yukinkin *to and fro, from side to side*
tobacco *n* : canli - Ptegleška Canli *Bull Durham tobacco*

- canli'icahiye *an additive to ~ to make it aromatic* - canliyatapi *chewing ~* - canliyukpanpi *a fine smoking tobacco* - canliyugmunpi *a cigar* - canli'iyopemni *or* iyopemni *or* mnihuha cannunpa *a cigarette* - canloguha *a ~ pouch* — cantojuha *a ~ bag* — canšaša *kiniknik* — wahpecanli *a vine similar to wintergreen* — wówinye *tobacco-ties* - canli wapahte séce *prayer offerings*

toe *n* : sihu - siocokan *the middle toe* - siokaza *the toes* - siokazunte *the toes taken together or singly* - sioko *the space between the toes* - sipagnagya *to or at the tip of the toes* - sipahunka *the big toe* - sipaiyokihe *the second toe* - sipinkpa *the toes* - sipinkpakpala *on tiptoe* - sišašte *the little toe* - sišašteiyokihe *the fourth toe* — naowinga *to turn the toes inward* — hminhmin *misshapen, or with the toes outward*

together *adv suff* : ...caska - Note: the *suff* is appended to numerals to make them *adv* — éciškanyankel *together* — gmuyapi s'e *with many things ~, bunched or crowded ~* — icagejuya ~ *or in company with* - icageya *together* — ogejuya ~ *with, among* — iyakijuya ~ *united* — kókiju *to come ~, to unite* — kašmeyalake s'e *with many sitting ~* — kawita *together* - wítakiya *en masse* - wítaya ~, *in company with* - wítayela *in the company with, en masse* — okijeya *together* - ptáptaya *or* ptáya *collectively* - sakib *together* — wokípuskica *to drive close ~*

toilet *n* : oiheya tipi *an outhouse* — oleja *a urinal, chamberpot*

tomorrow *n* : hínhanna kin *or* hínhanna kinhan *or* hanyankeci

tongue *n* : ceji - tacejiokaslute *~ cutting* - tacejisu *dribblings*

tool *n* : wíkicanyanpi *tools or a tool* - wíkicaye *implements* — wówinyeyapi *tools, instruments* — wícage *a ~ with which to make something, an implement* - wówinyeya *to use as a tool or instrument*

SOME TOOLS:

adz *or* **adze** *n* : can'icakan *any tool used for hewing wood* - icakan *an adze*
anvil *n* : mázaaglehan
arrow maker *n* : wan'iyukeze
auger *n* : can'iyuhloke *a drill for wood* — can'iyumni *an auger for boring holes in wood* — wícahloke *a tool with which to make holes* — makaiyuhloke *or* makiyuhloke *a post hole*
awl *n* : tahinšpa
ax *or* axe *n* : nazonspe *or* nazunspe *or* nasonspe — opetanka *a broad axe*
bailer *n* : ipahte
battery *n* : kan'ínaškaškan *a medical battery*
bellows *n* : pelipogan
beetle *v* : icaškice *a hammer*
binder *n* : wícaške
brush *n* : wícasto — wícacice *a ~ for clothes and furs* — wícaguke *a clothes brush*
brush-breaker *n* : conwiyugoge *i.e. underbrush*
can-opener *n* : mazíyuhloke
cement mixer *n* : makikacoco
chain *n* : mas'ícicahaha *i.e. with steel links*
chisel *n* : maz'icakse *or* masicašpe
clamp *or* press *n* : wícaskice *or* wícaškice
clippers *n* : iwicakcašla
compass *n* : makiwanyanke
crusher *n* : wícawege
cultivator *n* : imah'akate *or* makaiyuksaksa *or* makiyuhinhe
cutter *n* : wícakse *or* wíyukse *a sissors or knife*
dashboard *n* : tokatahan canblaska
draw-knife *n* : canwicajipe
drill *n* : can'iyuhomni ciscila maziyuhomni *a too with which to make holes*
extractor *n* : iyušloka
fan *n* : wícalu
file *n* : iyume *something with which to grind or ~, as a file or stone* - mas'iyume *to ~ to form wood or metal* — apaman *to ~ or polish on* — wípame *a tool to smoothen surfaces* - can'ipame *a ~ to make smooth wood surfaces, a rasp* - maz'ipame *a tool to make smooth metal surfaces*
filter *or* strainer *n* : wínaze
flatiron *n* : mázablaska
flattener *n* : pahinpabla *a ~ for quills*
gouge *n* : wícapote *a tool used to tear apart, rend a thing*
grappler *n* : wícahpu *a tool for picking up* — wícahpe *an instrument for throwing something, e.g. a sling* - Cf hook, reach
grinder *n* : wíyukpan *a grinding mill*
grindstone *n* : míliyuma
hammer *n* : mazíyapa — hohuicate *a primitive ~* - ihohucate *a large stone ~ to break bones to get marrow* — ihonicata *a ~ to pound meat and cherries* — imaziyapa *an iron ~* — wícaškin *a ~ to pound cherries* — wakat'ozapi *a stone ~*
harrow *n* : iyuhinhe *or* makinaksaksa *or* makiyuhinte *or* magiyuhinte — magicahinte *a rake or harrow* - Cf rake
hatchet *n* : wícat'e *a killing tool*
hayrack *n* : pejiitokšu
hayrake *n* : pejiiyuhinte
hoe *n* : magicamna
hook *n* : mázaškopa - Cf grappler
hose *n* : tašupa
incisor *n* : wíyukeze — wan'iyugola *a tool to incise arrows*
knife *n* : míla — kan'iwapsake *a ~ to cut sinew* — míyokšijapi *a pocket-knife* — wahinpahpa *a fleshing-knife*
lancet *n* : wícakpe *or* kan'icakpe
lister *n* : makiyublu iwoju - Cf plow
marker *n* : wícago *a marking instrument*
microscope *n* : masiwanyanke - Cf telescope
mill *n* : onakpan
mower *n* : pejiinakse
nozzle *n* : mníwosli i
opener *n* : maziyuhloke
pickaxe *n* : makaik'e *or* makikašpe
pitch-fork *n* : pejiicape
pincers *n* : imasoyuze *or* mázawoyuspa *tongs*
plane *n* : wícajipe *a shaving tool to make smooth wood*
planter *n* : iwoju *a drill for planting seed*
pliers *n* : mazoyuspe
plow *n* : mahiyublu *or* makiyublu *or* magiyublu — makaiyupte *or* makiyupte *or* makateca iyublu *a breaking ground plow*
plowshare *n* : opé
poker *n* : winuhcala tacanpetipiye
press *n* : wípaškice *a washboard, a sort of press*
rake *n* : iyuhinte *or* wíyuhinte *or* owankiyuhinte
reach *n* : iyuhpe *something with which to pull down*
roller *n* : makinaskilye
rounding tool *n* : wan'ipame *used in arrow-making*

saw *n* : wícakse *a tool used to cut off* — talicakse *a ~ used to cut meat*
scissors *n* : iyušla
scope *n* : maziwanyanke
scraper *n* : iyuk'eze *or* wícakince *or* wíyukince — mínska *or* wahintka *a ~ for hides* — wípaguke *a ~ used in scraping down skins*
screw *or* nail tightener *n* : wícat'inze *a screwdriver or hammer* - Cf wrench
screw-jack *or* jack-screw *n* : mázawiyuhomni *or* mázawiyuwanka àya *a jack-screw*
scythe *n* : pejiicašla *or* wícašla
shears *n* : wíyušla
shovel *n* : pelicu *a coal ~* - Cf spade
sickle *n* : mílakaš'in — pejiicašlaope *a mower* — wagmezeicakse *a corn sickle*
single-tree *or* double-tree *n* : canpagmiyutitan
sledge *n* : wícablece *a ~ hammer*
sling *n* : iyuhmun
snippers *or* snips *n* : iyuksa *or* maziyukce
snowplow *n* : waipate
spade *n* : makinapte - makipapte *a shovel*
spring *n* : wícapsice *anything used to make one jump*
square *n* : mázawiyute *a carpenter's ~*
strainer *n* : - Cf filter
syringe *n* : mníwosli
telescope *or* scope *or* field-glass *n* : masiwanke
threshing machine *or* combine *n* : wínakanye *or* icapan
tongs *n* : maziyujipe
trap *n* : maz'iyugmunke *or* mas'igmunke
tree *n* : - Cf single-tree, double-tree
trowel *n* : tiicaskapi *or* tiakašluta
tweezers *n* : ištaȟeyušla
washboard *n* : wípaškite
wedge *n* : can'icašlece *or* icasleca *or* wícaslece
wheelbarrow *n* : wípaslohan
whetstone *or* razor strop *n* : míogle
wreckingbar *n* : wícaȟuge
wrench *or* screwdrive *or* drill *n* : maziyuhomni — wíyuhomni *a wrench* — wiiyúhlate *a pipe ~*

tooth *n* : hi - hiakigle *to set the teeth firmly* — hiipajaja *a toothbrush* — hiipašpu *to pick the teeth* — hiišta *the eyetooth* — hímaza *a gold tooth* — hinske *the front, the canine teeth* — híonah'ayela *showing the teeth* — hípašku *to pick the teeth* — hípsonpsonla *teeth on edge* — hiuya *to grow teeth, as do children* — híyazan *to have a toothache* - híyazanpi *a toothache* — híyuskablu *a dental powder*
toothpick *n* : heyotake ipašpu
top *n* : cánwacikiyapi *or* canyuwacikizapi *a toy top* - cányuwacipi *a top spun with two fingers* — hutiyagleya *from top to bottom* — ícitakignag *on top of each other* - itagnaka *to put one on top of the other* - itagnagye *placed one on top of another* - itakignag *with one on top of another* — ipa *the top of anything, as the high hill at the end of a ridge etc.* — pínkpa *the top e.g. of a tower*
topple *v* : kaptuja *to ~ over* — naitunkab *to ~ over backwards*
torch *n* : pelijanjanpi
tornado *n* : owámniomni *a cyclone*
toss *v* : pakapa *to bat e.g. a pitched ball* — paškehan *to toss aside, away*
totter *adv* : nat'ope s'e *in a tottering manner* — woháhayela *to make something ~ by shooting it* — wóškehan *to make something ~ and fall by shooting*

touch *va* : putaka *to ~ with the hand when bracing for a fall* - aputaka *to lay on hands* - aputagya *to make ~, or in a a way of touching* - iputaka *to kiss touching* - kputaka *to ~ one's own* - oputaka *to ~ in* — ayutan *to put the hand upon* - épatan *to touch with the hand, to feel* - éyutan *to go near and ~* - iglutantan *to ~ often* - iyatan *to ~ with the mouth* - kíciyutan *to ~ for one* - natan *to ~ or feel with the foot* - oyutan *to ~, to feel by hand* - yutan *to ~, to feel* — ékahtaka *to barely ~ there* - icahtagya *touching as a person leaning against a wall* - icahtaka *to come in contact on passing another* — igluš'inš'in *to tickle one's self repeatedly* — napiškan *to ~ with evil intent* - napiškankiya *to caress one* — pajunta *to ~, as hair in one's eyes* — yuni *to ~ one to call attention to something*
touchwood *or* **punk** *n* : cankagica *tinder*
touchy *vn* : wakiniya *to be or get out of humor*
tough *or* **hard** *adj* : sutá *durable, hardy, firm* - kasuta *to make ~ by pounding* — oyataka *to be ~ eating*
toward *adv* : aitkokib *facing toward* — tanyatakiya *toward one*
towel *n* : itepakinte *or* itipakinte
tower *n* : tiipasotka
town *n* : otonwahe, a village, a city - otonwahetu *at or to ~* — wašicuta *or* wašiyuta *at or to a white man's place of living*

toy *n* : inapiškanyanpi *or* wínapinškaye *or* wínapiškanye *toy, toys, playthings*
cík'ala škátapi *girls' toys, little playthings*
cunkšila *a toy bow and arrows*
hohuyuhmunpi *a boys' toy, i.e. a bone for tossing*
ipahotonpi *a pop-gun*
kinyekiyapi *a kite*
makapte *a toy clay buffalo*
makašunkawakan *a toy clay horse*
napobyapi *fire-crackers*
okawinȟela *a merry-go-round*
tate kahwogyapi *a toy let on water to drift with the wind*
unhcelapte *a toy cactus buffalo*
wanapohyapi *a balloon*

track *or* **trail** *n* : okaslohe — okasto *leaving a track* — oyé *a track, made by a foot etc.* - oyehan *to leave tracks* — oyuslohe *a mark left by dragging something* — oguhan *a track or trail*
trade *vn* : ítokiyopeya *to exchange*
tradition *n* : okiciyak aupi — wicocajeyate *traditions*
trail *v* : nacankuton *to make a ~* — ptántacanku *a ~ of small animals* — okaslohan *to leave a trail by dragging something along* - Cf track
train *v* : iglaonspe *to teach one's own* - kaonspe *to ~ or teach e.g. a horse* — uncihiya *to raise and ~ one to maturity*
tramp *n* : tókiiyaye s'a *a tramp, one who is gone always* — waun'unka *a vagabond*
trample *vn* : inablaska *to ~ under foot* — nakicija *to ~ out for* - nakija *to ~ one's own* — našnija *to kill* — nakicipan *to ~ for* — napan *to ~ out fine* — nakicisuta *to tread hard for one* — nawanica *to ~ to nothing, to destroy by trampling on, to evaporate* — onak'oza *to tread on and make hard* — onasto *to trample down and make bare*
transgression *n* : wókape
translate *v* : wayuieska *to interpret, or an interpreter* — wayuieskapi *an interpretation*
transport *v* : tokícikšu *to carry or port*
transverse *adv* : glakinyan

trap *v* : iyokalic'iya *to ~ in one's speech* — gmunka *to set a ~* - wagmunka *to ~ , to hunt with traps* - gmunk wacin *to think of trapping*
travel *vn* : ogligla *to go on a journey, make a trip* - oiglagya *travelling in* — wagligla *to ~ about* — wagligleca *a bum, one who is foot-loose* — oicimani *travelers, one's travelling* - ícimani *a single traveler* - oic'imani *a trip* — waomani *to ~ in snow* — iyunkel *travelling by foot* — okahwoka *a floater, a bum*
travois *n* : šun'onkonpa *or* šun'unkonpa *a pony or dog ~ i.e. a drag used for transport* — tušuheyunpi *the travois* — šunktacangleška *a carriage* — initiyuktan *a ~ booth for the transport of a baby*
treat *va* : iwištan *to ~ well e.g. the sick* — kiyúše *to maltreat one* — okih'anšunkeca *to ~ badly by depriving one of things* — ošung ihpeya *to ~ one badly, to maltreat one* — kúwa *to deal with one*
tree *n* : can - cangleglega *trees scattered* - can'ohlogeca *a hollow tree* - canpata *a clump of trees* - canpšunka *big and large trees* - canskiskeya *trees to grow in thickets* - canswoju *a grove of trees, a timber* - canšabšapa oju *trees standing against the bank of stream* - canwojupi *a tree nursery, a park, an orchard* - canohanzi *a bower*

KINDS :
apple tanspanhu can
ash psehte can - psehtin can *the green ash*
aspen can'itazipa
bass hínta
birch canhasan
boxelder canšuška
brambles canpepe
camomile cansinsila
cedar ȟante *or the* ȟanteša
cottonwood canyah'u *or* wágacan
dogwood canšaša *the red dogwood*
elm p'e
false indigo zintkalatacan
fig tamniohpi can *or* witanšnahu
hackberry agugugapi can *or* yamnumnugapi can
hawthorn taspanhu
hickory cansuhu
honeysuckle can'iskuye *or* cunwiskuya
ironwood ispanspanheca
lime and *linden* hínta
maple canhasan - Cf birch
mulberry canska
mushroom cannakpa
oak ituhu *the black oak* - útahu *the oak tree* - útahu can *oak wood, the burr oak and scrub oak*
pine wazi *or* wazican *the western pine*
poplar wahcinca
soft-wood cankap'ojela
spruce wazihcaka *the Black Hills spruce*
sumac canzi *or* can'unkcemna
walnut cansapa
willow cohwanjica *or* wahpepopa can *or* wahpewizilya *the sandbar willow*
wolf-berry zuzecatawote *or* ónšunk'nasapi hu

TREE PARTS :
bark canha *or simply* ha
bud cínkpa
resin canšin
sprout can'opamna
stump canpaksa
treetop cán'inkpa

TREE-RELATED EXPRESSIONS :
can'akansmiyan *to prune*
can'akit'a *with much brush*
cán'inkpata *at the top of a tree*
hánahpuhpu *to appear ready to peel bark, skin etc.*

trial *n* : wakiyapi *i.e. a ~ of a case*
tribe *n* : oyate *a group, a clan, tribe, nation, each distinguished as to the width and depth of social integration*
tributary *v* : oic'ipa *to be ~ to*
trick *v* : wakan'econ *to do tricks of jugglery* - wakan'econpila *magic and other tricks*
trickle *v* : š'éš'e
tricky *adv* : osinkpekpeyakel *in a ~ complicated way*
trifles *n* : - Cf trinkets
trigger *n* : inahpe *the ~ of a trap*
trim *or* **prune** *v* : kasnasna *to ~ , cut off* — oyus'o *to ~ off* — wapta *to ~ an edge* - wakicipta *to ~ off for one*
trinkets *n* : takuku *small articles* - takukukel *any or all sorts of things* - tákušnišni *or* tutka *trifles* — otutka *small articles, trifles, crumbs*
trip *v* : weiglak *to take a camping trip*
trippling *adv* : naoksaksala s'e *to be ~ along* — napsapsakela s'e *like a rope tearing apart, fig trippling along*
trite phrases *n* : wóštepi
triumph *v* : wakte *to kill in triumph* - iwaktekiyagla *to cause to go home in ~* — waktukiye *to come in triumph, or a triumph* - Cf kill
trot *v* : ikacancan *the trot of a horse* - kacancan *or* nacapcapa *to trot as a horse* - kacanglegleya *to stride* — yucabluzahan *to ~ rapidly, fast trotting as a horse*
trouble *v* : aiglušica *to make ~ for one's self* — hníyan *to be troubled, to have a stomachache* - hníyanyan *quaking for fear* - ihniyanyan *to be troubled with, to be excited about* — h'ánh'anka *one who creates disorder, an imp or villain* — iyagleic'iya *to get one's self into trouble, as a thief* — iyotiyekiya *to have or find something troublesome or hard* - iyotiyeic'iciya *to bring troubles on one's self* — nagiyeya *to vex, to bother, to trouble one* — pageya *threatening, bullyingly, troublesome* - wapageyeca *to cause trouble* — tókašniyan *without difficulties, untroubled* — wayuhika *troublesome, disturbing* — wópinta *causing ~ to one*
trough *n* : cankaškokpapi
truant *n* : kigle s'a *a stay-at-home person, esp a child* — wanajica *a run-away*
true *v* : wicaka *to be ~ , to speak in truth* - wicakala *to hold something to be true* - wicakaya *in truth* - awicaka *to tell the truth* - áwicakehan *truly, of a truth* - áwicakeya *truly* - áwicakeyahan *of a truth* - áwicakeyakel *in earnest* - iawicaka *to speak the truth* - iawicakehan *truly, in truth* - iewicaka *to tell the truth* - iewicakeya *truly* - tówicake *his truth or truthfulness* - wówicakeya *truthfully* - yawicakeyehci *making appear as true* - yuwicakeya *telling as true* — ehan'un *truly* - ehaš *certainly, truly* — itešniyan *indeed, in reality* — iton *to tell the truth* — itukaleš *truly, indeed* — waeyeca *to tell the facts*
trunk *or* **chest** *n* : can'opiye *a storage ~* — ognagnakapi *a chest*
trust *va* : awacin *confidence* - awacinpi *a thinking upon, a trusting in* - awakicin *to give one's attention to* - iwacinyan *to ~ in for or in ref to, or trustingly* - wacinkiya *to have confidence in* - wacinyanpi *confidence, trustiness* inakipa *to ~ in what makes for a good relationship with*

one's self — ínapeya *or* inápeya *trusting in* - kinihan *to have confidence in* — waceyapica *trustworthy* - zónta *honest, trustworthy*

truth *n* : - Cf true

try *v* : wakiya *to try a case* — okinica *to strive for, to try, attempt*

tub *n* : onunwe *a bathtub* — wóijajapi *a tub*

tube *adv* : nawoholyeya *in the shape of a tube*

tug *adv* : wayatiktil *tugging on something with the teeth*

tumble *v* : awocangle

tumult *n* : wawok'oya *to be tumultuous*

tune *or* **air** *n* : oahiyaye

turbid *adj* : šošá ~ *or muddy* - kašoša *to make* ~ - našoša *to make* ~ *or dirty* — kpukpa *full of dirt, mixed up*

turn *vn* : aicaptanptan *to roll over and over* - aigluptanyan *to turn over on or roll over on* - apaptan *to roll over on anything* - áptan *to roll over, as when shot* - áptanyan *to roll about or fall over on* - ayuptanptan *to turn or roll back and forth* - ayuptanyan *to turn or roll over on* - icaptankic'un *to roll over much, to roll about* - igluptan *to roll over* - ikpaptan *to turn one's self over, to roll over* - ikpaptanyela *in the manner of rolling over* - ipaptan *to turn over* - kaptanptan *to turn over and over* - kaptanya *to be upset* - paptan *to turn over* - woptányan *to turn over by shooting e.g. into a boat* - yaptanyan *to turn over with the mouth* — agluhomni *they all turn around to see* - ayuhomni *to turn around e.g. a gun on one* - yuhomni *to turn e.g. a grindstone* - iglahomni *to change one's own opinion* - igluhomni *to turn one's self around, to twirl* - igluhomniya *to cause one to turn himself around, fig to be converted* - ítohomni *to turn round, end around* - kíciyuhomni *to* ~ *around for one* - yuhomni *to* ~ *around, to turn e.g. a grindstone* — aopemni *to roll up in* - ayupemni *to twist or turn to one side on* — apagmigma *to roll over on* - iyugmigma *a rotator* — yueciya *to* ~ *inside out* — ayueciya *to* ~ *the wrong side out* — égluk̇šan *or* ékawinga *to turn arouind, to return* — iglamna *to* ~ *one's self arouind, to get back one's own, to gain one's own* — iyaglapšinyan *to* ~ *over upon upon anything* — naglapšunyan *to* ~ *bottom-up* — yaoglapšun *or* yuoglapšun *to* ~ *over* - yuoglapšunyan *turning over* — iyokawinga *to* ~ *round and round* - pawinhya *veering from a straight direction* — iyumni *that which turns* - namni *to* ~ *back, to return* - yumni *to* ~ *round something* - yumnimniyan *turning round and round* — katanblablas *on both sides of the back, to turn over and over as does a horse itching itself* — nahmin *to* ~ *outward* — paohaha *to* ~ *or flip over* — wanjitoktog *by turns, one by one* - unmatoktok *by turns one after another* - únmatoktok *by turns two by two* — yahaiyeya *to* ~ *aside with the mouth, to stagger* — yunakeya *to tip, to* ~ *on one side, to* ~ *over partly* — yuwaza *to rotate the hands as in running*

turtle *or* **tortoise** *n* : kéya *or* ke... - kecanh'a *a* ~ *smelling of wood* - keglezela *a spotted or striped* ~ - kéha *a tortoise shell* - keh'ánla *a small* ~ - kenunnuja *the soft-shell* ~ - képa *a tortoise head* - kes'amna *the stink turtle* - keškokpa *a species of* ~ - kéya *the large* ~ - kewoyuspa s'e *as a* ~ *dragged from the mud* — patkaša *or* patkašala *a small* ~ *that lives in water* - tatkaša *a species of* ~ *, the same as* keglezela, the mud-turtle

twin *n* : cekpa - cekapapi *twins*

twinkle *v* : - Cf shine

twist *adj* : pemni *warped, twisted, crooked, also, to warp, twist, to become crooked or entrangled* — ayapemni *to* ~ *esp with the mouth* - ayupemni *to* ~ *or turn to one side on* - kícipemni *to become twisted for one* - napemni *to* ~ *of itself* — ayaškopa *to make crooked or twisted by biting on* — ayuškopa *to make* ~ *or warp on anything* — kaškopa *to make crooked or twisted by striking* - naškopa *to* ~ *with the foot, or to* ~ *or become crooked of itself* — ayušuja *to sliver up on by twisting* - ayušušuja *to keep meandering* — gmun *twisted* - glugmun *to* ~ *one's own* - iciyugmun *to* ~ *together as two braids* - iciyugmunyan *twisted together* - pagmun *to* ~ *or roll up by hand* - kíciyugmun *to* ~ *for one* - kpagmun *to* ~ *one's own* - nakicigmun *to* ~ *for one* - nakigmun *to be twist* — íciyumnahe s'e *in various directions* — iyukin *to wrench, to pry* — oglapšun *to* ~ *off*

twitch *vn* : naka — céyanaka *to* ~ *under the eyes or about the mouth* - ištanaka *to have the eye* ~ *only once* — ínagnaka *to have the lips* ~ — ištanagnanka *to have the eye* ~ *repeatedly*

two *pron* : henayos *or* heniyos *or* henayoza *or* heniyoza *these two* - hénayuza *those two* - henáyuzakiya *or* heníyozakiya *these or those two times*

typewriter *n* : wówapiinahtagye *or* wínahtagye - nahtagya *to type e.g. a letter*

U

ugly *adj* : owanyangšica — tanšica *deformed*

umbrella *n* : oiyohanzi *an* ~ *erected on a wagon*

unable *v* : inakinta *to brush off for a reason, fig to be unable to finish a job* — iyejakakeš *unable or failing by a little* — okikpani *to be* ~ *for, to be impotent, to make* ~ - Cf able

unaided *vn* : akpaha *to be without help* — hoikceyakel *having not been educated or instructed, on the spur of the moment*

unarmed *adj* : iyayuscola

unbelief *n* : wacet'unglapi ~ or doubt

unchanging *adv* : yahomnipicašniyan *unchangeably*

unclean *adj* : wašepa

uncoil *vn* : nagla *to* ~ *of itself* - yaglagla *to unwind by mouth and stretch out* — yuglakiya *to make unroll or stretch out* - yuglaya *to cause to uncoil* - Cf coil

unconcerned *adv* : kas'alakel — tokecaca *unconcernedly* - toké ecáca *without specific purpose* - tókecakacel *for no reason* — wínkcekce *or* wínkcekceya *unconcerned, to no purpose*

uncouth *adv* : okišyakel *being uncouth, coarse, crude, heavy-handed*

uncover *adj* : zamnimni *uncovered* - zamniyahan without a cover - zamniyan *uncovered* - ayazamni *to open or uncover by speaking* - kazamni *to open* - kíciyuzamni *to open out or uncover for one* - yazamni *to* ~ *by mouth* — yuitešla *uncovering the face* - yuzamni *to* ~ *by pulling something away* - yuzamnihan *standing uncovered* — wakaajaja *to lay bare* — wakaašlaya *to uncover as by sweeping*

undaunted *adj* : hetonton *fearless, faces up to difficulties* - hetontonka *one who is steady and sturdy,* ~

undecided *adj* : wacinjata *hesitating* - wacinnunpa ~ *as to doing or not doing*

under *adv* : kul - kutanhan *from beneath or below* - hukuta *below, under, at the lowest place* — hukuya *at the lowest places* - ihukul *or* ihukuya ~ *or beneath, down be-*

low — ihutawab *prep or adv* : *downstream beyond, below, i.e. locally, at the end as of the month* — iyohlate *or* ohlate *under, beneath, underneath* - kahlate *below, undermining*

underbrush *adv* : can'akit'a *with much ~* — pazanyan *with the head beneath the bushes, as in sleeping*

understand *v* : iyukcan *to ~ or comprehend* - aglukcan *to ~ one's own upon or in relationg to* - iyukcankel *guessing* — wableza *to see clearly, understand* - aic'ibleza *to realize concerning one's self, to notice on one's behalf* - ibleza *to be enlightened about, as on waking* — okahniga *or* okicahniga *to understand or comprehend* - okiglahniga *to know and ~ what pertains to one's self* - okikahniga *to ~ one's own* - oglahniga *to ~ one's own affairs* - aokahniga *to ~ about* — aištaecelya *to catch a glimpse of* — aslolya *to know all about something* — owacinksapa *comprehending, intelligent, wise, understanding* - wacinton *to have understanding, have a mind of one's own, to be wise*

undo *va* : yuipahtu *to reverse*

unequal *adj* : aocikpani *uneven* - kaiyokpaniyan *unevenly* - kaocikpani *to make ~* - ocikpani *unequal in length* - wayaokpaniyan *to speak of as ~* — ociptetu *~ in length, space, time* - aociptetu *unequal, different* - aociptelya *not equal to, lacking* - kaocipteca — nah'eh'eyakel *unevenly* — ocihišnišniyan *unequally spaced or so in size* — onakikiyakel *unevenly as grass cut on a lawn* — wanwancašni *uneven as to size, kind, character, etc.*

unexpected *adv* : iyapakel *all of a sudden* — han'iyacinke *unexpectedly during the night* — kanšnišnilak *not to expect one*

unfold *vn* : kagla *to ~ of itself, to stretch out to full length, to uncoil*

unfortunate *vn* : íksapa *to be occupied with many things*

unfurl *va* : yublaga *to spread out*

uniform *or* **alike** *adv* : ókiwanjila *always, continually*

unimpeded *adv* : okawatonyan *without hindrance or obstruction, also in ref to weather, hence in clear weather*

unimportant *n* : ah'eca *things of minor importance*

unite *v* : ayukca *to untie* — ikoyaka *to stick or adhere to* - ikoyagya *to make adhere to, adhering to* - icikoyagya *to fasten one to another, sticking together* - icikoyaka *to be adhering together, fastened together* — ícipaja *dove-tailed, inserted, laminated, fitted* — íciyakaška *to tie or untie things mutually* - íciyaglaška *to ~ together another of one's own* - íciyaiglaškapi *they ~, bond together as man an wife* — kíyakiju *to unite* - ókiju *to have a reunion, be reunited* — kókiciyas'in *uniting, sticking together, tied together, flowing together as at a confluence* - ókiciyas'in *together united in copulation* — kokiyuhci *to make e.g. two holes into one by tearing out what separates them* - wóokiju *unity*

universal *pron* : ... eša *or* ... ešaš *or* ... šaš - Note: one of these follows the *pron* expressed, as in *táku ke eša* anything, whatever

unkempt *adj* : nahpihpiya *slouchy* — pehintuta *dishevelled* — póha *hair aflying or to make the hair stand* - pó haha s'e *shaking as would a buffalo shaking its head* - póha s'e *having bushy hair* — pšapša s'e *disorderly, ragged, dishevelled*

unnoticed *adv* : oslolyapišniyankel *not recognized* — tántan'inšniyan *in a way ~* — wamakamani šni *suddenly and ~ not having one's footsteps heard*

unpleasant *vn* : ašica *to become bad, unpleasant on or for* - ašicaya *or* ašicayakel *unpleasantly* - oašica *disagreeable* - oašilya *not standing well on, not up to standard* - ošicecake *rainy and unpleasant in ref to weather or country*

unravel *va* : yuswa

unrestrained *adj* : okiun šíca *hard to handle, as a lively horse or a child tossing about*

unrestricted *adv* : oikpaptanwašteya *rolling back and forth, as is said of one who doubts*

unroll *or* **untwist** *v* : kagla *to uncoil or unfold* - kícagla *to ~ for one, or to fall out* - yugla *to untwist, uncoil; stretch, unwind*

unscathed *adv* : tanyekel *whole, without injury*

unsettle *va* : yuhahalab

unsociable *adv* : ot'inhyakel *unsociably*

unsteady *adj* : ptanptan *rocking* - ptanptanla *unsteady in mind* — apajejeya *likely to fall, ~ at standing*

unsubstantial *vn* : tantonšni *~ as are certain foods* - tantonšniyan *unsubstantially, destitute of*

unsuccessful *v* : wawokpani *to be unlucky*

untangle *adv* : okakseya *hard to untangle*

untie *va* : ayakca - kcawahan *to come untied* — ayugla *to uncoil or untwist* — iyuška *to use to ~* - naška *to ~ by foot, or to come untied of itself* - naškahan *or* naškawahan *untied, loose* - yaška *or* yaškeškeke *to ~ by mouth, i.e. with the teeth* - yuška *to loosen*

until *adv* : lehinyagleya *until this day*

untrained *adj* : watogla *wild, skittish*

unused *vn* : yuowišni *to be ~ and thus to accumulate*

unwilling *adv* : mak'eyake s'e *apparently ~* — taunkašni *to be ~ to do* — t'ungyakel *unwillingly* - tawat'elyešni *unwilling to do or suffer*

up *or* **upward** *or* **on high** *adv* : iyuwanka *up, in an upward position* - kawankab *upward* - kawakaka *jolted up and down, bounced* - wankatu *or* wankal *up above* - kawankalwapa *a little up* - pawankal *upward, up high* - wankaltkiya *upwards, uphill* - wankatkiya *upward* — owoslal *straight up* - Cf high, height

uphill *adv* : kaiyakapteya *or* wankaltkiya

upper *v* : payapa *to be of the upper part*

upright *n* : wóiyecetu *honesty, uprightness* — iwosla *in an ~ manner* — woslá *~ or straight up, erect* - wosláhan *~, up* - wosláta *on end* — katowotanla *knocked upright*

uproot *va* : ayujun *to pull out* — kaju *to ~ something* - kíciyujun *to pull up by the roots for one* — ayupšun *to pull out by the roots on, to extract as teeth*

upset *vn* : iwasaza *to take hard, to get sick over* — kaptanyan *to cause to fall over* - naptanyan *to ~ by kicking*

upside-down *adv* : aglapšunyan *or* íyaglapšinyan *bottom upwards*

upstream *adv* : ínkpata *at the head, source, at any head* - íkpatahan *from the end or head of e.g. a stream* - ínkpatakiya *toward the top, upstream* - ínkpatakiyalas'e *upstream, toward the head of a stream* — tatowapa *upstream, up-river, up-wind*

urge *va* : pa *to push one* — wawiyopaštaka *to ~ one on* — iyonatan *to ~ one on, as with the foot*

urine *n* : taleja - léja *or* leš *to urinate or hold one's own urine* - léjapišni *inability to urinate* - oleja *to urinate in* - Cf excrete

use *va* : iwaši *to employ for a purpose* — un *to use* - nun *you use or have for use* — sóta *used up, gone, hazy* - agluso-ta *to use up one's own on* - aiglusota *to use up one's own, or to go all the way, to migrate* - awosota *to use all up by shooting upon* - iglusota *to use up one's own or one's self* - iyusota *to use all up with or for* - kíciyusota *to use up for one* - kasota *to use up, as by felling trees, by killing off cattle, by men falling in battle, or by the weather clearing off* - okasota *to destroy* - kísota *to use for* - oki-sota *to be used up, all are gone* - osota *they are all gone* - solya *to have used up e.g. one's wood supply* — apotan *used up on one, worn out as a coat on* — hékicinakeca *to have used up all to or for one* — peaglatata *or* wójuhaglatata *to exhaust one's supply giving it away* — šwéka *having used up everything, become "broke"*

useful *adj* : tokónpiça *good for something* — itanyešni *to be useless*

utensils *n* : - *i.e. in cooking and in use on the table* :

wíyatke *cup*
tatokahe cinška *dipper*
wícape *or* wícabwotapi *or* wícabyutapi *fork*
mílapaksa *knife*
iyuze *or* wícaȟepa *ladle*
mniognake *pitcher*
wíkalye *pot for tea or coffee*
wíyatke aglehe *saucer*
mniskuyaognake *shaker for salt*
wícacan *or* wíyucan *sieve*
cinška cík'ala *teaspoon*
cinška túkila *spoon from clam shell*
ptehecinška *spoon from buffalo or cow's horn*
mazakinška *or* maskinška *or* mazkinška *or* kinška *a metal spoon*

V

vacant *vn* : ocokaka *to be a vacancy*

vaccinate *v* : kago - kícago *to ~ one's own*

vacillate *adj* : oietatuyeyeke *or* tatuyeke *to waver or fluctuate* — psanpsanka *easily changing views*

vain *adv* : itokašniyan *in ~ , without reason* — makoškan *for naught, in ~* - itumakoskan *to no purpose* — otanla *to be vain, or to be attached to* — otuhci *in vain, for nothing* - ituhci *gratuitously* - otuya *groundlessly* - otuyacin *at random, for nought*

valley *n* : oblaye — osmaka *a ravine* - Cf gulch, hollow, plain

valuable *adj* : yušpika *worth buying or keeping, or a valuable thing*

value *va* : tákukiya *to ~ one's own* — teȟila *to love, to ~ one highly* - teȟikekila *to love one's own* - teȟikila *to ~ much* - tekiciȟila *to hold precious*

vanish *v* : kíwanice *to turn to nothing* — šníyeca *to ~ , to fade away*

variety *n* : watokeca *a ~ of things* — wanlwanlwancašniyan *in great variety*

varnish *n* : wíziye

veer *v* : gluna s'a *to go fowl as a ball when struck turns, veers suddenly in its course*

vegetable *n* : wójuhala *a vegetable pod* — Pangi Tankinkinyan Wakpala *the Great Artichoke Creek*

SOME VEGETABLES :
pangi *artichoke*
omnica *bean* - makatomnica *wild bean* - makomnicahu *earth bean* - omnica tankinyan *large bean*
pangipepe šaša *or* tínpsinla šaša *beet*
wahpeyutapi *cabbage*
tínpsinla zizi *carrot*
wagmeza špankagapi *green corn dried* - Cf grain
omnicahu *legumen*
wahpeinkpajiji *lettuce* - Note: the blue lettuce reminds one of a very hairy insect, *wabluškahinšma iyececa*
pšin *onion, leek* - pšinšicamna *wild onion* - pšinhubloka *poison onion, luks*
Šahiyela tatinpsinla *parsley*
pangihanska *parsnip*
omnicagmigmi *pea*
blo *potato*
pangipepe šaša *or* tínpsinla šaša *raddish* - Cf *beet*
unjinjintka *tomato* tínpsila *or* tinpsinla skaska *a turnip*

vegetation *n* : watoka

veil *n* : iteakahpe *a face cover*

vengeance *n* : watokiconpi *retaliation* - watogya *to take ~ on* - watogyapi *reprisal* - tokicic'on *to take ~ on for* - tokic'un *to revenge, take revenge on*

verse *n* : ošpe *a saying, a sentence* - Cf piece

very *adj* or *adv* : lila *or* liglila *or* lilahci *or* lilakel — iyotan *most, very great* — *postp* or *suff* : hca *or* hcahca *or* hcin *or* hcaka *or* hce *or* hci *very* — aiyuȟeya *extremely, wonderfully* — ícat'a *very* — tan... *very* — ...la *or* ...ka *or* ...lahcaka *or* ...lahcakaka *very*

Viaticum *np* : - Cf sacrament

victim *va* : wóunyeya *to have for a ~*

victory *n* : oohiye

vigilant *v* : nagiksabic'ila *to consider one's self ~*

villain *n* : wicowicašašni *one who is no-man*

vindicate *n* : wayuskapi *one who is vindicated, proved right*

vine *n* : can'iyuwi *or* can'iyuwiwi *or* canwiyuwi *or* iyuwi *or* wiyuwi *vine* - oyuwi *vine-like*

vinegar *n* : minískuya *or* mnískuya

violate *v* : wahtani *to ~ a law*

violent *adv* : ošungšungye *violently* - Cf much

virgin *n* : hokšiwinla *a ~ according to the flesh, having had no husband* — winyan cokab ti win *a woman who lives among women* — witanšna un *a woman who always lives alone*

visible *vn* kitán'in *to appear, to be visible for* - kitán'inšni *to be invisible, to be lost for* — okopeya *seen as through a hole* wanyangpica *visible* - owanyankešniyan *invisibly* — ozanyela *only a little ~*

vision *n* : owanyanke - wakanya wówanyanke *a sacred vision*

visit *v* : **hosanpata ya** *to go visiting* — tikicii *to visit one another* - tilehanyang ya *to pay one a visit* — tiunma k'el ya *to go visiting* — íci-mani *a traveler* - ícimanipi *traveling or visiting* — wankiciyankapi *to see one another, or a visit*

vivacious *adv* : otantonyan *vivaciously, lively, excited*

voice *n* : hóbu *a rough unpleasant ~* - hógahan *a rough loud ~* - hógata *or* hóȟapa *a rough ~* — hokiiyokpaza *to speak indistinctly* - hópiza *a small squeaking ~* - hó tanka *a great or loud ~* - hógluwankal with a high pitch ~ - hópiskiya *to speak with a squeaking ~* - hóš'agya *or* hótankakiya *or* hótankaya *with a loud or great ~* — hówašteya *to have a fine ~ , or speaking well*

void *va* : yujuju *to make ~ e.g. an agreement*

vomit *va* : glépa *to puke* - aglepa *to ~ on* - akigleglepa *to ~ on one's own on reaching home* - glebkiya *to cause to ~* - iglebkiya *to cause to ~ what one had eaten* - igleglepa *to ~, throw up, what one had eaten* - kaglepa *to make one throw up*

vote *n* : wówapioihpeya

vow *v* : awasuic'iya *to make a pledge* — wíic'iglukcan *to make a ~, a promise, a resolution* — wóiglaka *to declare one's purpose*

V-shape *n* : yušun'onpa *as the spread of two fingers, or the leges, or the branching stick or tree*

W

wad *v* : imnicoyapa *to use for wadding*

wade *va* : copá *to go into water* – acopa *to ~ into water for something* – copekiya *to make one ~ in water* — waayus'o *to ~ in after something*

wag *v* : sintonpsanpsan *or* sitonpsan *or* sintupsanpsan *fig or* situpsan *or* yupsanpsan *to wag the tail*

wage *n* : wíši *pay, remuneration* – wíšikahya *in lieu of wages* – wíšiton olotapi *a hireling* – wíšitonyan *for wages* – wíšiyukeya *for payment* — iyuwin *one's pay* — okamna *earnings*

wagon *n* : canpagmiyanpi – cankincipagmiyan *or* canpagmiyanpi hugageca *a ~ without a box* – canpagmiyanpi cík'ala *a buggy without a top* – canpagmiyanpi hununpa *a two-wheeled cart* – canpagmiya tànka *a lumber ~* – canpagmiyanpi cankahu *the underboard* – canpagmiyanpi hugmiyan *a wagon wheel* – canpagmiyanpi ihupa *a wagon pole* – canpagmiyanpi ipahunhunze *a wagon spring* – canpagmiyanpi škokpa *a wagon box* – canpagmiya ipatan *a spoke* – canpagmiyanpi oaye *a train*

wail *v* : wicakicilowan — wíwakonza *to ~ for those at war*

waist *adv* : pagoptan *around the ~*

wait *v* : ahanhepiic'iya *to ~ until night overtakes one* — apé *to ~ or hope for one* – aiyape *to lie in wait for* – akicipe *to wait for one* – akipe *to ~ for or expect one* – apekiya *to cause to ~ for* – gliape *to ~ one's coming home* – hiape *to await one's coming* – iyakipe *to ~ for, to befall one, to happen to* – iyakipeya *waiting for* – íyape *to ambush one* – iyapeya *to cause or have one lie in wait for* – kiápe *to ~ until one reaches home* – yeape *to ~ for one to come along* — ayuhel *waiting for* — glucantat'u yanka *to have to ~ long for something impatiently* — Itohínyanka yo *Well, wait!* – Itohiyanki yeto *Well now, wait!* — kta *to ~ for one to act* – ktáka *to wait on one to act* – owakta *to ~ for, look out for one* – waihakta *to make one ~ and follow* – wawiwaktaya *to make ~ for*

wake *n* : ahankiktapi *a wake, a watch for the dead*

waken *or* **awaken** *va* : ayuȟica *to awaken one upon* – agluȟica *to ~ one's own upon* – gluȟica *to wake up one's own* – igluȟica *to ~ one's self* – oikpaȟica *to come awake* – wakaȟica *to ~ one by striking* – wanaȟica *to ~ with the foot* – wayuȟica *to cause one to ~* — éyugica *to awaken right there* – ikpagica *to awake one's self* – kagica *or* kaȟica *to wake up by striking* – nagica *to ~ one by foot* – yagica *to ~ one by talking* – yugica *to arouse one from sleep* — ayanbic'iya *to keep awake all night for some purpose* – ayanpa *to spend a sleepless night* — kikta *to be awaken, to awaken from sleep* – hankikta *to wake while it is still night* — kagopa *to strike one asleep, to awake one partly and make snore* — nonhkatiya *to ~ one with a sudden noise* – otuyubleza *to ~ one by shaking*

walk *v* : máni – mániye s'e *as though taking a ~* – ákatinmàni *to walk moving the arms sideways outstretched on, as in measuring* – amani *to ~ on* – hanmani *to walk in the night, not to understand* – han'omani *to ~ at night* – ȟemani *to ~ on dry land* – htaomani *to ~ about at night* – imani *to ~ to or for a thing* – ímani *to go home* – omani *to ~ in according to, or one's travel* – omaniyan *to go on a ~ or trip* – omaniyankel walking — onaslata *to ~ slowly* – oomani *a sidewalk* – amakini *to walk or travel on one's own* – wamanika *one who likes to ~* — anahaha *to ~ or run noiselessly after one* — ayuceka *to make stagger on any place* — cahanskaska máni *to take long steps in walking* — cah'ali *to ~ on ice* — cákazigzitkiya *to make large strides* — gegeic'iyela *pacing back and forth* — icopa *to wade in, as in moccasins*

wallow *vn* : paptanptan *to ~ about* — ptemakokawaze *or* pteówaci *a buffalo ~*

wampum *n* : wíyokihehela

wander *v* : núni *to roam about, rove, miss the road* – onuni *to ~ in* – onuniya *to cause to ~ in* – onuniyata *wandering* – wayuwignuni *to make wander* — oyumni *to roam or rove about*

want *v* : kajinica šni *to be apparently not in want of anything* – Cf desire, insufficient, lack

war *vn* : zuyá *to make war* – ákiciyuza *to make ~ on one another* – azuya *or* azuyeya *to go to war against a people* – ozuye *a war, warparty, an army* — okicize *a fighting a battle, a war* — waktoglaka *to tell over one's military exploits* — wayaka *a captive or prisoner* — wapaha *a feather headdress* – wápaha *a staff used as a standard, flag, or banner* — wapáha iyusloheton *a headdress with one trailing tail* – wapaha mima *a headdress without a tail* – wapaha okijata *a headdress with two tails* – wapaha yuslohe *a headdress trailer*

warble *v* : wahognugnu *to yodel*

ward *or* **drive off** *n* : ocankoze *a warding off*

warm *adj* : káta – akalya *to cause to heat upon* – akata *to be hot on* – aokata *to be ~ on* – iglakata *to ~ one's self by moving the arms* – iyokataya *by heat* – iyokata *to be ~ inside as from liquor* – okataya *to make hot in* – okaltkiya *towards a ~ place* – petokali-c'iya *to ~ one's self at a fire* – petokalya *to ~ up a fire* — cóza *warm, comfortable* – coscoza *oppressive in warmth* – acosya *warmly* – acoza *to be warm on, to be comfortable* – aicoza *to be ~ on or with* – ayucoza *to make ~ on a place* – cosic'iya *to ~ one's self* – cosya *to cause to ~ a thing* – cos'igluza *to dress up warmly one's own or one's self* – glacoza *to ~ by striking* – icosya *to make ~ with* – icoza *to be ~ with clothing* – iglaocoza *to make one's self ~ by moving the arms* – igluocoscoza *to make one's self ~ by wearing much clothing* – iyocoza *to be ~ in as in a coat* – kacoza *to make ~ by striking* – naic'iocoza *to warm one's self by running* – ocoza *to be ~ in as in a house well built, or the warmth or heat* – pacoza *to make ~ by rubbing* — amašte *to be ~ on* – amašteic'iya yanka *to sit to sun and ~ one's self* – amaštenaptapta *rays in the sun, to one's self appearing on the ground's surface to be unsteady* – amaštet'a *to have a sun-stroke* – amašteya *exposed to the heat of the sun* – amašteyakel *hotly* — t'éca *lukewarm, tepid* – t'écaya *still warm as one dead* – at'éca *lukewarm as water* – it'éca *slightly ~, i.e. in ref to fluids only* – it'elya *to make tepid* – iškan *to move for a purpose, as to warm something* – kas'akiya *to extend one's hands over as over a stove to warm them*

warn *adv* : kaiyab *without warning*

warp *or* **twist** *vn* : naopa *to draw together as does a flower that shuts up* - paopo *to push and make a hollow place, to warp* — pemni *warped* — wapaškopa *to become warped*
wart *n* : wicošpi
wash *va* : apajaja *to ~ by rubbing or mopping on* - ayujaja *to wash on* - éiglujaja to ~ one's self right there - glujaja *to wash one's own* - icajaja *to wash by shaking* - iglujaja *to ~ one' self* - iyujaja *to ~ with* - jajahan *to be in need of washing* - kajaja *to ~ away* - kícipajaja *to ~ out* - kíciyujaja *to ~ for one* - kiyújaja *to ~ for another* - kpajaja *to ~ out one's own* - najaja *to ~ by trampling on* - napoyujaja *a wash basin* - onajaja *to cleanse or ~ out e.g. clothes by boiling* - ón'iglujajapi *a basin* - owayujaja *a tub* - wojája *a washtub* - wójajapi a *washing* - yujaja *to ~ clothes* — kasepa *to ~ off* — mniohpaya *or* ópsunpsun *to rinse* — pašpu *or* wapašpa *to ~ out stains* — woská *to ~ off by the rain*
waste *n* : igluwahpanica *one who is a spend-thrift, a squanderer* — inapiškan *to squander, to ~ things foolishly* — oyuponwaya *to scatter and thus waste*
watch *or* **attend** *v* : awanglakato oversee, take care of one's own - iwan'iglaka *to look at one's self* - wanyanka *to see* - awankiciyanka *to ~ or oversee for one* - awanyanka *to keep an eye on* - awanyangkiya *to cause to attend to or oversee* - awankiciyanka *to ~ for one* - iwankiciyanka *to give surveillance to* - iwanyanka *or* iwanyank *to look at, to surveil, examine, to spy on, to watch one* - iwanyangya *being careful* - owanyangšica *to be hard to ~* — íyakita *to keep ~ on* - wákita *to ~ out for* — ihakta *to be intent upon, to guard, to follow, obey, to regard highly or with love* - ihaktaya *to cause to have regard for, having regard for* — ištiyagna *closely watching, observing* — iyableza *to be on the ~ for something* - wáwanke *a watchman* — wayunka *to stand over and ~*
water *n* : mni *or* miní - imnija *full of ~* - mniali *to travel over the ~* - mnihaha *to run with ~* - mniohcaya *full of ~* - mniyosniya *to cool water*

BODIES OF WATER:
mniowamniyomni *an eddy*
mniowanca *or* mniwanca *an ocean, a sea*
mniskanmni *melted snow*
mniwancaokahmin *a bay, a gulf*
mniyušpala *a puddle*
mniyušpaye *a pool*
mniap'eyela *a shallow*
mnicapi *a well, a spring* — mnioicu *a made welli*

WATER FLOWING:
mnicaluza *rapid flow*
mnicašniyanyanla *rippling flow*
mnihiyaya *flooding flow* — mniokablaya *inundation*
mnitan *a flood*
wiwila *a spring*

TOOLS:
mniapahta *a skin bottle*
mniiwosli *a spout*
mniiyuhlogyapi *a flume*
mniiyusli *a faucet* — mniyutajapi *a pump, a faucet*
mnioškokpa *a gutter*
mnipasli *or* mnipatajapi *or* mniptaje *a pump*

MISCELLANIOUS:
kaištaminihanpi *to make eyes water*
mniapahta *to bottle water*
mnic'a *to dig for water*
mnil *in the water*
mniyapatanhan *by the water, river*
mniyušpašpayela *in puddles of water*
mnicagla *by the water*
mnicaškilyela *soaked with water*
mnih'eh'eyela *with dripping water*

wave *n* : tája *waves of water, or rough as agitated water* - kataja *to make rough, i.e. the water's surface* — mnikahmun *the roar of waves* — kakicipehan *to form waves* - mnikakicipehan *rolling waves* - mnitate *waves* — maštenaptapta *a ~ of hot air* — kahwoka *to ~ e.g. a flag in the wind* — kayeya *to ~ a blanket* — kóza *to ~ a signal* - mniakaštan *to pour or spill ~ on*
waver *v* : wayahahayela *to make falter, hesitate* - wayahahake *one that makes ~ by biting*
wax *n* : gageca *dross, scum, waste matter* — ginginca *ear ~* — tuhmungawigli *bees' ~*
way *or* **direction** *adv* : hétkiya *or* kátkiya *in that direction* - létkiya *or* lecetkiya *in this way* - leciyotan *in this way, direction* - onamniyeta *being off on one's own way* — otokiyotan *a way i.e. to travel* — ocanku *a roadway* — tuktognakel *in no way*
we *pron* 1st *pers pl* : - Cf I
weak *adj* : ahtata *feeble* - ahahtatešniyan *non-stop, without rest* — bleca *getting poorer and poorer as from sickness* - blebleca *with or in declining health* — húnkešniya *to render powerless* - ohunkešni *to be ~* — hustaka — hpéla *weak* — htata *or* htateca *languid, ~* — tónla s'e un *to be unwell and idle* — wankala *tender, easily torn or broken* — wašagkiciya *to make ~ for* - waš iyeya *to find weaker than one's self*
weapon *n* : wípe

WEAPONS:
ikute *ammunition*
wótawe *armor consecrated, or a charm*
hinajin *the arrow jaws holding the point* - histola *an arrowhead without barbs* - míwostake *a weakness of an arrow for me, i.e. with a blunt head* — kehuku *an arrowhead, diamond-shaped* — keston *an arrowhead,* barbed
canmilokatanpi *or* mítahe *a battle-axe*
icunkšila *a toy bow* - itazipa *the common bow* - takanitazipe *a bow overlaid with sinew* - takintazipa *or* titazipe *his bow*
kiínyeyapi *bowshot*
mázasu *bullet*
wahinša *a cap*
suto *a cartridge loaded*
hútela *a pistol*
cahli *gunpowder*
napakaha *a wrist guard*
ikteka *a killing instrument*
mázasuišloya *a lead smelter*
oyutanwankala *a powder loader*
mázasuiyokaštan *the bullet mold*
pahuzi *an old-time pistol*
mázawakan *or* íwogaga *or* sušašala *a rifle*
sukpanla *a shotgun*
išakpe *a six-shooter pistol*
ikancola *or* wahukeza *a spear or lance*
miwakan *a sword*
canhpi *tomahawk*
iyutan *a trigger*

cannaksa *or* ínyankapemni *a warclub* — tahezeze *a horn club to kill little animals*
iyopuhli *wadding*

ET CETERA :
hitakanyuwi *to bind the arrowhead on a shaft*
hiwajatapi *the arrowhead jaws*
napiyun *or* napinyun *without weapons*

wear *va* : icoma *or* icomi *to clothe, draw up around* — in *or* un *to ~ around the shoulders* — nap'in *to ~ around the neck* — únkiya *to make one ~* — kic'un *to put on, wear e.g. a hat* — koyaka *to ~ something* — mignáka *to ~ about the loins* - pégnaka *or* pegnagkiya *to ~ in the hair* - óglunge *to put on, ~ one's own* — ohan *or* oton *to put on, to ~ e.g. socks* — owin *to ~ ornaments as a pin or earrings etc.* — póštan *to ~ a head-covering* — *n* : *a hood or cloak with a hood* — tešlaka *to ~ about the head* - tešlagton *to ~ a fillet around the head* — onahloka *to ~ holes in* - inahloka *to ~ a hole with the foot* - opahloka *to pierce or wear holes in* — tépa *to ~ off* - tepahan *wearing off, worn off* - apatepa *to ~ off short, as in using a pencil* - atébtepaheyakel *tattered, threadbare, worn short* - atepahan *worn off short on* - ayutepa *to ~ off on* - glatepa *to ~ off one's own, as one's teeth* - iyutepa *to be worn out by anything* - oyutepa *to wear off* - katepa *to ~ out by itself striking against* - natepa *to ~ off with the foot one's shoes or a horse's hoof, worn off or out, worn short* - patepa *to ~ off by rubbing, or ~ out by pressure, as by a spring* - wotépa *to ~ off short by shooting e.g. an arrow* — ašpahan *threadbare, worn out* — ayupota *to ~ out on, to tear to pieces or destroy on* - inapota *to ~ out one's moccasins* - kíciyupota *to ~ out for one* - nakicipota *to ~ out e.g. shoes for one* - nakpota *to ~ out one's own shoes* - napota *to ~ out by foot* — húte *worn dull, as an axe* - kahute *to ~ to a stump* — icahci *to ~ out and come off* - icahciya *to make come off by wearing out* — inajapa *to ~ out the tip of one's shoes* — inapta *to ~ out one's shoes* — inašloka *to ~ through or ~ out* — kahunta *to ~ out gradually* — kakonta *to fray, ~ out thin* - nakonta *to ~ out* - pakonta *to ~ out partly , to fray* - yakonta *to ~ out chewing e.g. a rope etc.* - yukonta *to ~ out from handling* — kuka *worn out as clothes* - kakuka *to ~ out by striking* - nakuka *to ~ out with the feet* - pakuka *to ~ out handling* — wanakukeca *one who is hard on shoes* — kipacica *to ~ off or out* — nasota *to use up with the feet* — tannini *worn out* - wakatanni *to ~ out by striking* — yusepa *to rub or ~ off skin etc.*
weary *adj* : stáka *or* stusta *tired out, exhausted* - stusteya *wearily, tired out, or to weaken one* — wówatuka *weariness* - watuka *~, exhausted*
weather *adj* : mašte *hot and unpleasant, damp and rainy climate* - mašteosni *clear and cold* — otate *climate or a clime*
weave *va* : opazan *to interlace, braid, plait* - okpazan *to ~ one's own into* — zúnta *woven together* - kazunta or kazonta *to ~ together* - onazon *to weave* — oblotopason *to weave four strings* - obloyamnilason *to weave three strings* - oson *to braid something, or a braid of hair*
web *n* : iktomi tawogmunke *a spider's web*
wedge *v* : kaokajayata *to get wedged in* - Cf tool
weed *n* : canhloh suta *a woody sort of ~* - canhloh šlušluta *tall and slick weeds* — iwízilye *incense* — magayušla *or* mah'yušla *to ~ a field* — waptaye *a weed in general* — watušetka *withered weeds*
weep *adv* : ohowakanyankel *weeping in sorrow* - Cf cry

weigh *v* : kaospeya *or* kaspeya *to ~ , to ~ down* - kaospeyeton *to ~ anything* - kaspeyela *rather heavy* — tkeiyuta *to try, to feel for weight* - tkeuta *to ~ anything* - otkeyute *a weight*
welcome *v* : cokanhiyuic'iya *to come uninvited, to thrust one's self into* — Hókahe! *Come join us! Welcome all!*
well *n* : ominíowe *a dug ~* - miníoicu *a well* — ihoeceš *just as well* — ito *Come! or Well now!* — kinaš *Well then !* — oigluha *to be well off* — osutonyan *fairly well* — picáya *or* wakicoyakel *well done* — ahecelya *fairly well* — oáhececa *pretty well* — opiye *to make one well or to mend* - pikiciya *to make one well* - wapiyahci *in a sound way* — itanyan *well done* - otanyan *to be ~ , feeling no pain* - tantan *very well, nicely, good* - tanyan *well done* - tanyakel *or* tanyekel *or* tanyela *nicely done* — tanyehci *very well* - tanyeni *not well* — tókecašni *recovered, nothing the matter* — akisniyan *getting well* — kawašte *to make well, make perfect*
wet *vn* : spáya *to be ~ as in one's clothes* - aspaya *to become wet on* - ayaspaya *to wet with the mouth* - ipaspaya *to become wet as in sitting on the ground* - kaspaya *to moisten by sprinkling* - kispaya *to be or become wet for one* - naspa *to get wet* - oyuspaya *to make wet with the hands in* - paspaya *to make wet* - stanka *or* stan *moist* - ayastanka *to moisten by mouth* - ícastanka *to moisten the mouth* - kastanka *to moisten by pounding* - nastanka *to moisten with the feet* — ayasto *to lick smooth on* — nahpanyan *to moisten with a foot* - ohpan *to be wet in* - ohpankiya *to wet or soak in* - ohpanyan *to soak e.g. a wash in water* - ohpankiya *to dabble, splash gently* — totopa *all wet*
wheat *n* : aguyapi *a ~ bread*
wheel *n* : cangleška *a hoop, or round, wheel-like* — hugmiyan *or* hukagmiya *a wagon wheel* — hulazata *the hind wheels* — icahomni *a wheel* — kamima *to form a ~* — akawinga *to ~ about,round and round as an eagle glides*
when *adv conj* : cána *or* cánna *or* cánnahan *or* can *whenever* — kinhán *or* cinhán *if when* — k'onhán *or* k'unhán *or* c'onhán *when, in ref to past time* — ehantanhanš *or* ehantanš *if being equivalent to when* - hantanhanš *when that is the case, i.e. if that is the case* — héceca kin *if so, when* - hécinahan *if it is so* — kinahán *if or when* — tohán *or* tohánl *when or where*
where *adv* : ítoki *or* ítokiya *or* ítokiyapa *or* ítokiyapatanhan *or* ítokiyatanhan *whither, where or which way from* — tóhan *or* tohán *when* - tohanyankel *to where, how far* — tókel *somewhere, whithersoever, as* - tókelkiyatanhan *where, from what direction, or on or from what side* — tókeni *whereas, by no means* — tóki *somewhere* - tókiyani *or* tukteni ... šni *nowhere* — tuktetu ka keš *wherever*
whet *va* : yuhtanyan *to ~ or do a rough edge* - izuza *a whetstone, a grindstone*
which *pron* : tukte e k'eyaš *whichever, anybody* - watukte *~ or whichever*
while *adv* : ican *or* icunhan — kaetulake el *in a little while* — nakenula *for a short time* — ociscila *for a little time*
whine *adv* : zankel *whimpering* - azangzanka *to ~ as do some babies* — hókapsanpsan ià *to whine* — kínja *to ~ for food*
whip *n* : iyusaka *a gad* - kasaka *to switch, whip* - yusaka *to snap a ~ to to work off its stiffness* — iyuskapa *to crack and strike with a ~* - yuskapa *to crack a whip* — kapsinta *to scourge, flog* - yupsinpsinta *to ~ some-*

thing - icapsinte *or* wicapsinte *a whip* — icaȟape *a driving whip* — ptepsinta *a blacksnake whip*
whirl *v* : awocangle *to ~ and tumble, to ricochet* — kaomnimni *to ~ around* - wamniomni *a whirlwind or whirlpool, a hurricane* - yumnimni *to turn round and round* - oyupemni *to whirl*
whiskers *n* : pehin - Cf hair
whisper *v* : oji to ~ about one - jiji *to whisper* - jijilowan *to sing in a low voice* - jijiyahan *whispering* - okiciji *to whisper to one another* - wawoji *to tell secretly* - wawojiji *to ~, or a whisper*
whistle *v* : jo *to whistle* - ajo *to ~ for* - ajojo *to call by whistling* - ajojokiya *to cause to ~ for* - ijokiya *to purse or pucker the lips to ~* - jójo *to ~ for* - jolowan *to ~ a tune* - jolowanwan *to whistle a tune* - kajo *to ~ as the wind* - kijo *to ~ calling for* — jinlhingla *to ~ exhaling of a sudden* — waglašlošlo *to ~ with one note* — tateka s'a *to ~ as the wind*
white man *n* : wašicun - oh'an wašickun *one who makes things like a ~* — lilita *a child's word for a white man* - Cf wašicun, man
whittle *v* : kaptuh'a *to ~ or scrape off for kindling*
whizz *adv* : kinšyela *or* konšyela *or* šliyela *whizzing* — tum *a whizzing sound*
who *rel pron* : túwa ... ca he *or* cána *who* — túwekaleš *or* túwekeša *whoever*
whole *adv* : ógeya *the ~ of it, just as is* - iyugeya *all of* — otoza *blunt, round and long* — walupišni *a thing complete* - yulupišni *a thing intact, fresh* — yuhtutešni icu *to take the ~ entirely*
wicked *adj* : wicašašni *mean, deceptive* — cantewanica *to be heartless* — wóših'an *wickedness*
wide *adj* : blaȟa *or* blaga *wide at one end, hence tapering* — oglakinyan *width, or in breadth* - otanglakinyan *the breadth, width*
widow *n* : wiwazica - wicawiwazica *a widower*
wife *v* : wakanyuza *to take a wife as christians are called to* — wiiyagleȟa *to tag along with one's wife* — wikte *to beat one's wife* — wínyancin *to buy a wife*
wig *n* : wicapehinkagapi
wild *vn* : gnaškinyan *to be ~, crazy, or frantic* — guguhan *senseless, witless, without respect given* — itu *untamed* - itu un *or* otuyaun *to be in a wild state* — škéhan *prancing, jumping around, ambitious* - škehéca *an unbroken, unsteady animal*
wilderness *n* : makoskan - makoskanl *in the desert* - makoskantu *desert-like* — tiwokitahena *being away from houses, homeless, from a woman lacking a sense of a mother's responsibilities*
will *n* : tawacin - Cf mind
willing *adv* : cantekic'unyan *willingly* — *pron...*cinka *pron...freely* — eca *or* ecakel *purposely* - ecakaleš *at any rate* — econwacinšni *to be unwilling to do* — iyowinic'iya *to declare one's self ~* otawat'elya *to be ~ to* — tawat'lkiya *to be willing to do, to suffer* — tawat'elya *to be ~ for anything, ~ to do or suffer* - witawat'elya *to be ~* — ot'ognakel *although unwilling*
win *v* : ak'a *to put a mark in winning a game* — apaksonlya *to win by talking, to have the last word* — glutinto *to take all staked in a game* — kapá *to beat the opponent* — ktéla *to win a game* — ohikiya *to ~ back one's own* — wašagya *to beat easily* — wónate *to win, excel in a game*
wind *n* : tate *the air in motion* - tatoheya *against the ~ or current, upstream* - itatowab *or* itatowal *or* itatowapa *or* itatowapatanhan *or* itatowata *against the wind, windward, upwind, in the direction from which the wind blows* - tateiyumni *whirlwind* - tatekajo *or* tatipogan *a wind storm* - tateyanpa *a blast of wind, or wind to blow* - tatohekiya *or* tatowapa *or* tatowab tatowata *against the current* — iyokaluza *breezy* — tatuyektašniyan *with a crosswind*
windmill *n* : mnicatomni
window *n* : ojanjanglepi - ojanjanglepi akahpe *a window shutter, curtain, or shade*
windpipe *n* : blobloska
wing *or* **fin** *n* : ape *a tree leaf* - hoápe *a fish fin* — ȟupáhu *a bird's wing* — ícalu *a wing used to fan one's self, a fan* — kinyanpi *the wingeds*
wink *v* : ištakakpan to ~ the eye - ištakakpanpi s'e *winking the eyes rapidly, fluttering the eyes* - glakpan *to wink or beat one's own*
winter *n* : waniyetu - ówaniyetu *wintertime* - waniyetuokisapa *a ~ with little snow* - wanicokanyan *mid-winter* - wanihan *last ~* - waniti *or* waniun *to ~, spend the ~* - wanitipi *a ~ camp*
wipe *n* : ipapuza *a towel, something used to wipe dry* — pakinta *to wipe dry or clean* - ípakinta *to ~ off, or a towel* - ikpakinta *to ~ one's own* - kícipakinta *to ~ for one* - kipakinta *to cleanse for one, to ~ off* - kpakinta *to ~ one's own* - nakinta *to brush on or off* - opakinslasla *wiping the dirt away* - opapinslasla iyeya *to rub clean* — yuwinta *to wipe another's face in gesture as a sign of a desire for peace*
wise *adj* : iaksape *wise in talking* - ikiciksapa *to be wise for one by instructing one in the right way* - ikiksapa *to be ~ for one, to consult* -ikiksabya *to cakuse one to be ~ in ref to one's own, or wisely, cautiously* - iksabya *to make ~ for or concerning, or wisely* - iksapa *wise, prudent* - okiksapa *to be ~ in regard to* - toksapa *his or her wisdom*
wish *vn* : ... nunwe *let it be so* — ... ni *partic postp* : may it be so
witch *n* : wíhmunge *a witch medicine* - Cf shoot
with *prep* : kicí *with one person* - ob *or* obtu *with more than one* — ópeya being with, or to make go with — aopeya *to make follow with, or* together with, included — kicica *to be ~ or on one's side* - kicicaya *to be ~ another* - kicila *only with* — égna *with, in amongst* — agnala *with only, with only so many* — ayuhlaganšni *not to forsake, to be with constantly* — iyayustaka *to hold one thing together with another*
wither *v* : šnija *withered, dried up* - ašnija *to be wilted or withered on or for* - kašnija *to make wiithered* - našnija to trample on, or to be withered as after a frost - šnišya *to make dry up, fig to disappoint one* — našeca to make wither by trampling on - našelya *to cause trample on and make wither* — oyasaka *dried hard or withered on or in* - Cf dry
withhold *va* : akicinica *to retain for one* — ípila *to deny, to refuse to give as too good for one*
within *adv* : imahetu *or* imaheta *or* ímahel *or* timahetu *within* - imahetanhan - timahetanhan *from within* - imahetuyakel *in the inside of, within* — óhan *prep* : *among, within, in*
without *adv* : yuhašniyan
witness *v* : waayatan'in *to bear witness, or a witness* — wóyagkiyapi *a witness*
woman *n* : winyan *woman or wife* - wikoškalaka *a young ~* - sintewi *fig a young woman* - wihignaton *a married ~* - wicaglata *women who follow men in singing at dances* - wiihpeya *to cast off a woman* - wiicohtakešni

not having known women — wakanka *an old woman* — hokewin s'e *like the woman, appearing bulky having on many clothes* — win *female, of woman or of wife* - yuwinyanke s'e *being a bad woman* — wiiyanajince *to run away holding a woman* - wikišleya *to insult a woman* - wiwoȟa *a woman who lives with her husband's relatives* — winyanyatapi *a queen* — wiwašteka *a beautiful ~* — winuhcala *an elderly lady*

wonder *partic* : eša *or* ešaš *or* šaš - Note: these *partic* occur in three cases. Case 1 : at the beginning of the sentence, rendering the meaning "I wonder if ... " Case 2 : at the end of the sentence, rendering the meaning "though *or* although" Case 3 : after a *n* , meaning "also" or after a *v* , meaning "some *or* any" — wawakankan *a wonder-worker* - wówanke *a wonder to see* — wówitonpa *a wonder to one's way of thinking*

wood *n* : can *a piece of wood, a tree* - canglepi *cord-wood, firewood* - cankit'a *for a wood bin* - canblaska *a board* - can'icoga *driftwood* - can'iyutapi *a cord of wood* - cankaga *a log* - cankagica *touchwood, punk* — cankaiciyopteya *with ~ crossed* - can'optuȟa *wood chips, kindling ~* - canwilute *logwood* - canyuktan *bent ~* - cunhlogeca *dry ~ rotten within* - cunk'in *a load of ~* - cunk'inta *a reserve of ~ , a place to gather ~*

word *n* : oie *a word, a saying, a speech* - oieya *to use words* - tóie *his or her words* - wóie *a word* - wóeye *a saying*

work *n* : wówaši *one's, or a hired person* - wówašiya *to make ~ , to have as a hired person* — oh'án *to work, or an action, occupation, custom, device, artifice* — kaoh'anko *to make ~ fast* - wah'an'ic'iya *to pretend much ~* - wah'anka *to do hard ~ well* — kawaja *to ~ at perseveringly* — econ *to do something* - oecon *a doing, a work* - oeconšilya *to make one do his ~ badly* - wóeconla *to consider something hard ~ whereas it is not* - wóeconlaka *a difficult ~* - wóeconyan *to do ~ , an always busy person* — patica *to ~ up* — toskinciye *his or her doing* — wicohtani *labor* — atatape šni *working up keeping something soft*

worry *v* : ik'o *to get worried* — ilita *to be worried*

worse *adv* : aonšiya - aonšiyakel *worse and worse, still worse* — kícih'anyan *to fail, to worsen for one*

worship *v* : wakankaga *to make wakán or ceremonial* - wakanla *to reckon as holy or sacred* — yugalyapi *worship* — akanl waunyanpi *an altar of worship*

worthless *adj* : ašinhte *of poor quality* - ašinhteyakel *in a less good condition* — ošikšicela *~ things* - šícit'e *~ and very bad* — šuška *good for nothing, tardy* - šuškaka *a ~ fellow* — wahtešni *~ or wicked, evil* — wawašgya *to render worthless*

wound *va* : o *to wound a person* - oó *a wound* - ópi *wounded, a wound, one wounded* - oiyeya *a wound, a hole made by shot* - tao *to wound but not kill* - taopi *a wound, a wounded person, wounded* - ocape — wípemnašni *not wounded, dead from unknown causes* - wípemnayan *wounded, with a wound* - wípeohloka *a wound from a spear* — wopínspinza *to inflict light wounds*

wrap *va* : yuwi *to wrap around, bind, bandage* - agluwi *to ~ one's own around* - ayuwi *to ~ on* - igluwi *to ~ on one's own e.g. one's leggings* — aipiyaka *to gird one's self* — iyapehan *to fold up with, to wind on e.g. thread on a spool* - iyaic'ikpehan *to ~ one's self around as does a snake* — aiyapemni *to ~ up with* - iyapemni *to ~ or wind up in* - okipemni *to ~ around one's own* - opemni *to ~ in a garment* — heyun *to ~ up a pack* - heyunpi *what is wrapped* - oheyun *a wrapping or wrapper* — opazonta *to wind up in* — ounpa *to lay in and bind* — oyuskita *to ~ up in*

wreath *n* : natiyuskite *a ~ or crown* — wateślake *a fillet*

wrestle *va* : kiškata *to play with* - kiciškata a playmate — kícikšan *to have love-play*

wriggle *or* **squirm** *vn* : kšánkšan *to ~ as fish do*

wring *va* : yuškica *to squeeze out* - wíyuškice *a press, a wringer* — yuškepa *to ~ out water from wet clothes*

wrinkle *vn* : ápija *to be wrinkled on* — opíjeca *wrinkled as the face of an old person* — pišpija *many-wrinkled, shriveled* — iyupiza *wrinkled* — kakipaš *or* opišyela *or* glesyela *loose-fitting, loosely wrinkled* — pagingin *to make wrinkles* — šinšin *wrinkled* - yušin *to wrinkle* - yušinkiya *to make ~ e.g. the face or forehead in frowning* - yušinpi *wrinkles* - yušinyan *folded*

write *va* : owa *to ~ , draw, paint* - owakiya *to make draw* - éya okiwa *to ~ saying* - oic'iwa *to ~ one's self* - oikwa *to ~ one's own name* - okiwa *or* okiciwa *to ~ for one* - wówapi icåge *a writing tool* - wówapi kåga *to write a book, or a clerk*

writhe *vn* : paptanptan *to ~ rolling over*

writing materials *n* : iyowa *or* iowa - Note: such as :
canwiyowa *a pencil*
mázawiyowa *a pen*
mniȟuha iyowa *a pen or pencil*
mniȟuha kakanka *or* mniȟuka ska *paper*
mnisapa *ink*
mnisapa ipapuza *a blotter*
mnisapa wícazo *a penholder*

wrong *v* : šiloh'an *to do wrong* — tókinš *carelessly*

yard *n* : cun'iyutapi *a ~ measure* — hócoka *a courtyard*

yawn *v* : iyoya *to ~ , or to gape* - iyoyaya *to make ~* - wayaiyoya *to make ~ by talking* - yaiyowa *or* yaioyaya *to make ~ by speaking to*

year *n* : íomaka *the next year* - Cf time

yelp *or* **yell** *v* : onzéš'aš'akiya *to ~ as do wolves and coyotes* — panpan *to ~ as do children*

yes *adv* : han *or* to *yes, as men affirm* - toš *or* tói *yes, as women say it* — tókeša *yes at any rate, or yes after a while*

yesterday *n* : ihtálehan *the day before, in ref to any given day*

yield *v* : aicaga *or* aicah *to grow, produce* - aicage *the interest as of money*

yoke *n* : canglakinyan *a neckyoke, part of the harness of horse or ox*

Yokomi *np* : Yokomi *a Zuni chief associated with the Comanche people in perhaps the nineteenth century*

you *pron* : níye *you, singular* - níyepi *you plural* - níyeš *or* niš *you emph* — niš níye *you yourself* - nišnála *you alone* — *pron in compos* : ...ya... *or* ...ni... *you, as subject or as object* — *pron plural in compos* : ...ya...pi *or* ...ni...pi — ...nic'i... *yourself as object* — nitawa *or* nita... *your* — ...nici... *for you* — ...nicica... *with you* — níyecuhcin *you at any rate* — níyekaleš *even you*

young *n* : ójilaka *the ~ of men or animals* — ókihan *to follow, be after one, to be younger than* - ókihe *next to, or following, second* - Cf follow, family

Z

zeal *n* : wówacin - wówacintanka yuhapi *having patience and perseverance, zealous*

zigzag *adj* : pakšikšan *crooked* - yuglakšikšan *in a crooked line* - yuglakšinkšin *in all kinds of ways*

Appendix

OGLALA TETON SOCIETY
as ordered in the nineteenth century

Political	*Military*	*Social Services*
naca	officers	hunters
wicahcala	pipe bearers	akicita
wicašayatapika	drummers	pejuta wicaša
	rattlers	witanšnaun
Oglala Naca Omniciye	lance bearers	
Itancanpi	whippers	Naca Omniciye
judges	witanšnaun	Societies
supervisors		Skayuha
appointees	Akicita Societies	Miwatani
alliances	Tokala	Wicila
policing	Sotkayuha	
sanitation	Badger	Religion
	Brave Heart	Wicaša Wakan
	Kangiyuha	Witanšnaun

THE SIOUX NATION
Seven Council Fires

West of the Missouri River		*East of the Missouri River*
Teton	**Saones**	**Santee**
Oglala	Hunkpapa	Mdewakanton
Sicangu	Sihasapa	Wahpeton
Mnikowoju	Itazipco	Wahpekute
	Yankton	Sisseton
	Yanktonais	
LAKOTA DIALECT	NAKOTA DIALECT	DAKOTA DIALECT

Bibliography

Boas, Franz, and Ella C. Deloria. *Dakota Grammar*. National Academy of Sciences. Washington D.C.: U.S. Government Printing Office, 1941.

Boas, Franz, and John R. Swanton. *Siouan Dakota (Teton and Santee Dialects)*. In *Handbook of American Indian Languages*. Smithsonian Institution. Bureau of American Ethnology. Bull. 40, pt. 1. Washington, D.C.: U.S. Government Printing Office, 1911.

Buechel, Eugene. *A Dictionary of the Teton Dakota Sioux Language: Lakota–English, English–Lakota, with considerations given to Yankton and Santee, Oie wowapi wan Lakota–Ieska, Ieska–Lakota*. Ed. by Paul Manhart. Pine Ridge, SD: Holy Rosary Mission. 1970.

———. *A Grammar of Lakota: The Language of the Teton Sioux Indians*. St. Louis: John S. Swift Co., 1939. (Gramm)

——— . *Lakota Tales and Text*. 2 vols. trans. by Paul Manhart. Chamberlain, SD: Tipi Press, 1998

———. *Wowapi Wakan Wicowoyake Yuptecelapi Kin: Bible History in the Language of the Teton Sioux Indians*. New York: Benziger Brothers, 1924. (B.H.)

Buechel, Eugene, Peter Iron Shell, and Ivan Stars. *Lakota Tales and Text: Wisdom Stories, Customs, Lives, and Instruction of the Dakota Peoples*. Ed. by Paul Manhart. Pine Ridge, 1978.

Deloria, Ella Cara. *Dakota Texts*. Publications of the American Ethnological Society. Vol. 14. New York: G. E. Stechert and Co., 1932. (D)

Densmore, Frances. *Teton Sioux Music*. Smithsonian Institution. Bureau of American Ethnology. Bull. 61. Washington, D.C.: U.S. Government Printing Office, 1918. (FD)

Hoebel, E. Adamson. *Anthropology: The Study of Man*. 3rd ed. New York: McGraw-Hill, 1966.

Hoijer, Harry, ed. *Language in Culture: Conference on the Interrelations of Language and Other Aspects of Culture*. Comparative Studies of Culture and Civilizations. Chicago: University of Chicago Press, 1954.

Hunt, Jerome, trans. *Catechism, Prayers and Instructions in the Sioux Indian Language*. Cincinnati: Joseph Berning Printing Co., c. 1910.

Lado, Robert. *Linguistics across Cultures: Applied Linguistics for Language Teachers*. Ann Arbor: Univerity of Michigan Press, 1957.

Perrig, E. *Lakota–English Dictionary*. MS. Milwaukee: Marquette University Library Archives. 1902. (P)

Pilling, James C. *Bibliography of the Siouan Languages*. Smithsonian Institution. Bureau of Ethnology. Bull. 5. Washington, D.C.: U.S. Government Printing Office, 1887.

Riggs, Stephen R. *A Dakota–English Dictionary*. Edited by J. O. Dorsey. Vol. 7 of *Contributions to North American Ethnology*. Edited by John W. Powell. Smithsonian Institution. Bureau of American Ethnology. Washington, D.C.: U.S. Government Printing Office, 1890. (R)

Walker, J. R. *The Sundance of the Teton Dakota*. Anthropolical Papers of the American Museum of Natural History. Vol. 16, pt. 2. New York: The Trustees of the American Museum of Natural History, 1917. (WJR)

Williamson, John P. *An English–Dakota Dictionary / Wašicun ka Dakota ieska wowapi*. New York: American Tract Society, 1902. 264. (WI)

Wissler, Clark. *Societies and Ceremonial Associations in the Oglala Division of the Teton Dakota*. Anthropological Papers, American Museum of Natural History. Vol. 11, pt. 1. New York. 1912.